P9-CKY-043

Every Thing in Dickens

Dickens in 1868
Photograph taken in New York City by Ben Gurney

EVERY THING IN DICKENS

Ideas and Subjects Discussed by Charles Dickens in His Complete Works

A Topicon

Compiled and Edited by

GEORGE NEWLIN

GREENWOOD PRESS
Westport, Connecticut • London

blication Data

jects discussed by Charles Dickens in his complete works: a topicon / compiled and edited by George Newlin.
p. cm.
Includes bibliographical references and index.
ISBN 0-313-29874-2 (alk. paper)
1. Dickens, Charles, 1812–1870—Quotations. 2. Dickens, Charles, 1812–1870—Indexes. 3. Quotations, English. I. Dickens, Charles, 1812–1870. II. Title.
PR4553.N48 1996
823′.8—dc20 96-6347

British Library Cataloguing in Publication Data is available.

Library of Congress Catalog Card Number: 96-6347
ISBN: 0-313-29874-2

First published in 1996

Greenwood Press, 88 Post Road West, Westport, CT 06881
An imprint of Greenwood Publishing Group, Inc.

Printed in the United States of America

The paper used in this book complies with the Permanent Paper Standard issued by the National Information Standards Organization (Z39.48–1984).

10 9 8 7 6 5 4 3 2 1

The endpapers are reproduced from the painting (detail) *The Empty Chair* by Luke Fildes, by permission of the Dickens House Museum, 48 Doughty Street, London WC1N 2LF.

The photograph of Dickens (1868), which is the frontispiece, served the same function when it appeared without indication of source in *Dickens the Dramatist: On Stage, Screen and Radio*, by F. Dubrez Fawcett. London: W. H. Allen, 1952.

Windows into® Dickens

Everyone in Dickens, Volume I: Plots, People and Publishing Particulars in the Complete Works, 1833–1849 [ISBN 0-313-29581-6 (v. 1)]
Everyone in Dickens, Volume II: Plots, People and Publishing Particulars in the Complete Works, 1850–1870 [ISBN 0-313-29582-4 (v. 2)]
Everyone in Dickens, Volume III: Characteristics and Commentaries, Tables and Tabulations: A Taxonomy [ISBN 0-313-29583-2 (v. 3)]
Every Thing in Dickens: Ideas and Subjects Discussed by Charles Dickens in His Complete Works: A Topicon [ISBN 0-313-29874-2]

This Work is dedicated to Toni Lawrence Putnam, my life companion, and to my other blessings: Colin, Ian, Colette, Jane and Elizabeth—not all children of my body, but all the precious offspring of my heart; to Toni's children Cate and Karl, Will and Eve, and Philip and Karon, and to Jane's Harry and Elizabeth's Jeff; to past blessings Pamela and Tim, and Jennifer; and to our Futures, represented so far by Whitney, Katie Lee, Brendan, Inigo, Jordan, Dylan, Rozele, Brittany, Calli, Camille, Clara and Phoebe.

GCN

This Work is also dedicated to two remarkable institutions, valuable and highly important to literature and to Dickens studies in particular: the Dickens House in London, David Parker, Curator; and the Dickens Project at the University of California at Santa Cruz, Murray Baumgarten, founder, and John Jordan, Director. Both have been of immense importance in both tangible and intangible ways to the Editor's efforts, and it is a particular source of pleasure and pride that Windows into® Dickens *(the series of which* Every Thing in Dickens *constitutes the fourth volume) has the Project's official endorsement.*

GCN

Contents

Illustrations

Foreword

The world that Charles Dickens created is palpable, material, and vividly substantive, and it is *also,* inevitably and necessarily, filled with ideas, organizing concepts and categories from Victorian daily life and thought. Every page of his fiction, his journalism and his speeches contributes to Dickens' expression of the plethoric fullness of ideas and organizing categories that the Victorian world provided—about love, life, politics, society, science, technology, religion—about almost everything.

In that sense, Dickens is one vast *Topicon* of the Victorian world, and George Newlin has created a *Topicon* of Dickens. *Every Thing in Dickens* is not a key to all Victorian mythologies, but it is, along with Newlin's *Everyone in Dickens,* the key to almost *all* of Dickens. Though no reference work could ever be totally comprehensive in regard to Dickens' ideas, Newlin's selections comprehend so much that the result is a vast panorama. Of course there is nothing small-scale about Dickens, and Newlin's scale mirrors Dickens' vastness.

Readers and scholars will not have to be Dickensians to find within this reference work a fascinating illumination of the Victorian world: though it takes Dickens as its text, it is an interdisciplinary cornucopia. Historians of every sort will be able readily to locate vivid Dickensian exemplifications of Victorian life: from "Adolescence" to "Zululand," from "Akashic Records" to "Zoological Gardens."

Every Thing in Dickens can be read for pleasure, for casual browsing in the distinctiveness of Victorian things and thoughts; but it can also be mined for selective gold by the social historian, the political historian, the literary historian, and by those who simply need or want to know something specific about Dickens himself or about Victorian manners, morals, thoughts, and things.

There are two important features that great reference works possess: information and access. If you know, even in a general way, what you are looking for, they make it possible for you to get there. Dickens scholars have previously made efforts to provide information and access; some of them are estimable. But they have taken the form of either lists of characters or summaries of plots or pithy collections of sayings. These efforts have been limited by their available technology: the pen, the notecard, the typewriter.

Now, with his hand commanding the computer to use its powers to encode and arrange information, Newlin has created a reference work which, when added to his *Everyone in Dickens,* supplants every other work that has attempted to be a *Dickens Encyclopedia* or a *Dickens Dictionary* or a *Guide to Dickens.* I don't need the previous ones anymore. I will never need them again.

—Fred Kaplan, Distinguished Professor, City University of New York

Preface

Every Thing in Dickens: A Topicon is the fourth volume of George Newlin's *Windows into® Dickens.* The first three went under the title *Everyone in Dickens,* a breathtaking piece of intellectual effrontery, if ever there was one. But there was reason to hope the effrontery might be justified, and it was. Limitless patience, racoon-like curiosity, deftness with language, and the organisational capacity of the computer, all combined to ensure that *Everyone in Dickens* lives up to its name. Or very nearly. Such errors and omissions as there are will yield the occasional footnote in years to come, but the triumph of the footnoting scholar will be proportionate to the triumph of *Everyone in Dickens.*

Everyone in Dickens was a compassable project. Vast, but compassable. Either a character is to be found in Dickens's works, or he is not. Or she is not. Questions about Montague Tigg and Tigg Montague, or the identity of Datchery, are likely to be trivial or, at best, easily set aside.

Ideas and subjects are different. They are less easily named. Aliases abound. And trying to enumerate ideas and subjects brings to mind Kant's critique of the concept of a finite universe. Go to its outermost limit, and poke a stick beyond the edge. Where does the stick go? When you are trying to enumerate ideas and subjects in Dickens's works, there is always somewhere to poke your stick.

George Newlin's *Topicon* of Dickens, then, is a project of a different order. It can never be complete in the way *Everyone in Dickens* can. And it will carry the mark of its day more distinctly. Every age perceives the world differently, perceives representations of the world differently. Future generations will find things in Dickens we cannot see, and miss things plain to us.

There are deterrents, then, in the way of this project, but should they be allowed to deter? The answer, clearly, is no. Talk to lovers of Dickens and scholars in the field. They want a guide through the ideas and subjects he offers us. Inevitably, it will be a different kind of instrument from *Everyone in Dickens.* Entries will provoke judgment. Thoughtful readers will not be content with every entry they find. Thoughtful readers will not find every entry they would like to find.

The answer to this, though, is plain. Thoughtful readers have no need to be content with every entry they find, no need to find every entry they would like to find. They are readers who like to find places to poke sticks, and should appreciate the stimulus to do so. The *Topicon* offers that stimulus. It presents us with ideas and subjects to be found in Dickens, far more copiously and systematically than hitherto, sometimes more provocatively. It is almost without precedent and entirely without competition. Now that it exists, it is hard to see how any serious student of Dickens can manage without using it.

—David Parker, Curator of the Dickens House, London

Editor's Foreword

and a Word about the Computer

Dickens was great, to begin with. There is no doubt whatever about that. The register of his immortality was signed by Thackeray, Chesterton, Shaw, Santayana, Orwell, Edmund Wilson and many, many more. Tolstoy signed it. And Tolstoy's name was good for anything he chose to put his hand to.

Dickens was greater than he knew—than we know—and in many spheres. He was and is seen whole by no one (even his best biographers not excepted, if we are to judge by what came to print). Still held to be the greatest writer of English prose fiction, he excelled in reporting, journalism, periodical editing, acting, theatrical producing and directing, and dramatic reading. He was a dominant mover and shaker in education, public health, and private philanthropy, and he made heroic efforts, with some success, to rescue a goodly number of its practitioners from the oldest profession.

Dickens would drop almost anything when his vulnerable heart was touched. Despite (or because of) a severe poverty consciousness which kept him working frantically and living with suppressed fear all his life, he devoted countless hours to helping the less fortunate and rallying friends to assist colleagues in trouble. He did not forget the poor, the confused, the sick, the miserable: especially women and children unjustly abused and exploited, crushed and lost in the cracks and chasms of a tectonically changing world.

He knew more what it was to be Homeless ('Houseless') than those wretched wanderers themselves, for he saw accurately (there was never a more acute observer) and looked courageously, and he had the clear, unflinching, empathetic humanity to apprehend what he saw. He had the facility to describe this and other terrible things forcefully, with the seductive power of a great enchanter. He wanted to make a difference: he did.

Charles Dickens has much to give us today. He can make us laugh, for a start: he was and is the supreme humourist in fiction. He can make the hardest-hearted cry. And, once moved, we find it easier to see with our own eyes some dreadful things in our own world.

Perhaps we may even begin to do something about that eternal Soul Jacob Marley reminds us we have and had better tend to.

A Word about the Computer

When I saw Fred Kaplan's Foreword and David Parker's Preface to *Everyone in Dickens* (Vols. I-III of *Windows into® Dickens:* hereafter EID), I realized that my use of the computer in this project had to be talked about.

First of all, and obvious enough, these four volumes could not have been attempted without electronic word-processing. That said, it might be important to explain, particularly for those who might want to try this themselves, what my computer did *not* do.

When I began this work in 1989, technology, while amazingly advanced already, had not achieved certain innovations which might have helped me greatly, principally the scanner. Every word, every punctuation mark, every margin, tab and space instruction in the early years was created by me "by hand," that is, by finger, punching a key. I had been a competent typist, and a serious concert pianist. My fingers became so fast that I outran the basic program I was working with and often had to wait for my screen to show me what I had already written. Had I known what was coming I might have been paralyzed by an insidious rationalization: "Wait a few years, and then you can do this much quicker." I felt something like John Henry, the man who outraced new technology for a moment, only to fall dead on his own hammer.

Also, from the outset, using the relatively elementary Macintosh SE and an ink-jet printer with a basic system and program, I found myself having to upgrade every year or so as systems and programs improved, often first undoing manually what I had earlier created that way, before I could exploit new possibilities. Only when, in 1994, I invested in a laser printer and installed a doubled memory and the top of the line (at that time) System 7.1 and Microsoft 5.0 for the Mac, did I really get to the threshold of effective computer work. But I had no customized program, and I am no computer maven: I'm a reader who types. Everything, tables and indexes included, in every volume was personally typed out by me, then perhaps moved or replicated elsewhere. In the words of my computer consultant, I "hand-carved" every page.

Probably I will use a scanner next time (I still do not own one), thereby sparing a lot of dogsbody time. (A scanner takes an electronic picture of a page placed on it and makes it instantly manipulable on a computer screen just as though input manually by keyboard.) But there has been a major benefit in typing everything myself: I have truly lived with what Dickens created, right down to the last detail, and I have edited—been forced to edit—discriminatingly as I went along. When it has seemed unbearably tedious and virtually endless, I have remembered that the Man Himself had only his pen, and he wrote on the order of eight million words with it (the first two volumes of EID contain about 840,000, Volume III 332,000, this volume 860,000).

There is reason to hope that someday the material I have arranged in a multiplicity of documents on my hard disk will find its way onto a CD-ROM, or its successor, and users will be able to do what I can do with the box on my desk, and much more. The cost of bringing that about at the moment runs healthily up in six figures. What I myself do have now is the ability to move around quickly, find anything in a document in seconds, transfer material in moments and generally luxuriate in the results of six years of base-building.

It has been my responsibility to give the publisher camera-ready copy, and all its flaws are mine. That said, I will affirm that what is printed in these volumes has been arranged with all the thought and skill I have in me to be accessible and useful for all us old-fashioned people who like and use books.

Acknowledgments

A fundamental point needs to be made at the outset. Although considerable, including primary, research has been involved, particularly bearing on what Dickens actually wrote, *Windows into® Dickens,* of which *Every Thing in Dickens* is the fourth volume, has not been made by a professional scholar, nor does it grow from any new scholarly premise. It is, rather, a devoted amateur's contribution to aid the work of the scholars he greatly admires. My occasional interpolations (largely in EID), though sincere, may look naive to those who have lived with the Inimitable much longer than I, but, as is inevitable when dealing with a personality like Dickens's, one develops a point of view. Thanks to the editors at Greenwood Publishing Group, I have had a signal chance to express mine. In a few places I have done so. I am deeply and especially grateful to Robert Hagelstein, President, and Lynn Taylor, Executive Editor, at Greenwood; and my creative, acute and considerate production editor, Jane Lerner, has been indispensable.

Imperfect as they are, these volumes have benefited from generous help from three people whose credentials in the world of scholarship are undeniable. Fred Kaplan, America's outstanding Dickens biographer, has given generously at every turn and upon any seeking for advice, regardless of the hour of the day. Two great Dickensians of the United Kingdom, Professor Michael Slater and Dickens House Curator David Parker, have reviewed and consulted. David and his lovely wife Elinor extended hospitality generously on my two recent trips to London on this project, and I owe the chapter *Transportation and Travel* to Michael's suggestion. Both David and Michael have conscientiously and promptly responded to my frequent calls for help and background information.

I express again my thanks for their help to the invariably courteous and patient staffs of the Dickens House in London (an international treasure which should be better known); the British Library and the Theatre Museum in London; the Henry W. and Albert A. Berg Collection at the New York Public Library; and the Sterling Library microform archive at Yale University. Linda Hooper, factotum and pillar of the Dickens Project at Santa Cruz, California, has been a source of friendship and support.

The word *Topicon,* denoting a topical concordance, will remind many of the *Syntopicon* idea index from *Great Books of the Western World*, copyright 1952,

1990 by Encyclopædia Britannica, Inc. The *Syntopicon* covers nearly 3,000 topics derived from 102 ideas and provides a subject-matter index to writings included in the *Great Books.* There is a cousinship between this work's scheme and the principle of the *Syntopicon,* and we are grateful to Encyclopædia Britannica, Inc., for confirming that it has no objection to our use of *Topicon* in this work's title.

Over the years since the *Windows into® Dickens* idea germinated, several people have made contributions, usually intangible and sometimes not highly specific but very important nevertheless. I wish to acknowledge them, for reasons each (I hope) remembers. They are Murray Baumgarten, Barbara Welter Blewer, Robert Brawer, Gilman Burke, Merrell M. Clark, Philip Collins, Kate Delano Condax, Jill Cowen, James W. Ellison, Edward Guiliano, Ada Louise Huxtable, John O. Jordan, J. Robert Maguire, Michael Meller, Donald Oresman, Clarkson and Helga Potter, Gordon Philo (Charles Forsyte), Mordecai Pomerantz, Arnold Roth, Carolyn Smith, Ralph Townley, Richard Walters, Aileen Ward, Rhoda Weyr and Beverley Zabriskie.

There is no way to measure my personal debt to Charles Dickens, my mentor, inspiration and friend for the last seven (going on eight) intense and joyful years.

Introduction

When I was being trained to be a lawyer, I heard a lot about the Law: about its theory and its rhetoric; but the essential insight of the case method, not always shared with me by my teachers, was that the accurate marshalling of all the relevant facts was the fundamental prerequisite to any useful work (there is an idealism implicit in this statement, now that I think of it, which might explain why I am no longer a lawyer). I learned, if I had not already known, that in life the facts are always surprising and fascinating, if not absolutely bizarre. They are far more interesting in their raw state than when interpreted, no matter how scrupulous and dispassionate the interpreter.

To answer the question,"What did he actually say about that?" *Every Thing in Dickens* organizes Dickens's editorial comments, descriptions and philosophizings for accessibility, utility to scholarship and pleasure to the amateur enthusiast as well as the professional scholar. The book exists for all who would like to be able to find well-remembered Dickens insights and opinions quickly, discover new ones, and have a trove of accessible data on the man and his creations to revel in for its own sake, or to use to embark on their own explorations and develop their own conclusions. The Indexes to Words and Phrases, and to Localities, are additional powerful tools to these ends.

Charles John Huffam Dickens (1812-1870) wrote fourteen complete novels and half of another. We know so far (scholars will go on discovering) and reflect below that he created five Christmas Books and twenty Christmas Stories, some in collaboration, plus nine independent interpolations, twelve frameworks and much transitional material, set forth below *in haec verba,* for his beloved Christmas Numbers; 56 *Sketches by Boz* ranging from pure reporting to incandescently imagining to sheer fun-making; twelve drama reviews and 25 reports, mostly political, on assignment from *The Morning Chronicle;* a three-part pamphlet opposing restrictions on Sunday pleasures for the working class; 23 facetious sketches and a "remonstrance" on the foibles of young gentlemen and young couples; and 47 pieces (three in collaboration) for the *Examiner,* his friend Forster's journal. There were four plays, a musical farce (fragments remain), a comedietta (lost) and three joint efforts, one adapting his own work. (Other adaptations are disregarded here.)

He led and wrote for four periodicals (he *wrote* for several more): *Bentley's Miscellany:* six pieces, four fragments and a collaboration; *Master Humphrey's*

Clock: ten fictional segments plus scaffolding, organized in six parts; *Household Words,* his preoccupation for ten years (1850-59, hereafter HW: 27 *Reprinted Pieces,* 87 pieces not otherwise collected, 49 collaborations, and the serialized book *A Child's History of England*); and, during his last decade, *All the Year Round* (hereafter AYR: 37 works collected as *The Uncommercial Traveller,* 17 other pieces and two collaborations) and a few fragments. There were 34* miscellaneous items, including letters to the press; three verse parodies and a two-part pamphlet, partly written in collaboration, on reforming the Royal Literary Fund.

Dickens wrote six short works, primarily fictional: *The Lamplighter, To Be Read at Dusk, A Lazy Tour of Two Idle Apprentices* (a collaboration with Wilkie Collins), *Hunted Down, George Silverman's Explanation,* and *A Holiday Romance;* and two book-length travel works: *American Notes* and *Pictures from Italy.* There were the unpublished *Mrs Gamp and the Strollers, Autobiographical Fragments,* and "The Life of Our Lord," named by his son.

There were 116 speeches (4 were not reported), a beautiful child's prayer, and *Lines Addressed to Mark Lemon* (all minimally in evidence in EID but reflected in this volume). Pro forma prefaces, verse prologues to others' works and some other little pieces drop through our screen.

The total of 646 works, big, medium, small and smaller, is tabulated:

Novels	15
Christmas Books	5
Christmas Stories (one a collaboration)	20
Christmas Story interpolations	9
Christmas Story frameworks	12
Sketches by Boz	56
The Morning Chronicle pieces so far identified	37
Sunday under Three Heads	3
Sketches of Young Gentleman, Young Couples	24
The Examiner	47
Plays (with collaborations; lost work included)	9
Bentley's Miscellany	11
Master Humphrey's Clock	10
Reprinted Pieces	27
Household Words not otherwise collected	87
Household Words collaborations	49
The Uncommercial Traveller	37
All the Year Round not otherwise collected	19
Miscellaneous articles, papers and pieces	34
Stand-alone short works, primarily fictional	6
Verse: three parodies, lines to Lemon	4
Travel volumes	2
Speeches (4 not reported; 19 brief acknowledgments)	116
A Child's History of England	1
Reformation of the Literary Fund	2
Mrs Gamp and the Strollers	1
Autobiographical Fragments	1
"The Life of Our Lord" and a child's prayer	2
	646

Of the four volumes of *Windows into® Dickens,* (the first three are *Everyone in Dickens*—EID) this was the first to be conceived. The entry which started it all is in the chapter on *Mind.* It is a passage on history and legend from *The Old Curiosity Shop.* It now appears under *History—truth and legend.* When I first read it, it struck me, an amateur historian, that it was very much worth "making a note on," but I could not decide how or where to make such a note, nor even how, once I had made it, I could reliably remind myself that I had done so. In the space of about twenty minutes thinking this over, I evolved the idea which became EID and the *Topicon.*

Compilations like the *Topicon* have been essayed in the past, but serious attempts have been rare. The first we know of was F. G. de Fontaine's 1873 *Cyclopedia* (deF on page lvii) It uses a straight "A to Z" approach, mixing subjects and characters (Cabs, Canal-boat, Candle, Captain Cuttle, Cards) made workable by a competent index. Densely packed in two-column small print over 543 pages, it is a formidable accomplishment for its day, though hard on our modern eyes and rife with citation mistakes. We stumbled on our copy in a rare book shop, and Carolyn Smith repaired it and made it usable.

A remarkable curiosity is Myron F. Brightfield's *Victorian England in its Novels (1840-1870)* (B on page lvii), a sort of Topicon covering over two thousand novels including several by Dickens. This three-volume work did not find a publisher but was issued in fifty photocopied sets of the typescript. Alerted to it by Michael Slater, we found, admired and shed a tear over it in the British Library. Had we another lifetime, we might try an *aggiornamento.*

The most recent effort, marred by a sketchy index, is that of Mollie and the late Michael Hardwick in 1973 (MMH on page lviii). Its principle of organization is the Work. The novels and the principal collections of the canon are presented chronologically. It amounts to a plotless super-abridgment of the generally known works. One can read it with pleasure as a series of highlights, but use of the index requires substantial initial familiarity with Dickens: more than most readers have these days.

None of these works covers the plays, uncollected journalism, speeches or collaborations. They omit much important socially-oriented material, and none gives any space to Dickens's descriptions of London neighbourhoods, America, or the other localities he knew, sometimes very well, and wrote about with his familiar graphic detail and flavour.

This has been strictly a "bottom-up" proceeding: if Dickens did not write on a particular subject the reader will find no mention of it. With few exceptions, no entry in this volume lacks typical Dickens aroma or flavour: on the contrary, his legendary ability to choose the apposite epithet is in evidence in virtually every paragraph.

In the last days before this work went to press, the editor woke in the night realizing for the first time that he had no captions related to the Monarchy. So a cross-reference appears in *Captions, and Their Locations in the Topicon.* We are trans-Atlantically bemused at the absence of any Dickensian animadversions to Monarchy's essential suitability, or lack of same, in human governance. Index IX in *A Taxonomy* (EID's Volume III), however, contains many of his pithy, often devastating summaries of the foibles and failures of particular monarchs, and a few of these have made their way into *From the Narration* in the Indexes of Words and Phrases.

We are sure we have omitted passages fondly remembered by those who, searching in vain, will want to burn the Editor in effigy or hang him at Newgate with his face to the wall. But we have tried our best not to do so, and it has been nearly endless (we had to stop some time) fun trying. We *know* we have occasionally duplicated an entry or part of it instead of making a cross-reference: that is usually inadvertence, not deliberation. There was a point when production considerations began to dictate leaving things alone.

A compilation such as this highlights Dickens's amazing genius for *language,* pure and simple, with greater intensity than can be shown in any other way. A few examples: *Death—dusty,* (page 28) gives Macbeth's phrase all the concreteness one could possibly require; Barkis's, Mrs Gradgrind's and Betty Higden's deaths (pages 42, 44 and 48), among many others; Dickens's description of the collective unconscious in 1844, 31 years before Jung's birth (page 248); the amazing way he makes manufacturing processes, as for porcelain and plate glass (pages 727 and 732), vivid and even comprehensible to mechanical duffers like this writer (yes, he had collaborators sometimes, but his magic is obvious in particular passages); for New Age enthusiasts, the remarkable description in *A Tale of Two Cities* of what are today called Akashic Records (page 1015); and his alchemical magic applied to a visit to a paper-mill, where the process of making paper from rags becomes a reflection on the Day of Judgment (page 1019).

What seems most extraordinary, however, is the amazing timeliness of Dickens's social commentary. One could find no more cogent and (to me) unanswerable argument for what we call "Affirmative Action" in the United States than the last paragraph of the passage quoted in the chapter *Fellow Man, in Relation* under *Blacks—education in America* (page 437). And there are many, many more: vital and compelling reminders of our human duty as sharers of the bounty of this planet to accept and implement the principle that, as G. K. Chesterton put it, "no one in the State must be too weak to influence the State." (GKC 174) I believe that if Dickens's commentaries on Slavery and Violence as he observed them in 1842 (*see* AN in EID Volume I as well as the relevant captions in this volume) were read and pondered today, the American social conscience, which has sometimes seemed dormant recently, could be energized, with powerful and beneficent effect.

There are some features in this compilation worth remark. In the chapter *Ages of Man,* we have presented all the fictional deaths in Dickens's work in a special section: *Last Lines of Death.* We had begun this assemblage when we discovered Garrett Stewart's *Death Sentences* (GS on page lviii) and this wonderful book confirmed our guess that this effort would be rewarding. In the second chapter, *Body,* we assemble a special section, *Smells,* which gives powerful evidence that Dickens had a preternaturally keen olfactory sense. In the chapter *London,* we provide Dickens's descriptions of the neighbourhoods he roamed and probably knew better than any other man of his time or since. In the penultimate chapter, *Charles Dickens Self-Revealed,* we collect examples of the nearest thing (to our mind) to a flaw in the Dickens use of English: his sometimes heavy-handed early use of the comic simile.

Dickens had much to say or illustrate relevant to the topics in this volume which does not appear here because it is associated with his characters. We have tried *not* to repeat here things extracted in EID but have added occasional commentary or cross-reference to make connections which seemed important.

In working with the *Topicon,* the Indexes in the *Taxonomy* might be very helpful: particularly Indexes IV and V (occupations), VI (relationships), VII (miscellaneous categories of named characters), VIII (generic characters) and XI (literary references). For example, to learn more about Dickens on Father and Fatherhood, one might turn to Index VI under that head and then go to the works cited. For Adolescence it would be Index VII; and so forth. Historical figures (given in **bold** in the text of this volume) will be found in Index IX or, in the case of most authors and composers, in Index XI part 1; and characters (italicized) in and quotations from others' fiction, mythology or the Bible will be found in Index XI part 2. The Glossary in Volume III will be a help for other references: usually, these are explained in notes in the body of this volume only when the Glossary lacks them.

Preparation of this volume has entailed a myriad of choices: of major subdivisions (our fifteen chapters); of captions (405, including 42 under *Charles Dickens Self-Revealed*); and, most especially, in assigning captions to particular chapters. It may not be obvious at first that some delicate, even profound, considerations were involved here, but we had to make working decisions: what is "body," what "mind," what "spirit"? How do we draw the line between "fellow man" and "humanity?"

Take the sensitive issue of homosexuality, for example. Is it somatically determined, or is it a spiritual issue involving a moral choice? We have opted for the chromosome school, but the reader is not obliged to agree with us. (We made an analogous decision on Hysteria.) On the other hand, we decided that addiction was more a matter of mind than of body, and that energy, as Dickens wrote about it, was a spiritual, not a physical, phenomenon. We hope readers will be philosophical about such things. We had to choose labels and group categories under them, for our and their convenience: there is no hidden agenda. The choices we made will be uncovered most efficiently by consulting *Captions, and Their Locations in the Topicon,* which follows.

Items cited with the prefixes HWC are from pieces CD explicitly acknowledged as written by him in concert with another. As Harry Stone notes (HS II p433), CD's "method of intensively editing, rewriting, and adding to what went into *Household Words* often made other sections [in addition to those he stated were his own] of articles as much his as the original author's. This is preeminently true of what Dickens called his 'composite' articles—that is, articles . . . which are listed in the *Household Words* Contributors' Book as jointly by Dickens and a collaborator . . . . " *But the reader is cautioned not to rely upon our inclusion of these items as meaning they are by CD.* Consult HS, or at least the entries in Vol. II, in each particular case: often, all one can say is that the words are "probably" by him, and in some cases one would not want to go even so far. We have them for their flavour, their quotability, their "aroma" of CD, and because it is certain, at the least, that he approved of the sentiments expressed, for he allowed nothing with which he did not agree to appear in any of the publications he edited. The same general comment applies to the collaborations in *Bentley's Miscellany* (prefix BC) and *All the Year Round* (prefix AYC).

Illustrations. Do pictures have a place in a volume like this? We wrestled with the question and discussed it with other Dickensians. We concluded that they would be a welcome diversion and a leaven to a very densely packed book. No illustration is included which CD did not approve or have the chance to approve, and all are associated with the earliest issuances of the works. We have chosen from among those not used in the earlier volumes, with the criteria that they had (i) archival significance, in the sense of being famous in their own right and historically significant (like *Mr Wardle and His Friends under the Influence of the Salmon,* almost Phiz's very first effort for a Dickens work; or (ii) precise connection with a passage in the *Topicon* (like *Mr Pickwick in Chase of his Hat,* which also has the interest of being one of the ill-fated

Robert Seymour's last works); or (iii) they added something which print lacked (like *Mr Chester's Chair,* where the picture has flavour Dickens's prose did not, or the illustration of the occupation Hairdresser). Others appear when the Editor could not resist them, the consideration sometimes being the inclusion of an artist not otherwise represented (as Buss, with a rather inferior depiction of a cricket match). Thomas Hatton (in NDP on page lviii) is our authority for illustrator attributions.

Extended Extracts. We have included some relatively lengthy examples of particularly marvellous, and in most but not all cases famous, scenes or discourses. They are the highest places in the Himalaya of the *oeuvre* and are listed in the Contents.

On the text: We have tried to avoid arcane though sometimes interesting questions concerning which texts ought to be considered the last word. Even in his journalism, when CD collected the *Sketches by Boz,* the *Reprinted Pieces* and *The Uncommercial Traveller* he made some textual changes and elisions and altered titles. Matters of this sort we have largely left to specialists. We have used the Charles Dickens edition (1868-1870) in several reincarnations: the 1894 Houghton Mifflin (New York), the 1895 Estes and Lauriat (Boston), the 1897 Gadshill (Chapman & Hall in London), the Oxford Illustrated (1957) and the Folio Society (the 1980's; London). We have delved into the Norton Critical and Clarendon (Oxford University Press) editions, but not to make text comparisons. Other sources are identified in particular cases.

On spelling and punctuation: English, as opposed to American, spellings are generally used, though we have not achieved complete consistency. Not all the texts were themselves consistent in such matters (certainly not with each other), and purity did not seem worth the nit-picking it would have required. Some archaisms, like ",—" have been modernized.

Indexes: Not fitting precisely within the scheme of this Volume, but likely to be useful to its readers and to those who possess EID, are the special Indexes: the two-part *Words and Phrases,* which cites this volume and EID Volumes I and II and Index IX in Volume III, and which we have deliberately sought to make a kind of "Index of Last Resort" where words and terms not fitting under any particular heading elsewhere are included; and *Localities,* where we try to cover every reference in the *oeuvre* other than the speeches, separately treating, and thus independently indexing, Dickens's two travel volumes, *American Notes* and *Pictures from Italy.*

There are two reasons for making a series like this. The first is obvious: to collect in one place and make accessible with indexes Dickens's great sayings and scenes, inimitable descriptions and character vignettes (these last, of course, are in EID)—the ones we remember, or wish we remembered, from our happy moments reading for pleasure. The other is rarer, and this book is probably the first example: to assemble for study and reflection all or substantially all Dickens's socially and psychologically (even spiritually) important observations, criticisms and recommendations.

We hope that, in reading and using ETD, the reader will find something approaching the pleasure and satisfaction we experienced creating it.

Garrison, N.Y. February 7, 1996 (Dickens's 184th birthday) George Newlin

How to Use This Book

Avoid making assumptions about how this work is organized and where particular subjects are to be found. Remember that its focus is, if you will, the Platonic Idea, concrete or abstract, illustrated in Dickens: not his characters (the three volumes of *Everyone in Dickens* are devoted to the characters), not their sayings (the Index at page 1040 is organized by sayings), not descriptions as such (the Index at page 1048 is organized by narrator's words and phrases).

Begin by surveying the book as a whole. Study the Table of Contents. Read the Introduction carefully. Cast your eye down *Captions, and Their Locations,* which follows, to get a detailed sense of what this book covers and for chapter and page locations. The 650 entries in this section constitute a Subject Index to this volume. We have tried to anticipate readers' interests in particular areas which, as CD dealt with them, did not rise to the status of an independent caption. We have done this usually by adding cross-references, either in the *Captions* section or in the tables of contents of the respective chapters.

The citation scheme we follow in the body of this work is that created for EID. The sections *Abbreviations and Dates* and *Titles Alphabetized* from those volumes are provided, beginning at pages xxxiii and xlv, respectively. The former is the place to identify the mysterious letters at the end of each quotation in the body of the volume. *Titles Alphabetized* is not essential to use of the *Topicon* but is provided for its general handiness to Dickensians. It provides EID page locations for all Dickens's works.

We apologise for those unprepossessing little squiggles, *And see, See also* and just *See.* Whether the reference runs on from consulted material or is paragraphed separately will usually suggest whether it relates to the caption or just to the sub-caption, but sometimes this treatment was influenced or determined by considerations of design and the justification of column-lengths.

Where a cross-reference is given, it means that the material then under the eye incompletely represents our assemblage of Dickens's thoughts on the particular subject. We have strenuously tried not to use material more than once, even when highly relevant under more than one caption (we have failed, by the way: the exercise of memory involved in articulating the components of this work would surprise and charm you). Take these suggestions seriously: a reader's review of a particular subject as covered herein will be incomplete otherwise. Look at the Index to *Words and Phrases* also.

When in the body of the *Topicon* we mention Indexes (Roman numbered), we mean those in Volume III of EID. To find a Work mentioned, look in *Abbreviations and Dates,* or *Titles Alphabetized.*

Key Words: The size of this work precluded inclusion of an exhaustive Key Words Index. The following section, *Captions, and Their Locations in the Topicon,* meets the need to some extent, and the nearly four thousand entries in the Indexes to Words and Phrases at the back of this volume have their own important utility in locating entries by key word, as well as by character and by idea. If you recall a wooden-legged man stamping along as though pounding in cribbage pegs, but you can't remember more about him, look for "cribbage" in *From the Narration.* Such statements as "I wants to make your flesh creep" will be in *Sayings of The Characters,* but remarks of Esther Summerson BH, Pip GE and other narrators will be in *From the Narration. From the Narration* should be consulted if a particular animal (as, hyena), body-part (as, tonsils and uvula), or other item is not found in the chapter caption lists where first sought. Where we have seen the opportunity, we have used this Index to fulfil more nearly the implication of this volume's slightly facetious title. The chapter caption lists are rich additional sources of key words. At page 1103, there is a Supplementary Index to Key Words, referencing entries in this volume.

(If the reader has Volume III of this series available, he will find "key word" help in the Indexes, particularly Index XI, which refers to works and quotations of others, and the Glossary.)

The Index to Localities has useful Sub-indexes (Battlefields, Castles and Forts; Hostelries; Places of Worship; Prisons; and Theatres) all limited to the historical as opposed to the fictional. Because it attempts to cover the entire *oeuvre,* it can be another way of focussing a misty memory. The two travel books, AN and PI, are independently indexed at pages 1198-1102.

We have supplied epigraphs for each Chapter, usually more than one. Where the reference is cited in brackets, it means that the quotation is elided or otherwise manipulated.

Captions, and Their Locations in the Topicon

Key to Chapters

A	Ages of Man
B	Body
CD	Charles Dickens revealed
F	Fellow Man, in Relation
FL	First and Last Things
H	Humankind, in Activity
IG	Industry and Government
L	London
LC	Letters and Communication
M	Mind
N	Nature
S	Spirit, and Moral Qualities
TP	Three Professions: clergy, law, medical
TT	Transportation and Travel
W	The Rest of the World

Abbreviations and Dates

Every novel, play, story, article, speech, preface, etc., of CD is given an abbreviation, used throughout. In this list, novels and Christmas Books are in chronological order. All other works are in alphabetical order of abbreviation. Page numbers cite locations of entries for the respective works in Volumes I or (beginning at p840) II, except those with a T prefix, which are to this volume. Absence of a page number means either that there is no entry in any of the volumes or (in the case of CHE) that there are many in this one.

			Date	Page
	NOVELS (N)			
PP	The Posthumous Papers of the Pickwick Club	1	1837	161
OT	The Adventures of Oliver Twist	2	1838	230
NN	The Life and Adventures of Nicholas Nickleby	3	1839	309
OCS	The Old Curiosity Shop	4	1841	426
BR	Barnaby Rudge: a Tale of the Riots of 'Eighty	5	1841	469
MC	The Life and Adventures of Martin Chuzzlewit	6	1844	546
DS	Dealings with the Firm of Dombey and Son	7	1847	708
DC	The Personal History of David Copperfield	8	1850	840
BH	Bleak House	9	1853	1044
HT	Hard Times for These Times	10	1854	1149
LD	Little Dorrit	11	1857	1201
TTC	A Tale of Two Cities	12	1859	1340
GE	Great Expectations	13	1861	1437
OMF	Our Mutual Friend	14	1865	1544
MED	The Mystery of Edwin Drood	15	1870	1673
	CHRISTMAS BOOKS (CB)	first collected in one volume	1852	
CC	A Christmas Carol	1	1843	615
C	The Chimes	2	1844	642
CH	The Cricket on the Hearth	3	1845	655
BL	The Battle of Life	4	1846	691
HM	The Haunted Man	5	1848	783
AF	Autobiographical Fragments		1847-49	803
AN	American Notes		1842	522
AN/C	Canada			541
AN/DT	The Democratic Tale of a Shoemaker			545
AN/ES	The East and the South			528
AN/S	Going to America: On Shipboard			526
AN/SI	A Suppressed Introduction			523
AN/SV	Slavery and Violence			542
AN/WM	The West and the Mid-west			536

	ALL THE YEAR ROUND			
AY/B	The Poor Man and His Beer	April 30	1859	1335
AY/C	Five New Points of Criminal Law	September 24	1859	1337
AY/D	Rather a Strong Dose	March 21	1863	1503
AY/DH	A Debt of Honour	June 6	1868	1658
AY/E	An Enlightened Clergyman	March 8	1862	1502
AY/H	Leigh Hunt: A Remonstrance	December 24	1859	1338
AY/K	Robert Keeley	April 10	1869	1644
AY/L	Landor's Life	July 24	1869	1645
AY/M	The Martyr Medium	April 4	1863	1503
AY/N	Address Intimating a New Series of *All the Year Round*	September 19, 26	1868	1650
AY/NS	A Neat Sample of Translation	January 27	1866	1657
AY/OR	Occasional Register (some entries are collaborations)	various dates	1859	1337
AY/Q	A Slight Question of Fact	February 13	1869	1644
AY/S	The Late Mr Stanfield	June 1	1867	1658
AY/T	The Tattlesnivel Bleater	December 31	1859	1338
AY/Y	The Young Man from the Country	March 1	1862	1502
AY/WN	Without a Name	January 21	1860	1339
AYC/C	Between the Cradle and the Grave (w Henry Morley)	February 1	1862	1501
AYC/WM	Working Men's Clubs (w Edmund Ollier)	March 26	1864	1504
	BENTLEY'S MISCELLANY			
B/A1	Address on the Completion of the First Volume of *Bentley's Miscellany*	June	1837	—
B/A2	Address on the Completion of the Second Volume of *Bentley's Miscellany*	November 30	1837	—
B/EG	Extraordinary Gazette: Speech of His Mightiness on Opening the Second Number of *Bentley's Miscellany*	March	1837	—
B/FE	Familiar Epistle from a Parent to a Child	February	1839	277
B/Ml	Full Report on the First Meeting of the Mudfog Association	October	1837	267
B/M2	Full Report on the Second Meeting of the Mudfog Association	September	1838	270
B/L	Some Particulars Concerning a Lion	May	1837	276
B/P	The Pantomime of Life	March	1837	274
B/T	Public Life of Mr Tulrumble, Once Mayor of Mudfog	January	1837	263
B/TA	Theatrical Advertisement: Extraordinary	February	1837	274
BC/RB	Mr Robert Bolton, the "Gentleman connected with the Press"	August	1838	277
CHE	A Child's History of England	January 1851 to October	1853	—
	THE CHRISTMAS STORIES (partial collection 1871)		December	957
CS/CS	The Child's Story	in order of publication, number 4	1852	1022
CS/CT	A Christmas Tree	1	1850	960
CS/DM	Doctor Marigold (includes *To be Taken with a Grain of Salt*)	18	1865	1622
CS/EP	The Perils of Certain English Prisoners	10	1857	1305
CS/GM	The Wreck of the Golden Mary	9	1856	1288
CS/GO	What Christmas Is as We Grow Older	2	1851	1000
CS/GS	Going into Society	11	1858	1320
CS/HH	The Haunted House (includes *The Ghost in Master B's Room*)	12	1859	1372
CS/HL	A House to Let (includes CS/GS)	11	1858	1320
CS/HT	The Holly-Tree (includes *The Boots*)	8	1855	1192
CS/L	Mrs Lirriper's Lodgings	16	1863	1513
CS/LL	Mrs Lirriper's Legacy	17	1864	1513
CS/MJ	Mugby Junction (incl *The Boy at Mugby* and *The Signal-man*)	19	1866	1629
CS/MS	A Message from the Sea	13	1860	1424
CS/NS	Nobody's Story	6	1854	1127
CS/NT	No Thoroughfare (a collaboration with Wilkie Collins)	20	1867	1640
CS/PR	The Poor Relation's Story	3	1852	1020
CS/PT	The Seven Poor Travellers (includes *Richard Doubledick*)	7	1854	1144
CS/SL	Somebody's Luggage (includes two independent stories)	15	1862	1489
CS/SS	The Schoolboy's Story	5	1853	1124
CS/TT	Tom Tiddler's Ground	14	1861	1481

	THE EXAMINER (not otherwise collected)			376
E/AE	An American in Europe	July 21	1849	405
E/AP	The American Panorama	December 16	1848	398
E/BJ	A Truly British Judge	August 19	1848	397
E/C	Central Criminal Court	December 8	1849	409
E/CA	Hoods' *Comic Annual for 1839,* reviewed	February 3	1839	383
E/CB	*The Boy's Country Book,* reviewed	April 7	1839	385
E/CC	Court Ceremonies	December 15	1849	409
E/CJ	The Chinese Junk	June 24	1848	394
E/CP	Capital Punishment	May 5	1849	404
E/DA	Demoralisation and Total Abstinence	October 27	1849	407
E/DC	Cruikshank's 'The Drunkard's Children'	July 8	1848	394
E/EA	Edinburgh Apprentice School Association	December 30	1848	399
E/FB	*The Ages of Female Beauty,* a collaboration reviewed	January 28	1838	381
E/FR	False Reliance	June 2	1849	405
E/IC	International Copyright: a Circular to British Authors	July 16	1842	387
E/I&C	Ignorance and Crime	April 22	1848	393
E/IR	Address/the Committee of the Italian Refugee Fund	September 9	1849	407
E/IV	Ignorance and its Victims	April 29	1848	394
E/JI	Juvenile Imprisonment in the Metropolis	September 16	1843	391
E/JP	Judicial Special Pleading	December 23	1848	399
E/L	Macready's *Lear* at Covent Garden	January 28	1838	382
E/LH	Macready's *Lear* at the Haymarket	October 27	1849	408
E/MB	Macready as 'Benedick'	March 4	1843	390
E/NE	The Niger Expedition	August 19	1848	395
E/NN	*The Night Side of Nature,* by Catherine Crowe	February 26	1848	392
E/PB	*Pierre Bertrand,* play by Frederic Lawrence	December 17	1837	381
E/PS	*The Poetry of Science,* reviewed	December 9	1848	398
E/PT	The Paradise at Tooting	January 20	1849	400
E/QC	The Queen's Coronation	July 1	1838	382
E/R	Rush's Conviction	April 7	1849	402
E/RC	A Recorder's Charge	March 3	1849	401
E/RG	Leech's 'The Rising Generation'	December 30	1848	399
E/S	*Sporting. Edited by Nimrod;* a book review	January 28	1838	381
E/SM	Snoring for the Million	December 24	1842	388
E/SP	Scott and his Publishers (three parts)	September 2, 1838; March 31 and September 29	1839	384
E/TE1	Theatrical Examiner: Serle's *The Maid of Orleans,* etc	December 3	1837	380
E/TE2	Theatrical Examiner: six theatre presentations	July 26	1840	386
E/TE3	Theatrical Examiner: *William Tell, Artaxerxes, Riquet*	December 31	1842	389
E/TE4	Theatrical Examiner: *La Favorita* in English, *Old Parr*	October 21	1843	391
E/TF	The Tooting Farm	January 27	1849	401
E/UO	Report of the Commissioners appointed to inquire into the Condition of the Persons variously engaged in the University of Oxford	June 3	1843	390
E/VD	The Verdict for Drouet	April 21	1849	403
E/VP	Three Verse Parodies	August 7, 14, 21	1841	386
E/VS	*Virginie* and *Black-Eyed Susan*	May 12	1849	404
EC/DH	Drainage and Health of the Metropolis (collaboration)	July 14	1849	405
EC/PC	Prison and Convict Discipline (collaboration)	March 10	1849	402
EC/SC	The Sewers' Commission (collaboration)	August 14	1849	407
GSE	George Silverman's Explanation		1868	1651
HD	Hunted Down		1859	1374
HR	A Holiday Romance		1868	1655
	HOUSEHOLD WORDS (not otherwise collected; largely assembled by B. W. Matz)			
HW/A	Our Almanac	November 24	1855	—
HW/AA	The Fine Arts in Australia (chip)	March 13	1852	—
HW/AP	The Amusements of the People (two parts)	March 30, April 13	1850	924
HW/AV	The Lost Arctic Voyagers (first two parts)	December 2, 9	1854	1141
HW/B	A Card from Mr Booley	May 18	1850	932
HW/BA	The Best Authority	June 20	1857	1305
HW/BS	Betting-Shops	June 26	1852	1012

HW/BV	Mr Booley's View of the Last Lord Mayor's Show	November 30	1850	953
HW/C	Chips (introductory)	July 6, 1850 through February 4	1854	940
HW/CB	A Crisis in the Affairs of Mr John Bull	November 23	1850	952
HW/CM	A Curious Misprint in the 'Edinburgh Review'	August 1	1857	1309
HW/CP	Cheap Patriotism	June 9	1855	1184
HW/DM	The Demeanour of Murderers	June 14	1856	1284
HW/DV	A December Vision	December 14	1850	953
HW/ES	A Narrative of Extraordinary Suffering	July 12	1851	987
HW/ET	Some Account of an Extraordinary Traveller	April 20	1850	928
HW/FC	A Few Conventionalities	June 28	1851	986
HW/FE	Chip: A Free (and Easy) School	December 6	1851	—
HW/FF	Frauds on the Fairies	October 1	1853	1040
HW/FL	Fast and Loose	March 24	1855	1282
HW/FS	The Finishing Schoolmaster	May 17	1851	979
HW/F&S	Fire and Snow	January 21	1854	1131
HW/GA	Gone Astray	August 13	1853	1039
HW/GB	The Great Baby	August 4	1855	1188
HW/GD	Gone to the Dogs	March 10	1855	1180
HW/GF	Gaslight Fairies	February 10	1855	1177
HW/GG	The Ghost of the Cock Lane Ghost Wrong Again (chip)	January 15	1853	—
HW/GH	The 'Good' Hippopotamus	October 12	1850	949
HW/GK	It is Not Generally Known	September 2	1854	1134
HW/GL	The Guild of Literature and Art	May 10	1851	977
HW/H	Homœopathy (chip)	November 15	1851	—
HW/HH	A Haunted House	July 23	1853	1038
HW/HN	The Household Narrative	April 13	1850	—
HW/HW	A Home for Homeless Women	April 23	1853	1033
HW/I	Insularities	January 19	1856	1278
HW/IL	The Individuality of Locomotives (chip)	September 21	1850	—
HW/IM	An Idea of Mine	March 13	1858	1319
HW/JB	Proposals for a National Jest-Book	May 3	1856	1282
HW/JT	The Late Mr Justice Talfourd	March 25	1854	1134
HW/L	The Friend of the Lions	February 2	1856	1280
HW/LE	Legal and Equitable Jokes	September 23	1854	1135
HW/LH	Address in Household Words: a Last Household Word	May 28	1859	1323
HW/LM	Reflections of a Lord Mayor	November 18	1854	1140
HW/LT	Lively Turtle	October 26	1850	951
HW/LW	The Last Words of the Old Year	January 4	1851	956
HW/MB	Mr Bull's Somnambulist	November 25	1854	1140
HW/ME	Murderous Extremes	January 3	1857	1303
HW/MP	The Murdered Person	October 11	1856	1287
HW/NE	Nobody, Somebody, and Everybody	August 30	1856	1286
HW/NY	New Year's Day	January 1	1859	1322
HW/OC	Our Commission	August 11	1855	1189
HW/OL	Old Lamps for New Ones	June 15	1850	937
HW/OP	That Other Public	February 3	1855	1177
HW/OS	On Strike	February 11	1854	1132
HW/P	Personal	June 12	1858	—
HW/PA	Proposals for Amusing Posterity	February 12	1853	1030
HW/PF	Perfect Felicity: in a Bird's Eye View	April 6	1850	928
HW/PP	Pet Prisoners	April 27	1850	929
HW/PW	A Preliminary Word: Address in the First Number of *Household Words*	March 30	1850	924
HW/R	From the Raven in the Happy Family	May 11, June 8, August 24	1850	931
HW/RD	Railway Dreaming	May 10	1856	1283
HW/RS	Railway Strikes	January 11	1851	967
HW/RT	Red Tape	February 15	1851	969
HW/RW	Ready Wit (chip)	February 4	1854	—
HW/S	Supposing (five parts)	April 20, 1850 through February 10	1855	929
HW/SA	Stores for the First of April	March 7	1857	1303
HW/SB	The Spirit Business	May 7	1853	1034
HW/SD	A Slight Depreciation of the Currency	November 3	1855	1190
HW/SG	Where We Stopped Growing	January 1	1853	1028
HW/SI	Chips: The Samaritan Institution	May 16	1857	1304

HW/SL	A Nightly Scene in London	January 26	1856	1279
HW/SP	Sucking Pigs	November 8	1851	995
HW/SR	Smuggled Relations	June 23	1855	1187
HW/SS	The Sunday Screw	June 22	1850	938
HW/SU	A Sleep to Startle Us	March 13	1852	1006
HW/TC	Things that Cannot be Done	October 8	1853	1042
HW/TD	Trading in Death	November 27	1852	1019
HW/TG	Footnote to "Three Graces of Christian Science"	May 20	1854	1134
HW/TH	The Thousand and One Humbugs	April 21, 28, May 5	1855	1182
HW/TM	To Working Men	October 7	1854	1136
HW/TT	The Toady Tree	May 26	1855	1183
HW/U	Please to Leave Your Umbrella	May 1	1858	1320
HW/UN	An Unsettled Neighbourhood	November 11	1854	1139
HW/W?	Why?	March 1	1856	1281
HW/WH	Whole Hogs	August 23	1851	990
HW/WM	The Worthy Magistrate	August 25	1855	1189
HW/WR	Well-Authenticated Rappings	February 20	1858	1319

Collaborations in *HOUSEHOLD WORDS* (largely assembled by Harry Stone)

HWC/AV	The Lost Arctic Voyagers (third part; with Dr John Rae)	December 23	1854	1143
HWC/B	Mr Bendigo Buster on Our National Defences Against Education (with Henry Morley)	December 28	1850	955
HWC/BC	Received: A Blank Child (W. H. Wills)	March 19	1853	1031
HWC/BE	A Black Eagle in a Bad Way (E. C. Grenville Murray and Henry Morley)	November 22	1851	997
HWC/BM	Boys to Mend (Henry Morley)	September 11	1852	1014
HWC/C	Common-Sense on Wheels (W. H. Wills and E. C. Grenville Murray)	April 12	1851	974
HWC/CD	A Curious Dance Round a Curious Tree (W. H. Wills)	January 17	1852	1004
HWC/CF	Cain in the Fields (R. H. Horne)	May 10	1851	977
HWC/D	One Man in a Dockyard (R. H. Horne)	September 6	1851	992
HWC/DB	Drooping Buds (Henry Morley)	April 3	1852	1009
HWC/DD	Doctor Dulcamara, M. P. (Wilkie Collins)	December 18	1858	1321
HWC/DF	Duelling in France (Eliza Lynn)	June 27	1857	1306
HWC/DS	The Tresses of the Day Star (Charles Knight)	June 21	1851	986
HWC/DT	Discovery of a Treasure Near Cheapside (Morley)	November 13	1852	1018
HWC/E	Epsom (W. H. Wills)	June 7	1851	979
HWC/EL	A Bundle of Emigrants' Letters (Caroline Chisholm)	March 30	1850	926
HWC/F	Two Chapters on Bank Note Forgeries: Chapter II (W. H. Wills)	September 21	1850	945
HWC/FE	A Free (and Easy) School (Henry Morley)	November 15	1851	996
HWC/FF	First Fruits (George Augustus Sala)	May 15	1852	1011
HWC/FP	Foreigners' Portraits of Englishmen (W. H. Wills and E. C. Grenville Murray)	September 21	1850	946
HWC/FR	Christmas in the Frozen Regions (Dr. Robert McCormick)	December 21	1850	954
HWC/GE	The Great Exhibition and the Little One (R. H. Horne)	July 5	1851	987
HWC/H	H. W. (Henry Morley)	April 16	1853	1032
HWC/HM	On Her Majesty's Service (E. C. Grenville Murray)	January 7	1854	1130
HWC/I	Idiots (W. H. Wills)	June 4	1853	1036
HWC/IJ	In and Out of Jail (Henry Morley and W. H. Wills)	May 14	1853	1035
HWC/LF	The Royal Literary Fund (Henry Morley)	March 8	1856	1282
HWC/MF	My Mahogany Friend (Mary Boyle)	March 8	1851	970
HWC/ML	The Heart of Mid-London (W. H. Wills)	May 4	1850	930
HWC/MP	The Metropolitan Protectives (W. H. Wills)	April 26	1851	975
HWC/N	North American Slavery (Henry Morley)	September 18	1852	1016
HWC/PA	A Plated Article (Henry Morley)	April 24	1852	1010
HWC/PD	A Popular Delusion (W. H. Wills)	June 1	1850	936
HWC/PG	Plate Glass (W. H. Wills)	February 1	1851	968
HWC/PI	Paris Improved (W. H. Wills)	November 17	1855	1190
HWC/PM	A Paper-Mill (Mark Lemon)	August 31	1850	943
HWC/PO	Post-Office Money-Orders (W. H. Wills)	March 20	1852	1008
HWC/RB	A Clause for the New Reform Bill (Wilkie Collins)	October 9	1858	1320

HWC/RP	By Rail to Parnassus (Henry Morley)	June 16	1855	1186
HWC/S	Spitalfields (W. H. Wills)	April 5	1851	973
HWC/SB	Chips: Small Beginnings (W. H. Wills)	April 5	1851	974
HWC/SN	Shakspeare and Newgate (R. H. Horne)	October 4	1851	992
HWC/T	The Old Lady in Threadneedle Street (W. H. Wills)	July 6	1850	939
HWC/U	My Uncle (W. H. Wills)	December 6	1851	998
HWC/V	Valentine's Day at the Post-Office (W. H. Wills)	March 30	1850	926
HWC/W	The Doom of English Wills (W. H. Wills)	September 28	1850	947
HWC/W2	The Doom of English Wills: Cathedral Number Two (with W. H. Wills)	October 5	1850	948
HWC/WM	Our Wicked Mis-statements (Henry Morley)	January 19	1856	1278
HWC/WR	The Wind and the Rain (Henry Morley)	May 31	1851	979
L	The Lamplighter (farce attempted 1838)		1841	466
LL	"The Life of Our Lord"		1849	793
LML	Lines to Mark Lemon		1851	1121
LT	The Lazy Tour of Two Idle Apprentices	October 3, 10, 17, 25, 31	1857	1293
MC	*THE MORNING CHRONICLE*			132
MC/BF	Buckstone Farce	October 14	1834	135
MC/BH	*Brown's Horse* (review of a burlesque)	January 19	1836	150
MC/BL	Meeting of Birmingham Liberals	November 29	1834	136
MC/C	Colosseum	July 8	1835	143
MC/CF	Grand Colosseum Fete	July 10	1835	143
MC/CN	*The Castilian Noble and the Contrabandista* (drama)	November 4	1835	145
MC/DB	Great Political Dinner at Bath	November 13	1835	146
MC/DS	*Dream of the Sea* (drama review)	November 24	1835	147
MC/E	General Elections in the Metropolis: Essex (Chlmsfrd)	January 13	1835	139
MC/EB1, 2	Express from Bristol: Grand Dinner	November 11 and 12	1835	145
MC/EC	General Elections in the Metropolis: Colchester	January 10	1835	138
MC/EE	General Elections in the Metropolis: Essex (Braintree)	January 12	1835	138
MC/EG1, 2	Reception of Earl Grey	September 17 and 18	1834	134
MC/ES	General Elections in the Metropolis: Sudbury	January 14	1835	140
MC/HH	Calamitous Event at Hatfield House	December 2, 3 and 4	1835	147
MC/JR	Express from Exeter: South Devon Election	May 2	1835	142
MC/KC	*The King's Command* (drama review)	October 27	1835	145
MC/LV	Licensed Victuallers' Charity School	January 22	1836	150
MC/MC	*The Maid of Castile* (drama review)	January 22	1835	142
MC/MN	Melbourne v Norton	June 23	1836	153
MC/NE1,2	Northamptonshire Election (the hustings)	December 16 and 17	1835	148
MC/NE3	Northamptonshire Election (post-election report)	December 19	1835	149
MC/OH	*One Hour; or, a Carnival Ball* (drama review)	January 12	1836	149
MC/R	*Rienzi, the last of the Tribunes* (drama review)	January 4	1836	152
MC/RC	The Reopening of the Colosseum	October 13	1835	144
MC/RD	Great Reform Dinner at Ipswich	May 28	1836	152
MC/RP	*The Rival Pages* (drama review)	October 9	1835	144
MC/S	General Elections in the Metropolis: Suffolk	January 17	1835	140
MC/SS	St Saviour's, Southwark	December 5	1834	137
MC/SW	The Story Without a Beginning	December 18	1834	137
MC/W	The Waterman (drama review)	January 15	1836	150
MC/YK	*The Yellow Kids* (drama review)	October 20	1835	144
MC/Z	*Zarah* (drama review)	September 8	1835	143
MC/ZR	*Zarah* revisited	November 17	1835	146
MGS	Mrs Gamp and the Strollers		1847	703
MHC	*MASTER HUMPHREY'S CLOCK*		1840-41	410
MH/C	The Clock-Case. A Confession found in a Prison in the Time of Charles the Second	April	1840	423
MH/DG	The Deaf Gentleman from his own Apartment	November	1841	T44
MH/F	The Clock-Case. First Night of the Giant Chronicles	April	1840	422
MH/I	The Clock-Case. Introduction to the Giant Chronicles	April	1840	421
MHC	Master Humphrey's Clock (including two Correspondents)	April	1840	412
MH/PT	Mr Pickwick's Tale	May	1840	424
MH/V	Master Humphrey's Visitor	May	1840	—
MH/W	Mr Weller's Watch	June	1840	T44

	MISCELLANEOUS PIECES			
MP/AI	The Agricultural Interest	March 9	1844	636
MP/AP	Introduction to the Legends and Lyrics of Adelaide Anne Procter		1866	1541
MP/CC	Elegy Written in a Country Churchyard (parody)	December 3	1849	802
MP/CE	Crime and Education	February 4	1846	639
MP/CG	Concerning Grimaldi		1838	633
MP/CP	Capital Punishment	Feb 23, 28; March 9, 13, 16	1846	640
MP/CT	Chauncy Hare Townshend		1869	1543
MP/DR	Dramatic Rights in Fiction	January 12	1861	—
MP/EC	The Early Closing Movement	March 28	1844	—
MP/EF	Address of the English Author to the French Public		1857	—
MP/ES	The Earthquake Shock in England	October 8	1863	—
MP/FA	On Mr Fechter's Acting	August	1869	1543
MP/FW	An Appeal to Fallen Women	October	1850	—
MP/JG	Introductory Chapter to Memoirs of Joseph Grimaldi		1838	633
MP/JO	Preface to Evenings of a Working Man, by John Overs		1844	638
MP/LA	Lord Londonderry to Lord Ashley	October 20	1842	636
MP/LB	Preface to The Loving Ballad of Lord Bateman	November	1837	632
MP/LM	Two Letters from "Manlius" to the Morning Chronicle	June 23, 29	1840	634
MP/MC	The Mines and Collieries Bill	July 25	1842	634
MP/PD	Prologue to The Patrician's Daughter		1842	—
MP/PE	Public Executions (two letters to the Times)	November 13, 17	1849	801
MP/PN	Prayer at Night (date uncertain)			—
MP/SC	The Spirit of Chivalry	August	1845	639
MP/TH	Threatening Letter to Thomas Hood, from an Ancient Gentleman	May	1844	634
MP/WH	Women in the Home (a revision of Angela Burdett Coutts's work?)		1856	—
MP/WM	The Great International Walking-Match	February	1868	1542
MP/WT	In Memoriam: W. M. Thackeray	February	1864	1540
	PLAYS			
P/L	The Lamplighter [never performed; *see* L]		1838	—
P/O'T	O'Thello [the Moor is an Irishman; only fragments survive]		1828	—
P/SG	The Strange Gentleman		1836	227
P/SR	The Stratagems of Rozanza, a "Venetian comedietta" [not extant]		1826?	—
P/VC	The Village Coquettes		1836	228
P/W?	Is She his Wife? or, Something Singular!		1837	229
PC/FD	The Frozen Deep (collaboration with Wilkie Collins)		1856	1121
PC/ND	Mr Nightingale's Diary (with Mark Lemon)		1851	1120
PC/NT	No Thoroughfare (with Wilkie Collins)		1867-8	1123
PI	Pictures from Italy		1846	669
PI/D	Diorama			687
PI/F	France			671
PI/G	Genoa and the North of Italy			675
PI/R	To Rome			682
RD	To be Read at Dusk		1852	1024
RLF	The Case of the Reformers in the Literary Fund		1858	1324
	REPRINTED PIECES (from *Household Words;* different original titles in brackets)			
	These pieces, together with five CS, were collected and published in		1858	
RP/AT	The Artful Touch	September 14	1850	944
RP/B	Our Bore	October 9	1852	1016
RP/BL	The Begging-Letter Writer	May 18	1850	933
RP/BM	"Births. Mrs. Meek, of a Son"	February 22	1851	969
RP/BS	Bill-sticking	March 22	1851	972
RP/DF	On Duty with Inspector Field	June 14	1851	982
RP/DP	The Detective Police [A Detective Police Party]	July 27, August 10	1850	941
RP/DS	A Child's Dream of a Star	April 6	1850	927
RP/DT	Down with the Tide	February 5	1853	1029
RP/EW	Our English Watering-Place [Our Watering-Place]	August 2	1851	989
RP/F	A Flight	August 30	1851	991
RP/FF	A Monument of French Folly	March 8	1851	971

RP/FW	Our French Watering-Place	November 4	1854	1136
RP/GA	The Ghost of Art	July 20	1850	940
RP/HF	Our Honourable Friend	July 31	1852	1013
RP/LA	Lying Awake	October 30	1852	1018
RP/LV	The Long Voyage	December 31	1853	1042
RP/NS	The Noble Savage	June 11	1853	1037
RP/OS	Out of Season [Out of the Season]	June 28	1856	1285
RP/OT	Out of Town	September 29	1855	1189
RP/PB	Prince Bull. A Fairy Tale	February 17	1855	1179
RP/PG	The Pair of Gloves	September 14	1850	943
RP/S	Our School	October 11	1851	993
RP/TP	Poor Man's Tale of a Patent	October 19	1850	949
RP/TS	The Sofa	September 14	1850	944
RP/V	Our Vestry	August 28	1852	1014
RP/WW	A Walk in a Workhouse	May 25	1850	935

	SPEECHES (as collected and dated, and mostly as captioned, in KFS in 1960)			seqnce
S/A1	Artists' Benevolent Fund: London [brief acknowledgment]	May 12	1838	2
S/A2	Artists' Benevolent Society [not reported]	May 11	1844	21
S/A3	Artists' Benevolent Fund	May 8	1858	75
S/A4	Artists' General Benevolent Fund	March 29	1862	87
S/AR	Administrative Reform Association: London	June 27	1855	55
S/B	At a Reading of *A Christmas Carol:* Bradford	December 28	1854	49
S/B1	Young Men of Boston: Banquet in His Honour	February 1	1842	8
S/B2	Farewell Reading in Boston	April 8	1868	107
S/BA	At a Reading for the Bristol Athenaeum [brief ackn]	January 19	1858	68
S/BM1	At a Reading of the *Carol:* Birmingham and Midland Institute	December 30	1853	48
S/BM2	Birmingham and Midland Institute: Annual Inaugural Meeting	September 27	1869	112
S/BM3	Birmingham and Midland Institute Prize-Giving	January 6	1870	113
S/BP	Conversazione: Birmingham Polytechnic Institution	February 28	1844	19
S/BS	Presentation to Dickens and Banquet to Literature and Art: Birmingham Society of Artists	January 6	1853	44
S/C	Presentation and Banquet in His Honour at Coventry	December 4	1858	80
S/CH	Presentation to Captain Hewett [of the *Britannia*]	January 29	1842	7
S/CL	Meeting for the Removal of Trade Restrictions on the Commerce of Literature [brief ackn]	May 4	1852	40
S/CM1	Lecture by A. H. Layard for the Chatham Mechanics' Institute [brief ackn]	April 17	1860	83
S/CM2	Reading: Chatham Mechanics' Institute [brief ackn]	December 18	1860	84
S/CM3	Reading: Chatham Mechanics' Institute [brief ackn]	January 16	1862	86
S/CT1	Commercial Travellers' Schools	December 30	1854	50
S/CT2	Commercial Travellers' Schools	December 22	1859	81
S/DC	Meeting for the Foundation of the Royal Dramatic College	July 21	1858	77
S/DD	Charitable Society for the Deaf and Dumb [brief ackn]	May 23	1843	15
S/DH	Dinner at Hartford in His Honour	February 7	1842	9
S/DM	Dramatic, Equestrian and Musical Sick Fund	February 14	1866	99
S/DP	Meeting of the Dramatic Profession on Dulwich College	March 13	1856	58
S/E	Public Dinner in Edinburgh in His Honour	June 25	1841	6
S/EP	At a Reading of the *Carol* for the Edinburgh Philosophical Institution [brief ackn]	March 26	1858	71
S/FB	Farewell Banquet Before Visit to the United States	November 2	1867	104
S/FD	After a Performance of *The Frozen Deep* [brief ackn]	August 24	1857	66
S/FR	The Farewell Reading	March 15	1870	114
S/GA	First Annual *Soirée* of the Glasgow Athenæum	December 28	1847	26
S/GB	Governesses' Benevolent Institution	April 20	1844	20
S/GI1	Gardeners' Benevolent Institution: London	June 9	1851	37
S/GI2	Gardeners' Benevolent Institution	June 14	1852	41
S/GL1	Banquet to Guild of Literature and Art: Manchester	August 31	1852	42
S/GL2	After the Opening of the Houses for the Guild of Literature and Art: Knebworth	July 21	1865	97
S/GS	Royal Geographical Society [brief ackn]	May 25	1857	64
S/H	Royal Free Hospital	May 6	1863	91

S/HC	Hospital for Consumption and Diseases of the Chest	May 6	1843	14
S/HI1	Royal Hospital for Incurables	June 5	1856	60
S/HI2	Royal Hospital for Incurables	May 21	1857	63
S/J	After Reading the *Carol*: Manchester [brief ackn]	July 31	1857	65
S/L	*Soirée* of the Liverpool Mechanics' Institution	February 26	1844	18
S/LB	Banquet in His Honour at St George's Hall, Liverpool	April 10	1869	110
S/LC	Prize-giving of the Institutional Association of Lancashire and Cheshire: Manchester	December 3	1858	79
S/LF1	Literary Fund: Anniversary Festival	May 8	1837	1
S/LF2	Literary Fund: Anniversary Festival [not reported]	May 12	1841	5
S/LF3	Royal Literary Fund: Annual General Meeting	March 14	1855	51
S/LF4	Royal Literary Fund: Special General Meeting	June 16	1855	54
S/LF5	Royal Literary Fund: Annual General Meeting	Marh 12	1856	57
S/LF6	Royal Literary Fund: Annual General Meeting	March 11	1857	61
S/LF7	Royal Literary Fund: Annual General Meeting	March 10	1858	70
S/LM	*Soirée* of the Leeds Mechanics' Institution	December 1	1847	25
S/LS	Southwark Literary and Scientific Institution	December 2	1840	4
S/M	Royal Society of Musicians	March 8	1860	82
S/M1	Banquet in Honour of W. C. Macready [not reported]	July 20	1839	3
S/M2	Banquet in Honour of W. C. Macready	March 1	1851	34
S/MA	First Annual *Soirée* of the Manchester Athenæum	October 5	1843	17
S/MF	Opening of the Manchester Free Library	September 2	1852	43
S/MH1	Banquet at the Mansion House: London [brief ackn]	July 7	1849	30
S/MH2	Banquet at the Mansion House [brief ackn]	May 2	1853	47
S/MH3	Banquet at the Mansion House	April 1	1861	85
S/MH4	Banquet at the Mansion House [unreported]	January 16	1866	98
S/N1	Newsvendors' Benevolent Institution: London	November 21	1849	31
S/N2	Newsvendors' Benevolent Institution	January 27	1852	38
S/N3	Newsvendors' Benevolent Institution	May 21	1855	53
S/N4	Newsvendors' Benevolent Institution	May 20	1862	88
S/N5	Newsvendors' Benevolent Institution	May 9	1865	95
S/N6	Newsvendors' Benevolent Institution	April 5	1870	115
S/NP	Newspaper Press Fund	May 20	1865	96
S/NY1	Banquet in His Honour: New York	February 18	1842	10
S/NY2	New York Farewell Dinner	April 18	1868	108
S/NY3	Farewell Reading in New York	April 20	1868	109
S/OH	Oxford and Harvard Boat Race Dinner: Sydenham	August 30	1869	111
S/P	Before a Reading in Providence, R. I. [brief ackn]	February 20	1868	106
S/PP1	Printers' Pension Society: London	April 4	1843	13
S/PP2	Printers' Pension Society	April 6	1864	92
S/PR	Playground and General Recreation Society:London	June 1	1858	76
S/PRA	Printers' Readers' Association: London	September 17	1867	103
S/R	Railway Benevolent Society	June 5	1867	102
S/RA1	Royal Academy Banquet [brief ackn]	April 30	1853	46
S/RA2	Royal Academy Banquet [brief ackn]	May 1	1858	74
S/RA3	Royal Academy Banquet (collected in 1988 reissue of KFS)	May 3	1862	88
S/RA4	Royal Academy Banquet [CD's last speech]	April 30	1870	116
S/RC	Metropolitan Rowing Clubs: London	May 7	1866	101
S/RE	At Two Readings at Edinburgh [brief ackn]	September 27and 28	1858	78
S/RP	At the First Reading for His Own Profit: London	April 29	1858	73
S/RS	'Social Supper' in His Honour: Richmond	March 18	1842	12
S/S1	The Sanatorium: London [brief ackn]	June 29	1843	16
S/S2	The Sanatorium	June 4	1844	22
S/SA1	Metropolitan Sanitary Association: London	February 6	1850	32
S/SA2	Metropolitan Sanitary Association	May 10	1851	36
S/SC	Hospital for Sick Children	February 9	1858	69
S/SM	After a Reading of the *Carol:* Sheffield Mechanics' Institute [brief ackn]	December 22	1855	56
S/SS	Meeting for the Establishment of the Shakespeare Foundation Schools	May 11	1864	94
S/TF1	General Theatrical Fund: London	April 6	1846	23
S/TF2	General Theatrical Fund	March 29	1847	24
S/TF3	General Theatrical Fund	April 17	1848	27
S/TF4	General Theatrical Fund	May 21	1849	28

S/TF5	General Theatrical Fund	March 25	1850	33
S/TF6	General Theatrical Fund	April 14	1851	35
S/TF7	General Theatrical Fund	April 5	1852	39
S/TF8	Royal General Theatrical Fund	March 22	1853	45
S/TF9	Royal General Theatrical Fund	April 2	1855	52
S/TF10	Royal General Theatrical Fund	March 17	1856	59
S/TF11	Royal General Theatrical Fund	April 6	1857	62
S/TF12	Royal General Theatrical Fund	March 29	1858	72
S/TF13	Royal General Theatrical Fund	April 4	1863	90
S/TF14	Royal General Theatrical Fund	March 28	1866	100
S/UH	University College Hospital	April 12	1864	93
S/UL	United Law Clerks' Society: London	June 19	1849	29
S/W1	Private Dinner in His Honour: Washington	March 14	1842	11
S/W2	First and Farewell Readings: Washington [no report]	February 3, 7	1868	105
S/WC	Warehousemen and Clerks' Schools	November 5	1857	67

	SKETCHES BY BOZ (different original titles in brackets)			page
SB/A	Astley's	May 9	1835	38
SB/B	The Beadle. The Parish Engine. The Schoolmaster.	February 28	1835	7
SB/BC	The Bloomsbury Christening	April	1834	124
SB/BH	The Boarding-House	May and August	1834	87
SB/BM	The Broker's Man	July 28	1835	13
SB/BS	Broker's and Marine-store Shops	December 15	1834	59
SB/BV	The Black Veil		1836	107
SB/C	The Curate The Old Lady The Half-pay Captain.	May 19	1835	8
SB/CC	The Criminal Courts [Old Bailey]	October 23	1835	62
SB/CD	A Christmas Dinner	December 27	1835	69
SB/DA	The Dancing Academy	October 11	1835	77
SB/DC	Doctors' Commons	October 11	1836	34
SB/DD	The Drunkard's Death		1837	130
SB/EB	The Election for Beadle	July 14	1835	11
SB/EC	Early Coaches	February 19	1835	46
SB/EE	Miss Evans and the Eagle	October 4	1835	71
SB/FM	The First of May [A Little Talk about Spring and the Sweeps]	May 31	1836	57
SB/FS	The Four Sisters	June 18	1835	10
SB/GF	Greenwich Fair	April 16	1835	40
SB/GS	Gin-shops	February 7	1835	59
SB/HC	Hackney-coach Stands	January 31	1835	32
SB/HP	The Hospital Patient	August 6	1835	73
SB/HS	Horatio Sparkins	February	1834	104
SB/JD	The Misplaced Attachment of Mr John Dounce [Love and Oysters]	November 25	1835	74
SB/JP	Mrs Joseph Porter	January	1834	116
SB/LC	The Last Cab-driver; the First Omnibus Cad [Hackney Cabs and their Drivers: September 17, 1836; Some Account of an Omnibus Cad: November 1, 1835]		1835	49
SB/LR	London Recreations	March 17	1835	35
SB/LS	The Ladies' Socictics	August 20	1835	14
SB/MC	Mr Minns and his Cousin [A Dinner at Poplar Walk]	December	1833	93
SB/MM	The Mistaken Milliner [The Vocal Dressmaker]	November 22	1835	76
SB/MN	Making a Night of it	October 18	1835	81
SB/MS	Meditations in Monmouth Street	October 11	1836	30
SB/NN	Our Next-door Neighbour	March 18	1836	15
SB/NY	The New Year	January 3	1836	70
SB/O	Omnibuses	September 26	1834	48
SB/P	A Parliamentary Sketch	March 7 and April 11	1835	52
SB/PD	Public Dinners	April 7	1835	54
SB/PO	The Parlour Orator	December 13	1835	72
SB/PS	The Pawnbroker's Shop	June 30	1835	60
SB/PT	Private Theatres	August 11	1835	43
SB/PV	The Prisoners' Van	November 19	1835	83
SB/R	The River	June 6	1835	37
SB/S	Sentiment	June 7	1834	96

SB/SD	Seven Dials	September 27	1835	28
SB/SE	The Steam Excursion	October	1834	109
SB/SG	Shabby-genteel People	November 5	1834	80
SB/SM	The Streets—Morning	July 21	1835	22
SB/SN	The Streets—Night	January 17	1836	24
SB/ST	Shops and their Tenants	October 10	1834	26
SB/SY	Scotland Yard	October 4	1836	27
SB/TP	Thoughts about People	April 23	1835	67
SB/TR	The Tuggses at Ramsgate	March 31	1836	99
SB/VG	Vauxhall Gardens by Day	October 26	1835	45
SB/V	A Visit to Newgate		1836	64
SB/WD	The Great Winglebury Duel		1836	114
SB/WT	A Passage in the Life of Mr Watkins Tottle	January, February	1835	120
STH	Sunday under Three Heads		1836	155
SH/AI	As It Is			157
SH/MM	As It Might Be Made			160
SH/SB	As Sabbath Bills Would Make It			159
SYC	Sketches of Young Couples (see YC/ below)		1840	294
SYG	Sketches of Young Gentlemen (see YG/ below)		1838	278

THE UNCOMMERCIAL TRAVELLER (from *All the Year Round;* different original titles in brackets) published in three volumes in 1860, 1863 and 1875

UT/AB	On an Amateur Beat [An Amateur Beat]	February 27	1869	1629
UT/AH	Titbull's Alms-houses	October 24	1863	1525
UT/AL	Arcadian London [London out of Season]	September 29	1860	1420
UT/AS	Aboard Ship [New Uncommercial Traveller]	December 5	1868	1664
UT/B	Mr Barlow	January 16	1869	1668
UT/BB	The Boiled Beef of New England	August 15	1863	1521
UT/BC	Birthday Celebrations	June 6	1865	1512
UT/C	Chambers	August 18	1860	1416
UT/CA	The City of the Absent	July 18	1863	1518
UT/CD	Chatham Dockyard	August 29	1863	1521
UT/CM	The Calais Night Mail	May 2	1863	1508
UT/DH	A Little Dinner in an Hour	January 2	1869	1668
UT/D	Dullborough Town	June 30	1860	1413
UT/FF	In the French-Flemish Country	September 12	1863	1522
UT/FL	A Fly-leaf in a Life	May 22	1869	1671
UT/GL	His General Line of Business	January 28	1860	1392
UT/GT	The Great Tasmania's Cargo	April 21	1860	1402
UT/IP	The Italian Prisoner	October 13	1860	1423
UT/LC	City of London Churches	May 5	1860	1403
UT/MJ	Poor Mercantile Jack	March 10	1860	1396
UT/MM	Medicine Men of Civilisation	September 26	1863	1524
UT/NS	Nurse's Stories	September 8	1860	1419
UT/NW	Night Walks	July 21	1860	1414
UT/PA	A Plea for Total Abstinence	June 5	1869	1672
UT/R	The Ruffian	October 10	1868	1663
UT/RM	Some Recollections of Mortality	May 16	1863	1509
UT/RT	Refreshments for Travellers	March 24	1860	1398
UT/S	The Shipwreck	January 28	1860	1392
UT/SC	An Old Stage-Coaching House	August 1	1863	1519
UT/SE	A Small Star in the East	December 19	1868	1665
UT/SL	Bound for the Great Salt Lake	July 4	1863	1515
UT/SN	Shy Neighbourhoods	May 26	1860	1406
UT/ST	The Short-timers	June 20	1863	1514
UT/T	Tramps	June 16	1860	1409
UT/TA	Travelling Abroad	April 7	1860	1399
UT/TV	Two Views of a Cheap Theatre	February 25	1860	1395
UT/W	Wapping Workhouse	February 18	1860	1394

	SKETCHES OF YOUNG COUPLES	sequence no.	1840	294
YC/C	The Contradictory Couple	4		299
YC/D	The Couple who Dote upon their Children	5		300
YC/E	The Egotistical Couple	9		305
YC/F	The Formal Couple	2		297
YC/H	The Couple who Coddle Themselves	10		306
YC/I	The Cool Couple	6		302
YC/L	The Loving Couple	3		298
YC/N	The Nice Little Couple	8		303
YC/O	The Old Couple	11		307
YC/P	The Plausible Couple	7		302
YC/R	Remonstrance (Introduction)	0		296
YC/X	Conclusion	0		—
YC/Y	The Young Couple	1		296

	SKETCHES OF YOUNG GENTLEMEN	sequence no.	1838	278
YG/B	The Bashful Young Gentleman	1		279
YG/C	The Censorious Young Gentleman	7		287
YG/D	The Domestic Young Gentleman	6		285
YG/F	The Funny Young Gentleman	8		288
YG/M	The Military Young Gentleman	4		283
YG/O	The Out-and-Out Young Gentleman	2		281
YG/P	The Political Young Gentleman	5		285
YG/T	The Theatrical Young Gentleman	9		288
YG/TO	The "Throwing-off" Young Gentleman	11		291
YG/V	The Poetical Young Gentleman	10		289
YG/VF	The Very Friendly Young Gentleman	3		282
YG/YL	The Young Ladies' Young Gentleman	12		292

Titles Alphabetized

Speeches are not included, but the story-interludes in PP, NN and the Christmas Stories are here. Page references are to Volumes I or (beginning at p840) II of *Everyone in Dickens.*

Bibliographic References

The following are the principal works we consulted in preparing *Windows into® Dickens* (four volumes to date). They are occasionally cited below. As with CD's works, we have used a shorthand abbreviation scheme.

ADFN Dunkling, Leslie and Gosling, William; eds. *New American Dictionary of First Names.* New York: Signet paperback [1983]

AYR/O Oppenlander, Ella Anne, ed. *Dickens' All the Year Round: Descriptive Index and Contributor List.* Troy, N.Y.: Whitston Publishing Co., 1984

B Brightfield, Myron F. *Victorian England in its Novels (1840-1870).* Los Angeles: University of California Library, 1968 (not published, but issued in 50 photocopied sets of the typescript, and consulted at the British Library, London)

BSB Bentley, Nicolas; Slater, Michael; and Burgis, Nina. *The Dickens Digest.* Oxford and New York: Oxford University Press, 1988

CN/AYR *Christmas Numbers from "All the Year Round," conducted by Charles Dickens.* London: 26, Wellington Street, Strand, W. C. and Messrs. Chapman and Hall, 193, Piccadilly, W. (undated; about 1868)

D *The Dickensian,* 1905-date; various editors, currently Malcolm Andrews; The Dickens Fellowships, Dickens House, London

deF de Fontaine, F. G. *A Cyclopedia of the Best Thoughts of Charles Dickens.* New York: E. J. Hale & Son, 1873

DP Paroissien, David, ed. *Selected Letters of Charles Dickens.* Boston: Twayne Publishers, 1985

DW Dickens, Cedric Charles; and Watts, Alan, eds. *The Sayings of Charles Dickens.* London: Gerald Duckworth & Co., Ltd., 1995

EJ Johnson, Edgar. *Charles Dickens: His Tragedy and Triumph.* 2 vols. New York: Simon and Schuster, 1952

FGK Kitton, F. G. *The Minor Writings of Charles Dickens.* London: E. Stock, 1900

FK Kaplan, Fred. *Dickens: A Biography.* New York: William Morrow, 1988

FKM —ed. *Charles Dickens' Book of Memoranda.* New York: The New York Public Library [c1981]

FS Dickens, Charles. The complete novels and Christmas Books. London: The Folio Society, 1981-88 (introductions by Christopher Hibbert)

GC Guiliano, Edward; and Collins, Philip; eds. *The Annotated Dickens.* 2 vols. New York: Clarkson N. Potter [c1986]

GCVA Chesterton, Gilbert Keith. *The Victorian Age in Literature.* New York: Henry Holt & Co., 1913

GKC —*Criticisms and Appreciations of the Works of Charles Dickens.* London: J. M. Dent & Sons Ltd., 1911

GS — Stewart, Garrett. *Death Sentences: Styles of Dying in British Fiction.* Cambridge, MA: Harvard University Press [c1984]

HMCD — *The Writings of Charles Dickens.* New York: Houghton Mifflin, 1894. Edwin Percy Whipple ("and others") provided critical and bibliographical introductions and notes; indexes by Gilbert A. Pierce and William A. Wheeler

HS — Stone, Harry, ed. *Charles Dickens' Uncollected Writings from Household Words 1850-1859.* 2 vols. Bloomington and London: Indiana University Press [c1968]

HSN — —ed. *Dickens' Working Notes for His Novels.* Chicago: University of Chicago [c1987]

HW/L — Lohrli, Anne, comp. *Household Words: Table of Contents, List of Contributors and their Contributions; based on the Household Words Office Book.* Toronto: University of Toronto Press, 1973

JC — Cook, James, ed. *Bibliography of the Writings of Charles Dickens, with many curious and interesting Particulars relating to His Works.* London: Frank Kerslake, 1879

JF — Forster, John. *The Life of Charles Dickens.* 3 vols. London: Chapman and Hall, 1872-1874

KFS — Fielding, K. J., ed. *The Speeches of Charles Dickens.* Oxford: Clarendon Press, 1960 [reissued with new frontmatter 1988]

LCD — *The London of Charles Dickens.* Speldhurst, Kent: Midas Books, 1979; first published 1970 by the London Transport Executive and Midas Books, with the assistance of the Dickens Fellowship, Doughty Street, London (John Greaves, Secretary and Mrs Gwen Major)

MA — Andrews, Malcolm. *Dickens and the Grown-up Child.* Iowa City: University of Iowa Press [c1994]

MMH — Hardwick, Michael and Mollie. *The Charles Dickens Encyclopedia.* New York and London: Scribners [c1973]

MS/DW — Slater, Michael. *Dickens and Women.* Stanford, CA: Stanford University Press [c1983]

MP — Charles Dickens. *Miscellaneous Papers from 'The Morning Chronicle', 'The Daily News', 'The Examiner', 'Household Words', 'All the Year Round', etc., as collected by B. M. Matz;* 2 vols. Millwood, N.Y.: Kraus Reprint, 1983

ND — Waugh, Arthur; Walpole, Hugh; Dexter, Walter; and Hatton, Thomas; eds. *The Nonesuch Edition of the complete works of Charles Dickens.* Bloomsbury. 16 vols, 1937-1938

NDP — *Nonesuch Dickensiana: Retrospectus and Prospectus: The Nonesuch Dickens.* Bloomsbury: The Nonesuch Press, 1937

OID — *The Oxford Illustrated Dickens.* Oxford and New York: Oxford University Press, first printing, 1936

PA — Ackroyd, Peter. *Dickens.* New York: HarperCollins, 1990

PE — House, Madeline; Storey, Graham; Tillotson, Kathleen; Fielding, K. J.; Burgis, Nina; and Easson, Angus; eds (to date). *The Pilgrim Edition of The Letters of Charles Dickens (1820-1855)* 7 vols. (to date). Oxford: Clarendon Press, 1965-1993

PF — Fitzgerald, Percy. *Memories of Charles Dickens: with an account of "Household Words," and "All the Year Round" and of the Contributors Thereto.* Bristol: Arrowsmith, 1913

QC — Quiller-Couch, Sir Arthur. *Charles Dickens and Other Victorians.* New York: G. P. Putnam's Sons, 1925

Many authors entertain, not only a foolish, but a really dishonest objection to acknowledge the sources from whence they derive much valuable information. We have no such feeling. We are merely endeavouring to discharge, in an upright manner, the responsible duties of our editorial functions; and whatever fantastical ambition we might have felt under other circumstances to lay claim to a creative role in connection with what follows, a regard for truth forbids us to do more than claim the merits of judicious arrangement and impartial commentary. The labours of another have raised for us an immense reservoir of important facts. We merely lay them on, and communicate them, in a clear and gentle stream, through the medium of these entries, to a world thirsting for Dickensian knowledge.

The Editor

[PP 4]

Ages of Man

From morning to night, as from the cradle to the grave, is but a succession of changes so gentle and easy, that we can scarcely mark their progress.

NN 22

"Three-score-and-ten's the mark; and no man with a conscience, and a proper sense of what's expected of him, has any business to live longer."

MC 11

Last Lines of Death: chronologically, all 185 fictional deaths in Dickens

Character	Work	Year
Grandmother	SB/BM	35
Mother	SB/BM	35
William	SB/NN	35
Patient	SB/HP	35
Hanged boy	SB/BV	35
Watkins Tottle	SB/WT	35
Warden	SB/DD	36
Chambers occupant	PP	36
Another	PP	36
Bardell	PP	36
Susan Weller	PP	36
Chancery prisoner	PP	36
Pantomime clown	PP	36
Mrs Edmunds	PP	36
Edmunds	PP	36
Madman's wife	PP	36
Poor child	PP	36
Mrs Bayton	OT	36
Sally	OT	36
Nancy	OT	36
Bill Sikes	OT	36
Bull's-eye	OT	37
White waistcoat man	OT	37
Dick	OT	37
Harvey children	YC/O	37
Anne	YC/O	37
Crofts forbear	YC/O	37
Nicholas Nickleby sr	NN	37
Dorker	NN	37
Dockworker	NN	37
Lord Verisopht	NN	37
Walter Bray	NN	37
Smike	NN	37
Ralph Nickleby	NN	37
Arthur Gride	NN	37
Sir Mulberry Hawk	NN	37
Alice of York	NN	37
Hugh Graham	MH/I	37
Master Humphrey	MH/DG	37
Jinkinson	MH/W	37
Hairdresser	MH/W	38
Nephew	MH/C	38
Harry	OCS	38
A little brother	OCS	38
Daniel Quilp	OCS	38
Nell Trent	OCS	38
Nell's grandfather	OCS	38
Stagg	BR	38
Ned Dennis	BR	38
Hugh	BR	38
Rioter	BR	38
Sir John Chester	BR	38
Sir George Gordon	BR	38
Gashford	BR	38
John Willet	BR	38
Anthony Chuzzlewit	MC	39
Tigg Montague	MC	39
Jonas Chuzzlewit	MC	39
Ebenezer Scrooge	CC	39
Deedles	C	39
Lilian Fern	C	39
Craggs	BL	39
Fanny Dombey	DS	39
Paul Dombey	DS	39
Mrs Skewton	DS	39
James Carker	DS	39
Alice Marwood	DS	40
David Copperfield sr	DC	40
Joe Peggotty	DC	40
Tom (Em'ly's father)	DC	40
Clara Copperfield	DC	40
Baby Murdstone	DC	40
Last occupant	DC	40
Barkis	DC	40
Francis Spenlow	DC	40
Dora Copperfield	DC	40
Jip	DC	40
Ham Peggotty	DC	40
James Steerforth	DC	40
A sister	RP/DS	40
A baby	RP/DS	41
A mother	RP/DS	41
Maiden daughter	RP/DS	41
The child, a man	RP/DS	41
A child	CS/CS	41
A wife	CS/CS	41
A twin brother	RD	41
Miss Barbary	BH	41
Tom Jarndyce	BH	41
Lady Dedlock	BH	41
Brickmaker's baby	BH	41
Peffer	BH	41
Captain Hawdon	BH	41
Mrs Turveydrop	BH	41
Neckett	BH	42
Tinker	BH	42
Krook	BH	42
Gridley	BH	42
Jo	BH	42
Tulkinghorn	BH	42
Lady Honoria	BH	42
Harold Skimpole	BH	42
Richard Carstone	BH	42
A wife and child	CS/NS	42
Captain Taunton	CS/PT	42
Mrs Gradgrind	HT	42
Stephen Blackpool	HT	42
Gordon	HT	42
Bounderby	HT	42
Bob Tample	HT	42
Henri Barronneau	LD	43
Mme Rigaud	LD	43
Lillie Meagles	LD	43
Gowan, sr	LD	43
Finching	LD	43
General	LD	43
Lion	LD	43
William Dorrit	LD	43
Frederick Dorrit	LD	43
Merdle	LD	43
Clennam's mother	LD	43
Clennam, sr	LD	43
Blandois	LD	44
Mrs Clennam	LD	44
Tip Dorrit	LD	44
Lucy Atherfield	CS/GM	44
Mrs Arthur Holliday	LT	44
Ellen's mother	LT	44
Ellen	LT	44
A lover murdered	LT	44
Murderer, hanged	LT	44
Charker	CS/EP	45
Mrs Venning	CS/EP	45
Christian King	CS/EP	45
Mr Chops	CS/GS	45
The Kirklands	CS/HL	45
George Forley	CS/HL	45
Gaspard's child	TTC	45
St Evrémonde	TTC	45
Bastille commander	TTC	45
Mob victims	TTC	45
Foulon	TTC	45
Foulon's son-in-law	TTC	46
Mme Defarge br'thr	TTC	46
Mme Defarge sister	TTC	46
Madame Defarge	TTC	46
Seamstress	TTC	46
Sydney Carton	TTC	46
Miss Niner	HD	46
Julius Slinkton	HD	46
Murderer's bride	UT/NS	46
Captain Murderer	UT/NS	46
Wopsle's great-aunt	GE	46
Mrs Joe Gargery	GE	46
Arthur Havisham	GE	47
Murdered woman	GE	47
Compeyson	GE	47
Magwitch	GE	47
Miss Havisham	GE	47
Bill Barley	GE	47
Bentley Drummle	GE	47
Cpl Théophile	CS/SL	47
Lirriper	CS/L	47
Peggy Edson	CS/L	47
Edson	CS/LL	47
Harmon daughter	OMF	48
Another	OMF	48
Harmon	OMF	48
Gaffer Hexam	OMF	48
Johnny	OMF	48
George Radfoot	OMF	48
Betty Higden	OMF	48
Cleaver (Mr Dolls)	OMF	48
Bradley Headstone	OMF	48
Rogue Riderhood	OMF	48
Sophy Marigold	CS/DM	48
Mrs Marigold	CS/DM	48
The Signal-man	CS/MJ	48
Walter Wilding	CS/NT	49
Jules Obenreizer	CS/NT	49
Ethelinda Sapsea	MED	49

The Children at Their Cousin's Grave OCS

Adolescence

" . . . the eldest son, a boy of fourteen years old, who was evidently trying to look as if he did not belong to the family . . . waxed indignant, and remonstrated in no very gentle terms on the gross impropriety of having his name repeated in so loud a voice at a public place, on which all the children laughed very heartily, and one of the little boys wound up by expressing his opinion, that 'George began to think himself quite a man now,' whereupon both pa and ma laughed too; and George (who carried a dress cane and was cultivating whiskers) muttered that 'William always was encouraged in his impertinence;' and assumed a look of profound contempt, which lasted the whole evening . . . .

" . . . the whole party seemed quite happy, except the exquisite in the back of the box, who, being too grand to take any interest in the children, and too insignificant to be taken notice of by anybody else, occupied himself, from time to time, in rubbing the place where the whiskers ought to be, and was completely alone in his glory." SB/A

Ancestry

—absence: "'I have only one thing more to say to you, Mr Harthouse . . . . You are a man of family. Don't you deceive yourself by supposing for a moment that I am a man of family. I am a bit of dirty riff-raff, and a genuine scrap of tag, rag, and bobtail.'

"If anything could have exalted Jem's interest in Mr Bounderby, it would have been this very circumstance. Or, so he told him.

"'So now,' said Bounderby, 'we may shake hands on equal terms. I say, equal terms, because although I know what I am, and the exact depth of the gutter I have lifted myself out of, better than any man does, I am as proud as you are. I am just as proud as you are.'" HT ii 2

—in a castle: "The Baron Von Koëldwethout, of Grogzwig in Germany . . . lived in an old castle; for what German baron ever lived in a new one? . . one of the baron's ancestors, being short of money, had inserted a dagger in a gentleman who called one night to ask his way . . . the baron's ancestor, who was an amiable man, felt very sorry afterwards for having been so rash, and laying violent hands upon a quantity of stone and timber which belonged to a weaker baron, built a chapel as an apology, and so took a receipt from Heaven, in full of all demands." NN 6

—checkered past: "Strangers of limited information and dull apprehension were sometimes observed not to know what a Powler was, and even to appear uncertain whether it might be a business, or a political party, or a profession of faith. The better class of minds, however, did not need to be informed that the Powlers were an ancient stock, who could trace themselves so exceedingly far back that it was not surprising if they sometimes lost themselves—which they had rather frequently done, as respected horse-flesh, blind-hookey, Hebrew monetary transactions, and the Insolvent Debtors' Court." HT i 7

—claimed falsely: "Detected as the Bully of humility, who had built his windy reputation upon lies, and in his boastfulness had put the honest truth as far away from him as if he had advanced the mean claim (there is no meaner) to tack himself on to a pedigree, [Bounderby] cut a most ridiculous figure." HT iii 5

—crest: " . . . the new Veneering crest, in gold and eke in silver, frosted and also thawed, a camel of all work. The Herald's College found out a Crusading ancestor for Veneering who bore a camel on his shield (or might have done it if he had thought of it), and a caravan of camels take charge of the fruits and flowers and candles, and kneel down to be loaded with the salt." OMF i 2

—patronage of literature: "That huckstering, peddling, pandering to patronage for the sale of a book, the offspring of intellect and genius . . . it was sickening to see a man whom God had made a poet, crouching to those whose only title to eminence was derived from the achievements of the great great grandfather of those little, little sons. The poet—for it was his natural avocation—was entitled to worship the stars; but when they contemplated him paying his adoration to stars and garters too, that was indeed a very different thing." S/LS (CD's speech reported in the *Morning Advertiser* December 3, 1840)

—portraits: "'If you have seen the picture-gallery of any one old family, you will remember how the same face and figure—often the fairest and slightest of them all—come upon you in different generations; and how you trace the same sweet girl through a long line of portraits—never growing old or changing—the Good Angel of the race—abiding by them in all reverses—redeeming all their sins . . . .'" OCS 69

"[Richard Carstone] had been over the Hall in the course of the morning, and whimsically described the family pictures as we walked. There were such portentous shepherdesses among the Ladies Dedlock dead and gone, he told us, that peaceful crooks became weapons of assault in their hands. They tended their flocks severely in buckram and powder, and put their sticking-plaster patches on to terrify commoners, as the chiefs of some other tribes put on their war-paint. There was a Sir Somebody Dedlock, with a battle, a sprung-mine, volumes of smoke, flashes of lightning, a town on fire, and a stormed fort, all in full action between his horse's two hind legs: showing, he supposed, how little a Dedlock made of such trifles. The whole race he represented as having evidently been, in life, what he called 'stuffed people,'—a large collection, glassy eyed, set up in the most approved manner on their various twigs and perches, very correct, perfectly free from animation, and always in glass cases." BH 37

"Dreary and solemn the old house looks, with so many appliances of habitation, and with no inhabitants except the pictured forms upon the walls. So did these come and go, a Dedlock in possession might have ruminated passing along; so did they see this gallery hushed and quiet, as I see it now; so think, as I think, of the gap that they would make in this domain when they were gone; so find it, as I find it, difficult to believe that it could be, without them; so pass from my world, as I pass from theirs, now closing the reverberating door; so leave no blank to miss them, and so die.

"Through some of the fiery windows, beautiful from without, and set, at this sunset hour, not in dull grey stone but in a glorious house of gold, the light excluded at other windows pours in, rich, lavish, overflowing like the summer plenty in the land. Then do the frozen Dedlocks thaw. Strange movements come upon their features, as the shadows of leaves play there. A dense Justice in a corner is beguiled into a wink. A staring Baronet, with a truncheon, gets a dimple in his chin. Down into the bosom of a stony shepherdess there steals a fleck of light and warmth, that would have done it good, a hundred years ago. One ancestress of Volumnia, in high-heeled shoes, very like her—casting the shadow of that virgin event before her full two centuries—shoots out into a halo and becomes a saint. A maid of honour of the court of Charles the Second, with large round eyes (and other charms to correspond), seems to bathe in glowing water, and it ripples as it glows." BH 40

—*pride in:* "As no lady or gentleman, with any claims to polite breeding, can possibly sympathise with the Chuzzlewit Family without being first assured of the extreme antiquity of the race, it is a great satisfaction to know that it undoubtedly descended in a direct line from Adam and Eve; and was, in the very earliest times, closely connected with the agricultural interest. If it should ever be urged by grudging and malicious persons, that a Chuzzlewit, in any period of the family history, displayed an overweening amount of family pride, surely the weakness will be considered not only pardonable but laudable, when the immense superiority of the house to the rest of mankind, in respect of this its ancient origin, is taken into account.

"It is remarkable that as there was, in the oldest family of which we have any record, a murderer and a vagabond, so we never fail to meet, in the records of all old families, with innumerable repetitions of the same phase of character. Indeed, it may be laid down as a general principle, that the more extended the ancestry, the greater the amount of violence and vagabondism; for in ancient days those two amusements, combining a wholesome excitement with a promising means of repairing shattered fortunes, were at once the ennobling pursuit and the healthful recreation of the Quality of this land." MC 1

"Talking of the baron's ancestor puts me in mind of the baron's great claims to respect on the score of his pedigree. I am afraid to say, I am sure, how many ancestors the baron had; but I know that he had a great many more than any other man of his time, and I only wish that he had lived in these latter days that he might have had more. It is a very hard thing upon the great men of past centuries, that they should have come into the world so soon, because a man who was born three or four hundred years ago, cannot reasonably be expected to have had as many relations before him as a man who is born now. The last man, whoever he is—and he may be a cobbler or some low vulgar dog for aught we know—will have a longer pedigree than the greatest nobleman now alive: and I contend that this is not fair." NN 6

—*1066 and all that:* "Perhaps in this place the history may pause to congratulate itself upon the enormous amount of bravery, wisdom, eloquence, virtue, gentle birth, and true nobility, that appears to have come into England with the Norman Invasion: an amount which the genealogy of every ancient family lends its aid to swell, and which would, beyond all question, have been found to be just as great, and to the full as prolific in giving birth to long lines of chivalrous descendants, boastful of their origin, even though William the Conqueror had been William the Conquered: a change of circumstances which, it is quite certain, would have made no manner of difference in this respect." MC 1

"Reginald Wilfer is a name with rather a grand sound, suggesting on first acquaintance brasses in country churches, scrolls in stained-glass windows, and generally the De Wilfers who came over with the Conqueror. For, it is a remarkable fact in genealogy that no De Any ones ever came over with Anybody else." OMF i 4

Baby

—all-consuming: "It was a very Moloch of a baby, on whose insatiate altar the whole existence of this particular young brother was offered up a daily sacrifice. Its personality may be said to have consisted in its never being quiet, in any one place, for five consecutive minutes, and never going to sleep when required." HM 2

—bran-new: ". . . Son [Paul Dombey] lay tucked up warm in a little basket bedstead, carefully disposed on a low settee immediately in front of the fire and close to it, as if his constitution were analogous to that of a muffin, and it was essential to toast him brown while he was very new . . . .

"Son was very bald, and very red, and though (of course) an undeniably fine infant, somewhat crushed and spotty in his general effect, as yet . . . the countenance of Son was crossed and recrossed with a thousand little creases, which . . . Time would take delight in smoothing out and wearing away with the flat part of his scythe, as a preparation of the surface for his deeper operations." ¶DS 1

—first: "The first baby! The doctor, the imperious nurse, the nervous walking up and down the parlour, the creaking stairs, the nurse again, imperious still, but now triumphant. The little stranger sparring like an infant **Tom Cribb** in long clothes. That baby's acts and deeds for months! His extraordinary shrewdness, his unexampled beauty, his superhuman capacity for 'taking notice,' his admirable **Crichton**ian qualities. He *was* a baby! Another and another little stranger have dropped in since then. Each was *a* baby, but not *the* baby!" HWC/FF

—going out: " . . . to get the [Peerybingle] baby under weigh took time. Not that there was much of the baby, speaking of it as a thing of weight and measure, but there was a vast deal to do about and about it, and it all had to be done by easy stages.

"For instance, when the baby was got, by hook and by crook, to a certain point of dressing, and you might have rationally supposed that another touch or two would finish him off, and turn him out a tip-top baby challenging the world, he was unexpectedly extinguished in a flannel cap, and hustled off to bed; where he simmered (so to speak) between two blankets for the best part of an hour.

"From this state of inaction he was then recalled, shining very much and roaring violently, to partake of—well? I would rather say, if you'll permit me to speak generally—of a slight repast. After which, he went to sleep again . . . the baby, being all alive again was invested . . . with a cream-coloured mantle for its body, and a sort of nankeen raised-pie for its head; and so in course of time they all three got down to the door . . . . " ¶CH 2

—out of the mouths . . . : "'Berry's very fond of you, ain't she?' Paul once asked Mrs Pipchin when they were sitting by the fire with the cat.

"'Yes,' said Mrs Pipchin.

"'Why?' asked Paul.

"'Why!' returned the disconcerted old lady. 'How can you ask such things, Sir! Why are you fond of your sister Florence?'

"'Because she's very good,' said Paul. 'There's nobody like Florence.'

"'Well!' retorted Mrs Pipchin, shirtly, 'and there's nobody like me, I suppose.'

"'Ain't there really though?' asked Paul, leaning forward in his chair, and looking at her very hard.

"'No,' said the old lady.

"'I am glad of that,' observed Paul, rubbing his hands thoughtfully. 'That's a very good thing.'" DS 11

—too much hat: "The ill-starred youngest Toodle but one . . . was prevented from his part in this general salutation [of Miss Tox]

by having fixed the sou'wester hat (with which he had been previously trifling) deep on his head, hind side before, and being unable to get it off again; which accident presenting to his terrified imagination a dismal picture of his passing the rest of his days in darkness, and in hopeless seclusion from his friends and family, caused him to struggle with great violence, and to utter suffocating cries. Being released, his face was discovered to be very hot, and red, and damp; and Miss Tox took him on her lap, much exhausted." DS 38

—transition: " . . . Paul's slumbers gradually changed. More and more light broke in upon them; distincter and distincter dreams disturbed them; an accumulating crowd of objects and impressions swarmed about his rest; and so he passed from babyhood to childhood, and became a talking, walking, wondering Dombey." DS 8

And see Childbirth, *and* LC:Communication

Bachelor

—on housekeeping: "Topper . . . answered that a bachelor was a wretched outcast, who had no right to express an opinion on the subject." CC 3

—an irritant: " . . . there is a time for all things, and the couple who happen to be always in a loving state before company, are well-nigh intolerable.

"And in taking up this position we would have it distinctly understood that we do not seek alone the sympathy of bachelors, in whose objection to loving couples we recognise interested motives and personal considerations. We grant that to that unfortunate class of society there may be something very irritating, tantalising, and provoking, in being compelled to witness those gentle endearments and chaste interchanges which to loving couples are quite the ordinary business of life.

"But while we recognise the natural character of the prejudice to which these unhappy men are subject, we can neither receive their biassed evidence, nor address ourself to their inflamed and angered minds. Dispassionate experience is our only guide . . . . " ¶YC/L

—sad habit: "]Morfin] handed [Harriet Carker] down to a coach . . . and if his landlady had not been deaf, she would have heard him muttering as he went back up stairs . . . that we were creatures of habit, and it was a sorrowful habit to be an old bachelor." DS 58

—a target: "'A bachelor is a miserable wretch, sir,' said Mr Lillyvick . . . . 'I have lived in the world for nigh sixty year, and I ought to know what it is . . . .

"'If a bachelor happens to have saved a little matter of money . . . his sisters and brothers, and nephews and nieces, look to that money, and not to him; even if by being a public character he is the head of the family, or as it may be the main from which all the other little branches are turned on, they still wish him dead all the while, and get low-spirited every time they see him looking in good health, because they want to come into his little property. You see that?' . . . " NN 25

And see Old Boy. Index VI *lists 80 named bachelors, many of them important in the works. There are nine more in* Index VIII, part 2, *including the archetypal Single Gentleman OCS.*

Birthday

—adult: "It is not Mr Bagnet's birthday. Mr Bagnet merely distinguishes that epoch in the musical instrument business, by kissing the children with an extra smack before breakfast, smoking an additional pipe after dinner, and wondering towards evening what his poor old mother is thinking about it—a subject of infinite speculation, and rendered so by his mother having departed this life, twenty years." BH 49

—celebrated in "Society:" "All this time and always, poor little Miss Podsnap, whose tiny efforts (if she had made any) were swallowed up in the magnificence of her mother's rocking, kept herself as much out of sight and mind as she could, and appeared to be counting on many dismal returns of the day. It was somehow understood, as a secret article in the state proprieties of Podsnappery, that nothing must be said about the day. Consequently this young damsel's nativity was hushed up and looked over, as if it were agreed on all hands that it would have been better that she had never been born." OMF i 11

—child: "Those occasions are kept with some marks of distinction, but they rarely overleap the bounds of happy returns and a pudding. On young Woolwich's last birthday, Mr Bagnet certainly did, after observing on his growth and general advancement, proceed, in a moment of profound reflection on the changes wrought by time, to examine him in the catechism; accomplishing with extreme accuracy the questions number one

and two, What is your name? and Who gave you that name? but there failing in the exact precision of his memory, and substituting for number three, the question And how do you like that name? which he propounded with a sense of its importance, in itself so edifying and improving, as to give it quite an orthodox air." BH 49

—*wife:* "It is the old girl's birthday; and that is the greatest holiday and reddest-letter day in Mr Bagnet's calendar. The auspicious event is always commemorated according to certain forms, settled and prescribed by Mr Bagnet some years since. Mr Bagnet being deeply convinced that to have a pair of fowls for dinner is to attain the highest pitch of imperial luxury, invariably goes forth himself very early in the morning of this day to buy a pair; he is, as invariably, taken in by the vendor, and installed in the possession of the oldest inhabitants of any coop in Europe. Returning with these triumphs of toughness tied up in a clean blue and white cotton handkerchief (essential to the arrangements), he in a casual manner invites Mrs Bagnet to declare at breakfast what she would like for dinner. Mrs Bagnet, by a coincidence never known to fail, replying Fowls, Mr Bagnet instantly produces his bundle from a place of concealment, amidst general amazement and rejoicing. He further requires that the old girl shall do nothing all day long, but sit in her very best gown, and be served by himself and the young people. As he is not illustrious for his cookery, this may be supposed to be matter of state rather than enjoyment on the old girl's part; but she keeps her state with all imaginable cheerfulness." BH 49

Boy

"Of the page I make no account, for, he is a boy, and therefore the natural enemy of Creation." UT/RT

—*as an audience:* "We had been obliged to turn away two hundred to-night, Friar Bacon said, for want of room, and that, not counting the boys, of whom we had taken in only a few picked ones, by reason of the boys, as a class, being given to too fervent a custom of applauding with their boot heels." AY/B

—*carefree:* "If Young John [Chivery] had ever slacked in his truth in the less penetrable days of his boyhood, when youth is prone to wear its boots unlaced and is happily unconscious of digestive organs, he had soon strung it up again and screwed it tight." LD i 18

—*classified:* "'I never see any difference in boys [said Mr Grimwig]. I only know two sorts of boys. Mealy boys, and beef-faced boys . . . . I know a friend who has a beef-faced boy; a fine boy, they call him; with a round head, and red cheeks, and glaring eyes; a horrid boy; with a body and limbs that appear to be swelling out of the seams of his blue clothes; with the voice of a pilot, and the appetite of a wolf. I know him! The wretch!'" OT 14

—*educated:* "I wonder by what ingenuity we brought on that confused state of mind when sense became nonsense, when figures wouldn't work, when dead languages wouldn't construe, when live languages wouldn't be spoken, when memory wouldn't come, when dulness and vacancy wouldn't go. I cannot remember that we ever conspired to be sleepy after dinner, or that we ever particularly wanted to be stupid, and to have flushed faces and hot beating heads, or to find blank hopelessness and obscurity this afternoon in what would become perfectly clear and bright in the freshness of to-morrow morning. We suffered for these things, and they made us miserable enough.

"Neither do I remember that we ever bound ourselves by any secret oath or other solemn obligation, to find the seats getting too hard to be sat upon after a certain time; or to have intolerable twitches in our legs, rendering us aggressive and malicious with those members; or to be troubled with a similar uneasiness in our elbows, attended with fistic consequences to our neighbours; or to carry two pounds of lead in the chest, four pounds in the head, and several active blue-bottles in each ear.

"Yet, for certain, we suffered under those distresses, and were always charged at for labouring under them, as if we had brought them on, of our own deliberate act and deed." ¶UT/ST

—*excited:* " . . . one of the little boys, running into the room as airily as little boys usually run who have an unlimited allowance of animal food in the holidays, and keep their hands constantly forced down to the bottoms of very deep trouser-pockets when they take exercise . . . . " YG/YL

—*exhorted:* "'My young friend,' says Chadband, 'it is because you know nothing that you are to us a gem and jewel. For what are you, my young friend? Are you a beast of the field? No. A bird of the air? No. A fish of the sea or river? No. You are a human boy, my young friend. A human boy. O glorious to be a human boy! And why glorious, my young friend? Because you are capable of receiving the lessons of wisdom, because you are capable of profiting by this discourse which I now deliver for your good, because you are not a stick, or a staff, or a stock, or a stone, or a post, or a pillar.

O running stream of sparkling joy
To be a soaring human boy!

And do you cool yourself in that stream now, my young friend? No. Why do you not cool yourself in that stream now? Because you are in a state of darkness, because you are in a state of obscurity, because you are in a state of sinfulness, because you are in a state of bondage. My young friend, what *is* bondage? Let us, in a spirit of love, inquire.'

"At this threatening stage of the discourse, Jo, who seems to have been gradually going out of his mind, smears his right arm over his face, and gives a terrible yawn. Mrs Snagsby indignantly expresses her belief that he is a limb of the archfiend." BH 19

—godfather of: " . . . I would rather incur the responsibility of being Godfather to a Bell than a Boy . . . ." C 1

—hair: see Child*—rumpled*

—a predilection: " . . . [Bailey] being of a playful temperament, and contemplating with a delight peculiar to his sex and time of life, any chance of dashing himself into small fragments, lingered behind . . . to walk upon the parapet." MC 9

—put down: "'When your opinion's wanted, you give it [said John Willet to his son Joe]. When you're spoke to, you speak. When your opinion's not wanted and you're not spoke to, don't give an opinion and don't you speak. The world's undergone a nice alteration since my time, certainly. My belief is that there an't any boys left—that there isn't such a thing as a boy—that there's nothing now between a male baby and a man—and that all the boys went out with his blessed Majesty King George the Second.'" BR 1

—reputed: "'Boy of the neighbourhood? Hey?' said [Mr Jaggers] . . . .

"'Well! Behave yourself. I have a pretty large experience of boys, and you're a bad set of fellows. Now mind! . . . you behave yourself.'" GE 11

—restless: " . . . the greater part of the observations made that evening, were interrupted by Mrs Micawber's discovering that Master Micawber was sitting on his boots, or holding his head on with both arms as if he felt it loose, or accidentally kicking Traddles under the table, or shuffling his feet over one another, or producing them at distances from himself apparently outrageous to nature, or lying sideways with his hair among the wineglasses, or developing his restlessness of limb in some other form incompatible with the general interests of society; and by Master Micawber's receiving those discoveries in a resentful spirit." DC 36

—Spartan: "' . . . with the fox biting him, which I hope you'll excuse my bringing up, for of all the tiresome boys that will go tumbling into every sort of company, that boy's the tiresomest.'" LD i 24

—ubiquity: ". . . we had no end of boys, but where *is* there any end of boys?" HW/UN

—wriggling: "Regardless of the fire, though it hits him more than once, [Jasper] rushes at Deputy, collars him, and tries to bring him across. But Deputy is not to be so easily brought across. With a diabolical insight into the strongest part of his position, he is no sooner taken by the throat than he curls up his legs, forces his assailant to hang him, as it were, and gurgles in his throat, and screws his body, and twists, as already undergoing the first agonies of strangulation. There is nothing for it but to drop him." MED 12

Childbirth

—aftermath: "The fatherless little stranger was welcomed by some grosses of prophetic pins in a drawer upstairs, to a world not at all excited on the subject of his arrival." DC 1

"I wish to know why, when my child, Augustus George [Meek], was expected in our circle, a provision of pins was made, as if the little stranger were a criminal who was to be put to the torture immediately on his arrival, instead of a holy babe? I wish to know why haste was made to stick those pins all over his innocent form, in every direction? I wish to be informed why light and air are excluded from Augustus George, like poisons? Why, I ask, is my unoffending infant so hedged into a basket-bedstead, with dimity and calico, with miniature sheets and blankets, that I can only hear him snuffle (and no wonder!) deep down under the pink hood of a little bathing-machine, and can never peruse even so much of his lineaments as his nose.

"Was I expected to be the father of a French Roll, that the brushes of All Nations were laid in, to rasp Augustus George? Am I to be told that his sensitive skin was ever intended by Nature to have rashes brought out upon it, by the premature and incessant use of those formidable little instruments?

"Is my son a Nutmeg, that he is to be grated on the stiff edges of sharp frills? Am I the parent of a Muslin boy, that his yielding surface is to be crimped and small plaited? Or is my child composed of Paper or of Linen, that impressions of the finer getting-up art, practised by the laundress, are to be printed off, all over his soft arms and legs, as I constantly observe them? The starch enters his soul; who can wonder that he cries?

"Was [he] intended to have limbs, or to be born a Torso? I presume that limbs were the intention, as they are the usual practice. Then, why are my poor child's limbs fettered and tied up? Am I to be told that there is any analogy between Augustus George Meek and **Jack Sheppard**?

"Analyse Castor Oil at any Institution of Chemistry that may be agreed upon, and inform me what resemblance, in taste, it bears to that natural provision which it is at once the pride and duty of Maria Jane [mother] to administer to Augustus George! Yet, I charge Mrs Prodgit [nurse] (aided and abetted by Mrs Bigby [grandmother]) with systematically forcing Castor Oil on my innocent son, from the first hour of his birth. When that medicine, in its efficient action, causes internal disturbance to Augustus George, I charge Mrs Prodgit (aided and abetted by Mrs Bigby) with insanely and inconsistently administering opium to allay the storm she has raised! What is the meaning of this?

"If the days of Egyptian Mummies are past, how dare Mrs Prodgit require, for the use of my son, an amount of flannel and linen that would carpet my humble roof? Do I wonder that she requires it? No! This morning, within an hour, I beheld this agonising sight. I beheld my son—Augustus George—in Mrs Prodgit's hands, and on Mrs Prodgit's knee, being dressed. He was at the moment, comparatively speaking, in a state of nature; having nothing on but an extremely short shirt, remarkably disproportionate to the length of his usual outer garments. Trailing from Mrs Prodgit's lap, on the floor, was a long narrow roller or bandage—I should say of several yards in extent. In this, I SAW Mrs Prodgit tightly roll the body of my unoffending infant, turning him over and over, now presenting his unconscious face upwards, now the back of his bald head, until the unnatural feat was accomplished, and the bandage secured by a pin, which I have every reason to believe entered the body of my only child. In this tourniquet, he passes the present phase of his existence. Can I know it, and smile!

"I fear I have been betrayed into expressing myself warmly, but I feel deeply. Not for myself; for Augustus George. I dare not interfere. Will any one? Will any publication? Any doctor? Any parent? Any body? . . . Augustus George is a production of Nature (I cannot think otherwise), and I claim that he should be treated with some remote reference to Nature . . . .

" . . . . Besides which, I learn from the statistical tables that one child in five dies within the first year of its life; and one child in three, within the fifth. That don't look as if we could never improve in these particulars, I think!

P.P.S. Augustus George is in convulsions." RP/BM

—birthmark: " . . . when [Mary Rudge's] son was born, upon the very day the deed [of double murder] was known, [Barnaby] bore upon his wrist what seemed a smear of blood but half washed out." BR 5

—a formality: "There are certain polite forms and ceremonies which must be observed in civilized life, or mankind relapse into their original barbarism. No genteel lady was ever yet confined—indeed, no genteel confinement can possibly take place —without the accompanying symbol of a muffled knocker. Mrs Kenwigs was a lady of some pretensions to gentility; Mrs Kenwigs was confined. And, therefore, Mr Kenwigs tied up the silent knocker on the premises in a white kid glove." NN 36

—glossed over: " . . . Mr William Barker was born——but why need we relate where Mr William Barker was born, or when? Why scrutinise the entries in parochial ledgers, or seek to penetrate the Lucinian mysteries of lying-in-hospitals? Mr William Barker *was* born, or he had never been. There is a son—there was a father. There is an effect—there was a cause. Surely this is suffi-

cient information for the most *Fatima*-like curiosity; and, if it be not, we regret our inability to supply any further evidence on the point. Can there be a more satisfactory, or more strictly parliamentary course? Impossible." SB/LC

—illegitimate: "For I saw very well [writes Esther Summerson] that I could not have been intended to die, or I should never have lived; not to say should never have been reserved for a such a happy life. I saw very well how many things had worked together, for my welfare; and that if the sins of the fathers were sometimes visited upon the children, the phrase did not mean what I had in the morning feared it meant. I knew I was as innocent of my birth as a queen of hers; and that before my Heavenly Father I should not be punished for birth, nor a queen rewarded for it. I had had experience, in the shock of that very day, that I could, even thus soon, find comforting reconcilements to the change that had fallen on me. I renewed my resolutions, and prayed to be strengthened in them; pouring out my heart for myself, and for my unhappy mother, and feeling that the darkness of the morning was passing away. It was not upon my sleep; and when the next day's light awoke me, it was gone." BH 36

—medical tact: "'It's a fine boy, Mr Kenwigs,' said Mr Lumbey, the doctor. . . It's the finest boy I ever saw in my life . . . .I never saw such a baby.'

"It is a pleasant thing to reflect upon, and furnishes a complete answer to those who contend for the gradual degeneration of the human species, that every baby born into the world is a finer one than the last. . . ." NN 36

—workhouse version: "Although I am not disposed to maintain that the being born in a workhouse, is in itself the most fortunate and enviable circumstance that can possibly befall a human being, I do mean to say that in this particular instance, it was the best thing for Oliver Twist that could by possibility have occurred. The fact is, that there was considerable difficulty in inducing Oliver to take upon himself the office of respiration—a troublesome practice, but one which custom has rendered necessary to our easy existence; and for some time he lay gasping on a little flock mattress, rather unequally poised between this world and the next: the balance being decidedly in favour of the latter.

"Now, if, during this brief period, Oliver had been surrounded by careful grandmothers, anxious aunts, experienced nurses, and doctors of profound wisdom, he would most inevitably and indubitably have been killed in no time. There being nobody by, however, but a pauper old woman, who was rendered rather misty by an unwonted allowance of beer; and a parish surgeon who did such matters by contract; Oliver and Nature fought out the point between them. The result was, that, after a few struggles, Oliver breathed, sneezed, and proceeded to advertise to the inmates of the workhouse the fact of a new burden having been imposed upon the parish, by setting up as loud a cry as could reasonably have been expected from a male infant who had not been possessed of that very useful appendage, a voice, for a much longer space of time than three minutes and a quarter." ¶OT 1

And see Baby

Child and Childhood

—accident saga: "It unfortunately happened as they quickened their pace, that the orphan, lost to considerations of personal safety in the ardour of the moment, overbalanced himself and toppled into the street. Being an orphan of a chubby conformation, he then took to rolling, and had rolled into the gutter before they could come up. From the gutter he was rescued by John Rokesmith, and thus the first meeting with Mrs Higden was inaugurated by the awkward circumstance of their being in possession—one would say at first sight unlawful possession—of the orphan upside down and purple in the countenance. The board across the doorway too, acting as a trap equally for the feet of Mrs Higden coming out, and the feet of Mrs Boffin and John Rokesmith going in, greatly increased the difficulty of the situation: to which the cries of the orphan imparted a lugubrious and inhuman character.

"At first, it was impossible to explain, on account of the orphan's 'holding his breath:' a most terrific proceeding, superinducing, in the orphan, lead-colour rigidity and a deadly silence, compared with which his cries were music yielding the height of enjoyment. But as he gradually recovered, Mrs Boffin gradually introduced herself, and smiling peace was gradually wooed back to Mrs Betty Higden's home." OMF i 16

—adult interest: "It is one of my rules in life not to believe a man who may happen to

tell me that he feels no interest in children . . . any heart which could really toughen its affections and sympathies against those dear little people must be wanting in so many humanizing experiences of innocence and tenderness, as to be quite an unsafe monstrosity among men." S/SC

—betrayed by materialism: "'Father, you have trained me from my cradle?'

"'Yes, Louisa.'

"'I curse the hour in which I was born to such a destiny.'

"'[Thomas Gradgrind] looked at her in doubt and dread, vacantly repeating: 'Curse the hour? Curse the hour?'

"'How could you give me life, and take from me all the inappreciable things that raise it from the state of conscious death? Where are the graces of my soul? Where are the sentiments of my heart? What have you done, O father, what have you done, with the garden that should have bloomed once, in this great wilderness here? . . .

"' . . . . I don't reproach you, father. What you have never nurtured in me, you have never nurtured in yourself; but O! if you had only done so, long ago, or if you had only neglected me, what a much better and much happier creature I should have been this day!'" HT ii 12

And see Matrimony*—betrayed by materialism;* M:Education*—materialistic, a failure; and* M:Mind*—Reason enthroned alone*

—breakfast: "The little Tetterbys were not habituated to regard that meal in the light of a sedentary occupation, but discussed it as a dance or trot; rather resembling a savage ceremony, in the occasional shrill whoops, and brandishings of bread and butter, with which it was accompanied, as well as in the intricate filings off into the street and back again, and the hoppings up and down the doorsteps, which were incidental to the performance. In the present instance, the contentions between these Tetterby children for the milk and water jug, common to all, which stood upon the table, presented so lamentable an instance of angry passions risen very high indeed, that it was an outrage on the memory of **Dr Watts**. It was not until Mr Tetterby had driven the whole herd out of the front door, that a moment's peace was secured; and even that was broken by the discovery that Johnny had surreptitiously come back, and was at that instant choking in the jug, like a ventriloquist, in his indecent and rapacious haste." HM 3

And see B:Food and drink*—bread and butter —and tea*

—in the city: "I don't know where [Charley Neckett] was going, but we saw her run, such a little, little creature, in her womanly bonnet and apron, through a covered way at the bottom of the court; and melt into the city's strife and sound, like a dewdrop in an ocean." BH 15

—confidence in adults: ". . . I [David Copperfield] am inclined to believe that with the simple confidence of a child, and the natural reliance of a child upon superior years (qualities I am very sorry any children should prematurely change for worldly wisdom), I had no serious mistrust of [the waiter who had eaten his food] on the whole, even then." DC 5

—corrupted: "The girl belonged to a class—unhappily but too extensive—the very existence of which should make men's hearts bleed. Barely past her childhood, it required but a glance to discover that she was one of those children, born and bred in neglect and vice, who have never known what childhood is: who have never been taught to love and court a parent's smile, or to dread a parent's frown. The thousand nameless endearments of childhood, its gaiety and its innocence, are alike unknown to them. They have entered at once upon the stern realities and miseries of life, and to their better nature it is almost hopeless to appeal in after-times, by any of the references which will awaken, if it be only for a moment, some good feeling in ordinary bosoms, however corrupt they may have become. Talk to *them* of parental solicitude, the happy days of childhood, and the merry games of infancy! Tell them of hunger and the streets, beggary and stripes, the gin-shop, the station-house, and the pawnbroker's, and they will understand you." SB/VN

—of doting parents: "The couple who dote upon their children have usually a great many of them: six or eight at least. The children are either the healthiest in all the world, or the most unfortunate in existence . . . the children of this couple can know no medium. They are either prodigies of good health or prodigies of bad health; whatever they are, they must be prodigies. Mr Whiffler must have to describe at his office such excruciating agonies constantly undergone by his eldest boy, as nobody else's eldest boy ever underwent; or he must be able to declare that there never was a child en-

dowed with such amazing health, such an indomitable constitution, and such a cast-iron frame, as his child. His children must be, in some respect or other, above and beyond the children of all other people. To such an extent is this feeling pushed, that we were once slightly acquainted with a lady and gentleman who carried their heads so high and became so proud after their youngest child fell out of a two-pair-of-stairs window without hurting himself much, that the greater part of their friends were obliged to forego their acquaintance." YC/D

—fear of not being understood: "If a dread of not being understood be hidden in the breasts of other young people to anything like the extent to which it used to be hidden in mine [Pip's]—which I consider probable, as I have no particular reason to suspect myself of having been a monstrosity—it is the key to many reservations." GE 9

—first play: "The first play! The promise; the hope deferred . . . scrutiny of the weather during the day! Willingly did we submit, at five o'clock that evening, to the otherwise, and at any other time, detestable ordeal of washing, and combing, and being made straight. We did not complain when the soap got into our eyes; we bore the scraping of the comb, and the rasping of the brush without a murmur: we were going to the play, and we were happy. Dressed, of course, an hour too soon; drinking tea as a mere form and ceremony—for the tea might have been hay and hot water (not impossible), and the bread and butter might have been sawdust, for anything we could taste of it; sitting with petful impatience in the parlour, trying on the first pair of white kid gloves, making sure that the theatre would be burnt down, or that papa would never come home from the office, or mamma prevented . . . from having her dress fastened; or that (to a positive certainty) a tremendous storm of hail, rain, sleet, and thunder would burst out as we stepped into the cab, and send us, theatreless, to bed.

"We went to the play, and were happy. The sweet, dingy, shabby little country theatre, we declared, and believed, to be much larger than either Drury Lane or Covent Garden . . . . Dear, narrow, uncomfortable, faded-cushioned, flea-haunted, single tier of boxes! The green curtain, with a hole in it, through which a bright eye peeped; the magnificent officers, in red and gold coats (it was a garrison town), in the stage-box, who volunteered, during the acts, [a] popular catch . . . for our special amusement and delectation, as we thought then, but, as we are inclined to fear now, under the influence of wine! The pit, with so few people in it; with the lady, who sold apples and oranges, sitting in a remote corner, like Pomona in the sulks.

"And the play when it did begin—stupid, badly acted, badly got up as it very likely was. Our intense, fear-stricken admiration of the heroine, when she let her back hair down, and went mad, in blue. The buff-boots of Digby the manager. The funny man (there never was such a funny man) in a red scratch wig, who, when imprisoned in the deepest dungeon beneath the castle moat, sang a comic song about a leg of mutton. The sorry quadrille band in the orchestra, to our ears as scientifically melodious as though **Costa** had been conductor; **Sivori**, first fiddle; **Richardson**, flute; or **Bottesini**, double bass. The refreshment, administered to us by kind hands during the intervals of performance, never to be forgotten—oranges, immemorial sponge-cakes. The admonitions to 'sit up,' the warnings not to 'talk loud,' in defiance of which (seeing condonatory smiles on the faces of those we loved) we screamed outright with laughter, when the funny man, in the afterpiece, essaying to scale a first floor front by means of a rope ladder, fell, ladder and all, to the ground.

"The final fall of the green curtain, followed by an aromatic perfume of orange-peel and lamp-oil, and the mysterious appearance of ghostly brown Holland draperies from the private boxes. Shawling, cloaking, home, and more primaries—for then it was when we for the first time 'sat up late,' and for the first time ever tasted sandwiches after midnight, or imbibed a sip, a very small sip, of hot something and water." ¶HWC/FF

—friends: "All the schoolfellows and others of old, whom I inquired about, had either done superlatively well or superlatively ill—had either become uncertificated bankrupts, or been felonious and got themselves transported; or had made great hits in life, and done wonders. And this is so commonly the case, that I never can imagine what becomes of all the mediocre people of people's youth—especially considering that we find no lack of the species in our maturity." UT/DT

—happiness in procreation: Humanity is indeed a happy lot, when we can repeat our-

selves in others, and still be young as they." BR 27

—idealism stultified: "Neither, as [Louisa Gradgrind] approached her old home now, did any of the best influences of old home descend upon her. The dreams of childhood—its airy fables; its graceful, beautiful, humane, impossible adornments of the world beyond: so good to be believed in once, so good to be remembered when outgrown, for then the least among them rises to the stature of a great Charity in the heart, suffering little children to come into the midst of it, and to keep with their pure hands a garden in the stony ways of this world, wherein it were better for all the children of Adam that they should oftener sun themselves, simple and trustful, and not worldly-wise—what had she to do with these?

"Remembrances of how she had journeyed to the little that she knew, by the enchanted roads of what she and millions of innocent creatures had hoped and imagined; of how, first coming upon Reason through the tender light of Fancy, she had seen it a beneficent GOD, deferring to GOD as great as itself: not a grim Idol, cruel and cold, with its victims bound hand to foot, and its big dumb shape set up with a sightless stare, never to be moved by anything but so many calculated tons of leverage—what had she to do with these?

"Her remembrances of home and childhood were remembrances of the drying up of every spring and fountain in her young heart as it gushed out. The golden waters were not there. They were flowing for the fertilization of the land where grapes are gathered from thorns, and figs from thistles." ¶HT ii 9

—impressionability: "It would be difficult to overstate the intensity and accuracy of an intelligent child's observation. At that impressible time of life, it must sometimes produce a fixed impression. If the fixed impression be of an object terrible to the child, it will be (for want of reasoning upon) inseparable from great fear. Force the child at such a time, be Spartan with it, send it into the dark against its will, leave it in a lonely bedroom against its will, and you had better murder it." UT/TA

—injustice: "In the little world in which children have their existence, whosoever brings them up, there is nothing so finely perceived and so finely felt, as injustice. It may be only small injustice that the child can be exposed to; but the child is small, and its world is small, and its rocking-horse stands as many hands high, according to scale, as a big-boned Irish hunter. Within myself, I [Pip] had sustained, from my babyhood, a perpetual conflict with injustice. I had known, from the time when I could speak, that my sister, in her capricious and violent coercion, was unjust to me. I had cherished a profound conviction that her bringing me up by hand, gave her no right to bring me up by jerks. Through all my punishments, disgraces, fasts and vigils, and other penitential performances, I had nursed this assurance; and to my communing so much with it, in a solitary and unprotected way, I in great part refer the fact that I was morally timid and very sensitive." GE 8

—memories

—churchyard and sundial: "There is nothing half so green that I know anywhere, as the grass of that churchyard; nothing half so shady as its trees; nothing half so quiet as its tombstones. The sheep are feeding there, when I kneel up, early in the morning, in my little bed in a closet within my mother's room, to look out at it; and I see the red light shining on the sun-dial, and think within myself, 'Is the sun-dial glad, I wonder, that it can tell the time again?'" DC 2

—the out-of-doors: "What man is there, over whose mind a bright spring morning does not exercise a magic influence—carrying him back to the days of his childish sports, and conjuring up before him the old green field with its gently-waving trees, where the birds sang as he has never heard them since—where the butterfly fluttered far more gaily than he ever sees him now, in all his ramblings—where the sky seemed bluer, and the sun shone more brightly—where the air blew more freshly over greener grass, and sweeter-smelling flowers—where everything wore a richer and more brilliant hue than it is ever dressed in now! Such are the deep feelings of childhood, and such are the impressions which every lovely object stamps upon its heart!

"The hardy traveller wanders through the maze of thick and pathless woods, where the sun's rays never shone, and heaven's pure air never played; he stands on the brink of the roaring waterfall, and, giddy and bewildered, watches the foaming mass as it leaps from stone to stone, and from crag to crag; he lingers in the fertile plains of a land of perpetual sunshine, and revels in the luxury of their balmy breath. But what are the deep forests, or the thundering waters, or the richest landscapes that bounteous nature ever spread, to charm the eyes, and captivate the sense of man, compared with the recollection of the old scenes of his early youth? Magic scenes indeed; for the fancies of childhood dressed them in colours brighter than the rainbow, and almost as fleeting!" ¶SB/FM

—*memory and death:* "Christmas Eve in Cloisterham. A few strange faces in the streets; a few other faces, half strange and half familiar, once the faces of Cloisterham children, now the faces of men and women who come back from the outer world at long intervals to find the city wonderfully shrunken in size, as if it had not washed by any means well in the meanwhile. To these, the striking of the Cathedral clock, and the cawing of the rooks from the Cathedral tower, are like voices of their nursery time. To such as these, it has happened in their dying hours afar off, that they have imagined their chamber floor to be strewn with the autumnal leaves fallen from the elm trees in the Close: so have the rustling sounds and fresh scents of their earliest impressions revived when the circle of their lives was very nearly traced, and the beginning and the end were drawing close together." MED 14

—*moral standing:* "'It is not much . . . for a blind and sinful man to invoke a blessing on something so far better than himself as a little child is . . . .'" CS/MJ 2

And see The Boys at Dotheboys Hall NN, and TP:Lawyer—*and children*

—*other people's:* " . . . the disagreeable children of our particular friends. We know by experience what it is to have them down after dinner, and across the rich perspective of a miscellaneous dessert, to see, as in a black dose darkly, the family doctor looming in the distance. We know—I have no doubt we all know—what it is to assist at those little maternal anecdotes and table entertainments illustrated with imitations and descriptive dialogue . . . . We know what it is when those children won't go to bed; we know how they prop their eyelids open with their forefingers when they will sit up; how, when they become fractious, they say aloud that they don't like us, and our nose is too long, and why don't we go? And we are perfectly acquainted with those kicking bundles which are carried off at last protesting." S/SC

—*play:* "Some majestic minds out of doors may, for anything I know, and certainly for anything I care, consider it a very humdrum and low proceeding to stop, in a country full of steam-engines, power-looms, big ships, monster mortars, and great guns of all sorts, to consider where the children are to play. Nevertheless, I know that the question is a very kind one, and a very necessary one. The surgeon and the recruiting sergeant will tell you with great emphasis, that the children's play is of immense importance to a community in the development of bodies; the clergyman, the schoolmaster, and the moral philosopher, in all degrees, will tell you with no less emphasis, that the children's play is of great importance to a community in the development of minds.

"I venture to assert that there can be no physical health without play; and there can be no efficient and satisfactory work without play; that there can be no sound and wholesome thought without play. A country full of dismal little old men and women who had never played would be in a mighty bad way indeed; and you may depend upon it that without play, and good play, too, those powerful English cheers which have driven the sand of Asia before them, and made the very ocean shake, would degenerate into a puling whimper, that would be the most consolatory sound that can possibly be conceived to all the tyrants on the face of the earth." ¶S/PR

—*power of observation:* " . . . I think the memory of most of us can go farther back . . . than many of us suppose; just as I believe the power of observation in numbers of very young children to be quite wonderful for its closeness and accuracy. Indeed, I think that most grown men who are remarkable in this respect, may with greater propriety be said not to have lost the faculty, than to have acquired it; the rather, as I generally observe such men to retain a certain freshness, and gentleness, and capacity of being pleased, which are also an inheritance they have preserved from their childhood." DC 1

"I could observe, in little pieces, as it were; but as to making a net of a number of these pieces, and catching anybody in it, that was, as yet, beyond me." DC 2

—*at prayer:* " . . . we made our camp [writes Gill Davis], and got our supper, and set our watch, and the children fell asleep. It was solemn and beautiful in those wild and solitary parts, to see them, every night before they lay down, kneeling under the bright sky, saying their little prayers at women's laps. At that time we men all uncovered, and mostly kept at a distance. When the innocent creatures rose up, we murmured 'Amen!' all together. For, though we had not heard what they said, we knew it must be good for us." CS/EP 3

—privileged at Christmas: " . . . [the daughter], soon beginning to mingle in the sports, got pillaged by the young brigands most ruthlessly. What would I not have given to be one of them! Though I never could have been so rude, no, no! I wouldn't for the wealth of all the world have crushed that braided hair, and torn it down; and for the precious little shoe, I wouldn't have plucked it off, God bless my soul! to save my life. As to measuring her waist in sport, as they did, bold young brood, I couldn't have done it; I should have expected my arm to have grown round it for a punishment, and never come straight again. And yet I should have dearly liked, I own, to have touched her lips; to have questioned her, that she might have opened them; to have looked upon the lashes of her downcast eyes, and never raised a blush; to have let loose waves of hair, an inch of which would be a keepsake beyond price; in short, I should have liked, I do confess, to have had the lightest license of a child, and yet to have been man enough to know its value." CC 2

—protected from a bully: "'Shall I go away, aunt?' I asked, trembling.

"'No, sir,' said my aunt. 'Certainly not!' With which she pushed me into a corner near her, and fenced me in with a chair, as if it were a prison or a bar of justice. This position I continued to occupy during the whole interview, and from it I now saw Mr and Miss Murdstone enter the room . . . .

"'Miss Trotwood!'

"'I beg your pardon,' observed my aunt with a keen look. 'You are the Mr Murdstone who married the widow of my late nephew, David Copperfield, of Blunderstone Rookery?—Though why Rookery, *I* don't know!'

"'I am,' said Mr Murdstone.

"'You'll excuse my saying, sir,' returned my aunt, 'that I think it would have been a much better and happier thing if you had left that poor child alone' . . . . My aunt inclined her head to Mr Murdstone, who went on:

"'Miss Trotwood. On the receipt of your letter, I considered it an act of greater justice to myself, and perhaps of more respect to you—'

"'Thank you,' said my aunt, still eyeing him keenly. 'You needn't mind me.'

"'To answer it in person, however inconvenient the journey,' pursued Mr Murdstone, "rather than by letter. This unhappy boy who has run away from his friends and his occupation . . . has been the occasion of much domestic trouble and uneasiness; both during the lifetime of my late dear wife, and since. He has a sullen, rebellious spirit; a violent temper; and an untoward, intractable disposition. Both my sister and myself have endeavoured to correct his vices, but ineffectually. And I have felt—we both have felt, I may say; my sister being fully in my confidence—that it is right you should receive this grave and dispassionate assurance from our lips.'

"'It can hardly be necessary for me to confirm anything stated by my brother,' said Miss Murdstone; 'but I beg to observe, that, of all the boys in the world, I believe this is the worst boy.'

"'Strong!' said my aunt, shortly.

"'But not at all too strong for the facts,' returned Miss Murdstone.

"'Ha!' said my aunt. 'Well, sir?'

"'I have my opinions,' resumed Mr Murdstone, whose face darkened more and more, the more he and my aunt observed each other, which they did very narrowly, 'as to the best mode of bringing him up; they are founded, in part, on my knowledge of him, and in part on my knowledge of my own means and resources. I am responsible for them to myself, I act upon them, and I say no more about them. It is enough that I place this boy under the eye of a friend of my own, in a respectable business; that it does not please him; that he runs away from it; makes himself a common vagabond about the country; and comes here, in rags, to appeal to you, Miss Trotwood. I wish to set before you, honourably, the exact consequences—so far as they are within my knowledge—of your abetting him in this appeal.'

"'But about the respectable business first,' said my aunt. 'If he had been your own boy, you would have put him to it, just the same, I suppose?'

"'If he had been my brother's own boy,' returned Miss Murdstone, striking in, 'his character, I trust, would have been altogether different.'

"'Or if the poor child, his mother, had been alive, he would still have gone into the respectable business, would he?' said my aunt.

"'I believe,' said Mr Murdstone, with an inclination of his head, 'that Clara would have disputed nothing which myself and my sister Jane Murdstone were agreed was for the best.'

"Miss Murdstone confirmed this with an audible murmur.

"'Humph!' said my aunt. 'Unfortunate baby! . . .

"'The poor child's annuity died with her?'

"'Died with her,' replied Mr Murdstone.

"'And there was no settlement of the little property—the house and garden—the what's-its-name Rookery without any rooks in it—upon her boy?'

"It had been left to her, unconditionally, by her first husband,' Mr Murdstone began, when my aunt caught him up with the greatest irascibility and impatience.

"'Good Lord, man, there's no occasion to say that. Left to her unconditionally! I think I see David Copperfield looking forward to any condition of any sort or kind, though it stared him point-blank in the face! Of course it was left to her unconditionally. But when she married again—when she took that most disastrous step of marrying you, in short,' said my aunt, 'to be plain—did no one put in a word for the boy at that time?'

"'My late wife loved her second husband, ma'am,' said Mr Murdstone, 'and trusted implicitly in him.'

"'Your late wife, sir, was a most unworldly, most unhappy, most unfortunate baby,' returned my aunt, shaking her head at him. 'That's what *she* was. And now, what have you got to say next?'

"'Merely this, Miss Trotwood,' he returned. 'I am here to take David back; to take him back unconditionally, to dispose of him as I think proper, and to deal with him as I think right. I am not here to make any promise, or give any pledge to anybody. You may possibly have some idea, Miss Trotwood, of abetting him in his running away, and in his complaints to you. Your manner, which I must say does not seem intended to propitiate, induces me to think it possible. Now I must caution you that if you abet him once, you abet him for good and all; if you step in between him and me, now, you must step in, Miss Trotwood, for ever. I cannot trifle, or be trifled with. I am here, for the first and last time, to take him away. Is he ready to go? If he is not—and you tell me he is not; on any pretence; it is indifferent to me what—my doors are shut against him henceforth, and yours, I take it for granted, are open to him.'

"To this address, my aunt had listened with the closest attention, sitting perfectly upright, with her hands folded on one knee, and looking grimly on the speaker. When he had finished, she turned her eyes so as to command Miss Murdstone, without otherwise disturbing her attitude, and said:

"'Well, ma'am, have *you* got anything to remark?'

"'Indeed, Miss Trotwood,' said Miss Murdstone, 'all that I could say has been so well said by my brother, and all that I know to be the fact has been so plainly stated by him, that I have nothing to add except my thanks for your politeness. For your very great politeness, I am sure,' said Miss Murdstone; with an irony which no more affected my aunt than it discomposed the cannon I had slept by at Chatham.

"'And what does the boy say?' said my aunt. 'Are you ready to go, David?'

"I answered no, and entreated her not to let me go. I said that neither Mr nor Miss Murdstone had ever liked me, or had ever been kind to me. That they had made my mama, who always loved me dearly, unhappy about me, and that I knew it well, and that Peggotty knew it. I said that I had been more miserable than I thought anybody could believe who only knew how young I was. And I begged and prayed my aunt—I forget in what terms now, but I remember that they affected me very much then—to befriend and protect me, for my father's sake.

"'Mr Dick,' said my aunt; 'what shall I do with this child?'

"Mr Dick considered, hesitated, brightened, and rejoined, 'Have him measured for a suit of clothes directly.'

"'Mr Dick,' said my aunt triumphantly, 'give me your hand, for your common sense is invaluable.' Having shaken it with great cordiality, she pulled me towards her and said to Mr Murdstone:

"'You can go when you like; I'll take my chance with the boy. If he's all you say he is, at least I can do as much for him then, as you have done. But I don't believe a word of it.'

"'Miss Trotwood,' rejoined Mr Murdstone, shrugging his shoulders, as he rose, 'if you were a gentleman—'

"'Bah! Stuff and nonsense!' said my aunt. 'Don't talk to me!'

"'How exquisitely polite!' exclaimed Miss Murdstone, rising. 'Overpowering, really!'

"'Do you think I don't know,' said my aunt, turning a deaf ear to the sister, and continuing to address the brother, and to shake her head at him with infinite expression, 'what kind of life you must have led that poor, unhappy, misdirected baby? Do you think I don't know what a woeful day it was for the soft little creature when *you* first came in her way—smirking and making great eyes at her, I'll be bound, as if you couldn't say boh! to a goose!'

"'I never heard anything so elegant!' said Miss Murdstone.

"'Do you think I can't understand you as well as if I had seen you,' pursued my aunt, 'now that I *do* see and hear you—which I tell you candidly, is anything but a pleasure to me? Oh yes, bless us! who so smooth and silky as Mr Murdstone at first! The poor, benighted innocent had never seen such a man. He was made of sweetness. He worshipped her. He doted on her boy—tenderly doted on him! He was to be another father to him, and they were all to live together in a garden of roses, weren't they? Ugh! Get along with you, do!' said my aunt.

"'I never heard anything like this person in my life!' exclaimed Miss Murdstone.

"'And when you had made sure of the poor little fool,' said my aunt—'GOD forgive me that I should call her so, and she gone where *you* won't go in a hurry—because you had not done wrong enough to her and hers, you must begin to train her, must you? begin to break her, like a poor caged bird, and wear her deluded life away, in teaching her to sing *your* notes?'

"'This is either insanity or intoxication,' said Miss Murdstone, in a perfect agony at not being able to turn the current of my aunt's address towards herself; 'and my suspicion is that it's intoxication.'

"Miss Betsey, without taking the least notice of the interruption, continued to address herself to Mr Murdstone as if there had been no such thing.

"'Mr Murdstone,' she said, shaking her finger at him, 'you were a tyrant to the simple baby, and you broke her heart. She was a loving baby—I know that; I knew it years before you ever saw her—and through the best part of her weakness you gave her the wounds she died of. There is the truth for your comfort, however you like it. And you and your instruments may make the most of it.'

"'Allow me to inquire, Miss Trotwood,' interposed Miss Murdstone, 'whom you are pleased to call, in a choice of words in which I am not experienced, my brother's instruments?'

"Still stone-deaf to the voice, and utterly unmoved by it, Miss Betsey pursued her discourse.

"'It was clear enough, as I have told you, years before you ever saw her—and why, in the mysterious dispensations of Providence, you ever did see her, is more than humanity can comprehend—it was clear enough that the poor soft little thing would marry somebody, at some time or other; but I did hope it wouldn't have been as bad as it has turned out. That was the time, Mr Murdstone, when she gave birth to her boy here,' said my aunt; 'to the poor child you sometimes tormented her through afterwards, which is a disagreeable remembrance, and makes the sight of him odious now. Aye, aye! you needn't wince!' said my aunt. 'I know it's true without that.'

"He had stood by the door, all this while, observant of her, with a smile upon his face, though his black eyebrows were heavily contracted. I remarked now, that, though the smile was on his face still, his colour had gone in a moment, and he seemed to breathe as if he had been running.

"'Good day, sir,' said my aunt, 'and good bye! Good day to you too, ma'am,' said my aunt, turning suddenly upon his sister. 'Let me see you ride a donkey over *my* green again, and as sure as you have a head upon your shoulders, I'll knock your bonnet off, and tread upon it!'

"It would require a painter, and no common painter too, to depict my aunt's face as she delivered herself of this very unexpected sentiment, and Miss Murdstone's face as she heard it. But the manner of the speech, no less than the matter, was so fiery, that Miss Murdstone, without a word in answer, discreetly put her arm through her brother's, and walked haughtily out of the cottage; my aunt remaining in the window looking after them; prepared, I have no doubt, in case of the donkey's reappearance, to carry her threat into execution.

"No attempt at defiance being made, however, her face gradually relaxed, and became so pleasant, that I was emboldened to kiss and thank her; which I did with great heartiness, and with both my arms clasped round her neck." DC 14

—*purgatory:* "The length of those five days I can convey no idea of to any one. They occupy the place of years in my remembrance. The way in which I listened to all the incidents of the house that made themselves audible to me; the ringing of bells, the opening and shutting of doors, the murmuring of voices, the footsteps on the stairs; to any laughing, whistling, or singing, outside, which seemed more dismal than anything else to me in my solitude and disgrace—the uncertain pace of the hours, especially at night, when I would wake thinking it was morning, and find that the family were not yet gone to bed, and that all the length of night had yet to come—the depressed dreams and nightmares I had—the return of day, noon, afternoon, evening, when the boys played in the churchyard, and I watched them from a distance within the room, being ashamed to show myself at the window lest they should know I was a prisoner—the strange sensation of never hearing myself speak—the fleeting intervals of something like cheerfulness, which came with eating and drinking, and went away with it—the setting in of rain one evening, with a fresh smell, and its coming down faster and faster between me and the church, until it and gathering night seemed to quench me in gloom, and fear, and remorse—all this appears to have gone round and round for years instead of days, it is so vividly and strongly stamped on my remembrance." DC 4

—*early responsibility in:* " 'It always grieves me,' I observed, roused by what I took to be [Nell's grandfather's] selfishness, 'it always grieves me to contemplate the initiation of children into the ways of life, when they are scarcely more than infants. It checks their confidence and simplicity—two of the best qualities that Heaven gives them—and demands that they share our sorrows before they are capable of entering into our enjoyments.'" OCS 1

—*rewarding a good man:* "'Good?' said Em'ly. 'If I was ever to be a lady, I'd give him a sky-blue coat with diamond buttons, nankeen trousers, a red velvet waistcoat, a cocked hat, a large gold watch, a silver pipe, and a box of money.'" DC 3

—*rumpled:* " . . . when Mr Wopsle referred to me, he considered it a necessary part of such reference to rumple my hair and poke it into my eyes. I cannot conceive why everybody of his standing who visited at our house should always have put me through the same inflammatory process under similar circumstances. Yet I do not call to mind that I was ever in my earlier youth the subject of remark in our social family circle, but some large-handed person took some such ophthalmic steps to patronise me." GE 10

—*scientifically reared:* "An eminent eye-witness told me that he was one of a company of learned pundits who assembled at the house of a very distinguished philosopher of the last generation, to hear him expound his stringent views concerning infant education and early mental development, and he told me that, while the philosopher did this in very beautiful and lucid language, the philosopher's little boy, for his part, edified the assembled sages by dabbling up to the elbows in an apple pie which had been provided . . . having previously anointed his hair with syrup, combed it with his fork, and brushed it with his spoon." S/SC

—secrecy, under terror: " . . . I [Pip] have often thought that few people know what secrecy there is in the young, under terror. No matter how unreasonable the terror, so that it be terror. I was in mortal terror of the young man who wanted my heart and liver; I was in mortal terror of my interlocutor with the iron leg; I was in mortal terror of myself, from whom an awful promise had been extracted; I had no hope of deliverance through my all-powerful sister, who repulsed me at every turn; I am afraid to think of what I might have done on requirement, in the secrecy of my terror." GE 2

—at the shore: "So many children are brought down to our watering-place [Broadstairs] that, when they are not out of doors, as they usually are in fine weather, it is wonderful where they are put: the whole village seeming much too small to hold them under cover. In the afternoons, you see no end of salt and sandy little boots drying on upper window-sills. At bathing-time in the morning, the little bay re-echoes with every shrill variety of shriek and splash—after which, if the weather be at all fresh, the sands teem with small blue mottled legs. The sands are the children's great resort. They cluster there, like ants: so busy burying their particular friends, and making castles with infinite labour which the next tide overthrows, that it is curious to consider how their play, to the music of the sea, foreshadows the realities of their after lives." RP/EW

"[Boulogne] is a place wonderfully populous in children; English children, with governesses reading novels as they walk down the shady lanes of trees, or nursemaids interchanging gossip on the seats; French children with their smiling bonnes in snow-white caps, and themselves—if little boys—in straw head-gear like beehives, work-baskets and church hassocks." RP/FW

—sick: "One of the little patients followed our movements with its eyes, with a sad, thoughtful, peaceful look; one indulged in a big stare of childish curiosity and wonder. They had toys strewn upon their counterpanes. A sick child is a contradiction of ideas, like a cold summer. But to quench the summer in a child's heart is, thank God! not easy. If we do not make a frost with wintry discipline, if we will use soft looks and gentle words; though such an hospital be full of sick and ailing bodies, the light, loving spirits of the children will fill its wards with pleasant sounds, contrasting happily with the complainings that abound among our sick adults. Suffer these little ones to come to such a Christian House, and forbid them not! They will not easily forget it." HWC/DB

—a spanking: "That dear child, it seemed, connecting a chapel with tombstones, when it was entered for any purpose apart from the ordinary religious exercises, could not be persuaded but that his mother was now to be decently interred, and lost to him for ever. In the anguish of this conviction, he screamed with astonishing force, and turned black in the face. However touching these marks of a tender disposition were to his mother, it was not in the character of that remarkable woman to permit her recognition of them to degenerate into weakness.

"Therefore, after vainly endeavouring to convince his reason by shakes, pokes, bawlings-out, and similar applications to his head, she led him into the air, and tried another method; which was manifested to the marriage party by a quick succession of sharp sounds, resembling applause, and subsequently, by their seeing Alexander [MacStinger] in contact with the coolest paving-stone in the court, greatly flushed, and loudly lamenting." ¶DS 60

—spoilt

—by indulgence: " . . . it is likely that even we are not without experience now and then of spoilt children. I do not mean of our own spoilt children, because nobody's own children ever were spoilt . . . " S/SC

See —other people's

—by poverty and neglect: "The spoilt children whom I must show you are spoilt children of the poor in this great city—the children who are, every year, for ever and ever irrevocably spoilt out of this breathing life of ours by tens of thousands, but who may in vast numbers be preserved, if you, assisting and not contravening the ways of Providence, will help to save them. The two grim nurses, Poverty and Sickness, who bring these children before you, preside over their births, rock their wretched cradles, nail down their little coffins, pile up the earth above their graves." S/SC

—of the underclass: "'Put the case that [a legal adviser] lived in an atmosphere of evil, and that all he saw of children was, their being generated in great numbers for certain destruction. Put the case that he often saw children solemnly tried at a criminal bar, where they were held up to be seen; put the

case that he habitually knew of their being imprisoned, whipped, transported, neglected, cast out, qualified in all ways for the hangman, and growing up to be hanged. Put the case that pretty nigh all the children he saw in his daily business life, he had reason to look upon as so much spawn, to develop into the fish that were to come to his net—to be prosecuted, defended, forsworn, made orphans, bedevilled somehow.'" GE 51 *And see* F:Crime—*the children*

"I could enter no other houses for that one while, for I could not bear the contemplation of the children. Such heart as I had summoned to sustain me against the miseries of the adults failed me when I looked at the children. I saw how young they were, how hungry, how serious and still. I thought of them, sick and dying in those lairs. I think of them dead without anguish; but to think of them so suffering and so dying quite unmanned me." UT/SE

—*unwelcome:* "What meals I had in silence and embarrassment, always feeling that there were a knife and fork too many, and those mine; an appetite too many, and that mine; a plate and chair too many, and those mine; a somebody too many, and that I!" DC 8

—*Utilitarian rearing:* "'What do *I* know, father, said Louisa [Gradgrind] in her quiet manner, 'of tastes and fancies; of aspirations and affections; of all that part of my nature in which such light things might have been nourished? What escape have I had from problems that could be demonstrated, and realities that could be grasped?' As she said it, she unconsciously closed her hand, as if upon a solid object, and slowly opened it as though she were releasing dust or ash . . . .

"'Why, father,' she pursued . . . . The baby-preference that even I have heard of as common among children, has never had its innocent resting-place in my breast. You have been so careful of me, that I never had a child's heart. You have trained me so well, that I never dreamed a child's dream. You have dealt so wisely with me, father, from my cradle to this hour, that I never had a child's belief or a child's fear.'

"Mr Gradgrind was quite moved by his success, and by this testimony to it." HT i 15

—*watching adults dancing:* "For quite a long time they would not be persuaded to take partners and dance. Most of the boys [adult men] said, 'Thanks; much! But not at present.' And most of the rest of the boys said, 'Thanks; much! But never do.' . . .

"At last they did begin in a slow and melancholy way to slide about to the music; though even then they wouldn't mind what they were told, but would have this partner, and wouldn't have that partner, and showed temper about it. And they wouldn't smile—no, not on any account they wouldn't; but, when the music stopped, went round and round the room in dismal twos, as if everybody else was dead." HR/4

—*what comes naturally:* "Treachery don't come natural to beaming youth; but trust and pity, love and constancy—they do, thank GOD!" CS/LL 2

—*willful:* "'A vexatious (do you hear, sir?), a vexatious, capricious, thankless, troublesome, Animal; but I hope you'll do better in the time to come, and I bless you and forgive you!' Here, [Bella] quite forgot that it was Pa's turn to make the responses, and clung to his neck. 'Dear Pa, if you knew how much I think this morning of what you told me once . . . when I stamped and screamed, and beat you with my detestable little bonnet! I feel as if I had been stamping and screaming and beating you with my hateful little bonnet, ever since I was born, darling!' . . .

"'Did I hurt you much, poor little Pa?' asked Bella, laughing (notwithstanding her repentance), with fantastic pleasure in the picture, 'when I beat you with my bonnet?'

"'No my child. Wouldn't have hurt a fly!'" OMF iv 4

—*young love:* "'You have loved [Arabella] from a child, my friend. You loved her when we were boys at school together, and, even then, she was wayward, and slighted your young feelings. Do you recollect, with all the eagerness of a child's love, one day pressing upon her acceptance, two small caraway-seed biscuits and one sweet apple, neatly folded into a circular parcel with the leaf of a copybook?'

"'I do,' replied Bob Sawyer.

"'She slighted that, I think?' said Ben Allen.

"'She did,' rejoined Bob. 'She said I had kept the parcel so long in the pockets of my corduroys, that the apple was unpleasantly warm.'

"'I remember,' said Mr Allen, gloomily. 'Upon which we ate it ourselves, in alternate bites.'" PP 48

Death

—of an abandoned child: "what was the matter with the nurse . . . ? Oh, 'the dropped child' was dead! Oh, the child that was found in the street, and she had brought up ever since, had died an hour ago, and see where the little creature lay, beneath this cloth! The dear, the pretty dear!

"The dropped child seemed too small and poor a thing for Death to be in earnest with, but Death had taken it; and already its diminutive form was neatly washed, composed, and stretched as if in sleep upon a box. I thought I heard a voice from Heaven saying, It shall be well for thee, O nurse of the itch-ward,* when some less gentle pauper does those offices to thy cold form, that such as the dropped child are the angels who behold my Father's face!" RP/WW

**a name chosen by William Hogarth for his etching of a workhouse*

—aged looks, its effect on: "Alas! How few of Nature's faces are left alone to gladden us with their beauty! The cares, and sorrows, and hungerings of the world, change them as they change hearts; and it is only when those passions sleep, and have lost their hold for ever, that the troubled clouds pass off, and leave Heaven's surface clear. It is a common thing for the countenances of the dead, even in that fixed and rigid state, to subside into the long-forgotten expression of sleeping infancy, and settle into the very look of early life; so calm, so peaceful, do they grow again, that those who knew them in their happy childhood, kneel by the coffin's side in awe, and see the Angel even upon earth." OT 24

But see Old Age*—second childhood*

—in an almshouse: "On the occurrence of a death in Titbull's, it is invariably agreed among the survivors—and it is the only subject on which they do agree—that the departed did something 'to bring it on.' Judging by Titbull's, I should say the human race need never die, if they took care." UT/AH

—a beginning: "'I have done you many wrongs, my own. I have fallen like a poor stray shadow on your way, I have married you to poverty and trouble, I have scattered your means to the winds. You will forgive me all this, my Ada, before I begin the world?'

"A smile irradiated [Richard Carstone's] face, as she bent to kiss him. He slowly laid his face down upon her bosom, drew his arms closer round her neck, and with one parting sob began the world. Not this world, O not this! The world that sets this right." BH 65

—bereavement: " . . . the blank that follows death—the weary void—the sense of desolation that will come upon the strongest minds, when something familiar and beloved is missed at every turn—the connexion between inanimate and senseless things, and the object of recollection, when every household GOD becomes a monument and every room a grave. . . ." OCS 72

"It was the first time that a grave had opened in my [Pip's] road of life, and the gap it made in the smooth ground was wonderful. The figure of my sister in her chair by the kitchen fire haunted me night and day. That the place could possibly be, without her, was something my mind seemed unable to compass; and whereas she had seldom or never been in my thoughts of late, I had now the strangest idea that she was coming towards me in the street, or that she would presently knock at the door. In my rooms too, with which she had never been at all associated, there was at once the blankness of death and a perpetual suggestion of the sound of her voice or the turn of her face or figure, as if she were still alive and had been often there." GE 35

And see S:Grief*—of the poor*

—of brothers: "[Amy and Frederick Dorrit] remained in a dim room near, until it was almost midnight, quiet and sad together. At times his grief would seek relief, in a burst like that in which it had found its earliest expression; but, besides that his little strength would soon have been unequal to such strains, he never failed to recall her words, and to reproach himself and calm himself. The only utterance with which he indulged his sorrow, was the frequent exclamation that his brother [William Dorrit] was gone, alone; that they had been together in the outset of their lives, that they had fallen into misfortune together, that they had kept together through their many years of poverty, that they had remained together to that day; and that his brother was gone alone, alone!" LD ii 19

"It was a moonlight night; but the moon rose late, being long past the full. When it was high in the peaceful firmament, it shone through half-closed lattice blinds into the solemn room where the stumblings and wanderings of a life had so lately ended.

Two quiet figures were within the room; two figures, equally still and impassive, equally removed by an untraversable distance from the teeming earth and all that it contains, though soon to lie in it.

"One figure reposed upon the bed. The other, kneeling on the floor, drooped over it; the arms easily and peacefully resting on the coverlet; the face bowed down, so that the lips touched the hand over which with its last breath it had bent. The two brothers were before their Father; far beyond the twilight judgments of this world; high above its mists and obscurities." LD ii 19

—capricious: "A candle faintly burned in the window, to which the black [undertaker's] ladder had often been raised for the sliding away of all that was most precious in this world to a striving wife and a brood of hungry babies; and Stephen [Blackpool] added to his other thoughts the stern reflection, that of all the casualties of this existence upon earth, not one was dealt out with so unequal a hand as Death. The inequality of Birth was nothing to it. For, say that the child of a King and the child of a Weaver were born to-night in the same moment, what was that disparity, to the death of any human creature who was serviceable to, or beloved by, another, while this abandoned woman [his abject, drunken wife] lived on!" HT i 13

—cause, speculated: "At first, [Merdle] was dead of all the diseases that ever were known, and of several bran-new maladies invented with the speed of Light to meet the demand of the occasion. He had concealed a dropsy from infancy, he had inherited a large estate of water on the chest from his grandfather, he had had an operation performed upon him every morning of his life for eighteen years, he had been subject to the explosion of important veins in his body after the manner of fireworks, he had had something the matter with his lungs, he had had something the matter with his heart, he had had something the matter with his brain.

"Five hundred people who sat down to breakfast entirely uninformed on the whole subject, believed before they had done breakfast, that they privately and personally knew Physician to have said to Mr Merdle, 'You must expect to go out, some day, like the snuff of a candle;' and that they knew [him] to have said to Physician, 'A man can die but once.'" ¶LD ii 25

—of a child: "'We know that when the young, the beautiful, and good, are visited with sickness, their pure spirits insensibly turn towards their bright home of lasting rest; we know, Heaven help us! that the best and fairest of our kind, too often fade in blooming.'" OT 35

"[Harry] was a very young boy; quite a child. His hair still hung in curls about his face, and his eyes were very bright; but their light was of Heaven, not earth . . . [Nell] thought as a child herself, and did not perhaps sufficiently consider to what a bright and happy existence those who die young are borne, and how in death they lose the pain of seeing others die around them, bearing to the tomb some strong affection of their hearts (which makes the old die many times in one long life) . . ." OCS 25, 26

—to a child: " . . . the sad scene [Nell] had witnessed, was not without its lesson of content and gratitude; of content with the lot which left her health and freedom; and gratitude that she was spared to the one relative and friend she loved, and to live and move in a beautiful world, when so many young creatures—as young and full of hope as she—were stricken down and gathered to their graves. How many of the mounds in that old churchyard where she had lately strayed, grew green above the graves of children! And though she thought as a child herself, and did not perhaps sufficiently consider to what a bright and happy existence those who die young are borne, and how in death they lose the pain of seeing others die around them, bearing to the tomb some strong affection of their hearts (which makes the old die many times in one long life), still she thought wisely enough, to draw a plain and easy moral from what she had seen that night, and to store it, deep in her mind." OCS 26

— a child, dying: "The morsel of burnt child . . . looked as if . . . he mused upon the Future of some older children lying around him in the same place, and thought it best, perhaps, all things considered, that he should die—as if he knew, without fear, of those many coffins, made and unmade, piled up in the store below—and of his unknown friend, 'the dropped child,' calm upon the box-lid covered with a cloth.

"But there was something wistful and appealing, too, in his tiny face, as if, in the midst of all the hard necessities and incongruities he pondered on, he pleaded, in behalf of the helpless and the aged poor, for a little more liberty—and a little more bread." RP/WW

—of a child-mother: "'She was never well,' said Peggotty, 'for a long time. She was uncertain in her mind, and not happy. When her baby was born, I thought at first she would get better, but she was more delicate, and sunk a little every day. She used to like to sit alone before her baby came, and then she cried; but afterwards she used to sing to it—so soft, that I once thought, when I heard her, it was like a voice up in the air, that was rising away.

"'I think she got to be more timid, and more frightened-like, of late; and that a hard word was like a blow to her. But she was always the same to me. She never changed to her foolish Peggotty, didn't my sweet girl.'

"Here Peggotty stopped, and softly beat upon my hand a little while.

"'The last time that I saw her like her own old self, was the night when you came home, my dear. The day you went away, she said to me, "I never shall see my pretty darling again. Something tells me so, that tells the truth, I know."

"'She tried to hold up after that; and many a time, when they told her she was thoughtless and light-hearted, made believe to be so; but it was all a bygone then. She never told her husband what she had told me—she was afraid of saying it to anybody else—till one night, a little more than a week before it happened, when she said to him: "My dear, I think I am dying."

"'It's off my mind now, Peggotty," she told me, when I laid her in her bed that night. "He will believe it more and more, poor fellow, every day for a few days to come; and then it will be past. I am very tired. If this is sleep, sit by me while I sleep: don't leave me. GOD bless both my children! GOD protect and keep my fatherless boy!"

"'I never left her afterwards,' said Peggotty. 'She often talked to them two down-stairs . . . but when they went away from her bedside, she always turned to me, as if there was rest where Peggotty was, and never fell asleep in any other way.

"'On the last night, in the evening, she kissed me, and said: "If my baby should die too, Peggotty, please let them lay him in my arms, and bury us together." (It was done; for the poor lamb lived but a day beyond her.) "Let my dearest boy go with us to our resting-place," she said, "and tell him that his mother, when she lay here, blessed him not once, but a thousand times."'

"Another silence followed this, and another gentle beating on my hand.

"'It was pretty far in the night,' said Peggotty, 'when she asked me for some drink; and when she had taken it, gave me such a patient smile, the dear!—so beautiful!

"'Daybreak had come, and the sun was rising, when she said to me, how kind and considerate Mr Copperfield had always been to her, and how he had borne with her, and told her, when she doubted herself, that a loving heart was better and stronger than wisdom, and that he was a happy man in hers. "Peggotty, my dear," she said then, "put me nearer to you," for she was very weak. "Lay your good arm underneath my neck," she said, "and turn me to you, for your face is going far off, and I want it to be near." I put it as she asked; and oh Davy! the time had come when my first parting words to you were true—when she was glad to lay her poor head on her stupid cross old Peggotty's arm—and she died like a child that had gone to sleep!'" DC 9

—defied: "'The sun sets every day [said Steerforth], and people die every minute, and we mustn't be scared by the common lot. If we failed to hold our own, because that equal foot at all men's doors was heard knocking somewhere, every object in this world would slip from us. No! Ride on! Rough-shod if need be, smooth-shod if that will do, but ride on! Ride on over all obstacles, and win the race!'" DC 28

—by drowning: " . . . [Quilp] staggered and fell; and next moment was fighting with the cold, dark water.

"For all its bubbling up and rushing in his ears, he could hear the knocking at the gate again—could hear a shout that followed it—could recognise the voice. For all his struggling and plashing, he could understand . . . that they were all but looking on while he was drowned; that they were close at hand, but could not make an effort to save him; that he himself had shut and barred them out. He answered the shout—with a yell, which seemed to make the hundred fires that danced before his eyes tremble and flicker as if a gust of wind had stirred them. It was of no avail. The strong tide filled his throat, and bore him on, upon its rapid current.

"Another mortal struggle, and he was up again, beating the water with his hands, and looking out with wild and glaring eyes that showed him some black object he was drifting close upon. The hull of a ship! He could touch its smooth and slippery surface with his hand. One loud cry now—but the resistless water bore him down before he could give it utterance, and, driving him under it, carried away a corpse.

"It toyed and sported with its ghastly freight, now bruising it against the slimy piles, now hiding it in mud or long rank grass, now dragging it heavily over rough stones and gravel, now feigning to yield it to its own element, and in the same action luring it away, until, tired of the ugly plaything, it flung it on a swamp—a dismal place where pirates had swung in chains, through many a wintry night—and left it there to bleach.

"And there it lay, alone. The sky was red with flame, and the water that bore it there had been tinged with the sullen light as it flowed along. The place the deserted carcase had left so recently, a living man, was now a blazing ruin. There was something of the glare upon its face. The hair, stirred by the damp breeze, played in a kind of mockery of death—such a mockery as the dead man himself would have revelled in when alive—about its head, and its dress fluttered idly in the night wind." OCS 67

And see S:Suicide—*regretted*

—supposedly: "'No, no; no more,' said Captain Cuttle, sorrowfully meditating; 'no more. There he lays, all his days—'

"Mr Bunsby, who had a musical ear, suddenly bellowed, 'In the Bays of Biscay, O!' which so affected the good Captain, as an appropriate tribute to departed worth, that he shook him by the hand in acknowledgment, and was fain to wipe his eyes.

"'Well, well!' said the Captain with a sigh, as the Lament of Bunsby ceased to ring and vibrate in the skylight. 'Affliction sore, long time he bore, and let us overhaul the wollume, and there find it.'

"'Physicians,' observed Bunsby, 'was in vain.'

"'Aye, aye, to be sure,' said the Captain, 'what's the good o' *them* in two or three hundred fathoms o' water!'" DS 39

—dusty: "The opening of the service recalls my wandering thoughts. I then find, to my astonishment, that I have been, and still am, taking a strong kind of invisible snuff, up my nose, into my eyes, and down my throat. I wink, sneeze, and cough. The clerk sneezes; the clergyman winks; the unseen organist sneezes and coughs (and probably winks); all our little party wink, sneeze, and cough.

"The snuff seems to be made of the decay of matting, wood, cloth, stone, iron, earth, and something else. Is the something else, the decay of dead citizens in the vaults below? As sure as Death it is! Not only in the cold damp February day, do we cough and sneeze dead citizens, all through the service, but dead citizens have got into the very bellows of the organ, and half choked the same.

"We stamp our feet to warm them, and dead citizens arise in heavy clouds. Dead citizens stick upon the walls, and lie pulverised on the sounding-board over the clergyman's head, and, when a gust of air comes, tumble down upon him." ¶UT/LC

—the 'Farmer': "It is likely enough that in the rough outhouses of some tillers of the heavy lands adjacent to Paris, there were [in 1775] sheltered from the weather that very day, rude carts, bespattered with rustic mire, snuffed about by pigs, and roosted in by poultry, which the Farmer, Death, had already set apart to be his tumbrils of the Revolution." TTC i 1

—foreshadowed: "Night after night, the lights burn in the window, and the figure lies upon the bed, and Edith sits beside it, and the restless waves are calling to them both the whole night long. Night after night, the waves are hoarse with repetition of their mystery; the dust lies piled upon the shore; the sea-birds soar and hover; the winds and clouds are on their trackless flight; the white arms beckon, in the moonlight, to the invisible country far away.

"And still the sick old woman looks into the corner, where the stone arm—part of a figure of some tomb, she says—is raised to strike her. At last it falls; and then a dumb old woman lies upon the bed, and she is crooked and shrunk up, and half of her is dead." DS 41

—of a good man: "Oh cold, cold, rigid, dreadful Death, set up thine altar here, and dress it with such terrors as thou hast at thy command: for this is thy dominion! But of the loved, revered, and honoured head, thou canst not turn one hair to thy dread purposes, or make one feature odious. It is not that the hand is heavy and will fall

down when released; it is not that the heart and pulse are still; but that the hand WAS open, generous, and true; the heart brave, warm, and tender; and the pulse a man's. Strike, Shadow, strike! And see his good deeds springing from the wound, to sow the world with life immortal!" CC 4

—to those about to be hanged: "Although one of these men displayed, in his speech and bearing, the most reckless hardihood; and the other, in his every word and action, testified such an extreme of abject cowardice that it was humiliating to see him; it would be difficult to say which of them would most have repelled and shocked an observer. Hugh's was the dogged desperation of a savage at the stake; the hangman was reduced to a condition little better, if any, than that of a hound with the halter round his neck. Yet, as Mr Dennis knew and could have told them, these were the two commonest states of mind in persons brought to their pass. Such was the wholesale growth of the seed sown by the law, that this kind of harvest was usually looked for, as a matter of course.

"In one respect they all agreed. The wandering and uncontrollable train of thought, suggesting sudden recollections of things distant and long forgotten and remote from each other—the vague restless craving for something undefined, which nothing could satisfy, the swift flight of the minutes, fusing themselves into hours, as if by enchantment—the rapid coming of the solemn night—the shadow of death always upon them, and yet so dim and faint, that objects the meanest and most trivial started from the gloom beyond, and forced themselves upon the view—the impossibility of holding the mind, even if they had been so disposed, to penitence and preparation, or of keeping it to any point while one hideous fascination tempted it away—these things were common to them all, and varied only in their outward tokens." BR 76

—ironic, of a river ghoul: "Soon the form of the bird of prey [Jesse Hexam], dead some hours, lay stretched upon the shore, with a new blast storming at it and clotting the wet hair with hailstones.

"Father, was that you calling me? Father! I thought I heard you call me twice before! Words never to be answered, those, upon the earth side of the grave. The wind sweeps jeeringly over Father, whips him with the frayed ends of his dress and his jagged hair, tried to turn him where he lies stark on his back, and force his face towards the rising sun, that he may be shamed the more.

"A lull, and the wind is secret and prying with him; lifts and lets fall a rag; hides palpitating under another rag; runs nimbly through his hair and beard. Then, in a rush, it cruelly taunts him. Father, was that you calling me? Was it you, the voiceless and the dead? Was it you, thus buffeted as you lie here in a heap? Was it you, thus baptized unto Death, with these flying impurities now flung upon your face?

"Why not speak, Father? Soaking into this filthy ground as you lie here, is your own shape. Did you never see such a shape soaked into your boat? Speak, Father. Speak to us, the winds, the only listeners left you!" ¶OMF i 14

—in a large house: "The funeral of [Fanny Dombey] having been 'performed' to the entire satisfaction of the undertaker, as well as of the neighbourhood at large, which is generally disposed to be captious on such a point, and is prone to take offence at any omissions or shortcomings in the ceremonies, the various members of [the] household subsided into their several places in the domestic system. That small world, like the great one out of doors, had the capacity of easily forgetting its dead; and when the cook had said she was a quiet-tempered lady, and the housekeeper had said it was the common lot, and the butler had said who'd have thought it, and the housemaid had said she couldn't hardly believe it, and the footman had said it seemed exactly like a dream, they had quite worn the subject out, and began to think their mourning was wearing rusty too." DS 3

"There is a hush through Mr Dombey's house. Servants gliding up and down-stairs rustle but make no sound of footsteps. They talk together constantly, and sit long at meals, making much of their meat and drink, and enjoying themselves after a grim, unholy fashion. Mrs Wickam, with her eyes suffused with tears, relates melancholy anecdotes; and tells them how she always said at Mrs Pipchin's that it would be so; and takes more table-ale than usual; and is very sorry but sociable. Cook's state of mind is similar. She promises a little fry for supper, and struggles about equally against her feelings and the onions. Towlinson begins to think there's a fate in it, and wants to know if anybody can tell him of any good that ever came of living in a corner house. It seems to all of them as having happened a long time ago; though yet the child lies, calm and beautiful, upon his little bed.

"After dark there come some visitors—noiseless visitors, with shoes of felt—who have been there before; and with them comes that bed of rest which is so strange a one for infant sleepers." DS 18

—literary: " . . . an incident in which I am happy to know you were interested and still more happy to know, though it may sound paradoxical, that you were disappointed: I mean the death of the little heroine [Nell]. When I first conceived the idea of conducting that simple story to its termination, I determined rigidly to adhere to it, and never to forsake the end I had in view. Not untried in the school of affliction, in the death of those we love, I thought what a good thing it would be if in my little work of pleasant amusement I could substitute a garland of fresh flowers for the sculptured horrors which disgrace the tomb." S/E

—and memory: "It was fine summer weather again, and, as I [Pip] walked along, the times when I was a little helpless creature, and my sister did not spare me, vividly returned. But they returned with a gentle tone upon them, that softened even the edge of Tickler. For now, the very breath of the beans and clover whispered to my heart that the day must come when it would be well for my memory that others walking in the sunshine should be softened as they thought of me." GE 35

—at the moment: "The boy was lying, fast asleep . . . so pale with anxiety, and sadness, and the closeness of his prison, that he looked like death; not death as it shows in shroud and coffin, but in the guise it wears when life has just departed; when a young and gentle spirit has, but an instant, fled to Heaven, and the gross air of the world has not had time to breathe upon the changing dust it hallowed." OT 19

—of a mother: "The lady lay upon her bed . . . clasping her little daughter to her breast. The child clung close about her, with the same intensity as before, and never raised her head . . . .

"There was such a solemn stillness round the bed; and the two medical attendants seemed to look on the impassive form with so much compassion and so little hope, that Mrs Chick was for the moment diverted from her purpose. But presently summoning courage, and what she called presence of mind, she sat down by the bedside, and said in the low precise tone of one who endeavours to awaken a sleeper:

"'Fanny! Fanny!'

"There was no sound in answer but the loud ticking of Mr Dombey's watch and Doctor Parker Peps's watch, which seemed in the silence to be running a race . . . .

"The two medical attendants exchanged a look across the bed; and the Physician, stooping down, whispered in the child's ear. Not having understood the purport of his whisper, the little creature turned her perfectly colourless face, and deep dark eyes towards him; but without loosening her hold in the least.

"The whisper was repeated.

"'Mama!' said the child.

"The little voice, familiar and dearly loved, awakened some show of consciousness, even at that ebb. For a moment, the closed eye-lids trembled, and the nostril quivered, and the faintest shadow of a smile was seen.

"'Mama!' cried the child sobbing aloud. 'Oh dear Mama! oh dear Mama!'

"The Doctor gently brushed the scattered ringlets of the child, aside from the face and mouth of the mother. Alas how calm they lay there; how little breath there was to stir them!

"Thus, clinging fast to that slight spar within her arms, the mother drifted out upon the dark and unknown sea that rolls round all the world." DS 1

—an old fashion: "The golden ripple on the wall came back again, and nothing else stirred in the room. The old, old fashion! The fashion that came in with our first garments, and will last unchanged until our race has run its course, and the wide firmament is rolled up like a scroll. The old, old fashion—Death!" DS 16

—of an old man: "[Anthony Chuzzlewit] had fallen from his chair in a fit, and lay there, battling for each gasp of breath, with every shrivelled vein and sinew starting in its place, as if it were bent on bearing witness to his age, and sternly pleading with Nature against his recovery. It was frightful to see how the principle of life, shut up within his withered frame, fought like a strong devil, made to be released, and rent its ancient prison-house. A young man in the fulness of his vigour, struggling with so

much strength of desperation, would have been a dismal sight; but an old, old shrunken body, endowed with preternatural might, and giving the lie in every motion of its every limb and joint to its enfeebled aspect, was a hideous spectacle indeed." MC 18

—of one the death of many: "'Because it an't one loss [said Captain Cuttle], but a round dozen. Where's that there young schoolboy, with the rosy face and curly hair, that used to be as merry in this here parlour, come round every week, as a piece of music? Gone down with Wal'r [Walter Gay]. Where's that there fresh lad, that nothing couldn't tire nor put out, and that sparkled up and blushed so, when we joked him about Heart's Delight, that he was beautiful to look at? Gone down with Wal'r. Where's that there man's spirit, all afire, that wouldn't see the old man hove down for a minute, and cared nothing for itself? Gone down with Wal'r. It an't one Wal'r. There was a dozen Wal'rs that I know'd and loved, all holding round his neck when he went down, and they're a-holding round mine now!'" DS 32

—premonition: " . . . an involuntary chill—a momentary feeling akin to fear—but vanishing directly, and leaving no alarm behind. Again, too, dreams of the little scholar; of the roof opening, and a column of bright faces, rising far away into the sky, as she had seen in some old scriptural picture once, and looking down on her, asleep. It was a sweet and happy dream. The quiet spot, music in the air, and a sound of angel's wings." OCS 52

"When I took [Dora] up, and felt that she was lighter in my arms, a dead, blank feeling came upon me, as if I were approaching to some frozen region yet unseen, that numbed my life." DC 48

—by pressure: "There was a general moralising upon Pressure, in every street. All the people who had tried to make money and had not been able to do it, said, There you were! You no sooner began to devote yourself to the pursuit of wealth, than you got Pressure. The idle people improved the occasion in a similar manner. See, said they, what you brought yourself to by work, work, work! You persisted in working, you overdid it, Pressure came on, and you were done for! This consideration was very potent in many quarters, but nowhere more so than among the young clerks and partners who had never been in the slightest danger of overdoing it. These one and all declared, quite piously, that they hoped they would never forget the warning as long as they lived, and that their conduct might be so regulated as to keep off Pressure, and preserve them, a comfort to their friends, for many years." LD ii 25

—of a prostitute: "[Meg Veck] saw the entering figure; screamed its name; cried 'Lilian!'

"It was swift, and fell upon its knees before her: clinging to her dress.

"'Up, dear! Up! Lilian! My own dearest!'

"'Never more, Meg; never more! Here! Here! Close to you, holding to you, feeling your dear breath upon my face!'

"'Sweet Lilian! Darling Lilian! Child of my heart—no mother's love can be more tender—lay your head upon my breast!'

"'Never more, Meg. Never more! When I first looked into your face, you knelt before me. On my knees before you, let me die. Let it be here!'

"'You have come back. My Treasure! We will live together, work together, hope together, die together!'

"'Ah! Kiss my lips, Meg; fold your arms about me; press me to your bosom; look kindly on me; but don't raise me. Let it be here. Let me see the last of your dear face upon my knees!'

"O Youth and Beauty, happy as ye should be, look at this! O Youth and Beauty, working out the ends of your Beneficent Creator, look at this!

"'Forgive me, Meg! So dear, so dear! Forgive me! I know you do, I see you do, but say so, Meg!'

"She said so, with her lips on Lilian's cheek. And with her arms twined round—she knew it now—a broken heart.

"'His blessing on you, dearest love. Kiss me once more! He suffered her to sit beside His feet, and dry them with her hair. O Meg, what Mercy and Compassion!'

"As she died, the Spirit of the child returning, innocent and radiant, touched the old man [Toby Veck] with its hand, and beckoned him away." C 3

—a release: "[Nell] was dead, and past all help, or need of it . . . .

"'It is not,' said the schoolmaster, as he bent down to kiss her on the cheek, and gave his tears free vent, 'it is not on earth that Heaven's justice ends. Think what it is compared with the World to which her young spirit has winged its early flight, and say, if one deliberate wish expressed in solemn terms above this bed could call her back to life, which of us would utter it!'" OCS 71

—and remorse: "We need be careful how we deal with those about us, when every death carries to some small circle of survivors, thoughts of so much omitted, and so little done—of so many things forgotten, and so many more which might have been repaired! There is no remorse so deep as that which is unavailing; if we would be spared its tortures, let us remember this, in time." OT 33

—resented: "The Honourable Mrs Skewton, like many genteel persons who have existed at various times, set her face against death altogether, and objected to the mention of any such low and levelling upstart." DS 30

—on the seacoast: "'People can't die, along the coast,' said Mr Peggotty, 'except when the tide's pretty nigh out. They can't be born, unless it's pretty nigh in—not properly born, till flood. He's a going out with the tide. It's ebb at half-arter three, slack water half-an-hour. If he lives till it turns, he'll hold his own till past the flood, and go out with the next tide.'

"We remained there, watching him, a long time—hours. What mysterious influence my presence had upon him in that state of his senses, I shall not pretend to say; but when he at last began to wander feebly, it is certain he was muttering about driving me to school.

"'He's coming to himself,' said Peggotty.

"Mr Peggotty touched me, and whispered with much awe and reverence, 'They are both a going out fast.'

"'Barkis, my dear!' said Peggotty.

"C. P. Barkis,' he cried faintly. 'No better woman anywhere!'

"'Look! Here's Master Davy!' said Peggotty. For he now opened his eyes.

"I was on the point of asking him if he knew me, when he tried to stretch out his arm, and said to me, distinctly, with a pleasant smile:

"'Barkis is willin'!'

"And, it being low water, he went out with the tide." DC 30

—of a son and a brother

—the sister: " . . . Floy could always soothe and reassure him; and it was his daily delight to make her lay her head down on his pillow, and take some rest.

"'You are always watching me, Floy. Let me watch *you*, now!' They would prop him up with cushions in a corner of his bed, and there he would recline the while she lay beside him: bending forward oftentimes to kiss her, and whispering to those who were near that she was tired, and how she had sat up so many nights beside him.

"Thus, the flush of the day, in its heat and light, would gradually decline; and again the golden water would be dancing on the wall . . . . " DS 16

—the father: " . . . this figure with its head upon its hand returned so often, and remained so long, and sat so still and solemn, never speaking, never being spoken to, and rarely lifting up its face, that Paul began to wonder languidly, if it were real; and in the night-time saw it sitting there, with fear.

"'Floy!' he said. 'What *is* that?'

"'Where, dearest?'

"'There! at the bottom of the bed.'

"'There's nothing there, except papa!'

"The figure lifted up its head, and rose, and coming to the bedside, said: 'My own boy! Don't you know me?'

"Paul looked it in the face, and thought, was this his father? But the face so altered to his thinking, thrilled while he gazed, as if it were in pain; and before he could reach out both his hands to take it between them, and draw it towards him, the figure turned away quickly from the little bed, and went out at the door . . . .

" . . . . The next time he observed the figure sitting at the bottom of the bed, he called to it.

"'Don't be so sorry for me, dear papa! Indeed I am quite happy!'

"His father coming and bending down to him—which he did quickly, and without first pausing by the bedside—Paul held him round the neck, and repeated those words to him several times, and very earnestly; and Paul never saw him in his room again at any time, whether it were day or night, but he called out, 'Don't be so sorry for me! Indeed I am quite happy!' This was the beginning of his always saying in the morning that he was a great deal better, and that they were to tell his father so." DS 16

—brother and sister together: "'Now lay me down,' he said, 'and, Floy, come close to me, and let me see you!'

"Sister and brother wound their arms around each other, and the golden light came streaming in, and fell upon them, locked together.

"'How fast the river runs, between its green banks and the rushes, Floy! But it's very near the sea. I hear the waves! They always said so!'

"Presently he told her that the motion of the boat upon the stream was lulling him to rest. How green the banks were now, how bright the flowers growing on them, and how tall the rushes! Now the boat was out at sea, but gliding smoothly on. And now there was a shore before him. Who stood on the bank!—

"He put his hands together, as he had been used to do at his prayers. He did not remove his arms to do it; but they saw him fold them so, behind her neck.

"'Mama is like you, Floy. I know her by the face! But tell them that the print upon the stairs at school is not divine enough. The light about the head is shining on me as I go!'" DS 16

The extraordinary Chapter 16 of DS may be found complete in Vol. I at pp775-778.

—by spontaneous combustion: "' . . . what on earth is going on in this [Krook's] house to-night? Is there a chimney on fire? . . . See how the soot's falling. See here, on my arm! See again, on the table here! Confound the stuff, it won't blow off—smears, like black fat!' . . .

" . . . . Look at my fingers!'

"A thick, yellow liquor defiles them, which is offensive to the touch and sight and more offensive to the smell. A stagnant, sickening oil, with some natural repulsion in it that makes them both shudder . . . .

"They go down, more dead than alive, and holding one another, push open the door of the back shop. The cat has retreated close to it, and stands snarling—not at them; at something on the ground, before the fire. There is a very little fire left in the grate, but there is a smouldering suffocating vapour in the room, and a dark greasy coating on the walls and ceiling . . . .

"What is it? Hold up the light.

"Here is a small burnt patch of flooring; here is the tinder from a little bundle of burnt paper, but not so light as usual, seeming to be steeped in something; and here is—is it the cinder of a small charred and broken log of wood sprinkled with white ashes, or is it coal? O Horror, he IS here! and this from which we run away, striking out the light and overturning one another into the street is all that represents him.

"Help, help, help! come into this house for Heaven's sake!

"Plenty will come in, but none can help. The Lord Chancellor of that court, true to his title in his last act, has died the death of all Lord Chancellors in all courts, and of all authorities in all places under all names soever, where false pretences are made, and where injustice is done. Call the death by any name Your Highness will, attribute it to whom you will, or say it might have been prevented how you will, it is the same death eternally—inborn, inbred, engendered in the corrupted humours of the vicious body itself, and that only—Spontaneous Combustion, and none other of all the deaths that can be died." BH 32

—in the underclass: " . . . the cart so hard to draw, is near its journey's end, and drags over stony ground. All round the clock it labours up the broken steps, shattered and worn. Not many times can the sun rise, and behold it still upon its weary road . . . .

"Jo is in a sleep or in a stupor to-day, and Allan Woodcourt, newly arrived, stands by him, looking down upon his wasted form. After a while, he softly seats himself upon the bedside with his face towards him . . . and touches his chest and heart. The cart had very nearly given up, but labours on a little more . . . . After a short relapse into sleep or stupor, he makes, of a sudden, a strong effort to get out of bed . . . .

"'It's time for me to go to that there berryin ground, sir . . . .

"'Where they laid him [Captain Hawdon] as wos wery good to me, wery good to me indeed, he wos. It's time fur me to go down to that there berryin ground, sir, and ask to be put along with him . . . . It's turned wery dark, sir. Is there any light a-comin?'

"'It is coming fast, Jo.'

"Fast. The cart is shaken all to pieces, and the rugged road is very near its end . . . .

"'Jo, can you say what I say?'

"'I'll say anythink as you say, sir, fur I knows it's good.'

"'OUR FATHER.'

"'Our Father!—yes, that's wery good, sir.'

"'WHICH ART IN HEAVEN.'

"'Art in Heaven—is the light a-comin, sir?'

"'It is close at hand. HALLOWED BE THY NAME!

"'Hallowed be—thy—'

"The light is come upon the dark benighted way. Dead!

"Dead, your Majesty. Dead, my lords and gentlemen. Dead, men and women, born with Heavenly compassion in your hearts. And dying thus around us every day." BH 47
—in a vision: "I saw a mighty Spirit, traversing the world without any rest or pause. It was omnipresent, it was all powerful, it had no compunction, no pity, no relenting sense that any appeal from any of the race of men could reach. It was invisible to every creature born upon the earth, save once to each. It turned its shaded face on whatsoever living thing, one time; and straight the end of that thing was come.

"It passed through the forest, and the vigorous tree it looked on shrunk away; through the garden, and the leaves perished and the flowers withered; through the air, and the eagles flagged upon the wing and dropped; through the sea, and the monsters of the deep floated, great wrecks, upon the waters. It met the eyes of lions in their lairs, and they were dust; its shadow darkened the faces of young children lying asleep, and they awoke no more.

"It had its work appointed; it inexorably did what was appointed to it to do; and neither sped nor slackened. Called to, it went on unmoved, and did not come. Besought, by some who felt that it was drawing near, to change its course, it turned its shaded face upon them, even while they cried, and they were dumb. It passed into the midst of palace chambers, where there were lights and music, pictures, diamonds, gold and silver; crossed the wrinkled and the grey, regardless of them; looked into the eyes of a bright bride; and vanished.

"It revealed itself to the baby on the old crone's knee, and left the old crone wailing by the fire. But, whether the beholder of its face were, now a king, or now a labourer, now a queen, or now a seamstress; let the hand it palsied be on the sceptre, or the plough, or yet too small and nerveless to grasp anything: the Spirit never paused in its appointed work, and sooner or later turned its impartial face on all." ¶HW/DV
—the watch: "It is a dreadful thing to wait and watch for the approach of a death; to know that hope is gone, and recovery impossible; and to sit and count the dreary hours through long, long nights—such nights as only watchers by the bed of sickness know.

"It chills the blood to hear the dearest secrets of the heart—the pent-up, hidden secrets of many years—poured forth by the unconscious helpless being before you; and to think how little the reserve and cunning of a whole life will avail, when fever and delirium tear off the mask at last. Strange tales have been told in the wanderings of dying men; tales so full of guilt and crime, that those who stood by the sick person's couch have fled in horror and affright, lest they should be scared to madness by what they heard and saw; and many a wretch has died alone, raving of deeds the very name of which has driven the boldest man away." ¶SB/DD

—of a young girl: They saw the vault covered, and the stone fixed down. Then, when the dusk of evening had come on, and not a sound disturbed the sacred stillness of the place—when the bright moon poured in her light on tomb and monument, on pillar, wall, and arch, and most of all (it seemed to them) upon [Nell's] quiet grave—in that calm time, when outward things and inward thoughts teem with assurances of immortality, and worldly hopes and fears are humbled in the dust before them—then, with tranquil and submissive hearts they turned away, and left the child with GOD.

"Oh! it is hard to take to heart the lesson that such deaths will teach, but let no man reject it, for it is one that all must learn, and is a mighty, universal Truth. When Death strikes down the innocent and young, for every fragile form from which he lets the panting spirit free, a hundred virtues rise, in shapes of mercy, charity, and love, to walk the world, and bless it. Of every tear that sorrowing mortals shed on such green graves, some good is born, some gentler nature comes. In the Destroyer's steps there spring up bright creations that defy his power, and his dark path becomes a way of light to Heaven." OCS 72

Nell is Dead OCS

The Last Lines of Death

CD described many deaths. In each case, the last paragraph, sometimes just the last sentence or phrase, stark or emotional, casual or intense, funny or tragic, coldly dismissive or evocative, is a telling summary and farewell. Here are those farewells in the chronological order of the fictional works in which they appear:

Grandmother. " . . . an old 'ooman—the ugliest and dirtiest I ever see . . . went into the infirmary, and very soon died." SB/BM

Mother. "'. . . she burst a blood-vessel one mornin', and died too; and a happy release it was . . . . '" SB/BM

William. " . . . a strange expression stole upon his features; not of pain or suffering, but an indescribable fixing of every line and muscle.

"The boy was dead." SB/NN

Patient. "'Some kind gentleman take my love to my poor old father. Five years ago, he said he wished I had died a child. Oh, I wish I had! I wish I had!'

"The nurse bent over the girl for a few seconds, and then drew the sheet over her face. It covered a corpse." SB/HP

Hanged boy. "The throat was swollen, and a livid mark encircled it. The truth flashed suddenly upon him.

"'This is one of the men who were hanged this morning! . . . Who was he? . . .

"'*My son,*' rejoined the woman; and fell senseless at his feet." SB/BV

Watkins Tottle. "A few weeks after . . . the body of a gentleman unknown was found in the Regent's canal. In the trousers-pockets were four shillings and threepence half-penny; a matrimonial advertisement from a lady, which appeared to have been cut out of a Sunday paper; a tooth-pick, and a card-case, which it is confidently believed would have led to the identification of the unfortunate gentleman, but for the circumstance of there being none but blank cards in it." SB/WT

Warden, hopeless drunk. " . . . the body was washed ashore, some miles down the river, a swollen and disfigured mass. Unrecognised and unpitied, it was borne to the grave; and there it has long since mouldered away!" SB/DD

Chambers occupant. "'He died one morning of apoplexy, as he was going to open his outer door. Fell with his head in his own letter-box, and there he lay for eighteen months. Every body thought he'd gone out of town . . . .

"'The benchers . . . . Forced the lock; and a very dusty skeleton in a blue coat, black knee-shorts, and silks, fell forward in the arms of the porter . . . . '" PP 21

Another. "'Tenant of a top set—bad character—shut himself up in his bed-room closet, and took a dose of arsenic . . . standing bolt upright in the corner, was the last tenant, with a little bottle clasped firmly in his hand, and his face—well!'" PP 21

Bardell. "'The late Mr Bardell . . . glided almost imperceptibly from the world, to seek elsewhere for that repose and peace which a custom-house can never afford.'

"At this pathetic description of the decease of Mr Bardell, who had been knocked on the head with a quart-pot in a public-house cellar, the learned serjeant's voice faltered . . . ." PP 34

Susan Clarke Weller. "' . . . just as she wos a turnen the corner my boy she took the wrong road and vent down hill vith a welocity you never see and notvithstanding that the drag wos put on drectly by the medikel man it wornt of no use at all for she paid the last pike at twenty minutes afore six o'clock yesterday evenin havin done the journey wery much under the reglar time vich praps was partly owen to her haven taken in wery little luggage . . . . '" PP 52

"'" . . . keep a good heart, my dear; and you'll live to see me punch that 'ere Stiggins's head yet." She smiled at this, Samivel,' said the old gentleman, stifling a sigh with his pipe, 'but she died arter all!'" PP 52

Chancery prisoner. " . . . the turnkey, stooping over the pillow, drew hastily back. 'He has got his discharge, by G——said the man.

"He had. But he had grown so like death in life, that they knew not when he died." PP 44

Pantomime clown. "He grasped my shoulder convulsively, and, striking his breast with the other hand, made a desperate attempt to articulate. It was unavailing—he extended his arm towards [his wife and child], and made another violent effort. There was a rattling noise in the throat—a glare of the eye—a short stifled groan—and he fell back—dead!'" PP 3 (interlude)

Mrs Edmunds. "' . . .the poor woman's soul took its flight, I confidently hope, and solemnly believe, to a place of eternal happiness and rest.'" PP 6 (interlude)

Edmunds. "'His face turned black: the gore rushed from his mouth and nose, and dyed the grass a deep dark red, as he staggered and fell. He had ruptured a blood-vessel: and he was a dead man before his son could raise him.'" PP 6 (interlude)

Madman's wife. "She lay bereft of animation for hours; and when life, look, and speech returned, her senses had deserted her, and she raved wildly and furiously . . . .

"She died next day . . . I had carried my object and killed her . . . ." PP 11 (interlude)

Poor child. "For two months, [the poor girl] and her little companion watched the opening of the [prison] gate as usual. One day she failed to come, for the first time. Another morning arrived, and she came alone. The child was dead." PP 21 (interlude)

Mrs Bayton. " . . . in a small recess, opposite the door, there lay upon the ground, something covered with an old blanket . . . . ' . . . she was dying; and all the blood in my heart has dried up, for they starved her to death.'" OT 5

Sally, a pauper crone. " . . . she once again rose, slowly and stiffly, into a sitting posture; then, clutching the coverlid with both hands, muttered some indistinct sounds in her throat, and fell lifeless on the bed." OT 24

Nancy, a prostitute. "The murderer staggering backward to the wall, and shutting out the sight with his hand, seized a heavy club and struck her down." OT 47

Bill Sikes. " . . . he lost his balance and tumbled over the parapet. The noose was on his neck. It ran up with his weight, tight as a bowstring, and swift as the arrow it speeds. He fell for five-and-thirty feet. There was a sudden jerk, a terrific convulsion of the limbs; and there he hung, with the open knife clenched in his stiffening hand." OT 50

Bull's-eye. "Missing his aim, he fell into the ditch, turning completely over as he went; and striking his head against a stone, dashed out his brains." OT 50

Man in white waistcoat. "'Ah! he went to heaven last week, in a oak coffin with plated handles . . . . '" OT 51

Dick. "It is a world of disappointment; often to the hopes we most cherish, and hopes that do our nature the greatest honour.

"Poor Dick was dead!" OT 52

Harvey children. "one was an infant—they wept for him; the next a girl, a slight young thing too delicate for earth—her loss was hard indeed to bear. The third, a man. That was the worst of all . . . . " YC/O

Anne, once a maidservant. " . . . [Jane Adams] knows she had a bad husband who used her ill, and that she died in Lambeth workhouse. Dear, dear, in Lambeth workhouse!" YC/O

Grandfather, of Crofts the barber. "'He died accidentally, Sir . . . he didn't mean to do it. He always would go a-running about the streets—walking never satisfied *his* spirit—and he run against a post and died of a hurt in his chest.'" YC/O

Nicholas Nickleby, sr. "Mr Nickleby . . . embraced his wife and children, and having pressed them by turns to his languidly beating heart, sunk exhausted on his pillow. They were concerned to find that his reason went astray after this; for he babbled, for a long time, about the generosity and goodness of his brother and the merry old times when they were at school together. This fit of wandering past, he solemnly commended them to One who never deserted the widow or her fatherless children, and, smiling gently on them, turned upon his face, and observed that he thought he could fall asleep." NN 1

Dorker, "'who unfortunately—'

'—unfortunately died at Dotheboys Hall' . . . . " NN 4

Dockworker. "'Smashed, sir, by a cask of sugar.'" NN 35

Lord Verisopht. "Two shots were fired . . . the young lord turned his head sharply round, fixed upon his adversary a ghastly stare, and, without a groan or stagger, fell down dead.

" . . . all the light and life of day came on; and, amidst it all, and pressing down the grass whose every blade bore twenty tiny lives, lay the dead man, with his stark and rigid face turned upward to the sky." NN 50

Walter Bray. " . . . some person going in and shaking him by the arm, he fell heavily to the ground and was discovered to be dead." NN 54

Smike. "He fell into a slight slumber, and waking smiled as before; then, spoke of beautiful gardens, which he said stretched out before him, and were filled with figures of men, women, and many children, all with light upon their faces; then, whispered that it was Eden—and so died." NN 58

Ralph Nickleby. "He had torn a rope from one of the old trunks, and hanged himself on an iron hook immediately below the trap-door in the ceiling—in the very place to which the eyes of his son, a lonely desolate little creature, had so often been directed in childish terror, fourteen years before." NN 62 *See* S:Suicide—*fatherhood discovered*

Arthur Gride. " . . . he was found murdered in his bed." NN 65

Sir Mulberry Hawk. " . . . he was thrown into jail for debt, and there perished miserably, as such high spirits generally do." NN 65

Alice of York. "'Four sisters sat there. Their black garments made their pale faces whiter still, and time and sorrow had worked deep ravages. They were stately yet; but the flush and pride of beauty were gone.

"'And Alice—where was she? In Heaven.'" NN 6 (interlude)

Hugh Graham. "At that moment a shot from an unseen hand . . . struck Graham in the brain, and he fell dead." MH/I

Master Humphrey. "Going up to him, we found him dead . . . I never saw him look so calm and tranquil . . . so very spiritual, so strangely and indefinably allied to youth, although his head was gray and venerable. . . . He had relapsed for a moment into his late train of meditation, and, with a thoughtful smile upon his face, had died." MH/DG

Jinkinson. " . . . at last vun day he has in all the children vun arter another, shaves each on 'em wery clean, and gives him vun kiss on the crown o' his head; then he has in the two assistants, and arter cuttin' and curlin' of 'em in the first style of elegance, says he should like to hear the woice o' the greasiest bear, vich rekvest is immediately complied with; then he says that he feels wery happy in his mind and vishes to be left alone; and then he dies, previously cuttin' his own hair and makin' one flat curl in the wery middle of his forehead.'" MH/W

Hairdresser. "It took a deal o' poetry to kill the hairdresser, and some people say arter all that it wos more the gin and water as caused him to be run over; p'r'aps it was a little o' both, and came o' mixing the two.'" MH/W

Nephew, of a condemned man. "The next I saw was my own sword naked in my hand, and he lying at my feet stark dead—dabbled here and there with blood, but otherwise no different from what I had seen him in his sleep—in the same attitude too, with his cheek resting upon his little hand." MH/C *Compare James Steerforth, below*

Harry. " . . . his eyes were very bright; but their light was of Heaven, not earth . . . the little scholar turned his face towards the wall, and fell asleep.

"The poor schoolmaster sat in the same place, holding the small cold hand in his, and chafing it. It was but the hand of a dead child. He felt that; and yet he chafed it still, and could not lay it down." OCS 25

A little brother. "[The children] had an infant with them, and had laid it down asleep upon a child's grave, in a little bed of leaves. It was a new grave—the resting-place, perhaps, of some little creature, who, meek and patient in his illness, had often sat and watched them, and now seemed, to their minds, scarcely changed." OCS 53

Daniel Quilp. "The hull of a ship! He could touch its smooth and slippery surface with his hand. One loud cry now—but the resistless water bore him down before he could give it utterance, and, driving him under it, carried away a corpse." OCS 67

See —by drowning

Nell Trent. "Opening her eyes at last, from a very quiet sleep . . . she turned to the old man with a lovely smile upon her face—such, they said, as they had never seen, and never could forget—and clung with both her arms about his neck. They did not know that she was dead, at first." OCS 72 *See —of a young girl; illustration p35*

Nell's grandfather. "He did not return at the usual hour, and they went to seek him. He was lying dead upon the stone.

"They laid him by the side of her whom he had loved so well; and, in the church where they had often prayed, and mused, and lingered hand in hand, the child and the old man slept together." OCS 72

Stagg. "The word was given, and the men fired . . . .

" . . . the smoke had not yet scattered, but curled slowly off in a little cloud, which seemed like the dead man's spirit moving solemnly away. There were a few drops of blood upon the grass—more, when they turned him over—that was all." BR 69

Ned Dennis, hanged. " . . . he continued to rave . . . until his voice failed him, and he sank down a mere heap of clothes between the two attendants." BR 77

Hugh, hanged. "He . . . moved onward in his place, with a careless air, though listening at the same time to the Service for the Dead, with something between sullen attention, and quickened curiosity. As soon as he had passed the door, his miserable associate [Ned Dennis] was carried out; and the crowd beheld the rest." BR 77

Rioter, hanged. "One young man was hanged . . . whose aged grey-headed father waited for him at the gallows, kissed him at its foot when he arrived, and sat there, on the ground, till they took him down. They would have given him the body of his child; but he had no hearse, no coffin, nothing to remove it in, being too poor—and walked meekly away beside the cart that took it back to prison, trying, as he went, to touch its lifeless hand." BR 77

Sir John Chester. "Raising himself upon his hands, he gazed at [Haredale] for an instant, with scorn and hatred in his look, but, seeming to remember, even then, that this expression would distort his features after death, he tried to smile, and faintly moving his right hand, as if to hide his bloody linen in his vest, fell back dead . . . ." BR 81

Lord George Gordon. "Deserted by his former friends, and treated in all respects like the worst criminal in the jail, he lingered on, quite cheerful and resigned, until the 1st of November 1793, when he died in his cell, being then only three-and-forty years of age." BR 82

Gashford. " . . . a meager, wan old man, diseased and miserably poor, was found dead in his bed at an obscure inn in the Borough, where he was quite unknown. He had taken poison." BR 82

John Willet "was one morning found speechless in his bed. He lay in this state, free from all tokens of uneasiness, for a whole week, when he was suddenly restored to consciousness by hearing the nurse whisper in his son's ears that he was going. 'I'm a-going, Joseph,' said Mr Willet, turning round upon the instant, 'to the Salwanners'*—and immediately gave up the ghost." BR 82

**His son Joe had lost his arm at Savannah, Georgia, in the American Revolution.*

Anthony Chuzzlewit. " . . . on his livid face, and on his horny hands, and in his glassy eyes, and traced by an eternal finger in the very drops of sweat upon his brow, was one word—Death.

"He spoke to them in something of his own voice too, but sharpened and made hollow, like a dead man's face . . . .

"They . . . exposed him to the free current of morning air. But not all the air that is, nor all the winds that ever blew 'twixt Heaven and earth, could have brought new life to him.

"Plunge him to the throat in gold pieces now, and his heavy fingers shall not close on one!" MC 18

Tigg Montague, murdered. "What had [Jonas] left within the wood, that he sprang out of it as if it were a hell!

"The body of a murdered man. In one thick solitary spot, it lay among the last year's leaves of oak and beech, just as it had fallen headlong down. Sopping and soaking in among the leaves that formed its pillow; oozing down into the boggy ground, as if to cover itself from human sight; forcing its way between and through the curling leaves, as if those senseless things rejected and forswore it, and were coiled up in abhorrence; went a dark, dark stain that dyed the whole summer night from earth to heaven." MC 47

Jonas Chuzzlewit. "'Stop the coach! He has poisoned himself! The smell comes from this bottle in his hand!'

"The hand had shut upon it tight. With that rigidity of grasp with which no living man, in the full strength and energy of life, can clutch a prize he has won.

"They dragged him out into the dark street; but jury, judge, and hangman, could have done no more, and could do nothing now. Dead, dead, dead." MC 51

Ebenezer Scrooge. "'How are you?' 'How are you?' 'Well! Old Scratch has got his own at last, hey?' 'So I am told. Cold, isn't it?' 'Seasonable for Christmas time. You're not a skater, I suppose?' 'No. No. Something else to think of. Good morning!'

"Not another word. That was their meeting, their conversation, and their parting." CC 4 *[elision indications omitted, paragraphs consolidated]*

Deedles, in a vision. "'Put a double-barrelled pistol to his mouth, in his own counting house . . . and blew his brains out. No motive. Princely circumstances!' . . .

"'Oh the brain, the brain! . . . . the nerves, the nerves; the mysteries of this machine called Man! Oh the little that unhinges it: poor creatures that we are! . . . But there is One above. We must submit, Mr Fish. We must submit!" C 3

Lilian Fern, in a vision. "'He suffered her to sit beside His feet, and dry them with her hair. O Meg, what Mercy and Compassion!'

"As she died, the Spirit of the child returning, innocent and radiant, touched the old man with its hand, and beckoned him away." C 3

See —of a prostitute

Craggs. "'Mr Craggs, sir,' said Snitchey, shutting tight for an instant, and opening them again, 'was struck off the roll of life too soon . . . . It's a great loss to me. He was my right arm, my right leg, my right ear, my right eye, was Mr Craggs. I am paralytic without him.'" BL 3

Fanny Dombey. "Thus, clinging fast to that slight spar within her arms, the mother drifted out upon the dark and unknown sea that rolls round all the world." DS 1

Paul Dombey. "The golden ripple on the wall came back again, and nothing else stirred in the room." DS 16 *See —an old fashion*

Mrs Skewton. "Edith touches the white lips, and for a moment all is still. A moment afterwards, her mother, with her girlish laugh, and the skeleton of the Cleopatra manner, rises in her bed.

"Draw the rose-coloured curtains. There is something else upon its flight besides the wind and clouds. Draw the rose-coloured curtains close!" DS 41

James Carker. "He heard a shout . . . felt the earth tremble—knew in a moment that the rush was come—uttered a shriek—looked round—saw the red eyes, bleared and dim, in the daylight, close upon him—was beaten down, caught up, and whirled away upon a jagged mill, that spun him round and round, and struck him limb from limb, and licked his stream of life up with its fiery heat, and cast his mutilated fragments in the air." DS 55

Alice Marwood: "'I shall come,' said Harriet [Carker], when she shut the book, 'very early in the morning.' . . .

"[Alice] laid her hand upon her breast, murmuring the sacred name that had been read to her; and life passed from her face, like light removed." DS 58

David Copperfield, sr. "I was a posthumous child. My father's eyes had closed upon the light of this world six months when mine opened on it." DC 1

Joe Peggotty. "'My brother Joe was *his* [Ham's] father,' said Mr Peggotty.

"'Dead?, Mr Peggotty?' I hinted, after a respectful pause.

"'Drowndead,' said Mr Peggotty." DC 3

Tom. "'My brother-in-law, Tom, was *her* [Little Em'ly's] father.'

"I couldn't help it. '—Dead, Mr Peggotty?' I hinted, after another respectful silence.

"'Drowndead,' said Mr Peggotty." DC 3

Clara Copperfield. "'"Lay your good arm underneath my neck," she said, "and turn me to you, for your face is going far off, and I want it to be near." I put it as she asked ... and she died like a child that had gone to sleep!'" DC 9 *And see —of a child mother*

Baby Murdstone. "The mother who lay in the grave, was the mother of my infancy; the little creature in her arms, was myself, as I had once been, hushed for ever on her bosom." DC 9

Last occupant. "'Hey! What did he die of?' asked my aunt.

"'Well, ma'am, he died of drink,' said Mrs Crupp, in confidence. 'And smoke.'" DC 23

Barkis. "I was on the point of asking him if he knew me, when he tried to stretch out his arm, and said to me, distinctly, with a pleasant smile:

"'Barkis is willin'!'

"And, it being low water, he went out with the tide." DC 30 *See —on the sea-coast*

Francis Spenlow. "'. . . . Whether he fell out in a fit, or got out, feeling ill before the fit came on—or even whether he was quite dead then, though there is no doubt he was quite insensible—no one appears to know. If he breathed, certainly he never spoke. Medical assistance was got as soon as possible, but it was quite useless.'" DC 38

Dora Copperfield. "'I said that it was better as it is!' she whispers, as she holds me in her arms. 'Oh, Doady, after more years, you never could have loved your child-wife better than you do; and, after more years, she would so have tried and disappointed you, that you might not have been able to love her half so well! I know I was too young and foolish. It is much better as it is! . . .

"It is over. Darkness comes before my eyes; and, for a time, all things are blotted out of my remembrance." DC 53

"When the Angel of Death alighted there, my child-wife fell asleep—they told me so when I could bear to hear it—on her [Agnes's] bosom with a smile." DC 54

Jip. "'Oh, Jip! It may be, never again!'

"He lies down at my feet, stretches himself out as if to sleep, and, with a plaintive cry, is dead." DC 53

Ham Peggotty. "At length he neared the wreck. He was so near, that with one more of his vigorous strokes he would be clinging to it—when a high, green, vast hill-side of water, moving on shoreward, from beyond the ship, he seemed to leap up into it with a mighty bound, and the ship was gone!

"Some eddying fragments I saw in the sea, as if a mere cask had been broken . . . where they were hauling in. Consternation was in every face. They drew him to my very feet—insensible—dead. He was carried to the nearest house . . . every means of restoration were tried; but he had been beaten to death by the great wave, and his generous heart was stilled for ever." DC 55

James Steerforth. "'Has a body come ashore?'

"[The fisherman] said, 'Yes.'

"'Do I know it?' I asked then.

"He answered nothing.

"But he led me to the shore. And on that part of it where she and I had looked for shells, two children . . . among the ruins of the home he had wronged—I saw him lying with his head upon his arm, as I had often seen him lie at school." DC 55

A sister. "But while she was still very young, oh very very young, the sister drooped . . . and a little weak voice used to say, 'God bless my brother and the star!'

"And so the time came all too soon! when the child looked out alone, and when there was no face on the bed; and when there was a little grave among the graves, not there before; and when the star made long rays down towards him, as he saw it through his tears." RP/DS

A baby. "There was a baby born to be a brother to the child; and while he was so little that he never yet had spoken word, he stretched his tiny form out on his bed, and died." RP/DS

A mother. " . . . an old servant came to him and said:

"'Thy mother is no more. I bring her blessing on her darling son!'" RP/DS

A maiden daughter. " . . . the man who had been the child saw his daughter, newly lost to him, a celestial creature . . . ." RP/DS

The child, now an old man. "They whispered one another, 'He is dying.'

"And he said, 'I am. My age is falling from me like a garment, and I move towards the star as a child. And O, my Father, now I thank thee that it has so often opened, to receive those dear ones who await me!'

"And the star was shining; and it shines upon his grave." RP/DS

A child. "' Father, I am going to Heaven! . . the child who went to Heaven, rose into the golden air and vanished." CS/CS

A wife. "'My husband,' said the lady. 'I am called' . . . .

"Then, the mother, who was already drawn into the shade of the dark avenue and moving away with her arms still round his neck, kissed him, and said, 'My dearest, I am summoned, and I go!' And she was gone." CS/CS

A twin brother, in a ghost story. "His brother lay upon his bed . . . . He was in white, like the figure—necessarily so, because he had his night-dress on. He looked like the figure—necessarily so, because he looked earnestly at his brother when he saw him come into the room.

"But, when his brother reached the bedside, he slowly raised himself in bed, and looking full upon him, said these words:

"'JAMES, YOU HAVE SEEN ME BEFORE, TO-NIGHT—AND YOU KNOW IT!'

"And so died!" RD

Miss Barbary. "She was laid upon her bed. For more than a week she lay there, little altered outwardly; with her old handsome resolute frown that I so well knew, carved upon her face . . . . Her face was immovable. To the very last, and even afterwards, her frown remained unsoftened." BH 3

Tom Jarndyce. "' . . . says he, "it's being ground to bits in a slow mill; it's being roasted at a slow fire; it's being stung to death by single bees; it's being drowned by drops; it's going mad by grains." . . . I hadn't hardly got back here, when I heard a shot go echoing and rattling right away into the inn. I ran out—neighbours ran out—twenty of us cried at once, "Tom Jarndyce!" BH 5

Lady Dedlock. "' . . . she repulsed him as he bent over her, and looking at him fixedly and coldly, said "I will die here where I have walked. And I will walk here, though I am in my grave. I will walk here, until the pride of this house is humbled . . . .

"'There and then she died.'" BH 7

Brickmaker's baby. "Ada, whose gentle heart was moved by its appearance, bent down to touch its little face. As she did so, I saw what happened and drew her back. The child died.

"'O Esther!' cried Ada, sinking on her knees beside it. 'Look here! O Esther, my love, the little thing! The suffering, quiet, pretty little thing! I am so sorry for it. I am so sorry for the mother. I never saw a sight so pitiful as this before! O baby, baby!'" BH 8

Peffer. "Peffer is never seen in Cook's court now. He is not expected there, for he has been recumbent this quarter of a century in the churchyard of St Andrew's, Holborn . . . . " BH 10

Captain Hawdon. "No curtain veils the darkness of the night, but the discoloured shutters are drawn together; and through the two gaunt holes pierced in them, famine might be staring in—the Banshee of the man upon the bed . . . .

"[Tulkinghorn] thinks he has awakened his friend. He lies a little turned away, but his eyes are surely open . . . .

" . . . . As the light goes in, the great eyes in the shutters, darkening, seem to close. Not so the eyes upon the bed.

"'God save us!' exclaims Mr Tulkinghorn. 'He is dead!'

"Krook drops the heavy hand he has taken up, so suddenly that the arm swings over the bedside." BH 10, 11

Mrs Turveydrop. "[Mr Turveydrop] had married a meek little dancing-mistress . . . and had worked her to death . . . his wife (overpowered by his Deportment) had, to the last, believed in him, and had, on her death-bed, in the most moving terms, confided him to their son . . . . " BH 14

Neckett. "'You remember our friend Coavinses, Miss Summerson?' . . .

"'O yes!' said I.

"'Coavinses has been arrested by the great Bailiff,' said Mr Skimpole. 'He will never do violence to the sunshine any more.'" BH 15

Tinker. "'Drink put him in the hospital, guv'ner, and the hospital put him—in a glass case, I *have* heerd,' Phil replies mysteriously.

"'By that means you got promotion? Took the business, Phil?'" BH 26

Krook. "O Horror, he IS here! and this from which we run away, striking out the light and overturning one another into the street is all that represents him. BH 32 *See —spontaneous combustion*

Gridley. "The roof rang with a scream from Miss Flite, which still rings in my ears.

"'O no, Gridley!' she cried, as he fell heavily and calmly back from before her, 'not without my blessing. After so many years!'" BH 36

Jo. "' . . . is the light a-comin, sir?'

"'It is close at hand. HALLOWED BE THY NAME!

"'Hallowed be—thy—'

"The light is come upon the dark benighted way. Dead!" BH 47 *See —in the underclass*

Tulkinghorn. "What's that? Who fired a gun or pistol? Where was it? . . .

" . . . . For Mr Tulkinghorn's time is over for evermore; and the Roman pointed at the murderous hand uplifted against his life, and pointed helplessly at him, from night to morning, lying face downward on the floor, shot through the heart." BH 48

Lady Honoria. "I saw before me, lying on the step, the mother of the dead child. She lay there, with one arm creeping round a bar of the iron gate, and seeming to embrace it . . . she lay there, and they stopped me! . . .

"I passed on to the gate, and stooped down. I lifted the heavy head, put the long dank hair aside, and turned the face. And it was my mother cold and dead." BH 59

Harold Skimpole. "He died some five years afterwards, and left a diary behind him . . . which showed him to have been the victim . . . [and] an amiable child." BH 61

Richard Carstone. "He slowly laid his face down upon her bosom, drew his arms closer round her neck, and with one parting sob began the world. Not this world, O not this! The world that sets this right." BH 65 *See —a beginning*

A wife and child. " . . . [Nobody's] Master came and stood near to him dressed in black. He, also, had suffered heavily. His young wife, his beautiful and good young wife, was dead; so, too, his only child . . . said he, 'O you labouring men! The calamity began among you. If you had but lived more healthily and decently, I should not be the widowed and bereft mourner that I am this day.'" CS/NS

Captain Taunton. "'Dear Doubledick,' said he, 'I am dying . . . . Write to my mother. You will see Home again . . . .

"He spoke no more, but faintly signed for a moment towards his hair as it fluttered in the wind . . . and, gently turning his face over on the supporting arm as if for rest, died, with his hand upon the breast in which he had revived a soul." CS/PT

Mrs Gradgrind. " . . . the light that had always been feeble and dim behind the weak transparency, went out; and even Mrs Gradgrind, emerged from the shadow in which man walketh and disquieteth himself in vain, took upon her the dread solemnity of the sages and patriarchs." HT ii 9

Stephen Blackpool. "They carried him very gently along the fields, and down the lanes, and over the wide landscape . . . . It was soon a funeral procession. The star had shown him where to find the GOD of the poor; and through humility, and sorrow, and forgiveness, he had gone to his Redeemer's rest." HT iii 6

Gordon. "'Emma, thee lotht her huthband. He wath throw'd a heavy backfall off a Elephant in a thort of a Pagoda thing ath the Thultan of the Indieth, and he never got the better of it . . . .'' HT iii 7

Bounderby. " . . . Josiah Bounderby of Coketown was to die of a fit in the Coketown street, and [his] same precious will was to begin its long career of quibble, plunder, false pretences, vile example, little service and much law . . . " HT iii 9

Bob Tample. "Oftentimes [his sister] comes back with bedridden lines from the brother, who is always nearly dead and never quite, until he does tardily make an end of it, and at last this Actæon* reversed has rung the Dogs wholly down and betaken himself to them finally . . . we bury Bob's memory with the epitaph that he

went to the Dogs." HW/GD
**the luckless mythical figure who surprised Diana bathing: she changed him into a stag; he was hunted to death by his own hounds.*

Henri Barronneau. "' . . . sixty-five at least, and in a failing state of health. I had lived in the house some four months, when Monsieur Henri Barronneau had the misfortune to die:—at any rate, not a rare misfortune, that. It happens without any aid of mine, pretty often.'" LD i 1

Mme Rigaud, formerly Barronneau. "'One night Madame Rigaud and myself were walking amicably—I may say like lovers—on a height overhanging the sea. An evil star occasioned Madame Rigaud to advert to her relations . . . I grew warm, and provoked her . . . in an access of fury that I must ever deplore, [she] threw herself upon me with screams of passion (no doubt those that were overheard at some distance), tore my clothes, tore my hair, lacerated my hands, trampled and trod the dust, and finally leaped over, dashing herself to death upon the rocks below. Such is the train of incidents which malice has perverted into my endeavouring to force from Madame Rigaud a relinquishment of her rights; and, on her persistence in a refusal to make the concession I required, struggling with her—assassinating her!'" LD i 1

Lillie Meagles, a twin sister "'who died when we could just see her eyes—exactly like Pet's—above the table, as she stood on tiptoe holding by it.'" LD i 2

Gowan, sr. " . . . the paternal Gowan, originally attached to a legation abroad, had been pensioned off as a Commissioner of nothing particular somewhere or other, and had died at his post with his drawn salary in his hand, nobly defending it to the last extremity." LD i 17

Finching. "' . . . ere we had yet fully detected the housemaid in selling the feathers out of the spare bed Gout flying upwards soared with Mr F to another sphere.'" LD i 24

General. " . . . the commissary took his seat behind the proprieties with great decorum, and Mrs General drove until the commissary died . . . [he] having been buried with all the decorations suitable . . . Mrs General began to inquire what quantity of dust and ashes was deposited at the bankers'. It then transpired that the commissary had so far stolen a march on Mrs General as to have bought himself an annuity some years before his marriage, and to have reserved that circumstance, in mentioning, at the period of his proposal, that his income was derived from the interest of his money." LD ii 2

Lion. "'Faith, dear ladies!' said Blandois, smiling and shrugging his shoulders, 'somebody has poisoned that noble dog. He is as dead as the Doges!'" LD ii 6

William Dorrit and

Frederick Dorrit. "Two quiet figures were within the room; two figures, equally still and impassive, equally removed by an untraversable distance from the teeming earth and all that it contains, though soon to lie in it.

"One figure reposed upon the bed. The other, kneeling on the floor, drooped over it; the arms easily and peacefully resting on the coverlet; the face bowed down, so that the lips touched the hand over which with its last breath it had bent. The two brothers were before their Father; far beyond the twilight judgments of this world; high above its mists and obscurities." LD ii 19

See —of brothers

Merdle. "There was a bath . . . from which the water had been hastily drained off. Lying in it, as in a grave or sarcophagus, with a hurried drapery of sheet and blanket thrown across it, was the body of a heavily-made man, with an obtuse head, and coarse, mean, common features.

"A sky-light had been opened to release the steam with which the room had been filled; but, it hung, condensed into water-drops, heavily upon the walls, and heavily upon the face and figure in the bath. The room was still hot, and the marble of the bath still warm; but, the face and figure were clammy to the touch. The white marble at the bottom of the bath was veined with a dreadful red. On the ledge at the side, were an empty laudanum-bottle and a tortoise-shell handled penknife—soiled, but not with ink." ¶LD ii 25

Arthur Clennam's mother. "'As well might it be charged upon me [said Mrs Clennam], that the stings of an awakened conscience drove her mad, and that it was the will of the Disposer of all things that she should live so, many years." LD ii 30

Clennam, sr. "'Arthur's father and I lived no further apart, with half the globe between us, than when we were together in this home. He died, and sent this watch back to me, with its Do not forget.'" LD ii 30

Blandois, formerly Rigaud. "In one swift instant, the old house was before them, with the man lying smoking in the window; another thundering sound, and it heaved, surged outward, opened asunder in fifty places, collapsed, and fell . . . the great pile of chimneys which was then alone left standing, like a tower in a whirlwind, rocked, broke, and hailed itself down upon the heap of ruin, as if every tumbling fragment were intent on burying the crushed wretch deeper . . . .

" . . . it was night for the second time when [the diggers] found the dirty heap of rubbish that had been the foreigner, before his head had been shivered to atoms, like so much glass, by the great beam that lay upon him, crushing him." LD ii 31

Mrs Clennam. " . . . [she] dropped upon the stones; and she never from that hour moved so much as a finger again, or had the power to speak one word. For upwards of three years she reclined in her wheeled chair, looking attentively at those about her, and appearing to understand what they said: but the rigid silence she had so long held was evermore enforced upon her, and, except that she could move her eyes and faintly express a negative and affirmative with her head, she lived and died a statue." LD ii 31

Tip Dorrit. "[Little Dorrit] . . . a tender nurse and friend to Tip for some few years, who was never vexed by the great exactions he made of her, in return for the riches he might have given her if he had ever had them, and who lovingly closed his eyes upon the Marshalsea and all its blighted fruits." LD ii 34

Lucy Atherfield. "I see the golden hair and the innocent face now, between me and the driving clouds, like an angel going to fly away . . . she lay in her mother's arms at my feet . . . the child died, very peacefully . . . which was known to all in the boat by the mother's breaking out into lamentations for the first time since the wreck . . . 'committed to His merciful goodness!'. . . I laid my rough face softly on the placid little forehead, and buried the Golden Lucy in the grave of the Golden Mary." CS/GM

Mrs Arthur Holliday. "It turned out to be a long, lingering, hopeless malady. I attended her throughout . . . [and] had many long and interesting conversations with her in the intervals when she suffered least . . .

"A fortnight after [one] conversation, she died." LT 2

Ellen's mother. "In one of her imperious states, she froze, and never thawed again. She put her hands to her head one night, uttered a cry, stiffened, lay in that attitude certain hours, and died." LT 4

Ellen. ""'O, forgive me! I will do anything. O, Sir, pray tell me I may live!'

""'Die!'

""'Are you so resolved? Is there no hope for me?'

""'Die!!'

"'Her large eyes strained themselves with wonder and fear; wonder and fear changed to reproach; reproach to blank nothing. It was done. He was not at first so sure it was done, but that the morning sun was hanging jewels in her hair—he saw the diamond, emerald, and ruby, glittering among it in little points, as he stood looking down at her—when he lifted her and laid her on her bed.

"'She was soon laid in the ground." LT 4

A lover, murdered. "[The murderer] faced round, now, to follow him with his eyes. As the back of the bare light-brown head was turned to him, he saw a red curve stretch from his hand to it. He knew, before he threw the bill-hook, where it had alighted—I saw, had alighted, and not, would alight; for, to his clear perception the thing was done before he did it. He cleft the head, and it remained there, and the boy lay on his face." LT 4

Murderer, hanged; in apparition. "A chilled, slow, earthy, fixed old man. A cadaverous old man of measured speech. An old man who seemed as unable to wink, as if his eyelids had been nailed to his forehead. An old man whose eyes—two spots of fire—had no more motion than if they had been connected with the back of his skull by screws driven through it, and rivetted and bolted outside, among his grey hair . . . .

"'Your face is turned . . . to the Castle wall. When you are tied up, you see its stones expanding and contracting violently, and a similar expansion and contraction seem to take place in your own head and breast. Then, there is a rush of fire and an earthquake, and the Castle springs into the air, and you tumble down a precipice.'

"'His cravat appeared to trouble him. He put his hand to his throat, and moved his neck from side to side. He was an old man of a swollen character of face, and his nose was immovably hitched up on one side, as if by a little hook inserted in that nostril . . . .

"'His money could do nothing to save him, and he was hanged. *I* am He, and I was hanged at Lancaster Castle with my face to the wall, a hundred years ago!'" LT 4

Charker. "He was cut to pieces . . . his hair was all singed off, and his face was blackened with the running pitch from a torch.

"He made no complaint of pain, or of anything. 'Good-bye, old chap,' was all he said, with a smile. 'I've got my death. And Death ain't life. Is it, Gill?'" CS/EP

Mrs Venning. " . . . [I saw her] standing upright on the top of the steps of the trench, with her gray hair and her dark eyes—hide her daughter's child behind her, among the folds of her dress, strike a pirate with her other hand, and fall, shot by his pistol." CS/EP

Christian George King. "Shot through the heart. Some of the people ran round to the spot, and drew him out, with the slime and wet trickling down his face; but his face itself would never stir any more to the end of time." CS/EP

Mr Chops. "'Toby,' he says, with a quiet smile, 'the little man will now walk three times round the Cairawan, and retire behind the curtain.'

"When we called him in the morning, we found him gone into a much better Society than mine or Pall Mall's." CS/GS

The Kirklands. "Mr Forley not only never forgave that marriage, but vowed that he would visit the scandal of it heavily in the future on husband and wife. Both escaped his vengeance, whatever he meant it to be. The husband was drowned on his first voyage after his marriage, and the wife died in child-bed." CS/HL

George Forley. "'Three hours before Mr Forley's death,' said Mr Dalcott, 'his medical attendant left him apparently in a fair way of recovery. The change for the worse took place so suddenly, and was accompanied by such severe suffering, as entirely to prevent him from communicating his last wishes to any one. When I reached his house, he was insensible.'" CS/HL

Gaspard's child. "At last, swooping at a street corner by a fountain, one of [the carriage's] wheels came to a sickening little jolt, and there was a loud cry from a number of voices, and the horses reared and plunged . . . .

". . . . As the tall man suddenly got up from the ground, and came running at the carriage, Monsieur the Marquis clapped his hand for an instant on his sword-hilt.

"'Killed!!' shrieked the man, in wild desperation, extending both arms at their length above his head, and staring at him. 'Dead!'" TTC ii 7

Marquis St Evrémonde. " . . . there was one stone face too many, up at the château.

"The Gorgon had surveyed the building again in the night, and had added the one stone face wanting; the stone face for which it had waited through about two hundred years.

"It lay back on the pillow of Monsieur the Marquis. It was like a fine mask, suddenly startled, made angry, and petrified. Drive home into the heart of the stone figure attached to it, was a knife. Round its hilt was a frill of paper, on which was scrawled:

"'*Drive him fast to his tomb. This, from JACQUES.*'" TTC ii 9

Bastille commander. "[Mme Defarge] stood immovable close to the grim old officer, and remained immovable close to him; remained immovable close to him through the streets, as Defarge and the rest bore him along; remained immovable close to him when he was got near his destination, and began to be struck at from behind; remained immovable close to him when the long-gathering rain of stabs and blows fell heavy; was so close to him when he dropped dead under it, that, suddenly animated, she put her foot upon his neck, and with her cruel knife—long ready—hewed off his head." TTC ii 21

Mob victims. "Other seven faces there were, carried higher, seven dead faces, whose drooping eyelids and half-seen eyes awaited the Last Day. Impassive faces, yet with a suspended—not an abolished—expression on them; faces, rather, in a fearful pause, as having yet to raise the dropped lids of the eyes, and bear witness with the bloodless lips, 'THOU DIDST IT!'" TTC ii 21

Foulon. "'Bring him out! Bring him to the lamp!' . . .

" . . . . Once, he went aloft, and the rope broke, and they caught him shrieking; twice, he went aloft, and the rope broke, and they caught him shrieking; then, the rope was merciful, and held him, and his head was soon upon a pike, with grass enough in the mouth for all Saint Antoine to dance at the sight of." TTC ii 22

See IG:Revolution—*a lynching*

Foulon's son-in-law. "Saint Antoine wrote his crimes on flaring sheets of paper, seized him—would have torn him out of the breast of an army to bear Foulon company—set his head and heart on pikes, and carried the three spoils of the day, in Wolf-procession, through the streets." TTC ii 22

Mme Defarge's brother. " . . . invested for the moment with extraordinary power, he raised himself completely . . . .

""Marquis," said the boy, turned to him with his eyes opened wide, and his right hand raised, "in the days when all these things are to be answered for, I summon you and yours, to the last of your bad race, to answer for them. I mark this cross of blood upon you, as a sign that I do it . . . .

"'Twice, he put his hand to the wound in his breast, and with his forefinger drew a cross in the air. He stood for an instant with the finger yet raised, and, as it dropped, he dropped with it, and I laid him down dead."'" TTC iii 10

Mme Defarge's sister. ""My patient died, two hours before midnight—at a time, by my watch, answering almost to the minute when I had first seen her. I was alone with her, when her forlorn young head drooped gently on one side, and all her earthly wrongs and sorrows ended." TTC iii 10

Madame Defarge. "Madame Defarge's hands were at her bosom. Miss Pross looked up, saw what it was, struck at it, struck out a flash and a crash, and stood alone—blinded with smoke.

"All this was in a second. As the smoke cleared, leaving an awful stillness, it passed out on the air, like the soul of the furious woman whose body lay lifeless on the ground." TTC iii 14

Seamstress. "The two stand in the fast-thinning throng of victims, but they speak as if they were alone. Eye to eye, voice to voice, hand to hand, heart to heart, these two children of the Universal Mother, else so wide apart and differing, have come together on the dark highway, to repair home together, and to rest in her bosom . . . .

"She kisses [Carton's] lips; he kisses hers; they solemnly bless each other. The spare hand does not tremble as he releases it; nothing worse than a sweet, bright constancy is in the patient face. She goes next before him—is gone; the knitting-women count Twenty-Two." TTC iii 15

Sydney Carton. "'I am the Resurrection and the Life, saith the Lord: he that believeth in me, though he were dead, yet shall he live: and whosoever liveth and believeth in me shall never die.'

"The murmuring of many voices, the upturning of many faces, the pressing on of many footsteps in the outskirts of the crowd, so that it swells forward in a mass, like one great heave of water, all flashes away. Twenty-three." TTC iii 15

His final soliloquy is in Vol. II at p1372.

Miss Niner. "The sister had wasted away very slowly, and wild and terrible fantasies had come over her toward the end . . . . " HD 4

Julius Slinkton. "' . . . the miscreant suddenly turned away his face, and seemed to strike his mouth with his open hand. At the same instant, the room was filled with a new and powerful odour, and, almost at the same instant, he broke into a crooked run, leap, start—I have no name for the spasm—and fell, with a dull weight that shook the heavy old doors and windows in their frames.

"That was a fitting end of him." HD 5

Captain Murderer's bride: " . . . when [the fair twin] had lined the dish with crust and had cut the crust all ready to fit the top, the Captain called out, '*I* see the meat in the glass!' And the bride looked up at the glass, just in time to see the Captain cutting her head off; and he chopped her in pieces, and peppered her, and salted her, and put her in the pie, and sent it to the baker's, and ate it all, and picked the bones." UT/NS

Captain Murderer, and another bride. " . . . before [the dark twin] began to roll out the paste she had taken a deadly poison of a most awful character, distilled from toads' eyes and spiders' knees; and Captain Murderer had hardly picked her last bone, when he began to swell, and to turn blue, and to be all over spots, and to scream. And he went on swelling and turning bluer, and being more all over spots and screaming, until he reached from floor to ceiling and from wall to wall; and then, at one o-clock in the morning, he blew up with a loud explosion." UT/NS

Mr Wopsle's great-aunt. "[She] conquered a confirmed habit of living into which she had fallen, and Biddy became a part of our establishment." GE 16

Mrs Joe Gargery. "'It's for you, Handel,' said Herbert . . . 'and I hope there is nothing the matter.' This was in allusion to its heavy black seal and border.

"The letter was signed TRABB & CO., and its contents were simply, that I was an honoured sir, and that they begged to inform me that Mrs J. Gargery had departed this life on Monday last at twenty minutes past six in the evening, and that my attendance was requested at the interment on Monday next at three o'clock in the afternoon." GE 34

Arthur Havisham. "' . . . he starts up with a scream, and screams out, "Here she [his betrayed sister] is! She's got the shroud again. She's unfolding it. She's coming out of the corner. She's coming to the bed. Hold me, both on you—one on each side—don't let her touch me with it. Hah! She missed me that time. Don't let her throw it over my shoulders. Don't let her lift me up to get it round me. She's lifting me up. Keep me down!" Then he lifted himself up hard, and was dead.'" GE 42

Murdered woman. "[She] was found dead in a barn near Hounslow Heath. There had been a violent struggle, perhaps a fight. She was bruised and scratched and torn, and had been held by the throat at last and choked." GE 48

Compeyson. " . . . . He told me in a whisper that they had gone down, fiercely locked in each other's arms, and that there had been a struggle under water, and that he had disengaged himself, struck out, and swam away." GE 54

" . . . Compeyson, who had meant to depose to [Magwitch's identity], was tumbling on the tides, dead . . . . " GE 55

Magwitch. "With a last faint effort, which would have been powerless but for my yielding to it, and assisting it, he raised my hand to his lips. Then he gently let it sink upon his breast again, with his own hands lying on it. The placid look at the white ceiling came back, and passed away, and his head dropped quietly on his breast." GE 56

Miss Havisham. "[Joe] shook his head when I then asked him if she had recovered?

"'Is she dead, Joe?"

"'Why, you see, old chap,' said Joe, in a tone of remonstrance, and by way of getting at it by degrees, 'I wouldn't go so far as to say that, for that's a deal to say, but she ain't—'

"'Living, Joe?'

"'That's nigher where it is,' said Joe; 'she ain't living.'" GE 57

Bill Barley. " . . . the beam across the parlour ceiling at Mill Pond Bank had then ceased to tremble under old Bill Barley's growls and was at peace . . . . " GE 57

Bentley Drummle. "And I had heard of the death of [Estella's] husband, from an accident consequent on his ill-treatment of a horse." GE 59

Corporal Théophile. "'Our Corporal. Hélas, our dear Corporal!' . . .

"'At the fire. But he was so brave, so ready. Ah, too brave, too ready!' . . .

"'And a falling beam——'

"'Good God!' exclaimed the Englishman. 'It was a private soldier who was killed?'

"'No. A Corporal, the same Corporal, our dear Corporal. Beloved by all his comrades. The funeral ceremony was touching—penetrating. Monsieur The Englishman, your eyes fill with tears.'" CS/SL 2

Lirriper. " . . . he had ever been a free liver being in the commercial travelling line and travelling what he called a limekiln road—'a dry road, Emma my dear,' my poor Lirriper says to me, 'where I have to lay the dust with one drink or another all day long and half the night, and it wears me Emma'—and this led to his running through a good deal and might have run through the turnpike too when that dreadful horse that never would stand still for a single instant set off, but for its being night and the gate shut, and consequently took his wheel, my poor Lirriper and the gig smashed to atoms and never spoke afterwards." CS/L 1

Peggy Edson. "Then I brought the baby in its wrappers from where it lay, and I says:

"'My dear this is sent to a childless old woman. This is for me to take care of.'

"The trembling lip was put up towards my face for the last time, and I dearly kissed it.

"'Yes my dear,' I says. 'Please God! Me and the Major.'

"I don't know how to tell it right, but I saw her soul brighten and leap up, and get free and fly away in the grateful look." CS/L 1

Edson. "' . . . which I think would ease his spirit in his last hour if you would lay your cheek against his forehead and say, "May God forgive you!"'

"'O Gran,' says Jemmy with a full heart 'I am not worthy!' But he leaned down and did it. Then the faltering fingers made out to catch hold of my sleeve at last, and I believe he was a-trying to kiss me when he died." CS/LL 1

Harmon daughter, and Another. "' . . . they lived in a humble dwelling, probably possessing a porch ornamented with honeysuckle and woodbine twining, until she died. I must refer you to the Registrar of the District in which the humble dwelling was situated, for the certified cause of death; but early sorrow and anxiety may have had to do with it, though they may not appear in the ruled pages and printed forms. Indisputably this was the case with Another, for he was so cut up by the loss of his young wife that if he outlived her a year it was as much as he did.'" OMF i 2

Harmon. "'Venerable parent dies . . . . He directs himself to be buried with certain eccentric ceremonies and precautions against his coming to life, with which I need not bore you . . . . '" OMF i 2

Gaffer Hexam. "Soon the form of the bird of prey, dead some hours, lay stretched upon the shore, with a new blast storming at it and clotting the wet hair with hailstones . . . The wind sweeps jeeringly over Father, whips him with the frayed ends of his dress and his jagged hair, tries to turn him where he lies stark on his back, and force his face towards the rising sun, that he may be shamed the more.

Johnny. "With a weary and yet a pleased smile, and with an action as if he stretched his little figure out to rest, the child heaved his body on the sustaining arm, and seeking Rokesmith's face with his lips, said:

"'A kiss for the boofer lady.'

"Having now bequeathed all he had to dispose of, and arranged his affairs in this world, Johnny, thus speaking, left it." OMF ii 9

George Radfoot. "'Death has come to him. Death came to him in an ugly shape. He looked,' said the man, 'very horrible after it.'

"'Arter what?' said Riderhood, with a frowning stare.

"'After he was killed.'" OMF ii 12

Betty Higden. "'What is your name, my dear?'

"'My name is Lizzie Hexam.'

"'I must be sore disfigured. Are you afraid to kiss me?'

"The answer is the ready pressure of her lips upon the cold but smiling mouth.

"'Bless ye! *Now* lift me, my love.'

"Lizzie Hexam very softly raised the weather-stained grey head, and lifted her as high as Heaven." OMF iii 8

Cleaver (Mr Dolls). "The medical testimony was more precise and more to the purpose than it sometimes is in a Court of Justice. 'You had better send for something to cover it. All's over.'

" . . . . It was carried home, and . . . put down in the parlour—the little working-bench being set aside to make room for it—and there, in the midst of the dolls with no speculation in their eyes, lay Mr Dolls with no speculation in his." OMF iv 9

Bradley Headstone and Rogue Riderhood. "'Let go!' said Riderhood. 'Stop! What are you trying at? You can't drown Me. Ain't I told you that the man as has come through drowning can never be drowned? I can't be drowned.'

"'I can be!' returned Bradley, in a desperate, clenched voice. 'I am resolved to be. I'll hold you living, and I'll hold you dead. Come down!'

"Riderhood went over the smooth pit backward, and Bradley Headstone upon him. When the two were found lying under the ooze and scum behind one of the rotting gates, Riderhood's hold had relaxed, probably in falling, and his eyes were staring upward. But he was girdled still with Bradley's iron ring, and the rivets of the iron ring held tight." OMF iv 15

Sophy. " . . . I felt her lift herself a little on my shoulder, to look across the dark street. 'What troubles you, darling?' 'Nothing troubles me, father. I am not at all troubled. But don't I see a pretty churchyard over there?' 'Yes, my dear.' 'Kiss me twice, dear father, and lay me down to rest upon that church-yard grass so soft and green.' I staggered back into the cart with her head dropped on my shoulder, and I says to her mother, 'Quick. Shut the door! Don't let those laughing people see!' 'What's the matter?' she cries. 'O woman, woman,' I tells her, 'you'll never catch my little Sophy by her hair again, for she has flown away from you!'" CS/DM 1

Mrs Marigold. " . . . we saw a woman beating a child in a cruel manner, who screamed, 'Don't beat me! O mother, mother, mother!' Then my wife stopped her ears, and ran away like a wild thing, and next day she was found in the river." CS/DM 1

The Signal-man. "'He was cut down by

an engine, Sir. No man in England knew his work better. But somehow he was not clear of the outer rail. It was just at broad day. He had struck the light, and had the lamp in his hand. As the engine came out of the tunnel, his back was towards her, and she cut him down.'" CS/MJ 4

Walter Wilding. " . . . he opened his eyes in his own character, and said: 'Don't move me, Sally, because of what I am going to say; I lie quite easily. I think my time is come. I don't know how it may appear to you, Sally, but ——

"Insensibility fell upon him for a few minutes; he emerged from it once more.

"—I don't know how it may appear to you, Sally, but so it appears to me.'

"When he had thus conscientiously finished his favourite sentence, his time came, and he died." CS/NT 1

Jules Obenreizer. "'He went on alone. He had passed the gallery when an avalanche—like that which fell behind you near the Bridge of the Ganther——

"'Killed him?'

"'We dug him out, suffocated and broken all to pieces!'" CS/NT 4

Ethelinda Sapsea. " . . . she never could, and she never did, find a phrase satisfactory to her perhaps-too-favorable estimate of my intellect [said Mr Sapsea]. To the very last (feeble action of liver), she addressed me in the same unfinished terms.'" MED 4

Divorce

—exhilaration after shock: "And it cannot be denied that, when [Tom Pinch] had made up his mind . . . he felt an unaccustomed sense of freedom—a vague and indistinct impression of holiday-making—which was very luxurious. He had his moments of depression and anxiety, and they were, with good reason, pretty numerous; but still, it was wonderfully pleasant to reflect that he was his own master, and could plan and scheme for himself. It was startling, thrilling, vast, difficult to understand; it was a stupendous truth, teeming with responsibility and self-distrust; but in spite of all his cares, it gave a curious relish to the viands at the Inn, and interposed a dreamy haze between him and his prospects, in which they sometimes showed to magical advantage." MC 36

—expense: "The Law of Divorce is in such condition that from the tie of marriage there is no escape to be had, no absolution to be got, except under certain proved circumstances not necessary to enter upon here, and then only on payment of an enormous sum of money.

"Ferocity, drunkenness, flight, felony, madness, none of these will break the chain, without the enormous sum of money. The husband who, after years of outrage, has abandoned his wife, may at any time claim her for his property and seize the earnings on which she subsists. The most profligate of women, an intolerable torment, torture, and shame to her husband, may nevertheless, unless he be a very rich man, insist on remaining handcuffed to him, and dragging him away from any happier alliance, from youth to old age and death.

"Out of this condition of things among the common people, out of the galling knowledge of the impossibility of relief—aggravated, in cottages and single rooms, to a degree not easily imaginable by ill-assorted couples who live in houses of many chambers, and who, both at home and abroad, can keep clear of each other and go their respective ways—vices and crimes arise which no one with open eyes and any fair experience of the people can fail often to trace . . . back to this source." ¶HW/MP

—for the poor: "'What do you mean?' said Bounderby, getting up to lean his back against the chimney piece. 'What are you talking about? You took her for better for worse.'

"'I mun be ridden o' her. I cannot bear 't nommore. I ha' lived under 't so long, for that I ha' had'n the pity and comforting words o' th' best lass living or dead. Haply, but for her, I should ha' gone hottering mad.'

"'He wishes to be free, to marry the female of whom he speaks, I fear, sir,' observed Mrs Sparsit in an undertone, and much dejected by the immorality of the people.

"'I do. The lady says what's right. I do. I were a coming to 't. I ha' read i' th' papers that great fok (fair faw 'em a'! I wishes 'em no hurt!) are not bonded together for better for worst so fast, but that they can be set free fro' *their* misfortnet marriages, an' marry ower agen. When they dunnot agree, for that their tempers is ill-sorted, they has rooms o' one kind an' another in their houses, above a bit, and they can live asunders. We fok ha' only one room, and we can't. When that won't do, they ha' gowd an' other cash, an' they can say, "This for yo' an' that for me," an' they can go their separate ways. We can't. Spite o' all that, they can be set free for smaller wrongs than mine. So, I mun be ridden o' this woman, and I want t' know how?'

"'No how,' returned Mr Bounderby.

"'If I do her any hurt, sir, there's a law to punish me?'

"'Of course there is.'

"'If I flee from her, there's a law to punish me?'

"'Of course there is.'

"'If I marry t'oother dear lass, there's a law to punish me?'

"'Of course there is.'

"'If I was to live wi' her an' not marry her—saying such a thing could be, which it never could or would, an' her so good—there's a law to punish me, in every innocent child belonging to me?'

"'Of course there is.'

"'Now, a' GOD's name,' said Stephen Blackpool, 'show me the law to help me!'

"'Hem! There's a sanctity in this relation of life,' said Mr Bounderby, 'and—and—it must be kept up.'" HT i 11

"O! Better to have no home in which to lay his head, than to have a home and dread to go to it, through such a cause. [Blackpool] ate and drank, for he was exhausted—but he little knew or cared what; and he wandered about in the chill rain, thinking and thinking, and brooding and brooding.

"No word of a new marriage had ever passed between them; but Rachael had taken great pity on him years ago, and to her alone he had opened his closed heart all this time, on the subject of his miseries; and he knew very well that if he were free to ask her, she would take him. He thought of the home he might at that moment have been seeking with pleasure and pride; of the different man he might have been that night; of the lightness then in his now heavy-laden breast; of the then restored honour, self-respect, and tranquillity all torn to pieces.

"He thought of the waste of the best part of his life, of the change it made in his character for the worse every day, of the dreadful nature of his existence, bound hand and foot, to a dead woman, and tormented by a demon in her shape. He thought of Rachael, how young when they were first brought together in these circumstances, how mature now, how soon to grow old. He thought of the number of girls and women she had seen marry, how many homes with children in them she had seen grow up around her, how she had contentedly pursued her own lone quiet path—for him—and how he had sometimes seen a shade of melancholy on her blessed face, that smote him with remorse and despair.

"He set the picture of her up, beside the infamous image of last night; and thought, Could it be, that the whole earthly course of one so gentle, good, and self-denying, was subjugate to such a wretch as that!

"Filled with these thoughts—so filled that he had an unwholesome sense of growing larger, of being placed in some new and diseased relation towards the objects among which he passed, of seeing the iris round every misty light turn red—he went home for shelter." ¶HT i 12

—for the rich: "'Tell him,' said Edith . . . 'that I wish for a separation between us. That there had better be one. That I recommend it to him . . . .

"'Good Heaven, Mrs Dombey!' said her husband, with supreme amazement, 'do you imagine it possible that I could ever listen to such a proposition? Do you know who I am, Madam? Do you know what I represent? Did you ever hear of Dombey and Son? People to say that Mr Dombey—Mr Dombey!—was separated from his wife! Common people to talk of Mr Dombey and his domestic affairs! Do you seriously think, Mrs Dombey, that I would permit my name to be handed about in such connexion? Pooh, pooh, Madam! Fie for shame! You're absurd.' Mr Dombey absolutely laughed." DS 47

Family

—getting to bed: "Softening more and more, as his own tender feelings and those of his injured son were worked on, Mr Tetterby concluded by embracing him, and immediately breaking away to catch one of the real delinquents. A reasonably good start occurring, he succeeded, after a short but smart run, and some rather severe cross-country work under and over the bedsteads, and in and out among the intricacies of the chairs, in capturing his infant, whom he condignly punished, and bore to bed.

"This example had a powerful, and apparently, mesmeric influence on him of the boots, who instantly fell into a deep sleep, though he had been, but a moment before, broad awake, and in the highest possible feather. Nor was it lost upon the two young architects, who retired to bed, in an adjoining closet, with great privacy and speed. The comrade of the Intercepted One also shrinking into his nest with similar discretion, Mr Tetterby, when he paused for breath, found himself unexpectedly in a scene of peace." ¶HM 2

—neglected: "'My dear!' said I, smiling. 'Your papa, no doubt, considers his family.'

"'O yes, his family is all very fine, Miss Summerson,' replied Miss Jellyby; 'but what comfort is his family to him? His family is nothing but bills, dirt, waste, noise, tumbles downstairs, confusion, and wretchedness.'" BH 14

—offending: "Fledgeby's mother offended her family by marrying Fledgeby's father. It is one of the easiest achievements in life to offend your family when your family want to get rid of you. Fledgeby's mother's family had been very much offended with her for being poor, and broke with her for becoming comparatively rich." OMF ii 5

—poor relations: "It is a melancholy truth that even great men have their poor relations. Indeed great men have often more than their fair share of poor relations; inasmuch as very red blood of the superior quality, like inferior blood unlawfully shed, *will* cry aloud, and *will* be heard. Sir Leicester's cousins, in the remotest degree, are so many Murders, in the respect that they 'will out.' Among whom there are cousins who are so poor, that one might almost dare to think it would have been the happier for them never to have been plated links upon the Dedlock chain of gold, but to have been made of common iron at first, and done base service.

"Service, however (with a few limited reservations; genteel but not profitable), they may not do, being of the Dedlock dignity. So they visit their richer cousins, and get into debt when they can, and live but shabbily when they can't, and find—the women no husbands, and the men no wives—and ride in borrowed carriages, and sit at feasts that are never of their own making, and so go through high life. The rich family sum has been divided by so many figures, and they are the something over that nobody knows what to do with." BH 28

"The rest of the cousins are ladies and gentlemen of various ages and capacities; the major part, amiable and sensible, and likely to have done well enough in life if they could have overcome their cousinship; as it is, they are almost all a little worsted by it, and lounge in purposeless and listless paths, and seem to be quite as much at a loss how to dispose of themselves, as anybody else can be how to dispose of them." BH 28

—lodged: "Volumnia [Dedlock], in her room up a retired landing on the staircase—the second turning past the end of the carving and gilding—a cousinly room containing a fearful abortion of a portrait of Sir Leicester, banished for its crimes, and commanding in the day a solemn yard, planted with dried-up shrubs like antediluvian specimens of black tea . . . . " BH 58

Father and Fatherhood

—bitter cold: "If anything had frightened her, it was the face he turned upon her. The glowing love within the breast of his young daughter froze before it, and she stood and looked at him as if stricken into stone.

"There was not one touch of tenderness or pity in it. There was not one gleam of interest, parental recognition, or relenting in it. There was a change in it, but not of that kind. The old indifference and cold constraint had given place to something: what, she never thought and did not dare to think, and yet she felt it in its force, and knew it well without a name: that as it looked upon her, seemed to cast a shadow on her head.

"Did he see before him the successful rival of son, in health and life? Did he look upon his own successful rival in that son's affection? Did a mad jealousy and withered pride, poison sweet remembrances that should have endeared and made her precious to him? Could it be possible that it was gall to him to look upon her in her beauty and her promise: thinking of his infant boy?

"Florence had no such thoughts. But love is quick to know when it is spurned and hopeless: and hope died out of hers, as she stood looking in her father's face." DS 18

—to a cynic: "'My good fellow,' interposed the parent hastily, as he set down his glass, and raised his eyebrows with a startled and horrified expression, 'for Heaven's sake don't call me by that obsolete and ancient name ["father"]. Have some regard for delicacy. Am I grey, or wrinkled, do I go on crutches,

have I lost my teeth, that you adopt such a mode of address? Good GOD, how very coarse!'" BR 32

—of daughters: "'You must see my daughters. I have a blue-eyed daughter who is my Beauty daughter, I have a Sentiment daughter, and I have a Comedy daughter. You must see them all. They'll be enchanted . . . . '

"'It is pleasant,' said Mr Skimpole, turning his sprightly eyes from one to the other of us, 'and it is whimsically interesting, to trace peculiarities in families. In this family we are all children, and I am the youngest.'

"The daughters, who appeared to be very fond of him, were amused by this droll fact; particularly the Comedy daughter." BH 43

—diffident: "Nor was it less agreeable to observe how John the Carrier, reference being made by Dot to the aforesaid baby, checked his hand when on the point of touching the infant, as if he thought he might crack it; and bending down, surveyed it from a safe distance, with a kind of puzzled pride, such as an amiable mastiff might be supposed to show, if he found himself, one day, the father of a young canary." CH 1

—fatherhood discovered: "As [the bearer of the news] quitted the room,. Sir John's face changed; and the smile gave place to a haggard and anxious expression, like that of a weary actor jaded by the performance of a difficult part. He rose from his bed with a heavy sigh, and wrapped himself in his morning-gown.

" . . . 'Extremely distressing to be the parent of such an uncouth creature! Still, I gave him very good advice. I told him he would certainly be hanged. I could have done no more if I had known of our relationship; and there are a great many fathers who have never done as much for their natural children.—The hairdresser may come in, Peak!'

"The hairdresser came in; and saw in Sir John Chester (whose accommodating conscience was soon quieted by the numerous precedents that occurred to him in support of his last observation), the same imperturbable, fascinating, elegant gentleman he had seen yesterday, and many yesterdays before." BR 75

And see S:Suicide—*on discovering fatherhood*

—grandfather: "'Samivel Veller, sir,' said the old gentleman, 'has conferred upon me the ancient title o' grandfather vich had long laid dormouse, and wos s'posed to be nearly hex-tinct in our family.'" MHC 3

—and mother

—belief in child: "'You have a bad father, have you [said James Carker]?'

"'No, Sir!' returned Rob [Toodle], amazed. 'There ain't a better nor a kinder father going, than mine is.'

"'Why don't you want to see him then?' inquired his patron.

"'There's such a difference between a father and a mother, Sir,' said Rob, after faltering for a moment. 'He couldn't hardly believe yet that I was going to do better—though I know he'd try to—but a mother—*she* always believes what's good, Sir; at least I know my mother does, GOD bless her!'" DS 22

—in memory: "Some men rarely revert to their father, but seem, in the bank-books of their remembrance, to have transferred all the stock of filial affection into their mother's name. Mr Bagnet is one of these. Perhaps his exalted appreciation of the merits of the old girl, causes him usually to make the noun-substantive, Goodness, of the feminine gender." BH 49

—substitute: "' . . . I cannot charge myself [said Haredale] with having . . . lost sight of a heartfelt desire for [a niece's] true happiness; or with having acted—however much I was mistaken—with any other impulse than the one pure, single, earnest wish to be to her, as far as in my inferior nature lay, the father she had lost.'" BR 79

—sympathies limited: "It was understood that nothing of a tender nature could possibly be confided to Old Barley, by reason of his being totally unequal to the consideration of any subject more psychological than Gout, Rum, and Purser's stores." GE 46

—tyrannical: "A homely proverb recognises the existence of a troublesome class of persons who, having an inch conceded them, will take an ell. Not to quote the illustrious examples of those heroic scourges of mankind, whose amiable path in life has been from birth to death through blood, and fire, and ruin, and who would seem to have existed for no better purpose than to teach mankind that as the absence of pain is pleasure, so the earth, purged of their presence, may be deemed a blessed place—not to quote such mighty instances, it will be sufficient to refer to old John Willet.

"Old John having long encroached a good standard inch, full measure, on the liberty of Joe, and having snipped off a Flemish ell in the matter of the parole, grew so despotic and so great, that his thirst for conquest knew no bounds. The more young Joe submitted, the more absolute old John became. The ell soon faded into nothing. Yards, furlongs, miles arose; and on went old John in the pleasantest manner possible, trimming off an exuberance in this place, shearing away some liberty of speech or action in that, and conducting himself in his small way with as much high mightiness and majesty, as the most glorious tyrant that ever had his statue reared in the public ways, of ancient or of modern times." BR 30

Index VI *has a list of all CD's named fathers.*

Funeral

—in England

—in a child's eyes

—the procession: "... the undertaker, who was handing us gloves on a tea-tray as if they were muffins, and tying us into cloaks (mine had to be pinned up all round, it was so long for me) . . . I knew . . . was making game. So, when we got out into the streets, and I constantly disarranged the procession by tumbling on the people before me because my handkerchief blinded my eyes, and tripping up the people behind me because my cloak was so long, I felt that we were all making game. I was truly sorry for [the deceased], but I knew that it was no reason why we should be trying (the women with their heads in hoods like coal-scuttles with the black side outward) to keep step with a man in a scarf, carrying a thing like a mourning spy-glass, which he was going to open presently and sweep the horizon with. I knew that we should not all have been speaking in one particular key-note struck by the undertaker, if we had not been making game. Even in our faces we were every one of us as like the undertaker as if we had been his own family, and I perceived that this could not have happened unless we had been making game." UT/MM

"'Pocket-handkerchiefs out, all!' cried Mr Trabb at this point, in a depressed business-like voice—'Pocket-handkerchiefs out! We are ready!'

"So, we all put our pocket-handkerchiefs to our faces, as if our noses were bleeding, and filed out two and two . . . . The remains of my [Pip's] poor sister [Mrs Joe Gargery] had been brought round by the kitchen door, and, it being a point of Undertaking ceremony that the six bearers must be stifled and blinded under a horrible black velvet housing with a white border, the whole looked like a blind monster with twelve human legs, shuffling and blundering along under the guidance of two keepers—the postboy and his comrade.

"The neighbourhood, however, highly approved of these arrangements, and we were much admired as we went through the village; the more youthful and vigorous part of the community making dashes now and then to cut us off, and lying in wait to intercept us at points of vantage. At such times the more exuberant among them called out in an excited manner on our emergence round some corner of expectancy, '*Here* they come!' '*Here* they are!' and we were all but cheered. In this progress I was much annoyed by the abject Pumblechook, who, being behind me, persisted all the way, as a delicate attention, in arranging my streaming hatband, and smoothing my cloak. My thoughts were further distracted by the excessive pride of Mr and Mrs Hubble, who were surpassingly conceited and vainglorious in being members of so distinguished a procession." GE 35

—the wake: "The continued impossibility of getting on without plum-cake; the ceremonious apparition of a pair of decanters containing port and sherry and cork; Sally's sister at the tea-table, clinking the best crockery and shaking her head mournfully every time she looked down into the teapot, as if it were the tomb; the Coat of Arms again, and Sally as before; lastly, the words of consolation administered to Sally when it was considered right that she should 'come round nicely:' which were, that the deceased had had 'as com-for-ta-ble a fu-ne-ral as comfortable could be!'" UT/MM

—to a grown-up: "Other funerals have I seen with grown-up eyes . . . of which the burden has been the same childish burden. Making game. Real affliction, real grief and solemnity, have been outraged, and the funeral has been 'performed.' The waste for which the funeral customs of many tribes of savages are conspicuous, has attended these civilised obsequies; and once, and twice, have I wished in my soul that if the waste must be, they would let the undertaker bury the money, and let me bury the friend." UT/MM

"Why should high civilisation and low savagery ever come together on the point of making [funerals] a wantonly wasteful and contemptible set of forms?" UT/MM

—*cheap: a professional critical:* "'You wouldn't be inclined to take a walking one of two, with the plain wood and a tin plate, I suppose?'

"'Certainly not,' replied Mr Mould, 'much too common. Nothing to say to it.'

"'I told 'em it was precious low' . . . .

"'Tell 'em to go somewhere else. We don't do that style of business here,' said Mr Mould. 'Like their impudence to propose it. Who is it?

"'Why . . . that's where it is, you see. It's the beadle's son-in-law.'

"'The beadle's son-in-law, eh?' said Mould. 'Well! I'll do it if the beadle follows in his cocked hat; not else. We carry it off that way, by looking official, but it'll be low enough then. His cocked hat, mind!'" MC 25

—*deep trimming:* "'Poor soul!' Camilla presently went on . . . 'he is so very strange! Would any one believe that when Tom's wife died, he actually could not be induced to see the importance of the children's having the deepest of trimmings to their mourning?' "Good Lord!" says he, "Camilla, what can it signify so long as the poor bereaved little things are in black?" So like Matthew! The idea!

"'Good points in him, good points in him,' said Cousin Raymond; 'Heaven forbid I should deny good points in him; but he never had, and he never will have, any sense of the proprieties.'

"'You know I was obliged,' said Camilla, 'I was obliged to be firm. I said, "It WILL NOT DO, for the credit of the family." I told him that, without deep trimmings, the family was disgraced. I cried about it from breakfast till dinner. I injured my digestion. And at last he flung out in his violent way, and said, with a D, "Then do as you like." Thank Goodness it will always be a consolation to me to know that I instantly went out in a pouring rain and bought the things.'" GE 11

—*a professional gratified:* "'This is one of the most impressive cases, sir . . . that I have seen in the whole course of my professional experience. . . . Such affectionate regret, sir, I never saw. There is no limitation, there is positively NO limitation:' opening his eyes wide, and standing on tiptoe: 'in point of expense! I have orders, sir, to put on my whole establishment of mutes; and mutes come very dear . . . not to mention their drink. To provide silver-plated handles of the very best description, ornamented with angels' heads from the most expensive dies. To be perfectly profuse in feathers. In short, sir, to turn out something absolutely gorgeous.'" MC 19

" . . . an afflicted gentleman, an affectionate gentleman, who knows what it is in the power of money to do, in giving him relief, and in testifying his love and veneration for the departed. It can give him . . . four horses to each vehicle; it can give him velvet trappings; it can give him drivers in cloth cloaks and top-boots; it can give him the plumage of the ostrich, dyed black; it can give him any number of walking attendants, dressed in the first style of funeral fashion, and carrying batons tipped with brass; it can give him a handsome tomb; it can give him a place in Westminster Abbey itself, if he choose to invest it in such a purchase. Oh! do not let us say that gold is dross, when it can buy such things as these.'" MC 19

And see H:Vocations—*undertaker*

—*to a raven:* "Oh my crop and feathers, what a scene it was! . . .

"First of all, two dressed-up fellows came—trying to look sober, but they couldn't do it—and stuck themselves outside the door. There they stood, for hours, with a couple of crutches covered over with drapery; cutting their jokes on the company as they went in, and breathing such strong rum and water into our establishment over the way. . . . As if a pair of respectable crows wouldn't have done it much better!

"By and by, there came a hearse and four, and then two carriages and four; and on the tops of 'em, and on all the horses' heads, were plumes of feathers, hired at so much per plume; and everything, horses and all, was covered over with black velvet, till you couldn't see it. Because there were not feathers enough yet, there was a fellow in the procession carrying a board of 'em on his head, like Italian images; and there were about five-and-twenty or thirty other fellows (all hot and red in the face with eating and drinking) dressed up in scarves and hatbands, and carrying—shut-up fishing-rods, I believe—who went draggling through the mud, in a manner that I thought would be the death of me . . . . As if any two-and-sixpenny masquerade, tumbled into a vat of blacking, wouldn't be quite as solemn, and immeasurably cheaper!" HW/R 2

—*to a severe critic:* "Several years have now elapsed since it began to be clear to the comprehension of most rational men that the English people had fallen into a condition much to be regretted, in respect of their funeral customs. A system of barbarous show and expense was found to have gradually erected itself above the grave, which, while it could possibly [*sic*] do no honour to the memory of the dead, did great dishonour to the living, as inducing them to associate the most solemn of human occasions with unmeaning mummeries, dishonest debt, profuse waste, and bad example in an utter oblivion of responsibility.

"The more the subject was examined, and the lower the investigation was carried, the more monstrous (as was natural) these usages appeared to be, both in themselves and in their consequences. No class of society escaped. The competition among the middle classes for superior gentility in funerals—the gentility being estimated by the amount of ghastly folly in which the undertaker was permitted to run riot—descended even to the very poor; to whom the cost of funeral customs was so ruinous and so disproportionate to their means that they formed clubs among themselves to defray such charges.

"Many of these clubs, conducted by designing villains who preyed upon the general infirmity, cheated and wronged the poor most cruelly; others, by presenting a new class of temptations to the wickedest natures among them, led to a new class of mercenary murders, so abominable in their iniquity that language cannot stigmatise them with sufficient severity.

"That nothing might be wanting to complete the general depravity, hollowness, and falsehood, of this state of things, the absurd fact came to light, that innumerable harpies assumed the titles of furnishers of funerals, who possessed no funeral furniture whatever, but who formed a long file of middlemen between the chief mourner and the real tradesman, and who hired out the trappings from one to another—passing them on like water-buckets at a fire—every one of them charging his enormous percentage on his share of the 'black job.'

"Add to all this, the demonstration, by the simplest and plainest practical science, of the terrible consequences to the living, inevitably resulting from the practice of burying the dead in the midst of crowded towns; and the exposition of a system of indecent horror, revolting to our nature and disgraceful to our age and nation, arising out of the confined limits of such burial-grounds and the avarice of their proprietors; and the culminating point of this gigantic mockery is at last arrived at." ¶HW/TD

—in France: "In France, upon the whole, these ceremonies are more sensibly regulated, because they are upon the whole less expensively regulated. I cannot say that I have ever been much edified by the custom of tying a bib and apron on the front of the house of mourning, or that I would myself particularly care to be driven to my grave in a nodding and bobbing car, like an infirm four-post bedstead, by an inky fellow-creature in a cocked-hat. But it may be that I am constitutionally insensible to the virtues of a cocked-hat.

"In provincial France, the solemnities are sufficiently hideous, but are few and cheap. The friends and townsmen of the departed, in their own dresses and not masquerading under the auspices of the African Conjurer, surround the hand-bier, and often carry it. It is not considered indispensable to stifle the bearers, or even to elevate the burden on their shoulders; consequently it is easily taken up, and easily set down, and is carried through the streets without the distressing floundering and shuffling that we see at home.

"A dirty priest or two, and a dirtier acolyte or two, do not lend any especial grace to the proceedings . . . . But there is far less of the Conjurer and the Medicine Man in the business than under like circumstances here. The grim coaches that we reserve expressly for such shows, are non-existent; if the cemetery be far out of the town, the coaches that are hired for other purposes of life are hired for this purpose; and although the honest vehicles make no pretence of being overcome, I have never noticed that the people in them were the worse for it." ¶UT/MM

—in good society: "A great crowd assembles in Lincoln's Inn Fields on the day of the [Tulkinghorn] funeral. Sir Leicester Dedlock attends the ceremony in person; strictly speaking, there are only three other human followers, that is to say, Lord Doodle, William Buffy, and the debilitated cousin (thrown in as a make-weight), but the amount of inconsolable carriages is immense.

"The Peerage contributes more four-wheeled affliction than has ever been seen in that neighbourhood. Such is the assemblage of armorial bearings on coach panels, that the Heralds' College might be supposed to have lost its father and mother at a blow.

"The Duke of Foodle sends a splendid pile of dust and ashes, with silver wheel-boxes, patent axles, all the last improvements, and three bereaved worms, six feet high, holding on behind, in a bunch of woe. All the state coachmen in London seem plunged into mourning; and if that dead old man of the rusty garb be not beyond a taste in horse-flesh (which appears impossible), it must be highly gratified this day." ¶BH 53

—*Mrs Grundy's expectations:* "Here's the plumber painter and glazier come to take the funeral order which he is going to give to the sexton, who is going to give it to the clerk, who is going to give it to the carpenter, who is going to give it to the haberdasher, who is going to give it to the furnishing undertaker, who is going to divide it with the Black Jobmaster.

"'Hearse and four, Sir?' says he. 'No, a pair will be sufficient.' 'I beg your pardon, sir, but when we buried Mr Grundy at number twenty, there was four on 'em, Sir; I think it right to mention it.' 'Well, perhaps there had better be four.' 'Thank you, Sir. Two coaches and four, Sir, shall we say?' 'No. Coaches and pair.' 'You'll excuse my mentioning it, Sir, but pairs to the coaches, and four to the hearse, would have a singular appearance to the neighbours. When we put four to anything, we always carry four right through.' 'Well! say four!' 'Thank you, Sir. Feathers of course?' 'No. No feathers. They're absurd.' 'Very good, Sir. *No* feathers?' 'No.' '*Very* good, Sir. We *can* do fours without feathers, Sir, but it's what we never do. When we buried Mr Grundy, there was feathers, and—I only throw it out, Sir—Mrs Grundy might think it strange.' 'Very well! Feathers!' 'Thank you, Sir,'—and so on." HW/R 2

—*interment of a pauper:* "Then the active and intelligent [beadle], who has got into the morning papers as such, comes with his pauper company to Mr Krook's, and bears off the body of our dear brother here departed, to a hemmed-in churchyard, pestiferous and obscene, whence malignant diseases are communicated to the bodies of our dear brothers and sisters who have not departed; while our dear brothers and sisters who hang about official backstairs—would to Heaven they *had* departed!—are very complacent and agreeable. Into a beastly scrap of ground which a Turk would reject as a savage abomination, and a Caffre would shudder at, they bring our dear brother here departed, to receive Christian burial.

"With houses looking on, on every side, save where a reeking little tunnel of a court gives access to the iron gate—with every villainy of life in action close on death, and every poisonous element of death in action close on life—here, they lower our dear brother down a foot or two: here, sow him in corruption, to be raised in corruption; an avenging ghost at many a sick-bedside: a shameful testimony to future ages, how civilisation and barbarism walked this boastful island together.

"Come night, come darkness, for you cannot come too soon, or stay too long, by such a place as this! Come, straggling lights into the windows of the ugly houses; and you who do iniquity therein, do it at least with this dread scene shut out! Come, flame of gas, burning so sullenly above the iron gate, on which the poisoned air deposits its witch-ointment slimy to the touch! It is well that you should call to every passerby, 'Look here!'" BH 11

—*in Italy*

—*church service:* "There is a ceremony when an old Cavaliere or the like, expires, of erecting a pile of benches in the cathedral, to represent his bier; covering them over with a pall of black velvet; putting his hat and sword on the top; making a little square of seats about the whole; and sending out formal invitations to his friends and acquaintances to come and sit there, and hear Mass: which is performed at the principal Altar, decorated with an infinity of candles for that purpose." PI 5

—*confraternities:* "When the better kind of people die, or are at the point of death, their nearest relations generally walk off: retiring into the country for a little change, and leaving the body to be disposed of, without any superintendence from them.

"The procession is usually formed, and the coffin borne, and the funeral conducted, by a body of persons called a Confraternita, who, as a kind of voluntary penance, undertake to perform these offices, in regular rotation, for the dead: but who, mingling something of pride with their humility, are dressed in a loose garment covering their whole person, and wear a hood concealing the face; with breathing-holes and apertures for the eyes.

"The effect of this costume is very ghastly: especially in the case of a certain Blue Confraternita belonging to Genoa, who, to say the least of them, are very ugly customers, and who look—suddenly encountered in their pious ministration in the streets—as if they were Ghoules or Demons, bearing off the body for themselves." ¶PI 5

"In Italy, the hooded Members of Confraternities who attend on funerals, are dismal and ugly to look upon; but the services they render are at least voluntarily rendered, and impoverish no one, and cost nothing." UT/MM

—of the poor: "It may be a consequence of the frequent direction of the popular mind, and pocket, to the souls in Purgatory, but there is very little tenderness for the *bodies* of the dead here. For the very poor, there are, immediately outside one angle of the walls, and behind a jutting point of the fortification, near the sea, certain common pits—one for every day in the year—which all remain closed up, until the turn of each comes for its daily reception of dead bodies. . . .

"Certainly, the effect of this promiscuous and indecent splashing down of dead people in so many wells, is bad. It surrounds Death with revolting associations, that insensibly become connected with those whom Death is approaching. Indifference and avoidance are the natural result; and all the softening influences of the great sorrow are harshly disturbed." PI 5

*—Nell's, in blank verse:**

"And now the bell—the bell
She had so often heard by night and day,
And listen'd to with solemn pleasure,
Almost as a living voice—
Rung its remorseless toll for her,
So young, so beautiful, so good.

"Decrepit age, and vigorous life.
And blooming youth, and helpless infancy,
Pour'd forth—on crutches, in the pride of strength
And health, in the full blush
Of promise, the mere dawn of life—
To gather round her tomb. Old men were there,
Whose eyes were dim
And senses failing—
Grandames, who might have died ten years ago,
And still been old—the deaf, the blind, the lame,
The palsied.
The living dead in many shapes and forms,
To see the closing of that early grave.
What was the death it would shut in
To that which still
Could crawl and creep above it?

"Along the crowded path they bore her now;
Pure as the new-fall'n snow
That covered it: whose day on earth
Had been as fleeting.
Under that porch, where she had sat when Heaven
In mercy brought her to that peaceful spot,
She pass'd again, and the old church
Received her in its quiet shade." OCS 72

*deF p204, *based on the work and insights of R. H. Horne in 1848*

Grave and Graveyard

—cemetery

—for the disregarded: "A churchyard. Here, then, the wretched man whose name [Scrooge] was now to learn, lay underneath the ground. It was a worthy place. Walled in by houses; overrun by grass and weeds, the growth of vegetation's death, not life; choked up with too much burying; fat with repleted appetite. A worthy place!" CC 4

—in France: "There was a Cemetery outside the town . . . . To be sure there were some wonderful things in it (from the Englishman's point of view), and of a certainty in all Britain you would have found nothing like it. Not to mention the fanciful flourishes of hearts and crosses in wood and iron, that were planted all over the place, making it look very like a Firework-ground, where a most splendid pyrotechnic display might be expected after dark, there were so many wreaths upon the graves, embroidered, as it might be, 'To my mother,' 'To my daughter,' 'To my father,' 'To my brother,' 'To my sister,' 'To my friend,' and those many wreaths were in so many stages of elaboration and decay, from the wreath of yesterday, all fresh colour and bright beads, to the wreath of last year, a poor mouldering wisp of straw!

"There were so many little gardens and grottoes made upon graves, in so many tastes, with plants and shells and plaster figures and porcelain pitchers, and so many odds and ends! There were so many tributes of remembrance hanging up, not to be discriminated by the closest inspection from little round waiters, whereon were depicted in glowing hues either a lady or a gentleman with a white pocket-handkerchief out of all proportion, leaning, in a state of the most faultless mourning and most profound affliction, on the most architectural and gorgeous urn!

"There were so many surviving wives who had put their names on the tombs of their deceased husbands, with a blank for the date of their own departure from this weary world; and there were so many surviving husbands who had rendered the same homage to their deceased wives; and out of the number there must have been so many who had long ago married again! In fine, there was so much in the place that would have seemed mere frippery to a stranger, save for the consideration that the lightest paper flower that lay upon the poorest heap of earth was never touched by a rude hand, but perished there, a sacred thing!" ¶CS/SL 2

—for paupers: "'He was put there,' says Jo, holding to the bars and looking in.

"'Where? O, what a scene of horror!'

"There!' says Jo, pointing. 'Over yinder. Among them piles of bones, and close to that there kitchin winder! They put him wery nigh the top. They was obliged to stamp upon it to get it in. I could unkiver it for you with my broom, if the gate was open. That's why they locks it, I s'pose,' giving it a shake. 'It's always locked: Look at the rat!' cries Jo, excited. 'Hi! look! There he goes! Ho! into the ground!'

"The servant [disguised; it is Lady Dedlock] shrinks into a corner—into a corner of that hideous archway, with its deadly stains contaminating her dress; and putting out her two hands, and passionately telling him to keep away from her, for he is loathsome to her, so remains for some moments. Jo stands staring, and is still staring when she recovers herself.

"'Is this place of abomination consecrated ground?'

"'I don't know nothink of consequential ground,' says Jo, still staring.

"'Is it blessed?'

"'WHICH?' says Jo, in the last degree amazed.

"'Is it blessed?'

"'I'm blest if I know,' says Jo, staring more than ever; 'but I shouldn't think it warn't. Blest?' repeats Jo, something troubled in his mind. 'It ain't done it much good if it is. Blest? I should think it was t'othered myself. But I don't know nothing!'" BH 16

"The gate was closed. Beyond it, was a burial-ground—a dreadful spot in which the night was very slowly stirring; but where I could dimly see heaps of dishonoured graves and stones, hemmed in by filthy houses, with a few dull lights in their windows, and on whose walls a thick humidity broke out like a disease." BH 59 *See also* F:Pauper—*burial*

—for the poor: Ralph Nickleby "had to pass a poor, mean burial-ground—a dismal place raised a few feet above the level of the street, and parted from it by a low parapet wall and an iron railing; a rank, unwholesome, rotten spot, where the very grass and weeds seemed in their frowsy growth, to tell that they had sprung from paupers' bodies, and struck their roots in the graves of men, sodden in steaming courts and drunken hungry dens. And here in truth they lay, parted from the living by a little earth and a board or two—lay thick and close—corrupting in body as they had in mind; a dense and squalid crowd. Here they lay cheek by jowl with life: no deeper down than the feet of the throng that passed there every day, and piled high as their throats. Here they lay, a grisly family, all those dear departed brothers and sisters of the ruddy clergyman who did his task so speedily when they were hidden in the ground!" NN 62

"The words were read above the ashes of Betty Higden, in a corner of a churchyard near the river; in a churchyard so obscure that there was nothing in it but grass-mounds, not so much as one single tombstone. It might not be to do an unreasonably great deal for the diggers and hewers, in a registering age, if we ticketed their graves at the common charge; so that a new generation might know which was which: so that the soldier, sailor, emigrant, coming home, should be able to identify the resting-place of father, mother, playmate, or betrothed. For we turn up our eyes and say that we are all alike in death, and we might turn them down and work the saying out in this world, so far. It would be sentimental, perhaps? But how say ye, my lords and gentlemen and honourable boards, shall we not find good standing-room left for a little sentiment, if we look into our crowds?" OMF iii 9

—visited by a raven: "Here again, the raven was in a highly reflective state; walking up and down when he had dined, with an air of elderly complacency which was strongly suggestive of his having his hands under his coat-tails; and appearing to read the tombstones with a very critical taste.

Sometimes, after a long inspection of an epitaph, he would strop his beak upon the grave to which it referred, and cry in his hoarse tones, 'I'm a devil, I'm a devil, I'm a devil!' but whether he addressed his observations to any supposed person below, or merely threw them off as a general remark, is matter of uncertainty." BR 25

—*city churchyard:* "Such strange churchyards hide in the City of London; churchyards sometimes so entirely detached from churches, always so pressed upon by houses; so small, so rank, so silent, so forgotten, except by the few people who ever look down into them from their smoky windows. As I stand peeping in through the iron gates and rails, I can peel the rusty metal off, like bark from an old tree.

"The illegible tombstones are all lopsided, the grave-mounds lost their shape in the rains of a hundred years ago, the Lombardy Poplar or Plane-Tree that was once a drysalter's daughter and several common-councilmen, has withered like those worthies, and its departed leaves are dust beneath it. Contagion of slow ruin overhangs the place. The discoloured tiled roofs of the environing buildings stand so awry, that they can hardly be proof against any stress of weather. Old crazy stacks of chimneys seem to look down as they overhang, dubiously calculating how far they will have to fall. In an angle of the walls, what was once the tool-house of the gravedigger rots away, encrusted with toadstools. Pipes and spouts for carrying off the rain from the encompassing gables, broken or feloniously cut for old lead long ago, now let the rain drip and splash as it list, upon the weedy earth." ¶UT/CA

And see N:Flora—*trees—in a city churchyard*

—*in cold weather:* "The bottom of the oldest grave about . . . was not more still and quiet, than the churchyard in the pale moonlight. The cold hoar-frost glistened on the tombstones, and sparkled like rows of gems, among the stone carvings of the old church. The snow lay hard and crisp upon the ground; and spread over the thickly-strewn mounds of earth so white and smooth a cover that it seemed as if corpses lay there, hidden only by their winding sheets. Not the faintest rustle broke the profound tranquillity of the solemn scene. Sound itself appeared to be frozen up, all was so cold and still." PP 29

—*dew in a churchyard:* ". . . the dew glistened on the green mounds, like tears shed by Good Spirits over the dead." OCS 53

—*epitaphs:* "Shunning the tombs, [the sun] crept about the mounds, beneath which slept poor humble men, twining for them the first wreaths they had ever won, but wreaths less liable to wither and far more lasting in their kind, than some which were graven deep in stone and marble, and told in pompous terms of virtues meekly hidden for many a year, and only revealed at last to executors and mourning legatees." OCS 16

"The court brought them to a churchyard; a paved square court, with a raised bank of earth about breast high, in the middle, enclosed by iron rails. Here, conveniently and healthfully elevated above the level of the living, were the dead, and the tombstones; some of the latter droopingly inclined from the perpendicular, as if they were ashamed of the lies they told." OMF ii 15

—*grave*

—*a child's:* "Some young children sported among the tombs, and hid from each other, with laughing faces. They had an infant with them, and had laid it down asleep upon a child's grave, in a little bed of leaves. It was a new grave—the resting-place, perhaps, of some little creature, who, meek and patient in its illness, had often sat and watched them, and now seemed to their minds, scarcely changed.

"She drew near and asked one of them whose grave it was. The child answered that that was not its name; it was a garden —his brother's. It was greener, he said, than all the other gardens, and the birds loved it better because he had been used to feed them. When he had done speaking, he looked at [Nell] with a smile, and kneeling down and nestling for a moment with his cheek against the turf, bounded merrily away." OCS 53 *See illustration, p6*

—*flowers:* "'Look at them. See how they hang their heads, and droop, and wither. Do you guess the reason?'

"'No,' [Nell] replied.

"'Because the memory of those who lie below passes away so soon. At first they tend them, morning, noon, and night; they soon begin to come less frequently; from once a day, to once a week; from once a week, to once a month; then, at long and uncertain intervals: then, not at all. Such tokens seldom flourish long. I have known the briefest summer flowers outlive them.'

"'I grieve to hear it,' said the child.

"'Ah! so say the gentlefolks who come down here to look about them,' returned the old man, shaking his head, 'but I say otherwise. "It's a pretty custom you have in this part of the country," they say to me sometimes, "to plant the graves, but it's melancholy to see these things all withering or dead." I crave their pardon and tell them that, as I take it, 'its a good sign for the happiness of the living. And so it is. It's nature.'

"'Perhaps the mourners learn to look to the blue sky by day, and to the stars by night, and to think that the dead are there, and not in graves,' said the child in an earnest voice." OCS 54

—*a girl's, errant and beloved:* "Within the altar of the old village church there stands a white marble tablet, which bears as yet but one word—'AGNES!' There is no coffin in that tomb; and may it be many, many years, before another name is placed above it! But if the spirits of the Dead ever come back to earth, to visit spots hallowed by the love—the love beyond the grave—of those whom they knew in life, I believe that the shade of Agnes [Fleming] sometimes hovers round that solemn nook. I believe it none the less because that nook is in a church, and she was weak and erring." OT 53

—*a youth's:* "The grave was green above the dead boy's grave, and trodden by feet so small and light, that not a daisy drooped its head beneath their pressure. Through all the spring and summer-time, garlands of fresh flowers, wreathed by infant hands, rested on the stone; and when the children came here to change them lest they should wither and be pleasant to [Smike] no longer, their eyes filled with tears, and they spoke low and softly of their poor dead cousin." NN 65

—*graverobbing*

—*in action:* "Crouching down . . . and looking in, [Young Jerry Cruncher] made out the three fishermen creeping through some rank grass, and all the gravestones in the churchyard—it was a large churchyard that they were in—looking on like ghosts in white, while the church tower itself looked on like the ghost of a monstrous giant. They did not creep far, before they stopped and stood upright. And then they began to fish.

"They fished with a spade, at first. Presently the honoured parent appeared to be adjusting some instrument like a great corkscrew. Whatever tools they worked with, they worked hard, until the awful striking of the church clock so terrified Young Jerry, that he made off . . . . They were still fishing perseveringly, when he peeped in at the gate for the second time; but, now they seemed to have got a bite. There was a screwing and complaining sound down below, and their bent figures were strained, as if by a weight. By slow degrees the weight broke away the earth upon it, and came to the surface. Young Jerry very well knew what it would be; but, when he saw it, and saw his honoured parent about to wrench it open, he was so frightened, being new to the sight, that he made off again . . . . " TTC ii 14

—*and a coffin:* "[Young Jerry Cruncher] had a strong idea that the coffin he had seen was running after him; and, pictured as hopping on behind him, bolt upright, upon its narrow end, always on the point of overtaking him and hopping on at his side—perhaps taking his arm—it was a pursuer to shun. It was an inconsistent and ubiquitous fiend too, for, while it was making the whole night behind him dreadful, he darted out into the roadway to avoid dark alleys, fearful of its coming hopping out of them like a dropsical boy's-Kite without tail and wings. It hid in doorways, too, rubbing its horrible shoulders against doors, and drawing them up to its ears, as if it were laughing. It got into shadows on the road, and lay cunningly on its back to trip him up. All this time it was incessantly hopping on behind and gaining on him, so that when the boy got to his own door he had reason for being half dead. And even then it would not leave him, but followed him up-stairs with a bump on every stair, scrambled into bed with him, and bumped down, dead and heavy, on his breast when he fell asleep." TTC ii 14

—*gravestone:* "'Durdles was making his reflections here . . . surrounded by his works, like a poplar Author.—Your own brother-in-law;' introducing a sarcophagus within the railing, white and cold in the moonlight. 'Mrs Sapsea;' introducing the monument of that devoted wife. 'Late Incumbent;' introducing the Reverend Gentleman's broken column. 'Departed Assessed Taxes;' introducing a vase and towel, standing on what might represent the cake of soap. 'Former pastrycook and Muffin-maker, much respected;' introducing gravestone. 'All safe and sound here, sir, and all Durdles's work.

Of the common folk, that is merely bundled up in turf and brambles, the less said the better. A poor lot, soon forgot.'" MED 5

Home

—abandoned: "God knows I had no part in it while [the Murdstones] remained there, but it pained me to think of the dear old place as altogether abandoned; of the weeds growing tall in the garden, and the fallen leaves lying thick and wet upon the paths. I imagined how the winds of winter would howl round it, how the cold rain would beat upon the window-glass, how the moon would make ghosts on the walls of the empty rooms, watching their solitude all night. I thought afresh of the grave in the churchyard, underneath the tree: and it seemed as if the house were dead too, now, and all connected with my father and mother were faded away." DC 17

—apotheosis: "Before marriage and afterwards, let [young ladies and gentlemen] learn to centre all their hopes of real and lasting happiness in their own fireside; let them cherish the faith that in home, and all the English virtues which the love of home engenders, lies the only true source of domestic felicity; let them believe that round the household GODs, contentment and tranquillity cluster in their gentlest and most graceful forms; and that many weary hunters of happiness through the noisy world, have learnt this truth too late, and found a cheerful spirit and a quiet mind only at home at last." YC/Conclusion

—ashamed of it: "It is a most miserable thing to feel ashamed of home. There may be black ingratitude in the thing, and the punishment may be retributive and well deserved; but, that it is a miserable thing, I can testify.

"Home had never been a very pleasant place to me, because of my sister's temper. But, Joe [Gargery] had sanctified it, and I believed in it. I had believed in the best parlour as a most elegant saloon; I had believed in the front door, as a mysterious portal of the Temple of State whose solemn opening was attended with a sacrifice of roast fowls; I had believed in the kitchen as a chaste though not magnificent apartment; I had believed in the forge as the glowing road to manhood and independence. Within a single year all this was changed. Now, it was all coarse and common, and I would not have had Miss Havisham and Estella see it on any account." GE 14

—be it ever: "'—Be it ever,' added Mr Wegg in prose as he glanced about [Mr Venus's] shop, 'ever so ghastly, all things considered there's no place like it.'" OMF iii 7

—chaotic: "[Mr Jellyby's] scrambling home, from week's end to week's end, is like one great washing-day—only nothing's washed!'" BH 14

—to a cynic: "' . . . a real home [said Doctor Jeddler] is only four walls; and a fictitious one, mere rags and ink.'" BL 2

—a definition: "'If it were defined by any particular four walls and a roof, GOD knows I should be sufficiently puzzled to say whereabouts it lay; but that is not what I mean. When I speak of home, I speak of the place where, in default of a better, those I love are gathered together; and if that place were a gipsy's tent, or a barn, I should call it by the same good name notwithstanding." NN 35

—destroyed: "The ashes of the commonest fire are melancholy things, for in them there is an image of death and ruin—of something that has been bright, and is but dull, cold, dreary dust—with which our nature forces us to sympathise. How much more sad the crumbled embers of a home: the casting down of that great altar, where the worst among us sometimes perform the worship of the heart; and where the best have offered up such sacrifices, and done such deeds of heroism, as, chronicled, would put the proudest temples of old Time, with all their vaunting annals, to the blush!" BR 81

—foreseen: "Upon another girl's face . . . a quiet and contented little face, we see Home fairly written. Shining from the word, as rays shine from a star, we see how, when our graves are old, other hopes than ours are young, other hearts than ours are moved; how other ways are smoothed; how other happiness blooms, ripens, and decays—no, not decays, for other homes and other bands of children, not yet in being nor for ages yet to be, arise, and bloom and ripen to the end of all!" CS/GO

—leaving and returning: "And now I find that all the French people on board begin to grow, and all the English people to shrink. The French are nearing home, and shaking off a disadvantage, whereas we are shaking it on. Zamiel is the same man, and Abd-el-Kader is the same man, but each seems to come into possession of an indescribable confidence that departs from us—from Monied Interest, for instance, and from me.

Just what they gain, we lose. Certain British 'Gents' about the steersman, intellectually nurtured at home on parody of everything and truth of nothing, become subdued, and in a manner forlorn . . . . " RP/F

—literary evocation: ""'And being in her own home,"' read Marion, from the book; '"her home made exquisitely dear by these remembrances, she now began to know that the great trial of her heart must soon come on, and could not be delayed. O Home, our comforter and friend when others fall away, to part with whom, at any step between the cradle and the grave"'—

"'Marion, my love!' said Grace.

"'Why, Puss!' exclaimed her father, 'what's the matter?'

"She put her hand upon the hand her sister stretched towards her, and read on; her voice still faltering and trembling, though she made an effort to command it when thus interrupted.

"'"To part with whom, at any step between the cradle and the grave, is always sorrowful. O Home, so true to us, so often slighted in return, be lenient to them that turn away from thee, and do not haunt their erring footsteps too reproachfully! Let no kind looks, no well-remembered smiles, be seen upon thy phantom face. Let no ray of affection, welcome, gentleness, forbearance, cordiality, shine from thy white head. Let no old loving word, or tone, rise up in judgment against thy deserter; but if thou canst look harshly and severely, do, in mercy to the Penitent!!"'

"'Dear Marion, read no more to-night,' said Grace—for she was weeping.

"'I cannot,' she replied, and closed the book. 'The words seem all on fire!'" BL 2

—of a miser: "A gloomy house the Bower, with sordid signs on it of having been, through its long existence as Harmony Jail, in miserly holding. Bare of paint, bare of paper on the walls, bare of furniture, bare of experience of human life . . . .

"A certain leanness falls upon houses not sufficiently imbued with life (as if they were nourished upon it), which was very noticeable here. The staircase, balustrades, and rails, had a spare look—an air of being denuded to the bone—which the panels of the walls and the jambs of the doors and windows also bore. The scanty moveables partook of it; save for the cleanliness of the place, the dust into which they were all resolving would have lain thick on the floors; and those, both in colour and in grain, were worn like old faces that had kept much alone.

"The bedroom where the clutching old man [Harmon] had lost his grip on life was left as he had left it. There was the old grisly four-post bedstead, without hanging, and with a jail-like upper rim of iron and spikes; and there was the old patch-work counterpane. There was the tight-clenched old bureau, receding atop like a bad and secret forehead; there was the cumbersome old table with twisted legs, at the bowed-side; and there was the box upon it, in which the will had lain. A few old chairs with patch-work covers, under which the more precious stuff to be preserved had slowly lost its quality of colour without imparting pleasure to any eye, stood against the wall. A hard family likeness was on all these things." OMF i 15

—nearly deserted: "Florence felt that, for her, there was greater peace within it than elsewhere. It was better and easier to keep her secret shut up there, among the tall dark walls, than to carry her abroad into the light, and try to hide it from a crowd of happy eyes. It was better to pursue the study of her loving heart, alone, and find no new discouragements in loving hearts about her. It was easier to hope, and pray, and love on, all uncared for, yet with constancy and patience, in the tranquil sanctuary of such remembrances, although it moulded, rusted, and decayed about her; than in a new scene, let its gayety be what it would. She welcomed back her old enchanted dream of life, and longed for the old dark door to close upon her, once again." DS 28

—returning: "At sunrise, one fair Monday morning—the twenty-seventh of June, I shall not easily forget the day—there lay before us old Cape Clear, God bless it, showing, in the mist of early morning, like a cloud; the brightest and most welcome cloud to us that ever hid the face of Heaven's fallen sister—Home." AN/C

"Bright as the scene was; fresh, and full of motion; airy, free, and sparkling; it was nothing to the life and exultation in the breasts of the two travellers, at sight of the old churches, roofs, and darkened chimney stacks of Home. The distant roar, that swelled up hoarsely from the busy streets, was music in their ears; the lines of people gazing from the wharves, were friends held dear; the canopy of smoke that overhung the town was brighter and more beautiful to them than if the richest silks of Persia had been waving in the air. And though the water going on its glistening track, turned, ever and again, aside to dance and sparkle round great ships, and swiftly passed, in many a sportive chase, through obdurate old iron rings, set deep into the stone-work of the quays; not even it was half so buoyant, and so restless, as their fluttering hearts, when yearning to set foot, once more, on native ground.

"A year had passed, since those same spires and roofs had faded from their eyes. It seemed, to them, a dozen years. Some trifling changes, here and there, they called to mind; and wondered that they were so few and slight. In health and fortune, prospect and resource, they came back poorer men than they had gone away. But it was home." MC 35

—revisited: "Of course the town had shrunk fearfully, since I was a child there. I had entertained the impression that the High-street was at least as wide as Regent-street, London, or the Italian Boulevard at Paris. I found it little better than a lane. There was a public clock in it, which I had supposed to be the finest clock in the world: whereas it now turned out to be as inexpressive, moon-faced, and weak a clock as ever I saw. It belonged to a Town Hall, where I had seen an Indian (who I now suppose wasn't an Indian) swallow a sword (which I now suppose he didn't). The edifice had appeared to me in those days so glorious a structure, that I had set it up in my mind as the model on which the Genie of the Lamp built the palace for Aladdin. A mean little brick heap, like a demented chapel, with a few yawning persons in leather gaiters, and in the last extremity for something to do, lounging at the door with their hands in their pockets, and calling themselves a Corn Exchange!" UT/DT

And see Child*—memory and death*

—its spirits: "And all was Caleb's doing; all the doing of [Bertha Plummer's] simple father! But he too had a Cricket on his Hearth; and listening sadly to its music when the motherless Blind Child was very young, that Spirit had inspired him with the thought that even her great deprivation might be almost changed into a blessing, and the girl made happy by these little means. For all the Cricket tribe are potent Spirits, even though the people who hold converse with them do not know it (which is frequently the case); and there are not, in the unseen world, voices more gentle and more true, that may be so implicitly relied on, or that are so certain to give none but tenderest counsel, as the Voices in which the Spirits of the Fireside and the Hearth address themselves to human kind." CH 2

—stately: "The saying is, that home is home, be it never so homely. If it hold good in the opposite contingency, and home is home be it never so stately, what an altar to the Household Gods is raised up here." DS 35

—unused: "Whatever is built by man for man's occupation, must, like natural creations, fulfil the intention of its existence, or soon perish. This old house had wasted more from desuetude than it would have wasted from use, twenty years for one." OMF i 15

"Within, I found it, as I had expected, transcendently dismal. The slowly changing shadows waved on it from the heavy trees, were doleful in the last degree; the house was ill-placed, ill-built, ill-planned, and ill-fitted. It was damp, it was not free from dry rot, there was a flavour of rats in it, and it was the gloomy victim of that indescribable decay which settles on all the work of man's hands whenever it is not turned to man's account." CS/HH

See also F:The Poor, Working*—household affections, and* LC:Words and Phrases

Matrimony

—advice

—John Chester: "Marriage is a civil contract: people marry to better their worldly condition and improve appearances; it is an affair of house and furniture, of liveries, servants, equipage, and so forth. The lady being poor and you poor also, there is an end of the matter. You cannot enter upon these considerations, and have no manner of business with the ceremony. I drink [Miss Haredale's] health in this glass, and respect and honour her for her extreme good sense. It is a lesson to you." BR 32

—Alderman Cute: "'You are going to be married you say,' pursued the Alderman. 'Very unbecoming and indelicate in one of your sex! But never mind that. After you are married, you'll quarrel with your husband and come to be a distressed wife. You may think not; but you will, because I tell you so. Now, I give you fair warning, that I have made up my mind to Put distressed wives Down. So, don't be brought before me.

"'You'll have children—boys. Those boys will grow up bad, of course, and run wild in the streets, without shoes and stockings. Mind, my young friend! I'll convict 'em summarily, every one, for I am determined to Put boys without shoes and stockings Down. Perhaps your husband will die young (most likely) and leave you with a baby. Then you'll be turned out of doors, and wander up and down the streets. Now, don't wander near me, my dear, for I am resolved to Put all wandering mothers Down.

"'All young mothers, of all sorts and kinds, it's my determination to Put Down. Don't think to plead illness as an excuse with me; or babies as an excuse with me; for all sick persons and young children (I hope you know the church-service, but I'm afraid not) I am determined to Put Down.

"'And if you attempt, desperately, and ungratefully, and impiously, and fraudulently attempt, to drown yourself, or hang yourself, I'll have no pity for you, for I have made up my mind to Put all suicide Down! If there is one thing,' said the Alderman, with his self-satisfied smile, 'on which I can be said to have made up my mind more than on another, it is to Put suicide Down. So don't try it on.'" ¶C 1

CD, probably correctly, ascribed these views to Sir Peter Laurie: see Vol. I p654

—Mrs Maylie, and reputation: "'Youth has many generous impulses which do not last; and among them are some which, being gratified, become only the more fleeting. Above all, I think,' said the lady, fixing her eyes on her son's face, 'that if an enthusiastic, ardent and ambitious man marry a wife on whose name there is a stain, which, though it originate in no fault of hers, may be visited by cold and sordid people upon her, and upon his children also; and, in exact proportion to his success in the world, be cast in his teeth and made the subject of sneers against him; he may, no matter how generous and good his nature, one day repent of the connection he formed in early life. And she may have the pain and torture of knowing that he does so.'" OT 34

—Mrs Merdle, and Society: "Mrs Merdle reviewed the bosom which Society was accustomed to review; and having ascertained that show-window of Mr Merdle's and the London jewellers to be in good order, replied [to Mrs Gowan]:

"'As to marriage on the part of a man, my dear, Society requires that he should retrieve his fortunes by marriage. Society requires that he should gain by marriage. Society requires that he should found a handsome establishment by marriage. Society does not see, otherwise, what he has to do with marriage.

"'Young men . . . I mean people's sons who have the world before them—must place themselves in a better position towards Society by marriage, or Society really will not have any patience with their making fools of themselves. Dreadfully worldly all this sounds,' said Mrs Merdle, leaning back in her nest and putting up her glass again, 'does it not?'

"'But it is true,' said Mrs Gowan, with a highly moral air.

"'My dear, it is not to be disputed for a moment,' returned Mrs Merdle; 'because Society has made up its mind on the subject, and there is nothing more to be said.'" LD 33

—Annie Strong: "'We had been little lovers once. If circumstances had not happened otherwise, I might have come to persuade myself that I really loved him, and might have married him, and been most wretched. There can be no disparity in marriage like unsuitability of mind and purpose. . . . '" DC 45

—Betsey Trotwood: "'These are early days, Trot,' she pursued, 'and Rome was not built in a day, nor in a year. You have chosen freely for yourself;' a cloud passed over her face for a moment, I thought; 'and you have a chosen a very pretty and a very affectionate creature.

"'It will be your duty, and it will be your pleasure too—of course I know that; I am not delivering a lecture—to estimate her (as you chose her) by the qualities she has, and not by the qualities she may not have. The latter you must develop in her, if you can.

"'And if you cannot, child,' here my aunt rubbed her nose, 'you must just accustom yourself to do without 'em. But remember, my dear, your future is between you two. No one can assist you; you are to work it out for yourselves. This is marriage, Trot; and Heaven bless you both in it, for a pair of babes in the wood as you are!'" ¶DC 44

—Tony Weller: "'I'm a goin' to leave you, Samivel my boy, and there's no telling ven I shall see you again. Your mother-in-law may ha' been too much for me, or a thousand things may have happened by the

time you next hears any news o' the celebrated Mr Veller o' the Bell Savage. The family name depends wery much upon you, Samivel, and I hope you'll do wot's right by it.

"'Upon all little pints o' breedin', I know I may trust you as vell as if it was my own self. So I've only this here one little bit of adwice to give you. If ever you gets to up-'ards o' fifty, and feels disposed to go a marryin' anybody—no matter who—jist you shut yourself up in your own room, if you've got one, and pison yourself off hand. Hangin's wulgar, so don't you have nothin' to say to that. Pison yourself, Samivel, my boy, pison yourself, and you'll be glad on it arterwards.' With these affecting words, Mr Weller looked steadfastly on his son, and turning slowly upon his heel, disappeared from his sight." ¶PP 23

—attraction: "'May I ask you if you have ever had an opportunity of remarking, down in your part of the country, that the children of not exactly suitable marriages, are always most particularly anxious to be married?'

"This was such a singular question, that I asked him, in return, 'Is it so?'

"'I don't know,' said Herbert; 'that's what I want to know. Because it is decidedly the case with us. My poor sister Charlotte, who was next me and died before she was fourteen, was a striking example.

"'Little Jane is the same. In her desire to be matrimonially established, you might suppose her to have passed her short existence in the perpetual contemplation of domestic bliss. Little Alick in a frock has already made arrangements for his union with a suitable young person at Kew. And, indeed, I think we are all engaged, except the baby.'" ¶GE 30

—the Banns: unsuccessful suitor: "When the clerk handed up a list to the clergyman, Mr Toots, being then seated, held on by the seat of the pew; but when the names of Walter Gay and Florence Dombey were read aloud as being in the third and last stage of that association, he was so entirely conquered by his feelings as to rush from the church without his hat, followed by the beadle and pew-opener, and two gentlemen of the medical profession, who happened to be present; of whom the first-named presently returned for that article, informing Miss Nipper in a whisper that she was not to make herself uneasy about the gentleman, as the gentleman said his indisposition was of no consequence.

"Miss Nipper, feeling that the eyes of that integral portion of Europe which lost itself weekly among the high-backed pews, were upon her, would have been sufficiently embarrassed by this incident, though it had terminated here; the more so, as the captain in the front row of the gallery, was in a state of unmitigated consciousness which could hardly fail to express to the congregation that he had some mysterious connexion with it.

"But the extreme restlessness of Mr Toots painfully increased and protracted the delicacy of her situation. That young gentleman, incapable, in his state of mind, of remaining alone in the churchyard, a prey to solitary meditation, and also desirous, no doubt of testifying his respect for the offices he had in some measure interrupted, suddenly returned—not coming back to the pew, but stationing himself on a free seat in the aisle, between two elderly females who were in the habit of receiving their portion of a weekly dole of bread then set forth on a shelf in the porch.

"In this conjunction Mr Toots remained, greatly disturbing the congregation, who felt it impossible to avoid looking at him, until his feelings overcame him again, when he departed silently and suddenly. Not venturing to trust himself in the church any more, and yet wishing to have some social participation in what was going on there, Mr Toots was after this, seen from time to time, looking in, with a lorn aspect, at one or other of the windows; and as there were several windows accessible to him from without, and as his restlessness was very great, it not only became difficult to conceive at which window he would appear next, but likewise became necessary, as it were, for the whole congregation to speculate upon the chances of the different windows, during the comparative leisure afforded them by the sermon.

"Mr Toots's movements in the churchyard were so eccentric, that he seemed generally to defeat all calculation, and to appear, like the conjuror's figure, where he was least expected; and the effect of these mysterious presentations was much increased by its being difficult to him to see in, and easy to everybody else to see out: which occasioned his remaining, every time, longer than might have been expected, with his face close to the glass, until he all at once became aware that all eyes were upon him, and vanished.

"These proceedings on the part of Mr Toots, and the strong individual consciousness of them that was exhibited by the captain, rendered Miss Nipper's position so responsible a one, that she was mightily relieved by the conclusion of the service; and was hardly so affable to Mr Toots as usual, when he informed her and the captain, on the way back, that now he was sure he had no hope, you know, he felt more comfortable—at least not exactly more comfortable, but more comfortably and completely miserable." DS ¶56

—beneath one's station: "'You see,' said Mr Toots, 'what *I* wanted in a wife was—in short, was sense. Money, Feeder, I had. Sense I—I had not, particularly . . . .

"'No, Feeder, I had *not*. Why should I disguise it? I had *not*. I knew that sense was There,' said Mr Toots, stretching out his hand towards his wife, 'in perfect heaps. I had no relation to object or be offended, on the score of station; for I had no relation. I have never had anybody belonging to me but my guardian, and him, Feeder, I have always considered as a Pirate and a Corsair . . . .

"'Accordingly,' resumed Mr Toots, 'I acted on my own. Bright was the day on which I did so! Feeder! Nobody but myself can tell what the capacity of that woman's mind is. If ever the Rights of Women, and all that kind of thing, are properly attended to, it will be through her powerful intellect.'" DS 60

"'The question before the Committee is, whether a young man of very fair family, good appearance, and some talent, makes a fool or a wise man of himself in marrying a female waterman, turned factory girl' . . . .

"'A gentleman can have no feelings who contracts such a marriage,' flushes Podsnap.

"'Pardon me, sir,' says Twemlow, rather less mildly than usual, 'I don't agree with you. If this gentleman's feelings of gratitude, of respect, of admiration, and affection, induced him (as I presume they did) to marry this lady——

"'This lady!' echoes Podsnap.

"'Sir,' returns Twemlow, with his wristbands bristling a little, '*you* repeat the word; *I* repeat the word. This lady. What else would you call her, if the gentleman were present?

"'This being something in the nature of a poser for Podsnap, he merely waves it away with a speechless wave.

"'I say,' resumes Twemlow, 'if such feelings on the part of this gentleman induced this gentleman to marry this lady, I think he is the greater gentleman for the action, and makes her the greater lady. I beg to say that when I use the word gentleman, I use it in the sense in which the degree may be attained by any man. The feelings of a gentleman I hold sacred, and I confess I am not comfortable when they are made the subject of sport or general discussion.'

"'I should like to know,' sneers Podsnap, 'whether your noble relation would be of your opinion.'

"'Mr Podsnap,' retorts Twemlow, 'permit me. He might be, or he might not be. I cannot say. But I could not allow even him to dictate to me on a point of great delicacy, on which I feel very strongly.'

"Somehow, a canopy of wet blanket seems to descend upon the company, and Lady Tippins was never known to turn so very greedy, or so very cross." OMF iv 17

—betrayed by materialism: "'Father . . . if you had known that there lingered in my breast, sensibilities, affections, weaknesses capable of being cherished into strength, defying all the calculations ever made by man, and no more known to his arithmetic than his Creator is—would you have given me to the husband whom I am now sure that I hate?' . . .

"'When I was irrevocably married, there rose up into rebellion against the tie, the old strife, made fiercer by all those causes of disparity which arise out of our two individual natures, and which no general laws shall ever rule or state for me, father, until they shall be able to direct the anatomist where to strike his knife into the secrets of my soul.'" HT ii 12

—bickering: "In their matrimonial bickerings [the Chicks] were, upon the whole, a well-matched, fairly-balanced, give-and-take couple. It would have been, generally speaking, very difficult to have betted on the winner. Often when Mr Chick seemed beaten, he would suddenly make a start, turn the tables, clatter them about the ears of Mrs Chick, and carry all before him. Being liable himself to similar unlooked-for checks from Mrs Chick, their little contests usually possessed a character of uncertainty that was very animating." DS 1

—caution advised: "'That young person [Mary],' said Mr Pickwick, 'is attached to your son.'

"'To Samivel Veller?' exclaimed the parent.

"'Yes,' said Mr Pickwick.

"'It's nat'ral,' said Mr Weller, after some consideration, 'nat'ral, but raythe alarmin. Sammy must be careful.'

"'How do you mean?' inquired Mr Pickwick.

"'Wery careful that he don't say nothin' to her,' responded Mr Weller. 'Wery careful that he ain't led away, in a innocent moment, to say anythink as may lead to a conwiction for breach. You're never safe with 'em, Mr Pickwick, ven they vunce has designs on you; there's no knowin' vere to have 'em; and vile you're a-considering of it, they have you. I wos married fust that vay myself, sir, and Sammy wos the consekens o' the manoover.'" PP 56

—complementarity: "Mrs Wilfer was, of course, a tall woman and an angular. Her lord being cherubic, she was necessarily majestic, according to the principle which matrimonially unites contrasts." OMF i 4

—diplomacy: "'Oh, don't tell me what you were going to say,' interposed Mrs. Sowerberry. 'I am nobody; don't consult me, pray. *I* don't want to intrude upon your secrets.' As Mrs. Sowerberry said this, she gave an hysterical laugh, which threatened violent consequences.

"'But my dear,' said Sowerberry, 'I want to ask your advice.'

"'No, no, don't ask mine,' replied Mrs. Sowerberry, in an affecting manner: 'ask somebody else's.' Here, there was another hysterical laugh, which frightened Mr. Sowerberry very much. This is a very common and much-approved matrimonial course of treatment, which is often very effective. It at once reduced Mr. Sowerberry to begging, as a special favour, to be allowed to say what Mrs. Sowerberry was most curious to hear. After a short altercation of less than three quarters of an hour's duration, the permission was most graciously conceded." OT 5

—engagement announced: "'Miss Dorrit has no doubt exercised the soundest discretion of which the circumstances admitted, and I trust will allow me to offer her my sincere congratulations. When free from the trammels of passion,' Mrs General closed her eyes at the word, as if she could not utter it, and see anybody; 'when occurring with the approbation of near relatives; and when cementing the proud structure of a family edifice; these are usually auspicious events. I trust Miss Dorrit will allow me to offer her my best congratulations.'" LD ii 15

—experience a teacher; "'I am ashamed on you!' said Sam, reproachfully: 'what do you let [Stiggins] show his red nose in the Markis o' Granby at all, for?'

"Mr Weller the elder fixed on his son an earnest look, and replied, ' 'Cause I'm a married man, Samivel, 'cause I'm a married man. Wen you're a married man, Samivel, you'll understand a good many things as you don't understand now; but vether it's worth while goin' through so much to learn so little, as the charity-boy said ven he got to the end of the alphabet, is a matter o' taste. *I* rayther think it isn't.'" PP 27

—fainting: "'Oh, Doll, Doll,' said her good-natured father [Gabriel Varden]. 'If you ever have a husband of your own . . . never faint, my darling. More domestic unhappiness has come of easy fainting, Doll, than from all the greater passions put together.'" BR 19

—later in life: " . . . I have heard [Master Humphrey] say, more than once, that he could not concur with the generality of mankind in censuring equal marriages made in later life, since there were many cases in which such unions could not fail to be a wise and rational source of happiness to both parties." MH/DG

—marriage

—loving: " . . . a worthy gentleman [Godfrey Nickleby], who taking it into his head rather late in life that he must get married, and not being young enough or rich enough to aspire to the hand of a lady of fortune, had wedded an old flame out of mere attachment, who in her turn had taken him for the same reason: thus two people who cannot afford to play cards for money, sometimes sit down to a quiet game for love." NN 1

—unhappy: "'I know the misery, the slow torture, the protracted anguish of that ill-assorted union. I know how listlessly and wearily each of that wretched pair dragged on their heavy chain through a world that was poisoned to them both. I know how cold formalities were succeeded by open taunts; how indifference gave place to dislike, dislike to hate, and hate to loathing, until at last they wrenched the clanking

bond asunder, and retiring a wide space apart, carried each a galling fragment, of which nothing but death could break the rivets, to hide it in new society beneath the gayest looks they could assume.'" OT 49

"The barrier between Mr Dombey and his wife was not weakened by time. Ill-assorted couple, unhappy in themselves and in each other, bound together by no tie but the manacle that joined their fettered hands, and straining that so harshly, in their shrinking asunder, that it wore and chafed to the bone. Time, consoler of affliction and softener of anger, could do nothing to help them. Their pride, however different in kind and object, was equal in degree; and, in their flinty opposition, struck out fire between them which might smoulder or might blaze, as circumstances were, but burned up everything within their mutual reach, and made their marriage way a road of ashes . . . .

"A marble rock could not have stood more obdurately in his way than she; and no chilled spring, lying uncheered by any ray of light in the depths of a deep cave, could be more sullen or more cold than he." DS 47

"Was it the speciality of Mr and Mrs Lammle, or does it ever obtain with other loving couples? In these matrimonial dialogues they never addressed each other, but always some invisible presence that appeared to take a station about midway between them. Perhaps the skeleton in the cupboard comes out to be talked to, on such domestic occasions? . . .

"'And what is to happen next?' asked Mrs Lammle of the skeleton.

"'Smash is to happen next,' said Mr Lammle to the same authority.

"After this, Mrs Lammle looked disdainfully at the skeleton—but without carrying the look on to Mr Lammle—and drooped her eyes. After that, Mr Lammle did exactly the same thing, and drooped *his* eyes. A servant then entering with toast, the skeleton retired into the closet, and shut itself up." OMF iii 12

—*young ladies' view:* " . . . young ladies will look forward to being married, and will jostle each other in the race to the altar, and will avail themselves of all opportunities of displaying their own attractions to the best advantage, down to the very end of time as they have done from its beginning." NN 9

—*prior research:* "Mr Bumble had re-counted the tea-spoons, re-weighed the sugar-tongs, made a closer inspection of the milk-pot, and ascertained to a nicety the exact condition of the furniture, down to the very horse-hair seats of the chairs; and had repeated each process full half-a-dozen times; before he began to think that it was time for Mrs Corney to return. Thinking begets thinking; as there were no sounds of Mrs Corney's approach, it occurred to Mr Bumble that it would be an innocent and virtuous way of spending the time, if he were further to allay his curiosity by a cursory glance at the interior of Mrs Corney's chest of drawers.

"Having listened at the keyhole, to assure himself that nobody was approaching the chamber, Mr Bumble, beginning at the bottom, proceeded to make himself acquainted with the contents of the three long drawers: which, being filled with various garments of good fashion and texture, carefully preserved between two layers of old newspapers, speckled with dried lavender: seemed to yield him exceeding satisfaction.

"Arriving, in course of time, at the right-hand corner drawer (in which was the key), and beholding therein a small padlocked box, which, being shaken, gave forth a pleasant sound, as of the chinking of coin, Mr Bumble returned with a stately walk to the fireplace; and, resuming his old attitude, said, with a grave and determined air, 'I'll do it!' He followed up this remarkable declaration, by shaking his head in a waggish manner for ten minutes, as though he were remonstrating with himself for being such a pleasant dog; and then, he took a view of his legs in profile, with much seeming pleasure and interest." OT 27

—*proposal misunderstood:* "To any one . . . conversant with the admirable regulation of Mr Pickwick's mind, his appearance and behaviour . . . would have been most mysterious and unaccountable . . . . It was evident that something of great importance was in contemplation, but what that something was, not even Mrs Bardell herself had been enabled to discover.

"'Mrs Bardell,' said Mr Pickwick, at last, as that amiable female approached the termination of a prolonged dusting of the apartment . . . .

"'Do you think it a much greater expense to keep two people, than to keep one?'

"'La, Mr Pickwick,' said Mrs Bardell colouring up to the very border of her cap, as she fancied she observed a species of matrimonial twinkle in the eyes of her lodger; 'La, Mr Pickwick, what a question!'

"'Well, but *do* you?' inquired Mr Pickwick.

"'That depends—' said Mrs Bardell, approaching the duster very near to Mr Pickwick's elbow, which was planted on the table—'that depends a good deal upon the person, you know, Mr Pickwick; and whether it's a saving and careful person, sir.'

"'That's very true,' said Mr Pickwick, 'but the person I have in my eye (here he looked very hard at Mrs Bardell) I think possesses these qualities; and has, moreover, a considerable knowledge of the world, and a great deal of sharpness, Mrs Bardell; which may be of material use to me.'

"'La, Mr Pickwick,' said Mrs Bardell; the crimson rising to her cap-border again.

"'I do,' said Mr Pickwick, growing energetic, as was his wont in speaking of a subject which interested him, 'I do, indeed; and to tell you the truth, Mrs Bardell, I have made up my mind.'

"'Dear me, sir,' exclaimed Mrs Bardell.

"'You'll think it very strange now,' said the amiable Mr Pickwick, with a good-humoured glance at his companion, 'that I never consulted you about this matter, and never even mentioned it, till I sent your little boy out this morning—eh?'

"Mrs Bardell . . . had long worshipped Mr Pickwick at a distance, but here she was, all at once, raised to a pinnacle to which her wildest and most extravagant hopes had never dared to aspire. Mr Pickwick was going to propose—a deliberate plan, too—sent her little boy to the Borough, to get him out of the way—how thoughtful—how considerate!

"'Well,' said Mr Pickwick, 'what do you think?'

"'Oh, Mr Pickwick,' said Mrs Bardell, trembling with agitation, 'you're very kind, sir.'

"'It'll save you a good deal of trouble, won't it?' said Mr Pickwick.

"'Oh, I never thought anything of the trouble, sir,' replied Mrs Bardell; 'and, of course, I should take more trouble to please you then, than ever; but it is so kind of you, Mr Pickwick, to have so much consideration for my loneliness.'

"'Ah, to be sure,' said Mr Pickwick; 'I never thought of that. When I am in town, you'll always have somebody to sit with you. To be sure, so you will.'

"'I'm sure I ought to be a very happy woman,' said Mrs Bardell.

"'And your little boy—' said Mr Pickwick.

"'Bless his heart!' interposed Mrs Bardell, with a maternal sob.

"'He, too, will have a companion,' resumed Mr Pickwick, 'a lively one, who'll teach him, I'll be bound, more tricks in a week than he would ever learn in a year.' And Mr Pickwick smiled placidly.

"'Oh you dear—' said Mrs Bardell.

"Mr Pickwick started.

"'Oh you kind, good, playful dear,' said Mrs Bardell; and without more ado, she rose from her chair, and flung her arms round Mr Pickwick's neck, with a cataract of tears and a chorus of sobs.

"'Bless my soul,' cried the astonished Mr Pickwick;—'Mrs Bardell my good woman—dear me, what a situation—pray consider.—Mrs Bardell, don't—if anybody should come—'

"'Oh, let then come,' exclaimed Mrs Bardell, frantically; 'I'll never leave you,—dear, kind, good, soul;' and, with these words, Mrs Bardell clung the tighter.

"'Mercy upon me,' said Mr Pickwick, struggling violently, 'I hear somebody coming up the stairs. Don't, don't, there's a good creature, don't.' But entreaty and remonstrance were alike unavailing; for Mrs Bardell had fainted in Mr Pickwick's arms; and before he could gain time to deposit her on a chair, Master Bardell entered the room, ushering in Mr Tupman, Mr Winkle, and Mr Snodgrass." PP 12

—risk: "Matrimony is proverbially a serious undertaking. Like an overweening predilection for brandy-and-water, it is a misfortune into which a man easily falls, and from which he finds it remarkably difficult to extricate himself. It is of no use telling a man who is timorous on these points, that it is but one plunge, and all is over. They say the same thing at the Old Bailey, and the unfortunate victims derive as much comfort from the assurance in the one case as in the other." SB/WT

—and spiritual growth: "'There might be some credit in being jolly with a wife, 'specially if the children had the measles and that, and was very fractious indeed. But I'm a'most afraid to try it [said Mark Tapley]. I don't see my way clear.'

"'You're not very fond of anybody, perhaps?' said Pinch.

"'Not particular, sir, I think.'

"'But the way would be, you know, Mark, according to your views of things,' said Mr Pinch, 'to marry somebody you didn't like and who was very disagreeable.'

"'So it would, sir; but that might be carrying out a principle a little too far, mightn't it?'" MC 5

—Victoria and Albert: "To that one young couple on whose bright destiny the thoughts of nations are fixed, may the youth of England look, and not in vain, for an example. From that one couple, blest and favoured as they are, may they learn, that even the glare and glitter of a court, the splendour of a palace, and the pomp and glory of a throne, yield in their power of conferring happiness to domestic worth and virtue. From that one young couple may they learn that the crown of a great empire, costly and jewelled though it be, gives place in the estimation of a Queen to the plain gold ring that links her woman's nature to that of tens of thousands of her humble subjects, and guards in her woman's heart one secret store of tenderness, whose proudest boast shall be that it knows no Royalty save Nature's own, and no pride of birth but being the child of Heaven!" YC/concl

—wedding

—all told: "'Whom Lady Tippins, standing on a cushion, surveying through the eyeglass, thus checks off: 'Bride; five-and-forty if a day, thirty shillings a yard, veil fifteen pounds, pocket-handkerchief a present. Bridesmaids; kept down for fear of outshining bride, consequently not girls, twelve and sixpence a yard, Veneering's flowers, snub-nosed one rather pretty but too conscious of her stockings, bonnets three pound ten. Twemlow; blessed release for the dear man if she really was his daughter, nervous even under the pretence that she is, well he may be. Mrs Veneering; never saw such velvet, say two thousand pounds as she stands, absolute jeweller's window, father must have been a pawnbroker, or how could these people do it? Attendant unknowns; pokey.'" OMF 10

—anniversary: "The noble lady's condition on these delightful occasions was one compounded of heroic endurance and heroic forgiveness. Lurid indications of the better marriages she might have made shone athwart the awful gloom of her composure, and fitfully revealed the cherub as a little monster unaccountably favoured by Heaven, who had possessed himself of a blessing for which many of his superiors had sued and contended in vain.

"So firmly had this his position towards his treasure become established, that when the anniversary arrived, it always found him in an apologetic state. It is not impossible that his modest penitence may have even gone the length of sometimes severely reproving him for that he ever took the liberty of making so exalted a character his wife." OMF iii 4

"'It was one of mamma's cherished hopes that I should become united to a tall member of society. It may have been a weakness, but if so, it was equally the weakness, I believe, of King Frederick of Prussia . . . . Mamma would appear to have had an indefinable foreboding of what afterwards happened, for she would frequently urge upon me, "Not a little man. Promise me, my child, not a little man. Never, never, never marry a little man!"

"Papa also would remark to me (he possessed extraordinary humour), "that a family of whales must not ally themselves with sprats." His company was eagerly sought, as may be supposed, by the wits of the day, and our house was their continual resort ....

"'Among the most prominent members of that distinguished circle, was a gentleman measuring six feet four in height . . . . This gentleman was so obliging as to honour me with attentions which I could not fail to understand. I immediately announced to both my parents that those attentions were misplaced, and that I could not favour his suit.

They inquired was he too tall? I replied it was not the stature, but the intellect was too lofty.

"'At our house, I said, the tone was too brilliant, the pressure was too high, to be maintained by me, a mere woman, in everyday domestic life. I well remember mamma's clasping her hands, and exclaiming, "This will end in a little man!" She afterwards went so far as to predict that it would end in a little man whose mind would be below the average, but that was in what I may denominate a paroxysm of maternal disappointment.

"'Within a month,' said Mrs Wilfer, deepening her voice, as if she were relating a terrible ghost story, 'within a month, I first saw R. W., my husband. Within a year I married him. It is natural for the mind to recall these dark coincidences on the present day.'" ¶OMF iii 4

—*enviable carriage;* "Horses prance and caper; coachmen and footmen shine in fluttering favors, flowers, and new-made liveries. Away they dash and rattle through the streets: and as they pass along, a thousand heads are turned to look at them, and a thousand sober moralists revenge themselves for not being married too, that morning, by reflecting that these people little think such happiness can't last." DS 31

—*licence:* "' . . . up comes the touter, touches his hat—"Licence, sir" says he.—"What licence?" says my father.—"Marriage licence," says the touter—"Dash my veskit," says my father, "I never thought o' that."—"I think you wants one, sir," says the touter. My father pulls up, and thinks a bit—"No," says he, "damme, I'm too old, b'sides I'm a many sizes too large," says he.—"Not a bit on it, sir," says the touter.—"Think not?" says my father.—"I'm sure not," says he; "we married a gen'lm'n twice your size, last Monday."—"Did you though," said my father.—"To be sure we did," says the touter, "you're a babby to him—this way, sir,—this way!"—and sure enough my father walks arter him, like a tame monkey behind a horgan, into a little back office, vere a feller sat among dirty papers and tin boxes, making believe he was busy. "Pray take a seat, vile I makes out the affidavit, sir," says the lawyer.—"Thankee, sir," says my father, and down he sat, and stared with all his eyes, and his mouth vide open, at the names on the boxes. "What's your name, sir," says the lawyer.—"Tony Weller," says my father.—"Parish?" says the lawyer.—"Belle Savage," says my father . . . . "And what's the lady's name?" says the lawyer. My father was struck all of a heap. "Blessed if I know," says he. "Not know!" says the lawyer.—"No more than you do," says my father, "can't I put that in arterwards?"—"Impossible!" says the lawyer.—"Wery well," says my father, after he'd thought a moment, "put down Mrs Clarke."—"What Clarke?" says the lawyer, dipping his pen in the ink.—"Susan Clarke, Markis o' Granby, Dorking," says my father; "she'll have me, if I ask, I des-say—I never said nothing to her, but she'll have me, I know." The licence was made out, and she *did* have him, and what's more she's got him now, and *I* never had any of the four hundred pound, worse luck.'" PP 10

"The realisation of my boyish day-dreams is at hand. I am going to take out the licence.

"It is a little document to do so much; and Traddles contemplates it, as it lies upon my desk, half in admiration, half in awe. There are the names in the sweet old visionary connexion, David Copperfield and Dora Spenlow; and there, in the corner, is that Parental Institution, the Stamp Office, which is so benignantly interested in the various transactions of human life, looking down upon our Union; and there is the Archbishop of Canterbury invoking a blessing on us in print, and doing it as cheap as could possibly be expected." DC 43

—*not a joking matter:* "A wedding is a licensed subject to joke upon, but there really is no great joke in the matter after all;—we speak merely of the ceremony, and beg it to be distinctly understood that we indulge in no hidden sarcasm upon a married life. Mixed up with the pleasure and joy of the occasion, are the many regrets at quitting home, the tears of parting between parent and child, the consciousness of leaving the dearest and kindest friends of the happiest portion of human life, to encounter the cares and troubles with others still untried and little known: natural feelings which we would not render this chapter mournful by describing, and which we should be still more unwilling to be supposed to ridicule." PP 28

—a particular Wedding: "I go home, more incredulous than ever, to a lodging that I have hard by; and get up very early in the morning, to ride to the Highgate road and fetch my aunt.

"I have never seen my aunt in such state. She is dressed in lavender-coloured silk, and has a white bonnet on, and is amazing. Janet has dressed her, and is there to look at me. Peggotty is ready to go to church, intending to behold the ceremony from the gallery. Mr Dick, who is to give my darling to me at the altar, has had his hair curled. Traddles, whom I have taken up by appointment at the turnpike, presents a dazzling combination of cream colour and light blue; and both he and Mr Dick have a general effect about them of being all gloves.

"No doubt I see this, because I know it is so; but I am astray, and seem to see nothing. Nor do I believe anything whatever. Still, as we drive along in an open carriage, this fairy marriage is real enough to fill me with a sort of wondering pity for the unfortunate people who have no part in it, but are sweeping out the shops, and going to their daily occupations.

"My aunt sits with my hand in hers all the way. When we stop a little way short of the church, to put down Peggotty, whom we have brought on the box, she gives it a squeeze, and me a kiss.

"'GOD bless you, Trot! My own boy never could be dearer. I think of poor dear Baby this morning.'

"'So do I. And of all I owe to you, dear aunt.'

"'Tut, child!' says my aunt; and gives her hand in overflowing cordiality to Traddles, who then gives his to Mr Dick, who then gives his to me, who then gives mine to Traddles, and then we come to the church door.

"The church is calm enough, I am sure; but it might be a steam-power loom in full action, for any sedative effect it has on me. I am too far gone for that.

"The rest is all a more or less incoherent dream.

"A dream of their coming in with Dora; of the pew-opener, arranging us, like a drill-sergeant, before the altar rails; of my wondering, even then, why pew-openers must always be the most disagreeable females procurable, and whether there is any religious dread of a disastrous infection of good humour which renders it indispensable to set those vessels of vinegar upon the road to Heaven.

"Of the clergyman and clerk appearing; of a few boatmen and some other people strolling in; of an ancient mariner behind me, strongly flavouring the church with rum; of the service beginning in a deep voice, and our all being very attentive.

"Of Miss Lavinia, who acts as a semi-auxiliary bridesmaid, being the first to cry, and of her doing homage (as I take it) to the memory of Pidger, in sobs; of Miss Clarissa applying a smelling-bottle; of Agnes taking care of Dora; of my aunt endeavouring to represent herself as a model of sternness, with tears rolling down her face; of little Dora trembling very much, and making her responses in faint whispers.

"Of our kneeling down together, side by side; of Dora's trembling less and less, but always clasping Agnes by the hand; of the service being got through, quietly and gravely; of our all looking at each other in an April state of smiles and tears, when it is over; of my young wife being hysterical in the vestry, and crying for her poor papa, her dear papa.

"Of her soon cheering up again, and our signing the register all round. Of my going into the gallery for Peggotty to bring *her* to sign it; of Peggotty's hugging me in a corner, and telling me she saw my own dear mother married; of its being over, and our going away.

"Of my walking so proudly and lovingly down the aisle with my sweet wife upon my arm, through a mist of half-seen people, pulpits, monuments, pews, fonts, organs, and church-windows, in which there flutter faint airs of association with my childish church at home, so long ago.

"Of their whispering, as we pass, what a youthful couple we are, and what a pretty little wife she is. Of our all being so merry and talkative in the carriage going back. Of Sophy telling us that when she saw Traddles (whom I had entrusted with the licence) asked for it, she almost fainted, having been convinced that he would contrive to lose it, or to have his pocket picked. Of Agnes laughing gaily; and of Dora being so fond of Agnes that she will not be separated from her, but still keeps her hand.

"Of there being a breakfast, with abundance of things, pretty and substantial, to eat and drink, whereof I partake, as I should do in any other dream, without the least perception of their flavour; eating and drinking, as I may say, nothing but love and marriage, and no more believing in the viands than in anything else.

"Of my making a speech in the same dreamy fashion, without having an idea of what I want to say, beyond such as may be comprehended in the full conviction that I haven't said it. Of our being very sociably and simply happy (always in a dream though); and of Jip's having wedding cake, and its not agreeing with him afterwards.

"Of the pair of hired post-horses being ready, and of Dora's going away to change her dress. Of my aunt and Miss Clarissa remaining with us; and our walking in the garden; and my aunt, who has made quite a speech at breakfast touching Dora's aunts, being mightily amused with herself, but a little proud of it too.

"Of Dora's being ready, and of Miss Lavinia's hovering about her, loth to lose the pretty toy that has given her so much pleasant occupation. Of Dora's making a long series of surprised discoveries that she has forgotten all sorts of little things; and of everybody's running everywhere to fetch them.

"Of their all closing about Dora, when at last she begins to say good-bye, looking with their bright colours and ribbons, like a bed of flowers. Of my darling being almost smothered among the flowers, and coming out, laughing and crying both together, to my jealous arms.

"Of my wanting to carry Jip (who is to go along with us), and Dora's saying, No, that she must carry him, or else he'll think she don't like him any more, now she is married, and will break his heart. Of our going, arm in arm, and Dora stopping and looking back, and saying, 'If I have ever been cross or ungrateful to anybody, don't remember it!' and bursting into tears.

"Of her waving her little hand, and our going away once more. Of her once more stopping and looking back, and hurrying to Agnes, and giving Agnes, above all the others, her last kisses and farewells.

"We drive away together, and I awake from the dream. I believe it at last. It is my dear, dear, little wife beside me, whom I love so well!

"'Are you happy now, you foolish boy?' says Dora, 'and sure you don't repent?'" DC 43

—*a less particular wedding:* "If [the noble savage] wants a wife he appears before the kennel of the gentleman whom he has selected for his father-in-law, attended by a party of male friends of a very strong flavour, who screech and whistle and stamp an offer of so many cows for the young lady's hand.

"The chosen father-in-law—also supported by a high-flavoured party of male friends—screeches, whistles, and yells (being seated on the ground, he can't stamp) that there never was such a daughter in the market as his daughter, and that he must have six more cows. The son-in-law and his select circle of backers screech, whistle, stamp, and yell in reply, that they will give three more cows.

"The father-in-law (an old deluder, overpaid at the beginning) accepts four, and rises to bind the bargain. The whole party, the young lady included, then falling into epileptic convulsions, and screeching, whistling, stamping, and yelling together—and nobody taking any notice of the young lady . . . the noble savage is considered married, and his friends make demoniacal leaps at him by way of congratulation." ¶RP/NS

—*a procession:* "[Captain Cuttle] was suddenly transfixed and rendered speechless by a triumphant procession that he beheld advancing towards him.

"This awful demonstration was headed by that determined woman, Mrs MacStinger, who, preserving a countenance of inexorable resolution, and wearing conspicuously attached to her obdurate bosom a stupendous watch and appendages, which the captain recognised at a glance as the property of Bunsby, conducted under her arm no other than that sagacious mariner;

he, with the distraught and melancholy visage of a captive borne into a foreign land, meekly resigning himself to her will. Behind them appeared the young MacStingers, in a body, exulting. Behind them, two ladies of a terrible and steadfast aspect, leading between them a short gentleman in a tall hat, who likewise exulted. In the wake, appeared Bunsby's boy, bearing umbrellas. The whole were in good marching order; and a dreadful smartness that pervaded the party would have sufficiently announced, if the intrepid countenances of the ladies had been wanting, that it was a procession of sacrifice, and that the victim was Bunsby." DS 60

—ring: "'Now here, my blooming English maidens, is an article, the last article of the present evening's sale, which I offer to only you, the lovely Suffolk Dumplings biling over with beauty, and I won't take a bid of a thousand pounds for from any man alive. Now what is it? Why, I'll tell you what it is. It's made of fine gold, and it's not broke, though there's a hole in the middle of it, and it's stronger than any fetter that ever was forged, though it's smaller than any finger in my set of ten . . . .

"Now what else is it? Come, I'll tell you. It's a hoop of solid gold, wrapped in a silver curl-paper, that I myself took off the shining locks of the ever-beautiful old lady in Threadneedle-street, London city; I wouldn't tell you so if I hadn't the paper to show, or you mightn't believe it even of me. Now what else is it? It's a man-trap and a handcuff, the parish stocks and a leg-lock, all in gold and all in one. Now what else is it? It's a wedding-ring.'" ¶CS/DM 1

—in the shadow of death: "Then they all stood around the bed, and Mr Milvey, opening his book, began the service; so rarely associated with the shadow of death; so inseparable in the mind from a flush of life and gaiety and hope and health and joy. Bella thought how different from her own sunny little wedding, and wept. Mrs Milvey overflowed with pity, and wept too. The dolls' dressmaker, with her hands before her face, wept in her golden bower. Reading in a low clear voice, and bending over Eugene [Wrayburn], who kept his eyes upon him, Mr Milvey did his office with suitable simplicity. As the bridegroom could not move his hand, they touched his fingers with the ring, and so put it on the bride [Lizzie Hexam]. When the two plighted their troth, she laid her hand on his, and kept it there. When the ceremony was done, and all the rest departed from the room, she drew her arm under his head, and laid her own head down upon the pillow by his side.

"'Undraw the curtains, my dear girl,' said Eugene, after a while, 'and let us see our wedding-day.'

"The sun was rising, and his first rays struck into the room as she came back and put her lips to his. 'I bless the day!' said Eugene. 'I bless the day!' said Lizzie." OMF iv 11

—unavoidable: "'Jack Bunsby,' whispered the captain [Cuttle], 'do you do this here, o' your own free will?'

"Mr Bunsby answered 'No.'

"'Why do you do it, then, my lad?' inquired the captain, not unnaturally.

"Bunsby, still looking, and always looking with an immovable countenance, at the opposite side of the world, made no reply.

"'Why not sheer off?' said the captain.

"'Eh?' whispered Bunsby, with a momentary gleam of hope.

"'Sheer off,' said the captain.

"'Where's the good?' retorted the forlorn sage. 'She'd capter me agen.'

"'Try!' replied the captain. 'Cheer up! Come! Now's your time. Sheer off, Jack Bunsby!' . . . .

"'Come!' said the captain, nudging him with his elbow, 'now's your time! Sheer off! I'll cover your retreat. The time's a flying. Bunsby! It's for liberty. Will you once?'

"Bunsby was immovable.

"'Bunsby!' whispered the captain, 'will you twice?'

"Bunsby wouldn't twice.

"'Bunsby!' urged the captain, 'it's for liberty; will you three times? Now or never!'

"Bunsby didn't then and didn't ever; for Mrs MacStinger immediately afterwards married him." DS 60

—wooden-legged observer: "Say, cherubic parent taking the lead, in what direction do we steer first? With some such inquiry in his thoughts, Gruff and Glum, stricken by so sudden an interest that he perked his neck and looked over the intervening people, as if he were trying to stand on tiptoe with his two wooden legs, took an observation of R. W. There was no 'first ' in the case, Gruff and Glum made out; the cherubic parent was bearing down and crowding on direct for Greenwich church, to see his relations.

"For Gruff and Glum, though most events acted on him simply as tobacco-stoppers, pressing down and condensing the quids within him, might be imagined to trace a family resemblance between the cherubs in the church architecture, and the cherub in the white waistcoat. Some resemblance of old Valentines, wherein a cherub, less appropriately attired for a proverbially uncertain climate, had been seen conducting lovers to the altar, might have been fancied to inflame the ardour of his timber toes. Be it as it might, he gave his moorings the slip, and followed in chase." OMF iv 4

—wished-for: "I concluded in my own mind that [Rosa Dartle] was about thirty years of age, and that she wished to be married. She was a little dilapidated—like a house—with having been so long to let; yet had, as I have said, an appearance of good looks." DC 20

Mother

—duty to: "'See there, my boy,' says George, very gently smoothing the mother's hair with his hand, 'there's a good loving forehead for you! All bright with love of you, my boy. A little touched by the sun and weather, through following your father about and taking care of you, but as fresh and wholesome as a ripe apple on a tree.'

"Mr Bagnet's face expresses, so far as in its wooden material lies, the highest approbation and acquiescence.

"'The time will come, my boy,' pursues the trooper, 'when this hair of your mother's will be grey, and this forehead all crossed and re-crossed with wrinkles—and a fine old lady she'll be then. Take care, while you are young, that you can think in those days, '*I* never whitened a hair of her dear head—*I* never marked a sorrowful line in her face!' For of all the many things that you can think of when you are a man, you had better have *that* by you, Woolwich!' BH 34

—and father: "'I think . . . it must be somewhere written that the virtues of the mothers shall, occasionally, be visited on the children, as well as the sins of the fathers.'" BH 17

—the hand that rocked: "But [King Alfred] had—as most men who grow up to be great and good are generally found to have had—an excellent mother . . . ." CHE 3

—learning at her knee: "I had been apt enough to learn, and willing enough, when my mother and I had lived alone together. I can faintly remember learning the alphabet at her knee. To this day, when I look upon the fat black letters in the primer, the puzzling novelty of their shapes, and the easy good-nature of O and Q and S, seem to present themselves again before me as they used to do. But they recall no feeling of disgust or reluctance. On the contrary, I seem to have walked along a path of flowers as far as the crocodile-book, and to have been cheered by the gentleness of my mother's voice and manner all the way." DC 4

—a model: "Miss Miggs . . . said that indeed Miss Dolly might take pattern by her blessed mother, who, she always had said, and always would say, though she were to be hanged, drawn, and quartered for it next minute, was the mildest, amiablest, forgivingest-spirited, longest-sufferingest female as ever she could have believed; the mere narration of whose excellencies had worked such a wholesome change in the mind of her own sister-in-law, that, whereas, before, she and her husband lived like cat and dog, and were in the habit of exchanging brass candlesticks, potlids, flatirons, and other such strong resentments, they were now the happiest and affectionatest couple upon earth; as could be proved any day on application Golden Lion Court, number twenty-sivin, second bell-handle on the right-hand door-post.

"After glancing at herself as a comparatively worthless vessel, but still as one of some desert, she besought her to bear in mind that her aforesaid dear and only mother was of a weakly constitution and excitable temperament, who had constantly to sustain afflictions in domestic life, compared with which thieves and robbers were as nothing, and yet never sunk down or gave way to despair or wrath, but, in prize-fighting phraseology, always came up to time with a cheerful countenance, and went in to win as if nothing had happened." ¶BR 22

—objectivity: " . . . many Chuzzlewits, both male and female, are proved to demonstration, on the faith of letters written by their own mothers, to have had chiselled noses, undeniable chins, forms that might have served the sculptor for a model, exquisitely-turned limbs, and polished foreheads of so transparent a texture that the blue veins might be seen branching off in various directions, like so many roads on an ethereal map." MC 1

Index VI *lists CD's 135 named mothers and highlights those who succeed or fail signally with sons or daughters.*

Nurse and nursery

—childrearing principles: " . . . said Susan Nipper; 'wish you good morning, Mrs Richards, now Miss Floy, you come along with me, and don't go hanging back like a naughty wicked child that judgments is no example to, don't.'

"In spite of being thus adjured, and in spite also of some hauling on the part of Susan Nipper, tending towards the dislocation of her right shoulder, little Florence [Dombey] broke away and kissed her new friend . . . .

"Spitfire seemed to be in the main a good-natured little body, although a disciple of that school of trainers of the young idea which holds that childhood, like money, must be shaken and rattled and jostled about a good deal to keep it bright . . . 'but goodness gracious ME, Miss Floy, you haven't got your things off yet, you naughty child, you haven't, come along!'

"With these words, Susan Nipper, in a transport of coercion, made a charge at her young ward, and swept her out of the room." DS 3

—effect on a child's mind: "If we all knew our own minds (in a more enlarged sense than the popular acceptation of that phrase), I suspect we should find our nurses responsible for most of the dark corners we are forced to go back to against our wills." UT/NS

—intent and method: "' . . . when a sweet young pretty innocent, that never ought to have a cross word spoken to or of it, is run down, the case is very different indeed. My goodness gracious me, Miss Floy, you naughty, sinful child, if you don't shut your eyes this minute, I'll call in them hob-goblins that lives in the cock-loft to come and eat you up alive!'

"Here Miss Nipper made a horrible lowing, supposed to issue from a conscientious goblin of the bull species, impatient to discharge the severe duty of his position. Having further composed her young charge by covering her head with the bed-clothes, and making three or four angry dabs at the pillow, she folded her arms, and screwed up her mouth, and sat looking at the fire for the rest of the evening." DS 5

—reading aloud: crocodiles: "'Now let me hear some more abut the Crorkindills,' said Peggotty, who was not quite right in the name yet, 'for I an't heard half enough.'

" . . . we returned to those monsters, with fresh wakefulness on my part, and we left their eggs in the sand for the sun to hatch; and we ran away from them, and baffled them by constantly turning, which they were unable to do quickly, on account of their unwieldy make; and we went into the water after them, as natives, and put sharp pieces of timber down their throats; and in short we ran the whole crocodile gauntlet." DC 2

Index VI *lists CD's 16 named nurserymaids, including Susan Nipper DS, Peggotty DC and Polly Toodle DS. Only the last nursed.*

—tales of inns and taverns: "My first impressions of an Inn dated from the Nursery; consequently I went back to the Nursery for a starting-point, and found myself at the knee of a sallow woman with a fishy eye, an aquiline nose, and a green gown, whose specialty was a dismal narrative of a landlord by the roadside, whose visitors unaccountably disappeared for many years, until it was discovered that the pursuit of his life had been to convert them into pies.

"For the better devotion of himself to this branch of industry, he had constructed a secret door behind the head of the bed; and when the visitor (oppressed with pie) had fallen asleep, this wicked landlord would look softly in with a lamp in one hand and a knife in the other, would cut his throat, and would make him into pies; for which purpose he had coppers, underneath a trapdoor, always boiling; and rolled out his pastry in the dead of the night. Yet even he was not insensible to the stings of conscience, for he never went to sleep without being heard to mutter, 'Too much pepper!' which was eventually the cause of his being brought to justice." ¶CS/HT 1

"I had no sooner disposed of this criminal than there started up another of the same period, whose profession was originally housebreaking; in the pursuit of which art he had had his right ear chopped off one night, as he was burglariously getting in at a window, by a brave and lovely servant-maid (whom the aquiline-nosed woman, though not at all answering the description, always mysteriously implied to be herself).

"After several years, this brave and lovely servant-maid was married to the landlord of a country Inn; which landlord had this remarkable characteristic, that he always wore a silk nightcap, and never would on any consideration take it off. At last, one night, when he was fast asleep, the brave and lovely woman lifted up his silk nightcap on the right side, and found that he had no ear there; upon which she sagaciously perceived that he was the clipped housebreaker, who had married her with the intention of putting her to death. She immediately heated the poker and terminated his career, for which she was taken to King George upon his throne, and received the compliments of royalty on her great discretion and valour." ¶CS/HT 1

"The [narrator's] brother-in-law . . . found himself benighted, and came to an Inn. A dark woman opened the door, and he asked her if he could have a bed there. She answered yes, and put his horse in the stable, and took him into a room where there were two dark men. While he was at supper, a parrot in the room began to talk, saying, 'Blood, blood! Wipe up the blood!' Upon which one of the dark men wrung the parrot's neck, and said he was fond of roasted parrots, and he meant to have this one for breakfast in the morning.

"After eating and drinking heartily, the immensely rich, tall brother-in-law went up to bed; but he was rather vexed, because they had shut his dog in the stable, saying that they never allowed dogs in the house. He sat very quiet for more than an hour, thinking and thinking, when, just as his candle was burning out, he heard a scratch at the door. He opened the door, and there was the Newfoundland dog! The dog came softly in, smelt about him, went straight to some straw in the corner which the dark men had said covered apples, tore the straw away, and disclosed two sheets steeped in blood.

"Just at that moment the candle went out, and the brother-in-law, looking through a chink in the door, saw the two dark men stealing upstairs; one armed with a dagger that long (about five feet); the other carrying a chopper, a sack, and a spade. Having no remembrance of the close of this adventure, I suppose my faculties to have been always so frozen with terror at this stage of it, that the power of listening stagnated within me for some quarter of an hour." ¶CS/HT 1

And see UT/NS

—volunteer: "At the little ceremonies of the bath and toilette, [Miss Tox] assisted with enthusiasm. The administration of infantine doses of physic awakened all the active sympathy of her character; and being on one occasion secreted in a cupboard (whither she had fled in modesty), when Mr Dombey was introduced into the nursery by his sister, to behold his son, in the course of preparation for bed, taking a short walk uphill over Richards's gown, in a short and airy linen jacket, Miss Tox was so transported beyond the ignorant present as to be unable to refrain from crying out, 'Is he not beautiful, Mr Dombey! Is he not a Cupid, Sir!' and then almost sinking behind the closet door with confusion and blushes." DS 5

Old Age

—alchemy of imagination: "We are men of secluded habits, with something of a cloud upon our early fortunes, whose enthusiasm, nevertheless, has not cooled with age, whose spirit of romance is not yet quenched, who are content to ramble through the world in a pleasant dream, rather than ever waken again to its harsh realities. We are alchemists who would extract the essence of perpetual youth from dust and ashes, tempt coy Truth in many light and airy forms from the bottom of her well, and discover one crumb of comfort or one grain of good in the commonest and least-regarded matter that passes through our crucible. Spirits of past times, creatures of imagination, and people of to-day are alike the objects of our seeking, and, unlike the objects of search with most philosophers, we can insure their coming at our command." MHC 1

—contented: "On a summer's evening, when the large watering-pot has been filled and emptied some fourteen times, and the old couple have quite exhausted themselves by trotting about, you will see them sitting happily together in the little summer-house, enjoying the calm and peace of the twilight, and watching the shadows as they fall upon the garden, and gradually growing thicker and more sombre, obscure the tints of their gayest flowers—no bad emblem of the years that have silently rolled over their heads, deadening in their course the brightest hues of early hopes and feelings which have long since faded away. These are their only recreations, and they require no more. They have within themselves the materials of comfort and content; and the only anxiety of each is to die before the other." SB/LR

And see H:Recreations*—gardening*

—discontented: "Grandmother Smallweed . . . screeches, like a horrible old parrot without any plumage, 'Ten ten-pound notes!'

"Grandfather Smallweed immediately throws the cushion at her.

"'Drat you, be quiet!' says the good old man.

"The effect of this act of jaculation is twofold. It not only doubles up Mrs Smallweed's head against the side of her porter's chair, and causes her to present, when extricated by her grand-daughter, a highly unbecoming state of cap, but the necessary exertion recoils on Mr Smallweed himself, whom it throws back into *his* porter's chair, like a broken puppet. The excellent old gentleman being, at these times, a mere clothes-bag with a black skull-cap on the top of it, does not present a very animated appearance, until he has undergone the two operations at the hands of his grand-daughter, of being shaken up like a great bottle, and poked and punched like a great bolster. Some indication of a neck being developed in him by these means, he and the sharer of his life's evening again sit fronting one another in their two porter's chairs, like a couple of sentinels long forgotten on their post by the Black Serjeant, Death." BH 21

—and the dying Year: "The Year was Old, that day. The patient Year had lived through the reproaches and misuses of its slanderers, and faithfully performed its work. Spring, summer, autumn, winter. It had laboured through the destined round, and now laid down its weary head to die. Shut out from hope, high impulse, active happiness, itself, but active messenger of many joys to others, it made appeal in its decline to have its toiling days and patient hours remembered, and to die in peace. Trotty might have read a poor man's allegory in the fading year; but he was past that, now.

"And only he? Or has the like appeal been ever made, by seventy years at once upon an English labourer's head, and made in vain!'" C 2

—embraced: "'You have wonderful energy,' returned Rokesmith. 'You are as young as I am.'

"Betty Higden gravely shook her head. 'I am strong for my time of life, sir, but not young, thank the Lord!'

"'Are you thankful for not being young?'

"'Yes, sir. If I was young, it would all have to be gone through again, and the end would be a weary way off, don't you see?'" OMF ii 14

—haunting scenes of youth: "The popular faith in ghosts has a remarkable affinity with the whole current of our thoughts at such an hour as this, and seems to be their necessary and natural consequence. For who can wonder that man should feel a vague belief in tales of disembodied spirits wandering through those places which they once dearly affected, when he himself, scarcely less separated from his old world than they, is for ever lingering upon past emotions and bygone times, and hovering, the ghost of his former self, about the places and people that warmed his heart of old?

"It is thus that at this quiet hour I haunt the house where I was born, the rooms I used to tread, the scenes of my infancy, my boyhood, and my youth; it is thus that I prowl around my buried treasure (though not of gold or silver), and mourn my loss; it is thus that I revisit the ashes of extinguished fires, and take my silent stand at old bedsides. If my spirit should ever glide back to this chamber when my body is mingled with the dust, it will but follow the course it often took in the old man's lifetime, and add but one more change to the subjects of its contemplation." MHC 2

—hearty: "[Gabriel Varden] was past the prime of life, but Father Time is not always a hard parent, and, though he tarries for none of his children, often lays his hand lightly upon those who have used him well; making them old men and women inexorably enough, but leaving their hearts and spirits young and in full vigour. With such people the grey head is but the impression of the old fellow's hand in giving them his blessing, and every wrinkle but a notch in the quiet calendar of a well-spent life." BR 2

—measured: "'Three score and ten,' said Chuffey, 'ought and carry seven. Some men are so strong that they live to four score—four times ought's an ought, four times two's an eight—eighty. Oh! why—why—why—didn't he [Anthony Chuzzlewit] live to four times ought's an ought, and four times two's an eight, eighty?'

"'Ah! what a wale of grief!' cried Mrs Gamp, possessing herself of the bottle and glass." MC 19

—old man, archetypal: "Anybody may pass, any day, in the thronged thoroughfares of the metropolis, some meagre, wrinkled, yellow old man (who might be supposed to have dropped from the stars, if there were any star in the heavens dull enough to be

suspected of casting off so feeble a spark), creeping along with a scared air, as though bewildered and a little frightened by the noise and bustle. This old man is always a little old man. If he were ever a big old man, he has shrunk into a little old man; if he were always a little old man, he has dwindled into a less old man . . . . And so, like the country mouse in the second year of a famine, come to see the town-mouse, and timidly threading his way to the town-mouse's lodging through a city of cats, this old man passes in the streets.

" . . . the old man is going home to the Workhouse; and on his good behaviour they do not let him out often (though methinks they might, considering the few years he has before him to go out in, under the sun); and on his bad behaviour they shut him up closer than ever, in a grove of two score and nineteen more old men, every one of whom smells of all the others." LD i 31

—*respected by the poor:* "Age, especially when it strives to be self-reliant and cheerful, finds much consideration among the poor. The old woman [Mrs Pegler] was so decent and contented, and made so light of her infirmities, though they had increased upon her since her former interview with Stephen [Blackpool], that they [he and Rachael] both took an interest in her." HT ii 6

—*at the seaside:* "Spectres of the George the Fourth days flitted unsteadily among the crowd, bearing the outward semblance of ancient dandies, of every one of whom it might be said, not that he had one leg in the grave, or both legs, but that he was steeped in grave to the summit of his high shirt-collar, and had nothing real about him but his bones." UT/DH

—*second childhood:*

—*cheerful:* "'Dear me!' said Mr Omer, 'when a man is drawing on to a time of life where the two ends of life meet; when he finds himself, however hearty he is, being wheeled about for the second time in a species of go-cart; he should be over-rejoiced to do a kindness if he can. He wants plenty. And I don't speak of myself, particular,' said Mr Omer, 'because, sir, the way I look at it is, that we are all drawing on to the bottom of the hill, whatever age we are, on account of time never standing still for a single moment. So let us always do a kindness, and be over-rejoiced. To be sure!'" DC 51

— *sad:* "We call this a state of childishness, but it is the same poor hollow mockery of it, that death is of sleep. Where, in the dull eyes of doating men, are the laughing light and life of childhood, the gaiety that has known no check, the frankness that has felt no chill, the hope that has never withered, the joys that fade in blossoming? Where, in the sharp lineaments of rigid and unsightly death, is the calm beauty of slumber, telling of rest for the waking hours that are past, and the gentle hopes and loves for those which are to come? Lay death and sleep down, side by side, and say who shall find the two akin. Send forth the child and childish man together, and blush for the pride that libels our own old happy state, and gives its title to an ugly and distorted image." OCS 12

—*senile:* "'Sit down, you dancing, prancing, shambling, scrambling poll-parrot! Sit down!'

"This little apostrophe to Mrs Smallweed is occasioned by a propensity on the part of that unlucky old lady, whenever she finds herself on her feet, to amble about and 'set' to inanimate objects, accompanying herself with a chattering noise, as in a witch dance. A nervous affection has probably as much to do with these demonstrations, as any imbecile intention in the poor old woman; but on the present occasion they are so particularly lively in connexion with the Windsor arm-chair, fellow to that in which Mr Smallweed is seated, that she only quite desists when her grandchildren have held her down in it: her lord in the meanwhile bestowing upon her, with great volubility, the endearing epithet of 'a pig-headed Jackdaw,' repeated a surprising number of times." BH 33

—*unpredictable:* "' . . . these old people—there's no trusting 'em, Fred [said Swiveller]. There's an aunt of mine down in Dorsetshire that was going to die when I was eight years old, and hasn't kept her word yet. They're so aggravating, so unprincipled, so spiteful. Unless there's apoplexy in the family, Fred, you can't calculate upon 'em, and even then they deceive you just as often as not.'" OCS 7

—*workhouse:* "Aged people were there in every variety. Mumbling, blear-eyed, spectacled, stupid, deaf, lame; vacantly winking in the gleams of sun that now and then crept in through the open doors from the paved yard; shading their listening ears or blinking eyes with their withered hands; poring over their books, leering at nothing, going to sleep, crouching and drooping in corners. There were weird old women, all skeleton within, all bonnet and cloak without, continually wiping their eyes with dirty dusters of pocket-handkerchiefs; and there were ugly old crones, both male and female, with a ghastly kind of contentment upon them which was not at all comforting to see. Upon the whole, it was the dragon, Pauperism, in a very weak and impotent condition; toothless, fangless, drawing his breath heavily enough, and hardly worth chaining up." RP/WW

—youthful: "'Brother Ned . . . I believe that Tim Linkinwater was born a hundred-and-fifty years old, and is gradually coming down to five-and-twenty; for he's younger every birthday than he was the year before.'" NN 37

'Old Boy'

"If we had to make a classification of society, there are a particular kind of men whom we should immediately set down under the head of 'Old Boys;' and a column of most extensive dimensions the old boys would require . . . the numbers of the old boys have been gradually augmenting within the last few years, and . . . they are at this moment alarmingly on the increase.

"Upon a general review of the subject, and without considering it minutely in detail, we should be disposed to subdivide the old boys into two distinct classes—the gay old boys, and the steady old boys. The gay old boys are paunchy old men in the disguise of young ones, who frequent the Quadrant and Regent Street in the daytime: the theatres (especially theatres under lady management) at night; and who assume all the foppishness and levity of boys, without the excuse of youth or inexperience. The steady old boys are certain stout old gentlemen of clean appearance, who are always to be seen in the same taverns, at the same hours every evening, smoking and drinking in the same company.

"There was once a fine collection of old boys to be seen round the circular table at Offley's every night, between the hours of half-past eight and half-past eleven. We have lost sight of them for some time. There were, and may be still, for aught we know, two splendid specimens in full blossom at the Rainbow Tavern in Fleet Street, who always used to sit in the box nearest the fire-place, and smoked long cherry-stick pipes which went under the table, with the bowls resting on the floor. Grand old boys they were—fat, red-faced, white-headed old fellows—always there—one on one side the table, and the other opposite—puffing and drinking away in great state. Everybody knew them, and it was supposed by some people that they were both immortal." SB/JD

And see Bachelor. Indexes VII *and* VIII *list more Old Boys.*

'Old Maid'

"The only great occasions for Volumnia [Dedlock] . . . are those occasions, rare and widely-separated, when something is to be done for the county or the country, in the way of gracing a public ball. Then, indeed, does the tuckered sylph come out in fairy form, and proceed with joy under cousinly escort to the exhausted old assembly-room. . . . Then does she twirl and twine, a pastoral nymph of good family, through the mazes of the dance . . . . Then is she kind and cruel, stately and unassuming, various, beautifully wilful.

"Then is there a singular kind of parallel between her and the little glass chandeliers of another age, embellishing that assembly-room; which, with their meagre stems, their spare little drops, their disappointing knobs where no drops are, their bare little stalks from which knobs and drops have both departed, and their little feeble prismatic twinkling, all seem Volumnias." ¶BH 66

Index VI *lists 20 single ladies and 17 spinsters. Rachael Wardle PP and Lucretia Tox DS are particularly fine Old Maids.*

Orphan and Orphanhood

—de facto: "' . . . not an orphan in the wide world can be so deserted as the child who is an outcast from a living parent's love.'" DS 24

"Yielding at once to the impulse of her affection, timid at all other times, but bold in its truth to him in his adversity, and undaunted by past repulse, Florence, dressed as she was, hurried down-stairs. As she set her light foot in the hall, he came out of his room. She hastened towards him unchecked, with her arms stretched out, and crying 'Oh dear, dear papa!' as if she would have clasped him round the neck.

"And so she would have done. But in his frenzy, he lifted up his cruel arm, and struck her, crosswise, with that heaviness, that she tottered on the marble floor; and as he dealt the blow, he told her what Edith was, and bade her follow her, since they had always been in league.

"She did not sink down at his feet; she did not shut out the sight of him with her trembling hands; she did not weep; she did not utter one word of reproach. But she looked at him, and a cry of desolation issued from her heart. For as she looked, she saw him murdering that fond idea to which she had held in spite of him. She saw his cruelty, neglect, and hatred dominant above it, and stamping it down. She saw she had no father upon earth, and ran out, orphaned, from his house." DS 47

—foundling: " . . . the maternal and paternal Slowboy were alike unknown to Fame, and Tilly had been bred by public charity, a foundling; which word, though only differing from fondling by one vowel's length, is very different in meaning, and expresses quite another thing." CH 1

—orphanhood discovered: "Mothers and children travelled with him; mothers and children met each other at the station; mothers and children were in the shops . . . . Everywhere, the nearest and dearest of human relations showed itself happily in the happy light of day. Everywhere, [Walter Wilding] was reminded of the treasured delusion from which he had been awakened so cruelly—of the lost memory which had passed from him like a reflection from a glass." CS/NT 1

"He might have overcome the shock he had sustained in the one great affection of his life, or he might have overcome his consciousness of being in the enjoyment of another man's property; but the two together were too much for him.

"A man haunted by twin ghosts, he became deeply depressed. The inseparable spectres sat at the board with him, ate from his platter, drank from his cup, and stood by his bedside at night. When he recalled his supposed mother's love, he felt as though he had stolen it. When he rallied a little under the respect and attachment of his dependants, he felt as though he were even fraudulent in making them happy, for that should have been the unknown man's duty and gratification.

"Gradually, under the pressure of his brooding mind, his body stooped, his step lost its elasticity, his eyes were seldom lifted from the ground. He knew he could not help the deplorable mistake that had been made, but he knew he could not mend it; for the days and weeks went by and no one claimed his name or his possessions.

"And now there began to creep over him a cloudy consciousness of often-recurring confusion in his head. He would unaccountably lose, sometimes whole hours, sometimes a whole day and night. Once, his remembrance stopped as he sat at the head of the dinner-table, and was blank until daybreak. Another time, it stopped as he was beating time to their singing, and went on again when he and his partner were walking in the courtyard by the light of the moon, half the night later." ¶CS/NT 1

—resentful: "'She is somebody's child—anybody's—nobody's. Put her in a room in London here with any six people old enough to be her parents, and her parents may be there for anything she knows. They may be in any house she sees, they may be in any churchyard she passes, she may run against 'em in any street, she may make chance acquaintances of 'em at any time; and never know it.

"'She knows nothing about 'em. She knows nothing about any relative whatever. Never did. Never will . . . . Sometimes she's proud and won't touch [her trust money] for a length of time; sometimes she's so poor, that she must have it. She writhes under her life. A woman more angry, passionate, reckless, and revengeful never lived.'" LD ii 11

—search for: "Mr and Mrs Milvey had found their search a difficult one. Either an eligible orphan was of the wrong sex (which almost always happened) or was too old, or too young, or too sickly, or too dirty, or too much accustomed to the streets, or too likely to run away; or it was found impossible to complete the philanthropic transaction without buying the orphan. For the instant it became known that anybody wanted the orphan, up started some affectionate relative of the orphan who put a price upon the orphan's head.

"The suddenness of an orphan's rise in the market was not to be paralleled by the maddest records of the Stock Exchange. He would be at five thousand per cent discount out at nurse making a mud pie at nine in the morning, and (being inquired for) would go up to five thousand per cent premium before noon.

"The market was 'rigged' in various artful ways. Counterfeit stock got into circulation. Parents boldly represented themselves as dead, and brought their orphans with them.

Genuine orphan-stock was surreptitiously withdrawn from the market.

"It being announced, by emissaries posted for the purpose, that Mr and Mrs Milvey were coming down the court, orphan scrip would be instantly concealed, and production refused, save on a condition usually stated by the brokers as a 'gallon of beer.' Likewise, fluctuations of a wild and South-Sea nature were occasioned by orphan-holders keeping back, and then rushing into the market a dozen together.

"But the uniform principle at the root of all these various operations was bargain and sale; and that principle could not be recognized by Mr and Mrs Milvey." ¶OMF i 16

—taking care of each other: " . . . we went up to the top room. I tapped at the door, and a little shrill voice inside said, 'We are locked in. Mrs Blinder's got the key!'

"I applied the key on hearing this, and opened the door. In a poor room, with a sloping ceiling, and containing very little furniture, was a mite of a boy, some five or six years old, nursing and hushing a heavy child of eighteen months. There was no fire, though the weather was cold; both children were wrapped in some poor shawls and tippets, as a substitute. Their clothing was not so warm, however, but that their noses looked red and pinched, and their small figures shrunken, as the boy walked up and down, nursing and hushing the child with its head on his shoulder.

"'Who has locked you up here alone?' we naturally asked.

"'Charley,' said the boy, standing still to gaze at us.

"'Is Charley your brother?'

"'No. She's my sister, Charlotte. Father called her Charley.'

"'Are there any more of you besides Charley?'

"'Me,' said the boy, 'and Emma,' patting the limp bonnet of the child he was nursing. 'And Charley.'

"'Where is Charley now?'

"'Out a-washing,' said the boy, beginning to walk up and down again, and taking the nankeen bonnet much too near the bedstead, by trying to gaze at us at the same time.

"We were looking at one another, and at these two children, when there came into the room a very little girl, childish in figure but shrewd and older-looking in the face—pretty-faced too—wearing a womanly sort of bonnet much too large for her, and drying her bare arms on a womanly sort of apron. Her fingers were white and wrinkled with washing, and the soap-suds were yet smoking which she wiped off her arms. But for this, she might have been a child, playing at washing, and imitating a poor working-woman with a quick observation of the truth.

"She had come running from some place in the neighbourhood, and had made all the haste she could. Consequently, though she was very light, she was out of breath, and could not speak at first, as she stood panting, and wiping her arms, and looking quietly at us.

"'O, here's Charley!' said the boy.

"The child he was nursing, stretched forth its arms, and cried out to be taken by Charley. The little girl took it, in a womanly sort of manner belonging to the apron and the bonnet, and stood looking at us over the burden that clung to her most affectionately.

"'Is it possible,' whispered my guardian, as we put a chair for the little creature, and got her to sit down with her load: the boy keeping close to her, holding to her apron, 'that this child works for the rest? Look at this! For GOD's sake look at this!'

"It was a thing to look at. The three children close together, and two of them relying solely on the third, and the third so young and yet with an air of age and steadiness that sat so strangely on the childish figure.

"'Charley, Charley!' said my guardian. 'How old are you?'

"'Over thirteen, sir,' replied the child.

"'O! What a great age!' said my guardian. 'What a great age, Charley!'

"I cannot describe the tenderness with which he spoke to her; half playfully, yet all the more compassionately and mournfully.

"'And do you live alone here with these babies, Charley?' said my guardian.

"'Yes, sir,' returned the child, looking up into his face with perfect confidence, 'since father died.'

"'And how do you live, Charley? O! Charley,' said my guardian, turning his face away for a moment, 'how do you live?'

"'Since father died, sir, I've gone out to work. I'm out washing to-day.'

"'GOD help you, Charley!' said my guardian. 'You're not tall enough to reach the tub!'

"'In pattens I am, sir,' she said quickly. 'I've got a high pair as belonged to mother.'

"'And when did mother die? Poor mother!'

"'Mother died just after Emma was born,' said the child, glancing at the face upon her bosom. 'Then father said I was to be as good a mother to her as I could. And so I tried. And so I worked at home, and did cleaning and nursing and washing, for a long time before I began to go out. And that's how I know how; don't you see, sir?'

"'And do you often go out?'

"'As often as I can,' said Charley, opening her eyes, and smiling, 'because of earning sixpences and shillings!'

"'And do you always lock the babies up when you go out?'

"'Top keep 'em safe, sir, don't you see?' said Charley. 'Mrs Blinder comes up now and then, and Mr Gridley comes up sometimes, and perhaps I can run in sometimes, and they can play, you know, and Tom an't afraid of being locked up, are you, Tom?'

"'No-o!' said Tom, stoutly.

"'When it comes on dark, the lamps are lighted down in the court, and they show up here quite bright—almost quite bright. Don't they, Tom?'

"'Yes, Charley,' said Tom, 'almost quite bright.'

"'Then he's as good as gold,' said the little creature—O! in such a motherly, womanly way! 'And when Emma's tired, he puts her to bed. And when he's tired he goes to bed himself. And when I come home and light the candle, and has a bit of supper, he sits up again and has it with me. Don't you, Tom?'

"'O yes, Charley!' said Tom. 'That I do!' And either in this glimpse of the great pleasure of his life, or in gratitude and love for Charley, who was all in all to him, he laid his face among the scanty folds of her frock, and passed from laughing into crying.

"It was the first time since our entry, that a tear had been shed among these children. The little orphan girl had spoken of their father and their mother, as if all that sorrow were subdued by the necessity of taking courage, and by her childish importance in being able to work, and by her bustling busy way. But now, when Tom cried; although she sat quite tranquil, looking quietly at us, and did not by any movement disturb a hair of the head of either of her little charges; I saw two silent tears fall down her face." BH 15

Orphanhood in Dickens is statistically reviewed in Vol. III p285. Index VI *lists 318 full and partial orphans named in the works.*

Parents

—indifferent: "'A stranger came into my father's place when I was but a child, and I was easily an alien from my mother's heart. My parents, at the best, were of that sort whose care soon ends, and whose duty is soon done; who cast their offspring loose, early, as birds do theirs; and, if they do well, claim the merit; and, if ill, the pity.'" HM 1

—overfond: "Doctor Johnson used to tell a story of a man who had but one idea, which was a wrong one. The couple who dote upon their children are in the same predicament: at home or abroad, at all times, and in all places, their thoughts are bound up in this one subject, and have no sphere beyond.

"They relate the clever things their offspring say or do, and weary every company with their prolixity and absurdity. Mr Whiffler takes a friend by the button at a street corner on a windy day to tell him a *bon mot* of his youngest boy's; and Mrs Whiffler, calling to see a sick acquaintance, entertains her with a cheerful account of all her own past sufferings and present expectations.

"In such cases the sins of the fathers indeed descend upon the children; for people soon come to regard them as predestined little bores. The couple who dote upon their children cannot be said to be actuated by a general love for these engaging little people (which would be a great excuse); for they are apt to underrate and entertain a jealousy of any children but their own.

"If they examined their own hearts, they would, perhaps, find at the bottom of all this, more self-love and egotism than they think of. Self-love and egotism are bad qualities, of which the unrestrained exhibition, though it may be sometimes amusing, never fails to be wearisome and unpleasant. Couples who dote upon their children, therefore, are best avoided." YC/D

Successful parents are few and far between in Dickens. Index VI *lists all named fathers and mothers, notes their respective success and failure rates with sons and daughters and at p283 lists all significant characters who grew up with two parents.*

Schooldays

—breaks

—Christmas: "School books are shut up; **Ovid** and **Virgil** silenced; the Rule of Three, with its cool impertinent inquiries, long disposed of; **Terence** and **Plautus** acted no more, in an arena of huddled desks and forms, all chipped, and notched, and inked; cricket-bats, stumps, and balls, left higher up, with the smell of trodden grass and the softened noise of shouts in the evening air; the tree is still fresh, still gay. If I no more come home at Christmas time, there will be girls and boys (thank Heaven) while the world lasts." CS/CT

—happy: "Oh, Saturdays! Oh, happy Saturdays, when Florence always came at noon, and never would, in any weather, stay away, though Mrs Pipchin snarled, and growled, and worried her bitterly. Those Saturdays were Sabbaths for at least two little Christians among all the Jews, and did the holy Sabbath work of strengthening and knitting up a brother's and a sister's love." DS 12

—indifferent: "When the Midsummer vacation approached, no indecent manifestations of joy were exhibited by the leaden-eyed young gentlemen assembled at Doctor Blimber's. Any such violent expression as 'break up,' would have been quite inapplicable to that polite establishment. The young gentlemen oozed away, semi-annually, to their own homes; but they never broke up. They would have scorned the action." DS 14

—happy retrospect of a head-boy: "My school-days! The silent gliding on of my existence—the unseen, unfelt progress of my life—from childhood up to youth! Let me think, as I look back upon that flowing water, now a dry channel overgrown with leaves, whether there are any marks along its course, by which I can remember how it ran.

"A moment, and I occupy my place in the Cathedral, where we all went together, every Sunday morning, assembling first at school for that purpose. The earthy smell, the sunless air, the sensation of the world being shut out, the resounding of the organ through the black and white arched galleries and aisles, are wings that take me back, and hold me hovering above those days, in a half-sleeping and half-waking dream.

"I am not the last boy in the school. I have risen, in a few months, over several heads. But the first boy seems to me a mighty creature, dwelling afar off, whose giddy height is unattainable. Agnes says, 'No,' but I say, 'Yes,' and tell her that she little thinks what stores of knowledge have been mastered by the wonderful Being, at whose place she thinks I, even I, weak aspirant, may arrive in time. He is not my private friend and public patron, as Steerforth was; but I hold him in a reverential respect. I chiefly wonder what he'll be, when he leaves Doctor Strong's, and what mankind will do to maintain any place against him. . . .

"I am higher in the school, and no one breaks my peace. I am not at all polite, now, to the Misses Nettingalls' young ladies, and shouldn't dote on any of them, if there were twice as many and twenty times as beautiful. I think the dancing-school a tiresome affair, and wonder why the girls can't dance by themselves and leave us alone. I am growing great in Latin verses, and neglect the laces of my boots. Doctor Strong refers to me in public as a promising young scholar. Mr Dick is wild with joy, and my aunt remits me a guinea by the next post . . . .

"Time has stolen on unobserved, for Adams is not the head-boy in the days that are come now, nor has he been this many and many a day. Adams has left the school so long, that when he comes back, on a visit to Doctor Strong, there are not many there, besides myself, who know him. Adams is going to be called to the bar almost directly, and is to be an advocate, and to wear a wig. I am surprised to find him a meeker man than I had thought, and less imposing in appearance. He has not staggered the world yet, either; for it goes on (as well as I can make out) pretty much the same as if he had never joined it.

"A blank, through which the warriors of poetry and history march on in stately hosts that seem to have no end—and what comes next! I am the head-boy, now! I look down on the line of boys below me, with a condescending interest in such of them as bring to my mind the boy I was myself, when I first came there. That little fellow seems to be no part of me; I remember him as something left behind upon the road of life—as something I have passed, rather than have actually been—and almost think of him as of some one else." DC 18

—routine: "The rest of the half-year is a jumble in my recollection of the daily strife and struggle of our lives; of the waning summer and the changing season; of the frosty mornings when we were rung out of bed, and the cold, cold smell of the dark nights when we were rung into bed; of the evening schoolroom dimly lighted and indifferently warmed, and the morning schoolroom which was nothing but a great shivering-machine; of the alternation of boiled beef with roast beef, and boiled mutton with roast mutton; of clods of bread-and-butter, dog's-eared lesson-books, cracked slates, tear-blotted copy-books, canings, rulerings, hair-cuttings, rainy Sundays, suet-puddings, and a dirty atmosphere of ink surrounding all.

"I well remember though, how the distant idea of the holidays, after seeming for an immense time to be a stationary speck, began to come towards us, and to grow and grow. How from counting months, we came to weeks, and then to days; and how I then began to be afraid that I should not be sent for and when I learnt from Steerforth that I *had* been sent for, and was certainly to go home, had dim forebodings that I might break my leg first. How the breaking-up day changed its place fast, at last, from the week after next to next week, this week, the day after to-morrow, to-morrow, to-day, to-night—when I was inside the Yarmouth mail, and going home." DC 7

—schoolroom during holiday: "I gazed upon the schoolroom into which [Mr Mell] took me, as the most forlorn and desolate place I had ever seen. I see it now. A long room, with three long rows of desks, and six of forms, and bristling all round with pegs for hats and slates. Scraps of old copy-books and exercises litter the dirty floor. Some silk-worms' houses, made of the same materials, are scattered over the desks. Two miserable little white mice, left behind by their owner, are running up and down in a fusty castle made of pasteboard and wire, looking in all the corners with their red eyes for anything to eat. A bird, in a cage very little bigger than himself, makes a mournful rattle now and then in hopping on his perch, two inches high, or dropping from it; but neither sings nor chirps. There is a strange unwholesome smell upon the room, like mildewed corduroys, sweet apples wanting air, and rotten books. There could not well be more ink splashed about it, if it had been roofless from its first construction, and the skies had rained, snowed, hailed, and blown ink through the varyng seasons of the year." DC 5

—a summer's day: "Oh! how some of those idle fellows longed to be outside, and how they looked at the open door and window, as if they half meditated rushing violently out, plunging into the woods, and being wild boys and savages from that time forth.

"What rebellious thoughts of the cool river, and some shady bathing-place beneath willow trees with branches dipping in the water, kept tempting and urging that sturdy boy, who, with his shirt-collar unbuttoned and flung back as far as it could go, sat fanning his flushed face with a spelling-book, wishing himself a whale, or a tittlebat, or a fly, or anything but a boy at school on that hot, broiling day!

"Heat! ask that other boy, whose seat being nearest to the door gave him opportunities of gliding out into the garden and driving his companions to madness by dipping his face into the bucket of the well and then rolling on the grass—ask him if there were ever such a day as that, when even the bees were diving deep down into the cups of flowers and stopping there, as if they had made up their minds to retire from business and be manufacturers of honey no more.

"The day was made for laziness, and lying on one's back in green places, and staring at the sky till its brightness forced one to shut one's eyes and go to sleep; and was this a time to be poring over musty books in a dark room, slighted by the very sun itself? Monstrous!" OCS 25

Widow

—*honourable:* "My poor Lirriper being behindhand with the world and being buried at Hatfield Church in Hertfordshire . . . I went round to the creditors and I says 'Gentlemen I am acquainted with the fact that I am not answerable for my late husband's debts but I wish to pay them for I am his lawful wife and his good name is dear to me. I am going into the Lodgings gentlemen as a business and if I prosper every farthing that my late husband owed shall be paid for the sake of the love I bore him, by this right hand.' It took a long time to do but it was done, and the silver cream-jug which is between ourselves and the bed and the mattress in my room up-stairs (or it would have found legs so sure as ever the Furnished bill was up) being presented by the gentlemen engraved 'To Mrs Lirriper a mark of grateful respect for her honourable conduct' gave me a turn which was too much for my feelings, till Mr Betley which at that time had the parlours and loved his joke says 'Cheer up Mrs Lirriper, you should feel as if it was only your christening and they were your godfathers and godmothers which did promise for you.' And it brought me round, and I don't mind confessing to you my dear that I then put a sandwich and a drop of sherry in a little basket and went down to Hatfield churchyard outside the coach and kissed my hand and laid it with a kind of proud and swelling love on my husband's grave, though bless you it had taken me so long to clear his name that my wedding-ring was worn quite fine and smooth when I laid it on the green green waving grass." CS/L 1

—*weeds:* "It was perhaps a part of Mrs Heep's humility, that she still wore weeds. Notwithstanding the lapse of time that had occurred since Mr Heep's decease, she still wore weeds. I think there was some compromise in the cap; but otherwise she was as weedy as in the early days of her mourning." DC 18

—*Tony Weller's view*

—*cure for gout:* "'Take care, old fellow, or you'll have a touch of your old complaint, the gout.'

"'I've found a sov'rin cure for that, Sammy, said Mr Weller, setting down the glass.

"'A sovereign cure for the gout,' said Mr Pickwick, hastily producing his note-book; 'what is it?'

"'The gout, sir,' replied Mr Weller, 'the gout is a complaint as arises from too much ease and comfort. If ever you're attacked with the gout, sir, jist you marry a widder as has got a good loud woice, with a decent notion of usin' it, and you'll never have the gout agin. It's a capital prescription, sir. I takes it reg'lar, and I can warrant it to drive away any illness as is caused by too much jollity.' Having imparted this valuable secret, Mr Weller drained his glass once more, produced a laboured wink, sighed deeply, and slowly retired." PP 20

—*dominant:* "'Widders . . . are 'ceptions to ev'ry rule. I have heerd how many ord'nary women, one widder's equal to, in pint o' comin' over you. I think it's five-and-twenty, but I don't rightly know vether it an't more . . . . You know what the counsel said . . . as defended the gen'l'm'n as beat his wife with the poker venever he got jolly. "And arter all, my Lord," says he, "it's a amable weakness." So I says respectin' widders, Sammy, and so you'll say, ven you gets as old as me.'" PP 23

And see TT:Railroad—*risk of Widow*

—*history of hospitality:* "'Take example by your father, my boy, and be wery careful o' widders all your life, specially if they've kept a public-house . . . .'" PP 20

The 92 named widows in Dickens are listed in Index VI.

Will and Testament

—*charity benefit:* "The maxim that out of evil cometh good, is strongly illustrated . . . . Some immensely rich old gentleman or lady, surrounded by needy relatives, makes, upon a low average, a will a-week. The old gentleman or lady, never very remarkable in the best of times for good temper, is full of aches and pains from head to foot; full of fancies and caprices; full of spleen, distrust, suspicion, and dislike.

"To cancel old wills, and invent new ones, is at last the sole business of such a testator's existence; and relations and friends (some of whom have been bred up distinctly to inherit a large share of the property, and have been, from their cradles, specially disqualified from devoting themselves to any useful pursuit, on that account) are so often and so unexpectedly and summarily cut off, and reinstated, and cut off again, that the whole family, down to the remotest cousin, is kept in a perpetual fever.

"At length it becomes plain that the old lady or gentleman has not long to live; and the plainer this becomes, the more clearly the old lady or gentleman perceives that everybody is in a conspiracy against their poor old dying relative; wherefore the old lady or gentleman makes another last will—positively the last this time—conceals the same in a china teapot, and expires next day. Then it turns out, that the whole of the real and personal estate is divided between half-a-dozen charities; and that the dead and gone testator has in pure spite helped to do a great deal of good, at the cost of an immense amount of evil passion and misery." AN 3

—emotions reflected: "We naturally fell into a train of reflection as we walked homewards, upon the curious old records of likings and dislikings; of jealousies and revenges; of affection defying the power of death, and hatred pursued beyond the grave, which these depositories contain; silent but striking tokens, some of them, of excellence of heart, and nobleness of soul; melancholy examples, others, of the worst passions of human nature. How many men as they lay speechless and helpless on the bed of death, would have given worlds but for the strength and power to blot out the silent evidence of animosity and bitterness, which now stands registered against them in Doctors' Commons!" SB/DC

—executorship's perils: "'Ah,' said the cobbler . . . . 'What do you suppose ruined me, now?'

"'Wy,' said Sam, trimming the rush-light, 'I s'pose the beginnin' wos, that you got into debt, eh?'

"'Never owed a farden,' said the cobbler; 'try again.' . . .

"'You didn't go to law, I hope?' said Sam, suspiciously.

"'Never in my life,' replied the cobbler. 'The fact is, I was ruined by having money left me . . . an old gentleman that I worked for, down in the country, and a humble relation of whose I married . . . was seized with a fit and went off . . . he left five thousand pound behind him . . . . One of which . . . he left to me, 'cause I'd married his relation, you see . . . .

"'And being surrounded by a great number of nieces and nevys, as was always a quarrelling and fighting among themselves for the property, he makes me his executor, and leaves the rest to me: in trust, to divide it among 'em as the will provided . . . when I was going to take out a probate of the will, the nieces and nevys, who was desperately disappointed at not getting all the money, enters a caveat against it . . . .

"'But . . . finding that they couldn't agree among themselves, and consequently couldn't get up a case against the will, they withdrew the caveat, and I paid all the legacies. I'd hardly done it, when one nevy brings an action to set the will aside. The case comes on, some months afterwards, afore a deaf old gentleman, in a back room somewhere down by Paul's Churchyard; and arter four counsels had taken a day a-piece to bother him regularly, he takes a week or two to consider, and read the evidence in six vollums, and then gives his judgment that how the testator was not quite right in his head, and I must pay all the money back again, and all the costs.

"'I appealed; the case come on before three or four very sleepy gentlemen, who had heard it all before in the other court, where they're lawyers without work; the only difference being, that, there, they're called doctors, and in the other place delegates, if you understand that; and they very dutifully confirmed the decision of the old gentleman below.

"'After that, we went into Chancery, where we are still, and where I shall always be. My lawyers have had all my thousand pound long ago; and what between the estate, as they call it, and the costs, I'm here for ten thousand, and shall stop here, till I die, mending shoes.

"'Some gentlemen have talked of bringing it afore parliament, and I dare say would have done it, only they hadn't time to come to me, and I hadn't power to go to them, and they got tired of my long letters, and dropped the business. And this is GOD's truth, without one word of suppression or exaggeration, as fifty people, both in this place and out of it, very well know.'

"The cobbler paused to ascertain what effect his story had produced on Sam; but finding that he had dropped asleep, knocked the ashes out of his pipe, sighed, put it down, drew the bed-clothes over his head, and went to sleep too." ¶PP 44

"A sallow prisoner has come up, in custody, for the half-dozenth time, to make a personal application 'to purge himself of his contempt;' which, being a solitary surviving executor who has fallen into a state of conglomeration about accounts of which it is not pretended that he had ever any knowledge, he is not at all likely ever to do. In the meantime his prospects in life are ended." BH 1

—legacy: "The minion of fortune and the worm of the hour [Noddy Boffin] . . . had become as much at home in his eminently aristocratic family mansion as he was likely ever to be. He could not but feel that, like an eminently aristocratic family cheese, it was much too large for his wants, and bred an infinite amount of parasites; but he was content to regard this drawback on his property as a sort of perpetual Legacy Duty." OMF ii 8

—shoemaker's children

—estate lawyer's stated policy: "'You are probably aware, Mr Copperfield, that I am not altogether destitute of worldly possessions, and that my daughter is my nearest and dearest relative? . . . And you can hardly think,' said Mr Spenlow, 'having experience of what we see, in the Commons here, every day, of the various unaccountable and negligent proceedings of men, in respect of their testamentary arrangements—of all subjects, the one on which perhaps the strangest revelations of human inconsistency are to be met with—but that mine are made?'

"I inclined my head in acquiescence.

"'I should not allow,' said Mr Spenlow, with an evident increase of pious sentiment, and slowly shaking his head as he poised himself upon his toes and heels alternately, 'my suitable provision for my child to be influenced by a piece of youthful folly like the present. It is mere folly. Mere nonsense. In a little while, it will weigh lighter than any feather.

"'But I might—I might—if this silly business were not completely relinquished altogether, be induced in some anxious moment to guard her from, and surround her with protections against, the consequences of any foolish step in the way of marriage.

"'Now, Mr Copperfield, I hope that you will not render it necessary for me to open, even for a quarter of an hour, that closed page in the book of life, and unsettle, even for a quarter of an hour, grave affairs long since composed.'

"There was a serenity, a tranquillity, a calm-sunset air about him, which quite affected me. He was so peaceful and resigned—clearly had his affairs in such perfect train, and so systematically wound up—that he was a man to feel touched in the contemplation of. I really think I saw tears rise to his eyes, from the depth of his own feeling of all this." ¶DC 38

—what he did: : "We had sealed up several packets; and were still going on dustily and quietly, when Mr Jorkins said to us, applying exactly the same words to his late partner as his late partner had applied to him:

"'Mr Spenlow was very difficult to move from the beaten track. You know what he was! I am disposed to think he had made no will.'

"'Oh, I know he had!' said I.

"They both stopped and looked at me.

"'On the very day when I last saw him,' said I, 'he told me that he had, and that his affairs were long since settled.'

"Mr Jorkins and old Tiffey shook their heads with one accord.

"'That looks unpromising,' said Tiffey.

"'Very unpromising,' said Mr Jorkins.

"'Surely you don't doubt—' I began.

"'My good Mr Copperfield!' said Tiffey, laying his hand upon my arm, and shutting up both his eyes as he shook his head: 'if you had been in the Commons as long as I have, you would know that there is no subject on which men are so inconsistent, and so little to be trusted.'

"'Why, bless my soul, he made that very remark!' I replied persistently.

"'I should call that almost final,' observed Tiffey. 'My opinion is—no will.'

"It appeared a wonderful thing to me, but it turned out that there *was* no will. He had never so much as thought of making one, so far as his papers afforded any evidence; for there was no kind of hint, sketch or memorandum, of any testamentary intention whatever . . . ." DC 38

—storage of: " . . . I submitted that I thought the Prerogative Office rather a queerly managed institution. Mr Spenlow inquired in what respect? I replied, with all due deference to his experience (but with more deference, I am afraid, to his being Dora's father), that perhaps it was a little nonsensical that the Registry of that Court, containing the original wills of all persons leaving effects within the immense province of Canterbury, for three whole centuries,

should be an accidental building, never designed for the purpose, leased by the registrars for their own private emolument, unsafe, not even ascertained to be fire-proof, choked with the important documents it held, and positively, from the roof to the basement, a mercenary speculation of the registrars, who took great fees from the public, and crammed the public's wills away anyhow and anywhere, having no other object than to get rid of them cheaply.

"That, perhaps it was a little unreasonable that these registrars in the receipt of profits amounting to eight or nine thousand pounds a year (to say nothing of the profits of the deputy registrars, and clerks of seats), should not be obliged to spend a little of that money, in finding a reasonably safe place for the important documents which all classes of people were compelled to hand over to them, whether they would or no.

"That, perhaps, it was a little unjust, that all the great offices in this great office should be magnificent sinecures, while the unfortunate working-clerks in the cold dark room upstairs were the worst rewarded, and the least considered men, doing important services, in London.

"That perhaps it was a little indecent that the principal registrar of all, whose duty it was to find the public, constantly resorting to this place, all needful accommodation, should be an enormous sinecurist in virtue of that post (and might be, besides, a clergyman, a pluralist, the holder of a stall in a cathedral, and what not), while the public was put to the inconvenience of which we had a specimen every afternoon when the office was busy, and which we knew to be quite monstrous.

"That, perhaps, in short, this Prerogative Office of the diocese of Canterbury was altogether such a pestilent job, and such a pernicious absurdity, that but for its being squeezed away in a corner of Saint Paul's Churchyard, which few people knew, it must have been turned completely inside out, and upside down, long ago.

"Mr Spenlow smiled as I became modestly warm on the subject, and then argued this question with me as he had argued the other. He said, what was it after all? It was a question of feeling. If the public felt that their wills were in safe keeping, and took it for granted that the office was not to be made better, who was the worse for it? Nobody. Who was the better for it? All the sinecurists.

"Very well. Then the good predominated. It might not be a perfect system; nothing *was* perfect; but what he objected to, was, the insertion of the wedge. Under the Prerogative Office, the country had been glorious. Insert the wedge into the Prerogative Office, and the country would cease to be glorious. He considered it the principle of a gentleman to take things as he found them; and he had no doubt the Prerogative Office would last our time.

"I deferred to his opinion, though I had great doubts of it myself. I find he was right, however; for it has not only lasted to the present moment, but has done so in the teeth of a great parliamentary report made (not too willingly) eighteen years ago, when all these objections of mine were set forth in detail, and when the existing stowage for wills was described as equal to the accumulation of only two years and a half more. What they have done with them since; whether they have lost many, or whether they sell any, now and then, to the butter shops; I don't know. I am glad mine is not there, and I hope it may not go there, yet awhile." ¶DC 33

—*strangely situated:* " . . . it was found . . . at the bottom of a horse's nose-bag; wherein (besides hay) there was discovered an old gold watch, with chain and seals, which Mr Barkis had worn on his wedding-day, and which had never been seen before or since; a silver tobacco-stopper, in the form of a leg; an imitation lemon, full of minute cups and saucers . . . an old horse-shoe, a bad shilling, a piece of camphor, and an oyster-shell. From the circumstance of the latter article having been much polished, and displaying prismatic colours on the inside, I conclude that Mr Barkis had some general ideas about pearls, which never resolved themselves into anything definite." DC 31

—*Testament missing:* "Taking the proffered packet from [Robin Toodle's[hand, the Captain opened it and read as follows:—

"'My dear Ned Cuttle. Enclosed is my will!' The Captain turned it over, with a doubtful look—'and Testament.—Where's the Testament?' said the Captain, instantly impeaching the ill-fated Grinder. 'What have you done with that, my lad?'

"'*I* never see it,' whimpered Rob. 'Don't keep on suspecting an innocent lad, Captain. *I* never touched the Testament.'

"Captain Cuttle shook his head, implying that somebody must be made answerable for it; and gravely proceeded . . . . " DS 25

—*"tight"*: "'Make me as compact a little will as can be reconciled with tightness, leaving the whole of the property to "my beloved wife, Henrietty Boffin, sole executrix." Make it as short as you can, using those words; but make it tight.'

"At some loss to fathom Mr Boffin's notions of a tight will, Lightwood felt his way.

"'I beg your pardon, but professional profundity must be exact. When you say tight——'

"'I mean tight,' Mr Boffin explained.

"'Exactly so. And nothing can be more laudable. But is the tightness to bind Mrs Boffin to any and what conditions?'

"'Bind Mrs Boffin?' interposed her husband. 'What are you thinking of? what I want is to make it all hers so tight as that her hold of it can't be loosed.'

"'Hers freely, to do what she likes with? Hers absolutely?'

"'Absolutely!' repeated Mr Boffin, with a short, sturdy laugh." OMF i 8

Youth

—*development of a selfish example:* "Time . . . presently turned out young Thomas a foot taller than when his father had last taken particular notice of him.

"'Thomas is becoming,' said Mr Gradgrind,' almost a young man.'

"Time passed Thomas on in the mill, while his father was thinking about it, and there he stood in a long-tailed coat and a stiff shirt-collar.

"'Really,' said Mr Gradgrind, 'the period has arrived when Thomas ought to go to Bounderby.'

"Time, sticking to him, passed him on into Bounderby's Bank, made him an inmate of Bounderby's house, necessitated the purchase of his first razor, and exercised him diligently in his calculations relative to number one." HT i 14

—*first inebriation:* "We hope and trust you may never have had this primary we are about to speak of? But there *are* some persons of the male sex who may remember with sufficient minuteness the first time they ever got—elevated. If *you* do, the impression will never be eradicated from your mind. Competent persons have declared you, on several subsequent occasions, to have been incapable of seeing a hole in a ladder. The earth seemed to spin round in an inconsistent manner; the pavement was soft—very soft—and felt, you said, as though you were walking on clouds; until suddenly, without the slightest provocation, it came up and smote you on the forehead. Of course, you didn't fall down—that would have been ridiculous.

"Slanderers declared that you attempted to climb up the gutter, under the impression that it was a lamp-post; and, being dissuaded therefrom vehemently endeavoured to play the harp upon the area-railings. How distinctly you remember to this day how completely you forgot everything; how you dreamt you were a water-jug with no water in it—*Tantalus, Prometheus, Ixion,* all rolled into one; how you awoke the next morning without the slightest idea of how you got into bed; how sick, sorry, and repentant you were!" ¶HWC/FF

David Copperfield's experience: Vol. II p856.

—*immaturity:* "I was very young, he was young too, and, in the ignorant hardihood of such a time of life, we don't know what we do to those who have undergone more discipline." CS/MJ 2

—*looks:* " . . . cheerfulness and content are great beautifiers, and are famous preservers of youthful looks, depend upon it." BR 73

—*missed:* "In the active superintendence of this young person [Charley Neckett], Judy Smallweed appears to attain a perfectly geological age, and to date from the remotest periods." BH 21

"'Young ways were never my ways [said Grewgious]. I was the only offspring of parents far advanced in life, and I half believe I was born advanced in life myself . . . while the general growth of people seem to have come into existence buds, I seem to have come into existence a chip. I was a chip—and a very dry one—when I first became aware of myself." MED 9

—*resilience:* " . . . [Nicholas Nickleby] hailed the morning on which he had resolved to quite London, with a light heart, and sprang from his bed with an elasticity of spirit which is happily the lot of young persons, or the world would never be stocked with old ones." NN 22

—*ruined:* "I found Richard thin and languid, slovenly in his dress, abstracted in his manner, forcing his spirits now and then, and at other intervals relapsing into a dull thoughtfulness. About his large bright eyes that used to be so merry, there was a wanness and a restlessness that changed them altogether. I cannot use the expression that he looked old. There is a ruin of youth which is not like age; and into such a ruin Richard's youth and youthful beauty had all fallen away." BH 60

—treated as a man: "O memorable occasion! It was after dinner somewhere (we had gone there with our sister; only a year older than ourself, but universally admitted to be a woman, while we unjustly laboured under the tremendous reproach of boyhood) and were left alone, with an aged Being—fifty, perhaps—who was our host, and another patriarch of forty or so. We were simpering behind the decanters, extremely doubtful of our having any business there, when the host uttered these remarkable expressions:

"'Mr Bud, will you help yourself, and pass the wine!'

"We did it, and felt that we had passed the Rubicon too. We helped ourself feebly, awkwardly, consciously. We felt that they were thinking 'Will he take more than is good for him? Will his eyes roll in his head? Will he disappear beneath the table?'

"But we did it, and bashfully sipped our wine, and even made impotent attempts to close our left eye critically, and look at it against the light.

"We have been promoted twice or thrice since, and have even sat in high places, and received honour; but our host has never said, with the same deep significance—

"'Mr Bud, will you help yourself and pass the wine?'" HWC/FF

Barnaby and his Father [in prison] BR
[The son mentally damaged in utero *by his mother's horror at Rudge's murder of a kind employer: extreme, but not really atypical of this relationship in Dickens]*

Mr Wardle and His Friends under the Influence of the Salmon PP

Body

Life must be held sacred among us in more ways than one—sacred, not merely from the murderous weapon, or the subtle poison, or the cruel blow, but sacred from preventible diseases, distortions, and pains. Physical life respected, moral life comes next.

[RP/BL]

"'*It's difficult to impart the receipt for Cobbler's Punch, sir,' said Venus, 'because, however particular you may be in allotting your materials, so much will still depend upon the indiwidual gifts, and there being a feeling thrown into it. But the groundwork is gin.*"

[OMF iv 14]

The Hamper Emptied in a Twinkling OCS

Ablutions

—adult: ". . . Mr Peggotty went out to wash himself in a kettleful of hot water, remarking that 'cold would never get *his* muck off.' He soon returned, greatly improved in appearance; but so rubicund, that I couldn't help thinking his face had this in common with the lobsters, crabs, and crawfish—that it went into the hot water very black and came out very red." DC 3

And see W:America and Americans—*ablutions; and* Jaggers GE Vol. II p1459

—childish: " . . . [Mrs Joe Gargery] pounced on me like an eagle on a lamb, and my face was squeezed into wooden bowls in sinks, and my head was put under taps of water-butts, and I was soaped, and kneaded, and towelled, and thumped, and harrowed, and rasped, until I really was quite beside myself. (I may here remark that I suppose myself to be better acquainted than any living authority, with the ridgy effect of a wedding-ring, passing unsympathetically over the human countenance.)" GE 7

—excited: "Shaving was not an easy task, for [Scrooge's] hand continued to shake very much; and shaving requires attention, even when you don't dance while you are at it. But if he had cut the end of his nose off, he would have put a piece of sticking-plaister over it, and been quite satisfied." CC 5

—a father by his daughter: "'He has been grubbing and grubbing at school,' said Bella [Wilfer], looking at her father's hand and lightly slapping it, 'till he's not fit to be seen. Oh what a grubby child!!'

"'Indeed, my dear,' said her father, 'I was going to ask to be allowed to wash my hands, only you find me out so soon.'

"'Come here, sir!' cried Bella, taking him by the front of his coat, 'come here and be washed directly. You are not to be trusted to do it for yourself. Come here, sir!'

"The cherub, to his genial amusement, was accordingly conducted to a little washing-room, where Bella soaped his face and rubbed his face, and soaped his hands and rubbed his hands, and splashed him and rinsed him and towelled him, until he was as red as beetroot, even to his very ears: 'Now you must be brushed and combed, sir,' said Bella, busily. 'Hold the light, John. Shut your eyes, sir, and let me take hold of your chin. Be good directly, and do as you are told!'

"Her father being more than willing to obey, she dressed his hair in her most elaborate manner, brushing it out straight, parting it, winding it over her fingers, sticking it up on end, and constantly falling back on John [Rokesmith] to get a good look at the effect of it . . . .

"'There!' said Bella, when she had at last completed the final touches. 'Now you are something like a genteel boy! Put your jacket on, and come and have your supper.'" OMF iv 5

—spartan: "Mr George, having shaved himself before a looking-glass of minute proportions, then marches out, bare-headed and bare-chested, to the Pump, in the little yard, and anon comes back shining with yellow soap, friction, drifting rain, and exceedingly cold water. As he rubs himself upon a large jack-towel, blowing like a military sort of diver just come up: his crisp hair curling tighter and tighter on his sunburnt temples, the more he rubs it, so that it looks as if it never could be loosened by any less coercive instrument than an iron rake or a curry-comb—as he rubs, and puffs, and polishes, and blows, turning his head from side to side, the more conveniently to excoriate his throat, and standing with his body well bent forward, to keep the wet from his martial legs—Phil [Squod], on his knees lighting a fire, looks round as if it were enough washing for him to see all that done, and sufficient renovation, for one day, to take in the superfluous health his master throws off.

"When Mr George is dry, he goes to work to brush his head with two hard brushes at once, to that unmerciful degree that Phil, shouldering his way round the gallery in the act of sweeping it, winks with sympathy. This chafing over, the ornamental part of Mr George's toilet is soon performed." BH 26

—toilette: " . . . Mrs Skewton's maid appeared, according to custom, to prepare her gradually for night. At night, she should have been a skeleton, with dart and hour-glass, rather than a woman, this attendant; for her touch was as the touch of Death. The painted object shrivelled underneath her hand; the form collapsed, the hair dropped off, the arched dark eyebrows changed to scanty tufts of grey; the pale lips shrunk, the skin became cadaverous and loose; an old, worn, yellow, nodding woman, with red eyes, alone remained in Cleopatra's place, huddled up, like a slovenly bundle, in a greasy flannel gown." DS 27

Alcohol and Alcoholism

—abstinence movement

—aboard ship: " . . . would I like to show the grog distribution in 'the fiddle' at noon to the Grand United Amalgamated Total Abstinence Society? Yes, I think I should. I think it would do them good to smell the rum, under the circumstances. Over the grog, mixed in a bucket, presides the boatswain's mate, small tin can in hand. Enter the crew, the guilty consumers, the grown-up brood of Giant Despair, in contradistinction to the band of youthful angel Hope . . . .

" . . . . As the first man, with a knowingly kindled eye, watches the filling of the poisoned chalice (truly but a very small tin mug, to be prosaic), and, tossing back his head, tosses the contents into himself, and passes the empty chalice and passes on, so the second man with an anticipatory wipe of his mouth on sleeve or handkerchief, bides his turn, and drinks and hands and passes on, in whom, and in each as his turn approaches, beams a knowingly kindled eye, a brighter temper, and a suddenly awaked tendency to be jocose with some shipmate . . . vastly comforted, I note them all to be, on deck presently, even to the circulation of redder blood in their cold blue knuckles; and when I look up at them lying out on the yards, and holding on for life among the beating sails, I cannot for my life see the justice of visiting on them—or on me—the drunken crimes of any number of criminals arraigned at the heaviest of assizes." UT/AS

—in an American inn: "We dine soon afterwards . . . and have nothing to drink but tea and coffee. As they are both very bad and the water is worse, I ask for brandy; but it is a Temperance Hotel, and spirits are not to be had for love or money.

"This preposterous forcing of unpleasant drinks down the reluctant throats of travellers is not at all uncommon in America, but I never discovered that the scruples of such wincing landlords induced them to preserve any unusually nice balance between the quality of their fare, and their scale of charges: on the contrary, I rather suspected them of diminishing the one and exalting the other, by way of recompence for the loss of their profit on the sale of spirituous liquors.

"After all, perhaps, the plainest course for persons of such tender consciences, would be, a total abstinence from tavern-keeping." ¶AN 14

—public demonstration: "It was a Teetotal procession, as I learnt from its banners, and was long enough to consume twenty minutes in passing. There were a great number of children in it, some of them so very young in their mothers' arms as to be in the act of practically exemplifying their abstinence from fermented liquors, and attachment to an unintoxicating drink, while the procession defiled." UT/TA

—use without abuse: "For so large a number of the people using draught-horses in [the procession] were so clearly unable to use them without abusing them, that I perceived total abstinence from horseflesh to be the only remedy of which the case admitted. As it is all one to teetotalers whether you take half a pint of beer or half a gallon, so it was all one here whether the beast of burden were a pony or a cart-horse . . . .

"Teetotal mathematics demonstrate that the less includes the greater; that the guilty include the innocent, the blind the seeing, the deaf the hearing, the dumb the speaking, the drunken the sober. If any of the moderate users of draught-cattle in question should deem that there is any gentle violence done to their reason by these elements of logic, they are invited to come out of the procession . . . and look at it from my window." ¶UT/TA

—workingman's restaurant: "[A] drawback on the Whitechapel establishment, is the absence of beer. Regarded merely as a question of policy, it is very impolitic, as having a tendency to send the working men to the public-house, where gin is reported to be sold.

"But, there is a much higher ground on which this absence of beer is objectionable. It expresses distrust of the working man. It is a fragment of that old mantle of patronage in which so many estimable Thugs, so darkly wandering up and down the moral world, are sworn to muffle him. Good beer is a good thing for him, he says, and he likes it; the Depot could give it him good, and he now gets it bad.

"Why does the Depot not give it him good? Because he would get drunk. Why does the Depot not let him have a pint with his dinner, which would not make him drunk? Because he might have had another pint, or another two pints, before he came.

"Now, this distrust is an affront, is exceedingly inconsistent with the confidence the managers express in their hand-bills, and is a timid stopping-short upon the straight highway. It is unjust and unreasonable, also. It is unjust, because it punishes the sober man for the vice of the drunken man. It is unreasonable, because any one at all experienced in such things knows that the drunken workman does not get drunk where he goes to eat and drink, but where he goes to drink—expressly to drink." ¶UT/BB *And see* IG:Labour—*patronised*

—*after-effect:* "How somebody, lying in my bed, lay saying and doing all this over again, at cross purposes, in a feverish dream all night—the bed a rocking sea that was never still! How, as that somebody slowly settled down into myself, did I begin to parch, and feel as if my outer covering of skin were a hard board; my tongue the bottom of an empty kettle, furred with long service, and burning up over a slow fire; the palms of my hands, hot plates of metal which no ice could cool!" DC 24

—*black-out:* "An old confusion in my mind, as if a body of Titans had taken an enormous lever and pushed the day before yesterday some months back." DC 25

—*conversation:* "[Dick Swiveller] began by remarking that soda-water, though a good thing in the abstract, was apt to lie cold upon the stomach unless qualified with ginger, or a small infusion of brandy, which latter article he held to be preferable in all cases, saving for the one consideration of expense. Nobody venturing to dispute these positions, he . . . went on to inform us that Jamaica rum, though unquestionably an agreeable spirit of great richness and flavour, had the drawback of remaining constantly present to the taste next day . . . ." OCS 2

—*crossing a street:* "A more ridiculous and feeble spectacle than this tottering wretch [Mr Dolls] making unsteady sallies into the roadway, and as often staggering back again, oppressed by terrors of vehicles that were a long way off or were nowhere, the streets could not have shown.

"Over and over again, when the course was perfectly clear, he set out, got half-way, described a loop, turned, and went back again, when he might have crossed and recrossed half-a-dozen times. Then he would stand shivering on the edge of the pavement, looking up the street and looking down, while scores of people jostled him, and crossed, and went on.

"Stimulated in course of time by the sight of so many successes, he would make another sally, make another loop, would all but have his foot on the opposite pavement, would see or imagine something coming, and would stagger back again. There he would stand making spasmodic preparations as if for a great leap, and at last would decide on a start at precisely the wrong moment, and would be roared at by drivers, and would shrink back once more, and stand in the old spot shivering, with the whole of the proceedings to go through again." ¶OMF iii 10

—*death:* " . . . going into a public-house, and being supplied in stress of business with his rum, and seeking to vanish without payment, he was collared, searched, found penniless, and admonished not to try that again, by having a pail of dirty water cast over him. This application superinduced another fit of the trembles, after which Mr Dolls, as finding himself in good cue for making a call on a professional friend, addressed himself to the Temple.

" . . . . Mr Dolls, accepting the shilling, promptly laid it out in two threepenny-worths of conspiracy against his life, and two threepenny-worths of raging repentance. Returning to the Chambers with which burden, he was descried coming round into the court by the wary young Blight watching from the window: who instantly closed the outer door, and left the miserable object to expend his fury on the panels.

"The more the door resisted him, the more dangerous and imminent became that bloody conspiracy against his life. Force of police arriving, he recognized in them the conspirators, and laid about him hoarsely, fiercely, staringly, convulsively, foamingly. A humble machine, familiar to the conspirators and called by the expressive name of Stretcher, being unavoidably sent for, he was rendered a harmless bundle of torn rags by being strapped down upon it, with voice and consciousness gone out of him, and life fast going . . . .

" . . . . A ghastly light shining upon him that he didn't need, the beast so furious but a few minutes gone was quiet enough now, with a strange mysterious writing on his face, reflected from one of the great bottles, as if Death had marked him: 'Mine.'

"The medical testimony was more precise

and more to the purpose than it sometimes is in a Court of Justice. 'You had better send for something to cover it. All's over.'

"Therefore the police sent for something to cover it, and it was covered and borne through the streets, the people falling away. After it went the dolls' dressmaker, hiding her face in the Jewish skirts, and clinging to them with one hand, while with the other she plied her stick. It was carried home, and, by reason that the staircase was very narrow, it was put down in the parlour—the little working-bench being set aside to make room for it—and there, in the midst of the dolls with no speculation in their eyes, lay Mr Dolls with no speculation in his." OMF iv 8

—*degradation:* "We will be bold to say, that there is scarcely a man in the constant habit of walking, day after day, through any of the crowded thoroughfares of London, who cannot recollect among the people whom he 'knows by sight,' to use a familiar phrase, some being of abject and wretched appearance whom he remembers to have seen in a very different condition, whom he has observed sinking lower and lower, by almost imperceptible degrees, and the shabbiness and utter destitution of whose appearance, at last, strike forcibly and painfully upon him, as he passes by.

"Is there any man who has mixed much with society, or whose avocations have caused him to mingle, at one time or other, with a great number of people, who cannot call to mind the time when some shabby, miserable wretch, in rags and filth, who shuffles past him now in all the squalor of disease and poverty, was a respectable tradesman, or clerk, or a man following some thriving pursuit, with good prospects, and decent means?—or cannot any of our readers call to mind from among the list of their *quondam* acquaintance, some fallen and degraded man, who lingers about the pavement in hungry misery—from whom every one turns coldly away, and who preserves himself from sheer starvation, nobody knows how?

"Alas! such cases are of too frequent occurrence to be rare items in any man's experience: and but too often arise from one cause—drunkenness—that fierce rage for the slow, sure poison, that oversteps every other consideration; that casts aside wife, children, friends, happiness, and station; and hurries its victims madly on to degradation and death." ¶SB/DD

—*delirium tremens:* "'Arthur [Havisham] . . . come a tearing down into Compeyson's parlour late at night, in only a flannel gown, with his hair all in a sweat, and he says to Compeyson's wife, "Sally, she really is upstairs alonger me, now, and I can't get rid of her. She's all in white," he says, "wi' white flowers in her hair, and she's awful mad, and she's got a shroud hanging over her arm, and she says she'll put it on me at five in the morning . . . .

"'"I don't know how she's there," says Arthur, shivering dreadful with the horrors, "but she's standing in the corner at the foot of the bed, awful mad. And over where her heart's broke—*you* broke it!—there's drops of blood" . . . .

"'Compeyson's wife and me took him up to bed agen, and he raved most dreadful. "Why look at her!" he cried out. "She's a shaking the shroud at me! Don't you see her? Look at her eyes! Ain't it awful to see her so mad?" Next, he cries, "She'll put it on me, and then I'm done for! Take it away from her, take it away!" And then he catched hold of us, and kep on a talking to her, and answering of her, till I half-believed I see her myself.'" GE 42

—*an embarrassing encounter:* "'Agnes!' I said, thickly, 'Lorblessmer! Agnes!'

"'Hush! Pray!' she answered, I could not conceive why. 'You disturb the company. Look at the stage!'

"I tried, on her injunction, to fix it, and to hear something of what was going on there, but quite in vain. I looked at her again by-and-bye, and saw her shrink into her corner, and put her gloved hand to her forehead.

"'Agnes!' I said. 'I'mafraidyou'renorwell.'

"'Yes, yes. Do not mind me, Trotwood,' she returned. 'Listen! Are you going away soon?'

"'Amigoarawaysoo?' I repeated.

"'Yes.'

"I had a stupid intention of replying that I was going to wait, to hand her downstairs. I suppose I expressed it somehow; for, after she had looked at me attentively for a little while, she appeared to understand, and replied in a low tone:

"'I know you will do as I ask you, if I tell you I am very earnest in it. Go away now, Trotwood, for my sake, and ask your friends to take you home.'" DC 24

"But the agony of mind, the remorse, and shame I felt, when I became conscious next day! My horror of having committed a thousand offences I had forgotten, and which nothing could ever expiate—my recollection of that indelible look which Agnes had given me—the torturing impossibility of communicating with her, not knowing, beast that I was, how she came to be in London, or where she stayed—my disgust of the very sight of the room where the revel had been held—my racking head—the smell of smoke, the sight of glasses, the impossibility of going out, or even getting up! Oh, what a day it was!" DC 24

—gin-shop neighbourhoods: "Although places of this description are to be met with in every second street, they are invariably numerous and splendid in precise proportion to the dirt and poverty of the surrounding neighbourhood. The gin-shops in and near Drury Lane, Holborn, St Giles's, Covent Garden, and Clare Market, are the handsomest in London. There is more of filth and squalid misery near those great thoroughfares than in any part of this mighty city." SB/GS

—in a graveyard: "'Let the old uns come out if they dare, when we go among their tombs. My spirit is ready for 'em.'

"'Do you mean animal spirits, or ardent?'

"'The one's the t'other,' answers Durdles, 'and I mean 'em both.'" MED 12

—hospitality: "'Now, just a leetle drop,' said Mrs Mann persuasively.

"'What is it?' inquired the beadle.

"'Why, it's what I'm obliged to keep a little of in the house, to put into the blessed infants' Daffy, when they ain't well, Mr Bumble,' replied Mrs Mann as she opened a corner cupboard, and took down a bottle and glass. 'It's gin. I'll not deceive you, Mr B. It's gin.'

"'Do you give the children Daffy, Mrs Mann?' inquired Bumble, following with his eyes the interesting process of mixing.

"'Ah, bless 'em, that I do, dear as it is,' replied the nurse. 'I couldn't see 'em suffer before my very eyes, you know, sir.'" OT 2

—inebriety in context: "Well-disposed gentlemen, and charitable ladies, would alike turn with coldness and disgust from a description of the drunken besotted men, and wretched broken-down miserable women, who form no inconsiderable portion of the frequenters of these haunts; forgetting, in the pleasant consciousness of their own rectitude, the poverty of the one, and the temptation of the other.

"Gin-drinking is a great vice in England, but wretchedness and dirt are a greater; and until you improve the homes of the poor, or persuade a half-famished wretch not to seek relief in the temporary oblivion of his own misery, with the pittance which, divided among his family, would furnish a morsel of bread for each, gin-shops will increase in number and splendour.

"If Temperance Societies would suggest an antidote against hunger, filth, and foul air, or could establish dispensaries for the gratuitous distribution of bottles of Lethe-water, gin-palaces would be numbered among the things that were." ¶SB/GS

"Drunkenness, as a national horror, is the effect of many causes. Foul smells, disgusting habitations, bad workshops and workshop customs, want of light, air, and water, the absence of all easy means of decency and health, are commonest among its common, everyday, physical causes.

"The mental weariness and languor so induced, the want of wholesome relaxation, the craving for *some* stimulus and excitement, which is as much a part of such lives as the sun is; and, last and inclusive of all the rest, ignorance, and the need there is amongst the English people of reasonable, rational training, in lieu of mere parrot-education, or none at all; are its most obvious moral causes." E/DC

—ingestion in a tower: "As aëronauts lighten the load they carry, when they wish to rise, similarly Durdles has lightened the wicker bottle in coming up. Snatches of sleep surprise him on his legs, and stop him in his talk. A mild fit of calenture [a delirium] seizes him, in which he deems that the ground so far below, is on a level with the tower, and would as lief walk off the tower into the air as not. Such is his state when they begin to come down. And as aëronauts make themselves heavier when they wish to descend, similarly Durdles charges himself with more liquid from the wicker bottle, that he may come down the better." MED 12

—and medical practice: "The special feature in Dr Haggage's treatment of the case, was his determination to keep Mrs Bangham up to the mark. As thus:

"'Mrs Bangham,' said the doctor, before he had been there twenty minutes, 'go outside and fetch a little brandy, or we shall have you giving in.'

"'Thank you, sir. But none on my accounts,' said Mrs Bangham.

"'Mrs Bangham,' returned the doctor, 'I am in professional attendance on this lady, and don't choose to allow any discussion on your part. Go outside and fetch a little brandy, or I foresee that you'll break down.'

"'You're to be obeyed, sir,' said Mrs Bangham, rising. 'If you was to put your own lips to it, I think you wouldn't be the worse, for you look but poorly, sir.'

"'Mrs Bangham,' returned the doctor, 'I am not your business, thank you, but you are mine. Never you mind *me*, if you please. What you have got to do, is, to do as you are told, and to go and get what I bid you.'

"Mrs Bangham submitted; and the doctor, having administered her potion, took his own. He repeated the treatment every hour, being very determined with Mrs Bangham." LD i 6

—medicinal: "Mrs Gamp, with the bottle on one knee, and the glass on the other, sat upon a stool, shaking her head for a long time, until, in a moment of abstraction, she poured out a dram of spirits, and raised it to her lips. It was succeeded by a second, and by a third, and then her eyes—either in the sadness of her reflections upon life and death, or in her admiration of the liquor—were so turned up, as to be quite invisible. But she shook her head still." MC 19

"She came up to me one evening . . . to ask . . . if I could oblige her with a little tincture of cardamums mixed with rhubarb, and flavoured with seven drops of the essence of cloves, which was the best remedy for her complaint;—or, if I had not such a thing by me, with a little brandy, which was the next best. It was not, she remarked, so palatable to her, but it was the next best. As I had never even heard of the first remedy, and always had the second in the closet, I gave Mrs Crupp a glass of the second, which (that I might have no suspicion of its being devoted to any improper use) she began to take in my presence." DC 26

—misunderstood: " . . . what did Mr Snevellicci do? He winked—winked, openly and undisguisedly; winked with his right eye—upon Henrietta Lillyvick!

"The collector fell back in his chair in the intensity of his astonishment. If anybody had winked at her as Henrietta Petowker, it would have been indecorous in the last degree; but as Mrs Lillyvick! While he thought of it in a cold perspiration, and wondered whether it was possible that he could be dreaming, Mr Snevellicci repeated the wink, and drinking to Mrs Lillyvick in dumb show, actually blew her a kiss! Mr Lillyvick left his chair, walked straight up to the other end of the table, and fell upon him—literally fell upon him—instantaneously. Mr Lillyvick was no light weight, and consequently when he fell upon Mr Snevellicci, Mr Snevellicci fell under the table. Mr Lillyvick followed him, and the ladies screamed." NN 30

—in moderation: ""Do you drink? said the baron [of Grogzwig], touching the bottle with the bowl of his pipe.

""Nine times out of ten, and then very hard," rejoined the [Genius of Despair and Suicide], drily.

""Never in moderation?" . . .

""Never," replied the figure, with a shudder; "that breeds cheerfulness."" NN 6

—morning after: "[Stryver] had that rather wild, strained, seared marking about the eyes, which may be observed in all free livers of his class, from the portrait of Jeffries downward, and which can be traced, under various disguises of Art, through the portraits of every Drinking Age." TTC ii 5

—old man: "Sometimes, on holidays, towards evening, he will be seen to walk with a slightly increased infirmity, and his old eyes will glimmer with a moist and marshy light. Then the little old man is drunk. A very small measure will over-set him: he may be bowled off his unsteady legs with a half-pint pot. Some pitying acquaintance—chance acquaintance, very often—has warmed up his weakness with a treat of beer, and the consequence will be the lapse of a longer time than usual before he shall pass again." LD i 31

—overdoing: "'It wasn't the wine,' murmured Mr Snodgrass, in a broken voice. 'It was the salmon.' (Somehow or other, it never is the wine, in these cases.)" PP 8 *This quotes an actual excuse CD once heard.*

Swiveller "chanced at the moment to be sprinkling a glass of warm gin and water on the dust of the law, and to be moistening his clay, as the phrase goes, rather copiously. But as clay in the abstract, when too much moistened, becomes of a weak and uncertain consistency, breaking down in unexpected places, retaining impressions but faintly, and preserving no strength or steadiness of character, so Mr Swiveller's clay, having imbibed a considerable quantity of moisture, was in a very loose and slippery state, insomuch that the various ideas impressed upon it were fast losing their distinctive character, and running into each other." OCS 48

—*praised:* "'Pour on. Fill high. A bumper with a bead in the middle! Give me enough of this . . . and I'll do murder if you ask me! . . .

"'I always am [drinking] when I can get it,' cried Hugh boisterously, waving the empty glass above his head, and throwing himself into a rude dancing attitude. 'I always am. Why not? Ha ha ha! What's so good to me as this? What has ever been? What else has kept away the cold on bitter nights, and driven hunger off in starving times? What else has given me the strength and courage of a man, when men would have left me to die, a puny child? I should never have had a man's heart but for this. I should have died in a ditch. Where's he who when I was a weak and sickly wretch, with trembling legs and fading sight, bade me cheer up, as this did? I never knew him; not I. I drink to the drink, master. Ha ha ha!'" BR 23

—*private difficulties:* "'She has her failings—as who has not? [said Mr Guppy speaking of his mother]—but I never knew her to do it when company was present; at which time you may freely trust her with wines, spirits, or malt liquors.'" BH 9

—*rationalized:* " . . . they both very gravely agreed that it was extremely unwise to eat so many pickled walnuts with the chops, as it was a notorious fact that they always made people queer and sleepy; indeed, if it had not been for the whiskey and cigars, there was no knowing what harm they mightn't have done 'em." SB/MN

—*resistance to injury:* "Drunken men, they say, may roll down precipices, and be quite unconscious of any serious personal inconvenience when their reason returns." NN 33

—*stages of intoxication:* " . . . Mr Snevellicci . . . was scarcely ever sober. He knew in his cups three distinct stages of intoxication—the dignified—the quarrelsome—the amorous. When professionally engaged he never got beyond the dignified; in private circles he went through all three, passing from one to another with a rapidity of transition often rather perplexing to those who had not the honour of his acquaintance." NN 30

—*young man about town:* "I began, by being singularly cheerful and light-hearted; all sorts of half-forgotten things to talk about, came rushing into my mind, and made me hold forth in a most unwonted manner. I laughed heartily at my own jokes, and everybody else's; called Steerforth to order for not passing the wine; made several engagements to go to Oxford; announced that I meant to have a dinner-party exactly like that, once a week, until further notice; and madly took so much snuff out of Grainger's box, that I was obliged to go into the pantry, and have a private fit of sneezing ten minutes long.

"I went on, by passing the wine faster and faster yet, and continually starting up with a corkscrew to open more wine, long before any was needed. I proposed Steerforth's health. I said he was my dearest friend, the protector of my boyhood, and the companion of my prime. I said I was delighted to propose his health. I said I owed him more obligations than I could ever repay, and held him in a higher admiration than I could ever express. I finished by saying, 'I'll give you Steerforth! God bless him! Hurrah!' We gave him three times three, and another, and a good one to finish with. I broke my glass in going round the table to shake hands with him, and I said (in two words) 'Steerforth, you'retheguidingstarofmyexistence.'"

"I went on, by finding suddenly that somebody was in the middle of a song. Markham was the singer, and he sang 'When the heart of a man is depressed with care'. He said, when he had sung it, he would give us 'Woman!' I took objection to that, and I couldn't allow it. I said it was not a respectful way of proposing the toast, and I would never permit that toast to be drunk in my house otherwise than as 'The Ladies!' I was very high with him, mainly I think because I saw Steerforth and Grainger laughing at me—or at him—or at both of us. He said a man was not to be dictated to. I said a man *was.* He said a man was not to be insulted, then. I said he was right there—never under my roof, where the Lares were sacred, and the laws of hospitality paramount. He said it was no derogation from a man's dignity to confess that I was a devilish good fellow. I instantly proposed his health.

"Somebody was smoking . . . *I* was smoking . . . Steerforth had made a speech about me, in the course of which I had been affected almost to tears. I returned thanks, and hoped the present company would dine with me to-morrow, and the day after—each day at five o'clock, that we might enjoy the pleasures of conversation and society through a long evening. I felt called upon to propose an individual. I would give them my aunt. Miss Betsey Trotwood, the best of her sex!" DC 24

"Owing to some confusion in the dark, the door was gone. I was feeling for it in the window-curtains, when Steerforth, laughing, took me by the arm and led me out. We went down-stairs, one behind another. Near the bottom, somebody fell, and rolled down. Somebody else said it was Copperfield. I was angry at that false report, until, finding myself on my back in the passage, I began to think there might be some foundation for it.

"A very foggy night, with great rings round the lamps in the streets! There was an indistinct talk of its being wet. I considered it frosty. Steerforth dusted me under a lamp-post, and put my hat into shape, which somebody produced from somewhere in a most extraordinary manner, for I hadn't had it on before. Steerforth then said, 'You are all right, Copperfield, are you not?' and I told him, 'Neverberrer.'" DC 24

And see —after-effect; B:Tobacco—*overdone; and* Drunkard *in* Indexes VII and VIII

Blindness

—beloved: "The Blind Girl never knew that ceilings were discoloured, walls blotched and bare of plaster here and there, high crevices unstopped and widening every day, beams mouldering and tending downward. The Blind Girl never knew that iron was rusting, wood rotting, paper peeling off; the size, and shape, and true proportion of the dwelling, withering away. The Blind Girl never knew that ugly shapes of delf and earthenware were on the board; that sorrow and faint-heartedness were in the house; that Caleb's scanty hairs were turning grayer and more gray, before her sightless face. The Blind Girl never knew they had a master, cold, exacting, and uninterested—never knew that Tackleton was Tackleton, in short; but lived in the belief of an eccentric humourist who loved to have his jest with them, and who, while he was the Guardian Angel of their lives, disdained to hear one word of thankfulness.

"And all was Caleb's doing; all the doing of her simple father! But he too had a Cricket on his Hearth; and listening sadly to its music when the motherless Blind Child was very young, that Spirit had inspired him with the thought that even her great deprivation might be almost changed into a blessing, and the girl made happy by these little means." CH 2

—candour of expression: "It is strange to watch the faces of the blind, and see how free they are from all concealment of what is passing in their thoughts; observing which, a man with eyes may blush to contemplate the mask he wears. Allowing for one shade of anxious expression which is never absent from their countenances, and the like of which we may readily detect in our own faces if we try to feel our way in the dark, every idea, as it rises within them, is expressed with the lightning's speed and nature's truth. If the company at a rout, or drawing-room at court, could only for one time be as unconscious of the eyes upon them as blind men and women are, what secrets would come out, and what a worker of hypocrisy this sight, the loss of which we so much pity, would appear to be!

"The thought occurred to me as I sat down in another room before a girl, blind, deaf, and dumb, destitute of smell, and nearly so of taste—before a fair young creature with every human faculty and hope and power of goodness and affection enclosed within her delicate frame, and but one outward sense—the sense of touch. There she was before me; built up, as it were, in a marble cell, impervious to any ray of light or particle of sound; with her poor white hand peeping through a chink in the wall, beckoning to some good man for help, that an immortal soul might be awakened.

"Long before I looked upon her, the help had come. Her face was radiant with intelligence and pleasure. Her hair, braided by her own hands, was bound about a head whose intellectual capacity and development were beautifully expressed in its graceful outline and its broad, open brow; her dress, arranged by herself, was a pattern of neatness and simplicity; the work she had knitted lay beside her; her writing-book was on the desk she leaned upon. From the mournful ruin of such bereavement there had slowly risen up this gentle, tender, guileless, grateful-hearted being." AN 3

—compensation: " . . . we are accustomed to see in those who have lost a human sense, something in its place almost divine . . . . " BR 46

—and conscience: "'I know what you would say: you have hinted at it once already. Have I no feeling for you, because I am blind? No, I have not. Why do you expect me, being in darkness, to be better than men who have their sight—why should you? Is the hand of Heaven more manifest in my having no eyes, than in your having two? It's the cant of you folks to be horrified if a blind man robs, or lies, or steals; oh yes, it's far worse in him, who can barely live on the few halfpence that are thrown to him in streets, than in you, who can see, and work, and are not dependent on the mercies of the world. A curse on you! You who have five senses may be wicked at your pleasure; we who have four, and want the most important, are to love and be moral on our affliction. The true charity and justice of rich to poor, all the world over!'" BR 46

—invoked by epithet: "A very common imprecation concerning the most beautiful of human features: which, if it were heard above, only once out of every fifty thousand times that it is uttered below, would render blindness as common a disorder as measles." OT 16

—a lesson to be learned: "Ye who have eyes and see not, and have ears and hear not; ye who are as the hypocrites, of sad countenances, and disfigure your faces that ye may seem unto men to fast; learn healthy cheerfulness and mild contentment, from the deaf, and dumb, and blind! Self-elected saints with gloomy brows, this sightless, careless, voiceless child may teach you lessons you will do well to follow. Let that poor hand of hers lie gently on your hearts, for there may be something in its healing touch akin to that of the Great Master, whose precepts you misconstrue, whose lessons you pervert, of whose charity and sympathy with all the world not one among you in his daily practice knows as much as many of the worst among those fallen sinners to whom you are liberal in nothing but the preachment of perdition." AN 3

—its varieties: "'There are various degrees and kinds of blindness, widow. There is the connubial blindness, ma'am, which perhaps you may have observed in the course of your own experience, and which is a kind of wilful and self-bandaging blindness. There is the blindness of party, ma'am, and public men, which is the blindness of a mad bull in the midst of a regiment of soldiers clothed in red. There is the blind confidence of youth, which is the blindness of young kittens, whose eyes have not yet opened on the world; and there is that physical blindness, ma'am, of which I am, contrary to my own desire, a most illustrious example. Added to these, ma'am, is that blindness of the intellect, of which we have a specimen in your interesting son, and which, having sometimes glimmerings and dawnings of the light, is scarcely to be trusted as a total darkness.'" BR 45

There are three blind named characters in the works: Sampson Dibble, a Mormon emigrant UT/SL; Bertha Plummer, an overprotected daughter CH; and the infamous Stagg BR. There are, however, 18 one- or game-eyed figures listed in Index VII, *and there is Laura Bridgman[H], discussed in AN: see above.*

Body

—barefoot: " . . . Mr Lobley mopped, and, arranging cushions, stretchers, and the like, danced the tight-rope the whole length of the boat like a man to whom shoes were a superstition and stockings slavery . . . . " MED 22

—blood: "[Mr Winkle] sat on the ground, staunching with a yellow silk handkerchief the stream of life which issued from his nose . . . ." PP 4

—cheek: "This,' said Mrs Wilfer, presenting a cheek to be kissed, as sympathetic and responsive as the back of the bowl of a spoon, 'is quite an honour!'" OMF ii 8

"'My child is welcome, though unlooked for,' said [Mrs Wilfer], at the time presenting her cheek as if it were a cool slate for visitors to enroll themselves upon." OMF iii 16

—chest, in cold weather: " . . . [Tom Pinch] made the discovery that the bosom of his companion's shirt was as much exposed as if it were Midsummer, and was ruffled by every breath of air, 'why don't you wear a waistcoat?'

"'What's the good of one, sir?' asked Mark.

"'Good of one?' said Mr Pinch. 'Why, to keep your chest warm.'

"'Lord love you, sir!' cried Mark, 'you don't know me. *My* chest don't want no warming. Even if it did, what would no waistcoat bring it to? Inflammation of the lungs, perhaps? Well, there'd be some credit in being jolly, with a inflammation of the lungs.'" MC 5

—chin: "'That,' repeated Mrs Gowan, furling her green fan for the moment, and tapping her chin with it (it was on the way to

being a double chin; might be called a chin and a half at present), 'that's all!'" LD i 33

Bunsby DS and Tugby C have notable chins.

—complexion

—blue: "The Major [Bagstock], with his complexion like a Stilton cheese, and his eyes like a prawn's, went roving about . . . ." DS 10

—blush: "Mr Watkins Tottle blushed up to the eyes and down to the chin, and exhibited a most extensive combination of colours as he confessed the soft impeachment." SB/WT

"'I will not look for blushes in such a quarter [as Matilda Browdie],' said Miss Squeers, haughtily, 'for that countenance is a stranger to everything but hignominiousness and red-faced boldness.'" NN 42

—florid: "[Fang's] face was stern, and much flushed. If he were really not in the habit of drinking rather more than was exactly good for him, he might have brought an action against his countenance for libel, and have recovered heavy damages." OT 11

Stryver TTC is conspicuously florid of face, and drink is apparently the reason.

—flush: "Mr Dorrit threw in another compliment here, to the effect that business, like the time which was precious in it, was made for slaves; and that it was not for Mrs Merdle, who ruled all hearts at her supreme pleasure, to have anything to do with it. Mrs Merdle laughed, and conveyed to Mr Dorrit an idea that the Bosom flushed—which was one of her best effects." LD ii 15

—digestion: "'The process of digestion, as I have been informed by anatomical friends, is one of the most wonderful works of nature. I do not know how it may be with others, but it is a great satisfaction to me to know, when regaling on my humble fare, that I am putting in motion the most beautiful machinery with which we have any acquaintance. I really feel at such times as if I was doing a public service. When I have wound myself up, if I may employ such a term,' said Mr. Pecksniff with exquisite tenderness, 'and know that I am Going, I feel that in the lesson afforded by the works within me, I am a Benefactor to my Kind!'" MC 8

"'You see this toothpick?' said Scrooge . . . .

"' . . . I see it,' said the Ghost . . . .

"'Well!' returned Scrooge, 'I have but to swallow this, and be for the rest of my days persecuted by a legion of goblins, all of my own creation. Humbug, I tell you! humbug!'" CC 1 *And see* Senses

"The Veneering dinners are excellent dinners . . . and all goes well. Notably, Lady Tippins has made a series of experiments on her digestive functions, so extremely complicated and daring, that if they could be published with their results it might benefit the human race. Having taken in provisions from all parts of the world, this hardy old cruiser has last touched at the North Pole . . . . " OMF i 2

—elbows: "Abrasions on the elbows are not generally understood, it is true, to range within that class of personal charms called beauty-spots. But it is better, going through the world, to have the arms chafed in that narrow passage, than the temper: and Clemency [Newcome]'s was sound and whole as any beauty's in the land." BL 2

And see F:Manners*—bashfulness at dinner*

—eye

—black: "'Waiter! raw beef-steak for the gentleman's eye—nothing like raw beef-steak for a bruise, sir; cold lamp-post very good, but lamp-post inconvenient—damned odd standing in the open street half an hour, with your eye against a lamp-post. . . .'" PP 2

—bright: "There was no flour on Ruth [Pinch]'s hands when she received them in the triangular parlour, but there were pleasant smiles upon her face, and a crowd of welcomes shining out of every smile, and gleaming in her bright eyes. By-the-bye, how bright they were! Looking into them for but a moment, when you took her hand, you saw, in each, such a capital miniature of yourself, representing you as such a restless, flashing, eager, brilliant little fellow—

"Ah! if you could only have kept them for your own miniature! But, wicked, roving, restless, too impartial eyes, it was enough for any one to stand before them, and straightway there he danced and sparkled quite as merrily as you!" MC 39

And see Meg Veck's bright eyes C

—a cast: "[Charles Kitterbell] had a cast in his eye which rendered it quite impossible for any one with whom he conversed to know where he was looking. His eyes appeared fixed on the wall, and he was staring you out of countenance: in short, there was no catching his eye, and perhaps it is a merciful dispensation of Providence that such eyes are not catching." SB/BC

—of the humble: "'Now I ain't one of your lady's men, Master Copperfield [said Uriah Heep]; but I've had eyes in my ed, a pretty long time back. We umble ones have got eyes, mostly speaking—and we look out of 'em.'" DC 42

—knowing: "Tackleton stood looking on maliciously with the half-closed eye; which, whenever it met [Dot Peerybingle's]—or caught it, for it can hardly be said to have ever met another eye: rather being a kind of trap to snatch it up—augmented her confusion in a most remarkable degree." CH 2

—military: " . . . the soft light of intelligence burnt rather feebly in the eyes of the warriors, inasmuch as the command 'eyes front' had been given, and all the spectator saw before him was several thousand pairs of optics, staring straight forward, wholly divested of any expression whatever." PP 4

—nautical: "'Captain Swosser loved that craft for my sake. When she was no longer in commission, he frequently said that if he were rich enough to buy her old hulk, he would have an inscription let into the timbers of the quarter-deck where we stood as partners in the dance, to mark the spot where he fell—raked fore and aft (Captain Swosser used to say) by the fire from my tops. It was his naval way of mentioning my eyes.'" BH 13

—philanthropic: " . . . [Mrs Pardiggle's] spectacles were made the less engaging by her eyes being what Ada [Clare] called 'choking eyes,' meaning very prominent . . . . " BH 8

—red: "[Solomon Gills] was a slow, quiet-spoken, thoughtful old fellow, with eyes as red as if they had been small suns looking at you through a fog; and a newly-awakened manner, such as he might have acquired by having stared for three or four days successively through every optical instrument in his shop, and suddenly came back to the world again, to find it green." DS 4

—sanctimonious: "'What,' [old Martin Chuzzlewit] asked of Mr Pecksniff, happening to catch his eye in its descent; for until now it had been piously upraised, with something of that expression which the poetry of ages has attributed to a domestic bird, when breathing its last amid the ravages of an electric storm: 'What are [your daughters'] names?'" MC 10

—shy: "Then why, whenever Ruth [Pinch] lifted up her eyes, did she let them fall again immediately, and seek the uncongenial pavement of the court? They were not such eyes as shun the light: they were not such eyes as require to be hoarded to enhance their value. They were much too precious and too genuine to stand in need of arts like those. Somebody must have been looking at them!" MC 45

—small: "Mr Gusher, being a flabby gentleman with a moist surface, and eyes so much too small for his moon of a face that they seemed to have been originally made for somebody else, was not at first sight prepossessing." BH 15

—with spectacles: " . . . the Captain [Cuttle] trimmed the candle, put on his spectacles—he had felt it appropriate to take to spectacles on entering into the Instrument Trade, though his eyes were like a hawk's . . . . " DS 32

—without spectacles: "[Crisparkle] had the eyes of a microscope and a telescope combined, when they were unassisted." MED 6

—sunken: "'Here, sir,' replied Job [Trotter], presenting himself on the staircase. We have described him, by-the-bye, as having deeply sunken eyes, in the best of times. In his present state of want and distress, he looked as if those features had gone out of town altogether." PP 42

Blandois/Lagnier/Rigaud LD and Jerry Cruncher TTC have flat or sharp, unprepossessing eyes. See also Blindness—note.

—face

—bifurcated: " . . . now [Scadder's] profile was towards them, and nothing but attentive thoughtfulness was written on it. Strangely different to the other side! He was not a man much given to laughing, and never laughed outright; but every line in the print of the crow's-foot, and every little wiry vein in that division of his head, was wrinkled up into a grin! The compound figure of death and the Lady at the top of the old ballad was not divided with a greater nicety, and hadn't halves more monstrously unlike each other, than the two profiles of Zephaniah Scadder." MC 21

—cruel: "[Gamfield's] villainous countenance was a regular stamped receipt for cruelty." OT 3

—healthy: "Mrs Meagles [had] a pleasant English face which had been looking at homely things for five-and-fifty years or more, and shone with a bright reflection of them." LD i 2

—Irish: "Such a thoroughly Irish face, that it seemed as if he ought, as a matter of right and principle, to be in rags, and could have no sort of business to be looking cheerfully at anybody out of a whole suit of clothes." MC 17

—long: "'Oh, do not say for ever, Belinda,' exclaimed the excitable Cymon, as two strongly-defined tears chased each other down his pale face—it was so long that there was plenty of room for a chase—'Do not say for ever!'" SB/TR

—made up: "How the fascinating Tippins gets on when arraying herself for the bewilderment of the senses of men, is known only to the Graces and her maid; but perhaps even that engaging creature . . . could dispense with a good deal of the trouble attendant on the daily restoration of her charms, seeing that as to her face and neck this adorable divinity is, as it were, a diurnal species of lobster—throwing off a shell every forenoon, and needing to keep in a retired spot until the new crust hardens." OMF ii 16

—pretty faces together: "You know sometimes, when you are used to a pretty face, how, when it comes into contact and comparison with another pretty face, it seems for the moment to be homely and faded, and hardly to deserve the high opinion you have had of it. Now, this was not at all the case, either with Dot [Peerybingle] or May [Fielding]; for May's face set off Dot's, and Dot's face set off May's, so naturally and agreeably, that, as John Peerybingle was very near saying when he came into the room, they ought to have been born sisters—which was the only improvement you could have suggested." CH 2

—relaxed: "[Britain] was much broader, much redder, much more cheerful, and much jollier in all respects. It seemed as if his face had been tied up in a knot before, and was now untwisted and smoothed out." BL 2

—repellent: "'To be plain with you [said Varden to Rudge], friend, you don't carry in your countenance a letter of recommendation.'" BR 2

"'What are you staring at?' said Jonas.

"'Not a handsome man,' returned the guard. 'If you want your fortune told, I'll tell you a bit of it. You won't be drowned. That's a consolation for you.'" MC 47

—shapeless, shifting: "[Molly] set on every dish; and I always saw in her face, a face rising out of the caldron. Years afterwards, I made a dreadful likeness of that woman, by causing a face that had no other natural resemblance to it than it derived from flowing hair, to pass behind a bowl of flaming spirits in a dark room." GE 26

—unflatteringly described: "'By my soul [said Boythorn], the countenance of that fellow, when he was a boy, was the blackest image of perfidy, cowardice, and cruelty ever set up as a scarecrow in a field of scoundrels. If I were to meet that most unparalleled despot in the streets to-morrow, I would fell him like a rotten tree.!'" BH 9

—fidgets: "'Years don't tell much in our firm, Master Copperfield, except in raising up the umble, namely mother and self—and in developing,' he added, as an afterthought, 'the beautiful, namely, Miss Agnes.'

"[Uriah Heep] jerked himself about, after this compliment, in such an intolerable manner, that my aunt, who had sat looking straight at him, lost all patience.

"'Deuce take the man!' said my aunt, sternly, 'what's he about? Don't be galvanic, sir!'

"'I ask your pardon, Miss Trotwood,' returned Uriah; 'I'm aware you're nervous.'

"'Go along with you, sir!' said my aunt, anything but appeased. 'Don't presume to say so! I am nothing of the sort. If you're an eel, sir, conduct yourself like one. If you're a man, control your limbs, sir! Good God!' said my aunt, with great indignation, 'I am not going to be serpentined and corkscrewed out of my senses!'

"Mr Heep was rather abashed, as most people might have been, by this explosion; which derived great additional force from the indignant manner in which my aunt afterwards moved in her chair, and shook her head as if she were making snaps or bounces at him." DC 35

And see Waiting—*and fidgeting*

—fingers: "Joe . . . secretly crossed his two forefingers, and exhibited them to me, as our token that Mrs Joe was in a cross temper. This was so much her normal state, that Joe and I would often, for weeks together, be, as to our fingers, like monumental Crusaders as to their legs." GE 4

—fingernails: "'Look here!' taking something out. 'Scraps of the Russian Prince's nails. Prince Alphabet turned topsy-turvey, *I* call him, for his name's got all the letters in it, higgledy-piggledy.'

"'The Russian Prince is a client of yours, is he?' said Steerforth.

"'I believe you, my pet,' replied Miss Mowcher. 'I keep his nails in order for him. Twice a week! Fingers *and* toes . . . .

"' . . . . I said, what a set of humbugs we were in general, and I showed you the scraps of the Prince's nails to prove it. The Prince's nails do more for me in private families of the genteel sort, than all my talents put together. I always carry 'em about. They're the best introduction. If Miss Mowcher cuts the Prince's nails, she *must* be all right. I give 'em away to the young ladies. They put 'em in albums, I believe. Ha! ha! ha! Upon my life, "the whole social system" (as the men call it when they make speeches in Parliament) is a system of Prince's nails' . . . . " DC 22

"Instead of putting on his coat and waistcoat with anything like the impetuousity that could alone have kept pace with Walter's mood, [Captain Cuttle] declined to invest himself with those garments at all at present; and informed Walter, that on such a serious matter, he must be allowed to 'bite his nails a bit.'

"'It's an old habit of mine, Wal'r,' said the Captain, 'any time these fifty year. When you see Ned Cuttle bite his nails, Wal'r, then you may know that Ned Cuttle's aground.'

"Thereupon the Captain put his iron hook between his teeth as if it were a hand; and with an air of wisdom and profundity that was the very concentration and sublimation of all philosophical reflection and grave inquiry, applied himself to the consideration of the subject [of Walter Gay's career] in its various branches." DS 15

—forefinger: "Mr Bucket and his fat forefinger are much in consultation together under existing circumstances. When Mr Bucket has a matter of this pressing interest under his consideration, the fat forefinger seems to rise to the dignity of a familiar demon. He puts it to his ears, and it whispers information; he puts it to his lips, and it enjoins him to secrecy; he rubs it over his nose, and it sharpens his scent; he shakes it before a guilty man, and it charms him to his destruction. The Augurs of the Detective Temple invariably predict, that when Mr Bucket and that finger are in much conference, a terrible avenger will be heard of before long.

"Otherwise mildly studious in his observation of human nature, on the whole a benignant philosopher, not disposed to be severe upon the follies of mankind, Mr Bucket pervades a vast number of houses, and strolls about an infinity of streets: to outward appearance rather languishing for want of an object. He is in the friendliest condition towards his species, and will drink with most of them. He is free with his money, affable in his manners, innocent in his conversation—but, through the placid stream of his life, there glides an under-current of forefinger." BH 53

"Just at dusk, Inspectors Wield and Stalker are announced; but we do not undertake to warrant the orthography* of any of the names here mentioned . . . . Inspector Wield [has] a habit of emphasising his conversation by the aid of a corpulent fore-finger, which is constantly in juxtatposition with his eyes or nose." RP/DP

**See* Index IX: *Inspector Charles Field*

—hands

—clammy: " . . . I saw Uriah Heep shutting up the office; and, feeling friendly towards everybody, went in and spoke to him, and at parting, gave him my hand. But oh, what a clammy hand his was! as ghostly to the touch as to the sight! I rubbed mine afterwards, to warm it, *and to rub his off.*

"It was such an uncomfortable hand, that, when I went to my room, it was still cold and wet upon my memory." DC 15

—gift of God: "Long may it remain in this mixed world a point not easy of decision, which is the more beautiful evidence of the Almighty's goodness—the delicate fingers that are formed for sensitiveness and sympathy of touch, and made to minister to pain and grief, or the rough, hard, Captain Cuttle hand, that the heart teaches, guides, and softens in a moment." DS 48

—a mother's: " . . . only her fluttering hands give utterance to her emotions. But they are eloquent, very, very eloquent . . . . They speak of gratitude, of joy, of grief, of hope; of inextinguishable affection, cherished with no return since this stalwart man was a stripling; of a better son loved less, and this son loved so fondly and so proudly; and they speak in such touching language, that Mrs Bagnet's eyes brim up with tears . . . ." BH 55

—observed: "The varieties of hands that hover about the [post-office] grating, and are thrust through the little doorways in it, are a continual study for [the clerks]—or would

be, if they had any time to spare . . . . The coarse-grained hand which seems all thumb and knuckle, and no nail, and which takes up money or puts it down with such an odd, clumsy, lumbering touch; the retail trader's hand which chinks it up and tosses it over with a bounce; the housewife's hand which has a lingering propensity to keep some of it back, and to drive a bargain by not paying in the last shilling or so of the sum for which her [money] order was obtained; the quick, the slow, the coarse, the fine, the sensitive and dull, the ready and unready; they are always at the grating all day long." HWC/PO

—prisoners': "'The child put all these things [lunch] between the bars into the soft, smooth, well-shaped hand, with evident dread—more than once drawing back her own and looking at the man [Rigaud] with her fair brow roughened into an expression half of fright and half of anger. Whereas she had put the lump of coarse bread into the swart, scaled, knotted hands of John Baptist [Cavalletto] (who had scarcely as much nail on his eight fingers and two thumbs as would have made out one for Monsieur Rigaud), with ready confidence; and when he kissed her hand, had herself passed it caressingly over his face." LD i 1

—resolute: "As [Daniel Peggotty] stood, looking at his cap for a little while before beginning to speak, I could not help observing what power and force of character his sinewy hand expressed, and what a good and trusty companion it was to his honest brow and iron-grey hair . . . . His hand upon the table rested there in perfect repose, with a resolution in it that might have conquered lions." DC 51

—strong and yet gentle: "Joe [Gargery] laid his hand upon my shoulder with the touch of a woman. I have often thought him since like the steam-hammer, that can crush a man or pat an egg-shell, in his combination of strength with gentleness . . . . O dear good faithful tender Joe, I feel the loving tremble of your hand upon my arm, as solemnly this day as if it had been the rustle of an angel's wing!" GE 18

—warm and cold: "Captain Cuttle . . . was so much struck by the magnanimity of Mr Dombey . . . he could not refrain from seizing that gentleman's right hand in his own solitary left, and while he held it open with his powerful fingers, bringing the hook down upon its palm in a transport of admiration. At this touch of warm feeling and cold iron, Mr Dombey shivered all over." DS 10

And see F:Manners—*shaking hands*

—head: "The shining bald head, which looked so very large because it shone so much; and the long grey hair at its sides and back, like floss silk or spun glass, which looked so very benevolent because it was never cut . . . . Philanthropists of both sexes . . . had cried in a rapture of disappointment, 'Oh! why, with that head, is he not a benefactor to his species! Oh! why, with that head, is he not a father to the orphan and a friend to the friendless!' With that head, however, he remained old Christopher Casby, proclaimed by common report rich in house property; and with that head, he now sat in his silent parlour. Indeed it would be the height of unreason to expect him to be sitting there without that head." LD i 13

—heart: "'We have too much reason to fear that he died of a broken heart.'

"'Pooh!' said Ralph, 'there's no such thing. I can understand a man's dying of a broken neck, or suffering from a broken arm, or a broken head, or a broken leg, or a broken nose; but a broken heart!—nonsense, it's the cant of the day. If a man can't pay his debts, he dies of a broken heart, and his widow's a martyr.'" NN 3

And see S:Heart—*literal and figurative*

—leg

—detached and missed: "'Where am I?' asks Mr Wegg.

"'You're somewhere in the back shop across the yard, sir; and speaking quite candidly, I wish I'd never bought you of the Hospital Porter.'

"'Now, look here, what did you give for me?'

"'Well . . . you were one of a warious lot, and I don't know.'

"Silas puts his point in the improved form of 'What will you take for me? . . . According to your own account, I'm not worth much . . . . '

"'Not for miscellaneous working in, I grant you, Mr Wegg; but you might turn out valuable yet, as . . . a Monstrosity, if you'll excuse me.'

"Repressing an indignant look, indicative of anything but a disposition to excuse him, Silas pursues his point . . . .

"'I have a prospect of getting on in life

and elevating myself by my own independent exertions,' says Wegg, feelingly, 'and I shouldn't like—I tell you openly I should *not* like—under such circumstances, to be what I may call dispersed, a part of me here, and a part of me there, but should wish to collect myself like a genteel person.'" OMF i 7

—large: " . . . very stout gentleman, whose body and legs looked like half a gigantic roll of flannel, elevated on a couple of inflated pillow-cases." PP 7

—long: "[Mary Ann Paragon] had a cousin in the Life Guards, with such long legs that he looked like the afternoon shadow of somebody else." DC 44

—subject to injury: "If I might be allowed to mention a young lady's legs, on any terms, I would observe of Miss Slowboy's, that there was a fatality about them which rendered them singularly liable to be grazed; and that she never effected the smallest ascent or descent, without recording the circumstance upon them with a notch, as *Robinson Crusoe* marked the days upon his wooden calendar. But as this might be considered ungenteel, I'll think of it." CH 2

"The children tumbled about, and notched memoranda of their accidents in their legs, which were perfect little calendars of distress." BH 5

—and vanity: "Stagg then dropped on one knee, and gently smoothed the calves of [Tappertit's] legs, with an air of humble admiration.

"'That I had but eyes!' he cried, 'to behold my captain's symmetrical proportions! That I had but eyes, to look upon these twin invaders of domestic peace!'" BR 8

"[Simon] . . . twisted his head round, and looked closely at his legs.

"'If they's a dream,' said Sim, 'let sculptures have such wisions, and chisel 'em out when they wake. This is reality. Sleep has no such limbs as them. Tremble, Willet, and despair.'" BR 31

—wooden: "Mr Wegg next modestly remarks on the want of adaptation in a wooden leg to ladders and such-like airy perches, and also hints at an inherent tendency in that timber fiction, when called into action for the purposes of a promenade on an ashy slope, to stick itself into the yielding foothold, and peg its owner to one spot." OMF ii 7

Index VII *lists nine named characters with wooden or cork legs, and* Index VIII *adds another seven generics. Only Wegg is important: the wooden leg amounts to much less in Dickens than, say, the game or missing eye.*

—lips: "'The word Papa [said Mrs General], besides, gives a pretty form to the lips. Papa, potatoes, poultry, prunes, and prism, are all very good words for the lips: especially prunes and prism. You will find it serviceable, in the formation of a demeanour, if you sometimes say to yourself in company—on entering a room, for instance—Papa, potatoes, poultry, prunes and prism, prunes and prism.'" LD ii 5

—nose

—to an artist: "'When I want a nose or an eye for any particular sitter, I have only to look out of window and wait till I get one.'

"'Does it take long to get a nose, now?' inquired Nicholas, smiling.

"'Why, that depends in a great measure on the pattern,' replied Miss La Creevy. 'Snubs and romans are plentiful enough, and there are flats of all sorts and sizes when there's a meeting at Exeter Hall;* but perfect aquilines, I am sorry to say, are scarce, and we generally use them for uniforms or public characters.'" NN 5

**venue of activist soial and political meetings.*

—cold: "Toby [Veck]'s nose was very red, and his eyelids were very red, and he winked very much, and his shoulders were very near his ears, and his legs were very stiff, and altogether he was evidently a long way upon the frosty side of cool . . . .

"'There's nothing,' said Toby, breaking forth afresh—but here he stopped short in his trot, and with a face of great interest and some alarm, felt his nose carefully all the way up. It was but a little way (not being much of a nose) and he had soon finished.

"'I thought it was gone,' said Toby, trotting off again. 'It's all right, however. I am sure I couldn't blame it if it was to go. It has a precious hard service of it in the bitter weather, and precious little to look forward to; for I don't take snuff myself. It's a good deal tried, poor creetur, at the best of times; for when it *does* get hold of a pleasant whiff or so (which an't too often), it's generally from somebody else's dinner, a-coming home from the baker's.'" C 1

"If Miss Tox could believe the evidence of one of her senses, it was a very cold day. That was quite clear. She took an early opportunity of promoting the circulation in the tip of her nose by secretly chafing it with her pocket-handkerchief, lest, by its very low temperature, it should disagreeably astonish the baby when she came to kiss it." DS 5

And see N:Times of Day—*morning—grumps*

—*nondescript:* "'What may you call his nose, now, my dear, pursued Mrs Nickleby, wishing to interest Nicholas in the subject [of her daughter's admirer] to the utmost.

"'Call it?' repeated Nicholas.

"'Ah!' returned his mother, 'what style of nose? what order of architecture, if one may say so? I am not very learned in noses. Do you call it a Roman or a Grecian?"

"'Upon my word, mother,' said Nicholas, laughing, 'as well as I remember, I should call it a kind of Composite, or mixed nose. But I have no very strong recollection on the subject. If it will afford you any gratification, I'll observe it more closely, and let you know.'" NN 55

—*Roman:* "I think the Romans must have aggravated one another very much, with their noses. Perhaps they became the restless people they were, in consequence. Anyhow, Mr Wopsle's Roman nose so aggravated me, during the recital of my misdemeanours, that I should have liked to pull it until he howled." GE 4

And see Waiting—*vigilance*

—*sharp:* " . . . a niece—a short, shrewd niece [later Mrs Snagsby], something too violently compressed about the waist, and with a sharp nose like a sharp autumn evening, inclining to be frosty towards the end." BH 10

—*obesity:* "'What do you think of him, sir, for a specimen of the Dotheboys Hall feeding? Ain't he fit to bust out of his clothes, and start the seams, and make the very buttons fly off with his fatness! Here's flesh!' cried Squeers, turning the boy about, and indenting the plumpest part of his figure with divers pokes and punches, to the great discomposure of his son and heir. 'Here's firmness, here's solidness! Why, you can hardly get up enough of him between your finger and thumb to pinch him anywheres.'" NN 34

—*physical resemblance*

—*environmental influence:* "In some of [Estella's] looks and gestures there was that tinge of resemblance to Miss Havisham which may often be noticed to have been acquired by children, from grown persons with whom they have been much associated and secluded, and which, when childhood is passed, will produce a remarkable occasional likeness of expression between faces that are otherwise quite different." GE 29

—*Napoleon in Italy:* "As usually happens in almost any collection of paintings, of any sort, in Italy, where there are many heads, there is, in one of them [at Pisa's Campo Santo], a striking accidental likeness of Napoleon. At one time, I used to please my fancy with the speculation whether these old painters, at their work, had a foreboding knowledge of the man who would one day arise to wreak such destruction upon art: whose soldiers would make targets of great pictures, and stable their horses among triumphs of architecture. But the same Corsican face is so plentiful in some parts of Italy at this day, that a more commonplace solution of the coincidence is unavoidable." PI 10 *Is the double-entendre intentional? No.*

—*ribs:* "When I prepare a miscellaneous one [skeleton], I know before hand that I can't keep to nature, and be miscellaneous with ribs, because every man has his own ribs, and no other man's will go with them [said Mr Venus]; but elseways I can be miscellaneous. I have just sent home a Beauty—a perfect Beauty—to a school of art. One leg Belgian, one leg English, and the pickings of eight other people in it. Talk of not being qualified to be miscellaneous!'" OMF i 7

—*shoulders:* " . . . with an impatient and petulant expression both in [Bella Wilfer's] face and in her shoulders (which in her sex and at her age are very expressive of discontent) . . . . " OMF i 4

Stryver TTC is noticeable for shouldering.

—*small stature*

—*dwarf's pluck:* "'I am surprised,' I began, 'to see you so distressed and serious'—when [Miss Mowcher] interrupted me.

"'Yes, it's always so!' she said. 'They are all surprised, these inconsiderate young people, fairly and full grown, to see any natural feeling in a little thing like me! They make a plaything of me, use me for their amusement, throw me away when they are tired, and wonder that I feel more than a toy horse or a wooden soldier! Yes, yes, that's the way. The old way! . . .

" . . . . I must live. I do no harm. If these are people so unreflecting or so cruel, as to make a jest of me, what is left for me to do but to make a jest of myself, them, and everything? If I do so, for the time, whose fault is that? Mine? . . .

"'Be thankful for me, if you have a kind heart, as I think you have,' she said, 'that while I know well what I am, I can be cheerful and endure it all. I am thankful for myself, at any rate, that I can find my tiny way through the world, without being beholden to any one; and that in return for all that is thrown at me, in folly or vanity, as I go along, I can throw bubbles back. If I don't brood over all I want, it is the better for me, and not the worse for any one. If I am a plaything for you giants, be gentle with me.'" DC 32

—good nature: "Whether it is that pleasant qualities, being packed more closely in small bodies than in large, come more readily to hand than when they are diffused over a wider space, and have to be gathered together for use, we don't know, but as a general rule—strengthened like all other rules by its exceptions—we hold that little people are sprightly and good-natured. The more sprightly and good-natured people we have, the better; therefore, let us wish well to all nice little couples, and hope that they may increase and multiply." YC/N

Dickens claimed a height of five feet nine inches. He liked little people. See Vol. III p.703: *Threads to Pull On*

—stomach, empty: "And now that the cloud settled on Saint Antoine, which a momentary gleam had driven from his sacred countenance, the darkness of it was heavy—cold, dirt, sickness, ignorance, and want, were the lords in waiting on the saintly presence—nobles of great power all of them; but, most especially the last. Samples of a people that had undergone a terrible grinding and re-grinding in the mill, and certainly not in the fabulous mill which ground old people young, shivered at every corner, passed in and out at every doorway, looked from every window, fluttered in every vestige of a garment that the wind shook.

"The mill which had worked them down, was the mill that grinds young people old; the children had ancient faces and grave voices; and upon them, and upon the grown faces, and ploughed into every furrow of age and coming up afresh, was the sign, Hunger. It was prevalent everywhere. Hunger was pushed out of the tall houses, in the wretched clothing that hung upon poles and lines; Hunger was patched into them with straw and rag and wood and paper; Hunger was repeated in every fragment of the small modicum of firewood that the man sawed off; Hunger stared down from the smokeless chimneys, and started up from the filthy street that had no offal, among its refuse, of anything to eat.

"Hunger was the inscription on the baker's shelves, written in every small loaf of his scanty stock of bad bread; at the sausage-shop, in every dead-dog preparation that was offered for sale. Hunger rattled its dry bones among the roasting chestnuts in the turned cylinder; Hunger was shred into atomies in every farthing porringer of husky chips of potato, fried with some reluctant drops of oil." ¶TTC i 5

"All the women knitted. They knitted worthless things; but, the mechanical work was a mechanical substitute for eating and drinking; the hands moved for the jaws and the digestive apparatus: if the bony fingers had been still, the stomachs would have been more famine-pinched." TTC ii 16

See also W:Cities and Towns*—Paris—Saint Antoine in 1775; and, as to hunger in England,* OT Vol.I p236

—teeth

—a baby's: "It was a peculiarity of this baby [Sally Tetterby] to be always cutting teeth. Whether they never came, or whether they came and went away again, is not in evidence; but it had certainly cut enough, on the showing of Mrs Tetterby, to make a handsome dental provision for the sign of the Bull and Mouth.

"All sorts of objects were impressed for the rubbing of its gums, notwithstanding that it always carried, dangling at its waist (which was immediately under its chin), a bone ring, large enough to have represented the rosary of a young nun. Knife-handles, umbrella-tops, the heads of walking-sticks selected from the stock, the fingers of the family in general, but especially of Johnny, nutmeg-graters, crusts, the handles of doors, and the cool knobs on the tops of pokers, were among the commonest instruments indiscriminately applied for this baby's relief.

"The amount of electricity that must have been rubbed out of it in a week, is not to be calculated. Still Mrs Tetterby always said 'it was coming through, and then the child would be herself;' and still it never did come through, and the child continued to be somebody else." ¶HM 3

—chattering: "'Ugh, you disgraceful boy!' exclaimed Miss Wren, attracted by the

sound of [her father's] chattering teeth. 'I wish they'd all drop down your throat and play at dice in your stomach!'" OMF iii 10

—dazzling: "Mr Carker the Manager did a great deal of business in the course of the day, and bestowed his teeth upon a great many people. In the office, in the court, in the street, and on 'Change, they glistened and bristled to a terrible extent. Five o'clock arriving, and with it Mr Carker's bay horse, they got on horseback, and went gleaming up Cheapside." DS 22

"But Withers, meeting [Carker] on the stairs, stood amazed at the beauty of his teeth, and at his brilliant smile; and as he rode away upon his white-legged horse, the people took him for a dentist, such was the dazzling show he made." DS 37

—displaced: "'And quite a family it is to make tea for,' said Mrs Gamp; 'and wot a happiness to do it! My good young 'ooman'—to the servant-girl—'p'raps somebody would like to try a new-laid egg or two, not biled too hard. Likeways, a few rounds o' buttered toast, first cuttin' off the crust, in consequence of tender teeth, and not too many of 'em; which Gamp himself, Mrs Chuzzlewit, at one blow, being in liquor, struck out four, two single and two double, as was took by Mrs Harris for a keepsake, and is carried in her pocket at this present hour, along with two cramp-bones, a bit o' ginger, and a grater like a blessed infant's shoe, in tin, with a little heel to put the nutmeg in: as many times I've seen and said, and used for caudle when required, within the month.'" MC 46

—displayed: " . . . the gentleman had very white teeth . . . when there was no excuse for laughing, he generally finished with the same monosyllable ['hey?'], which he uttered so as to display them." NN 50

—dominant: "A cat, or a monkey, or a hyena, or a death's-head, could not have shown the Captain more teeth at one time, than Mr Carker showed him at this period of their interview." DS 17

—voice

—abused: " . . . the Major's voice, what with talking and eating and chuckling and choking, appeared to be in the box under the rumble, or in some neighbouring haystack. Nor did the Major improve it at the Royal Hotel, where rooms and dinner had been ordered, and where he so oppressed his organs of speech by eating and drinking, that when he retired to bed he had no voice at all, except to cough with, and could only make himself intelligible to the dark servant by gasping at him." DS 20

—adenoidal: "I have never yet ascertained in the course of my uncommercial travels, why a Refractory habit should affect the tonsils and uvula; but, I have always observed that Refractories of both sexes and every grade, between a Ragged School and the Old Bailey, have one voice, in which the tonsils and uvula gain a diseased ascendancy." UT/WW

—audible Above: "Little Dorrit turned at the door to say 'God bless you!' She said it very softly, but perhaps she may have been as audible above—who knows?—as a whole cathedral choir." LD i 14

—breathless: "'I called in consequence of an advertisement,' said the stranger, in a voice as if she had been playing a set of Pan's pipes for a fortnight without leaving off." SB/BH

"When [Toby Veck] had found his voice—which it took him some time to do, for it was a long way off, and hidden under a load of meat . . . ." C 2

—at childbirth: "'Well, sir,' said Doctor Parker Peps in a round, deep, sonorous voice, muffled for the occasion, like the knocker; 'do you find that your dear lady is at all roused by your visit?'" DS 1

—choked by a name: "' . . . they may be happy wives and mothers; they may be handsome like my darling M—e—

"He couldn't finish the name. The final letter [g] swelled in his throat, to the size of the whole alphabet." C 2

—harsh: "If an iron door could be supposed to quarrel with its hinges, and to make a firm resolution to open with slow obstinacy, and grind them to powder in the process, it would emit a pleasanter sound in so doing, than did these words in the rough and bitter voice in which they were uttered by Ralph [Nickleby]. Even Mr Mantalini felt their influence, and turning affrighted round, exclaimed—'What a demd horrid croaking!'" NN 10

—heartening: "'But you says to me, says you, delivering it out of your chest as hearty as possible, so that it was like a glass of something hot, "What accident have you met with? You have been badly hurt. What's amiss, old boy? Cheer up, and tell us about it!" Cheer up! I was cheered already!'" BH 26

—homelike: "[Dot's] pleasant voice—O what a voice it was, for making household

music at the fireside of an honest man!" CH 3

—a hurricane: "The interview with Mr Boythorn was a long one—and a stormy one too, I should think; for although his room was at some distance, I heard his loud voice rising every now and then like a high wind, and evidently blowing perfect broadsides of denunciation." BH 9

—imitative? "'No, I will *not.*' This was said with a most determined air, and in a voice which might have been taken for an imitation of anything; it was quite as much like a Guinea-pig as a bassoon." SB/SE

—literary, of an old friend: "'His wery woice,' said the Captain, looking round with an exultation to which even his face could hardly render justice—'his wery woice, as chock full o' science as ever it was! Sol Gills, lay to, my lad, upon your own wines and fig-trees, like a taut ould patriark as you are, and overhaul them there adwentures o' yourn, in your own formilior woice. 'Tis *the* voice,' said the Captain, impressively, and announcing a quotation with his hook, 'of the sluggard, I heerd him complain, you have woke me too soon, I must slumber again. Scatter his enemies, and make 'em fall!'" DS 56

—mellow: "My poor Lirriper was a handsome figure of a man, with a beaming eye and a voice as mellow as a musical instrument made of honey and steel . . . . " CS/L i

—mind: "Mrs Chick herself lost, for a moment, the presence of mind on which she so much prided herself; and remained mute . . . . But recovering her voice—which was synonymous with her presence of mind, indeed they were one and the same thing—she replied with dignity . . . . " DS 18

—muffled: "'Mind you!' returned [Rogue Riderhood], stretching forward over the half-door to throw his words into the bar; for his voice was as if the head of his boat's mop were down his throat; 'I say so, Miss Abbey!'" OMF i 6

—penetrating: "' . . . when I let the upper floor to Cap'en Cuttle, oh I do a thankless thing, and cast pearls before swine!'

"Mrs MacStinger pitched her voice for the upper windows in offering these remarks, and cracked off each clause sharply by itself as if from a rifle possessing an infinity of barrels." DS 23

" . . . Edith stopped [Mr Dombey], in a voice which, although not raised in the least, was so clear, emphatic, and distinct, that it might have been heard in a whirlwind.

"'I tell you I will speak to you alone,' she said. 'If you are not mad, heed what I say.'" DS 47

—portentous: "Mr Craggs seemed positively to grate upon his own hinges, as he delivered this opinion." BL 1

—signalling: "As soon as [Arabella Allen] came nearly below the tree, Sam began, by way of gently indicating his presence, to make sundry diabolical noises similar to those which would probably be natural to a person of middle age who had been afflicted with a combination of inflammatory sore throat, croup, and hooping-cough [*sic.*], from his earliest infancy." PP 39

—smothered: "'No,' returned Dumps . . . speaking in a voice like Desdemona with the pillow over her mouth." SB/BC

—squeezed: "Mother had the gripe and clutch of poverty . . . not least of all upon her voice. Her sharp and high-pitched words were squeezed out of her, as by the compression of bony fingers on a leathern bag; and she had a way of rolling her eyes about and about the cellar, as she scolded, that was gaunt and hungry." GSE 3

—strident: "'Mrs Jellyby,' pursued [Mrs Pardiggle], always speaking in the same demonstrative, loud, hard tone, so that her voice impressed my fancy as if it had a sort of spectacles on too . . . 'Mrs Jellyby is a benefactor to society, and deserves a helping hand.'" BH 8

—suppressed: "Mr Vholes, after glancing at the official cat, who is patiently watching a mouse's hole, fixes his charmed gaze again on his young client, and proceeds in his buttoned-up half-audible voice, as if there were an unclean spirit in him that will neither come out nor speak out." BH 39

—whisper: "One disagreeable result of whispering is, that it seems to evoke an atmosphere of silence, haunted by the ghosts of sound—strange cracks and tickings, the rustling of garments that have no substance in them, and the tread of dreadful feet that would leave no mark on the sea-sand or the winter snow." BH 32

Closet

—mess: " . . . such wonderful things came tumbling out of the closets when they were opened—bits of mouldy pie, sour bottles, Mrs Jellyby's caps, letters, tea, forks, odd

boots and shoes of children, firewood, wafers, saucepan-lids, damp sugar in odds and ends of paper bags, footstools, black-lead brushes, bread, Mrs Jellyby's bonnets, books with butter sticking to the binding, guttered candle-ends put out by being turned upside down in broken candlesticks, nut-shells, heads and tails of shrimps, dinner-mats, gloves, coffee-grounds, umbrellas—that [Mr Jellyby] looked frightened, and left off again." BH 30

—pantry: "It was a most wonderful closet, worthy of Cloisterham and of Minor Canon Corner. Above it, a portrait of Handel in a flowing wig beamed down at the spectator, with a knowing air of being up to the contents of the closet, and a musical air of intending to combine all its harmonies in one delicious fugue.

"No common closet with a vulgar door on hinges, openable all at once, and leaving nothing to be disclosed by degrees, this rare closet had a lock in mid-air, where two perpendicular slides met: the one falling down, and the other pushing up. The upper slide, on being pulled down (leaving the lower a double mystery), revealed deep shelves of pickle-jars, jam-pots, tin canisters, spice boxes, and agreeably outlandish vessels of blue and white, the luscious lodgings of preserved tamarinds and ginger.

"Every benevolent inhabitant of this retreat had his name inscribed upon his stomach. The pickles, in a uniform of rich brown double-breasted buttoned coat, and yellow or sombre drab continuations, announced their portly forms, in printed capitals, as Walnut, Gherkin, Onion, Cabbage, Cauliflower, Mixed, and other members of that noble family. The jams, as being of a less masculine temperament, and as wearing curl-papers, announced themselves in feminine calligraphy, like a soft whisper, to be Raspberry, Gooseberry, Apricot, Plum, Damson, Apple, and Peach.

"The scene closing on these charmers, and the lower slide ascending, oranges were revealed, attended by a mighty japanned sugar-box, to temper their acerbity if unripe. Home-made biscuits waited at the Court of these Powers, accompanied by a goodly fragment of plum-cake, and various slender ladies' fingers, to be dipped into sweet wine and kissed. Lowest of all, a compact leaden vault enshrined the sweet wine and a stock of cordials: whence issued whispers of Seville Orange, Lemon, Almond, and Caraway-seed.

"There was a crowning air upon this closet of closets, of having been for ages hummed through by the Cathedral bell and organ, until those venerable bees had made sublimated honey of everything in store; and it was always observed that every dipper among the shelves (deep, as has been noticed, and swallowing up head, shoulders, and elbows) came forth again mellow-faced, and seeming to have undergone a saccharine transfiguration." ¶MED 10

—punishment: ". . . there was the old dark closet, also with nothing in it, of which he had been many a time the sole contents, in days of punishment, when he had regarded it as the veritable entrance to that bourne to which the tract had found him galloping." LD i 3

Dress

—apron: ". . . I venture to breathe to the quiet bricks and stones my confidential wonderment why a ticket-porter, who never does any work with his hands, is bound to wear a white apron, and why a great Ecclesiastical Dignitary, who never does any work with his hands either, is equally bound to wear a black one." UT/CA

And see H:Housewife—*cooking*

—baby clothes: ". . . mantua-making and millinery, on the smallest scale imaginable, appeared to have become the favourite amusement of the whole family. The parlour wasn't quite as tidy as it used to be, and if you called in the morning, you would see lying on a table, with an old newspaper carelessly thrown over them, two or three particularly small caps, rather larger than if they had been made for a moderate-sized doll, with a small piece of lace, in the shape of a horse-shoe, let in behind: or perhaps a white robe, not very large in circumference, but very much out of proportion in point of length, with a little tucker round the top, and a frill round the bottom; and once when we called, we saw a long white roller, with a kind of blue margin down each side, the probable use of which, we were at a loss to conjecture." SB/FS

—for cold: ". . . the weight of Moloch [Sally Tetterby] being much increased by a complication of defences against the cold, composed of knitted worsted-work, and forming a complete suit of chain-armour, with a head-piece and blue gaiters." HM 3

—of the blind: ". . . no uniform is worn; and I was very glad of it, for two reasons. Firstly, because I am sure that nothing but

senseless custom and want of thought would reconcile us to the liveries and badges we are so fond of at home. Secondly, because the absence of these things presents each child to the visitor in his or her own proper character, with its individuality unimpaired; not lost in a dull, ugly, monotonous repetition of the same unmeaning garb: which is really an important consideration. The wisdom of encouraging a little harmless pride in personal appearance even among the blind, or the whimsical absurdity of considering charity and leather breeches inseparable companions, as we do, requires no comment." AN 3

—*boot, of a graverobber:* "'What!' said Mr Cruncher, looking out of bed for a boot. 'You're at it agin, are you?'

"After hailing the morn with this second salutation, he threw a boot at the woman as a third. It was a very muddy boot, and may introduce the odd circumstance connected with Mr Cruncher's domestic economy, that, whereas he often came home after banking hours with clean boots, he often got up next morning to find the same boots covered with clay." TTC ii 1

—*cane:* " . . . like a little finger-post, surmounted by an ivory hand marshalling [young John Chivery] the way that he should go . . . . " LD i 18

—*at a carnival:* "Every sort of bewitching madness of dress was there. Little preposterous scarlet jackets; quaint old stomachers, more wicked than the smartest bodies; Polish pelisses, strained and tight as ripe gooseberries; tiny Greek caps, all awry, and clinging to the dark hair, Heaven knows how; every wild, quaint, bold, shy, pettish, madcap fancy had its illustration in a dress; and every fancy was as dead forgotten by its owner, in the tumult of merriment, as if the three old aqueducts that still remain entire had brought Lethe into Rome, upon their sturdy arches, that morning." PI 11

—*changing fashion:* "'A Monmouth Street laced coat' was a by-word a century ago; and still we find Monmouth Street the same. Pilot great-coats with wooden buttons have usurped the place of the ponderous laced coats with full skirts; embroidered waistcoats with large flaps have yielded to double-breasted checks with roll-collars; and three-cornered hats of quaint appearance have given place to the low crowns and broad brims of the coachman school . . . . " SB/MS

"After showing me a roll of cloth which he said was extra super, and too good mourning for anything short of parents, [Mr Omer] took my various dimensions, and put them down in a book. While he was recording them he called my attention to his stock in trade, and to certain fashions which he said had 'just come up,' and to certain other fashions which he said had 'just gone out.'

"'And by that sort of thing we very often lose a little mint of money,' said Mr Omer. 'But fashions are like human beings. They come in, nobody knows when, why, or how; and they go out, nobody knows when, why, or how. Everything is like life, in my opinion, if you look at it in that point of view.'" DC 9

—*for a christening:* "'Miss Tox!'

"And enter that fair enslaver, with a blue nose and indescribably frosty face, referable to her being very thinly clad in a maze of fluttering odds and ends, to do honour to the ceremony . . . . " DS 5

—*close-fitting:* "'Stop!' cried the gentleman, stretching forth his right arm, which was so tightly wedged into his threadbare sleeve that it looked like a cloth sausage." MC 4

—*a coachman's grandson:* "'Tony, my boy, tell the lady wot them clothes are, as grandfather says, father ought to let you vear.'

"'A little white hat and a little sprig weskut and little knee cords and little top-boots and a little green coat with little bright buttons and a little welwet collar,' replied Tony, with great readiness and no stops.

"'That's the cos-toom, mum . . . . 'Once make sich a model on him as that, and you'd say he *wos* a angel!'" MHC 6

—*collars:* "I knew [Joe] made himself so dreadfully uncomfortable entirely on my account, and that it was for me he pulled up his shirt-collar so very high behind, that it made the hair on the crown of his head stand up like a tuft of feathers" GE 13

"As to his shirt-collar, and his coat-collar, they were perplexing to reflect upon—insoluble mysteries both. Why should a man scrape himself to that extent, before he could consider himself full-dressed? Why should he suppose it necessary to be purified by suffering for his holiday clothes?" GE 27

—conventional in England: "Some years ago, we, the writer . . . took the liberty of buying a great-coat which we saw exposed for sale . . . which appeared to be in our eyes the most sensible great-coat we had ever seen. Taking the further liberty to wear this great-coat after we had bought it, we became a sort of Spectre, eliciting the wonder and terror of our fellow creatures as we flitted along the streets. We accompanied the coat to Switzerland for six months; and, although it was perfectly new there, we found it was not regarded as a portent of the least importance. We accompanied it to Paris for another six months; and, although it was perfectly new there too, nobody minded it. This coat so intolerable to Britain, was nothing more nor less than the loose wide-sleeved mantle, easy to put on, easy to put off, and crushing nothing beneath it, which everybody now wears." HW/I

—descending fashion: "Probably there are not more second-hand clothes sold in London than in Paris, and yet the mass of the London population have a second-hand look which is not to be detected on the mass of the Parisian population. I think this is mainly because a Parisian workman does not in the least trouble himself about what is worn by a Parisian idler, but dresses in the way of his own class, and for his own comfort. In London, on the contrary, the fashions descend; and you never fully know how inconvenient or ridiculous a fashion is, until you see it in its last descent.

"It was but the other day, on a racecourse, that I observed four people in a barouche deriving great entertainment from the contemplation of four people on foot. The four people on foot were two young men and two young women; the four people in the barouche were two young men and two young women. The four young women were dressed in exactly the same style; the four young men were dressed in exactly the same style. Yet the two couples on wheels were as much amused by the two couples on foot, as if they were quite unconscious of having themselves set those fashions, or of being at that very moment engaged in the display of them." ¶UT/BB

"Whatsoever fashion is set in England, is certain to descend. This is a text for a perpetual sermon on care in setting fashions. When you find a fashion low down, look back for the time (it will never be far off) when it was the fashion high up. This is the text for a perpetual sermon on social justice. From imitations of Ethiopian Serenaders, to imitations of Prince's coats and waistcoats, you will find the original model in St James's Parish. When the Serenaders become tiresome, trace them beyond the Black Country; when the coats and waistcoats become insupportable, refer them to their source in the Upper Toady Regions." UT/BB

—disguise: "As [Magwitch] was at present dressed in a seafaring slop suit, in which he looked as if he had some parrots and cigars to dispose of, I next discussed with him what dress he should wear. He cherished an extraordinary belief in the virtues of 'shorts' as a disguise, and had in his own mind sketched a dress for himself that would have made him something between a dean and a dentist." GE 40

—duplicated: "The ladies, it seems, 'never wear a pair of white satin shoes or white gloves more than once.' And we have a dim vision of the agitation of the tremendous depths of this social sea which looks so smooth at top, when we are informed that 'some of them (the ladies) if they find, on going into society, *another person of inferior rank wearing the same dress as themselves* '—which would certainly appear an inconvenient proceeding—'the dress, upon being taken off, is at once thrown aside, and the lady's maid perfectly understands her perquisite.'

"Having recovered our breath, impeded in the contemplation of this awful picture, and the mysterious shadow thrown around the lady's maid, we expect to find our American friend in some new scene . . . . " E/AE

"'The Duke,' meantime, it is to be presumed, keeping his noble eyes on Mr Colman's waistcoat, until he satisfies his noble mind that it is not a waistcoat, like his waistcoat; which would render it indispensable for his Grace instantly to depart from table, take it off in desperation, and bestow it on his valet." E/AE

—early Nineteenth Century: "There is no King George the Fourth now (more's the pity!) to set the dandy fashion; there are no clear-starched jack-towel neckcloths, no short-waisted coats, no false calves, no stays. There are no caricatures, now, of effeminate Exquisites so arrayed, swooning in opera boxes with excess of delight, and being revived by other dainty creatures, poking long-necked scent-bottles at their noses. There is no beau whom it takes four men at once to shake into his buckskins, or who goes to see all the executions, or who is troubled with the self-reproach of having once consumed a pea." BH 12

—ensemble of a struggler: "So poor a clerk, through having a limited salary and an unlimited family, that [Reginald Wilfer] had never yet attained the modest object of his ambition: which was, to wear a complete new suit of clothes, hats and boots included, at one time. His black hat was brown before he could afford a coat, his pantaloons were white at the seams and knees before he could buy a pair of boots, his boots had worn out before he could treat himself to new pantaloons, and by the time he worked round to the hat again, that shining modern article roofed-in an ancient ruin of various periods." OMF i 4

—foreigner in English clothes: " . . . the Native, who wore a pair of ear-rings in his dark-brown ears, and on whom his European clothes sat with an outlandish impossibility of adjustment—being, of their own accord, and without any reference to the tailor's art, long where they ought to be short, short where they ought to be long, tight where they ought to be loose, and loose where they ought to be tight—and to which he imparted a new grace, whenever the Major attacked him, by shrinking into them like a shrivelled nut, or a cold monkey . . . . " DS 20

—gloves: "That discreet damsel [Miss Skiffins] was attired as usual, except that she was now engaged in substituting for her green kid gloves, a pair of white. The Aged [Parent] was likewise occupied in preparing a similar sacrifice for the altar of Hymen. The old gentlemen, however, experienced so much difficulty in getting his gloves on, that Wemmick found it necessary to put him with his back against a pillar, and then to get behind the pillar himself and pull away at them, while I for my part held the old gentleman round the waist, that he might present an equal and safe resistance. By dint of this ingenious scheme, his gloves were got on to perfection." GE 55

And see A:Matrimony*—wedding—a particular wedding*

" . . . with his hands in his pockets, [Bounderby] sauntered out into the hall. 'I never wear gloves,' it was his custom to say. 'I didn't climb up the ladder in *them*. Shouldn't be so high up, if I had.'" HT i 4

—gowns for a wedding: "Florence was to cast off her mourning, and to wear a brilliant dress on the occasion. The milliner's intentions on the subject of this dress—the milliner was a Frenchwoman, and greatly resembled Mrs Skewton—were so chaste and elegant, that Mrs Skewton bespoke one like it for herself. The milliner said it would become her to admiration, and that all the world would take her for the young lady's sister . . . .

"Mrs Skewton rang for candles . . . . With the candles appeared her maid, with the juvenile dress that was to delude the world to-morrow. The dress had savage retribution in it, as such dresses ever have, and made her infinitely older and more hideous than her greasy flannel gown. But Mrs Skewton tried it on with mincing satisfaction; smirked at her cadaverous self in the glass, as she thought of its killing effect upon the Major; and suffering her maid to take it off again, and prepare her for repose, tumbled into ruins like a house of painted cards." DS 30

—handkerchief: " . . . Mr Tigg took from his hat what seemed to be the fossil remains of an antediluvian pocket-handkerchief, and wiped his eyes therewith." MC 7

—a hangman's: "'These smalls,' said Dennis, rubbing his legs; 'these very smalls—they belonged to a friend of mine that's left off sich incumbrances for ever: this coat too—I've often walked behind this coat, in the street, and wondered whether it would ever come to me; this pair of shoes have danced a hornpipe for another man, afore my eyes, full half a dozen times at least: and as to my hat,' he said, taking it off, and whirling it round upon his fist—Lord! I've seen this hat go up Holborn on the box of a hackney-coach—ah, many and many a day!'" BR 39

—hat

—chasing: "There are very few moments in a man's existence when he experiences so much ludicrous distress, or meets with so little charitable commiseration, as when he is in pursuit of his own hat. A vast deal of coolness, and a peculiar degree of judgment, are requisite in catching a hat. A man must not be precipitate, or he runs over it; he must not rush into the opposite extreme, or he loses it altogether. The best way is, to keep gently up with the object of pursuit, to be wary and cautious, to watch your opportunity well, get gradually before it, then make a rapid dive, seize it by the crown, and stick it firmly on your head: smiling pleasantly all the time, as if you thought it as good a joke as anybody else." PP 4

Mr Pickwick in Chase of his Hat PP

—conventional: "The hermetically-sealed, black, stiff, chimney-pot, a foot and a half high, which we call a hat, is generally admitted to be neither convenient nor graceful; but, there are very few middle-aged gentlemen . . . who would bestow their daughters on wide-awakes, however estimable the wearers. **Smith Payne and Smith**, or **Ransom and Co.**, would probably consider a run upon the house not at all unlikely, in the event of their clerks coming to business in caps, or with such felt-fashions on their heads as didn't give them the headache, and as they could wear comfortably and cheaply." HW/I

—on a formal call: " . . . Joe took his hat off and stood weighing it by the brim in both his hands: as if he had some urgent reason in his mind for being particular to half a quarter of an ounce . . . .When I looked back at Joe in the long passage, he was still weighing his hat with the greatest care, and was coming after us in long strides on the tips of his toes." GE 13

"' . . . Joe, taking it up carefully with both hands, like a bird's-nest with eggs in it, wouldn't hear of parting with that piece of property, and persisted in standing talking over it in a most uncomfortable way . . . getting the bird's-nest under his left arm for the moment, and groping in it for an egg with his right . . . .

" . . . Joe, being invited to sit down to table, looked all round the room for a suitable spot on which to deposit his hat—as if it were only on some few very rare substances in nature that it could find a resting-place—and ultimately stood it on an extreme corner of the chimney-piece, from which it ever afterwards fell off at intervals . . . .

" . . . his attention being providentially attracted by his hat, which was toppling. Indeed, it demanded from him a constant attention, and a quickness of eye and hand, very like that exacted by wicket-keeping. He made extraordinary play with it, and showed the greatest skill; now, rushing at it and catching it neatly as it dropped; now, merely stopping it midway, beating it up, and humouring it in various parts of the room and against a good deal of the pattern of the paper on the wall, before he felt it safe to close with it; finally splashing it into the slop-basin, where I took the liberty of laying hands upon it." GE 27

—of a self-made man: "So, Mr Bounderby threw on his hat—he always threw it on, as expressing a man who had been far too busily employed in making himself, to acquire any fashion of wearing his hat . . . . " HT i 4

See also Sam Weller PP—*hat,* Vol. I p183

—head-dress: "Spezzia [La Spezia] is a good place to tarry at; by reason . . . of the head-dress of the women, who wear, on one side of their head, a small doll's straw hat, stuck on to the hair; which is certainly the oddest and most roguish head-gear that ever was invented." PI 10

—jewels: "'I must tell you first, that there is a threatening appearance in your manner, Madam . . . which does not become you.'

"She laughed. The shaken diamonds in her hair started and trembled. There are fables of precious stones that would turn pale, their wearer being in danger. Had these been such, their imprisoned rays of light would have taken flight that moment, and they would have been as dull as lead." DS 47

""This great and fortunate man had provided that extensive bosom, which required so much room to be unfeeling enough in, with a nest of crimson and gold some fifteen years before. It was not a bosom to repose upon, but it was a capital bosom to hang jewels upon. Mr Merdle wanted something to hang jewels upon, and he bought it for the purpose. **Storr and Mortimer** might have married on the same speculation.

"Like all his other speculations, it was sound and successful. The jewels showed to the richest advantage. The bosom moving in Society with the jewels displayed upon it, attracted general admiration. Society approving, Mr Merdle was satisfied." LD i 21

—labourers': " . . . I like to see the humbler classes of society careful of their dress and appearance, and even, if they please, decorated with such little trinkets as come within the compass of their means . . . I would always encourage this kind of pride, as a worthy element of self-respect, in any person I employed . . . . " AN 4

—and love: "Within the first week of my passion, I bought four sumptuous waistcoats—not for myself: *I* had no pride in them; for Dora—and took to wearing straw-coloured kid gloves in the streets, and laid the foundations of all the corns I have ever had. If the boots I wore at that period could only be produced and compared with the natural size of my feet, they would show what the state of my heart was, in a most affecting manner." DC 26

—mittens: "Making, with his leaky shoes, a crooked line of slushy footprints in the mire; and blowing on his chilly hands and rubbing them against each other, poorly defended from the searching cold by threadbare mufflers of grey worsted, with a private apartment only for the thumb, and a common room or tap for the rest of the fingers; Toby [Veck], with his knees bent and his cane beneath his arm, still trotted." C 1

—mourning

—test of friendship: "Kate might have said, that mourning is sometimes the coldest wear which mortals can assume; that it not only chills the breasts of those it clothes, but extending its influence to summer friends, freezes up their sources of good-will and kindness, and withering all the buds of promise they once so liberally put forth, leaves nothing but bared and rotten hearts exposed. There are few who have lost a friend or relative constituting in life their sole dependence, who have not keenly felt this chilling influence of their sable garb." NN 17

—test of tailoring: "The consideration of Mrs Boffin had clothed Mr Sloppy in a suit of black, on which the tailor had received personal directions from Rokesmith to ex-

pend the utmost cunning of his art, with a view to the concealment of the cohering and sustaining buttons. But so much more powerful were the frailties of Sloppy's form than the strongest resources of tailoring science, that he now stood before the Council, a perfect Argus in the way of buttons: shining and winking and gleaming and twinkling out of a hundred of those eyes of bright metal, at the dazzled spectators. The artistic taste of some unknown hatter had furnished him with a hatband of wholesale capacity which was fluted behind, from the crown of his hat to the brim, and terminated in a black bunch, from which the imagination shrunk discomfited and the reason revolted. Some special powers with which his legs were endowed had already hitched up his glossy trousers at the ankles, and bagged them at the knees: while similar gifts in his arms had raised his coat-sleeves from his wrists and accumulated them at his elbows. Thus set forth, with the additional embellishments of a very little tail to his coat, and a yawning gulf at his waistband, Sloppy stood confessed." OMF ii 10

—new clothes: "My clothes were rather a disappointment, of course. Probably every new and eagerly expected garment ever put on since clothes came in, fell a trifle short of the wearer's expectation. But after I had had my new suit on, some half an hour, and had gone through an immensity of posturing with Mr Pumblechook's very limited dressing-glass, in the futile endeavour to see my legs, it seemed to fit me better." GE 19

—night-cap: "'People may say what they like,' observed Mrs Nickleby, 'but there's a great deal of comfort in a night-cap, as I'm sure you would confess, Nicholas my dear, if you would only have strings to yours, and wear it like a Christian, instead of sticking it upon the very top of your head like a blue-coat boy; you needn't think it an unmanly or quizzical thing to be particular about your night-cap, for I have often heard your poor dear papa, and the reverend Mr what's his name . . . . I have often heard them say, that the young men at college are uncommonly particular about their nightcaps, and that the Oxford nightcaps are quite celebrated for their strength and goodness; so much so, indeed, that the young men never dream of going to bed without 'em, and I believe it's admitted on all hands that *they* know what's good, and don't coddle themselves.'" NN 37

"Having lent [Uriah Heep] a night-cap, which he put on at once, and in which he made such an awful figure, that I have never worn one since, I left him to his rest." DC 25

" . . . it happened to me the other night to be lying: not with my eyes half closed, but with my eyes wide open; not with my night-cap drawn almost down to my nose, for on sanitary principles I never wear a nightcap: but with my hair pitchforked and touzled all over the pillow. . . . " RP/LA

—nun's: " . . . could they . . . look upon her grave, in garbs which would chill the very ashes within it? Could they bow down in prayer, and when all Heaven turned to hear them, bring the dark shade of sadness on one angel's face? No." NN 6

—old man's: "His coat is of a colour, and cut, that never was the mode anywhere, at any period. Clearly, it was not made for him, or for any individual mortal. Some wholesale contractor measured Fate for five thousand coats of such quality, and Fate has lent this old coat to this old man, as one of a long unfinished line of many old men. It has always large dull metal buttons, similar to no other buttons. The old man wears a hat, a thumbed and napless and yet an obdurate hat, which has never adapted itself to the shape of his poor head. His coarse shirt and his coarse neckcloth have no more individuality than his coat and hat: they have the same character of not being his—of not being anybody's. Yet this old man wears these clothes with a certain unaccustomed air of being dressed and elaborated for the public ways; as though he passed the greater part of his time in a nightcap and gown." LD i 31

—for a party: "Mrs Blimber appeared, looking lovely, Paul thought; and attired in such a number of skirts that it was quite an excursion to walk round her. Miss Blimber came down soon after her mamma; a little squeezed in appearance, but very charming. . . . There was a good array of white waistcoats and cravats in the young gentlemen's bedrooms as evening approached . . . ." DS 14

—pauper child: "What an excellent example of the power of dress young Oliver Twist was! Wrapped in the blanket which had hitherto formed his only covering, he might have been the child of a nobleman or a beggar; it would have been hard for the haughtiest stranger to have assigned him his

proper station in society. But now that he was enveloped in the old calico robes which had grown yellow in the same service, he was badged and ticketed, and fell into his place at once—a parish child—the orphan of a workhouse—the humble, half-starved drudge—to be cuffed and buffeted through the world—despised by all, and pitied by none." OT 1

—in a pawnshop: "The background, composed of handkerchiefs, coats, shirts, hats, and other old articles 'On Leaving,' had a general dim resemblance to human listeners; especially where a shiny black sou'-wester suit and hat hung, looking very like a clumsy mariner with his back to the company, who was so curious to overhear, that he paused for the purpose with his coat half pulled on, and his shoulders up to his ears in the uncompleted action." OMF ii 12

—petticoat: "'I wish to goodness, Ma . . . that you'd loll a little.' . . .

"'I hope,' said the impressive lady, 'I am incapable of it.'

"'I am sure you look so, Ma. But why one should go out to dine with one's own daughter or sister, as if one's under-petticoat was a backboard, I do *not* understand.'

"'Neither do I understand,' retorted Mrs Wilfer, with deep scorn, 'how a young lady can mention the garment in the name in which you have indulged. I blush for you.'

"'Thank you, Ma,' said Lavvy, yawning, 'but I can do it for myself, I am obliged to you, when there's any occasion.'

"Here, Mr Sampson, with the view of establishing harmony, which he never under any circumstances succeeded in doing, said with an agreeable smile: 'After all, you know, ma'am, we know it's there.' And immediately felt that he had committed himself." OMF iv 16

—pocket: "How Clemency [Newcome] . . . held one pocket open, and looked down into its yawning depths for the thimble which wasn't there—and how she then held an opposite pocket open, and seeming to descry it, like a pearl of great price, at the bottom, cleared away such intervening obstacles as a handkerchief, an end of wax candle, a flushed apple, an orange, a lucky penny, a cramp bone, a padlock, a pair of scissors in a sheath more expressively describable as promising young shears, a handful or so of loose beads, several balls of cotton, a needle-case, a cabinet collection of curl-papers, and a biscuit . . . is of no consequence.

"Nor how, in her determination to grasp this pocket by the throat and keep it prisoner (for it had a tendency to swing, and twist itself round the nearest corner), she assumed and calmly maintained, an attitude apparently inconsistent with the human anatomy and the laws of gravity. It is enough that at last she triumphantly produced the thimble . . . . " BL 1

—politicians': "It is not at first sight a very rational custom to paint a broad blue stripe across one's nose and both cheeks, and a broad red stripe from the forehead to the chin, to attach a few pounds of wood to one's under lip, to stick fish-bones in one's ears and a brass curtain-ring in one's nose, and to rub one's body all over with rancid oil, as a preliminary to entering on business. But this is a question of taste and ceremony, and so is the Windsor Uniform. The manner of entering on the business itself is another question. A council of six hundred savage gentlemen entirely independent of tailors, sitting on their hams in a ring, smoking, and occasionally grunting, seem to me, according to the experience I have gathered in my voyages and travels, somehow to do what they come together for; whereas that is not at all the general experience of a council of six hundred civilised gentlemen very dependent on tailors and sitting on mechanical contrivances." UT/MM

—professional: "I wonder, is the Medicine-Man of the North American Indians never to be got rid of, out of the North American country? He comes into my Wigwam on all manner of occasions, and with the absurdest 'Medicine.' I always find it extremely difficult, and I often find it simply impossible, to keep him out of my Wigwam. For his legal 'Medicine' he sticks upon his head the hair of quadrupeds, and plasters the same with fat, and dirty-white powder, and talks a gibberish quite unknown to the men and squaws of his tribe. For his religious 'Medicine' he puts on puffy white sleeves, little black aprons, large black waistcoats of a peculiar cut, collarless coats, with Medicine button-holes, Medicine stockings and gaiters and shoes, and tops the whole with a highly grotesque Medicinal hat." UT/MM

—rustling: " . . . the matronly Tisher heaves in sight, rustling through the room like the legendary ghost of a dowager in silken skirts." MED 3

—sailors: "Some in boots, some in leggings, some in tarpaulin overalls, some in frocks,

some in pea-coats, a very few in jackets, most with sou'wester hats, all with something rough and rugged round the throat; all dripping salt water where they stand; all pelted by weather, besmeared with grease, and blackened by the sooty rigging." UT/AS

—second-hand: "There was the man's whole life written as legibly on those clothes, as if we had his autobiography engrossed on parchment before us.

"The first was a patched and much-soiled skeleton suit; one of those straight blue cloth cases in which small boys used to be confined, before belts and tunics had come in, and old notions had gone out: an ingenious contrivance for displaying the full symmetry of a boy's figure, by fastening him into a very tight jacket, with an ornamental row of buttons over each shoulder, and then buttoning his trousers over it, so as to give his legs the appearance of being hooked on, just under the armpits."

"They were decent people, but not overburdened with riches, or he would not have so far outgrown the suit when he passed into those corduroys with the round jacket; in which he went to a boys' school, however, and learnt to write—and in ink of pretty tolerable blackness, too, if the place where he used to wipe his pen might be taken as evidence.

"A black suit and the jacket changed into a diminutive coat. His father had died, and the mother had got the boy a message-lad's place in some office. A long-worn suit that one; rusty and threadbare before it was laid aside, but clean and free from soil to the last . . . .

" . . . we felt as much sorrow when we saw . . . the change that began to take place now . . . . The next suit, smart but slovenly; meant to be gay, and yet not half so decent as the threadbare apparel; redolent of the idle lounge, and the blackguard companions, told us, we thought, that the widow's comfort had rapidly faded away."

"A long period had elapsed, and a greater change had taken place, by the time of casting off the suit that hung above. It was that of a stout, broad-shouldered, sturdy-chested man; and we knew at once, as anybody would, who glanced at that broad-skirted green coat, with the large metal buttons, that its wearer seldom walked forth without a dog at his heels, and some idle ruffian, the very counterpart of himself, at his side. The vices of the boy had grown with the man . . . .

"A coarse round frock, with a worn cotton neckerchief, and other articles of clothing of the commonest description, completed the history. A prison, and the sentence—banishment or the gallows." SB/MS

—self-respecting poor: "There are many grave old persons, I know, who shake their heads with an air of profound wisdom, and tell you that poor people dress too well now-a-days; that when they were children, folks knew their stations in life better; that you may depend upon it, no good will come of this sort of thing in the end—and so forth: but I fancy I can discern in the fine bonnet of the working-man's wife, or the feather-bedizened hat of his child, no inconsiderable evidence of good feeling on the part of the man himself, and an affectionate desire to expend the few shillings he can spare from his week's wages, in improving the appearance and adding to the happiness of those who are nearest and dearest to him.

"This may be a very heinous and unbecoming degree of vanity, perhaps, and the money might possibly be applied to better uses; it must not be forgotten, however, that it might very easily be devoted to worse: and if two or three faces can be rendered happy and contented, by a trifling improvement of outward appearance, I cannot help thinking that the object is very cheaply purchased, even at the expense of a smart gown, or a gaudy riband.

"There is a great deal of very unnecessary cant about the over-dressing of the common people. There is not a manufacturer or tradesman in existence, who would not employ a man who takes a reasonable degree of pride in the appearance of himself and those about him, in preference to a sullen slovenly fellow, who works doggedly on, regardless of his own clothing and that of his wife and children, and seeming to take pleasure or pride in nothing." ¶STH/1

—shabby: "Mr Jobling is buttoned up closer than mere adornment might require. His hat presents at the rims a peculiar appearance of a glistening nature, as if it had been a favourite snail-promenade. The same phenomenon is visible on some parts of his coat, and particularly at the seams. He has the faded appearance of a gentleman in embarrassed circumstances; even his light whiskers droop with something of a shabby air." BH 20

—for shipboard: "Mr Micawber, I must ob-

serve, in his adaptation of himself to a new state of society, had acquired a bold buccaneering air, not absolutely lawless, but defensive and prompt. One might have supposed him a child of the wilderness, long accustomed to live out of the confines of civilisation, and about to return to his native wilds.

"He had provided himself, among other things, with a complete suit of oil-skin, and a straw hat with a very low crown, pitched or caulked on the outside. In this rough clothing, with a common mariner's telescope under his arm, and a shrewd trick of casting up his eye at the sky as looking out for dirty weather, he was far more nautical, after his manner, than Mr Peggotty.

"His whole family, if I may so express it, were cleared for action. I found Mrs Micawber in the closest and most uncompromising of bonnets, made fast under the chin; and in a shawl which tied her up . . . like a bundle, and was secured behind at the waist, in a strong knot.

"Miss Micawber I found made snug for stormy weather, in the same manner, with nothing superfluous about her. Master Micawber was hardly visible in a Guernsey shirt, and the shaggiest suit of slops I ever saw; and the children were done up, like preserved meats, in impervious cases.

"Both Mr Micawber and his eldest son wore their sleeves loosely turned back at the wrists, as being ready to lend a hand in any direction, and to 'tumble up,' or sing out, 'Yeo—Heave—Yeo!' on the shortest notice." ¶DC 57

—shoes

—professionally viewed: "TOM . . . I may as vell go my rounds, and glean for the deputy. (*Pulls out a piece of chalk from his pocket, and takes up boots from No. 23.*) Twenty-three. It's difficult to tell what a fellow is ven he hain't got his senses, but I think this here twenty-three's a timorious, faint-hearted genus. (*Examines the boots.*) You want new soleing, No. 23. (*Goes to No. 24, takes up boots, and looks at them.*) Hallo! here's a bust; and there's been a piece put on in the corner.—I must let my missis know. The bill's always doubtful ven there's any mending. (*Goes to No. 21, takes up boots.*) French calf Vellingtons. —All's right here. These here French calves always comes it strong—light vines, and all that 'ere. (*Looking round.*) Wery happy to see there ain't no high-lows—they never drinks nothing but gin and vater. Them and the cloth boots is the vurst customers an inn has.—The cloth boots is always obstemious, only drinks sherry vine and vater, and never eats no suppers. (*He chalks the number of the room on each pair of boots as he takes them up.*) Lucky for you, my French calves, that you ain't done with the patent polish, or you'd ha' been witrioled in no time. I don't like to put oil o'witriol on a well-made pair of boots; but ven they're rubbed vith that 'ere polish, it must be done, or the profession's ruined." P/SG 2 ii

—second-hand: "We . . . began fitting visionary feet and legs into a cellar-board full of boots and shoes, with a speed and accuracy that would have astonished the most expert artist in leather, living.

"There was one pair of boots in particular—a jolly, good-tempered, hearty-looking, pair of tops, that excited our warmest regard; and we had got a fine, red-faced, jovial fellow of a market-gardener into them, before we had made their acquaintance half a minute.

"They were just the very thing for him. There were his huge fat legs bulging over the tops, and fitting them too tight to admit of his tucking in the loops he had pulled them on by; and his knee-cords with an interval of stocking; and his blue apron tucked up round his waist; and his red neckerchief and blue coat, and a white hat stuck on one side of his head; and there he stood with a broad grin on his great red face, whistling away, as if any other idea but that of being happy and comfortable had never entered his brain."

" . . . the form of a coquettish servant-maid suddenly sprung into a pair of Denmark satin shoes . . . .

"A very smart female, in a showy bonnet, stepped into a pair of grey cloth boots, with black fringe and binding, that were studiously pointing out their toes on the other side of the top-boots, and seemed very anxious to engage his attention . . . .

" . . . excessive gallantry of a very old gentleman with a silver-headed stick, who tottered into a pair of large list shoes, that were standing in one corner of the board, and indulged in a variety of gestures expressive of his admiration of the lady in the cloth boots . . . .

" . . . immeasurable amusement of a young fellow we put into a pair of long-quartered pumps . . . . " SB/MS

—*small boy:* " . . . I date from the period when small boys had a dreadful high-shouldered sleeved strait-waistcoat put upon them by their keepers, over which their dreadful little trousers were buttoned tight, so that they roamed about disconsolate, with their hands in their pockets, like dreadful little pairs of tongs that were vainly looking for the rest of the fire-irons. . . . " HW/NY

—*for society dinner:* "Mr Merdle took down a countess who was secluded somewhere in the core of an immense dress, to which she was in the proportion of the heart to the overgrown cabbage. If so low a simile may be admitted, the dress went down the staircase like a richly brocaded Jack in the Green, and nobody knew what sort of small person carried it." LD i 21

—*starch:* "There was a good deal of competition in the [Doctors] Commons on all points of display, and it turned out some very choice equipages then; though I always have considered, and always shall consider, that in my time the great article of competition there was starch: which I think was worn among the proctors to as great an extent as it is in the nature of man to bear." DC 26

—*umbrella*

—*alert:* "Mrs Sanders, whose eyes were intently fixed on the judge's face, planted herself close by [the witness-box], with the large umbrella: keeping her right thumb pressed on the spring with an earnest countenance, as if she were fully prepared to put it up at a moment's notice." PP 34

—*commercial:* "When the weather was wet, [Silas Wegg] put up his umbrella over his stock-in-trade, not over himself; when the weather was dry, he furled that faded article, tied it round with a piece of yarn, and laid it cross-wise under the trestles: where it looked like an unwholesomely-forced lettuce that had lost in colour and crispness what it had gained in size." OMF i 5

—*psychological:* "What is the moral support derived by some sea-going amateurs from an umbrella? Why do certain voyagers across the Channel always put up that article, and hold it up with a grim and fierce tenacity? . . . Is there any analogy, in certain constitutions, between keeping an umbrella up, and keeping the spirits up?" UT/CM

—*versatile:* "The latter faithful appendage is also invariably a part of the old girl's [Mrs Bagnet] presence out of doors. It is of no colour known in this life, and has a corrugated wooden crook for a handle, with a metallic object let into its prow or beak, resembling a little model of a fan-light over a street door, or one of the oval glasses out of a pair of spectacles: which ornamental object has not that tenacious capacity of sticking to its post that might be desired in an article long associated with the British army. The old girl's umbrella is of a flabby habit of waist, and seems to be in need of stays—an appearance that is possibly referable to its having served, through a series of years, at home as a cupboard, and on journeys as a carpet bag. She never puts it up . . . but generally uses the instrument as a wand with which to point out joints of meat or bunches of greens in marketing, or to arrest the attention of tradesmen by a friendly poke." BH 34

—*the uniform:* "There are some promotions in life, which, independent of the more substantial rewards they offer, acquire peculiar value and dignity from the coats and waistcoats connected with them. A field-marshal has his uniform; a bishop his silk apron; a counsellor his silk gown; a beadle his cocked-hat. Strip the bishop of his apron, or the beadle of his hat and lace; what are they? Men. Mere men." OT 37

—*waistcoat*

—*a cage:* "'It isn't the waistcoat that I look at [said Brass]. It is the heart. The checks in the waistcoat are but the wires of the cage. But the heart is the bird. Ah! How many sich birds are perpetually moulting, and putting their beaks through the wires to peck at all mankind!'" OCS 56

—*stiff:* " . . . an East India Director, of immense wealth, in a waistcoat apparently constructed in serviceable deal by some plain carpenter, but really engendered in the tailor's art, and composed of the material called nankeen . . . ." DS 36

—*and wristbands:* " . . . Mr Toots appeared to be involved in a good deal of uncertainty whether, on the whole, it was judicious to button the bottom button of his waistcoat, and whether, on a calm revision of all the circumstances, it was best to wear his wristbands turned up or turned down. Observing that Mr Feeder's were turned up, Mr Toots turned his up; but the wristbands of the next arrival being turned down, Mr Toots turned his down. The differences in point of waistcoat buttoning, not only at the bottom, but at the top too, became so numerous and complicated as the arrivals thickened, that Mr Toots was continually fingering that article of dress, as if he were performing on some instrument; and appeared to find the incessant execution it demanded, quite bewildering." DS 14

—for a wedding: "Mr Barkis bloomed in a new blue coat, of which the tailor had given him such good measure, that the cuffs would have rendered gloves unnecessary in the coldest weather, while the collar was so high that it pushed his hair up on end on the top of his head. His bright buttons, too, were of the largest size. Rendered complete by drab pantaloons and a buff waistcoat, I thought Mr Barkis a phenomenon of respectability." DC 10

—of a wooer: "I scarcely knew [Mr Guppy] again, he was so uncommonly smart. He had an entirely new suit of glossy clothes on, a shining hat, lilac-kid gloves, a neckerchief of a variety of colours, a large hot-house flower in his button-hole, and a thick gold ring on his little finger. Besides which, he quite scented the dining-room with bear's-grease and other perfumery. He looked at me with an attention that quite confused me . . . I never looked at him, but I found him looking at me, in the same scrutinising and curious way." BH 9 *And see John Chivery LD* Vol. II p1243

Food and Drink

At the Coffee-house (The Jolly Sandboys) OCS

"'Come, hand in the eatables.'

"'There was something in the sound of the last word which roused the unctuous boy. He jumped up: and the leaden eyes, which twinkled behind his mountainous cheeks, leered horribly upon the food as he unpacked it from the basket." PP 4

—ale, mulled: " . . . the landlord retired to draw the beer, and presently returning with it, applied himself to warm the same in a small tin vessel shaped funnel-wise, for the convenience of sticking it far down in the fire and getting at the bright places. This was soon done, and he handed it over to Mr Codlin with that creamy froth upon the surface which is one of the happy circumstances attendant upon mulled malt." OCS 18

—appetite

—and attire: "I have my doubts, too, founded on the acute experience acquired at this period of my life, whether a sound enjoyment of animal food can develop itself freely in any human subject who is always in torment from tight boots. I think the extremities require to be at peace before the stomach will conduct itself with vigour." DC 28

—and love: "'Dear Mr Toots,' said Florence, 'you are so friendly to me, and so honest, that I am sure I may ask a favour of you.'

"'Miss Dombey,' returned Mr Toots, 'if you'll only name one, you'll—you'll give me an appetite. To which,' said Mr Toots, with some sentiment, 'I have long been a stranger.'" DS 61

"In my love-lorn condition, my appetite languished; and I was glad of it, for I felt as though it would have been an act of perfidy towards Dora to have a natural relish for my dinner." DC 28

—suppressed: "'That's right,' said Squeers, calmly getting on with his breakfast; 'keep ready till I tell you to begin. Subdue your appetites, my dears, and you've conquered human natur. This is the way we inculcate strength of mind, Mr Nickleby,' said the schoolmaster, turning to Nicholas, and speaking with his mouth very full of beef and toast." NN 5

—baked potato: "'May the present moment,' said Dick [Swiveller], sticking his fork into a large carbuncular potato, 'be the worst of our lives! I like this plan of sending 'em with the peel on; there's a charm in drawing a potato from its native element (if I may so express it) to which the rich and powerful are strangers. Ah! "Man wants but little here below, nor wants that little long!"* How true that is!—after dinner.'" OCS 8

**Oliver Goldsmith's* The Vicar of Wakefield, ch 8: The Hermit (Edwin and Angelina, st 8)

—beefsteak pudding: "I knocked up a beefsteak-pudding for one, with two kidneys, a dozen oysters, and a couple of mushrooms thrown in. It's a pudding to put a man in good humour with everything, except the two bottom buttons of his waistcoat." CS/DM

—beer: "The first ingredient in the making of glass, to which we were introduced, was contained in a goodly row of barrels in full tap, marked with the esteemed brand of '**Truman, Hanbury, Buxton, & Co.**' It is the well-known fermented extract of malt and hops, which is, it seems, nearly as necessary to the production of good plate glass, as flint and soda. To liquefy the latter materials by means of fire, is, in truth, dry work; and our *cicerone* explained, that seven pints per day, per man, of Messrs. Truman, Hanbury, Buxton, and Company's entire, has been found, after years of thirsty experience, to be absolutely necessary to moisten human clay, hourly baked at the mouths of blazing furnaces." HWC/PG

—blackberries "are melancholy things; they take our thoughts back to the days of trustful childhood, when we could crop those little joys by the wayside, and did not know that they are only safe while they are sour, and that the over-sweet have constantly a maggot coiled within. Alas for the experience of life!" HWC/FE

—bread and butter: "My sister [Mrs Joe Gargery] had a trenchant way of cutting our bread-and-butter for us, that never varied. First, with her left hand she jammed the loaf hard and fast against her bib—where it sometimes got a pin into it, and sometimes a needle, which we afterwards got into our mouths. Then she took some butter (not too much) on a knife and spread it on the loaf, in an apothecary kind of way, as if she were making a plaister—using both sides of the knife with a slapping dexterity, and trimming and moulding the butter off round the crust. Then, she gave the knife a final smart wipe on the edge of the plaister, and then sawed a very thick round off the loaf: which she finally, before separating from the loaf, hewed into two halves, of which Joe got one, and I the other." GE 2

"Mr Trabb had sliced his hot roll into three feather beds, and was slipping butter in between the blankets, and covering it up." GE 19

—and tea: " . . . Mr Toodle washed down with a pint mug of tea, and proceeded to solidify with a great weight of bread and butter; charging his young daughters, meanwhile, to keep plenty of hot water in the pot, as he was uncommon dry, and should take the indefinite quantity of 'a sight of mugs,' before his thirst was appeased.

"In satisfying himself, however, Mr Toodle was not regardless of the younger branches about him, who, although they had made their own evening repast, were on the look-out for irregular morsels as possessing a relish. These he distributed now and then to the expectant circle, by holding out great wedges of bread and butter, to be bitten at by the family in lawful succession, and by serving out small doses of tea in like manner with a spoon; which snacks had such a relish in the mouths of these young Toodles, that, after partaking of the same, they performed private dances of ecstasy among themselves, and stood on one leg apiece, and hopped, and indulged in other saltatory tokens of gladness. These vents for their excitement found, they gradually closed about Mr Toodle again, and eyed him hard as he got through more bread and butter, and tea; affecting, however, to have no further expectations of their own in reference to those viands, but to be conversing on foreign subjects, and whispering confidentially.

"Mr Toodle, in the midst of this family group, and setting an awful example to his children in the way of appetite, was conveying the two young Toodles on his knees to Birmingham by special engine, and was contemplating the rest over a barrier of bread and butter . . . . " DS 38

—breakfast

—of an active detective: "Mr Bucket lays into a breakfast of two mutton chops as a foundation to work upon, together with tea, eggs, toast, and marmalade, on a corresponding scale." BH 44

—of an aesthete: "'Here I am! This is my frugal breakfast. Some men want legs of beef and mutton for breakfast; I don't. Give me my peach, my cup of coffee, and my claret; I am content. I don't want them for themselves, but they remind me of the sun. There's nothing solar about legs of beef and mutton. Mere animal satisfaction!'" BH 43

—in America: " . . . breakfast would have been no breakfast unless the principal dish were a deformed beef-steak with a great flat bone in the centre, swimming in hot butter, and sprinkled with the very blackest of all possible pepper." AN 3

—of a dwarf: " . . . [Quilp] ate hard eggs, shell and all, devoured gigantic prawns with the heads and tails on, chewed tobacco and water-cresses at the same time and with extraordinary greediness, drank boiling tea without winking, bit his fork and spoon till they bent again, and in short performed so many horrifying and uncommon acts that the women were nearly frightened out of their wits, and began to doubt if he were really a human creature." OCS 5

—of a large family: "In this mood they sat down to breakfast. The little Tetterbys were not habituated to regard that meal in the light of a sedentary occupation, but discussed it as a dance or trot; rather resembling a savage ceremony, in the occasional shrill whoops, and brandishings of bread and butter, with which it was accompanied, as well as in the intricate filings off into the street and back again, and the hoppings up and down the doorsteps, which were incidental to the performance. In the present instance, the contentions between these Tetterby children for the milk-and-water jug, common to all, which stood upon the table, presented so lamentable an instance of angry passions risen very high indeed, that it was an outrage on the memory of Doctor Watts. It was not until Mr Tetterby had driven the whole herd out at the front door, that a moment's peace was secured; and even that was broken by the discovery that Johnny had surreptitiously come back, and was at that instant choking in the jug like a ventriloquist, in his indecent and rapacious haste." HM 3

—at a locksmith's: "It was a substantial meal; for, over and above the ordinary tea equipage, the board creaked beneath the weight of a jolly round of beef, a ham of the first magnitude, and sundry towers of buttered Yorkshire cake, piled slice upon slice in most alluring order. There was also a goodly jug of well-browned clay, fashioned into the form of an old gentleman, not by any means unlike the locksmith [Gabriel Varden], atop of whose bald head was a fine white froth answering to his wig, indicative, beyond dispute, of sparkling home-brewed ale. But, better far than fair home-brewed, or Yorkshire cake, or ham, or beef,

or anything to eat or drink that earth or air or water can supply, there sat, presiding over all, the locksmith's rosy daughter [Dolly], before whose dark eyes even beef grew insignificant, and malt became as nothing." BR 4

—and the mind: "As to breakfast. I could get a variety of delicacies for breakfast at the Clarendon, that are out of the question at Mrs Skim's. Granted. But I don't want to have them! My opinion is, that we are not entirely animal and sensual. Man has an intellect bestowed upon him. If he clogs that intellect by too good a breakfast, how can he properly exert that intellect in meditation, during the day, upon his dinner? That's the point. We are not to enchain the soul. We are to let it soar. It is expected of us." HW/LT

—restorative: "[Mr Micawber] wept; but so far recovered, almost immediately, as to ring the bell for the waiter, and bespeak a hot kidney pudding and a plate of shrimps for breakfast in the morning." DC 17

—carving a goose: " . . . if there be one branch of housekeeping in which [Mrs Chirrup] excels to an utterly unparalleled and unprecedented extent, it is in the important one of carving. A roast goose is universally allowed to be the great stumbling-block in the way of young aspirants to perfection in this department of science; many promising carvers, beginning with legs of mutton, and preserving a good reputation through fillets of veal, sirloins of beef, quarters of lamb, fowls, and even ducks, have sunk before a roast goose, and lost caste and character for ever.

"To Mrs Chirrup the resolving a goose into its smallest component parts is a pleasant pastime—a practical joke—a thing to be done in a minute or so, without the smallest interruption to the conversation of the time. No handing the dish over to an unfortunate man upon her right or left, no wild sharpening of the knife, no hacking and sawing at an unruly joint, no noise, no splash, no heat, no leaving off in despair; all is confidence and cheerfulness.

"The dish is set upon the table, the cover is removed; for an instant, and only an instant, you observe that Mrs Chirrup's attention is distracted; she smiles, but heareth not. You proceed with your story; meanwhile the glittering knife is slowly upraised, both Mrs Chirrup's wrists are slightly but not ungracefully agitated, she compresses her lips for an instant, then breaks into a smile, and all is over. The legs of the bird slide gently down into a pool of gravy, the wings seem to melt from the body, the breast separates into a row of juicy slices, the smaller and more complicated parts of his anatomy are perfectly developed, a cavern of stuffing is revealed, and the goose is gone!" ¶YC/N

—casters/cruets: " . . . I held up before [Bullfinch] in succession the cloudy oil and furry vinegar, the clogged cayenne, the dirty salt, the obscene dregs of soy, and the anchovy sauce in a flannel waistcoat of decomposition." UT/DH

—cheese: " . . . like an eminently aristocratic family cheese, [Mr Boffin's house] was much too large for his wants, and bred an infinite amount of parasites . . . ." OMF ii 8

—Christmas pudding: "Hallo! A great deal of steam! The pudding was out of the copper. A smell like a washing-day! That was the cloth. A smell like an eating-house and a pastrycook's next door to each other, with a laundress's next door to that! That was the pudding! In half a minute Mrs Cratchit entered—flushed, but smiling proudly—with the pudding, like a speckled cannon-ball, so hard and firm, blazing in half of half-a-quartern of ignited brandy, and bedight with Christmas holly stuck into the top.

"Oh, a wonderful pudding! Bob Cratchit said, and calmly too, that he regarded it as the greatest success achieved by Mrs Cratchit since their marriage." CC 3

—cobbler's punch: "'You don't use lemon in your business, do you?' asked Wegg, sniffing again.

"'No, Mr Wegg,' said Venus. 'When I use it at all, I mostly use it in cobblers' punch.'

"'What do you call cobblers' punch?' demanded Wegg, in a worse humour than before.

"'It's difficult to impart the receipt for it, sir,' returned Venus, 'because, however particular you may be in allotting your materials, so much will still depend upon the individual gifts, and there being a feeling thrown into it. But the groundwork is gin.'" OMF iv 14

—cod-fish: " . . . Mr Weller and the guard are endeavouring to insinuate into the fore-boot [of the Muggleton Telegraph] a huge cod-fish several sizes too large for it—which is snugly packed up, in a long brown basket, with a layer of straw over the top, and which has been left to the last, in order that

he may repose in safety on the half-dozen barrels of real native oysters, all the property of Mr Pickwick, which have been arranged in regular order at the bottom of the receptacle. The interest displayed in Mr Pickwick's countenance is most intense, as Mr Weller and the guard try to squeeze the cod-fish into the boot, first head first, and then tail first, and then top upward, and then bottom upward, and then side-ways, and then long-ways, all of which artifices the implacable cod-fish sturdily resists, until the guard accidentally hits him in the very middle of the basket, whereupon he suddenly disappears into the boot, and with him, the head and shoulders of the guard himself, who, not calculating upon so sudden a cessation of the passive resistance of the cod-fish, experiences a very unexpected shock, to the unsmotherable delight of all the porters and bystanders." PP 28

—*collation:* "The 'sit-down supper' was excellent; there were four barley-sugar temples on the table, which would have looked beautiful if they had not melted away when the supper began; and a water-mill, whose only fault was that instead of going round, it ran over the table-cloth. Then there were fowls, and tongue, and trifle, and sweets, and lobster salad, and potted beef—and everything.

"And little Kitterbell kept calling out for clean plates, and the clean plates did not come; and then the gentlemen who wanted the plates said they didn't mind, they'd take a lady's; and then Mrs Kitterbell applauded their gallantry, and the greengrocer ran about till he thought his seven and sixpence was very hardly earned; and the young ladies didn't eat much for fear it shouldn't look romantic, and the married ladies eat as much as possible, for fear they shouldn't have enough; and a great deal of wine was drunk, and everybody talked and laughed considerably." ¶SB/BC

—*afloat:* "The throbbing motion of the engine was but too perceptible. There was a large, substantial, cold boiled leg of mutton, at the bottom of the table, shaking like blanc-mange; a previously hearty sirloin of beef looked as if it had been suddenly seized with the palsy; and some tongues, which were placed on dishes rather too large for them, went through the most surprising evolutions; darting from side to side, and from end to end, like a fly in an inverted wine-glass. Then, the sweets shook and trembled, till it was quite impossible to help them, and people gave up the attempt in despair; and the pigeon-pies looked as if the birds, whose legs were stuck outside, were trying to get them in. The table vibrated and started like a feverish pulse, and the very legs were convulsed—everything was shaking and jarring . . . . Several ominous demands were made for small glasses of brandy; the countenances of the company gradually underwent most extraordinary changes; one gentleman was observed suddenly to rush from table without the slightest ostensible reason, and dart up the steps with incredible swiftness: thereby greatly damaging both himself and the steward, who happened to be coming down at the same moment.

"The cloth was removed; the dessert was laid on the table; and the glasses were filled. The motion of the boat increased; several members of the party began to feel rather vague and misty, and looked as if they had only just got up." SB/SE

—*cooking*

—*English / French:* " . . . Miss Pross took charge of the lower regions, and always acquitted herself marvellously. Her dinners, of a very modest quality, were so well cooked and so well served, and so neat in their contrivances, half English and half French, that nothing could be better. Miss Pross's friendship being of the thoroughly practical kind, she had ravaged Soho and the adjacent provinces, in search of impoverished French, who, tempted by shillings and half-crowns, would impart culinary mysteries to her. From these decayed sons and daughters of Gaul, she had acquired such wonderful arts, that the woman and girl who formed the staff of domestics regarded her as quite a Sorceress, or Cinderella's Godmother: who would send out for a fowl, a rabbit, a vegetable or two from the garden, and change them into anything she pleased." TTC ii 6

—*melodious:* "Mrs Wilfer then solemnly divested herself of her handkerchief and gloves, as a preliminary sacrifice to preparing the frying-pan, and R. W. himself went out to purchase the viand. He soon returned, bearing the same in a fresh cabbage-leaf, where it coyly embraced a rasher of ham. Melodious sounds were not long in rising from the frying-pan on the fire, or in seeming, as the firelight danced in the mellow halls of a couple of full bottles on the table, to play appropriate dance-music." OMF i 4

—cutlet: " . . . [the waiter] will not take the sham silver cover off, without a pause for a flourish, and a look at the musty cutlet as if he were surprised to see it—which cannot possibly be the case, he must have seen it so often before. A sort of fur has been produced upon its surface by the cook's art, and in a sham silver vessel staggering on two feet instead of three, is a cutaneous kind of sauce, of brown pimples and pickled cucumber." UT/RT

—dining

—in a bank: " . . . 'present my compliments to young Mr Thomas, and ask him if he would step up and partake of a lamb chop and walnut ketchup, with a glass of India ale?'" HT ii 11

—in a boarding house: "The boarders were seated, a lady and gentleman alternately, like the layers of bread and meat in a plate of sandwiches; and then Mrs Tibbs directed James to take off the covers. Salmon, lobster-sauce, giblet-soup, and the usual accompaniments were *dis*-covered: potatoes like petrifactions, and bits of toasted bread, the shape and size of blank dice." SB/BH

—with Croesus: "It was a dinner to provoke an appetite, though he had not had one. The rarest dishes, sumptuously cooked and sumptuously served; the choicest fruits; the most exquisite wines; marvels of workmanship in gold and silver, china and glass; innumerable things delicious to the senses of taste, smell, and sight, were insinuated into its composition. O, what a wonderful man this Merdle, what a great man, what a master man, how blessedly and enviably endowed—in a word, what a rich man!" LD ii 12

—entertaining at home: "'Take off the covers, Martha,' said Mrs Parsons, directing the shifting of the scenery with great anxiety. The order was obeyed, and a pair of boiled fowls, with tongue and et ceteras, were displayed at the top, and a fillet of veal at the bottom. On one side of the table two green sauce-tureens, with ladles of the same, were setting to each other in a green dish; and on the other was a curried rabbit, in a brown suit, turned up with lemon." SB/WT

—of hypochondriacs: "Now, the dinner is always a good one, the appetites of the diners being delicate, and requiring a little of what Mrs Merrywinkle calls 'tittivation' the secret of which is understood to lie in good cookery and tasteful spices, and which process is so successfully performed in the present instance, that both Mr and Mrs Merrywinkle eat a remarkably good dinner, and even the afflicted Mrs Chopper wields her knife and fork with much of the spirit and elasticity of youth.

"But Mr Merrywinkle, in his desire to gratify his appetite, is not unmindful of his health, for he has a bottle of carbonate of soda with which to qualify his porter, and a little pair of scales in which to weigh it out. Neither in his anxiety to take care of his body is he unmindful of the welfare of his immortal part, as he always prays that for what he is going to receive he may be made truly thankful; and in order that he may be as thankful as possible, eats and drinks to the utmost." ¶YC/H

—at a wedding: "Then the dinner. There was baked leg of mutton at the top, boiled leg of mutton at the bottom, pair of fowls and leg of pork in the middle; porter-pots at the corners; pepper, mustard, and vinegar in the centre; vegetables on the floor: and plum-pudding and apple-pie and tartlets without number: to say nothing of cheese, and celery, and water-cresses, and all that sort of thing." SB/MM

—on the wife's birthday: "Further conversation is prevented, for the time, by the necessity under which Mr Bagnet finds himself of directing the whole force of his mind to the dinner, which is a little endangered by the dry humour of the fowls in not yielding any gravy, and also by the made-gravy acquiring no flavour, and turning out of a flaxen complexion.

"With a similar perverseness, the potatoes crumble off forks in the process of peeling, upheaving from their centres in every direction, as if they were subject to earthquakes. The legs of the fowls, too, are longer than could be desired, and extremely scaly. Overcoming these disadvantages to the best of his ability, Mr Bagnet at last dishes, and they sit down at table; Mrs Bagnet occupying the guest's place at his right hand.

"It is well for the old girl that she has but one birthday in a year, for two such indulgences in poultry might be injurious. Every kind of finer tendon and ligament that is in the nature of poultry to possess, is developed in these specimens in the singular form of guitar-strings. Their limbs appear to have struck roots into their breasts and bodies, as aged trees strike roots into the earth. Their legs are so hard, as to encourage the idea that they must have devoted the greater part of their long and arduous lives to pedestrian exercises, and the walking of matches.

"But Mr Bagnet, unconscious of these little defects, sets his heart on Mrs Bagnet eating a most severe quantity of the delicacies before her; and as that good old girl would not cause him a moment's disappointment on any day, least of all on such a day, for any consideration, she imperils her digestion fearfully. How young Woolwich cleans the drumsticks without being of ostrich descent, his anxious mother is at a loss to understand." ¶BH 49

—dinner-time: "'There's nothing,' said Toby [Veck], 'more regular in its coming round than dinner-time, and nothing less regular in its coming round than dinner. That's the great difference between 'em. It's took me a long time to find it out. I wonder whether it would be worth any gentleman's while, now, to buy that obserwation for the Papers; or the Parliament!'" C 1

—drinks, in America: " . . . the stranger is initiated into the mysteries of Gin-sling, Cocktail, Sangaree, Mint Julep, Sherry-cobbler, Timber Doodle, and other rare drinks." AN 3

—egg: "'Its very easy to talk,' said Mrs Mantalini.

"'Not so easy when one is eating a demnition egg,' replied Mr Mantalini; 'for the yolk runs down the waistcoat, and yolk of egg does not match any waistcoat but a yellow waistcoat, demmit.'" NN 17

—fish: "What a dinner! Specimens of all the fishes that swim in the sea, surely had swum their way to it, and if samples of the fishes of divers colours that made a speech in the Arabian Nights (quite a ministerial explanation in respect of cloudiness), and then jumped out of the frying-pan, were not to be recognised, it was only because they had all become of one hue by being cooked in batter among the whitebait." OMF iv 4

—flip: " . . . a good-humoured comely woman of some fifty years of age . . . came running in, attended by a man bearing a stone pitcher of terrific size . . . .

"Mrs Chickenstalker's notion of a little flip did honour to her character. The pitcher steamed and smoked and reeked like a volcano; and the man who had carried it was faint." C 4

—of French children: "At three years old the Mooninian babies [*CD dreams he has just been on the Moon*] grow up. They are by that time familiar with coffee-houses, and used up as to truffles. They dine at six. Soup, fish, two entrées, a vegetable, a cold dish, or pâté-de-foie-gras, a roast, a salad, a sweet, and a preserved peach or so, form (with occasional whets of sardines, radishes, and Lyons sausage) their frugal repast.

"They breakfast at eleven, on a light beefsteak with Madeira sauce, a kidney steeped in champagne, a trifle of sweetbread, a plate of fried potatoes, and a glass or two of wholesome Bordeaux wine. I have seen a marriageable young female aged five, in a mature bonnet and crinoline, finish off at a public establishment with her amiable parents, on coffee that would consign a child of any other nation to the family undertaker in one experiment.

"I have dined at a friendly party, sitting next to a Mooninian baby, who ate of nine dishes besides ice and fruit, and, wildly stimulated by sauces, in all leisure moments flourished its spoon about its head in the manner of a pictorial glory." ¶HW/RD

—goose, at Christmas: "There never was such a goose. Bob [Cratchit] said he didn't believe there ever was such a goose cooked. Its tenderness and flavour, size and cheapness, were the themes of universal admiration. Eked out by apple-sauce and mashed potatoes, it was a sufficient dinner for the whole family; indeed, as Mrs Cratchit said with great delight (surveying one small atom of a bone upon the dish), they hadn't ate it all at last!" CC 3

—gourmandise: "If [the Peer] really be eating his supper now, at what hour can he possibly have dined! A second solid mass of rump-steak has disappeared, and he eat [*sic.*] the first in four minutes and three quarters, by the clock over the window. Was there ever such a personification of Falstaff! Mark the air with which he gloats over that Stilton, as he removed the napkin which has been placed beneath his chin to catch the superfluous gravy of the steak, and with what gusto he imbibes the porter which has been fetched, expressly for him, in the pewter pot. Listen to the hoarse sound of that voice, kept down as it is by layers of solids, and deep draughts of rich wine, and tell us if you ever saw such a perfect picture of a regular *gourmand* . . . ." SB/P

And see Bagstock DS Vol. I pp728-9

—gravy: "'Presiding over an establishment like this, makes sad havoc with the features, my dear Miss Pecksniffs,' said Mrs. Todgers. 'The gravy alone, is enough to add twenty years to one's age, I do assure you'. . . . 'The anxiety of that one item . . . keeps the mind continually upon the stretch. There is no such passion in human nature, as the passion for gravy among commercial gentlemen. It's nothing to say a joint won't yield—a whole animal wouldn't yield—the amount of gravy they expect each day at dinner. And what I have undergone in consequence,' cried Mrs. Todgers, raising her eyes and shaking her head, 'no one would believe!'" MC 9

" . . . the 'young gal' had dropped it all upon the stairs—where it remained, by-the-bye, in a long train, until it was worn out." DC 28

—leg of mutton: "The leg of mutton came up very red within, and very pale without: besides having a foreign substance of a gritty nature sprinkled over it, as if it had had a fall into the ashes of that remarkable kitchen fireplace." DC 28

—for a little brother: "I was regaled with the scaly tips of the drumsticks of the fowls, and with those obscure corners of pork of which the pig, when living, had had the least reason to be vain." GE 4

—meat: "To see the butcher slap the steak, before he laid it on the block, and give his knife a sharpening, was to forget breakfast instantly. It was agreeable, too—it really was—to see him cut it off, so smooth and juicy. There was nothing savage in the act, although the knife was large and keen; it was a piece of art, high art; there was delicacy of touch, clearness of tone, skilful handling of the subject, fine shading. It was the triumph of mind over matter, quite.

"Perhaps the greenest cabbage-leaf ever grown in a garden was wrapped about this steak, before it was delivered over to Tom. But the butcher had a sentiment for his business, and knew how to refine upon it. When he saw Tom putting the cabbage-leaf into his pocket awkwardly, he begged to be allowed to do it for him; 'for meat,' he said with some emotion, 'must be humoured, not drove.'" MC 39

—meat pie: "'I lodged in the same house vith a pieman once, sir [said Sam Weller] and a wery nice man he was—reg'lar clever chap, too—make pies out o' anything, he could. "What a number o' cats you keep, Mr Brooks," says I, when I'd got intimate with him. "Ah," says he, "I do—a good many," says he. "You must be wery fond o' cats," says I. "Other people is," says he, a winkin' at me; "they an't in season till the winter though," says he. "Not in season!" says I. "No," says he, "fruits is in, cats is out." "Why, what do you mean?" says I. "Mean?" says he. "That I'll never be a party to the combination o' the butchers, to keep up the prices o' meat," says he. "Mr Weller," says he, a squeezing my hand wery hard, and vispering in my ear—"don't mention this here agin—but it's the seasonin' as does it. They're all made o' them noble animals," says he, a pointin' to a wery nice little tabby kitten, "and I seasons 'em for beefsteak, weal, or kidney, 'cordin' to the demand. And more than that," says he, "I can make a weal a beef-steak, or a beef-steak a kidney, or any one on 'em a mutton, at a minute's notice, just as the market changes, and appetites wary!"'" PP 19

"'*Do* my eyes deceive me, or is that object up there a—a pie? It can't be a pie.'

"'Yes, it's a pie, Wegg,' replied Mr Boffin, with a glance of some little discomfiture at the Decline and Fall.

"'*Have* I lost my smell for fruits, or is it a apple pie, sir?' asked Wegg.

"'It's a veal and ham pie,' said Mr Boffin.

"'Is it indeed, sir? And it would be hard, sir, to name the pie that is a better pie than a weal and hammer,' said Mr Wegg, nodding his head emotionally.

"'Have some, Wegg?'

"'Thank you, Mr Boffin, I think I will, at your invitation. I wouldn't at any other party's at the present juncture; but at yours, sir—And meaty jelly too, especially when a little salt, which is the case where there's ham, is mellering to the organ, is very mellering to the organ.' Mr Wegg did not say what organ, but spoke with a cheerful generality." OMF i 5

—milk: "It is pastoral to feel the freshness of the air in the uninhabited town, and to appreciate the shepherdess character of the few milkwomen who purvey so little milk that it would be worth nobody's while to adulterate it, if anybody were left to undertake the task. On the crowded sea-shore, the great demand for milk, combined with the strong local temptation of chalk, would betray itself in the lowered quality of the article. In Arcadian London I derive it from the cow." UT/AL

—*muffins:* "'Blowing and sleeting hard . . . and threatening snow. Dark. And very cold.'

"'I'm glad to think we had muffins,' said the former porter [Tugby], in the tone of one who had set his conscience at rest. 'It's a sort of night that's meant for muffins. Likewise crumpets. Also Sally Lunns.'

"The former porter mentioned each successive kind of eatable, as if he were musingly summing up his good actions. After which he rubbed his fat legs as before, and jerking them at the knees to get the fire upon the yet unroasted parts, laughed as if somebody had tickled him.

"'You're in spirits, Tugby, my dear,' observed his wife.

"The firm was Tugby, late Chickenstalker.

"'No,' said Tugby. 'No. Not particular. I'm a little elewated. The muffins came so pat!'" C 4

—*ordered by an out-patient:* 'Very good, said the old gentleman, raising his voice, 'then bring in the bottled lightning, a clean tumbler, and a corkscrew.'

"Nobody executing this order, the old gentleman, after a short pause, raised his voice again and demanded a thunder sandwich. This article not being forthcoming either, he requested to be served with a fricassee of boot-tops and goldfish sauce, and then, laughing heartily, gratified his hearers with a very long, very loud, and most melodious bellow." NN 49

—*oysters, in America:* " . . . a guest . . . is certain to see, at every dinner, an unusual amount of poultry on the table; and at ever supper, at least two mighty bowls of hot stewed oysters, in any one of which a half-grown Duke of Clarence might be smothered easily." AN 3

"At other downward flights of steps, are other lamps, marking the whereabouts of oyster-cellars—pleasant retreats, say I: not only by reason of their wonderful cookery of oysters, pretty nigh as large as cheese-plates . . . but because of all kinds of eaters of fish, or flesh, or fowl, in these latitudes, the swallowers of oysters alone are not gregarious; but subduing themselves, as it were, to the nature of what they work in, and copying the coyness of the thing they eat, do sit apart in curtained boxes, and consort by twos, not by two hundreds." AN 6

—*a child's first:* " . . . we tasted our first oyster. A remarkable sensation! We feel it slipping down our throat now, like a sort of maritime castor-oil, and are again bewildered by an unsatisfactory doubt whether it really *was* the oyster which made that mysterious disappearance, or whether we are going to begin to taste it presently." HWC/FF

—*and poverty:* "'It's a wery remarkable circumstance, sir,' said Sam, 'that poverty and oysters always seems to go together.'

"'I don't understand you, Sam,' said Mr Pickwick.

"'What I mean, sir,' said Sam, 'is, that the poorer a place is, the greater call there seems to be for oysters. Look here, sir: here's a oyster stall to every half-dozen houses. The street's lined vith 'em. Blessed if I don't think that ven a man's wery poor, he rushes out of his lodgings, and eats oysters in reg'lar desperation.'

"'To be sure he does,' said Mr Weller senior; 'and it's just the same vith pickled salmon!'

"'Those are two very remarkable facts, which never occurred to me before,' said Mr Pickwick." PP 22

—*a pie:* "Once I passed a fortnight at an Inn in the North of England, where I was haunted by the ghost of a tremendous pie. It was a Yorkshire pie, like a fort—an abandoned fort with nothing in it; but the waiter had a fixed idea that it was a point of ceremony at every meal to put the pie on the table. After some days I tried to hint, in several delicate ways, that I considered the pie done with; as, for example, by emptying fag-ends of glasses of wine into it; putting cheese-plates and spoons into it, as into a basket; putting wine-bottles into it, as into a cooler; but always in vain, the pie being invariably cleaned out again and brought up as before. At last, beginning to be doubtful whether I was not the victim of a spectral illusion, and whether my health and spirits might not sink under the horrors of an imaginary pie, I cut a triangle out of it, fully as large as the musical instrument of that name in a powerful orchestra. Human prevision could not have foreseen the result—but the waiter mended the pie. With some effectual species of cement, he adroitly fitted the triangle in again, and I paid my reckoning and fled." CS/HT 1

—*pigeon-pie:* "The pigeon-pie was not bad, but it was a delusive pie: the crust being like a disappointing head, phrenologically speaking: full of lumps and bumps, with nothing particular underneath." DC 28

—pig's knuckle: " . . . 'here's your mother [said Mr Tetterby] been and bought, at the cook's shop, besides pease pudding a whole knuckle of a lovely roast leg of pork, with lots of crackling left upon it, and with seasoning gravy and mustard quite unlimited. Hand in your plate, my boy, and begin while it's simmering' . . . .

"There might have been more pork on the knucklebone—which knuckle-bone the carver at the cook's shop had assuredly not forgotten in carving for previous customers—but there was no stint of seasoning, and that is an accessory dreamily suggesting pork, and pleasantly cheating the sense of taste. The pease pudding, too, the gravy and mustard, like the Eastern rose in respect of the nightingale, if they were not absolutely pork, had lived near it; so, upon the whole, there was the flavour of a middle-sized pig." HM 2

—pineapple: " . . . I suppose there never were so many pine-apples in a Train as there appear to be in this Train.

"'Whew! The hot-house air is faint with pine-apples. Every French citizen or citizeness is carrying pine-apples home. The compact little Enchantress in the corner . . . has a pine-apple in her lap. Compact Enchantress's friend . . . has two pine-apples in her lap, and a bundle of them under the seat. Tobacco-smoky Frenchman . . . carries pine-apples in a covered basket. Tall, grave, melancholy Frenchman . . . has the green end of a pine-apple sticking out of his neat valise." RP/F

" . . . . Compact Enchantress . . . gives a little scream; a sound that seems to come from high up in her precious little head; from behind her bright little eyebrows. 'Great Heaven, my pine-apple! My Angel! It is lost!' Mystery is desolated. A search made. It is not lost. Zamiel finds it." RP/F

—in preacherly perspective: "'My friends . . . what is this which we now behold as being spread before us? Refreshment. Do we need refreshment then, my friends? We do. And why do we need refreshment, my friends? Because we are but mortal, because we are but sinful, because we are but of the earth, because we are not of the air.

"'Can we fly, my friends? We cannot. Why can we not fly, my friends? . . . Is it because we are calculated to walk? It is. Could we walk, my friends, without strength? We could not. What should we do without strength, my friends? Our legs would refuse to bear us, our knees would double up, our ankles would turn over, and we should come to the ground.

"'Then from whence, my friends, in a human point of view, do we derive the strength that is necessary to our limbs? Is it . . . from bread in various forms, from butter which is churned from the milk which is yielded unto us by the cow, from the eggs which are laid by the fowl, from ham, from tongue, from sausage, and from such like? It is. Then let us partake of the good things which are set before us!'" ¶BH 19

—preparation: "'Now, Ma,' said Bella . . . 'you and Lavvy think magnificent me fit for nothing, but I intend to prove the contrary. I mean to be Cook to-day.'

"'Hold!' rejoined her majestic mother. 'I cannot permit it. Cook, in that dress!'

"'As for my dress, Ma,' returned Bella, merrily searching in a dresser-drawer, 'I mean to apron it and towel it all over the front; and as to permission, I mean to do without.'

"'*You* cook?' said Mrs Wilfer. '*You* who never cooked when you were at home?'

"'Yes, Ma,' returned Bella; 'that is precisely the state of the case.'

"She girded herself with a white apron, and busily with knots and pins contrived a bib to it, coming close and tight under her chin, as if it had caught her round the neck to kiss her. Over this bib her dimples looked delightful, and under it her pretty figure not less so. 'Now, Ma,' said Bella, pushing back her hair from her temples with both hands, 'what's first?'

"'First,' returned Mrs Wilfer solemnly, 'if you persist in what I cannot but regard as conduct utterly incompatible with the equipage in which you arrived—'

('Which I do, Ma.')

"'First, then, you put the fowls down to the fire.'

"'To—be—sure!' cried Bella; 'and flour them, and twirl them round, and there they go!' sending them spinning at a great rate. 'What's next, Ma?'

"'Next,' said Mrs Wilfer with a wave of her gloves, expressive of abdication under protest from the culinary throne, 'I would recommend examination of the bacon in the saucepan on the fire, and also of the potatoes by the application of a fork. Preparation of the greens will further become necessary if you persist in this unseemly demeanour.'

"'As of course I do, Ma.'

"Persisting, Bella gave her attention to one thing and forgot the other, and gave her attention to the other and forgot the third, and remembering the third was distracted by the fourth, and made amends whenever she went wrong by giving the unfortunate fowls an extra spin, which made their chance of ever getting cooked exceedingly doubtful. But it was pleasant cookery too." OMF iii 4 *See —underdone poultry* p 143

—punch

—cheering: To divert his thoughts . . . I informed Mr Micawber that I relied upon him for a bowl of punch, and led him to the lemons. His recent despondency, not to say despair, was gone in a moment. I never saw a man so thoroughly enjoy himself amid the fragrance of lemon-peel and sugar, the odour of burning rum, and the steam of boiling water, as Mr Micawber did that afternoon. It was wonderful to see his face shining at us out of a thin cloud of these delicate fumes, as he stirred, and mixed, and tasted, and looked as if he were making, instead of punch, a fortune for his family down to the latest posterity." DC 28

And see Tobacco*—post-prandially*

—domestic centrepiece: "Mr Mould was surrounded by his household gods. He was enjoying the sweets of domestic repose, and gazing on them with a calm delight. The day being sultry, and the window open, the legs of Mr Mould were on the window-seat, and his back reclined against the shutter. Over his shining head a handkerchief was drawn, to guard his baldness from the flies. The room was fragrant with the smell of punch, a tumbler of which grateful compound stood upon a small round table, convenient to the hand of Mr Mould; so deftly mixed, that as his eye looked down into the cool transparent drink, another eye, peering brightly from behind the crisp lemon-peel, looked up at him, and twinkled like a star." MC 25

—medically festive: "After dinner, Mr Bob Sawyer ordered in the largest mortar in the shop, and proceeded to brew a reeking jorum of rum-punch therein; stirring up and amalgamating the materials with a pestle in a very creditable and apothecary-like manner. Mr Sawyer, being a bachelor, had only one tumbler in the house, which was assigned to Mr Winkle as a compliment to the visitor; Mr Ben Allen being accommodated with a funnel with a cork in the narrow end; and Bob Sawyer contented himself with one of those wide-lipped crystal vessels inscribed with a variety of cabalistic characters, in which chemists are wont to measure out their liquid drugs in compounding prescriptions. These preliminaries adjusted, the punch was tasted, and pronounced excellent; and it having been arranged that Bob Sawyer and Ben Allen should be considered at liberty to fill twice to Mr Winkle's once, they started fair, with great satisfaction and good-fellowship." PP 38

—at a wake: ". . . [Quilp] descried Mr. Brass seated at the table with pen, ink, and paper, and the case-bottle of rum—his own case-bottle, and his own particular Jamaica—convenient to his hand; with hot water, fragrant lemons, white lump sugar, and all things fitting; from which choice materials, Sampson, by no means insensible to their claims upon his attention, had compounded a mighty glass of punch reeking hot; which he was at that very moment stirring up with a teaspoon, and contemplating with looks in which a faint assumption of sentimental regret struggled but weakly with a bland and comfortable joy." OCS 49

—rabbit pie: "'Such a rabbit pie, Bill,' exclaimed [Charley Bates], disclosing to view a huge pasty; 'sitch delicate creeturs, with sitch tender limbs, Bill, that the wery bones melt in your mouth, and there's no occasion to pick 'em . . . . '" OT 39

—roast pig: "'I don't know how it is, but a fine warm summer day like this, with the birds singing in every direction, always puts me in mind of roast pig, with sage and onion sauce, and made gravy.'

"'That's a curious association of ideas, is it not, mama?'

"'Upon my word, my dear, I don't know,' replied Mrs Nickleby. 'Roast pig; let me see. On the day five weeks after you were christened, we had a roast—no, that couldn't have been a pig, either, because I recollect there were a pair of them to carve, and your poor papa and I could never have thought of sitting down to two pigs—they must have been partridges. Roast pig! I hardly think we ever could have had one . . . for your papa could never bear the sight of them in the shops, and used to say that they always put him in mind of very little babies, only the pigs had much fairer complexions . . . . " NN 41

—roast pork: "' . . . here's your mother been and bought . . . a whole knuckle of a lovely roast leg of pork, with lots of crackling left upon it, and with seasoning gravy and mustard quite unlimited. Hand in your plate, my boy, and begin while it's simmering.'" HM 2

—rum, in shipwreck: "We had nothing else whatever, but half a pint of water each per day, and sometimes, when we were coldest and weakest, a teaspoonful of rum each, served out as a dram. I know how learnedly it can be shown that rum is poison, but I also know that in this case, as in all similar cases I have ever read of—which are numerous—no words can express the comfort and support derived from it. Nor have I the least doubt that it saved the lives of far more than half our number." CS/GM

—salad: "'I know'd she wouldn't have a cowcumber!'

"Mrs Gamp changed colour, and sat down upon the bedstead.

"'Lord bless you, Betsey Prig, your words is true. I quite forgot it!'

"'Mrs Prig, looking steadfastly at her friend, put her hand in her pocket, and with an air of surly triumph drew forth either the oldest of lettuces or youngest of cabbages, but at any rate, a green vegetable of an expansive nature, and of such magnificent proportions that she was obliged to shut it up like an umbrella before she could pull it out. She also produced a handful of mustard and cress, a trifle of the herb called dandelion, three bunches of radishes, an onion rather larger than an average turnip, three substantial slices of beetroot, and a short prong or antler of celery; the whole of this garden-stuff having been publicly exhibited, but a short time before, as a twopenny salad, and purchased by Mrs Prig on condition that the vendor could get it all into her pocket. Which had been happily accomplished, in High Holborn, to the breathless interest of a hackney-coach stand. And she laid so little stress on this surprising forethought, that she did not even smile, but returning her pocket into its accustomed sphere, merely recommended that these productions of nature should be sliced up, for immediate consumption, in plenty of vinegar." MC 49

—sandwich

—an accolade: " . . . crowds of us had sandwiches and ginger-beer at the refreshment-bars established for us in the Theatre. The sandwich—as substantial as was consistent with portability, and as cheap as possible—we hailed as one of our greatest institutions. It forced its way among us at all stages of the entertainment, and we were always delighted to see it; its adaptability to the varying moods of our nature was surprising; we could never weep so comfortably as when our tears fell on our sandwich; we could never laugh so heartily as when we choked with sandwich; Virtue never looked so beautiful or Vice so deformed as when we paused, sandwich in hand, to consider what would come of that resolution of Wickedness in boots, to sever Innocence in flowered chintz from Honest Industry in striped stockings. When the curtain fell for the night, we still fell back upon sandwich, to help us through the rain and mire, and home to bed." UT/TV

—French version: "'Well,' said Our Missis, with dilated nostrils. 'Take a fresh, crisp, long, crusty, penny loaf made of the whitest and best flour. Cut it longwise through the middle. Insert a fair and nicely fitting slice of ham. Tie a smart piece of ribbon round the middle of the whole to bind it together. Add at one end a neat wrapper of clean white paper by which to hold it. And the universal French Refreshment sangwich busts on your disgusted vision'" CS/MJ

—sober realism: " . . . I ask myself the question, What am I to do? How am I to live? Ill fo manger, you know,' says Mr Jobling, pronouncing that word as if he meant a necessary fixture in an English stable. 'Ill fo manger. That's the French saying, and mangering is as necessary to me as it is to a Frenchman. Or more so.'" BH 20

—soup: "From a beetle-haunted kitchen . . . fumes arose, suggestive of a class of soup which Mr Grazinglands knew, from painful experience, enfeebles the mind, distends the stomach, forces itself into the complexion, and tried to ooze out at the eyes." UT/RT

—*stew:* "'It's a stew of tripe,' said the landlord, smacking his lips, 'and cow-heel,' smacking them again, 'and bacon,' smacking them once more, 'and steak,' smacking them for the fourth time, 'and peas, cauliflowers, new potatoes, and sparrow-grass, all working up together in one delicious gravy.' Having come to the climax, he smacked his lips a great many times, and taking a long hearty sniff of the fragrance that was hovering about, put on the cover again with the air of one whose toils on earth were over." OCS 18

Mr Codlin's Heart is Touched OCS

—*surprising chef*

—*devil of mutton (Mr Micawber):* "'If you will allow me to take the liberty of remarking that there are few comestibles better, in their way, than a Devil, and that I believe, with a little division of labour, we could accomplish a good one if the young person in attendance could produce a gridiron, I would put it to you, that this little misfortune may be easily repaired.'

"There was a gridiron in the pantry, on which my morning rasher of bacon was cooked. We had it in, in a twinkling, and immediately applied ourselves to carrying Mr Micawber's idea into effect. The division of labour to which he had referred was this:—Traddles cut the mutton into slices; Mr Micawber (who could do anything of this sort to perfection) covered them with pepper, mustard, salt, and cayenne; I put them on the gridiron, turned them with a fork, and took them off, under Mr Micawber's direction; and Mrs Micawber heated, and continually stirred, some mushroom ketchup in a little saucepan. When we had slices enough done to begin upon, we fell-to, with our sleeves still tucked up at the wrist, more slices sputtering and blazing on the fire, and our attention divided between the mutton on our plates, and the mutton then preparing

"What with the novelty of this cookery, the excellence of it, the bustle of it, the frequent starting up to look after it, the frequent sitting down to dispose of it as the crisp slices came off the gridiron hot and hot, the being so busy, so flushed with the fire, so amused, and in the midst of such a tempting noise and savour, we reduced the leg of mutton to the bone . . . I dare say there never was a greater success." DC 28

—dinner of fowl and sausage (Captain Cuttle): "The Captain had spread the cloth with great care, and was making some egg-sauce in a little saucepan: basting the fowl from time to time during the process with a strong interest, as it turned and browned on a string before the fire. Having propped Florence up with cushions on the sofa . . . the Captain pursued his cooking with extraordinary skill, making hot gravy in a second little saucepan, boiling a handful of potatoes in a third, never forgetting the egg-sauce in the first, and making an impartial round of basting and stirring with the most useful of spoons every minute.

"Besides these cares, the Captain had to keep his eye on a diminutive frying-pan, in which some sausages were hissing and bubbling in a most musical manner; and there was never such a radiant cook as the Captain looked, in the height and heat of these functions: it being impossible to say whether his face or his glazed hat shone the brighter.

"The dinner being at length quite ready, Captain Cuttle dished and served it up, with no less dexterity than he had cooked it. He then dressed for dinner, by taking off his glazed hat and putting on his coat. That done, he wheeled the table close against Florence on the sofa, said grace, unscrewed his hook, screwed his fork into its place, and did the honours of the table." ¶DS 49

—underdone poultry (Reginald Wilfer): "'But what,' said Bella, as she watched the carving of the fowls, 'makes them pink inside, I wonder, Pa! Is it the breed?'

"'No, I don't think it's the breed, my dear,' returned Pa. 'I rather think it is because they are not done.'

"'They ought to be,' said Bella.

"'Yes, I'm aware they ought to be, my dear,' rejoined her father, 'but they—ain't.'

"So the gridiron was put in requisition, and the good-tempered cherub . . . undertook to grill the fowls." OMF iii 4

—sweetbread: "'In yielding up my trust here, I shall not be freed from the necessity of eating the bread of dependence:' [Mrs Sparsit] might have said the sweetbread, for that delicate article in a savoury brown sauce was her favourite supper: 'and I would rather receive it from your hand, than from any other.'" HT i 16

—sycophantic: "Mr Pumblechook helped me to the liver wing, and to the best slice of tongue (none of those out-of-the-way No Thoroughfares of Pork now), and took, comparatively speaking, no care of himself at all. 'Ah! poultry, poultry! You little thought,' said Mr Pumblechook, apostrophising the fowl in the dish, 'when you was a young fledgling, what was in store for you. You little thought you was to be refreshment beneath this humble roof for one as—Call it a weakness, if you will,' said Mr Pumblechook, getting up again, 'but may I? *may* I—[taking Pip by both hands]?'" GE 19

—Tea

—in a caravan: " . . . that it was not an unprovided or destitute caravan was clear from this lady's occupation, which was the very pleasant and refreshing one of taking tea. The tea-things, including a bottle of rather suspicious character and a cold knuckle of ham, were set forth upon a drum, covered with a white napkin; and there, as if at the most convenient round-table in all the world, sat this roving lady, taking her tea and enjoying the prospect." OCS 26

—in a castle: "We returned into the Castle, where we found Miss Skiffins preparing tea. The responsible duty of making the toast was delegated to the Aged, and that excellent old gentleman was so intent upon it that he seemed to be in some danger of melting his eyes. It was no nominal meal that we were going to make, but a vigorous reality. The Aged prepared such a haystack of buttered toast, that I could scarcely see him over it as it simmered on an iron stand hooked on to the top-bar; while Miss Skiffins brewed such a jorum of tea, that the pig in the back premises became strongly excited, and repeatedly expressed his desire to participate in the entertainment." GE 37

—in a hotel: "I rang for the tea, and the waiter . . . brought in by degrees some fifty adjuncts to that refreshment, but of tea not a glimpse. A tea-board, cups and saucers, plates, knives and forks (including carvers), spoons (various), salt-cellars, a meek little muffin confined with the utmost precaution under a strong iron cover, Moses in the bulrushes typified by a soft bit of butter in a quantity of parsley, a pale loaf with a powdered head, two proof impressions of the bars of the kitchen fireplace on triangular bits of bread, and ultimately a fat family urn: which the waiter staggered in with, expressing in his countenance burden and suffering. After a prolonged absence at this stage of the entertainment, he at length

came back with a casket of precious appearance containing twigs. These I steeped in hot water, and so from the whole of these appliances extracted one cup of I don't know what, for Estella." GE 33

—indulged: "'Sammy,' whispered Mr Weller, 'if some o' these here people don't want tappin' to-morrow mornin', I ain't your father, and that's wot it is. Why, this here old lady next me is a drowndin' herself in tea.'

"'Be quiet, can't you?' murmured Sam.

"'Sam,' whispered Mr Weller, a moment afterwards, in a tone of deep agitation, 'mark my vords, my boy. If that 'ere secretary fellow keeps on for only five minutes more, he'll blow hisself up with toast and water.'

"'Well, let him, if he likes,' replied Sam; 'it ain't no bis'ness o' yourn.'

"'If this here lasts much longer, Sammy,' said Mr Weller, in the same low voice, 'I shall feel it my duty, as a human bein', to rise and address the cheer. There's a young 'ooman on the next form but two, as has drunk nine breakfast cups and half: and she's a swellin' wisibly before my wery eyes.'" PP 33

"'Brother,' said Wegg . . . 'I should like to ask you something. You remember the night when I first looked in here, and found you floating your powerful mind in tea?'

"Still swilling tea, Mr Venus nodded assent.

"'And there you sit, sir,' pursued Wegg with an air of thoughtful admiration, 'as if you had never left off! There you sit, sir, as if you had an unlimited capacity of assimilating the fragrant article! There you sit, sir, in the midst of your works, looking as if you'd been called upon for Home, Sweet Home, and was obleeging the company!'" OMF iii 7

—and malediction: "There was no one with Flora but Mr F's Aunt, which respectable gentlewoman, basking in a balmy atmosphere of tea and toast, was ensconced in an easy chair by the fireside, with a little table at her elbow, and a clean white handkerchief spread over her lap on which two pieces of toast at that moment awaited consumption. Bending over a steaming vessel of tea, and looking through the steam, and breathing forth the steam, like a malignant Chinese enchantress engaged in the performance of unholy rites, Mr F's Aunt put down her great teacup and exclaimed, 'Drat him, if he an't come back again!'" LD ii 9

—one for the pot: " . . . one little pot of tea, wherein was infused one little silver scoopful of that herb on behalf of Miss Tox, and one little silver scoopful on behalf of the teapot—a flight of fancy in which good housekeepers delight . . . . " DS 29

—spiritual: "'My little woman,' says Mr Snagsby to the sparrows in Staple Inn, 'likes to have her religion rather sharp, you see!'

"So Guster, much impressed by regarding herself for the time as the handmaid of Chadband, whom she knows to be endowed with the gift of holding forth for four hours at a stretch, prepares the little drawing-room for tea. All the furniture is shaken and dusted, the portraits of Mr and Mrs Snagsby are touched up with a wet cloth, the best tea-service is set forth, and there is excellent provision made of dainty new bread, crusty twists, cool fresh butter, thin slices of ham, tongue and German sausage, and delicate little rows of anchovies nestling in parsley; not to mention new-laid eggs, to be brought up warm in a napkin, and hot buttered toast. For Chadband is rather a consuming vessel—the persecutors say a gorging vessel; and can wield such weapons of the flesh as a knife and fork, remarkably well." BH 19

—stimulated: "As the privileges of the side-table—besides including the small prerogatives of sitting next the toast, and taking two cups of tea to other people's one, and always taking them at a crisis, that is to say, before putting fresh water into the teapot, and after it had been standing for some time—also comprehended a full view of the company, and an opportunity of addressing them as from a rostrum, Mrs. Gamp discharged the functions entrusted to her with extreme good-humour and affability. Sometimes resting her saucer on the palm of her outspread hand, and supporting her elbow on the table, she stopped between her sips of tea to favour the circle with a smile, a wink, a roll of the head, or some other mark of notice; and at those periods her countenance was lighted up with a degree of intelligence and vivacity, which it was almost impossible to separate from the benignant influence of distilled waters." MC 46

—a toast: "'With you. Hob and nob,' returned the sergeant. 'The top of mine to the foot of yours—the foot of yours to the top of

mine—Ring once, ring twice—the best tune on the Musical Glasses! Your health. May you live a thousand years, and never be a worse judge of the right sort than you are at the present moment of your life!'" GE 5

—tripe, to a statistician: "'Come here. What's that? Your dinner?'

"'Yes, sir,' said Trotty [Veck], leaving it behind him in a corner.

"'Don't leave it there,' exclaimed the gentleman [Alderman Cute]. 'Bring it here, bring it here. So! This is your dinner, is it?'

"'Yes sir,' repeated Trotty, looking with a fixed eye and a watery mouth, at the piece of tripe he had reserved for a last delicious tit-bit; which the gentleman was now turning over and over on the end of the fork . . . .

"'This is a description of animal food, Alderman,' said Filer, making little punches in it with a pencil-case, 'commonly known to the labouring population of this country, by the name of tripe . . . .

"'But who eats tripe?' said Mr Filer, looking round. 'Tripe is without an exception the least economical, and the most wasteful article of consumption that the markets of this country can by possibility produce. The loss upon a pound of tripe has been found to be, in the boiling, seven-eights [*sic*..] of a fifth more than the loss upon a pound of any other animal substance whatever. Tripe is more expensive, properly understood, than the hot-house pine-apple. Taking into account the number of animals slaughtered yearly within the bills of mortality alone; and forming a low estimate of the quantity of tripe which the carcases of those animals, reasonably well butchered, would yield; I find that the waste on that amount of tripe, if boiled, would victual a garrison of five hundred men for five months of thirty-one days each, and a February over. The Waste, the Waste!'

"Trotty [Veck] stood aghast, and his legs shook under him. He seemed to have starved a garrison of five hundred men with his own hand.

"'Who eats tripe?' said Mr Filer, warmly. 'Who eats tripe?'

"Trotty made a miserable bow.

"'You do, do you?' said Mr Filer. 'Then I'll tell you something. You snatch your tripe, my friend, out of the mouths of widows and orphans.'

"'I hope not, sir,' said Trotty faintly. 'I'd sooner die of want!'

"'Divide the amount of tripe before-mentioned, Alderman,' said Mr Filer, 'by the estimated number of existing widows and orphans, and the result will be one pennyweight of tripe to each. Not a grain is left for that man. Consequently, he's a robber.'

"Trotty was so shocked, that it gave him no concern to see the Alderman finish the tripe himself. It was a relief to get rid of it, anyhow." C 1

—turkey, for Christmas: "'Here's the Turkey. Hallo! Whoop! How are you! Merry Christmas!'

"It *was* a Turkey! He never could have stood upon his legs, that bird. He would have snapped 'em short off in a minute, like sticks of sealing-wax.

"'Why, it's impossible to carry that to Camden Town,' said Scrooge. 'You must have a cab.'" CC 5

—vegetarian: " . . . an elderly, pimply-faced, vegetable-diet sort of man, in a black coat, dark mixture trousers, and small black gaiters; a kind of being who seemed to be an essential part of the desk at which he was writing, and to have as much thought or sentiment." PP 20

—extreme view: "Mankind can only be regenerated by dining on Vegetables. Why? Certain worthy gentlemen have dined, it seems, on vegetables for ever so many years, and are none the worse for it. Straightway, these excellent men, excited to the highest pitch, announce themselves by public advertisement as 'DISTINGUISHED VEGETARIANS,' vault upon a platform, hold a vegetable festival, and proceed to show, not without prolixity and weak jokes, that a vegetable diet is the only true faith, and that, in eating meat, mankind is wholly mistaken and partially corrupt.

"Distinguished Vegetarians. As the men who wear Nankeen trousers might hold a similar meeting, and become Distinguished Nankeenarians! But am I to have NO meat? If I take a pledge to eat three cauliflowers daily in the cauliflower season, a peck of peas daily in the pea time, a gallon of broad Windsor beans daily when beans are 'in,' and a young cabbage or so every morning before breakfast, with perhaps a little ginger between meals (as a vegetable substance, corrective of that windy diet), may I not be allowed half an ounce of gravy-beef to flavour my potatoes? Not a shred? Distinguished Vegetarians can acknowledge no imperfect animal.

Their Hog must be a Whole Hog, according to the fashion of the time." ¶HW/WH

—wassail: "It was high time to make the Wassail now; therefore I had up the materials (which, together with their proportions and combinations, I must decline to impart, as the only secret of my own I was ever known to keep), and made a glorious jorum. Not in a bowl; for a bowl anywhere but on a shelf is a low superstition, fraught with cooling and slopping; but in a brown earthenware pitcher, tenderly suffocated, when full, with a coarse cloth. It being now upon the stroke of nine, I set out for Watts's Charity, carrying my brown beauty in my arms. I would trust Ben, the waiter, with untold gold; but there are strings in the human heart which must never be sounded by another, and drinks that I make myself are those strings in mine." CS/PT

"Having deposited my brown beauty in a red nook of the hearth, inside the fender, where she soon began to sing like an ethereal cricket, diffusing at the same time odours as of ripe vineyards, spice forests, and orange groves—I say, having stationed my beauty in a place of security and improvement, I introduced myself to my guests by shaking hands all round, and giving them a hearty welcome." CS/PT

—welcome home: "The kitchen fire burnt clear and red, the table was spread out, the kettle boiled; the slippers were there, the boot-jack too, sheets of ham were there, cooking on the gridiron; half-a-dozen eggs were there, poaching in the frying-pan; a plethoric cherry-brandy bottle was there, winking at a foaming jug of beer upon the table; rare provisions were there, dangling from the rafters as if you had only to open your mouth, and something exquisitely ripe and good would be glad of the excuse for tumbling into it. Mrs Lupin, who for [Martin and Mark's] sakes had dislodged the very cook, high priestess of the temple, with her own genial hands was dressing their repast." MC 43

Furniture

—bed

—in debtor's prison: "Mr Weller proceeded to inquire which was the individual bedstead that Mr Roker had so flatteringly described as an out-an-outer to sleep in.

"That's it,' replied Mr Roker, pointing to a very rusty one in a corner. 'It would make any one go to sleep, that bedstead would, whether they wanted to or not.'

"'I should think,' said Sam, eyeing the piece of furniture in question with a look of excessive disgust, 'I should think poppies was nothing to it.'" PP 41

"'Will you allow me to in-quire wy you make up your bed under that 'ere deal table?' said Sam.

"' 'Cause I was always used to a fourposter afore I came here, and I find the legs of the table answer just as well,' replied the cobbler." PP 44

—despotic: "[The bedroom] was a sort of vault on the ground floor at the back, with a despotic monster of a fourpost bedstead in it, straddling over the whole place, putting one of his arbitrary legs into the fireplace, and another into the doorway, and squeezing the wretched little washing-stand in quite a Divinely Righteous manner." GE 45

—dominant: "Mrs Gamp's apartment was not a spacious one, but, to a contented mind, a closet is a palace; and the first-floor front at Mr Sweedlepipe's may have been, in the imagination of Mrs Gamp, a stately pile. If it were not exactly that, to restless intellects, it at least comprised as much accommodation as any person, not sanguine to insanity, could have looked for in a room of its dimensions. For only keep the bedstead always in your mind; and you were safe. That was the grand secret. Remembering the bedstead, you might even stoop to look under the little round table for anything you had dropped, without hurting yourself much against the chest of drawers, or qualifying as a patient of Saint Bartholomew, by falling into the fire.

"Visitors were much assisted in their cautious efforts to preserve an unflagging recollection of this piece of furniture, by its size: which was great. It was not a turn-up bedstead, nor yet a French bedstead, nor yet a four-post bedstead, but what is poetically called a tent: the sacking whereof was low and bulgy, insomuch that Mrs Gamp's box would not go under it, but stopped halfway, in a manner which, while it did violence to the reason, likewise endangered the legs of a stranger. The frame too, which would have supported the canopy and hangings if there had been any, was ornamented with divers pippins carved in timber, which on the slightest provocation, and frequently on none at all, came tumbling down; harassing the peaceful guest with inexplicable terrors.

"The bed itself was decorated with a patchwork quilt of great antiquity; and at the upper end, upon the side nearest to the door, hung a scanty curtain of blue check, which prevented the Zephyrs that were abroad in Kingsgate Street, from visiting Mrs Gamp's head too roughly. Some rusty gowns and other articles of that lady's wardrobe depended from the posts; and these had so adapted themselves by long usage to her figure, that more than one impatient husband coming in precipitately, at about the time of twilight, had been for an instant stricken dumb by the supposed discovery that Mrs Gamp had hanged herself. One gentleman, coming on the usual hasty errand, had said indeed, that they looked like guardian angels 'watching of her in her sleep.' But that, as Mrs Gamp said, 'was his first;' and he never repeated the sentiment, though he often repeated his visit." MC 49

—usual: "When we talk of beds we think of a well-appointed and long-established home—we think of a luxurious room, grown to be an old and dear companion—we think, perhaps, of a number of pretty rooms surrounding it, where we have watched our children sleeping from their cradles upward." S/H

And see Illness and Injury—*hospital bed*

—carpet: " . . . Mrs General was accessible to the valet. That envoy found her on a little square of carpet, so extremely diminutive in reference to the size of her stone and marble floor, that she looked as if she might have had it spread for the trying on of a ready-made pair of shoes; or as if she had come into possession of the enchanted piece of carpet, bought for forty purses by one of the three princes in the Arabian Nights, and had that moment been transported on it, at wish, into a palatial saloon with which it had no connexion." LD ii 5

—convertible bookcase: " . . . [Swiveller] never failed to speak of . . . his rooms, his lodgings, or his chambers, conveying to his hearers a notion of indefinite space, and leaving their imaginations to wander through long suites of lofty halls, at pleasure.

"In this flight of fancy, Mr Swiveller was assisted by a deceptive piece of furniture, in reality a bedstead, but in semblance a bookcase, which occupied a prominent situation in his chamber and seemed to defy suspicion and challenge inquiry. There is no doubt that by day Mr Swiveller firmly believed this secret convenience to be a bookcase and nothing more; that he closed his eyes to the bed, resolutely denied the existence of the blankets, and spurned the bolster from his thoughts. No word of its real use, no hint of its nightly service, no allusion to its peculiar properties, had ever passed between him and his most intimate friends. Implicit faith in the deception was the first article of his creed. To be the friend of Swiveller you must reject all circumstantial evidence, all reason, observation, and experience, and repose a blind belief in the bookcase. It was his pet weakness and he cherished it." OCS 7

—convertible sofa: "How different [from a turn-up bedstead] is the demeanour of a sofa bedstead! Ashamed of its real use, it strives to appear an article of luxury and gentility—an attempt in which it miserably fails. It has neither the respectability of a sofa, nor the virtues of a bed; every man who keeps a sofa bedstead in his house, becomes a party to a wilful and designing fraud—we question whether you could insult him more, than by insinuating that you entertain the least suspicion of its real use." SB/BM

—in a country house: "The furniture, old-fashioned rather than old, like the house, was as pleasantly irregular. Ada's sleeping-room was all flowers—in chintz and paper, in velvet, in needlework, in the brocade of two stiff courtly chairs, which stood, each attended by a little page of a stool for greater state, on either side of the fireplace.

"Our sitting-room was green; and had, framed and glazed, upon the walls, numbers of surprising and surprised birds, staring out of pictures at a real trout in a case, as brown and shining as if it had been served with gravy; at the death of Captain Cook; and at the whole process of preparing tea in China, as depicted by Chinese artists.

"In my room there were oval engravings of the months—ladies haymaking, in short waists, and large hats tied under the chin, for June—smooth-legged noblemen, pointing, with cocked-hats, to village steeples, for October. Half-length portraits, in crayons, abounded all through the house; but were so dispersed that I found the brother of a youthful officer of mine in the china-closet, and the grey old age of my pretty young bride, with a flower in her bodice, in the breakfast-room. As substitutes, I had four angels, of Queen Anne's reign, taking a complacent gentleman to heaven, in festoons, with some difficulty; and a composition in needlework, representing fruit, a kettle, and an alphabet.

"All the movables, from the wardrobes to the chairs and tables, hangings, glasses, even to the pincushions and scent-bottles on the dressing-tables, displayed the same quaint variety. They agreed in nothing but their perfect neatness, their display of the whitest linen, and their storing-up, wheresoever the existence of a drawer, small or large, rendered it possible, of quantities of rose-leaves and sweet lavender." BH 6

—covered: "Within a few hours the cottage furniture began to be wrapped up for preservation in the family absence—or, as Mr Meagles expressed it, the house began to put its hair in papers." LD ii 9

—a debtor's: "[Skimpole's] furniture had been all cleared off, it appeared, by the person who took possession of it on his blue-eyed daughter's birthday; but he seemed quite relieved to think that it was gone. Chairs and tables, he said, were wearisome objects; they were monotonous ideas, they had no variety of expression, they looked you out of countenance, and you looked them out of countenance. How pleasant, then, to be bound to no particular chairs and tables, but to sport like a butterfly among all the furniture on hire, and to flit from rosewood to mahogany, and from mahogany to walnut, and from this shape to that, as the humour took one!" BH 17

—decrepit: " . . . a large garret bed-room. Meagre and spare, like all the other rooms, it was even uglier and grimmer than the rest, by being the place of banishment for the worn-out furniture. Its movables were ugly old chairs with worn-out seats, and ugly old chairs without any seats; a threadbare patternless carpet, a maimed table, a crippled wardrobe, a lean set of fire-irons like the skeleton of a set deceased, a washing-stand that looked as if it had stood for ages in a hail of dirty soapsuds, and a bedstead with four bare atomies of posts, each terminating in a spike, as if for the dismal accommodation of lodgers who might prefer to impale themselves." LD i 3

—at an inn: "It was the grimmest room I have ever had a nightmare in; and all the furniture, from the four posts of the bed to the two old silver candlesticks, was tall, high-shouldered, and spindle-waisted." CS/PT

—kettle

—at first: " . . . the kettle was aggravating and obstinate. It wouldn't allow itself to be adjusted on the top bar; it wouldn't hear of accommodating itself kindly to the knobs of coal; it *would* lean forward with a drunken air, and dribble, a very Idiot of a kettle, on the hearth. It was quarrelsome, and hissed and spluttered morosely at the fire. To sum up all, the lid, resisting Mrs Peerybingle's fingers, first of all turned topsy-turvy, and then, with an ingenious pertinacity deserving of a better cause, dived sideways in—down to the very bottom of the kettle. And the hull of the *Royal George** has never made half the monstrous resistance to coming out of the water, which the lid of that kettle employed against Mrs Peerybingle, before she got it up again.

"It looked sullen and pig-headed enough, even then; carrying its handle with an air of defiance, and cocking its spout pertly and mockingly at Mrs Peerybingle, as if it said, 'I won't boil. Nothing shall induce me!'" CH 1

**Warship which sank in Portsmouth Harbour in 1782; there had been repeated failed attempts to raise her.*

—at last: "Now it was . . . that the kettle began to spend the evening. Now it was that the kettle, growing mellow and musical, began to have irrepressible gurglings in its throat, and to indulge in short vocal snorts, which it checked in the bud, as if it hadn't quite made up its mind yet to be good company. Now it was that after two or three such vain attempts to stifle its convivial sentiments, it threw off all moroseness, all reserve, and burst into a stream of song so cosy and hilarious, as never maudlin nightingale yet formed the least idea of.

" . . . . With its warm breath gushing forth in a light cloud which merrily and gracefully ascended a few feet, then hung about the chimney-corner as its own domestic Heaven, it trolled its song with that strong energy of cheerfulness, that its iron body hummed and stirred upon the fire; and the lid itself, the recently rebellious lid—such is the influence of a bright example—performed a sort of jig, and clattered like a deaf and dumb young cymbal that had never known the use of its twin brother." CH 1

—its song:

"It's a dark night . . . and the rotten leaves are lying by the way;

And, above, all is mist and darkness, and, below, all is mire and clay;

And there's only one relief in all the sad and murky air;

And I don't know that it is one, for it's nothing but a glare;

Of deep and angry crimson, where the sun and wind together;

Set a brand upon the clouds for being guilty of such weather;

And the widest open country is a long dull streak of black;

And there's hoar-frost on the finger-post, and thaw upon the track;

And the ice it isn't water, and the water isn't free;

And you couldn't say that anything is what it ought to be . . . . " CH 1

—mirror: "The chimney-piece was very high, and there was a bad glass—what I may call a wavy glass—above it, which, when I stood up, just showed me my anterior phrenological developments—and these never look well in any subject, cut short off at the eyebrow." CS/HT

"In what had once been a drawing-room, there were a pair of meagre mirrors, with dismal processions of black figures carrying black garlands, walking round the frames; but even these were short of heads and legs, and one undertaker-like Cupid had swung round on his own axis and got upside down, and another had fallen off altogether." LD i 5

—of a miser: "Meagre old chairs and tables, of spare and bony make, and hard and cold as misers' hearts, were ranged in grim array against the gloomy walls; attenuated presses, grown lank and lantern-jawed in guarding the treasures they enclosed, and tottering, as though from constant fear and dread of thieves, shrunk up in dark corners, whence they cast no shadows on the ground, and seemed to hide and cower from observation. A tall grim clock upon the stairs, with long lean hands and famished face, ticked in cautious whispers; and when it struck the time, in thin and piping sounds like an old man's voice, it rattled, as if it were pinched with hunger.

"No fireside couch was there, to invite repose and comfort. Elbow-chairs there were, but they looked uneasy in their minds, cocked their arms suspiciously and timidly, and kept upon their guard. Others were fantastically grim and gaunt, as having drawn themselves up to their utmost height, and put on their fiercest looks to stare all comers out of countenance. Others again knocked up against their neighbours, or leant for support against the wall, somewhat ostentatiously, as if to call all men to witness that they were not worth the taking. The dark square lumbering bedsteads seemed built for restless dreams; the musty hangings to creep in scanty folds together, whispering among themselves, when rustled by the wind, their trembling knowledge of the tempting wares that lurked within the dark and tight-locked closets." NN 51

—old-fashioned: "It came on darker and darker. The old-fashioned furniture of the chamber, which was a kind of hospital for all the invalided movables in the house, grew indistinct and shadowy in its many shapes; chairs and tables, which by day were as honest cripples as need be, assumed a doubtful and mysterious character; and one old leprous screen of faded India leather and gold binding, which had kept out many a cold breath of air in days of yore and shut in many a jolly face, frowned on him with a spectral aspect, and stood at full height in its allotted corner, like some gaunt ghost who waited to be questioned. A portrait opposite the window—a queer, old gray-eyed general, in an oval frame—seemed to wink and doze as the light decayed, and at length, when the last faint glimmering speck of day went out, to shut its eyes in good earnest, and fall sound asleep." BR 31

—an old lawyer's: "Like as he is to look at, so is his apartment in the dusk of the present afternoon. Rusty, out of date, withdrawing from attention, able to afford it. Heavy, broad-backed, old-fashioned mahogany and horsehair chairs, not easily lifted, obsolete tables with spindle legs and dusty baize covers, presentation prints of the holders of great titles in the last generation, or the last but one, environ him. A thick and dingy Turkey carpet muffles the floor where he sits, attended by two candles in old-fashioned silver candlesticks, that give a very insufficient light to his large room. The titles on the backs of his books have retired into the binding; everything that can have a lock has got one; no key is visible." BH 10

—ostentatious plate: "Hideous solidity was the characteristic of the Podsnap plate. Everything was made to look as heavy as it

could, and to take up as much room as possible. Everything said boastfully, 'Here you have as much of me in my ugliness as if I were only lead; but I am so many ounces of precious metal worth so much an ounce;—wouldn't you like to melt me down? A corpulent straddling épergne, blotched all over as if it had broken out in an eruption rather than been ornamented, delivered this address from an unsightly silver platform in the centre of the table. Four silver wine-coolers, each furnished with four staring heads, each head obtrusively carrying a big silver ring in each of its ears, conveyed the sentiment up and down the table, and handed it on to the pot-bellied silver salt-cellars. All the big silver spoons and forks widened the mouths of the company expressly for the purpose of thrusting the sentiment down their throats with every morsel they ate." OMF 11

—*securing possessions:* "What Mrs. Gamp wanted in chairs she made up in bandboxes; of which she had a great collection, devoted to the reception of various miscellaneous valuables, which were not, however, as well protected as the good woman, by a pleasant fiction, seemed to think: for, though every bandbox had a carefully closed lid, not one among them had a bottom: owing to which cause the property within was merely, as it were, extinguished.

"The chest of drawers having been originally made to stand upon the top of another chest, had a dwarfish, elfin look, alone; but in regard of its security it had a great advantage over the bandboxes, for as all the handles had been long ago pulled off, it was very difficult to get at its contents. This indeed was only to be done by one or two devices; either by tilting the whole structure forward until all the drawers fell out together, or by opening them singly with knives, like oysters." ¶MC 49

—*turn-up bedstead:* "A turn-up bedstead is a blunt, honest piece of furniture; it may be slightly disguised with a sham drawer; and sometimes a mad attempt is even made to pass it off for a book-case; ornament it as you will, however, the turn-up bedstead seems to defy disguise, and to insist on having it distinctly understood that he is a turn-up bedstead, and nothing else—that he is indispensably necessary, and that being so useful, he disdains to be ornamental." SB/BM

" . . . so hastily and recently turned up that the blankets were boiling over, as it were, and keeping the lid open . . . . " LD i 9

And see H:Auction, *and* Shop—*second-hand furniture*

Hair

—*'aggerawators':* " . . . [Wilkins's] hair [was] carefully twisted into the outer corner of each eye, till it formed a variety of that description of semi-curls usually known as 'aggerawators.'" SB/EE

—*arranged in abstraction:* "Mr Pancks listened with such interest that . . . [he] occupied his hands during the whole recital in so erecting the loops and hooks of hair all over his head, that he looked, when it came to a conclusion, like a journeyman Hamlet in conversation with his father's spirit." LD ii 13

—*beard in the American West:* "The traveller was an old man with a grey grizzly beard two inches long, a shaggy moustache of the same hue, and enormous eyebrows. . . . On being addressed by one of the party, he drew nearer, and said, rubbing his chin (which scraped under his horny hand like fresh gravel beneath a nailed shoe), that he was from Delaware . . . . " AN 13

—*beard in art:* "'The German taste came up,' said [the model], 'and threw me out of bread. I am ready for the taste now.'

" . . . I saw that the lower part of his face was tied up, in what is commonly called a Belcher handkerchief. He slowly removed this bandage, and exposed to view a long dark beard, curling over his upper lip, twisting about the corners of his mouth, and hanging down upon his breast . . . .

"He made his beard a little jagged with his hands, folded his arms, and said,

"'Severity!'

"I shuddered. It was so severe.

"He made his beard flowing on his breast, and, leaning both hands on the staff of a carpet-broom . . . said:

"'Benevolence.'

"I stood transfixed. The change of sentiment was entirely in the beard. The man might have left his face alone, or had no face. The beard did everything.

"He lay down, on his back, on my table, and with that action of his head threw up his beard at the chin.

"'That's death!' said he.

"'He got off my table and, looking up at the ceiling, cocked his beard a little awry; at the same time making it stick out before him.

"'Adoration, or a vow of vengeance,' he observed.

"He turned his profile to me, making his upper lip very bulky with the upper part of his beard.

"'Romantic character,' said he.

"He looked sideways out of his beard, as if it were an ivy-bush. 'Jealousy,' said he. He gave it an ingenious twist in the air, and informed me that he was carousing. He made it shaggy with his fingers—and it was Despair; lank—and it was avarice; tossed it all kinds of ways—and it was rage. The beard did everything." RP/GA

—before a party: "There was something queer, too, about Mrs Blimber's head at dinner-time, as if she had screwed her hair up too tight; and though Miss Blimber showed a graceful bunch of plaited hair on each temple, she seemed to have her own little curls in paper underneath, and in a play-bill too: for Paul read 'Theatre Royal' over one of her sparkling spectacles, and 'Brighton' over the other." DS 14

" . . . and such a smell of singed hair, that Doctor Blimber sent up the footman with his compliments, and wished to know if the house was on fire. But it was only the hair-dresser curling the young gentlemen, and overheating his tongs in the ardor of business." DS 14

—a desperate resort: "To my unutterable amazement, I now, for the first time, saw Mr Pocket relieve his mind by going through a performance that struck me as very extraordinary . . . . He laid down the carving-knife and fork—being engaged in carving at the moment—put his two hands into his disturbed hair, and appeared to make an extraordinary effort to lift himself up by it. When he had done this, and had not lifted himself up at all, he quietly went on with what he was about." GE 23

—dressing: " . . . [Veneering] finds Twemlow in his lodgings, fresh from the hands of a secret artist who has been doing something to his hair with yolks of eggs. The process requiring that Twemlow shall, for two hours after the application, allow his hair to stick upright and dry gradually, he is in an appropriate state for the receipt of startling intelligence; looking equally like the Monument on Fish Street Hill, and King Priam on a certain incendiary occasion not wholly unknown as a neat point from the classics." OMF ii 3

—on end with terror: "At times, I thought [says Pip], What if the young man who was with so much difficulty restrained from imbruing his hands in me, should yield to a constitutional impatience, or should mistake the time, and should think himself accredited to my heart and liver to-night, instead of to-morrow! If ever anybody's hair stood on end with terror, mine must have done so then. But, perhaps, nobody's ever did?" GE 2

—on the head: "Excellent fellow as I knew Traddles to be, and warmly attached to him as I was, I could not help wishing . . . that he had never contracted the habit of brushing his hair so very upright. It gave him a surprised look—not to say a hearth-broomy kind of expression . . . .

"'I took the liberty of mentioning it to Traddles . . . and saying that if he *would* smooth it down a little—

"'But it won't.'

"'Won't be smoothed down?' said I.

"'No,' said Traddles. 'Nothing will induce it. If I was to carry a half-hundredweight upon it, all the way to Putney, it would be up again the moment the weight was taken off. You have no idea what obstinate hair mine is, Copperfield. I am quite a fretful porcupine.'

"I was a little disappointed, I must confess, but thoroughly charmed by his good-nature too. I told him how I esteemed his good-nature; and said that his hair must have taken all the obstinacy out of his character for *he* had none." DC 41

—moustache: " . . . his tears dropped down on the moustachio which it was a credit to him to have done his best to grow, but it is not in mortals to command success . . . . " CS/GS

—shaving: "Whereas, in almost all the other countries of Europe, more or less of moustache and beard was habitually worn, it came to be established in this speck of an island, as an Insularity from which there was no appeal, that an Englishman, whether he liked it or not, must hew, hack, and rasp his chin and upper lip daily. The inconvenience of this infallible test of British respectability was so widely felt, that fortunes were made by razors, razor-strops, hones, pastes, shaving-soaps, emollients for the soothing of the tortured skin, all sorts of contrivances to lessen the misery of the shaving process and diminish the amount of time it occupied." HW/I

—spiritual connection: " . . . [Doctor Manette] put his hand to his neck, and took off a blackened string with a scrap of folded rag attached to it. He opened this, carefully, on his knee, and it contained a very little quantity of hair; not more than one or two long golden hairs, which he had, in some old day, wound off upon his finger.

"He took [Lucie Manette's] hair into his hand again, and looked closely at it. 'It is the same. How can it be! When was it! How was it!'

"As the concentrating expression returned to his forehead, he seemed to become conscious that it was in hers too. He turned her full to the light and looked at her.

"'She had laid her head upon my shoulder, that night when I was summoned out—she had a fear of my going, though I had none—and when I was brought to the North Tower they found these upon my sleeve. "You will leave me them? They can never help me escape in the body, though they may in the spirit." Those were the words I said. I remember them very well.'" TTC i 6

—straitened circumstances: "'This is another of the consequences of being poor! The idea of a girl with a really fine head of hair, having to do it by one flat candle and a few inches of looking-glass!'" OMF i 4

—in the sun: " . . . whereas [Sissy] was so dark-eyed and dark-haired, that she seemed to receive a deeper and more lustrous colour from the sun, when it shone upon her, the boy [Bitzer] was so light-eyed and light-haired, that the selfsame rays appeared to draw out of him what little colour he ever possessed." HT i 2

—tearing: "With an imprecation Slinkton put his hand to his head, tore out some hair, and flung it to the ground. It was the end of the smooth walk [up his parting]; he destroyed it in the action, and it will soon be seen that his use for it was past." HD

—whiskers

—assumed: "[Poll Sweedlepipe] happened to have been sharpening his razors, which were lying open in a row, while a huge strop dangled from the wall. Glancing at these preparations, Mr Bailey stroked his chin, and a thought appeared to occur . . . .

"'Poll,' he said, 'I ain't as neat as I could wish about the gills. Being here, I may as well have a shave, and get trimmed close.'

"'The barber stood aghast; but Mr Bailey divested himself of his neck-cloth, and sat down in the easy shaving chair with all the dignity and confidence in life. There was no resisting his manner. The evidence of sight and touch became as nothing. His chin was as smooth as a new-laid egg or a scraped Dutch cheese; but Poll Sweedlepipe wouldn't have ventured to deny, on affidavit, that he had the beard of a Jewish rabbi.

"'Go *with* the grain, Poll, all round, please,' said Mr Bailey, screwing up his face for the reception of the lather. 'You may do wot you like with the bits of whisker. I don't care for 'em.'

"The meek little barber stood gazing at him with the brush and soap-dish in his hand, stirring them round and round in a ludicrous uncertainty, as if he were disabled by some fascination from beginning. At last he made a dash at Mr Bailey's cheek. Then he stopped again, as if the ghost of a beard had suddenly receded from his touch; but receiving mild encouragement from Mr Bailey, in the form of an adjuration to 'Go in and win,' he lathered him bountifully. Mr Bailey smiled through the suds in his satisfaction.

"'Gently over the stones, Poll. Go a tiptoe over the pimples!'

"Poll Sweedlepipe obeyed, and scraped the lather off again with particular care. Mr Bailey squinted at every successive dab, as it was deposited on a cloth on his left shoulder, and seemed, with a microscopic eye, to detect some bristles in it; for he murmured more than once, 'Reether redder than I could wish, Poll.' The operation being concluded, Poll fell back and stared at him again, while Mr Bailey, wiping his face on the jack-towel, remarked, 'that arter late hours nothing freshened up a man so much as a easy shave.'" MC 29

—longed-for: "While feeling for the whisker that he anxiously expected, Fledgeby underwent remarkable fluctuations of spirits, ranging along the whole scale from confidence to despair. There were times when he started, as exclaiming, 'By Jupiter, here it is at last!' There were other times when, being equally depressed, he would be seen to shake his head and give up hope. To see him at those periods leaning on a chimneypiece, like as on an urn containing the ashes of his ambition, with the cheek, that would not sprout, upon the hand on which that cheek had forced conviction, was a distressing sight." OMF ii 4

"Fledgeby presented, has the air of going to say something, has the air of going to say nothing, has an air successively of meditation, of resignation, and of desolation . . . and fades into the extreme background, feeling for his whisker, as if it might have turned up since he was there five minutes ago . . . [he] has devoted the interval to taking an observation of Boots's whiskers, Brewer's whiskers, and Lammle's whiskers, and considering which pattern of whisker he would prefer to produce out of himself by friction, if the Genie of the cheek would only answer to his rubbing." OMF ii 16

And see A:Adolescent

—prized: "But what Mr Weevle [Jobling] prizes most, of all his few possessions (next after his light whiskers, for which he has an attachment that only whiskers can awaken in the breast of man). . . . " BH 20

Extremely spiky heads of hair are worn by Jerry Cruncher TTC and Pancks LD; Bunsby DS is especially shaggy.

Homosexuality

—address: "[Mr Wilfer] was shy, and unwilling to own to the name of Reginald, as being too aspiring and self-assertive a name. In his signature he used only the initial R . . . .

"Out of this, the facetious habit had arisen in the neighbourhood surrounding Mincing Lane of making Christian names for him of adjectives and participles beginning with R." OMF i 4

And see LC:Names and naming*—fitting*

—monarch: " . . . [Edward II] seemed to care little or nothing for his beautiful wife; but was wild with impatience to meet Gaveston again.

"When he landed at home, he paid no attention to anybody else, but ran into the favourite's arms before a great concourse of people, and hugged him, and kissed him, and called him his brother . . . the besotted King . . . not only disgusted the Court and the people by his doting folly, but offended his beautiful wife too, who never liked him afterwards." CHE 17

"One night—it was the night of September the twenty-first, one thousand three hundred and twenty-seven—dreadful screams were heard, by the startled people in the neighbouring town, ringing through the thick walls of the Castle . . . . Next morning [Edward] was dead—not bruised, or stabbed, or marked upon the body, but much distorted in the face: and it was whispered afterwards that those two villains, Gournay and Ogle, had burnt up his inside with a red-hot iron." CHE 17

Great for a children's book! History does not confirm the story: Edward may have starved himself, or been starved, to death. Violence has not been completely ruled out.

—in naming: "Sergeant Mith, a smooth-faced man with a fresh bright complexion, and a strange air of simplicity . . . and in a soft, wheedling tone of voice . . . . " RP/DP

A case can be made for Fagin's boys' having an extracurricular function; and Michael Slater pointed out to us CD's adroit suggestion in a boy-child and another, older:

—waiting: "It was clear that there was no such thing as a nightcap to this baby's head, and that even he never went to bed, but was always kept up—and would grow up, kept up—waiting for [sailor] Jack . . . .

" . . . a stout old lady—**Hogarth** drew her exact likeness more than once—and a boy who was carefully writing a copy in a copybook . . . .

"'Why, this is a strange time for this boy to be writing his copy. In the middle of the night!'. . .

" . . . . There she sat, rosily beaming at the copy-book and the boy . . . when we left her in the middle of the night, waiting for Jack." UT/MJ *And see* SB/V Vol. I p65

House

—affinity for bad weather: " . . . its sundial in a little bricked-up corner, where no sun had straggled for a hundred years, but where, in compensation for the sun's neglect, the snow would lie for weeks when it lay nowhere else, and the black east wind would spin like a huge humming-top, when in all other places it was silent and still." HM 1

"The debilitated old house in the city,

wrapped in its mantle of soot, and leaning heavily on the crutches that had partaken of its decay and worn out with it, never knew a healthy or a cheerful interval, let what would betide. If the sun ever touched it, it was but with a ray, and that was gone in half an hour; if the moonlight ever fell upon it, it was only to put a few patches on its doleful cloak, and make it look more wretched. The stars, to be sure, coldly watched it when the nights and the smoke were clear enough; and all bad weather stood by it with a rare fidelity. You should alike find rain, hail, frost, and thaw lingering in that dismal enclosure, when they had vanished from other places; and as to snow, you should see it there for weeks, long after it had changed from yellow to black, slowly weeping away its grimy life. The place had no other adherents." LD i 15

—*alms-house, superannuated:* " . . . those common-place, smoky-fronted London Alms-Houses, with a little paved court-yard in front enclosed by iron railings, which have got snowed up, as it were, by bricks and mortar; which were once in a suburb, but are now in the densely populated town; gaps in the busy life around them, parentheses in the close and blotted texts of the streets." UT/AH *And see* H:Architect

—*ancient:* "[Redlaw's] dwelling was so solitary and vault-like—an old, retired part of an ancient endowment for students, once a brave edifice planted in an open place, but now the obsolete whim of forgotten architects; smoke-age-and-weather-darkened, squeezed on every side by the overgrowing of the great city, and choked, like an old well, with stones and bricks; its small quadrangles, lying down in very pits formed by the streets and buildings, which, in course of time, had been constructed above its heavy chimney stacks; its old trees, insulted by the neighbouring smoke, which deigned to droop so low when it was very feeble and the weather very moody; its grass-plots, struggling with the mildewed earth to be grass, or to win any show of compromise; its silent pavements, unaccustomed to the tread of feet, and even to the observation of eyes . . . . " HM 1

"An old brick house, so dingy as to be all but black, standing by itself within a gateway. Before it, a square court-yard where a shrub or two and a patch of grass were as rank (which is saying much) as the iron railings inclosing them were rusty; behind it, a jumble of roots. It was a double house, with long, narrow, heavily-framed windows. Many years ago it had had it in its mind to slide down sideways; it had been propped up, however, and was leaning on some half-dozen gigantic crutches; which gymnasium for the neighbouring cats, weather-stained, smoke-blackened, and overgrown with weeds, appeared in these latter days to be no very sure reliance." LD i 3

—*renovated:* "Some attempts had been made . . . to infuse new blood into this dwindling frame, by repairing the costly old wood-work here and there with common deal; but it was like the marriage of a reduced old noble to a plebeian pauper, and each party to the ill assorted union shrunk away from the other." DC 50

—*balcony:* "The [Roman] Corso is . . . a street of shops, and palaces, and private houses . . . . There are verandahs and balconies, of all shapes and sizes, to almost every house—not on one story alone, but often to one room or another on every story—put there in general with so little order or regularity, that if, year after year, and season after season, it had rained balconies, hailed balconies, snowed balconies, blown balconies, they could scarcely have come into existence in a more disorderly manner." PI 11

—*bleak, in Chancery:* "'There is, in that city of London there, some property of ours . . . meaning of the Suit's, but I ought to call it the property of Costs; for Costs is the only power on earth that will ever get anything out of it now, or will ever know it for anything but an eyesore and a heartsore. It is a street of perishing blind houses, with their eyes stoned out; without a pane of glass, without so much as a window-frame, with the bare blank shutters tumbling from their hinges and falling asunder; the iron rails peeling away in flakes of rust; the chimneys sinking in; the stone steps to every door (and every door might be Death's Door) turning stagnant green; the very crutches on which the ruins are propped, decaying.'" BH 8

—*chimney:* "In that quarter of London in which Golden Square is situated, there is a bygone, faded, tumble-down street, with two irregular rows of tall meagre houses, which seem to have stared each other out of countenance years ago. The very chimneys appear to have grown dismal and melancholy, from having had nothing better to look at than the chimneys over the way. Their tops are battered, and broken, and blackened with smoke; and, here and there, some taller stack than the rest, inclining heavily to one side and toppling over the roof, seems to meditate taking revenge for half a century's neglect by crushing the inhabitants of the garrets beneath." NN 14

—*clothes lines:* " . . . other houses . . . with poles and lines thrust out of them, on which unsightly linen hung: as if the inhabitants were angling for clothes, and had had some wretched bites not worth attending to." LD i 9 *And see* LC:Fairy-tale—*vision of a defective*

—*country*

—*by day:* " . . . a mighty grim red-brick quadrangle, guarded by stone lions disrespectfully throwing somersaults over the escutcheons of the noble family." UT/T

—*by night:* " . . . I passed before the terrace garden with its fragrant odours, and its broad walks, and its well-kept beds and smooth turf; and I saw how beautiful and grave it was, and how the old stone balustrades and parapets, and wide flights of shallow steps, were seamed by time and weather; and how the trained moss and ivy grew about them, and around the old stone pedestal of the sun-dial; and I heard the fountain falling.

"Then the way went by long lines of dark windows, diversified by turreted towers, and porches, of eccentric shapes, where old stone lions and grotesque monsters bristled outside dens of shadow, and snarled at the evening gloom over the escutcheons they held in their grip. Thence the path wound underneath a gateway, and through a courtyard where the principal entrance was . . . and by the stables where none but deep voices seemed to be, whether in the murmuring of the wind through the strong mass of ivy holding to a high red wall, or in the low complaining of the weathercock, or in the barking of the dogs, or in the slow striking of a clock." ¶BH 36

—*old-fashioned:* " . . . with three peaks in the roof in front, and a circular sweep leading to the porch . . . .

"It was one of those delightfully irregular houses where you go up and down steps out of one room into another, and where you come upon more rooms when you think you have seen all there are, and where there is a bountiful provision of little halls and passages, and where you find still older cottage-rooms in unexpected places, with lattice windows and green growths pressing through them.

"Mine, which we entered first, was of this kind, with an up-and-down roof, that had more corners in it than I ever counted afterwards, and a chimney (there was a wood-fire on the hearth) paved all around with pure white tiles, in every one of which a bright miniature of the fire was blazing. Out of this room, you went down two steps, into a charming little sitting-room, looking down upon a flower-garden, which room was henceforth to belong to Ada [Clare] and me [Esther Summerson]. Out of this you went up three steps, into Ada's bed-room, which had a fine broad window, commanding a beautiful view (we saw a great expanse of darkness lying underneath the stars), to which there was a hollow window-seat, in which, with a spring-lock, three dear Adas might have been lost at once.

"Out of this room, you passed into a little gallery, with which the other best rooms (only two) communicated, and so, by a little staircase of shallow steps, with a number of corner stairs in it, considering its length, down into the hall. But if, instead of going out at Ada's door, you came back into my room, and went out at the door by which you had entered it, and turned up a few crooked steps that branched off in an unexpected manner from the stairs, you lost yourself in passages, with mangles in them, and three-cornered tables, and a Native-Hindoo chair, which was also a sofa, a box, and a bedstead, and looked in every form, something between a bamboo skeleton and a great bird-cage, and had been brought from India nobody knew by whom or when.

"From these, you came on Richard [Carstone]'s room, which was part library, part sitting-room, part bed-room, and seemed indeed a comfortable compound of many rooms. Out of that, you went straight, with a little interval of passage, to the plain room where Mr Jarndyce slept, all the year round, with his window open, his bedstead without any furniture standing in the middle of the floor for more air, and his cold-bath gaping for him in a smaller room adjoining.

"Out of that, you came into another passage, where there were back-stairs, and where you could hear the horses being rubbed down, outside the stable, and being told to Hold up, and Get over, as they slipped about very much on the uneven stones. Or you might, if you came out at another door (every room had at least two doors), go straight down to the hall again by half-a-dozen steps and a low archway, wondering how you got back there, or had ever got out of it . . . .

"Such, with its illuminated windows, softened here and there by shadows of curtains, shining out upon the star-light night; with its light, and warmth, and comfort; with its hospitable jingle, at a distance, of preparations for dinner; with the face of its generous master brightening everything we saw; and just wind enough without to sound a low accompaniment to everything we heard; were our first impressions of Bleak House." BH ¶6 *And see* Furniture—*in a country house*

—*in the rain:* "The waters are out in Lincolnshire. An arch of the bridge in the park has been sapped and sopped away. The adjacent low-lying ground, for a half a mile in breadth, is a stagnant river, with melancholy trees for islands in it, and a surface punctured all over, all day long, with falling rain.

"My Lady Dedlock's 'place' has been extremely dreary. The weather, for many a day and night, has been so wet that the trees seem wet through, and the soft loppings and prunings of the woodman's axe can make no crash or crackle as they fall. The deer, looking soaked, leave quagmires, where they pass. The shot of a rifle loses its sharpness in the moist air, and its smoke moves in a tardy little cloud towards the green rise, coppice-topped, that makes a background for the falling rain.

"The view from my Lady Dedlock's own windows is alternately a lead-coloured view, and a view in Indian ink. The vases on the stone terrace in the foreground catch the rain all day; and the heavy drops fall, drip, drip, drip, upon the broad flagged pavement, called, from old time, the Ghost's Walk, all night. On Sundays, the little church in the park is mouldy; the oaken pulpit breaks out into a cold sweat; and there is a general smell and taste as of the ancient Dedlocks in their graves." ¶BH 2

—*shut up:* "Chesney Wold is shut up, carpets are rolled into great scrolls in corners of comfortless rooms, bright damask does penance in brown holland, carving and gilding puts on mortification, and the Dedlock ancestors retire from the light of day again. Around and around the house the leaves fall thick—but never fast, for they come circling down with a dead lightness that is sombre and slow. Let the gardener sweep and sweep the turf as he will, and press the leaves into full barrows, and wheel them off, still they lie ankle-deep. Howls the shrill wind round Chesney Wold; the sharp rain beats, the windows rattle, and the chimneys growl. Mists hide in the avenues, veil the points of view, and move in funeral-wise across the rising grounds. On all the house there is a cold, blank smell, like the smell of a little church, though something dryer: suggesting that the dead and buried Dedlocks walk there, in the long nights, and leave the flavour of their graves behind them." BH 29

—*in the sun:* "It was a picturesque old house, in a fine park richly wooded. Among the trees, and not far from the residence, [Mr Boythorn] pointed out the spire of the little church of which he had spoken.

"O, the solemn woods over which the light and shadow travelled swiftly, as if Heavenly wings were sweeping on benignant errands, through the summer air; the smooth green slopes, the glittering water, the garden where the flowers were so symmetrically arranged in clusters of the richest colours, how beautiful they looked!

"The house, with gable and chimney, and tower, and turret, and dark doorway, and broad terrace-walk, twining among the balustrades of which, and lying heaped upon the vases, there was one great flush of roses, seemed scarcely real in its light solidity, and in the serene and peaceful hush that rested on all around it.

"To Ada and to me, that, above all, appeared the pervading influence. On everything, house, garden, terrace, green slopes, water, old oaks, fern, moss, woods again, and far away across the openings in the prospect, to the distance lying wide before us with a purple bloom upon it, there seemed to be such undisturbed repose." ¶BH 18

—*underused:* "Thus Chesney Wold. With so much of itself abandoned to darkness and vacancy; with so little change under the summer shining or the wintry lowering; so sombre and motionless always—no flag flying now by day, no rows of lights sparkling by night; with no family to come and go, no visitors to be the souls of pale cold shapes of rooms, no stir of life about it;—passion and pride, even to the stranger's eye, have died away from the place in Lincolnshire, and yielded it to dull repose." BH 66

—cramped: "Arthur Clennam came to a squeezed house, with a ramshackle bowed front, little dingy windows, and a little dark area like a damp waistcoat-pocket, which he found to be number twenty-four, Mews Street, Grosvenor Square . . . .

"The footman . . . said, 'walk in.' It required some judgment to do it without butting the inner hall-door open, and in the consequent mental confusion and physical darkness slipping down the kitchen stairs. The visitor, however, brought himself up safely on the door-mat.

"Still the footman said 'Walk in,' so the visitor followed him . . . . After a skirmish in the narrow passage, occasioned by the footman's opening the door of the dismal dining-room with confidence, finding some one there with consternation, and backing on the visitor with disorder, the visitor was shut up, pending his announcement, in a close back parlour. There he had an opportunity of . . . looking out at a low blinding back wall three feet off, and speculating on the number of Barnacle families within the bills of mortality who lived in such hutches of their own free flunkey choice." LD i 10

—door-knocker

—characteristic: "The various expressions of the human countenance afford a beautiful and interesting study; but there is something in the physiognomy of street-door knockers, almost as characteristic, and nearly as infallible. Whenever we visit a man for the first time, we contemplate the features of his knocker with the greatest curiosity, for we well know, that between the man and his knocker, there will inevitably be a greater or less degree of resemblance and sympathy.

"For instance, there is one description of knocker that used to be common enough, but which is fast passing away—a large round one, with the jolly face of a convivial lion smiling blandly at you, as you twist the sides of your hair into a curl or pull up your shirt-collar while you are waiting for the door to be opened; we never saw that knocker on the door of a churlish man—so far as our experience is concerned, it invariably bespoke hospitality and another bottle.

"No man ever saw this knocker on the door of a small attorney or bill-broker; they always patronise the other lion; a heavy ferocious-looking fellow, with a countenance expressive of savage stupidity—a sort of grand master among the knockers, and a great favourite with the selfish and brutal.

"Then there is a little pert Egyptian knocker, with a long thin face, a pinched-up nose, and a very sharp chin; he is most in vogue with your government-office people, in light drabs and starched cravats; little spare priggish men, who are perfectly satisfied with their own opinions, and consider themselves of paramount importance.

"We were greatly troubled a few years ago, by the innovation of a new kind of knocker, without any face at all, composed of a wreath, depending from a hand or small truncheon. A little trouble and attention, however, enabled us to overcome this difficulty, and to reconcile the new system to our favourite theory. You will invariably find this knocker on the doors of cold and formal people, who always ask you why you *don't* come, and never say *do*.

"Everybody knows the brass knocker is common to suburban villas, and extensive boarding-schools . . . we have recapitulated all the most prominent and strongly-defined species." SB/NN

—haunted: " . . . let any man explain to me, if he can, how it happened that Scrooge, having his key in the lock of the door, saw in the knocker, without its undergoing any intermediate process of change—not a knocker, but Marley's face.

"Marley's face. It was not in impenetrable shadow as the other objects in the yard were, but had a dismal light about it, like a bad lobster in a dark cellar. It was not angry or ferocious, but looked at Scrooge as Marley used to look: with ghostly spectacles turned up on its ghostly forehead. The hair was curiously stirred, as if by breath or hot air; and, though the eyes were wide open, they were perfectly motionless. That, and its livid colour, made it horrible; but its horror seemed to be in spite of the face and beyond its control, rather than a part of its own expression." CC 1

—muffled: " . . . Mr Kenwigs sent out for a pair of the cheapest white kid gloves—those at fourteenpence—and selecting the strongest, which happened to be the right-hand one, walked downstairs with an air of pomp and much excitement, and proceeded to muffle the knob of the street-door knocker therein. Having executed this task with great nicety, Mr Kenwigs pulled the door to, after him, and just stepped across the road to try the effect from the opposite side of the street . . . .

"Now, considered as an abstract circumstance, there was no more obvious cause or reason why Mr Kenwigs should take the trouble of muffling this particular knocker, than there would have been for his muffling the knocker of any nobleman or gentleman resident ten miles off; because, for the greater convenience of the numerous lodgers, the street-door always stood wide open, and the knocker was never used at all . . . .

"But knockers may be muffled for other purposes than those of mere utilitarianism, as, in the present instance, was clearly shown. There are certain polite forms and ceremonies which must be observed in civilised life, or mankind relapse into their original barbarism. No genteel lady was ever yet confined—indeed, no genteel confinement can possibly take place—without the accompanying symbol of a muffled knocker." NN 36

—dull and dead, in Calais: "A dead sort of house, with a dead wall over the way and a dead gateway at the side, where a pendant bell-handle produced two dead tinkles, and a knocker produced a dead, flat, surface-tapping, that seemed not to have depth enough in it to penetrate even the cracked door. However, the door jarred open on a dead sort of spring; and [Clennam] closed it behind him as he entered a dull yard, soon brought to a close at the back by another dead wall, where an attempt had been made to train some creeping shrubs, which were dead; and to make a little fountain in a grotto, which was dry, and to decorate that with a little statue, which was gone." LD ii 20

—factual, in the provinces: "A very regular feature on the face of the country, Stone Lodge was. Not the least disguise toned down or shaded off that uncompromising fact in the landscape. A great square house, with a heavy portico darkening the principal windows, as its master's heavy brows overshadowed his eyes. A calculated, cast up, balanced, and proved house. Six windows on this side of the door, six on that side; a total of twelve in this wing, a total of twelve in the other wing; four-and-twenty carried over to the back wings. A lawn and garden and an infant avenue, all ruled straight like a botanical account-book. Gas and ventilation, drainage and water-service, all of the primest quality. Iron clamps and girders, fireproof from top to bottom; mechanical lifts for the housemaids, with all their brushes and brooms; everything that heart could desire." HT i 3

—fashionable: "Upon that establishment of state, the Merdle establishment in Harley Street, Cavendish Square, there was the shadow of no more common wall than the fronts of other establishments of state on the opposite side of the street. Like unexceptionable Society, the opposing rows of houses in Harley Street were very grim with one another. Indeed, the mansions and their inhabitants were so much alike in that respect, that the people were often to be found drawn up on opposite sides of dinner-tables, in the shade of their own loftiness, staring at the other side of the way with the dulness of the houses.

"Everybody knows how like the street, the two dinner-rows of people who take their stand by the street will be. The expressionless uniform twenty houses, all to be knocked at and rung at in the same form, all approachable by the same dull steps, all fended off by the same pattern of railing, all with the same impracticable fire-escapes, the same inconvenient fixtures in their heads, and everything without exception to be taken at a high valuation—who has not dined with these? The house so drearily out of repair, the occasional bow-window, the stuccoed house, the newly-fronted house, the corner house with nothing but angular rooms, the house with the blinds always down, the house with the hatchment always up, the house where the collector has called for one quarter of an Idea, and found nobody at home—who has not dined with these? The house that nobody will take, and is to be had a bargain—who does not know her? The showy house that was taken for life by the disappointed gentleman, and which does not suit him at all—who is unacquainted with that haunted habitation?" LD i 21

—once: " . . . a house by the Green: a staid old house, where hoops and powder and patches, embroidered coats, rolled stockings, ruffles, and swords, had had their court days many a time . . . .

"A bell with an old voice—which I dare say in its time had often said to the house, Here is the green farthingale, Here is the diamond-hilted sword, Here are the shoes with red heels and the blue solitaire—sounded gravely in the moonlight . . . . " GE 33

—fireplace: "The fireplace was an old one, built by some Dutch merchant long ago, and

paved all round with quaint Dutch tiles, designed to illustrate the Scriptures. There were Cains and Abels, Pharaoh's daughters, Queens of Sheba, Angelic messengers descending through the air on clouds like feather-beds, Abrahams, Belshazzars, Apostles putting off to sea in butter-boats, hundreds of figures . . . . " CC 1

—of a hedonist: "It is not a mansion; it is of no pretensions as to size; but it is beautifully arranged, and tastefully kept. The lawn, the soft, smooth slope, the flower-garden, the clumps of trees where graceful forms of ash and willow are not wanting, the conservatory, the rustic verandah with sweet-smelling creeping plants entwined about the pillars, the simple exterior of the house, the well-ordered offices, though all upon the diminutive scale proper to a mere cottage, bespeak an amount of elegant comfort within, that might serve for a palace.

"This indication is not without warrant; for within it is a house of refinement and luxury. Rich colours, excellently blended, meet the eye at every turn; in the furniture—its proportions admirably devised to suit the shapes and sizes of the small rooms; on the walls; upon the floors; tingeing and subduing the light that comes in through the odd glass doors and windows here and there. There are a few choice prints and pictures too; in quaint nooks and recesses there is no want of books; and there are games of skill and chance set forth on tables—fantastic chessmen, dice, backgammon, cards, and billiards.

"And yet amidst this opulence of comfort, there is something in the general air that is not well. Is it that the carpets and the cushions are too soft and noiseless, so that those who move or repose among them seem to act by stealth? Is it that the prints and pictures do not commemorate great thoughts or deeds, or render nature in the poetry of landscape, hall, or hut, but are of one voluptuous cast—mere shows of form and colour—and no more?

"Is it that the books have all their gold outside, and that the titles of the greater part qualify them to be companions of the prints and pictures? Is it that the completeness and the beauty of the place are here and there belied by an affectation of humility, in some unimportant and inexpensive regard, which is as false as the face of the too truly painted portrait hanging yonder, or its original at breakfast in his easy chair below it? Or is it that, with the daily breath of that original and master of all here, there issues forth some subtle portion of himself, which gives a vague expression of himself to everything about him?" ¶DS 33

—intimidating: "[The Brass and Copper family] lived at Camberwell; in a house so big and fierce, that its mere outside, like the outside of a giant's castle, struck terror into vulgar minds and made bold persons quail. There was a great iron gate; with a great bell, whose handle was in itself a note of admiration; and a great lodge; which, being close to the house, rather spoilt the look out certainly, but made the look-in tremendous. At this entry, a great porter kept constant watch and ward; and when he gave the visitor high leave to pass, he rang a second great bell, responsive to whose note a great footman appeared in due time at the great hall-door, with such great tags upon his liveried shoulder that he was perpetually entangling and hooking himself among the chairs and tables . . . ." MC 9

—kitchen: " . . . a little narrow room—which was very completely and neatly fitted as a kitchen. 'See,' said Eugene [Wrayburn], 'miniature flour-barrel, rolling-pin, spice-box, shelf of brown jars, chopping-board, coffee-mill, dresser elegantly furnished with crockery, saucepans and pans, roasting-jack, a charming kettle, an armoury of dish-covers. The moral influence of these objects, in forming the domestic virtues, may have an immense influence upon me . . . . " OMF ii 5

—little: " . . . a little cracked nutshell of a wooden house, which was, in truth, no better than a pimple on the prominent red-brick nose of Gruff and Tackleton. The premises of Gruff and Tackleton were the great feature of the street; but you might have knocked down Caleb Plummer's dwelling with a hammer or two, and carried off the pieces in a cart.

"If any one had done the dwelling-house of Caleb Plummer the honour to miss it after such an inroad, it would have been, no doubt, to commend its demolition as a vast improvement. It stuck to the premises of Gruff and Tackleton, like a barnacle to a ship's keel, or a snail to a door, or a little bunch of toadstools to the stem of a tree." CH 2

—as metaphor: "It stood in a garden, no doubt as fresh and beautiful in the May of the Year, as Pet now was in the May of her life; and it was defended by a goodly show of handsome trees and spreading ever-

greens, as Pet was by Mr and Mrs Meagles. It was made out of an old brick house, of which a part had been altogether pulled down, and another part had been changed into the present cottage; so there was a hale elderly portion, to represent Mr and Mrs Meagles, and a young picturesque, very pretty portion to represent Pet. There was even the later addition of a conservatory sheltering itself against it, uncertain of hue in its deep-stained glass, and in its more transparent portions flashing to the sun's rays, now like fire and now like harmless water drops; which might have stood for Tattycoram." LD i 16

—modest: "In one of these streets, the cleanest of them all, and on the shady side of the way . . . was a modest building, not very straight, not large, not tall; not bold-faced, with great staring windows, but a shy, blinking house, with a conical roof going up into a peak over its garret window of four small panes of glass, like a cocked hat on the head of an elderly gentleman with one eye. It was not built of brick or lofty stone, but of wood and plaster; it was not planned with a dull and wearisome regard to regularity, for no one window matched the other, or seemed to have the slightest reference to anything besides itself." BR 4

—monocled: "The house-front, is so old and worn, and the brass plate is so shining and staring, that the general result has reminded imaginative strangers of a battered old beau with a large modern eye-glass stuck in his blind eye." MED 3

—old-fashioned, in Canterbury: "At length we stopped before a very old house bulging out over the road; a house with long, low, lattice-windows bulging out still farther, and beams with carved heads on the ends bulging out too, so that I fancied the whole house was leaning forward, trying to see who was passing on the narrow pavement below. It was quite spotless in its cleanliness. The old-fashioned brass knocker on the low arched door, ornamented with carved garlands of fruit and flowers, twinkled like a star; the two stone steps descending to the door were as white as if they had been covered with fair linen; and all the angles and corners, and carvings and mouldings, and quaint little panes of glass, and quainter little windows, though as old as the hills, were as pure as any snow that ever fell upon the hills." DC 15

—palazzo: "We all know what an old palace in or near Genoa is—how time and the sea air have blotted it—how the drapery painted on the outer walls has peeled off in great flakes of plaster—how the lower windows are darkened with rusty bars of iron—how the courtyard is overgrown with grass—how the outer buildings are dilapidated—how the whole pile seems devoted to ruin.

"Our palazzo was one of the true kind. It had been shut up close for months. Months?—years!—it had an earthy smell, like a tomb. The scent of the orange trees on the broad back terrace, and of the lemons ripening on the wall, and of some shrubs that grew around a broken fountain, had got into the house somehow, and had never been able to get out again. There was, in every room, an aged smell, grown faint with confinement. It pined in all the cup-boards and drawers. In the little rooms of communication between great rooms, it was stifling. If you turned a picture . . . there it still was, clinging to the wall behind the frame, like a sort of bat." RD

—back court: " . . . passing out at a great crazy door in the back of the hall, instead of turning the other way, to get into the street again; it bangs behind you, making the dismalest and most lonesome echoes, and you stand in a yard (the yard of the same house) which seems to have been unvisited by human foot, for a hundred years.

"Not a sound disturbs its repose. Not a head, thrust out of any of the grim, dark, jealous windows, within sight, makes the weeds in the cracked pavement faint of heart, by suggesting the possibility of there being hands to grub them up. Opposite to you, is a giant figure carved in stone, reclining, with an urn, upon a lofty piece of artificial rockwork; and out of the urn, dangles the fag end of a leaden pipe, which, once upon a time, poured a small torrent down the rocks. But the eye-sockets of the giant are not drier than this channel is now. He seems to have given his urn, which is nearly upside down, a final tilt; and after crying, like a sepulchral child, 'All gone!' to have lapsed into a stony silence." ¶PI 5

—plural, in Genoa: "The endless details of these rich Palaces: the walls of some of them, within, alive with masterpieces by Vandyke! The great, heavy, stone balconies, one above another, and tier over tier: with here and there, one larger than the rest, towering high up—a huge marble platform; the doorless vestibules, massively barred lower windows, immense public

staircases, thick marble pillars, strong dungeon-like arches, and dreary, dreaming, echoing vaulted chambers . . . the terrace gardens between house and house, with green arches of the vine, and groves of orange-trees, and blushing oleander in full bloom, twenty, thirty, forty feet above the street—the painted halls, mouldering, and blotting, and rotting in the damp corners, and still shining out in beautiful colours and voluptuous designs, where the walls are dry—the faded figures on the outsides of the houses, holding wreaths, and crowns, and flying upward, and downward, and standing in niches, and here and there looking fainter and more feeble than elsewhere, by contrast with some fresh little Cupids, who on a more recently decorated portion of the front, are stretching out what seems to be the semblance of a blanket, but is, indeed, a sun-dial—the steep, steep, up-hill streets of small palaces (but very large palaces for all that), with marble terraces looking down into close by-ways . . . ." PI 5

—of the past: "It was a dreary, silent building, with echoing courtyards, desolated turret-chambers, and whole suites of rooms shut up and mouldering to ruin.

"The terrace-garden, dark with the shades of overhanging trees, had an air of melancholy that was quite oppressive. Great iron gates, disused for many years, and red with rust, drooping on their hinges and overgrown with long rank grass, seemed as though they tried to sink into the ground, and hide their fallen state among the friendly weeds. The fantastic monsters on the walls, green with age and damp, and covered here and there with moss, looked grim and desolate.

"There was a sombre aspect even on that part of the mansion which was inhabited and kept in good repair, that struck the beholder with a sense of sadness; of something forlorn and failing, whence cheerfulness was banished. It would have been difficult to imagine a bright fire blazing in the dull and darkened rooms, or to picture any gaiety of heart or revelry that the frowning walls shut in. It seemed a place where such things had been, but could be no more—the very ghost of a house, haunting the old spot in its old outward form, and that was all." ¶BR 13

—quiet: "[Arthur Clennam] stepped into the sober, silent, air-tight house—one might have fancied it to have been stifled by Mutes in the Eastern manner—and the door, closing again, seemed to shut out sound and motion. The furniture was formal, grave, and quaker-like, but well-kept; and had as prepossessing an aspect as anything, from a human creature to a wooden stool, that is meant for much use and is preserved for little, can ever wear. There was a grave clock, ticking somewhere up the staircase; and there was a songless bird in the same direction, pecking at his cage, as if he were ticking too. The parlour-fire, ticked in the grate. There was only one person on the parlour-hearth, and the loud watch in his pocket ticked audibly." LD i 13

—rooms, deserted: "'Rooms get an awful look about them [said George Rouncewell] when they are fitted up, like these, for one person you are used to see in them, and that person is away under any shadow: let alone being God knows where.'

"He is not far out. As all partings foreshadow the great final one—so, empty rooms, bereft of a familiar presence, mournfully whisper what your room and what mine must one day be. My Lady [Dedlock]'s state has a hollow look, thus gloomy and abandoned; and in the inner apartment . . . the traces of her dresses and her ornaments, even the mirrors accustomed to reflect them when they were a portion of herself, have a desolate and vacant air. Dark and cold as the wintry day is, it is darker and colder in these deserted chambers than in many a hut that will barely exclude the weather; and though the servants heap fires in the grates, and set the couches and the chairs within the warm glass screens that let their ruddy light shoot through to the furthest corners, there is a heavy cloud upon the rooms which no light will dispel." BH 58

—tall: "On either side of [the bagman's uncle], there shot up against the dark sky, tall, gaunt, straggling houses, with time-stained fronts, and windows that seemed to have shared the lot of eyes in mortals, and to have grown dim and sunken with age. Six, seven, eight stories high, were the houses; story piled above story, as children build with cards—throwing their dark shadows over the roughly paved road, and making the dark night darker." PP 49

—town

—dining-room: " . . . Mr Dombey . . . finding no uncongeniality in an air of scant and gloomy state that pervaded the room, in colour a dark brown, with black hatchments of pictures blotching the walls, and twenty-four black chairs, with almost as

many nails in them as so many coffins, waiting like mutes, upon the threshold of the Turkey carpet; and two exhausted negroes holding up two withered branches of candelabra on the sideboard, and a musty smell prevailing as if the ashes of ten thousand dinners were entombed in the sarcophagus below it . . . [he] looked down into the cold depths of the dead sea of mahogany on which the fruit dishes and decanters lay at anchor. . . ." DS 30

—its mistress dead: "It was as blank a house inside as outside. When the funeral was over, Mr Dombey ordered the furniture to be covered up . . . and the rooms to be ungarnished, saving such as he retained for himself on the ground floor. Accordingly, mysterious shapes were made of tables and chairs, heaped together in the middle of rooms, and covered over with great winding-sheets. Bell-handles, window-blinds, and looking-glasses, being papered up in journals, daily and weekly, obtruded fragmentary accounts of deaths and dreadful murders. Every chandelier or lustre, muffled in holland, looked like a monstrous tear depending from the ceiling's eye. Odours, as from vaults and damp places, came out of the chimneys. The dead and buried lady was awful in a picture-frame of ghastly bandages. Every gust of wind that rose, brought eddying round the corner from the neighbourhood mews, some fragments of the straw that had been strewn before the house when she was ill, mildewed remains of which were still cleaving to the neighbourhood; and these, being always drawn by some invisible attraction to the threshold of the dirty house to let immediately opposite, addressed a dismal eloquence to Mr Dombey's windows." DS 3

—neglected: "Florence [Dombey] lived alone in the great dreary house, and day succeeded day, and still she lived alone; and the blank walls looked down upon her with a vacant stare, as if they had a Gorgon-like mind to stare her youth and beauty into stone.

"No magic dwelling-place in magic story, shut up in the heart of a thick wood, was ever more solitary and deserted to the fancy, than was her father's mansion in its grim reality, as it stood lowering on the street: always by night, when lights were shining from neighbouring windows, a blot upon its scanty brightness; always by day, a frown upon its never-smiling face.

"There were not two dragon sentries keeping ward before the gate of this abode, as in magic legend are usually found on duty over the wronged innocence imprisoned; but besides a glowering visage, with its thin lips parted wickedly, that surveyed all comers from above the archway of the door, there was a monstrous fantasy of rusty iron, curling and twisting like a petrifaction of an arbour over the threshold, budding in spikes and corkscrew points, and bearing, one on either side, two ominous extinguishers, that seemed to say, 'Who enter here, leave light behind!'

"There were no talismanic characters engraven on the portal, but the house was now so neglected in appearance, that boys chalked the railings and the pavement—particularly round the corner where the side wall was—and drew ghosts on the stable door; and being sometimes driven off by Mr Towlinson, made portraits of him, in return, with his ears growing out horizontally from under his hat.

"Noise ceased to be, within the shadow of the roof. The brass band that came into the street once a week, in the morning, never brayed a note in at those windows; but all such company, down to a poor little piping organ of weak intellect, with an imbecile party of automaton dancers, waltzing in and out at folding-doors, fell off from it with one accord, and shunned it as a hopeless place.

"The spell upon it was more wasting than the spell that used to set enchanted houses sleeping once upon a time but left their waking freshness unimpaired.

"The passive desolation of disuse was everywhere silently manifest about it. Within doors, curtains, drooping heavily, lost their old folds and shapes, and hung like cumbrous palls. Hecatombs of furniture, still piled and covered up, shrunk like imprisoned and forgotten men, and changed insensibly. Mirrors were dim as with the breath of years. Patterns of carpets faded and became perplexed and faint, like the memory of those years' trifling incidents. Boards, starting at unwonted footsteps, creaked and shook. Keys rusted in the locks of doors.

"Damp started on the walls, and as the stains came out, the pictures seemed to go in and secrete themselves. Mildew and mould began to lurk in closets. Fungus trees grew in corners of the cellars. Dust accumulated, nobody knew whence nor how; spiders, moths, and grubs were heard of every day. An exploratory black-beetle now and then was found immovable upon the stairs, or in an upper room, as wondering how he got there. Rats began to squeak and scuffle in the night time, through dark galleries they mined behind the panelling.

"The dreary magnificence of the state rooms, seen imperfectly by the doubtful light admitted through closed shutters, would have answered well enough for an enchanted abode. Such as the tarnished paws of gilded lions, stealthily put out from beneath their wrappers; the marble lineaments of busts on pedestals, fearfully revealing themselves through veils; the clocks that never told the time, or, if wound up by any chance, told it wrong, and struck unearthly numbers, which are not upon the dial; the accidental tinklings among the pendant lustres, more startling than alarm-bells; the softened sounds and laggard air that made their way among these objects, and a phantom crowd of others, shrouded and hooded, and made spectral of shade.

"But, besides, there was the great staircase, where the lord of the place so rarely set his foot, and by which his little child had gone up to Heaven. There were other staircases and passages where no one went for weeks together; there were two closed rooms associated with dead members of the family, and with whispered recollections of them; and to all the house but Florence, there was a gentle figure moving through the solitude and gloom, that gave to every lifeless thing a touch of present human interest and wonder.

"For Florence lived alone in the deserted house, and day succeeded day, and still she lived alone, and the cold walls looked down upon her with a vacant stare, as if they had a Gorgon-like mind to stare her youth and beauty into stone." ¶DS 23

"In the course of the day too, Arthur [Clennam] looked through the whole house. Dull and dark he found it. The gaunt rooms, deserted for years upon years, seemed to have settled down into a gloomy lethargy from which nothing could rouse them again. The furniture, at once spare and lumbering, hid in the rooms rather than furnished them, and there was no colour in all the house; such colour as had ever been there, had long ago started away on lost sunbeams—got itself absorbed, perhaps, into flowers, butterflies, plumage of birds, precious stones, what not.

"There was no one straight floor, from the foundation to the roof; the ceilings were so fantastically clouded by smoke and dust, that old women might have told fortunes in them better than in grouts of tea; the dead-cold hearths showed no traces of having ever been warmed, but in heaps of soot that had tumbled down the chimneys, and eddied about in little dusky whirlwinds when the doors were opened . . . .

"Down in the cellars, as up in the bed-chambers, old objects that he well remembered were changed by age and decay, but were still in their old places; even to empty beer-casks hoary with cobwebs, and empty wine-bottles with fur and fungus choking up their throats. There, too, among unused bottle-racks and pale slants of light from the yard above, was the strong room stored with old ledgers, which had as musty and corrupt a smell as if they were regularly balanced, in the dead small hours, by a nightly resurrection of old book-keepers." ¶LD 1 5

—uniform: " . . . they were all built on one monotonous pattern, and looked like the early copies of a blundering boy who was learning to make houses, and had not yet got out of his cramped brick-and-mortar pothooks . . . . " DC 27

—unused: "A gloomy house the Bower, with sordid signs on it of having been, through its long existence as Harmony Jail, in miserly holding. Bare of paint, bare of paper on the walls, bare of furniture, bare of experience of human life. Whatever is built by man for man's occupation, must, like natural creations, fulfil the intention of its existence, or soon perish. This old house had wasted more from desuetude than it would have wasted from use, twenty years for one.

"A certain leanness falls upon houses not sufficiently imbued with life (as if they were nourished upon it), which was very noticeable here. The staircase, balustrades, and rails, had a spare look—an air of being denuded to the bone—which the panels of the walls and the jambs of the doors and windows also bore. The scanty moveables partook of it; save for the cleanliness of the place, the dust into which they were all resolving would have lain thick on the floors; and those, both in colour and in grain, were worn like old faces that had kept much alone." OMF i 15

—in Venice: "Notwithstanding that its walls were blotched, as if missionary maps

were bursting out of them to impart geographical knowledge; notwithstanding that its weird furniture was forlornly faded and musty, and that the prevailing Venetian odour of bilge water and an ebb-tide on a weedy shore was very strong; the place was better within than it promised." LD ii 6

—up a yard: "They were a gloomy suite of rooms, in a lowering pile of building up a yard, where it had so little business to be, that one could scarcely help fancying it must have run there when it was a young house, playing at hide-and-seek with other houses, and have forgotten the way out again." CC 1

Hurry

—absence: "Sir Leicester is content enough that the ironmaster should feel that there is no hurry there; there, in that ancient house, rooted in that quiet park, where the ivy and the moss have had time to mature, and the gnarled and warted elms, and the umbrageous oaks, stand deep in the fern and leaves of a hundred years; and where the sun-dial on the terrace has dumbly recorded for centuries that Time, which was as much the property of every Dedlock—while he lasted—as the house and lands. Sir Leicester sits down in an easy-chair, opposing his repose and that of Chesney Wold to the restless flights of ironmasters." BH 28

—illusion: "More is done, or considered to be done—which does as well—by taking cabs, and 'going about,' than the fair Tippins knew of. Many vast vague reputations have been made, solely by taking cabs and going about. This particularly obtains in all Parliamentary affairs. Whether the business in hand be to get a man in, or get a man out, or get a man over, or promote a railway, or jockey a railway, or what else, nothing is understood to be so effectual as scouring nowhere in a violent hurry—in short, as taking cabs and going about." OMF ii 3

—obstacles: "When a man is in a violent hurry to get on, and has a specific object in view, the attainment of which depends on the completion of his journey, the difficulties which interpose themselves in his way appear not only to be innumerable, but to have been called into existence especially for the occasion." SB/WT

Hysterics

—angry: "'Have I lived to this day to be called a fright!' cried Miss Knag, suddenly becoming convulsive, and making an effort to tear her front off . . . .

"'Have I deserved to be called an elderly person?' screamed Miss Knag . . . .

"'I hate her,' cried Miss Knag; 'I detest and hate her. Never let her speak to me again; never let anybody who is a friend of mine speak to her; a slut, a hussy, an impudent artful hussy!' Having denounced the object of her wratch, in these terms, Miss Knag screamed once, hiccupped thrice, gurgled in her throat several times, slumbered, shivered, woke, came to, composed her headdress, and declared herself quite well again." NN 18

"'Like you, you fool! said [Mrs Joe Gargery] to Joe, 'giving holidays to great idle hulkers like that. You are a rich man, upon my life, to waste wages in that way. I wish *I* was his master!'

"'You'd be everybody's master if you durst,' retorted Orlick, with an ill-favoured grin.

"('Let her alone,' said Joe.)

"'I'd be a match for all noodles and all rogues,' returned my sister, beginning to work herself into a mighty rage. 'And I couldn't be a match for the noodles, without being a match for your master, who's the dunderheaded king of the noodles. And I couldn't be a match for the rogues, without being a match for you, who are the blackest-looking and the worst rogue between this and France. Now!'

"'You're a foul shrew, Mother Gargery,' growled the journeyman. 'If that makes a judge of rogues, you ought to be a good 'un.'

"('Let her alone, will you?' said Joe.)

"'What did you say? What did that fellow Orlick say to me, Pip? What did he call me, with my husband standing by? O! O! O! Each of these exclamations was a shriek; and I must remark of my sister, what is equally true of all the violent women I have ever seen, that passion was no excuse for her, because it is undeniable that instead of lapsing into passion, she consciously and deliberately took extraordinary pains to force herself into it, and became blindly furious by regular stages; 'what was the name that he gave me before the base man who swore to defend me? O! Hold me! O!'

"'Ah-h-h! growled the journeyman, between his teeth, 'I''d hold you, if you was my wife. I'd hold you under the pump, and choke it out of you.'

"('I tell you, let her alone,' said Joe.)

"'Oh! To hear him!' cried my sister, with a clap of her hands and a scream together—which was her next stage. 'To hear the names he's giving me! That Orlick! In my own house! Me, a married woman! With my husband standing by! O! O!' Here my sister, after a fit of clappings and screamings, beat her hands upon her bosom and upon her knees, and threw her cap off, and pulled her hair down—which were the last stages on her road to frenzy. Being by this time a perfect Fury and a complete success, she made a dash at the door, which I had fortunately locked." GE 15

—*fainting:* "'Mr Tupman has met with a little accident; that's all.'

"The spinster aunt uttered a piercing scream, burst into an hysteric laugh, and fell backwards in the arms of her nieces.

"'Throw some cold water over her,' said the old gentleman.

"'No, no,' murmured the spinster aunt; 'I am better now. Bella, Emily—a surgeon! Is he wounded?—Is he dead?—Is he—ha, ha, ha!' Here the spinster aunt burst into fit number two, of hysteric laughter interspersed with screams.

"'Calm yourself,' said Mr Tupman . . . . 'Dear, dear madam, calm yourself.'"

"'It is his voice!' exclaimed the spinster aunt; and strong symptoms of fit number three developed themselves forthwith.

"'Do not agitate yourself, I entreat you. . . . I am very little hurt, I assure you'

"'Then you are not dead! ejaculated the hysterical lady. 'Oh, say you are not dead!'

"'Don't be a fool, Rachael,' interposed Mr Wardle, rather more roughly than was quite consistent with the poetic nature of the scene. 'What the devil's the use of his *saying* he isn't dead?'

"'No, no, I am not' . . . ." PP 7

" . . . [Arabella] would most certainly have decamped, and alarmed the house, had not fear fortunately deprived her of the power of moving, and caused her to sink down on a garden seat; which happened by good luck to be near at hand.

"'She's a going' off,' soliloquised Sam in great perplexity. 'Wot a thing it is, as these here young creeturs *will* go a faintin' avay just wen they oughtn't to. Here, young 'ooman, Miss Sawbones, Mrs Vinkle, don't!'

"Whether it was the magic of Mr Winkle's name, or the coolness of the open air, or some recollection of Mr Weller's voice, that revived Arabella, matters not." PP 39

And see A:Matrimony

—*marital politics:* "Mrs Pott . . . uttered a loud shriek, and threw herself at full length on the hearth-rug, screaming, and tapping it with the heels of her shoes, in a manner which could leave no doubt of the propriety of her feelings on the occasion . . . .

"So, as the hysterics were still hovering about, Mr Pott said once more that he would [horsewhip the rival editor]; but Mrs Pott was so overcome at the bare idea of having ever been suspected, that she was half-a-dozen times on the very verge of a relapse, and most unquestionably would have gone off, had it not been for the . . . repeated entreaties for pardon from the conquered Pott; and finally, when that unhappy individual had been frightened and snubbed down to his proper level, Mrs Pott recovered, and they went to breakfast." PP 18

—*protective agitation:* "'My own unnatural mother,' screamed [Lavinia], 'wants to annihilate George! But you shan't be annihilated, George. I'll die first!' . . . . Ma shall destroy me first, and then she'll be contented. Oh, oh, oh! Have I lured George from his happy home to expose him to this? George dear, be free! Leave me, ever dearest George to Ma and to my fate. Give my love to your aunt, George dear, and implore her not to curse the viper that has crossed your path and blighted your existence. Oh, oh, oh!' The young lady, who, hysterically speaking, was only just come of age, and had never gone off yet, here fell into a highly creditable crisis, which, regarded as a first performance, was very successful; Mr Sampson, bending over the body meanwhile, in a state of distraction, which induced him to address Mrs Wilfer in the inconsistent expressions: 'Demon—with the highest respect for you—behold your work!'

" . . . the Irrepressible gradually coming to herself, and asking with wild emotion, 'George dear, are you safe?' and further, 'George love, what has happened? Where is Ma?' Mr Sampson, with words of comfort, raised her prostrate form, and handed her to Mrs Wilfer as if the young lady were something in the nature of refreshments. Mrs Wilfer, with dignity partaking of the refreshments, by kissing her once on the brow (as if accepting an oyster), Miss Lavvy, tottering, returned to the protection of Mr Sampson: to whom she said, 'George dear, I am afraid I have been foolish; but I am still a little weak and giddy; don't let go my hand, George!' And whom she afterwards greatly agitated at intervals, by giving utterance, when least expected to, to a sound between a sob and a bottle of soda-water, that seemed to rend the bosom of her frock." OMF iv 5

—relief: " . . . Barbara—that soft-hearted, gentle, foolish little Barbara—is suddenly missed, and found to be in a swoon by herself in the back parlour, from which swoon she falls into hysterics, and from which hysterics into a swoon again, and is, indeed, so bad, that despite a mortal quantity of vinegar and cold water she is hardly a bit better at last than she was at first." OCS 68

—spousal: "Mrs Snagsby replies by delivering herself a prey to spasms; not an unresisting prey, but a crying and a tearing one, so that Cook's Court re-echoes with her shrieks. Finally, becoming cataleptic, she has to be carried up the narrow staircase like a grand piano. After unspeakable suffering, productive of the utmost consternation, she is pronounced, by expresses from the bedroom, free from pain, though much exhausted; in which state of affairs Mr Snagsby, trampled and crushed in the pianoforte removal, and extremely timid and feeble, ventures to come out from behind the door in the drawing-room." BH 25

—tactical: "Mrs Varden wept, and laughed, and sobbed, and shivered, and hiccoughed, and choaked, and said she knew it was very foolish, but she couldn't help it; and that when she was dead and gone, perhaps they would be sorry for it—which really, under the circumstances, did not appear quite so probable as she seemed to think—with a great deal more to the same effect. In a word, she passed with great decency through all the ceremonies incidental to such occasions; and being supported upstairs, was deposited in a highly spasmodic state on her own bed, where Miss Miggs shortly afterwards flung herself upon the body.

"The philosophy of all this was, that Mrs Varden wanted to go to Chigwell; that she did not want to make any concession or explanation; that she would only go on being implored and entreated so to do; and that she would accept no other terms. Accordingly, after a vast amount of moaning and crying upstairs, and much dampening of foreheads, and vinegaring of temples, and hartshorning of noses, and so forth; and after most pathetic adjurations from Miggs, assisted by warm brandy-and-water not over-weak, and divers other cordials also of a stimulating quality, administered at first in teaspoonsful, and afterwards in increasing doses, and of which Miss Miggs herself partook as a preventive measure (for fainting is infectious); after all these remedies, and many more too numerous to mention, but not to take, had been applied; and many verbal consolations, moral, religious, and miscellaneous, had been superadded thereto, the locksmith humbled himself, and the end was gained." BR 19

Illness and Injury

—apoplexy disregarded: "'If a man don't wrap up,' said the Major, taking in another button of his buff waistcoat, 'he has nothing to fall back upon. But some people *will* die. They *will* do it. Damme, they *will*. They're obstinate. I tell you what, Dombey, it may not be ornamental; it may not be refined; it may be rough and tough; but a little of the genuine old English Bagstock stamina, Sir, would do all the good in the world to the human breed.'

"After imparting this precious piece of information, the Major, who was certainly true-blue, whatever other endowments he may have possessed or wanted, coming within the 'genuine old English' classification, which has never been exactly ascertained, took his lobster-eyes and his apoplexy to the club, and choked there all day." DS 40

—asthma: "'I smoke on srub and water myself,' said Mr Omer, taking up his glass, 'because it's considered softening to the passages, by which this troublesome breath of mine gets into action. But, Lord bless you,' said Mr Omer, huskily, 'it ain't the passages that's out of order! "Give me breath enough," says I to my daughter Minnie, "and *I*'ll find passages, my dear!"'" CD 30

—breathing difficulty: "'Last night, said Sloppy, 'when I was a-turning at the wheel pretty late, the mangle seemed to go like our Johnny's breathing. It began beautiful, then as it went out it shook a little and got unsteady, then as it took the turn to come home it had a rattle-like and lumbered a bit, then it come smooth, and so it went on till I scarce know'd which was mangle and which was Our Johnny. Nor Our Johnny, he scarce know'd either, for sometimes when the mangle lumbers he says, 'Me choking, Granny!' and Mrs Higden holds him up, in her lap and says to me, 'Bide a bit, Sloppy,'

and we all stops together. And when Our Johnny gets his breathing again, I turns again, and we all goes on together.'" OMF ii 9

—childhood: "'Indeed,' said Mrs Nickleby, 'I don't think [Kate] ever was better, since she had the hooping-cough, scarlet fever and measles, all at the same time, and that's the fact.'" NN 26

"Every tooth was a break-neck fence, and every pimple in the measles a stone-wall to [little Paul Dombey]. He was down in every fit of the whooping-cough, and rolled upon and crushed by a whole field of small diseases, that came trooping on each other's heels to prevent his getting up again. Some bird of prey got into his throat instead of the thrush; and the very chickens, turning ferocious—if they have anything to do with that infant malady to which they lend their name—worried him like tiger-cats." DS 8

—cold: "'I had a cold once,' said Mrs Nickleby. 'I think it was in the year eighteen hundred and seventeen . . . that I thought I never should get rid of; actually and seriously that I thought I should never get rid of; I was only cured at last by a remedy that I don't know whether you ever happened to hear of, Mr Pluck. You have a gallon of water as hot as you can possibly bear it, with a pound of salt and six pen'orth of the finest bran, and sit with your head in it for twenty minutes every night just before going to bed; at least, I don't mean your head—your feet. It's a most extraordinary cure—a most extraordinary cure. I used it for the first time, I recollect, the day after Christmas Day, and by the middle of April following the cold was gone. It seems quite a miracle, when you come to think of it, for I had it ever since the beginning of September.'"

"'What an afflicting calamity!' said Mr Pyke.

"'Perfectly horrid!' exclaimed Mr Pluck.

"'But it's worth the pain of hearing, only to know that Mrs Nickleby recovered it, isn't it, Pluck?' cried Mr Pyke.

"'That is the circumstance which gives it such a thrilling interest,' replied Mr Pluck." NN 27

—crippled boy: "' . . . no one seems to care much for the poor sickly cripple. I have asked him, very often, if I can do nothing for him; his answer is always the same, "Nothing." His voice is growing weak of late, but I can *see* that he makes the old reply. He can't leave his bed now, so they have moved it close beside the window, and there he lies all day; now looking at the sky, and now at his flowers, which he still makes shift to trim and water, with his own thin hands. At night, when he sees my candle, he draws back his curtain, and leaves it so, till I am in bed. It seems such company to him to know that I am there, that I often sit at my window for an hour or more, that he may see that I am still awake; and sometimes I get up in the night to look at the dull melancholy light in his little room, and wonder whether he is awake or sleeping.

"'The night will not be long coming,' said Tim, 'when he will sleep, and never wake again on earth. We have never so much as shaken hands in all our lives, and yet I shall miss him like an old friend.'" NN 40

—disorientation: "'Not at all well, Louisa. Very faint and giddy.'

"'Are you in pain, dear mother?'

"'I think there's a pain somewhere in the room,' said Mrs Gradgrind, 'but I couldn't positively say that I have got it.'" HT ii 9

—fever: "The worm does not his work more surely on the dead body, than does this slow creeping fire upon the living frame." OT 12

"Tossing to and fro upon his hot, uneasy bed; tormented by a fierce thirst which nothing could appease; unable to find, in any change of posture, a moment's peace or ease; and rambling for ever through deserts of thought where there was no resting-place, no sight or sound suggestive of refreshment or repose, nothing but a dull eternal weariness, with no change but the restless shiftings of his miserable body, and the weary wanderings of his mind, constant still to one ever-present anxiety—to a sense of something left undone, of some fearful obstacle to be surmounted, of some carking care that would not be driven away and haunted the distempered brain, now in this form, now in that—always shadowy and dim, but recognisable for the same phantom in every shape it took, darkening every vision like an evil conscience, and making slumber horrible; in these slow tortures of his dread disease, the unfortunate Richard [Swiveller] lay wasting and consuming inch by inch, until at last, when he seemed to fight and struggle to rise up, and to be held down by devils, he sunk into a deep sleep, and dreamed no more." OCS 44

"That I had a fever and was avoided,

that I suffered greatly, that I often lost my reason, that the time seemed interminable, that I confounded impossible existences with my own identity; that I was a brick in the house wall, and yet entreating to be released from the giddy place where the builders had set me; that I was a steel beam of a vast engine, clashing and whirling over a gulf, and yet that I implored in my own person to have the engine stopped, and my part in it hammered off; that I passed through these phases of disease, I know of my own remembrance, and did in some sort know at the time. That I sometimes struggled with real people, in the belief that they were murderers, and that I would all at once comprehend that they meant to do me good, and would then sink exhausted in their arms, and suffer them to lay me down, I also knew at the time." GE 57

—hospital bed: "The hospital bed is a poor little frame of iron, some four feet wide, in a great bare ward the patients never saw before—a little space not much larger than a grave, in a long perspective of unrest and pain.

"But to the body stretched upon that little bed, come the ready hand, the soothing touch, the knowledge that can relieve pain within that suffering body; and to the softened mind within it come, at the best time, the words of the Great Friend of the sick in body, and the sick in spirit, who never raised His hand upon earth except to heal." S/H

—restless night: "Oh weary, weary hour! Oh, haggard mind, groping darkly through the past; incapable of detaching itself from the miserable present; dragging its heavy chain of care through imaginary feasts and revels, and scenes of awful pomp; seeking but a moment's rest among the long-forgotten haunts of childhood, and the resorts of yesterday; and dimly finding fear and horror everywhere! Oh, weary, weary hour! What were the wanderings of Cain, to these!

"Still, without a moment's interval, the burning head tossed to and fro. Still, from time to time, fatigue, impatience, suffering, and surprise, found utterance upon that rack, and plainly too, though never once in words. At length, in the solemn hour of midnight, he began to talk; waiting awfully for answers sometimes; as though invisible companions were about his bed; and so replying to their speech and questioning again." MC 25

—gout

—aristocratic: "Even Sir Leicester's gallantry has some trouble to keep pace with [Lady Dedlock]. It would have more, but that his other faithful ally, for better and for worse—the gout—darts into the old oak bedchamber at Chesney Wold, and grips him by both legs.

"Sir Leicester receives the gout as a troublesome demon, but still a demon of the patrician order. All the Dedlocks, in the direct male line, through a course of time during and beyond which the memory of man goeth not to the contrary, have had the gout. It can be proved, sir. Other men's fathers may have died of the rheumatism, or may have taken base contagion from the tainted blood of the sick vulgar, but the Dedlock family have communicated something exclusive, even to the levelling process of dying, by dying of their own family gout. It has come down, through the illustrious line, like the plate, or the pictures, or the place in Lincolnshire. It is among their dignities. Sir Leicester is, perhaps, not wholly without an impression, though he has never resolved it into words, that the angel of death in the discharge of his necessary duties may observe to the shades of the aristocracy, 'My lords and gentlemen, I have the honour to present to you another Dedlock certified to have arrived per the family gout.'" BH 16

—hallucination: "In falling ill, I seemed to have crossed a dark lake, and to have left all my experiences, mingled together by the great distance, on the healthy shore . . . .

" . . . I am almost afraid to hint at that time in my disorder—it seemed one long night, but I believe there were both nights and days in it—when I laboured up colossal staircases, ever striving to reach the top, and ever turned, as I have seen a worm in a garden path, by some obstruction, and labouring again . . . .

"Dare I hint at that worse time when, strung together somewhere in great black space, there was a flaming necklace, or ring, or starry circle of some kind, of which *I* was one of the beads! And when my only prayer was to be taken off from the rest, and when it was such inexplicable agony and misery to be a part of the dreadful thing?" BH 35

—head injury: "In the act of turning his eyes gratefully towards his friend, [Eugene Wrayburn] wandered away. His eyes stood still, and settled into that former intent unmeaning stare.

"Hours and hours, days and nights, he remained in this same condition. There were times when he would calmly speak to his friend after a long period of unconsciousness, and would say he was better, and would ask for something. Before it could be given him, he would be gone again . . . .

"The one word, Lizzie, he muttered millions of times. In a certain phase of his distressful state, which was the worst to those who tended him, he would roll his head upon the pillow, incessantly repeating the name in a hurried and impatient manner, with the misery of a disturbed mind, and the monotony of a machine. Equally, when he lay still and staring, he would repeat it for hours without cessation, but then, always in a tone of subdued warning and horror. Her presence and her touch upon his breast or face would often stop this, and then they learned to expect that he would for some time remain still, with his eyes closed, and that he would be conscious on opening them. But the heavy disappointment of their hope—revived by the welcome silence of the room—was, that his spirit would glide away again and be lost, in the moment of their joy that it was there.

"This frequent rising of a drowning man from the deep, to sink again, was dreadful to the beholders. But gradually the change stole upon him that it became dreadful to himself. His desire to impart something that was on his mind, his unspeakable yearning to have speech with his friend and make a communication to him, so troubled him when he recovered consciousness, that its term was thereby shortened. As the man rising from the deep would disappear the sooner for fighting with the water, so he in his desperate struggle went down again." OMF iv 10

—*rheumatism:* "'You will excuse her infirmities [said John Chester]? If she were in a more elevated station of society, she would be gouty. Being but a hewer of wood and drawer of water, she is rheumatic.'" BR 26

"'I've got a touch of the Tombatism on me, Mr Jasper, but that I must expect.'

"'You mean the Rheumatism', says Sapsea, in a sharp tone . . . .

"'No, I don't. I mean, Mr Sapsea, the Tombatism. It's another sort of Rheumatism. Mr Jasper knows what Durdles means. You get among them Tombs afore it's well light on a winter morning, and keep on, as the Catechism says, a-walking in the same all the days of your life, and *you*'ll know what Durdles means.'" MED 4

—*smallpox:* "Mr Sloppy . . . proceeded to remark that he thought Johnny 'must have took 'em from the Minders.' Being asked what he meant, he answered, them that come out upon him and partickler his chest. Being requested to explain himself, he stated that there was some of 'em wot you couldn't kiver with a sixpence. Pressed to fall back upon a nominative case, he opined that they wos about as red as ever red could be. 'But as long as they strikes out'ards, sir,' continued Sloppy, 'they ain't so much. It's their striking in'ards that's to be kep off.'" OMF ii 9

—*antivenereal effect:* "I could hardly have believed that anybody could in a moment have turned so red, or changed so much, as Mr Guppy did when I now put up my veil . . . I am sure I never saw such faltering, such confusion, such amazement and apprehension . . . .

"Something seemed to rise in his throat that he could not possibly swallow. He put his hand there, coughed, made faces, tried again to swallow it, coughed again, made faces again, looked all round the room, and fluttered his papers . . . .

"' . . . . I regret that my arrangements in life, combined with circumstances over which I have no control, will put it out of my power ever to fall back upon that offer, or to renew it in any shape or form whatever; but it will ever be a retrospect entwined—er—with friendship's bowers.'" BH 38

—*starvation:* "In [the hospital's] seven-and-thirty beds I saw but little beauty, for starvation in the second or third generation takes a pinched look; but I saw the sufferings both of infancy and childhood tenderly assuaged; I heard the little patients answering to pet, playful names; the light touch of a delicate lady laid bare the wasted sticks of arms for me to pity; and the claw-like little hands, as she did so, twined themselves lovingly around her wedding-ring." UT/SE

And see Body—*stomach, empty*

—*stroke:* "Cleopatra was arrayed in full dress, with the diamonds, short sleeves, rouge, curls, teeth, and other juvenility all complete; but Paralysis was not to be deceived, had known her for the object of its errand, and had struck her at her glass, where she lay like a horrible doll that had tumbled down.

"They took her to pieces in very shame, and put the little of her that was real on a bed. Doctors were sent for, and soon came. Powerful remedies were resorted to; opinions given that she would rally from this shock, but would not survive another; and there she lay speechless, and staring at the ceiling for days; sometimes making inarticulate sounds in answer to such questions as did she know who were present, and the like: sometimes giving no reply either by sign or gesture, or in her unwinking eyes." DS 37

—tuberculosis: "There is a dread disease which so prepares its victim, as it were, for death; which so refines it of its grosser aspect, and throws around familiar looks unearthly indications of the coming change—a dread disease, in which the struggle between soul and body is so gradual, quiet, and solemn, and the result so sure, that day by day and grain by grain, the mortal part wastes and withers away, so that the spirit grows slight and sanguine with its lightening load and feeling immortality at hand, deems it but a new term of mortal life—a disease in which death and life are so strangely blended, that death takes the glow and hue of life, and life the gaunt and grisly form of death—a disease which medicine never cured, wealth warded off, or poverty could boast exemption from—which sometimes moves in giant strides, and sometimes at a tardy sluggish pace, but, slow or quick, is ever sure and certain." NN 49

—withheld from officialdom: "To conceal herself in sickness, like a lower animal; to creep out of sight and coil herself away, and die; had become [Mrs Higden's] instinct. To catch up in her arms the sick child who was dear to her, and hide it as if it were a criminal, and keep off all ministration but such as her own ignorant tenderness and patience could supply, had become this woman's idea of maternal love, fidelity, and duty. The shameful accounts we read, every week in the Christian year, my Lords and Gentlemen and Honourable Boards, the infamous records of small official inhumanity, do not pass by the people as they pass by us. And hence these irrational, blind, and obstinate prejudices, so astonishing to our magnificence, and having no more reason in them—God save the Queen and confound their politics—no, than smoke has in coming from fire!" OMF ii 9

Fanny Cleaver OMF, Tiny Tim Cratchit CC, Master Humphrey MHC and Phoebe CS/MJ are notable named cripples. There are 15 named invalids and nine patients in Index VII, *and 21 patients in* Index VIII.

Illumination

—candle: "'*There's* a blessed-looking candle!' says Tony, pointing to the heavily burning taper on his table with a great cabbage head and a long winding-sheet.

"'That's easily improved,' Mr Guppy observed, as he takes the snuffers in hand.

"'*Is* it?' returns his friend. 'Not so easily as you think. It has been smouldering like that, ever since it was lighted.'" BH 32

"As I stood idle by Mr Jaggers's fire, its rising and falling flame made the two casts on the shelf look as if they were playing a diabolical game at bo-peep with me; while the pair of coarse fat office candles that dimly lighted Mr Jaggers as he wrote in a corner, were decorated with dirty winding-sheets, as if in remembrance of a host of hanged clients." GE 48

"The wretched candle burns down; the woman takes its expiring end between her fingers, lights another at it, crams the guttering, frying morsel deep into the candlestick, and rams it home with the new candle, as if she were loading some ill-savoured and unseemly weapon of witchcraft." MED 23

—friction match: "Durdles has lighted his lantern, by drawing from the cold hard wall a spark of that mysterious fire which lurks in everything . . . . " MED 12

—gaslight: "Gas looming through the fog in divers places in the streets, much as the sun may, from the spongy fields, be seen to loom by husband-man and ploughboy. Most of the shops lighted two hours before their time—as the gas seems to know, for it has a haggard and unwilling look." BH 1

And see LC:Adages—*cutting off your nose*

—rushlight: "As I had asked for a night-light, the chamberlain had brought me in, before he left me, the good old constitutional rush-light of those virtuous days—an object like the ghost of a walking-cane, which instantly broke its back if it were touched, which nothing could ever be lighted at, and which was placed in solitary confinement at the bottom of a high tin tower, perforated with round holes that made a staringly wide-awake pattern on the walls. When I had got into bed, and lay there, footsore, weary, and wretched, I found that I could no more close my own eyes than I could close

the eyes of this foolish Argus. And thus, in the gloom and death of the night, we stared at one another." GE 45

—whale oil: "Here and there a weak little iron hoop, through which bold boys aspire to throw their friends' caps (its only present use) retains its place among the rusty foliage, sacred to the memory of departed oil. Nay, even oil itself, yet lingering at long intervals in a little absurd glass pot, with a knob in the bottom like an oyster, blinks and sulks at newer lights every night, like its high and dry master in the House of Lords." BH 48

Miser and miserliness

—comforts provided: "Business, as may be readily supposed, was the main thing in this establishment; insomuch indeed that it shouldered comfort out of doors, and jostled the domestic arrangements at every turn. Thus in the miserable bedrooms there were files of moth-eaten letters hanging up against the walls; and linen rollers, and fragments of old patterns, and odds and ends of spoiled goods, strewed upon the ground; while the meagre bedsteads, washing-stands, and scraps of carpet, were huddled away into corners as objects of secondary consideration, not to be thought of but as disagreeable necessities, furnishing no profit, and intruding on the one affair of life.

"The single sitting-room was on the same principle, a chaos of boxes and old papers, and had more counting-house stools in it than chairs: not to mention a great monster of a desk straddling over the middle of the floor, and an iron safe sunk into the wall above the fire-place. The solitary little table for purposes of refection and social enjoyment, bore as fair a proportion to the desk and other business furniture, as the graces and harmless relaxations of life had ever done, in the persons of the old man [Anthony Chuzzlewit] and his son [Jonas], in their pursuit of wealth." MC 11

—home: "In an old house, dismal, dark and dusty, which seemed to have withered, like himself, and to have grown yellow and shrivelled in hoarding him from the light of day, as he had in hoarding his money, lived Arthur Gride." NN 51 *See* Furniture*—of a miser.*

—miser summarized

—in adjectives: " . . . a squeezing, wrenching, grasping, scraping, clutching, covetous, old sinner!" CC 1

—in nouns: "' . . . he's a leech in his dispositions, he's a screw and a wice in his actions, a snake in his twistings, and a lobster in his claws.'" BH 34

—money-lender: "' . . . when that young fellow [Fledgeby]'s interest is concerned, he holds as tight as a horse-leech. When money is in question with that fellow, he is a match for the Devil . . . . He has no quality of youth in him . . . . Touch him upon money, and you touch no booby then. He really is a dolt, I suppose, in other things; but it answers his own purpose very well.'" OMF ii 4

"Whether this young gentleman [Fledgeby] (for he was but three-and-twenty) combined with the miserly vice of an old man, any of the open-handed vices of a young one, was a moot point; so very honourably did he keep his own counsel.

"He was sensible of the value of appearances as an investment, and liked to dress well; but he drove a bargain for every moveable about him, from the coat on his back to the china on his breakfast-table; and every bargain, by representing somebody's ruin or somebody's loss, acquired a peculiar charm for him.

"It was a part of his avarice to take, within narrow bounds, long odds at races; if he won, he drove harder bargains; if he lost, he half starved himself until next time.

"Why money should be so precious to an Ass too dull and mean to exchange it for any other satisfaction, is strange; but there is no animal so sure to get laden with it, as the Ass who sees nothing written on the face of the earth and sky but the three letters L. S. D.—not Luxury, Sensuality, Dissoluteness, which they often stand for, but the three dry letters. Your concentrated fox is seldom comparable to your concentrated Ass in money-breeding." ¶OMF ii 5

—parsimony in entertaining: "Mr Jonas [Chuzzlewit] inquired in the first instance if [Charity and Mercy Pecksniff] were good walkers, and being answered, 'Yes,' submitted their pedestrian powers to a pretty severe test; for he showed them as many sights, in the way of bridges, churches, streets, outsides of theatres, and other free spectacles, in that one forenoon, as most people see in a twelvemonth. It was observable in this gentleman, that he had an insurmountable distaste to the insides of buildings; and that he was perfectly acquainted with the merits of all shows, in re-

spect of which there was any charge for admission, which it seemed were every one detestable, and of the very lowest grade of merit." MC 11

—*a saving grace:* This fine young man [Jonas Chuzzlewit] had all the inclination to be a profligate of the first water, and only lacked the one good trait in the common catalogue of debauched vices—open-handedness—to be a notable vagabond. But there his griping and penurious habits stepped in; and as one poison will sometimes neutralise another, when wholesome remedies would not avail, so he was restrained by a bad passion from quaffing his full measure of evil, when virtue might have sought to hold him back in vain." MC 11

Barkis DC, Chill CS/PR, Gride NN, Scrooge CC and Joshua Smallweed BH are fine specimens. Boffin OMF fakes the role convincingly. And see Index VII.

Money and Finance

—*acquisitiveness:* "The education of Mr. Jonas had been conducted from his cradle on the strictest principles of the main chance. The very first word he learnt to spell was 'gain' and the second (when he got into two syllables), 'money.'" MC 8

"All his life long, [Mr Pecksniff] had been walking up and down the narrow ways and by-places, with a hook in one hand and a crook in the other, scraping all sorts of valuable odds and ends into his pouch. Now, there being a special Providence in the fall of a sparrow, it follows (so Mr Pecksniff would have reasoned), that there must also be a special Providence in the alighting of the stone, or stick, or other substance which is aimed at the sparrow. And Mr Pecksniff's hook, or crook, having invariably knocked the sparrow on the head and brought him down, that gentleman may have been led to consider himself as specially licensed to bag sparrows, and as being specially seised and possessed of all the birds he had got together." MC 20

—*avarice*

—*effect:* "[G]old conjures up a mist about a man more destructive of all his old senses and lulling to his feelings than the fumes of charcoal . . . " NN 1

"'Before my eyes [Mr Boffin] grows suspicious, capricious, hard, tyrannical, unjust. If ever a good man were ruined by good fortune, it is my benefactor. And yet, Pa [said Bella Wilfer], think how terrible the fascination of money is! I see this, and hate this, and dread this, and don't know but that money might make a much worse change in me. And yet I have money always in my thoughts and my desires; and the whole life I place before myself is money, money, money, and what money can make of life!'" OMF iii 4

—*a raven's comment:* "[**Buffon**] finds us Ravens to be most extraordinary creatures. We have properties so remarkable, that you'd hardly believe it. 'A piece of money, a teaspoon, or a ring,' he says, 'are always tempting baits to our avarice. These we will slily seize upon; and, if not watched, carry to our favourite hole.' How odd!

"Did you ever hear of a place called California? *I* have. I understand there are a number of animals over there, from all parts of the world, turning up the ground with their bills, grubbing under the water, sickening, moulting, living in want and fear, starving, dying, tumbling over on their backs, murdering one another, and all for what? Pieces of money that they want to carry to their favourite holes. Ravens every one of 'em! Not a man among 'em, bless you!" HW/R 1

—*bankruptcy*

—*cause:* "The sea had ebbed and flowed, through a whole year. Through a whole year, the winds and clouds had come and gone; the ceaseless work of Time had been performed, in storm and sunshine. Through a whole year, the tides of human chance and change had set in their allotted courses.

"Through a whole year, the famous house of Dombey and Son had fought a fight for life, against cross accidents, doubtful rumours, unsuccessful ventures, unpropitious times, and most of all, against the infatuation of its head, who would not contract its enterprises by a hair's breadth, and would not listen to a word of warning that the ship he strained so hard against the storm, was weak, and could not bear it.

"The year was out, and the great house was down." DS 58

—*embarrassment:* "To Major Bagstock, the bankruptcy was quite a calamity. The major was not a sympathetic character—his attention being wholly concentrated on J. B.—nor was he a man subject to lively emotions, except in the physical regards of gasping and choking. But he had so paraded his friend Dombey at the club; had so flourished him at the heads of the members in general, and so put them down by continual assertion of his riches; that the club, being but human, was delighted to retort upon the major, by asking him, with a show of great concern, whether this tremendous smash had been at all expected, and how his friend Dombey bore it.

"To such questions, the major, waxing very purple, would reply that it was a bad world, sir, altogether; that Joey knew a thing or two, but had been done, sir, done like an infant; that if you had foretold this, sir, to J. Bagstock, when he went abroad with Dombey and was chasing that vagabond up and down France, J. Bagstock would have pooh-pooh'd you—would have pooh-pooh'd you, sir, by the Lord!

"That Joe had been deceived, sir, taken in, hoodwinked, blindfolded, but was broad awake again and staring; insomuch, sir, that if Joe's father were to rise up from the grave to-morrow, he wouldn't trust the old blade with a penny piece, but would tell him that his son Josh was too old a soldier to be done again, sir. That he was a suspicious, crabbed, cranky, used-up, J. B. infidel, sir; and that if it were consistent with the dignity of a rough and tough old major, of the old school, who had had the honour of being personally known to, and commended by, their late Royal Highnesses the Dukes of Kent and York, to retire to a tub and live in it, by Gad sir, he'd have a tub in Pall Mall to-morrow, to show his contempt for mankind!

"Of all this, and many variations of the same tune, the major would deliver himself with so many apoplectic symptoms, such rollings of his head, and such violent growls of ill usage and resentment, that the younger members of the club surmised he had invested money in his friend Dombey's house, and lost it; though the old soldiers and deeper dogs, who knew Joe better, wouldn't hear of such a thing.

"The unfortunate Native, expressing no opinion, suffered dreadfully; not merely in his moral feelings, which were regularly fusilladed by the major every hour in the day, and riddled through and through, but in his sensitiveness to bodily knocks and bumps, which was kept continually on the stretch. For six entire weeks after the bankruptcy, this miserable foreigner lived in a rainy season of boot-jacks and brushes." ¶DS 58

—professional gusto: "Mr Rugg's enjoyment of embarrassed affairs was like a housekeeper's enjoyment in pickling and preserving, or a washerwoman's enjoyment of a heavy wash, or a dustman's enjoyment of an overflowing dust-bin, or any other professional enjoyment of a mess in the way of business." LD ii 28

—resented by the holier: "The world was very busy now, in sooth, and had a deal to say. It was an innocently credulous and a much ill-used world. It was a world in which there was no other sort of bankruptcy whatever. There were no conspicuous people in it, trading far and wide on rotten banks of religion, patriotism, virtue, honour. There was no amount worth mentioning of mere paper in circulation, on which anybody lived pretty handsomely, promising to pay great sums of goodness with no effects. There were no shortcomings anywhere, in anything but money. The world was very angry indeed; and the people especially, who, in a worse world, might have been supposed to be bankrupt traders themselves in shows and pretences, were observed to be mightily indignant." DS 58

—sale preparation: "The [Dombey] house stands, large and weather-proof, in the long dull street; but it is a ruin, and the rats fly from it.

"The men in the carpet caps go on tumbling the furniture about; and the gentlemen with the pens and ink make out inventories of it, and sit upon pieces of furniture never made to be sat upon, and eat bread and cheese from the public-house on other pieces of furniture never made to be eaten on, and seem to have a delight in appropriating precious articles to strange uses.

"Chaotic combinations of furniture also take place. Mattresses and bedding appear in the dining-room; the glass and china get into the conservatory; the great dinner service is set out in heaps on the long divan in the large drawing-room; and the stair-wires, made into fasces, decorate the marble chimney pieces. Finally, a rug, with a printed bill upon it, is hung out from the balcony; and a similar appendage graces either side of the hall door.

"Then, all day long, there is a retinue of mouldy gigs and chaise-carts in the street; and herds of shabby vampires, Jew and Christian, over-run the house, sounding the plate-glass mirrors with their knuckles, striking discordant octaves on the Grand Piano, drawing wet forefingers over the pictures, breathing on the blades of the best dinner-knives, punching the squabs of chairs and sofas with their dirty fists, touzling the feather beds, opening and shutting all the drawers, balancing the silver spoons and forks, looking into the very threads of the drapery and linen, and disparaging everything.

"There is not a secret place in the whole house. Fluffy and snuffy strangers stare into the kitchen-range as curiously as into the attic clothes-press. Stout men with napless hats on, look out of the bedroom windows, and cut jokes with friends in the street. Quiet, calculating spirits withdraw into the dressing-rooms with catalogues, and make marginal notes thereon, with stumps of pencils. Two brokers invade the very fire-escape, and take a panoramic survey of the neighbourhood from the top of the house. The swarm and buzz, and going up and down, endure for days. The Capital Modern Household Furniture &c, is on view." ¶DS 59

—*sale proper:* "Then there is a palisade of tables made in the best drawing-room; and on the capital, french-polished, extending, telescopic range of Spanish mahogany dining-tables with turned legs, the pulpit of the auctioneer is erected; and the herds of shabby vampires, Jew and Christian, the strangers fluffy and snuffy, and the stout men with the napless hats, congregate about it and sit upon everything within reach, mantel-pieces included, and begin to bid. Hot, humming, and dusty are the rooms all day; and—high above the heat, hum, and dust—the head and shoulders, voice and hammer, of the auctioneer, are ever at work. The men in the carpet caps get flustered and vicious with tumbling the lots about, and still the lots are going, going, gone; still coming on. Sometimes there is joking and a general roar. This lasts all day and three days following. The Capital Modern Household Furniture, &c, is on sale." DS 59

—*sale removal:* "Then the mouldy gigs and chaise-carts reappear; and with them come spring-vans and waggons, and an army of porters with knots. All day long, the men with carpet caps are screwing at screw-drivers and bed-winches, or staggering by the dozen together on the staircase under heavy burdens, or upheaving perfect rocks of Spanish mahogany, best rosewood, or plate-glass, into the gigs and chaise-carts, vans and waggons. All sorts of vehicles of burden are in attendance, from a tilted waggon to a wheelbarrow. Poor Paul's little bedstead is carried off in a donkey-tandem. For nearly a whole week, the Capital Modern Household furniture, &c, is in course of removal.

"At last it is all gone. Nothing is left about the house but scattered leaves of catalogues, littered scraps of straw and hay, and a battery of pewter pots behind the hall-door. The men with the carpet caps gather up their screw-drivers and bed-winches into bags, shoulder them, and walk off. One of the pen-and-ink gentlemen goes over the house as a last attention; sticking up bills in the windows respecting the lease of this desirable family mansion, and shutting the shutters. At length he follows the men with the carpet caps. None of the invaders remain. The house is a ruin, and the rats fly from it." ¶DS 59

—*upper class:* "The Bank had foreclosed a mortgage effected on the property . . . by one of the Coketown magnates, who, in his determination to make a shorter cut than usual to an enormous fortune, overspeculated himself by about two hundred thousand pounds. These accidents did sometimes happen in the best regulated families of Coketown, but the bankrupts had no connexion whatever with the improvident classes." HT ii 7

—*its burden:* "'For the same reason that I am not a hoarder of money,' said [old Martin Chuzzlewit], 'I am not lavish of it. Some people find their gratification in storing it up: and others theirs in parting with it; but I have no gratification connected with the thing. Pain and bitterness are the only goods it ever could procure for me. I hate it. It is a spectre walking before me through the world, and making every social pleasure hideous.'" MC 3

—*for charity:* " . . . when men had to deal with the large sums of money so often contributed with such ready hands, and with such unlimited generosity, towards the relief of distress—and oftentimes, mayhap, of misery—it became more than ever essential to be assured that such money was faithfully expended, and not diverted into other channels than those for which it was legitimately designed. In any other case, though flowing knee-deep with all the cardinal virtues, and chin-deep with all the gentilities and respectabilities, and with all the red and blue books that were ever published, it would but be like the unhappy man on whom a verdict was delivered, 'found drowned'." S/A4

—crash: " . . . the Bank was broken, the other model structures of straw had taken fire and were turned to smoke. The admired piratical ship had blown up, in the midst of a vast fleet of ships of all rates, and boats of all sizes; and on the deep was nothing but ruin: nothing but burning hulls, bursting magazines, great guns self-exploded tearing friends and neighbours to pieces, drowning men clinging to unseaworthy spars and going down every minute, spent swimmers floating dead, and sharks." LD ii 26

—the burned: "' . . . the human bees will swarm to the beating of any old tin kettle; in that fact lies the complete manual of governing them. When they can be got to believe that the kettle is made of the precious metals, in that fact lies the whole power of men like our late lamented [Merdle]'" LD ii 28 *And see* F:Fraud—*the gulled*

—effect on people: "At every small deprivation or discomfort which presented itself . . . to remind her of her straitened and altered circumstances, peevish visions of her dower of one thousand pounds had arisen before Mrs Nickleby's mind, until, at last, she had come to persuade herself that of all her late husband's creditors she was the worst used and the most to be pitied. And yet, she had loved him dearly for many years, and had no greater share of selfishness than is the usual lot of mortals. Such is the irritability of sudden poverty." NN 10

—and the dead: "'Has a dead man any use for money [said Gaffer Hexam]? Is it possible for a dead man to have money? What world does a dead man belong to? T'other world. What world does money belong to? This world. How can money be a corpse's? Can a corpse own it, want it, spend it, claim it, miss it?'" OMF i 1

—discounting bills: "'It is to melt some scraps of dirty paper into bright, shining, chinking, tinkling, demd mint sauce.'" NN 34

—dreamt of: "'As I walk along [said Barnaby], I try to find, among the grass and moss, some of that small money for which [my mother] works so hard and used to shed so many tears. As I lie asleep in the shade, I dream of it—dream of digging it up in heaps; and spying it out, hidden under bushes; and seeing it sparkle, as the dew-drops do, among the leaves.'" BR 46

—and dust: "'[Harmon] grew rich as a Dust Contractor, and lived in a hollow in a hilly country entirely composed of Dust. On his own small estate the growling old vagabond threw up his own mountain range, like an old volcano, and its geological formation was Dust. Coal-dust, vegetable-dust, bone-dust, crockery dust, rough dust, and sifted dust—all manner of Dust.'" OMF 2

—and duty: " . . . if every man drawn in a conscription paid a fine instead of going for a soldier, the country in which that happened would have no defenders . . . . Money is great, but it is not omnipotent. All the Money that could be piled up between this and the moon would not fill the place of one little grain of duty." HW/SD

—empty purse: "Joe [Willet] bought a roll, and reduced his purse to the condition (with a difference) of that celebrated purse of *Fortunatus,* which, whatever were its favoured owner's necessities, had one unvarying amount in it. In these real times, when all the Fairies are dead and buried, there are still a great many purses which possess that quality. The sum-total they contain is expressed in arithmetic by a circle, and whether it be added to or multiplied by its own amount, the result of the problem is more easily stated than any known in figures." BR 31

—how defined? "'Papa! what's money?'

"The abrupt question had such immediate reference to the subject of Mr Dombey's thoughts, that Mr Dombey was quite disconcerted.

"'What is money, Paul?' he answered. 'Money?'

"'Yes,' said the child, laying his hands upon the elbows of his little chair, and turning the old face up towards Mr Dombey's; 'what is money?'

"Mr Dombey was in a difficulty. He would have liked to give him some explanation involving the terms circulating-medium, currency, depreciation of currency, paper, bullion, rates of exchange, value of precious metals in the market, and so forth; but looking down at the little chair, and seeing what a long way down it was, he answered: 'Gold, and silver, and copper. Guineas, shillings, half-pence. You know what they are?'

"'Oh, yes, I know what they are,' said Paul. 'I don't mean that, Papa. I mean what's money after all?'

"Heaven and Earth, how old his face was as he turned it up again towards his father's!

"'What is money after all!' said Mr Dombey, backing his chair a little, that he might the better gaze in sheer amazement at the presumptuous atom that propounded such an inquiry.

"'I mean, Papa, what can it do?' . . .

"Mr Dombey . . . expounded to him how that money, though a very potent spirit, never to be disparaged on any account whatever, could not keep people alive whose time was come to die; and how that we must all die, unfortunately, even in the City, though we were never so rich. But how that money caused us to be honoured, feared, respected, courted, and admired, and made us powerful and glorious in the eyes of all men; and how that it could, very often, even keep off death, for a long time together . . . . And how it could do all, that could be done." DS 8

—independent income: "'My own small income (I devoutly wish that my grandfather had left it to the Ocean rather than to me!) has been an effective Something, in the way of preventing me from turning to at Anything. And I think yours has been much the same [said Mortimer Lightwood].'

"'There spake the voice of wisdom,' said Eugene [Wrayburn]. 'We are shepherds both. In turning to at last, we turn to in earnest. Let us say no more of that, for a few years to come.'" OMF iv 16

See also S:Happiness—*defined*

"Alfred [Starling] is a young fellow who pretends to be 'fast' (another word for loose, as I understand the term), but who is much too good and sensible for that nonsense, and who would have distinguished himself before now, if his father had not unfortunately left him a small independence of two hundred a year, on the strength of which his only occupation in life has been to spend six. I am in hopes, however, that his Banker may break, or that he may enter into some speculation guaranteed to pay twenty percent.; for, I am convinced that if he could only be ruined, his fortune is made." CS/HH 1

—innocence, purported: "'He's a queer bird, is Harold,' said Mr Bucket, eyeing me with great expression.

"'He is a singular character,' said I.

"'No idea of money,' observed Mr Bucket.—'He takes it though!' . . .

"'Then says [Skimpole], lifting up his eyebrows in the gayest way, "it's no use mentioning a fypunnote to me, my friend, because I'm a mere child in such matters, and have no idea of money." Of course I understood what his taking it so easy meant; and being now quite sure he was the man for me, I wrapped the note round a little stone and threw it up to him. Well! He laughs and beams, and looks as innocent as you like, and says, "But I don't know the value of these things. What am I to *do* with this?" "Spend it, sir," says I. "But I shall be taken in," he says, "they won't give me the right change, I shall lose it, it's no use to me." Lord, you never saw such a face as he carried it with! . . .

"' . . . . Now, Miss Summerson, I'll give you a piece of advice that your husband will find useful when you are happily married and have got a family about you. Whenever a person says to you that they are as innocent as can be in all concerning money, look well after your own money, for they are dead certain to collar it, if they can. Whenever a person proclaims to you "In worldly matters I'm a child," you consider that that person is only a-crying off from being held accountable, and that you have got that person's number, and it's Number One. Now, I am not a poetical man myself . . . but I'm a practical one, and that's my experience. So's this rule. Fast and loose in one thing, Fast and loose in everything. I never knew it to fail.'" BH 57

—investment

—illiquid: "'You've got *some* money, haven't you?' whispered the Captain.

"'Yes, yes—oh yes—I've got some,' returned old Sol, first putting his hands into his empty pockets, and then squeezing his Welsh wig between them, as if he thought he might wring some gold out of it; 'but I—the little I have got, isn't convertible, Ned; it can't be got at. I have been trying to do something with it for Wally, and I'm old fashioned, and behind the time. It's here and there, and—and, in short, it's as good as nowhere,' said the old man, looking in bewilderment about him.

"He has so much the air of a half-witted person who had been hiding his money in a variety of places, and had forgotten where, that the Captain followed his eyes, not without a faint hope that he might remember some few hundred pounds concealed up the chimney, or down in the cellar. But Solomon Gills knew better than that." DS 9

"' . . . some of our lost ships, freighted with gold, have come home, truly,' returns old Sol, laughing. 'Small craft, Mr Toots, but serviceable to my boy!'" DS 62

—speculative: "Speculation is a round game; the players see little or nothing of their cards at first starting; gains *may* be great—and so may losses. The run of luck went against Mr Nickleby. A mania prevailed, a bubble burst, four stockbrokers took villa residences at Florence, four hundred nobodies were ruined, and among them Mr Nickleby." NN 1

"This narrow thoroughfare . . . is Wall Street: the Stock Exchange and Lombard Street of New York. Many a rapid fortune has been made in this street, and many a no less rapid ruin. Some of these very merchants whom you see hanging about here now, have locked up money in their strong-boxes, like the man in the Arabian Nights, and opening them again, have found but withered leaves." AN 6

"'Well! Then, Betsey had to look about her, for a new investment. She thought she was wiser, now, than her man of business [Mr Wickfield], who was not such a good man of business by this time, as he used to be—I am alluding to your father, Agnes—and she took it into her head to lay it out for herself. So she took her pigs,' said my aunt, 'to a foreign market; and a very bad market it turned out to be. First, she lost in the mining way, and then she lost in the diving way—fishing up treasure, or some such *Tom Tidler* [*sic.*] nonsense,' explained my aunt, rubbing her nose; 'and then she lost in the mining way again, and, last of all, to set the thing entirely to rights, she lost in the banking way. I don't know what the Bank shares were worth for a little while,' said my aunt; 'cent per cent was the lowest of it, I believe; but the Bank was at the other end of the world, and tumbled into space, for what I know; anyhow, it fell to pieces, and never will and never can pay sixpence; and Betsey's sixpences were all there, and there's an end of them.'" DC 35

—its power: "'In other hands, I have known money do good; in other hands I have known it triumphed in, and boasted of, with reason, as the master-key to all the brazen gates that close upon the paths to worldly honour, fortune, and enjoyment.'" MC 3

—reduced circumstances

—cast out: "'A curse,' [Geoffrey Haredale] muttered, 'upon the wretched state of us proud beggars, from whom the poor and rich are equally at a distance; the one being forced to treat us with a show of cold respect, the other condescending to us in their every deed and word, and keeping more aloof, the nearer they approach us." BR 25

—ostentatious: "'Thank you very much, Sir,' that discreet lady observed, 'but pray do not let My comfort be a consideration. Anything will do for Me.'

"It soon appeared that if Mrs Sparsit had a failing in her association with that [Bounderby] domestic establishment, it was that she was so excessively regardless of herself and regardful of others, as to be a nuisance. On being shown her chamber, she was so dreadfully sensible of its comforts as to suggest the inference that she would have preferred to pass the night on the mangle in the laundry.

"True, the Powlers and the Scadgerses were accustomed to splendour, 'but it is my duty to remember,' Mrs Sparsit was fond of observing with a lofty grace: particularly when any of the domestics were present, 'that what I was, I am no longer. Indeed,' said she, 'if I could altogether cancel the remembrance that Mr Sparsit was a Powler, or that I myself am related to the Scadgers family; or if I could even revoke the fact, and make myself a person of common descent and ordinary connexions; I would gladly do so. I should think it, under existing circumstances, right to do so.'

"The same Hermitical state of mind led to her renunciation of made dishes and wines at dinner, until fairly commanded by Mr Bounderby to take them; when she said, 'Indeed you are very good, Sir;' and departed from a resolution of which she had made rather formal and public announcement, to 'wait for the simple mutton.' She was likewise deeply apologetic for wanting the salt; and, feeling amiably bound to bear out Mr Bounderby to the fullest extent in the testimony he had borne to her nerves, occasionally sat back in her chair and silently wept; at which periods a tear of large dimensions, like a crystal earring, might be observed (or rather, must be, for it insisted on public notice) sliding down her Roman nose." ¶HT ii 8

—riches a curse: "'The curse of my existence [said old Martin Chuzzlewit], and the realisation of my own mad desire, is that by the golden standard which I bear about me, I am doomed to try the metal of all other men, and find it false and hollow . . . I have

gone, a rich man, among people of all grades and kinds; relatives, friends, and strangers; among people in whom, when I was poor, I had confidence, and justly, for they never once deceived me then, or, to me, wronged each other. But I have never found one nature, no, not one, in which, being wealthy and alone, I was not forced to detect the latent corruption that lay hid within it, waiting for such as I to bring it forth.

"'Treachery, deceit, and low design; hatred of competitors, real or fancied, for my favour; meanness, falsehood, baseness, and servility; or . . . an assumption of honest independence, almost worse than all; these are the beauties which my wealth has brought to light. Brother against brother, child against parent, friends treading in the faces of friends, this is the social company by whom my way has been attended.

"'There are stories told—they may be true or false—of rich men who, in the garb of poverty, have found out virtue and rewarded it. They were dolts and idiots for their pains. They should have made the search in their own characters. They should have shown themselves fit objects to be robbed and preyed upon and plotted against and adulated by any knaves, who, but for joy, would have spat upon their coffins when they died their dupes; and then their search would have ended as mine has done, and they would be what I am.'" ¶MC 3

—a philosophic view: "'I will not deny,' said Mrs Gamp with meekness, 'that I am but a poor woman, and that the money is a object; but do not let that act upon you, Mr Mould. Rich folks may ride on camels, but it ain't so easy for 'em to see out of a needle's eye. That is my comfort, and I hope I knows it.'" MC 25

—stock market

—denizens: "There were friends who seemed to be always coming and going across the Channel, on errands about the Bourse, and Greek and Spanish and India and Mexican and par and premium and discount and three quarters and seven eighths. There were other friends who seemed to be always lolling and lounging in and out of the City, on questions of the Bourse, and Greek and Spanish and India and Mexican and par and premium and discount and three quarters and seven eighths.

"They were all feverish, boastful, and indefinably loose; and they all ate and drank a great deal; and made bets in eating and drinking. They all spoke of sums of money, and only mentioned the sums and left the money to be understood; as 'five and forty thousand Tom,' or 'Two hundred and twenty-two on every individual share in the lot Joe.'

"They seemed to divide the world into two classes of people; people who were making enormous fortunes, and people who were being enormously ruined. They were always in a hurry, and yet seemed to have nothing tangible to do; except a few of them (these, mostly asthmatic and thick-lipped) who were for ever demonstrating to the rest, with gold pencil-cases which they could hardly hold because of the big rings on their forefingers, how money was to be made.

"Lastly, they all swore at their grooms, and the grooms were not quite as respectful or complete as other men's grooms; seeming somehow to fall short of the groom point as their masters fell short of the gentleman point." ¶OMF ii 4

—shares: "The mature young gentleman is a gentleman of property. He invests his property. He goes, in a condescending amateurish way, into the City, attends meetings of Directors, and has to do with traffic in Shares.

"As is well known to the wise in their generation, traffic in Shares is the one thing to have to do with in this world. Have no antecedents, no established character, no cultivation, no ideas, no manners; have Shares. Have Shares enough to be on Boards of Direction in capital letters, oscillate on mysterious business between London and Paris, and be great.

"Where does he come from? Shares. Where is he going to? Shares. What are his tastes? Shares. Has he any principles? Shares. What squeezes him into Parliament? Shares. Perhaps he never of himself achieved success in anything, never originated anything, never produced anything! Sufficient answer to all; Shares. O mighty Shares!

"To set those blaring images so high, and to cause us smaller vermin, as under the influence of henbane or opium, to cry out night and day, 'Relieve us of our money, scatter it for us, buy us and sell us, ruin us, only we beseech ye take rank among the powers of the earth, and fatten on us!'" ¶OMF i 10

—talked about: "It was said by the wise and witty **Sydney Smith**, that many

Englishmen appear to have a remarkable satisfaction in even speaking of large sums of money; and that when men of this stamp say of Mr So-and-So, 'I am told he is worth two HUN-dred THOU-sand POUNDS,' there is a relish in their emphasis, an unctuous appetite and zest in their open-mouthed enunciation, which nothing but the one inspiring theme, Money, develops in them." HW/SD

—*usurer's lament:* "'Ten thousand pounds! And only lying there for a day—for one day! How many anxious years, how many pinching days and sleepless nights, before I scraped together that ten thousand pounds! —Ten thousand pounds! How many proud painted dames would have fawned and smiled, and how many spendthrift blockheads done me lip-service to my face and cursed me in their hearts, while I turned that ten thousand pounds into twenty! While I ground, and pinched, and used these needy borrowers for my pleasure and profit, what smooth-tongued speeches, and courteous looks, and civil letters, they would have given me! The cant of the lying world is, that men like me compass our riches by dissimulation and treachery: by fawning, cringing, and stooping. Why, how many lies, what mean evasions, what humbled behaviour from upstarts who, but for my money, would spurn me aside as they do their betters every day, would that ten thousand pounds have brought me in! Grant that I had doubled it—made cent. per cent.—for every sovereign told another—there would not be one piece of money in all the heap which wouldn't represent ten thousand mean and paltry lies, told, not by the money-lender, oh no! but by the money-borrowers, your liberal thoughtless generous dashing folks, who wouldn't be so mean as save a sixpence for the world!'" NN 56

—*wealth worshipped:* "The famous name of Merdle became, every day, more famous in the land. Nobody knew that the Merdle of such high renown had ever done any good to any one, alive or dead, or to any earthly thing . . . nobody had the smallest reason for supposing the clay of which this object of worship was made, to be other than the commonest clay, with as clogged a wick smouldering inside of it as ever kept an image of humanity from tumbling to pieces.

"All people knew (or thought they knew) that he had made himself immensely rich; and, for that reason alone, prostrated themselves before him, more degradedly and less excusably than the darkest savage creeps out of his hole in the ground to propitiate, in some log or reptile, the Deity of his benighted soul.

"Nay, the high priests of this worship had the man before them as a protest against their meanness. The multitude worshipped on trust—though always distinctly knowing why—but the officiators at the altar had the man habitually in their view. They sat at his feasts, and he sat at theirs.

"There was a spectre always attendant on him, saying to these high priests, 'Are such the signs you trust, and love to honour; this head, these eyes, this mode of speech, the tone and manner of this man? You are the levers of the Circumlocution Office, and the rulers of men. When half-a-dozen of you fall out by the ears, it seems that mother earth can give birth to no other rulers.

"Does your qualification lie in the superior knowledge of men, which accepts, courts, and puffs this man? Or, if you are competent to judge aright the signs I never fail to show you when he appears among you, is your superior honesty your qualification?' Two rather ugly questions these, always going about town with Mr Merdle; and there was a tacit agreement that they must be stifled." ¶LD ii 12

"Tradesmen's books hunger, and Tradesmen's mouths water, for the gold dust of the Golden Dustman. As Mrs Boffin and Miss Wilfer drive out, or as Mr Boffin walks out at his jog-trot pace, the fishmonger pulls of his hat with an air of reverence founded on conviction. His men cleanse their fingers on their woollen aprons before presuming to touch their foreheads to Mr Boffin or Lady. The gaping salmon and the golden mullet lying on the slab seem to turn up their eyes sideways, as they would turn up their hands, if they had any, in worshipping admiration. The butcher, though a portly and a prosperous man, doesn't know what to do with himself, so anxious is he to express humility when discovered by the passing Boffins taking the air in a mutton grove. Presents are made to the Boffin servants, and bland strangers with business-cards, meeting said servants in the street, offer hypothetical corruption." OMF i 17

And see H:Bank—*its money,* S:Degeneration—*moral; and* Index VII, *listing some of CD's rich; others include* Podsnap OMF and Malderton SB/HS

Restaurant

—bachelor patronage: "Mr Thomas Potter and Mr Robert Smithers met by appointment to begin the evening with a dinner; and a nice, snug, comfortable dinner they had, consisting of a little procession of four chops and four kidneys, following each other, supported on either side by a pot of the real draught stout, and attended by divers cushions of bread and wedges of cheese.

"When the cloth was removed, Mr Thomas Potter ordered the waiter to bring in two goes of his best Scotch whiskey, with warm water and sugar, and a couple of his 'very mildest' Havannahs, which the waiter did. Mr Thomas Potter mixed his grog, and lighted his cigar; Mr Robert Smithers did the same. . . . " SB/MN

—a catered repast: " . . . while the table was . . . the lap of luxury—being entirely furnished forth from the coffee-house—the circumjacent region of sitting-room was of a comparatively pastureless and shifty character: imposing on the waiter the wandering habits of putting the covers on the floor (where he fell over them), the melted butter in the armchair, the bread on the bookshelves, the cheese in the coal-scuttle, and the boiled fowl into my bed in the next room—where I found much of its parsley and butter in a state of congelation when I retired for the night. All this made the feast delightful, and when the waiter was not there to watch me, my pleasure was without alloy." GE 21

—a chop-house: "I dined at what Herbert [Pocket] and I used to call a Geographical chop-house—where there were maps of the world in porter-pot rims on every half-yard of the table-cloths, and charts of gravy on every one of the knives—to this day there is scarcely a single chop-house within the Lord Mayor's dominions which is not Geographical—and wore out the time in dozing over crumbs, staring at gas, and baking in a hot blast of dinners." GE 47

—a coffee-house experience: " . . . a look at the musty cutlet as if [the waiter] were surprised to see it—which cannot possibly be the case, he must have seen it so often before . . . your waiter cannot bring your bill yet, because he is bringing, instead, three flinty-hearted potatoes and two grim head of broccoli, like the occasional ornaments on area railings, badly boiled." UT/RT

—fast food: "Accordingly they betake themselves to a neighbouring dining-house, of the class known among its frequenters by the denomination Slap-Bang . . . .

"Into the dining-house, unaffected by the seductive show in the window, of artificially whitened cauliflowers and poultry, verdant baskets of peas, coolly blooming cucumbers, and joints ready for the spit, Mr Smallweed leads . . . .

"Conscious of his elfin power, and submitting to his dread experience, Mr Guppy consults him in the choice of that day's banquet; turning an appealing look towards him as the waitress repeats the catalogue of viands, and saying 'What do *you* take, Chick?' Chick, out of the profundity of his artfulness, preferring 'veal and ham and French beans—and don't you forget the stuffing, Polly,' (with an unearthly cock of his venerable eye); Mr Guppy and Mr Jobling give the like order. Three pint pots of half-and-half are superadded.

"Quickly the waitress returns, bearing what is apparently a model of the tower of Babel, but what is really a pile of plates and flat tin dish-covers. Mr Smallweed, approving of what is set before him, conveys intelligent benignity into his ancient eye, and winks upon her. Then, amid a constant coming in, and going out, and running about, and a clatter of crockery, and a rumbling up and down of the machine which brings the nice cuts from the kitchen, and a shrill crying for more nice cuts down the speaking-pipe, and a shrill reckoning of the cost of nice cuts that have been disposed of, and a general flush and steam of hot joints, cut and uncut, and a considerably heated atmosphere in which the soiled knives and tablecloths seem to break out spontaneously into eruptions of grease and blotches of beer, the legal triumvirate appease their appetites." BH 20

—French, contrasted with English: "And as to lunch why bless you if I kept a man-cook and two kitchen-maids I couldn't get it done for twice the money, and no injured young woman a glaring at you and grudging you and acknowledging your patronage by wishing that your food might choke you, but so civil and so hot and attentive and every way comfortable . . . . " CS/LL 1

And see W:France and the French—*railroad restaurant report*

—in Italy: " . . . there is a fair specimen of a real Genoese tavern, where the visitor may derive good entertainment from real

Genoese dishes, such as Tagliarini; Ravioli; German sausages, strong of garlic, sliced and eaten with fresh green figs; cocks' combs and sheep-kidneys, chopped up with mutton chops and liver; small pieces of some unknown part of a calf, twisted into small shreds, fried, and served up in a great dish like white-bait; and other curiosities of that kind.

"They often get wine at these suburban Trattorie, from France and Spain and Portugal, which is brought over by small captains in little trading-vessels. They buy it at so much a bottle, without asking what it is, or caring to remember if anybody tells them, and usually divide it into two heaps; of which they label one Champagne, and the other Madeira. The various opposite flavours, qualities, countries, ages, and vintages that are comprised under these two general heads is quite extraordinary. The most limited range is probably from cool Gruel up to old Marsala, and down again to apple Tea." PI 5

—*country inn:* "We had the usual dinner in this solitary house; and a very good dinner it is, when you are used to it. There is something with a vegetable or some rice in it, which is a sort of shorthand or arbitrary character for soup, and which tastes very well, when you have flavoured it with plenty of grated cheese, lots of salt, and abundance of pepper. There is the half-fowl of which this soup has been made. There is a stewed pigeon, with the gizzards and livers of himself and other birds stuck all round him. There is a bit of roast beef, the size of a small French roll. There are a scrap of Parmesan cheese, and five little withered apples, all huddled together on a small plate, and crowding one upon the other, as if each were trying to save itself from the chance of being eaten. Then there is coffee; and then there is bed." PI 10

—*at a pastrycook's:* "He beheld nothing to eat, but butter in various forms, slightly charged with jam, and languidly frizzling over tepid water. Two ancient turtle-shells, on which was inscribed the legend, 'SOUPS,' decorated a glass partition within, enclosing a stuffy alcove, from which a ghastly mockery of a marriage-breakfast spread on a rickety table, warned the terrified traveller. An oblong box of stale and broken pastry at reduced prices, mounted on a stool, ornamented the doorway . . . .

"From a beetle-haunted kitchen below this institution, fumes arose, suggestive of a class of soup which Mr Grazinglands knew, from painful experience, enfeebles the mind, distends the stomach, forces itself into the complexion, and tries to ooze out at the eyes . . . [he[looked in at a cold and floury baker's shop, where utilitarian buns, unrelieved by a currant, consorted with hard biscuits, a stone filter of cold water, a hard pale clock, and a hard little old woman, with flaxen hair, of an undeveloped-farinaceous aspect, as if she had been fed upon seeds." ¶UT/RT

—*prepared food shop:* " . . . a dirty shop-window in a dirty street, which was made almost opaque by the steam of hot meats, vegetables, and puddings. But glimpses were to be caught of a roast leg of pork bursting into tears of sage and onion in a metal reservoir full of gravy, of an unctuous piece of roast beef and blisterous Yorkshire pudding, bubbling hot in a similar receptacle, of a stuffed fillet of veal in rapid cut, of a ham in a perspiration with the pace it was going at, of a shallow tank of baked potatoes glued together by their own richness, of a truss or two of boiled greens, and other substantial delicacies. Within, were a few wooden partitions, behind which such customers as found it more convenient to take away their dinners in stomachs than in their hands, packed their purchases in solitude." LD i 20

—*in public gardens:* "It was rumoured . . . that Vauxhall Gardens by day were the scene of secret and hidden experiments; that there, carvers were exercised in the mystic art of cutting a moderate-sized ham into slices thin enough to pave the whole of the grounds; that beneath the shade of the tall trees, studious men were constantly engaged in chemical experiments, with the view of discovering how much water a bowl of negus could possibly bear; and that in some retired nooks, appropriated to the study of ornithology, other sage and learned men were, by a process known only to themselves, incessantly employed in reducing fowls to a mere combination of skin and bone." SB/VG

—*railroad:* "I travel by railroad. I start from home at seven or eight in the morning, after breakfasting hurriedly. What with skimming over the open landscape, what with mining in the damp bowels of the earth, what with banging, booming, and shrieking the scores of miles away, I am hungry when I arrive at the 'Refreshment' station where I am expected.

"Please observe—expected. I have said I am hungry; perhaps I might say, with greater point and force, that I am to some extent exhausted, and that I need—in the expressive French sense of the word—to be restored. What is provided for my restoration?

"The apartment that is to restore me is a wind-trap, cunningly set to inveigle all the draughts in that country-side, and to communicate a special intensity and velocity to them as they rotate in two hurricanes—one about my wretched head, one about my wretched legs.

"The training of the young ladies behind the counter who are to restore me has been from their infancy directed to the assumption of a defiant dramatic show that I am *not* expected. It is in vain for me to represent to them, by my humble and conciliatory manners, that I wish to be liberal. It is in vain for me to represent to myself, for the encouragement of my sinking soul, that the young ladies have a pecuniary interest in my arrival. Neither my reason nor my feelings can make head against the cold, glazed glare of eye with which I am assured that I am not expected, and not wanted.

"The solitary man among the bottles would sometimes take pity on me, if he dared, but he is powerless against the rights and mights of Woman . . . . Chilling fast in the deadly tornadoes to which my upper and lower extremities are exposed, and subdued by the moral disadvantage at which I stand, I turn my disconsolate eyes on the refreshments that are to restore me.

"I find that I must either scald my throat by insanely ladling into it, against time and for no wager, brown hot water stiffened with flour; or I must make myself flaky and sick with Banbury cake; or, I must stuff into my delicate organisation, a currant pin-cushion which I know will swell into immeasurable dimensions when it has got there; or, I must extort from an iron-bound quarry, with a fork, as if I were farming an inhospitable soil, some glutinous lumps of gristle and grease, called pork-pie.

"While thus forlornly occupied, I find that the depressing banquet on the table is, in every phase of its profoundly unsatisfactory character, so like the banquet at the meanest and shabbiest of evening parties, that I begin to think I must have 'brought down' to supper, the old lady unknown, blue with cold, who is setting her teeth on edge with a cool orange at my elbow—that the pastrycook who has compounded for the company on the lowest terms per head, is a fraudulent bankrupt, redeeming his contract with the stale stock from his window—that, for some unexplained reason, the family giving the party have become my mortal foes, and have given it on purpose to affront me."

"You present to your mind, a picture of the refreshment-table at that terminus. The conventional shabby evening-party supper—accepted as the model for all termini and all refreshment stations, because it is the last repast known to this state of existence of which any human creature would partake, but in the direst extremity—sickens your contemplation, and your words are these: 'I cannot dine on stale sponge-cakes that turn to sand in the mouth. I cannot dine on shining brown patties, composed of unknown animals within, and offering to my view the device of an indigestible star-fish in leaden pie-crust without. I cannot dine on a sandwich that has long been pining under an exhausted receiver. I cannot dine on barley-sugar. I cannot dine on Toffee.' You repair to the nearest hotel . . . . " ¶UT/RT

—shipboard: "At one, a bell rings, and the stewardess comes down with a steaming dish of baked potatoes, and another of roasted apples; and plates of pig's face, cold ham, salt beef; or perhaps a smoking mess of rare hot collops. We fall to upon these dainties; eat as much as we can (we have great appetites now); and are as long as possible about it." AN 2

And see Food and Drink*—collation—afloat;* H:Vocations*—waiter,* TT:In America*—meals, and* W:Inns

Senses

—fallible: "'You don't believe in me,' observed [Marley's] Ghost.

"'I don't,' said Scrooge.

"'Why do you doubt your senses?'

"'Because,' said Scrooge, 'a little thing affects them. A slight disorder of the stomach makes them cheats. You may be an undigested bit of beef, a blot of mustard, a crumb of cheese, a fragment of an underdone potato. There's more of gravy than of grave about you, whatever you are!'" CC 1

And see Body*—digestion*

—three of the five: "How well I recollect the kind of day it was! I smell the fog that hung about the place; I see the hoar frost,

ghostly, through it; I feel my rimy hair fall clammy on my cheek; I look along the dim perspective of the schoolroom, with a sputtering candle here and there to light up the foggy morning, and the breath of the boys wreathing and smoking in the raw cold as they blow upon their fingers, and tap their feet upon the floor." DC 9 *Smell is mentioned first: see* Smell

Sleep

" . . . Heaven's gift to all its creatures . . . . " BR 18

—balmy: "'In the meantime, as it's rather late, I'll try and get a wink or two of the balmy.'

"'The balmy' came almost as soon as it was courted. In a very few minutes Mr Swiveller was fast asleep, dreaming that he had married Nelly Trent, and come into the property, and that his first act of power was to lay waste the market-garden of Mr Cheggs, and turn it into a brick field." OCS 8

—breathing: "The room was so very warm, the tobacco so very good, and the fire so very soothing, that Mr Willet by degrees began to doze; but as he had perfectly acquired, by dint of long habit, the art of smoking in his sleep, and as his breathing was pretty much the same, awake or asleep, saving that in the latter case he sometimes experienced a slight difficulty in respiration (such as a carpenter meets with when he is planing and comes to a knot), neither of his companions was aware of the circumstance, until he met with one of these impediments and was obliged to try again.

"'Johnny's dropped off,' said Mr Parkes in a whisper.

"'Fast as a top,' said Mr Cobb.

"Neither of them said any more until Mr Willet came to another knot—one of surpassing obduracy—which bade fair to throw him into convulsions, but which he got over at last without waking, by an effort quite superhuman.

"'He sleeps uncommon hard,' said Mr Cobb." BR 33

—in a church: "There are not many people—and as it is desirable that a story-teller and a story-reader should establish a mutual understanding as soon as possible, I beg it to be noticed that I confine this observation neither to young people nor to little people, but extend it to all conditions of people: little and big, young and old: yet growing up, or already growing down again —there are not, I say, many people who would care to sleep in a church. I don't mean at sermon-time in warm weather (when the thing has actually been done, once or twice), but in the night, and alone. A great multitude of persons will be violently astonished, I know, by this position, in the broad bold Day. But it applies to Night. It must be argued by night, and I will undertake to maintain it successfully on any gusty winter's night appointed for the purpose, with any one opponent chosen from the rest, who will meet me singly in an old churchyard, before an old church-door; and will previously empower me to lock him in, if needful to his satisfaction, until morning." C 1

—in a coach: "At last the sun rose, and then my companions seemed to sleep easier. The difficulties under which they had laboured all night, and which had found utterance in the most terrific gasps and snorts, are not to be conceived. As the sun got higher, their sleep became lighter, and so they gradually one by one awoke. I recollect being very much surprised by the feint everybody made, then, of not having been to sleep at all, and by the uncommon indignation with which every one repelled the charge. I labour under the same kind of astonishment to this day, having invariably observed that of all human weaknesses, the one to which our common nature is the least disposed to confess (I cannot imagine why) is the weakness of having gone to sleep in a coach." DC 5

"The tendency of mankind when it falls asleep in coaches, is to wake up cross; to find its legs in its way; and its corns an aggravation. Mr Pecksniff not being exempt from the common lot of humanity, found himself, at the end of his nap, so decidedly the victim of these infirmities, that he had an irresistible inclination to visit them upon his daughters . . . . " MC 8

—insomnia: "What a doleful night! How anxious, how dismal, how long! There was an inhospitable smell in the room, of cold soot and hot dust; and, as I looked up into the corners of the tester over my head, I thought what a number of blue-bottle flies from the butcher's, and earwigs from the market, and grubs from the country, must be holding on up there, lying by for next summer. This led me to speculate whether any of them ever tumbled down, and then I fancied that I felt light falls on my face—a

disagreeable turn of thought, suggesting other and more objectionable approaches up my back.

"When I had lain awake a little while, those extraordinary voices with which silence teems, began to make themselves audible. The closet whispered, the fireplace sighed, the little washing-stand ticked, and one guitar-string played occasionally in the chest of drawers. At about the same time, the eyes on the wall acquired a new expression, and in every one of those staring rounds I saw written, DON'T GO HOME." GE 45

" . . . Benjamin Franklin's paper on the art of procuring pleasant dreams, which would seem necessarily to include the art of going to sleep, came into my head. Now, as I often used to read that paper when I was a very small boy, and as I recollect everything I read then as perfectly as I forget everything I read now, I quoted 'Get out of bed, beat up and turn your pillow, shake the bed-clothes well with at least twenty shakes, then throw the bed open and leave it to cool; in the meanwhile, continuing undrest, walk about your chamber. When you begin to feel the cold air unpleasant, then return to your bed, and you will soon fall asleep, and your sleep will be sweet and pleasant.' Not a bit of it! I performed the whole ceremony, and if it were possible to me to be more saucer-eyed than I was before, that was the only result that came of it." RP/LA

And see F:Guest—*unwelcome*

—*out of bed:* "With the peculiar sensitiveness on the subject of the disgraceful action of going to sleep out of bed, which is the lot of all mankind . . . . " LT 3

—*preferable to waking?* "Gradually [Oliver] fell into that deep tranquil sleep which ease from recent suffering alone imparts; that calm and peaceful rest which it is pain to wake from. Who, if this were death, would be roused again to all the struggles and turmoils of life; to all its cares for the present; its anxieties for the future; more than all, its weary recollections of the past!" OT 12

And see FL:Life—*its restoration regretted, and* N:Time of Day—*morning in time of trial*

—*in prison:* "The prison of La Force was a gloomy prison, dark and filthy, and with a horrible smell of foul sleep in it. Extraordinary how soon the noisome flavour of imprisoned sleep, becomes manifest in all such places that are ill cared for!" TTC iii 1

—*refreshing:* "'And if I might adwise, sir,' added Mr Weller, 'I'd just have a good night's rest arterwards, and not begin inquiring arter this here deep 'un 'till mornin'. There's nothin' so refreshin' as sleep, sir, as the servant-girl said afore she drank the egg-cupful o' laudanum.'" PP 16

—*repulsive:* "I stole into the next room to look at [Heep]. There I saw him, lying on his back, with his legs extending to I don't know where, gurglings taking place in his throat, stoppages in his nose, and his mouth open like a post-office. He was so much worse in reality than in my distempered fancy, that afterwards I was attracted to him in very repulsion, and could not help wandering in and out every half hour or so, and taking another look at him." DC 25

—*sitting up:* "Mr Riderhood poetically remarking that he would pick the bones of his night's rest, in his wooden chair, sat in the window." OMF iv 7

—*snoring:* "'It's enough to be robbed while you're snoring because you're too comfortable . . . . I didn't snore, myself, when I was your age [said Bounderby], let me tell you. I hadn't victuals enough to snore.'" HT ii 8

—*after wine:* "The wine, which had exerted its somniferous influence over Mr Snodgrass and Mr Winkle, had stolen upon the senses of Mr Pickwick. That gentleman had gradually passed through the various stages which precede the lethargy produced by dinner, and its consequences. He had undergone the ordinary transitions from the height of conviviality to the depth of misery, and from the depth of misery to the height of conviviality. Like a gas-lamp in the street, with the wind in the pipe, he had exhibited for a moment an unnatural brilliancy; then sunk so low as to be scarcely discernible: after a short interval he had burst out again, to enlighten for a moment, then flickered with an uncertain, staggering sort of light, and then gone out altogether. His head was sunk upon his bosom; and perpetual snoring, with a partial choke occasionally, were the only audible indications of the great man's presence." PP 2

"Mr Spenlow being a little drowsy after the champagne—honour to the soil that grew the grape, to the grape that made the wine, to the sun that ripened it, and to the merchant who adulterated it—and being fast asleep in a corner of the carriage, I rode by the side and talked to Dora." DC 33

—for a wounded mind: "'Sleep is what you want [said Captain Cuttle], afore all other things, and may you be able to show yourself smart with that there balsam for the still small woice of a wownded mind!'" DS 48

—in a Yorkshire school: "It needed a quick eye to detect, from among the huddled mass of sleepers, the form of any given individual. As they lay closely packed together, covered, for warmth's sake, with their patched and ragged clothes, little could be distinguished but the sharp outlines of pale faces, over which the sombre light shed the same dull heavy colour, with here and there a gaunt arm thrust forth; its thinness hidden by no covering, but fully exposed to view, in all its shrunken ugliness.

"There were some who, lying on their backs with upturned faces and clenched hands, just visible in the leaden light, bore more the aspect of dead bodies than of living creatures; and there were others coiled up into strange and fantastic postures; such as might have been taken for the uneasy efforts of pain to gain some temporary relief, rather than the freaks of slumber.

"A few—and these were among the youngest of the children—slept peacefully on, with smiles upon their faces, dreaming perhaps of home; but ever and again a deep and heavy sigh, breaking the stillness of the room, announced that some new sleeper had awakened to the misery of another day; and, as morning took the place of night, the smiles gradually faded away, with the friendly darkness which had given them birth." ¶NN 13

Smells

CD's sense of smell was so particular and acute, and his descriptions so graphic, that it seemed worthwhile to highlight this faculty by collecting here some brief descriptions, even though they may be part of longer extracts given elsewhere. See also cross-references in the captions index above in this chapter.

—abandoned schoolroom: "There is a strange unwholesome smell upon the room, like mildewed corduroys, sweet apples wanting air, and rotten books." DC 5

—adhesive cement: "Until old Hungerford-market was pulled down, until old Hungerford-stairs were destroyed, and the very nature of the ground changed, I never had the courage to go back to the place where my [blacking-factory] servitude began. I never saw it. I could not endure to go near it. For many years, when I came near to Robert Warren's in the Strand, I crossed over to the opposite side of the way, to avoid a certain smell of the cement they put upon the blacking-corks, which reminded me of what I was once." AF

—associated with taste: ". . . we all three dined together off a beefsteak pie . . . which was curiously flavoured on this occasion, I recollect well, by a miscellaneous taste of tea, coffee, butter, bacon, cheese, new loaves, firewood, candles, and walnut ketchup, continually ascending from the [chandler's] shop." DC 32

—Barnard's Inn: ". . . dry rot and wet rot and all the silent rots that rot in neglected roof and cellar—rot of rat and mouse and bug and coaching stables near at hand besides—addressed themselves faintly to my sense of smell, and moaned, 'Try Barnard's Mixture.'" GE 21

—book: ". . . a pleasant smell of paper freshly pressed came issuing forth, awakening instant recollections of some new grammar had at school, long time ago . . . . " MC 5

—cadger: ". . . something which smelt like several damp umbrellas, a barrel of beer, a cask of warm brandy-and-water, and a small parlour-full of stale tobacco-smoke mixed . . . . " MC 4

—cheap hotel room: "There was an inhospitable smell in the room, of cold soot and hot dust . . . . " GE 45

—cheap theatre: "My sense of smell, without being particularly delicate, has been so offended in some of the commoner places of public resort, that I have often been obliged to leave them when I have made an uncommercial journey expressly to look on." UT/TV

—Christmas pudding: "A smell like a washing-day! That was the cloth. A smell like an eating-house and a pastrycook's next door to each other, with a laundress's next door to that! That was the pudding!" CC 3

—churches: ". . . rot and mildew and dead citizens formed the uppermost scent, while, infused into it in a dreamy way not at all displeasing, was the staple character of the neighbourhood. In the churches about Mark-lane, for example, there was a dry whiff of wheat; and I accidentally struck an airy sample of barley out of an aged hassock in one of them. From Rood-lane to Tower-street, and thereabouts, there was often a

subtle flavour of wine: sometimes, of tea. One church near Mincing-lane smelt like a druggist's drawer. Behind the Monument the service had a flavour of damaged oranges, which, a little further down towards the river, tempered into herrings, and gradually toned into a cosmopolitan blast of fish. In one church, the exact counterpart of the church in the Rake's Progress where the hero is being married to the horrible old lady, there was no speciality of atmosphere, until the organ shook a perfume of hides all over us from some adjacent warehouse." UT/LC

—Covent Garden Market: " . . . at the herbalists' doors, gratefully inhaling scents as of veal-stuffing yet uncooked, dreamily mixed up with capsicums, brown-paper, seeds: even with hints of lusty snails and fine young curly leeches." MC 40

—equestrian performer: "[Childers] smelt of lamp-oil, straw, orange-peel, horses' provender, and sawdust . . . . " HT 6

—evoking a corpse: "There was a rather a sickly smell . . . in the little anteroom of my apartment at the [Paris] hotel. The large dark creature in the Morgue was by no direct experience associated with my sense of smell, because, when I came to the knowledge of him, he lay behind a wall of thick plate-glass, as good as a wall of steel or marble, for that matter. Yet the whiff of the room never failed to reproduce him." UT/TA

—express train: "It bore through the harvest country a smell like a large washing-day, and a sharp issue of steam as from a huge brazen tea-urn." LT 1

—Genoa shopping district: "In the streets of shops, the houses . . . are very dirty: quite undrained, if my nose be at all reliable: and emit a peculiar fragrance, like the smell of very bad cheese, kept in very hot blankets." PI 5

—hackney-coach: " . . . with the peculiar smell of which the present generation is unacquainted, but to which I am again ready to swear as a combination of stable, dog with the mange, and very old bellows." CS/HH 2

—ham, in a prison: "Clennam tried to do honour to the meal, but unavailingly. The ham sickened him, the bread seemd to turn to sand in his mouth . . . .

"He took a sprig or so of water-cress, and tried again; but, the bread turned to a heavier sand than before, and the ham (though it was good enough of itself) seemed to blow a faint simoom of ham through the whole Marshalsea." LD ii 27

—hatter's: "There were two or three hat-manufactories there, then (I think they are there still); and among the things which, encountered anywhere, or under any circumstances, will instantly recall that time, is the smell of hat-making." AF 2

—house in a mews: "To the sense of smell, the house was like a sort of bottle filled with a strong distillation of mews; and when the footman opened the door, he seemed to take the stopper out . . . .

"Still the footman said 'Walk in,' so the visitor followed him. At the inner hall—door, another bottle seemed to be presented filled with concentrated provisions, and extract of Sink from the pantry . . . the visitor was shut up, pending his announcement, in a close back parlour. There he had an opportunity of refreshing himself with both the bottles at once . . . ." LD i 10

—Hulks prisoner: " . . . the prisoners had come over with their keeper—bringing with them that curious flavour of bread-poultice, baize, rope-yarn, and hearthstone, which attends the convict presence." GE 28

—Italian palazzo: "There was, in every room, an aged smell, grown faint with confinement. It pined in all the cupboards and drawers. In the little rooms of communication between great rooms, it was stifling. If you turned a picture . . . there it still was, clinging to the wall behind the frame, like a sort of bat." RD

—law-office: "A smell as of unwholesome sheep, blending with the smell of must and dust, is referable to the nightly (and often daily) consumption of mutton fat in candles, and to the fretting of parchment forms and skins in greasy drawers. The atmosphere is otherwise stale and close." BH 39

—a library: " . . . a library, which was in fact a dressing-room, so that the smell of hot-pressed paper, vellum, morocco, and Russia leather, contended in it with the smell of divers pairs of boots . . . . " DS 3

—prison, in America: " . . . gentle odours, such as would arise from a thousand mildewed umbrellas, wet through, and a thousand buck-baskets, full of half-washed linen . . . ." AN 6

—punch: "The latter perfume, with the fostering aid of boiling water and lemon-peel, diffused itself throughout the room, and became so highly concentrated around the warm fireside, that the wind passing over

the house-roof must have rushed off charged with a delicious whiff of it, after buzzing like a great bee at that particular chimney-pot." OMF 4

—shop: "Mr Wegg sits down on a box in front of the fire, and inhales a warm and comfortable smell which is not the smell of the shop. 'For that,' Mr Wegg inwardly decides, as he takes a corrective sniff or two, 'is musty, leathery, feathery, cellary, gluey, gummy, and,' with another sniff, 'as it might be, strong of old pairs of bellows.'" OMF i 7

—shore guide: "[Glubb was] a weazen, old, crab-faced man, in a suit of battered oilskin, who had got tough and stringy from long pickling in salt water, and who smelt like a weedy sea-beach when the tide is out." DS 8

—shut-up house: "On all the house there is a cold, blank smell, like the smell of a little church, though something dryer: suggesting that the dead and buried Dedlocks walk there, in the long nights, and leave the flavour of their graves behind them." BH 29

—store-room: "A dark store-room . . . letting a mouldy air come out at the door, in which there is the smell of soap, pickles, pepper, candles, and coffee, all at one whiff." DC 2

—Venetian canal: " . . . the grip of the watery odours on one particular little bit of the bridge of your nose (which is never released while you stay there) . . . . " CS/HT 1

—wine: "'Now, Mrs Gamp, what's *your* news?'

"The lady in question was by this time in the doorway, curtseying to Mrs Mould. At the same moment a peculiar fragrance was borne upon the breeze, as if a passing fairy had hiccoughed, and had previously been to a wine-vault." MC 25

Timepiece

—Dutch clock: " . . . little waxy-faced Dutch clock in the corner . . . .

" . . . the jolly blaze uprose and fell, flashing and gleaming on the little Haymaker at the top of the Dutch clock, until one might have thought he stood stock still before the Moorish Palace, and nothing was in motion but the flame.

"He was on the move, however; and had his spasms, two to the second, all right and regular. But his sufferings, when the clock was going to strike, were frightful to behold; and when a Cuckoo looked out of a trapdoor in the Palace, and gave note six times, it shook him, each time, like a spectral voice—or like a something wiry, plucking at his legs.

"It was not until a violent commotion and a whirring noise among the weights and ropes below him had quite subsided, that this terrified Haymaker became himself again. Nor was he startled without reason; for these rattling, bony skeletons of clocks are very disconcerting in their operation, and I wonder very much how any set of men, but most of all how Dutchmen, can have had a liking to invent them. There is a popular belief that Dutchmen love broad cases and much clothing for their own lower selves; and they might know better than to leave their clocks so very lank and unprotected, surely." CH 1

—eight-day clock: " . . . [the half-pay Captain] took to pieces the eight-day clock on the front landing, under pretence of cleaning the works, which he put together again, by some undiscovered process, in so wonderful a manner, that the large hand has done nothing but trip up the little one ever since." SB/C

—first watch: "Who can lay his hand upon his waistcoat pocket, and say he has forgotten his first watch? Ours was a dumpy silver one, maker's name **Snoole**, of Chichester, number seventeen thousand three hundred and ten. Happy Snoole, to have made so many watches; yet we were happy—oh, how happy! to possess even one of them. We looked at that watch continually; we set it at every clock, and consulted it every five minutes; we opened and shut it, we wound it up, we regulated it, we made it do the most amazing things, and suddenly run a little chain off a wheel in a tearing manner—after which it stopped.

"How obliging we were to everybody who wished to know what o'clock it was! Did we ever go to bed without that watch snug under the pillow? Did not a lock of our sweetheart's hair have a sweet lurking place between the inner and outer cases? Where is that dumpy silver watch—where the more ambitious pinchbeck (there are no pinchbeck watches now) that followed? Where is the gold Geneva, the silver lever? How many watches have we bought, sold, swopped and bartered since then; and which of them do we remember half so well as the dumpy silver, maker's name **Snoole**, Chicester, seventeen thousand three hundred and ten!" ¶HWC/FF

—*friendly:* ". . . my old, cheerful, companionable Clock. How can I ever convey to others an idea of the comfort and consolation that this old Clock has been for years to me!

"It is associated with my earliest recollections . . . but it is not on that account, nor because it is a quaint old thing in a huge oaken case curiously and richly carved, that I prize it as I do. I incline to it as if it were alive, and could understand and give me back the love I bear it.

" . . . what other thing that has not life (I will not say how few things that have) could have proved the same patient, true, untiring friend? How often have I sat in the long winter evenings feeling such society in its cricket-voice, that raising my eyes from my book and looking gratefully towards it, the face reddened by the glow of the shining fire has seemed to relax from its staid expression and to regard me kindly! how often in the summer twilight, when my thoughts have wandered back to a melancholy past, have its regular whisperings recalled them to the calm and peaceful present! how often in the dead tranquillity of night has its bell broken the oppressive silence, and seemed to give me assurance that the old clock was still a faithful watcher at my chamber-door! My easy-chair, my desk, my ancient furniture, my very books, I can scarcely bring myself to love even these last like my old clock." MH 1

Master Humphrey's Room MHC

—*gloating:* " . . . the large, hard-featured clock on the sideboard, which [Clennam] used to see bending its figured brows upon him with a savage joy when he was behind-hand with his lessons, and which, when it was wound up once a week with an iron handle, used to sound as if it were growling in ferocious anticipation of the miseries into which it would bring him." LD i 3

—*inexorable:* " . . . a stern room, with a deadly statistical clock in it, which measured every second with a beat like a rap upon a coffin-lid . . . . " HT i 15

—*inquisitive:* "'And how do you do, Sir?' [Doctor Blimber] said to Mr Dombey; 'and how is my little friend?' Grave as an organ was the Doctor's speech; and when he ceased, the great clock in the hall seemed (to Paul at least) to take him up, and to go on saying, 'how, is, my, lit, tle, friend? how, is, my, lit, tle, friend?' over and over and over again . . . .

"'Ha!' said the Doctor . . . . How do you do, my little friend?'

"The clock in the hall wouldn't subscribe to this alteration in the form of words, but continued to repeat 'how, is, my, lit, tle, friend? how, is, my, lit, tle, friend?'" DS 11

—*medicinal:* "At this stage of her recovery, Captain Cuttle, with an imperfect association of a Watch with a Physician's treatment of a patient, took his own down from the mantel-shelf, and holding it out on his hook, and taking Florence's hand in his, looked steadily from one to the other, as expecting the dial to do something.

"'What cheer, my pretty?' said the Captain. 'What cheer now? You've done her some good, my lad, I believe,' said the Captain, under his breath, and throwing an approving glance upon his watch. 'Put you back half-an-hour every morning, and about another quarter towards the afternoon, and you're a watch as can be ekalled by few and excelled by none. What cheer, my lady lass?'" DS 48

—*in silence:* "Any such invasion of a dead stillness as the striking of distant clocks, causes it to appear the more intense and insupportable when the sound has ceased." MH 3

—*in solitude:* "Then, the school-room clock conducted itself in a way in which it had never conducted itself before—fell lame, somehow, and yet persisted in running on as hard and as loud as it could: the consequence of which behaviour was, that it staggered among the minutes in a state of the greatest confusion, and knocked them about in all directions without appearing to get on with its regular work." CS/TT 6

—*in St Paul's:* " . . . a complicated crowd of wheels and chains in iron and brass—great, sturdy, rattling engines—suggestive of breaking a finger put in here or there, and grinding the bone to powder—and these were the Clock! Its very pulse, if I may use the word, was like no other clock. It did not mark the flight of every moment with a gentle second stroke, as though it would check old Time, and have him stay his pace in pity, but measured it with one sledge-hammer beat, as if its business were to crush the seconds as they came trooping on, and remorselessly to clear a path before the Day of Judgment." MH 14

—*statistical:* "The deadly statistical recorder in the Gradgrind observatory knocked every second on the head as it was born, and buried it with his accustomed regularity." HT i 16

—*unhealthy* " . . . an unearthly collection of clocks, purporting to be the work of Parisian and Genevese artists—chiefly bilious-faced clocks, supported on sickly white crutches, with their pendulums dangling like lame legs . . . ." RP/EW

Tobacco

—*the best of pipes:* " . . . when Florence, taking down his pipe from the mantel-shelf, gave it into his hand, and entreated him to smoke it, the good Captain was so bewildered by her attention that he held it as if he had never held a pipe in all his life . . . . When he had filled his pipe in an absolute reverie of satisfaction, Florence lighted it for him—the Captain having no power to object, or to prevent her—and resuming her place on the old sofa, looked at him with a smile so loving and so grateful, a smile that showed him so plainly how her forlorn heart turned to him, as her face did, through grief, that the smoke of the pipe got into the Captain's throat and made him cough, and got into the Captain's eyes, and made them blink and water.

"The manner in which the Captain tried to make believe that the cause of these effects lay hidden in the pipe itself, and the way in which he looked into the bowl for it, and not finding it there, pretended to blow it out of the stem, was wonderfully pleasant. The pipe soon getting into better condition, he fell into that state of repose becoming a good smoker; but sat with his eyes fixed on Florence, and, with a beaming placidity not to be described, and stopping every now and then to discharge a little cloud from his lips, slowly puffed it forth. . . . " DS 49

—*chewed*

—*by a guest:* "[Hannibal Chollop] sat smoking and improving the circle [of spit], without making any attempts either to converse or to take leave, apparently labouring under the not uncommon delusion that for a free and enlightened citizen of the United States to convert another man's house into a spittoon for two or three hours together, was a delicate attention, full of interest and politeness, of which nobody could ever tire." MC 33

—marksmanship: "I was surprised to observe that even steady old chewers of great experience are not always good marksmen, which has rather inclined me to doubt that general proficiency with the rifle of which we have heard so much in England. Several gentlemen called upon me who, in the course of conversation, frequently missed the spittoon at five paces, and one (but he was certainly short-sighted) mistook the closed sash for the open window, at three. On another occasion, when I dined out, and was sitting with two ladies and some gentlemen round a fire before dinner, one of the compay fell short of the fireplace, six distinct times. I am disposed to think, however, that this was occasioned by his not aiming at that object, as there was a white marble hearth before the fender, which was more convenient, and may have suited his purpose better." AN 8

—nocturnal: "Either they carry their restlessness to such a pitch that they never sleep at all, or they expectorate in dreams, which would be a remarkable mingling of the real and ideal. All night long, and every night, on this canal, there was a perfect storm and tempest of spitting; and once, my coat being in the very centre of a hurricane sustained by five gentlemen (which moved vertically, strictly carrying out **Reid**'s Theory of the Law of Storms), I was fain the next morning to lay it on the deck, and rub it down with fair water before it was in a condition to be worn again." AN 10

—Senatorial: "The Senate is a dignified and decorous body, and its proceedings are conducted with much gravity and order. Both houses are handsomely carpeted; but the state to which these carpets are reduced by the universal disregard of the spittoon with which every honourable member is accommodated, and the extraordinary improvements on the patterns which are squirted and dabbled upon it in every direction, do not admit of being described. I will merely observe, that I strongly recommend all strangers not to look at the floor; and if they happen to drop anything, though it be their purse, not to pick it up with ungloved hand on any account.

"It is somewhat remarkable too, at first, to say the least, to see so many honourable members with swelled faces; and it is scarcely less remarkable to discover that this appearance is caused by the quantity of tobacco they contrive to stow within the hollow of the cheek. It is strange enough, too, to see an honourable gentleman leaning back in his tilted chair, with the legs on the desk before him, shaping a convenient 'plug' with his penknife, and when it is quite ready for use, shooting the old one from his mouth, as from a popgun, and clapping the new one in its place." AN 8

—on a train: " . . . my attention was attracted to a remarkable appearance issuing from the windows of the gentleman's car immediately in front of us, which I supposed for some time was occasioned by a number of industrious persons inside, ripping open feather-beds, and giving the feathers to the wind. At length it occurred to me that they were only spitting, which was indeed the case; though how any number of passengers which it was possible for that car to contain, could have maintained such a playful and incessant shower of expectoration, I am still at a loss to understand: notwithstanding the experience in all salivatory phenomena which I afterwards acquired." AN 7

—ubiquitous spitting: "As Washington may be called the head-quarters of tobacco-tinctured saliva, the time is come when I must confess, without any disguise, that the prevalence of those two odious practices of chewing and expectorating began about this time to be anything but agreeable, and soon became most offensive and sickening. In all the public places of America this filthy custom is recognised.

"In the courts of law the judge has his spittoon, the crier his, the witness his, and the prisoner his; while the jurymen and spectators are provided for, as so many men who in the course of nature must desire to spit incessantly. In the hospitals the students of medicine are requested, by notices upon the wall, to eject their tobacco-juice into the boxes provided for that purpose, and not to discolour the stairs. In public buildings, visitors are implored, through the same agency, to squirt the essence of their quids, or 'plugs,' as I have heard them called by gentlemen learned in this kind of sweetmeat, into the national spittoons, and not about the bases of the marble columns.

"But in some parts this custom is inseparably mixed up with every meal and morning call, and with all the transactions of social life. The stranger who follows in the track I took myself will find it in its full bloom and glory, luxuriant in all its alarming recklessness, at Washington. And let him not persuade himself (as I once did, to my shame), that previous tourists have exaggerated its extent. The thing itself is an exaggeration of nastiness which cannot be outdone." ¶AN 8

—youths on shipboard: "On board this steamboat there were two young gentlemen, with shirt-collars reversed as usual, and armed with very big walking-sticks, who planted two seats in the middle of the deck, at a distance of some four paces apart, took out their tobacco-boxes, and sat down opposite each other to chew. In less than a quarter of an hour's time, these hopeful youths had shed about them on the clean boards a copious shower of yellow rain; clearing, by that means, a kind of magic circle, within whose limits no intruders dared to come, and which they never failed to refresh and re-refresh before a spot was dry. This, being before breakfast, rather disposed me, I confess, to nausea; but looking attentively at one of the expectorators, I plainly saw that he was young in chewing, and felt inwardly uneasy himself. A glow of delight came over me at this discovery; and as I marked his face turn paler and paler, and saw the ball of tobacco in his left cheek quiver with his suppressed agony, while yet he spat and chewed and spat again, in emulation of his older friend, I could have fallen on his neck and implored him to go on for hours." AN 8

—depended on: "'You don't find this sort of thing disagreeable, I hope, sir?' said his right-hand neighbour, a gentleman in a checked shirt, and Mosaic studs, with a cigar in his mouth.

"'Not in the least,' replied Mr Pickwick, 'I like it very much, although I am no smoker myself.'

"'I should be very sorry to say I wasn't' interposed another gentleman on the opposite side of the table. 'It's board and lodging to me, is smoke.'

"Mr Pickwick glanced at the speaker, and thought that if it were washing too, it would be all the better." PP 20

—detectable: " . . . [Swiveller] proceeded to observe that the human hair was a great retainer of tobacco-smoke, and that the young gentlemen of Westminster and Eton, after eating vast quantities of apples to conceal any scent of cigars from their anxious friends, were usually detected in consequence of their heads possessing this remarkable property; whence he concluded that if the Royal Society would turn their attention to the circumstance, and endeavour to find in the resources of science a means of preventing such untoward revelations, they might indeed be looked upon as benefactors to mankind." OCS 2

—as a disinfectant: "The apartment was very far removed from the old man's chamber, but Mr Quilp deemed it prudent, as a precaution against infection from fever, and a means of wholesome fumigation, not only to smoke, himself, without cessation, but to insist upon it that his legal friend did the like. Moreover, he sent an express to the wharf for the tumbling boy, who arriving with all despatch, was enjoined to sit himself down in another chair just inside the door, continually to smoke a great pipe which the dwarf had provided for the purpose, and to take it from his lips under any pretence whatever, were it only for one minute at a time, if he dared." OCS 11

—enjoyed: "The smoke came crookedly out of Mr Flintwinch's mouth, as if it circulated through the whole of his wry figure and came back by his wry throat, before coming forth to mingle with the smoke from the crooked chimneys and the mists from the crooked river." LD ii 23

—essential: "' . . . I must have my smoke [said Magwitch]. When I was first hired out as shepherd t'other side of the world, it's my belief I should ha' turned into a molloncolly-mad sheep myself, if I hadn't a had my smoke.'" GE 40

—lethal: "'Hey! What did [the last occupant] die of?' asked my aunt.

"'Well, ma'am, he died of drink,' said Mrs Crupp, in confidence. 'And smoke.'

"'Smoke? You don't mean chimneys?' said my aunt.

"'No, ma'am,' returned Mrs Crupp. 'Cigars and pipes.'

"'*That's* not catching, Trot, at any rate,' remarked my aunt, turning to me.

"'No, indeed,' said I." DC 23

—lighting a pipe: "[Dot Peerybingle] was, out and out, the very best filler of a pipe, I should say, in the four quarters of the globe. To see her put that chubby little finger in the bowl, and then blow down the pipe to clear the tube, and, when she had done so, affect to think that there was really something in the tube, and blow a dozen times, and hold it to her eye like a telescope, with a most provoking twist in her capital little face, as she looked down it, was quite a brilliant thing. As to the tobacco, she was perfect mistress of the subject; and her lighting of the pipe, with a wisp of paper,

when the Carrier had it in his mouth—going so very near his nose, and yet not scorching it—was Art, high Art." CH 1

And see H:Woman—*home-making instinct*

—*overdone:* "Somebody was smoking. We were all smoking. *I* was smoking, and trying to suppress a rising tendency to shudder . . . .

"Somebody was leaning out of my bedroom window, refreshing his forehead against the cool stone of the parapet, and feeling the air upon his face. It was myself. I was addressing myself as 'Copperfield,' and saying, 'Why did you try to smoke? You might have known you couldn't do it.' Now, somebody was unsteadily contemplating his features in the looking-glass. That was I too. I was very pale in the looking-glass; my eyes had a vacant appearance; and my hair—only my hair, nothing else—looked drunk." DC 24

—*plant:* "I saw . . . the whole process of picking, rolling, pressing, drying, packing in casks, and branding. All the tobacco thus dealt with, was in course of manufacture for chewing; and one would have supposed there was enough in that one storehouse to have filled even the comprehensive jaws of America. In this form, the weed looks like the oil-cake on which we fatten cattle; and even without reference to its consequences, is sufficiently uninviting." AN 9

—*post-prandial:* " . . . the cloth, the plates, the salt-cellars, the knives and forks, the glasses and pewter-pots, being all that the guests had not eaten or drunk, were cleared; bunches of pipes were laid upon the table; and everybody ordered what he liked to drink, or went his way. Mr Simpson . . . himself consorted with a company of generous spirits—connected with a Brewery, perhaps—and smoked a mild cigar . . . .

" . . . . Deep in the oiled depths of the old-fashioned table, a reflection of every man's face appeared below him, beaming. Many pipes were lighted, the windows were opened at top, and a fragrant cloud enwrapped the company, as if they were all being carried upward together. The undertaker laughed monstrously at a joke, and the agriculturist thought the country might go on, say ten years, with good luck." ¶HWC/PD

—*recreation:* "Mr Quilp . . . shut himself up in his Bachelor's Hall, which, by reason of its newly-erected chimney depositing the smoke inside the room and carrying none of it off, was not quite so agreeable as more fastidious people might have desired. Such inconveniences, however, instead of disgusting the dwarf with his new abode, rather suited his humour . . . he lighted his pipe, and smoked against the chimney until nothing of him was visible through the mist but a pair of red and highly inflamed eyes, with sometimes a dim vision of his head and face, as, in a violent fit of coughing, he slightly stirred the smoke and scattered the heavy wreaths by which they were obscured.

"In the midst of this atmosphere, which must infallibly have smothered any other man, Mr Quilp passed the evening with great cheerfulness; solacing himself all the time with the pipe and the case-bottle . . . ." OCS 50

And see H:Recreation—*taking snuff*

Toys

—*in a children's hospital:* " . . . Johnny came to himself, out of a sleep or a swoon or whatever it was, to find himself lying in a little quiet bed, with a little platform over his breast, on which were already arranged, to give him heart and urge him to cheer up, the Noah's ark, the noble steed, and the yellow bird, with the officer in the Guards doing duty over the whole, quite as much to the satisfaction of his country as if he had been upon Parade.

"And at the bed's head was a coloured picture beautiful to see, representing as it were another Johnny seated on the knee of some Angel surely who loved little children. And marvellous fact to lie and stare at: Johnny had become one of a little family, all in little quiet beds (except two playing dominoes in little arm-chairs at a little table on the hearth): and on all the little beds were little platforms whereon were to be seen dolls' houses, woolly dogs with mechanical barks in them not very dissimilar from the artificial voice pervading the bowels of the yellow bird, tin armies, Moorish tumblers, wooden tea-things, and the riches of the earth." OMF ii 9

—*at Christmas:* "Then the shouting and the struggling, and the onslaught that was made on the defenceless porter! The scaling him, with chairs for ladders, to dive into his pockets, despoil him of brown-paper parcels, hold on tight by his cravat, hug him round the neck, pommel his back, and kick his legs in irrepressible affection. The shouts of wonder and delight with which the development of every package was received! The terrible announcement that the baby had been taken in the act of putting a doll's frying-pan into his mouth, and was more than suspected of having swallowed a fictitious turkey, glued on a wooden platter! The immense relief of finding this a false alarm! The joy, and gratitude, and ecstasy! They are all indescribable alike." CC 2

—dolls and dolls' houses: "Caleb [Plummer] and his daughter [Bertha] were at work together in their usual working-room, which served them for their ordinary living-room as well; and a strange place it was. There were houses in it, finished and unfinished, for dolls of all stations in life. Suburban tenements for dolls of moderate means; kitchens and single apartments for dolls of the lower classes; capital town residences for dolls of high estate.

"Some of these establishments were already furnished according to estimate, with a view to the convenience of dolls of limited income; others could be fitted on the most expensive scale, at a moment's notice, from whole shelves of chairs and tables, sofas, bedsteads, and upholstery. The nobility and gentry, and public in general, for whose accommodation these tenements were designed, lay, here and there, in baskets, staring straight up at the ceiling; but in denoting their degrees in society, and confining them to their respective stations (which experience shows to be lamentably difficult in real life), the makers of these dolls had far improved on Nature, which is often froward and perverse; for they, not resting on such arbitrary marks as satin, cotton-print, and bits of rag, had superadded striking personal differences which allowed of no mistake.

"Thus, the doll-lady of distinction had wax limbs of perfect symmetry; but only she and her compeers. The next grade in the social scale being made of leather, and the next of coarse linen stuff. As to the common-people, they had just so many matches out of tinder-boxes, for their arms and legs, and there they were—established in their sphere at once, beyond the possibility of getting out of it." ¶CH 2

—not ugly enough: "'Who's that with the grey hair?'

"'I don't know, sir, returned Caleb in a whisper. 'Never see him before, in all my life. A beautiful figure for a nut-cracker; quite a new model. With a screw-jaw opening down into his waistcoat, he'd be lovely.'

"'Not ugly enough,' said Tackleton.

"'Or for a firebox, either,' observed Caleb, in deep contemplation, 'what a model! Unscrew his head to put the matches in; turn him heels up'ards for the light; and what a firebox for a gentleman's mantel-shelf, just as he stands!'

"'Not half ugly enough,' said Tackleton. 'Nothing in him at all!'" CH 1

—variety as in life: "There were various other examples of this handicraft, besides dolls, in Caleb Plummer's room. There were Noah's Arks, in which the birds and beasts were an uncommonly tight fit, I assure you; though they could be crammed in anyhow, at the roof, and rattled and shaken into the smallest compass. By a bold poetical licence, most of these Noah's Arks had knockers on the doors; inconsistent appendages, perhaps, as suggestive of morning callers and a postman, yet a pleasant finish to the outside of the building.

"There were scores of melancholy little carts which, when the wheels went round, performed most doleful music. Many small fiddles, drums, and other instruments of torture; no end of cannon, shields, swords, spears, and guns. There were little tumblers in red breeches, incessantly swarming up high obstacles of red-tape, and coming down, head first, on the other side; and there were innumerable old gentlemen of respectable, not to say venerable, appearance, insanely flying over horizontal pegs, inserted, for the purpose, in their own street doors. There were beasts of all sorts; horses, in particular, of every breed, from the spotted barrel on four pegs, with a small tippet for a mane, to the thorough-bred rocker on his highest mettle.

"As it would have been hard to count the dozens upon dozens of grotesque figures that were ever ready to commit all sorts of absurdities on the turning of a handle, so it would have been no easy task to mention any human folly, vice, or weakness, that had not its type, immediate or remote, in Caleb Plummer's room. And not in an exaggerated form, for very little handles will move men and women to as strange performances as any toy was ever made to undertake." ¶CH 2 *And see* CD:Nursery toys

Waiting

—and fidgeting: "It struck eleven, and [Eugene Wrayburn] made believe to compose himself patiently. But gradually he took the fidgets in one leg, and then in the

other leg, and then in one arm, and then in the other arm, and then in his chin, and then in his back, and then in his forehead, and then in his hair, and then in his nose; and then he stretched himself recumbent on two chairs, and groaned; and then he started up.

"'Invisible insects of diabolical activity swarm in this place. I am tickled and twitched all over. Mentally, I have now committed a burglary under the meanest circumstances, and the myrmidons of justice are at my heels.'

"'I am quite as bad,' said [Mortimer] Lightwood, sitting up facing him, with a tumbled head, after going through some wonderful evolutions, in which his head had been the lowest part of him. 'This restlessness began, with me, long ago. All the time you were out, I felt like *Gulliver* with the Lilliputians firing upon him.'" OMF i 13

—and itching: "There are few things more worrying than sitting up for somebody, especially if that somebody be at a party. You cannot help thinking how quickly the time passes with them, which drags so heavily with you; and the more you think of this, the more your hopes of their speedy arrival decline.

"Clocks tick so loud, too, when you are sitting up alone, and you seem as if you had an under garment of cobwebs on. First, something tickles your right knee, and then the same sensation irritates your left. You have no sooner changed your position, than it comes again in the arms; when you have fidgeted your limbs into all sorts of odd shapes, you have a sudden relapse in the nose, which you rub as if to rub it off—as there is no doubt you would, if you could.

"Eyes, too, are mere personal inconveniences; and the wick of one candle gets an inch and a half long, while you are snuffing the other. These, and various other little nervous annoyances, render sitting up for a length of time after everybody else has gone to bed, anything but a cheerful amusement." ¶PP 36

—staying awake: " . . . with an expression of face in which a great number of opposite ingredients, such as mischief, cunning, malice, triumph, and patient expectation, were all mixed up together in a kind of physiognomical punch, Miss Miggs composed herself to wait and listen, like some fair ogress who had set a trap and was watching for a nibble from a plump young traveller." BR 9

" . . . Miss Miggs, who, having arrived at that restless state and sensitive condition of the nervous system which are the result of long watching, did, by a constant rubbing and tweaking of her nose, a perpetual change of position (arising from the sudden growth of imaginary knots and knobs in her chair), a frequent friction of her eyebrows, the incessant recurrence of a small cough, a small groan, a gasp, a sigh, a sniff, a spasmodic start, and by other demonstrations of that nature, so file down and rasp, as it were, the patience of the locksmith, that after looking at her in silence for some time, he at last broke out . . . .

" . . . to be quiet with such a basilisk before him was impossible. If he looked another way, it was worse to feel that she was rubbing her cheek, or twitching her ear, or winking her eye, or making all kinds of extraordinary shapes with her nose, than to see her do it. If she was for a moment free from any of these complaints, it was only because of her foot being asleep, or of her arm having got the fidgets, or of her leg being doubled up with the cramp, or of some other horrible disorder which racked her whole frame.

"If she did enjoy a moment's ease, then with her eyes shut and her mouth wide open, she would be seen to sit very stiff and upright in her chair; then to nod a little way forward, and stop with a jerk; then to nod a little farther forward, and stop with another jerk; then to recover herself; then to come forward again—lower—lower—lower—by very slow degrees, until, just as it seemed impossible that she could preserve her balance for another instant, and the locksmith was about to call out in an agony, to save her from dashing down upon her forehead and fracturing her skull, then all of a sudden and without the smallest notice, she would come upright and rigid again with her eyes open, and in her countenance an expression of defiance, sleepy but yet most obstinate, which plainly said 'I've never once closed 'em since I looked at you last, and I'll take my oath of it!'" ¶BR 51

—on the street: "Two hours were a long stretch of lounging about, after a long day's labour. Stephen sat upon the step of a door, leaned against a wall under an archway, strolled up and down, listened for the church clock, stopped and watched children playing in the street. Some purpose or other is so natural to every one, that a mere loiterer always looks and feels remarkable.

When the first hour was out, Stephen even began to have an uncomfortable sensation upon him of being for the time a disreputable character." HT ii 6

"Being something too soon in their arrival, [Charley Hexam and Headstone] lurked at a corner, waiting for [Lizzie] to appear. The best-looking among us will not look very well, lurking at a corner, and Bradley came out of that disadvantage very poorly indeed." OMF ii 15

—vigilance: "Mrs Sparsit, lying by to recover the tone of her nerves in Mr Bounderby's retreat, kept such a sharp look-out, night and day, under her Coriolanian eyebrows, that her eyes, like a couple of lighthouses on an iron-bound coast, might have warned all prudent mariners from that bold rock her Roman nose and the dark and craggy region in its neighbourhood, but for the placidity of her manner. Although it was hard to believe that her retiring for the night could be anything but a form, so severely wide awake were those classical eyes of hers, and so impossible did it seem that her rigid nose could yield to any relaxing influence, yet her manner of sitting, smoothing her uncomfortable, not to say, gritty mittens (they were constructed of a cool fabric like a meat-safe), or of ambling to unknown places of destination with her foot in her cotton stirrup, was so perfectly serene, that most observers would have been constrained to suppose her a dove, embodied by some freak of nature, in the earthly tabernacle of a bird of the hook-beaked order.

"She was a most wonderful woman for prowling about the house. How she got from story to story was a mystery beyond solution. A lady so decorous in herself, and so highly connected, was not to be suspected of dropping over the banisters or sliding down them, yet her extraordinary facility of locomotion suggested the wild idea. Another noticeable circumstance in Mrs Sparsit was, that she was never hurried. She would shoot with consummate velocity from the roof to the hall, yet would be in full possession of her breath and dignity on the moment of her arrival there. Neither was she ever seen by human vision to go at a great pace." HT ii 9

—rained-on: "Mrs Sparsit saw [Louisa] out of the wood, and saw her enter the house. What to do next? It rained now, in a sheet of water. Mrs Sparsit's white stockings were of many colours, green predominating; prickly things were in her shoes; caterpillars slung themselves, in hammocks of their own making, from various parts of her dress; rills ran from her bonnet, and her Roman nose. In such condition, Mrs Sparsit stood hidden in the density of the shrubbery, considering what next . . . .

"The black eyes kept upon the railroad-carriage in which [Louisa] had travelled, settled upon it a moment too late. The door not being opened after several minutes, Mrs Sparsit passed it and repassed it, saw nothing, looked in, and found it empty. Wet through and through: with her feet squelching and squashing in her shoes whenever she moved; with a rash of rain upon her classical visage; with a bonnet like an over-ripe fig; with all her clothes spoiled; with damp impressions of every button, string, and hook-and-eye she wore, printed off upon her highly connected back; with a stagnant verdure on her general exterior, such as accumulates on an old park fence in a mouldy lane; Mrs Sparsit had no resource but to burst into tears of bitterness and say, 'I have lost her!'" HT ii 11

—and watching: "None are so anxious as those who watch and wait; and at these times, mournful fancies came flocking on [Nell's] mind, in crowds.

"She would take her station here, at dusk, and watch the people as they passed up and down the street, or appeared at the windows of the opposite houses; wondering whether those rooms were as lonesome as that in which she sat, and whether those people felt it company to see her sitting there, as she did only to see them look out and draw in their heads again.

"There was a crooked stack of chimneys on one of the roofs, in which, by often looking at them, she had fancied ugly faces that were frowning over at her and trying to peer into the room . . . she would draw in her head to look round the room and see that everything was in its place and hadn't moved; and looking out into the street again, would perhaps see a man passing with a coffin on his back, and two or three others silently following him to a house where somebody lay dead; which made her shudder and think of such things until they suggested afresh the old man's altered face and manner, and a new train of fears and speculations.

"If he were to die—if sudden illness had happened to him, and he were never to come home again, alive—if, one night, he should come home, and kiss and bless her as usual, and after she had gone to bed and had fallen asleep and was perhaps dreaming pleasantly, and smiling in her sleep, he should kill himself and his blood come creeping, creeping, on the ground to her own bed-room door!" ¶OCS 9

Walking

—advice: "'Walk fast, Wal'r, my lad,' returned the Captain, mending his pace; 'and walk the same all the days of your life. Overhaul the catechism for that advice, and keep it!'" DS 9

—compared to riding: " . . . they set off on foot; which was, after all, a better mode of travelling than in the gig, as the weather was very cold and very dry.

"Better! A rare strong, hearty, healthy walk—four statute miles an hour—preferable to that rumbling, tumbling, jolting, shaking, scraping, creaking, villanous old gig? Why, the two things will not admit of comparison. It is an insult to the walk, to set them side by side. Where is an instance of a gig having ever circulated a man's blood, unless when, putting him in danger of his neck, it awakened in his veins and in his ears, and all along his spine, a tingling heat, much more peculiar than agreeable? When did a gig ever sharpen anybody's wits and energies, unless it was when the horse bolted, and, crashing madly down a steep hill with a stone wall at the bottom, his desperate circumstances suggested to the only gentleman left inside, some novel and unheard-of mode of dropping out behind? Better than the gig!

"The air was cold, Tom [Pinch]; so it was, there was no denying it; but would it have been more genial in the gig? The blacksmith's fire burned very bright, and leaped up high, as though it wanted men to warm; but would it have been less tempting, looked at from the clammy cushions of a gig? The wind blew keenly, nipping the features of the hardy wight who fought his way along; blinding him with his own hair if he had enough of it, and wintry dust if he hadn't; stopping his breath as though he had been soused in a cold bath; tearing aside his wrappings-up, and whistling in the very marrow of his bones; but it would have done all this a hundred times more fiercely to a man in a gig, wouldn't it? A fig for gigs!

"Better than the gig! When were travellers by wheels and hoofs seen with such red-hot cheeks as those? when were they so good-humouredly and merrily bloused? when did their laughter ring upon the air, as they turned them round, what time the stronger gusts came sweeping up; and, facing round again as they passed by, dashed on, in such a glow of ruddy health as nothing could keep pace with, but the high spirits it engendered? Better than the gig! Why, here *is* a man in a gig coming the same way now. Look at him as he passes his whip into his left hand, chafes his numbed right fingers on his granite leg, and beats those marble toes of his upon the foot-board. Ha, ha, ha! Who would exchange this rapid hurry of the blood for yonder stagnant misery, though its pace were twenty miles for one?

"Better than the gig! No man in a gig could have such interest in the milestones. No man in a gig could see, or feel, or think, like merry users of their legs. How, as the wind sweeps on, upon these breezy downs, it tracks its flight in darkening ripples on the grass, and smoothest shadows on the hills! Look round and round upon this bare bleak plain, and see even here, upon a winter's day, how beautiful the shadows are! Alas! it is the nature of their kind to be so. The loveliest things in life, Tom, are but shadows; and they come and go, and change and fade away, as rapidly as these!

"Another mile, and then begins a fall of snow, making the crow, who skims away so close above the ground to shirk the wind, a blot of ink upon the landscape. But though it drives and drifts against them as they walk, stiffening on their skirts, and freezing in the lashes of their eyes, they wouldn't have it fall more sparingly, no, not so much as by a single flake, although they had to go a score of miles. And, lo! the towers of the Old [Salisbury] Cathedral rise before them, even now! and by-and-bye they come into the sheltered streets, made strangely silent by their white carpet; and so to the Inn for which they are bound; where they present such flushed and burning faces to the cold waiter, and are so brimful of vigour, that he almost feels assaulted by their presence; and, having nothing to oppose to the attack (being fresh, or rather stale, from the blazing fire in the coffee-room), is quite put out of his pale countenance." MC 12

—complacent: "'What's the matter, what's the matter?' said the gentleman for whom the door was opened; coming out of the house at that kind of light-heavy pace—that peculiar compromise between a walk and a jog-trot—with which a gentleman upon the smooth down-hill of life, wearing creaking

boots, a watch-chain, and clean linen, *may* come out of his house; not only without any abatement of his dignity, but with an expression of having important and wealthy engagements elsewhere." C 1

—ostentatious: "The Major, more blue-faced and staring—more over-ripe, as it were, than ever—and giving vent, every now and then, to one of the horse's coughs, not so much of necessity as in a spontaneous explosion of importance, walked arm-in-arm with Mr Dombey up the sunny side of the way, with his cheeks swelling over his tight stock, his legs majestically wide apart, and his great head wagging from side to side, as if he were remonstrating within himself for being such a captivating object." DS 21

—self-satisfied: "The Doctor's walk was stately, and calculated to impress the juvenile mind with solemn feelings. It was a sort of march; but when the Doctor put out his right foot, he gravely turned upon his axis, with a semicircular sweep towards the left; and when he put out his left foot, he turned in the same manner towards the right. So that he seemed, at every stride he took, to look about him, as though he were saying, 'Can anybody have the goodness to indicate any subject, in any direction, on which I am uninformed? I rather think not.'" DS 12

Wine

—appreciated: "Making a stiff arm to the elbow, [Riderhood] poured the wine into his mouth, tilted it into his right cheek, as saying, 'What do you think of it?' tilted it into his left cheek, as saying, 'What do *you* think of it?' jerked it into his stomach, as saying, 'What do *you* think of it?' To conclude, smacked his lips, as if all three replied, 'We think well of it.'" OMF i 12

—cellarman's perspective: "'I have said to Pebbleson Nephew many a time, when they have said to me, "Put a livelier face upon it, Joey"—I have said to them, "gentlemen, it is all wery well for you that has been accustomed to take your wine into your systems by the conwivial channel of your throttles, to put a lively face upon it; but," I says, "I have been accustomed to take *my* wine in at the pores of the skin, and, took that way, it acts different. It acts depressing. It's one thing, gentlemen," I says to Pebbleson Nephew, "to charge your glasses in a dining-room with a Hip Hurrah and a Jolly Companions Every One, and it's another thing to be charged yourself, through the pores, in a low dark cellar and a mouldy atmosphere. It makes all the difference betwixt bubbles and wapours," I tells Pebbleson Nephew. And so it do. I've been a cellarman my life through, with my mind fully given to the business. What's the consequence? I'm as muddled a man as lives—you won't find a muddleder man than me—nor yet you won't find my equal in molloncolly. Sing of Filling the bumper fair, Every drop you sprinkle, O'er the brow of care, Smooths away a wrinkle? Yes. P'raps so. But try filling yourself through the pores, underground, when you don't want to do it!'" CS/NT 1

—cross-examined: "[Jaggers] cross-examined his very wine when he had nothing else in hand. He held it between himself and the candle, tasted the port, rolled it in his mouth, swallowed it, looked at his glass again, smelt the port, tried it, drank it, filled again, and cross-examined the glass again, until I was as nervous as if I had known the wine to be telling him something to my disadvantage. Three or four times I feebly thought I would start conversation; but whenever he saw me going to ask him anything, he looked at me with his glass in his hand, and rolling his wine about in his mouth, as if requesting me to take notice that it was of no use, for he couldn't answer." GE 29

—in England: "'Wine [says Obenreizer]? Is it trade in England, or profession? Not a fine art?'" PC/NT I iii

—harvest: "It was vintage time in the valleys on the Swiss side of the Pass of the Great Saint Bernard, and along the banks of the Lake of Geneva. The air there was charged with the scent of gathered grapes. Baskets, troughs, and tubs of grapes, stood in the dim village door-ways, stopped the steep and narrow village streets, and had been carrying all day along the roads and lanes. Grapes, split and crushed under foot, lay about everywhere.

"The child carried in a sling by the laden peasant woman toiling home, was quieted with picked-up grapes; the idiot sunning his big goitre under the eaves of the wooden chalet by the way to the waterfall, sat munching grapes; the breath of the cows and goats was redolent of leaves and stalks of grapes; the company in every little cabaret were eating, drinking, talking grapes. A pity that no ripe touch of this generous abundance could be given to the thin, hard, stony wine, which after all was made from the grapes!" ¶LD ii 1

—*indulged:* " . . . I began to observe that [Mr Pumblechook] was getting flushed in the face; as to myself, I felt all face, steeped in wine and smarting." GE 19

—*and integrity:* "' . . . the stock was higgledy-piggledy, and I haven't yet tasted my way quite through it with a view to sorting it. Therefore, if you order one kind and get another, change till it comes right. For what,' said Mellows, unloading his hat as before, 'what would you or any gentleman do, if you ordered one kind of wine and was required to drink another? Why, you'd (and naturally and properly, having the feelings of a gentleman), you'd take and drown yourself in a pail!'" UT/SC

—*old port:*"In his lowering magazine of dust, the universal article into which his papers and himself, and all his clients, and all things of earth, animate and inanimate, are resolving, Mr Tulkinghorn sits at one of the open windows, enjoying a bottle of old port.

"Though a hard-grained man, close, dry, and silent, [Mr Tulkinghorn] can enjoy old wine with the best. He has a priceless binn of port in some artful cellar under the [Lincoln's Inn] Fields, which is one of his many secrets. When he dines alone in chambers, as he has dined to-day, and has his bit of fish and his steak or chicken brought in from the coffee-house, he descends with a candle to the echoing regions below the deserted mansion, and, heralded by a remote reverberation of thundering doors, comes gravely back, encircled by an earthy atmosphere, and carrying a bottle from which he pours a radiant nectar, two score and ten years old, that blushes in the glass to find itself so famous, and fills the whole room with the fragrance of southern grapes." BH 22

—*old and precious:* "The host had gone below to the cellar, and had brought up bottles of ruby, straw-coloured, and golden drinks, which had ripened long ago in lands where no fogs are, and had since lain slumbering in the shade. Sparkling and tingling after so long a nap, they pushed at their corks to help the corkscrew (like prisoners helping rioters to force their gates), and danced out gaily. If P.J.T. in seventeen-forty-seven, or in any other year of his period, drank such wines—then, for a certainty, P.J.T. [inscribed over the Staple Inn door] was Pretty Jolly Too." MED 11

—*praised:* "'You do wrong not to fill your glass,' said Mr Chester, holding up his own before the light. 'Wine in moderation—not in excess, for that makes men ugly—has a thousand pleasant influences. It brightens the eye, improves the voice, imparts a new vivacity to one's thoughts and conversation: you should try it, Ned.'" BR 32

—*sherry*

—*appreciated:* "Mr Bucket frequently observes, in friendly circles where there is no restraint, that he likes a toothful of your fine old brown East Inder sherry better than anything you can offer him. Consequently he fills and empties his glass, with a smack of his lips . . . . " BH 53

—*cobbler:* Mark Tapley "produced a very large tumbler, piled up to the brim with little blocks of clear transparent ice, through which one or two thin slices of lemon, and a golden liquid of delicious appearance, appeared from the still depths below, to the loving eye of the spectator.

"'What do you call this?' said Martin.

"But Mr Tapley made no answer: merely plunging a reed into the mixture—which caused a pleasant commotion among the pieces of ice—and signifying by an expressive gesture that it was to be pumped up through that agency by the enraptured drinker.

"Martin took the glass, with an astonished look; and applied his lips to the reed; and cast up his eyes once in ecstasy. He paused no more until the goblet was drained to the last drop . . . .

"'This wonderful invention, sir,' said Mark, tenderly patting the empty glass, 'is called a cobbler. Sherry cobbler when you name it long; cobbler, when you name it short." MC 17

And see W:America—*plantation*

—*at the Dodo:* "I wonder where it gets its Sherry? If I were to send my pint of wine to some famous chemist to be analysed, what would it turn out to be made of? It tastes of pepper, sugar, bitter-almonds, vinegar, warm knives, any flat drinks, and a little brandy. Would it unman a Spanish exile by reminding him of his native land at all? I think not. If there really be any townspeople out of the churchyards, and if a caravan of them ever do dine, with a bottle of wine per man, in this desert of the Dodo, it must make good for the doctor next day!" RP/PA

—*effect:* "One of the very tall young men already smells of sherry, and his eyes have a tendency to become fixed in his head, and to stare at objects without seeing them. The very tall young man is conscious of this failing in himself; and informs his comrade that it's his 'exciseman.' The very tall young man would say excitement, but his speech is hazy." DS 31

—*at evening:* "Everybody else within the bills of mortality was hot; but the Patriarch [Christopher Casby] was perfectly cool. Everybody was thirsty, and the Patriarch was drinking. There was a fragrance of limes or lemons about him; and he had made a drink of golden sherry, which shone in a large tumbler, as if he were drinking the evening sunshine." LD ii 32

—*medicinal:* "'If my friend Dombey suffers from bodily weakness, and would allow me [Lord Feenix] to recommend what has frequently done myself good, as a man who has been extremely queer at times, and who lived pretty freely in the days when men lived very freely, I should say, let it be in point of fact the yolk of an egg, beat up with sugar and nutmeg, in a glass of sherry, and taken in the morning with a slice of dry toast. Jackson, who kept the boxing-rooms in Bond Street . . . used to mention that in training for the ring they substituted rum for sherry. I should recommend sherry in this case, on account of my friend Dombey being in an invalided condition; which might occasion rum to fly—in point of fact to his head—and throw him into a devil of a state.'" DS 61

—*mulled:* "'They burn sherry very well here,' said Mr Inspector, as a piece of local intelligence. 'Perhaps you gentlemen might like a bottle?'

"The answer being By all means, Bob Gliddery received his instructions from Mr Inspector, and departed in a becoming state of alacrity engendered by reverence for the majesty of the law . . . .

"Bob's reappearance with a steaming jug broke off the conversation. But although the jug steamed forth a delicious perfume, its contents had not received that last happy touch which the surpassing finish of the Six Jolly Fellowship-Porters imparted on such momentous occasions.

"Bob carried in his left hand one of those iron models of sugar-loaf hats before mentioned, into which he emptied the jug, and the pointed end of which he thrust deep down into the fire, so leaving it for a few moments while he disappeared and reappeared with three bright drinking-glasses. Placing these on the table and bending over the fire, meritoriously sensible of the trying nature of his duty, he watched the wreaths of steam, until at the special instant of projection he caught up the iron vessel and gave it one delicate twirl, causing it to send forth one gentle hiss.

"Then he restored the contents to the jug; held over the steam of the jug each of the three bright glasses in succession; finally filled them all, and with a clear conscience awaited the applause of his fellow creatures." ¶OMF i 13

—*sommelier:* "The appearance of dinner here cut Bella short . . . because it was put on under the auspices of a solemn gentleman in black clothes and a white cravat, who looked much more like a clergyman than *the* clergyman, and seemed to have mounted a great deal higher in the church: not to say, scaled the steeple. This dignitary, conferring in secrecy with John Rokesmith on the subject of punch and wines, bent his head as though stooping to the Papistical practice of receiving auricular confession. Likewise, on John's offering a suggestion which didn't meet his views, his face became overcast and reproachful, as enjoining penance." OMF iv 4

And see Restaurant—*in Italy*

Doctor Blimber's Young Gentlemen as They Appeared When Enjoying Themselves DS

Mind

The one serviceable, safe, certain, remunerative, attainable quality in every study and in every pursuit is the quality of attention. My own invention or imagination would never have served me as it has, but for the habit of commonplace, humble, patient, daily, toiling, drudging attention. Genius, vivacity, quickness of penetration, brilliancy in association of ideas—such mental qualities will not be commanded; but attention, after due term of submissive service, always will.

[S/BM2]

"I was thinking of one thing and thinking of another. Just as you yourself might. Just as anybody might. And when I do think of one thing and do think of another, I hardly need to tell you that I think of the family. Because, dear me! a person's thoughts," Mrs Tickit said this with an argumentative and philosophic air, "however they may stray, will go more or less on what is uppermost in their minds. They will do it, sir, and a person can't prevent them."

[LD ii 9]

The School OCS

Addiction

—enabling: "What could the child [Nell] do, with the knowledge she had, but give him every penny that came into her hands, lest he should be tempted on to rob their benefactress? If she told the truth (so thought the child) he would be treated as a madman; if she did not supply him with money, he would supply himself; supplying him, she fed the fire that burnt him up, and put him perhaps beyond recovery." OCS 31

—an end: "The air of the room is almost bad enough to have extinguished [the candle], if [Tulkinghorn] had not. It is a small room, nearly black with soot, and grease, and dirt. In the rusty skeleton of a grate, pinched at the middle as if Poverty had gripped it, a red coke fire burns low. In the corner by the chimney, stand a deal table and a broken desk; a wilderness marked with a rain of ink. In another corner, a ragged old portmanteau on one of the two chairs, serves for cabinet or wardrobe; no larger one is needed, for it collapses like the cheeks of a starved man. The floor is bare; except that one old mat, trodden to shreds of rope-yard, lies perishing upon the hearth. No curtain veils the darkness of the night, but the discoloured shutters are drawn together; and through the two gaunt holes pierced in them, famine might be staring in—the Banshee of the man upon the bed.

"For, on a low bed opposite the fire—a confusion of dirty patch-work, lean-ribbed ticking, and coarse sacking—the lawyer, hesitating just within the doorway, sees a man. He lies there, dressed in shirt and trousers, with bare feet. He has a yellow look in the spectral darkness of a candle that has guttered down, until the whole length of its wick (still burning) has doubled over, and left a tower of winding-sheet above it. His hair is ragged, mingling with his whiskers and his beard—the latter, ragged too, and grown, like the scum and mist around him, in neglect. Foul and filthy as the room is, foul and filthy as the air is, it is not easy to perceive what fumes those are which most oppress the senses in it; but through the general sickliness and faintness, and the odour of stale tobacco, there comes into the lawyer's mouth the bitter, vapid taste of opium.

"'Hallo, my friend!' he cries, and strikes his iron candlestick against the door.

"He thinks he has awakened his friend. He lies a little turned away, but his eyes are surely open . . . .

"As he rattles on the door, the candle which has drooped so long, goes out, and leaves him in the dark; with the gaunt eyes in the shutters staring down upon the bed." BH 10

—a trance: " . . . he sees that the woman is of a haggard appearance, and that her weazen chin is resting on her hands, and that her eyes are staring—with an unwinking, blind sort of steadfastness—before her . . . .

"'Are you ill?'

"'No, deary,' she answers, without looking at him, and with no departure from her strange blind stare.

"'Are you blind?'

"'No, deary.'

"'Are you lost, homeless, faint? What is the matter, that you stay here in the cold so long, without moving?'

"By slow and stiff efforts, she appears to contract her vision until it can rest upon him; and then a curious film passes over her, and she begins to shake." MED 14

—visible: " . . . [his] whole appearance had undergone a complete change. His face was flushed and eager, his eyes were strained, his teeth set, his breath came short and thick, and the hand he laid upon [Nell's] arm trembled so violently that she shook beneath its grasp . . . . Exulting in some brief triumph, or cast down by a defeat, there he sat so wild and restless, so feverishly and intensely anxious, so terribly eager, so ravenous for the paltry stakes, that she could have almost better borne to see him dead. And yet she was the innocent cause of all this torture, and he, gambling with such a savage thirst for gain as the most insatiable gambler never felt, had not one selfish thought!" OCS 19

Associations, mental

—on an anniversary: "'I well remember mamma's clasping her hands, and exclaiming, "This will end in a little man!" . . . She afterwards went so far as to predict that it would end in a little man whose mind would be below the average, but that was in what I may denominate a paroxysm of maternal disappointment. Within a month,' said Mrs Wilfer, deepening her voice, as if she were relating a terrible ghost story, 'within a month, I first saw R. W., my husband. Within a year I married him. It is natural for the mind to recall these dark

coincidences on the present day.'" OMF iii 4

—for an author: "I began this book [*Dombey & Son*] by the Lake of Geneva, and went on with it for some months in France, before pursuing it in England. The association between the writing and the place of writing is so curiously strong in my mind, that at this day, although I know, in my fancy, every stair in the little midshipman's house, and could swear to every pew in the church in which Florence was married, or to every young gentleman's bedstead in Doctor Blimber's establishment, I yet confusedly imagine Captain Cuttle as secluding himself from Mrs MacStinger among the mountains of Switzerland. Similarly, when I am reminded by any chance of what it was that the waves were always saying, my remembrance wanders for a whole winter night about the streets of Paris—as I restlessly did with a heavy heart, on the night when I had written the chapter in which my little friend [Paul Dombey] and I parted company." DS Preface

—gravestones: "As I never saw my father or my mother, and never saw any likeness of either of them . . . my first fancies regarding what they were like, were unreasonably derived from their tombstones. The shape of the letters on my father's, gave me an odd idea that he was a square, stout, dark man, with curly black hair. From the character and turn of the inscription, '*Also Georgiana Wife of the Above,*' I drew a childish conclusion that my mother was freckled and sickly. To five little stone lozenges, each about a foot and a half long, which were arranged in a neat row beside their grave, and wre sacred to the memory of five little brothers of mine . . . I am indebted for a belief I religiously entertained that they had all been born on their backs with their hands in their trousers-pockets, and had never taken them out in this state of existence." GE 1

—a meal: "'Edward, my father had a son, who being a fool like you, and, like you, entertaining low and disobedient sentiments, he disinherited and cursed one morning after breakfast. The circumstance occurs to me with a singular clearness of recollection this evening. I remember eating muffins at the time, with marmalade.'" BR 32

—for a railroad worker: "'I starts light with Rob only; I comes to a branch; I takes on what I finds there; and a whole train of ideas gets coupled on to him, afore I knows where I am, or where they comes from. What a Junction a man's thoughts is,' said Mr Toodle, 'to-be-sure!'" DS 38

—for a reader: "'And since I've took to general reading, you've took to general writing, eh, sir?' said Mr Omer, surveying me [David Copperfield] admiringly. 'What a lovely work that was of yours! What expressions in it! I read it every word—every word. And as to feeling sleepy! Not at all!'

"I laughingly expressed my satisfaction, but I must confess that I thought this association of ideas significant." DC 51

—at sea at night: "At first, too, and even when the hour, and all the objects it exalts, have come to be familiar, it is difficult, alone and thoughtful, to hold them to their proper shapes and forms. They change with the wandering fancy; assume the semblance of things left far away; put on the well-remembered aspect of favourite places dearly loved; and even people them with shadows. Streets, houses, rooms; figures so like their usual occupants, that they have startled me by their reality, which far exceeded, as it seemed to me, all power of mine to conjure up the absent; have, many and many a time, at such an hour, grown suddenly out of objects with whose real look, and use, and purpose, I was as well acquainted as with my own two hands." AN 2

—unconscious: "There are strange chords in the human heart, which will lie dormant through years of depravity and wickedness, but which will vibrate at last to some slight circumstance apparently trivial in itself, but connected by some undefined and indistinct association with past days that can never be recalled, and with bitter recollections from which the most degraded creature in existence cannot escape." SB/PS

—unsought: "There are chords in the human heart—strange, varying strings—which are only struck by accident; which will remain mute and senseless to appeals the most passionate and earnest, and respond at last to the slightest casual touch. In the most insensible or childish minds, there is some train of reflection which art can seldom lead, or skill assist, but which will reveal itself, as great truths have done, by chance; and when the discoverer has the plainest and simplest end in view." OCS 55

And see B:Food and drink—*roast pig*

Curiosity

—the beyond: "'Do you know,' simpered Cleopatra [Mrs Skewton], reversing the knave of clubs, who had come into her game

with his heels uppermost, 'that if anything could tempt me to put a period to my life, it would be curiosity to find out what it's all about and what it means; there are so many provoking mysteries, really, that are hidden from us." DS 21

—compulsive: "'Well, sir,' returns Mr Snagsby, 'you see my little woman is—not to put too fine a point upon it—inquisitive. She's inquisitive. Poor little thing, she's liable to spasms, and it's good for her to have her mind employed. In consequence of which she employs it—I should say upon every individual thing she can lay hold of, whether it concerns her or not—especially not. My little woman has a very active mind, sir.'" BH 22

—manipulated: "To surround anything, however monstrous or ridiculous, with an air of mystery, is to invest it with a secret charm and power of attraction which to the crowd is irresistible. False priests, false prophets, false doctors, false patriots, false prodigies of every kind, veiling their proceedings in mystery, have always addressed themselves at an immense advantage to the popular credulity, and have been, perhaps, more indebted to that resource in gaining and keeping for a time the upper hand of Truth and Common Sense, than to any half-dozen items in the whole catalogue of imposture.

"Curiosity is, and has been from the creation of the world, a master-passion. To awaken it, to gratify it by slight degrees, and yet leave something always in suspense, is to establish the surest hold that can be had, in wrong, on the unthinking portion of mankind." BR 37

—servants': " . . . I was looked after by an inflammatory old female, assisted by an animated rag-bag whom she called her niece; and to keep a room secret from them would be to invite curiosity and exaggeration. They both had weak eyes, which I had long attributed to their chronically looking in at keyholes, and they were always at hand when not wanted; indeed that was their only reliable quality besides larceny." GE 40

And see FL:Life—*mystery*

Day-dreaming

—in a deprived life: He leaned upon the sill of the long low window, and looking out upon the blackened forest of chimneys again, began to dream. For, it had been the uniform tendency of this man's life—so much was wanting in it to think about, so much that might have been better directed and happier to speculate upon—to make him a dreamer, after all." LD i 3

—on the ocean: "And so, with the watch aloft setting all the sails, and with the screw below revolving at a mighty rate, and occasionally giving the ship an angry shake for resisting, I fell into my idlest ways, and lost myself.

"As, for instance, whether it was I lying there, or some other entity even more mysterious, was a matter I was far too lazy to look into. What did it signify to me if it were I? or to the more mysterious entity, if it were he? Equally as to the remembrances that drowsily floated by me, or by him, why ask when or where the things happened? Was it not enough that they befell at some time, somewhere?" UT/AS

—on a river: "There are some small out-of-the-way landing-places on the Thames and the Medway, where I do much of my summer idling. Running water is favourable to day-dreams, and a strong tidal river is the best of running water for mine . . . .

"Watching these [ships and other vessels], I still am under no obligation to think about them, or even so much as to see them, unless it perfectly suits my humour. As little am I obliged to hear the plash and flop of the tide, the ripple at my feet, the clinking windlass afar off, or the humming steam-ship paddles further away yet. These, with the creaking little jetty on which I sit, and the gaunt high-water marks and low-water marks in the mud, and the broken causeway, and the broken bank, and the broken stakes and piles leaning forward as if they were vain of their personal appearance and looking for their reflection in the water, will melt into any train of fancy.

"Equally adaptable to any purpose or to none, are the pasturing sheep and kine upon the marshes, the gulls that wheel and dip around me, the crows (well out of gunshot) going home from the rich harvest-fields, the heron that has been out a-fishing and looks as melancholy, up there in the sky, as if it hadn't agreed with him. Everything within the range of the senses will, by the aid of the running water, lend itself to everything beyond that range, and work into a drowsy whole, not unlike a kind of tune, but for which there is no exact definition." ¶UT/CD

—on the shore: So dreamy is the murmur of

the sea below my window, that may have been here, for anything I know, one hundred years. Not that I have grown old, for, daily on the neighbouring downs and grassy hill-sides, I find that I can still in reason walk any distance, jump over anything, and climb up anywhere; but that the sound of the ocean seems to have become so customary to my musings, and other realities seem so to have gone aboard ship and floated away over the horizon, that, for aught I will undertake to the contrary, I am the enchanted son of the King my father, shut up in a tower on the sea-shore, for protection against an old she-goblin who insisted on being my godmother, and who foresaw at the font—wonderful creature!—that I should get into a scrape before I was twenty-one." RP/OT

And see Mind—*effect of solitude—illness*

Dreams and Dreaming

—*bad, of America:* "The log-house, with the open door, and drooping trees about it; the stagnant morning mist, and red sun, dimly seen beyond; the vapour rising up from land and river; the quick stream making the loathsome banks it washed more flat and dull: how often they returned in dreams! How often it was happiness to wake and find them Shadows that had vanished!'" MC 33

—*in bereavement:* "It is not in my power to retrace, one by one, all the weary phases of distress of mind through which I passed. There are some dreams that can only be imperfectly and vaguely described; and when I oblige myself to look back on this time of my life, I seem to be recalling such a dream. I see myself passing on among the novelties of foreign towns, palaces, cathedrals, temples, pictures, castles, tombs, fantastic streets—the old abiding places of History and Fancy—as a dreamer might; bearing my painful load through all, and hardly conscious of the objects as they fade before me. Listlessness to everything but brooding sorrow, was the night that fell on my undisciplined heart. Let me look up from it—as at last I did, thank Heaven!—and from its long, sad, wretched dream, to dawn." DC 58

—*of a condemned man:* "Worn with watching and excitement, he sleeps, and the same unsettled state of mind pursues him in his dreams. An insupportable load is taken from his breast; he is walking with his wife in a pleasant field, with the bright sky above them, and a fresh and boundless prospect on every side—how different from the stone walls of Newgate! She is looking—not as she did when he saw her for the last time in that dreadful place, but as she used when he loved her—long, long ago, before misery and ill-treatment had altered her looks, and vice had changed his nature, and she is leaning upon his arm, and looking up into his face with tenderness and affection—and he does *not* strike her now, nor rudely shake her from him. And oh! how glad he is to tell her all he had forgotten in that last hurried interview, and to fall on his knees before her and fervently beseech her pardon for all the unkindness and cruelty that wasted her form and broke her heart! The scene suddenly changes. He is on his trial again: there are the judge and jury, and prosecutors, and witnesses, just as they were before. How full the court is—what a sea of heads—with a gallows, too, and a scaffold—and how all those people stare at *him!* Verdict, 'Guilty.' No matter; he will escape.

"The night is dark and cold, the gates have been left open, and in an instant he is in the street, flying from the scene of his imprisonment like the wind. The streets are cleared, the open fields are gained and the broad wide country lies before him. Onward he dashes in the midst of darkness, over hedge and ditch, through mud and pool, bounding from spot to spot with a speed and lightness, astonishing even to himself. At length he pauses; he must be safe from pursuit now; he will stretch himself on that bank and sleep till sunrise.

"A period of unconsciousness succeeds. He wakes . . . the condemned felon again, guilty and despairing; and in two hours more will be dead." SB/VN

—*defined:* "Dreams are the bright creatures of poem and legend, who sport on earth in the night season, and melt away in the first beam of the sun, which lights grim care and stern reality on their daily pilgrimage through the world." NN 13

—*a dreamer's condition:* " . . . Bella [Wilfer] was in the state of a dreamer; perfectly unable to account for her being there, perfectly unable to forecast what would happen next, or whither she was going, or why; certain of nothing in the immediate present, but that she confided in John, and that John seemed somehow to be getting more triumphant. But what a certainty was that!" OMF iv 12

—equalizing effect: "It would be curious, as illustrating the equality of sleep, to inquire how many of its phenomena are common to all classes, to all degrees of wealth and poverty, to every grade of education and ignorance.

"Here, for example, is her Majesty Queen Victoria in her palace, this present blessed night, and here is Winking Charley, a sturdy vagrant, in one of her Majesty's jails. Her majesty has fallen, many thousands of times, from that same Tower, which *I* claim a right to tumble off now and then. So has Winking Charley.

"Her Majesty in her sleep has opened or prorogued Parliament, or has held a Drawing Room, attired in some very scanty dress, the deficiencies and improprieties of which have caused her great uneasiness. I, in my degree, have suffered unspeakable agitation of mind from taking the chair at a public dinner at the London Tavern in my night-clothes, which not all the courtesy of my kind friend and host **Mr Bathe** could persuade me were quite adapted to the occasion.

"Winking Charley has been repeatedly tried in a worse condition. Her Majesty is no stranger to a vault or firmament, of a sort of floorcloth, with an indistinct pattern distantly resembling eyes, which occasionally obtrudes itself on her repose. Neither am I. Neither is Winking Charley.

"It is quite common to all three of us to skim along with airy strides a little above the ground; also to hold, with the deepest interest, dialogues with various people, all represented by ourselves; and to be at our wit's end to know what they are going to tell us; and to be indescribably astonished by the secrets they disclose.

"It is probable that we have all three committed murders and hidden bodies. It is pretty certain that we have all desperately wanted to cry out, and have had no voice; that we have all gone to the play and not been able to get in; that we have all dreamed much more of our youth than of our later lives; that—I have lost it! The thread's broken." ¶RP/LA

—presentiment: "'I dreamt [said Walter Bray] that it was this morning, and you and I had been talking, as we have been this minute; that I went up stairs, for the very purpose for which I am going now; and that as I stretched out my hand to take Madeline's, and lead her down, the floor sank with me, and after falling from such an indescribable and tremendous height as the imagination scarcely conceives except in dreams, I alighted in a grave.'" NN 53 [*Bray died upstairs a moment later.*]

—remembered: "'A few hours more,' thought Walter, 'and no dream I ever had here when I was a school-boy will be so little mine as this old room. The dream may come back in my sleep, and I may return waking to this place, it may be: but the dream at least will serve no other master, and the room may have a score, and every one of them may change, neglect, misuse it.'" DS 19

—the sane and the insane: "Are not the sane and the insane equal at night as the sane lie a dreaming? Are not all of us outside this hospital, who dream, more or less in the condition of those inside it, every night of our lives? Are we not nightly persuaded, as they daily are, that we associate preposterously with kings and queens, emperors and empresses, and notabilities of all sorts? Do we not nightly jumble events and personages and times and places, as these do daily? Are we not sometimes troubled by our own sleeping inconsistencies; and do we not vexedly try to account for them or excuse them, just as these do sometimes in respect of their waking delusions?

"Said an afflicted man to me, when I was last in a hospital like this, 'Sir, I can frequently fly.' I was half ashamed to reflect that so could I—by night. Said a woman to me on the same occasion, 'Queen Victoria frequently comes to dine with me, and her Majesty and I dine off peaches and maccaroni in our night-gowns, and his Royal Highness the Prince Consort does us the honour to make a third on horseback in a Field-Marshal's uniform.' Could I refrain from reddening with consciousness when I remembered the amazing royal parties I myself had given (at night), the unaccountable viands I had put on table, and my extraordinary manner of conducting myself on those distinguished occasions? I wonder that the great master who knew everything, when he called Sleep the death of each day's life, did not call Dreams the insanity of each day's sanity." UT/NW

—of several: "If Martin dreamed at all, some clue to the matter of his visions may possibly be gathered from the after-pages of this history. Those of Thomas Pinch were all of holidays, church organs, and seraphic Pecksniffs. It was some time before Mr

Pecksniff dreamed at all . . . . But he, too, slept and dreamed at last. Thus in the quiet hours of the night, one house shuts in as many incoherent and incongruous fancies as a madman's head." MC 5

—in words: "It is very remarkable, that as we dream in words, and carry on imaginary conversations, in which we speak both for ourselves and for the shadows who appear to us in those visions of the night, so [Laura Bridgman], having no words, uses her finger alphabet in her sleep. And it has been ascertained that when her slumber is broken, and is much disturbed by dreams, she expresses her thoughts in an irregular and confused manner on her fingers: just as we should murmur and mutter them indistinctly, in the like circumstances." AN 3

And see W:America—*covered bridge*

Education

—adult: "[American] Ladies who have a passion for attending lectures are to be found among all classes and all conditions . . . it has at least the merit of being always new. One lecture treads so quickly on the heels of another, that none are remembered; and the course of this month may be safely repeated next, with its charm of novelty unbroken, and its interest unabated." AN 3

—aggressive: "Master Bitherstone read aloud to the rest a pedigree from Genesis (judiciously selected by Mrs Pipchin), getting over the names with the ease and clearness of a person tumbling up the treadmill . . . . About noon Mrs Pipchin presided over some Early Readings. It being a part of Mrs Pipchin's system not to encourage a child's mind to develop and expand itself like a young flower, but to open it by force like an oyster, the moral of these lessons was usually of a violent and stunning character: the hero—a naughty boy—seldom, in the mildest catastrophe being finished off by anything less than a lion, or a bear." DS 8

"'There is a great deal of nonsense—and worse—talked about young people not being pressed too hard at first, and being tempted on, and all the rest of it, Sir,' said Mrs Pipchin, impatiently rubbing her hooked nose. 'It never was thought of in my time, and it has no business to be thought of now. My opinion is, "Keep 'em at it."'" DS 11

—the bad kind: " . . . I don't like that sort of school . . . where the bright childish imagination is utterly discouraged, and where those bright childish faces, which it is so very good for the wisest among us to remember in after life, when the world is too much with us early and late, are gloomily and grimly scared out of countenance; where I have never seen among the pupils, whether boys or girls, anything but little parrots and small calculating machines." S/WC

—the best kind: " . . . the best of education: that which the grown man from day to day and year to year furnishes for himself and maintains for himself, and in right of which his education goes on all his life, instead of leaving off, complacently, just when he begins to live in the social system." S/LM

"Mere reading and writing are not education. It would be quite as reasonable to call bricks and mortar, architecture; oils and colours, art; reeds and cat-gut, music; or a child's spelling-book the works of **Shakespeare**, **Milton** or **Bacon**, as to call the lowest rudiments of education, 'education', and to visit upon that much abused and slandered word their failure in any instance.

"To my thinking it is precisely because they are not education: because, generally speaking, the word has been misunderstood in that sense a great deal too long; because education for the business of life, and for the due cultivation of the domestic virtues, is at least as important from day to day to the grown person as to the child; because real education amidst the strife and contention for a livelihood, and the consequent necessity incumbent on a great number of young persons to go into the world when they are very young and having had no adequate opportunity for mental culture, is extremely difficult—it is because of these things that I look upon Mechanics' Institutions and Athenaeums as vitally important to the well-being of society; and it is because the rudiments of education may there be turned to good account in the acquisition of sound principles, and in the practice of the great virtues of Faith, Hope, and Charity, to which all our knowledge tends: it is because of that, I take it, that we are met here in Education's name tonight." ¶S/GA

—charity school

—exposure to Church: "Rob the Grinder, whose reverence for the inspired writings, under the admirable system of the Grinders' School, had been developed by a perpetual bruising of his intellectual shins against all the proper names of all the tribes of Judah, and by the monotonous repetition of hard

verses, expecially by way of punishment, and by the parading of him at six years old in leather breeches, three times a Sunday, very high up, in a very hot church, with a great organ buzzing against his drowsy head, like an exceedingly busy bee—Rob the Grinder made a mighty show of being edified when the Captain ceased to read, and generally yawned and nodded while the reading was in progress." DS 39

—faculty: " . . . the master, a superannuated old Grinder of savage disposition, who had been appointed schoolmaster because he didn't know anything, and wasn't fit for anything, and for whose cruel cane all chubby little boys had a perfect fascination." DS 5"

". . . the quondam grinder [Biler Toodle], huffed and cuffed, and flogged and badged, and taught, as parrots are, by a brute jobbed into his place of schoolmaster with as much fitness for it as a hound, might not have been educated on quite a right plan in some undiscovered respect . . . ." DS 20

—purpose: "'I am far from being friendly,' pursued Mr Dombey, 'to what is called by persons of levelling sentiments, general education. But it is necessary that the inferior classes should continue to be taught to know their position, and to conduct themselves properly. So far I approve of schools. . . . " DS 5

—regimented: "Again, I don't by any means like schools in leather breeches, and with mortified straw baskets for bonnets, which file along the streets to churches in long melancholy rows under the escort of that surprising British monster, a beadle, whose system of instruction, I am afraid, but too often presents that happy union of sound with sense, of which a very remarkable instance is given in a grave report of a trustworthy school inspector, to the effect that a boy in great repute at school for his learning, presented on his slate, as one of the ten commandments, the perplexing prohibition, 'Thou shalt not commit doldrum'." S/WC

—the right sort: " . . . perhaps you will permit me to sketch in a few words the sort of school that I do like. It is a school established by the members of an industrious and useful order, which supplies the comforts and graces of life at every familiar turning in the road of our existence; it is a school established by them for the Orphan and Necessitous Children of their own brethren and sisterhood; it is a place of education where, while the beautiful history of the Christian religion is daily taught, and while the life of that Divine teacher who Himself took little children on His knees is daily studied, no sectarian ill will nor narrow human dogma is permitted to darken the face of the clear heaven which they disclose.

"It is a children's school, which is at the same time no less a children's home, a home not to be confided to the care of cold or ignorant strangers, nor, by the nature of its foundation, in the course of ages to pass into hands that have as much natural right to deal with it as [with] the peaks of the highest mountains or with the depths of the sea, but to be from generation to generation administered by men living in precisely such homes as those poor children have lost; by men always bent upon making that replacement, such a home as their own dear children might find a happy refuge in if they themselves were taken early away." ¶S/WC

—tribulation: " . . . poor Biler's life had been . . . rendered weary by the costume of the Charitable Grinders. The youth of the streets could not endure it. No young vagabond could be brought to bear its contemplation for a moment, without throwing himself upon the unoffending wearer, and doing him a mischief. His social existence had been more like that of an early Christian, than an innocent child of the nineteenth century. He had been stoned in the streets. He had been overthrown into gutters; bespattered with mud; violently flattened against posts. Entire strangers to his person had lifted his yellow cap off his head and cast it to the winds. His legs had not only undergone verbal criticisms and revilings, but had been handled and pinched." DS 6

—uniform described: "'The dress . . . is a nice, warm, blue baize tailed coat and cap, turned up with orange-coloured binding; red worsted stockings; and very strong leather small-clothes. One might wear the articles one's-self,' said Mrs Chick, with enthusiasm, 'and be grateful.'" DS 5

—vindication: " . . . they never taught honour at the Grinders' School, where the system that prevailed was particularly strong in the engendering of hypocrisy. Insomuch, that many of the friends and masters of past grinders said, if this were what came of education for the common

people, let us have none. Some more rational said, let us have a better one. But the governing powers of the Grinders' Company were always ready for them, by picking out a few boys who had turned out well, in spite of the system, and roundly asserting that they could have only turned out well because of it. Which settled the business of those objectors out of hand, and established the glory of the Grinders' Institution." DS 38

—*classical:* "I thought it much to be regretted that Richard [Carstone]'s education had not counteracted those influences ["the habit of putting off—and trusting to this, that, and the other chance, without knowing what chance"] or directed his character.

"He had been eight years at a public school, and had learnt, I understood, to make Latin verses of several sorts, in the most admirable manner. But I never heard that it had been anybody's business to find out what his natural bent was, or where his failings lay, or to adapt any kind of knowledge to *him. He* had been adapted to the verses, and learnt the art of making them to such perfection, that if he had remained at school until he was of age, I suppose he could only have gone on making them over and over again, unless he had enlarged his education by forgetting how to do it.

"Still, although I had no doubt that they were very beautiful, and very improving, and very sufficient for a great many purposes of life, and always remembered all through life, I did doubt whether Richard would not have profited by some one studying him a little, instead of his studying them quite so much. ¶BH 13 *And see Tozer and Tozer's uncle DS* Vol. I p770

—*and common sense:* "[William] Laud, who was a sincere man, of large learning but small sense—for the two things sometimes go together in very different quantities . . . . " CHE 33 i

—*counterproductive:* "That I am particularly ignorant what most things in the universe are made of, and how they are made, is another of my charges against *Mr Barlow.* With the dread upon me of developing into a *Harry* and with a further dread upon me of being Barlowed if I made inquiries, by bringing down upon myself a cold shower-bath of explanations and experiments, I forbore enlightenment in my youth, and became, as they say in melodramas, 'the wreck you now behold.' That I consorted with idlers and dunces is another of the melancholy facts for which I hold *Mr Barlow* responsible . . . . So I took the path, which, but for *Mr Barlow,* I might never have trodden." UT/B

—*country ("dame") school:* "The Educational scheme or Course established by Mr Wopsle's great-aunt may be resolved into the following synopsis. The pupils ate apples and put straws down one another's backs, until Mr Wopsle's great-aunt collected her energies, and made an indiscriminate totter at them with a birch-rod. After receiving the charge with every mark of derision, the pupils formed in line and buzzingly passed a ragged book from hand to hand. The book had an alphabet in it, some figures and tables, and a little spelling—that is to say, it had had once. As soon as this volume began to circulate, Mr Wopsle's great-aunt fell into a state of coma; arising either from sleep or a rheumatic paroxysm.

"The pupils then entered among themselves upon a competitive examination on the subject of Boots, with the view of ascertaining who could tread the hardest upon whose toes. This mental exercise lasted until Biddy made a rush at them and distributed three defaced Bibles (shaped as if they had been unskilfully cut off the chump-end of something), more illegibly printed at the best than any curiosities of literature I have since met with, speckled all over with iron-mould, and having various specimens of the insect world smashed between their leaves. This part of the Course was usually lightened by several single combats between Biddy and refractory students.

"When the fights were over, Biddy gave out the number of a page, and then we all read aloud what we could—or what we couldn't—in a frightful chorus; Biddy leading with a high shrill monotonous voice, and none of us having the least notion of, or reverence for, what we were reading about. When this horrible din had lasted a certain time, it mechanically awoke Mr Wopsle's great-aunt, who staggered at a boy fortuitously, and pulled his ears. This was understood to terminate the Course for the evening, and we emerged into the air with shrieks of intellectual victory.

"It is fair to remark that there was no prohibition against any pupil's entertaining himself with a slate or even with the ink (when there was any), but that it was not easy to pursue that branch of study in the winter season, on account of the little general shop in which the classes were holden—and which was also Mr Wopsle's great-aunt's sitting-room and bed-chamber—being but faintly illuminated through the agency of one low-spirited dip-candle and no snuffers." ¶GE 10

—dangers of bad: "Utilitarian economists, skeletons of schoolmasters, Commissioners of Fact, genteel and used-up infidels, gabblers of many little dog's-eared creeds, the poor you will have always with you. Cultivate in them, while there is yet time, the utmost graces of the fancies and affections, to adorn their lives so much in need of ornament; or, in the day of your triumph, when romance is utterly driven out of their souls, and they and a bare existence stand face to face, Reality will take a wolfish turn, and make an end of you." HT ii 6

—deaf/dumb/blind: "'After a while, instead of labels, the individual letters were given to [Laura Bridgman] on detached bits of paper: they were arranged side by side so as to spell *book, key, &c;* then they were mixed up in a heap and a sign was made for her to arrange them herself so as to express the words *book, key &c;* and she did so.

"'Hitherto, the process had been mechanical, and the success about as great as teaching a very knowing dog a variety of tricks. The poor child had sat in mute amazement, and patiently imitated everything her teacher did; but now the truth began to flash upon her: her intellect began to work: she perceived that here was a way by which she could herself make up a sign of anything that was in her own mind, and show it to another mind; and at once her countenance lighted up with a human expression: it was no longer a dog, or parrot: it was an immortal spirit, eagerly seizing upon a new link of union with other spirits! I could almost fix upon the moment when this truth dawned upon her mind, and spread its light to her countenance . . . . '" AN 3

—discipline

—beneficial: "'Atten-tion!' Instantly a hundred boys stood forth in the paved yard as one boy;' bright, quick, eager, steady, watchful for the look of command, instant and ready for the word. Not only was there complete precision—complete accord to the eye and to the ear—but an alertness in the doing of the thing which deprived it, curiously, of its monotonous or mechanical character. There was perfect uniformity, and yet an individual spirit and emulation. No spectator could doubt that the boys liked it." UT/ST

—uncomfortable: " . . . I don't like that sort of school . . . where memory always depicts the youthful enthraller of my first affection as for ever standing against a wall, in a curious machine of wood, which confined her innocent feet in the first dancing position, while those arms, which should have encircled my jacket, those precious arms, I say, were pinioned behind her by an instrument of torture called a backboard, fixed in the manner of a double direction post." S/WC

—in England: "Who, knowing England at this time, would wish to utter with his last breath a more righteous warning than that its curse is ignorance, or a miscalled education which is as bad or worse . . .? Well will it be for us and for our children, if those dying words be never henceforth forgotten on the Judgment Seat." HW/JT

And see W:America—*education*

"Schools are intolerable follies [says Bendigo Buster]; and of all schools the most foolish is the German School. England is acting, in regard to schools, as becomes her practical good sense. Her boys are in the gutters, growing up to manly independence; they swear well, fight like bricks, and have game in 'em. By her boys, I mean the multitude, the children of the people. I know that in the upper classes there are children more or less demoralized by education, and that the same evil influence is sometimes brought to bear upon the poor. But, England, as a nation, don't trouble herself much about the education of the masses; something like forty-five out of a hundred of 'em can't read and write. That's what I call being practical." HWC/B

—a forcing house

—early stages: "The young gentlemen were prematurely full of carking anxieties. They knew no rest from the pursuit of stony-hearted verbs, savage noun-substantives, inflexible syntactic passages, and ghosts of exercises that appeared to them in their dreams. Under the forcing system, a young gentleman usually took leave of his spirits in three weeks. He had all the cares of the world on his head in three months. He conceived bitter sentiments against his parents or guardians in four; he was an old misanthrope, in five; envied Curtius that blessed

refuge in the earth, in six; and at the end of the first twelvemonth had arrived at the conclusion, from which he never afterwards departed, that all the fancies of the poets, and lessons of the sages, were a mere collection of words and grammar, and had no other meaning in the world." DS 11

—*method:* "Whenever a young gentleman was taken in hand by Doctor Blimber, he might consider himself sure of a pretty tight squeeze. The doctor only undertook the charge of ten young gentlemen, but he had, always ready, a supply of learning for a hundred, on the lowest estimate; and it was at once the business and delight of his life to gorge the unhappy ten with it.

"In fact, Doctor Blimber's establishment was a great hot-house, in which there was a forcing apparatus incessantly at work. All the boys blew before their time. Mental green-peas were produced at Christmas, and intellectual asparagus all the year round. Mathematical gooseberries (very sour ones too) were common at untimely seasons, and from mere sprouts of bushes, under Doctor Blimber's cultivation. Every description of Greek and Latin vegetable was got off the driest twigs of boys, under the frostiest circumstances. Nature was of no consequence at all. No matter what a young gentleman was intended to bear, Doctor Blimber made him bear to pattern, somehow or other.

"This was all very pleasant and ingenious, but the system of forcing was attended with its usual disadvantages. There was not the right taste about the premature productions, and they didn't keep well." DS 11

—*results:* "Mr Tozer, now a young man of lofty stature, in Wellington boots, was so extremely full of antiquity as to be nearly on a par with a genuine ancient Roman in his knowledge of English: a triumph that affected his good parents with the tenderest emotions, and caused the father and mother of Mr Briggs (whose learning, like ill-arranged luggage, was so tightly packed that he couldn't get at anything he wanted) to hide their diminished heads. The fruit laboriously gathered from the tree of knowledge by this latter young gentleman, in fact, had been subject to so much pressure, that it had become a kind of intellectual Norfolk Biffin, and had nothing of its original form or flavour remaining. Master Bitherstone now, on whom the forcing system had the happier and not uncommon effect of leaving no impression whatever, when the forcing apparatus ceased to work, was in a much more comfortable plight; and being then on shipboard, bound for Bengal, found himself forgetting, with such admirable rapidity, that it was doubtful whether his declensions of noun-substantives would hold out to the end of the voyage." DS 60

—*a good school:* "Doctor Strong's was an excellent school; as different from Mr Creakle's as good is from evil. It was very gravely and decorously ordered, and on a sound system; with an appeal, in everything, to the honour and good faith of the boys, and an avowed intention to rely on their possession of those qualities unless they proved themselves unworthy of it, which worked wonders. We all felt that we had a part in the management of the place, and in sustaining its character and dignity. Hence, we soon became warmly attached to it—I am sure I did for one, and I never knew, in all my time, of any other boy being otherwise—and learnt with a good will, desiring to do it credit. We had noble games out of hours, and plenty of liberty; but even then, as I remember, we were well spoken of in the town, and rarely did any disgrace, by our appearance or manner, to the reputation of Doctor Strong and Doctor Strong's boys." DC 16

—*government officer:* "A mighty man at cutting and drying, he was; a government officer; in his way (and in most other people's too), a professed pugilist; always in training, always with a system to force down the general throat like a bolus, always to be heard of at the bar of his little Public-office, ready to fight all England. To continue in fistic phraseology, he had a genius for coming up to the scratch, wherever and whatever it was, and proving himself an ugly customer. He would go in and damage any subject whatever with his right, follow up with his left, stop, exchange, counter, bore his opponent (he always fought All England) to the ropes, and fall upon him neatly. He was certain to knock the wind out of common sense, and render that unlucky adversary deaf to the call of time." HT i 2

—*grammar:* "'Mark!' said Tom Pinch, energetically: 'if you don't sit down this minute, I'll swear at you!'

"'Well, sir,' returned Mr Tapley, 'sooner than you should do that, I'll comply. It's a considerable invasion of a man's jollity to be made so partickler welcome, but a Werb is a word as signified to be, to do, or to suffer (which is all the grammar, and enough too, as ever I wos taught); and if there's a Werb alive, I'm it. For I'm always a-bein', sometimes a-doin', and continually a-sufferin'.'" MC 48

—*innovative scheme:* " . . . a hideous small boy in rags flinging stones at [Durdles] as a well-defined mark in the moonlight . . . whenever he hits Durdles, [he] blows a whistle of triumph through a jagged gap, convenient for the purpose, in the front of his mouth, where half his teeth are wanting; and whenever he misses him, yelps out 'Mulled agin!' and tried to atone for the failure by taking a more correct and vicious aim . . . .

"'Own brother, sir,' observes Durdles . . . 'own brother to **Peter the Wild Boy**! But I gave him an object in life . . . . I took him in hand and gave him an object. What was he before? A destroyer. What work did he do? Nothing but destruction. What did he earn by it? Short terms in Cloisterham Jail. Not a person, not a piece of property, not a winder, not a horse, nor a dog, nor a cat, nor a bird, nor a fowl, nor a pig, but what he stoned, for want of an enlightened object. I put that enlightened object before him, and now he can turn his honest halfpenny by the three penn'orth a week.'

"'I wonder he has no competitors.'

"'He has plenty, Mr Jasper, but he stones 'em all away. Now, I don't know what this scheme of mine comes to,' pursues Durdles, considering about it with the same sodden gravity; 'I don't know what you may precisely call it. It ain't a sort of a—scheme of a—National Education?'

"'I should say not,' replies Jasper.

"'*I* should say not,' assents Durdles; 'then we won't try to give it a name.'" MED 5

—*languages:* " . . . those terrible old Scalds who seem to have existed for the express purpose of addling the brains of mankind when they begin to investigate languages. . . ." UT/NS

—"*a little learning*": "How often have we heard, from that large class of men, wise in their generation, who would really seem to be born and bred for no other purpose than to pass into currency counterfeit and mischievous scraps of wisdom, as it is the sole pursuit of some other criminals to utter base coin—how often have we heard from them as an all-convincing and self-evident argument, that 'A little learning is a dangerous thing'? Why, a little hanging was considered a very dangerous thing, according to the same authorities, with this difference, that because a little hanging was dangerous, we had a great deal of it; and because a little learning was dangerous, we were to have none at all.

"Why, when I hear such cruel absurdities gravely reiterated, I do sometimes begin to doubt whether the parrots of society are not more pernicious to its interests than its birds of prey. I should be glad to hear such people's estimate of the comparative danger of 'a little learning' and a vast amount of ignorance; I should be glad to know which they consider the most prolific parent of misery and crime.

"Descending a little lower in the social scale, I should be glad to assist them in their calculations, by carrying them into certain jails and nightly refuges I know of, where my own heart dies within me when I see thousands of immortal creatures condemned, without alternative or choice, to tread, not what our great poet [in *Macbeth*] calls 'the primrose path [*sic.*] to the everlasting bonfire', but one of jagged flints and stones, laid down by brutal ignorance, and held together like the solid rocks by years of this most wicked axiom." ¶S/MA

—*materialistic, a failure:* "'Would you have doomed me, at any time, to the frost and blight that have hardened and spoiled me? Would you have robbed me—for no one's enrichment—only for the greater desolation of this world—of the immaterial part of my life, the spring and summer of my belief, my refuge from what is sordid and bad in the real things around me, my school in which I should have learned to be more humble and more trusting with them, and to hope in my little sphere to make them better?'

"'O no, no. No, Louisa.'

"'Yet, father, if I had been stone blind; if I had groped my way by my sense of touch, and had been free, while I knew the shapes and surfaces of things, to exercise my fancy somewhat, in regard to them; I should have been a million times wiser, happier, more loving, more contented, more innocent and human in all good respects, than I am with the eyes I have . . . .

"'With a hunger and thirst upon me, father, which have never been for a moment appeased; with an ardent impulse towards some region where rules, and figures, and definitions were not quite absolute; I have grown up, battling every inch of my way.'

"'I never knew you were unhappy, my child.'

"'Father, I always knew it. In this strife I have almost repulsed and crushed my better angel into a demon. What I have learned has left me doubting, misbelieving, despising, regretting, what I have not learned; and my dismal resource has been to think that life would soon go by, and that nothing in it could be worth the pain and trouble of a contest.'" HT ii 12

See Mind—*Reason enthroned alone;* A:Child and Childhood—*betrayed by materialism; and* A:Matrimony—*betrayed by materialism*

"'I had proved my—my system to myself, and I have rigidly administered it; and I must bear the responsibility of its failures. I only entreat you to believe, my favourite child, that I have meant to do right.'

"He said it earnestly, and to do him justice he had. In gauging fathomless deeps with his little mean excise-rod, and in staggering over the universe with his rusty stiff-legged compasses, he had meant to do great things. Within the limits of his short tether he had tumbled about, annihilating the flowers of existence with greater singleness of purpose than many of the blatant personages whose company he kept." HT iii 1

—a poor school: "The school at which young Charley Hexam had first learned from a book—the streets being, for pupils of his degree, the great Preparatory Establishment in which very much that is never unlearned is learned without and before book—was a miserable loft in an unsavoury yard. Its atmosphere was oppressive and disagreeable; it was crowded, noisy, and confusing; half the pupils dropped asleep, or fell into a state of waking stupefaction; the other half kept them in either condition by maintaining a monotonous droning noise, as if they were performing, out of time and tune, on a ruder sort of bagpipe. The teachers, animated solely by good intentions, had no idea of execution, and a lamentable jumble was the upshot of their kind endeavours.

"It was a school for all ages, and for both sexes. The latter were kept apart, and the former were partitioned off into square assortments. But all the place was pervaded by a grimly ludicrous pretence that every pupil was childish and innocent. This pretence, much favoured by the lady-visitors, led to the ghastliest absurdities.

"Young women old in the vices of the commonest and worst life, were expected to profess themselves enthralled by the good child's book, the Adventures of Little Margery, who resided in the village cottage by the mill; severely reproved and morally squashed the miller when she was five and he was fifty; divided her porridge with singing birds; denied herself a new nankeen bonnet, on the ground that the turnips did not wear nankeen bonnets, neither did the sheep who ate them; who plaited straw and delivered the dreariest orations to all comers, at all sorts of unseasonable times.

"So unwieldy young dredgers and hulking mudlarks were referred to the experiences of *Thomas Twopence,* who, having resolved not to rob (under circumstances of uncommon atrocity) his particular friend and benefactor, of eighteenpence, presently came into supernatural possession of three and sixpence, and lived a shining light ever afterwards. (Note that the benefactor came to no good.) Several swaggering sinners had written their own biographies in the same strain; it always appearing from the lessons of those very boastful persons, that you were to do good, not because it *was* good, but because you were to make a good thing of it.

"Contrariwise, the adult pupils were taught to read (if they could learn) out of the New Testament; and by dint of stumbling over the syllables and keeping their bewildered eyes on the particular syllables coming round to their turn, were as absolutely ignorant of the sublime history, as if they had never seen or heard of it. An exceedingly and confoundingly perplexing jumble of a school, in fact, where black spirits and grey, red spirits and white, jumbled jumbled jumbled jumbled, jumbled every night.

"And particularly every Sunday night. For then, an inclined plane of unfortunate infants would be handed over to the prosiest and worst of all the teachers with good intentions, whom nobody older would endure. Who, taking his stand on the floor before them as chief executioner, would be attended by a conventional volunteer boy as executioner's assistant.

"When and where it first became the conventional system that a weary or inattentive infant in a class must have its face smoothed downward with a hot hand, or when and where the conventional volunteer boy first beheld such system in operation, and became inflamed with a sacred zeal to administer it, matters not. It was the function of the chief executioner to hold forth, and it was the function of the acolyte to dart at sleeping infants, yawning infants, restless infants, whimpering infants, and smooth their wretched faces; sometimes with one hand, as if he were anointing them for a whisker; sometimes with both hands, applied after the fashion of blinkers.

"And so the jumble would be in action in this department for a mortal hour; the exponent drawling on to My Dearerr Childerreneer, let us say, for example, about the beautiful coming to the Sepulchre; and repeating the word Sepulchre (commonly used among infants) five hundred times, and never once hinting what it meant; the conventional boy smoothing away right and left, as an infallible commentary; the whole hot-bed of flushed and exhausted infants exchanging measles, rashes, whooping-cough, fever, and stomach disorders, as if they were assembled in High Market for the purpose." ¶OMF ii 1

—of the poor: "His children, stunted in their growth, bore traces of unwholesome nurture: but they had beauty in his sight. Above all other things, it was an earnest desire of this man's soul that his children should be taught. 'If I am sometimes misled,' said he, 'for want of knowledge, at least let them know better, and avoid my mistakes. If it is hard to me to reap the harvest of pleasure and instruction that is stored in books, let it be easier to them.'

"But the Bigwig family broke out into violent family quarrels concerning what it was lawful to teach to this man's children. Some of the family insisted on such a thing being primary and indispensable above all other things; and others of the family insisted on such another thing being primary and indispensable above all other things; and the Bigwig family, rent into factions, wrote pamphlets, held convocations, delivered charges, orations, and all varieties of discourses; impounded one another in courts Lay and courts Ecclesiastical; threw dirt, exchanged pummelings, and fell together by the ears in unintelligible animosity. Meanwhile, this man, in his short evening snatches at his fireside, saw the demon Ignorance arise there, and take his children to itself. He saw his daughter perverted into a heavy slatternly drudge; he saw his son go moping down the ways of low sensuality, to brutality and crime; he saw the dawning light of intelligence in the eyes of his babies so changing into cunning and suspicion, that he could have rather wished them idiots." CS/NS

See F:The Poor, Working*—their education*

—public school: " . . . I believe there is not in England any institution so socially liberal as a public school. It has been called a little cosmos of life outside, and I think it is so, with the exception of one of life's worst foibles—for as far as I know, nowhere in this country is there so complete an absence of servility to mere rank, to mere position, to mere riches as in a public school. A boy there is always what his abilities or his personal qualities make him. We may differ about the curriculum and other matters, but of the frank, free, manly, independent spirit preserved in our public schools, I apprehend there can be no kind of question." S/SS

—retribution if neglected: "I hold that for any fabric of society to go on day after day, and year after year, from father to son, and from grandfather to grandson, unceasingly punishing men for not engaging in the pursuit of virtue and the practice of crime, without showing them the way to virtue, has no foundation in justice, has no foundation in religion, has no foundation in truth, and has only one parallel in fiction that I know of . . . [in the *Arabian Nights*] there is the case of a powerful spirit who had been imprisoned at the bottom of the sea, shut up in a casket with a leaden cover, sealed with the seal of Solomon upon it. There he lay neglected for many centuries, and during that period made many different vows: at first, that he would reward magnificently those who should release him, and, at last, that he would destroy them. Now, there is a spirit of great power, the Spirit of Ignorance, long shut up in a vessel of Obstinate Neglect, with a great deal of lead in its composition, and sealed with the seal of many, many Solomons, and which is exactly in the same position. Release it in time, and it will bless, restore, and reanimate society; but let it lie under the rolling waves of years, and its blind revenge at last will be destruction." S/BP

—schoolbooks: "They comprised a little English, and a deal of Latin—names of things, declensions of articles and substantives, exercises thereon, and preliminary rules—a trifle of orthography, a glance at ancient history, a wink or two at modern ditto, a few tables, two or three weights and measures, and a little general information. When poor Paul had spelt out number two,

he found he had no idea of number one; fragments whereof afterwards obtruded themselves into number three, which slided into number four, which grafted itself on to number two. So that whether twenty *Romulus*es made a *Remus*, or hic hæc hoc was troy weight, or a verb always agreed with an ancient Briton, or three times four was Taurus, a bull, were open questions with him." DS 12

The Breaking-up at Dotheboys Hall NN

—schoolmaster, unqualified in Yorkshire: "Although any man who had proved his unfitness for any other occupation in life, was free, without examination or qualification, to open a school anywhere; although preparation for the functions he undertook, was required in the surgeon who assisted to bring a boy into the world, or might one day assist perhaps, to send him out of it—in the chemist, the attorney, the butcher, the baker, the candle-stick maker—the whole round of crafts and trades, the schoolmaster excepted; and although schoolmasters, as a race, were the blockheads and impostors that might naturally be expected to arise from such a state of things, and to flourish in it; these Yorkshire schoolmasters were the lowest and most rotten round in the whole ladder.

"Traders in the avarice, indifference, or imbecility of parents, and the helplessness of children; ignorant, sordid, brutal men, to whom few considerate persons would have entrusted the board and lodging of a horse or a dog; they formed the worthy cornerstone of a structure, which, for absurdity and a magnificent high-handed *laissez-aller* neglect, has rarely been exceeded in the world.

"We hear sometimes of an action for damages against the unqualified medical practitioner, who has deformed a broken limb in pretending to heal it. But, what about the hundreds of thousands of minds that have been deformed for ever by the incapable pettifoggers who have pretended to form them!" NN pref.

"'I have been that chap's [Smike] benefactor, feeder, teacher, and clother. I have been that chap's classical, commercial, mathematical, philosophical, and trigonomical friend. My son—my only son, Wackford—has been his brother. Mrs Squeers has been his mother, grandmother, aunt—Ah! and I may say uncle too, all in one . . . What's my return? What's come of my milk of human kindness? It turns into curds and whey when I look at him.'" NN 38

And see H:Vocations—*school proprietor*

—*of a self-made man:* "'I pulled through it, though nobody threw me out a rope. Vagabond, errand boy, vagabond, labourer, porter, clerk, chief manager, small partner, Josiah Bounderby of Coketown. Those are the antecedents and the culmination. Josiah Bounderby of Coketown learned his letters from the outsides of the shops . . . and was first able to tell the time upon a dial-plate, from studying the steeple-clock of St Giles's Church, London, under the direction of a drunken cripple, who was a convicted thief, and an incorrigible vagrant. Tell Josiah Bounderby of Coketown, of your district schools, and your model schools, and your training schools, and your whole kettle-of-fish of schools; and Josiah Bounderby of Coketown tells you plainly, all right all correct—he hadn't such advantages—but let us have hard-headed, solid-fisted people—the education that made him won't do for everybody, he knows well—such and such his education was, however, and you may force him to swallow boiling fat, but you shall never force him to suppress the facts of his life.'" HT i 4

—*self-teaching:* "The man who lives from day to day by the daily exercise in his sphere of hand or head, and seeks to improve himself . . . acquires for himself that property of soul which has in all times upheld struggling men in every degree, but self-made men especially and always. He secures to himself that faithful companion which, while it has ever lent the light of its countenance to men of rank and eminence who have deserved it, has ever shed its brightest consolations on men of low estate and almost hopeless means. It took its patent seat beside **Sir Walter Raleigh** in his dungeon-study in the Tower; and it laid its head upon the block with [**Sir Thomas**] **More**. But it did not disdain to watch the stars with [**James**] **Ferguson**, the shepherd's boy; it walked the streets in mean attire with [**George**] **Crabbe**; it was a poor barber here in Lancashire with [**Sir Richard**] **Arkwright**; it was a tallow-chandler's son with [**Benjamin**] **Franklin;** it worked at shoemaking with [**Robert**] **Bloomfield** in his garret; it followed the plough with [**Robert**] **Burns**; and, high above the noise of loom and hammer, it whispers courage, even at this day, in ears that I could name in [the factories of] Sheffield and Manchester." S/MA

—*teaching*

—*good master:* "The usher at Our School, who was considered to know everything as opposed to the Chief, who was considered to know nothing, was a bony, gentle-faced, clerical-looking young man in rusty black. It was whispered that he was sweet upon one of Maxby's sisters (Maxby lived close by, and was a day pupil), and further that he 'favoured Maxby.' As we remember, he taught Italian to Maxby's sisters on half-holidays. He once went to the play with them, and wore a white waistcoat and a rose: which was considered among us equivalent to a declaration.

" . . . we all liked him; for he had a good knowledge of boys, and would have made it a much better school if he had had more power. He was writing master, mathematical master, English master, made out the bills, mended the pens, and did all sorts of things. He divided the little boys with the Latin master (they were smuggled through their rudimentary books, at odd times when there was nothing else to do), and he always called at parents' houses to inquire after sick boys, because he had gentlemanly manners.

"He was rather musical, and on some remote quarter-day had bought an old trombone; but a bit of it was lost, and it made the most extraordinary sounds when he sometimes tried to play it of an evening.

"His holidays never began (on account of the bills) until long after ours; but in the summer vacations he used to take pedestrian excursions with a knapsack; and at Christmas time he went to see his father at Chipping Norton, who we all said (on no authority) was a dairy-fed pork-butcher.

"Poor fellow! He was very low all day on Maxby's sister's wedding-day, and afterwards was thought to favour Maxby more than ever, though he had been expected to spite him. He has been dead these twenty years. Poor fellow!" ¶RP/OS

—great: "'You remember me, Mr Young Jackson?' . . .

"'Most gratefully, Sir. You were the ray of hope and prospering ambition in my life. When I attended your course, I believed that I should come to be a great healer, and I felt almost happy . . . .

"'You are like a Superior Being to me. You are like Nature beginning to reveal herself to me. I hear you again, as one of the hushed crowd of young men kindling under the power of your presence and knowledge, and you bring into my eyes the only exultant tears that ever stood in them.'" CS/MJ 1

—through singing: "'Very fond of them,' she said . . . 'but I know nothing of teaching, beyond the interest I have in it, and the pleasure it gives me when they learn. Perhaps your overhearing my little scholars sing some of their lessons has led you so far astray as to think me a grand teacher? Ah! I thought so! No, I have only read and been told about that system. It seemed so pretty and pleasant, and to treat them so like the merry Robins they are, that I took up with it in my little way.'" CS/MJ 3

—worthy of respect: "'My meaning is [said Tom Pinch], that no man can expect his children to respect what he degrades . . . . Your governess cannot win the confidence and respect of your children . . . . Let her begin by winning yours, and see what happens then . . . .

"'Respect! I believe young people are quick enough to observe and imitate; and why or how should they respect whom no one else respects, and everybody slights? And very partial they must grow—oh, very partial!—to their studies, when they see to what a pass proficiency in those same tasks has brought their governess! Respect! Put anything the most deserving of respect before your daughters in the light in which you place her, and you will bring it down as low, no matter what it is! . . .

"'Why, how can you, as an honest gentleman, profess displeasure or surprise at your daughter telling my sister she is something beggarly and humble, when you are for ever telling her the same thing yourself in fifty plain, outspeaking ways, though not in words; and when your very porter and footman make the same delicate announcement to all comers? As to your suspicion and distrust of her: even of her word: if she is not above their reach, you have no right to employ her.'

"'No right!' said the brass-and-copper founder.

"'Distinctly not . . . if you imagine that the payment of an annual sum of money gives it to you, you immensely exaggerate its power and value. Your money is the least part of your bargain in such a case. You may be punctual in that to half a second on the clock, and yet be Bankrupt.'" MC 36

See H:Vocations*—governess; and —school teacher*

—Utilitarian: "'You are to be in all things regulated and governed,' said the [government] gentleman, 'by fact. We hope to have, before long, a board of fact, composed of commissioners of fact, who will force the people to be a people of fact, and of nothing but fact. You must discard the word Fancy altogether. You have nothing to do with it. You are not to have, in any object of use or ornament, what would be a contradiction in fact. You don't walk upon flowers in fact; you cannot be allowed to walk upon flowers in carpets. You don't find foreign birds and butterflies come and perch upon your crockery; you cannot be permitted to paint foreign birds and butterflies upon your crockery. You never meet with quadrupeds going up and down walls; you must not have quadrupeds represented upon walls. You must see,' said the gentleman, 'for all these purposes, combinations and modifications (in primary colours) of mathematical figures which are susceptible of proof and demonstration. This is the new discovery. This is fact. This is taste.'" HT i 2

And see Facts*—and nursery tales*

—unscientific: "Mrs Gradgrind . . . looked (as she always did) like an indifferently executed transparency of a small female figure, without enough light behind it . . . . 'Go and be somethingological directly.' [She]

was not a scientific character, and usually dismissed her children to their studies with this general injunction to choose their pursuit." HT i 4

—when lacking: "I am getting on in years now [writes Gill Davis], though I am able and hearty. I was recommended for promotion, and everything was done to reward me that could be done; but my total want of all learning stood in my way, and I found myself so completely out of the road to it, that I could not conquer any learning, though I tried." CS/EP 2

—of women: "Whether the course female education has taken of late days—whether the pursuit of giddy frivolities, and empty nothings, has tended to unfit women for that quiet domestic life, in which they show far more beautifully than in the most crowded assembly, is a question we should feel little gratification in discussing: we hope not." SB/LR

Example

—benign: "I pray Heaven that I never may forget the dear girl [Agnes Wickfield] in her love and truth, at that time of my life; for if I should, I must be drawing near the end, and then I would desire to remember her best! She filled my heart with such good resolutions, strengthened my weakness so, by her example, so directed—I know not how, she was too modest and gentle to advise me in many words—the wandering ardour and unsettled purpose within me, that all the little good I have done, and all the harm I have forborne, I solemnly believe I may refer to her." DC 35

"It is dreadful to observe how long a bad example will be followed; but, it is encouraging to know that a good example is never thrown away." CHE 21

—malign: "I conceive that the sordid coarseness and brutality of Jonas would be unnatural, if there had been nothing in his early education, and in the precept and example always before him, to engender and develop the vices that make him odious. But, so born and so bred; admired for that which made him hateful, and justified from his cradle in cunning, treachery, and avarice; I claim him as the legitimate issue of the father upon whom those vices are seen to recoil. And I submit that their recoil upon that old man in his unhonoured age is not a mere piece of poetical justice, but is the extreme exposition of a direct truth." MC preface

Experience

—unconscious influence: ". . . observe how many things were to be considered according to her own unfortunate experience. Show Pleasant Riderhood a Wedding in the street, and she only saw two people taking out a regular license to quarrel and fight. Show her a Christening, and she saw a little heathen personage having a quite superfluous name bestowed upon it, inasmuch as it would be commonly addressed by some abusive epithet; which little personage was not in the least wanted by anybody, and would be shoved and banged out of everybody's way, until it should grow big enough to shove and bang. Show her a Funeral, and she saw an unremunerative ceremony in the nature of a black masquerade, conferring a temporary gentility on the performers, at an immense expense, and representing the only formal party ever given by the deceased. Show her a live father, and she saw but a duplicate of her own father, who from her infancy had been taken with fits and starts of discharging his duty to her, which duty was always incorporated in the form of a fist or a leathern strap, and being discharged hurt her." OMF ii 12

Facts

—a burden borne upward: "'What do you think of that for a kite?' [Mr Dick] said.

"I answered that it was a beautiful one. I should think it must have been as much as seven feet high.

"'I made it. We'll go and fly it, you and I,' said Mr Dick. 'Do you see this?'

"He showed me that it was covered with manuscript, very closely and laboriously written; but so plainly, that as I looked along the lines, I thought I saw some allusion to King Charles the First's head again, in one or two places.

"'There's plenty of string,' said Mr Dick, 'and when it flies high, it takes the facts a long way. That's my manner of diffusing 'em. I don't know where they may come down. It's according to circumstances, and the wind, and so forth; but I take my chance of that.'" DC 14

"It was quite an affecting sight, I used to think, to see [Mr Dick] with the kite when it was up a great height in the air. What he had told me, in his room, about his belief in its disseminating the statements pasted on it, which were nothing but old leaves of abortive Memorials, might have been a fancy with him sometimes; but not when he was out, looking up at the kite in the sky, and feeling it pull and tug at his hand. He never looked so serene as he did then. I used to fancy, as I sat by him of an evening, on a green slope, and saw him watch the kite high in the quiet air, that it lifted his mind out of its confusion, and bore it (such was my boyish thought) into the skies. As he wound the string in, and it came lower and lower down out of the beautiful light, until it fluttered to the ground, and lay there like a dead thing, he seemed to wake gradually out of a dream; and I remember to have seen him take it up, and look about him in a lost way, as if they had both come down together, so that I pitied him with all my heart." DC 15

—and morality: "Then came the Teetotal Society, who complained that these same [Coketown] people *would* get drunk, and showed in tabular statements that they did get drunk, and proved at tea parties that no inducement, human or Divine (except a medal), would induce them to forego their custom of getting drunk.

"Then came the chemist and druggist, with other tabular statements, showing that when they didn't get drunk, they took opium. Then came the experienced chaplain of the jail, with more tabular statements, outdoing all the previous tabular statements, and showing that the same people *would* resort to low haunts, hidden from the public eye, where they heard low singing and saw low dancing, and mayhap joined in it; and where A. B., aged twenty-four next birthday, and committed for eighteen months' solitary, had himself said (not that he had ever shown himself particularly worthy of belief) his ruin began, as he was perfectly sure and confident that otherwise he would have been a tip-top moral specimen." HT i 5

—and nursery tales: "No little Gradgrind had ever seen a face in the moon; it was up in the moon before it could speak distinctly. No little Gradgrind had ever learned the silly jingle, Twinkle, twinkle, little star; how I wonder what you are! No little Gradgrind had ever known wonder on the subject, each little Gradgrind having at five years old dissected the Great Bear like a Professor **Owen**, and drive Charles's Wain like a locomotive engine-driver. No little Gradgrind had ever associated a cow in a field with that famous cow with the crumpled horn who tossed the dog who worried the cat who killed the rat who ate the malt, or with that yet more famous cow who swallowed *Tom Thumb:* it had never heard of those celebrities, and had only been introduced to a cow as a gramnivorous, ruminating quadruped with several stomachs." HT i 3

—and religion: "You saw nothing in Coketown but what was severely workful. If the members of a religious persuasion built a chapel there—as the members of eighteen religious persuasions had done—they made it a pious warehouse of red brick, with sometimes (but this is only in highly ornamental examples) a bell in a birdcage on the top of it.

"The solitary exception was the New Church; a stuccoed edifice with a square steeple over the door, terminating in four short pinnacles like florid wooden legs. All the public inscriptions in the town were painted alike, in severe characters of black and white. The jail might have been the infirmary, the infirmary might have been the jail, the town-hall might have been either, or both, or anything else, for anything that appeared to the contrary in the graces of their construction. Fact, fact, fact, everywhere in the material aspect of the town; fact, fact, fact . . . in the immaterial . . . .

" . . . . Coketown did not come out of its own furnaces, in all respects like gold that had stood the fire. First, the perplexing mystery of the place was, Who belonged to the eighteen denominations? Because, whoever did, the labouring people did not. It was very strange to walk through the streets on a Sunday morning, and note how few of *them* the barbarous jangling of bells that was driving the sick and nervous mad, called away from their own quarter, from their own close rooms, from the corners of their own streets, where they lounged listlessly, gazing at all the church and chapel going, as at a thing with which they had no manner of concern.

"Nor was it merely the stranger who noticed this, because there was a native organization in Coketown itself, whose members were to be heard of in the House of Commons every session, indignantly petitioning for acts of parliament that should make these people religious by main force." ¶HT i 5

"'I am the only child [said Arthur Clennam] of parents who weighed, measured, and priced everything; for whom what could not be weighed, measured, and priced, had no existence. Strict people as the phrase is, professors of a stern religion, their very religion was a gloomy sacrifice of tastes and sympathies that were never their own, offered up as a part of a bargain for the security of their possessions. Austere faces, inexorable discipline, penance in this world and terror in the next—nothing graceful or gentle anywhere, and the void in my cowed heart everywhere—this was my childhood, if I may so misuse the word as to apply it to such a beginning of life.'" LD i 2

—of science: "To show that the facts of science are at least as full of poetry, as the most poetical fancies ever founded on an imperfect observation and a distant suspicion of them . . . to show that if the Dryades no longer haunt the woods, there is, in every forest, in every tree, in every leaf, and in every ring on every sturdy trunk, a beautiful and wonderful creation, always changing, always going on, always bearing testimony to the stupendous workings of Almighty Wisdom, and always leading the student's mind from wonder on to wonder, until he is wrapt and lost in the vast worlds of wonder by which he is surrounded from his cradle to his grave; it is a purpose worthy of the natural philosopher, and salutary to the spirit of the age." E/PS

See N:Nature—*myth and science—statistics*

—evidence: "'The side that can prove anything [said James Harthouse] in a line of units, tens, hundreds, and thousands, Mrs Bounderby, seems to me to afford the most fun, and to give a man the best chance. I am quite as much attached to it as if I believed it. I am quite ready to go in for it, to the same extent as if I believed it. And what more could I possibly do, if I did believe it!'" HT ii 2

—exculpatory: "'If a thunderbolt had fallen on me,' said the father, 'it would have shocked me less than this [Tom Gradgrind's bank robbery].'

"'I don't see why,' grumbled the son. 'So many people are employed in situations of trust; so many people, out of so many, will be dishonest. I have heard you talk, a hundred times, of its being a law. How can I help laws? You have comforted others with such things, father. Comfort yourself!'" HT iii 7

—and national prosperity: "'And [Mr M'Choakumchild] said, Now, this schoolroom is a Nation. And in this nation, there are fifty millions of money. Isn't this a prosperous nation? Girl number twenty, isn't this a prosperous nation, and a'n't you in a thriving state?'

"'What did you say?' asked Louisa.

"'Miss Louisa, I said I didn't know. I thought I couldn't know whether it was a prosperous nation or not, and whether I was in a thriving state or not, unless I knew who had got the money, and whether any of it was mine. But that had nothing to do with it. It was not in the figures at all,' said Sissy, wiping her eyes.

"'That was a great mistake of yours,' observed Louisa." HT i 9

—Parliamentary: "'MR KWAKLEY stated the result of some most ingenious statistical inquiries relative to the difference between the value of the qualification of several members of Parliament as published to the world, and its real nature and amount. After reminding the section that every member of Parliament for a town or borough was supposed to possess a clear freehold estate of three hundred pounds per annum, the honourable gentleman excited great amusement and laughter by stating the exact amount of freehold property possessed by a column of legislators, in which he had included himself. It appeared from this table, that the amount of such income possessed by each was 0 pounds, 0 shillings, and 0 pence, yielding an average of the same. (Great laughter.) It was pretty well known that there were accommodating gentlemen in the habit of furnishing new members with temporary qualifications to the ownership of which they swore solemnly—of course as a mere matter of form. He argued from these *data* that it was wholly unnecessary for members of Parliament to possess any property at all, especially as when they had none the public could get them so much cheaper." B/M2

—readership: "'Mr Gradgrind greatly tormented his mind about what the people read in [the Coketown] library: a point whereon little rivers of tabular statements periodically flowed into the howling ocean of tabular statements, which no diver ever got to any depth in and came up sane." HT i 8

"MR SLUG stated to the section the result of some calculations he had made with great difficulty and labour, regarding the state of infant education among the middle classes of London. He found that, within a circle of three miles from the Elephant and Castle, the following were the names and numbers of children's books principally in circulation:—

"Jack the Giant-killer	7,943
Ditto and Bean-stalk	8,621
Ditto and Eleven Brothers	2,845
Ditto and Jill	1,998
Total	21,407

"He found that the proportion of *Robinson Crusoes* to *Philip Quarlls* was as four and a half to one; and that the preponderance of *Valentine and Orsons* over *Goody Two Shoeses* was as three and an eighth of the former to half a one of the latter; a comparison of Seven Champions* with *Simple Simons* gave the same result. The ignorance that prevailed was lamentable. One child, on being asked whether he would rather be Saint George of England or a respectable tallow-chandler, instantly replied, 'Taint George of Ingling.' Another, a little boy of eight years old, was found to be firmly impressed with a belief in the existence of dragons, and openly stated that it was his intention when he grew up, to rush forth sword in hand for the deliverance of captive princesses, and the promiscuous slaughter of giants. Not one child among the number interrogated had ever heard of **Mungo Park**,—some inquiring whether he was at all connected with the black man that swept the crossing; and others whether he was in any way related to the Regent's Park. They had not the slightest conception of the commonest principles of mathematics, and considered *Sindbad the Sailor* the most enterprising voyager that the world had ever produced." B/M1

**The patron saints of England (St George), Scotland (St Andrew), Wales (St David), Ireland (St Patrick), France (St Denys), Spain (St James), and Italy (St Anthony)*

—*sociological:* "Although Mr Gradgrind did not take after Blue Beard, his room was quite a blue chamber in its abundance of blue books. Whatever they could prove (which is usually anything you like), they proved there, in an army constantly strengthening by the arrival of new recruits. In that charmed apartment, the most complicated social questions were cast up, got into exact totals, and finally settled—if those concerned could only have been brought to know it. As if an astronomical observatory should be made without any windows, and the astronomer within should arrange the starry universe solely by pen, ink, and paper, so Mr Gradgrind, in *his* Observatory (and there are many like it), had no need to cast an eye upon the teeming myriads of human beings around him, but could settle all their destinies on a slate, and wipe out all their tears with one dirty little bit of sponge." HT i 15

—*starvation:* "'Then Mr M'Choakumchild said he would try me again. And he said, This schoolroom is an immense town, and in it there are a million of inhabitants, and only five-and-twenty are starved to death in the streets, in the course of a year. What is your remark on that proportion? And my remark was—for I couldn't think of a better one—that I thought it must be just as hard upon those who were starved, whether the others were a million, or a million million. And that was wrong too.'

"'Of course it was.'" HT i 9

—*stutterings:* "'Then Mr M'Choakumchild said he would try me once more. And he said, Here are the stutterings——'

"'Statistics,' said Louisa.

"'Yes, Miss Louisa—they always remind me of stutterings, and that's another of my mistakes . . . . " HT i 9

—*and taste:* "' . . . you are not to see anywhere [said the government gentleman], what you don't see in fact; you are not to have anywhere, what you don't have in fact. What is called Taste, is only another name for Fact.'" HT i 2

—*and theories:* " . . . Affery [Flintwinch], like greater people, had always been right in her facts, and always wrong in the theories she deduced from them." LD ii 31

First Impression

—*bluster:* "He had a certain air of being a handsome man—which he was not; and a certain air of being a well-bred man—which he was not. It was mere swagger and challenge; but in this particular, as in many others, blustering assertion goes for proof, half over the world." LD i 1

—*of dishonesty:* "The partition which separated my own office from our general outer office in the City was of thick plate-glass. I could see through it what passed in the outer office, without hearing a word. I had it put up in place of a wall that had been there for years—ever since the house was built. It is no matter whether I did or did not make the change in order that I might derive my first impression of strangers, who came to us on business, from their faces alone, without being influenced by anything they said. Enough to mention that I turned my glass partition to that account, and that a Life-Assurance Office is at all times exposed to be practised upon by the most crafty and cruel of the human race." HD

"I took [Slinkton's] face to pieces in my mind, like a watch, and examined it in detail. I could not say much against any of his features separately; I could say even less against them when they were put together. 'Then is it not monstrous,' I asked myself, 'that because a man happens to part his hair straight up the middle of his head, I should permit myself to suspect, and even to detest him?'

"(I may stop to remark that this was no proof of my sense. An observer of men who finds himself steadily repelled by some apparently trifling thing in a stranger is right to give it great weight. It may be the clue to the whole mystery. A hair or two will show where a lion is hidden. A very little key will open a very heavy door.)" HD

Habit

—adversity as: "Mr Micawber pressed my hand, and groaned, and afterwards shed tears. I was greatly touched, and disappointed too, for I had expected that we should be quite gay on this happy and long-looked-for occasion. But Mr and Mrs Micawber were so used to their old difficulties, I think, that they felt quite shipwrecked when they came to consider that they were released from them. All their elasticity was departed, and I never saw them half so wretched as on this night . . . ." DC 12

—Chancery and Fashion: "Both the world of fashion and the Court of Chancery are things of precedent and usage; oversleeping Rip Van Winkles, who have played at strange games through a deal of thundery weather; sleeping beauties, whom the Knight will wake one day, when all the stopped spits in the kitchen shall begin to turn prodigiously!" BH 2

—indifference to transformation: "'Your brother is an altered man,' returned the gentleman [Morfin], compassionately. 'I assure you I don't doubt it.'

"'He was an altered man when he did wrong,' said Harriet [Carker]. 'He is an altered man again, and is his true self now, believe me, Sir.'

"'But we go on,' said her visitor, rubbing his forehead, in an absent manner, with his hand, and then drumming thoughtfully on the table, 'we go on in our clockwork routine, from day to day, and can't make out, or follow, these changes. They—they're a metaphysical sort of thing. We—we haven't leisure for it. We—we haven't courage. They're not taught at schools or colleges, and we don't know how to set about it. In short, we are so d—d business-like,' said the gentleman, walking to the window, and back, and sitting down again, in a state of extreme dissatisfaction and vexation." DS 33

—inertia: "Mr Stryver shouldered his way through the law, like some great engine forcing itself through turbid water, and dragged his useful friend in his wake, like a boat towed astern. As the boat so favoured is usually in a rough plight, and mostly under water, so, Sydney [Carton] had a swamped life of it. But, easy and strong custom, unhappily so much easier and stronger in him than any stimulating sense of desert or disgrace, made it the life he was to lead; and he no more thought of emerging from his state of lion's jackal, than any real jackal may be supposed to think of rising to be a lion." TTC ii 21

—numbing effect: "'I am sure,' said [Mr Morfin], rubbing his forehead again; and drumming on the table as before, 'I have good reason to believe that a jog-trot life, the same from day to day, would reconcile one to anything. One don't see anything, one don't hear anything, one don't know anything; that's the fact. We go on taking everything for granted, and so we go on, until whatever we do, good, bad, or indifferent, we do from habit. Habit is all I shall have to report, when I am called upon to plead to my conscience, on my death-bed. "Habit," says I; "I was deaf, dumb, blind, and paralytic, to a million things, from habit." "Very business-like indeed, Mr What's-your-name," says Conscience, "but it won't do here!"'" DS 33

—precedent: "As this excellent woman [Mrs Gamp] had been formally entrusted with the care of Mr Chuffey on a previous occasion, neither Mr Jonas [Chuzzlewit] nor anybody else had the resolution to interfere directly with her [callous] mode of treatment: though all present (Tom Pinch and his sister especially) appeared to be disposed to differ from her views. For such is the rash boldness of the uninitiated, that they will frequently set up some monstrous abstract principle, such as humanity, or tenderness, or the like idle folly, in obstinate defiance of all precedent and usage;

and will even venture to maintain the same against the persons who have made the precedents and established the usage, and who must therefore be the best and most impartial judges of the subject." MC 46

—*sensitive to shock:* "'I observe you [John Carker] are more astonished at present. Well! That's reasonable enough under existing circumstances. If we were not such creatures of habit as we are, we shouldn't have reason to be astonished half so often [said Morfin] . . . .

"Putting his hands into his pockets, and leaning back in his chair, he . . . went on to say, with a kind of irritable thoughtfulness: 'It's this same habit that confirms some of us, who are capable of better things, in Lucifer's own pride and stubbornness—that confirms and deepens others of us in villany—more of us in indifference—that hardens us from day to day, according to the temper of our clay, like images, and leaves us as susceptible as images to new impressions and convictions." DS 53

And see A:Bachelor—*a sad habit; and* LC: Words and Phrases—*"force of habit"*

Handwriting

—*calligraphy:* "In his epistolary communciation, as in his dialogues and discourses on the great question to which it related, Mr Dorrit surrounded the subject with flourishes, as writing-masters embellish copy-books and ciphering-books: where the titles of the elementary rules of arithmetic diverge into swans, eagles, griffins, and other caligraphic recreations, and where the capital letters go out of their minds and bodies into ecstasies of pen and ink. Nevertheless, he did render the purport of his letter sufficiently clear . . . . " LD ii 15

—*cursive:* "'The wind blew—not up the road or down it, though that's bad enough, but sheer across it, sending the rain slanting down like the lines they used to rule in the copy-books at school, to make the boys slope well.'" PP 14

—*figures:* "—'I kept my housekeeping-book regularly, and balanced it with Mr Copperfield every night,' cried my mother in another burst of distress, and breaking down again . . . .

"—'And I am sure we never had a word of difference respecting it, except when Mr Copperfield objected to my threes and fives being too much like each other, or to my putting curly tails to my sevens and nines,' resumed my mother in another burst, and breaking down again." DC 2

—*ink:* "Mr and Mrs Boffin sat, after breakfast, in the Bower, a prey to prosperity. Mr Boffin's face denoted Care and Complication. Many disordered papers were before him, and he looked at them about as hopefully as an innocent civilian might look at a crowd of troops whom he was required at five minutes' notice to manœvre and review. He had been engaged in some attempts to make notes of these papers; but being troubled (as men of his stamp often are) with an exceedingly distrustful and corrective thumb, that busy member had so often interposed to smear his notes, that they were little more legible than the various impressions of itself, which blurred his nose and forehead. It is curious to consider, in such a case as Mr Boffin's, what a cheap article ink is, and how far it may be made to go.

"As a grain of musk will scent a drawer for many years, and still lose nothing appreciable of its original weight, so a half-pennyworth of ink would blot Mr Boffin to the roots of his hair and the calves of his legs, without inscribing a line on the paper before him, or appearing to diminish in the inkstand." ¶OMF i 15

"He was a smeary writer, and wrote a dreadful bad hand. Utterly regardless of ink, he lavished it on every undeserving object—on his clothes, his desk, his hat, the handle of his tooth brush, his umbrella. Ink was found freely on the coffee-room carpet, by No. 4 table, and two blots were on his restless couch . . . on the morning of the third of February, eighteen fifty-six, he procured his no less than fifth pen and paper. To whatever deplorable act of ungovernable composition he immolated those materials obtained from the bar, there is no doubt that the fatal deed was committed in bed, and that it left its evidences but too plainly, long afterwards, upon the pillow-case." CS/SL 1 *CD spoofs himself here.*

—*a lesson:* "To relate how it was a long time before [Kit Nubbles'] modesty could be so far prevailed upon as to admit of his sitting down in the parlour . . . how when he did sit down, he tucked up his sleeves and squared his elbows and put his face close to the copy-book and squinted horribly at the lines—how from the very first moment of having the pen in his hand, he began to wallow in blots, and to daub himself with ink up to the very roots of his hair—how if he did by accident form a letter properly, he immediately smeared it out again with his arm in his preparations to make another—how at every fresh mistake, there was a fresh burst of merriment from [Nell] and a louder and not less hearty laugh from poor Kit himself—and how there was all the way through, notwithstanding, a gentle wish on her part to teach, and an anxious desire on his to learn—to relate all these particulars would no doubt occupy more space and time than they deserve." OCS 3

—a missive: "The writing looked like a skein of thread in a tangle, and the note was ingeniously folded into a perfect square, with the direction squeezed up into the right-hand corner, as if it were ashamed of itself. The back of the epistle was pleasingly ornamented with a large red wafer, which, with the addition of divers ink-stains bore a marvellous resemblance to a black beetle trodden upon." SB/BH 2

—notes of a spy: "Rob [Toodle] sat down behind the desk with a most assiduous demeanour; and in order that he might forget nothing of what had transpired, made notes of it on various small scraps of paper, with a vast expenditure of ink. There was no danger of these documents betraying anything, if accidentally lost; for long before a word was dry, it became as profound a mystery to Rob, as if he had had no part whatever in its production." DS 23

—signature: "How [Britain] laboured under an apprehension not uncommon to persons in his degree, to whom the use of pen and ink is an event, that he couldn't append his name to a document, not of his own writing, without committing himself in some shadowy manner, or somehow signing away vague and enormous sums of money; and how he approached the deeds under protest, and by dint of the Doctor [Jeddler]'s coercion, and insisted on pausing to look at them before writing (the cramped hand, to say nothing of the phraseology, being so much Chinese to him), and also on turning them round to see whether there was anything fraudulent underneath; and how, having signed his name, he became desolate as one who had parted with his property and rights; I want the time to tell.

"Also, how the blue bag containing his signature, afterwards had a mysterious interest for him, and he couldn't leave it; also, how Clemency Newcome, in an ecstasy of laughter at the idea of her own importance and dignity, brooded over the whole table with her two elbows, like a spread eagle, and reposed her head upon her left arm as a preliminary to the formation of certain cabalistic characters, which required a deal of ink, and imaginary counterparts whereof she executed at the same time with her tongue. Also, how, having once tasted ink, she became thirsty in that regard, as tame tigers are said to be after tasting another sort of fluid, and wanted to sign everything, and put her name in all kinds of places." ¶BL 1

—struggles: " . . . Sam Weller sat himself down in a box near the stove, and pulled out the sheet of gilt-edged letter-paper, and the hard-nibbed pen. Then looking carefully at the pen to see that there were no hairs in it, and dusting down the table, so that there might be no crumbs of bread under the paper, Sam tucked up the cuffs of his coat, squared his elbows, and composed himself to write.

"To ladies and gentlemen who are not in the habit of devoting themselves practically to the science of penmanship, writing a letter is no very easy task; it being always considered necessary in such cases for the writer to recline his head on his left arm, so as to place his eyes as nearly as possible on a level with the paper, while glancing sideways at the letters he is constructing, to form with his tongue imaginary characters to correspond. These motions, although unquestionably of the greatest assistance to original composition, retard in some degree the progress of the writer; and Sam [Weller] had unconsciously been a full hour and half writing words in small text, smearing out wrong letters with his little finger, and putting in new ones which required going over very often to render them visible through the old blots, when he was roused by the opening of the door and the entrance of his parent." PP 33

"Writing was a trying business to Charley, who seemed to have no natural power over a pen, but in whose hand every pen appeared to become perversely animated, and to go wrong and crooked, and to stop, and splash, and sidle into corners, like a saddle-donkey. It was very odd, to see what old letters Charley's young hand had made; they, so wrinkled, and shrivelled, and tottering; it, so plump and round." BH 31

"Evidently Biddy had taught Joe to write . . . Joe now sat down to his great work, first choosing a pen from the pen-tray as if it were a chest of large tools, and tucking up his sleeves as if he were going to wield a crowbar or sledge-hammer. It was necessary for Joe to hold on heavily to the table with his left elbow, and to get his right leg well out behind him, before he could begin, and when he did begin he made every downstroke so slowly that it might have been six feet long, while at every upstroke I could hear his pen spluttering extensively.

"He had a curious idea that the inkstand was on the side of him where it was not, and constantly dipped his pen into space, and seemed quite satisfied with the result. Occasionally, he was tripped up by some orthographical stumbling-block, but on the whole he got on very well indeed, and when he had signed his name, and had removed a finishing blot from the paper to the crown of his head with his two forefingers, he got up and hovered about the table, trying the effect of his performance from various points of view as it lay there, with unbounded satisfaction." ¶GE 57

History

—convulsion imminent: "It was the best of times, it was the worst of times, it was the age of wisdom, it was the age of foolishness, it was the epoch of belief, it was the epoch of incredulity, it was the season of Light, it was the season of Darkness, it was the spring of hope, it was the winter of despair, we had everything before us, we had nothing before us, we were all going direct to Heaven, we were all going direct the other way—in short, the period was so far like the present period [1859], that some of its noisiest authorities insisted on its being received, for good or for evil, in the superlative degree of comparison only.

"There were a king with a large jaw and a queen with a plain face, on the throne of England; there were a king with a large jaw and a queen with a fair face, on the throne of France. In both countries it was clearer than crystal to the lords of the State preserves of loaves and fishes, that things in general were settled for ever." TTC i 1

—ecclesiastical enclave: " . . . Minor Canon Corner was a quiet place in the shadow of the Cathedral, which the cawing of the rooks, the echoing footsteps of rare passers, the sound of the Cathedral bell, or the roll of the Cathedral organ, seemed to render more quiet than absolute silence. Swaggering fighting men had had their centuries of ramping and raving about Minor Canon Corner, and beaten serfs had had their centuries of drudging and dying there, and powerful monks had had their centuries of being sometimes useful and sometimes harmful there, and behold they were all gone out of Minor Canon Corner, and so much the better. Perhaps one of the highest uses of their ever having been there, was, that there might be left behind, that blessed air of tranquillity which pervaded Minor Canon Corner, and that serenely romantic state of the mind—productive for the most part of pity and forbearance—which is engendered by a sorrowful story that is all told, or a pathetic play that is played out." MED 6

—Middle Ages: "'Oh!' cried Mrs Skewton, with a faded little scream of rapture, 'the Castle is charming!—associations of the Middle Ages—and all that—which is so truly exquisite. Don't you doat upon the Middle Ages, Mr Carker?'

"'Very much, indeed,' said Mr Carker.

"'Such charming times!' cried Cleopatra. 'So full of faith! So vigorous and forcible! So picturesque! So perfectly removed from commonplace! Oh dear! If they would only leave us a little more of the poetry of existence in these terrible days! . . .

"'Those darling byegone times, Mr Carker,' said Cleopatra, 'with their delicious fortresses, and their dear old dungeons, and their delightful places of torture, and their romantic vengeances, and their picturesque assaults and sieges, and everything that makes life truly charming! How dreadfully we have degenerated!'

"'Yes, we have fallen off deplorably,' said Mr Carker." DS 27

—politic: Even . . . great personages dying in bed, making exemplary ends and sounding speeches; and polite history, more servile than their instruments, embalming them!" LD i 1

—route to Dover: "Over the road where the old Romans used to march, over the road where the old Canterbury pilgrims used to go, over the road where the travelling trains of the old imperious priests and princes used to jingle on horseback between the continent and this Island through the mud and water, over the road where **Shakespeare** hummed to himself, 'Blow, blow, thou winter wind,' as he sat in the saddle at the gate of the inn yard noticing the carriers; all among the cherry orchards, apple orchards, corn-fields, and hop-gar-

dens; so went I, by Canterbury to Dover." UT/TA

—*truth and legend:* The bachelor " . . . was not one of those rough spirits who would strip fair Truth of every little shadowy vestment in which time and teeming fancies love to array her—and some of which become her pleasantly enough, serving, like the waters of her well, to add new graces to the charms they half conceal and half suggest, and to awaken interest and pursuit rather than languour and indifference—as, unlike this stern and obdurate class, he loved to see the goddess crowned with those garlands of wild flowers which tradition wreathes for her gentle wearing, and which are often freshest in their homeliest shapes—he trod with a light step and bore with a light hand upon the dust of centuries, unwilling to demolish any of the airy shrines that had been raised above it, if one good feeling or affection of the human heart were hiding thereabouts.

"Thus, in the case of an ancient coffin of rough stone, supposed for many generations to contain the bones of a certain baron, who, after ravaging, with cut, and thrust, and plunder, in foreign lands, came back with a penitent and sorrowing heart to die at home, but which had been lately shown by learned antiquaries to be no such thing, as the baron in question (so they contended) had died hard in battle, gnashing his teeth and cursing with his latest breath—the bachelor stoutly maintained that the old tale was the true one; that the baron, repenting him of the evil, had done great charities and meekly given up the ghost; and that if ever baron went to heaven, that baron was then at peace.

"In like manner, when the aforesaid antiquaries did argue and contend that a certain secret vault was not the tomb of a grey-haired lady who had been hanged and drawn and quartered by glorious Queen Bess for succouring a wretched priest who fainted of thirst and hunger at her door, the bachelor did solemnly maintain against all comers that the church was hallowed by the said poor lady's ashes; that her remains had been collected in the night from four of the city's gates, and thither in secret brought, and there deposited: and the bachelor did further (being highly excited at such times) deny the glory of Queen Bess, and assert the immeasurably greater glory of the meanest woman in her realm who had a merciful and tender heart.

"As to the assertion that the flat stone near the door was not the grave of the miser who had disowned his only child and left a sum of money to the church to buy a peal of bells, the bachelor did readily admit the same, and that the place had given birth to no such man. In a word, he would have had every stone and plate of brass, the monument only of deeds whose memory should survive. All others he was willing to forget. They might be buried in consecrated ground, but he would have had them buried deep, and never brought to light again." ¶OCS 54

"The opinion of the [Bleeding Heart] Yard was divided respecting the derivation of its name. The more practical of its inmates abided by the tradition of a murder; the gentler and more imaginative inhabitants, including the whole of the tender sex, were loyal to the legend of a young lady of former times closely imprisoned in her chamber by a cruel father for remaining true to her own true love, and refusing to marry the suitor he chose for her.

"The legend related how that the young lady used to be seen up at her window behind the bars, murmuring a love-lorn song of which the burden was, 'Bleeding Heart, Bleeding Heart, bleeding away,' until she died. It was objected by the murderous party that this Refrain was notoriously the invention of a tambour-worker, a spinster and romantic, still lodging in the Yard. But, forasmuch as all favourite legends must be associated with the affections, and as many more people fall in love than commit murder—which it may be hoped, howsoever bad we are, will continue until the end of the world to be the dispensation under which we shall live—the Bleeding Heart, Bleeding Heart, bleeding away story, carried the day by a great majority.

"Neither party would listen to the antiquaries who delivered learned lectures in the neighbourhood, showing the Bleeding Heart to have been the heraldic cognizance of the old family to whom the property had once belonged. And, considering that the hour-glass they turned from year to year was filled with the earthiest and coarsest sand, the Bleeding Heart Yarders had reason enough for objecting to be despoiled of the one little golden grain of poetry that sparkled in it." LD i 12

"There is an old tune yet known . . . by this this King is said to have been discovered in his captivity. BLONDEL, a favourite Minstrel of King Richard, as the story relates, faithfully seeking his Royal master, went singing it outside the gloomy walls of many foreign fortresses and prisons; until at last he heard it echoed from within a dungeon, and knew the voice, and cried out in ecstasy, 'O Richard, O my King!' You may believe it, if you like; it would be easy to believe worse things." CHE 13

"There is a legend that to prevent the people from being incited to rebellion by the songs of their bards and harpers, Edward [I] had them all put to death. Some of them may have fallen among other men who held out against the King; but this general slaughter is, I think, a fancy of the harpers themselves, who, I dare say, made a song about it many years afterwards, and sang it by the Welsh firesides until it came to be believed." CHE 16

—the Tudors: "'We have no Faith . . . even in the days of that inestimable Queen Bess, upon the wall there, which were so extremely golden. Dear creature! She was all Heart! And that charming father of hers! I hope you doat on Harry the Eighth!'

"'I admire him very much,' said Carker.

"'So bluff!' cried Mrs Skewton, 'wasn't he? So burly. So truly English. Such a picture, too, he makes, with his dear little peepy eyes, and his benevolent chin!'" DS 27

Hypnagogic state

"There is a drowsy state, between sleeping and waking, when you dream more in five minutes with your eyes half open, and yourself half conscious of everything that is passing around you, than you would in five nights with your eyes fast closed, and your senses wrapt in perfect unconsciousness. At such times, a mortal knows just enough of what his mind is doing, to form some glimmering conception of its mighty powers, its bounding from earth and spurning time and space, when freed from the restraint of its corporeal associate." OT 9

"There is a kind of sleep that steals upon us sometimes, which, while it holds the body prisoner, does not free the mind from a sense of things about it, and enable it to ramble at its pleasure. So far as an overpowering heaviness, a prostration of strength, and an utter inability to control our thoughts or power of motion, can be called sleep, this is it; and yet, we have a consciousness of all that is going on about us, and, if we dream at such a time, words which are really spoken, or sounds which really exist at the moment, accommodate themselves with surprising readiness to our visions, until reality and imagination become so strangely blended that it is afterwards almost matter of impossibility to separate the two.

"Nor is this, the most striking phenomenon incidental to such a state. It is an undoubted fact, that although our senses of touch and sight be for the time dead, yet our sleeping thoughts, and the visionary scenes that pass before us, will be influenced and materially influenced, by the *mere silent presence* of some external object; which may not have been near us when we closed our eyes: and of whose vicinity we have had no waking consciousness." ¶OT 34

"A man may be very sober—or at least firmly set upon his legs on that neutral ground which lies between the confines of perfect sobriety and slight tipsiness—and yet feel a strong tendency to mingle up present circumstances with others which have no manner of connection with them; to confound all consideration of persons, things, times, and places; and to jumble his disjointed thoughts together in a kind of mental kaleidoscope, producing combinations as unexpected as they are transitory. This was Gabriel Varden's state, as, nodding in his dog sleep, and leaving his horse to pursue a road with which he was well acquainted, he got over the ground unconsciously, and drew nearer and nearer home. He had roused himself once, when the horse stopped until the turnpike gate was opened, and had cried a lusty 'good night!' to the toll-keeper; but then he awoke out of a dream about picking a lock in the stomach of the Great Mogul, and even when he did wake, mixed up the turnpike man with his mother-in-law who had been dead twenty years. It is not surprising, therefore, that he soon relapsed, and jogged heavily along, quite insensible to his progress." BR 3

"As Mortimer Lightwood sat before the blazing fire, conscious of drinking brandy and water then and there in his sleep, and yet at one and the same time drinking burnt sherry at the Six Jolly Fellowships, and lying under the boat on the river shore, and sitting in the boat that Riderhood rowed, and listening to the lecture recently concluded, and having to dine in the Temple with an unknown man who described himself as M. R. F. Eugene Gaffer Harmon, and said he lived at Hailstorm—as he passed through these curious vicissitudes of fatigue and slumber, arranged upon the scale of a dozen hours to the second, he became aware of answering aloud a commnication of pressing importance that had never been made to him, and then turned it into a cough . . . [he] stumbled in his sleep to a cab-stand, called a cab, and had entered the army and committed a capital military offence and been tried by court-martial and found guilty and had arranged his affairs and been marched out to be shot, before the door banged." OMF i 14

And see Mind—*thinking—in a hypnagogic state*

Ignorance

—and crime: "The notion that education for the general people is comprised in the faculty of tumbling over words, letter by letter, and syllable by syllable, like the learned pig, or of making staggering pothooks and hangers inclining to the right, has surely had its day by this time, and a long day too. The comfortable conviction that a parrot acquaintance with the Church Catechism and the Commandments is enough shoe-leather for poor pilgrims by the Slough of Despond, sufficient armour against the *Giants Slay-Good* and *Despair,* and a sort of Parliamentary train for third-class passengers to the beautiful Gate of the City, must be pulled up by the roots, as its growth will overshadow this land.

"Side by side with Crime, Disease, and Misery in England, Ignorance is always brooding, and is always certain to be found. The union of Night with Darkness is not more certain and indisputable." E/IC

—and death: "I saw a Minister of State, sitting in his Closet; and round about him, rising from the country which he governed, up to the Eternal Heavens, was a low dull howl of Ignorance. It was a wild, inexplicable mutter, confused, but full of threatening, and it made all hearers' hearts to quake within them. But few heard. In the single city where this Minister of State was seated, I saw Thirty Thousand children, hunted, flogged, imprisoned, but not taught—who might have been nurtured by the wolf or bear, so little of humanity had they within them or without—all joining in this doleful cry. And, ever among them, as among all ranks and grades of mortals, in all parts of the globe, the Spirit [of Death] went; and ever by thousands, in their brutish state, with all the gifts of God perverted in their breasts or trampled out, they died." HW/DV

—its power: "Look where we will, do we not find it powerful for every kind of wrong and evil? Powerful to take its enemies to its heart, and strike its best friends down; powerful to fill the prisons, the hospitals, and the graves; powerful for blind violence, prejudice, and error, in all their gloomy and destructive shapes." S/LM

—and Want: "'This boy is Ignorance. This girl is Want. Beware them both, and all of their degree, but most of all beware this boy, for on his brow I see that written which is Doom, unless the writing be erased. Deny it!' cried the Spirit, stretching out its hand towards the city. 'Slander those who tell it ye! Admit it for your factious purposes, and make it worse. And bide the end!'" CC 3

And see IG:Labour—*its 'station'*

Illusion and Disillusion

—in prison: "To save her life, [Joan] signed a declaration prepared for her . . . that all her visions and Voices had come from the Devil . . . she was condemned to imprisonment for life, 'on the bread of sorrow and the water of affliction.'

"But, on the bread of sorrow and the water of affliction, the visions and the Voices soon returned. It was quite natural that they should do so, for that kind of disease is much aggravated by fasting, loneliness, and anxiety of mind." CHE 22 ii

—at night in the snow: "[Kit] could descry objects enough . . . but none correctly. Now, a tall church spire appeared in view, which presently became a tree, a barn, a shadow on the ground, thrown on it by their own bright lamps. Now, there were horsemen, foot-passengers, carriages, going on before, or meeting them in narrow ways; which, when they were close upon them, turned to shadows too. A wall, a ruin, a sturdy gable end, would rise up in the road; and, when they were plunging headlong at it, would be the road itself. Strange turnings, too, bridges, and sheets of water, appeared to start up here and there, making the way doubtful and uncertain; and yet they were on the same bare road, and these things, like the others, as they were passed, turned into dim illusions." OCS 70

—young love reencountered: "In his youth [Arthur Clennam] had ardently loved this woman [Flora Finching, *née* Casby], and had heaped upon her all the locked-up wealth of his affection and imagination.

That wealth had been, in his desert home, like Robinson Crusoe's money; exchangeable with no one, lying idle in the dark to rust, until he poured it out for her. Ever since that memorable time, though he had, until the night of his arrival, as completely dismissed her from any association with his Present or Future as if she had been dead (which she might easily have been for anything he knew), he had kept the old fancy of the Past unchanged, in its old sacred place. And now, after all, the last of the Patriarchs [Christopher Casby] coolly walked into the parlour, saying in effect, 'Be good enough to throw it down and dance upon it. This is Flora.'

"Flora, always tall, had grown to be very broad too, and short of breath; but that was not much. Flora, whom he had left a lily, had become a peony; but that was not much. Flora, who had seemed enchanting in all she said and thought, was diffuse and silly. That was much. Flora, who had been spoiled and artless long ago, was determined to be spoiled and artless now, That was a fatal blow." LD i 13

Imagination

—*castle in the air:* "I really do not know, in my Castle, what loneliness is. Some of our children or grandchildren are always about it, and the young voices of my descendants are delightful—O, how delightful!—to me to hear. My dearest and most devoted wife, ever faithful, ever loving, ever helpful and sustaining and consoling, is the priceless blessing of my house; from whom all its other blessings spring . . . .

"Such is my Castle, and such are the real particulars of my life therein preserved. I often take Little Frank home there. He is very welcome to my grandchildren, and they play together. At this time of the year—the Christmas and New Year time—I am seldom out of my Castle. For, the associations of the season seem to hold me there, and the precepts of the season seem to teach me that it is well to be there.

"'And the Castle is—' observed a grave, kind voice among the company.

"'Yes. My Castle,' said the poor relation, shaking his head as he still looked at the fire, 'is in the Air. John our esteemed host suggests its situation accurately. My Castle is in the Air. I have done." CS/PR

—*in fear:* "Hark! A footstep on the stairs, and now the door was slowly opening. It was but imagination, yet imagination had all the terrors of reality; nay, it was worse, for the reality would have come and gone, and there an end, but in imagination it was always coming, and never went away." OCS 31

—*indispensable:* "But, happy Sissy's happy children loving [Louisa]; all children loving her; she, grown learned in childish lore; thinking no innocent and pretty fancy ever to be despised; trying hard to know her humbler fellow-creatures, and to beautify their lives of machinery and reality with those imaginative graces and delights, without which the heart of infancy will wither up, the sturdiest physical manhood will be morally stark death, and the plainest national prosperity figures can show, will be the Writing on the Wall. . . . " HT iii 9

—*and sectarian religion:* "These portentous infants [the adult population of Coketown] being alarming creatures to stalk about in any human society, the eighteen denominations incessantly scratched one another's faces and pulled one another's hair by way of agreeing on the steps to be taken for their improvement—which they never did; a surprising circumstance, when the happy adaptation of the means to the end is considered. Still, although they differed in every other particular, conceivable and inconceivable (especially inconceivable), they were pretty well united on the point that these unlucky infants were never to wonder.

"Body number one, said they must take everything on trust. Body number two, said they must take everything on political economy. Body number three, wrote leaden little books for them, showing how the good grown-up baby invariably got to the Savings-bank, and the bad grown-up baby invariably got transported. Body number four, under dreary pretences of being droll (when it was very melancholy indeed), made the shallowest pretences of concealing pitfalls of knowledge, into which it was the duty of these babies to be smuggled and inveigled. But, all the bodies agreed that they were never to wonder." ¶HT i 8

—*stimulated by the press:* "To show to all, that in all familiar things, even in those which are repellent on the surface, there is Romance enough, if we will find it out:—to teach the hardest workers at this whirling wheel of toil, that their lot is not necessarily a moody, brutal fact, excluded from the sympathies and graces of imagination; to bring the greater and the lesser in degree, together, upon that wide field, and mutually dispose them to a better acquaintance and a kinder understanding—is one main object of our *Household Words.*" HW/PW

—stunted: " . . . struggling through the dissatisfaction of [Louisa Gradgrind's] face, there was a light with nothing to rest upon, a fire with nothing to burn, a starved imagination keeping life in itself somehow, which brightened its expression. Not with the brightness natural to cheerful youth, but with uncertain, eager, doubtful flashes, which had something painful in them, analogous to the changes on a blind face groping its way." HT i 3

—and understanding: "Do not let us, in the midst of the visible objects of nature, whose workings we can tell off in figures, surrounded by machines that can be made to the thousandth part of an inch, acquiring every day knowledge which can be proved upon a slate or demonstrated by a microscope—do not let us, in the laudable pursuit of the facts that surround us, neglect the fancy and the imagination which equally surround us as part of the great scheme.

"Let the child have its fables; let the man or woman into which it changes, always remember these fables tenderly. Let numerous graces and ornaments that cannot be weighed and measured, and that seem at first sight idle enough, continue to have their places about us, be we never so wise. The hardest head may co-exist with the softest heart. The union and just balance of those two is always a blessing to the possessor, and always a blessing to mankind." S/LC

—in worry: " . . . Florence suffered the added pain of thinking that she had been, perhaps, the innocent occasion of involving Walter [Gay] in peril, and all to whom he was dear, herself included, in an agony of suspense. For the rest, uncertainty and danger seemed written upon everything. The weathercocks on spires and housetops were mysterious with hints of stormy wind, and pointed, like so many ghostly fingers, out to dangerous seas, where fragments of great wrecks were drifting, perhaps, and helpless men were rocked upon them into a sleep as deep as the unfathomable waters. When Florence came into the City, and passed gentlemen who were talking together, she dreaded to hear them speaking of the ship, and saying it was lost. Pictures and prints of vessels fighting with the rolling waves filled her with alarm. The smoke and clouds, though moving gently, moved too fast for her apprehensions, and made her fear there was a tempest blowing at that moment on the ocean." DS 23

Insanity and the Insane

" . . . the absence of the soul is far more terrible in a living man than in a dead one . . . . " BR 3

—asylum at Lancaster: "'The usual thing,' said Francis Goodchild, with a sigh. 'Long groves of blighted men-and-women trees, interminable avenues of hopeless faces; numbers, without the slightest power of really combining for any earthly purpose; a society of human creatures who have nothing in common but that they have all lost the power of being humanly social with one another.'" LT 4

—in childhood: "How often . . . had [Mary Rudge] sat beside [Barnaby] night and day, watching for the dawn of mind that never came; how had she feared, and doubted, and yet hoped, long after conviction forced itself upon her! The little stratagems she had devised to try him, the little tokens he had given in his childish way—not of dullness but of something infinitely worse, so ghastly and unchild-like in its cunning—came back as vividly as if but yesterday had intervened . . . he, old and elfin-like in face, but ever dear to her, gazing at her with a wild and vacant eye, and crooning some uncouth song . . . .

"His older childhood, too; the strange imaginings he had; his terror of certain senseless things—familiar objects he endowed with life; the slow and gradual breaking out of that one horror, in which, before his birth, his darkened intellect began; how, in the midst of all, she had found some hope and comfort in his being unlike another child, and had gone on almost believing in the slow development of his mind until he grew a man, and then his childhood was complete and lasting . . . . " BR 25

—stereotypes: "The popular notion of an Idiot would probably be found to vary very little essentially, in different places, however modified by local circumstances. To the traveller in France or Italy, the name recalls a vacant creature all in rags, gibbering and blinking in the sun with a distorted face, and led about as a possession and a stock-in-trade by some phenomenon of filth and ugliness in the form of an old woman. In association with Switzerland, it suggests a horrible being, seated at a châlet door

(perhaps possessing sense enough to lead the way to a neighbouring waterfall), of stunted and misshapen form, with a pendulous excrescence dangling from his throat, like a great skin bag with a weight in it.* In the highlands of Scotland, or on the roads of Ireland, he becomes a red-haired Celt, rather more unreasonable than usual, plunging ferociously out of a mud cabin, and casting stones at the stranger's head. As a remembrance of our own childhood in an English country town, he is a shambling knock-kneed man who was never a child, with an eager utterance of discordant sounds which he seemed to keep in his protruding forehead, a tongue too large for his mouth, and a dreadful pair of hands that wanted to ramble over everything—our own face included. But in all these cases the main idea of an idiot would be of a hopeless, irreclaimable, unimprovable being. And if he be further recalled as under restraint in a workhouse or lunatic asylum, he will still come upon the imagination as wallowing in the lowest depths of degradation and neglect: a miserable monster, whom nobody may put to death, but whom every one must wish dead, and be distressed to see alive." HWC/I

**goiter: this depiction is echoed in PC/NT, even to the waterfall. See* Volume II p 1123

—treatment: " . . . I am not sure but that many people expect far too much. I have known some, after visiting the noblest of our Institutions for this terrible calamity, express their disappointment at the many deplorable cases they had observed with pain, and hint that, after all, the better system could do little. . . . Wonderful things have been done for the Blind, and for the Deaf and Dumb; but, the utmost is necessarily far inferior to the restoration of the senses of which they are deprived. To lighten the affliction of insanity by all human means, is not to restore the greatest of the Divine gifts; and those who devote themselves to the task do not pretend that it is. They find their sustainment and reward in the substitution of humanity for brutality, kindness for maltreatment, peace for raging fury; in the acquisition of love instead of hatred; and in the knowledge that, from such treatment, improvement, and hope of final restoration will come, if such hope be possible. It may be little to have abolished from mad-houses all that is abolished, and to have substituted all that is substituted. Nevertheless, reader, if you can do a little in any good direction—do it. It will be much, some day." HWC/CD

—uncomfortable to some: "That class of persons, unhappily always too large a one for this world, who are so desperately careful to receive no uncomfortable emotions from sad realities or pictures of sad realities, that they become the incarnation of the demon selfishness, and are, by their sickly letting-alone, the most intolerably mischievous people in the community, will probably exclaim, 'O, but all this must be excessively painful!' To which we reply, that such an affliction considered by itself is very painful; but that, considered with a rational reference to the alleviations and improvements of which it is plainly susceptible under such treatment, it ought to become the reverse of painful, and ought to do the visitor good.

"Madam you are a lady of very fine feelings, you are very easily shocked, you 'can't bear' a great deal that a higher wisdom than yours would seem to have contemplated your bearing when your little place was allotted to you on this ball. This idiot child of thirteen, sitting in its little chair before the fire—as to its bodily growth, a child of six; as to its mental development, nothing—is an odious sight to you. This idiot old man of eight, with the extraordinarily small head, the paralytic gestures, and the half-palsied forefinger, eternally shaking before his hatchet face as he chatters and chatters, disturbs you very much. But, madam, it were worth while to enquire while the brazen head is yet saying unto 'Time is!'* how much of the putting away of these unfortunates in past years, and how much of the putting away of many kinds of unfortunates at any time, may be attributable to that same refinement which cannot endure to be told about them. And, madam, if I may make so bold, I will venture to submit whether such delicate persons as your ladyship may not be laying up a rather considerable stock of responsibility; and you will excuse my saying that I would not have so sensitive a heart in my bosom for the dignity of the whole corporation." HWC/I

**In Robert Greene's play, the head pronounced: "Time is, time was, time is past."*

—wooing: "'Queen of my soul,' replied the stranger, folding his hands together, 'this goblet sip!'

"'Nonsense, sir,' said Mrs Nickleby . . . .

"'Won't you sip the goblet?' urged the stranger, with his head imploringly on one side, and his right hand on his breast. 'Oh, do sip the goblet!' . . .

"'Why is it,' said the old gentleman, coming up a step higher, and leaning his elbows on the wall, with as much complacency as if he were looking out of a window, 'why is it that beauty is always obdurate, even when admiration is as honourable and respectful as mine?' Here he smiled, kissed his hand, and made several low bows. 'Is it owing to the bees, who, when the honey season is over, and they are supposed to have been killed with brimstone, in reality fly to Barbary and lull the captive Moors to sleep with their drowsy songs? Or is it,' he added, dropping his voice almost to a whisper, 'in consequence of the statue at Charing Cross having been lately seen, on the Stock Exchange at midnight, walking arm-in-arm with the Pump from Aldgate, in a riding-habit? . . .'

"' . . . this is a sacred and enchanted spot, where the most divine charms'—here he kissed his hand and bowed again—'waft mellifluousness over the neighbours' gardens, and force the fruit and vegetables into premature existence.'" NN 41

"'She is come!' said the old gentleman, laying his hand upon his heart. 'Cormoran and Blunderbore! She is come! All the wealth I have is hers if she will take me for her slave. Where are grace, beauty, and blandishments, like those? In the Empress of Madagascar? No. In the Queen of Diamonds? No. In Mrs **Rowland**, who every morning bathes in Kalydor for nothing? No. Melt all these down into one, with the three Graces, the nine Muses, and fourteen biscuit-bakers' daughters from Oxford Street, and make a woman half as lovely. Pho! I defy you.'" NN 49

And see Dreams and dreaming—*the sane and the insane; and* S:Weeping—*exciting*

Invention and inventor

—*earnestness:* " . . . one who worthily invents must be in earnest, and the Barnacles abhorred and dreaded nothing half so much. That again was very reasonable; since in a country suffering under the affliction of a great amount of earnestness, there might, in an exceeding short space of time, be not a single Barnacle left sticking to a post." LD ii 8

—*and government:* " . . . the established narrative, which has become tiresome; the matter-of-course narrative which we all know by heart. How, after interminable attendance and correspondence, after infinite impertinences, ignorances, and insults, my lords made a Minute, number three thousand four hundred and seventy-two, allowing the culprit to make certain trials of his invention at his own expense. How the trials were made in the presence of a board of six, of whom two ancient members were too blind to see it, two other ancient members were too deaf to hear it, one other ancient member was too lame to get near it, and the final ancient member was too pigheaded to look at it.

"How there were more years; more impertinences, ignorances, and insults. How my lords then made a Minute, number five thousand one hundred and three, whereby they resigned the business to the Circumlocution Office. How the Circumlocution Office, in course of time, took up the business as if it were a bran new thing of yesterday, which had never been heard of before; muddled the business, addled the business, tossed the business in a wet blanket. How the impertinences, ignorances, and insults went through the multiplication table.

"How there was a reference of the invention to three Barnacles and a Stiltstalking, who knew nothing about it; into whose heads nothing could be hammered about it; who got bored about it, and reported physical impossibilities about it. How the Circumlocution Office, in a Minute, number eight thousand seven hundred and forty, 'saw no reason to reverse the decision at which my lords had arrived.' How the Circumlocution Office, being reminded that my lords had arrived at no decision, shelved the business. How there had been a final interview with the head of the Circumlocution Office that very morning, and how the Brazen Head* had spoken, and had been, upon the whole, and under all the circumstances, and looking at it from the various points of view, of opinion that one of two courses was to be pursued in respect of the business: that was to say, either to leave it alone for evermore, or to begin it all over again." ¶LD i 10

**See* Insanity—*uncomfortable to some:* note

—*and humbug:* "'And the invention?' said [Arthur] Clennam.

"'My good fellow,' returned Ferdinand [Barnacle], 'if you'll excuse the freedom of that form of address, nobody wants to know of the invention, and nobody cares two-pence-halfpenny about it.'

"'Nobody in the Office, that is to say?'

"'Nor out of it. Everybody is ready to dislike and ridicule any invention. You have no idea how many people want to be left alone. You have no idea how the Genius of the country (overlook the Parliamentary nature of the phrase, and don't be bored by it) tends to being left alone. Believe me, Mr Clennam,' said the sprightly young Barnacle, in his pleasantest manner, 'our place is not a wicked Giant to be charged at full tilt; but, only a wind-mill showing you, as it grinds immense quantities of chaff, which way the country wind blows.'

"'If I could believe that,' said Clennam, 'it would be a dismal prospect for all of us.'

"'Oh! don't say so!' returned Ferdinand. 'It's all right. We must have humbug, we all like humbug, we couldn't get on without humbug. A little humbug, and a groove, and everything goes on admirably, if you leave it alone.'" LD ii 28

—its obligation: "'But what is a man to do? If he has the misfortune to strike out something serviceable to the nation, he must follow where it leads him.'

"'Hadn't he better let it go?' asked Clennam.

"'He can't do it,' said Doyce, shaking his head with a thoughtful smile. 'It's not put into his head to be buried. It's put into his head to made useful. You hold your life on the condition that to the last you shall struggle hard for it. Every man holds a discovery on the same terms.'" LD i 16

—obstacles: "As an ingenious man, [Daniel Doyce] had necessarily to encounter every discouragement that the ruling powers for a length of time had been able by any means to put in the way of this class of culprits; but that was only reasonable self-defence in the powers, since How to do it must obviously be regarded as the natural and mortal enemy of How not to do it. In this was to be found the basis of the wise system, by tooth and nail upheld by the Circumlocution Office, of warning every ingenious British subject to be ingenious at his peril: of harassing him, obstructing him, inviting robbers (by making his remedy uncertain, difficult, and expensive) to plunder him, and at the best of confiscating his property after a short term of enjoyment, as though invention were on a par with felony." LD ii 8

—patent system: "William Butcher and me had a long talk, Christmas Day, respecting of the Model. William is very sensible. But sometimes cranky. William said, 'What will you do with it, John?' I said, 'Patent it.' William said, "How patent it, John?' I said, 'By taking out a Patent.' William then delivered that the law of Patent was a cruel wrong. William said, 'John, if you make your invention public, before you get a Patent, any one may rob you of the fruits of your hard work. You are put in a cleft stick, John. Either you must drive a bargain very much against yourself, by getting a party to come forward beforehand with the great expenses of the Patent; or, you must be put about, from post to pillar, among so many parties, trying to make a better bargain for yourself, and showing your invention, that your invention will be took from you over your head . . . I tell you the truth;' which he then delivered more at length. I said to W. B. I would Patent the invention myself . . . .

" . . . I put this: Is it reasonable to make a man feel as if, in inventing an ingenious inprovement meant to do good, he had done something wrong? How else can a man feel, when he is met by such difficulties at every turn? All inventors taking out a Patent MUST feel so . . . .

" . . . . Look at the Home Secretary, the Attorney-General, the Patent Office, the Engrossing Clerk, the Lord Chancellor, the Privy Seal, the Clerk of the Patents, the Lord Chancellor's Purse-bearer, the Clerk of the Hanaper, the Deputy Clerk of the Hanaper, the Deputy Sealer, and the Deputy Chaff-wax. No man in England could get a Patent for an Indian-rubber band, or an iron-hoop, without feeing all of them. Some of them, over and over again. I went through thirty-five stages. I began with the Queen upon the Throne. I ended with the Deputy Chaff-wax. Note. I should like to see the Deputy Chaff-wax. Is it a man, or what is it?

" . . . . Thomas [Joy] said to me, when we parted, 'John, if the laws of this country were as honest as they ought to be, you would have come to London—registered an exact description and drawing of your invention—paid half-a-crown or so for doing of it—and therein and thereby have got your Patent.'

"My opinion is the same as Thomas Joy. Further. In William Butcher's delivering 'that the whole gang of Hanapers and Chaff-waxes must be done away with, and that England has been chaffed and waxed sufficient.' I agree." RP/TP

—red tape: " . . in the dominions of Prince Bull, among the great mass of the community . . . were a number of very ingenious men, who were always busy with some invention or other, for promoting the prosperity of the Prince's subjects, and augmenting the Prince's power. But, whenever they submitted their models for the Prince's approval, his godmother stepped forward, laid her hand upon them, and said 'Tape.' Hence it came to pass, that when any particularly good discovery was made, the discoverer usually carried it off to some other Prince, in foreign parts, who had no old godmother who said Tape. This was not on the whole an advantageous state of things for Prince Bull, to the best of my understanding." RP/PB

The background, training and mind of CD's great exemplar, Daniel Doyce, are at Vol. II pp1233-34

Knowledge

—its absence: "'I say, we know that we exist,' repeated Horatio . . . 'but there we stop; there, is an end to our knowledge; there, is the summit of our attainments; there, is the termination of our ends. What more do we know?'

"'Nothing,' replied Mr Frederick—than whom no one was more capable of answering for himself in that particular." SB/HS

—head and heart: "Knowledge, as all followers of it must know, has a very limited power indeed when it informs the head alone; but when it informs the head and heart too, it has a power over life and death, the body and the soul, and dominates the universe." S/LC

—its power: " . . . the power of knowledge, if I understand it, is to bear and forbear; to learn the path of duty and to tread it; to engender that self-respect which does not stop at self, but cherishes the best respect for the best objects; to turn an always enlarging acquaintance with the joys and sorrows, capabilities and imperfections of our race to daily account in mildness of life and gentleness of construction, and humble efforts for the improvement, stone by stone, of the whole social fabric." S/LM

Letters of the alphabet

—"A": "'Next day, Sir,' said Joe, looking at me as if I were a long way off, 'having cleaned myself, I go and I see Miss A.'

"'Miss A., Joe? Miss Havisham?'

"'Which I say, Sir,' replied Joe, with an air of legal formality, as if he were making his will, 'Miss A., or otherways Havisham.'" GE 27

—"B": "My speculations about [Master B] were uneasy and manifold. Whether his Christian name was Benjamin, Bissextile (from his having been born in Leap Year), Bartholomew, or Bill. Whether the initial letter belonged to his family name, and that was Baxter, Black, Brown, Barker, Buggins, Baker, or Bird. Whether he was a foundling, and had been baptized B. Whether he was a lion-hearted boy, and B. was short for Briton, or for Bull." CS/HH 2

"I also carried the mysterious letter into the appearance and pursuits of the deceased; wondering whether he dressed in Blue, wore Boots (he couldn't have been Bald), was a boy of Brains, liked Books, was good at Bowling, had any skill as a Boxer, even in his Buoyant Boyhood Bathed from a Bathing-machine at Bognor, Bangor, Bournemouth, Brighton, or Broadstairs, like a Bounding Billiard Ball?

"So, from the first, I was haunted by the letter B." CS/HH 2

CD is probably spoofing himself and his own sobriquet, 'Boz.'

—"D": ". . . that very evening Biddy entered on our special agreement, by . . . lending me, to copy at home, a large old English D which she had imitated from the heading of some newspaper, and which I supposed, until she told me what it was, to be a design for a buckle." GE 10

—"E": "'What's the game at forfeits [said Miss Mowcher]? I love my love with an E, because she's enticing; I hate her with an E, because she's engaged. I took her to the sign of the exquisite, and treated her with an elopement; her name's Emily, and she lives in the east? Ha! ha! ha! Mr Copperfield, ain't I volatile?'" DC 22

—learned as a child: " . . . I have a distinct recollection (in my early days at school, when under the dominion of an old lady, who to my mind ruled the world with the birch) of feeling an intense disgust with printers and printing. I thought the letters were printed and sent there to plague me, and I looked upon the printer as my enemy. When I was taught to say my prayers I was told to pray for my enemies, and I distinctly remember praying especially for the printer

as my greatest enemy. I never now see a row of large, black, fat, staring Roman capitals, but this reminiscence rises up before me . . . .

"But this feeling of dislike to the printer altogether disappeared from the time I saw my own name in print. I now feel gratified at looking at the jolly letter O, the crooked S, with its full benevolent turns, the curious G, and the Q with its comical tail, that first awoke in me a sense of the humourous." S/PP2

"O": "'Well, Charley,' said I, looking over a copy of the letter O in which it was represented as square, triangular, pear-shaped, and collapsed in all kinds of ways, 'we are improving.'" BH 31

Literacy

—absence

—animalistic: "' . . . that chap that can't read nor write, and has never had much to do with anything but animals, and has never lived in any way but like the animals he has lived among, *is* a animal. And,' said Mr Willet, arriving at his logical conclusion, 'is to be treated accordingly.'" BR 11

—evil: "The factory-bells had need to ring their loudest that morning to disperse the groups of workers who stood in the tardy day-break, collected round the placards, devouring them with eager eyes. Not the least eager of the eyes assembled, were the eyes of those who could not read. These people, as they listened to the friendly voice that read aloud—there was always some such ready to help them—stared at the characters which meant so much with a vague awe and respect that would have been half ludicrous, if any aspect of public ignorance could ever be otherwise than threatening and full of evil." HT iii 4

—impact in profession: "'Are there any bill-stickers who can't read?' I took the liberty of inquiring.

"'Some,' said the King [of Bill-Stickers]. 'But they know which is the right side up-'ards of their work. They keep it as it's given out to 'em. I have seen a bill or so stuck wrong side up'ards. But it's very rare.'" RP/BS

—in numbers: "'How old are you, Phil?' asks the trooper . . . .

"'I'm something with a eight in it,' says Phil. 'It can't be eighty. Nor yet eighteen. It's betwixt 'em, somewheres.'

"Mr George, slowly putting down his saucer without tasting its contents, is laughingly beginning, 'Why, what the deuce, Phil,' —when he stops, seeing that Phil is counting on his dirty fingers.

"'I was just eight,' says Phil, 'agreeable to the parish calculation, when I went with the tinker . . . . That was April Fool Day. I was able to count up to ten; and when April Fool Day come round again, I says to myself, "Now, old chap, you're one and a eight in it." April Fool Day after that, "Now, old chap, you're two and a eight in it." In course of time, I come to ten and a eight in it; two tens and a eight in it. When it got so high, it got the upper hand of me; but this is how I always know there's a eight in it.'" BH 26

—shaming: "Very few could write their names; all who could not, pleaded that they could not, more or less sorrowfully, and always with a shake of the head, and in a lower voice than their natural speaking voice. Crosses could be made standing; signatures must be sat down to. There was no exception to this rule." AY/B

—admired: "' . . . I listened with hadmiration amounting to haw. I thought to myself, "Here's a man with a wooden leg—a literary man with—"'

"'N—not exactly so, sir,' said Mr Wegg.

"'Why, you know every one of these songs by name and by tune, and if you want to read or to sing any one on 'em off straight, you've only to whip on your spectacles and do it!' cried Mr Boffin. 'I see you at it!'

"'Well, sir,' returned Mr Wegg, with a conscious inclination of the head; 'we'll say literary, then.'

"'"A literary man—*with* a wooden leg—and all Print is open to him!" That's what I thought to myself, that morning,' pursued Mr Boffin, leaning forward to describe, uncramped by the clothes-horse, as large an arc as his right arm could make; '"all print is open to him!" And it is ain't it?'

"'Why, truly, sir,' Mr [Silas] Wegg admitted with modesty; 'I believe you couldn't show me the piece of English print, that I wouldn't be equal to collaring and throwing.'

"'On the spot?' said Mr [Noddy] Boffin.

"'On the spot.'" OMF i 5

—beginning at the beginning: "'You are oncommon in some things. You're oncommon small. Likewise, you're a oncommon scholar.'

"'No; I am ignorant and backward, Joe.'

"'Well, Pip,' said Joe, 'be it so or be it son't, you must be a common scholar afore you can be a oncommon one, I should hope! The king upon his throne, with his crown upon his 'ed, can't sit and write his acts of Parliament in print, without having begun, when he were a unpromoted prince, with the alphabet—ah!' added Joe, with a shake of the head that was full of meaning, 'and begun at A too, and worked his way to Z. And *I* know what that is to do, though I can't say I've exactly done it.'" GE 7

—and books: " . . . he [Charley Hexam] glanced at the backs of the books, with an awakened curiosity that went below the binding. No one who can read, ever looks at a book, even unopened on a shelf, like one who cannot." OMF i 3

—borderline: "'I only reads a thimble.'

"'Read a thimble!' echoed Snitchey. 'What are you talking about, young woman?'

"Clemency nodded. 'And a nutmeg-grater' . . . .

" . . . at last she triumphantly produced the thimble on her finger, and rattled the nutmeg-grater: the literature of both those trinkets being obviously in course of wearing out and wasting away, through excessive friction.

"'That's the thimble, is it, young woman?' said Mr Snitchey, diverting himself at her expense. 'And what does the thimble say?'

"'It says,' replied Clemency, reading slowly round as if it were a tower, 'For-get and For-give.'

" . . . 'And the nutmeg-grater?' inquired the head of the Firm.

"'The grater says,' returned Clemency, 'Do as you—would—be—done by.'" BL 1

—concealed: "The bridegroom, to whom the pen was handed first, made a rude cross for his mark; the bride, who came next, did the same. Now, I had known the bride when I was last there, not only as the prettiest girl in the place, but as having quite distinguished herself in the school; and I could not help looking at her with some surprise. She came aside and whispered to me, while tears of honest love and admiration stood in her bright eyes, 'He's a dear good fellow, miss; and I wouldn't shame him for the world!'" BH 36

—early stage: "One night, I [Pip] was sitting in the chimney-corner with my slate, expending great efforts on the production of a letter to Joe [Gargery] . . . . With an alphabet on the hearth at my feet for reference, I contrived in an hour or two to print and smear this epistle:

"'MI DEER JO i OPE U R KRWITE WELL i OPE i SHAL SON B HABELL 4 2 TEEDGE U JO AN THEN WE SHORL B SO GLODD AN WEN i M PRENGTD ['prenticed] 2 U JO WOT LARX AN BLEVE ME INF XN PIP.'

"There was no indispensable necessity for my communicating with Joe by letter, inasmuch as he sat beside me and we were alone. But, I delivered this written communication (slate and all) with my own hand, and Joe received it, as a miracle of erudition.

"'I say, Pip, old chap!' cried Joe, opening his blue eyes wide, 'what a scholar you are! Ain't you?'

"'I should like to be,' said I glancing at the slate as he held it: with a misgiving that the writing was rather hilly.

"'Why, here's a J,' said Joe, 'and a O equal to anythink! Here's a J and a O, Pip, and a J-O, Joe.'

"I had never heard Joe read aloud to any greater extent than this monosyllable, and I had observed at church last Sunday, when I accidentally held our Prayer-book upside down, that it seemed to suit his convenience quite as well as if it had been all right. Wishing to embrace the present occasion of finding out whether in teaching Joe, I should have to begin quite at the beginning, I said, 'Ah! But read the rest, Joe.'

"'The rest, eh, Pip?' said Joe, looking at it with a slowly searching eye. 'One, two, three. Why, here's three Js, and three Os, and three J-O, Joes, in it Pip!'

"I leaned over Joe, and, with the aid of my forefinger, read him the whole letter.

"'Astonishing!' said Joe, when I had finished. 'You ARE a scholar.'

"'How do you spell Gargery, Joe?' I asked him, with modest patronage.

"'I don't spell it at all,' said Joe.

"'But supposing you did?'

"'It *can't* be supposed,' said Joe. 'Tho' I'm oncommon fond of reading, too.'

"'Are you, Joe?'

"'On-common. Give me,' said Joe, 'a good book, or a good newspaper, and sit me down afore a good fire, and I ask no better. Lord!' he continued, after rubbing his knees a little, 'when you *do* come to a J and a O, and says you, "Here, at last, is a J-O, Joe," how interesting reading is!'

"I derived from this last, that Joe's education, like Steam, was yet in its infancy." GE 7

—marking with a cross: "[Edward the Confessor] attached a great seal to his state documents, instead of merely marking them, as the Saxon Kings had done, with the sign of the cross—just as poor people who have never been taught to write, now make the same mark for their names." CHE 6

—parental influence: "'My father, Pip [said Joe Gargery], he were given to drink, and when he were overtook with drink, he hammered away at my mother most onmerciful. It were a'most the only hammering he did, indeed, 'xcepting at myself . . . .

"'Consequence, my mother and me we ran away from my father several times; and then my mother she'd go out to work, and she'd say, "Joe," she'd say, "now, please God, you shall have some schooling, child," and she'd put me to school. But my father were that good in his hart that he couldn't abear to be without us. So, he'd come with a most tremenjous crowd and make such a row at the doors of the houses where we was, that they used to be obligated to have no more to do with us and to give us up to him. And then he took us home and hammered us. Which, you see, Pip,' said Joe, pausing in his meditative raking of the fire, and looking at me, 'were a drawback on my learning.'" GE 7

—reading aloud: "'Bought him at a sale,' said Mr [Noddy] Boffin. 'Eight wollumes. Red and gold. Purple ribbon in every wollume, to keep the place where you leave off. Do you know him?'

"'The book's name, sir?' inquired Silas [Wegg].

"'I thought you might have know'd him without it,' said Mr Boffin, slightly disappointed. 'His name is Decline-and-Fall-Off-The Rooshan-Empire.' (Mr Boffin went over these stones slowly and with much caution.)

"'Ay indeed!' said Mr Wegg, nodding his head with an air of friendly recognition.

"'You know him, Wegg?'

"'I haven't been not to say right slap through him, very lately,' Mr Wegg made answer, 'having been otherways employed, Mr Boffin. But know him? Old familiar declining and falling off the Rooshan? Rather, sir! Ever since I was not so high as your stick . . . .'" OMF i 5

"And now, Mr Wegg at length pushed away his plate and put on his spectacles, and Mr Boffin lighted his pipe and looked with beaming eyes into the opening world before him, and Mrs Boffin reclined in a fashionable manner on her sofa: as one who would be part of the audience if she found she could, and would go to sleep if she found she couldn't.

"'Hem!' began Wegg. 'This, Mr Boffin and Lady, is the first chapter of the first wollume of the Decline and Fall off——' here he looked hard at the book, and stopped.

"'What's the matter, Wegg?'

"'Why, it comes into my mind, sir, do you know, sir,' said Wegg with an air of insinuating frankess (having first again looked hard at the book), 'that you made a little mistake this morning, which I had meant to set you right in, only something put it out of my head. I think you said Rooshan Empire, sir?'

"'It is Rooshan; ain't it, Wegg?'

"'No, sir. Roman, Roman.'

"'What's the difference, Wegg?'

"'The difference, sir?' Mr Wegg was faltering and in danger of breaking down, when a bright thought flashed upon him. 'The difference, sir? There you place me in a difficulty, Mr Boffin. Suffice it to observe, that the difference is best postponed to some other occasion when Mrs Boffin does not honour us with her company. In Mrs Boffin's presence, sir, we had better drop it.'

"Mr Wegg thus came out of his disadvantage with quite a chivalrous air, and not only that, but by dint of repeating with a manly delicacy, 'In Mrs Boffin's presence, sir, we had better drop it!' turned the disadvantage on Boffin, who felt that he had committed himself in a very painful manner.

"Then, Mr Wegg, in a dry unflinching way, entered on his task going straight across country at everything that came before him; taking all the hard words, biographical and geographical; getting rather shaken by Hadrian, Trajan, and the Antonines; stumbling at Polybius (pronounced Polly Beeious, and supposed by Mr Boffin to be a Roman virgin, and by Mrs Boffin to be responsible for that necessity of dropping it); heavily unseated by Titus Antoninus Pius; up again and galloping smoothly with Augustus; finally, getting over the ground well with Commodus, who, under the appellation of Commodious, was held by Mr Boffin to have been quite unworthy of his English origin, and 'not to have acted up to his name' in his government of the Roman people . . . . Mr Wegg having read on by rote and attached as few ideas as possible to the text, came out of the encounter fresh; but, Mr Boffin, who had soon laid down his eyes and mind at the confounding enormities of the Romans, was so severely punished that he could hardly wish his literary friend Good-night, and articulate 'To-morrow.'

"'Commodious,' gasped Mr Boffin, staring at the moon, after letting Wegg out of the gate and fastening it: 'Commodious fights in that wild-beast-show, seven hundred and thirty-five times, in one character only! As if that wasn't stunning enough, a hundred lions is turned into the same wild-beast-show all at once! As if that wasn't stunning enough, Commodious, in another character, kills 'em all off in a hundred goes! As if that wasn't stunning enough, Vittle-us (and well named too) eat six millions' worth, English money, in seven months! Wegg takes it easy, but upon-my-soul to a old bird like myself these are scarers. And even now that Commodious is strangled, I don't see a way to our bettering ourselves.' Mr Boffin added as he turned his pensive steps towards the Bower and shook his head, 'I didn't think this morning there was half so many Scarers in Print. But I'm in for it now!'" OMF i 5

—*spelling:* "'What's your name, sir?' inquired the judge.

"'Sam Weller, my lord,' replied that gentleman.

"'Do you spell it with a "V" or a "W?"' inquired the judge.

"'That depends upon the taste and fancy of the speller, my lord,' replied Sam; 'I never had occasion to spell it more than once or twice in my life, but I spells it with a "V."'

"Here a voice in the gallery exclaimed aloud, 'Quite right too, Samivel, quite right. Put it down a we, my lord, put it down a we.'" PP 34

In April 1848, CD wrote an article for the Examiner summarizing some statistics on individuals arrested, tried and convicted of sundry crimes in 1847 in London. These showed that 11,100 men out of 41,000 (27%) and 17,100 women out of 25,500 (67%) reported no trade or occupation. Of the 25,500 women, 9,000 (35%) could neither read nor write and fourteen could read and write well. Of the men, 13,000 (32%) could neither read nor write, and 150 could do both well. His comment:

"This state of mental comparison is what has been commonly called 'education' in England for a good many years. And that ill-used word might, quite as reasonably, be employed to express a teapot." E/IC

Memory and memories

"'She [Bertha] never forgets, returned Caleb [Plummer]. 'It's one of the few things she an't clever in.'" CH 2

"'Memory is sometimes like a half-forgotten dream.'" CS/NT 1

—*in absence of heart:* "I showed [Estella] to a nicety where I had seen her walking on the casks, that first old day, and she said with a cold and careless look in that direction, 'Did I?' I reminded her where she had come out of the house and given me my meat and drink, and she said, 'I don't remember.' 'Not remember that you made me cry?' said I. 'No,' said she, and shook her head and looked about her . . . .

"'You must know,' said Estella, condescending to me as a brilliant and beautiful woman might, 'that I have no heart—if that has anything to do with my memory.'" GE 29

—*evaded:* "'I am the Ghost of Christmas Past.'

"'Long past?' inquired Scrooge: observant of its dwarfish stature.

"'No. Your past.'

"Perhaps Scrooge could not have told anybody why, if anybody could have asked him; but he had a special desire to see the Spirit in his cap, and begged him to be covered.

"'What!' exclaimed the Ghost, 'would you so soon put out, with worldly hands, the light I give? Is it not enough that you are one of those whose passions made this cap, and force me through whole trains of years to wear it low upon my brow!'" CC 1

—*of happiness:* "'Take any subject of sorrowful regret, and see with how much of pleasure it is associated. The recollection of past pleasure may become pain . . . it does. To remember happiness which cannot be restored is pain, but of a softened kind. Our recollections are unfortunately mingled with much that we deplore, and with many actions which we bitterly repent; still in the most chequered life I firmly think there are so many little rays of sunshine to look back upon, that I do not believe any mortal (unless he had put himself without the pale of hope) would deliberately drain a goblet of the waters of Lethe, if he had it in his power . . . .

"'Why, then, the good in this state of existence preponderates over the bad, let miscalled philosophers tell us what they will. If our affections be tried, our affections are our consolation and comfort; and memory, however sad, is the best and purest link between this world and a better.'" ¶NN 6

—law of conservation: "'In the material world, as I have long taught [said Redlaw], nothing can be spared; no step or atom in the wondrous structure could be lost, without a blank being made in the great universe. I know, now, that it is the same with good and evil, happiness and sorrow, in the memories of men.'" HM 2

—a metaphor: "Many and many a time in after years did Nicholas look back to this period of his life, and tread again the humble quiet homely scenes that rose up as of old before him . . . every little incident, and even slight words and looks of those old days, little heeded then, but well remembered when busy cares and trials were quite forgotten; came fresh and thick before him many and many a time, and, rustling above the dusty growth of years, came back green boughs of yesterday." NN 49

—of mother lost "Can I say of her face—altered as I have reason to remember it, perished as I know it is—that it is gone, when here it comes before me at this instant, as distinct as any face that I may choose to look on in a crowded street? Can I say of her innocent and girlish beauty, that it faded, and was no more, when its breath falls on my cheek now, as it fell that night? Can I say she ever changed, when my remembrance brings her back to life, thus only; and, truer to its loving youth than I have been, or man ever is, still holds fast what it cherished then?" DC 2

—in the old: "'I should like to ask you:— Does your childhood seem far off? Do the days when you sat at your mother's knee, seem days of very long ago?'

"Responding to [Carton's] softened manner, Mr Lorry answered:

"'Twenty years back, yes; at this time of my life, no. For, as I draw closer and closer to the end, I travel in the circle, nearer and nearer to the beginning. It seems to be one of the kind smoothings and preparings of the way. My heart is touched now, by many remembrances that had long fallen asleep, of my pretty young mother (and I so old!), and by many associations of the days when what we call the World was not so real with me, and my faults were not confirmed in me.'" TTC iii 9

—and pain: " . . . the windows of the house of Memory, and the windows of the house of Mercy, are not so easily closed as windows of glass and wood. They fly open unexpectedly; they rattle in the night; they must be nailed up. Mr The Englishman [Langley] had tried nailing them, but had not driven the nails quite home. So he passed but a disturbed evening and a worse night." CS/SL 2

—of people: "After musing for some minutes, the old gentleman [Brownlow] walked, with the same meditative face, into a back ante-room opening from the yard; and there, retiring into a corner, called up before his mind's eye a vast amphitheatre of faces over which a dusky curtain had hung for many years. 'No,' said the old gentleman, shaking his head; 'it must be imagination.'

"He wandered over them again. He had called them into view; and it was not easy to replace the shroud that had so long concealed them. There were the faces of friends, and foes: and of many that had been almost strangers: peering intrusively from the crowd; there were the faces of young and blooming girls that were now old women; there were faces that the grave had changed and closed upon, but which the mind, superior to its power, still dressed in their old freshness and beauty: calling back the lustre of the eyes, the brightness of the smile, the beaming of the soul through its mask of clay: and whispering of beauty beyond the tomb, changed but to be heightened, and taken from earth only to be set up as a light, to shed a soft and gentle glow upon the path to Heaven." OT 11

—reminiscence late at night: "My old companion tells me it is midnight . . . I always love this peaceful time of night, when long-buried thoughts, favoured by the gloom and silence, steal from their graves, and haunt the scenes of faded happiness and hope.

"The popular faith in ghosts has a remarkable affinity with the whole current of our thoughts at such an hour as this, and seems to be their necessary and natural consequence. For who can wonder that man should feel a vague belief in tales of disembodied spirits wandering through those places which they once dearly affected, when he himself, scarcely less separated from his old world than they, is for ever lingering upon past emotions and bygone times, and hovering, the ghost of his former self, about the places and people that warmed his heart of old?

"It is thus that at this quiet hour I haunt the house where I was born, the rooms I used to tread, the scenes of my infancy, my boyhood, and my youth; it is thus that I prowl around my buried treasure (though not of gold or silver), and mourn my loss; it is thus that I revisit the ashes of extinguished fires, and take my silent stand at old bedsides. If my spirit should ever glide back to this chamber when my body is mingled with the dust, it will but follow the course it often took in the old man's lifetime, and add but one more change to the subjects of its contemplation." MH 6

—remorse: "We need be careful how we deal with those about us, when every death carries to some small circle of survivors, thoughts of so much omitted, and so little done—of so many things forgotten, and so many more which might have been repaired! There is no remorse so deep as that which is unavailing; if we would be spared its tortures, let us remember this, in time." OT 33

"'Let him remember it in that room, years to come. The rain that falls upon the roof, the wind that mourns outside the door, may have foreknowledge in their melancholy sound. Let him remember it in that room, years to come!'

"He did remember it. In the miserable night he thought of it; in the dreary day, the wretched dawn, the ghostly, memory-haunted twilight. He did remember it. In agony, in sorrow, in remorse, in despair! 'Papa! papa! Speak to me, dear papa!' He heard the words again and saw the face. He saw it fall upon the trembling hands, and heard the one prolonged low cry go upward.

"Oh! He did remember it! The rain that fell upon the roof, the wind that mourned outside the door that night, had had foreknowledge in their melancholy sound. He knew, now, what he had done. He knew, now, that he had called down that upon his head, which bowed it lower than the heaviest stroke of fortune. He knew, now, what it was to be rejected and deserted; now, when every loving blossom he had withered in his innocent daughter's heart was snowing down in ashes on him." DS 59

"Haggard anxiety and remorse are bad companions to be barred up with. Brooding all day, and resting very little indeed at night, will not arm a man against misery. Next morning, Clennam felt that his health was sinking, as his spirits had already sunk, and that the weight under which he bent was bearing him down." LD ii 29

And see A:Death*—and remorse*

—sad, by the sea: "All is going on as it was wont. The wave are hoarse with repetition of their mystery; the dust lies piled upon the shore; the sea-birds soar and hover; the winds and clouds go forth upon their trackless flight; the white arms beckon, in the moonlight, to the invisible country far away.

"With a tender, melancholy pleasure, Florence finds herself again on the old ground so sadly trodden, yet so happily, and thinks of him in the quiet place where he and she have many and many a time conversed together, with the water welling up about his couch. And now, as she sits pensive there, she hears in the wild low murmur of the sea, his little story told again, his very words repeated; and finds that all her life, and hopes, and griefs, since—in the solitary house, and in the pageant it has changed to—have a portion in the burden of the marvellous song." DS 41

See A:The Dead*—remembered;* IG: Capital and Labour; *and* S:Happiness*—remembered —of unhappiness*

—obliterated: "' . . . I would not deprive myself [said Redlaw] of any kindly recollection, or any sympathy that is good for me, or others. What shall I lose, if I assent to this? What else will pass from my remembrance?'

"'No knowledge; no result of study; nothing but the intertwisted chain of feelings and associations, each in its turn dependent on, and nourished by, the banished recollections. Those will go.'

"'Are they so many?' said the haunted man, reflecting in alarm.

"'They have been wont to show themselves in the fire, in music, in the wind, in the dead stillness of the night, in the revolving years,' returned the Phantom scornfully.

"'In nothing else?'

"The Phantom held its peace . . . .

"'A moment! I call Heaven to witness,' said the agitated man, 'that I have never been a hater of my kind—never morose, indifferent, or hard, to anything around me. If, living here alone, I have made too much of all that was and might have been, and too little of what is, the evil, I believe, has fallen on me, and not on others. But, if there were poison in my body, should I not, possessed of antidotes and knowledge how to use them, use them? If there be poison in my mind, and through this fearful shadow I can cast it out, shall I not cast it out?'

"'Say,' said the Spectre, 'is it done?'

"'A moment longer!' he answered hurriedly. *'I would forget it if I could!* Have *I* thought that, alone, or has it been the thought of thousands upon thousands, generation after generation? All human memory is fraught with sorrow and trouble. My memory is as the memory of other men, but other men have not this choice. Yes, I close the bargain. Yes! I WILL forget my sorrow, wrong, and trouble!'" HM 1

"'It is only since last night,' [Redlaw] muttered gloomily, 'that I have remained shut up, and yet all things are strange to me. I am strange to myself. I am here, as in a dream. What interest have I in this place, or in any place that I can bring to my remembrance? My mind is going blind!'" HM 2

—recovered: "The abiding change that had come upon him since the influence of the music, and the Phantom's reappearance, was, that now he truly felt how much he had lost, and could compassionate his own condition, and contrast it, clearly, with the natural state of those who were around him. In this, an interest in those who were around him was revived, and a meek, submissive sense of his calamity was bred, resembling that which sometimes obtains in age, when its mental powers are weakened, without insensibility or sullenness being added to the list of its infirmities . . . .

"Redlaw fell upon his knees, with a loud cry.

"'O Thou,' he said, 'who through the teaching of pure love, has graciously restored me to the memory which was the memory of Christ upon the cross, and of all the good who perished in His cause, receive my thanks . . . .'" HM 3

Mind

—achievements commemorated: " . . . when he looked among the images in iron, marble, bronze, and brass, he failed to find a rather meritorious countryman of his, once the son of a Warwickshire wool-dealer [**Shakespeare**], or any single countryman whomsoever of that kind. He could find none of the men whose knowledge had rescued him and his children from terrific and disfiguring disease, whose boldness had raised his forefathers from the condition of serfs, whose wise fancy had opened a new and high existence to the humblest, whose skill had filled the working man's world with accumulated wonders." CS/NS

—attention: "The one serviceable, safe, certain, remunerative, attainable quality in every study and in every pursuit is the quality of attention. My own invention or imagination, such as it is, I can most truthfully assure you, would never have served me as it has, but for the habit of commonplace, humble, patient, daily, toiling, drudging attention. Genius, vivacity, quickness of penetration, brilliancy in association of ideas—such mental qualities, like the qualities of the apparition of the externally armed head in *Macbeth,* will not be commanded; but attention, after due term of submissive service, always will. Like certain plants which the poorest peasant may grow in the poorest soil, it can be cultivated by anyone, and it is certain in its own good season to bring forth flowers and fruit." S/BM2

—and contrast: "Everything in our lives, whether of good or evil, affects us most by contrast. If the peace of the simple village had moved [Nell] more strongly, because of the dark and troubled ways that lay beyond and through which she had journeyed with such failing feet . . . . " OCS 53

—effect of solitude

—illness: "The wheeled chair had its associated remembrances and reveries, one may suppose, as every place that is made the station of a human being has. Pictures of demolished streets and altered houses, as they formerly were when the occupant of the chair was familar with them; images of people as they too used to be, with little or no allowance made for the lapse of time since they were seen; of these, there must have been many in the long routine of gloomy days. To stop the clock of busy existence, at the hour when we were personally sequestered from it; to suppose mankind stricken motionless, when we were brought to a stand-still; to be unable to measure the changes beyond our view, by any larger standard than the shrunken one of our own uniform and contracted existence; is the infirmity of many invalids, and the mental unhealthiness of almost all recluses." LD i 29

—prison: "I believe that very few men are capable of estimating the immense amount of torture and agony which this dreadful punishment, prolonged for years, inflicts upon the sufferers; and in guessing at it myself, and in reasoning from what I have seen written upon their faces, and what to my certain knowledge they feel within, I am only the more convinced that there is a depth of terrible endurance in it which none but the sufferers themselves can fathom, and which no man has a right to inflict upon his fellow-creature.

"I hold this slow and daily tampering with the mysteries of the brain, to be immeasurably worse than any torture of the body: and because its ghastly signs and tokens are not so palpable to the eye and sense of touch as scars upon the flesh; because its wounds are not upon the surface, and it extorts few cries that human ears can hear; therefore I the more denounce it, as a secret punishment which slumbering humanity is not roused up to stay." ¶AN 7

"My firm conviction is that, independent of the mental anguish it occasions—an anguish so acute and so tremendous, that all imagination of it must fall far short of the reality—it wears the mind into a morbid state, which renders it unfit for the rough contact and busy action of the world. It is my fixed opinion that those who have undergone this punishment, MUST pass into society again morally unhealthy and diseased. There are many instances on record, of men who have chosen, or have been condemned, to lives of perfect solitude, but I scarcely remember one, even among sages of strong and vigorous intellect, where its effect has not become apparent, in some disordered train of thought, or some gloomy hallucination. What monstrous phantoms, bred of despondency and doubt, and born and reared in solitude, have stalked upon the earth, making creation ugly, and darkening the face of Heaven!

"Suicides are rare among these prisoners: are almost, indeed, unknown. But no argument in favour of the system, can reasonably be deduced from this circumstance, although it is very often urged. All men who have made diseases of the mind their study, know perfectly well that such extreme depression and despair as will change the whole character, and beat down all its powers of elasticity and self-resistance, may be at work within a man, and yet stop short of self-destruction." AN 7

—focused under stress: "There are times when the mind, being painfully alive to receive impressions, a great deal may be noted at a glance." NN 53

"Perhaps a man never sees so much at a glance as when he is in a situation of extremity. The chances are a hundred to one, that if Barnaby [Rudge] had lounged in at the gate to look about him, he would have lounged out again with a very imperfect idea of the place, and would have remembered very little about it.

"But as he was taken handcuffed across the gravelled area, nothing escaped his notice. The dry, arid look of the dusty square, and of the bare brick building; the clothes hanging at some of the windows; and the men in their shirt-sleeves and braces, lolling with half their bodies out of the others; the green sun-blinds at the officers' quarters, and the little scanty trees in front; the drummer-boys practising in a distant court-yard; the men at drill on the parade; the two soldiers carrying a basket between them, who winked to each other as he went by, and slily pointed to their throats; the spruce serjeant who hurried past with a cane in his hand, and under his arm a clasped book with a vellum cover; the fellows in the ground-floor rooms, furbishing and brushing up their different articles of dress, who stopped to look at him, and whose voices as they spoke together echoed loudly through the empty galleries and passages;—everything, down to the stand of muskets before the guard-house, and the drum with a pipe-clayed belt attached, in one corner, impressed itself upon his observation, as though he had noticed them in the same place a hundred times, or had been a whole day among them, in place of one brief hurried minute." BR 58

"[Orlick] drank again, and became more ferocious. I saw by his tilting of the bottle that there was no great quantity left in it. I distinctly understood that he was working himself up with its contents, to make an end of me. I knew that every drop it held was a drop of my life. I knew that when I was changed into a part of the vapour that had crept towards me but a little while before, like my own warning ghost, he would do as he had done in my sister's case—make all haste to the town, and be seen slouching about there, drinking at the alehouses. My rapid mind pursued him to the town, made a picture of the street with him in it, and contrasted its lights and life with the lonely marsh and the white vapour creeping over it, into which I should have dissolved.

"It was not only that I could have summed up years and years and years while he said a dozen words, but that what he did say presented pictures to me, and not mere words. In the excited and exalted state of my brain, I could not think of a place without seeing it, or of persons without seeing them. It is impossible to overstate the vividness of these images, and yet I was so intent, all the time, upon him himself—who would not be intent on the tiger crouching to spring!—that I knew of the slightest action of his fingers." GE 13

—gift of God: "Wherever hammers beat, or wherever factory chimneys smoke; wherever hands are busy, or the clanking of machinery resounds; wherever, in a word, there are masses of industrious beings whom their wise Creator did not see fit to constitute all body, but into each and every one of whom He breathed a mind—there, I would fain believe, some touch of sympathy and encouragement is felt from our collective pulse now beating in this Hall." S/LM

—of the heart: "What was strangest of all was, that the only real relief which seemed to make its way into the secret region of [the Strongs'] domestic unhappiness, made its way there in the person of Mr Dick.

"What his thoughts were on the subject, or what his observation was, I am as unable to explain, as I dare say he would have been to assist me in the task. But, as I have recorded in the narrative of my school days, his veneration for the Doctor was unbounded; and there is a subtlety of perception in real attachment, even when it is borne towards man by one of the lower animals, which leaves the highest intellect behind. To this mind of the heart, if I may call it so, in Mr Dick, some bright ray of the truth shot straight.

"He had proudly resumed his privilege, in many of his spare hours, of walking up and down the garden with the Doctor; as he had been accustomed to pace up and down The Doctor's Walk at Canterbury. But matters were no sooner in this state, than he devoted all his spare time (and got up earlier to make it more) to these perambulations. If he had never been so happy as when the Doctor read that marvellous performance, the Dictionary, to him; he was now quite miserable unless the Doctor pulled it out of his pocket, and began. When the Doctor and I were engaged, he now fell into the custom of walking up and down with Mrs Strong, and helping her to trim her favourite flowers, or weed the beds. I dare say he rarely spoke a dozen words in an hour: but his quiet interest, and his wistful face, found immediate response in both their breasts; each knew that the other liked him, and that he loved both; and he became what no one else could be—a link between them." DC 42

"[Mrs Higden was] an active old woman, with a bright dark eye and a resolute face, yet quite a tender creature too; not a logically-reasoning woman, but God is good, and hearts may count in Heaven as high as heads." OMF i 16

"Mrs Lammle's manner changed under the poor silly girl [Georgiana Podsnap]'s embraces, and she turned extremely pale: directing one appealing look, first to Mrs Boffin, and then to Mr Boffin. Both understood her instantly, with a more delicate subtlety than much better educated people, whose perception came less directly from the heart, could have brought to bear upon the case." OMF iv 2

—ideas: "Ideas, like ghosts (according to the common notion of ghosts), must be spoken to a little before they will explain themselves . . . . " DS 12

—and meanness: "[Fascination Fledgeby] was the meanest cur existing, with a single pair of legs. and instinct (a word we all clearly understand) going largely on four legs, and reason always on two, meanness on four legs never attains the perfection of meanness on two." OMF ii 5

—opinions: "It is much easier to burn men than to burn their opinions . . . . " CHE 21

—overindulged " . . . certain it is that minds, like bodies, will often fall into a pimpled ill-conditioned state from mere excess of comfort, and like them, are often successfully cured by remedies in themselves very nauseous and unpalatable." BR 7

—Reason enthroned alone: "Neither, as [Louisa] approached her old home now, did any of the best influences of old home descend upon her. The dreams of childhood—its airy fables; its graceful, beautiful, humane, impossible adornments of the world beyond: so good to be believed in once, so good to be remembered when outgrown, for then the least among them rises to the stature of a great Charity in the heart, suf-

fering little children to come into the midst of it, and to keep with their pure hands a garden in the stony ways of this world, wherein it were better for all the children of Adam that they should oftener sun themselves, simple and trustful, and not worldly-wise—what had she to do with these?

"Remembrances of how she had journeyed to the little that she knew, by the enchanted roads of what she and millions of innocent creatures had hoped and imagined; of how, first coming upon Reason through the tender light of Fancy, she had seen it a beneficent god, deferring to gods as great as itself: not a grim Idol, cruel and cold, with its victims bound hand to foot, and its big dumb shape set up with a sightless stare, never to be moved by anything but so many calculated tons of leverage—what had she to do with these?

"Her remembrances of home and childhood were remembrances of the drying up of every spring and fountain in her young heart as it gushed out. The golden waters were not there. They were flowing for the fertilization of the land where grapes are gathered from thorns, and figs from thistles." ¶HT ii 9

—reasoning: "'My sweet, I am only going to reason.'

"'Oh, but reasoning is worse than scolding!' exclaimed Dora, in despair. 'I didn't marry to be reasoned with. If you meant to reason with such a poor little thing as I am, you ought to have told me so, you cruel boy!'

"I tried to pacify Dora, but she turned away her face, and shook her curls from side to side, and said, 'You cruel, cruel boy!' so many times, that I really did not exactly know what to do: so I took a few turns up and down the room in my uncertainty, and came back again.

"'Dora, my darling!'

"'No, I am not your darling. Because you *must* be sorry that you married me, or else you wouldn't reason with me!' returned Dora." DC 43

—simplicity deceptive: "[Mr Dick] was a universal favourite, and his ingenuity in little things was transcendent. He could cut oranges into such devices as none of us had an idea of. He could make a boat out of anything, from a skewer upwards. He could turn crampbones into chessmen; fashion Roman chariots from old court cards; make spoked wheels out of cotton reels, and bird-cages of old wire. But he was greatest of all, perhaps, in the articles of string and straw; with which we were all persuaded he could do anything that could be done by hands." DC 17

And see —of the heart; and Facts*—a burden borne upward*

—staying power of its creation: "What light is shed upon the world, at this day, from amidst these rugged Palaces of Florence! Here, open to all comers, in their beautiful and calm retreats, the ancient Sculptors are immortal, side by side with **Michael Angelo**, **Canova**, **Titian**, **Rembrandt**, **Raphael**, Poets, Historians, Philosophers—those illustrious men of history, beside whom its crowned heads and harnessed warriors show so poor and small, and are so soon forgotten.

"Here, the imperishable part of noble minds survives, placid and equal, when strongholds of assault and defence are overthrown; when the tyranny of the many, or the few, or both, is but a tale; when Pride and Power are so much cloistered dust.

"The fire within the stern streets, and among the massive Palaces and Towers, kindled by rays from Heaven, is still burning brightly, when the flickering of war is extinguished and the household fires of generations have decayed; as thousands upon thousands of faces, rigid with the strife and passion of the hour, have faded out of the old Squares and public haunts, while the nameless Florentine Lady [Leonardo's Mona Lisa], preserved from oblivion by a Painter's hand, yet lives on, in enduring grace and youth." ¶PI 19

—succumbing to stress: "The sudden and terrible shock she had received, combined with the great affliction and anxiety of mind which she had for a long time endured, proved too much for Madeline's strength. Reovering from the state of stupefaction into which the sudden death of her father happily plunged her, she only exchanged that condition for one of dangerous and active illness. When the delicate physical powers which have been sustained by an unnatural strain upon the mental energies and a resolute determination not to yield, at last give way, their degree of prostration is usually proportionate to the strength of the effort which has previously upheld them. Thus it was that the illness which fell on Madeline was of no slight or temporary nature, but one which, for a time threatened her reason, and—scarcely worse—her life itself." NN 53

—*thinking*

—*in the dock:* "The jailer touched [Fagin] on the shoulder. He followed mechanically to the end of the dock, and sat down on a chair. The man pointed it out, or he would not have seen it. . . . There was one young man sketching his face in a little note-book. He wondered whether it was like, and looked on when the artist broke his pencil-point, and made another with his knife, as any idle spectator might have done.

"In the same way, when he turned his eyes towards the judge, his mind began to busy itself with the fashion of his dress, and what it cost, and how he put it on. There was an old fat gentleman on the bench, too, who had gone out, some half an hour before, and now come back. He wondered within himself whether this man had been to get his dinner, what he had had, and where he had had it; and pursued this train of careless thought until some new object caught his eye and roused another.

"Not that, all this time, his mind was, for an instant, free from one oppressive overwhelming sense of the grave that opened at his feet; it was ever present to him, but in a vague and general way, and he could not fix his thoughts upon it. Thus, even while he trembled, and turned burning hot at the idea of speedy death, he fell to counting the iron spikes before him, and wondering how the head of one had been broken off, and whether they would mend it, or leave it as it was. Then, he thought of all the horrors of the gallows and the scaffold—and stopped to watch a man sprinkling the floor to cool it—and then went on to think again." OT 52

—*in a hypnagogic state:* Well, sir, proceeded Mrs Tickit, 'I was thinking of one thing and thinking of another. Just as you yourself might. Just as anybody might.'

"'Precisely so,' said Clennam. 'Well?'

"'And when I do think of one thing and do think of another,' pursued Mrs Tickit, 'I hardly need to tell you, Mr Clennam, that I think of the [Meagles] family. Because, dear me! a person's thoughts,' Mrs Tickit said this with an argumentative and philosophic air, 'however they may stray, will go more or less on what is uppermost in their minds. They *will* do it, sir, and a person can't prevent them.'

"Arthur subscribed to this discovery with a nod.

"'You find it so yourself, sir, I'll be bold to say,' said Mrs Tickit, 'and we all find it so. It an't our stations in life that changes us, Mr Clennam; thoughts is free!—As I was saying, I was thinking of one thing and thinking of another, and thinking very much of the family. Not of the family in the present times only, but in the past times too. For when a person does begin thinking of one thing and thinking of another, in that manner as it's getting dark, what I say is, that all times seem to be present, and a person must get out of that state and consider before they can say which is which.'" LD ii 9

—*when perplexed and disoriented:* "'It is a sensation not experienced by many mortals,' said he, 'to be looking into a churchyard on a wild windy night, and to feel that I no more hold a place among the living than these dead do, and even to know that I lie buried somewhere else, as they lie buried here. Nothing uses me to it. A spirit that was once a man could hardly feel stranger or lonelier, going unreocgnised among mankind than I feel.

"'But this is the fanciful side of the situation. It has a real side, so difficult that, though I think of it every day, I never thoroughly think it out. Now, let me determine to think it out as I walk home. I know I evade it, as many men—perhaps most men—do evade thinking their way through their greatest perplexity. I will try to pin myself to mine. Don't evade it, John Harmon; don't evade it; think it out!'" OMF ii 13

—*when talking:* "Not being of a very speculative character, however, save under circumstances when her speculations could be put into words and uttered aloud . . . . " NN 49

—*uncertain:* "'My lad,' said the Captain . . . 'a man's thoughts is like the winds, and nobody can't answer for 'em for certain, any length of time together." DS 39

—*the Unconscious:* "Black are the brooding clouds and troubled the deep waters, when the Sea of Thought, first heaving from a calm, gives up its Dead. Monsters uncouth and wild, arise in premature, imperfect resurrection; the several parts and shapes of different things are joined and mixed by chance; and when, and how, and by what wonderful degrees, each separates from each, and every sense and object of the mind resumes its usual form and lives again, no man—though every man is every day the casket of this type of the Great

Mystery—can tell." C 3

—unconscious affinity: "Perhaps [Toby Veck] was the more curious about these Bells, because there were points of resemblance between themselves and him. They hung there, in all weathers, with the wind and rain driving in upon them; facing only the outsides of all those houses; never getting any nearer to the blazing fires that gleamed and shone upon the windows, or came puffing out of the chimney tops; and incapable of participation in any of the good things that were constantly being handed, through the street doors and the area railings, to prodigious cooks. Faces came and went at many windows: sometimes pretty faces, youthful faces, pleasant faces: sometimes the reverse: but Toby knew no more (though he often speculated on these trifles, standing idle in the streets) whence they came, or where they went, or whether, when the lips moved, one kind word was said of him in all the year, than did the Chimes themselves.

"Toby was not a casuist—that he knew of, at least—and I don't mean to say that when he began to take to the Bells, and to knit up his first rough acquaintance with them into something of a closer and more delicate woof, he passed through these considerations one by one, or held any formal review or great field-day in his thoughts. But what I mean to say, and do say is, that as the functions of Toby's body, his digestive organs for example, did of their own cunning, and by a great many operations of which he was altogether ignorant, and the knowledge of which would have astonished him very much, arrive at a certain end; so his mental faculties, without his privity or concurrence, set all these wheels and springs in motion, with a thousand others, when they worked to bring about his liking for the Bells." C 1

And see Associations, mental; *and* Hypnagogic State

Parapsychology

—déjà vu: "'Oh, Master Copperfield [said Uriah Heep], with what a pure affection do I love the ground my Agnes walks on!'

"I believe I had a delirious idea of seizing the red-hot poker out of the fire, and running him through with it. It went from me with a shock, like a ball fired from a rifle: but the image of Agnes, outraged by so much as a thought of this red-headed animal's, remained in my mind (when I looked at him, sitting all awry as if his mean soul griped his body), and made me giddy. He seemed to swell and grow before my eyes; the room seemed full of the echoes of his voice; and the strange feeling (to which, perhaps, no one is quite a stranger) that all this had occurred before, at some indefinite time, and that I knew what he was going to say next, took possession of me." DC 35

"'Upon my honour,' said Mr Micawber, indefinitely kissing his hand and bowing with his genteelest air, 'I do Homage to Miss Wickfield! Hem!'

"'I am glad of that, at least,' said I.

"'If you had not assured us, my dear Copperfield, on the occasion of that agreeable afternoon we had the happiness of passing with you, that D. was your favourite letter,' said Mr Micawber, 'I should unquestionably have supposed that A. had been so.'

"We have all some experience of a feeling, that comes over us occasionally, of what we are saying and doing having been said and done before, in a remote time—of our having been surrounded, dim ages ago, by the same faces, objects, and circumstances—of our knowing perfectly what will be said next, as if we suddenly remembered it! I never had this mysterious impression more strongly in my life, than before he uttered those words." DC 39

"At sunset, when I was walking on alone [toward Bologna], while the horses rested, I arrived upon a little scene, which, by one of those singular mental operations of which we are all conscious, seemed perfectly familiar to me, and which I see distinctly now.

"There was not much in it. In the blood red light, there was a mournful sheet of water, just stirred by the evening wind; upon its margin a few trees. In the foreground was a group of silent peasant girls leaning over the parapet of a little bridge, and looking, now up at the sky, now down into the water; in the distance, a deep bell; the shade of approaching night on everything.

"If I had been murdered there, in some former life, I could not have seemed to remember the place more thoroughly, or with a more emphatic chilling of the blood; and the mere remembrance of it acquired in that minute, is so strengthened by the imaginary recollection, that I hardly think I could forget it." ¶PI 7

—experiences told: "I have always noticed a prevalent want of courage, even among per-

sons of superior intelligence and culture, as to imparting their own psychological experiences when those have been of a strange sort. Almost all men are afraid that what they could relate in such wise would find no parallel or response in a listener's internal life, and might be suspected or laughed at.

"A truthful traveller, who should have seen some extraordinary creature in the likeness of a sea-serpent, would have no fear of mentioning it; but the same traveller, having had some singular presentiment, impulse, vagary of thought, vision (so called), dream, or other remarkable mental impression, would hesitate considerably before he would own to it.

"To this reticence I attribute much of the obscurity in which such subjects are involved. We do not habitually communicate our experiences of these subjective things as we do our experiences of objective creation. The consequence is, that the general stock of experience in this regard appears exceptional, and really is so, in respect of being miserably imperfect." ¶CS/DM 2

—precognition

—of death: "'. . . I have such a fear and dread upon me to-night [said Nancy] that I can hardly stand . . . I scarcely know of what . . . . I wish I did. Horrible thoughts of death, and shrouds with blood upon them, and a fear that has made me burn as if I was on fire, have been upon me all day. I was reading a book to-night, to wile the time away, and the same things came into the print.'

"'Imagination,' said the gentleman [Brownlow], soothing her.

"'No imagination,' replied the girl in a hoarse voice. 'I'll swear I saw "coffin" written in every page of the book in large black letters—aye, and they carried one close to me, in the streets tonight.'

"'There is nothing unusual in that,' said the gentleman. 'They have passed me often.'

"'*Real ones,*' rejoined the girl. 'This was not.'" OT 46

"[Tigg] was flushed with wine, but not gay. His scheme had succeeded, but he showed no triumph. The effort of sustaining his difficult part before his late companion had fatigued him, perhaps, or it may be that the evening whispered to his conscience, or it may be (as it *has* been) that a shadowy veil was dropping round him, closing out all thoughts but the presentiment and vague foreknowledge of impending doom.

"If there be fluids, as we know there are, which, conscious of a coming wind, or rain, or frost, will shrink and strive to hide themselves in their glass arteries; may not that subtle liquor of the blood perceive, by properties within itself, that hands are raised to waste and spill it; and in the veins of men run cold and dull as his did, in that hour!" MC 47

"Some other terror came upon [James Carker] quite removed from this of being pursued, suddenly, like an electric shock, as he was creeping through the streets. Some visionary terror, unintelligible and inexplicable, associated with a trembling of the ground—a rush and sweep of something through the air, like death upon the wing. He shrunk, as if to let the thing go by. It was not gone, it never had been there, yet what a startling horror it had left behind." DS 55 *Carker is killed later by a train*

"In common with the generality of people [the surgeon] had often heard and read of singular instances, in which a presentiment of death, at a particular day, or even minute, had been entertained and realised." SB/BV *See also* CS/MJ 4 *The Signal-man*

—of illness: "It was a cold, wild night, and the trees shuddered in the wind. The rain had been thick and heavy all day, and with little intermission for many days. None was falling just then, however. The sky had partly cleared, but was very gloomy—even above us, where a few stars were shining. In the north and north-west, where the sun had set three hours before, there was a pale dead light both beautiful and awful; and into it long sullen lines of cloud waved up, like a sea stricken immovable as it was heaving. Towards London, a lurid glare overhung the whole dark waste; and the contrast between these two lights, and the fancy which the redder light engendered of an unearthly fire, gleaming on all the unseen buildings of the city, and on all the faces of its many thousands of wondering inhabitants, was as solemn as might be.

"I had no thought, that night—none, I am quite sure—of what was soon to happen to me. But I have always remembered since, that when we had stopped at the garden-gate to look up at the sky, and when we went upon our way, I had for a moment an undefinable impression of myself as being something different from what I then was. I know it was then, and there, that I had it. I have ever since connected the feeling with that spot and time, and with everything associated with that spot and time, to the distant voices in the town, the barking of a dog, and the sound of wheels coming down the miry hill." BH 31

—mystery of the future: "The room in which they were, communicating with that in which [Jarndyce] stood, was only lighted by the fire. Ada sat at the piano; Richard stood beside her, bending down. Upon the wall, their shadows blended together, surrounded by strange forms, not without a ghostly motion caught from the unsteady fire, though reflecting from motionless objects. Ada touched the notes so softly, and sang so low, that the wind, sighing away to the distant hills, was as audible as the music. The mystery of the future, and the little clue afforded to it by the voice of the present, seemed expressed in the whole picture." BH 6

See Dreams and dreaming—*presentiment*

Philosophy

—acceptance: "'I see more of the world, I can assure you,' said Mr Omer, 'in this chair, than ever I see out of it. You'd be surprised at the number of people that looks in of a day to have a chat. You really would! There's twice as much in the newspaper, since I've taken to this chair, as there used to be. As to general reading, dear me, what a lot of it I do get through! That's what I feel so strong, you know! If it had been my eyes, what should I have done? If it had been my ears, what should I have done? Being my limbs, what does it signify? Why, my limbs only made my breath shorter when I used 'em. And now, if I want to go out into the street or down to the sands, I've only got to call Dick, Joram's youngest 'prentice, and away I go in my own carriage, like the Lord Mayor of London.'

"He half suffocated himself with laughing here.

"'Lord bless you!' said Mr Omer, resuming his pipe, 'a man must take the fat with the lean; that's what he must make up his mind to, in this life.'" DC 51

—disappointment borne: "'You think of me, Ruth,' said Tom [Pinch], 'and it is very natural that you should, as if I were a character in a book; and you make it a sort of poetical justice that I should, by some impossible means or other, come, at last, to marry the person I love. But there is a much higher justice than poetical justice, my dear, and it does not order events upon the same principle.

"'Accordingly, people who read about heroes in books, and choose to make heroes of themselves out of books, consider it a very fine thing to be discontented and gloomy, and misanthropical, and perhaps a little blasphemous, because they cannot have everything ordered for their individual accommodation. Would you like me to become one of that sort of people?

"'No, Tom. But still I know,' she added timidly, 'that this is a sorrow to you in your own better way.'

"Tom thought of disputing the position. But it would have been mere folly, and he gave it up.

"'My dear,' said Tom, 'I will repay your affection with the Truth, and all the Truth. It is a sorrow to me. I have proved it to be so sometimes, though I have always striven against it. But somebody who is precious to you may die, and you may dream that you are in heaven with the departed spirit, and you may find it a sorrow to wake to the life on earth, which is no harder to be borne than when you fell asleep.

"'It is sorrowful to me to contemplate my dream, which I always knew was a dream, even when it first presented itself; but the realities about me are not to blame. They are the same as they were. My sister, my sweet companion, who makes this place so dear, is she less devoted to me, Ruth, than she would have been, if this vision had never troubled me? My old friend John [Westlock], who might so easily have greeted me with coldness and neglect, is he less cordial to me? The world about me, is there less good in that?

"'Are my words to be harsh and my looks to be sour, and is my heart to grow cold, because there has fallen in my way a good and beautiful creature, who but for the selfish regret that I cannot call her my own, would, like all other good and beautiful creatures, make me happier and better! No, my dear sister. No,' said Tom stoutly. 'Remembering all my means of happiness, I hardly dare to call this lurking something a sorrow; but whatever name it may justly bear, I thank Heaven that it renders me more sensible of affection and attachment, and softens me in fifty ways. Not less happy. Not less happy, Ruth!'" MC 50

—*in essence:* " . . . philosophers are only men in armour, after all." PP 10

—*forbearance:* "'[Philosophy] runs in the family, I b'lieve, sir,' replied Mr [Sam] Weller. 'My father's wery much in that line, now. If my mother-in-law blows him up, he whistles. She flies in a passion, and breaks his pipe; he steps out, and gets another. Then she screams wery loud, and falls into 'sterics: and he smokes wery comfortably 'till she comes to agin. That's philosophy, sir, an't it?'

"'A very good substitute for it, at all events,' replied Mr Pickwick, laughing." PP 16

—*a gift of the spirit:* "In the exhaustless catalogue of Heaven's mercies to mankind, the power we have of finding some germs of comfort in the hardest trials must ever occupy the foremost place; not only because it supports and upholds us when we most require to be sustained, but because in this source of consolation there is something, we have reason to believe, of the divine spirit; something of that goodness which detects amidst our own evil doings, a redeeming quality; something which, even in our fallen nature, we possess in common with the angels; which had its being in the old time when they trod the earth, and lingers on it yet, in pity.

"How often, on their journey, did the widow [Mary Rudge] remember with a grateful heart, that out of his deprivation Barnaby's cheerfulness and affection sprung! How often did she call to mind that but for that, he might have been sullen, morose, unkind, far removed from her—vicious, perhaps, and cruel! How often had she cause for comfort, in his strength, and hope, and in his simple nature! Those feeble powers of mind which rendered him so soon forgetful of the past, save in brief gleams and flashes—even they were a comfort now. The world to him was full of happiness; in every tree, and plant, and flower, in every bird, and beast, and tiny insect whom a breath of summer wind laid low upon the ground, he had delight. His delight was hers; and where many a wise son would have made her sorrowful, this poor light-hearted idiot filled her breast with thankfulness and love." BR 47

—*the Golden Rule:* "'Do as you would, you know, and cetrer, eh!' observed Clemency [Newcome] . . . . 'Such a short cut, an't it?'

"'I'm not sure,' said Mr Britain, 'that it's what would be considered good philosophy. I've my doubts about that; but it wears well, and saves a quantity of snarling, which the genuine article don't always.'" BL 2 *And see* Scholarship—*unenthusiastic*

—*at mealtime:* "Boiled beef and greens constitute the day's variety on the former repast of boiled pork and greens; and Mrs Bagnet serves out the meal in the same way, and seasons it with the best of temper: being that rare sort of old girl that she receives Good to her arms without a hint that it might be Better; and catches light from any little spot of darkness near her." BH 34

—*mistaken resistance:* "'I have had my share of sorrows [said Geoffrey Haredale]—more than the common lot, perhaps, but I have borne them ill. I have broken where I should have bent; and have mused and brooded, when my spirit should have mixed with all God's great creation. The men who learn endurance, are they who call the whole world, brother." BR 79

—*resignation:* "'Lookee, rascal,' said Hugh [to Dennis], contracting his brows, 'I'm not altogether such a shallow blade but I know you expected to get something by [treachery], or you wouldn't have done it. But it's done, and you're here, and it will soon be all over with you and me; and I'd die as soon as live, or live as die. Why should I trouble myself to have revenge on you? To eat, and drink, and go to sleep, as long as I stay here, is all I care for. If there was but a little more sun to bask in, than can find its way into this cursed place, I'd lie in it all day, and not trouble myself to sit or stand up once. That's all the care I have for myself. Why should I care for you ?'" BR 74

—*ups and downs:* "Mr Plornish amiably growled, in his philosophical but not lucid manner, that there was ups you see, and there was downs. It was in wain to ask why ups, why downs; there they was, you know. He had heerd it given for a truth that accordin' as the world went round, which round it did rewolve undoubted, even the best of gentlemen must take his turn of standing with his ed upside down and all his air a-flying the wrong way into what you might call Space. Wery well then. What Mr Plornish said was, wery well then. That gentleman's ed would come up'ards when his turn come, that gentleman's air would be a pleasure to look upon being all smooth again, and wery well then!" LD ii 27

—useful to a schoolmaster: "'What's the reason,' said Mr Squeers . . . 'what's the reason for rheumatics? What do they mean? What do people have 'em for—eh?

"Mrs Sliderskew didn't know, but suggested that it was possibly because they couldn't help it.

"'Measles, rheumatics, hooping-cough, fevers, agers, and lumbagers,' said Mr Squeers, 'is all philosophy together; that's what it is. The heavenly bodies is philosophy, and the earthly bodies is philosophy. If there's a screw loose in a heavenly body, that's philosopohy; and if there's a screw loose in a earthly body, that's philosophy too; or it may be that sometimes there's a little metaphysics in it, but that's not often. Philosophy's the chap for me. If a parent asks a question in the classical, commercial, or mathematical line, says I, gravely, "Why, sir, in the first place, are you a philosopher?" "No, Mr Squeers," he says, I an't." "Then, sir," says I, "I am sorry for you, for I shan't be able to explain it." Naturally, the parent goes away, and wishes he was a philosopher, and, equally naturally, thinks I'm one.'" NN 57

—Utilitarianism: "It was a fundamental principle of the Gradgrind philosophy that everything was to be paid for. Nobody was ever on any account to give anybody anything, or render anybody help without purchase. Gratitude was to be abolished, and the virtues springing from it were not to be. Every inch of the existence of mankind, from birth to death, was to be a bargain across a counter. And if we didn't get to Heaven, that way, it was not a politico-economical place, and we had no business there." HT iii 8

And see Education*—materialistic, a failure; —Utilitarian; and* Facts*—statistics, and —and taste*

Psychology

—fixation: "It was in vain that he tried to control his attention, by directing it to any business occupation or thought; it rode at anchor by the haunting topic, and would hold to no other idea. As though a criminal should be chained in a stationary boat on a deep clear river, condemned, whatever countless leagues of water flowed past him, always to see the body of the fellow-creature he had drowned lying at the bottom, immovable, and unchangeable, except as the eddies made it broad or long, now expanding, now contracting its terrible lineaments; so Arthur, below the shifting current of transparent thoughts and fancies which were gone and succeeded by others as soon as come, saw, steady and dark, and not to be stirred from its place, the one subject that he endeavoured with all his might to rid himself of, and that he could not fly from." LD ii 23

—perception influenced by mood: "The melancholy which had seemed to the sad eyes of the anxious [Oliver] to hang, for days past, over every object, beautiful as all were, was dispelled by magic. The dew seemed to sparkle more brightly on the green leaves; the air to rustle among them with a sweeter music; and the sky itself to look more blue and bright. Such is the influence which the condition of our own thoughts, exercises, even over the appearance of external objects. Men who look on nature, and their fellow-men, and cry that all is dark and gloomy, are in the right; but the sombre colours are reflections from their own jaundiced eyes and hearts. The real hues are delicate, and need a clearer vision." OT 34 *And see* N:Nature*—perverted*

—perception and memory: "We are so much in the habit of allowing impressions to be made upon us by external objects, which should be produced by reflection alone, but which, without such visible aids, often escape us; that I am not sure I should have been so thoroughly possessed by this one subject [the face of Nell], but for the heaps of fantastic things I had seen huddled together in the curiosity-dealer's warehouse.

"These, crowding upon my mind, in connection with the child, and gathering round her, as it were, brought her condition palpably before me. I had her image, without any effort of imagination, surrounded and beset by everything that was foreign to its nature, and furthest removed from the sympathies of her sex and age.

"If these helps to my fancy had all been wanting, and I had been forced to imagine her in a common chamber, with nothing unusual or uncouth in its appearance, it is very probable that I should have been less impressed with her strange and solitary state. As it was, she seemed to exist in a kind of allegory; and having these shapes about her, claimed my interest so strongly, that (as I have already remarked) I could not dismiss her from my recollection, do what I would." OCS 1

—projection: "Was there nothing jarring and discordant even in [young Martin Chuzzlewit's] tone of courage, with this one note 'self' for ever audible, however high the strain? Not in her ears. It had been better otherwise, perhaps, but so it was. She heard the same bold spirit which had flung away as dross all gain and profit for her sake, making light of peril and privation that she might be calm and happy; and she heard no more. That heart where self has found no place and raised no throne, is slow to recognise its ugly presence when it looks upon it. As one possessed of an evil spirit was held in old time to be alone conscious of the lurking demon in the breasts of other men, so kindred vices know each other in their hiding places every day, when Virtue is incredulous and blind." MC 14 *And see* S:Cynic*—projection*

—prophecy fulfilled: "The firm of Barbox Brothers had been some offshoot or irregular branch of the Public Notary and bill-broking tree. It had gained for itself a griping reputation before the days of Young Jackson, and the reputation had stuck to it and to him.

"As he had imperceptibly come into possession of the dim den up in the corner of a court off Lombard Street, on whose grimy windows the inscription Barbox Brothers had for many long years daily interposed itself between him and the sky, so he had insensibly found himself a personage held in chronic distrust, whom it was essential to screw tight to every transaction in which he engaged, whose word was never to be taken without his attested bond, whom all dealers with [will?] openly set up guards and wards against.

"This character had come upon him through no act of his own. It was as if the original Barbox had stretched himself down upon the office floor, and had thither caused to be conveyed Young Jackson in his sleep, and had there effected a metempsychosis and exchange of persons with him.

"The discovery—aided in its turn by the deceit of the only woman he had ever loved, and the deceit of the only friend he had ever made; who eloped from him to be married together—the discovery, so followed up, completed what his earliest rearing had begun. He shrank, abashed, within the form of Barbox, and lifted up his head and heart no more." ¶CS/MJ 1 ii

See also Mind*—the Unconscious;* Parapsychology; F:Prisoner*—preoccupation; and* LC: Ghost, Goblin*—human psychology,*

Scholarship

—research: " . . . a work on Chinese metaphysics, sir.' said Pott . . . .

"'An abstruse subject I should conceive,' said Mr Pickwick.

"'Very, sir,' responded Pott, looking intensely sage. '[My critic] *crammed* for it, to use a technical but expressive term; he read up for the subject, at my desire, in the *Encyclopædia Britannica.*'

"'Indeed!' said Mr Pickwick; 'I was not aware that that valuable work contained any information respecting Chinese metaphysics.'

"'He read, sir,' rejoined Pott, laying his hand on Mr Pickwick's knee, and looking round with a smile of intellectual superiority, 'he read for metaphysics under the letter M, and for China under the letter C, and combined his information, sir!'" PP 51

—tutor: "A certain portion of [Darnay's] time was passed at Cambridge, where he read with undergraduates as a sort of tolerated smuggler who drove a contraband trade in European languages, instead of conveying Greek and Latin through the Custom House." TTC ii 10

—unenthusiastic: "M'Choakumchild reported that [Sissy] had a very dense head for figures; that, once possessed with a general idea of the globe, she took the smallest conceivable interest in its exact measurements; that she was extremely slow in the acquisition of dates, unless some pitiful incident happened to be connected therewith; that she would burst into tears on being required (by the mental process) immediately to name the cost of two hundred and forty-seven muslin caps at fourteenpence halfpenny; that she was as low down, in the school, as low could be; that after eight weeks of induction into the elements of Political Economy, she had only yesterday been set right by a prattler three feet high, for returning to the question, 'What is the first principle of this science?' the absurd answer, 'To do unto others as I would that they should do unto me.'

"Mr Gradgrind observed, shaking his head, that all this was very bad; that it showed the necessity of infinite grinding at the mill of knowledge, as per system, schedule, blue book, report, and tabular statements A to Z; and that Jupe 'must be kept to it.' So Jupe was kept to it, and became low-spirited, but no wiser." HT i 9

Solitude

—accustomed: "Solitary men [writes Master Humphrey] are accustomed, I suppose, unconsciously to look upon solitude as their own peculiar property. I had sat alone in my room on many, many anniversaries of this great holiday [Christmas Day], and had never regarded it but as one of universal assemblage and rejoicing. I had excepted, and with an aching heart, a crowd of prisoners and beggars . . . . " MH 6

—in age: "[Geoffrey Haredale] was not the less alone for having spent so many years in seclusion and retirement. This was not better preparation than a round of social cheerfulness: perhaps it even increased the keenness of his sensibility. He had been so dependent upon [his niece Emma] for companionship and love; she had come to be so much a part and parcel of his existence; they had had so many cares and thoughts in common, which no one else had shared; that losing her was beginning life anew, and being required to summon up the hope and elasticity of youth, amid the doubts, distrusts, and weakened energies of age." BR 81

—its blessings: "Here was one of the advantages of having lived alone so long! The little, bustling, active, cheerful creature existed entirely within herself, talked to herself, made a confidant of herself, was as sarcastic as she could be, on people who offended her, by herself; pleased herself, and did no harm. If she indulged in scandal, nobody's reputation suffered; and if she enjoyed a little bit of revenge, no living soul was one atom the worse. One of the many to whom, from straitened circumstances, a consequent inability to form the associations they would wish, and a disinclination to mix with the society they could obtain . . . the humble artist had pursued her lonely, but contented way for many years; and, until the peculiar misfortunes of the Nickleby family attracted her attention, had made no friends, though brimfull of the friendliest feelings to all mankind. There are many warm hearts in the same solitary guise as poor little Miss La Creevy's." NN 20

—its danger: "That [Miss Havisham] had done a grievous thing in taking an impressionable child [Estella] to mould into the form that her wild resentment, spurned affection, and wounded pride found vengeance in, I knew full well. But that, in shutting out the light of day, she had shut out infinitely more; that, in seclusion, she had secluded herself from a thousand natural and healing influences; that her mind, brooding solitary, had grown diseased, as all minds do and must and will that reverse the appointed order of their Maker, I knew equally well." GE 49

—in London: "London is as complete a solitude as the plains of Syria . . . ." NN 20

—in youth: "When the house door closed with a bang and a shake . . . Miss Kimmeens being, as before stated, of a self-reliant and methodical character, presently began to parcel out the long summer-day before her.

"And first she thought she would go all over the house, to make quite sure that nobody with a great-coat on and a carving-knife in it, had got under one of the beds or into one of the cupboards. Not that she had ever before been troubled by the image of anybody armed with a great-coat and a carving-knife, but that it seemed to have been shaken into existence by the shake and the bang of the great street door, reverberating through the solitary house.

"So, little Miss Kimmeens looked under the five empty beds of the five departed pupils, and looked under her own bed, and looked under Miss Pupford's bed, and looked under Miss Pupford's assistant's bed. And when she had done this, and was making the tour of the cupboards, the disagreeable thought came into her young head, What a very alarming thing it would be to find somebody with a mask on, like Guy Fawkes, hiding bolt upright in a corner and pretending not to be alive! However, Miss Kimmeens having finished her inspection without making any such uncomfortable discovery, sat down in her tidy little manner to needlework, and began stitching away at a great rate.

"The silence all about her soon grew very oppressive, and the more so because of the odd inconsistency that the more silent it was, the more noises there were. The noise of her own needle and thread as she stitched, was infinitely louder in her ears than the stitching of all the six pupils, and of Miss Pupford, and of Miss Pupford's assistant, all stitching away at once on a highly emulative afternoon . . . .

" . . . the stairs . . . began to creak in a most unusual manner, and then the furniture began to crack, and then poor little Miss Kimmeens, not liking the furtive aspect of things in general, began to sing as she stitched. But it was not her own voice that she heard—it was somebody else making believe to be Kitty, and singing excessively flat, without any heart—so as that would never mend matters, she left off again.

"By and by, the stitching became so palpable a failure that Miss Kitty Kimmeens folded her work neatly, and put it away in its box, and gave it up. Then the question arose about reading. But no; the book that was so delightful when there was somebody she loved for her eyes to fall on when they rose from the page, had not more heart in it than her own singing now. The book went to its shelf as the needlework had gone to its box, and, since something *must* be done—thought the child, 'I'll go put my room to rights.'

"She shared her room with her dearest little friend among the other five pupils, and why then should she now conceive a lurking dread of the little friend's bedstead? But she did. There was a stealthy air about its innocent white curtains, and there were even dark hints of a dead girl lying under the coverlet.

"The great want of human company, the great need of a human face, began now to express itself in the facility with which the furniture put on strange exaggerated resemblances to human looks. A chair with a menacing frown was horribly out of temper in a corner; a most vicious chest of drawers snarled at her from between the windows. It was no relief to escape from those monsters to the looking-glass, for the reflection said, 'What? Is that you all alone there? How you stare!' And the background was all a great void stare as well.

"The day dragged on, dragging Kitty with it very slowly by the hair of her head, until it was time to eat. There were good provisions in the pantry, but their right flavour and relish had evaporated . . . . Where was the use of laying the cloth symmetrically for one small guest, who had gone on ever since the morning growing smaller and smaller, while the empty house had gone on swelling larger and larger? The very Grace came out wrong, for who were 'we' who were going to receive and be thankful? So, Miss Kimmeens was *not* thankful, and found her-self taking her dinner in very slovenly style—gobbling it up, in short, rather after the manner of the lower animals, not to particularise the pigs.

"But, this was by no means the worst of the change wrought out in the naturally loving and cheery little creature as the solitary day wore on. She began to brood and be suspicious. She discovered that she was full of wrongs and injuries. All the people she knew, got tainted by her lonely thoughts and turned bad . . . .

" . . . it began to be obvious that this was a plot. They had said to one another, 'Never mind Kitty; you get off, and I'll get off; and we'll leave Kitty to look after herself. Who cares for *her?*' To be sure they were right in that question; for who *did* care for her, a poor little lonely thing against whom they all planned and plotted? Nobody, nobody! Here Kitty sobbed . . . .

" . . . . They thought they were enjoying themselves, but it would come home to them one day to have thought so. They would all be dead in a few years, let them enjoy themselves ever so much. It was a religious comfort to know that.

"It was such a comfort to know it, that little Miss Kitty Kimmeens suddenly sprang from the chair in which she had been musing in a corner, and cried out, 'O those envious thoughts are not mine, O this wicked creature isn't me! Help me, somebody! I go wrong, alone by my weak self! Help me, anybody!'" ¶CS/TT 6

Stupidity

—*in brief:* " . . . Mr Sparkler would probably be the last person, in any assemblage of the human species, to receive an impression from anything that passed in his presence." LD i 33

—*inarticulate:* "The exquisitely bold and original thought presented itself to Mr Sparkler, that there was an opening here for saying there were some of the family (emphasising 'some' in a marked manner) to whom no painter could render justice. But, for want of a form of words in which to express the idea, it returned to the skies." LD ii 6

—*suppressed:* "Mr Sparkler . . . made a brief though pertinent rejoinder; the same being neither more nor less than that he had long perceived Miss Fanny to have no nonsense about her, and that he had no doubt of its being all right with his Governor. At that point, the object of his affections shut him up like a box with a spring lid, and sent him away." LD ii 15

True and false

—falsehood

—boastful: "Some of [Stryver's] King's Bench familiars, who were occasionally parties to the full-bodied wine and the lie, excused him for the latter by saying that he had told it so often, that he believed it himself—which is surely such an incorrigible aggravation of an originally bad offence, as to justify any such offender's being carried off to some suitably retired spot, and there hanged out of the way." TTC ii 21

—homely advice: "'There's one thing you may be sure of, Pip,' said Joe [Gargery], after some rumination, 'namely, that lies is lies. Howsever they come, they didn't ought to come, and they come from the father of lies, and work round to the same. Don't you tell no more of 'em, Pip. *That* ain't the way to get out of being common, old chap . . . . Lookee here, Pip, at what is said to you by a true friend. Which this to you the true friend say. If you can't get to be oncommon through going straight, you'll never get to do it through going crooked. So don't tell no more on 'em, Pip, and live well and die happy.'" GE 9

—whopper in white: "Well, well! not much, but Tom's all. The half-sovereign. He had wrapped it hastily in a piece of paper, and pinned it to the leaf. These words were scrawled in pencil on the inside: 'I don't want it, indeed. I should not know what to do with it if I had it.'

"There are some falsehoods, Tom, on which men mount, as on bright wings, towards Heaven. There are some truths, cold bitter taunting truths, wherein your worldly scholars are very apt and punctual, which bind men down to earth with leaden chains. Who would not rather have to fan him, in his dying hour, the lightest feather of a falsehood such as thine, than all the quills that have been plucked from the sharp porcupine, reproachful truth, since time began!" MC 13

—'honesty in dishonesty': "Mr James Harthouse, 'going in' for his adopted party, soon began to score. With the aid of a little more coaching for the political sages, a little more genteel listlessness for the general society, and a tolerable management of the assumed honesty in dishonesty, most effective and most patronized of the polite deadly sins, he speedily came to be considered of much promise. The not being troubled with earnestness was a grand point in his favour, enabling him to take to the hard Fact fellows with as good a grace as if he had been born one of the tribe, and to throw all other tribes overboard, as conscious hypocrites.

"'Whom none of us believe, my dear Mrs Bounderby, and who do not believe themselves. The only difference between us and the professors of virtue or benevolence, or philanthropy—never mind the name—is, that we know it is all meaningless, and say so; while they know it equally and will never say so.'" HT ii 7 *And see* S:Apathy—*amorality*

—real and unreal: "'We are dreadfully real, Mr Carker,' said Mrs Skewton; 'are we not?'

"Few people had less reason to complain of their reality than Cleopatra, who had as much that was false about her as could well go to the composition of anybody with a real individual existence. But Mr Carker commiserated with our reality nevertheless, and agreed that we were very hardly used in that regard." DS 27

—serenity of truth: "A composed and unobtrusive self-sustainment was noticeable in Daniel Doyce—a calm knowledge that what was true must remain true, in spite of all the Barnacles in the family ocean, and would be just the truth, and neither more nor less, when even that sea had run dry—which had a kind of greatness in it, though not of the official quality." LD i 16

—and taxes: "'Do you remember what you told me once, about her making all the apple parsties and doing all the cooking?'

"'Yes, very well,' I returned.

"'It was as true,' said Mr Barkis, 'as turnips is. It was as true,' said Mr Barkis, nodding his nightcap, which was his only means of emphasis, 'as taxes is. And nothing's truer than them.'" DC 21

And see W:America—*press—toasted*

Wits

—lived upon: "'And I'll tell you what,' said Mr Pyke; 'if you'll send round to the public-house for a pot of mild half-and-half, positively and actually I'll drink it.'

"And positively and actually Mr Pyke *did* drink it, and Mr Pluck helped him, while Mrs Nickleby looked on in divided admiration of the condescension of the two, and the aptitude with which they accommodated themselves to the pewter-pot . . . gentlemen who, like Messrs Pyke and Pluck, live upon their wits (or not so much, perhaps, upon the presence of their own wits as upon the absence of wits in other people) are occasionally reduced to very narrow shifts and straits, and are at such periods accustomed to regale themselves in a very simple and primitive manner." NN 27

"'If you try to prejudice me, by making out that I have lived by my wits—how do your lawyers live—your politicians—your intriguers—your men of the Exchange?' . . . " LD i 1

—polished: "'I have knocked about harder than you, and have got along further than you. I have had, all my sea-going life long, to keep my wits polished bright with acid and friction, like the brass cases of the ship's instruments.. I'll keep you company on this expedition. Now you don't live by talking any more than I do. Clench that hand of yours in this hand of mine, and that's a speech on both sides.'" CS/MS 2

Wonder

—its absence: "There has been only one child in the Smallweed family for several generations. Little old men and women there have been, but no child, until Mr [Bart] Smallweed's grandmother, now living, became weak in her intellect, and fell (for the first time) into a childish state. With such infantine graces as a total want of observation, memory, understanding and interest, and an eternal disposition to fall asleep over the fire and into it, Mr Smallweed's grandmother has undoubtedly brightened the family.

"Mr Smallweed's grandfather is likewise of the party. He is in a helpless condition as to his lower, and nearly so as to his upper limbs; but his mind is unimpaired. It holds, as well as it ever held, the first four rules of arithmetic, and a certain small collection of the hardest facts. In respect of ideality, reverence, wonder, and other such phrenological attributes, it is no worse off than it used to be. Everything that Mr Smallweed's grandfather ever put away in his mind was a grub at first, and is a grub at last. In all his life he has never bred a single butterfly." BH 21

—necessity: "In an utilitarian age, of all other times, it is a matter of grave importance that fairy tales should be respected. Our English red tape is too magnificently red ever to be employed in the tying up of such trifles, but every one who has considered the subject knows full well that a nation without fancy, without some romance, never did, never can, never will, hold a great place under the sun." HW/FF *And see* A:Child

—negated: "Now, besides very many babies just able to walk, there happened to be in Coketown a considerable population of babies who had been walking against time towards the infinite world, twenty, thirty, forty, fifty years and more. These portentous infants being alarming creatures to stalk about in any human society, the eighteen denominations incessantly scratched one another's faces and pulled one another's hair by way of agreeing on the steps to be taken for their improvement—which they never did; a surprising circumstance, when the happy adaptation of the means to the end is considered.

"Still, although they differed in every other particular, conceivable and inconceivable (especially inconceivable), they were pretty well united on the point that these unlucky infants were never to wonder.

"Body number one, said they must take everything on trust. Body number two, said they must take everything on political economy. Body number three, wrote leaden little books for them, showing how the good grown-up baby invariably got to the Savings-bank, and the bad grown-up baby invariably got transported. Body number four, under dreary pretences of being droll (when it was very melancholy indeed), made the shallowest pretences of concealing pitfalls of knowledge, into which it was the duty of these babies to be smuggled and inveigled. But, all the bodies agreed that they were never to wonder." ¶HT i 8

And see Education—*Utilitarian*

Addendum

—and "X," 'Y" and "Z": "'A was an archer, and shot at a frog.' Of course he was. He was an apple-pie also, and there he is! He was a good many things in his time, was A, and so were most of his friends, except X, who had so little versatility, that I never knew him to get beyond Xerxes or Xantippe—like Y, who was always confined to a Yacht or Yew Tree; and Z condemned for ever to be a Zebra or a Zany." CS/CT

Letters and Communication

It is not easy for a man to speak of his own books. I dare say that few persons have been more interested in mine than I; and if it be a general principle in nature that a lover's love is blind, and that a mother's love is blind, I believe it may be said of an author's attachment to the creatures of his own imagination, that it is a perfect model of constancy and devotion, and is the blindest of all.

S/B1

"You know him, Wegg?"

"I haven't been not say right slap through him, very lately . . . having been otherways employed, Mr Boffin. But know him? Old familiar declining and falling off the Rooshan? Rather, sir! Ever since I was not so high as your stick."

OMF i 5

A Cheap Theatre on Saturday Night UT/CT

Adages, Maxims and Proverbs

—brag: "'Very well,' said Mr Jaggers. 'Recollect the admission you have made, and don't try to go from it presently.

"'Who's a-going to try?' retorted Joe [Gargery].

"'I don't say anybody is. Do you keep a dog?'

"'Yes, I do keep a dog.'

"'Bear in mind then, that Brag is a good dog, but that Holdfast is a better. Bear that in mind, will you?' repeated Mr Jaggers, shutting his eyes and nodding his head at Joe, as if he were forgiving him something." GE 18

—cutting of your nose: "Such of the No Gas party, however, as have got shops, remain in opposition and burn tallow—exhibiting in their windows the very picture of the sulkiness that punishes itself, and a new illustration of the old adage about cutting off your nose to be revenged on your face, in cutting off their gas to be revenged on their business." RP/EW

—honesty and policy: "'Ah!' rejoins Mr Brass, brimful of moral precepts and love of virtue. 'A charming subject of reflection for you, very charming. A subject of proper pride and congratulation, Christopher. Honesty is the best policy.—I always find it so myself. I lost forty-seven pound ten by being honest this morning. But it's all gain, it's gain!'

"Mr Brass slyly tickles his nose with his pen, and looks at Kit with the water standing in his eyes. Kit thinks that if ever there was a good man who belied his appearance, that man is Sampson Brass.

"'A man,' says Sampson, 'who loses forty-seven pound ten in one morning by his honesty, is a man to be envied. If it had been eighty pounds, the luxuriousness of feeling would have been increased. Every pound lost, would have been a hundredweight of happiness gained. The still small voice, Christopher,' cries Brass, smiling, and tapping himself on the bosom, 'is a singing comic songs within me, and all is happiness and joy!'" OCS 57

—just and generous: "'Hold! There is a most remarkably long-headed, flowing-bearded, and patriarchal proverb, which observes that it is the duty of a man to be just before he is generous. Be just now [said Tigg], and you can be generous presently.'" MC 13

—little pitchers: "Charley [Neckett] verified the adage about little pitchers, I am sure; for she heard of more sayings and doings, in a day, than would have come to my ears in a month." BH 37

—maxims of virtue: " . . . Mr [John] Chester followed . . . by propounding certain virtuous maxims, somewhat vague and general in their nature, doubtless, and occasionally partaking of the character of truisms, worn a little out at elbow, but delivered in so charming a voice and with such uncommon serenity and peace of mind, that they answered as well as the best.

"Nor is this to be wondered at; for as hollow vessels produce a far more musical sound in falling than those which are substantial, so it will oftentimes be found that sentiments which have nothing in them make the loudest ringing in the world, and are the most relished." ¶BR 27

—misfortunes: "Misfortunes, saith the adage, never come singly. There is little doubt that troubles are exceedingly gregarious in their nature, and flying in flocks, are apt to perch capriciously; crowding on the heads of some poor wights until there is not an inch of room left on their unlucky crowns, and taking no more notice of others who offer as good resting-places for the soles of their feet, than if they had no existence." BR 32

—out of sight: "'Out of sight, out of mind,' is well enough as a proverb applicable to cases of friendship, though absence is not always necessary to hollowness of heart, even between friends, and truth and honesty, like precious stones, are perhaps most easily imitated at a distance, when the counterfeits often pass for real." NN 40

—procrastination: "'At present, and until something turns up (which I am, I may say, hourly expecting), I have nothing to bestow but advice. Still, my advice is so far worth taking that—in short, that I have never taken it myself, and am the . . . miserable wretch you behold . . . . My advice is, never do to-morrow what you can do to-day. Procrastination is the thief of time. Collar him.'

"'My poor papa's maxim,' Mrs Micawber observed.

"'My dear,' said Mr Micawber, 'your papa was very well in his way . . . . But he applied that maxim to our marriage, my dear; and that was so far prematurely entered into, in consequence, that I never recovered the expense.'" DC 12

—Rome wasn't built: "'Rome, brother,' re-

turned Wegg: 'a city which (it may not be generally known) originated in twins and a wolf, and ended in Imperial marble, wasn't built in a day.'

"'Did I say it was?' asked Venus.

"'No, you did not, brother. Well inquired.'" OMF iii 6

—when in Rome: "'If I [Jerry Cruncher], as a honest tradesman, succeed in providing a jinte of meat or two, none of your not touching of it, and sticking to bread. If I, as a honest tradesman, am able to provide a little beer, none of your declaring on water. When you go to Rome, do as Rome does. Rome will be a ugly customer to you, if you don't. *I*'m your Rome, you know.'" TTC ii 14

Advertisement

—bill-sticking

—historical: "'When my father was Engineer, Beadle, and Bill-Sticker to the parish of St Andrew's, Holborn, he employed women to post bills for him. He employed women to post bills at the time of the riots of London . . . .

"'The bills being at that period mostly proclamations and declarations, and which were only a demy size, the manner of posting the bills (as they did not use brushes) was by means of a piece of wood which they called a "dabber." Thus things continued till such time as the State Lottery was passed, and then the printers began to print larger bills, and men were employed instead of women, as the State Lottery Commissioners then began to send men all over England to post bills, and would keep them out for six or eight months at a time, and they were called by the London bill-stickers "trampers," their wages at the time being ten shillings per day, besides expenses. They used sometimes to be stationed in large towns for five or six months together, distributing the schemes to all the houses in the town. And then there were more caricature wood-block engravings for posting-bills than there are at the present time . . . . The largest bills printed at that period were a two-sheet double crown; and when they commenced printing four-sheet bills, two bill-stickers would work together. . . .

"'A two-sheet double crown . . . is a bill thirty-nine inches wide by thirty inches high.'" RP/BS

—rivalry: "'Since the abolishing of the State Lottery all that good feeling has gone [said the King], and nothing but jealousy exists, through the rivalry of each other. Several bill-sticking companies have started, but have failed. The first party that started a company was twelve year ago; but what was left of the old school and their dependants joined together and opposed them. And for some time were quiet again, till a printer of Hatton Garden formed a company by hiring the sides of houses; but he was not supported by the public, and he left his wooden frames fixed up for rent.

"'The last company that started, took advantage of the New Police Act, and hired . . . the hoarding of Trafalgar Square, and established a bill-sticking office . . . and engaged some of the new bill-stickers to do their work, and for a time got the half of all our work, and with such spirit did they carry on their opposition towards us, that they used to give us in charge before the magistrate and get us fined; but they found it so expensive that they could not keep it up, for they were always employing a lot of ruffians from the Seven Dials to come and fight us; and on one occasion the old bill-stickers went to Trafalgar Square to attempt to post bills, when they were given in custody by the watchman in their employ, and fined at Queen Square five pounds . . . . During the time the men were waiting for the fine, this company started off to a public-house that we were in the habit of using, and waited for us coming back, where a fighting scene took place that beggars description." ¶RP/BS

—a warehouse, postered: " . . . I contemplated . . . an old warehouse which rotting paste and rotting paper had brought down to the condition of an old cheese. It would have been impossible to say, on the most conscientious survey, how much of its front was brick and mortar, and how much decaying and decayed plaster. It was so thickly encrusted with fragments of bills, that no ship's keel after a long voyage could be half so foul. All traces of the broken windows were billed out, the doors were billed across, the water-spout was billed over.

"The building was shored up to prevent its tumbling into the street; and the very beams erected against it were less wood than paste and paper, they had been so continually posted and reposted. The forlorn dregs of old posters so encumbered this wreck, that there was no hold for new posters, and the stickers had abandoned the place in despair, except one enterprising man who had hoisted the last masquerade to a clear spot near the level of the stack of chimneys, where it waved and drooped like a shattered flag.

"Below the rusty cellar-grating, crumpled remnants of old bills torn down rotted away in wasting heaps of fallen leaves. Here and there, some of the thick rind of the house had peeled off in strips, and fluttered heavily down, littering the street; but still, below these rents and gashes, layers of decomposing posters showed themselves, as if they were interminable. I thought the building could never even be pulled down, but in one adhesive heap of rottenness and poster. As to getting in—I don't believe that if the Sleeping Beauty and her Court had been so billed up, the young Prince could have done it." ¶RP/BS

—boarding-house: "Answers out of number were received, with all sorts of initials; all the letters of the alphabet seemed to be seized with a sudden wish to go out boarding and lodging; voluminous was the correspondence between Mrs Tibbs and the applicants; and most profound was the secrecy observed. 'E.' didn't like this; 'I.' couldn't think of putting up with that; 'I.O.U.' didn't think the terms would suit him; and 'G.R' had never slept in a French bed." SB/BH

—boot-blacking: "'For years upon years, the only pictures in my possession . . . were the engravings of a man shaving himself in a boot, on the blacking bottles that I was overjoyed to use in cleaning boots with . . . .' HT ii 7

—carnival attractions: "The neighbours cut up rough, and made complaints; but Mr Magsman don't know what they *would* have had. It was a lovely thing. First of all, there was the canvass, representin the picter of the Giant, in Spanish trunks and a ruff, who was himself half the heighth of the house, and was run up with a line and pulley to a pole on the roof, so that his Ed was coeval with the parapet. Then, there was the canvass, representin the picter of the Albina lady, showing her white air to the Army and Navy in correct uniform. Then, there was the canvass, representin the picter of the Wild Indian a scalpin a member of some foreign nation. Then, there was the canvass, representin the picter of a child of a British Planter, seized by two Boa Constrictors . . . . Similarly, there was the canvass, representin the picter of the Wild Ass of the Prairies . . . . Last, there was the canvass, representin the picter of the Dwarf, and like him too (considerin), with **George the Fourth** in sych a state of astonishment at him as His Majesty couldn't with his utmost politeness and stoutness express. The front of the House was so covered with canvasses, that there wasn't a spark of daylight ever visible on that side. 'MAGSMAN'S AMUSEMENTS,' fifteen foot long by two foot high, ran over the front door and parlour winders." CS/GS

—hairdressers' print: " . . . upon his own ground, he was not; nor was there any more distinct trace of him to assist the imagination of an inquirer, than a professional print or emblem of his calling (much favoured in the trade), representing a hair-dresser of easy manners curling a lady of distinguished fashion, in the presence of a patent upright grand pianoforte.'" MC 19

—mode of revenge: "If I had an enemy whom I hated—which Heaven forbid!—and if I knew of something that sat heavy on his conscience, I think I would introduce that something into a Posting-Bill, and place a large impression in the hands of an active sticker. I can scarcely imagine a more terrible revenge. I should haunt him, by this means, night and day.

"I do not mean to say that I should publish his secret, in red letters two feet high, for all the town to read: I would darkly refer to it. It should be between him, and me, and the Posting-Bill. Say, for example, that, at a certain period of his life, my enemy had surreptitiously possessed himself of a key. I would then embark my capital in the lock business, and conduct that business on the advertising principle. In all my placards and advertisements, I would throw up the line SECRET KEYS.

"Thus, if my enemy passed an uninhabited house, he would see his conscience glaring down on him from the parapets, and peeping up at him from the cellars. If he took a dead-wall in his walk, it would be alive with reproaches. If he sought refuge in an omnibus, the panels thereof would become Belshazzar's palace to him. If he took a boat, in a wild endeavour to escape, he would see the fatal words lurking under the arches of the bridges over the Thames. If he walked the streets with down-cast eyes, he would recoil from the very stones of the pavement, made eloquent by lampblack lithograph. If he drove or rode, his way would be blocked up by enormous vans, each proclaiming the same words over and over again from its whole extent of surface.

"Until, having gradually grown thinner and paler, and having at last totally rejected food, he would miserably perish, and I should be revenged." ¶RP/BS

—"*Personals:*" "'No,' said [Tom] Pinch. 'No. I have been looking over the advertising sheet, thinking there might be something in it, which would be likely to suit me. But, as I often think, the strange thing seems to be that nobody is suited. Here are all kinds of employers wanting all sorts of servants, and all sorts of servants wanting all kinds of employers, and they never seem to come together. Here is a gentleman in a public office in a position of temporary difficulty, who wants to borrow five hundred pounds; and in the very next advertisement here is another gentleman who has got exactly that sum to lend. But he'll never lend it to him, John [Westlock], you'll find!

"'Here is a lady possessing a moderate independence, who wants to board and lodge with a quiet, cheerful family; and here is a family describing themselves in those very words, "a quiet, cheerful family," who want exactly such a lady to come and live with them. But she'll never go, John! Neither do any of these single gentlemen who want an airy bedroom, with the occasional use of a parlour, ever appear to come to terms with these other people who live in a rural situation, remarkable for its bracing atmosphere, within five minutes' walk of the Royal Exchange.

"'Even those letters of the alphabet, who are always running away from their friends and being entreated at the tops of columns to come back, never *do* come back, if we may judge from the number of times they are asked to do it and don't. It really seems,' said Tom, relinquishing the paper with a thoughtful sigh, 'as if people had the same gratification in printing their complaints as in making them known by word of mouth; as if they found it a comfort and consolation to proclaim "I want such and such a thing, and I can't get it, and I don't expect I ever shall!"'" ¶MC 36

—*poetical:* " . . . handbills, some of which were couched in the form of parodies on popular melodies, as 'Believe me if all Jarley's wax-work so rare'—'I saw thy show in youthful prime'—'Over the water to Jarley'; while, to consult all tastes, others wre composed with a view to the lighter and more facetious spirits, as a parody on the favourite air of 'If I had a donkey,' beginning

'If I know'd a donkey wot wouldn't go
To see Mrs JARLEY's wax-work show
Do you think I'd acknowledge him?"
  Oh no no!
    Then run to Jarley's . . . . " OCS 27

—*the Public:* "FOUND—ALWAYS. An immense flock of gulls to believe in preposterous advertisements." AY/OR

—*shop signs in Paris:* "The trade signs (and they were almost as many as the shops) were, all, grim illustrations of Want. The butcher and the porkman painted up, only the leanest scrags of meat; the baker, the coarsest of meagre loaves. The people rudely pictured as drinking in the wine-shops, croaked over their scanty measures of thin wine and beer, and were gloweringly confidential together. Nothing was represented in a flourishing condition, save tools and weapons; but, the cutler's knives and axes were sharp and bright, the smith's hammers were heavy, and the gunmaker's stock was murderous." TTC i 5

—*theatrical:* "Next day the posters appeared in due course, and the public were informed, in all the colours of the rainbow, and in letters afflicted with every possible variation of spinal deformity, how that Mr Johnson would have the honour of making his last appearance that evening, and how that an early application for places was requested, in consequence of the extraordinary overflow attendant on his performances. It being a remarkable fact in theatrical history, but one long since established beyond dispute, that it is a hopeless endeavour to attract people to a theatre unless they can be first brought to believe that they will never get into it." NN 30

—*walking:* " . . . unstamped advertisement—an animated sandwich, composed of a boy between two boards." SB/DA

And see IG:Capital and Labour

American language

—*confusing:* "'Dinner, if you please,' said I to the waiter.

"'When?' said the waiter.

"'As quick as possible,' said I.

"'Right away?' said the waiter.

"After a moment's hesitation, I answered 'No,' at hazard.

"'*Not* right away?' cried the waiter, with an amount of surprise that made me start.

"I looked at him doubtfully, and returned, 'No; I would rather have it in this private room. I like it very much.'

"At this, I really thought the waiter must have gone out of his mind: as I believe he would have done, but for the interposition of another man, who whispered in his ear, 'Directly.'

"'Well! and that's a fact!' said the waiter, looking helplessly at me: 'Right away.'

"I saw now that 'Right away" and 'Directly' were one and the same thing. So I reversed my previous answer, and sat down to dinner in ten minutes afterwards . . . . " AN 2

—disregarded: " . . . a bravura concert, solely sustained by the Misses Norris, presently began. They sang in all languages—except their own. German, French, Italian, Spanish, Portuguese, Swiss [*sic.*]; but nothing native; nothing so low as native. For, in this respect, languages are like many other travellers: ordinary and commonplace enough at home, but specially genteel abroad." MC 17

And see Words and Phrases—*'fix'; and —'Yes, Sir'*

Argument

—ad hominem

"'Heaven forbid,' said Mr Crisparkle, 'that in my desire to clear one man I should lightly criminate another! I accuse no one.'

"'Tcha!' ejaculated Mr Honeythunder with great disgust; for this was by no means the principle on which the Philanthropic Brotherhood usually proceeded. 'And, sir, you are not a disinterested witness, we must bear in mind.'

"'How am I an interested one?' enquired Mr Crisparkle, smiling innocently, at a loss to imagine.

"'There was a certain stipend, sir, paid to you for your pupil, which may have warped your judgment a bit,' said Mr Honeythunder, coarsely.

"'Perhaps I expect to retain it still?' Mr Crisparkle returned, enlightened; 'do you mean that too?'

"'Well, sir,' returned the professional Philanthropist, getting up, and thrusting his hands down into his trousers pockets; 'I don't go about measuring people for caps. If people find I have any about me that fit 'em, they can put 'em on and wear 'em, if they like. That's their look out: not mine.'

"Mr Crisparkle eyed him with a just indignation, and took him to task thus:

"'Mr Honeythunder, I hoped when I came in here that I might be under no necessity of commenting on the introduction of platform manners or platform manoeuvres among the decent forbearances of private life. But you have given me such a specimen of both, that I should be a fit subject for both if I remained silent respecting them. They are detestable.'

"'They don't suit *you,* I dare say, sir.'

"'They are,' repeated Mr Crisparkle, without noticing the interruption, 'detestable. They violate equally the justice that should belong to Christians, and the restraints that should belong to gentlemen. You assume a great crime to have been committed by one whom I, acquainted with the attendant circumstances, and having numerous reasons on my side, devoutly believe to be innocent of it. Because I differ from you on that vital point, what is your platform resource? Instantly to turn upon me, charging that I have no sense of the enormity of the crime itself, but am its aider and abettor!

"'So, another time—taking me as representing your opponent in other cases—you set up a platform credulity: a moved and seconded and carried unanimously profession of faith in some ridiculous delusion or mischievous imposition. I decline to believe it, and you fall back upon your platform resource of proclaiming that I believe nothing; that because I will not bow down to a false God of your making, I deny the true God!

"'Another time, you make the platform discovery that War is a calamity, and you propose to abolish it by a string of twisted resolutions tossed into the air like the tail of a kite. I do not admit the discovery to be yours in the least, and I have not a grain of faith in your remedy. Again, your platform resource of representing me as revelling in the horrors of a battle field like a fiend incarnate!

"'Another time, in another of your undiscriminating platform rushes, you would punish the sober for the drunken. I claim consideration for the comfort, convenience, and refreshment of the sober; and you presently make platform proclamation that I have a depraved desire to turn Heaven's creatures into swine and wild beasts!

"'In all such cases your movers, and your seconders, and your supporters—your regular Professors of all degrees—run amuck like so many mad Malays, habitually attributing the lowest and basest motives with the utmost recklessness . . . and quoting figures which you know to be as wilfully onesided as a statement of any complicated account that should be all Creditor side and no Debtor, or all Debtor side and no Creditor. Therefore it is, Mr Honeythunder, that I consider the platform a sufficiently bad example and a sufficiently bad school, even in public life; but hold that, carried into private life, it becomes an unendurable nuisance.'

"'These are strong words, sir!' exclaimed the Philanthropist.

"'I hope so,' said Mr Crisparkle. 'Good morning.'" ¶MED 17

—contradiction: " . . . [Miggs's] vexation and chagrin being of that internally bitter sort which finds no relief in words, and is aggravated to madness by want of contradiction, she could hold out no longer, and burst into a storm of sobs and tears." BR 80

—for its own sake: "Our bore is also great in argument. He infinitely enjoys a long humdrum, drowsy interchange of words of dispute about nothing. He considers that it strengthens the mind, consequently, he 'don't see that,' very often. Or, he would be glad to know what you mean by that. Or, he doubts that. Or, he has always understood exactly the reverse of that. Or, he can't admit that. Or, he begs to deny that. Or, surely you don't mean that. And so on. He once advised us; offered us a piece of advice, after the fact, totally impracticable and wholly impossible of acceptance, because it supposed the fact, then eternally disposed of, to be yet in abeyance. It was a dozen years ago, and to this hour our bore benevolently wishes, in a mild voice, on certain regular occasions, that we had thought better of his opinion." RP/B

—a gift of Nature: "'For the matter o' that [said John Willet], Phil [Parkes], argeyment is a gift of Natur. If Natur has gifted a man with powers of argeyment, a man has a right to make the best of 'em, and has not a right to stand on false delicacy, and deny that he is so gifted; for that is a turning of his back on Natur, a flouting of her, a slighting of her precious caskets, and a proving of one's self to be a swine that isn't worth her scattering pearls before.'" BR 1

Authorship

—acknowledged:

"'TO DAVID COPPERFIELD, ESQUIRE
"'THE EMINENT AUTHOR

"'MY DEAR SIR,

"'Years have elapsed, since I had an opportunity of ocularly perusing the lineaments, now familiar to the imaginations of a considerable portion of the civilized world.

"'But, my dear sir, though estranged (by the force of circumstances, over which I have had no control) from the personal society of the friend and companion of my youth, I have not been unmindful of his soaring flight. Nor have I been debarred,

Though seas between us braid ha' roared,

(**Burns**) from participating in the intellectual feasts he has spread before us.

"'I cannot, therefore, allow of the departure from this place of an individual whom we mutually respect and esteem, without, my dear sir, taking this public opportunity of thanking you, on my own behalf, and, I may undertake to add on that of the whole of the Inhabitants of Port Middlebay, for the gratification of which you are the ministering agent.

"'Go on, my dear sir! You are not unknown here, you are not unappreciated. Though "remote", we are neither "unfriended", "melancholy", nor (I may add) "slow". Go on, my dear sir, in your Eagle course! The inhabitants of Port Middlebay may at least aspire to watch it, with delight, with entertainment, with instruction!

"'Among the eyes elevated towards you from this portion of the globe, will ever be found, while it has light and life,

"'The
"'Eye
"'Appertaining to
"'WILKINS MICAWBER,
"'Magistrate.'" DC 63

—authors: There is a popular prejudice, a kind of superstition, to the effect that authors are not a particularly united body, that they are not invariably and inseparably attached to each other." S/M2

—characters: "It is the fate of most men who mingle with the world, and attain even the prime of life, to make many real friends, and lose them in the course of nature. It is the fate of all authors or chroniclers to create imaginary friends, and lose them in the course of art. Nor is this the full extent of their misfortunes; for they are required to furnish an account of them besides." PP 57

"It is not easy for a man to speak of his own books. I dare say that few persons have been more interested in mine than I;

and if it be a general principle in nature that a lover's love is blind, and that a mother's love is blind, I believe it may be said of an author's attachment to the creatures of his own imagination, that it is a perfect model of constancy and devotion, and is the blindest of all." S/B1

—*connections:* "'If I send him, in my own name, verses that he does not honestly like, either it will be very painful to him to return them, or he will print them for papa's sake, and not for their own. So I have made up my mind [said Adelaide Procter] to take my chance fairly with the unknown volunteers.'

"Perhaps it requires an editor's experience of the profoundly unreasonable grounds on which he is often urged to accept unsuitable articles—such as having been to school with the writer's husband's brother-in-law, or having lent an alpenstock in Switzerland to the writer's wife's nephew, when that interesting stranger had broken his own—fully to appreciate the delicacy and the self-respect of this resolution." AYR/P

—*copyright, domestic:* "' . . . if any preposterous bill were brought forward, for giving poor grubbing devils of authors a right to their own property, I should like to say [said Gregsbury], that I for one would never consent to opposing an insurmountable bar to the diffusion of literature among *the people*—you understand?—that the creations of the pocket, being man's., might belong to one man, or one family; but that the creations of the brain, being God's, ought as a matter of course to belong to the people at large . . . those who wrote for posterity should be content to be rewarded by the approbation of posterity . . . and you could be as funny as you liked about the authors; because I believe the greater part of them live in lodgings, and are not voters.'" NN 16

—*copyright, international:* " . . . to its literature every country must look for one great means of refining and improving its people, and one great source of national pride and honour. You have in America great writers—great writers—who will live in all time, and are as familiar to our lips as household words. Deriving (as they all do in a greater or less degree, in their several walks) their inspiration from the stupendous country which gave them birth, they diffuse a better knowledge of it, and a higher love for it, all over the civilized world. I take leave to say, in the presence of some of those gentlemen, that I hope the time is not far distant when they, in America, will receive of right some substantial profit and return in England from their labours; and when we, in England, shall receive some substantial profit and return for ours. Pray do not misunderstand me. Securing for myself from day to day the means of an honourable subsistence, I would rather have the affectionate regard of my fellow men, than I would have heaps and mines of gold. But the two things do not seem to me incompatible. They cannot be, for nothing good is incompatible with justice. There must be an international arrangement in this respect: England has done her part, and I am confident that the time is not far distant when America will do hers. It becomes the character of a great country; *firstly,* because it is justice; *secondly,* because without it you never can have, and keep, a literature of your own." S/B1

" . . . if there had existed any law in this respect, [**Sir Walter**] **Scott** might not have sunk beneath the mighty pressure on his brain, but might have lived to add new creatures of his fancy to the crowd which swarm about you in your summer walks and gather round your winter evening hearths.

" . . . there came back fresh upon me, that touching scene in the great man's life, when he lay upon his couch surrounded by his family, and listened, for the last time, to the rippling of the river he had so well loved, over its stony bed. I pictured him to myself, faint, wan, dying, crushed both in mind and body by his honourable struggle, and hovering round him the ghosts of his own imagination—*Waverly, Ravenswood, Jeannie Deans, Rob Roy, Caleb Balderstone, Dominie Sampson*—all the familiar throng—with cavaliers, and Puritans, and Highland chiefs innumerable overflowing the chamber, and fading away in the dim distance beyond.

"I pictured them, fresh from traversing the world, and hanging down their heads in shame and sorrow that, from all those lands into which they had carried gladness, instruction, and delight for millions, they had brought him not one friendly hand to help to raise him from that sad, sad bed. No, nor brought him from that land in which his own language was spoken, and in every house and hut of which his own books were read in his own tongue, one grateful dollar-piece to buy a garland for his grave." S/DH

—*distraction:* "'Do you recollect the date,' said Mr Dick, looking earnestly at me, and taking up his pen to note it down, 'when

King Charles the First had his head cut off?'

"I said I believed it happened in the year sixteen hundred and forty-nine.

"'Well,' returned Mr Dick, scratching his ear with his pen, and looking dubiously at me. 'So the books say; but I don't see how that can be. Because, if it was so long ago, how could the people about him have made that mistake of putting some of the trouble out of *his* head, after it was taken off, into *mine?*'

"I was very much surprised by the inquiry; but could give no information on this point . . . .

"'Is it a Memorial about his own history that he is writing, aunt?'

"'Yes, child,' said my aunt, rubbing her nose again. 'He is memorialising the Lord Chancellor, or the Lord Somebody or other—one of those people, at all events, who are paid to *be* memoralised—about his affairs. I suppose it will go in, one of these days. He hasn't been able to draw it up yet, without introducing that mode of expressing himself; but it don't signify; it keeps him employed.'

"In fact, I found out afterwards that Mr Dick had been for upwards of ten years endeavouring to keep King Charles the First out of the Memorial; but he had been constantly getting into it, and was there now." DC 14

—exaggeration: "What is exaggeration to one class of minds and perceptions, is plain truth to another. That which is commonly called a long-sight, perceives in a prospect innumerable features and bearings nonexistent to a short-sighted person. I sometimes ask myself whether there may occasionally be a difference of this kind between some writers and some readers; whether it is always the writer who colours highly, or whether it is now and then the reader whose eye for colour is a little dull.

"On this head of exaggeration I have a positive experience, more curious than the speculation I have just set down. It is this:—I have never touched a character precisely from the life, but some counterpart of that character has incredulously asked me: 'Now really, did I ever really, see one like it?'

"All the Pecksniff family upon earth are quite agreed, I believe, that Mr Pecksniff is an exaggeration, and that no such character ever existed. I will not offer any plea on his behalf to so powerful and genteel a body. . . . " MC pref

—and fashion: "Mr Simpson . . . being disinherited by his father, who died soon afterwards, was fortunate enough to obtain a permanent engagement at a fashionable haircutter's; hairdressing being a science to which he had frequently directed his attention. In this situation he had necessarily many opportunities of making himself acquainted with the habits, and style of thinking, of the exclusive portion of the nobility of this kingdom. To this fortunate circumstance are we indebted for the production of those brilliant efforts of genius, his fashionable novels, which so long as good taste, unsullied by exaggeration, cant, and quackery, continues to exist, cannot fail to instruct and amuse the thinking portion of the community." SB/BH

—finding readers: "[Oliver] found himself in a little back room, quite full of books . . . marvelling where the people could be found to read such a great number of books as seemed to be written to make the world wiser. Which is still a marvel to more experienced people than Oliver Twist, every day of their lives." OT 14

—frustrated: "'Why isn't he contented?' was the natural enquiry.

"'Misplaced,' said Mr Grewgious, with great mystery . . . . What do you think Mr Bazzard has done? . . . He has written a play,' said Mr Grewgious, in a solemn whisper. 'A tragedy . . . . And nobody,' pursued Mr Grewgious in the same tone, 'will hear, on any account whatever, of bringing it out'. . . .

"'Mr Bazzard's father, being a Norfolk farmer, would have furiously laid about him with a flail, a pitchfork, and every agricultural implement available for assaulting purposes, on the slightest hint of his son's having written a play. So the son, bringing to me the father's rent (which I receive), imparted his secret, and pointed out that he was determined to pursue his genius, and that it would put him in peril of starvation, and that he was not formed for it.'

"'For pursuing his genius, sir?'

"'No, my dear,' said Mr Grewgious, 'for starvation. It was impossible to deny the position that Mr Bazzard was not formed to be starved, and Mr Bazzard then pointed out that it was desirable that I should stand between him and a fate so perfectly unsuited to his formation. In that way Mr Bazzard became my clerk, and . . . he feels the degradation.

"There are some other geniuses that Mr

Bazzard has become acquainted with, who have also written tragedies, which likewise nobody will on any account whatever hear of bringing out, and these choice spirits dedicate their plays to one another in a highly panegyrical manner. Mr Bazzard has been the subject of one of these dedications. Now, you know, *I* never had a play dedicated to *me* ! . . .

"He is very short with me sometimes, and then I feel that he is meditating "This blockhead is my master! A fellow who couldn't write a tragedy on pain of death, and who will never have one dedicated to him with the most complimentary congratulations on the high position he has taken in the eyes of posterity!" Very trying, very trying. However, in giving him directions, I reflect beforehand: "Perhaps he may not like this," or "He might take it ill if I asked that," and so we get on very well. Indeed better than I could have expected.'" ¶MED 20

—*humble:* "'Where will you sit, uncle?' said Mrs Kenwigs, in the full glow of family pride, which the appearance of her distinguished relation occasioned.

"'Anywheres, my dear,' said the collector, 'I am not particular.'

"Not particular! What a meek collector. If he had been an author, who knew his place, he couldn't have been more humble." NN 14

—*interaction of drama and fiction:* " . . . I think it is a most appropriate and fit thing to have such a writer [as **Thackeray**] as my friend, and such an art as the dramatic brought face to face, as we see them here tonight. Every good actor plays direct to every good author, and every writer of fiction, though he may not adopt the dramatic form, writes in effect for the stage. He may write novels always, and plays never, but the truth and wisdom that are in him must permeate the art of which truth and passion are the life, and must be more or less reflected in that great mirror which he holds up to nature.

"Now, gentlemen, actors and managers and authors are all represented in this present company. We may, without any great effort of imagination, suppose that all of them have studied the mighty deep secrets of the human heart in many theatres of many kinds, great and small, but I am sure that none of them can have studied those mysterious workings in any theatre from the stage wagon of Thespis downwards, to greater advantage, to greater profit, and to greater contentment than in the airy booths of *Vanity Fair.* To this skilful showman, who has so much delighted us, and whose words have so charmed us tonight, we are now to express our gratitude . . . . " S/TF12

—*lionized:* "The lion was a literary one. Of course there were a vast number of people present who had admired his roarings, and were anxious to be introduced to him; and very pleasant it was to see them brought up for the purpose, and to observe the patient dignity with which he received all their patting and caressing. This brought forcibly to our mind what we had so often witnessed at country fairs, where the other lions are compelled to go through as many forms of courtesy as they chance to be acquainted with, just as often as admiring parties happen to drop in upon them." B/L

—*magniloquent:* "The individual in question, Mr Theodosius [Butler], had written a pamphlet containing some very weighty considerations on the expediency of doing something or other; and as every sentence contained a good many words of four syllables, his admirers took it for granted that he meant a good deal." SB/S

—*objectivity:* " . . . a gentleman of a literary turn, who wrote squibs upon the rest, and knew the weak side of everybody's character but his own." MC 9

—*patronage:* "To the great compact phalanx of the people, by whose industry, perseverance, and intelligence, and their result in money-wealth, such places as Birmingham, and many others like it, have arisen—to that great centre of support, that comprehensive experience, and that beating heart —Literature has turned happily from individual patrons, sometimes munificent, often sordid, always few, and has found there at once its highest purpose, its natural range of action, and its best reward . . . .

"From the shame of the purchased dedication, from the scurrilous and dirty work of Grub Street, from the dependent seat on sufferance at my Lord Duke's table today, and from the sponging-house and Marshalsea tomorrow, from that venality which, by a fine moral retribution, has degraded statesmen even to a greater extent than authors, because the statesman entertained a low belief in the universality of corruption, while the author yielded only to the dire necessity of his calling—from all such evils the people have set Literature free." ¶S/BS

And see A:Ancestry—*patronage of literature*

"I went last year to a highly respectable place of resort, Willis's Rooms, in St. James's, to a Special General meeting of [the Royal Literary Fund] . . . the general appearance of the place was very much like Almack's in the morning. A number of stately old dowagers were ranged in a row on one side, and old gentlemen sat on the other. The ball was opened with due solemnity by a real marquis, who walked a minuet with the Secretary, at which the audience were much affected. Then another party advanced, who, I am sorry to say, was only a member of the House of Commons—but a gentleman highly connected—and he gracefully took the floor. To him, however, succeeded a distinguished lord, then a bishop, then the son of a distinguished lord; after which the minor church rose, with a member of the Stock Exchange and the Bar; and, at last, in an interval of the theatricals, a man more immediately connected with Literature [**Robert Bell**], though not of course considered very respectable, was allowed to step in and sustain the part of *Pangloss,* in the adventures of *Candide,* and delight the audience by explaining that this was the best of all possible societies, conducted under the best of all possible managements, at the least of all possible expenditure from the best of all possible funds.

"It is in these things—it is in our fondness for being so stupendously genteel, by keeping up such a fashionable appearance, by giving way to the vulgar and common social vice of hanging on to great connexions at any price—that the money goes. Why, sir, the very last distinguished writer of fiction [**Thackeray**] whom you caught for your public dinner, told you, in return for drinking his health, somewhere towards the small hours of the morning, that he felt like the servant in plush who is permitted to sweep the stage down, when there are no more great people to come on; and I myself, at a dinner some twelve years ago, felt like a sort of *Rip Van Winkle* reversed, who had gone to sleep backwards for a hundred years; and, waking, found that Literature instead of being emancipated, had to endure all manner of aristocratic patrons, and was lying at the feet of people who did nothing for it, instead of standing alone and appealing to the public for support." S/LF5

—*playwright, reluctant:* "'If I was under sentence of decapitation, and was about to be instantly decapitated, and an express arrived with a pardon for the condemned convict Grewgious if he wrote a play, I should be under the necessity of resuming the block, and begging the executioner to proceed to extremities—meaning,' said Mr Grewgious, passing his hand under his chin, 'the singular number, and this extremity.'" MED 20

—*product read aloud:* "To everybody in succession, Captain Hopkins said: 'Have you read it?'—'No.' 'Would you like to hear it read?' If he weakly showed the least disposition to hear it, Captain Hopkins, in a loud sonorous voice, gave him every word of it. The Captain would have read it twenty thousand times, if twenty thousand people would have heard him, one by one. I remember a certain luscious roll he gave to such phrases as 'The people's representatives in Parliament assembled,' 'Your petitioners therefore humbly approach your honourable house,' 'His gracious Majesty's unfortunate subjects,' as if the words were something real in his mouth, and delicious to taste; Mr Micawber, meanwhile, listening with a little of an author's vanity, and contemplating (not severely) the spikes on the opposite wall." DC 11

—*self-description:* "My conclusion was that I would begin her [Sophy Marigold's] book with some account of myself. So that, through reading a specimen or two of me on the footboard, she might form an idea of my merits there. I was aware that I couldn't do myself justice. A man can't write his eye (at least I don't know how to), nor yet can a man write his voice, nor the rate of his talk, nor the quickness of his action, nor his general spicy way. But he can write his turns of speech, when he is a public speaker—and indeed I have heard that he very often does, before he speaks 'em." CS/DM 1

—*status in Austria:* " . . . not one of the noble millions may exercise a trade for bread: may practise law or medicine, or sink down into authorship." HWC/BE

—*and suffering:* "'[Mortimer Knag] has a most romantic heart . . . and the disappointment was a dreadful blow. He is a wonderfully accomplished man—most extraordinarily accomplished—reads—hem—reads every novel that comes out; I mean every novel that—hem—that has any fashion in it, of course. The fact is, that he did find so much in the books he read, applicable to his own misfortunes, and did find himself in every respect so much like the heroes—because of course he is conscious of his own superiority, as we all are, and very naturally—that he took to scorning everything, and became a genius; and I am quite sure that he is, at this very present moment, writing another book . . . .

"' . . . I think his disappointment a great thing for him, because if he hadn't been disappointed he couldn't have written about blighted hopes and all that; and the fact is, if it hadn't happened as it has, I don't believe his genius would ever have come out at all.'" ¶NN 18

—*taking pains:* "The results of his researches . . . occupied a much longer time in the getting together than they ever will in the perusal. And this is probably the case with most reading matter, except when it is of that highly beneficial kind (for Posterity) which is 'thrown off in a few moments of leisure' by the superior poetic geniuses who scorn to take prose pains." CS/MJ 2

—*unrecognized:* "If such institutions [as the Southwark Literary and Scientific] had existed in times gone by, **Milton** might have been appreciated in the age which he adorned, [**Thomas**] **Otway** might have lived and dined a few years longer, and he [CD] knew not but that even **Wordsworth** might have been drawn from the dust of those shelves where until lately he had lain unnoticed and unremarked. Many, many of the illustrious dead, whose works were destined to illuminate posterity, might not have died the wretched inmates of the madhouse, or the asylum for the destitute." S/LS (in the *Morning Advertiser,* December 3, 1840)

—*urge to be published:* "'Is this [his wife's epitaph] to be put in hand at once, Mr Sapsea?'

"Mr Sapsea, with an Author's anxiety to rush into publication, replies that it cannot be out of hand too soon." MED 4

—*voluntary correspondent, male:* "His name is Legion. He writes everything—on every description of paper, and with every conceivable and inconceivable quality of illegible ink. Like the players in Hamlet, nothing comes amiss to him; 'tragedy, comedy, history, pastoral, pastoral-comical, historical-pastoral, tragical-historical, tragical-comical, historical-pastoral, scene individable, or poem unlimited.' But if he particularly excel in any one species of composition, it is perhaps, as to our experience, in the poem unlimited.

"He has a general idea that literature is the easiest amusement in the world. He figures a successful author as a radiant personage whose whole time is devoted to idleness and pastime—who keeps a prolific mind in a sort of corn-sieve, and lightly shakes a bushel of it out sometimes, in an odd half hour after breakfast.

"It would amaze his incredulity beyond all measure, to be told that such elements as patience, study, punctuality, determination, self-denial, training of mind and body, hours of application and seclusion to produce what he reads in seconds, enter into such a career. He has no more conception of the necessity of entire devotion to it, than he has of an eternity from the beginning. Correction and recorrection in the blotted manuscript, consideration, new observation, the patient massing of many reflections, experiences and imaginings for one minute purpose, and the patient separation from the heap of all the fragments that will unite to serve it—these would be Unicorns or Griffins to him—fables altogether. Hence, he can often afford to dispense with the low rudiments of orthography; and of the principles of composition it is obvious that he need know nothing.

"He is fond of applying himself to literature in a leisure hour, or 'a few leisure moments.' He 'throws his thoughts' upon paper. He rarely sends what he considers his best production. His best production is not copied—somehow, it seldom is. He is aware that there are many remarkable defects in the manuscript he encloses, but if we will insert that, 'on the usual terms' he has another at home that will astonish us. He is not at all vain, but he 'knows he has it in him.' It is possible that it may be in him; but it is certain that under these circumstances it very, very, seldom comes out.

"Sometimes he will write, without sending anything, to know 'if we are open to voluntary contributors?' He will be informed 'Yes, decidedly. If their contributions be adapted to these pages.' He will then write again, to know what style of contribution would be preferred? He will be informed in answer that he had better try his own style. He writes back, to the effect that he has no style, no subject, no knowledge, and nothing to tell; and will therefore feel obliged to us for a few suggestions.

"He calls sometimes. When he calls, he has often been a captain or a major. He comes with a foregone conclusion that we are always sitting in a padded chair (after a little early corn-sieve practice) open, like some competition of a sporting nature, to All England. He takes it very ill that we don't see him. Considers it ungentlemanly. Had supposed we were a public character, and doesn't understand it. He comes on behalf of a gifted friend, with a tragedy in five acts, a poem in twelve books, or a story that would occupy a volume or two of this publication. He brings it out of a cab, and leaves it in the office, rolled up in paper like a whitey-brown bolster. It bears evident traces of having been in every other office in the wide world, whence any composition in the English language is disseminated through the agency of print and paper.

"He is written to, and politely informed that the excessive bulk of this treasure renders it (without reference to its intrinsic merits or demerits) quite unsuitable as a blessing to the unhappy H.W.* He reappears with all speed, red-faced and ireful, reproduces card, demands explanatory interview, and terrifies publisher. Nothing coming of it, he, on the spot, indites a letter, wherein he communicates to us that as we decline to accept the contribution of his gifted friend, he requires to be informed in writing, for the information of his gifted friend, what our critical opinion is, in detail, of the bolster, and what publisher we recommend for it; for which critical opinion he will call to-morrow afternoon at four precisely.

"He is again politely written to and informed that we cannot undertake to form and deliver such opinion, having our little hallucinations and labouring under the delusion that we have something else to do. Then he reappears with the cab, and takes the bolster away in extraordinary dudgeon; protesting to the last that he had supposed we were a public character, and that he don't understand it." ¶HWC/H

**Household Words*

—female: "(God bless her!—Mrs or Miss Legion) is not so angry, but she is an unreasonable Angel, too. She brings little beneficent schemes in bags of Berlin wool, and, though they won't suit us, thinks they will suit our friends: among whom she begs us to distribute two hundred and fifty copies. She is the most amiable woman in the world—but she is impracticable; she is, indeed, though we love her! She brings the flattest and thinnest of little crimson or blue books, published by subscription, and wants to read them to us aloud. When she writes, it is on scented paper, highly glazed, over which all the letters seem to skate, and all the looped letters to tumble down.

"Her favorite title for poetry is 'To a Child,' or 'To——.' We don't know who —— is, but we wish he would lead her to the altar. In prose, she addresses the Gentle Reader constantly, and sprinkles with French words. She is invariably persuaded that blanks heighten the interest, and convey an air of reality. She generally begins, 'It was on a summer evening in the year eighteen hundred and (blank), near the pretty little town of (blank), where the (blank) river murmurs its rippling way among the rushes, that a youth of handsome mien and fine figure, who might have numbered two-and-twenty summers, and whose expressive countenance was cast in the pure Greek mould.'

"Occasionally, she presents herself in the serious aspect of having some relative to support, and is particularly deserving of the gentlest consideration and respect. Then it is our misery to endeavour to explain to her that what is written for publication can be read for its own merits only; and that it would be as hopeful a resource to play a church organ without any knowledge of, or aptitude for, the instrument, as to play the muse's lyre. In any case and every case, she always forms a profound conviction (and will die in it) that we have never read her manuscript." HWC/H

—the writing trade: "'How should you like to grow up a clever man, and write books, eh? [said Mr Brownlow].

"'I think I would rather read them, sir,' replied Oliver.

"'What! wouldn't you like to be a book-writer? said the old gentleman.

"Oliver considered a little while; and at last said, he should think it would be a much better thing to be a bookseller; upon which the old gentleman laughed heartily, and declared he had said a very good thing. Which Oliver felt glad to have done, though he by no means knew what it was.

"'Well, well,' said the old gentleman, composing his features. 'Don't be afraid! We won't make an author of you, while there's an honest trade to be learnt, or brickmaking to turn to.'

"'Thank you, sir,' said Oliver. At the earnest manner of his reply, the old gentleman laughed again; and said something about a curious instinct, which Oliver, not understanding, paid no very great attention to." OT 14

And see Mrs Hominy MC. Indexes IV *and* V *list, respectively, 18 male and 4 female authors named in the works.* Index VIII *has 5 examples, including the* Somebody CS/SL *who is a CD self-portrait.*

Books

—*Arabian Nights:* "'I used to read to [my father] to cheer his courage [said Sissy Jupe], and he was very fond of that. They were wrong books—I am never to speak of them here—but we didn't know there was any harm in them.'

"'And he liked them?' said Louisa [Gradgrind], with a searching gaze on Sissy all this time.

"'O very much! They kept him, many times, from what did him real harm. And often and often of a night, he used to forget all his troubles in wondering whether the Sultan would let the lady go on with the story, or would have her head cut off before it was finished.'" HT i 9

"*Fortunatus* had only a life interest in his purse; and we all know too well that when he died, it vanished with him. *Sinbad the Sailor,* a munificent merchant in his way, gave the porter of Bagdad only a poor one hundred sequins every day after dinner. *Aladdin* sent his mother to propose for the Sultan's daughter, with a tolerable present of jewels, but still with no more than could be spread forth on a china dish and tied up in a napkin. The *Genie of the Lamp* considered it a reasonable exercise of his supernatural power, to serve refreshments on a 'large silver tray holding twelve covered dishes of the same metal, two flagons of wine, and two silver cups.'

"*Ali Baba* beheld in the robbers' cavern what his limited ideas conceived to be a pretty large amount of ready money in gold coin; yet he thought it a wonderful thing to carry off no more than his three asses could bear, under an outer load of wood and green boughs; and there was not so much of it but that his wife borrowed 'a small measure'—about the size of a banker's shovel, say—to measure it out. *Prince Camaralzaman* (not to be learned, and call him Kummir al Zummaun) found, in the cave he accidentally opened on the gardener's ground, fifty brass urns, each with a cover on it, all full of gold dust. But, his share of gold dust, when he divided it with the gardener, was not such a great share after all, for it only half filled fifty olive pots; and *that's* not much—in these times." ¶HWC/DT

CD often cited the Nights, *perhaps (with* Crusoe) *his favourite childhood reading. A list of his references is in* Index XI part 2.

—*character in love:* "'You think of me, Ruth,' said Tom, 'and it is very natural that you should, as if I were a character in a book; and you make it a sort of poetical justice that I should, by some impossible means or other, come, at last, to marry the person I love. But there is a much higher justice than poetical justice, my dear, and it does not order events upon the same principle. Accordingly, people who read about heroes in books, and choose to make heroes of themselves out of books, consider it a very fine thing to be discontented and gloomy, and misanthropical, and perhaps a little blasphemous, because they cannot have everything ordered for their individual accommodation." MC 50

—*illustrated:* " . . . I am in a position to offer a friendly remonstrance . . . to the designers and engravers of the pictures . . . . Have they considered the awful consequences likely to flow from their representations of Virtue? Have they asked themselves the question, whether the terrific prospect of acquiring that fearful chubbiness of head, unwieldiness of arm, feeble dislocation of leg, crispiness of hair, and enormity of shirt-collar, which they represent as inseparable from Goodness, may not tend to confirm sensitive waverers, in Evil?

"A most impressive example (if I had believed it) of what a Dustman and a Sailor may come to, when they mend their ways, was presented to me in this same [bookseller's] shopwindow. When they were leaning (they were intimate friends) against a post, drunk and reckless, with surpassingly bad hats on, and their hair over their foreheads, they were rather picturesque, and looked as if they might be agreeable men, if they would not be beasts. But, when they had got over their bad propensities, and when, as a consequence, their heads had swelled alarmingly, their hair had got so curly that it lifted their blown-out cheeks up, their coat-cuffs were so long that they never could do any work, and their eyes were so wide open that they never could do any sleep, they presented a spectacle calculated to plunge a timid nature into the depths of Infamy." ¶UT/DT

—library

—in an industrial town: "There was a library in Coketown, to which general access was easy. Mr Gradgrind greatly tormented his mind about what the people read in this library: a point whereon little rivers of tabular statements periodically flowed into the howling ocean of tabular statements, which no diver ever got to any depth in and came up sane.

"It was a disheartening circumstance, but a melancholy fact, that even these readers persisted in wondering. They wondered about human nature, human passions, human hopes and fears, the struggles, triumphs and defeats, the cares and joys and sorrows, the lives and deaths of common men and women! They sometimes, after fifteen hours' work, sat down to read mere fables about men and women, more or less like themselves, and about children, more or less like their own. They took **De Foe** to their bosoms, instead of **Euclid**, and seemed to be on the whole more comforted by **Goldsmith** than by **Cocker**. Mr Gradgrind was for ever working, in print and out of print, at this eccentric sum, and he never could make out how it yielded this unaccountable product." HT i 8

—at an inn: "There were books, too, in this room; books on the table, books on the chimneypiece, books in an open press in the corner. **Fielding** was there, and **Smollett** was there, and **Steele** and **Addison** were there, in dispersed volumes; and there were tales of those who go down to the sea in ships, for windy nights; and there was really a choice of good books for rainy days or fine.

"It was so very pleasant to see these things in such a lonesome by-place—so very agreeable to find these evidences of a taste, however homely, that went beyond the beautiful cleanliness and trimness of the house—so fanciful to imagine what a wonder the room must be to the little children born in the gloomy village—what grand impressions of it those of them who became wanderers over the earth would carry away; and how, at distant ends of the world, some old voyagers would die, cherishing the belief that the finest apartment known to men was once in the Hesket-Newmarket Inn, in rare old Cumberland—it was such a charmingly lazy pursuit to entertain these rambling thoughts over the choice oatcake and the genial whiskey . . . ." ¶LT 1

—in a mansion: "They were black, cold rooms; and seemed to be in mourning, like the inmates of the house. The books precisely matched as to size, and drawn up in line, like soldiers, looked in their cold, hard, slippery uniforms, as if they had but one idea among them, and that was a freezer. The bookcase, glazed and locked, repudiated all familiarities. Mr **Pitt**, in bronze on the top, with no trace of his celestial origin about him, guarded the unattainable treasure like an enchanted Moor. A dusty urn at each high corner, dug up from an ancient tomb, preached desolation and decay, as from two pulpits; and the chimney-glass, reflecting Mr Dombey and his portrait at one blow, seemed fraught with melancholy meditations." DS 5

—a lifesaver: "My [David Copperfield's] father had left a small collection of books in a little room upstairs, to which I had access (for it adjoined my own) and which nobody else in our house ever troubled. From that blessed little room, *Roderick Random, Peregrine Pickle, Humphrey Clinker, Tom Jones, the Vicar of Wakefield, Don Quixote, Gil Blas,* and *Robinson Crusoe,* came out, a glorious host, to keep me company. They kept alive my fancy, and my hope of something beyond that place and time—they, and the Arabian Nights, and the Tales of the Genii—and did me no harm; for whatever harm was in some of them was not there for me; *I* knew nothing of it.

"It is astonishing to me now, how I found time, in the midst of my porings and blunderings over heavier themes, to read those books as I did. It is curious to me how I could ever have consoled myself under my small troubles (which were great troubles to me), by impersonating my favourite characters in them—as I did—and by putting Mr and Miss Murdstone into all the bad ones—which I did too. I have been *Tom Jones* (a child's Tom Jones, a harmless creature) for a week together. I have sustained my own idea of *Roderick Random* for a month at a stretch, I verily believe.

"I had a greedy relish for a few volumes of Voyages and Travels—I forget what, now—that were on those shelves; and for days and days I can remember to have gone about my region of our house, armed with the centre-piece out of an old set of boot-trees—the perfect realisation of Captain Somebody, of the Royal British Navy, in danger of being beset by savages, and resolved to sell his life at a great price. The Captain never lost dignity, from having his ears boxed with the Latin Grammar. I did; but the Captain was a Captain and a hero; in despite of all the grammars of all the languages in the world, dead or alive.

"This was my only and my constant comfort. When I think of it, the picture always rises in my mind, of a summer evening, the boys at play in the churchyard, and I sitting on my bed, reading as if for life." DC ¶4

—looked-at: "No one who can read, ever looks at a book, even unopened on a shelf, like one who cannot." OMF i 3

—love of: "There are not many places that I find it more agreeable to revisit when I am in an idle mood, than some places to which I have never been. For, my acquaintance with those spots is of such long standing, and has ripened into an intimacy of so affectionate a nature, that I take a particular interest in assuring myself that they are unchanged.

"I never was in *Robinson Crusoe*'s Island, yet I frequently return there. The colony he established on it soon faded away, and it is uninhabited by any descendants of the grave and courteous Spaniards, or of *Will Atkins* and the other mutineers, and has relapsed into its original condition . . . though his track on the memorable evening of his landing to set his captain ashore, when he was decoyed about and round about until it was dark, and his boat was stove, and his strength and spirits failed him, is yet plainly to be traced . . . . So is the sandy beach on which the memorable footstep was impressed, and where the savages hauled up their canoes when they came ashore for those dreadful public dinners, which led to a dancing worse than speech-making . . . .

"Neither was I ever belated among wolves, on the borders of France and Spain; nor did I ever, when night was closing in and the ground was covered with snow, draw up my little company among some felled trees which served as a breast-work, and there fire a train of gunpowder so dexterously that suddenly we had three or four score blazing wolves illuminating the darkness around us . . . .

"I was never in the robbers' cave, where *Gil Blas* lived, but I often go back there and find the trapdoor just as heavy to raise as it used to be, while that wicked old disabled Black lies everlastingly cursing in bed. I was never in *Don Quixote*'s study, where he read his books of chivalry until he rose and hacked at imaginary giants, and then refreshed himself with great draughts of water, yet you couldn't move a book in it without my knowledge, or with my consent.

"I was never (thank Heaven) in company with the little old woman who hobbled out of the chest and told the merchant *Abudah* to go in search of the Talisman of *Oromanes,* yet I make it my business to know that she is well preserved and as intolerable as ever. I was never at the school where the boy **Horatio Nelson** got out of bed to steal the pears: not because he wanted any, but because every other boy was afraid: yet I have several times been back to this Academy, to see him let down out of window with a sheet.

"So with Damascus, and Bagdad, and Brobdingnag (which has the curious fate of being usually misspelt when written), and Lilliput, and Laputa, and the Nile, and Abyssinia, and the Ganges, and the North Pole, and many hundreds of places—I was never at them, yet it is an affair of my life to keep them intact, and I am always going back to them." ¶UT/NS

"I am a poor clerk, who, being out of employment, was on that morning travelling to Southampton . . . in some little hope of procuring occupation in [a] counting-house. . . .

"The first bell had rung. Suddenly it occurred to me that I would have a book. It was long since I had added one to the small stock from which I got solace of evenings in my lodgings . . . .

"For a time my sad thoughts were my only company. I paid no attention to . . . the talisman against dulness that reposed upon my lap . . . .

" . . . . I smiled faintly and opened my book, to begin **Leigh Hunt**'s 'Story of Rimini' . . . ." HWC/RP

—and the printer: " . . . by the printers' means [CD's hearers] were enabled to scatter throughout the world the loftiest efforts of intellect—the 'thoughts that breathe, the words that burn'*—to send to every part of the universe the great imaginings of the most accomplished minds, to instruct and regenerate mankind." S/PP1

**Thomas Gray: see* Index XI

—reading, at arm's length: " . . . the Doctor [Blimber], leaning back in his chair, with his hand in his breast as usual, held a book from him at arm's length, and read. There

was something very awful in this manner of reading. It was such a determined, unimpassioned, inflexible, cold-blooded way of going to work. It left the Doctor's countenance exposed to view; and when [he] smiled auspiciously at his author, or knit his brows, or shook his head and made wry faces at him, as much as to say, 'Don't tell me, Sir; I know better,' it was terrific." DS 11

—reference: ". . . Bitherstone, born beneath some Bengal star of ill-omen, is extremely inky; and his Lexicon has got so dropsical from constant reference, that it won't shut, and yawns as if it really could not bear to be so bothered." DS 41

—in sum: " . . . a book, in spite of the old proverb, is a cake that you can eat and have. . . . " HWC/IJ

And see S:Bible and Prayer-book

Communication

—with a baby: A mechanical power of reproducing scraps of current conversation for the delectation of the baby, with all the sense struck out of them, and all the nouns changed into the plural number." CH 1

—a contribution: " . . . a ray of light on any path of duty or diversion, pain or pleasure, toil or rest, fact or fancy, among the multiplicity of paths in the labyrinth trodden by the sons of Adam . . . . " LD ii 12

—by expression

—arch: "'Now that you *can* begin, sir,' returned Bella, with a look as if she italicised the word by putting one of her dimples under it, 'what were you going to say?'" OMF iii 9

—a clue, or not: "The expression of a man's face is commonly a help to his thoughts, or glossary on his speech; but the countenance of Newman Noggs, in his ordinary moods, was a problem which no stretch of ingenuity could solve." NN 3

—cruel: "[Gamfield's] countenance was a regular stamped receipt for cruelty." OT 3

—emulated: "Any strongly marked expression of face on the part of a chief actor in a scene of great interest, to whom many eyes are directed, will be unconsciously imitated by the spectators." TTC ii 3

—fierce: "The old lady . . . drew herself up, and looked carving-knives at the hard-headed delinquent." PP 6

—frowning: " , , , [Mrs Clennam] turned her eyes momentarily upon her son, with a dark frown, as if the sculptor of old Egypt had indented it in the hard granite face, to frown for ages." LD i 5

"[Hexam] had the special peculiarity of some birds of prey, that when he knitted his brow, his ruffled crest stood highest." OMF i 3

—furious: "[Lammle's] colour has turned to a livid white, and ominous marks have come to light about his nose, as if the finger of the very devil himself had, within the last few moments, touched it here and there." OMF i 10

—gloomy: "A pale, puffy-faced, dark-haired person of thirty [Bazzard], with big dark eyes that wholly wanted lustre, and a dissatisfied, doughy complexion, that seemed to ask to be sent to the baker's. A gloomy person, with tangled locks, and a general air of having been reared under the shadow of that baleful tree of Java* which has given shelter to more lies than the whole botanical kingdom." MED 11

**the upas tree, of miasmically virulent qualities: its sap is poisonous.*

—impassive: "'Have you just come here, sir?' inquired Mr Tupman, with a piercing look.

"'Just,' replied the fat boy [Joe Lambert].

"Mr Tupman looked at him very hard again; but there was not a wink in his eye, or a curve in his face: there was not a gleam of mirth, or anything but feeding in his whole visage." PP 8

"[Mr Lillyvick's] face . . . might have been carved out of *lignum vitae*, for anything that appeared to the contrary." NN 14

"What my aunt saw, or did not see, I defy the science of physiognomy to have made out, without her own consent. I believe there never was anybody with such an imperturbable countenance when she chose. Her face might have been a dead wall on the occasion in question, for any light it threw upon her thoughts." DC 35

"His imperturbable face has been as inexpressive as his rusty clothes. One could not even say he has been thinking all this while. He has shown neither patience nor impatience, nor attention nor abstraction. He has shown nothing but his shell. As easily might the tone of a delicate musical instrument be inferred from its case, as the tone of Mr Tulkinghorn from his case." BH 11

—irritated: "'I told you not to bang the door so!' repeated Dumps, with an expression of countenance like the knave of clubs, in convulsions." SB/BC

—of passers-by: "Some frowned, some smiled, some muttered to themselves, some made slight gestures, as if anticipating the conversation in which they would shortly be engaged, some wore the cunning look of bargaining and plotting, some were anxious and eager, some slow and dull; in some countenances, were written gain; in others, loss. It was like being in the confidence of all these people to stand quietly there, looking into their faces as they flitted past. In busy places, where each man has an object of his own, and feels assured that every other man has his, his character and purpose are written broadly in his face. In the public walks and lounges of a town, people go to see and to be seen, and there the same expression, with little variety, is repeated a hundred times. The working-day faces come nearer to the truth, and let it out more plainly." OCS 44

And see CD:Esoteric science—*physiognomy*

—plotting: ". . . an expression of face in which a great number of opposite ingredients, such as mischief, cunning, malice, triumph, and patient expectation, were all mixed up together in a kind of physiognomical punch, Miss Miggs composed herself to wait and listen, like some fair ogress who had set a trap and was watching for a nibble from a plump young traveller." BR 9

—poker-faced, briefly: ". . . Mr Tapley for a moment presented . . . an utterly stolid and expressionless face: a perfect dead wall of countenance. But opening window after window in it, with asonishing rapidity, and lighting them all up as for a general illumination, he repeated [his speculation]." MC 7

—portentous: "Mrs Varden slightly raised her hands, shook her head, and looked at the ground, as though she saw straight through the globe, out at the other end, and into the immensity of space beyond." BR 27

—sarcastic: "The thin straight lines of the setting of the eyes, and the thin straight lips, and the markings in the nose, curved with a sarcasm that looked handsomely diabolic." TTC ii 9

—self-important: ". . . a little man with a puffy Say-nothing-to-me, or-I'll-contradict-you sort of countenance, who remained very quiet; occasionally looking round him when the conversation slackened as if he contemplated putting in something very weighty; and now and then bursting into a short cough of inexpressible grandeur." PP 7

—self-indulged: "[Tugby's] great broad chin, with creases in it large enough to hide a finger in; the astonished eyes, that seemed to expostulate with themselves for sinking deeper and deeper into the yielding fat of the soft face; the nose, afflicted with that disordered action of its functions which is generally termed The Snuffles; the short thick throat and labouring chest, with other beauties of the like description . . . ." C 4

—severe: "[Mrs Clennam's] severe face had no thread of relaxation in it, by which any explorer could have been guided to the gloomy labyrinth of her thoughts." LD i 5

—simian: ". . . with a grin upon his features altogether indescribable, but which seemed to be compounded of every monstrous grimace of which men or monkeys are capable, the dwarf slowly retreated . . . . " OCS 48

—sour: "Bella playfully setting herself about the task, Mrs Wilfer's impressive countenance followed her with glaring eyes, presenting a combination of the once popular sign of the Saracen's Head, with a piece of Dutch clockwork, and suggesting to an imaginative mind that from the composition of the salad, her daughter might prudently omit the vinegar. But no word issued from the majestic matron's lips. And this was more terrific to her husband (as perhaps she knew) than any flow of eloquence with which she could have edified the company." OMF iii 16

—terrified: "There is no sort of whiteness in all the hues under the sun, at all like the whiteness of Monsieur Rigaud's face as it was then [summoned to trial for murder]. Neither is there any expression of the human countenance at all like that expression, in every little line of which the frightened heart is seen to beat. Both are conventionally compared with death; but the difference is the whole deep gulf between the struggle done, and the fight at its most desperate extremity." LD i 1

—triumphant: "The hard-headed man looked triumphantly round, as if he had been very much contradicted by somebody, but had got the better of him at last." PP 6

—after a tussle: "In the weak eyes of Venus, and in every reddish dust-coloured hair in his shock of hair, there was a marked distrust of Wegg and an alertness to fly at him on perceiving the smallest occasion. In the hard-grained face of Wegg, and in his stiff knotty figure (he looked like

a German wooden toy), there was expressed a politic conciliation, which had no spontaneity in it. Both were flushed, flustered, and rumpled, by the late scuffle . . . . " OMF iii 7

—*unhappy:* "Mr Winkle responded with a forced smile, and took up the spare gun with an expression of countenance which a metaphysical rook, impressed with a foreboding of his approaching death by violence, may be supposed to assume. It might have been keenness, but it looked remarkably like misery." PP 7

—*vacuous:* "Here Bazzard awoke himself by his own snoring; and, as is usual in such cases, sat apoplectically staring at vacancy, as defying vacancy to accuse him of having been asleep." MED 11

—*yawn:* "Mr Jasper, in the act of yawning behind his wineglass, puts down that screen and calls up a look of interest. It is a little impaired in its expressiveness by his having a shut-up gape still to dispose of, with watering eyes." MED 4

—*by gesture:* " . . . Walter . . . was too much occupied . . . to observe either that his uncle was evidently unacquainted with the intelligence the Captain had undertaken to impart, or that the Captain made signals with his hook, warning him to avoid the subject. Not that the Captain's signals were calculated to have proved very comprehensible, however attentively observed; for, like those Chinese sages who are said in their conferences to write certain learned words in the air that are wholly impossible of pronunciation, the Captain made such waves and flourishes as nobody without a previous knowledge of his mystery, would have been at all likely to understand." DS 17

"'Have you ever thought of looking to me to do any kind of work?'

"John Baptist answered with that peculiar backhanded shake of the right forefinger which is the most expressive negative in the Italian language." LD i 1

And see W:Italy—*beggary—at Naples*

—*grammar:* "In the grammar of Mrs Merdle's verbs on this momentous subject [a job for her son], there was only one Mood, the Imperative; and that Mood had only one tense, the Present. Mrs Merdle's verbs were so pressingly presented to Mr Merdle to conjugate, that his sluggish blood and long coat-cuffs became quite agitated." LD ii 12

"'Is any gentleman present . . . acquainted with the English Grammar?'

"Bleeding Heart Yard was shy of claiming that acquaintance.

"'It's no matter,' said Mr Pancks. 'I merely wish to remark that the task this Proprietor has set me, has been never to leave off conjugating the Imperative Mood Present Tense of the verb To keep always at it. Keep thou always at it. Let him keep always at it. Keep we or do we keep always at it. Keep ye or do ye keep always at it. Let them keep always at it. Here is your benevolent Patriarch of a Casby, and there is his golden rule." LD ii 32

"'[Jasper] has been took a little poorly.'

"'Say "taken," Tope—to the Dean,' the younger rook interposes in a low tone with this touch of correction, as who should say, 'You may offer bad grammar to the laity, or the humbler clergy, not to the Dean.'" MED 2

And see IG: Government—*mayors*

—*heart to heart:* "As [Gradgrind] now leaned back in his chair, and bent his deep-set eyes upon [Louisa] in his turn, perhaps he might have seen one wavering moment in her, when she was impelled to throw herself upon his breast, and give him the pent-up confidences of her heart. But, to see it, he must have overleaped at a bound the artificial barriers he had for many years been erecting, between himself and all those subtle essences of humanity which will elude the utmost cunning of algebra until the last trumpet ever to be sounded shall blow even algebra to wreck. The barriers were too many and too high for such a leap. With his unbending, utilitarian, matter-of-fact face, he hardened her again; and the moment shot away into the plumbless depths of the past, to mingle with all the lost opportunities that are drowned there." HT i 15

—*irrelevant:* "As these remarks were quite unanswerable—which is the happy property of all remarks that are sufficiently wide of the purpose—they changed the current of the conversation . . . . " CH 2

—*by knitting:* "'Are you sure,' asked Jacques Two, of Defarge, 'that no embarrassment can arise from our manner of keeping the register? Without doubt it is safe, for no one beyond ourselves can decipher it; but shall we always be able to decipher it—or, I ought to say, will she?

"'Jacques,' returned Defarge, drawing himself up, 'if madame my wife undertook to keep the register in her memory alone, she would not lose a word of it—not a syllable of it. Knitted, in her own stitches and her own symbols, it will always be as plain to her as the sun. Confide in Madame Defarge, it would be easier for the weakest poltroon that lives, to erase himself from existence, than to erase one letter of his name or crimes from the knitted register of Madame Defarge.'" TTC ii 15

—by letter: "Now, although Mr Bucket walks upstairs to the little library within the larger one, with the face of a man who receives some scores of letters every day, it happens that much correspondence is not incidental to his life. He is no great scribe; rather handling his pen like the pocket-staff he carries about with him always convenient to his grasp; and discourages correspondence with himself in others, as being too artless and direct a way of doing delicate business. Further, he often sees damaging letters produced in evidence, and has occasion to reflect that it was a green thing to write them. For these reasons he has very little to do with letters, either as sender or receiver." BH 53

For the archetypal author of the begging-letter, see Southcote RP/BL Vol. II p933

—letters in a lawsuit: "'And now, gentlemen, but one word more. Two letters have passed between these parties, letters which are admitted to be in the handwriting of the defendant, and which speak volumes indeed. These letters, too, bespeak the character of the man. They are not open, fervent, eloquent epistles, breathing nothing but the language of affectionate attachment. They are covert, sly, underhanded communications, but, fortunately, far more conclusive than if couched in the most glowing language and the most poetic imagery—letters that must be viewed with a cautious and suspicious eye—letters that were evidently intended at the time, by Pickwick, to mislead and delude any third parties into whose hands they might fall.

"'Let me read the first:—"Garraway's, twelve o'clock. Dear Mrs. B.—Chops and Tomata sauce. Yours, PICKWICK." Gentlemen, what does this mean? Chops and Tomata sauce! Yours, Pickwick! Chops! Gracious heavens! and Tomata sauce! Gentlemen, is the happiness of a sensitive and confiding female to be trifled away, by such shallow artifices as these?

"'The next has no date whatever, which is in itself suspicious. "Dear Mrs B., I shall not be at home till to-morrow. Slow coach." And then follows this very remarkable expression. "Don't trouble yourself about the warming-pan." The warming-pan! Why, gentlemen, who *does* trouble himself about a warming-pan? When was the peace of mind of man or woman broken or disturbed by a warming-pan, which is in itself a harmless, a useful, and I will add, gentlemen, a comforting article of domestic furniture? Why is Mrs Bardell so earnestly entreated not to agitate herself about this warming-pan, unless (as is no doubt the case) it is a mere cover for hidden fire—a mere substitute for some endearing word or promise, agreeably to a preconcerted system of correspondence, artfully contrived by Pickwick with a view to his contemplated desertion, and which I am not in a condition to explain?

"'And what does this allusion to the slow coach mean? For aught I know, it may be a reference to Pickwick himself, who has most unquestionably been a criminally slow coach during the whole of this transaction, but whose speed will now be very unexpectedly accelerated, and whose wheels, gentlemen, as he will find to his cost, will very soon be greased by you!' . . . " PP 34

—lovers: " . . . though lovers are remarkable for leaving a great deal unsaid on all occasions, and very properly desiring to come back and say it, they are remarkable also for a wonderful power of condensation; and can, in one way or other, give utterance to more language—eloquent language—in any given short space of time, than all the six hundred and fifty-eight members of the Commons House of Parliament of the United Kingdom of Great Britain and Ireland; who are strong lovers, no doubt, but of their country only, which makes all the difference; for in a passion of that kind (which is not always returned), it is the custom to use as many words as possible, and express nothing whatever." MC 43

—moving lips: " . . . [Clemency Britain] made some eager signs to her husband, and pointed to the bill, and moved her mouth as if she were repeating with great energy, one word or phrase to him over and over again. As she uttered no sound, and as her dumb motions like most of her gestures were of a very extraordinary kind, this unintelligible conduct reduced Mr Britain to the confines of despair. He stared at the table, at the stranger, at the spoons, at his wife—followed her pantomime with looks of deep amazement and perplexity—asked in the

same language, was it property in danger, was it he in danger, was it she—answered her signals with other signals expressive of the deepest distress and confusion—followed the motions of her lips—guessed half aloud 'milk and water,' 'monthly warning,' 'mice and walnuts'—and couldn't approach her meaning." BL 3 [*She is saying 'Michael Warden.'*]

—silent, in Italy: "Why do the beggars rap their chins constantly, with their right hands, when you look at them? Everything is done in pantomime in Naples, and that is the conventional sign for hunger.

"A man who is quarrelling with another, yonder, lays the palm of his right hand on the back of his left, and shakes the two thumbs—expressive of a donkey's ears—whereat his adversary is goaded to desperation.

"Two people bargaining for fish, the buyer empties an imaginary waistcoat pocket when he is told the price, and walks away without a word: having thoroughly conveyed to the seller that he considers it too dear.

"Two people in carriages, meeting, one touches his lips, twice or thrice, holding up the five fingers of his right hand, and gives a horizontal cut in the air with the palm. The other nods briskly, and goes his way. He has been invited to a friendly dinner at half-past five o'clock, and will certainly come.

"All over Italy, a peculiar shake of the right hand from the wrist, with the forefinger stretched out, expresses a negative—the only negative beggars will ever understand. But, in Naples, those five fingers are a copious language." ¶PI 13

—turgid, in Parliament: "Then again, how did it come to be necessary to the Constitution that I should be such a very circuitous and prolix peer as to 'take leave to remind you, my Lords, of what fell from the noble and learned lord on the opposite side of your Lordships' house, who preceded my noble and learned friend on the cross Benches when he addressed himself with so much ability to the observations of the Right Reverend Prelate near me, in reference to the measure now brought forward by the Noble Baron'—when, all this time, I mean, and only want to say, **Lord Brougham**?" HW/FC

—winking

—identifying a boy: "He was a secret-looking man whom I [Pip] had never seen before. His head was all on one side, and one of his eyes was half shut up, as if he were taking aim at something with an invisible gun . . . he gave me only a look with his aiming eye—no, not a look, for he shut it up, but wonders may be done with an eye by hiding it." GE 10

—in a pub: "'We were quite alone there, except that a few hovellers' (the Kentish name for longshore boatmen like his companions) 'were hanging about their lugs, waiting while the tide made, as hovellers will.' (One of the two boatmen, thoughtfully regarding me, shut up one eye; this I understood to mean: first, that he took me into the conversation: secondly, that he confirmed the proposition: thirdly, that he announced himself as a hoveller.)" RP/OS

—secret: "Mr Weller communicated this secret with great glee, and winked so indefatigably after doing so, that Sam began to think he must have got the *tic douleureux* in his right eye-lid." PP 33

—slow: This was said with a mysterious wink; or what would have been a wink if, in Mr Grewgious's hands, it could have been quick enough." MED 11

Conversation

—baby-talk: "A mechanical power of reproducing scraps of current conversation for the delectation of the baby, with all the sense struck out of them, and all the nouns changed into the plural number." CH 1

—give and take: "This skilful see-saw of Mr Dorrit and Mrs Merdle, so that each of them sent the other up, and each of them sent the other down, and neither had the advantage, acted as a sedative on Mr Dorrit's cough." LD ii 15

—gracious: "I [Sampson] listened to [Slinkton's] talk at dinner, and observed how readily other men responded to it, and with what a graceful instinct he adapted his subjects to the knowledge and habits of those he talked with. As, in talking with me, he had easily started the subject I might be supposed to understand best, and to be the most interested in, so, in talking with others, he guided himself by the same rule. The company was of a varied character; but he was not at fault, that I could discover, with any member of it. He knew just as much of each man's pursuit as made him agreeable to that man in reference to it, and just as little as made it natural in him to seek modestly for information when the theme was broached." HD 2

—interrogation: "I found that Mrs Heep gradually got nearer to me, and that Uriah gradually got opposite to me, and that they respectfully plied me with the choicest of the eatables on the table. There was nothing particularly choice there, to be sure; but I took the will for the deed, and felt that they were very attentive. Presently they began to talk about aunts, and then I told them about mine; and about fathers and mothers, and then I told them about mine; and then Mrs Heep began to talk about fathers-in-law [step-fathers], and then I began to tell her about mine; but stopped, because my aunt had advised me to observe a silence on that subject.

"A tender young cork, however, would have had no more chance against a pair of corkscrews, or a tender young tooth against a pair of dentists, or a little shuttlecock against two battledores, than I had against Uriah and Mrs Heep. They did just what they liked with me; and wormed things out of me that I had no desire to tell, with a certainty I blush to think of: the more especially as, in my juvenile frankness, I took some credit to myself for being so confidential, and felt that I was quite the patron of my two respectful entertainers." DC 17

—opener: " . . . a mild and modest young Quaker, who opened the discourse by informing me, in a grave whisper, that his grandfather was the inventor of cold-drawn castor-oil. I mention the circumstance here, thinking it probable that this is the first occasion on which the valuable medicine in question was ever used as a conversational aperient." AN 7 *'aperient': opener, laxative —Webster's Unabridged Dictionary 2d ed.*

—persiflage: "'I say,' quoth Miss Brass, abruptly breaking silence, 'you haven't seen a silver pencil-case this morning, have you?'

"'I didn't meet many in the street,' rejoined Mr Swiveller. 'I saw one—a stout pencil-case of respectable appearance—but as he was in company with an elderly penknife, and a young toothpick with whom he was in earnest conversation, I felt a delicacy in speaking to him.'" OCS 58

Double-entendre

"She touched his organ, and from that bright epoch, even it, the old companion of his happiest hours, incapable as he had thought of elevation, began a new and deified existence." MC 24

Well, of course CD didn't mean it, but it is irresistible. W. S. Gilbert gives us another instance of the treachery of a changing vernacular: "Is this the Court of the Exchequer? Be firm, be firm my pecker! Your evil star's in the ascendant." *—Trial by Jury*

CD must have meant the following, however:

"The spirit being set before him in a huge case-bottle ... [Quilp] ordered cold water and the box of cigars; and these being supplied, he settled himself in an arm-chair . . . .

"'Now, Mrs Quilp,' he said; 'I feel in a smoking humour, and shall probably blaze away all night. But sit where you are, if you please, in case I want you.'

"His wife returned no other reply than the customary 'Yes, Quilp,' and the small lord of the creation took his first cigar and mixed his first glass of grog. The sun went down and the stars peeped out . . . the room became perfectly dark and the end of the cigar a deep fiery red, but still Mr Quilp went on smoking and drinking in the same poistion, and staring listlessly out of the window with the dog-like smile always on his face, save when Mrs Quilp made some involuntary movement of restlessness or fatigue; and then it expanded into a grin of delight. [chapter break]

"Whether Mr Quilp took any sleep by snatches of a few winks at a time, or whether he sat with his eyes wide open all night long, certain it is that he kept his cigar alight, and kindled every fresh one from the ashes of that which was nearly consumed, without requiring the assistance of a candle . . . .

"At length the day broke, and poor Mrs Quilp, shivering with the cold of early morning and harassed by fatigue and want of sleep, was discovered sitting patiently on her chair, raising her eyes at intervals in mute appeal . . . . But her dwarfish spouse still smoked his cigar and drank his rum without heeding her . . . .

"His obedient wife withdrew the bolt, and her lady mother entered . . . .

"'Why, Betsy,' said the old woman, 'you haven't been a—you don't mean to say you've been a—'

"'Sitting up all night?' said Quilp, supplying the conclusion of the sentence. 'Yes she has!'

"'All night!' cried Mrs Jiniwin.

"'Aye all night . . . Who says man and wife are bad company? Ha ha! The time has flown.'

"'You're a brute!' exclaimed Mrs Jiniwin.

"'Come, come,' . . . you mustn't call her names. She's married now, you know. And though she *did* beguile the time and keep me from my bed, you must not be so tenderly careful of me as to be out of humour with her. Bless you for a dear old lady.'" OCS 4-5

Debatable? Christopher Hibbert calls the foregoing a "scene of concupiscence" and quotes Gabriel Pearson's view that it is "the nearest we get to downright copulation in early-Victorian fiction." FS pref to OCS xv

Fairy-tale and Fantasy

—ghost

—amenable to reason: "' . . . one of the glass doors slowly opening, disclosed a pale and emaciated figure in soiled and worn apparel, standing erect in the press. The figure was tall and thin, and the countenance expressive of care and anxiety; but there was something in the hue of the skin, and gaunt and unearthly appearance of the whole form, which no being of this world was ever seen to wear.

"'"Who are you?" said the new tenant, turning very pale: poising the poker in his hand, however, and taking a very decent aim at the countenance of the figure. "Who are you?" "Don't throw that poker at me," replied the form; "If you hurled it with ever so sure an aim, it would pass through me, without resistance, and expend its force on the wood behind. I am a spirit." "And, pray, what do you want here?" faltered the tenant. "In this room" replied the apparition, "my worldly ruin was worked, and I and my children beggared. In this press, the papers in a long, long suit, which accumulated for years, were deposited. In this room, when I had died of grief, and long-deferred hope, two wily harpies divided the wealth for which I had contested during a wretched existence, and of which, at last, not one farthing was left for my unhappy descendants. I terrified them from the spot, and since that day have prowled by night—the only period at which I can revisit the earth—about the scenes of my long-protracted misery. This apartment is mine: leave it to me."

"'"If you insist upon making your appearance here," said the tenant, who had had time to collect his presence of mind during this prosy statement of the ghost's, "I shall give up possession with the greatest pleasure; but I should like to ask you one question, if you will allow me." "Say on," said the apparition, sternly. "Well," said the tenant, "I don't apply the observation personally to you, because it is equally applicable to most of the ghosts I ever heard of; but it does appear to me somewhat inconsistent, that when you have an opportunity of visiting the fairest spots of earth—for I suppose space is nothing to you—you should always return exactly to the very places where you have been most miserable."

"'"Egad, that's very true; I never thought of that before," said the ghost. "You see, sir," pursued the tenant, "this is a very uncomfortable room. From the appearance of that press, I should be disposed to say that it is not wholly free from bugs; and I really think you might find much more comfortable quarters: to say nothing of the climate of London, which is extremely disagreeable." "You are very right, sir," said the ghost, politely, "it never struck me till now; I'll try change of air directly."

"In fact, he began to vanish as he spoke: his legs, indeed had quite disappeared. "And if, sir," said the tenant calling after him, "if you *would* have the goodness to suggest to the other ladies and gentlemen who are now engaged in haunting old empty houses, that they might be much more comfortable elsewhere, you will confer a very great benefit on society." "I will," replied the ghost; "we must be dull fellows, very dull fellows, indeed; I can't imagine how we can have been so stupid." With these words, the spirit disappeared; and . . . he never came back again.'" ¶PP 21

—anniversary: "'I [Solomon Daisy] have heard it said that as we keep our birthdays when we are alive, so the ghosts of dead people, who are not easy in their graves, keep the day they died upon.'" BR 33

—disbelieved, but . . . : "Ask the first hundred citizens of Cloisterham, met at random in the streets at noon, if they believed in Ghosts, they would tell you no; but put them to choose at night between these eerie Precincts and the thoroughfare of shops, and you would find that ninety-nine declared for the longer round and the more frequented way." MED 12

—father, early morning: ". . . I once saw the apparition of my father, at this hour. He was alive and well, and nothing ever came of it, but I saw him in the daylight, sitting with his back towards me, on a seat that stood beside my bed. His head was resting on his hand, and whether he was

slumbering or grieving, I could not discern. Amazed to see him there, I sat up, moved my position, leaned out of bed, and watched him. As he did not move, I spoke to him more than once. As he did not move then, I became alarmed and laid my hand upon his shoulder, as I thought—and there was no such thing." CS/HH 1

—frisson fomented: " . . . I had remarked that we were at our ghostliest whenever he came up in the evening to comfort the servants. Let me do Ikey no injustice. He was afraid of the house, and believed in its being haunted; and yet he would play false on the haunting side, so surely as he got an opportunity. The Odd Girl's case was exactly similar. She went about the house in a state of real terror, and yet lied monstrously and wilfully, and invented many of the alarms she spread, and made many of the sounds we heard. I had had my eye on the two, and I know it.

"It is not necessary for me, here, to account for this preposterous state of mind; I content myself with remarking that it is familiarly known to every intelligent man who has had fair medical, legal, or other watchful experience; that it is as well established and as common a state of mind as any with which observers are acquainted; and that it is one of the first elements, above all others, rationally to be suspected in, and strictly looked for, and separated from, any question of this kind." ¶CS/HH

—social attribute: "'Sir Morbury Dedlock was the owner of Chesney Wold. Whether there was any account of a ghost in the family before those days, I can't say. I should think it very likely, indeed.'

"Mrs Rouncewell holds this opinion, because she considers that a family of such antiquity and importance has a right to a ghost. She regards a ghost as one of the privileges of the upper classes; a genteel distinction to which the common people have no claim." BH 7

—unoriginal: " . . . ghosts have little originality, and 'walk' in a beaten track. Thus, it comes to pass, that a certain room in a certain old hall, where a certain bad lord, baronet, knight, or gentleman, shot himself, has certain planks in the floor from which the blood *will not* be taken out. You may scrape and scrape, as the present owner has done, or plane and plane, as his father did, or scrub and scrub, as his grandfather did, or burn and burn with strong acids, as his great-grandfather did, but there the blood will still be—no redder and no paler—no more and no less—always just the same. Thus, in such another house there is a haunted door, that never will keep open; or another door that never will keep shut; or a haunted sound of a spinning-wheel, or a hammer, or a footstep, or a cry, or a sigh, or a horse's tramp, or the rattling of a chain. Or else, there is a turret-clock, which, at the midnight hour, strikes thirteen when the head of the family is going to die; or a shadowy, immovable black carriage which at such a time is always seen by somebody, waiting near the great gates in the stable-yard." CS/CT

And see A:Death—*Last Lines of Death—Murderer, hanged, in apparition;* B:Body—*digestion, and* S:Church—*cathedral, at night*

—giant: "There never was a race of people who so completely gave the lie to history as these giants, or whom all the chroniclers have so cruelly libelled. Instead of roaring and ravaging about the world, constantly catering for their cannibal larders, and perpetually going to market in an unlawful manner, they are the meekest people in any man's acquaintance: rather inclining to milk and vegetable diet, and bearing anything for a quiet life.

"So decidedly are amiability and mildness their characteristics, that I confess I look upon that youth who distinguished himself by the slaughter of these inoffensive persons, as a false-hearted brigand, who, pretending to philanthropic motives, was secretly influenced only by the wealth stored up within their castles, and the hope of plunder.

"And I lean the more to this opinion from finding that even the historian of those exploits, with all his partiality for his hero, is fain to admit that the slaughtered monsters in question were of a very innocent and simple turn; extremely guileless and ready of belief; lending a credulous ear to the most improbable tales; suffering themselves to be easily entrapped into pits; and even (as in the case of the Welsh Giant) with an excess of the hospitable politeness of a landlord, ripping themselves open, rather than hint at the possibility of their guests being versed in the vagabond arts of sleight-of-hand and hocus-pocus." ¶AN 12

—goblins of the Bells: "Then . . . did Trotty [Veck] see in every Bell a bearded figure of the bulk and stature of the Bell—incomprehensibly, a figure and the Bell itself. Gigantic, grave, and darkly watchful of him, as he stood rooted to the ground.

"Mysterious and awful figures! Resting on nothing; poised in the night air of the tower, with their draped and hooded heads merged in the dim roof; motionless and shadowy. Shadowy and dark, although he saw them by some light belonging to themselves—none else was there—each with its muffled hand upon its goblin mouth." C 3

And see Gabriel Grub's goblin PP

—haunted house: "There is no end to the old houses, with resounding galleries, and dismal state-bedchambers, and haunted wings shut up for many years, through which we may ramble, with an agreeable creeping up our back, and encounter any number of ghosts, but (it is worthy of remark perhaps) reducible to a very few general types and classes . . . . " CS/CT

—household spirits: "For all the Cricket tribe are potent Spirits, even though the people who hold converse with them do not know it (which is frequently the case); and there are not, in the unseen world, voices more gentle and more true, that may be so implicitly relied on, or that are so certain to give none but tenderest counsel, as the Voices in which the Spirits of the Fireside and the Hearth address themselves to human kind." CH 2

—phantoms and elves: "[Toby] saw the tower, whither his charmed footsteps had brought him, swarming with dwarf phantoms, spirits, elfin creatures of the Bells. He saw them leaping, flying, dropping, pouring from the Bells without a pause. He saw them, round him on the ground; above him, in the air; clambering from him, by the ropes below; looking down upon him, from the massive iron-girded beams; peeping in upon him, through the chinks and loopholes in the walls; spreading away and away from him in enlarging circles, as the water ripples give way to a huge stone that suddenly comes plashing in among them.

"He saw them, of all aspects and all shapes. He saw them ugly, handsome, crippled, exquisitely formed. He saw them young, he saw them old, he saw them kind, he saw them cruel, he saw them merry, he saw them grim; he saw them dance, and heard them sing; he saw them tear their hair, and heard them howl. He saw the air thick with them. He saw them come and go, incessantly. He saw them riding downward, soaring upward, sailing off afar, perching near at hand, all restless and all violently active.

"Stone, and brick, and slate, and tile, became transparent to him as to them. He saw them *in* the houses, busy at the sleepers' beds. He saw them soothing people in their dreams; he saw them beating them with knotted whips; he saw them yelling in their ears; he saw them playing softest music on their pillows; he saw them cheering some with the songs of birds and the perfume of flowers; he saw them flashing awful faces on the troubled rest of others, from enchanted mirrors which they carried in their hands.

"He saw these creatures, not only among sleeping men but waking also, active in pursuits irreconcilable with one another, and possessing or assuming natures the most opposite. He saw one buckling on innumerable wings to increase his speed; another loading himself with chains and weights, to retard him. He saw some putting the hands of clocks forward, some putting the hands of clocks backward, some endeavouring to stop the clock entirely. He saw them representing, here a marriage ceremony, there a funeral; in this chamber an election, in that a ball; he saw, everywhere, restless and untiring motion . . . .

"As he gazed, the Chimes stopped. Instantaneous change! The whole swarm fainted! their forms collapsed, their speed deserted them; they sought to fly, but in the act of falling died and melted into air. No fresh supply succeeded them. One straggler leaped down pretty briskly from the surface of the Great Bell, and alighted on his feet, but he was dead and gone before he could turn round.

"Some few of the late company who had gambolled in the tower, remained there, spinning over and over a little longer; but these became at every turn more faint, and few, and feeble, and soon went the way of the rest. The last of all was one small hunchback, who had got into an echoing corner, where he twirled and twirled, and floated by himself a long time; showing such perseverance, that at last he dwindled to a leg and even to a foot, before he finally retired; but he vanished in the end, and then the tower was silent." ¶C 3

—spirit of the dead: "Marley was dead, to begin with. There is no doubt whatever about that. . . . This must be distinctly understood, or nothing wonderful can come of the story I am going to relate. If we were not perfectly convinced that *Hamlet*'s Father died before the play began, there would be nothing more remarkable in his taking a stroll at night, in an easterly wind, upon his own ramparts, than there would be in any other middleaged gentleman rashly turning out after dark in a breezy spot—say Saint Paul's Churchyard for instance—literally to astonish his son's weak mind." CC 1

—vision of a defective: "'Look down there,' [Barnaby] said softly; 'do you mark how they whisper in each other's ears; then dance and leap, to make believe they are in sport? Do you see how they stop for a moment, when they think there is no one looking, and mutter among themselves again; and then how they roll and gambol, delighted with the mischief they've been plotting? Look at 'em now. See how they whirl and plunge. And now they stop again, and whisper cautiously together—little thinking, mind, how often I have lain upon the grass and watched them. I say—what is it that they plot and hatch?—Do you know?'

"'They are only clothes,' returned the guest, 'such as we wear; hanging on those lines to dry, and fluttering in the wind.'

"'Clothes!' echoed Barnaby, looking close into his face, and falling quickly back. 'Ha ha! Why, how much better to be silly, than as wise as you! You don't see shadowy people there, like those that live in sleep—not you. Nor eyes in the knotted panes of glass, nor swift ghosts when it blows hard, nor do you hear voices in the air, nor see men stalking in the sky—not you! I lead a merrier life than you, with all your cleverness. You're the dull men. We're the bright ones. Ha! ha! I'll not change with you, clever as you are—not I!' . . .

"'He wants imagination,' said Mr Willet, very slowly, and after a long silence; 'that's what he wants. I've tried to instil it into him, many and many's the time; but'—John added this in confidence—'he an't made for it; that's the fact.'" BR 10

—witch and familiar: "The good old lady might have been—not to record it disrespectfully—a witch, and Paul and the cat her two familiars, as they all sat by the fire together. It would have been quite in keeping with the appearance of the party if they had all sprung up the chimney in a high wind one night, and never been heard of any more.

"This, however, never came to pass. The cat, and Paul, and Mrs Pipchin, were constantly to be found in their usual places after dark; and Paul, eschewing the companionship of Master Bitherstone, went on studying Mrs Pipchin, and the cat, and the fire, night after night, as if they were a book of necromancy, in three volumes." DS 8

Literary uplift

—clemency: "'If you're in 'arnest, you see, my lad,' said the Captain, 'you're a object of clemency, and clemency is the brightest jewel in the crown of a Briton's head, for which you'll overhaul the constitution as laid down in Rule Britannia, and, when found, *that* is the charter as them garden angels was a singing of, so many times over. Stand by!'" DS 39

Did the Captain read Spinoza? Ethics pt III 59 note: *I refer those actions which work out the good of the agent to courage, and those which work out the good of others to nobility. Therefore temperance, sobriety, and presence of mind in danger, etc., are species of courage; but modesty, clemency, etc., are species of nobility.*

—fauna and Hercules: "'Moralise as we will, the world goes on. As *Hamlet* says,* *Hercules* may lay about him with his club in every possible direction, but he can't prevent the cats from making a most intolerable row on the roofs of the houses, or the dogs from being shot in the hot weather if they run about the streets unmuzzled.'" MC 4

**I loved you ever: but it is no matter.*
Let Hercules himself do what he may,
The cat will mew and dog will have his day.
—Hamlet V i

—fig-tree: "'Hear him!' cried the Captain. 'Good morality! Wal'r, my lad. Train up a fig-tree in the way it should go, and when you are old sit under the shade on it. Overhaul the—'Well,' said the Captain on second thoughts, 'I an't quite certain where that's to be found, but when found, make a note of.'" DS 19

A conflation of Proverbs 22:6: *Train up a child in the way he should go: and when he is old, he will not depart from it; and* I Kings 4:25: *And Judah and Israel dwelt safely, every man under his vine and under his fig tree (and see* Micah 4:4).

—friend in need: "'Wal'r, my boy,' replied the Captain, 'in the Proverbs of Solomon you will find the following words, "May we never want a friend in need, nor a bottle to give him!' When found, make a note of'" DS 15

Hazlitt, English Proverbs: *A friend in need is a friend indeed, derived from* Plautus's Epidicus III iii: *Nothing is there more friendly to a man than a friend in need.* Proverbs 27: 6: *Faithful are the wounds of a friend; but the kisses of an enemy are deceitful.*

—voice of the sluggard: "'His wery woice,' said the Captain . . . his wery woice as chock full o' science as ever it was! Sol Gills, lay to, my lad, upon your own wines and fig-trees, like a taut ould patriark as you are, and overhaul them adwentures o' yourn, in your own formilior woice. 'Tis *the* woice,' said the Captain, impressively, and announcing a quotation with his hook,' of the sluggard, I heerd him complain, you have woke me too soon, I must slumber again. Scatter his enemies, and make 'em fall!'" DS 56

See Index XI; Luke 1:51: *He hath scattered the proud in the imagination of their hearts.*

Names and Naming

—"Aaron:" " . . . that I have the honour and pleasure [said Eugene Wrayburn] of a speaking acquaintance with such a Patriarch [Riah] as you describe, and that I address him as Mr Aaron, because it appears to me Hebraic, expressive, appropriate, and complimentary. Notwithstanding which strong reasons for its being his name, it may not be his name.'" OMF iii 10

—"Boz": "'Boz,' my signature in the Morning Chronicle, and in the Old Monthly Magazine, appended to the monthly cover of this book, and retained long afterwards, was the nick-name of a pet child, a younger brother, whom I dubbed Moses, in honour of the *Vicar of Wakefield;* which being facetiously pronounced through the nose, became Boses, and, being shortened, became Boz. Boz was a very familiar household word to me, long before I was an author, and so I came to adopt it." PP pref

—"Edwin": "'Hark'ee, dear genl'mn. What's your Chris'en name?'

"'Edwin.'

"'Edwin, Edwin, Edwin,' she repeats, trailing off into a drowsy repetition of the word; and then asks suddenly: 'Is the short of that name Eddy?'

"'It is sometimes called so,' he replies....

" . . . . You be thankful that your name ain't Ned.'

"He looks at her quite steadily, as he asks: 'Why?'

"'Because it's a bad name to have just now.'

"'How a bad name?'

"'A threatened name. A dangerous name.'

"'The proverb says that threatened men live long,' he tells her, lightly.

"'Then Ned—so threatened is he, wherever he may be while I am a-talking to you, deary—should live to all eternity!' replies the woman." MED 14

—Englishman handling Italian: "'Now I think of it,' returned [Arthur] Clennam, 'there's Cavalletto. He shall go with you, if you like . . . . '

"' . . . . No, I think I'll be pulled through by Mother [said Meagles]. Cavallooro (I stick at his very name to start with, and it sounds like the chorus to a comic song) is so necessary to you, that I don't like the thought of taking him away.'" LD ii 9

—family name, disliked: "'Babley—Mr Richard Babley—that's the gentleman's true name.'

"'But don't you call him by it, whatever you do. He can't bear his name. That's a peculiarity of his. Though I don't know that it's much of a peculiarity, either; for he has been ill-used enough, by some that bear it, to have a mortal antipathy for it, Heaven knows. Mr Dick is his name here, and everywhere else, now—if he ever went anywhere else, which he don't. So take care, child, you don't call him anything *but* Mr Dick.'" DC 14

—fitting; and the letter "R": "[Mr Wilfer] was shy, and unwilling to own to the name of Reginald, as being too aspiring and self-assertive a name. In his signature he used only the initial R., and imparted what it really stood for, to none but chosen friends, under the seal of confidence.

"Out of this, the facetious habit had arisen in the neighbourhood surrounding Mincing Lane of making Christian names for him of adjectives and participles beginning with R. Some of these were more or less appropriate: as Rusty, Retiring, Ruddy, Round, Ripe, Ridiculous, Ruminative; others derived their point from their want of application: as Raging, Rattling, Roaring, Raffish.

"But, his popular name was Rumty, which in a moment of inspiration had been bestowed upon him by a gentleman of convivial habits connected with the drug market, as the beginning of a social chorus, his leading part in the execution of which had led this gentleman to the Temple of Fame, and of which the whole expressive burden ran:

Rumty iddity, row dow dow.
Sing toodlely, teedlely, bow wow wow.

Thus he was constantly addressed, even in minor notes on business, as 'Dear Rumty;' in answer to which, he sedately signed himself, 'Yours truly, R. Wilfer.'" OMF i 4 *And see* B:Homosexuality*—and naming*

—free association and "Little Dorrit:" "'Why yes of course,' returned Flora; 'and of all the strangest names I ever heard the strangest, like a place down in the country with a turnpike, or a favourite pony or a puppy or a bird or something from a seed-shop to be put in a garden or a flower-pot and come up speckled.'" LD i 23

—importance: ""Swidge" is the appellation by which they speak of Mrs William in general, among themselves, I'm told; but that's what I say, sir [said William Swidger]. Better be called ever so far out of your name, if it's done in real liking, than have it made ever so much of, and not cared about! What's a name for? To know a person by. If Mrs William is known by something better than her name—I allude to Mrs William's qualities and disposition—never mind her name, though it *is* Swidger, by rights. Let 'em call her Swidge, Widge, Bridge—Lord! London Bridge, Blackfriars, Chelsea, Putney, Waterloo or Hammersmith Suspension—if they like!'" HM 1

—"John": " . . . in and out, under the figure-head of the John of Sunderland making a speech to the winds (as is done by many Johns) . . . . " GE 54

—missing 'H': "'Then there's the sea; and the boats and ships; and the fishermen; and the beach; and Am to play with——'

"Peggotty meant her nephew Ham . . . but she spoke of him as a morsel of English Grammar." DC 2

—mnemonic ineptitude: "'But Geor—is the right name Georgina or Georgiana?

"'Georgiana.'

"'I was thinking yesterday, I didn't know there was such a name. I thought it must end in ina.'

"'Why?'

"'Why, you play—if you can—the Concertina, you know,' replied Fledgeby, meditating very slowly. 'And you have—when you catch it—the Scarlatina. And you can come down from a balloon in a parach—no, you can't, though. Well, say Georgeute—I mean Georgiana.'" OMF ii 5

This is an inside joke, playing on Georgina Hogarth. See Index II.

—by a mother-in-law: "'And now you see,' whimpered Mrs Gradgrind, adjusting her shawls after the affectionate ceremony, 'I shall be worrying myself, morning, noon, and night, to know what I am to call him!'

"'Mrs Gradgrind,' said her husband, solemnly, 'what do you mean?'

"'Whatever I am to call him, Mr Gradgrind, when he is married to Louisa! I must call him something. It's impossible,' said Mrs Gradgrind, with a mingled sense of politeness and injury, 'to be constantly addressing him and never giving him a name. I cannot call him Josiah, for the name is insupportable to me. You yourself wouldn't hear of Joe, you very well know. Am I to call my own son-in-law, Mister! Not, I believe, unless the time has arrived when, as an invalid, I am to be trampled upon by my relations. Then, what am I to call him!'" HT i 15

She decides to call him 'J.'

—Peggotty: "'Peggotty!' repeated Miss Betsey [Trotwood], with some indignation. 'Do you mean to say, child, that any human being has gone into a Christian church, and got herself named Peggotty?' DC 1

"'You remember my aunt, Peggotty?' . . .

"'For the love of goodness, child,' exclaimed my aunt, 'don't call the woman by that South Sea Island name! If she married and got rid of it, which was the best thing she could do, why don't you give her the benefit of the change? What's your name now,—P?' said my aunt, as a compromise for the obnoxious appellation.

"'Barkis, ma'am,' said Peggotty, with a curtsey.

"'Well! That's human,' said my aunt. 'It sounds less as if you wanted a Missionary. How d'ye do, Barkis? I hope you're well?'" DC 34

—*"Philip"*: "'I don't take to Philip,' said [Herbert Pocket], smiling, 'for it sounds like a moral boy out of the spelling-book, who was so lazy that he fell into a pond, or so fat that he couldn't see out of his eyes, or so avaricious that he locked up his cake till the mice ate it, or so determined to go a bird's-nesting that he got himself eaten by bears who lived handy in the neighbourhood.'" GE 22

—*private theatres:* "With the double view of guarding against the discovery of friends or employers, and enhancing the interest of an assumed character, by attaching a high-sounding name to its representative, these geniuses [the amateurs] assume fictitious names, which are not the least amusing part of the playbill of a private theatre. Belville, Melville, Treville, Berkeley, Randolph, Byron, St Clair, and so forth, are among the humblest; and the less imposing titles of Jenkins, Walker, Thomson, Barker, Solomons, &c., are completely laid aside. There is something imposing in this, and it is an excellent apology for shabbiness into the bargain." SB/PT

—*Skylark:* "They left me . . . with a very nice man, with a very large head of red hair, and a very small shiny hat upon it, who had got a cross-barred shirt or waistcoat on, with 'Skylark' in capital letters across the chest. I thought it was his name; and that as he lived on board ship, and hadn't a street-door to put his name on, he put it there instead; but when I called him Mr Skylark, he said it meant the vessel." DC 2

Notable individuals

—*Sir Edward Bulwer Lytton:* " . . . there hardly can have been, among the followers of literature, a man of more high standing further above those little grudging jealousies, which do sometimes disparage its brightness, than **Sir Edward Bulwer Lytton**." S/M2

—*Daniel Maclise:* "Of his genius in his chosen art I will venture to say nothing here, but of his prodigious fertility of mind and wonderful wealth of intellect, I may confidently assert that they would have made him, if he had been so minded, at least as great a writer as he was a painter. The gentlest and most modest of men, the freshest as to his generous appreciation of young aspirants, and the frankest and largest-hearted as to his peers, incapable of a sordid or ignoble thought, gallantly sustaining the true dignity of his vocation, without one grain of self-ambition, wholesomely natural at the last as at the first, 'in wit a man, simplicity a child', no Artist, of whatever denomination, I make bold to say, ever went to his rest leaving a more golden memory pure from dross, or having devoted himself with a truer chivalry to the Art-Goddess whom he worshipped." S/RA4

—*Charles Macready:* " . . . in the path we both tread I have uniformly found him from the first the most generous of men; quick to encourage, slow to disparage, ever anxious to assert the order of which he is so great an ornament; never condescending to shuffle it off, and leave it outside state rooms, as a Mussulman might leave his slippers outside a mosque." S/M2

—*Sir Thomas More:* " . . . the best, and wisest, and the greatest of men, who . . . died what was almost the natural death of the good, and the wise and the great . . . ." S/PP1 *And see* The Press—*its power*

—*Harriet Beecher Stowe:* "Interest in the subject of slavery has during the present year been reawakened by an admirable book,* in which its main features—as they exist in North America—are painted in the freshest colours. *Uncle Tom's Cabin* with all its faults (and it is not free from the fault of overstrained conclusions and violent extremes) is a noble work; full of high power, lofty humanity; the gentlest, sweetest, and yet boldest, writing. Its authoress, **Harriet Beecher Stowe**, is an honour to the time that has produced her, and will take her place among the best writers of fiction, inspired by the best and noblest purpose. *Uncle Tom* and *Aunt Chloe, George Harris,* and the other negroes with whom Mrs Stowe has by this time made most of us acquainted, are, no doubt, rare specimens of slaves; but, the details of the slave system among which they live have been carefully collected, and are represented, bright or black, fairly and with all due variety, so that they may be generally accepted as remarkable pictures of the every day truth. The subject thus reintroduced is one that it becomes all men to discuss, since the extinction of slavery in America by any other than the old process that has held good since the world began [unexplained], can take place only by the infection of slaveholders with the epidemic of a very prevalent opinion." HWC/N

**Mrs Stowe (1811-1896) published Uncle Tom's Cabin in 1852.*

—*William Makepeace Thackeray:* ". . . [CD] has the privilege of being sometimes called upon to propose the health of the chairman at the annual dinner; and when that chairman is a man for whose genius he has a warm admiration and the most earnest respect, when that chairman is a gentleman who is an honour to literature, and in whom literature is honoured, when that is the case he feels that last privilege to be a great and high one . . . [this dinner] never can have, a gentleman in that position shedding a greater lustre upon it than the noble English writer who fills this Chair tonight." S/TF12

And see Authorship—*interaction of drama and fiction;* MP/WT; *and introductory quotation to* MED

Oratory

—*American:* ". . . 'if, sir [said General Choke], in such a place, and at such a time, I might venture to conclude with a sentiment, glancing—however slantin'dicularly—at the subject in hand, I would say, sir, may the British Lion have his talons eradicated by the noble bill of the American Eagle, and be taught to play upon the Irish Harp and the Scotch Fiddle that music which is breathed in every empty shell that lies upon the shores of green Co-lumbia!'

"Here the lank gentleman sat down again, amidst a great sensation; and every one looked very grave." MC 21

—*for a Cause:* "Now, the Monomaniacs, being by their disease impelled to clamber upon platforms, and there squint horribly under the strong possession of an unbalanced idea, will of course be out of reason and go wrong." HW/GB

—*in Congress:* "There are more quarrels than with us, and more threatenings than gentlemen are accustomed to exchange in any civilised society of which we have record: but farm-yard imitations have not as yet been imported from the Parliament of the United Kingdom. The feature in oratory which appears to be the most practised, and most relished, is the constant repetition of the same idea or shadow of an idea in fresh words; and the inquiry out of doors is not, 'What did he say?' but, 'How long did he speak?' These, however, are but enlargements of a principle which prevails elsewhere." AN 8

—*dinner table:* "Nobody could talk to anybody, because [Luke Honeythunder] held forth to everybody at once, as if the company had no individual existence, but were a Meeting. He impounded the Reverend Mr Septimus, as an official personage to be addressed, or kind of human peg to hang his oratorical hat on, and fell into the exasperating habit, common among such orators, of impersonating him as a wicked and weak opponent. Thus, he would ask: 'And will you, sir, now stultify yourself by telling me'—and so forth, when the innocent man had not opened his lips, nor meant to open them." MED 6

—*enunciation:* ". . . the Lord Mayor of London, who was in the habit of practising oratory when alone, as **Demosthenes** did, and with the somewhat similar object of correcting a curious impediment in his speech, which always thrust the letter H upon him when he had no business with it, and always took it away from him when it was indispensable . . . . " HW/LM *And see* B:Money and Finance—*talked about*

—*Irish:* "And when the petition had been read and was about to be adopted, there came forward the Irish member (who was a young gentleman of ardent temperament), with such a speech as only an Irish member can make, breathing the true soul and spirit of poetry, and poured forth with such fervour, that it made one warm to look at him." NN 2

—*kitchen:* "Mr Giles, pulling out his shirt-frill . . . made a great many other remarks, no less illustrative of his humility, which were received with equal favour and applause, and were, withal, as original and as much to the purpose, as the remarks of great men commonly are." OT 34

—*Mayors' Addresses:* "Must we look at these Addresses as specimens of composition? If we do, we find them to be a species of literary hunting-field, in which every substantive is a terrified stag, run down by a pack of yelping tautological adjectives. For the sake of the mayor—a man and a brother; a human being who has surely done us no serious harm—for the sake of the mayor, who comes up innocently to her Majesty's carriage window, the unconscious bearer of a document which accredits him as a mauler of her Majesty's English, suppress the further production of Municipal Addresses!" HWC/RB

—*Parliamentary:* "And there, with his noble friend and relative Lord Decimus, was William Barnacle, who . . . always kept ready his own particular recipe for How not to do it; sometimes tapping the Speaker, and drawing it fresh out of him, with a 'First, I will beg you, sir, to inform the House what Precedent we have for the course into which the honourable gentleman would precipitate us;' sometimes asking the honourable gentleman to favour him with his own version of the Precedent; sometimes telling the honourable gentleman that he (William Barnacle) would search for a Precedent; and oftentimes crushing the honourable gentleman flat on the spot, by telling him there *was* no Precedent. But, Precedent and Precipitate were, under all circumstances, the well-matched pair of battle-horses of this able Circumlocutionist." LD i 34

—*political:* "'My conduct as been, and ever well be, regulated by a sincere regard for the true and real interests of this great and happy country. Whether I look at home, or abroad; whether I behold the peaceful industrious communities of our island home: her rivers covered with steamboats, her roads with locomotives, her streets with cabs, her skies with balloons of a power and magnitude hitherto unknown in the history of aeronautics in this or any other nation—I say, whether I look merely at home, or, stretching my eyes farther, contemplate the boundless prospect of conquest and possession—achieved by British perseverance and British valour—which is outspread before me, I clasp my hands, and turning my eyes to the broad expanse above my head, exclaim, "Thank Heaven, I am a Briton!"'" NN 16

"He might be asked, he observed, in a peroration of great power, what were his principles? His principles were what they always had been. His principles were written in the countenances of the lion and unicorn; were stamped indelibly upon the royal shield which those grand animals supported, and upon the free words of fire which that shield bore. His principles were, Britannia and her sea-king trident! His principles were, commercial prosperity co-existently with perfect and profound agricultural contentment; but short of this he would never stop.

"His principles were these—with the addition of his colours nailed to the mast, every man's heart in the right place, every man's eye open, every man's hand ready, every man's mind on the alert. His principles were these, concurrently with a general revision of something—speaking generally—and a possible re-adjustment of something else, not to be mentioned more particularly. His principles, to sum up all in a word, were, Hearths and Altars, Labour and Capital, Crown and Sceptre, Elephant and Castle." RP/HF

—*at a public dinner:* " . . . why must Mr Wilson refer to Mr Jackson as 'my honourable friend, if he will permit me to call him so'? Has Wilson any doubt about it? Why does Mr Smithers say that he is sensible he has already detained you too long, and why *you* say, 'No, no; go on!' when you know you are sorry for it directly afterwards? . . .

"No man could ever say why he was greatly refreshed and fortified by forms of words, as 'Resolved. That this meeting respectfully but firmly views with sorrow and apprehension, not unmixed with abhorrence and dismay'—but they *do* invigorate the patient, in most cases, like a cordial.

"It is a strange thing that the chairman is obliged to refer to 'the present occasion';—that there is a horrible fascination in the phrase which he can't elude. Also, that there should be an unctuous smack and relish in the enunciation of titles, as 'And I may be permitted to inform this company that when I had the honour of waiting on His Royal Highness, to ask His Royal Highness to be pleased to bestow his gracious patronage on our excellent Institution, His Royal Highness did me the honour to reply, with that condescension which is ever His Royal Highness's most distinguishing characteristic'—and so forth.

"As to the singular circumstance that such and such a duty should not have been entrusted to abler hands than mine, everybody is familiar with that phenomenon, but it's very strange that it *must* be so!" HW/FC

—*public-house:* "'What is a man?' continued the red-faced specimen of the species, jerking his hat indignantly from its peg on the wall. 'What is an Englishman? Is he to be trampled upon by every oppressor? Is he to be knocked down at everybody's bidding? What's freedom? Not a standing army. What's a standing army? Not freedom. What's general happiness? Not universal misery. Liberty ain't the window-tax, is it? The Lords ain't the Commons, are they?' And the red-faced man, gradually bursting into a radiating sentence, in which such adjectives as 'dastardly,' 'oppressive,' 'violent,' and 'sanguinary,' formed the most conspicuous words, knocked his hat indignantly over his eyes, left the room, and slammed the door after him.

"'Wonderful man!' said he of the sharp nose.

"'Splendid speaker!' added the broker.

"'Great power!' said everybody . . . ." SB/PO

—*temperance society:* "The speeches, judging from the little I could hear of them, were certainly adapted to the occasion, as having that degree of relationship to cold water which wet blankets may claim . . . . " AN 1

—*union organizer:* "Oh my friends and fellow-countrymen, the down-trodden operatives of Coketown, oh my fellow-brothers and fellow-workmen and fellow-citizens and fellow-men, what a to-do was there, when Slackbridge unfolded what he called 'that damning document [a placard offering £20 for apprehension of Stephen Blackpool],' and held it up to the gaze, and for the execration of the working-man community! 'Oh my fellow-men, behold of what a traitor in the camp of those great spirits who are enrolled upon the holy scroll of Justice and of Union, is appropriately capable! Oh my prostrate friends, with the galling yoke of tyrants on your necks and the iron foot of despotism treading down your fallen forms into the dust of the earth, upon which right glad would your oppressors be to see you creeping on your bellies all the days of your lives, like the serpent in the garden . . . my friends—my labouring friends, for I rejoice and triumph in that stigma—my friends whose hard but honest beds are made in toil, and whose scanty but independent pots are boiled in hardship . . . my band of brothers in a sacred bond, to which your children and your children's children yet unborn have set their infant hands and seals, I propose to you on the part of the United Aggregate Tribunal, ever watchful for your welfare, ever zealous for your benefit, that this meeting does Resolve: That Stephen Blackpool, weaver, referred to in this placard, having been already solemnly disowned by the community of Coketown Hands, the same are free from the shame of his misdeeds, and cannot as a class be reproached with his dishonest actions!'" HT iii 4

—*wedding:* "'Ladies and gentlemen, I am Josiah Bounderby of Coketown. Since you have done my wife and myself the honour of drinking our healths and happiness, I suppose I must acknowledge the same; though, as you all know me, and know what I am, and what my extraction was, you won't expect a speech from a man who, when he sees a Post, says "that's a Post," and when he sees a Pump, says "that's a Pump," and is not to be got to call a Post a Pump, or a Pump a Post, or either of them a Toothpick. If you want a speech this morning, my friend and father-in-law, Tom Gradgrind, is a Member of Parliament, and you know where to get it. I am not your man. However, if I feel a little independent when I look around this table today, and reflect how little I thought of marrying Tom Gradgrind's daughter when I was a ragged street-boy, who never washed his face unless it was at a pump, and that not oftener than once a fortnight, I hope I may be excused. So, I hope you like my feeling independent; if you don't, I can't help it. I *do* feel independent. Now I have mentioned, and you have mentioned, that I am this day married to Tom Gradgrind's daughter. I am very glad to be so. It has long been my wish to be so. I have watched her bringing-up, and I believe she is worthy of me. At the same time—not to deceive you—I believe I am worthy of her. So, I thank you, on both our parts, for the goodwill you have shown towards us; and the best wish I can give the unmarried part of the present company, is this: I hope every bachelor may find as good a wife as I have found. And I hope every spinster may find as good a husband as my wife has found.'" HT i 16

"Then Lord Decimus, who was a wonder on his own Parliamentary pedestal, turned out to be the windiest creature here: proposing happiness to the bride and bridegroom in a series of platitudes, that would have made the hair of any sincere disciple and believer stand on end; and trotting, with the complacency of an idiotic elephant, among howling labyrinths of sentences which he seemed to take for high roads, and never so much as wanted to get out of." LD i 34

Pantomime

—in a cheap theatre: "We began at half-past six with a pantomime—with a pantomime so long, that before it was over I felt as if I had been travelling for six weeks—going to India, say, by the Overland Mail. The Spirit of Liberty was the principal personage in the Introduction, and the Four Quarters of the World came out of the globe, glittering, and discoursed with the Spirit, who sang charmingly.

"We were delighted to understand that there was no liberty anywhere but among ourselves, and we highly applauded the agreeable fact. In an allegorical way . . . we and the Spirit of Liberty got into a kingdom of Needles and Pins, and found them at war with a potentate who called in to his aid their old arch enemy Rust, and who would have got the better of them if the Spirit of Liberty had not in the nick of time transformed the leaders into Clown, Pantaloon, Harlequin, Columbine, Harlequina, and a whole family of Sprites, consisting of a remarkably stout father and three spineless sons.

"We all knew what was coming when the Spirit of Liberty addressed the king with a big face, and His Majesty backed to the side-scenes and began untying himself behind, with his big face all on one side. Our excitement at that crisis was great, and our delight unbounded. After this era in our existence, we went through all the incidents of a pantomime; it was not by any means a savage pantomime, in the way of burning or boiling people, or throwing them out of window, or cutting them up; was often very droll; was always liberally got up, and cleverly presented." ¶UT/TV

—in life

—age seeking youth: "[The pantaloon's] amorous propensities, too, are eminently disagreeable; and his mode of addressing ladies in the open street at noonday is downright improper, being usually neither more nor less than a perceptible tickling of the aforesaid ladies in the waist, after committing which, he starts back, manifestly ashamed (as well he may be) of his own indecorum and temerity; continuing, nevertheless, to ogle and beckon to them from a distance in a very unpleasant and immoral manner.

"Is there any man who cannot count a dozen pantaloons in his own social circle? Is there any man who has not seen them swarming at the west end of the town on a sunshiny day or a summer's evening, going through the last-named pantomimic feats with as much liquorish energy, and as total an absence of reserve, as if they were on the very stage itself?

"We can tell upon our fingers a dozen pantaloons of our acquaintance at this moment—capital pantaloons, who have been performing all kinds of strange freaks, to the great amusement of their friends and acquaintance, for years past: and who to this day are making such comical and ineffectual attempts to be young and dissolute, that all beholders are like to die with laughter." ¶B/P

—humbling of the great: "In the fulness of his heart, in the fancied security of wealth, in the possession and enjoyment of all the good things of life, the elderly gentleman suddenly loses his footing and stumbles. How the audience roar! He is set upon by a noisy and officious crowd, who buffet and cuff him unmercifully.

"They scream with delight! Every time the elderly gentleman struggles to get up, his relentless persecutors knock him down again. The spectators are convulsed with merriment! And when at last the elderly gentleman does get up, and staggers away, despoiled of hat, wig, and clothing, himself battered to pieces, and his watch and money gone, they are exhausted with laughter, and express their merriment and admiration in rounds of applause

"Is this like life? Change the scene to any real street;—to the Stock Exchange, or the City banker's; the merchant's counting-house, or even the tradesman's shop. See any one of these men fall—the more suddenly, and the nearer the zenith of his pride and riches, the better. What a wild hallo is raised over his prostrate carcase by the shouting mob; how they whoop and yell as he lies humbled beneath them! Mark how eagerly they set upon him when he is down; and how they mock and deride him as he slinks away. Why, it is the pantomime to the very letter." ¶B/P

—unreality relished: "This particular public have inherently a great pleasure in the contemplation of physical difficulties overcome; mainly, as I take it, because the lives of a large majority of them are exceedingly monotonous and real, and further, are a struggle against continual difficulties, and further still, because anything in the form of

accidental injury, or any kind of illness or disability is so very serious in their own sphere.

"I will explain this seeming paradox of mine. Take the case of a Christmas Pantomime. Surely nobody supposes that the young mother in the pit who falls into fits of laughter when the baby is boiled or sat upon, would be at all diverted by such an occurrence off the stage. Nor is the decent workman in the gallery, who is transported beyond the ignorant present by the delight with which he sees a stout gentleman pushed out of a two pair of stairs window, to be slandered by the suspicion that he would be in the least entertained by such a spectacle in any street in London, Paris, or New York.

"It always appears to me that the secret of this enjoyment lies in the temporary superiority to the common hazards and mischances of life; in seeing casualties, attended when they really occur with bodily and mental suffering, tears, and poverty, happen through a very rough sort of poetry without the least harm being done to any one—the pretence of distress in a pantomime being so broadly humorous as to be no pretence at all.

"Much as in the comic fiction I can understand the mother with a very vulnerable baby at home, greatly relishing the invulnerable baby on the stage, so in the Cremorne reality I can understand the mason who is always liable to fall off a scaffold in his working jacket and to be carried to the hospital, having an infinite admiration of the radiant personage in spangles who goes into the clouds upon a bull, or upside down, and who, he takes it for granted—not reflecting upon the thing—has, by uncommon skill and dexterity, conquered such mischances as those to which he and his acquaintance are continually exposed." ¶RP/LA

See also Shakespeare—*and the Pantomime;* S:Christmas—*in a cathedral town; and* IG:Politics—*Electioneering; and —Parliamentary—opening, —atmosphere, and —party discipline*

Poet and Poetry

—*accidental:* "'In time I were able to keep [my father, said Joe Gargery], and I kep him till he went off in a purple leptic fit. And it were my intentions to have had put upon his tombstone that Whatsume'er the failings on his part, Remember reader he were that good in his hart.'

"Joe recited this couplet with such manifest pride and careful perspicuity, that I asked him if he had made it himself.

"'I made it,' said Joe, 'my own self. I made it in a moment. It was like striking out a horseshoe complete, in a single blow. I never was so much surprised in all my life—couldn't credit my own ed—to tell you the truth, hardly believed it were my own ed. As I was saying, Pip, it were my intentions to have had it cut over him; but poetry costs money, cut it how you will, small or large, and it were not done." GE 7

—*broadly defined:* "'Miss Tox, Paul [said Louisa Chick] . . . has been working at a little gift for Fanny, which I promised to present. It is only a pin-cushion for the toilette table, Paul, but I do say, and will say, and must say, that Miss Tox has very prettily adapted the sentiment to the occasion. I call "Welcome little Dombey" Poetry, myself!'" DS 1

—*commercial:* "'Ask the perfumers, ask the blacking-makers, ask the hatters, ask the old lottery-office keepers—ask any man among 'em what my poetry has done for him, and mark my words, he blesses the name of Slum.'" OCS 28

—*convivial context:* "'We'll devote the evening, brother,' exclaimed Wegg, 'to prosecute our friendly move. And arterwards, crushing a flowing wine-cup—which I allude to brewing rum-and-water—we'll pledge one another. For what says the Poet?

"And you needn't, Mr Venus, be your
 black bottle,
For surely I'll be mine,
And we'll take a glass with a slice of
 lemon in it to which you're partial,
For auld lang syne."'" OMF iii 6

—*an effusion:* "'Mrs Leo Hunter . . . doats on poetry, sir. She adores it. I may say that her whole soul and mind are wound up, and entwined with it. She has produced some delightful pieces, herself, sir. You may have met with her "Ode to an Expiring Frog," sir.'

"'I don't think I have,' said Mr Pickwick.

"'You astonish me, sir,' said Mr Leo Hunter. 'It created an immense sensation. It was signed with an "L" and eight stars, and appeared originally in a Lady's Magazine. It commenced

"*Can I view thee panting, lying
On thy stomach, without sighing;*

Can I unmoved see thee dying
On a log,
Expiring frog!"'

"'Beautiful!' said Mr Pickwick.

"'Fine,' said Mr Leo Hunter, 'so simple.'

"'Very,' said Mr Pickwick.

"'The next verse is still more touching. Shall I repeat it?'

"'If you please,' said Mr Pickwick.

"'It runs thus,' said the grave man, still more gravely.

"Say, have fiends in shape of boys,
With wild halloo, and brutal noise,
Hunted thee from marshy joys,
With a dog,
Expiring frog!"'

"'Finely expressed,' said Mr Pickwick." PP 15

—epic: "'Epic poem—ten thousand lines—revolution of July—composed it on the spot—*Mars* by day, *Apollo* by night—bang the field-piece, twang the lyre.'

"'You were present at that glorious scene, sir?' said Mr Snodgrass.

"'Present! think I was;* fired a musket—fired with an idea—rushed into wine shop—wrote it down—back again—whiz, bang—another idea—wine shop again—pen and ink—back again—cut and slash—noble time, sir.'" PP 2

**Mr Jingle refers to the 1830 Paris Revolution, but he is speaking in 1827.*

—foibles: "No claim can be set up for [Adelaide Procter], thank God! to the possession of any of the conventional poetical qualities. She never by any means held the opinion that she was among the greatest of human beings; she never suspected the existence of a conspiracy on the part of mankind against her; she never recognised in her best friends her worst enemies; she never cultivated the luxury of being misunderstood and unappreciated; she would far rather have died without seeing a line of her composition in print, than that I should have maundered about her, here, as 'the Poet,' or 'the Poetess.'" AYR/P

—from the graveyard: (by Gabriel Grub, gravedigger)

Brave lodgings for one, brave lodgings for one,
A few feet of cold earth, when life is done;
A stone at the head, a stone at the feet,
A rich, juicy meal for the worms to eat;
Rank grass over head, and damp clay around,
Brave lodgings for one, these, in holy ground! PP 29

—lodger: "[Mr Minns looked] forward to his visit on the following Sunday, with the feelings of a penniless poet to the weekly visit of his Scotch landlady." SB/MC

—mortal effect: "'It took a deal o' poetry to kill the hairdresser, and some people say arter all that it was more the gin and water as caused him to be run over; p'r'aps it was a little o' both, and came o' mixing the two.'" MHC 5

—in peroration: "'I *could* end with a werse; what do you think?'

"'I don't like it, Sam,' rejoined Mr Weller. 'I never know'd a respectable coachman as wrote poetry, 'cept one, as made an affectin' copy o' werses the night afore he wos hung for a highway robbery; and *he* wos only a Cambervell man, so even that's no rule.'

"But Sam was not to be dissuaded from the poetical idea that occurred to him, so he signed the letter,

Your love-sick
Pickwick.'"

PP 33

—and prose: "He was often near to something or other very clever, by his own account: this lumbering, slow, honest John; this John so heavy, but so light of spirit; so rough upon the surface, but so gentle at the core; so dull without, so quick within; so stolid, but so good! Oh Mother Nature, give thy children the true poetry of heart that hid itself in this poor Carrier's breast—he was but a Carrier by the way—and we can bear to have them talking prose, and leading lives of prose; and bear to bless thee for their company!" CH 1

—sonnet "A young gentleman with a sonnet, the retention of which for two years had enfeebled his mind and undermined his knees, got the sonnet into the Dullborough Warden and gained flesh." UT/DT

—three opinions

—Lamps: "Oh! I'll tell of you, father, as the gentleman has asked about you. He is a poet, Sir.'

"'I shouldn't wish the gentleman, my dear,' observed Lamps, for the moment turning grave, 'to carry away that opinion of your father, because it might look as if I was given to asking the stars in a mollon-colly manner what they was up to. Which I wouldn't at once waste the time, and take the liberty, my dear.'" CS/MJ 1

—Tony Weller: "'Poetry's unnat'ral; no man ever talked poetry 'cept a beadle on boxin' day, or Warren's blackin', or Rowland's oil, or some o' them low fellows; never you let yourself down to talk poetry, my boy.'" PP 33 *And see —in peroration*

—Silas Wegg: "'Was you thinking at all of poetry?' Mr Wegg inquired, musing.

"'Would it come dearer?' Mr Boffin asked.

"'It would come dearer,' Mr Wegg returned. 'For when a person comes to grind off poetry night after night, it is but right he should expect to be paid for its weakening effect on his mind.'" OMF i 5

And see A:Funeral—*Nell's, in blank verse; and* YG/V

Press

—in a country inn: "Pretending to read a smeary newspaper long out of date, which had nothing half so legible in its local news, as the foreign matter of coffee, pickles, fish-sauces, gravy, melted butter, and wine, with which it was sprinkled all over, as if it had taken the measles in a highly irregular form . . . . " GE 43

—criticism: "Any individual or body of individuals made the subject of uncomplimentary newspaper remark *is* ill-used as a matter of course. It never was otherwise. The precedents are numerous." E/TF

—enemy of tyrants: "The tyrants and humbugs . . . would gladly pension off all the printers throughout the world and have done with them; but let the friends of education and progress unite in pensioning off the worn out and afflicted printers, and the remainder would ultimately press the tyrants and humbugs off the face of the earth. For if ever they were to be pressed out, the printer's is the press that will do it. The printer is the friend of intelligence, of thought; he is the friend of liberty, of freedom, of law; indeed, the printer is the friend of every man who is the friend of order; the friend of every man who can read. Of all inventions, of all the discoveries in science or art, of all the great results in the wonderful progress of mechanical energy and skill, the printer is the only product of civilization necessary to the existence of free man." S/PP2

—history: "It was no more than two hundred and fifty years since the first idea of a newspaper was conceived in this island, to stimulate the people to resist the Spanish Armada.* It was not more than two hundred years since the first notion of a regular newspaper, in anything like its present form, was reduced to practice. One hundred and fifty years ago there did not appear to have been a single daily paper in England, and ten years later only one." S/N1

**KJF p102n: "English Mercurie, 1588: it had been shown to be an eighteenth century forgery, in 1839."*

—importance of reporters: "I would venture to remind you, if I delicately may, in the august presence of members of Parliament, how much we, the public, owe to the reporters, if it were only for their skill in the two great successes of condensation and rejection. Conceive what our sufferings, under an Imperial Parliament however popularly constituted, under however glorious a constitution, would be if the reporters could not skip." S/N5

For CD's own reporting experience, see CD: Young reporter

—liberty of: "[The public] has been a maze of doubt and confusion, for the last three or four years, on that vexed question, the Liberty of the Press. It has been told by Noble Lords that the said Liberty is vastly inconvenient. No doubt it is. No doubt all Liberty is—to some people. Light is highly inconvenient to such as have their sufficient reasons for preferring darkness; and soap and water is observed to be a particular inconvenience to those who would rather be dirty than clean." HW/OP

—mission: "The intimate connexion between the facts and realities of the time, and the means by which we aim, in Household Words, to soften what is hard in them, to exalt what is held in little consideration, and to show the latent hope there is in what may seem unpromising, needs not to be pointed out . . . . As another humble means of enabling those who accept us for their friend, to bear the world's rough-cast events to the anvil of courageous duty, and there beat them into shape, we enter on the project, and confide in its success." HW/HN

—in New York (actual): "No amusements? . . . What are the fifty newspapers, which those precocious urchins are bawling down the street, and which are kept filed within, what are they but amusements? Not vapid waterish amusements, but good strong stuff; dealing in round abuse and blackguard names; pulling off the roofs of private houses, as the Halting Devil did in Spain; pimping and pandering for all degrees of vicious taste, and gorging with coined lies the

most voracious maw; imputing to every man in public life the coarsest and the vilest motives; scaring away from the stabbed and prostrate body-politic, every Samaritan of clear conscience and good deeds; and setting on, with yell and whistle and the clapping of foul hands, the vilest vermin and worst birds of prey.—No amusements!" AN 6

—in New York (fictional): "'Here's this morning's New York Sewer!' cried [a newsboy]. 'Here's this morning's New York Stabber! Here's the New York Family Spy! Here's the New York Private Listener! Here's the New York Peeper! Here's the New York Plunderer! Here's the New York Keyhole Reporter! Here's the New York Rowdy Journal! Here's all the New York papers!

"'Here's full particulars of the patriotic loco-foco movement yesterday, in which the whigs was so chawed up; and the last Alabama gouging case; and the interesting Arkansas dooel with Bowie knives; and all the Political, Commercial, and Fashionable News. Here they are! Here they are! Here's the papers, here's the papers!'

"'Here's the Sewer!' cried another. 'Here's the New York Sewer! Here's some of the twelfth thousand of today's Sewer, with the best accounts of the markets, and all the shipping news, and four whole columns of country correspondence, and a full account of the Ball at Mrs White's last night, where all the beauty and fashion of New York was assembled; with the Sewer's own particulars of the private lives of all the ladies that was there!

"'Here's the Sewer! Here's some of the twelfth thousand of the New York Sewer! Here's the Sewer's exposure of the Wall Street Gang, and the Sewer's exposure of the Washington Gang, and the Sewer's exclusive account of a flagrant act of dishonesty committed by the Secretary of State when he was eight years old; now communicated, at a great expense, by his own nurse.

"'Here's the Sewer! Here's the New York Sewer, in its twelfth thousand, with a whole column of New Yorkers to be shown up, and all their names printed! Here's the Sewer's article upon the Judge that tried him, day afore yesterday, for libel, and the Sewer's tribute to the independent Jury that didn't convict him, and the Sewer's account of what they might have expected if they had!

"'Here's the Sewer, here's the Sewer! Here's the wide-awake Sewer; always on the lookout; the leading Journal of the United States, now in its twelfth thousand, and still a-printing off. Here's the New York Sewer!'

"'It is in such enlightened means,' said a voice almost in Martin's ear, 'that the bubbling passions of my country find a vent.'" ¶MC 16

"'Pray,' said Martin, after some hesitation, 'may I venture to ask, with reference to a case I observe in this paper of yours, whether the Popular Instructor often deals in—I am at a loss to express it without giving you offence—in forgery? In forged letters, for instance,' he pursued, for the Colonel [Diver] was perfectly calm and quite at his ease, 'solemnly purporting to have been written at recent periods by living men?'

"'Well, sir!' replied the colonel. 'It does, now and then.'

"'And the popular instructed; what do they do?' asked Martin.

"'Buy 'em,' said the colonel . . . 'Buy 'em by hundreds of thousands,' resumed the colonel. 'We are a smart people here, and can appreciate smartness.'

"'Is smartness American for forgery?' asked Martin.

"'Well!' said the colonel, 'I expect it's American for a good many things that you call by other names. But you can't help yourselves in Europe. We can.' . . . At all events, whatever name we choose to employ . . . I suppose the art of forgery was not invented here, sir?'" MC 16

—newspaper

—classified notices: " . . . there pass by fleets of ships bound to all parts of the earth, all going to have immediate dispatch, all with a little more stowage for a little more cargo, and a few more berths for a few more passengers, that they all have the most spacious cabins, all teak-built and copper-fastened, all carrying surgeons of experience, and having elevated space between decks—all, in short, A.1. at Lloyd's and everywhere else.

" . . . I find I am offered every kind of house, lodging, clerk, servant, situation, that I can possibly or impossibly want, with everything to eat, drink, wear, and use. I learned to my intense gratification—for I begin to have some doubts upon the subject myself—that I need never grow old; that I may preserve the juvenile bloom of my complexion to any period of life; that I need never more have any grey hairs; that if I ever cough again it is entirely my own fault; that I need never be ill of any complaint; that if I want brown cod liver oil I know where to find it; that if I want a Turkish bath I know where to get it; and that if I want an income of seven pounds a week for life for 2*s.* 6*d.* down, I have only to send the postage stamps and there it is." S/N4

—foreign news: " . . . this one glance over my newsman's shoulder gives me the comprehensive knowledge of what is going on over the great continent of Europe, over the great continent of America to boot, to say nothing of such little-known geographical regions as India and China; for Reuter's telegrams come straight to me . . . . All these topics are ready sifted for me in sharp, terse, pointed, leading articles. In a word, every morning before my breakfast is done, I can put a girdle round the earth, like *Ariel,* and come up to the time of high water at London Bridge, and the arrival of the Japanese ambassadors." S/N4

—government news: " . . . my eye rests on the Imperial Parliament, and there I read among other stereotyped passages, which I am always sure to find there, how the hon. member for somewhere, asked the Right hon. gentleman the Secretary of State for the Home Department, whether he had any intelligence to communicate respecting that last outrage, or that last railway accident, or that last mine explosion, or that last case of police justice; and I always read how the Right hon. gentleman said in reply, rather magnificently, that 'he knew nothing whatever about the matter except what he had read in the newspapers'. Which stereotyped reply I observe to be received universally with a 'Hear, hear', which is, to me, perfectly incomprehensible; because I can read such things in a paper without drawing a salary for doing it." S/N4

—large: "The daily papers are so very large in proportion to [Bart Smallweed], shorn of his hat, that when he holds up the Times to run his eye over the columns, he seems to have retired for the night, and to have disappeared under the bed-clothes." BH 20

—personals: "Well, the first thing that occurs to me in taking up the newspaper every morning is that we are born every day, that every day we—or at least some of us—are married, and that every day we die. Consequently my first glimpse over the newsman's shoulder instructs me that Atkins is born, Catkins is married, and that Datkins is dead. But one of the most remarkable circumstances connected with the sheet is, that Atkin's [*sic.*] infancy seems to be surpringly brief, for I immediately discover in the very next column that he has grown up to be seventeen years old, and has run away from his mother.

"At least I see that, 'if W. A.', which stands for William Atkins, 'who is seventeen years old, in a dress suit, with one front tooth missing, will only return to his disconsolate parents, everything will be arranged to the satisfaction of everyone'. I am afraid he never will return, for the reason, amongst others perhaps, that if he had ever meant to come back he never would have gone away. Immediately below, I find a mysterious character, in a position of such mysterious difficulty, that it is only to be expressed by several disjointed letters, several figures, several stars, and some such adjuration as, 'Amelia write instantly. Destruction, all is lost! The canary bird has made over his property to his uncle. The elephant is on the wing.'" ¶S/N4

—police intelligence: ". . . that teaches me that if I want to bite off a woman's nose I can do it very cheap, but if I want surreptitiously to make off with the salted nose of a pig or calf from a shop window, it will cost me exceedingly dear. And, also, that if I allow myself to be betrayed into the folly, say, of killing an inoffensive tradesman on his own doorstep, that little act of indiscretion will not in the least interfere with my triumphant production of testimonials to character as a most amiable young man, particularly to be esteemed in all respects, but above all things remarkable for the singular inoffensiveness of my character and disposition." S/N4

—at the post-office: "It was then just drizzling newspapers. The great window . . . being thrown open, the first black fringe of a thunder-cloud of newspapers impending over the Post-Office was discharging itself fitfully—now in large drops, now in little; now in sudden plumps, now stopping altogether. By degrees it began to rain hard; by fast degrees the storm came on harder and harder, until it blew, rained, hailed, snowed, newspapers. A fountain of newspapers played in at the window. Waterspouts of newspapers broke from enormous sacks, and engulphed the men inside. A prodigious main of newspapers, at the Newspaper River Head, seemed to be turned on, threatening destruction to the

miserable Post-Office.

"The Post-Office was so full already, that the window foamed at the mouth with newspapers. Newspapers flew out like froth, and wre tumbled in again by the by-standers. All the boys in London seemed to have gone mad, and to be besieging the Post-Office with newspapers. Now and then there was a girl; now and then a woman; now and then a weak old man: but as the minute hand of the clock crept near to six, such a torrent of boys, and such a torrent of newspapers came tumbling in together pell-mell, head over heels, one above another, that the giddy head looking on chiefly wondered why the boys springing over one another's heads, and flying the garter into the Post-Office with the enthusiasm of the corps of acrobats at **M. Franconi**'s, didn't post themselves nightly, along with the newspapers, and get delivered all the world.

"Suddenly it struck six. Shut Sesame! Perfectly still weather. Nobody there. No token of the late storm—Not a soul, too late!

"But what a chaos within! Men up to their knees in newspapers on great platforms; men gardening among newspapers with rakes; men digging and delving among newspapers as if a new description of rock had been blasted into those fragments; men going up and down a gigantic trap—an ascending and descending-room worked by a steam engine—still taking with them nothing but newspapers!

"All the history of the time, all the chronicled births, deaths, and marriages, all the crimes, all the accidents, all the vanities, all the changes, all the realities, of all the civilised earth, heaped up, parcelled out, carried about, knocked down, cut, shuffled, dealt, played, gathered up again, and passed from hand to hand, in an apparently interminable and hopeless confusion, but really in a system of admirable order, certainty, and simplicity, pursued six nights every week, all through the rolling year! Which of us, after this, shall find fault with the rather more extensive system of good and evil, when we don't quite understand it at a glance; or set the stars right in their spheres?" ¶HWC/V

—theatre: " . . . there, perhaps, I read the gratifying announcement, which is no news to anyone, that the true spirit of a picturesque artist has again been displayed by Mr **Benjamin Webster**, and that another most subtle and delicate piece of genuine comedy has bgeen achieved by my friend Mr **Alfred Wigan**." S/N4

—periodical, abandoned: "The first chapter of this tale appeared in the fourth number of [MHC], when I had already been made uneasy by the desultory character of that work, and when I believe, my readers had thoroughly participated in the feeling . . . .

"When the story was finished, that it might be freed from the incumbrance of associations and interruptions with which it had no kind of concern, I caused the few sheets of [MHC],which had been printed in connection with it, to be cancelled; and . . . they became the property of the trunkmaker and the butter-man. I was especially unwilling, I confess, to enrich those respectable trades with the opening paper of the abandoned design, in which [the protagonist] described himself and his manner of life. Though I now affect to make the confession philosophically, as referring to a bygone emotion, I am conscious that my pen winces a little even while I write these words. But it was done, and wisely done, and [MHC], as originally constructed, became one of the lost books of the earth—which, we all know, are far more precious than any that can be read for love or money." OCS pref.

—its power: "The beadle is very careful that two gentlemen not very neat about the cuffs and buttons (for whose accommodation he has provided a special little table near the Coroner, in the Harmonic Meeting Room) should see all that is to be seen. For they are the public chroniclers of such inquiries, by the line; and he is not superior to the universal human infirmity, but hopes to read in print what 'Mooney, the active and intelligent beadle of the district,' said and did; and even aspires to see the name of Mooney as familiarly and patronisingly mentioned as the name of the Hangman is, according to the latest examples." BH 11

"I now give 'The Press', that wonderful lever **Archimedes** wished for, and which *has* moved the world! which has impelled it onward in the path of knowledge, of mercy, and of human improvement so far that nothing in the world can ever roll it back! The mass of the people, said **Dr Johnson** very truly, in any country where printing is unknown, must be barbarous; and **Sir Thomas More** . . . so clearly saw into futurity, and descried from afar off the stupendous influence of the press, that he went out of his way to set up a printing-press in Utopia, knowing that without it even the people of that fancied land would not bear competition in the course of years with the real nations of the earth." S/PP1

"I know that to some its power is obnoxious . . . . But as we have means of judging for ourselves every morning and evening of the newspaper literature, it is satisfactory to know that there never was a righteous cause but the same men have hated it; and there never was a disappointed man or a discontented patriot, anxious to pass upon a people determined not to recognize him as such, but he has bemoaned the privileges of the press in the same crocodile's tears." S/PP 1

—*read aloud:* "A highly popular murder had been committed, and Mr Wopsle was imbrued in blood to the eyebrows. He gloated over every abhorrent adjective in the description, and identified himself with every witness at the Inquest. He faintly moaned, 'I am done for,' as the victim, and he barbarously bellowed, 'I'll serve you out,' as the murderer. He gave the medical testimony, in pointed imitation of our local practitioner; and he piped and shook, as the aged turnpike-keeper who had heard blows, to an extent so very paralytic as to suggest a doubt regarding the mental competency of that witness. The coroner, in Mr Wopsle's hands, became *Timon of Athens;* the beadle, *Coriolanus.* He enjoyed himself thoroughly, and we all enjoyed ourselves, and were delightfully comfortable. In this cozy state of mind we came to the verdict of Wilful Murder." GE 18

"Wemmick explained to me while the Aged got his spectacles, out, that this was according to custom, and that it gave the old gentleman infinite satisfaction to read the news aloud . . . .

"'Only tip him a nod every now and then when he looks off his paper,' said Wemmick, 'and he'll be as happy as a king. We are all attention, Aged One' . . . .

"The Aged's reading reminded me of the classes at Mr Wopsle's great-aunt's, with the pleasanter peculiarity that it seemed to come through a keyhole. As he wanted the candles close to him, and as he was always on the verge of putting either his head or the newspaper into them, he required as much watching as a powder-mill. But Wemmick was equally untiring and gentle in his vigilance, and the Aged read on, quite unconscious of his many rescues. Whenever he looked at us, we all expressed the greatest interest and amazement, and nodded until he resumed again." GE 37

—*source of information:* " . . . probably not one single individual in this great company has failed today to see a newspaper, or has failed today to hear something derived from a newspaper which was quite unknown to him or her yesterday. Of all those restless crowds that have this day thronged through the streets of this enormous city, the same may be said as the general gigantic rule. It may be said almost equally of the brightest and the dullest, the largest and the least provincial town in the empire; and this, observe, not only as to the active, the industrious, and the healthy among the population, but also to the bedridden, the idle, the blind, and the deaf and dumb." S/N5

—*strike imagined:* "Imagine all the morning trains waiting in vain for all the newspapers. Imagine all sorts and conditions of men dying to know the shipping news, the commercial news, the legal news, the criminal news, the foreign news and domestic news—paralysis on all the provincial exchanges, the silence and desertion on the newsmen's exchange in London, the circulation of the blood of the country standing still, the clock of the world stopped! Why, even Mr **Reuter**, the great Reuter whom I am always glad to imagine slumbering at night by the side of Mrs Reuter, with a galvanic battery under the bolster, telegraph wires to the head of his bed, and an electric bell at each ear[:] even he would click and flash those wondrous dispatches of his to little purpose, if it were not for the humble, and by comparison, slow activity, which gathers up the stitches of the electric needle, and scatters them over the land." S/N5

—*yellow:* "Some tillers of the field, into which we now come, have been before us, and some are here whose high usefulness we readily acknowledge, and whose company it is an honour to join. But there are others here—Bastards of the Mountain, draggled fringe on the Red Cap, Panders to the basest passions of the lowest natures—whose existence is a national reproach. And these we should consider it our highest service to displace." HW/PW

Rumour

—*current sensation:* "Thus, like the tides on which it had been borne to the knowledge of men, the Harmon Murder—as it came to be popularly called—went up and down, and ebbed and flowed, now in the town, now in the country, now among palaces, now among hovels, now among lords and ladies and gentlefolks, now among labourers and hammerers and ballast-heavers, until at last, after a long interval of slack water, it got out to sea and drifted away." OMF i 3

—*in emulation:* "And not the least amazing circumstance connected with [Lady Dedlock's] being vaguely the town talk, is, that people hovering on the confines of Mr Sladdery's high connexion, people who know nothing and ever did know nothing about her, think it essential to their reputation to pretend that she is their topic too; and to retail her at second-hand with the last new word and the last new manner, and the last new drawl, and the last new polite indifference, and all the rest of it, all at second-hand but considered equal to new, in inferior systems and to fainter stars. If there be any man of letters, art, or science among these little dealers, how noble in him to support the feeble sisters on such majestic crutches!" BH 58

—*inaccurate:* " . . . your popular rumour, unlike the rolling stone of the proverb, is one which gathers a deal of moss in its wanderings up and down . . . . " OCS 48

—*mode of transmission:* "Rumour, always flying, bat-like, about Cook's Court, and skimming in and out at everybody's windows, does say that Mrs Snagsby is jealous and inquisitive . . . . " BH 10

"'There is one of those odd impressions in my house, which do mysteriously get into houses sometimes, which nobody seems to have picked up in a distant form from anybody, and yet which everybody seems to have got hold of loosely from somebody and let go again . . . . '" LD i 27

"By what means the news that there had been a quarrel between the two young men overnight, involving even some kind of onslaught by Mr Neville upon Edwin Drood, got into Miss Twinkleton's establishment before breakfast, it is impossible to say. Whether it was brought in by the birds of the air, or came blowing in with the very air itself, when the casement windows were set open; whether the baker brought it kneaded into the bread, or the milkman delivered it as part of the adulteration of his milk; or the housemaids, beating the dust out of their mats against the gateposts, received it in exchange deposited on the mats by the town atmosphere; certain it is that the news permeated every gable of the old building before Miss Twinkleton was down. . . . " MED 9

—*suppressing it:* "'You know what Rumour, is Mr Sampson [said Mr Slinkton]. I never repeat what I hear; it is the only way of paring the nails and shaving the head of Rumour.'" HD 2

And see F:Blacks—*vague rumour*

Secret

—*depositories:* "As [Clennam] went along, upon a dreary night, the dim streets by which he went seemed all depositories of oppressive secrets. The deserted counting-houses, with their secrets of books and papers locked up in chests and safes; the banking houses, with their secrets of strong rooms and wells, the keys of which were in a very few secret pockets and a very few secret breasts; the secrets of all the dispersed grinders in the vast mill, among whom there were doubtless plunderers, forgers, and trust-betrayers of many sorts, whom the light of any day that dawned might reveal; he could have fancied that these things, in hiding, imparted a heaviness to the air. The shadow thickening and thickening as he approached its source, he thought of the secrets of the lonely church-vaults, where the people who had hoarded and secreted in iron coffers were in their turn similarly hoarded, not yet at rest from doing harm; and then of the secrets of the river, as it rolled its turbid tide between two frowning wildernesses of secrets, extending, thick and dense, for many miles, and warding off the free air and the free country, swept by winds and wings of birds.

"The shadow still darkening as he drew near the house, the melancholy room which his father had once occupied, haunted by the appealing face he had himself seen fade away with him when there was no other watcher by the bed, arose before his mind. Its close air was secret. The gloom, and must, and dust of the whole tenement, were secret. At the heart of it his mother presided, inflexible of face, indomitable of will, firmly holding all the secrets of her own and his father's life, and austerely opposing herself, front to front, to the great final secret of all life." LD ii 10

—*longevity:* "'Such matters keep well, and, like good wine, often double their value in course of time,' answered the matron [Mrs

Bumble], still preserving the resolute indifference she had assumed. 'As to lying dead, there are those who will lie dead for twelve thousand years to come, or twelve million, for anything you or I know, who will tell strange tales at last!'" OT 38

—*protected:* "STRANGE GENTLEMAN. Can —can—you be secret, Boots?

"TOM [SPARKS]. That depends entirely on accompanying circumstances;—see the point?

"S. G. [*abbrev provided*]. I think I comprehend your meaning, Boots. You insinuate that you could be secret (*putting his hand in his pocket*) if you had—five shillings, for instance—isn't that it, Boots?

"TOM. That's the line o' argument I should take up; but that ain't exactly my meaning.

"S. G. No!

"TOM. No. A secret's a thing as is always a rising to one's lips. It requires an astonishing weight to keep one on 'em down.

"S. G. Ah!

"'TOM. Yes; I don't think I could keep one snug—reg'lar snug, you know—

"S. G. Yes, regularly snug, of course.

"TOM. If it had a less weight atop on it than ten shillin's.

"S. G. You don't think three half-crowns would do it?

"TOM. It might, I won't say it wouldn't, but I couldn't warrant it.

"S. G. You could the other!

"TOM. Yes.

"S. G. Then there it is." P/SG I i

—*secretiveness and candour:* "'I suppose,' said Mr Toodle, relishing his meal infinitely, 'as our Biler is a doin' now about, as well as a boy *can* do, eh, Polly!'

"'Oh! he's a doing beautiful!' responded Polly.

"'He an't got to be at all secret-like—has he, Polly?' inquired Mr Toodle.

"'No!' said Mrs Toodle, plumply . . . .

"'You see, my boys and gals,' said Mr Toodle, looking round upon his family, 'wotever you're up to in a honest way, it's my opinion as you can't do better than be open. If you find yourselves in cuttings or in tunnels, don't you play no secret games. Keep your whistles going, and let's know where you are.'" DS 38

—*uncomfortable:* "To know that he is always keeping a secret from her; that he has, under all circumstances, to conceal and hold fast a tender double tooth, which her sharpness is ever ready to twist out of his head; gives Mr Snagsby, in her dentistical presence, much of the air of a dog, who has a reservation from his master, and will look anywhere rather than meet his eye." BH 25

See Nadgett MC, *who "was born to be a secret," and* Tulkinghorn BH, *"a great reservoir of confidences."*

Shakespeare

—*absence of leg:* "'Shakspeare's an infernal humbug, Pip! [quoting a Viscount] What's the good of Shakspeare, Pip? I never read him. What the devil is it all about, Pip? There's a lot of feet in Shakspeare's verse, but there ain't any legs worth mentioning in Shakspeare's plays, are there, Pip? *Juliet, Desdemona, Lady Macbeth,* and all the rest of 'em, whatever their names are, might as well have no legs at all, for anything the audience know about it, Pip. Why, in that respect they're all Miss **Biffin**s to the audience, Pip. I'll tell you what it is. What the people call dramatic poetry is a collection of sermons. Do I go to the theatre to be lectured? No, Pip. If I wanted that, I'd go to church. What's the legitimate object of the drama, Pip? Human nature. What are legs? Human nature. Then let us have plenty of leg pieces, Pip, and I'll stand by you, my buck!'" MC 28

—*analyzed:* "[Curdle] had likewise proved, that by altering the received mode of punctuation, any one of Shakespeare's plays could be made quite different, and the sense completely changed; it is needless to say, therefore, that he was a great critic, and a very profound and most original thinker." NN 24

—*cited to praise:* "'Sir [said Tigg], if there is a man on earth whom a gentleman would feel proud and honoured to be mistaken for, that man is my friend Slyme. For he is, without an exception, the highest-minded, the most independent-spirited, most original, spiritual, classical, talented, the most thoroughly Shakespearian, if not **Milton**ic, and at the same time the most disgustingly-unappreciated dog I know.'" MC 4

—*commercial:* "An Immortal Somebody was wanted in Dullborough, to dimple for a day the stagnant face of the waters; he was rather wanted by Dullborough generally, and much wanted by the principal hotel-keeper . . . it is hardly necessary to record that Dullborough did what ever man does when he wants to write a book or deliver a lecture, and is provided with all the materials except a subject. It fell back upon Shakespeare.

"No sooner was it resolved to celebrate Shakespeare's birthday in Dullborough, than the popularity of the immortal bard became surprising. You might have supposed the first edition of his works to have been published last week, and enthusiastic Dullborough to have got half through them. (I doubt, by the way, whether it had ever done half that, but this is a private opinion.)

"Portraits of Shakespeare broke out in the bookshop windows, and our principal artist painted a large original portrait in oils for the decoration of the dining-room. It was not in the least like any of the other portraits, and was exceedingly admired, the head being much swollen.

"At the Institution, the Debating Society discussed the new question, Was there sufficient ground for supposing that the Immortal Shakespeare ever stole deer? This was indignantly decided by an overwhelming majority in the negative; indeed, there was but one vote on the Poaching side, and that was the vote of the orator who had undertaken to advocate it, and who became quite an obnoxious character. . . . " ¶UT/DT

—in conversation: "'I'm always ill after Shakespeare,' said Mrs Wititterly. 'I scarcely exist the next day; I find the reaction so very great after a tragedy, my lord, and Shakespeare is such a delicious creature.'

"'Ye—es!' replied Lord Verisopht. 'He was a clayver man.'" NN 27

—in a dream: . . . I recollect [said Mrs Nickleby] that all night long I dreamt of nothing but a black gentleman, at full length, in plaster-of-Paris, with a lay down collar tied with two tassels, leaning against a post and thinking; and when I woke in the morning and described him to Mr Nickleby, he said it was Shakespeare just as he had been when he was alive, which was very curious indeed . . . I recollect I was in the family way with my son Nicholas at the time . . . it was quite a mercy . . . that my son didn't turn out to be a Shakspeare, and what a dreadful thing that would have been!'" NN 27

—the Fool in Lear: " . . . one of the most wonderful creations of Shakespeare's genius. The picture of his quick and pregnant sarcasm, of his loving devotion, of his acute sensibility, of his despairing mirth, of his heartbroken silence—contrasted with the rigid sublimity of *Lear's* suffering, with the huge desolation of *Lear's* sorrow, with the vast and outraged image of *Lear's* madness —is the noblest thought that ever entered into the heart and mind of man." E/RL

—Hamlet evoked: "The room Arthur Clennam's deceased father had occupied for business purposes, when he first remembered him, was so unaltered that he might have been imagined still to keep it invisibly . . . . His picture, dark and gloomy, earnestly speechless on the wall, with the eyes intently looking at his son as they had looked when life departed from them, seemed to urge him awfully to the task he had attempted; but as to any yielding on the part of his mother, he had now no hope, and as to any other means of setting his distrust at rest, he had abandoned hope a long time." LD i 5

—Hamlet's aunt: "[Mr Waterbrook] . . . presented me, with much ceremony, to a very awful lady in a black velvet dress, and a great black velvet hat, whom I remember as looking like a near relation of *Hamlet*'s—say his aunt . . . .

" . . . [she] had the family failing of indulging in soliloquy, and held forth in a desultory manner, by herself, on every topic that was introduced. These were few enough, to be sure; but as we always fell back upon Blood, she had as wide a field for abstract speculation as her nephew himself." DC 25

—life a dream: "'And in regard to the changes of human life [said Lord Feenix], and the extraordinary manner in which we are perpetually conducting ourselves, all I can say is, with my friend Shakespeare—man who wasn't for an age but for all time, and with whom my friend Gay is no doubt acquainted—that it's like the shadow of a dream.'" DS 61

—and Pantomime: "A gentleman, not altogether unknown as a dramatic poet, wrote thus a year or two ago—

> *'All the world's a stage*
> *And all the men and women merely players:'*

and we, tracking out his footsteps at the scarcely-worth-mentioning little distance of a few millions of leagues behind, venture to add, by way of new reading, that he meant a Pantomime, and that we are all actors in

The Pantomime of Life." B/P

—in pedagogy: "When Dora was very childish, and I would have infinitely preferred to humour her, I tried to be grave—and disconcerted her, and myself too. I talked to her on the subjects which occupied my thoughts; and I read Shakespeare to her—and fatigued her to the last degree. I accustomed myself to giving her, as it were quite casually, little scraps of useful information, or sound opinion—and she started from them when I let them off, as if they had been crackers.

"No matter how incidentally or naturally I endeavoured to form my little wife's mind, I could not help seeing that she always had an instinctive perception of what I was about, and became a prey to the keenest apprehensions. In particular, it was clear to me, that she thought Shakespeare a terrible fellow." ¶DC 48

—questionably quoted: "'Slyme's biographer, sir, whoever he may be, resumed the gentleman, 'must apply to me; or, if I am gone to that what's-his-name from which no thingumbob comes back,* he must apply to my executors for leave to search among my papers.'" MC 4

**The undiscovered country from whose bourn / no traveller returns:* Hamlet III i

—for a tourist: "'I find [said Mrs Wititterly] I take so much more interest in his plays, after having been to that dear little dull house he was born in! . . . I don't know how it is, but after you've seen the place and written your name in the little book, somehow or other you seem to be inspired; it kindles up quite a fire within one.'" NN 27

See also CD:Exploited

Smile

—counterproductive: "[Brass] had a cringing manner, but a very harsh voice; and his blandest smiles were so extremely forbidding that to have had his company under the least repulsive circumstances, one would have wished him to be out of temper that he might only scowl." OCS 11

—cruel: " . . . a smile that is only seen on cruel faces: a very faint smile, lifting the nostril, scarcely touching the lips, and not breaking away gradually, but instantly dismissed when done with . . . . " LD i 27

—cunning: "[Boffin's] very smile was cunning, as if he had been studying smiles among the portraits of his misers." OMF iii 5

—deceptive: "[Wemmick's] mouth was such a post-office of a mouth that he had a mechanical appearance of smiling. We had got to the top of Holborn Hill before I knew that it was merely a mechanical appearance, and that he was not smiling at all." GE 21

—at a good smell: " . . . Toby, putting a hand on each knee, bent down his nose to the basket, and took a long inspiration at the lid; the grin upon his withered face expanding in the process, as if he were inhaling laughing gas." C

—imbecile: "He was a weak-eyed young man, with the first faint streaks or early dawn of a grin on his countenance. It was mere imbecility; but Mrs Pipchin took it into her head that it was impudence, and made a snap at him directly." DS 11

—rare: "[Phil] was an impenetrable man . . . morose, even to the Chief, and never smiled, except at breaking-up, when in acknowledgment of the toast, 'Success to Phil! Hooray!' he would slowly carve a grin out of his wooden face, where it would remain until we were all gone." RP/OS

—sadistic: "Miss Wren had a reasonably good eye for smiles, being well accustomed to them on the part of her young friends [dolls], though their smiles mostly ran smaller than in nature. But she had never seen so singular a smile as that upon this lady [Sophronia Lammle]'s face. It twitched her nostrils open in a remarkable manner, and contracted her lips and eyebrows. It was a smile of enjoyment too, though of such a fierce kind that Miss Wren thought she would rather not enjoy herself than do it in that way." OMF iv 8

—slow: " . . . [Bunsby's] smile which had been at first but three specks—one at the right-hand corner of his mouth, and one at the corner of each eye—gradually overspread his whole face, and rippling up into his forehead, lifted the glazed hat . . . ." DS 15

—twilight: " . . . 'there are no people here just now with whom we care to associate.'

"'They have not enough heart,' said Edith [Granger], with a smile. The very twilight of a smile: so singularly were its light and darkness blended . . . a multitude of expressions, among which that of the twilight smile, without the smile itself, overshadowed all the rest . . . . " DS 21

—unaccustomed: "'Now, said Ralph, with a smile, which, in common with all other tokens of emotion, seemed to skulk under his face, rather than play boldly over it . . . ." DS 19

"'Six years old!' said Mr Dombey, settling his neckcloth—perhaps to hide an irrepressible smile that rather seemed to strike upon the surface of his face and glance away, as finding no resting-place, than to play there for an instant." DS 11

—*welcoming:* "There was no flour on Ruth [Pinch]'s hands when she received them in the triangular parlour, but there were pleasant smiles upon her face, and a crowd of welcomes shining out of every smile, and gleaming in her bright eyes." MC 39

—*wooden:* " . . . I observed that [Uriah Heep] had not such a thing as a smile about him, and that he could only widen his mouth and make two hard creases down his cheeks, one on each side, to stand for one." DC 16

Talk

—*abrupt:* "[Pancks] was a singular man in all respects; he might not have been quite in earnest, but that the short, hard, rapid manner in which he shot out these cinders of principles, as if it were done by mechanical revolvency, seemed irreconcilable with banter." LD i 13

—*authoress:* "There was the horrible Hominy, talking deep truths in a melodious snuffle, and pouring forth her mental endowments to such an extent that the Major's bitterest enemy, hearing her, would have forgiven him from the bottom of his heart . . . .

"It would be difficult to give an adequate idea of Mrs Hominy's freshness next day, or of the avidity with which she went headlong into moral philosophy, at breakfast . . . she quoted interminable passages from certain essays on government, written by herself . . . Martin quite settled it between himself and his conscience, that in any new settlement it would be absolutely necessary to have such a person knocked on the head for the general peace of society." MC 22

—*boasting:* "It does not follow in the case of such a person [as Jonas Chuzzlewit] that the more talkative he becomes, the more agreeable he is; on the contrary, his merits show to most advantage, perhaps, in silence. Having no means, as he thought, of putting himself on an equality with the rest, but by the assertion of that depth and sharpness on which he had been complimented, Jonas exhibited that faculty to the utmost; and was so deep and sharp that he lost himself in his own profundity, and cut his fingers with his own edge-tools." MC 28

—*enthusiastic:* " . . . the hall-door suddenly burst open, and the hall resounded with these words, uttered with the greatest vehemence and in a stentorian tone:

"'We have been misdirected, Jarndyce, by a most abandoned ruffian, who told us to take the turning to the right instead of to the left. He is the most intolerable scoundrel on the face of the earth. His father must have been a most consummate villain, ever to have such a son. I would have had that fellow shot without the least remorse!'

"'Did he do it on purpose?' Mr Jarndyce inquired.

"'I have not the slightest doubt that the scoundrel has passed his whole existence in misdirecting travellers!' returned the other. 'By my soul, I thought him the worst-looking dog I had ever beheld, when he was telling me to take the turning to the right. And yet I stood before that fellow face to face, and didn't knock his brains out!'

"'Teeth, you mean?' said Mr Jarndyce.

"'Ha, ha, ha!' laughed Mr Lawrence Boythorn, really making the whole house vibrate. 'What, you have not forgotten [that schooldays incident] yet! Ha, ha, ha!—And that was another most consummate vagabond! By my soul, the countenance of that fellow, when he was a boy, was the blackest image of perfidy, cowardice, and cruelty ever set up as a scarecrow in a field of scoundrels. If I were to meet that most unparalleled despot in the streets tomorrow, I would fell him like a rotten tree!'

"'I have no doubt of it,' said Mr Jarndyce. 'Now, will you come upstairs?'

"'By my soul, Jarndyce,' returned his guest, who seemed to refer to his watch, 'if you had been married, I would have turned back at the garden-gate, and gone away to the remotest summits of the Himalaya Mountains, sooner than I would have presented myself at this unseasonable hour.'

"'Not quite so far, I hope?' said Mr Jarndyce.

"'By my life and honour, yes!' cried the visitor. 'I wouldn't be guilty of the audacious insolence of keeping a lady of the house waiting all this time, for any earthly consideration. I would infinitely rather destroy myself—infinitely rather!'

"Talking thus, they went upstairs; and presently we heard him in his bedroom thundering 'Ha, ha, ha!' and again 'Ha, ha, ha!' until the flattest echo in the neighbourhood seemed to catch the contagion, and to laugh as enjoyingly as he did, or as we did when we heard him laugh." BH 9

—*enunciation:* "Both the [Cheeryble] brothers . . . had a very emphatic and earnest delivery; both had lost nearly the same teeth, which imparted the same peculiarity to their speech; and both spoke as if, besides possessing the utmost serenity of mind that the kindliest and most unsuspecting nature could bestow, they had, in collecting the plums from Fortune's choicest pudding, retained a few for present use, and kept them in their mouths." NN 35

—*"Freudian" slip:* "'But I have ever,' said Mr Pecksniff, 'sacrificed my children's happiness to my own—I mean my own happiness to my children's—and I will not begin to regulate my life by other rules of conduct now." MC 30

—*loquacity:* "After sundry accounts of himself, his family, his connexions, his friends, his jokes, his business, and his brothers (most talkative men have a great deal to say about their brothers), Mr Peter Magnus took a blue view of Mr Pickwick through his coloured spectacles . . . . " PP 22

—*magniloquence*

—*exemplified:* "'Under the impression . . . that your peregrinations in this metropolis have not as yet been extensive, and that you might have some difficulty in penetrating the arcana of the Modern Babylon in the direction of the City Road—in short,' said Mr Micawber, in another burst of confidence, 'that you might lose yourself—I shall be happy to call this evening, and instal you in the knowledge of the nearest way.'" DC 11 *"Yet I do fear thy nature; It is too full o' the milk of human kindness To catch the nearest way.* Macbeth I v

"'My dear Copperfield,' said Mr Micawber, putting out his hand, 'this is indeed a meeting which is calculated to impress the mind with a sense of the instability and uncertainty of all human—in short, it is a most extraordinary meeting. Walking along the street, reflecting upon the probability of something turning up (of which I am at present rather sanguine), I find a young but valued friend turn up, who is connected with the most eventful period of my life; I may say, with the turning-point of my existence. Copperfield, my dear fellow, how do you do?'" DC 17

"'I beg your pardon, Mr Traddles,' said Mr Micawber, with the old roll in his voice, as he checked himself in humming a soft tune. 'I was not aware that there was any individual, alien to this tenement, in your sanctum.'

"Mr Micawber slightly bowed to me, and pulled up his shirt-collar.

"'How do you do, Mr Micawber?' said I.

"'Sir,' said Mr Micawber, 'you are exceedingly obliging. I am *in statu quo.*'

"'And Mrs Micawber?' I pursued.

"'Sir,' said Mr Micawber, 'she is also, thank God, *in statu quo*'

"'And the children, Mr Micawber?'

"'Sir,' said Mr Micawber, 'I rejoice to reply that they are, likewise, in the enjoyment of salubrity.'" DC 27

—*to impress:* ". . . [Mr Pecksniff] was in the frequent habit of using any word that occurred to him as having a good sound, and rounding a sentence well, without much care for its meaning. And he did this so boldly, and in such an imposing manner, that he would sometimes stagger the wisest people with his eloquence, and make them gasp again.

"His enemies asserted, by the way, that a strong trustfulness in sounds and forms was the master-key to Mr. Pecksniff's character." MC 2

—*poetic:* "' . . . there an't a 'ousekeeper, no nor a lodger in our street, don't know that I lost money by that man, and by his guzzlings and his muzzlings'—Mrs MacStinger used the last word for the joint sake of alliteration [*sic.;* assonance?] and aggravation, rather than for the expression of any idea . . . . '" DS 39

—*Parliamentary:* "It is my impression that much of its [autumn London's] serene and peaceful character is attributable to the absence of customary Talk. How do I know but there may be subtle influences in Talk, to vex the souls of men who don't hear it? How do I know but that Talk, five, ten, twenty miles off, may get into the air and disagree with me?

"If I rise from my bed, vaguely troubled and wearied and sick of my life, in the session of Parliament, who shall say that my noble friend, my right reverend friend, my right honourable friend, my honourable friend, my honourable and learned friend, or my honourable and gallant friend, may not be responsible for that effect upon my nervous system?

"Too much Ozone in the air, I am informed and fully believe (though I have no idea what it is), would affect me in a marvellously disagreeable way; why may not too much Talk? I don't see or hear the Ozone; I don't see or hear the Talk.

"And there is so much Talk; so much too much; such loud cry, and such scant supply of wool; such a deal of fleecing, and so little fleece! Hence, in the Arcadian season, I find it a delicious triumph to walk down to deserted Westminster, and see the Courts shut up; to walk a little further and see the Two Houses shut up; to stand in the Abbey Yard . . . and gloat upon the ruins of Talk . . . my grateful heart expands with the consciousness that there is no adjourned Debate, no ministerial explanation, nobody to give notice of intention to ask the noble Lord at the head of her Majesty's Government five-and-twenty bootless questions in one, no term time with legal argument, no Nisi Prius with eloquent appeal to British Jury; that the air will to-morrow, and to-morrow, and to-morrow, remain untroubled by this superabundant generating of Talk.

"In a minor degree it is a delicious triumph to me to go into the club, and see the carpets up, and the Bores and the other dust dispersed to the four winds. Again New Zealander-like, I stand on the cold hearth, and say in the solitude, 'Here I watched Bore A 1, with voice always mysteriously low and head always mysteriously drooped, whispering political secrets into the ears of Adam's confiding children. Accursed be his memory for ever and a day!'" ¶UT/AL

—*silence:* "'Sam, be quiet,' said Mr Pickwick.

"'Dumb as a drum vith a hole in it, sir,' replied Sam." PP 25

—*words*

—*dictionary:* "'What a useful work a Dictionary is [cried Mrs Markleham]! What a necessary work! The meanings of words! Without Doctor Johnson, or somebody of that sort, we might have been at this present moment calling an Italian-iron a bedstead.'" DC 45

—*earnest:* "'A word in earnest [said John Jarndyce] is as good as a speech.'" BH 6

—*the English language:* "We talk about the tyranny of words, but we like to tyrannise over them too; we are fond of having a large superfluous establishment of words to wait upon us on great occasions; we think it looks important, and sounds well. As we are not particular about the meaning of our liveries on state occasions, if they be but fine and numerous enough, so the meaning or necessity of our words is a secondary consideration, if there be but a great parade of them. And as individuals get into trouble by making too great a show of liveries, or as slaves when they are too numerous rise against their masters, so I think I could mention a nation that has got into many great difficulties, and will get into many greater, from maintaining too large a retinue of words." DC 52

—*influence:* "'Words, sir [said Blandois] never influence the course of the cards, or the course of the dice. Do you know that? You do? I also play a game, and words are without power over it.'" LD ii 28

—*and oaths:* "The horses arrive in about an hour. In the interval, the driver swears; sometimes Christian oaths, sometimes Pagan oaths. Sometimes, when it is a long, compound oath, he begins with Christianity and merges into Paganism." PI 6

"'I give you my word, constable—' said Brass. But here the constable interposed with the constitutional principle 'words be blowed;' observing that words were but spoon-meat for babes and sucklings, and that oaths were the food for strong men." OCS 60

—*the slang of pugilism:* "The Chicken himself attributed [his] punishment to his having had the misfortune to *get into Chancery* early in the proceedings, when he was severely *fibbed* by the Larkey one, and heavily *grassed.* But it appeared from the published records of that great contest that the Larkey Boy had had it all his own way from the beginning, and that the Chicken had been *tapped,* and *bunged,* and had *received pepper,* and had been *made groggy,* and had *come up piping,* and had endured a complication of similar strange inconveniences, until he had been *gone into and finished.*" DS 44

—*used economically:* " . . . I never wanted two or three words in my life that I didn't know where to lay my hand upon 'em [Captain Cuttle] observed . . . . It comes of not wasting language as some do.'

"The reflection perhaps reminded him that he had better, like young Norval's father, 'increase his store.' At any rate he became silent, and remained so . . . ." DS 4

Theatre and Spectacle

—abandoned: "There is the Farnese palace, too [in Parma]; and in it one of the dreariest spectacles of decay that ever was seen—a grand, old, gloomy theatre, mouldering away.

"It is a large wooden structure, of the horse-shoe shape; the lower seats arranged upon the Roman plan, but above them, great heavy chambers, rather than boxes, where the Nobles sat, remote in their proud state.

Such desolation as has fallen on this theatre, enhanced in the spectator's fancy by its gay intention and design, none but worms can be familiar with. A hundred and ten years have passed since any play was acted here. The sky shines in through the gashes in the roof; the boxes are dropping down, wasting away, and only tenanted by rats; damp and mildew smear the faded colours, and make spectral maps upon the panels; lean rags are dangling down where there were gay festoons on the proscenium; the stage has rotted so, that a narrow wooden gallery is thrown across it, or it would sink beneath the tread, and bury the visitor in the gloomy depths beneath. The desolation and decay impress themselves on all the senses. The air has a mouldering smell, and an earthy taste; any stray outer sounds that struggle in with some lost sunbeam, are muffled and heavy; and the worm, the maggot, and the rot have changed the surface of the wood beneath the touch, as time will seam and roughen a smooth hand. If ever Ghosts act plays, they act them on this ghostly stage." PI 6

—access to seat: " . . . we paid five shillings, at nine o'clock in the evening, for our one seat at a pantomime; after our cheerful compliance with which demand, a hungry footpad clapped a rolled-up playbill to our breast, like the muzzle of a pistol, and positively stood before the door of which he was the keeper, to prevent our access (without forfeiture of another shilling for his benefit) to the seat we had purchased." HW/OP

—acting styles: "The theatrical young gentleman is a great advocate for violence of emotion and redundancy of action. If a father has to curse a child upon the stage, he likes to see it done in the thoroughgoing style, with no mistake about it: to which end it is essential that the child should follow the father on her knees, and be knocked violently over on her face by the old gentleman as he goes into a small cottage, and shuts the door behind him.

"He likes to see a blessing invoked upon the young lady, when the old gentleman repents, with equal earnestness, and accompanied by the usual conventional forms, which consist of the old gentleman looking anxiously up into the clouds, as if to see whether it rains, and then spreading an imaginary tablecloth in the air over the young lady's head—soft music playing all the while.

"Upon these, and other points of a similar kind, the theatrical young gentleman is a great critic indeed. He is likewise very acute in judging of natural expressions of the passions, and knows precisely the frown, wink, nod, or leer, which stands for any one of them, or the means by which it may be converted into any other: as jealousy, with a good stamp of the right foot, becomes anger; or wildness, with the hands clasped before the throat, instead of tearing the wig, is passionate love.

"If you venture to express a doubt of the accuracy of any of these portraitures, the theatrical young gentleman assures you, with a haughty smile, that it always has been done in that way, and he supposes they are not going to change it at this time of day to please you; to which, of course, you meekly reply that you suppose not." ¶YG/T

"Until, having gradually grown thinner and paler, and having at last totally rejected food, [my enemy] would miserably perish, and I should be revenged. This conclusion I should, no doubt, elaborate by laughing a hoarse laugh in three syllables, and folding my arms tight upon my chest agreeably to most of the examples of glutted animosity that I have had an opportunity of observing in connexion with the Drama—which, by the by, as involving a good deal of noise, appears to me to be occasionally confounded with the Drummer." RP/BS

—acting technique: "Judging of it by analogy; by comparison with anything we know in nature, literature, art; by any test we can apply to it, from within us or without, we can imagine no purer or higher piece of genuine comedy than Mr Macready's performance . . . .

"The nice distinction between such an aspect of the character as this, and the after love scenes . . . was such as none but a master could have expressed, though the veriest tyro in the house might feel its truth when presented to him." E/MB

—athleticism: "It is observable that when people upon the stage are in any strait involving the very last extremity of weakness and exhaustion, they invariably perform feats of strength requiring great ingenuity and muscular power. Thus, a wounded prince or bandit-chief, who is bleeding to death and too faint to move, except to the softest music (and then only upon his hands and knees), shall be seen to approach a cottage door for aid, in such a series of writhings and twistings, and with such curlings up of the legs, and such rollings over and over, and such gettings up and tumblings down again, as could never be achieved save by a very strong man skilled in posture-making." NN 48

—elocution: " . . . I had a latent impression that there was something decidedly fine in Mr Wopsle's elocution . . . because it was very slow, very dreary, very up-hill and down-hill, and very unlike any way in which any man in any natural circumstances of life or death ever expressed himself about anything." GE 31

—makeup: "'We had a first-tragedy man in our company once, who, when he played Othello, used to black himself all over. But that's feeling a part and going into it as if you meant it; it isn't usual; more's the pity.'" NN 48

—actor in his profession

—benefitting mankind: "Let any of us look back upon his past life, and say whether he owes no gratitude to the actor's art! Not because it is often exercised in the midst of sickness, poverty, and misfortune—other arts, God knows, are liable to the like distresses! Not because the actor sometimes comes from scenes of affliction and misfortune—even from death itself—to play his part before us; all men must do that violence to their feelings, in passing on to the fulfilment of their duties in the great strife and fight of life. But because in the relief afforded to us by the actor's act, we always find some reflection, humorous or pathetic, sombre or grotesque, of all the best things that we feel and know." S/TF6

—career in decline: "I was aware that Mr Wopsle had not succeeded in reviving the Drama, but, on the contrary, had rather partaken of its decline. He had been ominously heard of, through the playbills, as a faithful Black, in connexion with a little girl of noble birth, and a monkey. And Herbert [Pocket] had seen him as a predatory Tartar of comic propensities, with a face like a red brick, and an outrageous hat all over bells." GE 47

—despite hardship: "He grinds hard at his vocation, is often steeped in direful poverty, and lives, at the best, in a little world of mockeries. It is bad enough to give away a great estate six nights a-week, and want a shilling; to preside at imaginary banquets, hungry for a mutton chop; to smack the lips over a tankard of toast and water, and declaim about the mellow produce of the sunny vineyard on the banks of the Rhine; to be a rattling young lover, with the measles at home; and to paint sorrow over, with burnt cork and rouge; without being called upon to despise his vocation too. If he can utter the trash to which he is condemned, with any relish, so much the better for him, Heaven knows; and peace be with him!" HW/AP 1

—innate gifts: "'There's genteel comedy in your walk and manner, juvenile tragedy in your eye, and touch-and-go farce in your laugh,' said Mr Vincent Crummles. 'You'll do as well as if you had thought of nothing else but the lamps, from your birth downwards.'" NN 22

"' . . . what a capital countenance your friend [Smike] has got!' . . . Why, as he is now,' said the manager, striking his knee emphatically; 'without a pad upon his body, and hardly a touch of paint upon his face, he'd make such an actor for the starved business as was never seen in this country. Only let him be tolerably well up in the *Apothecary* in Romeo and Juliet with the slightest possible dab of red on the tip of his nose, and he'd be certain of three rounds the moment he put his head out of the practicable door in the front grooves O. P. . . . I never saw a young fellow so regularly cut out for that line since I've been in the profession, and I played the heavy children when I was eighteen months old.'" NN 22

—his knees: " . . . Mr Crummles put on his other eyebrow, and the calves of his legs, and then put on his legs, which were of a yellowish flesh-colour, and rather soiled about the knees, from frequent going down upon those joints, in curses, prayers, last struggles, and other strong passages." NN 48

—*rehearsal:* "'Now then. "Who calls so loud?"'

"'"Who calls so loud"' said Smike.

"'"Who calls so loud?"' repeated Nicholas.

"'"Who calls so loud?"' cried Smike.

"Thus they continued to ask each other who called so loud, over and over again; and when Smike had that by heart, Nicholas went to another sentence, and then to two at a time, and then to three, and so on, until at midnight poor Smike found to his unspeakable joy that he really began to remember something about the text.

"Early in the morning they went to it again, and Smike, rendered more confident by the progress he had already made, got on faster and with better heart. As soon as he began to acquire the words pretty freely, Nicholas showed him how he must come in with both hands spread out upon his stomach, and how he must occasionally rub it, in compliance with the established form by which people on the stage always denote that they want something to eat. After the morning's rehearsal they went to work again, nor did they stop, except for a hasty dinner, until it was time to repair to the theatre at night . . . .

"As soon as they were dressed, and at every interval when he was not upon the stage, Nicholas renewed his instructions. They prospered well. The *Romeo* was received with hearty plaudits and unbounded favour, and Smike was pronounced unanimously, alike by audience and actors, the very prince and prodigy of *Apothecaries.*" NN 25

Nicholas instructs Smike in the Art of Acting NN

—actors, off-duty: " . . . an indescribable public-house-parlour swagger, and a kind of conscious air . . . . " SB/A *See* Vol.I p38ff

—amateur debut: " . . . when Nicholas [Nickleby] came on for his crack scene with Mrs Crummles, what a clapping of hands there was! When Mrs Crummles (who was his unworthy mother), sneered, and called him 'presumptuous boy', and he defied her, what a tumult of applause came on!

"When he quarrelled with the other gentleman about the young lady, and producing a case of pistols, said, that if he *was* a gentleman, he would fight him in the drawing-room, till the furniture was sprinkled with the blood of one, if not of two—how boxes, pit, and gallery joined in one most vigorous cheer!

"When he called his mother names, because she wouldn't give up the young lady's property, and she relenting, caused him to relent likewise, and fall down on one knee and ask her blessing, how the ladies in the audience sobbed! When he was hid behind the curtain in the dark, and the wicked relation poked a sharp sword in every direction, save where his legs were plainly visible, what a thrill of anxious fear ran through the house!

"His air, his figure, his walk, his look, everything he said or did, was the subject of commendation. There was a round of applause every time he spoke. And when at last, in the pump-and-tub scene, Mrs Grudden lighted the blue fire, and all the unemployed members of the company came in, and tumbled down in various directions—not because that had anything to do with the plot, but in order to finish off with a tableau—the audience (who had by this time increased considerably) gave vent to such a shout of enthusiasm, as had not been heard in those walls for many and many a day." NN 24

—amateur Hamlet: "On our arrival in Denmark [to see Wopsle], we found the king and queen of that country elevated in two arm-chairs on a kitchen-table, holding a Court. The whole of the Danish nobility were in attendance; consisting of a noble boy in the wash-leather boots of a gigantic ancestor, a venerable Peer with a dirty face, who seemed to have risen from the people late in life, and the Danish chivalry with a comb in its hair and pair of white silk legs, and presenting on the whole a feminine appearance. My gifted townsman stood gloomily apart, with folded arms, and I could have wished that his curls and forehead had been more probable.

"Several curious little circumstances transpired as the action proceeded. The late king of the country not only appeared to have been troubled with a cough at the time of his decease, but to have taken it with him to the tomb, and to have brought it back. The royal phantom also carried a ghostly manuscript round its truncheon, to which it had the appearance of occasionally referring, and that, too, with an air of anxiety and a tendency to lose the place of reference which were suggestive of a state of mortality. It was this, I conceive, which led to the Shade's being advised by the gallery to 'turn over!'—a recommendation which it took extremely ill.

"It was likewise to be noted of this majestic spirit that whereas it always appeared with an air of having been out a long time and walked an immense distance, it perceptibly came from a closely contiguous wall. This occasioned its terrors to be received derisively. The *Queen of Denmark,* a very buxom lady, though no doubt historically brazen, was considered by the public to have too much brass about her; her chin being attached to her diadem by a broad band of that metal (as if she had a gorgeous toothache), her waist being encircled by another, and each of her arms by another, so that she was openly mentioned as 'the kettle-drum.'

"The noble boy in the ancestral boots, was inconsistent; representing himself, as it were in one breath, as an able seaman, a strolling actor, a gravedigger, a clergyman, and a person of the utmost importance at a Court fencing-match, on the authority of whose practised eye and nice discrimination the finest strokes were judged. This gradually led to a want of toleration for him, and even—on his being detected in holy orders, and declining to perform the funeral service—to the indignation taking the form of nuts.

"Lastly, *Ophelia* was a prey to such slow musical madness, that when, in course of time, she had taken off her white muslin scarf, folded it up, and buried it, a sulky man who had been long cooling his impatient nose against an iron bar in the front row of the gallery, growled, 'Now the baby's put to bed, let's have supper!' Which, to say the least of it, was out of keeping.

"Upon my unfortunate townsman all these incidents accumulated with playful effect. Whenever that undecided Prince had to ask a question or state a doubt, the public helped him out with it. As for example; on the question whether 'twas nobler in the mind to suffer,' some roared yes, and some no, and some inclining to both opinions said 'toss up for it;' and quite a Debating Society arose.

"When he asked what should such fellows as he do crawling between earth and heaven, he was encouraged with loud cries of 'Hear, hear!' When he appeared with his stocking disordered (its disorder expressed, according to usage, by one very neat fold in the top, which I suppose to be always got up with a flat iron), a conversation took place in the gallery respecting the paleness of his leg, and whether it was occasioned by the turn the ghost had given him. On his taking the recorders—very like a little black flute that had just been played in the orchestra and handed out at the door—he was called upon unanimously for Rule Britannia. When he recommended the player not to saw the air thus, the sulky man said, 'And don't *you* do it, neither; you're a deal worse than *him!*' and I grieve to add that peals of laughter greeted Mr Wopsle on every one of these occasions.

"But his greatest trials were in the churchyard: which had the appearance of a primeval forest, with a kind of small ecclesiastical wash-house on one side, and a turnpike gate on the other. Mr Wopsle, in a comprehensive black cloak, being descried entering at the turnpike, the gravedigger was admonished in a friendly way, 'Look out! Here's the undertaker a coming, to see how you're getting on with your work!'

"I believe it is well known in a constitutional country that Mr Wopsle could not possibly have returned the skull, after moralising over it, without dusting his fingers on a white napkin taken from his breast; but even that innocent and indispensable action did not pass without the comment 'Waiter!' The arrival of the body for interment (in an empty black box with the lid tumbling open), was the signal for a general joy which was much enhanced by the discovery, among the bearers, of an individual obnoxious to identification. The joy attended Mr Wopsle through his struggle with *Laertes* on the brink of the orchestra and the grave, and slackened no more until he had tumbled the king off the kitchen-table, and had died by inches from the ankles upward.

"We had made some pale efforts in the beginning to applaud Mr Wopsle; but they were too hopeless to be persisted in. Therefore we had sat, feeling keenly for him, but laughing, nevertheless, from ear to ear. I laughed in spite of myself all the time, the whole thing was so droll; and yet I had a latent impression that there was something decidedly fine in Mr Wopsle's elocution—not for old associations' sake, I am afraid, but because it was very slow, very dreary, very up-hill and down-hill, and very unlike any way in which any man in any natural circumstances of life or death ever expressed himself about anything." ¶GE 31

—audience

—at a cheap theatre: "We were a motley assemblage of people, and we had a good many boys and young men among us; we had also many girls and young women. To represent, however, that we did not include a very great number, and a very fair proportion of family groups, would be to make a gross mis-statement. Such groups were to be seen in all parts of the house; in the boxes and stalls particularly, they were composed of persons of very decent appearance, who had many children with them.

"Among our dresses there were most kinds of shabby and greasy wear, and much fustian and corduroy that was neither sound nor fragrant. The caps of our young men were mostly of a limp character, and we who wore them, slouched, high-shouldered, into our places with our hands in our pockets, and occasionally twisted our cravats about our necks like eels, and occasionally tied them down our breasts like links of sausages, and occasionally had a screw in our hair over each cheek-bone with a slight Thief-flavour in it.

"Besides prowlers and idlers, we were mechanics, dock-labourers, costermongers, petty tradesmen, small clerks, milliners, stay-makers, shoe-binders, slop-workers, poor workers in a hundred highways and byways. Many of us—on the whole, the majority—were not at all clean, and not all choice in our lives or conversation. But we had all come together in a place where our convenience was well consulted, and where we were well looked after, to enjoy an evening's entertainment in common. We were not going to lose any part of what we had paid for through anybody's caprice, and as a community we had a character to lose. So, we were closely attentive, and kept excellent order; and let the man or boy who did otherwise instantly get out from this place, or we would put him out with the greatest expedition." ¶UT/TV

—lower classes: "The play . . . was performed amidst the usual hideous medley of fights, foul language, catcalls, shrieks, yells, oaths, blasphemy, obscenity, apples, oranges, nuts, biscuits, ginger-beer, porter, and pipes—not that there was any particular objection to the Play, but that the audience were, on the whole, in a condition of mind, generally requiring such utterance. Pipes of all lengths were at work in the gallery; several were displayed in the pit. Cans of beer, each with a pint measure to drink from (for the convenience of gentlemen who had neglected the precaution of bringing their own pots in their bundles), were carried through the dense crowd at all stages of the tragedy. Sickly children in arms were squeezed out of shape, in all parts of the house. Fish was fried at the entrance doors. Barricades of oyster-shells encumbered the pavement. Expectant half-price visitors to the gallery, howled defiant impatience up the stairs, and danced a sort of Carmagnole all round the building." HWC/SN

"Instead of being at a great disadvantage in comparison with the mass of the audience, they were here *the* audience, for whose accommodation the place was made. We believe this to be one great cause of the success of these speculations. In whatever way the common people are addressed, whether in churches, chapels, schools, lecture-rooms, or theatres, to be successfully addressed they must be directly appealed to. No matter how good the feast, they will not come to it on mere sufferance. If, on looking round us, we find that the only things plainly and personally addressed to them, from quack medicines upwards, be bad or very defective things—so much the worse for them and for all of us, and so much the more unjust and absurd the system which has haughtily abandoned a strong ground to such occupation.

"We will add that we believe these people have a right to be amused. A great deal that we consider to be unreasonable, is written and talked about not licensing these places of entertainment. We have already intimated that we believe a love of dramatic representations to be an inherent principle in human nature." HW/AP 2

—hint of censorship: "The people who now resort here, *will be* amused somewhere. It is of no use to blink that fact, or to make pretences to the contrary. We had far better apply ourselves to improving the character of their amusement. It would not be exacting much, or exacting anything very difficult, to require that the pieces represented in these Theatres should have, at least, a good, plain, healthy purpose in them." HW/AP 2

—upper classes: " . . . the nobility and gentry . . . who seldom enter a theatre unless it be a foreign one; or who, when they do repair to an English temple of the drama, would seem to be attracted thither solely by an amiable desire to purify, by their presence, a scene of vice and indecorum; and who select their place of entertainment accordingly." E/MB

—backstage: "At last they came into a maze of dust, where a quantity of people were tumbling over one another, and where there was such a confusion of unaccountable shapes of beams, bulkheads, brick walls, ropes, and rollers, and such a mixing of gaslight and daylight, that they seemed to have got on the wrong side of the pattern of the universe." LD i 20

—ballet

—conventionalities: "Who knows how it came about that the young Swiss maiden . . . should, as an established custom, revolve, on her nuptial morning, so airily and often, that at length she stands before us, for some seconds, like a beautiful white muslin pen-wiper? Why is her bed-chamber always immediately over the cottage-door? Why is she always awakened by three taps of her lover's hands? Why does her mother always spin? Why is her residence invariably near a bridge? In what Swiss canton do the hardy mountaineers pursue the chamois in silk stockings, pumps, blue breeches, cherry-coloured bows, and their shirt-sleeves?" HW/FC

—in England: " . . . there bounded on to the stage from some mysterious inlet, a little girl in a dirty white frock with tucks up to the knees, short trousers, sandaled shoes, white spencer, pink gauze bonnet,

green veil and curl-papers; who turned a pirouette, cut twice in the air, turned another pirouette, then, looking off at the opposite wing, shrieked, bounded forward to within six inches of the footlights, and fell into a beautiful attitude of terror, as a shabby gentleman in an old pair of buff slippers came in at one powerful slide, and chattering his teeth, fiercely brandished a walking-stick.

"'They are going through the Indian Savage and the Maiden,' said Mrs Crummles . . . .

"The manager clapped his hands as a signal to proceed, and the savage, becoming ferocious, made a slide towards the maiden; but the maiden avoided him in six twirls, and came down, at the end of the last one, upon the very points of her toes [in sandaled shoes?]. This seemed to make some impression upon the savage; for, after a little more ferocity and chasing of the maiden into corners, he began to relent, and stroked his face several times with his right thumb and four fingers, thereby intimating that he was struck with admiration of the maiden's beauty. Acting upon the impulse of this passion, he (the savage) began to hit himself severe thumps in the chest, and to exhibit other indications of being desperately in love, which being rather a prosy proceeding, was very likely the cause of the maiden's falling asleep; whether it was or no, asleep she did fall, sound as a church, on a sloping bank, and the savage perceiving it, leant his left ear on his left hand, and nodded sideways, to intimate to all whom it might concern that she *was* asleep, and no shamming. Being left to himself, the savage had a dance, all alone. Just as he left off, the maiden woke up, rubbed her eyes, got off the bank, and had a dance all alone too—such a dance that the savage looked on in ecstasy all the while, and when it was done, plucked from a neighbouring tree some botanical curiosity, resembling a small pickled cabbage, and offered it to the maiden, who at first wouldn't have it, but on the savage shedding tears relented. Then the savage and the maiden danced violently together, and, finally, the savage dropped on on one knee, and the maiden stood on one leg upon his other knee; thus concluding the ballet, and leaving the spectators in a state of pleasing uncertainty, whether she would ultimately marry the savage, or return to her friends." NN 23

—in Italy: "In the splendid theatre of La Scala, there was a ballet of action performed after the opera, under the title of Prometheus: in the beginning of which, some hundred or two of men and women represented our mortal race before the refinements of the arts and sciences, and loves and graces, came on earth to soften them. I never saw anything more effective.

"Generally speaking, the pantomimic action of the Italians is more remarkable for its sudden and impetuous character than for its delicate expression; but, in this case, the drooping monotony: the weary, miserable, listless, moping life: the sordid passions and desires of human creatures, destitute of those elevating influences to which we owe so much, and to whose promoters we render so little: were expressed in a manner really powerful and affecting. I should have thought it almost impossible to present such an idea so strongly on the stage, without the aid of speech." PI 9

—circus: "Dear, dear, what a place it looked, that Astleys; with all the paint, gilding, and looking-glass; the vague smell of horses suggestive of coming wonders; the curtain that hid such gorgeous mysteries; the clean white sawdust down in the circus; the company coming in and taking their places, the fiddlers looking carelessly up at them while they tuned their instruments, as if they didn't want the play to begin, and knew it all beforehand! What a glow was that, which burst upon them all, when that long, clear, brilliant row of lights came slowly up; and what the feverish excitement when the little bell rang and the music began in good earnest, with strong parts for the drums, and sweet effects for the triangles! . . .

"Then the play itself! the horses which little Jacob believed from the first to be alive, and the ladies and gentlemen of whose reality he could be by no means persuaded, having never seen or heard anything at all like them—the firing, which made Barbara wink—the forlorn lady, who made her cry—the tyrant, who made her tremble—the man who sang the song with the lady's maid and danced the chorus, who made her laugh—the pony who reared upon his hind-legs when he saw the murderer, and wouldn't hear of walking on all fours again until he was taken into custody—the clown who ventured on such familiarities with the military man in boots—the lady who jumped over the nine-and-twenty ribbons and came down safe upon the horse's back—everything was delightful, splendid, and surprising!" OCS 39

—clichés of situation: "In our theatrical experience as playgoers, we are all, I have no doubt, pretty equally accustomed to predict from certain little signs and tokens on the stage, what is going to happen there. For example, when the young lady, the admiral's daughter, is left alone to relieve her feelings with certain general observations not particularly connected with the subject, and when a certain smart, spiritual rapping is heard to proceed from the depths of the earth immediately before her feet, we foretell that a song is intended. When two gentlemen enter for whom, by a happy coincidence, exactly two chairs, and neither fewer nor more, are waiting, we augur that a conversation will probably ensue, and that it is far from impossible that that conversation will assume a retrospectively biographical character. In like manner when two other gentlemen, particularly if they belong to the seafaring, the marauding, or smuggling professions, are observed to have armed themselves since their last appearance with a very short sword with a very large hilt, we predict with some confidence that this cautious preparation will end in a combat." S/TF12

—comic relief: "It is the custom on the stage: in all good, murderous melodramas: to present the tragic and the comic scenes, in as regular alternation, as the layers of red and white in a side of streaky, well-cured bacon. The hero sinks upon his straw bed, weighed down by fetters and misfortunes; and, in the next scene, his faithful but unconscious squire regales the audience with a comic song.

"We behold, with throbbing bosoms, the heroine in the grasp of a proud and ruthless baron: her virtue and her life alike in danger; drawing forth her dagger to preserve the one at the cost of the other; and, just as our expectations are wrought up to the highest pitch, a whistle is heard; and we are straightway transported to the great hall of the castle; where a grey-headed seneschal sings a funny chorus with a funnier body of vassals, who are free of all sorts of places from church vaults to palaces, and roam about in company, carolling perpetually.

"Such changes appear absurd, but they are not so unnatural as they would seem at first sight. The transitions in real life from well-spread boards to death-beds, and from mourning weeds to holiday garments, are not a whit less startling; only, there, we are busy actors, instead of passive lookers-on; which makes a vast difference. The actors in the mimic life of the theatre, are blind to violent transitions and abrupt impulses of passion or feeling, which, presented before the eyes of mere spectators, are at once condemned as outrageous and preposterous." OT 17

—a compliment: "'And oh ain't it a Ev'nly place,' suddenly interrupted Maggy . . . .. 'Almost as good as a hospital. Only there ain't no Chicking in it.'" LD i 14

"'How did you like my reading. . . gentlemen?' said Mr Waldengarver [Mr Wopsle's stage identity], almost, if not quite, with patronage.

"Herbert said from behind (again poking me), 'massive and concrete.' So I said boldly, as if I had originated it, and must beg to insist upon it, 'massive and concrete.'

"'I am glad to have your approbation, gentlemen,' said Mr Waldengarver, with an air of dignity . . . . " GE 31

—at a country fair: "This immense booth, with the large stage in front, so brightly illuminated with variegated lamps, and pots of burning fat, is 'Richardson's,' where you have a melodrama (with three murders and a ghost), a pantomime, a comic song, an overture, and some incidental music, all done in five-and-twenty minutes." SB/GF

And see —melodrama

—deserted: "Between the bridge and the two great theatres there was but the distance of a few hundred paces, as the theatres came next. Grim and black within, at night, those great dry Wells, and lonesome to imagine, with the rows of faces faded out, the lights extinguished, and the seats all empty. One would think that nothing in them knew itself at such a time but Yorick's skull. In one of my night walks, as the church steeples were shaking the March winds and rain with the strokes of Four, I passed the outer boundary of one of these great deserts, and entered it. With a dim lantern in my hand, I groped my well-known way to the stage, and looked over the orchestra—which was like a great grave dug for a time of pestilence—into the void beyond.

"A dismal cavern of an immense aspect, with the chandelier gone dead like everything else, and nothing visible through mist and fog and space but tiers of winding-sheets. The ground at my feet where, when last there, I had seen the peasantry of Naples dancing among the vines, reckless of the burning mountain which threatened to overwhelm them, was now in possession of a strong serpent of engine-hose, watchfully lying in wait for the serpent Fire, and ready to fly at it if it showed its forked tongue. A ghost of a watchman, carrying a faint corpse candle, haunted the distant upper gallery and flitted away.

"Retiring within the proscenium, and holding my light above my head towards the rolled-up curtain—green no more, but black as ebony—my sight lost itself in a gloomy vault, showing faint indications in it of a shipwreck of canvas and cordage. Methought I felt much as a diver might at the bottom of the sea." ¶UT/NW

—fathers on stage: "By the way, talking of fathers, we should very much like to see some piece in which all the dramatis personae were orphans. Fathers are invariably great nuisances on the stage, and always have to give the hero or heroine a long explanation of what was done before the curtain rose, usually commencing with 'It is now nineteen years, my dear child, since your blessed mother (here the old villain's voice falters) confided you to my charge. You were then an infant,' &c., &c.

"Or else they have to discover, all of a sudden, that somebody whom they have been in constant communication with, during three long acts, without the slightest suspicion, is their own child: in which case they exclaim, 'Ah! what do I see? This bracelet! That smile! These documents! Those eyes! Can I believe my senses?—It must be!—Yes—it is, it is my child!'—'My father!' exclaims the child; and they fall into each other's arms, and look over each other's shoulders, and the audience gives three rounds of applause." ¶SB/A

"It is customary with fathers in stage-plays, after giving their daughters to the men of their hearts, to congratulate themselves on having no other business on their hands but to die immediately: though it is rarely found that they are in a hurry to do it." MC 30

—fight scene: " . . . everybody knows what an effect may be produced by a good combat. One—two—three—four—over; then, one—two—three—four—under; then thrust; then dodge and slide about; then fall down on one knee; then fight upon it, and then get up again and stagger.

"You may keep on doing this, as long as it seems to take—say ten minutes—and then fall down (backwards, if you can manage it without hurting yourself), and die game: nothing like it for producing an effect. They always do it at Astley's and Sadler's Wells, and if they don't know how to do this sort of thing, who in the world does?

"A small child, or a female in white, increases the interest of a combat materially—indeed, we are not aware that a regular legitimate terrific broadsword combat could be done without; but it would be rather difficult, and somewhat unusual, to introduce this effect in the last scene of Richard the Third, so the only thing to be done is, just to make the best of a bad bargain, and be as long as possible fighting it out." ¶SB/PT

—first impression: "It was Covent Garden Theatre that I [David Copperfield] chose; and there, from the back of a centre box, I saw Julius Caesar and the new Pantomime. To have all those noble Romans alive before me, and walking in and out for my entertainment, instead of being the stern taskmasters they had been at school, was a most novel and delightful effect.

"But the mingled reality and mystery of the whole show, the influence upon me of the poetry, the lights, the music, the company, the smooth stupendous changes of glittering and brilliant scenery, were so dazzling, and opened up such illimitable regions of delight, that when I came out into the rainy street, at twelve o'clock at night, I felt as if I had come from the clouds, where I had been leading a romantic life for ages, to a bawling, splashing, link-lighted, umbrella-struggling, hackney-coach-jostling, patten-clinking, muddy, miserable world." DC 19

—free tickets: "What was the most absorbing and longest-lived passion in the human breast? What was the passion so powerful that it would almost induce the generous to be mean, the careless to be cautious, the guileless to be deeply designing, the dove to emulate the serpent? A daily editor of vast experience and great acuteness, who was one of the company, considerably surprised us by saying, with the greatest confidence, that the passion in question was the passion of getting orders for the play." S/N6

—hangers-on: "'Everybody who is at all acquainted with theatrical matters knows what a host of shabby, poverty-stricken men hang about the stage of a large establish-

ment—not regularly engaged actors, but ballet people, procession men, tumblers, and so forth, who are taken on during the run of a pantomime, or an Easter piece, and are then discharged, until the production of some heavy spectacle occasions a new demand for their services.'" PP 3

—high praise: " . . . the most intellectual and rational of all our amusements" YG/T

—an ideal playhouse: "To every part of this Theatre, spacious fire-proof ways of ingress and egress. For every part of it, convenient places of refreshment and retiring rooms. Everything to eat and drink carefully supervised as to quality, and sold at an appointed price; respectable female attendants ready for the commonest women in the audience; a general air of consideration, decorum, and supervision, most commendable; an unquestionably humanising influence in all the social arrangements of the place . . . .

" . . . Magnificently lighted by a firmament of sparkling chandeliers, the building was ventilated to perfection. My sense of smell, without being particularly delicate, has been so offended in some of the commoner places of public resort, that I have often been obliged to leave them when I have made an uncommercial journey expressly to look on. The air of this Theatre was fresh, cool, and wholesome.

"To help towards this end, very sensible precautions had been used, ingeniously combining the experience of hospitals and railway stations. Asphalt pavements substituted for wooden floors, honest bare walls of glazed brick and tile—even at the back of the boxes—for plaster and paper, no benches stuffed, and no carpeting or baize used; a cool material with a light glazed surface, being the covering of the seats.

" . . . It has been constructed from the ground to the roof, with a careful reference to sight and sound in every corner; the result is, that its form is beautiful, and that the appearance of the audience, as seen from the proscenium—with every face in it commanding the stage, and the whole so admirably raked and turned to that centre, that a hand can scarcely move in the great assemblage without the movement being seen from thence—is highly remarkable in its union of vastness with compactness.

"The stage itself, and all its appurtenances of machinery, cellarage, height and breadth, are on a scale more like the Scala at Milan . . . than any notion a stranger would be likely to form of the Britannia Theatre . . . . The Forty Thieves might be played here, and every thief ride his real horse, and the disguised captain bring in his oil jars on a train of real camels, and nobody be put out of the way. This really extraordinary place is the achievement of one man's enterprise . . . ." ¶UT/TV

—horse-riding troupe: "There were two or three handsome young women among them, with their two or three husbands, and their two or three mothers, and their eight or nine little children, who did the fairy business when required. The father of one of the families was in the habit of balancing the father of another of the families on the top of a great pole; the father of a third family often made a pyramid of both those fathers, with Master Kidderminster for the apex, and himself for the base; all the fathers could dance upon rolling casks, stand upon bottles, catch knives and balls, twirl hand-basins, ride upon anything, jump over everything, and stick at nothing. All the mothers could (and did) dance, upon the slack wire and tight rope, and perform rapid acts on bare-backed steeds; none of them were at all particular in respect of showing their legs; and one of them, alone in a Greek chariot, drove six in hand into every town they came to.

"They all assumed to be mighty rakish and knowing, they were not very tidy in their private dresses, they were not at all orderly in their domestic arrangements, and the combined literature of the whole company would have produced but a poor letter on any subject. Yet there was a remarkable gentleness and childishness about these people, a special inaptitude for any kind of sharp practice, and an untiring readiness to help and pity one another, deserving often of as much respect, and always of as much generous construction, as the everyday virtues of any class of people in the world." ¶HT i 6

—illusion: "I noticed that the people who kept the shops, and who represented the passengers in the thoroughfares, and so forth, had no conventionality in them, but were unusually like the real thing—from which I infer that you may take that audience in (if you wish to) concerning Knights and Ladies, Fairies, Angels, or such like, but they are not to be done as to anything in the streets." UT/TV

—*improbabilities:* "Such changes [cited under *comic relief*] appear absurd; but they are not so unnatural as they would seem at first sight. The transitions in real life from well-spread boards to death-beds, and from mourning weeds to holiday garments, are not a whit less startling; only, there, we are busy actors, instead of passive lookers-on; which makes a vast difference.

"The actors in the mimic life of the theatre, are blind to violent transitions and abrupt impulses of passion or feeling, which, presented before the eyes of mere spectators, are at once condemned as outrageous and preposterous." ¶OT 17

—*inauspicious debut:* " . . . Wopsle: he's had a drop . . . .

"'. . . he's left the Church and went into the playacting . . . .

"I took what Joe gave me, and found it to be the crumpled playbill of a small metropolitan theatre, announcing the first appearance, in that very week, of 'the celebrated Provincial Amateur of Roscian renown, whose unique performance in the highest tragic walk of our National Bard has lately occasioned so great a sensation in local dramatic circles' . . .

"'Was there a great sensation?'

"'Why,' said Joe, 'yes, there certainly were a peck of orange-peel. Partickler when he see the ghost. Though I put it to yourself, sir, whether it were calc'lated to keep a man up to his work with a good hart, to be continiwally cutting in betwixt him and the Ghost with "Amen!" A man may have had a misfortun' and been in the Church . . . but that is no reason why you should put him out at such a time. Which I meantersay, if the ghost of a man's own father cannot be allowed to claim his attention, what can, Sir? Still more, when his mourning 'at is unfortunately made so small as that the weight of the black feathers brings it off, try to keep it on how you may.'" GE 27

—*mannerisms:* "No man ever knew yet, no man ever will know, why a stage-nobleman is bound to go to execution with a stride and a stop alternately, and cannot proceed on any other terms. It is not within the range of the loftiest intellect to explain why a stage-letter, before it can be read by the recipient, must be smartly rapped back, after being opened, with the knuckles of one hand. It is utterly unknown why choleric old gentlemen always have a trick of carrying their canes behind them, between the waist-buttons of their coat." HW/FC

"Why does the baron, or the general, or the venerable steward, or the amiable old farmer, talk about his chee-ilde? He knows of no such thing as a chee-ilde anywhere else; what business has he with a chee-ilde on the boards alone? I never knew an old gentleman to hug himself with his left arm, fall into a comic fit of delirium tremens, and say to his son, 'Damme, you dog, will you marry her?' Yet, the moment I see an old gentleman on the stage with a small cape to his coat, I know of course that this will infallibly happen. Now, why should I be under the obligation to be always entertained by this spectacle, however refreshing, and why should I never be surprised?" HW/W?

And see YG/T

—*melodrama:* "A change of performance takes place every day during the fair, but the story of the tragedy is always pretty much the same. There is a rightful heir, who loves a young lady, and is beloved by her; and a wrongful heir, who loves her too, and isn't beloved by her; and the wrongful heir gets hold of the rightful heir, and throws him into a dungeon, just to kill him off when convenient, for which purpose he hires a couple of assassins—a good one and a bad one—who, the moment they are left alone, get up a little murder on their own account, the good one killing the bad one, and the bad one wounding the good one.

"Then the rightful heir is discovered in prison, carefully holding a long chain in his hands, and seated despondingly in a large armchair; and the young lady comes in to two bars of soft music, and embraces the rightful heir; and then the wrongful heir comes in to two bars of quick music (technically called 'a hurry'), and goes on in the most shocking manner, throwing the young lady about as if she was nobody, and calling the rightful heir 'Ar-recreant—ar-wretch!' in a very loud voice, which answers the double purpose of displaying his passion, and preventing the sound being deadened by the sawdust.

"The interest becomes intense; the wrongful heir draws his sword, and rushes on the rightful heir; a blue smoke is seen, a gong is heard, and a tall white figure (who has been all this time, behind the armchair, covered over with a tablecloth), slowly rises to the tune of 'Oft in the stilly night.' This is no other than the ghost of the rightful heir's father, who was killed by the wrongful heir's father, at sight of which the wrongful heir becomes apoplectic, and is literally 'struck all of a heap,' the stage not being large enough to admit of his falling down at full length.

"Then the good assassin staggers in, and says he was hired in conjunction with the bad assassin, by the wrongful heir, to kill the rightful heir; and he's killed a good many people in his time, but he's very sorry for it, and won't do so any more—a promise which he immediately redeems, by dying off hand without any nonsense about it.

"Then the rightful heir throws down his chain; and then two men, a sailor, and a young woman (the tenantry of the rightful heir) come in, and the ghost makes dumb motions to them, which they, by supernatural interference, understand—for no one else can; and the ghost (who can't do anything without blue fire) blesses the rightful heir and the young lady, by half suffocating them with smoke: and then a muffin-bell rings, and the curtain drops." ¶SB/GF

"Now if Mr Pecksniff knew, from anything Martin Chuzzlewit [the elder] had expressed in gestures, that he wanted to speak to him, he could only have found it out on some such principle as prevails in melodramas, and in virtue of which the elderly farmer with the comic son always knows what the dumb girl means when she takes refuge in his garden, and relates her personal memoirs in incomprehensible pantomime." MC 3

"[At the play], I found a virtuous boatswain in his Majesty's service—a most excellent man, though I could have wished his trousers not quite so tight in some places and not quite so loose in others—who knocked all the little men's hats over their eyes, though he was very generous and brave, and who wouldn't hear of anybody's paying taxes, though he was very patriotic. He had a bag of money in his pocket, like a pudding in the cloth, and on that property married a young person in bed-furniture, with great rejoicings; the whole population of Portsmouth (nine in number at the last Census) turning out on the beach, to rub their own hands and shake everybody else's, and sing, 'Fill, fill!'

"A certain dark-complexioned Swab, however, who wouldn't fill, or do anything else that was proposed to him, and whose heart was openly stated (by the boatswain) to be as black as his figurehead, proposed to two other Swabs to get all mankind into difficulties; which was so effectually done (the Swab family having considerable political influence) that it took half the evening to set things right, and then it was only brought about through an honest little grocer with a white hat, black gaiters, and red nose, getting into a clock, with a gridiron, and listening, and coming out, and knocking everybody down from behind with the gridiron whom he couldn't confute with what he had overheard.

"This led to Mr Wopsle's (who had never been heard of before) coming in with a star and garter on, as plenipotentiary of great power direct from the Admiralty, to say that the Swabs were all to go to prison on the spot, and that he had brought the boatswain down the Union Jack, as a slight acknowledgment of his public services. The boatswain, unmanned for the first time, respectfully dried his eyes on the Jack, and then cheering up and addressing Mr Wopsle as Your Honour, solicited permission to take him by the fin. Mr Wopsle conceding his fin with a gracious dignity, was immediately shoved into a dusty corner while everybody danced a hornpipe; and from that corner, surveying the public with a discontented eye, became aware of me." ¶GE 47

—orchestra pit: "With a dim lantern in my hand, I groped my well-known way to the stage and looked over the orchestra—which was like a great grave dug for a time of pestilence—into the void beyond." UT/NW

—Punch: "When they came to any town or village, or even to a detached house of good appearance, Short blew a blast upon the brazen trumpet and carolled a fragment of a song in that hilarious tone common to Punches and their consorts. If people hurried to the windows, Mr Codlin pitched the temple, and hastily unfurling the drapery and concealing Short therewith, flourished hysterically on the Pipes and performed an air.

"Then the entertainment began as soon as might be; Mr Codlin having the responsibility of deciding on its length and of protracting or expediting the time for the hero's final triumph over the enemy of mankind, according as he judged that the after-crop of half-pence would be plentiful or scant. When it had been gathered in to the last farthing, he resumed his load and on they went again.

"Sometimes they played out the toll across a bridge or ferry, and once exhibited by particular desire at a turnpike, where the collector, being drunk in his solitude, paid down a shilling to have it to himself. There was one small place of rich promise in which their hopes were blighted, for a favourite character in the play having gold-lace upon his coat and being a meddling wooden-headed fellow was held to be a libel on the beadle, for which reason the authorities enforced a quick retreat; but they were generally well received, and seldom left a town without a troop of ragged children shouting at their heels." ¶OCS 17

—puppets in Italy: "The Theatre of Puppets, or Marionetti—a famous company from Milan—is, without any exception, the drollest exhibition I ever beheld in my life. I never saw anything so exquisitely ridiculous. They *look* between four and five feet high, but are really much smaller; for when a musician in the orchestra happens to put his hat on the stage, it becomes alarmingly gigantic, and almost blots out an actor.

"They usually play a comedy, and a ballet. The comic man in the comedy I saw one summer night, is a waiter in an hotel. There never was such a locomotive actor, since the world began. Great pains are taken with him. He has extra joints in his legs: and a practical eye, with which he winks at the pit, in a manner that is absolutely insupportable to a stranger, but which the initiated audience, mainly composed of the common people, receive (so they do everything else) quite as a matter of course, and as if he were a man.

"His spirits are prodigious. He continually shakes his legs, and winks his eye. And there is a heavy father with grey hair, who sits down on the regular conventional stage-bank, and blesses his daughter in the regular conventional way, who is tremendous. No one would suppose it possible that anything short of a real man could be so tedious. It is the triumph of art."

"In the ballet, an Enchanter runs away with the Bride, in the very hour of her nuptials. He brings her to his cave, and tries to soothe her. They sit down on a sofa (the regular sofa! in the regular place, O.P. Second Entrance!) and a procession of musicians enters; one creature playing a drum, and knocking himself off his legs at every blow. These failing to delight her, dancers appear. Four first; then two; *the* two; the flesh-coloured two.

"The way in which they dance; the height to which they spring; the impossible and inhuman extent to which they pirouette; the revelation of their preposterous legs; the coming down with a pause, on the very tips of their toes, when the music requires it; the gentleman's retiring up, when it is the lady's turn; and the lady's retiring up, when it is the gentleman's turn; the final passion of a pas-de-deux; and the going off with a bound!—I shall never see a real ballet, with a composed countenance again." ¶PI 5

—roles of an actor: "'You may be the Brigand, or the *Hamlet,* or the Ghost, or the Court Physician, or the King's whole army; you may do the light business, or the heavy business, or the comic business, or the serious business, or the eccentric business; you may be the captain who courts the young lady, whose guardian unaccountably persists in dressing himself a hundred years behind the time; or you may be the lady's young brother, in white kid gloves and trousers, whose position in the family would appear to be to listen to all the female members of it when they sing, and to shake hands with them between all the verses; or you may be the Baron who gives the *fête,* and who sits on the sofa under the canopy, with the Baroness, to behold the *fête;* or you may be the peasant who swells the drinking chorus at the *fête,* and who may usually be observed to turn his glass upside-down immediately before drinking the Baron's health; or you may be the Clown who takes away the doorstep of the house where there's a dinner party; or you may be the first stout gentleman who issues forth out of that house, on the false alarm of fire, and precipitates himself into the area; or you may be a Fairy, residing for ever in a revolving Star, in the Regions of Pleasure, or the Palace of Delight; or you may even be a Witch in *Macbeth,* bearing a marvellous resemblance to the *Malcolm* or *Donaldbain* [*sic.*] of the previous scenes with his wig hindside before." S/TF6

—stage-door atmosphere: ". . . when [Little Dorrit] was directed to a furtive sort of door, with a curious up-all-night air about it, that appeared to be ashamed of itself and to be hiding in an alley, she hesitated to approach it; being further deterred by the sight of some half-dozen close-shaved gentlemen, with their hats very strangely on, who were lounging about the door, looking not at all unlike Collegians [imprisoned debtors].

"On her applying to them, reassured by

this resemblance, for a direction . . . they made way for her to enter a dark hall—it was more like a great grim lamp gone out than anything else—where she could hear the distant playing of music and the sound of dancing feet. A man so much in want of airing that he had a blue mould upon him, sat watching this dark place from a hole in a corner, like a spider . . . . " LD i 20

"Did any of our readers ever notice the class of people, who hang about the stage-doors of our minor theatres in the daytime? You will rarely pass one of these entrances without seeing a group of three or four men conversing on the pavement, with an indescribable public-house-parlour swagger, and a kind of conscious air, peculiar to people of this description.

"They always seem to think they are exhibiting; the lamps are ever before them . . . . There is generally a groom or two, sitting on the window-sill, and two or three dirty shabby-genteel men in checked neckerchiefs, and sallow linen, lounging about, and carrying, perhaps, under one arm, a pair of stage shoes badly wrapped up in a piece of old newspaper.

"Some years ago we used to stand looking, open-mouthed, at these men, with a feeling of mysterious curiosity, the very recollection of which provokes a smile at the moment we are writing. We could not believe that the beings of light and elegance, in milk-white tunics, salmon-coloured legs, and blue scarfs, who flitted on sleek cream-coloured horses before our eyes at night, with all the aid of lights, music, and artificial flowers, could be the pale, dissipated-looking creatures we beheld by day." ¶SB/A

—stock plots: "'What do you mean to do for me, old fellow?' asked Mr Lenville . . . . 'Anything in the gruff and grumble way?'

"'You turn your wife and child out of doors,' said Nicholas; 'and in a fit of rage and jealousy, stab your eldest son in the library.'

"'Do I though!' exclaimed Mr Lenville. 'That's very good business.'

"'After which,' said Nicholas, 'you are troubled with remorse till the last act, and then you make up your mind to destroy yourself. But, just as you are raising the pistol to your head, a clock strikes—ten.'

"'I see,' cried Mr Lenville. 'Very good.'

"'You pause,' said Nicholas; 'you recollect to have heard a clock strike ten in your infancy. The pistol falls from your hand—you are overcome—you burst into tears, and become a virtuous and exemplary character for ever afterwards.'

"'Capital!' said Mr Lenville: 'that's a sure card, a sure card. Get the curtain down with a touch of nature like that, and it'll be a triumphant success.'

"'Is there anything good for me?' inquired Mr Folair, anxiously.

"'Let me see,' said Nicholas. 'You play the faithful and attached servant; you are turned out of doors with the wife and child.'

"'Always coupled with that infernal [Infant] phenomenon,' sighed Mr Folair; 'and we go into poor lodgings, where I won't take any wages, and talk sentiment, I suppose?'

"'Why—yes,' replied Nicholas: 'that is the course of the piece.'

"'I must have a dance of some kind, you know,' said Mr Folair. "You'll have to introduce one for the phenomenon, so you'd better make a *pas de deux,* and save time.'

"'There's nothing easier than that,' said Mr Lenville, observing the disturbed looks of the young dramatist.

"'Upon my word I don't see how it's to be done,' rejoined Nicholas.

"'Why, isn't it obvious?' reasoned Mr Lenville. 'Gadzooks, who can help seeing the way to do it?—you astonish me! You get the distressed lady, and the little child, and the attached servant, into the poor lodgings, don't you?—Well, look here. The distressed lady sinks into a chair and buries her face in her pocket-handkerchief—"What makes you weep, mama?" says the child. "Don't weep, mama, or you'll make we weep too!"—"And me!" says the faithful servant, rubbing his eyes with his arm. "What can we do to raise your spirit, dear mama?" says the little child. "Aye, what *can* we do?" says the faithful servant. "Oh, Pierre!" says the distressed lady; "would that I could shake off these painful thoughts."—"Try, ma'am, try," says the faithful servant; "rouse yourself, ma'am; be amused."—"I will," says the lady, "I will learn to suffer with fortitude. Do you remember that dance, my honest friend, which, in happier days, you practised with this sweet angel? It never failed to calm my spirits then. Oh! let me see it once again before I die!"—There it is—cue for the band, *before I die,*—and off they go. That's the regular thing; isn't it, Tommy?'

"'That's it,' replied Mr Folair. 'The distressed lady, overpowered by old recollections, faints at the end of the dance, and you close in with a picture.'" NN 24

—*in time of war:* " . . . in the midst of wars and tumults the humanizing arts are not forgotten. Least of all, as is natural, that art, that through the means of one little play, has made the battles of Poitiers and Agincourt more renowned than all the chroniclers and historians put together, and which . . . has done more to stir the bold English blood in a just cause, than all the parliamentary speeches that were ever delivered, than all the debates which ever made the night hideous. Surely you are not inappropriately asked to remember this object in a time of war, when it can present to you tangibly and in its glowing pictures the joys of military triumph, the sorrows of defeat, the constancy of noble minds, the misfortunes and unspeakable calamities of war, and the inappreciable blessings of peace." S/TF9

—*the unities:* "'The unities of the drama before everything [said Mr Curdle].'

"'Might I ask you,' said Nicholas, hesitating between the respect he ought to assume, and his love of the whimsical, 'might I ask you what the unities are?'

"Mr Curdle coughed and considered. 'The unities, sir,' he said, 'are a completeness—a kind of universal dove-tailedness with regard to place and time—a sort of general oneness, if I may be allowed to use so strong an expression. I take those to be the dramatic unities, so far as I have been enabled to bestow attention upon them, and I have read much upon the subject, and thought much.

"'I find, running through the performances of this child,' said Mr Curdle, turning to the [Infant] phenomenon, 'a unity of feeling, a breadth, a light and shade, a warmth of colouring, a tone, a harmony, a glow, an artistical development of original conceptions, which I look for in vain among older performers—I don't know whether I make myself understood?'

"'Perfectly,' replied Nicholas." ¶NN 24

Words and Phrases

—*conventional phrases:* "They presented their compliments to Mr Copperfield, and informed him that they had given his letter their best consideration, 'with a view to the happiness of both parties'—which I thought rather an alarming expression . . . because I had (and have all my life) observed that conventional phrases are a sort of fireworks, easily let off, and liable to take a great variety of shapes and colours not at all suggested by their original form." DC 41

—*"all a-tauto"* " . . . within a few minutes of the first alarm, we had wore ship and got her off, and were all a-tauto—which I felt very grateful for: not that I knew what it was, but that I perceived that we had not been all a-tauto lately." UT/ST

—*"aristocratic"* "'What do you call it when Lords break off door-knockers and beat policemen, and play at coaches with other people's money, and all that sort of thing?

"'Aristocratic?' suggested the collector.

"'Ah! aristocratic,' replied Miss Petowker; 'something very aristocratic about him, isn't there?'" NN 15

—*"boy"* "This word is much used as a term of reproach by elderly gentlemen towards their juniors, probably with the view of deluding society into the belief that if they could be young again, they wouldn't on any account." NN 3

—*"butter wouldn't melt"* "It would be no description of Mr. Pecksniff's gentleness of manner to adopt the common parlance, and say that he looked at this moment as if butter wouldn't melt in his mouth. He rather looked as if any quantity of butter might have been made out of him, by churning the milk of human kindness, as it spouted upwards from his heart." MC 3

—*"chaise"* "'How shall we go?' inquired the captain; 'it's too warm to walk.'

"'A shay?' suggested Mr Joseph Tuggs.

"'Chaise,' whispered Mr Cymon.

"'I should think one would be enough,' said Mr Joseph Tuggs aloud, quite unconscious of the meaning of the correction. 'However, two shays if you like.'" SB/TR

—*"commonplace"* "I will not say that everything was utterly commonplace, because I doubt if anything can be that, except to utterly commonplace people . . . . " CS/HH 1

—*"cool"* "'And a cool four thousand, Pip!'

"I never discovered from whom Joe [Gargery] derived the conventional temperature of the four thousand pounds, but it appeared to make the sum of money more to him, and he had a manifest relish in insisting on its being cool." GE 17

—*"darn"* "'If here ain't the Harrisburg mail at last, and dreadful bright and smart to look at too,' cried an elderly gentleman in some excitement, 'darn my mother!'

"I don't know what the sensation of being darned may be, or whether a man's mother has a keener relish or disrelish of the process than anybody else; but if the endurance of this mysterious ceremony by the old lady in question had depended on the accuracy of her son's vision in respect to the abstract brightness and smartness of the Harrisburg mail, she would certainly have undergone its infliction." AN 9

—"*dead as a doornail*" "Mind! I don't mean to say that I know, of my own knowledge, what there is particularly dead about a door-nail. I might have been inclined, myself, to regard a coffin-nail as the deadest piece of ironmongery in the trade. But the wisdom of our ancestors is in the simile; and my unhallowed hands shall not disturb it, or the Country's done for. You will therefore permit me to repeat, emphatically, that Marley was as dead as a door-nail." CC 1

—"*eccentricity*" "As [penniless boasters] are equally gentlemanly, clever, witty, intelligent, wise, and well-bred, we need scarcely have recommended them to the peculiar consideration of the young ladies, if it were not that some of the gentle creatures whom we hold in such high respect, are perhaps a little too apt to confound a great many heavier terms with the light word eccentricity, which we beg them henceforth to take in a strictly **Johnson**ian sense, without any liberality or latitude of construction." YG/OO

—"*fame*" "'Did you ever hear a definition of fame, sir?' 'I have heard several,' replied Nicholas, with a smile. What is yours?' 'When I dramatise a book, sir,' said the literary gentleman, '*that's* fame. For its author.'" NN 48 [*paragraphs elided*]

—"*farewell*" "Why is it that we can better bear to part in spirit than in body, and while we have the fortitude to act farewell have not the nerve to say it? On the eve of long voyages or an absence of many years, friends who are tenderly attached will separate with the usual look, the usual pressure of the hand, planning one final interview for the morrow, while each well knows that it is but a poor feint to save the pain of uttering that one word, and that the meeting will never be. Should possibilities be worse to bear than certainties? We do not shun our dying friends; the not having distinctly taken leave of one among them, whom we left in all kindness and affection, will often embitter the whole remainder of a life." OCS 15

"There are those in this city [New York] who would brighten, to me, the darkest winter-day that ever glimmered and went out in Lapland; and before whose presence even Home grew dim, when they and I exchanged that painful word which mingles with our every thought and deed; which haunts our cradle-heads in infancy, and closes up the vista of our lives in age." AN 6

—"*fix:*" "'Will you try,' said my opposite neighbour, handing me a dish of potatoes, broken up in milk and butter, 'will you try some of these fixings?'

"There are few words which perform such various duties as this word 'fix.' It is the Caleb Quotem of the American vocabulary. You call upon a gentleman in a country town, and his help informs you that he is 'fixing himself' just now, but will be down directly: by which you are to understand that he is dressing. You inquire, on board a steamboat, of a fellow-passenger, whether breakfast will be ready soon, and he tells you he should think so, for when he was last below, they were 'fixing the tables:' in other words, laying the cloth. You beg a porter to collect your luggage, and he entreats you not to be uneasy, for he'll 'fix it presently:' and if you complain of indisposition, you are advised to have recourse to Doctor So-and-so, who will 'fix you' in no time.

"One night, I ordered a bottle of mulled wine at an hotel where I was staying, and waited a long time for it; at length it was put upon the table with an apology from the landlord that he feared it wasn't 'fixed properly.' And I recollect once, at a stagecoach dinner, overhearing a very stern gentleman demand of a waiter who presented him with a plate of underdone roast-beef, 'whether he called that, fixing God A'mighty's vittles?'" AN 10

—"*force of habit:*" "'The force of habit' is a trite phrase in everybody's mouth; and it is not a little remarkable that those who use it most as applied to others, unconsciously afford in their own persons singular examples of the power which habit and custom exercise over the minds of men, and of the little reflection they are apt to bestow on subjects with which every day's experience has rendered them familiar." SB/VN

—"*foundering:* " . . . he first went a seafaring and was near foundering (what a terrific sound that word had for me when I was a boy!) in his first gale of wind." UT/CM

—"*foundling:*" "For the maternal and paternal Slowboy were alike unknown to Fame, and Tilly had been bred by public charity, a foundling; which word, though only differing from fondling by one vowel's length, is very different in meaning, and expresses quite another thing." CH 1

—"*gammon*" "'The meaning of that term—gammon,' said Mr Gregsbury, 'is unknown to me. If it means that I grow a little too fervid, or perhaps even hyperbolical, in extolling my native land, I admit the full justice of the remark. I *am* proud of this free and happy country. My form dilates, my eye glistens, my breast heaves, my heart swells, my bosom burns, when I call to mind her greatness and her glory.'" NN 16

—"*gormed:*" " . . . [Daniel Peggotty] swore a dreadful oath that he would be 'Gormed' if he didn't cut and run for good, if [his generosity] was ever mentioned again. It appeared, in answer to my inquiries, that nobody had the least idea of the etymology of this terrible verb passive to be gormed; but that they all regarded it as constituting a most solemn imprecation." DC 3

—"*great girl:*" "' . . . a point that, even at the present moment, makes me take out my pocket-handkerchief like a great girl, as people say [said John Chivery]: though I am sure I don't know why a great girl should be a term of reproach, for every rightly constituted male mind loves 'em great and small.'" LD ii 27

—"*greatest happiness of the greatest number*" "'I owe it to my fellow-creatures [said Sapsea] that [Neville Landless] should be, in the words of **Bentham**, where he is the cause of the greatest danger to the smallest number.'" MED 16

—"*home*" ". . . though home is a name, a word, it is a strong one; stronger than magician ever spoke, or spirit answered to, in strongest conjuration." MC 35

And see A:Home—*a definition*

—"*jiggered*"" "'Well, then,' said [Orlick], 'I'm jiggered if I don't see you home!'

"This penalty of being jiggered was a favourite supposititious case of his. He attached no definite meaning to the word that I am aware of, but used it . . . to affront mankind, and convey an idea of something savagely damaging. When I was younger, I had had a general belief that if he jiggered me personally, he would have done it with a sharp and twisted hook." GE 17

—"*kinfreederel*" "'I'd only jist come out for my 'elth [said Deputy Winks] when I see you two a-coming out of the Kinfreederel.'" [Cloisterham cathedral] MED 12

—'"*labour*" " . . . Mrs Gamp had ben up all the previous night, in attendance upon a ceremony to which the usage of gossips has given that name which expresses, in two syllables, the curse pronounced on Adam." MC 19

—*legal terms:* "'Wot do you mean by leavin' it on trust?' inquired Sam, waking up a little. 'If it ain't ready money, were's the use on it?'

"'It's a law term, that's all,' said the cobbler.

"'I don't think that,' said Sam, shaking his head. 'There's wery little trust in that shop. Hows'ever, go on.'

"'Well,' said the cobbler: 'when I was going to take out a probate of the will, the nieces and nevys, who was desperately disappointed at not getting all the money, enters a caveat against it.'

"'What's that?' inquired Sam.

"'A legal instrument, which is as much as to say, it's no go,' replied the cobbler.

"'I see,' said Sam, 'a sort of brother-in-law o' the have-his carcase.'" PP 44

—"*living by one's wits*" "— which means by the abuse of every faculty that worthily employed raises man above the beasts, and so degraded, sinks him far below them." OCS 73 *And see* M:Wits—*lived upon*

—"*making a night of it*" " . . . an expressive term, implying the borrowing of several hours from tomorrow morning, adding them to the night before, and manufacturing a compound night of the whole." SB/MN

—"*a match with the constable*" "'Wy, he did wot many men as has been much better know'd has done in their time, sir,' replied Sam, 'he run a match agin the constable, and vun it.'

"'In other words, I suppose,' said Mr Pickwick, 'he got into debt.'" PP 41

—"*monsters of affection*" "'You never saw [Hugh], living?' asked the clergyman, of Edward [at Hugh's interment after hanging].

"'Often, years ago; not knowing him for my brother.'

"'Never since?'

"'Never. Yesterday, he steadily refused to see me. It was urged upon him, many times, at my desire.'

"'Still he refused? That was hardened and unnatural.'

"'Do you think so?'

"'I infer that you do not?'

"'You are right. We hear the world wonder, every day, at monsters of ingratitude. Did it never occur to you that it often looks for monsters of affection, as though they were things of course?'" BR 79

—"*morning paper*" "[Master Adolphus Tetterby's] juvenility might have been at some loss for a harmless outlet, in his early application to traffic, but for a fortunate discovery he made of a means of entertaining himself, and of dividing the long day into stages of interest, without neglecting business. This ingenious invention, remarkable, like many great discoveries, for its simplicity, consisted in varying the first vowel in the word 'paper,' and substituting, in its stead, at different periods of the day, all the other vowels in grammatical succession. Thus, before daylight in the winter time, he went to and fro, in his little oilskin cap and cape, and his big comforter, piercing the heavy air with his cry of 'Morn-ing Pa-per!' which, about an hour before noon, changed to 'Morn-ing Pep-per!' which, at about two, changed to 'Morn-ing Pip-per!' which, in a couple of hours, changed to 'Morn-ing Pop-per!' and so declined with the sun into 'Eve-ning Pup-per!' to the great relief and comfort of this young gentleman's spirits." HM 2

—"*never mind*" [Mr Magnus] repeated the sneer with increased effect. 'But you shall answer it, sir.'

"'Answer what?' said Mr Pickwick.

"'Never mind, sir,' replied Mr Magnus, striding up and down the room. 'Never mind.'

"There must be something very comprehensive in this phrase of 'Never mind,' for we do not recollect to have ever witnessed a quarrel in the street, at a theatre, public room, or elsewhere, in which it has not been the standard reply to all belligerent inquiries. 'Do you call yourself a gentleman, sir?'—'Never mind, sir.' 'Did I offer to say anything to the young woman, sir?'—'Never mind, sir.' 'Do you want your head knocked up against that wall, sir?'—'Never mind, sir.' It is observable, too, that there would appear to be some hidden taunt in this universal 'Never mind,' which rouses more indignation in the bosom of the individual addressed, than the most lavish abuse could possibly awaken." PP 24

—"*obstinate*" "'And you mean to say you are still obstinate?'

"'Not obstinate, Miss, I hope.'

"'Firm (I suppose you call it) then?'

"'Yes, Miss. Fixed like.'

"'Never was an obstinate person yet, who would own to the word!' remarked Miss Potterson, rubbing her vexed nose: 'I'm sure I would, if I was obstinate; but I am a pepperer, which is different.'" OMF 6

—"*old school*" "He is of what is called the old school—a phrase generally meaning any school that seems never to have been young . . . ." BH 2

—"*Pickwickian*" Blotton, a member of the Pickwick Club, "' . . . would only say . . . that he repelled the hon. gent's false and scurrilous accusation, with profound contempt. (Great cheering) The hon. gent. was a humbug. (Immense confusion and loud cries of "Chair" and "Order.") . . . .

"'The CHAIRMAN felt it his imperative duty to demand of the honourable gentleman, whether he had used the expression which had just escaped him in a common sense.

"'Mr BLOTTON had no hesitation in saying that he had not—he had used the word in its Pickwickian sense. (Hear, hear.) He was bound to acknowledge that, personally, he entertained the highest regard and esteem for the honourable gentleman; he had merely considered him a humbug in a Pickwickian point of view. (Hear, hear.)'" PP 1
This lampoon of the then-common mode of explaining insults in the House of Commons as meant "only in a Parliamentary sense" is said to have led to the great decline and ultimate disappearance of this fiction.

—"*rallying*" "It is likewise agreed that they are all so exhausted with the work behind them, and need to be so fortified for the work before them, as to require peculiar strengthening from Veneering's cellar. Therefore, the Analytical has orders to produce the cream of the cream of his bins, and therefore it falls out that rallying becomes rather a trying word for the occasion: Lady Tippins being observed gamely to inculcate the necessity of rearing round their dear Veneering; Podsnap advocating roaring round him; Boots and Brewer declaring their intention of reeling round him; and Veneering thanking his devoted friends one and all, with great emotion, for rarullarulling round him." OMF ii 3

—"*reading*" "'You charm me, Mortimer, with

your reading of my weaknesses [said Eugene Wrayburn]. (By-the-bye, that very word, Reading, in its critical use, always charms me. An actress's Reading of a chambermaid, a dancer's Reading of a hornpipe, a singer's Reading of a song, a marine painter's Reading of the sea, the kettledrum's Reading of an instrumental passage, are phrases ever youthful and delightful.)" OMF iii 10

—"*sober as a judge*" "Mr Twigger at once solemnly pledged himself to be as sober as a judge, and Nicholas Tulrumble was satisfied, although, had we been Nicholas, we should certainly have exacted some promise of a more specific nature; inasmuch as, having attended the Mudfog assizes in the evening more than once, we can solemnly testify to having seen judges with very strong symptoms of dinner under their wigs. However, that's neither here nor there." B/T

—"*study*" ". . . who ever knew a man who never read or wrote either who hadn't got some small back parlour which he would call a study!" PP 35

—"*swarming*" ". . . the smallest boy but one divining [his mother's] intent, immediately began swarming upstairs after her—if that word of doubtful etymology be admissible—on his arms and legs . . . . " DS 2

—"*theatrical*" "Conceiving the difference between a dramatic picture and a theatrical picture, to be, that in the former case a story is strikingly told, without apparent consciousness of a spectator, and that in the latter case the groups are obtrusively conscious of a spectator, and are obviously dressed up, and doing (or not doing) certain things with an eye to the spectator, and not for the sake of the story . . . . " HW/I

—"*time is money*" "' . . . they're a wise people, the Scotch. [Nickleby] will talk about business, and won't give away his time for nothing. He's very right. Time is money, time is money.'

"'He was one of us who made that saying, I should think,' said Ralph. 'Time is money, and very good money too, to those who reckon interest by it. Time *is* money! Yes, and time costs money; it's rather an expensive article to some people we could name, or I forget my trade.'" NN 47

—"*To wit, in manner following, that is to say*" "Again, Mr Micawber had a relish in this formal piling up of words, which, however ludicrously displayed in his case, was, I must say, not at all peculiar to him. I have observed it, in the course of my life, in numbers of men. It seems to me to be a general rule. In the taking of legal oaths, for instance, deponents seem to enjoy themselves mightily when they come to several good words in succession, for the expression of one idea; as, that they utterly detest, abominate, and abjure, or so forth; and the old anathemas were made relishing on the same principle." DC 52

—"*un-English*" "Why does that word 'un-English,' always act as a spell upon me, and why do I suffer it to settle any question? Twelve months ago, it was un-English to abstain from throttling our soldiers. Thirty years ago, it was un-English not to hang people up by scores every Monday. Sixty years ago, it was un-English to be sober after dinner. A hundred years ago, it was un-English not to love cock-fighting, prize-fighting, dog-fighting, bull-baiting, and other savageries. Why do I submit to the word as a clincher, without asking myself whether it has any meaning? I don't dispute that I do so, every day of my life; but I want to know why I do so?" HW/W?

—"*uncertain temper*" "—a phrase which being interpreted signifies a temper tolerably certain to make everybody more or less uncomfortable." BR 7

—"*upon my word*": "'Upon my word, sir,' said the astonished Mrs Pott, stooping to pick up the paper. 'Upon my word, sir!'

"Mr Pott winced beneath the contemptuous gaze of his wife. He had made a desperate struggle to screw up his courage, but it was fast coming unscrewed again.

"There appears nothing very tremendous in this little sentence, 'Upon my word, sir' when it comes to be read; but the tone of voice in which it was delivered, and the look that accompanied it, both seeming to bear reference to some revenge to be thereafter visited upon the head of Pott, produced their full effect upon him." PP 18

—"*work*" "'But my school is a pleasure to me,' [Phoebe] interrupted, opening her brown eyes wider, as if surprised to find [her father] so obtuse. 'I began it when I was but a child, because it brought me and other children into company, don't you see? *That* was not work. I carry it on still, because it keeps children about me. *That* is not work. I do it as love, not as work. Then my lace-pillow;' her busy hands had stopped, as if her argument required all her cheerful earnestness, but now went on again at the name; 'it goes with my thoughts when I think, and it goes with my tunes when I hum any, and *that's* not work. Why, you yourself thought it was music, you know, Sir. And so it is to me.'" CS/MJ 1

—*"Yes:"* "'Traddles was recommended to me by a professional friend. Oh, yes. Yes. He has a kind of talent for drawing briefs, and stating a case in writing, plainly. I am able to throw something in Traddles's way, in the course of the year; something—for him—considerable. Oh yes. Yes.'

"I was much impressed by the extremely comfortable and satisfied manner in which Mr Waterbrook delivered himself of this little word 'Yes,' every now and then. There was wonderful expression in it. It completely conveyed the idea of a man who had been born, not to say with a silver spoon, but with a scaling-ladder, and had gone on mounting all the heights of life one after another, until now he looked, from the top of the fortifications, with the eye of a philosopher and a patron, on the people down in the trenches." DC 25

—*"Yes, Sir"* "Whenever the coach [to Columbus, Ohio] stops, and you can hear the voices of the inside passengers; or whenever any bystander addresses them, or any one among them; or they address each other; you will hear one phrase repeated over and over and over again to the most extraordinary extent. It is an ordinary and unpromising phrase enough, being neither more nor less than 'Yes, Sir;' but it is adapted to every variety of circumstance, and fills up every pause . . . .

"STRAW HAT. There was a snap of cold, last week.

"BROWN HAT. Yes, Sir.

"STRAW HAT. Yes, Sir.

"A pause. They look at each other, very seriously.

"STRAW HAT. I calculate you'll have got through that case of the corporation, Judge, by this time, now?

"B.H. Yes, Sir.

"S.H. How did the verdict go, Sir?

"B.H. For the defendant, Sir.

"S.H. (Interrogatively.) Yes, Sir?

"B.H. (Affirmatively.) Yes, Sir.

BOTH. (Musingly, as each gazes down the street.) Yes, Sir . . . . " AN 14

Truth Prevails, and Virtue is Triumphant MC

Spirit, and Moral Qualities

Ages of incessant labour by immortal creatures for this earth must pass into eternity before the good of which it is susceptible is all developed. Any spirit working kindly in its little sphere, whatever it may be, will find its mortal life too short for its vast means of usefulness.

[CC 1]

"There are some upon this earth of yours," said the Spirit, "who lay claim to know us, and who do their deeds of passion, pride, ill-will, hatred, envy, bigotry, and selfishness in our name, who are as strange to us as if they had never lived. Remember that, and charge their doings on themselves, not us."

[CC 3]

The Church OCS

Adversity

—and good nature: "[Gabriel Grub] saw that men who worked hard, and earned their scanty bread with lives of labour, were cheerful and happy; and that to the most ignorant, the sweet face of nature was a never-failing source of cheerfulness and joy. He saw those who had been delicately nurtured, and tenderly brought up, cheerful under privations, and superior to suffering that would have crushed many of a rougher grain, because they bore within their own bosoms the materials of happiness, contentment, and peace. He saw that women, the tenderest and most fragile of all God's creatures, were the oftenest superior to sorrow, adversity, and distress; and he saw that it was because they bore, in their own hearts, an inexhaustible well-spring of affection and devotion. Above all, he saw that men like himself, who snarled at the mirth and cheerfulness of others, were the foulest weeds on the fair surface of the earth; and setting all the good of the world against the evil, he came to the conclusion that it was a very decent and respectable sort of world after all." PP 30

—its use: " . . . in the hideous solitude of that most hideous place, with Hope so far removed, Ambition quenched, and Death beside [Martin Chuzzlewit] rattling at the very door, reflection came, as in a plague-beleaguered town; and so he felt and knew the failing of his life, and saw distinctly what an ugly spot it was.

"Eden was a hard school to learn so hard a lesson in; but there were teachers in the swamp and thicket, and the pestilential air, who had a searching method of their own.

"He made a solemn resolution that when his strength returned he would not dispute the point or resist the conviction, but would look upon it as an established fact, that selfishness was in his breast, and must be rooted out. He was so doubtful (and with justice) of his own character, that he determined not to say one word of vain regret or good resolve to Mark, but steadily to keep his purpose before his own eyes solely: and there was not a jot of pride in this; nothing but humility and stead-fastness: the best armour he could wear. So low had Eden brought him down. So high had Eden raised him up." MC 33

"'I know how obdurate I was [said Mercy Pecksniff]! I never thought at all; dear Mr Chuzzlewit, I never thought at all; I had no thought, no heart, no care to find one; at that time. It has grown out of my trouble. I have felt it in my trouble. I wouldn't recall my trouble, such as it is and has been—and it is light in comparison with trials which hundreds of good people suffer every day, I know—I wouldn't recall it to-morrow, if I could. It has been my friend, for without it no one could have changed me; nothing could have changed me. Do not mistrust me because of these tears; I cannot help them. I am grateful for it, in my soul. Indeed I am!'" MC 54

"Taking into account where [Arthur Clennam] was, the interest that had first brought him there when he had been free to keep away, and the gentle presence that was equally inseparable from the walls and bars about him and from the impalpable remembrances of his later life which no walls or bars could imprison, it was not remarkable that everything his memory turned upon should bring him round again to Little Dorrit. Yet it was remarkable to him; not because of the fact itself; but because of the reminder it brought with it, how much the dear little creature had influenced his better resolutions.

"None of us clearly know to whom or to what we are indebted in this wise, until some marked stop in the whirling wheel of life brings the right perception with it. It comes with sickness, it comes with sorrow, it comes with the loss of the dearly loved, it is one of the most frequent uses of adversity." LD ii 37

And see FL:Angel—*a shared attribute*

—war between the sexes: "It is a dangerous thing to see anything in the sphere of a vain blusterer, before the vain blusterer sees it himself. Mr Bounderby felt that Mrs Sparsit had audaciously anticipated him, and presumed to be wiser than he. Inappeasably indignant with her for her triumphant discovery of Mrs Pegler, he turned this presumption, on the part of a woman in her dependent position, over and over in his mind, until it accumulated with turning like a great snowball.

"At last he made the discovery that to discharge this highly connected female—to have it in his power to say, 'She was a woman of family, and wanted to stick to me, but I wouldn't have it, and got rid of her'—would be to get the utmost possible amount of crowning glory out of the connexion, and at the same time to punish Mrs Sparsit according to her deserts.

"Filled fuller than ever, with this great idea, Mr Bounderby came in to lunch, and sat himself down in the dining-room of former days, where his portrait was. Mrs Sparsit sat by the fire, with her foot in her cotton stirrup, little thinking whither she was posting.

"Since the Pegler affair, this gentlewoman had covered her pity for Mr Bounderby with a veil of quiet melancholy and contrition. In virtue thereof, it had become her habit to assume a woeful look, which woeful look she now bestowed upon her patron.

"'What's the matter now, ma'am?' said Mr Bounderby, in a very short, rough way.

"'Pray, sir,' returned Mrs Sparsit, 'do not bite my nose off.'

"'Bite your nose off, ma'am?' repeated Mr Bounderby. '*Your* nose!' meaning, as Mrs Sparsit conceived, that it was too developed a nose for the purpose. After which offensive implication, he cut himself a crust of bread, and threw the knife down with a noise.

"Mrs Sparsit took her foot out of her stirrup, and said, 'Mr Bounderby, sir!'

"'Well, ma'am?' retorted Mr Bounderby. 'What are you staring at?'

"'May I ask, sir,' said Mrs Sparsit, 'have you been ruffled this morning?'

"'Yes, ma'am.'

"'May I inquire, sir,' pursued the injured woman, 'whether *I* am the unfortunate cause of your having lost your temper?'

"'Now, I'll tell you what, ma'am,' said Bounderby, 'I am not come here to be bullied. A female may be highly connected, but she can't be permitted to bother and badger a man in my position, and I am not going to put up with it.' (Mr Bounderby felt it necessary to get on: foreseeing that if he allowed of details, he would be beaten.)

"Mrs Sparsit first elevated, then knitted, her Coriolanian eyebrows; gathered up her work into its proper basket; and rose.

"'Sir,' said she, majestically. 'It is apparent to me that I am in your way at present. I will retire to my own apartment.'

"'Allow me to open the door, ma'am.'

"'Thank you, sir; I can do it for myself.'

"'You had better allow me, ma'am,' said Bounderby, passing her, and getting his hand upon the lock; 'because I can take the opportunity of saying a word to you, before you go. Mrs Sparsit, ma'am, I rather think you are cramped here, do you know? It appears to me, that, under my humble roof, there's hardly opening enough for a lady of your genius in other people's affairs.'

"Mrs Sparsit gave him a look of the darkest scorn, and said with great politeness, 'Really, sir?'

"'I have been thinking it over, you see, since the late affairs have happened, ma'am,' said Bounderby, 'and it appears to my poor judgment—'

"'Oh! Pray, sir,' Mrs Sparsit interposed, with sprightly cheerfulness, 'don't disparage your judgment. Everybody knows how unerring Mr Bounderby's judgment is. Everybody has had proofs of it. It must be the theme of general conversation. Disparage anything in yourself but your judgment, sir,' said Mrs Sparsit, laughing.

"Mr Bounderby, very red and uncomfortable, resumed:

"'It appears to me, ma'am, I say, that a different sort of establishment altogether would bring out a lady of *your* powers. Such an establishment as your relation, Lady Scadgers's, now. Don't you think you might find some affairs there, ma'am, to interfere with?'

"'It never occurred to me before, sir,' returned Mrs Sparsit; 'but now you mention it, I should think it highly probable.'

"'Then suppose you try, ma'am,' said Bounderby, laying an envelope with a cheque in it in her little basket. 'You can take your own time for going, ma'am' but perhaps in the meanwhile, it will be more agreeable to a lady of your powers of mind, to eat her meals by herself, and not to be intruded upon. I really ought to apologize to you—being only Josiah Bounderby of Coketown—for having stood in your light so long.'

"'Pray don't name it, sir,' returned Mrs Sparsit. 'If that portrait could speak, sir—but it has the advantage over the original of not possessing the power of committing itself and disgusting others—it would testify, that a long period has elapsed since I first habitually addressed it as the picture of a Noodle. Nothing that a Noodle does, can awaken surprise or indignation; the proceedings of a Noodle can only inspire contempt.'

"Thus saying, Mrs Sparsit, with her Roman features like a medal struck to commemorate her scorn of Mr Bounderby, surveyed him fixedly from head to foot, swept disdainfully past him, and ascended the staircase." ¶HT iii 9

Apathy

—amorality: "Mrs Bounderby,' [James Harthouse] returned, laughing, 'upon my honour, no. I will make no such pretence to you. I have seen a little, here and there, up and down; I have found it all to be very worthless, as everybody has, and as some confess they have, and some do not; and I am going in for your respected father's opinions—really because I have no choice of opinions, and may as well back them as anything else.'

"'Have you none of your own?' asked Louisa.

"'I have not so much as the slightest predilection left. I assure you I attach not the least importance to any opinions. The result of the varieties of boredom I have undergone, is a conviction (unless conviction is too industrious a word for the lazy sentiment I entertain on the subject), that any set of ideas will do just as much good as any other set, and just as much harm as any other set. There's an English family with a charming Italian motto. What will be, will be. It's the only truth going!'

"This vicious assumption of honesty in dishonesty—a vice so dangerous, so deadly, and so common—seemed, he observed, a little to impress her in his favour." HT ii 2

And see M:True and false—*'honesty in dishonesty'*

—blasé: "'Mr Jack!' said the Doctor [Strong]. 'Copperfield!'

"Mr Jack Maldon shook hands with me; but not very warmly, I believed; and with an air of languid patronage, at which I secretly took great umbrage. But his languor altogether was quite a wonderful sight; except when he addressed himself to his cousin Annie.

"'Have you breakfasted this morning, Mr Jack?' said the Doctor.

"'I hardly ever take breakfast, sir,' he replied, with his head thrown back in an easy-chair. 'I find it bores me.'

"'Is there any news to-day?' inquired the Doctor.

"'Nothing at all, sir,' replied Mr Maldon. 'There's an account about the people being hungry and discontented down in the North, but they are always being hungry and discontented somewhere.'

"The Doctor looked grave, and said, as though he wished to change the subject, 'Then there's no news at all; and no news, they say, is good news.'

"'There's a long statement in the papers, sir, about a murder,' observed Mr Maldon. 'But somebody is always being murdered, and I didn't read it.'

"A display of indifference to all the actions and passions of mankind was not supposed to be such a distinguished quality at that time, I think, as I have observed it to be considered since. I have known it very fashionable indeed. I have seen it displayed with such success, that I have encountered some fine ladies and gentlemen who might as well have been born caterpillars. Perhaps it impressed me the more then, because it was new to me, but it certainly did not tend to exalt my opinion of, or to strengthen my confidence in, Mr Jack Maldon." DC 36

—of the comfortable, excoriated: "'Who hears in us, the Chimes, one note bespeaking disregard, or stern regard, of any hope, or joy, or pain, or sorrow, of the many-sorrowed throng; who hears us make response to any creed that gauges human passions and affections, as it gauges the amount of miserable food on which humanity may pine and wither; does us wrong . . . .

"'Who hears us echo the dull vermin of the earth: the Putters Down of crushed and broken natures, formed to be raised up higher than such maggots of the time can crawl or can conceive,' pursued the Goblin of the Bell; 'who does so, does us wrong . . . .

"'Lastly, and most of all,' pursued the Bell, 'Who turns his back upon the fallen and disfigured of his kind; abandons them as vile; and does not trace and track with pitying eyes the unfenced precipice by which they fell from good—grasping in their fall some tufts and shreds of that lost soil, and clinging to them still when bruised and dying in the gulf below; does wrong to

Heaven and man, to time and to eternity.'" C 3

—*coolness:* "There is an old-fashioned weather-glass representing a house with two doorways, in one of which is the figure of a gentleman, in the other the figure of a lady. When the weather is to be fine the lady comes out and the gentleman goes in; when wet, the gentleman comes out and the lady goes in. They never seek each other's society, are never elevated and depressed by the same cause, and have nothing in common. They are the model of a cool couple, except that there is something of politeness and consideration about the behaviour of the gentleman in the weather-glass, in which neither of the cool couple can be said to participate.

"The cool couple are seldom alone together, and when they are, nothing can exceed their apathy and dulness: the gentleman being for the most part drowsy, and the lady silent. If they enter into conversation, it is usually of an ironical or recriminatory nature . . . .

"Thus, a great many cool couples go on until they are cold couples, and the grave has closed over their folly and indifference. Loss of name, station, character, life itself, has ensued from causes as slight as these. . . . " YC/I

—*to egregious political appointment:* "When it became known to the Britons on the shore of the yellow Tiber that their intelligent compatriot Mr Sparkler was made one of the Lords of their Circumlocution Office, they took it as a piece of news with which they had no nearer concern than with any other piece of news—any other Accident or Offence—in the English papers. Some laughed; some said, by way of complete excuse, that the post was virtually a sinecure, and any fool who could spell his name was good enough for it; some, and these were the more solemn political oracles, said that Decimus did wisely to strengthen himself, and that the sole constitutional purpose of all places within the gift of Decimus, was, that Decimus *should* strengthen himself. A few bilious Britons there were who would not subscribe to this article of faith; but their objection was purely theoretical. In a practical point of view, they listlessly abandoned the matter, as being the business of some other Britons unknown, somewhere, or nowhere.

"In like manner, at home, great numbers of Britons maintained, for as long as four-and-twenty consecutive hours, that those invisible and anonymous Britons 'ought to take it up;' and that if they quietly acquiesced in it, they deserved it. But of what class the remiss Britons were composed, and where the unlucky creatures hid themselves, and why they hid themselves, and how it constantly happened that they neglected their interests, when so many other Britons were quite at a loss to account for their not looking after those interests, was not, either upon the shore of the yellow Tiber or the shore of the black Thames, made apparent to men." ¶LD ii 14

—*indifference:* ". . . [old Martin Chuzzlewit's] character seemed to have modified by regular degrees, and to have softened down into a dull indifference . . . . His looks were much the same as ever, but his mind was singularly altered. It was not that this or that passion stood out in brighter or in dimmer hues; but that the colour of the whole man was faded. As one trait disappeared, no other trait sprung up to take its place. His senses dwindled too. He was less keen of sight; was deaf sometimes; took little notice of what passed before him; and would be profoundly taciturn for days together." MC 30

Bible and Prayer-book

—*catechism:* "'Look at him! Love! Honour! And Obey! Overhaul your catechism till you find that passage, and when found turn the leaf down. Success, my boy!'

"[Captain Cuttle] was so perfectly satisfied both with his quotation and his reference to it, that he could not help repeating the words again in a low voice, and saying he had forgotten 'em these forty year.

"'But I never wanted two or three words in my life that I didn't know where to lay my hand upon 'em . . . . It comes of not wasting language as some do.'" DS 4

"'Walk fast, Wal'r, my lad . . . and walk the same all the days of your life. Overhaul the catechism for that advice, and keep it!'" DS 9

Psalms 23:6: *Surely goodness and mercy shall follow me all the days of my life (and see* Psalms 27:4 *and* Proverbs 31:12)

—*as comfort:* "'Lay my head so, dear, that as you read I may see the words in your kind face.'

"Harriet [Carker] complied and read—read the eternal book for all the weary and the heavy-laden; for all the wretched, fallen, and neglected of this earth—read the blessed history, in which the blind lame palsied beggar, the criminal, the woman stained with shame, the shunned of all our dainty clay, has each a portion, that no human pride, indifference, or sophistry, through all the ages that this world shall last, can take away, or by the thousandth atom of a grain reduce—read the ministry of Him who, through the round of human life, and all its hopes and griefs, from birth to death, from infancy to age, had sweet compassion for, and interest in, its every scene and stage, its every suffering and sorrow.

"'I shall come,' said Harriet, when she shut the book, 'very early in the morning.'

"The lustrous eyes, yet fixed upon her face, closed for a moment, then opened; and Alice [Marwood] kissed and blest her.

"The same eyes followed her to the door; and in their light, and on the tranquil face, there was a smile when it was closed.

"They never turned away. She laid her hand upon her breast, murmuring the sacred name that had been read to her; and life passed from her face, like light removed." DS 58

—as punishment: "Rob the Grinder, whose reverence for the inspired writings, under the admirable system of the Grinders' School, had been developed by a perpetual bruising of his intellectual shins against all the proper names of all the tribes of Judah, and by the monotonous repetition of hard verses, especially by way of punishment. . . . " DS 39

—regularly read: "On Sunday nights, the Captain [Cuttle] always read for himself, before going to bed, a certain Divine Sermon once delivered on a Mount; and although he was accustomed to quote the text, without book, after his own manner, he appeared to read it with as reverent an understanding of its heavenly spirit, as if he had got it all by heart in Greek, and had been able to write any number of fierce theological disquisitions on its every phrase." DS 39

—for swearing: "'And even then, dear boy,' said [Magwitch], pulling a greasy little clasped black Testament out of his pocket, 'we'll have him on his oath.'

"To state that my terrible patron carried this little black book about the world solely to swear people on in cases of emergency, would be to state what I never quite established—but this I can say, that I never knew him put it to any other use. The book itself had the appearance of having been stolen from some court of justice, and perhaps his knowledge of its antecedents, combined with his own experience in that wise, gave him a reliance on its powers as a sort of legal spell or charm." GE 40

—as threat: "There was the dreary Sunday of [Arthur Clennam's] childhood, when he sat with his hands before him, scared out of his senses by a horrible tract which commenced business with the poor child by asking him in its title, why he was going to Perdition?—a piece of curiosity that he really in a frock and drawers was not in a condition to satisfy—and which, for the further attraction of his infant mind, had a parenthesis in every other line with some such hiccupping reference as 2 Ep. Thess. c. iii v. 6 & 7.*" LD 1 3

**Not a novice, lest being lifted up with pride he fall into the condemnation of the devil. / Moreover he must have a good report of them which are without: lest he fall into reproach and the snare of the devil.*

"There was the interminable Sunday of [Arthur Clennam's] nonage; when his mother, stern of face and unrelenting of heart, would sit all day behind a bible—bound, like her own construction of it, in the hardest, barest, and straitest boards, with one dinted ornament on the cover like the drag of a chain, and a wrathful sprinkling of red upon the edges of the leaves—as if it, of all books! were a fortification against sweetness of temper, natural affection, and gentle intercourse." LD 1 3

Chapel (Dissenting)

—contrasted with fashionable observance: "A small close chapel with a white-washed wall, and plain deal pews and pulpit, contains a closely-packed congregation, as different in dress as they are opposed in manner, to that we have just quitted. The hymn is sung—not by paid singers, but by the whole assembly at the loudest pitch of their voices, unaccompanied by any musical instrument, the words being given out, two lines at a time, by the clerk.

"There is something in the sonorous quavering of the harsh voices, in the lank and hollow faces of the men, and the sour solemnity of the women, which bespeaks this a stronghold of intolerant zeal and ignorant enthusiasm. The preacher enters the pulpit . . . . The congregation fall upon their knees, and are hushed into profound stillness as he delivers an extempore prayer, in which he calls upon the Sacred Founder of the Christian faith to bless his ministry, in terms of disgusting and impious familiarity not to be described . . . . The congregation murmur their acquiescence in his doctrines: and a short groan occasionally bears testimony to the moving nature of his eloquence . . . .

"A low moaning is heard, the women rock their bodies to and fro, and wring their hands; the preacher's fervour increases . . . . A great excitement is visible among his hearers, a scream is heard, and some young girl falls senseless on the floor . . . the girl is removed, a hymn is sung, a petition for some measure for securing the better observance of the Sabbath, which has been prepared by the good man, is read; and his worshipping admirers struggle who shall be the first to sign it" ¶STH/1

—proliferation: "There are two dissenting chapels, besides, in our small watering-place; being in about the proportion of a hundred and twenty guns to a yacht." RP/EW *And see* M:Wonder*—negated*

—venality: "All through my time as a foundation boy, I was within a few miles of Brother Hawkyard's congregation; and whenever I was what we called a leave-boy on a Sunday, I went over there at his desire.

"Before the knowledge became forced upon me that outside their place of meeting these brothers and sisters were no better than the rest of the human family, but on the whole were, to put the case mildly, as bad as most, in respect of giving short weight in their shops, and not speaking the truth—I say, before this knowledge became forced upon me, their prolix addresses, their inordinate conceit, their daring ignorance, their investment of the Supreme Rule of heaven and earth with their own miserable meannesses and littlenesses, greatly shocked me.

"Still, as their term for the frame of mind that could not perceive them to be in an exalted state of grace was the 'worldly' state, I did for a time suffer tortures under my inquiries of myself whether that young worldly-devilish spirit of mine could secretly be lingering at the bottom of my non-appreciation." ¶GSE 6

Index IV *lists six colourfully named preachers, including Boanerges Boiler UT/LC, Jabez Fireworks HW/WH, and Melchisedech Howler DS; and* Index VIII *has eight figures.*

Christianity

—born again: "'How's mother-in-law this mornin'?'

"'Queer, Sammy, queer,' replied the elder Mr Weller, with impressive gravity. 'She's been gettin' rayther in the Methodistical order lately, Sammy; and she is uncommon pious, to be sure. She's too good a creetur for me, Sammy. I feel I don't deserve her.'

"'Ah,' said Mr Samuel, 'that's wery self-denyin' o' you.'

"'Wery,' replied his parent, with a sigh. 'She's got hold o' some inwention for grown-up people being born again, Sammy; the new birth, I thinks they calls it. I should wery much like to see that system in haction, Sammy. I should wery much like to see your mother-in-law born again. Wouldn't I put her out to nurse!'" PP 22

—canine example: "'He's a rum dog. Don't he look fierce at any strange cove that laughs or sings when he's in company! . . . . Won't he growl at all, when he hears a fiddle playing! And don't he hate other dogs as ain't of his breed! Oh, no!'

"'He's an out-and-out Christian,' said Charley.

"This was merely intended as a tribute to the animal's abilities, but it was an appropriate remark in another sense, if Master Bates had only known it; for there are a good many ladies and gentlemen, claiming to be out-and-out Christians, between whom, and Mr Sikes's dog, there exist strong and singular points of resemblance." OT 18

—fused with the 'false': "But whether, in this ride [in Rome], you pass by obelisks, or columns: ancient temples, theatres, houses, porticoes, or forums: it is strange to see, how every fragment, whenever it is possible, has been blended into some modern structure, and made to serve some modern purpose—a wall, a dwelling-place, a granary, a stable—some use for which it never was designed, and associated with which it cannot otherwise than lamely assort. It is stranger still, to see how many ruins of the old mythology: how many fragments of obsolete legend and observance: have been incorporated into the worship of Christian altars here; and how, in numberless respects, the false faith and the true are fused into a monstrous union." PI 11

—genuine: "Many a time had that kind creature [Reverend Milvey] got up, and gone out to Mrs Sprodgkin . . . suppressing a strong

sense of her comicality by his strong sense of duty, and perfectly knowing that nothing but a cold would come of it. However, beyond themselves, the Reverend Frank Milvey and Mrs Milvey seldom hinted that Mrs Sprodgkin was hardly worth the trouble she gave; but both made the best of her, as they did of all their troubles." OMF iv 11

"So cheerful of spirit and guiltless of affectation, as true practical Christianity ever is! I read more of the New Testament in the fresh frank face going up the village beside me, in five minutes, than I have read in anathematising discourses (albeit put to press with enormous flourishing of trumpets), in all my life. I heard more of the Sacred Book in the cordial voice that had nothing to say about its owner, than in all the would-be celestial pairs of bellows that have ever blown conceit at me . . . .

"In this noble modesty, in this beautiful simplicity, in this serene avoidance of the least attempt to 'improve' an occasion which might be supposed to have sunk of its own weight into my heart, I seemed to have happily come, in a few steps, from the churchyard with its open grave, which was the type of Death, to the Christian dwelling side by side with it, which was the type of Resurrection." UT/S

—hypocritical: "Muggleton is an ancient and loyal borough, mingling a zealous advocacy of Christian principles with a devoted attachment to commercial rights; in demonstration whereof, the mayor, corporation, and other inhabitants, have presented at divers times, no fewer than one thousand four hundred and twenty petitions against the continuance of negro slavery abroad, and an equal number against any interference with the factory system at home; sixty-eight in favour of the sale of livings in the Church, and eighty-six for abolishing Sunday trading in the street." PP 7

—inconvenient congregant: "She was a member of the Reverend Frank [Milvey]'s congregation, and made a point of distinguishing herself in that body, by conspicuously weeping at everything, however cheering, said by the Reverend Frank in his public ministration; also by applying to herself the various lamentations of David, and complaining in a personally injured manner (much in arrear of the clerk and the rest of the respondents) that her enemies were digging pit-falls about her, and breaking her with rods of iron. Indeed, this old widow discharged herself of that portion of the Morning and Evening Service as if she were lodging a complaint on oath and applying for a warrant before a magistrate. But this was not her most inconvenient characteristic, for that took the form of an impression, usually recurring in inclement weather and at about daybreak, that she had something on her mind, and stood in immediate need of the Reverend Frank to come and take it off." OMF iv 11

—prayer: "'Jo! Did you ever know a prayer?' [said Allan Woodcourt]

"'Never knowd nothink, sir.'

"'Not so much as one short prayer?'

"'No, sir. Nothink at all. Mr Chadbands he wos a-prayin wunst at Mr Sangsby's and I heerd him, but he sounded as if he wos a-speakin to hisself, and not to me. He prayed a lot, but *I* couldn't make out nothink on it. Different times, there was other genlmen come down Tom-all-Alone's a-prayin, but they all mostly sed as the t'other wuns prayed wrong, and all mostly sounded to be a-talkin to theirselves, or a-passin blame on the t'others, and not a-talkin to us. *We* never knowd nothink. *I* never knowd what it wos all about.'" BH 47

—pre-French Revolution: "Under the guidance of her Christian pastors, she entertained herself, besides, with such humane achievements as sentencing a youth to have his hands cut off, his tongue torn out with pincers, and his body burned alive, because he had not kneeled down in the rain to do honour to a dirty procession of monks which passed within his view at a distance of some fifty or sixty yards." TTC i 1

—sanctimonious: "'A Turk turns his face, after washing it well, to the East, when he says his prayers; these ['your haughty religious'] good people, after giving their faces such a rub against the World as to take the smiles off, turn with no less regularity, to the darkest side of Heaven. Between the Mussulman and the Pharisee, commend me to the first!'" OT 46

—what the martyrs would think: "'The Triumphs of the Faith are not above ground in our splendid churches,' said the friar, looking round upon us, as we stopped to rest in one of the low passages, with bones and dust surrounding us on every side. 'They are here! Among the Martyrs' Graves!'

"He was a gentle, earnest man, and said it from his heart; but when I thought how Christian men have dealt with one another; how, perverting our most merciful religion, they have hunted down and tortured, burnt and beheaded, strangled, slaughtered, and oppressed each other; I pictured to myself an agony surpassing any that this Dust had suffered with the breath of life yet lingering in it, and how these great and constant hearts would have been shaken—how they would have quailed and drooped—if a foreknowledge of the deeds that professing Christians would commit in the great Name for which they died, could have rent them with its own unutterable anguish, on the cruel wheel, and bitter cross, and in the fearful fire." ¶PI 11

For rigid Christianity, see, for example, Miss Barbary BH and Mrs Clennam LD

See also N:Nature—*perverted*

Christmas

—in a cathedral town: "Seasonable tokens are about. Red berries shine here and there in the lattices of Minor Canon Corner; Mr and Mrs Tope are daintily sticking sprigs of holly into the carvings and sconces of the Cathedral stalls, as if they were sticking them into the coat-buttonholes of the Dean and Chapter.

"Lavish profusion is in the shops: particularly in the articles of currants, raisins, spices, candied peel, and moist sugar. An unusual air of gallantry and dissipation is abroad; evinced in an immense bunch of mistletoe hanging in the greengrocer's shop doorway, and a poor little Twelfth Cake, culminating in the figure of a Harlequin—such a very poor little Twelfth Cake, that one would rather call it a Twenty-Fourth Cake, or a Forty-Eighth Cake—to be raffled for at the pastry-cook's, terms one shilling per member.

"Public amusements are not wanting. The Wax-Work which made so deep an impression on the reflective mind of the Emperor of China is to be seen by particular desire during Christmas Week only, on the premises of the bankrupt livery-stable keeper up the lane; and a new grand comic Christmas pantomime is to be produced at the Theatre: the latter heralded by the portrait of Signor Jacksonini the clown, saying 'How do you do to-morrow?' quite as large as life, and almost as miserably. In short, Cloisterham is up and doing . . . . " ¶MED 14

—and family: "Who can be insensible to the outpourings of good feeling, and the honest interchange of affectionate attachment, which abound at this season of the year? A Christmas family-party! We know nothing in nature more delightful!

"There seems a magic in the very name of Christmas. Petty jealousies and discords are forgotten; social feelings are awakened, in bosoms to which they have long been strangers; father and son, or brother and sister, who have met and passed with averted gaze, or a look of cold recognition, for months before, proffer and return the cordial embrace, and bury their past animosities in their present happiness.

"Kindly hearts that have yearned towards each other, but have been withheld by false notions of pride and self-dignity, are again reunited, and all is kindness and benevolence! Would that Christmas lasted the whole year through (as it ought), and that the prejudices and passions which deform our better nature, were never called into action among those to whom they should ever be strangers!

"The Christmas family-party that we mean, is not a mere assemblage of relations, got up at a week or two's notice, and not likely to be repeated in the next. No. It is an annual gathering of all the accessible members of the family, young or old, rich or poor; and all the children look forward to it, for two months beforehand, in a fever of anticipation.

"Formerly, it was held at grandpapa's; but grandpapa getting old, and grandmamma getting old too, and rather infirm, they have given up house-keeping, and domesticated themselves with uncle George; so the party always takes place at uncle George's house . . . . " ¶SB/CD

"The noise in this room was perfectly tumultuous, for there were more children there than Scrooge, in his agitated state of mind, could count; and, unlike the celebrated herd in the poem, they were not forty children conducting themselves like one, but every child was conducting itself like forty. The consequences were uproarious beyond belief; but no one seemed to care; on the contrary, the mother and daughter laughed heartily, and enjoyed it very much, and the latter, soon beginning to mingle in the sports, got pillaged by the young brigands most ruthlessly . . . .

"But now a knocking at the door was heard, and such a rush immediately ensued that she, with laughing face and plundered dress, was borne towards it in the centre of a flushed and boisterous group, just in time to greet the father, who came home attended by a man laden with Christmas toys and presents . . . . The joy, and gratitude, and ecstasy! They are all indescribable alike. It is enough that, by degrees, the children and their emotions got out of the parlour, and, by one stair at a time, up to the top of the house, where they went to bed, and so subsided." CC 2

And see B:Toys—*at Christmas*

—*fellow-feeling:* "And thus the evening passes, in a strain of rational good-will and cheerfulness, doing more to awaken the sympathies of every member of the party in behalf of his neighbour, and to perpetuate their good feeling during the ensuing year, than half the homilies that have ever been written, by half the Divines that have ever lived." SB/CD

—*the 'founder' and Nature:* "And now the mists began to rise in the most beautiful manner, and the sun to shine; and as I went on through the bracing air, seeing the hoar-frost sparkle everywhere, I felt as if all Nature shared in the joy of the great Birthday.

"Going through the woods, the softness of my tread upon the mossy ground and among the brown leaves enhanced the Christmas sacredness by which I felt surrounded. As the whitened stems environed me, I thought how the Founder of the time had never raised his benignant hand, save to bless and heal, except in the case of one unconscious tree. By Cobham Hall, I came to the village, and the churchyard where the dead had been quietly buried, 'in the sure and certain hope' which Christmas-time inspired.

"What children could I see at play, and not be loving of, recalling who had loved them! No garden that I passed was out of unison with the day, for I remembered that the tomb was in a garden, and that 'she, supposing him to be the gardener,' had said, 'Sir, if thou have borne him hence, tell me where thou hast laid him, and I will take him away.'

"In time, the distant river with the ships came full in view, and with it pictures of the poor fishermen, mending their nets, who arose and followed him—of the teaching of the people from a ship pushed off a little way from shore, by reason of the multitude—of a majestic figure walking on the water, in the loneliness of night.

"My very shadow on the ground was eloquent of Christmas; for did not the people lay their sick where the mere shadows of the men who had heard and seen him might fall as they passed along?" ¶CS/PT 3

—*and healing:* "Then, as Christmas is a time in which, of all times in the year, the memory of every remediable sorrow, wrong, and trouble in the world around us, should be active with us, not less than our own experiences, for all good, [Redlaw] laid his hand upon the [Child], and, silently calling Him to witness who laid His hand on children in old time, rebuking, in the majesty of His prophetic knowledge, those who kept them from Him, vowed to protect him, teach him, and reclaim him." HM 3

—*homecoming:* "School-books shut up; **Ovid** and **Virgil** silenced; the Rule of Three, with its cool impertinent inquiries, long disposed of; **Terence** and **Plautus** acted no more, in an arena of huddled desks and forms, all chipped, and notched, and inked; cricket-bats, stumps, and balls, left higher up, with the smell of trodden grass and the softened noise of shouts in the evening air; the tree is still fresh, still gay. If I no more come home at Christmas-time, there will be boys and girls (thank Heaven!) while the World lasts; and they do! Yonder they dance and play upon the branches of my Tree, God bless them, merrily, and my heart dances and plays too!

"And I *do* come home at Christmas. We all do, or we all should. We all come home, or ought to come home, for a short holiday—the longer, the better—from the great boarding-school, where we are for ever working at our arithmetical slates, to take, and give a rest. As to going a visiting, where can we not go, if we will; where have we not been when we would; starting our fancy from our Christmas Tree?" CS/CT

—*irksome*

—*to one:* "'Don't be cross, uncle!' said the nephew.

"'What else can I be,' returned the uncle, 'when I live in such a world of fools as this? Merry Christmas! Out upon merry Christmas! What's Christmas time to you but a time for paying bills without money; a time for finding yourself a year older, and not an hour richer; a time for balancing your books and having every item in 'em through a round dozen of months presented dead against you? If I could work my will,' said Scrooge indignantly, 'every idiot who goes about with "Merry Christmas" on his lips should be boiled with his own pudding, and buried with a stake of holly through his heart.'" CC 1

—not to another: "' . . . I have always thought of Christmas time [said Fred], when it has come round—apart from the veneration due to its sacred name and origin, if anything belonging to it can be apart from that—as a good time; a kind, forgiving, charitable, pleasant time; the only time I know of, in the long calendar of the year, when men and women seem by one consent to open their shut-up hearts freely, and to think of people below them as if they really were fellow-passengers to the grave, and not another race of creatures bound on other journeys. And therefore, uncle, though it has never put a scrap of gold or silver in my pocket, I believe that it *has* done me good, and *will* do me good; and I say, God bless it!'" CC 1

—joy: "And numerous indeed are the hearts to which Christmas brings a brief season of happiness and enjoyment. How many families, whose members have been dispersed and scattered far and wide, in the restless struggles of life, are then reunited, and meet once again in that happy state of companionship and mutual good-will, which is a source of such pure and unalloyed delight, and one so incompatible with the cares and sorrows of the world, that the religious belief of the most civilised nations, and the rude traditions of the roughest savages, alike number it among the first joys of a future condition of existence, provided for the blest and happy! How many old recollections, and how many dormant sympathies, does Christmas time awaken!" PP 27

—in a lighthouse: "Built upon a dismal reef of sunken rocks, some league or so from shore, on which the waters chafed and dashed the wild year through, there stood a solitary lighthouse. Great heaps of seaweed clung to its base, and storm-birds—born of the wind one might suppose, as seaweed of the water—rose and fell about it, like the waves they skimmed.

"But even here, two men who watched the light had made a fire, that through the loophole in the thick stone wall shed out a ray of brightness on the awful sea. Joining their horny hands over the rough table at which they sat, they wished each other Merry Christmas in their can of grog; and one of them—the elder too, with his face all damaged and scarred with hard weather, as the figure-head of an old ship might be—struck up a sturdy song that was like a gale in itself." CC 3

—in London: "The house fronts looked black enough, and the windows blacker, contrasting with the smooth white sheet of snow upon the roofs, and with the dirtier snow upon the ground; which last deposit had been ploughed up in deep furrows by the heavy wheels of carts and waggons; furrows that crossed and recrossed each other hundreds of times where the great streets branched off; and made intricate channels, hard to trace in the thick yellow mud and icy water.

"The sky was gloomy, and the shortest streets were choked up with a dingy mist, half thawed, half frozen, whose heavier particles descended in a shower of sooty atoms, as if all the chimneys in Great Britain had, by one consent, caught fire, and were blazing away to their dear hearts' content. There was nothing very cheerful in the climate or the town, and yet was there an air of cheerfulness abroad that the clearest summer air and brightest summer sun might have endeavoured to diffuse in vain.

"For the people who were shovelling away on the house-tops were jovial and full of glee; calling out to one another from the parapets, and now and then exchanging a facetious snowball—better-natured missile far than many a wordy jest—laughing heartily if it went right and not less heartily if it went wrong.

"The poulterers' shops were still half open, and the fruiterers' were radiant in their glory. There were great, round, pot-bellied baskets of chestnuts, shaped like the waistcoats of jolly old gentlemen, lolling at the doors, and tumbling out into the street in their apoplectic opulence. There were ruddy, brown-faced, broad-girthed Spanish Onions, shining in the fatness of their growth like Spanish Friars, and winking from their shelves in wanton slyness at the girls as they went by, and glanced demurely at the hung-up mistletoe.

"There were pears and apples, clustered high in blooming pyramids; there were bunches of grapes, made in the shopkeepers' benevolence to dangle from conspicuous hooks, that people's mouths might water gratis as they passed; there were piles of filberts, mossy and brown, recalling, in their fragrance, ancient walks among the woods, and pleasant shufflings ankle deep through withered leaves; there were Norfolk Biffins, squab and swarthy, setting off the yellow of the oranges and lemons, and, in the great compactness of their juicy persons, urgently entreating and beseeching to be carried home in paper bags and eaten after dinner.

"The very gold and silver fish, set forth among these choice fruits in a bowl, though members of a dull and stagnant-blooded race, appeared to know that there was something going on; and, to a fish, went gasping round and round their little world in slow and passionless excitement.

"The Grocers'! oh the Grocers'! nearly closed, with perhaps two shutters down, or one; but through those gaps such glimpses! It was not alone that the scales descending on the counter made a merry sound, or that the twine and roller parted company so briskly, or that the canisters were rattled up and down like juggling tricks, or even that the blended scents of tea and coffee were so grateful to the nose, or even that the raisins were so plentiful and rare, the almonds so extremely white, the sticks of cinnamon so long and straight, the other spices so delicious, the candied fruits so caked and spotted with molten sugar as to make the coldest lookers-on feel faint and subsequently bilious.

"Nor was it that the figs were moist and pulpy, or that the French plums blushed in modest tartness from their highly-decorated boxes, or that everything was good to eat and in its Christmas dress; but the customers were all so hurried and so eager in the hopeful promise of the day, that they tumbled up against each other at the door, crashing their wicker baskets wildly, and left their purchases upon the counter, and came running back to fetch them, and committed hundreds of the like mistakes, in the best humour possible; while the Grocer and his people were so frank and fresh that the polished hearts with which they fastened their aprons behind might have been their own, worn outside for general inspection, and for Christmas daws to peck at if they chose.

"But soon the steeples called good people all, to church and chapel, and away they came, flocking through the streets in their best clothes, and with their gayest faces. And at the same time there emerged from scores of bye-streets, lanes, and nameless turnings, innumerable people, carrying their dinners to the bakers' shops.

"The sight of these poor revellers appeared to interest the [Ghost of Christmas Present] very much, for he stood with Scrooge beside him in a baker's doorway, and taking off the covers as their bearers passed, sprinkled incense on their dinners from his torch. And it was a very uncommon kind of torch, for once or twice when there were angry words between some dinner-carriers who had jostled each other, he shed a few drops of water on them from it, and their good humour was restored directly. For they said it was a shame to quarrel upon Christmas Day. And so it was! God love it, so it was!" ¶CC 3

—mistletoe: "From the centre of the ceiling of this kitchen, old Wardle had just suspended, with his own hands, a huge branch of mistletoe, and this same branch of mistletoe instantaneously gave rise to a scene of general and delightful struggling and confusion; in the midst of which, Mr Pickwick, with a gallantry that would have done honour to a descendant of Lady Tollimglower herself, took the old lady by the hand, led her beneath the mystic branch, and saluted her in all courtesy and decorum.

"The old lady submitted to this piece of practical politeness with all the dignity which befitted so important and serious a solemnity, but the younger ladies, not being so thoroughly imbued with a superstitious veneration for the custom: or imagining that the value of a salute is very much enhanced if it cost a little trouble to obtain it: screamed and struggled, and ran into corners, and threatened and remonstrated, and did everything but leave the room, until some of the less adventurous gentlemen were on the point of desisting, when they all at once found it useless to resist any longer, and submitted to be kissed with a good grace.

"Mr Winkle kissed the young lady with the black eyes, and Mr Snodgrass kissed Emily, and Mr [Sam] Weller, not being particular about the form of being under the mistletoe, kissed Emma and the other female servants, just as he caught them. As to the poor relations, they kissed everybody, not even excepting the plainer portions of the young-lady visitors, who, in their excessive confusion, ran right under the mistletoe, as soon as it was hung up, without knowing it!

"Wardle stood with his back to the fire, surveying the whole scene, with the utmost satisfaction; and the fat boy took the opportunity of appropriating to his own use, and summarily devouring, a particularly fine mince-pie, that had been carefully put by for somebody else." PP 28

—and present blessings: "Christmas time! That man must be a misanthrope indeed, in whose breast something like a jovial feeling is not roused—in whose mind some pleasant associations are not awakened—by the recurrence of Christmas. There are people who will tell you that Christmas is not to them what it used to be; that each succeeding Christmas has found some cherished hope, or happy prospect, of the year before, dimmed or passed away; that the present only serves to remind them of reduced circumstances and straitened incomes—of the feasts they once bestowed on hollow friends, and of the cold looks that meet them now, in adversity and misfortune.

"Never heed such dismal reminiscences. There are few men who have lived long enough in the world, who cannot call up such thoughts any day in the year. Then do not select the merriest of the three hundred and sixty-five, for your doleful recollections, but draw your chair nearer the blazing fire—fill the glass and send round the song—and if your room be smaller than it was a dozen years ago, or if your glass be filled with reeking punch, instead of sparkling wine, put a good face on the matter, and empty it off-hand, and fill another, and troll off the old ditty you used to sing, and thank God it's no worse.

"Look on the merry faces of your children (if you have any) as they sit round the fire. One little seat may be empty; one slight form that gladdened the father's heart, and roused the mother's pride to look upon, may not be there. Dwell not upon the past; think not that one short year ago, the fair child now resolving into dust, sat before you, with the bloom of health upon its cheek, and the gaiety of infancy in its joyous eye. Reflect upon your present blessings—of which every man has many—not on your past misfortunes, of which all men have some. Fill your glass again, with a merry face and contented heart. Our life on it, but your Christmas shall be merry, and your new year a happy one!" ¶SB/CD

—reminiscence: "We write these words now, many miles distant from the spot at which, year after year, we met on that day, a merry and joyous circle. Many of the hearts that throbbed so gaily then, have ceased to beat; many of the looks that shone so brightly then, have ceased to glow; the hands we grasped have grown cold; the eyes we sought have hid their lustre in the grave; and yet the old house, the room, the merry voices and smiling faces, the jest, the laugh, the most minute and trivial circumstances connected with those happy meetings, crowd upon our mind at each recurrence of the season, as if the last assemblage had been but yesterday! Happy, happy Christmas, that can win us back to the delusions of our childish days; that can recall to the old man the pleasures of his youth; that can transport the sailor and the traveller, thousands of miles away, back to his own fireside and his quiet home!" PP 28

—at sea: ". . . they lighted on a ship. They stood beside the helmsman at the wheel, the look-out in the bow, the officers who had the watch; dark ghostly figures in their several stations; but every man among them hummed a Christmas tune, or had a Christmas thought, or spoke below his breath to his companion of some by-gone Christmas Day, with homeward hopes belonging to it. And every man on board, waking or sleeping, good or bad, had had a kinder word for one another on that day than on any day in the year; and had shared to some extent in its festivities; and had remembered those he cared for at a distance, and had known that they delighted to remember him." CC 3

—the Season: "Christmas was close at hand, in all his bluff and hearty honesty; it was the season of hospitality, merriment, and open-heartedness; the old year was preparing, like an ancient philosopher, to call his friends around him, and amidst the sound of feasting and revelry to pass gently and calmly away. Gay and merry was the time . . . ." PP 28

—strengthening spirit: "And is our life here, at the best, so constituted that, pausing as we advance at such a noticeable milestone in the track as this great birthday, we look back on the things that never were, as naturally and full as gravely as on the

things that have been and are gone, or have been and still are? If it be so, and so it seems to be, must we come to the conclusion that life is little better than a dream, and little worth the loves and strivings that we crowd into it?

"No! Far be such miscalled philosophy from us, dear Reader, on Christmas Day! Nearer and closer to our hearts be the Christmas spirit, which is the spirit of active usefulness, perseverance, cheerful discharge of duty, kindness and forbearance! It is in the last virtues especially, that we are, or should be, strengthened by the unaccomplished visions of our youth; for, who shall say that they are not our teachers to deal gently even with the impalpable nothings of the earth!" CS/GO

—at sunset: "The winter sun goes down over town and village; on the sea it makes a rosy path, as if the Sacred tread were fresh upon the water. A few more moments, and it sinks, and night comes on, and lights begin to sparkle in the prospect.

"On the hill-side beyond the shapelessly-diffused town, and in the quiet keeping of the trees that gird the village-steeple, remembrances are cut in stone, planted in common flowers, growing in grass, entwined with lowly brambles around many a mound of earth. In town and village, there are doors and windows closed against the weather, there are flaming logs heaped high, there are joyful faces, there is healthy music of voices.

"Be all ungentleness and harm excluded from the temples of the Household Gods, but be those remembrances admitted with tender encouragement! They are of the time and all its comforting and peaceful reassurances; and of the history that reunited even upon earth the living and the dead; and of the broad beneficence and goodness that too many men have tried to tear to narrow shreds." ¶CS/GO

—a transformation: "'Now, I'll tell you what, my friend,' said Scrooge, 'I am not going to stand this sort of thing any longer. And therefore . . . I am about to raise your salary!'

"Bob trembled, and got a little nearer to the ruler. He had a momentary idea of knocking Scrooge down with it, holding him, and calling to the people in the court for help and a strait-waistcoat.

"'A merry Christmas, Bob!' said Scrooge, with an earnestness that could not be mistaken, as he clapped him on the back. "A merrier Christmas, Bob, my good fellow, than I have given you for many a year! I'll raise your salary, and endeavour to assist your struggling family, and we will discuss your affairs this very afternoon, over a Christmas bowl of smoking bishop, Bob! Make up the fires and buy another coal-scuttle before you dot another i, Bob Cratchit!'

"Scrooge was better than his word. He did it all, and infinitely more; and to Tiny Tim, who did NOT die, he was a second father. He became as good a friend, as good a master, and as good a man as the good old city knew, or any other good old city, town, or borough in the good old world. Some people laughed to see the alteration in him, but he let them laugh, and little heeded them; for he was wise enough to know that nothing ever happened on this globe, for good, at which some people did not have their fill of laughter in the outset . . . . His own heart laughed: and that was quite enough for him.

"He had no further intercourse with Spirits . . . it was always said of him, that he knew how to keep Christmas well, if any man alive possessed the knowledge." CC 5

—the tree and a prayer: "Encircled by the social thoughts of Christmas-time, still let the benignant figure of my childhood stand unchanged! In every cheerful image and suggestion that the season brings, may the bright star that rested above the poor roof, be the star of all the Christian world! A moment's pause, O vanishing tree, of which the lower boughs are dark to me as yet, and let me look once more! I know there are blank spaces on thy branches, where eyes that I have loved, have shone and smiled; from which they are departed. But, far above, I see the raiser of the dead girl, and the Widow's Son; and God is good! If Age be hiding for me in the unseen portion of thy downward growth, O may I, with a grey head, turn a child's heart to that figure yet, and a child's trustfulness and confidence!

"Now, the tree is decorated with bright merriment, and song, and dance, and cheerfulness. And they are welcome. Innocent and welcome be they ever held, beneath the branches of the Christmas Tree, which cast no gloomy shadow! But, as it sinks into the ground, I hear a whisper going through the leaves. 'This, in commemoration of the law of love and kindness, mercy and compassion. This, in remembrance of Me!'" CS/CT

Church

—art in Italy: " . . . St Stefano Rotondo, a damp, mildewed vault of an old church in the outskirts of Rome, will always struggle uppermost in my mind, by reason of the hideous paintings with which its walls are covered. These represent the martyrdoms of saints and early Christians; and such a panorama of horror and butchery no man could imagine in his sleep, though he were to eat a whole pig raw, for supper.

"Grey-bearded men being boiled, fried, grilled, crimped, singed, eaten by wild beasts, worried by dogs, buried alive, torn asunder by horses, chopped up small with hatchets: women having their breasts torn with iron pinchers, their tongues cut out, their ears screwed off, their jaws broken, their bodies stretched upon the rack, or skinned upon the stake, or crackled up and melted in the fire: these are among the mildest subjects.

"So insisted on, and laboured at, besides, that every sufferer gives you the same occasion for wonder as poor old *Duncan* awoke, in *Lady Macbeth,* when she marvelled at his having so much blood in him." ¶PI 11

—bells

—chimes: "They were old Chimes, trust me. Centuries ago, these bells had been baptized by bishops: so many centuries ago, that the register of their baptism was lost long, long before the memory of man, and no one knew their names. They had had their Godfathers and Godmothers, these Bells . . . and had their silver mugs no doubt, besides. But Time had mowed down their sponsors, and Henry the Eighth had melted down their mugs; and they now hung, nameless and mugless, in the church-tower.

"Not speechless, though. Far from it. They had clear, loud, lusty, sounding voices, had these Bells; and far and wide they might be heard upon the wind. Much too sturdy Chimes were they, to be dependent on the pleasure of the wind, moreover; for, fighting gallantly against it when it took an adverse whim, they would pour their cheerful notes into a listening ear right royally; and bent on being heard on stormy nights, by some poor mother watching a sick child, or some lone wife whose husband was at sea, they had been sometimes known to beat a blustering Nor'Wester . . . . " C 1

—defied: "The sound of a deep bell came along the wind. One.

"'Lie on, cried the usurer [Nickleby], 'with your iron tongue! Ring merrily for births that make expectants writhe, and marriages that are made in hell, and toll ruefully for the dead whose shoes are worn already! Call men to prayers who are godly because not found out, and ring chimes for the coming in of every year that brings this cursed world nearer to its end. No bell or book for me; throw me on a dunghill, and let me rot there to infect the air!'" NN 62

—exasperating: "Mr Arthur Clennam sat in the window of the coffee-house on Ludgate Hill, counting one of the neighbouring bells, making sentences and burdens of songs out of it in spite of himself, and wondering how many sick people it might be the death of in the course of the year. As the hour approached, its changes of measure made it more and more exasperating. At the quarter, it went off into a condition of deadly-lively importunity, urging the populace in a voluble manner to Come to church, Come to church! At the ten minutes, it became aware that the congregation would be scanty, and slowly hammered out in low spirits, They *won't* come, they *won't* come, they *won't* come! At the five minutes, it abandoned hope, and shook every house in the neighbourhood for three hundred seconds, with one dismal swing per second, as a groan of despair.

"'Thank Heaven!' said Clennam, when the hour struck, and the bell stopped." LD i 2

And see L:Times of Day—*dusk on a Sunday*

—in Italy: "Meanwhile (and especially on festa-days) the bells of the churches ring incessantly; not in peals, or any known form of sound, but in a horrible, irregular, jerking, dingle, dingle, dingle: with a sudden stop at every fifteenth dingle or so, which is maddening. This performance is usually achieved by a boy up in the steeple, who takes hold of the clapper, or a little rope attached to it, and tries to dingle louder than every other boy similarly employed. The noise is supposed to be particularly obnoxious to Evil Spirits; but looking up into the steeples, and seeing (and hearing) these young Christians thus engaged, one might very naturally mistake them for the Enemy." PI 5

—in London: "London Time by the great clock of Saint Paul's, ten at night. All the lesser London churches strain their metallic throats. Some, flippantly begin before the heavy bell of the great cathedral; some,

tardily begin three, four, five, half-a-dozen, strokes behind it; all are in sufficiently near accord, to leave a resonance in the air, as if the winged father who devours his children, had made a sounding sweep with his gigantic scythe in flying over the city." CS/NT

"The church bells began to ring . . . but they by no means improved the case, for they said, in a petulant way, and speaking with some difficulty in their irritation, WHAT'S-be-come-of-THE-coach-ES!' Nor would they (I found on listening) ever vary their emphasis, save in respect of growing more sharp and vexed, but invariably went on, WHAT'S-be-come-of-THE-coach-ES!'—always beginning the inquiry with an unpolite abruptness. Perhaps from their elevation they saw the railway, and it aggravated them." UT/SC

"Westminster Abbey was fine gloomy society for another quarter of an hour; suggesting a wonderful procession of its dead among the dark arches and pillars, each century more amazed by the century following it than by all the centuries going before. And indeed it was a solemn consideration what enormous hosts of dead belong to one old great city, and how, if they were raised while the living slept, there would not be the space of a pin's point in all the streets and ways for the living to come out into. Not only that, but the vast armies of dead would overflow the hills and valleys beyond the city, and would stretch away all round it, God knows how far." UT/NW

—*worldly:* " . . . there were no voices in the bells to make [Joe Willet] turn. Since the time of noble Whittington, fair flower of merchants, bells have come to have less sympathy with humankind. They only ring for money and on state occasions. Wanderers have increased in number; ships leave the Thames for distant regions, carrying from stem to stern no other cargo; the bells are silent; they ring out no entreaties or regrets; they are used to it and have grown worldly." BR 31

—*cathedral, at night:* "Among those secluded nooks [near Minor Canon Corner] there is very little stir or movement after dark. There is little enough in the high tide of the day, but there is next to none at night. Besides that the cheerfully frequent High Street lies nearly parallel to the spot (the old Cathedral rising between the two), and is the natural channel in which the Cloisterham traffic flows, a certain awful hush pervades the ancient pile, the cloisters, and the churchyard, after dark, which not many people care to encounter. Ask the first hundred citizens of Cloisterham, met at random in the streets at noon, if they believed in Ghosts, they would tell you no; but put them to choose at night between these eerie Precincts and the thoroughfare of shops, and you would find that ninety-nine declared for the longer round and the more frequent way. The cause of this is not to be found in any local superstition that attaches to the Precincts—albeit a mysterious lady, with a child in her arms and a rope dangling from her neck, has been seen flitting about there by sundry witnesses as intangible as herself—but it is to be sought in the innate shrinking of dust with the breath of life in it from dust out of which the breath of life has passed; also, in the widely diffused, and almost as widely unacknowledged, reflection: 'If the dead do, under any circumstances, become visible to the living, these are such likely surroundings for the purpose that I, the living, will get out of them as soon as I can.'" MED 12

And see W:Cities and towns—*Rochester (the cathedral)*

—*and a child:* "Here is our pew in church. What a high-backed pew! With a window near it, out of which our house can be seen, and *is* seen many times during the morning's service, by Peggotty, who likes to make herself as sure as she can that it's not being robbed, or is not in flames.

"But though Peggotty's eye wanders, she is much offended if mine does, and frowns to me, as I stand upon the seat, that I am to look at the clergyman. But I can't always look at him—I know him without that white thing on, and I am afraid of his wondering why I stare so, and perhaps stopping the service to inquire—and what am I to do?

"It's a dreadful thing to gape, but I must do something. I look at my mother, but *she* pretends not to see me. I look at a boy in the aisle, and *he* makes faces at me. I look at the sunlight coming in at the open door through the porch, and there I see a stray sheep—I don't mean a sinner, but mutton—half making up his mind to come into the church.

"I feel that if I looked at him any longer, I might be tempted to say something out loud; and what would become of me then? I look up at the monumental tablets on the wall, and try to think of Mr Bodgers, late of this parish, and what the feelings of Mrs

Bodgers must have been, when affliction sore, long time Mr Bodgers bore, and physicians were in vain.

"I wonder whether they called in Mr Chillip, and he was in vain; and if so, how he likes to be reminded of it once a week. I look from Mr Chillip, in his Sunday neckcloth, to the pulpit; and think what a good place it would be to play in, and what a castle it would make, with another boy coming up the stairs to attack it, and having the velvet cushion with the tassels thrown down on his head.

"In time my eyes gradually shut up; and, from seeming to hear the clergyman singing a drowsy song in the heat, I hear nothing, until I fall off the seat with a crash, and am taken out, more dead than alive, by Peggotty." ¶DC 2

—dismal: "The tall shrouded pulpit and reading desk; the dreary perspective of empty pews stretching away under the galleries, and empty benches mounting to the roof and lost in the shadow of the great grim organ; the dusty matting and cold stone slabs; the grisly free seats in the aisles; and the damp corner by the bell-rope, where the black trestles used for funerals were stowed away, along with some shovels and baskets, and a coil or two of deadly-looking rope; the strange, unusual, uncomfortable smell, and the cadaverous light; were all in unison. It was a cold and dismal scene." DS 5

—dusty: "There is a dusty old clerk, who keeps a sort of evaporated news-shop underneath an archway opposite, behind a perfect fortification of posts. There is a dusty old pew-opener who only keeps herself, and finds that quite enough to do. There is a dusty old beadle . . . who has something to do with a worshipful Company who have got a Hall in the next yard . . . . There are dusty wooden ledges and cornices poked in and out over the altar, and over the screen, and round the gallery, and over the inscription about what the Master and Wardens of the Worshipful Company did in one thousand six hundred and ninety-four. There are dusty old sounding-boards over the pulpit and reading-desk, looking like lids to be let down on the officiating ministers, in case of their giving offence. There is every possible provision for the accommodation of dust, except in the churchyard, where the facilities in that respect are very limited." DS 57

—hemmed in: "The church was a mouldy old church in a yard, hemmed in by a labyrinth of back streets and courts, with a little burying-ground round it, and itself buried in a kind of vault, formed by the neighbouring houses, and paved with echoing stones. It was a great, dim, shabby pile, with high old oaken pews, among which about a score of people lost themselves every Sunday; while the clergyman's voice drowsily resounded through the emptiness, and the organ rumbled and rolled as if the church had got the colic, for want of a congregation to keep the wind and damp out. But so far was this city church from languishing for the company of other churches, that spires were clustered round it, as the masts of shipping cluster on the river. It would have been hard to count them from its steeple-top, they were so many. In almost every yard and blind-place near, there was a church. The confusion of bells . . . was deafening. There were twenty churches close together, clamouring for people to come in." DS 56

—in London: "There were churches also by the dozens, with many a ghostly little churchyard, all overgrown with such straggling vegetation as springs up spontaneously from damp, and graves, and rubbish. In some of these dingy resting-places, which bore much the same analogy to green churchyards, as the pots of earth for mignonette and wall-flower in the windows overlooking them did to rustic gardens, there were trees; tall trees; still putting forth their leaves in each succeeding year, with such a languishing remembrance of their kind (so one might fancy, looking on their sickly boughs) as birds in cages have of theirs. Here, paralysed old watchmen guarded the bodies of the dead at night, year after year, until at last they joined that solemn brotherhood; and, saving that they slept below the ground a sounder sleep than even they had ever known above it, and were shut up in another kind of box, their condition can hardly be said to have undergone any material change when they in turn were watched themselves." MC 9

—City: " . . . I came upon one obscure church which had broken out in the melodramatic style, and was got up with various tawdry decorations, much after the manner of the extinct London Maypoles. These attractions had induced several young priests or deacons, in black bibs for waistcoats, and several young ladies interested in that holy

order (the proportion being, as I estimated, seventeen young ladies to a deacon), to come into the City as a new and odd excitement. It was wonderful to see how these young people played out their little play in the heart of the City, all among themselves, without the deserted City's knowing anything about it. It was as if you should take an empty counting-house on a Sunday, and act one of the old Mysteries there . . . . There was a remarkably agreeable smell of pomatum in this congregation." UT/LC

—empty: "Whether I think of the church where the sails of the oyster-boats in the river almost flapped against the windows, or of the church where the railroad made the bells hum as the train rushed by above the roof, I recall a curious experience. On summer Sundays, in the gentle rain or the bright sunshine—either deepening the idleness of the idle city—I have sat, in that singular silence which belongs to resting-places usually astir, in scores of buildings, at the hearts of the world's metropolis, unknown to far greater numbers of people speaking the English tongue than the ancient edifices of the Eternal City, or the Pyramids of Egypt." UT/LC

—memorials: "The dark vestries and registries into which I have peeped, and the little hemmed-in churchyards that have echoed to my feet, have left impressions on my memory as distinct and quaint as any it has in that way received. In all those dusty registers that the worms are eating, there is not a line but made some hearts leap, or some tears flow, in their day. Still and dry now, still and dry! and the old tree at the window, with no room for its branches, has seen them all out. So with the tomb of the old Master of the old Company, on which it drips. His son restored it and died, his daughter restored it and died, and then he had been remembered long enough, and the tree took possession of him, and his name cracked out." UT/LC

—steeple: " . . . where the belfry is, and iron rails are ragged with rust, and sheets of lead and copper, shrivelled by the changing weather, crackle and heave beneath the unaccustomed tread; and birds stuff shabby nests into corners of old oaken joists and beams; and dust grows old and grey . . . . High up in the steeple of an old church, far above the light and murmur of the town and far below the flying clouds that shadow it, is the wild and dreary place at night: and high up in the steeple of an old church, dwelt the Chimes I tell of." C 1

—vestry: "[The sexton] ushers them into an old, brown, panelled, dusty vestry, like a corner-cupboard with the shelves taken out; where the wormy registers diffuse a smell like faded snuff . . . . " DS 57

—window: "The westering sun slants into the churchyard by some unwonted entry, a few prismatic tears drop on an old tombstone, and a window that I thought was only dirty is for the moment all bejewelled. Then the light passes, and the colours die." UT/CA

Compassion

—pitilessness: "Both [Madame Defarge's] hearers derived a horrible enjoyment from the deadly nature of her wrath—the listener could feel how white she was, without seeing her—and both highly commended it. . . . 'Tell the Wind and the Fire where to stop; not me!'" TTC iii 12

—pity: "'Reduced—I should say poor people . . . must live where they can.'

"'Ah! very true, so they must; very proper indeed!' rejoined Miss Knag with that sort of half-sigh, which, accompanied by two or three slight nods of the head, is pity's small change in general society; 'and that's what I very often tell my brother, when our servants go away ill, one after another, and he thinks the back-kitchen's rather too damp for 'em to sleep in. These sort of people, I tell him, are glad to sleep anywhere! Heaven suits the back to the burden. What a nice thing it is to think that it should be so, isn't it?'" NN 18

"'My son is getting on, Mrs Pipchin. Really he is getting on.'

"There was something melancholy in the triumphant air with which Mr Dombey said this. It showed how long Paul's childish life had been to him, and how his hopes were set upon a later stage of his existence. Pity may appear a strange word to connect with any one so haughty and so cold, and yet he seemed a worthy subject for it at that moment." DS 11

—woman for her beloved: "And now, indeed, I began to think that in my old association of her with the stained-glass window in the church, a prophetic foreshadowing of what she would be to me, in the calamity that was to happen in the fulness of time, had found a way into my mind. In all that sorrow, from the moment, never to be forgotten, when she stood before me with her upraised hand, she was like a sacred presence in my

lonely house. When the Angel of Death alighted there, my child-wife fell asleep—they told me so when I could bear to hear it—on her bosom, with a smile. From my swoon, I first awoke to a consciousness of her compassionate tears, her words of hope and peace, her gentle face bending down as from a purer region nearer Heaven, over my undisciplined heart, and softening its pain." DC 54

Conscience

—elasticity: ". . . in the majority of cases, conscience is an elastic and very flexible article, which will bear a deal of stretching and adapt itself to a great variety of circumstances. Some people by prudent management and leaving it off piece by piece like a flannel waistcoat in warm weather, even contrive, in time, to dispense with it altogether, but there be others who can assume this garment and throw it off at pleasure; and this being the great and most convenient improvement, is the one most in vogue." OCS 6

—guilt

—body language: ". . . Mr Lorry looked at Jerry [Cruncher] in considerable doubt and mistrust. That honest tradesman's manner of receiving the look, did not inspire confidence; he changed the leg on which he rested, as often as if he had fifty of those limbs, and were trying them all; he examined his finger-nails with a very questionable closeness of attention; and whenever Mr Lorry's eye caught his, he was taken with that peculiar kind of short cough requiring the hollow of a hand before it, which is seldom, if ever, known to be an infirmity attendant on perfect openness of character." TTC iii 9

—of the condemned: "Although at the bottom of [Rudge's] every thought there was an uneasy sense of guilt, and dread of death, he felt no more than that vague consciousness of it, which a sleeper has of pain. It pursues him through his dreams, gnaws at the heart of all his fancied pleasures, robs the banquet of its taste, music of its sweetness, makes happiness itself unhappy, and yet is no bodily sensation, but a phantom without shape, or form, or visible presence; pervading everything, but having no existence; recognizable everywhere, but nowhere seen, or touched, or met with face to face, until the sleep is past, and waking agony returns." BR 62

"Still listening attentively, [Rudge] made out, in course of time, that the jail was besieged by a furious multitude. His guilty conscience instantly arrayed these men against himself, and brought the fear upon him that he would be singled out, and torn to pieces.

"Once impressed with the terror of this conceit, everything tended to confirm and strengthen it. His double crime, the circumstances under which it had been committed, the length of time that had elapsed, and its discovery in spite of all, made him, as it were, the visible object of the Almighty's wrath. In all the crime and vice and moral gloom of the great pest-house of the capital, he stood alone, marked and singled out by his great guilt, a Lucifer among the devils. The other prisoners were a host, hiding and sheltering each other—a crowd like that without the walls. He was one man against the whole united concourse; a single, solitary, lonely man, from whom the very captives in the jail fell off and shrunk appalled." BR 65

—foreknowledge: "Conscience is a dreadful thing when it accuses man or boy; but when, in the case of a boy, that secret burden cooperates with another secret burden down the leg of his trousers [bread for Magwitch], it is (as I can testify) a great punishment. The guilty knowledge that I was going to rob Mrs Joe—I never thought I was going to rob Joe, for I never thought of any of the housekeeping property as his—united to the necessity of always keeping one hand on my bread-and-butter as I sat, or when I was ordered about the kitchen on any small errand, almost drove me out of my mind." GE 2

—irrational: "'If the real man feels as guilty as I do,' said Eugene, 'he is remarkably uncomfortable.'"

"'Influence of secrecy,' suggested Lightwood.

"'I am not at all obliged to it for making me Guy Fawkes in the vault and a Sneak in the area both at once,' said Eugene." OMF i 13

—a murderer's: "The night had now come, when the old clerk was to be delivered over to his keepers. In the midst of his guilty distractions, Jonas [Chuzzlewit] had not forgotten it.

"It was a part of his guilty state of mind to remember it; for on his persistence in the scheme depended one of his precautions for his own safety. A hint, a word, from the old

man, uttered at such a moment in attentive ears, might fire the train of suspicion, and destroy him. His watchfulness of every avenue by which the discovery of his guilt might be approached, sharpened with his sense of the danger by which he was encompassed. With murder on his soul, and its innumerable alarms and terrors dragging at him night and day, he would have repeated the crime, if he had seen a path of safety stretching out beyond. It was in his punishment; it was in his guilty condition. The very deed which his fears rendered insupportable, his fears would have impelled him to commit again." MC 51
And see F:Murderer—*haunted*

—*seen in an angel's mirror:* "'I am not a moral sort of fellow,' [James Harthouse] said, 'and I never make any pretensions to the character of a moral sort of fellow. I am as immoral as need be. At the same time, in bringing any distress upon the lady who is the subject of the present conversation [Louisa Bounderby], or in unfortunately compromising her in any way, or in committing myself by any expression of sentiments towards her, not perfectly reconcilable with—in fact with—the domestic hearth; or in taking any advantage of her father's being a machine, or of her brother's being a whelp, or of her husband's being a bear; I beg to be allowed to assure you that I have had no particularly evil intentions, but have glided on from one step to another with a smoothness so perfectly diabolical, that I had not the slightest idea the catalogue was half so long until I began to turn it over. Whereas I find,' said Mr James Harthouse, in connclusion, 'that it is really in several volumes.'" HT iii 2 *And see* FL: Angel—*a visitation*
And see Hypocrite—*guilt suppressed*

Courage

—*absent:* "In a word, I [Pip] was too cowardly to do what I knew to be right, as I had been too cowardly to avoid doing what I knew to be wrong. I had had no intercourse with the world at that time, and I imitated none of its many inhabitants who act in this manner. Quite an untaught genius, I made the discovery of the line of action for myself." GE 6

—*best aroused:* "I [Captain Ravender] have heard it broached that orders should be given in great new ships by electric telegraph. I admire machinery as much as any man, and am as thankful to it as any man can be for what it does for us. But it will never be a substitute for the face of a man, with his soul in it, encouraging another man to be brave and true. Never try it for that. It will break down like a straw." CS/GM

"In endeavouring to inspire her with some fortitude, she increased her own . . . . " BR 71

—*in the cowardly:* " . . . this gentleman's stoicism was of that not uncommon kind, which enables a man to bear with exemplary fortitude the afflictions of his friends, but renders him, by way of counterpoise, rather selfish and sensitive in respect of any that happen to befall himself." BR 74

—*innate:* "'Aboard o' that there unfort'nate vessel . . . was a lady, a gallant lad [Walter Gay] . . . when the stoutest hearts and oldest hands was hove down, he was firm and cheery. It warn't the want of objects to like and love ashore that gave him courage, it was his nat'ral mind. I've seen it in his face, when he was no more than a child . . . and when I thought it nothing but his good looks, bless him!'" DS 49

—*morale affected by weather:* "It was a chill dark autumn evening . . . . The rain fell fast, and the wind blew hard; and straying out on the house-top by that stormy bedroom of his old friend, to take an observation of the weather, the Captain's heart died within him, when he saw how wild and desolate it was. Not that he associated the weather of that time with poor Walter [Gay]'s destiny, or doubted that if Providence had doomed him to be lost and shipwrecked, it was over, long ago; but that beneath an outward influence, quite distinct from the subject-matter of his thoughts, the Captain [Cuttle]'s spirits sank, and his hopes turned pale, as those of wiser men had often done before him, and will often do again." DS 32

—*in the peaceful:* " . . . it being the manner of peaceful men to be very bold when the danger is over, they were abundantly fierce and daring; not scrupling to question the stoutest passenger with great severity, and carrying it with a very high hand over all errand-boys, servant-girls, and 'prentices." BR 73

—*and tears:* "'I am a Briton,' said Miss Pross, 'I am desperate. I don't care an English Twopence for myself. I know that the longer I keep you here, the greater hope there is for my Ladybird. I'll not leave a handful of that dark hair upon your head, if you lay a finger on me!'

"Thus Miss Pross, with a shake of her head and a flash of her eyes between every rapid sentence, and every rapid sentence a whole breath. Thus Miss Pross, who had never struck a blow in her life.

"But her courage was of that emotional nature that it brought the irrepressible tears into her eyes. This was a courage that Madame Defarge so little comprehended as to mistake for weakness. 'Ha, ha!' she laughed, 'you poor wretch! What are you worth!'" TTC iii 14

Cruelty

—to animals: "All this [driving animals to market] was being done, in a deep red glare of burning torches, which were in themselves a strong addition to the horrors of the scene; for the men who were arranging the sheep and lambs in their miserably confined pens, and forcing them to their destination through alleys of the most preposterously small dimensions, constantly dropped gouts of the blazing pitch upon the miserable creatures' backs; and to smell the singeing and burning, and to see the poor things shrinking from this roasting, inspired a sickness, a disgust, a pity and an indignation, almost insupportable. To reflect that the gate of St. Bartholomew's Hospital was in the midst of this devilry, and that such a monument of years of sympathy for human pain should stand there, jostling this disgraceful record of years of disregard of brute endurance—to look up at the faint lights in the windows of the houses where the people were asleep, and to think that some of them had been to Public Prayers that Sunday, and had typified the Divine love and gentleness, by the panting, footsore creature, burnt, beaten, and needlessly tormented there, that night, by thousands—suggested truths so inconsistent and so shocking, that the Market of the Capital of the World seemed a ghastly and blasphemous Nightmare." HWC/ML

And see N:Animals *—cattle; and —oxen*

"'We are not a heavy load, George?'

"'That's always what the ladies say,' replied the man, looking a long way round, as if he were appealing to Nature in general against such monstrous propositions. 'If you see a woman a driving, you'll always perceive that she will never keep her whip still; the horse can't go fast enough for her. If cattle have got their proper load, you can never persuade a woman that they'll not bear something more.'" OCS 26

—an impression: "As Arthur came over the stile and down to the water's edge, the lounger glanced at him for a moment, and then resumed his occupation of idly tossing stones into the water with his foot. There was something in his way of spurning them out of their places with his heel, and getting them into the required position, that Clennam thought had an air of cruelty in it. Most of us have more or less frequently derived a similar impression, from a man's manner of doing some very little thing: plucking a flower, clearing away an obstacle, or even destroying an insentient object." LD i 17

—influence in school: "In a school carried on by sheer cruelty, whether it is presided over by a dunce or not, there is not likely to be much learned. I believe our boys were, generally, as ignorant a set as any schoolboys in existence; they were too much troubled and knocked about to learn: they could no more do that to advantage, than any one can do anything to advantage, in a life of constant misfortune, torment, and worry." DC 7

And see Soul-Murder

Cunning

—and credulity: " . . . there is a simplicity of cunning no less than a simplicity of innocence; and in all matters where a lively faith in knavery and meanness was required as the ground-work of belief, Mr Jonas [Chuzzlewit] was one of the most credulous of men. His ignorance, which was stupendous, may be taken into account, if the reader pleases, separately." MC 11

""[Montague] had said, in the outset, that Jonas was too sharp for him; and Jonas, who would have been sharp enough to believe him in nothing else, though he had solemnly sworn it, believed him in that, instantly." MC 28

—and greed: "'As I think I told you once before,' said I, 'it is you [Uriah Heep] who have been, in your greed and cunning, against all the world. It may be profitable to you to reflect, in future, that there never were greed and cunning in the world yet, that did not do too much, and over-reach themselves. It is as certain as death.'" DC 52

—and simplicity: "The man of low cunning had, of course, acquired a mastery over the

man of high simplicity. The mean man had, of course, got the better of the generous man. How long such conquests last is another question; that they are achieved is every-day experience, not even to be flourished away by Podsnappery itself. The undesigning Boffin had become so far immeshed by the wily Wegg that his mind misgave him he was a very designing man indeed in purposing to do more for Wegg. It seemed to him (so skilful was Wegg) that he was plotting darkly, when he was contriving to do the very thing that Wegg was plotting to get him to do. And thus, while he was mentally turning the kindest of kind faces on Wegg this morning, he was not absolutely sure but that he might somehow deserve the charge of turning his back on him." OMF i 15

Cynic and Cynicism

—*"Always suspect everybody":* "With deference to the better opinion of Mr. Brass, and more particularly to the authority of his Great Ancestor, it may be doubted with humility whether the elevating principle laid down by the latter gentleman and acted upon by his descendant, is always a prudent one, or attended in practice with the desired results. This is beyond question a bold and presumptuous doubt, inasmuch as many distinguished characters, called men of the world, long-headed customers, knowing dogs, shrewd fellows, capital hands at business, and the like, have made, and do daily make, this axiom their polar star and compass. Still the doubt may be gently insinuated . . . it will always happen that these men of the world, who go through it in armour, defend themselves from quite as much good as evil; to say nothing of the inconvenience and absurdity of mounting guard with a microscope at all times, and of wearing a coat of mail on the most innocent occasions." OCS 66

—*in America:* "One great blemish in the popular mind of America, and the prolific parent of an innumerable brood of evils, is Universal Distrust. Yet the American citizen plumes himself upon this spirit, even when he is sufficiently dispassionate to perceive the ruin it works; and will often adduce it, in spite of his own reason, as an instance of the great sagacity and acuteness of the people, and their superior shrewdness and independence.

"'You carry,' says the stranger, 'this jealousy and distrust into every transaction of public life . . . . It has rendered you so fickle, and so given to change, that your inconstancy has passed into a proverb; for you no sooner set up an idol firmly, than you are sure to pull it down and dash it into fragments: and this, because directly you reward a benefactor, or a public servant, you distrust him, merely because he *is* rewarded; and immediately apply yourselves to find out, either that you have been too bountiful in your acknowledgements, or he remiss in his deserts.

"Any man who attains a high place among you, from the President downwards, may date his downfall from that moment; for any printed lie that any notorious villain pens, although it militate directly against the character and conduct of a life, appeals at once to your distrust, and is believed.

"You will strain at a gnat in the way of trustfulness and confidence, however fairly won and well deserved; but you will swallow a whole caravan of camels, if they be laden with unworthy doubts and mean suspicions. Is this well, think you, or likely to elevate the character of the governors or the governed, among you?'" AN 18

—*danger to society:* "Publicly and privately, it were much better for the age in which [Harthouse] lived, that he and the legion of whom he was one were designedly bad, than indifferent and purposeless. It is the drifting icebergs setting with any current anywhere, that wreck the ships." HT ii 8

—*fortune-hunting*

—*for a daughter:* " . . . Mrs Skewton turned her head languidly towards the Major, without otherwise moving, and asked him how his friend was?

"'Dombey, Ma'am,' returned the Major, with a facetious gurgling in his throat, 'is as well as a man in his condition *can* be. His condition is a desperate one, Ma'am. He is touched, is Dombey! Touched!' cried the Major. 'He is bayonetted through the body.'

"Cleopatra cast a sharp look at the Major, that contrasted forcibly with the affected drawl in which she presently said—

"'Major Bagstock, although I know but little of the world—nor can I really regret my inexperience, for I fear it is a false place, full of withering conventionalities; where Nature is but little regarded, and where the music of the heart, and the gushing of the soul, and all that sort of thing, which is so truly poetical, is seldom heard—I cannot misunderstand your meaning. There is an allusion to Edith [Granger]—to my extremely dear child,' said Mrs Skewton, tracing the outline of her eyebrows with her forefinger, 'in your words, to which the tenderest of chords vibrates excessively! . . .

"'And that allusion,' pursued Cleopatra, 'would involve one of the most—if not positively *the* most—touching, and thrilling, and sacred emotions of which our sadly-fallen nature is susceptible, I conceive . . . .

"'I feel that I am weak. I feel that I am wanting in that energy, which should sustain a mama: not to say a parent: on such a subject,' said Mrs Skewton, trimming her lips with the laced edge of her pocket-handkerchief; 'but I can hardly approach a topic so excessively momentous to my dearest Edith without a feeling of faintness. Nevertheless, bad man, as you have boldly remarked upon it, and as it has occasioned me great anguish:' Mrs Skewton touched her left side with her fan: 'I will not shrink from my duty.'" DS 26

—in love: "Tellson's [Bank] had whitewashed the Cupid, but he was still to be seen on the ceiling, in the coolest linen, aiming (as he very often does) at money from morning to night." TTC iii 1

—pervasive: "'All men are fortune-hunters, are they not [said John Chester]? The law, the church, the court, the camp—see how they are all crowded with fortune-hunters, jostling each other in the pursuit. The Stock Exchange, the pulpit, the counting-house, the royal drawing-room, the senate—what but fortune-hunters are they filled with? A fortune-hunter! Yes. You *are* one; and you would be nothing else, my dear Ned, if you were the greatest courtier, lawyer, legislator, prelate, or merchant, in existence. If you are squeamish and moral, Ned, console yourself with the reflection that at the very worst your fortune-hunting can make but one person miserable or unhappy. How many people do you suppose these other kinds of huntsmen crush in following their sport—hundreds at a step? Or thousands?'" BR 15

—levelling the world: "'I am not a great impostor [said Henry Gowan]. Buy one of my pictures, and I assure you, in confidence, it will not be worth the money. Buy one of another man's—any great professor who beats me hollow—and the chances are that the more you give him, the more he'll impose upon you. They all do it.'

"'All painters?' [said Arthur Clennam]

"'Painters, writers, patriots, all the rest who have stands in the market. Give almost any man I know, ten pounds, and he will impose upon you to a corresponding extent; a thousand pounds—to a corresponding extent; ten thousand pounds—to a corresponding extent. So great the success, so great the imposition. But what a capital world it is!' cried Gowan with warm enthusiasm. 'What a jolly, excellent, lovable world it is! . . .

"'And after all,' cried Gowan, with the characteristic balancing of his which reduced everything in the wide world to the same light weight, 'though I can't deny that the Circumlocution Office may ultimately shipwreck everybody and everything, still, that will probably not be in our time . . . .'" LD i 26 *And see* FL:Life—*a joke*

—projection: "[Ralph Nickleby] knew himself well, and choosing to imagine that all mankind were cast in the same mould, hated them; for, though no man hates himself—the coldest among us having too much self-love for that—yet most men unconsciously judge the world from themselves, and it will be very generally found that those who sneer habitually at human nature, and affect to despise it, are among its worst and least pleasant samples." NN 44

—and virtue: "'Virtuous and gifted animals [said John Chester], whether man or beast, always are so very hideous.'" BR 23

—the world: "'The world is a lively place enough [said John Chester], in which we must accommodate ourselves to circumstances, sail with the stream as glibly as we can, be content to take froth for substance, the surface for the depth, the counterfeit for the real coin. I wonder no philosopher has ever established that our globe itself is hollow. It should be, if Nature is consistent in her works.'" BR 12

Degeneration

—adventurer in a laundry: "'You're never to be trusted . . . . Isn't it enough that I paid two pound fourteen for you, and took you out of prison and let you live here like a gentleman, but must you go on like this: breaking my heart besides?'

"'I will never break its heart, I will be a good boy, and never do so any more; I will never be naughty again: I beg its little pardon,' said Mr Mantalini, dropping the handle of the mangle, and folding his palms together, 'it is all up with its handsome friend! He has gone to the demnition bow-wows. It will have pity? It will not scratch and claw, but pet and comfort? Oh demmit.'" NN 64

—*"Dry Rot"*: " . . . I made a new start with a new heart, setting the old King's Bench prison before me for my next object, and resolving, when I should come to the wall, to think of poor Horace Kinch, and the Dry Rot in men.

"A very curious disease the Dry Rot in men, and difficult to detect the beginning of . . . . The first strong external revelation of the Dry Rot in men, is a tendency to lurk and lounge; to be at street-corners without intelligible reason; to be going anywhere when met; to be about many places rather than at any; to do nothing tangible, but to have an intention of performing a variety of intangible duties to-morrow or the day after. When this manifestation of the disease is observed, the observer will usually connect it with a vague impression once formed or received, that the patient was living a little too hard.

"He will scarcely have had leisure to turn it over in his mind and form the terrible suspicion 'Dry Rot,' when he will notice a change for the worse in the patient's appearance: a certain slovenliness and deterioration, which is not poverty, nor dirt, nor intoxication, nor ill-health, but simply Dry Rot. To this, succeeds a smell as of strong waters, in the morning; to that, a looseness respecting money; to that, a stronger smell as of strong waters, at all times; to that, a looseness respecting everything; to that, a trembling of the limbs, somnolency, misery, and crumbling to pieces.

"As it is in wood, so it is in men. Dry Rot advances at a compound usury quite incalculable. A plank is found infected with it, and the whole structure is devoted. Thus it had been with the unhappy Horace Kinch, lately buried by a small subscription. Those who knew him had not nigh done saying, 'So well off, so comfortably established, with such hope before him—and yet, it is feared, with a slight touch of Dry Rot!' when lo! the man was all Dry Rot and dust." ¶UT/NW

—*moral:* "That it is at least as difficult to stay a moral infection as a physical one; that such a disease will spread with the malignity and rapidity of the Plague; that the contagion, when it has once made head, will spare no pursuit or condition, but will lay hold on people in the soundest health, and become developed in the most unlikely constitutions; is a fact as firmly established by experience as that we human creatures breathe an atmosphere.

"A blessing beyond appreciation would be conferred upon mankind, if the tainted, in whose weakness or wickedness these virulent disorders are bred, could be instantly seized and placed in close confinement (not to say summarily smothered) before the poison is communicable." ¶LD ii 13

"Of whom Mr Pancks had taken the prevalent disease, he could no more have told than if he had unconsciously taken a fever. Bred at first, as many physical diseases are, in the wickedness of men, and then disseminated in their ignorance, these epidemics, after a period, get communicated to many sufferers who are neither ignorant nor wicked. Mr Pancks might, or might not, have caught the illness himself from a subject of this class; but, in this category he appeared before Clennam, and the infection he threw off was all the more virulent." LD ii 13

—*pawnshop:* "And it was strange, very strange, even to [young Martin Chuzzlewit], to find how, by quick though almost imperceptible degrees, he lost his delicacy and self-respect, and gradually came to do that as a matter of course, without the least compunction, which but a few short days before had galled him to the quick. The first time he visited the pawnbroker's, he felt on his way there as if every person whom he passed suspected whither he was going; and on his way back again, as if the whole human tide he stemmed, knew well where he had come from. When did he care to think of their discernment now!

"In his first wanderings up and down the weary streets, he counterfeited the walk of one who had an object in his view; but soon there came upon him the sauntering, slipshod gait of listless idleness and the lounging at street-corners, and plucking and biting of stray bits of straw, and strolling up and down the same place, and looking into the same shop-windows, with a miserable indifference, fifty times a day. At first, he came out from his lodging with an uneasy sense of being observed—even by those chance passers-by, on whom he had never looked before, and hundreds to one would never see again—issuing in the morning from a public-house; but now, in his comings-out and goings-in he did not mind to lounge about the door, or to stand sunning himself in careless thought beside the wooden stem, studded from head to heel with pegs, on which the beer-pots dangled like so many boughs upon a pewter-tree. And yet it took but five weeks to reach the lowest round of this tall ladder!" ¶MC 13

See also N:Nature—*perverted*

Diffidence

—*bashfulness:* "I felt very lonely. Yet I could no more have proposed to the landlord and landlady to admit me to their society (though I should have liked it very much) than I could have asked them to present me with a piece of plate. Here my great secret, the real bashfulness of my character, is to be observed. Like most bashful men, I judge of other people as if they were bashful too. Besides being far too shamefaced to make the proposal myself, I really had a delicate misgiving that it would be in the last degree disconcerting to them." CS/HT

"If the bashful young gentleman, in turning a street corner, chance to stumble suddenly upon two or three young ladies of his acquaintance, nothing can exceed his confusion and agitation. His first impulse is to make a great variety of bows, and dart past them, which he does until, observing that they wish to stop, but are uncertain whether to do so or not, he makes several feints of returning, which causes them to do the same; and at length, after a great quantity of unnecessary dodging and falling up against the other passengers, he returns and shakes hands most affectionately with all of them, in doing which he knocks out of their grasp sundry little parcels, which he hastily picks up, and returns very muddy and disordered. The chances are that the bashful young gentleman then observes it is very fine weather, and being reminded that it has only just left off raining for the first time these three days, he blushes very much, and smiles as if he had said a very good thing." YG/B

—*modesty*

—*gratuitous:* "'I wouldn't,' cried Miggs, folding her hands and looking upwards with a kind of devout blankness, 'I wouldn't lay myself out as she does; I wouldn't be as bold as her; I wouldn't seem to say to all male creeturs "come and kiss me"'—and here a shudder quite convulsed her frame—'for any earthly crowns as might be offered. Worlds,' Miggs added solemnly, 'should not reduce me. No. Not if I was Wenis.'

"'Well, but you *are* Wenus, you know,' said Mr Dennis, confidentially.

"'No, I am not, good gentlemen,' answered Miggs, shaking her head with an air of self-denial which seemed to imply that she might be if she chose, but she hoped she knew better. 'No, I am not, good gentlemen. Don't charge me with it.' BR 70

—*total:* "To say that Tom [Pinch] had no idea of playing first fiddle in any social orchestra, but was always quite satisfied to be set down for the hundred and fiftieth violin in the band, or thereabouts, is to express his modesty in very inadequate terms." MC 12

—*in young men:* "Young Mr [Frank] Cheeryble then earnestly entreated old Mr Cheeryble to confess that it was all a jest [that Frank had a love abroad], which old Mr Cheeryble at last did, young Mr Cheeryble being so much in earnest about it, that—as Mrs Nickleby said many thousand times afterwards in recalling the scene—he 'quite coloured', which she rightly considered a memorable circumstance, and one worthy of remark, young men not being as a class remarkable for modesty or self-denial, especially when there is a lady in the case, when, if they colour at all, it is rather their practice to colour the story, and not themselves." NN 43

Duty

—*activity:* "'Rattle me out of bed early [said Pancks], set me going, give me as short a time as you like to bolt my meals in, and keep me at it. Keep me always at it, I'll keep you always at it, you keep somebody else always at it. There you are, with the Whole Duty of Man in a commercial country.'" LD i 13

—*in the army:* "Any animated description of a modern battle, any private soldier's letter published in the newspapers, any page of the records of the Victoria Cross, will show that in the ranks of the army, there exists under all disadvantages as fine a sense of duty as is to be found in any station on earth. Who doubts that if we all did our duty as faithfully as the soldier does his, this world would be a better place? There may be greater difficulties in our way than in the soldier's. Not disputed. But, let us at least do our duty towards *him.*" UT/GT

And see B:Money and Finance—*and duty*

—*benign influence:* "It was not because I [Pip] was faithful, but because Joe [Gargery] was faithful, that I never ran away and went for a soldier or a sailor. It was not because I had a strong sense of the virtue of industry, but because Joe had a strong sense of the virtue of industry, that I worked with tolerable zeal against the grain. It is not possible to know how far the influence of any amiable honest-hearted duty-doing man flies out into the world; but it is very possible to know how it has touched one's self in going by, and I know right well that any good that intermixed itself with my apprenticeship came of plain contented Joe, and not of restless aspiring discontented me." GE 14

—*of and to a child:* "'I went away undutiful enough, and have come back no better, you may swear. But have you been very dutiful to me?'

"'I?' cried the old woman. 'To my gal! A mother dutiful to her own child!'

"'It sounds unnatural, don't it?' returned the daughter, looking coldly on her with her stern, regardless, hardy, beautiful face; 'but I have thought of it sometimes, in the course of *my* lone years, till I have got used to it. I have heard some talk about duty first and last; but it has always been of my duty to other people. I have wondered now and then—to pass away the time—whether no one ever owed any duty to me.'" DS 34

—*doing it:* "'You see that young lady [Amy Dorrit] who was here just now [said Mr Meagles]—that little, quiet, fragile figure passing along there, Tatty? Look. The people stand out of the way to let her go by. The men—see the poor, shabby fellows—pull off their hats to her quite politely, and now she glides in at that doorway. See her, Tattycoram?'

"'Yes, sir.'

"'I have heard tell, Tatty, that she was once regularly called the child of this place. She was born here, and lived here many years. I can't breathe here. A doleful place, to be born and bred in, Tattycoram?'

"'Yes indeed, sir!'

"'If she had constantly thought of herself, and settled with herself that everybody visited this place upon her, turned it against her, and cast it at her, she would have led an irritable and probably an [*sic.*] useless existence. Yet I have heard tell, Tattycoram, that her young life has been one of active resignation, goodness, and noble service. Shall I tell you what I consider those eyes of hers that were here just now, to have always looked at, to get that expression?'

"'Yes, if you please, sir.'

"'Duty, Tattycoram. Begin it early, and do it well; and there is no antecedent to it, in any origin or station, that will tell against us with the Almighty, or with ourselves.'" LD ii 33 *And see* Pride—*as duty*

"[Charker] was one of the best of men, and, in a certain sort of a way, one with the least to say for himself. I qualify it, because, besides being able to read and write like a Quarter-master, he had always one most excellent idea in his mind. That was, Duty. Upon my soul, I don't believe, though I admire learning beyond everything, that he could have got a better idea out of all the books in the world, if he had learnt them every word, and been the cleverest of scholars." CS/EP 1

—*done:* "The Reverend Frank Milvey, comforting Sloppy, expounded to him how the best of us were more or less remiss in our turnings at our respective Mangles—some of us very much so—and how we were all a halting, failing, feeble, and inconstant crew.

"'*She* warn't, sir,' said Sloppy, taking this ghostly counsel rather ill, in behalf of his late benefactress. 'Let us speak for ourselves, sir. She went through with whatever duty she had to do. She went through with me, she went through with the Minders, she went through with herself, she went through with everything. O Mrs Higden, Mrs Higden, you was a woman and a mother and a mangler in a million million!'

"With those heartfelt words, Sloppy removed his dejected head from the church door, and took it back to the grave in the corner and laid it down there, and wept alone." OMF iii 9

—*filial:* "'I am very glad to see that you have so high a sense of your duties as a son, Sam,' said Mr Pickwick.

"'I always had, sir,' replied Mr Weller.

"'That's a very gratifying reflection, Sam,' said Mr Pickwick, approvingly.

"'Wery, sir,' replied Mr Weller; 'if ever I wanted anything' o' my father, I always asked for it in a wery 'spectful and obligin' manner. If he didn't give it me, I took it, for fear I should be led to do anythin' wrong, through not havin' it. I saved him a world o' trouble in this vay, sir.'

"'That's not precisely what I meant, Sam,' said Mr Pickwick, shaking his head, with a slight smile.

"'All good feelin', sir—the wery best intentions, as the gen'l'm'n said ven he run away from his wife 'cos she seemed unhappy with him,' replied Mr Weller." PP 27

—*and greatness:* "[Crisparkle] was simply and stanchly true to his duty, alike in the large case and in the small. So all true souls ever are. So every true soul ever was, ever is, and ever will be. There is nothing little to the really great in spirit." MED 17

—*and inclination:* "As it was very easy for Kit [Nubbles] to persuade himself that the old house was in his way, his way being anywhere, he tried to look upon his passing it once more as a matter of imperative and disagreeable necessity, quite apart from any desire of his own, to which he could not choose but yield. It is not uncommon for people who are much better fed and taught than Christopher Nubbles had ever been, to make duties of their inclinations in matters of more doubtful propriety, and to take great credit for the self-denial with which they gratify themselves." OCS 14

—*of man:* " . . . [Bitzer's] only reasonable transaction in [tea] would have been to buy it for as little as he could possibly give, and sell it for as much as he could possibly get; it having been clearly ascertained by philosophers that in this is comprised the whole duty of man—not a part of man's duty, but the whole." HT ii 1

—*mouthing it:* "'. . . I have a duty to discharge which I owe to society [said Mr Pecksniff]; and it shall be discharged, my friend, at any cost!'

"Oh late-remembered, much-forgotten, mouthing, braggart duty, always owed, and seldom paid in any other coin than punishment and wrath, when will mankind begin to know thee! When will men acknowledge thee in thy neglected cradle, and thy stunted youth, and not begin their recognition in thy sinful manhood and thy desolate old age!

"Oh ermined Judge whose duty to society is, now, to doom the ragged criminal to punishment and death, hadst thou never, Man, a duty to discharge in barring up the hundred open gates that wooed him to the felon's dock, and throwing but ajar the portals to a decent life!

"Oh prelate, prelate, whose duty to society it is to mourn in melancholy phrase the sad degeneracy of these bad times in which thy lot of honours has been cast, did nothing go before thy elevation to the lofty seat, from which thou dealest out thy homilies to other tarriers for dead men's shoes, whose duty to society has not begun!

"Oh magistrate, so rare a country gentleman and brave a squire, had you no duty to society, before the ricks were blazing and the mob were mad; or did it spring up, armed and booted from the earth, a corps of yeomanry, full-grown!" ¶MC 31

—*a principle:* "As the fierce dark teaching of [Arthur Clennam's] childhood had never sunk into his heart, so the first article in his code of morals was, that he must begin in practical humility, with looking well to his feet on earth, and that he could never mount on wings of words to Heaven. Duty on earth, restitution on earth, action on earth; these first, as the first steep steps upward. Strait was the gate and narrow was the way; far straiter and narrower than the broad high road paved with vain professions and vain repetitions, motes from other men's eyes and liberal delivery of others to the judgment—all cheap materials costing absolutely nothing." LD i 27

—*and self-respect:* "'But a man in any station can do his duty,' said the young Captain [Taunton], 'and, in doing it, can earn his own respect, even if his case should be so very unfortunate and so very rare that he can earn no other man's. A common soldier, poor brute though you called him just now, has this advantage in the stormy times we live in, that he always does his duty before a host of sympathising witnesses. Do you doubt that he may so do it as to be extolled through a whole regiment, through a whole army, through a whole country? Turn while you may yet retrieve the past, and try.'" CS/PT

—*unadorned:* " . . . she holding this course as part of no fantastic vow, or bond, or brotherhood, or sisterhood, or pledge, or covenant, or fancy dress, or fancy fair; but simply as a duty to be done . . . . " HT iii 9

—*unscrupulous schoolmaster's:* "'Ah! Mrs Squeers, sir, was as partial to that lad [Dorker] as if he had been her own; the attention, sir, that was bestowed upon that boy in his illness! Dry toast and warm tea offered him every night and morning, when he couldn't swallow anything—a candle in his bed-room on the very night he died—the best dictionary sent up for him to lay his head upon. I don't regret it though. It is a pleasant thing to reflect that one did one's duty by him.'" NN 4

Emotions

—anger of a gentle man: "Filled with these thoughts [of his drunken wife and wasted life]—so filled that he had an unwholesome sense of growing larger, of being placed in some new and diseased relation towards the objects among which he passed, of seeing the iris round every misty light turn red—[Stephen Blackpool] went home for shelter." HT ii 12

—anger softened by grief: "The association of ideas . . . did the Captain [Cuttle] a great deal of good; it softened him in the very height of his anger, and brought the tears into his eyes.

"Arrived at the Wooden Midshipman's again, and sitting down in a corner of the dark shop, the Captain's indignation, strong as it was, could make no head against his grief. Passion seemed not only to do wrong and violence to the memory of the dead, but to be infected by death, and to droop and decline beside it. All the living knaves and liars in the world, were nothing to the honesty and truth of one dead friend." DS 32

—Anglo-Saxon: "'Gentlemen,' said the cherub, inaudibly addressing, in his Anglo-Saxon tendency to throw his feelings into the form of a speech, the boys down below, who were bidding against each other to put their heads in the mud for sixpence . . . ." OMF iv 4

—contempt: "' . . . if I hadn't more manliness [said Susan Nipper] than that insipidest of his sex [Mr Perch], I'd never take pride in my hair again, but turn it up behind my ears, and wear coarse caps, without a bit of border, until death released me from my insignificance.'" DS 23

—disappointment: "As I have known legatees deeply injured by a bequest of five hundred pounds because it was not five thousand, and as I was once acquainted with a pensioner on the Public to the extent of two hundred a year, who perpetually anathematised his Country because he was not in the receipt of four, having no claim whatever to sixpence: so perhaps it usually happens, within certain limits, that to get a little help is to get a notion of being defrauded of more." UT/AH

—irrepressible: "'My feelings, Mrs Todgers [said Pecksniff], will not consent to be entirely smothered, like the young children in the Tower. They are grown up, and the more I press the bolster on them, the more they look round the corner of it.'" MC 9

—relieved: "There was anything but solitude in the nursery; for there, Mrs Chick and Miss Tox were enjoying a social evening, so much to the disgust of Miss Susan Nipper, that that young lady embraced every opportunity of making wry faces behind the door. Her feelings were so much excited on the occasion, that she found it indispensable to afford them this relief, even without having the comfort of any audience or sympathy whatever. As the knight-errants of old relieved their minds by carving their mistress's names in deserts, and wildernesses, and other savage places where there was no probability of there ever being anybody to read them, so did Miss Susan Nipper curl her snub nose into drawers and wardrobes, put away winks of disparagement in cupboards, shed derisive squints into stone pitchers, and contradict and call names out in the passage." DS 4

—resentment: "'I couldn't forgive myself at such a time as this . . . and when there's so much serious distress to think about, if I rested hard on any one, especially on them that little darling Paul speaks well of, but I *may* wish that the family was set to work in a stony soil to make new roads, and that Miss Blimber went in front, and had the pickaxe!'" DS 15

"'How do they pass their lives in this beautiful and peaceful place?' was the subject of my speculation with a visitor who once accompanied me to a charming rustic retreat for old men and women: a quaint ancient foundation in a pleasant English county, behind a picturesque church and among rich old convent gardens . . . [the inhabitants] passed their lives in considering themselves mulcted of certain ounces of tea by a deaf old steward who lived among them in the quadrangle. There was no reason to suppose that any such ounces of tea had ever been in existence, or that the old steward so much as knew what was the matter;—he passed *his* life in considering himself periodically defrauded of a birch-broom by the beadle." UT/AH

—spite: "Spite is a little word; but it represents as strange a jumble of feelings, and compound of discords, as any polysyllable in the language. Miss [Fanny] Squeers knew as well in her heart of hearts, that what the miserable serving girl had said was sheer, coarse, lying flattery, as did the girl herself; yet the mere opportunity of venting a little ill-nature against the offending Miss Price, and affecting to compassionate her weak-

nesses and foibles, though only in the presence of a solitary dependant, was almost as great a relief to her spleen as if the whole had been gospel truth. Nay, more. We have such extraordinary powers of persuasion when they are exerted over ourselves, that Miss Squeers felt quite high-minded and great after her noble renunciation of John Browdie's hand, and looked down upon her rival with a kind of holy calmness and tranquillity, that had a mighty effect in soothing her ruffled feelings." NN 12

—suppressed: "In truth [Lady Dedlock] is not a hard lady naturally; and the time has been when the sight of the venerable figure [Mrs Rouncewell] suing to her with such strong earnestness would have moved her to great compassion. But so long accustomed to suppress emotion, and keep down reality; so long schooled for her own purposes, in that destructive school which shuts up the natural feelings of the heart, like flies in amber, and spreads one uniform and dreary gloss over the good and bad, the feeling and the unfeeling, the sensible and the senseless; she had subdued even her wonder until now." BH 55

—suppression relieved: "[Louisa Gradgrind] did not raise her head. A dull anger that she should be seen in her distress, and that the involuntary look she had so resented should come to this fulfilment, smouldered within her like an unwholesome fire. All closely imprisoned forces rend and destroy. The air that would be healthful to the earth, the water that would enrich it, the heat that would ripen it, tear it when caged up. So in her bosom even now; the strongest qualities she possessed, long turned upon themselves, became a heap of obduracy, that rose against a friend.

"It was well that soft touch came upon her neck, and that she understood herself to be supposed to have fallen asleep. The sympathetic hand did not claim her resentment. Let it lie there, let it lie.

"It lay there, warming into life a crowd of gentler thoughts; and she rested. As she softened with the quiet, and the consciousness of being so watched, some tears made their way into her eyes. The face touched hers, and she knew that there were tears upon it too, and she the cause of them." HT iii 1

—terror: "A more complete picture of terror than the little man [Solomon Daisy] presented, it would be difficult to imagine. The perspiration stood in beads upon his face, his knees knocked together, his every limb trembled, the power of articulation was quite gone; and there he stood, panting for breath, gazing on [the Maypolers] with such livid ashy looks, that they were infected with his fear, though ignorant of its occasion, and, reflecting his dismayed and horror-stricken visage, stared back again without venturing to question him . . . " BR 33

"'I am to depart in state, I see?'

"'Why, unless you did,' returned the jailer, 'you might depart in so many pieces that it would be difficult to get you together again. There's a crowd, Monsieur Rigaud, and it doesn't love you.'

"He passed on out of sight, and unlocked and unbarred a low door in the corner of the chamber. 'Now,' said he, as he opened it and appeared within, 'come out.'

"There is no sort of whiteness in all the hues under the sun at all like the whiteness of Monsieur Rigaud's face as it was then. Neither is there any expression of the human countenance at all like that expression, in every little line of which the frightened heart is seen to beat. Both are conventionally compared with death; but the difference is the whole deep gulf between the struggle done, and the fight at its most desperate extremity." LD i 1

—vengefulness: "'I would trample on them all,' [Rosa Dartle] answered. 'I would have [Daniel Peggotty's] house pulled down. I would have [Little Em'ly] branded on the face, drest in rags, and cast out in the streets to starve. If I had the power to sit in judgment on her, I would see it done. See it done? I would do it! I detest her. If I ever could reproach her with her infamous condition, I would go anywhere to do so. If I could hunt her to her grave, I would. If there was any word of comfort that would be a solace to her in her dying hour, and only I possessed it, I wouldn't part with it for life itself.'

"The mere vehemence of her words can convey, I am sensible, but a weak impression of the passion by which she was possessed, and which made itself articulate in her whole figure, though her voice, instead of being raised, was lower than usual. No description I could give of her would do justice to my recollection of her, or to her entire deliverance of herself to her anger. I have seen passion in many forms, but I have never seen it in such a form as that." DC 32

Energy

—absence rationalized: "'Then idiots talk,' said Eugene [Wrayburn], leaning back, folding his arms, smoking with his eyes shut, and speaking slightly through his nose, 'of Energy. If there is a word in the dictionary under any letter from A to Z that I abominate, it is energy. It is such a conventional superstition, such parrot gabble! What the deuce! Am I to rush out into the street, collar the first man of a wealthy appearance that I meet, shake him, and say, "Go to law upon the spot, you dog, and retain me, or I'll be the death of you"? Yet that would be energy.'

"'Precisely my view of the case, Eugene [said Mortimer Lightwood]. But show me a good opportunity, show me something really worth being energetic about, and *I* 'll show you energy.'

"'And so will I,' said Eugene.

"And it is likely enough that ten thousand other young men, within the limits of the London Post-office town-delivery, made the same hopeful remark in the course of the same evening." OMF i 3

—idleness "I am a young man of that easy disposition, that I lie abed till it's absolutely necessary to get up and earn something, and then I lie abed again till I have spent it." CS/SL 3

" . . . he had . . . nobody to speak to who really felt . . . the unutterable folly of climbing, undriven, up any steep place in the world, when there is level ground within reach to walk on instead. Was it for this that Thomas [Idle] had left London? London, where there are nice short walks in level public gardens, with benches of repose set up at convenient distances for weary travellers—London, where rugged stone is humanely pounded into little lumps for the road, and intelligently shaped into smooth slabs for the pavement!" LT 1

"Prone on the sofa, Thomas [Idle] made no attempt to get through the hours, but passively allowed the hours to get through *him.* Where other men in his situation would have read books and improved their minds, Thomas slept and rested his body. Where other men would have pondered anxiously over their future prospects, Thomas dreamed lazily of his past life.

"The one solitary thing he did, which most other people would have done in his place, was to resolve on making certain alterations and improvements in his mode of existence, as soon as the effects of the misfortune that had overtaken him had all passed away. Remembering that the current of his life had hitherto oozed along in one smooth stream of laziness, occasionally troubled on the surface by a slight passing ripple of industry, his present ideas on the subject of self-reform, inclined him—not as the reader may be disposed to imagine, to project schemes for a new existence of enterprise and exertion—but, on the contrary, to resolve that he would never, if he could possibly help it, be active or industrious again, throughout the whole of his future career.

"It is due to Mr Idle to relate that his mind sauntered towards this peculiar conclusion on distinct and logically-producible grounds. After reviewing, quite at his ease, and with many needful intervals of repose, the generally-placid spectacle of his past existence, he arrived at the discovery that all the great disasters which had tried his patience and equanimity in early life, had been caused by his having allowed himself to be deluded into imitating some pernicious example of activity and industry that had been set him by others.

"The first disaster occurred after Thomas had been an idle and a popular boy at school, for some happy years. One Christmas-time, he was stimulated by the evil example of a companion, whom he had always trusted and liked, to be untrue to himself, and to try for a prize at the ensuing half-yearly examination. He did try, and he got a prize—how, he did not distinctly know at the moment, and cannot remember now.

"No sooner, however, had the book—Moral Hints to the Young on the Value of Time—been placed in his hands, than the first troubles of his life began. The idle boys deserted him, as a traitor to their cause. The industrious boys avoided him, as a dangerous interloper; one of their number, who had always won the prize on previous occasions, expressing just resentment at the invasion of his privileges by calling Thomas into the playground, and then and there administering to him the first sound and genuine thrashing that he had ever received in his life.

"Unpopular from that moment, as a beaten boy, who belonged to no side and was rejected by all parties, young Idle soon lost caste with his masters, as he had previously lost caste with his schoolfellows. He had forfeited the comfortable reputation of being the one lazy member of the youthful community whom it was quite hopeless to punish. Never again did he hear the headmaster say reproachfully to an industrious boy who had committed a fault, 'I might have expected this in Thomas Idle, but it is inexcusable, Sir, in you, who know better.' Never more, after winning that fatal prize, did he escape the retributive imposition, or the avenging birch. From that time, the masters made him work, and the boys would not let him play. From that time his social position steadily declined, and his life at school became a perpetual burden to him." ¶LT 3

See also A:Death—*by pressure*

—*procrastination:* " . . . to beat about the bush till the bush is withered and dead . . . . " S/DM

—*value unperceived:* "'Guppy,' says Mr Jobling, 'I will not deny it. I was on the wrong side of the post. But I trusted to things coming round.'

"That very popular trust in flat things coming round! Not in their being beaten round, or worked round, but in their 'coming' round! As though a lunatic should trust in the world's 'coming' triangular!" BH 20

Envy

—*of accomplishment:* "The worst class of sum worked in the every-day world, is cyphered by the diseased arithmeticians who are always in the rule of Subtraction as to the merits and successes of others, and never in Addition as to their own.

"The habit, too, of seeking some sort of recompense in the discontented boast of being disappointed, is a habit fraught with degeneracy. A certain idle carelessness and recklessness of consistency soon comes of it. To bring deserving things down by setting undeserving things up, is one of its perverted delights; and there is no playing fast and loose with the truth, in any game, without growing the worse for it." LD ii 6

—*of a benefactor:* "'What? Was it outside the house at present ockypied, to its disgrace, by that minion of fortune and worm of the hour,' said Wegg, falling back upon his strongest terms of reprobation, and slapping the counter, 'that I, Silas Wegg, five hundred times the man he ever was, sat in all weathers, waiting for a errand or a customer? Was it outside that very house as I first set eyes upon him, rolling in the lap of luxury, when I was a-selling halfpenny ballads there for a living? And am I to grovel in the dust for *him* to walk over? No!'

"There was a grin upon the ghastly countenance of the French gentleman under the influence of the firelight, as if he were computing how many thousand slanderers and traitors array themselves against the fortunate, on premises exactly answering to those of Mr Wegg. One might have fancied that the big-headed babies were toppling over with their hydrocephalic attempts to reckon up the children of men who transform their benefactors into their injurers by the same process. The yard or two of smile on the part of the alligator might have been invested with the meaning, 'All about this was quite familiar knowledge down in the depths of the slime, ages ago.'" OMF iii 14

—*and indolence:* "He might have added that he hated two sorts of men; all those who did him favours, and all those who were better off than himself; as in either case their position was an insult to a man of his stupendous merits. But he did not; for . . . Mr Slyme; of too haughty a stomach to work, to beg, to borrow, or to steal; yet mean enough to be worked or borrowed, begged or stolen for, by any catspaw that would serve his turn; too insolent to lick the hand that fed him in his need, yet cur enough to bite and tear it in the dark . . . Mr Slyme fell forward with his head upon the table, and so declined into a sodden sleep." MC 7

Evil

—*the Devil in human affairs:* "When the Devil goeth about like a roaring lion, he goeth about in a shape by which few but savages and hunters are attracted. But, when he is trimmed, smoothed, and varnished, according to the mode; when he is aweary of vice, and aweary of virtue, used up as to brimstone, and used up as to bliss; then, whether he take to the serving out of red tape, or to the kindling of red fire, he is the very Devil." HT ii 8

—*in human nature:* "Is it the interest of any man to steal, to game, to waste his health and mental faculties by drunkenness, to lie, forswear himself, indulge hatred, seek desperate revenge, or do murder? No. All these are roads to ruin. And why, then, do men tread them? Because such inclinations are among the vicious qualities of mankind.

"Blot out, ye friends of slavery, from the

catalogue of human passions, brutal lust, cruelty, and the abuse of irresponsible power (of all earthly temptations the most difficult to be resisted), and when ye have done so, and not before, we will inquire whether it be the interest of a master to lash and maim the slaves, over whose lives and limbs he has an absolute control!" ¶AN 17

—in a man's face: "On this man, with his moustache going up and his nose coming down in that most evil of smiles, and with his surface eyes looking as if they belonged to his dyed hair, and had had their natural power of reflecting light stopped by some similar process, Nature, always true, and never working in vain, had set the mark, Beware! It was not her fault, if the warning were fruitless. She is never to blame in any such instance." LD i 30

—man's capacity for: "Not all the rain that ever fell, or ever will fall, will put as much of hell's fire out, as a man can carry about with him." OT 38

—in particular people: "'He [Rigaud] was a wicked wretch,' said the landlady, 'and well merited what he had the good fortune to escape. So much the worse.'

"'Stay, madame! Let us see,' returned the Swiss, argumentatively turning his cigar between his lips. 'It may have been his unfortunate destiny. He may have been the child of circumstances. It is always possible that he had, and has, good in him if one did but know how to find it out. Philosophical philanthropy teaches—'

"The rest of the little knot about the stove murmured an objection to the introduction of that threatening expression. Even the two players at dominoes glanced up from their game, as if to protest against philosophical philanthropy being brought by name into the Break of Day.

"'Hold there, you and your philanthropy,' cried the smiling landlady, nodding her head more than ever. 'Listen then. I am a woman, I. I know nothing of philosophical philanthropy. But I know what I have seen, and what I have looked in the face, in this world here, where I find myself. And I tell you this, my friend, that there are people (men and women both, unfortunately) who have no good in them—none. That there are people whom it is necessary to detest without compromise. That there are people who must be dealt with as enemies of the human race. That there are people who have no human heart, and who must be crushed like savage beasts and cleared out of the way. They are but few, I hope; but I have seen (in this world here where I find myself, and even at the little Break of Day) that there are such people. And I do not doubt that this man—whatever they call him, I forget his name [Rigaud]—is one of them.'

"The landlady's lively speech was received with greater favour at the Break of Day, than it would have elicited from certain amiable white-washers of the class she so unreasonably objected to, nearer Great Britain." LD i 11

—purposes: "' . . . all good things perverted to evil purposes, are worse than those which are naturally bad [said Gabriel Varden]. A thoroughly wicked woman is wicked indeed. When religion goes wrong, she is very wrong, for the same reason.'" BR 51

And see Good*—and Evil, and* N:Nature*—perverted*

Fidelity and Loyalty

—to an accused: "' . . . I feel certain that [Neville Landless's] tale is true [said Septimus Crisparkle]. Feeling that certainty, I befriend him. As long as that certainty shall last, I will befriend him. And if any consideration could shake me in this resolve, I should be so ashamed of myself for my meanness that no man's good opinion—no, nor no woman's—so gained, could compensate me for the loss of my own.'

"Good fellow! Manly fellow! And he was so modest, too. There was no more self-assertion in the Minor Canon than in the schoolboy who had stood in the breezy playing-fields keeping a wicket. He was simply and staunchly true to his duty alike in the large case and in the small. So all true souls ever are. So every true soul ever was, ever is, and ever will be. There is nothing little to the really great in spirit." MED 17

—a daughter's: "She could go down to her father's rooms now, and think of him, and suffer her loving heart humbly to approach him, without fear of repulse. She could look upon the objects that had surrounded him in his sorrow, and could nestle near his chair, and not dread the glance that she so well remembered. She could render him such little tokens of her duty and service, as putting everything in order for him with her own hands, binding little nosegays for his

table, changing them as one by one they withered, and he did not come back, preparing something for him every day, and leaving some timid mark of her presence near his usual seat. To-day, it was a little painted stand for his watch; to-morrow she would be afraid to leave it, and would substitute some other trifle of her making not so likely to attract his eye. Waking in the night, perhaps, she would tremble at the thought of his coming home and angrily rejecting it, and would hurry down with slippered feet and quickly beating heart, and bring it away. At another time, she would only lay her face upon his desk, and leave a kiss there, and a tear." DS 23

—*of daughter to father:* "There was a classical daughter once—perhaps [Euphrasia, in Byron's *Childe Harold*]—who ministered to her father in his prison as her mother had ministered to her. Little Dorrit, though of the unheroic modern stock, and mere English, did much more, in comforting her father's wasted heart upon her innocent breast, and turning to it a fountain of love and fidelity that never ran dry or waned, through all his years of famine." LD i 19

—*disarming trust:* "It may have been that Mrs Lammle tried in some manner to excuse her conduct to herself by depreciating the poor little victim of whom she spoke with acrimonious contempt. It may have been too that in this she did not quite succeed, for it is very difficult to resist confidence, and she knew she had Georgiana [Podsnap]'s." OMF ii 4

—*of husband to wife:* "'My Lady is too high in position, too handsome, too accomplished, too superior in most respects to the best of those by whom she is surrounded, not to have her enemies and traducers, I dare say. Let it be known to them, as I make it known to you, that being of sound mind, memory, and understanding, I revoke no disposition I have made in her favour. I abridge nothing I have ever bestowed upon her. I am on unaltered terms with her, and I recall—having the full power to do it if I were so disposed, as you see—no act I have done for her advantage and happiness.'

"[Sir Leicester Dedlock's] formal array of words might have at any other time, as it has often had, something ludicrous in it; but at this time it is serious and affecting. His noble earnestness, his fidelity, his gallant shielding of her, his general conquest of his own wrong and his own pride for her sake, are simply honourable, manly, and true. Nothing less worthy can be seen through the lustre of such qualities in the commonest mechanic, nothing less worthy can be seen in the best-born gentleman. In such a light both aspire alike, both rise alike, both children of the dust shine equally." BH 58

—*lack of it:* "'I have had disappointments to contend against,' said Squeers, looking very grim; 'Bolder's father was two pound ten short. Where is Bolder?'

"'Here he is, please sir,' rejoined twenty officious voices. Boys are very like men to be sure." NN 7

"They threw [Joan's] ashes into the river Seine; but they will rise against her murderers on the last day.

"From the moment of her capture, neither the French King nor one single man in all his court raised a finger to save her. It is no defence of them that they may have never really believed in her, or that they may have won her victories by their skill and bravery. The more they pretended to believe in her, the more they had caused her to believe in herself; and she had ever been true to them, ever brave, ever nobly devoted. But, it is no wonder, that they, who were in all things false to themselves, false to one another, false to their country, false to Heaven, false to Earth, should be monsters of ingratitude and treachery to a helpless peasant girl." CHE 21 ii

See M:Illusion—*young love reencountered*

—*of an old retainer:* "'It's forty-four year,' said Tim, making a calculation in the air with his pen, and drawing an imaginary line before he cast it up, 'forty-four year, next May, since I first kept the books of Cheeryble Brothers. I've opened the safe every morning all that time (Sundays excepted) as the clock struck nine, and gone over the house every night at half-past ten (except on Foreign Post nights, and then twenty minutes before twelve) to see the doors fastened, and the fires out. I've never slept out of the back attic one single night. . . . I have slept in that room,' added Tim, sinking his voice a little, 'for four-and-forty year; and if it wasn't inconvenient, and didn't interfere with business, I should request leave to die there.'

"'Damn you, Tim Linkinwater, how dare you talk about dying?' roared the twins by one impulse, and blowing their old noses violently.

"'That's what I've got to say, Mr Edwin and Mr Charles,' said Tim, squaring his shoulders again. 'This isn't the first time you've talked about superannuating me; but, if you please, we'll make it the last, and drop the subject for evermore.'

"With those words, Tim Linkinwater stalked out, and shut himself up in his glass-case, with the air of a man who had had his say, and was thoroughly resolved not to be put down.

"The brothers interchanged looks, and coughed some half-dozen times without speaking.

"'He must be done something with, brother Ned,' said the other warmly; 'we must disregard his old scruples; they can't be tolerated or borne. He must be made a partner, brother Ned; and if he won't submit to it peaceably, we must have recourse to violence.'" NN 35

—a sister's: "This slight, small, patient figure, neatly dressed in homely stuffs, and indicating nothing but the dull, household virtues, that have so little in common with the received idea of heroism and greatness, unless, indeed, any ray of them should shine through the lives of the great ones of the earth, when it becomes a constellation and is tracked in Heaven straightway—this slight, small, patient figure, leaning on the man still young but worn and grey, is she, his sister, who, of all the world, went over to him in his shame and put her hand in his, and with a sweet composure and determination, led him hopefully upon his barren way." DS 33

—among theatre people: " . . . there is no class of society the members of which so well help themselves or so well help each other. Not in the whole grand chapters of Westminster Abbey and York Minster, not in the whole quadrangle of the Royal Exchange, not in the whole list of members of the Stock Exchange, not in the Inns of Court, not in the College of Physicians, not in the College of Surgeons, can there possibly be found more remarkable instances of uncomplaining poverty, of cheerful, constant self-denial, or the generous remembrance of the claims of kindred and professional brotherhood, than will certainly be found in the dingiest and dirtiest concert room, in the least lucid theatre, even in the raggedest tent circus that was ever stained by weather." S/DM

—to a trust: "Many accounts and account-books, many files of correspondence, and several strong boxes, garnished Mr Grewgious's room. They can scarcely be represented as having lumbered it, so conscientious and precise was their orderly arrangement. The apprehension of dying suddenly, and leaving one fact or one figure with any incompleteness or obscurity attaching to it, would have stretched Mr Grewgious stone dead any day. The largest fidelity to a trust was the life-blood of the man. There are sorts of life-blood that course more quickly, more gayly, more attractively; but there is no better sort in circulation." MED 11

—a wife and mother's: "'George, you know the old girl —she's as sweet and as mild as milk. But touch her on the children—or myself—and she's off like gun-powder.'

"'It does her credit, Mat!'

"'George,' says Mr Bagnet, looking straight before him, 'the old girl—can't do anything—that don't do her credit. More or less. I never say so. Discipline must be maintained.'

"'She's worth her weight in gold,' says the trooper.

"'In gold?' says Mr Bagnet. 'I'll tell you what. The old girl's weight—is twelve stone six. Would I take that weight—in any metal—*for* the old girl? No. Why not? Because the old girl's metal is far more precious—than the preciousest metal. And she's *all* metal!'

"'You are right, Mat!'

"'When she took me—and accepted of the ring—she 'listed under me and the children—heart and head; for life. She's that earnest,' says Mr Bagnet, 'and true to her colours—that, touch us with a finger—and she turns out—and stands to her arms. If the old girl fires wide—once in a way—at the call of duty—look over it, George. For she's loyal!'" BH 34

Generosity

—elicited craftily: "'Mr Skimpole,' said Richard to me, 'has a delicacy in applying to my cousin Jarndyce, because he has lately—I think, sir, I understood you that you had lately——'

"'Oh, yes!' returned Mr Skimpole, smiling. 'Though I forget how much it was, and when it was. Jarndyce would readily do it again; but I have the epicure-like feeling that would prefer a novelty in help; that I would rather,' and he looked at Richard and me, 'develop generosity in a new soil, and in a new form of flower . . . .

"Richard and I looked at one another again. It was a most singular thing that the arrest was our embarrassment, and not Mr Skimpole's. He observed us with a genial interest; but there seemed, if I may venture on such a contradiction, nothing selfish in it. He had entirely washed his hands of the difficulty, and it had become ours." BH 6

—innate: "[Arthur Clennam's nature] saved him still from the whimpering weakness and cruel selfishness of holding that because such a happiness or such a virtue had not come into his little path, or worked well for him, therefore it was not in the great scheme, but was reducible, when found in appearance, to the basest elements. A disappointed mind he had, but a mind too firm and healthy for such unwholesome air. Leaving himself in the dark, it could rise into the light, seeing it shine on others and hailing it.

"Therefore, he sat before his dying fire, sorrowful to think upon the way by which he had come to that night, yet not strewing poison on the way by which other men had come to it." LD i 13

—perturbed: " . . . [there was] a contention, always waging within [Arthur Clennam's heart], between a tendency to dislike Mr Henry Gowan, if not to regard him with positive repugnance, and a whisper that the inclination was unworthy. A generous nature is not prone to strong aversions, and is slow to admit them even dispassionately; but when it finds ill-will gaining upon it, and can discern between-whiles that its origin is not dispassionate, such a nature becomes distressed." LD i 26

—self-sacrifice: Sir Philip Sidney "had to ride back wounded, a long distance, and was very faint with fatigue and loss of blood, when some water, for which he had eagerly asked, was handed to him. But he was so good and gentle even then, that seeing a poor badly wounded common soldier lying on the ground, looking at the water with longing eyes, he said, 'Thy necessity is greater than mine,' and gave it up to him.

"This touching action of a noble heart is perhaps as well known as any incident in history—is as famous far and wide as the blood-stained Tower of London, with the axe, and block, and murders out of number. So delightful is an act of true humanity, and so glad are mankind to remember it." ¶CHE 31 ii

Good

—doing it

—on the bench: "Lingering in the bright moonlight at the close of a happy day, [Thomas Talfourd] spoke of his new functions, of his sense of the great responsibility he undertook, and of his placid belief that the habits of his professional life rendered him equal to their efficient discharge; but, above all, he spoke with an earnestness, never more to be separated in his friend's mind from the murmur of the sea upon a moonlight night, of his reliance on the strength of his desire to do right before God and man. He spoke with his own singleness of heart, and his solitary hearer knew how deep and true his purpose was." HW/JT

—for its own sake: "' . . . this little death has made me ask myself the question, seriously, whether I wasn't too bent upon pleasing myself. Else why did I seek out so much for a pretty child, and a child quite to my liking? Wanting to do good, why not do it for its own sake, and put my taste and likings by? . . . I have been thinking if I take any orphan to provide for, let it not be a pet and a plaything for me, but a creature to be helped for its own sake.'" OMF ii 10

—and Evil

—classification: "It appeared . . . that everybody whom this Gowan knew was either more or less of an ass, or more or less of a knave; but was, notwithstanding, the most lovable, the most engaging, the simplest, truest, kindest, dearest, best fellow that ever lived.

"The process by which this unvarying result was attained, whatever the premises, might have been stated by Mr Henry Gowan thus: 'I claim to be always bookkeeping, with a peculiar nicety, in every man's case, and posting up a careful little account of Good and Evil with him. I do this so conscientiously, that I am happy to tell you I find the most worthless of men to be the dearest old fellow too; and am in a condition to make the gratifying report, that there is much less difference than you are inclined to suppose between an honest man and a scoundrel.' The effect of this cheering discovery happened to be, that while he seemed to be scrupulously finding good in most men, he did in reality lower it where it was, and set it up where it was not; but that was its only disagreeable or dangerous feature." LD i 17

—eternal law: " . . . the hard, wrathful and sordid nature that had wrung as much work out of [the Boffins] as could be got in their best days, for as little money as could be paid to hurry on their worst, had never been so warped but that it knew their moral straightness and respected it. In its own despite, in a constant conflict with itself and them, it had done so. And this is the eternal law. For, Evil often stops short at itself and dies with the doer of it! but Good, never." OMF i 8

—lesson of marble sculpture: "Standing in one of the many studii of Carrara, that afternoon—for it is a great workshop, full of beautifully-finished copies of marble, of almost every figure, group, and bust, we know—it seemed, at first, so strange to me that those exquisite shapes, replete with grace, and thought, and delicate repose, should grow out of all this toil, and sweat, and torture! [*See* N:Animal—*oxen*] But I soon found a parallel to it, and an explanation of it, in every virtue that springs up in miserable ground, and every good thing that has its birth in sorrow and distress.

"And, looking out of the sculptor's great window, upon the marble mountains, all red and glowing in the decline of day, but stern and solemn to the last, I thought, my God! how many quarries of human hearts and souls, capable of far more beautiful results, are left shut up and mouldering away: while pleasure-travellers through life, avert their faces, as they pass, and shudder at the gloom and ruggedness that conceal them!" ¶PI 10

—humour: "'I don't believe, mother [said Kit Nubbles], that harmless cheerfulness and good humour are thought greater sins in Heaven than shirt-collars are, and I do believe that those chaps are just about as right and sensible in putting down the one as in leaving off the other—that's my belief. Whenever a Little Bethel parson calls you a precious lamb, or says your brother's one, you tell him it's the truest thing he's said for a twelvemonth, and that if he'd got a little more of the lamb himself, and less of the mint-sauce—not being quite so sharp and sour over it—I should like him all the better.'" OCS 41 *And see* Laughter

—intentions: "It was a snug little room, Mr Feeder's, with his bed in another little room inside of it; and a flute, which Mr Feeder couldn't play yet, but was going to make a point of learning, he said, hanging up over the fireplace. There were some books in it, too, and a fishing-rod; for Mr Feeder said he should certainly make a point of learning to fish, when he could find time. Mr Feeder had amassed, with similar intentions, a beautiful little curly secondhand key-bugle, a chessboard and men, a Spanish Grammar, a set of sketching materials, and a pair of boxing-gloves. The art of self-defence Mr Feeder said he should undoubtedly make a point of learning, as he considered it the duty of every man to do; for it might lead to the protection of a female in distress." DS 14 *And see* Duty—*filial; and* Honour—*ends and means*

—kindness from the uncouth: " . . . it is not surprising that the affectionate heart of the child should have been touched to the quick by one kind and generous spirit, however uncouth the temple in which it dwelt. Thank Heaven that the temples of such spirits are not made with hands, and that they may be more worthily hung with poor patchwork than with purple and fine linen." OCS 11

—its propagation: "Any propagation of goodness and benevolence is no small addition to the aristocracy of nature, and no small subject of rejoicing for mankind at large." OCS 73

And see FL:The Dead—*influence for good*

Gratitude

—complacent: "For, as Mr. Pecksniff justly observed . . . it is always satisfactory to feel, in keen weather, that many other people are not as warm as you are. And this, he said, was quite natural, and a very beautiful arrangement; not confined to coaches, but extending itself into many social ramifications. 'For' (he observed), 'if every one were warm and well-fed, we should lose the satisfaction of admiring the fortitude with which certain conditions of men bear cold and hunger. And if we were not better off than anybody else, what would become of our sense of gratitude; which,' said Mr. Pecksniff with tears in his eyes, as he shook his fist at a beggar who wanted to get up behind, 'is one of the holiest feelings of our common nature' . . . . " MC 8

—a mother's: "Polly [Toodle], who had passed Heaven knows how many sleepless nights on account of this her dissipated firstborn, and had not seen him for weeks and weeks, could have almost kneeled to Mr Carker the Manager, as to a Good Spirit—in

spite of his teeth. But Mr Carker rising to depart, she only thanked him with her mother's prayers and blessings: thanks so rich when paid out of the heart's mint, especially for any service Mr Carker had rendered, that he might have given back a large amount of change, and yet been overpaid." DS 22

—racial characteristic: "[Fledgeby's] grateful servant [Riah]—in whose race gratitude is deep, strong, and enduring—bowed his head, and actually did now put the hem of his coat to his lips: though so lightly that the wearer knew nothing of it." OMF ii 5

Greatness

—illusory: "so modest was Mr Merdle withal, in the midst of these splendid achievements, that he looked more like a man in possession of his house under a distraint, than a commercial Colossus bestriding his own hearth-rug while the little ships were sailing in to dinner." LD ii 12

—surprising: "'Well, but suppose he wasn't a hairdresser,' suggested Sam [Weller].

"'Wy then, sir, be parliamentary and call him vun all the more,' returned his father [Tony Weller]. 'In the same vay as ev'ry gen'lman in another place is a *h*onourable, ev'ry barber in this place is a hairdresser. Ven you read the speeches in the papers, and see as vun gen'lman says of another, "the *h*onourable member, if he vill allow me to call him so," you vill understand, sir, that that means "if he vill allow me to keep up that 'ere pleasant and uniwersal fiction."'

"It is a common remark, confirmed by history and experience, that great men rise with the circumstances in which they are placed. Mr Weller came out so strong in his capacity of chairman, that Sam was for some time prevented from speaking by a grin of surprise, which held his faculties enchained, and at last subsided in a long whistle of a single note. Nay, the old gentleman appeared even to have astonished himself, and that to no small extent, as was demonstrated by the vast amount of chuckling in which he indulged, after the utterance of these lucid remarks." MH 5

—undermined: "Towards his first wife, Mr Dombey, in his cold and lofty arrogance, had borne himself like the removed Being he almost conceived himself to be. He had been 'Mr Dombey' with her when she first saw him, and he was 'Mr Dombey' when she died. He had asserted his greatness during their whole married life, and she had meekly recognised it. He had kept his distant seat of state on the top of his throne, and she her humble station on its lowest step; and much good it had done him, so to live in solitary bondage to his one idea!

"He had imagined that the proud character of his second wife would have been added to his own—would have merged into it, and exalted his greatness. He had pictured himself haughtier than ever, with Edith's haughtiness subservient to his. He had never entertained the possibility of its arraying itself against him. And now, when he found it rising in his path at every step and turn of his daily life, fixing its cold, defiant, and contemptuous face upon him, this pride of his, instead of withering, or hanging down its head beneath the shock, put forth new shoots, became more concentrated and intense, more gloomy, sullen, irksome, and unyielding, than it had ever been before." ¶DS 40

And see Duty—*and the great*

Grief

—and healing: "It was a long and gloomy night that gathered on me [David Copperfield], haunted by the ghosts of many hopes, of many dear remembrances, many errors, many unavailing sorrows and regrets.

"I went away from England; not knowing, even then, how great the shock was that I had to bear. I left all who were dear to me, and went away; and believed that I had borne it, and it was past. As a man upon a field of battle will receive a mortal hurt, and scarcely know that he is struck, so I, when I was left alone with my undisciplined heart, had no conception of the wound with which it had to strive.

"The knowledge came upon me, not quickly, but little by little, and grain by grain. The desolate feeling with which I went abroad, deepened and widened hourly. At first it was a heavy sense of loss and sorrow, wherein I could distinguish little else. By imperceptible degrees, it became a hopeless consciousness of all that I had lost—love, friendship, interest; of all that had been shattered—my first trust, my first affection, the whole airy castle of my life; of all that remained—a ruined blank and waste, lying wide around me, unbroken, to the dark horizon.

"If my grief were selfish, I did not know it to be so. I mourned for my child-wife, taken from her blooming world, so young. I mourned for him who might have won the love and admiration of thousands, as he had won mine long ago. I mourned for the broken heart that had found rest in the stormy sea; and for the wandering remnants of the simple home, where I had heard the night-wind blowing when I was a child.

"From the accumulated sadness into which I fell, I had at length no hope of ever issuing again. I roamed from place to place, carrying my burden with me everywhere. I felt its whole weight now; and I drooped beneath it, and I said in my heart that it could never be lightened.

"When this despondency was at its worst, I believed that I should die. Sometimes, I thought that I would like to die at home; and actually turned back on my road, that I might get there soon. At other times, I passed on farther away, from city to city, seeking I know not what, and trying to leave I know not what behind.

"It is not in my power to retrace, one by one, all the weary phases of distress of mind through which I passed. There are some dreams that can only be imperfectly and vaguely described; and when I oblige myself to look back on this time of my life, I seem to be recalling such a dream. I see myself passing on among the novelties of foreign towns, palaces, cathedrals, temples, pictures, castles, tombs, fantastic streets—the old abiding places of History and Fancy—as a dreamer might; bearing my painful load through all, and hardly conscious of the objects as they fade before me. Listlessness to everything, but brooding sorrow, was the night that fell on my undisciplined heart. Let me look up from it—as at last I did, thank Heaven!—and from its long, sad, wretched dream, to dawn.

"For many months I travelled with this ever-darkening cloud upon my mind. Some blind reasons that I had for not returning home—reasons then struggling within me, vainly, for more distinct expression—kept me on my pilgrimage. Sometimes, I had proceeded restlessly from place to place, stopping nowhere; sometimes, I had lingered long in one spot. I had had no purpose, no sustaining soul within me, anywhere.

"I was in Switzerland. I had come out of Italy, over one of the great passes of the Alps, and had since wandered with a guide among the by-ways of the mountains. If those awful solitudes had spoken to my heart, I did not know it. I had found sublimity and wonder in the dread heights and precipices, in the roaring torrents, and the wastes of ice and snow; but as yet, they had taught me nothing else.

"I came, one evening before sunset, down into a valley, where I was to rest. In the course of my descent to it, by the winding track along the mountain-side, from which I saw it shining far below, I think some long-unwonted sense of beauty and tranquillity, some softening influence awakened by its peace, moved faintly in my breast. I remember pausing once, with a kind of sorrow that was not all oppressive, not quite despairing. I remember almost hoping that some better change was possible within me.

"I came into the valley, as the evening sun was shining on the remote heights of snow, that closed it in like eternal clouds. The bases of the mountains forming the gorge in which the little village lay, were richly green; and high above this gentler vegetation, grew forests of dark fir, cleaving the wintry snow-drift, wedge-like, and stemming the avalanche. Above these, were range upon range of craggy steeps, grey rock, bright ice, and smooth verdure-specks of pasture, all gradually blending with the crowning snow.

"Dotted here and there on the mountain's side, each tiny dot a home, were lonely wooden cottages, so dwarfed by the towering heights that they appeared too small for toys. So did even the clustered village in the valley, with its wooden bridge across the stream, where the stream tumbled over broken rocks, and roared away among the trees. In the quiet air, there was a sound of distant singing—shepherd voices; but, as one bright evening cloud floated midway along the mountain's side, I could almost have believed it came from there, and was not earthly music. All at once, in this serenity, great Nature spoke to me;—and soothed me to lay down my weary head upon the grass, and weep as I had not wept yet, since Dora died!" ¶DC 58

—*need for:* "'Oh my brother! oh my brother!'

"It was a natural emotion, not to be suppressed; and it would make way even between the fingers of the hands with which [Florence Dombey] covered up her face. The overcharged and heavy-laden breast must sometimes have that vent, or the poor wounded solitary heart within it would have fluttered like a bird with broken wings, and sunk down in the dust." DS 18

—*ostentatious:* "As Oliver accompanied his master in most of his adult expeditions, too, in order that he might acquire that equanimity of demeanour and full command of nerve which are essential to a finished undertaker, he had many opportunities of observing the beautiful resignation and fortitude with which some strong-minded people bear their trials and losses.

"For instance; when Sowerberry had an order for the burial of some rich old lady or gentleman, who was surrounded by a great number of nephews and nieces, who had been perfectly inconsolable during the previous illness, and whose grief had been wholly irrepressible even on the most public occasions, they would be as happy among themselves as need be—quite cheerful and contented—conversing together with as much freedom and gaiety, as if nothing whatever had happened to disturb them. Husbands, too, bore the loss of their wives with the most heroic calmness. Wives, again, put on weeds for their husbands, as if, so far from grieving in the garb of sorrow, they had made up their minds to render it as becoming and attractive as possible. It was observable, too, that ladies and gentlemen who were in passions of anguish during the ceremony of interment, recovered almost as soon as they reached home, and became quite composed before the tea-drinking was over. All this was very pleasant and improving to see; and Oliver beheld it with great admiration." OT 6

—*of the poor:* "'They little know, who coldly talk of the poor man's bereavements, as a happy release from pain to the departed, and a merciful relief from expense to the survivor—they little know, I say, what the agony of those bereavements is. A silent look of affection and regard when all other eyes are turned coldly away—the consciousness that we possess the sympathy and affection of one being when all others have deserted us—is a hold, a stay, a comfort, in the deepest affliction, which no wealth could purchase, or power bestow. The child had sat at his parents' feet for hours together, with his little hands patiently folded in each other, and his thin wan face raised towards them. They had seen him pine away, from day to day; and though his brief existence had been a joyless one, and he was now removed to that peace and rest which, child as he was, he had never known in this world, they were his parents, and his loss sunk deep into their souls.'" PP 21

—*purified by love:* " . . . Florence could do nothing but weep, and wander up and down, and sometimes, in a sudden pang of desolate remembrance, fly to her own chamber, wring her hands, lay her face down on her bed, and know no consolation: nothing but the bitterness and cruelty of grief. This commonly ensued upon the recognition of some spot or object very tenderly associated with [little Paul Dombey]; and it made the miserable house, at first, a place of agony.

"But it is not in the nature of pure love to burn so fiercely and unkindly long. The flame that in its grosser composition has the taint of earth, may prey upon the breast that gives it shelter; but the sacred fire from heaven is as gentle in the heart, as when it rested on the heads of the assembled twelve, and showed each man his brother, brightened and unhurt. The image conjured up, there soon returned the placid face, the softened voice, the loving looks, the quiet trustfulness and peace; and Florence, though she wept still, wept more tranquilly, and courted the remembrance." DS 18

And see Happiness—*and grief; and* A:Death—*bereavement*

Happiness

—*complacency:* "Mr Dombey's cup of satisfaction was so full at this moment, however, that he felt he could afford a drop or two of its contents, even to sprinkle on the dust in the by-path of his little daughter." DS 5

"Complacent and affable as man could be, Mr Carker picked his way along the streets and hummed a soft tune as he went. He seemed to purr, he was so glad." DS 22

—*contentment:* "'If there's little business today, there'll be more tomorrow [said Brass]. A contented spirit, Mr Richard, is the sweetness of existence.'" OCS 56

And see Adversity—*and good nature*

—*defined:* "'Annual income twenty pounds [said Mr Micawber], annual expenditure nineteen nineteen six, result happiness. Annual income twenty pounds, annual expenditure twenty pounds ought and six, result misery. The blossom is blighted, the leaf is withered, the God of day goes down upon the dreary scene, and—and in short you are for ever floored. As I am!'

"To make his example the more impressive, Mr Micawber drank a glass of punch with an air of great enjoyment and satisfaction, and whistled the College Hornpipe.

"I did not fail to assure him that I would store these precepts in my mind, though indeed I had no need to do so, for, at the time, they affected me visibly." DC 12

—gained in usefulness: " . . . [Jackson] now had eyes and thoughts for a new external world. How the many toiling people lived, and loved, and died; how wonderful it was to consider the various trainings of eye and hand, the nice distinctions of sight and touch, that separated them into classes of workers, . . . which combined their many intelligences and forces . . . . 'I too am but a little part of a great whole,' he began to think; 'and to be serviceable to myself and others, or to be happy, I must cast my interest into, and draw it out of, the common stock.'" CS/MJ 2

—and grief: "'Do you think the sisters who loved [Alice of York] so well, would have grieved the less if her life had been one of gloom and sadness? If anything could soothe the first sharp pain of a heavy loss, it would be—with me—the reflection, that those I mourned, by being innocently happy here, and loving all about them, had prepared themselves for a purer and happier world. The sun does not shine upon this fair earth to meet frowning eyes, depend upon it.'" NN 6

And see A:The Dead—*remembered; and* M:Memory—*of happiness*

—to a housemaid: "What day-dreams of hope and happiness—of life being one perpetual holiday, with no master and no mistress to grant or withhold it—of every Sunday being a Sunday out—of pure freedom as to curls and ringlets, and no obligation to hide fine heads of hair in caps—what pictures of happiness, vast and immense to her, but utterly ridiculous to us, bewilder the brain of the little housemaid at number six, all called into existence by the wedding at the corner!" YC/Y

—of an idiot: "It is something to look upon enjoyment, so that it be free and wild and in the face of nature, though it is but the enjoyment of an idiot. It is something to know that Heaven has left the capacity of gladness in such a creature's breast; it is something to be assured that, however lightly men may crush that faculty in their fellows, the Great Creator of mankind imparts it even to his despised and slighted work. Who would not rather see a poor idiot happy in the sunlight, than a wise man pining in a darkened jail!" BR 25

—jolly against odds: "'Lookin' on the bright side of human life [said Mark Tapley], in short, one of my hopeful wisions is, that there's a deal of misery a'waitin' for me; in the midst of which I may come out tolerable strong, and be jolly under circumstances as reflects some credit. I goes into the world, sir, wery boyant, and I tries this. I goes aboard ship first, and wery soon discovers (by the ease with which I'm jolly, mind you) as there's no credit to be got *there.* I might have took warning by this, and gave it up; but I didn't. I gets to the U-nited States; and then I *do* begin, I won't deny it, to feel some little credit in sustaining my spirits. What follows? Jest as I'm a beginning to come out, and am a treadin' on the werge, my master deceives me'

"'Deceives you!' cried Tom.

"'Swindles me,' retorted Mr Tapley, with a beaming face. 'Turns his back on ev'rything as made his service a creditable one, and leaves me, high and dry, without a leg to stand upon. In which state I returns home. Wery good. Then all my hopeful wisions bein' crushed; and findin' that there ain't no credit for me nowhere; I abandons myself to despair, and says, "Let me do that as has the least credit in it, of all; marry a dear, sweet creetur, as is wery fond of me: me being, at the same time, wery fond of her: lead a happy life, and struggle no more again' the blight which settles on my prospects."'" MC 48

And see H:Vocations—*gloomy*

—in love: "Blessed Sunday Bells, ringing so tranquilly in their entranced and happy ears! Blessed Sunday peace and quiet, harmonizing with the calmness in their souls, and making holy air around them! Blessed twilight stealing on, and shading [Florence] so soothingly and gravely, as she falls asleep, like a hushed child, upon the bosom she has clung to!" DS 50

—matter of trifles: "The friends of the contradictory couple often deplore their frequent disputes, though they rather make light of

them at the same time: observing, that there is no doubt they are very much attached to each other, and that they never quarrel except about trifles. But neither the friends of the contradictory couple, nor the contradictory couple themselves, reflect, that as the most stupendous objects in nature are but vast collections of minute particles, so the slightest and least considered trifles make up the sum of human happiness or misery." YC/C

"'A small matter,' said the Ghost, 'to make these silly folks so full of gratitude.'

"'Small!' echoed Scrooge . . . .

"'Why! Is it not? He has spent but a few pounds of your mortal money: three or four, perhaps. Is that so much that he deserves this praise?'

"'It isn't that,' said Scrooge, heated by the remark, and speaking unconsciously like his former, not his latter self. 'It isn't that, Spirit. He has the power to render us happy or unhappy; to make our service light or burdensome; a pleasure or a toil. Say that his power lies in words and looks; in things so slight and insignificant that it is impossible to add and count 'em up: what then? The happiness he gives is quite as great as if it cost a fortune.'" CC 2

—in marriage: "'Remember that [to avoid easy fainting], my dear [said Varden], if you would be really happy, which you never can be, if your husband isn't.'" BR 19

—utter joy: "You never in all your life saw anything like Trotty [Veck] . . . . I don't care where you have lived or what you have seen; you never in all your life saw anything at all approaching him! He sat down in his chair and beat his knees and cried; he sat down in his chair and beat his knees and laughed; he sat down in his chair and beat his knees and laughed and cried together; he got out of his chair and hugged Meg; he got out of his chair and hugged Richard; he got out of his chair and hugged them both at once; he kept running up to Meg, and squeezing her fresh face between his hands and kissing it, going from her backwards not to lose sight of it, and running up again like a figure in a magic lantern; and whatever he did, he was constantly sitting himself down in his chair, and never stopping in it for one single moment; being—that's the truth—beside himself with joy." C 4

—on a wedding day: "So, [Bella] leaning on her husband's arm, they turned homeward by a rosy path which the gracious sun struck out for them in its setting. And oh, there are days in this life, worth life and worth death. And oh, what a bright old song it is, that oh, 'tis love, 'tis love, 'tis love, that makes the world go round!" OMF iv 4

Hatred

—for one we have injured: "So long as he had been a passive instrument in his hands, Sir Mulberry had regarded [Lord Verisopht] with no other feeling than contempt; but now that he presumed to avow opinions in opposition to his, and even to turn upon him with a lofty tone and an air of superiority, he began to hate him. Conscious that in the vilest and most worthless sense of the term, he was dependent upon the weak young lord, Sir Mulberry could the less brook humiliation at his hands, and when he began to dislike him he measured his dislike—as men often do—by the extent of the injuries he had inflicted upon its object. When it is remembered that Sir Mulberry Hawk had plundered, duped, deceived, and fooled his pupil in every possible way, it will not be wondered at that beginning to hate him, he began to hate him cordially." NN 50

—of the superior: " . . . apart from all the grace of youth and comeliness, there was an emanation from the warm young heart in [Nicholas's] look and bearing which kept the old man down.

"However striking such a contrast as this may be to lookers-on, none ever feel it with half the keenness or acuteness of perfection with which it strikes to the very soul of him whose inferiority it marks. It galled Ralph to the heart's core, and he hated Nicholas from that hour." NN 3

"And now, to be defied and spurned, to be held up to [Kate] in the worst and most repulsive colours, to know that she was taught to hate and despise him; to feel that there was infection in his touch and taint in his companionship—to know all this, and to know that the mover of it all, was that same boyish poor relation who had twitted him in their very first interview, and openly bearded and braved him since, wrought [Ralph Nickleby's] quiet and stealthy malignity to such a pitch, that there was scarcely anything he would not have hazarded to gratify it, if he could have seen his way to some immediate retaliation . . . ." NN 34

Heart

—apparent to another: "It was the liveliest room in the building . . . . Birds, flowers, books, drawing, music, and a hundred such graceful tokens of feminine loves and cares, filled it with more of life and human sympathy than the whole house besides seemed made to hold. There was heart in the room; and who that has a heart, ever fails to recognise the silent presence of another!" BR 20

—a bird in a cage: "'It isn't the waistcoat that I look at [said Brass]. It is the heart. The checks in the waistcoat are but the wires of the cage. But the heart is the bird. Ah! How many sich birds are perpetually moulting, and putting their beaks through the wires to peck at all mankind!'" OCS 56

—changing: "God help the man whose heart ever changes with the world, as an old mansion when it becomes an inn!" BR 10

—contents hidden: "'I speak as I find, Mr Sweedlepipes,' said Mrs Gamp. 'Forbid it should be otherways! But we never knows wot's hidden in each other's hearts; and if we had glass winders there, we'd need keep the shetters up, some on us, I do assure you!'" MC 29

—contrasting: " . . . it would have been a stranger contrast still, to have read the hearts that were beating side by side; to have had laid bare the gentle innocence of the one, and the rugged villainy of the other; to have hung upon the guileless thoughts of the affectionate girl [Kate Nickleby], and been amazed that among all the wily plots and calculations of the old man [Ralph Nickleby], there should not be one word or figure denoting thought of death or of the grave. But so it was; and stranger still—though this is a thing of every day—the warm young heart palpitated with a thousand anxieties and apprehensions, while that of the old worldly man lay rusting in its cell, beating only as a piece of cunning mechanism, and yielding no one throb of hope, or fear, or love, or care, for any living thing." NN 10

—a coquette's: "Dolly had [a heart] undoubtedly, and it was not a tough one, either, though there was a little mist of coquettishness about it, such as sometimes surrounds that sun of life in its morning, and slightly dims its lustre . . . the tears stood in Dolly's eyes, and she felt more sorry than she could tell; but next moment she happened to raise them to the glass, and really there was something there so exceedingly agreeable, that as she sighed, she smiled, and felt surprisingly consoled." BR 20

—financially speaking: "'The heart is not always a royal mint [said Pecksniff], with patent machinery to work its metal into current coin. Sometimes it throws it out in strange forms, not easily recognised as coin at all. But it is sterling gold. It has at least that merit. It is sterling gold.'" MC 20

—heavy: " . . . feeling as if my [Doctor Marigold's] heart was a heavy weight at the end of a broken sashline . . . . " CS/DM

—innocent: "'If we all had hearts like those which beat so lightly in the bosoms of the young and beautiful [said the grey-haired gentleman], what a heaven this earth would be! If, while our bodies grow old and withered, our hearts could but retain their early youth and freshness, of what avail would be our sorrows and sufferings! But, the faint image of Eden which is stamped upon them in childhood, chafes and rubs in our rough struggles with the world, and soon wears away: too often to leave nothing but a mournful blank remaining.'" NN 6

—inspired: "What [Little Dorrit's] pitiful look saw, at that early time, in her father, in her sister, in her brother, in the jail; how much, or how little of the wretched truth it pleased God to make visible to her; lies hidden with many mysteries. It is enough that she was inspired to be something which was not what the rest were, and to be that something, different and laborious, for the sake of the rest. Inspired? Yes. Shall we speak of the inspiration of a poet or a priest, and not of the heart impelled by love and self-devotion to the lowliest work in the lowliest way of life!

"With no earthly friend to help her, or so much as to see her, but the one so strangely assorted [Bob, the turnkey]; with no knowledge even of the common daily tone and habits of the common members of the free community who are not shut up in prisons; born and bred, in a social condition, false even with a reference to the falsest condition outside the walls; drinking from infancy of a well whose waters had their own peculiar stain, their own unwholesome and unnatural taste; the Child of the Marshalsea began her womanly life." LD i 7

—liability when soft: "'Do you know how pinched and destitute I am?' [Mary Rudge] retorted. 'I do not think you do, or can. If

you had eyes, and could look around you on this poor place, you would have pity on me. Oh! let your heart be softened by your own affliction, friend, and have some sympathy with mine.'

"The blind man snapped his fingers as he answered:

"'—Beside the question, ma'am, beside the question. I have the softest heart in the world, but I can't live upon it. Many a gentleman lives well upon a soft head, who would find a heart of the same quality a very great drawback.'" BR 45

—*light:* "Light hearts, light hearts, that float so gaily on a smooth stream, that are so sparkling and buoyant in the sunshine—down upon fruit, bloom upon flowers, blush in summer air, life of the winged insect, whose whole existence is a day—how soon ye sink in troubled water! Poor Dolly [Varden]'s heart—a little, gentle, idle, fickle thing; giddy, restless, fluttering; constant to nothing but bright looks, and smiles and laughter—Dolly's heart was breaking." BR 71

—*literal and figurative:* "'Now do, Ned, do not,' said Mr [John] Chester, raising his delicate hand imploringly, 'talk in that monstrous manner. About to speak from your heart. Don't you know that the heart is an ingenious part of our formation—the centre of the blood-vessels and all that sort of thing—which has no more to do with what you say or think, than your knees have? How can you be so very vulgar and absurd? These anatomical allusions should be left to gentlemen of the medical profession. They are really not agreeable in society. You quite surprise me, Ned.'

"'Well! there are no such things to wound, or heal, or have regard for. I know your creed, sir, and will say no more,' returned his son.

"'There again,' said Mr Chester, sipping his wine, 'you are wrong. I distinctly say there are such things. We know there are. The hearts of animals—of bullocks, sheep, and so forth—are cooked and devoured, as I am told, by the lower classes, with a vast deal of relish. Men are sometimes stabbed to the heart, shot to the heart; but as to speaking from the heart, or to the heart, or being warm-hearted, or cold-hearted, or broken-hearted, or being all heart, or having no heart—pah! these things are nonsense, Ned.'" BR 32

—*missing:* "'All sorts of traps as Compeyson could set with his head, and keep his own legs out of and get the profits from and let another man in for, was Compeyson's business. He'd no more heart than a iron file, he was as cold as death, and he had the head of the Devil afore mentioned.'" GE 42

—*openness contagious:* "'Let me hear it all [said Charles Cheeryble]. No impertinent curiosity—no, no, no.'

"There was something so earnest and guileless in the way in which all this was said, and such a complete disregard of all conventional restraints and coldnesses, that Nicholas [Nickleby] could not resist it. Among men who have any sound and sterling qualities, there is nothing so contagious as pure openness of heart. Nicholas took the infection instantly . . . . " NN 35

—*in the right place:* "'Mr Clennam [said Chivery], don't you take no notice of my son . . . in case you find him cut up any ways difficult. My son has a 'art, and my son's 'art is in the right place. Me and his mother knows where to find it, and we find it sitiwated correct.'" LD ii 27

—*of a shallow man:* "[Harthouse] was touched in the cavity where his heart should have been—in that nest of addled eggs, where the birds of heaven would have lived if they had not been whistled away . . . ." HT iii 2

—*to a shallow woman:* "'Really,' cried Mrs Skewton, who had taken this opportunity of inspecting Mr Carker through her glass, and satisfying herself (as she lisped audibly to the Major) that he was all heart; 'really now, this [Carker's freeing her daughter of an annoyance] is one of the most enchanting coincidences that I ever heard of. The idea! My dearest Edith, there is such an obvious destiny in it, that really one might almost be induced to cross one's arms upon one's frock, and say, like those wicked Turks, there is no What's-his-name but Thingummy, and What-you-may-call-it is his prophet!'" DS 27

—*understood:* "'I shall bless your name,' sobbed the locksmith's little daughter, 'as long as I live. I shall never hear it spoken without feeling as if my heart would burst. I shall remember it in my prayers, every night and morning till I die!' . . . .

"Oh! how much, and how keenly, the little coquette of five years ago, felt now! [Dolly] had found her heart at last. Never having known its worth till now, she had never known the worth of his. How priceless it appeared!" BR 72

—vibrating: "There are chords in the human heart—strange, varying strings—which are only struck by accident; which will remain mute and senseless to appeals the most passionate and earnest, and respond at last to the slightest casual touch. In the most insensible or childish minds, there is some train of reflection which art can seldom lead, or skill assist, but which will reveal itself, as great truths have done, by chance, and when the discoverer has the plainest end in view." OCS 55

—wounded: "If the little Haymaker had been armed with the sharpest of scythes, and had cut at every stroke into the Carrier's heart, he never could have gashed and wounded it as Dot had done.

"It was a heart so full of love for her; so bound up and held together by innumerable threads of winning remembrance, spun from the daily working of her many qualities of endearment; it was a heart in which she had enshrined herself so gently and so closely; a heart so single and so earnest in its Truth, so strong in right, so weak in wrong, that it could cherish neither passion nor revenge at first, and had only room to hold the broken image of its Idol." CH 3

Hope

—a debtor's: "' . . . despair seldom comes with the first severe shock of misfortune. A man has confidence in untried friends, he remembers the many offers of service so freely made by his boon companions when he wanted them not; he has hope—the hope of happy inexperience—and however he may bend beneath the first shock, it springs up in his bosom, and flourishes there for a brief space, until it droops beneath the blight of disappointment and neglect." PP 21

—and despair: "There is one among the many forms of despair—perhaps the most pitiable of all—which persists in disguising itself as Hope." CS/NT1

—destroyed: "It is when our budding hopes are nipped beyond recovery by some rough wind, that we are the most disposed to picture to ourselves what flowers they might have borne, if they had flourished . . . . " DS 10

"Captain Cuttle, like all mankind, little knew how much hope had survived within him under discouragement, until he felt its death-shock." DS 32

And see M:Illusion and Disillusion

—elusive: "If there were any Hope alive that evening, the Captain thought, as he held his hat on, it certainly kept house, and wasn't out of doors; so the Captain, shaking his head in a despondent manner, went in to look for it.

"Captain Cuttle descended slowly to the little back parlour, and, seated in his accustomed chair, looked for it in the fire; but it was not there, though the fire was bright. He took out his tobacco-box and pipe, and composing himself to smoke, looked for it in the red glow from the bowl, and in the wreaths of vapour that curled upward from his lips: but there was not so much as an atom of the rust of Hope's anchor in either. He tried a glass of grog; but melancholy truth was at the bottom of that well, and he couldn't finish it. He made a turn or two in the shop, and looked for Hope among the instruments; but they obstinately worked out reckonings for the missing ship, in spite of any opposition he could offer, that ended at the bottom of the lone sea." DS 32

—pervasive: "Such is hope, Heaven's own gift to struggling mortals; pervading, like some subtle essence, from the skies, all things, both good and bad; as universal as death, and more infectious than disease." NN 19

—vulnerability: "And all the way to the [Eden] landing-place and back, Mark [Tapley] talked incessantly: as if he would infuse into his partner's breast some faint belief that they had arrived under the most auspicious and cheerful of all imaginable circumstances.

"But many a man who would have stood within a home dismantled, strong in his passion and design of vengeance, has had the firmness of his nature conquered by the razing of an air-built castle. When the log-hut received them for the second time, Martin [Chuzzlewit] lay down upon the ground, and wept aloud." MC 23

—without facts: "'Hope, you see, Wal'r,' said the Captain [Cuttle], sagely, 'Hope. It's that as animates you. Hope is a buoy, for which you overhaul your Little Warbler, sentimental diwision, but Lord, my lad, like any other buoy, it only floats; it can't be steered nowhere. Along with the figure-head of Hope,' said the Captain, 'there's a anchor; but what's the good of my having a anchor, if I can't find no bottom to let it go in?'" DS 50

And see Pride—*a mother's*

Humility

—*apparent:* " . . . . The stiffness and nicety of Mr Carker's dress, and a certain arrogance of manner, either natural to him or imitated from a pattern not far off, gave great additional effect to his humility. He seemed a man who would contend against the power that vanquished him, if he could, but who was utterly borne down by the greatness and superiority of Mr Dombey." DS 13

—*a principle:* "'All along you've thought me too umble now, I shouldn't wonder?'

"'I am not fond of professions of humility,' I returned . . . .

"'There now!' said Uriah, looking flabby and lead-coloured in the moonlight. 'Didn't I know it! But how little you think of the rightful umbleness of a person in my station, Master Copperfield! Father and me was both brought up at a foundation school for boys . . . . They taught us all a deal of umbleness—not much else that I know of, from morning to night. We was to be umble to this person, and umble to that; and to pull off our caps here, and to make bows there; and always to know our place, and abase ourselves before our betters. And we had such a lot of betters! Father got the monitor-medal by being umble. So did I. Father got made a sexton by being umble. He had the character, among the gentlefolks, of being such a well-behaved man, that they were determined to bring him in. 'Be umble, Uriah,' says father to me, 'and you'll get on. It was what was always being dinned into you and me at school; it's what goes down best. Be umble,' says father, 'and you'll do!' And really it ain't done bad!'

"It was the first time it had ever occurred to me, that this detestable cant of false humility might have originated out of the Heep family. I had seen the harvest, but had never thought of the seed.

"'When I was quite a young boy,' said Uriah, 'I got to know what umbleness did, and I took to it. I ate umble pie with an appetite. I stopped at the umble point of my learning, and says I, "Hold hard!" When you offered to teach me Latin, I knew better. 'People like to be above you,' says father, 'keep yourself down.' I am very umble to the present moment, Master Copperfield, but I've got a little power!'" DC 39

False humility is a recurrent theme in Dickens's art: see James Carker DS, Uriah Heep DC and Josiah Bounderby HT

Hypocrite and Hypocrisy

—*its absence raising a son:* " . . . [Jonas's] coarse allusions, even to himself, filled [Anthony Chuzzlewit] with a stealthy glee; causing him to rub his hands and chuckle covertly, as if he said in his sleeve, '*I* taught him. *I* trained him. This is the heir of my bringing-up. Sly, cunning, and covetous, he'll not squander my money. I worked for this; I hoped for this; it has been the great end and aim of my life.'

"What a noble end and aim it was to contemplate in the attainment, truly! But there be some who manufacture idols after the fashion of themselves, and fail to worship them when they are made: charging their deformity on outraged nature. Anthony was better than these at any rate." MC 11

—*in action and at rest:* "Leaving the favoured, and well-received, and flattered of the world; [John Chester] of the world most worldly, who never compromised himself by an ungentlemanly action, and never was guilty of a manly one; to lie smilingly asleep—for even sleep, working but little change in his dissembling face, became with him a piece of cold conventional hypocrisy. . . . " BR 25

—*aggrandizing:* "There are some men, who, living with the one object of enriching themselves, no matter by what means, and being perfectly conscious of the baseness and rascality of the means which they will use every day towards this end, affect nevertheless—even to themselves—a high tone of moral rectitude, and shake their heads and sigh over the depravity of the world. Some of the craftiest scoundrels that ever walked this earth, or rather—for walking implies, at least, an erect position and the bearing of a man—that ever crawled and crept through life by its dirtiest and narrowest ways, will gravely jot down in diaries the events of every day, and keep a regular debtor and creditor account with Heaven, which shall always show a floating balance in their own favour.

"Whether this is a gratuitous (the only gratuitous) part of the falsehood and trickery of such men's lives, or whether they really hope to cheat Heaven itself, and lay up treasure in the next world by the same process which has enabled them to lay up treasure in this—not to question how it is, so it is. And, doubtless, such book-keeping (like certain autobiographies which have enlightened the world) cannot fail to prove serviceable, in the one respect of sparing the recording Angel some time and labour." ¶NN 44

—Lord Chesterfield: "'Upon my honour . . . the most masterly composition, the most delicate thoughts, the finest code of morality, and the most gentlemanly sentiments in the universe! . . . .

"'My **Lord Chesterfield**,' [John Chester] said, pressing his hand tenderly upon the book as he laid it down, 'if I could but have profited by your genius soon enough to have formed my son on the model you have left to all wise fathers, both he and I would have been rich men. **Shakespeare** was undoubtedly very fine in his way; **Milton** good, though prosy; **Lord Bacon** deep, and decidedly knowing; but the writer who should be his country's pride, is my Lord Chesterfield . . . .

"'I thought I was tolerably accomplished as a man of the world,' he continued, 'I flattered myself that I was pretty well versed in all those little arts and graces which distinguish men of the world from boors and peasants, and separate their character from those intensely vulgar sentiments which are called the national character. Apart from any natural prepossession in my own favour, I believed I was. Still, in every page of this enlightened writer, I find some captivating hypocrisy which has never occurred to me before, or some superlative piece of selfishness to which I was utterly a stranger. I should quite blush for myself before this stupendous creature, if, remembering his precepts, one might blush at anything. An amazing man! a nobleman indeed! any King or Queen may make a Lord, but only the Devil himself—and the Graces—can make a Chesterfield.'" BR 23

—conscience: " 'For myself, my conscience is my bank. I have a trifle invested there, a mere trifle, Mr Jonas [Chuzzlewit]; but I prize it as a store of value, I assure you.'

"The good man's enemies would have divided upon this question into two parties. One would have asserted without scruple that if Mr Pecksniff's conscience were his bank, and he kept a running account there, he must have overdrawn it beyond all mortal means of computation. The other would have contended that it was a mere fictitious form; a perfectly blank book; or one in which entries were only made with a peculiar kind of invisible ink to become legible at some indefinite time; and that he never troubled it at all." MC 20

—cure proposed: "'If I'd my vay, Samivel, I'd just stick some o' these here lazy shepherds behind a heavy wheelbarrow, and run 'em up and down a fourteen-inch-wide plank all day. That 'ud shake the nonsense out of 'em, if anythin' vould.'" PP 27

—egotistical: "Perhaps this is the worst kind of egotism. It has not even the poor excuse of being spontaneous, but is the result of a deliberate system and malice aforethought. Mere empty-headed conceit excites our pity, but ostentatious hypocrisy awakens our disgust." YC/E

See also Christianity—*hypocritical*

—elaborate characterisation: " . . . Mrs Weller, being wholly unable to suppress her feelings, sobbed aloud, and stated her conviction that the red-nosed man was a saint; whereupon Mr Weller, senior, ventured to suggest in an undertone, that he must be the representative of the united parishes of Saint Simon Without, and St. Walker Within." PP 45

BSB p226 explains that such a representative is "a hypocrite. 'Without' and 'Within' refer to the City boundaries, and are found as parts of names of streets and churches. Stiggins is Simon (St Simon the Zealot or perhaps Simon Pure) to all appearances, but Walker (. . . 'humbug') in reality."

—frankly foreshadowing: "'What are we?' said Mr Pecksniff, 'but coaches? Some of us are slow coaches'—

"'Goodness, pa!' cried Charity.

"'Some of us, I say,' resumed her parent with increased emphasis, 'are slow coaches; some of us are fast coaches. Our passions are the horses; and rampant animals too!'—

"'Really, pa!' cried both the daughters at once. 'How very unpleasant.'

"'And rampant animals too!' repeated Mr Pecksniff, with so much determination, that he may be said to have exhibited, at the moment, a sort of moral rampancy himself: 'and Virtue is the drag. We start from The Mother's Arms, and we run to The Dust Shovel.'" MC 8

—gloomy: "Ye who have eyes and see not, and have ears and hear not; ye who are as the hypocrites of sad countenances, and disfigure your faces that you may seem unto men to fast; learn healthy cheerfulness, and mild contentment, from the deaf, and dumb, and blind!

"Self-elected saints with gloomy brows, this sightless, earless, voiceless child may teach you lessons you will do well to follow. Let that poor hand of hers lie gently on your hearts; for there may be something in its healing touch akin to that of the Great Master whose precepts you misconstrue, whose lessons you pervert, of whose charity and sympathy with all the world, not one among you in his daily practice knows as much as many of the worst among those fallen sinners, to whom you are liberal in nothing but the preachment of perdition!" AN 3

—guilt suppressed: "When men are about to commit, or to sanction the commission of some injustice, it is not uncommon for them to express pity for the object either of that or some parallel proceeding, and to feel themselves, at the time, quite virtuous and moral, and immensely superior to those who express no pity at all. This is a kind of upholding of faith above works, and is very comfortable." NN 54

—Uriah Heep: " 'Do you suppose he has any money, Traddles?' I asked.

"'Oh dear, yes, I should think so,' he replied, shaking his head, seriously. 'I should say he must have pocketed a good deal, in one way or other. But I think you would find, Copperfield, if you had an opportunity of observing his course, that money would never keep that man out of mischief. He is such an incarnate hypocrite, that whatever object he pursues, he must pursue crookedly. It's his only compensation for the outward restraints he puts upon himself. Always creeping along the ground to some small end or other, he will always magnify every object in the way; and consequently will hate and suspect everybody that comes, in the most innocent manner, between him and it. So the crooked courses will become crookeder, at any moment, for the least reason, or for none. It's only necessary to consider his history here,' said Traddles, 'to know that.'" DC 53

—honesty despised: "'This Kit [said Quilp] is one of your honest people; one of your fair characters; a prowling, prying hound; a hypocrite: a double-faced, white-livered, sneaking spy; a crouching cur to those that feed and coax him, and a barking, yelping dog to all besides.'" OCS 51

—a humbug's comeuppance: "The Last of the Patriarchs [Christopher Casby] had been so seized by assault, and required so much room to catch an idea in, and so much more room to turn it in, that he had not a word to offer in reply. He appeared to be meditating some Patriarchal way out of his delicate position, when Mr Pancks, once more suddenly applying the trigger to his hat, shot it off again with his former dexterity. On the preceding occasion, one or two of the Bleeding Heart Yarders had obsequiously picked it up and handed it to its owner; but Mr Pancks had now so far impressed his audience, that the Patriarch had to turn and stoop for it himself.

"Quick as lightning, Mr Pancks, who, for some moments, had had his right hand in his coat pocket, whipped out a pair of shears, swooped upon the Patriarch behind, and snipped off short the sacred locks that flowed upon his shoulders. In a paroxysm of animosity and rapidity, Mr Pancks then caught the broad-brimmed hat out of the astounded Patriarch's hand, cut it down into a mere stewpan, and fixed it on the Patriarch's head.

"Before the frightful results of this desperate action, Mr Pancks himself recoiled in consternation. A bare-polled, goggle-eyed, big-headed lumbering personage stood staring at him, not in the least impressive, not in the least venerable, who seemed to have started out of the earth to ask what was become of Casby." LD ii 32

—messenger of peace: "If ever Mr Pecksniff wore an apostolic look, he wore it on this memorable day. If ever his unruffled smile proclaimed the words, 'I am a messenger of peace!' that was its mission now. If ever man combined within himself all the mild qualities of the lamb with a considerable touch of the dove, and not a dash of the crocodile, or the least possible suggestion of the very mildest seasoning of the serpent, that man was he." MC 4

—resilience: "It was a special quality, among the many admirable qualities possessed by Mr Pecksniff, that the more he was found out, the more hypocrisy he practised. Let him be discomfited in one quarter, and he refreshed and recompensed himself by carrying the war into another. If his workings and windings were detected by A, so much the greater reason was there for practising without loss of time on B, if it were only to keep his hand in. He had never been such a saintly and improving spectacle to all about him, as after his detection by

Thomas Pinch. He had scarcely ever been at once so tender in his humanity, and so dignified and exalted in his virtue, as when young Martin's scorn was fresh and hot upon him.

"Having this large stock of superfluous sentiment and morality on hand, which must positively be cleared off at any sacrifice, Mr Pecksniff no sooner heard his son-in-law announced, than he regarded him as a kind of wholesale or general order, to be immediately executed." MC 44

—smooth-faced "His meditations . . . kept close to their nest upon the earth, and looked about, among the dust and worms. But there was not a bird in the air, singing unseen, farther beyond the reach of human eye than Mr Carker's thoughts. He had his face so perfectly under control, that few could say more, in distinct terms of its expression, than that it smiled or that it pondered . . . he sprang up from his reverie, and looked around with a sudden smile, as courteous and as soft as if he had numerous observers to propitiate: nor did he relapse, after being thus awakened; but clearing his face, like one who bethought himself that it might otherwise wrinkle and tell tales, went smiling on, as if for practice." DS 27

—spuriously reformed: "To these [supporters of the Sabbath law] may be added another class of men—the stern and gloomy enthusiasts, who would make earth a hell, and religion a torment: men who, having wasted the earlier part of their lives in dissipation and depravity, find themselves when scarcely past its meridian, steeped to the neck in vice, and shunned like a loathsome disease. Abandoned by the world, having nothing to fall back upon, nothing to remember but time mis-spent, and energies misdirected, they turn their eyes and not their thoughts to Heaven, and delude themselves into the impious belief, that in denouncing the lightness of heart of which they cannot partake, and the rational pleasures from which they never derived enjoyment, they are more than remedying the sins of their old career, and—like the founders of monasteries and builders of churches, in ruder days—establishing a good set claim upon their Maker." STH/2

—spuriously sincere "Men who are thoroughly false and hollow [like John Chester], seldom try to hide those vices from themselves; and yet in the very act of avowing them, they lay claim to the virtues they feign most to despise. 'For,' they say, 'this is honesty, this is truth. All mankind are like us, but they have not the candour to avow it.' The more they affect to deny the existence of any sincerity in the world, the more they would be thought to possess it in its boldest shape; and this is an unconscious compliment to Truth on the part of these philosophers, which will turn the laugh against them to the Day of Judgment." BR 23

—unobserved: "Mr Carker bowed his head, and rising from the table, and standing thoughtfully before the fire . . . looked down at Mr Dombey with the evil slyness of some monkish carving, half human and half brute; or like a leering face on an old waterspout." DS 42

And see B:Blindness—*candour*

Integrity

—abandoned to please: "'But is it really possible to please the world?' says some doubting reader. It is indeed. Nay, it is not only very possible, but very easy. The ways are crooked, and sometimes foul and low. What then? A man need but crawl upon his hands and knees, know when to close his eyes and when his ears, when to stoop and when to stand upright; and if by the world is meant that atom of it in which he moves himself, he shall please it, never fear." YC/P

—earnestness: "'It was a maxim of Captain Swosser's,' said Mrs Badger, 'speaking in his figurative naval manner, that when you make pitch hot, you cannot make it too hot; and that if you only have to swab a plank, you should swab it as if Davy Jones were after you. It appears to me that this maxim is applicable to the medical, as wel as to the nautical profession.'" BH 17

And see M:Invention

—honesty: "'I tell you, ma'am,' said Mr Witherden, 'what I think as an honest man, which, as the poet observes, is the noblest work of God. I agree with the poet in every particular, ma'am. The mountainous Alps on the one hand, or a humming-bird on the other, is nothing, in point of workmanship, to an honest man—or woman." OCS 14

"'A man,' says Sampson [Brass], 'who loses forty-seven pound ten in one morning by his honesty, is a man to be envied. If it had been eighty pound, the luxuriousness of feeling would have been increased. Every pound lost, would have been a hundredweight of happiness gained. The still small voice, Christopher,' cried Brass, smiling, and tapping himself on the bosom, 'is a-singing comic songs within me, and all is happiness and joy!'" OCS 57

—honour

—commitment: "'I have your word and honour, sir [said Silas Wegg]?'

"'My good fellow,' retorted Mr Boffin, 'you have my word; and how you can have that, without my honour too, I don't know. I've sorted a lot of dust in my time, but I never knew the two things go into separate heaps.'" OMF iii 14

—end and means: "'Let no man turn aside, ever so slightly, from the broad path of honour [said Geoffrey Haredale], on the plausible pretence that he is justified by the goodness of his end. All good ends can be worked out by good means. Those that cannot, are bad; and may be counted so at once, and left alone.'" BR 79

—keeping her promise: "'Whatever the old girl says, do. Do it! Whenever the old girl says, *I*'ll do it. She does it.'

"'Then she is as honest and genuine as she looks . . . and it is impossible to say more for her.'

"'She's Colour-Serjeant of the Nonpareil battalion,' said Mr Bagnet . . . . And there's not such another." BH 52

—in old age: "'I can still walk twenty mile if I am put to it. I'd far better be a-walking than a-getting numbed and dreary. I'm a good fair knitter, and can make many little things to sell. The loan from your lady and gentleman of twenty shillings to fit out a basket with would be a fortune for me. Trudging round the country and tiring of myself out, I shall keep the deadness off, and get my own bread by my own labour. And what more can I want? . . . . Why, I know very well,' said old Betty Higden, 'and you know very well, that your lady and gentleman would set me up like a queen for the rest of my life, if so be that we could make it right among us to have it so. But we can't make it right among us to have it so.

"'I've never took charity yet, nor yet has any one belonging to me. And it would be forsaking of myself indeed, and forsaking of my children dead and gone, and forsaking of their children dead and gone, to set up a contradiction now at last . . . . It ain't that I mean to give offence by being anyways proud,' said the old creature simply, 'but that I want to be of a piece like, and helpful of myself right through to my death.'" ¶OMF ii 14

—principle: "'But excellent Boythorn might say,' returned our host, swelling and growing very red, 'I'll be—'

"'I understand,' said Mr Skimpole. 'Very likely he would.'

"'—if I *will* go to dinner!' cried Mr Boythorn, in a violent burst, and stopping to strike his stick upon the ground. 'And he would probably add, "Is there such a thing as principle, Mr Harold Skimpole?"

"'To which Harold Skimpole would reply, you know,' he returned in his gayest manner, and with his most ingenuous smile, "'Upon my life I have not the least idea! I don't know what it is you call by that name, or where it is, or who possessed it. If you possess it, and find it comfortable, I am quite delighted, and congratulate you heartily. But I know nothing about it, I assure you; for I am a mere child, and I lay no claim to it, and I don't want it!" So, you see, excellent Boythorn and I would go to dinner after all!'" BH 18

—resposnsibility: "'Now when you mention responsibility,' [Skimpole] resumed, 'I am disposed to say, that I never had the happiness of knowing any one whom I should consider so refreshingly responsible as yourself. You appear to me to be the very touchstone of responsibility. When I see you, my dear Miss Summerson, intent upon the perfect working of the whole little orderly system of which you are the centre, I feel inclined to say to myself—in fact I do say to myself, very often—*that's* responsibility!" BH 37

—self-trust: "A composed and unobtrusive self-sustainment was noticeable in Daniel Doyce—a calm knowledge that what was true must remain true, in spite of all the Barnacles in the family ocean, and would be just the truth, and neither more nor less, when even that sea had run dry—which had a kind of greatness in it, though not of the official quality." LD i 16

—true to onself: "Most men will be found sufficiently true to themselves to be true to an old idea. It is no proof of an inconstant mind, but exactly the opposite, when the idea will not bear close comparison with the reality, and the contrast is a fatal shock ot it." LD 13

—weakness of character: " . . . it is the unhappy lot of thoroughly weak men, that their very sympathies, affections, confidences—all the qualities which in better constituted minds are virtues—dwindle into foibles, or turn into downright vices." BR 36

Jesus Christ

—blended intellect and imagination: "The Divine Teacher was as gentle and considerate as He was powerful and wise. You all know how He could still the raging of the sea, and could hush a little child. As the utmost results of the wisdom of men can only be at last to help to raise this earth to that condition to which His doctrine, untainted by the blindnesses and passions of men, would have exalted it long ago; so let us always remember that He set us the example of blending the understanding and the imagination, and that, following it ourselves, we tread in His steps, and help our race on to its better and best days." S/LC

—and the Cross: "Redlaw fell upon his knees, with a loud cry.

"'O Thou,' he said, 'who through the teaching of pure love, has graciously restored me to the memory [of sadness and grief] which was the memory of Christ upon the cross, and of all the good who perished in His cause, receive my thanks, and bless her!'" HM 3

—forgiveness: "'O, Mrs Clennam, Mrs Clennam,' said Little Dorrit, 'angry feelings and unforgiving deeds are no comfort and no guide to you and me. My life has been passed in this poor prison, and my teaching has been very defective; but, let me implore you to remember later and better days. Be guided only by the healer of the sick, the raiser of the dead, the friend of all who were afflicted and forlorn, the patient Master who shed tears of compassion for our infirmities. We cannot but be right if we put all the rest away, and do everything in remembrance of Him. There is no vengeance and no infliction of suffering in His life, I am sure. There can be no confusion in following Him, and seeking for no other footsteps, I am certain!'" LD ii 31 *And see* Selfishness*—of a murderer*

—and the Inquisition: "Mash, mash, mash! An endless routine of heavy hammers. Mash, mash, mash! upon the sufferer's limbs. See the stone trough! says Goblin. For the water torture! Gurgle, swill, bloat, burst, for the Redeemer's honour! Suck the bloody rag, deep down into your unbelieving body, Heretic, at every breath you draw! And when the executioner plucks it out, reeking with the smaller mysteries of God's own Image, know us for His chosen servants, true believers in the Sermon on the Mount, elect disciples of Him who never did a miracle but to heal: who never struck a man with palsy, blindness, deafness, dumbness, madness, any one affliction of mankind; and never stretched His blessed hand out, but to give relief and ease!" PI 3

—invoked in great trial: "'I'm a going to seek my niece through the wureld. I'm a going to find my poor niece [Em'ly] in her shame, and bring her back. No one stop me! I tell you I'm a going to seek my niece!'

"'No, no!' cried Mrs Gummidge . . . . 'No, no, Dan'l, not as you are now. Seek her in a little while, my lone lorn Dan'l, and that'll be but right! but not as you are now. Sit ye down, and give me your forgiveness for having ever been a worrit to you, Dan'l—what have *my* contrairies ever been to this!—and let us speak a word about them times when she was first an orphan, and when Ham was too, and when I was a poor widder woman, and you took me in. It'll soften your poor heart, Dan'l,' laying her head upon his shoulder, 'and you'll bear your sorrow better; for you know the promise, Dan'l, "As you have done it unto one of the least of these, you have done it unto me"; and that can never fail under this roof, that's been our shelter for so many, many year!'

"He was quite passive now; and when I heard him crying, the impulse that had been upon me to go down upon my knees, and ask their pardon for the desolation I had caused, and curse Steerforth, yielded to a better feeling. My over-charged heart found the same relief, and I cried too." DC 31

—life summarized: "The Waits are playing, and they break my childish sleep! What images do I associate with the Christmas music . . . . An angel, speaking to a group of shepherds in a field; some travellers, with eyes uplifted, following a star; a baby in a manger; a child in a spacious temple, talking with grave men; a solemn figure, with a mild and beautiful face, raising a dead girl by the hand; again, near a city gate, calling back the son of a widow, on his bier, to life; a crowd of people looking through the opened roof of a chamber where he sits, and letting down a sick person on a bed, with ropes; the same, in a tempest, walking on the water to a ship; again, on a sea-shore, teaching a great multitude; again, with a child upon his knee, and other children round; again, restoring sight to the blind, speech to the dumb, hearing to the deaf, health to the sick, strength to the lame,

knowledge to the ignorant; again, dying upon a Cross, watched by armed soldiers, a thick darkness coming on, the earth beginning to shake, and only one voice heard, 'Forgive them, for they know not what they do.'" CS/CT

—a little child: " . . . [Lucie Manette's] little Lucie lay on her bosom. Then, among the advancing echoes, there was the tread of her tiny feet and the sound of her prattling words. Let greater echoes resound as they would, the young mother at the cradle side could always hear those coming. They came, and the shady house was sunny with a child's laugh, and the Divine friend of children, to whom in her trouble she had confided hers, seemed to take her child in His arms, as He took the child of old, and made it a sacred joy to her." TTC ii 21

—a little child, crippled: "'Somehow [Tiny Tim] gets thoughtful, sitting by himself so much, and thinks the strangest things you ever heard. He told me, coming home, that he hoped the people saw him in the church, because he was a cripple, and it might be pleasant to them to remember upon Christmas Day, who made lame beggars walk, and blind men see.'" CC 3

—a little child, dead: "Presently I took the light burden from [Jenny's] lap; did what I could to make the baby's rest the prettier and gentler; laid it on a shelf, and covered it with my own handkerchief. We tried to comfort the mother, and we whispered to her what Our Saviour said of children. She answered nothing, but sat weeping—weeping very much." BH 8

—remembered, after a death: "Quiet. Very quiet. The noisy little Cratchits were as still as statues in one corner, and sat looking up at Peter, who had a book before him. The mother and her daughters were engaged in sewing. But surely they were very quiet!

"'"And He took a child, and set him in the midst of them."' [Matt 18:2]

"Where had Scrooge heard those words? He had not dreamed them. The boy must have read them out, as he and the Spirit crossed the threshold. Why did he not go on?

"The mother laid her work upon the table, and put her hand up to her face.

"'The colour hurts my eyes,' she said.

"The colour? Ah, poor Tiny Tim!" CC 4

—remembered, by a hero: "Long ago, when [Carton] had been famous among his earliest competitors as a youth of great promise, he had followed his father to the grave. His mother had died, years before. These solemn words, which had been read at his father's grave, arose in his mind as he went down the dark streets, among the heavy shadows, with the moon and the clouds sailing on high above him. 'I am the resurrection and the life, saith the Lord: he that believeth in me, though he were dead, yet shall he live: and whosoever liveth and believeth in me, shall never die.'" TTC iii 9

—and woman: " . . . I used to fancy that next to what was taught upon the Mount [Mrs Edson] took most of all to His gentle compassion for us poor women and to His young life and to how His mother was proud of Him and treasured His sayings in her heart." CS/L 1

See also Bible—*as comfort, and —regularly read;* Christmas—*'founder' and nature; and* Hypocrite—*gloomy*

Laughter

—apoplectic: "Here the old gentleman [Tony Weller] shook his head from side to side, and was seized with a hoarse internal rumbling, accompanied with a violent swelling of the countenance, and a sudden increase in the breadth of all his features; symptoms which alarmed his son not a little.

"'Don't be frightened, Sammy, don't be frightened,' said the old gentleman, when, by dint of much struggling, and various convulsive stamps upon the ground, he had recovered his voice. 'It's only a kind o' quiet laugh as I'm a tryin' to come, Sammy.'

"'Well, if that's wot it is,' said Sam, 'you'd better not try to come it agin. You'll find it raythor a dangerous inwention.'

"'Don't you like it, Sammy?' inquired the old gentleman.

"'Not at all,' replied Sam.

"'Well,' said Mr Weller, with the tears still running down his cheeks, 'it 'ud ha' been a wery great accommodation to me if I could ha' done it, and 'ud ha' saved a good many vords atween your mother-in-law and me, sometimes; but I am afeered you're right, Sammy: it's too much in the appleplexy line—a deal too much, Samivel.'" PP 45

"' . . . . I'm a little elewated. The muffins came so pat!'

"With that [Tugby] chuckled until he was black in the face; and had so much ado to become any other colour, that his fat legs took the strangest excursions into the air. Nor were they reduced to anything like decorum until Mrs Tugby had thumped him violently on the back, and shaken him as if he were a great bottle.

"'Good gracious, goodness, lord-a-mercy bless and save the man!' cried Mrs Tugby, in great terror. 'What's he doing?'

"Mr Tugby wiped his eyes, and faintly repeated that he found himself a little elewated.

"'Then don't be so again, that's a dear good soul,' said Mrs Tugby, 'if you don't want to frighten me to death, with your struggling and fighting!'

"Mr Tugby said he wouldn't; but his whole existence was a fight, in which, if any judgment might be founded on the constantly-increasing shortness of his breath, and the deepening purple of his face, he was always getting the worst of it." C 4

" . . . [Major Bagstock] sat down in a chair, and fell into a silent fit of laughter, with which he was sometimes seized, and which was always particularly awful. It held him so long on this occasion that the dark servant, who stood watching him at a distance, but dared not for his life approach, twice or thrice gave him over for lost. His whole form, but especially his face and head, dilated beyond all former experience; and presented to the dark man's view, nothing but a heavy mass of indigo. At length he burst into a violent paroxysm of coughing, and when that was a little better burst into such ejaculations . . . . " DS 10

—asthmatic: "'What is there that any woman couldn't do, that she shouldn't do—especially on the subject of another woman's good looks?'

"I really thought it was all over with Mr Omer, after he had uttered this libellous pleasantry. He coughed to that extent, and his breath eluded all his attempts to recover it with that obstinacy, that I fully expected to see his head go down behind the counter, and his little black breeches, with the rusty little bunches of ribbons at the knees, come quivering up in a last ineffectual struggle. At length, however, he got better, though he still panted hard, and was so exhausted that he was obliged to sit on the stool of the shop-desk." DC 21

—derisive: "Some people laughed to see the alteration in [Scrooge], but he let them laugh, and little heeded them; for he was wise enough to know that nothing ever happened on this globe, for good, at which some people did not have their fill of laughter in the outset; and knowing that such as these would be blind anyway, he thought it quite as well that they should wrinkle up their eyes in grins, as have the malady in less attractive forms. His own heart laughed; and that was quite enough for him." CC 5

—expressionless: "'One must either laugh or cry at such stupendous inconsistencies; and I prefer to laugh [said Doctor Jeddler].'

"Britain, who had been paying the profoundest and most melancholy attention to each speaker in his turn, seemed suddenly to decide in favour of the same preference, if a deep sepulchral sound that escaped him might be construed into a demonstration of risibility. His face, however, was so perfectly unaffected by it, both before and afterwards, that although one or two of the breakfast party looked round as being startled by a mysterious noise, nobody connected the offender with it." BL 1

—forced: "In persons who were so soon to part, and to interpose between their else daily communication the formidable barrier of many thousand miles of stormy space, and who were for that reason anxious to cast no other cloud, not even the passing shadow of a moment's disappointment or discomfiture, upon the short interval of happy companionship that yet remained to them—in persons so situated, the natural transition from these first surprises [at meagre accommodations] was obviously into peals of hearty laughter . . . . " AN 1

"When the morning—*the* morning—came, and we met at breakfast, it was curious to see how eager we all were to prevent a moment's pause in the conversation, and how astoundingly gay everybody was: the forced spirits of each member of the little party having as much likeness to his natural mirth, as hot-house peas at five guineas the quart, resemble in flavour the growth of the dews, and air, and rain of Heaven." AN 1

—infectious: "If you should happen, by any unlikely chance, to know a man more blest in a laugh than Scrooge's nephew, all I can say is, I should like to know him too. Introduce him to me, and I'll cultivate his acquaintance.

"It is a fair, even-handed, noble adjustment of things, that while there is infection in disease and sorrow, there is nothing in the world so irresistibly contagious as laughter and good-humour. When Scrooge's nephew laughed in this way: holding his sides, rolling his head, and twisting his face into the most extravagant contortions: Scrooge's niece, by marriage, laughed as heartily as he. And their assembled friends being not a bit behindhand, roared out lustily." CC 3 *And see* LC:Talk—*enthusiastic*

—*inward:* ". . . the Serjeant's clerk laughed again; not a noisy, boisterous laugh, but a silent, internal chuckle, which Mr Pickwick disliked to hear. When a man bleeds inwardly, it is a dangerous thing for himself; but when he laughs inwardly, it bodes no good to other people." PP 31

—*of a large man:* "If there could only have been somebody by, to see how the bedclothes shook, and to see the Yorkshireman's great red face and round head appear above the sheets, every now and then, like some jovial monster coming to the surface to breathe, and once more dive down convulsed with the laughter which came bursting forth afresh—that somebody would have been scarcely less amused than John Browdie himself." NN 39

"Never was man so tickled with a respectable old joke, as John Browdie . . . . He chuckled, roared, half suffocated himself by laughing large pieces of beef into his windpipe, roared again, persisted in eating at the same time, got red in the face and black in the forehead, coughed, cried, got better, went off again laughing inwardly, got worse, choked, had his back thumped, stamped about, frightened his wife, and at last recovered in a state of the last exhaustion and with the water streaming from his eyes . . . ." NN 42

—*lawyer's:* "Mr Jaggers never laughed; but he wore great bright creaking boots; and, in poising himself on those boots, with his large head bent down and his eyebrows joined together, awaiting an answer, he sometimes caused the boots to creak, as if *they* laughed in a dry and suspicious way." GE 24

—*maternal:* "'Could I speak to you alone for a moment?' said I [Esther Summerson].

"Anything like the jocoseness of Mr Guppy's mother just now, I think I never saw. She made no sound of laughter; but she rolled her head, and shook it, and put her handkerchief to her mouth, and appealed to Caddy with her elbow, and her hand, and her shoulder, and was so unspeakably entertained altogether that it was with some difficulty she could marshal Caddy through the little folding-door into her bedroom adjoining.

"'Miss Summerson,' said Mr Guppy, 'you will excuse the waywardness of a parent ever mindful of a son's happiness. My mother, though highly exasperating to the feelings, is actuated by maternal dictates.'" BH 38

—*melodramatic:* "It may be necessary to observe, lest there should appear any incongruity in the close of this soliloquy, that Mr Swiveller did not wind up with a cheerful hilarious laugh, which would have been undoubtedly at variance with his solemn reflections, but that, being in a theatrical mood, he merely achieved that performance which is designated in melodramas 'laughing like a fiend,'—for it seems that your fiends always laugh in syllables, and always in three syllables, never more or less, which is a remarkable property in such gentry, and one worthy of remembrance." OCS 56

—*a natural good:* "'Can you suppose there's any harm in looking as cheerful and being as cheerful as our poor circumstances will permit? Do I see anything in the way I'm made, which calls upon me to be a snivelling, solemn, whispering chap, sneaking about as if I couldn't help it, and expressing myself in a most unpleasant snuffle? On the contrary, don't I see every reason why I shouldn't? Just hear this! Ha ha ha! Ain't that as nat'ral as walking, and as good for the health? Ha ha ha! Ain't that as nat'ral as a sheep's bleating, or a pig's grunting, or a horse's neighing, or a bird's singing? Ha ha ha! Isn't it, mother?'" OCS 22

—*silent:* "Job [Trotter], rubbing his hands with delight, uttered the first sound he had given vent to, since he entered the house—a light, noiseless chuckle, which seemed to intimate that he enjoyed his laugh too much to let any of it escape in sound." PP 25

"'Is that Mr Maldon a-horseback, ringing at the gate, sir?'

"'It looks like him,' I replied, as carelessly as I could.

"Uriah [Heep] stopped short, put his hands between his great knobs of knees, and doubled himself up with laughter. With perfectly silent laughter. Not a sound escaped from him. I was so repelled by his odious behaviour, particularly by this concluding instance, that I turned away without any ceremony; and left him doubled up in the middle of the garden, like a scarecrow in want of support." DC 42

—suppressed: "The Major, under cover of the dimness, swelled, and swelled, and rolled his purple face about, and winked his lobster eye, until he fell into a fit of wheezing, which obliged him to rise and take a turn or two about the room . . . ." DS 26

Melancholy

—cheap: " . . . that cheapest and most accessible of luxuries . . . . " DS 8

—irrational: "And Mr Jaggers made not me alone intensely melancholy, because, after he was gone, Herbert said of himself, with his eyes fixed on the fire, that he thought he must have committed a felony and forgotten the details of it, he felt so dejected and guilty." GE 36

—mispronounced: " . . . there was a something touching in [Sophy Marigold's] looks that made the cart most peaceful and most quiet, though not at all melancholy. ["N.B. In the Cheap Jack patter, we generally sound it lemonjolly, and it gets a laugh."]" CS/DM

—overcome: "'And my advice to all men is, that if ever they become hipped and melancholy from similar causes (as very many men do), they look at both sides of the question, applying a magnifying glass to the best one; and if they still feel tempted to retire without leave, that they smoke a large pipe and drink a full bottle first, and profit by the laudable example of the baron of Grogzwig.'" NN 6

Music: its effect

—associations: "For all that the child observed, and felt, and thought, that night—the present and the absent; what was then and what had been—were blended like the colours in the rainbow, or in the plumage of rich birds when the sun is shining on them, or in the softening sky when the same sun is setting. The many things he had had to think of lately, passed before him in the music; not as claiming his attention over again, or as likely ever more to occupy it, but as peacefully disposed of and gone." DS 14

—a crippling immunity: " . . . [Redlaw] stopped to listen to a plaintive strain of music, but could only hear a tune, made manifest to him by the dry mechanism of the instruments and his own ears, with no address to any mystery within him, without a whisper in it of the past, or of the future, powerless upon him as the sound of last year's running water, or the rushing of last year's wind." HM 2

—despised by gloomy religion: "'That Frederick Dorrit was the beginning of it all. If he had not been a player of music, and had not kept, in those days of his youth and prosperity, an idle house where singers, and players, and such-like children of Evil, turned their backs on the Light and their faces to the Darkness, [Arthur's mother] might have remained in her lowly station, and might not have been raised out of it to be cast down. But, no. Satan entered into that Frederick Dorrit, and counselled him that he was a man of innocent and laudable tastes who did kind actions, and that here was a poor girl with a voice for singing music with. Then he is to have her taught. Then Arthur's father, who has all along been secretly pining in the ways of virtuous ruggedness, for those accursed snares which are called the Arts, becomes acquainted with her. And so, a graceless orphan, training to be a singing girl, carries it, by that Frederick Dorrit's agency, against me, and I am humbled and deceived!—Not I, that is to say,' [Mrs Clennam] added quickly, as colour flushed into her face; 'a greater than I. What am I?'" LD ii 30

—dog and boy: "[The drover's dog] and Jo listen to the music, probably with much the same amount of animal satisfaction; likewise, as to awakened association, aspiration, or regret, melancholy or joyful reference to things beyond the senses, they are probably upon a par." BH 16

—healing penetration: " . . . the Christmas music [Redlaw] had heard before, began to play. He listened to it at first, as he had listened in the churchyard; but presently—it playing still, and being borne towards him on the night-air, in a low, sweet, melancholy strain—he rose, and stood stretching his hands about him, as if there were some friend approaching within his reach, on whom his desolate touch might rest, yet do no harm. As he did this, his face became less fixed and wondering; a gentle trembling came upon him; and at last his eyes filled with tears, and he put his hands before them, and bowed down his head.

"His memory of sorrow, wrong, and trouble, had not come back to him; he knew that it was not restored; he had no passing belief or hope that it was. But some dumb stir within him made him capable, again, of being moved by what was hidden, afar off, in the music. If it were only that it told him sorrowfully the value of what he had lost, he thanked Heaven for it with a fervent gratitude." HM 3

—'heart' in it: "'You are fond of music, Mr Dombey?'

"'Eminently so,' was Mr Dombey's answer.

"'Yes. It's very nice,' said Cleopatra [Mrs Skewton], looking at her cards. 'So much heart in it—undeveloped recollections of a previous state of existence—and all that—which is so truly charming." DS 21

—at the organ: " . . . Tom [Pinch] took the organ himself. It was then turning dark, and the yellow light that streamed in through the ancient windows in the choir was mingled with a murky red. As the grand tones resounded through the church, they seemed, to Tom, to find an echo in the depth of every ancient tomb, no less than in the deep mystery of his own heart.

"Great thoughts and hopes came crowding on his mind as the rich music rolled upon the air, and yet among them—something more grave and solemn in their purpose, but the same—were all the images of that day, down to its very lightest recollection of childhood.

"The feeling that the sounds awakened, in the moment of their existence, seemed to include his whole life and being; and as the surrounding realities of stone and wood and glass grew dimmer in the darkness, these visions grew so much the brighter that Tom might have . . . sat there pouring out his grateful heart till midnight . . . . " ¶MC 5

—protean power: "You know it can give back the dead; it can place at your side the congenial creature dear to you who never lived. You know that the blind see in it; the bed-ridden have hope in it; the dead hear it. We all hear it from the sound of the varying seasons, to the beating of the waters upon which our Saviour walked." S/M

—on the savage breast: "After tea, they had some music. For they were a musical family, and knew what they were about, when they sung a Glee or Catch, I can assure you: especially Topper, who could growl away in the bass like a good one, and never swell the large veins in his forehead, or get red in the face over it.

"Scrooge's niece played well upon the harp; and played among other tunes a simple little air (a mere nothing: you might learn to whistle it in two minutes), which had been familiar to the child who fetched Scrooge from the boarding-school, as he had been reminded by the Ghost of Christmas Past.

"When this strain of music sounded, all the things that Ghost had shown him, came upon his mind; he softened more and more; and thought that if he could have listened to it often, years ago, he might have cultivated the kindnesses of life for his own happiness with his own hands, without resorting to the sexton's spade that buried Jacob Marley." CC 3

—soporific: "[Pecksniff] had not what may be called a fine ear for music, but he knew when it had a tranquillising influence on his soul; and that was the case now, for it sounded to him like a melodious snore." MC 31

—staying power: " . . . a sorrowful air will sometimes outlive many generations of strong men, and even last longer than battle-axes with twenty pounds of steel in the head . . . . " CHE 13

" . . . as long as mankind lived, and loved, and hoped, so long music, which draws them upward in all their varying and erring moods, could never cease out of the world." S/M

New Year

—gay: "Next to Christmas-day, the most pleasant annual epoch in existence is the advent of the New Year. There are a lachrymose set of people who usher in the New Year with watching and fasting, as if they were bound to attend as chief mourners at the obsequies of the old one. Now, we cannot but think it a great deal more complimentary, both to the old year that has rolled away, and to the New Year that is just beginning to dawn upon us, to see the old fellow out, and the new one in, with gaiety and glee.

"There must have been some few occurrences in the past year to which we can look back, with a smile of cheerful recollection, if not with a feeling of heartfelt thankfulness. And we are bound by every rule of justice and equity to give the New Year credit for being a good one, until he proves himself unworthy the confidence we repose in him." SB/NY

"The toast is drunk with acclamation; Dobble returns thanks, and the whole party rejoin the ladies in the drawing-room. Young men who were too bashful to dance before supper, find tongues and partners; the musicians exhibit unequivocal symptoms of having drunk the new year in, while the company were out; and dancing is kept up until far in the first morning of the new year." SB/NY

"The streets were full of motion, and the shops were decked out gaily. The New Year, like an Infant Heir to the whole world, was waited for, with welcomes, presents, and rejoicings. There were books and toys for the New Year, glittering trinkets for the New Year, dresses for the New Year, schemes of fortune for the New Year; new inventions to beguile it. Its life was parcelled out in almanacks and pocket-books; the coming of its moons, and stars, and tides, was known beforehand to the moment; all the workings of its seasons in their days and nights, were calculated with as much precision as Mr Filer could work sums in men and women." C 2

—Old Year: "The Year was Old, that day. The patient Year had lived through the reproaches and misuses of its slanderers, and faithfully performed its work. Spring, summer, autumn, winter. It had laboured through the destined round, and now laid down its weary head to die. Shut out from hope, high impulse, active happiness, itself, but active messenger of many joys to others, it made appeal in its decline to have its toiling days and patient hours remembered, and to die in peace. Trotty [Veck] might have read a poor man's allegory in the fading year; but he was past that, now . . . .

"The New Year, the New Year. Everywhere the New Year! The Old Year was already looked upon as dead; and its effects were selling cheap, like some drowned mariner's aboardship. Its patterns were Last Year's, and going at a sacrifice, before its breath was gone. Its treasures were mere dirt, beside the riches of its unborn successor!" C 2

—serious: " . . . the first stroke of twelve peals from the neighbouring churches. There certainly—we must confess it now—is something awful in the sound. Strictly speaking, it may not be more impressive now than at any other time; for the hours steal as swiftly on at other periods, and their flight is little heeded.

"But we measure man's life by years, and it is a solemn knell that warns us we have passed another of the landmarks which stand between us and the grave. Disguise it as we may, the reflection will force itself on our minds, that when the next bell announces the arrival of a new year, we may be insensible alike of the timely warning we have so often neglected, and of all the warm feelings that glow within us now." ¶SB/NY

—transition: "'Hard weather indeed,' returned [Tugby's] wife, shaking her head.

"'Aye, aye! Years,' said Mr Tugby, 'are like Christians in that respect. Some of 'em die hard; some of 'em die easy. This one hasn't many days to run, and is making a fight for it. I like him all the better.'" C 4

—the Wish: "So may the New Year be a happy one to you, happy to many more whose happiness depends on you! So may each year be happier than the last, and not the meanest of our brethren or sisterhood debarred their rightful share, in what our Great Creator formed them to enjoy." C 4

Perseverance

—its absence: "' . . . [Richard Carstone] has not chosen his profession advisedly [said Mrs Bayham Badger] . . . . He is of such a very easy disposition, that probably he would never think it worth while to mention how he really feels; but he feels languid about the profession. He has not that positive interest in it which makes it his vocation. If he has any decided impression in reference to it, I should say it was that it is a tiresome pursuit. Now, this is not promising. Young men, like Mr Allan Woodcourt, who take it from a strong interest in all that it can do, will find some reward in it through a great deal of work for a very little money, and through years of considerable endurance and disappointment. But I am quite convinced that this would never be the case with Mr Carstone.'" BH 17

—advice: "'Rick, the world is before you [said John Jarndyce]; and it is most probable that as you enter it, so it will receive you. Trust in nothing but in Providence and your own efforts. Never separate the two, like the heathen waggoner. Constancy in love is a good thing; but it means nothing, and is nothing, without constancy in every kind of effort. If you had the abilities of all the great men, past and present, you could do nothing well, without sincerely meaning it, and setting about it. If you entertain the

supposition that any real success, in great things or in small, ever was or could be, ever will or can be, wrested from Fortune by fits and starts, leave that wrong idea here, or leave your cousin Ada [Clare] here.'" BH 13

—in education: " . . . 'Courage, Persevere'. This is the motto of a friend and worker. Not because the eyes of Europe are upon them, for I don't in the least believe it; nor because the eyes of even England are upon them, for I don't in the least believe it; not because their doings will be proclaimed with blast of trumpet at the street corners, for no such musical performance will take place; not because self-improvement is at all certain to lead to worldly success, but because it is good and right of itself; and because, being so, it does assuredly bring with it, its own resources and its own rewards." S/BM2

—essential ingredient: "I [David Copperfield] feel as if it were not for me to record, even though this manuscript is intended for no eyes but mine, how hard I worked at that tremendous shorthand, and all improvement appertaining to it, in my sense of responsibility to Dora and her aunts. I will only add, to what I have already written of my perseverance at this time of my life, and of a patient and continuous energy which then began to be matured within me, and which I know to be the strong part of my character, if it have any strength at all, that there, on looking back, I find the source of my success." ¶DC 42

And see H:Stenography

—of a lover: "'You are aware, Captain Gills, that I, too, have adored Miss Dombey.'

"'Cheer up!' said the Captain, laying his hand on Mr Toots's shoulder. 'Stand by, boy!'

"'It is my intention, Captain Gills,' returned the spirited Mr Toots, '*to* cheer up. Also to stand by, as much as possible. When the silent tomb shall yawn, Captain Gills, I shall be ready for burial; not before.'" DS 56

Pretension

—of apprentices: "We may smile at such people, but they can never excite our anger. They are usually on the best terms with themselves, and it follows almost as a matter of course, in good humour with every one about them. Besides, they are always the faint reflection of higher lights; and, if they do display a little occasional foolery in their own proper persons, it is surely more tolerable than precocious puppyism in the Quadrant, whiskered dandyism in Regent Street and Pall Mall, or gallantry in its dotage anywhere." SB/TP

—imitative folding of one's arms: "Why have six hundred men been trying through several generations to fold their arms? The last twenty Parliaments have directed their entire attention to this graceful art . . . a certain ex-senator still producible, 'folded his arms better than any man in the house.' I have seen aspirants inflamed with a lofty ambition, studying through whole sessions the folded arms on the Treasury Bench, and trying to fold their arms according to the patterns there presented. I have known neophytes far more distracted about the folding of their arms than about the enunciation of their political views, or the turning of their periods.

"The injury inflicted on the nation by Mr Canning, when he folded his arms and got his portrait taken, is not to be calculated. Every member of Parliament from that hour to the present has been trying to fold his arms. It is a graceful, a refined, a decorative art; but, I doubt if its results will bear comparison with the infinite pains and charges bestowed upon its cultivation." HW/W?

—of the genteel: "'My mother lives in the most primitive manner down in that dreary red-brick dungeon at Hampton Court,' said Gowan. 'If you would make your own appointment, suggest your own day for permitting me to take you there to dinner, you would be bored and she would be charmed. Really that's the state of the case.' . . .

"The venerable inhabitants of that venerable pile seemed, in those times, to be encamped there like a sort of civilised gipsies. There was a temporary air about their establishments, as if they were going away the moment they could get anything better; there was also a dissatisfied air about themselves, as if they took it very ill that they had not already got something much better.

"Genteel blinds and makeshifts were more or less observable as soon as their doors were opened; screens not half high enough, which made dining-rooms out of arched passages, and warded off obscure corners where footboys slept at night with their heads among the knives and forks; curtains which called upon you to believe that they didn't hide anything; panes of glass which requested you not to see them; many objects of various forms, feigning to have no connection with their guilty secret, a bed; disguised traps in walls, which were clearly coal-cellars; affectations of no thoroughfares, which were evidently doors to little kitchens.

"Mental reservations and artful mysteries grew out of these things. Callers looking steadily into the eyes of their receivers, pretended not to smell cooking three feet off; people, confronting closets accidentally left open, pretended not to see bottles; visitors, with their heads against a partition of thin canvas and a page and a young female at high words on the other side, made believe to be sitting in a primeval silence. There was no end to the small social accommodation-bills of this nature which the gipsies of gentility were constantly drawing upon, and accepting for, one another." LD i 26

—*of imprisoned debtors:* "If Young John Chivery had had the inclination, and the power, to write a satire on family pride, he would have had no need to go for an avenging illustration out of the family of his beloved. He would have found it amply in that gallant brother and that dainty sister, so steeped in mean experiences, and so loftily conscious of the family name; so ready to beg or borrow from the poorest, to eat of anybody's bread, spend anybody's money, drink from anybody's cup and break it afterwards. To have painted the sordid facts of their lives, and they throughout invoking the death's head apparition of the family gentility to come and scare their benefactors, would have made Young John a satirist of the first water." LD i 20

"When this spirited young man [Tip Dorrit], and his sister [Fanny], had begun systematically to produce the family skeleton for the overawing of the College, this narrative cannot precisely state. Probably at about the period when they began to dine on the College charity. It is certain that the more reduced and necessitous they were, the more pompously the skeleton emerged from its tomb; and that when there was anything particularly shabby in the wind, the skeleton always came out with the ghastliest flourish." LD i 20

Pride

—*arrogant:* "Towards his first wife, Mr Dombey, in his cold and lofty arrogance, had borne himself like the removed Being he almost conceived himself to be. He had been 'Mr Dombey' with her when she first saw him, and he was 'Mr Dombey' when she died. He had asserted his greatness during their whole married life, and she had meekly recognised it. He had kept his distant seat of state on the top of his throne, and she her humble station on its lowest step; and much good it had done him, so to live in solitary bondage to his one idea! He had imagined that the proud character of his second wife would have been added to his own—would have merged into it, and exalted his greatness.

"He had pictured himself haughtier than ever, with Edith's haughtiness subservient to his. He had never entertained the possibility of its arraying itself against him. And now, when he found it rising in his path at every step and turn of his daily life, fixing its cold, defiant, and contemptuous face upon him, this pride of his, instead of withering, or hanging down its head beneath the shock, put forth new shoots, became more concentrated and intense, more gloomy, sullen, irksome, and unyielding, than it had ever been before." ¶DS 40 *And see* B:Body—*facial expression*

—*dignity:* "[Simon Tappertit] threw himself on a bench with the air of a man who was faint with dignity." BR 8

"[Sir Leicester Dedlock] carried himself like an eight-day clock at all times: like one of a race of eight-day clocks in gorgeous cases, that never go and never went—Ha ha ha!—but he will have some extra stiffness." BH 18

—*impact of dress:* "Dignity, and even holiness too, sometimes, are more questions of coat and waistcoat than some people imagine." OT 37

—*as duty:* "'There is a kind of pride, Sir,' [Harriet Carker] returned, after a moment's silence, 'or what may be supposed to be pride, which is mere duty; I hope I cherish no other.'" DS 33

—*egotistical:* "'He is, if I may so, the slave of his own greatness, and goes yoked to his own triumphal car like a beast of burden, with no idea on earth but that it is behind him and is to be drawn on, over everything and through everything.'" DS 45

—*false:* "[Nancy] felt burdened with the sense of her own deep shame, and shrunk as though she could scarcely bear the presence of her with whom she had sought this interview.

"But struggling with these better feelings was pride—the vice of the lowest and most debased creatures no less than of the high and self-assured. The miserable companion of thieves and ruffians, the fallen outcast of low haunts, the associate of the scourings of the jails and hulks, living within the shadow of the gallows itself—even this degraded being felt too proud to betray a feeble gleam of the womanly feeling which she thought a weakness, but which alone connected her with that humanity, of which her wasting life had obliterated so many, many traces when a very child." OT 40

"Once, it had seemed to me that when I should at last roll up my shirt-sleeves and go into the forge, Joe [Gargery]'s 'prentice, I should be distinguished and happy. Now the reality was in my hold, I only felt that it was dusty with the dust of the small coal, and that I had a weight upon my daily remembrance to which the anvil was a feather. . . .

"What I wanted, who can say? How can I say, when I never knew? What I dreaded was, that in some unlucky hour I, being at my grimiest and commonest, should lift up my eyes and see Estella [Havisham] looking in at one of the wooden windows of the forge. I was haunted by the fear that she would, sooner or later, find me out, with a black face and hands, doing the coarsest part of my work, and would exult over me and despise me." GE 14

"Let me confess exactly, with what feelings I looked forward to Joe [Gargery]'s coming.

"Not with pleasure, though I was bound to him by so many ties; no; with considerable disturbance, some mortification, and a keen sense of incongruity. If I could have kept him away by paying money, I certainly would have paid money. My greatest reassurance was, that he was coming to Barnard's Inn, not to Hammersmith, and consequently would not fall in Bentley Drummle's way . . . I had the sharpest sensitiveness as to his being seen by Drummle, whom I held in contempt. So, throughout life, our worst weaknesses and meannesses are usually committed for the sake of the people whom we most despise." GE 27

—"false": "'I propose [said Wrayburn to Lizzie] to be of some use . . . by paying some qualified person of your own sex and age to come here, certain nights in the week, and give you certain instruction which you wouldn't want if you hadn't been a self-denying daughter and sister. You know that it's good to have it, or you would never have so devoted yourself to your brother's having it. Than why not have it . . . .

"'Your false pride does wrong to yourself and does wrong to your dead father . . . . By perpetuating the consequences of his ignorant and blind obstinacy. By resolving not to set right the wrong he did you. By determining that the deprivation to which he condemned you, and which he forced upon you, shall always rest upon his head.'" ¶OMF ii 2

—and friendship: "Mr Dombey, in his friendlessness, inclined to the Major. It cannot be said that he warmed towards him, but he thawed a little. The Major . . . was a man of the world, and knew some great people. He talked much, and told stories; and Mr Dombey was disposed to regard him as a choice spirit who shone in society; and who had not that poisonous ingredient of poverty with which choice spirits in general are too much adulterated. His station was undeniable. Altogether the Major was a creditable companion, well accustomed to a life of leisure, and to such places as that they were about to visit, and having an air of gentlemanly ease about him that mixed well enough with his own City character, and did not compete with it at all." DS 20

—happy: "I [Doctor Marigold] was as pleased and as proud as a Pug-Dog with his muzzle black-leaded for a evening party, and his tail extra curled by machinery." CS/DM 3

—innocent: "'He [William Dorrit] is very much respected. Everybody who comes in, is glad to know him. He is more courted than any one else. He is far more thought of than the Marshal is.'

"If ever pride were innocent, it was innocent in Little Dorrit when she grew boastful of her father." LD i 9

—meeting resistance: It is not in the nature of things that a man of Mr Dombey's mood, opposed to such a spirit as he had raised against himself, should be softened in the imperious asperity of his temper; or that the

cold hard armour of pride in which he lived encased, should be made more flexible by constant collision with haughty scorn and defiance.

"It is the curse of such a nature—it is a main part of the heavy retribution on itself it bears within itself—that while deference and concession swell its evil qualities, and are the food it grows upon, resistance and questioning of its exacting claims, foster it too, no less. The evil that is in it finds equally its means of growth and propagation in opposites. It draws support and life from sweets and bitters; bowed down before, or unacknowledged, it still enslaves the breast in which it has its throne; and, worshipped or rejected, is as hard a master as the Devil in dark fables." ¶DS 40

—a mother's: "Pride is one of the seven deadly sins; but it cannot be the pride of a mother in her children, for that is a compound of two cardinal virtues—faith and hope. That was the pride which swelled Mrs Nickleby's heart that night, and this it was which left upon her face, glistening in the light when they returned home, traces of the most grateful tears she had ever shed." NN 43

—what is obnoxious to it: "I suppose there is nothing Pride can so little bear with, as Pride itself . . . . " BH 18

—its other side: "[Mr Dombey] is a gentleman of high honour and integrity. Any man in his position could, and many a man in his position would, have saved himself, by making terms which would have very slightly, almost insensibly, increased the losses of those who had had dealings with him, and left him a remnant to live upon. But he is resolved on payment to the last farthing of his means.

"'His own words are, that they will clear, or nearly clear, the house, and that no one can lose much. Ah, Miss Harriet , it would do us no harm to remember oftener than we do, that vices are sometimes only virtues carried to excess! His pride shows well in this.'" ¶DS 58

—personal: "We have been, indeed, for some days unable to determine who will transmit the greatest name to posterity; ourselves, who sent our correspondent down; our correspondent, who wrote an account of the matter; or the association, who gave our correspondent something to write about. We rather incline to the opinion that we are the greatest man of the party, inasmuch as the notion of an exclusive and authentic report originated with us; this may be prejudice: it may arise from a prepossession on our part in our own favour. Be it so. We have no doubt that every gentleman concerned in this mighty assemblage is troubled with the same complaint in a greater or less degree; and it is a consolation to us to know that we have at least this feeling in common with the great scientific stars, the brilliant and extraordinary luminaries, whose speculations we record." B/M1

—of place: " . . . one man's a blacksmith, and one's a whitesmith, and one's a goldsmith, and one's a coppersmith. Diwisions among such must come, and must be met as they come. If there's been any fault at all to-day [said Joe Gargery], it's mine. You and me is not two figures to be together in London; nor yet anywheres else but what is private, and beknown, and understood among friends.

"'It ain't that I am proud, but that I want to be right, as you shall never see me no more in these clothes. I'm wrong in these clothes. I'm wrong out of the forge, the kitchen, or off th' meshes. You won't find half so much fault in me if you think of me in my forge dress, with my hammer in my hand, or even my pipe. You won't find half so much fault in me if, supposing as you should ever wish to see me, you come and put your head in at the forge window and see Joe the blacksmith, there, at the old anvil, in the old burnt apron, sticking to the old work. I'm awful dull, but I hope I've beat out something nigh the rights of this at last. And so GOD bless you, dear old Pip, old chap, GOD bless you!'

"I had not been mistaken in my fancy that there was a simple dignity in him. The fashion of his dress could no more come in its way when he spoke these words, than it could come in its way in Heaven." ¶GE 27

—self-destructive: "'I have dreamed,' said Edith in a low voice, 'of a pride that is all powerless for good, all powerful for evil; of a pride that has been galled and goaded, through many shameful years, and has never recoiled except upon itself; a pride that has debased its owner with the consciousness of deep humiliation, and never

helped its owner boldly to resent it or avoid it, or to say, "This shall not be!" a pride that, rightly guided, might have led perhaps to better things, but which, misdirected and perverted, like all else belonging to the same possessor, has been self-contempt, mere hardihood, and ruin.'" DS 43

—spiritual: "More than forty years had passed over the grey head of this determined woman [Mrs Clennam], since the time she recalled. More than forty years of strife and struggle with the whisper that, by whatever name she called her vindictive pride and rage, nothing through all eternity could change their nature.

"Yet, gone those more than forty years, and come this Nemesis now looking her in the face, she still abided by her old impiety—still reversed the order of Creation, and breathed her own breath into a clay image of her Creator. Verily, verily, travellers have seen many monstrous idols in many countries; but no human eyes have ever seen more daring, gross, and shocking images of the Divine nature, than we creatures of the dust make in our own likeness of our own bad passions." ¶LD ii 30 *And see* H:Man*—relationship to God*

—a stimulant: "Prying and tormenting as the world was, it did Mr Dombey the service of nerving him to pursuit and revenge. It roused his passion, stung his pride, twisted the one idea of his life into a new shape, and made some gratification of his wrath, the object into which his whole intellectual existence resolved itself. All the stubbornness and implacability of his nature, all its hard impenetrable quality, all its gloom and moroseness, all its exaggerated sense of personal importance, all its jealous disposition to resent the least flaw in the ample recognition of his importance by others, set this way like many streams united into one, and bore him on upon their tide. The most impetuously passionate and violently impulsive of mankind would have been a milder enemy to encounter than the sullen Mr Dombey wrought to this. A wild beast would have been easier turned or soothed than the grave gentleman without a wrinkle in his starched cravat." DS 53

—vulnerable: "Who wears such armour, too, bears with him every another heavy retribution. It is of proof against conciliation, love, and confidence: against all gentle sympathy from without, all trust, all tenderness, all soft emotion; but to deep stabs in the self-love it is as vulnerable as the bare breast to steel; and such tormenting festers rankle there, as follow on no other wounds, no, though dealt with the mailed hand of Pride itself, on weaker pride, disarmed and thrown down." DS 40

"He silenced the distant thunder with the rolling of his sea of pride. He would bear nothing but his pride. And in his pride, a heap of inconsistency, and misery, and self-inflicted torment, he hated her." DS 40

Purity

—in the innocent: "A change had been gradually stealing over [Nell], in the time of her loneliness and sorrow. With failing strength and heightening resolution, there had sprung up a purified and altered mind; there had grown in her bosom blessed thoughts and hopes, which are the portion of few but the weak and drooping." OCS 52

—simplicity: "Tom, Tom [Pinch]! The man in all this world most confident in his sagacity and shrewdness; the man in all this world most proud of his distrust of other men, and having most to show in gold and silver as the gains belonging to his creed; the meekest favourer of that wise doctrine, Every man for himself, and God for us all (there being high wisdom in the thought that the Eternal Majesty of Heaven ever was, or can be, on the side of selfish lust and love!); shall never find, oh, never find, be sure of that, the time come home to him, when all his wisdom is an idiot's folly, weighed against a simple heart!" MC 39

Religion

—basic: "' . . of course it would be hopeless to help [the allotment-holders] to be happier and better if they had no religious feeling at all.'" AY/B

—and cleanliness: "Mrs Joe [Gargery] was a very clean housekeeper, but had an exquisite art of making her cleanliness more uncomfortable and unacceptable than dirt itself. Cleanliness is next to Godliness, and some people do the same by their religion." GE 3

—and digestion: "[Georgiana] was a cousin —an indigestive single woman, who called her rigidity religion, and her liver love." GE 25

—Druids

—earlier: "The [ancient] Britons had a strange and terrible religion, called the Religion of the Druids . . . mixed up the worship of the Serpent, and of the Sun and Moon, with the worship of some of the Heathen

Gods and Goddesses. Most of its ceremonies were kept secret by the priests, the Druids, who pretended to be enchanters, and who carried magicians' wands, and wore, each of them, about his neck, what he told the ignorant people was a Serpent's egg in a golden case . . . they were very powerful, and very much believed in, and as they made and executed the laws, and paid no taxes, I don't wonder that they liked their trade.

"And, as they persuaded the people the more Druids there were, the better off the people would be, I don't wonder that there were a good many of them. But it is pleasant to think that there are no Druids, *now,* who go on in that way, and pretend to carry Enchanters' Wands and Serpents' Eggs—and of course there is nothing of the kind, anywhere." CHE 1

—later: " . . . it was in the Roman time, and by means of Roman ships, that the Christian Religion was first brought into Britain, and its people first taught the great lesson that, to be good in the sight of GOD, they must love their neighbours as themselves, and do unto others as they would be done by.

"The Druids declared that it was very wicked to believe in any such thing, and cursed all the people who did believe it, very heartily. But, when the people found that they were none the better for the blessings of the Druids, and none the worse for the curses of the Druids, but, that the sun shone and the rain fell without consulting the Druids at all, they just began to think that the Druids were mere men, and that it signified very little whether they cursed or blessed. After which, the pupils of the Druids fell off greatly in numbers, and the Druids took to other trades." CHE 1

—excommunication: "[It] was . . . the great weapon of the clergy. It consisted in declaring the person who was excommunicated, an outcast from the Church and from all religious offices; and in cursing him all over, from the top of his head to the sole of his foot, whether he was standing up, lying down, sitting, kneeling, walking, running, hopping, jumping, gaping, coughing, sneezing, or whatever else he was doing. This unchristian nonsense would of course have made no sort of difference to the person cursed—who could say his prayers at home if he were shut out of church, and whom none but GOD could judge—but for the fears and superstitions of the people, who avoided excommunicated persons, and made their lives unhappy." CHE 12

—and humanity: "Is it necessary or advisable to address such an audience continually as 'fellow-sinners'? Is it not enough to be fellow-creatures, born yesterday, suffering and striving to-day, dying tomorrow? By our common humanity, my brothers and sisters, by our common capacities for pain and pleasure, by our common laughter and our common tears, by our common aspiration to reach something better than ourselves, by our common tendency to believe in something good, and to invest whatever we love or whatever we lose with some qualities that are superior to our own failings and weaknesses as we know them in our own poor hearts—by these, Hear me!—Surely, it is enough to be fellow-creatures. Surely, it includes the other designation, and some touching meanings over and above." UT/TV

—hypocrisy: "[The Gordon Riots] teach a good lesson. That what we falsely call a religious cry is easily raised by men who have no religion, and who in their daily practice set at nought the commonest principles of right and wrong; that it is begotten of intolerance and persecution; that it is senseless, besotted, inveterate and unmerciful; all History teaches us. But perhaps we do not know it in our hearts too well, to profit by even so humble an example as the 'No Popery' riots of Seventeen Hundred and Eighty." BR pref

—Inquisition: "'I speak as I find . . . . 'Forbid it should be otherways! But we never knows wot's hidden in each other's hearts; and if we had glass winders there, we'd need keep the shetters up, some on us, I do assure you!

"'But you don't mean to say' . . . .

"' No,' said Mrs Gamp . . . . I don't. Don't think I do. The torters of the Imposition shouldn't make me own I did.'" MC 29

" . . . [Henry IV] first established in England the detestable and atrocious custom, brought from abroad, of burning [heretics] as a punishment for their opinions. It was the importation into England of one of the practices of what was called the Holy Inquisition: which was the most *un*holy and the most infamous tribunal that ever disgraced mankind, and made men more like demons than followers of Our Saviour." CHE 20

—Islam: "'My dearest Edith, there is such an obvious destiny in it, that really one

might almost be induced to cross one's arms upon one's frock, and say, like those wicked Turks, there is no What's-his-name but Thingummy, and What-you-may-call-it is his prophet!'

"Edith deigned no revision of this extraordinary quotation from the Koran . . . . " DS 27

—joyless: "'I am the only child [said Arthur Clennam] of parents who weighed, measured, and priced everything; for whom what could not be weighed, measured, and priced, had no existence. Strict people as the phrase is, professors of a stern religion, their very religion was a gloomy sacrifice of tastes and sympathies that were never their own, offered up as a part of a bargain for the security of their possessions. Austere faces, inexorable discipline, penance in this world and terror in the next—nothing graceful or gentle anywhere, and the void in my cowed heart everywhere—this was my childhood, if I may so misuse the word as to apply it to such a beginning of life.'" LD i 2

"'I hope plays mayn't be sinful, Kit, but I'm a'most afraid,' said Mrs Nubbles.

"'I know who has been putting that in your head,' rejoined her son disconsolately; 'that's Little Bethel again. Now I say, mother, pray don't take to going there regularly, for if I was to see your good-humoured face that has always made home cheerful, turned into a grievous one, and the baby trained to look grievous too, and to call itself a young sinner (bless its heart) and a child of the devil (which is calling its dead father names); if I was to see this, and see little Jacob looking grievous likewise, I should so take it to heart that I'm sure I should go and list for a soldier, and run my head on purpose against the first cannonball I saw coming my way.'" OCS 22

And see CD:Opinions

—disproved: "Ye men of gloom and austerity, who paint the face of Infinite Benevolence with an eternal frown; read in the Everlasting Book, wide open to your view, the lesson it would teach. Its pictures are not in black and sombre hues, but bright and glowing tints; its music—save when ye drown it—is not in sighs and groans, but songs and cheerful sounds. Listen to the million voices in the summer air, and find one dismal as your own. Remember, if ye can, the sense of hope and pleasure which every glad return of day awakens in the breast of all your kind who have not changed their nature; and learn some wisdom even from the witless, when their hearts are lifted up they know not why, by all the mirth and happiness it brings." BR 25

—view of children: "As to any recreation with other children of my age, I had very little of that; for the gloomy theology of the Murdstones made all children out to be a swarm of little vipers (though there *was* a child once set in the midst of the Disciples), and held that they contaminated one another." DC 4

—misanthropic: "'I hope I know my own unworthiness [said Miggs], and that I hate and despise myself and all my fellow-creatures as every practicable Christian should.'" BR 13

"'What such people miscall their religion, is a vent for their bad-humours and arrogance. And do you know I must say, sir,' he continued, mildly laying his head on one side, 'that I *don't* find authority for Mr and Miss Murdstone in the New Testament?'

"'I never found it either!' said I.

"'In the meantime, sir,' said Mr Chillip, 'they are much disliked; and as they are very free in consigning everybody who dislikes them to perdition, we really have a good deal of perdition going on in our neighbourhood! However, as Mrs Chillip says, sir, they undergo a continual punishment; for they are turned inward, to feed upon their own hearts, and their own hearts are very bad feeding.'" DC 59

—missionary work

—futility: "The history of this Expedition [to the Niger] is the history of the Past, in reference to the heated visions of philanthropists for the railroad Christianisation of Africa . . . . Such means are useless, futile, and we will venture to add—in despite of hats broad-brimmed or shovel-shaped, and coats of drab or black, with collars or without—wicked. No amount of philanthropy has a right to waste such valuable life as was squandered here, in the teeth of all experience and feasible pretence of hope. Between the civilised European and the barbarous African there is a great gulf set.

"The air that brings life to the latter brings death to the former. In the mighty revolutions of the wheel of time, some change in this regard may come about; but in this age of the world, all the white armies and white missionaries of the world would fall, as withered reeds, before the rolling of one African river.

"To change the customs even of civilised and educated men, and impress them with new ideas is—we have good need to know it—a most difficult and slow proceeding; but to do this by ignorant and savage races is a work which, like the progressive changes of the globe itself, requires a stretch of years that dazzles in the looking at.

"It is not, we conceive, within the likely providence of God, that Christianity shall start to the banks of the Niger, until it shall have overflowed all intervening space. The stone that is dropped into the ocean of ignorance at Exeter Hall, must make its widening circles, one beyond another, until they reach the negro's country in their natural expansion.

"There is a broad, dark sea between the Strand in London and the Niger, where those rings are not yet shining; and through all that space they must appear, before the last one breaks upon the shore of Africa. Gently and imperceptibly the widening circle of enlightenment must stretch and stretch, from man to man, from people on to people, until there is a girdle round the earth; but no convulsive effort, or far-off aim, can make the last great outer circle first, and then come home at leisure to trace out the inner one.

"Believe it, African Civilisation, Church of England Missionary, and all other Missionary Societies! The work at home must be completed thoroughly, or there is no hope abroad. To your tents, O Israel! but see they are your own tents! Set *them* in order; leave nothing to be done *there;* and outpost will convey your lesson on to outpost, until the naked armies of King Obi and King Boy are reached and taught. Let a knowledge of the duty that man owes to man, and to his God, spread thus, by natural degrees and growth of example, to the outer shores of Africa, and it will float in safety up the rivers, never fear!" E/NE

—to the poor: "What avails it to send a Missionary to me, a miserable man or woman living in a fœtid Court where every sense bestowed upon me for my delight becomes a torment, and every minute of my life is new mire added to the heap under which I lie degraded? To what natural feeling within me is he to address himself? What ancient chord within me can he hope to touch? Is it my remembrance of my children? It is a remembrance of distortion and decay, scrofula and fever? Would he address himself to my hopes of immortality? I am so surrounded by material filth that my Soul can not rise to the contemplation of an immaterial existence!

"Or, if I be a miserable child, born and nurtured in the same wretched place, and tempted, in these better times, to the Ragged School, what can the few hours' teaching that I get there do for me, against the noxious, constant, ever-renewed lesson of my whole existence[?] But, give me my first glimpse of Heaven through a little of its light and air—give me water—help me to be clean—lighten this heavy atmosphere in which my spirit droops and I become the indifferent and callous creature that you see me—gently and kindly take the body of my dead relation out of the small room where I grow to be so familiar with the awful change that even *its* sanctity is lost to me—and, Teacher, then I'll hear, you know how willingly, of Him whose thoughts were so much with the Poor, and who had compassion for all human sorrow!" ¶S/SA1

—Mormon: "I, Uncommercial Traveller for the firm of Human Interest Brothers, had come aboard this Emigrant Ship to see what Eight hundred Latter-day Saints were like, and I found them (to the rout and overthrow of all my expectations) like what I now describe . . . .

"UNCOMMERCIAL. These are a very fine set of people you have brought together here.

"MORMON AGENT. Yes, sir, they are a *very* fine set of people.

"UNCOMMERCIAL (looking about). Indeed, I think it would be difficult to find Eight hundred people together anywhere else, and find so much beauty and so much strength and capacity for work among them." UT/SL

"I afterwards learned that a Despatch was sent home by the captain before he struck out into the wide Atlantic, highly extolling the behaviour of these Emigrants, and the perfect order and propriety of all their social arrangements.

"What is in store for the poor people on the shores of the Great Salt Lake, what happy delusions they are labouring under now, on what miserable blindness their eyes may be opened then, I do not pretend to say. But I went on board their ship to bear testimony against them if they deserved it, as I fully believed they would; to my great astonishment they did not deserve it; and my predispositions and tendencies must not affect me as an honest witness.

"I went over the Amazon's side, feeling it impossible to deny that, so far, some remarkable influence had produced a remarkable result, which better known influences have often missed." ¶UT/SL

—*Oxford Movement:* "The brilliant and distinguished circle comprehends within it, no contracted amount of education, sense, courage, honour, beauty, and virtue. Yet there is something a little wrong about it, in despite of its immense advantages. What can it be?

". . . is there Dandyism . . . that has got below the surface and is doing less harmless things than jack-towelling itself and stopping its own digestion, to which no rational person need particularly object?

"Why, yes. It cannot be disguised. There *are,* at Chesney Wold this January week, some ladies and gentlemen of the newest fashion, who have set up a Dandyism—in Religion, for instance. Who, in mere lackadaisical want of an emotion, have agreed upon a little dandy talk about the Vulgar wanting faith in things in general; meaning, in the things that have been tried and found wanting, as though a low fellow should unaccountably lose faith in a bad shilling, after finding it out! Who would make the Vulgar very picturesque and faithful, by putting back the hands upon the Clock of Time, and cancelling a few hundred years of history." BH 12

—*prayer of a castaway child:* "'There's a child's hymn I and Tom used to say at my mother's knee when we were little ones keeps running through my thoughts . . . . It's as clear in my mind at this minute as if my mother was here listening to me,' said Dick, and he repeated:

"'Hear my prayer, O! Heavenly father,
Ere I lay me down to sleep;
Bid thy Angels, pure and holy,
Round my bed their vigil keep.

"'My sins are heavy, but Thy mercy
Far outweighs them every one;
Down before Thy Cross I cast them,
Trusting in Thy help alone.

"'Keep me through this night of peril
Underneath its boundless shade;
Take me to Thy rest, I pray Thee,
When my pilgrimage is made.

"'None shall measure out Thy patience
By the span of human thought;
None shall bound the tender mercies
Which Thy Holy Son has bought.

"'Pardon all my past transgressions,
Give me strength for days to come;
Guide and guard me with Thy blessing
Till Thy Angels bid me home.'"

CS/GM*br: Poor Dick's story*

—*and prejudice:* " . . . some of you Protestants of promise [said Geoffrey Haredale] are at this moment leagued in yonder building, to prevent [Roman Catholics'] having the surpassing and unheard-of privilege of teaching our children to read and write—here—in this land, where thousands of us enter your service every year, and to preserve the freedom of which, we die in bloody battles abroad, in heaps: and that others of you, to the number of some thousands as I learn, are led on to look on all men of my creed as wolves and beasts of prey . . . .'" BR 43

—*procession in France:* "The procession was a very long one, and included an immense number of people divided into small parties; each party chanting nasally, on its own account, without reference to any other, and producing a most dismal result. There were angels, crosses, Virgins carried on flat boards surrounded by Cupids, crowns, saints, missals, infantry, tapers, monks, nuns, relics, dignitaries of the church in green hats, walking under crimson parasols: and, here and there, a species of sacred street-lamp hoisted on a pole." PI 5

—*Protestantism*

—*and bad temper:* " . . . a message arrived from Mrs Varden, making known to all whom it might concern, that she felt too much indisposed to rise . . . and therefore desired to be immediately accommodated with the little black tea-pot of strong mixed tea, a couple of rounds of buttered toast, a middling-sized dish of beef and ham cut thin, and the Protestant Manual in two volumes post octavo. Like some other ladies who in remote ages flourished upon this globe, Mrs Varden was most devout when most ill-tempered. Whenever she and her husband were at unusual variance, then the Protestant Manual was in high feather." BR 4

—*and Bloody Mary:* "'At a crisis like the present, when Queen Elizabeth, that maiden monarch, weeps within her tomb, and Bloody Mary, with a brow of gloom and shadow, stalks triumphant—'

"'Oh sir,' cried [Grueby], gruffly, 'where's the use of talking of Bloody Mary, under such circumstances as the present, when my lord's wet through, and tired with hard riding? Let's either go on to London, sir, or put up at once; or that unfort'nate Bloody Mary will have more to answer for—and she's done a deal more harm in her grave than she ever did in her lifetime, I believe.'" BR 35

—faint beginning: 1215 AD: " . . . the Pope, coming to the aid of his precious friend [King John], laid the kingdom under an Interdict again, because the people took part with the Barons. It did not much matter, for the people had grown so used to it now, that they had begun to think nothing about it. It occurred to them . . . that they could keep their churches open, and ring their bells, without the Pope's permission as well as with it. So they tried the experiment—and found that it succeeded perfectly." CHE 14

—in the streets: "' . . . they're all mixed up somehow or another [said John Grueby] with that unfort'nate Bloody Mary, and call her name out till they're hoarse. They're all Protestants too—every man and boy among 'em: and Protestants are very fond of spoons I find, and silver-plate in general, whenever area-gates is left open accidentally . . . . One of these evenings, when the weather gets warmer and Protestants are thirsty, they'll be pulling London down—and I never heard that Bloody Mary went as far as *that.*'" BR 35

And see Sincerity—*missing*

The No-Popery Dance BR

—Puritanism

—late 16th century: " . . . [they] were called the Puritans, because they said that they wanted to have everything very pure and plain in all the Church service. These last were for the most part an uncomfortable people, who thought it highly meritorious to dress in a hideous manner, talk through their noses, and oppose all harmless enjoyments . . . they were powerful too, and very much in earnest . . . . " CHE 31 ii

—mid-17th century: "The Puritans of that time were as much opposed to harmless recreations and healthful amusements as those of the present day, and it is amusing to observe that each in their generation advance precisely the same description of arguments . . . .

"'A woman about Northampton . . . fell a dauncing, which continued within night; at which time shee was got with child, which at the birth shee murthering, was detected and apprehended, and being convented before the justice, shee confess it, and withal told the occasion of it, saying it was her falling to sport on the Sabbath . . . which brought her adultory and that murther.'" STH/3

" . . . the Scottish sort of Puritan religion . . . was then exceedingly popular among the soldiers. They were as much opposed to the Bishops as to the Pope himself; and the very privates, drummers, and trumpeters, had such an inconvenient habit of starting up and preaching long-winded discourses, that I would not have belonged to that army on any account." CHE 33 iv

—mid-19th century: "[Hartford} is the seat of the local legislature of Connecticut, which sage body enacted, in bygone times, the renowned code of 'Blue Laws,' in virtue whereof, among other enlightened provisions, any citizen who could be proved to have kissed his wife on Sunday, was punishable, I believe, with the stocks. Too much of the old Puritan spirit exists in these parts to the present hour; but its influence has not tended, that I know, to make the people less hard in their bargains, or more equal in their dealings.

"As I never heard of its working that effect anywhere else, I infer that it never will, here. Indeed, I am accustomed, with reference to great professions and severe faces, to judge of the goods of the other world pretty much as I judge of the goods of this; and whenever I see a dealer in such commodities with too great a display of them in his window, I doubt the quality of the article within." ¶AN 4

—Quaker

—kite-flying:: "' . . . [Mr Dick]'s the most amenable and friendly creature in existence [said Betsey Trotwood]. If he likes to fly a kite sometimes, what of that! Franklin used to fly a kite. He was a Quaker, or something of that sort, if I am not mistaken. And a Quaker flying a kite is a much more ridiculous object than anybody else.'" DC 14

And see F:Courtier*—in Africa;* LC:Conversation*—opener; and* W:Cities and towns—*Philadelphia*

—reformed, in Scotland: "This obdurate and harsh spirit of the Scottish reformers (the Scotch have always been rather a sullen and frowning people in religious matters) put up the blood of the Romish French court . . . . " CHE 31

—retribution embraced: "'Not to obtrude doctrine upon you,' [Mrs Clennam] looked at the rigid pile of hard pale books before her . . . 'I will say this much: that I shape my course by pilots, strictly by proved and tried pilots, under whom I cannot be shipwrecked—can not be—and that if I were unmindful of the admonition conveyed in those three letters [D.N.F.—Do Not Forget], I should not be half as chastened as I am ....

"'If I forgot my ignorances in my life of health and freedom, I might complain of the life to which I am now condemned. I never do: I never have done. If I forgot that this scene, the Earth, is expressly meant to be a scene of gloom, and hardship, and dark trial, for the creatures who are made out of its dust, I might have some tenderness for its vanities. But I have no such tenderness. If I did not know that we are, every one, the subject (most justly the subject) of a wrath that must be satisfied, and against which mere actions are nothing, I might repine at the difference between me, imprisoned here, and the people who pass the gateway yonder. But I take it as a grace and favour to be elected to make the satisfaction I am making here, to know what I know for certain here, and to work out what I have worked out here. My affliction might otherwise have had no meaning to me. Hence I would forget, and I do forget, nothing. Hence I am contented, and say it is better with me than with millions.'" LD i 30

—sainthood: "When he died, the monks settled that he was a Saint, and called him Saint Dunstan ever afterwards. They might just as well have settled that he was a coach-horse, and could just as easily have called him one." CHE 4

—Shakers: " . . . a party of Shakers, who were at work upon the road; who wore the broadest of all broad-brimmed hats; and were in all visible respects such very wooden men, that I felt about as much sympathy for them, and as much interest in them, as if they had been so many figure-heads of ships . . . . " AN 15

—furniture: " . . . we walked into a grim room, where several grim hats were hanging on grim pegs, and the time was grimly told by a grim clock which uttered every tick with a kind of struggle, as if it broke the grim silence reluctantly, and under protest. Ranged against the wall were six or eight stiff high-backed chairs, and they partook so strongly of the general grimness that one

would much rather have sat on the floor than incurred the smallest obligation to any of them." AN 15

—people: "Presently there stalked into this apartment, a grim old Shaker, with eyes as hard, and dull, and cold, as the great round metal buttons on his coat and waistcoat; a sort of calm goblin . . . we requested leave to make some trifling purchases of Shaker goods; which was grimly conceded . . . the stock was presided over by something alive in a russet case, which the elder said was a woman; and which I suppose *was* a woman, though I should not have suspected it." AN 15

"They eat and drink together, after the Spartan model, at a great public table. There is no union of the sexes, and every Shaker, male and female, is devoted to a life of celibacy. Rumour has been busy upon this theme, but here again I must refer to the lady of the store, and say, that if many of the sister Shakers resemble her, I treat all such slander as bearing on its face the strongest marks of wild improbability." AN 15

—worship: "These people are called Shakers from their peculiar form of adoration, which consists of a dance, performed by the men and women of all ages, who arrange themselves for that purpose in opposite parties: the men first divesting themselves of their hats and coats, which they gravely hang against the wall before they begin; and tying a ribbon round their shirt-sleeves, as though they were going to be bled.

"They accompany themselves with a droning, humming noise, and dance until they are quite exhausted, alternately advancing and retiring in a preposterous sort of trot. The effect is said to be unspeakably absurd: and if I may judge from a print of this ceremony which I have in my possession; and which I am informed by those who have visited the chapel, is perfectly accurate; it must be infinitely grotesque." AN 15

And see CD:View of Joyless Religion

—shrine

—in Flanders: "Little whitewashed black holes of chapels, with barred doors and Flemish inscriptions, abound at roadside corners, and often they are garnished with a sheaf of wooden crosses, like children's swords; or, in their default, some hollow old tree with a saint roosting in it, is similarly decorated, or a pole with a very diminutive saint enshrined aloft in a sort of sacred pigeon-house.

"Not that we are deficient in such decoration in the town here, for, over at the church yonder, outside the building, is a scenic representation of the Crucifixion, built up with old bricks and stones, and made out with painted canvas and wooden figures: the whole surmounting the dusty skull of some holy personage (perhaps), shut up behind a little ashy iron grate, as if it were originally put there to be cooked, and the fire had long gone out." ¶UT/FF

—in Italy: "The roadside crosses in this part of Italy [Tuscany] are numerous and curious. There is seldom a figure on the cross, though there is sometimes a face; but they are remarkable for being garnished with little models in wood, of every possible object that can be connected with the Saviour's death.

"The cock that crowed when Peter had denied his Master thrice, is usually perched on the tip-top; and an ornithological phenomenon he generally is. Under him, is the inscription. Then, hung on to the cross-beam, are the spear, the reed with the sponge of vinegar and water at the end, the coat without seam for which the soldiers cast lots, the dice-box with which they threw for it, the hammer that drove in the nails, the pincers that pulled them out, the ladder which was set against the cross, the crown of thorns, the instrument of flagellation, the lantern with which Mary went to the tomb (I suppose), and the sword with which Peter smote the servant of the high priest—a perfect toy-shop of little objects, repeated at every four or five miles, all along the highway." ¶PI 10

—spurious: "'Ah, dear!' moaned Mrs Gamp, sinking into the shaving chair, 'that there blessed Bull [Lewsome], Mr Sweedlepipe, has done his wery best to conker me. Of all the trying inwalieges in this walley of the shadder, that one beats 'em black and blue' . . . .

"'Talk of constitooshun!' Mrs Gamp observed. 'A person's constitooshun need be made of bricks to stand it. Mrs Harris jestly says to me, but t'other day, "Oh! Sairey Gamp," she says, "how is it done?" "Mrs Harris, ma'am," I says to her, "we gives no trust ourselves, and puts a deal o' trust elsevere; these is our religious feelins, and we finds 'em answer." "Sairey," says Mrs

Harris, "sech is life. Vich likeways is the hend of all things!"'" MC 29

—*superstition:* "It is a good example of the superstitions of the monks, that this Missal [on which **Harold** took an oath in 1066], instead of being placed upon a table, was placed upon a tub; which, when Harold had sworn, was uncovered, and shown to be full of dead men's bones—bones, as the monks pretended, of saints. This was supposed to make Harold's oath a great deal more impressive and binding. As if the great name of the Creator of Heaven and earth could be made more solemn by a knuckle-bone, or a double-tooth, or a finger-nail, of **Dunstan**!" CHE 6

—*suppression of monasteries:* "There is no doubt that many of these religious establishments were religious in nothing but in name, and were crammed with lazy, indolent, and sensual monks. There is no doubt that they imposed upon the people in every possible way; that they had images moved by wires, which they pretended were miraculously moved by Heaven; that they had among them a whole tun measure full of teeth, all purporting to have come out of the head of one saint, who must indeed have been a very extraordinary person with that enormous allowance of grinders: that they had bits of coal which they said had fried **Saint Lawrence**, and bits of toe-nails which they said belonged to other famous saints; penknives, and boots, and girdles, which they said belonged to others; and that all these bits of rubbish were called Relics, and adored by the ignorant people.

"But, on the other hand, there is no doubt either, that the King's officers and men punished the good monks with the bad; did great injustice; demolished many beautiful things and many valuable libraries; destroyed numbers of paintings, stained glass windows, fine pavements, and carvings; and that the whole court were ravenously greedy and rapacious for the division of this great spoil among them." CHE 28

—*Transcendentalism:* "On inquiring what this appellation might be supposed to signify, I was given to understand that whatever was unintelligible would be certainly transcendental. Not deriving much comfort from this elucidation, I pursued the inquiry still further . . . . Transcendentalism has its occasional vagaries (what school has not?), but it has good healthful qualities in spite of them; not least among the number a hearty disgust of Cant, and an aptitude to detect her in all the million varieties of her everlasting wardrobe. And therefore if I were a Bostonian, I think I would be a Transcendentalist." AN 3

—*Trappists:* "Looming in the distance, as we rode along [in Missouri], was another of the ancient Indian burial-places, called The Monks' Mound; in memory of a body of fanatics of the order of La Trappe, who founded a desolate convent [?] there, many years ago, when there were no settlers within a thousand miles, and were all swept off by the pernicious climate: in which lamentable fatality, few rational people will suppose, perhaps that society experienced any very severe deprivation." AN 13

—*Unitarianism:* "The Unitarian church is represented, in this remote place [St Louis], as in most other parts of America, by a gentleman of great worth and excellence. The poor have good reason to remember and bless it; for it befriends them, and aids the cause of rational education, without any sectarian or selfish views. It is liberal in all its actions; of kind construction; and of wide benevolence." AN 12

And see W:America—*diversion: religion*

CD's nearest approach personally to organized religion was Unitarianism. And see Religion—*joyless—in America*

—*universality:* " . . . the Pacific Ocean, with its lovely islands, where the savage girls plait flowers, and the savage boys carve cocoa-nut shells, and the grim blind idols muse in their shady groves to exactly the same purpose as the priests and chiefs." UT/SL

—*wrathful:* "The gloomy taint that was in the Murdstone blood, darkened the Murdstone religion, which was austere and wrathful. I have thought, since, that its assuming that character was a necessary consequence of Mr Murdstone's firmness, which wouldn't allow him to let anybody off from the utmost weight of the severest penalties he could find any excuse for. Be this as it may, I well remember the tremendous visages with which we used to go to church, and the changed air of the place . . . I wonder with a sudden fear whether it is likely that our good old clergyman can be wrong, and Mr and Miss Murdstone right, and that all the angels in Heaven can be destroying angels." DC 4

"[Mrs Clennam] then put on the spectacles and read certain passages aloud from a book—sternly, fiercely, wrathfully—praying that her enemies (she made them by her tone and manner expressly hers) might be put to the edge of the sword, consumed by fire, smitten by plagues and leprosy, that their bones might be ground to dust, and that they might be utterly exterminated. As she read on, years seemed to fall away from her son like the imaginings of a dream, and all the old dark horrors of his usual preparation for the sleep of an innocent child to overshadow him." LD i 3

"Woe to the suppliant, if such a one there were or ever had been, who had any concession to look for in the inexorable face at the cabinet. Woe to the defaulter whose appeal lay to the tribunal where those severe eyes presided. Great need had the rigid woman of her mystical religion, veiled in gloom and darkness, with lightnings of cursing, vengeance, and destruction, flashing through the sable clouds. Forgive us our debts as we forgive our debtors, was a prayer too poor in spirit for her. Smite thou my debtors, Lord, wither them, crush them; do Thou as I would do, and Thou shalt have my worship: this was the impious tower of stone she built up to scale Heaven." LD i 5

And see Christianity, *and* F:The Poor, Working—*religion, and —visited*

Religious observance

—in the country: "I was travelling in the west of England a summer or two back, and was induced by the beauty of the scenery, and the seclusion of the spot, to remain for the night in a small village, distant about seventy miles from London. The next morning was Sunday; and I walked out towards the church. Groups of people—the whole population of the little hamlet apparently—were hastening in the same direction. Cheerful and good-humoured congratulations were heard on all sides, as neighbours overtook each other, and walked on in company.

"Occasionally I passed an aged couple, whose married daughter and her husband were loitering by the side of the old people, accommodating their rate of walking to their feeble pace, while a little knot of children hurried on before; stout young labourers in clean round frocks; and buxom girls with healthy, laughing faces, were plentifully sprinkled about in couples, and the whole scene was one of quiet and tranquil contentment, irresistibly captivating.

"The morning was bright and pleasant, the hedges were green and blooming, and a thousand delicious scents were wafted on the air, from the wild flowers which blossomed on either side of the footpath. The little church was one of those venerable simple buildings which abound in the English counties; half overgrown with moss and ivy, and standing in the centre of a little plot of ground, which, but for the green mounds with which it was studded, might have passed for a lovely meadow.

"I fancied that the old clanking bell which was now summoning the congregation together, would seem less terrible when it rung out the knell of a departed soul, than I had ever deemed possible before—that the sound would tell only of a welcome to calmness and rest, amidst the most peaceful and tranquil scene in nature.

"I followed into the church—a low-roofed building with small arched windows, through which the sun's rays streamed upon a plain tablet on the opposite wall, which had once recorded names, now as undistinguishable on its worn surface, as were the bones beneath, from the dust into which they had resolved.

"The impressive service of the Church of England was spoken—not merely *read*—by a grey-headed minister, and the responses delivered by his auditors, with an air of sincere devotion as far removed from affectation or display, as from coldness or indifference. The psalms were accompanied by a few instrumental performers, who were stationed in a small gallery extending across the church at the lower end, over the door: and the voices were led by the clerk . . . .

"The discourse was plain, unpretending, and well adapted to the comprehension of the hearers. At the conclusion of the service, the villagers waited in the churchyard to salute the clergyman as he passed; and two or three, I observed, stepped aside, as if communicating some little difficulty, and asking his advice. This, to guess from the homely bows, and other rustic expressions of gratitude, the old gentleman readily conceded." ¶STH/3

—early Christianity: " . . . the islanders . . . quarrelled bitterly among themselves as to what prayers they ought to say, and how they ought to say them. The priests, being very angry with one another on these questions, cursed one another in the heartiest manner; and (uncommonly like the old Druids) cursed all the people whom they

could not persuade." CHE 2

—established church: "It was comfortably settled that there was to be only one form of religion, and that all men were to think exactly alike. But, although this was arranged two centuries and a half ago [in the time of James I], and although the arrangement was supported by much fining and imprisonment, I do not find that it is quite successful, even yet." CHE 32

—fashionable: "Here is a fashionable church, where the service commences at a late hour, for the accommodation of such members of the congregation—and they are not a few—as may happen to have lingered at the Opera far into the morning of the Sabbath; an excellent contrivance for poising the balance between God and Mammon, and illustrating the ease with which a man's duties to both may be accommodated and adjusted.

"How the carriages rattle up, and deposit their richly-dressed burdens beneath the lofty portico! The powdered footmen glide along the aisle, place the richly-bound prayer-books on the pew desks, slam the doors, and hurry away, leaving the fashionable members of the congregation to inspect each other through their glasses, and to dazzle and glitter in the eyes of the few shabby people in the free seats. The organ peals forth, the hired singers commence a short hymn, and the congregation condescendingly rise, stare about them, and converse in whispers.

"The clergyman enters the reading-desk. . . . Observe the graceful emphasis with which he offers up the prayers for the King, the Royal Family, and all the Nobility; and the nonchalance with which he hurries over the more uncomfortable portions of the service, the seventh commandment [adultery] for instance, with a studied regard for the taste and feeling of his auditors, only to be equalled by that displayed by the sleek divine who succeeds him . . . and then arrives at the anxiously expected 'Now to God,' which is the signal for the dismissal of the congregation.

"The organ is again heard; those who have been asleep wake up, and those who have kept awake, smile and seem greatly relieved; bows and congratulations are exchanged, the livery servants are all bustle and commotion, bang go the steps, up jump the footmen, and off rattle the carriages: the inmates discoursing on the dresses of the congregation, and congratulating themselves on having set so excellent an example to the community in general, and Sunday-pleasurers in particular." ¶STH/1

—high church: William Laud "looked upon vows, robes, lighted candles, images, and so forth, as amazingly important in religious ceremonies; and he brought in an immensity of bowing and candle-snuffing. He also regarded archbishops and bishops as a sort of miraculous persons, and was inveterate in the last degree against any who thought otherwise." CHE 33 i

—monk: "Dotted here and there [at St Peter's], were little knots of friars (Francescani, or Cappuccini, in their coarse brown dresses and peaked hoods) making a strange contrast to the gaudy ecclesiastics of higher degree, and having their humility gratified to the utmost, by being shouldered about, and elbowed right and left, on all sides. Some of these had muddy sandals and umbrellas, and stained garments: having trudged in from the country. The faces of the greater part were as coarse and heavy as their dress; their dogged, stupid, monotonous stare at all the glory and splendour, having something in it, half miserable, and half ridiculous." PI 11

—prayer: "[Jerry Cruncher] devoted himself during the remainder of the evening to keeping a most vigilant watch on Mrs Cruncher, and sullenly holding her in conversation that she might be prevented from meditating any petitions to his disadvantage. With this view, he urged his son to hold her in conversation also, and led the unfortunate woman a hard life by dwelling on any causes of complaint he could bring against her, rather than he would leave her for a moment to her own reflections. The devoutest person could have rendered no greater homage to the efficacy of an honest prayer than he did in this distrust of his wife. It was as if a professed unbeliever in ghosts should be frightened by a ghost story." TTC ii 14

—Roman Catholic practice in Italy

—burial: "Though such a custom [as the confraternity for burial] may be liable to the abuse attendant on many Italian customs, of being recognised as a means of establishing a current account with Heaven, on which to draw, too easily, for future bad actions, or as an expiation for past misdeeds, it must be admitted to be a good one, and a practical one, and one involving unquestionably

good works.

"A voluntary service like this, is surely better than the imposed penance (not at all an infrequent one) of giving so many licks to such and such a stone in the pavement of the cathedral; or than a vow to the Madonna to wear nothing but blue for a year or two. This is supposed to give great delight above; blue being (as is well known) the Madonna's favourite colour. Women who have devoted themselves to this act of Faith, are very commonly seen walking in the streets." PI 5

—churches generally: "The scene in all the churches is the strangest possible. The same monotonous, heartless, drowsy chaunting, always going on; the same dark building, darker from the brightness of the street without; the same lamps dimly burning; the self-same people kneeling here and there; turned towards you, from one altar or other, the same priest's back, with the same large cross embroidered on it; however different in size, in shape, in wealth, in architecture, this church is from that, it is the same thing still.

"There are the same dirty beggars stopping in their muttered prayers to beg; the same miserable cripples exhibiting their deformity at the doors; the same blind men, rattling little pots like kitchen pepper-castors: their depositories for alms; the same preposterous crowns of silver stuck upon the painted heads of single saints and Virgins in crowded pictures, so that a little figure on a mountain has a head-dress bigger than the temple in the foreground, or adjacent miles of landscape; the same favourite shrine or figure, smothered with little silver hearts and crosses, and the like: the staple trade and show of all the jewellers; the same odd mixture of respect and indecorum, faith and phlegm: kneeling on the stones, and spitting on them, loudly; getting up from prayers to beg a little, or to pursue some other worldly matter: and then kneeling down again, to resume the contrite supplication at the point where it was interrupted . . . .

"Above all, there is always a receptacle for the contributions of the Faithful, in some form or other. Sometimes, it is a money-box, set up between the worshipper, and the wooden life-size figure of the redeemer; sometimes, it is a little chest for the maintenance of the Virgin; sometimes, an appeal on behalf of a popular Bambino; sometimes, a bag at the end of a long stick, thrust among the people here and there, and vigilantly jingled by an active Sacristan; but there it always is, and, very often, in many shapes in the same church, and doing pretty well in all." ¶PI 11

—compared with the railroad: " . . . the railroad between Leghorn and Pisa, which is a good one, and has already begun to astonish Italy with a precedent of punctuality, order, plain dealing, and improvement—the most dangerous and heretical astonisher of all. There must have been a slight sensation, as of earthquake, surely, in the Vatican, when the first Italian railroad was thrown open." PI 10

—the miraculous: "The cathedral [at Naples] . . . contains the famous sacred blood of San Gennaro or Januarius: which is preserved in two phials in a silver tabernacle, and miraculously liquefies three times a-year, to the great admiration of the people. At the same moment, the stone (distant some miles) where the Saint suffered martyrdom, becomes faintly red. It is said that the officiating priests turn faintly red also, sometimes, when these miracles occur." PI 13

—the Scala Sancta: "I never, in my life, saw anything at once so ridiculous, and so unpleasant, as this sight—ridiculous in the absurd incidents inseparable from it; and unpleasant in its senseless and unmeaning degradation.

"There are two steps to begin with, and then a rather broad landing. The more rigid climbers went along this landing on their knees, as well as up the stairs; and the figures they cut, in their shuffling progress over the level surface, no description can paint.

"Then, to see them watch their opportunity from the porch, and cut in where there was a place next the wall! And to see one man with an umbrella (brought on purpose, for it was a fine day) hoisting himself, unlawfully, from stair to stair! And to observe a demure lady of fifty-five or so, looking back, every now and then, to assure herself that her legs were properly disposed!

"There were such odd differences in the speed of different people, too. Some got on as if they were doing a match against time; others stopped to say a prayer on every step. This man touched every stair with his forehead, and kissed it; that man scratched his head all the way.

"The boys got on brilliantly, and were up

and down again before the old lady had accomplished her half-dozen stairs. But most of the penitents came down, very sprightly and fresh, as having done a real good substantial deed which it would take a good deal of sin to counterbalance; and the old gentleman in the watch-box was down upon them with his canister while they were in this humour, I promise you.

"As if such a progress were not in its nature inevitably droll enough, there lay, on the top of the stairs, a wooden figure on a crucifix, resting on a sort of great iron saucer: so rickety and unsteady, that whenever an enthusiastic person kissed the figure, with more than usual devotion, or threw a coin into the saucer, with more than common readiness (for it served in this respect as a second or supplementary canister), it gave a great leap and rattle, and nearly shook the attendant lamp out; horribly frightening the people further down, and throwing the guilty party into unspeakable embarrassment." ¶PI 11

—at St Peter's: "At last [the candles] were all blessed; and then they were all lighted; and then the Pope was taken up, chair and all, and carried round the church.

"I must say, that I never saw anything, out of November, so like the popular English commemoration of the fifth of that month [Guy Fawkes' Day]. A bundle of matches and a lantern, would have made it perfect. Nor did the Pope, himself, at all mar the resemblance, though he has a pleasant and venerable face; for as this part of the ceremony makes him giddy and sick, he shuts his eyes when it is performed: and having his eyes shut and a great mitre on his head, and his head itself wagging to and fro as they shook him in carrying, he looked as if his mask were going to tumble off.

"The two immense fans which are always borne, one on either side of him, accompanied him, of course, on this occasion. As they carried him along, he blessed the people with the mystic sign; and as he passed them, they kneeled down. When he had made the round of the church, he was brought back again, and if I am not mistaken, this performance was repeated, in the whole, three times.

"There was, certainly, nothing solemn or effective in it; and certainly very much that was droll and tawdry. But this remark applies to the whole ceremony, except the raising of the Host, when every man in the guard dropped on one knee instantly, and dashed his naked sword on the ground; which had a fine effect.

"The next time I saw the cathedral, was some two or three weeks afterwards, when I climbed up into the ball; and then, the hangings being taken down, and the carpet taken up, but all the framework left, the remnants of these decorations looked like an exploded cracker." ¶PI 11

—tomb of a saint: "The subterranean chapel in which the body of San Carlo Borromeo is preserved, presents as striking and as ghastly a contrast, perhaps, as any place can show. The tapers which are lighted down there, flash and gleam on alti-rilievi in gold and silver, delicately wrought by skilful hands, and representing the principal events in the life of the saint. Jewels, and precious metals, shine and sparkle on every side.

"A windlass slowly removes the front of the altar; and, within it, in a gorgeous shrine of gold and silver, is seen, through alabaster, the shrivelled mummy of a man: the pontifical robes with which it is adorned, radiant with diamonds, emeralds, rubies: every costly and magnificent gem. The shrunken heap of poor earth in the midst of this great glitter, is more pitiful than if it lay upon a dunghill. There is not a ray of imprisoned light in all the flash and fire of jewels, but seems to mock the dusty holes where eyes were, once. Every thread of silk in the rich vestments seems only a provision from the worms that spin, for the behoof of worms that propagate in sepulchres." ¶PI 9

—the Sabbath

—enforced in London: "'Spirit,' said Scrooge, after a moment's thought, 'I wonder you, of all the beings in the many worlds about us, should desire to cramp these people's opportunities of innocent enjoyment.'

"'I!' cried the Spirit.

"'You would deprive them of their means of dining every seventh day, often the only day on which they can be said to dine at all,' said Scrooge. 'Wouldn't you?'

"'I!' cried the Spirit.

"'You seek to close these places on the Seventh Day?' said Scrooge. 'And it comes to the same thing.

"'*I* seek!' exclaimed the Spirit.

"'Forgive me if I am wrong. It has been

done in your name, or at least in that of your family,' said Scrooge.

"'There are some upon this earth of yours,' returned the Spirit, 'who lay claim to know us, and who do their deeds of passion, pride, ill-will, hatred, envy, bigotry, and selfishness in our name, who are as strange to us and all our kith and kin, as if they had never lived. Remember that, and charge their doings on themselves, not us.'" CC 3

—joyless: "There was the interminable Sunday of [Arthur Clennam's] nonage; when his mother, stern of face and unrelenting of heart, would sit all day behind a bible—bound, like her own construction of it, in the hardest, barest, and straitest boards, with one dinted ornament on the cover like the drag of a chain, and a wrathful sprinkling of red upon the edge of the leaves—as if it, of all books! were a fortification against sweetness of temper, natural affection, and gentle intercourse.

"There was the resentful Sunday of a little later, when he sat glowering and glooming through the tardy length of the day, with a sullen sense of injury in his heart, and no more real knowledge of the beneficent history of the New Testament, than if he had been bred among idolaters. There was a legion of Sundays, all days of unserviceable bitterness and mortification, slowly passing before him." ¶LD i

—of workers: "The wise and beneficent Creator who places men upon earth, requires that they shall perform the duties of that station of life to which they are called, and He can never intend that the more a man strives to discharge those duties, the more he shall be debarred from happiness and enjoyment.

"Let those who have six days in the week for all the world's pleasures, appropriate the seventh to fasting and gloom, either for their own sins or those of other people, if they like to bewail them; but let those who employ their six days in a worthier manner, devote their seventh to a different purpose.

"Let divines set the example of true morality: preach it to their flocks in the morning, and dismiss them to enjoy true rest in the afternoon; and let them select for their text, and let Sunday legislators take for their motto, the words which fell from the lips of that Master, whose precepts they misconstrue, and whose lessons they pervert—'The Sabbath was made for man, and not man to serve the Sabbath.'" ¶STH/3

And see IG:Government—*Sunday-observance*

—service ends: " . . . we receive the signal to make that unanimous dive which surely is a little conventional—like the strange rustlings and settlings and clearings of throats and noses, which are never dispensed with, at certain points of the Church service, and are never held to be necessary under any other circumstances. In a minute more it is all over, and the organ expresses itself to be as glad of it as it can be of anything in its rheumatic state . . . . " UT/LC

Self-confidence

"Gentlemen of the free-and-easy sort, who plume themselves on being acquainted with a move or two, and being usually equal to the time-of-day, express the wide range of their capacity for adventure by observing that they are good for anything from pitch-and-toss to manslaughter; between which opposite extremes, no doubt, there lies a tolerably wide and comprehensive range of subjects. Without venturing for Scrooge quite as hardily as this, I don't mind calling on you to believe that he was ready for a good broad field of strange appearances, and that nothing between a baby and [a] rhinoceros would have astonished him very much." CC 3

Self-consciousness

"Serjeant Buzfuz and Mr Skimpin for the plaintiff,' said the judge [Stareleigh], writing down the names in his note-book, and reading as he wrote; 'for the defendant, Serjeant Snubbin and Mr Monkey.'

"'Beg your Lordship's pardon, Phunky.'

"'Oh, very good,' said the judge; 'I never had the pleasure of hearing the gentleman's name before.' Here Mr Phunky bowed and smiled, and the judge bowed and smiled too, and then Mr Phunky, blushing into the very whites of his eyes, tried to look as if he didn't know that everybody was gazing at him: a thing which no man ever succeeded in doing yet, or in all reasonable probability, ever will." PP 34

Self-deception

" . . . Miss [Fanny] Squeers, looking in her own little glass, where, like most of us, she saw—not herself, but the reflection of some pleasant image in her own brain." NN 12 *And see* Spitefulness—*soothed*

" . . . persuading himself that he was a most conscientious and glorious martyr, [Nicholas] nobly resolved to do what, if he had examined his own heart a little more carefully, he would have found he could not resist. Such is the sleight of hand by which we juggle with ourselves, and change our very weaknesses into most magnanimous virtues!" NN 46

"'I am in the twenty-third year of my life here,' [William Dorrit] said, with a catch in his breath that was not so much a sob as an irrepressible sound of self-approval, the momentary outburst of a noble consciousness. 'It is all I could do for my children—I have done it. Amy, my love, you are by far the best loved of the three; I have had you principally in my mind—whatever I have done for your sake, my dear child, I have done freely and without murmuring.'

"Only the wisdom that holds the clue to all hearts and all mysteries, can surely know to what extent a man, especially a man brought down as this man had been, can impose upon himself. Enough, for the present place, that he lay down with wet eyelashes, serene, in a manner majestic, after bestowing his life of degradation as a sort of portion on the devoted child upon whom its miseries had fallen so heavily, and whose love alone had saved him to be even what he was." LD i 19

"All the swindlers upon earth are nothing to the self-swindlers, and with such pretences did I [Pip] cheat myself. Surely a curious thing. That I should innocently take a bad half-crown of somebody else's manufacture, is reasonable enough; but that I should knowingly reckon the spurious coin of my own make, as good money! An obliging stranger, under pretence of compactly folding up my bank-notes for security's sake, abstracts the notes and gives me nutshells; but what is his sleight of hand to mine, when I fold up my own nutshells and pass them on myself as notes!" GE 28

"See into what wonderful maudlin refuges featherless ostriches plunge their heads! It is such unspeakable moral compensation to Wegg to be overcome by the consideration that Mr Rokesmith has an underhanded mind!" OMF ii 7

And see F:Condescension—*patronising*

Self-dread

"[Florence] dared not look into the glass; for the sight of the darkening mark upon her bosom [where her father had struck her] made her afraid of herself, as if she bore about her something wicked. She covered it up, with a hasty, faltering hand, and in the dark; and laid her weary head down, weeping." DS 49

"Suddenly I came upon a pasteboard placard, beautifully written, which was lying on the desk, and bore these words:'*Take care of him. He bites*' . . . .

"What I suffered from that placard nobody can imagine. Whether it was possible for people to see me or not, I always fancied that somebody was reading it . . . wherever my back was, there I imagined somebody always to be . . . everybody, in a word, who came backwards and forwards to the house, of a morning when I was ordered to walk there, read that I was to be taken care of, for I bit. I recollect that I positively began to have a dread of myself, as a kind of wild boy who did bite." DC 5

" . . . I was passing quickly on [writes Esther Summerson], and in a few moments should have passed the lighted window, when my echoing footsteps brought it suddenly into my mind that there was a dreadful truth in the legend of the Ghost's Walk; that it was I, who was to bring calamity upon the stately house; and that my warning feet were haunting it even then. Seized with an augmented terror of myself which turned me cold, I ran from myself and everything, retraced the way by which I had come, and never paused until I had gained the lodge-gate, and the park lay sullen and black behind me." BH 36

And see F:Murderer—*self-dread*

Self-importance

—*buttoned-up:* "Mr Tite Barnacle was a buttoned-up man, and consequently a weighty one. All buttoned-up men are weighty. All buttoned-up men are believed in. Whether or no the reserved and never-exercised power of unbuttoning, fascinates mankind; whether or no wisdom is supposed to condense and augment when buttoned up, and to evaporate when unbuttoned; it is certain that the man to whom importance is accorded is the buttoned-up man. Mr Tite Barnacle never would have passed for half his current value, unless his coat had been always buttoned up to his white cravat." LD ii 12

—*city squire:* "Mr Podsnap was well to do, and stood very high in Mr Podsnap's opinion. Beginning with a good inheritance, he had married a good inheritance, and had thriven exceedingly in the Marine Insurance way, and was quite satisfied. He never could make out why everybody was not quite satisfied, and he felt conscious that he set a brilliant social example in being particularly well satisfied with most things, and, above all other things, with himself....

"As a so eminently respectable man, Mr Podsnap was sensible of its being required of him to take Providence under his protection. Consequently he always knew exactly what Providence meant. Inferior and less respectable men might fall short of that mark, but Mr Podsnap was always up to it. And it was very remarkable (and must have been very comfortable) that what Providence meant was invariably what Mr Podsnap meant." OMF i 11

"That they, when unable to lay hold of him, should respectfully grasp at the hem of his mantle; that they, when they could not bask in the glory of him, the sun, should take up with the pale reflected light of the watery young moon, his daughter, appeared quite natural, becoming, and proper. It gave him a better opinion of the discretion of the Lammles than he had heretofore held, as showing that they appreciated the value of the connection. So, Georgiana repairing to her friend, Mr Podsnap went out to dinner, and to dinner, and yet to dinner, arm in arm with Mrs Podsnap; settling his obstinate head in his cravat and shirt-collar, much as if he were performing on the Pandean pipes, in his own honour, the triumphal march, See the conquering Podsnap comes, Sound the trumpets, beat the drums!*" OMF ii 4

**Thomas Morell's libretto for Handel's oratorios* Judas Maccabeus *and* Joshua.

—country squire: " . . . this gentleman [Squire Kennet] had various endearing appellations among his intimate friends. By some he was called 'a country gentleman of the true school,' by some 'a fine old country gentleman,' by some 'a sporting gentleman,' by some 'a thorough-bred Englishman,' by some 'a genuine John Bull;' but they all agreed in one respect, and that was, that it was a pity there were not more like him, and that because there were not, the country was going to rack and ruin every day.

"He was in the commission of the peace, and could write his name almost legibly; but his greatest qualifications were, that he was more severe with poachers, was a better shot, a harder rider, had better horses, kept better dogs, could eat more solid food, drink more strong wine, go to bed every night more drunk and get up every morning more sober, than any man in the county. In knowledge of horseflesh he was almost equal to a farrier, in stable learning he surpassed his own head groom, and in gluttony not a pig on his estate was a match for him.

"He had no seat in Parliament himself, but he was extremely patriotic, and usually drove his voters up to the poll with his own hands. He was warmly attached to church and state, and never appointed to the living in his gift any but a three-bottle man and a first-rate fox-hunter. He mistrusted the honesty of all poor people who could read and write, and had a secret jealousy of his own wife (a young lady whom he had married for what his friends called 'the good old English reason,' that her father's property adjoined his own) for possessing those accomplishments in a greater degree than himself. In short, Barnaby being an idiot, and Grip a creature of mere brute instinct, it would be very hard to say what this gentleman was." ¶BR 47

—egotism: "In all these ceremonies the noble savage holds forth to the utmost possible extent about himself; from which (to turn him to some civilised account) we may learn, I think, that as egotism is one of the most offensive and contemptible littlenesses a civilised man can exhibit, so it is really incompatible with the interchange of ideas; inasmuch as if we all talked about ourselves we should soon have no listeners, and must be all yelling and screeching at once on our own separate accounts: making society hideous." RP/NS

And see Pride, *passim.*

Self-pity

"'I know what I am. I know that I am a lone lorn creetur', and not only that everythink goes contrairy with me, but that I go contrairy with everybody. Yes, yes, I feel more than other people do, and I show it more. It's my misfortun'.'

"I really couldn't help thinking. . . that the misfortune extended to some other members of that family besides Mrs Gummidge. But Mr Peggotty made no such retort, only answering with another entreaty to Mrs Gummidge to cheer up.

"'I an't what I could wish myself to be,' said Mrs Gummidge. 'I am far from it. I know what I am. My troubles has made me contrairy. I feel my troubles, and they make me contrairy. I wish I didn't feel 'em, but I do. I wish I could be hardened to 'em, but I an't. I make the house uncomfortable. I don't wonder at it. I've made your sister so all day, and Master Davy.'

"Here I was suddenly melted, and roared out, 'No, you haven't, Mrs Gummidge,' in great mental distress.

"'It's far from right that I should do it,' said Mrs Gummidge. 'It an't a fit return. I had better go into the house and die. I am a lone lorn creetur', and had much better not make myself contrairy here. If thinks must go contrairy with me, and I must go contrairy myself, let me go contrairy in my parish. Dan'l, I'd better go into the house, and die and be a riddance!'

"Mrs Gummidge retired with these words, and betook herself to bed." DC 3

Self-reliance

"'Johnny, my pretty,' continued old Betty [Higden], caressing the child, and rather mourning over it than speaking to it, 'your old Granny Betty is nigher fourscore year than threescore and ten. She never begged nor had a penny of the Union money in all her life. She paid scot and she paid lot when she had money to pay; she worked when she could, and she starved when she must. You pray that your Granny may have strength enough left her at the last (she's strong for an old one, Johnny), to get up from her bed and run and hide herself, and swown to death in a hole, sooner than fall into the hands of those Cruel Jacks we read of, that dodge and drive, and worry and weary, and scorn and shame, the decent poor.'

"A brilliant success, my Lords and Gentlemen and Honourable Boards, to have brought it to this in the minds of the best of the poor! Under submission might it be worth thinking of, at any odd time?

"The fright and abhorrence that Mrs Betty Higden smoothed out of her strong face as she ended this diversion, showed how seriously she had meant it." OMF i 16

"The morning found her afoot again, but fast declining as to the clearness of her thoughts, though not as to the steadiness of her purpose. Comprehending that her strength was quitting her, and that the struggle of her life was almost ended, she could neither reason out the means of getting back to her protectors, nor even form the idea. The overmastering dread, and the proud stubborn resolution it engendered in her to die undegraded, were the two distinct impressions left in her failing mind. Supported only by a sense that she was bent on conquering in her life-long fight, she went on.

"The time was come, now, when the wants of this little life were passing away from her. She could not have swallowed food, though a table had been spread for her in the next field. The day was cold and wet, but she scarcely knew it. She crept on, poor soul, like a criminal afraid of being taken, and felt little beyond the terror of falling down while it was yet daylight, and being found alive. She had no fear that she would live through another night.

"Sewn in the breast of her gown, the money to pay for her burial was still intact. If she could wear through the day, and then lie down to die under cover of darkness, she would die independent. If she were captured previously, the money would be taken from her as a pauper who had no right to it, and she would be carried to the accursed workhouse." OMF iii 8

"'As you must grow old in time, and come to your dying hour, my dear, you'll not give [the letter and money] up to any one but them?'

"'No. Most solemnly.'

"'Never to the Parish?' with a convulsed struggle.

"'No. Most solemnly.'

"'Nor let the Parish touch me, nor yet so much as look at me?' with another struggle.

"'No. Faithfully.'

"A look of thankfulness and triumph lights the worn old face. The eyes, which have been darkly fixed upon the sky, turn with meaning in them towards the compassionate face from which the tears are dropping, and a smile is on the aged lips as they ask:

"'What is your name, my dear?'

"'My name is Lizzie Hexam.'

"'I must be sore disfigured. Are you afraid to kiss me?'

"The answer is the ready pressure of her lips upon the cold but smiling mouth.

"'Bless ye! *Now* lift me, my love.'

"Lizzie Hexam very softly raised the weather-stained grey head, and lifted her as high as Heaven." OMF iii 8

See also F:Poor-House and Poor Law

Self-respect

—modesty: "I [David Copperfield] laboured hard at my book, without allowing it to interfere with the punctual discharge of my newspaper duties; and it came out and was very successful. I was not stunned by the praise which sounded in my ears, notwithstanding that I was keenly alive to it, and thought better of my own performance, I have little doubt, than anybody else did.

"It has always been my observation of human nature, that a man who has any good reason to believe in himself never flourishes himself before the faces of other people in order that they may believe in him. For this reason, I retained my modesty in very self-respect; and the more praise I got, the more I tried to deserve." DC 48

—risk in its absence: "Oh, moralists, who treat of happiness and self-respect, innate in every sphere of life, and shedding light on every grain of dust in God's highway, so smooth below your carriage-wheels, so rough beneath the tread of naked feet, bethink yourselves, in looking on the swift descent of men who *have* lived in their own esteem, that there are scores of thousands breathing now, and breathing thick with painful toil, who in that high respect have never lived at all, nor had a chance of life! Go ye, who rest so placidly upon the sacred Bard* who had been young, and when he strung his harp was old, and had never seen the righteous forsaken, or his seed begging their bread; go, Teachers of content and honest pride, into the mine, the mill, the forge, the squalid depths of deepest ignorance, and uttermost abyss of man's neglect, and say can any hopeful plant spring up in air so foul that it extinguishes the soul's bright torch as fast as it is kindled! And, oh! ye Pharisees of the nineteen hundredth year of Christian Knowledge, who soundingly appeal to human nature, see first that it be human. Take heed it has not been transformed, during your slumber and the sleep of generations, into the nature of the Beasts." MC 13 *And see* Pride—*a fall*

**King David: Psalms 37:25*

Self-transformation

"'I have turned from the world [said Geoffrey Haredale], and I pay the penalty. . . . It is too late to evade it now. I sometimes think, that if I had to live my life once more, I might amend this fault—not so much, I discover when I search my mind, for the love of what is right, as for my own sake. But even when I make these better resolutions, I instinctively recoil from the idea of suffering again what I have undergone; and in this circumstance I find the unwelcome assurance that I should still be the same man, though I could cancel the past, and begin anew, with its experience to guide me.'" BR 79

Selfishness

—analyzed: "In every single circumstance, whether it were cruel, cowardly, or false, [Martin Chuzzlewit, the elder] saw the flowering of the same pregnant seed. Self; grasping, eager, narrow-ranging, over-reaching self; with its long train of suspicions, lusts, deceits, and all their growing consequences; was the root of the vile tree . . . ." MC 52

"'There is a kind of selfishness,' said Martin [Chuzzlewit,the elder] 'I have learned it in my experience of my own breast: which is constantly upon the watch for selfishness in others; and holding others at a distance by suspicions and distrusts, wonders why they don't approach, and don't confide, and calls that selfishness in them. Thus I once doubted those about me—not without reason in the beginning—and thus I once doubted you, Martin.'" MC 52

—basis of better things: "Some philosophers tell us that selfishness is at the root of our best loves and affections. Mr Dombey's young child was, from the beginning, so distinctly important to him as a part of his own greatness, or (which is the same thing) of the greatness of Dombey and Son, that there is no doubt his parental affection might have been easily traced, like many a goodly superstructure of fair fame, to a very low foundation. But he loved his son with all the love he had. If there were a warm place in his frosty heart, his son occupied it; if its very hard surface could receive the impression of any image, the image of that son was there; though not so much as an infant, or as a boy, but as a grown man—the 'Son' of the Firm." DS 8

—blind: "'I am going on, Mr Headstone, don't you be afraid [said Charley Hexam]. I am going on to the end, and I have told you beforehand what the end is. Now you know my story. You are as well aware as I am that I have had many disadvantages to leave behind me in life. You have heard me mention my father, and you are sufficiently

acquainted with the fact that the home from which I, as I may say, escaped, might have been a more creditable one than it was. My father died, and then it might have been supposed that my way to respectability was pretty clear. No. For then my sister [Lizzie] begins.'

"He spoke as confidently, and with as entire an absence of any tell-tale colour in his cheek, as if there were no softening old time behind him. Not wonderful, for there *was* none in his hollow empty heart. What is there but self, for selfishness to see behind it?

"'When I speak of my sister, I devoutly wish that you had never seen her, Mr Headstone. However, you did see her, and that's useless now. I confided in you about her. I explained her character to you, and how she interposed some ridiculous fanciful notions in the way of our being as respectable as I tried for. You fell in love with her, and I favoured you with all my might. She could not be induced to favour you, and so we came into collision with this Mr Eugene Wrayburn.

"'Now, what have you done? Why, you have justified my sister in being firmly set against you from first to last, and you have put me in the wrong again! and why have you done it? Because, Mr Headstone, you are in all your passions so selfish, and so concentrated upon yourself, that you have not bestowed one proper thought on me.'

"The cool conviction with which the boy took up and held his position could have been derived from no other vice in human nature.

"'It is,' he went on, actually with tears, 'an extraordinary circumstance attendant on my life, that every effort I make towards perfect respectability is impeded by somebody else through no fault of mine! Not content with doing what I have put before you, you will drag my name into notoriety through dragging my sister's—which you are pretty sure to do, if my suspicions have any foundation at all—and the worse you prove to be, the harder it will be for me to detach myself from being associated with you in people's minds.'

"While he had dried his eyes and heaved a sob over his injuries, he began moving towards the door.

"'However, I have made up my mind that I will become respectable in the scale of society, and that I will not be dragged down by others. I have done with my sister as well as with you. Since she cares so little for me as to care nothing for undermining my respectability, she shall go her way and I will go mine. My prospects are very good, and I mean to follow them alone." ¶OMF iv 7

—in the high-spirited: " . . . Nicholas [Nickleby] was not, in the ordinary sense of the word, a young man of high spirit. He would resent an affront to himself, or interpose to redress a wrong offered to another, as boldly and freely as any knight that ever set lance in rest; but he lacked that peculiar excess of coolness and great-minded selfishness, which invariably distinguished gentlemen of high spirit. In truth, for our own part, we are disposed to look upon such gentlemen as being rather incumbrances than otherwise in rising families: happening to be acquainted with several whose spirit prevents their settling down to any grovelling occupation, and only displays itself in a tendency to cultivate mustachios, and look fierce; and although mustachios and ferocity are both very pretty things in their way, and very much to be commended, we confess to a desire to see them bred at the owner's proper cost, rather than at the expense of low-spirited people." NN 16

—in the highly strung: " . . . when your finely strung people are out of sorts they must have everybody else unhappy likewise . . . . " OCS 14

—personified: "[Mr Turveydrop] had married a meek little dancing-mistress, with a tolerable connexion (having never in his life before done anything but deport himself), and had worked her to death, or had, at the best, suffered her to work herself to death, to maintain him in those expenses which were indispensable to his position.

"At once to exhibit his Deportment to the best models, and to keep the best models constantly before himself, he had found it necessary to frequent all public places of fashionable and lounging resort; to be seen at Brighton and elsewhere at fashionable times; and to lead an idle life in the very best clothes. To enable him to do this, the affectionate little dancing-mistress had toiled and laboured, and would have toiled and laboured to that hour, if her strength had lasted so long.

"For the mainspring of the story was that, in spite of the man's absorbing selfishness, his wife (overpowered by his Deportment) had, to the last, believed in him, and had, on her death-bed, in the most moving terms, confided him to their son as one who had an inextinguishable claim upon him, and whom he could never regard with too much pride and deference. The son, inheriting his mother's belief, and having the Deportment always before him, had lived and grown in the same faith, and now, at thirty years of age, worked for his father twelve hours a-day, and looked up to him with veneration on the old imaginary pinnacle." BH ¶14

—rationalized: "Martin [Chuzzlewit, the younger]'s nature was a frank and generous one; but he had been bred up in his grandfather's house; and it will usually be found that the meaner domestic vices propagate themselves to be their own antagonists. Selfishness does this especially; so do suspicion, cunning, stealth, and covetous propensities. Martin had unconsciously reasoned as a child, 'My guardian takes so much thought of himself, that unless I do the like by *myself*, I shall be forgotten.' So he had grown selfish." MC 33

Sensitivity

—dulled: "I left the last of [Richmond slaves] behind me in the person of a wretched drudge, who, after running to and fro all day till midnight, and moping in his stealthy winks of sleep upon the stairs betweenwhiles, was washing the dark passages at four o'clock in the morning; and went upon my way with a grateful heart that I was not doomed to live where slavery was, and had never had my senses blunted to its wrongs and horrors in a slave-rocked cradle." AN 9

—of a murderer: "This was the young, smooth-faced farmer [**Thomas Drory**], the selfish and illiterate fiend of the fields, who displayed no remorse for his crime, and made no confession until all chance of escape was gone, even out of his dazed mind, and the day for his execution fixed. This was he, who, when the cord was about to be passed round his own throat, advanced with drooping head, a ghastly paleness, closed eyes, quivering in every limb and every joint, and ejaculating in broken accents, 'This is a faithful saying, and *worthy of all acceptation,* that Jesus Christ came into the world to save sinners—of whom *I* am the chief, of whom *I* am the chief!'

"It was, probably, worthy of acceptation, in the mind of this most selfish and cruel beast, because the person to be saved was himself; nay, we may conjecture that there was within him a vague, blasphemous notion, that Our Saviour came into the world, solely for the purpose of saving such wretches as he—and, as he was the chief of wretches, then chiefly for his especial salvation. . . . The life of another was nothing when it stood in the way of his least personal interest or inconvenience. If he must suffer death for taking care of himself, then he considers that, in proportion to the greatness of his assumed offence, so great is his claim to the benefits derivable from the death of the Saviour. And, at the last, he no more cares for, or thinks of, the death of his victim, or the mediation that shall be made for *her,* than he thought of her love or of her agony, when he twisted the neck that bent itself to his pretended embrace." ¶HWC/CF

—to nature: "A soft air stirred the leaves of the fresh green trees, and passed like a smooth shadow over the river, and like a smoother shadow over the yielding grass. The voice of the falling water, like the voices of the sea and the wind, was an outer memory to a contemplative listener; but not particularly so to Mr Riderhood, who sat on one of the blunt wooden levers of his lock-gates, dozing. Wine must be got into a butt by some agency before it can be drawn out: and the wine of sentiment never having been got into Mr Riderhood by any agency, nothing in nature tapped him." OMF iv 1

Sincerity

—absence bemoaned: "'What I want,' drawled Mrs Skewton, pinching her shrivelled throat, 'is heart.' It was frightfully true in one sense, if not in that in which she used the phrase. 'What I want, is frankness, confidence, less conventionality, and freer play of soul. We are so dreadfully artificial.'" DS 21

"Why are we not more natural! Dear me! With all those yearnings, and gushings, and impulsive throbbings that we have implanted in our souls, and which are so very charming, why are we not more natural?'

"Mr Dombey said it was very true, very true.

"'We could be more natural, I suppose, if we tried?' said Mrs Skewton.

"Mr Dombey thought it possible.

"'Devil a bit, Ma'am,' said the Major. 'We couldn't afford it. Unless the world was peopled with J.B.'s—tough and blunt old Joes, Ma'am, plain red herrings with hard noses, Sir—we couldn't afford it. It wouldn't do.'" DS 21

—*earnestness* "All were very earnest over this; and earnestness in men, when they are right and true, is so impressive, that Mr Pettifer deserted his cookery and looked on quite moved." CS/MS *And see* M:Invention—*earnest*

—*exemplified:* "Miss Tox's sympathy is such that she can scarcely speak. She is no chicken, but she has not grown tough with age and celibacy. Her heart is very tender, her compassion very genuine, her homage very real. Beneath the locket with the fishy-eye in it, Miss Tox bears better qualities than many a less whimsical outside; such qualities as will outlive, by many courses of the sun, the best outsides and brightest husks that fall in the harvest of the great reaper." DS 59

—*missing:* "'Let us be sincere [said John Chester], my dear madam—'

"'—and Protestant,' murmured Mrs Varden.

"'—and Protestant above all things. Let us be sincere and Protestant, strictly moral, strictly just (though always with a leaning towards mercy), strictly honest, and strictly true, and we gain—it is a slight point, certainly, but still it is something tangible; we throw up a groundwork and foundation, so to speak, of goodness, on which we may afterwards erect some worthy superstructure.'

"Now, to be sure, Mrs Varden thought, here is a perfect character. Here is a meek, righteous, thoroughgoing Christian, who, having mustered all these qualities so difficulty of attainment; who, having dropped a pinch of salt on the tails of all the cardinal virtues, and caught them every one; makes light of their possession, and pants for more morality. For the good woman never doubted (as many good men and women never do), that this slighting kind of profession, this setting so little store by great matters, this seeming to say 'I am not proud, I am what you hear, but I consider myself no better than other people; let us change the subject, pray'—was perfectly genuine and true. He so contrived it, and said it in that way that it appeared to have been forced from him, and its effect was marvellous." BR 27

Soul-murder

—*of a little boy:* "A worldly little devil was mother's usual name for me. Whether I cried for that I was in the dark, or for that it was cold, or for that I was hungry, or whether I squeezed myself into a warm corner when there was a fire, or ate voraciously when there was food, she would still say, 'O you worldly little devil!' And the sting of it was, that I quite well knew myself to be a worldly little devil. Worldly as to wanting to be housed and warmed, worldly as to wanting to be fed, worldly as to the greed with which I inwardly compared how much I got of those good things with how much father and mother got, when, rarely, those good things were going.

"Sometimes they both went away seeking work; and then I would be locked up in the cellar for a day or two at a time. I was at my worldliest then. Left alone, I yielded myself up to a worldly yearning for enough of anything (except misery). . . . Worldly little devil, I would stand about, musingly fitting my cold bare feet into cracked bricks and crevices of the damp cellar-floor . . . . " GSE 3

—*of a little girl:* "I happened to look timidly up from my stitching, across the table, at my godmother, and I saw in her face, looking gloomily at me, 'It would have been far better, little Esther, that you had had no birthday; that you had never been born!'

"I broke out crying and sobbing, and I said 'O, dear godmother, tell me, pray do tell me, did mama die on my birthday?'

"'No,' she returned. 'Ask me no more, child!'

"'O, do pray tell me something of her. Do now, at last, dear godmother, if you please! What did I do to her? How did I lose her? Why am I so different from other children, and why is it my fault, dear godmother? No, no, no, don't go away. O, speak to me!'

"I was in a kind of fright beyond my grief; and I caught hold of her dress, and was kneeling to her. She had been saying all the while, 'Let me go!' But now she stood still.

"Her darkened face had such power over me, that it stopped me in the midst of my vehemence. I put up my trembling little hand to clasp hers, or to beg her pardon with what earnestness I might, but withdrew it as she looked at me, and laid it on my fluttering heart. She raised me, sat in her chair, and standing me before her, said slowly, in a cold, low voice—I see her knitted brow, and pointed finger:

"'Your mother, Esther, is your disgrace, and you were hers. The time will come—and soon enough—when you will understand this better, and will feel it too, as no one save a woman can. I have forgiven her;' but her face did not relent; 'the wrong she did to me, and I say no more of it, though it was greater than you will ever know—than any one will ever know, but I, the sufferer. For yourself, unfortunate girl, orphaned and degraded from the first of these evil anniversaries, pray daily that the sins of others be not visited upon your head, according to what is written. Forget your mother, and leave all other people to forget her who will do her unhappy child that greatest kindness. Now, go!'

"She checked me, however, as I was about to depart from her—so frozen as I was!—and added this:

"'Submission, self-denial, diligent work, are the preparations for a life begun with such a shadow on it. You are different from other children, Esther, because you were not born, like them, in common sinfulness and wrath. You are set apart.'

"I went up to my room, and crept to bed, and laid my doll's cheek against mine wet with tears; and holding that solitary friend upon my bosom, cried myself to sleep. Imperfect as my understanding of my sorrow was, I knew that I had brought no joy, at any time, to anybody's heart, and that I was to no one upon earth what Dolly was to me." BH 3

" . . . I fell asleep . . . and dreamed of the days when I lived in my godmother's house. I am not sufficiently acquainted with such subjects to know whether it is at all remarkable that I almost always dreamed of that period of my life." BH 9

—of the mind: "To prepare the mind for such a heavy sleep, its growth must be stopped by rigor and cruelty in childhood; there must be years of misery and suffering, lightened by no ray of hope; the chords of the heart, which beat a quick response to the voice of gentleness and affection, must have rusted and broken in their secret places, and bear the lingering echo of no old word of love or kindness. Gloomy, indeed, must have been the short day, and dull the long, long twilight, preceding such a night of intellect as [Smike's]." NN 38

Spiritualism

—sects in France: "The leprosy of unreality disfigured every human creature in attendance upon Monseigneur [the pre-Revolution aristocracy]. In the outermost room were half a dozen exceptional people who had had, for a few years, some vague misgiving in them that things in general were going rather wrong. As a promising way of setting them right, half of the half-dozen had become members of a fantastic sect of Convulsionists, and were even then considering within themselves whether they should foam, rage, roar, and turn cataleptic on the spot—thereby setting up a highly intelligible finger-post to the Future, for Monseigneur's guidance. Besides these Dervishes, were other three who had rushed into another sect, which mended matters with a jargon about 'the Centre of Truth:' holding that Man had got out of the Centre of Truth—which did not need much demonstration—but had not got out of the Circumference, and that he was to be kept from flying out of the Circumference, and was even to be shoved back into the Centre, by fasting and seeing of spirits. Among these, accordingly, much discoursing with spirits went on—and it did a world of good which never became manifest." TTC ii 7

—spoofed: " . . . . 'I have passed the night—as indeed I pass the whole of my time now—in spiritual intercourse.'

"'O!' said I, something snappishly.

"'The conferences of the night began,' continued the gentleman, turning several leaves of his note-book, 'with this message: "Evil communications corrupt good manners" . . . .

"'"A bird in the hand,"'said the gentleman, reading his last entry with great solemnity, '"is worth two in the Bosh."'

"'Truly I am of the same opinion,' said I; 'but shouldn't it be Bush?'

"'It came to me, Bosh,' returned the gentleman." CS/HH 1

Dickens had strong views on Spiritualism: see E/NN, HW/SB and HW/WR.

Suffering

—as teacher: "' . . . suffering has been stronger than all other teaching [said Estella Havisham], and has taught me to understand what your heart used to be. I have been bent and broken, but—I hope—into a better shape.'" GE 59

—and Time: "'We all change, but that's with Time; Time does his work honestly, and I don't mind him [said Gabriel Varden]. A fig for Time, sir. Use him well, and he's a hearty fellow, and scorns to have you at a disadvantage. But care and suffering (and those have changed her [Mary Rudge]) are devils, sir—secret, stealthy, undermining devils—who tread down the brightest flowers in Eden, and do more havoc in a month than Time does in a year.'" BR 26

Suicide

—compulsion: " . . . a species of fervour or intoxication, known, without doubt, to have led some persons to brave the guillotine unnecessarily, and to die by it, was not mere boastfulness, but a wild infection of the wildly shaken public mind. In seasons of pestilence, some of us will have a secret attraction to the disease—a terrible passing inclination to die of it. And all of us have like wonders hidden in our breasts, only needing circumstances to evoke them." TTC iii 6

—contemplated: "'Did it ever strike you [said Dismal Jemmy], on such a morning as this, that drowning would be happiness and peace?'

"'God bless me, no!' replied Mr. Pickwick, edging a little from the balustrade, as the possibility of the dismal man's tipping him over, by way of experiment, occurred to him rather forcibly.

"'I have thought so, often,' said the dismal man, without noticing the action. 'The calm, cool water seems to me to murmur an invitation to repose and rest. A bound, a splash, a brief struggle; there is an eddy for an instant, it gradually subsides into a gentle ripple; the waters have closed above your head, and the world has closed upon your miseries and misfortunes for ever.' The sunken eye of the dismal man flashed brightly as he spoke, but the momentary excitement quickly subsided; and he turned calmly away . . . ." PP 5

"Not one other word did Bradley [Headstone] utter all that night. Not once did he change his attitude, or loosen his hold upon his wrist. Rigid before the fire, as if it were a charmed flame that was turning him old, he sat, with the dark lines deepening in his face, its stare becoming more and more haggard, its surface turning whiter and whiter as if it were being overspread with ashes, and the very texture and colour of his hair degenerating.

"Not until the late daylight made the window transparent did this decaying statue move. Then it slowly arose, and sat in the window looking out." OMF iv 15

And see FL:Life*—mystery*

—fatherhood discovered: "'. . . .You had better hear this now than at any other time, said Tim [Linkinwater], 'it may have some influence with you. For Heaven's sake come!'

". . . after a moment's hesitation, [Ralph Nickleby] went into the hall for his hat, and returning got into the coach without speaking a word.

"Tim well remembered afterward and often said, that as Ralph Nickleby went into the house for this purpose, he saw him by the light of the candle which he had set down upon a chair, reel and stagger like a drunken man. He well remembered, too, that when he had placed his foot upon the coach steps, he turned round and looked upon him with a face so ashy pale and so very wild and vacant that it made him shudder, and for the moment almost afraid to follow. People were fond of saying that he had some dark presentiment upon him then, but his emotion might perhaps, with greater show of reason, be referred to what he had undergone that day . . . .

"'What if we tell you that a poor unfortunate boy, a child in everything but ever having known one of those tender endearments, or one of those lightsome hours which make our childhood a time to be remembered like a happy dream through all our after life—a warm-hearted, harmless, affectionate creature, who never offended you or did you wrong, but on whom you have vented the malice and hatred you have conceived for your nephew, and whom you have made an instrument for wreaking your bad passions upon him—what if we tell you that, sinking under your persecution, long in suffering, this poor creature has gone to tell his sad tale where, for your part in it, you must surely answer?'

"'. . . . You did well to send. I would have travelled a hundred miles afoot, through mud, mire, and darkness, to hear this news just at this time.'

"Even then, moved as he was by this savage joy, Ralph could see in the faces of the two [Cheeryble] brothers, mingling with their look of disgust and horror, something of that indefinable compassion for himself which he had noticed before . . . .

"'That boy,' said [Brooker], 'that these gentlemen have been talking of—'

"'That boy,' repeated Ralph, looking vacantly at him.

"'Whom I saw stretched dead and cold upon his bed, and who is now in his grave —'

"'Who is now in his grave,' echoed Ralph, like one who talks in his sleep.

"The man raised his eyes, and clasped his hands solemnly together:

"'—Was your only son, so help me God in heaven!'

"In the midst of a dead silence, Ralph sat down, pressing his two hands upon his temples. He removed them after a minute, and never was there seen part of a living man, undisfigured by any wound, such a ghastly face as he then disclosed. He looked fixedly at Brooker, who was by this time standing at a short distance from him, but did not say one word or make the slightest sound or gesture . . . .

"'. . . . I have been made the instrument of working out this dreadful retribution upon the head of a man who, in the hot pursuit of his bad ends, has persecuted and hunted down his own child to death . . . .'

"He had hardly spoken, when the lamp, which stood upon the table close to where Ralph was seated, and which was the only one in the room, was thrown to the ground and left them in utter darkness. There was some trifling confusion in obtaining another light; the interval was a mere nothing; but when it appeared, Ralph Nickleby was gone" NN 60

"Creeping from the house and slinking off like a thief; groping with his hand when first he got into the street as if he were a blind man, and looking often over his shoulder while he hurried away, as though he were followed in imagination or reality by some one anxious to question or detain him, Ralph Nickleby left the city behind him and took the road to his own home.

"The night was dark, and a cold wind blew, driving the clouds furiously and fast before it. There was one black, gloomy mass that seemed to follow him; not hurrying in the wild chase with the others, but lingering sullenly behind, and gliding darkly and stealthily on. He often looked back at this, and more than once stopped to let it pass over, but somehow, when he went forward again it was still behind him, coming mournfully and slowly up like a shadowy funeral train . . . .

"As he passed [the cemetery], Ralph called to mind that he had been one of a jury long before, on the body of a man who had cut his throat; and that he was buried in this place. He could not tell how he came to recollect it now, when he had so often passed and never thought about him, or how it was that he felt an interest in the circumstance, but he did both, and stopping, and clasping the iron railings with his hands, looked eagerly in, wondering which might be his grave . . . .

"He could not fix upon the spot among such a heap of graves, but he conjured up a strong and vivid idea of the man himself, and how he looked, and what had led him to do it, all of which he recalled with ease. By dint of dwelling upon this theme, he carried the impression with him when he went away, as he remembered when a child to have had frequently before him the figure of some goblin he had once seen chalked upon a door. But as he drew nearer and nearer home he forgot it again, and began to think how very dull and solitary the house would be inside.

"This feeling became so strong at last, that when he reached his own door, he could hardly make up his mind to turn the key and open it—when he had done that and gone into the passage, he felt as though to shut it again would be to shut out the world. But he let it go, and it closed with a loud noise. There was no light. How very dreary, cold, and still it was!

"Shivering from head to foot he made his way up-stairs into the room where he had been last disturbed. He had made a kind of compact with himself that he would not think of what had happened until he got home. He was at home now, and suffered himself for the first time to consider it.

"His own child—his own child! He never doubted the tale; he felt it was true, knew it as well now as if he had been privy to it all along. His own child! And dead too. Dying beside Nicholas—loving him, and looking upon him as something like an angel! That was the worst . . . .

"If he had known his child to be alive, if no deceit had been ever practised and he had grown up beneath his eye, he might have been a careless, indifferent, rough, harsh father—like enough—he felt that; but the thought would come that he might have been otherwise, and that his son might have been a comfort to him and they two happy together. He began to think now, that his supposed death and his wife's flight had had some share in making him the morose, hard man he was. He seemed to remember a time when he was not quite so rough and obdurate . . . .

"But one tender thought, or one of natural regret in that whirlwind of passion and remorse, was a drop of calm water in a stormy maddened sea. His hatred of Nicholas had been fed upon his own defeat, nourished on his interference with his schemes, fattened upon his old defiance and success. There were reasons for its increase; it had grown and strengthened gradually. Now it attained a height which was sheer wild lunacy . . . .

"The dead boy's love for Nicholas, and the attachment of Nicholas to him, was insupportable agony. The picture of his death-bed, with Nicholas at his side tending and supporting him, and he breathing out his thanks, and expiring in his arms, when he would have had them mortal enemies and hating each other to the last, drove him frantic. He gnashed his teeth and smote the air, and looking wildly round, with eyes which gleamed through the darkness, cried aloud:

"'I am trampled down and ruined. The wretch told me true. The night has come! Is there no way to rob them of further triumph, and spurn their mercy and compassion? Is there no devil to help me?

"Swiftly there glided again into his brain the figure he had raised that night. It seemed to lie before him. The head was covered now. So it was when he first saw it. The rigid, up-turned, marble feet too, he remembered well.

"Then came before him the pale and trembling relatives who had told their tale upon the inquest—the shrieks of women—the silent dread of men—the consternation and disquiet—the victory achieved by that heap of clay which with one motion of its hand had let out the life and made this stir among them—

"He spoke no more, but after a pause softly groped his way out of the room, and up the echoing stairs—up to the top—to the front garret—where he closed the door be-hind him, and remained.

"It was a mere lumber-room now, but it yet contained an old dismantled bedstead: the one on which his son had slept, for no other had ever been there. He avoided it hastily, and sat down as far from it as he could.

"The weakened glare of the lights in the street below, shining through the window which had no blind or curtain to intercept it, was enough to show the character of the room . . . . It had a shelving roof; high in one part, and at another descending almost to the floor.

"It was towards the highest part that Ralph directed his eyes, and upon it he kept them fixed steadily for some minutes, when he rose, and dragging thither an old chest upon which he had been seated, mounted upon it, and felt along the wall above his head with both hands. At length they touched a large iron hook firmly driven into one of the beams.

"At that moment he was interrupted by a loud knocking at the door below. After a little hesitation he opened the window . . . . He listened to the man's retreating footsteps until the sound had passed, and then gazing up into the sky saw, or thought he saw, the same black cloud that had seemed to follow him home, and which now appeared to hover directly above the house.

"'I know its meaning now,' he muttered, 'and the restless nights, the dreams, and why I have quailed of late;—all pointed to this. Oh! if men by selling their own souls could ride rampant for a term, for how short a term would I barter mine to-night! . . . .

"With a wild look around, in which frenzy, hatred, and despair, were horribly mingled, he shook his clenched hand at the sky above him, which was still dark and threatening, and closed the window.

"The rain and hail pattered against the glass, the chimneys quaked and rocked; the crazy casement rattled with the wind as though an impatient hand inside were striving to burst it open. But no hand was there, and it opened no more . . . .

"He had torn a rope from one of the old trunks and hanged himself on an iron hook immediately below the trap-door in the ceiling—in the very place to which the eyes of his son, a lonely, desolate, little creature, had so often been directed in childish terror fourteen years before." ¶NN 62

—intimated: "'Copperfield, you are a true friend; but when the worst comes to the worst, no man is without a friend who is possessed of shaving materials.' At this dreadful hint Mrs Micawber threw her arms round Mr Micawber's neck and entreated him to be calm. He wept; but so far recovered, almost immediately, as to ring the bell for the waiter, and bespeak a hot kidney pudding and a plate of shrimps for breakfast in the morning." DC 17

—of a murderer: "He whined, and cried, and cursed, and entreated them, and struggled, and submitted, in the same breath, and had no power to stand . . . one of the [police] remarked how faint the peaches smelt.

"The other assented at the moment, but presently stooped down in quick alarm, and looked at the prisoner.

"'Stop the coach! He has poisoned himself! The smell comes from this bottle in his hand!'

"The hand had shut upon it tight. With that rigidity of grasp with which no living man, in the full strength and energy of life, can clutch a prize he has won." MC 51

—regretted: "[Warden] retreated a few paces, took a short run, desperate leap, and plunged into the river.

"Not five seconds had passed when he rose to the water's surface—but what a change had taken place in that short time, in all his thoughts and feelings! Life—life in any form, poverty, misery, starvation—anything but death. He fought and struggled with the water that closed over his head, and screamed in agonies of terror. The curse of his own son rang in his ears. The shore—but one foot of dry ground—he could almost touch the step. One hand's breadth nearer, and he was saved—but the tide bore him onward, under the dark arches of the bridge, and he sank to the bottom.

"Again he rose, and struggled for life. For one instant—for one brief instant—the buildings on the river's banks, the lights on the bridge through which the current had borne him, the black water, and the fast-flying clouds, were distinctly visible—once more he sunk, and once again he rose. Bright flames of fire shot up from earth to heaven, and reeled before his eyes, while the water thundered in his ears, and stunned him with its furious roar.

"A week afterwards the body was washed ashore . . . . " SB/DD

—by social class

—for the Poor: " . . . if you attempt, desperately, and ungratefully, and impiously, and fraudulently attempt, to drown yourself, or hang yourself, I'll have no pity for you, for I have made up my mind to Put all suicide Down! If there is one thing,' said the Alderman [Cute], with his self-satisfied smile, 'on which I can be said to have made up my mind more than on another, it is to Put suicide Down. So don't try it on.'" C 1

—for the Rich: "'Oh the brain, the brain!' exclaimed the pious Alderman [Cute], lifting up his hands. 'Oh the nerves, the nerves; the mysteries of this machine called Man! Oh the little that unhinges it: poor creatures that we are! Perhaps a dinner, Mr Fish. Perhaps the conduct of his son, who, I have heard, ran very wild . . . . A most respectable man. One of the most respectable men I ever knew! A lamentable instance, Mr Fish. A public calamity! I shall make a point of wearing the deepest mourning. A most respectable man! But there is One above. We must submit, Mr Fish. We must submit!'

"What, Alderman! No word of Putting Down? Remember, Justice, your high moral boast and pride. Come, Alderman! Balance those scales. Throw me into this, the empty one, no dinner, and Nature's founts in some poor woman, dried by starving misery and rendered obdurate to claims for which her offspring *has* authority in holy mother Eve. Weigh me the two, you *Daniel,* going to judgment, when your day shall come! Weigh them, in the eyes of suffering thousands, audience (not unmindful) of the grim farce you play. Or supposing that you strayed from your five wits—it's not so far to go, but that it might be—and laid hands upon that throat of yours, warning your fellows (if you have a fellow) how they croak their comfortable wickedness to raving heads and stricken hearts. What then?" C 3

—spurious: "The dressing-room door being hastily flung open, Mr Mantalini was disclosed to view, with his shirt-collar symmetrically thrown back: putting a fine edge to a breakfast knife by means of his razor strop.

"'Ah!' cried Mr Mantalini. 'Interrupted!' and whisk went the breakfast knife into Mr Mantalini's dress-gown pocket, while Mr Mantalini's eyes rolled wildly, and his hair floating in wild disorder, mingled with his whiskers.

"'Alfred,' cried his wife, flinging her arms about him, 'I didn't mean to say it, I didn't mean to say it!'

"'Ruined!' cried Mr Mantalini. 'Have I brought ruin upon the best and purest creature that ever blessed a demnition vagabond! Demmit, let me go.' At this crisis of his ravings Mr Mantalini made a pluck at the breakfast knife, and being restrained by his wife's grasp, attempted to dash his head against the wall—taking very good care to be at least six feet from it." NN 21

Indexes VII *(16 named) and* VIII *(8 unnamed) list the suicides in Dickens. Allan Woodcourt BH thought Captain Hawdon died accidentally: see* M:Addiction*—an end.*

Superficiality

—creed of a master: "'The world is a lively place enough [said John Chester], in which we must accommodate ourselves to circumstances, sail with the stream as glibly as we can, be content to take froth for substance, the surface for the depth, the counterfeit for the real coin. I wonder no philosopher has ever established that our globe itself is hollow. It should be, if Nature is consistent in her works.'" BR 12

—lack of understanding: " . . . Mr Gowan treated his wife, even in his very fondness, too much like a beautiful child. He seemed so unsuspicious of the depths of feeling which [Little Dorrit] knew must lie below that surface, that she doubted if there could be any such depths in himself. She wondered whether his want of earnestness might be the natural result of his want of such qualities, and whether it was with people as with ships, that, in too shallow and rocky waters, their anchors had no hold, and they drifted anywhere." LD ii 6

Temper

—in close quarters: "She [the late Mrs Marigold] wasn't a bad wife, but she had a temper. If she could have parted with that one article at a sacrifice, I wouldn't have swopped her away in exchange for any other woman in England. Not that I ever did swop her away, for we lived together till she died, and that was thirteen year.

"Now, my lords and ladies and gentlefolks all, I'll let you into a secret, though you won't believe it. Thirteen year of temper in a Palace would try the worst of you, but thirteen year of temper in a Cart would try the best of you. You are kept so very close to it in a cart, you see. There's thousands of couples among you getting on like sweet ile upon a whetstone in houses five and six pairs of stairs high, that would go to the Divorce Court in a cart. Whether the jolting makes it worse, I don't undertake to decide; but in a cart it does come home to you, and stick to you. Wiolence in a cart is so wiolent, and aggrawation in a cart is *so* aggrawating." CS/DM 1

—epithet: "'Sir,' said Mr Tupman, 'you're a fellow!'

"'Sir,' said Mr Pickwick, 'you're another!'" PP 5

—indulged: I [Pip] must remark of my sister [Mrs Joe Gargery], what is equally true of all the violent women I have ever seen, that passion was no excuse for her, because it is undeniable that instead of lapsing into passion, she consciously and deliberately took extraordinary pains to force herself into it, and became blindly furious by regular stages . . . . " GE 15

—sublimation: " . . . my sister 'went on the Rampage,' in a more alarming degree than at any previous period. She asked me and Joe whether we supposed she was doormats under our feet, and how we dared to use her so, and what company we graciously thought she *was* fit for? When she had exhausted a torrent of such inquiries, she threw a candlestick at Joe, burst into a loud sobbing, got out the dustpan—which was always a very bad sign—put on her coarse apron, and began cleaning up to a terrible extent. Not satisfied with a dry cleaning, she took to a pail and scrubbing brush, and cleaned us out of house and home, so that we stood shivering in the back yard." GE 12

See Religion*—Protestantism—bad temper*

—variable: ""The proceedings of such a day occasioned various fluctuations in the human thermometer, and especially in instruments so sensitively and delicately constructed as Mrs Varden. Thus, at dinner Mrs V. stood at summer heat; genial, smiling, and delightful. After dinner, in the sunshine of the wine, she went up at least

half-a-dozen degrees, and was perfectly enchanting. As its effect subsided, she fell rapidly, went to sleep for an hour or so at temperate, and woke at something below freezing. Now she was at summer heat again, in the shade; and when tea was over, and old John, producing a bottle of cordial from one of the oaken cases, insisted on her sipping two glasses thereof in slow succession, she stood steadily at ninety for one hour and a quarter. Profiting by experience, the locksmith took advantage of this genial weather to smoke his pipe in the porch, and in consequence of this prudent management, he was fully prepared, when the glass went down again, to start homewards directly." BR 21

Valentine

—card: "The particular picture on which Sam Weller's eyes were fixed . . . was a highly coloured representation of a couple of human hearts skewered together with an arrow, cooking before a cheerful fire, while a male and female cannibal in modern attire: the gentleman being clad in a blue coat and white trousers, and the lady in a deep red pelisse with a parasol of the same: were approaching the meal with hungry eyes, up a serpentine gravel path leading thereunto.

"A decidedly indelicate young gentleman, in a pair of wings and nothing else, was depicted as superintending the cooking; a presentation of the spire of the church in Langham Place, London, appeared in the distance; and the whole formed a 'valentine,' of which, as a written inscription in the window testified, there was a large assortment within, which the shopkeeper pledged himself to dispose of, to his countrymen generally, at the reduced rate of one and sixpence each." PP 33

—father's reaction: "'It's a walentine.'

"A what!' exclaimed Mr [Tony] Weller, apparently horror-stricken by the word.

"'A walentine,' replied Sam.

"'Samivel, Samivel,' said Mr Weller, in reproachful accents, 'I didn't think you'd ha' done it. Arter the warnin' you've had o' your father's wicious propensities; arter all I've said to you upon this here wery subject; arter actiwally seein' and bein' in the company o' your own mother-in-law, vich I should ha' thought wos a moral lesson as no man could never ha' forgotten to his dyin' day! I didn't think you'd ha' done it, Sammy, I didn't think you'd ha' done it!' These objections were too much for the good old man. He raised Sam's tumbler to his lips and drank off its contents." PP 33

—and the ladies: "I believe that as little is known of the saint whose name is written here as can well be known of any saint or sinner. We, your loyal servants, are deeply thankful to him for having somehow gained possession of one day in the year—for having, as no doubt he has, arranged the almanac for 1866 expressly to delight us with the enchanting fiction that we have some tender proprietorship in you which we should scarcely dare to claim on a less auspicious occasion. Ladies, the utmost devotion sanctioned by the saint we beg to lay at your feet, and any little innocent privileges to which we may be entitled by the same authority we beg respectfully but firmly to claim at your hands." S/DM

—text: "Sam dipped his pen into the ink to be ready for any corrections, and began with a very theatrical air.

"'"Lovely——"'

"'Stop,' said Mr Weller, ringing the bell. 'A double glass o' the inwariable, my dear . . . I've been here before, in my time. Go on, Sammy.'

"'"Lovely creetur,"' repeated Sam.

"'Tain't in poetry, is it' interposed his father.

"'No, no,' replied Sam . . .

"'"Lovely creetur I feel myself a dammed —"'

"'That ain't proper,' said Mr Weller, taking his pipe from his mouth.

"'No; it ain't "dammed,"' observed Sam, holding the letter up to the light, 'It's "shamed," there's a blot there—"I feel myself ashamed."'

"'Wery good,' said Mr Weller. 'Go on.'

"'"Feel myself ashamed, and completely cir—" I forget what this here word is,' said Sam, scratching his head with the pen, in vain attempts to remember.

"'Why don't you look at it, then?' inquired Mr Weller.

"'So I *am* a lookin' at it,' replied Sam, 'but there's another blot. Here's a "c," and a "i," and a "d."'

"'Circumwented, p'haps,' suggested Mr Weller.

"'No, it ain't that,' said Sam, '"circumscribed;" that's it.'

"'That ain't as good a word as circumwented, Sammy,' said Mr Weller, gravely.

"'Think not?' said Sam.

"'Nothin' like it,' replied his father.

"'But don't you think it means more?' inquired Sam.

"'Vell, p'raps it is a more tenderer word,' said Mr Weller, after a few moments' reflection. 'Go on, Sammy.'

"'"Feel myself ashamed and completely circumscribed in a dressin' of you, for you *are* a nice gal and nothin' but it."'

"'That's a wery pretty sentiment,' said the elder Mr Weller, removing his pipe to make way for the remark.

"'Yes, I think it is rayther good,' observed Sam, highly flattered.

"'Wot I like in that 'ere style of writin',' said the elder Mr Weller, 'is, that there ain't no callin' names in it—no Wenuses, nor nothin' o' that kind. Wot's the good o' callin' a young 'ooman a Wenus or a angel, Sammy?'

"'Ah! what indeed?' replied Sam.

"'You might jist as well call her a griffin, or a unicorn, or a king's arms at once, which is wery well known to be a col-lection o' fabulous animals,' added Mr Weller.

"'Just as well,' replied Sam.

"'Drive on, Sammy,' said Mr Weller.

"Sam complied with the request, and proceeded as follows:—his father continuing to smoke, with a mixed expression of wisdom and complacency, which was particularly edifying.

"'"Afore I see you, I thought all women was alike."'

"'So they are,' observed the elder Mr Weller, parenthetically.

"'"But now,"' continued Sam, '"now I find what a reg'lar soft-headed, inkred'lous turnip I must ha' been: for there ain't nobody like you, though *I* like you better than nothin' at all." I thought it best to make that rayther strong,' said Sam, looking up.

"Mr Weller nodded approvingly, and Sam resumed.

"'"So I take the privilidge of the day, Mary, my dear—as the gen'l'm'n in difficulties did, ven he valked out of a Sunday—to tell you that the first and only time I see you, your likeness was took on my hart in much quicker time and brighter colours than ever a likeness was took by the profeel macheen (wich p'raps you may have heerd on Mary my dear) altho it *does* finish a portrait and put the frame and glass on complete, with a hook at the end to hang it up by, and all in two minutes and a quarter."'

"'I am afeerd that werges on the poetical, Sammy,' said Mr Weller, dubiously.

"'No it don't,' replied Sam, reading on very quickly, to avoid contesting the point:

"'"Except of me Mary my dear as your walentine and think over what I've said. My dear Mary, I will now conclude." That's all,' said Sam.

"'That's rather a sudden pull up, ain't it, Sammy?' inquired Mr Weller.

"'Not a bit on it,' said Sam; 'she'll vish there wos more, and that's the great art o' letter writin'.'" PP 33

And see LC:Poet and Poetry—*in peroration, and —three opinions*

Vanity

—*of age:* "'I have been thinking, Davy,' replied the sexton, 'that she,' he pointed to the grave, 'must have been a deal older than you or me.'

"'Seventy-nine,' answered the old man with a shake of the head, 'I tell you that I saw it.'

"'Saw it?' replied the sexton; 'aye, but, Davy, women don't always tell the truth about their age.'

"'That's true, indeed,' said the other old man, with a sudden sparkle in his eye. 'She might have been older.'

"'I am sure she must have been. Why, only think how old she looked. You and I seemed but boys to her.'

"'She did look old,' rejoined David. 'You're right. She did look old.'

"'Call to mind how old she looked for many a long, long year, and say if she could be but seventy-nine at last—only our age,' said the sexton.

"'Five year older at the very least!'. . .

"'Five!' retorted the sexton. 'Ten. Good eighty-nine. I call to mind the time her daughter died. She was eighty-nine if she was a day, and tries to pass upon us now for ten year younger. Oh! human vanity ....

"And so they parted; each persuaded that the other had less life in him than himself; and both greatly consoled and comforted by the little fiction that they had agreed upon, respecting Becky Morgan, whose decease was no longer a precedent of uncomfortable application, and would be no business of theirs for half a score of years to come." OCS 54

—of deep injury: "That [Miss Havisham] had done a grievous thing in taking an impressionable child to mould into the form that her wild resentment, spurned affection, and wounded pride found vengeance in, I knew full well. But that, in shutting out the light of day, she had shut out infinitely more; that, in seclusion, she had secluded herself from a thousand natural and healing influences; that her mind, brooding solitary, had grown diseased, as all minds do and must and will that reverse the appointed order of their Maker, I knew equally well. And could I look upon her without compassion, seeing her punishment in the ruin she was, in her profound unfitness for this earth on which she was placed, in the vanity of sorrow which had become a master mania, like the vanity of penitence, the vanity of remorse, the vanity of unworthiness, and other monstrous vanities that have been curses in this world? GE 49

—an older woman's: " . . . Sam followed up his advantage by kissing his mother-in-law.

"'Get along with you!' said Mrs Weller, pushing him away.

"'For shame, young man!' said the gentleman with the red nose.

"'No offence, sir, no offence,' replied Sam; 'you're wery right, though; it ain't the right sort o' thing, wen mothers-in-law is young and good looking, is it sir?'

"'It's all vanity,' said Mr Stiggins.

"'Ah, so it is,' said Mrs Weller, setting her cap to rights.

"Sam thought it was, too, but he held his peace." PP 27

—on a sickbed: "At length [Mrs Skewton] began to recover consciousness, and in some degree the power of motion, though not yet of speech. One day the use of her right hand returned; and showing it to her maid who was in attendance on her, and appearing very uneasy in her mind, she made signs for a pencil and some paper . . . .

"After much painful scrawling and erasing, and putting in of wrong characters, which seemed to tumble out of the pencil of their own accord, the old woman produced this document:

"'Rose-coloured curtains.'

"The maid being perfectly transfixed, and with tolerable reason, Cleopatra amended the manuscript by adding two words more, when it stood thus:

"'Rose-coloured curtains for doctors.'

"The maid now perceived remotely that she wished these articles to be provided for the better presentation of her complexion to the faculty; and as those in the house who knew her best, had no doubt of the correctness of this opinion, which she was soon able to establish for herself, the rose-coloured curtains were added to her bed, and she mended with increased rapidity from that hour. She was soon able to sit up, in curls and a laced cap and night-gown, and to have a little artificial bloom dropped into the hollow caverns of her cheeks.

"It was a tremendous sight to see this old woman in her finery leering and mincing at Death, and playing off her youthful tricks upon him as if he had been the Major . . . . " DS 37

Weeping

—exciting: "'Tears!' cried the old gentleman. . . . 'Catch the crystal globules—catch 'em—bottle 'em up—cork 'em tight—put sealing-wax on the top—seal 'em with a cupid—label 'em "Best quality"—and stow 'em away in the fourteen bin, with a bar if iron on the top to keep the thunder off!'" NN 41

—healing: "'If you hear in my voice [said Lucie Manette to her father]—I don't know that it is so, but I hope it is—if you hear in my voice any resemblance to a voice that once was sweet music in your ears, weep for it, weep for it! If you touch, in touching my hair, anything that recalls a beloved head that lay on your breast when you were young and free, weep for it, weep for it! If, when I hint to you of a Home that is before us, where I will be true to you with all my duty and with all my faithful service, I bring back the remembrance of a Home long desolate, while your poor heart pined away, weep for it, weep for it!'

"She held him closer round the neck, and rocked him on her breast like a child.

"'If, when I tell you, dearest dear, that your agony is over, and that I have come here to take you from it, and that we go to England to be at peace and at rest, I cause you to think of your useful life laid waste, and of our native France so wicked to you, weep for it, weep for it! And if, when I shall tell you of my name, and of my father who is living, and of my mother who is dead, you learn that I have to kneel to my honoured father, and implore his pardon for having never for his sake striven all day and lain awake and wept all night, because the love of my poor mother hid his torture from me, weep for it, weep for it! Weep for her, then, and for me! Good gentlemen, thank God! I feel his sacred tears upon my face, and his sobs strike against my heart. O, see! Thank God for us, thank God!'

"He had sunk in her arms, and his face dropped on her breast: a sight so touching, yet so terrible in the tremendous wrong and suffering which had gone before it, that the two beholders [Lorry and Defarge] covered their faces." TTC i 6

—inwardly: "I [Pip] verily believe that her [Estella Havisham's] not remembering and not minding in the least, made me cry again, inwardly—and that is the sharpest crying of all." GE 29

—for joy: "She sat down on the little sofa, and untied her bonnet-strings. He sat down by her side, and very near her: very, very near her. Oh, rapid, swelling, bursting little heart, you knew that it would come to this, and hoped it would. Why beat so wildly, heart!

"'Dear Ruth! Sweet Ruth! If I had loved you less, I could have told you that I loved you, long ago. I have loved you from the first. There never was a creature in the world more truly loved than you, dear Ruth, by me!'

"She clasped her little hands before her face. The gushing tears of joy, and pride, and hope, and innocent affection, would not be restrained. Fresh from her full young heart they came to answer him." MC 53

—in parting: "Heaven knows we need never be ashamed of our tears, for they are rain upon the blinding dust of earth, overlying our hard hearts. I [Pip] was better after I had cried, than before—more sorry, more aware of my own ingratitude, more gentle. If I had cried before, I should have had Joe [Gargery] with me then." GE 19

—in rejection: "'And good-bye, John,' said little Dorrit. 'And I hope you will have a good wife one day, and be a happy man. I am sure you will deserve to be happy, and you will be, John.'

"As she held out her hand to him with these words, the heart that was under the waistcoat of sprigs—mere slop-work, if the truth must be known—swelled to the size of the heart of a gentleman; and the poor, common little fellow, having no room to hold it, burst into tears." LD i 18

—in religious posture: "'I'll tell you wot it is, Samivel, my boy,' whispered the old gentleman into his son's ear, after a long and steadfast contemplation of his lady and Mr Stiggins; 'I think there must be somethin' wrong in your mother-in-law's inside, as vell as in that o' the red-nosed man.'

"'Wot do you mean?' said Sam.

"'I mean this here, Sammy,' replied the old gentleman, 'that wot they drink, don't seem no nourishment to 'em; it all turns to warm water, and comes a pourin' out o' their eyes. 'Pend upon it, Sammy, it's a constitootional infirmity.'" PP 45

And see F:Love—*unrequited—tombstone*

—sentimental diary: "'D. fondled J. Associations thus awakened, opened floodgates of sorrow. Rush of grief admitted. (Are tears the dewdrops of the heart? J.M.)" DC 38

D. is David Copperfield, J. is Dora Spenlow's dog Jip, and the diarist is Julia Mills.

—Sam Weller's view: "'Come, come,' interposed Sam, who had witnessed Mr Trotter's tears with considerable impatience, 'blow this here water-cart bis'ness. It won't do no good, this won't.'

"'Sam,' said Mr Pickwick reproachfully, 'I am sorry to find that you have little respect for this young man's feelings.'

"'His feelings is all wery well, sir,' replied Mr Weller; 'and as they're so wery fine, and it's a pity he should lose 'em, I think he'd better keep 'em in his own buzzum, than let 'em ewaporate in hot water, 'specially as they do no good. Tears never yet wound up a clock, or worked a steam ingen'. The next time you go out to a smoking party, young fellow, fill your pipe with that 'ere reflection; and for the present just put that bit of pink gingham into your pocket. 'Tan't so handsome that you need keep waving it about, as if you was a tight-rope dancer.'" PP 16

Champion crier Florence Dombey DS weeps fifty-seven times, the last five for joy.

Will

—its loss: "'I have no will. That is to say,' [Clennam] coloured a little, 'next to none that I can put in action now. Trained by main force; broken, not bent; heavily ironed with an object on which I was never consulted and which was never mine; shipped away to the other end of the world before I was of age, and exiled there until my father's death there . . . always grinding in a mill I always hated; what is to be expected from me in middle life? Will, purpose, hope? All those lights were ex-inguished before I could sound the words.'" LD i 2

And see Soul-murder, and M:Facts—*and religion*

—and power: "'I wish I could do you, or any of you, a greater [service],' said Miss La Creevy; 'but the power to serve is as seldom joined with the will, as the will is with the power, *I* think.'" NN 20

Worldliness

—calculation: "[Jonas Chuzzlewit] appeared to be steadily engaged in subjecting some given amount [his wife's dowry] to the operation of every known rule of figures; adding to it, taking from it, multiplying it, reducing it by long and short division; working it by the rule-of-three direct and inversed; exchange or barter; practice; simple interest; compound interest; and other means of arithmetical calculation." MC 20

—interest and convenience: "Our interest and convenience commonly oblige many of us to make professions that we cannot feel. We have partnerships of interest and convenience, friendships of interest and convenience, dealings of interest and convenience, marriages of interest and convenience, every day." DS 45

—priorities: "'Have you no taste for anything, Mr Pancks?'

"'What's taste?' dryly retorted Pancks.

"'Let us say inclination.'

"'I have an inclination to get money, sir,' said Pancks, 'if you'll show me how' . . . .

"'You are no great reader, I suppose?' said Clennam

"'Never read anything but letters and accounts. Never collect anything but advertisements relative to next of kin. If *that's* a taste, I have got that.'" LD i 13

—and a simple heart: "The man in all this world most confident in his sagacity and shrewdness; the man in all this world most proud of the distrust of other men, and having most to show in gold and silver as the gains belonging to his creed; the meekest favourer of that wise doctrine, Every man for himself, and God for us all (there being high wisdom in the thought that the Eternal Majesty of Heaven ever was, or can be, on the side of selfish lust and love!); shall never find, oh, never find, be sure of that, the time come home to him, when all his wisdom is an idiot's folly, weighed against a simple heart!" MC 39

—and the universe: "The thoughts of worldly men are for ever regulated by a moral law of gravitation, which, like the physical one, holds them down to earth. The bright glory of day, and the silent wonders of a starlit night, appeal to their minds in vain. There are no signs in the sun, or in the moon, or in the stars, for their reading.

"They are like some wise men, who, learning to know each planet by its Latin name, have quite forgotten such small heavenly constellations as Charity, Forbearance, Universal Love, and Mercy, although they shine by night and day so brightly that the blind may see them; and who, looking upward at the spangled sky, see nothing there but the reflection of their own great wisdom and book-learning.

"It is curious to imagine these people of the world, busy in thought, turning their eyes towards the countless spheres that shine above us, and making them reflect the only images their minds contain. The man who lives but in the breath of princes, has nothing in his sight but stars for courtiers' breasts. The envious man beholds his neighbours' honours even in the sky; to the money-hoarder, and the mass of worldly folk, the whole great universe above glitters with sterling coin—fresh from the mint—stamped with the sovereign's head coming always between them and heaven, turn where they may. So do the shadows of our own desires stand between us and our better angels, and thus their brightness is eclipsed." BR 29

And see Cynic—*'always suspect everybody'*

—unjustly imputed: "Brother Gimblet came forward, and took (as I knew he would) the text, 'My kingdom is not of this world.' Ah! but whose was, my fellow-sinners? Whose? Why, our brother's here present was . . . .

"Brother Gimblet then groaned and bellowed his way through my composition . . . . The service closed with a hymn, in which the brothers unanimously roared, and the sisters unanimously shrieked at me, That I by wiles of worldly gain was mocked, and they on waters of sweet love were rocked; that I with mammon struggled in the dark, while they were floating in a second ark.

"I went out from all this with an aching heart and a weary spirit: not because I was quite so weak as to consider these narrow creatures interpreters of the Divine Majesty and Wisdom, but because I was weak enough to feel as though it were my hard fortune to be misrepresented and misunderstood, when I most tried to subdue any risings of mere worldliness within me, and when I most hoped that, by dint of trying earnestly, I had succeeded." GSE 6

Mr Tapley Succeeds in Finding a "Jolly" Subject for Contemplation MC

Fellow Man, in Relation

Mankind is my business. The common welfare is my business; charity, mercy, forbearance, and benevolence, are all my business. The dealings of my trade are but a drop of water in the comprehensive ocean of my business.

[CC 1]

All men and women who fall into exclusive habits of self-indulgence, and forget their natural sympathy and close connexion with everybody and everything in the world around them, not only neglect the first duty of life, but, by a happy retributive justice, deprive themselves of its truest and best enjoyment.

YC/H

Appearances

—*beauty:* "'I am not a man to be moved by a pretty face,' muttered Ralph [Nickleby] sternly. 'There is a grinning skull beneath it, and men like me, who look and work below the surface, see that, and not its delicate covering.'" NN 31

—*'coming out':* "Now, 'coming out,' either in acting, or singing, or society, or facetiousness, or anything else, is all very well, and remarkably pleasant to the individual principally concerned, if he or she can but manage to come out with a burst, and being out to keep out, and not go in again; but it does unfortunately happen that both consummations are extremely difficult to accomplish, and that the difficulties of getting out at all in the first instance, and if you surmount them, of keeping out in the second, are pretty much on a par, and no slight ones either . . . . " SB/MM

—*deceiving:* "Now, in the old days at home, certain audacious doubts respecting the last of the Patriarchs, which were afloat in the air, had, by some forgotten means, come in contact with Arthur [Clennam]'s sensorium. He was aware of motes and specks of suspicion, in the atmosphere of that time; seen through which medium, Christopher Casby was a mere Inn signpost without any Inn—an invitation to rest and be thankful, when there was no place to put up at, and nothing whatever to be thankful for.

"He knew that some of these specks even represented Christopher as . . . being a crafty impostor. Other motes there were which showed him as a heavy, selfish, drifting Booby, who, having stumbled, in the course of his unwieldy jostlings against other men, on the discovery that to get through life with ease and credit, he had but to hold his tongue, keep the bald part of his head well polished, and leave his hair alone, had had just cunning enough to seize the idea and stick to it.

"It was said that his being town-agent to Lord Decimus Tite Barnacle was referable, not to his having the least business capacity, but to his looking so supremely benignant that nobody could suppose the property screwed or jobbed under such a man; also, that for similar reasons he now got more money out of his own wretched lettings, unquestioned, than anybody with a less nobby and less shining crown could possibly have done.

"In a word, it was represented . . . that many people select their models, much as the painters . . . select theirs; and that, whereas in the Royal Academy some evil old ruffian of a Dog-stealer will annually be found embodying all the cardinal virtues, on account of his eyelashes, or his chin, or his legs (thereby planting thorns of confusion in the breasts of the more observant students of nature), so, in the great social Exhibition, accessories are often accepted in lieu of the internal character." ¶LD i 13

"'It's a mighty fine sign-post, is The Casby's Head,' said Mr Pancks, surveying it with anything rather than admiration; 'but the real name of the House is the Sham's Arms.'" LD ii 32

" . . . he compromised himself by no admission that his new engagement was at all out of his way, or involved the least element of the ridiculous. Mr Wegg would even have picked a handsome quarrel with any one who should have challenged his deep acquaintance with those aforesaid eight volumes of Decline and Fall. His gravity was unusual, portentous, and immeasurable, not because he admitted any doubt of himself, but because he perceived it necessary to forestall any doubt of himself in others. And herein he ranged with that very numerous class of impostors, who are quite as determined to keep up appearances to themselves, as to their neighbours." OMF i 5

"' . . . you don't want to exchange words of mistrust with me; and if you did, you couldn't, because I wouldn't. You and I are old enough to know better than to judge against experience from surfaces and appearances; and if you haven't lived to find out the evil and injustice of such judgments, you are a lucky man.'" CS/MS

—*deportment:* "'My children,' said Mr Turveydrop, paternally encircling Caddy with his left arm as she sat beside him, and putting his right hand gracefully on his hip. 'My son and daughter, your happiness shall be my care. I will watch over you. You shall always live with me'; meaning, of course, I will always live with you; 'this house is henceforth as much yours as mine; consider it your home. May you long live to share it with me!'

"The power of his Deportment was such, that they really were as much overcome with thankfulness as if, instead of quartering himself upon them for the rest of his life, he were making some munificent sacrifice in their favour.

"'For myself, my children,' said Mr Turveydrop, 'I am falling into the sear [*sic.*] and yellow leaf, and it is impossible to say how long the last feeble traces of gentlemanly Deportment may linger in this weaving and spinning age. But, so long, I will do my duty to society, and will show myself, as usual, about town. My wants are few and simple. My little apartment here, my few essentials for the toilet, my frugal morning meal, and my little dinner, will suffice. I charge your dutiful affection with the supply of these requirements, and I charge myself with all the rest.'

"They were overpowered afresh by his uncommon generosity." BH 23

—embarrassing: "Let me confess exactly, with what feelings I looked forward to Joe [Gargery]'s coming.

"Not with pleasure . . . with considerable disturbance, some mortification, and a keen sense of incongruity. If I could have kept him away by paying money, I certainly would have paid money. My greatest reassurance was, that he was coming to Barnard's Inn, not to Hammersmith, and consequently would not fall in Bentley Drummle's way. I had little objection to his being seen by Herbert [Pocket] or his father, for both of whom I had a respect; but I had the sharpest sensitiveness as to his being seen by Drummle, whom I held in contempt. So, throughout life, our worst weaknesses and meannesses are usually committed for the sake of the people whom we most despise." GE 27

—the emperor's clothes: "The multitude worshipped on trust—though always distinctly knowing why—but the officiators at the altar had the man [Merdle] habitually in their view. They sat at his feasts, and he sat at theirs. There was a spectre always attendant on him, saying to these high priests, 'Are such the signs you trust, and love to honour; this head, these eyes, this mode of speech, the tone and manner of this man? You are the levers of the Circumlocution Office, and the rulers of men. When half-a-dozen of you fall out by the ears, it seems that mother earth can give birth to no other rulers. Does your qualification lie in the superior knowledge of men, which accepts, courts, and puffs this man? Or, if you are competent to judge aright the signs I never fail to show you when he appears among you, is your superior honesty your qualification? Two rather ugly questions these, always going about town with Mr Merdle; and there was a tacit agreement that they must be stifled." LD ii 12

—evaluated: " . . . the faculty (or the habit) of correctly observing the characters of men, is a rare one. I have not even found, within my experience, that the faculty (or the habit) of correctly observing so much as the faces of men, is a general one by any means. The two commonest mistakes in judgement that I suppose to arise from the former default, are, the confounding of shyness with arrogance—a very common mistake indeed—and the not understanding that an obstinate nature exists in a perpetual struggle with itself." DS preface

—evidence: "'Not a particle of evidence, Pip,' said Mr Jaggers, shaking his head and gathering up his skirts. 'Take nothing on its looks; take everything on evidence. There's no better rule.'" GE 40

—manipulated: "It is wonderful how Virtue turns from dirty stockings; and how Vice, married to ribbons and a little gay attire, changes her name, as wedded ladies do, and becomes Romance." OT pref 3d ed

—rough outside: " . . . a cheerful landscape, prominent in which the old Abbey Church, with its massive tower, threw a softer train of shadow on the view than seemed compatible with its rugged character. But so from rough outsides (I hope I have learnt), serene and gentle influences often proceed." BH 8

Begging

—appeals to the Golden Dustman: " . . . they all enclose documents (they call their scraps documents; but they are, as to papers deserving the name, what minced veal is to a calf), the non-return of which would be their ruin. That is to say, they are utterly ruined now, but they would be more utterly ruined then.

"Among these correspondents are several daughters of general officers, long accustomed to every luxury of life (except spelling), who little thought, when their gallant fathers waged war in the Peninsula, that they would ever have to appeal to those whom Providence, in its inscrutable wisdom, has blessed with untold gold, and from among whom they select the name of Nicodemus Boffin, Esquire, for a maiden effort in this wise, understanding that he has such a heart as never was.

"The Secretary [Rokesmith] learns, too, that confidence between man and wife would seem to obtain but rarely when virtue is in distress, so numerous are the wives who take up their pens to ask Mr Boffin for money without the knowledge of their devoted husbands, who would never permit it; while, on the other hand, so numerous are the husbands who take up their pens to ask Mr Boffin for money without the knowledge of their devoted wives, who would instantly go out of their senses if they had the least suspicion of the circumstance.

"There are the inspired beggars, too. These were sitting, only yesterday evening, musing over a fragment of candle which must soon go out and leave them in the dark for the rest of their nights, when surely some angel whispered the name of Nicodemus Boffin, Esquire, to their souls, imparting rays of hope, nay confidence, to which they had long been strangers!

"Akin to these are the suggestively-befriended beggars. They were partaking of a cold potato and water by the flickering and gloomy light of a lucifer match, in their lodgings (rent considerably in arrear, and heartless landlady threatening expulsion 'like a dog' into the streets), when a gifted friend happening to look in, said, 'Write immediately to Nicodemus Boffin, Esquire,' and would take no denial.

"There are the nobly independent beggars, too. These, in the days of their abundance, ever regarded gold as dross, and have not yet got over that only impediment in the way of their amassing wealth, but they want no dross from Nicodemus Boffin, Esquire. No, Mr Boffin; the world may term it pride, paltry pride if you will, but they wouldn't take it if you offered it; a loan, sir—for fourteen weeks to the day, interest calculated at the rate of five per cent per annum, to be bestowed upon any charitable institution you may name—is all they want of you, and if you have the meanness to refuse it, count on being despised by these great spirits.

"There are the beggars of punctual business-habits, too. These will make an end of themselves at a quarter to one P.M. on Tuesday, if no Post-office order is in the interim received from Nicodemus Boffin, Esquire; arriving after a quarter to one P.M. on Tuesday, it need not be sent; as they will then (having made an exact memorandum of the heartless circumstances) be 'cold in death.'

"There are the beggars on horseback, too, in another sense of the proverb. These are mounted and ready to start on the highway to affluence. The goal is before them, the road is in the best condition, their spurs are on, the steed is willing, but at the last moment, for want of some special thing—a clock, a violin, an astronomical telescope, an electrifying machine—they must dismount for ever, unless they receive its equivalent in money from Nicodemus Boffin, Esquire.

"Less given to detail are the beggars who make sporting ventures. These, usually to be addressed in reply under initials at a country post office, inquire in feminine hands, Dare one who cannot disclose herself to Nicodemus Boffin, Esquire, but whose name might startle him were it revealed, solicit the immediate advance of two hundred pounds from unexpected riches exercising their noblest privilege in the trust of a common humanity?" ¶OMF i 17

—former employer: "For a drunken, squalid, begging-letter-writing man, called Pecksniff (with a shrewish daughter), haunts thee, Tom; and when he makes appeals to thee for cash, reminds thee that he built thy fortunes better than his own; and when he spends it, entertains the alehouse company with tales of thine ingratitude and his munificence towards thee once upon a time; and then he shows his elbows, worn in holes, and puts his soleless shoes up on a bench, and begs his auditors look there, while thou art comfortably housed and clothed. All known to thee, and yet all borne with, Tom!" MC 54

—fraudulent: "The amount of money he annually diverts from wholesome and useful purposes in the United Kingdom, would be a set-off against the Window Tax. He is one of the most shameless frauds and impositions of this time. In his idleness, his mendacity, and the immeasurable harm he does to the deserving—dirtying the stream of true benevolence, and muddling the brains of foolish justices, with inability to distinguish between the base coin of distress, and the true currency we have always among us—he is more worthy of Norfolk Island than three-fourths of the worst characters who are sent there. Under any rational system, he would have been sent there long ago." RP/BL

"That the calling is a successful one, and that large sums of money are gained by it, must be evident to anybody who reads the Police Reports of such cases. But prosecutions are of rare occurrence, relatively to the extent to which the trade is carried on. The cause of this is to be found (as no one knows better than the Begging-Letter Writer, for it is a part of his speculation) in the aversion people feel to exhibit themselves as having been imposed upon, or as having weakly gratified their consciences with a lazy, flimsy substitute for the noblest of all virtues.

"There is a man at large . . . who, within these twelve months, has been probably the most audacious and the most successful swindler that even this trade has ever known. There has been something singularly base in this fellow's proceedings; it has been his business to write to all sorts and conditions of people, in the names of persons of high reputation and unblemished honour, professing to be in distress—the general admiration and respect for whom has ensured a ready and generous reply." ¶RP/BL

And see FL:Life—*impaired by fraud*

Blacks

—*in Africa: their dress:* "'I don't know whether you happen to have read many books of African Travel, Mr Rokesmith?' said R. W. [Reginald Wilfer].

"'I have read several.'

"'Well, you know, there's usually a King George, or a King Boy, or a King Sambo, or a King Bill, or Bull, or Rum, or Junk, or whatever name the sailors may have happened to give him.'

"'Where?' asked Rokesmith.

"'Anywhere. Anywhere in Africa, I mean. Pretty well everywhere, I may say; for black kings are cheap—and *I* think'—said R. W., with an apologetic air, 'nasty.'

"'I am much of your opinion, Mr Wilfer. You were going to say—?'

"'I was going to say, the king is generally dressed in a London hat only, or a Manchester pair of braces, or one epaulette, or a uniform coat, with his legs in the sleeves, or something of that kind.'

"'Just so,' said the Secretary.

"'In confidence, I assure you, Mr Rokesmith,' observed the cheerful cherub, 'that when more of my family were at home and to be provided for, I used to remind myself immensely of that king. You have no idea, as a single man, of the difficulty I have had in wearing more than one good article at a time.'" OMF ii 14

—*at Almack's in New York:* "Heyday! the landlady of Almack's thrives! A buxom fat mulatto woman, with sparkling eyes, whose head is daintily ornamented with a handkerchief of many colours. Nor is the landlord much behind her in his finery, being attired in a smart blue jacket, like a ship's steward, with a thick gold ring upon his little finger, and round his neck a gleaming golden watch-guard. How glad he is to see us! what will we please to call for? A dance? It shall be done directly, Sir: 'a regular breakdown.'" AN 6

And see H:Dance and dancing—*at Almack's in New York City; and* H:Recreation—*minstrel show*

—*and beauty:* "In reference to the ridiculous assertion that Mr Dickens in his book termed a woman 'quite beautiful' who was a Negress, he positively believes that he was shown no Negress in the Prison . . . but he has not the least doubt of having been guilty of the (American) enormity of detecting beauty in a pensive quadroon or mulatto girl . . . . " HW/PP

—*benign hope:* "Of these negroes [from Sierra Leone]—a faithful, cheerful, active, affectionate race—a very interesting account is given; which seems to render it clear that they, under civilised direction, are the only hopeful human agents to whom recourse can ultimately be had for aid in working out the slow and gradual raising up of Africa" E/NE

—*education in America:* "No doubt it has been true that negroes, set to work by any motive which called out their higher feelings as men, would become ambitious and acquire a thirst for freedom in the end. So it is, so let it be. Educate the negroes on plantations, make them intelligent men and women, let them imbibe in their full freedom the doctrines of Christianity.

"It has been true that it was not safe to give knowledge to men who were placed in a position which the faintest flash of reason would resent. We have been told by a Christian minister, who laboured in his way to elevate the minds of negroes in some North American plantations, that his permission to preach was clogged with many stipulations as to what he should not say; that he was expressly forbidden to teach anything which might induce a slave to question his position or wish to be free; and that, in consequence, he found himself unable to preach even man's duty to his neighbour.

"So it has been and must be; the slave who acquires education and religious principle must desire to be free: let it be so.

Cultivate the slave's best feelings, teach him, awaken him to manhood; and do this fearlessly because you are determined that he shall attain what will become the object of his wishes. When you have taught him to desire his proper place among his fellows, let him take it; let him work for you as a free man, and be well assured that he will work . . . . If, step by step, the degraded race be raised, their higher impulses awakened, their minds developed, their moral ties religiously respected, there will arise out of the present multitude of slaves, by slow degrees, a race of free labourers far more efficient than the present gangs, while the yearly increasing surplus of black population educated into love of freedom would pass over to Liberia, and form a nation on the coast of Africa, whereof America might boast for ever.

"Americans might so abolish slavery as to produce with little or no cost—probably with profit to themselves—results incomparably greater than have been attained by England with a vast expenditure of money. Our cousins are capable of great works, and a great work lies at their door. Heartily glad shall we be when they shall begin to leave off whipping their negroes, and shall set steadily to work to whip the Britishers in the results to be obtained out of enlightened efforts to give to the slave freedom both of mind and body. This victory over ourselves America may win, and England shall be foremost in the celebration of her triumph." ¶HWC/N

—and missionaries: "That model missionary [**Dr Livingstone**] and good brave man found at least one tribe of blacks with a very strong sense of the ridiculous, insomuch that although an amiable and docile people, they never could see the Missionaries dispose of their legs in the attitude of kneeling, or hear them begin a hymn in chorus, without bursting into roars of irrepressible laughter." UT/MM

—sailors dancing in Liverpool: "The male dancers were all blacks, and one was an unusually powerful man of six feet three or four. The sound of their flat feet on the floor was as unlike the sound of white feet as their faces were unlike white faces. They toed and heeled, shuffled, double-shuffled, double-double-shuffled, covered the buckle, and beat the time out rarely, dancing with a great show of teeth, and with a childish good-humoured enjoyment that was very prepossessing. They generally kept together, these poor fellows, said Mr Superintendent, because they were at a disadvantage singly, and liable to slights in the neighbouring streets. But if I were Light Jack, I should be very slow to interfere oppressively with Dark Jack; for, whenever I have had to do with him, I have found him a simple and a gentle fellow. Bearing this in mind, I asked his friendly permission to leave him restoration of beer, in wishing him good night, and thus it fell out that the last words I heard him say, as I blundered down the worn stairs, were 'Jeblem's elth! Ladies drinks fust!'" UT/MJ

And see H:Dance and dancing*—at Almack's in New York City; and —calling a dance in Liverpool*

—slum: Five Points, New York: "What place is this, to which the squalid street conducts us? A kind of square of leprous houses, some of which are attainable only by crazy wooden stairs without. What lies beyond this tottering flight of steps, that creak beneath our tread? —a miserable room, lighted by one dim candle, and destitute of all comfort, save that which may be hidden in a wretched bed . . . .

"Ascend these pitch-dark stairs, heedful of a false footing on the trembling boards, and grope your way with me into this wolfish den, where neither ray of light nor breath of air, appears to come. A negro lad, startled from his sleep by the officer's voice —he knows it well—but comforted by his assurance that he has not come on business, officiously bestirs himself to light a candle. The match flickers for a moment, and shows great mounds of dusty rags upon the ground; then dies away and leaves a denser darkness than before, if there can be degrees in such extremes. He stumbles down the stairs and presently comes back, shading a flaring taper with his hand. Then the mounds of rags are seen to be astir, and rise slowly up, and the floor is covered with heaps of negro women, waking from their sleep: their white teeth chattering, and their bright eyes glistening and winking on all sides with surprise and fear, like the countless repetition of one astonished African face in some strange mirror.

"Mount up these other stairs with no less caution . . . into the housetop; where the bare beams and rafters meet overhead, and calm night looks down through the crevices in the roof. Open the door of one of these cramped hutches full of sleeping negroes. Pah! They have a charcoal fire within; there is a smell of singeing clothes, or flesh, so close they gather round the brazier; and vapours issue forth that blind and suffocate. From every corner, as you glance about you in these dark retreats, some figure crawls half-awakened, as if the judgment-hour were near at hand, and every obscene grave were giving up its dead. Where dogs would howl to lie, women, and men, and boys slink off to sleep, forcing the dislodged rats to move away in quest of better lodgings." AN 6

And compare Irish—*in London*

—*vague rumour:* " . . . the wildest frenzy and fatuity of evil report rose against [Neville Landless] . . . he had caused to be whipped to death sundry 'Natives'—nomadic persons, encamping now in Asia, now in Africa, now in the West Indies, and now at the North Pole—vaguely supposed in Cloisterham to be always black, always of great virtue, always calling themselves Me, and everybody else Massa or Missie (according to sex), and always reading tracts of the obscurest meaning, in broken English, but always accurately understanding them in the purest mother tongue." MED 16

—*white racism:* "In truth, it must be acknowledged, that the free Americans, the very abolitionists themselves, are stout supporters of the slave system in act, whatever they may be in theory. In the free states of America, the negro is no less forced down out of his just position as a man than when he works under the planter's whip. Even in an English drawing-room, the American who meets by chance a guest with negro blood marked on his forehead, feels like a cat upon whose domain some strange dog has intruded, and is not easily restrained by the rules of English courtesy from spitting. However respectable the position earned by a free negro—and, as **Mrs [Harriet Beecher] Stowe** truly points out, free negroes know how to come by the respectabilities of money—though he be clean of body, neatly dressed, and by the colour of his mind a man of sense and honour: there is not a white fellow, black with dirt in his body, and black with rascality in his mind, who would not scorn to sit beside him on an omnibus; there is not a kitchen scullion claiming to be white under his grease and soot, who would not consider it an insult to be told that he must dine at the same table with the negro gentleman." HWC/N

And see W:America—*freedom generally*

Cannibalism

—*forestalled:* "Foreseeing that if the boat lived through the stormy weather, the time must come, and soon come, when we should have absolutely no morsel to eat, I [Captain Ravender] had one momentous point often in my thoughts. Although I had, years before that, fully satisfied myself that the instances in which human beings in the last distress have fed upon each other, are exceedingly few, and have very seldom indeed (if ever) occurred when the people in distress, however dreadful their extremity, have been accustomed to moderate forbearance and restraint; I say, though I had long before quite satisfied my mind on this topic, I felt doubtful whether there might not have been in former cases some harm and danger from keeping it out of sight and pretending not to think of it.

"I felt doubtful whether some minds, growing weak with fasting and exposure and having such a terrific idea to dwell upon in secret, might not magnify it until it got to have an awful attraction about it. This was not a new thought of mine, for it had grown out of my reading. However, it came over me stronger than it had ever done before—as it had reason for doing—in the boat, and on the fourth day I decided that I would bring to the light that unformed fear which must have been more or less darkly in every brain among us.

"Therefore, as a means of beguiling the time and inspiring hope, I gave them the best summary in my power of **Bligh**'s voyage of more than three thousand miles, in an open boat, after the Mutiny of the Bounty, and of the wonderful preservation of that boat's crew. They listened throughout with great interest, and I concluded by telling them, that, in my opinion, the happiest circumstance in the whole narrative was, that Bligh, who was no delicate man either, had solemnly placed it on record therein that he was sure and certain that under no conceivable circumstances whatever would that emaciated party, who had gone through all the pains of famine, have preyed on one another.

"I cannot describe the visible relief which this spread through the boat, and how the tears stood in every eye. From that time I was as well convinced as Bligh himself that there was no danger, and that this phantom, at any rate, did not haunt us." ¶CS/GM

—practiced: "A convict . . . escapes with other prisoners from a penal settlement. It is an island, and they seize a boat, and get to the main land. Their way is by a rugged and precipitous sea-shore, and they have no earthly hope of ultimate escape . . . . Famine, as they all must have foreseen, besets them early in their course. Some of the party die and are eaten; some are murdered by the rest and eaten.

"This one awful creature eats his fill, and sustains his strength, and lives on to be recaptured and taken back. The unrelateable experiences through which he has passed have been so tremendous, that he is not hanged as he might be, but goes back to his old chained-gang work.

"A little time, and he tempts one other prisoner away, seizes another boat, and flies once more—necessarily in the old hopeless direction, for he can take no other. He is soon cut off, and met by the pursuing party face to face, upon the beach. He is alone. In his former journey he acquired an inappeasable relish for his dreadful food. He urged the new man away, expressly to kill him and eat him. In the pockets on one side of his coarse convict-dress, are portions of the man's body, on which he is regaling; in the pockets on the other side is an untouched store of salted pork (stolen before he left the island) for which he has no appetite.

"He is taken back, and he is hanged. But I shall never see that sea-beach on the wall or in the fire, without him, solitary monster, eating as he prowls along, while the sea rages and rises at him." ¶RP/LV

Capital Punishment

—appalling character: "Contact with death, even in its least terrible shape, is solemn and appalling. How much more awful is it to reflect on this near vicinity to the dying—to men in full health and vigour, in the flower of youth or the prime of life, with all their faculties and perceptions as acute and perfect as your own; but dying, nevertheless—dying as surely—with the hand of death imprinted upon them as indelibly—as if mortal disease had wasted their frames to shadows, and corruption had already begun!" SB/VN *See also —proximity and public indifference*

—atrocity in punishment

—for religion: "Under the guidance of her Christian pastors, [France] entertained herself, besides, with such human achievements as sentencing a youth to have his hands cut off, his tongue torn out with pincers, and his body burned alive, because he had not kneeled down in the rain to do honour to a dirty procession of monks which passed within his view, at a distance of some fifty or sixty yards." TTC i 1

—for the State: "'One old man says . . . that his right hand, armed with the knife, will be burnt off before his face; that, into wounds which will be made in his arms, his breast, and his legs, there will be poured boiling oil, melted lead, hot resin, wax, and sulphur; finally, that he will be torn limb from limb by four strong horses. That old man says, all this was actually done to a prisoner who made an attempt on the life of the late King, Louis Fifteen.'" TTC ii15

—the condemned: "Conceive the situation of a man, spending his last night on earth in this cell. Buoyed up with some vague and undefined hope of reprieve, he knew not why—indulging in some wild and visionary idea of escaping, he knew not how—hour after hour of the three preceding days allowed him for preparation, has fled with a speed which no man living would deem possible, for none but this dying man can know. He has wearied his friends with entreaties, exhausted the attendants with importunities, neglected in his feverish restlessness the timely warnings of his spiritual consoler; and, now that the illusion is at last dispelled, now that eternity is before him and guilt behind, now that his fears of death amount almost to madness, and an overwhelming sense of his helpless, hopeless state rushes upon him, he is lost and stupefied, and has neither thoughts to turn to, nor power to call upon, the Almighty Being, from whom alone he can seek mercy and forgiveness, and before whom his repentance can alone avail." SB/VN

—to a cynic: "'I [John Chester] do not like their having hanged his mother. The fellow has a fine eye, and I am sure she was handsome. But very probably she was coarse—red-nosed perhaps, and had clumsy feet. Aye, it was all for the best, no doubt.'" BR 23

—deterrent effect: "Some murders are committed in hot blood and furious rage; some, in deliberate revenge; some, in terrible despair; some (but not many) for mere gain; some, for the removal of an object dangerous to the murder's peace or good name; some, to win a monstrous notoriety.

"On murders committed in rage, in the despair of strong affection (as when a starving child is murdered by its parent) or for gain, I believe the punishment of death to have no effect in the least. In the two first cases, the impulse is a blind and wild one, infinitely beyond the reach of any reference to the punishment. In the last, there is little calculation beyond the absorbing greed of the money to be got." MP/CP iii

—*effect on the executioner:* "Barnaby [Rudge] was to die. There was no hope. It is not the least evil attendant upon the frequent exhibition of this last dread punishment, of Death, that it hardens the minds of those who deal it out, and makes them, though they be amiable men in other respects, indifferent to, or unconscious of, their great responsibility. The word had gone forth that Barnaby was to die. It went forth, every month, for lighter crimes. It was a thing so common, that very few were startled by the awful sentence, or cared to question its propriety. Just then, too, when the law had been so flagrantly outraged, its dignity must be asserted. The symbol of its dignity—stamped upon every page of the criminal statute-book—was the gallows; and Barnaby was to die." BR 76

—*fundamentally:* " . . . this last dreadful and repulsive penalty; which never turned a man inclined to evil, and has hardened thousands who were half inclined to good." BR 65

—*hanging of women:* "'I tell you what though, brother,' said Dennis, cocking his hat for the convenience of scratching his head . . . 'it's worthy of notice, as a proof of the amazing equalness and dignity of our law, that it don't make no distinction between men and women. I've heerd the judge say, sometimes, to a highwayman or housebreaker as had tied the ladies neck and heels . . . and put 'em in a cellar, that he showed no consideration to women.

"'Now, I say that there judge didn't know his business, brother; and that if I had been that there highwayman or housebreaker, I should have made answer: "What are you talking of, my lord? I showed the women as much consideration as the law does, and what more would you have me do?"

"'If you was to count up in the newspapers the number of females as have been worked off in this here city alone, in the last ten year . . . you'd be surprised at the total—quite amazed, you would. There's a dignified and equal thing; a beautiful thing! But we've no security for its lasting. Now that they've begun to favour these here Papists, I shouldn't wonder if they went and altered even *that*, one of these days. Upon my soul, I shouldn't.'" ¶BR 59

—*human interest:* "'Ah!' returned the man, with a relish; 'he'll be drawn on a hurdle to be half hanged, and then he'll be taken down and sliced before his own face, and then his inside will be taken out and burnt while he looks on, and then his head will be chopped off, and he'll be cut into quarters. That's the sentence.' . . .

"Everybody present, except the one wigged gentleman who looked at the ceiling, stared at [Darnay]. All the human breath in the place, rolled at him, like a sea, or a wind, or a fire. Eager faces strained round pillars and corners, to get a sight of him; spectators in back rows stood up, not to miss a hair of him; people on the floor of the court, laid their hands on the shoulders of the people before them, to help themselves, at anybody's cost, to a view of him—stood a-tiptoe, got upon ledges, stood upon next to nothing, to see every inch of him. Conspicuous among these latter, like an animated bit of the spiked wall of Newgate, Jerry [Cruncher] stood: aiming at the prisoner the beery breath of a whet he had taken as he came along, and discharging it to mingle with the waves of other beer, and gin, and tea, and coffee, and what not, that flowed at him, and already broke upon the great windows behind him in an impure mist and rain . . . .

"The sort of interest with which this man was stared and breathed at, was not a sort that elevated humanity. Had he stood in peril of a less horrible sentence—had there been a chance of any one of its savage details being spared—by just so much would he have lost in his fascination. The form that was to be doomed to be so shamefully mangled, was the sight; the immortal creature that was to be so butchered and torn asunder, yielded the sensation. Whatever gloss the various spectators put upon the interest, according to their several arts and powers of self-deceit, the interest was, at the root of it, Ogreish." TTC ii 2

—*impact on childish observer:* " . . . while I lie awake . . . the Mannings, husband and wife, hanging on the top of Horsemonger Lane Jail. In connexion with which dismal spectacle, I recall this curious fantasy of the mind. That, having beheld that execution, and having left those two forms dangling on the top of the entrance gateway—the man's a limp, loose suit of clothes as if the man had gone out of them; the woman's, a fine shape, so elaborately corseted and artfully dressed, that it was quite unchanged in its trim appearance as it slowly swung from side to side—I never could, by my uttermost efforts, for some weeks, present the outside of that prison to myself (which the terrible impression I had received continually obliged me to do) without presenting it with the two figures still hanging in the morning air. Until, strolling past the gloomy place one night, when the street was deserted and quiet, and actually seeing that the bodies were not there, my fancy was persuaded, as it were, to take them down and bury them within the precincts of the jail, where they have lain ever since." RP/LA

—national methodology

—in America: "The prison-yard in which [the guard] pauses now, has been the scene of terrible performances. Into this narrow, grave-like place, men are brought out to die. The wretched creature stands beneath the gibbet on the ground; the rope about his neck, and when the sign is given, a weight at its other end comes running down, and swings him up into the air—a corpse.

"The law requires that there be present at this dismal spectacle, the judge, the jury, and citizens to the amount of twenty-five. From the community it is hidden. To the dissolute and bad, the thing remains a frightful mystery. Between the criminal and them, the prison-wall is interposed as a thick gloomy veil. It is the curtain to his bed of death, his winding-sheet, and grave. From him it shuts out life, and all the motives to unrepenting hardihood in that last hour, which its mere sight and presence is often all-sufficient to sustain. There are no bold eyes to make him bold; no ruffians to uphold a ruffian's name before. All beyond the pitiless stone wall, is unknown space." AN 6

—in England: "When [Dennis the hangman] remembered the great estimation in which his office was held, and the constant demand for his services; when he bethought himself, how the Statute Book regarded him as a kind of Universal Medicine applicable to men, women, and children, of every age and variety of criminal constitution; and how high he stood, in his official capacity, in the favour of the Crown, and both Houses of Parliament, the Mint, the Bank of England, and the judges of the land; when he recollected that whatever ministry was in or out, he remained their peculiar pet and panacea, and that for his sake England stood single and conspicuous among the civilised nations of the earth: when he called these things to mind and dwelt upon them, he felt certain that the national gratitude *must* relieve him from the consequences of his late proceedings, and would certainly restore him to his old place in the happy social system." BR 74

" . . . the hangman, ever busy and ever worse than useless, was [in 1775] in constant requisition; now, stringing up long rows of miscellaneous criminals; now, hanging a housebreaker on Saturday who had been taken on Tuesday; now, burning people in the hand at Newgate by the dozen, and now burning pamphlets at the door of Westminster Hall; to-day, taking the life of an atrocious murderer, and to-morrow of a wretched pilferer who had robbed a farmer's boy of sixpence." TTC i 1

—in Italy: "His neck fitting into a hole, made for the purpose, in a cross plank, was shut down, by another plank above; exactly like the pillory. Immediately below him was a leathern bag. And into it his head rolled instantly.

"The executioner was holding it by the hair, and walking with it round the scaffold, showing it to the people, before one quite knew that the knife had fallen heavily, and with a rattling sound.

"When it had travelled round the four sides of the scaffold, it was set upon a pole in front—a little patch of black and white, for the long street to stare at, and the flies to settle on. The eyes were turned upward, as if he had avoided the sight of the leathern bag, and looked to the crucifix. Every tinge and hue of life had left it in that instant. It was dull, cold, livid, wax. The body also.

"There was a great deal of blood. When we left the window, and went close up to the scaffold, it was very dirty; one of the two men who were throwing water over it, turning to help the other lift the body into a shell . . . . A strange appearance was the apparent annihilation of the neck. The head was taken off so close, that it seemed as if the knife had narrowly escaped crushing the jaw, or shaving off the ear; and the body looked as if there were nothing left above the shoulder." PI 11

—in Switzerland: "In that Canton the headsman still does his office with a sword; and I came upon this murderer sitting bound to a chair, with his eyes bandaged, on a scaffold in a little market-place. In that instant, a great sword (loaded with quicksilver in the thick part of the blade) swept round him like a gust of wine or fire, and there was no such creature in the world. My wonder was, not that he was so suddenly dispatched, but that any head was left unreaped, within a radius of fifty yards of that tremendous sickle." CS/HT

—needful apparatus: "A great multitude had already assembled; the windows were filled with people, smoking and playing cards to beguile the time; the crowd were pushing, quarrelling, and joking. Everything told of life and animation, but one dark cluster of objects in the very centre of all—the black stage, the cross-beam, the rope, and all the hideous apparatus of death." OT 52

"Into the street outside the jail's main wall, workmen came straggling at this solemn hour, in groups of two or three, and meeting in the centre, cast their tools upon the ground and spoke in whispers. Others soon issued from the jail itself, bearing on their shoulders planks and beams; these materials being all brought forth, the rest bestirred themselves, and the dull sound of hammers began to echo through the stillness.

"Here and there among this knot of labourers, one, with a lantern or a smoky link, stood by to light his fellows at their work; and by its doubtful aid, some might be dimly seen taking up the pavement of the road, while others held great upright posts, or fixed them in the holes thus made for their reception. Some dragged slowly on towards the rest an empty cart, which they brought rumbling from the prison yard; while others erected strong barriers across the street. All were busily engaged. Their dusky figures moving to and fro, at that unusual hour, so active and so silent, might have been taken for those of shadowy creatures toiling at midnight on some ghostly, unsubstantial work, which, like themselves, would vanish with the first gleam of day, and leave but morning mist and vapour.

"While it was yet dark, a few lookers-on collected, who had plainly come there for the purpose and intended to remain: even those who had to pass the spot on their way to some other place, lingered yet, as though the attraction of that were irresistible. Meanwhile the noise of saw and mallet went on briskly, mingled with the clattering of boards on the stone pavement of the road, and sometimes with the workmen's voices as they called to one another . . . .

"By-and-bye, the feeble light grew stronger, and the houses, with their sign boards and inscriptions, stood plainly out, in the dull gray morning. Heavy stage waggons crawled from the inn-yard opposite, and travellers peeped out; and as they rolled sluggishly away, cast many a backward look towards the jail. And now the sun's first beams came glancing into the street; and the night's work, which, in its various stages and in the varied fancies of the lookers-on had taken a hundred shapes, wore its own proper form—a scaffold and a gibbet." BR 77

"All was brightness and promise, excepting in the street below, into which (for it yet lay in shadow) the eye looked down as into a dark trench, where, in the midst of so much life, and hope, and renewal of existence, stood the terrible instrument of death. It seemed as if the very sun forebore to look upon it.

"But it was better, grim and sombre in the shade, than when, the day being more advanced, it stood confessed in the full glare and glory of the sun, with its black paint blistering, and its nooses dangling in the light like loathsome garlands. It was better in the solitude and gloom of midnight, with a few forms clustering about it, than in the freshness and the stir of morning, the centre of an eager crowd. It was better haunting the street like a spectre, when men were in their beds, and influencing perchance the city's dreams, than braving the broad day, and thrusting its obscene presence upon their waking senses." BR 77

And see IG:Revolution*—the Guillotine*

—prison chapel: "There is one object, too, which rivets the attention and fascinates the gaze, and from which we may turn horror-stricken in vain, for the recollection of it will haunt us, waking and sleeping, for a long time afterwards. Immediately below the reading-desk, on the floor of the chapel, and forming the most conspicuous object in its little area, is *the condemned pew;* a huge black pen, in which the wretched people, who are singled out for death, are placed on the Sunday preceding their execution, in

sight of all their fellow-prisoners, from many of whom they may have been separated but a week before, to hear prayers for their own souls, to join in the responses of their own burial service, and to listen to an address, warning their recent companions to take example by their fate, and urging themselves, while there is yet time—nearly four-and-twenty hours—to 'turn, and flee from the wrath to come!'

"Imagine what have been the feelings of the men whom that fearful pew has enclosed, and of whom, between the gallows and the knife, no mortal remnant may now remain! Think of the hopeless clinging to life to the last, and the wild despair, far exceeding in anguish the felon's death itself, by which they have heard the certainty of their speedy transmission to another world, with all their crimes upon their heads, rung into their ears by the officiating clergyman!

"At one time—and at no distant period either—the coffins of the men about to be executed, were placed in that pew, upon the seat by their side, during the whole service. It may seem incredible, but it is true. Let us hope that the increased spirit of civilisation and humanity which abolished this frightful and degrading custom, may extend itself to other usages equally barbarous; usages which have not even the plea of utility in their defence, as every year's experience has shown them to be more and more inefficacious." ¶SB/VN

—prisoner's viewpoint: "[Fagin] sat down on a stone bench opposite the door, which served for seat and bedstead; and casting his bloodshot eyes upon the ground, tried to collect his thoughts. After a while, he began to remember a few disjointed fragments of what the judge had said: though it had seemed to him, at the time, that he could not hear a word. These gradually fell into their proper places, and by degrees suggested more; so that in a little time he had the whole, almost as it was delivered. To be hanged by the neck, till he was dead—that was the end. To be hanged by the neck till he was dead.

"As it came on very dark, he began to think of all the men he had known who had died upon the scaffold; some of them through his means. They rose up in such quick succession, that he could hardly count them. He had seem some of them die—and had joked, too, because they died with prayers upon their lips. With what a rattling noise the drop went down; and how suddenly they changed, from strong and vigorous men to dangling heaps of clothes!

"Some of them might have inhabited that very cell—sat upon that very spot. It was very dark; why didn't they bring a light? The cell had been built for many years. Scores of men must have passed their last hours there. It was like sitting in a vault strewn with dead bodies—the cap, the noose, the pinioned arms, the faces that he knew, even beneath that hideous veil.—Light, light!

"At length, when his hands were raw with beating against the heavy door and walls, two men appeared: one bearing a candle, which he thrust into an iron candlestick fixed against the wall: the other dragging in a mattress on which to pass the night; for the prisoner was to be left alone no more . . . .

"It was not until the night of this last awful day, that a withering sense of his helpless, desperate state came in its full intensity upon his blighted soul; not that he had ever held any defined or positive hope of mercy, but that he had never been able to consider more than the dim probability of dying so soon. He had spoken little to either of the two men who relieved each other in their attendance upon him, and they, for their parts, made no effort to rouse his attention. He had sat there, awake, but dreaming. Now, he started up, every minute, and with gasping mouth and burning skin, hurried to and fro, in such a paroxysm of fear and wrath that even they—used to such sights—recoiled from him with horror. He grew so terrible, at last, in all the tortures of his evil conscience, that one man could not bear to sit there, eying him alone; and so the two kept watch together . . . . OT 52

And see Prisoner*—condemned; and* N:Times of Day*—night—before an execution*

—proximity and public indifference: "If Bedlam could be suddenly removed like another *Aladdin*'s palace, and set down on the space now occupied by Newgate, scarcely one man out of a hundred, whose road to business every morning lies through Newgate Street, or the Old Bailey, would pass the building without bestowing a hasty glance on its small, grated windows, and a transient thought upon the condition of the unhappy beings immured in its dismal cells; and yet these same men, day by day, and hour by hour, pass and repass this gloomy depository of the guilt and misery of

London, in one perpetual stream of life and bustle, utterly unmindful of the throng of wretched creatures pent up within it—nay, not even knowing, or if they do, not heeding, the fact, that as they pass one particular angle of the massive wall with a light laugh or a merry whistle, they stand within one yard of a fellow-creature, bound and helpless, whose hours are numbered, from whom the last feeble ray of hope has fled for ever, and whose miserable career will shortly terminate in a violent and shameful death.

"Contact with death, even in its least terrible shape, is solemn and appalling. How much more awful is it to reflect on this near vicinity to the dying—to men in full health and vigour, in the flower of youth or the prime of life, with all their faculties and perceptions as acute and perfect as your own; but dying, nevertheless—dying as surely—with the hand of death imprinted upon them as indelibly—as if mortal disease had wasted their frames to shadows, and corruption had already begun!" ¶SB/VN

—and religious politics: "'If these Papists gets into power [said Dennis], and begins to boil and roast instead of hang, what becomes of my work! If they touch my work that's a part of so many laws, what becomes of the laws in general, what becomes of the religion, what becomes of the country! . . . I mustn't have no Papists interfering with me, unless they come to be worked off in course of law; I mustn't have no biling, no roasting, no frying—nothing but hanging. My lord may well call me an earnest fellow. In support of the great Protestant principle of having plenty of that, I'll,' and here [Dennis the hangman] beat his club upon the ground, 'burn, fight, kill—do anything you bid me, so that it's bold and devilish—though the end of it was, that I got hung myself.'" BR 37

—its sweep in 1780: "'Parliament says this here—says Parliament, "If any man, woman, or child, does anything which goes again a certain number of our acts"—how many hanging laws may there be at this present time, Muster Gashford? Fifty?'

"'I don't exactly know how many,' replied Gashford, leaning back in his chair and yawning; 'a great number though.'

"'Well, say fifty. Parliament says, "If any man, woman, or child, does anything again any one of them fifty acts, that man, woman, or child, shall be worked off by Dennis." George the Third steps in when they number very strong at the end of a sessions, and says, "These are too many for Dennis. I'll have half for *my* self and Dennis shall have half for *him* self;" and sometimes he throws me in one over that I don't expect, as he did three year ago, when I got **Mary Jones**, a young woman of nineteen who come up to Tyburn with a infant at her breast, and was worked off for taking a piece of cloth off the counter of a shop in Ludgate Hill, and putting it down again when the shopman see her; and who had never done any harm before, and only tried to do that, in consequence of her husband having been pressed three weeks previous, and she being left to beg, with two young children—as was proved upon the trial.

"'Ha ha!—Well! That being the law and the practice of England, is the glory of England, an't it, Muster Gashford?'" ¶BR 37

"But indeed, at that time, putting to death was a recipe much in vogue with all trades and professions . . . . Death is Nature's remedy for all things, and why not Legislation's? Accordingly, the forger was put to death; the utterer of a bad note was put to Death; the unlawful opener of a letter was put to Death; the purloiner of forty shillings and sixpence was put to Death; the holder of a horse . . . who made off with it, was put to Death; the coiner of a bad shilling was put to Death; the sounders of three-fourths of the notes in the whole gamut of Crime, were put to Death. Not that it did the least good in the way of prevention—it might almost have been worth remarking that the fact was exactly the reverse—but, it cleared off (as to this world) the trouble of each particular case, and left nothing else connected with it to be looked after." TTC ii 1

—of traitors: "[David of Wales] was sentenced to be hanged, drawn, and quartered; and from that time [about 1300] this became the established punishment of Traitors in England—a punishment wholly without excuse, as being revolting, vile, and cruel, after its object is dead; and which has no sense in it, as its only real degradation (and that nothing can blot out) is to the country that permits on any consideration such abominable barbarity." CHE 16

And see TP:Courts of Law*—criminal courts —collective sentencing; and* TP:Judge

Charity

—*appeal by the Dream-Children:* "The most delightful paper, the most charming essay, which the tender imagination of **Charles Lamb** conceived, represents him as sitting by his fireside on a winter night, telling stories to his own dear children, and delighting in their society, until he suddenly comes to his old, solitary, bachelor self, and finds that they were but dream-children, who might have been, but never were. 'We are nothing', they say to him; 'less than nothing, and dreams. We are only what might have been, and we must wait upon the tedious shore of Lethe, millions of ages, before we have existence and a name.' 'And immediately awakening', he says, 'I found myself in my arm-chair.'

"The dream-children whom I would now raise, if I could, before every one of you, according to your various circumstances, should be the dear child you love, the dearer child you have lost, the child you might have had, the child you certainly have been. Each of these dream-children should hold in its powerful hand one of the little children now lying in the Child's Hospital, or now shut out of it to perish. Each of these dream-children should say to you, 'O help this little suppliant in my name; O, help it for my sake!'" ¶S/SC

—*beginner:* " . . . I then said, more particularly, that I was not sure of my qualifications. That I was inexperienced in the art of adapting my mind to minds very differently situated, and addressing them from suitable points of view. That I had not that delicate knowledge of the heart which must be essential to such a work. That I had much to learn, myself, before I could teach others, and that I could not confide in my good intentions alone. For these reasons, I thought it best to be as useful as I could, and to render what kind services I could, to those immediately about me; and to try to let that circle of duty gradually and naturally expand itself. All this I said, with anything but confidence; because Mrs Pardiggle was much older than I, and had great experience, and was so very military in her manners." BH 8

—*committees:* "It amazed us . . . to find how the great object of the lives of nearly all [Mr Jarndyce's] correspondents appeared to be to form themselves into committees for getting in and laying out money. The ladies were as desperate as the gentlemen; indeed, I think they were even more so. They threw themselves into committees in the most impassioned manner, and collected subscriptions with a vehemence quite extraordinary. It appeared to us that some of them must pass their whole lives in dealing out subscription-cards to the whole post-office directory—shilling cards, half-crown cards, half-sovereign cards, penny cards.

"They wanted everything. They wanted wearing apparel, they wanted linen rags, they wanted money, they wanted coals, they wanted soup, they wanted interest, they wanted autographs, they wanted flannel, they wanted whatever Mr Jarndyce had—or had not.

"Their objects were as various as their demands. They were going to raise new buildings, they were going to pay off debts on old buildings, they were going to establish in a picturesque building (engraving of proposed West Elevation attached) the Sisterhood of Mediaeval Marys; they were going to give a testimonial to Mrs Jellyby; they were going to have their Secretary's portrait painted, and presented to his mother-in-law, whose deep devotion to him was well known; they were going to get up everything, I really believe, from five hundred thousand tracts to an annuity, and from a marble monument to a silver teapot.

"They took a multitude of titles. They were the Women of England, the Daughters of Britain, the Sisters of all the Cardinal Virtues separately, the Females of America, the Ladies of a hundred denominations. They appeared to be always excited about canvassing and electing. They seemed to our poor wits, and according to their own accounts, to be constantly polling people by tens of thousands, yet never bringing their candidates in for anything. It made our heads ache to think, on the whole, what feverish lives they must lead." ¶BH 8

"[Mr Jarndyce] remarked that there were two classes of charitable people; one, the people who did a little and made a great deal of noise; the other, the people who did a great deal and made no noise at all." BH 8

—*at home:* "Jo is brought in. He is not one of Mrs Pardiggle's Tockahoopo Indians; he is not one of Mrs Jellyby's lambs; being wholly unconnected with Borrioboola-Gha; he is not softened by distance and unfamiliarity; he is not a genuine foreign-grown savage; he is the ordinary home-made article. Dirty, ugly, disagreeable to all the senses, in body a common creature of the common streets, only in soul a heathen. Homely filth begrimes him, homely parasites devour him, homely sores are in him, homely rags are on him: native ignorance, the growth of English soil and climate, sinks his immortal nature lower than the beasts that perish. Stand forth, Jo, in uncompromising colours! From the sole of thy foot to the crown of thy head there is nothing interesting about thee." BH 47

—home missionaries: "'The worst o' these here shepherds is, my boy, that they reg'larly turns the heads of all the young ladies about here. Lord bless their little hearts, they thinks it's all right, and don't know no better; but they're the wictims o' gammon, Samivel, they're the wictims o' gammon . . . and wot aggrawates me, Samivel, is to see 'em a wastin' all their time and labour in making clothes for copper-coloured people as don't want 'em, and taking no notice of flesh-coloured Christians as do.'" PP 27

"'So you vouldn't subscribe to the flannel veskits?' said Sam, after another interval of smoking.

"'Cert'nly not,' replied Mr Weller: 'what's the good o' flannel veskits to the young niggers abroad? But I'll tell you what it is, Sammy,' said Mr Weller, lowering his voice, and bending across the fire-place; 'I'd come down wery handsome towards straight veskits for some people at home.'

"As Mr Weller said this, he slowly recovered his former position, and winked at his first-born, in a profound manner.

"'It cert'nly seems a queer start to send out pocket ankerchers to people as don't know the use on 'em,' observed Sam.

"'They're always a doin' some gammon of that sort, Sammy,' replied his father." PP 27

"In short, we heard of a great many Missions, of various sorts, among this set of people; but, nothing respecting them was half so clear to us, as that it was Mr Quale's mission to be in ecstasies with everybody else's mission, and that it was the most popular mission of all.

"Mr Jarndyce had fallen into this company, in the tenderness of his heart and his earnest desire to do all the good in his power; but that he felt it to be too often an unsatisfactory company, where benevolence took spasmodic forms; where charity was assumed, as a regular uniform, by loud professors and speculators in cheap notoriety, vehement in profession, restless and vain in action, servile in the last degree of meanness to the great, adulatory of one another, and intolerable to those who were anxious quietly to help the weak from falling, rather than with a great deal of bluster and self-laudation to raise them up a little way when they were down; he plainly told us.

"When a testimonial was originated to Mr Quale, by Mr Gusher (who had already got one, originated by Mr Quale), and when Mr Gusher spoke for an hour and a half on the subject to a meeting, including two charity schools of small boys and girls, who were specially reminded of the widow's mite, and requested to come forward with halfpence and be acceptable sacrifices; I think the wind was in the east for three whole weeks." ¶BH 15

And see H:Philanthropist—*a project*

—need for romance: "There are many lives of much pain, hardship, and suffering, which, having no stirring interest for any but those who lead them, are disregarded by persons who do not want thought or feeling, but who pamper their compassion and need high stimulants to rouse it.

"There are not a few among the disciples of charity who require in their vocation scarcely less excitement than the votaries of pleasure in theirs; and hence it is that diseased sympathy and compassion are every day expended on out-of-the-way objects, when only too many demands upon the legitimate exercise of the same virtues in a healthy state, are constantly within the sight and hearing of the most unobservant person alive. In short, charity must have its romance, as the novelist or playwright must have his. A thief in fustian is a vulgar character, scarcely to be thought of by persons of refinement; but dress him in green velvet, with a high-crowned hat, and change the scene of his operations from a thickly-peopled city to a mountain road, and you shall find in him the very soul of poetry and adventure. So it is with the one great cardinal virtue, which, properly nourished and exercised leads to, if it does not necessarily include, all the others. It must have its romance; and the less of real hard struggling work-a-day life there is in that romance, the better." NN 18

—officiousness: "The business was carried on by [the shopman's] eldest daughter . . . we never passed at night without seeing the eldest girl at work . . . . We often thought,

as her pale face looked more sad and pensive in the dim candle-light, that if those thoughtless females who interfere with the miserable market of poor creatures such as these knew but one-half of the misery they suffer, and the bitter privations they endure, in their honourable attempts to earn a scanty subsistence, they would, perhaps, resign even opportunities for the gratification of vanity, and an immodest love of self-display, rather than drive them to a last dreadful resource, which it would shock the delicate feelings of these *charitable* ladies to hear named." SB/ST

—pontifical: "'I don't like it, Mr Venus. I don't like to have the life knocked out of former inhabitants of this house, in the gloomy dark, and not know who did it.'

"'Might you have any suspicions, Mr Wegg?'

"'No,' returns that gentleman. 'I know who profits by it. But I have no suspicions.'

"Having said which, Mr Wegg smokes and looks at the fire with a most determined expression of Charity; as if he had caught that cardinal virtue by the skirts, as she felt it her painful duty to depart from him, and held her by main force." OMF ii 7

—from the poor: " . . . before [Nell and her grandfather] reached the corner of the lane, the [furnace-watcher] came running after them, and, pressing her hand, left something in it—two old, battered, smoke-encrusted penny pieces. Who knows but they shone as brightly in the eyes of angels, as golden gifts that have been chronicled on tombs?" OCS 44

—puffery of patrons: "'Patrons and Patronesses, and Vice-Patrons and Vice-Patronesses, and Deceased Patrons and Deceased Patronesses, and Ex-Vice-Patrons and Ex-Vice-Patronesses, what does it all mean in the books of the Charities that come pouring in on Rokesmith as he sits among 'em pretty well up to his neck! If Mr Tom Noakes gives his five shillings, ain't he a Patron, and if Mrs Jack Styles gives her five shillings, ain't she a Patroness? What the deuce is it all about? If it ain't stark staring impudence, what do you call it?'

"'Don't be warm, Noddy,' Mrs Boffin urged.

"'Warm!' cried Mr Boffin. 'It's enough to make a man smoking hot. I can't go anywhere without being Patronized. I don't want to be Patronized. If I buy a ticket for a Flower Show, or a Music Show, or any sort of Show, and pay pretty heavy for it, why am I to be Patroned and Patronessed as if the Patrons and Patronesses treated me? If there's a good thing to be done, can't it be done on its own merits? If there's a bad thing to be done, can it ever be Patroned and Patronessed right? Yet when a new Institution's going to be built, it seems to me that the bricks and mortar ain't made of half so much consequence as the Patrons and Patronesses; no, nor yet the objects. I wish somebody would tell me whether other countries get Patronized to anything like the extent of this one! And as to the Patrons and Patronesses themselves, I wonder they're not ashamed of themselves. They ain't Pills, or Hair-Washes, or Invigorating Nervous Essences, to be puffed in that way!'" OMF ii 14

—self-display: "Aspiring young ladies, who read flaming accounts of some 'fancy fair in high life,' suddenly grow desperately charitable; visions of admiration and matrimony float before their eyes; some wonderfully meritorious institution, which by the strangest accident in the world, has never been heard of before, is discovered to be in a languishing condition: Thomson's great room, or Johnsons' nursery-ground, is forthwith engaged, and the aforesaid young ladies, from mere charity, exhibit themselves for three days, from twelve to four, for the small charge of one shilling per head!" SB/LR

—sincerity: "'Whether that species of benevolence which is so very cautious and long-sighted that it is seldom exercised at all, lest its owner should be imposed upon, and so wounded in his self-love, be real charity or a worldly counterfeit, I leave to wiser heads than mine to determine.'" PP 53

—solicitation

—church: "Oh the varieties of dust for ocular use, offered in exchange for the gold dust of the Golden Dustman! Fifty-seven churches to be erected with half-crowns, forty-two parsonage houses to be repaired with shillings, seven-and-twenty organs to be built with halfpence, twelve hundred children to be brought up on postage stamps. Not that a half-crown, shilling, halfpenny, or postage stamp, would be particularly acceptable from Mr Boffin, but that it is so obvious he is the man to make up the deficiency." OMF i 17

—corporate: ". . . mostly in difficulties, yet mostly lavish, too, in the expensive arti-

cles of print and paper. Large fat private double letter, sealed with ducal coronet. 'Nicodemus Boffin, Esquire. My dear Sir,—Having consented to preside at the forthcoming Annual Dinner of the Family Party Fund, and feeling deeply impressed with the immense usefulness of that noble Institution and the great importance of its being supported by a List of Stewards that shall prove to the public the interest taken in it by popular and distinguished men, I have undertaken to ask you to become a Steward on that occasion. Soliciting your favourable reply before the 14th instant, I am, My Dear sir, Your faithful servant, LINSEED.

P. S. The Steward's fee is limited to three Guineas.'

"Friendly this, on the part of the Duke of Linseed (and thoughtful in the postscript), only lithographed by the hundred and presenting but a pale individuality of address to Nicodemus Boffin, Esquire, in quite another hand. It takes two noble Earls and a Viscount, combined, to inform Nicodemus Boffin, Esquire, in an equally flattering manner, that an estimable lady in the West of England has offered to present a purse containing twenty pounds, to the Society for Granting Annuities to Unassuming Members of the Middle Classes, if twenty individuals will previously present purses of one hundred pounds each. And those benevolent noblemen very kindly point out that if Nicodemus Boffin, Esquire, should wish to present two or more purses, it will not be inconsistent with the design of the estimable lady in the West of England, provided each purse be coupled with the name of some member of his honoured and respected family." ¶OMF i 17

—the squeamish: ". . . there are people of so refined and delicate a nature, that they cannot bear the contemplation of [hunger, disease, vice]. Not that they turn instinctively from crime; but that criminal characters, to suit them, must be, like their meat, in delicate disguise . . . a Sikes in fustian is insupportable . . . if I turn back to the days in which [**William Hogarth**] or any of [**Fielding**, **De Foe**, **Goldsmith**, **Smollett**, etc.] flourished, I find the same reproach levelled against them every one, each in his turn, by the insects of the hour, who raised their little hum, and died, and were forgotten." OT pref 3d ed

—testamentary: "Did he see any faint reflection of his own image making a vainglorious will, whereby five-and-twenty Humbugs, past five-and-fifty years of age, each taking upon himself the name, Josiah Bounderby of Coketown, should for ever dine in Bounderby Hall, for ever lodge in Bounderby buildings, for ever attend a Bounderby chapel, for ever go to sleep under a Bounderby chaplain, for ever be supported out of a Bounderby estate, and for ever nauseate all healthy stomachs, with a vast amount of Bounderby balderdash and bluster?" HT iii 9

—true: "And as true charity not only covers a multitude of sins, but includes a multitude of virtues, such as forgiveness, liberal construction, gentleness and mercy to the faults of others, and the remembrance of our own imperfections and advantages, [Master Humphrey] bade us not inquire too closely into the venial errors of the poor, but finding that they *were* poor, first to relieve and then endeavour—at an advantage—to reclaim them." MH 15

—trust administration: " . . . I gathered that the greater part of the property bequeathed by the Worshipful Master Richard Watts for the maintenance of this foundation was, at the period of his death, mere marshland; but that, in course of time, it had been reclaimed and built upon, and was very considerably increased in value. I found, too, that about a thirtieth part of the annual revenue was now expended on the purposes commemorated in the inscription over the door; the rest being handsomely laid out in Chancery, law expenses, collectorship, receivership, poundage, and other appendages of management, highly complimentary to the importance of the six Poor Travellers. In short, I made the not entirely new discovery that it may be said of an establishment like this, in dear old England, as of the fat oyster in the American story, that it takes a good many men to swallow it whole." CS/PT

Charm

—conciliating: "'You'll mention that I called, perhaps?' said Dick . . . .

"'And say,' added Mr Swiveller, 'say, sir, that I was wafted here upon the pinions of concord; that I came to remove, with the rake of friendship, the seeds of mutual wiolence and heart-burning, and to sow in their place, the germs of social harmony. Will you have the goodness to charge yourself with that commission, sir?'" OCS 13

Dick does not strike us as a reader of Goethe,

but the latter's remark that "Pleasure and love are the pinions of great deeds" (Iphigenie auf Tauris II i) *suggests that Dickens was.*

—manipulating: "If any one had told me, then, that all this was a brilliant game, played for the excitement of the moment, for the employment of high spirits, in the thoughtless love of superiority, in a mere wasteful careless course of winning what was worthless to him [Steerforth], and next minute thrown away: I say, if any one had told me such a lie that night, I wonder in what manner of receiving it my indignation would have found a vent!" DC 21

—overwhelming: " . . . [Steerforth's] easy, spirited good humour; his genial manner, his handsome looks, his natural gift of adapting himself to whomsoever he pleased, and making direct, when he cared to do it, to the main point of interest in anybody's heart; bound [Peggotty] to him wholly in five minutes. His manner to me, alone, would have won her. But, through all these causes combined, I sincerely believe she had a kind of adoration for him before he left the house that night.

"He stayed there with me to dinner—if I were to say willingly, I should not half express how readily and gaily. He went into Mr Barkis's room like light and air, brightening and refreshing it as if he were healthy weather. There was no noise, no effort, no consciousness, in anything he did; but in everything an indescribable lightness, a seeming impossibility of doing anything else, or doing anything better, which was so graceful, so natural and agreeable, that it overcomes me, even now, in the remembrance. . . .

"He maintained all his delightful qualities to the last . . . . Indeed, they were more and more brightly exhibited as the hours went on; for I thought even then, and I have no doubt now, that the consciousness of success in his determination to please, inspired him with a new delicacy of perception, and made it, subtle as it was, more easy to him . . . .

"As to Mrs Gummidge, he roused that victim of despondency with a success never attained by any one else (so Mr Peggotty informed me), since the decease of the old one. He left her so little leisure for being miserable, that she said next day she thought she must have been bewitched." DC 21

[*CD deleted the specifics of this last in proof, but we cannot resist restoring this "proof" of what Steerforth could do when faced with a real challenge:*

"Mrs Gummidge, as usual, was taken poorly in her spirits when we showed a disposition to be merry, and was as usual adjured by Mr Peggotty to cheer up.

"'No, Dan'l,' said Mrs Gummidge, shaking her head, 'I gets worse and worse. I had far better go into the [Work] House to-morrow morning afore breakfast.'

"'No, no,' cried Steerforth, 'don't say so! what's the matter?'

"'You don't know me, sir,' said the doleful Gummidge, 'or you wouldn't ask.'

"'The loss is mine,' said Steerforth, coaxingly, 'but let us know each other better. What's the matter?'

"Mrs Gummidge shed tears, and stated her unfortunate condition in the usual terms. 'I'm a lone lorn creetur, and everythink goes contrairy with me!'

"'No?' cried Steerforth. 'Why, we must be designed by Heaven for one another. I'm a lone lorn creature myself, and everything has gone contrairy with me from my cradle. Mr Peggotty, will you change places, and allow me to sit next her?'

"The immediate effect of this on Mrs Gummidge was to make her laugh. '*You* lone and lorn!' cried Mrs Gummdige, peevishly. 'Yes! Your looks is like it!'

"'They are as like it as yours are,' said Steerforth, taking his seat beside her.

"'Indeed!' said Mrs Gummidge, with another laugh.

"'Aye, indeed!' cried Steerforth. 'Come! Let us be lone and lorn together. Everything shall go contrairy with us both, and we'll go contrairy with al' the world.'

"It was in vain for Mrs Gummidge to resist this league, or to try to push him away. He sat there all the rest of the evening; and whenever Mrs Gummidge began to shake her head, repeated his proposal. The consequence was, that Mrs Gummidge was continually laughing and pushing him . . . ." GC II 220]

—seductive: "Presently, they brought [little Em'ly] to the fireside, very much confused, and very shy—but she soon became more assured when she found how gently and respectfully Steerforth spoke to her; how skilfully he avoided anything that would embarrass her; how he talked to Mr Peggotty of boats, and ships, and tides, and fish; how he referred to me about the time when

he had seen Mr Peggotty at Salem House; how delighted he was with the boat and all belonging to it; how lightly and easily he carried on, until he brought us, by degrees, into a charmed circle, and we were all talking away without any reserve.

"Em'ly, indeed, said little all the evening; but she looked, and listened, and her face got animated, and she was charming. Steerforth told a story of a dismal shipwreck . . . as if he saw it all before him—and little Em'ly's eyes were fastened on him all the time, as if she saw it too. He told us a merry adventure of his own, as a relief to that, with as much gaiety as if the narrative were as fresh to him as it was to us—and little Em'ly laughed until the boat rang with the musical sounds, and we all laughed (Steerforth too), in irresistible sympathy with what was so pleasant and light-hearted. He got Mr Peggotty to sing, or rather to roar, 'When the stormy winds do blow, do blow, do blow;' and he sang a sailor's song himself, so pathetically and beautifully, that I could have almost fancied that the real wind creeping sorrowfully round the house, and murmuring low through our unbroken silence, was there to listen." DC 21

—a step-son's: "'Mother-in-law,' said Sam, 'how are you?'

"'Why, I do believe he is a Weller!' said Mrs W., raising her eyes to Sam's face, with no very gratified expression of countenance.

"'I rather think he is,' said the imperturbable Sam; 'and I hope this here reverend gen'l'm'n 'll excuse me saying that I vish I was *the* Weller as owns you, mother-in-law.'

"This was a double-barrelled compliment. It implied that Mrs Weller was a most agreeable female, and also that Mr Stiggins had a clerical appearance. It made a visible impression at once . . . . " PP 27

—tough subject: "During the whole of this day . . . Steerforth exerted himself with his utmost skill, and that was with his utmost ease, to charm this singular creature [Rosa Dartle] into a pleasant and pleased companion. That he should succeed, was no matter of surprise to me. That she should struggle against the fascinating influence of his delightful art—delightful nature I thought it then—did not surprise me either; for I knew that she was sometimes jaundiced and perverse. I saw her features and her manner slowly change; I saw her look at him with growing admiration; I saw her try, more and more faintly, but always angrily, as if she condemned a weakness in herself, to resist the captivating power that he possessed; and finally, I saw her sharp glance soften, and her smile become quite gentle, and I ceased to be afraid of her as I had really been all day, and we all sat about the fire, talking and laughing together, with as little reserve as if we had been children." DC 29

Condescension

—misplaced: "Though the host of the Nutmeg-Grater had a lively regard for his good-wife, it was of the old patronising kind, and she amused him mightily. Nothing would have astonished him so much, as to have known for certain from any third party, that it was she who managed the whole house, and made him, by her plain straightforward thrift, good-humour, honesty, and industry, a thriving man. So easy it is, in any degree of life (as the world very often finds it), to take those cheerful natures that never assert their merit, at their own modest valuation; and to conceive a flippant liking of people for their outward oddities and eccentricities, whose innate worth, if we would look so far, might make us blush in the comparison!" BL 3

—patronising: "What a satisfaction it was to Mrs Chick—a common-place piece of folly enough, compared with whom her sister-in-law had been a very angel of womanly intelligence and gentleness—to patronise and be tender to the memory of that lady: in exact pursuance of her conduct to her in her lifetime: and to thoroughly believe herself, and take herself in, and make herself uncommonly comfortable on the strength of her toleration! What a mighty pleasant virtue toleration should be when we are right, to be so very pleasant when we are wrong, and quite unable to demonstrate how we come to be invested with the privilege of exercising it!" DS 4

Courtier

—in Africa: "There is a frantic wickedness in [the Praiser's] manner of worrying the air, and gnashing out, 'O what a delightful chief he is! O what a delicious quantity of blood he sheds! O how majestically he laps it up! O how charmingly cruel he is! O how he tears the flesh of his enemies and crunches the bones! O how like the tiger and the leopard and the wolf and the bear he is! O, row row row row, how fond I am of him!'

which might tempt the Society of Friends to charge at a hand-gallop into the Swartz-Kop location and exterminate the whole kraal." RP/NS

—*of Canute:* ". . . Canute was one day disgusted with his courtiers for their flattery . . . he caused his chair to be set on the seashore, and feigned to command the tide as it came up not to wet the edge of his robe, for the land was his . . . . I fancy I see them all on the sea-shore together; the King's chair sinking in the sand; the King in a mighty good humour with his own wisdom, and the courtiers pretending to be quite stunned by it!" CHE 5

—*deference:* "When Perch, the messenger, whose place was on a little bracket, like a timepiece, saw Mr Dombey come in—or rather when he felt that he was coming, for he had usually an instinctive sense of his approach—he hurried into Mr Dombey's room, stirred the fire, quarried fresh coals from the bowels of the coal-box, hung the newspaper to air upon the fender, put the chair ready, and the screen in its place, and was round upon his heel on the instant of Mr Dombey's entrance, to take his great-coat and hat, and hang them up.

"Then Perch took the newspaper, and gave it a turn or two in his hands before the fire, and laid it, deferentially, at Mr Dombey's elbow. And so little objection had Perch to doing deferential in the last degree, that if he might have laid himself at Mr Dombey's feet, or might have called him by some such title as used to be bestowed upon the Caliph **Haroun Alraschid**, he would have been all the better pleased.

"As this honour would have been an innovation and an experiment, Perch was fain to content himself by expressing as well as he could, in his manner, You are the light of my Eyes. You are the Breath of my Soul. You are the commander of the Faithful Perch! With this imperfect happiness to cheer him, he would shut the door softly, walk away on tiptoe, and leave his great chief . . . ." ¶DS 13

" . . . Mr Perch the messenger knocked softly at the door, and coming in on tiptoe, bending his body at every step as if it were the delight of his life to bow, laid some papers on the table.

"'Would you please to be engaged, sir?' asked Mr Perch [of Carker the manager], rubbing his hands, and deferentially putting his head on one side, like a man who felt he had no business to hold it up in such a presence, and would keep it as much out of the way as possible." DS 22

—*dissembling:* "Mrs Sparsit was so much affected . . . that, assisting Mr Bounderby to his hat after breakfast, and being then alone with him in the hall, she imprinted a chaste kiss upon his hand, murmured 'My benefactor!' and retired, overwhelmed with grief. Yet it is an indubitable fact, within the cognizance of this history, that five minutes after he had left the house in the self-same hat, the same descendant of the Scadgerses and connexion by matrimony of the Powlers, shook her right-hand mitten at his portrait, made a contemptuous grimace at that work of art, and said 'Serve you right, you Noodle, and I am glad of it.'" HT ii 9

—*of Edward II:* "[Despenser's] poor old father and he were innocent enough of any worse crimes than the crime of having been friends of a King, on whom, as a mere man, they would never have deigned to cast a favourable look. It is a bad crime, I know, and leads to worse; but, many lords and gentlemen—I even think some ladies, too, if I recollect right—have committed it in England, who have neither been given to the dogs, nor hanged up fifty feet high." CHE 17

—*money a consideration:* "'The profit!' repeated Mr Pecksniff. 'The profit of dissimulation! To worship the golden calf of Baal, for eighteen shillings a week!' . . .

"'Oh Calf, Calf!' cried Mr Pecksniff mournfully. 'Oh, Baal, Baal! Oh my friend, Mrs Todgers! To barter away that precious jewel, self-esteem, and cringe to any mortal creature—for eighteen shillings a week!' . . .

"Eighteen shillings a week! Just, most just, thy censure, upright Pecksniff! Had it been for the sake of a ribbon, star, or garter; sleeves of lawn, a great man's smile, a seat in parliament, a tap upon the shoulder from a courtly sword; a place, a party, or a thriving lie, or eighteen thousand pounds, or even eighteen hundred;—but to worship the golden calf for eighteen shillings a week! Oh pitiful, pitiful!" MC 10

—*in North America:* "On one respect, to be sure, I am quite free from [the Medicine-Man]. On occasions when the Medicine-Man in general, together with a large number of the miscellaneous inhabitants of his village, both male and female, are presented to the principal Chief, his native 'Medicine' is a comical mixture of old odds and ends (hired of traders), and new things in antiquated shapes, and pieces of red cloth (of which he is particularly fond), and white and red and blue paint for the face. The irrationality of this particular Medicine culminates in a mock battle-rush, from which many of the squaws are borne out much dilapidated. I need not observe how unlike this is to a Drawing-Room at St James's Palace." UT/MM

—of the rich: "The famous name of Merdle became, every day, more famous in the land. Nobody knew that the Merdle of such high renown had ever done any good to any one, alive or dead, or to any earthly thing . . . nobody had the smallest reason for supposing the clay of which this object of worship was made, to be other than the commonest clay, with as clogged a wick smouldering inside of it as ever kept an image of humanity from tumbling to pieces. All people knew (or thought they knew) that he had made himself immensely rich; and, for that reason alone, prostrated themselves before him, more degradedly and less excusably than the darkest savage creeps out of his hole in the ground to propitiate, in some log or reptile, the Deity of his benighted soul." LD ii 12

—of Richard II: "As to the lords and ladies about the Court, they declared him to be the most beautiful, the wisest, and the best—even of princes—whom the lords and ladies about the Court, generally declare to be the most beautiful, the wisest, and the best of mankind. To flatter a poor boy in this base manner was not a very likely way to develop whatever good was in him; and it brought him to anything but a good or happy end." CHE 19

—schoolchildren: "'A Member of Parliament's daughter!' ejaculated Amelia, in an ecstatic tone.

"'A Member of Parliament's daughter!' repeated Miss Maria, with a smile of delight, which, of course, elicited a concurrent titter of pleasure from all the young ladies.

"'It's exceedingly delightful!' said Miss Amelia; whereupon all the young ladies murmured their admiration again. Courtiers are but school-boys, and court-ladies school-girls." SB/S

—supernatural: " . . . all the goblins in waiting, crowded round the wretched sexton, and kicked him without mercy: according to the established and invariable custom of courtiers upon earth, who kick whom royalty kicks, and hug whom royalty hugs." PP 29

—sycophancy: "Mrs Todgers vowed that anything one quarter as angelic she had never seen. 'She wanted but a pair of wings, a dear,' said that good woman, 'to be a young syrup:' meaning, possibly, young sylph, or seraph." MC 9

" . . . false and subtle men will always secretly despise and dislike the object upon which they fawn, and always resent the payment and receipt of homage that they know to be worthless . . . . " DS 55

"Dobbs is perfectly clear . . . that men are to be deferred to for their capacity for what they undertake, for their talents and worth, and for nothing else . . . . But I have seen Dobbs dive and double about that Royal Academy Exhibition, in pursuit of a nobleman, in a marvellously small way. I have stood with Dobbs examining a picture, when the Marquis has entered, and I have known of the Marquis's entrance without lifting my eyes or turning my head, solely by the increased gentility in the audible tones of Dobbs's critical observation . . . until the Marquis has said, 'Ha, Dobbs?' and Dobbs, with his face folded into creases of deference, has piloted that illustrious nobleman away, to the contemplation of some pictorial subtleties of his own discovery." HW/TT

And see TF:Lawyer—*flatterer*

—tact and tactlessness: "Not an opinion could be elicited from the Long-lost [brother], in unison with the sentiments of any individual present. He contradicted Flipfield dead, before he had eaten his salmon . . . . He was an antipathetical being, with a peculiar power and gift of treading on everybody's tenderest place. They talk in America of a man's 'Platform.' I should describe the Platform of the Long-lost as a Platform composed of other people's corns, on which he had stumped his way, with all his might and main, to his present position." UT/BC

Crime and Criminal

—against children: "'What do you think, then? asked Noah, anxiously regarding [Fagin]. 'Something in the sneaking way, where it was pretty sure work, and not much more risk than being at home.'

"'What do you think of the old ladies?' asked Fagin. 'There's a good deal of money made in snatching their bags and parcels, and running round the corner.'

"'Don't they holler out a good deal, and scratch sometimes?' asked Noah, shaking his head. 'I don't think that would answer my purpose. Ain't there any other line open?'

"'Stop!' said Fagin, laying his hand on Noah's knee. 'The kinchin lay.'

"'What's that?' demanded Mr Claypole.

"'The kinchins, my dear,' said Fagin, 'is the young children that's sent on errands by their mothers, with sixpences and shillings; and the lay is just to take their money away—they've always got it ready in their hands—then knock 'em into the kennel, and walk off very slow, as if there were nothing else the matter but a child fallen down and hurt itself. Ha! ha! ha!'

"'Ha! ha!' roared Mr Claypole, kicking up his legs in an ecstasy. 'Lord, that's the very thing!' OT 42

—*the children:* "I looked at [the constable], and I looked about at the disorderly traces in the mud, and I thought of the drops of rain and the footprints of an extinct creature, hoary ages upon ages old, that geologists have identified on the face of a clift; and this speculation came over me: If this mud could petrify at this moment, and could lie concealed here for ten thousand years, I wonder whether the race of men then to be our successors on the earth could, from these or any marks, by the utmost force of the human intellect, unassisted by tradition, deduce such an astounding inference as the existence of a polished state of society that bore with the public savagery of neglected children in the streets of its capital city, and was proud of its power by sea and land, and never used its power to seize and save them!" UT/AB *And see* N:Nature—*perverted*

"I know . . . that if the State would begin its work and duty at the beginning, and would with the strong hand take those children out of the streets, while they are yet children, and wisely train them, it would make them a part of England's glory, not its shame—of England's strength, not its weakness—would raise good soldiers and sailors, and good citizens, and many great men, out of the seeds of its criminal population.

"Yet . . . I concern myself far more about one railway-bridge across a public thoroughfare, than about a dozen generations of scrofula, ignorance, wickedness, prostitution, poverty, and felony. I can slip out at my door, in the small hours after any midnight, and, in one circuit of the purlieus of Covent-garden Market, can behold a state of infancy and youth, as vile as if a Bourbon sat upon the English throne; a great police force looking on with authority to do no more than worry and hunt the dreadful vermin into corners and there leave them." ¶UT/ST

" . . . let me say, that I know the prisons of London well . . . and that the children in them are enough to break the heart and hope of any man." MP/CE *And see —and poverty*

—*education:* "[Prison governors] know perfectly well, that these children pass and repass through the prisons all their lives; that they are never taught; that the first distinctions between right and wrong are, from their cradles, perfectly confounded and perverted in their minds; that they come of untaught parents, and will give birth to another untaught generation; that in exact proportion to their natural abilities, is the extent and scope of their depravity; and that there is no escape or chance for them in any ordinary revolution of human affairs." MP/CE *And see* M:Education—*ignorance*

—*as we sow . . .* "As we sow, we reap. Let the reader go into the children's side of any prison in England, or, I grieve to add, of many workhouses, and judge whether those are monsters who disgrace our streets, people our hulks and penitentiaries, and overcrowd our penal colonies, or are creatures whom we have deliberately suffered to be bred for misery and ruin." MC pref

—*criminal mind:* "The state of the man [Bradley Headstone] was murderous, and he knew it. More; he irritated it, with a kind of perverse pleasure akin to that which a sick man sometimes has in irritating a wound upon his body. Tied up all day with his disciplined show upon him, subdued to the performance of his routine of educational tricks, encircled by a gabbling crowd, he broke loose at night like an ill-tamed wild animal. Under his daily restraint, it was his compensation, not his trouble, to give a glance towards his state at night, and to the freedom of its being indulged.

"If great criminals told the truth—which, being great criminals, they do not—they would very rarely tell of their struggles against the crime. Their struggles are towards it. They buffet with opposing waves to gain the bloody shore, not to recede from it.

"This man perfectly comprehended that he hated his rival with his strongest and worst forces, and that if he tracked him to Lizzie Hexam, his so doing would never serve himself with her, or serve her. All his pains were taken, to the end that he might incense himself with the sight of the detested figure in her company and favour, in her place of concealment. And he knew as well what act of his would follow if he did, as he knew that his mother had borne him. Granted, that he may not have held it necessary to make express mention to himself of the one familiar truth any more than of the other.

"He knew equally well that he fed his wrath and hatred, and that he accumulated provocation and self-justification, by being made the nightly sport of the reckless and insolent Eugene. Knowing all this, and still always going on with infinite endurance, pains, and perseverance, could his dark soul doubt whither he went?" ¶OMF iii 11

"What could [Rosa Bud] know of the criminal intellect, which its own professed students perpetually misread, because they persist in trying to reconcile it with the average intellect of average men, instead of identifying it as a horrible wonder apart. . . . " MED 20

—in England in 1775: "In England, there was scarcely an amount of order and protection to justify much national boasting. Daring burglaries by armed men, and highway robberies, took place in the capital itself every night; families were publicly cautioned not to go out of town without removing their furniture to upholsterers' warehouses for security; the highwayman in the dark was a City tradesman in the light, and, being recognised and challenged by his fellow-tradesman whom he stopped in his character of 'the Captain', gallantly shot him through the head and rode away; the mail was waylaid by seven robbers, and the guard shot three dead, and then got shot dead himself by the other four, 'in consequence of the failure of his ammunition:' after which the mail was robbed in peace; that magnificent potentate, the Lord Mayor of London, was made to stand and deliver on Turnham Green, by one highwayman, who despoiled the illustrious creature in sight of all his retinue; prisoners in London gaols fought battles with their turnkeys, and the majesty of the law fired blunderbusses in among them, loaded with rounds of shot and ball; thieves snipped off diamond crosses from the necks of noble lords at Court drawing-rooms; musketeers went into St Giles's, to search for contraband goods, and the mob fired on the musketeers, and the musketeers fired on the mob, and nobody thought any of these occurrences much out of the common way." BR 4

—and environment: "O honorable friend, member for Verbosity, your boy of fourteen—who brought home his prize from school this Midsummer, and told you with some glee of his boyish escapades—is a fine fellow; in spite of his juvenile offences he will grow up one of these days, to be a noble, honest man. But, had he been deprived of your assistance, O honorable friend, of your good thought on his behalf and your wife's tender solicitude; had your birthplace been a filthy fever-breeding alley; had no voice of teacher ever sounded in your ears; had you been made a callous man by rubbing constantly against the hardest side of society; had your wife died of the gin with which she sought to drown the despondent sense of a most wretched existence; had you gone to your daily work, leaving your boy in the pestiferous alley; what would he, what could he, have been!" HWC/BM

—false front: "Wintry morning, looking with dull eyes and sallow face upon the neighbourhood of Leicester Square, finds its inhabitants unwilling to get out of bed. Many of them are not early risers at the brightest of times, being birds of night who roost when the sun is high, and are wide awake and keen for prey when the stars shine out. Behind dingy blind and curtain, in upper story and garret, skulking more or less under false names, false hair, false titles, false jewellery, and false histories, a colony of brigands lie in their first sleep.

"Gentlemen of the green baize road who could discourse, from personal experience, of foreign galleys and home treadmills; spies of strong governments that eternally quake with weakness and miserable fear, broken traitors, cowards, bullies, gamesters, shufflers, swindlers, and false witnesses; some not unmarked by the branding-iron, beneath their dirty braid; all with more cruelty in them than was in **Nero**, and more crime than is in Newgate.

"For, howsoever bad the devil can be in fustian or smock-frock (and he can be very bad in both), he is a more designing, callous, and intolerable devil when he sticks a pin in his shirt-front, calls himself a gentleman, backs a card or colour, plays a game or so of billiards, and knows a little about bills and promissory notes, than in any other form he wears. And in such form Mr Bucket shall find him, when he will, still pervading the tributary channels of Leicester Square." ¶BH 26

—*gentlemanly:* " . . . I have read of practised thieves with the appearance and manners of gentlemen—a popular phenomenon which never existed on earth out of fiction and a police report." UT/RT

—*observer inured:* "The [turnkey] was not unnaturally cruel or hard-hearted. He had come to look upon felony as a kind of disorder, like the scarlet fever or erysipelas; some people had it—some hadn't—just as it might be." OCS 61

—*petty thievery:* "Whoever would begin to be worried with letting Lodgings that wasn't a lone woman with a living to get is a thing inconceivable to me, my dear; excuse the familiarity, but it comes natural to me in my own little room, when wishing to open my mind to those that I can trust, and I should be truly thankful if they were all mankind, but such is not so, for have but a Furnished bill in the window and your watch on the mantelpiece, and farewell to it if you turn your back for but a second, however gentlemanly the manners; nor is being of your own sex any safeguard, as I have reason, in the form of sugar-tongs, to know, for that lady (and a fine woman she was) got me to run for a glass of water, on the plea of going to be confined, which certainly turned out true, but it was in the Stationhouse." CS/L 1

—*pickpocket:* "In several parts of the house we noticed some young pickpockets of our acquaintance; but as they were evidently there as private individuals, and not in their public capacity, we were little disturbed by their presence. For we consider the hours of idleness passed by this class of society as so much gain to society at large. . . . " HW/AP 1

—*and poverty:* " . . . an effort [the Ragged Schools] . . . to introduce among the miserable and neglected outcasts in London, some knowledge of the commonest principles of morality and religion; to commence their recognition as immortal human creatures, before the Gaol Chaplain becomes their only schoolmaster; to suggest to Society that its duty to this wretched throng, foredoomed to crime and punishment, rightfully begins at some distance from the police office; and that the careless maintenance from year to year, in this the capital city of the world, of a vast hopeless nursery of ignorance, misery, and vice; a breeding place for the hulks and jails: is horrible to contemplate." MP/CE

—*punishment in former times:* "Facing eastward, I left behind me Smithfield and Old Bailey—fire and faggot, condemned hold, public hanging, whipping through the city at the cart-tail, pillory, branding-iron, and other beautiful ancestral landmarks, which rude hands have rooted up, without bringing the stars quite down upon us as yet . . . . " UT/AB

—*revival of whipping:* "The late brutal assaults. I strongly question the expediency of advocating the revival of whipping for those crimes. It is a natural and generous impulse to be indignant at the perpetration of inconceivable brutality, but I doubt the whipping panacea gravely. Not in the least regard or pity for the criminal, whom I hold in far lower estimation than a mad wolf, but in consideration for the general tone and feeling, which is very much improved since the whipping times.

"It is bad for a people to be familiarised with such punishments. When the whip went out of Bridewell, and ceased to be flourished at the cart's tail and at the whipping-post, it began to fade out of madhouses, and workhouses, and schools and families, and to give place to a better system everywhere, than cruel driving. It would be hasty, because a few brutes may be inadequately punished, to revive, in any aspect, what, in so many aspects, society is hardly yet happily rid of.

"The whip is a very contagious kind of thing, and difficult to confine within one set of bounds . . . at least quadruple the term of imprisonment for aggravated assaults—and above all let us, in such cases, have no Pet Prisoning, vain glorifying, strong soup, and roasted meats, but hard work, and one unchanging and uncompromising dietary of bread and water, well or ill; and we shall do much better than by going down into the dark to grope for the whip among the rusty fragments of the rack, and the branding iron, and the chains and gibbet from the public roads, and the weights that pressed men to death in the cells of Newgate." ¶RP/LA

—*on the river:* "And as to the various kinds of water-thieves . . . there were the Tier-rangers, who silently dropped alongside the tiers of shipping in the Pool, by night, and who, going to the companion-head, listened for two snores—snore number one, the skipper's; snore number two, the mate's—mates and skippers always snoring great guns, and being dead sure to be hard at it if they had turned in and were asleep. Hearing the double fire, down went the Rangers into the skippers' cabins; groped for the skippers' inexpressibles, which it was the custom of those gentlemen to shake off, watch, money, braces, boots, and all together, on the floor; and therewith made off as silently as might be.

"Then there were the Lumpers, or labourers employed to unload vessels. They wore loose canvas jackets with a broad hem in the bottom, turned inside, so as to form a large circular pocket in which they could conceal, like clowns in pantomimes, packages of surprising sizes. A great deal of property was stolen in this manner . . . from steamers; first, because steamers carry a larger number of small packages than other ships; next, because of the extreme rapidity with which they are obliged to be unladen for their return voyages.

"The Lumpers dispose of their booty easily to marine store dealers, and the only remedy to be suggested is that marine store shops should be licensed, and thus brought under the eye of the police as rigidly as public-houses. Lumpers also smuggle goods ashore for the crews of vessels. The smuggling of tobacco is so considerable, that it is well worth the while of the sellers of smuggled tobacco to use hydraulic presses, to squeeze a single pound into a package small enough to be contained in an ordinary pocket.

"Next . . . there were the Truckers—less thieves than smugglers, whose business it was to land more considerable parcels of goods than the Lumpers could manage. They sometimes sold articles of grocery and so forth, to the crews, in order to cloak their real calling, and get aboard without suspicion.

"Besides these, there were the Dredgermen, who, under pretence of dredging up coals and such like from the bottom of the river, hung about barges and other undecked craft, and when they saw an opportunity, threw any property they could lay their hands on overboard: in order slyly to dredge it up when the vessel was gone. Sometimes, they dexterously used their dredges to whip away anything that might lie within reach. Some of them were mighty neat at this, and the accomplishment was called dry dredging.

"Then, there was a vast deal of property, such as copper nails, sheathing, hardwood &c., habitually brought away by shipwrights and other workmen from their employers' yards, and disposed of to marine store dealers, many of whom escaped detection through hard swearing, and their extraordinary artful ways of accounting for the possession of stolen property.

"Likewise, there were special-pleading practitioners, for whom barges 'drifted away of their own selves'—they having no hand in it, except first cutting them loose, and afterwards plundering them—innocents, meaning no harm, who had the misfortune to observe those foundlings wandering about the Thames." ¶RP/DT

And see Capital punishment, Murderer, Prison, Prisoner, Public execution

Debt and Debtor

—constrained about town: "'I enter in this little book the names of the streets that I can't go down while the shops are open [said Richard Swiveller]. This dinner to-day closes Long Acre. I bought a pair of boots in Great Queen Street last week, and made that no thoroughfare too. There's only one avenue to the Strand left open now, and I shall have to stop up that to-night with a pair of gloves. The roads are closing so fast in every direction, that in about a month's time, unless my aunt sends me a remittance, I shall have to go three or four miles out of town to get over the way.'" OCS 8

—detained at a public-house: "'There is at this present moment in this very place, a perfect constellation of talent and genius, who is involved . . . in a situation as tremendous, perhaps, as the social intercourse of the nineteenth century will readily admit of. There is actually at this instant, at the Blue Dragon in this village—an alehouse, observe: a common, paltry, low-minded, clodhopping, pipe smoking alehouse—an individual, of whom it may be said, in the language of the Poet, that nobody but himself can in any way come up to him; who is detained there for his bill. Ha! ha! For his bill. I repeat it. For his bill.

Now,' said Mr Tigg, 'we have heard of Fox's Book of Martyrs, I believe, and we have heard of the Court of Requests, and the Star Chamber; but I fear the contradiction of no man alive or dead, when I assert that my friend Chevy Slyme being held in pawn for a bill, beats any amount of cock-fighting with which I am acquainted.'" MC 7

—*discharged by I.O.U.:* "'To leave this metropolis,' said Mr Micawber, 'and my friend Mr Thomas Traddles, without acquitting myself of the pecuniary part of this obligation, would weigh upon my mind to an insupportable extent. I have, therefore, prepared for my friend Mr Thomas Traddles, and I now hold in my hand a document, which accomplishes the desired object. I beg to hand to my friend Mr Thomas Traddles my I.O.U. for forty-one, ten, eleven and a half, and I am happy to recover my moral dignity, and to know that I can once more walk erect before my fellow-man.'

"With this introduction (which greatly affected him), Mr Micawber placed his I.O.U. in the hands of Traddles, and said he wished him well in every relation of life. I am persuaded, not only that this was quite the same to Mr Micawber as paying the money, but that Traddles himself hardly knew the difference until he had had time to think about it.

"Mr Micawber walked so erect before his fellow-man on the strength of this virtuous action, that his chest looked half as broad again when he lighted us down the stairs." DC 36

—*his furniture:* "'The oddity of the thing is,' said Mr Skimpole, with a quickened sense of the ludicrous, 'that my chairs and tables were not paid for, and yet my landlord walks off with them as composedly as possible. Now, that seems droll! There is something grotesque in it. The chair and table merchant never engaged to pay my landlord my rent. Why should my landlord quarrel with *him?* If I have a pimple on my nose which is disagreeable to my landlord's peculiar ideas of beauty, my landlord has no business to scratch my chair and table merchant's nose, which has no pimple on it. His reasoning seems defective!'" BH 17

And see B:Furniture—*a debtor's*

—*genius humiliated:* "'I swear,' cried Mr Slyme, giving the table an imbecile blow with his fist, and then feebly leaning his head upon his hand, while some drunken drops oozed from his eyes, 'that I am the wretchedest creature on record. Society is in a conspiracy against me. I'm the most literary man alive. I'm full of scholarship; I'm full of genius; I'm full of information; I'm full of novel views on every subject; yet look at my condition! I'm at this moment obliged to two strangers for a tavern bill!'" MC 7

—*landlady's bill:* "'She says that if I can afford to give a party I ought to be able to pay her confounded "little bill."'

"'How long has it been running?' inquired Mr Ben Allen. A bill, by the bye, is the most extraordinary locomotive engine that the genius of man ever produced. It would keep on running during the longest lifetime, without ever once stopping of its own accord." PP 32

—*ordained:* "'He relies upon everybody!' said Mr Jarndyce . . . .

"'Everybody! And he'll be in the same scrape again, next week! . . . He's always in the same scrape. He was born in the same scrape. I verily believe that the announcement in the newspapers when his mother was confined, was "On Tuesday last, at her residence in Botheration Building, Mrs Skimpole of a son in difficulties"'" BH 6

—*a spunging-house:* "The room—which was a small, confined den—was partitioned off into boxes, like the common-room of some inferior eating-house. The dirty floor had evidently been as long a stranger to the scrubbing-brush as to carpet or floor-cloth: and the ceiling was completely blackened by the flare of the oil-lamp by which the room was lighted at night. The grey ashes on the edges of the tables, and the cigar ends which were plentifully scattered about the dusty grate, fully accounted for the intolerable smell of tobacco which pervaded the place; and the empty glasses and half-saturated slices of lemon on the tables, together with the porter pots beneath them, bore testimony to the frequent libations in which the individuals who honoured Mr Solomon Jacobs by a temporary residence in his house indulged. Over the mantel-shelf was a paltry looking-glass, extending about half the width of the chimney-piece; but by way of counterpoise, the ashes were confined by a rusty fender about twice as long as the hearth." SB/WT

—*spurious helplessness:* "[Harold Skimpole] particularly requested to see Little Coavinses (meaning Charley [Neckett]), and told her, with a patriarchal air, that he had given her late father all the business in his power; and that if one of her little brothers would make haste to get set-up in the same profession, he hoped he should still be able to put a good deal of employment in his way.

"'For I am constantly being taken in these nets,' said Mr Skimpole, looking beamingly at us over a glass of wine-and-water, 'and am constantly being bailed out—like a boat. Or paid off—like a ship's company. Somebody always does it for me. I can't do it, you know, for I never have any money. But Somebody does it. I get out by Somebody's means; I am not like the starling; I get out. If you were to ask me who Somebody is, upon my word I couldn't tell you. Let us drink to Somebody. God bless him!'" BH 37

—young men about town: "I [Pip] established with myself, on these occasions, the reputation of a first-rate man of business—prompt, decisive, energetic, clear, cool-headed. When I had got all my responsibilities down upon my list, I compared each with the bill, and ticked it off. My self-approval when I ticked an entry was quite a luxurious sensation. When I had no more ticks to make, I folded all my bills up uniformly, docketed each on the back, and tied the whole into a symmetrical bundle. Then I did the same for Herbert (who modestly said he had not my administrative genius), and felt that I had brought his affairs into a focus for him.

"My business habits had one other bright feature, which I called 'leaving a Margin.' For example: supposing Herbert's debts to be one hundred and sixty-four pounds four-and-twopence, I would say, 'Leave a margin, and put them down at two hundred.' Or, supposing my own to be four times as much, I would leave a margin, and put them down at seven hundred.

"I had the highest opinion of the wisdom of this same Margin, but I am bound to acknowledge that, on looking back, I deem it to have been an expensive device. For we always ran into new debt immediately, to the full extent of the margin, and sometimes, in the sense of freedom and solvency it imparted, got pretty far on into another margin.

"But there was a calm, a rest, a virtuous hush, consequent on these examinations of our affairs, that gave me, for the time, an admirable opinion of myself. Soothed by my exertions, my method, and Herbert's compliments, I would sit with his symmetrical bundle and my own on the table before me among the stationery, and feel like a Bank of some sort, rather than a private individual." ¶GE 34

And see H:Vocations—*broker's man*

Debtor's Prison

—on first entering: "Many eyes, that have long since been closed in the grave, have looked round upon that scene lightly enough, when entering the gate of the old Marshalsea Prison for the first time . . . . How soon have those same eyes, deeply sunken in the head, glared from faces wasted with famine, and sallow from confinement, in days when it was no figure of speech to say that debtors rotted in prison, with no hope of release, and no prospect of liberty!" PP 21 *And see* S:Hope—*a debtor's*

—death: "'I hope,' [the Chancery prisoner] gasped after a while: so faintly that they bent their ears close over the bed to catch the half-formed sounds his pale lips gave vent to: 'I hope my merciful Judge will bear in mind my heavy punishment on earth. Twenty years, my friend, twenty years in this hideous grave! My heart broke when my child died, and I could not even kiss him in his little coffin. My loneliness since then, in all this noise and riot, has been very dreadful. May God forgive me! He has seen my solitary, lingering death.'

"He folded his hands, and murmuring something more they could not hear, fell into a sleep—only a sleep at first, for they saw him smile.

"They whispered together for a little time, and the turnkey, stooping over the pillow, drew hastily back. 'He has got his discharge, by G—! 'said the man.

"He had. But he had grown so like death in life, that they knew not when he died." PP 44

" . . . in a miserable shed a few yards off . . . lay, all quiet and ghastly, the body of the Chancery prisoner who had died the night before, awaiting the mockery of an inquest. The body! It is the lawyer's term for the restless whirling mass of cares and anxieties, affections, hopes, and griefs, that make up the living man. The law had his body; and there it lay, clothed in grave clothes, an awful witness to its tender mercy." PP 45

—the Fleet: "It was getting dark; that is to say, a few gas jets were kindled in this place which was never light, by way of compliment to the evening, which had set in outside. As it was rather warm, some of the tenants of the numerous little rooms which opened into the gallery on either hand, had set their doors ajar.

"Mr Pickwick peeped into them as he passed along, with great curiosity and interest. Here four or five great hulking fellows, just visible through a cloud of tobacco-smoke, were engaged in noisy and riotous conversation over half-emptied pots of beer, or playing at all-fours with a very greasy pack of cards.

Discovery of Jingle at the Fleet PP

"In the adjoining room, some solitary tenant might be seen, poring, by the light of a feeble tallow candle, over a bundle of soiled and tattered papers, yellow with dust and dropping to pieces from age: writing, for the hundredth time, some lengthened statement of his grievances, for the perusal of some great man whose eyes it would never reach, or whose heart it would never touch.

"In a third, a man, with his wife and a whole crowd of children, might be seen making up a scanty bed on the ground, or upon a few chairs, for the younger ones to pass the night in. And in a fourth, and a fifth, and a sixth, and a seventh, the noise, and the beer, and the tobacco-smoke, and the cards, all came over again in greater force than before.

"In the galleries themselves, and more especially on the staircases, there lingered a great number of people, who came there, some because their rooms were empty and lonesome, others because their rooms were full and hot: the greater part because they were restless and uncomfortable, and not possessed of the secret of exactly knowing what to do with themselves.

"There were many classes of people here, from the labouring man in his fustian jacket, to the broken-down spendthrift in his shawl dressing-gown, most appropriately out at elbows; but there was the same air about them all—a listless jail-bird careless swagger, a vagabondish who's-afraid sort of bearing, which is wholly indescribable in words, but which any man can understand in one moment if he wish, by setting foot in the nearest debtor's prison, and looking at the very first group of people he sees there, with the same interest as Mr Pickwick did." ¶PP 41

—inmate

—discomfort: "For a burning restlessness set in, an agonised impatience of the prison, and a conviction that he [Arthur Clennam] was going to break his heart and die there, which caused him indescribable suffering. His dread and hatred of the place became so intense that he felt it a labour to draw his breath in it. The sensation of being stifled sometimes so overpowered him, that he would stand at the window holding his throat and gasping. At the same time a longing for other air, and a yearning to be beyond the blind blank wall, made him feel as if he must go mad with the ardour of the desire." LD ii 29

—general attitude: "It was evident from the general tone of the whole party, that they had come to regard insolvency as the normal state of mankind, and the payment of debts as a disease that occasionally broke out." LD i 8

—when one is freed: "There, were the people who were always going out to-morrow, and always putting it off; there, were the people who had come in yesterday and who were much more jealous and resentful of this freak of fortune than the seasoned birds. There, were some who, in pure meanness of spirit, cringed and bowed before the enriched Collegian [William Dorrit] and his family; there, were others who did so really because their eyes, accustomed to the gloom of their imprisonment and poverty, could not support the light of such bright sunshine.

"There, were many whose shillings had gone into his pocket to buy him meat and drink; but none who were now obtrusively Hail fellow well met! with him, on the strength of that assistance. It was rather to be remarked of the caged birds, that they were a little shy of the bird about to be so grandly free, and that they had a tendency to withdraw themselves towards the bars, and seem a little fluttered as he passed." ¶LD i 36

—the Marshalsea: "Thirty years ago [1825] there stood, a few doors short of the church of Saint George, in the borough of Southwark, on the left-hand side of the way going southward, the Marshalsea Prison. It had stood there many years before, and it remained there some years afterwards; but it is gone now, and the world is none the worse without it.

"It was an oblong pile of barrack building, partitioned into squalid houses standing back to back, so that there were no back rooms; environed by a narrow paved yard, hemmed in by high walls duly spiked at top. Itself a close and confined prison for debtors, it contained within it a much closer and more confined jail for smugglers. Offenders against the revenue laws, and defaulters to excise or customs, who had incurred fines which they were unable to pay, were supposed to be incarcerated behind an iron-plated door, closing up a second prison, consisting of a strong cell or two, and a blind alley some yard and a half wide, which formed the mysterious termination of the very limited skittle-ground in which the Marshalsea debtors bowled down their troubles.

"Supposed to be incarcerated there, because the time had rather outgrown the strong cells and the blind alley. In practice they had come to be considered a little too bad, though in theory they were quite as good as ever; which may be observed to be the case at the present day with other cells that are not at all strong, and with other blind alleys that are stone-blind. Hence the smugglers habitually consorted with the debtors (who received them with open arms), except at certain constitutional moments when somebody came from some Office, to go through some form of overlooking something, which neither he nor anybody else knew anything about. On those truly British occasions, the smugglers, if any, made a feint of walking into the strong cells and the blind alley, while this somebody pretended to do his something; and made a reality of walking out again as soon as he hadn't done it—neatly epitomising the administration of most of the public affairs, in our right little, tight little, island." LD i 6

—*messengers:* "There was a string of people already straggling in, whom it was not difficult to identify as the nondescript messengers, go-betweens, and errand-bearers of the place. Some of them had been lounging in the rain until the gate should open; others, who had timed their arrival with greater nicety, were coming up now, and passing in with damp whitey-brown paper bags from the grocers, loaves of bread, lumps of butter, eggs, milk, and the like.

"The shabbiness of these attendants upon shabbiness, the poverty of these insolvent waiters upon insolvency, was a sight to see. Such threadbare coats and trousers, such fusty gowns and shawls, such squashed hats and bonnets, such boots and shoes, such umbrellas and walking-sticks, never were seen in Rag Fair. All of them wore the cast-off clothes of other men and women; were made up of patches and pieces of other people's individuality, and had no sartorial existence of their own proper.

"Their walk was the walk of a race apart. They had a peculiar way of doggedly slinking round the corner, as if they were eternally going to the pawnbroker's. When they coughed, they coughed like people accustomed to be forgotten on door-steps and in draughty passages, waiting for answers to letters in faded ink, which gave the recipients of those manuscripts great mental disturbance and no satisfaction.

"As they eyed the stranger in passing, they eyed him with borrowing eyes—hungry, sharp, speculative as to his softness if they were accredited to him, and the likelihood of his standing something handsome. Mendicity on commission stopped in their high shoulders, shambled in their unsteady legs, buttoned and pinned and darned and dragged their clothes, frayed their buttonholes, leaked out of their figures in dirty little ends of tape, and issued from their mouths in alcoholic breathings." ¶LD i 9

—*nourishment:* "'Gone, my dear sir—last coat—can't help it. Lived on a pair of boots—whole fortnight. Silk umbrella—ivory handle—week—fact—honour—ask Job—knows it.'

"'Lived for three weeks upon a pair of boots, and a silk umbrella with an ivory handle!' exclaimed Mr Pickwick, who had only heard of such things in shipwrecks, or read of them in Constable's Miscellany."* PP 42

**During 1826-35, Archibald Constable published* Constable's Miscellany of Original and Selected Publications in the Various Departments of Literature, the Sciences, and the Arts. *BSB p62*

—*the poor side:* "The poor side of a debtor's prison, is, as its name imports, that in which the most miserable and abject class of debtors are confined. A prisoner having declared upon the poor side, pays neither rent nor chummage. His fees, upon entering and leaving the gaol, are reduced in amount, and he becomes entitled to a share of some small quantities of food: to provide which, a few charitable persons have, from time to time, left trifling legacies in their wills. Most of our readers will remember, that, until within a very few years past, there was a kind of iron cage in the wall of the Fleet Prison, within which was posted some man of hungry looks, who, from time to time, rattled a money-box, and exclaimed in a mournful voice, 'Pray, remember the poor debtors; pray, remember the poor debtors.' The receipts of this box, when there were any, were divided among the poor prisoners; and the men on the poor side relieved each other in this degrading office.

"Although this custom has been abolished, and the cage is now boarded up, the miserable and destitute condition of these unhappy persons remains the same. We no longer suffer them to appeal at the prison gates to the charity and compassion of the passers by: but we still leave unblotted in the leaves of our statute book, for the reverence and admiration of succeeding ages, the just and wholesome law which declares that the sturdy felon shall be fed and clothed, and that the penniless debtor shall be left to die of starvation and nakedness. This is no fiction. Not a week passes over our heads, but, in every one of our prisons for debt, some of these men must inevitably expire in the slow agonies of want, if they were not relieved by their fellow-prisoners." PP 42

—*the population:* "The great body of the prison population appeared to be Mivins, and Smangle, and the parson, and the butcher, and the leg, over and over, and over again. There were the same squalor, the same turmoil and noise, the same general characteristics, in every corner; in the best and the worst alike. The whole place seemed restless and troubled; and the people were crowding and flitting to and fro, like the shadows in an uneasy dream." PP 45

—the principle questioned: "'It seems to be hard,' said Little Dorrit, 'that he [her father] should have lost so many years and suffered so much, and at last pay all the debts as well. It seems to me hard that he should pay in life and money both.'" LD i 35

—its punishment: "'It strikes me, Sam,' said Mr Pickwick, leaning over the iron-rail at the stairhead, 'it strikes me, Sam, that imprisonment for debt is scarcely any punishment at all.'

"'Think not, sir?' inquired Mr Weller.

"'You see how these fellows drink, and smoke, and roar,' replied Mr Pickwick. 'It's quite impossible that they can mind it much.'

"'Ah, that's just the wery thing, sir,' rejoined Sam, '*they* don't mind it; it's a regular holiday to them—all porter and skittles. It's the t'other vuns as gets done over, vith this sort o' thing: them down-hearted fellers as can't svig avay at the beer, nor play at skittles neither; them as vould pay if they could, and gets low by being boxed up. I'll tell you wot it is, sir; them as is always a idlin' in public-houses it don't damage at all, and them as is always a workin' wen they can, it damages too much. "It's unekal," as my father used to say wen his grog warn't made half-and-half: "It's unekal, and that's the fault on it."'" PP 41

—the Rules: "The Rules are a certain liberty adjoining the [King's Bench] prison, and comprising some dozen streets in which debtors who can raise money to pay large fees, from which their creditors do *not* derive any benefit, are permitted to reside by the wise provisions of the same enlightened laws which leave the debtor who can raise no money to starve in jail, without the food, clothing, lodging, or warmth, which are provided for felons convicted of the most atrocious crimes that can disgrace humanity. There are many pleasant fictions of the law in constant operation, but there is not one so pleasant or practically humorous as that which supposes every man to be of equal value in its impartial eye, and the benefits of all laws to be equally attainable by all men, without the smallest reference to the furniture of their pockets." NN 46

—its shops: "Cross over to the Surrey side, and look at such shops of this description as are to be found near the King's Bench prison, and in 'the Rules.' How different, and how strikingly illustrative of the decay of some of the unfortunate residents in this part of the metropolis! Imprisonment and neglect have done their work. There is contamination in the profligate denizens of a debtor's prison; old friends have fallen off; the recollection of former prosperity has passed away; and with it all thoughts for the past, all care for the future.

"First, watches and rings, then cloaks, coats, and all the more expensive articles of dress, have found their way to the pawnbroker's. That miserable resource has failed at last, and the sale of some trifling article at one of these shops has been the only mode left of raising a shilling or two, to meet the urgent demands of the moment. Dressing-cases and writing-desks, too old to pawn but too good to keep; guns, fishing-rods, musical instruments, all in the same condition; have first been sold, and the sacrifice has been but slightly felt.

"But hunger must be allayed, and what has already become a habit is easily resorted to, when an emergency arises. Light articles of clothing, first of the ruined man, then of his wife, at last of their children, even of the youngest, have been parted with, piecemeal. There they are, thrown carelessly together until a purchaser presents himself, old, and patched and repaired, it is true; but the make and materials tell of better days; and the older they are, the greater the misery and destitution of those whom they once adorned." ¶SB/BM

—a shelter: "'I ain't seen the market outside, Bill,' he says, 'for seventeen year.' 'I know you ain't,' says the turnkey, smoking his pipe. 'I should like to see it for a minit, Bill,' he says. 'Wery probable,' says the turnkey, smoking his pipe wery fierce, and making believe he warn't up to what the little man wanted. 'Bill,' says the little man more abrupt than afore, 'I've got the fancy in my head. Let me see the public streets once more afore I die; and if I ain't struck with apoplexy, I'll be back in five minits by the clock.' 'And wot 'ud become o' me if you *was* struck with apoplexy?' said the turnkey. 'Wy,' says the little creetur, 'whoever found me 'ud bring me home, for I have got my card in my pocket, Bill,' he says, 'No. 20, Coffee-room Flight;' and that was true, sure enough . . . . The turnkey takes a fixed look at him, and at last he says in a solemn

manner, 'Tventy,' he says, 'I'll trust you; you won't get your old friend into trouble.' 'No, my boy; I hope I've somethin' better behind here,' says the little man, and as he said it he hit his little veskit wery hard, and then a tear started out o' each eye, which wos wery extraordinary, for it wos supposed as water never touched his face. He shook the turnkey by the hand; our he vent——

"'And never came back again,' said Mr Pickwick.

"'Wrong for vunce, sir,' replied Mr Weller, 'for back he come, two minits afore the time, a bilin' with rage; sayin' how he'd been nearly run over by a hackney-coach; that he warn't used to it: and he was blowed if he wouldn't write to the Lord Mayor. They got him pacified at last; and for five years arter that, he never even so much as peeped out o' the lodge-gate.'" PP 41

"'He got a curiosity to go and taste the beer at a new public-house over the way, and it wos such a wery nice parlour, that he took it into his head to go there every night. . . . At last he began to get so precious jolly, that he used to forget how the time vent, or care nothin' at all about it, and he vent on gettin' later and later, till vun night his old friend wos just a shuttin' the gate—had turned the key in fact—wen he come up. 'Hold hard, Bill,' he says. 'Wot, ain't you come home yet, Tventy?' says the turnkey, 'I thought you wos in, long ago.' 'No I wasn't,' says the little man, vith a smile. 'Well then, I'll tell you wot it is, my friend,' says the turnkey, openin' the gate very slow and sulky, 'it's my 'pinion as you've got into bad company o' late, which I'm wery sorry to see. Now, I don't wish to do nothing harsh,' he says, 'but if you can't confine yourself to steady circles, and find your vay back at reglar hours, as sure as you're a standin' there, I'll shut you out altogether!' The little man was seized with a wiolent fit o' tremblin', and never vent outside the prison walls artervards!'" PP 41

—*the Yard at the Fleet:* "The area formed by the wall in that part of the Fleet in which Mr Pickwick stood, was just wide enough to make a good racket-court; one side being formed, of course, by the wall itself and the other by that portion of the prison which looked (or rather would have looked, but for the wall) toward St Paul's Cathedral. Sauntering or sitting about, in every possible attitude of listless idleness, were a great number of debtors, the major part of whom were waiting in prison until their day of 'going up' before the Insolvent Court should arrive; while others had been remanded for various terms, which they were idling away, as they best could. Some were shabby, some were smart, many dirty, a few clean; but there they all lounged, and loitered, and slunk about, with as little spirit or purpose as the beasts in a menagerie.

"Lolling from the windows which commanded a view of this promenade, were a number of persons, some in noisy conversation with their acquaintance below, others playing at ball with some adventurous throwers outside, others looking on at the racket-players, or watching the boys as they cried the game. Dirty slipshod women passed and re-passed, on their way to the cooking-house in one corner of the yard; children screamed, and fought, and played together, in another; the tumbling of the skittles, and the shouts of the players, mingled perpetually with these and a hundred other sounds; and all was noise and tumult . . . . " PP 45

Detection

—*appearance and reality:* " . . . we burrow for information on such points as the following. Whether there really are any highway robberies in London, or whether some circumstances not convenient to be mentioned by the aggrieved party, usually precede the robberies complained of, under that head, which quite change their character? Certainly the latter, almost always.

"Whether in the case of robberies in houses, where servants are necessarily exposed to doubt, innocence under suspicion ever becomes so like guilt in appearance, that a good officer need be cautious how he judges it? Undoubtedly. Nothing is so common or deceptive as such appearances at first.

"Whether in a place of public amusement, a thief knows an officer, and an officer knows a thief—supposing them, beforehand, strangers to each other—because each recognises in the other, under all disguise, an inattention to what is going on, and a purpose that is not the purpose of being entertained? Yes. That's the way exactly.

"Whether it is reasonable or ridiculous to trust to the alleged experiences of thieves as narrated by themselves, in prisons, or penitentiaries, or anywhere? In general, nothing more absurd. Lying is their habit and their trade; and they would rather lie—even if they hadn't an interest in it, and didn't want to make themselves agreeable—than tell the truth." ¶RP/DP

—classes of criminal activity: "From the swell mob, we diverge to the kindred topics of cracksmen, fences, public-house dancers, area-sneaks, designing young people who go out 'gonophing,' and other 'schools.'" RP/DP

—in London: " . . . the Detective Force organised since the establishment of the existing Police, is so well chosen and trained, proceeds so systematically and quietly, does its business in such a workmanlike manner, and is always so calmly and steadily engaged in the service of the public, that the public really do not know enough of it, to know a tithe of its usefulness." RP/DP

" . . . such is the peculiar ability, always sharpening and being improved by practice, and always adapting itself to every variety of circumstances, and opposing itself to every new device that perverted ingenuity can invent, for which this important social branch of the public service is remarkable! For ever on the watch, with their wits stretched to the utmost, these officers have, from day to day and year to year, to set themselves against every novelty of trickery and dexterity that the combined imaginations of all the lawless rascals in England can devise, and to keep pace with every such invention that comes out." RP/DP

—theorizing: "Within eight-and-forty hours, a reward of One Hundred Pounds was proclaimed, together with a free pardon to any person or persons not the actual perpetrator or perpetrators, and so forth in due form.

"This Proclamation rendered Mr Inspector additionally studious, and caused him to stand meditating on river-stairs and causeways, and to go lurking about in boats, putting this and that together. But, according to the success with which you put this and that together, you get a woman and a fish apart, or a Mermaid in combination. And Mr Inspector could turn out nothing better than a Mermaid, which no Judge and Jury would believe in." OMF i 3

—undivulged process: "In the Courts of Justice, the materials of thousands of such stories as we have narrated—often elevated into the marvellous and romantic, by the circumstances of the case—are dryly compressed into the set phrase, 'in consequence of information I received, I did so and so.' Suspicion was to be directed, by careful inference and deduction, upon the right person; the right person was to be taken, wherever he had gone, or whatever he was doing to avoid detection; he is taken; there he is at the bar; that is enough. From information I, the officer, received, I did it; and, according to the custom in these cases, I say no more.

"These games of chess, played with live pieces, are played before small audiences, and are chronicled nowhere. The interest of the game supports the player. Its results are enough for Justice. To compare great things with small, suppose **Leverrier** or **Adams** informing the public that from information he had received he had discovered a new planet; or **Columbus** informing the public of his day that from information he had received he had discovered a new continent; so the Detectives inform it that they have discovered a new fraud or an old offender, and the process is unknown." RP/DP

And see Police; *and* B:Body—*forefinger*

For detectives, police and private, see Indexes IV *and* VIII

Fraud

—its blind spot: "As [Jonas Chuzzlewit] made no attempt to conciliate Mr Pecksniff, but, on the contrary, was more boorish and rude to him than usual, that gentleman, so far from suspecting his real design, laid himself out to be attacked with advantage. For it is in the nature of a knave to think the tools with which he works indispensable to knavery; and knowing what he would do himself in such a case, Mr Pecksniff argued, 'if this young man wanted anything of me for his own ends, he would be polite and deferential.'" MC 44

—diagnosed: " . . . the late Mr Merdle's complaint had been, simply, Forgery and Robbery. He, the uncouth object of such wide-spread adulation, the sitter at great men's feasts, the roc's egg of great ladies' assemblies, the subduer of exclusiveness, the leveller of pride, the patron of patrons, the bargain-driver with a Minister for Lordships of the Circumlocution Office, the recipient of more acknowledgment within some ten or fifteen years, at most, than had been bestowed in England upon all peaceful public benefactors, and upon all the leaders of all the Arts and Sciences, with all their works to testify for them, during two centuries at least—he, the shining wonder, the new constellation to be followed by the wise men bringing gifts, until it stopped over cer-

tain carrion at the bottom of a bath and disappeared—was simply the greatest Forger and the greatest Thief that ever cheated the gallows." LD ii 25

—the gulled: "'A consummate rascal of course,' said Ferdinand [Barnacle], 'but remarkably clever! One cannot help admiring the fellow. Must have been such a master of humbug. Knew people so well—got over them so completely—did so much with them!'

"In his easy way, he was really moved to genuine admiration.

"'I hope,' said Arthur [Clennam], 'that [Merdle] and his dupes may be a warning to people not to have so much done with them again.'

"'My dear Mr Clennam,' returned Ferdinand, laughing, 'have you really such a verdant hope? The next man who has as large a capacity and as genuine a taste for swindling, will succeed as well. Pardon me, but I think you really have no idea how the human bees will swarm to the beating of any old tin kettle . . . . No doubt there are here and there,' said Ferdinand politely, 'exceptional cases, where people have been taken in for what appeared to them to be much better reasons; and I need not go far to find such a case; but they don't invalidate the rule." LD ii 28

—from a height: "'There's a surprisin' number of men, sir [said Mark Tapley], who as long as they've only got their own shoes and stockings to depend upon, will walk downhill, along the gutters quiet enough, and by themselves, and not do much harm. But set any on 'em up with a coach and horses, sir; and it's wonderful what a knowledge of drivin' he'll show, and how he'll fill his wehicle with passengers, and start off in the middle of the road, neck or nothing, to the Devil! Bless your heart, sir, there's ever so many Tiggs a-passin' this here Temple-gate any hour in the day, that only want a chance to turn out full-blown Montagues every one!'" MC 52

—unmasked:

—introductory: "'How is our friend Heep, Mr Micawber?' said I, after a silence.

"'My dear Copperfield,' returned Mr Micawber, bursting into a state of much excitement, and turning pale, 'if you ask after my employer as your friend, I am sorry for it; if you ask after him as my friend, I sardonically smile at it. In whatever capacity you ask after my employer, I beg, without offence to you, to limit my reply to this—that whatever his state of health may be, his appearance is foxy: not to say diabolical. You will allow me, as a private individual, to decline pursuing a subject which has lashed me to the utmost verge of desperation in my professional capacity.'" DC 49

"'I'll put my hand in no man's hand,' said Mr Micawber, gasping, puffing, and sobbing, to that degree that he was like a man fighting with cold water, 'until I have—blown to fragments—the—a—destestable—serpent—HEEP! I'll partake of no one's hospitality, until I have—a—moved Mount Vesuvius—to eruption—on—a—the abandoned rascal—HEEP! Refreshment—a—underneath this roof—particularly punch—would—a—choke me—unless—I had—previously—choked the eyes—out of the head—a—of—interminable cheat, and liar—HEEP! I—a—I'll know nobody—and—a—say nothing—and—a—live nowhere—until I have crushed—to—a—undiscoverable atoms—the—transcendent and immortal hypocrite and perjurer—HEEP!'

"I really had some fear of Mr Micawber's dying on the spot. The manner in which he struggled through these inarticulate sentences, and, whenever he found himself getting near the name of Heep, fought his way on to it, dashed at it in a fainting state, and brought it out with a vehemence little less than marvellous, was frightful; but now, when he sank into a chair, steaming, and looked at us, with every possible colour in his face that had no business there, and an endless procession of lumps following one another in hot haste up his throat, whence they seemed to shoot into his forehead, he had the appearance of being in the last extremity. I would have gone to his assistance, but he waved me off, and wouldn't hear a word." DC 49

—nemesis: "'Don't wait, Micawber,' said Uriah.

"Mr Micawber, with his hand upon the ruler in his breast, stood erect before the door, most unmistakably contemplating one of his fellow-men, and that man his employer.

"'What are you waiting for?' said Uriah. 'Micawber! did you hear me tell you not to wait?'

"'Yes!' replied the immovable Mr Micawber.

"'Then why *do* you wait?' said Uriah.

"'Because I—in short, choose,' replied Mr Micawber, with a burst.

"Uriah's cheeks lost colour, and an unwholesome paleness, still faintly tinged by his pervading red, overspread them. He looked at Mr Micawber attentively, with his whole face breathing short and quick in every feature.

"'You are a dissipated fellow, as all the world knows,' he said, with an effort at a smile, 'and I am afraid you'll oblige me to get rid of you. Go along! I'll talk to you presently.'

"'If there is a scoundrel on this earth,' said Mr Micawber, suddenly breaking out again with the utmost vehemence, 'with whom I have already talked too much, that scoundrel's name is—HEEP!'

"Uriah fell back, as if he had been struck or stung. Looking slowly round upon us with the darkest and wickedest expression that his face could wear, he said, in a lower voice:

"'Oho! This is a conspiracy! You have met here by appointment! You are playing Booty with my clerk, are you, Copperfield? Now, take care. You'll make nothing of this. We understand each other, you and me. There's no love between us. You were always a puppy with a proud stomach, from your first coming here; and you envy me my rise, do you? None of your plots against me; I'll counterplot you! Micawber, you be off. I'll talk to you presently.'

"'Mr Micawber,' said I, 'there is a sudden change in this fellow, in more respects than the extraordinary one of his speaking the truth in one particular, which assures me that he is brought to bay. Deal with him as he deserves!'". . .

"Mr Micawber, whose impetuousity I had restrained thus far with the greatest difficulty, and who had repeatedly interposed with the first syllable of SCOUN-drel! without getting to the second, now burst forward, drew the ruler from his breast (apparently as a defensive weapon), and produced from his pocket a foolscap document, folded in the form of a large letter. Opening this packet, with his old flourish, and glancing at the contents, as if he cherished an artistic admiration of their style of composition, he began to read as follows:

"'"Dear Miss Trotwood and gentlemen——"'

"'Bless and save the man!' exclaimed my aunt in a low voice. 'He'd write letters by the ream, if it was a capital offence!'

"Mr Micawber, without hearing her, went on.

"'"In appearing before you to denounce probably the most consummate Villain that has ever existed,"' Mr Micawber, without looking off the letter, pointed the ruler, like a ghostly truncheon, at Uriah Heep, '"I ask no consideration for myself. The victim, from my cradle, of pecuniary liabilities to which I have been unable to respond, I have ever been the sport and toy of debasing circumstances. Ignominy, Want, Despair, and Madness, have, collectively or separately, been the attendants of my career."'

"The relish with which Mr Micawber described himself as a prey to these dismal calamities was only to be equalled by the emphasis with which he read his letter; and the kind of homage he rendered to it with a roll of his head, when he thought he had hit a sentence very hard indeed.

"'"In an accumulation of Ignominy, Want, Despair, and Madness, I entered the office—or, as our lively neighbour the Gaul would term it, the Bureau—of the Firm, nominally conducted under the appellation of Wickfield and—HEEP, but, in reality, wielded by—HEEP alone. HEEP, and only HEEP, is the mainspring of that machine. HEEP, and only HEEP, is the Forger and the Cheat."'

"Uriah, more blue than white at these words, made a dart at the letter, as if to tear it in pieces. Mr Micawber, with a perfect miracle of dexterity or luck, caught his advancing knuckles with the ruler, and disabled his right hand. It dropped at the wrist, as if it were broken. The blow sounded as if it had fallen on wood.

"'The Devil take you!' said Uriah, writhing in a new way with pain. 'I'll be even with you.'

"'Approach me again, you—you—you HEEP of infamy,' gasped Mr Micawber, 'and if your head is human, I'll break it. Come on, come on!'

"I think I never saw anything more ridiculous—I was sensible of it, even at the time—than Mr Micawber making broad-sword guards with the ruler, and crying, 'Come on!' while Traddles and I pushed him back into a corner, from which, as often as we got him into it, he persisted in emerging again.

"His enemy, muttering to himself, after wringing his wounded hand for some time, slowly drew off his neckerchief and bound it up; then held it in his other hand, and sat upon his table with his sullen face looking down.

"Mr Micawber, when he was sufficiently cool, proceeded with his letter.

"'"The stipendiary emoluments in consideration of which I entered into the service of—HEEP,"' always pausing before that word and uttering it with astonishing vigour, '"were not defined, beyond the pittance of twenty-two shillings and six per week. The rest was left contingent on the value of my professional exertions; in other and more expressive words, on the baseness of my nature, the cupidity of my motives, the poverty of my family, the general moral (or rather immoral) resemblance between myself and—HEEP. Need I say that it soon became necessary for me to solicit from—HEEP—pecuniary advances towards the support of Mrs Micawber, and our blighted but rising family? Need I say that this necessity had been foreseen by—HEEP? That those advances were secured by I. O. U.'s and other similar acknowledgements, known to the legal institutions of this country? And that I thus became immeshed in the web he had spun for my reception?"'

"Mr Micawber's enjoyment of his epistolary powers, in describing this unfortunate state of things, really seemed to outweigh any pain or anxiety that the reality could have caused him. He read on:

"'"Then it was that—HEEP—began to favour me with just so much of his confidence as was necessary to the discharge of his infernal business. Then it was that I began, if I may so Shakespearianly express myself, to dwindle, peak, and pine. I found that my services were constantly called into requisition for the falsification of business, and the mystification of an individual whom I will designate as Mr W. That Mr W. was imposed upon, kept in ignorance, and deluded, in every possible way; yet, that all this while, the ruffian—HEEP—was professing unbounded gratitude to, and unbounded friendship for, that much-abused gentleman. This was bad enough; but, as the philosophic Dane observes, with that universal applicability which distinguishes the illustrious ornament of the Elizabethan Era, worse remains behind!" '

"Mr Micawber was so very much struck by this happy rounding off with a quotation, that he indulged himself, and us, with a second reading of the sentence, under pretence of having lost his place.

"'"It is not my intention,"' he continued, reading on, '"to enter on a detailed list, within the compass of the present epistle (though it is ready elsewhere), of the various malpractices of a minor nature, affecting the individual whom I have denominated Mr W., to which I have been a tacitly consenting party. My object, when the contest within myself between stipend and no stipend, baker and no baker, existence and non-existence, ceased, was to take advantage of my opportunities to discover and expose the major malpractices committed, to that gentleman's grievous wrong and injury, by—HEEP. Stimulated by the silent monitor within, and by a no less touching and appealing monitor without—to whom I will briefly refer as Miss W.—I entered on a not unlaborious task of clandestine investigation, protracted now, to the best of my knowledge, information, and belief, over a period exceeding twelve calendar months."'

"He read this passage as if it were from an Act of Parliament; and appeared majestically refreshed by the sound of the words.

"'"My charges against—HEEP,"' he read on, glancing at him, and drawing the ruler into a convenient position under his left arm, in case of need, '"are as follows."'

"We all held our breath, I think. I am sure Uriah held his.

"'"First,"'said Mr Micawber. '"When Mr W.'s faculties and memory for business became, through causes into which it is not necessary or expedient for me to enter, weakened and confused—HEEP—designedly perplexed and complicated the whole of the official transactions. When Mr W. was least fit to enter on business—HEEP was always at hand to force him to enter on it. He obtained Mr W.'s signature under such circumstances to documents of importance, representing them to be other documents of no importance. He induced Mr W. to empower him to draw out, thus, one particular sum of trust-money, amounting to twelve six fourteen, two and nine, and employed it to meet pretended business charges and deficiencies which were either already provided for, or had never really existed. He gave this proceeding, throughout, the appearance of having originated in Mr W.'s own dishonest intention, and of having been accomplished by Mr W.'s own dishonest act; and has used it, ever since, to torture and constrain him."'

"'You shall prove this, you Copperfield!' said Uriah, with a threatening shake of the head. 'All in good time!'

"'Ask—HEEP—Mr Traddles, who lived in his house after him,' said Mr Micawber, breaking off from the letter; 'will you?'

"'The fool himself—and lives there now,' said Uriah, disdainfully.

"'Ask HEEP—if he ever kept a pocket-book in that house,' said Mr Micawber; 'will you?'

"I saw Uriah's lank hand stop, involuntarily, in the scraping of his chin.

"'Or ask him,' said Mr Micawber, 'if he ever burnt one there. If he says Yes, and asks you where the ashes are, refer him to Wilkins Micawber, and he will hear of something not at all to his advantage!'

"The triumphant flourish with which Mr Micawber delivered himself of these words, had a powerful effect in alarming the mother; who cried out in much agitation:

"'Ury, Ury! Be umble, and make terms my dear!'

"'Mother!' he retorted, 'will you keep quiet? You're in a fright, and don't know what you say or mean. Umble!' he repeated, looking at me, with a snarl; 'I've umbled some of 'em for a pretty long time back, umble as I was!'

"Mr Micawber, genteelly adjusting his chin in his cravat, presently proceeded with his composition.

"'"Second. HEEP has, on several occasions, to the best of my knowledge, information, and belief—" '

"'But *that* won't do,' muttered Uriah, relieved. 'Mother, you keep quiet.'

"'We will endeavour to provide something that WILL do, and do for you finally, sir, very shortly,' replied Mr Micawber.

"'"Second. HEEP has, on several occasions, to the best of my knowledge, information, and belief, systematically forged, to various entries, books, and documents, the signature of Mr W.; and has distinctly done so in one instance, capable of proof by me. To wit, in manner following, that is to say. . . . Mr W. being infirm, and it being within the bounds of probability that his decease might lead to some discoveries, and to the downfall of—HEEP's—power over the W. family—as I, Wilkins Micawber, the undersigned, assume—unless the filial affection of his daughter could be secretly influenced from allowing any investigation of the partnership affairs to be ever made, the said—HEEP—deemed it expedient to have a bond ready by him, as from Mr W., for the before-mentioned sum of twelve six fourteen, two and nine, with interest, stated therein to have been advanced by—HEEP—to Mr W. to save Mr W. from dishonour; though really the sum was never advanced by him, and has long been replaced. The signatures to this instrument purporting to be executed by Mr W. and attested by Wilkins Micawber, are forgeries by—HEEP. I have, in my possession, in his hand and pocket-book, several similar imitations of Mr W.'s signature, here and there defaced by fire, but legible to any one. I never attested any such document. And I have the document itself, in my possession."'

"Uriah Heep, with a start, took out of his pocket a bunch of keys, and opened a certain drawer; then, suddenly bethought himself of what he was about, and turned again towards us, without looking in it.

"'"And I have the document,"' Mr Micawber read again, looking about as if it were the text of a sermon, '"in my possession,"—that is to say, I had, early this morning, when this was written, but have since relinquished it to Mr Traddles.'

"'It is quite true,' assented Traddles.

"'Ury, Ury!' cried the mother, 'be umble and make terms. I know my son will be umble, gentlemen, if you'll give him time to think. Mr Copperfield, I'm sure you know that he was always very umble, sir!'

"It was singular to see how the mother still held to the old trick, when the son had abandoned it as useless.

"'Mother,' he said, with an impatient bite at the handkerchief in which his hand was wrapped, 'you had better take and fire a loaded gun at me . . . .

"'What more have you got to bring forward? If anything, go on with it. What do you look at me for?'

"Mr Micawber promptly resumed his letter, glad to revert to a performance with which he was so highly satisfied.

"'"Third. And last. I am now in a condition to show, by—HEEP's—false books and—HEEP's real memoranda, beginning with the partially destroyed pocket-book (which I was unable to comprehend, at the time of its accidental discovery by Mrs Micawber, on our taking possession of our present abode, in the locker or bin devoted to the reception of the ashes calcined on our domestic hearth), that the weaknesses, the faults, the very virtues, the parental affections, and the sense of honour of the unhappy Mr W. have been for years acted on by, and warped to the base purposes of—HEEP. That Mr W. has been for years deluded and plundered, in every conceivable manner, to the pecuniary aggrandisement of the avaricious, false, and grasping—HEEP. That the engrossing object of—HEEP—was, next to gain, to subdue Mr and Miss W. (of his ulterior views in reference to the latter I say nothing) entirely to himself. That his last act, completed but a few months since, was to induce Mr W. to execute a relinquishment of his share in the partnership, and even a bill of sale on the very furniture of his house, in consideration of a certain annuity, to be well and truly paid by—HEEP—on the four common quarter-days in each and every year. That these meshes; beginning with alarming and falsified accounts of the estate of which Mr W. is the receiver, at a period when Mr W. had launched into imprudent and ill-judged speculations, and may not have had the money, for which he was morally and legally responsible, in hand; going on with pretended borrowings of money at enormous interest, really coming from—HEEP—and by—HEEP—fraudulently obtained or withheld from Mr W. himself, on pretence of such speculations or otherwise perpetuated by a miscellaneous catalogue of unscrupulous chicaneries—gradually thickened, until the unhappy Mr W. could see no world beyond. Bankrupt, as he believed, alike in circumstances, in all other hope, and in honour, his sole reliance was upon the monster in the garb of man"'—Mr Micawber made a good deal of this, as a new turn of expression—'"who, by making himself necessary to him, had achieved his destruction. All this I undertake to show. Probably much more!"'

"I whispered a few words to Agnes, who was weeping, half joyfully, half sorrowfully, at my side; and there was a movement among us, as if Mr Micawber had finished. He said, with exceeding gravity, 'Pardon me,' and proceeded, with a mixture of the lowest spirits and the most intense enjoyment, to the peroration of his letter.

"'"I have now concluded. It merely remains for me to substantiate these accusations; and then, with my ill-starred family, to disappear from the landscape on which we appear to be an incumbrance. That is soon done. It may be reasonably inferred that our baby will first expire of inanition, as being the frailest member of our circle; and that our twins will follow next in order. So be it! For myself, my Canterbury Pilgrimage has done much; imprisonment on civil process, and want, will soon do more. I trust that the labour and hazard of an investigation—of which the smallest results have been slowly pieced together, in the pressure of arduous avocations, under grinding penurious apprehensions, at rise of morn, at dewy eve, in the shadows of night, under the watchful eye of one whom it were superfluous to call Demon—combined with the struggle of parental Poverty to turn it, when completed, to the right account, may be as the sprinkling of a few drops of sweet water on my funereal pyre. I ask no more. Let it be, in justice, merely said of me, as of a gallant and eminent naval Hero, with whom I have no pretensions to cope, that what I have done, I did, in despite of mercenary and selfish objects,

For England, home, and Beauty.

"'"Remaining always, &c &c.,
WILKINS MICAWBER."'"

"Much affected, but still intensely enjoying himself, Mr Micawber folded up his letter, and handed it with a bow to my aunt, as something she might like to keep.

"There was, as I had noticed on my first visit long ago, an iron safe in the room. The key was in it. A hasty suspicion seemed to strike Uriah; and, with a glance at Mr Micawber, he went to it, and threw the doors clanking open. It was empty.

"'Where are the books?' he cried, with a frightful face. 'Some thief has stolen the books!'

"Mr Micawber tapped himself with the ruler. 'I did, when I got the key from you as usual—but a little earlier—and opened it this morning.'

"'Don't be uneasy,' said Traddles. 'They have come into my possession. I will take care of them., under the authority I mentioned.'

"'You receive stolen goods, do you?' cried Uriah.

"'Under such circumstances,' answered Traddles, 'yes.'" DC 52

Friend and Friendship

—absence of affinity: "' . . . O, as you are a kind, true man [said Minnie Meagles to Arthur Clennam]! when I am first separated from home . . . try to reconcile papa to him [her intended, Henry Gowan] a little more, and use your great influence to keep him before papa's mind, free from prejudice and in his real form. Will you do this for me, as you are a noble-hearted friend?'

"Poor Pet! Self-deceived, mistaken child! When were such changes ever made in men's natural relations to one another: when was such reconcilement of ingrained differences ever effected! It has been tried many times by other daughters, Minnie; it has never succeeded; nothing has ever come of it but failure." LD i 28

—acquaintance: "'Captain Gills,' blurted out Mr Toots . . . 'do you think you could think favourably of that proposition of mine, and give me the pleasure of your acquaintance?'

"'Why I tell you what it is, my lad,' replied the Captain, who had at length concluded on a course of action; 'I've been turning that there over.'

"'Captain Gills, it's very kind of you,' retorted Mr Toots. 'I'm much obliged to you. Upon my word and honour, Captain Gills, it would be a charity to give me the pleasure of your acquaintance. It really would.'

"'You see, brother,' argued the Captain slowly, 'I don't know you.'

"'But you never *can* know me, Captain Gills,' replied Mr Toots, steadfast to his point, 'if you don't give me the pleasure of your acquaintance.'

"The Captain seemed struck by the originality and power of this remark, and looked at Mr Toots as if he thought there was a great deal more in him than he had expected." DS 39

—crowd: "' . . . *I* didn't want to make a triumph of it [said Varden]. But, directly we got into the street we were known, and this hubbub began. Of the two,' he added, as he wiped his crimson face, 'and after experience of both, I think I'd rather be taken out of my house by a crowd of enemies, than escorted home by a mob of friends!'" BR 79

And see H:Mob—*of friends*

—Damon and Pythias: "[They] were undoubtedly very good fellows in their way: the former for his extreme readiness to put in special bail for a friend: and the latter for a certain trump-like punctuality in turning up just in the very nick of time, scarcely less remarkable. Many points in their character have, however, grown obsolete. *Damon*s are rather hard to find, in these days of imprisonment for debt (except the sham ones, and they cost half-a-crown); and, as to the *Pythias*es, the few that have existed in these degenerate times, have had an unfortunate knack of making themselves scarce, at the very moment when their appearance would have been strictly classical. If the actions of these heroes, however, can find no parallel in modern times, their friendship can." SB/MN

—helping: "'Mr Wemmick,' said I, 'I want to ask your opinion. I am very desirous to serve a friend.'

"Wemmick tightened his post-office and shook his head, as if his opinion were dead against any fatal weakness of that sort.

"'This friend,' I pursued, 'is trying to get on in commercial life, but has no money, and finds it difficult and disheartening to make a beginning. Now, I want somehow to help him to a beginning.'

"'With money down?' said Wemmick, in a tone drier than any sawdust . . . .

"'Mr Pip,' said Wemmick, 'I should like

just to run over with you on my fingers, if you please, the names of the various bridges up as high as Chelsea Reach. Let's see: there's London, one; Southwark, two; Blackfriars, three; Waterloo, four; Westminister, five; Vauxhall, six.' He had checked off each bridge in its turn, with the handle of his safe-key on the palm of his hand. 'There's as many as six, you see, to choose from.'

"'I don't understand you,' said I.

"'Choose your bridge, Mr Pip,' returned Wemmick, 'and take a walk upon your bridge, and pitch your money into the Thames over the centre arch of your bridge, and you know the end of it. Serve a friend with it, and you may know the end of it too—but it's a less pleasant and profitable end.' . . .

"'Then is it your opinion,' I inquired, with some little indignation, 'that a man should never——'

"'—Invest portable property in a friend?' said Wemmick. 'Certainly he should not. Unless he wants to get rid of the friend—and then it becomes a question how much portable property it may be worth to get rid of him.'" GE 36

—not overdone: "'[Trotter] says that [Jingle's] the only friend he ever had, and he's attached to him, and all that. Friendship's a very good thing in its way; we are all very friendly and comfortable at the Stump, for instance, over our grog, where every man pays for himself; but damn hurting yourself for anybody else, you know! No man should have more than two attachments—the first, to number one, and the second to the ladies; that's what I say—ha! ha!' Mr Lowten concluded with a loud laugh, half in jocularity, and half in derision . . . ." PP 53

—purported: "'And did you hear [Pecksniff] say that he could have shed his blood for me?' [asked Tom Pinch]

"'Do you *want* any blood shed for you?' returned [Westlock], with considerable irritation. 'Does he shed anything for you that you *do* want? Does he shed employment for you, instruction for you, pocket-money for you? Does he shed even legs of mutton for you in any decent proportion to potatoes and garden stuff?'" MC 2

—rapport: "Whether people, by dint of sitting together in the same place and the same relative positions, and doing exactly the same things for a great many years, acquire a sixth sense, or some unknown power of influencing each other which serves them in its stead, is a question for philosophy to settle. But certain it is that old John Willet, Mr Parkes, and Mr Cobb, were one and all firmly of opinion that they were very jolly companions—rather choice spirits than otherwise; that they looked at each other every now and then as if there were a perpetual interchange of ideas going on among them; that no man considered himself or his neighbour by any means silent; and that each of them nodded occasionally when he caught the eye of another, as if he would say, 'You have expressed yourself extremely well, sir, in relation to that sentiment, and I quite agree with you.'" BR 33

—schoolmate: "'Where is my little sister,' said the ghost, 'and where my angelic little wife, and where is the boy I went to school with?'

"I entreated the phantom to be comforted, and above all things to take heart respecting the loss of the boy he went to school with. I represented to him that probably that boy never did, within human experience, come out well, when discovered. I urged that I myself had, in later life, turned up several boys whom I went to school with, and none of them had at all answered.

"I expressed my humble belief that that boy never did answer. I represented that he was a mythic character, a delusion, and a snare. I recounted how, the last time I found him, I found him at a dinner party behind a wall of white cravat, with an inconclusive opinion on every possible subject, and a power of silent boredom absolutely Titanic.

"I related how, on the strength of our having been together at 'Old Doylance's,' he had asked himself to breakfast with me (a social offence of the largest magnitude); how, fanning my weak embers of belief in Doylance's boys, I had let him in; and how, he had proved to be a fearful wanderer about the earth, pursuing the race of Adam with inexplicable notions concerning the currency, and with a proposition that the Bank of England should, on pain of being abolished, instantly strike off and circulate, God knows how many thousand millions of ten-and-sixpenny notes." ¶CS/HH 1

—sold: "'Do you sell all your friends?'

"Rigaud took his cigarette from his mouth, and eyed him with a momentary revelation of surprise. But he put it between his lips again, as he answered with coolness:

"'I sell anything that commands a price. How do your lawyers live, your politicians, your intriguers, your men of the Exchange? How do you live? How do you come here? Have you sold no friend? Lady of mine! I rather think, yes!'

"Clennam turned away from him towards the window, and sat looking out at the wall.

"'Effectively, sir,' said Rigaud, 'Society sells itself and sells me; and I sell Society.'" LD ii 28

—unequal: ". . . it may be observed of this friendship [between Martin Chuzzlewit and Tom Pinch], such as it was, that it had within it more likely materials of endurance than many a sworn brotherhood that has been rich in promise; for so long as the one party found a pleasure in patronising, and the other in being patronised (which was in the very essence of their respective characters), it was of all possible events among the least probable, that the twin demons, Envy and Pride, would ever arise between them. So in very many cases of friendship, or what passes for it, the old axiom is reversed, and like clings to unlike more than to like." MC 7

—untrue: "Friendships which are founded on a partnership in doing wrong, are never true . . . . " CHE 13

Fugitive

—giving enjoyment: "As I [Pip] watched [the soldiers] while they all stood clustering about the forge, enjoying themselves so much, I thought what terrible good sauce for a dinner my fugitive friend [Abel Magwitch] on the marshes was. They had not enjoyed themselves a quarter so much, before the entertainment was brightened with the excitement he furnished. And now, when they were all in lively anticipation of 'the two villains' being taken, and when the bellows seemed to roar for the fugitives, the fire to flare for them, the smoke to hurry away in pursuit of them, Joe [Gargery] to hammer and clink for them, and all the murky shadows on the wall to shake at them in menace as the blaze rose and sank and the red-hot sparks dropped and died, the pale afternoon outside almost seemed in my pitying young fancy to have turned pale on their account, poor wretches." GE 5

—hue and cry: "'Stop thief! Stop thief!' There is a magic in the sound. The tradesman leaves his counter, and the carman his waggon; the butcher throws down his tray; the baker his basket; the milkman his pail; the errand-boy his parcels; the school-boy his marbles; the paviour his pick-axe; the child his battledore. Away they run, pell-mell, helter-skelter, slap-dash: tearing, yelling, screaming, knocking down the passengers as they turn the corners, rousing up the dogs, and astonishing the fowls: and streets, squares, and courts, re-echo with the sound.

"'Stop thief! Stop thief! The cry is taken up by a hundred voices, and the crowd accumulate at every turning. Away they fly, splashing through the mud, and rattling along the pavements: up go the windows, out run the people, onward bear the mob, a whole audience desert Punch in the very thickest of the plot, and, joining the rushing throng, swell the shout, and lend fresh vigour to the cry, 'Stop thief! Stop thief!'

"'Stop thief! Stop thief!' There is a passion *for hunting something* deeply implanted in the human breast. One wretched breathless child [Oliver Twist], panting with exhaustion; terror in his looks; agony in his eyes; large drops of perspiration streaming down his face; strains every nerve to make head upon his pursuers; and as they follow on his track, and gain upon him every instant, they hail his decreasing strength with still louder shouts, and whoop and scream with joy. 'Stop thief!' Ay, stop him for God's sake, were it only in mercy!" OT 10

And see Police—*criminal viewpoint*

Gipsy

—children: "Even the sunburnt faces of gipsy children, half naked though they be, suggest a drop of comfort. It is a pleasant thing to see that the sun has been there; to know that the air and light are on them every day; to feel that they *are* children, and lead children's lives; that if their pillows be damp, it is with the dews of Heaven, and not with tears; that the limbs of their girls are free, and that they are not crippled by distortions, imposing an unnatural and horrible penance upon their sex; that their lives are spent, from day to day, at least among the waving trees, and not in the midst of dreadful engines which make young children old before they know what childhood is, and give them the exhaustion and infirmity of age, without, like age, the privilege to die. God send that old nursey-tales were true, and that gipsies stole such children by the score!" NN 50

—fortune-teller: "Munching, like that sailor's wife of yore, who had chestnuts in her lap, and scowling like the witch who asked for some in vain, the old woman ['Good Mrs Brown' disguised] picked the shilling up, and going backwards, like a crab, or like a heap of crabs: for her alternately expanding and contracting hands might have represented two of that species, and her creeping face, some half-a-dozen more: crouched on the veinous root of an old tree, pulled out a short black pipe from within the crown of her bonnet, lighted it with a match, and smoked in silence, looking fixedly at her questioner.

"Mr Carker laughed, and turned upon his heel.

"'Good!' said the old woman. 'One child dead, and one child living: one wife dead, and one wife coming. Go and meet her!'

"In spite of himself, the Manager looked round again, and stopped. The old woman, who had not removed her pipe, and was munching and mumbling while she smoked, as if in conversation with an invisible familiar, pointed with her finger in the direction he was going and laughed.

"'What was that you said, Bedlamite?' he demanded.

"The woman mumbled, and chattered, and smoked, and still pointed before him; but remained silent." DS 27

And see H:Race-meeting *and* HWC/E

Guest

—attendant unknowns: "Pokey unknowns, amazed to find how intimately they know Veneering, pluck up spirit, fold their arms, and begin to contradict him before breakfast . . . [they] are exceedingly benevolent to one another in invitations to take glasses of champagne . . . [and] support each other in being unimpressible. They persist in not being frightened by the gold and silver camels, and they are banded together to defy the elaborately chased ice-pails. They even seem to unite in some vague utterance of the sentiment that the landlord and landlady will make a pretty good profit out of this, and they almost carry themselves like customers . . . .

"So they all go up again into the gorgeous drawing-rooms—all of them flushed with breakfast, as having taken scarlatina sociably—and there the combined unknowns do malignant things with their legs to ottomans, and take as much as possible out of the splendid furniture." OMF i 10

—after dinner: "And now the haunch of mutton vapour-bath having received a gamey infusion, and a few last touches of sweets and coffee, was quite ready, and the bathers came . . . .

"There was not much youth among the bathers . . . . Bald bathers folded their arms and talked to Mr Podsnap on the hearthrug; sleek-whiskered bathers, with hats in their hands, lunged at Mrs Podsnap and retreated; prowling bathers went about looking into ornamental boxes and bowls as if they had suspicions of larceny on the part of the Podsnaps, and expected to find something they had lost at the bottom; bathers of the gentler sex sat silently comparing ivory shoulders." OMF i 11

—fashionable: "All the mirrors in the house are brought into action now: many of them after a long blank. They reflect handsome faces, simpering faces, youthful faces, faces of threescore-and-ten that will not submit to be old; the entire collection of faces that have come to pass a January week or two at Chesney Wold, and which the fashionable intelligence, a mighty hunter before the Lord, hunts with a keen scent, from their breaking cover at the Court of St James's to their being run down to Death." BH 12

And see B:House*—fashionable*

—unwelcome: "As no arguments I could urge, in my bewildered condition, had the least effect upon his modesty in inducing [Uriah Heep] to accept my bedroom, I was obliged to make the best arrangements I could, for his repose before the fire. The mattress of the sofa (which was a great deal too short for his lank figure), the sofa pillows, a blanket, the table-cover, a clean breakfast-cloth, and a great-coat made him a bed and covering, for which he was more than thankful . . . .

"I never shall forget that night. I never shall forget how I turned and tumbled; how I wearied myself with thinking about Agnes and this creature; how I considered what could I do, and what ought I to do; how I could come to no other conclusion than that the best course for her peace was to do nothing, and to keep to myself what I had heard. If I went to sleep for a few moments, the image of Agnes with her tender eyes, and of her father looking fondly on her, as I had so often seen him look, arose before me with appealing faces, and filled me with vague terrors. When I awoke, the recollection that Uriah was lying in the next room, sat heavy on me like a waking nightmare; and oppressed me with a leaden dread, as if I had had some meaner quality of devil for a lodger.

"The poker got into my dozing thoughts besides, and wouldn't come out. I thought, between sleeping and waking, that it was still red hot, and I had snatched it out of the fire, and run him through the body . . . .

"When I saw him going down-stairs early in the morning (for, thank Heaven! he would not stay to breakfast), it appeared to me as if the night was going away in his person. When I went out to the Commons, I charged Mrs Crupp with particular directions to leave the windows open, that my sitting-room might be aired, and purged of his presence." DC 25 *And see* B:Sleep—*repulsive*

Homeless

—*in the city:* "To be shelterless and alone in the open country, hearing the wind moan and watching for day through the whole long weary night; to listen to the falling rain, and crouch for warmth beneath the lee of some old barn or rick, or in the hollow of a tree; are dismal things—but not so dismal as the wandering up and down where shelter is, and beds and sleepers are by thousands; a houseless rejected creature.

"To pace the echoing stones from hour to hour, counting the dull chimes of the clocks; to watch the lights twinkling in chamber windows, to think what happy forgetfulness each house shuts in; that here are children coiled together in their beds, here youth, here age, here poverty, here wealth, all equal in their sleep, and all at rest; to have nothing in common with the slumbering world around, not even sleep, Heaven's gift to all its creatures, and be akin to nothing but despair; to feel, by the wretched contrast with everything on every hand, more utterly alone and cast away than in a trackless desert; this is a kind of suffering, on which the rivers of great cities close full many a time, and which the solitude in crowds alone awakens." ¶BR 18

"It was a large room with a small fire, and there was a great bay window in it which the rain had marked in the night as if with the tears of houseless people." CS/PR

"There are some few people well to do, who remember to have heard it said, that numbers of men and women—thousands, they think it was—get up in London every day, unknowing where to lay their heads at night; and that there are quarters of the town where misery and famine always are.

"They don't believe it quite—there may be some truth in it, but it is exaggerated, of course. So, each of these thousand worlds goes on, intent upon itself, until night comes again—first with its lights and pleasures, and its cheerful streets; then with its guilt and darkness.

"Heart of London [the clock in St Paul's], there is a moral in thy every stroke! as I look on at thy indomitable working, which neither death, nor press of life, nor grief, nor gladness out of doors will influence one jot, I seem to hear a voice within thee which sinks into my heart, bidding me, as I elbow my way among the crowd, have some thought for the meanest wretch that passes, and, being a man, to turn away with scorn and pride from none that bear the human shape." MH 14

—*in the cold:* "Bleak, dark, and piercing cold, it was a night for the well-housed and fed to draw round the bright fire and thank God they were at home; and for the homeless starving wretch to lay him down and die. Many hunger-worn outcasts close their eyes in our bare streets, at such times, who, let their crimes have been what they may, can hardly open them in a more bitter world." OT 23

—*drunkard:* "[Warden] begged his bread from door to door. Every halfpenny he could wring from the pity or credulity of those to whom he addressed himself, was spent in the old way. A year passed over his head; the roof of a jail was the only one that had sheltered him for many months. He slept under archways, and in brickfields—anywhere, where there was some warmth or shelter from the cold and rain. But in the last stage of poverty, disease, and houseless want, he was a drunkard still.

"At last, one bitter night, he sunk down on a door-step faint and ill. The premature decay of vice and profligacy had worn him to the bone. His cheeks were hollow and livid; his eyes were sunken, and their sight was dim. His legs trembled beneath his weight, and a cold shiver ran through every limb.

"And now the long-forgotten scenes of a misspent life crowded thick and fast upon him. He thought of the time when he had a home—a happy, cheerful home—and of those who peopled it, and flocked about him then, until the forms of his elder children seemed to rise from the grave, and stand about him—so plain, so clear, and so distinct they were that he could touch and feel them. Looks that he had long forgotten were fixed upon him once more; voices long since hushed in death sounded in his ears like the music of village bells. But it was only for an instant. The rain beat heavily upon him; and cold and hunger were gnawing at his heart again." SB/DD

—dying: "Sometimes [Betty Higden] would hear a newspaper read out, and would learn how the Registrar General cast up the units that had within the last week died of want and of exposure to the weather: for which that Recording Angel seemed to have a regular fixed place in his sum, as if they were its halfpence." OMF iii 8

WE GIVE THEE HEARTY THANKS FOR THAT IT HATH PLEASED THEE TO DELIVER THIS OUR SISTER OUT OF THE MISERIES OF THIS SINFUL WORLD.'" So read the Reverend Frank Milvey in a not untroubled voice, for his heart misgave him that all was not quite right between us and our sister—or say our sister in Law—Poor Law—and that we sometimes read these words in an awful manner, over our Sister and our Brother too." OMF iii 9

—at night: " . . . I finished my education in a fair amateur experience of houselessness. My principal object being to get through the night, the pursuit of it brought me into sympathetic relations with people who have no other object every night in the year . . . .

"At length . . . London would sink to rest. And then the yearning of the houseless mind would be for any sign of company, any lighted place, any movement, anything suggestive of any one being up—nay, even so much as awake, for the houseless eye looked out for lights in windows.

"Walking the streets under the pattering rain, Houselessness would walk and walk and walk, seeing nothing but the interminable tangle of streets, save at a corner, here and there, two policemen in conversation, or the sergeant or inspector looking after his men . . . .

"When a church clock strikes, on houseless ears in the dead of the night, it may be at first mistaken for company and hailed as such. But, as the spreading circles of vibration, which you may perceive at such a time with great clearness, go opening out, for ever and ever afterwards widening perhaps (as the philosopher has suggested) in eternal space, the mistake is rectified and the sense of loneliness is profounder. Once . . . I came to the great steps of St. Martin's church as the clock was striking Three. Suddenly, a thing that in a moment more I should have trodden upon without seeing, rose up at my feet with a cry of loneliness and houselessness, struck out of it by the bell, the like of which I never heard. We then stood face to face looking at one another, frightened by one another." UT/NW

In Dickens's terms, 'homeless' was usually 'houseless.' He calls himself 'Houselessness' in UT/NW

—no longer: "I turned my eyes away, yielded to the sensation of gratitude and rest which the sight of the white-curtained bed—and how much more the lying softly down upon it, nestling in the snow-white sheets!—inspired. I remember how I thought of all the solitary places under the night sky where I had slept, and how I prayed that I never might be houseless any more, and never might forget the houseless. I remember how I seemed to float, then, down the melancholy glory of that track upon the sea, away into the world of dreams." DC 13

—prisoner: "There were other prisoners . . . a houseless vagrant, going joyfully to prison as a place of food and shelter . . . . " SB/PV

—at a shelter: "They passed to their different sleeping-places, quietly and in good order. Every one sat down in his own crib, where he became presented in a curiously foreshortened manner; and those who had shoes took them off, and placed them in the adjoining path. There were, in the assembly, thieves, cadgers, trampers, vagrants, common outcasts of all sorts. In casual wards and many other Refuges, they would have been very difficult to deal with; but they were restrained here by the law of kindness, and had long since arrived at the knowledge that those who gave him [*sic*] that shelter could have no possible inducement save to do them good. Neighbours spoke little together—they were almost as uncompanionable as mad people—but everybody took his small loaf when the baskets went round, with a thankfulness more or less cheerful, and immediately ate it up." HW/SU

—on the street outside: "Crouched against the wall of the Workhouse, in the dark street, on the muddy pavement-stones, with the rain raining upon them, were five bundles of rags. They were motionless, and had no resemblance to the human form. Five great beehives, covered with rags—five

dead bodies taken out of graves, tied neck and heels, and covered with rags—would have looked like those five bundles upon which the rain rained down in the public street.

"'What is this!' said my companion [the writer **Albert Smith**]. 'What *is* this!'

"'Some miserable people shut out of the Casual Ward, I think,' said I.

"We had stopped before the five ragged mounds, and were quite rooted to the spot by their horrible appearance. Five awful Sphinxes by the wayside, crying to every passer-by, 'Stop and guess! What is to be the end of a state of society that leaves us here!' . . .

"We went to the ragged bundle nearest to the Workhouse-door, and I touched it. No movement replying, I gently shook it. The rags began to be slowly stirred within, and by little and little a head was unshrouded. The head of a young woman of three or four and twenty, as I should judge; gaunt with want, and foul with dirt; but not naturally ugly . . . .

"She spoke in a faint dull way, and had no curiosity or interest left. She looked dreamily at the black sky and the falling rain, but never looked at me or my companion . . . .

"'If you had a shilling to get some supper and a lodging should you know where to get it?'

"'Yes, I could do that.'

"'For God's sake get it then!'

"I put the money into her hand, and she feebly rose up and went away. She never thanked me, never looked at me—melted away into the miserable night, in the strangest manner I ever saw. I have seen many strange things, but not one that has left a deeper impression on my memory than the dull impassive way in which that worn-out heap of misery took that piece of money, and was lost." HW/SL

And see CD: Angry

—unfurnished lodgings: "'Arter I ran away from the carrier [said Sam Weller], and afore I took up with the vagginer, I had unfurnished lodgin's for a fortnight.'

"'Unfurnished lodgings?' said Mr Pickwick.

"'Yes—the dry arches of Waterloo Bridge. Fine sleeping-place—within ten minutes' walk of all the public offices—only if there is any objection to it, it is that the sitivations's *rayther* too airy. I see some queer sights there.'

"'I suppose you did,' said Mr Pickwick, with an air of considerable interest.

"'Sights, sir,' resumed Mr Weller, 'as 'ud penetrate your benevolent heart, and come out on the other side. You don't see the reg'lar wagrants there; trust 'em, they knows better than that. Young beggars, male and female, as hasn't made a rise in their profession, takes up their quarters there sometimes; but it's generally the worn-out, starving, houseless creeturs as rolls themselves in the dark corners o' them lonesome places . . . .'" PP 16

And see Loneliness; IG:Government *and* TP:Clergy—*Oxford Movement*

Impostor

—amateur: "There is a certain kind of impostor—a bragging, vaunting, puffing young gentleman—against whom we are desirous to warn that fairer part of creation . . . .

"The throwing-off young gentleman has so often a father possessed of vast property in some remote district of Ireland, that we look with some suspicion upon all young gentlemen who volunteer this description of themselves. The deceased grandfather of the throwing-off young gentleman was a man of immense possessions, and untold wealth; the . . . gentleman remembers, as well as if it were only yesterday, the deceased baronet's library, with its long rows of scarce and valuable books in superbly embossed bindings, arranged in cases, reaching from the lofty ceiling to the oaken floor; and the fine antique chairs and tables, and the noble old castle of Ballykillbabaloo, with its splendid prospect of hill and dale, and wood, and rich wild scenery, and the fine hunting stables and the spacious courtyards, 'and—and—everything upon the same magnificent scale,' says the throwing-off young gentleman, 'princely; quite princely. 'Ah!' And he sighs as if mourning over the fallen fortunes of his noble house.

"The throwing-off young gentleman is a universal genius; at walking, running, rowing, swimming, and skating, he is unrivalled; at all games of chance or skill, at hunting, shooting, fishing, riding, driving, or amateur theatricals, no one can touch him—that is could not, because he gives you carefully to understand, lest there should be any opportunity of testing his skill, that he is quite out of practice just now, and has been for some years.

"If you mention any beautiful girl of your common acquaintance in his hearing, the throwing-off young gentleman starts, smiles, and begs you not to mind him, for it was quite involuntary: people do say indeed that they were once engaged, but no—although she is a very fine girl, he was so situated at that time that he couldn't possibly encourage the—'but it's of no use talking about it!' he adds, interrupting himself. 'She has got over it now, and I firmly hope and trust is happy.' With this benevolent aspiration he nods his head in a mysterious manner, and whistling the first part of some popular air, thinks perhaps it will be better to change the subject.

"There is another great characteristic of the throwing-off young gentleman, which is, that he 'happens to be acquainted' with a most extraordinary variety of people in all parts of the world. Thus in all disputed questions, when the throwing-off young gentleman has no argument to bring forward, he invariably happens to be acquainted with some distant person, intimately connected with the subject, whose testimony decides the point against you, to the great—may we say it—to the great admiration of three young ladies out of every four, who consider the throwing-off young gentleman a very highly-connected young man, and a most charming person." ¶YG/TO

—beginning with No. 1: "[Wegg's] gravity was unusual, portentous, and immeasurable, not because he admitted any doubt of himself, but because he perceived it necessary to forestall any doubt of himself in others. And herein he ranged with that very numerous class of impostors, who are quite as determined to keep up appearances to themselves, as to their neighbours." OMF i 5

—commemorated: "In the picturesque old town of Rouen, where weeds and grass grow high on the cathedral towers, and the venerable Norman streets are still warm in the blessed sunlight though the monkish fires that once gleamed horribly upon them have long grown cold, there is a statue of Joan of Arc, in the scene of her last agony, in the square to which she has given its present name. I know some statues of modern times—even in the World's metropolis, I think—which commemorate less constancy, less earnestness, smaller claims upon the world's attention, and much greater impostors." CHE 22 ii

—to a cynic: "'I am not a great impostor. Buy one of my pictures, and I assure you, in confidence, it will not be worth the money. Buy one of another man's—any great professor who beats me hollow—and the chances are that the more you give him, the more he'll impose upon you. They all do it.'

"'All painters?'

"'Painters, writers, patriots, all the rest who have stands in the market. Give almost any man I know, ten pounds, and he will impose upon you to a corresponding extent; a thousand pounds—to a corresponding extent; ten thousand pounds—to a corresponding extent; ten thousand pounds—to a corresponding extent. So great the success, so great the imposition. But what a capital world it is!' cried Gowan with warm enthusiasm. 'What a jolly, excellent loveable world it is!'" LD i 26

And see Appearances—*deceiving*

Irish

—in London: "Ten, twenty, thirty—who can count them! Men, women, children, for the most part naked, heaped upon the floor like maggots in a cheese! Ho! In that dark corner yonder! Does anybody lie there? Me sir, Irish me, a widder, with six children. And yonder? Me sir, Irish me, with me wife and eight poor babes. And to the left there? Me sir, Irish me, along with two more Irish boys as is me friends. And to the right there? Me sir and the Murphy fam'ly, numbering five blessed souls.

"And what's this, coiling, now, about my foot? Another Irish me, pitifully in want of shaving, whom I have awakened from sleep—and across my other foot lies his wife—and by the shoes of Inspector Field lie their three eldest—and their three youngest are at present squeezed between the open door and the wall. And why is there no one on that little mat before the sullen fire? Because O'Donovan, with his wife and daughter, is not come in from selling Lucifers! Nor on the bit of sacking in the nearest corner? Bad luck! Because that Irish family is late to-night, a-cadging in the streets!" ¶RP/DF

"After council holden in the street, we enter other lodging-houses, public-houses, many lairs and holes; all noisome and offensive; none so filthy and so crowded as where Irish are." RP/DF *And see* SB/GS

Jews

—blanket judgment: " . . . what could I suppose, when you were a silent party to all

[Fledgeby] said? It did look bad; now didn't it?'

"'It looked so bad, Jenny,' responded the old man [Riah], with gravity, 'that I will straightway tell you what an impression it wrought upon me. I was hateful in mine own eyes. I was hateful to myself, in being so hateful to the debtor and to you.

"But more than that, and worse than that, and to pass out far and broad beyond myself—I reflected that evening, sitting alone in my garden on the housetop, that I was doing dishonour to my ancient faith and race. I reflected—clearly reflected for the first time, that in bending my neck to the yoke I was willing to wear, I bent the unwilling necks of the whole Jewish people.

"For it is not, in Christian countries, with the Jews as with other peoples. Men say, "This is a bad Greek, but there are good Greeks. This is a bad Turk, but there are good Turks." Not so with the Jews. Men find the bad among us easily enough—among what peoples are the bad not easily found?—but they take the worst of us as samples of the best; they take the lowest of us as presentations of the highest; and they say, "All Jews are alike."

"If, doing what I was content to do here, because I was grateful for the past and have small need of money now, I had been a Christian, I could have done it, compromising no one but my individual self. But doing it as a Jew, I could not choose but compromise the Jews of all conditions and all countries. It is a little hard upon us, but it is the truth. I would that all our people remembered it! Though I have little right to say so, seeing that it came home so late to me.

" . . . passing the painful scene of that day in review before me many times, I always saw that the poor gentleman believed the story readily, because I was one of the Jews—that you believed my story readily, my child, because I was one of the Jews—that the story itself first came into the invention of the originator thereof, because I was one of the Jews. This was the result of my having had you three before me, face to face, and seeing the thing visibly presented as upon a theatre. Wherefore I perceived that the obligation was upon me to leave this service." ¶OMF iv 9

—diet and commercial reputation: "' . . . if you don't like either cold fowl or hot boiled ham which many people don't I dare say besides Jews and theirs are scruples of conscience which we must all respect though I must say I wish they had them equally strong when they sell us false articles for real that certainly ain't worth the money I shall be quite vexed,' said Flora." LD i 24

—and finance: "'I propose,' said Mr Micawber, 'Bills—a convenience to the mercantile world, for which, I believe, we are originally indebted to the Jews, who appear to me to have had a devilish deal too much to do with them ever since—because they are negotiable." DC 54

—letting live: "' . . . I should not have had the power, without our managing partner.'

"'Surely not the Jew who received us?' said Mrs Milvey.

"('My dear,' observed her husband, in parenthesis, 'why not?')

"'The gentleman certainly is a Jew,' said Lizzie [Hexam], 'and the lady, his wife, is a Jewess, and I was first brought to their notice by a Jew. But I think there cannot be kinder people in the world.'

"'But suppose they try to convert you!' suggested Mrs Milvey, bristling in her good little way, as a clergyman's wife.

"'To do what, ma'am?' asked Lizzie, with a modest smile.

"'To make you change your religion,' said Mrs Milvey.

"Lizzie shook her head, still smiling. 'They have never asked me what my religion is. They asked me what my story was, and I told them. They asked me to be industrious and faithful, and I promised to be so. They most willingly and cheerfully do their duty to all of us who are employed here, and we try to do ours to them. Indeed they do much more than their duty to us, for they are wonderfully mindful of us in many ways.'

"'It is easy to see you're a favourite, my dear,' said little Mrs Milvey, not quite pleased.

"'It would be very ungrateful in me to say I am not,' returned Lizzie, 'for I have been already raised to a place of confidence here. But that makes no difference in their following their own religion and leaving all of us to ours. They never talk of theirs to us, and they never talk of ours to us. If I was the last in the mill it would be just the same. They never asked me what religion that poor thing [Betty Higden] had followed.'" OMF iii 9

—in Mantua: "The marshy town was so intensely dull and flat, that the dirt upon it seemed not to have come there in the ordinary course, but to have settled and mantled on its surface as on standing water. And yet there were some business-dealings going on, and some profits realising; for there were arcades full of Jews, where those extraordinary people were sitting outside their shops, contemplating their stores of stuffs, and woollens, and bright handkerchiefs, and trinkets: and looking, in all respects, as wary and business-like as their brethren in Houndsditch, London." PI 9

—persecution

—in the time of Henry III: "I am sorry to say, however, that instead of falling upon the King's party with whom their quarrel was [the Londoners] fell upon the miserable Jews, and killed at least five hundred of them. They pretended that some of these Jews were on the King's side, and that they kept hidden in their houses, for the destruction of the people, a certain terrible composition called Greek Fire, which could not be put out with water, but only burnt the fiercer for it. What they really did keep in their houses was money; and this their cruel enemies wanted, and this their cruel enemies took, like robbers and murderers." CHE 15

—under Edward I: " . . . I am sorry to add that in this reign [late 13th century] they were most unmercifully pillaged. They were hanged in great numbers, on accusations of having clipped the King's coin—which all kinds of people had done. They were heavily taxed; they were disgracefully badged; they were, on one day, thirteen years after the coronation, taken up with their wives and children and thrown into beastly prisons, until they purchased their release by paying to the King twelve thousand pounds.

"Finally, every kind of property belonging to them was seized by the King, except so little as would defray the charge of their taking themselves away into foreign countries. Many years elapsed before the hope of gain induced any of their race to return to England, where they had been treated so heartlessly and had suffered so much." ¶CHE 16

—poor: "'Can't be buyer and seller too. That's what the Jews say; ain't it?'

"'At least we say truly, if we say so,' answered the old man with a smile.

"'Your people need speak the truth sometimes, for they lie enough,' remarked Fascination Fledgeby.

"'Sir, there is,' returned the old man with quiet emphasis, 'too much untruth among all denominations of men.'

"Rather dashed, Fascination Fledgeby took another scratch at his intellectual head with his hat, to gain time for rallying.

"'For instance,' he resumed, as though it were he who had spoken last, 'who but you and I ever heard of a poor Jew?'

"'The Jews,' said the old man, raising his eyes from the ground with his former smile. 'They hear of poor Jews often, and are very good to them.'" OMF ii 5

—in Rome: "The little town of miserable houses, walled, and shut in by barred gates, is the quarter where the Jews are locked up nightly [in 1845], when the clock strikes eight—a miserable place, densely populated, and reeking with bad odours, but where the people are industrious and money-getting. In the daytime, as you make your way along the narrow streets, you see them all at work; upon the pavement, oftener than in their dark and frowzy shops: furbishing old clothes, and driving bargains." PI 11

Loneliness

—of chambers: "It is to be remarked of chambers in general, that they must have been built for chambers, to have the right kind of loneliness. You may make a great dwelling-house very lonely, by isolating suites of rooms and calling them chambers, but you cannot make the true kind of loneliness. In dwelling-houses, there have been family festivals; children have grown in them, girls have bloomed into women in them, courtships and marriages have taken place in them.

"True chambers never were young, childish, maidenly; never had dolls in them, or rocking-horses, or christenings, or betrothals, or little coffins. Let Gray's Inn identify the child who first touched hands and hearts with *Robinson Crusoe,* in any one of its many 'sets,' and that child's little statue, in white marble with a golden inscription, shall be at its service, at my cost and charge, as a drinking fountain for the spirit, to freshen its thirsty square.

"Let Lincoln's produce from all its houses, a twentieth of the procession derivable from any dwelling-house one-twentieth of its age, of fair young brides who married for love and hope, not settlements, and all the Vice-Chancellors shall thenceforward be kept in nosegays for nothing, on application to the writer hereof.

"It is not denied that on the terrace of the Adelphi, or in any of the streets of that sub-terranean-stable-haunted spot, or about Bedford-row, or James-street of that ilk (a grewsome place), or anywhere among the neighbourhoods that have done flowering and have run to seed, you may find Chambers replete with the accommodations of Solitude, Closeness, and Darkness, where you may be as low-spirited as in the genuine article, and might be as easily murdered, with the placid reputation of having merely gone down to the sea-side. But, the many waters of life did run musical in those dry channels once;—among the Inns, never." UT/C

—of a cheapjack: "Being naturally of a tender turn, I had dreadful lonely feelings on me arter this [his dog's death]. I conquered 'em at selling times, having a reputation to keep (not to mention keeping myself), but they got me down in private, and rolled upon me. That's often the way with us public characters. See us on the foot-board, and you'd give pretty well anything you possess to be us. See us off the footboard, and you'd add a trifle to be off your bargain." CS/DM 1

—in a crowd: "Middle-aged men, whose salaries have by no means increased in the same proportion as their families, plod steadily along, apparently with no object in view but the counting-house; knowing by sight almost everybody they meet or overtake, for they have seen them every morning (Sundays excepted) during the last twenty years, but speaking to no one. If they do happen to overtake a personal acquaintance, they just exchange a hurried salutation, and keep walking on, either by his side or in front of him, as his rate of walking may chance to be. As to stopping to shake hands, or to take the friend's arm, they seem to think that as it is not included in their salary, they have no right to it." SB/SM

"Thus easily did Stephen Blackpool fall into the loneliest of lives, the life of solitude among a familiar crowd. The stranger in the land who looks into ten thousand faces for some answering look and never finds it, is in cheering society as compared with him who passes ten averted faces daily, that were once the countenances of friends. Such experience was to be Stephen's now, in every waking moment of his life; at his work, on his way to it and from it, at his door, at his window, everywhere. By general consent, they even avoided that side of the street on which he habitually walked; and left it, of all the working men, to him only.

"He had been for many years, a quiet silent man, associating but little with other men, and used to companionship with his own thoughts. He had never known before the strength of the want in his heart for the frequent recognition of a nod, a look, a word; or the immense amount of relief that had been poured into it by drops through such small means. It was even harder than he could have believed possible, to separate in his own conscience his abandonment by all his fellows from a baseless sense of shame and disgrace." HT ii 4

—of the homeless: "He raised his head, and looked up the long dismal street. He recollected that outcasts like himself, condemned to wander day and night in those dreadful streets, had sometimes gone distracted with their own loneliness. He remembered to have heard many years before that a homeless wretch had once been found in a solitary corner, sharpening a rusty knife to plunge into his own heart, preferring death to that endless, weary, wandering to and fro. In an instant his resolve was taken, his limbs received new life: he ran quickly from the spot, and paused not for breath until he reached the river-side." SB/DD

—in a hospital: "Who can tell the anguish of those weary hours, when the only sound the sick man hears is the disjointed wanderings of some feverish slumberer near him, the low moan of pain, or perhaps the muttered, long-forgotten prayer of a dying man? Who, but they who have felt it, can imagine the sense of loneliness and desolation which must be the portion of those who in the hour of dangerous illness are left to be tended by strangers; for what hands, be they ever so gentle, can wipe the clammy brow, or smooth the restless bed, like those of mother, wife, or child?" SB/HP

—at school: " . . . Florence ran back to throw her arms round his neck, and . . . hers was the last face in the doorway: turned towards him with a smile of encouragement, the brighter for the tears through which it beamed.

"It made his childish bosom heave and swell when it was gone; and sent the globes, the books, blind **Homer** and

Minerva, swimming round the room. But they stopped, all of a sudden; and then he heard the loud clock in the hall still gravely inquiring 'how, is, my, lit, tle, friend?' how, is, my, lit, tle, friend? as it had done before.

"He sat, with folded hands, upon his pedestal, silently listening. But he might have answered 'weary, weary! very lonely, very sad!' And there, with an aching void in his young heart, and all outside so cold, and bare, and strange, Paul sat as if he had taken life unfurnished, and the upholsterer were never coming." DS 11

—in a word: "'Company, you see—company is—is—it's a very different thing from solitude—ain't it?'

"'There's no denying that 'ere,' said Mr Weller, joining in the conversation, with an affable smile. 'That's what I call a self-evident proposition, as the dog's-meat man said, when the housemaid told him he warn't a gentleman.'" PP 22

And see Homeless; and CD:Authorship—*similes, comical*

Love

—absence and mystery: "Mystery and disappointment are not absolutely indispensable to the growth of love, but they are very often its powerful auxiliaries . . . . Love . . . is very materially assisted by a warm and active imagination, which has a long memory, and will thrive for a considerable time on a very slight and sparing food. Thus it is that it often attains its most luxuriant growth in separation and under circumstances of the utmost difficulty . . . . " NN 40

—absent mind: " . . . there is a subtlety of perception in real attachment, even when it is borne towards man by one of the lower animals, which leaves the highest intellect behind. To this mind of the heart, if I may call it so, in Mr Dick, some bright ray of the truth shot straight . . . . " DC 42

—affection wounded: [Haredale] looked much older, and more care-worn. Agitation and anxiety of mind scattered wrinkles and grey hairs with no unsparing hand; but deeper traces follow on the silent uprooting of old habits, and severing of dear, familiar ties. The affections may not be so easily wounded as the passions, but their hurts are deeper, and more lasting. He was now a solitary man, and the heart within him was dreary and lonesome." BR 81

—and ambition: "'The beautiful young lady at Miss Havisham's, and she's more beautiful than anybody ever was, and I admire her dreadfully, and I want to be a gentleman on her account.' Having made this lunatic confession, I began to throw my torn-up grass into the river, as if I had some thoughts of following it.

"'Do you want to be a gentleman, to spite her or to gain her over?' Biddy quietly asked me, after a pause.

"'I don't know,' I moodily answered.

"'Because, if it is to spite her,' Biddy pursued, 'I should think—but you know best—that might be better and more independently done by caring nothing for her words. And if it is to gain her over, I should think—but you know best—she was not worth gaining over.'

"Exactly what I myself had thought, many times. Exactly what was perfectly manifest to me at the moment. But how could I, a poor dazed village lad, avoid that wonderful inconsistency into which the best and wisest of men fall every day?

"'It may be all quite true,' said I to Biddy, 'but I admire her dreadfully.'"

"In short, I turned over on my face when I came to that, and got a good grasp on the hair, on each side of my head, and wrenched it well. All the while knowing the madness of my heart to be so very mad and misplaced, that I was quite conscious it would have served my face right, if I had lifted it up by my hair, and knocked it against the pebbles as a punishment for belonging to such an idiot.'" GE 17

—and attire: "Within the first week of my passion, I bought four sumptuous waistcoats—not for myself; I had no pride in them; for Dora—and took to wearing straw-coloured kid gloves in the streets, and laid the foundations of all the corns I have ever had. If the boots I wore at that period could only be produced and compared with the natural size of my feet, they would show what the state of my heart was, in a most affecting manner." DC 26

—besotted: "I shall never have such a ride. I have never had such another . . . the phaeton was open; and I rode behind it, and Dora sat with her back to the horses, looking towards me. She kept the bouquet close to her on the cushion, and wouldn't allow Jip to sit on that side of her at all, for fear he should crush it. She often carried it in her hand, often refreshed herself with its fragrance. Our eyes at those times often

met; and my great astonishment is that I didn't go over the head of my gallant grey into the carriage.

"There was dust, I believe. There was a good deal of dust, I believe. I have a faint impression that Mr Spenlow remonstrated with me for riding in it; but I knew of none. I was sensible of a mist of love and beauty about Dora, but of nothing else. He stood up sometimes, and asked me what I thought of the prospect. I said it was delightful, and I dare say it was; but it was all Dora to me. The sun shone Dora, and the birds sang Dora. The south wind blew Dora, and the wild flowers in the hedges were all Doras, to a bud." DC 33

—between children: "Of all the company [at the wedding] though, none are more pleasant to behold or better pleased with themselves than two young children, who, in honour of the day, have seats among the guests. Of these, one is a little fellow of six or eight years old, brother to the bride—and the other a girl of the same age, or something younger, whom he calls 'his wife.'

"The real bride and bridegroom are not more devoted than they: he all love and attention, and she all blushes and fondness, toying with a little bouquet which he gave her this morning, and placing the scattered rose-leaves in her bosom with nature's own coquettishness. They have dreamt of each other in their quiet dreams, these children, and their little hearts have been nearly broken when the absent one has been dispraised in jest. When will there come in after-life a passion so earnest, generous, and true as theirs; what, even in its gentlest realities, can have the grace and charm that hover round such fairy lovers!" YC/Y

—of children: "I really felt ashamed to take advantage of the ingenuousness or grateful feeling of the child for the purpose of gratifying my curiosity. I love these little people; and it is not a slight thing when they, who are so fresh from God, love us." OCS 1

—commitment overdone: "'Hear me, Pip! [said Miss Havisham] I adopted [Estella] to be loved. I bred her and educated her, to be loved, I developed her into what she is, that she might be loved. Love her!'

"She said the word often enough, and there could be no doubt that she meant to say it; but if the often repeated word had been hate instead of love—despair—revenge—dire death—it could not have have sounded from her lips more like a curse.

"'I'll tell you,' said [Miss Havisham], in the same hurried passionate whisper, 'what real love is. It is blind devotion, unquestioning self-humiliation, utter submission, trust and belief against yourself and against the whole world, giving up your whole heart and soul to the smiter—as I did!'" GE 29

—compensation: "'Don't go yet,' urged the fat boy.

"'I must,' replied Mary. 'Good-bye, for the present.'

"The fat boy, with elephantine playfulness, stretched out his arms to ravish a kiss; but as it required no great agility to elude him, his fair enslaver had vanished before he closed them again; upon which the apathetic youth ate a pound or so of steak with a sentimental countenance, and fell fast asleep." PP 54 *And see* Vol. I pp192-3

—courtship

—advice: "'I should commence, sir, with a tribute to the lady's beauty and excellent qualities; from them, sir, I should diverge to my own unworthiness.'

"'Very good,' said Mr Magnus.

"'Unworthiness for *her* only, mind, sir,' resumed Mr Pickwick; 'for to show that I was not wholly unworthy, sir, I should take a brief review of my past life, and present condition. I should argue, by analogy, that to anybody else, I must be a very desirable object. I should then expatiate on the warmth of my love, and the depth of my devotion. Perhaps I might then be tempted to seize her hand.'

"'Yes, I see,' said Mr Magnus: 'that would be a very great point.'

"'I should then, sir,' continued Mr Pickwick, growing warmer as the subject presented itself in more glowing colours before him: 'I should then, sir, come to the plain and simple question, "Will you have me!? I think I am justified in assuming that, upon this, she would turn away her head.'

"'You think that may be taken for granted?' said Mr Magnus; 'because, if she did not do that at the right place, it would be embarrassing.'

"'I think she would,' said Mr Pickwick. 'Upon this, sir, I should squeeze her hand, and I think—I *think,* Mr Magnus—that after I had done that, supposing there was no refusal, I should gently draw away the handkerchief, which my slight knowledge of human nature leads me to suppose the lady would be applying to her eyes at the moment, and steal a respectful kiss. I think I should kiss her, Mr Magnus; at this particular point, I am decidedly of opinion that if the lady were going to take me at all, she would murmur into my ears a bashful acceptance.'" PP 24

—blissful: "What an idle time it was! What an unsubstantial, happy, foolish time it was!

"When I [David Copperfield] measured Dora [Spenlow]'s finger for a ring that was to be made of Forget-me-nots, and when the jeweller, to whom I took the measure, found me out, and laughed over his order-book, and charged me anything he liked for the pretty little toy, with its blue stones—so associated in my remembrance with Dora's hand, that yesterday, when I saw such another, by chance, on the finger of my own daughter, there was a momentary stirring in my heart, like pain!

"When I walked about, exalted with my secret, and full of my own interest, and felt the dignity of loving Dora, and of being beloved, so much, that if I had walked the air, I could not have been more above the people not so situated, who were creeping on the earth!

"When we had those meetings in the garden of the square, and sat within the dingy summer-house, so happy, that I love the London sparrows to this hour, for nothing else, and see the plumage of the tropics in their smoky feathers!

"When we had our first great quarrel (within a week of our betrothal), and when Dora sent me back the ring, enclosed in a despairing cocked-hat note, wherein she used the terrible expression that 'our love had begun in folly, and ended in madness!' which dreadful words occasioned me to tear my hair, and cry that all was over!

"When, under cover of the night, I flew to Miss Mills, whom I saw by stealth in a back kitchen where there was a mangle, and implored Miss Mills to interpose between us and avert insanity. When Miss Mills undertook the office and returned with Dora, exhorting us, from the pulpit of her own bitter youth, to mutual concession, and the avoidance of the desert of Sahara!

"When we cried, and made it up, and were so blest again, that the back kitchen, mangle and all, changed to Love's own temple, where we arranged a plan of correspondence through Miss Mills, always to comprehend at least one letter on each side every day!

"What an idle time! What an unsubstantial, happy, foolish time! Of all the times of mine that Time has in his grip, there is none that in one retrospect I can smile at half so much, and think of half so tenderly." DC 33

—factual: " . . . Mr Bounderby went every evening to Stone Lodge, as an accepted wooer. Love was made on these occasions in the form of bracelets; and, on all occasions during the period of betrothal, took a manufacturing aspect. Dresses were made, jewellery was made, cakes and gloves were made, settlements were made, and an extensive assortment of Facts did appropriate honour to the contract. The business was all Facts, from first to last." HT i 16

—rustic: "On the very first evening after our arrival, Mr Barkis appeared in an exceedingly vacant and awkward condition, and with a bundle of oranges tied up in a handkerchief. As he made no allusion of any kind to this property, he was supposed to have left it behind him by accident when he went away; until Ham [Peggotty], running after him to restore it, came back with the information that it was intended for Peggotty. After that occasion he appeared every evening at exactly the same hour, and always with a little bundle, to which he never alluded, and which he regularly put behind the door, and left there. These offerings of affection were of a most various and eccentric description. Among them I remember a double set of pigs' trotters, a huge pin-cushion, half a bushel or so of apples, a pair of jet earrings, some Spanish onions, a box of dominoes, a canary bird and cage, and a leg of pickled pork.

"Mr Barkis's wooing, as I remember it, was altogether of a peculiar kind. He very seldom said anything; but would sit by the fire in much the same attitude as he sat in his cart, and stare heavily at Peggotty, who was opposite. One night, being, as I suppose, inspired by love, he made a dart at the bit of wax-candle she kept for her thread, and put it in his waistcoat-pocket and carried it off. After that, his great delight was to produce it when it was wanted, sticking to the lining of his pocket, in a partially melted state, and pocket it again when it was done with. He seemed to enjoy himself very much, and not to feel at all called upon to talk. Even when he took Peggotty out for a walk on the flats, he had no uneasiness on that head, I believe; contenting himself with now and then asking her if she was pretty comfortable; and I remember that sometimes, after he was gone, Peggotty would throw her apron over her face, and laugh for half-an-hour." DC 10

—a cynic's view: " . . . Ralph [Nickleby] saw clearly enough that Mr Mantalini had gained a fresh lease of his easy life, and that, for some time longer at all events, his degradation and downfall were postponed.

"'But it will come soon enough,' thought Ralph; 'all love—bah! that I should use the cant of boys and girls—is fleeting enough; though that which has its sole root in the admiration of a whiskered face like that of yonder baboon, perhaps lasts the longest, as it originates in the greater blindness and is fed by vanity.'" NN 34

—a daughter's

—admiring and ashamed: "[Little Dorrit's] look at her father, half admiring him and proud of him, half ashamed for him, all devoted and loving, went to [Arthur's] inmost heart." LD i 8

—injured but steadfast: "Her father did not know . . . how much she loved him. She was very young, and had no mother, and had never learned, by some fault or misfortune, how to express to him that she loved him. She would be patient, and would try to gain that art in time, and win him to a better knowledge of his only child.

"This became the purpose of her life. The morning sun shone down upon the faded house, and found the resolution bright and fresh within the bosom of its solitary mistress. Through all the duties of the day it animated her; for Florence hoped that the more she knew, and the more accomplished she became, the more glad he would be when he came to know and like her. Sometimes she wondered, with a swelling heart and rising tear, whether she was proficient enough in anything to surprise him when they should become companions. Sometimes she tried to think if there were any kind of knowledge that would bespeak his interest more readily than another. Always—at her books, her music, and her work: in her morning walks, and in her nightly prayers—she had her engrossing aim in view. Strange study for a child, to learn the road to a hard parent's heart!" DS 24

"'[Sissy] keeps the bottle that he sent her for, to this hour; and she will believe in his affection to the last moment of her life,' said Mr Gradgrind." HT iii 8

—killed: " . . . in her lonely yearning to the dead [Walter Gay] whom she had loved, no thought of home—no possibility of going back—no presentation of it as yet existing, or as sheltering her father—once entered her thoughts. She had seen the murder done. In the last lingering natural aspect in which she had cherished [her father] through so much, he had been torn out of her heart, defaced, and slain. The thought of it was so appalling to her, that she covered her eyes, and shrunk trembling from the least remembrance of the deed, or of the cruel hand that did it. If her fond heart could have held his image after that, it must have broken; but it could not; and the void was filled with a wild dread that fled from all confronting with its shattered fragments—with such a dread as could have risen out of nothing but the depths of such a love, so wronged." DS 49

—from the dead: "Into her mind, as into all others contending with the great affliction of our mortal nature, there had stolen solemn wonderings and hopes, arising in the dim world beyond the present life, and murmuring, like faint music, of recognition in the far-off land between her brother and her mother; of some present consciousness in both of her: some love and commiseration for her: and some knowledge of her as she went her way upon the earth. It was a soothing consolation to Florence to give shelter to these thoughts, until one day—it was soon after she had last seen her father in his own room, late at night—the fancy came upon her, that, in weeping for his alienated heart, she might stir the spirits of the dead against him. Wild, weak, childish, as it may have been to think so, and to tremble at the half-formed thought, it was the impulse of her loving nature; and from that hour Florence strove against the cruel wound in her breast, and tried to think of him whose hand had made it only with hope." DS 24

—dealing with a 'pass': "As Wemmick and Miss Skiffins sat side by side, and as I sat in a shadowy corner, I observed a slow and gradual elongation of Mr Wemmick's mouth, powerfully suggestive of his slowly and gradually stealing his arm round Miss Skiffins's waist. In course of time I saw his

hand appear on the other side of Miss Skiffins; but at that moment Miss Skiffins neatly stopped him with the green glove, unwound his arm again as if it were an article of dress, and with the greatest deliberation laid it on the table before her. Miss Skiffins's composure while she did this was one of the most remarkable sights i have ever seen, and if I could have thought the act consistent with abstraction of mind, I should have deemed that Miss Skiffins performed it mechanically.

"By and by, I noticed Wemmick's arm beginning to disappear again, and gradually fading out of view. Shortly afterwards his mouth began to widen again. After an interval of suspense on my part that was quite enthralling and almost painful, I saw his hand appear on the other side of Miss Skiffins. Instantly, Miss Skiffins stopped it with the neatness of a placid boxer, took off that girdle or cestus as before, and laid it on the table. Taking the table to represent the path of virtue, I am justified in stating that during the whole time of the Aged's reading, Wemmick's arm was straying from the path of virtue and being recalled to it by Miss Skiffins." GE 37

—*declared:* "'And you, dear Florence? are you nothing? he returned.

"'No, nothing, Walter. Nothing but your wife.' The light hand stole about his neck, and the voice came nearer—nearer. 'I am nothing any more, that is not you. I have no earthly hope any more, that is not you. I have nothing dear to me any more, that is not you!'" DS 56

"'You [Estella] are part of my existence [said Pip], part of myself. You have been in every line I have ever read, since I first came here, the rough common boy whose poor heart you wounded even then. You have been in every prospect I have ever seen since—on the river, on the sails of the ships, on the marshes, in the clouds, in the light, in the darkness, in the wind, in the woods, in the sea, in the streets.

"'You have been the embodiment of every graceful fancy that my mind has ever become acquainted with. The stones of which the strongest London buildings are made, are not more real, or more impossible to be displaced by your hands, than your presence and influence have been to me, there and everywhere, and will be. Estella, to the last hour of my life, you cannot choose but remain part of my character, part of the little good in me, part of the evil. But, in this separation I associate you only with the good, and I will faithfully hold you to that always, for you must have done me far more good than harm, let me feel now what sharp distress I may. O God bless you, God forgive you!'

"In what ecstasy of unhappiness I got these broken words out of myself, I don't know. The rhapsody welled up within me, like blood from an inward wound, and gushed out. I held her hand to my lips some lingering moments, and so I left her." GE 44

—*diffident:* "'Affection,' said Miss Lavinia, glancing at her sister for corroboration, which she gave in the form of a little nod to every clause, 'mature affection, homage, devotion, does not easily express itself. Its voice is low. It is modest and retiring, it lies in ambush, waits and waits. Such is the mature fruit. Sometimes a life glides away, and finds it still ripening in the shade.'

"Of course I did not understand then that this was an allusion to her supposed experience of the stricken Pidger; but I saw, from the gravity with which Miss Clarissa nodded her head, that great weight was attached to these words." DC 41

—*effect on the beloved's children:* "No man ever really loved a woman, lost her, and knew her with a blameless though an unchanged mind, when she was a wife and a mother, but her children had a strange sympathy with him—an instinctive delicacy of pity for him. What fine hidden sensibilities are touched in such a case, no echoes tell; but it is so, and it was so here. Carton was the first stranger to whom little Lucie held out her chubby arms, and he kept his place with her as she grew. The little boy had spoken of him, almost at the last. 'Poor Carton! Kiss him for me!'" TTC ii 21

—*effect on the heart:* " . . . it came into my mind, now, that I might try to prevent [Silvy's] taking the fever by keeping away from her . . . .

"Out of this holding her in my thoughts, to the humanising of myself, I suppose some childish love arose within me. I felt, in some sort, dignified by the pride of protecting her—by the pride of making the sacrifice for her. As my heart swelled with that new feeling, it insensibly softened about mother and father. It seemed to have been frozen before, and now to be thawed. The old ruin and all the lovely things that haunted it were not sorrowful for me only, but sorrowful for mother and father as well. Therefore did I cry again, and often too." GSE

—embrace: "You never will derive so much delight from seeing a glorious little woman in the arms of a third party, as you would have felt if you had seen Dot run into the Carrier's embrace. It was the most complete, unmitigated, soul-fraught little piece of earnestness that ever you beheld in all your days." CH 3

—a father's: "I have said that Caleb [Plummer] and his poor Blind Daughter lived here. I should have said that Caleb lived here, and his poor Blind Daughter somewhere else—in an enchanted home of Caleb's furnishing, where scarcity and shabbiness were not, and trouble never entered. Caleb was no sorcerer, but in the only magic art that still remains to us, the magic of devoted, deathless love, Nature had been the mistress of his study; and from her teaching all the wonder came." CH 2 *And see* B:Blindness—*beloved*

—at first sight: " . . . I heard a voice say, 'Mr Copperfield, my daughter Dora, and my daughter Dora's confidential friend!' It was, no doubt, Mr Spenlow's voice, but I didn't know it, and I didn't care whose it was. All was over in a moment. I had fulfilled my destiny. I was a captive and a slave. I loved Dora Spenlow to distraction!

"She was more than human to me. She was a Fairy, a Sylph, I don't know what she was—anything that no one ever saw, and everything that everybody ever wanted. I was swallowed up in an abyss of love in an instant. There was no pausing on the brink; no looking down, or looking back; I was gone, headlong, before I had sense to say a word to her." DC 24

"[Bradley Headstone] held as straight a course . . . as the wisdom of his ancestors, exemplified in the construction of the intervening streets, would let him, and walked with a bent head hammering at one fixed idea. It had been an immovable idea since he first set eyes upon her. It seemed to him as if all that he could suppress in himself he had suppressed, as if all that he could restrain in himself he had restrained, and the time had come—in a rush, in a moment—when the power of self-command had departed from him.

"Love at first sight is a trite expression quite sufficiently discussed; enough that in certain smouldering natures like this man's, that passion leaps into a blaze, and makes such head as fire does in a rage of wind, when other passions, but for its mastery, could be held in chains. As a multitude of weak, imitative natures are always lying by, ready to go mad upon the next wrong idea that may be broached—in these times, generally some form of tribute to Somebody for something that never was done, or if ever done, that was done by Somebody Else—so these less ordinary natures may lie by for years, ready on the touch of an instant to burst into flame." OMF ii 11

—folding a carpet: "It is not half as innocent a thing as it looks, that shaking little pieces of carpet—at least, there may be no great harm in the shaking, but the folding is a very insidious process. So long as the shaking lasts, and the two parties are kept the carpet's length apart, it is as innocent an amusement as can well be devised; but when the folding begins, and the distance between them gets gradually lessened from one half its former length to a quarter, and then to an eighth, and then to a sixteenth, and then to a thirty-second, if the carpet be long enough: it becomes dangerous. We do not know, to a nicety, how many pieces of carpet were folded in this instance, but we can venture to state that as many pieces as there were, so many times did Sam kiss the pretty housemaid." PP 39

—frivolity remarked: "No! Dash it, Tony,' says [Mr Guppy], 'you really ought to be careful how you wound the feelings of a man, who has an unrequited image imprinted on his art, and who is *not* altogether happy in those chords which vibrate to the tenderest emotions. You, Tony, possess in yourself all that is calculated to charm the eye, and allure the taste. It is not—happily for you, perhaps, and I may wish that I could say the same—it is not your character to hover around the flower. The ole garden is open to you, and your airy pinions carry you through it. Still, Tony, far be it from me, I am sure, to wound even your feelings without a cause!'" BH 32

—in a gondola: "As this gondola attended [the Dorrit girls'] progress in various artful ways; sometimes shooting on ahead, and stopping to let them pass; sometimes, when the way was broad enough, skimming along side by side with them; and sometimes following close astern; and as Fanny gradually made no disguise that she was playing off graces upon somebody within it, of whom

she at the same time feigned to be unconscious; Little Dorrit at length asked who it was? . . .

"Mr Sparkler had, undeniably, a weak appearance; with his eye in the window like a knot in the glass, and no reason on earth for stopping his bark suddenly, except the real reason . . . .

"' . . . here we are at home. And Young Sparkler at the door, inquiring who is within. By the merest accident, of course!'

"In effect, the swain was standing up in his gondola, card-case in hand, affecting to put the question to a servant. This conjunction of circumstances led to his immediately afterwards presenting himself before the young ladies in a posture, which in ancient times would not have been considered one of favourable augury for his suit; since the gondoliers of the young ladies, having been put to some inconvenience by the chase, so neatly brought their own boat in the gentlest collision with the bark of Mr Sparkler, as to tip that gentleman over like a larger species of ninepin, and cause him to exhibit the soles of his shoes to the object of his dearest wishes: while the nobler portions of his anatomy struggled at the bottom of his boat, in the arms of one of his men." LD ii 6

—and grooming: "'Sir,' said Mrs Crupp, in a tone approaching to severity, 'I've laundressed other young gentlemen besides yourself. A young gentleman may be over-careful of himself, or he may be under-careful of himself. He may brush his hair too regular, or too unregular. He may wear his boots much too large for him, or much too small. That is according as the young gentleman has his original character formed. But let him go to which extreme he may, sir, there's a young lady in both of 'em.'" DC 26

—and a hairdresser's dummy: "'Vunce upon a time there wos a young hairdresser as opened a wery smart little shop vith four wax dummies in the winder, two gen'lmen and two ladies—the gen'lmen vith blue dots for their beards, wery large viskers, oudacious heads of hair, uncommon clear eyes, and nostrils of amazin' pinkness; the ladies vith their heads o' one side, their right forefingers on their lips, and their forms deweloped beautiful, in vich last respect they had the adwantage over the gen'lmen, as wasn't allowed but wery little shoulder, and terminated rayther abrupt in fancy drapery . . . .

"'Vun o' these dummies wos a fav'rite vith him beyond the others; and ven any of his acquaintance asked him wy he didn't get married—and the young ladies he know'd, in partickler, often did—he used to say, "Never! I never vill enter into the bonds of vedlock," he says, "until I meet vith a young 'ooman as realises my idea o' that 'ere fairest dummy vith the light hair. Then, and not till then," he says, "I vill approach the altar." All the young ladies he know'd as had got dark hair told him this wos wery sinful, and that he wos wurshippin' a idle; but them as wos at all near the same shade as the dummy coloured up wery much, and wos observed to think him a wery nice young man . . . .

"'The young hairdresser hadn't been in the habit o' makin' this avowal above six months, ven he encountered a young lady as wos the wery picter o' the fairest dummy. "Now," he says, "it's all up. I am a slave!" The young lady wos not only the picter o' the fairest dummy, but she was wery romantic, as the young hairdresser was, too, and he says, "O!" he says, "here's a community o' feelin', here's a flow o' soul!" he says, "here's a interchange o' sentiment!" The young lady didn't say much, o' course, but she expressed herself agreeable, and shortly artervards vent to see him vith a mutual friend. The hairdresser rushes out to meet her, but d'rectly she sees the dummies she changes colour and falls a tremblin' wiolently.

"'Look up, my love," says the hairdresser, "behold your imige in my winder, but not correcter than in my art!" "My imige!" she says. "Yourn!" replies the hairdresser. "But whose imige is *that?*" she says, a pinting at vun o' the gen'lmen. "No vun's, my love," he says, "it is but a idea." "A idea!" she cries: "it is a portrait, I feel it is a portrait, and that 'ere noble face must be in the millingtary!" "Wot do I hear!" says he, a crumplin' his curls. "Villiam Gibbs," she says, quite firm, "never renoo the subject. I respect you as a friend," she says, "but my affections is set upon that manly brow." "This," says the hairdresser, "is a reg'lar blight, and in it I perceive the hand of Fate. Farevell!" Vith these vords he rushes into the shop, breaks the dummy's nose vith a blow of his curlin'-irons, melts him down at the parlour fire, and never smiles artervards.'

"'The young lady, Mr Weller?' said the housekeeper.

"'Why, ma'am,' said Sam, 'finding that Fate had a spite agin her, and everybody she come into contact vith, she never smiled neither, but read a deal o' poetry and pined avay—by rayther slow degrees, for she ain't dead yet.'" ¶MHC 5

—kiss

—affectionate: It was a remarkably small corner, and so—it was nobody's fault but the man's who built the house—Sam and the pretty housemaid were necessarily very close together . . . .

"'Good bye!' said Sam; and as he said it, he dropped the hat that had cost so much trouble in looking for.

"'How awkward you are,' said the pretty housemaid. 'You'll lose it again, if you don't take care.'

"So, just to prevent his losing it again, she put it on for him.

"Whether it was that the pretty housemaid's face looked prettier still, when it was raised towards Sam's, or whether it was the accidental consequence of their being so near to each other, is matter of uncertainty to this day; but Sam kissed her.

"'You don't mean to say you did that on purpose,' said the pretty housemaid, blushing.

"'No, I didn't then,' said Sam; 'but I will now.'

"So he kissed her again . . . .

"And this was the first passage of Mr Weller's first love." PP 25

"'The young lady put up her hand as if to caution my uncle not to do so, and said—no, she didn't say anything—she smiled. When you are looking at a pair of the most delicious lips in the world, and see them gently break into a roguish smile—if you are very near them, and nobody else by—you cannot better testify your admiration of their beautiful form and colour than by kissing them at once. My uncle did so, and I honour him for it.'" PP 49

—bony: "At the close of the evening when [Mrs General] rose to retire, Mr Dorrit took her by the hand, as if he were going to lead her out into the Piazza of the People to walk a minuet by moonlight, and with great solemnity conducted her to the room door, where he raised her knuckles to his lips. Having parted from her with what may be conjectured to have been a rather bony kiss, of a cosmetic flavour, he gave his daughter his blessing, graciously. And having thus hinted that there was something remarkable in the wind, he again went to bed." LD ii 19

—cold: "[Miss Barbary] gave me one cold parting kiss upon my forehead, like a thaw-drop from the stone porch." BH 3

—instructional: "'What's the matter, Barbara?' said Kit.

"'Nothing,' cried Barbara. And Barbara pouted—not sulkily, or in an ugly manner, but just enough to make her look more cherry-lipped than ever.

"There is no school in which a pupil gets on so fast, as that in which Kit became a scholar when he gave Barbara the kiss. He saw what Barbara meant now—he had his lesson by heart all at once—she was the book—there it was before him, as plain as print." OCS 69

—not invited: "'Now, I'll tell you what, young man; I'll trouble you not to repeat the impertinence you were guilty of, on the morning you went away.'

"'You would not be very angry, would you? asked Nicholas.

"'Wouldn't I!' said Miss La Creevy. 'You had better try; that's all!'

"Nicholas, with becoming gallantry, immediately took Miss La Creevy at her word, who uttered a faint scream and slapped his face; but it was not a very hard slap, and that's the truth.

"'I never saw such a rude creature!' exclaimed Miss La Creevy.

"'You told me to try,' said Nicholas.

"'Well; but I was speaking ironically,' rejoined Miss La Creevy.

"'Oh! that's another thing,' said Nicholas; 'you should have told me that, too.'" NN 20

—patriotic: " . . . the traveller caught [Mrs Lupin] in his arms, and she uttered a glad cry of recognition.

"'Yes, I will!' cried Mark, 'another—one more—twenty more! You didn't know me in that hat and coat? I thought you would have known me anywheres! Ten more!' . . .

"'Fifteen more!' said Mr Tapley. 'How handsome and how young you look! Six more! The last half-dozen warn't a fair one, and must be done over again. Lord bless you, what a treat it is to see you! One more! Well, I never was so jolly. Just a few more, on account of there not being any credit in it!' . . . One more! Won't you? Not a very little one, to finish off with?'

"'You have had plenty, I am sure,' said the hostess. 'Go along with your foreign manners!'

"'That ain't foreign, bless you!' cried Mark. 'Native as oysters, that is! One more, because it's native! As a mark of respect for the land we live in! This don't count as between you and me, you understand,' said Mr Tapley. 'I ain't a kissing you now, you'll observe. I have been among the patriots! I'm a kissin' my country!'" MC 43

—of the lonely: "We [Doctor Marigold and Sophy] soon made out to begin to understand one another, through the goodness of the Heavens, when she knowed that I meant true and kind by her. In a very little time she was wonderful fond of me. You have no idea what it is to have anybody wonderful fond of you, unless you have been got down and rolled upon by the lonely feelings that I have mentioned as having once got the better of me." CS/DM 1

And see S:Hope—*disappointed*

—murderous: "'You know what I am going to say. I love you. What other men may mean when they use that expression, I cannot tell; what *I* mean is, that I am under the influence of some tremendous attraction which I have resisted in vain, and which overmasters me. You could draw me to fire, you could draw me to water, you could draw me to the gallows, you could draw me to any death, you could draw me to anything I have most avoided, you could draw me to any exposure and disgrace. This and the confusion of my thoughts, so that I am fit for nothing, and the confusion of my thoughts, so that I am fit for nothing, is what I mean by your being the ruin of me.

"'But if you would return a favourable answer to my offer of myself in marriage, you could draw me to any good—every good—with equal force. My circumstances are quite easy, and you would want for nothing. My reputation stands quite high, and would be a shield for yours. If you saw me at my work, able to do it well and respected in it, you might even come to take a sort of pride in me:—I would try hard that you should. Whatever considerations I may have thought of against this offer, I have conquered, and I make it with all my heart. . . . I don't know that I could say more if I tried. I might only weaken what is ill enough said as it is. I only add that if it is any claim on you to be in earnest, I am in thorough earnest, dreadful earnest.'

"The powdered mortar from under the stone at which [Bradley Headstone] wrenched, rattled on the pavement to confirm his words." ¶OMF ii 15

"She would have gone once more—was all but gone—and once more his face, darkly threatening what would follow if she went, has stopped her. Looking at him with the expression of the instant frozen on her face, she sits down on the seat again.

"'Rosa, even when my dear boy was affianced to you, I loved you madly; even when I thought his happiness in having you for his wife was certain, I loved you madly; even when I strove to make him more ardently devoted to you, I loved you madly; even when he gave me the picture of your lovely face so carelessly traduced by him, which I feigned to hang always in my sight for his sake, but worshipped in torment for years, I loved you madly; in the distasteful work of the day, in the wakeful misery of the night, girded by sordid realities, or wandering through Paradises and Hells of visions into which I rushed, carrying your image in my arms, I loved you madly.'

"If anything could make his words more hideous to her than they are in themselves, it would be the contrast between the violence of his look and delivery, and the composure of his assumed attitude . . . .

"'Reckon up nothing at this moment, angel, but the sacrifices that I lay at those dear feet, which I could fall down among the vilest ashes and kiss, and put upon my head as a poor savage might. There is my fidelity to my dear boy after death. Tread upon it!'

"With an action of his hands, as though he cast down something precious.

"'There is the inexpiable offence against my adoration of you. Spurn it!'

"With a similar action.

"'There are my labours in the cause of a just vengeance for six toiling months. Crush them!'

"With another repetition of the action.

"'There is my past and my present wasted life. There is the desolation of my heart and my soul. There is my peace; there is my despair. Stamp them into the dust; so that you take me, were it even mortally hating me!' . . .

"'I love you, love you, love you! If you were to cast me off now—but you will not—

you would never be rid of me. No one should come between us. I would pursue you to the death.'" MED 19

—a mystery: "'We were getting up our Children in the Wood one morning, when there cometh into our Ring, by the thtage door, a dog. He had travelled a long way, he wath in very bad condition, he wath lame, and pretty well blind. He went round to our childrn, one after another, as if he wath a theeking for a child he know'd; and then he come to me, and throwd hithelf up behind, and thtood on hith two forelegth, weak ath he wath, and then he wagged hith tail and died. Thquire, that dog wath Merrylegth.

"'Sissy's father's dog!'

"'Thethilia'th father'th old dog. Now, Thquire, I can take my oath, from my knowledge of that dog, that that man wath dead—and buried—afore that dog came back to me . . . whether her father bathely detherted her; or whether he broke hith own heart alone, rather than pull her down along with him; never will be known, now, Thquire, till—no, not till we know how the dogth findth uth out!'" UT iii 8

—a necessity: "'She [Clara Copperfield] often talked to them two down-stairs—for she loved them; she couldn't bear not to love any one who was about her . . . . " DC 9

—nurturing and nurtured: "Who [Madeline Bray], slowly recovering from a disorder so severe and dangerous, could be insensible to the unremitting attentions of such a nurse as gentle, tender, earnest Kate? On whom could the sweet soft voice, the light step, the delicate hand, the quiet, cheerful, noiseless discharge of those thousand little offices of kindness and relief which we feel so deeply when we are ill, and forget so lightly when we are well—on whom could they make so deep an impression as on a young heart stored with every pure and true affection that women cherish; almost a stranger to the endearments and devotion of its own sex, save as it learnt them from itself; rendered, by calamity and suffering, keenly susceptible of the sympathy so long unknown and so long sought in vain! What wonder that days became as years in knitting them together!" NN 55

—of one who does not exist: "Florence loved [her father] still, but, by degrees, had come to love him rather as some dear one who had been, or who might have been, than as the hard reality before her eyes. Something of the softened sadness with which she loved the memory of little Paul, or of her mother, seemed to enter now into her thoughts of him, and to make them, as it were, a dear remembrance. Whether it was that he was dead to her, and that partly for this reason, partly for his share in those old objects of her affection, and partly for the long association of him with hopes that were withered and tendernesses he had frozen, she could not have told; but the father whom she loved began to be a vague and dreamy idea to her: hardly more substantially connected with her real life, than the image she would sometimes conjure up, of her dear brother yet alive, and growing to be a man, who would protect and cherish her." DS 47

—of other people's property: "If Mr Barker can be fairly said to have had any weakness in his earlier years, it was an amiable one—love; love in its most comprehensive form—a love of ladies, liquids, and pocket-handkerchiefs. It was no selfish feeling; it was not confined to his own possessions, which but too many men regard with exclusive complacency. No; it was a nobler love—a general principle. It extended itself with equal force to the property of other people.

"There is something very affecting in this. It is still more affecting to know, that such philanthropy is but imperfectly rewarded. Bow Street, Newgate, and Millbank, are a poor return for general benevolence, evincing itself in an irrepressible love for all created objects. Mr Barker felt it so. After a lengthened interview with the highest legal authorities, he quitted his ungrateful country, with the consent, and at the expense, of its Government; proceeded to a distant shore; and there employed himself, like another Cincinnatus, in clearing and cultivating the soil—a peaceful pursuit, in which a term of seven years glided almost imperceptibly away." SB/LC

—persistent proposals: "' . . . [Mr Finching] proposed to me once in a hackney-coach once in a boat once in a pew once on a donkey at Tunbridge Wells and the rest on his knees. . . . '" LD i 24

—Platonic: "'Walter will return to-morrow,' said Mrs Captain Waters, mournfully breaking silence.

"Mr Cymon Tuggs sighed like a gust of wind through a forest of gooseberry bushes, as he replied, 'Alas, he will.'

"'Oh, Cymon!' resumed Belinda, 'the chaste delight, the calm happiness, of this one week of Platonic love is too much for me!'

"Cymon was about to suggest that it was too little for him, but he stopped himself, and murmured unintelligibly.'" SB/TR

—to a poetical young gentleman: "'Mr Milkwash,' says a young lady as she unlocks her album to receive the young gentleman's original impromptu contribution, 'how very silent you are! I think you must be in love.' 'Love!' cries the poetical young gentleman, starting from his seat by the fire and terrifying the cat who scampers off at full speed, 'Love! that burning consuming passion; that ardour of the soul, that fierce glowing of the heart. Love! The withering, blighting influence of hope misplaced and affection slighted. Love, did you say! Ha! ha! ha!'

"With this, the poetical young gentleman laughs a laugh belonging only to poets and Mr **O. Smith** of the Adelphi Theatre, and sits down, pen in hand, to throw off a page or two of verse in the biting, semi-atheistical demoniac style, which, like the poetical young gentleman himself, is full of sound and fury, signifying nothing." YG/V

—possession, irresistible: " . . . though [Estella] had taken such strong possession of me, though my fancy and my hope were so set upon her, though her influence on my boyish life and character had been all-powerful, I did not . . . invest her with any attributes save those she possessed . . . .

"According to my experience, the conventional notion of a lover cannot be always true. The unqualified truth is, that when I loved Estella with the love of a man, I loved her simply because I found her irresistible. Once for all; I knew to my sorrow, often and often, if not always, that I loved her against reason, against promise, against peace, against hope, against happiness, against all discouragement that could be. Once for all; I loved her none the less because I knew it, and it had no more influence in restraining me, than if I had devoutly believed her to be human perfection." GE 29

The Dance at the Seminary OCS

—rivals confront: "'Did you speak to me, sir?' said Mr Cheggs, following [Richard Swiveller] into a corner. 'Have the kindness to smile, sir, in order that we may not be suspected. Did you speak to me, sir?'

"Mr Swiveller looked with a supercilious smile at Mr Cheggs's toes, then raised his eyes from them to his ankle, from that to his shin, from that to his knee, and so on very gradually, keeping up his right leg, until he reached his waistcoat, when he raised his eyes from button to button until he reached his chin, and travelling straight up the middle of his nose came at last to his eyes, when he said abruptly,

"'No, sir, I didn't.'

"'Hem!' said Mr Cheggs, glancing over his shoulder, 'have the goodness to smile again, sir. Perhaps you wished to speak to me, sir.'

"'No, sir, I didn't do that, either.'

"'Perhaps you may have nothing to say to me *now*, sir,' said Mr Cheggs fiercely.

"At these words Richard Swiveller withdrew his eyes from Mr Cheggs's face, and travelling down the middle of his nose and down his waistcoat and down his right leg reached his toes again, and carefully surveyed them; this done, he crossed over, and coming up the other leg and thence approaching by the waistcoat as before, said when he had got to his eyes, 'No, sir, I haven't.'

"'Oh, indeed sir!' said Mr Cheggs. 'I'm glad to hear it. You know where I'm to be found, I suppose, sir, in case you *should* have anything to say to me?'

"'I can easily inquire, sir, when I want to know.'

"'There's nothing more we need say, I believe, sir?'

"'Nothing more, sir.'—With that they closed the tremendous dialogue by frowning mutually, Mr Cheggs hastened to tender his hand to Miss Sophy, and Mr Swiveller sat himself down in a corner in a very moody state." OCS 8

—sad outcome: "'You needn't mention her name. There's no such name now. Her name is Cheggs now, Sophy Cheggs. Yet love I as man never loved that hadn't wooden legs, and my heart, my heart is breaking for the love of Sophy Cheggs.'" OCS 50

"' 'Twas ever thus, from childhood's hour I've seen my fondest hopes decay, I never loved a tree or flower but 'twas the first to fade away; I never nursed a dear Gazelle, to glad me with its soft black eye, but when it came to know me well, and love me, it was sure to marry a market-gardener .... *

" . . . 'I shall wear this emblem of woman's perfidy, in remembrance of her with whom I shall never again thread the windings of the mazy; whom I shall never more pledge in the rosy; who, during the short remainder of my existence, will murder the balmy.'" OCS 56

**See Thomas Moore's* Lalla Rookh, Index XI

—schoolteacher preoccupied: "'Though all unseen and unsuspected by the pupils, Bradley Headstone even pervaded the school exercises. Was Geography in question? He would come triumphantly flying out of Vesuvius and Ætna ahead of the lava, and would boil unharmed in the hot springs of Iceland, and would float majestically down the Ganges and the Nile. Did History chronicle a king of men? Behold him in pepper-and-salt pantaloons, with his watch-guard round his neck. Were copies to be written? In capital B's and H's most of the girls under Miss Peecher's tuition were half a year ahead of every other letter in the alphabet. And Mental Arithmetic, administered by Miss Peecher, often devoted itself to providing Bradley Headstone with a wardrobe of fabulous extent; fourscore and four neck-ties at two and ninepence-halfpanny, two gross of silver watches at four pounds fifteen and six-pence, seventy-four black hats at eighteen shillings; and many similar superfluities." OMF ii 11

—and selfishness: "Is selfishness a necessary ingredient in the composition of that passion called love, or does it deserve all the fine things which poets, in the exercise of their undoubted vocation, have said of it? There are, no doubt, authenticated instances of gentlemen having given up ladies and ladies having given up gentlemen to meritorious rivals, under circumstances of great high-mindedness; but is it quite established that the majority of such ladies and gentlemen have not made a virtue of necessity, and nobly resigned what was beyond their reach; as a private soldier might register a vow never to accept the order of the Garter, or a poor curate of great piety and learning, but of no family—save a very large family of children—might renounce a bishopric?

"Here was Nicholas Nickleby, who would have scorned the thought of counting how the chances stood of his rising in favour or fortune with the Brothers Cheeryble, now that their nephew had returned, already deep in calculations whether that same nephew was likely to rival him in the affections of the fair unknown—discussing the matter with himself too, as gravely as if, with that one exception, it were all settled; and recurring to the subject again and again, and feeling quite indignant and ill-used at the notion of anybody else making love to one with whom he had never exchanged a word in all his life.

"To be sure, he exaggerated rather than depreciated the merits of his new acquaintance; but still he took it as a kind of personal offence that he should have any merits at all—in the eyes of this particular young lady, that is; for elsewhere he was quite welcome to have as many as he pleased.

"There was undoubted selfishness in all this, and yet Nicholas was of a most free and generous nature, with as few mean or sordid thoughts, perhaps, as ever fell to the lot of any man; and there is no reason to suppose that, being in love, he felt and thought differently from other people in the like sublime condition." ¶NN 43

—*suffusing an atmosphere:* "[Nicholas Nickleby] felt as though the smile of Heaven were on the little chamber; as though the beautiful devotion of so young and weak a creature [Madeline Bray], had shed a ray of its own on the inanimate things around, and made them beautiful as itself; as though the halo with which old painters surround the bright angels of a sinless world, played about a being akin in spirit to them, and its light were visibly before him.

"And yet Nicholas was in the Rules of the King's Bench Prison! If he had been in Italy indeed, and the time had been sunset, and the scene a stately terrace! But, there is one broad sky over all the world, and, whether it be blue or cloudy, the same Heaven beyond it; so, perhaps, he had no need of compunction for thinking as he did." NN 46

—*a teacher:* " . . . Mrs John Rokesmith stitched . . . with so dexterous a hand, that she must have taken lessons of somebody. Love is in all things a most wonderful teacher, and perhaps love from a pictorial point of view, with nothing on but a thimble, had been teaching this branch of needlework to Mrs John Rokesmith.

"Placidly, though rather consequentially smiling, she sat stitching away with a regular sound, like a sort of dimpled little charming Dresden-china clock by the very best maker." OMF iv 11

—*at twilight:* "No doubt, there are a great many things to be said appropriate to a summer evening, and no doubt they are best said in a low voice, as being most suitable to the peace and serenity of the hour; long pauses, too, at times, and then an earnest word or so, and then another interval of silence which, somehow, does not seem like silence either, and perhaps now and then a hasty turning away of the head, or drooping of the eyes towards the ground, all these minor circumstances, with a disinclination to have candles introduced and a tendency to confuse hours with minutes, are doubtless mere influences of the time, as many lovely lips can clearly testify.

"Neither was there the slightest reason why Mrs Nickleby should have expressed surprise when, candles being at length brought in, Kate's bright eyes were unable to bear the light which obliged her to avert her face, and even to leave the room for some short time; because when one has sat in the dark so long, candles *are* dazzling, and nothing can be more strictly natural than that such results should be produced, as all well-informed young people know. For that matter, old people know it too, or did know it once, but they forget these things sometimes, and more's the pity." ¶NN 49

—*unrequited*

—*amidst the laundry:* " . . . she preceded the visitor into a little parlour behind the shop, with a little window in it commanding a very little dull back-yard. In this yard, a wash of sheets and table-cloths tried (in vain, for want of air) to get itself dried on a line or two; and among those flapping articles was, sitting in a chair, like the last mariner left alive on the deck of a damp ship without the power of furling the sails, a little woebegone young man.

"'Our John,' said Mrs Chivery.

"Not to be deficient in interest, Clennam asked what he might be doing there?

"'It's the only change he takes,' said Mrs Chivery, shaking her head afresh. 'He won't go out, even in the back-yard, when there's no linen; but when there's linen to keep the neighbours' eyes off, he'll sit there, hours. Hours he will. Says he feels as if it was groves!'" LD i 22

—*deterioration:* "'The state of my feelings towards Miss Dombey [said Mr Toots] is of that unspeakable description, that my heart is a desert island, and she lives in it alone. I'm getting more used up every day, and I'm proud to be so. If you could see my legs when I take my boots off, you'd form some idea of what unrequited affection is. I have been prescribed bark, but I don't take it, for I don't wish to have any tone whatever given to my constitution.'" DS 48

"'I beg your pardon, Captain Gills, but you don't happen to see anything particular in me, do you?'

"'No, my lad,' returned the captain. 'No.'

"'Because you know,' said Mr Toots with a chuckle, 'I KNOW I'm wasting away. You needn't at all mind alluding to that. I—I should like it. Burgess and Co., have altered my measure, I'm in that state of thinness. It's a gratification to me. I—I'm glad of it. I—I'd a great deal rather go into a decline, if I could. I'm a mere brute you know, grazing upon the face of the earth, Captain Gills.'" DS 48

—letting go: "'Arthur,' said [Meagles], using that familiar address for the first time in their communication, 'do you remember my telling you . . . that Pet's baby sister who was dead seemed to Mother and me to have grown as she had grown, and changed as she had changed?'

"'Very well.'

"'You remember my saying that our thoughts had never been able to separate those twin sisters, and that in our fancy whatever Pet was, the other was?'

"'Yes, very well.'

"'Arthur,' said Mr Meagles, much subdued, 'I carry that fancy further to-night. I feel to-night, my dear fellow, as if you had loved my dead child very tenderly, and had lost her when she was like what Pet is now.'

"'Thank you!' murmured Clennam, 'thank you!' And pressed his hand.

"'Will you come in?' said Mr Meagles, presently.

"'In a little while.'

"Mr Meagles fell away, and he was left alone. When he had walked on the river's brink in the peaceful moonlight for some half-an-hour, he put his hand in his breast and tenderly took out the handful of roses. Perhaps he put them to his heart, perhaps he put them to his lips, but certainly he bent down on the shore, and gently launched them on the flowing river. Pale and unreal in the moonlight, the river floated them away.

"The lights were bright within doors when he entered, and the faces on which they shone, his own face not excepted, were soon quietly cheerful. They talked of many subjects . . . and so to bed, and to sleep. While the flowers, pale and unreal in the moonlight, floated away upon the river; and thus do greater things that once were in our breasts, and near our hearts, flow from us to the eternal seas." LD i 28

—self-immolating: "'If I could be dyed black, and made Miss Dombey's slave, I should consider it a compliment. If, at the sacrifice of all my property, I could get transmigrated into Miss Dombey's dog—I—I really think I should never leave off wagging my tail . . . if I could swear to it upon a hot piece of iron, or a live coal, or melted lead, or burning sealing-wax, or anything of that sort, I should be glad to hurt myself, as a relief to my feelings.' And Mr Toots looked hurriedly about the room, as if for some sufficiently painful means of accomplishing his dread purpose." DS 39

—sleepless: "'As to sleep, you know, I never sleep now. I might be a Watchman, except that I don't get any pay, and he's got nothing on his mind.'" DS 48

—tombstone: "'Here lie the mortal remains of JOHN CHIVERY, Never anything worth mentioning, Who died about the end of the year one thousand eight hundred and twenty-six, Of a broken heart, Requesting with his last breath that the word AMY might be inscribed over his ashes, Which was accordingly directed to be done, By his afflicted Parents.'" LD i 18

And see S:Weeping*—in rejection*

—unselfish: "'Mine an't a selfish affection, you know . . . . It's the sort of thing with me, Captain Gills, that if I could be run over—or—or trampled upon—or—or thrown off a very high place—or anything of that sort—for Miss Dombey's sake, it would be the most delightful thing that could happen to me.'" DS 32

—vegetable expression: "'But when he began to throw his cucumbers over our wall . . . . And vegetable-marrows likewise' . . . .

"'You know, there is no language of vegetables, which converts a cucumber into a formal declaration of attachment.'

"'My dear,' replied Mrs Nickleby, tossing her head and looking at the ashes in the grate, 'he has done and said all sorts of things . . . .

"'Every time I go to the window,' said Mrs Nickleby, 'he kisses one hand, and lays the other upon his heart—of course it's very foolish of him to do so, and I dare say you'll say it's very wrong, but he does it very respectfully—very respectfully indeed—and very tenderly, extremely tenderly. So far, he deserves the greatest credit; there can be no doubt about that. Then, there are the presents which come pouring over the wall every day, and very fine they certainly are, very fine; we had one of the cucumbers at dinner yesterday, and think of pickling the rest for next winter.'" NN 37

—*what might have been:* " . . . [Mr Twemlow] is low . . . and is distinctly aware of a dint in his heart, made by the most adorable of the adorable bridesmaids. For, the poor little harmless gentleman once had his fancy, like the rest of us, and she didn't answer (as she often does not), and he thinks the adorable bridesmaid is like the fancy as she was then (which she is not at all), and that if the fancy had not married some one else for money, but had married him for love, he and she would have been happy (which they wouldn't have been), and that she has a tenderness for him still (whereas her toughness is a proverb). Brooding over the fire, with his dried little head in his dried little hands, and his dried little elbows on his dried little knees, Twemlow is melancholy. 'No Adorable to bear me company here!' thinks he. 'No Adorable at the club! A waste, a waste, a waste, my Twemlow!' And so drops asleep, and has galvanic starts all over him." OMF i 10

"Ah! my Twemlow! Say, little feeble grey personage, what thoughts are in thy breast to-day, of the Fancy—so still to call her who bruised thy heart when it was green and thy head brown—and whether it be better or worse, more painful or less, to believe in the Fancy to this hour, than to know her for a greedy armour-plated crocodile, with no more capacity of imagining the delicate and sensitive and tender spot behind thy waistcoat, than of going straight at it with a knitting-needle." OMF ii 16

—*wooing practically:* " . . . Mr Bounderby went every evening to Stone Lodge, as an accepted wooer. Love was made on these occasions in the form of bracelets; and, on all occasions during the period of betrothal, took a manufacturing aspect. Dresses were made, jewellery was made, cakes and gloves were made, settlements were made, and an extensive assortment of Facts did appropriate honour to the contract. The business was all Facts, from first to last. The Hours did not go through any of those rosy performances, which foolish poets have ascribed to them at such times; neither did the clocks go any faster, or any slower, than at other seasons." HT i 16

—*in the world:* [Merrylegs has tracked down the circus and then died.] "'It theemth to prethent two thingth to a perthon, don't it, thquire?' said Mr Sleary, musing as he looked down into the depths of his brandy and water: 'one, that there ith a love in the world, not all Thelf-intereth after all, but thomething very different; t'other, that it hath a way of ith own of calculating or not calculating, whith thomehow or another ith at leatht ath hard to give a name to, ath the wayth of the dogth ith!'" HT iii 8

—*young:* "Of course I was in love with little Em'ly. I am sure I loved that baby quite as truly, quite as tenderly, with greater purity and more disinterestedness, than can enter into the best love of a later time of life, high and ennobling as it is. I am sure my fancy raised up something round that blue-eyed mite of a child, which etherealised, and made a very angel of her. If, any sunny forenoon, she had spread a little pair of wings, and flown away before my eyes, I don't think I should have regarded it as much more than I had had reason to expect.

"We used to walk about that dim old flat at Yarmouth in a loving manner, hours and hours. The days sported by us, as if Time had not grown up himself yet, but were a child too, and always at play. I told Em'ly I adored her, and that unless she confessed she adored me I should be reduced to the necessity of killing myself with a sword. She said she did, and I have no doubt she did.

"As to any sense of inequality, or youthfulness, or other difficulty in our way, little Em'ly and I had no such trouble, because we had no future. We made no more provision for growing older, than we did for growing younger. We were the admiration of Mrs Gummidge and Peggotty, who used to whisper of an evening when we sat lovingly, on our little locker side by side, 'Lor! wasn't it beautiful!' Mr Peggotty smiled at us from behind his pipe, and Ham [Peggotty] grinned all the evening and did nothing else. They had something of the sort of pleasure in us, I suppose, that they might have had in a pretty toy, or a pocket model of the Colosseum." DC 3

Manners

—bashfulness at dinner: "Fledgeby and Georgiana [Podsnap] not only struck each other speechless, but struck each other into astonishing attitudes; Georgiana, as she sat facing Fledgeby, making such efforts to conceal her elbows as were totally incompatible with the use of a knife and fork; and Fledgeby, as he sat facing Georgiana, avoiding her countenance by every possible device, and betraying the discomposure of his mind in feeling for his whiskers with his spoon, his wine-glass, and his bread." OMF ii 4

—bowing: "Then Mr Stryver turned and burst out of the Bank, causing such a concussion of air on his passage through, that to stand up against it bowing behind the two counters, required the utmost remaining strength of the two ancient clerks.

"Those venerable and feeble persons were always seen by the public in the act of bowing, and were popularly believed, when they had bowed a customer out, still to keep on bowing in the empty office until they bowed another customer in." TTC ii 12

"'And a very good [motto] it is, gentlemen,' said Bob [Gliddery], receiving his fee, and drawing a bow out of his head with his right hand, very much as he would have drawn a pint of beer out of the beer-engine." OMF i 13

—curtsey: "Miss Tox, in the midst of her spreading gauzes, went down altogether like an opera-glass shutting-up; she curtseyed so low, in acknowledgement of Mr Dombey's advancing a step or two to meet her." DS 5

—drinking wine: "'Take another glass of wine [said Herbert Pocket], and excuse my mentioning that society as a body does not expect one to be so strictly conscientious in emptying one's glass, as to turn it bottom upwards with the rim on one's nose.'" GE 22

—frankness: "Whenever a frank manner is offensive, it is because it is strained or feigned; for there may be quite as much intolerable affectation in plainness as in mincing nicety. All that the captain [Jorgan] said and did was honestly according to his nature; and his nature was open nature and good nature; therefore, when he paid this little compliment, and expressed with a sparkle or two of his knowing eye, 'I see how it is, and nothing could be better,' he had established a delicate confidence on that subject with the family." CS/MS 1

—good form: "Everything with the formal couple resolves itself into a matter of form. They don't call upon you on your account, but their own; not to see how you are, but to show how they are: it is not a ceremony to do honour to you, but to themselves—not due to your position, but to theirs. If one of a friend's children die, the formal couple are as sure and punctual in sending to the house as the undertaker; if a friend's family be increased, the monthly nurse is not more attentive than they. The formal couple, in fact, joyfully seize all occasions of testifying their good-breeding and precise observance of the little usages of society; and for you, who are the means to this end, they care as much as a man does for the tailor who has enabled him to cut a figure, or a woman for the milliner who has assisted her to a conquest." YC/F

—insincere: "'How d'ye do, dear?' said the Misses Briggs to the Misses Taunton. (The word 'dear' among girls is frequently synonymous with 'wretch.')" SB/SE

—perversely admired: "When they had first met this gallant gentleman at Geneva, Gowan had been undecided whether to kick him or encourage him; and had remained, for about four-and-twenty hours, so troubled to settle the point to his satisfaction, that he had thought of tossing up a five-franc piece on the terms, 'Tails, kick; heads, encourage,' and abiding by the voice of the oracle. It chanced, however, that his wife expressed a dislike to the engaging Blandois, and that the balance of feeling in the hotel was against him. Upon that, Gowan resolved to encourage him.

"Why this perversity, if it were not in a generous fit? . . . He found a pleasure in declaring that a courtier with the refined manners of Blandois ought to rise to the greatest distinction in any polished country. He found a pleasure in setting up Blandois as the type of elegance, and making him a satire upon others who piqued themselves on personal graces. He seriously protested that the bow of Blandois was perfect, that the address of Blandois was irresistible, and that the picturesque ease of Blandois would be cheaply purchased (if it were not a gift, and unpurchasable) for a hundred thousand francs.

"That exaggeration in the manner of the man, which has been noticed as appertaining to him and to every such man, whatever his original breeding, as certainly as the sun belongs to this system, was acceptable to Gowan as a caricature, which he found it a humorous resource to have at hand for the ridiculing of numbers of people who necessarily did more or less of what Blandois overdid." ¶LD ii 6

—punctilio: "Mrs Nickleby, knowing of her son's obligations to the honest Yorkshireman, had, after some demur, yielded her consent to Mr and Mrs Browdie being invited out to tea; in the way of which arrangement, there were at first sundry difficulties and obstacles, arising out of her not having had an opportunity of 'calling' upon Mrs Browdie first; for although Mrs Nickleby very often observed with much complacency (as most punctilious people do), that she had not an atom of pride or formality about her, still she was a great stickler for dignity and ceremonies; and as it was manifest that, until a call had been made, she could not be (politely speaking, and according to the laws of society) even cognizant of the fact of Mrs Browdie's existence, she felt her situation to be one of peculiar delicacy and difficulty.

"The call must originate with me, my dear.' said Mrs Nickleby, 'that's indispensable. The fact is, my dear, that it's necessary there should be a sort of condescension on my part, and that I should show this young person that I am willing to take notice of her.'" NN 45

—shaking hands: "[Mr Chick] gave Mr Dombey his hand, as if he feared it might electrify him. Mr Dombey took it as if it were a fish, or seaweed, or some such clammy substance, and immediately returned it to him with exalted politeness." DS 5

"With great heartiness . . . the Captain once again extended his enormous hand (not unlike an old block in colour), and gave [Carker] a grip that left upon his smoother flesh a proof impression of the chinks and crevices with which the Captain's palm was liberally tattooed." DS 17

"Mr Merdle was slinking about the hearth-rug, waiting to welcome Mrs Sparkler. His hand seemed to retreat up his sleeve as he advanced to do so, and he gave her such a superfluity of coat cuff that it was like being received by the popular conception of Guy Fawkes. When he put his lips to hers, besides, he took himself into custody by the wrists, and backed himself among the ottomans and chairs and tables as if he were his own Police officer, saying to himself, 'Now, none of that! Come! I've got you, you know, and you go quietly along with me!'" LD ii 16

"And [William Dorrit] offered his hand. Mr Merdle looked at the hand for a little while, took it on his for moment as if his were a yellow salver or fish-slice, and then returned it to Mr Dorrit." LD ii 16

"'As a mortal equally with myself, whose hand I take in mine for the first time this day, having unaccountably overlooked that act so full of boundless confidence binding a fellow-creetur to a fellow-creetur,' says Wegg, holding Mr Venus's palm out, flat and ready for smiting, and now smiting it; 'as such—and no other—for I scorn all lowlier ties betwixt myself and the man walking with his face erect that alone I call my Twin—regarded and regarding in this trustful bond—what do you think [Boffin] might have hid?'" OMF ii 7

—bank employee: "The discreet Mr Lorry . . . shook hands. There was a peculiarity in his manner of shaking hands, always to be seen in any clerk at Tellson's who shook hands with a customer when the House pervaded the air. He shook in a self-abnegating way, as one who shook for Tellson and Co." TTC ii 12

And see B:Body—*hand*

—table: "'Let me [said Herbert Pocket] introduce the topic, Handel [Pip], by mentioning that in London it is not the custom to put the knife in the mouth—for fear of accidents—and that while the fork is reserved for that use, it is not put further in than necessary. It is scarcely worth mentiooning, only it's as well to do as other people do. Also, the spoon is not generally used overhand, but under. This has two advantages. You get at your mouth better (which after all is the object), and you save a good deal of the attitude of opening oysters, on the part of the right elbow.'" GE 22

"[Magwitch] ate in a ravenous way that was very disagreeable, and all his actions were uncouth, noisy, and greedy. Some of his teeth had failed him since I saw him eat on the marshes, and as he turned his food in his mouth, and turned his head sideways to bring his strongest fangs to bear upon it, he looked terribly like a hungry old dog.

"If I had begun with any appetite, he would have taken it away, and I should have sat much as I did—repelled from him by an insurmountable aversion, and gloomily looking at the cloth.

"'I'm a heavy grubber, dear boy,' he said, as a polite kind of apology when he had made an end of his meal, 'but I always was. If it had been in my constitution to be a lighter grubber, I might ha' got into lighter trouble.'" GE 40

—theatrical farewell: " . . . Mr Crummles, who could never lose any opportunity for professional display, had turned out for the express purpose of taking a public farewell of Nicholas; and to render it the more imposing, he was now, to that young gentleman's most profound annoyance, inflicting upon him a rapid succession of stage embraces, which, as everybody knows, are performed by the embracer's laying his or her chin on the shoulder of the object of affection, and looking over it. . . . the elder Master Crummles was going through a similar ceremony with Smike; while Master Percy Crummles, with a very little second-hand camlet cloak, worn theatrically over his left shoulder, stood by, in the attitude of an attendant officer, waiting to convey the two victims to the scaffold." NN 31

Theatrical Emotion of Mr Vincent Crummles NN

Murder

—*crime of passion:* ". . . when [Dot Perrybingle] rose and left [John], sobbing as she went, he felt it a relief to have the vacant place beside him rather than her so long-cherished presence. This in itself was anguish keener than all, reminding him how desolate he was become, and how the great bond of his life was rent asunder.

"The more he felt this, and the more he knew he could have better borne to see her lying prematurely dead before him with their little child upon her breast, the higher and the stronger rose his wrath against his enemy. He looked about him for a weapon.

"There was a gun, hanging on the wall. He took it down, and moved a pace or two towards the door of the perfidious Stranger's room. He knew the gun was loaded. Some shadowy idea that it was just to shoot this man like a wild beast, seized him, and dilated in his mind until it grew into a monstrous demon in complete possession of him, casting out all milder thoughts and setting up its undivided empire.

"That phrase is wrong. Not casting out his milder thoughts, but artfully transforming them. Changing them into scourges to drive him on. Turning water into blood, love into hate, gentleness into blind ferocity. Her image, sorrowing, humbled, but still pleading to his tenderness and mercy with resistless power, never left his mind; but, staying there, it urged him to the door; raised the weapon to his shoulder; fitted and nerved his finger to the trigger; and cried 'Kill him! In his bed!'" CH 3

—*in the first degree:*

—*motivated:* "'Chuzzlewit!' replied Montague, leaning forward, with his arms upon his knees, and looking full into his face. 'Strange things have been done, and are done every day; not only in our way, but in a variety of other ways; and no one suspects them. But ours, as you say, my good friend, is a strange way; and we strangely happen, sometimes, to come into the knowledge of very strange events.

"He beckoned to Jonas to bring his chair nearer; and looking slightly round, as if to remind him of the presence of Nadgett, whispered in his ear.

"From red to white; from white to red again; from red to yellow; then to a cold, dull, awful, sweat-bedabbled blue. In that short whisper, all these changes fell upon the face of Jonas Chuzzlewit; and when at last he laid his hand upon the whisperer's mouth, appalled, lest any syllable of what he said should reach the ears of the third person present, it was as bloodless and as heavy as the hand of Death.

"He drew his chair away, and sat a spectacle of terror, misery, and rage. He was afraid to speak, or look, or move, or sit still. Abject, crouching, and miserable, he was a greater degradation to the form he bore, than if he had been a loathsome wound from head to heel.

"His companion leisurely resumed his dressing, and completed it, glancing sometimes with a smile at the transformation he had effected, but never speaking once.

"'You'll not object,' he said, when he was quite equipped, 'to venture further with us, Chuzzlewit, my friend?'

"His pale lips faintly stammered out a 'No.'" MC 38

—*a murderer steeling himself:* "[Jonas] had the aspect of a man found out and held at bay; of being baffled, hunted, and beset; but there was now a dawning and increasing purpose in his face, which changed it very much. It was gloomy, distrustful, lowering; pale with anger and defeat; it still was humbled, abject, cowardly, and mean; but, let the conflict go on as it would, there was one strong purpose wrestling with every emotion of his mind, and casting the whole series down as they arose.

"Not prepossessing in appearance at the best of times, it may be readily supposed that he was not so now. He had left deep marks of his front teeth in his nether lip; and those tokens of the agitation he had lately undergone improved his looks as little as the heavy corrugations in his forehead. But he was self-possessed now; unnaturally self-possessed, indeed, as men quite otherwise than brave are known to be in desperate extremities; and when the carriage stopped, he waited for no invitation, but leapt hardily out, and went upstairs . . . .

"Jonas left the window, and walked up close to [Montague]. He did not look him in the face; it was not his habit to do that; but he kept his eyes towards him—on his breast, or thereabouts—and was at great pains to speak slowly and distinctly in reply. Just as a man in a state of conscious drunkenness might be.

" . . . It might have struck a close observer that this fixed and steady glance of Jonas's was a part of the alteration which had taken place in his demeanour. He kept it rivetted on one spot, with which his thoughts had manifestly nothing to do; like as a juggler walking on a cord or wire to any dangerous end, holds some object in his sight to steady him, and never wanders from it, lest he trip." MC 41

—a murderer steeled: "The boisterous manner which Jonas had exhibited during the latter part of this conversation, and which had gone on rapidly increasing with almost every word he had spoken; from the time when he looked his honourable friend in the face until now; did not now subside, but, remaining at its height, abided by him. Most unusual with him at any period; most inconsistent with his temper and constitution; especially unnatural it would appear in one so darkly circumstanced; it abided by him. It was not like the effect of wine, or any ardent drink, for he was perfectly coherent. It even made him proof against the usual influence of such means of excitement; for, although he drank deeply several times that day, with no reserve or caution, he remained exactly the same man, and his spirits neither rose nor fell in the least observable degree." MC 41

—preparing: "[Jonas] paced the room again in the same restless and unsteady way; and then sat down upon the bedstead, leaning his chin upon his hand, and looking at the table. When he had looked at it for a long time, he remembered his supper; and resuming the chair he had first occupied, began to eat with great rapacity: not like a hungry man, but as if he were determined to do it. He drank too, roundly; sometimes stopping in the middle of a draught to walk, and change his seat and walk again, and dart back to the table and fall to, in a ravenous hurry, as before.

"It was now growing dark. As the gloom of evening, deepening into night, came on, another dark shade emerging from within him seemed to overspread his face, and slowly change it. Slowly, slowly; darker and darker; more and more haggard; creeping over him by little and little; until it was black night within him and without." MC 46

"[The bells] ceased at last, and then the silence was so new and terrible that it seemed the prelude to some dreadful noise. Footsteps in the court! Two men. [Jonas] fell back from the door on tiptoe, as if they could have seen him through its wooden panels.

"They passed on, talking (he could make out) about a skeleton which had been dug up yesterday, in some work of excavation near at hand, and was supposed to be that of a murdered man. 'So murder is not always found out, you see,' they said to one another as they turned the corner." MC 46

—a plan implemented: "Did no men passing through the dim streets shrink without knowing why, when he came stealing up behind them? As he glided on, had no child in its sleep an indistinct perception of a guilty shadow falling on its bed, that troubled its innocent rest? Did no dog howl, and strive to break its rattling chain, that it might tear him; no burrowing rat, scenting the work he had in hand, essay to gnaw a passage after him, that it might hold a greedy revel at the feast of his providing? When he looked back, across his shoulder, was it to see if his quick footsteps still fell dry upon the dusty pavement, or were already moist and clogged with the red mire that stained the naked feet of *Cain*?" MC 46

"[Jonas] bargained for a seat outside this coach, and took it. And he . . . occupied the same place all night . . . .

"And yet he slept. Riding on among those sentinels of God, he slept, and did not change the purpose of his journey. If he forgot it in his troubled dreams, it came up steadily, and woke him. But it never woke him to remorse, or to abandonment of his design." MC 47 *And see* N:Nature—*and a murderer*

"The sun was welcome to [Jonas]. There were life and motion, and a world astir, to divide the attention of Day. It was the eye of Night: of wakeful, watchful, silent, and attentive Night, with so much leisure for the observation of his wicked thoughts: that he dreaded most. There is no glare in the night. Even Glory shows to small advantage in the night, upon a crowded battlefield. How then shows Glory's blood-relation, bastard Murder!

"Aye! He made no compromise, and held no secret with himself now. Murder. He had come to do it." MC 47

—*execution:* "As the sunlight died away, and evening fell upon the wood, [Tigg Montague] entered it. Moving, here and there, a bramble or a drooping bough which stretched across his path, he slowly disappeared. At intervals a narrow opening showed him passing on, or the sharp cracking of some tender branch denoted where he went; then he was seen or heard no more.

"Never more beheld by mortal eye or heard by mortal ear: one man excepted. That man, parting the leaves and branches on the other side, near where the path emerged again, came leaping out soon afterwards.

"What had he left within the wood, that he sprang out of it as if it were a hell!

"The body of a murdered man. In one thick solitary spot, it lay among the last year's leaves of oak and beech, just as it had fallen headlong down. Sopping and soaking in among the leaves that formed its pillow; oozing down into the boggy ground, as if to cover itself from human sight; forcing its way between and through the curling leaves, as if those senseless things rejected and forswore it, and were coiled up in abhorrence; went a dark, dark stain that dyed the whole summer night from earth to heaven." MC 47

—*returned:* "[Jonas] listened. Not a sound. As he turned the key with a trembling hand, and pushed the door softly open with his knee, a monstrous fear beset his mind.

"What if the murdered man were there before him!

"He cast a fearful glance all round. But there was nothing there.

". . . . The raging thirst, the fire that burnt within him as he lay beneath the clothes, the augmented horror of the room when they shut it out from his view; the agony of listening, in which he paid enforced regard to every sound, and thought the most unlikely one the prelude to that knocking which should bring the news; the starts with which he left his couch, and looking in the glass, imagined that his deed was broadly written in his face and lying down and burying himself once more beneath the blankets, heard his own heart beating Murder, Murder, Murder, in the bed; what words can paint tremendous truths like these!" MC 47 *See* Murderer—*dread of self; and* S:Self-dread

—*waiting:* "In [Jonas's] secret dread of meeting the household for the first time, after what he had done, he lingered at the door on slight pretexts that they might see him without looking in his face; and left it ajar while he dressed; and called out to have the windows opened, and the pavement watered, that they might become accustomed to his voice. Even when he had put off the time, by one means or other, so that he had seen or spoken to them all, he could not muster courage for a long while to go in among them, but stood at his own door listening to the murmur of their distant conversation.

"He could not stop there for ever, and so joined them. His last glance at the glass had seen a tell-tale face, but that might have been because of his anxious looking in it. He dared not look at them to see if they observed him, but he thought them very silent.

"And whatsoever guard he kept upon himself, he could not help listening, and showing that he listened. Whether he attended to their talk, or tried to think of other things, or talked himself, or held his peace, or resolutely counted the dull tickings of a hoarse clock at his back, he always lapsed, as if a spell were on him, into eager listening. For he knew it must come; and his present punishment, and torture, and distraction, were, to listen for its coming.

"Hush!" MC 47

"[Jonas's] watchfulness of every avenue by which the discovery of his guilt might be approached, sharpened with his sense of the danger by which he was encompassed. With murder on his soul, and its innumerable alarms and terrors dragging at him night and day, he would have repeated the crime, if he had seen a path of safety stretching out beyond. It was in his punishment; it was in his guilty condition. The very deed which his fears rendered insupportable, his fears would have impelled him to commit again." MC 51

"Hush!

"Still listening! To every sound. [Jonas] had listened ever since and it had not come yet . . . he thought—of his own controlling power and direction he thought—of the one dread question only. When they would find the body in the wood.

"He tried—he had never left off trying—not to forget it was there, for that was impossible, but to forget to weary himself by drawing vivid pictures of it in his fancy; by going softly about it and about it among the leaves, approaching it nearer and nearer through a gap in the boughs, and startling the very flies that were thickly sprinkled all over it, like heaps of dried currants.

"His mind was fixed and fastened on the discovery, for intelligence of which he listened intently to every cry and shout; listened when any one came in or went out; watched from the window the people who passed up and down the street; mistrusted his own looks and words. And the more his thoughts were set upon the discovery, the stronger was the fascination which attracted them to the thing itself: lying alone in the wood.

"He was for ever showing and presenting it, as it were, to every creature whom he saw. 'Look here! Do you know of this? Is it found? Do you suspect *me?*' If he had been condemned to bear the body in his arms, and lay it down for recognition at the feet of every one he met, it could not have been more constantly with him, or a cause of more monotonous and dismal occupation than it was in this state of his mind.

"Still he was not sorry. It was no contrition or remorse for what he had done that moved him; it was nothing but alarm for his own security. The vague consciousness he possessed of having wrecked his fortune in the murderous venture, intensified his hatred and revenge, and made him set the greater store by what he had gained. The man was dead; nothing could undo that. He felt a triumph yet, in the reflection . . . .

—discovery: "An irrepressible exclamation burst from the lips of Jonas, as Lewsome entered at the door. It was not a groan, or a shriek, or a word, but was wholly unlike any sound that had ever fallen on the ears of those who heard it, while at the same time it was the most sharp and terrible expression of what was working in his guilty breast, that nature could have invented . . . .

"He knew that they were on his heels, and felt that they were resolute to run him to destruction. Inch by inch the ground beneath him was sliding from his feet; faster and faster the encircling ruin contracted and contracted towards himself, its wicked centre, until it should close in and crush him . . . .

"He tried to deny [the truth], but his tongue would not move. He conceived some desperate thoughts of rushing away, and tearing through the streets; but his limbs would as little answer to his will as his stark, stiff, staring face . . . . It was as if every drop of blood in the wood had found a voice to jeer him with . . . .

—apparently reprieved: "[Jonas's] base triumph, struggling with his cowardice, and shame, and guilt, was so detestable, that they turned away from him, as if he were some obscene and filthy animal, repugnant to the sight. And here that last black crime was busy with him too; working within him to his perdition . . . with that unnecessary wasteful danger haunting him; despair was in his very triumph and relief; wild, ungovernable, raging despair, for the uselessness of the peril into which he had plunged; despair that hardened him and maddened him, and set his teeth a-grinding in a moment of his exultation . . . .

—conclusion: "'I have not been watching him so long for nothing,' returned Nadgett. 'I never watched a man so close as I have watched him.'

"Another of the phantom forms of this terrific Truth! Another of the many shapes in which it started up about him, out of the vacancy. This man, of all men in the world, a spy upon him; this man, changing his identity: casting off his shrinking, purblind, unobservant character, and springing up into a watchful enemy! The dead man might have come out of his grave, and not confounded and appalled him more.

"The game was up. The race was at an end; the rope was woven for his neck. If, by a miracle, he could escape from this strait, he had but to turn his face another way, no matter where, and there would rise some new avenger front to front with him; some infant in an hour grown old, or old man in an hour grown young, or blind man with his sight restored, or deaf man with his hearing given him. There was no chance. He sank down in a heap against the wall, and never hoped again from that moment." MC 51

—museum inspiration: " . . . the reverend Ordinary of Newgate . . . writes (in singular English):

"'I have often thought, and still think, that the origin of garotte robberies took place from the exhibition of the way the Thugs in India strangle and plunder passengers, as exhibited in the British Museum . . . [which has] been, the means of giving to men addicted to crime and violence an idea how their evil purposes may be accomplished.'

"Now, setting aside the fact notorious to all men . . . that the desperate characters of the metropolis are in the habit of fatiguing themselves with the study of the British Museum, and that the worst of the Ticket-of-leave men may be invariably found there, between the hours of ten and four, annotating their catalogues with great diligence, we take leave to protest against this reverend gentleman's doctrine, as utterly nonsensical in itself, and surpassingly insulting to the people." HW/SA

—social disqualifier: "All the circumstances after a murder . . . must be dreadfully unpleasant [said John Chester]—so much bustle and disturbance—no repose—a constant dwelling upon one subject—and the running in and out, and up and down stairs, intolerable. I wouldn't have such a thing happen to anybody I was nearly interested in, on any account. 'Twould be enough to wear one's life out.'" BR 10

"' . . . The very idea of marrying a girl whose father was killed, like meat [said John Chester]! Good God, Ned, how disagreeable! Consider the impossibility of having any respect for your father-in-law under such unpleasant circumstances—think of his having been "viewed" by jurors, and "sat upon" by coroners, and of his very doubtful position in the family ever afterwards. It seems to me such an indelicate sort of thing that I really think the girl ought to have been put to death by the state to prevent its happening.'" BR 15

Murderer

—assassins in Italy: "Leghorn had a bad name in connexion with stabbers, and with some justice it must be allowed; for, not many years ago, there was an assassination club there, the members of which bore no ill-will to anybody in particular, but stabbed people (quite strangers to them) in the streets at night, for the pleasure and excitement of the recreation. I think the president of this amiable society was a shoemaker. He was taken, however, and the club was broken up." PI 10

—blind spot: "Bradley [Headstone] was suspicious of every sound he heard, and of every face he saw, but was under a spell which very commonly falls upon the shedder of blood, and had no suspicion of the real danger that lurked in his life, and would have it yet. Riderhood was much in his thoughts—had never been out of his thoughts since the night-adventure of their first meeting; but Riderhood occupied a very different place there, from the place of pursuer; and Bradley had been at the pains of devising so many means of fitting that place to him, and of wedging him into it, that his mind could not compass the possibility of his occupying any other. And this is another spell against which the shedder of blood for ever strives in vain. There are fifty doors by which discovery may enter. With infinite pains and cunning, he double locks and bars forty-nine of them, and cannot see the fiftieth standing wide open." OMF iv 7

—drawn back: "'Why did you return?' said the blind man [Stagg].

"'Why is blood red [said Rudge]? I could no more help it, than I could live without breath. I struggled against the impulse, but I was drawn back, through every difficult and adverse circumstance, as by a mighty engine. Nothing could stop me. The day and hour were none of my choice. Sleeping and waking, I had been among the old haunts for years—had visited my own grave. Why did I come back? Because this jail was gaping for me, and he [the victim] stood beckoning at the door.'" BR 62

—dread of self: " . . . he was not sorry for what he had done. He was frightened when he thought of it—when did he not think of it!—but he was not sorry. He had had a terror and dread of the wood when he was in it; but being out of it, and having committed the crime, his fears were now diverted, strangely, to the dark room he had left shut up at home. He had a greater horror, infinitely greater, of that room than of the wood. Now that he was on his return to it, it seemed beyond comparison more dismal and more dreadful than the wood. His hideous secret was shut up in the room, and all its terrors were there; to his thinking it was not in the wood at all." MC 47

"Dread and fear were upon him, to an extent he had never counted on, and could not manage in the least degree. He was so horribly afraid of that infernal room at home. This made him, in a gloomy, murderous, mad way, not only fearful *for* himself but *of* himself; for being, as it were, a part of the room: a something supposed to be there, yet missing from it: he invested himself with its mysterious terrors; and when he pictured in his mind the ugly chamber, false and quiet, false and quiet, through the dark hours of two nights; and the tumbled bed, and he not in it, though believed to be; he became in a manner his own ghost and phantom, and was at once the haunting spirit and the haunted man." MC 47

—facing death: "[Gabriel Varden] had seen [Rudge] pass along the crowded street, amidst the execration of the throng; and marked his quivering lip, and trembling limbs; the ashy hue upon his face, his clammy brow, and wild distraction of his eye—the fear of death that swallowed up all other thoughts, and gnawed without cessation at his heart and brain.

"He had marked the wandering look, seeking for hope, and finding, turn where it would, despair. He had seen the remorseful, pitiful, desolate creature, riding, with his coffin by his side, to the gibbet. He knew that, to the last, he had been an unyielding, obdurate man; that in the savage terror of his condition he had hardened, rather than relented, to his wife and child; and that the last words which had passed his white lips were curses on them as his enemies." ¶BR 76

—flight and end: "The sun—the bright sun, that brings back, not light alone, but new life, and hope, and freshness to man—burst upon the crowded city in clear and radiant glory. Through costly-coloured glass and paper-mended window, through cathedral dome and rotten crevice, it shed its equal ray. It lighted up the room where the murdered woman [Nancy] lay. It did. [Sikes] tried to shut it out, but it would stream in. If the sight had been a ghastly one in the dull morning, what was it, now, in all that brilliant light!

"He had not moved; he had been afraid to stir. There had been a moan and motion of the hand; and, with terror added to rage, he had struck and struck again. Once he threw a rug over it; but it was worse to fancy the eyes, and imagine them moving towards him, than to see them glaring upward, as if watching the reflection of the pool of gore that quivered and danced in the sunlight on the ceiling. He had plucked it off again. And there was the body—mere flesh and blood, no more—but such flesh, and so much blood!

"He struck a light, kindled a fire, and thrust the club into it. There was hair upon the end, which blazed and shrunk into a light cinder, and, caught by the air, whirled up the chimney. Even that frightened him, sturdy as he was; but he held the weapon till it broke, and then piled it on the coals to burn away, and smoulder into ashes. He washed himself, and rubbed his clothes; there were spots that would not be removed, but he cut the pieces out, and burnt them. How those stains were dispersed about the room! The very feet of the dog were bloody.

"All this time he had never once turned his back upon the corpse; no, not for a moment. Such preparations completed, he moved, backward, towards the door: dragging the dog with him, lest he should soil his feet anew and carry out new evidences of the crime into the streets. He shut the door softly, locked it, took the key, and left the house." OT 48

"Where could he go, that was near and not too public, to get some meat and drink? Hendon. That was a good place, not far off, and out of most people's way. Thither he directed his steps—running sometimes, and sometimes, with a strange perversity, loitering at a snail's pace, or stopping altogether and idly breaking the hedges with his stick. But when he got there, all the people he met—the very children at the doors— seemed to view him with suspicion. Back he turned again, without the courage to purchase bit or drop, though he had tasted no food for many hours; and once more he lingered on the Heath, uncertain where to go . . . .

"It was nine o'clock at night, when the man, quite tired out, and the dog, limping and lame from the unaccustomed exercise, turned down the hill by the church of the quiet village, and plodding along the little street, crept into a small public-house . . . .

" . . . . The robber, after paying his reckoning, sat silent and unnoticed in his corner, and had almost dropped asleep, when he was half wakened by the noisy entrance of a new-comer . . . .

"'And what be that stoof? Good to eat, Harry?' asked a grinning countryman, pointing to some composition cakes in one corner.

"'This,' said the fellow, producing one, 'is the infallible and invaluable composition for removing all sorts of stain, rust, dirt, mildew, spick, speck, spot, or spatter, from silk, satin, linen, cambric, cloth, crape, stuff, carpet, merino, muslin, bombazeen, or woollen stuff. Wine-stains, fruit-stains, beer-stains, water-stains, paint-stains, pitch-stains, any stains, all come out at one rub with the infallible and invaluable composition. If a lady stains her honour, she has only need to swallow one cake and she's cured at once—for it's poison. If a gentleman wants to prove this, he has only need to bolt one little square, and he has put it beyond question—for it's quite as satisfactory as a pistol-bullet, and a great deal nastier in the flavour, consequently the more credit in taking it. . . .

"'One penny a square! Two halfpence is all the same, and four farthings is received with joy. One penny a square! Wine-stains, fruit-stains, beer-stains, water-stains, paint-stains, pitch-stains, mud-stains, blood-stains! Here is a stain upon the hat of a gentleman in company, that I'll take clean out, before he can order me a pint of ale.'

"'Hah!' cried Sikes, starting up. 'Give that back.'

"'I'll take it clean out, sir,' replied the man, winking to the company, 'before you can come across the room to get it. Gentlemen, all, observe the dark stain upon this gentleman's hat, not wider than a shilling, but thicker than a half-crown. Whether it is a wine-stain, fruit-stain, beer-stain, water-stain, paint-stain, pitch-stain, mud-stain, or blood-stain—'

"The man got no further, for Sikes with a hideous imprecation overthrew the table, and tearing the hat from him, burst out of the house." OT 48

"He went on doggedly; but as he left the town behind him, and plunged into the solitude and darkness of the road, he felt a dread and awe creeping upon him which shook him to the core. Every object before him, substance or shadow, still or moving, took the semblance of some fearful thing; but these fears were nothing compared to the sense that haunted him of that morning's ghastly figure following at his heels. He could trace its shadow in the gloom, supply the smallest item of the outline, and note how stiff and solemn it seemed to stalk along. He could hear its garments rustling in the leaves, and every breath of wind came laden with that last low cry. If he stopped it did the same. If he ran, it followed—not running too: that would have been a relief: but like a corpse endowed with the mere machinery of life, and borne on one slow melancholy wind that never rose or fell.

"At times he turned, with desperate determination, resolved to beat this phantom off, though it should look him dead; but the hair rose on his head, and his blood stood still, for it had turned with him, and was behind him then. He had kept it before him that morning, but it was behind now—always. He leaned his back against a bank, and felt that it stood above him, visibly out against the cold night-sky. He threw himself upon the road—on his back upon the road. At his head it stood, silent, erect, and still—a living grave-stone, with its epitaph in blood.

"Let no man talk of murderers escaping justice, and hint that Providence must sleep. There were twenty score of violent deaths in one long minute of that agony of fear.

"There was a shed in a field he passed, that offered shelter for the night. Before the door, were three tall poplar trees, which made it very dark within; and the wind moaned through them with a dismal wail. He could not walk on, till daylight came again; and here he stretched himself close to the wall—to undergo new torture.

"For now, a vision came before him, as constant and more terrible than that from which he had escaped. Those widely staring eyes, so lustreless and so glassy, that he had better borne to see them than think upon them, appeared in the midst of the darkness; light in themselves, but giving light to nothing. There were but two, but they were everywhere. If he shut out the sight, there came the room with every well-known object—some, indeed, that he would have forgotten, if he had gone over its contents from memory—each in its accustomed place. The body was in its place, and its eyes were as he saw them when he stole away. He got up, and rushed into the field without. The figure was behind him. He re-entered the shed, and shrunk down once more. The eyes were there, before he had laid himself along.

"And here he remained in such terror as none but he can know, trembling in every limb, and the cold sweat starting from every pore . . . . " OT 48

"The broad sky seemed on fire. Rising into the air with showers of sparks, and rolling one above the other, were sheets of flame, lighting the atmosphere for miles round . . . .

"He came upon the spot . . . . He shouted, too, till he was hoarse; and flying from memory and himself, plunged into the thickest of the throng.

"Hither and thither he dived that night: now working at the pumps, and now hurrying through the smoke and flame . . . .

"This mad excitement over, there returned, with tenfold force, the dreadful consciousness of his crime. He looked suspiciously about him, for the men were conversing in groups, and he feared to be the subject of their talk. The dog obeyed the significant beck of his finger, and they drew off, stealthily, together . . . .

"He hurried off, and walked till he almost dropped upon the ground; then lay down in a lane, and had a long, but broken and uneasy sleep. He wandered on again, irresolute and undecided, and oppressed with the fear of another solitary night.

"Suddenly, he took the desperate resolution of going back to London." OT 48

"Crackit went down to the door, and returned followed by a man with the lower part of his face buried in a handkerchief, and another tied over his head under his hat. He drew them slowly off. Blanched face, sunken eyes, hollow cheeks, beard of three days' growth, wasted flesh, short thick breath; it was the very ghost of Sikes." OT 50

"Crackit . . . directly came back with Charley Bates behind him. Sikes sat opposite the door, so that the moment the boy entered the room he encountered his figure.

"'Toby,' said the boy, falling back, as Sikes turned his eyes towards him, 'why didn't you tell me this, down-stairs?'" OT 50

"'Help!' shrieked Charley Bates] in a voice that rent the air. 'He's here! Break down the door!'

"'In the King's name,' cried the voices without; and the hoarse cry arose again, but louder . . . .

"'Damn you!' cried the desperate ruffian, throwing up the sash and menacing the crowd. 'Do your worst! I'll cheat you yet!'" OT 50

"Roused into new strength and energy, and stimulated by the noise within the house which announced that an entrance had really been effected, [Sikes] set his foot against the stack of chimneys, fastened one end of the rope tightly and firmly round it, and with the other made a strong running noose by the aid of his hands and teeth almost in a second. He could let himself down by the cord to within a less distance of the ground than his own height, and had his knife ready in his hand to cut it then and drop.

"At the very instant when he brought the loop over his head previous to slipping it beneath his arm-pits . . . at that very instant the murderer, looking behind him on the roof, threw his arms above his head, and uttered a yell of terror.

"'The eyes again!' he cried in an unearthly screech.

"Staggering as if struck by lightning, he lost his balance and tumbled over the parapet. The noose was on his neck. It ran up with his weight, tight as a bowstring, and swift as the arrow it speeds. He fell for five-and-thirty feet. There was a sudden jerk, a terrific convulsion of the limbs; and there he hung, with the open knife clenched in his stiffening hand.

"The old chimney quivered with the shock, but stood it bravely. The murderer swung lifeless against the wall; and the boy, thrusting aside the dangling body which obscured his view, called to the people to come and take him out, for God's sake.

"A dog [Bull's-eye], which had lain concealed till now, ran backwards and forwards on the parapet with a dismal howl, and collecting himself for a spring, jumped for the dead man's shoulders. Missing his aim, he fell into the ditch, turning completely over as he went; and striking his head against a stone, dashed out his brains." OT 50

The Last Chance OT

—haunted: "The man was hurrying to the door, when suddenly there came towards them on the wind, the loud and rapid tolling of an alarm-bell, and then a bright and vivid glare streamed up, which illumined, not only the whole chamber, but all the country.

"It was not the sudden change from darkness to this dreadful light, it was not the sound of distant shrieks and shouts of triumph, it was not this dread invasion of the serenity and peace of night, that drove the man back as though a thunderbolt had struck him. It was the Bell. If the ghastliest shape the human mind has ever pictured in its wildest dreams had risen up before him, he could not have staggered backward from its touch, as he did from the first sound of that loud iron voice. With eyes that started from his head, his limbs convulsed, his face most horrible to see, he raised one arm high up into the air, and holding something visionary back and down, with his other hand, drove at it as though he held a knife and stabbed it to the heart. He clutched his hair, and stopped his ears, and travelled madly round and round; then gave a frightful cry, and with it rushed away: still, still, the Bell tolled on and seemed to follow him—louder and louder, hotter and hotter yet. The glare grew brighter, the roar of voices deeper; the crash of heavy bodies falling, shook the air; bright streams of sparks rose up into the sky; but louder than them all—rising faster far, to Heaven—a million times more fierce and furious—pouring forth dreadful secrets after its long silence—speaking the language of the dead—the Bell—the Bell!" BR 55

"'You have a strong fancy,' said the blind man, with a smile.

"'Strengthen yours with blood, and see what it will come to.'

"[Rudge] groaned and rocked himself, and looking up for the first time, said, in a low, hollow voice:

"'Eight-and-twenty years! Eight-and-twenty years! He has never changed in all that time, never grown older, nor altered in the least degree. He has been before me in the dark night, and the broad sunny day; in the twilight, the moonlight, the sunlight, the light of fire, and lamp, and candle, and in the deepest gloom. Always the same! In company, in solitude, on land, on shipboard; sometimes leaving me alone for months, and sometimes always with me. I have seen him at sea, come gliding in the dead of night along the bright reflection of the moon in the calm water; and I have seen him, on quays and market-places, with his hand uplifted, towering, the centre of a busy crowd, unconscious of the terrible form that had its silent stand among them. Fancy! Are you real? Am I? Are these iron fetters, riveted on me by the smith's hammer, or are they fancies I can shatter at a blow?'" BR 62

And see —flight and end

—self-possession: " . . . there is no greater mistake than to suppose that a man who is a calculating criminal, is, in any phase of his guilt, otherwise than true to himself, and perfectly consistent with his whole character. Such a man commits murder, and murder is the natural culmination of his course; such a man has to outface murder, and will do it with hardihood and effrontery. It is a sort of fashion to express surprise that any notorious criminal, having such crime upon his conscience, can so brave it out. Do you think that if he had it on his conscience at all, or had a conscience to have it upon, he would ever have committed the crime?" HD

—state of mind: "Now, too, was [Bradley Headstone] cursed with a state of mind more wearing and more wearisome than remorse. He had no remorse; but the evildoer who can hold that avenger at bay, cannot escape the slower torture of incessantly doing the evil deed again and doing it more efficiently. In the defensive declarations and pretended confessions of murderers, the pursuing shadow of this torture may be traced through every lie they tell.

"If I had done it as alleged, is it conceivable that I would have made this and this mistake? If I had done it as alleged, should I have left that unguarded place which that false and wicked witness against me so infamously deposed to?

"The state of that wretch who continually finds the weak spots in his own crime, and strives to strengthen them when it is unchangeable, is a state that aggravates the offence by doing the deed a thousand times instead of once; but it is a state, too, that tauntingly visits the offence upon a sullen unrepentant nature with its heaviest punishment every time.

"Bradley toiled on, chained heavily to the idea of his hatred and his vengeance, and thinking how he might have satiated both in many better ways than the way he had taken. The instrument might have been better, the spot and the hour might have been better chosen.

"To batter a man down from behind in the dark, on the brink of a river, was well enough, but he ought to have been instantly disabled, whereas he had turned and seized his assailant; and so, to end it before chance help came, and to be rid of him, he had been hurriedly thrown backward into the river before the life was fully beaten out of him.

"Now if it could be done again, it must not be so done. Supposing his head had been held down under water for a while. Supposing the first blow had been truer. Supposing he had been shot. Supposing he had been strangled. Suppose this way, that way, the other way. Suppose anything but getting unchained from the one idea, for that was inexorably impossible." ¶OMF iv 7

—viewed poetically: " . . . when the sickening murder and mangling of a wretched woman was affording delicious food wherewith to gorge the insatiable curiosity of the public, our friend the poetical young gentleman was in ecstasies—not of disgust, but admiration. 'Heavens!' cried the poetical young gentleman, 'how grand; how great!' . . . and thereupon it came out, in a fine torrent of eloquence, that the murderer was a great spirit, a bold creature full of daring and nerve, a man of dauntless heart and determined courage, and withal a great casuist and able reasoner, as was fully demonstrated in his philosophical colloquies with the great and noble of the land. We held our peace, and meekly signified our in-

disposition to controvert these opinions . . . being perfectly convinced that the respectable and immoral hero in question is not the first and will not be the last hanged gentleman upon whom false sympathy or diseased curiosity will be plentifully expended." YG/V

—his violence: "'Hell's fire! cried Sikes, breaking fiercely from the Jew. 'Let me go!'

"Flinging the old man from him, he rushed from the room, and darted, wildly and furiously, up the stairs.

"'Bill, Bill!' cried Fagin, following him hastily. 'A word. Only a word.'

"The word would not have been exchanged, but that the housebreaker was unable to open the door: on which he was expending fruitless oaths and violence, when the Jew came panting up.

"'Let me out,' said Sikes. 'Don't speak to me; it's not safe. Let me out, I say!'

"'Hear me speak a word,' rejoined Fagin, laying his hand upon the lock. 'You won't be—'. . .

"'You won't be—too—violent, Bill?'

"The day was breaking, and there was light enough for the men to see each other's faces. They exchanged one brief glance; there was a fire in the eyes of both, which could not be mistaken.

"'I mean,' said Fagin, showing that he felt all disguise was not useless, 'not too violent for safety. Be crafty, Bill, and not too bold.'

"Sikes made no reply; but, pulling open the door, of which Fagin had turned the lock, dashed into the silent streets.

"Without one pause, or moment's consideration; without once turning his head to the right or left, or raising his eyes to the sky, or lowering them to the ground, but looking straight before him with savage resolution: his teeth so tightly compressed that the strained jaw seemed starting through his skin; the robber held on his headlong course, nor muttered a word, nor relaxed a muscle, until he reached his own door. He opened it, softly, with a key; strode lightly up the stairs; and entering his own room, double-locked the door, and lifting a heavy table against it, drew back the curtain of the bed.

"The girl was lying, half-dressed, upon it. He had roused her from her sleep, for she raised herself with a hurried and startled look.

"'Get up!' said the man." OT 47

"'You know, you she devil!' returned the robber [Sikes], suppressing his breath. 'You were watched to-night; every word you said was heard.'

"'Then spare my life for the love of Heaven, as I spared yours,' rejoined the girl [Nancy], clinging to him . . . .

"The man struggled violently to release his arms; but those of the girl were clasped round his, and tear her as he would, he could not tear them away . . . .

"The housebreaker freed one arm, and grasped his pistol. The certainty of immediate detection if he fired, flashed across his mind even in the midst of his fury; and he beat it twice with all the force he could summon, upon the upturned face that almost touched his own.

"She staggered and fell: nearly blinded with the blood that rained down from a deep gash in her forehead; but raising herself, with difficulty, on her knees, drew from her bosom a white handkerchief—Rose Maylie's own—and holding it up, in her folded hands, as high towards Heaven as her feeble strength would allow, breathed one prayer for mercy to her Maker.

"It was a ghastly figure to look upon. The murderer staggering backward to the wall, and shutting out the sight with his hand, seized a heavy club and struck her down." OT 47

Native American

—evaluated: "The Indians of North America—a very inferior people to the Saxons . . . ." CHE 2

—exploited: "I was very much interested in looking over a number of treaties made from time to time with the poor Indians, signed by the different chiefs at the period of their ratification, and preserved in the office of the Secretary to the Commonwealth [of Pennsylvania]. These signatures, traced of course by their own hands, are rough drawings of the creatures or weapons they were called after. Thus, the Great Turtle makes a crooked pen-and-ink outline of a great turtle; the Buffalo sketches a buffalo; the War Hatchet sets a rough image of that weapon for his mark. So with the Arrow, the Fish, the Scalp, the Big Canoe, and all of them.

"I could not but think—as I looked at these feeble and tremulous productions of hands which could draw the longest arrow to the head in a stout elk-horn bow, or split a bead or feather with a rifle-ball—of Crabbe's* musings over the Parish Register, and the irregular scratches made with a pen, by men who would plough a lengthy furrow straight from end to end.

"Nor could I help bestowing many sorrowful thoughts upon the simple warriors whose hands and hearts were set there, in all truth and honesty; and who only learned in course of time from white men how to break their faith, and quibble out of forms and bonds. I wonder, too, how many times the credulous Big Turtle, or trusting Little Hatchet, had put his mark to treaties which were falsely read to him; and had signed away, he knew not what, until it went and cast him loose upon the new possessors of the land, a savage indeed." ¶AN9

**George Crabbe's poem* The Parish Register (1807): *how strange that men / Who guide the plough, should fail to guide the pen*

—*"progress":* "Among the blazing grass, and herds of buffaloes and wild horses, and among the wigwams of the fast-declining Indians [Mr Booley] began to consider how, in the eternal current of progress setting across this globe in one unchangeable direction, like the unseen agency that points the needle to the Pole, the Chiefs who only dance the dances of their fathers, and will never have a new figure for a new tune, and the Medicine men who know no Medicine but what was medicine a hundred years ago, must be surely and inevitably swept from the earth, whether they be Choctawas, Mandans, Britons, Austrians, or Chinese." HW/ET

And see Courtier—*in North America; and* B: Dress—*medicine man magic; and Dickens's encounter with the impressive Pitchlynn AN*

Nuisance

—*classic:* "'The fact is, Mr Mopes, that you are not only a Nuisance—'

"'A Nuisance?' repeated the Hermit, fiercely.

"'What is a place in this obscene state of dilapidation but a Nuisance? What is a man in your obscene state of dilapidation but a Nuisance? Then, as you very well know, you cannot do without an audience, and your audience is a Nuisance.

"'You attract all the disreputable vagabonds and prowlers within ten miles around, by exhibiting yourself to them in that objectionable blanket, and by throwing copper money among them, and giving them drink out of those very dirty jars and bottles that I see in there (their stomachs need be strong!); and in short,' said Mr Traveller, summing up in a quietly and comfortably settled manner, 'you are a Nuisance, and this kennel is a Nuisance, and the audience that you cannot possibly dispense with is a Nuisance, and the Nuisance is not merely a local Nuisance, because it is a General Nuisance to know that there *can be* such a Nuisance left in civilisation so very long after its time.'" ¶CS/TT 1

—*dealt with:* "'I've only got to say this here,' said Sam, stopping short, 'that if *I* was the properiator o' the Markis o' Granby, and that 'ere Stiggins came and made toast in *my* bar, I'd—'

"'What?' interposed Mr Weller, with great anxiety. 'What?'

"'—Pison his rum-and-water,' said Sam.

"'No!' said Mr Weller, shaking his son eagerly by the hand, 'would you raly, Sammy; would you, though?'

"'I would,' said Sam. 'I wouldn't be too hard upon him at first. I'd drop him in the water-butt, and put the lid on; and if I found he was insensible to kindness, I'd try the other persvasion.'" PP 27

Pauper

—*burial:* "Then the active and intelligent [Beadle], who has got into the morning papers as such, comes with his pauper company . . . and bears off the body of our dear brother [Captain Hawdon] here departed, to a hemmed-in churchyard, pestiferous and obscene, whence malignant diseases are communicated to the bodies of our dear brothers and sisters who have not departed; while our dear brothers and sisters who hang about official back-stairs—would to Heaven they *had* departed!—are very complacent and agreeable. Into a beastly scrap of ground which a Turk would reject as a savage abomination, and a Caffre would shudder at, they bring our dear brother here departed, to receive Christian burial.

"With houses looking on, on every side, save where a reeking little tunnel of a court gives access to the iron gate—with every villainy of life in action close on death, and every poisonous element of death in action close on life—here, they lower our dear brother down a foot or two: here, sow him in corruption, to be raised in corruption: an avenging ghost at many a sick bedside: a shameful testimony to future ages, how civilisation and barbarism walked this boastful island together.

"Come night, come darkness, for you cannot come too soon, or stay too long, by such a place as this! Come, straggling lights, into the windows of the ugly houses; and you who do iniquity therein, do it at least with this dread scene shut out! Come, flame of gas, burning so sullenly above the iron gate, on which the poisoned air deposits its witch-ointment, slimy to the touch! It is well that you should call to every passer-by, 'Look here!'" BH 11

"'There!' says Jo, pointing. ' Over yinder. Among them piles of bones, and close to that there kitchin winder! They put him wery nigh the top. They was obliged to stamp upon it to git it in. I could unkiver it for you with my broom, if the gate was open. That's why they locks it, I s'pose,' giving it a shake. 'It's always locked. Look at the rat!' cried Jo, excited. 'Hi! Look! There he goes! Ho! Into the ground!'" BH 16

—care compared with U.S.: "At Boston, in the State of Massachusetts, this poor creature would have been individually addressed, would have been tended in her own room, and would have had her life gently assimilated to a comfortable life out of doors. When Britain first, at Heaven's command, arose, with a great deal of allegorical confusion, from out the azure main, did her guardian angels positively forbid it in the Charter which has been so much besung?" UT/WW

—management: "The members of this board were very sage, deep, philosophical men; and when they came to turn their attention to the workhouse, they found out at once, what ordinary folks would never have discovered—the poor people liked it! It was a regular place of public entertainment for the poorer classes; a tavern where there was nothing to pay; a public breakfast, dinner, tea, and supper all the year round; a brick and mortar elysium, where it was all play and no work.

"'Oho!' said the board, looking very knowing; 'we are the fellows to set this to rights; we'll stop it all, in no time.' So, they established the rule, that all poor people should have the alternative (for they would compel nobody, not they), of being starved by a gradual process in the house, or by a quick one out of it. With this view, they contracted with the water-works to lay on an unlimited supply of water; and with a corn-factor to supply periodically small quantities of oatmeal; and issued three meals of thin gruel a day, with an onion twice a week, and half a roll on Sundays.

"They made a great many other wise and humane regulations, having reference to the ladies, which it is not necessary to repeat; kindly undertook to divorce poor married people, in consequence of the great expense of a suit in Doctors' Commons; and, instead of compelling a man to support his family, as they had theretofore done, took his family away from him, and made him a bachelor!

"There is no saying how many applicants for relief, under these last two heads, might have started up in all classes of society, if it had not been coupled with the workhouse; but the board were long-headed men, and had provided for this difficulty. The relief was inseparable from the workhouse and the gruel; and that frightened people." OT 2

—shelter: "[Jenny's] friend had been here and there, and had been played about from hand to hand, and had come back as she went. At first it was too early for the boy [Jo] to be received into the proper refuge, and at last it was too late. One official sent her to another, and the other sent her back again to the first, and so backward and forward; until it appeared to me as if both must have been appointed for their skill in evading their duties, instead of performing them." BH 31

—variety: A-bed in these miserable rooms, here on bedsteads, there . . . on the floor were women in every stage of distress and disease. None but those who have attentively observed such scenes, can conceive the extraordinary variety of expression still latent under the general monotony and uniformity of colour, attitude, and condition. The form a little coiled up and turned away, as though it had turned its back on this world for ever; the uninterested face at once lead-coloured and yellow, looking passively upward from the pillow; the haggard mouth a little dropped, the hand outside the coverlet, so dull and indifferent, so light, and yet so heavy; these were on every pallet; but when I stopped beside a bed, and said ever so slight a word to the figure lying there, the ghost of the old character came into the face, and made the Foul ward as various as the fair world." UT/WW

See also Poor-house and Poor Law

Police

—Bow Street: "The Constables, and the Bow Street men from London—for this happened in the days of the extinct red-waistcoated police—were about the house for a week or two, and did pretty much what I have heard and read of like authorities doing in other such cases.

"They took up several obviously wrong people, and they ran their heads very hard against wrong ideas, and persisted in trying to fit the circumstances to the ideas, instead of trying to extract ideas from the circumstances. Also, they stood about the door of the Jolly Bargemen, with knowing and reserved looks that filled the whole neighbourhood with admiration; and they had a mysterious manner of taking their drink, that was almost as good as taking the culprit. But not quite, for they never did it." GE 16

—criminal viewpoint: "What is the inscription, Deputy, on all the discoloured sheets? A precaution against loss of linen. Deputy turns down the rag of an unoccupied bed and discloses it, STOP THIEF!

"To lie at night, wrapped in the legend of my slinking life; to take the cry that pursues me, waking, to my breast in sleep; to have it staring at me, and clamouring for me, as soon as consciousness returns; to have it for my first-foot on New Year's day, my Valentine, my Birthday salute, my Christmas greeting, my parting with the old year. STOP THIEF!

"And to know that I *must* be stopped, come what will. To know that I am no match for this individual energy and keenness, or this organized and steady system! Come across the street, here, and, entering by a little shop, and yard, examine these intricate passages and doors, contrived for escape, flapping and counter-flapping, like the lids of the conjuror's boxes. But what avail they? Who gets in by a nod, and shows their secret working to us? Inspector Field." RP/DF

And see Fugitive—*hue and cry*

—criticized: "To tell us in open court, until it has become as trite a feature of news as the great gooseberry, that a costly police-system such as was never before heard of, has left in London, in the days of steam and gas and photographs of thieves and electric telegraphs, the sanctuaries and stews of the Stuarts! Why, a parity of practice, in all departments, would bring back the Plague in two summers, and the Druids in a century!" UT/AB

—in 1800: "The police of London were a very different body in that day; the isolated position of the suburbs, when the rage for building and the progress of improvement had not yet begun to connect them with the main body of the city and its environs, rendered many of them (and [Walworth] in particular) a place of resort for the worst and most depraved characters. Even the streets in the gayest parts of London were imperfectly lighted at that time; and such places as these were left entirely to the mercy of the moon and stars. The chances of detecting desperate characters, or of tracing them to their haunts, were thus rendered very few, and their offences naturally increased in boldness, as the consciousness of comparative security became the more impressed upon them by daily experience." SB/BV

—escorting a criminal: "It is impossible to describe how Mr Bucket gets her [Hortense] out, but he accomplishes that feat in a manner so peculiar to himself; enfolding and pervading her like a cloud, and hovering away with her as if he were a homely Jupiter, and she the object of his affections." BH 54

—French: " . . . like the old French Police—quick at detection, but very weak as a preventive power." MC 40

—inured: "This functionary [police constable], being, of course, well used to such scenes; looking upon all kinds of robbery, from petty larceny up to housebreaking or ventures on the highway, as matters in the regular course of business; and regarding the perpetrators in the light of so many customers coming to be served at the wholesale and retail shop of criminal law where he stood behind the counter; received Mr Brass's statement of facts with about as much interest and surprise, as an undertaker might evince if required to listen to a circumstantial account of the last illness of a person whom he was called in to wait upon professionally; and took Kit into custody with a decent indifference." OCS 60

—at a public meeting: " . . . pending the arrangement of the proceedings, and a fair division of the speechifying, the public in the large room were eyeing, by turns, the empty platform, and the ladies in the Music Gallery. In these amusements the greater portion of them had been occupied for a cou-

ple of hours before, and as the most agreeable diversions pall upon the taste on a too protracted enjoyment of them, the sterner spirits now began to hammer the floor with their boot-heels, and to express their dissatisfaction by various hoots and cries.

"These vocal exertions, emanating from the people who had been there longest, naturally proceeded from those who were nearest to the platform and furthest from the policemen in attendance, who having no great mind to fight their way through the crowd, but entertaining nevertheless a praiseworthy desire to do something to quell the disturbance, immediately began to drag forth by the coat tails and collars all the quiet people near the door; at the same time dealing out various smart and tingling blows with their truncheons, after the manner of that ingenious actor, Mr Punch, whose brilliant example, both in the fashion of his weapons and their use, this branch of the executive occasionally follows." ¶NN 2

—*social status of:* "'Look here at me! [said old Martin Chuzzlewit's nephew Chevy Slyme] Can you see the man of your family who has more talent in his little finger than all the rest in their united brains, dressed as a police officer without being ashamed? I took up with this trade on purpose to shame you. . . .' 'If your debauchery, and that of your chosen friends, has really brought you to this level,' returned the old man, 'keep it. You are living honestly, I hope, and that's something.'" MC 51

—*a station:* "The whitewashed room was pure white as of old, the methodical book-keeping was in peaceful progress as of old, and some distant howler was banging against a cell-door as of old. The sanctuary was not a permanent abiding-place, but a kind of criminal Pickford's. The lower passions and vices were regularly ticked off in the books, warehoused in the cells, carted away as per accompanying invoice, and left little mark upon it." OMF iv 12

The Poor, Abject

—*and animals:* "To be hustled, and jostled, and moved on; and really to feel that it would appear to be perfectly true that I have no business, here, or there, or anywhere; and yet to be perplexed by the consideration that I *am* here somehow, too, and everybody overlooked me until I became the creature that I am! It must be a strange state, not merely to be told that I am scarcely human . . . but to feel it of my own knowledge all my life! To see the horses, dogs, and cattle, go by me, and to know that in ignorance I belong to them, and not to the superior beings in my shape, whose delicacy I offend! . . .

"[Jo] goes to his crossing, and begins to lay it out for the day. The town awakes; the great tee-totum is set up for its daily spin and whirl; all that unaccountable reading and writing, which has been suspended for a few hours, recommences. Jo, and the other lower animals, get on in the unintelligible mess as they can. It is market-day. The blinded oxen, over-goaded, over-driven, never guided, run into wrong places and are beaten out; and plunge, red-eyed and foaming, at stone walls; and often sorely hurt the innocent, and often sorely hurt themselves. Very like Jo and his order; very, very like!" BH 16

—*deceptiveness of the picturesque:* " . . . maccaroni-eating at sunset, and flower-selling all day long, and begging and stealing everywhere and at all hours, you see upon the bright sea-shore, where the waves of the bay sparkle merrily. But, lovers and hunters of the picturesque, let us not keep too studiously out of view the miserable depravity, degradation, and wretchedness, with which this gay Neapolitan life is inseparably associated!

"It is not well to find Saint Giles's so repulsive, and the Porta Capuana so attractive. A pair of naked legs and a ragged red scarf, do not make *all* the difference between what is interesting and what is coarse and odious! Painting and poetising for ever, if you will, the beauties of this most beautiful and lovely spot of earth, let us, as our duty, try to associate a new picturesque with some faint recognition of man's destiny and capabilities; more hopeful, I believe, among the ice and snow of the North Pole, than in the sun and bloom of Naples." ¶PI 13

"In the closes and wynds of that picturesque place [Edinburgh slums]—I am sorry to remind you what fast friends picturesqueness and typhus often are—we saw more poverty and sickness in an hour than many people would believe in a life." S/SC

And see H:Race Meeting—*at Hampton*

—*a dying child:* "Our way [in Edinburgh] lay from one to another of the most wretched dwellings—reeking with horrible odours—shut out from the sky—shut out from the air—mere pits and dens. In a room in one of these places, where there was an empty porridge-pot on the cold hearth, with a ragged woman and some ragged children crouching on the bare ground near it—where, I remember as I speak, that very light, reflected from a high damp-stained and time-stained house wall, came trembling in, as if the fever which had shaken everything else there had shaken even it—there lay, in an old egg-box which the mother had begged from a shop, a little feeble, wasted, wan, sick child. With his little wasted face, and his little hot worn hands folded over his breast, and his little bright attentive eyes, I can see him now, as I have seen him for several years, looking steadily at us.

"There he lay in his little frail box, which was not at all a bad emblem of the little body from which he was slowly parting—there he lay, quite quiet, quite patient, saying never a word. He seldom cried, the mother said; he seldom complained; 'he lay there, seeming to wonder what it was a' aboot'. God knows I thought, as I stood looking at him, he had his reasons for wondering—reasons for wondering how it could possibly come to be that he lay there, left alone, feeble and full of pain, when he ought to have been as bright and as brisk as the birds that never got near him—reasons for wondering how he came to be left there, a little decrepit old man, pining to death, quite a thing of course, as if there were no crowds of healthy and happy children playing on the grass under the summer's sun within a stone's throw of him, as if there were no bright moving sea on the other side of the great hill overhanging the city; as if there were no great clouds rushing over it; as if there were no life, and movement, and vigour anywhere in the world—nothing but stoppage and decay.

"There he lay looking at us, saying in his silence, more pathetically than I have ever heard anything said by any orator in my life, 'Will you please to tell us what this means, strange man? and if you can give me any good reason why I should be so soon, so far advanced on my way to Him who said that children were to come into His presence, and were not to be forbidden, but who scarcely meant, that they should come by this hard road by which I am travelling—pray give that reason to me, for I seek it very earnestly and wonder about it very much'; and to my mind he has been wondering about it ever since." ¶S/SC

—*"move on":* "'He's as obstinate a young gonoph as I know. He WON'T move on.'

"'O my eye! Where can I move to!' cries the boy, clutching quite desperately at his hair, and beating his bare feet upon the floor . . . .

"'Don't you come none of that, or I shall make blessed short work of you!' says the constable, giving him a passionless shake. 'My instructions are, that you are to move on. I have told you so five hundred times.'

"'But where?' cries the boy.

"'Well! Really, constable, you know,' says Mr Snagsby wistfully . . . 'really that does seem a question. Where, you know?'

"'My instructions don't go to that,' replies the constable. 'My instructions are that this boy is to move on.'

"Do you hear, Jo? It is nothing to you or to any one else, that the great lights of the parliamentary sky have failed for some few years, in this business, to set you the example of moving on. The one grand recipe remains for you—the profound philosophical prescription—the be-all and the end-all of your strange existence upon earth. Move on! You are by no means to move off, Jo, for the great lights can't at all agree about that. Move on!" BH 19

—*music as a plea:* "That wretched woman with the infant in her arms, round whose meagre form the remnant of her own scanty shawl is carefully wrapped, has been attempting to sing some popular ballad, in the hope of wringing a few pence from the compassionate passerby.

"A brutal laugh at her weak voice is all she has gained. The tears fall thick and fast down her own pale face; the child is cold and hungry, and its low half-stifled wailing adds to the misery of its wretched mother, as she moans aloud, and sinks despairingly down, on a cold damp doorstep.

"Singing! How few of those who pass such a miserable creature as this, think of the anguish of heart, the sinking of soul and spirit, which the very effort of singing produces. Bitter mockery! Disease, neglect, and starvation, faintly articulating the words of the joyish ditty, that has enlivened your hours of feasting and merriment, God knows how often! It is no subject of jeering. The weak tremulous voice tells a fearful tale of want and famishing; and the feeble singer of this roaring song may turn away, only to die of cold and hunger." ¶SB/SN

—their neighbourhoods

—Ratcliff and Stepney: "I had been looking, yesternight, through the famous 'Dance of Death,' and to-day the grim old woodcuts arose in my mind with the new significance of a ghastly monotony not to be found in the original. The weird skeleton rattled along the streets before me, and struck fiercely; but it was never at the pains of assuming a disguise. It played on no dulcimer here, was crowned with no flowers, waved no plume, minced in no flowing robe or train, lifted no wine-cup, sat at no feast, cast no dice, counted no gold. It was simply a bare, gaunt, famished skeleton, slaying his way along.

"The borders of Ratcliff and Stepney, eastward of London, and giving on the impure river, were the scene of this uncompromising dance of death, upon a drizzling November day. A squalid maze of streets, courts, and alleys of miserable houses let out in single rooms. A wilderness of dirt, rags, and hunger. A mud-desert, chiefly inhabited by a tribe from whom employment has departed, or to whom it comes but fitfully and rarely." UT/SE

—Seven Dials: "How many people may there be in London, who, if we had brought them deviously and blindfold, to this street, fifty paces from the Station House, and within call of Saint Giles's church, would know it for a not remote part of the city in which their lives are passed? How many, who amidst this compound of sickening smells, these heaps of filth, these tumbling houses, with all their vile contents, animate and inanimate, slimily overflowing into the black road, would believe that they breathe *this* air?

"How much Red Tape may there be, that could look round on the faces which now hem us in—for our appearance here has caused a rush from all points to a common centre—the lowering foreheads, the sallow cheeks, the brutal eyes, the matted hair, the infected, vermin-haunted heaps of rags—and say, 'I have thought of this. I have not dismissed the thing. I have neither blustered it away, nor frozen it away, nor tied it up and put it away, nor smoothly said pooh, pooh! to it when it has been shown to me?'" ¶RP/DF

—overwhelmed

—dying: "I asked [Jo] to come with us, and we could take care that he had some shelter for the night.

"'I don't want no shelter,' he said; 'I can lay amongst the warm bricks.'

"'But don't you know that people die there?' replied Charley [Neckett].

"'They dies everywheres,' said the boy. 'They dies in their lodgings—she knows where; I showed her—and they dies down in Tom-all-Alone's in heaps. They dies more than they lives, according to what I see.'" BH 31

—prototype: "' . . . a creature more like a young wild beast than a young child, shivering upon a door-step . . . . A bundle of tatters, held together by a hand, in size and form almost an infant's, but, in its greedy, desperate little clutch, a bad old man's.

"A face rounded and smoothed by some half-dozen years, but pinched and twisted by the experiences of a life. Bright eyes, but not youthful. Naked feet, beautiful in their childish delicacy—ugly in the blood and dirt that cracked upon them. A baby-savage, a young monster, a child who had never been a child, a creature who might live to take the outward form of man, but who, within, would live and perish a mere beast.

"Used, already, to be worried and hunted like a beast, the boy crouched down as he was looked at, and looked back again, and interposed his arm to ward off the expected blow.

"'I'll bite,' he said, 'if you hit me!'" HM 1

"'This,' said the Phantom [to Redlaw], pointing to the boy, 'is the last, completest illustration of a human creature, utterly bereft of such remembrances as you [Redlaw] have yielded up. No softening memory of sorrow, wrong, or trouble enters here, because this wretched mortal from his birth has been abandoned to a worse condition than the beasts, and has, within his knowledge, no one contrast, no humanising touch, to make a grain of such a memory spring up in his hardened breast. All within this desolate creature is barren wilderness. All within the man bereft of what you have resigned, is the same barren wilderness. Woe to such a man! Woe, tenfold, to the nation that shall count its monsters such as this, lying here, by hundreds, and by thousands! . . .

"'There is not . . . one of these—not one—but shows a harvest that mankind MUST REAP. From every seed of evil in this boy, a field of ruin is grown that shall be gathered in, and garnered up, and sown again in many places in the world, until regions are overspread with wickedness enough to raise the waters of another Deluge. Open and unpunished murder in a city's streets would be less guilty in its daily toleration, than one such spectacle as this . . . .

"'There is not a father . . . by whose side in his daily or nightly walk, these creatures pass; there is not a mother among all the ranks of loving mothers in this land;' there is no one risen from the state of childhood, but shall be responsible in his or her degree for this enormity. There is not a country throughout the earth on which it would not bring a curse. There is no religion upon earth that it would not deny; there is no people upon earth it would not put to shame . . . ." HM 3

—slum: "Again, in these confined intolerable rooms, burrowed out like the holes of rats or the nests of insect-vermin, but fuller of intolerable smells, are crowds of sleepers, each on his foul truckle-bed coiled up beneath a rug. Halloa here! Come! Let us see you! Show your face! . . .

"Thus, we make our New Oxford Streets, and our other new streets, never heeding, never asking, where the wretches whom we clear out, crowd. With such scenes at our doors, with all the plagues of Egypt tied up with bits of cob-web in kennels so near our homes, we timorously make our Nuisance Bills and Boards of Health nonentities, and think to keep away the Wolves of Crime and Filth by our electioneering ducking to little vestrymen and our gentlemanly handling of Red Tape!" RP/DF

—spoken to: "A habit in [Allan Woodcourt] of speaking to the poor, and of avoiding patronage or condescension, or childishness (which is the favourite device, many people deeming it quite a subtlety to talk to them like little spelling books), has put him on good terms with [Jenny] easily." BH 46

—we have always with us: "Jo is brought in. He is not one of Mrs Pardiggle's Tockahoopo Indians; he is not one of Mrs Jellyby's lambs; being wholly unconnected with Borrioboola-Gha; he is not softened by distance and unfamiliarity; he is not a genuine foreign-grown savage; he is the ordinary home-made article. Dirty, ugly, disagreeable to all the senses, in body a common creature of the common streets, only in soul a heathen. Homely filth begrimes him, homely parasites devour him, homely sores are in him, homely rags are on him: native ignorance, the growth of English soil and climate, sinks his immortal nature lower than the beasts that perish. Stand forth, Jo, in uncompromising colours! From the sole of thy foot to the crown of thy head there is nothing interesting about thee." BH 47

The Poor, Working

—basically:"They are not skilled mechanics in any wise. They are but labourers—dock-labourers, water-side labourers, coal-porters, ballast-heavers, such-like hewers of wood and drawers of water. But they have come into existence, and they propagate their wretched race." UT/SE

—in bereavement: "An ugly woman, very poorly clothed, hurried in while I [Esther Summerson] was glancing at them, and coming straight up to the mother, said, 'Jenny! Jenny!' The mother rose on being so addressed, and fell upon the woman's neck.

"She also had upon her face and arms the marks of ill-usage. She had no kind of grace about her, but the grace of sympathy; but when she condoled with the woman, and her own tears fell, she wanted no beauty. I say condoled, but her only words were 'Jenny! Jenny!' All the rest was in the tone in which she said them.

"I thought it very touching to see these two women, coarse and shabby and beaten, so united; to see what they could be to one another; to see how they felt for one another; how the heart of each to each was softened by the hard trials of their lives. I think the best side of such people is almost hidden from us. What the poor are to the poor is little known, excepting to themselves and GOD." BH 8

—cleanliness: "The Right Rev. [**Dr Charles Blomfield**, Bishop of London] prelate in the chair had referred . . . to that charge frequently made, among other ill-considered charges, against the poor, that they liked to be dirty and to lead degraded lives. Now if that charge were true it would only present to [CD] another proof of our living in a very alarming and a most unnatural state of society. But it was no more true of them than that when they first had public baths they would not bathe, and that when they first had washhouses their wives would not wash. We could not expect to gather 'grapes from thorns nor figs from thistles'; and we could not be surprised if the poor were not sensible of the decencies of life when they had no opportunity of being made ac-

quainted with them. The main wonder in connexion with the poor was that they did so soon esteem what was really for their good when they had any fair experience of it." S/SA1 (third person report) *And see* S:Religion—*Missionary work—to the poor*

—dignified: "[Stephen Blackpool] was neither courtly, nor handsome, nor picturesque, in any respect; and yet his manner of accepting it, and of expressing his thanks without more words, had a grace in it that Lord Chesterfield could not have taught his son in a century." HT ii 6

—disease: " . . . the news began to spread that a pestilence had appeared among the labourers, and was slaying them by the thousands. Going forth to look about him, [Nobody] soon found this to be true. The dying and the dead were mingled in the close and tainted houses among which his life was passed. New poison was distilled into the always murky, always sickening air. The robust and the weak, old age and infancy, the father and the mother, all were stricken down alike.

"What means of flight had he? He remained there, where he was, and saw those who were dearest to him die." CS/NS

—dress: There is a dapper smartness, struggling through very limited means, about the young man, which induces one to set him down at once as a junior clerk to a tradesman or attorney. The girl no one could possibly mistake. You may tell a young woman in the employment of a large dress-maker, at any time, by a certain neatness of cheap finery and humble following of fashion which pervade her whole attire . . . . " STH/1

—education: "'And won't you give me back *my* son! said the other woman . . . 'Won't you give me back *my* son, sir, who was transported for the same offence?'

"'Was *he* deaf and dumb, woman?' asked the gentleman sternly.

"'Was he not, sir?'

"'You know he was not.'

"'He was,' cried the woman. 'He was deaf, dumb, and blind, to all that was good and right, from his cradle. Her boy may have learnt no better! where did mine learn better? where could he? who was there to teach him better, or where was it to be learnt?'

"'Peace, woman,' said the gentleman, 'your boy was in possession of all his senses.'

"'He was,' cried the mother; 'and he was the more easy to be led astray because he had them. If you save this boy because he may not know right from wrong, why did you not save mine who was never taught the difference? You gentlemen have as good a right to punish her boy, that God has kept in ignorance of sound and speech, as you have to punish mine, that you kept in ignorance yourselves. How many of the girls and boys—ah, men and women too—that are brought before you, and you don't pity, are deaf and dumb in their minds, and go wrong in that state, and are punished in that state, body and soul, while you gentlemen are quarrelling among yourselves whether they ought to learn this or that?—Be a just man, sir, and give me back my son.'" OCS 45

—epidemic: "[Nobody] was at work again, solitary and sad, when his Master came and stood near to him dressed in black. He, also, had suffered heavily. His young wife, his beautiful and good young wife, was dead; so, too, his only child.

"'Master, 'tis hard to bear—I know it—but be comforted. I would give you comfort, if I could.'

"The Master thanked him from his heart, but, said he, 'O you labouring men! The calamity began among you. If you had but lived more healthily and decently, I should not be the widowed and bereft mourner that I am this day.... O you labouring men! How seldom do we ever hear of you, except in connexion with some trouble!'

"'Master,' he replied, 'I am Nobody, and little likely to be heard of (nor yet much wanted to be heard of, perhaps), except when there is some trouble. But it never begins with me, and it never can end with me. As sure as Death, it comes down to me, and it goes up from me.'

"There was so much reason in what he said, that the Bigwig family, getting wind of it, and being horribly frightened by the late desolation, resolved to unite with him to do the things that were right—at all events, so far as the said things were associated with the direct prevention, humanly speaking, of another pestilence.

"But, as their fear wore off, which it soon began to do, they resumed their falling out among themselves, and did nothing. Consequently the scourge appeared again—low down as before—and spread avengingly upward as before, and carried off vast numbers of the brawlers. But not a man among them ever admitted, if in the least degree he ever perceived, that he had anything to do with it." CS/NS

—exhaustion: " . . . unfortunately there are other tokens [besides dress] not to be misunderstood—the pale face with its hectic bloom, the slight distortion of form which no artifice of dress can wholly conceal, the unhealthy stoop, and the short cough—the effects of hard work and close application to a sedentary employment, upon a tender frame . . . .

"I would to God, that the iron-hearted man who would deprive such people as these of their only pleasures [by enactment of the Sabbath Bill], could feel the sinking of heart and soul, the wasting exhaustion of mind and body, the utter prostration of present strength and future hope, attendant upon that incessant toil which lasts from day to day, and from month to month; that toil which is too often protracted until the silence of midnight, and resumed with the first stir of morning." STH/1

—factory hands: "For the first time in her life Louisa had come into one of the dwellings of the Coketown Hands; for the first time in her life she was face to face with anything like individuality in connexion with them. She knew of their existence by hundreds and by thousands. She knew what results in work a given number of them would produce in a given space of time. She knew them in crowds passing to and from their nests, like ants or beetles. But she knew from her reading infinitely more of the ways of toiling insects than of these toiling men and women.

"Something to be worked so much and paid so much, and there ended; something to be infallibly settled by laws of supply and demand; something that blundered against those laws, and floundered into difficulty; something that was a little pinched when wheat was dear, and over-ate itself when wheat was cheap; something that increased at such a rate of percentage, and yielded such another percentage of crime, and such another percentage of pauperism; something wholesale, of which vast fortunes were made; something that occasionally rose like a sea, and did some harm and waste (chiefly to itself), and fell again; this she knew the Coketown Hands to be. But, she had scarcely thought more of separating them into units, than of separating the sea itself into its component drops." HT ii 6

—habitation: "Great heaps of ashes; stagnant pools, overgrown with rank grass and duckweed; broken turnstiles; and the upright posts of palings long since carried off for firewood, which menaced all heedless walkers with their jagged and rusty nails, were the leading features of the landscape; while here and there a donkey, or a ragged horse, tethered to a stake, and cropping off a wretched meal from the coarse, stunted turf, were quite in keeping with the scene, and would have suggested (if the houses had not done so sufficiently, of themselves) how very poor the people were who lived in the crazy huts adjacent, and how foolhardy it might prove for one who carried money, or wore decent clothes, to walk that way alone, unless by daylight.

"Poverty has its whims and shows of taste, as wealth has. Some of these cabins were turreted, some had false windows painted on their rotten walls; one had a mimic clock, upon a crazy tower of four feet high, which screened the chimney; each in its little patch of ground had a rude seat or arbour. The population dealt in bones, in rags, in broken glass, in old wheels, in birds, and dogs. These, in their several ways of stowage, filled the gardens; and shedding a perfume, not of the most delicious nature, in the air, filled it besides with yells, and screams, and howling." BR 44

—heroic: "Cant as we may, and as we shall to the end of all things, it is very much harder for the poor to be virtuous than it is for the rich; and the good that is in them, shines the brighter for it.

"In many a noble mansion lives a man, the best of husbands and of fathers, whose private worth in both capacities is justly lauded to the skies. But bring him here, upon this crowded deck [bearing emigrants to Canada]. Strip from his fair young wife her silken dress and jewels, unbind her braided hair, stamp early wrinkles on her brow, pinch her pale cheek with care and much privation, array her faded form in coarsely patched attire, let there be nothing but his love to set her forth or deck her out, and you shall put it to the proof indeed.

"So change his station in the world, that he shall see in those young things who climb upon his knee: not records of his wealth and name: but little wrestlers with him for his daily bread; so many poachers on his scanty meal; so many units to divide his every sum of comfort, and farther to reduce its small amount.

"In lieu of the endearments of childhood in its sweetest aspect, heap upon him all its pains and wants, its sicknesses and ills, its fretfulness, caprice, and querulous endurance: let its prattle be, not of engaging infant fancies, but of cold, and thirst, and hunger: and if his fatherly affection outlive all this, and he be patient, watchful, tender; careful of his children's lives, and mindful always of their joys and sorrows; then send him back to Parliament, and Pulpit, and to Quarter Sessions, and when he hears fine talk of the depravity of those who live from hand to mouth, and labour hard to do it, let him speak up, as one who knows, and tell those holders forth that they, by parallel with such a class, should be High Angels in their daily lives, and lay but humble siege to Heaven at last.

"Which of us shall say what he would be, if such realities with small relief or change all through his days, were his! Looking round upon these people: far from home, houseless, indigent, wandering, weary with travel and hard living: and seeing how patiently they nursed and tended their young children: how they consulted ever their wants first, then half supplied their own; what gentle ministers of hope and faith the women were; how the men profited by their example; and how very, very seldom even a moment's petulance or harsh complaint broke out among them: I felt a stronger love and honour of my kind come glowing on my heart, and wished to God there had been many Atheists in the better part of human nature there, to read this simple lesson in the book of Life." ¶AN 15

—household affections: ". . . if ever household affections and loves are graceful things, they are graceful in the poor. The ties that bind the wealthy and the proud to home may be forged on earth, but those which link the poor man to his humble hearth are of the true metal and bear the stamp of Heaven.

"The man of high descent may love the halls and lands of his inheritance as a part of himself, as trophies of his birth and power; his associations with them are associations of pride and wealth and triumph; the poor man's attachment to the tenement he holds, which strangers have held before, and may to-morrow occupy again, has a worthier root, struck deep into a purer soil.

"His household gods are of flesh and blood, with no alloy of silver, gold or precious stone; he has no property but in the affections of his own heart; and when they endear bare floors and walls, despite of rags and toil and scanty meals, that man has his love of home from God, and his rude hut becomes a solemn place.

"Oh! if those who rule the destinies of nations would but remember this—if they would but think how hard it is for the very poor to have engendered in their hearts that love of home from which all domestic virtues spring, when they live in dense and squalid masses where social decency is lost, or rather never found—if they would but turn aside from the wide thoroughfares and great houses, and strive to improve the wretched dwellings in bye-ways where only Poverty may walk—many low roofs would point more truly to the sky, than the loftiest steeple that now rears proudly up from the midst of guilt, and crime, and horrible disease, to mock them by its contrast.

"In hollow voices from Workhouse, Hospital, and Jail, this truth is preached from day to day, and has been proclaimed for years. It is no light matter—no outcry from the working vulgar, no mere question of the people's health and comforts that may be whistled down on Wednesday nights." ¶OCS 38

—patriotism: "In love of home, the love of country has its rise; and who are truer patriots or the best in time of need—those who venerate the land, owning its wood, and stream, and earth, and all that they produce? or those who love their country, boasting not a foot of ground in all its wide domain?" OCS 38

"If you were ever in the Belgian villages near the field of Waterloo, you will have seen, in some quiet little church, a monument erected by faithful companions in arms to the memory of Colonel A, Major B, Captains C, D and E, Lieutenants F and G, Ensigns H, I and J, seven non-commissioned officers, and one hundred and thirty rank and file, who fell in the discharge of their duty on the memorable day.

"The story of Nobody is the story of the rank and file of the earth. They bear their share of the battle; they have their part in the victory; they fall; they leave no name but in the mass. The march of the proudest of us, leads to the dusty way by which they go. O! Let us think of them this year at the Christmas fire, and not forget them when it is burnt out." CS/NS

But see CD:The Poor—*fear of uprising*

—*recreation*

—*in idleness:* "In addition to the numerous groups who are idling about the ginshops and squabbling in the centre of the road, every post in the open space has its occupant, who leans against it for hours, with listless perseverance. It is odd enough that one class of men in London appear to have no enjoyment beyond leaning against posts.

"We never saw a regular bricklayer's labourer take any other recreation, fighting excepted. Pass through St Giles's in the evening of a week-day, there they are in their fustian dresses, spotted with brick-dust and whitewash, leaning against posts. Walk through Seven Dials on Sunday morning: there they are again, drab or light corduroy trousers, Blucher boots, blue coats, and great yellow waistcoats, leaning against posts. The idea of a man dressing himself in his best clothes, to lean against a post all day!" ¶SB/SD

—*needed:* " . . . he looked about him on his Sundays and holidays, and he saw how much monotony and weariness there was, and thence how drunkenness arose with all its train of ruin. Then he appeared to the Bigwig family, and said, 'We are a labouring people, and I have a glimmering suspicion in me that labouring people of whatever condition were made—by a higher intelligence than yours, as I poorly understand it—to be in need of mental refreshment and recreation. See what we fall into, when we rest without it. Come! Amuse me harmlessly, show me something, give me an escape!

"But here the Bigwig family fell into a state of uproar absolutely deafening. When some few voices were faintly heard, proposing to show him the wonders of the world, the greatness of creation, the mighty changes of time, the workings of nature and the beauties of art—to show him these things, that is to say, at any period of his life when he could look upon them—there arose among the Bigwigs such roaring and raving, such pulpiting and petitioning, such maundering and memorialising, such name-calling and dirt-throwing, such a shrill wind of parliamentary questioning and feeble replying—where 'I dare not' waited on 'I would'—that the poor fellow stood aghast, staring wildly around.

"'Have I provoked all this,' said he, with his hands to his affrighted ears, 'by what was meant to be an innocent request, plainly arising out of my familiar experience, and the common knowledge of all men who choose to open their eyes? I don't understand, and I am not understood. What is to come of such a state of things?" CS/NS *And see* H:Recreation—*needed*

"That these Sunday [preaching] meetings in Theatres are good things, I do not doubt. Nor do I doubt that they will work lower and lower down in the social scale, if those who preside over them will be very careful on two heads: firstly, not to disparage the places in which they speak, or the intelligence of their hearers; secondly, not to set themselves in antagonism to the natural inborn desire of the mass of mankind to recreate themselves and to be amused." UT/TV

—*paltry:* "Fearful to relate, there was even a sort of little Fair in the village. Some despairing gingerbread that had been vainly trying to dispose of itself all over the country, and had cast a quantity of dust upon its head in its mortification, again appealed to the public from an infirm booth.

"So did a heap of nuts, long, long, exiled from Barcelona, and yet speaking English so indifferently as to call fourteen of themselves a pint. A peep-show which had originally started with the Battle of Waterloo, and had since made it every other battle of later date by altering the Duke of Wellington's nose, tempted the student of illustrated history.

"A Fat Lady, perhaps in part sustained upon postponed pork, her professional associate being a Learned Pig, displayed her life-size picture in a low dress, as she appeared when presented at Court, several yards round. All this was a vicious spectacle, as any poor idea of amusement on the part of the rougher hewers of wood and drawers of water in this land of England ever is and shall be.

"They *must not* vary the rheumatism with amusement. They may vary it with fever and ague, or with as many rheumatic variations as they have joints; but positively not with entertainment after their own manner." ¶OMF iv 6

—*reliability:* " . . . whenever the working classes enjoy an opportunity of effectually rebutting accusations which falsehood or thoughtlessness have brought against them, they always avail themselves of it, and show themselves in their true characters . . . any number of thousands of persons of the humblest condition of life in this country, can pass through [the] National Gallery, or the British Museum, in seasons of holiday making, without damaging in the slightest degree, the smallest rarity, in either wonderful collection." S/BP

—religion: "'Jo! Did you ever know a prayer [asked Allan Woodcourt]?'

"'Never knowd nothink, sir.'

"'Not so much as one short prayer?

"'No, sir. Nothink at all. Mr Chadbands he wos a-prayin wunst at Mr Sangsby's and I heerd him, but he sounded as if he wos a-speakin to hisself, and not to me. He prayed a lot, but *I* couldn't make out nothink on it. Different times, there was other genlmen come down Tom-all-Alone's a-prayin, but they all mostly sed as the t'other wuns prayed wrong, and all mostly sounded to be a-talkin to theirselves, or a-passin blame on the t'others, and not a-talkin to us. We never knowd nothink. I never knowd what it wos all about.'" BH 47

"A kind preacher came to [Nobody], and would have said some prayers to soften his heart in his gloom, but he replied:

"'O what avails it, missionary, to come to me, a man condemned to residence in this fœtid place, where every sense bestowed upon me for my delight becomes a torment, and where every minute of my numbered days is new mire added to the heap under which I lie oppressed!

"'But, give me my first glimpse of Heaven, through a little of its light and air; give me pure water; help me to be clean; lighten this heavy atmosphere and heavy life, in which our spirits sink, and we become the indifferent and callous creatures you too often see us; gently and kindly take the bodies of those who die among us, out of the small room where we grow to be so familiar with the awful change that even ITS sanctity is lost to us; and, Teacher, then I will hear—none know better than you, how willingly—of Him whose thoughts were so much with the poor, and who had compassion for all human sorrow!'" CS/NS

"That the crowning miracle of all the miracles summed up in the New Testament, after the miracle of the blind seeing, and the lame walking, and the restoration of the dead to life, was the miracle that the poor had the Gospel preached to them. That while the poor were unnaturally and unnecessarily cut off by the thousand, in the prematurity of their age, or in the rottenness of their youth—for of flower or blossom such youth has none—the Gospel was NOT preached to them, saving in hollow and unmeaning voices. That of all wrongs, this was the first mighty wrong the Pestilence warned us to set right." RP/BL

—subsistence: "'Such work, such work! So many hours, so many days, so many long, long nights of hopeless, cheerless, never-ending work—not to heap up riches, not to live grandly or gaily, not to live upon enough, however coarse; but to earn bare bread; to scrape together just enough to toil upon, and want upon, and keep alive in us the consciousness of our hard fate! Oh Meg [Veck], Meg!' [Lilian Fern] raised her voice and twined her arms about her as she spoke, like one in pain. 'How can the cruel world go round, and bear to look upon such lives?'" C 3

—in a trap: "'Now, gentlemen,' said Will Fern, holding out his hands, and flushing for an instant in his haggard face, 'see how your laws are made to trap and hunt us when we're brought to this. I tries to live elsewhere. And I'm a vagabond. To jail with him! I comes back here. I goes a-nutting in your woods, and breaks—who don't—a limber branch or two. To jail with him!

"One of your keepers sees me in the broad day, near my own patch of garden, with a gun. To jail with him! I has a nat'ral angry word with that man, when I'm free again. To jail with him! I cuts a stick. To jail with him! I eats a rotten apple or a turnip. To jail with him! It's twenty mile away; and coming back I begs a trifle on the road. To jail with him! At last, the constable, the keeper—anybody—finds me anywhere, a-doing anything. To jail with him, for he's a vagrant, and jail-bird known; and jail's the only home he's got.

"The Alderman [Cute] nodded sagaciously, as who should say, 'A very good home too!'

"'Do I say this to serve MY cause?' cried Fern. 'Who can give me back my liberty, who can give me back my good name, who can give me back my innocent niece? Not all the Lords and Ladies in wide England.

"'But, gentlemen, gentlemen, dealing with other men like me, begin at the right end. Give us, in mercy, better homes when we're a-lying in our cradles; give us better food when we're a-working for our lives; give us kinder laws to bring us back when we're a-going wrong; and don't set Jail, Jail, Jail, afore us, everywhere we turn.

"'There an't a condescension you can show the Labourer then, that he won't take, as ready and as grateful as a man can be; for he has a patient, peaceful, willing heart. But you must put his rightful spirit in him first; for whether he's a wreck and ruin such as me, or is like one of them that stand here now, his spirit is divided from you at this time.

"'Bring it back, gentlefolks, bring it back! Bring it back, afore the day comes when even his Bible changes in his altered mind, and the words seem to him to read, as they have sometimes read in my own eyes—in Jail: "Whither thou goest, I can Not go; where thou lodgest, I do Not lodge; thy people are Not my people; Nor thy God my God!"'" ¶C 3

—and the Underclass: "And now let me close this terrible account with a redeeming and beautiful trait of the poorest of the poor. When we came out of the Workhouse, we had gone across the road to a public-house, finding ourselves without silver, to get change for a sovereign. I held the money in my hand while I was speaking to the five apparitions.

"Our being so engaged attracted the attention of many people of the very poor sort usual to that place; as we leaned over the mounds of rags, they eagerly leaned over us to see and hear; what I had in my hand, and what I said, and what I did, must have been plain to nearly all the concourse. When the last of the five had got up and faded away, the spectators opened to let us pass; and not one of them, by word, or look, or gesture, begged of us.

"Many of the observant faces were quick enough to know that it would have been a relief to us to have got rid of the rest of the money with any hope of doing good with it. But there was a feeling among them all, that their necessities were not to be placed by the side of such a spectacle; and they opened a way for us in profound silence, and let us go." ¶HW/SL

"No one who had any experience of the poor could fail to be deeply affected by their patience, by their sympathy with one another, and by the beautiful alacrity with which they helped each other in toil, in the day of suffering, and at the hour of death. It hardly ever happened that any case of extreme protracted destitution found its way into the public prints without our reading at the same time of some ragged Samaritan sharing his last loaf or spending his last penny to relieve the poor miserable in the little room upstairs, or in the cellar underground." S/SA1 (third person report)

—and the upper classes: "'I have begun to understand a little that most calamities will come from us, as this one did, and that none will stop at our poor doors, until we are united with that great squabbling family yonder, to do the things that are right.

"We cannot live healthily and decently, unless they who undertook to manage us provide the means. We cannot be instructed unless they will teach us; we cannot be rationally amused, unless they will amuse us; we cannot but have some false gods of our own, while they set up so many of theirs in all the public places.

"The evil consequences of imperfect instruction, the evil consequences of pernicious neglect, the evil consequences of unnatural restraint and the denial of humanising enjoyments, will all come from us, and none of them will stop with us. They will spread far and wide. They always do; they always have done . . . .'" ¶CS/NS

—visited: "'I wants it done and over [said the bricklayer]. I wants a end of these liberties took with my place. I wants a end of being drawed like a badger. Now you're a-going to poll-pry and question according to custom—I know what you're a-going to be up to. Well! You haven't got no occasion to be up to it.

"'I'll save you the trouble. Is my daughter a-washin? Yes, she is a-washin. Look at the water. Smell it! That's wot we drinks. How do you like it, and what do you think of gin, instead! An't my place dirty? Yes, it is dirty—it's nat'rally dirty, and it's nat'rally onwholesome; and we've had five dirty and onwholesome children, as is all dead infants, and so much the better for them, and for us besides.

"'Have I read the little book wot you left? No, I an't read the little book wot you left. There an't nobody here as knows how to read it; and if there wos, it wouldn't be suitable to me. It's a book fit for a babby, and I'm not a babby. If you was to leave me a doll, I shouldn't nuss it.

"'How have I been conducting of myself?

Why, I've been drunk for three days; and I'd a been drunk four, if I'd a had the money. Don't I never mean for to go to church? No, I don't never mean for to go to church. I shouldn't be expected there, if I did; the beadle's too genteel for me. And how did my wife get that black eye? Why, I giv' it her; and if she says I didn't, she's a Lie!'

"He had pulled his pipe out of his mouth to say all this, and he now turned over on his other side, and smoked again. Mrs Pardiggle, who had been regarding him through her spectacles with a forcible composure, calculated, I could not help thinking, to increase his antagonism, pulled out a good book, as if it were a constable's staff, and took the whole family into custody. I mean into religious custody, of course; but she really did it, as if she were an inexorable moral Policeman carrying them all off to a station-house." ¶BH 8

"Knowing that I could compensate myself thereafter for my self-denial, if I saw fit, I had resolved that I would give nothing in the course of these visits. I did this to try the people. I may state at once that my closest observation could not detect any indication whatever of an expectation that I would give money: they were grateful to be talked to about their miserable affairs, and sympathy was plainly a comfort to them; but they neither asked for money in any case, nor showed the least trace of surprise or disappointment or resentment at my giving none." UT/SE

—*virtue:* "I believe that Virtue shows quite as well in rags and patches as she does in purple and fine linen. I believe that she and every beautiful object in external nature, claim some sympathy in the breast of the poorest man who breaks his scanty loaf of daily bread. I believe that she goes barefoot as well as shod. I believe that she dwells rather oftener in alleys and by-ways than she does in courts and palaces, and that it is good, and pleasant, and profitable to track her out, and follow her. I believe that to lay one's hand upon some one of those rejected ones whom the world has too long forgotten, and too often mis-used, and to say to the proudest and most thoughtless—these creatures have the same elements and capacities of goodness as yourselves, they are moulded in the same form, and made of the same clay; and though ten times worse than you, may, in having retained anything of their original nature amidst the trials and distresses of their condition, be really ten times better." S/B1

—*work, and reward:* "They was all hard up there [in Bleeding Heart Yard], Mr Plornish said, uncommon hard up, to be sure. Well, he couldn't say how it was; he didn't know as anybody *could* say how it was; all he know'd was, that so it was. When a man felt, on his back and in his own belly, that poor he was, that man (Mr Plornish gave it as his decided belief) know'd well that he was poor somehow or another, and you couldn't talk it out of him, no more than you could talk Beef into him.

"Then you see, some people as was better off said, and a good many such people lived pretty close up to the mark themselves if not beyond it so he'd heerd, that they was 'improvident' (that was the favourite word) down the Yard. For instance, if they see a man with his wife and children going to Hampton Court in a Wan, perhaps once in a year, they says, 'Hallo! I thought you was poor, my improvident friend!' Why, Lord, how hard it was upon a man! What was a man to do? He couldn't go mollancholly mad, and even if he did, you wouldn't be the better for it. In Mr Plornish's judgment you would be the worse for it.

"Yet you seemed to want to make a man mollancholly mad. You was always at it—if not with your right hand, with your left. What was they a doing in the Yard? Why, take a look at 'em and see. There was the girls and their mothers a working at their sewing, or their shoe-binding, or their trimming, or their waistcoat making, day and night and night and day, and not more than able to keep body and soul together after all—often not so much. There was people of pretty well all sorts of trades you could name, all wanting to work, and yet not able to get it. There was old people, after working all their lives, going and being shut up in the workhouse, much worse fed and lodged and treated altogether, than—Mr Plornish said manufacturers, but appeared to mean malefactors.

"Why, a man didn't know where to turn himself, for a crumb of comfort. As to who was to blame for it, Mr Plornish didn't know who was to blame for it. He could tell you who suffered, but he couldn't tell you whose fault it was. It wasn't *his* place to find out, and who'd mind what he said, if he did find out? He only know'd that it wasn't put right by them what undertook that line of business, and that it didn't come right of itself. And in brief his illogical opinion was, that if you couldn't do nothing for him, you had better take nothing from him for doing of it; so far as he could make out, that was about what it come to." ¶LD i 12

Poor-house and Poor Law

—administration: "[Meg Veck] dressed the child next morning with unusual care . . . and once more tried to find some means of life. It was the last day of the Old Year. She tried till night, and never broke her fast. She tried in vain.

"She mingled with an abject crowd, who tarried in the snow, until it pleased some officer appointed to dispense the public charity (the lawful charity; not that once preached upon a Mount), to call them in, and question them, and say to this one, 'Go to such a place,' to that one, 'Come next week;' to make a football of another wretch, and pass him here and there, from hand to hand, from house to house, until he wearied and lay down to die; or started up and robbed, and so became a higher sort of criminal, whose claims allowed of no delay. Here, too, she failed." C 4

—clients: "And what was very curious, was, that these dim old women had one company notion which was the fashion of the [workhouse]. Every old woman who became aware of a visitor and was not in bed hobbled over a form into her accustomed seat, and became one of a line of dim old women confronting another line of dim old women across a narrow table. There was no obligation whatever upon them to range themselves in this way; it was their manner of 'receiving.' As a rule, they made no attempt to talk to one another, or to look at the visitor, or to look at anything, but sat silently working their mouths, like a sort of poor old Cows." UT/WW

And see A:Old Age—*workhouse*

—dreaded: "'The Poor-house?' said the Secretary.

"Mrs Higden set that resolute old face of hers, and darkly nodded yes.

"'You dislike the mention of it.'

"'Dislike the mention of it?' answered the old woman. 'Kill me sooner than take me there. Throw this pretty child under cart-horses' feet and a loaded waggon, sooner than take him there. Come to us and find us all a-dying, and set a light to us all where we lie, and let us all blaze away with the house into a heap of cinders, sooner than move a corpse of us there!'

"A surprising spirit in this lonely woman after so many years of hard working and hard living, my Lords and Gentlemen and Honourable Boards! What is it that we call it in our grandiose speeches? British independence, rather perverted? Is that, or something like it, the ring of the cant?

"'Do I never read in the newspapers,' said the dame, fondling the child—'God help me and the like of me!—how the worn-out people that do come down to that, get driven from post to pillar, and pillar to post, a-purpose to tire them out! Do I never read how they are put off, put off, put off—how they are grudged, grudged, grudged the shelter, or the doctor, or the drop of physic, or the bit of bread? Do I never read how they grow heartsick of it and give it up, after having let themselves drop so low, and how they after all die out for want of help? Then I say, I hope I can die as well as another, and I'll die without that disgrace.'

"Absolutely impossible, my Lords and Gentlemen and Honourable Boards, by any stretch of legislative wisdom to set these perverse people right in their logic?" OMF i 16

"To conceal herself in sickness, like a lower animal; to creep out of sight and coil herself away and die, had become this woman [Betty Higden]'s instinct. To catch up in her arms the sick child who was dear to her, and hide it as if it were a criminal, and keep off all ministration but such as her own ignorant tenderness and patience could supply, had become this woman's idea of maternal love, fidelity, and duty.

"The shameful accounts we read, every week in the Christian year, my lords and gentlemen and honourable boards, the infamous records of small official inhumanity, do not pass by the people as they pass by us. And hence these irrational, blind, and obstinate prejudices, so astonishing to our magnificence, and having no more reason in them—God save the Queen and Con-found their politics—no, than smoke has in coming from fire!" ¶OMF ii 8

"My lords and gentlemen and honourable boards, when you in the course of your dust-shovelling and cinder-raking have piled up a mountain of pretentious failure, you must off with your honourable coats for the removal of it, and fall to the work with the power of all the queen's horses and all the queen's men, or it will come rushing down and bury us alive.

"Yes, verily, my lords and gentlemen and honourable boards, adapting your Catechism to the occasion, and by God's help so you must. For when we have got things to the pass that with an enormous treasure at disposal to relieve the poor, the best of the poor detest our mercies, hide their heads from us, and shame us by starving to death in the midst of us, it is a pass impossible of prosperity, impossible of continuance.

"It may not be so written in the Gospel according to Podsnappery; you may not 'find these words' for the text of a sermon, in the Returns of the Board of Trade; but they have been the truth since the foundations of the universe were laid, and they will be the truth until the foundations of the universe are shaken by the Builder.

"This boastful handiwork of ours, which fails in its terrors for the professional pauper, the sturdy breaker of windows and the rampant tearer of clothes, strikes with a cruel and a wicked stab at the stricken sufferer, and is a horror to the deserving and unfortunate. We must mend it, lords and gentlemen and honourable boards, or in its own evil hour it will mar every one of us." ¶OMF iii 8

" . . . the old abhorrence grew stronger on [Betty Higden] as she grew weaker, and it found more sustaining food than she did in her wanderings. Now, she would light upon the shameful spectacle of some desolate creature—or some wretched ragged groups of either sex, or of both sexes, with children among them, huddled together like the smaller vermin, for a little warmth—lingering and lingering on a doorstep, while the appointed evader of the public trust did his dirty office of trying to weary them out and so get rid of them.

"Now, she would light upon some poor decent person, like herself, going afoot on a pilgrimage of many weary miles to see some worn-out relative or friend who had been charitably clutched off to a great blank barren Union House, as far from old home as the County Jail . . . and in its dietary, and in its lodging, and in its tending of the sick, a much more penal establishment . . . .

"This is not to be received as a figure of speech. Old Betty Higden, however tired, however footsore, would start up and be driven away by her awakened horror of falling into the hands of Charity. It is a remarkable Christian improvement, to have made a pursuing Fury of the Good Samaritan; but it was so in this case, and it is a type of many, many, many." ¶OMF iii 8 *And see* S:Self-reliance

"'Have you nothing by you to eat but the piece of bread I see there?'

"'Nothing. And we had the rest of the loaf for our breakfast, with water. I don't know what's to come of it.'

"'Have you no prospect of improvement?'

"'If my eldest son earns anything to-day, he'll bring it home. Then we shall have something to eat to-night, and may be able to do something towards the rent. If not, I don't know what's to come of it.' . . . .

"These people had a mortal dread of entering the work-house, and received no out-of-door relief." UT/SE *And see* Homeless

—food: "'A MEMBER begged to be informed whether it would be possible to administer—say, the twentieth part of a grain of bread and cheese to all grown-up paupers, and the fortieth part to children, with the same satisfying effect as their present allowance.

"'PROFESSOR MUFF was willing to stake his professional reputation on the perfect adequacy of such a quantity of food to the support of human life—in workhouses; the addition of the fifteenth part of a grain of pudding twice a week would render it a high diet." B/M1

—the infirm: "Groves of babies in arms; groves of mothers and other sick women in bed; groves of lunatics; jungles of men in stone-paved down-stairs day-rooms, waiting for their dinners; longer and longer groves of old people, in up-stairs Infirmary wards, wearing out life, God knows how . . . .

"In all these Long Walks of aged and infirm, some old people were bed-ridden, and had been for a long time; some were sitting on their beds half-naked; some dying in their beds; some out of bed, and sitting at a table near the fire. A sullen or lethargic indifference to what was asked, a blunted sensibility to everything but warmth and food, a moody absence of complaint as being of no use, a dogged silence and resentful desire to be left alone again, I thought were generally apparent." RP/WW

Power

—aristocratic, pre-1789: "'We were so robbed by that man who stands there, as all we common dogs are by those superior Beings—taxed by him without mercy,

obliged to work for him without pay, obliged to grind our corn at his mill, obliged to feed scores of his tame birds on our wretched crops, and forbidden for our lives to keep a single tame bird of our own, pillaged and plundered to that degree that when we chanced to have a bit of meat, we ate it in fear, with the door barred and the shutters closed, that his people should not see it and take it from us—I say, we were so robbed, and hunted, and were made so poor, that our father told us it was a dreadful thing to bring a child into the world, and that what we should most pray for, was, that our women might be barren and our miserable race die out!'" TTC iii 10

"'You know, Doctor [Manette], that it is among the Rights of these Nobles to harness us common dogs to carts, and drive us . . . that it is among their Rights to keep us in their grounds all night, quieting the frogs, in order that their noble sleep may not be disturbed.'" TTC iii 10

—its attraction: "Power (unless it be the power of intellect or virtue) has ever the greatest attraction for the lowest natures; and the mere defiance of the unconscious house-front, with his power to strip the roof off the inhabiting family like the roof of a house of cards, was a treat which had a charm for Silas Wegg." OMF iii 7

—cruelty and retribution: "Oh! if when we oppress and grind our fellow-creatures, we bestowed but one thought on the dark evidences of human error, which, like dense and heavy clouds, are rising, slowly it is true, but not less surely, to Heaven, to pour their after-vengeance on our heads; if we heard but one instant, in imagination, the deep testimony of dead men's voices, which no power can stifle, and no pride shut out; where would be the injury and injustice, the suffering, misery, cruelty, and wrong, that each day's life brings with it!" OT 30

—despotism: it's 'demise': "The endurance of despotism is one great distinguishing mark of a savage always. The improving world has quite got the better of that too." RP/NS

—exploitation: "'[Laura Bridgman, deaf, dumb and blind] chooses for her friends and companions, those children who are intelligent, and talk best with her; and she evidently dislikes to be with those who are deficient in intellect, unless, indeed, she can make them serve her purposes, which she is evidently inclined to do. She takes advantage of them, and makes them wait upon her, in a manner that she knows she could not exact of others; and in various ways shows her Saxon blood.'" AN 3

—to make happy "'A small matter,' said the Ghost, 'to make these silly folks so full of gratitude.'

"'Small!' echoed Scrooge . . . .

"'Why! Is it not? He has spent but a few pounds of your mortal money: three or four perhaps. Is that so much that he deserves this praise?'

"'It isn't that,' said Scrooge, heated by the remark, and speaking unconsciously like his former, not his latter, self. 'It isn't that, Spirit. He has the power to render us happy or unhappy; to make our service light or burdensome; a pleasure or a toil. Say that his power lies in words and looks; in things so slight and insignificant that it is impossible to add and count 'em up: what then? The happiness he gives, is quite as great as if it cost a fortune.'

"He felt the Spirit's glance, and stopped." CC 2

And see S:Will—*and power*

Prison

—absence of green: "It was a large prison, with many courts and passages so like one another, and so uniformly paved, that I seemed to gain a new comprehension, as I passed along, of the fondness that solitary prisoners, shut up among the same staring walls from year to year, have had—as I have read—for a weed, or a stray blade of grass. In an arched room by himself, like a cellar upstairs: with walls so glaringly white, that they made the massive iron window-bars and iron-bound door even more profoundly black than they were: we found the trooper [Mr George] standing in a corner." BH 52

—before trial: "'Must go before the magistrate now, sir . . . . His worship will be disengaged in half a minute. Now, young gallows!'

"This was an invitation for Oliver [Twist] to enter through a door which he unlocked as he spoke, and which led into a stone cell. Here he was searched; and nothing being found upon him, locked up.

"This cell was in shape and size something like an area cellar, only not so light. It was most intolerably dirty; for it was Monday morning; and it had been tenanted by six drunken people, who had been locked up, elsewhere, since Saturday night. But this is little. In our station-houses, men and women are every night confined on the most trivial *charges* —the word is worth noting—in dungeons, compared with which, those in Newgate, occupied by the most atrocious felons, tried, found guilty, and under sentence of death, are palaces. Let any one who doubts this, compare the two." OT 11

—essential ingredient: ". . . one of the first essentials and requirements of a well-regulated Prison is, that its inmates should be worse off in every imaginable respect than the bulk of honest paupers and honest labouring men. Taking every precaution to ensure the cleanliness and health of criminals—for it is of great importance to society that they should not engender disease—I require that their condition shall, in no particular, present a favorable comparison with the pauper's or the labourer's. Let it do so under any system, and I call that system, however plausible in theory, a manifestly false and absurd one in its practical operation." HWC/IJ

—French: "In Marseilles that day there was a villainous prison. In one of its chambers, so repulsive a place that even the obtrusive stare [of the sun] blinked at it, and left it to such refuse of reflected light as it could find for itself, were two men. Besides the two men, a notched and disfigured bench, immovable from the wall, with a draught-board rudely hacked upon it with a knife, a set of draughts, made of old buttons and soup bones, a set of dominoes, two mats, and two or three wine bottles. That was all the chamber held, exclusive of rats and other unseen vermin, in addition to the seen vermin, the two men.

"It received such light as it got, through a grating of iron bars, fashioned like a pretty large window, by means of which it could be always inspected from the gloomy staircase on which the grating gave. There was a broad strong ledge of stone to this grating, where the bottom of it was let into the masonry, three or four feet above the ground. . . .

"A prison taint was on everything there. The imprisoned air, the imprisoned light, the imprisoned damps, the imprisoned men, were all deteriorated by confinement. As the captive men were faded and haggard, so the iron was rusty, the stone was slimy, the wood was rotten, the air was faint, the light was dim. Like a well, like a vault, like a tomb, the prison had no knowledge of the brightness outside; and would have kept its polluted atmosphere intact, in one of the spice islands of the Indian ocean." LD i 1

—hard labour: ". . . I think it right and necessary that there should be in jails some degraded kind of hard and irksome work, belonging only to jails . . . . What kind of work does the determined thief, or the determined swindler, or the determined vagrant, most abhor? Find me that work; and to it, in preference to any other, I set that man relentlessly . Now, I make bold to whisper . . . the inquiry whether the work best answering to this description is not almost invariably found to be useless work? And to such useless work, I plainly say, I desire to set that determined thief, swindler, or vagrant, *for his punishment.* I have not the least hesitation in avowing . . . that it is a satisfaction to me to see that determined thief . . . sweating profusely at the treadmill or the crank, and extremely galled to know that he is doing nothing all the time but undergoing *punishment.* I have a very strong idea that he is sent to prison, rightfully, for that purpose; and I have no idea whatever that he is yet entitled to the privilege of being taught a trade, or that his life out of that place has established his claim within that place to work as men work who are not despoilers of their kind." HWC/IJ

—the Hulks: "'What might be your opinion of the place?'

"'A most beastly place. Mudbank, mist, swamp, and work: work, swamp, mist, and mudbank.'" GE 28

—Old Bailey: "They hanged at Tyburn, in those days, so the street outside Newgate had not obtained one infamous notoriety that has since attached to it. But, gaol was a vile place, in which most kinds of debauchery and villainy were practised, and where dire diseases were bred, that came into court with the prisoners, and sometimes rushed straight from the dock at my Lord Chief Justice himself, and pulled him off the bench. It had more than once happened, that the Judge in the black cap pronounced his own doom as certainly as the prisoner's, and even died before him.

"For the rest, the Old Bailey was famous as a kind of deadly inn-yard, from which pale travellers set out continually, in carts and coaches, on a violent passage into the other world: traversing some two miles and a half of public street and road, and shaming few good citizens, if any.

"So powerful is use, and so desirable to be good use in the beginning. It was famous, too, for the pillory, a wise old institution, that inflicted a punishment of which no one could foresee the extent; also, for the whipping-post, another dear old institution, very humanising and softening to behold in action; also, for extensive transactions in blood-money, another fragment of ancestral wisdom, systematically leading to the most frightful mercenary crimes that could be committed under Heaven.

"Altogether, the Old Bailey, at that date, was a choice illustration of the precept, that 'Whatever is is right;' an aphorism that would be as final as it is lazy, did it not include the troublesome consequence, that nothing that ever was, was wrong." ¶TTC ii 2

—*reform:* "We [Pip and Wemmick] were at Newgate in a few minutes, and we passed through the lodge where some fetters were hanging up on the bare walls among the prison rules, into the interior of the jail. At that time, jails were much neglected, and the period of exaggerated reaction consequent on all public wrong-doing—and which is always its heaviest and longest punishment—was still far off. So, felons were not lodged and fed better than soldiers (to say nothing of paupers), and seldom set fire to their prisons with the excusable object of improving the flavour of their soup." GE 32

—*silent system:* " . . . where many prisoners are . . . locked up alone, for twelve hours out of every twenty-four, and where, while preserved from contamination, he is still one of a society of men, and not an isolated being, filling his whole sphere of view with a diseased dilation of himself." HW/PP

—*treadmill:* "'I have been walking these seven days.'

"'Walking for sivin days!' said the young gentleman. 'Oh, I see. Beak's order, eh? But,' he added, noticing Oliver's look of surprise, 'I suppose you don't know what a beak is, my flash com-pan-i-on.'

"Oliver mildly replied, that he had always heard a bird's mouth described by the term in question.

"'My eyes, how green!' exclaimed the young gentleman. 'Why, a beak's a madgst'rate; and when you walk by a beak's order, it's not straight forerd, but always agoing up, and nivir a coming down agin. Was you never on the mill?'

"'What mill?' inquired Oliver.

"'What mill! Why, *the* mill—the mill as takes up so little room that it'll work inside a Stone Jug; and always goes better when the wind's low with people, than when it's high; acos then they can't get workmen.'" OT 8

" . . . [Sampson Brass] was permitted to grace the mother country, under certain insignificant restrictions.

"These were, that he should, for a term of years, reside in a spacious mansion where several other gentlemen were lodged and boarded at the public charge, who went clad in a sober uniform of grey turned up with yellow, had their hair cut extremely short, and chiefly lived on gruel and light soup. It was also required of him that he should partake of their exercise of constantly ascending an endless flight of stairs; and, lest his legs, unused to such exertion, should be weakened by it, that he should wear upon one ankle an amulet or charm of iron" OCS 73

Prisoner

—*agitated:* "Still, in his captivity, like a lower animal—like some impatient ape, or roused bear of the smaller species—the prisoner [Cavalletto], now left solitary, had jumped upon the ledge . . . .

"Excited into a still greater resemblance to a caged wild animal by his anxiety to know more, the prisoner leaped nimbly down, ran round the chamber, leaped nimbly up again, clasped the grate and tried to shake it, leaped down and ran, leaped up and listened, and never rested until the noise, becoming more and more distant, had died away. How many better prisoners have worn their noble hearts out so; no man thinking of it; not even the beloved of their souls realising it; great kings and governors, who had made them captive, careering in the sunlight jauntily, and men cheering them on." LD i 1

—*condemned*

—*his cell:* "We entered the first cell. It was a stone dungeon, eight feet long by six wide, with a bench at the upper end, under which were a common rug, a Bible, and prayer-book. An iron candle-stick was fixed into the wall at the side; and a small high window at the back admitted as much air and light as could struggle in between a double row of heavy, crossed iron bars. It contained no other furniture of any description." SB/VN

—*dreadful sight:* "He cowered down upon his stone bed, and thought of the past. He had been wounded with some missiles from the crowd on the day of his capture, and his head was bandaged with a linen cloth. His red hair hung down upon his bloodless face; his beard was torn, and twisted into knots; his eyes shone with a terrible light; his unwashed flesh crackled with the fever that burnt him up . . . .

"Those dreadful walls of Newgate, which have hidden so much misery and such unspeakable anguish, not only from the eyes, but, too often, and too long, from the thoughts, of men, never held so dread a spectacle as that. The few who lingered as they passed, and wondered what the man was doing who was to be hung to-morrow, would have slept but ill that night, if they could have seen him . . . .

"The condemned criminal was seated on his bed, rocking himself from side to side, with a countenance more like that of a snared beast than the face of a man. His mind was evidently wandering to his old life, for he continued to mutter, without appearing conscious of [visitors'] presence otherwise than as a part of his vision . . . .

"'Fagin,' said the jailer.

"'That's me!' cried the Jew, falling, instantly, into the attitude of listening he had assumed upon his trial. 'An old man, my Lord; a very old, old man!'

"'Here,' said the turnkey, laying his hand upon his breast to keep him down. 'Here's somebody wants to see you, to ask you some questions, I suppose. Fagin, Fagin! Are you a man?'

"'I shan't be one long,' he replied, looking up with a face retaining no human expression but rage and terror. 'Strike them all dead! What right have they to butcher me?'" OT 52

—*his last night:* "Hours have glided by, and still he sits upon the same stone bench with folded arms, heedless alike of the fast decreasing time before him, and the urgent entreaties of the good man at his side. The feeble light is wasting gradually, and the deathlike stillness of the street without, broken only by the rumbling of some passing vehicle which echoes mournfully through the empty yards, warns him that the night is waning fast away. The deep bell of St Paul's strikes—one! He heard it; it has roused him. Seven rapid strides, cold drops of terror starting on his forehead, and every muscle of his frame quivering with agony. Seven hours! He suffers himself to be led to his seat, mechanically takes the bible which is placed in his hand, and tries to read and listen. No: his thoughts will wander. The book is torn and soiled by use—and like the book he read his lessons in, at school, just forty years ago. He has never bestowed a thought upon it, perhaps, since he left it as a child: and yet the place, the time, the room—nay, the very boys he played with, crowd as vividly before him as if they were scenes of yesterday; and some forgotten phrase, some childish word, rings in his ears like the echo of one uttered but a minute since. The voice of the clergyman recalls him to himself. He is reading from the sacred book its solemn promises of pardon for repentance, and its awful denunciation of obdurate men. He falls upon his knees and clasps his hands to pray. Hush! what sound was that? He starts upon his feet. It cannot be two yet. Hark! Two quarters have struck;—the third—the fourth. It is! Six hours left. Tell him not of repentance! Six hours' repentance for eight times six years of guilt and sin! He buries his face in his hands, and throws himself on the bench . . . .

"A period of unconsciousness succeeds. He wakes, cold and wretched. The dull grey light of morning is stealing into the cell, and falls upon the form of the attendant turnkey. Confused by his dreams, he starts from his uneasy bed in momentary uncertainty. It is but momentary. Every object in the narrow cell is too frightfully real to admit of doubt or mistake. He is the condemned felon again, guilty and despairing; and in two hours more will be dead." SB/VN

And see M:Dreams and dreaming—*of a condemned man*

—*mental preparation:* "[Charles Darnay] had never seen the instrument that was to terminate his life. How high it was from the ground, how many steps it had, where he would be stood, how he would be touched, whether the touching hands would be dyed red, which way his face would be turned, whether he would be the first, or might be the last: these and many similar questions, in no wise directed by his will, obtruded themselves over and over again, countless times. Neither were they connected with fear: he was conscious of no fear. Rather, they originated in a strange besetting desire to know what to do when the time came; a desire gigantically disproportionate to the few swift moments to which it referred; a wondering that was more like the wondering of some other spirit within his, than his own." TTC iii 13

—repentance? "It may be urged that, in the preparation of a criminal for death, and in his devout reception of religious comfort, and in his full confession and late repentance, his reformation is achieved and worked out . . . . Hosts of angels have been imagined, in enthusiastic sermons, waiting to conduct the murderer to Heaven; and strange parallels have even been suggested, in such discourses, between the Scaffold and the Cross . . . I do distinctly challenge and dispute this kind of reformation. Besides that the reformation brought about by legal punishment, should be, to be satisfactory, a living, lasting, growing one: working on, in degradation and humility, from day to day; and striving, in its chains, and labour, and long-distant Hope, to make some atonement always;—besides this, I doubt the possibility of a great change being wrought in any man's heart and nature, in the flush and fever of that flying interval between the Warrant and the Noose." MP/CP i

—reprieve? "I see Hope living on, and know it must live on, in some faint shape, until the Bell begins to toll. I see the restless mind wandering away, miserably, from the main theme of the repentant letter, written in the cell; and while it tells of trust and steadfastness, having power to settle nowhere. I see the abject clinging on to life, which clutches at the hangman's hand, and blesses him beneath the beam. I see, in everything, the same wild, rapid, incoherent dream . . . .

"'I can give you no hope of life,' said a gentleman to a criminal . . . .'Unless I had solemnly given the promise elsewhere, that I would tell you so, I should not be here. But, by much entreaty, I have obtained a respite: that there may be time to inquire into what I have represented as a doubtful point. Can you bear the thought of living, only for another week?' 'O God, sir!' cried the man, 'a week is a long time to live!' And being smitten, as if he were only a week old then, he fell down, senseless . . . ." MP/CP i
Dickens added a note: "In consequence of new proof elicited by this new inquiry, the man was saved." DP p217

—in the dock: " . . . you can scarcely believe that the result of the trial is a matter of life or death to one wretched being present. But turn your eyes to the dock; watch the prisoner attentively for a few moments; and the fact is before you, in all its painful reality. Mark how restlessly he has been engaged for the last ten minutes, in forming all sorts of fantastic figures with the herbs which are strewed upon the ledge before him; observe the ashy paleness of his face when a particular witness appears, and how he changes his position and wipes his clammy forehead and feverish hands, when the case for the prosecution is closed, as if it were a relief to him to feel that the jury knew the worst.

"The defence is concluded; the judge proceeds to sum up the evidence; and the prisoner watches the countenances of the jury, as a dying man, clinging to life to the very last, vainly looks in the face of his physician for a slight ray of hope. They turn round to consult; you can almost hear the man's heart beat, as he bites the stalk of rosemary, with a desperate effort to appear composed." SB/CC

—moved by coach: "At that time it was customary to carry Convicts down to the dockyards by stage-coach. As I had often heard of them in the capacity of outside passengers, and had more than once seen them on the high road dangling their ironed legs over the coach roof, I had no cause to be surprised when Herbert [Pocket], meeting me in the yard, came up and told me that there were two convicts going down with me . . . .

"They had been treating their guard, I suppose, for they had a gaoler with them, and all three came out wiping their mouths on their hands. The two convicts were handcuffed together, and had irons on their legs—iron of a pattern that I knew well. They wore the dress that I likewise knew well. Their keeper had a brace of pistols, and carried a thick-knobbed bludgeon under his arm; but he was on terms of good understanding with them, and stood, with them beside him, looking on at the putting-to of the horses, rather with an air as if the convicts were an interesting Exhibition not formally open at the moment, and he the Curator." GE 28

—occupation: "'You see,' said Doctor Manette, turning to [Mr Lorry] after an uneasy pause, 'it is very hard to explain, consistently, the innermost workings of this poor man's mind. He once yearned so frightfully for that occupation, and it was so welcome when it came; no doubt it relieved his pain so much, by substituting the perplexity

of the fingers for the perplexity of the brain, and by substituting, as he became more practised, the ingenuity of the hands, for the ingenuity of the mental torture; that he has never been able to bear the thought of putting it quite out of his reach. Even now, when I believe he is more hopeful of himself than he has ever been, and even speaks of himself with a kind of confidence, the idea that he might need that old employment, and not find it, gives him a sudden sense of terror, like that which one may fancy strikes to the heart of a lost child.'" TTC ii 19

—preoccupation: "The prisoner [Rudge], left to himself, sat down upon his bedstead: and resting his elbows on his knees, and his chin upon his hands, remained in that attitude for hours.

"It would be hard to say, of what nature his reflections were. They had no distinctness, and, saving for some flashes now and then, no reference to his condition or the train of circumstances by which it had been brought about. The cracks in the pavement of his cell, the chinks in the wall where stone was joined to stone, the bars in the window, the iron ring upon the floor—such things as these, subsiding strangely into one another, and awakening an indescribable kind of interest and amusement, engrossed his whole mind; and although at the bottom of his every thought there was an uneasy sense of guilt, and dread of death, he felt no more than that vague consciousness of it, which a sleeper has of pain.

"It pursues him through his dreams, gnaws at the heart of all his fancied pleasures, robs the banquet of its taste, music of its sweetness, makes happiness itself unhappy, and yet is no bodily sensation, but a phantom without shape, or form, or visible presence; pervading everything, but having no existence; recognisable everywhere, but nowhere seen, or touched, or met with face to face, until the sleep is past, and waking agony returns." ¶BR 62

—solitary confinement

—in America: "On the haggard face of every man among these prisoners, the same expression sat. I know not what to liken it to. It had something of that strained attention which we see upon the faces of the blind and deaf, mingled with a kind of horror, as though they had all been secretly terrified. In every little chamber that I entered, and at every grate through which I looked, I seemed to see the same appalling countenances. It lives in my memory, with the fascination of a remarkable picture. Parade before my eyes, a hundred men, with one among them newly released from this solitary suffering, and I would point him out." AN 7 *See* M:Mind*—effect of solitude*

—in England: ". . . he writes to me [David Copperfield] here, that he will be glad to show me, in operation, the only true system of prison discipline; the only unchallengeable way of making sincere and lasting converts and penitents—which, you know, is by solitary confinement . . . .

"As we were going through some of the magnificent passages, I inquired of Mr Creakle and his friends what were supposed to be the main advantages of this all-governing and universally over-riding system? I found them to be the perfect isolation of prisoners—so that no one man in confinement there, knew anything about another; and the reduction of prisoners to a wholesome state of mind, leading to sincere contrition and repentance.

"Now, it struck me, when we began to visit individuals in their cells, and to traverse the passages in which those cells were, and to have the manner of the going to chapel and so forth, explained to us, that there was a strong probability of the prisoners knowing a good deal about each other, and of their carrying on a pretty complete system of intercourse. This, at the time I write, has been proved, I believe, to be the case; but as it would have been flat blasphemy against the system to have hinted such a doubt then, I looked out for the penitence as diligently as I could . . . .

"We had now seen all there was to see. It would have been in vain to represent to such a man as the worshipful Mr Creakle, that Twenty Seven and Twenty Eight were perfectly consistent and unchanged; that exactly what they were then, they had always been; that the hypocritical knaves were just the subjects to make that sort of profession in such a place; that they knew its market-value at least as well as we did, in the immediate service it would do them when they were expatriated; in a word, that it was a rotten, hollow, painfully suggestive piece of business altogether. We left them to their system and themselves, and went home wondering.

"'Perhaps it's a good thing, Traddles,' said I, 'to have an unsound Hobby ridden hard; for it's the sooner ridden to death.'

"'I hope so,' replied Traddles." DC 61

—in France: effect on voice: "The faintness of [Dr Manette's] voice was pitiable and dreadful. It was not the faintness of physical weakness, though confinement and hard fare no doubt had their part in it. Its deplorable peculiarity was, that it was the faintness of solitude and disuse. It was like the last feeble echo of a sound made long and long ago.

"So entirely had it lost the life and resonance of the human voice, that it affected the senses like a once beautiful colour faded away into a poor weak stain. So sunken and suppressed it was, that it was like a voice underground. So expressive it was, of a hopeless and lost creature, that a famished traveller, wearied out by lonely wandering in a wilderness, would have remembered home and friends in such a tone before lying down to die." ¶TTC i 6

—spurious penitence: "I found as prevalent a fashion in the form of the penitence, as I had left outside in the forms of the coats and waistcoats in the windows of the tailors' shops. I found a vast amount of profession, varying very little in character: varying very little (which I thought exceedingly suspicious) even in words. I found a great many foxes, disparaging whole vineyards of inaccessible grapes; but I found very few foxes whom I would have trusted within reach of a bunch.

" . . . I found that the most professing men were the greatest objects of interest: and that their conceit, their vanity, their want of excitement, and their love of deception (which many of them possessed to an almost incredible extent, as their histories showed), all prompted to these professions, and were all gratified by them." DC 61

Public execution

—the audience

—in 1780: "As the warmth of the cheerful day began to shed itself upon the scanty crowd, the murmur of tongues was heard, shutters were thrown open and blinds drawn up, and those who had slept in rooms over against the prison, where places to see the execution were let at high prices, rose hastily from their beds. In some of the houses, people were busy taking out the window sashes for the better accommodation of spectators; in others, the spectators were already seated, and beguiling the time with cards, or drinks, or jokes among themselves. Some had purchased seats upon the house-tops, and were already crawling to their stations from parapet and garret window. Some were yet bargaining for good places, and stood in them in a state of indecision; gazing at the slowly-swelling crowd, and at the workmen as they rested listlessly against the scaffold—affecting to listen with indifference to the proprietor's eulogy of the commanding view his house afforded, and the surpassing cheapness of his terms . . . .

"Five o'clock had struck—six—seven—and eight. Along the two main streets . . . a living stream had now set in, rolling towards the marts of gain and business. Carts, coaches, wagons, trucks, and barrows, forced a passage through the outskirts of the throng, and clattered onward in the same direction. Some of these, which were public conveyances and had come from a short distance in the country, stopped; and the driver pointed to the gibbet with his whip, though he might have spared himself the pains, for the heads of all the passengers were turned that way without his help, and the coach windows were stuck full of staring eyes. In some of the carts and wagons, women might be seen, glancing fearfully at the same unsightly thing; and even little children were held up above the people's heads to see what kind of toy a gallows was, and learn how men were hanged. . . .

"As the hour approached, a buzz and hum arose, which, deepening every moment, soon swelled into a roar, and seemed to fill the air. No words or even voices could be distinguished in this clamour, nor did they speak much to each other; though such as were better informed upon the topic than the rest, would tell their neighbours, perhaps, that they might know the hangman [Ned Dennis] when he came out, by his being the shorter one: and that the man who was to suffer with him was named Hugh: and that it was Barnaby Rudge who would be hanged in Bloomsbury Square.

"The hum grew, as the time drew near, so loud, that those who were at the windows could not hear the church-clock strike, though it was close at hand. Nor had they any need to hear it, either, for they could see it in the people's faces. So surely as another quarter chimed, there was a movement in the crowd—as if something had passed over it—as if the light upon them had been changed—in which the fact was readable as on a brazen dial, figured by a giant's hand.

"Three quarters past eleven! The murmur now was deafening, yet every man seemed mute. Look where you would among the crowd, you saw strained eyes and lips compressed; it would have been difficult for the most vigilant observer to point this way or that, and say that yonder man had cried out. It were as easy to detect the motion of lips in a sea-shell.

"Three quarters past eleven! Many spectators who had retired from the windows came back refreshed, as though their watch had just begun. Those who had fallen asleep roused themselves; and every person in the crowd made one last effort to better his position—which caused a press against the sturdy barriers that made them bend and yield like twigs . . . . Then, a profound silence replaced the tumult that had so long been gathering and a breathless pause ensued. Every window was now choked up with heads; the house-tops teemed with people—clinging to chimneys, peering over gable-ends, and holding on where the sudden loosening of any brick or stone would dash them down into the street. The church-tower, the church-roof, the churchyard, the prison-leads, the very waterspouts and lamp-posts—every inch of room—swarmed with human life.

"At the first stroke of twelve the prison-bell began to toll. Then the roar—mingled now with cries of 'Hats off!' and 'Poor fellows!' and, from some specks in the great concourse, with a shriek or groan—burst forth again. It was terrible to see—if any one in that distraction of excitement could have seen—the world of eager eyes, all strained upon the scaffold and the beam." ¶BR 77

—*in 1849:* "I believe that a sight so inconceivably awful as the wickedness and levity of the immense crowd collected at that execution this morning [the Mannings', at Horsemonger Lane] could be imagined by no man, and could be presented in no heathen land under the sun. The horrors of the gibbet and of the crime which brought the wretched murderers to it faded in my mind before the atrocious bearing, looks, and language of the assembled spectators.

"When I came upon the scene at midnight, the shrillness of the cries and howls that were raised from time to time, denoting that they came from a concourse of boys and girls already assembled in the best places, made my blood run cold. As the night went on, screeching, and laughing, and yelling in strong chorus of parodies on negro melodies, with substitutions of 'Mrs Manning' for 'Susannah,' and the like, were added to these.

"When the day dawned, thieves, low prostitutes, ruffians, and vagabonds of every kind, flocked on to the ground, with every variety of offensive and foul behaviour. Fightings, faintings, whistlings, imitations of Punch, brutal jokes, tumultuous demonstrations of indecent delight when swooning women were dragged out of the crowd by the police, with their dresses disordered, gave a new zest to the general entertainment. When the sun rose brightly—as it did—it gilded thousands upon thousands of upturned faces, so inexpressibly odious in their brutal mirth or callousness, that a man had cause to feel ashamed of the shape he wore, and to shrink from himself, as fashioned in the image of the Devil.

"When the two miserable creatures who attracted all this ghastly sight about them were turned quivering into the air, there was no more emotion, no more pity, no more thought that two immortal souls had gone to judgment, no more restraint in any of the previous obscenities, than if the name of Christ had never been heard in this world, and there were no belief among men but that they perished like the beasts." ¶MP/PE

"There never is (and there never was) an execution at the Old Bailey in London, but the spectators include two large classes of thieves—one class who go there as they would go to a dog-fight, or any other brutal sport, for the attraction and excitement of the spectacle; the other who make it a dry matter of business, and mix with the crowd, solely to pick pockets.

"Add to these, the dissolute, the drunken, the most idle, profligate, and abandoned of both sexes—some moody, ill-conditioned minds, drawn thither by a fearful interest—and some impelled by curiosity; of whom the greater part are of an age and temperament rendering the gratification of that curiosity highly dangerous to themselves and to society—and the great elements of the concourse are stated." ¶MP/CP iv

Dickens campaigned all his life against public executions: see MP/PE, /CP and E/CP

—*in Italy:* "Nobody cared, or was at all affected. There was no manifestation of disgust, or pity, or indignation, or sorrow . . . .

It was an ugly, filthy, careless, sickening spectacle; meaning nothing but butchery beyond the momentary interest to the one wretched actor. Yes! Such a sight has one meaning and one warning. Let me not forget it. The speculators in the lottery, station themselves at favourable points for counting the gouts of blood that spirt out, here or there; and buy that number. It is pretty sure to have a run upon it." PI 11

Slavery

—in America: "'And may I ask,' said Martin, glancing, but not with any displeasure, from Mark to the negro [Cicero], 'who this gentleman is? Another friend of yours?'

"'Why, sir,' returned Mark, taking him aside, and speaking confidentially in his ear, 'he's a man of colour, sir!'

"'Do you take me for a blind man,' asked Martin, somewhat impatiently, 'that you think it necessary to tell me that, when his face is the blackest that ever was seen?'

"'No, no, when I say a man of colour,' returned Mark, 'I mean that he's been one of them as there's picters of in the shops. A man and a brother, you know, sir,' said Mr Tapley, favouring his master with a significant indication of the figure so often represented in tracts and cheap prints.

"'A slave!' cried Martin, in a whisper.

"'Ah!' said Mark in the same tone. 'Nothing else. A slave. Why, when that there man was young—don't look at him while I'm a-telling it—he was shot in the leg; gashed in the arm; scored in his live limbs, like crimped fish; beaten out of shape; had his neck galled with an iron collar, and wore iron rings upon his wrists and ankles. The marks are on him to this day. When I was having my dinner just now, he stripped of his coat, and took away my appetite.'

"'Is *this* true?' asked Martin of [Bevan], who stood beside them.

"'I have no reason to doubt it. . . . It very often is.'

"'Bless you,' said Mark [Tapley], 'I know it is, from hearing his whole story. That master died; so did his second master from having his head cut open with a hatchet by another slave, who, when he'd done it, went and drowned himself: then he got a better one. In years and years he saved up a little money, and bought his freedom, which he got pretty cheap at last, on account of his strength being nearly gone, and he being ill. Then he come here. And now he's a-saving up to treat himself, afore he dies, to one small purchase; it's nothing to speak of; only his own daughter; that's all!' cried Mr Tapley, becoming excited. 'Liberty for ever! Hurrah! Hail, Columbia!'

"'Hush!' cried Martin, clapping his hand upon his mouth: 'and don't be an idiot. What is he doing here?'

"'Waiting to take our luggage off upon a truck,' said Mark. 'He'd have come for it by-and-bye, but I engaged him for a very reasonable charge (out of my own pocket) to sit along with me and make me jolly; and I *am* jolly; and if I was rich enough to contract with him to wait upon me once a day, to be looked at, I'd never be anything else.'

"The fact may cause a solemn impeachment of Mark's veracity, but it must be admitted nevertheless, that there was that in his face and manner at the moment, which militated strongly against this emphatic declaration of his state of mind." MC 17 *See* W:America*—freedom generally; and —liberty*

And see —'A man and a brother'

"The sensation of exacting any service from human creatures who are bought and sold, and being, for the time, a party as it were to their condition, is not an enviable one. The institution exists, perhaps, in its least repulsive and most mitigated form in such a town as this [Baltimore]; but it *is* slavery; and though I was, with respect to it, an innocent man, its presence filled me with a sense of shame and self-reproach." AN 7

And see W:America*—freedom generally*

—effect on land: "The tract of country [in Virginia] . . . was once productive; but the soil has been exhausted by the system of employing a great amount of slave labour in forcing crops, without strengthening the land: and it is now little better than a sandy desert overgrown with trees. Dreary and uninteresting as its aspect is, I was glad to the heart to find anything on which one of the curses of this horrible institution has fallen; and had greater pleasure in contemplating the withered ground, than the richest and most thriving cultivation in the same place could possibly have afforded me." AN 9

—effect on mind: "To those who are happily unaccustomed to them, the countenances in the streets and labouring-places [of Richmond, VA], too, are shocking. All men who know that there are laws against in-

structing slaves, of which the pains and penalties greatly exceed in their amount the fines imposed on those who maim and torture them, must be prepared to find their faces very low in the scale of intellectual expression.

"But the darkness—not of skin, but mind—which meets the stranger's eye at every turn; the brutalizing and blotting out of all fairer characters traced by Nature's hand; immeasurably outdo his worst belief. That travelled creation of the great satirist's brain [**Swift**'s *Gulliver*], who fresh from living among horses, peered from a high casement down upon his own kind with trembling horror, was scarcely more repelled and daunted by the sight, than those who look upon some of these faces for the first time must surely be." AN 9 *And see* S:Sensitivity—*dulled*

" . . . taken from a half-barbarous condition and educated by the whites, for their own purposes, down into the ways of brutes instead of up into the feelings of developed men; with no high purpose in life ever set before them; with no higher motive of existence than the fattening of their white masters; insulted (if they only knew it) by a lurking contumely even in the kindest accents; the great mass of the negro population has become infected with the universal feeling, and has fallen so low as to accept and share the prejudice against itself . . . .

"We think, too, that it is possible to combine with the duty of emancipation the not less important duty of undoing the evil that has been done to the slaves' minds, and of doing them some good service by way of atonement. When we have clipped men's minds and made them slavish, it is poor compensation that their bodies should be set at large. We believe that earnest and dispassionate inquiry among men experienced in all the details of the question, would lead eventually to a performance by America of the moral duty of emancipation in a way that might wipe out every reproach for the past treatment of the negroes, and reflect eternal honour on the stars and stripes." HWC/N

—*in England:* "And Mr Goodchild adds that the stones of Lancaster do sometimes whisper, even yet, of rich men passed away—upon whose great prosperity some of these old doorways frowned sullen in the brightest weather—that their slave-gain turned to curses, as the Arabian Wizard's money turned to leaves, and that no good ever came of it, even unto the third and fourth generations, until it was wasted and gone." LT 3 *See* W:Cities and Towns—*Lancaster*

—*'A man and a brother:'* "'I have no peace of my life [said Caddy Jellyby]. Talk of Africa! I couldn't be worse off if I was a what's-his-name—man and a brother!'" BH 14

"[Mr Dorrit's] health being drunk with acclamations, he was not so baronial after all but that in trying to return thanks he broke down, in the manner of a mere serf with a heart in his breast, and wept before [the Marshalsea collegians] all. After this great success, which he supposed to be a failure, he gave them 'Mr Chivery and his brother officers;' whom he had beforehand presented with ten pounds each, and who were all in attendance. Mr Chivery spoke to the toast, saying, What you undertake to lock up, lock up; but remember that you are, in the words of the fettered African, a man and a brother ever." LD i 36

"Where they pick the black up is a mystery I cannot solve, as in the case of the willingest girl that ever came into a house halfstarved poor thing, a girl so willing that I called her Willing Sophy down upon her knees scrubbing early and late and ever cheerful but always smiling with a black face . . . there it was and always on her nose, which turning up and being broad at the end seemed to boast of it and caused warning from a steady gentleman and excellent lodger with breakfast by the week but a little irritable and use of a sitting-room when required, his words being 'Mrs Lirriper I have arrived at the point of admitting that the Black is a man and a brother, but only in a natural form and when it can't be got off.'" CS/L

"'Now, Mortimer,' says Lady Tippins, rapping the sticks of her closed green fan upon the knuckles of her left hand—which was particularly rich in knuckles, 'I insist upon your telling all that is to be told about the man from Jamaica.'

"'Give you my honour I never heard of any man from Jamaica, except the man who was a brother,' replies Mortimer." OMF i 2

Britain's Anti-Slavery Society disseminated the picture of a slave being whipped, with the caption, "Am I not a man and a brother?" The Wedgwood porcelain factory in 1768 made a medallion showing a negro in chains with the same motto. And see —*in America*

—*public opinion:* "Public opinion! Why, public opinion in the slave States *is* slavery, is it not? Public opinion, in the slave States, has delivered the slaves over, to the gentle mercies of their masters. Public opinion has made the laws, and denied the slaves legislative protection.

"Public opinion has knotted the lash, heated the branding-iron, loaded the rifle, and shielded the murderer. Public opinion threatens the abolitionist with death, if he venture to the South . . . . Public opinion has, within a few years, burned a slave alive at a slow fire in the city of St. Louis; and public opinion has to this day maintained upon the bench that estimable Judge who charged the Jury, impanelled there to try his murderers, that their most horrid deed was an act of public opinion, and being so, must not be punished by the laws the public sentiment had made.

"Public opinion hailed this doctrine with a howl of wild applause, and set the prisoners free, to walk the city, men of mark, and influence, and station, as they had been before." AN 17

—seen from England: "'[Mark Tapley] went,' said Mrs. Lupin, with increased distress, 'to America. He was always tender-hearted and kind, and perhaps at this moment may be lying in prison under sentence of death, for taking pity on some miserable black, and helping the poor runaway creetur to escape. How could he ever go to America! Why didn't he go to some of those countries where the savages eat each other fairly, and give an equal chance to every one!'" MC 43

—servility ingrained: "It is no mitigation of the inhuman character of slavery to say, that in the majority of cases, negroes have been depressed so far towards the state of simple beasts of burden, that they have acquired the hearts and brains of horses and of oxen. Rational education of their minds is jealously withheld. They are taught to regard, as the sole object of their lives, not the advance of their own souls, but the increase of their master's cotton.

"Every look they get, even the kindest, every tone they hear, confirms their knowledge of the fact that they are chattels. 'A slave,' says one of the codes, 'is in the power of the master to whom he belongs. The master may sell him, dispose of his person, his industry, his labour; he can do nothing, possess nothing, nor acquire any thing, but which must belong to his master.'

"It is the greatest horror of the slave system to our minds, when men can live contented under so complete an abnegation of their manhood. Born to the system, bred to the system, degraded by being set to labour in sight of a whip, like the brutes, so working on a motive against which even a well-bred brute comes to rebel—thousands of negroes are content to be well fed and housed, occasionally patted on the head or played with, and, when their master finds it needful to reduce his stock, part with a mere transitory brutish pang from a contented wife in Maryland, perhaps, to lie down content with a new wife in a new stall in Tennessee.

"Burning alive, and all the tortures that were racked out of ingenious brains, are the most trumpery of wrongs compared with this treading of all things that are precious out of human hearts. It is pleasanter to think of slaves in Cuba flying before bloodhounds, than to know that the slaves of North America learn to identify themselves with their masters, and to lie down contented with their place among farm animals, because they are well fed; and that in the year 1850, out of three million slaves only a thousand fled away in search of liberty: the greater part even of that thousand seeking not liberty for its own sake, but as a means of escape from the punishments incurred by theft and other crime." ¶HWC/N

—upholders: "The upholders of slavery in America . . . may be divided into three great classes.

"The first, are those more moderate and rational owners of human cattle, who have come into possession of them as so many coins in their trading capital, but who admit the frightful nature of the Institution . . . .

"The second, consists of all those owners, breeders, users, buyers and sellers of slaves, who will, until the bloody chapter has a bloody end, own, breed, use, buy, and sell them at all hazards . . . who would at this or any other moment, gladly involve America in a war, civil or foreign, provided that it had for its sole end and object the assertion of their right to perpetuate slavery, and to whip and work and torture slaves, unquestioned by any human authority, and unassailed by any human power; who, when they speak of Freedom, mean the Freedom to oppress their kind, and to be savage, merciless, and cruel . . . .

"The third, and not the least numerous or influential, is composed of all that delicate gentility which cannot bear a superior, and cannot brook an equal; of that class whose Republicanism means, 'I will not tolerate a man above me: and of those below, none must approach too near;' whose pride, in a land where voluntary servitude is shunned as a disgrace, must be ministered to by slaves; and whose inalienable rights can only have their growth in negro wrongs." AN 17

And see Violence; LC:Notable individuals—*Harriet Beecher Stowe; and* W:America—*freedom generally, —plantation, and —values*

Violence

—endemic: "Do we not know that the man who has been born and bred among [slavery's] wrongs; who has seen in his childhood husbands obliged at the word of command to flog their wives; women, indecently compelled to hold up their own garments that men might lay the heavier stripes upon their legs, driven and harried by brutal overseers in their time of travail, and becoming mothers on the field of toil, under the very lash itself; who has read in youth, and seen his virgin sisters read, descriptions of runaway men and women, and their disfigured persons, which could not be published elsewhere, of so much stock upon a farm, or at a show of beasts:—do we not know that that man, whenever his wrath is kindled up, will be a brutal savage?

"Do we not know that as he is a coward in his domestic life, stalking among his shrinking men and women slaves armed with his heavy whip, so he will be a coward out of doors, and carrying cowards' weapons hidden in his breast, will shoot men down and stab them when he quarrels?

"And if our reason did not teach us this and much beyond; if we were such idiots as to close our eyes to that fine mode of training which rears up such men; should we not know that they who among their equals stab and pistol in the legislative halls, and in the counting-house, and on the marketplace, and in all the elsewhere peaceful pursuits of life, must be to their dependants, even though they were free servants, so many merciless and unrelenting tyrants?" ¶AN 17

"'What an extraordinary people you are!' cried Martin [Chuzzlewit]. 'Are Mr Chollop and the class he represents, an Institution here? Are pistols with revolving barrels, sword-sticks, bowie-knives, and such things, Institutions on which you pride yourselves? Are bloody duels, brutal combats, savage assaults, shooting down and stabbing in the streets, your Institutions! Why, I shall hear next that Dishonour and Fraud are among the Institutions of the great republic . . . the greater part of these things are one Institution with us, and we call it by the generic name of Old Bailey!'" MC 34

—engendered by slavery: "What! shall we declaim against the ignorant peasantry of Ireland, and mince the matter when these American [slave] taskmasters are in question? Shall we cry shame on the brutality of those who ham-string cattle: and spare the lights of Freedom upon earth who notch the ears of men and women, cut pleasant posies in the shrinking flesh, learn to write with pens of red-hot iron on the human face, rack their poetic fancies for liveries of mutilation which their slaves shall wear for life and carry to the grave, breaking living limbs as did the soldiery who mocked and slew the Saviour of the world, and set defenceless creatures up for targets!

"Shall we whimper over legends of the tortures practised on each other by the Pagan Indians, and smile upon the cruelties of Christian men! Shall we, so long as these things last, exult above the scattered remnants of that race, and triumph in the white enjoyment of their possessions?

"Rather, for me, restore the forest and the Indian village; in lieu of stars and stripes, let some poor feather flutter in the breeze; replace the streets and squares by wigwams; and though the death-song of a hundred haughty warriors fill the air, it will be music to the shriek of one unhappy slave." ¶AN 17

—an infection: "On one theme, which is commonly before our eyes, and in respect of which our national character is changing fast, let the plain Truth be spoken, and let us not, like dastards, beat about the bush by hinting at the Spaniard and the fierce Italian.

"When knives are drawn by Englishmen in conflict let it be said and known: 'We owe this change to Republican Slavery. These are the weapons of Freedom. With sharp points and edges such as these, Liberty in America hews and hacks her slaves; or, failing that pursuit, her sons devote them to a better use, and turn them on each other.'" ¶AN 17

And see Vol. I pp542-44

Humankind, in Activity

There are quiet victories and struggles, great sacrifices of self, and noble acts of heroism, in Life, not the less difficult to achieve, because they have no earthly chronicle or audience—done every day in nooks and corners, and in little households, and in men's and women's hearts—any one of which might reconcile the sternest man to such a world, and fill him with belief and hope in it.

[BL 1]

Her name was Paragon. Her nature was represented to us, when we engaged her, as being feebly expressed in her name. We should have been at her mercy, if she had had any; but she was a remorseless woman, and had none.

[DC 44]

Martin meets an Acquaintance
in the House of a Mutual Relation MC

Architect and Architecture

"' . . . we didn't find that [the blacking warehouse] come up to its likeness in the red bills at the shop doors: which I meantersay,' added Joe [Gargery], in an explanatory manner, 'as it is there drawd too architectooralooral.'

"I really believe Joe would have prolonged this word (mightily expressive to my mind of some architecture that I know) into a perfect Chorus, but for his attention being providentially attracted by his hat, which was toppling." GE 27

—ancient building: "The room into which they entered was a vaulted chamber once nobly ornamented by cunning architects, and still retaining, in its beautiful groined roof and rich stone tracery, choice remnants of its ancient splendour. Foliage carved in the stone, and emulating the master of Nature's hand, yet remained to tell how many times the leaves outside had come and gone, while it lived on unchanged. The broken figures supporting the burden of the chimney-piece, though mutilated, were still distinguishable for what they had been—far different from the dust without—and showed sadly by the empty hearth, like creatures who had outlived their kind, and mourned their own too slow decay." OCS 52

—attic: " . . . it was but a little place, with a sliding window, and a phrenological ceiling expressive of all the peculiarities of the house-roof." CS/MS 2

—builder: "'Well, perhaps,' said Sam, 'you bought houses, wich is delicate English for goin' mad: or took to buildin', wich is a medical term for bein' incurable.'

"'The cobbler shook his head and said, 'Try again.'" PP 44

" . . . why kitchen stairs should all be corner stairs is for the builders to justify though I do not think they fully understand their trade and never did, else why the sameness and why not more conveniences and fewer draughts and likewise making a practice of laying the plaster on too thick I am well convinced which holds the damp, and as to chimney-pots putting them on by guesswork like hats at a party and no more knowing what their effect will be upon the smoke bless you than I do if so much, except that it will mostly be either to send it down your throat in a straight form or give it a twist before it goes there.

"And what I says speaking as I find of those new metal chimneys all manner of shapes . . . is that they only work your smoke into artificial patterns for you before you swallow it and that I'd quite as soon swallow mine plain, the flavour being the same, not to mention the conceit of putting up signs on the top of your house to show the forms in which you take your smoke into your inside." ¶CS/LL 1

—castle in Walworth: "Wemmick's house was a little wooden cottage in the midst of plots of garden, and the top of it was cut out and painted like a battery mounted with guns.

"'My own doing,' said Wemmick. 'Looks pretty; don't it?'

"I highly commended it. I think it was the smallest house I ever saw: with the queerest gothic windows (by far the greater part of them sham), and a gothic door, almost too small to get in it.

"'That's a real flagstaff, you see,' said Wemmick, 'and on Sundays I run up a real flag. Then look here. After I have crossed this bridge, I hoist it up—so—and cut off the communication.'

"The bridge was a plank, and it crossed a chasm about four feet wide and two deep. But it was very pleasant to see the pride with which he hoisted it up, and made it fast; smiling as he did so, with a relish, and not merely mechanically.

"'At nine o'clock every night, Greenwich time,' said Wemmick, 'the gun fires. There he is, you see! And when you hear him go, I think you'll say he's a Stinger.'

"The piece of ordnance referred to was mounted in a separate fortress, constructed of lattice-work. It was protected from the weather by an ingenious little tarpaulin contrivance in the nature of an umbrella.

"'Then, at the back,' said Wemmick, 'out of sight, so as not to impede the idea of fortifications—for it's a principle with me, if you have an idea, carry it out and keep it up—I don't know whether that's your opinion——'

"I said, decidedly.

"'—At the back, there's a pig, and there are fowls and rabbits; then I knock together my own little frame, you see, and grow cucumbers; and you'll judge at supper what sort of a salad I can raise. So, sir,' said Wemmick, smiling again, but seriously, too, as he shook his head, 'if you can suppose the little place besieged, it would hold out a devil of a time in point of provisions.'

"Then, he conducted me to a bower about a dozen yards off, but which was approached by such ingenious twists of path that it took quite a long time to get at; and in this retreat our glasses were already set forth. Our punch was cooling in an ornamental lake, on whose margin the bower was raised. This piece of water (with an island in the middle which might have been the salad for supper) was of a circular form, and he had constructed a fountain in it, which, when you set a little mill going and took a cork out of a pipe, played to that powerful extent that it made the back of your hand quite wet.

"'I am my own engineer, and my own carpenter, and my own plumber, and my own gardener, and my own Jack of all Trades,' said Wemmick, in acknowledging my compliments." GE 25

—*church:* "A very hideous church with four towers at the four corners, generally resembling some petrified monster, frightful and gigantic, on its back, with its legs in the air." OMF ii 1

—*enclave at Pisa:* "It was a surprise to me to find [the leaning tower] in a grave retired place, apart from the general resort, and carpeted with smooth green turf. But, the group of buildings, clustered on and about this verdant carpet: comprising the Tower, the Baptistery, the Cathedral, and the Church of the Campo Santo: is perhaps the most remarkable and beautiful in the whole world; and from being clustered there, together, away from the ordinary transactions and details of the town, they have a singularly venerable and impressive character. It is the architectural essence of a rich old city, with all its common life and common habitations pressed out, and filtered away." PI 10

—*fortifications:* " . . . I saw the artfullest pits and drawbridges, the slyest batteries, the most unexpected angles and turnings; the loneliest, deep-set, beetle-browed little windows, down among the stinging-nettles at the bottoms of trenches, indicative of subterranean passages and bomb-proof rooms. Here I saw forts, and citadels, and great-guns hiding their muzzles deceitfully behind mounds of earth; and the low flat tops of inner buildings crouching out of the range of telescopes and aim of shells; and mysterious gateways and archways, honeycombed with loopholes for small arms; and tokens of undermined communication between place and place; and narrow passages beset by dark vaults with gratings to fire through, that one would like to see the inside of, they are so mysterious, and smell so chill and earthy." HWC/D

—*illusory production:* "Of his architectural doings, nothing was clearly known, except that he had never designed or built anything; but it was generally understood that his knowledge of the science was almost awful in its profundity.

"Mr Pecksniff's professional engagements, indeed, were almost, if not entirely, confined to the reception of pupils . . . . A young gentleman's premium being paid, and the young gentleman come to Mr Pecksniff's house, Mr Pecksniff borrowed his case of mathematical instruments (if silver-mounted or otherwise valuable) . . . and turned him loose in a spacious room on the two-pair front; where, in the company of certain drawing-boards, parallel rulers, very stiff-legged compasses, and two, or perhaps three, other young gentlemen, he improved himself, for three or five years, according to his articles, in making elevations of Salisbury Cathedral from every possible point of sight; and in constructing in the air a vast quantity of Castles, Houses of Parliament, and other Public Buildings. Perhaps in no place in the world were so many gorgeous edifices of this class erected as under Mr Peckniff's auspices; and if but one-twentieth part of the churches which were built in that front room, with one or other of the Miss Pecksniffs at the altar in the act of marrying the architect, could only be made available by the parliamentary commissioners, no more churches would be wanted for at least five centuries." MC 2

—*military:* "What would the sleepy old town have been without the soldiers, seeing that even with them it had so overslept itself as to have slept its echoes hoarse, its defensive bars and locks and bolts and chains all rusty, and its ditches stagnant! From the days when **Vauban** engineered it to that perplexing extent that to look at it was like being knocked on the head with it, the stranger becoming stunned and stertorous under the shock of its incomprehensibility—from the days when **Vauban** made it the express incorporation of every substantive and adjective in the art of military engineering, and not only twisted you into it and twisted you out of it, to the right, to the left, opposite, under here, over there, in the dark, in the dirt, by the gateway, archway, covered way, dry way, wet way, fosse, portcullis, drawbridge, sluice, squat tower, pierced wall, and heavy battery, but likewise took a fortifying dive under the neighbouring country, and came to the surface three or four miles off, blowing out incomprehensible mounds and batteries among the quiet crops of chicory and beet-root—from those days to these the town had been asleep, and dust and rust and must had settled on its drowsy Arsenals and Magazines, and grass had grown up in its silent streets." CS/SL 2

—monotonous, in Camden Town: "The general air of the place reminded me forcibly of the days when I lived with Mr and Mrs Micawber. An indescribable character of faded gentility that attached to the house I sought, and made it unlike all the other houses in the street—though they were all built on one monotonous pattern, and looked like the early copies of a blundering boy who was learning to make houses, and had not yet got out of his cramped brick-and-mortar pothooks—reminded me still more of Mr and Mrs Micawber." DC 27

—ornament: " . . . the door, which had a projecting canopy in carved work, of festooned jack-towels and children's heads with water on the brain, designed after a once-popular monumental pattern . . . . " LD 1 3

—railway alms-house: "By the side of most railways out of London, one may see Alms-Houses and Retreats (generally with a Wing or a Centre wanting, and ambitious of being much bigger than they are), some of which are newly-founded Institutions, and some old establishments transplanted. There is a tendency in these pieces of architecture to shoot upward unexpectedly, like Jack's bean-stalk, and to be ornate in spires of Chapels and lanterns of Halls, which might lead to the embellishment of the air with many castles of questionable beauty but for the restraining consideration of expense. However, the managers, being always of a sanguine temperament, comfort themselves with plans and elevations of Loomings in the future, and are influenced in the present by philanthropy towards the railway passengers. For, the question how prosperous and promising the buildings can be made to look in their eyes, usually supersedes the lesser question how they can be turned to the best account for the inmates." UT/AH

—stairs: "'Mr Grewgious,' replied Mrs Billickin, 'pardon me, there is the stairs. Unless your mind is prepared for the stairs, it will lead to inevitable disappointment. You cannot, Miss,' said Mrs Billickin, addressing Rosa reproachfully, 'place a first floor, and far less a second, on the level footing of a parlour. No, you cannot do it, Miss, it is beyond your power, and wherefore try?'

"Mrs Billickin put it very feelingly, as if Rosa had shown a headstrong determination to hold the untenable position . . . .

" . . . . She made various genteel pauses on the stairs for breath, and clutched at her heart in the drawing-room as if it had very nearly got loose, and she had caught it in the act of taking wing.

"'And the second floor?' said Mr Grewgious, on finding the first satisfactory.

"'Mr Grewgious,' replied Mrs Billickin, turning upon him with ceremony, as if the time had now come when a distinct understanding on a difficult point must be arrived at, and a solemn confidence established, 'the second floor is over this.'" MED 22

—suggested assignments: "'Do you know, now,' said Mr Pecksniff, folding his hands, and looking at his young relation with an air of pensive interest, 'that I should very much like to see your notion of a cow-house?'

"But Martin by no means appeared to relish this suggestion.

"'A pump,' said Mr Pecksniff, 'is very chaste practice. I have found that a lamp-post is calculated to refine the mind and give it a classical tendency. An ornamental turnpike has a remarkable effect upon the imagination. What do you say to beginning with an ornamental turnpike?'" MC 6

—unawares, at work: "Mr Pecksniff had clearly not expected [Tom and Martin] for hours to come: for he was surrounded by open books, and was glancing from volume to volume, with a black-lead pencil in his mouth, and a pair of compasses in his hand, at a vast number of mathematical diagrams, of such extraordinary shapes that they looked like designs for fireworks." MC 5

—understated: "We have a pier—a queer old wooden pier, fortunately without the slightest pretensions to architecture, and very picturesque in consequence. Boats are hauled up upon it, ropes are coiled all over it; lobster-pots, nets, masts, oars, spars, sails, ballast, and rickety capstans, make a perfect labyrinth of it." RP/EW

And see W:Crities and Towns, fictionally named—*Mudfog*

Artists and Their Work

—*autonomy:* ". . . [CD] presented the artist as one to whom the finest and frailest of the five senses was essential to the achievement of every business of his life. He could not gain wealth or fame by buying something he never touched or saw, or selling to another man something he might never touch or see. No! he must strike out of himself every spark of the fire which warmed and lighted—aye, and perhaps consumed him. He must win the great battle of life with his own hands and by his own eyes, and he could not choose but be in the hot encounter, General Commander-in-Chief, Captain, Ensign, non-commissioned-officer, private, drummer, all, in one short word, in his own unaided self." S/A4 (third person report)

—*classical style:* ". . . painted ceilings, where Allegory, in Roman helmet and celestial linen, sprawls among balustrades and pillars, flowers, clouds, and big-legged boys, and makes the head ache—as would seem to be Allegory's object always, more or less." BH 10

—*the cherub (by contrast):* ". . the good-tempered cherub [Wilfer], who was often as uncherubically employed in his own family as if he had been in the employment of some of the Old Masters, undertook to grill the fowls. Indeed, except in respect of staring about him (a branch of the public service to which the pictorial cherub is much addicted), this domestic cherub discharged as many odd functions as his prototype; with the difference, say, that he performed with a blacking-brush on the family's boots, instead of performing on enormous wind instruments and double-basses, and that he conducted himself with cheerful alacrity to much useful purpose, instead of foreshortening himself in the air with the vaguest intentions." OMF iii 4

—*with a critic:* "'Do you know what my points are? [said the model]'

"No,' said I.

"'My throat and my legs,' said he. 'When I don't set for a head, I mostly sets for a throat and a pair of legs. Now, granted you was a painter, and was to work at my throat for a week together, I suppose you'd see a lot of lumps and bumps there, that would never be there at all, if you looked at me, complete, instead of only my throat. Wouldn't you?'

"'Probably,' said I, surveying him.

"'Why, it stands to reason,' said the Model. 'Work another week at my legs, and it'll be the same thing. You'll make 'em out as knotty and as knobby, at last, as if they was the trunks of two old trees. Then, take and stick my legs and throat on to another man's body, and you'll make a reg'lar monster. And that's the way the public gets their reg'lar monsters, every first Monday in May, when the Royal Academy Exhibition opens.'

"'You are a critic,' said I, with an air of deference." RP/GA

—*dealing with colour:* "A painter who has gazed too long upon some glaring colour, refreshes his dazzled sight by looking upon a darker and more sombre tint; but everything that met Mr [Godfrey] Nickleby's gaze wore so black and gloomy a hue, that he would have been beyond description refreshed by the very reverse of the contrast." NN 1

—*fancy ball school:* "And Sir Leicester is glad to repose in dignified contentment before the great fire in the library . . . honouring the fine arts with a glance of approbation. For he has his pictures, ancient and modern. Some of the Fancy Ball School in which Art occasionally condescends to become a master, which would be best catalogued like the miscellaneous articles in a sale. As, 'Three high-backed chairs, a table and cover, long-necked bottle (containing wine), one flask, one Spanish female's costume, three-quarter face portrait of Miss Jogg the model, and a suit of armour containing *Don Quixote.*' Or, 'One stone terrace (cracked), one gondola in distance, one Venetian senator's dress complete, richly embroidered white satin costume with profile portrait of Miss Jogg the model, one scimitar superbly mounted in gold with jewelled handle, elaborate Moorish dress (very rare), and *Othello.*'" BH 29

" . . . the portrait of Lady Dedlock over the mantel-shelf, in which she is represented on a terrace, with a pedestal upon the terrace, and a vase upon the pedestal, and her shawl upon the vase, and a prodigious piece of fur upon the shawl, and her arm on the prodigious piece of fur, and a bracelet on her arm." BH 32

—*fashionable engraving:* " . . . a choice collection of copper-plate impressons from that truly national work, The Divinities of Albion, or Galaxy Gallery of British Beauty, representing ladies of title and fashion in every variety of smirk that art, combined with capital, is capable of producing. With these magnificent portraits . . . [Weevle/ Jobling] decorates his apartment; and as the Galaxy Gallery of British Beauty wears every variety of fancy dress, plays every variety of musical instrument, fondles every variety of dog, ogles every variety of prospect, and is backed up by every variety of flower-pot and balustrade, the result is very imposing." BH 20

—fresco

—cartoon for: [Maclise's cartoon] is a design, intended to be afterwards copied and painted in fresco; and certain finish must be had at last, if not at first. It is very well to take it for granted in a Cartoon that a series of cross-lines, almost as rough and apart as the lattice-work of a garden summer-house, represents the texture of the human face; but the face cannot be painted so. A smear upon the paper may be understood, by virtue of the context . . . to stand for a limb, or a body, or a cuirass, or a hat and feathers, or a flat, or a boot, or an angel. But when the time arrives for rendering these things in colours on a wall, they must be grappled with, and cannot be slurred over in this wise." MP/SC

—deteriorating: "The decayed and mutilated paintings with which this church [at Parma] is covered, have, to my thinking, a remarkably mournful and depressing influence. It is miserable to see great works of art—something of the Souls of Painters—perishing and fading away, like human forms. This cathedral is odorous with the rotting of Correggio's frescoes in the Cupola. Heaven knows how beautiful they may have been at one time. Connoisseurs fall into raptures with them now; but such a labyrinth of arms and legs: such heaps of foreshortened limbs, entangled and involved and jumbled together; no operative surgeon, gone mad, could imagine in his wildest delirium." PI 6

—and the general welfare: "I am strongly disposed to believe there are very few debates in Parliament so important to the public welfare as a really good picture. I have also a notion that any number of bundles of the driest legal chaff that was ever chopped would be cheaply exchanged for one really accessible, really humanizing, really meritorious engraving . . . I sometimes observe that great ministers of state and other such exalted characters have a strange delight in rather ostentatiously declaring that they have no knowledge whatever of art, and particularly of impressing on the company that they have passed their lives in severe studies. It strikes me when I hear these things as if these great men looked upon the arts as a sort of dancing dogs, or Punch's show, to be turned to for amusement when one has nothing else to do.

"Now I always take the opportunity on these occasions of entertaining my humble opinion that all this is complete 'bosh'; and of asserting to myself my strong belief that the neighbourhoods of Trafalgar Square [the Royal Academy], or Suffolk Street [the British Artists' Society], rightly understood, are quite as important to the welfare of the empire as those of Downing Street or Westminster Hall." ¶S/A3

—on location: "In case of your being a pictorial artist, desirous of studying at small expense the physiognomies and beards of different nations, come, on receipt of this, to Pavilionstone [Folkestone]. You shall find all the nations of the earth, and all the styles of shaving and not shaving, hair cutting and hair letting alone, for ever flowing through our hotel." RP/OT

—models

—in London: "I am unable to silence the still small voice which tells me that I am tired to death of that young man with the large chest, and that I would thankfully accept a less symmetrical young man with a smaller chest, or even with a chest in which the stethoscope might detect a weakness. Immaculate as that other young man's legs are, I am sick of his legs. A novelty, even though it were bandy, would be a sweet and soothing relief to me." HW/IM

—on the Spanish Steps: " . . . these steps are the great place of resort for the artists' 'Models,' and there they are constantly waiting to be hired. The first time I went up there, I could not conceive why the faces seemed familiar to me; why they appeared to have beset me, for years, in every possible variety of action and costume; and how it came to pass that they started up before me, in Rome, in the broad day, like so many saddled and bridled nightmares.

"I soon found that we had made acquaintance, and improved it, for several years, on the walls of various Exhibition Galleries. There is one old gentleman, with long white hair and an immense beard, who, to my knowledge, has gone half through the catalogue of the Royal Academy. This is the venerable, or patriarchal model. He carries a long staff; and every knot and twist in that staff I have seen, faithfully delineated, innumerable times.

"There is another man in a blue cloak, who always pretends to be asleep in the sun (when there is any), and who, I need but say, is always very wide awake, and very attentive to the disposition of his legs. This is the *dolce far niente* model. There is another man in a brown cloak, who leans against a wall, with his arms folded in his mantle, and looks out of the corners of his eyes; which are just visible beneath his broad slouched hat. This is the assassin model. There is another man, who constantly looks over his own shoulder, and is always going away, but never does. This is the haughty, or scornful model.

"As to Domestic Happiness, and Holy Families, they should come very cheap, for there are lumps of them, all up the steps; and the cream of the thing is, that they are all the falsest vagabonds in the world, especially made up for the purpose, and having no counterparts in Rome or any other part of the habitable globe." ¶PI 11

—*with a model:* "'You, then,' said I . . . 'are the gentleman whom I have so frequently contemplated, in connection with a high-backed chair with a red cushion, and a table with twisted legs.'

"'I am that Model,' he rejoined moodily, 'and I wish I was anything else.'

"'Say not so,' I returned. 'I have seen you in the society of many beautiful young women;' as in truth I had, and always (I now remember) in the act of making the most of his legs.

"'No doubt,' said he. 'And you've seen me along with warses of flowers, and any number of table-kivers, and antique cabinets, and warious gammon.'

"'Sir?' said I.

"'And warious gammon,' he repeated, in a louder voice. 'You might have seen me in armour, too, if you had looked sharp. Blessed if I ha'n't stood in half the suits of armour as ever came out of **Pratt**'s shop: and sat, for weeks together, a-eating nothing, out of half the gold and silver dishes as has ever been lent for the purpose out of **Storr**ses, **and Mortimer**ses, or **Garrard**-ses, **and Davenport**seseses.'

"Excited, as it appeared, by a sense of injury, I thought he would never have found an end for the last word. But at length it rolled sullenly away with the thunder." RP/GA

"'As if warn't bad enough for a bob a-hour, for a man to be mixing himself up with that there jolly old furniter that one 'ud think the public know'd the wery nails in by this time—or to be putting on greasy old 'ats and cloaks, and playing tambourines in the Bay o' Naples, with Wesuvius a smokin' according to pattern in the background, and the wines a bearing wonderful in the middle distance—or to be unpolitely kicking up his legs among a lot o' gals, with no reason whatever in his mind, but to show 'em . . . . " RP/GA

—*mural:* "Mrs Plornish's shop-parlour had been decorated under her own eye, and presented, on the side towards the shop, a little fiction in which Mrs Plornish unspeakably rejoiced. This poetical heightening of the parlour consisted in the wall being painted to represent the exterior of a thatched cottage; the artist having introduced (in as effective a manner as he found compatible with their highly disproportioned dimensions) the real door and window.

"The modest sunflower and hollyhock were depicted as flourishing with great luxuriance on this rustic dwelling, while a quantity of dense smoke issuing from the chimney indicated good cheer within, and also, perhaps, that it had not been lately swept. A faithful dog was represented as flying at the legs of the friendly visitor, from the threshold; and a circular pigeon-house, enveloped in a cloud of pigeons, arose from behind the garden-paling. On the door (when it was shut) appeared the semblance of a brass-plate, presenting the inscription, Happy Cottage, T. and M. Plornish; the partnership expressing man and wife.

"No Poetry and no Art ever charmed the imagination more than the union of the two in this counterfeit cottage charmed Mrs Plornish. It was nothing to her that Plornish had a habit of leaning against it as he smoked his pipe after work, when his hat blotted out the pigeon-house and all the pigeons, when his back swallowed up the dwelling, when his hands in his pockets uprooted the blooming garden and laid waste the adjacent country. To Mrs Plornish, it was still a most beautiful cottage, a most wonderful deception; and it made no difference that Mr Plornish's eye was some inches above the level of the gable bed-room in the thatch." ¶LD ii 13

—in museums and galleries: "It is necessary that I should observe that I have a great delight in pictures. I am no painter myself, but I have studied pictures and written about them. I have seen all the most famous pictures in the world; my education and reading have been sufficiently general to possess me beforehand with a knowledge of most of the subjects to which a Painter is likely to have recourse; and, although I might be in some doubt as to the rightful fashion of the scabbard of King Lear's sword, for instance, I think I should know King Lear tolerably well, if I happened to meet with him.

"I go to all the Modern Exhibitions every season, and of course I revere the Royal Academy. I stand by its forty Academical articles almost as firmly as I stand by the thirty-nine Articles of the Church of England. I am convinced that in neither case could there be, by any rightful possibility, one article more or less." RP/GA

—the obscure discovered: "Our bore . . . being in Italy, made a discovery of a dreadful picture, which has been the terror of a large portion of the civilized world ever since. We have seen the liveliest men paralysed by it, across a broad dining-table. He was lounging among the mountains, sir, basking in the mellow influences of the climate, when he came to *una piccola chiesa*—a little church—or perhaps it would be more correct to say *una piccolissima cappella*—the smallest chapel you can possibly imagine . . . there hung a painting (subject, Virgin and Child) so divine in its expression, so pure and yet so warm and rich in its tone, so fresh in its touch, at once so glowing in its colour and so statuesque in its repose, that our bore cried out in an ecstasy, 'That's the finest picture in Italy!' And so it is, sir. There is no doubt of it. It is astonishing that that picture is so little known. Even the painter is uncertain. He afterwards took Blumb, of the Royal Academy . . . and you never saw a man so affected in your life as Blumb was. He cried like a child! And then our bore begins his description in detail—for all this is introductory—and strangles his hearers with the folds of the purple drapery." RP/B

—in personification: "So unmated were [Paul and Edith Dombey], and opposed, so forced and linked together by a chain which adverse hazard and mischance had forged: that fancy might have imagined the pictures on the walls around them, startled by the unnatural conjunction, and observant of it in their several expressions. Grim knights and warriors looked scowling on them. A churchman, with his hand upraised, denounced the mockery of such a couple coming to God's altar. Quiet waters in landscapes, with the sun reflected in their depths, asked, if better means of escape were not at hand, was there no drowning left? Ruins cried, 'Look here, and see what we are, wedded to uncongenial time!' Animals, opposed by nature, worried one another, as a moral to them. Loves and cupids took to flight afraid, and martyrdom had no such torment in its painted history of suffering." DS 27

—on porcelain and china: "I had been shown, at **Copeland**'s, patterns of beautiful design, in faultless perspective, which are causing the ugly old willow to wither out of public favour; and which, being quite as cheap, insinuate good wholesome natural art into the humblest households. When Mr and Mrs Sprat have . . . 'licked the platter clean,' they can—thanks to modern artists in clay—feast their intellectual tastes upon excellent delineations of natural objects." RP/PA

—portrait: "'Ah! The difficulties of Art, my dear, are great . . . . What with bringing out eyes with all one's power, and keeping down noses with all one's force, and adding to heads, and taking away teeth altogether, you have no idea of the trouble one little miniature is . . . and then people are so dissatisfied and unreasonable, that, nine times out of ten, there's no pleasure in painting them. Sometimes they say, "Oh, how very serious you have made me look, Miss La Creevy!" and at others, "La, Miss La Creevy, how very smirking!" when the very essence of a good portrait is, that it must be either serious or smirking, or it's no portrait at all.'" NN 10

"'Look at the Royal Academy [said Miss La Creevy]! All those beautiful shiny portraits of gentlemen in black velvet waistcoats, with their fists doubled up on round tables, or marble slabs, are serious, you know; and all the ladies who are playing with little parasols, or little dogs, or little children—it's the same rule in art, only varying the objects—are smirking. In fact . . . there are only two syles of portrait painting; the serious and the smirk; and we always use the serious for professional people (except actors sometimes), and the smirk for private ladies and gentlemen who don't care so much about looking clever.'" NN 10

"[Mrs Guppy's] close little sitting-room was prepared for a visit; and there was a portrait of her son in it, which, I had almost written here, was more like than life: it insisted upon him with such obstinacy, and was so determined not to let him off . . . ." BH 38

"'Portrait of Mr F behind the door and very like though too much forehead and as to a pillar with a marble pavement and balustrades and a mountain I never saw him near it nor not likely in the wine trade, excellent man but not at all in that way. . . .

"Little Dorrit glanced at the portrait again. The artist had given it a head that would have been, in an intellectual point of view, top-heavy for Shakespeare." LD i 24

" . . . a full-length engraving of the sublime Snigsworth over the chimney-piece, snorting at a Corinthian column, with an enormous roll of paper at his feet, and a heavy curtain going to tumble down on his head; those accessories being understood to represent the noble lord as somehow in the act of saving his country." OMF iii 17

—unlike: " . . . just as certain caricaturists and painters professedly making a portrait of some public man, which was not in the least like him, to begin with, have gone on repeating it and repeating it, until the public came to believe that it must be exactly like him, simply because it was *like itself,* and really have at last, in the fullness of time, grown almost to resent upon him their tardy discovery that he was not *like it.*" S/BM2

—practicalities: "There had been [said CD], and perhaps were, those of certain conventional ideas, who present Art as a mere child: a poor moon-striken [*sic.*] creature unable to take care of itself waiting as it were, to be safely conducted over the great crossings of life by some professional sweepers; as a miserable, slovenly slattern, down-at-heel and out-at-elbows, with no appreciation of the value of a home, no knowledge whatever of the value of money—and so on; but with these popular and still lingering hallucinations he had nothing whatever to do. He altogether renounced them.

"He represented the artist in a widely different light. Yes! as a reasonable creature; a sensible, practical, responsible gentleman; as one quite as well acquainted with the value of his own time and money as though he were 'on high "Change"' every day; as steadfast and methodical as if he had even a Bank or Life-office of his own to attend to; who lived in a house as well as others who were not artists; who enjoyed the pleasures of his wife, and home, and children, as other men; the former of whom not only attended properly to the ordinary matters of dress and curling of hair but, in short, was usually to be found marked by an association with a decorous amount of drapery." S/A4 (third person report)

—professional jealousy: "'Thomas, I find it necessary to be plain with you. I don't like the envious man. I have identified the cankerworm that's pegging away at your vitals, and it's envy, Thomas . . . . Whilst you contemplated the works of a gifted rival, and whilst you heard that rival's praises, and especially whilst you met his humble glance as he put that card away, your countenance was so malevolent as to be terrific. Thomas, I have heard of the envy of them that follows the Fine-Art line, but I never believed it could be what yours is. I wish you well, but I take my leave of you. And if you should ever get into trouble through knifeing—or say, garotting—a brother artist, as I believe you will, don't call me to character, Thomas, or I shall be forced to injure your case.'" CS/SL 3

—public sculpture in London: "At the corner of Wood Street, Cheapside, London, there is a tree. I suppose it has not the least business to be there, but it is pleasant there. It is a far better thing than a statue, to my thinking, as statues go. I have the greatest admiration for King George the Fourth, but I should prefer an elm tree in Trafalgar Square.* A pigtail in any material, but especially in stone, strikes me as a pretty object; still, I think a poplar would be on the whole more ornamental in Pall Mall East.* And anybody will concede that, in place of the frightful abortion of the top of the arch at Hyde Park Corner,* the commonest cabbage-stalk ever grown would be a blessed substitution." HWC/DT

**Bronze equestrian statues of George IV and George III, by Sir Francis Chantrey and Matthew Wyatt respectively, stood at the first two locations. One of Wellington, to the distress of many, had been put on top of the triumphal arch instead of the chariot and four horses originally intended by architect Decimus Burton. HS: "The arch and its statue became the butt of all sorts of gibes and witticisms. One French officer, upon* *viewing the structure, exclaimed,* 'Nous somme vengés!'" *(II 446n)*

—recently collected: ". . . the boy looked at the bran-new pilgrims on the wall, going to Canterbury in more gold frame than procession, and more carving than country." OMF i 3

—on the sidewalk: "The subjects consisted of a fine fresh salmon's head and shoulders, supposed to have been recently sent home from the fishmonger's; a moonlight night at sea (in a circle); dead game; scroll-work; the head of a hoary hermit engaged in devout contemplation; the head of a pointer smoking a pipe; and a cherubim, his flesh creased as in infancy, going on a horizontal errand against the wind." CS/SL 3

—tourist's acquisitions: "There were views, like and unlike, of a multitude of places; and there was one little picture-room devoted to a few of the regular sticky old Saints, with sinews like whipcord, hair like Neptune's, wrinkles like tattooing, and such coats of varnish that every holy personage served for a fly-trap, and became what is now called in the vulgar tongue a Catch-em-alive O.

"Of these pictorial acquisitions Mr Meagles spoke in the usual manner. He was no judge, he said, except of what pleased himself; he had picked them, up, dirt-cheap, and people *had* considered them rather fine. One man, who at any rate ought to know something of the subject, had declared that 'Sage, Reading' (a specially oily old gentleman in a blanket, with a swan's-down tippet for a beard, and a web of cracks all over him like rich pie-crust), to be a fine **Guercino**. As for **Sebastian del Piombo** there, you would judge for yourself; if it were not his later manner, the question was, Who was it? Titian, that might or might not be—perhaps he had only touched it. Daniel Doyce said perhaps he hadn't touched it, but Mr Meagles rather declined to overhear the remark." ¶LD i 16

—Leonardo's 'The Last Supper': "In the old refectory of the dilapidated Convent of Santa Maria delle Grazie, is the work of art, perhaps, better known than any other in the world: the Last Supper, by **Leonardo da Vinci**—with a door cut through it by the intelligent Dominican friars, to facilitate their operations at dinner-time." PI 9 *And see* CD:View of Painting and Sculpture

—for a vulgarian: Mr Podsnap's notions of the Arts in their integrity might have been stated thus. Literature; large print, respectively descriptive of getting up at eight, shaving close at a quarter-past, breakfasting at nine, going to the City at ten, coming home at half-past five, and dining at seven. Painting and Sculpture; models and portraits representing Professors of getting up at eight, shaving close at a quarter-past, breakfasting at nine, going to the City at ten, coming home at half-past five, and dining at seven. Music; a respectable performance (without variations) on stringed and wind instruments, sedately expressive of getting up at eight, shaving close at a quarter-past, breakfasting at nine, going to the City at ten, coming home at half-past five, and dining at seven. Nothing else to be permitted to those same vagrants the Arts, on pain of excommunication. Nothing else To Be—anywhere!" OMF i 11

—wax-works figures: "When the festoons were all put up as tastily as they might be, the stupendous collection was uncovered, and there were displayed, on a raised platform some two feet from the floor, running round the room and parted from the rude public by a crimson rope breast-high, divers sprightly effigies of celebrated characters, singly and in groups, clad in glittering dresses of various climes and times, and standing more or less unsteadily upon their legs, with their eyes very wide open, and their nostrils very much inflated, and the muscles of their legs and arms very strongly developed, and all their countenances expressing great surprise. All the gentlemen were very pigeon-breasted and very blue about the beards; and all the ladies were miraculous figures; and all the ladies and all the gentlemen were looking intensely nowhere, and staring with extraordinary earnestness at nothing." OCS 28

Auction

—at Broadstairs: "But the most wonderful feature of our Assembly Rooms, is, that an annual sale of 'Fancy and other China' is announced here with mysterious constancy and perseverance. Where the china comes from, where it goes to, why it is annually put up to auction when nobody ever thinks of bidding for it, how it comes to pass that it is always the same china, whether it would not have been cheaper, with the sea at hand, to have thrown it away, say in eighteen hundred and thirty, are standing enigmas.

"Every year the bills come out, every year

the Master of the Rooms gets into a little pulpit on a table, and offers it for sale, every year nobody buys it, every year it is put away somewhere till next year, when it appears again as if the whole thing were a new idea.

"We have a faint remembrance of an unearthly collection of clocks, purporting to be the work of Parisian and Genevese artists—chiefly bilious-faced clocks, supported on sickly white crutches, with their pendulums dangling like lame legs—to which a similar course of events occurred for several years, until they seemed to lapse away, of mere imbecility." ¶RP/EW

Bank

—of England's records: "Here, standing in a great long building of divers stories, looking dimly upward through iron gratings, and dimly downward through iron gratings, and into musty chambers diverging into the walls on either hand, you may muse upon the National Debt. All the sheep that ever came out of Northamptonshire, seem to have yielded up their skins to furnish the registers in which its accounts are kept. Sweating and wasting in this vast silent library, like manuscripts in a mouldy old convent, are the records of the Dividends that are, and have been, and of the Dividends unclaimed. Some men would sell their fathers into slavery, to have the rummaging of these old volumes. Some, who would let the Tree of Knowledge wither while they lay contemptuously at its feet, would bestir themselves to pluck at these leaves, like shipwrecked mariners. These are the books to profit by. This is the place for X. Y. Z. to hear of something to his advantage . . . . Oh, wonderful Old Lady! threading the needle with the golden eye all through the labyrinth of the National Debt, and hiding it in such dry hay-stacks as are rotting here!" HWC/TS

—in London: " . . . it gives one as good as a rich feeling to think of the broad counters with a rim along the edge, made for telling money out on, the scales for weighing precious metals, the ponderous ledgers, and, above all, the bright copper shovels for shovelling gold. When I draw money, it never seems as much money as when it is shovelled at me out of a bright copper shovel. I like to say, 'In gold,' and to see seven pounds musically pouring out of the shovel, like seventy; the Bank appearing to remark to me—I italicise appearing —'if you want more of this yellow earth, we keep it in barrows at your service.' To think of the banker's clerk with his deft finger turning the crisp edges of the Hundred-Pound Notes he has taken in a fat roll out of a drawer, is again to hear the rustling of that delicious south-cash wind." UT/CA

—its money: "The music of golden thousands clattered in the ear, as they jingled on counters until its last echoes were strangled in the puckers of tightened money-bags, or died under the clasps of purses. Wherever the eye turned, it rested on money; money of every possible variety; money in all shapes; money of all colours. There was yellow money, white money, brown money, gold money, silver money, copper money; paper money, pen and ink money. Money was wheeled about in trucks; money was carried about in bags; money was scavengered about with shovels. Thousands of sovereigns were jerked hither and thither from hand to hand—grave games of pitch and toss were played with staid solemnity; piles of bank notes—competent to buy whole German dukedoms and Italian principalities—hustled to and fro with as much indifference as if they were (as they had been) old rags." HWC/TS

—old-fashioned : "Tellson's Bank by Temple Bar was an old-fashioned place, even in the year one thousand seven hundred and eighty. It was very small, very dark, very ugly, very incommodious. It was an old-fashioned place, moreover, in the moral attribute that the partners in the House were proud of its smallness, proud of its darkness, proud of its ugliness, proud of its incommodiousness. They were even boastful of its eminence in those particulars, and were fired by an express conviction that, if it were less objectionable, it would be less respectable. This was no passive belief, but an active weapon which they flashed at more convenient places of business. Tellson's (they said) wanted no elbow-room, Tellson's wanted no light, Tellson's wanted no embellishment. Noakes and Co.'s might, or Snooks Brothers' might; but Tellson's, thank Heaven!—

"Any one of these partners would have disinherited his son on the question of rebuilding Tellson's. In this respect the House was much on a par with the Country; which did very often disinherit its sons for suggesting improvements in laws and customs that had long been highly objectionable, but were only the more respectable.

"Thus it had come to pass, that Tellson's was the triumphant perfection of inconvenience. After bursting open a door of idiotic obstinacy with a weak rattle in its throat, you fell into Tellson's down two steps, and came to your senses in a miserable little shop, with two little counters, where the oldest of men made your cheque shake as if the wind rustled it, while they examined the signature by the dingiest of windows, which were always under a shower-bath of mud from Fleet-street, and which were made the dingier by their own iron bars proper, and the heavy shadow of Temple Bar.

"If your business necessitated your seeing 'the House', you were put into a species of Condemned Hold at the back, where you meditated on a misspent life, until the House came with its hands in its pockets, and you could hardly blink at it in the dismal twilight.

"Your money came out of, or went into, wormy old wooden drawers, particles of which flew up your nose and down your throat when they were opened and shut. Your bank-notes had a musty odour, as if they were fast decomposing into rags again. Your plate was stowed away among the neighbouring cesspools, and evil communications corrupted its good polish in a day or two.

"Your deeds got into extemporised strong-rooms made of kitchens and sculleries, and fretted all the fat out of their parchments into the banking-house air. Your lighter boxes of family papers went up-stairs into a Barmecide room, that always had a great dining-table in it and never had a dinner, and where, even in the year one thousand seven hundred and eighty, the first letters written to you by your old love, or by your little children, were but newly released from the horror of being ogled through the windows, by the heads exposed on Temple Bar with an insensate brutality and ferocity worthy of Abyssinia or Ashantee." ¶TTC ii 1

—*youth:* "Cramped in all kinds of dim cupboards and hutches at Tellson's, the oldest of men carried on the business gravely. When they took a young man into Tellson's London house, they hid him somewhere till he was old. They kept him in a dark place, like a cheese, until he had the full Tellson flavour and blue-mould upon him. Then only was he permitted to be seen, spectacularly poring over large books, and casting his breeches and gaiters into the general weight of the establishment." TTC ii 1

And see F:Manners—*shaking hands—bank employee*

Business and commerce

—*office:* "Such vapid and flat daylight as filtered through the ground-glass windows and skylights, leaving a black sediment upon the panes, showed the books and papers, and the figures bending over them, enveloped in a studious gloom, and as much abstracted in appearance, from the world without, as if they wre assembled at the bottom of the sea; while a mouldy little strong room in the obscure perspective, where a shady lamp was always burning, might have represented the cavern of some ocean-monster, looking on with a red eye at these mysteries of the deep." DS 13

—*political economy:* "Mr Baps was a very grave gentleman, with a slow and measured manner of speaking; and before he had stood under the lamp five minutes, he began to talk to Toots (who had been silently comparing pumps with him) about what you were to do with your raw materials when they came into your ports in return for your drain of gold. Mr Toots, to whom the question seemed perplexing, suggsted 'Cook 'em.' But Mr Baps did not appear to think that would do . . . .

" . . . [Paul] observed Mr Baps the dancing-master get into conversation with Sir Barnet Skettles, and very soon ask him, as he had asked Mr Toots, what you were to do with your raw materials, when they came into your ports in return for your drain of gold—which was such a mystery to Paul that he was quite desirous to know what ought to be done with them. Sir Barnet Skettles had much to say upon the question, and said it; but it did not appear to solve the question, for Mr Baps retorted, Yes, but supposing Russia stepped in with her tallows; which struck Sir Barnet almost dumb, for he could only shake his head after that, and say, Why then you must fall back upon your cottons, he supposed." DS 14

Clubs

—*the Athenæum:* "One day, upon the steps of the Athenæum, of which eminent institution I have the honour to be a member, I found a fellow-member, Mr Prowler, of the Royal Society of Arts, lying in wait, under the portico, to pour a drop of special information into the ear of every man and brother who approached the temple. Mr Prowler is a grave and secret personage, always specially informed, who whispers his way through life; incessantly acting Midas to everybody else's Reed. He goes about, like a lukewarm draught of air, breathing intelligence into the ears of his fellow-men, and passing on." HW/BA

—*background:* "Gentlemen's clubs were once maintained for purposes of savage party warfare; working men's clubs of the same day assumed the same character. Gentlemen's clubs became places of quiet inoffensive recreation; working men's clubs began to follow suit." UT/BB

—*district:* "In that portion of Pall Mall, London, which is bounded on the east by the Senior United Service Club House, and on the west by the Carlton Club House—a miasmatic spot, in which I suppose more boredom to be babbled daily, than in any two thousand square miles on the surface of the earth—into that dismal region I had sometimes tracked [the Best Authority], and there lost him." HW/BA

—*the Reform:* "As I know the Best Authority to pervade that building constantly, my eye had frequently sought him, with a vague sense of the supernatural and an irresistible feeling of dread, in the galleries overhanging the hall where I had but too often heard him quoted. No trace of his form, however, had revealed itself to me ....

"I should explain that in the palatial establishment of which I write, there is a dreadful little vault on the left of the Hall, where we hang up our hats and coats; the gloom and closeness of which vault, shade the imagination." HW/BA

Crowd

—*city:* "Who could sit upon anything in Fleet Street during the busy hours of the day, and not be dazed and deafened by two immense processions, one ever tending westward with the sun, the other ever tending eastward from the sun, both ever tending to the plains beyond the range of red and purple where the sun goes down!

"With his straw in his mouth, Mr Cruncher sat watching the two streams, like the heathen rustic who has for several centuries been on duty watching one stream—saving that Jerry had no expectation of their ever running dry." TTC ii 14

—*creation:* "Now, we were perfectly aware that if two men stop in the street to look at any given object, or even to gaze in the air, two hundred men will be assembled in no time; but as we knew very well that no crowd of people could by possibility remain in a street for five minutes without getting up a little amusement among themselves, unless they had some absorbing object in view, the natural inquiry next in order was, 'What are all these people waiting here for?' . . . " SB/PV

—*its faces:* "The throng of people hurried by, in two opposite streams, with no symptom of cessation or exhaustion; intent upon their own affairs, and undisturbed in their business speculations, by the roar of carts and waggons laden with clashing wares, the slipping of horses' feet upon the wet and greasy pavement, the rattling of the rain on windows and umbrella-tops, the jostling of the more impatient passengers, and all the noise and tumult of a crowded street in the high tide of its occupation ....

"Some frowned, some smiled, some muttered to themselves; some made light gestures, as if anticipating the conversation in which they would shortly be engaged; some wore the cunning look of bargaining and plotting, some were anxious and eager, some slow and dull; in some countenances were written gain, in others loss.

"It was like being in the confidence of all these people to stand quietly there, looking into their faces as they flitted past. In busy places, where each man has an object of his own, and feels assured that every other man has his, his character and purpose are written broadly in his face. In the public walks and lounges of a town, people go to see and to be seen, and there the same expression, with little variety, is repeated a hundred times. The working-day faces come nearer to the truth, and let it out more plainly." ¶OCS 44

—*noise:* "'The world has gone mad, I think,' said the single gentleman, pressing through the concourse with his supposed bride. 'Stand back here, will you, and let me knock.'

"Anything that makes a noise is satisfactory to a crowd. A score of dirty hands were raised directly to knock for him, and seldom has a knocker of equal powers been made to produce more deafening sounds than this particular engine on the occasion in question. Having rendered these voluntary services, the throng modestly retired a little, preferring that the single gentleman should bear their consequences alone." OCS 47

—*outside a theatre:* "Having nothing to look at but the mud and the closed doors, they looked at me, and highly enjoyed the comic spectacle. My modesty inducing me to draw off, some hundreds of yards, into a dark corner, they at once forgot me, and applied themselves to their former occupation of looking at the mud and looking in at the closed doors: which, being of grated ironwork, allowed the lighted passage within to be seen. They were chiefly people of respectable appearance, odd and impulsive as most crowds are, and making a joke of being there as most crowds do." UT/TV

—and the river: "The roar soon grew more loud, the passengers more numerous, the shops more busy, until [Florence] was carried onward in a stream of life setting that way, and flowing, indifferently, past marts and mansions, prisons, churches, marketplaces, wealth, poverty, good, and evil, like the broad river side by side with it, awakened from its dreams of rushes, willows, and green moss, and rolling on, turbid and troubled, among the works and cares of men, to the deep sea." DS 48

Dance and Dancing

—with an agenda: " . . . determining to show the family what quality of man they trifled with, and influenced perhaps by his late libations, [Richard Swiveller] performed such feats of agility and such spins and twirls as filled the company with astonishment, and in particular caused a very long gentleman who was dancing with a very short scholar, to stand quite transfixed by wonder and admiration. Even Mrs Wackles forgot for the moment to snub three small young ladies who were inclined to be happy, and could not repress a rising thought that to have such a dancer as that in the family would be a pride indeed." OCS 8

—at Almack's in New York City: "Five or six couples come upon the floor, marshalled by a lively young negro, who is the wit of the assembly, and the greatest dancer known. He never leaves off making queer faces, and is the delight of all the rest, who grin from ear to ear incessantly. Among the dancers are two young mulatto girls, with large, black, drooping eyes, and head-gear after the fashion of the hostess, who are as shy, or feign to be, as though they never danced before, and so look down before the visitors, that their partners can see nothing but the long fringed lashes.

"But the dance commences. Every gentleman sets as long as he likes to the opposite lady, and the opposite lady to him, and all are so long about it that the sport begins to languish, when suddenly the lively hero dashes in to the rescue. Instantly the fiddler grins, and goes at it tooth and nail; there is new energy in the tambourine; new laughter in the dancers; new smiles in the landlady, new confidence in the landlord; new brightness in the very candles.

"Single shuffle, double shuffle, cut and cross-cut; snapping his fingers, rolling his eyes, turning in his knees, presenting the backs of his legs in front, spinning about on his toes and heels like nothing but the man's fingers on the tambourine; dancing with two left legs, two right legs, two wooden legs, two wire legs, two spring legs—all sorts of legs and no legs—what is this to him? And in what walk of life, or dance of life, does man ever get such stimulating applause as thunders about him, when, having danced his partner off her feet, and himself too, he finishes by leaping gloriously on the bar-counter, and calling for something to drink, with the chuckle of a million of counterfeit Jim Crows, in one inimitable sound!" ¶AN 6

—apprentices: "The notion of apprentices was still so odd to me, that I asked Caddy if there were many of them?

"'Four,' said Caddy. 'One in-door, and three out. They are very good children; only when they get together they *will* play—children like—instead of attending to their work. So the little boy you saw just now waltzes by himself in the empty kitchen, and we distribute the others over the house as well as we can.'

"'That is only for their steps, of course?' said I.

"'Only for their steps,' said Caddy. 'In that way they practise, so many hours at a time, whatever steps they happen to be upon. They dance in the academy; and at this time of year we do Figures at five every morning.'

"'Why, what a laborious life!' I exclaimed.

"'I assure you, my dear,' returned Caddy, smiling, 'when the out-door apprentices ring us up in the morning . . . and when I put up the window, and see them standing on the door-step with their little pumps under their arms, I am actually reminded of the Sweeps.'" BH 38

—calling a dance in Liverpool: "As master of the ceremonies, [the landlord] called all the figures, and occasionally addressed himself parenthetically after this manner. When he was very loud, I use capitals.

"'Now den! Hoy! ONE. Right and left. (Put a steam on, gib 'um powder.) LA-dies' chail. BAL-loon say. Lemonade! TWO. ADwarnse and go back (gib 'ell a breakdown, shake it out o' yerselbs, keep a movil). SWING-corners, BAL-loon say, and Lemonade! (Hoy!) THREE. GENT come for'ard with a lady and go back, hoppersite come for'ard and do what yer can (Aeiohoy!) BAL-loon say, and leetle lemonade (Dat hair nigger by 'um fireplace 'hind a' time, shake it out o' yerselbs, gib 'ell a breakdown). Now den! Hoy! FOUR! Lemonade. BAL-loon say, and swing. FOUR ladies meets in 'um middle, FOUR gents goes round 'um ladies, FOUR gents passes out under 'um ladies' arms, SWING—and lemonade till 'a moosic can't play no more! (Hoy, Hoy!)'" UT/MJ

—*la Carmagnole:* " . . . presently [Lucie Manette] heard a troubled movement and a shouting coming along, which filled her with fear. A moment afterwards, and a throng of people came pouring round the corner by the prison wall, in the midst of whom was the wood-sawyer hand in hand with The Vengeance. There could not be fewer than five hundred people, and they were dancing like five thousand demons.

"There was no other music than their own singing. They danced to the popular Revolution song, keeping a ferocious time that was like a gnashing of teeth in unison. Men and women danced together, women danced together, men danced together, as hazard had brought them together.

"At first, they were a mere storm of coarse red caps and coarse woollen rags; but, as they filled the place, and stopped to dance about Lucie, some ghastly apparition of a dance-figure gone raving mad arose among them. They advanced, retreated, struck at one another's hands, clutched at one another's heads, spun round alone, caught one another and spun round in pairs, until many of them dropped. While those were down, the rest linked hand in hand, and all spun round together: then the ring broke, and in separate rings of two and four they turned and turned until they all stopped at once, began again, struck, clutched, and tore, and then reversed the spin, and all spun round another way. Suddenly they stopped again, paused, struck out the time afresh, formed into lines the width of the public way, and, with their heads low down and their hands high up, swooped screaming off.

"No fight could have been half so terrible as this dance. It was so emphatically a fallen sport—a something, once innocent, delivered over to all devilry—a healthy pastime changed into a means of angering the blood, bewildering the senses, and steeling the heart. Such grace as was visible in it, made it the uglier, showing how warped and perverted all things good by nature were become. The maidenly bosom bared to this, the pretty almost-child's head thus distracted, the delicate foot mincing in this slough of blood and dirt, were types of the disjointed time.

"This was the Carmagnole." ¶TTC iii 5

—*Christmas party:* "Away they all went, twenty couple at once; hands half round and back again the other way; down the middle and up again; round and round in various stages of affectionate grouping; old top couple always turning up in the wrong place; new top couple starting off again, as soon as they got there; all top couples at last, and not a bottom one to help them! . . .

" . . . the fiddler . . . struck up 'Sir Roger de Coverley.' Then old Fezziwig stood out to dance with Mrs Fezziwig. Top couple, too; with a good stiff piece of work cut out for them; three or four and twenty pair of partners; people who were not to be trifled with; people who *would* dance, and had no notion of walking." CC 1

"Now, too, the lively air that fanned [the fire], grew less gentle as the music quickened and the dance proceeded with new spirit; and a breeze arose that made the leaves and berries dance upon the wall, as they had often done upon the trees; and the breeze rustled in the room as if an invisible company of fairies, treading in the footsteps of the good substantial revellers, were whirling after them. Now, too, no feature of the Doctor [Jeddler]'s face could be distinguished as he spun and spun; and now there seemed a dozen Birds of Paradise in fitful flight; and now there were a thousand little bells at work; and now a fleet of flying skirts was ruffled by a little tempest, when the music gave in, and the dance was over." BL 2

—*imagined:* "We had been looking on at this little pantomime with great satisfaction for some time, when, to our unspeakable astonishment, we perceived that the whole of the characters, including a numerous corps de ballet of boots and shoes in the background, into which we had been hastily thrusting as many feet as we could press into the service, were arranging themselves in order for dancing; and some music striking up at the moment, to it they went without delay.

"It was perfectly delightful to witness the agility of the market-gardener. Out went the boots, first on one side, then on the other, then cutting, then shuffling, then setting to the Denmark satins, then advancing, then retreating, then going round, and then repeating the whole of the evolutions again, without appearing to suffer in the least from the violence of the exercise.

"Nor were the Denmark satins a bit behindhand, for they jumped and bounded about in all directions; and though they were neither so regular, nor so true to the time as the cloth boots, still, as they seemed to do it from the heart, and to enjoy it more, we candidly confess that we preferred their style of dancing to the other.

"But the old gentleman in the list shoes was the most amusing object in the whole party: for besides his grotesque attempts to appear youthful, and amorous, which were sufficiently entertaining in themselves, the young fellow in the pumps managed so artfully that every time the old gentleman advanced to salute the lady in the cloth boots, he trod with his whole weight on the old fellow's toes, which made him roar with anguish, and rendered all the others like to die of laughing." SB/MS

—*in politics:* "The uselessness of arguing with any supporter of a Government or of an Opposition, is well known. Try dancing. It is a better exercise, and has the unspeakable recommendation that it couldn't be reported." UT/MM

—*school party:* "Mr Feeder, after imbibing several custard-cups of negus, began to enjoy himself. The dancing in general was ceremonious, and the music rather solemn—a little like church music in fact—but after the custard-cups Mr Feeder told Mr Toots that he was going to throw a little spirit into the thing. After that, Mr Feeder not only began to dance as if he meant dancing and nothing else, but secretly to stimulate the music to perform wild tunes. Further, he became particular in his attentions to the ladies; and dancing with Miss Blimber, whispered to her—whispered to her!—though not so softly but that Paul heard him say this remarkable poetry,

'Had I a heart for falsehood framed,
I ne'er could injure YOU!'

This, Paul heard him repeat to four young ladies in succession. Well might Mr Feeder say to Mr Toots, that he was afraid he should be worse for it tomorrow!" DS 14

—*solemn:* " . . . [Tracy Tupman] hopping about, with a face expressive of the most intense solemnity, dancing (as a good many people do) as if a quadrille were not a thing to be laughed at, but a severe trial to the feelings, which it requires inflexible resolution to encounter." PP 2

"We danced for an hour with great gravity; the melancholy child doing wonders with his lower extremities, in which there appeared to be some sense of enjoyment though it never rose above his waist." BH 38

—*unaffected:* "If there were no such thing as display in the world, my private opinion is, and I hope you agree with me, that we might get on a great deal better than we do, and might be infinitely more agreeable company than we are. It was charming to see how these girls danced. They had no spectators but the apple-pickers on the ladders. They were very glad to please them, but they danced to please themselves (or at least you would have supposed so); and you could no more help admiring, than they could help dancing. How they did dance!

"Not like opera-dancers. Not at all. And not like Madame Anybody's finished pupils. Not the least. It was not quadrille dancing, nor minuet dancing, nor even country-dance dancing. It was neither in the old style, nor the new style, nor the French style, nor the English style: though it may have been by accident, a trifle in the Spanish style, which is a free and joyous one, I am told, deriving a delightful air of off-hand inspiration, from the chirping little castanets.

"As they danced among the orchard trees, and down the groves of stems and back again, and twirled each other lightly round and round, the influence of their airy motion seemed to spread and spread, in the sunlighted scene, like an expanding circle in the water. Their streaming hair and fluttering skirts, the elastic grass beneath their feet, the boughs that rustled in the morning air—the flashing leaves, the speckled shadows on the soft green ground—the balmy wind that swept along the landscape, glad to turn the distant windmill, cheerily—everything between the two girls, and the man and team at plough upon the ridge of land, where they showed against the sky as if they were the last things in the world—seemed dancing too." ¶BL 1

—after a wedding: "There was a dance in the evening. With which general mention of that recreation, I should have left it alone, if I had not some reason to suppose that it was quite an original dance, and one of a most uncommon figure. It was formed in an odd way; in this way. Edward [Plummer], that sailor-fellow—a good free dashing sort of a fellow he was—had been telling them various marvels concerning parrots, and mines, and Mexicans, and gold dust, when all at once he took it in his head to jump up from his seat and propose a dance; for Bertha's harp was there, and she had such a hand upon it as you seldom hear. Dot (sly little piece of affectation when she chose) said her dancing days were over; *I* think because the carrier was smoking his pipe, and she liked sitting by him, best. Mrs Fielding had no choice, of course, but to say *her* dancing days were over, after that; and everybody said the same, except May; May was ready.

"So, May and Edward get up, amid great applause, to dance alone; and Bertha plays her liveliest tune.

"Well! if you'll believe me, they have not been dancing five minutes, when suddenly the carrier flings his pipe away, takes Dot round the waist, dashes out into the room, and starts off with her, toe and heel, quite wonderfully. Tackleton no sooner sees this, than he skims across to Mrs Fielding, takes her round the waist, and follows suit. Old Dot no sooner sees this, than up he is, all alive, whisks off Mrs Dot in the middle of the dance, and is the foremost there. Caleb [Plummer] no sooner sees this, than he clutches Tilly Slowboy by both hands and goes off at score; Miss Slowboy, firm in the belief that diving hotly in among the other couples, and effecting any number of concussions with them, is your only principle of footing it." CH 3

Dilettante

—an amateur: "'[Harold Skimpole] is grown up—he is at least as old as I am—but in simplicity, and freshness, and enthusiasm, and a fine guileless inaptitude for all worldly affairs, he is a perfect child . . . . He is a musical man; an Amateur, but might have been a Professional. He is an Artist, too; an Amateur, but might have been a Professional. He is a man of attainments and of captivating manners. He has been unfortunate in his affairs, and unfortunate in his pursuits, and unfortunate in his family; but he don't care—he's a child!' . . .

" . . . he must confess to two of the oldest infirmities in the world: one was, that he had no idea of time; the other, that he had no idea of money. In consequence of which he never kept an appointment, never could transact any business, and never knew the value of anything! Well! So he had got on in life, and here he was!

"He was very fond of reading the papers, very fond of making fancy sketches with a pencil, very fond of nature, very fond of art. All he asked of society was, to let him live. *That* wasn't much. His wants were few. Give him the papers, conversation, music, mutton, coffee, landscape, fruit in the season, a few sheets of Bristol-board, and a little claret, and he asked no more. He was a mere child in the world, but he didn't cry for the moon. He said to the world, 'Go your several ways in peace! Wear red coats, blue coats, lawn sleeves, put pens behind your ears, wear aprons; go after glory, holiness, commerce, trade, any object you prefer; only—let Harold Skimpole live!'" BH ¶6

—in art: "'An artist, I infer from what he says?'

"'A sort of a one,' said Daniel Doyce, in a surly tone.

"'What sort of a one?' asked Clennam, with a smile.

"'Why, he has sauntered into the Arts at a leisurely Pall-Mall pace,' said Doyce, 'and I doubt if they care to be taken quite so coolly.'" LD i 17

" . . . Henry Gowan, inheriting from his father, the Commissioner, that very questionable help in life, a very small independence, had been difficult to settle; the rather, as public appointments chanced to be scarce, and his genius, during his earlier manhood, was of that exclusively agricultural character which applies itself to the cultivation of wild oats.

"At last he had declared that he would become a Painter; partly because he had always had an idle knack that way, and partly to grieve the souls of the Barnacles-in-chief who had not provided for him. So it had come to pass successively, first, that several distinguished ladies had been frightfully shocked; then, that portfolios of his performances had been handed about o'nights, and declared with ecstasy to be perfect **Claudes**, perfect **Cuyps**, perfect phænomena; then, that Lord Decimus had bought his picture, and had asked the President and Council to dinner at a blow, and had said, with his own magnificent gravity, 'Do you know, there appears to me to be really immense merit in that work?' and, in short, that people of condition had absolutely taken pains to bring him into fashion.

"But, somehow it had all failed. The prejudiced public had stood out against it obstinately. They had determined not to admire Lord Decimus's picture. They had determined to believe that in every service, except their own, a man must qualify himself, by striving, early and late, and by working heart and soul, might and main. So now Mr Gowan, like that worn-out old coffin which never was Mahomet's nor anybody else's, hung midway between two points: jaundiced and jealous as to the one he had left: jaundiced and jealous as to the other that he couldn't reach." ¶LD i 17

—dabbler: "[Mrs Bayham Badger] was surrounded in the drawing-room by various objects, indicative of her painting a little, playing the piano a little, playing the guitar a little, playing the harp a little, singing a little, working a little, reading a little, writing poetry a little, and botanising a little . . . . If I add, to the little list of her accomplishments, that she rouged a little, I do not mean that there was any harm in it." BH 13

—exemplar of taste: "[Chevy Slyme] was brooding over the remains of yesterday's decanter of brandy, and was engaged in the thoughtful occupation of making a chain of rings on the top of the table with the wet foot of his drinking-glass. Wretched and forlorn as he looked, Mr Slyme had once been, in his way, the choicest of swaggerers; putting forth his pretensions, boldly, as man of infinite taste and most undoubted promise. The stock-in-trade requisite to set up an amateur in this department of business is very slight, and easily got together: a trick of the nose and a curl of the lip sufficient to compound a tolerable sneer, being ample provision for any exigency. But, in an evil hour, this off-shoot of the Chuzzlewit trunk, being lazy, and ill qualified for any regular pursuit, and having dissipated such means as he ever possessed, had formally established himself as a professor of Taste for a livelihood; and finding, too late, that something more than his old amount of qualifications was necessary to sustain him in this calling, had quickly fallen to his present level, where he retained nothing of his old self but his boastfulness and his bile, and seemed to have no existence separate or apart from his friend Tigg. And now, so abject and so pitiful was he—at once so maudlin, insolent, beggarly, and proud—that even his friend and parasite, standing erect beside him, swelled into a Man by contrast." MC 7 *And see* LC:Shakespeare—*cited to praise*

—good intentions: "It was a snug room, Mr Feeder's, with his bed in another little room inside of it; and a flute, which Mr Feeder couldn't play yet, but was going to make a point of learning, he said, hanging up over the fireplace. There were some books in it, too, and a fishing-rod; for Mr Feeder said he should certainly make a point of learning to fish, when he could find time. Mr Feeder had amassed, with similar intentions, a beautiful little curly secondhand key-bugle, a chessboard and men, a Spanish Grammar, a set of sketching materials, and a pair of boxing-gloves." DS 14

Emigrant

—aboard ship: "It was such a strange scene to me, and so confined and dark, that, at first, I could make out hardly anything; but, by degrees, it cleared, as my eyes became more accustomed to the gloom, and I seemed to stand in a picture by **Ostade**.

"Among the great beams, bulks, and ringbolts of the ship, and the emigrant-berths, and chests, and bundles, and barrels, and heaps of miscellaneous baggage—lighted up, here and there, by dangling lanterns; and elsewhere by the yellow daylight straying down a windsail or a hatchway—were crowded groups of people, making new friendships, taking leave of one another, talking, laughing, crying, eating and drinking; some, already settled down into the possession of their few feet of space, with their little households arranged, and tiny children established on stools, or in dwarf elbow-chairs; others, despairing of a resting-place, and wandering disconsolately.

"From babies who had but a week or two of life behind them, to crooked old men and women who seemed to have but a week or two of life before them; and from ploughmen bodily carrying out soil of England on their boots, to smiths taking away samples of its soot and smoke upon their skins; every age and occupation appeared to be crammed into the narrow compass of the 'tween decks." ¶DC 57

"There were English people, Irish people, Welsh people, and Scotch people there; all with their little store of coarse food and shabby clothes; and nearly all with their families of children. There were children of all ages; from the baby at the breast, to the slattern-girl who was as much a grown woman as her mother. Every kind of domestic suffering that is bred in poverty, illness, banishment, sorrow, and long travel in bad weather, was crammed into the little space; and yet was there infinitely less of complaint and querulousness, and infinitely more of mutual assistance and general kindness to be found in that unwholesome ark, than in many brilliant ball-rooms.

"Mark [Tapley] looked about him wistfully, and his face brightened as he looked. Here an old grandmother was crooning over a sick child, and rocking it to and fro, in arms hardly more wasted than its own young limbs; here a poor woman with an infant in her lap, mended another little creature's clothes, and quieted another who was creeping up about her from their scanty bed upon the floor. Here were old men awkwardly engaged in little household offices, wherein they would have been ridiculous but for their good-will and kind purpose; and here were swarthy fellows—giants in their way—doing such little acts of tenderness for those about them, as might have belonged to gentlest-hearted dwarfs. The very idiot in the corner who sat mowing there, all day, had his faculty of imitation roused by what he saw about him; and snapped his fingers to amuse a crying child." MC 15

—embarking: "My Emigrant Ship lies broadside-on to the wharf. Two great gangways made of spars and planks connect her with the wharf; and up and down these gangways, perpetually crowding to and fro and in and out, like ants, are the Emigrants who are going to sail in my Emigrant Ship. Some with cabbages, some with loaves of bread, some with cheese and butter, some with milk and beer, some with boxes, beds, and bundles, some with babies—nearly all with children—nearly all with bran-new tin cans for their daily allowance of water, uncomfortably suggestive of a tin flavour in the drink.

"To and fro, up and down, aboard and ashore, swarming here and there and everywhere, my Emigrants. And still as the Dock-Gate swings upon its hinges, cabs appear, and carts appear, and vans appear, bringing more of my Emigrants, with more cabbages, more loaves, more cheese and butter, more milk and beer, more boxes, beds, and bundles, more tin cans, and on those shipping investments accumulated compound interest of children." ¶UT/SL

—poignance: "It was then calm, radiant sunset. She lay between us and the red light; and every taper line and spar was visible against the glow. A sight at once so beautiful, so mournful, and so hopeful, as the glorious ship, lying still on the flushed water, with all the life on board her crowded at the bulwarks, and there clustering, for a moment, bare-headed and silent, I never saw." DC 57

—practical preparation: "'In reference to our domestic preparations, madam,' said Mr Micawber, with some pride, 'for meeting the destiny to which we are now understood to be self-devoted, I beg to report them. My eldest daughter attends at five every morning in a neighbouring establishment, to acquire the process—if process it may be called—of milking cows. My younger children are instructed to observe, as closely as circumstances will permit, the habits of the pigs and poultry maintained in the poorer parts of this city; a pursuit from which they have, on two occasions, been brought home, within an inch of being run over. I have myself directed some attention, during the past week, to the art of baking; and my son Wilkins has issued forth with a walking-stick and driven cattle, when permitted, by the rugged hirelings who had them in charge, to render any voluntary service in that direction—which I regret to say, for the credit of our nature, was not often; he being generally warned, with imprecations, to desist.'" DC 54

And see IG:Government—*call for protective regulation*

Gambling

—ambience: "The excitement of play, hot rooms, and glaring lights, was not calculated to allay the fever of the time. In that giddy whirl of noise and confusion, the men were delirious. Who thought of money, ruin, or the morrow, in the savage intoxication of the moment? More wine was called for, glass after glass was drained, their parched and scalding mouths were cracked with thirst. Down poured the wine like oil on blazing fire. And still the riot went on. The debauchery gained its height; glasses were dashed upon the floor by hands that could

not carry them to lips; oaths were shouted out by lips which could scarcely form the words to vent them in; drunken losers cursed and roared; some mounted on the tables, waving bottles above their heads, and bidding defiance to the rest; some danced, some sang, some tore the cards and raved." NN 50

—cards: " . . . [Godfrey Nickleby] had wedded an old flame out of mere attachment, who in her turn had taken him for the same reason. Thus two people who cannot afford to play cards for money, sometimes sit down to a quiet game for love." NN 1

—croupier: "The [man] presided over the rouge-et-noir table. He was probably some ten years younger [than the proprietor], and was a plump, paunchy, sturdy-looking fellow, with his under-lip a little pursed from a habit of counting money inwardly as he paid it, but with no decidedly bad expression in his face, which was rather an honest and jolly one than otherwise. He wore no coat, the weather being hot, and stood behind the table with a huge mound of crowns and half-crowns before him, and a cash-box for notes.

"This game was constantly playing. Perhaps twenty people would be staking at the same time. This man had to roll the ball, to watch the stakes as they were laid down, to gather them off the colour which lost, to pay those who won, to do it all with the utmost despatch, to roll the ball again, and to keep this game perpetually alive. He did it all with a rapidity absolutely marvellous; never hesitating, never making a mistake, never stopping, and never ceasing to repeat . . . [certain] unconnected phrases . . . which, partly from habit, and partly to have something appropriate and business-like to say, he constantly poured out with the same monotonous emphasis, and in nearly the same order, all day long . . . . " ¶NN 50

—the lottery in Italy: "There is one extraordinary feature in the real life of Naples, at which we may take a glance before we go—the Lotteries.

"They prevail in most parts of Italy, but are particularly obvious, in their effects and influences here. They are drawn every Saturday. They bring an immense revenue to the Government; and diffuse a taste for gambling among the poorest of the poor, which is very comfortable to the coffers of the State, and very ruinous to themselves.

"The lowest stake is one grain; less than a farthing. One hundred numbers—from one to a hundred, inclusive—are put into a box. Five are drawn. Those are the prizes. I buy three numbers. If one of them comes up, I win a small prize. If two, some hundreds of times my stake. If three, three thousand five hundred times my stake. I stake (or play as they call it) what I can upon my numbers, and buy what numbers I please . . . .

"Every lottery office keeps a printed book, as Universal Lottery Diviner, where every possible accident and circumstance is provided for, and has a number against it . . . .

"If the roof of the theatre of San Carlo were to fall in, so many people would play upon the numbers attached to such an accident in the Diviner, that the Government would soon close those numbers, and decline to run the risk of losing any more upon them. This often happens. Not long ago, when there was a fire in the King's Palace, there was such a desperate run on fire, and king, and palace, that further stakes on the numbers attached to those words in the Golden Book were forbidden. Every accident or event, is supposed, by the ignorant populace, to be a revelation to the beholder, or party concerned, in connexion with the lottery . . . .

"I heard of a horse running away with a man, and dashing him down, dead, at the corner of a street. Pursuing the horse with incredible speed, was another man, who ran so fast, that he came up, immediately after the accident. He threw himself upon his knees beside the unfortunate rider, and clasped his hand with an expression of the wildest grief. 'If you have life,' he said, 'speak one word to me! If you have one gasp of breath left, mention your age for Heaven's sake, that I may play that number in the lottery.'" PI 17

—proprietor: " . . . a man of six or eight and fifty, who sat on a chair near one of the entrances of the booth, with his hands folded on the top of his stick and his chin appearing above them. He was a tall, fat, long-bodied man, buttoned up to the throat in a light green coat, which made his body look still longer than it was, and wore besides drab breeches and gaiters, a white neckerchief, and a broad-brimmed white hat. Amid all the buzzing noise of the games and the perpetual passing in and out of people, he seemed perfectly calm and abstracted, without the smallest particle of excitement in his composition.

"He exhibited no indication of weariness, nor, to a casual observer, of interest either. There he sat, quite still and collected. Sometimes, but very rarely, he nodded to some passing face, or beckoned to a waiter to obey a call from one of the tables. The next instant he subsided into his old state. He might have been some profoundly deaf old gentleman, who had come in to take a rest, or he might have been patiently waiting for a friend without the least consciousness of anybody's presence, or fixed in a trance, or under the influence of opium.

"People turned round and looked at him; he made no gesture, caught nobody's eye—let them pass away, and others come on and be succeeded by others, and took no notice. When he did move, it seemed wonderful how he could have seen anything to occasion it. And so, in truth, it was. But there was not a face that passed in or out this man failed to see, not a gesture at any one of the three tables that was lost upon him, not a word spoken by the bankers but reached his ear, not a winner or loser he could not have marked; and he was the proprietor of the place." ¶NN 50

—rationalized: "'I am no gambler . . . . I call Heaven to witness that I never played for gain of mine, or love of play; that at every piece I staked, I whispered to myself that orphan's name and called on Heaven to bless the venture, which it never did. Whom did it prosper? Who were those with whom I played? Men who lived by plunder, profligacy, and riot, squandering their gold in doing ill and propagating vice and evil. My winnings would have been from them, my winnings would have been bestowed to the last farthing on a young sinless child whose life they would have sweetened and made happy. What would they have contracted? The means of corruption, wretchedness, and misery. Who would not have hoped in such a cause . . . who would not have hoped as I did?'" OCS 9

Games and sports

—backgammon: "Miss Dartle played backgammon as eagerly as she did everything else. If I had seen her, first, at the board, I should have fancied that her figure had got thin, and her eyes had got large, over that pursuit, and no other in the world." DC 20

—Blind Man's Buff: "And I no more believe Topper was really blind than I believe he had eyes in his boots. My opinion is, that it was a done thing between him and Scrooge's nephew [Fred]; and that the Ghost of Christmas Present knew it. The way he went after that plump sister in the lace tucker, was an outrage on the credulity of human nature. Knocking down the fire-irons, tumbling over the chairs, bumping against the piano, smothering himself among the curtains, wherever she went, there went he!

"He always knew where the plump sister was. He wouldn't catch anybody else. If you had fallen up against him (as some of them did), on purpose, he would have made a feint of endeavouring to seize you, which would have been an affront to your understanding, and would instantly have sidled off in the direction of the plump sister. She often cried out that it wasn't fair; and it really was not.

"But when at last, he caught her; when, in spite of all her silken rustlings, and her rapid flutterings past him, he got her into a corner whence there was no escape; then his conduct was the most execrable. For his pretending not to know her; his pretending that it was necessary to touch her head-dress, and further to assure himself of her identity by pressing a certain ring upon her finger, and a certain chain about her neck; was vile, monstrous! No doubt she told him her opinion of it, when, another blind-man being in office, they were so very confidential together, behind the curtains." ¶CC 3

—bowls, in Italy: "The men, in red caps, and with loose coats hanging on their shoulders (they never put them on), were playing bowls, and buying sweetmeats, immediately outside the church. When half-a-dozen of them finished a game, they came into the aisle, crossed themselves with the holy water, knelt on one knee for an instant, and walked off again to play another game at bowls. They are remarkably expert at this diversion, and will play in the stony lanes and streets, and on the most uneven and disastrous ground for such a purpose, with as much nicety as on a billiard-table." PI 5

—cricket: "All-Muggleton had the first innings; and the interest became intense when Mr Dumkins and Mr Podder, two of the most renowned members of that most distinguished club, walked, bat in hand, to their respective wickets. Mr Luffey, the highest ornament of Dingley Dell, was pitched to bowl against the redoubtable Dumkins, and Mr Struggles was selected to do the same kind office for the hitherto un-

conquered Podder. Several players were stationed, to 'look out,' in different parts of the field, and each fixed himself into the proper attitude by placing one hand on each knee, and stooping very much as if he were 'making a back' for some beginner at leap-frog. All the regular players do this sort of thing;—indeed it's generally supposed that it is quite impossible to look out properly in any other position.

The Cricket Match PP

"The umpires were stationed behind the wickets; the scorers were prepared to notch the runs; a breathless silence ensued. Mr Luffey retired a few paces behind the wicket of the passive Podder, and applied the ball to his right eye for several seconds. Dumkins confidently awaited its coming with his eyes fixed on the motions of Luffey.

"'Play!' suddenly cried the bowler. The ball flew from his hand straight and swift towards the centre stump of the wicket. The wary Dumkins was on the alert; it fell upon the tip of his bat, and bounded far away over the heads of the scouts, who had just stooped low enough to let it fly over them.

"'Run—run—another.—Now, then, throw her up—up with her—stop there—another—no—yes—no—throw her up, throw her up!'—Such were the shouts which followed the stroke; and, at the conclusion of which All-Muggleton had scored two. Nor was Podder behindhand in earning laurels wherewith to garnish himself and Muggleton. He blocked the doubtful balls, missed the bad ones, took the good ones, and sent them flying to all parts of the field. The scouts were hot and tired; the bowlers were changed and bowled till their arms ached; but Dumkins and Podder remained unconquered.

"Did an elderly gentleman essay to stop

the progress of the ball, it rolled between his legs or slipped between his fingers. Did a slim gentleman try to catch it, it struck him on the nose, and bounded pleasantly off with redoubled violence, while the slim gentleman's eye filled with water, and his form writhed with anguish. Was it thrown straight up to the wicket, Dumkins had reached it before the ball.

"In short, when Dumkins was caught out, and Podder stumped out, All-Muggleton had notched some fifty-four, while the score of the Dingley Dellers was as blank as their faces. The advantage was too great to be recovered. In vain did the eager Luffey, and the enthusiastic Struggles, do all that skill and experience could suggest, to regain the ground Dingley Dell had lost in the contest;—it was of no avail; and in an early period of the winning game Dingley Dell gave in, and allowed the superior prowess of All-Muggleton." ¶PP 7

—at home: ". . . there was Mr Gabriel Parsons in a flannel jacket, running backwards and forwards, from a wicket to two hats piled on each other, and from the two hats to the wicket, in the most violent manner, while another gentleman with his coat off was getting down the area of the house, after a ball. When the gentleman without the coat had found it—which he did in less than ten minutes—he ran back to the hats, and Gabriel Parsons pulled up. Then the gentleman without the coat called out 'play,' very loudly, and bowled. Then Mr Gabriel Parsons knocked the ball several yards, and took another run. Then the other gentleman aimed at the wicket and didn't hit it; and Mr Gabriel Parsons, having finished running on his own account, laid down the bat and ran after the ball, which went into a neighbouring field. They called this cricket." SB/WT

—inexperienced at bat: "Shortly after leaving school, [Thomas Idle] accompanied a party of friends to a cricket-field, in his natural and appropriate character of spectator only. On the ground it was discovered that the players fell short of the required number, and facile Thomas was persuaded to assist in making up the complement. At a certain appointed time, he was roused from peaceful slumber in a dry ditch, and placed before three wickets with a bat in his hand. Opposite to him, behind three more wickets, stood one of his bosom friends, filling the situation (as he was informed) of bowler . . . . Stimulated to preternatural activity of body and sharpness of eye by the instinct of self-preservation, Mr Idle contrived, by jumping deftly aside at the right moment, and by using his bat (ridiculously narrow as it was for the purpose) as a shield, to preserve his life and limbs from the dastardly attack that had been made on both, to leave the full force of the deadly missile to strike his wicket instead of his leg; and to end the innings, so far as his side was concerned, by being immediately bowled out." LT 3

—inexperienced in the field: "[Idle's] conception of the whole art and mystery of 'fielding,' may be summed up in the three words of serious advice which he privately administered to himself on that trying occasion—avoid the ball. Fortified by this sound and salutary principle, he took his own course, impervious alike to ridicule and abuse. Whenever the ball came near him, he thought of his shins, and got out of the way immediately. 'Catch it!' 'Stop it!' 'Pitch it up!' were cries that passed by him like the idle wind that he regarded not. He ducked under it, he jumped over it, he whisked himself away from it on either side. Never once, through the whole innings did he and the ball come together on anything approaching to intimate terms." LT 3

—West Indian exploit: "'Warm!—red hot—scorching—glowing. Played a match once—single wicket—friend the Colonel—Sir Thomas Blazo—who should get the greatest number of runs.—Won the toss—first innings—seven o'clock A. M.—six natives to look out—went in; kept in—heat intense—natives all fainted—taken away—fresh half-dozen ordered—fainted also—Blazo bowling—supported by two natives—couldn't bowl me out—fainted too—cleared away the Colonel—wouldn't give in—faithful attendant—Quanko Samba—last man left—sun so hot, bat in blisters, ball scorched brown—five hundred and seventy runs—rather exhausted—Quanko mustered up last remaining strength—bowled me out—had a bath, and went out to dinner . . . .

"'Poor Quanko—never recovered it—bowled on, on my account—bowled off, on his own—died, sir.'" PP 7

—Mora, in Italy: "The most favourite game is the national one of Mora, which they pursue with surprising ardour, and at which they will stake everything they possess. It is a destructive kind of gambling, requiring no accessories but the ten fingers, which are always—I intend no pun—at hand. Two men play together. One calls a number—

say the extreme one, ten. He marks what portion of it he pleases by throwing out three, or four, or five fingers; and his adversary has, in the same instant, at hazard, and without seeing his hand, to throw out as many fingers, as will make the exact balance.

"Their eyes and hands become so used to this, and act with such astonishing rapidity, that an uninitiated bystander would find it very difficult, if not impossible, to follow the progress of the game. The initiated, however, of whom there is always an eager group looking on, devour it with the most intense avidity; and as they are always ready to champion one side or the other in case of a dispute, and are frequently divided in their partisanship, it is often a very noisy proceeding.

"It is never the quietest game in the world; for the numbers are always called in a loud sharp voice, and follow as close upon each other as they can be counted. On a holiday evening . . . you will hear this game in progress in a score of wine-shops at once; and looking over any vineyard walk, or turning almost any corner, will come upon a knot of players in full cry.

"It is observable that most men have a propensity to throw out some particular number oftener than another: and the vigilance with which two sharp-eyed players will mutually endeavour to detect this weakness, and adapt their game to it, is very curious and entertaining. The effect is greatly heightened by the universal suddenness and vehemence of gesture; two men playing for half a farthing with an intensity as all-absorbing as if the stake were life." ¶PI 5

—*schoolboys'*: "These Wednesdays were the happiest days of Mr Dick's life . . . though he never took an active part in any game but kite-flying, [he] was as deeply interested in all our sports as any one among us. How often have I seen him, intent upon a match at marbles or pegtop, looking on with a face of unutterable interest, and hardly breathing at the critical times! How often, at hare and hounds, have I seen him mounted on a little knoll, cheering the whole field on to action. . . ! How many a summer-hour have I known to be but blissful minutes to him in the cricket-field! How many winter days have I seen him, standing blue-nosed, in the snow and east wind, looking at the boys going down the long slide, and clapping his worsted gloves in rapture!" DC 17

—*whist:* "The rubber was conducted with all that gravity of deportment and sedateness of demeanour which befit the pursuit entitled 'whist'—a solemn observance, to which, as it appears to us, the title of 'game' has been very irreverently and ignominiously applied . . . Mr Miller . . . not being quite so much absorbed as he ought to have been, contrived to commit various high crimes and misdemeanours, which excited the wrath of the fat gentleman to a very great extent, and called forth the good-humour of the old lady in a proportionate degree.

"'There!' said the criminal Miller triumphantly, as he took up the odd trick at the conclusion of a hand; 'that could not have been played better, I flatter myself;—impossible to have made another trick!'

"'Miller ought to have trumped the diamond, oughtn't he, sir?' said the old lady.

"Mr Pickwick nodded assent.

"'Ought I, though?' said the unfortunate, with a doubtful appeal to his partner.

"'You ought, sir,' said the fat gentleman, in an awful voice.

"'Very sorry,' said the crestfallen Miller.

"'Much use that,' growled the fat gentleman.

"'Two by honours makes us eight,' said Mr Pickwick.

"Another hand. 'Can you one?' inquired the old lady.

"'I can,' replied Mr Pickwick. 'Double, single, and the rub.'

"'Never was such luck,' said Mr Miller.

"'Never was such cards,' said the fat gentleman.

"A solemn silence: Mr Pickwick humorous, the old lady serious, the fat gentleman captious, and Mr Miller timorous.

"'Another double,' said the old lady: triumphantly making a memorandum of the circumstance, by placing one sixpence and a battered half-penny under the candlestick.

"'A double, sir,' said Mr Pickwick.

"'Quite aware of the fact, sir,' replied the fat gentleman, sharply.

"Another game, with a similar result, was followed by a revoke from the unlucky Miller; on which the fat gentleman burst into a state of high personal excitement which lasted until the conclusion of the game, when he retired into a corner, and remained perfectly mute for one hour and twenty-seven minutes; at the end of which time he emerged from his retirement, and offered Mr Pickwick a pinch of snuff with the air of a man who had made up his mind to a Christian forgiveness of injuries sustained. The old lady's hearing decidedly improved, and . . . Miller felt as much out of his element as a dolphin in a sentry-box." PP 6

The Card-room at Bath PP

"Poor Mr Pickwick! he had never played with three thorough-paced female card-players before. They were so desperately sharp, that they quite frightened him. If he played a wrong card, Miss Bolo looked a small armoury of daggers; if he stopped to consider which was the right one, Lady Snuphanuph would throw herself back in her chair, and smile with a mingled glance of impatience and pity to Mrs Colonel Wugsby; at which Mrs Colonel Wugsby would shrug up her shoulders, and cough, as much as to say she wondered whether he ever would begin. Then, at the end of every hand, Miss Bolo would inquire with a dismal countenance and reproachful sigh, why Mr Pickwick had not returned that diamond, or led the club, or roughed the spade, or finessed the heart, or led through the honour, or brought out the ace, or played up to the king, or some such thing; and in reply to all these grave charges, Mr Pickwick would be wholly unable to plead any justification whatever, having by this time forgotten all about the game. People came and looked on, too, which made Mr Pickwick nervous. Besides all this, there was a great deal of distracting conversation near the table . . . . All these things, combined with the noises and interruptions of constant comings in and goings out, made Mr Pickwick play rather badly; the cards were against him, also; and when they left off at ten minutes past eleven, Miss Bolo rose from the table considerably agitated, and went straight home, in a flood of tears and a sedan-chair." PP 35

Housewife

—cooking: "First, [Ruth Pinch] tripped down-stairs into the kitchen for the flour, then for the pie-board, then for the eggs, then for the butter, then for a jug of water, then for the rolling pin, then for a pudding-basin, then for the pepper, then for the salt; making a separate journey for everything, and laughing every time she started off afresh.

"When all the materials were collected, she was horrified to find she had no apron on, and so ran *up*-stairs, by way of variety, to fetch it. She didn't put it on up-stairs, but came dancing down with it in her hand; and being one of those little women to whom an apron is a most becoming little vanity, it took an immense time to arrange; having to be carefully smoothed down beneath—Oh, heaven, what a wicked little stomacher! and to be gathered up into little plaits by the strings before it could be tied, and to be tapped, rebuked, and wheedled, at the pockets, before it would set right, which at last it did, and when it did—but never mind; this is a sober chronicle.

"And then, there were her cuffs to be tucked up, for fear of flour; and she had a little ring to pull off her finger, which wouldn't come off . . . and during the whole of these preparations she looked demurely every now and then at Tom, from under her dark eye-lashes, as if they were all a part of the pudding and indispensable to its composition . . . .

"Such a busy little woman as she was! So full of self-importance, and trying so hard not to smile, or seem uncertain about anything! It was a perfect treat to Tom to see her with her brows knit, and her rosy lips pursed up, kneading away at the crust, rolling it out, cutting it up into strips, lining the basin with it, shaving it off fine round the rim, chopping up the steak into small pieces, raining down pepper and salt upon them, packing them into the basin, pouring in cold water for gravy, and never venturing to steal a look in his direction, lest her gravity should be disturbed; until, at last, the basin being quite full and only wanting the top crust, she clapped her hands all covered with paste and flour, at Tom, and burst out heartily into such a charming little laugh of triumph, that the pudding need have had no other seasoning to commend it to the taste of any reasonable man on earth." ¶MC 39

—coping: " . . . the dress would be lain aside, trim little wrappers and aprons would be substituted, and Bella [Rokesmith], putting back her hair with both hands, as if she were making the most business-like arrangements for going dramatically distracted, would enter on the household affairs of the day. Such weighing and mixing and chopping and grating, such dusting and washing and polishing, such snipping and weeding and trowelling and other small gardening, such making and mending and folding and airing, such diverse arrangements, and above all such severe study!

"For Mrs J. R., who had never been wont to do too much at home as Miss B. W., was under the constant necessity of referring for advice and support to a sage volume entitled The Complete British Family Housewife, which she would sit consulting, with her elbows on the table and her temples on her hands, like some perplexed enchantress poring over the Black Art. This, principally because the Complete British Housewife, however sound a Briton at heart, was by no means an expert Briton at expressing herself with clearness in the British tongue, and sometimes might have issued her directions to equal purpose in the Kamskatchan language. In any crisis of this nature, Bella would suddenly exclaim aloud, 'Oh, you ridiculous old thing, what do you mean by that? You must have been drinking!' And having made this marginal note, would try the Housewife again, with all her dimples screwed into an expression of profound research.

"There was likewise a coolness on the part of the British Housewife, which Mrs John Rokesmith found highly exasperating. She would say, 'Take a salamander,' as if a general should command a private to catch a Tartar. Or, she would casually issue the order, 'Throw in a handful—' of something entirely unattainable. In these, the Housewife's most glaring moments of unreason, Bella would shut her up and knock her on the table, apostrophizing her with the compliment, 'Oh you ARE a stupid old donkey! Where am I to get it, do you think?'" ¶OMF iii 5

Knighthood

—*erroneous:* " . . . the late Sir Thomas Tippins, knighted in mistake for somebody else by His Majesty King George the Third, who, while performing the ceremony, was graciously pleased to observe, 'What, what, what? Who, who, who? Why, why, why?. . . " OMF i 10

—*hope for mayors:* "Mayors have been knighted for 'going up' with addresses: explosive machines intrepidly discharging shot and shell into the English Grammar. Mr Sapsea may 'go up' with an address. Rise, Sir Thomas Sapsea! Of such is the salt of the earth." MED 12

—*resentful:* " . . . Mrs Pocket was the only daughter of a certain quite accidental deceased Knight, who had invented for himself a conviction that his deceased father would have been made a Baronet but for somebody's determined opposition arising out of entirely personal motives—I forget whose, if I ever knew—the Sovereign's, the Prime Minister's, the Lord Chancellor's, the Archbishop of Canterbury's, anybody's—and had tacked himself on to the nobles of the earth in right of this quite supposititious fact. I believe he had been knighted himself for storming the English grammar at the point of the pen, in a desperate address engrossed on vellum, on the occasion of the laying of the first stone of some building or other, and for handing some Royal Personage either the trowel or the mortar." GE 23

—*reward of merit:* "But how Sir John? Nothing so simple, or so easy . . . . John Chester, Esquire, M. P., attended court—went up with an address—headed a deputation. Such elegance of manner, so many graces of deportment, such powers of conversation, could never pass unnoticed. Mr was too common for such merit. A man so gentlemanly should have been—but Fortune is capricious—born a Duke: just as some dukes should have been born labourers. He caught the fancy of the king, knelt down a grub, and rose a butterfly.." BR 40

Lodger

—*on cleaning day:* "The Captain in his own apartment was sitting with his hands in his pockets and his legs drawn up under his chair, on a very small desolate island, lying about midway in an ocean of soap and water. The Captain's windows had been cleaned, the walls had been cleaned, the stove had been cleaned, and everything, the stove excepted, was wet, and shining with soft soap and sand: the smell of which drysaltery impregnated the air. In the midst of the dreary scene, the Captain, cast away upon his island, looked round on the waste of waters with a rueful countenance, and seemed waiting for some friendly bark to come that way, and take him off." DS 23

—*intimidated:* "The door opening, without any note of preparation, and apparently of itself, the hard glazed hat in question skimmed into the room like a bird, and alighted heavily at the Captain's feet . . . .

"'You see I should have bore down on Sol Gills yesterday, and this morning, but she—she took it away and kep it. That's the long and short of the subject.'

"'Who did, for goodness sake? asked Susan Nipper.

"'The lady of the house, my dear,' returned the Captain, in a gruff whisper, and making signals of secrecy. 'We had some words about the swabbing of these here planks, and she—in short,' said the Captain, eyeing the door, and relieving himself with a long breath, 'she stopped my liberty.'

"' . . . . It's difficult navigation. She's very hard to carry on with, my dear. You never can tell how she'll head, you see. She's full one minute, and round upon you next. And when she *is* a tartar,' said the Captain, with the perspiration breaking out upon his forehead—. There was nothing but a whistle emphatic enough for the conclusion of the sentence, so the Captain whistled tremulously." DS 23

—*a landlady's view:* "It is a hardship hurting to the feelings that Lodgers open their minds so wide to the idea that you are trying to get the better of them and shut their minds so close to the idea that they are trying to get the better of you . . . . " CS/L 1

—*"wandering Christian":* " . . . why *they* should roam the earth looking for bills and then coming in and viewing the apartments and stickling about terms and never at all wanting them or dreaming of taking them being already provided, is a mystery I should be thankful to have explained if by any miracle it could be.

"It's wonderful they live so long and thrive so on it but I suppose the exercise makes it healthy, knocking so much and going from house to house and up and down stairs all day, and then their pretending to be so particular and punctual is a most astonishing thing, looking at their watches and saying 'Could you give me the refusal of the rooms till twenty minutes past eleven the day after to-morrow in the forenoon, and supposing it to be considered essential by my friend from the country could there be a small iron bedstead put in the little room upon the stairs?'

"Why when I was new to it my dear I used to consider before I promised and to make my mind anxious with calculations and to get quite wearied out with disappointments, but now I says 'Certainly by all means' well knowing it's a Wandering Christian and I shall hear no more about it, indeed by this time I know most of the Wandering Christians by sight as well as they know me, it being the habit of each individual revolving round London in that capacity to come back about twice a year, and it's very remarkable that it runs in families and the children grow up to it, but even were it otherwise I should no sooner hear of the friend from the country which is a certain sign than I should nod and say to myself You're a Wandering Christian, though whether they are (as I have heard) persons of small property with a taste for regular employment and frequent change of scene I cannot undertake to tell you." ¶CS/L 1

See also B:Food and Drink—*gravy*

Man

—*depth of passion:* "'No man knows till the time comes [said Headstone], what depths are within him. To some men it never comes; let them rest and be thankful. To me, you brought it; on me, you forced it; and the bottom of this raging sea,' striking himself upon the breast, 'has been heaved up ever since.'" OMF ii 15

—*distractible:* "The Analytical Chemist [butler] returning, everybody looks at him. Not because anybody wants to see him, but because of that subtle influence in nature which impels humanity to embrace the slightest opportunity of looking at anything, rather than the person who addresses it." OMF i 2

—*and machine:* "A clattering of clogs upon the pavement; a rapid ringing of bells; and all the melancholy mad elephants, polished and oiled up for the day's monotony, were at their heavy exercise again.

"Stephen [Blackpool] bent over his loom, quiet, watchful, and steady. A special contrast, as every man was in the forest of looms where Stephen worked, to the crashing, smashing, tearing piece of mechanism at which he laboured. Never fear, good people of an anxious turn of mind, that Art will consign Nature to oblivion. Set anywhere, side by side, the work of GOD and the work of man; and the former, even though it be a troop of Hands of very small account, will gain in dignity from the comparison.

"So many hundred Hands in this Mill; so many hundred horse Steam Power. It is known, to the force of a single pound weight, what the engine will do; but, not all the calculators of the National Debt can tell me the capacity for good or evil, for love or hatred, for patriotism or discontent, for the decomposition of virtue into vice, or the reverse, at any single moment in the soul of one of these its quiet servants, with the composed faces and the regulated actions. There is no mystery in it; there is an unfathomable mystery in the meanest of them, for ever.—Supposing we were to reverse our arithmetic for material objects, and to govern these awful unknown quantities by other means!" HT i 11

—*misanthrope*

—*classified:* "The despisers of mankind—apart from the mere fools and mimics, of that creed—are of two sorts. They who believe their merit neglected and unappreciated, make up one class; they who receive adulation and flattery, knowing their own worthlessness, compose the other. Be sure that the coldest-hearted misanthropes are ever of this last order." BR 24

—*hermitage:* "It was a nook in a rustic by-road, which the genius of Mopes had laid waste as completely, as if he had been born an Emperor and a Conqueror. Its centre object was a dwelling-house, sufficiently substantial, all the window-glass of which had been long ago abolished by the surprising genius of Mopes, and all the windows of which were barred across with rough-split logs of trees nailed over them on the outside.

"A rickyard, hip-high in vegetable rankness and ruin, contained outbuildings, from which the thatch had lightly fluttered away, on all the winds of all the seasons of the year, and from which the planks and beams had heavily dropped and rotted. The frosts and damps of winter, and the heats of summer, had warped what wreck remained, so that not a post or a board retained the position it was meant to hold, but everything was twisted from its purpose, like its owner, and degraded and debased.

"In this homestead of the sluggard, behind the ruined hedge, and sinking away among the ruined grass and the nettles, were the last perishing fragments of certain ricks: which had gradually mildewed and collapsed, until they looked like mounds of rotten honeycomb, or dirty sponge.

"Tom Tiddler's ground could even show its ruined water; for there was a slimy pond into which a tree or two had fallen—one soppy trunk and branches lay across it then—which in its accumulation of stagnant weed, and in its black decomposition, and in all its foulness and filth, was almost comforting, regarded as the only water that could have reflected the shameful place without seeming polluted by that low office." ¶CS/TT

—ostentatious: "'What *is* a Hermit?' asked the Traveller . . . .

"'I'll tell you what I suppose it to be,' said the Traveller. 'An abominably dirty thing.'

"'Mr Mopes is dirty, it cannot be denied,' said the Landlord.

"'Intolerably conceited.'

"'Mr Mopes is vain of the life he leads, some do say,' replied the Landlord, as another concession.

"'A slothful, unsavoury, nasty reversal of the laws of human nature,' said the Traveller; 'and for the sake of GOD's working world and its wholesomeness, both moral and physical, I would put the thing on the treadmill (if I had my way) wherever I found it; whether on a pillar, or in a hole; whether on Tom Tiddler's ground, or the Pope of Rome's ground, or a Hindoo fakeer's ground, or any other ground.'" CS/TT 1

—at table: Codlin "talked very slowly and ate very greedily, as is not uncommon with philosophers and misanthropes . . . he had already eat [*sic.*]as much as he could possibly carry and was now moistening his clay with strong ale, whereof he took deep draughts with a silent relish and invited nobody to partake—thus again strongly indicating his misanthropical turn of mind.

"Breakfast being at length over, Mr Codlin called the bill, and charging the ale to the company generally (a practice also savouring of misanthropy) divided the sum-total into two fair and equal parts . . . . " OCS 16, 17

—turnpike men: "'They're all on 'em men as has met vith some disappointment in life,' said Mr [Tony] Weller senior.

"'Ay, ay?' said Mr Pickwick.

"'Yes, Consequence of vich, they retires from the world, and shuts themselves up in pikes; partly vith the view of being solitary, and partly to rewenge themselves on mankind, by takin' tolls.'

"'Dear me,' said Mr Pickwick, 'I never knew that before.'

"'Fact, sir,' said Mr Weller; 'if they was gen'l'm'n you'd call 'em misanthropes, but as it is, they only takes to pike-keepin.'" PP 22

See also Hermit

—relationship to God: "' . . . let him look at me, in prison, and in bonds here. I endure without murmuring, because it is appointed that I shall so make reparation for my sins. Reparation! Is there none in this room? Has there been none here these fifteen years?'

"Thus was [Mrs Clennam] always balancing her bargain with the Majesty of heaven, posting up the entries to her credit, strictly keeping her set-off, and claiming her due. She was only remarkable in this, for the force and emphasis with which she did it. Thousands upon thousands do it, according to their varying manner, every day." LD i 5

—social nature: "'Now that a man,' [Mr Traveller] said, appealing to the summer sky as he did so, 'that a man—even behind bars, in a blanket and skewer—should tell me that he can see, from day to day, any orders or conditions of men, women, or children, who can by any possibility teach him that it is anything but the miserablest drivelling for a human creature to quarrel with his social nature—not to go so far as to say, to renounce his common human decency, for that is an extreme case; or who can teach him that he can in any wise separate himself from his kind and the habits of his kind, without becoming a deteriorated spectacle calculated to give the Devil (and perhaps the monkeys) pleasure,—is something wonderful!'" CS/TT 1

"'You are an arrogant and boastful hero,'

said the Hermit. 'You think yourself profoundly wise.'

"'Bah!' returned Mr Traveller, quietly smoking. 'There is little wisdom in knowing that every man must be up and doing, and that all mankind are made dependent on one another.'" CS/TT 1

"'What I have told you is, that it is a moral impossibility that any son or daughter of Adam can stand on this ground that I put my foot on, or on any ground that mortal treads, and gainsay the healthy tenure on which we hold our existence.'

"'Which is,' sneered the Hermit, 'according to you—'

"'Which is,' returned the other, 'according to Eternal Providence, that we must arise and wash our faces and do our gregarious work and act and re-act on one another, leaving only the idiot and the palsied to sit blinking in the corner.'" CS/TT 1

—superficial: "[James Harthouse] was quick enough to observe; he had a good memory, and did not forget a word of the brother's revelations. He interwove them with everything he saw of the sister [Louisa Bounderby], and he began to understand her. To be sure, the better and profounder part of her character was not within his scope of perception; for in natures, as in seas, depth answers unto depth; but he soon began to read the rest with a student's eye." HT ii 7

—true nature: "'And after all, sir, what is man?' said the metaphysical Sparkins. 'I say, what is man?'

"'Ah! very true,' said Mr Malderton; 'very true.'

"'We know that we live and breathe,' continued Horatio; 'that we have wants and wishes, desires and appetites——'

"'Certainly,' said Mr Frederick Malderton, looking profound.

"'I say, we know that we exist,' repeated Horatio, raising his voice, 'but there we stop. . . . Tom was about to hazard something, but, fortunately for his reputation, he caught his father's angry eye . . . ." SB/HS

And see M:Knowledge—*its absence*

—varied fates: "Which of the vast multitude of travellers, under the sun and the stars, climbing the dusty hills and toiling along the weary plains, journeying by land and journeying by sea, coming and going so strangely, to meet and to act and re-act on one another, which of the host may, with no suspicion of the journey's end, be travelling surely hither?

"Time shall show us. The post of honour and the post of shame, the general's station and the drummer's, a peer's statue in Westminster Abbey and a seaman's hammock in the bosom of the deep, the mitre and the workhouse, the woolsack and the gallows, the throne and the guillotine—the travellers to all are on the great high road; but it has wonderful divergences, and only Time shall show us whither each traveller is bound." LD i 15

Master/Mistress and servant

—the butler: "'Mrs Merdle's maid must be called, and told to get Mrs Merdle up, and prepare her as gently as she can, to see me. I have dreadful news to break to her.'

"Thus, Physician to the Chief Butler. The latter, who had a candle in his hand, called his man to take it away. Then he approached the window with dignity; looking on at Physician's news exactly as he had looked on at the dinners in that very room.

"'Mr Merdle is dead.'

"'I should wish,' said the Chief Butler, 'to give a month's notice.'

"'Mr Merdle has destroyed himself.'

"'Sir,' said the Chief Butler, 'that is very unpleasant to the feelings of one in my position, as calculated to awaken prejudice; and I should wish to leave immediately.'

"'If you are not shocked, are you not surprised, man?' demanded the Physician, warmly.

"The Chief Butler, erect and calm, replied in these memorable words. 'Sir, Mr Merdle never was the gentleman, and no ungentlemanly act on Mr Merdle's part would surprise me. Is there anybody else I can send to you, or any other directions I can give before I leave, respecting what you would wish to be done?'" LD ii 25

—manservants classified: "Mr Lammle's own particular servant behind his chair; the Analytical behind Veneering's chair; instances in point that such servants fall into two classes: one mistrusting the master's acquaintances, and the other mistrusting the master. Mr Lammle's servant, of the second class. Appearing to be lost in wonder and low spirits because the police are so long in coming to take his master up on some charge of the first magnitude." OMF ii 16

—resentful

—incompetence: "If [Silas] Wegg had been worse paid for his office, or better qualified to discharge it, he would have considered [his master's] visits complimentary and agreeable; but, holding the position of a handsomely-remunerated humbug, he resented them.

"This was quite according to rule, for the incompetent servant, by whomsoever employed, is always against his employer. Even those born governors, noble and right honourable creatures, who have been the most imbecile in high places, have uniformly shown themselves the most opposed (sometimes in belying distrust, sometimes in vapid insolence) to *their* employer. What is in such wise true of the public master and servant, is equally true of the private master and servant all the world over." OMF ii 7

And see S:Cunning—*and simplicity*

—sycophancy: ". . . false and subtle men will always secretly despise and dislike the object upon which they fawn, and always resent the payment and receipt of homage that they know to be worthless . . . ." DS 55

Mob

—burning a house: "It was not an easy task to draw off such a throng. If Bedlam gates had been flung open wide, there would not have issued forth such maniacs as the frenzy of that night had made. There were men there, who danced and trampled on the beds of flowers as though they trod down human enemies, and wrenched them from the stalks, like savages who twisted human necks. There were men who cast their lighted torches in the air, and suffered them to fall upon their heads and faces, blistering the skin with deep unseemly burns. There were men who rushed up to the fire, and paddled in it with their hands as if in water; and others who were restrained by force from plunging in, to gratify their deadly longing. On the skull of one drunken lad—not twenty, by his looks—who lay upon the ground with a bottle to his mouth, the lead from the roof came streaming down in a shower of liquid fire, white hot; melting his head like wax. When the scattered parties were collected, men—living yet, but singed as with hot irons—were plucked out of the cellars, and carried off upon the shoulders of others, who strove to wake them as they went along, with ribald jokes, and left them, dead, in the passages of hospitals. But of all the howling throng not one learnt mercy from, nor sickened at, these sights; nor was the fierce, besotted senseless rage of one man glutted." BR 55

—coordinate murder: the Grindstone: "The people in possession of the house had let them in at the gate, and they had rushed in to work at the grindstone; it had evidently been set up there for their purpose, as in a convenient and retired spot.

"But, such awful workers, and such awful work!

"The grindstone had a double handle, and, turning at it madly were two men, whose faces, as their long hair flapped back when the whirlings of the grindstone brought their faces up, were more horrible and cruel than the visages of the wildest savages in their most barbarous disguise. False eye-brows and false moustaches were stuck upon them, and their hideous countenances were all bloody and sweaty, and all awry with howling, and all staring and glaring with beastly excitement and want of sleep.

"As these ruffians turned and turned, their matted locks now flung forward over their eyes, now flung backward over their necks, some women held wine to their mouths that they might drink; and what with dropping blood, and what with dropping wine, and what with the stream of sparks struck out of the stone, all their wicked atmosphere seemed gore and fire.

"The eye could not detect one creature in the group free from the smear of blood. Shouldering one another to get next at the sharpening-stone, were men stripped to the waist, with the stain all over their limbs and bodies; men in all sorts of rags, with the stain upon those rags; men devilishly set off with spoils of women's lace and silk and ribbon, with the stain dyeing those trifles through and through.

"Hatchets, knives, bayonets, swords, all brought to be sharpened, were all red with it. Some of the hacked swords were tied to the wrists of those who carried them, with strips of linen and fragments of dress: ligatures various in kind, but all deep of the one colour. And as the frantic wielders of these weapons snatched them from the stream of sparks and tore away into the streets, the same red hue was red in their frenzied eyes;—eyes which any unbrutalised beholder would have given twenty years of life, to petrify with a well-directed gun.

"All this was seen in a moment, as the

vision of a drowning man, or of any human creature at any very great pass, could see a world if it were there . . . .

"'They are,' Mr Lorry whispered the words . . . 'murdering the prisoners.'" ¶TTC iii 2

—of friends: "Among a dense mob of persons, of whom not one was for an instant still, the locksmith's ruddy face and burly form could be descried, beating about as though he was struggling with a rough sea. Now, he was carried back a score of yards, now onward nearly to the door, now back again, now forced against the opposite houses, now against those adjoining his own: now carried up a flight of steps, and greeted by the outstretched hands of half a hundred men, while the whole tumultuous concourse stretched their throats, and cheered with all their might. Though he was really in a fair way to be torn to pieces in the general enthusiasm, the locksmith, nothing discomposed, echoed their shouts till he was as hoarse as they . . . .

"'Such is the blessed end, sir,' cried the panting locksmith . . .'of the best day's work we ever did. The rogues! it's been hard fighting to get away from 'em. I almost thought, once or twice, they'd have been too much for us with their kindness!'" BR 79

—individual psychology: "The leaders of the [1780] riot . . . kept steadily together, and only thought of implicating the mass of their followers so deeply that no hope of pardon or reward might tempt them to betray their more notorious confederates into the hands of justice.

"Indeed, the sense of having gone too far to be forgiven, held the timid together no less than the bold. Many who would readily have pointed out the foremost rioters and given evidence against them, felt that escape by that means was hopeless, when their every act had been observed by scores of people who had taken no part in the disturbances; who had suffered in their persons, peace, or property, by the outrages of the mob; who would be most willing witnesses; and whom the government would, no doubt, prefer to any King's evidence that might be offered.

"Many of this class had deserted their usual occupations on the Saturday morning; some had been seen by their employers active in the tumult; others knew they must be suspected, and that they would be discharged if they returned; others had been desperate from the beginning, and comforted themselves with the homely proverb, that, being hanged at all, they might as well be hanged for a sheep as a lamb.

"They all hoped and believed, in a greater or less degree, that the government they seemed to have paralysed, would, in its terror, come to terms with them in the end, and suffer them to make their own conditions. The least sanguine among them reasoned with himself that, at the worst, they were too many to be all punished, and that he had as good a chance of escape as any other man. The great mass never reasoned or thought at all, but were stimulated by their own headlong passions, by poverty, by ignorance, by the love of mischief, and the hope of plunder." ¶BR 53

—revulsion of feeling: "Then, began one of those extraordinary scenes with which the populace sometimes gratified their fickleness, or their better impulses towards generosity and mercy, or which they regarded as some set-off against their swollen account of cruel rage. No man can decide now to which of these motives such extraordinary scenes were referable; it is probable, to a blending of all the three, with the second predominating. No sooner was the acquittal pronounced, than tears were shed as freely as blood at another time, and such fraternal embraces were bestowed upon the prisoner by as many of both sexes as could rush at him, that after his long and unwholesome confinement he was in danger of fainting from exhaustion; none the less because he knew very well, that the very same people, carried by another current, would have rushed at him with the very same intensity, to rend him to pieces and strew him over the streets." TTC iii 6

—roaring: "'Slumkey for ever!' echoed Mr Pickwick, taking off his hat.

"'No Fizkin!' roared the crowd.

"'Certainly not!' shouted Mr Pickwick.

"'Hurrah!' And then there was another roaring like that of a whole menagerie when the elephant has rung the bell for the cold meat.

"'Who is Slumkey?' whispered Mr Tupman.

"'I don't know,' replied Mr Pickwick, in the same tone. 'Hush. Don't ask any questions. It's always best on these occasions to do what the mob do.'

"'But suppose there are two mobs?' suggested Mr Snodgrass.

"'Shout with the largest,' replied Mr Pickwick.

"Volumes could not have said more." PP 13

—*spontaneity:* "Thus, with beer-drinking, pipe-smoking, song-roaring, and infinite caricaturing of woe, the disorderly procession went its way, recruiting at every step, and all the shops shutting up before it . . . .

"The dead man disposed of, and the crowd being under the necessity of providing some other entertainment for itself, [someone] conceived the humour of impeaching casual passers-by, as Old Bailey spies, and wreaking vengeance on them. Chase was given to some scores of inoffensive persons who had never been near the Old Bailey in their lives, in the realisation of this fancy, and they were roughly hustled and maltreated. The transition to the sport of window-breaking, and thence to the plundering of public-houses, was easy and natural. At last, after several hours, when sundry summer-houses had been pulled down, and some area-railings had been torn up, to arm the more belligerent spirits, a rumour got about that the Guards were coming. Before this rumour, the crowd gradually melted away, and perhaps the Guards came, and perhaps they never came, and this was the usual progress of a mob." TTC ii 14

—*unpredictable:* "A mob is usually a creature of very mysterious existence, particularly in a large city. Where it comes from or whither it goes, few men can tell. Assembling and dispersing with equal suddenness, it is as difficult to follow to its various sources as the sea itself; nor does the parallel stop here, for the ocean is not more fickle and uncertain, more terrible when roused, more unreasonable, or more cruel." BR 52

See the Panorama of the Gordon Riots of 1780 BR Vol. I pp508-21, *considered by students of the 'madness of crowds' to have profoundly influenced, if not actually formed, modern views on mobs and their behaviour.*

Music-making

—*amateur orchestra:* "The overture, in fact, was not unlike a race between the different instruments; the piano came in first by several bars, and the violoncello next, quite distancing the poor flute; for the deaf gentleman *too-too'd* away, quite unconscious that he was at all wrong, until apprised, by the applause of the audience, that the overture was concluded." SB/JP

—*barrel-organ:* "[Major Tpschoffki] had what I consider a fine mind—a poetic mind. His ideas respectin his property never come upon him so strong as when he sat upon a barrel-organ and had the handle turned. Arter the wibration had run through him a little time, he would screech out, 'Toby, I feel my property coming—grind away! I'm counting my guineas by thousands, Toby—grind away! Toby, I shall be a man of fortun! I feel the Mint a jingling in me, Toby, and I'm swelling out into the Bank of England!' Such is the influence of music on a poetic mind. Not that he was partial to any other music but a barrel-organ; on the contrairy, hated it." CS/GS

—*bassoon:* "[Bagnet's] voice, short, deep, and resonant, is not at all unlike the tones of the instrument to which he is devoted. Indeed there may be generally observed in him an unbending, unyielding, brass-bound [*sic.*] air, as if he were himself the bassoon of the human orchestra . . . . 'It was the old girl that brought out my musical abilities. I should have been in the artillery now, but for the old girl. Six years I hammered at the fiddle. Ten at the flute. The old girl said it wouldn't do; intention good, but want of flexibility; try the bassoon. The old girl borrowed a bassoon from the bandmaster of the Rifle Regiment. I practised in the trenches. Got on, got another, get a living by it!'" BH 27

" . . . I regard with personal animosity the bassoon [at a French funeral], which is blown at intervals by the big-legged priest (it is always a big-legged priest who blows the bassoon), when his fellows combine in a lugubrious stalwart drawl." UT/MM

—*boy soprano:* "On looking at Master Micawber again, I saw that he had a certain expression of face, as if his voice were behind his eyebrows; where it presently appeared to be, on his singing us (as an alternative between that and bed), 'The Wood-Pecker tapping.'" DC 36

—*on the canal:* " . . . the man on deck, in whom the sentimental stage of drunkenness had now succeeded to the boisterous . . . requested that she would oblige him with a song . . . . Not knowing what might be the consequences of irritating her friend, and trembling with the fear of doing so, poor Nell sang him some little ditty which she had learned in happier times, and which was so agreeable to his ear, that on its conclusion he . . . requested to be favoured with another, to which he was so obliging as to roar a chorus to no particular tune, and with no words at all, but which amply made up in its amazing energy for its deficiency in other respects.

"The noise of this vocal performance awakened the other man, who, staggering upon deck and shaking his late opponent by the hand, swore that singing was his pride and joy and chief delight, and that he desired no better entertainment. With a third call, more imperative than either of the two former, Nell felt obliged to comply, and this time a chorus was maintained not only by the two men together, but also by the third man on horseback, who, being by his position debarred from a nearer participation in the revels of the night, roared when his companions roared, and rent the very air.

"In this way, with little cessation, and singing the same songs again and again, the tired and exhausted child kept them in good humour all that night; and many a cottager, who was roused from his soundest sleep by the discordant chorus as it floated away upon the wind, hid his head beneath the bed-clothes and trembled at the sounds." ¶OCS 43

—*in a cathedral:* " . . . one feeble voice, rising and falling in a cracked monotonous mutter, could at intervals be faintly heard . . . [it] went on like a dying voice, until the organ and the choir burst forth, and drowned it in a sea of music. Then, the sea fell, and the dying voice made another feeble effort, and then the sea rose high, and beat its life out, and lashed the roof, and surged among the arches, and pierced the heights of the great tower; and then the sea was dry, and all was still." MED 9

"Mr Jasper is in beautiful voice this day. In the pathetic supplication to have his heart inclined to keep this law, he quite astonishes his fellows by his melodious power. He has never sung difficult music with such skill and harmony, as in this day's Anthem. His nervous temperament is occasionally prone to take difficult music a little too quickly; to-day, his time is perfect." MED 14

—*children's band:* " . . . I saw with astonishment that several musical instruments, brazen and of great size, appeared to have suddenly developed two legs each, and to be trotting about a yard. And my astonishment was heightened when I observed a large drum, that had previously been leaning helpless against a wall, taking up a stout position on four legs. Approaching this drum and looking over it, I found two boys behind it (it was too much for one), and then I found that each of the brazen instruments had brought out a boy, and was going to discourse sweet sounds." UT/ST

—*children's chorus:* "As if the band had blown me into a great class-room out of their brazen tubes, in a great class-room I found myself now, with the whole choral force . . . singing the praises of a summer's day to the harmonium, and my small but highly respected friend the fifer blazing away vocally, as if he had been saving up his wind for the last twelvemonth; also the whole crew of the good ship Nameless swarming up and down the scale as if they had never swarmed up and down the rigging." UT/ST

—*in a Ragged School:* " . . . a moving of feet overhead announced that the School was breaking up for the night. It was succeeded by profound silence, and then by a hymn, sung in a subdued tone, and in very good time and tune, by the learners we had lately seen. Separated from their miserable bodies, the effect of their voices, united in this strain, was infinitely solemn. It was as if their souls were singing—as if the outward differences that parted us had fallen away, and the time was come when all the perverted good that was in them, or that ever might have been in them, arose imploringly to Heaven." HW/SU

—*in church*

—*in Genoa:* " . . . the organ played away, lustily, and a full band did the like; while a conductor, in a little gallery opposite to the band, hammered away on the desk before him, with a scroll; and a tenor, without any voice, sang. The band played one way, the organ played another, the singer went a third, and the unfortunate conductor banged and banged, and flourished his scroll on some principle of his own: apparently well satisfied with the whole performance." PI 5

—*in Rome:* "The singers were in a crib of wirework (like a large meat-safe or birdcage) in one corner; and sang most atrociously." PI 11

—*congenial:* ". . . John Browdie proceeded to consider the words of some north-country ditty, and to take his wife's recollection respecting the same. This done, he made divers ungainly movements in his chair, and singling out one particular fly on the ceiling from the other flies there asleep, fixed his eyes upon him, and began to roar a meek sentiment (supposed to be uttered by a gentle swain fast pining away with love and despair) in a voice of thunder." NN 45

—*depressing, in the street:* "There was music playing here and there, but it did not enliven the case. No barrel-organ mended the matter, and no big drum beat dull care away. Like the chapel bells that were also going here and there, they only seemed to evoke echoes from brick surfaces, and dust from everything. As to the flat wind-instruments, they seemed to have cracked their hearts and souls in pining for the country." MED 20

—*duet:* "It was a beautiful duet: first the small gentleman asked a question, and then the tall lady answered it; then the small gentleman and the tall lady sang together most melodiously; then the small gentleman went through a little piece of vehemence by himself, and got very tenor indeed, in the excitement of his feelings, to which the tall lady responded in a similar manner; then the small gentleman had a shake or two, after which the tall lady had the same, and then they both merged imperceptibly into the original air: and the band wound themselves up to a pitch of fury, and the small gentleman handed the tall lady out, and the applause was rapturous." SB/VG

—*fiddle:* "In came a fiddler with a music-book, and went up to the lofty desk, and made an orchestra of it, and tuned like fifty stomach-aches . . . and the fiddler plunged his hot face into a pot of porter, especially provided for that purpose. But scorning rest, upon his reappearance, he instantly began again, though there were no dancers yet, as if the other fiddler had been carried home, exhausted, on a shutter, and he were a bran-new man resolved to beat him out of sight, or perish." CC 2

Swiveller Fluting in Bed OCS

—*flute:* "Some men in [Richard Swiveller's] blighted position would have taken to drinking; but as Mr. Swiveller had taken to that before, he only took, on receiving the news that Sophy Wackles was lost to him for ever, to playing the flute; thinking after mature consideration that it was a good, sound, dismal occupation, not only in unison with his own sad thoughts, but calculated to awaken a fellow-feeling in the bosoms of his neighbours.

"In pursuance of this resolution, he now drew a little table to his bedside, and arranging the light and a small oblong music-book to the best advantage, took his flute from its box, and began to play most mournfully. The air was 'Away with melancholy'—a composition, which, when it is played very slowly on the flute in bed, with the further disadvantage of being performed by a gentleman but imperfectly acquainted with the instrument, who repeats one note a great many times before he can find the next, has not a lively effect.

"Yet for half the night, or more, Mr. Swiveller, lying sometimes on his back with his eyes upon the ceiling, and sometimes half out of bed to correct himself by the book, played this unhappy tune over and over again; never leaving off, save for a minute or two at a time to take breath . . . and then beginning again with renewed vigour. It was not until he had quite exhausted his several subjects of meditation, and had breathed into the flute the whole sentiment of the purl down to its very dregs, and had nearly maddened the people of the house, and at both the next doors, and over the way—that he shut up the music-book, extinguished the candle, and finding himself greatly lightened and relieved in his mind, turned round and fell asleep." ¶OCS 58

"The Master [Mell] . . . put his hand underneath the skirts of his coat, and brought out his flute in three pieces, which he screwed together, and began immediately to play. My impression is, after many years of consideration, that there never can have been anybody in the world who played worse. He made the most dismal sounds I have ever heard produced by any means, natural or artificial. I don't know what the tunes were—if there were such things in the performance at all, which I doubt—but the influence of the strain upon me was, first, to make me think of all my sorrows until I could hardly keep my tears back; then to take away my appetite; and lastly, to make me so sleepy that I couldn't keep my eyes open." DC 5 *And see —serenade*

—guitar and voice: "All I know of the rest of the evening is, that I heard the empress of my heart [Dora Spenlow] sing enchanted ballads in the French language, generally to the effect that, whatever was the matter, we ought always to dance, Ta ra la, Ta ra la! accompanying herself on a glorified instrument, resembling a guitar. That I was lost in blissful delirium. That I refused refreshment. That my soul recoiled from punch particularly . . . That I caught a view of myself in a mirror, looking perfectly imbecile and idiotic. That I retired to bed in a most maudlin state of mind, and got up in a crisis of feeble infatuation." DC 26

"On the pier, there is usually a guitar, which seems presumptuously enough to set its tinkling against the deep hoarseness of the sea, and there is always some boy or woman who sings, without any voice, little songs without any tune: the strain we have most frequently heard being an appeal to 'the sportsman' not to bag that choicest of game, the swallow." RP/FW

—harmonic meeting

—in a prison: "The occasional rattle of applause upon the tables of the Snuggery, denoted the successful termination of a morsel of Harmony; or the responsive acceptance, by the united children, of some toast or sentiment offered to them by their Father [William Dorrit]. Occasionally, a vocal strain more sonorous than the generality informed the listener that some boastful bass was in blue water, or in the hunting field, or with the reindeer, or on the mountain, or among the heather; but the Marshal of the Marshalsea knew better, and had got him hard and fast." LD i 22

—at a private party: "'Now,' said Jack Hopkins, 'just to set us going again, Bob, I don't mind singing a song.' And Hopkins, incited thereto, by tumultuous applause, plunged himself at once into 'The King, God bless him,' which he sang as loud as he could, to a novel air, compounded of the 'Bay of Biscay,' and 'A Frog he would.' The chorus was the essence of the song; and, as each gentleman sang it to the tune he knew best, the effect was very striking indeed." PP 32

—in town: "The more musical portion of the play-going community betake themselves to some harmonic meeting. As a matter of curiosity let us follow them thither for a few moments.

"In a lofty room of spacious dimensions, are seated some eighty or a hundred guests knocking little pewter measures on the tables, and hammering away, with the handles of their knives, as if they were so many trunk-makers. They are applauding a glee, which has just been executed by the three 'professional gentlemen' . . . . " SB/SN

—harp: "[Rosa Dartle] stood beside it for some little while, in a curious way, going

through the motion of playing it with her right hand, but not sounding it. At length she sat down, and drew it to her with one sudden action, and played and sang.

"I don't know what it was, in her touch or voice, that made that song the most unearthly I have ever heard in my life, or can imagine. There was something fearful in the reality of it. It was as if it had never been written, or set to music, but sprung out of the passion within her; which found imperfect utterance in the low sounds of her voice, and crouched again when all was still." DC 29

—humming: "Sampson Brass was no sooner left alone than he began to write with extreme cheerfulness and assiduity; humming as he did so, in a voice that was anything but musical, certain vocal snatches which appeared to have reference to the union between Church and State, inasmuch as they were compounded of the Evening Hymn and God save the King." OCS 56

"A certain skilful action of his fingers as [Morfin] hummed some bars, and beat time on the seat beside him, seemed to denote the musician; and the extraordinary satisfaction he derived from humming something very slow and long, which had no recognisable tune, seemed to denote that he was a scientific one." DS 33

—by Italians

—at Carrara: "It contains a beautiful little Theatre, newly built; and it is an interesting custom there, to form the chorus of labourers in the marble quarries, who are self-taught and sing by ear. I heard them in a comic opera, and in an act of 'Norma;' and they acquitted themselves very well; unlike the common people of Italy generally, who (with some exceptions among the Neapolitans) sing vilely out of tune, and have very disagreeable singing voices." PI 10

—at Naples: "Our English dilettanti would be very pathetic on the subject of the national taste, if they could hear an Italian opera half as badly sung in England as we may hear the Foscari [Verdi] performed, to-night, in the splendid theatre of San Carlo. But, for astonishing truth and spirit in seizing and embodying the real life about it, the shabby little San Carlino Theatre—the rickety house one story high, with a staring picture outside: down among the drums and trumpets, and the tumblers, and the lady conjurer—is without a rival anywhere." PI 17

—in a lifeboat: "Spectres as we soon were in our bodily wasting, our imaginations did not perish like the gross flesh upon our bones. Music and Adventure, two of the great gifts of Providence to mankind, could charm us long after that was lost." CS/GM 1

—opera in England: "Whereas, as mere animals, [the Indians] were wretched creatures, very low in the scale and very poorly formed; and as men and women possessing any power of truthful dramatic expression by means of action, they were no better than the chorus at an Italian Opera in England—and would have been worse if such a thing were possible." RP/NS

—serenade: "[The Pecksniff daughters] were, moreover, not ecstatically charmed to be awakened . . . by certain dulcet strains breaking in upon the silent watches of the night.

"It was very affecting, very. Nothing more dismal could have been desired by the most fastidious taste. The gentleman of a vocal turn was head mute, or chief mourner; Jinkins took the bass; and the rest took anything they could get.

"The youngest gentleman [Augustus Moddle] blew his melancholy into a flute. He didn't blow much out of it, but that was all the better. If the two Miss Pecksniffs and Mrs. Todgers had perished by spontaneous combustion, and the serenade had been in honour of their ashes, it would have been impossible to surpass the unutterable despair expressed in that one chorus, 'Go where glory waits thee!' It was a requiem, a dirge, a moan, a howl, a wail, a lament, an abstract of everything that is sorrowful and hideous in sound.

"The flute of the youngest gentleman was wild and fitful. It came and went in gusts, like the wind. For a long time together he seemed to have left off, and when it was quite settled by Mrs. Todgers and the young ladies that, overcome by his feelings, he had retired in tears, he unexpectedly turned up again at the very top of the tune, gasping for breath. He was a tremendous performer. There was no knowing where to have him; and exactly when you thought he was doing nothing at all, then was he doing the very thing that ought to astonish you most.

"There were several of these concerted pieces; perhaps two or three too many . . . . But even then, even at that solemn moment, when the thrilling sounds may be presumed to have penetrated into the very depths of his nature, if he had any depths, Jinkins couldn't leave the youngest gentleman alone. He asked him distinctly, before the second song began—as a personal favour too, mark the villain in that—not to play. Yes; he said so; not to play. The breathing of the youngest gentleman was heard through the key-hole of the door. He didn't play. What vent was a flute for the passions swelling up within his breast? A trombone would have been a world too mild." ¶MC 11

—*on shipboard:* "We had no lack of music, for one played the accordion, another the violin, and another (who usually began at six o'clock A.M.) the key-bugle: the combined effect of which instruments, when they all played different tunes in different parts of the ship, at the same time, and within hearing of each other, as they sometimes did (everybody being intensely satisfied with his own performance), was sublimely hideous." AN 16

" . . . we fell upon the dangerous and perfectly unnecessary experiment of striking up a hymn. After it was given out, we all rose, but everybody left it to somebody else to begin. Silence resulting, the officer (no singer himself) rather reproachfully gave us the first line again, upon which a rosy pippin of an old gentleman . . . gave a little stamp with his boot (as if he were leading off a country dance), and blithely warbled us into a show of joining.

"At the end of the first verse we became, through these tactics, so much refreshed and encouraged, that none of us, howsoever unmelodious, would submit to be left out of the second verse; while as to the third we lifted up our voices in a sacred howl that left it doubtful whether we were the more boastful of the sentiments we united in professing, or of professing them with a most discordant defiance of time and tune." ¶UT/AS

—*singing Bass:* "'Bass!' as the young gentlemen . . . forcibly remarks to his companion, 'bass!' I b'lieve you; he can go down lower than any man: so low sometimes that you can't hear him.' And so he does. To hear him growling away, gradually lower and lower down, till he can't get back again, is the most delightful thing in the world, and it is quite impossible to witness unmoved the impressive solemnity with which he pours forth his soul in 'My 'art's in the 'ighlands,' or 'The brave old Hoak.'" SB/SN

"After a great deal of preparatory crowing and humming, the captain began the duet from the opera of 'Paul and Virginia,' in that grunting tone in which a man gets down, Heaven knows where, without the remotest chance of ever getting up again. This, in private circles, is frequently designated 'a bass voice.'" SB/SE

" . . . they were a musical family, and knew what they were about, when they sung a Glee or Catch, I can assure you: especially Topper, who could growl away in the bass like a good one, and never swell the large veins in his forehead, or get red in the face over it." CC 3

—*singing for friends:* "So down [Ruth Pinch] sat, and in a pleasant voice began to sing the ballads Tom loved well. Old rhyming stories, with here and there a pause for a few simple chords, such as a harper might have sounded in the ancient time while looking upward for the current of some half-remembered legend; words of old poets, wedded to such measures that the strain of music might have been the poet's breath, giving utterance and expression to his thoughts; and now a melody so joyous and light-hearted, that the singer seemed incapable of sadness, until in her inconstancy (oh wicked little singer!) she relapsed, and broke the listeners' hearts again: these were the simple means she used to please them." MC 45

—*singing Soprano:* " . . . Mrs Micawber was good enough to sing us (in a small, thin, flat voice, which I remembered to have considered, when I first knew her, the very table-beer of acoustics) the favourite ballads of 'The Dashing White Serjeant', and 'Little Tafflin' . . . . Mr Micawber told us, that when he heard her sing the first one, on the first occasion of his seeing her beneath the parental roof, she had attracted his attention in an extraordinary degree; but that when it came to Little Tafflin, he had resolved to win that woman or perish in the attempt." DC 28

—*a sister singing:* ""When they all drew a little away, that Paul might see her; and when he saw her sitting there alone, so young, and good, and beautiful, and kind to him; and heard her thrilling voice, so natural and sweet, and such a golden link between him and all his life's love and happiness, rising out of the silence; he turned his face away and hid his tears. Not, as he told them when they spoke to him, not that the music was too plaintive or too sorrowful, but was so dear to him." DS 14

"It was not very long before, in the midst of the dismal house so wide and dreary, her low voice in the twilight, slowly and stopping sometimes, touched the old air to which he had so often listened, with his drooping head upon her arm. And after that, and when it was quite dark, a little strain of music trembled in the room: so softly played and sung, that it was more like the mournful recollection of what she had done at his request on that last night, than the reality repeated. But it was repeated, often—very often, in the shadowy solitude; and broken murmurs of the strain still trembled on the keys, when the sweet voice was hushed in tears." DS 18

—*on a train:* " . . . the manufacturing bosom of Yorkshire. A mysterious bosom it appeared, upon a damp, dark, Sunday night, dashed through in the train to the music of the whirling wheels, the panting of the engine, and the part-singing of hundreds of third-class excursionists, whose vocal efforts 'bobbed arayound' from sacred to profane, from hymns, to our transatlantic sisters the Yankee Gal and Mairy Anne, in a remarkable way.

"There seemed to have been some large vocal gathering near to every lonely station on the line. No town was visible, no village was visible, no light was visible; but, a multitude got out singing, and a multitude got in singing, and the second multitude took up the hymns, and adopted our transatlantic sisters, and sang of their own egregious wickedness, and of their bobbing arayound, and of how the ship it was ready and the wind it was fair, and they were bayound for the sea, Mairy Anne, until they in their turn became a getting-out multitude, and were replaced by another getting-in multitude, who did the same.

"And at every station, the getting-in multitude, with an artistic reference to the completeness of their chorus, incessantly cried, as with one voice while scuffling into the carriages, 'We mun aa' gang toogither!'" ¶LT 5

—*tuning up:* "The musicians are scraping and grating and screwing tremendously—playing no notes but notes of preparation. . . . " SB/PD

—*the uninitiated:* "Not even over Vendale himself did these songs of [Marguerite Obenreizer] cast a more potent spell than over Joey Ladle in his different way. Steadily refusing to muddle the harmony by taking any share in it, and evincing the supremest contempt for scales and such-like rudiments of music—which, indeed, seldom captivate mere listeners—Joey did at first give up the whole business for a bad job, and the whole of the performers for a set of howling Dervishes.

"But, descrying traces of unmuddled harmony in a part-song one day, he gave his two under cellarmen faint hopes of getting on towards something in course of time. An anthem of Handel's led to further encouragement from him: though he objected that that great musician must have been down in some of them foreign cellars pretty much, for to go and say the same thing so many times over; which, took it in how you might, he considered a certain sign of your having took it in somehow.

"On a third occasion . . . he became inspired with the words, 'Ann Koar!' . . . . But this was his final testimony to the merits of his mates, for, the instrumental duet being performed at the first Wednesday concert, and being presently followed by the voice of Marguerite Obenreizer, he sat with his mouth wide open, entranced, until she had finished; when, rising in his place with much solemnity, and prefacing what he was about to say with a bow . . . he delivered himself of the gratifying sentiment: 'Arter that, ye may all on ye get to bed!' And ever afterwards declined to render homage in any other words to the musical powers of the family." ¶CS/NT 1

—*violoncello:* "[Mr Morfin] was a great musical amateur in his way—after business; and had a paternal affection for his violoncello, which was once in every week transported from Islington, his place of abode, to a certain club-room hard by the bank, where quartettes of the most tormenting and excruciating nature were executed every Wednesday evening by a private party." DS 13

"The violoncello lying on the sofa between the two chairs, he took it up, without putting away the vacant chair, and sat droning on it, and slowly shaking his head at the vacant chair, for a long, long time. The expression he communicated to the instrument at first, though monstrously pathetic and bland, was nothing to the expression he communicated to his own face, and bestowed upon the empty chair; which was so sincere, that he was obliged to have recourse to Captain Cuttle's remedy more than once, and to rub his face with his sleeve.

"By degrees, however, the violoncello, in unison with his own frame of mind, glided melodiously into the Harmonious Blacksmith, which he played over and over again, until his ruddy and serene face gleamed like true metal on the anvil of a veritable blacksmith. In fine, the violoncello and the empty chair were the companions of his bachelorhood until nearly midnight; and when he took his supper, the violoncello, set up on end in the sofa corner, big with the latent harmony of a whole family full of harmonious blacksmiths, seemed to ogle the empty chair out of its crooked eyes, with unutterable intelligence." DS 58

"It was pleasant to observe that Mrs Wemmick no longer unwound Wemmick's arm when it adapted itself to her figure, but sat in a high-backed chair against the wall, like a violoncello in its case, and submitted to be embraced as that melodious instrument might have done." GE 55

—for a wedding: "The men who play the bells have got scent of the marriage; and the marrow-bones and cleavers too; and a brass band too. The first, are practising in a back settlement near Battlebridge; the second, put themselves in communication, through their chief, with [footman] Mr Towlinson, to whom they offer terms to be bought off; and the third in the person of an artful trombone, lurks and dodges round the corner, waiting for some traitor tradesman to reveal the place and hour of breakfast, for a bribe." DS 31

And see S:Music: its effect

Nobility

—achievement irrelevant: "' . . . my brave physician ought to have a Title bestowed upon him. And no doubt he will. You are of that opinion?'

"That he well deserved one, yes. That he would ever have one, no . . . .

"'I said it was not the custom in England to confer titles on men distinguished by peaceful services, however good and great; unless occasionally, when they consisted of the accumulation of some very large amount of money.

"'Why, good gracious,' said Miss Flite, 'how can you say that? Surely you know, my dear, that all the greatest ornaments of England in knowledge, imagination, active humanity, and improvement of every sort, are added to its nobility! Look round you, my dear, and consider. *You* must be rambling a little now, I think, if you don't know that this is the great reason why titles will always last in the land!'

"'I am afraid she believed what she said; for there were moments when she was very mad indeed." BH 35

—and an American: "Why an honest republican, coming from the United States to England on a mission of inquiry into ploughs, turnips, mangel-wurzel, and live stock, cannot be easy unless he is for ever exhibiting himself to his admiring countrymen, with a countess hanging on each arm, a duke or two walking deferentially behind, and a few old English barons (all his very particular friends) going on before, we cannot, to our satisfaction, comprehend.

"Neither is his facility of getting into such company quite intelligible; unless something of the spirit which rushes into print with a record of these genteel processions, pervades the aristocratic as well as the republican breast, and tickles the noble fancy with a bird's-eye view of some thousands of American readers across the water, poring, with open mouths and goggle-eyes, over descriptions of its owner's domestic magnificence. We are bound to confess . . . that we are not altogether free from a suspicion of this kind." ¶E/AE

—career: "'These dear, wild young noblemen, you know, Overton—'

"'Aye, aye, I see,' replied the mayor.—'Horses and dogs, play and wine—grooms, actresses, and cigars—the stable, the greenroom, the saloon, and the tavern; and the legislative assembly at last.'" SB/WD

—French, in prison: "In the instinctive association of prisoners with shameful crime and disgrace, the new comer recoiled from this company. But the crowning unreality of his long unreal ride, was, their all at once rising to receive him, with every refinement of manner known to the time, and with all the engaging graces and courtesies of life.

"So strangely clouded were these refinements by the prison manners and gloom, so spectral did they become in the inappropriate squalor and misery through which they were seen, that Charles Darnay seemed to stand in a company of the dead. Ghosts all! The ghost of beauty, the ghost of stateliness, the ghost of elegance, the ghost of pride, the ghost of frivolity, the ghost of wit, the ghost of youth, the ghost of age, all waiting their dismissal from the desolate shore, all turning on him eyes that were changed by the death they had died in coming there.

"It struck him motionless. The gaoler standing at his side, and the other gaolers . . . looked so extravagantly coarse contrasted with sorrowing mothers and blooming daughters who were there—with the apparitions of the coquette, the young beauty, and the mature woman delicately bred—that the inversion of all experience and likelihood which the scene of shadows presented, was heightened to its utmost. Surely, ghosts all. Surely, the long unreal ride some progress of disease that had brought him to these gloomy shades!

"'In the name of the assembled companions in misfortune,' said a gentleman of courtly appearance and address, coming forward, 'I have the honour of giving you welcome to La Force . . . . '" TTC iii 1

—new peerage: "That illustrious man, and great national ornament, Mr Merdle, continued his shining course. It began to be widely understood that one who had done society the admirable service of making so much money out of it, could not be suffered to remain a commoner. A baronetcy was spoken of with confidence; a peerage was frequently mentioned. Rumour had it that Mr Merdle had set his golden face against a baronetcy; that he had plainly intimated to Lord Decimus that a baronetcy was not enough for him; that he had said, 'No: a Peerage, or plain Merdle.' This was reported to have plunged Lord Decimus as nigh to his noble chin in a slough of doubts as so lofty a person could be sunk. For, the Barnacles, as a group of themselves in creation, had an idea that such distinctions belonged to them; and that when a soldier, sailor, or lawyer, became ennobled, they let him in, as it were, by an act of condescension, at the family door, and immediately shut it again." LD ii 24

—title: "'It is odd enough, but certain people seem to have as great a pleasure in pronouncing titles as their owners have in wearing them.'" BR 35

" . . . **Nell Gwyn**, first an orange girl and then an actress, who really had good in her, and of whom one of the worst things I know is, that actually she does seem to have been fond of the King [Charles II]. The first **Duke of St Albans** was this orange girl's child. In like manner the son of a merry waiting-lady, whom the King created **Duchess of Portsmouth**, became the **Duke of Richmond**. Upon the whole it is not so bad a thing to be a commoner." CHE 35

Noble savage

—ceremonial: "In the Tonga Island . . . there are a set of personages called Mataboos . . . who are the masters of all the public ceremonies, and who know the exact place in which every chief must sit down when a solemn public meeting takes place: a meeting which bears a family resemblance to our own Public Dinner, in respect of its being a main part of the proceedings that every gentleman present is required to drink something nasty." UT/MM

—a fiction: "[Booley] was struck, too, by the reflection that savage nature was not by any means such a fine and noble spectacle as some delight to represent it. He found it a poor, greasy, paint-plastered, miserable thing enough; but a very little way above the beasts in most respects; in many customs a long way below them. It occurred to him that . . . [he] was a troublesome braggart after all; making a mighty whooping and halloaing about nothing in particular, doing very little for science, not much more than the monkeys for art, scarcely anything worth mentioning for letters, and not often making the world greatly better than he found it. Civilisation, Mr Booley concluded, was, on the whole, with all its blemishes, a more imposing sight, and a far better thing to stand by." HW/ET

" . . . possibly the parrots don't know, possibly they do, that the noble savage is a wearisome impostor wherever he is, and has five hundred thousand volumes of indifferent rhyme, and no reason, to answer for." UT/SL

"To come to the point at once, I beg to say that I have not the least belief in the Noble Savage. I consider him a prodigious nuisance, and an enormous superstition. His calling rum fire-water, and me a pale face, wholly fail to reconcile me to him. I don't care what he calls me. I call him a savage, and I call a savage a something highly desirable to be civilised off the face of the earth.

"I think a mere gent (which I take to be the lowest form of civilisation) better than a howling, whistling, clucking, stamping, jumping, tearing savage. It is all one to me, whether he sticks a fish-bone through his visage, or bits of trees through the lobes of his ears, or bird's feathers in his head; whether he flattens his hair between two boards, or spreads his nose over the breadth of his face, or drags his lower lip down by great weights, or blackens his teeth, or knocks them out, or paints one cheek red and the other blue, or tattoos himself, or oils himself, or rubs his body with fat, or crimps it with knives.

"Yielding to whichsoever of these agreeable eccentricities, he is a savage—cruel, false, thievish, murderous; addicted more or less to grease, entrails, and beastly customs; a wild animal with the questionable gift of boasting; a conceited, tiresome, bloodthirsty, monotonous humbug." ¶RP/NS

But see F:Native American

—at heart: "There are pious persons who, in their practice, with a strange inconsistency, claim for every child born to civilisation all innate depravity, and for every savage born to the woods and wilds all innate virtue. We believe every savage to be in his heart covetous, treacherous, and cruel; and we have yet to learn what knowledge the white man—lost, houseless, shipless, apparently forgotten by his race, plainly famine-stricken, weak, frozen, helpless, and dying—has of the gentleness of Esquimaux nature." HW/AV 1

Occupations

See Indexes IV *and* V *for practicing examples*

"For myself, I know no station in which, the occupation of to-day cheerfully done, and the occupation of to-morrow cheerfully looked to, any one of these pursuits is not most humanising and laudable. I know no station which is rendered more endurable to the person in it or more safe to the person out of it, by having ignorance for its associate. I know no station which has a right to monopolise the means of mutual instruction, improvement, and rational entertainment, or which has ever continued to be a station very long, after seeking to do so." AN 4

—actor (minor): " . . . [they] do not win the great prizes, but . . . are nevertheless an essential part of the theatrical system, and by consequence bear a part in contributing to our pleasure . . . . The beds of such men are not of roses, but of very artificial flowers indeed. Their lives are full of care and privation, and hard struggles with very stern realities. It is from among the poor actors who drink wine from goblets, in colour marvellously like toast and water, and who preside at Barmecide feasts with wonderful appetites for steaks—it is from their ranks that the most triumphant favourites have sprung." S/TF1

—agent in monetary matters: "Mr Rugg's enjoyment of embarrassed affairs was like a housekeeper's enjoyment in pickling and preserving, or a washer-woman's enjoyment of a heavy wash, or a dustman's enjoyment of an overflowing dust-bin, or any other professional enjoyment of a mess in the way of business." LD ii 28

—blacksmith: "Then the village forge came out in all its bright importance. The lusty bellows roared Ha ha! to the clear fire, which roared in turn, and bade the shining sparks dance gaily to the merry clinking of the hammers on the anvil. The gleaming iron, in its emulation, sparkled too, and shed its red-hot gems around profusely. The strong smith and his men dealt such strokes upon their work, as made even the melancholy night rejoice, and brought a glow

into its dark face as it hovered about the doors and windows . . . . " MC 2

"' . . . unless you was to turn her out a set of shoes all four round [said Joe Gargery]—and which I meantersay as even a set of shoes all four round might not act acceptable as a present in a total wacancy of hoofs . . . [or] if you was helped to knocking her up a new chain for the front door—or say a gross or two of shark-headed screws for general use—or some light fancy article, such as a toasting-fork when she took her muffins—or a gridiron when she took a sprat or such like . . . .

"' . . . . For what's a door-chain when she's got one always up? And shark-headers is open to misrepresentations. And if it was a toasting-fork, you'd go into brass and do yourself no credit. And the oncommonest workman can't show himself oncommon in a gridiron—for a gridiron IS a gridiron . . . and you may haim at what you like, but a gridiron it will come out, either by your leave or again your leave, and you can't help yourself . . . . '" GE 15

—boatman: "For ever hovering about this pier, with their hands in their pockets, or leaning over the rough bulwark it opposes to the sea, gazing through telescopes which they carry about in the same profound receptacles, are the Boatmen of our watering-place. Looking at them, you would say that surely these must be the laziest boatmen in the world. They lounge about, in obstinate and inflexible pantaloons that are apparently made of wood, the whole season through. Whether talking together about the shipping in the Channel, or gruffly unbending over mugs of beer at the public-house, you would consider them the slowest of men.

"The chances are a thousand to one that you might stay here for ten seasons, and never see a boatman in a hurry. A certain expression about his loose hands, when they are not in his pockets, as if he were carrying a considerable lump of iron in each, without any inconvenience, suggests strength, but he never seems to use it.

"He has the appearance of perpetually strolling—running is too inappropriate a word to be thought of—to seed. The only subject on which he seems to feel any approach to enthusiasm, is pitch. He pitches everything he can lay hold of—the pier, the palings, his boat, his house—when there is nothing else left he turns to and even pitches his hat, or his rough-weather clothing.

"Do not judge him by deceitful appearances. These are among the bravest and most skilful mariners that exist. Let a gale arise and swell into a storm, let a sea run that might appal the stoutest heart that ever beat, let the Light-boat on these dangerous sands throw up a rocket in the night, or let them hear through the angry roar the signal-guns of a ship in distress, and these men spring up into activity so dauntless, so valiant, and heroic, that the world cannot surpass it.

"Cavillers may object that they chiefly live upon the salvage of valuable cargoes. So they do, and God knows it is no great living that they get out of the deadly risks they run. But put that hope of gain aside. Let these rough fellows be asked, in any storm, who volunteers for the life-boat to save some perishing souls, as poor and empty-handed as themselves, whose lives the perfection of human reason does not rate at the value of a farthing each; and that boat will be manned, as surely and as cheerfully, as if a thousand pounds were told down on the weather-beaten pier.

"For this, and for the recollection of their comrades whom we have known, whom the raging sea has engulfed before their children's eyes in such brave efforts, whom the secret sand has buried, we hold the boatmen of our watering-place in our love and honour, and are tender of the fame they well deserve." ¶RP/EW

And see A:Child and Childhood*—at the shore*

—bone articulator: "' . . . not to name myself as a workman without an equal [said Mr Venus], I've gone on improving myself in my knowledge of Anatomy, till both by sight and by name I'm perfect. Mr Wegg, if you was brought here loose in a bag to be articulated, I'd name your smallest bones blindfold equally with your largest, as fast as I could pick 'em out, and I'd sort 'em all, and sort your wertebræ, in a manner that would equally surprise and charm you.'" OMF i 7

—boots: "Sam!'

"'Hallo,' replied the man with the white hat.

"'Number twenty-two wants his boots.'

"'Ask number twenty-two, vether he'll have 'em now, or vait till he gets 'em,' was the reply.

"'Come, don't be a fool, Sam,' said the girl, coaxingly, 'the gentleman wants his boots directly.'

"'Well, you *are* a nice young 'ooman for a musical party, you are,' said the boot-cleaner. 'Look at these here boots—eleven pair o' boots; and one shoe as b'longs to number six, with the wooden leg. The eleven boots is to be called at half-past eight and the shoe at nine. Who's number twenty-two, that's to put all the others out? No, no; reg'lar rotation, as Jack Ketch said, wen he tied the men up. Sorry to keep you a waitin', sir, but I'll attend to you directly.'" PP 10

—breakfast-seller: "At the corner of a by-street, near Temple Bar, was stationed a 'street-breakfast.' The coffee was boiling over a charcoal fire, and large slices of bread and butter were piled one upon the other, like deals in a timber-yard. The company were seated on a form, which, with a view both to security and comfort, was placed against a neighbouring wall." SB/SE

The Professional Gentlemen at Madame Mantalini's NN

—broker's man: "' . . . a broker's man's is not a life to be envied [said Bung]; and . . . people hate and scout 'em because they're the ministers of wretchedness, like, to poor people. But what could I do, sir? The thing was no worse because I did it, instead of somebody else; and if putting me in possession of a house would put me in possession of three and sixpence a day, and levying a distress on another man's good would relieve my distress and that of my family, it can't be expected but what I'd take the job

and go through with it.

"'I never liked it, God knows; I always looked out for something else, and the moment I got other work to do, I left it. If there is anything wrong in being the agent in such matters—not the principal, mind you—I'm sure the business, to a beginner like I was, at all events, carries its own punishment along with it.

"'I wished again and again that the people would only blow me up, or pitch into me—that I wouldn't have minded, it's all in my way; but it's the being shut up by yourself in one room for five days, without so much as an old newspaper to look at, or anything to see out o' the winder but the roofs and chimneys at the back of the house, or anything to listen to but the ticking, perhaps, of an old Dutch clock, the sobbing of the missis now and then, the low talking of friends in the next room, who speak in whispers, lest "the man" should overhear them, or perhaps the occasional opening of the door, as a child peeps in to look at you, and then runs half-frightened away—it's all this, that makes you feel sneaking somehow, and ashamed of yourself . . . .

"' . . . there you are, without being washed or shaved all the time, shunned by everybody, and spoken to by no one, unless some one comes in at dinner-time, and asks you whether you want any more, in a tone as much as to say, "I hope you don't," or, in the evening, to inquire whether you wouldn't rather have a candle, after you've been sitting in the dark half the night. When I was left in this way, I used to sit, think, think, thinking . . . but I believe the old brokers' men who are regularly trained to it, never think at all. I have heard some on 'em say, indeed, that they don't know how!'" ¶SB/BM

" . . . [Kate's] attention was attracted by Mr Scaley himself, who, walking up to one of the cheval glasses, gave it a hard poke in the centre with his stick, as coolly as if it had been made of cast iron.

"'Good plate this here, Tix,' said Mr Scaley to his friend.

"'Ah!' rejoined Mr Tix, placing the marks of his four fingers, and a duplicate impression of his thumb on a piece of sky-blue silk; 'and this here article warn't made for nothing, mind you . . . .

"'It is Madame Mantalini,' said Kate

"'Then, said Mr Scaley, producing a small document from his pocket and unfolding it very slowly, 'this is a writ of execution, and if it's not conwenient to settle we'll go over the house at wunst, please, and take the inwentory . . . .

"'Well;' said the gentleman, after a pause, 'Wot's to be done—anything? Is it only a small crack, or a out-and-out smash? A break-up of the constitootion is it—werry good. Then Mr Tom Tix, esk-vire, you must inform your angel wife and lovely family as you won't sleep at home for three nights to come, along of being in possession here.'" NN 21

—butler: " . . . all the arrangements were stately and handsome. In particular, there was a butler in a blue coat and bright buttons, who gave quite a winey flavour to the table-beer; he poured it out so superbly." DS 12

"The chief butler was the next [to Mrs Merdle] magnificent institution of the day. He was the stateliest man in company. He did nothing, but he looked on as few other men could have done." LD i 21

—cab-driver: "Fifteen cabs on the rank, and three piratical cabs hovering about the street, on kidnapping expeditions. One of the fifteen is a Hansom—clean and well-built, but with a perilous driver up behind—a reckless man at street-corners—not at all accustomed to the care of children—a neck or nothing sort of fellow, and much more neck than nothing. Of the other fourteen drivers, eight don't know how to drive, and six don't care." HWC/C

—chambermaid: "I rang the chambermaid's bell; and Mrs Pratchett marched in, according to custom, demurely carrying a lighted flat candle before her, as if she was one of a long public procession, all the other members of which were invisible." CS/SL 3

—chimney-sweep

—risk: "'It's a nasty trade,' said Mr Limbkins, when Gamfield had again stated his wish [for a "' 'prentis'"].

"'Young boys have been smothered in chimneys before now,' said another gentleman.

"'That's acause they damped the straw afore they lit it in the chimbley to make 'em come down agin,' said Gamfield; 'that's all smoke, and no blaze; vereas smoke ain't o' no use at all in making a boy come down, for it only sinds him to sleep, and that's wot he likes. Boys is wery obstinit, and wery lazy, gen'l'men, and there's nothink like a good hot blaze to make 'em come down vith a run. It's humane too, gen'l'men, acause, even if they've stuck in the chimbley, roasting their feet makes 'em struggle to hextricate theirselves' . . . .

"[His request disapproved,] "As Mr Gamfield did happen to labour under the slight imputation of having bruised three or four boys to death already, it occurred to him that the board had, perhaps, in some unaccountable freak, taken it into their heads that this extraneous circumstance ought to influence their proceedings." OT 3

—romance: " . . . many years ago we began to be a steady and matter-of-fact sort of people, and dancing in spring being beneath our dignity, we gave it up, and in course of time it descended to the sweeps—a fall certainly, because, though sweeps are very good fellows in their way, and moreover very useful in a civilised community, they are not exactly the sort of people to give the tone to the little elegances of society. The sweeps, however, got the dancing to themselves, and they kept it up, and handed it down.

"This was a severe blow to the romance of spring-time, but it did not entirely destroy it either; for a portion of it descended to the sweeps with the dancing, and rendered them objects of great interest. A mystery hung over the sweeps in those days. Legends were in existence of wealthy gentlemen who had lost children, and who, after many years of sorrow and suffering, had found them in the character of sweeps. Stories were related of a young boy who, having been stolen from his parents in his infancy, and devoted to the occupation of chimney-sweeping, was sent, in the course of his professional career, to sweep the chimney of his mother's bedroom; and how, being hot and tired when he came out of the chimney, he got into the bed he had so often slept in as an infant, and was discovered and recognised therein by his mother, who once every year of her life, thereafter, requested the pleasure of the company of every London sweep, at half-past one o'clock, to roast beef, plum-pudding, porter, and sixpence.

"Such stories as these, and there were many such, threw an air of mystery round the sweeps, and produced for them some of those good effects which animals derive from the doctrine of the transmigration of souls. No one (except the masters) thought of ill-treating a sweep, because no one knew who he might be, or what nobleman's or gentleman's son he might turn out. Chimney-sweeping was, by many believers in the marvellous, considered as a sort of probationary term, at an earlier or later period of which, divers young noblemen were to come into possession of their rank and titles: and the professional was held by them in great respect accordingly." ¶SB/FM

—romance departed: "The romance of spring having gone out before our time, we were fain to console ourselves as we best could with the uncertainty that enveloped the birth and parentage of its attendant dancers, the sweeps; and we *did* console ourselves with it, for many years. But even this wretched source of comfort received a shock from which it has never recovered—a shock which has been in reality its death-blow. We could not disguise from ourselves the fact that whole families of sweeps were regularly born of sweeps, in the rural districts of Somers Town and Camden Town—that the eldest son succeeded to the father's business, that the other branches assisted him therein, and commenced on their own account; that their children again, were educated to the profession; and that about their identity there could be no mistake whatever." SB/FM

—coal-whipper: " . . . here, were colliers by the score and score, with the coal-whippers plunging off stages on deck, as counterweights to measures of coal swinging up, which were then rattled over the side into barges . . . . " GE 54

—cook: "Nor yet can you lay down the gentleman's-service when stimulated by prolonged incompatibility on the part of Cooks (and here it may be remarked that Cooking and Incompatibility will be mostly found united), and take up Waitering." CS/SL 1
And see Housewife*—cooking*

—corrector of the press (proofreader): " . . . I know from some slight practical experience, what the duties of the correctors of the press are . . . and I can testify . . . that they are not mechanical, that they are not mere matters of manipulation and routine, but that they require from those who perform them much natural intelligence, much superadded cultivation, considerable readiness of reference, quickness of resource, an excellent memory, and a clear understanding." S/PRA

—dancing-master: "The sister [Fanny Dorrit] was so apt a pupil, and the dancing-master had such abundant leisure to bestow upon her (for it took him a matter of ten weeks to set to his creditors, lead off, turn the Commissioners, and right and left back to his professional pursuits), that

wonderful progress was made. Indeed the dancing-master was so proud of it, and so wishful to display it before he left, to a few select friends among the [Marshalsea] collegians, that at six o'clock on a certain fine morning, a minuet de la cour came off in the yard—the college-rooms being of too confined proportions for the purpose—in which so much ground was covered, and the steps were so consciousticusly executed, that the dancing-master, having to play the kit besides, was thoroughly blown." LD i 7

—dentist, on vacation: "The dentists' instruments are rusting in their drawers, and their horrible cool parlours, where people pretend to read the Every-Day Book and not to be afraid, are doing penance for their grimness in white sheets." UT/AL

—detective: "Time and place cannot bind Mr Bucket. Like man in the abstract, he is here to-day and gone to-morrow—but, very unlike man indeed, he is here again the next day. This evening he will be casually looking into the iron extinguishers at the door of Sir Leicester Dedlock's house in town; and to-morrow morning he will be walking on the leads at Chesney Wold, where erst the old man [Tulkinghorn] walked whose ghost is propitiated with a hundred guineas. Drawers, desks, pockets, all things belonging to him, Mr Bucket examines. A few hours afterwards, he and the Roman will be alone together, comparing forefingers." BH 53

—drayman: "There were two good-tempered, burly draymen letting down big butts of beer into a cellar; and when John [Westlock] helped [Ruth Pinch]—almost lifted her—the lightest, easiest, neatest thing you ever saw—across the rope, they said he owed them a good turn for giving him the chance. Celestial draymen!" MC 53

—drover: Mixed up with these oxen, were great flocks of sheep, whose respective drovers were in agonies of mind to prevent their being intermingled in the dire confusion; and who raved, shouted, screamed, swore, whooped, whistled, danced like savages; and, brandishing their cudgels, laid about them most remorselessly." HWC/ML

—dustman: "'On his own small estate the growling old vagabond [Harmon] threw up his own mountain range, like an old volcano, and its geological formation was Dust. Coal-dust, vegetable-dust, bone-dust, crockery-dust, rough dust, and sifted dust—all manner of Dust.'" OMF i 2

—engraver: " . . whose work for popular approval was necessarily hard and slow—and for which, by the way, he was not always munificently paid—and which was not usually recommended by the faculty either for improving the eye or opening the chest." S/A4

—fireman-waterman: "'Do you want to be put on board a steamer, sir?' inquired an old fireman-waterman, very confidentially. He was dressed in a faded red suit, just the colour of the cover of a very old Court-guide." SB/SE

"[CD] could not get on in the beginning without being a pupil under an anomalous creature called a 'fireman-waterman', who wore an eminently tall hat, and a perfectly unaccountable uniform, of which it might be said that if it were less adapted for one thing than another, that thing was fire." S/RC (third person report)

—footman: "Powder! There was so much Powder in waiting, that it flavoured the dinner. Pulverous particles got into the dishes, and Society's meats had a seasoning of first-rate footmen." LD i 21

—gardener: "His gains are not great; he often knows gold and silver better as the colours of fruit and flowers, than by their presence in his pockets; and it is easy to see how his exposure to changes of weather may render him peculiarly liable to sickness and infirmity." S/GI2

—gloomy: "'I was thinking,' Mark replied, 'of something in the grave-digging way.'

"'Good Gracious, Mark!' cried Mr Pinch.

"'It's a good, damp, wormy sort of business, sir,' said Mark, shaking his head argumentatively, 'and there might be some credit in being jolly, with one's mind in that pursuit, unless grave diggers is usually given that way; which would be a drawback. You don't happen to know how that is, in general, do you, sir?' . . .

"'In case of that not turning out as well as one could wish, you know,' said Mark, musing again, 'there's other businesses. Undertaking now. That's gloomy. There might be credit to be gained there. A broker's man in a poor neighbourhood wouldn't be bad perhaps. A jailor sees a deal of misery. A doctor's man is in the very midst of murder. A bailiff's an't a live office nat'rally. Even a tax-gatherer must find his feelings rather worked upon, at times. There's lots of trades, in which I should have an opportunity, I think.'" MC 5

—*governess:* "To take the case of those ladies in comparison with menial servants: they were worse paid than the cook; their salaries would bear poor comparison with the wages of the butler; they would appear but shabbily with the remuneration of the lady's-maid; and they were even lower than those paid to liveried footmen. The power of governesses was acknowledged by the middle-aged lady in a turban—she felt the power of the governess's knowledge in the education of her daughters; gentlemen also felt the power of the governess's knowledge; but nobody thought of the poor fagged knowledge herself, her eyes red with poring over advertisements in search of a new situation; and, after having faithfully accomplished her task in one family, being thrown upon the world, and going forth again among strangers to educate others." S/GB

"Let us suppose . . . that a lady who lives by imparting to others the accomplishments that she acquired in happier and more prosperous days . . . is stricken down by illness. It is part of the lady's position that she should have no home to repair to . . . for her profession leads her, of necessity, to establish herself in the homes of others. It is, therefore, almost a part of that lady's position, very often to have no right to be ill; but, as that implied contract is an artificial one in which nature has no very great share, ill she is—and seriously." S/S2

—*gunsmith:* "Meanwhile, Phil [Squod] has fallen to work at his usual table, where he screws and unscrews, and cleans, and files, and whistles into small apertures, and blackens himself more and more, and seems to do and undo everything that can be done and undone about a gun." BH 26

Great Excitement of Miss Kénwigs at the Hair Dresser's Shop NN

—*hostler/ostler:* "A busy little man [Phil Squod] always is, in the polishing at harness-house doors, of stirrup-irons, bits, curb-chains, harness bosses, anything in the way of a stable-yard that will take a polish: leading a life of friction." BH 66

—*housekeeper applicant:* "There were the usual species of profoundly unsympathetic women, and the usual species of much too sympathetic women. There were buccaneering widows who came to seize [Walter Wilding], and who griped umbrellas under their arms, as if each umbrella were he, and each griper had got him.

"There were towering maiden ladies who had seen better days, and who came armed with clerical testimonials to their theology, as if he were Saint Peter with his keys. There were gentle maiden ladies who came to marry him. There were professional housekeepers, like non-commissioned officers, who put him through his domestic exercise, instead of submitting themselves to catechism.

"There were languid invalids, to whom salary was not so much an object as the comforts of a private hospital. There were sensitive creatures who burst into tears on being addressed, and had to be restored with glasses of cold water. There were some respondents who came two together, a highly promising one and a wholly unpromising: of whom the promising one answered all questions charmingly, until it would at last appear that she was not a candidate at all, but only the friend of the unpromising one, who had glowered in absolute silence and apparent injury." ¶CS/NT1

—*innkeeper* "[The landlord] opportunely appeared at this moment, to confirm Mr [Sam] Weller's statement relative to the accommodations of the establishment, and to back his entreaties with a variety of dismal conjectures regarding the state of the roads, the doubt of fresh horses being to be had at the next stage, the dead certainty of its raining all night, the equally moral certainty of its clearing up in the morning, and other topics of inducement familiar to innkeepers." PP 51

—*lamplighter*

—*in action:* " . . . the lights were springing up brilliantly in the shop windows, and the street lamp-lighters, scarcely finding ground enough to plant their ladders on in the midst of the afternoon's bustle, were skipping up and down and running in and out, opening more red eyes in the gathering fog than my rushlight tower at the Hummums had opened white eyes in the ghostly wall." GE 48

—*in the rain:* "The lamplighter was going his rounds now; and as the fiery jets sprang up under his touch, one might have fancied them astonished at being suffered to introduce any show of brightness into such a dismal scene." LD i 3

—*risks:* "Within a quarter of a century, [Pavilionstone] was a little fishing town, and they do say, that the time was, when it was a little smuggling town. I have heard that it was rather famous in the hollands and brandy way, and that coevally with that reputation the lamplighter's was considered a bad life at the Assurance Offices. It was observed that if he were not particular about lighting up, he lived in peace; but that, if he made the best of the oil-lamps in the steep and narrow streets, he usually fell over the cliff at an early age." RP/OT *And see* Vocation—*illicit—smuggler*

—*sacrosanct:* "The lamplighter now dotting the quiet Close with specks of light, and running at a great rate up and down his little ladder with that object—his little ladder under the sacred shadow of whose inconvenience generations had grown up, and which all Cloisterham would have stood aghast at the idea of abolishing . . . . " MED 12

—*traditions:* "If any of our readers have had the good fortune to behold a lamplighter's funeral, they will not be surprised to learn that lamplighters are a strange and primitive people; that they rigidly adhere to old ceremonies and customs which have been handed down among them from father to son since the first public lamp was lighted out of doors; that they intermarry, and betroth their children in infancy; that they enter into no plots or conspiracies (for who ever heard of a traitorous lamplighter?); that they commit no crimes against the laws of their country (there being no instance of a murderous or burglarious lamplighter); that they are, in short, notwithstanding their apparently volatile and restless character, a highly moral and reflective people: having among themselves as many traditional observances as the Jews, and being, as a body, if not as old as the hills, at least as old as the streets.

"It is an article of their creed that the first faint glimmering of true civilization shone in the first street-light maintained at the public expense. They trace their existence and high position in the public esteem, in a direct line to the heathen mythology; and hold that the history of *Prometheus* himself is but a pleasant fable, whereof the true hero is a lamplighter." ¶L

—land surveyor: "In one sense, and only one, [Pecksniff] may be said to have been a Land Surveyor on a pretty large scale, as an extensive prospect lay stretched out before the windows of his house." MC 2

—landlady: "It happened by evil chance to be one of Mrs MacStinger's great cleaning days. On these occasions, Mrs MacStinger was knocked up by the policeman at a quarter before three in the morning, and rarely succumbed before twelve o'clock next night. The chief object of this institution appeared to be, that Mrs MacStinger should move all the furniture into the back garden at early dawn, walk about the house in pattens all day, and move the furniture back again after dark . . . .

"' . . . . I said it wasn't Cap'en Cuttle's house—and it ain't his house—and forbid it, that it ever should be his house—for Cap'en Cuttle don't know how to keep a house—and don't deserve to have a house—it's *my* house—and when I let the upper floor to Cap'en Cuttle, oh I do a thankless thing, and cast pearls before swine!'" DS 23

"'My ward and an elderly lady,' said Mr Grewgious, 'wish to find a genteel lodging for a month or so. Have you any apartments available, ma'am?'

"'Mr Grewgious,' returned Mrs Billickin, 'I will not deceive you; far from it. I *have* apartments available.'

"This with the air of adding: 'Convey me to the stake, if you will; but while I live, I will be candid.'

"' . . . there is two bedrooms at the top of the 'ouse with gas laid on. I do not tell you that your bedroom floors is firm, for firm they are not. The gas-fitter himself allowed, that to make a firm job, he must go right under your jistes, and it were not worth the outlay as a yearly tenant so to do. The piping is carried above your jistes, and it is best that it should be made known to you.'

"Mr Grewgious and Rosa exchanged looks of some dismay . . . .

"Well! The roof is all right, no doubt,' said Mr Grewgious, plucking up a little.

"'Mr Grewgious,' returned Mrs Billickin, 'if I was to tell you, sir, that to have nothink above you is to have a floor above you, I should put a deception upon you which I will not do. No, sir. Your slates WILL rattle loose at that elewation in windy weather, do your utmost, best or worst! I defy you, sir, be you what you may, to keep your slates tight, try how you can . . . consequent it would be worse than of no use for me to trapse and travel up to the top of the 'ouse with you, and for you to say, "Mrs Billickin, what stain do I notice in the ceiling, for a stain I do consider it?" and for me to answer, "I do not understand you, sir." No, sir, I will not be so underhand. I *do* understand you before you pint it out. It is the wet, sir. It do come in, and it do not come in. You may lay dry there half your lifetime; but the time will come, and it is best that you should know it, when a dripping sop would be no name for you.'

"Mr Grewgious looked much disgraced by being prefigured in this pickle.

"'Have you any other apartments, ma'am?' he asked.

"'Mr Grewgious,' returned Mrs Billickin, with much solemnity, 'I have. You ask me have I, and my open and my honest answer air, I have. The first and second floors is wacant, and sweet rooms.'" MED 22

And see Architect and Architecture—*stairs*

—laundress, at Inns of Court "The genuine laundress, too, is an institution not to be had in its entirety out of and away from the genuine Chambers. Again, it is not denied that you may be robbed elsewhere. Elsewhere you may have—for money—dishonesty, drunkenness, dirt, laziness, and profound incapacity.

"But the veritable shining-red-faced shameless laundress; the true Mrs Sweeney—in figure, colour, texture, and smell, like the old damp family umbrella; the tip-top complicated abomination of stockings, spirits, bonnet, limpness, looseness, and larceny; is only to be drawn at the fountain-head. Mrs Sweeney is beyond the reach of individual art. It requires the united efforts of several men to ensure that great result, and it is only developed in perfection under an Honourable Society and in an Inn of Court." ¶UT/C

—mail guard: " . . . anybody on the road might be a robber . . . . So the guard of the Dover mail thought to himself . . . as he stood on his own particular perch behind the mail, beating his feet, and keeping an eye and a hand on the arm-chest before

him, where a loaded blunderbuss lay at the top of six or eight loaded horse-pistols, deposited on a substratum of cutlass." TTC i 2

—newsvendor: "It was not that they toiled in all weathers—it was not that they were up early and late—that they were watching while others slept—that they were at our doors daily throughout the year ministering to our requirements . . . it was because they were connected with that great power which had become the axis on which the moral world turned round.—Humbly connected no doubt, but most usefully and inseparably. They were, to that fountain of knowledge to all men which was popularly called 'the Press', as conduits to a well of water; or what the pipes which undermined the streets of this city were to the great gas works from which the lights proceeded which turned our night into day. It was that they went on for ever between us and those mighty engines which, working night by night, and all night long, were felt in their faintest throb througout the civilized world." S/N1

"The newsman is to be met with at every turn, on steamboats, and in railway stations. His profits are small, he has a great amount of anxiety and care, and no little amount of personal wear and tear. He is indispensable to civilization and freedom, and he is looked for with pleasurable excitement every day, except when he lends the paper for an hour, and then his punctuality in calling for it is anything but agreeable. I think the lesson we can learn from the newsman is some new illustration of the uncertainty of life, some illustration of its vicissitudes and fluctuations." S/N4

—photographer and photography

—professional: "Then do I speculate, What have those seam-worn artists been who stand at the photograph doors in Greek caps, sample in hand, and mysteriously salute the public—the female public with a pressing tenderness—to come in and be 'took'?

"What did they do with their greasy blandishments, before the era of cheap photography? Of what class were their previous victims, and how victimised? And how did they get, and how did they pay for, that large collection of likenesses, all purporting to have been taken inside, with the taking of none of which had that establishment any more to do than with the taking of Delhi?" ¶UT/AL

—state of the art: "'Ah,' said [Mrs Bedwin], 'painters always make ladies out prettier than they are, or they wouldn't get any custom, child. The man that invented the machine for taking likenesses might have known *that* would never succeed; it's a deal too honest. A deal,' said the old lady, laughing very heartily at her own acuteness." OT 12

" . . . indeed I consider photographs wanting in mellowness as a general rule and making you look like a new-ploughed field." CS/L 1

—porter, in the theatre: " . . . the hall porter who passes his life in a thorough 'draft', and, to the best of my observation, in perpetually interrupted endeavours to eat something with a knife and fork out of a basin, by a dusty fire, in that extraordinary little gritty room, upon which the sun never shines, and on the portals of which are inscribed the magic words, 'Stage Door'." S/DM

—printer: " . . . the printers were peculiarly liable to premature decay, to injury to their faculties when many others were still able to earn their daily bread . . . from the character of their occupation—the late and arduous hours during which they were obliged to tax powers that were often of the most delicate nature." S/PP1

—compositor: For quickness of perception, amount of endurance, and willingness to oblige, I have ever found the compositor pre-eminent. His labour is of a nature calling for the sympathy of all." S/PP2

—journeyman: "Often labouring under an avalanche of work, carried through half the night—often through the whole night—working in an unnatural and unwholesome atmosphere produced by artificial light, and exposed to sudden changes from heat to cold, the journeyman printer is rendered peculiarly liable to pulmonary complaints, blindness, and other serious diseases." S/PP2

—professional gentleman manqué: "'It was my hope when I came here [to Canterbury],' said Mr Micawber, 'to have got Wilkins into the Church: or perhaps I shall express my meaning more strictly, if I say the Choir. But there was no vacancy for a tenor in the venerable Pile for which this city is so justly eminent; and he has—in short, he has contracted a habit of singing in public-houses, rather than in sacred edifices.'

"'But he means well,' said Mrs Micawber,

tenderly.

"'I dare say, my love,' rejoined Mr Micawber, 'that he means particularly well; but I have not yet found that he carries out his meaning, in any given direction whatsoever.'

"Master Micawber's moroseness of aspect returned upon him again, and he demanded, with some temper, what he was to do? Whether he had been born a carpenter, or a coach-painter, any more than he had been born a bird? Whether he could go into the next street, and open a chemist's shop? Whether he could rush to the next assizes, and proclaim himself a lawyer? Whether he could come out by force at the opera, and succeed by violence? Whether he could do anything, without being brought up to something?" DC 52

—*rag and bone man:* "'You see I have so many things here,' [Krook] resumed, holding up the lantern, 'of so many kinds, and all, as the neighbours think (but *they* know nothing) wasting away and going to rack and ruin, that that's why they have given me and my place a christening. And I have so many old parchmentses and papers in my stock. And I have a liking for rust and must and cobwebs. And all's fish that comes to my net. And I can't abear to part with anything I once lay hold of (or so my neighbours think, but what do *they* know?) or to alter anything, or to have any sweeping, nor scouring, nor cleaning, nor repairing going on about me. That's the way I've got the ill name of Chancery.'" BH 5

—*railway employee:* "Here he is, in velveteen or in a policeman's dress, scaling cabs, storming carriages, finding lost articles by a kind of instinct, binding up lost umbrellas and walking sticks, wheeling trucks, counselling old ladies, with a wonderful interest in their affairs—mostly very complicated—and sticking labels upon all sorts of articles. I look around me. There he is again, in a station-master's uniform, directing and overseeing, with the head of a general, and the manners of a courteous host. There he is again in a guard's belt and buckle, with a handsome figure, inspiring confidence in timid passengers. He is as gentle to the weak people as he is bold to the strong, and he has not a single hair in his beard that is not up to its work.

"I glide out of the station, there he is again, with flags in his hands. There he is again, in the open country, at a level crossing. There he is again at the entrance to the tunnel. At every station that I stop at, there he is again as alert as usual. There he is again at the arrival platform, getting me out of the carriage as if I was his only charge upon earth." S/R

—*school proprietor:* "I don't like the sort of school to which I once went myself, the respected proprietor of which [**William Jones**] was by far the most ignorant man I have ever had the pleasure to know, who was one of the worst-tempered men perhaps that ever lived, whose business it was to make as much out of us and to put as little into us as possible, and who sold us at a figure which I remember we used to delight to estimate, as amounting to exactly £2. 4*s.* 6*d.* a head . . . . I do not like that sort of school, because I have never yet lost my ancient suspicion touching that curious coincidence that the boy with four brothers to come always got the prizes. In fact, and in short, I do not like that sort of school, which is a pernicious and abominable humbug altogether." S/WC

—*schoolteacher:* " . . . I never could understand the wholesomeness of the moral preached by the abject appearance and degraded condition of the teachers who plainly said to us by their looks every day of their lives, 'Boys, never be learned; whatever you are, above all things, be warned from that in time by our sunken cheeks, by our poor pimply noses so cruelly eruptive in the frosty mornings, by our meagre diet, by our acid beer, and by our extraordinary suits of clothes, of which no human being can say whether they are snuff-coloured turned black, or black turned snuff-coloured, a point upon which we ourselves are perfectly unable to offer any ray of enlightenment, it is so very long since they were undarned and new'." S/WC

—*scientist:* "'People objected to Professor Dingo, when we were staying in the North of Devon, after our marriage,' said Mrs Badger, 'that he disfigured some of the houses and other buildings, by chipping off fragments of those edifices with his little geological hammer. But the Professor replied, that he knew of no building, save the Temple of Science. The principle is the same, I think?'

"'Precisely the same,' said Mr Badger. 'Finely expressed! The Professor made the same remark . . . in his last illness; when (his mind wandering) he insisted on keeping his little hammer under the pillow, and chipping at the countenances of the attendants. The ruling passion!'" BH 17

The professor's specialty is vague: his wife went on his botanical expeditions. BH 11

—*sexton, undertaker:* "It by no means follows that because a man is a sexton, and constantly surrounded by the emblems of mortality, therefore he should be a morose and melancholy man; your undertakers are the merriest fellows in the world . . . . " PP 29

—*sherry trade:* " . . . somebody not wholly unconnected with the sherry trade whom [Spenlow] remembered by the remarkable circumstance that he had a Straduarius [*sic.*] violin to dispose of, and also a Madonna. . . . " OMF iii 13

—*ship's steward:* "'Lord bless my soul and body!' cried Mr Inspector. 'Talk of trades, Miss Abbey [Potterson], and the way they set their marks on men' (a subject which nobody had approached); 'who wouldn't know your brother [Job] to be a Steward! There's a bright and ready twinkle in his eye, there's a neatness in his action, there's a smartness in his figure, there's an air of reliability about him in case you wanted a basin, which points out the steward!'" OMF iv 12

—*shoemaker*: "He was a sallow man—all cobblers are; and had a strong bristly beard—all cobblers have." PP 44

"'I am sure there was a case in the day before yesterday's paper . . . about a journeyman shoe-maker who was jealous of a young girl in an adjoining village, because she wouldn't shut herself up in an air-tight three-pair of stairs, and charcoal herself to death with him; and who went and hid himself in a Wood with a sharp-pointed knife, and rushed out, as she was passing by with a few friends, and killed himself first and then all the friends, and then her —no, killed all the friends first, and then herself, and them *him*self—which is quite frightful to think of. Somehow or other,' added Mrs Nickleby . . . 'they always *are* journeymen shoe-makers who do these things in France, according to the papers. I don't know how it is—something in the leather, I suppose.'" NN 37

" . . . he sat himself down on a chair opposite to me; rested an arm on each knee, and, leaning forward very much, took from the ground, by a great effort, the specimen of metropolitan workmanship which I had just pulled off: whistling, pleasantly, as he did so. He turned it over and over; surveyed it with a contempt no language can express; and inquired if I wished him to fix me a boot like *that?* . . . .

"When he had finished, he fell into his old attitude, and taking up the boot again, mused for some time. 'And this,' he said, at last, 'is an English boot, is it? This is a London boot, eh?' 'That, Sir,' I replied, 'is a London boot.' He mused over it again, after the manner of Hamlet with Yorick's skull; nodded his head, as who should say, 'I pity the Institutions that led to the production of this boot;' rose; put up his pencil, notes, and paper—glancing at himself in the glass, all the time—put on his hat; drew on his gloves very slowly; and finally walked out." ¶AN 18

—*sick-nurse:* "A nurse attended her, who might have been the figure-head of a pauper-ship." UT/RM

" . . . an odious anomaly . . . who is a creature of that sort who never could continue to exist but for our deplorable propensity to take whatever does exist for granted, and to rest comfortably satisfied that, because it is very bad, it cannot be better." S/S2

—*stenographer:* "Traddles now informed me, as the result of his inquiries, that the mere mechanical acquisition necessary, except in rare cases, for thorough excellence in it, that is to say, a perfect and entire command of the mystery of short-hand writing and reading, was about equal in difficulty to the mastery of six languages; and that it might perhaps be attained, by dint of perseverance, in the course of a few years . . . ." DC 36

"I bought an approved scheme of the noble art and mystery of stenography (which cost me ten and sixpence), and plunged into a sea of perplexity that brought me, in a few weeks, to the confines of distraction. The changes that were rung upon dots, which in such a position meant such a thing, and in such another position something else, entirely different; the wonderful vagaries that were played by circles; the unaccountable consequences that resulted from marks like flies' legs; the tremendous effects of a curve in a wrong place; not only troubled my waking hours, but reappeared before me in my sleep.

"When I had groped my way, blindly, through these difficulties, and had mastered the alphabet, which was an Egyptian Temple in itself, there then appeared a procession of new horrors, called arbitrary characters; the most despotic characters I have ever known; who insisted, for instance, that a thing like the beginning of a cobweb, meant expectation, and that a pen-and-ink sky-rocket stood for disadvantageous. When I had fixed these wretches in my mind, I found that they had driven everything else out of it; then, beginning again, I forgot them; while I was picking them up, I dropped the other fragments of the system; in short, it was almost heart-breaking." ¶DC 38

—street opportunist: "The person, who is one of those extraordinary specimens of human fungus that spring up spontaneously in the western streets of London, ready dressed in an old red jacket, with a 'Mission' for holding horses and calling coaches, receives his twopence with anything but transport, tosses the money into the air, catches it over-handed, and retires." BH 26

—teacher of drawing: " . . . it might be that he was merely but a humble teacher of drawing, whose business it was to infuse into the rising generation a better appreciation of the labours of more richly gifted men . . . . " S/A4

—tour guide: "It seemed to be his duty to describe the monuments to the people . . . . He had no pace at all; no more than a tortoise. He loitered as the people loitered, that they might gratify their curiosity; and positively allowed them, now and then, to read the inscriptions of the tombs. He was neither shabby, nor insolent, nor churlish, nor ignorant. He spoke his own language with perfect propriety, and seemed to consider himself, in his way, a kind of teacher of the people, and to entertain a just respect both for himself and them. They would no more have such a man for a Verger in Westminster Abbey, than they would let the people in (as they do at Bologna) to see the monuments for nothing." PI 7

CD adds a footnote: "A far more liberal and just recognition of the public has arisen in Westminster Abbey since this was written."

—toymaker: "The care imprinted in the lines of Caleb's face, and his absorbed and dreamy manner, which would have sat well on some alchemist or abstruse student, were at first sight an odd contrast to his occupation, and the trivialities about him. But trivial things, invented and pursued for bread, become very serious matters of fact; and, apart from this consideration, I am not at all prepared to say, myself, that if Caleb had been a Lord Chamberlain, or a Member of Parliament, or a lawyer, or even a great speculator, he would have dealt in toys one whit less whimsical, while I have a very great doubt whether they would have been as harmless." CH 2

—undertaker: "'I wos a thinkin', Sammy, that upon the whole I wos wery sorry she wos gone . . . .

"Mr Weller . . . again fastening his eyes on the fire, shrouded himself in a cloud, and mused deeply . . . .

"'Vell,' said Sam, venturing to offer a little homely consolation, after the lapse of three or four minutes, consumed by the old gentleman in slowly shaking his head from side to side, and solemnly smoking; 'vell, gov'ner, ve must all come to it, one day or another.'

"'So we must, Sammy,' said Mr Weller the elder.

"'There's a Providence in it all,' said Sam.

"'O' course there is,' replied his father, with a nod of grave approval. 'Wot 'ud become of the undertakers vithout it, Sammy?'

"Lost in the immense field of conjecture opened by this reflection, the elder Mr Weller laid his pipe on the table, and stirred the fire with a meditative vision." PP 52

"Now I don't love many people; but I do love the undertakers . . . . They know you so well, that I look upon 'em as a sort of Ravens. They are so certain of your being genteel parties, that they stick at nothing. They are sure they've got the upper hand of you . . . . It's nothing to him that [funerals'] being unnecessarily expensive is a fact within the experience of all of you as glaring as the sun when there's not a cloud. He is certain that when you want a funeral 'performed,' he has only to be down upon you with Mrs Grundy, to do what he likes with you—and then he'll go home, and laugh like a Hyæna . . . .

"But . . . it *is* these undertakers' men to whom, in the last trying, bitter grief of life, you confide the loved and honoured forms of your sisters, mothers, daughters, wives. It is to these delicate gentry, and to their solemn remarks, and decorous behaviour, that you entrust the sacred ashes of all that has been the purest to you, and the dearest to you, in this world. Don't improve the breed! Don't change the custom! Be true to my opinion of you, and to Mrs Grundy!" HW/R 2

And see A:Funeral

—veterinary: "... [Traddles] lived in a little street near the Veterinary College at Camden Town, which was principally tenanted ... by gentlemen students who bought live donkeys, and made experiments on those quadrupeds in their private apartments." DC 27

—waterman (hackney): "... that wonderful character the waterman, in a suit of doormat. What is the fiction concerning this mysterious waterman? Is he supposed to be the father of the stand? Has he any place of residence besides the stand? Has he any relations or friends? Had he any youth? Was he ever anything but a waterman? Was his father a waterman? Was his mother the bride of a waterman? Will his son (if he have one) be a waterman? Was he always red in the face, and full of gin and beer? What does he do here? What does he mean? Is he what [Mr **Carlyle**]* calls a self-constituted Impostor, or did anybody ever constitute him what he is? And if so, why so, and what is he?" HWC/C

**Thomas Carlyle's* Latter-day Pamphlets (1850), Pamphlet No. 1, *"contains almost identical phrases and dwells on the same idea." HS I p242*

Occupations—illicit

—bird-catching: "... a round-headed lad, with his chubby face addressed towards the sky, who ... suddenly thrust into his capacious mouth two fingers of each hand, and with the assistance of that machinery whistled, with astonishing shrillness, to some pigeons at a considerable elevation in the air .... [He] again whistled with his utmost might, and then yelled in a rapture of excitement, 'Strays! Whoo-oop! Strays!' which identification had such an effect upon the conscious-stricken pigeons, that instead of going direct to some town in the North of England, as appeared to have been their original intention, they began to wheel and falter; whereupon Mrs Richards' firstborn pierced them with another whistle, and again yelled, in a voice that rose above the turmoil of the street, 'Strays! Whoo-oop! Strays!'" DS 23

—decoy: "Now, a shabby man, with an overhanging forehead, and a slinking eye, produces a small board, and invites your attention to something novel and curious—three thimbles and one little pea—with a one, two, three—and a two, three, one—and a one—and a two—in the middle—right hand, left hand—go you any bet from a crown to five sovereigns you don't lift the thimble the pea's under! Now, another gentleman (with a stick) much interested in the experi-ment, will 'go' two sovereigns that he does lift the thimble, provided strictly, that the shabby man holds his hand still, and don't touch 'em again. Now, the bet's made, and the gentleman with the stick, lifts obviously the wrong thimble, and loses. Now it is as clear as day to an innocent bystander, that the loser must have won if he had not blindly lifted the wrong thimble—in which he is strongly confirmed by another gentleman with a stick, also much interested, who proposes to 'go him' halves—a friendly sovereign to *his* sovereign—against the bank. Now, the innocent agrees, and loses;—and so the world turns round bringing innocents with it in abundance, though the three confederates are wretched actors, and could live by no other trade if they couldn't do it better." HWC/E

—graverobber: "'It's the damp, sir, what settles on my chest and voice,' said Jerry. 'I leave you to judge what a damp way of earning a living mine is.'

"'Well, well,' said the old clerk; 'we all have our various ways of gaining a livelihood. Some of us have damp ways, and some of us have dry ways.'" TTC ii 2

And see A:Grave and Graveyard

—prostitution:

—experience contrasted: "These two girls had been thrown upon London streets, their vices and debauchery, by a sordid and rapacious mother. What the younger girl was then, the elder had been once; and what the elder then was, the younger must soon become. A melancholy prospect, but how surely to be realised; a tragic drama, but how often acted!

"Turn to the prisons and police offices of London—nay, look into the very streets themselves. These things pass before our eyes, day after day, and hour after hour—they have become such matters of course, that they are utterly disregarded. The progress of these girls in crime will be as rapid as the flight of a pestilence, resembling it too in its baneful influence and wide-spreading infection.

"Step by step, how many wretched females, within the sphere of every man's observation, have become involved in a career of vice, frightful to contemplate; hopeless at its commencement, loathsome and repulsive in its course; friendless, forlorn, and unpitied, at its miserable conclusion!" ¶SB/PV

—memory evoked: "'What are you?' said Redlaw, pausing, with his hand upon the broken stair-rail.

"'What do you think I am?' she answered, showing him her face again.

"He looked upon the ruined Temple of God, so lately made, so soon disfigured . . . .

"He had a perception that she was one of many, and that he saw the type of thousands, when he saw her, drooping at his feet.

"'What are your parents?' he demanded.

"'I had a good home once. My father was a gardener, far away, in the country.'

"'Is he dead?'

"'He's dead to me. All such things are dead to me . . . . '

"'Girl!' said Redlaw, sternly, 'before this death, of all such things, was brought about, was there no wrong done to you? In spite of all that you can do, does no remembrance of wrong cleave to you? Are there not times upon times when it is misery to you?'

"So little of what was womanly was left in her appearance, that now, when she burst into tears, he stood amazed. But he was more amazed, and much disquieted, to note that in her awakened recollection of this wrong, the first trace of her old humanity and frozen tenderness appeared to show itself." HM 2

—river scavenger: "He had no net, hook, or line, and he could not be a fisherman; his boat had no cushion for a sitter, no paint, no inscription, no appliance beyond a rusty boat-hook and a coil of rope, and he could not be a waterman; his boat was too crazy and too small to take in a cargo for delivery, and he could not be a lighterman or river-carrier; there was no clue to what he looked for, but he looked for something, with a most intent and searching gaze The tide, which had turned an hour before, was runnng down, and his eyes watched every little race and eddy in its broad sweep, as the boat made slight headway against it, or drove stern foremost before it, according as he directed his daughter by a movement of his head. She watched his face as earnestly as she watched the river. But, in the intensity of her look there was a touch of dread or horror." OMF i 1

—smuggler: "A little fishing was done in the port [of Dover], and a quantity of strolling about by night, and looking seaward: particularly at those times when the tide made, and was near flood. Small tradesmen, who did no business whatever, sometimes unaccountably realised large fortunes, and it was remarkable that nobody in the neighbourhood could endure a lamplighter." TTC i 4 *And see —lamplighter—risk*

"The Porto Franco, or Free Port (where goods brought in from foreign countries pay no duty until they are sold and taken out, as in a bonded warehouse in England), is down here also; and two portentous officials, in cocked hats, stand at the gate to search you if they choose, and to keep out Monks and Ladies. For, Sanctity as well as Beauty has been known to yield to the temptation of smuggling, and in the same way: that is to say, by concealing the smuggled property beneath the loose folds of its dress. So Sanctity and Beauty may, by no means, enter." PI 5

—spy: "He knew, as every one employed as he was did, that he was never safe; that flight was impossible; that he was tied fast under the shadow of the axe; and that in spite of his utmost tergiversation and treachery in furtherance of the reigning terror, a word might bring it down upon him. Once denounced, and on such grave grounds as had just now been suggested to his mind, he foresaw that the dreadful woman of whose unrelenting character he had seen many proofs, would produce against him that register, and would quash his last chance of life. Besides that all secret men are men soon terrified, here were surely cards enough of one black suit, to justify the holder in growing rather livid as he turned them over." TTC iii 8

Peace

—enjoying it: "Travelling through all that extent of country [near Aix en Provence] after three years of Peace, [Captain Doubledick] blessed the better days on which the world had fallen. The corn was golden, not drenched in unnatural red; was bound in sheaves for food, not trodden underfoot by men in mortal fight. The smoke rose up from peaceful hearths, not blazing ruins. The carts were laden with the fair fruits of the earth, not with wounds and death. To him who had so often seen the terrible reverse, these things were beautiful indeed; and they brought him in a softened spirit to the old chateau near Aix upon a deep blue evening." CS/PT 2

—in hospital: "'When Maggy was ten years old . . . she had a bad fever, sir, and she has never grown any older ever since.'

"'Ten years old,' said Maggy, nodding her head. 'But what a nice hospital! So comfortable, wasn't it? Oh so nice it was. Such a Ev'nly place!'

"'She had never been at peace before, sir . . . and she always runs off upon that.'

"'Such beds there is there!' cried Maggy. 'Such lemonades! Such oranges! Such d'licious broth and wine! Such Chicking! Oh, AIN'T it a delightful place to go and stop at!'" LD i 9

—keeping it: "PERSON OF QUALITY. The better for a firm, and durable, and glorious peace; eh, Bull?

"BULL. . . . I was thinking (by your lordship's favour) how best to keep it.

"PERSON OF Q. Be easy on that point. There shall be a great standing army, and a great navy, and your relations and friends shall have more than their share of the bad, doubtful, and indifferent posts in both . . . .

"BULL. With your noble lordship's magnificent toleration, I would respectfully crave leave to scatter a few deferential syllables in the radiancy of your noble countenance. I find that this characteristic [the ability to move in concert in large bodies, accustomed to the use of arms] is not peculiar to my friends the French, but belongs, more or less, to all the peoples of Europe: whereof the English are the only people possessing the peculiarity of being quite untrained in the power of associating to defend themselves, their children, their women, and their native land. Will your noble honour's magnanimity bear with me if I represent that your noble lordship has, for some years now, discouraged the old British spirit, and disarmed the British hand? Your noble honour's game preserves and political sentiments have been the cause of—

"PERSON OF Q. (interrupting). S'death, Bull, I am bored. Make an end of this.

"BULL. . . if your honourable grace could find it in your benignity to take the occasion of this Peace [following the Crimean War] to trust your countrymen a little—to show some greater confidence in their love of their country and their loyalty to their sovereign—to think more of the peasants and less of the pheasants, and if your worship's loftiness could deign to encourage the common English clay to become moulded into so much of a soldierly shape as would make it a rampart for the whole empire, and place the Englishman on an equality with the Frenchman, the Piedmontese, the German, the American, the Swiss, your noble honour would therein do a great right, timely, which you will otherwise, as certain as Death (if your noble lordship will excuse that levelling word), at last condescend to try to do in a hurry when it shall be too late." HW/JB

—in prison: "'A little more elbow-room is all we want here [said Doctor Haggage]. We are quiet here; we don't get badgered here; there's no knocker here, sir, to be hammered at by creditors and bring a man's heart into his mouth. Nobody comes here to ask if a man's at home, and to say he'll stand on the door mat till he is. Nobody writes threatening letters about money to this place. It's freedom, sir, it's freedom! I have had to-day's practice at home and abroad, on a march, and abroad ship, and I'll tell you this: I don't know that I have ever pursued it under such quiet circumstances, as here this day. Elsewhere, people are restless, worried, hurried about, anxious respecting one thing, anxious respecting another. Nothing of the kind here, sir. we have done all that—we know the worst of it; we have got to the bottom, we can't fall, and what have we found? Peace. That's the word of it. Peace.'" LD i 6

Philanthropist

—adulatory: "[Mr Quale] seemed to project those two shining knobs of temples of his into everything that went on, and to brush his hair farther and farther back, until the very roots were almost ready to fly out of his head in inappeasable philanthropy. All objects were alike to him, but he was always particularly ready for anything in the way of a testimonial to any one. His great power seemed to be his power of indiscriminate admiration. He would sit, for any length of time, with the utmost enjoyment, bathing his temples in the light of any order of luminary. Having first seen him perfectly swallowed up in admiration of Mrs Jellyby, I had supposed her to be the absorbing object of his devotion. I soon discovered my mistake, and found him to be train-bearer and organ-blower to a whole procession of people." BH 15

—aggressive: "'And it is another most extraordinary thing,' remarked the Minor Canon [Septimus Crisparkle] in the same tone as before, 'that these Philanthropists are so given to seizing their fellow-creatures

by the scruff of the neck, and (as one may say) bumping them into the paths of peace.'" MED 6

"There were several Professors passing in and out, with exactly the aggressive air upon them of being ready for a turn-up with any Novice who might happen to be on hand, that Mr Crisparkle well remembered in the circles of the Fancy. Preparations were in progress for a moral little Mill somewhere on the rural circuit, and other Professors were backing this or that Heavy-Weight as good for such or such speech-making hits, so very much after the manner of the sporting publicans, that the intended Resolutions might have been Rounds.

"In an official manager of these displays much celebrated for his platform tactics, Mr Crisparkle recognized (in a suit of black) the counterpart of a deceased benefactor of his species, an eminent public character, once known to fame as Frosty-faced Fogo, who in days of yore superintended the formation of the magic circle with the ropes and stakes.

"There were only three conditions of resemblance wanting between these Professors and those. Firstly, the Philanthropists were in very bad training: much too fleshy, and presenting, both in face and figure, a superabundance of what is known to Pugilistic Experts as Suet Pudding. Secondly, the Philanthropists had not the good temper of the Pugilists, and used worse language. Thirdly, their fighting code stood in great need of revision, as empowering them not only to bore their man to the ropes, but to bore him to the confines of distraction; also to hit him when he was down, hit him anywhere and anyhow, kick him, stamp upon him, gouge him, and maul him behind his back without mercy. In these last particulars the Professors of the Noble Art were much nobler than the Professors of Philanthropy.

"Mr Crisparkle was so completely lost in musing on these similarities and dissimilarities, at the same time watching the crowd which came and went, always, as it seemed, on errands of antagonistically snatching something from somebody, and never giving anything to anybody: that his name was twice called before he heard it." ¶MED 17

—aggrieved: "'It is a most extraordinary thing,' interposed the gentle Minor Canon [Crisparkle], laying down his knife and fork to rub his ear in a vexed manner, 'that these Philanthropists are always denouncing somebody. And it is another most extraordinary thing that they are always so violently flush of miscreants!'" MED 6

—erratic: "Always impelled by an intense conviction that her life must not be dreamed away, and that her indulgence in her favourite pursuits must be balanced by action in the real world around her, [Adelaide Procter] was indefatigable in her endeavours to do some good. Naturally enthusiastic, and conscientiously impressed with a deep sense of her Christian duty to her neighbour, she devoted herself to a variety of benevolent objects.

"Now, it was the visitation of the sick that had possession of her; now, it was the sheltering of the houseless; now, it was the elementary teaching of the densely ignorant; now, it was the raising up of those who had wandered and got trodden under foot; now, it was the wider employment of her own sex in the general business of life; now, it was all these things at once.

"Perfectly unselfish, swift to sympathise and eager to relieve, she wrought at such designs with a flushed earnestness that disregarded season, weather, time of day or night, food, rest. Under such a hurry of the spirits, and such incessant occupation, the strongest constitution will commonly go down. Hers, neither of the strongest nor the weakest, yielded to the burden, and began to sink.

"To have saved her life, then, by taking action on the warning that shone in her eyes and sounded in her voice, would have been impossible without changing her nature. As long as the power of moving about in the old way was left to her, she must exercise it, or be killed by the restraint. And so the time came when she could move about no longer, and took to her bed." ¶AY/P

—husband: "'And Mr Jellyby, sir?' suggested Richard.

"'Ah! Mr Jellyby,' said Mr Kenge, 'is—a—I don't know that I can describe him to you better than by saying that he is the husband of Mrs Jellyby.'

"'A nonentity, sir?' said Richard, with a droll look.

"'I don't say that,' returned Mr Kenge, gravely. 'I can't say that, indeed, for I know nothing whatever *of* Mr Jellyby. I never, to my knowledge, had the pleasure of seeing Mr Jellyby. He may be a very superior man; but he is, so to speak, merged—Merged—in the more shining qualities of his wife.'" BH 4

—intolerant: "Though it was not literally true, as was facetiously charged against [Luke Honeythunder] by public unbelievers, that he called aloud to his fellow-creatures: 'Curse your souls and bodies, come here and be blessed!' still his philanthropy was of that gunpowderous sort that the difference between it and animosity was hard to determine.

"You were to abolish military force, but you were first to bring all commanding officers who had done their duty, to trial by court martial for that offence, and shoot them. You were to abolish war, but were to make converts by making war upon them, and charging them with loving war as the apple of their eye.

"You were to have no capital punishment, but were first to sweep off the face of the earth all legislators, jurists, and judges, who were of the contrary opinion. You were to have universal concord, and were to get it by eliminating all the people who wouldn't, or conscientiously couldn't, be concordant.

"You were to love your brother as yourself, but after an indefinite interval of maligning him (very much as if you hated him), and calling him all manner of names . . . the unanimously carried resolution under hand and seal, to the effect: 'That this assembled Body of Professing Philanthropists views, with indignant scorn and contempt, not unmixed with utter detestation and loathing abhorrence,'—in short, the baseness of all those who do not belong to it, and pledges itself to make as many obnoxious statements as possible about them, without being at all particular as to facts." MED 6

—phrenology: "In his college-days of athletic exercises, Mr Crisparkle had known professors of the Noble Art of fisticuffs, and had attended two or three of their gloved gatherings. He had now an opportunity of observing that as to the phrenological formation of the backs of their heads, the Professing Philanthropists were uncommonly like the Pugilists. In the development of all those organs which constitute, or attend, a propensity to 'pitch into' your fellow-creatures, the Philanthropists were remarkably favored." MED 17

—a project: "'Mrs Jellyby,' said Mr Kenge, standing with his back to the fire, and casting his eyes over the dusty hearth-rug, as if it were Mrs Jellyby's biography, 'is a lady of very remarkable strength of character, who devotes herself entirely to the public. She has devoted herself to an extensive variety of public subjects at various times, and is at present (until something else attracts her) devoted to the subject of Africa; with a view to the general cultivation of the coffee berry—*and* the natives—and the happy settlement, on the banks, of the African rivers, of our superabundant home population." BH 4

The Public

—distractible: " . . . the Public will turn away, at any time, to look at anything in preference to the thing showed 'em; and if you doubt it, get 'em together for any indiwidual purpose on the face of the earth, and send only two people in late, and see if the whole company an't far more interested in takin particular notice of them two than of you . . . . " CS/GS

—diverted: " . . . in connexion with these [ballooning] and similar dangerous exhibitions, it strikes me that that portion of the public whom they entertain, is unjustly reproached. Their pleasure is in the difficulty overcome. They are a public of great faith, and are quite confident that the gentleman will not fall off the horse, or the lady off the bull or out of the parachute, and that the tumbler has a firm hold with his toes. They do not go to see the adventurer vanquished, but triumphant.

"There is no parallel in public combats between men and beasts, because nobody can answer for the particular beast—unless it were always the same beast, in which case it would be a mere stage-show, which the same public would go in the same state of mind to see, entirely believing in the brute being beforehand safely subdued by the man.

"That they are not accustomed to calculate hazards and dangers with any nicety, we may know from their rash exposure of themselves in overcrowded steamboats, and unsafe conveyances and places of all kinds. And I cannot help thinking that instead of railing, and attributing savage motives to a people naturally well disposed and humane, it is better to teach them, and lead them argumentatively and reasonably—for they are very reasonable, if you will discuss a matter with them—to more considerate and wise conclusions." ¶RP/LA

And see LC:Theatre—*Pantomime—unreality relished*

—refreshed on the railroad: "'Fancy the Beast travelling six hundred miles on end, very fast, and with great punctuality, yet being taught to expect all this [French catering] to be done for it!'

"A spirited chorus of 'The Beast!'" CS/MJ 3

Race-Meeting

—arrivals: "Meanwhile, they were drawing near the town where the races were to begin next day; for, from passing numerous groups of gipsies and trampers on the road, wending their way towards it, and straggling out from every by-way and cross-country lane, they gradually fell into a stream of people, some walking by the side of covered carts, others with horses, others with donkeys, other toiling on with heavy loads upon their backs, but all tending to the same point. The public-houses by the wayside, from being empty and noiseless as those in the remoter parts had been, now sent out boisterous shouts and clouds of smoke; and, from the misty windows, clusters of broad red faces looked down upon the road. On every piece of waste or common ground, some small gambler drove his noisy trade, and bellowed to the idle passers-by to stop and try their chance; the crowd grew thicker and more noisy; gilt ginger-bread in blanket-stalls exposed its glories to the dust; and often a four-horse carriage, dashing by, obscured all objects in the gritty cloud it raised, and left them, stunned and blinded, far behind.

"It was dark before they reached the town itself . . . . Here all was tumult and confusion; the streets were filled with throngs of people—many strangers were there, it seemed, by the looks they cast about—the church-bells rang out their noisy peals, and flags streamed from windows and housetops. In the large inn-yards waiters flitted to and fro and ran against each other, horses clattered on the uneven stones, carriage steps fell rattling down, and sickening smells from many dinners came in a heavy lukewarm breath upon the sense. In the small public-houses, fiddlers with all their might and main were squeaking out the tune to staggering feet; drunken men, oblivious of the burden of their song, joined in a senseless howl, which drowned the tinkling of the feeble bell and made them savage for their drink; vagabond groups assembled round the doors to see the stroller woman dance, and add their uproar to the shrill flageolet and deafening drum." OCS 19

—Derby Day at Epsom: "Amidst the hum of voices a bell rings. What's that? What's the matter? They are clearing the course. Never mind. Try the pigeon-pie. A roar. What's the matter? It's only the dog upon the course. Is that all? Glass of wine. Another roar. What's that? It's only the man who wants to cross the course, and is intercepted, and brought back. Is that all? I wonder whether it is always the same dog and the same man, year after year! A great roar. What's the matter? By Jupiter, they are going to start.

"A deeper hum and a louder roar. Everybody standing on **Fortnum and Mason**. Now they're off! No. *Now* they're off! No. *Now* they're off. No. *Now* they are! Yes!

"There they go! Here they come! Where? Keep your eye on Tattenham Corner, and you'll see 'em coming round in half a minute. Good gracious, look at the Grand Stand, piled up with human beings to the top, and at the wonderful effect of changing light as all their faces and uncovered heads turn suddenly this way! Here they are! Who is? The horses! Where? Here they come! Green first. No: Red first. No: Blue first. No: the Favorite first. Who says so? Look! Hurrah! Hurrah! All over. Glorious race. Favorite wins! Two hundred thousands pounds lost and won. You don't say so? Pass the pie!" HWC/E

"The crowd thickens on both sides of the road. All London appears to have come out to see us. It is like a triumphant entry—except that, on the whole, we rather amuse than impress the populace. There are little love-scenes among the chestnut trees by the roadside—young gentlemen in gardens resentful of glances at young ladies from coach-tops—other young gentlemen in other gardens, minding young ladies, whose arms seem to be trained like the vines. There are good family pictures—stout fathers and jolly mothers—rosy cheeks squeezed in between the rails—and infinitesimal jockeys winning in canters on walking-sticks. There are smart maid-servants among the grooms at stable-doors, where Cook looms large and glowing. There is plenty of smoking and drinking among the tilted vans and at the public-houses, and some singing, but general order and good-humour. So, we leave the gardens and come into the streets, and if we there encounter a few ruffians throwing flour and chalk about, we know them for the dregs and refuse of a fine, trustworthy people, deserving of all confidence and honor." HWC/E *And see* TT:Chaises, Flys and Gigs

—at Doncaster

—grandstand: "Francis [Goodchild] much delights to be, not in the Grand Stand, but where he can see it, rising against the sky with its vast tiers of little white dots of faces, and its last high rows and corners of people, looking like pins stuck into an enormous pincushion—not quite so symmetrically as his orderly eye could wish, when people change or go away.

"When the race is nearly run out, it is as good as the race to him to see the flutter among the pins, and the change in them from dark to light, as hats are taken off and waved. Not less full of interest, the loud anticipation of the winner's name, the swelling, and the final roar; then, the quick dropping of all the pins out of their places, the revelation of the shape of the bare pincushion, and the closing-in of the whole host of Lunatics and Keepers, in the rear of the three horses with bright-coloured riders, who have not yet quite subdued their gallop though the contest is over." ¶LT 5

—town: "Monday, mid-day. Races not to begin until to-morrow, but all the mob-Lunatics out, crowding the pavements of the one main street of pretty and pleasant Doncaster, crowding the road, particularly crowding the outside of the Betting Rooms, whooping and shouting loudly after all passing vehicles.

"Frightened lunatic horses occasionally running away, with infinite clatter. All degrees of men, from peers to paupers, betting incessantly. Keepers very watchful, and taking all good chances. An awful family likeness among the Keepers, to **Mr Palmer** and **Mr Thurtell**.*

"With some knowledge of expression and some acquaintance with heads (thus writes Mr Goodchild), I never have seen anywhere, so many repetitions of one class of countenance and one character of head (both evil) as in this street at this time. Cunning, covetousness, secrecy, cold calculation, hard callousness and dire insensibility, are the uniform Keeper characteristics. Mr Palmer passes me five times in five minutes, and, as I go down the street, the back of Mr Thurtell's skull is always going on before me.

"Monday evening. Town lighted up; more Lunatics out than ever; a complete choke and stoppage of the thoroughfare outside the Betting Rooms. Keepers, having dined, pervade the Betting Rooms, and sharply snap at the moneyed Lunatics. Some Keepers flushed with drink, and some not, but all close and calculating.

"A vague echoing roar of 't'harses' and 't'races' always rising in the air, until midnight, at about which period it dies away in occasional drunken songs and straggling yells. But, all night, some unmannerly drinking-house in the neighbourhood opens its mouth at intervals and spits out a man too drunk to be retained: who thereupon makes what uproarious protest may be left in him, and either falls asleep where he tumbles, or is carried off in custody." ¶LT 5

**William Palmer and John Thurtell were famous contemporary murderers.*

—at Hampton: "The little race-course at Hampton was in the full tide and height of its gaiety, the day as dazzling as day could be, the sun high in the cloudless sky and shining in its fullest splendour. Every gaudy colour that fluttered in the air from carriage seat and garish tent top, shone out in its gaudiest hues. Old dingy flags gew new again, faded gilding was re-burnished, stained rotten canvas looked a snowy white; the very beggars' rags were freshened up, and sentiment quite forgot its charity in its fervent admiration of poverty so picturesque.

"It was one of those scenes of life and animation, caught in its very brightest and freshest moments, which can scarcely fail to please; for if the eye be tired of show and glare, or the ear be weary with a ceaseless round of noise, the one may repose, turn almost where it will, on eager happy and expectant faces, and the other deaden all consciousness of more annoying sounds in those of mirth and exhilaration . . . .

"The great race of the day had just been run; and the close lines of people on either side of the course suddenly breaking up and pouring into it, imparted a new liveliness to the scene, which was again all busy movement. Some hurried eagerly to catch a glimpse of the winning horse, others darted to and fro searching no less eagerly for the carriages they had left in quest of better stations. Here a little knot gathered round a pea and thimble table to watch the plucking of some unhappy greenhorn, and there another proprietor with his confederates....

"These would be hanging on the outskirts of a wide circle of people assembled round some itinerant juggler, opposed in his turn by a noisy band of music, or the classic game of 'Ring the Bull', while ventriloquists holding dialogues with wooden dolls, and fortune-telling women smothering the cries of real babies, divided with them, and many more, the general attention of the company.

"Drinking-tents were full, glasses began to clink in carriages, hampers to be unpacked, tempting provisions to be set forth, knives and forks to rattle, champagne corks to fly, eyes to brighten that were not dull before, and pickpockets to count their gains during the last heat. The attention so recently strained on one object of interest, was now divided among a hundred; and look where you would, was a motley assemblage of feasting, laughing, talking, begging, gambling, and mummery.

"Of the gambling-booths there was plentiful show, flourishing in all the splendour of carpeted ground, striped hangings, crimson cloth, pinnacled roofs, geranium pots, and livery servants. There were the Strangers' club-house, the Athenaeum club-house, the Hampton club-house, the Saint James's club-house, and half-a-mile of club-houses to play *in* ; and there was *rouge-et-noir*, French hazard, and *La Merveille*, to play *at*." ¶NN 50

Recreation

"I entertain a weak idea that the English people are as hard-worked as any people upon whom the sun shines. I acknowledge to this ridiculous idiosyncrasy, as a reason why I would give them a little more play." HT i 10

—balloonist

—variety: "The balloon ascents of last season. Let me reckon them up. There were the horse, the bull, the parachute, and the tumbler hanging on—chiefly by his toes, I believe—below the car. Very wrong, indeed, and decidedly to be stopped." RP/LA
And see The Public—*diverted*

—at Vauxhall Gardens: "Some half-dozen men were restraining the impetuousity of one of the balloons, which was completely filled, and had the car already attached; and as rumours had gone abroad that a Lord was 'going up,' the crowd were more than usually anxious and talkative. . . .

"' . . . isn't it a lovely thing to see him and his wife a-going up in one balloon, and his own son and *his* wife a-jostling up against them in another, and all of them going twenty or thirty mile in three hours or so, and then coming back in pochayses? I don't know where this here science is to stop, mind you; that's what bothers me.' . . .

"Just at this moment all eyes were directed to the preparations which were being made for starting. The car was attached to the second balloon, the two were brought pretty close together, and a military band commenced playing, with a zeal and fervour which would render the most timid man in existence but too happy to accept any means of quitting that particular spot of earth on which they were stationed . . . then the balloons went up, and the aerial travellers stood up, and the crowd outside roared with delight, and the two gentlemen who had never ascended before, tried to wave their flags, as if they were not nervous, but held on very fast all the while; and the balloons were wafted gently away. . . . The gardens disgorged their multitudes, boys ran up and down screaming 'bal-loon;' and in all the crowded thoroughfares people rushed out of their shops into the middle of the road, and having stared up in the air at two little black objects till they almost dislocated their necks, walked slowly in again, perfectly satisfied.

"The next day there was a grand account of the ascent in the morning papers, and the public were informed how it was the finest day but four in Mr **Green**'s remembrance; how they retained sight of the earth till they lost it behind the clouds; and how the reflection of the balloon on the undulating masses of vapour was gorgeously picturesque; together with a little science about the refraction of the sun's rays, and some mysterious hints respecting atmospheric heat and eddying currents of air . . . all of which was very instructive and very amusing, as our readers will see if they look to the papers. If we have forgotten to mention the date, they have only to wait till next summer, and take the account of the first ascent, and it will answer the purpose equally well." SB/VG

—bathing at Ramsgate: "'Well, I never!' exclaimed Mrs Tuggs, as she and Mr Joseph Tuggs, and Miss Charlotta Tuggs, and Mr Cymon Tuggs, with their eight feet in a corresponding number of yellow shoes, seated themselves on four rush-bottomed chairs, which, being placed in a soft part of the

sand, forthwith sunk down some two feet and a half—'Well, I never!'

"Mr Cymon, by an exertion of great personal strength, uprooted the chairs, and removed them further back.

"'Why, I'm blessed if there ain't some ladies a-going in!' exclaimed Mr Joseph Tuggs, with intense astonishment.

"'Lor, pa!' excalimed Miss Charlotta.

"'There *is,* my dear,' said Mr Joseph Tuggs. And, sure enough, four young ladies, each furnished with a towel, tripped up the steps of a bathing-machine. In went the horse, floundering about in the water; round turned the machine; down sat the driver; and presently out burst the young ladies aforesaid, with four distinct splashes.

"'Well, that's sing'ler, too!' ejaculated Mr Joseph Tuggs, after an awkward pause. Mr Cymon coughed slightly.

"'Why, here's some gentlemen a-going in on this side!' exclaimed Mrs Tuggs, in a tone of horror.

"Three machines—three horses—three flounderings—three turnings round—three splashes—three gentlemen, disporting themselves in the water like so many dolphins.

"'Well, *that's* singl'ler!' said Mr Joseph Tuggs again. Miss Charlotta coughed this time, and another pause ensued." SB/TR

—carnival

—decorations in Rome: " . . . anything so gay, so bright, and lively as the whole scene [in the Corso], it would be difficult to imagine. From all the innumerable balconies: from the remotest and highest, no less than from the lowest and nearest: hangings of bright red, bright green, bright blue, white and gold, were fluttering in the brilliant sunlight. From windows, and from parapets, and tops of houses, streamers of the richest colours, and draperies of the gaudiest and most sparkling hues, were floating out upon the street.

"The buildings seemed to have been literally turned inside out, and to have all their gaiety towards the highway. Shop-fronts were taken down, and the windows filled with company, like boxes at a shining theatre; doors were carried off their hinges, and long tapestried groves, hung with garlands of flowers and evergreens, displayed within; builder's scaffoldings were gorgeous temples, radiant in silver, gold, and crimson; and in every nook and corner, from the pavement to the chimney-tops, where women's eyes could glisten, there they danced, and laughed, and sparkled, like the light in water." PI 11

—Moccoletti: " . . . the diversion of the Moccoletti, the last gay madness of the Carnival, is now at hand . . . lights begin flashing, here and there; in the windows, on the house-tops, in the balconies, in the carriages, in the hands of the foot-passengers: little by little: gradually, gradually: more and more: until the whole long street is one great glare and blaze of fire.

"Then, everybody present has but one engrossing object; that is, to extinguish other people's candles, and to keep his own alight; and everybody: man, woman, or child, gentleman or lady, prince or peasant, native or foreigner: yells and screams, and roars incessantly, as a taunt to the subdued, 'Senza Moccolo, Senza Moccolo!' (Without a light! Without a light!) until nothing is heard but a gigantic chorus of those two words, mingled with peals of laughter.

"The game of the Moccoletti (the word, in the singular, Moccoletto, is the diminutive of Moccolo, and means a little lamp or candle-snuff) is supposed by some to be a ceremony of burlesque mourning for the death of the Carnival: candles being indispensable to Catholic grief. But whether it be so, or be a remnant of the ancient Saturnalia, or an incorporation of both, or have its origin in anything else, I shall always remember it, and the frolic, as a brilliant and most captivating sight: no less remarkable for the unbroken good-humour of all concerned, down to the very lowest . . . than for its innocent vivacity.

"For, odd as it may seem to say so, of a sport so full of thoughtlessness and personal display, it is as free from any taint of immodesty as any general mingling of the two sexes can possibly be; and there seems to prevail, during its progress, a feeling of general, almost childish, simplicity and confidence, which one thinks of with a pang, when the Ave Maria has rung it away, for a whole year." PI 11

—country fair: "The entrance is occupied on either side by the vendors of gingerbread and toys: the stalls are gaily lighted up, the most attractive goods profusely disposed, and unbonneted young ladies, in their zeal for the interest of their employers, seize you by the coat, and use all the blandishments

of 'Do, dear'—'There's a love'—'Don't be cross, now,' &c., to induce you to purchase half a pound of the real spice nuts, of which the majority of the regular fair-goers carry a pound or two as a present supply, tied up in a cotton pocket-handkerchief. Occasionally you pass a deal table, on which are exposed penn'orths of pickled salmon (fennel included), in little white saucers: oysters, with shells as large as cheese-plates, and divers specimens of a species of snail (*wilks,* we think they are called), floating in a somewhat bilious-looking green liquid. Cigars, too, are in great demand; gentlemen must smoke, of course, and here they are, two a penny, in a regular authentic cigar-box, with a lighted tallow candle in the centre.

"Imagine yourself in an extremely dense crowd, which swings you to and fro, and in and out, and every way but the right one; add to this the screams of women, the shouts of boys, the clanging of gongs, the firing of pistols, the ringing of bells, the bellowings of speaking-trumpets, the squeaking of penny dittoes, the noise of a dozen bands, with three drums in each, all playing different tunes at the same time, the hallooing of showmen, and an occasional roar from the wild-beast shows; and you are in the very centre and heart of the fair." SB/GF

—the professionals: "As the morning wore on, the tents assumed a gayer and more brilliant appearance, and long lines of carriages came rolling softly on the turf. Men who had lounged about all night in smock-frocks and leather leggings, came out in silken vests and hats and plumes, as jugglers or mountebanks; or in gorgeous liveries as soft-spoken servants at gambling booths; or in sturdy yeoman dress as decoys at unlawful games. Black-eyed gipsy girls, hooded in showy handkerchiefs, sallied forth to tell fortunes, and pale slender women with consumptive faces lingered upon the footsteps of ventriloquists and conjurors, and counted the sixpences with anxious eyes long before they were gained.

"As many of the children as could be kept within bounds, were stowed away, with all the other signs of dirt and poverty, among the donkeys, carts, and horses; and as many as could not be thus disposed of ran in and out in all intricate spots, crept between people's legs and carriage wheels, and came forth unharmed from under horses' hoofs. The dancing-dogs, the stilts, the little lady and the tall man, and all the other attractions, with organs out of number and bands innumerable, emerged from the holes and corners in which they had passed the night, and flourished boldly in the sun." ¶OCS 19

—disguised: "On referring to lists of the courses of lectures that had been given . . . I fancied I detected a shyness in admitting that human nature when at leisure has any desire whatever to be relieved and diverted; and a furtive sliding in of any poor make-weight piece of amusement, shamefacedly and edgewise. Thus, I observed that it was necessary for the members to be knocked on the head with Gas, Air, Water, Food, the Solar System, the Geological periods, Criticism on Milton, the Steam-engine, **John Bunyan**, and Arrow-Headed Inscriptions, before they might be tickled by those unaccountable choristers, the negro singers in the court costume of the reign of George the Second.

"Likewise, that they must be stunned by a weighty inquiry whether there was internal evidence in **Shakespeare**'s works, to prove that his uncle by the mother's side lived for some years at Stoke Newington, before they were brought-to by a Miscellaneous Concert. But, indeed, the masking of entertainment, and pretending it was something else—as people mask bedsteads when they are obliged to have them in sitting-rooms, and make believe that they are book-cases, sofas, chests of drawers, anything rather than bedsteads—was manifest even in the pretence of dreariness that the unfortunate entertainers themselves felt obliged in decency to put forth when they came here." ¶UT/DT

—fishing: "I have assisted at innumerable feats of angling by lying in the bottom of the boat, whole summer days, doing nothing with the greatest perseverance; which I have generally found to be as effectual towards the taking of fish as the finest tackle and the utmost science . . . . " CS/HT

—gardening: "If the regular City man who . . . drives home to Hackney, Clapton, Stamford Hill, or elsewhere, can be said to have any daily recreation beyond his dinner, it is his garden. He never does anything to it with his own hands; but he takes great pride in it notwithstanding . . . his delight in his garden appears to arise more from the consciousness of possession than actual enjoyment of it . . . .

" . . . when the cloth is removed, and he has drunk three or four glasses of his favourite port, he orders the French windows of his dining-room (which of course look into the garden) to be opened, and throwing a silk handkerchief over his head, and leaning back in his armchair, descants at considerable length upon its beauty, and the cost of maintaining it . . . when he has exhausted the subject, he goes to sleep.

"There is another and a very different class of men, whose recreation is their garden. An individual of this class resides some short distance from town—say in the Hampstead Road, or the Kilburn Road, or any other road where the houses are small and neat, and have little slips of back garden. He and his wife—who is as clean and compact a little body as himself—have occupied the same house ever since he retired from business twenty years ago . . . .

"In fine weather the old gentleman is almost constantly in the garden; and when it is too wet to go into it, he will look out of the window at it, by the hour together. He has always something to do there, and you will see him digging, and sweeping, and cutting, and planting, with manifest delight. In spring-time, there is no end to the sowing of seeds, and sticking little bits of wood over them, with labels, which look like epitaphs to their memory; and in the evening, when the sun has gone down, the perseverance with which he lugs a great watering-pot about is perfectly astonishing.

"The only other recreation he has is the newspaper, which he peruses every day, from beginning to end, generally reading the most interesting pieces of intelligence to his wife during breakfast. The old lady is very fond of flowers, as the hyacinth-glasses in the parlour-window, and geranium-pots in the little front court, testify. She takes great pride in the garden too: and when one of the four fruit-trees produces rather a larger gooseberry than usual, it is carefully preserved under a wine-glass in the sideboard, for the edification of visitors, who are duly informed that Mr So-and-so planted the tree which produced it, with his own hands." SB/LR

And see A:Old Age—*contented;* B:House—*country—garden; and* M: Mind—*of the heart*

—*hobby:* "When a man rides an amiable hobby that shies at nothing and kicks nobody, it is only agreeable to find him riding it with a humorous sense of the droll side of the creature. When the man is a cordial and an earnest man by nature, and withal is perfectly fresh and genuine, it may be doubted whether he is ever seen to greater advantage than at such a time." MED 22

—*knitting:* "All the women knitted. They knitted worthless things; but the mechanical work was a mechanical substitute for eating and drinking; the hands moved for the jaws and the digestive apparatus; if the bony fingers had been still, the stomachs would have been more famine-pinched . . . .

"Darkness closed around, and then came the ringing of church bells and the distant beating of the military drums in the Palace Court-Yard, as the women sat knitting, knitting. Darkness encompassed them. Another darkness was closing in as surely, when the church bells, then ringing pleasantly in many an airy steeple over France, should be melted into thundering cannon; when the military drums should be beating to drown a wretched voice, that night all potent as the voice of Power and Plenty, Freedom and Life. So much was closing in about the women who sat knitting, knitting, that they their very selves were closing around a structure yet unbuilt, where they were to sit knitting, knitting, counting dropping heads." TTC ii 16

—*lounging:* " . . . a dozen loungers. As to this idle company, there they stood, spellbound by the place [a blacksmith's forge], and, casting now and then a glance upon the darkness in their rear, settled their lazy elbows more at ease upon the sill, and leaned a little further in: no more disposed to tear themselves away than if they had been born to cluster round the blazing hearth like so many crickets." MC 2

—*minstrel show:* "My object was to hear and see the Mississippi Momuses in what the bills described as their 'National ballads, plantation break-downs, nigger part-songs, choice conundrums, sparkling repartees, &c.'

"I found the nine dressed alike, in the black coat and trousers, white waistcoat, very large shirt-front, very large shirt-collar, and very large white tie and wristbands, which constitute the dress of the mass of the African race, and which has been observed by travellers to prevail over a vast number of degrees of latitude. All the nine rolled their eyes exceedingly, and had very red lips.

"At the extremities of the curve they formed, seated in their chairs, were the performers on the tambourine and bones. The centre Momus, a black of melancholy aspect (who inspired me with a vague uneasiness for which I could not then account), performed on a Mississippi instrument closely resembling what was once called in this island a hurdy-gurdy. The Momuses on either side of him had each another instrument peculiar to the Father of Waters, which may be likened to a stringed weather-glass held upside down. There were likewise a little flute and a violin.

"All went well for awhile, and we had had several sparkling repartees exchanged between the performers on the tambourine and bones, when the black of melancholy aspect, turning to the latter, and addressing him in a deep and improving voice as 'Bones, sir,' delivered certain grave remarks to him concerning the juveniles present, and the season of the year; whereon I perceived that I was in the presence of *Mr Barlow*—corked!" ¶UT/B

Kit and Barbara at the Play OCS

—the morning after: "Oh these holidays! why will they leave us some regret? why cannot we push them back, only a week or two in our memories, so as to put them at once at that convenient distance whence they may be regarded either with a calm indifference or a pleasant effort of recollection? Why will they hang about us, like the flavour of yesterday's wine, suggestive of headaches and lassitude, and those good intentions for the future, which, under the earth, form the everlasting pavement of a large estate, and, upon it, usually endure until dinner-time or thereabouts?

"Who will wonder that Barbara had a headache, or that Barbara's mother was disposed to be cross, or that she slightly underrated Astley's, and thought the clown was older than they had taken him to be last night? Kit [Nubbles] was not surprised to hear her say so—not he. He had already had a misgiving that the inconstant actors in that dazzling vision had been doing the same thing the night before last, and would do it again that night, and the next, and for weeks and months to come, though he would not be there. Such is the difference between yesterday and to-day. We are all going to the play, or coming home from it." OCS 40

—necessity: "We know that the effect of prolonged and arduous labour is to produce, when a period of rest does arrive, a sensation of lassitude which it requires the reapplication of some stimulus to overcome. What stimulus have they? . . .

"But you hold out no inducement, you offer no relief from listlessness, you provide nothing to amuse his mind, you afford him no means of exercising his body. Unwashed and unshaven, he saunters moodily about, weary and dejected. In lieu of the wholesome stimulus he might derive from nature, you drive him to the pernicious excitement to be gained from art. He flies to the gin-shop as his only resource; and when, reduced to a worse level than the lowest brute in the scale of creation, he lies wallowing in the kennel, your saintly lawgivers lift up their hands to heaven, and exclaim for a law which shall convert the day intended for rest and cheerfulness, into one of universal gloom, bigotry, and persecution." STH/1

"Surely, none of us in our sober senses and acquainted with figures, are to be told at this time of day, that one of the foremost elements in the existence of the Coketown working-people had been for scores of years deliberately set at nought? That there was any Fancy in them demanding to be brought into healthy existence instead of struggling on in convulsions? That exactly in the ratio as they worked long and monotonously, the craving grew within them for some physical relief—some relaxation, encouraging good humour and good spirits, and giving them a vent—some recognized holiday, music—some occasional light pie in which even M'Choakumchild had no finger—which craving must and would be satisfied aright, or must and would inevitably go wrong, until the laws of the Creation were repealed?" HT i 4

"'Thquire, thak handth, firtht and latht! Don't be croth with uth poor vagabondth. People mutht be amuthed. They can't be alwayth a learning, nor yet they can't be alwayth a working, they an't made for it. You mutht have uth, thquire. Do the withe thing and the kind thing too, and make the betht of uth; not the wurtht!'

"'And I never thought before,' said Mr Sleary, putting his head in at the door again to say it, 'that I wath tho muth of a Cackler!'" HT iii 8

—*Saturday night* "There was a delicious sense of cleaning-up and making a quiet pause before going on in life afresh, in our village on Saturday nights, which stimulated Joe [Gargery] to dare to stay out half an hour longer on Saturdays than at other times." GE 10

—*seaside resort:* "If the pier had presented a scene of life and bustle to the Tuggses on their first landing at Ramsgate, it was far surpassed by the appearance of the sands on the morning after their arrival. It was a fine, bright, clear day, with a light breeze from the sea. There were the same ladies and gentlemen, the same children, the same nursemaids, the same telescopes, the same portable chairs. The ladies were employed in needlework, or watch-guard making, or knitting, or reading novels; the gentlemen were reading newspapers and magazines; the children were digging holes in the sand with wooden spades, and collecting water therein; the nursemaids, with their youngest charges in their arms, were running in after the waves, and then running back with the waves after them; and, now and then, a little sailing-boat either departed with a gay and talkative cargo of passengers, or returned with a very silent and particularly uncomfortable-looking one." SB/TR

"As we walked by the softly-lapping sea, all the notabilities of Namelesston, who are for ever going up and down with the changelessness of the tides, passed to and fro in procession. Pretty girls on horseback, and with detested riding-masters; pretty girls on foot; mature ladies in hats—spectacled, strong-minded, and glaring at the opposite or weaker sex. The Stock Exchange was strongly represented, Jerusalem was strongly represented, the bores of the prosier London clubs were strongly represented. Fortune-hunters of all denominations were there, from hirsute insolvency, in a curricule, to closely-buttoned swindlery in doubtful boots, on the sharp look-out for any likely young gentleman disposed to play a game at billiards round the corner. Masters of languages, their lessons finished for the day, were going to their homes out of sight of the sea; mistresses of accomplishments, carrying small portfolios, likewise tripped homeward; pairs of scholastic pupils, two and two, went languidly along the beach, surveying the face of the waters as if waiting for some Ark to come and take them off. . . . Alone stationary in the midst of all the movements, the Namelesston boat-men leaned against the railings and yawned, and looked out to sea, or looked at the moored fishing-boats and at nothing. Such is the unchanging manner of life with this nursery of our hardy seamen; and very dry nurses they are, and always wanting something to drink. The only two nautical personages detached from the railing were the two fortunate possessors of the celebrated monstrous unknown barking-fish, just caught (frequently just caught off Namelesston), who carried him about in a hamper, and pressed the scientific to look in at the lid." UT/DH

—*taking snuff:* "But Mr Feeder's great possession was a large green jar of snuff, which Mr Toots had brought down as a present, at the close of the last vacation; and for which he had paid a high price, as having been the genuine property of the Prince Regent. Neither Mr Toots nor Mr Feeder could partake of this or any other snuff, even in the most stinted and moderate degree, without being seized with convulsions of sneezing. Nevertheless it was their great delight to moisten a box-full with cold tea, stir it up on a piece of parchment with a paper-knife, and devote themselves to its consumption then and there. In the course of which cramming of their noses, they endured surprising torments with the constancy of martyrs: and, drinking table-beer at intervals, felt all the glories of dissipation." DS 14

And see W:Scotland and Scots—*taking snuff*

—*Vauxhall Gardens*

—*by day:* "We paid our shilling at the gate, and then we saw for the first time, that the entrance, if there had been any magic about it at all, was now decidedly disenchanted, being, in fact, nothing more nor less than a combination of very roughly-painted boards and sawdust. We glanced at the orchestra and supper-room as we hurried past—we just recognised them, and that was all.

"We bent our steps to the firework-ground; there, at least, we should not be disappointed. We reached it, and stood rooted to the spot with mortification and astonishment. *That* the Moorish tower—that wooden shed with a door in the centre, and daubs of crimson and yellow all round, like a gigantic watch-case! *That* the place where night after night we had beheld the undaunted Mr **Blackmore** make his terrific ascent, surrounded by flames of fire, and peals of artillery, and where the white garments of Madame Somebody (we forget even her name now), who nobly devoted her life to the manufacture of fireworks, had so often been seen fluttering in the wind, as she called up a red, blue, or parti-coloured light to illumine her temple!" SB/VG

—*by night:* "We loved to wander among these illuminated groves, thinking of the patient and laborious researches which had been carried on there during the day, and witnessing their results in the suppers which were served up beneath the light of lamps and to the sound of music at night. The temples and saloons and cosmoramas and fountains glittered and sparkled before our eyes; the beauty of the lady singers and the elegant deportment of the gentlemen, captivated our hearts; a few hundred thousand of additional lamps dazzled our senses; a bowl or two of punch bewildered our brains; and we were happy." SB/VG

—*walking:* "The weather being fine and dry, and any English road abounding in interest for him who had been so long away, [Arthur Clennam] sent his valise on by the coach, and set out to walk. A walk was in itself a new enjoyment to him, and one that had rarely diversified his life afar off.

"He went by Fulham and Putney, for the pleasure of strolling over the heath. It was bright and shining there; and when he found himself so far on his road to Twickenham, he found himself a long way on his road to a number of airier and less substantial destinations. They had risen before him fast, in the healthful exercise and the pleasant road. It is not easy to walk alone in the country without musing upon something. And he had plenty of unsettled subjects to meditate upon, though he had been walking to the Land's End." LD i 16

—*water-party:* "'Are you fond of the water?' is a question very frequently asked, in hot summer weather, by amphibious-looking young men. 'Very,' is the general reply. 'An't you?'—'Hardly ever off it,' is the response, accompanied by sundry adjectives, expressive of the speaker's heartfelt admiration of that element.

"Now, with all respect for the opinion of society in general, and cutter clubs in particular, we humbly suggest that some of the most painful reminiscences in the mind of every individual who has occasionally disported himself on the Thames, must be connected with his aquatic recreations.

"Who ever heard of a successful water-party?—or to put the question in a still more intelligible form, who ever saw one? We have been on water excursions out of number, but we solemnly declare that we cannot call to mind one single occasion of the kind, which was not marked by more miseries than any one would suppose could be reasonably crowded into the space of some eight or nine hours.

"Something has always gone wrong. Either the cork of the salad-dressing has come out, or the most anxiously expected member of the party has not come out, or the most disagreeable man in company would come out, or a child or two have fallen into the water, or the gentleman who undertook to steer has endangered everybody's life all the way, or the gentlemen who volunteered to row have been 'out of practice,' and performed very alarming evolutions, putting their oars down into the water and not being able to get them up again, or taking terrific pulls without putting them in at all; in either case, pitching over on the backs of their heads with startling violence, and exhibiting the soles of their pumps to the 'sitters' in the boat, in a very humiliating manner." SB/R

"There has evidently been up to this period no inconsiderable degree of boasting on everybody's part relative to his knowledge of navigation; the sight of the water rapidly cools their courage, and the air of self-denial with which each of them insists on somebody else's taking an oar, is perfectly delightful. At length, after a great deal of changing and fidgeting, consequent upon the election of a stroke-oar, the inability of one gentleman to pull on this side, of another to pull on that, and of a third to pull at all, the boat's crew are seated. 'Shove her off!' cries the coxswain, who looks as easy and comfortable as if he were steering in the Bay of Biscay. The order is obeyed; the boat is immediately turned completely round, and proceeds towards Westminster Bridge, amidst such a splashing and struggling as never was seen before, except when the Royal George went down. 'Back w'ater, sir,' shouts Dando, 'Back wa'ater, you sir, aft;' upon which everybody thinking he must be the individual referred to, they all back water, and back comes the boat, stern first, to the spot whence it started. 'Back water, you sir, aft; pull round you sir, for'ad, can't you?' shouts Dando, in a frenzy of excitement. 'Pull round, Tom, can't you?' re-echoes one of the party. 'Tom an't for'ad' replies another. 'Yes, he is,' cries a third; and the unfortunate young man, at the imminent risk of breaking a blood-vessel, pulls and pulls until the head of the boat fairly lies in the direction of Vauxhall Bridge. 'That's right—now pull all on you!' shouts Dando again, adding, in an under-tone, to somebody by him, 'Blowed if hever I see sich a set of muffs!' and away jogs the boat in a zigzag direction, every one of the six oars dipping into the water at a different time; and the yard is once more clear, until the arrival of the next party." SB/R

"There was a great water-party made up to go to Twickenham and dine, and afterwards dance in an empty villa by the riverside, hired expressly for the purpose. Mr and Mrs Leaver were of the company; and it was our fortune to have a seat in the same boat, which was an eight-oared galley, manned by amateurs, with a blue striped awning of the same pattern as their Guernsey shirts, and a dingy red flag of the same shade as the whiskers of the stroke oar.

"A coxswain being appointed, and all other matters adjusted, the eight gentlemen threw themselves into strong paroxysms, and pulled up with the tide, stimulated by the compassionate remarks of the ladies, who one and all exclaimed, that it seemed an immense exertion—as indeed it did. At first we raced the other boat, which came alongside in gallant style; but this being found an unpleasant amusement, as giving rise to a great quantity of splashing, and rendering the cold pies and other viands very moist, it was unanimously voted down, and we were suffered to shoot ahead, while the second boat followed ingloriously in our wake.

"It was at this time that we first recognised Mr Leaver. There were two firemen-watermen in the boat, lying by until somebody was exhausted; and one of them, who had taken upon himself the direction of affairs, was heard to cry in a gruff voice, 'Pull away, number two—give it her, number two—take a longer reach, number two—now, number two, sir, think you're winning a boat.'

"The greater part of the company had no doubt begun to wonder which of the striped Guernseys it might be that stood in need of such encouragement, when a stifled shriek from Mrs Leaver confirmed the doubtful and informed the ignorant; and Mr Leaver, still further disguised in a straw hat and no neckcloth, was observed to be in a fearful perspiration, and failing visibly.

"Nor was the general consternation diminished at this instant by the same gentleman (in the performance of an accidental aquatic feat, termed 'catching a crab') plunging suddenly backward, and displaying nothing of himself to the company, but two violently struggling legs . . . Mr Leaver was replaced in a sitting posture, and his oar (which had been going through all kinds of wrong-headed performances on its own account) was once more put in his hand, by the exertions of the two firemen-watermen . . . the company generally, who seemed to be apprehensive that if Mr Leaver remained where he was, he might contribute more than his proper share towards the drowning of the party, disinterestedly took part with Mrs Leaver, and said he really ought to go. . . . " YC/L

And see Gambling, Games, Race-Meeting, *and* LC:Theatre

Reputation

—absent: "'Are you the landlord?' inquired the gentleman.

"'I am, sir,' replied the landlord.

"'Do you know me?' demanded the gentleman.

"'I have not that pleasure, sir,' rejoined the landlord.

"'My name is Slurk,' said the gentleman.

"The landlord slightly inclined his head.

"'Slurk, sir,' repeated the gentleman, haughtily. 'Do you know me now, man?'

"The landlord made a strong effort, and at length replied: 'Well, sir, I do *not* know you.'"

"'Great Heaven!' said the stranger, dashing his clenched first upon the table. 'And this is popularity!'

"The landlord took a step or two towards the door; the stranger, fixing his eyes upon him, resumed.

"'This,' said the stranger, 'this is gratitude for years of labour and study in behalf of the masses. I alight wet and weary; no enthusiastic crowds press forward to greet their champion; the church-bells are silent; the very name elicits no responsive feeling in their torpid bosoms. It is enough,' said the agitated Mr Slurk, pacing to and fro, 'to curdle the ink in one's pen, and induce one to abandon their cause forever.'" PP 51

—fame: "It may have required a stronger effort on Tom Pinch's part to leave the seat on which he sat, and shake his friend [young Martin Chuzzlewit] by both hands, with nothing but serenity and grateful feeling painted on his face; it may have required a stronger effort to perform this simple act [in effect one of congratulation on Martin's relationship with Mary Graham] with a pure heart, than to achieve many and many a deed to which the doubtful trumpet blown by Fame has lustily resounded. Doubtful, because from its long hovering over scenes of violence, the smoke and steam of death have clogged the keys of that brave instrument; and it is not always that its notes are either true or tuneful." MC 12

—gained by going about: "Now the point of view seized by the bewitching Tippins, that this same working and rallying round is to keep up appearances, may have something in it, but not all the truth. More is done, or considered to be done—which does as well—by taking cabs, and 'going about,' than the fair Tippins knew of. Many vast vague reputations have been made, solely by taking cabs and going about. This particularly obtains in all Parliamentary affairs. Whether the business in hand be to get a man in, or get a man out, or get a man over, or promote a railway, or jockey a railway, or what else, nothing is understood to be so effectual as scouring nowhere in a violent hurry—in short, as taking cabs and going about." OMF ii 3

—literary: "Mr Snodgrass, being occasionally abstracted and melancholy, is to this day reputed a great poet among his friends and acquaintance, although we do not find that he has ever written anything to encourage the belief. There are many celebrated characters, literary, philosophical, and otherwise, who hold a high reputation on a similar tenure." PP 57

—obsessive preoccupation: "Though [Dombey] hide the world within him from the world without—which he believes has but one purpose for the time, and that, to watch him eagerly wherever he goes—he cannot hide those rebel traces of it, which escape in hollow eyes and cheeks, a haggard forehead, and a moody, brooding air. Impenetrable as before, he is still an altered man: and, proud as ever, he is humbled, or those marks would not be there.

"The world. What the world thinks of him, how it looks at him, what it sees in him, and what it says—this is the haunting demon of his mind. It is everywhere where he is; and, worse than that, it is everywhere where he is not. It comes out with him among his servants, and yet he leaves it whispering behind; he sees it pointing after him in the street; it is waiting for him in his counting-house; it leers over the shoulders of rich men among the merchants; it goes beckoning and babbling among the crowd; it always anticipates him, in every place; and is always busiest, he knows, when he has gone away. When he is shut up in his room at night, it is in his house, outside it, audible in footsteps on the pavement, visible in print upon the table, steaming to and fro on railroads and in ships: restless and busy everywhere, with nothing else but him." DS 51 *And see* A:Divorce—*for the rich*

—*posthumous:* "My mind, with inconceivable rapidity, followed out all the consequences of such a death. Estella's father would believe I had deserted him, would be taken, would die accusing me; even Herbert [Pocket] would doubt me . . . Joe and Biddy would never know how sorry I had been that night, none would ever know what I had suffered, how true I had meant to be, what an agony I had passed through. The death close before me was terrible, but far more terrible than death was the dread of being misremembered after death. And so quick were my thoughts, that I saw myself despised by unborn generations—Estella's children, and their children—while the wretch [Orlick]'s words were yet on his lips." GE 53

—*respectability:* "There was a servant in that house, a man [Littimer] who . . . was in appearance the pattern of respectability. I believe there never existed in his station a more respectable-looking man . . . his great claim to consideration was his respectability . . . every peculiarity that he had he made respectable. If his nose had been upside-down, he would have made that respectable. He surrounded himself with an atmosphere of respectability, and walked secure in it. It would have been next to impossible to suspect him of anything wrong, he was so thoroughly respectable. Nobody could have thought of putting him in a livery, he was so highly respectable." DC 21

"Mr Vholes is a very respectable man. He has not a large business, but he is a very respectable man. He is allowed by the greater attorneys who have made good fortunes, or are making them, to be a most respectable man. He never misses a chance in his practice; which is a mark of respectability. He never takes any pleasure; which is another mark of respectability. He is reserved and serious; which is another mark of respectability. His digestion is impaired, which is highly respectable." BH 39

—*selective:* " . . .the reflections of Sir Mulberry Hawk turned upon Kate Nickleby, and were, in brief, that she was undoubtedly handsome; that her coyness must be easily conquerable by a man of his address and experience, and that the pursuit was one which could not fail to redound to his credit, and greatly to enhance his reputation with the world. And lest this last consideration—no mean or secondary one with Sir Mulberry—should sound strangely in the ears of some, let it be remembered that most men live in a world of their own, and that in that limited circle alone are they ambitious for distinction and applause. Sir Mulberry's world was peopled with profligates, and he acted accordingly.

"Thus, cases of injustice, and oppression, and tyranny, and the most extravagant bigotry, are in constant occurrence among us every day. It is the custom to trumpet forth much wonder and astonishment at the chief actors therein setting at defiance so completely the opinion of the world; but there is no greater fallacy; it is precisely because they do consult the opinion of their own little world that such things take place at all, and strike the great world dumb with amazement." NN 28

—*in sport:* "With the quickness and penetration of a man of genius, [Tupman] had at once observed that the two great points to be attained were—first, to discharge his piece without injury to himself, and, secondly, to do so, without danger to the bystanders;—obviously, the best thing to do, after surmounting the difficulty of firing at all, was to shut his eyes firmly, and fire into the air.

"On one occasion, after performing this feat, Mr Tupman, on opening his eyes, beheld a plump partridge in the act of falling wounded to the ground. He was on the point of congratulating Mr Wardle on his invariable success, when that gentleman advanced towards him, and grasped him warmly by the hand.

"'Tupman,' said the old gentleman, 'you singled out that particular bird?'

"'No,' said Mr Tupman—'no.'

"'You did,' said Wardle. 'I saw you do it—I observed you pick him out—I noticed you, as you raised your piece to take aim; and I will say that the best shot in existence could not have done it more beautifully. You are an older hand at this, than I thought you, Tupman; you have been out before.'

"It was in vain for Mr Tupman to protest,

with a smile of self-denial that he never had. The very smile was taken as evidence to the contrary; and from that time forth, his reputation was established. It is not the only reputation that has been acquired as easily, nor are such fortunate circumstances confined to partridge-shooting." PP 19

Sailor

—a hard life: " . . . there Mercantile Jack was, and very busy he was, and very cold he was . . . the north-east winds snipping off the tops of the little waves in the Mersey, and rolling them into hailstones to pelt him with. Mercantile Jack was hard at it, in the hard weather: as he mostly is in all weathers, poor Jack.

"He was girded to ships' masts and funnels of steamers, like a forester to a great oak, scraping and painting; he was lying out on yards, furling sails that tried to beat him off; he was dimly discernible up in a world of giant cobwebs, reefing and splicing; he was faintly audible down in holds, stowing and unshipping cargo; he was winding round and round at capstans melodious, monotonous, and drunk; he was of a diabolical aspect, with coaling for the Antipodes; he was washing decks barefoot, with the breast of his red shirt open to the blast, though it was sharper than the knife in his leathern girdle; he was looking over bulwarks, all eyes and hair; he was standing by at the shoot of the Cunard steamer, off to-morrow, as the stocks in trade of several butchers, poulterers, and fishmongers, poured down into the icehouse; he was coming aboard of other vessels, with his kit in a tarpaulin bag, attended by plunderers to the very last moment of his shore-going existence . . . he stood swaying about, with his hair blown all manner of wild ways, rather crazedly taking leave of his plunderers, all the rigging in the docks was shrill in the wind, and every little steamer coming and going across the Mersey was sharp in its blowing off, and every buoy in the river bobbed spitefully up and down, as if there were a general taunting chorus of 'Come along, Mercantile Jack! Ill-lodged, ill-fed, ill-used, hocussed, entrapped, anticipated, cleaned out. Come along, Poor Mercantile Jack, and be tempest-tossed till you are drowned!'" ¶UT/MJ

—at home on land: "Mr Tartar's chambers were the neatest, the cleanest, and the best-ordered chambers ever seen under the sun, moon, and stars. The floors were scrubbed to that extent, that you might have supposed the London blacks emancipated for ever, and gone out of the land for good. Every inch of brass-work in Mr Tartar's possession was polished and burnished, till it shone like a brazen mirror. No speck, nor spot, nor spatter soiled the purity of any of Mr Tartar's household gods, large, small, or middle sized. His sitting-room was like the admiral's cabin, his bath room was like a dairy, his sleeping chamber, fitted all about with lockers and drawers, was like a seedsman's shop; and his nicely-balanced cot just stirred in the midst, as if it breathed.

"Everything belonging to Mr Tartar had quarters of its own assigned to it: his maps and charts had their quarters; his books had theirs; his brushes had theirs; his boots had theirs; his clothes had theirs; his case-bottles had theirs; his telescopes and other instruments had theirs.

"Everything was readily accessible. Shelf, bracket, locker, hook, and drawer were equally within reach, and were equally contrived with a view to avoiding waste of room, and providing some snug inches of stowage for something that would have exactly fitted nowhere else. His gleaming little service of plate was so arranged upon his side-board as that a slack salt-spoon would have instantly betrayed itself; his toilet implements were so arranged upon his dressing-table as that a toothpick of slovenly deportment could have been reported at a glance.

"So with the curiosities he had brought home from various voyages. Stuffed, dried, repolished, or otherwise preserved, according to their kind; birds, fishes, reptiles, arms, articles of dress, shells, seaweeds, grasses, or memorials of coral reef; each was displayed in its especial place, and each could have been displayed in no better place.

"Paint and varnish seemed to be kept somewhere out of sight, in constant readiness to obliterate stray finger-marks wherever any might become perceptible in Mr Tartar's chambers. No man-of-war was ever kept more spick and span from careless touch.

"On this bright summer day, a neat awning was rigged over Mr Tartar's flower-garden as only a sailor could rig it; and there was a sea-going air upon the whole effect, so delightfully complete, that the flower-garden might have appertained to stern-windows afloat, and the whole concern might have bowled away gallantly with all on board, if Mr Tartar had only clapped to his lips the speaking trumpet that was slung in a corner, and given hoarse orders to have the anchor up, look alive there, men, and get all sail upon her!" MED ¶21

—identification: "A sailor had these devices on his right arm. 'Our Saviour on the Cross, the forehead of the Crucifix and the vesture stained red; on the lower part of the arm, a man and woman; on one side of the Cross, the appearance of a half moon, with a face; on the other side, the sun; on the top of the Cross, the letters I.H.S.; on the left arm, a man and woman dancing, with an effort to delineate the female's dress; under which, initials.'

"Another seaman 'had, on the lower part of the right arm, the device of a sailor and a female; the man holding the Union Jack with a streamer, the folds of which waved over her head, and the end of it was held in her hand. On the upper part of the arm, a device of Our Lord on the Cross, with stars surrounding the head of the Cross, and one large star on the side in Indian ink. On the left arm, a flag, a true lover's knot, a face, and initials.'

"This tattooing was found still plain, below the discoloured outer surface of a mutilated arm, when such surface was carefully scraped away with a knife. It is not improbable that the perpetuation of this marking custom among seamen, may be referred back to their desire to be identified, if drowned and flung ashore." UT/S

And see Occupations—*boatman*

Servant problem

—in a boarding-house: "Girls as I was beginning to remark are one of your first and your lasting troubles, being like your teeth which begin with convulsions and never cease tormenting you from the time you cut them till they cut you, and then you don't want to part with them which seems hard but we must all succumb or buy artificial, and even where you get a will nine times out of ten you'll get a dirty face with it and naturally lodgers do not like good society to be shown in with a smear of black across the nose or a smudgy eyebrow . . . I says to Sophy, 'Now Sophy my good girl have a regular day for your stoves and keep the width of the Airy between yourself and the blacking and do not brush your hair with the bottoms of the saucepans and do not meddle with the snuffs of the candles and it stands to reason that it can no longer be' yet there it was . . . .

"Well consequently I put poor Sophy on to other work and forbid her answering the door or answering a bell on any account but she was so unfortunately willing that nothing would stop her flying up the kitchen-stairs whenever a bell was heard to tingle. I put it to her 'O Sophy Sophy for goodness' goodness' sake where does it come from?' To which that poor unlucky willing mortal bursting out crying to see me so vexed replied 'I took a deal of black into me ma'am when I was a small child being much neglected and I think it must be, that it works out' . . . ." ¶CS/L 1

"My dear I do assure you it's a harassing thing to know what kind of girls to give the preference to, for if they are lively they get bell'd off their legs and if they are sluggish you suffer from it yourself in complaints and if they are sparkling-eyed they get made love to, and if they are smart in their persons they try on your Lodgers' bonnets and if they are musical I defy you to keep them away from bands and organs, and allowing for any difference you like in their heads their heads will be always out of window just the same. And then what the gentlemen like in girls the ladies don't, which is fruitful hot water for all parties . . . ." CS/L 1

—in chambers: " . . . I was looked after by an inflammatory old female, assisted by an animated rag-bag whom she called her niece; and to keep a room secret from them would be to invite curiosity and exaggeration. They both had weak eyes, which I had long attributed to their chronically looking in at keyholes, and they were always at hand when not wanted; indeed that was their only reliable quality besides larceny." GE 40

"[Joe Gargery] did everything for me except the household work, for which he had engaged a very decent woman, after paying off the laundress on his first arrival. 'Which I do assure you, Pip,' he would often say, in explanation of that liberty; 'I found her a tapping the spare bed, like a cask of beer, and drawing off the feathers in a bucket, for sale. Which she would have tapped yourn next, and draw'd it off with you a laying on it, and was then a carrying away the coals gradiwally in the soup-tureen and wegetable dishes, and the wine and spirits in your Wellington boots.'" GE 57

—in a commercial boarding-house: " . . . [Bailey] . . . expressed his belief that the approaching collation would be of 'rather a spicy sort.'

"'Will it be long before it's ready, Bailey?' asked Mercy [Pecksniff].

"'No,' said Bailey, 'it *is* cooked. When I come up, she was dodging among the tender pieces with a fork, and eating of 'em.'

"But he had scarcely achieved the utterance of these words, when he received a manual compliment on the head, which sent him staggering against the wall; and Mrs Todgers, dish in hand, stood indignantly before him.

"'Oh you little villain!' said that lady. 'Oh you bad, false boy!'

"'No worse than yerself,' retorted Bailey, guarding his head, on a principle invented by Mr **Thomas Cribb**. 'Ah! Come now! Do that agin, will yer?'

"'He's the most dreadful child,' said Mrs Todgers, setting down the dish, 'I ever had to deal with. The gentlemen spoil him to that extent, and teach him such things, that I'm afraid nothing but hanging will ever do him any good . . . .

" . . . this remarkable boy . . . nothing disconcerted or put out of his way. If any piece of crockery, a dish or otherwise, chanced to slip through his hands (which happened once or twice), he let it go with perfect good breeding, and never added to the painful emotions of the company by exhibiting the least regret. Nor did he, by hurrying to and fro, disturb the repose of the assembly, as many well-trained servants do; on the contrary, feeling the hopelessness of waiting upon so large a party, he left the gentlemen to help themselves to what they wanted, and seldom stirred from behind Mr Jinkins's chair: where, with his hands in his pockets, and his legs planted pretty wide apart, he led the laughter, and enjoyed the conversation." MC 9

"This ancient female [Mrs Tamaroo] . . . was chiefly remarkable for a total absence of all comprehension upon every subject whatever. She was a perfect Tomb for messages and small parcels; and when dispatched to the Post Office with letters, had been frequently seen endeavouring to insinuate them into casual chinks in private doors, under the delusion that any door with a hole in it would answer the purpose. . . . She was on all occasions chary of opening the street-door, and ardent to shut it again; and she waited at table in a bonnet." MC 32

—for newlyweds: "Her name was Paragon. Her nature was represented to us, when we engaged her, as being feebly expressed in her name. She had a written character, as large as a proclamation; and, according to this document, could do everything of a domestic nature that ever I heard of, and a great many things that I never did hear of. . . .

"Our treasure was warranted sober and honest. I am therefore willing to believe that she was in a fit when we found her under the boiler; and that the deficient tea-spoons were attributable to the dustman.

"But she preyed upon our minds dreadfully. We felt our inexperience, and were unable to help ourselves. We should have been at her mercy, if she had had any; but she was a remorseless woman, and had none." DC 44

"The next domestic trial we went through, was the Ordeal of Servants. Mary Anne's cousin deserted into our coal-hole, and was brought out, to our great amazement, by a picquet of his companions in arms, who took him away handcuffed in a procession that covered our front-garden with ignominy. This nerved me to get rid of Mary Anne, who went so mildly, on receipt of wages, that I was surprised, until I found out about the tea-spoons, and also about the little sums she had borrowed in my name of the tradespeople without authority.

"After an interval of Mrs Kidgerbury—the oldest inhabitant of Kentish Town, I believe, who went out charing, but was too feeble to execute her conceptions of that art—we found another treasure, who was one of the most amiable of women, but who generally made a point of falling either up or down the kitchen stairs with the tray, and almost plunged into the parlour, as into a bath, with the tea-things. The ravages committed by this unfortunate rendering her dismissal necessary, she was succeeded (with intervals of Mrs Kidgerbury) by a long line of Incapables; terminating in a young person of genteel appearance, who went to Greenwich Fair in Dora's bonnet. After whom I remember nothing but an average equality of failure." ¶DC 44

"As to the washerwoman pawning the clothes, and coming in a state of penitent intoxication to apologise, I suppose that might have happened several times to anybody . . . . But I apprehend that we were personally fortunate in engaging a servant with a taste for cordials, who swelled our running account for porter at the public-house by such inexplicable items as 'quartern rum shrub (Mrs C.);' 'Half-quartern gin and cloves (Mrs C.);' 'Glass rum and peppermint (Mrs C.)'—the parentheses always referring to Dora, who was supposed, it appeared on explanation, to have imbibed the whole of these refreshments." DC 44

—*problems with a page:* "After several varieties of experiment, we had given up the housekeeping as a bad job. The house kept itself, and we kept a page. The principal function of this retainer was to quarrel with the cook; in which respect he was a perfect Whittington, without his cat, or the remotest chance of being made Lord Mayor.

"He appears to me to have lived in a hail of saucepan-lids. His whole existence was a scuffle. He would shriek for help on the most improper occasions—as when we had a little dinner party, or a few friends in the evening—and would come tumbling out of the kitchen, with iron missiles flying after him. We wanted to get rid of him, but he was very much attached to us, and wouldn't go. He was a tearful boy, and broke into such deplorable lamentations, when a cessation of our connexion was hinted at, that we were obliged to keep him.

"He had no mother—no anything in the way of a relative, that I could discover, except a sister, who fled to America the moment we had taken him off her hands; and he became quartered on us like a horrible young changeling. He had a lively perception of his own unfortunate state, and was always rubbing his eyes with the sleeve of his jacket, or stooping to blow his nose on the extreme corner of a little pocket-handkerchief, which he never *would* take completely out of his pocket, but always economised and secreted.

"This unlucky page, engaged in an evil hour at six pounds ten per annum, was a source of continual trouble to me. I watched him as he grew—and he grew like scarlet beans—with painful apprehensions of the time when he would begin to shave; even of the days when he would be bald or grey. I saw no prospect of ever getting rid of him; and, projecting myself into the future, used to think what an inconvenience he would be when he was an old man.

"I never expected anything less, than this unfortunate's manner of getting me out of my difficulty. He stole Dora's watch, which, like everything else belonging to us, had no particular place of its own; and, converting it into money, spent the produce (he was always a weak-minded boy) in incessantly riding up and down between London and Uxbridge outside the coach. He was taken to Bow Street, as well as I remember, on the completion of his fifteenth journey; when four-and-sixpence, and a second-hand fife which he couldn't play, were found upon his person.

"The surprise and its consequences would have been much less disagreeable to me if he had not been penitent. But he was very penitent indeed, and in a peculiar way—not in the lump, but by instalments. For example: the day after that on which I was obliged to appear against him, he made certain revelations touching a hamper in the cellar, which we believed to be full of wine, but which had nothing in it except bottles and corks. We supposed he had now eased his mind, and told the worst he knew of the cook; but, a day or two afterwards, his conscience sustained a new twinge, and he disclosed how she had a little girl, who, early every morning, took away our bread; and also how he himself had been suborned to maintain the milkman in coals.

"In two or three days more, I was informed by the authorities of his having led to the discovery of sirloins of beef among the kitchen-stuff, and sheets in the rag-bag. A little while afterwards, he broke out in an entirely new direction, and confessed to a knowledge of burglarious intentions as to our premises, on the part of the pot-boy, who was immediately taken up. I got to be so ashamed of being such a victim, that I would have given him any money to hold his tongue, or would have offered a round bribe for his being permitted to run away. It was an aggravating circumstance in the case that he had no idea of this, but conceived that he was making me amends in every new discovery: not to say, heaping obligations on my head.

"At last I ran away myself, whenever I saw an emissary of the police approaching wth some new intelligence; and lived a stealthy life until he was tried and ordered to be transported. Even then he couldn't be quiet, but was always writing us letters; and wanted so much to see Dora before he went away, that Dora went to visit him, and fainted when she found herself inside the iron bars. In short, I had no peace of my life until he was expatriated, and made (as I afterwards heard) a shepherd of, 'up the country' somewhere; I have no geographical idea where." ¶DC 44

"I had got on so fast of late, that I had even started a boy [Pepper: the Avenger] in boots—top boots—in bondage and slavery to whom I might be said to pass my days. For, after I had made this monster (out of the refuse of my washerwoman's family) and had clothed him with a blue coat, canary waistcoat, white cravat, creamy breeches, and the boots already mentioned, I had to find him a little to do and a great deal to eat; and with both of these horrible requirements he haunted my existence." GE 27

—visitors: "'Ah!' said Mr Bucket. 'Here we are, and a nice retired place it is. Puts a man in mind of the country house in the Woodpecker-tapping, that was known by the smoke which so gracefully curled. They're early with the kitchen fire, and that denotes good servants. But what you've always got to be careful of with servants is, who comes to see 'em; you never know what they're up to, if you don't know that. And another thing, my dear. Whenever you find a young man behind the kitchen-door, you give that young man in charge on suspicion of being secreted in a dwelling-house with an unlawful purpose.'" BH 57

Shop

—bone articulator: ". . . Mr Wegg selects one dark shop-window with a tallow candle dimly burning in it, surrounded by a muddle of objects, vaguely resembling pieces of leather and dry stick, but among which nothing is resolvable into anything distinct, save the candle itself in its old tin candlestick, and two preserved frogs fighting a small-sword duel . . . .

"'You're casting your eye round the shop, Mr Wegg. Let me show you a light. My working bench. My young man's bench. A Wice. Tools. Bones, warious. Skulls, warious. Preserved Indian baby. African ditto. Bottled preparations, warious. Everything within reach of your hand, in good preservation. The mouldy ones a-top. What's in those hampers over them again, I don't quite remember. Say, human warious. Cats. Articulated English baby. Dogs. Ducks. Glass eyes, warious. Mummied bird. Dried cuticle, warious. Oh dear me! That's the general panoramic view.'" OMF i 7

—book: "But what were even gold and silver, precious stones and clockwork, to the bookshops, whence a pleasant smell of paper freshly pressed came issuing forth, awakening instant recollections of some new grammar had at school, long time ago, with 'Master Pinch, Grove House Academy,' inscribed in faultless writing on the fly-leaf!

"That whiff of russia leather, too, and all those rows on rows of volumes, neatly ranged within: what happiness did they suggest! And in the window were the spick-and-span new works from London, with the title-pages, and sometimes even the first page of the first chapter, laid wide open: tempting unwary men to begin to read the book, and then, in the impossibility of turning over, to rush blindly in, and buy it!

"Here too were the dainty frontispiece and trim vignette, pointing like handposts on the outskirts of great cities, to the rich stock of incident beyond; and store of books, with many a grave portrait and time-honoured name, whose matter he knew well, and would have given mines to have, in any form, upon the narrow shelf beside his bed at Mr. Pecksniff's. What a heart-breaking shop it was!" ¶MC 5

—broker/appraiser: ". . . one Brogley, sworn broker and appraiser, who kept a shop where every description of second-hand furniture was exhibited in the most uncomfortable aspect, and under circumstances and in combinations the most completely foreign to its purpose. Dozens of chairs hooked on to washing-stands, which with difficulty posed themselves on the shoulders of sideboards, which in their turn stood upon the wrong side of dining-tables, gymnastic with their legs upward on the tops of other dining-tables, were among its most reasonable arrangements.

"A banquet array of dish-covers, wine-glasses, and decanters was generally to be seen, spread forth upon the bosom of a four-post bedstead, for the entertainment of such genial company as half-a-dozen pokers, and a hall lamp. A set of window curtains with no windows belonging to them, would be seen gracefully draping a barricade of chests of drawers, loaded with little jars from chemists' shops; while a homeless hearthrug severed from its natural companion the fireside, braved the shrewd east wind in its adversity, and trembled in melancholy accord with the shrill complainings of a cabinet piano, wasting away, a string a day, and faintly resounding to the noises of the street in its jangling and distracted brain.

"Of motionless clocks that never stirred a finger, and seemed as incapable of being successfully wound up, as the pecuniary affairs of their former owners, there was always great choice in Mr Brogley's shop; and various looking-glasses, accidentally placed at compound interest of reflection and refraction, presented to the eye an eternal perspective of bankruptcy and ruin." ¶DS 9

"On a board, at the side of the door, are placed about twenty books—all odd volumes; and as many wine-glasses—all different patterns; several locks, an old earthenware pan, full of rusty keys; two or three gaudy chimney-ornaments—cracked, of course; the remains of a lustre, without any drops; a round frame like a capital O, which has once held a mirror; a flute, complete with the exception of the middle joint; a pair of curling-irons; and a tinder-box.

"In front of the shop window are ranged some half-dozen high-backed chairs, with spinal complaints and wasted legs; a corner cupboard; two or three very dark mahogany tables with flaps like mathematical problems; some pickle-jars, some surgeons' ditto, with gilt labels and without stoppers, an unframed portrait of some lady who flourished about the beginning of the thirteenth century, by an artist who never flourished at all; an incalculable host of miscellanies of every description, including bottles and cabinets, rags and bones, fenders and street-door knockers, fire-irons, wearing apparel and bedding, a hall-lamp, and a room-door.

"Imagine, in addition to this incongruous mass, a black doll in a white frock, with two faces—one looking up the street, and the other looking down, swinging over the door; a board with the squeezed-up inscription 'Dealer in marine stores,' in lanky white letters, whose height is strangely out of proportion to their width; and you have before you precisely the kind of shop to which we wish to direct your attention." ¶SB/BS

—children's books: " . . . where poor *Robinson Crusoe* stood alone in his might, with dog and hatchet, goat-skin cap and fowling-pieces; calmly surveying *Philip Quarll* and the host of imitators round him, and calling Mr. Pinch to witness that he, of all the crowd, impressed one solitary footprint on the shore of boyish memory, whereof the tread of generations should not stir the lightest grain of sand.

"And there too were the Persian tales, with flying chests and students of enchanted books shut up for years in caverns: and there too was *Abudah,* the merchant, with the terrible little old woman hobbling out of the box in his bedroom: and there the mighty talisman, the rare Arabian Nights, with *Cassim Baba,* divided by four, like the ghost of a dreadful sum, hanging up, all gory, in the robbers' cave." ¶MC 5

—curiosity: "[It] was one of those receptacles for old and curious things which seem to crouch in odd corners of this town and to hide their musty treasures from the public eye in jealousy and distrust. There were suits of mail standing like ghosts in armour here and there, fantastic carvings brought from monkish cloisters, rusty weapons of various kinds, distorted figures in china and wood and iron and ivory: tapestry and strange furniture that might have been designed in dreams.

"The haggard aspect of the little old man [Nell's grandfather] was wonderfully suited to the place; he might have groped among old churches and tombs and deserted houses and gathered all the spoils with his own hands. There was nothing in the whole collection but was in keeping with himself; nothing that looked older or more worn than he." ¶OCS 1

—general (food and sundry): "A little shop, quite crammed and choked with the abundance of its stock; a perfectly voracious little shop, with a maw as accommodating and full as any shark's. Cheese, butter, firewood, soap, pickles, matches, bacon, table-beer, peg-tops, sweetmeats, boys' kites, bird-seed, cold ham, birch brooms, hearth-stones, salt, vinegar, blacking, red-herrings, stationery, lard, mushroom-ketchup, stay-laces, loaves of bread, shuttle-cocks, eggs, and slate pencil; everything was fish that came to the net of this greedy little shop, and all articles were in its net.

"How many other kinds of petty merchandise were there, it would be difficult to say; but balls of packthread, ropes of onions, pounds of candles, cabbage-nets, and brushes, hung in bunches from the ceiling, like extraordinary fruit; while various odd canisters emitting aromatic smells, established the veracity of the inscription over the outer door, which informed the public that the keeper of this little shop was a licensed dealer in tea, coffee, tobacco, pepper, and snuff." ¶C 4

—iron-ware: " . . . there was a low-browed, beetling shop, below a pent-house roof, where iron, old rags, bottles, bones, and greasy offal, were bought. Upon the floor within, were piled up heaps of rusty keys, nails, chains, hinges, files, scales, weights, and refuse iron of all kinds. Secrets that few would like to scrutinise were bred and hidden in mountains of unseemly rags, masses of corrupted fat, and sepulchres of bones." CC 4

—law-stationer: "Mr Snagsby has dealt in all sorts of blank forms of legal process; in skins and rolls of parchment; in paper—foolscap, brief, draft, brown, white, whitey-brown, and blotting; in stamps; in office-quills, pens, ink, India-rubber, pounce, pins, pencils, sealing-wax, and wafers; in red tape and green ferret; in pocket-books, almanacks, diaries, and law lists; in string boxes, rulers, ink-stands—glass and leaden, penknives, scissors, bodkins and other small office-cutlery; in short, in articles too numerous to mention; ever since he was out of his time, and went into partnership with Peffer." BH 10

—marine stores: "Here [in Ratcliff Highway], the wearing apparel is all nautical. Rough blue jackets, with mother-of-pearl buttons, oil-skin hats, coarse checked shirts, and large canvas trousers that look as if they were made for a pair of bodies instead of a pair of legs, are the staple commodities. Then, there are large bunches of cotton pocket-handkerchiefs, in colour and pattern unlike any one ever saw before, with the exception of those on the backs of the three young ladies without bonnets who passed just now.

"The furniture is much the same as elsewhere, with the addition of one or two models of ships, and some old prints of naval engagements in still older frames. In the window are a few compasses, a small tray containing silver watches in clumsy thick cases; and tobacco-boxes, the lid of each ornamented with a ship, or an anchor, or some such trophy. A sailor generally pawns or sells all he has before he has been long ashore, and if he does not, some favoured companion kindly saves him the trouble. In either case, it is an even chance that he afterwards unconsciously repurchases the same things at a higher price than he gave for them at first." SB/BS

—musical instrument: " . . . a musician's shop, having a few fiddles in the window, and some Pan's pipes and a tambourine, and a triangle, and certain elongated scraps of music . . . . " BH 27

"That wonderful mystery, the music-shop, carried it off as usual (except that it had more cabinet pianos in stock), as if season or no season were all one to it. It made the same prodigious display of bright brazen wind-instruments, horribly twisted, worth, as I should conceive, some thousands of pounds, and which it is utterly impossible that anybody in any season can ever play or want to play. It had five triangles in the window, six pairs of castanets, and three harps; likewise every polka with a coloured frontispiece that ever was published; from the original one where a smooth male and female Pole of high rank are coming at the observer with their arms a-kimbo, to the Ratcatcher's Daughter. Astonishing establishment, amazing enigma!" RP/OS

—nautical instrument

—inside contents: "The stock-in-trade of this old gentleman [Solomon Gills] comprised chronometers, barometers, telescopes, compasses, charts, maps, sextants, quadrants, and specimens of every kind of instrument used in the working of a ship's course, or the keeping of a ship's reckoning, or the prosecuting of a ship's discoveries.

"Objects in brass and glass were in his drawers and on his shelves, which none but the initiated could have found the top of, or guessed the use of, or having once examined, could have ever got back again into their mahogany nests without assistance.

"Everything was jammed into the tightest cases, fitted into the narrowest corners, fenced up behind the most impertinent cushions, and screwed into the acutest angles, to prevent its philosophical composure from being disturbed by the rolling of the sea. Such extraordinary precautions were taken in every instance to save room, and keep the thing compact; and so much practical navigation was fitted, and cushioned, and screwed into every box (whether the box was a mere slab, as some were, or something between a cocked hat and a star-fish, as others were, and those quite mild and modest boxes as compared with others); that the shop itself, partaking of the general infection, seemed almost to become a snug, sea-going, ship-shape concern, wanting only good sea-room, in the event of an unexpected launch, to work its way securely to any desert island in the world.

"Many minor incidents in the household life of the Ships' Instrument-maker who was proud of his little midshipman, assisted and bore out this fancy. His acquaintance lying chiefly among ship-chandlers and so forth, he had always plenty of the veritable ships' biscuit on his table. It was familiar with dried meats and tongues, possessing an extraordinary flavour of rope yard. Pickles were produced upon it, in great wholesale jars, with 'dealer in all kinds of Ships' Provisions' on the label: spirits were set forth in case bottles with no throats. Old prints of ships with alphabetical references to their various mysteries, hung in frames upon the walls; the Tartar Frigate under weigh, was on the plates; outlandish shells, seaweeds, and mosses, decorated the chimney-piece; the little wainscotted back parlour was lighted by a sky-light, like a cabin." ¶DS 4

—outside totem: " . . . little timber midshipmen in obsolete naval uniforms, eternally employed outside the shop doors of nautical instrument-makers in taking observations of the hackney coaches.

"Sole master and proprietor of one of these effigies—of that which might be called, familiarly, the woodenest—of that which thrust itself out above the pavement, right leg foremost, with a suavity the least endurable, and had the shoe buckles and flapped waistcoat the least reconcileable to human reason, and bore at its right eye the most offensively disproportionate piece of machinery—sole master and proprietor of that midshipman, and proud of him too, an elderly gentleman in a Welsh wig had paid house-rent, taxes, and dues, for more years than many a full-grown midshipman of flesh and blood has numbered in his life; and midshipmen who have attained a pretty green old age, have not been wanting in the English navy." DS 4

"The Wooden Midshipman at the Instrument-maker's door, like the hard-hearted little midshipman he was, remained supremely indifferent to Walter's going away . . . . With his quadrant at his round black knob of an eye, and his figure in his old attitude of indomitable alacrity, the midshipman displayed his elfin small-clothes to the best advantage, and, absorbed in scientific pursuits, had no sympathy with wordly concerns. He was so far the creature of circumstances, that a dry day covered him with dust, and a misty day peppered him with little bits of soot, and a wet day brightened up his tarnished uniform for the moment, and a very hot day blistered him; but otherwise he was a callous, obdurate, conceited midshipman, intent on his own discoveries, and caring as little for what went on about him, terrestrially, as **Archimedes** at the taking of Syracuse." DS 19

—pawnbroking

—in an ancient city:"Even [Cloisterham's] single pawnbroker takes in no pledges, nor has he for a long time, but offers vainly an unredeemed stock for sale, of which the costlier articles are dim and pale old watches apparently in a slow perspiration, tarnished sugar-tongs with ineffectual legs, and odd volumes of dismal books." MED 6

—classified: "There are some pawnbrokers' shops of a very superior description. There are grades in pawning as in everything else, and distinctions must be observed even in poverty. The aristocratic Spanish cloak and the plebeian calico shirt, the silver fork and the flat iron, the muslin cravat and the Belcher neckerchief, would but ill assort together; so the better sort of pawnbroker calls himself a silversmith, and decorates his shop with handsome trinkets and expensive jewellery, while the more humble money-lender boldly advertises his calling and invites observation." SB/PS

—client: ". . . we find [Diggory Chuzzlewit] making constant reference to an uncle, in respect of whom he would seem to have entertained great expectations, as he was in the habit of seeking to propitiate his favour by presents of plate, jewels, books, watches, and other valuable articles. Thus, he writes on one occasion to his brother in reference to a gravy-spoon, the brother's property, which he (Diggory) would appear to have borrowed or otherwise possessed himself of: 'Do not be angry, I have parted with it—to my uncle.'

"On another occasion he expresses himself in a similar manner with regard to a child's mug which had been entrusted to him to get repaired. On another occasion he says, 'I have bestowed upon that irresistible uncle of mine everything I ever possessed.' . . . Still it does not appear (which is strange) to have procured for him any lucrative post at court or elsewhere, or to have conferred upon him any other distinction than . . . the being invited by [his uncle] to certain entertainments, so splendid and costly in their nature, that he calls them 'Golden Balls.'" ¶MC 1

—contents: "A few old china cups; some modern vases, adorned with paltry paintings of three Spanish cavaliers playing three Spanish guitars; or a party of boors carousing: each boor with one leg painfully elevated in the air, by way of expressing his perfect freedom and gaiety; several sets of chessmen, two or three flutes, a few fiddles, a round-eyed portrait staring in astonishment from a very dark ground; some gaudily-bound prayer-books and testaments, two rows of silver watches quite as clumsy and almost as large as **Ferguson**'s first; numerous old-fashioned table and tea spoons, displayed, fan-like, in half-dozens; strings of coral with great broad gilt snaps; cards of rings and brooches, fastened and labelled separately, like the insects in the British Museum; cheap silver penholders and snuff-boxes, with a masonic star, complete the jewellery department; while five or six beds in smeary clouded ticks, strings of blankets and sheets, silk and cotton handkerchiefs, and wearing apparel of every description, form the more useful, though even less ornamental, part, of the articles exposed for sale. An extensive collection of planes, chisels, saws, and other carpenters' tools, which have been pledged, and never redeemed, form the foreground of the picture . . . . " SB/PS

—outside appearance: "It is a low, dirty-looking, dusty shop, the door of which stands always doubtfully a little way open: half inviting, half repelling the hesitating visitor, who, if he be as yet uninitiated, examines one of the old garnet brooches in the window for a minute or two with affected eagerness, as if he contemplated making a purchase; and then looking cautiously round to ascertain that no one watches him, hastily slinks in: the door closing of itself after him, to just its former width.

"The shop front and the window-frames bear evident marks of having been once painted; but what the colour was originally, or at what date it was probably laid on, are at this remote period questions which may be asked, but cannot be answered.

"Tradition states that the transparency in the front door, which displays at night three red balls on a blue ground, once bore also, inscribed in graceful waves, the words 'Money advanced on plate, jewels, wearing apparel, and every description of property,' but a few illegible hieroglyphics are all that now remain to attest the fact. The plate and jewels would seem to have disappeared, together with the announcement, for the articles of stock, which are displayed in some profusion in the window, do not include any very valuable luxuries of either kind." ¶SB/PS

—rag and bone: "[Miss Flite] had stopped at a shop, over which was written, KROOK, RAG AND BOTTLE WAREHOUSE. Also, in long thin letters, KROOK, DEALER IN MARINE STORES. In one part of the window was a picture of a red paper mill, at which a cart was unloading a quantity of sacks of old rags. In another, was the inscription, BONES BOUGHT. In another, KITCHEN-STUFF BOUGHT. In another, OLD IRON BOUGHT. In another, WASTE PAPER BOUGHT. In another, LADIES' AND GENTLEMEN'S WARDROBES BOUGHT.

"Everything seemed to be bought, and nothing to be sold there. In all parts of the window were quantities of dirty bottles; blacking bottles, medicine bottles, ginger-beer and soda-water bottles, pickle bottles, wine bottles, ink bottles.

"I am reminded by mentioning the latter, that the shop had, in several little particulars, the air of being in a legal neighbourhood, and of being, as it were, a dirty hanger-on and disowned relation of the law. There were a great many ink bottles. There was a little tottering bench of shabby old volumes, outside the door, labelled 'Law Books, all at 9d.' . . . . There were several second-hand bags, blue and red, hanging up. A little way within the shop-door, lay heaps of old crackled parchment scrolls, and discoloured and dog's-eared law-papers. I could have fancied that all the rusty keys, of which there must have been hundreds huddled together as old iron, had once belonged to doors of rooms or strong chests in lawyers' offices.

"The litter of rags tumbled partly into and partly out of a one-legged wooden scale, hanging without any counterpoise from a beam, might have been counsellors' bands and gowns torn up. One had only to fancy, as Richard whispered to Ada and me while we all stood looking in, that yonder bones in a corner, piled together and picked very clean, were the bones of clients, to make the picture complete." ¶BH 5 *And see—iron-ware*

—in a small town: " . . . Mr Pumblechook appeared to conduct his business by looking across the street at the saddler, who appeared to transact his business by keeping

his eye on the coach-maker, who appeared to get on in life by putting his hands in his pockets and contemplating the baker, who in his turn folded his arms and stared at the grocer, who stood at his door and yawned at the chemist. The watch-maker, always poring over a little desk with a magnifying glass at his eye, and always inspected by a group in smock-frocks poring over him through the glass of his shop-window, seemed to be about the only person in the High-street whose trade engaged his attention." GE 8

—*tobacconist:* "The tobacco business round the corner of Horsemonger Lane was carried on in a rural establishment one story high, which had the benefit of the air from the yards of Horsemonger Lane Jail, and the advantage of a retired walk under the wall of that pleasant establishment. The business was of too modest a character to support a life-size Highlander, but it maintained a little one on a bracket on the door-post, who looked like a fallen Cherub that had found it necessary to take to a kilt." LD i 18

—*unsuccessful:* "The small man . . . was . . . the chief of the firm described in the inscription of the little shop front, by the name and title of A. TETTERBY AND CO., NEWSMEN. Indeed, strictly speaking, he was the only personage answering to that designation; as Co. was a mere poetical abstraction, altogether baseless and impersonal.

"Tetterby's was the corner shop in Jerusalem Buildings. There was a good show of literature in the window, chiefly consisting of picture-newspapers out of date, and serial pirates, and foot-pads. Walking-sticks, likewise, and marbles, were included in the stock in trade. It had once extended into the light confectionery line; but it would seem that those elegancies of life were not in demand about Jerusalem Buildings, for nothing connected with that branch of commerce remained in the window, except a sort of small glass lantern containing a languishing mass of bull's-eyes, which had melted in the summer and congealed in the winter until all hope of ever getting them out, or of eating them without eating the lantern too, was gone for ever.

"Tetterby's had tried its hand at several things. It had once made a feeble little dart at the toy business; for, in another lantern, there was a heap of minute wax dolls, all sticking together upside down, in the direst confusion, with their feet on one another's heads, and a precipitate of broken arms and legs at the bottom. It had made a move in the millinery direction, which a few dry, wiry bonnet-shapes remained in a corner of the window to attest.

"It had fancied that a living might lie hidden in the tobacco trade, and had stuck up a representation of a native of each of the three integral portions of the British empire, in the act of consuming that fragrant weed; with a poetic legend attached, importing that in one cause they sat and joked, one chewed tobacco, one took snuff, one smoked; but nothing seemed to come of it—except flies.

"Time had been when it had put a forlorn trust in imitative jewellery, for in one pane of glass there was a card of cheap seals, and another of pencil-cases, and a mysterious black amulet of inscrutable intention, labelled ninepence. But, to that hour, Jerusalem Buildings had bought none of them.

"In short, Tetterby's had tried so hard to get a livelihood out of Jerusalem Buildings in one way or other, and appeared to have done so indifferently in all, that the best position in the firm was too evidently Co.'s; Co., as a bodiless creation, being untroubled with the vulgar inconveniences of hunger and thirst, being chargeable neither to the poor's-rates nor the assessed taxes, and having no young family to provide for." ¶HM 2

Social class

—"*Blood:*" "We might have been a party of Ogres, the conversation assumed such a sanguine complexion.

"'I confess I am of Mrs Waterbrook's opinion,' said Mr Waterbrook, with his wine-glass at his eye. 'Other things are all very well in their way, but give me Blood!'

"'Oh! There is nothing,' observed *Hamlet*'s aunt, 'so satisfactory to one! There is nothing that is so much one's *beau-ideal* of—of all that sort of thing, speaking generally. There are some low minds (not many, I am happy to believe, but there are *some*) that would prefer to do what *I* should call bow down before idols. Positively Idols! Before services, intellect, and so on. But these are intangible points. Blood is not so. We see Blood in a nose, and we know it. We meet with it in a chin, and we say, "There it is! That's Blood!" It is an actual matter of fact. We point it out. It admits of no doubt."

"The simpering fellow with the weak legs, who had taken Agnes down, stated the question more decisively yet, I thought.

"'Oh, you know, deuce take it,' said this gentleman, looking round the board with an imbecile smile, 'we can't forego Blood, you know. We must have Blood, you know. Some young fellows, you know, may be a little behind their station, perhaps, in point of education and behaviour, and may go a little wrong, you know, and get themselves and other people into a variety of fixes—and all that—but deuce take it, it's delightful to reflect that they've got Blood in 'em! Myself, I'd rather at any time be knocked down by a man who had got Blood in him, than I'd be picked up by a man who hadn't!'" DC 25

—distinctions: "' . . . fun presently—nobs not come yet—queer place—Dock-yard people of upper rank don't know Dock-yard people of lower rank—Dock-yard people of lower rank don't know small gentry—small gentry don't know tradespeople—Commissioner don't know anybody . . . .

" . . . . Mr Smithie bowed deferentially to Sir Thomas Clubber; and Sir Thomas Clubber acknowledged the salute with conscious condescension. Lady Clubber took a telescopic view of Mrs Smithie and family through her eye-glass, and Mrs Smithie stared in her turn at Mrs Somebody else, whose husband was not in the Dock-yard at all . . . .

'Miss Bulder was warmly welcomed by the Miss Clubbers; the greeting between Mrs Colonel Bulder and Lady Clubber was of the most affectionate description; Colonel Bulder and Sir Thomas Clubber exchanged snuff-boxes, and looked very much like a pair of **Alexander Selkirk**s—'Monarchs of all they surveyed.'

"While the aristocracy of the place—the Bulders, and Clubbers, and Snipes—were thus preserving their dignity at the upper end of the room, the other classes of society were imitating their example in other parts of it. The less aristocratic officers of the 97th devoted themselves to the families of the less important functionaries from the Dock-yard. The solicitors' wives, and the wine-merchant's wife, headed another grade (the brewer's wife visited the Bulders): and Mrs Tomlinson, the post-office keeper, seemed by mutual consent to have been chosen the leader of the trade party." PP 2

"[Kate Nickleby] had, it is true, quailed at the prospect of drudgery and hard service; but she had felt no degradation in working for her bread, until she found herself exposed to insolence and pride. Philosophy would have taught her that the degradation was on the side of those who had sunk so low as to display such passions habitually, and without cause; but she was too young for such consolation, and her honest feeling was hurt. May not the complaint, that common people are above their station, often take its rise in the fact of *un*common people being below theirs?" NN 17

"'Adieu, Miss Dorrit, with best wishes,' said Mrs Merdle. 'If we could only come to a Millennium, or something of that sort, I for one might have the pleasure of knowing a number of charming and talented persons from whom I am at present excluded. A more primitive state of society would be delicious to me. There used to be a poem when I learnt lessons, something about Lo the poor Indian whose something mind! If a few thousand persons moving in Society, could only go and be Indians, I would put my name down directly; but as, moving in Society, we can't be Indians, unfortunately—Good morning!'" LD i 20

—in the know: " . . . Mr Gulpidge and Mr Henry Spiker, who had hitherto been very distant, entered into a defensive alliance against us, the common enemy, and exchanged a mysterious dialogue across the table for our defeat and overthrow.

"'That affair of the first bond for four thousand five hundred pounds has not taken the course that was expected, Spiker,' said Mr Gulpidge.

"'Do you mean the D. of A.'s?' said Mr Spiker.

"'The C. of B.'s!' said Mr Gulpidge.

"Mr Spiker raised his eyebrows, and looked much concerned.

"'When the question was referred to Lord—I needn't name him; said Mr Gulpidge, checking himself—

"'I understand,' said Mr Spiker, 'N.'

"Mr Gulpidge darkly nodded—'was referred to him, his answer was, "Money or no release."'

"'Lord bless my soul!' cried Mr Spiker.

"'"Money, or no release,"' repeated Mr Gulpidge, firmly. 'The next in reversion—you understand me?'

"'K,' said Mr Spiker, with an ominous look.

"'—K. then positively refused to sign. He

was attended at Newmarket for that purpose, and he point-blank refused to do it.'

"'Mr Spiker was so interested, that he became quite stony.

"'So the matter rests at this hour,' said Mr Gulpidge, throwing himself back in his chair. 'Our friend Waterbrook will excuse me if I forbear to explain myself generally, on account of the magnitude of the interests involved.'

"Mr Waterbrook was only too happy, as it appeared to me, to have such interests, and such names, even hinted at, across his table. He assumed an expression of gloomy intelligence (though I am persuaded he knew no more about the discussion than I did), and highly approved of the discretion that had been observed. Mr Spiker, after the receipt of such a confidence, naturally desired to favour his friend with a confidence of his own; therefore the foregoing dialogue was succeeded by another, in which it was Mr Gulpidge's turn to be surprised, and that by another in which the surprise came round to Mr Spiker's turn again, and so on, turn and turn about. All this time we, the outsiders, remained oppressed by the tremendous interests involved in the conversation; and our host regarded us with pride, as the victims of a salutary awe and astonishment." DC 25

—its illusion: "Were this miserable mother ["Good Mrs Brown"], and this miserable daughter [Alice Marwood], only the reduction to their lowest grade, of certain social vices sometimes prevailing higher up? In this round world of many circles within circles, do we make a weary journey from the high grade to the low, to find at last that they lie close together, that the two extremes touch, and that our journey's end is but our starting-place? Allowing for great difference of stuff and texture, was the pattern of this woof repeated among gentle blood at all?

"Say, Edith Dombey [Alice's cousin]! And Cleopatra [Mrs Skewton; whose late husband's brother was Alice's father], best of mothers, let us have your testimony!" DS 34

—noblesse oblige: "The present representative of the Dedlocks is an excellent master. He supposes all his dependants to be utterly bereft of individual characters, intentions, or opinions, and is persuaded that he was born to supersede the necessity of their having any. If he were to make a discovery to the contrary, he would be simply stunned—would never recover himself, most likely, except to gasp and die. But he is an excellent master still, holding it a part of his state to be so." BH 7

—pecking order: "Noah [Claypole] was a charity-boy, but not a workhouse orphan. No chance-child was he, for he could trace his genealogy all the way back to his parents, who lived hard by; his mother being a washerwoman, and his father a drunken soldier, discharged with a wooden leg, and a diurnal pension of twopence-halfpenny and an unstateable fraction.

"The shop-boys in the neighborhood had long been in the habit of branding Noah, in the public streets, with the ignominious epithets of 'leathers,' 'charity,' and the like; and Noah had borne them without reply. But now that fortune had cast in his way a nameless orphan, at whom even the meanest could point the finger of scorn, he retorted on him with interest.

"This affords charming food for contemplation. It shows us what a beautiful thing human nature may be made to be; and how impartially the same amiable qualities are developed in the finest lord and the dirtiest charity-boy." ¶OT 5

—stratification: "Who, knowing England at this time [1854], would wish to utter with his last breath a more righteous warning than that its curse is ignorance, or a miscalled education which is as bad or worse, and a want of the exchange of innumerable graces and sympathies among the various orders of society, each hardened unto each and holding itself aloof? Well will it be for us and for our children, if those dying words be never henceforth forgotten on the Judgment Seat." HW/JT

—warfare: "Forth from her back parlor issued the Billickin to receive Miss Twinkleton, and War was in the Billickin's eye from that fell moment.

"Miss Twinkleton brought a quantity of luggage with her, having all Rosa [Bud]'s as well as her own. The Billickin took it ill that Miss Twinkleton's mind, being sorely disturbed by this luggage, failed to take in her personal identity with that clearness of perception which was due to its demands. Stateliness mounted her gloomy throne upon the Billickin's brow in consequence. And when Miss Twinkleton, in agitation taking stock of her trunks and packages, of which she had seventeen, particularly counted in the

Billickin herself as number eleven, the B found it necessary to repudiate.

"'Things cannot too soon be put upon the footing,' said she, with a candour so demonstrative as to be almost obtrusive, 'that the person of the Ouse is not a box nor yet a bundle, nor a carpet bag—no, I am ily obleeged to you, Miss Twinkleton, nor yet a beggar.' This last disclaimer had reference to Miss Twinkleton's distractedly pressing two and sixpence on her, instead of the cabman . . . .

" . . . the Billickin had somehow come to the knowledge that Miss Twinkleton kept a school. The leap from that knowledge to the inference that Miss Twinkleton would set herself to teach *her* something, was easy. 'But you don't do it,' soliloquized the Billickin; '*I* am not your pupil, whatever she,' meaning Rosa, 'may be, poor thing!'

"Miss Twinkleton, on the other hand, having changed her dress and recovered her spirits, was animated by a bland desire to improve the occasion in all ways, and to be as serene a model as possible. In a happy compromise between her two states of existence, she had already become, with her work-basket before her, the equably vivacious companion with a slight judicious flavoring of information, when the Billickin announced herself.

"'I will not hide from you, ladies,' said the B, enveloped in the shawl of state, 'for it is not my character to hide neither my motives nor my actions, that I take the liberty to look in upon you to express a ope that your dinner was to your liking. Though not Professed but Plain, still her wages should be a sufficient object to her to stimilate to soar above mere roast and biled.'

"'We dined very well indeed,' said Rosa, 'thank you.'

"'Accustomed,' said Miss Twinkleton, with a gracious air which to the jealous ears of the Billickin seemed to add 'my good woman':—'Accustomed to a liberal and nutritious, yet plain and salutary diet, we have found no reason to bemoan our absence from the ancient city, and the methodical household, in which the quiet routine of our lot has been hitherto cast.'

"'I did think it well to mention to my cook,' observed the Billickin with a gush of candour, 'which I ope you will agree with me, Miss Twinkleton, was a right precaution, that the young lady being used to what we should consider here but poor diet, had better be brought forard by degrees. For a rush from scanty feeding to generous feeding, and from what you may call messing to what you may call method, do require a power of constitution which is not often found in youth, particular when undermined by boarding-school.'

"It will be seen that the Billickin now openly pitted herself against Miss Twinkleton, as one whom she had fully ascertained to be her natural enemy.

"'Your remarks,' returned Miss Twinkleton, from a remote moral eminence, 'are well meant, I have no doubt; but you will permit me to observe that they develop a mistaken view of the subject, which can only be imputed to your extreme want of accurate information.'

"'My informiation,' retorted the Billickin, throwing in an extra syllable for the sake of an emphasis at once polite and powerful; 'my informiation, Miss Twinkleton, were my own experience, which I believe is usually considered to be good guidance. But whether so or not, I was put in youth to a very genteel boarding-school, the mistress being no less a lady than yourself, of about your own age or it may be some years younger, and a poorness of blood flowed from the table which has run through my life.'

"'Very likely,' said Miss Twinkleton, still from her distant eminence; 'and very much to be deplored. Rosa, my dear, how are you getting on with your work?'

"'Miss Twinkleton,' resumed the Billickin, in a courtly manner, 'before retiring on the Int, as a lady should, I wish to ask of yourself, as a lady, whether I am to consider that my words is doubted?'

"'I am not aware on what ground you cherish such a supposition,' began Miss Twinkleton, when the Billickin neatly stopped her.

"'Do not, if you please, put suppositions betwixt my lips where none such have been imported by myself. Your flow of words is great, Miss Twinkleton, and no doubt is expected from you by your pupils, and no doubt is considered worth the money. *No* doubt, I am sure. But not paying for flows of words, and not asking to be faviored with them here, I wish to repeat my question.'

"'If you refer to the poverty of your circulation—' began Miss Twinkleton again, when again the Billickin neatly stopped her.

"'I have used no such expressions.'

"'If you refer, then, to the poorness of your blood—'

"'Brought upon me,' stipulated the Billickin, expressly, 'at a boarding-school.'

"'Then,' resumed Miss Twinkleton, 'all I can say is, that I am bound to believe, on your asseveration, that it is very poor indeed. I cannot forbear adding, that if that unfortunate circumstance influences your conversation, it is much to be lamented, and it is eminently desirable that your blood were richer. Rosa, my dear, how are you getting on with your work?'

"'Hem! Before retiring, Miss,' proclaimed the Billickin to Rosa, loftily cancelling Miss Twinkleton, 'I should wish it to be understood between yourself and me that my transactions in future is with you alone. I know no elderly lady here, Miss; none older than yourself.'

"'A highly desirable arrangement, Rosa my dear,' observed Miss Twinkleton.

"'It is not, Miss,' said the Billickin, with a sarcastic smile, 'that I possess the Mill I have heard of, in which old single ladies could be ground up young (what a gift it would be to some of us!), but that I limit myself to you totally.'

"'When I have any desire to communicate a request to the person of the house, Rosa my dear,' observed Miss Twinkleton with majestic cheerfulness, 'I will make it known to you, and you will kindly undertake, I am sure, that it is conveyed to the proper quarter.'

"'Good-evening, Miss,' said the Billickin, at once affectionately and distantly. 'Being alone in my eyes, I wish you good-evening with best wishes, and do not find myself drove, I am truly 'appy to say, into expressing my contempt for any indiwidual, unfortunately for yourself, belonging to you.'

"The Billickin gracefully withdrew with this parting speech, and from that time Rosa occupied the restless position of shuttlecock between these two battledores. Nothing could be done without a smart match being played out." MED 21

"Society"

—abroad: "It appeared on the whole, to Little Dorrit herself, that this same society in which they lived, greatly resembled a superior sort of Marshalsea. Numbers of people seemed to come abroad, pretty much as people had come into the prison; through debt, through idleness, relationship, curiosity, and general unfitness for getting on at home.

"They were brought into these foreign towns in the custody of couriers and local followers, just as the debtors had been brought into the prison. They prowled about the churches and picture-galleries, much in the old, dreary, prison-yard manner. They were usually going away again to-morrow or next week, and rarely knew their own minds, and seldom did what they said they would do, or went where they said they would go: in all this again, very like the prison debtors.

"They paid high for poor accommodation, and disparaged a place while they pretended to like it: which was exactly the Marshalsea custom. They were envied when they went away, by people left behind feigning not to want to go: and that again was the Marshalsea habit invariably.

"A certain set of words and phrases, as much belonging to tourists as the College and the Snuggery belonged to the jail, was always in their mouths. They had precisely the same incapacity for settling down to anything, as the prisoners used to have; they rather deteriorated one another, as the prisoners used to do; and they wore untidy dresses, and fell into a slouching way of life; still, always like the people in the Marshalsea." ¶LD ii 7

"Everybody was walking about St Peter's and the Vatican on somebody else's cork legs, and straining every visible object through somebody else's sieve. Nobody said what anything was, but everybody said what the Mrs Generals, Mr **Eustace**, or somebody else said it was.

"The whole body of travellers seemed to be a collection of voluntary human sacrifices, bound hand and foot, and delivered over to Mr Eustace and his attendants, to have the entrails of their intellects arranged according to the taste of that sacred priesthood. Through the rugged remains of temples and tombs and palaces and senate halls and theatres and amphitheatres of ancient days, hosts of tongue-tied and blindfolded moderns were carefully feeling their way, incessantly repeating Prunes and Prism, in the endeavour to set their lips according to the received form.

"Mrs General was in her pure element. Nobody had an opinion. There was a formation of surface going on around her on an amazing scale, and it had not a flaw of courage or honest free speech in it." ¶LD ii 7
And see W: Cities and Towns—*Paris—in Society*

—its arts and letters: "There are also ladies and gentlemen . . . . On whom even the Fine Arts, attending in powder and walking backward like the Lord Chamberlain, must array themselves in the milliners' and tailors' patterns of past generations, and be particularly careful not to be in earnest, or to receive any impress from the moving age." BH 12
And see Artists and their work—*fancy ball*

—class emulation: "The wish of persons in the humbler classes of life, to ape the manners and customs of those whom fortune has placed above them, is often the subject of remark, and not unfrequently of complaint. The inclination may, and no doubt does, exist to a great extent, among the small gentility—the would-be aristocrats—of the middle classes. Tradesmen and clerks, with fashionable novel-reading families, and circulating-library-subscribing daughters, get up small assemblies in humble imitation of Almack's, and promenade the dingy 'large room' of some second-rate hotel with as much complacency as the enviable few who are privileged to exhibit their magnificence in that exclusive haunt of fashion and foolery." SB/LR

"Mr Malderton was a man whose whole scope of ideas was limited to Lloyd's, the Exchange, the India House, and the Bank. A few successful speculations had raised him from a situation of obscurity and comparative poverty, to a state of affluence.

"As frequently happens in such cases, the ideas of himself and his family became elevated to an extraordinary pitch as their means increased; they affected fashion, taste, and many other fooleries, in imitation of their betters, and had a very decided and becoming horror of anything which could, by possibility, be considered *low*.

"He was hospitable from ostentation, illiberal from ignorance, and prejudiced from conceit. Egotism and the love of display induced him to keep an excellent table: convenience, and a love of good things of this life, ensured him plenty of guests. He liked to have clever men, or what he considered such, at his table, because it was a great thing to talk about; but he never could endure what he called 'sharp fellows.' Probably he cherished this feeling out of compliment to his two sons, who gave their respected parent no uneasiness in that particular . . . .

"The family were ambitious of forming acquaintances and connexions in some sphere of society superior to that in which they themselves moved; and one of the necessary consequences of this desire, added to their utter ignorance of the world beyond their own small circle, was, that any one who could lay claim to an acquaintance with people of rank and title, had a sure passport to the table at Oak Lodge, Camberwell." ¶SB/HS

"The Gradgrind party wanted assistance in cutting the throats of the Graces. They went about recruiting; and where could they enlist recruits more hopefully, than among the fine gentlemen who, having found out everything to be worth nothing, were equally ready for anything?

"Moreoever, the healthy spirits who had mounted to this sublime height were attractive to many of the Gradgrind school. They liked fine gentlemen; they pretended that they did not, but they did. They became exhausted in imitation of them; and they yaw-yawed in their speech like them; and they served out, with an enervated air, the little mouldy rations of political economy, on which they regaled their disciples. There never before was seen on earth such a wonderfully hybrid race as was thus produced." HT ii 2

—to be consulted: "'Society,' said Mrs Merdle, with another curve of her little finger, 'is so difficult to explain to young persons (indeed is so difficult to explain to most persons) . . . . I wish Society was not so arbitrary, I wish it was not so exacting—Bird, be quiet!'

"The parrot had given a most piercing shriek, as if its name were Society, and it asserted its right to its exactions.

"'But,' resumed Mrs Merdle, 'we must take it as we find it. We know it is hollow and conventional and worldly and very shocking, but unless we are Savages in the Tropical seas (I should have been charmed to be one myself—most delightful life and perfect climate, I am told), we must consult it.'" LD i 20

—cost: "' . . . I'll impart to you a discovery I've made [said Chops]. It's wallable; it's cost twelve thousand five hundred pound; it may do you good in life.—The secret of this matter is, that it ain't so much that a person goes into Society, as that Society goes into a person . . . . Society has gone into me, to the tune of every penny of my property.'" CS/GS

"'When I was out of Society, I was paid light for being seen [said the dwarf]. When I went into Society, I paid heavy for being seen. I prefer the former, even if I wasn't forced upon it.'" CS/GS

—denizens: "'Society, taken in the lump, is all dwarfs [said Chops]. At the court of St. James's, they was all a doing my old business—all a goin three times round the Cairawan, in the hold court-suits and properties. Elsewheres, they was most of 'em ringin their little bells out of make-believes. Everywheres, the sarser was a goin round. Magsman, the sarser is the uniwersal Institution!'" CS/GS

"'As to Fat Ladies,' says [the dwarf], giving his head a tremendious one agin the wall, 'there's lots of *them* in Society, and worse than the original. *Hers* was a outrage upon Taste—simply a outrage upon Taste—awakenin contempt—carryin its own punishment in the form of a Indian!' Here he giv himself another tremendious one.

"'But *theirs,* Magsman [said Chops], *theirs* is mercenary outrages. Lay in Cashmeer shawls, buy bracelets, strew 'em and a lot of 'andsome fans and things about your rooms, let it be known that you give away like water to all as come to admire, and the Fat Ladies that don't exhibit for so much down upon the drum, will come from all the pints of the compass to flock about you, whatever you are. They'll drill holes in your 'art, Magsman, like a Cullender. And when you've no more left to give, they'll laugh at you to your face, and leave you to have your bones picked dry by Wulturs, like the dead Wild Ass of the Prairies that you deserve to be!'" ¶CS/GS

—a desert: "What ship comes sailing home from India, and what English lady is this, married to a growling old Scotch Crœsus with great flaps of ears? Can this be Julia Mills?

"Indeed it is Julia Mills, peevish and fine . . . . But Julia keeps no diary in these days; never sings Affection's Dirge; eternally quarrels with the old Scotch Crœsus, who is a sort of yellow bear with a tanned hide. Julia is steeped in money to the throat, and talks and thinks of nothing else. I liked her better in the Desert of Sahara.

"Or perhaps this *is* the Desert of Sahara! For, though Julia has a stately house, and mighty company, and sumptuous dinners every day, I see no green growth near her; nothing that can ever come to fruit or flower. What Julia calls 'society,' I see; among it Mr Jack Maldon, from his Patent Place, sneering at the hand that gave it him, and speaking to me of the Doctor as 'so charmingly antique.' But when society is the name for such hollow gentlemen and ladies, Julia, and when its breeding is professed indifference to everything that can advance or can retard mankind, I think we must have lost ourselves in that same Desert of Sahara, and had better find the way out." DC 64

—disastrous dinner-party: " . . . Mr Dombey's list (still constantly in difficulties) were, as a body, indignant with Mrs Dombey's list, for looking at them through eye-glasses, and audibly wondering who all those people were; while Mrs Dombey's list complained of weariness, and the young thing with the shoulders, deprived of the attentions of that gay youth Cousin Feenix (who went away from the dinner-table), confidentially alleged to thirty or forty friends that she was bored to death.

"All the old ladies with the burdens on their heads, had greater or less cause of complaint against Mrs Dombey; and the directors and chairmen coincided in thinking that if Dombey must marry, he had better have married somebody nearer his own age, not quite so handsome, and a little better off. The general opinion among this class of gentlemen was, that it was a weak thing in Dombey, and he'd live to repent it.

"Hardly anybody there, except the mild men, stayed, or went away, without considering himself or herself neglected and aggrieved by Mr Dombey or Mrs Dombey; and the speechless female in the black velvet hat was found to have been stricken mute, because the lady in the crimson velvet had been handed down before her. The nature even of the mild men got corrupted, either from their curdling it with too much lemonade, or from the general inoculation that prevailed; and they made sarcastic jokes to one another, and whispered disparagement on stairs and in bye-places.

"The general dissatisfaction and discomfort so diffused itself, that the assembled footmen in the hall were as well acquainted with it as the company above. Nay, the very linkmen outside got hold of it, and compared the party to a funeral out of mourning, with none of the company remembered in the will." ¶DS 36

—in French: "The fashionable intelligence has . . . found out that [the Dedlocks] will entertain a brilliant and distinguished circle of the *élite* of the *beau monde* (the fashionable intelligence is weak in English, but a giant refreshed in French), at the ancient and hospitable family seat in Lincolnshire." BH 12

—getting in: "Helves was the sole lion for the remainder of the day—impudence and the marvellous are pretty sure passports to any society." SB/SE

—giving dinners: "For it is by this time noticeable that, whatever befalls, the Veneerings must give a dinner upon it. Lady Tippins lives in a chronic state of invitation to dine with the Veneerings, and in a chronic state of inflammation arising from the dinners. Boots and Brewer go about in cabs, with no other intelligible business on earth than to beat up people to come and dine with the Veneerings. Veneering pervades the legislative lobbies, intent upon entrapping his fellow-legislators to dinner. Mrs Veneering dined with five-and-twenty bran-new faces over-night; calls upon them all to-day; sends them every one a dinner-card tomorrow, for the week after next; before that dinner is digested, calls upon their brothers and sisters, their sons and daughters, and invites them all to dinner. And still, as at first, howsoever the dining circle widens, it is to be observed that all the diners are consistent in appearing to go to the Veneerings', not to dine with Mr and Mrs Veneering (which would seem to be the last thing in their minds), but to dine with one another." OMF iii 17

—lion

—exemplar: "How the accomplished gentleman [Sir John Chester] spent the evening in the midst of a dazzling and brilliant circle; how he enchanted all those with whom he mingled by the grace of his deportment, the politeness of his manner, the vivacity of his conversation, and the sweetness of his voice; how it was observed in every corner, that Chester was a man of that happy disposition that nothing ruffled him, that he was one on whom the world's cares and errors sat lightly as his dress, and in whose smiling face a calm and tranquil mind was constantly reflected; how honest men, who by instinct knew him better, bowed down before him nevertheless, deferred to his every word, and courted his favourable notice; how people, who really had good in them, went with the stream, and fawned and flattered, and approved, and despised themselves while they did so, and yet had not the courage to resist; how, in short, he was one of those who are received and cherished in society (as the phrase is) by scores who individually would shrink from and be repelled by the object of their lavish regard; are things of course, which will suggest themselves. Matter so commonplace needs but a passing glance, and there an end." BR 24

—management: "The worthy gentleman [Lillyvick] then became once more the life and soul of the society; being again reinstated in his old post of lion, from which high station the temporary distraction of [the Kenwigs'] thoughts had for a moment dispossessed him.

"Quadruped lions are said to be savage, only when they are hungry; biped lions are rarely sulky longer than when their appetite for distinction remains unappeased. Mr Lillyvick stood higher than ever; for he had shown his power; hinted at his property and testamentary intentions; gained great credit for disinterestedness and virtue; and, in addition to all, was finally accommodated with a much larger tumbler of punch than that which Newman Noggs had so feloniously made off with." ¶NN 15

" . . . there is this remarkable circumstance to be noted in everything associated with my Lady Dedlock as one of a class—as one of the leaders and representatives of her little world. She supposes herself to be an inscrutable Being, quite out of the reach and ken of ordinary mortals—seeing herself in her glass, where indeed she looks so.

"Yet, every dim little star revolving about her, from her maid to the manager of the Italian Opera, knows her weaknesses, prejudices, follies, haughtinesses, and caprices; and lives upon as accurate a calculation and as nice a measure of her moral nature, as her dressmaker takes of her physical proportions.

"Is a new dress, a new custom, a new singer, a new dancer, a new form of jewellery, a new dwarf or giant, a new chapel, a new anything, to be set up? There are deferential people, in a dozen callings, whom my Lady Dedlock suspects of nothing but prostration before her, who can tell you how to manage her as if she were a baby; who do nothing but nurse her all their lives; who, humbly affecting to follow with profound subservience, lead her and her whole troop after them; who, in hooking one, hook all and bear them off, as *Lemuel Gulliver* bore away the stately fleet of the majestic Lilliput." ¶BH 2

—*and matrimony:* "Now, Mrs Merdle, who really knew her friend Society pretty well, and who knew what Society's mothers were, and what Society's daughters were, and what Society's matrimonial market was, and how prices ruled in it, and what scheming and counter-scheming took place for the high buyers, and what bargaining and huckstering went on, thought in the depths of her capacious bosom that [Minnie Meagles] was a sufficiently good catch. Knowing, however, what was expected of her, and perceiving the exact nature of the fiction to be nursed, she took it delicately in her arms, and put her required contribution of gloss upon it.

"'And that is all, my dear?' said she, heaving a friendly sigh. 'Well, well! The fault is not yours. You have nothing to reproach yourself with. You must exercise the strengh of mind for which you are renowned, and make the best of it.'" LD i 20

And see A:Matrimony—*advice—Mrs Merdle*

Podsnappery OMF

—*obligations:* "So it came to pass that Mr and Mrs Podsnap requested the honour of the company of seventeen friends of their souls at dinner; and that they substituted other friends of their souls for such of the seventeen original friends of their souls as deeply regretted that a prior engagement prevented their having the honor of dining with Mr and Mrs Podsnap, in pursuance of their kind invitation; and that Mrs Podsnap said of all these inconsolable personages, as she checked them off with a pencil in her list, 'Asked, at any rate, and got rid of;' and that they successfully disposed of a good many friends of their souls in this way, and felt their consciences much lightened." OMF i 11

—snobbery

—name-dropping: "It is so pleasant to find real merit appreciated, whatever its particular walk in life may be, that the general harmony of the company was doubtless much promoted by their knowing that the two men of the world were held in great esteem by the upper classes of society, and by the gallant defenders of their country in the army and navy, but particularly the former. The least of their stories had a colonel in it; lords were as plentiful as oaths; and even the Blood Royal ran in the muddy channel of their personal recollections." MC 28

—superannuated: "Carriages rattle, doors are battered at, the world exchanges calls; ancient charmers with skeleton throats, and peachy cheeks that have a rather ghastly bloom upon them seen by daylight, when indeed these fascinating creatures look like Death and the Lady fused together, dazzle the eyes of men." BH 56

" . . . the three expensive Miss Tite Barnacles, double-loaded with accomplishments and ready to go off, and yet not going off with the sharpness of flash and bang that might have been expected, but rather hanging fire." LD i 34

—and trade: "'[Miss Havisham's] father was a country gentleman . . . and was a brewer. I don't know why it should be a crack thing to be a brewer; but it is indisputable that while you cannot possibly be genteel and bake, you may be as genteel as never was and brew. You see it every day.'

"'Yet a gentleman may not keep a public-house; may he?' said I.

"'Not on any account,' returned Herbert [Pocket]; 'but a public-house may keep a gentleman.'" GE 22

—and wealth: "True, the Hampton Court Bohemians, without exception, turned up their noses at Merdle as an upstart; but they turned them down again, by falling flat on their faces to worship his wealth. In which compensating adjustment of their noses, they were pretty much like Treasury, Bar, and Bishop, and all the rest of them." LD i 33

—world of fashion: "Both the world of fashion and the Court of Chancery are things of precedent and usage; oversleeping *Rip Van Winkles,* who have played at strange games through a deal of thundery weather; sleeping beauties, whom the Knight will wake one day, when all the stopped spits in the kitchen shall begin to turn prodigiously!

"It is not a large world. Relatively even to this world of ours, which has its limits too (as your Highness shall find when you have made the tour of it, and are come to the brink of the void beyond), it is a very little speck. There is much good in it; there are many good and true people in it; it has its appointed place. But the evil of it is, that it is a world wrapped up in too much jeweller's cotton and fine wool, and cannot hear the rushing of the larger worlds, and cannot see them as they circle round the sun. It is a deadened world, and its growth is sometimes unhealthy for want of air." BH 2

"All the mirrors in the [Dedlock] house [Chesney Wold] are brought into action now; many of them after a long blank. They reflect handsome faces, simpering faces, youthful faces, faces of threescore-and-ten that will not submit to be old . . . there is something a little wrong about [this circle], in despite of its immense advantages. What can it be?

"Dandyism? There is no King George the Fourth now (more's the pity!) to set the dandy fashion; there are no clear-starched jack-towel neck-cloths, no short-waisted coats, no false calves, no stays. There are no caricatures, now, of effeminate Exquisites so arrayed, swooning in opera boxes with excess of delight, and being revived by other dainty creatures, poking long-necked scent-bottles at their noses.

"There is no beau whom it takes four men at once to shake into his buckskins, or who goes to see all the executions, or who is troubled with the self-reproach of having once consumed a pea. But is there Dandyism in the brilliant and distinguished circle notwithstanding . . . ?

"Why, yes. It cannot be disguised [*see* S:Religion—*Oxford Movement*] . . . .

"There are also ladies and gentlemen of another fashion, not so new, but very elegant, who have agreed to put a smooth glaze on the world, and to keep down all its realities. For whom everything must be languid and pretty. Who have found out the perpetual stoppage.

"Who are to rejoice at nothing, and be sorry for nothing. Who are not to be disturbed by ideas." ¶BH 12

—in France, before the Revolution: " . . . the rooms, though a beautiful scene to look at, and adorned with every device of decoration that the taste and skill of the time

could achieve, were, in truth, not a sound business; considered with any reference to the scarecrows in the rags and nightcaps elsewhere (and not so far off, either, but that the watching towers of Notre Dame, almost equidistant from the two extremes, could see them both), they would have been an exceedingly uncomfortable business—if that could have been anybody's business, at the house of Monseigneur.

"Military officers destitute of military knowledge; naval officers with no idea of a ship; civil officers without a notion of affairs; brazen ecclesiastics, of the worst world worldly, with sensual eyes, loose tongues, and looser lives; all totally unfit for their several callings, all lying horribly in pretending to belong to them, but all nearly or remotely of the order of Monseigneur, and therefore foisted on all public employments from which anything was to be got; these were to be told off by the score and the score.

"People not immediately connected with Monseigneur or the State, yet equally unconnected with anything that was real, or with lives passed in travelling by any straight road to any true earthly end, were no less abundant. Doctors who made great fortunes out of dainty remedies for imaginary disorders that never existed, smiled upon their courtly patients in the antechambers of Monseigneur. Projectors who had discovered every kind of remedy for the little evils with which the State was touched, except the remedy of setting to work in earnest to root out a single sin, poured their distracting babble into any ears they could lay hold of, at the reception of Monseigneur.

"Unbelieving Philosophers who were remodelling the world with words, and making card-towers of Babel to scale the skies with, talked with Unbelieving Chemists who had an eye on the transmutation of metals, at this wonderful gathering accumulated by Monseigneur. Exquisite gentlemen of the finest breeding, which was at that remarkable time—and has been since—to be known by its fruits of indifference to every natural subject of human interest, were in the most exemplary state of exhaustion, at the hotel of Monseigneur.

"Such homes had these various notabilities left behind them in the fine world of Paris, that the spies among the assembled devotees of Monseigneur—forming a goodly half of the polite company—would have found it hard to discover among the angels of that sphere one solitary wife, who, in her manners and appearance, owned to being a Mother. Indeed, except for the mere act of bringing a troublesome creature into this world—which does not go far towards the realisation of the name of mother—there was no such thing known to the fashion. Peasant women kept the unfashionable babies close, and brought them up, and charming grandmammas of sixty dressed and supped as at twenty." ¶TTC ii 7

And see B:Body—*fingernails; and* F:Friend—*sold*

Soldier

—*French recruits:* "I went by a train which was heavy with third-class carriages, full of young fellows (well guarded) who had drawn unlucky numbers in the last conscription, and were on their way to a famous French garrison town where much of the raw military material is worked up into soldiery.

"At the station they had been sitting about, in their threadbare homespun blue garments, with their poor little bundles under their arms, covered with dust and clay, and the various soils of France; sad enough at heart, most of them, but putting a good face upon it, and slapping their breasts and singing choruses on the smallest provocation; the gayer spirits shouldering half loaves of black bread speared upon their walking-sticks. As we went along, they were audible at every station, chorusing wildly out of tune, and feigning the highest hilarity. After a while, however, they began to leave off singing, and to laugh naturally . . . ." ¶UT/FF

—*Glory:* "'Is he recruiting for a—for a fine regiment?' said Joe, glancing at a little round mirror that hung in the bar.

"'I believe he is,' replied the host. 'It's much the same thing, whatever regiment he's recruiting for. I'm told there an't a deal of difference between a fine man and another one, when they're shot through and through.'

"'They're not all shot,' said Joe.

"'No,' the Lion answered, 'not all. Those that are—supposing it's done easy—are the best off, in my opinion.'

"'Ah!' retorted Joe, 'but you don't care for glory.'

"'For what?' said the Lion.

"'Glory.'

"'No,' returned the Lion, with supreme

indifference. 'I don't. You're right in that, Mr Willet. When Glory comes here, and calls for anything to drink and changes a guinea to pay for it, I'll give it him for nothing. It's my belief, sir, that the Glory's Arms wouldn't do a very strong business.'" BR 31

—the life disliked: "'For a soldier!' cried [Mantalini]. 'For a soldier! Would his joy and gladness see him in a coarse red coat with a little tail? Would she hear of his being slapped and beat by drummers demnebly? Would she have him fire off real guns, and have his hair cut, and his whiskers shaved, and his eyes turned right and left, and his trousers pipeclayed?'" NN 64

—recruitment: "The serjeant was describing a military life. It was all drinking, he said, except that there frequent intervals of eating and love-making. A battle was the finest thing in the world—when your side won it—and Englishmen always did that. 'Supposing you should be killed, sir?' said a timid voice in one corner. 'Well, sir, supposing you should be,' said the serjeant, 'what then? Your country loves you, sir; his Majesty King George the Third loves you; your memory is honoured, revered, respected; everybody's fond of you, and grateful to you; your name's wrote down at full length in a book in the War-office. Damme, gentlemen, we must all die some time, or another, eh?'

"The voice coughed, and said no more ....

"'. . . . I don't want to inveigle you. The king's not come to that, I hope. Brisk young blood is what we want; not milk and water. We won't take five men out of six. We want top--sawyers, we do. I'm not a-going to tell tales out of school, but, damme, if every gentleman's son that carries arms in our corps, through being under a cloud and having little differences with his relations, was counted up' . . . ." BR 31

—review: "A grand review was to take place upon the Lines. The manœuvres of half-a-dozen regiments were to be inspected by the eagle eye of the commander-in-chief; temporary fortifications had been erected, the citadel was to be attacked and taken, and a mine was to be sprung.

"Mr Pickwick was . . . an enthusiastic admirer of the army. Nothing could have been more delightful to him . . . .

" . . . . A few moments of eager expectation, and colours were seen fluttering gaily in the air, arms glistened brightly in the sun, column after column poured on to the plain. The troops halted and formed; the word of command rung through the line, there was a general clash of muskets as arms were presented; and the commander-in-chief, attended by Colonel Bulder and numerous officers, cantered to the front. The military bands struck up all together; the horses stood upon two legs each, cantered backwards, and whisked their tails about in all directions: the dogs barked, the mob screamed, the troops recovered, and nothing was to be seen on either side, as far as the eye could reach, but a long perspective of red coats and white trousers, fixed and motionless." PP 4

"Astounding evolutions they were, one rank firing over the heads of another rank, and then running away; and then the other rank firing over the heads of another rank, and running away in their turn; and then forming squares, with officers in the centre; and then descending the trench on one side with scaling ladders, and ascending it on the other again by the same means; and knocking down barricades of baskets, and behaving in the most gallant manner possible. Then there was such a ramming down of the contents of enormous guns on the battery, with instruments like magnified mops; such a preparation before they were let off, and such an awful noise when they did go, that the air resounded with the screams of ladies." PP 4

—in training in France: " . . . though there was a great agglomeration of soldiers in the town and neighbouring country, you might have held a grand Review and Field-day of them every one, and looked in vain among them all for a soldier choking behind his foolish stock, or a soldier lamed by his ill-fitting shoes, or a soldier deprived of the use of his limbs by straps and buttons, or a soldier elaborately forced to be self-helpless in all the small affairs of life. A swarm of brisk, bright, active, bustling, handy, odd, skirmishing fellows, able to turn cleverly at anything, from a siege to soup, from great guns to needles and thread, from the broadsword exercise to slicing an onion, from making war to making omelets, was all you would have found.

"What a swarm! From the Great Place under the eye of Mr The Englishman, where a few awkward squads from the last conscription were doing the goose-step—some members of those squads still as to their bodies, in the chrysalis peasant-state of

Blouse, and only military butterflies as to their regimentally-clothed legs—from the Great Place, away outside the fortifications, and away for miles along the dusty roads, soldiers swarmed. All day long, upon the grass-grown ramparts of the town, practising soldiers trumpeted and bugled; all day long, down in angles of dry trenches, practising soldiers drummed and drummed. Every forenoon, soldiers burst out of the great barracks into the sandy gymnasium-ground hard by, and flew over the wooden horse, and hung on to flying ropes, and dangled upside-down, between parallel bars, and shot themselves off wooden platforms—splashes, sparks, coruscations, showers of soldiers. At every corner of the town-wall, every guard-house, every gateway, every sentry-box, every drawbridge, every reedy ditch, and rushy dike, soldiers, soldiers, soldiers. And the town being pretty well all wall, guard-house, gateway, sentry-box, drawbridge, reedy ditch, and rushy dike, the town was pretty well all soldiers." CS/SL 2

—*viewed poetically:* "'It is indeed a noble and a brilliant sight,' said Mr Snodgrass, in whose bosom a blaze of poetry was rapidly bursting forth, 'to see the gallant defenders of their country drawn up in brilliant array before its peaceful citizens; their faces beaming—not with warlike ferocity, but with civilised gentleness; their eyes flashing—not with the rude fire of rapine or revenge, but with the soft light of humanity and intelligence.'" PP 4

—*wounded:* "'It's been took off!' . . .

"'Yes, sir,' said Mr Willet, with the look of a man who felt that he had earned a compliment, and deserved it. 'That's where it is. It's been took off' . . . .

"'At the defence of the Savannah, father.'

"'At the defence of the Salwanners,' repeated Mr Willet, softly; again looking round the table.

"'In America, where the war is,' said Joe.

"'In America, where the war is,' repeated Mr Willet. 'It was took off in the defence of the Salwanners in America where the war is.' Continuing to repeat these words to himself in a low tone of voice (the same information had been conveyed to him in the same terms, at least fifty times before), Mr Willet arose from table, walked round to Joe, felt his empty sleeve all the way up, from the cuff to where the stump of his arm remained; shook his hand; lighted his pipe at the fire, took a long whiff, walked to the door, turned round once when he had reached it, wiped his left eye with the back of his forefinger, and said, in a faltering voice: 'My son's arm—was took off—at the defence of the—Salwanners—in America—where the war is'—with which words he withdrew, and returned no more that night.'" BR 72

And see B:Body—*eye—military*

Traffic

—*city:* "Peffer . . . has been recumbent this quarter of a century in the churchyard of St Andrew's, Holborn, with the waggons and hackney-coaches roaring past him, all the day and half the night, like one great dragon." BH 10

—*"jam":* "There are three classes of animated objects which prevent your driving with any degree of comfort or celerity through streets which are but little frequented—they are pigs, children, and old women.

"On the occasion we are describing, the pigs were luxuriating on cabbage-stalks, and the shuttlecocks fluttered from the little deal battledores, and the children played in the road; and women, with a basket in one hand, and the street-door key in the other, would cross just before the horse's head, until Mr Gabriel Parsons was perfectly savage with vexation, and quite hoarse with hoi-ing and imprecating.

"Then, when he got into Fleet Street, there was 'a stoppage,' in which people in vehicles have the satisfaction of remaining stationary for half an hour, and envying the slowest pedestrians; and where policemen rush about, and seize hold of horses' bridles, and back them into shop-windows, by way of clearing the road and preventing confusion." SB/WT 2

Waiter

—*activity and mystery:* " . . . (waiters always speak in hints, and never utter complete sentences) . . . . The waiter pulled down the window-blind, and then pulled it up again—for a regular waiter must do something before he leaves the room—adjusted the glasses on the sideboard, brushed a place that was *not* dusty, rubbed his hands very hard, walked stealthily to the door, and evaporated." SB/WD

—breeding of: "You were conveyed [says Christopher]—ere your dawning powers were otherwise developed than to harbour vacancy in your inside—you were conveyed, by surreptitious means, into a pantry adjoining the Admiral Nelson, Civic and General Dining Rooms, there to receive by stealth that healthful sustenance which is the pride and boast of the British female constitution.

"Your mother was married to your father (himself a distant Waiter) in the profoundest secrecy; for a Waitress known to be married would ruin the best of businesses—it is the same as on the stage. Hence your being smuggled into the pantry, and that—to add to the infliction—by an unwilling grandmother.

"Under the combined influence of the smells of roast and boiled, and soup, and gas, and malt liquors, you partook of your earliest nourishment; your unwilling grandmother sitting prepared to catch you when your mother was called and dropped you; your grandmother's shawl ever ready to stifle your natural complainings; your innocent mind surrounded by uncongenial cruets, dirty plates, dish-covers, and cold gravy; your mother calling down the pipe for veals and porks, instead of soothing you with nursery rhymes.

"Under these untoward circumstances you were early weaned. Your unwilling grandmother, ever growing more unwilling as your food assimilated less, then contracted habits of shaking you till your system curdled, and your food would not assimilate at all. At length she was no longer spared, and could have been thankfully spared much sooner.

"When your brothers began to appear in succession, your mother retired, left off her smart dressing (she had previously been a smart dresser), and her dark ringlets (which had previously been flowing), and haunted your father late of nights, lying in wait for him, through all weathers, up the shabby court which led to the back door of the Royal Old Dust-Bin (said to have been so named by George the Fourth), where your father was Head. But the Dust-Bin was going down then, and your father took but little—excepting from a liquid point of view. Your mother's object in those visits was of a housekeeping character, and you was set on to whistle your father out Sometimes he came out, but generally not.

"Come or not come, however, all that part of his existence which was unconnected with open Waitering was kept a close secret, and was acknowledged by your mother to be a close secret, and you and your mother flitted about the court, close secrets both of you, and would scarcely have confessed under torture that you knew your father, or that your father had any name than Dick (which wasn't his name, though he was never known by any other), or that he had kith or kin or chick or child.

"Perhaps the attraction of this mystery, combined with your father's having a damp compartment to himself, behind a leaky cistern, at the Dust-Bin—a sort of a cellar compartment, with a sink in it, and a smell, and a plate-rack, and a bottle-rack, and three windows that didn't match each other or anything else, and no daylight—caused your young mind to feel convinced that you must grow up to be a Waiter too; but you did feel convinced of it, and so did all your brothers, down to your sister. Every one of you felt convinced that you was born to the Waitering.

"At this stage of your career, what was your feelings one day when your father came home to your mother in open broad daylight—of itself an act of Madness on the part of a Waiter—and took to his bed (leastwise, your mother and family's bed), with the statement that his eyes were devilled kidneys.

"Physicians being in vain, your father expired, after repeating at intervals for a day and a night, when gleams of reason and old business fitfully illuminated his being, 'Two and two is five. And three is sixpence.' Interred in the parochial department of the neighbouring churchyard, and accompanied to the grave by as many Waiters of long standing as could spare the morning time from their soiled glasses (namely, one), your bereaved form was attired in a white neckankecher, and you was took on from motives of benevolence at The George and Gridiron, theatrical and supper.

"Here, supporting nature on what you found in the plates (which was as it happened, and but too often thoughtlessly, immersed in mustard) and on what you found in the glasses (which rarely went beyond driblets and lemon), by night you dropped asleep standing, till you was cuffed awake, and by day was set to polishing every individual article in the coffee-room.

"Your couch being sawdust; your counterpane being ashes of cigars. Here, frequently hiding a heavy heart under the smart tie of your white neckankecher (or correctly speaking lower down and more to the left), you picked up the rudiments of knowledge from an extra, by the name of Bishops, and by calling plate-washer, and gradually elevating your mind with chalk on the back of the corner-box partition, until such time as you used the inkstand when it was out of hand, attained to manhood, and to be the Waiter that you find yourself." ¶CS/SL 1

—*demeanour:* "Rounding his mouth and both his eyes, as he stepped backward from the table, the waiter shifted his napkin from his right arm to his left, dropped into a comfortable attitude, and stood surveying the guest while he ate and drank, as from an observatory or watch-tower. According to the immemorial usage of waiters in all ages." TTC i 4

—*imputed expertise:* " . . . look what you are expected to know. You are never out, but they seem to think you regularly attend everywhere. 'What's this, Christopher, that I hear about the smashed Excursion Train?'—'How are they doing at the Italian Opera, Christopher?'—'Christopher, what are the real particulars of this business at the Yorkshire Bank?'

"Similarly a ministry gives me more trouble than it gives the Queen. As to Lord Palmerston, the constant and wearing connexion into which I have been brought with his lordship during the last few years is deserving of a pension." ¶CS/SL 1

—*leg:* " . . . the leg of this young man [the flying waiter], in its application to the door, evinced the finest sense of touch: always preceding himself and tray (with something of an angling air about it), by some seconds: and always lingering after he and the tray had disappeared, like *Macbeth*'s leg when accompanying him off the stage with reluctance to the assassination of *Duncan*." MED 11

—*misunderstood:* "I could wish here [says Christopher] to offer a few respectful words on behalf of the calling so long the calling of myself and family, and the public interest in which is but too often very limited.

"We are not generally understood. No, we are not. Allowance enough is not made for us. For, say that we ever show a little drooping listlessness of spirits, or what might be termed indifference or apathy. Put it to yourself what would your own state of mind be, if you was one of an enormous family every member of which except you was always greedy, and in a hurry. Put it to yourself that you was regularly replete with animal food at the slack hours of one in the day and again at nine P.M., and that the repleter you was, the more voracious all your fellow-creatures came in.

"Put it to yourself that it was your business, when your digestion was well on, to take a personal interest and sympathy in a hundred gentlemen fresh and fresh (say, for the sake of argument, only a hundred), whose imaginations was given up to grease and fat and gravy and melted butter, and abandoned to questioning you about cuts of this, and dishes of that—each of 'em going on as if him and you and the bill of fare was alone in the world." ¶CS/SL 1

—*movement* "Waiters never walk or run. They have a peculiar and mysterious power of skimming out of rooms, which other mortals possess not." PP 50

—*outdoorsman:* " . . . look at the Hypocrites we are made, and the lies (white, I hope) that are forced upon us! Why must a sedentary-pursuited Waiter be considered to be a judge of horseflesh, and to have a most tremenjous interest in horse-training and racing? Yet it would be half our little incomes out of our pockets if we didn't take on to have those sporting tastes.

"It is the same (inconceivable why!) with Farming. Shooting, equally so. I am sure that so regular as the months of August, September, and October come round, I am ashamed of myself in my own private bosom for the way in which I make believe to care whether or not the grouse is strong on the wing (much their wings, or drumsticks either, signifies to me, uncooked!), and whether the partridges is plentiful among the turnips, and whether the pheasants is shy or bold, or anything else you please to mention.

"Yet you may see me [Christopher], or any other Waiter of my standing, holding on by the back of the box, and leaning over a gentleman with his purse out and his bill before him, discussing these points in a confidential tone of voice, as if my happiness in life entirely depended on 'em." ¶CS/SL

—*a profession:* "In case confusion should

arise in the public mind (which it is open to confusion on many subjects) respecting what is meant or implied by the term Waiter, the present humble lines would wish to offer an explanation [writes Christopher].

"It may not be generally known that the person as goes out to wait is *not* a Waiter. It may not be generally known that the hand as is called in extra, at the Freemasons' Tavern, or the London, or the Albion, or otherwise, is *not* a Waiter. Such hands may be took on for Public Dinners by the bushel (and you may know them by their breathing with difficulty when in attendance, and taking away the bottle ere yet it is half out); but such are *not* Waiters.

"For you cannot lay down the tailoring, or the shoemaking, or the brokering, or the green-grocering, or the pictorial-periodicalling, or the second-hand wardrobe, or the small fancy businesses—you cannot lay down those lines of life at your will and pleasure by the half-day or evening, and take up Waitering. You may suppose you can, but you cannot; or you may go so far as to say you do, but you do not . . . . Then, what is the inference to be drawn respecting true Waitering? You must be bred to it. You must be born to it." ¶CS/SL 1

—team of two in a coffee-room: "It is a most astonishing fact that the waiter is very cold to you. Account for it how you may, smooth it over how you will, you cannot deny that he is cold to you. He is not glad to see you, he does not want you, he would much rather you hadn't come. He opposes to your flushed condition, an immovable composure.

"As if this were not enough, another waiter, born, as it would seem, expressly to look at you in this passage of your life, stands at a little distance, with his napkin under his arm and his hands folded, looking at you with all his might.

"You impress on your waiter that you have ten minutes for dinner, and he proposes that you shall begin with a bit of fish which will be ready in twenty. That proposal declined, he suggests—as a neat originality—'a weal or mutton cutlet.' You close with either cutlet, any cutlet, anything.

"He goes, leisurely, behind a door and calls down some unseen shaft. A ventriloquial dialogue ensues, tending finally to the effect that weal only, is available on the spur of the moment. You anxiously call out, 'Veal, then!' Your waiter having settled that point, returns to array your tablecloth, with a table napkin folded cocked-hat-wise (slowly, for something out of window engages his eye), a white wine-glass, a green wine-glass, a blue finger-glass, a tumbler, and a powerful field battery of fourteen casters with nothing in them; or at all events—which is enough for your purpose—with nothing in them that will come out.

"All this time, the other waiter looks at you—with an air of mental comparison and curiosity, now, as if it had occurred to him that you are rather like his brother. Half your time gone, and nothing come but the jug of ale and the bread, you implore your waiter to 'see after that cutlet, waiter; pray do!' He cannot go at once, for he is carrying in seventeen pounds of American cheese for you to finish with, and a small Landed Estate of celery and water-cresses.

"The other waiter changes his leg, and takes a new view of you, doubtfully, now, as if he had rejected the resemblance to his brother, and had begun to think you more like his aunt or his grandmother. Again you beseech your waiter with pathetic indignation, to 'see after that cutlet!' He steps out to see after it, and by-and-by, when you are going away without it, comes back with it.

"Even then, he will not take the sham silver cover off, without a pause for a flourish . . . you imperatively demand your bill; but, it takes time to get, even when gone for, because your waiter has to communicate with a lady who lives behind a sash-window in a corner, and who appears to have to refer to several Ledgers before she can make it out—as if you had been staying there a year.

"You become distracted to get away, and the other waiter, once more changing his leg, still looks at you—but suspiciously, now, as if you had begun to remind him of the party who took the great-coats last winter." ¶UT/RT *And see* B:Restaurant*—a coffee-shop experience*

—wealth: "Look at the most unreasonable point of all [says Chrisopher], and the point on which the greatest injustice is done us! Whether it is owing to our always carrying so much change in our right-hand trousers-pocket, and so many halfpence in our coat-tails, or whether it is human nature (which I were loth to believe), what is meant by the everlasting fable that Head Waiters is rich? How did that fable get into circulation? Who first put it about, and what are the facts to establish the unblushing statement?

"Come forth, thou slanderer, and refer the public to the Waiter's will in Doctors' Commons supporting thy malignant hiss! Yet this is so commonly dwelt upon—especially by the screws who give Waiters the least—that denial is vain; and we are obliged, for our credit's sake, to carry our heads as if we were going into a business, when of the two we are much more likely to go into a union.

"There was formerly a screw as frequented the Slamjam ere yet the present writer had quitted that establishment on a question of tea-ing his assistant staff out of his own pocket, which screw carried the taunt to its bitterest height. Never soaring above threepence, and as often as not grovelling on the earth a penny lower, he yet represented the present writer as a large holder of Consols, a lender of money on mortgage, a Capitalist. He has been overheard to dilate to other customers on the allegation that the present writer put out thousands of pounds at interest in Distilleries and Breweries. 'Well, Christopher,' he would say (having grovelled his lowest on the earth, half a moment before), 'looking out for a House to open, eh? Can't find a business to be disposed of on a scale as is up to your resources, humph?'

"To such a dizzy precipice of falsehood has this misrepresentation taken wing, that the well-known and highly-respected OLD CHARLES, long eminent at the West Country Hotel, and by some considered the Father of the Waitering, found himself under the obligation to fall into it through so many years that his own wife (for he had an unbeknown old lady in that capacity towards himself) believed it!

"And what was the consequence? When he was borne to his grave on the shoulders of six picked Waiters, with six more for change, six more acting as pall-bearers, all keeping step in a pouring shower without a dry eye visible, and a concourse only inferior to Royalty, his pantry and lodgings was equally ransacked high and low for property, and none was found!

"How could it be found, when, beyond his last monthly collection of walking-sticks, umbrellas, and pocket-handkerchiefs (which happened to have been not yet disposed of, though he had ever been through life punctual in clearing off his collections by the month), there was no property existing? Such, however, is the force of this universal libel, that the widow . . . expects John's [*sic.*] hoarded wealth to be found hourly!" ¶CS/SL

War

—battlefield : "Once upon a time, it matters little when, and in stalwart England, it matters little where, a fierce battle was fought. It was fought upon a long summer day when the waving grass was green. Many a wild flower formed by the Almighty Hand to be a perfumed goblet for the dew, felt its enamelled cup filled high with blood that day, and shrinking dropped. Many an insect deriving its delicate colour from harmless leaves and herbs, was stained anew that day by dying men, and marked its frightened way with an unnatural track. The painted butterfly took blood into the air upon the edges of its wings. The stream ran red. The trodden ground became a quagmire, whence, from sullen pools collected in the prints of human feet and horses' hoofs, the one prevailing hue still lowered and glimmered at the sun.

"Heaven keep us from a knowledge of the sights the moon beheld upon that field, when, coming up above the black line of distant rising-ground, softened and blurred at the edge by the trees, she rose into the sky and looked upon the plain, strewn with upturned faces that had once at mothers' breasts sought mothers' eyes, or slumbered happily. Heaven keep us from a knowledge of the secrets whispered afterwards upon the tainted wind that blew across the scene of that day's work and that night's death and suffering! Many a lonely moon was bright upon the battle-ground, and many a star kept mournful watch upon it, and many a wind from every quarter of the earth blew over it, before the traces of the fight were worn away.

"They lurked and lingered for a long time, but survived in little things; for Nature, far above the evil passions of men, soon recovered Her serenity, and smiled upon the guilty battle-ground as she had done before, when it was innocent. The larks sang high above it; the swallows skimmed and dipped and flitted to and fro; the shadows of the flying clouds pursued each other swiftly, over grass and corn and turnip-field and wood, and over roof and church-spire in the nestling town among the trees, away into the bright distance on the borders of the sky and earth, where the red sunsets faded.

"Crops were sown, and grew up, and were gathered in; the stream that had been crimsoned, turned a water-mill; men whistled at the plough; gleaners and haymakers were seen in quiet groups at work; sheep and oxen pastured; boys whooped and called, in fields, to scare away the birds; smoke rose from cottage chimneys; sabbath bells rang peacefully; old people lived and died; the timid creatures of the field, and simple flowers of the bush and garden, grew and withered in their destined terms: and all upon the fierce and bloody battle-ground, where thousands upon thousands had been killed in the great fight.

"But there were deep green patches in the growing corn at first, that people looked at awfully. Year after year they reappeared; and it was known that underneath those fertile spots, heaps of men and horses lay buried, indiscriminately, enriching the ground. The husbandmen who ploughed those places, shrunk from the great worms abounding there; and the sheaves they yielded were, for many a long year, called the Battle Sheaves, and set apart; and no one ever knew a Battle Sheaf to be among the last load at a Harvest Home.

"For a long time, every furrow that was turned, revealed some fragments of the fight. For a long time, there were wounded trees upon the battleground; and scraps of hacked and broken fence and wall, where deadly struggles had been made; and trampled parts where not a leaf or blade would grow. For a long time, no village girl would dress her hair or bosom with the sweetest flower from that field of death: and after many a year had come and gone, the berries growing there, were still believed to leave too deep a stain upon the hand that plucked them.

"The Seasons in their course, however, though they passed as lightly as the summer clouds themselves, obliterated, in the lapse of time, even these remains of the old conflict; and wore away such legendary traces of it as the neighbouring people carried in their minds, until they dwindled into old wives' tales, dimly remembered round the winter fire, and waning every year.

"Where the wild flowers and berries had so long remained upon the stem untouched, gardens arose, and houses were built, and children played at battles on the turf. The wounded trees had long ago made Christmas logs, and blazed and roared away. The deep green patches were no greener now than the memory of those who lay in dust below. The ploughshare still turned up from time to time some rusty bits of metal, but it was hard to say what use they had ever served, and those who found them wondered and disputed.

"An old dinted corselet, and a helmet, had been hanging in the church so long, that the same weak half-blind old man who tried in vain to make them out above the whitewashed arch, had marvelled at them as a baby. If the host slain upon the field, could have been for a moment reanimated in the forms in which they fell, each upon the spot that was the bed of his untimely death, gashed and ghastly soldiers would have stared in, hundreds deep, at household door and window; and would have risen on the hearths of quiet homes; and would have been the garnered store of barns and granaries; and would have started up between the cradled infant and its nurse; and would have floated with the stream, and whirled round on the mill, and crowded with orchard, and burdened the meadow, and piled the rickyard high with dying men. So altered was the battle-ground, where thousands upon thousands had been killed in the great fight." ¶BL 1

—and social class: "The end of this victory . . . was the usual one in those times [1216 AD]—the common men were slain without any mercy, and the knights and gentlemen paid ransom and went home." CHE 15

—Crimean incompetence: " . . . *our* public have got to the marrow of the true question arising out of the condition of the British Army before Sabastopol. *Our* Public know perfectly, that making every deduction for haste, obstruction, and natural strength of feeling in the midst of goading experiences, the correspondence of the *Times* has revealed a confused heap of mismanagement, imbecility, and disorder, under which the nation's bravery lies crushed and withered." HW/OP

"Consider the last possession that have gone to the Dogs. Consider, friends and countrymen, how the Dogs have been enriched, by your despoilment at the hands of your own blessed governors—to whom be honour and renown, stars and garters, for ever and ever!—on the shores of a certain obscure spot called Balaklava, where Britannia rules the waves in such an admirable manner, that she slays her children (who never never never will be slaves, but very very very often will be dupes), by the thousand, with every movement of her glorious trident! When shall there be added to the possessions of the Dogs, those columns of talk, which, let the columns of British soldiers vanish as they may, still defile before us wearily, wearily, leading to nothing, doing nothing, for the most part even saying nothing, openly enshrouding us in a mist of idle breath that obscures the events which are forming themselves—not into playful shapes, believe me—beyond." HW/GD

"It was [Nobody] who left the tents behind, who left the baggage behind, who chose the worst possible ground for encampments, who provided no means of transport, who killed the horses, who paralysed the commissariat, who knew nothing of the business he professed to know and monopolised, who decimated the English army. It was Nobody who gave out the famous unroasted coffee, it was Nobody who made the hospitals more horrible than language can describe, it was Nobody who occasioned all the dire confusion of Balaklava harbour, it was even Nobody who ordered the fatal Balaklava cavalry charge. The non-relief of Kars was the work of Nobody, and Nobody has justly and severely suffered for that infamous transaction." HW/NE

—Parliamentary inquiry: "At the Old Bailey, when a person under strong suspicion of malpractices is tried, it is the custom . . . to conduct the trial on stringent principles, and to confide it to impartial hands. It has not yet become the practice of the criminal, or even of the civil courts—but they, indeed, are constituted for the punishment of Somebody—to invite the prisoner's or defendant's friends to talk the matter over with him in a cosy, tea-and-muffin sort of way, and make out a verdict together . . . called making things 'pleasant.'

"But, when Nobody was shown within these few weeks to have occasioned intolerable misery and loss in the late war, and to have incurred a vast amount of guilt in bringing to pass results which all morally sane persons can understand to be fraught with fatal consequences, far beyond present calculation, this cosy course of proceeding was the course pursued.

"My Lord, intent upon establishing the responsibility of Nobody, walked into court as he would walk into a ball-room; and My Lord's friends and admirers toadied and fawned upon him in court, as they would toady him and fawn upon him in the other assembly. My Lord carried his head very high, and took a mighty great tone with the common people; and there was no question as to anything My Lord did or said, and Nobody got triumphantly fixed.

"Ignorance enough and incompetency enough to bring any country that the world has ever seen to defeat and shame, and to lay any head that ever was in it low, were proved beyond question; but, My Lord cried, 'On Nobody's eyes be it!' and My Lord's impaneled chorus cried, 'There is no impostor but Nobody; on him be the shame and blame!'" ¶HW/NE

—deterrence: " . . . because there are . . . oppressors and oppressed, arrayed against each other—that it is because there are, beyond his Dove Delegate and his Mouse Delegate, the wild beasts of the Forest—that it is because I dread and hate the miseries of tyranny and war—that it is because I would not be soldier-ridden, nor have other men so—that I am not for the disarming of England, and cannot be a member of his Peace Society . . . . " HW/WH

—horror: "War is a dreadful thing; and it is appalling to know how the English were obliged, next morning [after Agincourt], to kill those prisoners mortally wounded, who yet writhed in agony upon the ground; how the dead upon the French side were stripped by their own countrymen and countrywomen, and afterwards buried in great pits; how the dead upon the English side were piled up in a great barn, and how their bodies and the barn were all burned together. It is in such things, and in many more much too horrible to relate, that the real desolation and wickedness of war consist. Nothing can make war otherwise than horrible. But the dark side of it was little thought of and soon forgotten; and it cast no shade of trouble on the English people, except on those who had lost friends or relations in the fight." CHE 21

"'Because War is frightful, ruinous, and unchristian. Because the details of one battle, because the horrors of one siege, would so appal you, if you knew them, that probably you never could be happy afterwards.

Because man was not created in the image of his Maker to be blasted with gunpowder, or pierced with bayonets, or gashed with swords, or trampled under iron hoofs of horses, into a puddle of mire and blood.

"Because War is a wickedness that always costs us dear. Because it wastes our treasure, hardens our hearts, paralyses our industry, cripples our commerce, occasions losses, ills, and devilish crimes, unspeakable and out of number.'" HW/WH

Woman

—amends for suffering: "' . . . I see so much in my poor mother [said Joe Gargery], of a woman drudging and slaving and breaking her honest hart and never getting no peace in her mortal days, that I'm dead afeerd of going wrong in the way of not doing what's right by a woman, and I'd fur rather of the two go wrong the t'other way, and be a little ill-conwenienced myself. I wish it was only me that got put out, Pip; I wish there warn't no Tickler for you, old chap; I wish I could take it all on myself; but this is the up-and-down-and-straight on it, Pip, and I hope you'll overlook shortcomings.'" GE 7

—aroused: "There is something about a roused woman: especially if she add to all her other strong passions, the fierce impulses of recklessness and despair: which few men like to provoke." OT 16

—awkward: "'There is no call for any hock-'erdness, mum,' said Mr [Tony] Weller with the utmost politeness; 'no call wotsumever. A lady,' added the old gentleman, looking about him with the air of one who establishes an incontrovertible position—'a lady can't be hock'erd. Natur' has otherwise purwided.'" MHC 5

—basic view: "Notwithstanding Mr Toodle's great reliance on Polly, she was perhaps in point of artificial accomplishments very little his superior. But she was a good plain sample of a nature that is ever, in the mass, better, truer, higher, nobler, quicker to feel, and much more constant to retain, all tenderness and pity, self-denial and devotion, than the nature of men." DS 3

"'Pray, what is your opinion of woman, Mr Sparkins?' inquired Mrs Malderton. The young ladies simpered.

"'Man,' replied Horatio, 'man, whether he ranged the bright, gay, flowery plains of a second Eden, or the more sterile, barren, and I may say, commonplace regions, to which we are compelled to accustom ourselves, in times such as these; man, under any circumstances, or in any place—whether he were bending beneath the withering blasts of the frigid zone, or scorching under the rays of a vertical sun—man, without woman, would be—alone.'

"'I am very happy to find you entertain such honourable opinions, Mr Sparkins,' said Mrs Malderton." SB/HS

See LC:Words and Phrases—*'great girl'*

—companion: "I believe that the sympathy and society of those who are our best and dearest friends in infancy, in childhood, in manhood, and in old age, the most devoted and least selfish natures that we know on earth, who turn to us always constant and unchanged, when others turn away, should greet us here, if anywhere, and go on with us side by side." S/LM

—complimented: "'Such a fine woman as her, so handsome and so graceful and so elegant, is like a fresh lemon on a dinner-table, ornamental wherever she goes.'" BH 53

"' . . . when a young lady is as mild as she's game, and as game as she's mild, that's all I ask, and more than I expect. She then becomes a Queen, and that's about what you are yourself.'" BH 59

—delicate: "'Mrs Wititterly is of a most excitable nature, Sir Mulberry. The snuff of a candle, the wick of a lamp, the bloom on a peach, the down on a butterfly You might blow her away, my lord; you might blow her away.'" NN 27

—demeanour

—belligerent: "To many a single combat with Mrs Pipchin, did Miss Nipper gallantly devote herself; and if ever Mrs Pipchin in all her life had found her match, she had found it now. Miss Nipper threw away the scabbard the first morning she arose in Mrs Pipchin's house. She asked and gave no quarter. She said it must be war, and war it was; and Mrs Pipchin lived from that time in the midst of surprises, harassings, and defiances, and skirmishing attacks that came bouncing in upon her from the passage, even in unguarded moments of chops, and carried desolation to her very toast." DS 12

—imperturbable: "How Alexander wept when he had no more worlds to conquer, everybody knows—or has some reason to know by this time, the matter having been rather frequently mentioned. My Lady Dedlock, having conquered *her* world, fell, not into the melting, but rather into the

freezing mood. An exhausted composure, a worn-out placidity, an equanimity of fatigue not to be ruffled by interest or satisfaction, are the trophies of her victory. She is perfectly well-bred. If she could be translated to Heaven to-morrow, she might be expected to ascend without any rapture." BH 2

—injured: "Indeed, the bearing of this impressive woman [Mrs Wilfer], throughout the day, was a pattern to all impressive women under similar circumstances. She renewed the acquaintance of Mr and Mrs Boffin, as if Mr and Mrs Boffin had said of her what she had said of them, and as if Time alone could quite wear her injury out. She regarded every servant who approached her as her sworn enemy, expressly intending to offer her affronts with the dishes, and to pour forth outrages on her moral feelings from the decanters. She sat erect at table, on the right hand of her son-in-law, as half suspecting poison in the viands, and as bearing up with native force of character against other deadly ambushes. Her carriage towards Bella was as a carriage towards a young lady of good position whom she had met in society a few years ago. Even when, slightly thawing under the influence of sparkling champagne, she related to her son-in-law some passages of domestic interest concerning her papa, she infused into the narrative such Arctic suggestions of her having been an unappreciated blessing to mankind, since her papa's days, and also of that gentleman's having been a frosty impersonation of a frosty race, as struck cold to the very soles of the feet of the hearers. The Inexhaustible [baby] being produced, staring, and evidently intending a weak and washy smile shortly, no sooner beheld her, than it was stricken spasmodic and inconsolable. When she took her leave at last, it would have been hard to say whether it was with the air of going to the scaffold herself, or of leaving the inmates of the house for immediate execution." OMF iv 16

—dominance: "We have purposely excluded from consideration the couple in which the lady reigns paramount and supreme, holding such cases to be of a very unnatural kind, and like hideous births and other monstrous deformities, only to be discreetly and sparingly exhibited." YC/X

—gentle influence: "Strange to say, that quiet influence which was inseparable in my mind from Agnes, seemed to pervade even the city where she dwelt. The venerable cathedral towers, and the old jackdaws and rooks whose airy voices made them more retired than perfect silence would have done; the battered gateways, once stuck full with statues, long thrown down, and crumbled away, like the reverential pilgrims who had gazed upon them; the still nooks, where the ivied growth of centuries crept over gabled ends and ruined walls; the ancient houses, the pastoral landscape of field, orchard, and garden: everywhere—on everything—I felt the same serener air, the same calm, thoughtful, softening spirit." DC 39

—to a hangman: "Mr Dennis received this part of the scheme [to carry off a woman] with a wry face, observing that as a general principle he objected to women altogether, as being unsafe and slippery persons on whom there was no calculating with any certainty, and who were never in the same mind for four-and-twenty hours at a stretch." BR 52

—heart: " . . . Nature often enshrines gallant and noble hearts in weak bosoms—oftenest, God bless her, in female breasts . . ." OCS 24

"'For you women,' said Tom [Pinch], 'you women, my dear, are so kind, and in your kindness have such nice perception; you know so well how to be affectionate and full of solicitude without appearing to be; your gentleness of feeling is like your touch: so light and easy, that the one enables you to deal with wounds of the mind as tenderly as the other enables you to deal with wounds of the body. You are such —'

"'My goodness, Tom!' his sister interposed. 'You ought to fall in love immediately.'" MC 46

" . . . the woman's heart of Florence [Dombey], with its undivided treasure, can be yielded only once, and under slight or change, can only droop and die." DS 57

—helpful: " . . . **Mungo Park** fainting under a tree and succoured by a woman, gratefully remembers how his Good Samaritan has always come to him in woman's shape, the wide world over." RP/LV

—ideal, in peroration: "And now, as I close my task, subduing my desire to linger yet, these faces fade away. But one face, shining on me like a Heavenly light by which I see all other objects, is above them and beyond them all. And that remains.

"I turn my head, and see it, in its beautiful serenity, beside me. My lamp burns low, and I have written far into the night; but the dear presence, without which I were nothing, bears me company.

"Oh Agnes, oh my soul, so may thy face be by me when I close my life indeed; so may I, when realities are melting from me like the shadows which I now dismiss, still find thee near me, pointing upward!" DC 64

—idealized: "God bless them for their tender mercies! The Professor [**John Wilson**] was quite right when he said that I had not reached to an adequate delineation of their virtues; and I fear that I must go on blotting their characters in endeavouring to reach the ideal in my mind." S/E

—indispensable: "Without the ladies little good could be done in the world. [CD] had once been reminded of all *Robinson Crusoe* had done in a state of single blessedness, but on careful investigation of the authorities he found that that worthy had, in reality, had two wives." S/SC (third person report)

—instinct

—to give comfort: "With her own sweet tranquillity she calmed my agitation; led me back to the time of our parting; spoke to me of Emily, whom she had visited, in secret, many times; spoke to me tenderly of Dora's grave. With the unerring instinct of her noble heart, she touched the chords of my memory so softly and harmoniously, that not one jarred within me; I could listen to the sorrowful, distant music, and desire to shrink from nothing it awoke. How could I, when, blended with it all, was her dear self, the better angel of my life?" DC 60

—for homemaking "The Captain's delight and wonder at the quiet housewifery of Florence in assisting to clear the table, arrange the parlour, and sweep up the hearth—only to be equalled by the fervency of his protest when she began to assist him—were gradually raised to that degree, that at last he could not choose but do nothing himself, and stand looking at her as if she were some Fairy, daintily performing these offices for him, the red rim on his forehead glowing again, in his unspeakable admiration . . . .

" . . . . Likewise, when Florence, looking into the little cupboard, took out the case-bottle and mixed a perfect glass of grog for him, unasked, and set it at his elbow, his ruddy nose turned pale, he felt himself so graced and honoured." DS 49 *And see* B: Tobacco—*the best of pipes*

—for wedding-cake: "'Why what's this round box? Heart alive, John, it's a wedding-cake!'

"'Leave a woman alone to find out that,' said John, admiringly. 'Now a man would never have thought of it. Whereas, it's my belief that if you was to pack a wedding-cake up in a tea-chest, or a turn-up bedstead, or a pickled salmon keg, or any unlikely thing, a woman would be sure to find it out directly.'" CH 1

—intuition irreversible: "' . . . still I do not see anything in it, to criminate the poor child.'

"'No,' replied the doctor, 'of course not! Bless the bright eyes of your sex! They never see, whether for good or bad, more than one side of any question; and that is, always, the one which first presents itself to them.'" OT 31

"It has been often enough remarked that women have a curious power of divining the characters of men, which would seem to be innate and instinctive; seeing that it is arrived at through no patient process of reasoning, that it can give no satisfactory or sufficient account of itself, and that it pronounces in the most confident manner even against accumulated observation on the part of the other sex.

"But it has not been quite so often remarked that this power (fallible, like every other human attribute) is for the most part absolutely incapable of self-revision; and that when it has delivered an adverse opinion which by all human lights is subsequently proved to have failed, it is undistinguishable from prejudice, in respect of its determination not to be corrected.

"Nay, the very possibility of contradiction or disproof, however remote, communicates to this feminine judgment from the first, in nine cases out of ten, the weakness attendant on the testimony of an interested witness: so personally and strongly does the fair diviner connect herself with her divination." MED 10

—mistreated: "'Was there anything in [the book], about a man's being determined to conquer his wife, break her spirit, bend her temper, crush all her humours like so many nut-shells—kill her, for aught I know?' said Jonas . . . .

" . . . . He answered with an imprecation, and—

"Not with a blow? Yes. Stern truth against the base-souled villain: with a blow.

"No angry cries; no loud reproaches. Even her weeping and her sobs were stifled by her clinging round him. She only said, repeating it in agony of heart, How could he, could he, could he! And lost utterance in tears.

"Oh woman, God beloved in old Jerusalem! The best among us need deal lightly with thy faults, if only for the punishment thy nature will endure, in bearing heavy evidence against us on the Day of Judgment!" MC 28

—mutual emulation: "'It's as much your interest as mine, you know [said Tackleton] that the women should persuade each other that they're quiet and contented, and couldn't be better off. I know their way. Whatever one woman says, another woman is determined to clinch, always. There's that spirit of emulation among 'em, sir, that if your wife says to my wife, "I'm the happiest woman in the world, and mine's the best husband in the world, and I dote on him," my wife will say the same to yours, or more, and half believe it.'" CH 1

—in myth: "We know that the Graces were all women; we know that the Muses were women, and we know every day of our lives that the Fates are women." S/C

—oriented: "Now, and not before, Miss Fanny burst upon the scene, completely arrayed for her new part. Now, and not before, she wholly absorbed Mr Sparkler in her light, and shone for both, and twenty more. No longer feeling that want of a defined place and character which had caused her so much trouble, this fair ship began to steer steadily on a shaped course, and to swim with a weight and balance that developed her sailing qualities." LD ii 15

—power of language: "'. . . women can always put things in the fewest words [said Sikes].—Except when it's blowing up; and then they lengthens it out.'" OT 20

—power of observation: "'Impossible!' cries Twemlow, standing aghast. 'How do you know it?'

"'I scarcely know how I know it. The whole train of circumstances seemed to take fire at once, and show it to me.'

"'Oh! Then you have no proof.'

"'It is very strange,' says Mrs Lammle, coldly and boldly, and with some disdain, 'how like men are to one another in some things, though their characters are as different as can be! No two men can have less affinity between them, one would say, than Mr Twemlow and my husband. Yet my husband replies to me, "You have no proof," and Mr Twemlow replies to me with the very same words!'

"'But why, madam?' Twemlow ventures gently to argue. 'Consider why the very same words? Because they state the fact. Because you *have* no proof.'

"'Men are very wise in their way,' quoth Mrs Lammle . . . 'but they have wisdom to learn. My husband, who is not over-confiding, ingenuous, or inexperienced, sees this plain thing no more than Mr Twemlow does—because there is no proof. Yet I believe five women out of six, in my place, would see it as clearly as I do.'" OMF iii 17

—proper role: " . . . should we love our Julia better, if she were a Member of Parliament, a Parochial Guardian, a High Sheriff, a Grand Juror, or a woman distinguished for her able conduct in the chair? Do we not, on the contrary, rather seek in the society of our Julia, a haven of refuge from Members of Parliament, Parochial Guardians, High Sheriffs, Grand Jurors, and able chairmen? Is not the home-voice of our Julia as the song of the bird, after considerable bowwowing out of doors?" HW/SP

—at public dinners: "When I have the honour to fill this or any similar place [chairman of a dinner], I never lend my poor aid to uphold the preposterous fiction that the brightest part of creation are not present, and that the stars of the firmament on my right, which shine upon our waking and sleeping dreams, are not distinctly visible in the sky. It seems to me the most inconsistent and ridiculous of all customs, when we come to propose the first lady of the land, to forget that ladies are present;* and I, therefore, setting an example, trust and hope that you will follow that example, when I address you as ladies and gentlemen. [*Loud cheers.*]

"Ladies and gentlemen, allow me to offer you a toast which includes a great deal more than the two syllabic words in themselves; which, whilst they express our loyalty towards the lady who rules England, hardly expresses its loyalty to the ladies who rule us." S/WC

**At the Playground and General Recreation Society dinner, June 1, 1858, chaired by CD, he announced he would not preside at another dinner unless the sexes dined together.*

"Why, [CD] asked, should the gentlemen be ensconced before their smoking edibles and glittering decanters, and the ladies be compelled to sit above, behind that 'blistering screen', and look on contentedly all the while? Even in the Sandwich Isles or Otaheite the savages would not expel the fair sex from their banquets. Why should not these things be altered? For his part, if the committee would promise to introduce ladies next year, or the year after,* to the dinner-table at the annual festival, and place one on each side of the Chair, he would not have the least objection to act as president. [*Cheers.*]" S/M

**The Times report said CD's talk encouraged a hope, fulfilled six years later in 1866, that the Royal Society of Musicians and the Royal Society of Female Musicians might be united.*

" . . . I think that if the male sex were fairly polled, they would arrive at an almost unanimous conclusion that we men were never so wearisome to ourselves, never so exceedingly uninteresting to each other, as when conventionally we were supposed to be left entirely at our ease." S/MH3

—'*Rights:*' . . . a young—at least, an unmarried—lady, a Miss Wisk . . . [whose] mission . . . was to show the world that woman's mission was man's mission; and that the only genuine mission of both man and woman, was to be always moving declaratory resolutions about things in general at public meetings . . . Miss Wisk informed us, with great indignation, before we sat down to breakfast, that the idea of woman's mission lying chiefly in the narrow sphere of Home was an outrageous slander on the part of her Tyrant, Man." BH 30

"Belinda Bates, bosom friend of my sister, and a most intellectual, amiable, and delightful girl . . . has a fine genius for poetry, combined with real business earnestness, and 'goes in'—to use an expression of Alfred's—for Woman's mission, Woman's rights, Woman's wrongs, and everything that is woman's with a capital W, or is not and ought to be, or is and ought not to be.

"'Most praiseworthy, my dear, and Heaven prosper you!' I whispered to her . . . 'but don't overdo it. And in respect of the great necessity there is, my darling, for more employments being within the reach of Woman than our civilisation has as yet assigned to her, don't fly at the unfortunate men, even those men who are at first sight in your way, as if they were the natural oppressors of your sex; for, trust me, Belinda, they do sometimes spend their wages among wives and daughters, sisters, mothers, aunts, and grandmothers; and the play is, really, not *all* Wolf and Red Riding-Hood, but has other parts in it.'" CS/HH

And see B:Restaurant—*railroad*

"'Tom's family, gentlemen, were all lamplighters.'

"'Not the ladies, I hope?' asked the vice.

"'They had talent enough for it, Sir', rejoined the chairman, 'and would have been, but for the prejudices of society. Let women have their rights, Sir, and the females of Tom's family would have been every one of 'em in office. But that emancipation hasn't come yet, and hadn't then, and consequently they confined themselves to the bosoms of their families, cooked the dinners, mended the clothes, minded the children, comforted their husbands, and attended to the house-keeping generally. It's a hard thing upon the women, gentlemen, that they are limited to such a sphere of action as this; very hard.'" L

"Cinderella, being now a queen, applied herself to the government of the country on enlightened, liberal, and free principles. All the people who ate anything she did not eat, or who drank anything she did not drink, were imprisoned for life. All the newspaper offices from which any doctrine proceeded that was not her doctrine were burnt down. All the public speakers proved to demonstration that if there were any individual on the face of the earth who differed from them in anything, that individual was a designing ruffian and an abandoned monster.

"She also threw open the right of voting, and of being elected to public offices, and of making the laws, to the whole of her sex; who thus came to be always gloriously occupied with public life, and whom nobody dared to love. And they all lived happily ever afterwards." ¶HW/FF

"Talking of missions, here's our Proprietor's Wife with a mission now! She has found out that she ought to go and vote at elections; ought to be competent to sit in Parliament; ought to be able to enter the learned professions—the army and navy, too, I believe. She has made the discovery that she has no business to be the comfort of our Proprietor's life, and to have the hold upon him of not being mixed up in all the janglings and wranglings of men, but is quite ill-used in being the solace of his home, and wants to go out speechifying. That's our Proprietor's Wife's new mission.

Why, you never heard the Dove go on in that ridiculous way. She knows her true strength better." HW/R 1

And see A:Matrimony—*beneath one's station*

—*sarcastic:* "'My thanks, and my congratulations, are equally the meed of Mr Dorrit and of Miss Dorrit.'

"'To me,' observed Miss Fanny, 'they are excessively gratifying—inexpressibly so. The relief of finding that you have no objection to make, Mrs General, quite takes a load off my mind, I am sure. I hardly know what I should have done,' said Fanny, 'if you had interposed any objection, Mrs General.'

"Mrs General changed her gloves, as to the right glove being uppermost and the left undermost, with a Prunes and Prism smile.

"'To preserve your approbation, Mrs General,' said Fanny, returning the smile with one in which there was no trace of those ingredients, 'will of course be the highest object of my married life; to lose it, would of course be perfect wretchedness. I am sure your great kindness will not object, and I hope papa will not object, to my correcting a small mistake you have made, however. The best of us are so liable to mistakes, that even you, Mrs General, have fallen into a little error. The attention and distinction you have so impressively mentioned, Mrs General, as attaching to this confidence, are, I have no doubt, of the most complimentary and gratifying description; but they don't at all proceed from me. The merit of having consulted you on the subject would have been so great in me, that I feel I must not lay claim to it when it really is not mine. It is wholly papa's. I am deeply obliged to you for your encouragement and patronage, but it was papa who asked for it. I have to thank you, Mrs General, for relieving my breast of a great weight by so handsomely giving your consent to my engagement, but you have really nothing to thank me for. I hope you will always approve of my proceedings after I have left home, and that my sister also may long remain the favoured object of your condescension, Mrs General.'" LD ii 15

—*spirit:* "The patience and good disposition aboard of us, was wonderful. I was not surprised by it in the women; for all men born of women know what great qualities they will show when men will fail . . . . " CS/GM *See* S:Adversity—*and good nature*

—*toasted:* "He had, [CD] said, but half a dozen words to say. The Muses were ladies; the Graces were ladies; some of the best writers were ladies; some of the best characters in tragedy and comedy were ladies; the brightest portion of our existence were ladies. He would, therefore, give 'The Ladies'." S/TF3 [as reported in the *Era,* April 22, 1848]

—*unselfishness:* "Mr Lorry knew Miss Pross to be very jealous, but he also knew her by this time to be, beneath the surface of her eccentricity, one of those unselfish creatures—found only among women—who will, for pure love and admiration, bind themselves willing slaves, to youth when they have lost it, to beauty that they never had, to accomplishments that they were never fortunate enough to gain, to bright hopes that never shone upon their own sombre lives. He knew enough of the world to know that there is nothing in it better than the faithful service of the heart; so rendered and so free from any mercenary taint, he had such an exalted respect for it, that, in the retributive arrangements made by his own mind—we all make such arrangements, more or less—he stationed Miss Pross much nearer to the lower Angels than many ladies immeasurably better got up both by Nature and Art, who had balances at Tellson's.'" TTC ii 6

—*unwelcome praise:* "'In some respects, [my son] treads in the footsteps of his sainted mother. She was a devoted creature. But Wooman, lovely Wooman,' said Mr Turveydrop, with very disagreeable gallantry, 'what a sex you are!'" BH 14

—*washing clothes:* "The Peasant Women, with naked feet and legs, are so constantly washing clothes, in the public tanks, and in every stream and ditch, that one cannot help wondering, in the midst of all this dirt, who wears them when they are clean. The custom is to lay the wet linen which is being operated upon, on a smooth stone, and hammer away at it, with a flat wooden mallet. This they do, as furiously as if they were revenging themselves on dress in general for being connected with the Fall of Mankind." PI 5

—*watchful:* "But what I particularly observed, before I had been half-an-hour in the house, was the close and attentive watch Miss Dartle kept upon me; and the lurking manner in which she seemed to compare my face with Steerforth's, and Steerforth's with mine, and to lie in wait for something to come out between the two. So surely as I looked towards her, did I see that eager visage, with its gaunt black eyes and searching brow, intent on mine; or passing suddenly from mine to Steerforth's; or comprehending both of us at once.

"In this lynx-like scrutiny she was so far from faltering when she saw I observed it, that at such a time she only fixed her piercing look on me with a more intent expression still. Blame-less as I was, and knew that I was, in reference to any wrong she could possibly suspect me of, I shrunk before her strange eyes, quite unable to endure their hungry lustre." DC 29 *And see* Mrs Sparsit HT

—wife admired: "'Talk of fairies! cried Mr Kenwigs. '*I* never see anybody so light to be alive, never. Such manners too; so playful, and yet so sewerely proper! As for her figure! It isn't generally known,' said Mr Kenwigs, dropping his voice; 'but her figure was such, at that time, that the sign of the Britannia over in the Holloway Road, was painted from it!'" NN 36

"'She is a treasure!' exclaims Mr George.

"'She's more. But I never own to it before her. Discipline must be maintained . . . .'

"George remarks that she looks as fresh as a rose, and as sound as an apple.

"'The old girl,' says Mr Bagnet in reply, is a thoroughly fine woman. Consequently, she is like a thoroughly fine day. Gets finer as she gets on. I never saw the old girl's equal. But I never own to it before her. Discipline must be maintained!'" BH 27

—her worst enemy: "'Your sex have such a surprising animosity against one another, when you do differ [said Mr Bucket].'" BH 54

Mr Pickwick and Sam in the Attorney's Office PP

Three Professions

I hear his lumbering jocularity and I behold his big round face, and I look up the inside of his outstretched coat sleeve, as if it were a telescope, with the stopper on, and I hate him with an unwholesome hatred for two hours. I knew the preacher from beginning to end, all over and all through, while I was very young, and I left him behind at an early period of life. Peace be with him! More peace than he brought to me.

[UT/LC]

The one great principle of the English law is, to make business for itself. There is no other principle distinctly, certainly, and consistently maintained through all its narrow turnings. Viewed by this light it becomes a coherent scheme, and not the monstrous maze the laity are apt to think it. Let them but once clearly perceive that its grand principle is to make business for itself at their expense, and surely they will cease to grumble.

BH 39

The doctor's prognostication in reference to the weather was speedily verified. Although it was not a patient of his, his prophecy's quick fulfilment may be taken as an instance of his professional tact; for, unless the threatening aspect of the night had been perfectly plain and unmistakable, he would never have compromised his reputation by delivering any sentiments on the subject. He used this principle in Medicine with too much success to be unmindful of it in his commonest transactions.

[MC 42]

Clergy and Preaching: Chapel

—in the bosom of the flock: "To do the red-nosed man [Mr Stiggins] justice, he would have been very far from wise if he had entertained any such intention [of going]: from all appearances, he must have been possessed of a most desirable circle of acquaintance, if he could have reasonably expected to be more comfortable anywhere else. The fire was blazing brightly under the influence of the bellows, and the kettle was singing gaily under the influence of both. A small tray of tea-things was arranged on the table, a plate of hot buttered toast was gently simmering before the fire, and the red-nosed man himself was busily engaged in converting a large slice of bread into the same agreeable edible, through the instrumentality of a long brass toasting-fork. Beside him stood a glass of reeking hot pine-apple rum and water, with a slice of lemon in it; and every time the red-nosed man stopped to bring the round of toast to his eye, with the view of ascertaining how it got on, he imbibed a drop or two of the hot pine-apple rum and water, and smiled upon the rather stout lady, as she blew the fire." PP 27

—a child and chapel: "Not that I have any curiosity to hear powerful preachers. Time was, when I was dragged by the hair of my head, as one may say, to hear too many. On summer evenings, when every flower and tree and bird might have better addressed my soft young heart, I have in my day been caught in the palm of a female hand by the crown, have been violently scrubbed from the neck to the roots of the hair as a purification for the Temple, and have then been carried off, highly charged with saponaceous electricity, to be steamed like a potato in the unventilated breath of the powerful Boanerges Boiler and his congregation, until what small mind I had was quite steamed out of me.

"In which pitiable plight I have been haled out of the place of meeting, at the conclusion of the exercises, and catechised respecting Boanerges Boiler, his fifthly, his sixthly, and his seventhly, until I have regarded that reverend person in the light of a most dismal and oppressive Charade.

"Time was, when I was carried off to platform assemblages at which no human child, whether of wrath or grace, could possibly keep its eyes open, and when I felt the fatal sleep stealing, stealing over me, and when I gradually heard the orator in possession spinning and humming like a great top, until he rolled, collapsed, and tumbled over, and I discovered, to my burning shame and fear, that as to that last stage it was not he, but I.

"I have sat under Boanerges when he has specifically addressed himself to us—us, the infants—and at this present writing I hear his lumbering jocularity (which never amused us, though we basely pretended that it did), and I behold his big round face, and I look up the inside of his outstretched coat sleeve, as if it were a telescope, with the stopper on, and I hate him with an unwholesome hatred for two hours.

"Through such means did it come to pass that I knew the powerful preacher from beginning to end, all over and all through, while I was very young, and that I left him behind at an early period of life. Peace be with him! More peace than he brought to me!" ¶UT/LC

—oleaginous: "'My friends,' says Mr Chadband, 'Peace be on this house! On the master thereof, on the mistress thereof, on the young maidens, and on the young men! My friends, why do I wish for peace? What is peace? Is it war? No. Is it strife? No. Is it lovely, and gentle, and beautiful, and pleasant, and serene, and joyful? O yes! Therefore, my friends, I wish for peace, upon you and upon yours.'

"In consequence of Mrs Snagsby looking deeply edified, Mr Snagsby thinks it expedient on the whole to say Amen, which is well received . . . Mr Chadband stalks to the table, and, before taking a chair, lifts up his admonitory hand.

"'My friends,' says he, 'what is this which we now behold as being spread before us? Refreshment. Do we need refreshment then, my friends? We do. And why do we need refreshment, my friends? Because we are but mortal, because we are but sinful, because we are but of the earth, because we are not of the air. Can we fly, my friends? We cannot. Why can we not fly, my friends?'

"Mr Snagsby, presuming on the success of his last point, ventures to observe in a cheerful and rather knowing tone, 'No wings.' But is immediately frowned down by Mrs Snagsby.

"'I say, my friends,' pursues, Mr Chadband, utterly rejecting and obliterating Mr Snagsby's suggestion, 'why can we not fly? Is it because we are calculated to walk? It is. Could we walk, my friends, without strength? We could not. What should we do without strength, my friends? Our legs would refuse to bear us, our knees would double up, our ankles would turn over, and we should come to the ground. Then from whence, my friends, in a human point of view, do we derive the strength that is necessary to our limbs? Is it,' says Chadband, glancing over the table, 'from bread in various forms, from butter which is churned from the milk which is yielded untoe us by the cow, from the eggs which are laid by the fowl, from ham, from tongue, from sausage, and from such like? It is. Then let us partake of the good things which are set before us!

"The persecutors denied that there was any particular gift in Mr Chadband's piling verbose flights of stairs, one upon another, after this fashion. But this can only be received as a proof of their determination to persecute, since it must be within everybody's experience, that the Chadband style of oratory is widely received and much admired." BH 19

—preacher in action: "I could not possibly say to myself as the discourse proceeded, that the minister was a good speaker. I could not possibly say to myself that he expressed an understanding of the general mind and character of his audience.

"There was a supposititious working-man introduced into the homily, to make supposititious objections to our Christian religion and be reasoned down, who was not only a very disagreeable person, but remarkably unlike life—very much more unlike it than anything I had seen in the pantomime. The native independence of character this artisan was supposed to possess, was represented by a suggestion of a dialect that I certainly never heard in my uncommercial travels, and with a coarse swing of voice and manner anything but agreeable to his feelings, I should conceive, considered in the light of a portrait, and as far away from the fact as a Chinese Tartar.

"There was a model pauper introduced in like manner, who appeared to me to be the most intolerably arrogant pauper ever relieved, and to show himself in absolute want and dire necessity of a course of Stone Yard. For, how did this pauper testify to his having received the gospel of humility? A gentleman met him in the workhouse, and said . . . 'I am sorry to see you here. I am sorry to see you so poor.' 'Poor, sir!' replied that man, drawing himself up, 'I am the son of a Prince! *My* father is the King of Kings. *My* father is the Lord of Lords. *My* father is the ruler of all the Princes of the Earth!' &c.

"And this was what all the preacher's fellow-sinners might come to, if they would embrace this blessed book—which I must say it did some violence to my own feelings of reverence, to see held out at arm's length at frequent intervals and soundingly slapped, like a slow lot at a sale.

"Now, could I help asking myself the question, whether the mechanic before me, who must detect the preacher as being wrong about the visible manner of himself and the like to himself, and about such a noisy lip-server as that pauper, might not, most unhappily for the usefulness of the occasion, doubt that preacher's being right about things not visible to human senses?" ¶UT/TV

—preaching technique: "It happens that Mr Chadband has a pulpit habit of fixing some member of his congregation with his eye, and fatly arguing his points with that particular person; who is understood to be expected to be moved to an occasional grunt, groan, gasp, or other audible expression of inward working; which expression of inward working, being echoed by some elderly lady in the next pew, and so communicated, like a game of forfeits, through a circle of the more fermentable sinners present, serves the purpose of parliamentary cheering, and gets Mr Chadband's steam up." BH 25

—the Ranting persuasion: " . . . Mrs MacStinger resorted to a great distance every Sunday morning, to attend the ministry of the Reverend Melchisedech Howler, who, having been one day discharged from the West India Docks on a false suspicion (got up expressly against him by the general enemy) of screwing gimlets into puncheons, and applying his lips to the orifice, had announced the destruction of the world for that day two years, at ten in the morning, and opened a front parlour for the reception of ladies and gentlemen of the Ranting persuasion, upon whom, on the first occasion of their assemblage, the admonitions of the Reverend Melchisedech had produced so powerful an effect, that, in their rapturous performance of a sacred jig, which closed the service, the whole flock broke through into a kitchen below, and disabled a mangle belonging to one of the fold." DS 15

—the right note: "But, in respect of the large Christianity of his general tone; of his re-

nunciation of all priestly authority; of his earnest and reiterated assurance to the people that the commonest among them could work out their own salvation if they would, by simply, lovingly, and dutifully following Our Saviour, and that they needed the mediation of no erring man; in these particulars, this gentleman deserved all praise.

"Nothing could be better than the spirit, or the plain emphatic words of his discourse in these respects. And it was a most significant and encouraging circumstance that whenever he struck that chord, or whenever he described anything which Christ himself had done, the array of faces before him was very much more earnest, and very much more expressive of emotion, than at any other time." ¶UT/TV

—*right preaching*

—*a prescription:* "In the New Testament there is the most beautiful and affecting history conceivable by man, and there are the terse models for all prayer and for all preaching. As to the models, imitate them, Sunday preachers—else why are they there, consider? As to the history, tell it.

"Some people cannot read, some people will not read, many people (this especially holds among the young and ignorant) find it hard to pursue the verse-form in which the book is presented to them, and imagine that those breaks imply gaps and want of continuity. Help them over that first stumbling-block, by setting forth the history in narrative, with no fear of exhausting it. You will never preach so well, you will never move them so profoundly, you will never send them away with half so much to think of.

"Which is the better interest: Christ's choice of twelve poor men to help in those merciful wonders among the poor and rejected; or the pious bullying of a whole Union-full of paupers? What is your changed philosopher to wretched me, peeping in at the door out of the mud of the streets and of my life, when you have the widow's son to tell me about, the ruler's daughter, the other figure at the door when the brother of the two sisters was dead, and one of the two ran to the mourner, crying, 'The Master is come, and calleth for thee'?—Let the preacher who will thoroughly forget himself and remember no individuality but one, and no eloquence but one, stand up before four thousand men and women at the Britannia Theatre any Sunday night, recounting that narrative to them as fellow creatures, and he shall see a sight!" ¶UT/TV

—*a seaman in America:* "[**Edward Thompson Taylor**] handled his text in all kinds of ways, and twisted it into all manner of shapes; but always ingeniously, and with a rude eloquence, well adapted to the comprehension of his hearers. Indeed if I be not mistaken, he studied their sympathies and understandings much more than the display of his own powers. His imagery was all drawn from the sea, and from the incidents of a seaman's life; and was often remarkably good . . . .

" . . . my favourable impression of him may have been greatly influenced and strengthened, firstly, by his impressing upon his hearers that the true observance of religion was not inconsistent with a cheerful deportment and an exact discharge of the duties of their station, which, indeed, it scrupulously required of them; and secondly, by his cautioning them not to set up any monopoly in Paradise and its mercies. I never heard these two points so wisely touched (if indeed I have ever heard them touched at all), by any preacher of that kind before." AN 3

—*rostrum:* "In the centre . . . in a desk or pulpit covered with red baize, was the presiding minister. The kind of rostrum he occupied will be very well understood, if I liken it to a boarded-up fireplace turned towards the audience, with a gentleman in a black surtout standing in the stove and leaning forward over the mantelpiece." UT/TV

Clergy and Preaching: Church

—*cathedral staff:* "[Mr Wallace] satisfied himself about the archbishop, the dean, the precentor, the chancellor, the sub-dean, the four arch-deacons, the twenty-eight prebendaries, the sub-chanter, the five priest-vicars, the seven lay-clerks, the six choristers, the four vergers, and the other officers and servants of the little staff . . . . " HWC/W2

—*uncooperative:* "Could [Mr Wallace] have access to the documents themselves?

"The effect which this simple request produced in the office, was prodigious! A small schoolboy who should, at dinner, ask for a piece of the master's apple-pie; or a drummer on parade, who should solicit from his captain a loan of five shillings, could not produce a more sublime degree of indignant astonishment, than that which glared through the smoke from the faces of the deputy-registrar, the surrogate, the chief clerk, and all the junior clerks, then and there assembled. The effect produced amounted to temporary petrefaction; the principals neither spoke nor moved; the subordinates left off writing and poking the fire. So superlative was the audacity of the request, that it paralysed the pendulum of that small, rusty, dusty, smoky old ecclesiastical clock, and stopped the works!

"Refusal in words was not vouchsafed to Mr William Wallace; neither did he need that condescension. The silent but expressive pantomime was enough. As the Eastern culprit receives his doom by the speechless gesture of the judge's hand across his own neck; so Mr William Wallace fully understood that access to the record depositories of the province appertaining to Cathedral number two, was nearly equivalent to getting into a freemason's lodge after it has been 'tiled,'* or to obtaining admission to St Paul's Cathedral without twopence." HWC/W2

**HS: "The Masonic 'Tiler' stands at the door to protect a lodge or meeting from interruption and to keep its proceedings secret or 'tiled.'" I p177*

—curate, on duty: "If his manner in the pulpit had created an impression in his favour, the sensation was increased tenfold, by his appearance in private circles. Pews in the immediate vicinity of the pulpit or reading-desk rose in value; sittings in the centre aisle were at a premium: an inch of room in the front row of the gallery could not be procured for love or money . . . .

"He began to preach extempore sermons, and even grave papas caught the infection. He got out of bed at half-past twelve o'clock on winter's night, to half-baptise a washerwoman's child in a slop-basin, and the gratitude of the parishioners knew no bounds—the very churchwardens grew generous, and insisted on the parish defraying the expense of the watch-box on wheels, which the new curate had ordered for himself, to perform the funeral service in, in wet weather.

"He sent three pints of gruel and a quarter of a pound of tea to a poor woman who had been brought to bed of four small children, all at once—the parish were charmed. He got up a subscription for her—the woman's fortune was made. He spoke for one hour and twenty-five minutes, at an anti-slavery meeting at the Goat and Boots—the enthusiasm was at its height.

"A proposal was set on foot for presenting the curate with a piece of plate, as a mark of esteem for his valuable services rendered to the parish. The list of subscriptions was filled up in no time; the contest was, not who should escape the contribution, but who should be the foremost to subscribe. A splendid silver inkstand was made, and engraved with an appropriate inscription; the curate was invited to a public breakfast, at the before-mentioned Goat and Boots; the inkstand was presented in a neat speech by Mr Gubbins, the ex-churchwarden, and acknowledged by the curate in terms which drew tears into the eyes of all present—the very waiters were melted." ¶SB/C

—dress: "For his religious 'Medicine' he puts on puffy white sleeves, little black aprons, large black waistcoats of a peculiar cut, collarless coats with Medicine button-holes, Medicine stockings and gaiters and shoes, and tops the whole with a highly grotesque Medicinal hat." UT/MM

" . . . we observe a certain sanctimonious waistcoat breaking out among the junior clergy of this realm, which we take the liberty to consider by far the most incensing garment ever cut: calculated to lead to breaches of the peace, as moving persons of a temperament open to aggravating influences, to seize the collar and shake off the buttons.

"Again, we cannot be unmindful of the popularity, among others of the junior clergy, of a meek, spare, large-buttoned, long-skirted, black frock coat, curiously fastened at the neck round a smooth white band . . . . Again, some clerical dignitaries are compelled (therefore they are to be sympathised with, and not condemned) to wear an apron: which few unaccustomed persons can behold with gravity." ¶HW/SP

And see B:Dress—*medicine man magic*

—on duty, apparently: " . . . there, sure enough, is Mr Sliverstone, with dishevelled hair, powdering away with pen, ink, and paper, at a rate which, if he has any power of sustaining it, would settle the longest sermon in no time. At first he is too much absorbed to be roused by this intrusion; but presently looking up, says faintly, 'Ah!' and pointing to his desk with a weary and languid smile, extends his hand, and hopes you'll forgive him.

"Then Mrs Sliverstone sits down beside

him, and taking his hand in hers, tells you how that Mr Sliverstone has been shut up there ever since nine o'clock in the morning, (it is by this time twelve at noon,) and how she knows it cannot be good for his health, and is very uneasy about it. Unto this Mr Sliverstone replies firmly, that 'It must be done;' which agonizes Mrs Sliverstone still more, and she goes on to tell you that such were Mr Sliverstone's labours last week—what with the buryings, marryings, churchings, christenings, and all together—that when he was going up the pulpit stairs on Sunday evening, he was obliged to hold on by the rails, or he would certainly have fallen over into his own pew.

"Mr Sliverstone, who has been listening and smiling meekly, says, 'Not quite so bad as that, not quite so bad!' he admits though, on cross-examination, that he *was* very near falling upon the verger who was following him up to bolt the door; but adds, that it was his duty as a Christian to fall upon him, if need were, and that he, Mr Sliverstone, (and possibly the verger too) ought to glory in it." ¶YC/E

—on duty, truly: "So cheerful of spirit and guiltless of affectation, as true practical Christianity ever is! I read more of the New Testament in the fresh frank face going up the village beside me, in five minutes, than I have read in anathematising discourses (albeit put to press with enormous flourishing of trumpets), in all my life. I heard more of the Sacred Book in the cordial voice that had nothing to say about its owner, than in all the would-be celestial pairs of bellows that have ever blown conceit at me." UT/S

"Down to yesterday's post outward, my clergyman alone had written one thousand seventy-five letters to relatives and friends of the lost people. In the absence of self-assertion, it was only through my now and then delicately putting a question as the occasion arose, that I became informed of these things . . .

"In this noble modesty, in this beautiful simplicity, in this serene avoidance of the least attempt to 'improve' an occasion which might be supposed to have sunk of its own weight into my heart, I seemed to have happily come, in a few steps, from the churchyard with its open grave, which was the type of Death, to the Christian dwelling side by side with it, which was the type of Resurrection." UT/S

—a flawed profession: "[Contemplation of the church] may not be improved by the drawling voice, without a heart, that drearily pursues the dull routine; by the avaricious functionary who lays aside the silver mace to take the silver pieces, and who races through the Show as if he were the hero of a sporting wager.

"Some uncomfortable doubts may . . . obtrude themselves, of the practical Christianity of the head of some particular Foundation. He may be a brawler, or a proud man, or a sleek, or an artful. He may be usually silent, in the House of Lords when a Christian minister should speak, and may make a point of speaking when he should be silent. He may even be oblivious of the truth; a stickler by the letter, not the spirit, for his own purposes; a pettifogger in the supreme court of GOD's high law, as there are pettifoggers in the lower courts administering the laws of mortal man.

"Disturbing recollections may arise, of a few isolated cases here and there, where country curates with small incomes and large families, poor gentlemen and scholars, are condemned to work, like blind horses in a mill, while others who do not work get their rightful pay; or of the inconsistency and indecorum of the Church being made a Robe and Candlestick question, while so many shining lights are hidden under bushels, and so many black-cloth coats are thread-bare.

"The question may present itself, by remote chance, whether some shovel-hats be not made too much on the model of the banker's shovel with which the gold is gathered on the counter, and too little in remembrance of that other kind of shovel that renders ashes unto ashes, and dust to dust." ¶HWC/W

—Oxford Movement

—parody: Finding "That the intellectual works in the University of Oxford are, in all essential particulars, precisely what they were when it was first established for the Manufacture of Clergymen. That they alone have stood still (or, in the very few instances in which they have moved at all, have moved backward), when all other works have advanced and improved . . . . And your Commissioners can truly add, that they found nothing in the avocations of the miners of Scotland, the knife-grinders of Sheffield, or the workers in iron of Wolverhampton, one-half so prejudicial to the persons engaged therein, or one-half so

injurious to society, as this fatal system of employment in the University of Oxford . . . .

"That . . . there is no doubt that the persons employed . . . can all spell Church with great readiness, and, indeed, very seldom spell anything else. But, on the other hand . . . such comprehensive words as justice, mercy, charity, kindness, brotherly love, forbearance, gentleness, and Good Works, awaken no ideas whatever; while the evidence shows that the most preposterous notions are attached to the mere terms Priest and Faith . . . . A vast number of witnesses being interrogated as to what they understood by the words Religion and Salvation, answered Lighted Candles. Some said water; some, bread; others, little boys; others mixed the water, lighted candles, bread, and little boys all up together, and called the compound, Faith.

"Others again, being asked if they deemed it to be a matter of great interest in Heaven, and of high moment in the vast scale of creation, whether a poor human priest should put on, at a certain time, a white robe or a black one; or should turn his face to the East or to the West; or would bend his knees of clay; or stand, or worm on end upon the earth, said 'Yes, they did': and being further questioned, whether a man could hold such mummeries in his contempt, and pass to everlasting rest, said boldly, 'No.'" ¶E/UO *And see* S:Religion

—and the poor: "Dearly beloved brethren . . . do you know that between Gorham controversies, and Pusey controversies, and Newman controversies, and twenty other edifying controversies, a certain large class of minds in the community is gradually being driven out of all religion? Would it be well, do you think, to come out of the controversies for a little while, and be simply Apostolic thus low down!" HW/SU

—passing by on the other side: "'Mr Crisparkle,' quoth the Dean, 'human justice may err, but it must act according to its lights. The days of taking sanctuary are past. This young man [Neville Landless] must not take sanctuary with us.'

"'You mean that he must leave my house, sir?'

"'Mr Crisparkle,' returned the prudent Dean, 'I claim no authority in your house. I merely confer with you, on the painful necessity you find yourself under, of depriving this young man of the great advantages of your counsel and instruction.

"'It is very lamentable, sir,' Mr Crisparkle represented.

"'Very much so,' the Dean assented.

"'And if it be a necessity—' Mr Crisparkle faltered.

"'As you unfortunately find it to be,' returned the Dean.

"Mr Crisparkle bowed submissively: 'It is hard to prejudge his case, sir, but I am sensible that—'

"'Just so. Perfectly. As you say, Mr Crisparkle,' interposed the Dean, nodding his head smoothly, 'there is nothing else to be done. No doubt, no doubt. There is no alternative, as your good sense has discovered.'

"'I am entirely satisfied of his perfect innocence, sir, nevertheless.'

"'We-e-ell!' said the Dean, in a more confidential tone, and slightly glancing around him, 'I would not say so, generally. Not generally. Enough of suspicion attaches to him to—no, I think I would not say so, generally.'

"Mr Crisparkle bowed again.

"'It does not become us, perhaps,' pursued the Dean, 'to be partisans. Not partisans. We clergy keep our hearts warm and our heads cool, and we hold a judicious middle course.'

"'I hope you do not object, sir, to my having stated in public, emphatically, that he will reappear here, whenever any new suspicion may be awakened, or any new circumstance may come to light in this extraordinary matter?'

"'Not at all,' returned the Dean. And yet, do you know, I don't think,' with a very nice and neat emphasis on those two words: 'I *don't think* I would state it emphatically. State it? Ye-e—es! But emphatically? No-o-o. I *think* not. In point of fact, Mr Crisparkle, keeping our hearts warm and our heads cool, we clergy need do nothing emphatically.'

"So Minor Canon Row knew Neville Landless no more; and he went whither-soever he would, or could, with a blight upon his name and fame." MED16

—and politics: "[Political young gentlemen] have recently had many favourable opportunities of opening in churches, but as there the clergyman has it all his own way, and must not be contradicted, whatever politics he preaches, they are fain to hold their tongues until they reach the outer door,

though at the imminent risk of bursting in the effort." YG/P

—*on shipboard:* "Thus the scene. Some seventy passengers assembled at the saloon tables. Prayer-books on tables. Ship rolling heavily. Pause. No minister. Rumour has related that a modest young clergyman on board has responded to the captain's request that he will officiate. Pause again, and very heavy rolling.

"Closed double doors suddenly burst open, and two strong stewards skate in, supporting minister between them. General appearance as of somebody picked up drunk and incapable, and under conveyance to station-house. Stoppage, pause, and particularly heavy rolling. Stewards watch their opportunity, and balance themselves, but cannot balance minister; who, struggling with a drooping head and a backward tendency, seems determined to return below, while they are as determined that he shall be got to the reading-desk in mid-saloon. Desk portable, sliding away down a long table, and aiming itself at the breasts of various members of the congregation . . . .

"All this time the congregation have been breaking up into sects—as the manner of congregations often is—each sect sliding away by itself, and all pounding the weakest sect which slid first into the corner. Utmost point of dissent soon attained in every corner, and violent rolling. Stewards at length make a dash; conduct minister to the mast in the centre of the saloon, which he embraces with both arms; skate out; and leave him in that condition to arrange affairs with flock." ¶UT/AS

—*well-nourished:* "The clergyman is, perhaps, the chaplain of a civic company; he has the moist and vinous look, and eke the bulbous boots, of one acquainted with 'Twenty port, and comet vintages . . . of a prandial presence, and a muffled voice, [he] may be scant of hearing as well as of breath, but he only glances up [at the banging of the door], as having an idea that somebody has said Amen in a wrong place, and continues his steady jog-trot, like a farmer's wife going to market. He does all he has to do, in the same easy way, and gives us a concise sermon, still like the jog-trot of the farmer's wife on a level road. Its drowsy cadence soon lulls the three old women asleep . . . .

"But, we receive the signal to make that unanimous dive which surely is a little conventional—like the strange rustlings and settlings and clearings of throats and noses, which are never dispensed with, at certain points of the Church service, and are never held to be necessary under any other circumstances." UT/LC

Judge

—*aroused:* "Serjeant Buzfuz, who had proceeded with such volubility that his face was perfectly crimson, here paused for breath. The silence awoke Mr Justice Stareleigh, who immediately wrote down something with a pen without any ink in it, and looked unusually profound, to impress the jury with the belief that he always thought most deeply with his eyes shut." PP 34

—*and capital punishment:* "It is certain that men contract a general liking for those things which they have studied at great cost of time and intellect, and their proficiency in which has led to their becoming distinguished and successful. It is certain that out of this feeling arises, not only that passive blindness to their defects . . . but an active disposition to advocate and defend them . . . . Thus the Lord Chancellor, in 1813, objected to the removal of the penalty of death from the offence of stealing to the amount of five shillings from a shop. Thus, Lord Ellenborough, in 1820, anticipated the worst effects from there being no punishment of death for stealing five shillings' worth of wet linen from a bleaching ground." AP/CP 3

"He is a chief actor in the terrible drama of a trial, where the life or death of a fellow creature is at issue. No one who has seen such a trial can fail to know, or can ever forget, its intense interest. I care not how painful this interest is, to the good, wise judge upon the bench. I admit its painful nature, and the judge's goodness and wisdom to the fullest extent—but I submit that his prominent share in the excitement of such a trial, and the dread mystery involved, has a tendency to bewilder and confuse the judge upon the general subject of that penalty . . . .

Not to contend that there is no amount of wig or ermine that can change the nature of the man inside; not to say that the nature of a judge may be, like the dyer's hand, subdued to what it works in, and may become too used to this punishment of death, to consider it quite dispassionately; not to say that it may possibly be inconsistent to have, deciding as calm authorities in favour of death, judges who have been constantly sentencing to death;—I contend that . . . a judge, and especially a criminal judge, is a bad witness for the punishment . . . . " MP/CP 3

—on vacation: "There is only one Judge in town. Even he only comes twice a week to sit in chambers. If the country folks of those assize towns on his circuit could see him now! No full-bottomed wig, no red petticoats, no fur, no javelin-men, no white wands. Merely a close-shaved gentleman in white trousers and a white hat, with sea-bronze on the judicial countenance, and a strip of bark peeled by the solar rays from the judicial nose, who calls in at the shell-fish shop as he comes along, and drinks iced ginger-beer!" BH 19

Jury

—criticised by a beadle: "'The jury brought it in, "Died from exposure to the cold, and want of the common necessaries of life," didn't they?'

"Mr Bumble nodded.

"'And they made it a special verdict, I think,' said the undertaker, 'by adding some words to the effect, that if the relieving officer had——'

"'Tush! Foolery! interposed the beadle. 'If the board attended to all the nonsense that ignorant jurymen talk, they'd had enough to do.'

"'Very true,' said the undertaker; 'they would indeed.'

"'Juries,' said Mr Bumble, grasping his cane tightly, as was his wont when working into a passion: 'juries is ineddicated, vulgar, grovelling wretches.'

"'So they are,' said the undertaker.

"'They haven't no more philosophy nor political economy about 'em than that,' said the beadle, snapping his fingers contemptuously.

"'No more they have,' acquiesced the undertaker.

"'I despise 'em,' said the beadle, growing very red in the face.

"'So do it,' rejoined the undertaker.

"'And I only wish we'd a jury of the independent sort, in the house for a week or two,' said the beadle; 'the rules and regulations of the board would soon bring their spirit down for 'em.'" OT 4

—empanelled: " . . . a gentleman in black, who sat below the judge, proceeded to call over the names of the jury; and after a great deal of bawling, it was discovered that only ten special jurymen were present. Upon this Mr Serjeant Buzfuz prayed a tales; the gentleman in black then proceeded to press into the special jury, two of the common jurymen; and a green-grocer and a chemist were caught directly.

"'Answer to your names, gentlemen, that you may be sworn,' said the gentleman in black. 'Richard Upwitch.'

"'Here,' said the green-grocer.

"'Thomas Groffin.'

"'Here,' said the chemist.

"'Take the book, gentlemen. You shall well and truly try—'

"'I beg this court's pardon,' said the chemist, who was a tall, thin, yellow-visaged man, 'but I hope this court will excuse my attendance.'

"'On what grounds, sir?' said Mr Justice Stareleigh.

"'I have no assistant, my Lord,' said the chemist.

"'I can't help that, sir,' replied Mr Justice Stareleigh. 'You should hire one.'

"'I can't afford it, my Lord,' rejoined the chemist.

"'Then you ought to be able to afford it, sir,' said the judge, reddening . . . .

"'I know I *ought* to do, if I got on as well as I deserved, but I don't, my Lord,' answered the chemist.

"'Swear the gentleman,' said the judge, peremptorily.

"The officer had got no further than the 'You shall well and truly try,' when he was again interrupted by the chemist.

"'I am to be sworn, my Lord, am I?' said the chemist.

"'Certainly, sir,' replied the testy little judge.

"'Very well, my Lord,' replied the chemist, in a resigned manner. 'Then there'll be murder before this trial's over; that's all. Swear me, if you please, sir;' and sworn the chemist was, before the judge could find words to utter.

"'I merely wanted to observe, my Lord,' said the chemist, taking his seat with great deliberation, 'that I've left nobody but an errand-boy in my shop. He is a very nice boy, my Lord, but he is not acquainted with drugs; and I know that the prevailing impression on his mind is, that Epsom salts means oxalic acid; and syrup of senna, laudanum. That's all, my Lord.' With this, the tall chemist composed himself into a comfortable attitude, and, assuming a pleasant expression of countenance, appeared to have prepared himself for the worst." PP 34

—invoked: "A difference of opinion had arisen between herself [Betsey Trotwood] and Mrs Crupp, on an abstract question (the propriety of chambers being inhabited by the gentler sex); and my aunt, utterly indifferent to spasms on the part of Mrs Crupp, had cut the dispute short, by informing that lady that she smelt of my brandy, and that she would trouble her to walk out. Both of these expressions Mrs Crupp considered actionable, and had expressed her intention of bringing before a 'British Judy'—meaning, it was supposed, the bulwark of our national liberties." DC 35

—and mealtime: "'A good, contented, well-breakfasted juryman, is a capital thing to get hold of [said Mr Perker]. Discontented or hungry jurymen, my dear sir, always find for the plaintiff.'

"'Bless my heart,' said Mr Pickwick, looking very blank; 'what do they do that for?'

"'Why, I don't know,' replied the little man, coolly; 'saves time, I suppose. If it's near dinner-time, the foreman takes out his watch when the jury has retired, and says, "Dear me, gentlemen, ten minutes to five, I declare! I dine at five, gentlemen." "So do I," says everybody else, except two men who ought to have dined at three, and seem more than half disposed to stand out in consequence. The foreman smiles, and puts up his watch:—"Well, gentlemen, what do we say, plaintiff or defendant, gentlemen? I rather think, so far as I am concerned, gentlemen—I say, I rather think—but don't let that influence you—I *rather* think the plaintiff's the man." Upon this, two or three other men are sure to say that they think so too—as of course they do; and then they get on very unanimously and comfortably.'" PP 34

—tribunal in France: "Every eye was turned to the jury. The same determined patriots and good republicans as yesterday and the day before, and to-morrow and the day after. Eager and prominent among them, one man with a craving face, and his fingers perpetually hovering about his lips, whose appearance gave great satisfaction to the spectators. A life-thirsting, cannibal-looking, bloody-minded juryman, the Jacques Three of St. Antoine. The whole jury, as a jury of dogs empannelled to try the deer." TTC iii 9

The Law

—admission to the Bar: "Having no interest in the Church, [Thomas Idle] appropriately selected the next best profession for a lazy man in England—the Bar.

"Although the Benchers of the Inns of Court have lately abandoned their good old principles, and oblige their students to make some show of studying, in Mr Idle's time no such innovation as this existed. Young men who aspired to the honourable title of barrister were, very properly, not asked to learn anything of the law, but were merely required to eat a certain number of dinners at the table of their Hall, and to pay a certain sum of money; and were called to the Bar as soon as they could prove that they had sufficiently complied with these extremely sensible regulations.

"Never did Thomas move more harmoniously in concert with his elders and betters than when he was qualifying himself for admission among the barristers of his native country. Never did he feel more deeply what real laziness was in all the serene majesty of its nature, than on the memorable day when he was called to the Bar, after having carefully abstained from opening his law-books during his period of probation, except to fall asleep over them." ¶LT 3

" . . . I myself was uncommercially preparing for the Bar—which is done, as everybody knows, by having a frayed old gown put on in a pantry by an old woman in a chronic state of Saint Anthony's fire and dropsy, and, so decorated, bolting a bad dinner in a party of four, whereof each individual mistrusts the other three . . . . " UT/C

—aesthetic considerations: "'. . . in [the world's] having gone to law, and in its legal system altogether, I do observe a serious side—now, really, a something tangible, and with a purpose and intention in it . . . that commands respect. Life a farce, Dr Jeddler? With law in it?. . . .

"'Granted, if your please, that war is foolish,' said Snitchey. 'There we agree. For example. Here's a smiling country,' pointing it out with his fork, 'once overrun by soldiers—trespassers every man of 'em—and laid waste by fire and sword. He, he he! The idea of any man exposing himself, voluntarily, to fire and sword! Stupid, wasteful, positively ridiculous; you laugh at your fellow-creatures, you know, when you think of it!

"'But take this smiling country as it stands. Think of the laws appertaining to real property; to the bequest and devise of real property; to the mortgage and redemption of real property; to leasehold, freehold, and copyhold estate; think,' said Mr Snitchey, with such great emotion that he actually smacked his lips, 'of the complicated laws relating to title and proof of title, with all the contradictory precedents and numerous acts of parliament connected with them; think of the infinite number of ingenious and interminable chancery suits, to which this pleasant prospect may give rise; and acknowledge, Dr Jeddler, that there is a green spot in the scheme about us!" ¶BL 1

—a bachelor: "'You were present on the occasion of the destruction of these trinkets, and, indeed, are the more guilty of the two, in the eye of the law; for the law supposes that your wife acts under your direction.'

"'If the law supposes that,' said Mr Bumble, squeezing his hat emphatically in both hands, 'the law is a ass—a idiot. If that's the eye of the law, the law's a bachelor; and the worst I wish the law is, that his eye may be opened by experience—by experience.'" OT 51

—bar examination: "'I am now admitted (after undergoing an examination that's enough to badger a man blue, touching a pack of nonsense that he don't want to know) on the roll of attorneys . . . . '" BH 64

—chess game: "'Strange, indeed! [said Richard Carstone] all this wasteful wanton chess-playing *is* very strange. To see that composed Court yesterday jogging on so serenely, and to think of the wretchedness of the pieces on the board, gave me the headache and the heartache both together. My head ached with wondering how it happened, if men were neither fools nor rascals; and my heart ached to think they could possibly be either.'" BH 5

—defended: "'We are a prosperous community, Mr Jarndyce, a very prosperous community. We are a great country, Mr Jarndyce, we are a very great country. This is a great system, Mr Jarndyce, and would you wish a great country to have a little system? Now, really, really!'

"[Mr Kenge] said this at the stair-head, gently moving his right hand as if it were a silver trowel, wth which to spread the cement of his words on the structure of the system, and consolidate it for a thousand ages." BH 62

—its delay: "'[Tom Jarndyce] got into a restless habit of strolling about when the cause was on, or expected, talking to the little shop-keepers, and telling 'em to keep out of Chancery, whatever they did. 'For,' says he, 'it's being ground to bits in a slow mill; it's being roasted at a slow fire; it's being stung to death by single bees; it's being drowned by drops; it's going mad by grains.'" BH 5

—Equity: "I saw a great library of laws and law-proceedings, so complicated, costly, and unintelligible, that, although numbers of lawyers united in a public fiction that these were wonderfully just and equal, there was scarcely an honest man among them, but who said to his friend, privately consulting him, 'Better put up with a fraud or other injury than grope for redress through the manifold blind turnings and strange chances of this system.'

"I saw a portion of the system, called (of all things) Equity, which was ruin to suitors, ruin to property, a shield for wrong-doers having money, a rack for right-doers having none: a by-word for delay, slow agony of mind, despair, impoverishment, trickery, confusion, insupportable injustice. A main part of it, I saw prisoners wasting in gaol; mad people babbling in hospitals; suicides chronicled in the yearly records; orphans robbed of their inheritance; infants righted (perhaps) when they were gray.

"Certain lawyers and laymen came together, and said to one another . . . . 'We must change this.'

"Uprose, immediately, a throng of others, Secretaries, Petty Bags, Hanapers, Chaffwaxes, and what not, singing (in answer) 'Rule Britannia,' and 'God save the Queen'; making flourishing speeches, pronouncing hard names, demanding committees, commissions, commissioners, and other scarecrows, and terrifying the little band of innovators out of their five wits." HW/DV

—its fictions: "There are many pleasant fictions of the law in constant operation, but there is not one so pleasant or practically humorous as that which supposes every man to be of equal value in its impartial eye, and the benefits of all laws to be equally attainable by all men, without the

smallest reference to the furniture of their pockets." NN 46

—*imposing cruel punishment:* "'I suppose theyll be trying Forgeries this morning?'

"'Treason!'

"'That's quartering,' said Jerry. 'Barbarous!'

"'It is the law,' remarked the ancient clerk, turning his surprised spectacles upon him. 'It is the law.'

"'It's hard in the law to spile a man, I think. It's hard enough to kill him, but it's wery hard to spile him, sir.'

"'Not at all,' returned the ancient clerk. 'Speak well of the law. Take care of your chest and voice, my good friend, and leave the law to take care of itself. I give you that advice.'" TTC ii 2

Cruncher's objection is professional, not humanitarian: as a 'resurrection man' he needs whole, unspoiled corpses to sell for science.

—*indenture:* "Mr Snagsby is behind his counter in his grey coat and sleeves, inspecting an indenture of several skins which has just come in from the engrosser's; an immense desert of law-hand and parchment, with here and there a resting-place of a few large letters, to break the awful monotony, and save the traveller from despair." BH 47

—*injustice:* "The world, being in constant commission of vast quantities of injustice, is a little too apt to comfort itself with the idea that if the victim of its falsehood and malice have a clear conscience, he cannot fail to be sustained under his trials, and somehow or other to come right at last—'in which case,' say they who have hunted him down,'—though we certainly don't expect it—nobody will be better pleased than we.' Whereas, the world would do well to reflect, that injustice is in itself, to every generous and properly constituted mind, an injury, of all others the most insufferable, the most torturing, and the most hard to bear; and that many clear consciences have gone to their account elsewhere, and many sound hearts have broken, because of this very reason; the knowledge of their own deserts only aggravating their suffering, and rendering them the less endurable." OCS 61

—*a joke?* "'What do you call law?'

"'A joke,' replied the Doctor [Jeddler].

"'Did you ever go to law?' asked Mr Snitchey, looking out of the blue bag.

"'Never,' returned the Doctor.

"'If you ever do,' said Mr Snitchey, 'perhaps you'll alter that opinion.'" BL 1

—*and justice:* "'It won't do to have truth and justice on his side; he [George Rouncewell] must have law and lawyers,' exclaims the old girl [Mrs Bagnet], apparently persuaded that the latter form a separate establishment, and have dissolved partnership with truth and justice for ever and a day." BH 55

—*and medicine:* "Bar's knowledge of that agglomeration of Jurymen which is called humanity was as sharp as a razor; yet a razor is not a generally convenient instrument, and Physician's plain bright scalpel, though far less keen, was adaptable to far wider purposes. Bar knew all about the gullibility and knavery of people; but Physician could have given him a better insight into their tendernesses and affections, in one week of his rounds, than Westminster Hall and all the circuits put together, in threescore years and ten. Bar always had a suspicion of this, and perhaps was glad to encourage it (for, if the world were really a great Law Court one would think that the last day of Term could not too soon arrive); and so he liked and respected Physician quite as much as any other kind of man did." LD ii 25

—*its minion:* "Mr Grummer's mode of proceeding was professional, but peculiar. His first act was to bolt the door on the inside; his second, to polish his head and countenance very carefully with a cotton handkerchief; his third, to place his hat, with the cotton handkerchief in it, on the nearest chair; and his fourth, to produce from the breast-pocket of his coat a short truncheon, surmounted by a brazen crown, with which he beckoned to Mr Pickwick with a grave and ghost-like air.

"Mr Snodgrass was the first to break the astonished silence. He looked steadily at Mr Grummer for a brief space, and then said emphatically: "'This is a private room, sir. A private room'

"Mr Grummer shook his head, and replied, 'No room's private to his Majesty when the street door's once passed. That's law. Some people maintains that an Englishman's house is his castle. That's gammon.'

"The Pickwickians gazed on each other with wondering eyes.

"'Which is Mr Tupman?' inquired Mr Grummer. He had an intuitive perception of Mr Pickwick; he knew *him* at once.

"'My name's Tupman,' said that gentleman.

"'My name's Law,' said Mr Grummer.

"'What?' said Mr Tupman.

"'Law,' replied Mr Grummer, 'law, civil power, and exekative; them's my titles; here's my authority. Blank Tupman, blank Pickvick—against the peace of our sufferin Lord the King——stattit in that case made and purwided—and all regular. I apprehend you, Pickvick! Tupman—the aforesaid.'" PP 24

—its nature: "'It is not enough that Justice should be morally certain; she must be *immorally* certain—legally, that is.'

"'His Honor,' said Mr Datchery, 'reminds me of the nature of the law. Immoral. How true!'

"'As I say, sir,' pompously went on the Mayor [Sapsea], 'the arm of the law is a strong arm, and a long arm. That is the way I put it. A strong arm and a long arm.'

"'How forcible!—And yet, again, how true!' murmured Mr Datchery." MED 18

—to a neophyte: "I am naturally of a dreamy turn of mind; and my abundant leisure—for I am called to the Bar—coupled with much lonely listening to the twittering of sparrows, and the pattering of rain, has encouraged that disposition . . . .

"I am in the Law, but not of it. I can't exactly make out what it means. I sit in Westminster Hall sometimes (in character) from ten to four; and when I go out of Court, I don't know whether I am standing on my wig or my boots.

"It appears to me (I mention this in confidence) as if there were too much talk and too much law—as if some grains of truth were started overboard into a tempestuous sea of chaff." RP/GA

—on the job training: "'This is Mr Swiveller, my intimate friend—a gentleman of good family and great expectations, but who, having rather involved himself by youthful indiscretion, is content for a time to fill the humble station of a clerk—humble, but here most enviable . . . .

"'Miss Sally will teach him law, the delightful study of the law,' said Quilp; 'she'll be his guide, his friend, his companion, his Blackstone, his Coke upon Littleton, his Young Lawyer's Best Companion' . . . .

"'With Miss Sally,' Quilp went on, 'and the beautiful fictions of the law, his days will pass like minutes. Those charming creations of the poet, John Doe and Richard Roe, when they first dawn upon him, will open a new world for the enlargement of his mind and the improvement of his heart.'" OCS 33

—one great principle: "The one great principle of the English law is, to make business for itself. There is no other principle distinctly, certainly, and consistently maintained through all its narrow turnings. Viewed by this light it becomes a coherent scheme, and not the monstrous maze the laity are apt to think it. Let them but once clearly perceive that its grand principle is to make business for itself at their expense, and surely they will cease to grumble." BH 39

—a practice, in the country: "Snitchey and Craggs had a snug little office on the old Battle Ground, where they drove a snug little business, and fought a great many small pitched battles for a great many contending parties. Though it could hardly be said of these conflicts that they were running fights—for in truth they generally proceeded at a snail's pace—the part the Firm had in them came so far within the general denomination, that now they took a shot at this Plaintiff, and now aimed a chop at that Defendant, now made a heavy charge at an estate in Chancery, and now had some light skirmishing among an irregular body of small debtors, just as the occasion served, and the enemy happened to present himself.

"The Gazette was an important and profitable feature in some of their fields, as in fields of greater renown; and in most of the Actions wherein they showed their generalship, it was afterwards observed by the combatants that they had had great difficulty in making each other out, or in knowing with any degree of distinctness what they were about, in consequence of the vast amount of smoke by which they were surrounded." ¶BL 2

—seen by lawyers for their own account: "It may at first sight be matter of surprise to the thoughtless few that . . . a professional gentleman, should not have legally indicted some party or parties, active in the promotion of the nuisance; but they will be good enough to remember that as Doctors seldom take their own prescriptions and Divines do not always practise what they preach, so Lawyers are shy of meddling with the Law on their own account, knowing it to be an edged tool of uncertain application, very ex-

pensive in the working, and rather remarkable for its properties of close shaving, than for its always shaving the right person." OCS 37

—on vacation: "The bar of England is scattered over the face of the earth. How England can get on through four long summer months without its bar—which is its acknowledged refuge in adversity, and its only legitimate triumph in prosperity—is beside the question; assuredly that shield and buckler of Britannia are not in present wear.

"The learned gentleman who is always so tremendously indignant at the unprecedented outrage committed on the feelings of his client by the opposite party, that he never seems likely to recover it, is doing infinitely better than might be expected, in Switzerland.

"The learned gentleman who does the withering business, and who blights all opponents with his gloomy sarcasm, is as merry as a grig at a French watering-place. The learned gentleman who weeps by the pint on the smallest provocation, has not shed a tear these six weeks.

"The very learned gentleman who has cooled the natural heat of his gingery complexion in pools and fountains of law, until he has become great in knotty arguments for term-time, when he poses the drowsy Bench with legal 'chaff,' inexplicable to the uninitiated and to most of the initiated too, is roaming, with a characteristic delight in aridity and dust, about Constantinople.

"Other dispersed fragments of the same great Palladium are to be found on the canals of Venice, at the second cataract of the Nile, in the baths of Germany, and sprinkled on the sea-sand all over the English coast. Scarcely one is to be encountered in the deserted region of Chancery Lane. If such a lonely member of the bar do flit across the water, and come upon a prowling suitor who is unable to leave off haunting the scenes of his anxiety, they frighten one another, and retreat into opposite shades." ¶BH 19

And see L:Neighbourhoods—*Chancery Lane*

—the wig: " . . . life in a wig is to a large class of people much more terrifying and impressive than life with its own head of hair . . . . " OCS 63

"' . . . I have always been of the opinion that Mr Micawber possesses what I have heard my papa call, when I lived at home, the judicial mind; and I hope Mr Micawber is now entering on a field where that mind will develop itself, and take a commanding station [said Mrs Micawber].'

"I quite believe that Mr Micawber saw himself, in his judicial mind's eye, on the woolsack. He passed his hand complacently over his bald head, and said with ostentatious resignation:

"'My dear, we will not anticipate the decrees of fortune. If I am reserved to wear a wig, I am at least prepared, externally,' in allusion to his baldness, 'for that distinction. I do not,' said Mr Micawber, 'regret my hair, and I may have been deprived of it for a specific purpose. I cannot say.'" DC 36

"For his legal 'Medicine' he sticks upon his head the hair of quadrupeds, and plasters the same with fat, and dirty white powder, and talks a gibberish quite unknown to the men and squaws of his tribe." UT/MM

—'wiglomeration:' "'[Richard Carstone] must have a profession; he must make some choice for himself. There will be a world more Wiglomeration about it, I suppose, but it must be done.'

"'More what, Guardian?' said I.

"'More Wiglomeration,' said [John Jarndyce]. 'It's the only name I know for the thing. He is a ward in Chancery, my dear. Kenge and Carboy will have something to say about it; Master Somebody—a sort of ridiculous Sexton, digging graves for the merits of causes in a back room at the end of Quality Court, Chancery Lane—will have something to say about it; Counsel will have something to say about it; the Chancellor will have something to say about it; the Satellites will have something to say about it; they will all have to be handsomely fee'd, all round, about it; the whole thing will be vastly ceremonious, wordy, unsatisfactory, and expensive, and I call it, in general, Wiglomeration. How mankind ever came to be afflicted with Wiglomeration, or for whose sins these young people ever fell into a pit of it, I don't know; so it is.'" BH 8

Law clerk

—ambition: "'Do I understand, my dear Mr Traddles, that at the expiration of that period [five years], Mr Micawber would be eligible as a Judge or Chancellor?'

"'He would be *eligible.*' returned Traddles, with a strong emphasis on that word.

"'Thank you,' said Mrs Micawber. 'That

is quite sufficient. If such is the case, and Mr Micawber forfeits no privilege by entering on these duties, my anxiety is set at rest. I speak,' said Mrs Micawber, 'as a female, necessarily: but I have always been of opinion that Mr Micawber possesses what I have heard my papa call, when I lived at home, the judicial mind; and I hope Mr Micawber is now entering on a field where that mind will develop itself, and take a commanding station.'" DC 36

—being sworn: "The man in the spectacles was hard at work, swearing the clerks: the oath being invariably administered, without any effort at punctuation, and usually in the following terms:—

"'Take the book in your right hand this is your name and handwriting you swear that the contents of this your affidavit are true so help you God a shilling you must get change I haven't got it.'" PP 40

—classified: "There are several grades of Lawyers' Clerks. There is the Articled Clerk, who has paid a premium, and is an attorney in perspective, who runs a tailor's bill, receives invitations to parties, knows a family in Gower Street, and another in Tavistock Square: who goes out of town every Long Vacation to see his father, who keeps live horses innumerable; and who is, in short, the very aristocrat of clerks.

"There is the salaried clerk—out of door, or in door, as the case may be—who devotes the major part of his thirty shillings a week to his personal pleasure and adornment, repairs half-price to the Adelphi Theatre at least three times a week, dissipates majestically at the cider cellars afterwards, and is a dirty caricature of the fashion which expired six months ago.

"There is the middle-aged copying clerk, with a large family, who is always shabby, and often drunk. And there are the office lads in their first surtouts, who feel a befitting contempt for boys at day-schools: club as they go home at night, for saveloys and porter: and think there is nothing like 'life.'" ¶PP 31

—missing: "Very few loose papers are about. He has some manuscript near him, but is not referring to it. With the round top of an ink-stand, and two broken bits of sealing-wax, he is silently and slowly working out whatever train of indecision is in his mind. Now, the ink-stand top is in the middle; now, the red bit of sealing-wax, now the black bit. That's not it. Mr Tulkinghorn must gather them all up and begin again.

"Here beneath the painted ceiling, with fore-shortened Allegory staring down at his intrusion as if it meant to swoop upon him, and he cutting it dead, Mr Tulkinghorn has at once his house and office. He keeps no staff; only one middle-aged man, usually a little out at elbows, who sits in a high Pew in the hall, and is rarely overburdened with business. Mr Tulkinghorn is not in a common way. He wants no clerks. He is a great reservoir of confidences, not to be so tapped. His clients want *him;* he is all in all. Drafts that he requires to be drawn, are drawn by special pleaders in the Temple on mysterious instructions; fair copies that he requires to be made, are made at the stationer's, expense being no consideration. The middle-aged man in the Pew knows scarcely more of the affairs of the Peerage, than any crossing sweeper in Holborn." BH 10

—underoccupied: "'I am . . . high up an awful staircase commanding a burial-ground, and I have a whole clerk to myself, and he has nothing to do but look at the burial-ground, and what he will turn out when arrived at maturity, I cannot conceive. Whether, in that shabby rook's nest, he is always plotting wisdom, or plotting murder; whether he will grow up, after so much solitary brooding, to enlighten his fellow-creatures, or to poison them; is the only speck of interest that presents itself to my professional view.'" OMF i 3

"'Would you take a seat . . . while I look over our Appointment Book?' Young Blight made a great show of fetching from his desk a long thin manuscript volume with a brown paper cover, and running his finger down the day's appointments, murmuring, 'Mr Aggs, Mr Baggs, Mr Caggs, Mr Daggs, Mr Faggs, Mr Gaggs, Mr Boffin. Yes, sir, quite right. You are a little before your time sir. Mr Lightwood will be in directly.'

"'I'm not in a hurry,' said Mr Boffin.

"'Thank you, sir. I'll take the opportunity, if you please, of entering your name in our Callers' Book for the day.' Young Blight made another great show of changing the volume, taking up a pen, sucking it, dipping it, and running over previous entries before he wrote. As, 'Mr Alley, Mr Balley, Mr Calley, Mr Dalley, Mr Falley, Mr Galley, Mr Halley, Mr Lalley, Mr Malley. And Mr Boffin.'

"'Strict system here; eh, my lad?' said Mr

Boffin, as he was booked.

"'Yes, sir,' returned the boy. 'I couldn't get on without it.'

"By which he probably meant that his mind would have been shattered to pieces without this fiction of an occupation. Wearing in his solitary confinement no fetters that he could polish, and being provided with no drinking-cup that he could carve, he had fallen on the device of ringing alphabetical changes into the two volumes in question, or of entering vast numbers of persons out of the Directory as transacting business with Mr Lightwood. It was the more necessary for his spirits, because, being of a sensitive temperament, he was apt to consider it personally disgraceful to himself that his master had no clients." OMF i 8

—*on vacation:* "It is the hottest long vacation known for many years. All the young clerks are madly in love, and, according to their various degrees, pine for bliss with the beloved object, at Margate, Ramsgate, or Gravesend. All the middle-aged clerks think their families too large . . . . Temple Bar gets so hot, that it is, to the adjacent Strand and Fleet Street, what a heater is in an urn, and keeps them simmering all night." BH 19

—*view of the work:* "'How do you like the law, Mr Micawber?'

"'My dear Copperfield,' he replied. 'To a man possessed of the higher imaginative powers, the objection to legal studies is the amount of detail which they involve. Even in our professional correspondence,' said Mr Micawber, glancing at some letters he was writing, 'the mind is not at liberty to soar to any exalted form of expression. Still, it is a great pursuit. A great pursuit!'" DC 39

There are 21 named clerks in Index IV *and 29 unnamed figures, singular and plural, in* Index VIII.

Law courts

" . . . we went out . . . leaving my aunt behind; who would trust herself, she said in no such place, and who, I think, regarded all Courts of Law as a sort of powder-mills that might blow up at any time." DC 23

—*in America:* "To an Englishman, accustomed to the paraphernalia of Westminster Hall, an American Court of Law, is as odd a sight as, I suppose, an English Court of Law would be to an American. Except in the Supreme Court at Washington (where the judges wear a plain black robe), there is no such thing as a wig or gown connected with the administration of justice.

"The gentlemen of the bar being barristers and attorneys too (for there is no division of those functions as in England) are no more removed from their clients than attorneys in our Court for the Relief of Insolvent Debtors are, from theirs. The jury are quite at home, and make themselves as comfortable as circumstances will permit. The witness is so little elevated above, or put aloof from, the crowd in the court, that a stranger entering during a pause in the proceedings would find it difficult to pick him out from the rest.

"And if it chanced to be a criminal trial, his eyes, in nine cases out of ten, would wander to the dock in search of the prisoner, in vain; for that gentleman would most likely be lounging among the most distinguished ornaments of the legal profession, whispering suggestions in his counsel's ear, or making a toothpick out of an old quill with his penknife." ¶AN 3

—*Chancery Court*

—*its destructiveness:* "This is the Court of Chancery; which has its decaying houses and its blighted lands in every shire; which has its worn-out lunatic in every madhouse, and its dead in every churchyard; which has its ruined suitor, with his slipshod heels and threadbare dress, borrowing and begging through the round of every man's acquaintance; which gives to monied might, the means abundantly of wearying out the right; which so exhausts finances, patience, courage, hope; so overthrows the brain and breaks the heart; that there is not an honourable man among its practitioners who would not give—who does not often give—the warning, 'Suffer any wrong that can be done you, rather than come here!'" BH 1

"To see everything going on so smoothly, and to think of the roughness of the suitors' lives and deaths; to see all that full dress and ceremony, and to think of the waste, and want, and beggared misery it represented; to consider that, while the sickness of hope deferred was raging in so many hearts, this polite show went calmly on from day to day, and year to year, in such good order and composure; to behold the Lord Chancellor, and the whole array of practitioners under him, looking at one another and at the spectators, as if nobody had ever heard that all over England the name in which they were assembled was a bitter jest: was held in universal horror, contempt, and indignation; was known for something so flagrant and bad, that little short of a miracle could bring any good out of it to any one: this was so curious and self-contradictory to me, who had no experience of it, that it was at first incredible, and I could not comprehend it." BH 24

And see B:House—*bleak, in Chancery*

—*in a fog:* "Never can there come fog too thick, never can there come mud and mire too deep, to assort with the groping and floundering condition which this High Court of Chancery, most pestilent of hoary sinners, holds, this day, in the sight of heaven and earth.

"On such an afternoon, if ever, the Lord High Chancellor ought to be sitting here—as here he is—with a foggy glory round his head, softly fenced in with crimson cloth and curtains, addressed by a large advocate with great whiskers, a little voice, and an interminable brief, and outwardly directing his contemplation to the lantern in the roof, where he can see nothing but fog.

"On such an afternoon, some score of members of the High Court of Chancery bar ought to be—as here they are—mistily engaged in one of the ten thousand stages of an endless cause, tripping one another up on slippery precedents, groping knee-deep in technicalities, running their goat-hair and horse-hair warded heads against walls of words, and making a pretence of equity with serious faces, as players might.

"On such an afternoon, the various solicitors in the cause, some two or three of whom have inherited it from their fathers, who made a fortune by it, ought to be—as are they not?—ranged in a line, in a long matted well (but you might look in vain for Truth at the bottom of it), between the registrar's red table and the silk gowns, with bills, cross-bills, answers, rejoinders, injunctions, affidavits, issues, references to masters, masters' reports, mountains of costly nonsense, piled before them.

"Well may the court be dim, with wasting candles here and there: well may the fog hang heavy in it, as if it would never get out; well may the stained glass windows lose their colour, and admit no light of day into the place; well may the uninitiated from the streets, who peep in through the glass panes in the door, be deterred from entrance by its owlish aspect, and by the drawl languidly echoing to the roof from the padded dais where the Lord High Chancellor looks into the lantern that has no light in it, and where the attendant wigs are all stuck in a fog-bank! " ¶BH 1

—*impact on litigants:* "'How can we stand amazed at poor Rick [Richard Carstone]? A young man so unfortunate,' here he fell into a lower tone, as if he were thinking aloud, 'cannot at first believe (who could?) that Chancery is what it is. He looks to it, flushed and fitfully, to do something with his interests, and bring them to some settlement. It procrastinates, disappoints, tries, tortures him; wears out his sanguine hopes and patience, thread by thread; but he still looks to it, and hankers after it, and finds his whole world treacherous and hollow.'" BH 35

—*proposal for reform:* "'There never was such an infernal cauldron as that Chancery, on the face of the earth!' said Mr Boythorn. 'Nothing but a mine below it on a busy day in term time, with all its records, rules, and precedents collected in it, and every functionary belonging to it also, high and low, upward and downward, from its son the Accountant-General to its father the Devil, and the whole blown to atoms with ten thousand hundred-weight of gunpowder, would reform it in the least!'" BH 9

—*its real estate:* "Jo lives—that is to say, Jo has not yet died—in a ruinous place, known to the like of him by the name of Tom-all-Alone's. It is a black, dilapidated street, avoided by all decent people; where the crazy houses were seized upon, when their decay was far advanced, by some bold vagrants, who, after establishing their own possession, took to letting them out in lodgings.

"Now, these tumbling tenements contain, by night, a swarm of misery. As, on the ruined human wretch, vermin parasites appear, so, these ruined shelters have bred a crowd of foul existence that crawls in and out of gaps in walls and boards; and coils itself to sleep, in maggot numbers, where the rain drips in; and comes and goes, fetching and carrying fever, and sowing more evil in its every footprint than Lord Coodle, and

Sir Thomas Doodle, and the Duke of Foodle, and the fine gentlemen in office, down to Zoodle, shall set right in five hundred years—though born expressly to do it.

"Twice, lately, there has been a crash and a cloud of dust, like the springing of a mine, in Tom-all-Alone's; and, each time, a house has fallen. These accidents have made a paragraph in the newspapers, and have filled a bed or two in the nearest hospital. The gaps remain, and there are not unpopular lodgings among the rubbish. As several more houses are nearly ready to go, the next crash in Tom-all-Alone's may be expected to be a good one." ¶BH 16

—workaday habit: "When we came to the court, there was the Lord Chancellor . . . sitting in great state and gravity, on the bench; with the mace and seals on a red table below him, and an immense flat nosegay, like a little garden, which scented the whole court. Below the table, again, was a long row of solicitors, with bundles of papers on the matting at their feet; and then there were the gentlemen of the bar in wigs and gowns—some awake and some asleep, and one talking, and nobody paying much attention to what he said. The Lord Chancellor leaned back in his very easy chair, with his elbow on the cushioned arm, and his forehead resting on his hand; some of those who were present, dozed; some read the newspapers; some walked about, or whispered in groups: all seemed perfectly at their ease, by no means in a hurry, very unconcerned, and extremely comfortable." BH 24

And see —Chancery Court—its destructiveness

—Coroner's inquest

—venue: "The Coroner is to sit in the first-floor room at the Sol's Arms, where the Harmonic Meetings take place twice a week, and where the chair is filled by a gentleman of professional celebrity, faced by Little Swills, the comic vocalist, who hopes (according to the bill in the window) that his friends will rally round him, and support first-rate talent. The Sol's Arms does a brisk stroke of business all the morning....

"At the appointed hour arrives the Coroner, for whom the Jurymen are waiting, and who is received with a salute of skittles from the good dry skittle-ground attached to the Sol's Arms.

"The Coroner frequents more public-houses than any man alive. The smell of sawdust, beer, tobacco-smoke, and spirits, is inseparable in his vocation from death in its most awful shapes. He is conducted by the beadle and the landlord to the Harmonic Meeting Room, where he puts his hat on the piano, and takes a Windsor-chair at the head of a long table, formed of several short tables put together, and ornamented with glutinous rings in endless involutions, made by pots and glasses.

"As many of the Jury as can crowd together at the table sit there. The rest get among the spittoons and pipes, or lean against the piano. Over the Coroner's head is a small iron garland, the pendant handle of a bell, which rather gives the Majesty of the Court the appearance of going to be hanged presently.

"Call over and swear the Jury! While the ceremony is in progress, sensation is created by the entrance of . . . Little Swills. It is considered not unlikely that he will get up an imitation of the Coroner, and make it the principal feature of the Harmonic Meeting in the evening." ¶BH 11

—witness: "I remember, too, how hard [the accused's] mistress was upon her (she was a servant-of-all-work), and with what a cruel pertinacity that piece of Virtue spun her thread of evidence double, by intertwisting it with the sternest thread of construction." UT/RM

—criminal courts

—bail, and trial: "Mr Sampson [Brass], then, being detained . . . by the justice upon whom he called, and being so strongly pressed to protract his stay that he could by no means refuse, remained under his protection for a considerable time, during which the great attention of his entertainer kept him so extremely close, that he was quite lost to society, and never even went abroad for exercise saving into a small paved yard. So well, indeed, was his modest and retiring temper understood by those with whom he had to deal, and so jealous were they of his absence, that they required a kind of friendly bond to be entered into by two substantial housekeepers, in the sum of fifteen hundred pounds a-piece, before they would

suffer him to quit their hospitable roof—doubting, it appeared, that he would return, if once let loose, on any other terms. Mr Brass, struck with the humour of this jest, and carrying out its spirit to the utmost, sought from his wide connection a pair of friends whose joint possessions fell some halfpence short of fifteen pence, and proffered them as bail—for that was the merry word agreed upon on both sides. These gentlemen being rejected after twenty-four hours' pleasantry, Mr Brass consented to remain, and did remain until a club of choice spirits called a Grand Jury (who were in the joke) summoned him to a trial before twelve other wags for perjury and fraud, who in their turn found him guilty with a most facetious joy . . . . " OCS 73

—collective sentencing: "At that time it was the custom (as I learnt from my terrible experience of that Sessions) to devote a concluding day to the passing of Sentences, and to make a finishing effect with the Sentence of Death. But for the indelible picture that my remembrance now holds before me, I could scarcely believe, even as I write these words, that I saw two-and-thirty men and women put before the Judge to receive that sentence together. Foremost among the two-and-thirty was [Magwitch]; seated, that he might get breath enough to keep life in him.

"The whole scene starts out again in the vivid colours of the moment, down to the drops of April rain on the windows of the court, glittering in the rays of April sun. Penned in the dock, as I again stood outside it at the corner with his hand in mine, were the two-and-thirty men and women; some defiant, some stricken with terror, some sobbing and weeping, some covering their faces, some staring gloomily about. There had been shrieks from among the women convicts, but they had been stilled, and a hush had succeeded. The sheriffs with their great chains and nosegays, other civic gewgaws and monsters, criers, ushers, a great gallery full of people—a large theatrical audience—looked on, as the two-and-thirty and the Judge were solemnly confronted....

"The sun was striking in at the great windows of the court, through the glittering drops of rain upon the glass, and it made a broad shaft of light between the two-and-thirty and the Judge, linking both together, and perhaps reminding some among the audience, how both were passing on, with absolute equality, to the greater Judgment that knoweth all things and cannot err." GE 56

—mirror: "Over the prisoner [Darnay]'s head there was a mirror, to throw the light down upon him. Crowds of the wicked and the wretched had been reflected in it, and had passed from its surface and this earth's together. Haunted in a most ghastly manner that abominable place would have been, if the glass could ever have rendered back its reflections, as the ocean is one day to give up its dead." TTC ii 2

—monotony: "Through all the monotony of six of those interminable ten days—the same Judges and others on the bench, the same Murderer in the dock, the same lawyers at the table, the same tones of question and answer rising to the roof of the Court, the same scratching of the Judge's pen, the same ushers going in and out, the same lights kindled at the same hour when there had been any natural light of day, the same foggy curtain outside the great windows when it was foggy, the same rain pattering and dropping when it was rainy, the same footmarks of turnkeys and prisoner day after day on the same sawdust, the same keys locking and unlocking the same heavy doors—through all the wearisome monotony which made me feel as if I had been Foreman of the Jury for a vast period of time, and Piccadilly had flourished coevally with Babylon, the murdered man never lost one trace of his distinctness in my eyes, nor was he at any moment less distinct than anybody else." CS/DM 2

—Old Bailey: "Curiosity has occasionally led us into both Courts at the Old Bailey. Nothing is so likely to strike the person who enters them for the first time, as the calm indifference with which the proceedings are conducted; every trial seems a mere matter of business. There is a great deal of form, but no compassion; considerable interest, but no sympathy.

"Take the Old Court for example. There sit the Judges, with whose great dignity everybody is acquainted, and of whom therefore we need say no more. Then, there is the Lord Mayor in the centre, looking as cool as a Lord Mayor can look, with an immense *bouquet* before him, and habited in all the splendour of his office. Then, there are the Sheriffs, who are almost as dignified as the

Lord Mayor himself; and the Barristers, who are quite dignified enough in their own opinion; and the spectators, who having paid for their admission, look upon the whole scene as if it were got up especially for their amusement.

"Look upon the whole group in the body of the Court—some wholly engrossed in the morning papers, others carelessly conversing in low whispers, and others, again, quietly dozing away an hour—and you can scarcely believe that the result of the trial is a matter of life or death to one wretched being present . . . .

"[The jury] resume their places—a dead silence prevails as the foreman delivers in the verdict—'Guilty!' A shriek bursts from a female in the gallery; the prisoner casts one look at the quarter from whence the noise proceeded; and is immediately hurried from the dock by the gaoler. The clerk directs one of the officers of the Court to 'take the woman out,' and fresh business is proceeded with, as if nothing had occurred." SB/CC

—typical specimen: "It was a dirty frowsy room, at the upper end of which was a raised platform railed off from the rest, with a dock for the prisoners on the left hand against the wall, a box for the witnesses in the middle, and a desk for the magistrates on the right; the awful locality last named, being screened off by a partition which concealed the bench from the common gaze, and left the vulgar to imagine (if they could) the full majesty of justice.

"There were only a couple of women in the dock, who were nodding to their admiring friends, while the clerk read some depositions to a couple of policemen and a man in plain clothes who leant over the table. A jailer stood reclining against the dockrail, tapping his nose listlessly with a large key, except when he repressed an undue tendency to conversation among the idlers, by proclaiming silence; or looked sternly up to bid some woman 'Take the baby out,' when the gravity of justice was disturbed by feeble cries, half-smothered in the mother's shawl, from some meagre infant.

"The room smelt close and unwholesome; the walls were dirt-discoloured; and the ceiling blackened. There was an old smoky bust over the mantel-shelf, and a dusty clock above the dock—the only thing present, that seemed to go on as it ought; for depravity, or poverty, or an habitual acquaintance with both, had left a taint on all the animate matter, hardly less unpleasant than the thick greasy scum on every inanimate object that frowned upon it." ¶OT 43

—Doctors' Commons

—appraisal: "Now Doctors' Commons being familiar by name to everybody, as the place where they grant marriage-licenses to love-sick couples, and divorces to unfaithful ones; register the wills of people who have any property to leave, and punish hasty gentlemen who call ladies by unpleasant names . . . . " SB/DC

—atmosphere: "Mr Spenlow conducted me through a paved courtyard formed of grave brick houses, which I inferred, from the Doctors' names upon the doors, to be the official abiding-places of the learned advocates of whom Steerforth had told me; and into a large, dull room, not unlike a chapel to my thinking, on the left hand. The upper part of this room was fenced off from the rest; and there, on the two sides of a raised platform of the horse-shoe form, sitting on easy old-fashioned dining-room chairs, were sundry gentlemen in red gowns and gray wigs, whom I found to be the Doctors aforesaid.

"Blinking over a little desk like a pulpit-desk, in the curve of the horseshoe, was an old gentleman, whom, if I had seen him in an aviary, I should certainly have taken for an owl, but who, I learned, was the presiding judge. In the space within the horse-shoe, lower than these, that is to say on about the level of the floor, were sundry other gentlemen of Mr Spenlow's rank, and dressed like him in black gowns with white fur upon them, sitting at a long green table. Their cravats were in general stiff, I thought, and their looks haughty; but in this last respect, I presently conceived I had done them an injustice, for when two or three of them had to rise and answer a question of the presiding dignitary, I never saw anything more sheepish.

"The public, represented by a boy with a comforter, and a shabby-genteel man secretly eating crumbs out of his coat pockets, was warming itself at a stove in the centre of the Court. The languid stillness of the place was only broken by the chirping of this fire and by the voice of one of the Doctors, who was wandering slowly through a perfect library of evidence, and stopping to put up, from time to time, at a little roadside inns of argument on the journey. Altogether, I have never, on any occasion, made one at such a cosey, dosey, old-fashioned, time-forgotten, sleepy-headed little family-party in all my life; and I felt it would be quite a soothing opiate to belong to it in any character—except perhaps as a suitor." DC 23

—a candid view: "I can tell you best what [a proctor] is, [said Steerforth] by telling you what Doctors' Commons is. It's a little out-of-the-way place, where they administer what is called ecclesiastical law, and play all kinds of tricks with obsolete old monsters of acts of Parliament, which three-fourths of the world know nothing about, and the other fourth supposes to have been dug up, in a fossil state, in the days of the Edwards. It's a place that has an ancient monopoly in suits about people's wills and people's marriages, and disputes among ships and boats.

"'Nonsense, Steerforth!' I exclaimed. 'You don't mean to say that there is any affinity between nautical matters and ecclesiastical matters?'

"'I don't indeed, my dear boy,' he returned; 'but I mean to say that they are managed and decided by the same set of people, down in that same Doctors' Commons. You shall go there one day, and find them blundering through half the nautical terms in Young's Dictionary, apropos of the "Nancy" having run down the "Sarah Jane", or Mr Peggotty and the Yarmouth boatmen having put off in a gale of wind with an anchor and cable to the "Nelson" Indiaman in distress; and you shall go there another day, and find them deep in the evidence, pro and con., respecting a clergyman who has misbehaved himself; and you shall find the judge in the nautical case, the advocate in the clergyman's case, or contrariwise. They are like actors: now a man's a judge, and now he is not a judge; now he's one thing, now he's another; now he's something else, change and change about; but it's always a very pleasant, profitable little affair of private theatricals, presented to an uncommonly select audience.'" DC 23

—and the national interest: "I asked Mr Spenlow what he considered the best sort of professional business? He replied, that a good case of a disputed will, where there was a neat little estate of thirty or forty thousand pounds was, perhaps, the best of all. In such a case, he said, not only were there very pretty pickings, in the way of arguments at every stage of the proceedings, and mountains upon mountains of evidence on interrogatory and counter-interrogatory (to say nothing of an appeal lying, first to the Delegates, and then to the Lords); but, the costs being pretty sure to come out of the estate at last, both sides went at it in a lively and spirited manner, and expense was no consideration.

"Then, he launched into a general eulogium on the Commons. What was to be particularly admired (he said) in the Commons, was its compactness. It was the most conveniently organised place in the world. It was the complete idea of snugness. It lay in a nut-shell. For example: You brought a divorce case, or a restitution case, into the Consistory. Very good. You tried it in the Consistory. You made a quiet little round game of it, among a family group, and you played it out at leisure. Suppose you were not satisfied with the Consistory, what did you do then? Why, you went into the Arches. What was the Arches? The same court, in the same room, with the same bar, and the same practitioners, but another judge, for there the Consistory judge could plead any court-day as an advocate.

"Well, you played your round game out again. Still you were not satisfied. Very good. What did you do then? Why, you went to the Delegates. Who were the Delegates? Why, the Ecclesiastical Delegates were the advocates without any business, who had looked on at the round game when it was playing in both courts, and had seen the cards shuffled, and cut, and played, and had talked to all the players about it, and now came fresh, as judges, to settle the matter to the satisfaction of everybody!

"'Discontented people might talk of corruption in the Commons, closeness in the Commons, and the necessity of reforming the Commons,' said Mr Spenlow solemnly, in conclusion; 'but when the price of wheat per bushel had been highest, the Commons had been busiest; and a man might lay his hand upon his heart, and say this to the whole world,—'Touch the Commons, and down comes the country!'

"I listened to all this with attention; and though, I must say, I had my doubts whether the country was quite as much obliged to the Commons as Mr Spenlow made out., I respectfully deferred to his opinion. That about the price of wheat per bushel, I modestly felt was too much for my strength, and quite settled the question.

"I have never, to this hour, got the better of that bushel of wheat. It has reappeared to annihilate me, all through my life, in connexion with all kinds of subjects. I don't know now, exactly, what it has to do with me, or what right it has to crush me, on an infinite variety of occasions; but whenever I see my old friend the bushel brought in by the head and shoulders (as he always is, I observe), I give up a subject for lost." ¶DC 26

—*habeas corpus:* "Well, Sam,' said Mr Pickwick, 'I suppose they are getting the habeas corpus ready.'

"'Yes,' said Sam, 'and I vish they'd bring out the have-his-carcase. It's wery unpleasant keepin' us vaitin' here. I'd ha' got half a dozen have-his-carcases ready, pack'd up and all, by this time.'" PP 40

—*Insolvent Court*

—*protagonists:* "In a lofty room, ill-lighted and worse ventilated, situate in Portugal Street, Lincoln's Inn Fields, there sit nearly the whole year round, one, two, three, or four gentlemen in wigs, as the case may be, with little writing desks before them, constructed after the fashion of those used by the judges of the land, barring the French polish. There is a box of barristers on their right hand; there is an inclosure of insolvent debtors on their left; and there is an inclined plane of most especially dirty faces in their front. These gentlemen are the Commissioners of the Insolvent Court, and the place in which they sit, is the Insolvent Court itself." PP 43

—*observers:* "It is, and has been, time out of mind, the remarkable fate of this Court to be, somehow or other, held and understood, by the general consent of all the destitute shabby-genteel people in London, as their common resort, and place of daily refuge. It is always full. The steams of beer and spirits perpetually ascend to the ceiling, and, being condensed by the heat, roll down the walls like rain; there are more old suits of clothes in it at one time, than will be offered for sale in all Houndsditch in a twelvemonth; more unwashed skins and grizzly beards than all the pumps and shaving-shops between Tyburn and Whitechapel could render decent, between sunrise and sunset.

"It must not be supposed that any of these people have the least shadow of business in, or the remotest connection with, the place they so indefatigably attend. If they had, it would be no matter of surprise, and the singularity of the thing would cease. Some of them sleep during the greater part of the sitting; others carry small portable dinners wrapped in pocket-handkerchiefs or sticking out of their worn-out pockets, and munch and listen with equal relish; but no one among them was ever known to have the slightest personal interest in any case that was ever brought forward. Whatever they do, there they sit from the first moment to the last. When it is heavy rainy weather, they all come in, wet through; and at such times the vapours of the Court are like those of a fungus-pit." PP 43

Lawsuits

—*Bardell against Pickwick*

—*plaintiff's entrance:* " . . . Mrs Bardell, supported by Mrs Cluppins, was led in, and placed, in a drooping state, at the other end of the seat on which Mr Pickwick sat . . . . Mrs Sanders then appeared, leading in Master Bardell. At sight of her child, Mrs Bardell started; suddenly recollecting herself, she kissed him in a frantic manner; then relapsing into a state of hysterical imbecility, the good lady requested to be informed where she was. In reply to this, Mrs Cluppins and Mrs Sanders turned their heads away and wept, while Messrs. Dodson and Fogg intreated the plaintiff to compose herself. Serjeant Buzfuz rubbed his eyes very hard with a large white handkerchief, and gave an appealing look towards the jury, while the judge was visibly affected, and several of the beholders tried to cough down their emotions.

"'Very good notion that, indeed,' whispered Perker to Mr Pickwick. 'Capital fellows those Dodson and Fogg; excellent ideas of effect, my dear sir, excellent.'

" . . . Mrs Bardell began to recover by slow degrees, while Mrs Cluppins, after a careful survey of Master Bardell's buttons and the button-holes to which they severally belonged, placed him on the floor of the court in front of his mother—a commanding position in which he could not fail to awaken the full commiseration and sympathy of both judge and jury. This was not done without considerable opposition, and many tears, on the part of the young gentleman himself, who had certain inward misgivings that the placing him within the full glare of the judge's eye was only a formal prelude to his being immediately ordered away for instant execution, or for transportation beyond the seas, during the whole term of his natural life, at the very least." PP 34

—a barrister speaks: "Serjeant Buzfuz began by saying, that never, in the whole course of his professional experience—never, from the very first moment of his applying himself to the study and practice of the law—had he approached a case with feelings of such deep emotion, or with such a heavy sense of the responsibility imposed upon him—a responsibility, he would say, which he could never have supported, were he not buoyed up and sustained by a conviction so strong, that it amounted to positive certainty that the cause of truth and justice, or, in other words, the cause of his much-injured and most oppressed client, must prevail with the high-minded and intelligent dozen of men whom he now saw in that box before him.

"Counsel usually begin in this way, because it puts the jury on the very best terms with themselves, and makes them think what sharp fellows they must be. A visible effect was produced immediately; several jurymen beginning to take voluminous notes with the utmost eagerness . . . .

"'The plaintiff, gentlemen,' continued Serjeant Buzfuz, in a soft and melancholy voice, 'the plaintiff is a widow; yes, gentlemen, a widow. The late Mr Bardell, after enjoying for many years, the esteem and confidence of his sovereign, as one of the guardians of his royal revenues, glided almost imperceptibly from the world, to seek elsewhere for that repose and peace which a custom-house can never afford.'

"At this pathetic description of the decease of Mr Bardell, who had been knocked on the head with a quart-pot in a public-house cellar, the learned serjeant's voice faltered, and he proceeded with emotion:

"'Some time before his death, he had stamped his likeness upon a little boy. With this little boy, the only pledge of her departed exciseman, Mrs Bardell shrunk from the world, and courted the retirement and tranquillity of Goswell Street; and here she placed in her front parlour-window a written placard, bearing this inscription—"Apartments furnished for a single gentleman. Inquire within . . . .

"'I intreat the attention of the jury to the wording of this document. "Apartments furnished for a single gentleman"! Mrs Bardell's opinions of the opposite sex, gentlemen, were derived from a long contemplation of the inestimable qualities of her lost husband. She had no fear, she had no distrust, she had no suspicion, all was confidence and reliance.

"'"Mr Bardell," said the widow; "Mr Bardell was a man of honour, Mr Bardell was a man of his word, Mr Bardell was no deceiver, Mr Bardell was once a single gentleman himself; *to* single gentlemen I look for protection, for assistance, for comfort, and for consolation; *in* single gentlemen I shall perpetually see something to remind me of what Mr Bardell was, when he first won my young and untried affections; to a single gentleman, then, shall my lodgings be let."

"'Actuated by this beautiful and touching impulse (among the best impulses of our imperfect nature, gentlemen), the lonely and desolate widow dried her tears, furnished her first floor, caught the innocent boy to her maternal bosom, and put the bill up in her parlour-window. Did it remain there long? No. The serpent was on the watch, the train was laid, the mine was preparing, the sapper and miner was at work. Before the bill had been in the parlour-window three days—three days—gentlemen—a Being, erect upon two legs, and bearing all the outward semblance of a man, and not of a monster, knocked at the door of Mrs Bardell's house. He inquired within; he took the lodgings; and on the very next day he entered into possession of them. This man was Pickwick—Pickwick, the defendant ....

"'Of this man Pickwick I will say little; the subject presents but few attractions; and I, gentlemen, am not the man, nor are you, gentlemen, the men, to delight in the contemplation of revolting heartlessness, and of systematic villany [*sic.*] . . . . " PP 34

And see LC:Communication—*letters in a lawsuit*

"'But enough of this, gentlemen,' said Mr Serjeant Buzfuz, 'it is difficult to smile with an aching heart; it is ill jesting when our deepest sympathies are awakened. My client's hopes and prospects are ruined, and it is no figure of speech to say that her occupation is gone indeed. The bill is down—but there is no tenant. Eligible single gentlemen pass and repass—but there is no invitation for them to inquire within or without. All is gloom and silence in the house; even the voice of the child is hushed; his infant sports are disregarded when his mother weeps . . . . But Pickwick, gentlemen, Pickwick, the ruthless destroyer of this domestic oasis in the desert of Goswell Street—Pickwick, who has choked up the well, and thrown ashes on the sward—Pickwick, who comes before you to-day with his heartless Tomata sauce and warming-pans—Pickwick still rears his head with unblushing effrontery, and gazes without a sigh on the ruin he has made.

"'Damages, gentlemen—heavy damages—is the only punishment with which you can visit him; the only recompence you can award to my client. And for those damages she now appeals to an enlightened, a high-minded, a right-feeling, a conscientious, a dispassionate, a sympathising, a contemplative jury of her civilised countrymen.' With this beautiful peroration, Mr Serjeant Buzfuz sat down, and Mr Justice Stareleigh woke up." ¶PP 34

—witnesses

—effective for the defense: "Serjeant Buzfuz now rose with more importance than he had yet exhibited, if that were possible, and vociferated: 'Call Samuel Weller.'

"It was quite unnecessary to call Samuel Weller; for Samuel Weller stepped briskly into the box the instant his name was pronounced; and placing his hat on the floor, and his arms on the rail, took a bird's-eye view of the bar, and a comprehensive survey of the bench, with a remarkably cheerful and lively aspect.

"'What is your name, sir?' inquired the judge.

"'Sam Weller, my lord,' replied the gentleman.

"'Do you spell it with a "V" or a "W?"' inquired the judge.

"'That depends upon the taste and fancy of the speller, my lord,' replied Sam. 'I never had occasion to spell it more than once or twice in my life, but I spells it with a "V."'

"Here a voice in the gallery exclaimed aloud, 'Quite right too, Samivel, quite right. Put it down a we, my lord, put it down a we.'

"'Who is that, who dares to address the court?' said the little judge, looking up. 'Usher.'

"'Yes, my lord.'

"'Bring that person here instantly.'

"'Yes, my lord.'

"But as the usher didn't find the person, he didn't bring him; and, after a great commotion, all the people who had got up to look for the culprit, sat down again. The little judge turned to the witness as soon as his indignation would allow him to speak, and said,

"'Do you know who that was, sir?'

"'I rayther suspect it was my father, my lord,' replied Sam.

"'Do you see him here now?' said the judge.

"'No, I don't, my lord,' replied Sam, staring right up into the lantern in the roof of the court.

"'If you could have pointed him out, I would have committed him instantly,' said the judge.

"Sam bowed his acknowledgments, and turned with unimpaired cheerfulness of countenance towards Serjeant Buzfuz.

"'Now, Mr Weller,' said Serjeant Buzfuz.

"'Now, sir,' replied Sam.

"'I believe you are in the service of Mr Pickwick, the defendant in this case. Speak up, if you please, Mr Weller.'

"'I mean to speak up, sir,' replied Sam; 'I am in the service o' that 'ere gen'l'man, and a wery good service it is.'

"'Little to do, and plenty to get, I suppose?' said Serjeant Buzfuz, with jocularity.

"'Oh, quite enough to get, sir, as the soldier said ven they ordered him three hundred and fifty lashes,' replied Sam.

"'You must not tell us what the soldier, or any other man, said, sir,' interposed the judge; 'it's not evidence.'

"'Wery good, my lord,' replied Sam.

"'Do you recollect anything particular happening on the morning when you were first engaged by the defendant; eh, Mr Weller?' said Serjeant Buzfuz.

"'Yes I do, sir,' replied Sam.

"'Have the goodness to tell the jury what it was.'

"'I had a reg'lar new fit out o' clothes that mornin', gen'l'men of the jury,' said Sam, 'and that was a wery partickler and uncommon circumstance vith me in those days.'

"Hereupon there was a general laugh; and the little judge, looking with an angry countenance over his desk, said, 'You had better be careful, sir.'

"'So Mr Pickwick said at the time, my lord,' replied Sam; 'and I was wery careful o' that 'ere suit o' clothes; wery careful indeed, my lord.'

"The judge looked sternly at Sam for full two minutes, but Sam's features were so perfectly calm and serene that the judge said nothing, and motioned Serjeant Buzfuz to proceed.

"'Do you mean to tell me, Mr Weller,' said Serjeant Buzfuz, folding his arms emphatically, and turning half-round to the jury, as if in mute assurance that he would bother the witness yet: 'Do you mean to tell me, Mr Weller, that you saw nothing of this fainting on the part of the plaintiff in the arms of the defendant, which you have heard described by the witnesses?'

"'Certainly not,' replied Sam. 'I was in the passage 'till they called me up, and then the old lady was not there.'

"'Now, attend, Mr Weller,' said Serjeant Buzfuz, dipping a large pen into the inkstand before him, for the purpose of frightening Sam with a show of taking down his answer. 'You were in the passage, and yet saw nothing of what was going forward. Have you a pair of eyes, Mr Weller?'

"'Yes, I have a pair of eyes,' replied Sam, 'and that's just it. If they wos a pair o' patent double million magnifyin' gas microscopes of hextra power, p'raps I might be able to see through a flight o' stairs and a deal door; but bein' only eyes, you see, my wision's limited.'

"At this answer, which was delivered without the slightest appearance of irritation, and with the most complete simplicity and equanimity of manner, the spectators tittered, the little judge smiled, and Serjeant Buzfuz looked particularly foolish. After a short consultation with Dodson and Fogg, the learned Serjeant again turned towards Sam, and said, with a painful effort to conceal his vexation, 'Now, Mr Weller, I'll ask you a question on another point, if you please.'

"'If you please, sir,' rejoined Sam, with the utmost good-humour.

"'Do you remember going up to Mrs Bardell's house, one night in November last?'

"'Oh yes, very well.'

"'Oh, you *do* remember that, Mr Weller,' said Serjeant Buzfuz, recovering his spirits; 'I thought we should get at something at last.'

"I rayther thought that, too, sir,' replied Sam; and at this the spectators tittered again.

"'Well; I suppose you went up to have a little talk about this trial—eh, Mr Weller?' said Serjeant Buzfuz, looking knowingly at the jury.

"'I went up to pay the rent; but we *did* get a talkin' about the trial, replied Sam.

"'Oh, you did get a talking about the trial,' said Serjeant Buzfuz, brightening up with the anticipation of some important discovery. 'Now what passed about the trial; will you have the goodness to tell us, Mr Weller?'

"'Vith all the pleasure in life, sir,' replied Sam. 'Arter a few unimportant observations from the two wirtuous females as has been examined here to-day, the ladies gets into a wery great state o' admiration at the honourable conduct of Mr Dodson and Fogg—them two gen'l'men as is settin' near you now.' This, of course, drew general attention to Dodson and Fogg, who looked as virtuous as possible.

"'The attorneys for the plaintiff,' said Mr Serjeant Buzfuz. 'Well! They spoke in high praise of the honourable conduct of Messrs Dodson and Fogg, the attorneys for the plaintiff, did they?'

"'Yes,' said Sam 'they said what a wery gen'rous thing it was o' them to have taken up the case on spec, and to charge nothing at all for costs, unless they got 'em out of Mr Pickwick.'

"At this very unexpected reply, the spectators tittered again, and Dodson and Fogg, turning very red, leant over to Serjeant Buzfuz, and in a hurried manner whispered something in his ear.

"'You are quite right,' said Serjeant Buzfuz aloud, with affected composure. 'It's perfectly useless, my lord, attempting to get any evidence through the impenetrable stupidity of the witness. I will not trouble the court by asking him any more questions. Stand down, sir.'

"'Would any other gen'l'man like to ask me anything'?' inquired Sam, taking up his hat, and looking round most deliberately.

"'Not I, Mr Weller, thank you,' said Serjeant Snubbin, laughing.

"'You may go down, sir,' said Serjeant Buzfuz, waving his hand impatiently. Sam went down accordingly, after doing Messrs Dodson and Fogg's case as much harm as he conveniently could, and saying just as little respecting Mr Pickwick as might be, which was precisely the object he had had in view all along.'" PP 34

—feckless for the defense: "'Now, sir,' said Mr Skimpin, 'have the goodness to let his Lordship and the jury know what your name is, will you?' and Mr Skimpin inclined his head on one side to listen with great sharpness to the answer, and glanced at the jury meanwhile, as if to imply that he rather expected Mr Winkle's natural taste for perjury would induce him to give some name which did not belong to him.

"'Winkle,' replied the witness.

"'What's your Christian name, sir?' angrily inquired the little judge.

"'Nathaniel, sir,'

"'Daniel—any other name?'

"'Nathaniel, sir—my Lord, I mean.'

"'Nathaniel Daniel, or Daniel Nathaniel?'

"'No, my Lord, only Nathaniel; not Daniel at all.'

"'What did you tell me it was Daniel for, then, sir?' inquired the judge.

"'I didn't, my Lord,' replied Mr Winkle.

"'You did, sir,' replied the judge, with a severe frown. 'How could I have got Daniel on my notes, unless you told me so, sir?'

"This argument, was, of course, unanswerable. PP 34

—for the plaintiff: " . . . when [Mrs Cluppins] was safely perched on the top step, Mrs Bardell stood on the bottom one, with the pocket-handkerchief and pattens in one hand, and a glass bottle that might hold about a quarter of a pint of smelling salts in the other, ready for any emergency. Mrs Sanders, whose eyes were intently fixed on the judge's face, planted herself close by, with the large umbrella: keeping her right thumb pressed on the spring with an earnest countenance, as if she were fully prepared to put it up at a moment's notice.

"'Mrs Cluppins,' said Serjeant Buzfuz, 'pray compose yourself, ma'am.' Of course, directly Mrs Cluppins was desired to compose herself she sobbed with increased vehemence, and gave divers alarming manifestations of an approaching fainting fit, or, as she afterwards said, of her feelings being too many for her . . . .

"'What were you doing in the back room, ma'am?' inquired the little judge.

"'My Lord and Jury,' said Mrs Cluppins, with interesting agitation, 'I will not deceive you.'

"'You had better not, ma'am,' said the little judge.

"'I was there,' resumed Mrs Cluppins, 'unbeknown to Mrs Bardell; I had been out with a little basket, gentlemen, to buy three pound of red kidney purtaties, which was three pound tuppence ha'penny, when I see Mrs Bardell's street door on the jar.'

"'On the what?' exclaimed the little judge.

"'Partly open, my Lord,' said Serjeant Snubbin.

"'She *said* on the jar,' said the little judge, with a cunning look.

"'It's all the same, my Lord,' said Serjeant Snubbin. The little judge looked doubtful, and said he'd make a note of it. Mrs Cluppins then resumed:

"'I walked in, gentlemen, just to say good mornin', and went, in a permiscuous manner, up stairs, and into the back room. Gentlemen, there was the sound of voices in the front room, and—'

"'And you listened, I believe, Mrs Cluppins?' said Serjeant Buzfuz.

"'Beggin' your pardon, sir,' replied Mrs

Cluppins, in a majestic manner, 'I would scorn the haction. The voices was very loud, sir, and forced themselves upon my ear.'" PP 34

—in Doctors' Commons

—ecclesiastical: "We had an adjourned cause in the Consistory that day—about excommunicating a baker who had been objecting in a vestry to a paving-rate—and as the evidence was just twice the length of *Robinson Crusoe,* according to a calculation I made, it was rather late in the day before we finished. However, we got him excommunicated for six weeks, and sentenced in no end of costs; and then the baker's proctor, and the judge, and the advocates on both sides (who were all nearly related), went out of town together . . . . " DC 29

" . . . as we had another little excommunication case in court that morning, which was called The office of the Judge promoted by Tipkins against Bullock for his soul's correction, I passed an hour or two in attendance on it with Mr Spenlow very agreeably. It arose out of a scuffle between two churchwardens, one of whom was alleged to have pushed the other against a pump; the handle of which pump projecting into a school-house, which school-house was under a gable of the church-roof, made the push an ecclesiastical offence.." DC 29

—matrimonial: " . . . we had a divorce-suit coming on, under an ingenious little statute (repealed now, I believe, but in virtue of which I have seen several marriages annulled), of which the merits were these. The husband, whose name was Thomas Benjamin, had taken out his marriage licence as Thomas only; suppressing the Benjamin, in case he should not find himself as comfortable as he expected. *Not* finding himself as comfortable as he expected, or being a little fatigued with his wife, poor fellow, he now came forward, by a friend, after being married a year or two, and declared that his name was Thomas Benjamin, and therefore he was not married at all. Which the Court confirmed, to his great satisfaction." DC 33

—Matter of Gridley

"'I am one of two brothers. My father (a farmer) made a will, and left his farm and stock, and so forth, to my mother, for her life. After my mother's death, all was to come to me, except a legacy of three hundred pounds that I was then to pay my brother. My mother died. My brother, some time afterwards, claimed his legacy. I, and some of my relations, said that he had had a part of it already, in board and lodging, and some other things. Now mind! That was the question, and nothing else. No one disputed the will; no one disputed anything but whether part of that three hundred pounds had been already paid or not. To settle that question, my brother filing a bill, I was obliged to go into this accursed Chancery; I was forced there, because the law forced me, and would let me go nowhere else.

"'Seventeen people were made defendants to that simple suit! It first came on, after two years. It was then stopped for another two years, while the Master (may his head rot off!) inquired whether I was my father's son—about which there was no dispute at all with any mortal creature. He then found out that there were not defendants enough—remember, there were only seventeen as yet!—but that we must have another who had been left out; and must begin all over again. The costs at that time—before the thing was begun!—were three times the legacy.

"My brother would have given up the legacy, and joyful, to escape more costs. My whole estate, left to me in that will of my father's, has gone in costs. The suit, still undecided, has fallen into rack, and ruin, and despair, with everything else . . . . '" ¶BH 15

—Jarndyce and Jarndyce

—called: "When we had been there half an hour or so, the case in progress—if I may use a phrase so ridiculous in such a connection—seemed to die out of its own vapidity, without coming, or being by anybody expected to come, to any result. The Lord Chancellor then threw down a bundle of papers from his desk to the gentlemen below him, and somebody said, 'JARNDYCE AND JARNDYCE.' Upon this there was a buzz, and a laugh, and a general withdrawal of the by-standers, and a bringing in of great heaps, and piles, and bags and bagsfull of papers." BH 24

—characterized by a party: "'I am grieved [said Ada Clare] that I should be the enemy—as I suppose I am—of a great number of relations and others; and that they should be my enemies—as I suppose they are; and that we should all be ruining one another, without knowing how or why, and be in constant doubt and discord all our

lives. It seems very strange, as there must be right somewhere, that an honest judge in real earnest has not been able to find out through all these years where it is.'" BH 5

—characterized by a suitor: "'I don't know who does [understand it],' [John Jarndyce] returned. 'The Lawyers have twisted it into such a state of bedevilment that the original merits of the case have long disappeared from the face of the earth. It's about a Will, and the trusts under a Will—or it was, once. It's about nothing but Costs, now. We are always appearing, and disappearing, and swearing, and interrogating, and filing, and cross-filing, and arguing, and sealing, and motioning, and referring, and reporting, and revolving about the Lord Chancellor and all his satellites, and equitably waltzing ourselves off to dusty death, about Costs. That's the great question. All the rest, by some extraordinary means, has melted away.'" BH 8

—confusion confounded: "Jarndyce and Jarndyce drones on. This scarecrow of a suit has, in course of time, become so complicated, that no man alive knows what it means. The parties to it understand it least; but it has been observed that no two Chancery lawyers can talk about it for five minutes, without coming to a total disagreement as to all the premises. Innumerable children have been born into the cause; innumerable young people have married into it; innumerable old people have died out of it. Scores of persons have deliriously found themselves made parties in Jarndyce and Jarndyce, without knowing how or why; whole families have inherited legendary hatreds with the suit.

"The little plaintiff or defendant, who was promised a new rocking-horse when Jarndyce and Jarndyce should be settled, has grown up, possessed himself of a real horse, and trotted away into the other world. Fair wards of court have faded into mothers and grandmothers; a long procession of Chancellors has come in and gone out; the legion of bills in the suit have been transformed into mere bills of mortality; there are not three Jarndyces left upon the earth perhaps, since old Tom Jarndyce in despair blew his brains out at a coffee-house in Chancery Lane; but Jarndyce and Jarndyce still drags its dreary length before the court, perennially hopeless.

"Jarndyce and Jarndyce has passed into a joke. That is the only good that has ever come of it. It has been death to many, but it is a joke in the profession. Every master in Chancery has had a reference out of it. Every Chancellor was 'in it,' for somebody or other, when he was counsel at the bar. Good things have been said about it by blue-nosed, bulbous-shoed old benchers, in select port-wine committee after dinner in hall. Articled clerks have been in the habit of fleshing their legal wit upon it. The last Lord Chancellor handled it neatly when, correcting Mr Blowers, the eminent silk gown who said that such a thing might happen when the sky rained potatoes, he observed, 'or when we get through Jarndyce and Jarndyce, Mr Blowers;'—a pleasantry that particularly tickled the maces, bags, and purses." ¶BH 1

—corrupting: "How many people out of the suit Jarndyce and Jarndyce has stretched forth its unwholesome hand to spoil and corrupt, would be a very wide question. From the master, upon whose impaling files reams of dusty warrants in Jarndyce and Jarndyce have grimly writhed into many shapes, down to the copying-clerk in the Six Clerks' Office, who has copied his tens of thousands of Chancery-folio-pages under that eternal heading; no man's nature has been made better by it. In trickery, evasion, procrastination, spoliation, botheration, under false pretences of all sorts, there are influences that can never come to good.

"The very solicitors' boys who have kept the wretched suitors at bay, by protesting time out of mind that Mr Chizzle, Mizzle, or otherwise, was particularly engaged, and had appointments until dinner, may have got an extra moral twist and shuffle into themselves out of Jarndyce and Jarndyce. The receiver in the cause has acquired a goodly sum of money by it, but has acquired too a distrust for his own mother, and a contempt for his own kind.

"Chizzle, Mizzle, and otherwise, have lapsed into a habit of vaguely promising themselves that they will look into that outstanding little matter, and see what can be done for Drizzle—who was not well used—when Jarndyce and Jarndyce shall be got out of the office. Shirking and sharking, in all their many varieties, have been sown broadcast by the ill-fated cause; and even those who have contemplated its history from the outermost circle of such evil, have been insensibly tempted into a loose way of letting bad things alone to take their own bad course, and a loose belief that if the world go wrong, it was, in some off-hand manner, never meant to go right." BH 1

—famous, and revered by some: "'Is it possible,' pursued Mr Kenge, putting up his eyeglasses, 'that our young friend [Esther Summerson] . . . never heard of Jarndyce and Jarndyce! . . . . Not of one of the greatest Chancery suits known? Not of Jarndyce and Jarndyce—the—a—in itself a monument of Chancery practice. In which (I would say) every difficulty, every contingency, every masterly fiction, every form of procedure known in that court, is represented over and over again? It is a cause that could not exist, out of this free and great country. I should say that the aggregate of costs in Jarndyce and Jarndyce, Mrs Rachael; I was afraid he addressed himself to her, because I appeared inattentive; 'amounts at the present hour to from SIX-ty to SEVEN-ty THOUSAND POUNDS!" said Mr Kenge, leaning back in his chair." BH 3

—history: "'A certain Jarndyce, in an evil hour, made a great fortune, and made a great will. In the question how the trusts under that will are to be administered, the fortune left by the will is squandered away; the legatees under the will are reduced to such a miserable condition that they would be sufficiently punished, if they had committed an enormous crime in having money left them; and the will itself is made a dead letter.

"All through the deplorable cause, everything that everybody in it, except one man, knows already, is referred to that only one man who don't know it, to find out—all through the deplorable cause, everybody must have copies, over and over again, of everything that has accumulated about it in the way of cartloads of papers (or must pay for them without having them, which is the usual course, for nobody wants them); and must go down the middle and up again, through such an infernal country-dance of costs and fees and nonsense and corruption, as was never dreamed of in the wildest visions of a Witch's Sabbath.

"Equity sends questions to Law, Law sends questions back to Equity; Law finds it can't do this, Equity finds it can't do that; neither can so much as say it can't do anything, without this solicitor instructing and this counsel appearing for A, and that solicitor instructing and that counsel appearing for B; and so on through the whole alphabet, like the history of the Apple Pie. And thus, through years and years, and lives and lives, everything goes on, constantly beginning over and over again, and nothing ever ends. And we can't get out of the suit on any terms, for we are made parties to it, and *must be* parties to it, whether we like it or not.'" ¶BH 8

—at last, for the nonce: "'Several members of the bar are still to be heard, I believe?' says the Chancellor, with a slight smile.

"Eighteen of Mr Tangle's learned friends, each armed with a little summary of eighteen hundred sheets, bob up like eighteen hammers in a pianoforte, make eighteen bows, and drop into their eighteen places of obscurity.

"'We will proceed with the hearing on Wednesday fortnight,' says the Chancellor. For the question at issue is only a question of costs, a mere bud on the forest tree of the parent suit, and really will come to a settlement one of these days.

"The Chancellor rises; the bar rises . . . . The man from Shropshire ventures another demonstrative 'My lord!' but the Chancellor, being aware of him, has dexterously vanished. Everybody else quickly vanishes too. A battery of blue bags is loaded with heavy charges of papers and carried off by clerks; the little mad old woman marches off with her documents; the empty court is locked up. If all the injustice it has committed, and all the misery it has caused, could only be locked up with it, and the whole burnt away in a great funeral pyre—why so much the better for other parties than the parties in Jarndyce and Jarndyce!." BH 1

—at last, truly: " . . . when we came to Westminster Hall, we found that the day's business was begun. Worse than that, we found such an unusual crowd in the Court of Chancery that it was full to the door, and we could neither see nor hear what was passing within. It appeared to be something droll, for occasionally there was a laugh, and a cry of 'Silence!' It appeared to be something interesting, for every one was pushing and striving to get nearer. It appeared to be something that made the professional gentlemen very merry, for there were several young counsellors in wigs and whiskers on the outside of the crowd, and when one of them told the others about it, they put their hands in their pockets, and quite doubled themselves up with laughter, and went stamping about the pavement of

the hall.

"We asked a gentleman by us, if he knew what cause was on? He told us Jarndyce and Jarndyce. We asked him if he knew what was doing in it? He said, really no he did not, nobody ever did; but as well as he could make out, it was over. Over for the day? we asked him. No, he said; over for good.

"Over for good!

"When we heard this unaccountable answer, we looked at one another quite lost in amazement. Could it be possible that the will had set things right at last, and that Richard and Ada were going to be rich? It seemed too good to be true. Alas, it was!

"Our suspense was short; for a break up soon took place in the crowd, and the people came streaming out looking flushed and hot, and bringing a quantity of bad air with them. Still they were all exceedingly amused, and were more like people coming out from a Farce or a Juggler than from a court of Justice. We stood aside, watching for any countenance we knew; and presently great bundles of paper began to be carried out—bundles in bags, bundles too large to be got into any bags, immense masses of papers of all shapes and no shapes, which the bearers staggered under, and threw down for the time being, anyhow, on the Hall pavement, while they went back to bring out more. Even these clerks were laughing. We glanced at the papers, and seeing Jarndyce and Jarndyce everywhere, asked an official-looking person who was standing in the midst of them, whether the cause was over. 'Yes,' he said; 'it was all up with it at last!' and burst out laughing too. . . .

"'You are to reflect, Mr Woodcourt,' observed Mr Kenge, using his silver trowel, persuasively and smoothingly, 'that this has been a great cause, that this has been a protracted cause, that this has been a complex cause. Jarndyce and Jarndyce has been termed, not inaptly, a Monument of Chancery practice.'

"'And Patience has sat upon it a long time,' said Allan.

"'Very well indeed, sir,' returned Mr Kenge, with a certain condescending laugh he had. 'Very well! You are further to reflect, Mr Woodcourt,' becoming dignified almost to severity, 'that on the numerous difficulties, contingencies, masterly fictions, and forms of procedure in this great cause, there has been expended study, ability, eloquence, knowledge, intellect, Mr Woodcourt, high intellect. For many years, the—a—I would say the flower of the Bar, and the—a—I would presume to add, the matured autumnal fruits of the Woolsack—have been lavished upon Jarndyce and Jarndyce. If the public have the benefit, and if the country have the adornment, of this great Grasp, it must be paid for in money or money's worth, sir.'

"'Mr Kenge,' said Allan, appearing enlightened all in a moment. 'Excuse me, our time presses. Do I understand that the whole estate is found to have been absorbed in costs?'

"'Hem! I believe so,' returned Mr Kenge. 'Mr Vholes, what do *you* say?'

"'I believe so,' said Mr Vholes.

"'And that thus the suit lapses and melts away?'

"'Probably,' returned Mr Kenge. 'Mr Vholes?'

"'Probably,' said Mr Vholes." BH 65

—a lawyer's breakthrough: "'You see, my dear Copperfield, [said Traddles]', falling into the low confidential tone, 'after I had delivered my argument in DOE *dem.* JIPES *versus* WIGZELL, which did me great service with the profession. . . .'" DC 59

Lawyer

—adaptable: "We were a little like undertakers, in the Commons, as regarded Probate transactions; generally making it a rule to look more or less cut up, when we had to deal with clients in mourning. In a similar feeling of delicacy, we were always blithe and light-hearted with the licence clients." DC 33

—adulated: " . . . Mr Spenlow's proctorial gown and stiff cravat took Peggotty down a little, and inspired her with a greater reverence for the man who was gradually becoming more and more etherealized in my eyes every day, and about whom a reflected radiance seemed to me to beam when he sat erect in Court among his papers, like a little lighthouse in a sea of stationery." DC 33

—advocate, in Doctors' Commons: "'But advocates and proctors are not one and the same?' said I, a little puzzled. 'Are they?'

"'No,' returned Steerforth, 'the advocates are civilians—men who have taken a doctor's degree at college—which is the first reason of my knowing anything about it. The proctors employ the advocates. Both get very comfortable fees, and altogether they make a mighty snug little party. On the whole, I would recommend you to take to Doctors' Commons kindly, David. They plume themselves on their gentility there, I can tell you, if that's any satisfaction.'" DC 23 *And see* SB/DC

—aged: "Like a dingy London bird among the birds at roost in these pleasant fields, where the sheep are all made into parchment, the goats into wigs, and the pasture into chaff, the lawyer [Tulkinghorn], smoke-dried and faded, dwelling among mankind but not consorting with them, aged without experience of genial youth, and so long used to make his cramped nest in holes and corners of human nature that he has forgotten its broader and better range, comes sauntering home. In the oven made by the hot pavements and hot buildings, he has baked himself dryer than usual; and he has, in his thirsty mind, his mellowed port-wine, half a century old." BH 42

—American: "The learned gentleman (like a few of his English brethren) was desperately long-winded, and had a remarkable capacity of saying the same thing over and over again . . . . I listened to him for about a quarter of an hour; and, coming out of court at the expiration of that time, without the faintest ray of enlightenment as to the merits of the case, felt as if I were at home again." AN 3

—business-getting: "There were a number of hangers-on and outsiders about the [Doctors'] Commons, who, without being proctors themselves, dabbled in common-form business, and got it done by real proctors, who lent their names in consideration of a share in the spoil;— and there were a good many of these too. As our house now wanted business on any terms, we joined this noble band; and threw out lures to the hangers-on and outsiders, to bring their business to us.

"Marriage licences and small probates were what we all looked for, and what paid us best; and the competition for these ran very high indeed. Kidnappers and inveiglers were planted in all the avenues of entrance to the Commons, with instructions to do their utmost to cut off all persons in mourning, and all gentlemen with anything bashful in their appearance, and entice them to the offices in which their respective employers were interested; which instructions were so well observed, that I myself, before I was known by sight, was twice hustled into the premises of our principal opponent.

"The conflicting interests of these touting gentlemen being of a nature to irritate their feelings, personal collisions took place; and the Commons was even scandalised by our principal inveigler (who had formerly been in the wine trade, and afterwards in the sworn brokery line) walking about for some days with a black eye. Any one of these scouts used to think nothing of politely assisting an old lady in black out of a vehicle, killing any proctor whom she inquired for, representing his employer as the lawful successor and representative of that proctor, and bearing the old lady off (sometimes greatly affected) to his employer's office. Many captives were brought to me in this way.

"As to marriage licences, the competition rose to such a pitch, that a shy gentleman in want of one, had nothing to do but submit himself to the first inveigler, or be fought for, and become the prey of the strongest. One of our clerks, who was an outsider, used, in the height of this contest, to sit with his hat on, that he might be ready to rush out and swear before a surrogate any victim who was brought in.

"The system of inveigling continues, I believe, to this day. The last time I was in the Commons, a civil able-bodied person in a white apron pounced out upon me from a doorway, and whispering the word 'Marriage-licence' in my ear, was with great difficulty prevented from taking me up in his arms and lifting me into a proctor's." DC ¶39 *And see* A:Matrimony—*licence*

—chambers

—converted: "Here, in a large house [in Lincoln's Inn Fields], formerly a house of state, lives Mr Tulkinghorn. It is let off in sets of chambers now; and in those shrunken fragments of its greatness, lawyers lie like maggots in nuts." BH 10

—exotic presence: "The fact is, when— was it you that tumbled up-stairs . . . ?

"'It was,' said I, laughing.

"'Well then, when you tumbled up-stairs,' said Traddles, 'I was romping with the girls. In point of fact, we were playing at Puss in the Corner. But as that wouldn't do in Westminster Hall, and as it wouldn't look quite professional if they were seen by a client, they decamped . . . . The society of girls is a very delightful thing, Copperfield. It's not professional, but it's very delightful'. . . .

"They were a perfect nest of roses; they looked so wholesome and fresh. They were all pretty, and Miss Caroline was very handsome . . . .

"Altogether, it was a scene I could not help dwelling on with pleasure, for a long time after I got back and had wished Traddles good-night. If I had beheld a thousand roses blowing in a top set of chambers, in that withered Gray's Inn, they could not have brightened it half so much. The idea of those Devonshire girls, among the dry law-stationers and the attorneys' offices; and of the tea and toast, and children's songs, in that grim atmosphere of pounce and parchment, red-tape, dusty wafers, ink-jars, brief and draft paper, law reports, writs, declarations, and bills of costs, seemed almost as pleasantly fanciful as if I had dreamed that the Sultan's famous family had been admitted on the roll of attorneys, and had brought the talking bird, the singing tree, and the golden water into Gray's Inn Hall." DC 59

—outer bulwark: "[The chambers] were an upper set on a rotten staircase, with a mysterious bunk or bulkhead on the landing outside them, of a rather nautical and Screw Collier-like appearance than otherwise, and painted an intense black. Many dusty years have passed since the appropriation of this Davy Jones's locker to any purpose, and during the whole period within the memory of living man, it has been hasped and padlocked. I cannot quite satisfy my mind whether it was originally meant for the reception of coals, or bodies, or as a place of temporary security for the plunder 'looted' by laundresses; but I incline to the last opinion. It is about breast high, and usually serves as a bulk for defendants in reduced circumstances to lean against and ponder at, when they come on the hopeful errand of trying to make an arrangement without money—under which auspicious circumstances it mostly happens that the legal gentleman they want to see, is much engaged, and they pervade the staircase for a considerable period." UT/C

—inner truth: "Against this opposing bulk [of bulkhead] . . . the tomb-like outer door of the solicitor's chambers (which is also of an intense black) stands in dark ambush, half open, and half shut, all day. The solicitor's apartments are three in number; consisting of a slice, a cell, and a wedge. The slice is assigned to the two clerks, the cell is occupied by the principal, and the wedge is devoted to stray papers, old game baskets from the country, a washing-stand, and a model of a patent Ship's Caboose which was exhibited in Chancery at the commencement of the present century on an application for an injunction to restrain infringement." UT/C

And see F:Loneliness—*of chambers; and* L:Law inns

—and children: "'Put the case that he lived in an atmosphere of evil, and that all he saw of children was, their being generated in great numbers for certain destruction. Put the case that he often saw children solemnly tried at a criminal bar, where they were held up to be seen; put the case that he habitually knew of their being imprisoned, whipped, transported, neglected, cast out, qualified in all ways for the hangman, and growing up to be hanged. Put the case that pretty nigh all the children he saw in his daily business life, he had reason to look upon as so much spawn, to develop into the fish that were to come to his net—to be prosecuted, defended, forsworn, made orphans, bedevilled somehow.'" GE 51

—and client: "Mr Vholes, and his young client, and several blue bags, hastily stuffed out of all regularity of form, as the larger sort of serpents are in their first gorged state, have returned to the official den. Mr Vholes, quiet and unmoved, as a man of so much respectability ought to be, takes off his close black gloves as if he were skinning his hands, lifts off his tight hat as if he were scalping himself, and sits down at his desk. The client throws his hat and gloves upon the ground—tosses them anywhere, without looking after them or caring where they go; flings himself into a chair, half-sighing and half-groaning; rests his aching head upon his hand, and looks the portrait of *Young Despair.*" BH 39

—in Common Pleas: " . . . a numerous muster of gentlemen in wigs, in the barristers' seats: who presented, as a body, all that pleasing and extensive variety of nose and whisker for which the bar of England is so justly celebrated. Such of the gentlemen as had a brief to carry, carried it in as conspicuous a manner as possible, and occasionally scratched their noses therewith, to impress the fact more strongly on the observation of the spectators.

"Other gentlemen, who had no briefs to show, carried under their arms goodly octavos, with a red label behind, and that underdone-pie-crust-coloured cover, which is technically known as 'law-calf.' Others, who had neither briefs nor books, thrust their hands into their pockets, and looked as wise as they conveniently could; others, again, moved here and there with great restlessness and earnestness of manner, content to awaken thereby the admiration and astonishment of the uninitiated strangers." PP 34

—cynical: "'Gentlemen of your profession, sir,' continued Mr Pickwick, 'see the worst side of human nature. All its disputes, all its ill-will and bad blood, rise up before you. You know from your experience of juries (I mean no disparagement to you, or them) how much depends upon *effect:* and you are apt to attribute to others, a desire to use, for purposes of deception and self-interest, the very instruments which you, in pure honesty and honour of purpose, and with a laudable desire to do your utmost for your client, know the temper and worth of so well, from constantly employing them yourselves. I really believe that to this circumstance may be attributed the vulgar but very general notion of your being, as a body, suspicious, distrustful, and over-cautious.'" PP 31

—despised by love: " . . . those dim old judges and doctors wouldn't have cared for Dora, if they had known her . . . Dora might have sung and played upon that glorified guitar, until she led *me* to the verge of madness, yet not have tempted one of those slow-goers an inch out of his road!

"I despised them, to a man. Frozen-out old gardeners in the flower-beds of the heart, I took a personal offence against them all. The Bench was nothing to me but an insensible blunderer. The Bar had no more tenderness or poetry in it than the bar of a public-house." DC 33

—devouring eyes: "'Sir,' returned Vholes, always looking at the client, as if he were making a lingering meal of him with his eyes as well as with his professional appetite." BH 39

—his dining-room: "There was a bookcase in [Jaggers's] room; I saw from the backs of the books, that they were about evidence, criminal law, criminal biography, trials, acts of parliament, and such things. The furniture was all very solid and good, like his watch-chain. It had an official look, however, and there was nothing merely ornamental to be seen. In a corner was a little table of papers with a shaded lamp; so that he seemed to bring the office home with him in that respect too, and to wheel it out of an evening and fall to work." GE 26

—discreet: "He comes towards them at his usual methodical pace, which is never quickened, never slackened. He wears his usual expressionless mask—if it be a mask—and carries family secrets in every limb of his body, and every crease of his dress. Whether his whole soul is devoted to the great, or whether he yields them nothing beyond the services he sells, is his personal secret. He keeps it, as he keeps the secrets of his clients; he is his own client in that matter, and will never betray himself." BH 12

—examining a witness: "Then up comes Mr Brass, very brisk and fresh; and, having bowed to the judge, like a man who has had the pleasure of seeing him before, and who hopes he has been pretty well since their last meeting, folds his arms, and looks at his gentleman as much as to say 'Here I am—full of evidence—Tap me!' And the gentleman does tap him presently, and with great discretion too; drawing off the evidence by little and little, and making it run quite clear and bright in the eyes of all present." OCS 63

"Mr Guppy, who has an inquiring mind in matters of evidence, and who has been suffering severely from the lassitude of the long vacation, takes that interest in the case, that he enters on a regular cross-examination of the witness . . . Jo is requested to follow into the drawing-room doorway, where Mr Guppy takes him in hand as a witness, patting him into this shape, that shape, and the other shape, like a butterman dealing with so much butter, and worrying him according to the best models. Nor is the examination unlike many such model displays, both in respect of its eliciting nothing, and of its being lengthy . . . . " BH 19

—flatterer: "It was a maxim with Mr Brass that the habit of paying compliments kept a man's tongue oiled without any expense; and, as that useful member ought never to grow rusty or creak in turning on its hinges in the case of a practitioner of the law, in whom it should be always glib and easy, he lost few opportunities of improving himself by the utterance of handsome speeches and eulogistic expressions. And this had passed into such a habit with him, that, if he could not be correctly said to have his tongue at

his fingers' ends, he might certainly be said to have it anywhere but in his face: which being . . . of a harsh and repulsive character, was not oiled so easily, but frowned above all the smooth speeches—one of nature's beacons, warning off those who navigated the shoals and breakers of the World, or of that dangerous strait the Law, and admonishing them to seek less treacherous harbours and try their fortune elsewhere." OCS 35

—*fomenting litigation:* "'And of them Dodson and Foggs, as does these sort o' things on spec,' continued Mr Weller, 'as well as for the other kind and gen'rous people o' the same purfession, as sets people by the ears, free gratis for nothin', and sets their clerks to work to find out little disputes among their neighbours and acquaintances as vants settlin' by means o' law-suits—all I can say o' them is, that I vish they had the revard I'd give 'em.'" PP 26

—*"gentleman:"* "'Gentlemen, I appeal to you—really, gentlemen—consider, I beg of you. I am of the law. I am styled "gentleman" by Act of Parliament. I maintain the title by the annual payment of twelve pound sterling for a certificate. I am not one of your players of music, stage actors, writers of books, or painters of pictures, who assume a station that the laws of their country don't recognise. I am none of your strollers or vagabonds. If any man brings his action against me, he must describe me as a gentleman, or his action is null and void.'" OCS 60

—*getting paid:* "' . . . when I ultimately congratulate you, sir [said Mr Vholes] , with all my heart, on your accession to fortune—which, but that I never give hopes, I might say something further about—you will owe me nothing, beyond whatever little balance may be then outstanding of the costs as between solicitor and client, not included in the taxed costs allowed out of the estate. I pretend to no claim upon you, Mr C., but for the zealous and active discharge—not the languid and routine discharge, sir: that much credit I stipulate for—of my professional duty. My duty prosperously ended, all between us is ended.'

"Vholes finally adds, by way of rider to this declaration of his principles, that as Mr Carstone is about to rejoin his regiment, perhaps Mr C. will favour him with an order on his agent for twenty pounds on account." BH 39

"The client, with his dejection insensibly relieved, and his vague hopes rekindled, takes pen and ink and writes the draft; not without perplexed consideration and calculation of the date it may bear, implying scant effects in the agent's hands. All the while, Vholes, buttoned up in body and mind, looks at him attentively. All the while, Vholes's official cat watches the mouse's hole.

" . . . . Thus they part; and Vholes, left alone, employs himself in carrying sundry little matters out of his diary into his draft bill book, for the ultimate behoof of his three daughters. So might an industrious fox, or bear, make up his account of chickens or stray travellers with an eye to his cubs; not to disparage by that word the three raw-visaged, lank, and buttoned-up maidens, who dwell with the parent Vholes in an earthy cottage situated in a damp garden at Kennington." BH 39

—*heartless:* "Whether he be cold and cruel, whether immovable in what he has made his duty, whether absorbed in love of power, whether determined to have nothing hidden from him in ground where he has burrowed among secrets all his life, whether he in his heart despises the splendour of which he is a distant beam, whether he is always treasuring up slights and offences in the affability of his gorgeous clients—whether he be any of this, or all of this, it may be that my Lady had better have five thousand pairs of fashionable eyes upon her, in distrustful vigilance, than the two eyes of this rusty lawyer, with his wisp of neckcloth and his dull black breeches tied with ribbons at the knees." BH 29

—*imperturbable:* "His imperturbable face has been as inexpressive as his rusty clothes. One could not even say he has been thinking all this while. He has shown neither patience nor impatience, nor attention nor abstraction. He has shown nothing but his shell. As easily might the tone of a delicate musical instrument be inferred from its case, as the tone of Mr Tulkinghorn from *his* case." BH 11

—*for an innocent:* "'I should have got a lawyer [said Mr George] and he would have said (as I have often read in the newspapers), "my client says nothing, my client reserves his defence—my client this, that, and t'other." Well, 'tis not the custom of that breed to go straight, according to my opinion, or to think that other men do. Say, I am innocent, and I get a lawyer. He would be as likely to believe me guilty as not; perhaps more. What would he do, whether or not? Act as if I was—shut my mouth up, tell me not to commit myself, keep circumstances back, chop the evidence small, quibble, and get me off perhaps! . . .

"'I would rather be hanged in my own way. And I mean to be! I don't intend to say . . . that I am more partial to being hanged than another man. What I say is, I must come off clear and full or not at all. Therefore, when I hear stated against me what is true, I say it's true; and when they tell me, "whatever you say will be used," I tell them I don't mind that; I mean it to be used. If they can't make me innocent out of the whole truth, they are not likely to do it out of anything less, or anything else. And if they are, it's worth nothing to me.'" BH 52

—inquisitive: "' . . . we lawyers are always curious, always inquisitive, always picking up odds and ends for our patchwork minds, since there is no knowing when and where they may fit into some corner . . . . '" LD ii 12

—for insolvents: " . . . the attorneys, who sit at a large bare table below the Commissioners [for the Insolvent Court] are, after all, the greatest curiosities. The professional establishment of the more opulent of these gentlemen, consists of a blue bag and a boy: generally a youth of the Jewish persuasion. They have no fixed offices, their legal business being transacted in the parlours of public-houses, or the yards of prisons: whither they repair in crowds, and canvass for customers after the manner of omnibus cads. They are of a greasy and mildewed appearance; and if they can be said to have any vices at all, perhaps drinking and cheating are the most conspicuous among them. Their residences are usually on the outskirts of 'the Rules,' chiefly lying within a circle of one mile from the obelisk in St George's Fields. Their looks are not prepossessing, and their manners are peculiar." PP 43

—intimidating: " . . . my guardian had a woman under examination or cross-examination—I don't know which—and was striking her, and the bench, and everybody with awe. If anybody, of whatsoever degree, said a word that he didn't approve of, he instantly required to have it 'taken down.' If anybody wouldn't make an admission, he said, 'I'll have it out of you!' and if anybody made an admission, he said, 'Now I have got you!' The magistrates shivered under a single bite of his finger. Thieves and thief-takers hung in dread rapture on his words, and shrank when a hair of his eyebrows turned in their direction. Which side he was on I couldn't make out, for he seemed to me to be grinding the whole place in a mill; I only know that when I stole out on tiptoe he was not on the side of the bench; for he was making the legs of the old gentleman who presided quite convulsive under the table, by his denunciations of his conduct as the representative of British law and justice in that chair that day." GE 24

—manner: " . . . I said to Wemmick that I hardly knew what to make of Mr Jaggers's manner.

"'Tell him that, and he'll take it as a compliment,' answered Wemmick; 'he don't mean that you *should* know what to make of it—Oh!' for I looked surprised, 'it's not personal; it's professional; only professional.'

"Wemmick was at his desk, lunching—and crunching—on a dry, hard biscuit; pieces of which he threw from time to time into his slit of a mouth, as if he were posting them.

"'Always seems to me,' said Wemmick, 'as if he had set a man-trap and was watching it. Suddenly—click—you're caught!'" GE 24

And see W:Australia*—in metaphor*

—in necessity "'I yielded from necessity to Quilp [said Brass], for though necessity has no law, she has her lawyers." OCS 66

—office

—city, borderline: "There was not much to look at. A rickety table, with spare bundles of papers, yellow and ragged from long carriage in the pocket, ostentatiously displayed upon its top; a couple of stools set face to face on opposite sides of this crazy piece of furniture; a treacherous old chair by the fireplace, whose withered arms had hugged full many a client and helped to squeeze him dry; a second-hand wig-box, used as a depository for blank writs and declarations and other small forms of law, once the sole contents of the head which belonged to the wig which belonged to the box, as they were now of the box itself; two or three common books of practice; a jar of ink, a pounce-box, a stunted hearth-broom, a carpet trodden to shreds but still clinging with the tightness of desperation to its tacks—these, with the yellow wainscot of the walls, the smoke-discoloured ceiling, the dust and cobwebs, were among the most

prominent decorations of the office of Mr Sampson Brass." OCS 33

—city, struggling: "Mr Vholes's office, in disposition retiring and in situation retired, is squeezed up in a corner, and blinks at a dead wall. Three feet of knotty floored dark passage bring the client to Mr Vholes's jet black door, in an angle profoundly dark on the brightest midsummer morning, and encumbered by a black bulk-head of cellarage staircase, against which belated civilians generally strike their brows.

"Mr Vholes's chambers are on so small a scale, that one clerk can open the door without getting off his stool, while the other who elbows him at the same desk has equal facilities for poking the fire. A smell as of unwholesome sheep, blending with the smell of must and dust, is referable to the nightly (and often daily) consumption of mutton fat in candles, and to the fretting of parchment forms and skins in greasy drawers. The atmosphere is otherwise stale and close.

"The place was last painted or whitewashed beyond the memory of man, and the two chimneys smoke, and there is a loose outer surface of soot everywhere, and the dull cracked windows in their heavy frames have but one piece of character in them, which is a determination to be always dirty, and always shut, unless coerced. This accounts for the phenomenon of the weaker of the two usually having a bundle of firewood thrust between its jaws in hot weather." ¶BH 39

—city, successful: " . . . within ten minutes after he had received the assurance that the thing was impossible, [Mr Pickwick] was conducted by his solicitor into the outer office of the great Serjeant Snubbin himself.

"It was an uncarpeted room of tolerable dimensions, with a large writing-table drawn up near the fire: the baize top of which had long since lost all claim to its original hue of green, and had gradually grown grey with dust and age, except where all traces of its natural colour were obliterated by ink-stains. Upon the table were numerous little bundles of papers tied with red tape; and behind it, sat an elderly clerk, whose sleek appearance, and heavy gold watch-chain, presented imposing indications of the extensive and lucrative practice of Mr Serjeant Snubbin . . . .

" . . . [Mallard] shortly returned on tiptoe, and informed Mr Perker and Mr Pickwick that the Serjeant had been prevailed upon, in violation of all established rules and customs, to admit them at once.

" . . . . Books of practice, heaps of papers, and opened letters, were scattered over the table, without any attempt at order or arrangement; the furniture of the room was old and ricketty; the doors of the book-case were rotting on their hinges; the dust flew out from the carpet in little clouds at every step; the blinds were yellow with age and dirt; the state of everything in the room showed, with a clearness not to be mistaken, that Mr Serjeant Snubbin was far too much occupied with his professional pursuits to take any great heed or regard of his personal comforts." PP 31

—country: "The offices of Messrs Snitchey and Craggs stood convenient, with an open door down two smooth steps, in the market-place; so that any angry farmer inclining towards hot water, might tumble into it at once.

"Their special council-chamber and hall of conference was an old back-room up-stairs, with a low dark ceiling, which seemed to be knitting its brows gloomily in the consideration of tangled points of law. It was furnished with some high-backed leathern chairs, garnished with great goggle-eyed brass nails, of which, every here and there, two or three had fallen out—or had been picked out, perhaps, by the wandering thumbs and forefingers of bewildered clients.

"There was a framed print of a great judge in it, every curl in whose dreadful wig had made a man's hair stand on end. Bales of papers filled the dusty closets, shelves, and tables; and round the wainscot there were tiers of boxes, padlocked and fire-proof, with people's names painted outside, which anxious visitors felt themselves, by a cruel enchantment, obliged to spell backwards and forwards, and to make anagrams of, while they sat, seeming to listen to Snitchey and Craggs, without comprehending one word of what they said." ¶BL 2

—dingy: "And a mighty yellow jaundiced little office Mr Fips had of it; with a great, black, sprawling splash upon the floor in one corner, as if some old clerk had cut his throat there years ago, and had let out ink instead of blood." MC 39

—proctor's: "Doctors' Commons was approached by a little low archway. Before we

had taken many paces down the street beyond it, the noise of the city seemed to melt, as if by magic, into a softened distance. A few dull courts and narrow ways brought us to the sky-lighted offices of Spenlow and Jorkins; in the vestibule of which temple, accessible to pilgrims without the ceremony of knockng, three or four clerks were at work as copyists . . . .

"As we were left to look about us while Mr Spenlow was fetched, I availed myself of the opportunity. The furniture of the room was old-fashioned and dusty; and the green baize on the top of the writing-table had lost all its colour, and was as withered and pale as an old pauper. There were a great many bundles of papers on it, some indorsed as Allegations, and some (to my surprise) as Libels, and some as being in the Consistory Court, and some in the Arches Court, and some in the Prerogative Court, and some in the Admiralty Court, and some in the Delegates' Court; giving me occasion to wonder much, how many Courts there might be in the gross, and how long it would take to understand them all. Besides these, there were sundry immense manuscript Books of Evidence taken on affidavit, strongly bound, and tied together in massive sets, a set to each cause, as if every cause were a history in ten or twenty volumes. All this looked tolerably expensive, I thought, and gave me an agreeable notion of a proctor's business." DC 23

And see L:Law inns

—persuasive: "The engaging young Barnacle was the first arrival; but Bar overtook him on the staircase. Bar, strengthened as usual with his double eye-glass and his little jury droop, was overjoyed to see the engaging young Barnacle . . . .

"Bar could be light in hand, or heavy in hand, according to the customer he had to deal with. With Ferdinand Barnacle he was gossamer. Bar was likewise always modest and self-depreciatory—in his way. Bar was a man of great variety; but one leading thread ran through the woof of all his patterns. Every man with whom he had to do was in his eyes, a juryman; and he must get that juryman over, if he could." LD ii 12

"Bar, who had a bit of one eye and a bit of his double eye-glass for every one who came in at the door, no matter with whom he was conversing or what he was talking about, got among them all by some skilful means, without being seen to get at them, and touched each individual gentleman of the jury on his own individual favourite spot." LD ii 12

—process and prerogative: "'Now, my dear sir—my dear sir . . . pray, allow me—my dear sir, the very first principle to be observed in these cases, is this: if you place a matter in the hands of a professional man, you must in no way interfere in the progress of the business; you must repose implicit confidence in him . . . I shall be happy to receive any private suggestions of yours, as *amicus curiae,* but you must see the impropriety of your interfering with my conduct in this case, with such an *ad capitandum* argument as the offer of half a guinea. Really, my dear sir, really;' and the little man took an argumentative pinch of snuff, and looked very profound.

"'My only wish, sir,' said Mr Pickwick, 'was to bring this very unpleasant matter to as speedy a close as possible . . . . With which view . . . I made use of the argument which my experience of men has taught me is the most likely to succeed in any case.'

"'Ay, ay,' said the little man, 'very good, very good, indeed; but you should have suggested it to *me.* My dear sir, I'm quite certain you cannot be ignorant of the extent of confidence which must be placed in professional men. If any authority can be necessary on such a point, my dear sir, let me refer you to the well-known case in Barnwell and—' " PP 10

—proctor, Doctors' Commons: "'What *is* a proctor, Steerforth?' said I.

"'Why, he is a sort of monkish attorney,' replied Steerforth. 'He is, to some faded courts held in Doctors' Commons—a lazy old nook near St Paul's Churchyard—what solicitors are to the courts of law and equity. He is a functionary whose existence, in the natural course of things, would have terminated about two hundred years ago." DC 23

—to be protected: "But, not perceiving [the great principle of the English law—to "make business for itself"] quite plainly—only seeing it by halves in a confused way—the laity sometimes suffer in peace and pocket, with a bad grace, and *do* grumble very much. Then this respectability of Mr Vholes is brought into powerful play against them. 'Repeal this statute, my good sir?' says Mr Kenge, to a smarting client, 'repeal it, my dear sir? Never, with my consent. Alter this law, sir, and what will be the effect of

your rash proceeding on a class of practitioners very worthily represented, allow me to say to you, by the opposite attorney in the case, Mr Vholes? Sir, that class of practitioners would be swept from the face of the earth.

"Now you cannot afford—I will say, the social system cannot afford—to lose an order of men like Mr Vholes. Diligent, persevering, steady, acute in business. My dear sir, I understand your present feelings against the existing state of things, which I grant to be a little hard in your case; but I can never raise my voice for the demolition of a class of men like Mr Vholes.'

"The respectability of Mr Vholes has even been cited with crushing effect before Parliamentary committees, as in the following blue minutes of a distinguished attorney's evidence. 'Question (number five hundred and seventeen thousand eight hundred and sixty-nine). If I understand you, these forms of practice indisputably occasion delay? Answer. Yes, some delay. Question. And great expense? Answer. Most assuredly they cannot be gone through for nothing. Question. And unspeakable vexation? Answer. I am not prepared to say that. They have never given *me* any vexation; quite the contrary. Question. But you think that their abolition would damage a class of practitioners? Answer. I have no doubt of it. Question. Can you instance any type of that class? Answer. Yes. I would unhesitatingly mention Mr Vholes. He would be ruined. Question. Mr Vholes is considered, in the profession, a respectable man? Answer'— which proved fatal to the inquiry for ten years—'Mr Vholes is considered, in the profession, a *most* respectable man.'

"So in familiar conversation, private authorities no less disinterested will remark that they don't know what this age is coming to; that we are plunging down precipices; that now here is something else gone; that these changes are death to people like Vholes: a man of undoubted respectability, with a father in the Vale of Taunton, and three daughters at home. Take a few steps more in this direction, say they, and what is to become of Vholes's father? Is he to perish? And of Vholes's daughters? Are they to be shirt-makers, or governesses? As though, Mr Vholes and his relations being minor cannibal chiefs, and it being proposed to abolish cannibalism, indignant champions were to put the case thus: Make man-eating unlawful, and you starve the Vholeses!

"In a word, Mr Vholes, with his three daughters and his father in the Vale of Taunton, is continually doing duty, like a piece of timber, to shore up some decayed foundation that has become a pitfall and a nuisance. And with a great many people in a great many instances, the question is never one of a change from Wrong to Right (which is quite an extraneous consideration), but is always one of injury or advantage to that eminently respectable legion, Vholes." ¶BH 39

—real estate practice: "In dirty upper casements, here and there, hazy little patches of candlelight reveal where some wise draughtsman and conveyancer yet toils for the entanglement of real estate in meshes of sheepskin, in the average ratio of about a dozen of sheep to an acre of land. Over which bee-like industry, these benefactors of their species linger yet, though office-hours be past; that they may give for every day, some good account at last." BH 32

—residence: "Like as [Mr Tulkinghorn] is to look at, so is his apartment in the dusk of the present afternoon. Rusty, out of date, withdrawing from attention, able to afford it. Heavy broad-backed old-fashioned mahogany and horsehair chairs, not easily lifted, obsolete tables with spindle-legs and dusty baize covers, presentation prints of the holders of great titles in the last generation, or the last but one, environ him. A thick and dingy Turkey-carpet muffles the floor where he sits, attended by two candles in old-fashioned silver candlesticks, that give a very insufficient light to his large room. The titles on the backs of his books have retired into the binding; everything that can have a lock has got one; no key is visible. Very few loose papers are about." BH 10

—sentimental: "[Mike] called to announce that his eldest daughter was taken up on suspicion of shop-lifting. As he imparted this melancholy circumstance to Wemmick, Mr Jaggers standing magisterially before the fire and taking no share in the proceedings, Mike's eye happened to twinkle with a tear.

"'What are you about?' demanded Wemmick, with the utmost indignation. 'What do you come snivelling here for?'

"'I didn't go to do it, Mr Wemmick.'

"'You did,' said Wemmick. 'How dare

you? You're not in a fit state to come here, if you can't come here without spluttering like a bad pen. What do you mean by it?'

"'A man can't help his feelings, Mr Wemmick,' pleaded Mike.

"'His what?' demanded Wemmick, quite savagely. 'Say that again!'

"'Now look here, my man,' said Mr Jaggers, advancing a step, and pointing to the door. 'Get out of this office. I'll have no feelings here. Get out.'

"'It serves you right,' said Wemmick. 'Get out.'

"So the unfortunate Mike very humbly withdrew, and Mr Jaggers and Wemmick appeared to have re-established their good understanding, and went to work again with an air of refreshment upon them as if they had just had lunch." GE 51

—spouses: "Snitchey and Craggs had each, in private life as in professional existence, a partner of his own. Snitchey and Craggs were the best friends in the world and had a real confidence in one another; but Mrs Snitchey, by a dispensation not uncommon in the affairs of life, was on principle suspicious of Mr Craggs; and Mrs Craggs was on principle suspicious of Mr Snitchey. 'Your Snitcheys indeed,' the latter lady would observe, sometimes, to Mr Craggs; using that imaginative plural as if in disparagement of an objectionable pair of pantaloons, or other articles not possessed of a singular number; 'I don't see what you want with your Snitcheys, for my part. You trust a great deal too much to your Snitcheys, *I* think, and I hope you may never find my words come true.'

"While Mrs Snitchey would observe to Mr Snitchey, of Craggs, 'that if ever he was led away by man he was led away by that man, and that if she read a double purpose in a mortal eye, she read that purpose in Craggs's eye. Notwithstanding this, however, they were all very good friends in general: and Mrs Snitchey and Mrs Craggs maintained a close bond of alliance against 'the office,' which they both considered the Blue chamber, and common enemy, full of dangerous (because unknown) machinations." ¶BL 2

"Neither Snitchey nor Craggs openly attempted to stem the current . . . but both were content to be carried gently along it, until its force abated. This happened at about the same time as a general movement for a country dance; when Mr Snitchey proposed himself as a partner to Mrs Craggs, and Mr Craggs gallantly offered himself to Mrs Snitchey; and after some such slight evasions as 'why don't you ask somebody else?' and 'you'll be glad, I know, if I decline,' and 'I wonder you can dance out of the office' (but this jocosely now), each lady graciously accepted, and took her place.

"It was an old custom among them, indeed, to do so, and to pair off, in like manner, at dinners and suppers; for they were excellent friends, and on a footing of easy familiarity. Perhaps the false Craggs and the wicked Snitchey were a recognised fiction with the two wives, as Doe and Roe, incessantly running up and down bailiwicks, were with the two husbands; or, perhaps the ladies had instituted, and taken upon themselves, these two shares in the business, rather than be left out of it altogether. But certain it is, that each wife went as gravely and steadily to work in her vocation as her husband did in his, and would have considered it almost impossible for the Firm to maintain a successful and respectable existence, without her laudable exertions." BL 2

—as trustee: "Coy Conveyancing would not come to Mr Grewgious. She was wooed, not won, and they went their several ways. But an Arbitration being blown towards him by some unaccountable wind, and he gaining great credit in it as one indefatigable in seeking out right and doing right, a pretty fat Receivership was next blown into his pocket by a wind more traceable to its source.

"So, by chance, he had found his niche. Receiver and Agent now, to two rich estates, and deputing their legal business, in an amount worth having, to a firm of solicitors on the floor below, he had snuffed out his ambition (supposing him to have ever lighted it) and had settled down with his snuffers for the rest of his life . . . . The apprehension of dying suddenly, and leaving one fact or one figure with any incompleteness or obscurity attaching to it, would have stretched Mr Grewgious stone dead any day. The largest fidelity to a trust was the life-blood of the man. There are sorts of life-blood that course more quickly, more gaily, more attractively; but there is no better sort in circulation." MED 11

—unimaginative: "Mr Samuel Briggs was a mere machine, a sort of self-acting legal walking-stick." SB/SE

—*viewed by a litigant:* "'Gentlemen of your profession, sir,' continued Mr Pickwick, 'see the worst side of human nature. All its disputes, all its ill-will and bad blood, rise up before you. You know from your experience of juries (I mean no disparagement to you, or them) how much depends upon *effect*: and you are apt to attribute to others, a desire to use, for purposes of deception and self-interest, the very instruments which you, in pure honesty and honour of purpose, and with a laudable desire to do your utmost for your client, know the temper and worth of so well, from constantly employing them yourselves. I really believe that to this circumstance may be attributed the vulgar but very general notion of your being, as a body, suspicious, distrustful, and over-cautious.'" PP 31

—*wise advice:* "'Battledore and shuttlecock's a wery good game, vhen you an't the shuttlecock and two lawyers the battledores, in which case it gets too excitin' to be pleasant.'" PP 20

—*and witnesses*

—*prospective.* "'Well?'

"'Well, Mas'r Jaggers,' returned Mike . . . 'arter a deal o' trouble, I've found one, sir, as might do.'

"'What is he prepared to swear?'

"'Well, Mas'r Jaggers,' said Mike . . . 'in a general way, anythink.'

"Mr Jaggers suddenly became most irate. 'Now, I warned you before,' said he throwing his forefinger at the terrified client, 'that if ever you presumed to talk in that way here, I'd make an example of you. You infernal scoundrel, how dare you tell ME that?

"The client looked scared, but bewildered too, as if he were unconscious what he had done.

"'Spooney!' said the clerk, in a low voice, giving him a stir with his elbow. 'Soft Head! Need you say it face to face?'

"'Now, I ask you, you blundering booby,' said my guardian, very sternly, 'once more and for the last time, what the man you have brought here is prepared to swear?'

"Mike looked hard at my guardian, as if he were trying to learn a lesson from his face, and slowly replied, 'Ayther to character, or to having been in his company and never left him all the night in question.'

"'Now, be careful. In what station of life is this man?'

"Mike looked at his cap, and looked at the floor, and looked at the ceiling, and looked at the clerk, and even looked at me, before beginning to reply in a nervous manner, 'We've dressed him up like——' when my guardian blustered out:

"'What? You WILL, will you?'

"('Spooney!' added the clerk again, with another stir.)

"After some helpless casting about, Mike brightened and began again:

"'He is dressed like a 'spectable pieman. A sort of a pastry-cook.'

"'Is he here?' asked my guardian.

"'I left him,' said Mike, 'a setting on some doorsteps round the corner.'

"'Take him past that window, and let me see him.'

"The window indicated was the office window. We all three went to it, behind the wire blind, and presently saw the client go by in an accidental manner, with a murderous-looking tall individual, in a short suit of white linen and a paper cap. This guileless confectioner was not by any means sober, and had a black eye in the green stage of recovery, which was painted over.

"'Tell him to take his witness away directly,' said my guardian to the clerk, in extreme disgust, 'and ask him what he means by bringing such a fellow as that.'" GE 20

—*unreliable:* "[Mr Winkle answered] with so much eagerness that Mr Phunky ought to have got him out of the box with all possible dispatch. Lawyers hold that there are two kinds of particularly bad witnesses: a reluctant witness, and a too-willing witness; it was Mr Winkle's fate to figure in both characters." PP 34

Indexes IV *and* VIII *show 55 named lawyers and 16 law partnerships, and unnamed listings in six categories: advocates (3), attorneys (11), barristers (9), legal counsel (3), lawyers (19) and solicitors (4).*

Magistrate

—*abusive:* "Now, it so happened that Mr Fang was at that moment perusing a leading article in a newspaper of the morning, adverting to some recent decision of his, and commending him, for the three hundred and fiftieth time, to the special and particular notice of the Secretary of State for the Home Department. He was out of temper; and he looked up with an angry scowl.'

"'Who are you?' said Mr Fang.

"The old gentleman pointed, with some surprise, to his card.

"'Officer!' said Mr Fang, tossing the card contemptuously away with the newspaper. 'Who is this fellow?'

"'My name, sir,' said the old gentleman, speaking *like* a gentleman, 'my name sir, is Brownlow. Permit me to inquire the name of the magistrate who offers a gratuitous and unprovoked insult to a respectable person, under the protection of the bench.' Saying this, Mr Brownlow looked round the office as if in search of some person who would afford him the required information.

"'Officer!' said Mr Fang, throwing the paper on one side, 'what's this fellow charged with?' . . .

"' . . . I really never, without actual experience, could have believed——'

"'Hold your tongue, sir!' said Mr Fang, peremptorily.

"'I will not, sir!' replied the old gentleman.

"'Hold your tongue this instant, or I'll have you turned out of the office!' said Mr Fang. You're an insolent, impertinent fellow. How dare you bully a magistrate!'

"'What!' exclaimed the old gentleman, reddening.

"'Swear this person!' said Fang to the clerk. 'I'll not hear another word. Swear him.'" OT 11

This gentleman was copied from the real thing. See Vol. III p63 note L

—in America: " . . . we passed a 'Magistrate's office' . . . this awful Institution was nothing but a little lazy, good-for-nothing front parlour, open to the street; wherein two or three figures (I presume the magistrate and his myrmidons) were basking in the sunshine, the very effigies of languor and repose. It was a perfect picture of Justice retired from business for want of customers; her sword and scales sold off; napping comfortably with her legs upon the table." AN 12

—blockhead: "Here is a magistrate tells me I am one of a nation of drunkards. All Englishmen are drunkards, is the judicial bray. Here is another magistrate propounding from the seat of justice the stupendous nonsense that it is desirable that every person who gives alms in the streets should be fined for that offence. This to a Christian people, and with the New Testament lying before him—as a sort of Dummy, I suppose, to swear witnesses on." HW/W?

—inaccessible: "Although the presiding Genii in such an office as this, exercise a summary and arbitrary power over the liberties, the good name, the character, almost the lives, of Her Majesty's subjects, especially of the poorer class; and although, within such walls, enough fantastic tricks are daily played to make the angels blind with weeping; they are closed to the public, save through the medium of the daily press.1 Mr Fang was consequently a little indignant to see an unbidden guest enter in such irreverent disorder. "

"1. Or were virtually, then." OT 11

And see F:Prison*—the treadmill*

Index IV *lists seven magistrates in three categories (city, country, police), and there are 22 entries in* Index VIII.

Medicine and Medical Men

—admired: "I never walk out with my husband, but I hear the people bless him. I never go into a house of any degree, but I hear his praises, or see them in grateful eyes. I never lie down at night, but I know that in the course of that day he has alleviated pain, and soothed some fellow-creature in the time of need. I know that from the beds of those who were past recovery, thanks have often, often gone up, in the last hour, for his patient ministration. Is not this to be rich?" BH 67

—diagnosis

—aesthetically pleasing: " . . . the disabled man was soon laid on a table in a cool, methodical way, and carefully examined by a surgeon: who was as near at hand, and as ready to appear, as Calamity herself. 'He hardly knows an English word,' said Clennam; 'is he badly hurt?' 'Let us know all about it first,' said the surgeon, continuing his examination with a business-like delight in it, 'before we pronounce.'

"After trying the leg with a finger and two fingers, and one hand and two hands, and over and under, and up and down, and in this direction and in that, and approvingly remarking on the points of interest to another gentleman who joined him, the surgeon at last clapped the patient on the shoulder, and said, 'He won't hurt. He'll do very well. It's difficult enough, but we shall not want him to part with his leg this time.' Which Clennam interpreted to the patient [Cavalletto], who was full of gratitutde, and, in his demonstrative way, kissed both the interpreter's hand and the surgeon's several times.

"'It's a serious injury, I suppose?' said Clennam.

"'Ye-es,' replied the surgeon, with the thoughtful pleasure of an artist, contemplating the work upon his easel. 'Yes, it's enough. There's a compound fracture above the knee, and a dislocation below. They are both of a beautiful kind.' He gave the patient a friendly clap on the shoulder again, as if he really felt that he was a very good fellow indeed, and worthy of all commendation for having broken his leg in a manner interesting to science." LD i 13
CD in a rare medical mistake seems to confuse complexity ("compound": more than one factor involved, i.e., a fracture and a wound) with the notion of multiple: as a bone broken in several places. See next entry.

—prejudiced: "Mr Dombey being insensible, and bleeding from the head and face [after falling from his horse], was carried . . . to the nearest public-house . . . where he was soon attended by divers surgeons, who arrived in quick succession from all parts, and who seemed to come by some mysterious instinct, as vultures are said to gather about a camel who dies in the desert. After being at some pains to restore him to consciousness, these gentlemen examined into the nature of his injuries. One surgeon who lived hard by was strong for a compound fracture of the leg, which was the landlord's opinion also; but two surgeons who lived at a distance, and were only in that neighbourhood by accident, combated this opinion so disinterestedly, that it was decided at last that the patient, though severely cut and bruised, had broken no bones but a lesser rib or so, and might be carefully taken home before night." DS 42
CD suggests that a surgeon's opinion might be calculated to get business; but his medical knowledge is at fault, since a "compound" fracture entails a bone's breaking through the skin—a condition not at all ambiguous.

—recounted at length: "At one period of his life, our bore had an illness. It was an illness of a dangerous character for society at large. Innocently remark that you are very well, or that somebody else is very well; and our bore, with a preface that one never knows what a blessing health is until one has lost it, is reminded of that illness, and drags you through the whole of its symptoms, progress, and treatment.

"Innocently remark that you are not well, or that somebody else is not well, and the same inevitable result ensues. You will learn how our bore felt a tightness about here, sir, for which he couldn't account, accompanied with a constant sensation as if he were being stabbed—or, rather, jobbed—that expresses it more correctly—jobbed—with a blunt knife.

"Well, sir! water-wheels to turn round in his head, and hammers to beat incessantly thump, thump, thump, all down his back—along the whole of the spinal vertebræ. Our bore, when his sensations had come to this, thought it a duty he owed to himself to take advice, and he said, Now, whom shall I consult?

"He naturally thought of Callow, at that time one of the most eminent physicians in London, and he went to Callow. Callow said, 'Liver!' and prescribed rhubarb and calomel, low diet, and moderate exercise. Our bore went on with this treatment, getting worse every day, until he lost confidence in Callow, and went to Moon, whom half the town was then mad about.

"Moon was interested in the case; to do him justice he was very much interested in the case; and he said, 'Kidneys!' He altered the whole treatment, sir—gave strong acids, cupped, and blistered. This went on, our bore still getting worse every day, until he openly told Moon it would be a satisfaction to him if he would have a consultation with Clatter.

"The moment Clatter saw our bore, he said, 'Accumulation of fat about the heart!' Snugglewood, who was called in with him, differed, and said, 'Brain!' But what they all agreed upon was, to lay our bore upon his back, to shave his head, to leech him, to administer enormous quantities of medicine, and to keep him low; so that he was reduced to a mere shadow, you wouldn't have known him, and nobody considered it possible that he could ever recover.

"This was his condition, sir, when he heard of Jilkins—at that period in a very small practice, and living in the upper part of a house in Great Portland Street; but still, you understand, with a rising reputation among the few people to whom he was known. Being in that condition in which a drowning man catches at a straw, our bore sent for Jilkins. Jilkins came. Our bore liked his eye, and said, 'Mr Jilkins, I have a presentiment that you will do me good.' Jilkins's reply was characteristic of the man. It was, 'Sir, I mean to do you good.' This confirmed our bore's opinion of his eye, and they went into the case together—went completely into it.

"Jilkins then got up, walked across the room, came back, and sat down. His words were these. 'You have been humbugged. This is a case of indigestion, occasioned by deficiency of power in the Stomach. Take a mutton chop in half-an-hour, with a glass of the finest old sherry that can be got for money. Take two mutton chops to-morrow, and two glasses of the finest old sherry. Next day, I'll come again.' In a week our bore was on his legs, and Jilkins's success dates from that period!" ¶RP/B

—dissection: "'Nothing like dissecting, to give one an appetite,' said Mr Bob Sawyer, looking round the table.

"Mr Pickwick slightly shuddered.

"'By the bye, Bob,' said Mr Allen, 'have you finished that leg yet?'

"'Nearly,' replied Sawyer, helping himself to half a fowl as he spoke. 'It's a very muscular one for a child's.'

"'Is it?' inquired Mr Allen, carelessly.

"'Very,' said Bob Sawyer, with his mouth full.

"'I've put my name down for an arm, at our place,' said Mr Allen. "'We're clubbing for a subject, and the list is nearly full, only we can't get hold of any fellow that wants a head. I wish you'd take it.'

"'No,' replied Bob Sawyer; 'can't afford expensive luxuries.'

"'Nonsense!' said Allen.

"'Can't indeed,' rejoined Bob Sawyer. 'I wouldn't mind a brain, but I couldn't stand a whole head.'" PP 30

—at the funeral: "'Cake and wine, eh? Which is port? Thank you.'

"Mr Pecksniff took some also.

"'At about half-past one o'clock in the morning, sir,' resumed the doctor [Jobling], 'I was called up to attend that case. At the first pull of the night-bell I turned out, threw up the window, and put out my head. Cloak, eh? Don't tie it too tight. That'll do.'

"Mr Pecksniff having been likewise inducted into a similar garment, the doctor resumed.

"'And put out my head. Hat, eh? My good friend, that is not mine. Mr Pecksniff, I beg your pardon, but I think we have unintentionally made an exchange. Thank you. Well, sir, I was going to tell you—'

"'We are quite ready,' interrupted Mould in a low voice.

"'Ready, eh?' said the doctor. 'Very good. Mr Pecksniff, I'll take an opportunity of relating the rest in the coach. It's rather curious. Ready, eh? No rain, I hope?'

"'Quite fair, sir,' returned Mould

"'I was afraid the ground would have been wet,' said the doctor, 'for my glass fell yesterday. We may congratulate ourselves on our good fortune.' But seeing by this time that Mr Jonas and Chuffey were going out at the door, he put a white pocket-handkerchief to his face as if a violent burst of grief had suddenly come upon him, and walked down side by side with Mr Pecksniff." MC 19

—getting business: "'Have you no feeling for your profession, you groveller? Did you leave all the medicine?' . . . .The powders for the child, at the large house with the new family, and the pills to be taken four times a day at the ill-tempered old gentleman's with the gouty leg?'

"'Yes, sir.'

"'Then shut the door, and mind the shop.'

"'Come, said Mr Winkle . . . .'There is some medicine being sent out.'

"Mr Bob Sawyer . . . leaning forward to Mr Winkle, said, in a low tone:

"'He leaves it all at the wrong houses.'

"Mr Winkle looked perplexed . . . .

"'Don't you see?' said Bob. 'He goes up to a house, rings the area bell, pokes a packet of medicine without a direction into the servant's hand, and walks off. Servant takes it into the dining-parlour; master opens it, and reads the label: "Draught to be taken at bed-time—pills as before—lotion as usual—the powder. From Sawyer's, late Nockemorf's. Physicians' prescriptions carefully prepared," and all the rest of it. Shows it to his wife—she reads the label; it goes down to the servants—they read the label.

"'Next day, boy calls: "Very sorry—his mistake—immense business—great many parcels to deliver—Mr Sawyer's compliments—late Nockemorf." The name gets known, and that's the thing, my boy, in the medical way. Bless your heart, old fellow, it's better than all the advertising in the world. We have got one four-ounce bottle that's been to half the houses in Bristol, and hasn't done yet.'

"'Dear me, I see,' observed Mr Winkle; 'what an excellent plan!'

"'Oh, Ben and I have hit upon a dozen such,' replied Bob Sawyer, with great glee. 'The lamplighter has eighteen-pence a week to pull the night-bell for ten minutes every time he comes round; and my boy always rushes into church, just before the psalms, when the people have got nothing to do but look about 'em, and calls me out, with horror and dismay depicted on his countenance. "Bless my soul," everybody says, "somebody taken suddenly ill! Sawyer, late Nockemorf, sent for. What a business that young man has!"'" ¶PP 38

—healing: " . . . a man might be a great healer, if he would, and yet not be a great doctor . . . . " CS/MJ 2

"The patient was a married lady in the middle rank of life, who, having seen another lady at an evening party in a full suit of pearls, was suddenly seized with a desire to possess a similar equipment, although her husband's finances were by no means equal to the necessary outlay. Finding her wish ungratified, she fell sick, and the symptoms soon became so alarming, that [Dr Grummidge] was called in. At this period the prominent tokens of the disorder were sullenness, a total indisposition to perform domestic duties, great peevishness, and extreme languor, except when pearls were mentioned, at which times the pulse quickened, the eyes grew brighter, the pupils dilated, and the patient, after various incoherent exclamations, burst into a passion of tears, and exclaimed that nobody cared for her, and that she wished herself dead.

"Finding that the patient's appetite was affected in the presence of company, he began by ordering a total abstinence from all stimulants, and forbidding any sustenance but weak gruel; he then took twenty ounces of blood, applied a blister under each ear, one upon the chest, and another on the back; having done which, and administered five grains of calomel, he left the patient to her repose. The next day she was somewhat low, but decidedly better, and all appearances of irritation were removed. The next day she improved still further, and on the next again. On the fourth there was some appearance of a return of the old symptoms, which no sooner developed themselves, than he administered another dose of calomel, and left strict orders that, unless a decidedly favourable change occurred within two hours, the patient's head should be immediately shaved to the very last curl.

"From that moment she began to mend, and, in less than four-and-twenty hours was perfectly restored. She did not now betray the least emotion at the sight or mention of pearls or any other ornaments. She was cheerful and good-humoured, and a most beneficial change had been effected in her whole temperament and condition.'" B/M2

—for indigestion: " . . . Mr Twemlow feels a little queer on the sofa at his lodgings over the stable-yard in Duke Street, Saint James's, in consequence of having taken two advertised pills at about mid-day, on the faith of the printed representation accompanying the box (price one and a penny halfpenny, government stamp included), that the same 'will be found highly salutary as a precautionary measure in connexion with the pleasures of the table.' To whom, while sickly with the fancy of an insoluble pill sticking in his gullet, and also with the sensation of a deposit of warm gum languidly wandering within him a little lower down, a servant enters . . . . " OMF iii 17

—infant ingestion: "'Child's parents were poor people who lived in a court. Child's eldest sister bought a necklace; common necklace, made of large black wooden beads. Child, being fond of toys, cribbed the necklace, hid it, played with it, cut the string, and swallowed a bead. Child thought it capital fun, went back next day, and swallowed another bead. . . . Next day, child swallowed two beads; the day after that, he treated himself to three, and so on, till in a week's time he had got through the necklace— five-and-twenty beads in all. The sister, who was an industrious girl, and seldom treated herself to a bit of finery, cried her eyes out, at the loss of the necklace; looked high and low for it; but, I needn't say, didn't find it.

"A few days afterwards, the family were at dinner—baked shoulder of mutton, and potatoes under it—the child, who wasn't hungry, was playing about the room, when suddenly there was heard a devil of a noise, like a small hailstorm. 'Don't do that, my boy," said the father. "I ain't doin' nothing," said the child. "Well, don't do it again," said the father.

"There was a short silence, and then the noise began again, worse than ever. "If you don't mind what I say, my boy," said the father, "you'll find yourself in bed, in something less than a pig's whisper."

"He gave the child a shake to make him obedient, and such a rattling ensued as nobody ever heard before. "Why, dam'me, it's in the child!" said the father, "he's got the croup in the wrong place!" "No I haven't father," said the child, beginning to cry, "it's the necklace; I swallowed it, father."—The father caught the child up, and ran with him to the hospital: the beads in the boy's stomach rattling all the way with the jolting; and the people looking up in the air, and down in the cellars, to see where the unusual sound came from. He's in the hospital now,' said Jack Hopkins, 'and he makes such a devil of a noise when he walks about, that they're obliged to muffle him in a watchman's coat, for fear he should wake the patients!'

"'That's the most extraordinary case I ever heard of,' said Mr Pickwick, with an emphatic blow on the table." ¶PP 32

—misunderstood: "'Sir!' said the Doctor, in an awful voice, producing a card . . . 'my name is Slammer, Doctor Slammer, sir—97th Regiment—Chatham Barracks—my card, sir, my card.' He would have added more, but his indignation [at being cut out on the dance floor] choked him.

"'Ah!' replied [Jingle], coolly, 'Slammer—much obliged—polite attention—not ill now, Slammer—but when I am—knock you up.'

"'You—you're a shuffler! sir,' gasped the furious Doctor, 'a poltroon—a coward—a liar—a—a—will nothing induce you to give me your card, sir!'

"'Oh! I see,' said the stranger, half aside, 'negus too strong here—liberal landlord—very foolish—very—lemonade much better—hot rooms—elderly gentlemen—suffer for it in the morning—cruel—cruel;' and he moved on a step or two.

"'You are stopping in this house, sir,' said the indignant little man; 'you are intoxicated now, sir; you shall hear from me in the morning, sir. I shall find you out, sir; I shall find you out.'

"'Rather you found me out than found me at home,' replied the unmoved stranger." PP 2

—patent medicine

—in the North of England: "On market morning, Carlisle woke up amazingly . . . . There was its general market in the street. . . . With Doctor Mantle's Dispensary for the cure of all Human Maladies and no charge for advice,' and with Doctor Mantle's 'Laboratory of Medical, Chemical, and Botanical Science—both healing institutions established on one pair of trestles, one board, and one sun-blind." LT 1

—in France: "And hark! fanfaronade of trumpets, and here into the Great Place, resplendent in an open carriage, with four gorgeously-attired servitors up behind, playing horns, drums, and cymbals, rolled 'the Daughter of a Physician' in massive golden chains and earrings, and blue-feathered hat, shaded from the admiring sun by two immense umbrellas of artificial roses, to dispense (from motives of philanthropy) that small and pleasant dose which had cured so many thousands! Toothache, earache, headache, heartache, stomachache, debility, nervousness, fits, fainting fever, ague, all equally cured by the small and pleasant dose of the great Physician's great daughter!

"The process was this—she . . . told you so: On the first day after taking the small and pleasant dose, you would feel no particular influence beyond a most harmonious sensation of indescribable and irresistible joy; on the second day you would be so astonishingly better that you would think youself changed into somebody else; on the third day you would be entirely free from your disorder, whatever its nature and however long you had had it, and would seek out the Physician's Daughter to throw yourself at her feet, kiss the hem of her garment, and buy as many more of the small and pleasant doses as by the sale of all your few effects you could obtain; but she would be inaccessible—gone for herbs to the Pyramids of Egypt—and you would be (though cured) reduced to despair!

"Thus would the Physician's Daughter drive her trade (and briskly too), and thus would the buying and selling and mingling of tongues and colours continue, until the changing sunlight, leaving the Physician's Daughter in the shadow of high roofs, admonished her to jolt out westward, with a departing effect of gleam and glitter on the splendid equipage and brazen blast." CS/SL 1

—prognostication: "'It will be a stormy night!' exclaimed the doctor, as they started.

"The Doctor's prognostication in reference to the weather was speedily verified. Although the weather was not a patient of his, and no third party had required him to give an opinion on the case, the quick fulfilment of his prophecy may be taken as an instance of his professional tact; for, unless the threatening aspect of the night had been perfectly plain and unmistakable, Mr Jobling would never have compromised his reputation by delivering any sentiments on the subject. He used this principle in Medicine with too much success to be unmindful of it in his commonest transactions." MC 41,42

—*reality:* "As no man of large experience of humanity, however quietly carried it may be, can fail to be invested with an interest peculiar to the possession of such knowledge, Physician was an attractive man. Even the daintier gentlemen and ladies who had no idea of his secret, and who would have been startled out of more wits than they had, by the monstrous impropriety of his proposing to them 'Come and see what I see!' confessed his attraction. Where he was, something real was. And half a grain of reality, like the smallest portion of some other scarce natural productions, will flavour an enormous quantity of diluent." LD ii 25

—*skill in murder:* "' . . . edge-tools, edge-tools; never play with 'em. A very remarkable instance of the skilful use of edge-tools, by the way, occurs to me at this moment [said Jobling]. It was a case of murder. I am afraid it was a case of murder, committed by a member of our profession; it was so artistically done . . . . A certain gentleman was found, one morning . . . in an upright position, in the angle of a doorway, and supported consequently *by* the doorway. Upon his waistcoat there was one solitary drop of blood. He was dead and cold; and had been murdered, sir.'

"'Only one drop of blood!' said Jonas.

"'Sir, that man,' replied the doctor, 'had been stabbed to the heart. Had been stabbed to the heart with such dexterity, sir, that he had died instantly, and had bled internally. It was supposed that a medical friend of his (to whom suspicion attached) had engaged him in conversation on some pretence; had taken him, very likely, by the button in a conversational manner; had examined his ground at leisure with his other hand; had marked the exact spot; drawn out the instrument, whatever it was, when he was quite prepared; and—

"'And done the trick,' suggested Jonas.

"'Exactly so,' replied the doctor. 'It was quite an operation in its way, and very neat. The medical friend never turned up; and, as I tell you, he had the credit of it. Whether he did it or not I can't say. But, having had the honour to be called in with two or three of my professional brethren on the occasion, and having assisted to make a careful examination of the wound, I have no hesitation in saying that it would have reflected credit on any medical man; and that in an unprofessional person it could not but be considered, either as an extraordinary work of art, or the result of a still more extraordinary, happy, and favourable conjunction of circumstances.'" MC 41

—*a sound practice:* "Doctor Manette received such patients here [in London] as his old reputation, and its revival in the floating whispers of his story, brought him. His scientific knowledge, and his vigilance and skill in conducting ingenious experiments, brought him otherwise into moderate request, and he earned as much as he wanted." TTC ii 6

—*a stubborn patient:* "'One night [the patient] wos took very ill; sends for a doctor. "Wot's the matter?" says the doctor. "Wery ill," says the patient. "Wot have you been a eatin' on?" says the doctor. "Roast weal," says the patient. "Wot's the last thing you dewoured?" says the doctor. "Crumpets," says the patient. "That's it" says the doctor. "I'll send you a box of pills directly, and don't you never take no more of 'em," he says. "No more o' wot?" says the patient—"Pills?" "No; crumpets," says the doctor.

"'"Why?" says the patient, starting up in bed; "I've eat four crumpets, ev'ry night for fifteen year, on principle." "Well, then, you'd better leave em' off, on principle," says the doctor. "Crumpets is wholesome, sir" says the patient. "Crumpets is *not* wholesome, sir," says the doctor, wery fierce. "But they're so cheap," says the patient, comin' down a little, "and so wery fillin' at the price." "They'd be dear to you, at any price; dear if you wos paid to eat 'em," says the doctor. "Four crumpets a night," he says, "vill do your business in six months!"

"'The patient looks him full in the face, and turns it over in his mind for a long time, and at last he says, "Are you sure o' that 'ere, sir?" "I'll stake my professional reputation on it," says the doctor. "How many crumpets, at a sittin', do you think 'ud kill me off at once?" says the patient. "I don't know," says the doctor. "Do you think half a crown's worth 'ud do it?" says the patient. "I think it might," says the doctor. "Three shillins' wurth 'ud be sure to do it, I s'pose?" says the patient; "Certainly," says the doctor. "Wery good," says the patient; "good night." Next mornin' he gets up, has a fire lit, orders in three shillins' wurth o' crumpets, toasts 'em all, eats 'em all, and blows his brains out'

"'What did he do that for?' inquired Mr Pickwick abruptly; for he was considerably startled by this tragical termination of the narrative.

"'Wot did he do it for, sir?' reiterated Sam. 'Why in support of his great principle that crumpets wos wholesome, and to show that he wouldn't be put out of his way for nobody!'" PP 44

—surgery: "'Anything new?'

"'No, nothing particular. rather a good accident brought into the casualty ward.'

"'What was that, sir?' inquired Mr Pickwick.

"'Only a man fallen out of a four pair of stairs' window;—but it's a very fair case—very fair case indeed.'

"'Do you mean that the patient is in a fair way to recover?' inquried Mr Pickwick.

"'No,' replied Hopkins, carelessly. 'No, I should rather say he wouldn't. There must be a splendid operation though, to-morrow—magnificent sight if Slasher does it.'

"'You consider Mr Slasher a good operator?' said Mr Pickwick.

"'Best alive,' replied Hopkins. 'Took a boy's leg out of the socket last week—boy ate five apples and a ginger-bread cake—exactly two minutes after it was all over, boy said he wouldn't lie there to be made game of, and he'd tell his mother if they didn't begin.'" PP 32

—treatment for contusion: "'I was one blessed bruise, sir,' said Squeers, touching first the roots of his hair, and then the toes of his boots, 'from *here* to *there.* Vinegar and brown paper, vinegar and brown paper, from morning to night. I suppose there was a matter of half a ream of brown paper stuck upon me, from first to last. As I laid all of a heap in our kitchen, plastered all over, you might have thought I was a large brown paper parcel, chock full of nothing but groans.'" NN 34

—walking a hospital: "'You never see a postboy in that 'ere hospital as you *walked* (as they says o' the ghosts), did you?' demanded Sam [Weller]." PP 51 *See* Glossary

—wise, apparently: "The doctor, who was a red-nosed gentleman with a great bunch of seals dangling below a waistcoat of ribbed black satin, arrived with all speed, and taking his seat by the bedside of poor Nell, drew out his watch, and felt her pulse. Then he looked at her tongue, then he felt her pulse again, and while he did so, he eyed the half-emptied wineglass as if in profound abstraction.

"'I should give her——' said the doctor at length, 'a teaspoonful, every now and then, of hot brandy and water.

"'Why, that's exactly what we've done, sir!' said the delighted landlady.

"'I should also,' observed the doctor, who had passed the foot-bath on the stairs, 'I should also,' said the doctor, in the voice of an oracle, 'put her feet in hot water, and wrap them up in flannel. I should likewise,' said the doctor with increased solemnity, 'give her something light for supper—the wing of a roasted fowl now——'

"'Why, goodness gracious me, sir, it's cooking at the kitchen fire this instant!' cried the landlady. And so indeed it was, for the schoolmaster had ordered it to be put on, and it was getting on so well that the doctor might have smelt it if he had tried; perhaps he did.

"'You may then,' said the doctor, rising gravely, 'give her a glass of hot mulled port wine, if she likes wine——'

"'And a toast, sir?' suggested the landlady.

"'Ay,' said the doctor, in the tone of a man who makes a dignified concession. 'And a toast—of bread. But be very particular to make it of bread, if you please, ma'am.'

"With which parting injunction, slowly and portentously delivered, the doctor departed, leaving the whole house in admiration of that wisdom which tallied so closely with their own. Everybody said he was a very shrewd doctor indeed, and knew perfectly what people's constitutions were; which there appears some reason to suppose he did." OCS 46

And see B:Timepiece—*medicinal*

The Election at Eatanswill PP

Industry and Government

If there ever was a time when any one class could of itself do much for its own good, and for the welfare of society—which I greatly doubt—that time is unquestionably past. It is in the fusion of different classes, without confusion; in the bringing together of employers and employed; in the creating of a better common understanding among those whose interests are identical, who depend upon each other, and who can never be in unnatural antagonism without deplorable results, that one of the chief principles of a Mechanics' Institution should consist. A great deal of the bitterness among us arises from an imperfect understanding of one another.

[S/BM1]

Wherever there was a square yard of ground in British occupation, under the sun or moon, with a public post upon it, sticking to that post was a Barnacle. No intrepid navigator could plant a flagstaff upon any spot of earth, and take possession of it in the British name, but to that spot of earth, so soon as the discovery was known, the Circumlocution Office sent out a Barnacle and a despatch-box. Thus the Barnacles were all over the world, in every direction—despatch-boxing the compass.

LD i 34

Meeting the 'Prentices BR

Army

—*administration:* "It is in the nature of things that such an institution as our English army should have many bad and troublesome characters in it. But, this is a reason for, and not against, its being made as acceptable as possible to well-disposed men of decent behaviour. Such men are assuredly not tempted into the ranks, by the beastly inversion of natural laws, and the compulsion to live in worse than swinish foulness. Accordingly, when any such Circumlocutional embellishments of the soldier's condition have of late been brought to notice, we civilians, seated in outer darkness cheerfully meditating on an Income Tax, have considered the matter as being our business, and have shown a tendency to declare that we would rather not have it misregulated, if such declaration may, without violence to the Church Catechism, be hinted to those who are put in authority over us." UT/GT

—*service risk:* "'Supposing you should be killed, sir?' said a timid voice in one corner. 'Well, sir, supposing you should be,' said the [recruiting] sergeant, 'what then? Your country loves you, sir; his Majesty King George the Third loves you; your memory is honoured, revered, respected; everybody's fond of you, and grateful to you; your name's wrote down at full length in a book in the War Office. Damme, gentlemen, we must all die some time, or another, eh?'" BR 31

See also S:Duty—*in the army;* F:The Poor, Working—*patriotism; and* H:Soldier

Capital and Labour

—*advertisement:* " . . . with one or two exceptions, there seemed to be the very same placards in the window that he had seen before. There were the same unimpeachable masters and mistresses in want of virtuous servants, and the same virtuous servants in want of unimpeachable masters and mistresses, and the same magnificent estates for the investment of capital, and the same enormous quantities of capital to be invested in estates, and, in short, the same opportunities of all sorts for people who wanted to make their fortunes. And a most extraordinary proof it was of the national prosperity, that people had not been found to avail themselves of such advantages long ago." NN 35

—*fundamentally:* " . . . capital and labour are not opposed, but are mutually dependent and mutually supporting . . . . " S/MF

—*the gulf between:* "'Sir [said Stephen Blackpool], I canna, wi' my little learning an' my common way, tell the genelman what will better aw this—though some working men o' this town could, above my powers—but I can tell him what I know will never do 't. The strong hand will never do't. Vict'ry and triumph will never do't. Agreeing fur to mak one side unnat'rally awlus and for ever right, and toother side unnat'rally awlus and for ever wrong, will never, never do't. Nor yet lettin alone will never do't.

"Let thousands upon thousands alone, aw leading the like lives and aw faw'en into the like muddle, and they will be as one, and yo will be as anoother, wi' a black unpassable world betwixt yo, just as long or short a time as sitchlike misery can last. Not drawin nigh to fok, wi' kindness and patience an' cheery ways, that so draws nigh to one another in their monny troubles, and so cherishes one another in their distresses wi' what they need themseln—like, I humbly believe, as no people the genelman ha' seen in aw his travels can beat—will never do 't till th' sun turns t' ice.

"Most o' aw, rating 'em as so much Power, and reg'latin 'em as if they was figures in a soom, or machines: wi'out loves and likens, wi'out memories and inclinations, wi'out souls to weary and souls to hope—when aw goes quiet, draggin on wi' 'em as if they'd nowt o' th' kind, and when aw goes onquiet, reproachin 'em for their want o' sitch humanly feelins in their dealins wi' yo—this will never do't, sir, till God's work is onmade.'" ¶HT ii 5

—*memory:* "'You have an accurate memory of your own,' said Mr Dombey.

"'Oh! *I*' returned the manager. It's the only capital of a man like *me.*'" DS 13

—*question of class:* "If there ever was a time when any one class could of itself do much for its own good, and for the welfare of society—which I greatly doubt—that time is unquestionably past. It is in the fusion of different classes, without confusion; in the bringing together of employers and employed; in the creating of a better common understanding among those whose interests are identical, who depend upon each other, and who can never be in unnatural antagonism without deplorable results, that one of the chief principles of a Mechanics' Institution should consist. In this world a great deal of the bitterness among us arises from an imperfect understanding of one another." S/BM1

—the railroad and the right to strike: "[The railroad] is the result of a vast system of skilful combination, and a vast expenditure of wealth. The construction of the line, alone, against all the engineering difficulties it presented, involved an amount of outlay that was wonderful, even in England. To bring it to its present state of working efficiency, a thousand ingenious problems have been studied and solved, stupendous machines have been constructed, a variety of plans and schemes have been matured with incredible labour: a great whole has been pieced together by numerous capacities and applicances, and kept incessantly in motion.

"Even the character of the men, which stands deservedly high, has not been set up by themselves alone, but has been assisted by large contributions from these various sources. Without a good permanent way, and good engine power, they could not have established themselves in the public confidence as good drivers.

"Without good business-management in the complicated arrangements of trains for goods and passengers, they could not possibly have avoided accidents. They have done their part manfully; but they could not have done it, without efficient aid in like manful sort, from every department of the great executive staff.

"And because it happens that the whole machine is dependent upon them in one important stage, and is delivered necessarily into their control—and because it happens that Railway accidents, when they do occur, are of a frightful nature, attended with horrible mutilation and loss of life—and because such accidents, with the best precautions, probably *must* occur, in the event of their resignation in a body—is it, therefore, defensible to strike? . . .

"To the men, we would submit, that if they fail in adjusting the difference to their complete satisfaction, the failure will be principally their own fault, as inseparable, in great measure, from the injudicious and unjustifiable threat into which the more sensible portion of them have allowed themselves to be betrayed. What the Directors might have conceded to temperate remonstrance, it is easy to understand they may deem it culpable weakness to yield to so alarming a combination against the public service and safety." ¶HW/RS

—union organizers: "'Sir,' returned Stephen [Blackpool], with a quiet confidence of absolute certainty, 'if yo was t' tak a hundred Slackbridges—aw as there is, an aw the number ten times towd—an' was t' sew 'em up in separate sacks, an' sink 'em in the deepest ocean as were made ere ever dry land coom to be, yo'd leave the muddle just wheer 'tis.

"'Mischeevous strangers!' said Stephen, with an anxious smile; 'when ha' we not heern, I am sure, sin ever we can call to mind, o' th' mischeevous strangers! 'Tis not by *them* the trouble's made, sir. 'Tis not wi' *them* 't commences. I ha' no favour for 'em—I ha' no reason to favour 'em—but 'tis hopeless and useless to dream o' takin them fro their trade, 'stead o' takin their trade fro them!

"'Aw that's now about me in this room were heer afore I coom, an' will be heer when I am gone. Put that clock aboard a ship an' pack it off to Norfolk Island, an' the time will go on just the same. So 'tis wi' Slackbridge every bit.'" ¶HT ii 5

"[The working-men] are laboriously and constantly employed; and it is the habit of many men, so engaged, to allow other men to think for them. these deputy-thinkers are not the most judicious order of intellects. They are something quick at grievances. They drive Express Trains to that point, and Parliamentary to all other points. They are not always, perhaps, the best workmen. They are, sometimes, not workmen at all, but designing persons, who have, for their own base purposes, immeshed the workmen in a system of tyranny and oppression." HW/RS

Capitalism

—the coal trade: "'Mr Micawber was induced to think, on inquiry, that there might be an opening for a man of his talent in the Medway Coal Trade. Then, as Mr Micawber very properly said, the first step to be taken clearly was, to come and *see* the Medway. Which we came and saw . . . .

"'We came,' repeated Mrs Micawber, 'and saw the Medway. My opinion of the coal trade on that river, is, that it may require talent, but that it certainly requires capital. Talent, Mr Micawber has; capital, Mr Micawber has not. We saw, I think, the greater part of the Medway; and that is my individual conclusion." DC 17

—profit motive: "That when the Dodger, and his accomplished friend Master Bates,

joined in the hue-and-cry which was raised at Oliver [Twist]'s heels, in consequence of their executing an illegal conveyance of Mr Brownlow's personal property, as has been already described, they were actuated by a very laudable and becoming regard for themselves; and forasmuch as the freedom of the subject and the liberty of the individual are among the first and proudest boasts of a true-hearted Englishman, so, I need hardly beg the reader to observe, that this action should tend to exalt them in the opinion of all public and patriotic men, in almost as great a degree as this strong proof of their anxiety for their own preservation and safety goes to corroborate and confirm the little code of laws which certain profound and sound-judging philosophers have laid down as the mainsprings of all Nature's deeds and actions: the said philosophers very wisely reducing the good lady's proceedings to matters of maxim and theory: and, by a very neat and pretty compliment to her exalted wisdom and understanding, putting entirely out of sight any considerations of heart; or generous impulse and feeling. For, these are matters totally beneath a female who is acknowledged by universal admission to be far above the numerous little foibles and weaknesses of her sex.

"If I wanted any further proof of the strictly philosophical nature of the conduct of these young gentlemen in their very delicate predicament, I should at once find it in the fact . . . of their quitting the pursuit, when the general attention was fixed upon Oliver; and making immediately for their home by the shortest possible cut.

"Although I do not mean to assert that it is usually the practice of renowned and learned sages, to shorten the road to any great conclusion (their course indeed being rather to lengthen the distance, by various circumlocutions and discursive staggerings, like unto those in which drunken men under the pressure of a too mighty flow of ideas, are prone to indulge); still, I do mean to say, and do say distinctly, that it is the invariable practice of many mighty philosophers, in carrying out their theories, to evince great wisdom and foresight in providing against every possible contingency which can be supposed at all likely to affect themselves.

"Thus, to do a great right, you may do a little wrong; and you may take any means which the end to be attained will justify; the amount of the right, or the amount of the wrong, or indeed the distinction between the two, being left entirely to the philosopher concerned, to be settled and determined by his clear, comprehensive, and impartial view of his own particular case." ¶OT 12

And see S:Duty—*activity*

Civil Service

". . . that great Circumlocution Office on which the sun never sets and the light of reason never rises . . . . " UT/GT

—*candidates:* "Who are you passing every day at your Competitive Excruciations? The fortunate candidates whose heads and livers you have turned upside down for life? Not you. You are really passing the Crammers and Coaches. If your principle is right, why don't you turn out to-morrow morning with the keys of your cities on velvet cushions, your musicians playing, and your flags flying, and read addresses to the Crammers and Coaches on your bended knees, beseeching them to come out and govern you?

"Then, again, as to your public business of all sorts, your Financial statements and your Budgets; the Public knows much, truly, about the real doers of all that! Your Nobles and Right Honourables are first-rate men? Yes, and so is a goose a first-rate bird. But I'll tell you this about the goose;—you'll find his natural flavour disappointing, without stuffing." ¶CS/SL 3

—*defended:* "[Lord Decimus Tite Barnacle] . . . had risen to official heights on the wings of one indignant idea, and that was, My Lords, that I am yet to be told that it behoves a Minister of this free country to set bounds to the philanthropy, to cramp the charity, to fetter the public spirit, to contract the enterprise, to damp the independent self-reliance, of its people. That was, in other words, that this great statesman was always yet to be told that it behoved the Pilot of the ship to do anything but prosper in the private loaf and fish trade ashore, the crew being able, by dint of hard pumping, to keep the ship above water without him.

"On this sublime discovery, in the great art How not to do it, Lord Decimus had long sustained the highest glory of the Barnacle family; and let any ill-advised member of either House but try How to do it, by bringing in a Bill to do it, that Bill was as good as dead and buried when Lord Decimus Tite Barnacle rose up in his place and solemnly said, soaring into indignant majesty as the Circumlocution cheering soared around him, that he was yet to be told, My Lords, that it behoved him as the Minister of this free country, to set bounds to the philanthropy, to cramp the charity, to fetter the public spirit, to contract the enterprise, to damp the independent self-reliance, of its people. The discovery of this Behoving Machine was the discovery of the political perpetual motion. It never wore out, though it was always going round and round in all the State Departments." LD i 34

"When that admirable Department got into trouble, and was, by some infuriated Member of Parliament, whom the smaller Barnacles almost suspected of labouring under diabolic possession, attacked on the merits of no individual case, but as an Institution wholly abominable and Bedlamite; then the noble or right honourable Barnacle who represented it in the House, would smite that member and cleave him asunder, with a statement of the quantity of business (for the prevention of business) done by the Circumlocution Office.

"Then would that noble or right honourable Barnacle hold in his hand a paper containing a few figures, to which, with the permission of the House, he would entreat its attention. Then would the inferior Barnacles exclaim, obeying orders, 'Hear, Hear, Hear!' and 'Read!' Then would the noble or right honourable Barnacle perceive, sir, from this little document, which he thought might carry conviction even to the perversest mind (Derisive laughter and cheering from the Barnacle fry), that within the short compass of the last financial half-year, this much-maligned Department (Cheers) had written and received fifteen thousand letters (Loud cheers), had made twenty-four thousand minutes (Louder cheers), and thirty-two thousand five hundred and seventeen memoranda (Vehement cheering).

"Nay, an ingenious gentleman connected with the Department, and himself a valuable public servant, had done him the favour to make a curious calculation of the amount of stationery consumed in it during the same period. It formed a part of this same short document; and he derived from it the remarkable fact that the sheets of foolscap paper it had devoted to the public service would pave the footways on both sides of Oxford Street from end to end, and leave nearly a quarter of a mile to spare for the park (Immense cheering and laughter); while of tape—red tape—it had used enough to stretch, in graceful festoons, from Hyde Park Corner to the General Post Office.

"Then, amidst a burst of official exultation, would the noble or right honourable Barnacle sit down, leaving the mutilated fragments of the Member on the field. No one, after that exemplary demolition of him, would have the hardihood to hint that the more the Circumlocution Office did, the less was done, and that the greatest blessing it could confer on an unhappy public would be to do nothing." ¶LD ii 8

—and Empire: " . . . wherever there was a square yard of ground in British occupation, under the sun or moon, with a public post upon it, sticking to that post was a Barnacle. No intrepid navigator could plant a flagstaff upon any spot of earth, and take possession of it in the British name, but to that spot of earth, so soon as the discovery was known, the Circumlocution Office sent out a Barnacle and a despatch-box. Thus the Barnacles were all over the world, in every direction—despatch-boxing the compass." LD i 34

—employees: " . . . what the Barnacles had to do, was to stick on to the national ship as long as they could . . . to trim the ship, lighten the ship, clean the ship, would be to knock them off: that they could but be knocked off once; and that if the ship went down with them yet sticking to it, that was the ship's look out, and not theirs." LD i 10

"[Prince Bull] had been for some time very doubtful of his servants, who, besides being indolent and addicted to enriching their families at his expense, domineered over him dreadfully; threatening to discharge themselves if they were found the least fault with, pretending that they had done a wonderful amount of work when they had done nothing, making the most unmeaning speeches that ever were heard in the Prince's name, and uniformly showing themselves to be very inefficient indeed. Though, that some of them had excellent characters from previous situations is not to be denied." RP/PB

—hiring a chucklehead: " . . . it became necessary for Mr Sparkler to repair to England, and take his appointed part in the expression and direction of its genius, learning, commerce, spirit, and sense. The land of **Shakespeare**, **Milton**, **Bacon**, **Newton**, **Watt**, the land of a host of past and present

abstract philosophers, natural philosophers, and subduers of Nature and Art in their myriad forms, called to Mr Sparkler to come and take care of it, lest it should perish. Mr Sparkler, unable to resist the agonised cry from the depths of his country's soul, declared that he must go." LD ii 15 *And see* Government—*by a hierarchy*

—and Parliament

"Chapter X

"Containing the Whole Science of Government

"The Circumlocution Office was (as everybody knows without being told) the most important Department under Government. No public business of any kind could possibly be done at any time, without the acquiescence of the Circumlocution Office. Its finger was in the largest public pie, and in the smallest public tart. It was equally impossible to do the plainest right and to undo the plainest wrong, without the express authority of the Circumlocution Office. If another Gunpowder Plot had been discovered half an hour before the lighting of the match, nobody would have been justified in saving the parliament until there had been half a score of boards, half a bushel of minutes, several sacks of official memoranda, and a family-vault full of ungrammatical correspondence, on the part of the Circumlocution Office.

"This glorious establishment had been early in the field, when the one sublime principle involving the difficult art of governing a country, was first distinctly revealed to statesmen. It had been foremost to study that bright revelation, and to carry its shining influence through the whole of the official proceedings. Whatever was required to be done, the Circumlocution Office was beforehand with all the public departments in the art of perceiving—HOW NOT TO DO IT.

"Through this delicate perception, through the tact with which it invariably seized it, and through the genius with which it always acted on it, the Circumlocution Office had risen to overtop all the public departments; and the public condition had risen to be—what it was.

"It is true that How not to do it was the great study and object of all public departments and professional politicians all round the Circumlocution Office. It is true that every new premier and every new government, coming in because they had upheld a certain thing as necessary to be done, were no sooner come in than they applied their utmost faculties to discovering How not to do it.

"It is true that from the moment when a general election was over, every returned man who had been raving on hustings because it hadn't been done, and who had been asking the friends of the honourable gentleman in the opposite interest on pain of impeachment to tell him why it hadn't been done, and who had been asserting that it must be done, and who had been pledging himself that it should be done, began to devise, How it was not to be done.

"It is true that the debates of both Houses of Parliament the whole session through uniformly tended to the protracted deliberation, How not to do it. It is true that the royal speech at the opening of such session virtually said, My lords and gentlemen, you have a considerable stroke of work to do, and you will please to retire to your respective chambers, and discuss, How not to do it.

"It is true that the royal speech, at the close of such session, virtually said, My lords and gentlemen, you have through several laborious months been considering with great loyalty and patriotism, How not to do it, and you have found out; and with the blessing of Providence upon the harvest (natural, not political), I now dismiss you. All this is true, but the Circumlocution Office went beyond it.

"Because the Circumlocution Office went on mechanically, every day, keeping this wonderful, all-sufficient wheel of statesmanship, How not to do it, in motion. Because the Circumlocution Office was down upon any ill-advised public servant who was going to do it, or who appeared to be by any surprising accident in remote danger of doing it, with a minute, and a memorandum, and a letter of instructions, that extinguished him.

"It was this spirit of national efficiency in the Circumlocution Office that had gradually led to its having something to do with everything. Mechanicians, natural philosophers, soldiers, sailors, petitioners, memorialists, people with grievances, people who wanted to prevent grievances, people who wanted to redress grievances, jobbing people, jobbed people, people who couldn't get rewarded for merit, and people who couldn't get punished for demerit, were all indiscriminately tucked up under the foolscap paper of the Circumlocution Office.

"Numbers of people were lost in the Circumlocution Office. Unfortunates with wrongs, or with projects for the general welfare (and they had better have had wrongs at first, than have taken that bitter English recipe for certainly getting them), who in slow lapse of time and agony had passed safely through other public departments; who, according to rule, had been bullied in this, over-reached by that, and evaded by the other; got referred at last to the Circumlocution Office, and never reappeared in the light of day.

"Boards sat upon them, secretaries minuted upon them, commissioners gabbled about them, clerks registered, entered, checked, and ticked them off, and they melted away. In short, all the business of the country went through the Circumlocution Office, except the business that never came out of it; and *its* name was Legion.

"Sometimes, angry spirits attacked the Circumlocution Office. Sometimes, parliamentary questions were asked about it, and even parliamentary motions made or threatened about it, by demagogues so low and ignorant as to hold that the real recipe of government was, How to do it. Then would the noble lord, or right honourable gentleman, in whose department it was to defend the Circumlocution Office, put an orange in his pocket, and make a regular field-day of the occasion. Then would he come down to that house with a slap upon the table, and meet the honourable gentleman foot to foot.

"Then would he be there to tell that honourable gentleman that the Circumlocution Office not only was blameless in this matter, but was commendable in this matter, was extollable to the skies in this matter. Then would he be there to tell that honourable gentleman, that, although the Circumlocution Office was invariably right and wholly right, it never was so right as in this matter.

"Then would he be there to tell that honourable gentleman that it would have been more to his honour, more to his credit, more to his good taste, more to his good sense, more to half the dictionary commonplaces, if he had left the Circumlocution Office alone, and never approached this matter. Then would he keep one eye upon a coach or crammer from the Circumlocution Office sitting below the bar, and smash the honourable gentleman with the Circumlocution Office account of this matter.

"And although one of two things always happened; namely, either that the Circumlocution Office had nothing to say and said it, or that it had something to say of which the noble lord, or right honourable gentleman, blundered one half and forgot the other; the Circumlocution Office was always voted immaculate, by an accommodating majority.

"Such a nursery of statesmen had the Department become in virtue of a long career of this nature, that several solemn lords had attained the reputation of being quite unearthly prodigies of business, solely from having practised, How not to do it, at the head of the Circumlocution Office. As to the minor priests and acolytes of that temple, the result of all this was that they stood divided into two classes, and, down to the junior messenger, either believed in the Circumlocution Office as a heaven-born institution, that had an absolute right to do whatever it liked; or took refuge in total infidelity, and considered it a flagrant nuisance." ¶LD i 10 *And see* LC:Oratory—*Parliamentary*

—*probationary:* "And there, too, was a sprinkling of less distinguished Parliamentary Barnacles, who had not as yet got anything snug, and were going through their probation to prove their worthiness. These Barnacles perched upon staircases and hid in passages, waiting their orders to make houses or not to make houses; and they did all their hearing, and ohing, and cheering, and barking, under directions from the heads of the family; and they put dummy motions on the paper in the way of other men's motions; and they stalled disagreeable subjects off until late in the night and late in the session, and then with virtuous patriotism cried out that it was too late; and they went down into the country, whenever they were sent, and swore that Lord Decimus had revived trade from a swoon, and commerce from a fit, and had doubled the harvest of corn, quadrupled the harvest of hay, and prevented no end of gold from flying out of the Bank.

"Also these Barnacles were dealt, by the heads of the family, like so many cards below the court-cards, to public meetings and dinners; where they bore testimony to all sorts of services on the part of their noble and honourable relatives, and buttered the Barnacles on all sorts of toasts. And they stood, under similar orders, at all sorts of elections; and they turned out of their own seats, on the shortest notice and the most unreasonable terms, to let in other men; and they fetched and carried, and toadied and jobbed, and corrupted, and ate heaps of dirt, and were indefatigable in the public service.

"And there was not a list, in all the Circumlocution Office, of places that might fall vacant anywhere within half a century, from a lord of the Treasury to a Chinese consul, and up again to a governor-general of India, but, as applicants for such places, the names of some or of every one of these hungry and adhesive Barnacles were down." ¶LD i 34

—*unapproachable:* "'Regard our place from the point of view that we only ask you to leave us alone, and we are as capital a Department as you'll find anywhere.'

"'Is your place there to be left alone?' asked Clennam.

"'You exactly hit it,' returned Ferdinand. 'It is there with the express intention that everything shall be left alone. That is what it means. That is what it's for. No doubt there's a certain form to be kept up that it's for something else, but it's only a form. Why, good Heaven, we are nothing but forms! Think what a lot of our forms you have gone through. And you have never got any nearer to an end?'

"'Never,' said Clennam.

"'Look at it from the right point of view, and there you have us—official and effectual. It's like a limited game of cricket. A field of outsiders are always going in to bowl at the Public Service, and we block the balls.'

"Clennam asked what became of the bowlers? The airy young Barnacle replied, that they grew tired, got dead beat, got lamed, got their backs broken, died off, gave it up, went in for other games . . . .

"'And the invention?' said Clennam.

"' . . . nobody wants to know of the invention, and nobody cares twopence-halfpenny about it.'

"'Nobody in the Office, that is to say?'

"'Nor out of it. Everybody is ready to dislike and ridicule any invention. You have no idea how many people want to be left alone. You have no idea how the Genius of the country . . . tends to being left alone. Believe me, Mr Clennam,' said the sprightly young Barnacle, in his pleasantest manner, 'our place is not a wicked Giant to be charged at full tilt; but, only a windmill showing you, as it grinds immense quantities of chaff, which way the country wind blows.'" LD ii 28

Government, local

—*alderman:* "Seen the Alderman? Oh, dear! Who could ever help seeing the Alderman? He was so considerate, so affable, he bore so much in mind the natural desire of folks to see him, that if he had a fault, it was the being constantly On View. And wherever the great people were, there, to be sure, attracted by the kindred sympathy between great souls, was Cute." C 3

—*beadle*

—*authority:* "I have yet to learn [writes Boz] that a beadle, without the precincts of a church, churchyard, or workhouse, and acting otherwise than under the express orders of churchwardens and overseers in council assembled, to enforce the law against people who come upon the parish, and other offenders, has any lawful authority whatever over the rising youth of this country. I have yet to learn that a beadle can be called out by any civilian to exercise a domination and despotism over the boys of Britain. I have yet to learn that a beadle will be permitted by the commissioners of poor law regulation to wear out the soles and heels of his boots in illegal interference with the liberties of people not proved poor or otherwise criminal. I have yet to learn that a beadle has power to stop up the Queen's highway at his will and pleasure, or that the whole width of the street is not free and open to any man, boy, or woman in existence, up to the very walls of the houses . . . . " B/M2

—*criticized:* "'As to Beadle [said Mr Meagles], that I needn't say was wholly out of the question. If there is anything that is not to be tolerated on any terms, anything that is a type of Jack-in-office insolence and absurdity, anything that represents in coats, waistcoats, and big sticks, our English holding-on by nonsense, after every one has found it out, it is a beadle. You haven't seen a beadle lately? . . . Don't you see a beadle, now, if you can help it. Whenever I see a beadle in full fig, coming down a street on a Sunday at the head of a charity school, I am obliged to turn and run away, or I should hit him." LD i 1

—figurative: " . . . they were received by a portentous beadle. Mr Dombey, dismounting first to help the ladies out, and standing near him at the church door, looked like another beadle. A beadle less gorgeous but more dreadful; the beadle of private life; the beadle of our business and our bosoms." DS 5

—parish workhouse: "The parish beadle is one of the most, perhaps *the* most, important member of the local administration. He is not so well off as the churchwardens, certainly, nor is he to so learned as the vestry-clerk, nor does he order things quite so much his own way as either of them. But his power is very great, notwithstanding; and the dignity of his office is never impaired by the absence of efforts on his part to maintain it. The beadle of our parish is a splendid fellow. It is quite delightful to hear him, as he explains the state of the existing poor laws to the deaf old women in the board-room passage on business nights; and to hear what he said to the senior churchwarden, and what the senior churchwarden said to him; and what 'we' (the beadle and the other gentlemen) came to the determination of doing." SB/B

"'Well, and good morning to *you,* sir,' replied Mrs Mann, with many smiles; 'and hoping you find yourself well, sir!'

"'So-so, Mrs Mann,' replied the beadle. 'A porochial life is not a bed of roses, Mrs Mann.'

"'Ah, that it isn't indeed, Mr Bumble,' rejoined the lady. And all the infant paupers might have chorused the rejoinder with great propriety, if they had heard it.

"'A porochial life, ma'am,' continued Mr Bumble, striking the table with his cane, 'is a life of worrit, and vexation, and hardihood; but all public characters, as I may say, must suffer prosecution.'" OT 17

The author "had purposed to introduce, in this place, a dissertation touching the divine right of beadles, and elucidative of the position, that a beadle can do no wrong: which could not fail to have been both pleasurable and profitable to the right-minded reader, but which he is unfortunately compelled, by want of time and space, to postpone to some more convenient and fitting opportunity; on the arrival of which, he will be prepared to show, that a beadle properly constituted: that is to say, a parochial beadle, attached to a parochial workhouse, and attending in his official capacity the parochial church: is, in right and virtue of his office, possessed of all the excellences and best qualities of humanity; and that to none of those excellences, can mere companies' beadles, or court-of-law beadles, or even chapel-of-ease beadles (save the last, and they in a very lowly and inferior degree), lay the remotest sustainable claim." OT 27

—tolerated: "The beadle, though generally understood in the neighbourhood to be a ridiculous institution, is not without a certain popularity for the moment, if it were only as a man who is going to see the body. The policeman considers him an imbecile civilian, a remnant of the barbarous watchmen-times; but gives him admission, as something that must be borne with until Government shall abolish him." BH 11

—usefulness: "I regard this as a very notable uncommercial experience [serving compassionately on a jury], because this good came of a Beadle. And to the best of my knowledge, information, and belief, it is the only good that ever did come of a Beadle since the first Beadle put on his cocked-hat." UT/RM

Index IV *has 11 named beadles, and* Index VIII *24 entries, of whom* one, *exhausted and very hungry* UT/LC, *is a sympathetic figure.*

—licensing: "Every [French] butcher must be licensed: which proves him at once to be a slave, for we don't license butchers in England—we only license apothecaries, attorneys, post-masters, publicans, hawkers, retailers of tobacco, snuff, pepper, and vinegar—and one or two other little trades, not worth mentioning." RP/FF

—master of the workhouse: "He is an admirable specimen of a small tyrant: morose, brutish, and ill-tempered; bullying to his inferiors, cringing to his superiors, and jealous of the influence and authority of the beadle." SB/B

—mayors: "The sports and feasts which took place [following Henry VII's accession] were followed by a terrible fever, called the Sweating Sickness; of which great numbers of people died. Lord Mayors and Aldermen are thought to have suffered most from it; whether, because they were in the habit of

over-eating themselves, or because they were very jealous of preserving filth and nuisances in the City (as they have been since), I don't know." CHE 26

" . . . the Fire [of 1666] was a great blessing to the City afterwards, for it arose from its ruins very much improved—built more regularly, more widely, more cleanly and carefully, and therefore much more healthily. It might be far more healthy than it is, but there are some people in it still—even now, at this time, nearly two hundred years later—so selfish, so pig-headed, and so ignorant, that I doubt if even another Great Fire would warm them up to do their duty." CHE 35 i

"Without mayors, and many of them, it cannot be disputed that the whole framework of society—Mr Sapsea is confident that he invented that forcible figure—would fall to pieces." MED 12

See H:Knighthood—*hope for mayors; and* L:Lord Mayor

—*office-holding:* "[Mr Bumble] had a decided propensity for bullying: derived no inconsiderable pleasure from the exercise of petty cruelty; and, consequently, was (it is needless to say) a coward. This is by no means a disparagement to his character; for many official personages, who are held in high respect and admiration, are the victims of similar infirmities. The remark is made, indeed, rather in his favour than otherwise, and with a view of impressing the reader with a just sense of his qualifications for office." OT 37

—*rate collection:* "' . . . upon my life, I thought you were the King's-taxes.'

"'No!' said Mr Winkle.

"'I did, indeed,' responded Bob Sawyer, 'and I was just going to say that I wasn't at home, but if you'd leave a message I'd be sure to give it to myself; for he don't know me; no more does the Lighting and Paving. I think the Church-rates guesses who I am, and I know the Water-works does, because I drew a tooth of his when I first came down here.'" PP 38

—*urban planning:* "In the hardest working part of Coketown; in the innermost fortifications of that ugly citadel, where Nature was as strongly bricked out as killing airs and gases were bricked in; at the heart of the labyrinth of narrow courts upon courts, and close streets upon streets, which had come into existence piecemeal, every piece in a violent hurry for some one man's purpose, and the whole an unnatural family, shouldering, and trampling, and pressing one another to death; in the last close nook of this great exhausted receiver, where the chimneys, for want of air to make a draught, were built in an immense variety of stunted and crooked shapes . . . . " HT i 10

—*vestry*

—*in London:* "You may recollect the Reports of the Board of Health on the subject of cholera, and you may recollect the Reports of the discussions on the same subject at some Vestry Meetings. I have the honor . . . to be one of the constituent body of the amazing Vestry of Marylebone; and if you chance to remember . . . what the Board of Health *did,* in Glasgow and other places, and what my vestry *said,* you will probably agree with me that between this so-called Centralization, and this Vestrylization, the former is by far the best thing to stand by in an emergency. My vestry even took the high ground of denying the existence of cholera in any unusual degree. And though that denial had no greater effect upon the disease than my vestry's denial of the existence of Jacob's Island had upon the Earth about Bermondsey, the circumstance may be suggestive to you in considering what Vestrylization is, when a few noisy little landlords interested in the maintenance of abuses, struggle to the foremost ranks; and what the so-called Centralization is when it is a combination of active business habits, sound medical knowledge, and a zealous sympathy with the sufferings of the people." S/AR

—*public health:* "On the least provocation, or on none, it will be clamorous to know whether it is to be 'dictated to,' or 'trampled on,' or 'ridden over rough-shod.'

"Its great watchword is Self-government. That is to say, supposing our Vestry to favour any little harmless disorder like Typhus Fever, and supposing the Government of the country to be, by any accident, in such ridiculous hands, as that any of its authorities should consider it a duty to object to Typhus Fever—obviously an unconstitutional objection—then, our Vestry cuts in with a terrible manifesto about Self-government, and claims its independent right to have as much Typhus Fever as pleases itself.

"Some absurd and dangerous persons have represented, on the other hand, that though our Vestry may be able to 'beat the bounds' of its own parish, it may not be able to beat the bounds of its own diseases; which (say they) spread over the whole land, in an ever-expanding circle of waste, and misery, and death, and widowhood, and orphanage, and desolation. But our Vestry makes short work of any such fellows as these.

"It was our Vestry—pink of Vestries as it is—that in support of its favourite principle took the celebrated ground of denying the existence of the last pestilence that raged in England, when the pestilence was raging at the Vestry doors. Dogginson said it was plums; Mr Wigsby (of Chumbledon Square) said it was oysters; Mr Magg (of Little Winkling Street) said, amid great cheering, it was the newspapers.

"The noble indignation of our Vestry with that un-English institution the Board of Health, under those circumstances, yields one of the finest passages in its history. It wouldn't hear of rescue. Like Mr Joseph Miller's Frenchman, it would be drowned and nobody should save it. Transported beyond grammar by its kindled ire, it spoke in unknown tongues, and vented unintelligible bellowings, more like an ancient oracle than the modern oracle it is admitted on all hands to be. Rare exigencies produce rare things; and even our Vestry, new hatched to the woful time, came forth a greater goose than ever." ¶RP/V

Government, national

—*a fundamental view:* "My faith in the people governing is, on the whole, infinitesimal; my faith in The People governed, is, on the whole illimitable." S/BM2

—*appropriations:*"FOUND—A GREAT DEAL OF MONEY belonging to nobody, on its way to boroughs and counties to do nothing." AY/OR

—*call for protective regulation:* "The whole system of shipping and conveying [poor emigrants] is one that stands in need of thorough revision. If any class deserve to be protected and assisted by the Government, it is that class who are banished from their native land in search of the bare means of subsistence . . . .

"The law is bound, at least upon the English side, to see that too many of them are not put on board one ship: and that their accommodations are decent; not demoralising and profligate. It is bound, too, in common humanity, to declare that no man shall be taken on board without his stock of provisions being previously inspected by some proper officer, and pronounced moderately sufficient for his support upon the voyage.

"It is bound to provide, or to require that there be provided, a medical attendant; whereas in these ships there are none, though sickness of adults, and deaths of children, on the passage, are matters of the very commonest occurrence.

"Above all, it is the duty of any Government, be it monarchy or republic, to interpose and put an end to that system by which a firm of traders in emigrants purchase of the owners the whole 'tween-decks of a ship, and send on board as many wretched people as they can lay hold of. . . . " ¶AN 16

—*conduct of war in the Crimea:* "I wish to avoid placing in opposition here, the two words Aristocracy and People. I am one of those who can believe in the virtues and uses of both, and, I would elevate or depress neither, at the cost of a single just right belonging to either. I will use, instead of these words, the terms, the governors and the governed. These two bodies the [Administrative Reform] Association finds with a gulf between them, in which lie, newly buried, thousands on thousands of the bravest and most devoted men that, even England ever bred . . . .

" . . . an illustration:—A respectable old gentleman with a large and costly establishment of servants, finds his household in complete disorder, and that he can get nothing done. When he asks his servants to give his children bread, they give them stones; when they are told to give those children fish, they give them serpents. What they are ordered to send to the East they send to the West; when they ought to be serving dinner in the North, they are consulting obsolete and exploded cookery books in the South; they break, lose, forget, waste, destroy; only tumble over one another when required to do anything; and make the respectable gentleman's house a scene of scandalous ruin.

"At last the respectable gentleman calls to him his house steward, and says, even then more in sorrow than in anger, 'This is a terrible business, no fortune can stand it—no mortal equanimity can bear it! I must change my system of appointing my servants; I must obtain servants who know and will do their duty.' The house steward throws up his eyes in pious horror, ejaculates 'Good God, here is my master setting class against class!' rushes off into the servants' hall, and delivers a long and melting oration on that wicked theme." ¶S/AR

And see —incompetent; and H:War—*Crimean War incompetence*

—crisis: "England has been a dreadful state for some weeks. Lord Coodle would go out, Sir Thomas Doodle wouldn't come in, and there being nobody in Great Britain (to speak of) except Coodle and Doodle, there has been no Government. It is a mercy that the hostile meeting between those two great men, which at one time seemed inevitable, did not come off; because if both pistols had taken effect, and Coodle and Doodle had killed each other, it is to be presumed that England must have waited to be governed until young Coodle and young Doodle, now in frocks and long stockings, were grown up.

"This stupendous national calamity, however, was averted by Lord Coodle's making the timely discovery, that if in the heat of debate he had said that he scorned and despised the whole ignoble career of Sir Thomas Doodle, he had merely meant to say that party differences should never induce him to withhold from it the tribute of his warmest admiration; while it as opportunely turned out, on the other hand, that Sir Thomas Doodle had in his own bosom expressly booked Lord Coodle to go down to posterity as the mirror of virtue and honour.

"Still England has been some weeks in the dismal strait of having no pilot . . . to weather the storm; and the marvellous part of the matter is, that England has not appeared to care very much about it, but has gone on eating and drinking and marrying and giving in marriage, as the old world did in the days before the flood. But Coodle knew the danger, and Doodle knew the danger, and all their followers and hangers-on had the clearest possible perception of the danger. At last Sir Thomas Doodle has not only condescended to come in, but has done it handsomely, bringing in with him all his nephews, all his male cousins, and all his brothers-in-law. So there is hope for the old ship yet." ¶BH 40

—custom-house: "The servile rapacity of the French officials is sufficiently contemptible; but there is a surly boorish incivility about our men, alike disgusting to all persons who fall into their hands, and discreditable to the nation that keeps such ill-conditioned curs snarling about its gates." AN 3

—discourse compared: "It is a widely diffused custom among savage tribes, when they meet to discuss any affair of public importance, to sit up all night making a horrible noise, dancing, blowing shells, and (in cases where they are familiar with fire-arms) flying out into open places and letting off guns. It is questionable whether our legislative assemblies might not take a hint from this. A shell is not a melodious wind-instrument, and it is monotonous; but it is as musical as, and not more monotonous than, my Honourable friend's own trumpet, or the trumpet that he blows so hard for the Minister . . . .

"The honourable and savage member who has a loaded gun, and has grown impatient of debate, plunges out of doors, fires in the air, and returns calm and silent to the Palaver. Let the honourable civilised member similarly charged with a speech dart into the cloisters of Westminster Abbey in the silence of night, let his speech off, and come back harmless." ¶UT/MM

—Foreign Office

—on duty: "It was not yet black dark, and the roll was only just gone through, when up comes Mr Commissioner Pordage with his Diplomatic coat on.

"'Captain Carton,' says he, 'Sir, what is this?'

"'This, Mr Commissioner" (he was very short with him), 'is an expedition against the Pirates. It is a secret expedition, so please to keep it a secret.'

"'Sir,' says Commissioner Pordage, 'I trust there is going to be no unnecessary cruelty committed?'

"'Sir,' returns the officer, 'I trust not.'

"'That is not enough, Sir,' cried Commissioner Pordage, getting wroth. 'Captain Carton, I give you notice. Government requires you to treat the enemy with great delicacy, consideration, clemency, and forbearance.'

"'Sir,' says Captain Carton, 'I am an English officer, commanding English Men, and I hope I am not likely to disappoint the Government's just expectations. But, I presume you know that these villains under their black flag have despoiled our countrymen of their property, burnt their homes, barbarously murdered them and their little children, and worse than murdered their wives and daughters?'

"'Perhaps I do, Captain Carton,' answers Pordage, waving his hand, with dignity; 'perhaps I do not. It is not customary, Sir, for Government to commit itself.'" CS/EP 1

—*in retirement:* " . . . the paternal Gowan, originally attached to a legation abroad, had been pensioned off as a Commissioner of nothing particular somewhere or other, and had died at his post with his drawn salary in his hand, nobly defending it to the last extremity." LD i 17

"[Mrs Gowan] was a little lofty with him; so was another old lady, dark-browed and high-nosed, and who must have had something real about her, or she could not have existed, but it was certainly not her hair or her teeth or her figure or her complexion; so was a grey old gentleman of dignified and sullen appearance; both of whom had come to dinner. But, as they had all been in the British Embassy way in sundry parts of the earth, and as a British Embassy cannot better establish a character with the Circumlocution Office than by treating its compatriots with illimitable contempt (else it would become like the Embassies of other countries), Clennam felt that on the whole they let him off lightly." LD i 26

And see Civil Service—*and Empire*

—*by gentlemen:* " . . . I am certainly am not content to have such tricks played in the execution of public work as have been played for years upon years, in this and every 'Yard' in England, by the eminent personages who have condescended to do the public the great honour of directing such operations. More obstruction of good things and patronage of bad things, more extravagance, jobbery, ignorance, conceit, saving of cheese-parings and waste of gold, have been committed in these Dockyards (as in everything connected with the misdirection of the Navy), than in every other branch of the public service put together, including even the Woods and Forests.

"And however conscious I may be that an individual can do little, I very heartily protest that I mean to do all the little I can, to have England governed by men of merit, and not by fine gentlemen. An individual opinion is of small consequence, I know; but my opinion may possibly be held by others—and it is, that no privileged class is, by a direct dispensation of Providence, born to the broad arrow.* Many people are born with silver spoons in their mouths, many more with wooden ladles, but I never did hear of two or three genteel families being expressly born to the broad arrow. They may have taken possession of it as a matter of course, but that is another thing. It shows us, the people, the effect of a little combination on their part; and I think it is almost time for us to show *them* the effect of a little combination on ours." HWC/D

**a mark placed on government property; by extension the right to enjoy the perquisites of office*

—*the homeless:* "It is an awful thing, looking round upon those one hundred and sixty-seven representatives [in a Ragged School shelter] of many thousands, to reflect that a Government, unable, with the least regard to truth, to plead ignorance of the existence of such a place, should proceed as if the sleepers never were to wake again. I do not hesitate to say . . . that an annual sum of money, contemptible in amount as compared with any charges upon any list, freely granted in behalf of these Schools, and shackled with no preposterous Red Tape conditions, would relieve the prisons, diminish county rates, clear loads of shame and guilt out of the streets, recruit the army and navy, waft to new countries, Fleets full of useful labour, for which their inhabitants would be thankful and beholden to us." HW/SU

—*House of Commons*

"There are two public bodies remarkable for knowing nothing of the people, and for perpetually interfering to put them right. The one is the House of Commons; the other the Monomaniacs." HW/GB

—*in brief, politely:* "'But you have not imparted to me,' remarks Veneering, 'what you think of my entering the House of Commons?'

"'I think,' rejoins Twemlow feelingly, 'that it is the best club in London.'" OMF ii 3

—*criticized:* "The specimen of Representative Chamber to which [Mr Bull] invited their anxious attention, was brought from Westminster Market. It had been collected there in the month of July in the present year. No particular counter had been resorted to more than another, but the whole market had been laid under contribution to furnish the sample. Its diseased condition would be apparent, without any scientific aids, to the most short-sighted individual.

"It was fearfully adulterated with Talk, stained with Job, and diluted with large quantities of colouring matter of a false and deceptive nature. It was thickly overlaid with a varnish which he had resolved into its component parts, and had found to be made of Trash (both maudlin and defiant), boiled up with large quantities of Party Turpitude, and a heap of Cant. Cant, he need not tell the Commission, was the worst of poisons. It was almost inconceivable to him how an article in itself so wholesome as Representative Chamber, could have been got into this disgraceful state. It was mere Carrion, wholly unfit for human consumption, and calculated to produce nausea and vomiting." ¶HW/OC

—in dustman's terms: "[Louisa's] father was usually sifting and sifting at his parliamentary cinder-heap in London (without being observed to turn up many precious articles among the rubbish), and was still hard at it in the national dust-yard." HT ii 9

"Mr Gradgrind, apprised of his wife's decease, made an expedition from London, and buried her in a business-like manner. He then returned with promptitude to the national cinder-heap, and resumed his sifting for the odds and ends he wanted, and his throwing of the dust about into the eyes of other people who wanted other odds and ends—in fact resumed his parliamentary duties." HT ii 11

—haunted: "The first supernatural persecution . . . was the sound of a tremendous quantity of oaths. This was succeeded by the dragging of great weights about the house at untimely hours, accompanied with fearful noises, such as shrieking, yelling, barking, braying, crowing, coughing, fiendish laughter, and the like . . . a gush of words incessantly pouring forth within the haunted premises, was even more distressing still.

"In the dead of night, words, words, words—words of laudation, words of vituperation, words of indignation, words of peroration, words of order, words of disorder; words, words, words—the same words in the same weary array, of little or no meaning, over and over again—resounded in the unhappy gentleman's ears. The Irish accent was very frequently detectible in these dreadful sounds, and Mr Bull considered it an aggravation of his misery.

"All this time, the strangest and wildest confusion reigned among the furniture. Seats were overturned and knocked about; papers of importance that were laid upon the table, unaccountably disappeared; large measures were brought in and dropped; Members of Mr Bull's family were repeatedly thrown from side to side, without appearing to know that they had changed sides at all; other Members were absurdly hoisted from surprising distances to foremost benches, where they tried to hold on tight, but couldn't by any means effect it; invisible kicks flew about with the utmost rapidity; the seals of Mr Bull's offices, though of some weight, were tossed to and fro, like shuttlecocks . . . .

"In addition to these fearful revels, it was found that a forest growth of cobweb and fungus, which in the course of many generations had accumulated in the lobbies and passages of Mr Bull's old house, supernaturally sprung up at compound interest in the lobbies and passages of the new one, which were further infested by swarms of (supposed) unclean spirits that took refuge in the said growth." HW/HH

—in literary terms: "I will not ask how it comes to pass that personal altercations, involving all the removes and definitions of **Shakespeare**'s *Touchstone*—the retort courteous—the reply churlish—the reproof valiant—the countercheck quarrelsome—the lie circumstantial and the lie direct—are always of immeasurably greater interest in the House of Commons than the health, the taxation, the education, of a whole people.

"I will not penetrate the mysteries of that secret chamber in which the Bluebeard, Party, keeps his strangled public questions, straitly charging his last bride, the new comer, on no account to open the door." ¶S/AR

—and neglected children: "There are six hundred and fifty-six gentlemen in the English House of Commons assembling in London. There is not one of those gentlemen who may not, in one week, if he choose, acquire as dismal a knowledge of the Hell upon earth in which he lives, in regard of these children, as this [police] Inspector has—as we have—as no man can by possibility shut out, who will walk this town with open eyes observant of what is crying to GOD in the streets.

"If we were one of those six hundred and fifty-six, and had the courage to declare that we know the day *must come* when these children must be taken, by the strong hand, out of our shameful public ways, and must be rescued—when the State must (no will, or will not, in the case, but must) take up neglected and ignorant children wheresoever they are found, severely punishing the parents when they can be found, too, and forcing them, if they have any means of existence, to contribute something towards the reclamation of their offspring, but never again entrusting them with the duties they have aban-doned;—if we were to say this, and were to add that as the day must come, it cannot come too soon, and had best come now—Red Tape would arise against us in ten thousand shapes of virtuous opposition, and cocks would crow, and donkeys would bray, and owls would hoot, and strangers would be espied, and houses would be counted out, and we should be satisfactorily put down.

"Meanwhile, in Aberdeen, the horror has risen to that height, that against the law, the authorities have by force swept their streets clear of these unchristian objects, and have, to the utmost extent of their illegal powers, successfully done this very thing.

"Do none of the six hundred and fifty-six know of it—do none of them look into it—do none of them lay down their newspapers when they read of a baby sentenced for the third, fourth, fifth, sixth, seventh time to imprisonment and whipping, and ask themselves the question, 'Is there any earthly thing this child can do when this new sentence is fulfilled, but steal again, and be again imprisoned and again flogged, until, a precocious human devil, it is shipped away to corrupt a new world?'

"Do none of the six hundred and fifty-six, care to walk from Charing Cross to Whitechapel—to look into Wentworth Street—to stray into the lanes of Westminster—to go into a prison almost within the shadow of their own Victoria Tower—to see with their eyes and hear with their ears, what such childhood is, and what escape it has from being what it is? Well! Red Tape is easier, and tells for more in blue books, and will give you a committee five years long if you like, to enquire whether the wind ever blows, or the rain ever falls—and then you can talk about it, and do nothing." HWC/MP

—in theatrical terms: "I will not say that if I wanted to form a company of Her Majesty's servants, I think I should know where to put my hand on 'the comic old gentleman'; nor, that if I wanted to get up a pantomime, I fancy I should know what establishment to go to for the tricks and changes; also, for a very extensive host of supernumeraries, to trip one another up in that scene of contention with which many of us are familiar, both on these and on other boards, in which the principal objects thrown about, are loaves and fishes . . . .

"The public theatricals which the noble lord [**Palmerston**] is so condescending as to manage, are so intolerably bad, the machinery is so cumbrous, the parts so ill distributed, the company so full of 'walking gentlemen', the managers have such large families, and are so bent upon putting those families into what is theatrically called 'first business'—not because of their aptitude for it, but because they *are* their families, that we find ourselves obliged to organize an opposition.

"We have seen the *Comedy of Errors* played so dismally like a tragedy that we cannot bear it. We are, therefore, making bold to get up the *School of Reform,* and we hope, before the play is out, to improve that noble lord by our performance very considerably. If he object that we have no right to improve him without his license, we venture to claim that right in virtue of his orchestra, consisting of a very powerful piper, whom we always pay." ¶S/AR

—unresponsive: "Time hustled him into a little noisy and rather dirty machinery, in a by-corner, and made [Gradgrind] Member of Parliament for Coketown: one of the respected members for ounce weights and measures, one of the representatives of the multiplication table, one of the deaf honourable gentlemen, dumb honourable gentlemen, blind honourable gentlemen, lame honourable gentlemen, dead honourable gentlemen, to every other consideration. Else wherefore live we in a Christian land, eighteen hundred and odd years after our Master?" HT i 14

"I will not ask how it happens that bills which cramp and worry the people, and restrict their scant enjoyments, are so easily smuggled through that place, and how it happens that measures for their real service are so very difficult to pass. I will not analyse the confined air of the lobby, or reduce to their primitive gases, its deadening influences . . . . I will merely put it . . . whether the House of Commons is not occasionally a little hard of hearing, not a little dim of sight, not a little slow of understanding: whether, in short, it is not in a sufficiently invalided state to require close watching, and the occasional application of sharp stimulants; and whether it is not capable of improvement?

"I believe that, in order to preserve it in a state of real usefulness and independence, the people must be ever watchful and ever jealous of it; and it must have its memory jogged; it must be kept awake; when it happens to have taken too much Ministerial narcotic, it must be trotted about, and must be hustled and pinched in a friendly way, as is the usage in such cases." ¶S/AR

—incompetent: "Analysis had detected in every one of [the Public Offices], from seventy-five to ninety-eight per cent. of Noodledom. Noodledom was a deadly poison. An over-dose of it would destroy a whole nation, and [there was] a recent case where it had caused the death of many thousand men [Crimean War]. It was sometimes called Routine, sometimes Gentlemanly Business, sometimes The Best Intentions, and sometimes Amiable Incapacity; but, call it what you would analysis always resolved it into Noodledom. There was nothing in the whole united domains of the animal, vegetable, and mineral kingdoms, so incompatible with all the function of life as Noodledom." HW/OC

" . . . the truth, that the system of administering [the public's] affairs is innately bad; that classes and families and interests, have brought them to a very low pass; that the intelligence, steadfastness, foresight, and wonderful power of resource, which in private undertakings distinguish England from all other countries, have no vitality in its public business; that while every merchant and trader has enlarged his grasp and quickened his faculties, the Public Departments have been drearily lying in state, a mere stupid pageant of gorgeous coffins and feebly-burning lights; and that the windows must now be opened wide, and the candles put out, and the coffins buried, and the dayhlight freely admitted, and the furniture made firewood, and the dirt clean swept away." HW/OP

" . . . if Mr **Wild**, for example, who is close to me, were a distributor of news for the two reasons that his great grandmother, the Dowager-dowager Mrs Wild had been a distributor of news, and that he himself had not the slightest knowledge of his own business, I should have slight hope of him. Or, if he had selected for his assistant a man who left me the *Morning Post* for the last Christmas Day twelve months, instead of *The Times* of this morning, sent my copy of the *Examiner* to Bengal instead of to Tavistock Square, and insisted in serving me with publications I never wished to see, while keeping back those I am dying to read, I should have very small hope of him; and I should take the liberty of saying of such a master and man—as I have taken the liberty of saying pretty often latterly of another master [**Lord Palmerston**] and man: 'It is perfectly clear that no good whatever can come out of these people; they are a scarcely animated heap of confusion and imbecility, and they can no more become better than roses can bloom in the Great Desert, or than the Great Pyramid can stand on its head.'" S/N3

—monkish influence: "The King was at first as blind and stubborn as kings usually have been whensoever they have been in the hands of monks." CHE 6

—narrow leadership: " . . . it is perfectly clear to the brilliant and distinguished circle, all round, that nobody is in question but Boodle and his retinue, and Buffy and *his* retinue. These are the great actors for whom the stage is reserved. A People there are, no doubt—a certain large number of supernumeraries, who are to be occasionally addressed, and relied upon for shouts and choruses, as on the theatrical stage; but Boodle and Buffy, their followers and families, their heirs, executors, administrators, and assigns, are the born first-actors, managers, and leaders, and no others can appear upon the scene for ever and ever.

"In this, too, there is perhaps more Dandyism at Chesney Wold than the brilliant and distinguished circle will find good for itself in the long run. For it is, even with the stillest and politest circles, as with the circle the necromancer draws around him—very strange appearances may be seen in active motion outside. With this difference; that, being realities and not phantoms, there is the greater danger of their breaking in." BH 12

—Parliament: " . . . I do not remember having ever fainted away, or having even been moved to tears of joyful pride, at sight of any legislative body. I have borne the House of Commons like a man, and have yielded to no weakness, but slumber, in the House of Lords. I have seen elections for borough and county, and have never been impelled (no matter which party won) to damage my hat by throwing it up into the air in triumph, or to crack my voice, by

shouting for any reference to our Glorious Constitution, to the noble purity of our independent voters, or, the unimpeachable integrity of our independent members. Having withstood such strong attacks upon my fortitude, it is possible that I may be of a cold and insensible temperament, amounting to iciness, in such matters . . . . " AN 8

And see —House of Commons; Civil Service—*and Parliament;* Member of Parliament; *and* W:America—*Congress*

—pension "'In this state of mind, he petitioned the government for—I want a word again, gentlemen—what do you call that which they give to people when it's found out, at last, that they've never been of any use, and have been paid too much for doing nothing?'

"'Compensation?' suggested the vice." L

—responsibility: "MISSING—ON ALL OCCASIONS, the man who is responsible for anything done ill in the public service. He will particularly oblige by coming forward." AY/OR

—a sneer and a response: "Said the noble lord at the head of the Government, when Mr [**Austen Henry**] **Layard** asked him for a day for his motion [to inquire into Crimean War management], Let the hon. gentleman find a day for himself.

"'Now, in the names of all the gods at once,
Upon what meat doth this our Caesar feed,
That he is grown so great?'

If our Caesar will excuse me, I would take the liberty of reversing that cool and lofty sentiment, and I would say, 'First Lord, it is your duty to see that no man is left to find a day for himself. See you, who take the responsibility of government, who aspire to it, live for it, intrigue for it, scramble for it, who hold to it tooth-and-nail when you can get it, see you that no man is left to find a day for himself. In this old country, with its seething hard-worked millions, its heavy taxes, its crowds of ignorant, its crowds of poor, its crowds of wicked, woe the day which the dangerous man shall find for himself, because the head of the Queen's Government failed in his duty of anticipating it by a brighter and better one! Name you the day, First Lord; make the day; work for a day beyond your little time, **Lord Palmerston**, and History in return may then—not otherwise—find a day for you; a day equally associated with the contentment of the loyal, patient, willing-hearted English people, and with the happiness of your Royal Mistress and her fair line of children.'" S/AR

—somnambulistic: "The patient in whom are manifested the distressing symptoms of somnambulism I shall describe, is an old woman—Mrs Abigail Dean . . . always known in the House as Abby Dean [**Lord Aberdeen**] . . . .

"As if everything about this old woman were destined to be strange and exceptional, it is remarkable that although Abby Dean is at the head of the Upper Servants' Hall, and occupies the post of housekeeper in Mr Bull's family, nobody has the least confidence in her, and even Mr Bull himself has not the slightest idea how she got into the situation . . . .

"The following extracts from my notes of the case will describe her in her normal condition: 'Abby Dean. Phlelgmatic temperament. Bilious habit. Circulation, very sluggish. Speech, drowsy, indistinct, and confused. Senses, feeble. Memory, short. Pulse, very languid. A remarkably slow goer. At all times a heavy sleeper, and difficult to awaken. When awakened, peevish. Earlier in life had fits, and was much contorted—first on one side, and then on the other.'" HW/MB

"She will get up and dress herself, and go to Mr Bull's Treasury, or take her seat on her usual Bench in the Upper Servants' Hall, avoiding on the way the knocking of her head against walls and doors, but giving no other sign of intellectual vigour. She will sometimes sit up very late at night, moaning and muttering, and occasionally rising on her legs to complain of being attacked by enemies. (The common delusion that people are conspiring against her, is, as might naturally be expected, a feature of her disease.)

"She will frequently cram into her pockets a large accumulation of Mr Bull's bills, plans for the improvement of his estate, and other documents of importance, and will drop the same without any reason, and refuse to take them up again when they are offered to her. Other similar papers she will hide in holes and corners, quickly forgetting what she has done with them.

"Sometimes, she will fall to wringing her hands in the course of her wanderings in the House, and to declaring that unless she is treated with greater deference she will 'go out.' But, it is a curious illustration of the cunning often mingled with this disorder that she has never stirred an inch beyond the door; having, evidently, some latent consciousness in the midst of her stupor, that if she once went out, no earthly consideration would prevail on Mr Bull to let her in again." ¶HW/MB

—*welfare:* " . . . a Public Charity is immeasurably better than a Private Foundation, no matter how munificently the latter may be endowed. In our own country, where it has not . . . been a very popular fashion with governments to display any extraordinary regard for the great mass of the people or to recognise their existence as improvable creatures, private charities, unexampled in the history of the earth, have arisen, to do an incalculable amount of good among the destitute and afflicted.

"But the government of the country, having neither act nor part in them, is not in the receipt of any portion of the gratitude they inspire; and, offering very little shelter or relief beyond that which is to be found in the workhouse and the jail, has come, not unnaturally, to be looked upon by the poor rather as a stern master, quick to correct and punish, than a kind protector, merciful and vigilant in their hour of need." AN 3

—*whitewash:* "' . . . what did [my friend *Pangloss*] say in defence of the officers condemned by the Coroner's Jury, who, by signing the General Inspection report relative to the ship Great Tasmania, chartered for these troops, had deliberately asserted all that bad and poisonous dunghill refuse, to be good and wholesome food?' My official friend replied that it was a remarkable fact, that whereas some officers were only positively good, and other officers only comparatively better, those particular officers were superlatively the very best of all possible officers." UT/GT

And see Charles Dickens: Angry

Industry

—*coalpit:* "'I ha' fell into th' pit, my dear [said Stephen Blackpool], as have cost wi'in the knowledge o' old fok now livin, hundreds and hundreds o' men's lives—fathers, sons, brothers, dear to thousands an' thousands, an' keeping 'em fro' want and hunger. I ha' fell into a pit that ha' been wi' th' Firedamp crueller than battle. I ha' read on 't in the public petition, as onny one may read, fro' the men that works in pits, in which they ha' pray'n and pray'n the lawmakers for Christ's sake not to let their work be murder to 'em, but to spare 'em for th' wives and children that they loves as well as gentlefok loves theirs. When it were in work, it killed wi'out need; when 'tis let alone, it kills wi'out need. See how we die an' no need, one way an' another—in a muddle—every day!'" HT iii 6

—*industry town:* "It was a town of red brick, or of brick that would have been red if the smoke and ashes had allowed it; but as matters stood it was a town of unnatural red and black like the painted face of a savage. It was a town of machinery and tall chimneys, out of which interminable serpents of smoke trailed themselves for ever and ever, and never got uncoiled.

"It had a black canal in it, and a river that ran purple with ill-smelling dye, and vast piles of building full of windows where there was a rattling and a trembling all day long, and where the piston of the steam-engine worked monotonously up and down like the head of an elephant in a state of melancholy madness.

"It contained several large streets all very like one another, and many small streets still more like one another, inhabited by people equally like one another, who all went in and out at the same hours, with the same sound upon the same pavements, to do the same work, and to whom every day was the same as yesterday and to-morrow, and every year the counterpart of the last and the next." ¶HT i 5

And see Government, Local—*urban planning*

"As Coketown cast ashes not only on its own head but on the neighbourhood's too—after the manner of those pious persons who do penance for their own sins by putting other people into sackcloth . . . . " HT ii 6

—*in summer:* "A sunny midsummer day. There was such a thing sometimes, even in Coketown.

"Seen from a distance in such weather, Coketown lay shrouded in a haze of its own, which appeared impervious to the sun's rays. You only knew the town was there, because you knew there could have been no such sulky blotch upon the prospect without a town. A blur of soot and smoke, now confusedly tending this way, now that way, now aspiring to the vault of Heaven, now murkily creeping along the earth, as the wind rose and fell, or changed its quarter: a dense formless jumble, with sheets of cross light in it, that showed nothing but masses of darkness:—Coketown in the distance was suggestive of itself, though not a brick of it could be seen." HT ii 1

See also W:Cities and Towns—*Birmingham*

—*landscape and people:* "A long suburb of red brick houses—some with patches of garden-ground, where coal-dust and factory smoke darkened the shrinking leaves, and coarse rank flowers; and where the struggling vegetation sickened and sank under the hot breath of kiln and furnace, making them by its presence seem yet more blighting and unwholesome than in the town itself—a long, flat, straggling suburb passed, they came by slow degrees upon a cheerless region, where not a blade of grass was seen to grow; where not a bud put forth its promise in the spring; where nothing green could live but on the surface of the stagnant pools, which here and there lay idly sweltering by the black roadside . . . .

"On every side, and far as the eye could see into the heavy distance, tall chimneys, crowding on each other, and presenting that endless repetition of the same dull, ugly form, which is the horror of oppressive dreams, poured out their plague of smoke, obscured the light, and made foul the melancholy air. On mounds of ashes by the wayside, sheltered only by a few rough boards, or rotten pent-house roofs, strange engines spun and writhed like tortured creatures; clanking their iron chains, shrieking in their rapid whirl from time to time as though in torment unendurable, and making the ground tremble with their agonies. Dismantled houses here and there appeared, tottering to the earth, propped up by fragments of others that had fallen down, unroofed, windowless, blackened, desolate, but yet inhabited. Men, women, children, wan in their looks and ragged in attire, tended the engines, fed their tributary fires, begged upon the road, or scowled half-naked from the doorless houses . . . .

"But night-time in this dreadful spot!—night, when the smoke was changed to fire; when every chimney spirted [*sic.*] up its flame; and places, that had been dark vaults all day, now shone red-hot, with figures moving to and fro within their blazing jaws, and calling to one another with hoarse cries—night, when the noise of every strange machine was aggravated by the darkness; when the people near them looked wilder and more savage; when bands of unemployed labourers paraded in the roads, or clustered by torchlight round their leaders, who told them in stern language of their wrongs, and urged them on to frightful cries and threats; when maddened men, armed with sword and firebrand, spurning the tears and prayers of women who would restrain them, rushed forth on errands of terror and destruction, to work no ruin half so surely as their own—night, when carts came rumbling by, filled with rude coffins (for contagious disease and death had been busy with the living crops); when orphans cried, and distracted women shrieked and followed in their wake—night, when some called for bread, and some for drink to drown their cares; and some with tears, and some with staggering feet, and some with bloodshot eyes, went brooding home—night, which unlike the night that Heaven sends on earth, brought with it no peace, nor quiet, nor signs of blessed sleep—" ¶OCS 45

"[Nell and her grandfather] had long since got clear of the smoke and furnaces, except in one or two solitary instances, where a factory planted among fields withered the space about it, like a burning mountain." OCS 46

—*'material age':* " . . . has electricity become more material in the mind of any sane, or moderately insane man, woman, or child, because of the discovery that in the good providence of God it was made available for the service and use of man to an immeasurably greater extent than for his destruction? Do I make a more material journey to the bedside of my dying parents or my dying child, when I travel there at the rate of sixty miles an hour, than when I travel thither at the rate of six?

"Rather, in the swift case, does not my agonized heart become overfraught with gratitude to that Supreme Beneficence from whom alone can have proceeded the wonderful means of shortening my suspense? What is the materiality of the cable or the wire, compared with the immateriality of the spark? What is the materiality of certain chemical substances that we can weigh or measure, imprison or release, compared with the immateriality of their appointed affinities and repulsions, prescribed to them from the instant of their creation to the day of judgement?

"When did this so-called material age begin? With the invention of the art of printing? Surely it has been a long time about; and which is the more material object, the farthing tallow candle that will not give me light, or that flame of gas that will?" ¶S/BM2

—*mill owners, delicate:* "Surely there never was such fragile china-ware as that of which the millers of Coketown were made. Handle them never so lightly, and they fell to pieces with such ease that you might suspect them of having been flawed before.

"They were ruined, when they were required to send labouring children to school; they were ruined when inspectors were appointed to look into their works; they were ruined, when such inspectors considered it doubtful whether they were quite justified in chopping people up with their machinery; they were utterly undone, when it was hinted that perhaps they need not always make quite so much smoke . . . .

"Whenever a Coketowner felt he was ill-used—that is to say, whenever he was not left entirely alone, and it was proposed to hold him accountable for the consequences of any of his acts—he was sure to come out with the awful menace, that he would 'sooner pitch his property into the Atlantic'. This had terrified the Home Secretary within an inch of his life, on several occasions." ¶HT ii 1

—*steam engine:* "But the power that sets in motion all these rolling-mills, and upright dancing saws, and circular spinning saws, and runs away with tall tree-trunks at the end of a rope, and bores holes in thick masses of cold iron, and cuts brass like cheese, or shaves a surface of it with far more ease and softness than most razors shave a beard—where is this power? Behold him yonder! There he is in his house—the black and oily Majesty of Steam-power.

"I approach his dingy, vibrating, ominous house, and look through his small, square, smutty, open window. There he is, all black and shiny, ponderously heaving and sliding up and down, and bowing like Pluto, and ducking under, and curtseying with coy retirement, and twirling iron dumb-bells in the air, as if in triumph, and panting, and gasping, and blowing and snorting, and puffing and working incessantly, and whistling and drinking, and smoking! Truly, a most wonderful fellow—a great savage king, or, rather, one of the savage Pagods,* civilised into reason and utility." HWC/D

**idols worshipped in the Orient*

Labour

—*hands of Coketown:* " . . . among the multitude of Coketown, generically called 'the Hands,'—a race who would have found more favour with some people, if Providence had seen fit to make them only hands, or, like the lower creatures of the seashore, only hands and stomachs . . . . " HT i 10

"For the first time in her life, Louisa had come into one of the dwellings of the Coketown hands; for the first time in her life, she was face to face with anything like individuality in connexion with them. She knew of their existence by hundreds and by thousands. She knew what results in work a given number of them would produce, in a given space of time. She knew them in crowds passing to and from their nests, like ants or beetles. But she knew from her reading infinitely more of the ways of toiling insects than of these toiling men and women.

"Something to be worked so much and paid so much, and there ended; something to be infallibly settled by laws of supply and demand; something that blundered against those laws, and floundered into difficulty; something that was a little pinched when wheat was dear, and over-ate itself when wheat was cheap; something that increased at such a rate of percentage, and yielded such another percentage of crime, and such another percentage of pauperism; something wholesale, of which vast fortunes were made; something that occasionally rose like a sea, and did some harm and waste (chiefly to itself), and fell again; this she knew the Coketown Hands to be. But, she had scarcely thought more of separating them into units, than of separating the sea itself into its component drops." HT ii 6

—*health risks:* " . . . the philosophy of the matter of lead-poisoning and workpeople seems to me to have been pretty fairly summed up by the Irish-woman . . . 'Some of them gets lead-pisoned soon, and some of them gets lead-pisoned later, and some, but not many niver; and 'tis all according to the constitooshun, sur; and some constitooshuns is strong and some is weak.'" UT/AB *And see* Manufacturing—*white lead*

—*home weaving:* "A weaving country too [Flanders], for in the wayside cottages the loom goes wearily—rattle and click, rattle and click—and, looking in, I see the poor weaving peasant, man or woman, bending at the work, while the child, working too, turns a little handwheel put upon the ground to suit its height. An unconscionable monster, the loom in a small dwelling, asserting himself ungenerously as the breadwinner, straddling over the children's straw beds, cramping the family in space and air, and making himself generally objectionable and tyrannical. He is tributary, too, to ugly mills and factories and bleaching-grounds, rising out of the sluiced fields in an abrupt bare way, disdaining, like himself, to be ornamental or accommodating." UT/FF

—leadership: "Perhaps the world could not afford a more remarkable contrast than between the deliberate collected manner of these men proceeding with their business, and the clash and hurry of the engines among which their lives are passed.

"Their astonishing fortitude and perseverance; their high sense of honour among themselves; the extent to which they are impressed with the responsibility that is upon them of setting a careful example, and keeping their order out of any harm and loss of reputation; the noble readiness in them to help one another, of which most medical practitioners and working clergymen can give so many affecting examples; could scarcely ever be plainer to an ordinary observer of human nature than in this cockpit." HW/OS

—and the machine: "The exquisite beauty and efficiency of this [oar-making] machinery need no illustration, but happen to have a pointed illustration to-day. A pair of oars of unusual size chance to be wanted for a special purpose, and they have to be made by hand. Side by side with the subtle and facile machine, and side by side with the fast-growing pile of oars on the floor, a man shapes out these special oars with an axe . . . chipping and dinting, by comparison as leisurely as if he were a labouring Pagan getting them ready against his decease at threescore and ten, to take with him as a present to *Charon* for his boat, the man (aged about thirty) plies his task. The machine would make a regulation oar while the man wipes his forehead. The man might be buried in a mound made of the strips of thin broad wooden ribbon torn from the wood whirled into oars as the minutes fall from the clock, before he had done a forenoon's work with his axe." UT/CD

But see H:Man *—and machine*

—migrant: "Later in the season, the whole countryside, for miles and miles, will swarm with hopping tramps. They come in families, men, women, and children, every family provided with a bundle of bedding, an iron pot, a number of babies, and too often with some poor sick creature quite unfit for the rough life, for whom they suppose the smell of the fresh hop to be a sovereign remedy.

"Many of these hoppers are Irish, but many come from London. They crowd all the roads, and camp under all the hedges and on all the scraps of common-land, and live among and upon the hops until they are all picked, and the hop-gardens, so beautiful through the summer, look as if they had been laid waste by an invading army. Then, there is a vast exodus of tramps out of the country; and if you ride or drive round any turn of any road, at more than a foot pace, you will be bewildered to find that you have charged into the bosom of fifty families, and that there are splashing up all around you, in the utmost prodigality of confusion, bundles of bedding, babies, iron pots, and a good-humoured multitude of both sexes and all ages, equally divided between perspiration and intoxication." UT/T

And see CI:Inns and Taverns*—a country tavern*

"Then, there are the tramp handicraft men. Are they not all over England, in this Midsummer time? Where does the lark sing, the corn grow, the mill turn, the river run, and they are not among the lights and shadows, tinkering, chair-mending, umbrella-mending, clock-mending, knife-grinding?

"Surely, a pleasant thing, if we were in that condition of life, to grind our way through Kent, Sussex, and Surrey. For the worst six weeks or so, we should see the sparks we ground off, fiery bright against a background of green wheat and green leaves. A little later, and the ripe harvest would pale our sparks from red to yellow, until we got the dark newly-turned land for a background again, and they were red once more. By that time, we should have ground our way to the sea cliffs, and the whirr of our wheel would be lost in the breaking of the waves.

"Our next variety in sparks would be derived from contrast with the gorgeous medley of colours in the autumn woods, and, by the time we had ground our way round to the heathy lands between Reigate and Croydon, doing a prosperous stroke of business all along, we should show like a little firework in the light frosty air, and be the next best thing to the blacksmith's forge." ¶UT/T

" . . . leading a gipsy life between haymaking time and harvest, and looking as if they were just made of the dust of the earth, so very dusty are they, lounge about on cool doorsteps, trying to mend their unmendable shoes, or giving them to the city kennels as a hopeless job . . . . At all the more public pumps there is much cooling of bare feet, together with much bubbling and gurgling of drinking with hand to spout on the part of these Bedouins . . . . " MED 19

—patronised: "'Your only business, my good fellow,' pursued Sir Joseph, looking abstractedly at Toby; 'your only business in life is with me. You needn't trouble yourself to think about anything. I will think for you; I know what is good for you; I am your perpetual parent. Such is the dispensation of an all-wise Providence! Now, the design of your creation is—not that you should swill, and guzzle, and associate your enjoyments, brutally, with food'; Toby thought remorsefully of the tripe; 'but that you should feel the Dignity of Labour. Go forth erect into the cheerful morning air, and—and stop there. Live hard and temperately, be respectful, exercise your self-denial, bring up your family on next to nothing, pay your rent as regularly as the clock strikes, be punctual in your dealings (I set you a good example; you will find Mr Fish, my confidential secretary, with a cash-box before him at all times); and you may trust to me to be your Friend and Father.'" C 2

"The instinctive revolt of his spirit against patronage, is a quality much to be respected in the English working man. It is the base of his best qualities. Nor is it surprising that he should be unduly suspicious of patronage, and sometimes resentful of it even where it is not, seeing what a flood of washy talk has been let loose on his devoted head, or with what complacent condescension the same devoted head has been smoothed and patted.

"It is a proof to me of his self-control that he never strikes out pugilistically, right and left, when addressed as one of 'My friends,' or 'My assembled friends;' that he does not become inappeasable, and run amuck like a Malay, whenever he sees a biped in broadcloth getting on a platform to talk to him; that any pretence of improving his mind, does not instantly drive him out of his mind, and cause him to toss his obliging patron like a mad bull.

"For, how often have I heard the unfortunate working man lectured, as if he were a little charity-child, humid as to his nasal development, strictly literal as to his Catechism, and called by Providence to walk all his days in a station in life represented on festive occasions by a mug of warm milk-and-water and a bun! What popguns of jokes have these ears tingled to hear let off at him, what asinine sentiments, what impotent conclusions, what spelling-book moralities, what adaptations of the orator's insufferable tediousness to the assumed level of his understanding!

"If his sledge-hammers, his spades and pick-axes, his saws and chisels, his paint-pots and brushes, his forges, furnaces, and engines, the horses that he drove at his work, and the machines that drove him at his work, were all toys in one little paper box, and he the baby who played with them, he could not have been discoursed to, more impertinently and absurdly than I have heard him discoursed to times innumerable." ¶UT/BB

"To suppose that the working man cannot state this question [of alcohol use and abuse] to himself quite as plainly as I state it here, is to suppose that he is a baby, and is again to tell him in the old wearisome condescending patronising way that he must be goody-poody, and do as he is toldy-poldy, and not be a manny-panny or a voter-poter, but fold his handy-pandys and be a childy-pildy." UT/BB

—specialized: " . . . [Jackson] now had eyes and thoughts for a new external world. How the many toiling people lived, and loved, and died; how wonderful it was to consider the various trainings of eye and hand, the nice distinctions of sight and touch, that separated them into classes of workers, and even into classes of workers at subdivisions of one complete whole which combined their many intelligences and forces, though of itself but some cheap object of use or ornament in common life; how good it was to know that such assembling in a multitude on their part, and such contribution of their several dexterities towards a civilising end, did not deteriorate them as it was the fashion of the supercilious Mayflies of humanity to pretend, but engendered among them a self-respect, and yet a modest desire to be much wiser than they were (the first evinced in their well-balanced bearing and manner of speech when he stopped to ask a ques-

tion; the second, in the announcements of their popular studies and amusements on the public walls); these considerations, and a host of such, made his walk a memorable one. 'I too am but a little part of a great whole,' he began to think; 'and to be serviceable to myself and others, or to be happy, I must cast my interest into, and draw it out of, the common stock.'" CS/MJ 2

—spectator sport: "Bricklaying is another of the occupations that can by no means be transacted in rural parts, without the assistance of spectators—of as many as can be convened. In thinly-peopled spots, I have known bricklayers on tramp, coming up with bricklayers at work, to be so sensible of the indispensability of lookers-on, that they themselves have sat up in that capacity, and have been unable to subside into the acceptance of a proffered share in the job, for two or three days together.

"Sometimes the 'navvy,' on tramp, with an extra pair of half-boots over his shoulder, a bag, a bottle, and a can, will take a similar part in a job of excavation, and will look at it without engaging in it, until all his money is gone. The current of my uncommercial pursuits caused me only last summer to want a little body of workmen for a certain spell of work in a pleasant part of the country; and I was at one time honoured with the attendance of as many as seven-and-twenty, who were looking at six." ¶UT/T

"Among all the innumerable occupations that cannot possibly be transacted without the assistance of lookers-on, chair-mending may take a station in the first rank. When we sat down with our backs against the barn or the public-house, and began to mend, what a sense of popularity would grow upon us! When all the children came to look at us, and the tailor, and the general dealer, and the farmer who had been giving a small order at the little saddler's, and the groom from the great house, and the publican, and even the two skittle-players (and here note that, howsoever busy all the rest of village human-kind may be, there will always be two people with leisure to play at skittles, wherever village skittles are), what encouragement would be on us to plait and weave! No one looks at us while we plait and weave these words." UT/T

—its 'station': "I am now going to state three facts, which will startle a large class of readers on this side of the Atlantic, very much.

"First, there is a joint-stock piano in a great many of the boarding-houses [in Lowell, Mass]. Secondly, nearly all these young ladies subscribe to circulating libraries. Thirdly, they have got up among themselves a periodical called THE LOWELL OFFERING, 'A repository of original articles, written exclusively by females actively employed in the mills' . . . .

"The large class of readers, startled by these facts, will exclaim, with one voice, 'How very preposterous!' On my deferentially inquiring why, they will answer, 'These things are above their station.' In reply to that objection, I would beg to ask what their station is.

"It is their station to work. And they *do* work. They labour in these mills, upon an average, twelve hours a day, which is unquestionably work, and pretty tight work too. Perhaps it is above their station to indulge in such amusements, on any terms. Are we quite sure that we in England have not formed our ideas of the 'station' of working people, from accustoming ourselves to the contemplation of that class as they are, and not as they might be? I think that if we examine our own feelings, we shall find that the pianos, and the circulating libraries, and even the Lowell Offering, startle us by their novelty, and not by their bearing upon any abstract question of right or wrong.

"For myself, I know no station in which, the occupation of to-day cheerfully done and the occupation of to-morrow cheerfully looked to, any one of these pursuits is not most humanising and laudable. I know no station which is rendered more endurable to the person in it, or more safe to the person out of it, by having ignorance for its associate. I know no station which has a right to monopolise the means of mutual instruction, improvement, and rational entertainment; or which has ever continued to be a station very long, after seeking to do so." AN 4

—vocational sea-change: "The old stage-coachman was a farmer's friend. He wore top-boots, understood cattle, fed his horses upon corn, and had a lively personal interest in malt. The engine-driver's garb, and sympathies, and tastes belong to the factory. His fustian dress, besmeared with coal-dust and begrimed with soot; his oily hands, his dirty face, his knowledge of machinery; all point him out as one devoted to the manufacturing interest. Fire and smoke, and red-hot cinders follow in his

wake. He has no attachment to the soil, but travels on a road of iron, furnace wrought." MP/AI

"Are the police agricultural? The watchmen were. They wore woollen nightcaps to a man; they encouraged the growth of timber, by patriotically adhering to staves and rattles of immense size; they slept every night in boxes, which were but another form of the celebrated wooden walls of Old England; they never woke up till it was too late—in which respect you might have thought them very farmers. How is it with the police? Their buttons are made at Birmingham; a dozen of their truncheons would poorly furnish forth a watchman's staff; they have no wooden walls to repose between; and the crowns of their hats are plated with cast-iron." MP/AI

—viewed by management: "'Now, you have heard a lot of talk about the work in our mills, no doubt. You have? Very good. I'll state the fact of it to you. It's the pleasantest work there is, and it's the lightest work there is, and it's the best-paid work there is. More than that, we couldn't improve the mills themselves, unless we laid down Turkey carpets on the floors. Which we're not a-going to do.'

"'Mr Bounderby, perfectly right [said James Harthouse].'

"'Lastly,' said Bounderby, 'as to our Hands. There's not a Hand in this town, Sir, man, woman, or child, but has one ultimate object in life. That object is, to be fed on turtle soup and venison with a gold spoon. Now, they're not a-going—none of 'em—ever to be fed on turtle soup and venison with a gold spoon. And now you know the place.'" HT ii 2

—working conditions: "'Sir [said Stephen Blackpool], I were never good at showin o' 't, though I ha' had'n my share in feeling o' 't. 'Deed we are in a muddle, sir. Look round town—so rich as 'tis—and see the numbers o' people as has been broughten into bein heer, fur to weave, an' to card, an' to piece out a livin', aw the same one way, somehows, 'twixt their cradles and their graves. Look how we live, an' wheer we live, an' in what numbers, an' by what chances, and wi' what sameness; and look how the mills is awlus a goin, and how they never works us no nigher to onny dis'ant object—ceptin awlus, Death.

"Look how you considers of us, and writes of us, and talks of us, and goes up wi' yor deputations to Secretaries o' State 'bout us, and how yo are awlus right, and we are awlus wrong, and never had'n no reason in us sin ever we were born. Look how this ha' growen an' growen, sir, bigger an' bigger, broader an' broader, harder an' harder, fro year to year, fro generation unto generation. Who can look on 't, sir, and fairly tell a man 'tis not a muddle?'" ¶HT ii 5

And see Manufacturing—*weaving mill*

Legislation

—chartist: "I am not a Chartist, and I never was. I don't mean to say but what I see a good many public points to complain of, still I don't think that's the way to set them right. If I did think so, I should be a Chartist. But I don't think so, and I am not a Chartist. I read the paper, and hear discussion, at what we call 'a parlour,' in Birmingham, and I know many good men and workmen who are Chartists. Note. Not Physical force." RP/TP

—Corn Laws: ". . . the agricultural interest, or what passes by that name . . . never thinks of the suffering world, or sees it, or cares to extend its knowledge of it; or, so long as it remains a world, cares anything about it. All those whom Dante placed in the first pit or circle of the doleful regions, might have represented the agricultural interest in the present Parliament, or at quarter sessions, or at meetings of the farmers' friends, or anywhere else." MP/AI

". . . the cry 'Repeal the Corn-laws!'* . . . may be heard, moaning at night, through the straw-littered wards of Refuges for the Destitute; it may be read in the gaunt and famished faces which make our streets terrible; it is muttered in the thankful grace pronounced by haggard wretches over their felon fare in gaols; it is inscribed in dreadful characters upon the walls of Fever Hospitals; and may be plainly traced in every record of mortality. All of which proves, that there is a vast conspiracy afoot, against the unfortunate agricultural interest." MP/AI (1844)

And see Labour—*vocational sea-change; and* TP:Law Courts—*Doctors' Commons—and the national interest*

**The laws, which propped grain prices, were repealed after the Irish Famine of 1845-7*

—Sunday-observance law: "It was Sunday evening in London, gloomy, close and stale. . . .

"Everything was bolted and barred that

could by possibility furnish relief to an overworked people. No pictures, no unfamiliar animals, no rare plants or flowers, no natural or artificial wonders of the ancient world—all *taboo* with that enlightened strictness that the ugly South Sea gods in the British Museum might have supposed themselves at home again.

"Nothing to see but streets, streets, streets. Nothing to breathe but streets, streets, streets. Nothing to change the brooding mind, or raise it up. Nothing for the spent toiler to do, but to compare the monotony of his seventh day with the monotony of his six days, think what a weary life he led, and make the best of it—or the worst, according to the probabilities.

" . . . . What secular want could the million or so of human beings whose daily labour, six days in the week, lay among these Arcadian objects, from the sweet sameness of which they had no escape between the cradle and the grave—what secular want could they possibly have upon their seventh day? Clearly they could want nothing but a stringent policeman." LD i 3

"For, it is in nations as in families. Too tight a hand in these respects, is certain to engender a disposition to break loose, and to run riot. If the private experience of any reader, pausing on this sentence, cannot furnish many unhappy illustrations of its truth, it is a very fortunate experience indeed. Our most notable public example of it, in England, is just two hundred years old"* HW/SS

**written in 1850: Charles I was beheaded in 1649.*

See S:Religion—*the Sabbath; and* W:The English—*common people and the Sabbath*

Manufacturing

—china

—factory: "**Copeland**! Stop a moment. Was it yesterday I visited Copeland's works, and saw them making plates? . . . The plate says, decidedly, yesterday. I find the plate, as I look at it, growing into a companion.

"Don't you remember (says the plate) how many kilns you flew past, looking like the bowls of gigantic tobacco-pipes, cut short off from the stem and turned upside down? . . .

"And don't you remember (says the plate) how you . . . proceeded to my father's, Copeland's, where the whole of my family, high and low, rich and poor, are turned out upon the world from our nursery and seminary, covering some fourteen acres of ground?

—materials processing: "And don't you remember what we spring from:—heaps of lumps of clay, partially prepared and cleaned in Devonshire and Dorsetshire, whence said clay principally comes—and hills of flint, without which we should want our tingling sound, and should never be musical?

"And as to the flint, don't you recollect that it is first burnt in kilns, and is then laid under the four iron feet of a demon slave, subject to violent stamping fits, who, when they come on, stamps away insanely with his four iron legs, and would crush all the flint in the Isle of Thanet to powder, without leaving off?

"And as to the clay, don't you recollect how it is put into mills or teazers, and is sliced, and dug, and cut at, by endless knives, clogged and sticky, but persistent—and is pressed out of that machine through a square trough, whose form it takes—and is cut off in square lumps and thrown into a vat, and there mixed with water, and beaten to a pulp by paddle-wheels—and is then run into a rough house, all rugged beams and ladders splashed with white—superintended by *Grindoff the Miller* in his working clothes, all splashed with white—where it passes through no end of machinery-moved sieves all splashed with white, arranged in an ascending scale of fineness (some so fine, that three hundred silk threads cross each other in a single square inch of their surface), and all in a violent state of ague with their teeth for ever chattering, and their bodies for ever shivering!

"And as to the flint again, isn't it mashed and mollified and troubled and soothed, exactly as rags are in a paper-mill, until it is reduced to a pap so fine that it contains no atom of 'grit' perceptible to the nicest taste? And as to the flint and the clay together, are they not, after all this, mixed in the proportion of five of clay to one of flint, and isn't the compound—known as 'slip'—run into oblong troughs, where its superfluous moisture may evaporate; and finally, isn't it slapped and banged and beaten and patted and kneaded and wedged and knocked about like butter, until it becomes a beautiful grey dough, ready for the potter's use?

—potter: "In regard of the potter, popularly so called (says the plate), you don't mean to say you have forgotten that a workman called a Thrower is the man under whose hand this grey dough takes the shapes of the simpler household vessels as quickly as the eye can follow? You don't mean to say you cannot call him up before you, sitting, with his attendant woman, at his potter's wheel—a disc about the size of a dinner-plate, revolving on two drums slowly or quickly as he wills—who made you a complete breakfast-set for a bachelor, as a good-humoured little off-hand joke.

"You remember how he took up as much dough as he wanted, and, throwing it on his wheel, in a moment fashioned it into a teacup—caught up more clay and made a saucer—a larger dab and whirled it into a teapot—winked at a smaller dab and converted it into the lid of the teapot, accurately fitting by the measurement of his eye alone—coaxed a middle-sized dab for two seconds, broke it, turned it over at the rim, and made a milkpot—laughed, and turned out a slop-basin—coughed, and provided for the sugar?

—mould: "Neither, I think, are you oblivious of the newer mode of making various articles, but especially basins, according to which improvement a mould revolves instead of a disc? For you *must* remember (says the plate) how you saw the mould of a little basin spinning round and round, and how the workman smoothed and pressed a handful of dough upon it, and how with an instrument called a profile (a piece of wood, representing the profile of a basin's foot) he cleverly scraped and carved the ring which makes the base of any such basin, and then took the basin off the lathe like a doughy skull-cap to be dried, and afterwards (in what is called a green state) to be put into a second lathe, there to be finished and burnished with a steel burnisher?

"And as to moulding in general (says the plate), it can't be necessary for me to remind you that all ornamental articles, and indeed all articles not quite circular, are made in moulds. For you must remember how you saw the vegetable dishes, for example, being made in moulds; and how the handles of teacups, and the spouts of teapots, and the feet of tureens, and so forth, are all made in little separate moulds, and are each stuck on to the body corporate, of which it is destined to form a part, with a stuff called 'slag,' as quickly as you can recollect it.

"Further, you learnt—you know you did—in the same visit, how the beautiful sculptures in the delicate new material called Parian, are all constructed in moulds; how, into that material, animal bones are ground up, because the phosphate of lime contained in bones makes it translucent; how everything is moulded, before going into the fire, one-fourth larger than it is intended to come out of the fire, because it shrinks in that proportion in the intense heat; how, when a figure shrinks unequally, it is spoiled—emerging from the furnace a misshapen birth; a big head and a little body, or a little head and a big body, or a *Quasimodo* with long arms and short legs, or a **Miss Biffin** with neither legs nor arms worth mentioning.

—kilns: "And as to the kilns, in which the firing takes place, and in which some of the more precious articles are burnt repeatedly, in various stages of their process towards completion—as to the kilns (says the plate, warming with the recollection), if you don't remember THEM with a horrible interest, what did you ever go to Copeland's for? When you stood inside of one of those inverted bowls of a pre-Adamite tobacco-pipe, looking up at the blue sky through the open top far off, as you might have looked up from a well, sunk under the centre of the pavement of the Pantheon at Rome, had you the least idea where you were? And when you found yourself surrounded, in that dome-shaped cavern, by innumerable columns of an unearthly order of architecture, supporting nothing, and squeezed close together as if a pre-Adamite *Samson* had taken a vast Hall in his arms and crushed it into the smallest possible space, had you the least idea what they were? No (says the plate), of course not!

"And when you found that each of those pillars was a pile of ingeniously made vessels of coarse clay—called Saggers—looking, when separate, like raised-pies for the table of the mighty *Giant Blunderbore,* and now all full of various articles of pottery ranged in them in baking order, the bottom of each vessel serving for the cover of the one below, and the whole kiln rapidly filling with these, tier upon tier, until the last workman should have barely room to crawl out, before the closing of the jagged aperture in the wall and the kindling of the gradual fire; did you not stand amazed to think that all the year round these dread chambers are heating, white hot—and cooling—and filling-and emptying—and being bricked up—and broken open—humanly speaking, for ever and ever? To be sure you did!

"And standing in one of those kilns nearly full, and seeing a free crow shoot across the aperture a-top, and learning how the fire would wax hotter and hotter by slow degrees, and would cool similarly through a space of from forty to sixty hours, did no remembrance of the days when human clay was burnt oppress you? Yes. I think so! I suspect that some fancy of a fiery haze and a shortening breath, and a growing heat, and gasping prayer; and a figure in black interposing between you and the sky (as figures in black are very apt to do), and looking down, before it grew too hot to look and live, upon the Heretic in his edifying agony—I say I suspect (says the plate) that some such fancy was pretty strong upon you when you went out into the air, and blessed God for the bright spring day and the degenerate times!

—plain decoration: "After that, I needn't remind you what a relief it was to see the simplest process of ornamenting this 'biscuit' (as it is called when baked) with brown circles and blue trees—converting it into the common crockery-ware that is exported to Africa, and used in cottages at home. For (says the plate) I am well persuaded that you bear in mind how those particular jugs and mugs were once more set upon a lathe and put in motion; and how a man blew the brown colour (having a strong natural affinity with the material in that condition) on them from a blowpipe as they twirled; and how his daughter, with a common brush, dropped blotches of blue upon them in the right places; and how, tilting the blotches upside down, she made them run into rude images of trees, and there an end.

"And didn't you see (says the plate) planted upon my own brother that astounding blue willow, with knobbed and gnarled trunk, and foliage of blue ostrich feathers, which gives our family the title of 'willow pattern'? And didn't you observe, transferred upon him at the same time, that blue bridge which spans nothing, growing out from the roots of the willow; and the three blue Chinese going over it into a blue temple, which has a fine crop of blue bushes sprouting out of the roof; and a blue boat sailing above them, the mast of which is burglariously sticking itself into the foundations of a blue villa, suspended sky-high, surmounted by a lump of blue rock, sky-higher, and a couple of billing blue birds, sky-highest—together with the rest of that amusing blue landscape, which has, in deference to our revered ancestors of the Cerulean Empire, and in defiance of every known law of perspective, adorned millions of our family ever since the days of platters?"

—engraving: "Didn't you inspect the copper-plate on which my pattern was deeply engraved? Didn't you perceive an impression of it taken in cobalt colour at a cylindrical press, upon a leaf of thin paper, streaming from a plunge-bath of soap and water? Wasn't the paper impression daintily spread, by a light-fingered damsel (you *know* you admired her!), over the surface of the plate, and the back of the paper rubbed prodigiously hard—with a long tight roll of flannel, tied up like a round of hung beef—without so much as ruffling the paper, wet as it was? Then (says the plate), was not the paper washed away with a sponge, and didn't there appear, set off upon the plate, this identical piece of pre-Raphaelite blue distemper which you now behold? Not to be denied! I had seen all this and more . . . .

—printing and painting: "This reflection prompts me to transfer my attention from the blue plate to the forlorn but cheerfully painted vase on the sideboard. And surely (says the plate) you have not forgotten how the outlines of such groups of flowers as you see there, are printed, just as I was printed, and are afterwards shaded and filled in with metallic colours by women and girls? As to the aristocracy of our order, made of the finer clay—porcelain peers and peeresses;—the slabs, and panels, and table-tops and tazze; the endless nobility and gentry of dessert, breakfast, and tea services; the gemmed perfume bottles, and scarlet and gold salvers; you saw that they were painted by artists, with metallic colours laid on with camel-hair pencils, and afterwards burnt in.

—glazing: "And talking of burning in (says the plate), didn't you find that every subject, from the willow pattern to the landscape after Turner—having been framed upon

clay or porcelain biscuit—has to be glazed? Of course, you saw the glaze—composed of various vitreous materials—laid over every article; and of course you witnessed the close imprisonment of each piece in saggers upon the separate system rigidly enforced by means of fine-pointed earthenware stilts placed between the articles to prevent the slightest communication or contact.

"We had in my time—and I suppose it is the same now—fourteen hours' firing to fix the glaze and to make it 'run' all over us equally, so as to put a good shiny and unscratchable surface upon us. Doubtless, you observed that one sort of glaze—called printing-body—is burnt into the better sort of ware *before* it is printed. Upon this you saw some of the finest steel engravings transferred, to be fixed by an after glazing—didn't you? Why, of course you did!

"Of course I did. I had seen and enjoyed everything that the plate recalled to me, and had beheld with admiration how the rotatory motion which keeps this ball of ours in its place in the great scheme, with all its busy mites upon it, was necessary throughout the process, and could only be dispensed with in the fire." ¶HWC/PA

—*ironworks:* "[George Rouncewell] comes to a gateway in the brick wall, looks in, and sees a great perplexity of iron lying about, in every stage, and in a vast variety of shapes; in bars, in wedges, in sheets; in tanks, in boilers, in axles, in wheels, in cogs, in cranks, in rails; twisted and wrenched into eccentric and perverse forms, as separate parts of machinery; mountains of it broken up, and rusty in its age; distant furnaces of it glowing and bubbling in its youth; bright fireworks of it showering about, under the blows of the steam hammer; red-hot iron, white-hot iron, cold-black iron; an iron taste, an iron smell, and a Babel of iron sounds." BH 63

—*oar-making:* " . . . I am going to see the workshops where they make all the oars used in the British Navy. A pretty large pile of building, I opine, and a pretty long job! As to the building, I am soon disappointed, because the work is all done in one loft. And as to a long job—what is this? Two rather large mangles with a swarm of butterflies hovering over them? What can there be in the mangles that attracts butterflies?

"Drawing nearer, I discern that these are not mangles, but intricate machines, set with knives and saws and planes, which cut smooth and straight here, and slantwise there, and now cut such a depth, and now miss cutting altogether, according to the predestined requirements of the pieces of wood that are pushed on below them: each of which pieces is to be an oar, and is roughly adapted to that purpose before it takes its final leave of far-off forests, and sails for England.

"Likewise I discern that the butterflies are not true butterflies, but wooden shavings, which, being spirted [*sic.*] up from the wood by the violence of the machinery, and kept in rapid and not equal movement by the impulse of its rotation on the air, flutter and play, and rise and fall, and conduct themselves as like butterflies as heart could wish. Suddenly the noise and motion cease, and the butterflies drop dead. An oar has been made since I came in, wanting the shaped handle. As quickly as I can follow it with my eye and thought, the same oar is carried to a turning lathe. A whirl and a Nick! Handle made. Oar finished." ¶UT/CD

—*paper-making:* "I am to go, as the rags go, regularly and systematically through the Mill. I am to suppose myself a bale of rags. I *am* rags.

" . . . women at little tables, each with an awful scythe-shaped knife standing erect upon it, and looking like the veritable tooth of time. I am distributed among these women, and worried into smaller shreds—torn cross-wise at the knives. Already I begin to lose something of my grosser nature. The room is filled with my finest dust, and, as gratings of me drop from the knives, they fall through the perforated surface of the tables into receptacles beneath. When I am small enough, I am bundled up, carried away in baskets, and stowed in immense binns, until they want me in the Boiling-Room.

"The Boiling-Room has enormous cauldrons in it, each with its own big lid, hanging to the beams of the roof, and put on by machinery when it is full. It is a very clean place, 'coddled' by much boiling, like a washerwoman's fingers, and looks as if the kitchen of the Parish Union had gone into partnership with the Church Belfry. Here, I am pressed, and squeezed, and jammed, a dozen feet deep, I should think, into my own particular cauldron; where I simmer, boil, and stew, a long, long time. Then, I am a dense, tight mass, cut out in pieces like so much clay—very clean—faint as to my colour—greatly purified—and gradually becoming quite ethereal.

"In this improved condition, I am taken to the Cutting-Room. I am very grateful to the clear fresh water, for the good it has done me; and I am glad to be put into some more of it, and subjected to the action of large rollers filled with transverse knives, revolving by steam power upon iron beds, which favour me with no fewer than two million cuts per minute, though, within the memory of man, the functions of this machine were performed by an ordinary pestle and mortar. Such a drumming and rattling, such a battering and clattering, such a delight in cutting and slashing, not even the Austrian part of me ever witnessed before. This continues, to my great satisfaction, until I look like shaving lather; when I am run off into chambers underneath, to have my friend the water, from whom I am unwilling to be separated, drained out of me.

"At this time, my colour is a slight blue, if I have indigo in me, or a pale fawn, if I am rags from which the dyes have been expelled. As it is necessary to bleach the fawn-coloured pulp (the blue being used for paper of that tint), and as I *am* fawn-coloured pulp, I am placed in certain stone chambers, like catacombs, hermetically sealed, excepting the first compartment, which communicates with a gasometer containing manganese, vitriol, and salt. From these ingredients, a strong gas (not agreeable, I must say, to the sense of smell) is generated, and forced through all the chambers, each of which communicates with the other. These continue closed, if I remember right, some four-and-twenty hours, when a man opens them and takes to his heels immediately to avoid the offensive gas that rushes out. After I have been aired a little, I am again conveyed (quite white now, and very spiritual indeed) to some more obliging rollers upstairs.

"At it these grinders go, 'Munch, munch, munch!' like the sailor's wife in MACBETH, who had chesnuts [*sic.*] in her lap. I look, at first, as if I were the most delicious curds and whey; presently, I find that I am changed to gruel—not thin oatmeal gruel, but rich, creamy, tempting, exalted gruel! As if I had been made from pearls, which some voluptuous Mr Emden had converted into groats!

"And now, I am ready to undergo my last astounding transformation, and be made into paper by the machine. Oh what can I say of the wonderful machine, which receives me, at one end of a long room, gruel, and dismisses me at the other, paper!

"Where is the subtle mind of this *Leviathan* lodged? It must be somewhere—in a cylinder, a pipe, a wheel—or how could it ever do with me the miracles it does! How could it receive me on a sheet of wire-gauze, in my gruel-form, and slide me on, gradually assuming consistency—gently becoming a little paper-like, a little more, a little more still, very paper-like, indeed—clinging to wet blankets, holding tight by other surfaces, smoothly ascending Witney hills, lightly coming down into a woolly open country, easily rolling over and under a planetary system of heated cylinders, large and small, and ever growing, as I proceed, stronger and more paper-like!

"How does the power that fights the wintry waves on the Atlantic, and cuts and drills adamantine slabs of metal like cheese, how does it draw me out, when I am frailest and most liable to tear, so tenderly and delicately, that a woman's hand—no, even though I were a man, very ill and helpless, and she my nurse who loved me—could never touch me with so light a touch, or with a movement so unerring!

"How can I believe, even on experience, that, being of itself insensible, and only informed with intellect at second hand, it changes me, in less time than I take to tell it, into any sort of paper that is wanted, dries me, cuts me into lengths, becomes charged, just before dismissing me, with electricity, and gathers up the hair of the attendant-watcher, as if with horror at the mischiefs and desertions from the right, in which I may be instrumental!

"Above all, how can I reconcile its being mere machinery, with its leaving off when it has cut me into sheets, and NOT conveying me to the Exciseman in the next room, whom it plainly thinks a most unnatural conclusion!

"I am carried thither on trucks. I am examined, and my defective portions thrown out, for the Mill, again; I am made up into quires and reams; I am weighed and excised by the hundredweight; and I am ready for my work." ¶HWC/PM

—plate glass: "A lofty and enormous hall, with windows in the high walls open to the rainy night. Down the centre, a fearful row of roaring furnaces, white-hot: to look at which, even through the chinks in the iron screens before them, and masked, seemed to scorch and splinter the very breath within one. At right angles with this hall, another, an immense building in itself, with unearthly-looking instruments hanging on the walls, and strewn about, as if for some diabolical cookery. In dark corners, where the furnaces redly glimmered on them, from time to time, knots of swarthy muscular men, with nets drawn over their faces, or hanging from their hats: confusedly grouped, wildly dressed, scarcely heard to mutter amidst the roaring of the fires, and mysteriously coming and going, like picturesque shadows, cast by the terrific glare.

"Such figures there must have been, once upon a time, in some such scene, ministering to the worship of fire, and feeding the altars of the cruel god with victims. Figures not dissimilar, alas! there have been, torturing and burning, even in Our Saviour's name. But, happily those bitter days are gone. The senseless world is tortured for the good of man, and made to take new forms in his service. Upon the rack, we stretch the ores and metals of the earth, and not the image of the Creator of all. These fires and figures are the agents of civilisation, and not of deadly persecution and black murder. Burn fires and welcome! making a light in England that shall not be quenched by all the monkish dreamers in the world!" HWC/PG

" . . . 'they are going to cast. This way, gentlemen!'

"The kitchen in which the *Ogre* threatened to cook *Jack* and his seven brothers could not have been half so formidable an apartment as the enormous cuisine into which we were led. One end was occupied with a row of awful ovens; in the midst, stood a stupendous iron table; and upon it lay a rolling-pin, so big, that it could only be likened to half-a-dozen garden-rollers joined together at their ends. Above, was an iron crane or gallows to lift the enormous messes of red-hot gruel, thick and slab, which were not to be brought from the furnaces.

"'Stand clear!' A huge basin, white with heat, approaches, on a sort of iron hurley; at one end of which sits, triumphant, a salamander, in human form, to balance the Plutonian mass, as it approaches on its wheeled car—playing with it—a game of see-saw. It stops at the foot of the iron gallows . . . . a cuvette filled with molten glass, glowing from the fiery furnace . . . . The dreadful pot is lifted by the crane. It is poised immediately over the table; a workman tilts it; and out pours a cataract of molten opal which spreads itself, deliberately, like infernal sweet-stuff, over the iron table; which is spilled and slopped about, in a crowd of men, and touches nobody . . . .

"When the roller has passed over the table, it leaves a sheet of red-hot glass, measuring some twelve feet by seven.

"This translucent confection is pushed upon a flat wooden platform on wheels—sparkling, as it touches the wood, like innumerable diamonds—and is then run rapidly to an oven, there to be baked or annealed. The bed or 'sole' of this *carquèse* is heated to a temperature exactly equal to that of the glass; which is now so much cooled that you can stand within a yard or so of it without fear of scorching off your eyelashes. The pot out of the furnace is cooled too, out in the rain, and lies there, burst into a hundred pieces. It has been a good one: for it has withstood the fire, seventy days . . . .

"When eight plates are put into the *carquèse* it is closed up hermetically; for the tiniest current of cold air would crack the glass. The fire is allowed to go out of its own accord, and the cooling takes place so gradually, that it is not completed until eight days are over. When drawn forth, the glass is that 'rough plate' which we see let into the doors of railway stations, and forming half-transparent floors in manufactories. To make it completely transparent for windows and looking-glasses, elaborate processes of grinding and polishing are requisite. They are three in number:—roughing down, smoothing and polishing." HWC/PG

—shipbuilding: " . . . the mechanical powers for piercing the iron plates—four inches and a half thick—for rivets, shaping them under hydraulic pressure to the finest tapering turns of the ship's lines, and paring them away, with knives shaped like the beaks of strong and cruel birds, to the nicest requirements of the design!

"These machines of tremendous force, so easily directed by one attentive face and presiding hand . . . . 'Obedient monster, please to bite this mass of iron through and through, at equal distances, where these regular chalk-marks are, all round.'

Monster looks at its work, and lifting its ponderous head, replies, 'I don't particularly want to do it; but if it must be done——!' The solid metal wriggles out, hot from the monster's crunching tooth, and it *is* done.

"'Dutiful monster, observe this other mass of iron. It is required to be pared away, according to this delicately lessening and arbitrary line, which please to look at.' Monster (who has been in a reverie) brings down its blunt head, and, much in the manner of Doctor Johnson, closely looks along the line—very closely, being somewhat near-sighted. 'I don't particularly want to do it; but if it must be done——!' Monster takes another near-sighted look, takes aim, and the tortured piece writhes off, and falls, a hot tight-twisted snake, among the ashes.

"The making of the rivets is merely a pretty round game, played by a man and a boy, who put red-hot barley sugar in a Pope Joan board, and immediately rivets fall out of window; but the tone of the great machines is the tone of the great Yard and the great country: 'We don't particularly want to do it; but if it must be done——!'" ¶UT/CD

—steel mill: "In a large and lofty building, supported by pillars of iron, with great black apertures in the upper walls, open to the external air; echoing to the roof with the beating of hammers and roar of furnaces, mingled with the hissing of red-hot metal plunged in water, and a hundred strange unearthly noises never heard elsewhere; in this gloomy place, moving like demons among the flame and smoke, dimly and fitfully seen, flushed and tormented by the burning fires, and wielding great weapons, a faulty blow from any one of which must have crushed some workman's skull, a number of men laboured like giants.

"Others, reposing upon heaps of coals or ashes with their faces turned to the black vault above, slept or rested from their toil. Others again, opening the white-hot furnace-doors, cast fuel on the flames, which came rushing and roaring forth to meet it, and licked it up like oil. Others drew forth, with clashing noise upon the ground, great sheets of glowing steel, emitting an insupportable heat, and a dull deep light like that which reddens in the eyes of savage beasts." ¶OCS 44

—weaving mill: "The fairy palaces burst into illumination, before pale morning showed the monstrous serpents of smoke trailing themselves over Coketown. A clattering of clogs upon the pavement; a rapid ringing of bells; and all the melancholy mad elephants, polished and oiled up for the day's monotony, were at their heavy exercise again . . . .

"The day grew strong, and showed itself outside, even against the flaming lights within. The lights were turned out, and the work went on. The rain fell, and the Smoke-serpents, submissive to the curse of all that tribe, trailed themselves upon the earth. In the waste-yard outside, the steam from the escape pipe, the litter of barrels and old iron, the shining heaps of coals, the ashes everywhere, were shrouded in a veil of mist and rain.

"The work went on, until the noon-bell rang. More clattering upon the pavements. The looms, and wheels, and Hands all out of gear for an hour." HT i 11

"Machinery slackened; throbbing feebly like a fainting pulse; stopped. The bell again; the glare of light and heat dispelled; the factories, looming heavy in the black wet night—their tall chimneys rising up into the air like competing Towers of Babel." HT i 12

—white lead: "The purport of such works is the conversion of pig-lead into white-lead. This conversion is brought about by the slow and gradual effecting of certain successive chemical changes in the lead itself. The processes are picturesque and interesting—the most so, being the burying of the lead, at a certain stage of preparation, in pots, each pot containing a certain quantity of acid besides, and all the pots being buried in vast numbers, in layers, under tan, for some ten weeks . . . .

"As is the case with most pulps or pigments, so in the instance of this white-lead, processes of stirring, separating, washing, grinding, rolling, and pressing succeed. Some of these are unquestionably inimical to health, the danger arising from inhalation of particles of lead, or from contact between the lead and the touch, or both . . . .

"At last this vexed white-lead, having been buried and resuscitated, and heated and cooled and stirred, and separated and washed and ground, and rolled and pressed, is subjected to the action of intense fiery heat. A row of women . . . stood, let us say, in a large stone bake-house, passing on the baking dishes as they were given out by the cooks, from hand to hand, into the ovens. The oven, or stove, cold as yet, looked as high as an ordinary house, and was full of men and women on temporary footholds, briskly passing up and stowing away the dishes. The door of another oven, or stove, about to be cooled and emptied, was opened from above, for the uncommercial countenance to peer down into . . . . American inventiveness would seem to indicate that before very long white-lead may be made entirely by machinery." UT/AB

And see Labour—*health risks*

Member of Parliament

—*a borough:* "He is the honourable member for Verbosity—the best represented place in England . . . . " RP/HF

—*debtor:* "[Sir John Chester] wrote himself M. P.—but how? Why, thus. It was a proud family—more proud, indeed, than wealthy. He had stood in danger of arrest; of bailiffs, and a jail—a vulgar jail, to which the common people with small incomes went. Gentlemen of ancient houses have no privilege of exemption from such cruel laws —unless they are of one great house, and then they have. A proud man of his stock and kindred had the means of sending him there. He offered—not indeed to pay his debts, but to let him sit for a close borough until his own son came of age . . . . It was quite as good as an Insolvent Act, and infinitely more genteel. So Sir John Chester was a member of Parliament." BR 40

—*duties of staff:* "'I should require to be crammed, sir . . . . My secretary would have to make himself master of the foreign policy of the world, as it is mirrored in the newspapers; to run his eye over all accounts of public meetings, all leading articles, and accounts of the proceedings of public bodies; and to make notes of anything which it appeared to him might be made a point of, in any little speech upon the question of some petition lying on the table, or anything of that kind. Do you understand?'

"'I think I do, sir,' replied Nicholas.

"'Then,' said Mr Gregsbury, 'it would be necessary for him to make himself acquainted, from day to day, with newspaper paragraphs on passing events; such as "Mysterious disappearance, and supposed suicide of a pot-boy," or anything of that sort, upon which I might found a question to the secretary of State for the Home Department. Then, he would have to copy the question, and as much as I remembered of the answer (including a little compliment about independence and good sense); and to send the manuscript in a frank to the local paper, with perhaps half a dozen lines of leader to the effect, that I was always to be found in my place in Parliament, and never shrunk from the responsible and arduous duties, and so forth. You see?'

"Nicholas bowed.

"'Besides which,' continued Mr Gregsbury, 'I should expect him, now and then, to go through a few figures in the printed tables, and to pick out a few results, so that I might come out pretty well on timber duty questions, and finance questions, and so on; and I should like him to get up a few little arguments about the disastrous effects of a return to cash payments and a metallic currency, with a touch now and then about the exportation of bullion, and the emperor of Russia, and bank notes, and all that kind of thing, which it's only necessary to talk fluently about, because nobody understands it. Do you take me?'" NN 16

—*example:* "That singularly awkward and ungainly-looking man . . . who is leaning against the meat-screen, apparently deluding himself into the belief that he is thinking about something, is a splendid sample of a Member of the House of Commons concentrating in his own person the wisdom of a constituency . . . remark how very materially the great blinker-like spectacles assist the expression of that most intelligent face. Seriously speaking, did you ever see a countenance so expressive of the most hopeless extreme of heavy dulness, or behold a form so strangely put together? He is no great speaker: but when he *does* address the House, the effect is absolutely irresistible." SB/P

—*inspiring effect:* "Our honourable friend cannot come in for Verbosity too often. It is a good sign; it is a great example. It is to men like our honourable friend, and to contests like those from which he comes triumphant, that we are mainly indebted for that ready interest in politics, that fresh enthusiasm in the discharge of the duties of citizenship, that ardent desire to rush to the poll, at present so manifest throughout England. When the contest lies (as it sometimes does) between two such men as our honourable friend, it stimulates the finest emotions of our nature, and awakens the highest admiration of which our heads and hearts are capable." RP/HF

—*qualifications:* "For a gentleman who was rejoiced to see a body of visitors, Mr

Gregsbury looked as uncomfortable as might be; but perhaps this was occasioned by senatorial gravity, and a statesmanlike habit of keeping his feelings under control. He was a tough, burly, thick-headed gentleman, with a loud voice, a pompous manner, a tolerable command of sentences with no meaning in them, and in short every requisite for a very good member indeed." NN 16

"Mr James Harthouse, 'going in' for his adopted party, soon began to score. With the aid of a little more coaching for the political sages, a little more genteel listlessness for the general society, and a tolerable management of the assumed honesty in dishonesty, most effective and most patronized of the polite deadly sins, he speedily came to be considered of much promise. The not being troubled with earnestness was a grand point in his favour, enabling him to take to the hard Fact fellows with as good a grace as if he had been born one of the tribe, and to throw all other tribes overboard, as conscious hypocrites." HT ii 7

And see M:Facts—*statistics—Parliamentary*

—voting: "Our honourable friend has sat in several parliaments, and given bushels of votes. He is a man of that profundity in the matter of vote-giving, that you never know what he means. When he seems to be voting pure white, he may be in reality voting jet black. When he says Yes, it is just as likely as not—or rather more so—that he means No.

"This is the statesmanship of our honourable friend. It is in this that he differs from mere unparliamentary men. You may not know what he meant then, or what he means now; but our honourable friend knows, and did from the first know, both what he meant then, and what he means now; and when he said he didn't mean it then, he did in fact say that he means it now.

"And if you mean to say that you did not then, and do not now, know what he did mean then, or does mean now, our honourable friend will be glad to receive an explicit declaration from you whether you are prepared to destroy the sacred bulwarks of our nationality." ¶RP/HF

Politics and Politicians

—adroit non-sequitur: "'My good friend . . . wishes to know what I mean when he asks me what we are driving at, and when I candidly tell him, at the illimitable perspective, he wishes (if I understand him) to know what I mean? . . . I will indulge my good friend Tipkisson by telling him both what I mean and what I don't mean. (Cheers and cries of 'Give it him!')

"'Be it known to him then, and to all whom it may concern, that I do mean altars, hearths, and homes, and that I don't mean mosques and Mohammedanism!' The effect of this home-thrust was terrific. Tipkisson (who is a Baptist) was hooted down and hustled out, and has ever since been regarded as a Turkish Renegade who contemplates an early pilgrimage to Mecca.

"Nor was he the only discomfited man. The charge, while it stuck to him, was magically transferred to our honourable friend's opponent . . . and the men of Verbosity were asked to choose between our honourable friend and the Bible, and our honourable friend's opponent and the Koran. They decided for our honourable friend, and rallied round the illimitable perspective." ¶RP/HF

—advance men: " . . . for some weeks, backward and forward rush mysterious men with no names, who fly about all those particular parts of the country on which Doodle is at present throwing himself in an auriferous and malty shower, but who are merely persons of a restless disposition and never do anything anywhere.

"On these national occasions, Sir Leicester [Dedlock] finds the cousins useful. A better man than the Honourable Bob Stables to meet the Hunt at dinner, there could not possibly be. Better got up gentlemen than the other cousins, to ride over to polling-booths and hustings here and there, and show themselves on the side of England, it would be hard to find." BH 40

—agenda "Pondering in my mind the far-seeing schemes of Thisman and Thatman, and of the public blessing called Party, for staying the degeneracy, physical and moral, of many thousands (who shall say how many?) of the English race; for devising employment useful to the community for those who want but to work and live; for equalising rates, cultivating waste lands, facilitating emigration, and, above all things, saving and utilising the oncoming generations, and thereby changing ever-growing national weakness into strength: pondering in my mind, I say, these hopeful exertions, I turned down a narrow street [in the east end of London] to look into a house or two." UT/SE

—*balderdash:* "We have the glorious privilege of being always in hot water if we like. We are a shareholder in a Great Parochial British Joint Stock Bank of Balderdash." RP/V

—*canvassing:* "Meanwhile Twemlow, in an increasing hurry of spirits . . . gets to the club by the appointed time. At the club he promptly secures a large window, writing materials, and all the newspapers, and establishes himself, immoveable, to be respectfully contemplated by Pall Mall. Sometimes, when a man enters who nods to him, Twemlow says, 'Do you know Veneering?' Man says, 'No; member of the club?' Twemlow says, 'Yes. Coming in for Pocket-Breaches.' Man says, 'Ah! Hope he may find it worth the money!' yawns, and saunters out. Towards six o'clock of the afternoon, Twemlow begins to persuade himself that he is positively jaded with work, and think it much to be regretted that he was not brought up a Parliamentary agent." OMF ii 3

—*election:* "Doodle has found that he must throw himself upon the country—chiefly in the form of sovereigns and beer. In this metamorphosed state he is available in a good many places simultaneously, and can throw himself upon a considerable portion of the country at one time. Britannia being much occupied in pocketing Doodle in the form of sovereigns, and swallowing Doodle in the form of beer, and in swearing herself black in the face that she does neither—plainly to the advancement of her glory and morality—the London season comes to a sudden end, through all the Doodleites and Coodleites dispersing to assist Britannia in those religious exercises." BH 40

—*electioneering*

—*analogy to pantomime:* "Perhaps the cast of our political pantomime never was richer than at this day. We are particularly strong in clowns. At no former time, we should say, have we had such astonishing tumblers, or performers so ready to go through the whole of their feats for the amusement of an admiring throng.

"Their extreme readiness to exhibit, indeed, has given rise to some ill-natured reflections; it having been objected that by exhibiting gratuitously through the country when the theatre is closed, they reduce themselves to the level of mountebanks, and thereby tend to degrade the respectability of the profession.

"Certainly **Grimaldi** never did this sort of thing; and though **Brown, King, and Gibson** have gone to the Surrey in vacation time, and Mr **C. J. Smith** has ruralised at Sadler's Wells, we find no theatrical precedent for a general tumbling through the country, except in the gentleman, name unknown, who threw summersets on behalf of the late Mr **Richardson**, and who is no authority either, because he had never been on the regular boards." ¶B/P

—*described by a cheap-jack:* "For look here! Say it's election time. I [Doctor Marigold] am on the footboard of my cart in the market-place, on a Saturday night. I put up a general miscellaneous lot. I say: 'Now here, my free and independent woters, I'm a going to give you such a chance as you never had in all your born days, nor yet the days preceding. Now I'll show you what I am a going to do with you. Here's a pair of razors that'll shave you closer than the Board of Guardians; here's a flat-iron worth its weight in gold; here's a frying-pan artificially flavoured with essence of beefsteaks to that degree that you've only got for the rest of your lives to fry bread and dripping in it and there you are replete with animal food; here's a genuine chronometer watch in such a solid silver case that you may knock at the door with it when you come home late from a social meeting, and rouse your wife and family, and save up your knocker for the postman; and here's half-a-dozen dinner plates that you may play the cymbals with to charm the baby when it's fractious. Stop! I'll throw you in another article, and I'll give you that, and it's a rolling-pin; and if the baby can only get it well into its mouth when its teeth is coming and rub the gums once with it, they'll come through double, in a fit of laughter equal to being tickled. Stop again! I'll throw you in another article, because I don't like the looks of you, for you haven't the appearance of buyers unless I lose by you, and because I'd rather lose than not take money to-night, and that's a looking-glass in which you may see how ugly you look when you don't bid. What do you say now? Come! Do you say a pound? Not you, for you haven't got it. Do you say ten shillings? Not you, for you owe more to the tallyman. Well then, I'll tell you what I'll do with you. I'll heap 'em all on the footboard of the cart—there they are! razors, flat-iron, frying-pan, chronometer watch, dinner plates, rolling-pin, and looking-glass—take 'em all away for four shillings, and I'll give you sixpence for your trouble!' This is me, the Cheap Jack. But on the Monday morning, in the same market-place, comes the Dear Jack on the hustings—*his* cart—and what does *he* say? 'Now my free and independent woters, I am a going to give you such a chance' (he begins it just like me) 'as you never had in all your born days, and that's the chance of sending Myself to Parliament. Now I'll tell you what I am a going to do for you. Here's the interests of this magnificent town promoted above all the rest of the civilised and uncivilised earth. Here's your railways carried, and your neighbours' railways jockeyed. Here's all your sons in the Post-office. Here's Britannia smiling on you. Here's the eyes of Europe on you. Here's uniwersal prosperity for you, repletion of animal food, golden cornfields, gladsome homesteads, and rounds of applause from your own hearts, all in one lot, and that's myself. Will you take me as I stand? You won't? Well, then, I'll tell you what I'll do with you. Come now! I'll throw you in anything you ask for. There! Church-rates, abolition of church-rates, more malt tax, no malt tax, uniwersal education to the highest mark, or uniwersal ignorance to the lowest, total abolition of flogging in the army or a dozen for every private once a month all round. Wrongs of Men or Rights of Women—only say which it shall be, take 'em or leave 'em, and I'm of your opinion altogether, and the lot's your own on your own terms. There! You won't take it yet! Well, then, I'll tell you what I'll do with you. Come! You *are* such free independent woters, and I *am* so proud of you —you *are* such a noble and enlightened constituency, and I *am* so ambitious of the honour and dignity of being your member, which is by far the highest level to which the wings of the human mind can soar—that I'll tell you what I'll do with you. I'll throw you in all the public-houses in your magnificent town for nothing. Will that content you? It won't? You won't take the lot yet? Well, then, before I put the horse in and drive away, and make the offer to the next most magnificent town that can be discovered, I'll tell you what I'll do. Take the lot, and I'll drop two thousand pound in the streets of your magnificent town for them to pick up that can. Not enough? Now look here. This is the very furthest that I'm a going to. I'll make it two thousand five hundred. And still you won't? Here, missis! Put the horse—no, stop half a moment, I shouldn't like to turn my back upon you neither for a trifle, I'll make it two thousand seven hundred and fifty pound. There! Take the lot on your own terms, and I'll count out two thousand seven hundred and fifty pound on the footboard of the cart, to be dropped in the streets of your magnificent town for them to pick up that can. What do you say? Come now? You won't do better, and you may do worse. You take it? Hooray! Sold again, and got the seat!" CS/DM 1

CD did not paragraph this entire discourse, and we have abided by this, to give the effect of the non-stop patter of the Cheap Jack

—kissing babies: "There was a moment of awful suspense as the procession waited for the Honourable Samuel Slumkey to step into his carriage. Suddenly the crowd set up a great cheering.

"'He has come out,' said little Mr Perker, greatly excited; the more so as their position did not enable them to see what was going forward.

"Another cheer, much louder.

"'He has shaken hands with the men,' cried the little agent.

"Another cheer, far more vehement.

"'He has patted the babies on the head,' said Mr Perker, trembling with anxiety.

"A roar of applause that rent the air.

"'He has kissed one of 'em!' exclaimed the delighted little man.

"A second roar.

"'He has kissed another,' gasped the excited manager.

"A third roar.

"'He's kissing 'em all!' screamed the enthusiastic little gentleman. And hailed by the deafening shouts of the multitude, the procession moved on." PP 13

—letters to the editor: "At these momentous crises of the national fate, we are much assisted in our deliberations by two eminent volunteers; one of whom subscribes himself A Fellow Parishioner, the other, A Rate-Payer. Who they are, or what they are, or where they are, nobody knows; but whatever one asserts, the other contradicts. They are both voluminous writers, indicting more epistles than **Lord Chesterfield** in a single week; and the greater part of their feelings are too big for utterance in anything less than capital letters. They require the additional aid of whole rows of notes of admiration, like balloons, to point their generous indignation; and they sometimes com-

municate a crushing severity to stars. As thus:

"MEN OF MOONEYMOUNT

"Is it, or is it not, a * * * to saddle the parish with a debt of £2,745,6s. 9d., yet claim to be a RIGID ECONOMIST?

"Is it, or is it not a * * * to state as a fact what is proved to be *both a moral and a* PHYSICAL IMPOSSIBILITY?

"Is it, or is it not, a * * * to call £2,745 6s. 9d. nothing; and nothing, something?

"Do you, or do you not want a * * * TO REPRESENT YOU IN THE VESTRY?

"Your consideration of these questions is recommended to you by

"A FELLOW PARISHIONER"
RP/V

—*professional efforts:* ". . . the Member of Mr Bull's family was discovered to be haunted, night and day, by two evil spirits who had come down with him (they being usually prowling about the lobbies and passages of the house, and other dry places), and who, under the names of an Attorney and a Parliamentary Agent, committed ravages truly diabolical.

"The first act of this infernal pair was, to throw open all the public-houses, and invite the people of Burningshame to drink themselves raving mad. They then compelled them, with banners, and with instruments of brass, and big drums, idiotically to parade the town, and fall foul of all other banners, instruments of brass, and big drums, that they met.

"In the meantime, they tortured and terrified all the small tradesmen, buzzed in their ears, dazzled their eyes, nipped their pockets, pinched their children, appeared to and alarmed their wives (many of them in the family way), broke the rest of whole families, and filled them with anxiety and dread.

"Not content with this, they tempted the entire town, got the people to sell their precious souls, put red-hot money into their hands while they were looking another way, made them forswear themselves, set father against son, brother against brother, friend against friend; and made the whole of Burningshame one sty of gluttony, drunkenness, avarice, lying, false-swearing, waste, want, ill-will, contention and depravity." ¶HW/HH

—*local*

—*a microcosm:* "In all [our Vestry's] debates, they are laudbly imitative of the windy and wordy slang of the real original, and of nothing that is better in it. They have headstrong party animosities, without any reference to the merits of questions; they tack a surprising amount of debate to a very little business; they set more store by forms than they do by substances:—all very like the real original! It has been doubted in our borough, whether our Vestry is of any utility; but our own conclusion is, that it is of the use to the Borough that a diminishing mirror is to a painter, as enabling it to perceive in a small focus of absurdity all the surface defects of the real original." RP/V

—*observer:* "He was a great politician of course, and explained his opinions at some length to one of our company; but I only remember that he concluded with two sentiments, one of which was, Somebody for ever; and the other, Blast everybody else! which is by no means a bad abstract of the general creed in these matters." AN 13

—*partisan:* "It appears, then, that the Eatanswill people, like the people of many other small towns, considered themselves of the utmost and most mighty importance, and that every man in Eatanswill, conscious of the weight that attached to his example, felt himself bound to unite heart and soul with one of the two great parties that divided the town—the Blues and the Buffs.

"Now the Blues lost no opportunity of opposing the Buffs, and the Buffs lost no opportunity of opposing the Blues; and the consequence was, that whenever the Buffs and Blues met together at public meeting, Town-Hall, fair, or market, disputes and high words arose between them.

"With these dissensions it is almost superfluous to say that everything in Eatanswill was made a party question. If the Buffs proposed to new skylight the market-place, the Blues got up public meetings, and denounced the proceeding; if the Blues proposed the erection of an additional pump in the High Street, the Buffs rose as one man and stood aghast at the enormity. There were Blue shops and Buff shops, Blue inns and Buff inns;—there was a Blue aisle and a Buff aisle in the very church itself." ¶PP 13

—*Vestry:* "We have a Vestry in our borough, and can vote for a vestryman . . . .

"To get into this Vestry in the eminent capacity of Vestryman, gigantic efforts are made, and Herculean exertions used. It is made manifest to the dullest capacity at every election, that if we reject Snozzle we are done for, and that if we fail to bring in Blunderbooze at the top of the poll, we are unworthy of the dearest rights of Britons. Flaming placards are rife on all the dead walls in the borough, public-houses hang out banners, hackney-cabs burst into full-grown flowers of type, and everybody is, or should be, in a paroxysm of anxiety." RP/V

—Parliamentary

—atmosphere: " . . . we may reflect with pride and gratification of heart on the proficiency of our clowns as exhibited in the season. Night after night will they twist and tumble about, till two, three, and four o'-clock in the morning; playing the strangest antics, and giving each other the funniest slaps on the face that can possibly be imagined, without evincing the smallest tokens of fatigue. The strange noises, the confusion, the shouting and roaring, amid which all this is done, too, would put to shame the most turbulent sixpenny gallery that ever yelled through a boxing-night." B/P

—Canadian: "The Governor . . . said what he had to say manfully and well . . . the people shouted; the in's rubbed their hands; the out's shook their heads; the Government party said there never was such a good speech; the Opposition declared there never was such a bad one; the Speaker and members of the House of Assembly withdrew from the bar to say a great deal among themselves and do a little; and, in short, everything went on, and promised to go on, just as it does at home upon the like occasions." AN 2

—opening: "We take it that the commencement of a Session of Parliament is neither more nor less than the drawing up of the curtain for a grand comic pantomime, and that his Majesty's most gracious speech on the opening thereof may be not inaptly compared to the clown's opening speech of 'Here we are!' 'My lords and gentlemen, here we are!' appears, to our mind at least, to be a very good abstract of the point and meaning of the propitiatory address of the ministry. When we remember how frequently this speech is made, immediately after *the change* too, the parallel is quite perfect, and still more singular." B/P

—party discipline: "It is especially curious to behold one of these clowns compelled to go through the most surprising contortions by the irresistible influence of the wand of office, which his leader or harlequin holds above his head. Acted upon by this wonderful charm he will become perfectly motionless, moving neither hand, foot, nor finger, and will even lose the faculty of speech at an instant's notice; or on the other hand, he will become all life and animation if required, pouring forth a torrent of words without sense or meaning, throwing himself into the wildest and most fantastic contortions, and even grovelling on the earth and licking up the dust. These exhibitions are more curious than pleasing; indeed, they are rather disgusting than otherwise, except to the admirers of such things, with whom we confess we have no fellow-feeling.

"Strange tricks—very strange tricks—are also performed by the harlequin who holds for the time being the magic wand which we have just mentioned. The mere waving it before a man's eyes will dispossess his brains of all the notions previously stored there, and fill it with an entirely new set of ideas; one gentle tap on the back will alter the colour of a man's coat completely; and there are some expert performers who, having this wand held first on one side and then on the other, will change from side to side, turning their coats at every evolution, with so much rapidity and dexterity, that the quickest eye can scarcely detect their motions. Occasionally, the genius who confers the wand, wrests it from the hand of the temporary possessor, and consigns it to some new performer; on which occasions all the characters change sides, and then the race and the hard knocks being anew." B/P

—party leaders and retinue: "Then there is my Lord Boodle, of considerable reputation with his party, who has known what office is, and who tells Sir Leicester Dedlock with much gravity, after dinner, that he really does not see to what the present age is tending. A debate is not what a debate used to be; the House is not what the House used to be; even a Cabinet is not what it formerly was.

"He perceives with astonishment, that supposing the present Government to be overthrown, the limited choice of the Crown, in the formation of a new Ministry, would lie between Lord Coodle and Sir Thomas Doodle—supposing it to be impossible for the Duke of Foodle to act with Goodle, which may be assumed to be the case in consequence of the breach arising out of that affair with Hoodle.

"Then, giving the Home Department and the Leadership of the House of Commons to Joodle, the Exchequer to Koodle, the Colonies to Loodle, and the Foreign Office to Moodle, what are you to do with Noodle? You can't offer him the Presidency of the Council; that is reserved for Poodle. You can't put him in the Woods and Forests; that is hardly good enough for Quoodle. What follows? That the country is shipwrecked, lost, and gone to pieces (as is made manifest to the patriotism of Sir Leicester Dedlock), because you can't provide for Noodle!

"On the other hand, the Right Honourable William Buffy, M. P., contends across the table with some one else, that the shipwreck of the country—about which there is no doubt; it is only the manner of it that is in question—is attributable to Cuffy. If you had done with Cuffy what you ought to have done when he first came into Parliament, and had prevented him from going over to Duffy, you would have got him into alliance with Fuffy, you would have had with you the weight attaching as a smart debater to Guffy, you would have brought to bear upon the elections the wealth of Huffy, you would have got in for three counties Juffy, Kuffy, and Luffy, and you would have strengthened your administration by the official knowledge and the business habits of Muffy. All this, instead of being as you now are, dependent on the mere caprice of Puffy!

"As to this point, and as to some minor topics, there are differences of opinion; but it is perfectly clear to the brilliant and distinguished circle, all round, that nobody is in question but Boodle and his retinue, and Buffy and his retinue. These are the great actors for whom the stage is reserved. A People there are, no doubt—a certain large number of supernumeraries, who are to be occasionally addressed, and relied upon for shouts and choruses, as on the theatrical stage; but Boodle and Buffy, their followers and families, their heirs, executors, administrators, and assigns, are the born first-actors, managers, and leaders, and no others can appear upon the scene for ever and ever." BH 12

—reported upon: "I [David Copperfield] have tamed that savage stenographic mystery. I make a respectable income by it. I am in high repute for my accomplishment in all pertaining to the art, and am joined with eleven others in reporting the debates in Parliament for a Morning Newspaper. Night after night, I record predictions that never come to pass, professions that are never fulfilled, explanations that are only meant to mystify. I wallow in words. Britannia, that unfortunate female, is always before me, like a trussed fowl: skewered through and through with office-pens, and bound hand and foot with red tape. I am sufficiently behind the scenes to know the worth of political life. I am quite an Infidel about it, and shall never be converted." DC 43

—under orders to cheer: "' . . . when a man had leave to let off any little private popgun, it was always considered a great point for him to say that he had the happiness of believing that his sentiments were not without an echo in the breast of Mr **Pitt**; the pilot, in point of fact, who had weathered the storm. Upon which, a devilish large number of fellows immediately cheered, and put him in spirits. Though the fact is, that these fellows, being under orders to cheer most excessively whenever Mr Pitt's name was mentioned, became so proficient that it always woke 'em. And they were so entirely innocent of what was going on, otherwise, that it used to be commonly said . . . that if a man had risen in his place, and said that he regretted to inform the house that there was an Honourable Member in the last stage of convulsions in the Lobby, and that the Honourable Member's name was Pitt, the approbation would have been vociferous.'" DS 61

And see Member of Parliament

—pocket boroughs: " . . . Sir Leicester [Dedlock] . . . always delivering in his own candidateship, as a kind of handsome wholesale order to be promptly executed. Two other little seats that belong to him, he treats as retail orders of less importance; merely sending down the men, and signifying to the tradespeople, 'You will have the goodness to make these materials into two members of parliament, and to send them home when done.'" BH 40

"' . . . the people of those other two places, now? Do they yield so laudably to the vast and cumulative influence of such enterprise and such renown; do those little rills become absorbed so quietly and easily, and, as it were by the influence of natural laws, so beautifully, in the swoop of the majestic stream as it flows upon its wondrous way enriching the surrounding lands; that their course is perfectly to be calculated, and distinctly to be predicated?'

"Mr Merdle, a little troubled by Bar's eloquence, looked fitfully about the nearest salt-cellar for some moments, and then said, hesitating:

"'They are perfectly aware, sir, of their duty to Society. They will return anybody I send to them for that purpose.'

"'Cheering to know,' said Bar. 'Cheering to know.'

"The three places in question were three little rotten holes in this Island, containing three little ignorant, drunken, guzzling, dirty, out-of-the-way constituencies, that had reeled into Mr Merdle's pocket." LD ii 12

—*"policy":* "You may perhaps hear the cunning and promise-breaking of King Henry the First, called 'policy' by some people, and 'diplomacy' by others. Neither of these fine words will in the least mean that it was true; and nothing that is not true can possibly be good." CHE 10

—*Presidential:* "Quiet people avoid the question of the Presidency, for there will be a new election in three years and a half, and party feelings runs very high [1842: **John Tyler** had succeeded **William Henry Harrison**, dead after one month in office]: the great constitutional feature of this institution being, that directly the acrimony of the last election is over, the acrimony of the next one begins; which is an unspeakable comfort to all strong politicians and true lovers of their country; that is to say, to ninety-nine men and boys out of every ninety-nine and a quarter." AN 4

—*Reaction:* "It was too much the way of Monseigneur under his reverses as a refugee, and it was much too much the way of native British orthodoxy, to talk of this terrible Revolution as if it were the one only harvest ever known under the skies that had not been sown—as if nothing had ever been done, or omitted to be done, that had led to it—as if observers of the wretched millions in France, and of the misused and perverted resources that should have made them prosperous, had not seen it inevitably coming, years before, and had not in plain words recorded what they saw. Such vapouring, combined with the extravagant plots of Monseigneur for the restoration of a state of things that had utterly exhausted itself, and worn out Heaven and earth as well as itself, was hard to be endured without some remonstrance by any sane man who knew the truth . . . .

"Among the talkers, was Stryver . . . broaching to Monseigneur, his devices for blowing the people up and exterminating them from the face of the earth, and doing without them: and for accomplishing many similar objects akin in their nature to the abolition of eagles by sprinkling salt on the tails of the race." TTC ii 24

Revolution

—*boastful participant:* "'He was not at Duke Stret, or at Warwick Street, G. Varden,' said Simon, sternly; 'but he *was* at Westminster. Perhaps, sir, he kicked a county member, perhaps, sir, he tapped a lord—you may stare, sir, I repeat it—blood flowed from noses, and perhaps he tapped a lord. Who knows? This,' he added, putting his hand into his waistcoat-pocket, and taking out a large tooth, at the sight of which both Miggs and Mrs Varden screamed, 'this was a bishop's. Beware, G. Varden!'" BR 51

—*breeding ground:* "[Hunger's] abiding place was in all things fitted to it. A narrow winding street, full of offence and stench, with other narrow winding streets diverging, all peopled by rags and nightcaps, and all smelling of rags and nightcaps, and all visible things with a brooding look upon them that looked ill.

"In the hunted air of the people there was yet some wild-beast thought of the possibility of turning at bay. Depressed and slinking though they were, eyes of fire were not wanting among them; nor compressed lips, white with what they suppressed; nor foreheads knitted into the likeness of the gallows-rope they mused about enduring, or inflicting . . . .

"The crippling stones of the pavement, with their many little reservoirs of mud and water, had no footways, but broke off abruptly at the doors. The kennel, to make amends, ran down the middle of the street—when it ran at all: which was only after heavy rains, and then it ran, by many eccentric fits, into the houses. Across the streets, at wide intervals, one clumsy lamp was slung by a rope and pulley; at night, when the lamplighter had let these down, and lighted, and hoisted them again, a feeble grove of dim wicks swung in a sickly manner overhead, as if they were at sea. Indeed they were at sea, and the ship and crew were in peril of tempest." ¶TTC i 5

And see LC:Advertisement—*shop signs of Paris*

—*effect on the arts:* "'Uneasy lies the head that wears a crown' indeed, in days when crowns of so many sorts, of gold, brass, and iron, are tumbling from the heads of the wearers; but the head that wears a mimic crown, and the hand that grasps a mimic sceptre, fare at such a season, worst of all; for then the peaceful, graceful arts of life go down, and the slighter ornaments of social existence are the first things crushed. Therefore, gentlemen, if the King of Sardinia cannot get into trouble without involving the King of Mr *Daggerwood*'s Company; and if the leader of the Austrian armies cannot make a movement without affecting the leader of the business at the Theatre Royal, Little Pedlington, so much the more have we reason to rejoice in the continued prosperity of [the General Theatrical Fund] . . . ." S/TF4

The Unemployed Rioters OCS

—*fall of the Bastille:* "Headlong, mad, and dangerous footsteps to force their way into anybody's life, footsteps not easily made clean again if once stained red, the footsteps raging in Saint Antoine . . . .

"Saint Antoine had been . . . a vast dusky mass of scarecrows heaving to and fro, with frequent gleams of light above the billowy heads, where steel blades and bayonets shone in the sun. A tremendous roar arose from the throat of Saint Antoine, and a forest of naked arms struggled in the air like shrivelled branches of trees in a winter wind: all the fingers convulsively clutching at every weapon or semblance of a weapon that was thrown up from the depths below, no matter how far off.

"Who gave them out, whence they last came, where they began, through what agency they crookedly quivered and jerked, scores at a time, over the heads of the crowd, like a kind of lightning, no eye in the throng could have told; but, muskets were being distributed—so were cartridges, powder, and ball, bars of iron and wood, knives, axes, pikes, every weapon that distracted ingenuity could discover or devise. People who could lay hold of nothing else, set themselves with bleeding hands to force stones and bricks out of their places in walls. Every pulse and heart in Saint Antoine was on high-fever strain and at high-fever heat. Every living creature there held life as of no account, and was demented with a passionate readiness to sacrifice it.

"As a whirlpool of boiling waters has a centre point, so, all this raging circled round Defarge's wine-shop, and every human drop in the caldron had a tendency to be sucked towards the vortex where Defarge himself, already begrimed with gunpowder and sweat, issued orders, issued arms, thrust this man back, dragged this man forward, disarmed one to arm another, laboured and strove in the thickest of the uproar." TTC ii 21

"'Come then!' cried Defarge, in a resounding voice. 'Patriots and friends, we are ready! The Bastille!'

"With a roar that sounded as if all the breath in France had been shaped into the detested word, the living sea rose, wave on wave, depth on depth, and overflowed the city to that point. Alarm-bells ringing, drums beating, the sea raging and thundering on its new beach, the attack begun.

"Deep ditches, double drawbridge, massive stone walls, eight great towers, cannon, muskets, fire and smoke. Through the fire and through the smoke—in the fire and in the smoke, for the sea cast him up against a cannon, and on the instant he became a cannonier—Defarge of the wine-shop worked like a manful soldier. Two fierce hours.

"Deep ditch, single drawbridge, massive stone walls, eight great towers, cannon, muskets, fire and smoke. One drawbridge down! 'Work, comrades all, work! Work, Jacques One, Jacques Two, Jacques One Thousand, Jacques Two Thousand, Jacques Five-and-Twenty Thousand; in the name of all the Angels or the Devils—which you prefer—work!' Thus Defarge of the wine-shop, still at his gun, which had long grown hot.

"'To me, women!' cried madame his wife. 'What! We can kill as well as the men when the place is taken!' And to her, with a shrill thirsty cry, trooping women variously armed, but all armed alike in hunger and revenge.

"Cannon, muskets, fire and smoke; but, still the deep ditch, the single drawbridge, the massive stone walls, and the eight great towers. Slight displacements of the raging sea, made by the falling wounded. Flashing weapons, blazing torches, smoking waggon-loads of wet straw, hard work at neighbouring barricades in all directions, shrieks, volleys, execrations, bravery without stint, boom, smash and rattle, and the furious sounding of the living sea; but, still the deep ditch, and the single drawbridge, and the massive stone walls, and the eight great towers, and still Defarge of the wine-shop at his gun, grown double hot by the service of Four fierce hours.

"A white flag from within the fortress, and a parley—this dimly perceptible through the raging storm, nothing audible in it—suddenly the sea rose immeasurably wider and higher, and swept Defarge of the wine-shop over the lowered drawbridge, past the massive stone outer walls, in among the eight great towers surrendered!

"So resistless was the force of the ocean bearing him on, that even to draw his breath or turn his head was as impracticable as if he had been struggling in the surf at the South Sea, until he was landed in the outer court-yard of the Bastille. There, against an angle of a wall, he made a struggle to look about him. Jacques Three was nearly at his side; Madame Defarge, still heading some of her women, was visible in the inner distance, and her knife was in her hand. Everywhere was tumult, exultation, deafening and maniacal bewilderment, astounding noise, yet furious dumb-show." TTC ii 21

—*the Guillotine:* "Above all, one hideous figure grew as familiar as if it had been before the general gaze from the foundation of the world—the figure of the sharp female called La Guillotine.

"It was the popular theme for jests; it was the best cure for headache, it infallibly prevented the hair from turning gray, it imparted a peculiar delicacy to the complexion, it was the National Razor which shaved close: who kissed La Guillotine, looked through the little window and sneezed into the sack. It was the sign of the regeneration of the human race. It superseded the Cross. Models of it were worn on breasts from which the Cross was discarded, and it was bowed down to and believed in where the Cross was denied.

"It sheared off heads so many, that it, and the ground it most polluted, were a rotten red. It was taken to pieces, like a toy-puzzle for a young Devil, and was put together again when occasion wanted it. It hushed the eloquent, struck down the powerful, abolished the beautiful and good. Twenty-two friends of high public mark, twenty-one living and one dead, it had lopped the heads off, in one morning, in as many minutes. The name of the strong man of Old Scripture had descended to the chief functionary [Sanson] who worked it; but, so armed, he was stronger than his namesake, and blinder, and tore away the gates of God's own Temple every day." TTC iii 4

—*a lynching:* "'Does everybody here recall old Foulon, who told the famished people that they might eat grass, and who died, and went to Hell?'

"'Everybody!' from all throats.

"'The news is of him. He is among us!'

"'Among us!' from the universal throat again. 'And dead?'

"'Not dead! He feared us so much—and with reason—that he caused himself to be represented as dead, and had a grand mock-funeral. But they have found him alive, hiding in the country, and have brought him in. I have seen him but now, on his way to the Hôtel de Ville, a prisoner. I have said that he had reason to fear us. Say All! *Had* he reason?'

"Wretched old sinner of more than three-score years and ten, if he had never known it yet, he would have known it in his heart of hearts if he could have heard the answering cry . . . .

"'Patriots!' said Defarge, in a determined voice, 'are we ready?'

"Instantly Madame Defarge's knife was in her girdle; the drum was beating in the streets, as if it and a drummer had flown together by magic; and The Vengeance, uttering terrific shrieks, and flinging her arms about her head like all the forty Furies at once, was tearing from house to house, rousing the women.

"The men were terrible, in the bloody-minded anger with which they looked from windows, caught up what arms they had, and came pouring down into the streets; but the women were a sight to chill the boldest. From such household occupations as their bare poverty yielded, from their children, from their aged and their sick crouching on the bare ground famished and naked, they ran out with streaming hair, urging one another, and themselves, to madness with the wildest cries and actions. Villain Foulon taken, my sister! Old Foulon taken, my mother! Miscreant Foulon taken, my daughter! Then, a score of others ran into the midst of these, beating their breasts, tearing their hair, and screaming, Foulon alive! Foulon who told the starving people they might eat grass! Foulon who told my old father that he might eat grass, when I had no bread to give him! Foulon who told my baby it might suck grass, when these breasts were dry with want! O mother of God, this Foulon! O Heaven, our suffering! Hear me, my dead baby and my withered father: I swear on my knees, on these stones, to avenge you on Foulon! Husbands, and brothers, and young men, Give us the blood of Foulon, Give us the head of Foulon, Give us the heart of Foulon, Give us the body and soul of Foulon, Rend Foulon to pieces, and dig him into the ground, that grass may grow from him! With these cries, numbers of the women, lashed into blind frenzy, whirled about, striking and tearing at their own friends until they dropped into a passionate swoon, and were only saved by the men belonging to them from being trampled under foot . . . .

"'See! cried madame, pointing with her knife. 'See the old villain bound with ropes. That was well done to tie a bunch of grass upon his back. Ha, ha! That was well done. Let him eat it now!' Madame put her knife under her arm, and clapped her hands as at a play . . . .

"At length the sun rose so high that it struck a kindly ray as of hope or protection, directly down upon the old prisoner's head. The favour was too much to bear; in an instant the barrier of dust and chaff that had stood surprisingly long, went to the winds, and Saint Antoine had got him! . . . the cry seemed to go up, all over the city, 'Bring him out! Bring him to the lamp!'

"Down, and up, and head foremost on the steps of the building; now, on his knees; now, on his feet; now, on his back; dragged, and struck at, and stifled by the bunches of grass and straw that were thrust into his face by hundreds of hands; torn, bruised, panting, bleeding, yet always entreating and beseeching for mercy; now full of vehement agony of action, with a small clear space about him as the people drew one another back that they might see; now, a log of dead wood drawn through a forest of legs; he was hauled to the nearest street corner where one of the fatal lamps swung, and there Madame Defarge let him go—as a cat might have done to a mouse—and silently and composedly looked at him while they made ready, and while he besought her: the women passionately screeching at him all the time, and the men sternly calling out to have him killed with grass in his mouth. Once, he went aloft, and the rope broke, and they caught him shrieking; twice, he went aloft, and the rope broke, and they caught him shrieking; then, the rope was merciful, and held him, and his head was soon upon a pike, with grass enough in the mouth for all Saint Antoine to dance at the sight of." TTC ii 22

—the Terror: "There was no pause, no pity, no peace, no interval of relenting rest, no measurement of time. Though days and nights circled as regularly as when time was young, and the evening and the morning were the first day, other count of time there was none. Hold of it was lost in the raging fever of a nation, as it is in the fever of one patient. Now, breaking the unnatural silence of a whole city, the executioner showed the people the head of the king—and now, it seemed almost in the same breath, the head of his fair wife, which had had eight weary months of imprisoned widowhood and misery to turn it gray.

"And yet, observing the strange law of contradiction which obtains in all such cases, the time was long, while it flamed by so fast. A revolutionary tribunal in the capital, and forty or fifty thousand revolutionary committees all over the land; a law of the Suspected, which struck away all security for liberty or life, and delivered over any good and innocent person to any bad and guilty one; prisons gorged with people who had committed no offence, and could obtain no hearing; these things became the established order and nature of appointed things, and seemed to be ancient usage before they were many weeks old." TTC iii 4

"Every day, through the stony streets, the tumbrils now jolted heavily, filled with Condemned. Lovely girls, bright women, brown-haired, black-haired, and gray; youths; stalwart men and old; gentle born and peasant born; all red wine for La Guillotine, all daily brought into light from the dark cellars of the loathsome prisons, and carried to her through the streets to slake her devouring thirst. Liberty, Equality, Fraternity, or Death;—the last, much the easiest to bestow, O Guillotine!" TTC iii 5

And see —the Guillotine

—a threat: "Utilitarian economists, skeletons of schoolmasters, Commissioners of Fact, genteel and used-up infidels, gabblers of many little dog's-eared creeds, the poor you will have always with you. Cultivate in them, while there is yet time, the utmost graces of the fancies and affections, to adorn their lives so much in need of ornament; or, in the day of your triumph, when romance is utterly driven out of their souls, and they and a bare existence stand face to face, Reality will take a wolfish turn, and make an end of you." HT ii 6

—vitality: "The new era began; the king was tried, doomed, and beheaded; the Republic of Liberty, Equality, Fraternity, or Death, declared for victory or death against the world in arms; the black flag waved night and day from the great towers of Notre Dame; three hundred thousand men, summoned to rise against the tyrants of the earth, rose from all the varying soils of France, as if the dragon's teeth had been sown broadcast, and had yielded fruit equally on hill and plain, on rock, in gravel, and alluvial mud, under the bright sky of the South and under the clouds of the North, in fell and forest, in the vineyards and the olive-grounds and among the cropped grass and the stubble of the corn, along the fruitful banks of the broad rivers, and in the sand of the sea-shore." TTC iii 4

And see Government*—a sneer and a response; and* H:Recreation*—knitting*

Sanitation

—disease endemic: "When they come at last to Tom-all-Alone's . . . Mr Snagsby passes along the middle of a villainous street, undrained, unventilated, deep in black mud and corrupt water—though the roads are dry elsewhere—and reeking with such smells and sights that he, who has lived in London all his life, can scarce believe his senses. Branching from this street and its heaps of ruins, are other streets and courts so infamous that Mr Snagsby sickens in body and mind, and feels as if he were going, every moment deeper down, into the in-

fernal gulf . . . .

"'Are those the fever-houses, Darby?' Mr Bucket coolly asks, as he turns his bull's-eye on a line of stinking ruins.

"Darby replies that 'all them are,' and further that in all, for months and months, the people 'have been down by dozens,' and have been carried out, dead and dying 'like sheep with the rot.' Bucket observing to Mr Snagsby as they go on again, that he looks a little poorly, Mr Snagsby answers that he feels as if he couldn't breathe the dreadful air." BH 22

"I saw a poisoned air, in which Life drooped. I saw Disease, arrayed in all its store of hideous aspects and appalling shapes, triumphant in every alley, by-way, court, back-street, and poor abode, in every place where human beings congregated—in the proudest and most boastful places, most of all. I saw innumerable hosts foredoomed to darkness, dirt, pestilence, obscenity, misery, and early death.

"I saw, wheresoever I looked, cunning preparations made for defacing the Creator's Image, from the moment of its appearance here on earth, and stamping over it the image of the Devil. I saw, from those reeking and pernicious stews, the avenging consequences of such Sin issuing forth, and penetrating to the highest places. I saw the rich struck down in their strength, their darling children weakened and withered, their marriageable sons and daughters perish in their prime. I saw that not one miserable wretch breathed out his poisoned life in the deepest cellar of the most neglected town, but, from the surrounding atmosphere, some particles of his infection were borne away, charged with heavy retribution on the general guilt." ¶HW/DV

—*epidemic:* ". . . but [Tom-all Alone's] has his revenge. Even the winds are his messengers, and they serve him in these hours of darkness. There is not a drop of Tom's corrupted blood but propagates infection and contagion somewhere. It shall pollute, this very night, the choice stream (in which chemists on analysis would find the genuine nobility) of a Norman house, and his Grace shall not be able to say Nay to the infamous alliance. There is not an atom of Tom's slime, not a cubic inch of any pestilential gas in which he lives, not one obscenity or degradation about him, not an ignorance, not a wickedness, not a brutality of his committing, but shall work its retribution, through every order of society, up to the proudest of the proud, and to the highest of the high. Verily, what with tainting, plundering, and spoiling, Tom has his revenge." BH 46

—*government incompetence:* "They were making late hay, somewhere out of town; and though the fragrance had a long way to come, and many counter fragrances to contend with among the dwellings of the poor (may God reward the worthy gentlemen who stickle for the Plague as part and parcel of the wisdom of our ancestors, and who do their little best to keep those dwellings miserable!), yet it was wafted faintly into Princess's Place, whispering of Nature and her wholesome air, as such things will, even unto prisoners and captives, and those who are desolate and oppressed, in very spite of aldermen and knights to boot: at whose sage nod—and how they nod!—the rolling world stands still!" DS 29

—*in London:* "It is a close night, though the damp cold is searching too; and there is a laggard mist a little way up in the air. It is a fine steaming night to turn the slaughterhouses, the unwholesome trades, the sewerage, bad water, and burial-grounds to account, and give the Registrar of Deaths some extra business." BH 32

" . . . [the meeting's] great object was to bring the metropolis within the provisions of the Public Health Act, from the operation of which it had been most absurdly and monstrously excluded—because it was their duty to diminish an amount of suffering and a waste of life which would be a disgrace to a heathen land, to atone for long years of neglect, of which they had all to a greater or less extent been guilty, and to redress a most grievous and cruel injustice.

"It was a common figure of speech when anything very important was left out of any great scheme, to say that it was the tragedy of *Hamlet* with *Hamlet* left out; but the existence of a Public Health Act with the metropolis excluded from its operation suggested something to [CD] even more sad, and that was the representation of *Hamlet* with nothing in it but the gravedigger. They had agreed that this was a state of things which must not be allowed to continue. They found every year 13,000 unfortunate persons dying unnaturally and prematurely around them. They found infancy was made stunted, ugly, and full of pain; maturity made old, and old age imbecile; and pauperism made hopeless every day. They claimed for the metropolis of a Christian country that this should be remedied, and that the capital should set an example of humanity and justice to the whole empire." S/SA1 (third person report)

"Of the sanitary condition of London at the present moment, [CD] solemnly believed it would be almost impossible to speak too ill. He knew of many places in it unsurpassed in the accumulated horrors of their neglect by the dirtiest old spots in the dirtiest old towns, under the worst old governments in Europe. Great contrasts of rank, great contrasts of wealth, and great contrasts of comfort must, as every man of sense was aware, exist among all civilized communities; but he sincerely believed that no such contrasts as were afforded by our handsome streets, our railroads and our electric telegraphs, in the year of our Lord 1850, as compared with the great mass of the dwellings of the poor in many parts of this metropolis, had ever before been presented on this earth." S/SA1 (third person report)

And see Government, Local—*Vestry*

—Ludgate Hill: "Fifty thousand lairs surrounded [Arthur Clennam] where people lived so unwholesomely, that fair water put into their crowded rooms on Saturday night, would be corrupt on Sunday morning; albeit my lord, their county member, was amazed that they failed to sleep in company with their butcher's meat. Miles of close wells and pits of houses, where the inhabitants gasped for air, stretched far away towards every point of the compass. Through the heart of the town a deadly sewer ebbed and flowed, in the place of a fine fresh river." LD i 3

And see N:Nature—*perverted,* F:The Poor, Abject—*epidemic, —their neighbourhoods; and* L:Neigbourhoods—*Jacob's Island, —Seven Dials, —Tom-all-Alone's*

—slaughter-house

" . . . let us compare ourselves, to our national delight and pride, as to these two subjects of slaughter-house and beast-market, with the outlandish foreigner.

—English: "The blessings of Smithfield are too well understood to need recapitulation . . . . Possibly the merits of our slaughter-houses are not yet quite so generally appreciated.

"Slaughter-houses, in the large towns of England, are always (with the exception of one or two enterprising towns) most numerous in the most densely crowded places, where there is the least circulation of air. They are often underground, in cellars; they are sometimes in close back yards; sometimes (as in Spitalfields) in the very shops where the meat is sold.

"Occasionally, under good private management, they are ventilated and clean. For the most part, they are unventilated and dirty; and, to the reeking walls, putrid fat and other offensive animal matter clings with a tenacious hold. The busiest slaughter-houses in London are . . . surrounded by houses of a poor description, swarming with inhabitants. Some of them are close to the worst burial-grounds in London.

"When the slaughter-house is below the ground, it is a common practice to throw the sheep down areas, neck and crop—which is exciting, but not at all cruel. When it is on the level surface, it is often extremely difficult of approach. Then, the beasts have to be worried, and goaded, and pronged, and tail-twisted, for a long time before they can be got in—which is entirely owing to their natural obstinacy When it is not difficult of approach, but is in a foul condition, what they see and scent makes them still more reluctant to enter—which is their natural obstinacy again.

"When they do get in at last, after no trouble and suffering to speak of (for there is nothing in the previous journey into the heart of London, the night's endurance in Smithfield, the struggle out again, among the crowded multitude, the coaches, carts, waggons, omnibuses, gigs, chaises, phaetons, cabs, trucks, dogs, boys, whoopings, roarings, and ten thousand other distractions), they are represented to be in a most unfit state to be killed, according to microscopic examinations made of their fevered blood by one of the most distinguished physiologists in the world, **Professor Owen**—but that's humbug.

"When they *are* killed, at last, their reeking carcases are hung in impure air, to become, as the same Professor will explain to you, less nutritious and more unwholesome—but he is only an *un*common counsellor, so don't mind *him.* In half a quarter of a mile's lengh of Whitechapel, at one time, there shall be six hundred newly slaughtered oxen hanging up, and seven hundred sheep—but the more the merrier—proof of prosperity.

"Hard by Snow Hill and Warwick Lane, you shall see the little children, inured to sights of brutality from their birth, trotting along the alleys, mingled with troops of horribly busy pigs, up to their ankles in blood—but it makes the young rascals hardy. Into the imperfect sewers of this overgrown city, you shall have the immense mass of corruption, engendered by these practices, lazily thrown out of sight, to rise, in poisonous gases, into your house at night, when your sleeping children will most readily absorb them, and to find its languid way, at last, into the river that you drink—but the French are a frog-eating people who wear wooden shoes, and it's O the roast beef of England, my boy, the jolly old English roast beef.

"It's quite a mistake—a new-fangled notion altogether—to suppose that there is any natural antagonism between putrefaction and health. They know better than that, in the Common Council. You may talk about Nature, in her wisdom, always warning man through his sense of smell, when he draws near to something dangerous; but that won't go down in the City. Nature very often don't mean anything. *Mrs Quickly* says that prunes [*sic.:* her recipe specified prawns] are ill for a green wound; but whosoever says that putrid animal substances are ill for a green wound, or for robust vigour, or for anything or for anybody, is a humanity-monger and a humbug. Britons never, never, never, &c, therefore.

"And prosperity to cattle-driving, cattle-slaughtering, bone-crushing, blood-boiling, trotter-scraping, tripe-dressing, paunch-cleaning, gut-spinning, hide-preparing, tallow-melting, and other salubrious proceedings, in the midst of hospitals, church-yards, workhouses, schools, infirmaries, refuges, dwellings, provision-shops, nurseries, sick-beds, every stage and baiting-place in the journey from birth to death!" ¶RP/FF

And see L:Neighbourhoods—*Smithfield*

—*French*

—*market at Poissy:* "There is little noise without, abundant space, and no confusion. The open area devoted to the market is divided into three portions: the Calf Market, the Cattle Market, the Sheep Market. Calves at eight, cattle at ten, sheep at mid-day. All is very clean.

"The Calf Market is a raised platform of stone, some three or four feet high, open on all sides, with a lofty over-spreading roof, supported on stone columns, which give it the appearance of a sort of vineyard from Northern Italy . . . . No other butcher jostles Monsieur François; Monsieur François jostles no other butcher. Nobody is flustered and aggravated. Nobody is savage. In the midst of the country blue frocks and red handkerchiefs, and the butchers' coats, shaggy, furry, and hairy: of calf-skin, cow-skin, horse-skin, and bear-skin: towers a cocked hat and a blue cloak. Slavery! For *our* Police wear great-coats and glazed hats. . . .

" . . . . We can neither choose our road, nor our pace, for that is all prescribed to us. The public convenience demands that our carts should get to Paris by such a route, and no other (Napoleon had leisure to find that out, while he had a little war with the world upon his hands), and woe betide us if we infringe orders.

"Droves of oxen stand in the Cattle Market, tied to iron bars fixed into posts of granite. Other droves advance slowly down the long avenue, past the second town-gate, and the first town-gate, and the sentry-box, and the bandbox, thawing the morning with their smoky breath as they come along. Plenty of room; plenty of time. Neither man nor beast is driven out of his wits by coaches, carts, waggons, omnibuses, gigs, chaises, phaetons, cabs, trucks, boys, whoopings, roarings, and multitudes. No tail-twisting is necessary—no iron pronging is necessary. There are no iron prongs here. The market for cattle is held as quietly as the market for calves . . . ." RP/FF

—*abattoir in Paris:* "The abattoirs are all within the walls of Paris . . . they stand in open places in the suburbs, removed from the press and bustle of the city . . . . While [the animals] rest here, before being slaughtered, they are required to be fed and watered, and the stalls must be kept clean ....

"[The first slaughterhouse] is firmly built and paved with stone. It is well lighted, thoroughly aired, and lavishly provided with fresh water . . . . The pavement . . . slopes downward to a gutter, for its being more easily cleansed . . . . Upon the pavement of this first stone chamber, lies an ox scarcely dead. If I except the blood draining from him, into a little stone well in a corner of the pavement, the place is free from offence as the Place de la Concorde. It is infinitely purer and cleaner, I know . . . than the Cathedral of Notre Dame . . . .

"I look into rows of slaughter-houses. In many, retail dealers . . . are making bargains for meat. There is killing enough, certainly, to satiate an unused eye; and there are steaming carcasses enough, to suggest the expediency of a fowl and salad for dinner; but everywhere, there is an orderly, clean, well-systematised routine of work in progress—horrible work at the best, if you please; but so much the greater reason why it should be made the best of. I don't know . . . that a Parisian of the lowest order is particularly delicate, or that his nature is remarkable for an infinitesimal infusion of ferocity; but I do know, my potent, grave, and common counselling Signors [in London], that he is forced, when at this work, to submit himself to a thoroughly good system, and to make an Englishman very heartily ashamed of you." RP/FF

The Rendezvous of the Mob BR
[The 1780 Gordon Rioters investing Parliament]

The Wooden Midshipman on the Lookout DS

London

It is strange with how little notice, good, bad, or indifferent, a man may live and die in London. He awakens no sympathy in the breast of any single person; his existence is a matter of interest to no one save himself; he cannot be said to be forgotten when he dies, for no one remembered him when he was alive.

SB/TP

The streets are filled with carriages, and people gaily clad. The jails are full, too, to the throat, nor have the workhouses or hospitals much room to spare. The courts of law are crowded. Taverns have their frequenters, and every mart of traffic has its throng. Each of these places is a world, and has its own inhabitants; each is distinct from and almost unconscious of the existence of any other.

[MHC 14]

As they passed along in sunshine and shade, the noisy and the eager, and the arrogant and the froward and the vain, fretted, and chafed, and made their usual uproar.

[LD ii 34]

The Turret: A House in Old London [circa 1780] BR

Boarding-house

—clean and residential: "Mrs Tibbs was, beyond all dispute, the most tidy, fidgety, thrifty little personage that ever inhaled the smoke of London; and the house of Mrs Tibbs was, decidedly, the neatest in all Great Coram Street. The area and the area-steps, and the street-door and the street-door steps, and the brass handle, and the door-plate, and the knocker, and the fan-light, were all as clean and bright, as indefatigable white-washing, and hearth-stoning, and scrubbing and rubbing, could make them. The wonder was, that the brass door-plate, with the interesting inscription 'MRS TIBBS' had never caught fire from constant friction, so perseveringly was it polished. There were meat-safe-looking blinds in the parlour-windows, blue and gold curtains in the drawing-room, and spring-roller blinds, as Mrs Tibbs was wont in the pride of her heart to boast, 'all the way up.' The bell-lamp in the passage looked as clear as a soap-bubble; you could see yourself in all the tables, and French-polish yourself on any one of the chairs. The banisters were bees-waxed; and the very stair-wires made your eyes wink, they were so glittering." SB/BH

—dingy and commercial:

—interior: "M. Todgers's Commercial Boarding-House was a house of that sort which is likely to be dark at any time; but that morning it was especially dark. There was an odd smell in the passage, as if the concentrated essence of all the dinners that had been cooked in the kitchen since the house was built, lingered at the top of the kitchen stairs to that hour, and, like the Black Friar in Don Juan, 'wouldn't be driven away.' In particular, there was a sensation of cabbage; as if all the greens that had ever been boiled there, were evergreens, and flourished in immortal strength.

"The parlour was wainscoted, and communicated to strangers a magnetic and instinctive consciousness of rats and mice. The staircase was very gloomy and very broad, with balustrades so thick and heavy that they would have served for a bridge. In a sombre corner on the first landing, stood a gruff old giant of a clock, with a preposterous coronet of three brass balls on his head; whom few had ever seen—none ever looked in the face—and who seemed to continue his heavy tick for no other reason than to warn heedless people from running into him accidentally.

"It had not been papered or painted, hadn't Todgers's, within the memory of man. It was very black, begrimed, and mouldy. And, at the top of the staircase, was an old, disjointed, rickety, ill-favoured skylight, patched and mended in all kinds of ways, which looked distrustfully down at everything that passed below, and covered Todgers's up as if it were a sort of human cucumber-frame, and only people of a peculiar growth were reared there." ¶MC 8

—lower regions: "There was one staircase-window in it: at the side of the house, on the ground-floor: which tradition said had not been opened for a hundred years at least, and which, abutting on an always dirty lane, was so begrimed and coated with a century's mud, that no one pane of glass could possibly fall out, though all were cracked and broken twenty times. But the grand mystery of Todgers's was the cellarage, approachable only by a little back door and a rusty grating: which cellarage within the memory of man had had no connexion with the house, but had always been the freehold property of somebody else, and was reported to be full of wealth: though in what shape—whether in silver, brass, or gold, or butts of wine, or casks of gunpowder—was matter of profound uncertainty and supreme indifference to Todgers's, and all its inmates." MC 9

—upper regions: "The top of the house was worthy of notice. There was a sort of terrace on the roof, with posts and fragments of rotten lines, once intended to dry clothes upon; and there were two or three tea-chests out there, full of earth, with forgotten plants in them, like old walking-sticks. Whoever climbed to this observatory was stunned at first from having knocked his head against the little door in coming out; and after that, was for the moment choked from having looked, perforce, straight down the kitchen chimney; but these two stages over, there were things to gaze at from the top of Todgers's, well worth your seeing too.

"For first and foremost, if the day were bright, you observed upon the housetops, stretching far away, a long dark path: the shadow of the Monument: and turning round, the tall original was close beside you, with every hair erect upon his golden head, as if the doings of the city frightened him. Then there were steeples, towers, belfries, shining vanes, and masts of ships . . . . Gables, housetops, garret-windows, wilderness upon wilderness. Smoke and noise enough for all the world at once." ¶MC 9

The City

"The City looked unpromising enough, as Bella [Wilfer] made her way along its gritty streets. Most of its money-mills were slackening sail, or had left off grinding for the day. The master-millers had already departed, and the journeymen were departing. There was a jaded aspect on the business lanes and courts, and the very pavements had a weary appearance, confused by the tread of a million of feet.

"There must be hours of night to temper down the day's distraction of so feverish a place. As yet the worry of the newly-stopped whirling and grinding on the part of the money-mills seemed to linger in the air, and the quiet was more like the prostration of a spent giant than the repose of one who was renewing his strength." ¶OMF iii 16

Environs

—*Clerkenwell:* "In the venerable suburb—it was a suburb once—of Clerkenwell, towards that part of its confines which is nearest to the Charter House, and in one of those cool, shady streets, of which a few, widely scattered and dispersed, yet remain in such old parts of the metropolis—each tenement quietly vegetating like an ancient citizen who long ago retired from business, and dozing on in its infirmity, until in course of time it tumbles down, and is replaced by some extravagant young heir, flaunting in stucco and ornamental work, and all the vanities of modern days—in this quarter, and in a street of this description, the business of the present chapter lies.

"At the time of which it treats, though only six-and-sixty years ago, a very large part of what is London now had no existence. Even in the brains of the wildest speculators, there had sprung up no long rows of streets connecting Highgate with Whitechapel, no assemblages of palaces in the swampy levels, nor little cities in the open field. Although this part of town was then, as now, parcelled out in streets, and plentifully peopled, it wore a different aspect. There were gardens to many of the houses, and trees by the pavement side; with an air of freshness breathing up and down, which in these days would be sought in vain. Fields were nigh at hand, through which the New River took its winding course, and where there was merry haymaking in the summer-time. Nature was not so far removed, or hard to get at, as in these days: and, although there were busy trades in Clerkenwell, and working jewelers by scores, it was a purer place, with farm-houses nearer to it than many modern Londoners would readily believe, and lovers' walks at no great distance, which turned into squalid courts, long before the lovers of this age were born, or, as the phrase goes, thought of." BR 4

—*Holloway:* "[R. Wilfer's] home was in the Holloway region north of London, and then divided from it by fields and trees. Between Battle Bridge and that part of the Holloway district in which he dwelt, was a tract of suburban Sahara, where tiles and bricks were burnt, bones were boiled, carpets were beat, rubbish was shot, dogs were fought, and dust was heaped by contractors." OMF i 4

—*Kent:* "'Kent, sir—everybody knows Kent—apples, cherries, hops, and women.'" PP 2

—*opposite Norwood:* " . . . near to where the busy great north road of bygone days is silent and almost deserted . . . . The neighbourhood in which [Harriet Carker's] house stands has as little of the country to recommend it, as it has of the town. It is neither of the town nor country. The former, like the giant in his travelling boots, has made a stride and passed it, and has set his brick-and-mortar heel a long way in advance; but the intermediate space between the giant's feet, as yet, is only blighted country, and not town; and, here, among a few tall chimneys belching smoke all day and night, and among the brick-fields and the lanes where turf is cut, and where the fences tumble down, and where the dusty nettles grow, and where a scrap or two of hedge may yet be seen, and where the bird-catcher still comes occasionally, though he swears every time to come no more—this second home is to be found." DS 33

—*penetrated:* "At length these streets, becoming more straggling yet, dwindled and dwindled away, until there were only small garden patches bordering the road, with many a summer-house innocent of paint and built of old timber or some fragments of a boat, green as the tough cabbage-stalks that grew about it, and grottoed at the seams with toad-stools and tight-sticking snails.

"To these succeeded pert cottages, two and two with plots of ground in front, laid out in angular beds with stiff box borders and narrow paths between, where footstep never strayed to make the gravel rough. Then came the public-house, freshly painted in green and white, with tea-gardens and a bowling-green, spurning its old neighbour with the horse-trough where the waggons stopped; then fields; and then some houses, one by one, of goodly size with lawns, some even with a lodge where dwelt a porter and his wife.

"Then came a turnpike; then fields again with trees and haystacks; then a hill; and on top of that the traveller might stop, and—looking back at old Saint Paul's looming through the smoke, its cross peeping above the cloud (if the day were clear) and glittering in the sun; and casting his eyes upon the Babel out of which it grew until he traced it down to the furthest outposts of the invading army of bricks and mortar whose station lay for the present nearly at his feet—might feel at last that he was clear of London." OCS 15

'The Boot' [in Lamb's Conduit Fields] BR

—the Surrey side: " . . . that district of the flat country tending to the Thames, where Kent and Surrey meet, and where the railways still bestride the market-gardens that will soon die under them . . . in a neighbourhood which looked like a toy neighbourhood taken in blocks out of a box by a child of particularly incoherent mind, and set up anyhow: here, one side of a new street; there, a large solitary public-house facing nowhere; here, another unfinished street already in ruins; there, a church; here, an immense new warehouse; there, a dilapidated old country villa; then, a medley of black ditch, sparkling cucumber-frame, rank field, richly cultivated kitchen-garden, brick viaduct, arch-spanned canal, and disorder of frowsiness and fog. As if the child had given the table a kick and gone to sleep." OMF ii 1

Inns and Taverns

—Blue Boar, Leadenhall Market: " . . . a sign-board on which the painter's art had delineated something remotely resembling a cerulean elephant with an aquiline nose in lieu of trunk." PP 33

—celebrated public-house: "When Herbert [Pocket] came, we went and had lunch at a celebrated house which I then quite venerated, but now believe to have been the most abject superstition in Europe, and where I could not help noticing, even then, that there was much more gravy on the tablecloths and knives and waiters' clothes, than in the steaks." GE 22

—George and Vulture, George Yard, Lombard Street: "very good, old-fashioned, and comfortable quarters. . . . " PP 26

—Golden Cross: "We went to the Golden Cross, at Charing Cross, then a mouldy sort

of establishment in a close neighbourhood. A waiter showed me into the coffee-room; and a chambermaid introduced me to my small bedchamber, which smelt like a hackney-coach, and was shut up like a family vault." DC 19

—hybrid, of a new sort: " . . . a hybrid hotel in a little square . . . . It is hotel, boarding-house, or lodging-house, at its visitor's option. It announces itself, in the new Railway Advertisers, as a novel enterprise, timidly beginning to spring up. It bashfully, almost apologetically, gives the traveller to understand that it does not expect him, on the good old constitutional hotel plan, to order a pint of sweet blacking for his drinking, and throw it away; but insinuates that he may have his boots blacked instead of his stomach, and maybe also have bed, breakfast, attendance, and a porter up all night, for a certain fixed charge. From these and similar premises, many true Britons in the lowest spirits deduce that the times are levelling times, except in the article of high roads, of which there will shortly be not one in England." MED 23

Swiveller Advising the Small Boy OCS

—a public-house: "But the choicest spot in all Scotland Yard was the old public-house in the corner. Here, in a dark wainscoted room of ancient appearance, cheered by the glow of a mighty fire, and decorated with an enormous clock, whereof the face was white, and the figures black, sat the lusty coal-heavers, quaffing large draughts of Barclay's best, and puffing forth volumes of smoke, which wreathed heavily above their heads, and involved the room in a thick dark cloud. From this apartment might their voices be heard on a winter's night, penetrating to the very bank of the river, as they shouted out some sturdy chorus, or roared forth the burden of a popular song; dwelling upon the last few words with a strength and length of emphasis which made the very roof tremble above them." SB/SY

Swiveller is in a generic bar, not this pub.

—*Six Jolly Fellowship-Porters,* the Thames

—*appearance:* " . . . already mentioned as a tavern of a dropsical appearance, [it] had long settled down into a state of hale infirmity. In its whole constitution it had not a straight floor, and hardly a straight line; but it had outlasted, and clearly would yet outlast, many a better-trimmed building, many a sprucer public-house.

"Externally, it was a narrow lop-sided wooden jumble of corpulent windows heaped one upon another as you might heap as many toppling oranges, with a crazy wooden verandah impending over the water; indeed the whole house, inclusive of the complaining flag-staff on the roof, impended over the water, but seemed to have got into the condition of a faint-hearted diver who has paused so long on the brink that he will never go in at all.

"This description applies to the river-frontage of the Six Jolly Fellowship-Porters. The back of the establishment, though the chief entrance was there, so contracted, that it merely represented in its connexion with the front, the handle of a flat-iron set upright on its broadest end. This handle stood at the bottom of a wilderness of court and alley: which wilderness pressed so hard and close upon the Six Jolly Fellowship-Porters as to leave the hostelry not an inch of ground beyond its door. For this reason, in combination with the fact that the house was all but afloat at high water, when the Porters had a family wash the linen subjected to that operation might usually be seen drying on lines stretched across the reception-rooms and bedchambers.

"The wood forming the chimney-pieces, beams, partitions, floors, and doors, of the Six Jolly Fellowship-Porters, seemed in its old age fraught with confused memories of its youth. In many places it had become gnarled and riven, according to the manner of old trees; knots started out of it; and here and there it seemed to twist itself into some likeness of boughs.

"In this state of second childhood, it had an air of being in its own way garrulous about its early life. Not without reason was it often asserted by the regular frequenters of the Porters, that when the light shone full upon the grain of certain panels, and particularly upon an old corner cupboard of walnut-wood in the bar, you might trace little forests there, and tiny trees like the parent-tree, in full umbrageous leaf." ¶OMF i 6

—*the bar:* "The bar of the Six Jolly Fellowship-Porters was a bar to soften the human breast. The available space in it was not much larger than a hackney-coach; but no one could have wished the bar bigger, that space was so girt in by corpulent little casks, and by cordial-bottles radiant with fictitious grapes in bunches, and by lemons in nets, and by biscuits in baskets, and by the polite beer-pulls that made low bows when customers were served with beer, and by the cheese in a snug corner, and by the landlady [Abbey Potterson]'s own small table in a snugger corner near the fire, with the cloth everlastingly laid.

"This haven was divided from the rough world by a glass partition and a half-door with a leaden sill upon it for the convenience of resting your liquor; but, over this half-door the bar's snugness so gushed forth, that, albeit customers drank there standing, in a dark and draughty passage where they were shouldered by other customers passing in and out, they always appeared to drink under an enchanting delusion that they were in the bar itself." OMF i 6

—*the rest:* "For the rest, both the tap and parlour of the Six Jolly Fellowship-Porters gave upon the river, and had red curtains matching the noses of the regular customers, and were provided with comfortable fire-side tin utensils, like models of sugar-loaf hats, made in that shape that they might, with their pointed ends, seek out for themselves glowing nooks in the depths of the red coals, when they mulled your ale, or heated for you those delectable drinks, Purl, Flip, and Dog's Nose.

"The first of these humming compounds was a speciality of the Porters, which, through an inscription on its door-posts, gently appealed to your feelings as, 'The Early Purl House.' For, it would seem that Purl must always be taken early; though whether for any more distinctly stomachic reason than that, as the early bird catches the worm, so the early purl catches the customer, cannot here be resolved. It only remains to add that in the handle of the flat-iron, and opposite the bar, was a very little room like a three-cornered hat, into which no direct ray of sun, moon, or star, ever penetrated, but which was superstitiously regarded as a sanctuary replete with comfort and retirement by gaslight, and on the door of which was therefore painted its alluring name: Cosy." ¶OMF i 6

—*The Inn of the Three Cripples,* Saffron Hill —*upper room:* "The room was illuminated by two gas-lights; the glare of which was prevented by the barred shutters, and closely-drawn curtains of faded red, from being visible outside. The ceiling was blackened, to prevent its colour from being injured by the flaring of the lamps; and the place was so full of dense tobacco smoke, that at first it was scarcely possible to discern anything more.

"By degrees, however, as some of it cleared away through the open door, an assemblage of heads, as confused as the noises that greeted the ear, might be made out; and as the eye grew more accustomed to the scene, the spectator gradually became aware of the presence of a numerous company, male and female, crowded round a long table: at the upper end of which, sat a chairman with a hammer of office in his hand; while a professional gentleman, with a bluish nose, and his face tied up for the benefit of a toothache, presided at a jingling piano in a remote corner . . . .

"It was curious to observe some faces which stood out prominently from among the group. There was the chairman himself, (the landlord of the house) a coarse, rough, heavy built fellow, who, while the songs were proceeding, rolled his eyes hither and thither, and, seeming to give himself up to joviality, had an eye for everything that was done, and an ear for everything that was said—and sharp ones, too.

"Near him were the singers: receiving, with professional indifference, the compliments of the company, and applying themselves, in turn, to a dozen proffered glasses of spirits and water, tendered by their more boisterous admirers; whose countenances, expressive of almost every vice in almost every grade, irresistibly attracted the attention, by their very repulsiveness.

"Cunning, ferocity, and drunkenness in all its stages, were there, in their strongest aspects; and women: some with the last lingering tinge of their early freshness almost fading as you looked: others with every mark and stamp of their sex utterly beaten out, and presenting but one loathsome blank of profligacy and crime; some mere girls, others but young women, and none past the prime of life; formed the darkest and saddest portion of this dreary picture." ¶OT 26

—*White Hart:* "There are in London several old inns, once the headquarters of celebrated coaches in the days when coaches performed their journeys in a graver and more solemn manner than they do in these times; but which have now degenerated into little more than the abiding and booking places of country waggons. The reader would look in vain for any of these ancient hostelries, among the Golden Crosses and Bull and Mouths, which rear their stately fronts in the improved streets of London. If he would light upon any of these old places, he must direct his steps to the obscurer quarters of the town; and there in some secluded nooks he will find several, still standing with a kind of gloomy sturdiness, amidst the modern innovations which surround them.

"In the Borough especially, there still remain some half dozen old inns, which have preserved their external features unchanged, and which have escaped alike the rage for public improvement, and the encroachments of private speculation. Great, rambling, queer, old places they are, with galleries, and passages, and staircases, wide enough and antiquated enough to furnish materials for a hundred ghost stories. . . . It was in the yard of one of these inns—of no less celebrated a one than the White Hart . . . ." PP 10

—*Wilderness:* "The summer-house . . . was a rugged wooden box, rotten and bare to see, which overhung the river's mud, and threatened to slide down into it. The tavern to which it belonged was a crazy building, sapped and undermined by the rats, and only upheld by great bars of wood which were reared against its walls, and had propped it up so long that even they were decaying and yielding with their load, and of a windy night might be heard to creak and crack as if the whole fabric were about to come toppling down.

"The house stood—if anything so old and feeble could be said to stand—on a piece of waste ground, blighted with the unwholesome smoke of factory chimneys, and echoing the clank of iron wheels and rush of troubled water. Its internal accommodations amply fulfilled the promise of the outside. The rooms were low and damp, and clammy walls were pierced with chinks and holes, the rotten floors had sunk from their level, the very beams started from their places and warned the timid stranger from their neighbourhood." ¶OCS 21

Law inns

—*Barnard's:* ". . . I now found Barnard to be a disembodied spirit, or a fiction, and his inn the dingiest collection of shabby buildings ever squeezed together in a rank corner as a club for Tom-cats.

"We entered this haven through a wicket-gate, and were disgorged by an introductory passage into a melancholy little square that looked to me like a flat burying-ground. I thought it had the most dismal trees in it, and the most dismal sparrows, and the most dismal cats, and the most dismal houses (in number half a dozen or so), that I had ever seen.

"I thought the windows of the sets of chambers into which those houses were divided, were in every stage of dilapidated blind and curtain, crippled flower-pot, cracked glass, dusty decay, and miserable makeshift; while To Let To Let To Let, glared at me from empty rooms, as if no new wretches ever came there, and the vengeance of the soul of Barnard were being slowly appeased by the gradual suicide of the present occupants and their unholy interment under the gravel.

"A frouzy mourning of soot and smoke attired this forlorn creation of Barnard, and it had strewed ashes on its head, and was undergoing penance and humiliation as a mere dust-hole. Thus far my sense of sight; while dry rot and wet rot and all the silent rots that rot in neglected roof and cellar—rot of rat and mouse and bug and coaching stables near at hand besides—addressed themselves faintly to my sense of smell, and moaned, 'Try Barnard's Mixture.'" ¶GE 21

—*drizzle:* "Unfortunately the morning was drizzly, and an angel could not have concealed the fact that Barnard was shedding sooty tears outside the window, like some giant of a Sweep." GE 27

—*Gray's:* "Indeed, I look upon Gray's Inn generally one of the most depressing institutions in brick and mortar, known to the children of men. Can anything be more dreary than its arid Square, Sahara Desert of the law, with the ugly old tiled-topped tenements, the dirty windows, the bills To Let, To Let, the door-posts inscribed like gravestones, the crazy gateway giving upon the filthy Lane, the scowling iron-barred prison-like passage into Verulam-buildings, the mouldy red-nosed ticket-porters with little coffin plates, and why with aprons, the dry hard atomy-like appearance of the whole dust-heap?

"When my uncommercial travels tend to this dismal spot, my comfort is its rickety state. Imagination gloats over the fulness of time when the staircases shall have quite tumbled down—they are daily wearing into an ill-savoured powder, but have not quite tumbled down yet—when the last old prolix bencher all of the older time, shall have been got out of an upper window by means of a Fire Ladder, and carried off to the Holborn Union; when the last clerk shall have engrossed the last parchment behind the last splash on the last of the mud-stained windows, which, all through the miry year, are pilloried out of recognition in Gray's Inn-lane.

"Then, shall a squalid little trench, with rank grass and a pump in it, lying between the coffee-house and South-square, be wholly given up to cats and rats, and not, as now, have its empire divided between those animals and a few briefless bipeds—surely called to the Bar by voices of deceiving spirits, seeing that they are wanted there by no mortal—who glance down, with eyes better glazed than their casements, from their dreary and lack-lustre rooms.

"Then shall the way Nor' Westward, now lying under a short grim colonnade where in summer-time pounce flies from law-stationering windows into the eyes of laymen, be choked with rubbish and happily become impassable. Then shall the gardens where turf, trees, and gravel wear a legal livery of black, run rank, and pilgrims go to Gorhambury to see Bacon's effigy as he sat, and not come here (which in truth they seldom do) to see where he walked." UT/C

—*the coffee-house:* "As I [David Copperfield] followed the chief waiter with my eyes, I could not help thinking that the garden in which he had gradually blown to be the flower he was, was an arduous place to rise in. It had such a prescriptive, stiff-necked, long-established, solemn, elderly air. I glanced about the room, which had had its sanded floor sanded, no doubt, in exactly the same manner when the chief waiter was a boy—if he ever was a boy, which appeared improbable; and at the shining tables, where I saw myself reflected, in unruffled depths of old mahogany; and at the lamps, without a flaw in their trimming or cleaning; and at the comfortable green curtains, with their pure brass rods, snugly enclosing the boxes; and at the two large coal fires, brightly burning; and at the rows of decanters, burly as if with the consciousness of pipes of expensive old port wine below; and both England and the law appeared to me to be very difficult indeed to be taken by storm." DC 59

—their grisly romance: "'I was observing what singular old places they are [said Mr Pickwick].

"'*You!*' said the old man, contemptuously, 'What do *you* know of the time when young men shut themselves up in those lonely rooms, and read and read, hour after hour, and night after night, till their reason wandered beneath their midnight studies; till their mental powers were exhausted; till morning's light brought no freshness or health to them; and they sank beneath the unnatural devotion of their youthful energies to their dry old books? Coming down to a later time, and a very different day, what do *you* know of the gradual sinking beneath consumption, or the quick wasting of fever—the grand results of 'life' and dissipation—which men have undergone in these same rooms? How many vain pleaders for mercy, do you think have turned away heart-sick from the lawyer's office, to find a resting-place in the Thames, or a refuge in the gaol? They are no ordinary houses, those. There is not a panel in the old waiscotting, but what, if it were endowed with the powers of speech and memory, could start from the wall, and tell its tale of horror—the romance of life, sir, the romance of life! Common-place as they may seem now, I tell you they are strange old places, and I would rather hear many a legend with a terrific sounding name, than the true history of one old set of chambers.' . . .

"'Look at them in another light: their most common-place and least romantic. What fine places of slow torture they are! Think of the needy man who has spent his all, beggared himself, and pinched his friends, to enter the profession, which will never yield him a morsel of bread. The waiting—the hope—the disappointment—the fear—the misery—the poverty—the blight on his hopes, and end to his career—the suicide perhaps, or the shabby, slipshod drunkard. Am I not right about them?'" PP 21

—Lincoln's, at night: "It is night in Lincoln's Inn—perplexed and troublous valley of the shadow of the law, where suitors generally find but little day—and fat candles are snuffed out in offices, and clerks have rattled down the crazy wooden stairs, and dispersed. The bell that rings at nine o'clock, has ceased its doleful clangour about nothing; the gates are shut; and the night-porter, a solemn warder with a mighty power of sleep, keeps guard in his lodge. From tiers of staircase windows, clogged lamps like the eyes of Equity, bleared Argus with a fathomless pocket for every eye and an eye upon it, dimly blink at the stars. In dirty upper casements, here and there, hazy little patches of candlelight reveal where some wise draughtsman and conveyancer yet toils for the entanglement of real estate in meshes of sheep-skin, in the average ratio of about a dozen of sheep to an acre of land. Over which bee-like industry, these benefactors of their species linger yet, though office-hours be past; that they may give, for every day, some good account at last." BH 32

—neighbourhood: "Jostling against clerks going to post the day's letters, and against counsel and attorneys going home to dinner, and against plaintiffs and defendants, and suitors of all sorts, and against the general crowd, in whose way the forensic wisdom of ages has interposed a million of obstacles to the transaction of the commonest business of life—diving through law and equity, and through that kindred mystery, the street mud . . . the lawyer and the law-stationer come to a Rag and Bottle shop, and general emporium of much disregarded merchandise, lying and being in the shadow of the wall of Lincoln's Inn . . . ." BH 10

—the Temple: "There are, still, worse places than the Temple, on a sultry day, for basking in the sun, or resting idly in the shade. There is yet a drowsiness in its courts, and a dreamy dulness in its trees and gardens; those who pace its lanes and squares may yet hear the echoes of their footsteps on the sounding stones, and read upon its gates, in passing from the tumult of the Strand or Fleet Street, 'Who enters here leaves noise behind.'

"There is still the plash of falling water in fair Fountain Court, and there are yet nooks and corners where dun-haunted students may look down from their dusty garrets, on a vagrant ray of sunlight patching the shade of the tall houses, and seldom troubled to reflect a passing stranger's form.

"There is yet, in the Temple, something of a clerkly monkish atmosphere, which public offices of law have not disturbed, and even legal firms have failed to scare away. In summer time, its pumps suggest to thirsty idlers, springs cooler, and more sparkling, and deeper than other wells; and as they trace the spillings of full pitchers on the heated ground, they snuff the freshness, and, sighing, cast sad looks towards the Thames, and think of baths and boats, and saunter on, despondent." ¶BR 15

And see F:Loneliness—*of chambers*

London

—*anonymity:*"It is strange with how little notice, good, bad, or indifferent, a man may live and die in London. He awakens no sympathy in the breast of any single person; his existence is a matter of interest to no one save himself; he cannot be said to be forgotten when he dies, for no one remembered him when he was alive. There is a numerous class of people in this great metropolis who seem not to possess a single friend, and whom nobody appears to care for. Urged by imperative necessity in the first instance, they have resorted to London in search of employment, and the means of subsistence.

"It is hard, we know, to break the ties which bind us to our homes and friends, and harder still to efface the thousand recollections of happy days and old times, which have been slumbering in our bosoms for years, and only rush upon the mind, to bring before it associations connected with the friends we have left, the scenes we have beheld too probably for the last time, and the hopes we once cherished, but may entertain no more.

"These men, however, happily for themselves, have long forgotten such thoughts. Old country friends have died or emigrated; former correspondents have become lost, like themselves, in the crowd and turmoil of some busy city; and they have gradually settled down into mere passive creatures of habit and endurance." ¶SB/TP

And see —wayfarer, and M:Solitude—*its blessings*

—*approached:* "And now [Varden] approached the great city, which lay outstretched before him like a dark shadow on the ground, reddening the sluggish air with a deep dull light, that told of labyrinths of public ways and shops, and swarms of busy people. Approaching nearer and nearer yet, this halo began to fade, and the cause which produced it slowly to develop themselves. Long lines of poorly lighted streets might be faintly traced, with here and there a lighter spot, where lamps were clustered round a square or market, or round some great building; after a time these grew more distinct, and the lamps themselves were visible; slight yellow specks, that seemed to be rapidly snuffed out, one by one, as intervening obstacles hid them from the sight. Then, sounds arose—the striking of church clocks, the distant bark of dogs, the hum of traffic in the streets; then outlines might be traced—tall steeples looming in the air, and piles of unequal roofs oppressed by chimneys; then, the noise swelled into a louder sound, and forms grew more distinct and numerous still, and London—visible in the darkness by its own faint light, and not by that of Heaven—was at hand." BR 3

—*coincidence:* "'Why, I don't believe now,' added Tim [Linkinwater] . . . 'that there's such a place in all the world for coincidences as London is! . . . let us know. If there is any better place for such things, where is it? Is it in Europe? No, that it isn't. Is it in Asia? Why, of course it's not. Is it in Africa? Not a bit of it. Is it in America? *You* know better than that, at all events. Well, then,' said Tim, folding his arms resolutely, 'where is it?'" NN 43

—*diversity:* "Calm and unmoved amidst the scenes that darkness favours, the great heart of London [the clock in St Paul's] throbs in its Giant breast. Wealth and beggary, vice and virtue, guilt and innocence, repletion and the direst hunger, all treading on each other and crowding together, are gathered round it. Draw but a little circle above the clustering housetops, and you shall have within its space everything, with its opposite extreme and contradiction, close beside.

"Where yonder feeble light is shining, a man is but this moment dead. The taper at a few yards' distance is seen by eyes that have this instant opened on the world. There are two houses separated by but an inch or two of wall. In one, there are quiet minds at rest; in the other, a waking conscience that one might think would trouble the very air.

"In that close corner where the roofs shrink down and cower together as if to hide their secrets from the handsome street hard by, there are such dark crimes, such miseries and horrors, as could be hardly told in whispers. In the handsome street, there are folks asleep who have dwelt there all their lives, and have no more knowledge of these things than if they had never been, or were transacted at the remotest limits of the world—who, if they were hinted at, would shake their heads, look wise, and frown, and say they were impossible, and out of Nature—as if all great towns were not . . . .

"The day begins to break, and soon there is the hum and noise of life. Those who have spent the night on doorsteps and cold stones crawl off to beg; they who have slept in beds come forth to their occupation, too, and business is astir. The fog of sleep rolls slowly off, and London shines awake. The streets are filled with carriages, and people gaily clad. The jails are full, too, to the throat, nor have the workhouses or hospitals much room to spare. The courts of law are crowded. Taverns have their regular frequenters by this time, and every mart of traffic has its throng.

"Each of these places is a world, and has its own inhabitants; each is distinct from, and almost unconscious of the existence of any other. There are some few people well to do, who remember to have heard it said, that numbers of men and women—thousands, they think it was—get up in London every day, unknowing where to lay their heads at night; and that there are quarters of the town where misery and famine always are. They don't believe it quite—there may be some truth in it, but it is exaggerated, of course.

"So, each of these thousand worlds goes on, intent upon itself, until night comes again—first with its lights and pleasures, and its cheerful streets; then with its guilt and darkness." ¶MHC 14

—dress: "The mass of London people are shabby. The absence of distinctive dress has, no doubt, something to do with it. The porters of the Vintners' Company, the draymen, and the butchers, are about the only people who wear distinctive dresses; and even these do not wear them on holidays. We have nothing which for cheapness, cleanliness, convenience, or picturesqueness, can compare with the belted blouse. As to our women;—next Easter or Whitsuntide look at the bonnets at the British Museum or the National Gallery, and think of the pretty white French cap, the Spanish mantilla, or the Genoese mezzero.

"Probably there are not more second-hand clothes sold in London than in Paris, and yet the mass of the London population have a second-hand look which is not to be detected on the mass of the Parisian population." UT/BB

—habitation: "Ten thousand responsible houses surrounded [Arthur Clennam], frowning as heavily on the streets they composed, as if they were every one inhabited by the ten young men of the [Third] Calender's story, who blackened their faces and bemoaned their miseries every night. Fifty thousand lairs surrounded him where people lived so unwholesomely that fair water put into their crowded rooms on Saturday night; albeit my lord, their county member, was amazed that they failed to sleep in company with their butcher's meat. Miles of close wells and pits of houses, where the inhabitants gasped for air, stretched far away towards every point of the compass. Through the heart of the town a deadly sewer ebbed and flowed, in the place of a fine fresh river." LD i 3

—mud: " . . . diving through law and equity, and through that kindred mystery, the street mud, which is made of nobody knows what, and collects about us nobody knows whence or how: we only knowing in general that when there is too much of it, we find it necessary to shovel it away . . . . " BH 10

"What the mud had been doing with itself, or where it came from, who could say? But it seemed to collect in a moment, as a crowd will, and in five minutes to have splashed all the sons and daughters of Adam." LD i 3

—shabbiness: "The shabbiness of our English capital, as compared with Paris, Bordeaux, Frankfort, Milan, Geneva—almost any important town on the continent of Europe—I find very striking after an absence of any duration in foreign parts. London is shabby in contrast with Edinburgh, with Aberdeen, with Exeter, with Liverpool, with a bright little town like Bury St. Edmunds. London is shabby in contrast with New York, with Boston, with Philadelphia. In detail, one would say it can rarely fail to be a disappointing piece of shabbiness to a stranger from any of those places. There is nothing shabbier than Drury-lane, in Rome itself. The meanness of Regent-street, set against the great line of Boulevards in Paris, is as striking as the abortive ugliness of Trafalgar-square, set against the gallant beauty of the Place de la Concorde. London is shabby by daylight, and shabbier by gaslight. No Englishman knows what gaslight is, until he sees the Rue de Rivoli and the Palais Royal after dark." UT/BB

—*the shabby-genteel:* "Now, shabby people, God knows, may be found anywhere, and genteel people are not articles of greater scarcity out of London than in it; but this compound of the two—this shabby-gentility —is as purely local as the statue at Charing Cross, or the pump at Aldgate. It is worthy of remark, too, that only men are shabby-genteel; a woman is always either dirty and slovenly in the extreme, or neat and respectable, however poverty-stricken in appearance. A very poor man, 'who has seen better days,' as the phrase goes, is a strange compound of dirty-slovenliness and wretched attempts at faded smartness." SB/SG

—*a street for a day:* "The summer sun was never on the street, but in the morning about breakfast-time, when it came with the water-carts and the old clothes-men, and the people with geraniums, and the umbrella-mender, and the man who trilled the little bell of the Dutch clock as he went along. It was soon gone again to return no more that day; and the bands of music and the straggling Punch's shows going after it, left it a prey to the most dismal of organs, and white mice; with now and then a porcupine, to vary the entertainments; until the butlers whose families were dining out, began to stand at the house-doors in the twilight, and the lamp-lighter made his nightly failure in attempting to brighten up the street with gas." DS 3

—*walking sounds:* "That constant pacing to and fro, that never-ending restlessness, that incessant tread of feet wearing the rough stones smooth and glossy—is it not a wonder how the dwellers in narrow ways can bear to hear it!

"Think of a sick man in such a place as Saint Martin's Court, listening to the footsteps, and in the midst of pain and weariness obliged, despite himself (as though it were a task he must perform) to detect the child's step from the man's, the slipshod beggar from the booted exquisite, the lounging from the busy, the dull heel of the sauntering outcast from the quick tread of an expectant pleasure-seeker—think of the hum and noise being always present to his senses, and of the stream of life that will not stop, pouring on, on, on, through all his restless dreams, as if he were condemned to lie dead but conscious, in a noisy church yard, and had no hope of rest for centuries to come." ¶OCS 1

—*wayfarer:* "[Harriet Carker] often looked with compassion . . . upon the stragglers who came wandering into London, by the great highway hard by, and who, footsore and weary, and gazing fearfully at the huge town before them, as if foreboding that their misery there would be but as a drop of water in the sea, or as a grain of sea-sand on the shore, went shrinking on, cowering before the angry weather, and looking as if the very elements rejected them.

"Day after day, such travellers crept past, but always, as she thought, in one direction—always towards the town. Swallowed up in one phase or other of its immensity, towards which they seemed impelled by a desperate fascination, they never returned. Food for the hospitals, the churchyards, the prisons, the river, fever, madness, vice, and death—they passed on to the monster, roaring in the distance, and were lost." ¶DS 33

Lord Mayor

—*and literature:* "The literature of English history, losing its Lord Mayors, would lose, I find on consideration, some of its most notable instances of the public spirit, the munificence, the personal bravery, and the prowess of the good old citizens on this side Temple Bar. The literature of English romance, losing its Lord Mayors, would lose at one blow its wealthiest of London merchants, and its most beautiful merchant's daughter, its crossest cook, its best known foreign adventurer, its most profitable investment on record, and its most wonderful cat. Similarly, English biography, losing its Lord Mayors, would lose some of its most notable examples of rewarded perseverance and integrity, and some of its highest illustrations of the nobility of self-made men.

"I find that even the greatest of English satirists [**Hogarth**], of whom it is well said that his pictures require to be read like books—I find that even he could no more dispense with his Lord Mayors than any of the rest; for without them he could neither have committed his 'idle apprentice' for trial, nor, under circumstances of very touching and powerful contrast, have rewarded his 'industrious apprentice' by presenting him at the height of his fame and fortune." S/MH3

Neighbourhoods

—characteristic, in general: "Facing eastward, I left behind me Smithfield and Old Bailey . . . and went my way upon my beat, noting how oddly characteristic neighbourhoods are divided from one another, hereabout, as though by an invisible line across the way. Here shall cease the bankers and the money-changers; here shall begin the shipping interest and the nautical-instrument shops; here shall follow a scarcely perceptible flavouring of groceries and drugs; here shall come a strong infusion of butchers; now, small hosiers shall be in the ascendant; henceforth, everything exposed for sale shall have its ticketed price attached. All this as if specially ordered and appointed.

"A single stride at Houndsditch Church, no wider than sufficed to cross the kennel at the bottom of the Canon-gate—a single stride, and everything is entirely changed in grain and character. West of the stride, a table, or a chest of drawers on sale, shall be of mahogany and French-polished; east of the stride, it shall be of deal, smeared with a cheap counterfeit resembling lip-salve. West of the stride, a penny loaf or bun shall be compact and self-contained; east of the stride, it shall be of a sprawling and splay-footed character, as seeking to make more of itself for the money." UT/AB

—Adelphi Terrace: "There is always, to this day [1855], a sudden pause in that place to the roar of the great thoroughfare. The many sounds become so deadened that the change is like putting cotton in the ears, or having the head thickly muffled. At that time [about 1828], the contrast was far greater; there being no small steam-boats on the river, no landing places but slippery wooden stairs and foot-causeways, no railroad on the opposite bank, no hanging bridge or fishmarket near at hand, no traffic on the nearest bridge of stone, nothing moving on the stream but watermen's wherries and coal-lighters. Long and broad black tiers of the latter, moored fast in the mud as if they were never to move again, made the shore funereal and silent after dark; and kept what little water-movement there was, far out towards mid-stream. At any hour later than sunset, and not least at that hour when most of the people who have anything to eat at home are going home to eat it, and when most of those who have nothing have hardly yet slunk out to beg or steal, it was a deserted place and looked on a deserted scene." LD ii 9

—Barbican: " . . . [Simon Tappertit] hurried on to Barbican, and turning into one of the narrowest of the narrow streets which diverged from that centre . . . . From the main street he had entered, itself little better than an alley, a low-browed doorway led into a blind court, or yard, profoundly dark, unpaved, and reeking with stagnant odours. Into this ill-favoured pit, the locksmith's vagrant 'prentice groped his way . . . . " BR 8

—Cadogan Place: "Cadogan Place is the one slight bond that joins two great extremes; it is the connecting link between the aristocratic pavements of Belgrave Square and the barbarism of Chelsea. It is in Sloane Street, but not of it. The people in Cadogan Place look down upon Sloane Street, and think Brompton low. They affect fashion too, and wonder where the New Road is.

"Not that they claim to be on precisely the same footing as the high folks of Belgrave Square and Grosvenor Place, but that they stand with reference to them rather in the light of those illegitimate children of the great who are content to boast of their connexions, although their connexions disavow them. Wearing as much as they can of the airs and semblances of loftiest rank, the people of Cadogan Place have the realities of middle station. It is the conductor which communicates to the inhabitants of regions beyond its limit, the shock of pride of birth and rank, which it has not within itself, but derives from a fountain-head beyond; or, like the ligament which unites the Siamese twins, it contains something of the life and essence of two distinct bodies, and yet belongs to neither." NN 21

—Camden Town: " . . . [Traddles] lived in a little street near the Veterinary College at Camden Town . . . .

"I found that the street was not as desirable a one as I could have wished it to be, for the sake of Traddles. The inhabitants appeared to have a propensity to throw any little trifles they were not in want of, into the road: which not only made it rank and sloppy, but untidy too, on account of the cabbage-leaves. The refuse was not wholly vegetable either, for I myself saw a shoe, a doubled-up saucepan, a black bonnet, and an umbrella, in various stages of decomposition, as I was looking out for the number I wanted." DC 27

And see —Staggs's Gardens

—Chancery Lane, on vacation: "It is the long vacation in the regions of Chancery Lane. The good ships Law and Equity, those teak-built, copper-bottomed, iron-fastened, brazen-faced, and not by any means fast-sailing Clippers, are laid up in ordinary. The Flying Dutchman, with a view of ghostly clients imploring all whom they may encounter to peruse their papers, has drifted, for the time being, Heaven knows where. The Courts are all shut up; the public offices lie in a hot sleep; Westminster Hall itself is a shady solitude where nightingales might sing, and a tenderer class of suitors than is usually found there, walk.

"The Temple, Chancery Lane, Serjeants' Inn, and Lincoln's Inn even unto the Fields, are like tidal harbours at low water; where stranded proceedings, offices at anchor, idle clerks lounging on lop-sided stools that will not recover their perpendicular until the current of Term sets in, lie high and dry upon the ooze of the long vacation. Outer doors of chambers are shut up by the score, messages and parcels are to be left at the Porter's Lodge by the bushel. A crop of grass would grow in the chinks of the stone pavement outside Lincoln's Inn Hall, but that the ticket-porters, who have nothing to do beyond sitting in the shade there, with their white aprons over their heads to keep the flies off, grub it up and eat it thoughtfully." BH 19

—a City Square: " . . . let not those Londoners whose eyes have been accustomed to the aristocratic gravity of Grosvenor Square and Hanover Square, the dowager barrenness and frigidity of Fitzroy Square, or the gravel walks and garden seats of the Squares of Russell and Euston, suppose that the affections of Tim Linkinwater, or the inferior lovers of this particular locality, had been awakened and kept alive by any refreshing associations with leaves, however dingy, or grass, however bare and thin.

"The City Square has no enclosure, save the lamp-post in the middle; and has no grass but the weeds which spring up round its base. It is a quiet, little-frequented, retired spot, favourable to melancholy and contemplation, and appointments of long-waiting; and up and down its every side the Appointed saunters idly by the hour together wakening the echoes with the monotonous sound of his footsteps on the smooth worn stones, and counting, first the windows, and then the very bricks of the tall silent houses that hem him round about.

"In the winter-time, the snow will linger there, long after it has melted from the busy streets and highways. The summer's sun holds it in some respect, and, while he darts his cheerful rays sparingly into the square, keeps his fiery heat and glare for noisier and less-imposing precincts. It is so quiet, that you can almost hear the ticking of your own watch when you stop to cool in its refreshing atmosphere.

"There is a distant hum—of coaches, not of insects—but no other sound disturbs the stillness of the square. The ticket porter leans idly against the post at the corner, comfortably warm, but not hot, although the day is broiling. His white apron flaps languidly in the air, his head gradually droops upon his breast, he takes very long winks with both eyes at once; even he is unable to withstand the soporific influence of the place, and is gradually falling asleep. But now, he starts into full wakefulness, recoils a step or two, and gazes out before him with eager wildness in his eye. Is it a job, or a boy at marbles? Does he see a ghost, or hear an organ? No; sight more unwonted still—there is a butterfly in the square—a real, live butterfly! Astray from flowers and sweets, and fluttering among the iron heads of the dusty area railings." NN 37

—Clifford's Inn: " . . . [Mr Boffin] glanced into the mouldy little plantation, or cat-preserve, of Clifford's Inn, as it was that day, in search of a suggestion. Sparrows were there, cats were there, dry-rot and wet-rot were there, but it was not otherwise a suggestive spot." OMF i 8

—commercial: "Several fruit-brokers had their marts near Todgers's; and one of the first impressions wrought upon the stranger's senses was of oranges—of damaged oranges, with blue and green bruises on them, festering in boxes, or mouldering

away in cellars. All day long, a stream of porters from the wharves beside the river, each bearing on his back a bursting chest of oranges, poured slowly through the narrow passages; while underneath the archway by the public-house, the knots of those who rested and regaled within, were piled from morning until night. Strange solitary pumps were found near Todgers's hiding themselves for the most part in blind alleys, and keeping company with fire-ladders . . . .

"Among the narrow thoroughfares at hand, there lingered here and there, an ancient doorway of carved oak, from which, of old, the sounds of revelry and feasting often came; but now these mansions, only used for storehouses, were dark and dull, and, being filled with wool, and cotton, and the like—such heavy merchandise as stifles sound and stops the throat of echo—had an air of palpable deadness about them which, added to their silence and desertion, made them very grim.

"In like manner, there were gloomy courtyards in these parts, into which few but belated wayfarers ever strayed, and where vast bags and packs of goods, upward or downward bound, were for ever dangling between heaven and earth from lofty cranes. There were more trucks near Todgers's than you would suppose a whole city could ever need; not active trucks, but a vagabond race, for ever lounging in the narrow lanes before their masters' doors and stopping up the pass; so that when a stray hackney-coach or lumbering waggon came that way, they were the cause of such an uproar as enlivened the whole neighbourhood and made the bells in the next church-tower vibrate again.

"In the throats and maws of dark no-thoroughfares near Todgers's, individual wine-merchants and wholesale dealers in grocery-ware had perfect little towns of their own; and, deep among the foundations of these buildings, the ground was undermined and burrowed out into stables, where cart-horses, troubled by rats, might be heard on a quiet Sunday rattling their halters, as disturbed spirits in tales of haunted houses are said to clank their chains." ¶MC 9 *And see* Boarding-house—*commercial*

—*confusing, near the Monument:* "You couldn't walk about in Todgers's neighbourhood, as you could in any other neighbourhood. You groped your way for an hour through lanes and bye-ways, and court-yards, and passages; and you never once emerged upon anything that might be reasonably called a street. A kind of resigned distraction came over the stranger as he trod those devious mazes, and, giving himself up for lost, went in and out and round about and quietly turned back again when he came to a dead wall or was stopped by an iron railing, and felt that the means of escape might possibly present themselves in their own good time, but that to anticipate them was hopeless.

"Instances were known of people who, being asked to dine at Todgers's, had travelled round and round for a weary time, with its very chimney-pots in view; and finding it, at last, impossible of attainment, had gone home again with a gentle melancholy on their spirits, tranquil and uncomplaining. Nobody had ever found Todgers's on a verbal direction, though given within a minute's walk of it. Cautious emigrants from Scotland or the North of England had been known to reach it safely, by impressing a charity-boy, town-bred, and bringing him along with them; or by clinging tenaciously to the postman; but these were rare exceptions, and only went to prove the rule that Todgers's was in a labyrinth, whereof the mystery was known but to a chosen few." ¶BH 9 *And see* Boarding-house—*commercial* —*Covent Garden*

—*for the drunken:* "This market of Covent Garden was quite out of the creature's [Mr Dolls] line of road, but it had the attraction for him which it has for the worst of the solitary members of the drunken tribe. It may be the companionship of the nightly stir, or it may be the companionship of the gin and beer that slop about among carters and hucksters, or it may be the companionship of the trodden vegetable refuse, which is so like their own dress that perhaps they take the Market for a great wardrobe; but be it what it may, you shall see no such individual drunkards on doorsteps anywhere as there. Of dozing women-drunkards especially, you shall come upon such specimens there, in the morning sunlight, as you might seek out of doors in vain through London. Such stale vapid rejected cabbage-leaf and cabbage-stalk dress, such damaged-orange countenance, such squashed pulp of humanity, are open to the day nowhere else . . . .

"There is a swarm of young savages always flitting about this same place, creeping off with fragments of orange-chests and mouldy litter—Heaven knows into what holes they can convey them, having no home!—whose bare feet fall with a blunt dull softness on the pavement as the policeman hunts them, and who are (perhaps for that reason) little heard by the Powers that be, whereas in top-boots they would make a deafening clatter." OMF iv 9

—*Market:* "Covent Garden market, and the avenues leading to it, are thronged with carts of all sorts, sizes, and descriptions, from the heavy lumbering waggon, with its four stout horses, to the jingling costermonger's cart, with its consumptive donkey. The pavement is already strewed with decayed cabbage-leaves, broken hay-bands, and all the indescribable litter of a vegetable market; men are shouting, carts backing, horses neighing, boys fighting, basket-women talking, piemen expatiating on the excellence of their pastry, and donkeys braying. These and a hundred other sounds form a compound discordant enough to a Londoner's ears, and remarkably disagreeable to those of country gentlemen who are sleeping at the Hummums for the first time." SB/SM

"Many and many a pleasant stroll [Ruth and Tom Pinch] had in Covent Garden Market: snuffing up the perfume of the fruits and flowers, wondering at the magnificence of the pine-apples and melons; catching glimpses down side avenues, of rows and rows of old women, seated on inverted baskets shelling peas; looking unutterable things at the fat bundles of asparagus with which the dainty shops were fortified as with a breastwork; and, at the herbalists' doors, gratefully inhaling scents as of veal-stuffing yet uncooked, dreamily mixed up with capsicums, brown-paper, seeds: even with hints of lusty snails and fine young curly leeches.

"Many and many a pleasant stroll they had among the poultry markets, where ducks and fowls, with necks unnaturally long, lay stretched out in pairs, ready for cooking; where there were speckled eggs in mossy baskets, white country sausages beyond impeachment by surviving cat or dog, or horse or donkey, new cheeses to any wild extent, live birds in coops and cages, looking much too big to be natural, in consequence of those receptacles being much too little; rabbits, alive and dead, innumerable.

"Many a pleasant stroll they had among the cool, refreshing, silvery fish-stalls, with a kind of moonlight effect about their stock-in-trade, excepting always for the ruddy lobsters. Many a pleasant stroll among the waggon-loads of fragrant hay, beneath which dogs and tired waggoners lay fast asleep, oblivious of the pieman and the public-house." MC 40

—*varied perspectives:* "Little Dorrit looked into a dim room, which seemed a spacious one to her, and grandly furnished. Courtly ideas of Covent Garden, as a place with famous coffee-houses, where gentlemen wearing gold-laced coats and swords had quarrelled and fought duels; costly ideas of Covent Garden, as a place where there were flowers in winter at guineas a-piece, pine-apples at guineas a pound, and peas at guineas a pint; picturesque ideas of Covent Garden, as a place where there was a mighty theatre, showing wonderful and beautiful sights to richly-dressed ladies and gentlemen, and which was for ever far beyond the reach of poor Fanny or poor uncle; desolate ideas of Covent Garden, as having all those arches in it, where the miserable children in rags among whom she had just now passed, like young rats, slunk and hid, fed on offal, huddled together for warmth, and were hunted about (look to the rats young and old, all ye Barnacles, for before God they are eating away our foundations, and will bring the roofs on our heads!); teeming ideas of Covent Garden, as a place of past and present mystery, romance, abundance, want, beauty, ugliness, fair country gardens, and foul street-gutters; all confused together—made the room dimmer than it was, in Little Dorrit's eyes, as they timidly saw it from the door." LD i 14

—*vulnerable to weather:* ". . . on a drizzling Saturday evening in the last past month of January all that neighbourhood of Covent-garden looked very desolate. It is so essentially a neighbourhood which has seen better days, that bad weather affects it sooner than another place which has not come down in the world. In its present reduced condition it bears a thaw almost worse than any place I know. It gets so dreadfully low-spirited when damp breaks forth. Those wonderful houses about Drury-lane Theatre, which in the palmy days of theatres were prosperous and long-settled places of business, and which now change hands every week, but never change their character of being divided and subdivided on the ground floor into mouldy dens of shops where an orange and half-a-dozen nuts, or a pomatum-pot, one cake of fancy soap, and a cigar box, are offered for sale and never sold, were most ruefully contemplated that evening, by the statue of Shakespeare, with the rain-drops coursing one another down its innocent nose." UT/TV

—*East London:* " . . . a poor busy and thronged neighbourhood. Old iron and fried fish, cough drops and artificial flowers, boiled pigs'-feet and household furniture that looks as if it were polished up with lip-salve, umbrellas full of vocal literature and saucers full of shell-fish in a green juice which I hope is natural to them when their health is good, garnish the paved sideways. . . . " UT/AH

—*Fleet Market:* "Fleet Market, at that time [1780] was a long irregular row of wooden sheds and penthouses, occupying the centre of what is now called Farringdon Street. They were jumbled together in a most unsightly fashion, in the middle of the road; to the great obstruction of the thoroughfare and the annoyance of passengers, who were fain to make their way, as they best could, among carts, baskets, barrows, trucks, casks, bulks, and benches, and to jostle with porters, hucksters, waggoners, and a motley crowd of buyers, sellers, pickpockets, vagrants, and idlers. The air was perfumed with the stench of rotten leaves and faded fruit; the refuse of the butchers' stalls, and offal and garbage of a hundred kinds. It was indispensable to most public conveniences in those days, that they should be public nuisances likewise; and Fleet Market maintained the principle to admiration." BR 60

—*Garden Court:* " . . . it was quite natural—nothing could be more so—that they should glance down Garden Court; because Garden Court ends in the Garden, and the Garden ends in the River, and that glimpse is very bright and fresh and shining on a summer's day." MC 53

—*Golden Square:* "Although a few members of the graver professions live about Golden Square, it is not exactly in anybody's way to or from anywhere. It is one of the squares that have been; a quarter of the town that has gone down in the world, and taken to letting lodgings. Many of its first and second floors are let, furnished, to single gentlemen; and it takes boarders besides.

"It is a great resort of foreigners. The dark-complexioned men who wear large rings, and heavy watch-guards, and bushy whiskers, and who congregate under the Opera colonnade, and about the box-office in the season, between four and five in the afternoon, when they give away the orders—all live in Golden Square, or within a street of it. Two or three violins and a wind instrument from the Opera band reside within its precincts. Its boarding-houses are musical, and the notes of pianos and harps float in the evening time round the head of the mournful statue, the guardian genius of a little wilderness of shrubs, in the centre of the square.

"On a summer's night, windows are thrown open, and groups of swarthy mustachioed men are seen by the passer-by, lounging at the casements and smoking fearfully. Sounds of gruff voices practising vocal music invade the evening's silence; and the fumes of choice tobacco scent the air. There, snuff and cigars, and German pipes and flutes, and violins and violoncellos, divide the supremacy between them. It is the region of song and smoke. Street bands are on their mettle in Golden Square; and itinerant glee-singers quaver involuntarily as they raise their voices within its boundaries." ¶NN 2

And see B:House—*chimney*

—*Gray's Inn Road:* "Mr Casby lived in a street in the Gray's Inn Road, which had set off from that thoroughfare with the intention of running at one heat down into the valley, and up again to the top of Pentonville Hill; but which had run itself out of breath in twenty yards, and had stood still ever since. There is no such place in that part now; but it remained there for many years, looking with a baulked countenance at the wilderness patched with unfruitful gardens and pimpled with eruptive summer-houses, that it had meant to run over in no time." LD i 13

—Great Ormond Street: "London, like a fine old oak, that has lived through some centuries, has its dead bits in the midst of foliage . . . . Great Ormond Street belonged to our great-grandfathers; it was a bit of London full of sap a great number of years ago. It is cut off, now, from the life of the town—in London, but not of it—a suburb left between the New Road and High Holborn. We turned out of the rattle of Holborn into King Street, and went up Southampton Row through a short passage which led us into a square, dozing over its own departed greatness. Solitude in a crowd is acknowledged by the poets to be extremely oppressive, and we felt so much scared in Queen Square at finding ourselves all alone there, that we had not enough presence of mind to observe more than space and houses, and (if our vague impression be correct) a pump. Moreover, there were spectral streets, down which the eye was drawn. Great Ormond Street was written on a corner house in one of them. It was the enchanter's label by which we were bidden forward . . . . " HWC/DB

—Green Lanes: "[Ned Dennis and Hugh] went up Parliament Street, past Saint Martin's church, and away by Saint Giles's to Tottenham Court Road, at the back of which, upon the western side, was then a place called the Green Lanes. This was a retired spot, not of the choicest kind, leading into the fields. Great heaps of ashes; stagnant pools, overgrown with rank grass and duckweed; broken turnstiles; and the upright posts of palings long since carried off for firewood, which menaced all heedless walkers with their jagged and rusty nails; were the leading features of the landscape: while here and there a donkey, or a ragged horse, tethered to a stake, and cropping off a wretched meal from the coarse stunted turf, were quite in keeping with the scene, and would have suggested (if the houses had not done so, sufficiently, of themselves) how very poor the people were who lived in the crazy huts adjacent, and how foolhardy it might prove for one who carried money, or wore decent clothes, to walk that way alone, unless by daylight.

"Poverty has its whims and shows of taste, as wealth has. Some of these cabins were turreted, some had false windows painted on their rotten walls; one had a mimic clock, upon a crazy tower of four feet high, which screened the chimney; each in its little patch of ground had a rude seat or arbour. The population dealt in bones, in rags, in broken glass, in old wheels, in birds, and dogs. These, in their several ways of stowage, filled the gardens; and shedding a perfume, not of the most delicious nature, in the air, filled it besides with yelps, and screams, and howling." BR 44

—Haymarket: " . . . that curious region lying about the Haymarket and Leicester Square, which is a centre of attraction to indifferent foreign hotels and indifferent foreigners, racket-courts, fighting-men, swordsmen, footguards, old china, gaming-houses, exhibitions, and a large medley of shabbiness and shrinking out of sight." BH 21

" . . . the worst kept part of London . . . . " UT/NW

—near the India Docks: "Captain Cuttle lived on the brink of a little canal near the India Docks, where there was a swivel bridge which opened now and then to let some wandering monster of a ship come roaming up the street like a stranded leviathan.

"The gradual change from land to water, on the approach to Captain Cuttle's lodgings, was curious. It began with the erection of flag-staffs, as appurtenances to public-houses; then came slop-sellers' shops, with Guernsey shirts, sou'wester hats, and canvas pantaloons, at once the tightest and loosest of their order, hanging up outside. These were succeeded by anchor and chain-cable forges, where sledge-hammers were dinging upon iron all day long. Then came rows of houses, with little vane-surmounted masts uprearing them-selves from among the scarlet beans. Then ditches. Then pollard willows. Then more ditches. Then unaccountable patches of dirty water, hardly to be descried, for the ships that covered them. Then, the air was perfumed with chips; and all other trades were swallowed up in mast, oar, and block-making, and boat-building. Then, the ground grew marshy and unsettled. Then, there was nothing to be smelt but rum and sugar. Then, Captain Cuttle's lodgings—at once a first floor and a top story, in Brig Place—were close before you." ¶DS 9

Mr Pecksniff on his Mission MC
[to Kingsgate Street, High Holborn]

—*Jacob's Island:* "Near to that part of the Thames on which the church at Rotherhithe abuts, where the buildings on the banks are dirtiest and the vessels on the river blackest with the dust of colliers and the smoke of close-built low-roofed houses, there exists the filthiest, the strangest, the most extraordinary of the many localities that are hidden in London, wholly unknown, even by name, to the great mass of its inhabitants.

"To reach this place, the visitor has to penetrate through a maze of close, narrow, and muddy streets, thronged by the roughest and poorest of waterside people, and devoted to the traffic they may be supposed to occasion. The cheapest and least delicate provisions are heaped in the shops; the coarsest and commonest articles of wearing apparel dangle at the salesman's door, and stream from the house-parapet and windows. Jostling with unemployed labourers of the lowest class, ballast-heavers, coal-whippers, brazen women, ragged children, and the raff and refuse of the river, [Sikes] makes his way with difficulty along, assailed by offensive sights and smells from the narrow alleys which branch off on the right and left, and deafened by the clash of ponderous waggons that bear great piles of merchandise from the stacks of warehouses that rise from every corner.

"Arriving, at length, in streets remoter and less-frequented than those through which he has passed, he walks beneath tottering house-fronts projecting over the pavement, dismantled walls that seem to totter as he passes, chimneys half crushed, half hesitating to fall, windows guarded by rusty iron bars that time and dirt have almost eaten away, every imaginable sign of desolation and neglect.

"In such a neighbourhood, beyond Dockhead in the Borough of Southwark, stands Jacob's Island, surrounded by a muddy ditch, six or eight feet deep and fifteen or twenty wide when the tide is in, once called Mill Pond, but known in the days of this story as Folly Ditch. It is a creek or inlet from the Thames, and can always be filled at high water by opening the sluices at the Lead Mills from which it took its old name. At such times, a stranger, looking from one of the wooden bridges thrown across it at Mill Lane, will see the inhabitants of the houses on either side lowering from their back doors and windows, buckets, pails, domestic utensils of all kinds, in which to haul the water up; and when his eye is turned from these operations to the houses themselves, his utmost astonishment will be excited by the scene before him.

"Crazy wooden galleries common to the backs of half-a-dozen houses, with holes from which to look upon the slime beneath; windows, broken and patched, with poles thrust out, on which to dry the linen that is never there; rooms so small, so filthy, so confined, that the air would seem too tainted even for the dirt and squalor which they shelter; wooden chambers thrusting themselves out above the mud, and threatening to fall into it—as some have done; dirt-besmeared walls and decaying foundations; every repulsive lineament of poverty, every loathsome indication of filth, rot, and garbage; all these ornament the banks of Folly Ditch.

"In Jacob's Island, the warehouses are roofless and empty; the walls are crumbling down; the windows are windows no more; the doors are falling into the streets; the chimneys are blackened, but they yield no smoke. Thirty or forty years ago, before losses and chancery suits came upon it, it was a thriving place; but now it is a desolate island indeed. The houses have no owners; they are broken open, and entered upon by those who have the courage; and there they live, and there they die. They must have powerful motives for a secret residence, or be reduced to a destitute condition indeed, who seek a refuge in Jacob's Island." ¶OT 50 *And see* Vol. I p654

—*Lant Street:* "There is a repose about Lant Street, in the Borough, which sheds a gentle melancholy upon the soul. There are always a good many houses to let in the street: it is a bye-street too, and its dulness is soothing.

"A house in Lant Street would not come within the denomination of a first-rate residence in the strict acceptation of the term; but it is a most desirable spot nevertheless. If a man wished to abstract himself from the world—to remove himself from within the reach of temptation—to place himself beyond the possibility of any inducement to look out of the window—he should by all means go to Lant Street.

"In this happy retreat are colonised a few clear-starchers, a sprinkling of journeymen bookbinders, one or two prison agents for the Insolvent Court, several small housekeepers who are employed in the Docks, a handful of mantua-makers, and a seasoning of jobbing tailors.

"The majority of the inhabitants either direct their energies to the letting of furnished apartments, or devote themselves to the healthful and invigorating pursuit of mangling. The chief features in the still life of the street are green shutters, lodging-bills, brass door-plates, and bell-handles; the principal specimens of animated nature, the pot-boy, the muffin youth, and the baked-potato man.

"The population is migratory, usually disappearing on the verge of quarter-day, and generally by night. His Majesty's revenues are seldom collected in this happy valley; the rents are dubious; and the water communication is very frequently cut off." ¶PP 32

—*Mews Street, Grosvenor Square:* "[It] was not absolutely Grosvenor Square itself, but it was very near it. It was a hideous little street of dead wall, stables, and dung-hills, with lofts over coach-houses inhabited by coachmen's families, who had a passion for drying clothes, and decorating their window-sills with miniature turnpike-gates.

"The principal chimney-sweep of that fashionable quarter lived at the blind end of Mews Street; and the same corner contained an establishment much frequented about early morning and twilight, for the purchase of wine-bottles and kitchen-stuff. Punch's shows used to lean against the dead wall in Mews Street, while their proprietors were dining elsewhere; and the dogs of the neighbourhood made appointments to meet in the same locality.

"Yet there were two or three small airless houses at the entrance end of Mews Street, which went at enormous rents on account of their being abject hangers-on to a fashionable situation; and whenever one of these fearful little coops was to be let (which seldom happened, for they were in great request), the house agent advertised it as a gentlemanly residence in the most aristocratic part of town, inhabited solely by the elite of the beau monde." ¶LD i 10

—*Mill Pond Bank:* "It was called Mill Pond Bank, Chinks's Basin; and I had no other guide to Chinks's Basin than the Old Green Copper Rope-Walk.

"It matters not what stranded ships repairing in dry docks I lost myself among, what old hulls of ships in course of being knocked to pieces, what ooze and slime and other dregs of tide, what yards of ship-builders and ship-breakers, what rusty anchors blindly biting into the ground though for years off duty, what mountainous country of accumulated casks and timber, how many rope-walks that were not the Old Green Copper. After several times falling short of my destination and as often overshooting it, I came unexpectedly round a corner, upon Mill Pond Bank. It was a fresh kind of place, all circumstances considered, where the wind from the river had room to turn itself round; and there were two or three trees in it, and there was a stump of a ruined windmill, and there was the Old Green Copper Rope-Walk—whose long and narrow vista I could trace in the moonlight, along a series of wooden frames set in the ground, that looked like superannuated haymaking-rakes which had grown old and lost most of their teeth." GE 46

—*Millbank:* "The neighbourhood was a dreary one at that time; as oppressive, sad, and solitary by night, as any about London. There were neither wharves nor houses on the melancholy waste of road near the great blank Prison. A sluggish ditch deposited its mud at the prison walls. Coarse grass and rank weeds straggled over all the marshy land in the vicinity. In one part, carcases of houses, inauspiciously begun and never finished, rotted away. In another, the ground was cumbered with rusty iron monsters of steam-boilers, wheels, cranks, pipes, furnaces, paddles, anchors, diving-bells, windmill-sails, and I know not what strange objects, accumulated by some speculator, and grovelling in the dust, underneath which—having sunk into the soil of their own weight in wet weather—they had the appearance of vainly trying to hide themselves.

"The clash and glare of sundry fiery Works upon the river-side, arose by night to disturb everything except the heavy and unbroken smoke that poured out of their chimneys. Slimy gaps and causeways, winding among old wooden piles, with a sickly substance clinging to the latter, like green hair, and the rags of last year's handbills offering rewards for drowned men fluttering above high-water mark, led down through the ooze and slush to the ebb-tide.

"There was a story that one of the pits dug for the dead in the time of the Great Plague was hereabout; and a blighting influence seemed to have proceeded from it over the whole place. Or else it looked as if it had gradually decomposed into that nightmare condition, out of the overflowings of the polluted stream." DC 47

—*Park Lane neighbourhood:* "They rode to the top of Oxford Street, and there alighting, dived in among the great streets of melancholy stateliness, and the little streets that try to be as stately and succeed in being more melancholy, of which there is a labyrinth near Park Lane.

"Wildernesses of corner houses, the barbarous old porticoes and appurtenances; horrors that came into existence under some wrong-headed person in some wrong-headed time, still demanding the blind admiration of all ensuing generations and determined to do so until they tumbled down; frowned upon the twilight.

"Parasite little tenements, with the cramp in their whole frame, from the dwarf hall-door on the giant model of His Grace's in the Square to the squeezed window of the boudoir commanding the dung-hills in the Mews, made the evening doleful. Rickety dwellings of undoubted fashion, but of a capacity to hold nothing comfortably except a dismal smell, looked like the last result of the great mansions breeding in-and-in; and, where their little supplementary bows and balconies were supported on thin iron columns, seemed to be scrofulously resting upon crutches. Here and there a Hatchment, with the whole science of Heraldry in it, loomed down upon the street, like an Archbishop discoursing on Vanity.

"The shops, few in number, made no show; for popular opinion was as nothing to them. The pastrycook knew who was on his books, and in that knowledge could be calm, with a few glass cylinders of dowager peppermint-drops in his window, and half-a-dozen ancient specimens of currant-jelly. A few oranges formed the greengrocer's whole concession to the vulgar mind. A single basket made of moss, once containing plovers' eggs, held all that the poulterer had to say to the rabble.

"Everybody in those streets seemed . . . to be gone out to dinner, and nobody seemed to be giving the dinners they had gone to . . . . Here and there was a retiring public-house which did not require to be supported on the shoulders of the people, and where gentlemen out of livery were not much wanted." LD i 27

—Saffron Hill the Great: "[Jack Dawkins and Oliver Twist] crossed from the Angel into St John's Road; struck down the small street which terminates at Sadler's Wells Theatre; through Exmouth Street and Coppice Row; down the little court by the side of the workhouse; across the classic ground which once bore the name of Hockley-in-the-Hole; thence into Little Saffron Hill; and so into Saffron Hill the Great . . . .

"A dirtier or more wretched place [Oliver] had never seen. The street was very narrow and muddy, and the air was impregnated with filthy odours. There were a good many small shops; but the only stock in trade appeared to be heaps of children, who, even at that time of night, were crawling in and out at the doors, or screaming from the inside.

"The sole places that seemed to prosper amid the general blight of the place, were the public-houses; and in them, the lowest orders of Irish were wrangling with might and main. Covered ways and yards, which here and there diverged from the main street, disclosed little knots of houses, where drunken men and women were positively wallowing in filth; and from several of the door-ways, great ill-looking fellows were cautiously emerging, bound, to all appearance, on no very well-disposed or harmless errands." OT 8

—Seven Dials: "Seven Dials! the region of song and poetry—first effusions, and last dying speeches: hallowed by the names of **Catnach** and of **Pitts**—names that will entwine themselves with costermongers and barrel-organs, when penny magazines shall have superseded penny yards of song, and capital punishment be unknown!

"Look at the construction of the place. The gordian knot was all very well in its way: so was the maze of Hampton Court: so is the maze at the Beulah Spa: so were the ties of stiff white neckcloths, when the difficulty of getting one on was only to be equalled by the apparent impossibility of ever getting it off again. But what involutions can compare with those of Seven Dials? Where is there such another maze of streets, courts, lanes, and alleys? Where such a pure mixture of Englishmen and Irishmen, as in this complicated part of London? . . .

"The stranger who finds himself in 'The Dials' for the first time, and stands **Belzoni**-like, at the entrance of seven obscure passages, uncertain which to take, will see enough around him to keep his curiosity and attention awake for no inconsiderable time. From the irregular square into which he has plunged, the streets and courts dart in all directions, until they are lost in the unwholesome vapour which hangs over the house-tops, and renders the dirty perspective uncertain and confined; and lounging at every corner, as if they came there to take a few gasps of such fresh air as has found its way so far, but is too much exhausted already, to be enabled to force itself into the narrow alleys around, are groups of people, whose appearance and dwellings would fill any mind but a regular Londoner's with astonishment." SB/SD

"The peculiar character of these streets, and the close resemblance each one bears to its neighbour, by no means tends to decrease the bewilderment in which the unexperienced wayfarer through 'the Dials' finds himself involved. He traverses streets of dirty, straggling houses, with now and then an unexpected court composed of buildings as ill-proportioned and deformed as the half-naked children that wallow in the kennels.

"Here and there, a little dark chandler's shop, with a cracked bell hung up behind the door to announce the entrance of a customer, or betray the presence of some young gentleman in whom a passion for shop tills has developed itself at an early age: others, as if for support, against some handsome lofty building, which usurps the place of a low dingy public-house; long rows of broken and patched windows expose plants that may have flourished when 'the Dials' were built, in vessels as dirty as 'the Dials' themselves; and shops for the purchase of rags, bones, old iron, and kitchen-stuff, vie in cleanliness with the bird-fanciers' and rabbit-dealers', which one might fancy so many arks, but for the irresistible conviction that no bird in its proper senses, who was permitted to leave one of them, would ever come back again.

"Brokers' shops, which would seem to have been established by humane individuals, as refuges for destitute bugs, interspersed with announcements of day-schools, penny theatres, petition-writers, mangles, and music for balls or routs, complete the still life of the subject; and dirty men, filthy women, squalid children, fluttering shuttlecocks, noisy battledores, reeking pipes, bad fruit, more than doubtful oysters, attenuated cats, depressed dogs, and anatomical fowls, are the cheerful accompaniments." SB/SD

And see F:The Poor, Abject—*their neighbourhoods*

—*shopping district:* "[Nicholas Nickleby and Smike] rattled on through the noisy, bustling, crowded streets of London, now displaying long double rows of brightly-burning lamps, dotted here and there with the chemists' glaring lights, and illuminated besides with the brilliant flood that streamed from the windows of the shops, where sparkling jewellery, silks and velvets of the richest colours, the most inviting delicacies, and most sumptuous articles of luxurious ornament, succeeded each other in rich and glittering profusion.

"Streams of people apparently without end poured on and on, jostling each other in the crowd and hurrying forward, scarcely seeming to notice the riches that surrounded them on every side; while vehicles of all shapes and makes, mingled up together in one moving mass like running water, lent their ceaseless roar to swell the noise and tumult.

"As they dashed by the quickly-changing and every-varying objects, it was curious to observe in what a strange procession they passed before the eye. Emporiums of splendid dresses, the materials brought from every quarter of the world; tempting stores of everything to stimulate and pamper the sated appetite and give new relish to the oft-repeated feast; vessels of burnished gold and silver, wrought into every exquisite form of vase, and dish, and goblet; guns, swords, pistols, and patent engines of destruction; screws and irons for the crooked, clothes for the newly-born, drugs for the sick, coffins for the dead, and churchyards for the buried—all these jumbled each with the other and flocking side by side, seemed to flit by in motley dance like the fantastic groups of the old Dutch painter, and with the same stern moral for the unheeding restless crowd.

"Nor were there wanting objects in the crowd itself to give new point and purpose to the shifting scene. The rags of the squalid ballad-singer fluttered in the rich light that showed the goldsmith's treasures, pale and pinched-up faces hovered about the windows where was tempting food, hungry eyes wandered over the profusion guarded by one thin sheet of brittle glass—an iron wall to them; half-naked shivering figures stopped to gaze at Chinese shawls and golden stuffs of India. There was a christening party at the largest coffin-maker's, and a funeral hatchment had stopped some great improvements in the bravest mansion. Life and death went hand in hand; wealth and poverty stood side by side; repletion and starvation laid them down together." ¶NN 32

—*a slum:* ". . . they came upon a straggling neighbourhood, where the mean houses parcelled off in rooms, and windows patched with rags and paper, told of the populous poverty that sheltered there. The shops sold goods that only poverty could buy, and sellers and buyers were pinched and griped alike. Here were poor streets where faded gentility essayed with scanty space and ship-wrecked means to make its last feeble stand, but tax-gatherer and creditor came there as elsewhere, and the poverty that yet faintly struggled was hardly less squalid and manifest than that which had long ago submitted and given up the game.

"This was a wide, wide track—for the humble followers of the camp of wealth pitch their tents round about it for many a mile—but its character was still the same. Damp rotten houses, many to let, many yet building, many half-built and mouldering away—lodgings, where it would be hard to tell which needed pity most, those who let or those who came to take—children, scantily fed and clothed, spread over every street, and sprawling in the dust—scolding mothers, stamping their slipshod feet with noisy threats upon the pavement—shabby fathers, hurrying with dispirited looks to the occupation which brought them 'daily bread' and little more—mangling-women, washer-women, cobblers, tailors, chandlers, driving their trades in parlours and kitchens and back rooms and garrets, and sometimes all of them under the same roof—brick-fields, skirting gardens paled with staves of old casks, or timber pillaged from houses burnt down and blackened and blistered by the flames—mounds of dock-weed, nettles, coarse grass and oyster shells, heaped in rank confusion—small dissenting chapels to teach, with no lack of illustration, the miseries of Earth, and plenty of new churches, erected with a little superfluous wealth, to show the way to Heaven." OCS 15

"They left the busy scene, and went into an obscure part of the town, where Scrooge had never penetrated before, although he recognised its situation, and its bad repute. The ways were foul and narrow; the shops and houses wretched; the people half-naked, drunken, slipshod, ugly. Alleys and archways, like so many cesspools, disgorged their offences of smell, and dirt, and life, upon the straggling streets; and the whole quarter reeked with crime, with filth, and misery." CC 4

—*Smithfield:* "Turning down Sun Street and Crown Street, and crossing Finsbury Square, Mr Sikes struck, by way of Chiswell Street, into Barbican: thence into Long Lane, and so into Smithfield; from which latter place arose a tumult of discordant sounds that filled Oliver Twist with amazement.

"It was market-morning. The ground was covered, nearly ankle-deep, with filth and mire; a thick steam, perpetually rising from the reeking bodies of the cattle, and mingling with the fog, which seemed to rest upon the chimney-tops, hung heavily above. All the pens in the centre of the large area, and as many temporary pens as could be crowded into the vacant space, were filled with sheep; tied up to posts by the gutter side were long lines of beasts and oxen, three or four deep.

"Countrymen, butchers, drovers, hawkers, boys, thieves, idlers, and vagabonds of every low grade, were mingled together in a mass; the whistling of drovers, the barking of dogs, the bellowing and plunging of oxen, the bleating of sheep, the grunting and squeaking of pigs, the cries of hawkers, the shouts, oaths, and quarrelling on all sides; the ringing of bells and roar of voices, that issued from every public-house; the crowding, pushing, driving, beating, whooping, and yelling; the hideous and discordant din that resounded from every corner of the market; and the unwashed, unshaven, squalid, and dirty figures constantly running to and fro, and bursting in and out of the throng; rendered it a stunning and bewildering scene, which quite confounded the senses." OT 21

"So, I came into Smithfield; and the shameful place, being all asmear with filth and fat and blood and foam, seemed to stick to me. So I rubbed it off with all possible speed by turning into a street where I saw the great black dome of Saint Paul's bulging at me from behind a grim stone building which a bystander said was Newgate Prison." GE 20

—*Soho Square vicinity:* "A quainter corner than the corner where the Doctor [Manette] lived, was not to be found in London. There was no way through it, and the front windows of the Doctor's lodgings commanded a pleasant little vista of street that had a congenial air of retirement on it. There were few buildings then [1780], north of the Oxford-road, and forest-trees flourished, and wild flowers grew, and the hawthorn blossomed, in the now vanished fields. As a consequence, country airs circulated in Soho with vigorous freedom, instead of languishing into the parish like stray paupers without a settlement; and there was many a good south wall, not far off, on which the peaches ripened in their season.

"The summer light struck into the corner brilliantly in the earlier part of the day; but, when the streets grew hot, the corner was in shadow, though not in shadow so remote but that you could see beyond it into a glare of brightness. It was a cool spot, staid but cheerful, a wonderful place for echoes, and a very harbour from the raging streets.

"There ought to have been a tranquil bark in such an anchorage, and there was. The Doctor occupied two floors of a large still house, where several callings purported to be pursued by day, but whereof little was audible any day, and which was shunned by all of them at night. In a building at the back, attainable by a court-yard where a plane-tree rustled its green leaves, church-organs claimed to be made, and silver to be chased, and likewise gold to be beaten by some mysterious giant who had a golden arm starting out of the wall of the front hall—as if he had beaten himself precious, and menaced a similar conversion of all visitors.

"Very little of these trades, or of a lonely lodger rumoured to live upstairs, or of a dim coach-trimming maker asserted to have a counting-house below, was ever heard or seen. Occasionally, a stray workman putting his coat on, traversed the hall, or a stranger peered about there, or a distant clink was heard across the court-yard, or a thump from the golden giant. These, however, were only the exceptions required to prove the rule that the sparrows in the plane-tree behind the house, and the echoes in the corner before it, had their own way from Sunday morning unto Saturday night." ¶TTC ii 6

—Spitalfields: "Have you any distinct idea of Spitalfields, dear reader? A general one, no doubt you have—an impression that there are certain squalid streets, lying like narrow black trenches, far below the steeples, somewhere about London—toward the East, perhaps—where sallow, unshorn weavers, who have nothing to do, prowl languidly about, or lean against posts, or sit brooding on door-steps, and occasionally assemble together in a crowd to petition Parliament or the Queen; after which there is a Drawing-Room, or a Court Ball, where all the great ladies wear dresses of Spitalfields manufacture; and then the weavers dine for a day or two, and so relapse into prowling about the streets, leaning against the posts, and brooding on the door-steps . . . you may connect with this impression, a general idea that many pigeons are kept in Spitalfields, and you may remember to have thought, as you rattled along the dirty streets, observing the pigeon-hutches and pigeon-traps on the tops of the poor dwellings, that it was a natural aspiration in the inhabitants to connect themselves with any living creatures that could get out of that, and take a flight into the air. The smoky little bowers of scarlet-runners that you may have sometimes seen on the house-tops, among the pigeons, may have suggested to your fancy . . . abortions of the bean-stalk that led Jack to fortune: by the slender twigs of which, the Jacks of Spitalfields will never, never, climb to where the giant keeps his money.

"Will you come to Spitalfields?

"Turning eastward out of the most bustling part of Bishopsgate, we suddenly lose the noise that has been resounding in our ears, and fade into the quiet churchyard of the Priory of St Mary, Spital, otherwise 'Domus Dei et Beatæ Mariæ, extra Bishopsgate, in the Parish of St Botolph.' Its modern name is Spital Square. Cells and cloisters were, at an early date, replaced by substantial burgher houses, which, since the Revocation of the Edict of Nantes, in 1685, have been chiefly the depositories of the silk manufacture introduced into London, by the French Huguenots, who flew from the perfidy of Louis the Fourteenth. But much of the old quiet cloistered air, still lingers in the place." HWC/S

"'These high gaunt houses, all window on the upper story, and that window all small diamond panes, are like the houses in some foreign town, and have no trace of London in them—except its soot, which is indeed a large exception. It is as if the Huguenots had brought their streets along with them, and dropped them down here.'" HWC/S

—Staggs's Gardens, Camden Town: "This euphonious locality was situated in a suburb, known by the inhabitants of Staggs's Gardens by the name of 'Camberling Town'; a designation which the Strangers' Map of London, as printed (with a view to pleasant and commodious reference) on pocket-handkerchiefs, condenses, with some show of reason, into Camden Town . . . .

—coming of the railroad: "The first shock of a great earthquake had, just at that period, rent the whole neighbourhood to its centre. Traces of its course were visible on every side. Houses were knocked down; streets broken through and stopped; deep pits and trenches dug in the ground; enor-

mous heaps of earth and clay thrown up; buildings that were undermined and shaking, propped by great beams of wood.

"Here, a chaos of carts, overthrown and jumbled together, lay topsy-turvy at the bottom of a steep unnatural hill; there, confused treasures of iron soaked and rusted in something that had accidentally become a pond. Everywhere were bridges that led nowhere; thoroughfares that were wholly impassable; Babel towers of chimneys, wanting half their height; temporary wooden houses and enclosures, in the most unlikely situations; carcases of ragged tenements, and fragments of unfinished walls and arches, and piles of scaffolding, and wildernesses of bricks, and giant forms of cranes, and tripods straddling above nothing.

"There were a hundred thousand shapes and substances of incompleteness, wildly mingled out of their places, upside down, burrowing in the earth, aspiring in the air, mouldering in the water, and unintelligible as any dream. Hot springs and fiery eruptions, the usual attendants upon earthquakes, lent their contributions of confusion to the scene. Boiling water hissed and heaved within dilapidated walls; whence, also, the glare and roar of flames came issuing forth; and mounds of ashes blocked up rights of way, and wholly changed the law and custom of the neighbourhood.

"In short, the yet unfinished and unopened railroad was in progress; and, from the very core of all this dire disorder, trailed smoothly away, upon its mighty course of civilisation and improvement.

"But as yet, the neighbourhood was shy to own the railroad. One or two bold speculators had projected streets; and one had built a little, but had stopped among the mud and ashes to consider further of it. A bran-new tavern, redolent of fresh mortar and size, and fronting nothing at all, had taken for its sign The Railway Arms; but that might be rash enterprise—and the old-established Ham and Beef Shop had become the Railway Eating House, with a roast leg of pork daily, through interested motives of a similar immediate and popular description.

"Lodging-house keepers were favourable in like manner; and for the like reasons were not to be trusted. The general belief was very slow. There were frowzy fields, and cow-houses, and dunghills, and dustheaps, and ditches, and gardens, and summerhouses, and carpet-beating grounds, at the very door of the railway.

"Little tumuli of oyster shells in the oyster season, and of lobster shells in the lobster season, and of broken crockery and faded cabbage leaves in all seasons, encroached upon its high places. Posts, and rails, and old cautions to trespassers, and backs of mean houses, and patches of wretched vegetation, stared it out of countenance. Nothing was the better for it, or thought of being so. If the miserable waste ground lying near it could have laughed, it would have laughed it to scorn, like many of the miserable neighbours.

"Staggs's Gardens was uncommonly incredulous. It was a little row of houses, with little squalid patches of ground before them, fenced off with old doors, barrel staves, scraps of tarpaulin, and dead bushes; with bottomless tin kettles and exhausted iron fenders, thrust into the gaps. Here, the Staggs's Gardeners trained scarlet beans, kept fowls and rabbits, erected rotten summer-houses (one was an old boat), dried clothes, and smoked pipes.

"Some were of opinion that Staggs's Gardens derived its name from a deceased capitalist, one Mr Staggs, who had built it for his delectation. Others, who had a natural taste for the country, held that it dated from those rural times when the antlered herd, under the familiar denomination of Staggses, had resorted to its shady precincts.

"Be this as it may, Staggs's Gardens was regarded by its population as a sacred grove not to be withered by railroads; and so confident were they generally of its long outliving any such ridiculous inventions, that the master chimney-sweeper at the corner, who was understood to take the lead in the local politics of the gardens, had publicly declared that on the occasion of the railroad opening, if ever it did open, two of his boys should ascend the flues of his dwelling, with instructions to hail the failure with derisive jeers from the chimney-pots." DS 6

—the railroad arrived: "There was no such place as Staggs's Gardens. It had vanished from the earth. Where the old rotten summer-houses once had stood, palaces now reared their heads, and granite columns of gigantic girth opened a vista to the railway world beyond. The miserable waste ground, where the refuse-matter had

been heaped of yore, was swallowed up and gone; and in its frowzy stead were tiers of warehouses, crammed with rich goods and costly merchandise.

"The old by-streets now swarmed with passengers and vehicles of every kind: the new streets that had stopped disheartened in the mud and waggon-ruts, formed towns within themselves, originating wholesome comforts and conveniences belonging to themselves, and never tried nor thought of until they sprung into existence. Bridges that had led to nothing, led to villas, gardens, churches, healthy public walks. The carcasses of houses, and beginnings of new thoroughfares, had started off upon the line at steam's own speed, and shot away into the country in a monster train.

"As to the neighbourhood which had hesitated to acknowledge the railroad in its straggling days, that had grown wise and penitent, as any Christian might in such a case, and now boasted of its powerful and prosperous relation. There were railway patterns in its drapers' shops, and railway journals in the windows of its newsmen. There were railway hotels, office-houses, lodging-houses, boarding-houses; railway plans, maps, views, wrappers, bottles, sandwich-boxes, and time-tables; railway hackney-coach and cabstands; railway omnibuses, railway streets and buildings, railway hangers-on and parasites, and flatterers out of all calculation.

"There was even railway time observed in clocks, as if the sun itself had given in. Among the vanquished was the master chimney-sweeper, whilome incredulous at Staggs's Gardens, who now lived in a stuccoed house three storeys high, and gave himself out, with golden flourishes upon a varnished board, as contractor for the cleansing of railway chimneys by machinery . . . .

"But Staggs's Gardens had been cut up root and branch. Oh woe the day when 'not a rood of English ground'—laid out in Staggs's Gardens—is secure!" ¶DS 15

And see TT:Railroad—*newly arrived*

—*Staple Inn, Holborn*: "Behind the most ancient part of Holborn, London, where certain gabled houses some centuries of age still stand looking on the public way, as if disconsolately looking for the Old Bourne that has long run dry, is a little nook composed of two irregular quadrangles, called Staple Inn.

"It is one of those nooks, the turning into which out of the clashing street, imparts to the relieved pedestrian the sensation of having put cotton in his ears, and velvet soles on his boots. It is one of those nooks where a few smoke sparrows twitter in smoky trees, as though they called to one another, 'Let us play at country,' and where a few feet of garden mould and a few yards of gravel enable them to do that refreshing violence to their tiny understandings. Moreover, it is one of those nooks which are legal nooks; and it contains a little Hall, with a little lantern in its roof: to what obstructive purposes devoted, and at whose expense, this history knoweth not." ¶MED 11

—*a Swiss quarter:* "A curious colony of mountaineers has long been enclosed within that small flat London district of Soho. Swiss watch-makers, Swiss silver-chasers, Swiss jewellers, Swiss importers of Swiss musical boxes and Swiss toys of various kinds, draw close together there. Swiss professors of music, painting, and languages; Swiss artificers in steady work; Swiss couriers, and other Swiss servants chronically out of place; industrious Swiss laundresses and clear-starchers; mysteriously existing Swiss of both sexes; Swiss creditable and Swiss discreditable; Swiss to be trusted by all means, and Swiss to be trusted by no means; these divers Swiss particles are attracted to a centre in the district of Soho.

"Shabby Swiss eating-houses, coffee-houses, and lodging-houses, Swiss drinks and dishes, Swiss service for Sundays, and Swiss schools for week-days, are all to be found there. Even the native-born English taverns drive a sort of broken-English trade; announcing in their windows Swiss whets and drams, and sheltering in their bars Swiss skirmishes of love and animosity on most nights in the year." ¶CS/NT 1

—*Temple Fountain:* "Brilliantly the Temple Fountain sparkled in the sun, and laughingly its liquid music played, and merrily the idle drops of water danced and danced, and peeping out in sport among the trees, plunged lightly down to hide themselves, as little Ruth and her companion came towards it." MC 53

—*Tom-all-Alone's:* "'There is, in that city of London there, some property of ours . . . I say property of ours, meaning of the Suit's, but I ought to call it the property of Costs; for Costs is the only power on earth that will ever get anything out of it now, or will ever know it for anything but an eyesore and a heartsore. It is a street of perishing blind houses, with their eyes stoned out; without a pane of glass, without so much as a window-frame, with the bare blank shutters tumbling from their hinges and falling asunder; the iron rails peeling away in flakes of rust; the chimneys sinking in; the stone steps to every door (and every door might be Death's Door) turning stagnant green; the very crutches on which the ruins are propped, decaying.'" BH 8

"It is a black, dilapidated street, avoided by all decent people; where the crazy houses were seized upon, when their decay was far advanced, by some bold vagrants, who, after establishing their own possession, took to letting them out in lodgings. Now, these tumbling tenements contain, by night, a swarm of misery.

"As, on the ruined human wretch, vermin parasites appear, so these ruined shelters have bred a crowd of foul existence that crawls in and out of gaps in walls and boards; and coils itself to sleep, in maggot numbers, where the rain drips in; and comes and goes, fetching and carrying fever, and sowing more evil in its every footprint than Lord Coodle, and Sir Thomas Doodle, and the Duke of Foodle, and all the fine gentlemen in office, down to Zoodle, shall set right in five hundred years—though born expressly to do it.

"Twice, lately, there has been a crash and a cloud of dust, like the springing of a mine, in Tom-all-Alone's; and, each time, a house has fallen. These accidents have made a paragraph in the newspapers, and have filled a bed or two in the nearest hospital. The gaps remain, and there are not unpopular lodgings among the rubbish. As several more houses are nearly ready to go, the next crash in Tom-all-Alone's may be expected to be a good one.

"This desirable property is in Chancery, of course. It would be an insult to the discernment of any man with half an eye, to tell him so. Whether 'Tom' is the popular representative of the original plaintiff or defendant in Jarndyce and Jarndyce; or whether Tom lived here when the suit had laid the street waste, all alone, until other settlers came to join him; or whether the traditional title is a comprehensive name for a retreat cut off from honest company and put out of the pale of hope; perhaps nobody knows." ¶BH 16

"Much mighty speech-making there has been, both in and out of Parliament, concerning Tom, and much wrathful disputation how Tom shall be got right. Whether he shall be put into the main road by constables, or by beadles, or by bell-ringing, or by force of figures, or by correct principles of taste, or by high church, or by low church, or by no church; whether he shall be set to splitting trusses of polemical straws with the crooked knife of his mind, or whether he shall be put to stone-breaking instead.

"In the midst of which dust and noise, there is but one thing perfectly clear, to wit, that Tom only may and can, or shall and will, be reclaimed according to somebody's theory but nobody's practice. And in the hopeful mean-time, Tom goes to perdition head foremost in his old determined spirit. . . .

"It is a moot point whether Tom-all-Alone's be uglier by day or by night; but on the argument that the more that is seen of it the more shocking it must be, and that no part of it left to the imagination is at all likely to be made so bad as the reality, day carries it. The day begins to break now; and in truth it might be better for the national glory even that the sun should sometimes set upon the British dominions, than that it should ever rise upon so vile a wonder as Tom." ¶BH 46

And see B:Illness—*disease endemic; and* B: Sanitation

—*Tottenham Court Road:* " . . . we will make for Drury Lane, through the narrow streets and dirty courts which divide it from Oxford Street, and that classical spot adjoining the brewery at the bottom of Tottenham Court Road, best known to the initiated as the 'Rookery.'

"The filthy and miserable appearance of this part of London can hardly be imagined by those (and there are many such) who have not witnessed it. Wretched houses with broken windows patched with rags and paper: every room let out to a different family, and in many instances to two or even three—fruit and 'sweet-stuff' manufacturers in the cellars, barbers and red-herring vendors in the front parlours, cobblers in the back; a bird-fancier in the first floor, three families on the second, starvation in the attics, Irishmen in the passage, a 'musician' in the front kitchen, and a charwoman and five hungry children in the back one—filth everywhere—a gutter before the houses and a drain behind—clothes drying and slops emptying, from the windows; girls of fourteen or fifteen, with matted hair, walking about barefoot, and in white great-coats, almost their only covering; boys of all ages, in coats of all sizes and no coats at all; men and women, in every variety of scanty and dirty apparel, lounging, scolding, drinking, smoking, squabbling, fighting, and swearing." SB/GS

—*Walworth:* "The back part of Walworth, at its greatest distance from town, is a straggling miserable place enough, even in these days; but, five-and-thirty years ago, the greater portion of it was little better than a dreary waste, inhabited by a few scattered people of questionable character, whose poverty prevented their living in any better neighbourhood, or whose pursuits and mode of life rendered its solitude desirable. Very many of the houses which have since sprung up on all sides, were not built until some years afterwards; and the great majority even of those which were sprinkled about, at irregular intervals, were of the rudest and most miserable description.

"The appearance of the place through which he walked in the morning, was not calculated to raise the spirits of the young surgeon, or to dispel any feeling of anxiety or depression which the singular kind of visit he was about to make, had awakened. Striking off from the high road, his way lay across a marshy common, through irregular lanes, with here and there a ruinous and dismantled cottage fast falling to pieces with decay and neglect.

"A stunted tree, or pool of stagnant water, roused into a sluggish action by the heavy rain of the preceding night, skirted the path occasionally; and, now and then, a miserable patch of garden-ground, with a few old boards knocked together for a summer-house, and old palings imperfectly mended with stakes pilfered from the neighbouring hedges, bore testimony, at once to the poverty of the inhabitants, and the little scruple they entertained in appropriating the property of other people to their own use." SB/BV *And see* Weather—*wind*

" . . . [Wemmick] gave me to understand that we had arrived in the district of Walworth.

"It appeared to be a collection of black lanes, ditches, and little gardens, and to present the aspect of a rather dull retirement. Wemmick's house was a little wooden cottage in the midst of plots of garden, and the top of it was cut out and painted like a battery mounted with guns." GE 25

—*Westminster, Manchester Buildings:* "Within the precincts of the ancient city of Westminster, and within half a quarter of a mile of its ancient sanctuary, is a narrow and dirty region, the sanctuary of the smaller members of Parliament in modern days. It is all comprised in one street of gloomy lodging-houses, from whose windows in vacation time there frown long melancholy rows of bills, which say as plainly as did the countenances of their occupiers, ranged on ministerial and opposition benches in the session which slumbers with its fathers, 'To Let'—'To Let'.

"In busier periods of the year these bills disappear, and the houses swarm with legislators. There are legislators in the parlours, in the first floor, in the second, in the third, in the garrets; the small apartments reek with the breath of deputations and delegates. In damp weather the place is rendered close by the steams of moist acts of parliament and frowsy petitions; general postmen grow faint as they enter its infected limits, and shabby figures in quest of franks, flit restlessly to and fro like the troubled ghosts of Complete Letter-writers departed.

"This is Manchester Buildings; and here, at all hours of the night, may be heard the rattling of latch-keys in their respective keyholes, with now and then—when a gust of wind sweeping across the water which washed the Buildings' feet, impels the sound towards its entrance—the weak, shrill voice of some young member practising the morrow's speech.

"All the livelong day there is a grinding of organs and clashing and clanging of little boxes of music, for Manchester Buildings is an eel-pot, which has no outlet but its awkward mouth—a case-bottle which has no thoroughfare, and a short and narrow neck—and in this respect it may be typical of the fate of some few among its more adventurous residents, who, after wriggling themselves into Parliament by violent efforts and contortions, find that it too is no thoroughfare for them; that, like Manchester Buildings, it leads to nothing beyond itself; and that they are fain at last to back out, no wiser, no richer, not one whit more famous, than they went in." ¶NN 16

—*Wood Street, Cheapside:* "[My friend] merely took me by the arm . . . and turned me straight down Wood Street, among the bales, and waggons, and business men, of a busy street not wider than many a dining-room, with a pavement no wider than many a dinner-table: we threatened with the descent of great woollen bales upon our heads, and saving ourselves by a leap from being crushed under an avalanche of empty hampers tumbling down a mountain of waggon." HWC/DT

In Westminster Hall BR

Seasons

—blustery spring: "It was not summer yet, but spring; and it was not gentle spring ethereally mild, as in Thomson's Seasons, but nipping spring with an easterly wind, as in Johnson's, Jackson's, Dickson's, Smith's, and Jones's Seasons. The grating wind sawed rather than blew; and as it sawed, the sawdust whirled about the sawpit. Every street was a sawpit, and there were no top-sawyers; every passenger was an under-sawyer, with the sawdust blinding him and choking him.

"That mysterious paper currency which circulates in London when the wind blows, gyrated here and there and everywhere. Whence can it come, whither can it go? It hangs on every bush, flutters in every tree, is caught flying by the electric wires, haunts every enclosure, drinks at every pump, cowers at every grating, shudders upon every plot of grass, seeks rest in vain behind the legions of iron rails. In Paris, where nothing is wasted, costly and luxurious city though it be, but where wonderful human ants creep out of holes and pick up every scrap, there is no such thing. There, it blows nothing but dust. There, sharp eyes and sharp stomachs reap even the east wind, and get something out of it.

"The wind sawed, and the sawdust whirled. The shrubs wrung their many hands, bemoaning that they had been over-persuaded by the sun to bud; the young leaves pined; the sparrows repented of their early marriages, like men and women; the colours of the rainbow were discernible, not in floral spring, but in the faces of the people whom it nibbled and pinched. And ever the wind sawed, and the sawdust whirled.

"When the spring evenings are too long and light to shut out, and such weather is rife, the city . . . is at its worst. Such a black shrill city, combining the qualities of a smoky house and scolding wife; such a gritty city; such a hopeless city, with no rent in the leaden canopy of its sky; such a beleaguered city, invested by the great Marsh Forces of Essex and Kent." OMF i 12

—June: "It was the beginning of a day in June; the deep blue sky unsullied by a cloud, and teeming with brilliant light. The streets were as yet nearly free from passengers, the houses and shops were closed, and the healthful air of morning feels like breath from angels, on the sleeping town . . . every object was bright and fresh . . . church towers and steeples, frowning and dark at other times, now shone and dazzled in the sun; each humble nook and corner rejoiced in light; and the sky, dimmed by excessive distance, shed its placid smile on everything beneath." OCS 12

—summer: "Through the half-opened window, the Temple Garden looks green and pleasant; the placid river, gay with boat and barge, and dimpled with the plash of many an oar, sparkles in the distance; the sky is blue and clear; and the summer air steals gentle in, filling the room with perfume. The very town, the smoky town, is radiant. High roofs and steeple tops, wont to look black and sullen, smile a cheerful grey; every old gilded vane, and ball, and cross, glitters anew in the bright morning sun; and, high among them all, St Paul's towers up, showing its lofty crest in burnished gold." BR 75

"Norfolk is a delightful street to lodge in—provided you don't go lower down—but of a summer evening when the dust and waste paper lie in it and stray children play in it and a kind of a gritty calm and bake settles on it and a peal of church-bells is practising in the neighbourhood it is a trifle dull . . . . " CS/L 1

"A dull mist of heat had taken possession of the streets. Through the warm mist we roll in a warm omnibus. Over the parapet of London Bridge we see London in a heavy lump with the hot mist about it, and almost expect that St Paul's presently will throw out a spark, and the whole town, like a firework, begin to fizz and crackle. There is nothing that we might not be permitted to expect as a result of heat, upon the hottest morning of the hottest dog-days within the memory of the oldest dog." HWC/BM

" . . . deserts of gritty streets, where many people crowded at the corners of courts and byways to get some air, and where many other people walked with a miserably monotonous noise of shuffling feet on hot paving-stones, and where all the people and all their surroundings were so gritty and so shabby." MED 20

—the doldrums (autumn)

—time of love: "But, I have all this time been coming to the point, that the happy nature of my retirement is most sweetly expressed in its being the abode of Love. It is, as it were, an expensive Agapemone: nobody's speculation: everybody's profit. The one great result of the resumption of primitive habits, and (convertible terms) the not having much to do, is, the abounding of Love . . . .

"Everybody loves, and openly and blamelessly loves. My landlord's young man loves the whole of one side of the way of Old Bond-street, and is beloved several doors up New Bond-street besides. I never look out of window but I see kissing of hands going on all around me. It is the morning custom to glide from shop to shop and exchange tender sentiments; it is the evening custom for couples to stand hand in hand at house doors, or roam, linked in that flowery manner, through the unpeopled streets. There is nothing else to do but love; and what there is to do, is done." UT/AL

—house-minders: " . . . in its Arcadian time all my part of London is indistinctly pervaded by the Klem species. They creep about with beds, and go to bed in miles of deserted houses. They hold no companionship except that sometimes, after dark, two of them will emerge from opposite houses, and meet in the middle of the road as on neutral ground, or will peep from adjoining houses over an interposing barrier of area railings, and compare a few reserved mistrustful notes respecting their good ladies or good gentlemen . . . [they] may be dimly observed, when the heavy shadows fall, flitting to and fro, putting up the door-chain, taking in the pint of beer, lowering like phantoms at the dark parlour windows, or secretly consorting underground with the dust-bin and the water-cistern." UT/AL

—November: "London. Michaelmas Term lately over, and the Lord Chancellor sitting in Lincoln's Inn Hall. Implacable November weather. As much mud in the streets, as if the waters had but newly retired from the face of the earth, and it would not be won-

derful to meet a megalosaurus, forty feet long or so, waddling like an elephantine lizard up Holborn Hill. Smoke lowering down from chimney-pots, making a soft black drizzle, with flakes of soot in it as big as full-grown snowflakes—gone into mourning, one might imagine, for the death of the sun. Dogs, undistinguishable in mire.

"Horses, scarcely better; splashed to their very blinkers. Foot passengers, jostling one another's umbrellas, in a general infection of ill-temper, and losing their foot-hold at street-corners, where tens of thousands of other foot passengers have been slipping and sliding since the day broke (if this day ever broke), adding new deposits to the crust upon crust of mud, sticking at those points tenaciously to the pavement, and accumulating at compound interest." ¶BH 1

—*winter:* " . . . the Park . . . was clad in the least engaging of the three hundred and sixty-five dresses in the wardrobe of the year. It was raw, damp, dark, and dismal; the clouds were as muddy as the ground; and the short perspective of every street and avenue was closed up by the mist as by a filthy curtain." MC 14

"The dead winter-time was in full dreariness when I left my chambers for ever, at five o'clock in the morning. I had shaved by candle-light, of course, and was miserably cold, and experienced that general all-pervading sensation of getting up to be hanged which I have usually found inseparable from untimely rising under such circumstances.

"How well I remember the forlorn aspect of Fleet-street when I came out of the Temple! The street-lamps flickering in the gusty north-east wind, as if the very gas were contorted with cold; the white-topped houses; the bleak, star-lighted sky; the market people and other early stragglers, trotting to circulate their almost frozen blood; the hospitable light and warmth of the few coffee-shops and public-houses that were open for such customers; the hard, dry, frosty rime with which the air was charged (the wind had already beaten it into every crevice), and which lashed my face like a steel whip." CS/HT 1

—*fog:* "It was cold, bleak, biting weather: foggy withal: and [Scrooge] could hear the people in the court outside, go wheezing up and down, beating their hands upon their breasts, and stamping their feet upon the pavement stones to warm them. The city clocks had only just gone three, but it was quite dark already—it had not been light all day—and candles were flaring in the windows of the neighbouring offices, like ruddy smears upon the palpable brown air. The fog came pouring in at every chink and keyhole, and was so dense without, that although the court was of the narrowest, the houses opposite were mere phantoms. To see the dingy cloud come drooping down, obscuring everything, one might have thought that Nature lived hard by, and was brewing on a large scale." CC 1

—*thaw:* "A thaw, by all that is miserable! The frost is completely broken up. You look down the long perspective of Oxford Street, the gas-lights mournfully reflected on the wet pavement, and can discern no speck in the road to encourage the belief that there is a cab or a coach to be had—the very coachmen have gone home in despair.

"The cold sleet is drizzling down with that gentle regularity, which betokens a duration of four-and-twenty hours at least; the damp hangs upon the house-tops and lamp-posts, and clings to you like an invisible cloak. The water is 'coming in' in every area, the pipes have burst, the water-butts are running over; the kennels seem to be doing matches against time, pump-handles descend of their own accord, horses in market-carts fall down, and there's no one to help them up again, policemen look as if they had been carefully sprinkled with powdered glass; here and there a milk-woman trudges slowly along, with a bit of list round each foot to keep her from slipping; boys who 'don't sleep in the house,' and are not allowed much sleep out of it, can't wake their masters by thundering at the shop-door, and cry with the cold—the compound of ice, snow, and water on the pavement, is a couple of inches thick—nobody ventures to walk fast to keep himself warm, and nobody could succeed in keeping himself warm if he did." ¶SB/EC

And see The Thames—*at night in winter*

In Seventeen-Eighty

—*chairmen:* "Long stands of hackney-chairs and groups of chairmen, compared with whom the coachmen of our day are gentle and polite, obstructed the way and filled the air with clamour. . . . The solitary passenger was startled by the chairmen's cry of 'By your leave there!' as two came trotting past him with their empty vehicle—carried backwards to show its being disengaged—

and hurried to the nearest stand." BR 16

—crime and retribution: " . . . heavy stage-coaches and scarce heavier waggons were lumbering slowly towards the city, the coachmen, guard, and passengers, armed to the teeth, and the coach—a day or so perhaps behind its time, but that was nothing—despoiled by highwaymen; who made no scruple to attack, alone and single handed, a whole caravan of goods and men, and sometimes shot a passenger or two, and were sometimes shot themselves, as the case might be.

"On the morrow, rumours of this new act of daring on the road yielded matter for a few hours' conversation through the town, and a Public Progress of some fine gentleman (half drunk) to Tyburn, dressed in the newest fashion, and damning the ordinary with unspeakable gallantry and grace, furnished to the populace, at once a pleasant excitement and a wholesome and profound example." BR 16

—drinking establishments: ". . . night-cellars, indicated by a little stream of light crossing the pavement, and stretching out half-way into the road, and by the stifled roar of voices from below, yawned for the reception and entertainment of the most abandoned of both sexes . . . . " BR 16

—link-boys [torch-bearing street guides]: " . . . under every shed and bulk small groups of link-boys gamed away the earnings of the day; or one more weary than the rest, gave way to sleep, and let the fragment of his torch fall hissing on the puddled ground." BR 16

—night watch: "Then there was the watch with staff and lantern crying the hour, and the kind of weather; and those who woke up at his voice and turned them round in bed, were glad to hear it rained, or snowed, or blew, or froze, for very comfort's sake." BR 16

—running footmen; their recreation: "It was not unusual for these running gentry, who carried it with a very high hand, to quarrel in the servants' hall while waiting for their masters and mistresses; and, falling to blows either there or in the street without, to strew the place of skirmish with hair-powder, fragments of bag-wigs, and scattered nosegays. Gaming, the vice which ran so high among all classes (the fashion being of course set by the upper), was generally the cause of these disputes; for cards and dice were as openly used, and worked as much mischief, and yielded as much excitement below stairs, as above." BR 16

—shop signs: "Some of the shops, especially those to the eastward of Temple Bar, still adhered to the old practice of hanging out a sign; and the creaking and swinging of these boards in their iron frames on windy nights, formed a strange and mournful concert for the ears of those who lay awake in bed or hurried through the streets." BR 16

—streets, and crime: "They were, one and all, from the broadest and best to the narrowest and least frequented, very dark. The oil and cotton lamps, though regularly trimmed twice or thrice in the long winter nights, burnt feebly at the best; and at a late hour, when they were unassisted by the lamps and candles in the shops, cast but a narrow track of doubtful light upon the footway, leaving the projecting doors and house-fronts in the deepest gloom.

"Many of the courts and lanes were left in total darkness; those of the meaner sort, where one glimmering light twinkled for a score of houses, being favoured in no slight degree. Even in these places, the inhabitants had often good reason for extinguishing their lamp as soon as it was lighted; and the watch being utterly inefficient and powerless to prevent them, they did so at their pleasure.

"Thus, in the lightest thoroughfares, there was at every turn some obscure and dangerous spot whither a thief might fly for shelter, and few would care to follow; and the city being belted round by fields, green lanes, waste grounds, and lonely roads, dividing it at that time from the suburbs that have joined it since, escape, even where the pursuit was hot, was rendered easy.

"It is no wonder that with these favouring circumstances in full and constant operation, street robberies, often accompanied by cruel wounds, and not unfrequently by loss of life, should have been of nightly occurrence in the very heart of London, or that quiet folks should have had great dread of traversing its streets after the shops were closed.

"It was not unusual for those who wended home alone at midnight, to keep the middle of the road, the better to guard against surprise from lurking footpads; few would venture to repair at a late hour to Kentish Town or Hampstead, or even to Kensington or Chelsea, unarmed and unattended; while he who had been loudest and most valiant at the supper-table or the tavern, and had but a mile or so to go, was glad to fee a link-boy to escort him home." ¶BR 16

—*transportation of the rich:* "Many a private chair, too, inclosing some fine lady, monstrously hooped and furbelowed, and preceded by running foot-men bearing flambeaux—for which extinguishers are yet suspended before the doors of a few houses of the better sort—made the way gay and light as it danced along, and darker and more dismal when it had passed." BR 16

Streets

—*before dawn:* "There is an air of cold, solitary desolation about the noiseless streets which we are accustomed to see thronged at other times by a busy, eager crowd, and over the quiet, closely-shut buildings, which throughout the day are swarming with life and bustle, that is very impressive.

" . . . The drunken, the dissipated, and the wretched have disappeared; the more sober and orderly part of the population have not yet awakened to the labours of the day, and the stillness of death is over the streets; its very hue seems to be imparted to them, cold and lifeless as they look in the grey, sombre light of daybreak. The coach-stands in the larger thoroughfares are deserted; the night-houses are closed; and the chosen promenades of profligate misery are empty." SB/SM

—*at dawn:* "An hour wears away; the spires of the churches and roofs of the principal buildings are faintly tinged with the light of the rising sun; and the streets, by almost imperceptible degrees, begin to resume their bustle and animation. Market-carts roll slowly along: the sleepy waggoner impatiently urging on his tired horses, or vainly endeavouring to awaken the boy, who, luxuriously stretched on the top of the fruit-baskets, forgets, in happy oblivion, his long-cherished curiosity to behold the wonders of London." SB/SM

—*gloomy:* "It was one of the parasite streets [near Park Lane]; long, regular, narrow, dull, and gloomy; like a brick and mortar funeral." LD i 27

—*at night:* "But the streets of London, to be beheld in the very height of their glory, should be seen on a dark, dull, murky winter's night, when there is just enough damp gently stealing down to make the pavement greasy, without cleansing it of any of its impurities; and when the heavy, lazy mist, which hangs over every object, makes the gas-lamps look brighter, and the brilliantly lighted shops more splendid, from the contrast they present to the darkness around. All the people who are at home on such a night as this, seem disposed to make themselves as snug and comfortable as possible; and the passengers in the streets have excellent reason to envy the fortunate individuals who are seated by their own firesides." SB/SN

"The streets in the vicinity of the Marsh Gate and Victoria Theatre present an appearance of dirt and discomfort on such a night, which the groups who lounge about them in no degree tend to diminish. Even the little block-tin temple sacred to baked potatoes, surmounted by a splendid design in variegated lamps, looks less gay than usual; and as to the kidney-pie stand, its glory has quite departed." SB/SN

—*wealthy:* "It is a dull street under the best conditions; where the two long rows of houses stare at each other with that severity, that half-a-dozen of its greatest mansions seem to have been slowly stared into stone, rather than originally built in that material. It is a street of such dismal grandeur, so determined not to condescend to liveliness, that the doors and windows hold a gloomy state of their own in black paint and dust, and the echoing mews behind have a dry and massive appearance, as if they were reserved to stable the stone chargers of noble statues. Complicated garnish of iron-work entwines itself over the flights of steps in this awful street; and, from these petrified bowers, extinguishers for obsolete flambeaux gasp at the upstart gas." BH 48

The Thames

—*at dawn:* "The winking lights upon the bridges were already pale, the coming sun was like a marsh of fire on the horizon. The river, still dark and mysterious, was spanned by bridges that were turning coldly grey, with here and there at top a warm touch from the burning in the sky.

"As I [Pip] looked along the clustered roofs, with church towers and spires shooting into the unusually clear air, the sun rose up, and a veil seemed to be drawn from the river, and millions of sparkles burst out upon its waters. From me, too, a veil seemed to be drawn, and I felt strong and well." ¶GE 53

—from London center: "The wheels rolled on, and rolled down by the Monument, and by the Tower, and by the Docks; down by Ratcliffe, and by Rotherhithe; down by where accumulated scum of humanity seemed to be washed from higher grounds, like so much moral sewage, and to be pausing until its own weight forced it over the bank and sunk it in the river. In and out among vessels that seemed to have got ashore, and houses that seemed to have got afloat—among bowsprits staring into windows, and windows staring into ships—the wheels rolled on, until they stopped at a dark corner, river-washed and otherwise not washed at all, where the boy [Charley Hexam] alighted and opened the door." OMF i 3

—the Middlesex shore: "Years before the year one thousand eight hundred and sixty-one, people had left off taking boat at Break-Neck-Stairs, and watermen had ceased to ply there. The slimy little causeway had dropped into the river by a slow process of suicide, and two or three stumps of piles and a rusty iron mooring-ring were all that remained of the departed Break-Neck glories.

"Sometimes, indeed, a laden coal barge would bump itself into the place, and certain laborious heavers, seemingly mud-engendered, would arise, deliver the cargo in the neighbourhood, shove off, and vanish; but at most times the only commerce of Break-Neck-Stairs arose out of the conveyance of casks and bottles, both full and empty, both to and from the cellars of Wilding and Co., Wine Merchants.

"Even that commerce was but occasional, and through three-fourths of its rising tides the dirty indecorous drab of a river would come solitarily oozing and lapping at the rusty ring, as if it had heard of the Doge and the Adriatic, and wanted to be married to the great conserver of its filthiness, the Right Honourable the Lord Mayor." ¶CS/NT 1

—at night: "But the river had an awful look, the buildings on the banks were muffled in black shrouds, and the reflected lights seemed to originate deep in the water, as if the spectres of suicides were holding them to show where they went down. The wild moon and clouds were as restless as an evil conscience in a tumbled bed, and the very shadow of the immensity of London seemed to lie oppressively upon the river." UT/NW

—in winter: "A very dark night it was, and bitter cold; the east wind blowing bleak, and bringing with it stinging particles from marsh, and moor, and fen—from the Great Desert and Old Egypt, may be. Some of the component parts of the sharp-edged vapour that came flying up the Thames at London might be mummy-dust, dry atoms from the Temple at Jerusalem, camels' foot-prints, crocodiles' hatching-places, loosened grains of expression from the visages of blunt-nosed sphynxes, waifs and strays from caravans of turbaned merchants, vegetation from jungles, frozen snow from the Himalayas. O! It was very very dark upon the Thames, and it was bitter bitter cold." RP/DT

"We had been lying here some half an hour. With our backs to the wind, it is true; but the wind being in a determined temper blew straight through us, and would not take the trouble to go round. I would have boarded a fireship to get into action . . . . " RP/DT

"Every colour but black seemed to have departed from the world. The air was black, the water was black, the barges and hulks were black, the piles were black, the buildings were black, the shadows were only a deeper shade of black upon a black ground. Here and there, a coal fire in an iron cresset blazed upon a wharf; but one knew that it too had been black a little while ago, and would be black again soon. Uncomfortable rushes of water suggestive of gurgling and drowning, ghostly rattlings of iron chains, dismal clankings of discordant engines, formed the music that accompanied the dip of our oars and their rattling in the rullocks. Even the noises had a black sound to me—as the trumpet sounded red to the blind man." RP/DT

—ominous: "[Inspector Bucket] stood up to look over the parapet; he alighted, and went back after a shadowy female figure that flitted past us; and he gazed into the profound black pit of water, with a face that made my heart die within me. The river had a fearful look, so overcast and secret, creeping away so fast between the low flat lines of shore: so heavy with indistinct and awful shapes, both of substance and shadow: so deathlike and mysterious. I have seen it many times since then, by sunlight and by moonlight, but never free from the impres-

sions of that journey. In my memory, the lights upon the bridge are always burning dim; the cutting wind is eddying round the homeless woman whom we pass; the monotonous wheels are whirling on; and the light of the carriage-lamps reflected back, looks palely in upon me—a face, rising out of the dread water." BH 57

—on the river: "It was flood tide when Daniel Quilp sat himself down in the wherry to cross to the opposite shore. A fleet of barges were coming lazily on, some sideways, some head first, some stern first; all in a wrong-headed, dogged, obstinate way, bumping up against the larger craft, running under the bows of steamboats, getting into every kind of nook and corner where they had no business, and being crunched on all sides like so many walnut-shells; while each with its pair of long sweeps struggling and splashing in the water looked like some lumbering fish in pain. In some of the vessels at anchor all hands were busily engaged in coiling ropes, spreading out sails to dry, taking in or discharging their cargoes; in others no life was visible but two or three tarry boys, and perhaps a barking dog running to and fro upon the deck or scrambling up to look over the side and bark the louder for the view.

"Coming slowly on through the forest of masts was a great steam ship, beating the water in short impatient strokes with her heavy paddles as though she wanted room to breathe, and advancing in her huge bulk like a sea monster among the minnows of the Thames. On either hand were long black tiers of colliers; between them vessels slowly working out of harbour with sails glistening in the sun, and creaking noise on board, re-echoed from a hundred quarters. The water and all upon it was in active motion, dancing and buoyant and bubbling up; while the old grey Tower and piles of building on the shore, with many a church-spire shooting up between, looked coldly on, and seemed to disdain their chafing, restless neighbour." ¶OCS 5

"I like to watch the great ships standing out to sea or coming home richly laden, the active little steam-tugs confidently puffing with them to and from the sea-horizon, the fleet of barges that seem to have plucked their brown and russet sails from the ripe trees in the landscape, the heavy old colliers, light in ballast, floundering down before the tide, the light screw barks and schooners imperiously holding a straight course while the others patiently tack and go about, the yachts with their tiny hulls and great white sheets of canvas, the little sailing-boats bobbing to and fro on their errands of pleasure or business, and—as it is the nature of little people to do—making a prodigious fuss about their small affairs." UT/CD

"Again among the tiers of shipping, in and out, avoiding rusty chain-cables, frayed hempen hawsers, and bobbing buoys, sinking for the moment floating broken baskets, scattering floating chips of wood and shaving, cleaving floating scum of coal, in and out, under the figure-head of the John of Sunderland making a speech to the winds (as is done by many Johns), and the Betsy of Yarmouth with a firm formality of bosom and her knobby eyes starting two inches out of her head; in and out, hammers going in shipbuilders' yards, saws going at timber, clashing engines going at things unknown, pumps going in leaky ships, capstans going, ships going out to sea, and unintelligible sea-creatures roaring curses over the bulwarks at respondent lightermen; in and out—out at last upon the clearer river, where the ships' boys might take their fenders in, no longer fishing in troubled waters with them over the side, and where the festooned sails might fly out to the wind." GE 14

"They were all shivering, and everything about them seemed to be shivering; the river itself, craft, rigging, sails, such early smoke as there yet was on the shore. Black with wet, and altered to the eye by white patches of hail and sleet, the huddled buildings looked lower than usual, as if they were cowering, and had shrunk with the cold. Very little life was to be seen on either bank, windows and doors were shut, and the staring black and white letters upon wharves and warehouses 'looked . . . like the inscriptions over the graves of dead businesses.'

"As they glided slowly on, keeping under the shore, and sneaking in and out among the shipping, by back-alleys of water, in a pilfering way that seemed to be their boatman's normal manner of progression, all the objects among which they crept were so huge in contrast with their wretched boat as to threaten to crush it.

"Not a ship's hull, with its rusty iron links of cable run out of hawse-holes long discoloured with the iron's rusty tears, but seemed to be there with a fell intention.

Not a figurehead but had the menacing look of bursting forward to run them down. Not a sluice-gate, or a painted scale upon a post or wall, showing the depth of water, but seemed to hint, like the dreadfully facetious Wolf in bed in Grandmamma's cottage, 'That's to drown *you* in, my dears!' Not a lumbering black barge, with its cracked and blistered side impending over them, but seemed to suck at the river with a thirst for sucking them under.

"And everything so vaunted the spoiling influences of water—discoloured copper, rotten wood, honey-combed stone, green dank deposit—that the after-consequences of being crushed, sucked under, and drawn down, looked as ugly to the imagination as the main event." ¶OMF i 14

And see Neighbourhoods—*Adelphi Terrace*

—sometimes inconvenient: "Sir Barnet and Lady Skettles . . . resided in a pretty villa at Fulham, on the banks of the Thames; which was one of the most desirable residences in the world when a rowing-match happened to be going past, but had its little inconveniences at other times, among which may be enumerated the occasional appearance of the river in the drawing-room, and the contemporaneous disappearance of the lawn and shrubbery." DS 24

—the Wharves: "There [the steam-boats] lay, alongside of each other; hard and fast for ever, to all appearance, but designing to get out somehow, and quite confident of doing it; and in that faith shoals of passengers, and heaps of luggage, were proceeding hurriedly on board.

"Little steam-boats dashed up and down the stream incessantly. Tiers upon tiers of vessels, scores of masts, labyrinths of tackle, idle sails, splashing oars, gliding row-boats, lumbering barges, sunken piles, with ugly lodgings for the water-rat within their mud-discoloured nooks; church steeples, warehouses, house-roofs, arches, bridges, men and women, children, casks, cranes, boxes, horses, coaches, idlers, and hard-labourers: there they were, all jumbled up together, any summer morning, far beyond Tom's power of separation.

"In the midst of all this turmoil, there was an incessant roar from every packet's funnel, which quite expressed and carried out the uppermost emotion of the scene. They all appeared to be perspiring and bothering themselves, exactly as their passengers did; they never left off fretting and chafing, in their own hoarse manner, once; but were always panting out, without any stops, 'Come along do make haste I'm very nervous come along oh good gracious we shall never get there how late you are do make haste I'm off directly come along!'

"Even when they had left off, and had got safely out into the current, on the smallest provocation they began again: for the bravest packet of them all, being stopped by some entanglement in the river, would immediately begin to fume and pant afresh, 'Oh here's a stoppage what's the matter do go on there I'm in a hurry it's done on purpose did you ever oh my goodness *do* go on there!' and so, in a state of mind bordering on distraction, would be last seen drifting slowly through the mist into the summer light beyond, that made it red." MC 48

Times of Day

—daybreak: "The town was glad with morning light; places that had shown ugly and distrustful all night long, now wore a smile; and sparkling sun-beams dancing on chamber windows, and twinkling through blind and curtain before sleepers' eyes, shed light even into dreams, and chased away the shadows of the night.

"Birds in hot rooms, covered up close and dark, felt it was morning, and chafed and grew restless in their little cells; bright-eyed mice crept back to their tiny homes and nestled timidly together; the sleek house-cat, forgetful of her prey, sat winking at the rays of sun starting through keyhole and cranny in the door, and longed for her stealthy run and warm sleek bask outside.

"The nobler beasts confined in dens stood motionless behind their bars, and gazed on fluttering boughs and sunshine peeping through some little window, with eyes in which old forests gleamed—then stopped and gazed again. Men in their dungeons stretched their cramped cold limbs and cursed the stone that no bright sky could warm. The flowers that sleep by night, opened their gentle eyes and turned them to the day. The light, creation's mind, was everywhere, and all things owned its power." ¶OCS 15

"Soon, now, the distant line on the horizon brightened, the darkness faded, the sun rose red and glorious, and the chimney stacks and gables of the ancient building gleamed in the clear air, which turned the smoke and vapour of the city into a cloud of gold. The very sun-dial in his shady corner, where the wind was used to spin with such un-windy constancy, shook off the finer particles of snow that had accumulated on his dull old face in the night, and looked out at the little white wreaths eddying round and round him. Doubtless some blind groping of the morning made its way down into the forgotten crypt so cold and earthy, where the Norman arches were half buried in the ground, and stirred the dull deep sap in the lazy vegetation hanging to the walls, and quickened the slow principle of life within the little world of wonderful and delicate creation which existed there, with some faint knowledge that the sun was up." HM 3

And see The Thames—*at dawn*

—*dusk*

—*on a Sunday:* "It was a Sunday evening in London, gloomy, close and stale. Maddening church bells of all degrees of dissonance, sharp and flat, cracked and clear, fast and slow, made the brick-and-mortar echoes hideous. Melancholy streets in a penitential garb of soot, steeped the souls of the people who were condemned to look at them out of windows, in dire despondency. In every thoroughfare, up almost every alley, and down almost every turning, some doleful bell was throbbing, jerking, tolling, as if the Plague were in the city and the dead-carts were going round." LD ii 3

—*on a workday:* "A grey dusty withered evening in London city has not a hopeful aspect. The closed warehouses and offices have an air of death about them, and the national dread of colour has an air of mourning. The towers and steeples of the many house-encompassed churches, dark and dingy as the sky that seems descending on them, are no relief to the general gloom; a sundial on a church-wall has the look, in its useless black shade, of having failed in its business enterprise and stopped payment for ever; melancholy waifs and strays of housekeepers and porters sweep melancholy waifs and strays of papers and pins into the kennels, and other more melancholy waifs and strays explore them, searching and stooping and poking for anything to sell. The set of humanity outward from the City is as a set of prisoners departing from gaol, and dismal Newgate seems quite as fit a stronghold for the mighty Lord Mayor as his own state-dwelling.

"On such an evening, when the City grit gets into the hair and eyes and skin, and when the fallen leaves of the few unhappy City trees grind down in corners under wheels of wind . . . ." OMF ii 15

—*evening in summer:* "It was one of those summer evenings when there is no greater darkness than a long twilight. The vista of street and bridge was plain to see, and the sky was serene and beautiful. People stood and sat at their doors, playing with children and enjoying the evening; numbers were walking for air; the worry of the day had almost worried itself out, and few but themselves were hurried. As [Mrs Clennam and Little Dorrit] crossed the bridge, the clear steeples of the many churches looked as if they had advanced out of the murk that usually enshrouded them and come much nearer. The smoke that rose into the sky had lost its dingy hue and taken a brightness upon it. The beauties of the sunset had not faded from the long light films of cloud that lay at peace in the horizon. From a radiant centre over the whole length and breadth of the tranquil firmament, great shoots of light streamed among the early stars, like signs of the blessed later covenant of peace and hope that changed the crown of thorns into a glory." LD ii 31

—*morning:* "A fairer morning never shone. From the roofs and upper stories of these buildings, the spires of city churches and the great cathedral dome were visible, rising up beyond the prison, into the blue sky, and clad in the colour of light summer clouds, and showing in the clear atmosphere their every scrap of tracery and fret-work, and every niche and loophole. All was brightness and promise . . . . " BR 77

—*at night:* "A dark and dreary night; people nestling in their beds or circling late about the fire; Want, colder than Charity, shivering at the street corners; church-towers humming with the faint vibration of their own tongues, but newly resting from the ghostly preachment 'One!' The earth covered with a sable pall as for the burial of yesterday; the clumps of dark trees, its giant plumes of funeral feathers, waving sadly to and fro; all hushed, all noiseless, and in deep repose, save the swift clouds that skim across the moon, and the cautious wind, as, creeping after them upon the ground, it stops to listen, and goes rustling on, and stops again, and follows, like a savage on the trail." MC 15

"A very quiet night. When the moon shines very brilliantly, a solitude and stillness seem to proceed from her, that influence even crowded places full of life. Not only is it a still night on dusty high roads and on hill-summits, whence a wide expanse of country may be seen in repose, quieter and quieter as it spreads away into a fringe of trees against the sky, with the grey ghost of a bloom upon them; not only is it a still night in gardens and in woods, and on the river where the water-meadows are fresh and green, and the stream sparkles on among pleasant islands, murmuring weirs, and whispering rushes; not only does the stillness attend it as it flows where houses cluster thick, where many bridges are reflected in it, where wharves and shipping make it black and awful, where it winds from these disfigurements through marshes whose grim beacons stand like skeletons washed ashore, where it expands through the bolder region of rising grounds, rich in corn-field, wind-mill and steeple, and where it mingles with the ever-heaving sea; not only is it a still night on the deep, and on the shore where the watcher stands to see the ship with her spread wings cross the path of light that appears to be presented to only him; but even on this stranger's wilderness of London there is some rest. Its steeples and towers, and its one great dome, grow more ethereal; its smoke housetops lose their grossness, in the pale effulgence; the noises that arise from the streets are fewer and are softened, and the footsteps on the pavements pass more tranquilly away." BH 48

—Little Dorrit's party: "It was a chill dark night, with a damp wind blowing . . . . 'In only five hours and a half,' said Little Dorrit, 'We shall be able to go home' . . . . While the street was empty and silent, Little Dorrit was not afraid; but when she heard a footstep at a distance, or saw a moving shadow among the street lamps, she was startled . . . they would wander about a little, and come back again.

" . . . . At last, in the dead of the night, when the street was very still indeed, Little Dorrit laid [Maggy's] heavy head upon her bosom, and soothed her to sleep. And thus she sat at the gate, as it were alone; looking up at the stars, and seeing the clouds pass over them in their wild flight—which was the dance at Little Dorrit's party . . . .

"Thee o'clock, and half-past three, and they had passed over London Bridge. They had heard the rush of the tide against obstacles; and looked down, awed, through the dark vapour on the river; had seen little spots of lighted water where the bridge lamps were reflected, shinng like demon eyes, with a terrible fascination in them for guilt and misery. They had shrunk past homeless people, lying coiled up in nooks. They had run from drunkards. They had started from slinking men, whistling and signing to one another at bye corners, or running away at full speed. Though everywhere the leader and the guide, Little Dorrit, happy for once in her youthful appearance, feigned to cling to and rely upon Maggy. And more than once some voice, from among a knot of brawling or prowling figures in their path, had called out to the rest, to 'let the woman and the child go by!'" LD i 14

And see London—*streets; and* The Thames

Weather

—dreary: "It was a sombre day, and drops of chill rain fell at intervals. It was one of those colourless days when everything looks heavy and harsh. The houses frowned at us, the dust rose at us, the smoke swooped at us, nothing made any compromise about itself, or wore a softened aspect. I fancied my beautiful girl quite out of place in the rugged streets; and I thought there were more funerals passing along the dismal pavements, than I had ever seen before." BH 51

—fine: "Monday was a fine day, Tuesday was delightful, Wednesday was equal to either, and Thursday was finer than ever; four successive fine days in London! Hackney-coachmen became revolutionary, and crossing-sweepers began to doubt the existence of a First Cause. The *Morning Herald* informed its readers that an old woman in Camden Town had been heard to say that the fineness of the season was 'unprecedented in the memory of the oldest inhabitant;' . . . ." SB/BC

—fog: "Fog everywhere. Fog up the river, where it flows among green aits and meadows; fog down the river, where it rolls defiled among the tiers of shipping, and the waterside pollutions of a great (and dirty) city. Fog on the Essex marshes, fog on the Kentish heights. Fog creeping into the cabooses of collier-brigs; fog lying out on the yards, and hovering in the rigging of great ships; fog drooping on the gunwales of barges and small boats. Fog in the eyes and throats of ancient Greenwich pensioners, wheezing by the firesides of their wards; fog in the stem and bowl of the afternoon pipe of the wrathful skipper, down

in his close cabin; fog cruelly pinching the toes and fingers of his shivering little 'prentice boy on deck. Chance people on the bridges peeping over the parapets into a nether sky of fog, with fog all round them, as if they were up in a balloon, and hanging in the misty clouds." BH 1

—and frost: "The fog and frost so hung about the black old gateway of the house, that it seemed as if the Genius of the Weather sat in mournful meditation on the threshold." CC 1

And see Seasons—*winter—fog*

—foul: "It had rained, without a moment's cessation, since eight o'clock; everybody that passed up Cheapside, and down Cheapside, looked wet, cold, and dirty. All sorts of forgotten and long-concealed umbrellas had been put into requisition. Cabs whisked about, with the 'fare' as carefully boxed up behind two glazed calico curtains as any mysterious picture in any one of Mrs Radcliffe's castles; omnibus horses smoked like steam-engines; nobody thought of 'standing up' under doorways or arches; they were painfully convinced it was a hopeless case; and so everybody went hastily along, jumbling and jostling, and swearing and perspiring, and slipping about, like amateur skaters behind wooden chairs on the Serpentine on a frosty Sunday." SB/BC

—particular: "The sky was gloomy, and the shortest streets were choked up with a dingy mist, half thawed, half frozen, whose heavier particles descended in a shower of sooty atoms, as if all the chimneys in Great Britain had, by one consent, caught fire, and were blazing away to their dear hearts' content." CC 3

"My aunt . . . could not relent towards the London smoke, which, she said, 'peppered everything.' A complete revolution, in which Peggotty bore a prominent part, was effected in every corner of my rooms, in regard of this pepper . . . . " DC 35

" . . . I asked [William Guppy] whether there was a great fire anywhere? For the streets were so full of dense brown smoke that scarcely anything was to be seen.

"'O dear no, miss,' he said. 'This is a London particular.'

"I had never heard of such a thing.

"'A fog, miss,' said the young gentleman." BH 3

"It was a foggy day in London, and the fog was heavy and dark. Animate London, with smarting eyes and irritated lungs, was blinking, wheezing, and choking; inanimate London was a sooty spectre, divided in purpose between being visible and invisible, and so being wholly neither. Gaslights flared in the shops with a haggard and unblest air, as knowing themselves to be night-creatures that had no business abroad under the sun; while the sun itself, when it was for a few moments dimly indicated through circling eddies of fog, showed as if it had gone out, and were collapsing flat and cold.

"Even in the surrounding country it was a foggy day, but there the fog was grey, whereas in London it was, at about the boundary line, dark yellow, and a little within it brown, and then browner, and then browner, until at the heart of the City—which call Saint Mary Axe—it was rusty-black. From any point of the high ridge of land northward, it might have been discerned that the loftiest buildings made an occasional struggle to get their heads above the foggy sea, and especially that the great dome of Saint Paul's seemed to die hard; but this was not perceivable in the streets at their feet, where the whole metropolis was a heap of vapour charged with muffled sound of wheels, and enfolding a gigantic catarrh." ¶OMF iii 1

"The appointed morning was a raw morning in the month of November. There was a dense brown fog in Piccadilly, and it became positively black and in the last degree oppressive East of Temple Bar. I found the passages and staircases of the Court-House flaringly lighted with gas, and the Court itself similarly illuminated . . . I looked about the Court as well as I could through the cloud of fog and breath that was heavy in it. I noticed the black vapour hanging like a murky curtain outside the great windows, and I noticed the stifled sound of wheels on the straw or tan that was littered in the street . . . . " CS/DM 2

—effect on manufacturing: "'I have also heard that the atmosphere of London is positively detrimental to the manufacture of silk. Is that so?'

"'Why, sir . . . the two-days' fog we had in December last, was a dead loss to me of one hundred pounds. The blacks (London genuine particular) got into the white satins, despite the best precautions of the workpeople, and put them into an ugly, foxy, unsaleable half-mourning, sir. They would not even take a dye, decently. I had to send down, express, to our Suffolk branch to supply the deficiency; and the white satins, partly woven there on the same days, came up as white as driven snow.'" HWC/S

—smoke: " . . . smoke, which is the London ivy, had so wreathed itself round Peffer's name, and clung to his dwelling-place, that the affectionate parasite quite overpowered the parent tree." BH 10

—snow: "There was a dense fog too: as if it were a city in the clouds, which they had been travelling to all night up a magic beanstalk; and there was a thick crust upon the pavement like oil-cake: which, one of the outsides (mad, no doubt) said to another (his keeper, of course), was Snow." MC 8

—wind: "I wonder why metropolitan gales always blow so hard at Walworth. I cannot imagine what Walworth has done, to bring such windy punishment upon itself, as I never fail to find recorded in the newspapers when the wind has blown at all hard.

"Brixton seems to have something on its conscience; Peckham suffers more than a virtuous Peckham might be supposed to deserve; the howling neighbourhood of Deptford figures largely in the accounts of the ingenious gentlemen who are out in every wind that blows, and to whom it is an ill high wind that blows no good; but, there can hardly be any Walworth left by this time. It must surely be blown away. I have read of more chimney-stacks and house-copings coming down with terrific smashes at Walworth, and of more sacred edifices being nearly (not quite) blown out to sea from the same accursed locality . . . .

"I wonder why people are always blown into the Surrey Canal, and into no other piece of water! Why do people get up early and go out in groups, to be blown into the Surrey Canal? Do they say to one another, 'Welcome death, so that we get into the newspapers?" Even that would be an insufficient explanation, because even then they might sometimes put themselves in the way of being blown into the Regent's Canal, instead of always saddling Surrey for the field. Some nameless policeman, too, is constantly, on the slightest provocation, getting himself blown into this same Surrey Canal. Will **Sir Richard Mayne** see to it, and restrain that weak-minded and feeble-bodied constable?" ¶UT/RT

—and wet: "It was wretched weather; stormy and wet, stormy and wet; mud, mud, mud, deep in all the streets. Day after day, a vast heavy veil had been driving over London from the East, and it drove still, as if in the East there were an eternity of cloud and wind. So furious had been the gusts, that high buildings in town had had the lead stripped off their roofs; and in the country, trees had been torn up, and sails of windmills carried away; and gloomy accounts had come in from the coast, of shipwreck and death. Violent blasts of rain had accompanied these rages of wind, and the day just closed as I sat down to read had been the worst of all." GE 39

The Thriving City of Eden as it Appeared in Fact MC
[Cairo, Illinois]

The Rest of the World

"We Englishmen are Very Proud of our Constitution, Sir. It Was Bestowed Upon Us by Providence. No Other Country is so Favoured as This Country." "And other countries," said the foreign gentleman. "They do how?" "They do, Sir," returned Mr Podsnap, gravely shaking his head; "they do—I am sorry to be obliged to say it—as they *do. So it is. It was the Charter of the Land. This island was Blest, Sir, to the Direct Exclusion of such Other Countries as—as there may happen to be."*

[OMF i 11]

"What's the water in French, sir?'" "L'Eau," *replied Nicholas. "Ah!" said Mr Lillyvick, shaking his head mournfully,"I thought as much. Lo, eh? I don't think anything of that language—nothing at all."*

NN 16

America and Americans

—ablutions: "The washing accommodations were primitive. There was a tin ladle chained to the deck, with which every gentleman who thought it necessary to cleanse himself (many were superior to this weakness), fished the dirty water out of the canal, and poured it into a tin basin, secured in like manner. There was also a jack-towel. And, hanging up before a little looking-glass in the bar, in the immediate vicinity of the bread and cheese and biscuits, were a public comb and hairbrush." AN 10

"In all modes of travelling, the American customs, with reference to the means of personal cleanliness and wholesome ablution, are extremely negligent and filthy; and I strongly incline to the belief that a considerable amount of illness is referable to this cause." AN 11

" . . . every gentleman on board appeared to have had a difference with his laundress, and to have left off washing himself in early youth." MC 34

—accents: "I may premise that the word Prairie is variously pronounced *paraaer, parearer,* and *paroarer.* The latter mode of pronunciation is perhaps the most in favour." AN 13

"'You have brought, I see sir,' [Colonel Diver] said, turning round towards Martin [Chuzzlewit], and resting his chin on the top of his stick, 'the usual amount of misery and poverty and ignorance and crime, to be located in the bosom of the great Republic. Well, sir! let 'em come on in ship-loads from the old country. When vessels are about to founder, the rats are said to leave 'em. There is considerable of truth, I find, in that remark.'

"'The old ship will keep afloat a year or two longer yet, perhaps,' said Martin with a smile, partly occasioned by what the gentleman said, and partly by his manner of saying it, which was odd enough, for he emphasised all the small words and syllables in his discourse, and left the others to take care of themselves: as if he thought the larger parts of speech could be trusted alone, but the little ones required to be constantly looked after." MC 16

"Another time, a merry, wideawake American gent had tried the sawdust and spit it out, and had tried the Sherry and spit that out, and had tried in vain to sustain exhausted natur upon Butter-Scotch . . . when, as the bell was ringing and he paid Our Missis, he says, very loud and good-tempered: 'I tell Yew what 'tis, ma'arm. I la'af. Theer! I la'af. I Dew. I oughter ha' seen most things, for I hail from the Onlimited side of the Atlantic Ocean, and I haive travelled right slick over the Limited, head on through Jeerusalemm and the East, and likeways France and Italy, Europe Old World, and am now upon the track to the Chief Europian Village; but such an Institution as Yew, and Yewer young ladies, and Yewer fixin's solid and liquid, afore the glorious Tarnal I never did see yet!

"'And if I hain't found the eighth wonder of monarchical Creation, in finding Yew, and Yewer young ladies, and Yewer fixin's solid and liquid, all as aforesaid, established in a country where the people air not absolute Loonaticks, I am Extra Double Darned with a Nip and Frizzle to the innermostest grit! Wheerfur—Theer!—I la'af! I Dew, ma'arm. I la'af!' And so he went, stamping and shaking his sides, along the platform all the way to his own compartment." ¶CS/MJ 3

—aristocracy: "'The New York Rowdy Journal, sir,' resumed the colonel [Diver], 'is, as I expect you know, the organ of our aristocracy in this city.'

"'Oh! there *is* an aristocracy here, then? said Martin [Chuzzlewit]. 'Of what is it composed?'

"'Of intelligence, sir,' replied the colonel; 'of intelligence and virtue. And of their necessary consequence in this republic. Dollars, sir.'

"Martin was very glad to hear this, feeling well assured that if intelligence and virtue led, as a matter of course, to the acquisition of dollars, he would speedily become a great capitalist." MC 16

—arts and letters: "Once or twice . . . Martin [Chuzzlewit] asked . . . about the national poets, the theatre, literature, and the arts. But the information which these gentlemen were in a condition to give him on such topics, did not extend beyond the effusions of such master-spirits of the time as Colonel Diver, Mr Jefferson Brick, and others; renowned, as it appeared, for excellence in the achievement of a peculiar style of broadside-essay called 'a screamer.'

"'We are a busy people, sir,' said one of the captains, who was from the West, 'and have no time for reading mere notions. We don't mind 'em if they come to us in newspapers along with almighty strong stuff of another sort, but darn your books.'

"Here the general, who appeared to grow quite faint at the bare thought of reading anything which was neither mercantile nor political, and was not in a newspaper, inquired 'if any gentleman would drink some?'" MC 16

—an author's sarcasm: "Mr Pecksniff's house is more than a thousand leagues away; and again this happy chronicle has Liberty and Moral Sensibility for its high companions. Again it breathes the blessed air of Independence; again it contemplates with pious awe that moral sense which renders unto Cæsar nothing that is his; again inhales that sacred atmosphere which was the life of him—oh noble patriot, with many followers!—who dreamed of Freedom in a slave's embrace, and waking sold her offspring and his own in public markets." MC 21

—and British Institutions: "'Hush! Pray, silence!' said General Choke, holding up his hand, and speaking with a patient and complacent benevolence that was quite touching. 'I have always remarked it as a very extraordinary circumstance, which I impute to the natur' of British Institutions and their tendency to suppress that popular inquiry and information which air so widely diffused even in the trackless forests of this vast Continent of the Western Ocean; that the knowledge of Britishers themselves on such points [as the Queen's residence] is not to be compared with that possessed by our intelligent and locomotive citizens. This is interesting, and confirms my observation. When you say, sir,' he continued, addressing Martin [Chuzzlewit], 'that your Queen does not reside in the Tower of London, you fall into an error, not uncommon to your countrymen, even when their abilities and moral elements air such as to command respect. But sir, you are wrong. She *does* live there—'

"'When she is at the Court of Saint James's;' interposed [La Fayette] Kettle.

"'When she is at the Court of Saint James's, of course,' returned the General, in the same benignant way: 'for if her location was in Windsor Pavilion it couldn't be in London at the same time. Your Tower of London, sir,' pursued the General, smiling with a mild consciousness of his knowledge, 'is nat'rally your royal residence. Being located in the immediate neighbourhood of your Parks, your Drives, your Triumphant Arches, your Opera, and your Royal Almacks, it nat'rally suggests itself as the place for holding a luxurious and thoughtless court. And consequently,' said the General, 'consequently, the court is held there.'

"'Have you been in England?' asked Martin.

"'In print I have, sir,' said the General, 'not otherwise. We air a reading people here, sir. You will meet with much information among us that will surprise you, sir.'

"'I have not the least doubt of it,' returned Martin." MC 21

—buildings: "All the buildings looked as if they had been built and painted that morning, and could be taken down on Monday with very little trouble. In the keen evening air, every sharp outline looked a hundred times sharper than ever. The clean cardboard colonnades had no more perspective than a Chinese bridge on a teacup, and appeared equally well calculated for use.

"The razor-like edges of the detached cottages seemed to cut the very wind as it whistled against them, and to send it smarting on its way with a shriller cry than before. Those slightly-built wooden dwellings behind which the sun was setting with a brilliant lustre, could be so looked through and through, that the idea of any inhabitant being able to hide himself from the public gaze, or to have any secrets from the public eye, was not entertainable for a moment.

"Even where a blazing fire shone through the uncurtained windows of some distant house, it had the air of being newly lighted, and of lacking warmth; and instead of awakening thoughts of a snug chamber, bright with faces that first saw the light round that same hearth, and ruddy with warm hangings, it came upon one suggestive of the smell of new mortar and damp walls." AN 4

—character: " . . . I drank my cobbler, julep, sling, or cocktail, in all good-will, to my friend the General, and my friends the Majors, Colonels, and civilians all; full well knowing that, whatever little motes my beamy eyes may have descried in theirs, they belong to a kind, generous, large-hearted, and great people." CS/HT 1

"[The American people] are, by nature, frank, brave, cordial, hospitable, and affectionate. Cultivation and refinement seem but to enhance their warmth of heart and ardent enthusiasm; and it is the possession of these latter qualities in a most remarkable degree, which renders an educated American one of the most endearing and most generous of friends. I never was so won upon, as by this class; never yielded up my full confidence and esteem so readily and pleasurably, as to them; never can make again, in half a year, so many friends for whom I seem to entertain the regard of half a life.

"These qualities are natural, I implicitly believe, to the whole people. That they are, however, sadly sapped and blighted in their growth among the mass; and that there are influences at work which endanger them still more, and give but little present promise of their healthy restoration; is a truth that ought to be told." AN 18

And see —cheating; —preoccupation; and S: Cynic and Cynicism

—cheating: "Another prominent feature is the love of 'smart' dealing: which gilds over many a swindle and gross breach of trust; many a defalcation, public and private; and enables many a knave to hold his head up with the best, who well deserves a halter; though it has not been without its retributive operation, for this smartness has done more in a few years to impair the public credit, and to cripple the public resources, than dull honesty, however rash, could have effected in a century . . . .

"The following dialogue I have held a hundred times: 'Is it not a very disgraceful circumstance that such a man as So-and-so should be acquiring a large property by the most infamous and odious means, and notwithstanding all the crimes of which he has been guilty, should be tolerated and abetted by your Citizens? He is a public nuisance, is he not?' 'Yes, Sir.' 'A convicted liar?' 'Yes, Sir.' 'He has been kicked, and cuffed, and caned?' 'Yes, Sir.' 'And he is utterly dishonourable, debased, and profligate?' 'Yes, Sir.' 'In the name of wonder, then, what is his merit?' 'Well, Sir, he is a smart man.'" AN 18

—chivalry: " . . . no man sat down until the ladies were seated; or omitted any little act of politeness which could contribute to their comfort. Nor did I ever once, on any occasion, anywhere, during my rambles in America, see a [white] woman exposed to the slightest act of rudeness, incivility, or even inattention." AN 10

—"*city:*" " . . . we stop . . . for passengers, at some small town or village (I ought to say city, every place is a city here) . . . . " AN 11

—civil war's effect in England: "When the American civil war rendered it necessary, first in Glasgow, and afterwards in Manchester, that the working people should be shown how to avail themselves of the advantages derivable from system, and from the combination of numbers, in the purchase and the cooking of their food . . . . " UT/BB

—Congress: "I was sometimes asked, in my progress through other places, whether I had not been very much impressed by the *heads* of the law-makers at Washington; meaning not their chiefs and leaders, but literally their individual and personal heads, whereon their hair grew, and whereby the phrenological character of each legislator was expressed: and I almost as often struck my questioner dumb with indignant consternation by answering 'No, that I didn't remember being at all overcome.' As I must, at whatever hazard, repeat the avowal here, I will follow it up by relating my impressions on this subject in as few words as possible . . . my impressions of the live pillars of the Capitol at Washington must be received with such grains of allowance as this free confession may seem to demand.

"Did I see in this public body an assemblage of men, bound together in the sacred names of Liberty and Freedom, and so asserting the chaste dignity of those twin goddesses, in all their discussions, as to exalt at once the Eternal Principles to which their names are given, and their own character and the character of their countrymen, in the admiring eyes of the whole world? . . .

"It was not a month, since this same body had sat calmly by, and heard a man, one of themselves, with oaths which beggars in their drink reject, threaten to cut another's throat from ear to ear . . . .

"Where sat the many legislators of coarse threats; of words and blows such as coal-heavers deal upon each other, when they forget their breeding? On every side. Every session had its anecdotes of that kind, and the actors were all there.

"Did I recognise in this assembly, a body of men, who, applying themselves in a new world to correct some of the falsehoods and vices of the old, purified the avenues to Public Life, paved the dirty ways to Place and Power, debated and made laws for the

Common Good, and had no party but their Country?

"I saw in them, the wheels that move the meanest perversion of virtuous Political Machinery that the worst tools ever wrought. Despicable trickery at elections; underhanded tamperings with public officers; cowardly attacks upon opponents, with scurrilous newspapers for shields, and hired pens for daggers; shameful trucklings to mercenary knaves, whose claim to be considered, is, that every day and week they sow new crops of ruin with their venal types, which are the dragon's teeth of yore, in everything but sharpness; aidings and abettings of every bad inclination in the popular mind, and artful suppressions of all its good influences: such things as these, and in a word, Dishonest Faction in its most depraved and most unblushing form, stared out from every corner of the crowded hall." AN 8

And see —politics—noble; and —venal

—diversion: religion and uplift: "The peculiar province of the Pulpit in New England (always excepting the Unitarian Ministry) would appear to be the denouncement of all innocent and rational amusements. The church, the chapel, and the lecture-room, are the only means of excitement excepted; and to the church, the chapel, and the lecture-room, the ladies resort in crowds.

"Wherever religion is resorted to, as a strong drink, and as an escape from the dull monotonous round of home, those of its ministers who pepper the highest will be the surest to please. They who strew the Eternal Path with the greatest amount of brimstone, and who most ruthlessly tread down the flowers and leaves that grow by the wayside, will be voted the most righteous; and they who enlarge with the greatest pertinacity on the difficulty of getting into heaven, will be considered by all true believers certain of going there: though it would be hard to say by what process of reasoning this conclusion is arrived at. It is so at home, and it is so abroad. With regard to the other means of excitement, the Lecture, it has at least the merit of being always new. One lecture treads so quickly on the heels of another, that none are remembered; and the course of this month may be safely repeated next, with its charm of novelty unbroken, and its interest unabated." AN 3 *And see —recreation*

—dress: "Heaven save the ladies, how they dress! We have seen more colours in these ten minutes, than we should have seen elsewhere, in as many days. What various parasols! what rainbow silks and satins! what pinking of thin stockings, and pinching of thin shoes, and fluttering of ribbons and silk tassels, and display of rich cloaks with gaudy hoods and linings!" AN 6

—education: "'Education?' suggested Martin [Chuzzlewit], faintly.

"'Pretty well on that head,' said [Mr Bevan], shrugging his shoulders, 'still no mighty matter to boast of; for old countries, and despotic countries too, have done as much, if not more, and made less noise about it. We shine out brightly in comparison with England, certainly; but hers is a very extreme case.'" MC 16

—and England: "Points of difference there have been, points of difference there are, points of difference there probably always will be between the two great peoples. But broadcast in England is sown the sentiment that those two peoples are essentially one, and that it rests with them jointly to uphold the great Anglo-Saxon race, to which our President has referred, and all its great achievements before the world. And if I know anything of my countrymen—and they give me credit for knowing something—if I know anything of my countrymen, gentlemen, the English heart is stirred by the fluttering of those Stars and Stripes, as it is stirred by no other flag that flies except its own. If I know my countrymen, in any and every relation towards America, they begin, not as *Sir Anthony Absolute* recommended that lovers should begin, with 'a little aversion', but with a great liking and profound respect; and whatever the little sensitiveness of the moment, or the little official passion, or the little official policy now, or then, or here, or there, may be, take my word for it, that the first enduring, great popular consideration in England is a generous construction of justice." S/NY2

—and English aristocracy: "The whole [Norris] family had been in England. There was a pleasant thing! But Martin was not quite so glad of this, when he found that they knew all the great dukes, lords, viscounts, marquesses, duchesses, knights, and baronets, quite affectionately and were beyond everything interested in the least particular concerning them . . . .

"Martin thought it rather strange, and in some sort inconsistent, that during the whole of these narrations, and in the very meridian of their enjoyment thereof, both Mr Norris the father, and Mr Norris Junior, the son (who corresponded, every post, with four members of the English Peerage), enlarged upon the inestimable advantage of having no such arbitrary distinctions in that enlightened land, where there were no noblemen but nature's noblemen, and where all society was based on one broad level of brotherly love and national equality." MC 17

—flowers: "The ship was fragrant with flowers. Something of the old Mexican passion for flowers may have gradually passed into North America, where flowers are luxuriously grown, and tastefully combined in the richest profusion; but, be that as it may, such gorgeous farewells in flowers had come on board, that the small officer's cabin on deck, which I tenanted, bloomed over into the adjacent scuppers, and banks of other flowers that it couldn't hold made a garden of the unoccupied tables in the passengers' saloon. These delicious scents of the shore, mingling with the fresh airs of the sea, made the atmosphere a dreamy, an enchanting one." UT/AS

—freedom generally: [from a letter to a Public Man in Ireland] ""Devoted, mind and body, heart and soul, to Freedom, sir—to Freedom, blessed solace to the snail upon the cellar-door, the oyster in his pearly bed, the still mite in his home of cheese, the very winkle of your country in his shelly lair—in her unsullied name, we offer you our sympathy. Oh, sir, in this our cherished and our happy land, her fires burn bright and clear and smokeless: once lighted up in yours, the [British] lion shall be roasted whole.

""I am sir, in Freedom's name,

""Your affectionate friend and faithful Sympathiser,

""CYRUS CHOKE, General, U.S.M."'

"It happened that just as the General began to read this letter, the railroad train arrived, bringing a new mail from England . . . [the General] had no sooner possessed himself of the contents of these documents, than a change came over his face, involving such a huge amount of choler and passion, that the noisy concourse were silent in a moment, in very wonder at the sight of him.

"'My friends!' cried the General, rising; 'my friends and fellow-citizens, we have been mistaken in this man.'

"'In what man?' was the cry.

"'In this,' panted the General, holding up the letter he had read aloud a few minutes before. 'I find that he has been, and is, the advocate—consistent in it always too—of Nigger emancipation!'

"If anything beneath the sky be real, those Sons of Freedom would have pistolled, stabbed—in some way slain—that man by coward hands and murderous violence, if he had stood among them at that time. The most confiding of their own countrymen would not have wagered then; no, nor would they ever peril one dung-hill straw, upon the life of any man in such a strait. They tore the letter, cast the fragments in the air, trod down the pieces as they fell; and yelled, and groaned, and hissed, till they could cry no longer.

""I shall move,' said the General, when he could make himself heard, 'that the Watertoast Association of United Sympathisers be immediately dissolved!'

"Down with it! Away with it! Don't hear of it! Burn its records! Pull the room down! Blot it out of human memory!

"'But, my fellow-countrymen!' said the General, 'the contributions. We have funds. What is to be done with the funds?'

"It was hastily resolved that a piece of plate should be presented to a certain constitutional Judge, who had laid down from the Bench the noble principle that it was lawful for any white mob to murder any black man: and that another piece of plate, of similar value, should be presented to a certain Patriot, who had declared from his high place in the Legislature, that he and his friends would hang, without trial, any Abolitionist who might pay them a visit. For the surplus, it was agreed that it should be devoted to aiding the enforcement of those free and equal laws, which render it incalculably more criminal and dangerous to teach a negro to read and write than to roast him alive in a public city. These points adjusted, the meeting broke up in great disorder, and there was an end of the Watertoast Sympathy." MC 21

—freedom of speech: "'Perhaps you don't know [said Bevan] that [Benjamin] Franklin, in very severe terms, published his opinion that those who were slandered by such fellows as this colonel [Diver], having no sufficient remedy in the administration of this country's laws or in the decent and right-minded feeling of its people, were justified in retorting on such public nui-

sances by means of a stout cudgel?'

"'I was not aware of that,' said Martin [Chuzzlewit], 'but I am very glad to know it, and I think it worthy of his memory; especially . . . as I can already understand that it may have required great courage, even in his time to write freely on any question which was not a party one in this very free country.'

"'Some courage, no doubt,' returned his new friend. 'Do you think it would require any to do so, now?'

"'Indeed I think it would; and not a little,' said Martin.

"'You are right. So very right, that I believe no satirist could breathe this air. If another **Juvenal** or **Swift** could rise up among us to-morrow, he would be hunted down. If you have any knowledge of our literature, and can give me the name of any man, American born and bred, who has anatomised our follies as a people, and not as this or that party; and who has escaped the foulest and most brutal slander, the most inveterate hatred and intolerant pursuit; it will be a strange name in my ears, believe me. In some cases I could name to you, where a native writer has ventured on the most harmless and good-humoured illustrations of our vices or defects, it has been found necessary to announce, that in a second edition the passage has been expunged, or altered, or explained away, or patched into praise.'" MC 16

—Harvard College: "There is no doubt that much of the intellectual refinement and superiority of Boston, is referable to the quiet influence of the University of Cambridge . . . . The resident professors at that university are gentlemen of learning and varied attainments: and are, without one exception that I can call to mind, men who would shed a grace upon, and do honour to, any society in the civilised world." AN 4

—heating: "[The hospital] had one fault, however, which is common to all American interiors: the presence of the eternal, accursed, suffocating, red-hot demon of a stove, whose breath would blight the purest air under Heaven." AN 3

—the Irish

—as labourers: Martin [Chuzzlewit, the younger] "then learned that the Watertoast Association sympathised with a certain Public Man in Ireland, who held a contest upon certain points with England: and that they did so, because they didn't love England at all—not by any means because they loved Ireland much; being indeed horribly jealous and distrustful of its people always, and only tolerating them because of their working hard, which made them very useful; labour being held in greater indignity in the simple republic than in any other country upon earth." MC 21

" . . . two labourers in holiday clothes . . . . Irishmen both! You might know them, if they were masked, by their long-tailed blue coats and bright buttons, and their drab trousers, which they wear like men well used to working dresses, who are easy in no others. It would be hard to keep your model republics going, without the countrymen and countrywomen of those two labourers. For who else would dig, and delve, and drudge, and do domestic work, and make canals and roads, and execute great lines of Internal Improvement!" AN 6

"They are partly American and partly Irish, and herd together on the lower deck; where they amused themselves last evening till the night was pretty far advanced, by alternately firing off pistols and singing hymns." AN 11

—as settlers: " . . . we came upon an Irish colony [in upper New York State]. With means at hand of building decent cabins, it was wonderful to see how clumsy, rough, and wretched, its hovels were. The best were poor protection from the weather; the worst let in the wind and rain through wide breaches in the roofs of sodden grass, and in the walls of mud; some had neither door nor window; some had nearly fallen down, and were imperfectly propped up by stakes and poles; all were ruinous and filthy. Hideously ugly old women and very buxom young ones, pigs, dogs, men, children, babies, pots, kettles, dunghills, vile refuse, rank straw, and standing water, all wallowing together in an inseparable heap, composed the furniture of every dark and dirty hut." AN 15

—Justice: "In one of the ornamented portions of the [library in the Capitol], there is a figure of Justice; whereunto the Guide Book says, 'the artist at first contemplated giving more of nudity, but he was warned that the public sentiment of this country would not admit of it, and in his caution he has gone, perhaps, into the opposite extreme.' Poor Justice! she has been made to wear much stranger garments in America than those she pines in, in the Capitol. Let us hope that she has changed her dressmaker since they were fashioned, and that

the public sentiment of the country did not cut out the clothes she hides her lovely figure in, just now." AN 8

—liberty: "'Lord love you, sir,' [Mark Tapley] added, 'they're so fond of Liberty in this part of the globe, that they buy her and sell her and carry her to market with 'em. They've such a passion for Liberty, that they can't help taking liberties with her. That's what it's owing to.'" MC 17

—manners

—in service: "When I say that [our landlord] constantly walked in and out of the room with his hat on; and stopped to converse in the same free-and-easy state; and lay down on our sofa, and pulled his newspaper out of his pocket, and read it at his ease; I merely mention these traits as characteristic of the country; not at all as being matter of complaint, or as having been disagreeable to me.

"I should undoubtedly be offended by such proceedings at home, because there they are not the custom, and where they are not, they would be impertinences; but in America, the only desire of a good-natured fellow of this kind, is to treat his guests hospitably and well; and I had no more right, and I can truly say no more disposition, to measure his conduct by our English rule and standard, than I had to quarrel with him for not being of the exact stature which would qualify him for admission into the Queen's Grenadier Guards.

"As little inclination had I to find fault with a funny old lady who was an upper domestic in this establishment, and who, when she came to wait upon us at any meal, sat herself down comfortably in the most convenient chair, and producing a large pin to pick her teeth with, remained performing that ceremony, and steadfastly regarding us meanwhile with much gravity and composure (now and then pressing us to eat a little more), until it was time to clear away.

"It was enough for us, that whatever we wished done was done with great civility and readiness, and a desire to oblige, not only here, but everywhere else; and that all our wants were, in general, zealously anticipated." AN 14

—staring: " . . . those men and boys who happened to have nothing particular to do, and were curious in foreigners, came (according to custom) round the carriage in which I sat; let down all the windows; thrust in their heads and shoulders; hooked themselves on conveniently, by their elbows; and fell to comparing notes on the subject of my personal appearance, with as much indifference as if I were a stuffed figure.

"I never gained so much uncompromising information with reference to my own nose and eyes, and various impressions wrought by my mouth and chin on different minds, and how my head looks when it is viewed from behind, as on these occasions. Some gentlemen were only satisfied by exercising their sense of touch; and the boys (who are surprisingly precocious in America) were seldom satisfied, even by that, but would return to the charge over and over again.

"Many a budding president has walked into my room with his cap on his head and his hands in his pockets, and stared at me for two whole hours: occasionally refreshing himself with a tweak of his nose, or a draught from the water-jug; or by walking to the windows and inviting other boys in the street below, to come up and do likewise: crying, 'Here he is!' 'Come on!' 'Bring all your brothers!' with other hospitable entreaties of that nature." ¶AN 8

—table: "There is no doubt that the meal . . . was disposed of somewhat ravenously; and that the gentlemen thrust the broad-bladed knives and the two-pronged forks further down their throats than I ever saw the same weapons go before, except in the hands of a skilful juggler . . . . " AN 10

"'Upon my life!' cried Martin . . . . 'This is the most wonderful community that ever existed. A man deliberately makes a hog of himself, and that's an Institution!'

"'We have no time to ac-quire forms, sir,' said Elijah Pogram.

"'Acquire! cried Martin. 'But it's not a question of acquiring anything. It's a question of losing the natural politeness of a savage, and that instinctive good breeding which admonishes one man not to offend and disgust another. Don't you think that man over the way, for instance, naturally knows better, but considers it a very fine and independent thing to be a brute in small matters?'

"'He is a na-tive of our country, and is nat'rally bright and spry, of course,' said Mr Pogram.

"'Now, observe what this comes to, Mr Pogram,' pursued Martin. 'The mass of your countrymen begin by stubbornly neglecting little social observances, which have nothing to do with gentility, custom, usage, government, or country, but are acts of common, decent, natural, human politeness. You abet them in this, by resenting all attacks upon their social offences as if they were a beautiful national feature. From disregarding small obligations they come in regular course to disregard great ones; and so refuse to pay their debts. What they may do, or what they may refuse to do next, I don't know; but any man may see if he will, that it will be something following in natural succession, and a part of one great growth, which is rotten at the root.'

"The mind of Mr Pogram was too philosophical to see this; so they went on deck again, where, resuming his former post, he chewed until he was in a lethargic state, amounting to insensibility." MC 34

And see Vol. I p597: "*Mealtime*"

—*the military / militia:* "'Who told you that?' asked Martin [Chuzzlewit], sternly.

"'A military officer,' said Mark [Tapley].

"'Confound you for a ridiculous fellow!' cried Martin, laughing heartily in spite of himself. 'What military officer? You know they spring up in every field.'

"'As thick as scarecrows in England, sir,' interposed Mark, 'which is a sort of militia themselves, being entirely coat and wescoat, with a stick inside.'" MC 21

—*money:* " . . . 'three days after sight of this First of Exchange pay to Mr Ebenezer Scrooge or his order,' and so forth, would have become a mere United States' security if there were no days to count by." CC 2

—*New Englanders:* "In shrewdness of remark, and a certain cast-iron quaintness, the Yankees, or people of New England, unquestionably take the lead [in humour]; as they do in most other evidences of intelligence." AN 18

—*people:* "The people are all like, too. There is no diversity of character. They travel about on the same errands, say and do the same things in exactly the same manner, and follow in the same dull cheerless round. All down the long table, there is scarcely a man who is in anything different from his neighbour." AN 11

" . . . in travelling about, out of the large cities . . . I was quite oppressed by the prevailing seriousness and melancholy air of business: which was so general and unvarying, that at every new town I came to, I seemed to meet the very same people whom I had left behind me, at the last." AN 18

—*plantation:* " . . . although I went down with the owner of the estate, to 'the quarter,' as that part of it in which the slaves live is called, I was not invited to enter into any of their huts. All I saw of them, was, that they were very crazy, wretched cabins, near to which groups of half-naked children basked in the sun, or wallowed on the dusty ground. But I believe that this gentleman is a considerate and excellent master, who inherited his fifty slaves, and is neither a buyer nor a seller of human stock; and I am sure, from my own observation and conviction, that he is a kind-hearted, worthy man.

"The planter's house was an airy rustic dwelling . . . . The day was very warm, but the blinds being all closed, and the windows and doors set wide open, a shady coolness rustled through the rooms, which was exquisitely refreshing after the glare and heat without. Before the windows was an open piazza, where, in what they call the hot weather—whatever that may be—they sling hammocks, and drink and doze luxuriously.

"I do not know how their cool refections may taste within the hammocks, but, having experience, I can report that, out of them, the mounds of ices and the bowls of mint-julep and sherry-cobbler they make in these latitudes, are refreshments never to be thought of afterwards, in summer, by those who would preserve contented minds." ¶AN 9 *See* F:Slavery

—*politician:* "[Major Pawkins] was a great politician; and the one article of his creed, in reference to all public obligations involving the good faith and integrity of his country, was, 'run a moist pen slick through everything, and start fresh.' This made him a patriot.

"In commercial affairs he was a bold speculator. In plainer words he had a most distinguished genius for swindling, and could start a bank, or negotiate a loan, or form a land-jobbing company (entailing ruin, pestilence, and death, on hundreds of families), with any gifted creature in the Union. This made him an admirable man of business.

"He could hang about a bar-room, discussing the affairs of the nation, for twelve hours together; and in that time could hold forth with more intolerable dulness, chew more tobacco, smoke more tobacco, drink more rum-toddy, mint-julep, gin-sling, and cock-tail, than any private gentleman of his acquaintance. This made him an orator and a man of the people.

"In a word, the major was a rising character, and a popular character, and was in a fair way to be sent by the popular party to the State House of New York, if not in the end to Washington itself." ¶MC 16

—politics

—deportment: "One who rides at all hazards of limb and life in the chase of a fox, will prefer to ride recklessly at most times. So it was with these gentlemen. He was the greatest patriot, in their eyes, who brawled the loudest, and who cared the least for decency. He was their champion who, in the brutal fury of his own pursuit, could cast no stigma upon them for the hot knavery of theirs. Thus Martin [Chuzzlewit] learned in the five minutes' straggling talk about the stove, that to carry pistols into legislative assemblies, and swords in sticks, and other such peaceful toys; to seize opponents by the throat, as dogs or rats might do; to bluster, bully, and overbear by personal assailment; were glowing deeds. Not thrusts and stabs at Freedom, striking far deeper into her House of Life than any sultan's scimitar could reach; but rare incense on her altars, having a grateful scent in patriotic nostrils, and curling upwards to the seventh heaven of Fame." MC 16

—at an insane asylum: " . . . will it be believed that the miserable strife of Party feeling is carried even into this sad refuge of afflicted and degraded humanity? Will it be believed that the eyes which are to watch over and control the wanderings of minds on which the most dreadful visitation to which our nature is exposed has fallen, must wear the glasses of some wretched side in Politics?

"Will it be believed that the governor of such a house as this, is appointed, and deposed, and changed perpetually, as Parties fluctuate and vary, and as their despicable weathercocks are blown this way or that? A hundred times in every week, some new most paltry exhibition of that narrow-minded and injurious Party Spirit, which is the Simoom of America, sickening and blighting everything of wholesome life within its reach, was forced upon my notice; but I never turned my back upon it with feelings of such deep disgust and measureless contempt, as when I crossed the threshold of this madhouse." ¶AN 6

—in New York City: "Some trifling excitement prevailed upon the very brink and margin of the land of liberty; for an alderman had been elected the day before; and Party Feeling naturally running rather high on such an exciting occasion, the friends of the disappointed candidate had found it necessary to assert the great principles of Purity of Election and Freedom of Opinion by breaking a few legs and arms, and furthermore pursuing one obnoxious gentleman through the streets with the design of slitting his nose.

"These good-humoured little outbursts of the popular fancy were not in themselves sufficiently remarkable to create any great stir, after the lapse of a whole night; but they found fresh life and notoriety in the breath of the newsboys, who not only proclaimed them with shrill yells in all the highways and byways of the town, upon the wharves and among the shipping, but on the deck and down in the cabins of the steamboat; which, before she touched the shore, was boarded and overrun by a legion of those young citizens." MC 16

—noble: "That there are, among the representatives of the people in both Houses, and among all parties, some men of high character and great abilities, I need not say . . . personal intercourse and free communication have bred within me, not the result predicted in the very doubtful proverb, but increased admiration and respect. They are striking men to look at, hard to deceive, prompt to act, lions in energy, **Crichton**s in varied accomplishments, Indians in fire of eye and gesture, Americans in strong and generous impulse; and they as well represent the honour and wisdom of their country . . . ." AN 8

—venal: "Did I see among [the congressmen] the intelligence and refinement: the true, honest, patriotic heart of America? Here and there, were drops of its blood and life, but they scarcely coloured the stream of desperate adventurers which sets that way for profit and for pay. It is the game of these men, and of their profligate organs, to make the strife of politics so fierce and brutal, and so destructive of all self-respect in worthy men, that sensitive and delicate-minded persons shall be kept aloof, and they, and such as they, be left to battle out their selfish views unchecked. And thus this lowest of all scrambling fights goes on, and they who in other countries would, from their intelligence and station, most aspire to make the laws, do here recoil the farthest

from that degradation." AN 8

—polity: "'If you ask me [said Mr Bevan] ... whether I came back here better satisfied with a state of things which broadly divides society into two classes—whereof one, the great mass, asserts a spurious independence, most miserably dependent for its mean existence on the disregard of humanising conventionalities of manner and social custom, so that the coarser a man is, the more distinctly it shall appeal to his taste; while the other, disgusted with the low standard thus set up and made adaptable to everything, takes refuge among the graces and refinements it can bring to bear on private life, and leaves the public weal to such fortune as may betide it in the press and uproar of a general scramble—then again I answer, No. . . . .

"'In a word . . . I do not find and cannot believe, and therefore will not allow, that we are a model of wisdom, and an example to the world, and the perfection of human reason, and a great deal more to the same purpose, which you may hear any hour in the day; simply because we began our political life with two inestimable advantages.'

"'What were they?' asked Martin.

"'One, that our history commenced at so late a period as to escape the ages of bloodshed and cruelty through which other nations have passed; and so had all the light of their probation, and none of its darkness. The other, that we have a vast territory, and not—as yet—too many people on it. These facts considered, we have done little enough, I think.'" MC 17

—preoccupation: dollars: "Martin [was] . . . anxious to hear, and inform himself by, the conversation of the busy gentlemen, who now lounged about the stove as if a great weight had been taken off their minds by the withdrawal of the other sex; and who made a plentiful use of the spittoons and their toothpicks.

"It was rather barren of interest, to say the truth; and the greater part of it may be summed up in one word. Dollars. All their cares, hopes, joys, affections, virtues, and associations, seemed to be melted down into dollars. Whatever the chance contributions that fell into the slow cauldron of their talk, they made the gruel thick and slab with dollars. Men were weighed by their dollars, measures gauged by their dollars; life was auctioneered, appraised, put up, and knocked down for its dollars.

"The next respectable thing to dollars was any venture having their attainment for its end. The more of that worthless ballast, honour and fair-dealing, which any man cast overboard from the ship of his Good Name and Good Intent, the more ample stowage-room he had for dollars. Make commerce one huge lie and mighty theft. Deface the banner of the nation for an idle rag: pollute it star by star; and cut out stripe by stripe as from the arm of a degraded soldier. Do anything for dollars! What is a flag to *them*!" ¶MC 16

—love of trade: " . . . all kinds of deficient and impolitic usages are referred to the national love of trade . . . . The love of trade is assigned as a reason for that comfortless custom, so very prevalent in country towns, of married persons living in hotels, having no fireside of their own, and seldom meeting from early morning until late at night, but at the hasty public meals. The love of trade is a reason why the literature of America is to remain for ever unprotected: 'For we are a trading people, and don't care for poetry:' though we *do,* by the way, profess to be very proud of our poets: while healthful amusements, cheerful means of recreation, and wholesome fancies, must fade before the stern utilitarian joys of trade." AN 18

—press

—fictional comment: "The captain, who had the Sewer below at that moment, lunching expensively in one cabin, while the amiable Stabber was drinking himself into a state of blind madness in another, took a cordial leave of his friend the colonel, and hurried away to dispatch the champagne: well knowing (as it afterwards appeared) that if he failed to conciliate the editor of the Rowdy Journal, that potentate would denounce him and his ship in large capitals before he was a day older; and would probably assault the memory of his mother also, who had not been dead more than twenty years." MC 16

—irresponsibility: "It was clear that Colonel Diver, in the security of his strong position, and in his perfect understanding of the public sentiment, cared very little what Martin [Chuzzlewit] or anybody else thought about him. His high-spiced wares were made to sell, and they sold; and his thousands of readers could as rationally charge their delight in filth upon him, as a glutton can shift upon his cook the responsibility of his beastly excess. Nothing would have de-

lighted the colonel more than to be told that no such man as he could walk in high success the streets of any other country in the world: for that would only have been a logical assurance to him of the correct adaptation of his labours to the prevailing taste, and of his being strictly and peculiarly a national feature of America." MC 16

Mr Jefferson Brick Proposes an Appropriate Sentiment MC

—observations of a visitor: "These three characteristics [automatic mistrust, love of the 'smart' and total preoccupation with business] are strongly presented at every turn, full in the stranger's view. But, the foul growth of America has a more tangled root than this; and it strikes its fibres, deep in its licentious Press.

"Schools may be erected, East, West, North, and South; pupils be taught, and masters reared, by scores upon scores of thousands; colleges may thrive, churches may be crammed, temperance may be diffused, and advancing knowledge in all other forms walk through the land with giant strides: but while the newspaper press of America is in, or near, its present abject state, high moral improvement in that country is hopeless . . . .

"When any man, of any grade of desert in intellect or character, can climb to any public distinction, no matter what, in America, without first grovelling down upon the earth, and bending the knee before this monster of depravity; when any private excellence is safe from its attacks; when any social confidence is left unbroken by it, or any tie of social decency and honour is held in the least regard; when any man in that free country has freedom of opinion, and presumes to think for himself, and speak for himself, without humble reference to a censorship which, for its rampant ignorance and base dishonesty, he utterly loathes and despises in his heart; when those who most acutely feel its infamy and the reproach it casts upon the nation, and who most denounce it to each other, dare to set their heels upon, and crush it openly, in the sight of all men: then, I will believe that its influence is lessening, and men are returning to their manly senses.

"But while that Press has its evil eye in every house, and its black hand in every appointment in the state, from a president to a postman; while, with ribald slander for its only stock-in-trade, it is the standard literature of an enormous class, who must find their reading in a newspaper, or they will not read at all; so long must its odium be upon the country's head, and so long must the evil it works, be plainly visible in the Republic.

"To those who are accustomed to the leading English journals, or to the respectable journals of the Continent of Europe—to those who are accustomed to anything else in print and paper—it would be impossible, without an amount of extract for which I have neither space nor inclination, to convey an adequate idea of this frightful engine in America." ¶AN 18

CD modifed his strictures radically on his return visit in 1868: see Vol. I p525

—toasted: "'Well, sir!' cried the war correspondent [Jefferson Brick], 'since you have concluded to call upon me, I will respond. I will give you, sir, The Rowdy Journal and its brethren; the well of Truth, whose waters are black from being composed of printers' ink, but are quite clear enough for my country to behold the shadow of her Destiny reflected in.'" MC 16 *Illustration on page 809*

And see —recreation

—protest: "Mere messages in the earthly order of events had [in 1775] lately come to the English Crown and People, from a congress of British subjects in America: which, strange to relate, have proved more important to the human race than any communications yet received through any of the chickens of the Cock-lane [spiritualistic] brood." TTC i 1

—pumpkins and Prohibition: "'Run into the garden, my dear, and fetch me an American Pumpkin! American, because in some parts of that independent country there are prohibitory laws against the sale of alcoholic drinks in any form. Also, because America produced (among many great pumpkins) the glory of her sex, Mrs Colonel Bloomer. None but an American Pumpkin will do, my child.'" HW/FF

—recreation: "Are there no amusements? Yes. There is a lecture-room across the way, from which that glare of light proceeds, and there may be evening service for the ladies thrice a week, or oftener. For the young gentlemen, there is the counting-house, the store, the bar-room: the latter, as you may see through these windows, pretty full. Hark! to the clinking sound of hammers breaking lumps of ice, and to the cool gurgling of the pounded bits, as, in the process of mixing, they are poured from glass to glass! No amusements? What are these suckers of cigars and swallowers of strong drinks, whose hats and legs we see in every possible variety of twist, doing, but amusing themselves?

"What are the fifty newspapers, which those precocious urchins are bawling down the street, and which are kept filed within, what are they but amusements? Not vapid waterish amusements, but good strong stuff; dealing in round abuse and blackguard names; pulling off the roofs of private houses, as the *Halting Devil* did in Spain; pimping and pandering for all degrees of vicious taste, and gorging with coined lies the most voracious maw; imputing to every man in public life the coarsest and the vilest motives; scaring away from the stabbed and prostrate body-politic, every Samaritan of clear conscience and good deeds; and setting on, with yell and whistle and the clapping of foul hands, the vilest vermin and worst birds of prey. —No amusements!" ¶AN 6

And see —diversion: religion and uplift

—rocking-chair: "Even in this chamber [a steamboat cabin] there was a rocking-chair. It would be impossible to get on anywhere, in America, without a rocking-chair." AN 4

—sculpture: "'May you ever be as firm, sir, as your marble statter! May it ever be as great a terror Toe its ene-mies as you.'

"There is some reason to suppose that it was rather terrible to its friends; being a statue of the Elevated or Goblin School, in which the Honourable Elijah Pogram was represented as in a very high wind, with his hair all standing on end, and his nostrils blown wide open." MC 34

—*suggested visit:* "'Have a passage ready taken for 'Merriker. The 'Merrikin gov'ment will never give him [Mr Pickwick] up, ven they find as he's got money to spend, Sammy. Let the gov'ner stop there . . . and then let him come back and write a book about the 'Merrikins as'll pay all his expenses and more, if he blows 'em up enough.'" PP 45

—*symbol: the Eagle:* "' . . . I was a-thinking, sir . . . that if I was a painter and was called upon to paint the American Eagle, how should I do it?'

"'Paint it as like an Eagle as you could, I suppose.'

"'No,' said Mark [Tapley]. 'That wouldn't do for me, sir. I should want to draw it like a Bat, for its short-sightedness; like a Bantam, for its bragging; like a Magpie, for its honesty; like a Peacock, for its vanity; like a Ostrich, for its putting its head in the mud, and thinking nobody sees it—

"'And like a Phoenix, for its power of springing from the ashes of its faults and vices, and soaring up anew into the sky!' said Martin. 'Well, Mark. Let us hope so.'" MC 34

—*universities:* "Whatever the defects of American universities may be, they disseminate no prejudices; rear no bigots; dig up the buried ashes of no old superstitions; never interpose between the people and their improvement; exclude no man because of his religious opinions; above all, in their whole course of study and instruction, recognise a world, and a broad one too, lying beyond the college walls." AN 3

—*values:* " . . . again this happy chronicle has Liberty and Moral Sensibility for its high companions. Again it breathes the blessed air of Independence; again it contemplates with pious awe that moral sense which renders unto Caesar nothing that is his; again inhales that sacred atmosphere which was the life of him—oh noble patriot, with many followers!—who dreamed of Freedom in a slave's embrace, and waking sold her offspring and his own in public markets.

"How the wheels clank and rattle, and the tram-road shakes, as the train rushes on! And now the engine yells, as it were lashed and tortured like a living labourer, and writhed in agony. A poor fancy; for steel and iron are of infinitely greater account, in this commonwealth, than flesh and blood. If the cunning work of man be urged beyond its power of endurance, it has within it the elements of its own revenge; whereas the wretched mechanism of the Divine Hand is dangerous with no such property, but may be tampered with, and crushed, and broken, at the driver's pleasure. Look at that engine! It shall cost a man more dollars in the way of penalty and fine, and satisfiaction of the outraged law, to deface in wantonness that senseless mass of metal, than to take the lives of twenty human creatures. Thus the stars wink upon the bloody stripes; and Liberty pulls down her cap upon her eyes, and owns Oppression in its vilest aspect, for her sister." MC 21

And see F:Slavery *and* F:Violence

—*virtue, ostentatious:* "'The best on it is,' said Mark [Tapley], 'that when they do happen to make a decent stroke; such as better workmen, with no such opportunities, make every day of their lives and think nothing of; they begin to sing out so surprising loud. Take notice of my words, sir. If ever the defaulting part of this here country pays its debts—along of finding that not paying 'em won't do in a commercial point of view, you see, and is inconvenient in its consequences—they'll take such a shine out of it, and make such bragging speeches, that a man might suppose no borrowed money had ever been paid afore, since the world was first befun. That's the way they gammon each other, sir. Bless you, *I* know 'em.'" MC 23

—*West Point:* "In this beautiful place: the fairest among the fair and lovely Highlands of the North River: shut in by deep green heights and ruined forts, and looking down upon the distant town of Newburgh, along a glittering path of sunlit water, with here and there a skiff, whose white sail often bends on some new tack as sudden flaws of wind come down upon her from the gullies in the hills: hemmed in, besides, all round with memories of Washington, and events of the revolutionary war: is the Military School of America.

"It could not stand on more appropriate ground, and any ground more beautiful can hardly be. The course of education is severe, but well devised, and manly. Through June, July, and August, the young men encamp upon the spacious plain whereon the college stands; and all the year their military exercises are performed there, daily. The term of study at this institution, which the State requires from all cadets, is four years; but, whether it be from the rigid nature of the discipline, or the national impatience of restraint, or both causes combined, not more than half the number who begin their studies here, ever remain to finish them." AN 15

Australia

—*demeanour:* "'Good-morning, my dear,' said the principal [Namby, a gorgeous bailiff], addressing the young lady at the bar, with Botany Bay ease, and New South Wales gentility; 'which is Mr Pickwick's room, my dear?'" PP 40

—*in metaphor:* " . . . I said I supposed [Jaggers] was very skilful?

"'Deep,' said Wemmick, 'as Australia.' Pointing with his pen at the office floor, to express that Australia was understood, for the purposes of the figure, to be symmetrically on the opposite spot of the globe. 'If there was anything deeper,' added Wemmick, bringing his pen to paper, 'he'd be it.'" GE 24

Canada

—*praised:* "But Canada has held, and always will retain, a foremost place in my remembrance. Few Englishmen are prepared to find it what it is. Advancing quietly; old differences settling down, and being fast forgotten; public feeling and private enterprise alike in a sound and wholesome state; nothing of flush or fever in its system, but health and vigorous throbbing in its steady pulse: it is full of hope and promise.

"To me—who had been accustomed to think of it as something left behind in the strides of advancing society, as something neglected and forgotten, slumbering and wasting in its sleep—the demand for labour and the rates of wages; the busy quays of Montreal; the vessels taking in their cargoes, and discharging them; the amount of shipping in the different ports; the commerce, roads, and public works, all made *to last;* the respectability and character of the public journals; and the amount of rational comfort and happiness which honest industry may earn: were very great surprises." ¶AN 15

China

—*foolishly pictured:* "' . . . do tell me something [said Flora Finching to Clennam] about the Chinese ladies whether their eyes are really so long and narrow always putting me in mind of mother-of-pearl fish at cards and do they really wear tails down their back and plaited too or is it only the men, and when they pull their hair so very tight off their foreheads don't they hurt themselves, and why do they stick little bells all over their bridges and temples and hats and things or don't they really do it! ...

"' . . . what a country to live in for so long a time, and with so many lanterns and umbrellas too how very dark and wet the climate ought to be and no doubt actually is, and the sums of money that must be made by those two trades where everybody carries them and hangs them everywhere, the little shoes too and the feet screwed back in infancy is quite surprising, what a traveller you are!'" LD i 13

Cities and Towns, Actual

—*Aix-en-Provence:* " . . . the town was very clean; but so hot, and so intensely light, that when I walked out at noon it was like coming suddenly from the darkened room into crisp blue fire. The air was so very clear, that distant hills and rocky points appeared within an hour's walk; while the town immediately at hand—with a kind of blue wind between me and it—seemed to be white hot, and to be throwing off a fiery air from the surface." PI 4

—*Avignon:* "There lay before us . . . the broken bridge of Avignon, and all the city baking in the sun; yet with an under-done-pie-crust, battlemented wall, that never will be brown, though it bake for centuries.

"The grapes were hanging in clusters in the streets, and the brilliant Oleander was in full bloom everywhere. The streets are old and very narrow, but tolerably clean, and shaded by awnings stretched from house to house. Bright stuffs and handkerchiefs, curiosities, ancient frames of carved wood, old chairs, ghostly tables, saints, virgins, angels, and staring daubs of portraits, being exposed for sale beneath, it was very quaint and lively. All this was much set off, too, by the glimpses one caught, through a rusty gate standing ajar, of quiet sleepy court-yards, having stately old houses within, as silent as tombs." PI 3

—*Birmingham:* "The straggling cottages by the roadside, the dingy hue of every object visible, the murky atmosphere, the paths of cinders and brick-dust, the deep-red glow of furnace fires in the distance, the volumes of dense smoke issuing heavily forth from high toppling chimneys, blackening and obscuring everything around; the glare of distant lights, the ponderous waggons which toiled along the road, laden with clashing rods of iron, or piled with heavy goods—all betokened their rapid approach to the great working town of Birmingham.

"As they rattled through the narrow thoroughfares leading to the heart of the turmoil, the sights and sounds of earnest occupation struck more forcibly on the senses. The streets were thronged with working-people. The hum of labour resounded from every house, lights gleamed from the long casement windows in the attic stories, and the whirl of wheels and noise of machinery shook the trembling walls. The fires, whose lurid sullen light had been visible for miles, blazed fiercely up, in the great works and factories of the town. The din of hammers, the rushing of steam, and the dead heavy clanking of engines, was the harsh music which arose from every quarter." PP 50

—*Bologna:* "Again an ancient sombre town, under the brilliant sky; with heavy arcades over the footways of the older streets, and lighter and more cheerful archways in the newer portions of the town. Again, brown piles of sacred buildings, with more birds flying in and out of chinks in the stones; and more snarling monsters for the bases of the pillars. Again, rich churches, drowsy Masses, curling incense, tinkling bells, priests in bright vestments: pictures, tapers, laced altar cloths, crosses, images, and artificial flowers.

"There is a grave and learned air about the city, and a pleasant gloom upon it, that would leave it, a distinct and separate impression in the mind, among a crowd of cities, though it were not still further marked in the traveller's remembrance by the two brick leaning towers . . . inclining cross-wise as if they were bowing stiffly to each other—a most extraordinary termination to the perspective of some of the narrow streets.

"The colleges, and churches, too, and palaces: and above all the academy of Fine Arts, where there are a host of interesting pictures . . . give it a place of its own in the memory. Even though these were not, and there were nothing else to remember it by, the great Meridian on the pavement of the church of San Petronio, where the sunbeams mark the time among the kneeling people, would give it a fanciful and pleasant interest." ¶PI 7

—*Boston:* " . . . the air was so clear, the houses were so bright and gay; the signboards were painted in such gaudy colours; the gilded letters were so very golden; the bricks were so very red, the stone was so very white, the blinds and area railings were so very green, the knobs and plates upon the street doors so marvellously bright and twinkling; and all so slight and unsubstantial in appearance—that every thoroughfare in the city looked exactly like a scene in a pantomime." AN 3

—*suburbs:* "The suburbs are, if possible, even more unsubstantial-looking than the city. The white wooden houses (so white that it makes one wink to look at them), with their green jalousie blinds, are so sprinkled and dropped about in all directions, without seeming to have any root at all in the ground; and the small churches and chapels are so prim, and bright, and highly varnished; that I almost believed the whole affair could be taken up piecemal like a child's toy, and crammed into a little box." AN 3

—*Boulogne:* " . . . we have dallied for two or three seasons with a French watering-place: once solely known to us as a town with a very long street, beginning with an abattoir and ending with a steam-boat . . . . "

"But our French watering-place, when it is once got into, is a very enjoyable place. It has a varied and beautiful country around it, and many characteristic and agreeable things within it. To be sure, it might have fewer bad smells and less decaying refuse, and it might be better drained, and much cleaner in many parts, and therefore infinitely more healthy. Still, it is a bright, airy, pleasant, cheerful town; and if you were to walk down either of its three well-paved main streets, towards five o'clock in the afternoon, when delicate odours of cookery fill the air, and its hotel windows (it is full of hotels) give glimpses of long tables set out for dinner, and made to look sumptuous by the aid of napkins folded fan-wise, you would rightly judge it to be an uncommonly good town to eat and drink in.

"There is a charming walk, arched and shaded by trees, on the old walls that form the four sides of this High Town, whence you get glimpses of the streets below, and changing views of the other town and of the river, and of the hills and of the sea. It is made more agreeable and peculiar by some of the solemn houses that are rooted in the deep streets below, bursting into a fresher existence a-top, and having doors and windows, and even gardens, on these ramparts." RP/FW *And see* Tourism—*guidebooks, and* H: Marketplace

—*market:* "In the Place d'Armes of this town, a little decayed market is held, which seems to slip through the old gateway, like water, and go rippling down the hill, to mingle with the murmuring market in the lower town, and get lost in its movement and bustle.

"It is very agreeable on an idle summer morning to pursue this market-stream from the hill-top. It begins, dozingly and dully, with a few sacks of corn; starts into a surprising collection of boots and shoes; goes brawling down the hill in a diversified channel of old cordage, old iron, old crockery, old clothes, civil and military, old rags, new cotton goods, flaming prints of saints, little looking-glasses, and incalculable lengths of tape; dives into a backway, keeping out of sight for a little while, as streams will, or only sparkling for a moment in the shape of a market drinking-shop; and suddenly reappears behind the great church, shooting itself into a bright confusion of white-capped women and blue-bloused men, poultry, vegetables, fruits, flowers, pots, pans, praying-chairs, soldiers, country butter, umbrellas and other sun-shades, girl-porters waiting to be hired with baskets at their backs . . . .

"Early in the afternoon, the whole course of the stream is dry. The praying-chairs are put back in the church, the umbrellas are folded up, the unsold goods are carried away, the stalls and stands disappear, the square is swept, the hackney coaches lounge there to be hired, and on all the country roads (if you walk about, as much as we do) you will see the peasant women, always neatly and comfortably dressed, riding home, with the pleasantest saddle-furniture of clean milk-pails, bright butter-kegs, and the like, on the jolliest little donkeys in the world." ¶RP/FW

—*Broadstairs:* "In truth, our watering-place itself has been left somewhat high and dry by the tide of years. Concerned as we are for its honour, we must reluctantly admit that the time when this pretty little semicircular sweep of houses tapering off at the end of the wooden pier into a point in the sea, was a gay place, and when the light-house overlooking it shone at daybreak on company dispersing from public balls, is but dimly traditional now . . . .

"As to subscription balls in the Assembly Rooms of our watering-place now red-hot cannon balls are less improbable . . . .

"You would hardly guess which is the main street of our watering-place, but you may know it by its being always stopped up with donkey-chaises. Whenever you come here, and see harnessed donkeys eating clover out of barrows drawn completely across a narrow thoroughfare, you may be quite sure you are in our High Street.

"Our Police you may know by his uniform, likewise by his never on any account interfering with anybody—especially the tramps and vagabonds. In our fancy shops we have a capital collection of damaged goods, among which the flies of countless summers 'have been roaming.'

"We are great in obsolete seals, and in faded pin-cushions, and in rickety camp-stools, and in exploded cutlery, and in miniature vessels, and in stunted little telescopes, and in objects made of shells that pretend not to be shells. Diminutive spades, barrows, and baskets, are our principal articles of commerce; but even they don't look quite new somehow. They always seem to have been offered and refused somewhere else, before they came down to our watering-place." ¶RP/EW

—*a view:* "Half awake and half asleep, this idle morning in our sunny window on the edge of a chalk-cliff in the old-fashioned watering-place to which we are a faithful resorter, we feel a lazy inclination to sketch its picture.

"The place seems to respond. Sky, sea, beach, and village, lie as still before us as if they were sitting for the picture. It is dead low-water. A ripple plays among the ripening corn upon the cliff, as if it were faintly trying from recollection to imitate the sea; and the world of butterflies hovering over the crop of radish-seed are as restless in their little way as the gulls are in their larger manner when the wind blows.

"But the ocean lies winking in the sunlight like a drowsy lion—its glassy waters scarcely curve upon the shore—the fishing-boats in the tiny harbour are all stranded in the mud—our two colliers . . . have not an inch of water within a quarter of a mile of them, and turn, exhausted, on their sides, like faint fish of an antediluvian species.

Rusty cables and chains, ropes and rings, undermost parts of posts and piles and confused timber-defences against the waves, lie strewn about, in a brown litter of tangled sea-weed and fallen cliff which looks as if a family of giants had been making tea here for ages, and had observed an untidy custom of throwing their tea-leaves on the shore." RP/EW

—*Cairo, Illinois:* " . . . we arrived at a spot so much more desolate than any we had yet beheld, that the forlornest places we had passed were, in comparison with it, full of interest. At the junction of the two rivers, on ground so flat and low and marshy, that at certain seasons of the year it is inundated to the house-tops, lies a breeding-place of fever, ague, and death; vaunted in England as a mine of Golden Hope, and speculated in, on the faith of monstrous representations, to many people's ruin.

"A dismal swamp, on which the half-built houses rot away: cleared here and there for the space of a few yards; and teeming, then, with rank unwholesome vegetation, in whose baleful shade the wretched wanderers who are tempted hither, droop, and die, and lay their bones; the hateful Mississippi circling and eddying before it, and turning off upon its southern course a slimy monster hideous to behold; a hotbed of disease, an ugly sepulchre, a grave uncheered by any gleam of promise: a place without one single quality, in earth or air or water, to commend it: such is this dismal Cairo." AN 12

"As [Martin Chuzzlewit and Mark Tapley] proceeded further on their track, and came more and more towards their journey's end, the monotonous desolation of the scene increased to that degree, that for any redeeming feature it presented to their eyes, they might have entered, in the body, on the grim domains of Giant Despair. A flat morass, bestrewn with fallen timber; a marsh on which the good growth of the earth seemed to have been wrecked and cast away, that from its decomposing ashes vile and ugly things might rise; where the very trees took the aspect of huge weeds, begotten of the slime from which they sprung, by the hot sun that burnt them up; where fatal maladies, seeking whom they might infect, came forth at night in misty shapes, and creeping out upon the water, hunted them like spectres until day; where even the blessed sun, shining down on festering elements of corruption and disease, became a horror; this was the realm of Hope through which they moved.

"At last they stopped. At Eden too. The waters of the Deluge might have left it but a week before: so choked with slime and matted growth was the hideous swamp which bore that name.

"There being no depth of water close in shore, they landed from the vessel's boat, with all their goods beside them. There were a few log-houses visible among the dark trees: the best, a cow-shed or a rude stable. But for the wharves, the market-place, the public buildings!" MC 23

—*Calais*

—*exiles:* "[Clennam] met new groups of his countrymen, who had all a straggling air of having at one time overblown themselves, like certain uncomfortable kinds of flowers, and of being, now, mere weeds. They had all an air, too, of lounging out a limited round, day after day, which strongly reminded him of the Marshalsea." LD ii 20

—*landing:* "The passengers were landing from the packet on the pier at Calais. A low-lying place and a low-spirited place Calais was, with the tide ebbing out towards low water-mark. There had been no more water on the bar than had sufficed to float the packet in; and now the bar itself, with a shallow break of sea over it, looked like a lazy marine monster just risen to the surface, whose form was indistinctly shown as it lay asleep . . . .

"The long rows of gaunt black piles, slimy and wet and weather-worn, with funeral garlands of seaweed twisted about them by the late tide, might have represented an unsightly marine cemetery. Every wave-dashed, storm-beaten object, was so low and so little, under the broad grey sky, in the noise of the wind and sea, and before the curling lines of surf, making at it ferociously, that the wonder was there was any Calais left, and that its low gates and low wall and low roofs and low ditches and low sand-hills and low ramparts and flat streets, had not yielded long ago to the undermining and besieging sea, like the fortifications children make on the sea-shore.

"After slipping among oozy piles and planks, stumbling up wet steps and encountering many salt difficulties, the passengers entered on their comfortless peregrination along the pier; where all the French vagabonds and English outlaws in the town (half the population) attended to prevent their recovery from bewilderment.

After being minutely inspected by all the English, and claimed and reclaimed and counter-claimed as prizes by all the French, in a hand-to-hand scuffle three quarters of a mile long, they were at last free to enter the streets, and to make off in their various directions, hotly pursued." ¶LD ii 20

—once safely debarked: "Calais up and doing at the railway station, and Calais down and dreaming in its bed; Calais with something of 'an ancient and fish-like smell' about it, and Calais blown and sea-washed pure; Calais represented at the Buffet by savoury roast fowls, hot coffee, cognac, and Bordeaux; and Calais represented everywhere by flitting persons with a monomania for changing money—though I never shall be able to understand in my present state of existence how they live by it, but I suppose I should, if I understood the currency question—Calais *en gros,* and Calais *en detail,* forgive one who has deeply wronged you.—I was not fully aware of it on the other side, but I meant Dover." UT/CM

—Camoglia: "There is one town, Camoglia, with its little harbour on the sea, hundreds of feet below the road; where families of mariners live, who, time out of mind, have owned coasting-vessels in that place, and have traded to Spain and elsewhere. Seen from the road above, it is like a tiny model on the margin of the dimpled water, shining in the sun.

"Descended into, by the winding mule-tracks, it is a perfect miniature of a primitive seafaring town; the saltest, roughest, most piratical little place that ever was seen. Great rusty iron rings and mooring-chains, capstans, and fragments of old masts and spars, choke up the way; hardy rough-weather boats, and seamen's clothing, flutter in the little harbour or are drawn out on the sunny stones to dry; on the parapet of the rude pier, a few amphibious-looking fellows lie asleep, with their legs dangling over the wall, as though earth or water were all one to them, and if they slipped in, they would float away, dozing comfortably among the fishes; the church is bright with trophies of the sea, and votive offerings in commemoration of escape from storm and shipwreck.

"The dwellings not immediately abutting on the harbour are approached by blind low archways, and by crooked steps, as if in darkness and in difficulty of access they should be like holds of ships, or inconvenient cabins under water; and everywhere, there is a smell of fish, and sea-weed, and old rope." ¶PI 10

—Canterbury: "Early in the morning, I [David Copperfield] sauntered through the dear old tranquil streets, and again mingled with the shadows of the venerable gateways and churches. The rooks were sailing about the cathedral towers; and the towers themselves, overlooking many a long unaltered mile of the rich country and its pleasant streams, were cutting the bright morning air, as if there were no such thing as change on earth. Yet the bells, when they sounded, told me sorrowfully of change in everything; told me of their own age, and my pretty Dora's youth; and of the many, never old, who had lived and loved and died, while the reverberations of the bells had hummed through the rusty armour of the Black Prince hanging up within, and, motes upon the deep of Time, had lost themselves in air, as circles do in water." DC 52

—Carrara

—marble quarry: "They are four or five great glens, running up into a range of lofty hills, until they can run no longer, and are stopped by being abruptly strangled by Nature. The quarries, 'or caves' as they call them here, are so many openings, high up in the hills, on either side of these passes, where they blast and excavate for marble: which may turn out good or bad: may make a man's fortune very quickly, or ruin him by the great expense of working what is worth nothing. Some of these caves were opened by the ancient Romans, and remain as they left them to this hour. Many others are being worked at this moment; others are to be begun to-morrow, next week, next month; others are unbought, unthought of; and marble enough for more ages than have passed since the place was resorted to, lies hidden everywhere: patiently awaiting its time of discovery." PI 1

And see IG:Railroad—*absence at Carrara;* N:Animal—*oxen; and* S:Good and Evil—*lesson of marble sculpture*

—Chalons: "Chalons is a fair resting-place, in right of its good inn on the bank of the river, and the little steamboats, gay with green and red paint, that come and go upon it: which make up a pleasant and refreshing scene, after the dusty roads. But, unless you would like to dwell on an enormous plain, with jagged rows of irregular poplars on it, that look in the distance like so many combs with broken teeth: and unless you would like to pass your life without the pos-

sibility of going up-hill, or going up anything but stairs: you would hardly approve of Chalons as a place of residence." PI 3 *And see* Rivers—*Saone*

—*Cincinnati:* "Cincinnati is a beautiful city; cheerful, thriving, and animated. I have not often seen a place that commends itself so favourably and pleasantly to a stranger at the first glance as this does: with its clean houses of red and white, its well-paved roads, and foot-ways of bright tile.

"Nor does it become less prepossessing on a closer acquaintance. The streets are broad and airy, the shops extremely good, the private residences remarkable for their elegance and neatness. There is something of invention and fancy in the varying styles of these latter erections, which, after the dull company of the steamboat, is perfectly delightful, as conveying an assurance that there are such qualities still in existence.

"The disposition to ornament these pretty villas and render them attractive, leads to the culture of trees and flowers, and the laying out of well-kept gardens, the sight of which, to those who walk along the streets, is inexpressibly refreshing and agreeable. I was quite charmed with the appearance of the town, and its adjoining suburb of Mount Auburn: from which the city, lying in an amphitheatre of hills, forms a picture of remarkable beauty, and is seen to great advantage . . . .

"The society with which I mingled, was intelligent, courteous, and agreeable. The inhabitants of Cincinnati are proud of their city as one of the most interesting in America: and with good reason: for beautiful and thriving as it is now, and containing, as it does, a population of fifty thousand souls, but two-and-fifty years have passed away since the ground on which it stands (bought at that time for a few dollars) was a wild wood, and its citizens were but a handful of dwellers in scattered log huts upon the river's shores." AN 11

—*Deal:* "At last we came into the narrow streets of Deal: and very gloomy they were, upon a raw misty morning. The long flat beach, with its little irregular houses, wooden and brick, and its litter of capstans, and great boats, and sheds, and bare upright poles with tackle and blocks, and loose gravelly waste places overgrown with grass and weeds, wore as dull an appearance as any place I ever saw. The sea was heaving under a thick white fog; and nothing else was moving but a few early ropemakers, who, with the yarn twisted round their bodies, looked as if, tired of their present state of existence, they were spinning themselves into cordage." BH 45

—*Dover:* "The little narrow, crooked town of Dover hid itself away from the beach, and ran its head into the chalk cliffs, like a marine ostrich. The beach was a desert of heaps of sea and stones tumbling wildly about, and the sea did what it liked, and what it liked was destruction. It thundered at the town, and thundered at the cliffs, and brought the coast down, madly. The air among the houses was of so strong a piscatory flavour that one might have supposed sick fish went up to be dipped in it, as sick people went down to be dipped in the sea." TTC i 4 *And see* H:Vocations—*illicit—smuggling*

—*Epsom:* A straggling street, an undue proportion of inns, a large pond, a pump, and a magnificent brick clock case, make up—with a few more touches not necessary to be given here—the picture of the metropolis of English racing, and the fountain of Epsom salts. For three hundred and sixty-four days in the year a cannon-ball might be fired from one end of Epsom to the other without endangering human life. On the three hundred and sixty-fifth, or Derby Day, a population surges and rolls, and scrambles through the place, that may be counted in millions.

"Epsom during the races, and Epsom at any other time, are things as unlike as the Desert of Saharah and the interior of the Palace of Glass in Hyde Park." HWC/E *And see* H:Race-meeting—*Derby Day*

—*Ferrara:* "More solitary, more depopulated, more deserted, old Ferrara, than any city of the solemn brotherhood! The grass so grows up in the silent streets, that any one might make hay there, literally, while the sun shines. But the sun shines with diminished cheerfulness in grim Ferrara; and the people are so few who pass and repass through the places, that the flesh of its inhabitants might be grass indeed, and growing in the squares." PI 7

—*Florence:* "Magnificently stern and sombre are the streets of beautiful Florence; and the strong old piles of building make such heaps of shadow, on the ground and in the river, that there is another and a different city of rich forms and fancies, always lying at our feet.

"Prodigious palaces, constructed for defence, with small distrustful windows heavily barred, and walls of great thickness formed of huge masses of rough stone, frown, in their old sulky state, on every street. In the midst of the city—in the Piazza of the Grand Duke, adorned with beautiful statues and the Fountain of Neptune—rises the Palazzo Vecchio, with its enormous overhanging battlements, and the Great Tower that watches over the whole town.

"In its court-yard—worthy of the Castle of Otranto in its ponderous gloom—is a massive staircase that the heaviest waggon and the stoutest team of horses might be driven up. Within it, is a Great Saloon, faded and tarnished in its stately decorations, and mouldering by grains, but recording yet, in pictures on its walls, the triumphs of the Medici and the wars of the old Florentine people." ¶PI 19

—Ponte Vecchio: "Among the four old bridges that span the river, the Ponte Vecchio—that bridge which is covered with the shops of Jewellers and Goldsmiths—is a most enchanting feature in the scene. The space of one house, in the centre, being left open, the view beyond is shown as in a frame; and that precious glimpse of sky, and water, and rich buildings, shining so quietly among the huddled roofs and gables on the bridge, is exquisite." PI 19

—Fondi: " . . . the first Neapolitan town—Fondi. Take note of Fondi, in the name of all that is wretched and beggarly.

"A filthy channel of mud and refuse meanders down the centre of the miserable streets, fed by obscene rivulets that trickle from the abject houses. There is not a door, a window, or a shutter; not a roof, a wall, a post, or a pillar, in all Fondi, but is decayed, and crazy, and rotting away. The wretched history of the town, with all its sieges and pillages by Barbarossa and the rest, might have been acted last year. How the gaunt dogs that sneak about the miserable streets, come to be alive, and undevoured by the people, is one of the enigmas of the world." PI 12 *And see* Italy—*beggary*

—Genoa: "We could see Genoa before three; and watching it as it gradually developed its splendid amphitheatre, terrace rising above terrace, garden above garden, palace above palace, height upon height, was ample occupation for us, till we ran into the stately harbour . . . .

"I never in my life was so dismayed! The wonderful novelty of everything, the unusual smells, the unaccountable filth (though it is reckoned the cleanest of Italian towns), the disorderly jumbling of dirty houses, one upon the roof of another; the passages more squalid and more close than any in St. Giles's or old Paris; in and out of which, not vagabonds, but well-dressed women, with white veils and great fans, were passing and repassing; the perfect absence of resemblance in any dwelling-house, or shop, or wall, or post, or pillar, to anything one had ever seen before; and the disheartening dirt, discomfort, and decay; perfectly confounded me.

"I fell into a dismal reverie. I am conscious of a feverish and bewildered vision of saints' and virgins' shrines at the street corners—of great numbers of friars, monks, and soldiers—of vast red curtains, waving in the doorways of the churches—of always going up hill, and yet seeing every other street and passage going higher up—of fruit-stalls, with fresh lemons and oranges hanging in garlands made of vine-leaves—of a guard-house, and a draw-bridge—and some gateways—and vendors of iced water, sitting with little trays upon the margin of the kennel—and this is all the consciousness I had, until I was set down in a rank, dull, weedy court-yard, attached to a kind of pink jail; and was told I lived there." ¶PI 4 *But see* CD:Happy in Italy

"The narrow lanes have great villas opening into them, whose walls (outside walls, I mean) are profusely painted with all sorts of subjects, grim and holy. But time and the sea-air have nearly obliterated them; and they look like the entrance to Vauxhall Gardens on a sunny day. The court-yards of these houses are overgrown with grass and weeds; all sorts of hideous patches cover the bases of the statues, as if they were afflicted with a cutaneous disorder; the outer gates are rusty; and the iron bars outside the lower windows are all tumbling down.

"Firewood is kept in halls where costly treasures might be heaped up, mountains high; water-falls are dry and choked; fountains, too dull to play, and too lazy to work, have just enough recollection of their identity, in their sleep, to make the neighbourhood damp; and the sirocco wind is often blowing over all these things for days together, like a gigantic oven out for a holiday." ¶PI 5

"It is a place that 'grows upon you' every day. There seems to be always something to find out in it. There are the most extraordinary alleys and by-ways to walk about in. You can lose your way (what a comfort that is, when you are idle!) twenty times a day, if you like; and turn up again, under the most unexpected and surprising difficulties. It abounds in the strangest contrasts; things that are picturesque, ugly, mean, magnificent, delightful, and offensive, break upon the view at every turn." PI 5

And see B:House—*palazzo*

—*shopping district:* "In the streets of shops, the houses are much smaller [than the palazzos], but of great size notwithstanding, and extremely high. They are very dirty: quite undrained, if my nose be at all reliable: and emit a peculiar fragrance, like the smell of very bad cheese, kept in very hot blankets. Notwithstanding the height of the houses, there would seem to have been a lack of room in the City, for new houses are thrust in everywhere.

"Wherever it has been possible to cram a tumble-down tenement into a crack or corner, in it has gone. If there be a nook or angle in the wall of a church, or a crevice in any other dead wall, of any sort, there you are sure to find some kind of habitation: looking as if it had grown there, like a fungus. Against the Government House, against the old Senate House, round about any large building, little shops stick so close, like parasite vermin to the great carcase. And for all this, look where you may: up steps, down steps, anywhere, everywhere: there are irregular houses, receding, starting forward, tumbling down, leaning against their neighbours, crippling themselves or their friends by some means or other, until one, more irregular than the rest, chokes up the way, and you can't see any further." ¶PI 5

—*Gravesend:* "Tracking our guide through dock gates, over narrow drawbridges, along quays; now, dodging the rigging of ships; now, tripping over cables, made 'taut' to rings; now, falling foul of warping-posts (for it was getting dusk); one minute, leaping over deserted timber; the next, doubling stray casks; the next, winding among the strangest ruins of dismantled steam-boats, for which a regular Hospital seemed established in that desolate region of mud and water; then, emerging into dirty lanes, and turning the corners of roofless houses; we finished an exciting game of Follow my Leader, at a pair of tall gates. One of these, admitted us into the precincts of the southernmost of the six manufactories of plate glass existing in this country." HWC/PG

—*Halifax, Nova Scotia:* "The town is built on the side of a hill, the highest point being commanded by a strong fortress . . . . The houses are chiefly of wood. The market is abundantly supplied; and provisions are exceedingly cheap. The weather being unusually mild at that time for the season of the year, there was no sleighing: but there were plenty of those vehicles in yards and by-places, and some of them, from the gorgeous quality of their decorations, might have 'gone on' without alteration as triumphal cars in a melodrama at Astley's . . . the whole aspect of the town cheerful, thriving, and industrious." AN 2

—*Lancaster:* "It is Mr Goodchild's opinion, that if a visitor on his arrival at Lancaster could be accommodated with a pole which would push the opposite side of the street some yards farther off, it would be better for all parties. Protesting against being required to live in a trench, and obliged to speculate all day upon what the people can possibly be doing within a mysterious opposite window, which is a shop-window to look at, but not a shop-window in respect of its offering nothing for sale and declining to give any account whatever of itself, Mr Goodchild concedes Lancaster to be a pleasant place.

"A place dropped in the midst of a charming landscape, a place with a fine ancient fragment of castle, a place of lovely walks, a place possessing staid old houses richly fitted with old Honduras mahogany, which has grown so dark with time that it seems to have got something of a retrospective mirror-quality into itself, and to show the visitor, in the depth of its grain, through all its polish, the hue of the wretched slaves who groaned long ago under old Lancaster merchants." ¶LT 3

—*Leghorn:* " . . . a thriving, business-like, matter-of-fact place, where regulations observed there, in reference to trade and merchants, are very liberal and free; and the town, of course, benefits by them." PI 10

And see CD: Chauvinist; *and* F:Assassin

—*Lowell, Massachusetts:* " . . . a very dirty winter's day, and nothing in the whole town looked old to me, except the mud, which in some parts was almost knee-deep, and might have been deposited there, on the subsiding of the waters after the Deluge.

"In one place, there was a new wooden church, which, having no steeple, and being yet unpainted, looked like an enormous packing-case without any direction upon it. In another there was a large hotel, whose walls and colonnades were so crisp, and thin, and slight, that it had exactly the appearance of being built with cards . . . .

"The very river that moves the machinery in the mills (for they are all worked by water power), seems to acquire a new character from the fresh buildings of bright red brick and painted wood among which it takes its course; and to be as light-headed, thoughtless, and brisk a young river, in its murmurings and tumblings, as one would desire to see . . . when I saw a baby of some week or ten days old in a woman's arms at a street corner, I found myself unconsciously wondering where it came from: never supposing for an instant that it could have been born in such a young town as that." ¶AN 4

—*Lyons:* "Talk about people feeling, at certain unlucky times, as if they had tumbled from the clouds! Here is a whole town that is tumbled, anyhow, out of the sky; having been first caught up, like other stones that tumble down from that region, out of fens and barren places, dismal to behold!

"The two great streets through which the two great rivers dash, and all the little streets whose name is Legion, were scorching, blistering, and sweltering. The houses, high and vast, dirty to excess, rotten as old cheeses, and as thickly peopled. All up the hills that hem the city in, these houses swarm; and the mites inside were lolling out of the windows, and drying their ragged clothes on poles, and crawling in and out at the doors, and coming out to pant and gasp upon the pavement, and creeping in and out among huge piles and bales of fusty, musty, stifling goods; and living, or rather not dying till their time should come, in an exhausted receiver.

"Every manufacturing town, melted into one, would hardly convey an impression of Lyons as it presented itself to me: for all the undrained, unscavengered qualities of a foreign town, seemed grafted, there, upon the native miseries of a manufacturing one; and it bears such fruit as I would go some miles out of my way to avoid encountering again." PI 3

—*Marseilles:* "Thirty years ago [1825], Marseilles lay burning in the sun, one day.

"A blazing sun upon a fierce August day was no greater rarity in southern France then, than at any other time, before or since. Everything in Marseilles, and about Marseilles, had stared at the fervid sky, and been stared at in return, until a staring habit had become universal there. Strangers were stared out of countenance by staring white houses, staring white walls, staring white streets, staring tracts of arid road, staring hills from which verdure was burnt away. The only things to be seen not fixedly staring and glaring were the vines drooping under their load of grapes. These did occasionally wink a little, as the hot air barely moved their faint leaves.

"There was no wind to make a ripple on the foul water within the harbour, or on the beautiful sea without. The line of demarcation between the two colours, black and blue, showed the point which the pure sea would not pass; but it lay as quiet as the abominable pool, with which it never mixed. Boats without awnings were too hot to touch; ships blistered at their moorings; the stones of the quays had not cooled, night or day, for months. Hindoos, Russians, Chinese, Spaniards, Portuguese, Englishmen, Frenchmen, Genoese, Neapolitans, Venetians, Greeks, Turks, descendants from all the builders of Babel, come to trade at Marseilles, sought the shade alike—taking refuge in any hiding-place from a sea too intensely blue to be looked at, and a sky of purple, set with one great flaming jewel of fire.

"The universal stare made the eyes ache. Towards the distant line of Italian coast, indeed, it was a little relieved by light clouds of mist, slowly rising from the evaporation of the sea, but it softened nowhere else. Far away the staring roads, deep in dust, stared from the hill-side, stared from the hollow, stared from the interminable plain. Far away the dusty vines overhanging wayside cottages, and the monotonous wayside avenues of parched trees without shade, drooped beneath the stare of earth and sky. So did the horses with drowsy bells, in long files of carts, creeping slowly towards the interior; so did their recumbent drivers, when they were awake, which rarely happened; so did the exhausted labourers in the fields. Everything that lived or grew, was oppressed by the glare; except the lizard, passing swiftly over the rough stone walls, and the cicala [*sic.*], chirping his dry hot chirp, like a rattle. The very dust was scorched brown, and something quivered in the atmosphere as if the air itself were panting.

"Blinds, shutters, curtains, awnings, were all closed and drawn to keep out the stare. Grant it but a chink or keyhole, and it shot in like a white-hot arrow. The churches were the freest from it. To come out of the twilight of pillars and arches—dreamily dotted with winking lamps, dreamily peopled with ugly old shadows piously dozing, spitting, and begging—was to plunge into a fiery river, and swim for life to the nearest strip of shade. So, with people lounging and lying wherever shade was, with but little hum of tongues or barking of dogs, with occasional jangling of discordant church bells, and rattling of vicious drums, Marseilles, a fact to be strongly smelt and tasted, lay broiling in the sun one day." LD i 1

"I was there, twice or thrice afterwards [1845], in fair weather and foul; and I am afraid there is no doubt that it is a dirty and disagreeable place. But the prospect, from the fortified heights, of the beautiful Mediterranean, with its lovely rocks and islands, is most delightful. These heights are a desirable retreat, for less picturesque reasons—as an escape from a compound of vile smells perpetually arising from a great harbour full of stagnant water, and befouled by the refuse of innumerable ships with all sorts of cargoes: which, in hot weather, is dreadful in the last degree.

"There were foreign sailors, of all nations, in the streets; with red shirts, blue shirts, buff shirts, tawny shirts, and shirts of orange colour; with red caps, blue caps, green caps, great beards, and no beards; in Turkish turbans, glazed English hats, and Neapolitan head-dresses. There were the townspeople sitting in clusters on the pavement, or airing themselves on the tops of their houses, or walking up and down the closest and least airy of Boulevards; and there were crowds of fierce-looking people of the lower sort, blocking up the way, constantly.

"In the very heart of all this stir and uproar, was the common madhouse; a low, contracted, miserable building, looking straight upon the street, without the smallest screen or court-yard; where chattering madmen and mad women were peeping out, through rusty bars, at the staring faces below, while the sun, darting fiercely aslant into their little cells, seemed to dry up their brains, and worry them, as if they were baited by a pack of dogs." ¶PI 4

—*Naples:* "It wakes again to Policinelli [Punch performers], and pickpockets, buffo singers and beggars, rags, puppets, flowers, brightness, dirt, and universal degradation; airing its Harlequin suit in the sunshine, next day and every day; singing, starving, dancing, gaming, on the sea-shore; and leaving all labour to the burning mountain, which is ever at its work." PI 17

" . . . our last visit to Naples within these twelve months, when we found only four conditions of men remaining in the whole city: to wit, lazzaroni, priests, spies, and soldiers, and all of them beggars; the paternal government having banished all its subjects except the rascals." RP/FW

—*New Haven, Connecticut:* "Many of its streets . . . are planted with rows of grand old elm-trees; and the same natural ornaments surround Yale College, an establishment of considerable eminence and reputation. The various departments of this Institution are erected in a kind of park or common in the middle of the town, where they are dimly visible among the shadowing trees. The effect is very like that of an old cathedral yard in England; and when their branches are in full leaf, must be extremely picturesque." AN 5

—*New York City:* "'. . . [Lummy Ned] sent word home that it brought Old York to his mind, quite vivid, in consequence of being so exactly unlike it in every respect . . . .'" MC 13

—*harbour:* " . . . a noble bay, whose waters sparkled in the now cloudless sunshine like Nature's eyes turned up to Heaven.

"Then there lay stretched out before us, to the right, confused heaps of buildings, with here and there a spire or steeple, looking down upon the herd below; and here and there, again, a cloud of lazy smoke; and in the foreground a forest of ships' masts, cheery with flapping sails and waving flags. Crossing from among them to the opposite shore, were steam ferry-boats laden with people, coaches, horses, waggons, baskets, boxes: crossed and recrossed by other ferry-boats: all travelling to and fro: and never idle.

"Stately among these restless Insects, were two or three large ships, moving with slow majestic pace, as creatures of a prouder kind, disdainful of their puny journeys, and making for the broad sea. Beyond, were shining heights, and islands in the glancing river, and a distance scarcely less blue and bright than the sky it seemed to meet.

"The city's hum and buzz, the clinking of capstans, the ringing of bells, the barking of dogs, the clattering of wheels, tingled in the listening ear. All of which life and stir, coming across the stirring water, caught new life and animation from its free companionship; and, sympathising with its buoyant spirits, glistened as it seemed in sport upon its surface, and hemmed the vessel round, and plashed the water high about her sides, and, floating her gallantly into the dock, flew off again to welcome other comers, and speed before them to the busy port." AN 5

—poor: " . . . it must be remembered that New York, as a great emporium of commerce, and as a place of general resort, not only from all parts of the States, but from most parts of the world, has always a large pauper population to provide for; and labours, therefore, under peculiar difficulties in this respect. Nor must it be forgotten that New York is a large town, and that in all large towns a vast amount of good and evil is intermixed and jumbled up together." AN 6

—prison: "The day being very wet indeed, this [stone-quarry] labour was suspended, and the prisoners were in their cells. Imagine these cells, some two or three hundred in number, and in every one a man locked up; this one at his door for air, with his hands thrust through the grate; this one in bed (in the middle of the day, remember); and this one flung down in a heap upon the ground, with his head against the bars, like a wild beast.

"Make the rain pour down, outside, in torrents. Put the everlasting stove in the midst; hot, and suffocating, and vaporous, as a witch's cauldron. Add a collection of gentle odours, such as would arise from a thousand mildewed umbrellas, wet through, and a thousand buck-baskets, full of half-washed linen—and there is the prison, as it was that day." ¶AN 6

—Paris

—a slum: " . . . the doorway . . . opened from a stinking little black court-yard, and was the general public entrance to a great pile of houses, inhabited by a great number of people. In the gloomy tile-paved entry to the gloomy tile-paved staircase . . . .

"Such a staircase, with its accessories, in the older and more crowded parts of Paris, would be bad enough now; but, at that time [1775], it was vile indeed to unaccustomed and unhardened senses. Every little habitation within the great foul nest of one high building—that is to say, the room or rooms within every door that opened on the general staircase—left its own heap of refuse on its own landing, besides flinging other refuse from its own windows. The uncontrollable and hopeless mass of decomposition so engendered, would have polluted the air, even if poverty and deprivation had not loaded it with their intangible impurities; the two bad sources combined made it almost insupportable.

"Through such an atmosphere, by a steep dark shaft of dirt and poison, the way lay . . . [they] twice stopped to rest. Each of these stoppages was made at a doleful grating, by which any languishing good airs that were left uncorrupted, seemed to escape, and all spoilt and sickly vapours seemed to crawl in. Through the rusted bars, tastes, rather than glimpses, were caught of the jumbled neighbourhood; and nothing within range, nearer or lower than the summits of the two great towers of Notre-Dame, had any promise on it of healthy life or wholesome aspirations." ¶TTC i 5

—in Society (boring): " . . . [the Dedlocks] rattle out of the yard of the Hotel Bristol in the Place Vendome, and canter between the sun-and-shadow-chequered colonnade of the Rue de Rivoli and the garden of the ill-fated palace of a headless king and queen, off by the Place of Concord, and the Elysian Fields, and the Gate of the Star, out of Paris.

"Sooth to say, they cannot go away too fast; for, even here, my Lady Dedlock has been bored to death. Concert, assembly, opera, theatre, drive, nothing is new to my Lady, under the worn-out heavens. Only last Sunday, when poor wretches were gay—within the walls, playing with children among the clipped trees and the statues in the Palace Garden; walking, a score abreast, in the Elysian Fields, made more Elysian by performing dogs and wooden horses; between whiles filtering (a few) through the gloomy Cathedral of our Lady, to say a word or two at the base of a pillar, within flare of a rusty little gridiron-full of gusty little tapers—without the walls, encompassing Paris with dancing, love-making, wine-drinking, tobacco-smoking, tomb-visiting, billiard, card, and domino playing, quackdoctoring, and much murderous refuse, animate and inanimate—only last Sunday, my Lady, in the desolation of Boredom and the clutch of Giant Despair, almost hated her own maid for being in spirits." BH 12

—out of Society: "And of Paris [writes Mrs Lirriper] I can tell you no more my dear than that it's town and country both in one, and carved stone and long streets of high houses and gardens and fountains and statues and trees and gold, and immensely big soldiers and immensely little soldiers and the pleasantest nurses with the whitest caps a playing at skipping-rope with the bunchiest babies in the flattest caps, and clean table-cloths spread everywhere for dinner and people sitting out of doors smoking and sipping all day long and little plays being acted in the open air for little people and every shop a complete and elegant room, and everybody seeming to play at everything in this world.

"And as to the sparkling lights my dear after dark, glittering high up and low down and on before and on behind and all round, and the crowd of theatres and the crowd of people and the crowd of all sorts, it's pure enchantment. And pretty well the only thing that grated on me was that whether you pay your fare at the railway or whether you change your money at a money-dealer's or whether you take your ticket at the theatre, the lady or gentleman is caged up (I suppose by government) behind the strongest iron bars having more of a Zoological appearance than a free country." ¶CS/LL 1

—on a Sunday: "There was, of course, very little in the aspect of Paris . . . to reproach us for our Sunday travelling. The wine-shops (every second house) were driving a roaring trade; awnings were spreading, and chairs and tables arranging, outside the cafés, preparatory to the eating of ices, and drinking of cool liquids, later in the day; shoeblacks were busy on the bridges; shops were open; carts and waggons clattered to and fro; the narrow, up-hill, funnel-like streets across the River, were so many dense perspectives of crowd and bustle, parti-coloured nightcaps, tobacco-pipes, blouses, large boots, and shaggy heads of hair; nothing at that hour denoted a day of rest, unless it were the appearance, here and there, of a family pleasure-party, crammed into a bulky old lumbering cab; or of some contemplative holiday-maker in the freest and easiest dishabille, leaning out of a low garret window, watching the drying of his newly polished shoes on the little parapet outside (if a gentleman), or the airing of her stockings in the sun (if a lady), with calm anticipation." PI 2

—for a traveller: "Surely, not the pavement of Paris? Yes, I think it is, too. I don't know any other place where there are all these high houses, all these haggard-looking wine shops, all these billiard tables, all these stocking-makers with flat red or yellow legs of wood for signboard, all these fuel shops with stacks of billets painted outside, and real billets sawing in the gutter, all these dirty corners of streets, all these cabinet pictures over dark doorways representing discreet matrons nursing babies." RP/F

"The crowds in the streets, the lights in the shops and balconies, the elegance, variety, and beauty of their decorations, the number of the theatres, the brilliant cafés with their windows thrown up high and their vivacious groups at little tables on the pavement, the light and glitter of the houses turned as it were inside out, soon convince me that it is no dream; that I am in Paris, howsoever I got here. I stroll down to the sparkling Palais Royal, up the Rue de Rivoli, to the Place Vendome . . . .

"I walk up to the Barriere de l'Étoile, sufficiently dazed by my flight to have a pleasant doubt of the reality of everything about me; of the lively crowd, the overhanging trees, the performing dogs, the hobby-horses, the beautiful perspectives of shining lamps: the hundred and one enclosures, where the singing is, in gleaming orchestras of azure and gold, and where a star-eyed Houri comes round with a box for voluntary offerings. So, I pass to my hotel, enchanted; sup, enchanted; go to bed, enchanted . . . . " RP/F

—windy, but neat: "In Paris, where nothing is wasted, costly and luxurious city though it be, but where wonderful human ants creep out of holes and pick up every scrap, there is no such thing [as blowing waste paper]. There, it blows nothing but dust. There, sharp eyes and sharp stomachs reap even the east wind, and get something out of it." OMF i 12

And see IG:Revolution—*breeding ground; and —fall of the Bastille*

—Parma: "Parma has cheerful, stirring streets, for an Italian town; and conse-

quently is not so characteristic as many places of less note. Always excepting the retired Piazza, where the Cathedral, Baptistery, and Campanile—ancient buildings, of a sombre brown, embellished with innumerable grotesque monsters and dreamy-looking creatures carved in marble and red stone—are clustered in a noble and magnificent repose." PI 6

—*Philadelphia:* "It is a handsome city, but distractingly regular. After walking about it for an hour or two, I felt that I would have given the world for a crooked street. The collar of my coat appeared to stiffen, and the brim of my hat to expand beneath its quakery influence. My hair shrunk into a sleek short crop, my hands folded themselves upon my breast of their own calm accord, and thoughts of taking lodgings in Mark Lane over against the Market Place, and of making a large fortune by speculations in corn, came over me involuntarily . . . I should be disposed to say that it is more provincial than Boston or New York, and that there is afloat in the fair city, an assumption of taste and criticism, savouring rather of those genteel discussions upon the same themes, in connexion with Shakspeare and the Musical Glasses, of which we read in the Vicar of Wakefield." AN 7

And see N:Water—*works*

—*Piacenza:* "A brown, decayed, old town, Piacenza is. A deserted, solitary, grass-grown place, with ruined ramparts; half-filled-up trenches, which afford a frowzy pasturage to the lean kine that wander about them; and streets of stern houses, moodily frowning at the other houses over the way. The sleepiest and shabbiest of soldiery go wandering about, with the double curse of laziness and poverty, uncouthly wrinkling their mis-fitting regimentals; the dirtiest of children play with their impromptu toys (pigs and mud) in the feeblest of gutters; and the gauntest of dogs trot in and out of the dullest of archways, in perpetual search of something to eat, which they never seem to find.

"A mysterious and solemn Palace, guarded by two colossal statues, twin Genii of the place, stands gravely in the midst of the idle town; and the king with the marble legs, who flourished in the time of the thousand and one Nights, might live contentedly inside of it, and never have the energy, in his upper half of flesh and blood, to want to come out." ¶PI 6

—*Pisa and the Tower:* "The moon was shining when we approached Pisa, and for a long time we could see, behind the wall, the leaning Tower, all awry in the uncertain light; the shadowy original of the old pictures in school-books, setting forth 'The Wonders of the World.' Like most things connected in their first associations with school-books and school-times, it was too small. I felt it keenly. It was nothing like so high above the wall as I had hoped . . . . Still, it looked very well, and very strange, and was quite as much out of the perpendicular as **Harris*** had represented it to be. The quiet air of Pisa too; the big guard-house at the gate, with only two little soldiers in it; the streets with scarcely any show of people in them; and the Arno, flowing quaintly through the centre of the town; were excellent . . . .

"**Simond**** compares the Tower to the usual pictorial representations in children's books of the Tower of Babel. It is a happy simile, and conveys a better idea of the building than chapters of laboured description. Nothing can exceed the grace and lightness of the structure; nothing can be more remarkable than its general appearance. In the course of the ascent to the top (which is by an easy staircase), the inclination is not very apparent; but, at the summit, it becomes so, and gives one the sensation of being in a ship that has heeled over, through the action of an ebb-tide.

"The effect *upon the low side,* so to speak—looking over from the gallery, and seeing the shaft recede to its base—is very startling; and I saw a nervous traveller hold on to the Tower involuntarily, after glancing down, as if he had some idea of propping it up.

"The view within, from the ground—looking up, as through a slanted tube—is also very curious. It certainly inclines as much as the most sanguine tourist could desire. The natural impulse of ninety-nine people out of a hundred, who were about to recline upon the grass below it, to rest, and contemplate the adjacent buildings, would probably be, not to take up their position under the leaning side; it is so very much aslant." ¶PI 10

**J. Harris published* Rev. Isaac Taylor's Scenes in Europe *in 1819.*

***Louis Simond's* Tour in Italy and Sicily *was published in 1828.*

"The beggars seem to embody all the trade and enterprise of Pisa. Nothing else is stirring, but warm air. Going through the streets, the fronts of the sleepy houses look like backs. They are all so still and quiet, and unlike houses with people in them, that the greater part of the city has the appearance of a city at daybreak, or during a general siesta of the population. Or it is yet more like those backgrounds of houses in common prints, or old engravings, where windows and doors are squarely indicated, and one figure (a beggar of course) is seen walking off by itself into illimitable perspective." PI 10 *And see* Italy—*Beggary, and* H: Architecture—*enclave at Pisa*

—*Poissy:* "Many a French town have I seen, between this spot of ground and Strasburgh or Marseilles, that might sit for your picture, little Poissy! Barring the details of your old church, I know you well, albeit we make acquaintance, now, for the first time.

"I know your narrow, straggling, winding streets, with a kennel in the midst, and lamps slung across. I know your picturesque street-corners, winding up-hill Heaven knows why or where! I know your tradesmen's inscriptions, in letters not quite fat enough; your barbers' brazen basins dangling over little shops; your Cafés and Estaminets, with cloudy bottles of stale syrup in the windows, and pictures of crossed billiard cues outside.

"I know this identical grey horse with his tail rolled up in a knot like the 'back hair' of an untidy woman, who won't be shod, and who makes himself heraldic by clattering across the street on his hind-legs, while twenty voices shriek and growl at him as a Brigand, an accursed Robber, and an everlastingly-doomed Pig. I know your sparkling town-fountain, too, my Poissy, and am glad to see it near a cattle-market, gushing so freshly, under the auspices of a gallant little sublimated Frenchman wrought in metal, perched upon the top." ¶RP/FF *And see* IG:Slaughterhouse—*French*

—*Richmond, Virginia:* "There are pretty villas and cheerful houses in its streets, and Nature smiles upon the country round; but jostling its handsome residences, like slavery itself going hand in hand with many lofty virtues, are deplorable tenements, fences unrepaired, walls crumbling into ruinous heaps. Hinting gloomily at things below the surface, these, and many other tokens of the same description, force themselves upon the notice, and are remembered with depressing influence, when livelier features are forgotten." AN 9 *See* F:Slavery

—*Rochester (the cathedral):* "There are few things in this beautiful country of England, more picturesque to the eye, and agreeable to the fancy, than an old Cathedral town. Seen in the distance, rising from among corn-fields, pastures, orchards, gardens, woods, the river, the bridge, the roofs of ancient houses, and haply the ruins of a castle or abbey, the venerable Cathedral spires, opposed for many hundred years to the winter wind and summer sun, tower, like a solemn historical presence, above the city, conveying to the rudest mind associations of interest with the dusky Past.

"On a nearer approach, this interest is heightened. Within the building, by the long perspectives of pillars and arches; by the earthy smell, preaching more eloquently than deans and chapters, of the common doom; by the praying figures of knights and ladies on the tombs, with little headless generations of sons and daughters kneeling around them; by the stained-glass windows, softening and mellowing the light; by the oaken carvings of the stalls, where the shorn monks told their beads; by the battered effigies of archbishops and bishops, found built up in the walls, when all the world had been unconscious, for centuries, of their blunt stone noses; by the mouldering chapter-room; the crypt, with its barred loopholes, letting in long gleams of slanting light from the Cloisters where the dead lie, and where the ivy, bred among the broken arches, twines about their graves; by the sound of the bells, high up in the massive tower; by the universal gravity, mystery, decay, and silence.

"Without, by the old environing Cathedral-close, with its red-brick houses and staid gardens; by the same stained glass, so dark on that side though so bright within; by the pavement of half-obliterated tombstones; by the long echoes of the visitors' footsteps; by the wicket gate, that seems to shut the moving world out of that retirement; by the grave rooks and jackdaws that have built their nests in steeple crevices, where the after-hum of the chimes reminds them, perhaps, of the wind among the boughs of lofty trees; by the ancient scraps of palace and gateway; by the ivy again, that has grown to be so thick and strong; by the oak, famous in all that part, which has struck its mighty root through the Bishop's wall; by the Cathedral organ, whose sound fills all that space, and all the space it opens in the charmed imagination." ¶HWC/W

—*Rome:* " . . . [the Dorrits] moved, with their retinue, to Rome. Through a repetition of the former Italian scenes, growing more dirty and more haggard as they went on, and bringing them at length to where the very air was diseased, they passed to their destination. A fine residence had been taken for them on the Corso, and there they took up their abode, in a city where everything seemed to be trying to stand still for ever on the ruins of something else—except the water, which, following eternal laws, tumbled and rolled from its glorious multitude of fountains." LD ii 7

—*at first sight:* " . . . the Eternal City appeared, at length, in the distance; it looked like—I am half afraid to write the word—like LONDON! ! ! There it lay, under a thick cloud, with innumerable towers, and steeples, and roofs of houses, rising up into the sky, and high above them all, one Dome. I swear, that keenly as I felt the seeming absurdity of the comparison, it was so like London, at that distance, that if you could have shown it me, in a glass, I should have taken it for nothing else." PI 10

—*Colosseum [CD spells it Coliseum]:* "It is no fiction, but plain, sober, honest Truth, to say: so suggestive and distinct is it at this hour: that, for a moment—actually in passing in—they who will, may have the whole great pile before them, as it used to be, with thousands of eager faces staring down into the arena, and such a whirl of strife, and blood, and dust going on there, as no language can describe. Its solitude, its awful beauty, and its utter desolation, strike upon the stranger the next moment, like a softened sorrow; and never in his life, perhaps, will he be so moved and overcome by any sight, not immediately connected with his own affections and afflictions.

"To see it crumbling there, an inch a year; its walls and arches overgrown with green; its corridors open to the day; the long grass growing in its porches; young trees of yesterday, springing up on its ragged parapets, and bearing fruit: chance produce of the seeds dropped there by the birds who build their nests within its chinks and crannies: to see its Pit of Fight filled up with earth, and the peaceful Cross planted in the centre; to climb into its upper halls, and look down on ruin, ruin, ruin, all about it; the triumphal arches of Constantine, Septimus Severus, and Titus; the Roman Forum; the Palace of the Cæsars; the temples of the old religion, fallen down and gone; is to see the ghost of old Rome, wicked wonderful old city, haunting the very ground on which its people trod.

"It is the most impressive, the most stately, the most solemn, grand, majestic, mournful sight, conceivable. Never, in its bloodiest prime, can the sight of the gigantic Coliseum, full and running over with the lustiest life, have moved one heart, as it must move all who look upon it now, a ruin. GOD be thanked: a ruin!" ¶PI 11

" . . . we rode out into old ruined Rome . . . to take our leave of the Coliseum. I had seen it by moonlight before (I could never get through a day without going back to it), but its tremendous solitude that night [Easter Monday] is past all telling." PI 11

—*people:* "As [the Colosseum] tops the other ruins: standing there, a mountain among graves: so do its ancient influences outlive all other remnants of the old mythology and old butchery of Rome, in the nature of the fierce and cruel Roman people. The Italian face changes as the visitor approaches the city; its beauty becomes devilish; and there is scarcely one countenance in a hundred, among the common people in the streets, that would not be at home and happy in a renovated Coliseum to-morrow." PI 11

—*St Peter's:* "It is not religiously impressive or affecting. It is an immense edifice, with no one point for the mind to rest upon; and it tires itself with wandering round and round. The very purpose of the place, is not expressed in anything you see there, unless you examine its details—and all examination of details is incompatible with the place itself.

"It might be a Pantheon, or a Senate House, or a great architectural trophy, having no other object than an architectural triumph. There is a black statue of St. Peter, to be sure, under a red canopy; which is larger than life, and which is constantly having its great toe kissed by good Catholics. You cannot help seeing that: it is so very prominent and popular. But it does not heighten the effect of the temple, as a work of art; and it is not expressive—to me at least—of its high purpose.

"The pavement [under the Pope's chair] was covered with a carpet of the brightest green; and what with this green, and the intolerable reds and crimsons, and gold borders of the hangings, the whole concern looked like a stupendous Bonbon." ¶PI 11

—streets and plazas: "The narrow streets, devoid of footways, and choked, in every obscure corner, by heaps of dunghill-rubbish, contrast so strongly, in their cramped dimensions, and their filth, and darkness, with the broad square before some haughty church: in the centre of which, a hieroglyphic-covered obelisk, brought from Egypt in the days of the Emperors, looks strangely on the foreign scene about it; or perhaps an ancient pillar, with its honoured statue overthrown, supports a Christian saint: Marcus Aurelius giving place to Paul, and Trajan to St Peter. Then, there are the ponderous buildings reared from the spoliation of the Coliseum, shutting out the moon, like mountains: while here and there, are broken arches and rent walls, through which it gushes freely, as the life comes pouring from a wound." PI 11

—Swiss guard: " . . . a broad lane was kept clear by the Pope's Swiss guard, who wear a quaint striped surcoat, and striped tight legs, and carry halberds like those which are usually shouldered by those theatrical supernumeraries, who never *can* get off the stage fast enough, and who may be generally observed to linger in the enemy's camp after the open country, held by the opposite forces, has been split up the middle by a convulsion of Nature." PI 11

—St Louis: "In the old French portion of the town, the thoroughfares are narrow and crooked, and some of the houses are very quaint and picturesque: being built of wood, with tumble-down galleries before the windows, approachable by stairs or rather ladders from the street. There are queer little barbers' shops and drinking-houses too, in this quarter; and abundance of crazy old tenements with blinking casements, such as may be seen in Flanders. Some of these ancient habitations, with high garret gable-windows perking into the roofs, have a kind of French shrug about them; and being lopsided with age, appear to hold their heads askew, besides, as if they were grimacing in astonishment at the American Improvements.

"It is hardly necessary to say, that these consist of wharfs and warehouses, and new buildings in all directions; and of a great many vast plans which are still 'progressing.'" AN 12

—Salisbury (market day): " . . .the thoroughfares about the market-place being filled with carts, horses, donkeys, baskets, waggons, garden-stuff, meat, tripe, pies, poultry, and huckster's wares of every opposite description and possible variety of character.

"Then there were young farmers and old farmers, with smock-frocks, brown great-coats, drab great-coats, red worsted comforters, leather leggings, wonderful shaped hats, hunting-whips, and rough sticks, standing about in groups, or talking noisily together on the tavern steps, or paying and receiving huge amounts of greasy wealth, with the assistance of such bulky pocket-books that when they were in their pockets it was apoplexy to get them out, and when they were out it was spasms to get them in again.

"Also, there were farmers' wives in beaver bonnets and red cloaks, riding shaggy horses purged of all earthly passions, who went soberly into all manner of places without desiring to know why, and who, if required, would have stood stock still in a china-shop, with a complete dinner-service at each hoof.

"Also a great many dogs, who were strongly interested in the state of the market and the bargains of their masters; and a great confusion of tongues, both brute and human." ¶MC 5

—Sens: "So at length and at last my dear we come to Sens, a pretty little town with a great two-towered cathedral and the rooks flying in and out of the loopholes and another tower atop of one of the towers like a sort of a stone pulpit. In which pulpit with the birds skimming below him if you'll believe me, I saw a speck while I was resting at the inn before dinner which they made signs to me was Jemmy and which really was." CS/LL 1

—Siena: " . . . we reached the beautiful old city of Siena . . . the Cathedral, which is wonderfully picturesque inside and out, especially the latter—also the market-place, or great Piazza, which is a large square, with a great broken-nosed fountain in it: some quaint Gothic houses: and a high square brick tower; *outside* the top of which —a curious feature in such views in Italy— hangs an enormous bell. It is like a bit of Venice, without the water. There are some curious old Palazzi in the town, which is very ancient; and without having (for me) the interest of Verona, or Genoa, it is very dreamy and fantastic, and most interesting." PI 10

—Venice

—bank: "On the first-floor of the house was a Bank—a surprising experience for any gentleman of commercial pursuits bringing laws for all mankind from a British city—where the two spare clerks, like dried dragoons, in green velvet caps adorned with golden tassels, stood, bearded, behind a small counter in a small room, containing no other visible objects than an empty iron safe, with the door open, a jug of water, and a papering of garlands of roses; but who, on lawful requisition, by merely dipping their hands out of sight, could produce exhaustless mounds of five-franc pieces." LD ii 6

—the bay: " . . . I looked down on boats and barks; on masts, sails, cordage, flags; on groups of busy sailors, working at the cargoes of these vessels; on wide quays, strewn with bales, casks, merchandise of many kinds; on great ships, lying near at hand in stately indolence; on islands, crowned with gorgeous domes and turrets: and where golden crosses glittered in the light, atop of wondrous churches, springing from the sea!" PI 8

—the canals: "In this crowning unreality, where all the streets were paved with water, and where the deathlike stillness of the days and nights was broken by no sound but the softened ringing of church-bells, the rippling of the current, and the cry of the gondoliers turning the corners of the flowing streets . . . . [Amy] would watch the sunset, in its long low lines of purple and red, and its burning flush high up into the sky; so glowing on the buildings, and so lightening their structure, that it made them look as if their strong walls were transparent, and they shone from within." LD ii 3

"It was quite a walk, by mysterious staircases and corridors, from Mrs General's apartment—hoodwinked by a narrow side street with a low gloomy bridge in it, and dungeon-like opposite tenements, their walls besmeared with a thousand downward stains and streaks, as if every crazy aperture in them had been weeping tears of rust into the Adriatic for centuries—to Mr Dorrit's apartment: with a whole English house-front of window, a prospect of beautiful church-domes rising into the blue sky sheer out of the water which reflected them, and a hushed murmur of the Grand Canal laving the doorways below, where his gondolas and gondoliers attended his pleasure, drowsily swinging in a little forest of piles." LD ii 5

—Piazza San Marco: "It was a great Piazza, as I thought: anchored, like all the rest, in the deep ocean. On its broad bosom, was a Palace, more majestic and magnificent in its old age, than all the buildings of the earth, in the high prime and fulness of their youth. Cloisters and galleries: so light, they might have been the work of fairy hands: so strong that centuries had battered them in vain: wound round and round this palace, and enfolded it with a Cathedral, gorgeous in the wild luxuriant fancies of the East.

"At no great distance from the porch, a lofty tower, standing by itself, and rearing its proud head, alone, into the sky, looked out upon the Adriatic Sea. Near to the margin of the stream, were two ill-omened pillars of red granite; one having on its top, a figure with a sword and shield; the other, a winged lion. Not far from these again, a second tower: richest of the rich in all its decorations: even here, where all was rich: sustained aloft, a great orb, gleaming with gold and deepest blue: the Twelve Signs painted on it, and a mimic sun revolving in its course around them: while above, two bronze giants hammered out the hours upon a sounding bell.

"An oblong square of lofty houses of the whitest stone, surrounded by a light and beautiful arcade, formed part of this enchanted scene; and, here and there, gay masts for flags rose, tapering, from the pavement of the unsubstantial ground." ¶PI 8

—a poor neighbourhood: "The house, on a little desert island, looked as if it had broken away from somewhere else, and had floated by chance into its present anchorage, in company with a vine almost as much in want of training as the poor wretches who were lying under its leaves. The features of the surrounding picture were, a church with hoarding and scaffolding about it, which had been under supposititious repair so long that the means of repair looked a hundred years old, and had themselves fallen into decay; a quantity of washed linen, spread to dry in the sun; a number of houses at odds with one another and grotesquely out of the perpendicular, like rotten pre-Adamite cheeses cut into fantastic shapes and full of mites; and a feverish bewilderment of windows, with their lattice-blinds all hanging askew, and something draggled and dirty dangling out of most of them." LD ii 6 *And see* B:House—*in Venice*

—Verona: "I had been half afraid to go to Verona, lest it should at all put me out of conceit with Romeo and Juliet. But, I was no sooner come into the old market-place, than the misgiving vanished. It is so fanciful, quaint, and picturesque a place, formed by such an extraordinary and rich variety of fantastic buildings, that there could be nothing better at the core of even this romantic town: scene of one of the most romantic and beautiful of stories." PI 9

"Pleasant Verona! With its beautiful old palaces, and charming country in the distance, seen from terrace walks, and stately, balustraded galleries. With its Roman gates, still spanning the fair street, and casting, on the sunlight of to-day, the shade of fifteen hundred years ago. With its marble-fitted churches, lofty towers, rich architecture, and quaint old quiet thoroughfares, where shouts of Montagues and Capulets once resounded,

And made Verona's ancient citizens
Cast by their grave, beseeming ornaments,
To wield old partizans.

With its fast-rushing river, picturesque old bridge, great castle, waving cypresses, and prospect so delightful, and so cheerful! Pleasant Verona!" PI 9

—Washington, D. C. "Take the worst parts of the City Road and Pentonville, or the straggling outskirts of Paris, where the houses are smallest, preserving all their oddities, but especially the small shops and dwellings . . . . Burn the whole down; build it up again in wood and plaster; widen it a little . . . put green blinds outside all the private houses, with a red curtain and a white one in every window; plough up all the roads; plant a great deal of coarse turf in every place where it ought *not* to be; erect three handsome buildings in stone and marble, anywhere, but the more entirely out of everybody's way the better; call one the Post Office, one the Patent Office, and one the Treasury; make it scorching hot in the morning, and freezing cold in the afternoon, with an occasional tornado of wind and dust; leave a brick-field without the bricks, in all central places where a street may naturally be expected; and that's Washington." AN 8

"It is sometimes called the City of Magnificent Distances, but it might with greater propriety be termed the City of Magnificent Intentions; for it is only on taking a bird's-eye view of it from the top of the Capitol, that one can at all comprehend the vast designs of its projector, an aspiring Frenchman.*

"Spacious avenues, that begin in nothing, and lead nowhere; streets, mile-long, that only want houses, roads and inhabitants; public buildings that need but a public to be complete; and ornaments of great thoroughfares, which only lack great thoroughfares to ornament—are its leading features. One might fancy the season over, and most of the houses gone out of town for ever with their masters.

"To the admirers of cities it is a Barmecide Feast: a pleasant field for the imagination to rove in; a monument raised to a deceased project, with not even a legible inscription to record its departed greatness." ¶AN 8

**Pierre Charles L'Enfant (1754-1825), architect born in France who served under George Washington and planned the new capital. High construction costs led to his dismissal in 1791, but a century later (fifty years after CD's visit) the city had been completed, substantially in accordance with his plans.*

—Yarmouth: "It looked rather spongy and soppy, I thought, as I carried my eye over the great dull waste that lay across the river; and I could not help wondering, if the world were really as round as my geography-book said, how any part of it came to be so flat. But I reflected that Yarmouth might be situated at one of the poles; which would account for it.

"As we drew a little nearer, and saw the whole adjacent prospect lying a straight low line under the sky, I hinted to Peggotty that a mound or so might have improved it; and also that if the land had been a little more separated from the sea, and the town and the tide had not been quite so much mixed up, like toast and water, it would have been nicer . . . .

"When we got into the street . . . and smelt the fish, and pitch, and oakum, and tar, and saw the sailors walking about, and the carts jingling up and down over the stones, I felt that I had done so busy a place an injustice; and said as much to Peggotty, who heard my expressions of delight with great complacency, and told me it was well known (I suppose to those who had the good fortune to be born Bloaters) that Yarmouth was, upon the whole, the finest place in the universe." DC 3

Cities and Towns, fictionally named

—*Cloisterham (Rochester):* "An ancient city, Cloisterham, and no meet dwelling place for any one with hankerings after the noisy world. A monotonous, silent city, deriving an earthy flavour throughout from its Cathedral crypt, and so abounding in vestiges of monastic graves, that the Cloisterham children grow small salad in the dust of abbots and abbesses, and make dirt-pies of nuns and friars; while every ploughman in its outlying fields renders to once puissant Lord Treasurers, Archbishops, Bishops, and such-like, the attention which the Ogre in the story-book desired to render to his unbidden visitor, and grinds their bones to make his bread.

" . . . . So silent are the streets of Cloisterham (though prone to echo on the smallest provocation), that of a summer-day the sunblinds of its shops scarce dare to flap in the south wind; while the sun-browned tramps, who pass along and stare, quicken their limp a little, that they may the sooner get beyond the confines of its oppressive respectability. This is a feat not difficult of achievement, seeing that the streets of Cloisterham city are little more than one narrow street by which you get into it and get out of it: the rest being mostly disappointing yards with pumps in them and no thoroughfare—exception made of the Cathedral-close, and a paved Quaker settlement, in colour and general conformation very like a Quakeress's bonnet, up in a shady corner.

"In a word, a city of another and a bygone time is Cloisterham, with its hoarse Cathedral bell, its hoarse rooks hovering about the Cathedral tower, its hoarser and less distinct rooks in the stalls far beneath. Fragments of old wall, saint's chapel, chapter-house, convent and monastery, have got incongruously or obstructively built into many of its houses and gardens, much as kindred jumbled notions have become incorporated into many of its citizens' minds. All things in it are of the past . . . . The most abundant and the most agreeable evidences of progressing life in Cloisterham are the evidences of vegetable life in many gardens; even its drooping and despondent little theatre has its poor strip of garden, receiving the foul fiend, when he ducks from its stage into the infernal regions, among scarlet-beans or oyster-shells, according to the season of the year." MED 3

—*Dullborough (Rochester):* "Of course the town had shrunk fearfully, since I was a child there. I had entertained the impression that the High-street was at least as wide as Regent-street, London, or the Italian Boulevard at Paris. I found it little better than a lane. There was a public clock in it, which I had supposed to be the finest clock in the world: whereas it now turned out to be as inexpressive, moon-faced, and weak a clock as ever I saw. It belonged to a Town Hall, where I had seen an Indian (who I now suppose wasn't an Indian) swallow a sword (which I now suppose he didn't). The edifice had appeared to me in those days so glorious a structure, that I had set it up in my mind as the model on which the Genie of the Lamp built the palace for Aladdin. A mean little brick heap, like a demented chapel, with a few yawning persons in leather gaiters, and in the last extremity for something to do, lounging at the door with their hands in their pockets, and calling themselves a Corn Exchange!" UT/DT

—*Mudfog (Chatham):* "The town of Mudfog is extremely picturesque. Limehouse and Ratcliff Highway are both something like it, but they give you a very faint idea of Mudfog. There are a great many more public-houses in Mudfog—more than in Ratcliff Highway and Limehouse put together. The public buildings, too, are very imposing. We consider the town-hall one of the finest specimens of shed architecture, extant: it is a combination of the pig-sty and tea-garden-box orders; and the simplicity of its design is of surpassing beauty. The idea of placing a large window on one side of the door, and a small one on the other, is particularly happy. There is a fine old Doric beauty, too, about the padlock and scraper, which is strictly in keeping with the general effect." B/T

—*Pavilionstone (Folkestone):* "Within a quarter of a century, it was a little fishing town, and they do say, that the time was, when it was a little smuggling town . . . . Now, gas and electricity run to the very water's edge, and the South-Eastern Railway Company screech at us in the dead of night.

"But the old little fishing and smuggling town remains, and is so tempting a place for the [smuggling] purpose, that I think of going out some night next week, in a fur cap and pair of petticoat trousers, and running an empty tub, as a kind of archæological pursuit. Let nobody with corns come to Pavilionstone, for there are breakneck flights of ragged steps, connecting the principal streets by back-ways, which will cripple that visitor in half an hour . . . . In connection with these breakneck steps I observe some wooden cottages, with tumble-down out-houses, and back-yards three feet square, adorned with garlands of dried fish . . . . " RP/OT *And see* H:Lamplighter*—risks*

"The South-Eastern Company have brought Pavilionstone into such vogue, with their tidal trains and splendid steampackets, that a new Pavilionstone is rising up. I am, myself, of New Pavilionstone. We are a little mortary and limey at present, but we are getting on capitally. Indeed, we were getting on so fast, at one time, that we rather overdid it, and built a street of shops, the business of which may be expected to arrive in about ten years.

"We are sensibly laid out in general; and with a little care and pains (by no means wanting, so far), shall become a very pretty place. We ought to be, for our situation is delightful, our air is delicious, and our breezy hills and downs, carpeted with wild thyme, and decorated with millions of wild flowers, are, on the faith of a pedestrian, perfect. In New Pavilionstone we are a little too much addicted to small windows with more bricks in them than glass, and we are not over-fanciful in the way of decorative architecture, and we get unexpected sea-views through cracks in the street doors; on the whole, however, we are very snug and comfortable, and well accommodated." RP/OT

—Steepways (Clovelly, Devon): "And a mighty sing'lar and pretty place it is, as ever I saw in all the days of my life!' said Captain Jorgan, looking up at it.

"Captain Jorgan had to look high to look at it, for the village was built sheer up the face of a steep and lofty cliff. There was no road in it, there was no wheeled vehicle in it, there was not a level yard in it. From the sea-beach to the cliff-top two irregular rows of white houses, placed opposite to one another, and twisting here and there, and there and here, rose, like the sides of a long succession of stages of crooked ladders, and you climbed up the village or climbed down the village by the staves between, some six feet wide or so, and made of sharp irregular stones.

"The old pack-saddle, long laid aside in most parts of England as one of the appendages of its infancy, flourished here intact. Strings of pack-horses and pack-donkeys toiled slowly up the staves of the ladders, bearing fish, and coal, and such other cargo as was unshipping at the pier from the dancing fleet of village boats, and from two or three little coasting traders. As the beasts of burden ascended laden, or descended light, they got so lost at intervals in the floating clouds of village smoke, that they seemed to dive down some of the village chimneys, and come to the surface again far off, high above others.

"No two houses in the village were alike, in chimney, size, shape, door, window, gable, roof-tree, anything. The sides of the ladders were musical with water, running clear and bright. The staves were musical with the clattering feet of the pack-horses and pack-donkeys, and the voices of the fishermen urging them up, mingled with the voices of the fishermen's wives and their many children.

"The pier was musical with the wash of the sea, the creaking of capstans and windlasses, and the airy fluttering of little vanes and sails. The rough, sea-bleached boulders of which the pier was made, and the whiter boulders of the shore, were brown with drying nets. The red-brown cliffs, richly wooded to their extremest verge, had their softened and beautiful forms reflected in the bluest water, under the clear North Devonshire sky of a November day without a cloud.

"The village itself was so steeped in autumnal foliage, from the houses lying on the pier to the topmost round of the topmost ladder, that one might have fancied it was out a bird's-nesting, and was (as indeed it was) a wonderful climber. And mentioning birds, the place was not without some music from them too; for the rook was very busy on the higher levels, and the gull with his flapping wings was fishing in the bay, and the lusty little robin was hopping among the great stone blocks and iron rings of the breakwater, fearless in the faith of his ancestors, and the Children in the Wood." ¶CS/MS1

Egypt

—in academic circles: "'But don't she hate Arabs, and Turks, and Fellahs, and people?'

"'Certainly not.' Very firmly.

"'At least she *must* hate the Pyramids? Come, Eddy?'

"'Why should she be such a little—tall, I

mean—goose, as to hate the Pyramids, Rosa?'

"'Ah! you should hear Miss Twinkleton . . . bore about them, and then you wouldn't ask. Tiresome old burying-grounds! Isises, and Ibises, and Cheopses, and Pharoahses; who cares about them? And then there was Belzoni, or somebody, dragged out by the legs, half-choked with bats and dust. All the girls say: Serve him right, and hope it hurt him, and wish he had been quite choked.'" MED 3

—*a branch office:* " . . . Herbert would come home of a night . . . and would sketch airy pictures of himself conducting Clara Barley to the land of the Arabian Nights[?], and of me going out to join them (with a caravan of camels, I believe), and of our all going up the Nile and seeing wonders." GE 52

—*undeveloped:* "'And this most sensible of creatures likes the idea of being carried off to Egypt; does she, Eddy?'

"'Yes. She takes a sensible interest in triumphs of engineering skill: especially when they are to change the whole condition of an undeveloped country.'" MED 3

—*visited by Panorama:* "Thebes rose before him. An avenue of two hundred sphinxes, with not a head among them . . . conducted to the Temple of Carnak: its walls, eighty feet high and twenty-five feet thick, a mile and three-quarters in circumference . . . . Obelisks he saw, thousands of years of age, as sharp as if the chisel had cut their edges yesterday . . . tombs cut high up in the rock, where European travellers live solitary, as in stony crows' nests, burning mummied Thebans, gentle and simple—of the dried blood-royal maybe—for their daily fuel, and making articles of furniture of their dusty coffins.

"Upon the walls of temples, in colours fresh and bright as those of yesterday, he read the conquests of great Egyptian monarchs; upon the tombs of humbler people in the same blooming symbols, he saw their ancient way of working at their trades . . . .

"He visited the quarries of Silsileh, whence nearly all the red stone used by the ancient Egyptian architects and sculptors came; and there beheld enormous single-stoned colossal figures, nearly finished—redly snowed up, as it were, and trying hard to break out—waiting for the finishing touches, never to be given by the mummied hands of thousands of years ago . . . .

"His last look of that amazing land was at the Great Sphinx, buried in the sand—sand in its eyes, sand in its ears, sand drifted on his broken nose, sand lodging, feet deep, in the ledges of its head—struggling out of a wide sea of sand, as if to look hopelessly forth for the ancient glories once surrounding it." ¶HW/ET

The English

—*abroad:*

—*in France:* "As I glance into a print-shop window, Monied Interest, my late travelling companion, comes upon me, laughing with the highest relish of disdain. 'Here's a people!' he says, pointing to Napoleon in the window and Napoleon on the column. 'Only one idea all over Paris! A monomania!' Humph! I THINK I have seen Napoleon's match? There WAS a statue, when I came away, at Hyde Park Corner, and another in the City, and a print or two in the shops." RP/F

" . . . the captives, being shut up in the gloomy dungeon, are strained, two or three at a time, into an inner cell, to be examined as to passports; and across the doorway of communication, stands a military creature making a bar of his arm.

"Two ideas are generally present to the British mind during these ceremonies; first, that it is necessary to make for the cell with violent struggles, as if it were a life-boat and the dungeon a ship going down; secondly, that the military creature's arm is a national affront, which the government at home ought instantly to 'take up.'

"The British mind and body becoming heated by these fantasies . . . . This brings him to . . . a state of mere idiotcy; and when he is . . . cast out at a little door into a howling wilderness of touters, he becomes a lunatic with wild eyes and floating hair until rescued and soothed. If friendless and unrescued, he is generally put into a railway omnibus and taken to Paris." ¶RP/FW

"As to the boarding-houses of our French watering-place, they are Legion, and would require a distinct treatise. It is not without a sentiment of national pride that we believe them to contain more bores from the shores of Albion than all the clubs in London. As you walk timidly in their neighbourhood, the very neckcloths and hats of your elderly compatriots cry to you from the stones of the streets, 'We are Bores—avoid us!'

"We have never overheard at street corners such lunatic scraps of political and social discussion as among these dear countrymen of ours. They believe everything that is impossible and nothing that is true. They carry rumours, and ask questions, and make corrections and improvements on one another, staggering to the human intellect. And they are for ever rushing into the English library, propounding such incomprehensible paradoxes to the fair mistress of that establishment, that we beg to recommend her to her Majesty's gracious consideration as a fit object for a pension." ¶RP/FW

"'Not like Marseilles, eh [said Meagles]? No allonging and marshonging here! . . ." LD i 16

" . . . with an unshaken confidence that the English tongue was somehow the mother tongue of the whole world, only the people were too stupid to know it, Mr Meagles harangued innkeepers in the most voluble manner, entered into loud explanations of the most complicated sort, and utterly renounced replies in the native language of the respondents, on the ground that they were 'all bosh.' Sometimes interpreters were called in; whom Mr Meagles addressed in such idiomatic terms of speech, as instantly to extinguish and shut up—which made the matter worse." LD ii 33

"Now the Englishman, in taking his Appartement—or, as one might say on our side of the Channel, his set of chambers,—had given his name, correct to the letter, LANGLEY. But as he had a British way of not opening his mouth very wide on foreign soil, except at meals, the Brewery had been able to make nothing of it but L'Anglais. So Mr The Englishman he had become and he remained.

"'Never saw such a people!' muttered Mr The Englishman, as he now looked out of window. 'Never did, in my life!'

"This was true enough, for he had never before been out of his own country—a right little island, a tight little island, a bright little island, a show-fight little island, and full of merit of all sorts; but not the whole round world." CS/SL 2

And see TT:Tourism

—the British farmer: "I lay a night upon the road [in France] and enjoyed delectable cookery of potatoes, and some other sensible things, adoption of which at home would inevitably be shown to be fraught with ruin, somehow or other, to that rickety national blessing, the British farmer . . . . " UT/TA

—cheering: "In truth, no men on earth can cheer like Englishmen, who do so rally one another's blood and spirit when they cheer in earnest, that the stir is like the rush of their whole history, with all its standards waving at once, from Saxon **Alfred**'s downward." LD ii 22

—common people on the Sabbath: "The English people have long been remarkable for their domestic habits, and their household virtues and affections. They are, now, beginning to be universally respected by intelligent foreigners who visit this country, for their unobtrusive politeness, their good-humour, and their cheerful recognition of all restraints that really originate in consideration for the general good.

"They deserve this testimony (which we have often heard, of late, with pride) most honourably. Long maligned and mistrusted, they proved their case from the very first moment of having it in their power to do so; and have never, on any single occasion within our knowledge, abused any public confidence that has been reposed in them.

"It is an extraordinary thing to know of a people, systematically excluded from galleries and museums for years, that their respect for such places, and for themselves as visitors to them, dates, without any period of transition, from the very day when their doors were freely opened.

"The national vices are surprisingly few. The people in general are not gluttons, nor drunkards, nor gamblers, nor addicted to cruel sports, nor to the pushing of any amusement to furious and wild extremes. They are moderate, and easily pleased, and very sensible to all affectionate influences. Any knot of holiday-makers, without a large proportion of women and children among them, would be a perfect phenomenon.

"Let us go into any place of Sunday enjoyment where any fair representation of the people resort, and we shall find them decent, orderly, quiet, sociable among their families and neighbours. There is a general feeling of respect for religion, and for religious observances. The churches and chapels are well filled. Very few people who keep servants or apprentices leave out of consideration their opportunities of attending church or chapel; the general demeanour within those edifices, is particularly grave and decorous; and the general recreations without, are of a harmless and simple kind.

"Lord Brougham never did Henry Brougham more justice, than in declaring to the House of Lords, after the success of this motion in the House of Commons, that there is no country where the Sabbath is, on the whole, better observed than in England." HW/SS

—communicating with foreigners: "They spoke to [Cavalletto] in very loud voices as if he were stone deaf. They constructed sentences, by way of teaching him the language in its purity, such as were addressed by the savages to **Captain Cook**, or by *Friday* to *Robinson Crusoe.* Mrs Plornish was particularly ingenious in this art; and attained so much celebrity for saying 'Me ope you leg well soon,' that it was considered in the Yard, but a very short remove indeed from speaking Italian. Even Mrs Plornish herself began to think that she had a natural call towards that language." LD i 25

—Constitution: "'We Englishmen are Very Proud of our Constitution, Sir. It Was Bestowed Upon Us by Providence. No Other Country is so Favoured as This Country ....

"'And *other* countries,' said the foreign gentleman. 'They do how?'

"'They do, Sir,' returned Mr Podsnap, gravely shaking his head; 'they do—I am sorry to be obliged to say it—*as* they do.'

"'It was a little particular of Providence,' said the foreign gentleman, laughing; 'for the frontier is not large.'

"'Undoubtedly,' assented Mr Podsnap; 'But So it is. It was the Charter of the Land. This island was Blest, Sir, to the Direct Exclusion of such Other Countries as—as there may happen to be. And if we were all Englishmen present, I would say . . . that there is in the Englishman a combination of qualities, a modesty, an independence, a responsibility, a repose, combined with an absence of everything calculated to call a blush into the cheek of a young person, which one would seek in vain among the Nations of the Earth.'" OMF i 11

—conventionality and Mrs Grundy: "When shall we [stop] being afraid to make the most of small resources, and the best of scanty means of enjoyment? In Paris (as in innumerable other places and countries) a man who has six square feet of yard, or six square feet of housetop, adorns it in his own poor way, and sits there in the fine weather because he likes to do it, because he chooses to do it, because he has got nothing better of his own, and has never been laughed out of the enjoyment of what he has got.

"Equally, he will sit at his door, or in his balcony, or out on the pavement, because it is cheerful and pleasant and he likes to see the life of the city. For the last seventy years his family have not been tormenting their lives with continual enquiries and speculations whether other families, above and below, to the right and to the left, over the way and round the corner, would consider these recreations genteel, or would do the like, or would not do the like. That abominable old Tyrant, Madame Grundy, has never been of his acquaintance.

'The result is, that, with a very small income and in a very dear city, he has more innocent pleasure than fifty Englishmen of the same condition; and is distinctly . . . a more domestic man than the Englishman, in regard of his simple pleasures being, to a much greater extent, divided with his wife and children. It is a natural consequence of their being easy and cheap, and profoundly independent of Madame Grundy." ¶HW/I

—crime and punishment: " . . . those good old customs of the good old times which made England, even so recently as in the reign of the Third King George, in respect of her criminal code and her prison regulations, one of the most bloody-minded and barbarous countries on the earth." AN 3

—and foreign residents: "It was up-hill work for a foreigner, lame or sound, to make his way with the Bleeding Hearts. In the first place, they were vaguely persuaded that every foreigner had a knife about him; in the second, they held it to be a sound constitutional national axiom that he ought to go home to his own country. They never thought of inquiring how many of their own countrymen would be returned upon their hands from divers parts of the world, if the principle were generally recognised; they considered it practically and peculiarly British.

"In the third place, they had a notion that it was a sort of Divine visitation upon a foreigner that he was not an Englishman, and that all kinds of calamities happened to his country because it did things that England did not, and did not do things that England did. In this belief, to be sure, they had long been carefully trained by the Barnacles and Stiltstalkings, who were always proclaiming to them, officially and unofficially, that no country which failed to submit itself to those two large families could possibly hope to be under the protection of Providence; and who, when they believed it, disparaged them in private as the most prejudiced people under the sun.

"This, therefore, might be called a political position of the Bleeding Hearts; but they entertained other objections to having foreigners in the Yard. They believed that foreigners were always badly off; and though they were as ill off themselves as they could desire to be, that did not diminish the force of the objection.

"They believed that foreigners were dragooned and bayoneted; and though they certainly got their own sculls [*sic.*] promptly fractured if they showed any ill-humour, still it was with a blunt instrument, and that didn't count. They believed that foreigners were always immoral; and though they had an occasional assize at home, and now and then a divorce case or so, that had nothing to do with it.

"They believed that foreigners had no independent spirit, as never being escorted to the poll in droves by Lord Decimus Tite Barnacle, with colours flying and the tune of Rule Britannia playing. Not to be tedious, they had many other beliefs of a similar kind." ¶LD i 25

And see France and the French—*an English view; and* LC:Names and naming—*an Englishman handling Italian*

—*hospitality:* " . . . it is a grave consideration that [the guests in a stately home] have water to wash in, sheets to sleep in, paper to write letters on, and allumettes to light their sealing-wax by;—it is a matter for a philosopher's reflection that at breakfast you find the cold beef on the sideboard, and at night the chamber candlestick in the entry;—but the distinctive mark of the national character, the centre prong in the trident of Britannia, the strong tuft in the mane of the British lion, is the national propensity to perform that humble household service which is familiarly called 'emptying the slops.' This, and the kindred national propensity to brush a man's clothes and polish his boots, whensoever and wheresoever the clothes and boots can be seized without the man, are the noteworthy things that can never be effaced from an observant traveller's remembrance." E/AE

—*language:* "'I was Inquiring,' said Mr Podsnap . . . 'Whether You Have Observed in our Streets as We should say, Upon our Pavvy as You would say, any Tokens—'

"The foreign gentleman with patient courtesy entreated pardon; 'But what was tokenz?'

"'Marks,' said Mr Podsnap; 'Signs, you know, Appearances—Traces.'

"'Ah! Of a Orse?' inquired the foreign gentleman.

"'We call it Horse,' said Mr Podsnap, with forbearance. 'In England, Angleterre, England, We Aspirate the "H," and We Say "Horse." Only our Lower Classes Say "Orse!"'

"'Pardon,' said the foreign gentleman; 'I am alwiz wrong!'

"'Our Language,' said Mr Podsnap, with a gracious consciousness of being always right, 'is Difficult. Ours is a Copious Language, and Trying to Strangers. I will not Pursue my Question.'" OMF i 11

—*migrated to America:* "Of all grades and kinds of men that jostle one in the public conveyances of the States, these are often the most intolerable and the most insufferable companions. United to every disagreeable characteristic that the worst kind of American travellers possess, these countrymen of ours display an amount of insolent conceit and cool assumption of superiority, quite monstrous to behold.

"In the coarse familiarity of their approach, and the effrontery of their inquisitiveness (which they are in great haste to assert, as if they panted to revenge themselves upon the decent old restraints of home), they surpass any native specimens that came within my range of observation: and I often grew so patriotic when I saw and heard them, that I would cheerfully have submitted to a reasonable fine, if I could have given any other country in the whole world, the honour of claiming them for his children." ¶AN 7

—*patriotism:* "[Jasper] sang to Mr Sapsea that evening no kickshaw ditties, favorites with national enemies, but gave him the genuine George the Third home-brewed; exhorting him (as 'my brave boys') to reduce to a smashed condition all other islands but this island, and all continents, peninsulas, isthmuses, promontories, and other geographical forms of land soever, besides sweeping the seas in all directions. In short, he rendered it pretty clear that Providence made a distinct mistake in originating so small a nation of hearts of oak, and so many other verminous peoples." MED 12

—*reticence:* "On the same staircase with my friend Parkle, and on the same floor, there lived a man of law . . . . For three or four years, Parkle rather knew of him than knew him, but after that—for Englishmen—short pause of consideration, they began to speak." UT/C

—*soldiers:* "In respect of an air of enjoyable understanding of what they were about, which seems to be forbidden to English soldiers, the boys might have been small French troops." UT/ST

—*taste in Art:* "One of our most remarkable Insularities is a tendency to be firmly persuaded that what is not English is not natural. In the Fine Arts department of the French Exhibition, recently closed, we repeatedly heard, even from the more educated and reflective of our countrymen, that certain pictures which appeared to possess great merit . . . were all very well, but were 'theatrical' . . . . Taking further pains then, to find out what was meant by the term theatrical, we found that the actions and gestures of the figures were not English. That is to say—the figures expressing themselves in the vivacious manner natural in a greater or less degree to the whole great continent of Europe, were overcharged and out of the truth, because they did not express themselves in the manner of our little Island—which is so very exceptional, that it always places an Englishman at a disadvantage, out of his own country, until his fine sterling qualities shine through his external formality and constraint." HW/I

—*undefeated:* "[John Grueby] was a square-built, strong-made, bull-necked fellow, of the true English breed . . . one of those self-possessed, hard-headed, imperturbable fellows, who, if they are ever beaten at fisticuffs, or other kind of warfare, never know it, and go on coolly till they win." BR 35

—*understatement:* "Everywhere, as I saunter up and down the [Chatham] Yard, I meet with tokens of its quiet and retiring character. There is a gravity upon its red brick offices and houses, a sad pretence of having nothing worth mentioning to do, an avoidance of display, which I never saw out of England . . . . The costly store of timber is stacked and stowed away in sequestered places, with the pervading avoidance of flourish or effect. It makes as little of itself as possible, and calls to no one 'Come and look at me!'" UT/CD

English Channel

—*crossing the bar:* "Early in the morning I was on the deck of the steam-packet, and we were aiming at the bar in the usual intolerable manner, and the bar was aiming at us in the usual intolerable manner, and the bar got by far the best of it, and we got by far the worst—all in the usual intolerable manner." SB/TA

—*no respecter of persons:* "The sea has no appreciation of great men, but knocks them about like the small fry. It is habitually hard upon Sir Leicester [Dedlock], whose countenance it greenly mottles in the manner of sage-cheese, and in whose aristocratic system it effects a dismal revolution. It is the Radical of Nature to him." BH 12

—*for the untried:* " . . . when we came to the sea which I had never seen but once in my life and that when my poor Lirriper was courting me, the freshness of it and the deepness and the airiness and to think that it had been rolling ever since and that it was always a rolling and so few of us minding, made me feel quite serious. But I felt happy too and so did Jemmy and the Major and not much motion on the whole, though me with a swimming in the head and a sinking but able to take notice that the foreign insides appear to be constructed hollower than the English, leading to much more tremenjous noises when bad sailors." CS/LL 1

France and the French

—*before the Revolution:* "Whether there is any record, in the world's history, of a people among whom the arts and sciences, and the refinements of civilised life existed, so oppressed, degraded, and utterly miserable, as the mass of the French population were before that Revolution? . . .

"They had died of sheer want and famine, in numbers. The hunting-trains of their kings had ridden over their bodies in the royal forests. Multitudes had gone about, crying and howling for bread, in the streets of Paris. The line of road from Versailles to the capital had been blocked up by starvation and nakedness pouring in from the departments. The tables spread by **Egalité Orleans** in the public streets had been besieged by the foremost stragglers of a whole nation of paupers, on the face of every one of whom the shadow of the coming guillotine was black." ¶E/JP

—a broken cask of wine: "A large cask of wine had been dropped and broken, in the street. The accident had happened in getting it out of a cart; the cask had tumbled out with a run, the hoops had burst, and it lay on the stones just outside the door of the wine-shop, shattered like a walnut-shell.

"All the people within reach had suspended their business or their idleness, to run to the spot and drink the wine. The rough, irregular stones of the street, pointing every way, and designed, one might have thought, expressly to lame all living creatures that approached them, had dammed it into little pools; these were surrounded, each by its own jostling group or crowd, according to its size. Some men kneeled down, made scoops of their two hands joined, and sipped, or tried to help women, who bent over their shoulders, to sip, before the wine had all run out between their fingers. Others, men and women, dipped in the puddles with little mugs of mutilated earthenware, or even with handkerchiefs from women's heads, which were squeezed dry into infants' mouths; others made small mud-embankments, to stem the wine as it ran; others, directed by lookers-on up at high windows, darted here and there, to cut off little streams of wine that started away in new directions; others devoted themselves to the sodden and lee-dyed pieces of the cask, licking, and even champing the moister wine-rotted fragments with eager relish. There was no drainage to carry off the wine, and not only did it all get taken up, but so much mud got taken up along with it, that there might have been a scavenger in the street, if anybody acquainted with it could have believed in such a miraculous presence.

"A shrill sound of laughter and of amused voices—voices of men, women, and children—resounded in the street while this wine-game lasted. There was little roughness in the sport, and much playfulness. There was a special companionship in it, an observable inclination on the part of every one to join some other one, which led, especially among the luckier or lighter-hearted, to frolicsome embraces, drinking of healths, shaking of hands, and even joining of hands and dancing, a dozen together. When the wine was gone, and the places where it had been most abundant were raked into a gridiron-pattern by fingers, these demonstrations ceased, as suddenly as they had broken out. The man who had left his saw sticking in the firewood he was cutting, set it in motion again; the woman who had left on a door-step the little pot of hot ashes, with which she had been trying to soften the pain in her own starved fingers and toes, or in those of her child, returned to it; men with bare arms, matted locks, and cadaverous faces, who had emerged into the winter light from cellars, moved away to descend again; and a gloom gathered on the scene that appeared more natural to it than sunshine.

"The wine was red wine, and had stained the ground of the narrow street in the suburb of Saint Antoine, in Paris, where it was spilled. It had stained many hands, too, and many faces, and many naked feet, and many wooden shoes. The hands of the man who sawed the wood, left red marks on the billets; and the forehead of the woman who nursed her baby, was stained with the stain of the old rag she wound about her head again. Those who had been greedy with the staves of the cask, had acquired a tigerish smear about the mouth; and one tall joker so besmeared, his head more out of a long squalid bag of a night-cap than in it, scrawled upon a wall with his finger dipped in muddy wine lees—BLOOD.

"The time was to come, when that wine too would be spilled on the street-stones, and when the stain of it would be red upon many there." TTC 5

—countryside: "Plenty of vines there are in the open fields, but of a short low kind, and not trained in festoons, but about straight sticks . . . . Queer old towns, drawbridged and walled: with odd little towers at the angles, like grotesque faces, as if the wall had put a mask on, and were staring down into the moat; other strange little towers, in gardens and fields, and down lanes, and in farm-yards: all alone, and always round, with a peaked roof, and never used for any purpose at all; ruinous buildings of all sorts; sometimes an hotel de ville, sometimes a guard-house, sometimes a dwelling-house, sometimes a chateau with a rank garden, prolific in dandelion, and watched over by extinguisher-topped turrets, and blink-eyed little casements; are the standard objects, repeated over and over again.

"Sometimes we pass a village inn, with a crumbling wall belonging to it, and a perfect town of out-houses; and painted over the gateway, 'Stabling for Sixty Horses;' as indeed there might be stabling for sixty score, were there any horses to be stabled there, or anybody resting there, or anything stirring about the place but a dangling bush, indicative of the wine inside: which flutters idly in the wind, in lazy keeping with everything else, and certainly is never in a green old age, though always so old as to be dropping to pieces.

"And all day long, strange little narrow waggons, in strings of six or eight, bringing cheese from Switzerland, and frequently in charge, the whole line, of one man, or even boy—and he very often asleep in the foremost cart—come jingling past: the horses drowsily ringing the bells upon their harness . . . . " ¶PI 2

—dress

—aristocracy: "But, the comfort was, that all the company at the grand hotel of Monseigneur were perfectly dressed. If the Day of Judgment had only been ascertained to be a dress day, everybody there would have been eternally correct. Such frizzling and powdering and sticking up of hair, such delicate complexions artificially preserved and mended, such gallant swords to look at, and such delicate honour to the sense of smell, would surely keep anything going, for ever and ever. The exquisite gentlemen of the finest breeding wore little pendent trinkets that chinked as they languidly moved; these golden fetters rang like precious little bells; and what with that ringing, and with the rustle of silk and brocade and fine linen, there was a flutter in the air that fanned Saint Antoine and his devouring hunger far away.

"Dress was the one unfailing talisman and charm used for keeping all things in their places. Everybody was dressed for a Fancy Ball that was never to leave off." TTC ii 7

—executioner: "From the Palace of the Tuileries, through Monseigneur and the whole Court, through the Chambers, the Tribunals of Justice, and all society (except the scarecrows), the Fancy Ball descended to the common Executioner: who, in pursuance of the charm, was required to officiate 'frizzled, powdered, in a gold-laced coat, pumps, and white silk stockings.' At the gallows and the wheel—the axe was a rarity—Monsieur Paris, as it was the episcopal mode among his brother Professors of the provinces, Monsieur Orleans, and the rest, to call him, presided in this dainty dress. And who among the company at Monseigneur's reception in that seventeen hundred and eightieth year of our Lord, could possibly doubt, that a system rooted in a frizzled hangman, powdered, gold-laced, pumped, and white-silk stockinged, would see the very stars out!" TTC ii 7

—independence: "If a man in Paris have an idiosyncrasy on the subject of any article of attire between his hat and his boots, he gratifies it without the least idea that it can be anybody's affair but his; nor does anybody else make it his affair. If, indeed, there be anything obviously convenient or tasteful in the peculiarity, then it soon ceases to be a peculiarity, and is adopted by others. If not, it is let alone. In the meantime, the commonest man in the streets does not consider it at all essential to his character as a true Frenchman, that he should howl, stare, jeer, or otherwise make himself offensive to the author of the innovation." HW/I

—knack: "What does [Compact Enchantress] do to be so neat? How is it that every trifle she wears belongs to her, and cannot choose but be a part of her? And even Mystery, look at *her!* A model. Mystery is not young, not pretty, though still of an average candle-light passability; but she does such miracles on her own behalf, that, one of these days, when she dies, they'll be amazed to find an old woman in her bed, distantly like her." RP/F

—Eagle as symbol: " . . . I might have circled all night on my hobby-horse in a stately cavalcade of hobby-horses four abreast . . . while above it, the Eagle of France, gas-outlined and apparently afflicted with the prevailing infirmities that have lighted on the poultry, is in a very undecided state of policy, and as a bird moulting." UT/FF

See N:Bird*—poultry—in Flanders*

—the English view: "It was profoundly observed by a witty member of the Court of Common Council, in Council assembled in the City of London, in the year of our Lord one thousand eight hundred and fifty, that the French are a frog-eating people, who wear wooden shoes.

"We are credibly informed, in reference to the nation whom this choice spirit so happily disposed of, that the caricatures and stage representations which were current in England some half a century ago, exactly depict their present condition. For example, we understand that every Frenchman, without exception, wears a pigtail and curl-papers. That he is extremely sallow, thin, long-faced, and lantern-jawed. That the calves of his legs are invariably undeveloped; that his legs fail at the knees, and that his shoulders are always higher than his ears.

"We are likewise assured that he rarely tastes any food but soup maigre, and an onion; that he always says, 'By Gar! Aha! Vat you tell me, sare?' at the end of every sentence he utters; and that the true generic name of his race is the Mounseers, or the Parly-voos. If he be not a dancing-master, or a barber, he must be a cook; since no other trades but those three are congenial to the tastes of the people, or permitted by the Institutions of the country.

"He is a slave, of course. The ladies of France (who are also slaves) invariably have their heads tied up in Belcher handkerchiefs, wear long earrings, carry tambourines, and beguile the weariness of their yoke by singing in head voices through their noses—principally to barrel-organs.

"It may be generally summed up, of this inferior people, that they have no idea of anything." ¶RP/FF

—*impervious to weather:* "If I am coming from the Moon, what an extraordinary people the Mooninians must be for sitting down in the open air! I have seen them wipe the hoar-frost off the seats in the public ways, on the faintest appearance of a gleam of sun, and sit down to enjoy themselves. I have seen them, two minutes after it has left off raining for the first time in eight-and-forty hours, take chairs in the midst of the mud and water, and begin to chat.

"I have seen them by the roadside, easily reclining on iron couches, when their beards have been all but blown off their chins by the east wind. I have seen them, with no protection from the black drizzle and dirt but a saturated canvas blind overhead, and a handful of sand underfoot, smoke and drink new beer, whole evenings.

"And the Mooninian babies. Heavens, what a surprising race are the Mooninian babies! Seventy-one of these innocents have I counted, with their nurses and chairs, spending the day outside the Café de la Lune, in weather that would have satisfied **Herod**. Thirty-nine have I beheld in that locality at once, with these eyes, partaking of their natural refreshment under umbrellas. Twenty-three have I seen engaged with skipping-ropes, in mire three inches thick." ¶HW/RD

—*'long':* "Do you know those rivers so long, so uniform in breadth, so dully gray in hue, that in despair at their regularity, you momentarily libel nature as being only a grand canal commissioner after all? Do you know the long funereal rows of poplars, or dreary parallelograms of osiers, that fringe those river banks; the long white roads, hedgeless, but, oh! so dismally ditchful; the long, low stone walls; the long farmhouses, without a spark of the robust, leafy, cheerful life of the English homesteads; the long fields, scarcely evergreen, but of an ashen tone, wearily furrowed, as though the earth had grown old and was beginning to show the crow's feet; the long, interminable gray French landscape?

"The sky itself seems longer than it ought to be; and the clouds stretch away to goodness knows where in long low banks, as if the heavens had been ruled with a parallel. If a vehicle passes you it is only a wofully long diligence, lengthened yellow ugliness long drawn out, with a seemingly endless team of horses, and a long, stifling cloud of dust behind it: a driver for the wheelers with a whip seven times as long as it ought to be; and a postilion for the leaders with boots long enough for seven-leaguers. His oaths are long; the horses' manes are long; their tails are so long that they are obliged to have them tied up with straw. The stages are long, the journey long, the fare long—the whole longitudinal carriage leaves a long melancholy jingle of bells behind it.

"Yes: French scenery is very lengthy; so I settled in my mind at least, as I walked with long strides along the white French road. A longer me—my shadow—walked before me, bending its back and drooping its arms, and angularising its elongated legs like drowsy compasses. The shadow looked tired: I felt so. I had been oppressed by length all day. I had passed a long procession—some hundreds of boys in gray great coats and red trowsers: soldiers. I had found their guns and bayonets too long, their coats disproportionately lengthy; the moustaches of their officers ridiculously elongated. There was no end of them—their rolling drums, baggage waggons, and led horses.

"I had passed a team of bullocks ploughing: they looked as long as the lane that hath no turning. A long man followed them smoking a long pipe. A wretched pig I saw, too—a long, lean, bristly, lanky-legged monstrosity, without even a curly tail, for his tail was long and pendent; a miserable pig, half-snouted greyhound, half-abashed weazel, whole hog, and an eyesore to me. I was a long way from home. I had the spleen I wanted something short—not to drink but a short break in the long landscape, a house, a knoll, a clump of trees—anything to relieve this long purgatory." ¶CS/PT

This is Dickens's uncollected bridge introduction to the tale of the Swiss watchmaker, the fifth poor traveller.

Making off [across the French countryside] LD

—*market town:* "On market-days alone, its Great Place suddenly leaped out of bed. On market-days, some friendly enchanter struck his staff upon the stones of the Great Place, and instantly arose the liveliest booths and stalls, and sittings and standings, and a pleasant hum of chaffering and huckstering from many hundreds of tongues, and a pleasant, though peculiar, blending of colours—white caps, blue blouses, and green vegetables—and at last the Knight destined for the adventure seemed to have come in earnest, and all the Vaubanois sprang up awake.

"And now, by long, low-lying avenues of trees, jolting in white-hooded donkey-cart, and on donkey-back, and in tumbril and wagon, and cart and cabriolet, and afoot with barrow and burden—and along the dikes and ditches and canals, in little peak-prowed country boats—came peasant-men and women in flocks and crowds, bringing articles for sale.

"And here you had boots and shoes, and sweetmeats and stuffs to wear, and here (in the cool shade of the Town-hall) you had milk and cream and butter and cheese, and here you had fruits and onions and carrots, and all things needful for your soup, and here you had poultry and flowers and protesting pigs, and here new shovels, axes, spades, and bill-hooks for your farming work, and here huge mounds of bread, and here your unground grain in sacks, and here your children's dolls, and here the cake-seller, announcing his wares by beat and roll of drum . . . .

"And now the enchanter struck his staff upon the stones of the Great Place once more, and down went the booths, the sittings and standings, and vanished the merchandise, and with it the barrows, donkeys, donkey-carts, and tumbrils, and all other things on wheels and feet, except the slow scavengers with unwieldy carts and meagre horses clearing up the rubbish, assisted by the sleek town pigeons, better plumped out than on non-market days.

"While there was yet an hour or two to wane before the autumn sunset, the loiterer outside town-gate and drawbridge, and postern and double-ditch, would see the last shadows of trees, or the last country boat, paddled by the last market-woman on her way home, showing black upon the reddening, long, low, narrow dike between him and the mill; and as the paddle-parted scum and weed closed over the boat's track, he might be comfortably sure that its sluggish rest would be troubled no more until next market-day." ¶CS/SL 2

And see TP:Medicine—*patent—in France*

—*money-loving:* "Will any Englishman undertake to match me that generic French old lady whom I will instantly produce against him, from the private life of any house of five floors in the French capital, and who is a mere gulf for swallowing my money, or any man's money? That generic French old lady who, whether she gives me her daughter to wife, or sits next me in a balcony at a theatre, or opposite to me in a public carriage, or lets me an apartment, or plays me a match at dominoes, or sells me an umbrella, equally absorbs my substance, calculates my resources with a fierce nicety, and is intent upon my ruin?

"That generic French old lady who is always in black, and always protuberant, and always complimentary, and who always eats up everything that is presented to her—almost eats her knife besides—and who has a supernatural craving after francs which fascinates me, and inclines me to pour out all I have at her feet, saying, 'Take them and twinkle at me with those hungry eyes no more? *We* eminently a money-loving people! Why do we talk such nonsense with this terrible old woman to contradict us?" ¶HW/W?

—*railroad restaurant report:* "'On my experience south of Paris,' said Our Missis, in a deep tone, 'I will not expatiate. Too loathsome were the task! But fancy this. Fancy a guard coming round, with the train at full speed, to inquire how many for dinner. Fancy his telegraphing forward the number of diners. Fancy every one expected, and the table elegantly laid for the complete party. Fancy a charming dinner, in a charming room, and the head-cook, concerned for the honour of every dish, superintending in his clean white jacket and cap. Fancy the Beast [the Public] travelling six hundred miles on end, very fast, and with great punctuality, yet being taught to expect all this to be done for it!' . . .

"'Putting everything together,' said Our Missis, 'French Refreshmenting comes to this, and O, it comes to a nice total! First: eatable things to eat, and drinkable things to drink.'

"A groan from the young ladies . . . .

"'Second: convenience, and even elegance.'

"Another groan . . . .

"'Third: moderate charges.'

"This time a groan from me . . . .

"'Fourth:—and here,' says Our Missis, 'I claim your angriest sympathy—attention, common civility, nay, even politeness!'

"Me and the young ladies regularly raging mad all together.

"'And I cannot in conclusion,' says Our Missis, with her spitefullest sneer, 'give you a completer pictur of that despicable nation (after what I have related), than assuring you that they wouldn't bear our constitutional ways and noble independence at Mugby Junction for a single month, and that they would turn us to the right about and put another system in our places, as soon as look at us; perhaps sooner, for I do not believe they have the good taste to care to look at us twice.'" CS/MJ 3

—*en route to Paris:* " . . . a bugle, the alarm, a crash! What is it? Death? No, Amiens.

"More fortifications, more soldiering and drumming, more basins of soup, more little loaves of bread, more bottles of wine, more caraffes of brandy, more time for refreshment. Everything good, and everything ready. Bright, unsubstantial-looking, scenic sort of station. People waiting. Houses, uniforms, beards, moustaches, some sabots, plenty of neat women, and a few old-visaged children. Unless it be a delusion born of my giddy flight, the grown-up people and the children seem to change places in France. In general, the boys and girls are little old men and women, and the men and women lively boys and girls." RP/F

—*simple enjoyment:* "I had formed quite a high opinion of the French nation and had noticed them to be much more homely and domestic in their families and far more simple and amiable in their lives than I had ever been led to expect, and it did strike me between ourselves that in one particular they might be imitated to advantage by another nation which I will not mention, and that is in the courage with which they take their little enjoyments on little means and with little things and don't let solemn big-wigs stare them out of countenance or speechify them dull, of which said solemn big-wigs I have ever had the one opinion that I wish they were all made comfortable separately in coppers with the lids on and never let out any more." CS/LL 2

See The English—*conventionality*

—*stature related to occupation:* ". . . I am [not bound] to assign a reason for all the little men in France being soldiers, and all the big men postillions; which is the invariable rule." PI 2

And see Cities and Towns, Actual, *passim;* TT:Travel—*in France: of a villain;* W:Inns and Taverns, Abroad—*in France*

French language

—*"lo":* 'What sort of language do you consider French, sir?'

"'How do you mean?' asked Nicholas.

"'Do you consider it a good language, sir?' said the collector; 'a pretty language, a sensible language?'

"'A pretty language, certainly,' replied Nicholas, 'and as it has a name for everything, and admits of elegant conversation about everything, I presume it is a sensible one.'

"'I don't know,' said Mr Lillyvick, doubtfully. 'Do you call it a cheerful language now?'

"'Yes,' replied Nicholas, 'I should say it was, certainly.'

"'It's very much changed since my time, then,' said the collector, 'very much.'

"'Was it a dismal one in your time?' asked Nicholas, scarcely able to repress a smile.

"'Very,' replied Mr Lillyvick, with some vehemence of manner. 'It's the war time that I speak of; the last war. It may be a cheerful language. I should be sorry to contradict anybody; but I can only say that I've heard the French prisoners, who were natives, and ought to know how to speak it, talking in such a dismal manner, that it made one miserable to hear them. Ay, that I have, fifty times, sir—fifty times!'

Mr Lillyvick was waxing so cross, that Mrs Kenwigs thought it expedient to motion to Nicholas not to say anything; and it was not until Miss Petowker had practised several blandishments, to soften the excellent old gentleman, that he deigned to break silence, by asking,

"'What's the water in French, sir?'

"'*L'Eau,*' replied Nicholas.

"'Ah!' said Mr Lillyvick, shaking his head mournfully,'I thought as much. Lo, eh? I don't think anything of that language—nothing at all.'" NN 16

—*not spoken, in France:* "Although Miss Pross, through her long association with a French family, might have known as much of their language as of her own, if she had had a mind, she had no mind in that direction; consequently she knew no more of that 'nonsense' (as she was pleased to call it) than Mr Cruncher did. So her manner of marketing was to plump a noun-substantive at the head of a shopkeeper without any introduction in the nature of an article, and, if it happened not to be the name of the thing she wanted, to look round for that thing, lay hold of it, and hold on by it until the bargain was concluded. She always made a bargain for it, by holding up, as a statement of its just price, one finger less than the merchant held up, whatever his number might be." TTC iii 7

—*spoken by an Englishman:* "'"Bob swore!"—as the Englishman said for "Good night," when he first learnt French, and thought it so like English [said Miss Mowcher]. "Bob swore," my ducks!'" DC 22

"'I ask myself the question, What am I to do? How am I to live? Ill fo manger, you know,' says Mr Jobling, pronouncing that word as if he meant a necessary fixture in an English stable. 'Ill fo manger. That's the French saying, and mangering is as necessary to me as it is to a Frenchman. Or more so.'" BH 20

"And the way in which Jemmy spoke his French was a real charm. It was often wanted of him, for whenever anybody spoke a syllable to me I says 'Non-comprenny, you're very kind, but it's no use—Now Jemmy!' and then Jemmy he fires away at 'em lovely, the only thing wanting in Jemmy's French being as it appeared to me that he hardly ever understood a word of what they said to him which made it scarcely of the use it might have been though in other respects a perfect Native, and regarding the Major's fluency I should have been of the opinion judging French by English that there might have been a greater choice of words in the language though still I must admit that if I hadn't known him when he asked a military gentleman in a grey cloak what o'clock it was I should have took him for a Frenchman born." CS/LL 1

"Mr The Englishman was not particularly strong in the French language as a means of oral communication, though he read it very well. It is with languages as with people—when you only know them by sight, you are apt to mistake them; you must be on speaking terms before you can be said to have established an acquaintance." CS/SL 2

—*taught, in England:* " . . . Mr Charles Darnay was established in England as a higher teacher of the French language who was conversant with French literature. In this age [1759], he would have been a Professor; in that age, he was a Tutor. He read with young men who could find any leisure and interest for the study of a living tongue spoken all over the world, and he cultivated a taste for its stores of knowledge and fancy . . . .

"A certain portion of his time was passed at Cambridge, where he read with undergraduates as a sort of tolerated smuggler who drove a contraband trade in European languages, instead of conveying Greek and Latin through the Custom-house." TTC ii 10

See also H:"Society"—*the world of fashion*

Inns and Taverns, Abroad

—*in America:* " . . . with their four hundred beds apiece, and their eight or nine hundred ladies and gentlemen at dinner every day." CS/HT 1 *See also* America—*hotels*

—*in France*

—*Paris:* " . . . with the pretty apartment of four pieces up one hundred and seventy-five waxed stairs, the privilege of ringing the bell all day long without influencing anybody's mind or body but your own, and the not-too-much-for-dinner, considering the price." CS/HT 1

—*Poissy:* "Throughout all the land of France I know this unswept room at The Glory, with its peculiar smell of beans and coffee, where the butchers crowd about the stove, drinking the thinnest of wine from the smallest of tumblers; where the thickest of coffee-cups mingle with the longest of loaves, and the weakest of lump sugar . . . where the billiard-table is covered up in the midst like a great bird-cage—but the bird may sing by-and-by!" RP/FF

—*provinces:* "Next to the provincial Inns of France, with the great church-tower rising above the courtyard, the horse-bells jingling merrily up and down the street beyond, and the clocks of all descriptions in all the rooms, which are never right, unless taken at the precise minute when, by getting exactly twelve hours too fast or too slow, they unintentionally become so." CS/HT 1

—*Sens:* "The pleasantest-situated inn my dear! Right under the two towers, with their shadows a changing upon it all day like a kind of a sundial, and country people driving in and out of the courtyard in carts and hooded cabriolets and such like, and a market outside in front of the cathedral, and all so quaint and like a picter." CS/LL

—*in Germany*

—*generally:* " . . . where all the eatables are soddened down to the same flavour, and where the mind is disturbed by the apparition of hot puddings, and boiled cherries, sweet and slab, at awfully unexpected periods of the repast . . . a draught of sparkling beer from a foaming glass jug, and a glance of recognition through the windows of the student beer-houses at Heidelberg and elsewhere . . . . " CS/HT 1

—*on the Rhine:* "Next I put up for a minute at the restless Inns upon the Rhine, where your going to bed, no matter at what hour, appears to be the tocsin for everybody else's getting up; and where, in the table-d'hote room at the end of the long table (with several Towers of Babel on it at the other end, all made of white plates), one knot of stoutish men, entirely dressed in jewels and dirt, and having nothing else upon them, *will* remain all night, clinking glasses, and singing about the river that flows, and the grape that grows, and Rhine wine that beguiles, and Rhine woman that smiles and hi drink drink my friend and ho drink drink my brother, and all the rest of it." CS/HT 1

—*in Italy*

—*on the Campagna:* " . . . we stopped to refresh the horses, and to get some lunch, in a common malaria-shaken, despondent little public-house, whose every inch of wall and beam, inside, was (according to custom) painted and decorated in a way so miserable that every room looked like the wrong side of another room, and, with its wretched imitation of drapery, and lop-sided little daubs of lyres, seemed to have been plundered from behind the scenes of some travelling circus." PI 10

—*converted:* "So to the old palace Inns and old monastery Inns, in towns and cities of the same bright country; with their massive quadrangular staircases, whence you may look from among clustering pillars high into the blue vault of heaven; with their stately banqueting-rooms, and vast refectories; with their labyrinths of ghostly bedchambers, and their glimpses into gorgeous streets that have no appearance of reality or possibility." CS/HT 1

—*La Scala, in Tuscany:* "We then went on again, through a region gradually becoming bleaker and wilder, until it became as bare and desolate as any Scottish moors. Soon after dark, we halted for the night, at the osteria of La Scala: a perfectly lone house, where the family were sitting round a great fire in the kitchen, raised on a stone platform three or four feet high, and big enough for the roasting of an ox. On the upper, and only other floor of this hotel, there was a great wild rambling sala, with one very little window in a by-corner, and four black doors opening into four black bedrooms in various directions.

"To say nothing of another large black door, opening into another large black sala, with the staircase coming abruptly through a kind of trap-door in the floor, and the rafters of the roof looming above: a suspicious little press skulking in one obscure corner: and all the knives in the house lying about in various directions.

"The fireplace was of the purest Italian architecture, so that it was perfectly impossible to see it for the smoke. The waitress was like a dramatic brigand's wife, and wore the same style of dress upon her head. The dogs barked like mad; the echoes returned the compliments bestowed upon them; there was not another house within twelve miles; and things had a dreary, and rather a cut-throat, appearance." ¶PI 10

—*at Radicofani, in Tuscany:* " . . . a ghostly, goblin inn . . . full of such rambling corridors, and gaunt rooms, that all the murdering and phantom tales that ever were written might have originated in that one house . . . there is a winding, creaking, wormy, rustling, door-opening, foot-on-staircase-falling character about this Radicofani Hotel, such as I never saw, anywhere else." PI 10

—*roadside:* " . . . the lesser roadside Inns of Italy; where all the dirty clothes in the house (not in wear) are always lying in your anteroom; where the mosquitoes make a raisin pudding of your face in summer, and the cold bites it blue in winter; where you get what you can, and forget what you can't; where I should again like to be boiling my tea in a pocket-handkerchief dumpling, for want of a teapot." CS/HT 1

—*below the Simplon:* "The painted room in which [Little Dorrit] awoke, often a humbled state-chamber in a dilapidated palace . . . with its wild red autumnal vine-leaves overhanging the glass, its orange-trees on the cracked white terrace outside the window, a group of monks and peasants in the little street below, misery and magnificence wrestling with each other upon every rood of ground in the prospect, no matter how widely diversified, and misery throwing magnificence with the strength of fate. To this would succeed a labyrinth of bare passages and pillared galleries, with the family procession already preparing in the quadrangle below, through the carriages and luggage being brought together by the servants for the day's journey. Then, breakfast in another painted chamber, damp-stained and of desolate proportions; and then the departure . . . . " LD ii 3

—*in the south:* " . . . the close little Inns of the Malaria districts, with their pale attendants, and their peculiar smell of never letting in the air." CS/HT 1

—*Venice:* " . . . the immense fantastic Inns of Venice, with the cry of the gondolier below, as he skims the corner; the grip of the watery odours on one particular little bit of the bridge of your nose (which is never released while you stay there); and the great bell of St Mark's Cathedral tolling midnight." CS/HT 1

—*in Scotland:* " . . . the Highland Inns, with the oatmeal bannocks, the honey, the venison steaks, the trout from the loch, the whisky, and perhaps (having the materials so temptingly at hand) the Athol brose [a mixture of oatmeal, honey and whisky]." CS/HT 1

—*in Switzerland:*

—*near Mont Blanc:* "That was a good Inn, too, with the kind, cheerful landlady and the honest landlord, where I lived in the shadow of Mont Blanc, and where one of the apartments has a zoological papering on the walls, not so accurately joined but that the elephant occasionally rejoices in a tiger's hind legs and tail, while the lion puts on a trunk and tusks, and the bear, moulting as it were, appears as to portions of himself like a leopard." CS/HT 1

—*village inn:* "It was a very homely place, in a village of one narrow zigzag street, among mountains, and you went in at the main door through the cow-house, and among the mules and the dogs and the fowls, before ascending a great bare staircase to the rooms; which were all of unpainted wood, without plastering or papering—like rough packing-cases. Outside there was nothing but the straggling street, a little toy church with a copper-coloured steeple, a pine forest, a torrent, mists, and mountainsides." CS/HT I

—*in Wales:* "This reminiscence brought the Welsh Inns in general before me; with the women in their round hats, and the harpers with their white beards (venerable, but humbugs, I am afraid), playing outside the door while I took my dinner." CS/HT 1

Inns and Taverns, English

—*Admiral Benbow,* on the Channel coast: "Admiral Benbow's cheese was out of the season, but his home-made bread was good, and his beer was perfect. Deluded by some earlier spring day which had been warm and sunny, the Admiral had cleared the firing out of his parlour stove, and had put some flower-pots in—which was amiable and hopeful in the Admiral, but not judicious: the room being, at that present visiting, transcendantly cold. I therefore took the liberty of peeping out across a little stone passage into the Admiral's kitchen, and, seeing a high settle with its back towards me drawn out in front of the Admiral's kitchen fire, I strolled in, bread and cheese in hand, munching and looking about. One landsman and two boatmen were seated on the settle, smoking pipes and drinking beer out of thick pint crockery mugs—mugs peculiar to such places, with parti-coloured rings round them, and ornaments between the rings like frayed-out roots." RP/OT

—*angler's inns:* ". . . the pleasant white, clean, flower-pot-decorated bedrooms of those inns, overlooking the river, and the ferry, and the green ait [river island], and the church-spire, and the country bridge . . . ." CS/HT 1

—*Blue Dragon,* near Salisbury

—*sign:* ". . . a certain Dragon who swung and creaked complainingly before the village ale-house door. A faded and an ancient dragon he was; and many a wintry storm of rain, snow, sleet, and hail, had changed his colour from a gaudy blue to a faint lack-lustre shade of grey. But there he hung; rearing, in a state of monstrous imbecility, on his hind legs; waxing, with every month that passed, so much more dim and shapeless, that as you gazed at him on one side of the sign-board it seemed as if he must be gradually melting through it, and coming out upon the other.

"He was a courteous and considerate dragon, too; or had been in his distincter days; for in the midst of his rampant feebleness, he kept one of his fore paws near his nose, as though he would say, 'Don't mind me—it's only my fun;' while he held out the other in polite and hospitable entreaty. " MC 3

—*soporific effect:* ". . . a large apartment, such as one may see in country places, with a low roof and a sunken flooring, all downhill from the door, and a descent of two steps on the inside so exquisitely unexpected, that strangers, despite the most elaborate cautioning, usually dived in head first, as into a plunging-bath. It was none of your frivolous and preposterously bright bedrooms, where nobody can close an eye with any kind of propriety or decent regard to the association of ideas; but it was a good, dull, leaden, drowsy place, where every article of furniture reminded you that you came there to sleep, and that you were expected to go to sleep.

"There was no wakeful reflection of the fire there, as in your modern chambers, which upon the darkest nights have a watchful consciousness of French polish; the old Spanish mahogany winked at it now and then, as a dozing cat or dog might, nothing more. The very size and shape, and hopeless immovability of the bedstead, and wardrobe, and in a minor degree of even the chairs and tables, provoked sleep; they were plainly apoplectic and disposed to snore.

"There were no staring portraits to remonstrate with you for being lazy; no round-eyed birds upon the curtains, disgustingly wide awake, and insufferably prying. The thick neutral hangings, and the dark blinds, and the heavy heap of bed-clothes, were all designed to hold in sleep, and act as non-conductors to the day and getting up. Even the old stuffed fox upon the top of the wardrobe was devoid of any spark of vigilance, for his glass eye had fallen out, and he slumbered as he stood.

"Indeed it must be conceded to the whole brood of dragons of modern times, that they have made a great advance in civilisation and refinement. They no longer demand a beautiful virgin for breakfast every morning, with as much regularity as any tame single gentleman expects his hot roll, but rest content with the society of idle bachelors and roving married men: and they are now remarkable rather for holding aloof from the softer sex and discouraging their visits (especially on Saturday nights), than for rudely insisting on their company without any reference to their inclinations, as they are known to have done in days of yore." ¶MC 3

—*Bull's Head,* old coaching inn: "Take the old-established Bull's Head with its old-established knife-boxes on its old-established sideboards, its old-established flue under its old-established four-post bedsteads in its old-established airless rooms, its old-established frouziness up-stairs and downstairs, its old-established cookery, and its old-established principles of plunder.

"Count up your injuries, in its side-dishes of ailing sweetbreads in white poultices, of apothecaries' powders in rice for curry, of pale stewed bits of calf ineffectually relying for an adventitious interest on forcemeat balls. You have had experience of the old-established Bull's Head stringy fowls, with lower extremities like wooden legs, sticking up out of the dish; of its cannibalic boiled mutton, gushing horribly among its capers, when carved; of its little dishes of pastry—roofs of spermaceti ointment, erected over half an apple or four gooseberries.

"Well for you if you have yet forgotten the old-established Bull's Head fruity port: whose reputation was gained solely by the old-established price the Bull's Head put upon it, and by the old-established air with which the Bull's Head set the glasses and D'Oyleys on, and held that Liquid Gout to the three-and-sixpenny wax-candle, as if its old-established colour hadn't come from the dyer's." ¶UT/RT

—*a country tavern:* " . . . a little hostelry which no man possessed of a penny was ever known to pass in warm weather. Before its entrance are certain pleasant trimmed limes; likewise a cool well, with so musical a bucket-handle that its fall upon the bucket rim will make a horse prick up his ears and neigh, upon the droughty road half a mile off. This is a house of great resort for hay-making tramps and harvest tramps, insomuch that as they sit within, drinking their mugs of beer, their relinquished scythes and reaping-hooks glare out of the open windows, as if the whole establishment were a family war-coach of Ancient Britons." UT/T

—*Crispin and Crispanus,* in a country town: "Then, should we make a burst to get clear of the trees, and should soon find ourselves in the open, with the town-lights bright ahead of us. So should we lie that night at the ancient sign of the Crispin and Crispanus, and rise early next morning to be betimes on tramp again." UT/T

—*Dodo,* in "one of the chiefest towns of Staffordshire:" " . . . the landlady of the Dodo in the empty bar, whose eye had trouble in it and no welcome, when I asked for dinner . . . .

"If the Dodo were only a gregarious bird—if he had only some confused idea of making a comfortable nest—I could hope to get through the hours between this and bedtime, without being consumed by devouring melancholy. But, the Dodo's habits are all wrong. It provides me with a trackless desert of sitting-room, with a chair for every day in the year, a table for every month, and a waste of sideboard where a lonely China vase pines in a corner for its mate long departed, and will never make a match with the candlestick in the opposite corner if it live till Doomsday.

"The Dodo has nothing in the larder . . . . The Dodo excludes the outer air. When I mount up to my bedroom, a smell of closeness and flue gets lazily up my nose like sleepy snuff. The loose little bits of carpet writhe under my tread, and take wormy shapes . . . . The Dodo is narrow-minded as to towels; expects me to wash on a freemason's apron without the trimming: when I asked for soap, gives me a stony-hearted something white, with no more lather in it than the Elgin marbles. The Dodo has seen better days, and possesses interminable stables at the back—silent, grass-grown, broken-windowed, horseless.

"This mournful bird can fry a sole, however, which is much. Can cook a steak, too, which is more." HWC/PA *And see* B:Food and Drink—*sherry at the Dodo*

—*Dolphin's Head,* in Doncaster, a former "great stage-coaching town": " . . . which everywhere expressed past coachfulness and present coachlessness. Coloured prints of coaches, starting, arriving, changing horses, coaches in the sunshine, coaches in the snow, coaches in the wind, coaches in the mist and rain, coaches on the King's birthday, coaches in all circumstances compatible with their triumph and victory, but never in the act of breaking down or overturning, pervaded the house.

"Of these works of art, some, framed and not glazed, had holes in them; the varnish of others had become so brown and cracked, that they looked like overdone pie-crust; the designs of others were almost obliterated by the flies of many summers. Broken glasses, damaged frames, lop-sided hanging, and consignment of incurable cripples to places of refuge in dark corners, attested the desolation of the rest.

"The old room on the ground floor where the passengers of the Highflyer used to dine, had nothing in it but a wretched show of twigs and flower-pots in the broad window to hide the nakedness of the land . . . . The old fraudulent candles which were always being paid for and never used, were burnt out at last; but their tall stilts of candlesticks still lingered, and still outraged the human intellect by pretending to be silver . . . the score or two of pigeons that remained true to their ancestral traditions and the place, had collected in a row on the roof-ridge of the only out-house retained by the Dolphin, where all the inside pigeons tried to push the outside pigeon off. This I accepted as emblementical of the struggle for post and place in railway times." ¶UT/SC

—George, at Grantham: ". . . one of the best inns in England . . . ." NN 5

—Great Pavilionstone Hotel: "If you are going to our Great Pavilionstone Hotel, the sprightliest porters under the sun, whose cheerful looks are a pleasant welcome, shoulder your luggage, drive it off in vans, bowl it away in trucks, and enjoy themselves in playing athletic games with it.

"If you are for public life at our great Pavilionstone Hotel, you walk into that establishment as if it were your club; and find ready for you, your news-room, dining-room, smoking-room, billiard-room, music-room, public breakfast, public dinner twice a-day (one plain, one gorgeous), hot baths and cold baths.

"If you want to be bored, there are plenty of bores always ready for you, and from Saturday to Monday in particular, you can be bored (if you like it) through and through.

"Should you want to be private at our Great Pavilionstone Hotel, say but the word, look at the list of charges, choose your floor, name your figure—there you are, established in your castle, by the day, week, month, or year, innocent of all comers or goers, unless you have my fancy for walking early in the morning down the groves of boots and shoes, which so regularly flourish at all the chamber-doors before breakfast, that it seems to me as if nobody ever got up or took them in.

"Are you going across the Alps, and would you like to air your Italian at our Great Pavilionstone Hotel? Talk to the Manager . . . . And when you pay your bill at our Great Pavilionstone Hotel, you will not be put out of humour by anything you find in it.

"A thoroughly good inn, in the days of coaching and posting, was a noble place. But no such inn would have been equal to the reception of four or five hundred people, all of them wet through, and half of them dead sick, every day in the year. This is where we shine, in our Pavilionstone Hotel.

"Again—who, coming and going, pitching and tossing, boating and training, hurrying in, and flying out, could ever have calculated the fees to be paid at an old-fashioned house? In our Pavilionstone Hotel vocabulary, there is no such word as fee. Everything is done for you; every service is provided at a fixed and reasonable charge; all the prices are hung up in all the rooms; and you can make out your own bill beforehand, as well as the book-keeper." ¶RP/OT

—Great White Horse: "In the main street of Ipswich, on the left-hand side of the way . . . stands an inn known far and wide by the appellation of The Great White Horse, rendered the more conspicuous by a stone statue of some rampacious animal with flowing mane and tail, distantly resembling an insane cart-horse, which is elevated above the principal door.

"The Great White Horse is famous in the neighborhood, in the same degree as a prize ox, or county paper-chronicled turnip, or unwieldy pig—for its enormous size. Never were such labyrinths of uncarpeted passages, such clusters of mouldy, ill-lighted rooms, such huge numbers of small dens for eating or sleeping in, beneath any one roof, as are collected together between the four walls of the Great White Horse at Ipswich." ¶PP 22

—*Hesket-Newmarket Inn,* on the Cumberland Fells: "[The landlord] had a drawing-room, too, upstairs, which was worth a visit to the Cumberland Fells. (This was Mr Francis Goodchild's opinion, in which Mr Thomas Idle did not concur.)

"The ceiling of this drawing-room was so crossed and recrossed by beams of unequal lengths, radiating from a centre, in a corner, that it looked like a broken star-fish. The room was comfortably and solidly furnished with good mahogany and horsehair. It had a snug fireside, and a couple of well-curtained windows, looking out upon the wild country behind the house.

"What it most developed was, an unexpected taste for little ornaments and nick-nacks, of which it contained a most surprising number. They were not very various, consisting in great part of waxen babies with their limbs more or less mutilated, appealing on one leg to the parental affections from under little cupping glasses; but, *Uncle Tom* was there, in crockery, receiving theological instructions from *Miss Eva,* who grew out of his side like a wen, in an exceedingly rough state of profile propagandism.

"Engravings of Mr Hunt's country boy, before and after his pie, were on the wall, divided by a highly-coloured nautical piece, the subject of which had all her colours (and more) flying, and was making great way through a sea of a regular pattern, like a lady's collar. A benevolent, elderly gentleman of the last century, with a powdered head, kept guard, in oil and varnish, over a most perplexing piece of furniture on a table; in appearance between a driving seat and an angular knife-box, but, when opened, a musical instrument of tinkling wires, exactly like David's harp packed for travelling.

"Everything became a nick-nack in this curious room. The copper tea-kettle, burnished up to the highest point of glory, took his station on a stand of his own at the greatest possible distance from the fire-place, and said: 'By your leave, not a kettle, but a bijou.' The Staffordshire-ware butter-dish with the cover on, got upon a little round occasional table in a window, with a worked top, and announced itself to the two chairs accidentally placed there, as an aid to polite conversation, a graceful trifle in china to be chatted over by callers, as they airily trifled away the visiting moments of a butterfly existence, in that rugged old village on the Cumberland Fells. The very footstool could not keep the floor, but got upon a sofa, and therefrom proclaimed itself, in high relief of white and liver-coloured wool, a favourite spaniel coiled up for repose. Though, truly, in spite of its bright glass eyes, the spaniel was the least successful assumption in the collection: being perfectly flat, and dismally suggestive of a recent mistake in sitting down on the part of some corpulent member of the family." ¶LT 1

See also M:Books—*at an Inn*

—*Holly-Tree Inn,* somewhere in Yorkshire: "I thought I had never seen such a large room as that into which they showed me. It had five windows, with dark red curtains that would have absorbed the light of a general illumination; and there were complications of drapery at the top of the curtains, that went wandering about the wall in a most extraordinary manner. I asked for a smaller room, and they told me there was no smaller room. They could screen me in, however, the landlord said. They brought a great old japanned screen, with natives (Japanese, I suppose) engaged in a variety of idiotic pursuits all over it; and left me roasting whole before an immense fire.

"My bedroom was some quarter of a mile off, up a great staircase at the end of a long gallery; and nobody knows what a misery this is to a bashful man who would rather not meet people on the stairs. It was the grimmest room I have ever had the nightmare in; and all the furniture, from the four posts of the bed to the two old silver candlesticks, was tall, high-shouldered, and spindle-waisted.

"Below, in my sitting-room, if I looked round my screen, the wind rushed at me like a mad bull; if I stuck to my armchair, the fire scorched me to the colour of a new brick. The chimney piece was very high, and there was a bad glass—what I may call a wavy glass—above it, which, when I stood up, just showed me my anterior phrenological developments—and these never look well, in any subject, cut short off at the eyebrow. If I stood with my back to the fire, a gloomy vault of darkness above and beyond the screen insisted on being looked at; and, in its dim remoteness, the drapery of the ten curtains of the five windows went twisting and creeping about, like a nest of gigantic worms." CS/HT 1

—*hotel with embraceable staff:* ". . . we could all be very eloquent on the comforts of our favourite hotel, wherever it was—its beds, its stables, its vast amount of posting, its excellent cheese, its head waiter, its capital dishes, its pigeon-pies, or its 1820 port. Or possibly we could recall our chaste and innocent admiration of its landlady, or our fraternal regard for its handsome chambermaid. A celebrated dramatic critic once writing of a famous actress, renowned for her virtue and beauty, gave her the character of being 'an eminently gatherable-to-one's-arms, sort of person'. Perhaps someone amongst us has borne a somewhat similar mental tribute to the charms of the ladies associated with the administration of our favourite hotel." S/CT1

—*Jairing's,* in a seaside town: "Now, Jairing's being an hotel for families and gentlemen, in high repute among the midland counties, Mr Grazinglands plucked up a great spirit when he told Mrs Grazinglands she should have a chop there. That lady likewise felt that she was going to see Life.

"Arriving on that gay and festive scene, they found the second waiter, in a flabby undress, cleaning the windows of the empty coffee-room; and the first waiter, denuded of his white tie, making up his cruets behind the Post-Office Directory. The latter (who took them in hand) was greatly put out by their patronage, and showed his mind to be troubled by a sense of the pressing necessity of instantly smuggling Mrs Grazinglands into the obscurest corner of the building.

"This slighted lady (who is the pride of her division of the county) was immediately conveyed, by several dark passages, and up and down several steps, into a penitential apartment at the back of the house, where five invalided old plate-warmers leaned up against one another under a discarded old melancholy sideboard, and where the wintry leaves of all the dining-tables in the house lay thick. Also, a sofa, of incomprehensible form regarded from any sofane point of view, murmured 'Bed;' while an air of mingled fluffiness and heeltaps, added, 'Second Waiter's.'

"Secreted in this dismal hold, objects of a mysterious distrust and suspicion, Mr Grazinglands and his charming partner waited twenty minutes for the smoke (for it never came to a fire), twenty-five minutes for the sherry, half an hour for the tablecloth, forty minutes for the knives and forks, three-quarters of an hour for the chops, and an hour for the potatoes.

"On settling the little bill—which was not much more than the day's pay of a Lieutenant in the navy—Mr Grazinglands took heart to remonstrate against the general quality and cost of his reception. To whom the waiter replied, substantially, that Jairing's made it a merit to have accepted him on any terms: 'for,' added the waiter . . . 'when indiwiduals is not staying in the 'Ouse, their favours is not as a rule looked upon as making it worth Mr Jairing's while; nor is it, indeed a style of business Mr Jairing wishes.'" ¶UT/RT

—*Jolly Boatmen* (also *Lighterman's Arms*), at Mudfog [Chatham]: "At the very end of the Mudfog High Street, and abutting on the river-side, stands the Jolly Boatmen, an old-fashioned low-roofed, bay-windowed house, with a bar, kitchen, and tap-room all in one, and a large fireplace with a kettle to correspond, round which the working men have congregated time out of mind on a winter's night, refreshed by draughts of good strong beer, and cheered by the sounds of a fiddle and tambourine: the Jolly Boatmen having been duly licensed by the Mayor and corporation, to scrape the fiddle and thumb the tambourine from time whereof the memory of the oldest inhabitants goeth not to the contrary." B/T

—*Jolly Sandboys*, some days' walk from London: "[It] was a small road-side inn of pretty ancient date, with a sign, representing three Sandboys increasing their jollity with as many jugs of ale and bags of gold, creaking and swinging on its post on the opposite side of the road. . . . A mighty fire was blazing on the [kitchen] hearth and roaring up the wide chimney with a cheerful sound, which a large iron cauldron, bubbling and simmering in the heat, lent its pleasant aid to swell. There was a deep red ruddy blush upon the room, and when the landlord stirred the fire, sending the flames skipping and leaping up—when he took off the lid of the iron pot and there rushed out a savoury smell, while the bubbling sound grew deeper and more rich, and an unctuous steam came floating out, hanging in a delicious mist above their heads—when he did this, Mr Codlin's heart was touched. He sat down in the chimney-corner and smiled." OCS 18

—*Lancaster Inn:* "The house was a genuine old house of a very quaint description, teeming with old carvings, and beams, and panels, and having an excellent old staircase, with a gallery or upper staircase, cut off from it by a curious fence-work of old oak, or of the old Honduras Mahogany wood. It was, and is, and will be, for many a long year to come, a remarkably picturesque house; and a certain grave mystery lurking in the depth of the old mahogany panels, as if they were so many deep pools of dark water—such, indeed, as they had been much among when they were trees—gave it a very mysterious character after nightfall." LT 4

—*Magpie and Stump,* at Ipswich: "This favoured tavern, sacred to the evening orgies of Mr Lowten and his companions, was what ordinary people would designate a public-house. That the landlord was a man of a money-making turn, was sufficiently testified by the fact of a small bulk-head beneath the tap-room window, in size and shape not unlike a sedan-chair, being underlet to a mender of shoes: and that he was a being of a philanthropic mind, was evident from the protection he afforded to a pieman, who vended his delicacies without fear of interruption on the very door-step.

"In the lower windows, which were decorated with curtains of a saffron hue, dangled two or three printed cards, bearing reference to Devonshire cyder and Dantzic spruce, while a large black board, announcing in white letters to an enlightened public that there were 500,000 barrels of double stout in the cellars of the establishment, left the mind in a state of not unpleasing doubt and uncertainty as to the precise direction in the bowels of the earth, in which this mighty cavern might be supposed to extend.

"When we add, that the weather-beaten sign-board bore the half-obliterated semblance of a magpie intently eyeing a crooked streak of brown paint, which the neighbours had been taught from infancy to consider as the 'stump,' we have said all that need be said of the exterior of the edifice." ¶PP 20

'Magpie' is slang for a halfpenny, 'stump' for making payment.

—*Marquis of Granby,* at Dorking: " . . . in Mrs [Susan] Weller's time [it] was quite a model of a road-side public house of the better class—just large enough to be convenient, and small enough to be snug. On the opposite side of the road was a large sign-board on a high post, representing the head and shoulders of a gentleman with an apoplectic countenance, in a red coat with deep blue facings, and a touch of the same blue over his three-cornered hat, for a sky. Over that again were a pair of flags; beneath the last button of his coat were a couple of cannon; and the whole formed an expressive and undoubted likeness of the Marquis of Granby of glorious memory.

"The bar window displayed a choice collection of geranium plants, and a well-dusted row of spirit phials. The open shutters bore a variety of golden inscriptions, eulogistic of good beds and neat wines; and the choice group of country-men and hostlers lounging about the stable-door and horse-trough, afforded presumptive proof of the excellent quality of the ale and spirits which were sold within." PP 27

—*Maypole,* at Chigwell: "In the year 1775, there stood upon the borders of Epping Forest, at a distance of about twelve miles from London . . . a house of public entertainment called the Maypole . . . .

"The Maypole . . . was an old building, with more gable ends than a lazy man would care to count on a sunny day; huge zig-zag chimneys, out of which it seemed as though even smoke could not choose but come in more than naturally fantastic shapes, imparted to it in its tortuous progress; and vast stables, gloomy, ruinous, and empty. The place was said to have been built in the days of King Henry the Eighth; and there was a legend, not only that Queen Elizabeth had slept there one night while upon a hunting excursion, to wit, in a certain oak-panelled room with a deep bay window, but that next morning, while standing on a mounting block before the door with one foot in the stirrup, the virgin monarch had then and there boxed and cuffed an unlucky page for some neglect of duty . . . .

"Whether these, and many other stories of the like nature, were true or untrue, the Maypole was really an old house, a very old house, perhaps as old as it claimed to be, and perhaps older, which will sometimes happen with houses of an uncertain, as with ladies of a certain, age. Its windows were old diamond-pane lattices, its floors were sunken and uneven, its ceilings blackened by the hand of time, and heavy with massive beams. Over the doorway was an ancient porch, quaintly and grotesquely carved; and here on summer evenings the more favoured customers smoked and drank—ay, and sang many a good song too, sometimes—reposing on two grim-looking high-backed settles, which, like the twin dragons of some fairy tale, guarded the entrance to the mansion . . . .

The Best Apartment BR

"With its overhanging stories, drowsy little panes of glass, and front bulging out and projecting over the pathway, the old house looked as if it were nodding in its sleep. Indeed, it needed no very great stretch of fancy to detect in it other resemblances of humanity. The bricks of which it was built had originally been a deep dark red, but had grown yellow and discoloured like an old man's skin; the sturdy timbers had decayed like teeth; and here and there the ivy, like a warm garment to comfort it in its age, wrapt its green leaves closely round the time-worn walls.

"It was a hale and hearty age though, still: and in the summer or autumn evenings, when the glow of the setting sun fell upon the oak and chestnut trees of the adjacent forest, the old house, partaking of its lustre, seemed their fit companion, and to have many good years of life in him yet." ¶BR 1

—converted; the best room: "It was spacious enough in all conscience, occupying the whole depth of the house, and having at either end a great bay window, as large as many modern rooms; in which some few panes of stained glass, emblazoned with fragments of armorial bearings, though cracked, and patched, and shattered, yet remained; attesting, by their presence, that the former owner had made the very light subservient to his state, and pressed the sun itself into his list of flatterers; bidding it, when it shone into his chamber, reflect the badges of his ancient family, and take new hues and

colours from their pride.

"But those were old days, and now every little ray came and went as it would; telling the plain, bare, searching truth. Although the best room of the inn, it had the melancholy aspect of grandeur in decay, and was much too vast for comfort. Rich rustling hangings, waving on the walls; and, better far, the rustling of youth and beauty's dress; the light of women's eyes, outshining the tapers and their own rich jewels; the sound of gentle tongues, and music, and the tread of maiden feet, had once been there, and filled it with delight. But they were gone, and with them all its gladness. It was no longer a home; children were never born and bred there; the fireside had become mercenary—a something to be bought and sold—a very courtezan: let who would die, or sit beside, or leave it, it was still the same—it missed nobody, cared for nobody, had equal warmth and smiles for all. God help the man whose heart ever changes with the world, as an old mansion when it becomes an inn!" BR 10

The Maypole's State Couch BR

—the bar: "All bars are snug places, but the Maypole's was the very snuggest, cosiest, and completest bar, that ever the wit of man devised. Such amazing bottles in old oaken pigeon-holes; such gleaming tankards dangling from pegs at about the same inclination as thirsty men would hold them to their lips; such sturdy little Dutch kegs ranged in rows on shelves; so many lemons hanging in separate nets, and forming the fragrant grove already mentioned in this chronicle, suggestive, with goodly loaves of snowy sugar stowed away hard by, of punch, idealised beyond all mortal knowledge; such closets, such presses, such drawers full of pipes, such places for putting things away in hollow window-seats, all crammed to the throat with eatables, drinkables, or savoury condiments; lastly, and to crown all, as typical of the immense resources of the

establishment, and its defiances to all visitors to cut and come again, such a stupendous cheese!

"It is a poor heart that never rejoices—it must have been the poorest, weakest, and most watery heart that ever beat, which would not have warmed towards the Maypole bar." BR 19

—seduction for a traveller: " . . . a delicious perspective of warmth and brightness—when the ruddy gleam of the fire, streaming through the old red curtains of the common room, seemed to bring with it, as part of itself, a pleasant hum of voices, and a fragrant odour of steaming grog and rare tobacco, all steeped as it were in the cheerful glow—when the shadows, flitting across the curtain, showed that those inside had risen from their snug seats, and were making room in the snuggest corner . . . and a broad glare, suddenly streaming up, bespoke the goodness of the crackling log from which a brilliant train of sparks was doubtless at that moment whirling up the chimney in honour of his coming—when, super-added to these enticements, there stole upon him from the distant kitchen a gentle sound of frying, with a musical clatter of plates and dishes, and a savoury smell that made even the boisterous wind a perfume—Gabriel felt his firmness oozing rapidly away . . . .

"And how unnatural it seemed for a sober man to be plodding wearily along through miry roads, encountering the rude buffets of the wind and pelting of the rain, when there was a clean floor covered with crisp white sand, a well swept hearth, a blazing fire, a table decorated with white cloth, bright pewter flagons, and other tempting preparations for a well-cooked meal—when there were these things, and company disposed to make the most of them, all ready to his hand, and entreating him to enjoyment!" ¶BR 2

—in winter: "Cheerily, though there were none abroad to see it, shone the Maypole light that evening. Blessings on the red—deep, ruby glowing red—old curtain of the window; blending into one rich stream of brightness, fire and candle, meat, drink, and company, and gleaming like a jovial eye upon the bleak waste out of doors! Within, what carpet like its crunching sand, what music merry as its crackling logs, what perfume like its kitchen's dainty breath, what weather genial as its hearty warmth!

"Blessings on the old house, how sturdily it stood! How did the vexed wind chafe and roar about its stalwart roof; how did it pant and strive with its wide chimneys, which still poured forth from their hospitable throats, great clouds of smoke, and puffed defiance in its face; how, above all, did it drive and rattle at the casement, emulous to extinguish that cheerful glow, which would not be put down and seemed the brighter for the conflict.

"The profusion too, the rich and lavish bounty, of that goodly tavern! It was not enough that one fire roared and sparkled on its spacious hearth; in the tiles which paved and compassed it, five hundred flickering fires burnt brightly also. It was not enough that one red curtain shut the wild night out, and shed its cheerful influence on the room. In every saucepan lid, and candlestick, and vessel of copper, brass, or tin that hung upon the walls, were countless ruddy hangings, flashing and gleaming with every motion of the blaze, and offering, let the eye wander where it might, interminable vistas of the same rich colour. The old oak wainscoting, the beams, the chairs, the seats, reflected it in a deep dull glimmer. There were fires and red curtains in the very eyes of the drinkers, in their buttons, in their liquor, in the pipes they smoked." BR 33

—zest in the chimney-corner: "For a little knot of smokers and solemn gossips, who had seldom any new topics of discussion, this was a perfect Godsend. Here was a good, dark-looking mystery progressing under that very roof—brought home to the fireside, as it were, and enjoyable without the smallest pains or trouble. It is extraordinary what a zest and relish it gave to the drink, and how it heightened the flavour of the tobacco. Every man smoked his pipe with a face of grave and serious delight, and looked at his neighbour with a sort of quiet congratulation.

"Nay, it was felt to be such a holiday and special night, that, on the motion of little Solomon Daisy, every man (including John himself) put down his sixpence for a can of flip, which grateful beverage was brewed with all despatch, and set down in the midst of them on the brick floor; both that it might simmer and stew before the fire, and that its fragrant steam, rising up among them, and mixing with the wreaths of vapour from their pipes, might shroud them in a delicious atmosphere of their own, and shut out all the world. The very furniture of the room seemed to mellow and deepen in its tone; the ceiling and walls looked blacker and more highly polished, the curtains of a ruddier red; the fire burnt clear and high, and the crickets in the hearth-stone chirped with a more than wonted satisfaction." ¶BR 11

—*Mitre,* at Rochester: "There was an Inn in the cathedral town where I went to school, which had pleasanter recollections about it . . . . It was the Inn where friends used to put up, and where we used to go to see parents, and to have salmon and fowls, and be tipped. It had an ecclesiastical sign—the Mitre—and a bar that seemed to be the next best thing to a bishopric, it was so snug. I loved the landlord's youngest daughter to distraction—but let that pass. It was in this Inn that I was cried over by my rosy little sister, because I had acquired a black eye in a fight. And though she had been . . . for many a long year where all tears are dried, the Mitre softened me yet." CS/HT 1

—*Nutmeg-Grater:* " . . . one little roadside inn, snugly sheltered behind a great elm-tree with a rare seat for idlers encircling its capacious bole, addressed a cheerful front towards the traveller, as a house of entertainment ought, and tempted him with many mute but significant assurances of a comfortable welcome.

"The ruddy sign-board perched up in the tree, with its golden letters winking in the sun, ogled the passer-by, from among the green leaves, like a jolly face, and promised good cheer. The horse-trough, full of clear fresh water, and the ground below it sprinkled with droppings of fragrant hay, made every horse that passed, prick up his ears. The crimson curtains in the lower rooms, and the pure white hangings in the little bed-chambers above, beckoned, Come in! with every breath of air.

"Upon the bright green shutters, there were golden legends about beer and ale, and neat wines, and good beds; and an affecting picture of a brown jug frothing over at the top. Under the window-sills were flowering plants in bright red pots, which made a lively show against the white front of the house; and in the darkness of the doorway there were streaks of light, which glanced off from the surfaces of bottles and tankards." ¶BL 3

—*old coaching inn:* "We can all discourse . . . upon our recollections of the 'Talbot', the 'King's Head', or the 'Lion' of those days. We have all been to that room on the ground floor on one side of the old inn yard, not quite free from a certain fragrant smell of tobacco, where the cruets on the sideboard were usually absorbed by the skirts of the box coats that hung from the wall, where driving-seats were laid out at every turn like so many human mantraps, where county members framed and glazed were eternally presenting that petition which somehow or other made their glory in the county, though nothing else ever came of it. Where the *Book of Roads,* the first and last thing always required, was always missing, and generally wanted the first and last dozen leaves, and where one man was always arriving at some unusual hour in the middle of the night, and requiring his breakfast at a similarly singular period of the day." S/CT1

—*Peacock,* at Eatanswill: "[The Pickwickians] beguiled their time chiefly with such amusements as the Peacock afforded, which were limited to a bagatelle-board in the first floor, and a sequestered skittle-ground in the back yard." PP 14

—*the commercial room* "was a large bare-looking room, the furniture of which had no doubt been better when it was newer, with a spacious table in the centre, and a variety of smaller dittos in the corners: an extensive assortment of variously shaped chairs, and an old Turkey carpet, bearing about the same relative proportion to the size of the room, as a lady's pocket-handkerchief might to the floor of a watch-box. The walls were garnished with one or two large maps; and several weather-beaten rough great coats, with complicated capes, dangled from a long row of pegs in one corner.

"The mantelshelf was ornamented with a wooden inkstand, containing one stump of a pen and half a wafer: a road-book and director: a county history minus the cover: and the mortal remains of a trout in a glass coffin. The atmosphere was redolent of tobacco-smoke, the fumes of which had communicated a rather dingy hue to the whole room, and more especially to the dusty red curtains which shaded the windows. On the sideboard a variety of miscellaneous articles were huddled together, the most conspicuous of which were some very cloudy fish-sauce-cruets, a couple of driving-boxes, two or three whips, and as many travelling shawls, a tray of knives and forks, and the mustard." ¶PP 14

—*Pegasus's Arms:* "[Sissy Jupe] stopped, at twilight, at the door of a mean little public-house, with dim red lights in it. As haggard and as shabby, as if, for want of custom, it had itself taken to drinking, and had gone the way all drunkards go, and was very near the end of it . . . .

"The name of the public-house was the Pegasus's Arms. The Pegasus's legs might have been more to the purpose; but, underneath the winged horse upon the signboard, The Pegasus's Arms was inscribed in Roman letters. Beneath that inscription again, in a flowing scroll, the painter had touched off the lines:

Good malt makes good beer,
Walk in, and they'll draw it here;
Good wine makes good brandy,
Gives us a call, and you'll find it handy.

"Framed and glazed upon the wall behind the dingy little bar, was another Pegasus—a theatrical one—with real gauze let in for his wings, golden stars stuck on all over him, and his ethereal harness made of red silk." HT i 5, 6

—*posting-(coaching) inns:* "Casting my eyes upon my Holly-Tree fire, I next discerned among the glowing coals the pictures of a score or more of those wonderful English posting-inns which we are all so sorry to have lost, which were so large and so comfortable, and which were such monuments of British submission to rapacity and extortion. He who would see these houses pining away, let him walk from Basingstoke, or even Windsor, to London, by way of Hounslow, and moralise on their perishing remains; the stables crumbling to dust; unsettled labourers and wanderers bivouacking in the outhouses; grass growing in the yards; the rooms, where erst so many hundred beds of down were made up, let off to Irish lodgers at eighteenpence a week; a little ill-looking beer-shop shrinking in the tap of former days, burning coach-house gates for firewood, having one of its two windows bunged up, as if it had received punishment in a fight with the Railroad; a low-bandy-legged, brick-making bulldog standing in the doorway." CS/HT 1

—*railroad hotel*

—*impersonally grand:* "We all know . . . the great station hotel belonging to the company of proprietors, which has suddenly sprung up in the back outskirts of any place we like to name, and where we look out of our palatial windows, at little back yards and gardens, old summer-houses, fowl-houses, pigeon-traps, and pigsties.

"We all know this hotel in which we can get anything we want, after its kind, for money; but where nobody is glad to see us, or sorry to see us, or minds (our bill paid) whether we come or go, or how, or when, or why, or cares about us. We all know this hotel, where we have no individuality, but put ourselves into the general post, as it were, and are sorted and disposed of according to our division. We all know that we can get on very well indeed at such a place, but still not perfectly well; and this may be, because the place is largely wholesale, and there is a lingering personal retail interest within us that asks to be satisfied." UT/RT

—*newly built:* "What could I next see in my fire so naturally as the new railway-house of these times near the dismal country station; with nothing particular on draught but cold air and damp, nothing worth mentioning in the larder but new mortar, and no business doing beyond a conceited affectation of luggage in the hall?" CS/HT 1

"We all know the new hotel near the station, where it is always gusty, going up the lane which is always muddy, where we are sure to arrive at night, and where we make the gas start awfully when we open the front door. We all know the flooring of the passages and staircases that is too new, and the walls that are too new, and the house that is haunted by the ghost of mortar. We all know the doors that have cracked, and the cracked shutters through which we get a glimpse of the disconsolate moon. We all know the new people, who have come to keep the new hotel, and who wish they had never come, and who (inevitable result) wish *we* had never come.

"We all know how much too scant and smooth and bright the new furniture is, and how it has never settled down, and cannot fit itself into right places, and will get into wrong places. We all know how the gas, being lighted, shows maps of Damp upon the walls. We all know how the ghost of mortar passes into our sandwich, stirs our negus, goes up to bed with us, ascends the pale bedroom chimney, and prevents the smoke from following." ¶UT/RT

—*in Salisbury:* Tom Pinch "went to the inn where he had waited for Martin, and . . .

ordered a bed . . . .

"It was a low four-poster shelving downward in the centre like a trough, and the room was crowded with impracticable tables and exploded chests of drawers, full of damp linen. A graphic representation in oil of a remarkably fat ox hung over the fireplace, and the portrait of some former landlord (who might have been the ox's brother, he was so like him) stared roundly in, at the foot of the bed. A variety of queer smells were partially quenched in the prevailing scent of very old lavender; and the window had not been opened for such a long space of time that it pleaded immemorial usage, and wouldn't come open now." MC 31

—*the Ship,* on the Thames near the sea: "At length we descried a light and a roof, and presently afterwards ran alongside a little causeway made of stones that had been picked up hard by. Leaving the rest in the boat, I stepped ashore, and found the light to be in the window of a public-house. It was a dirty place enough, and I dare say not unknown to smuggling adventurers; but there was a good fire in the kitchen, and there were eggs and bacon to eat, and various liquors to drink. Also, there were two double-bedded rooms—'such as they were,' the landlord said . . .

" . . . . We found the air as carefully excluded from both [rooms] as if air were fatal to life; and there were more dirty clothes and bandboxes under the beds, than I should have thought the family possessed." GE 54

—*the Swan,* at Wolverhampton: "The Swan is a bird of a good substantial brood, worthy to be a country cousin of the hospitable Hen and Chickens, whose company we have deserted for only a few hours and with whom we shall roost again at Birmingham to-night. The Swan has bountiful coal-country notions of firing, snug homely rooms, cheerful windows looking down upon the clusters of snowy umbrellas in the market-place, and on the chaffering and chattering which is pleasantly hushed by the thick white down lying so deep, and softly falling still.

"Neat bright-eyed waitresses do the honours of the Swan. The Swan is confident about its soup, is troubled with no distrust concerning cod-fish, speaks the word of promise in relation to an enormous chine of roast beef, one of the dishes at 'the Ironmasters' dinner,' which will be disengaged at four. The Ironmasters' dinner! It has an imposing sound. We think of the Ironmasters joking, drinking to their Ironmistresses, clinking their glasses with a metallic ring, and comporting themselves at the festive board with the mighty men who have mastered Iron." ¶HW/F&S

"The Swan is rich in slippers—in those good old flip-flap inn slippers which nobody can keep on, which knock double knocks on every stair as their wearer comes downstairs, and fly away over the banisters before they have brought him to level ground. Rich also is the Swan in wholesome well-cooked dinner, and in tender chine of beef, so brave in size that the mining of all the powerful Ironmasters is but a sufficient outlet for its gravy. Rich in things wholesome and sound and unpretending is the Swan, except that we would recommend the good bird not to dip its beak into its sherry . . . finding that the Swan's ideas of something hot to drink are just and laudable, we adopt the same, with emendations (in the matter of lemon chiefly) of which modesty and total abstinence principles forbid the record." HW/F&S

—*tavern snuggery,* in a seaport town: "It was one of those unaccountable little rooms which are never seen anywhere but in a tavern, and are supposed to have got into taverns by reason of the facilities afforded to the architect for getting drunk while engaged in their construction. It had more corners in it than the brain of an obstinate man; was full of mad closets, into which nothing could be put that was not specially invented and made for that purpose; had mysterious shelvings and bulk-heads, and indications of stair-cases in the ceiling; and was elaborately provided with a bell that rung in the room itself, about two feet from the handle, and had no connection whatever with any other part of the establishment.

"It was a little below the pavement, and abutted close upon it; so that passengers grated against the window-panes with their buttons, and scraped it with their baskets; and fearful boys suddenly coming between a thoughtful guest and the light, derided him, or put out their tongues as if he were a physician; or made white knobs on the ends of their noses by flattening the same against the glass, and vanished awfully, like spectres." ¶MC 25

—*Temeraire,* in a seaside town: "The lonely traveller with the stomach-ache had all this time suffered severely, drawing up a leg now and then, and sipping hot brandy-and-water with grated ginger in it. When we tasted our (very) mock-turtle soup, and were instantly seized with symptoms of some disorder simulating apoplexy, and occasioned by the surcharge of nose and brain with lukewarm dish-water holding in solution sour flour, poisonous condiments, and (say) seventy-five per cent. of miscellaneous kitchen stuff rolled into balls, we were inclined to trace his disorder to that source.

"On the other hand, there was a silent anguish upon him too strongly resembling the results established within ourselves by the sherry, to be discarded from alarmed consideration. Again, we observed him, with terror, to be much overcome by our sole's being aired in a temporary retreat close to him, while the waiter went out (as we conceived) to see his friends. And when the curry made its appearance he suddenly retired in great disorder.

"In fine, for the uneatable part of this little dinner (as contradistinguished from the undrinkable) we paid only seven shillings and sixpence each. And Bullfinch and I agreed unanimously, that no such ill-served, ill-appointed, ill-cooked, nasty little dinner could be got for the money anywhere else under the sun. With that comfort to our backs, we turned them on the dear old Temeraire, the charging Temeraire, and resolved (in the Scotch dialect) to gang nae mair to the flabby Temeraire." ¶UT/DH

As to its casters, see TT:Travel—*hotel character: infallible test*

—*Three Jolly Hedgers,* in Hertfordshire: ". . . you find [a tramp] lying drunk that same evening in the wheelwright's sawpit under the shed where the felled trees are, opposite the sign of the Three Jolly Hedgers." UT/T

—*Tilted Wagon,* near Cloisterham: "Indeed, The Tilted Wagon, as a cool establishment on the top of a hill, where the ground before the door was puddled with damp hoofs and trodden straw . . . where the cheese was cast aground upon a shelf, in company with a mouldy tablecloth and a green-handled knife, in a sort of cast-iron canoe; where the pale-faced bread shed tears of crumb over its shipwreck in another canoe; where the family linen, half washed and half dried, led a public life of lying about; where everything to drink was drunk out of mugs, and everything else was suggestive of a rhyme to mugs; The Tilted Wagon, all these things considered, hardly kept its painted promise of providing good entertainment for Man and Beast." MED 15

—*Valiant Soldier:* "It was a great, rambling house, with dull corridors and wide staircases which the flaring candles seemed to make more gloomy." OCS 30

—*in Wiltshire:* "That was a good Inn down in Wiltshire where I put up once, in the days of the hard Wiltshire ale, and before all beer was bitterness. It was on the skirts of Salisbury Plain, and the midnight wind that rattled my lattice window came moaning at me from Stonehenge . . . I awoke one night to find [a weird shepherd] in the dark at my bedside, repeating the Athanasian Creed in a terrific voice. I paid my bill next day, and retired from the county with all possible precipitation." CS/HT

—*Winglebury Arms:* "The little town of Great Winglebury is exactly forty-two miles and three-quarters from Hyde Park corner. It has a long, straggling, quiet High Street, with a great black and white clock at a small red Town Hall, half-way up—a market-place—a cage—an assembly-room—a church—a bridge—a chapel—a theatre—a library—an inn—a pump—and a Post Office . . . .

"The Winglebury Arms, in the centre of the High Street, opposite the small building with the big clock, is the principal inn of Great Winglebury;—the commercial-inn, posting-house, and excise-office; the 'Blue' house at every election, and the Judges' house at every assizes.

"It is the head-quarters of the Gentlemen's Whist Club of Winglebury Blues (so called in opposition to the Gentlemen's Whist Club of Winglebury Buffs, held at the other house, a little further down): and whenever a juggler, or wax-work man, or concert-giver, takes Great Winglebury in his circuit, it is immediately placarded all over the town that Mr So-and-so, 'trusting to that liberal support which the inhabitants of Great Winglebury have long been so liberal in bestowing, has at a great expense engaged the elegant and commodious assembly-rooms, attached to the Winglebury Arms.'

"The house is a large one, with a red brick and stone front; a pretty spacious hall, ornamented with evergreen plants, terminates in a perspective view of the bar, and a glass case, in which are displayed a choice variety of delicacies ready for dressing, to catch the eye of a newcomer the moment he enters, and excite his appetite to the highest possible pitch.

"Opposite doors lead to the 'coffee' and 'commercial' rooms; and a great wide, rambling staircase—three stairs and a landing—four stairs and another landing—one step and another landing—half-a-dozen stairs and another landing—and so on—conducts to galleries of bedrooms, and labyrinths of sitting-rooms, denominated 'private,' where you may enjoy yourself, as privately as you can in any place where some bewildered being walks into your room every five minutes, by mistake, and then walks out again, to open all the doors along the gallery until he finds his own." ¶SB/WD

The Irish

—in Parliament: " . . . after the performance of an Umsebeuza, or war song—which is exactly like all the other songs—the [savage] chief makes a speech to his brothers and friends, arranged in single file. No particular order is observed during the delivery of this address, but every gentleman who finds himself excited by the subject, instead of crying 'Hear, hear!' as is the custom with us, darts from the rank and tramples out the life, or crushes the skull, or mashes the face, or scoops out the eyes, or breaks the limbs, or performs a whirlwind of atrocities on the body, of an imaginary enemy.

"Several gentlemen becoming thus excited at once, and pounding away without the least regard to the orator, that illustrious person is rather in the position of an orator in an Irish House of Commons. But several of these scenes of savage life bear a strong generic resemblance to an Irish election, and I think would be extremely well received and understood at Cork." ¶RP/NS

—patriotism: "'I never saw an object stand out so beautifully against the clear sky in my life,' ejaculated Alfred . . . .

"'I have frequently observed a chimney-pot in College Green, Dublin, which has a much better effect,' said the patriotic O'Bleary, who never allowed Ireland to be outdone on any point." SB/BH

And see America—*the Irish,* B:Body—*face—Irish,* F:Irish, *and* TT:Ship

Italy and things Italian

—beggary

—at Fondi: "A hollow-cheeked and scowling people they are! All beggars; but that's nothing. Look at them as they gather round. Some, are too indolent to come downstairs, or are too wisely mistrustful of the stairs, perhaps, to venture: so stretch out their lean hands from upper windows, and howl; others, come flocking about us, fighting and jostling one another, and demanding, incessantly, charity for the love of God charity for the love of the Blessed Virgin, charity for the love of all the Saints.

"A group of miserable children, almost naked, screaming forth the same petition, discover that they can see themselves reflected in the varnish of the carriage, and begin to dance and make grimaces, that they may have the pleasure of seeing their antics repeated in this mirror. A crippled idiot, in the act of striking one of them who drowns his clamorous demand for charity, observes his angry counterpart in the panel, stops short, and thrusting out his tongue, begins to wag his head and chatter.

"The shrill cry raised at this, awakens half-a-dozen wild creatures wrapped in frowzy brown cloaks, who are lying on the church-steps with pots and pans for sale. These, scrambling up, approach, and beg defiantly. 'I am hungry. Give me something. Listen to me, Signor. I am hungry!'

"Then, a ghastly old woman, fearful of being too late, comes hobbling down the street, stretching out one hand, and scratching herself all the way with the other, and screaming, long before she can be heard, 'Charity, charity! I'll go and pray for you directly, beautiful lady, if you'll give me charity!'" PI 12

—at Naples: "Why do the beggars rap their chins constantly, with their right hands, when you look at them? Everything is done in pantomime in Naples, and that is the conventional sign for hunger." PI 13

—at Parma: "There is a very interesting subterranean church here: the roof supported by marble pillars, behind each of which there seemed to be at least one beggar in ambush: to say nothing of the tombs and secluded altars. From every one of these lurking-places, such crowds of phantom-looking men and women, leading other men and women with twisted limbs or chattering jaws, or paralytic gestures, or idiotic heads, or some other sad infirmity, came hobbling out to beg, that if the ruined frescoes in the cathedral above, had been suddenly animated, and had retired to this lower church, they could hardly have made a greater confusion, or exhibited a more confounding display of arms and legs." PI 6

—*at Pisa:* If Pisa be the seventh wonder of the world in right of its Tower, it may claim to be, at least, the second or third in right of its beggars. They waylay the unhappy visitor at every turn, escort him to every door he enters at, and lie in wait for him, with strong reinforcements, at every door by which they know he must come out. The grating of the portal on its hinges is the signal for a general shout, and the moment he appears, he is hemmed in, and fallen on, by heaps of rags and personal distortions." PI 10

—*the Campagna:* " . . . an undulating flat . . . where few people can live; and where, for miles and miles, there is nothing to relieve the terrible monotony and gloom. Of all kinds of country that could, by possibility, lie outside the gates of Rome, this is the aptest and fittest burial-ground for the Dead City. So sad, so quiet, so sullen; so secret in its covering up of great masses of ruin, and hiding them; so like the waste places into which the men possessed with devils used to go and howl, and rend themselves, in the old days of Jerusalem." PI 10

—*a long walk:* "One day we walked out, a little party of three, to Albano, fourteen miles distant; possessed by a great desire to go there by the ancient Appian way, long since ruined and overgrown. We started at half-past seven in the morning, and within an hour or so were out upon the open Campagna.

"For twelve miles we went climbing on, over an unbroken succession of mounds, and heaps, and hills, of ruin. Tombs and temples, overthrown and prostrate; small fragments of columns, friezes, pediments; great blocks of granite and marble; mouldering arches, grass-grown and decayed; ruin enough to build a spacious city from; lay strewn about us.

"Sometimes, loose walls, built up from these fragments by the shepherds, came across our path; sometimes, a ditch between two mounds of broken stones, obstructed our progress; sometimes, the fragments themselves, rolling from beneath our feet, made it a toilsome matter to advance; but it was always ruin.

"Now, we tracked a piece of the old road, above the ground; now traced it, underneath a grassy covering, as if that were its grave; but all the way was ruin. In the distance, ruined aqueducts went stalking on their giant course along the plain; and every breath of wind that swept towards us, stirred early flowers and grasses, springing up, spontaneously, on miles of ruin.

"The unseen larks above us, who alone disturbed the awful silence, had their nests in ruin; and the fierce herdsmen, clad in sheepskins, who now and then scowled out upon us from their sleeping nooks, were housed in ruin.

"The aspect of the desolate Campagna in one direction, where it was most level, reminded me of an American prairie; but what is the solitude of a region where men have never dwelt, to that of a Desert, where a mighty race have left their footprints in the earth from which they have vanished; where the resting-places of their Dead, have fallen like their Dead; and the broken hourglass of Time is but a heap of idle dust!

"Returning, by the road, at sunset, and looking, from the distance, on the course we had taken in the morning, I almost feel (as I had felt when I first saw it, at that hour) as if the sun would never rise again, but looked its last, that night, upon a ruined world." PI 11

—*the past:* "When we have traversed it, and look back from Albano, its dark undulating surface lies below us like a stagnant lake, or like a broad dull Lethe flowing round the walls of Rome, and separating it from all the world! How often have the Legions, in triumphant march, gone glittering across that purple waste, so silent and unpeopled now! How often has the train of captives looked, with sinking hearts, upon the distant city, and beheld its population pouring out, to hail the return of their conqueror! What riot, sensuality and murder, have run mad in the vast palaces now heaps of brick and shattered marble! What glare of fires, and roar of popular tumult, and wail of pestilence and famine, have come sweeping over the wild plain where nothing is now heard but the wind, and where the solitary lizards gambol unmolested in the sun!" PI 12

—*character:* "In [Cavalletto's] submission, in his lightness, in his good humour, in his short-lived passion, in his easy contentment with hard bread and hard stones, in his ready sleep, in his fits and starts altogether, a true son of the land that gave him birth." LD i 1

—*churches:* " . . . [they] rested in dark corners of great churches; where there were winking lamps of gold and silver among pillars and arches, kneeling figures dotted about at confessionals and on the pavements; where there was the mist and scent of incense; where there were pictures, fantastic images, gaudy altars, great heights and distances, all softly lighted through stained glass, and the massive curtains that hung in the doorways." LD ii 3

—*countryside:* "Among the day's unrealities would be, roads where the bright red vines were looped and garlanded together on trees for many miles; woods of olives; white villages and towns on hill-sides, lovely without, but frightful in their dirt and poverty within; crosses by the way; deep blue lakes with fairy islands, and clustering boats with awnings of bright colours and sails of beautiful forms; vast piles of building mouldering to dust; hanging-gardens where the weeds had grown so strong that their stems, like wedges driven home, had split the arch and rent the wall; stone-terraced lanes, with the lizards running into and out of every chink. . . . " LD ii 3

—*foolishly pictured:* "'In Italy is she really?' said Flora,' with the grapes and figs growing everywhere and lava necklaces and bracelets too that land of poetry with burning mountains picturesque beyond belief though if the organ-boys come away from the neighbourhood not to be scorched nobody can wonder being so young and bringing their white mice with them most humane, and is she really in that favoured land with nothing but blue about her and dying gladiators and Belvederas though Mr F himself did not believe for his objection when in spirits was that the images could not be true there being no medium between expensive quantities of linen badly got up and all in creases and none whatever, which certainly does not seem probable though perhaps in consequence of the extremes of rich and poor which may account for it.'" LD ii 5

—*national spirit:* " . . . the mountain rivers of Italy, which are like the national spirit—very tame, or chafing suddenly and bursting bounds, only to dwindle away again." RP/DT

—*travels of a bottle:* ". . . one of those immense bottles in which the Italian peasants store their wine—a bottle holding some half-dozen gallons—bound round with basket-work for greater safety on the journey . . . what disquiet of mind this dearly beloved and highly treasured Bottle began to cost me, no man knows. It was my precious charge through a long tour; and for hundreds of miles I never had it off my mind by day or by night. Over bad roads—and they were many—I clung to it with affectionate desperation. Up mountains, I looked in at it, and saw it helplessly tilting over on its back, with terror. At innumerable inn doors, when the weather was bad, I was obliged to be put into my vehicle before the Bottle could be got in, and was obliged to have the Bottle lifted out before human aid could come near me. The Imp of the same name, except that his associations were all evil and these associations were all good, would have been a less troublesome travelling companion. I might have served Mr **Cruikshank*** as a subject for a new illustration of the miseries of the Bottle. The National Temperance Society might have made a powerful Tract of me.

"The suspicions that attached to this innocent Bottle greatly aggravated my difficulties. It was like the apple-pie in the child's book. Parma pouted at it, Modena mocked it, Tuscany tackled it, Naples nibbled it, Rome refused it, Austria accused it, Soldiers suspected it, Jesuits jobbed it. I composed a neat Oration, developing my inoffensive intentions in connection with this Bottle, and delivered it in an infinity of guardhouses, at a multitude of town gates, and on every drawbridge, angle, and rampart of a complete system of fortifications. Fifty times a day, I got down to harangue an infuriated soldiery about the Bottle.

"Through the filthy degradation of the abject and vile Roman States, I had as much difficulty in working my way with the Bottle, as if it had bottled up a complete system of heretical theology. In the Neapolitan country, where everybody was a spy, a soldier, a priest, or a lazzarone, the shameless beggars of all four denominations incessantly pounced on the Bottle, and made it a pretext for extorting money from me. Quires—quires do I say? Reams—of forms illegibly printed on whitey-brown paper were filled up about the Bottle, and it was the subject of more stamping and sanding than I had ever seen before. In consequence of which haze of sand, perhaps, it was always irregular, and always latent with dismal penalties of going back or not going forward, which were only to be abated by the silver crossing of a base hand, poked, shirtless, out of a ragged uniform sleeve. Under all discouragements, however, I stuck to my Bottle, and held firm to my resolution that every drop of its contents should reach the Bottle's destination.

"The latter refinement cost me a separate heap of troubles on its own separate account. What corkscrews did I see the military power bring out against that Bottle; what gimlets, spikes, diving-rods, gauges, and unknown tests and instruments! At some places they persisted in declaring that the wine must not be passed without being opened and tasted; I, pleading to the contrary, used then to argue the question, seated on the Bottle, lest they should open it in spite of me. In the southern parts of Italy, more violent shrieking, face-making, and gesticulating, greater vehemence of speech and countenance and action, went on about that Bottle than would attend fifty murders in a northen latitude. It raised important functionaries out of their beds in the dead of night. I have known half a dozen military lanterns to disperse themselves at all points of a great sleeping Piazza, each lantern summoning some official creature to get up, put on his cocked hat instantly, and come and stop the Bottle. It was characteristic that while this innocent Bottle had such immense difficulty in getting from little town to town, Signor **Mazzini** and the fiery cross were traversing Italy from end to end." UT/IP

Famous illustrator* ***George Cruikshank* *had become a campaigner against all forms of alcohol. See* HW/FF

—women: "The young women [in Genoa] are not generally pretty, but they walk remarkably well, and in their personal carriage and the management of their veils, display much innate grace and elegance." PI 5

—years of neglect: a summary: " . . . let us part from Italy, with all its miseries and wrongs, affectionately, in our admiration of the beauties, natural and artificial, of which it is full to overflowing, and in our tenderness towards a people, naturally well-disposed, and patient, and sweet-tempered.

"Years of neglect, oppression, and misrule, have been at work, to change their nature and reduce their spirit; miserable jealousies, fomented by petty Princes to whom union was destruction, and division strength, have been a canker at their root of nationality, and have barbarized their language; but the good that was in them ever, is in them yet, and a noble people may be, one day, raised up from these ashes. Let us entertain that hope!" ¶PI 19

And see: Cities and Towns, Actual, *passim;* Inns and Taverns, Abroad, *passim;* S: Religion—*Roman Catholic practice in Italy; and* TT:Tourism, *passim*

Lighthouse

—Calais: "The meagre lighthouse all in white, haunting the seaboard, as if it were the ghost of an edifice that had once had colour and rotundity, dripped melancholy tears after its late buffeting by the waves." LD ii 20

—Cape Grinez: "There [at Dover], the sea was tumbling in, with deep sounds, after dark, and the revolving French light on Cape Grinez was seen regularly bursting out and becoming obscured, as if the head of a gigantic light-keeper in an anxious state of mind were interposed every half-minute, to look how it was burning." UT/TA

—Folkestone: " . . . the very little wooden lighthouse . . . when it is lighted at night—red and green—it looks so like a medical man's, that several distracted husbands have at various times been found on occasions of premature domestic anxiety, going round and round it, trying to find the Night-bell." RP/OT

—Holyhead: " . . . there shone out from the haze and mist ahead, a gleaming light, which presently was gone, and soon returned, and soon was gone again. Whenever it came back, the eyes of all on board, brightened and sparkled like itself: and there we all stood, watching this revolving light upon the rock at Holyhead, and praising it for its brightness and its friendly warning, and lauding it, in short, above all other signal lights that ever were displayed, until it once more glimmered faintly in the distance, far behind us." AN 16

Niagara

—for insomnia: " . . . there I was, and the Horse-shoe Fall was thundering and tumbling in my eyes and ears, and the very rainbows that I left upon the spray when I really did last look upon it, were beautiful to see. The night-light being quite as plain, however, and sleep seeming to be many thousand miles further off than Niagara, I made up my mind to think a little about Sleep . . . . " RP/LA *And see* FL:Creation

Rivers

—Mississippi: "But what words shall describe the Mississippi, great father of rivers, who (praise be to Heaven) has no young children like him! An enormous ditch, sometimes two or three miles wide, running

liquid mud, six miles an hour: its strong and frothy current choked and obstructed everywhere by huge logs and whole forest trees: now twining themselves together in great rafts, from the interstices of which a sedgy lazy foam works up, to float upon the water's top; now rolling past like monstrous bodies, their tangled roots showing like matted hair; now glancing singly by like giant leeches; and now writhing round and round in the vortex of some small whirlpool, like wounded snakes.

"The banks low, the trees dwarfish, the marshes swarming with frogs, the wretched cabins few and far apart, their inmates hollow-cheeked and pale, the weather very hot, mosquitoes penetrating into every crack and crevice of the boat, mud and slime on everything: nothing pleasant in its aspect, but the harmless lightning which flickers every night upon the dark horizon.

"For two days we toiled up this foul stream, striking constantly against the floating timber, or stopping to avoid those more dangerous obstacles, the snags, or sawyers, which are the hidden trunks of trees that have their roots below the tide." AN 12

" . . . looking southward from [Cairo], we had the satisfaction of seeing that intolerable river dragging its slimy length and ugly freight abruptly off towards New Orleans; and passing a yellow line which stretched across the current, were again upon the clear Ohio, never, I trust, to see the Mississippi more, saving in troubled dreams and nightmares. Leaving it for the company of its sparkling neighbour, was like the transition from pain to ease, or the awakening from a horrible vision to cheerful realities." AN 14

—*sunset:* "The decline of day here was very gorgeous, tingeing the firmament deeply with red and gold up to the very keystone of the arch above us. As the sun went down behind the bank, the slightest blades of grass upon it seemed to become as distinctly visible as the arteries in the skeleton of a leaf, and when, as it slowly sank, the red and golden bars upon the water grew dimmer and dimmer yet, as if they were sinking too, and all the glowing colours of departing day paled, inch by inch, before the sombre night, the scene became a thousand times more lonesome and more dreary than before, and all its influences darkened with the sky." AN 12

—*Nile:* "Along that wonderful river, associated with such stupendous fables, and with a history more prodigious than any fancy of man, in its vast and gorgeous facts; among temples, palaces, pyramids, colossal statues, crocodiles, tombs, obelisks, mummies, sand and ruin; he proceeded, like an opium-eater in a mighty dream." HW/ET

—*Saone:* "A late, dull autumn night, was closing in upon the river Saone. The stream, like a sulllied looking-glass in a gloomy place, reflected the clouds heavily; and the low banks leaned over here and there, as if they were half curious, and half afraid, to see their darkening pictures in the water. The flat expanse of country about Chalons lay a long heavy streak, occasionally made a little ragged by a row of poplar trees, against the wrathful sunset. On the banks of the river Saone it was wet, depressing, solitary; and the night deepened fast." LD i 11

—*St Lawrence and the Thousand Islands:* "The beauty of this noble stream at almost any point, but especially in the commencement of this journey when it winds its way among the thousand Islands, can hardly be imagined. The number and constant successions of these islands, all green and richly wooded; their fluctuating sizes, some so large that for half an hour together one among them will appear as the opposite bank of the river, and some so small that they are mere dimples on its broad bosom; their infinite variety of shapes; and the numberless combinations of beautiful forms which the trees growing on them present: all form a picture fraught with uncommon interest and pleasure.

"In the afternoon we shot down some rapids where the river boiled and bubbled strangely, and where the force and headlong violence of the current were tremendous. At seven o'clock we reached Dickenson's Landing, whence travellers proceed for two or three hours by stage-coach: the navigation of the river being rendered so dangerous and difficult in the interval, by rapids, that steamboats do not make the passage. The number and length of those portages, over which the roads are bad, and the travelling slow, render the way between the towns of Montreal and Kingston, somewhat tedious." AN 15

And see L:The Thames

Scotland and Scots

—*and Mormonism:* "UNCOMMERCIAL. Do you get many Scotch?

"MORMON AGENT. Not many.

"UNCOMMERCIAL. Highlanders, for instance?

"MORMON AGENT. No, not Highlanders. They ain't interested enough in universal brotherhood and peace and good will.

"UNCOMMERCIAL. The old fighting blood is strong in them?

MORMON AGENT. Well, yes. And besides; they've no faith." UT/SL

—*and the Reformation:* "Now, the reformed religion, under the guidance of a stern and powerful preacher, named **John Knox**, and other such men, had been making fierce progress in Scotland. It was still a half savage country, where there was a great deal of murdering and rioting continually going on; and the Reformers, instead of reforming those evils as they should have done, went to work in the ferocious old Scottish spirit, laying churches and chapels waste, pulling down pictures and altars, and knocking about . . . friars of all sorts of colours, in all directions." CHE 31

—*taking snuff:* " . . . we *do* find [our American friend], for a little time, in the company of Scotch gentlemen, who keep small ivory spoons in their pockets 'to shove their snuff up their noses,' and who likewise carry small brushes in their pockets to sweep their noses and upper lips with afterwards—which is well known to be a practice universal with the bench and bar of Scotland, and with the principal members of the Scottish Universities, whose snuff is for the most part carried after them in coal-scuttles by Highlanders, who cannot be made to sneeze by any artificial process whatever." E/AE

Switzerland and things Swiss

—*Alps:* "The air had been warm and transparent through the whole of the bright day. Shining metal spires and church-roofs, distant and rarely seen, had sparkled in the view; and the snowy mountain-tops had been so clear that unaccustomed eyes, cancelling the intervening country, and slighting their rugged height for something fabulous, would have measured them as within a few hours' easy reach. Mountain-peaks of great celebrity in the valleys, whence no trace of their existence was visible sometimes for months together, had been since morning plain and near, in the blue sky. And now, when it was dark below, though they seemed solemnly to recede, like spectres who were going to vanish, as the red dye of the sunset faded out of them and left them coldly white, they were yet distinctly defined in their loneliness, above the mists and shadows." LD ii 1

" . . . here I enjoyed a dozen climates a day; being now (like *Don Quixote* on the back of the wooden horse) in the region of wind, now in the region of fire, now in the region of unmelting ice and snow. Here, I passed over trembling domes of ice, beneath which the cataract was roaring; and here was received under arches of icicles, of unspeakable beauty; and here the sweet air was so bracing and so light, that at halting-times I rolled in the snow when I saw my mule do it, thinking that he must know best." UT/TA

—*in brief:* "And now I came to the land of wooden houses, innocent cakes, thin butter soup, and spotless little inn bedrooms with a family likeness to Dairies." UT/TA

—*business office*: "An oddly pastoral kind of office it was, and one that would never have answered in England. It stood in a neat back yard, fenced off from a pretty flower-garden. Goats browsed in the doorway, and a cow was within half-a-dozen feet of keeping company with the clerk.

"Maître [Notary] Voigt's room was a bright and varnished little room, with panelled walls, like a toy-chamber. According to the seasons of the year, roses, sunflowers, hollyhocks, peeped in at the windows. Maître Voigt's bees hummed through the office all the summer, in at this window and out at that, taking it frequently in their day's work, as if honey were to be made from Maître Voigt's sweet disposition.

"A large musical box on the chimney-piece often trilled away at the Overture to Fra Diavolo, or a Selection from William Tell, with a chirruping liveliness that had to be stopped by force on the entrance of a client, and irrepressibly broke out again the moment his back was turned." ¶CS/NT

—*decor:* " . . . he passed at once into domestic Switzerland. A white-tiled stove for winter-time filled the fireplace of the room into which he was shown, the room's bare floor was laid together in a neat pattern of several ordinary woods, the room had a prevalent air of surface bareness and much scrubbing; and the little square of flowery carpet by the sofa, and the velvet chimney-board with its capacious clock and vases of artificial flowers, contended with that tone, as if, in bringing out the whole effect, a

Parisian had adapted a dairy to domestic purposes." CS/NT 1

—landscape, and habitation: " . . . how the Swiss villages, clustered at the feet of Giant mountains, looked like playthings; or how confusedly the houses were heaped and piled together; or how there were very narrow streets to shut the howling winds out in the winter-time; and broken bridges, which the impetuous torrents, suddenly released in spring, had swept away.

"Or how there were peasant women here, with great round fur caps: looking, when they peeped out of casements and only their heads were seen, like a population of Sword-bearers to the Lord Mayor of London; or how the town of Vevay, lying on the smooth lake of Geneva, was beautiful to see . . . .

"Or how, between [Fribourg] and Basle, the road meandered among thriving villages of wooden cottages, with overhanging thatched roofs, and low protruding windows, glazed with small round panes of glass like crown-pieces; or how, in every little Swiss homestead, with its cart or waggon carefully stowed away beside the house, its little garden, stock of poultry, and groups of red-cheeked children, there was an air of comfort, very new and very pleasant after Italy; or how the dresses of the women changed again, and there were no more sword-bearers to be seen; and fair white stomachers, and great black, fan-shaped, gauzy-looking caps, prevailed instead.

"Or how the country by the Jura mountains, sprinkled with snow, and lighted by the moon, and musical with falling water, was delightful; or how, below the windows of the great hotel of the Three Kings at Basle, the swollen Rhine ran fast and green . . . . " ¶PI 9

—mountain rivers: "Commend me to the beautiful waters among these mountains! Though I was not of their mind: they, being inveterately bent on getting down into the level country, and I ardently desiring to linger where I was. What desperate leaps they took, what dark abysses they plunged into, what rocks they wore away, what echoes they invoked! In one part where I went, they were pressed into the service of carrying wood down, to be burnt next winter, as costly fuel, in Italy. But, their fierce savage nature was not to be easily constrained, and they fought with every limb of the wood; whirling it round and round, stripping its bark away, dashing it against pointed corners, driving it out of the course, and roaring and flying at the peasants who steered it back again from the bank with long stout poles." UT/TA

—mountain towns: " . . . I would come down into picturesque little towns with gleaming spires and odd towers; and would stroll afoot into market-places in steep winding streets, where a hundred women in bodices, sold eggs and honey, butter and fruit, and suckled their children as they sat by their clean baskets, and had such enormous goitres (or glandular swellings in the throat) that it became a science to know where the nurse ended and the child began." UT/TA

—near the Simplon Pass: "No human creature had come across the Pass for four days. The snow above the snow-line was too soft for wheeled carriage, and not hard enough for sledge. There was snow in the sky. There had been snow in the sky for days past, and the marvel was that it had not fallen, and the certainty was that it must fall. No vehicle could cross . . . .

"The road was fair enough for stout walkers, and the air grew lighter and easier to breathe as [Obenreizer and Vendale] ascended. But the settled gloom remained as it had remained for days back. Nature seemed to have come to a pause. The sense of hearing, no less than the sense of sight, was troubled by having to wait so long for the change, whatever it might be, that impended. The silence was as palpable and heavy as the lowering clouds—or rather cloud, for there seemed to be but one in all the sky, and that one covering the whole of it.

"Although the light was thus dismally shrouded, the prospect was not obscured. Down in the valley of the Rhone behind them, the stream could be traced through all its many windings, oppressively sombre and solemn in its one leaden hue, a colourless waste.

"Far and high above them, glaciers and suspended avalanches overhung the spots where they must pass, by and by; deep and dark below them on their right, were awful precipice and roaring torrent; tremendous mountains arose in every vista. The gigantic landscape, uncheered by a touch of changing light or a solitary ray of sun, was yet terribly distinct in its ferocity.

"The hearts of two lonely men might

shrink a little, if they had to win their way for miles and hours among a legion of silent and motionless men—mere men like themselves—all looking at them with fixed and frowning front. But how much more, when the legion is of Nature's mightiest works, and the frown may turn to fury in an instant!" ¶CS/NT 3

—over the Simplon: "It was late in November; and the snow lying four or five feet thick in the beaten road on the summit (in other parts the new drift was already deep), the air was piercing cold. But, the serenity of the night, and the grandeur of the road, with its impenetrable shadows, and deep glooms, and its sudden turns into the shining of the moon and its incessant roar of falling water, rendered the journey more and more sublime at every step.

"Soon leaving the calm Italian villages below us, sleeping in the moonlight, the road began to wind among dark trees, and after a time emerged upon a barer region, very steep and toilsome, where the moon shone bright and high. By degrees, the roar of water grew louder; and the stupendous track, after crossing the torrent by a bridge, struck in between two massive perpendicular walls of rock that quite shut out the moonlight, and only left a few stars shining in the narrow strip of sky above.

"Then, even this was lost, in the thick darkness of a cavern in the rock, through which the way was pierced; the terrible cataract thundering and roaring close below it, and its foam and spray hanging, in a mist, about the entrance.

"Emerging from this cave, and coming again into the moonlight, and across a dizzy bridge, it crept and twisted upward, through the Gorge of Gondo, savage and grand beyond description, with smooth-fronted precipices, rising up on either hand, and almost meeting overhead. Thus we went, climbing on our rugged way, higher and higher all night, without a moment's weariness: lost in the contemplation of the black rocks, the tremendous heights and depths, the fields of smooth snow lying, in the clefts and hollows, and the fierce torrents thundering headlong down the deep abyss.

"Towards daybreak, we came among the snow, where a keen wind was blowing fiercely. . . . A sledge being then made ready, and four horses harnessed to it, we went, ploughing, through the snow. Still upward, but now in the cold light of morning, and with the great white desert on which we travelled, plain and clear.

"We were well upon the summit of the mountain: and had before us the rude cross of wood, denoting its greatest altitude above the sea: when the light of the rising sun, struck, all at once, upon the waste of snow, and turned it a deep red. The lonely grandeur of the scene, was then at its height." ¶PI 9

"Taking to our wheels again, soon afterwards, we began rapidly to descend; passing under everlasting glaciers, by means of arched galleries, hung with clusters of dripping icicles; under and over foaming waterfalls; near places of refuge, and galleries of shelter against sudden danger; through caverns over whose arched roofs the avalanches slide, in spring, and bury themselves in the unknown gulf beneath.

"Down, over lofty bridges, and through horrible ravines: a little shifting speck in the vast desolation of ice and snow, and monstrous granite rocks; down through the deep Gorge of the Saltine, and deafened by the torrent plunging madly down, among the riven blocks of rock, into the level country, far below. Gradually down, by zig-zag roads, lying between an upward and a downward precipice, into warmer weather, calmer air, and softer scenery, until there lay before us, glittering like gold or silver in the thaw and sunshine, the metal-covered, red, green, yellow, domes and church-spires of a Swiss town." ¶PI 9

—St Bernard: " . . . I make that journey . . . with the same happy party—ah! two since dead, I grieve to think—and there is the same track, with the same black wooden arms to point the way, and there are the same storm-refuges here and there; and there is the same snow falling at the top, and there are the same frosty mists, and there is the same intensely cold convent with its menagerie smell, and the same breed of dogs fast dying out, and the same breed of jolly young monks whom I mourn to know as humbugs, and the same convent parlour with its piano and the sitting round the fire, and the same supper, and the same lone night in a cell, and the same bright fresh morning when going out into the highly rarefied air was like a plunge into an icy bath." RP/LA

—storm: "At first, but a few flakes descended slowly and steadily. After a little

while the fall grew much denser, and suddenly it began without apparent cause to whirl itself into spiral shapes. Instantly ensuing upon this last change, an icy blast came roaring at them, and every sound and force imprisoned until now was let loose.

"One of the dismal galleries through which the road is carried at that perilous point, a cave eked out by arches of great strength, was near at hand. They struggled into it, and the storm raged wildly. The noise of the wind, the noise of the water, the thundering down of displaced masses of rock and snow, the awful voices with which not only that gorge but every gorge in the whole monstrous range seemed to be suddenly endowed, the darkness as of night, the violent revolving of the snow which beat and broke it into spray and blinded them, the madness of everything around insatiate for destruction, the rapid substitution of furious violence for unnatural calm, and hosts of appalling sounds for silence; these were things, on the edge of a deep abyss, to chill the blood, though the fierce wind, made actually solid by ice and snow, had failed to chill it." CS/NT 3

—*sunset:* "Five couriers . . . on the summit of the Great St. Bernard . . . looking at the remote heights, stained by the setting sun, as if a mighty quantity of red wine had been broached upon the mountain top, and had not yet had time to sink into the snow . . . .

"The wine upon the mountain top soaked in as we looked; the mountain became white; the sky, a very dark blue; the wind rose; and the air turned piercing cold." RD

And see: F:Capital Punishment—*national methodologies; and* L:Neighbourhoods—*a Swiss Quarter*

Wales and the Welsh

"The faces of some of the Welsh people, among whom there were many old persons, were certainly the least intelligent. Some of these [Mormon] emigrants would have bungled sorely, but for the directing hand that was always ready. The intelligence here was unquestionably of a low order, and the heads were of a poor type." UT/SL

" . . . the Welsh, although they were naturally a gentle, quiet, pleasant people, who liked to receive strangers in their cottages among the mountains, and to set before them with free hospitality whatever they had to eat and drink, and to play to them on their harps, and sing their native ballads to them, were a people of great spirit when their blood was up. Englishmen [late 13th century] . . . began to be insolent in Wales, and to assume the air of master; and the Welsh pride could not bear it." CHE 16

Addendum

Antarctica

" . . . Mr Booley accompanied the expedition under Sir James Ross . . . which sailed from the River Thames on the 12th of May 1848, and which, on the 11th of September, entered Port Leopold Harbour.

"In this inhospitable region, surrounded by eternal ice, cheered by no glimpse of the sun, shrouded in gloom and darkness . . . . The ships were covered in, and fortified all round with walls of ice and snow; the masts were frozen up; hoar frost settled on the yards, tops, shrouds, stays, and rigging; around, in every direction, lay an interminable waste, on which only the bright stars, the yellow moon, and the vivid Aurora Borealis looked, by night or day . . . .

" . . . . And now, at midnight, all was bright and shining. Mountains of ice, wedged and broken into the strangest forms —jagged points, spires, pinnacles, pyramids, turrets, columns in endless succession and in infinite variety, flashing and sparkling with ten thousand hues, as though the treasures of the earth wre frozen up in all that water—appeared on every side. Masses of ice, floating and driving hither and thither, menaced the hardy voyagers with destruction; and threatened to crush their strong ships, like nutshells. But, below those ships was clear sea-water, now; the fortifying walls were gone; the yards, tops, shrouds and rigging, free from that hoary rust of long inaction, showed like themselves again; and the sails, bursting from the masts, like foliage which the welcome sun at length developed, spread themselves to the wind, and wafted the travellers away." HW/ET

The Thriving City of Eden as it Appeared on Paper MC

My First Fall in Life DC

Transportation and Travel

The four greys skimmed along; the bugle was in as high spirits as the greys; the coachman chimed in sometimes; the wheels hummed cheerfully in unison; the brass work on the harness was an orchestra of little bells; and thus the whole concern, from the buckles of the leader's coupling-reins to the handle of the hind boot, was one great instrument of music.

[MC 36]

The whole business of the human race between London and Dover, being spoliation, Mr Dorrit was waylaid at Dartford, pillaged at Gravesend, rifled at Rochester, fleeced at Sittingbourne, and sacked at Canterbury. However, it being the Courier's business to get him out of the hands of the banditti, the Courier bought him off at every stage.

LD ii 18

In America

—*canal boat:* " . . . a barge with a little house in it, viewed from the outside; and a caravan at a fair, viewed from within: the gentlemen being accommodated, as the spectators usually are, in one of those locomotive museums of penny wonders; and the ladies being partitioned off by a red curtain, after the manner of the dwarfs and giants in the same establishments, whose private lives are passed in rather close exclusiveness." AN 9

—*sleeping-hammock:* " . . . I found suspended on either side of the cabin, three long tiers of hanging book-shelves, designed apparently for volumes of the small octavo size. Looking with greater attention at these contrivances (wondering to find such literary preparations in such a place), I descried on each shelf a sort of microscopic sheet and blanket; then I began dimly to comprehend that the passengers were the library, and that they were to be arranged, edge-wise, on these shelves, till morning.

"I was assisted to this conclusion by seeing some of them gathered round the master of the boat, at one of the tables, drawing lots with all the anxieties and passions of gamesters depicted in their countenances; while others, with small pieces of cardboard in their hands, were groping among the shelves in search of numbers corresponding with those they had drawn. As soon as any gentleman found his number, he took possession of it by immediately undressing himself and crawling into bed. The rapidity with which an agitated gambler subsided into a snoring slumberer, was one of the most singular effects I have ever witnessed . . . .

"The politeness of the person in authority had secured to me a shelf in a nook . . . I found it, on after-measurement, just the width of an ordinary sheet of Bath post letter-paper; and I was at first in some uncertainty as to the best means of getting into it. But the shelf being a bottom one, I finally determined on lying upon the floor, rolling gently in, stopping immediately I touched the mattress, and remaining for the night with that side uppermost, whatever it might be. Luckily, I came upon my back at exactly the right moment.

"I was much alarmed on looking upward, to see, by the shape of his half-yard of sacking (which his weight had bent into an exceedingly tight bag), that there was a very heavy gentleman above me, whom the slender cords seemed quite incapable of holding; and I could not help reflecting upon the grief of my wife and family in the event of his coming down in the night. But as I could not have got up again without a severe bodily struggle, which might have alarmed the ladies; and as I had nowhere to go to, even if I had; I shut my eyes upon the danger, and remained there." ¶AN 10

—*coach:* "'I expect we shall want *the big* coach.'

"I could not help wondering within myself what the size of this big coach might be, and how many persons it might be designed to hold; for the vehicle which was too small for our purpose was something larger than two English heavy night coaches, and might have been the twin-brother of a French Diligence. My speculations were speedily set at rest, however, for as soon as we had dined, there came rumbling up the street, shaking its sides like a corpulent giant, a kind of barge on wheels. After much blundering and backing, it stopped at the door: rolling heavily from side to side when its other motion had ceased, as if it had taken cold in its damp stable, and between that, and the having been required in its dropsical old age to move at any faster pace than a walk, were distressed by shortness of wind." AN 9

"The coach holds nine inside, having a seat across from door to door, where we in England put our legs: so that there is only one feat more difficult in the performance than getting in, and that is getting out again." AN 14

—*coachman*

—*black, coping:* "A tremendous place is close before us, the black driver rolls his eyes, screws his mouth up very round, and looks straight between the two leaders, as if he were saying to himself, 'We have done this often before, but *now* I think we shall have a crash.' He takes a rein in each hand; jerks and pulls at both; and dances on the splashboard with both feet (keeping his seat, of course) like the late lamented **Ducrow** on two of his fiery coursers. We come to the spot, sink down in the mire nearly to the coach windows, tilt on one side at an angle of forty-five degrees, and stick there. The insides scream dismally; the coach stops; the horses flounder; all the other six coaches stop; and the four-and-twenty horses flounder likewise: but merely for company, and in sympathy with ours. Then the following circumstances occur.

"BLACK DRIVER (to the horses). 'Hi!'

"Nothing happens. Insides scream again.

"BLACK DRIVER (to the horses). 'Ho!'

"Horses plunge, and splash the black driver . . . .

"BLACK DRIVER (still to horses). 'Jiddy! Jiddy!'

"Horses pull violently, drag the coach out of the hole, and draw it up a bank; so steep, that the black driver's legs fly up into the air, and he goes back among the luggage on the roof. But he immediately recovers himself, and cries (still to the horses),

"'Pill!'

"No effect. On the contrary, the coach begins to roll back upon No. 2, which rolls back upon No. 3, which rolls back upon No. 4 and so on, until No. 7 is heard to curse and swear, nearly a quarter of a mile behind.

"BLACK DRIVER (louder than before). 'Pill!'

"Horses make another struggle to get up the bank, and again the coach rolls backward.

"BLACK DRIVER (louder than before). 'Pe-e-e-ill!'

"Horses make a desperate struggle.

" BLACK DRIVER (recovering spirits). 'Hi, Jiddy, Jiddy, Pill!'

"Horses make another effort.

"BLACK DRIVER (with great vigour). 'Ally Loo! Hi. Jiddy, Jiddy. Pill. Ally Loo!'

"Horses almost do it.

" BLACK DRIVER (with his eyes starting out of his head), 'Lee, den. Lee, dere. Hi. Jiddy, Jiddy. Pill. Ally Loo. Lee-e-e-e-e!'

"They run up the bank, and go down again on the other side at a fearful pace. It is impossible to stop them, and at the bottom there is a deep hollow, full of water. The coach rolls frightfully. The insides scream. The mud and water fly about us. The black driver dances like a madman. Suddenly we are all right by some extraordinary means, and stop to breathe." AN 9

—dress: "Negro coachmen and white; in straw hats, black hats, white hats, glazed caps, fur caps; in coats of drab, black, brown, green, blue nankeen, striped jean and linen; and there, in that one instance (look while it passes, or it will be too late), in suits of livery. Some southern republican that, who puts his blacks in uniform, and swells with Sultan pomp and power." AN 6

"The coachmen always change with the horses, and are usually as dirty as the coach. The first was dressed like a very shabby English baker; the second like a Russian peasant: for he wore a loose purple camlet robe, with a fur collar, tied round his waist with a parti-coloured worsted sash; grey trousers; light blue gloves: and a cap of bear-skin." AN 9

—interest in his work: "The landlord of the inn [in Ohio] is usually among [the loafers], and seems, of all the party, to be the least connected with the business of the house. Indeed he is with reference to the tavern, what the driver is in relation to the coach and passengers: whatever happens in his sphere of action, he is quite indifferent, and perfectly easy in his mind." AN 14

—covered bridge: "We crossed [the Susquehanna River] by a wooden bridge, roofed and covered in on all sides, and nearly a mile in length. It was profoundly dark; perplexed, with great beams, crossing and recrossing it at every possible angle; and through the broad chinks and crevices in the floor, the rapid river gleamed, far down below, like a legion of eyes. We had no lamps; and as the horses stumbled and floundered through this place, towards the distant speck of dying light, it seemed interminable. I really could not at first persuade myself as we rumbled heavily on, filling the bridge with hollow noises, and I held down my head to save it from the rafters above, but that I was in a painful dream; for I have often dreamed of toiling through such places, and as often argued, even at the time, 'this cannot be reality.'" AN 9

—hotels: " . . . I put out to sea for the Inns of America, with their four hundred beds apiece, and their eight or nine hundred ladies and gentlemen at dinner every day. Again I stood in the bar-rooms thereof, taking my evening cobbler, julep, sling, or cocktail.

"Again I listened to my friend the General—whom I had known for five minutes, in the course of which period he had made me intimate for life with two Majors, who again had made me intimate for life with three Colonels, who again had made me brother to twenty-two civilians,—again, I say, I listened to my friend the General, leisurely expounding the resources of the establishment, as to gentlemen's morning-room, Sir; ladies' morning-room, Sir; gentlemen's evening-room, Sir; ladies' evening-room, Sir; ladies' and gentlemen's evening reuniting-room, Sir; music-room, Sir; reading-room, Sir; over four hundred sleeping-rooms, Sir; and the entire planned and finished within twelve calendar months from the first clearing off of the old encumbrances on the plot, at a cost of five hundred thousand dollars, Sir.

"Again I found, as to my individual way of thinking, that the greater, the more gorgeous, and the more dollarous the establishment was, the less desirable it was." ¶CS/HT1

—accommodations: " . . . [we] straightway repaired to an extremely comfortable hotel: except, as usual, in the article of bedrooms, which, in almost every place we visited, were very conducive to early rising." AN 4

—Barnum's, Baltimore: "The most comfortable of all the hotels of which I had any experience in the United States, and they were not a few, is Barnum's . . . where the English traveller will find curtains to his bed, for the first and probably the last time in America (this is a disinterested remark, for I never use them); and where he will be likely to have enough water for washing himself, which is not at all a common case." AN 9

—in Belleville, Missouri: "There was an hotel in this place, which, like all hotels in America, had its large dining-room for the public table. It was an odd, shambling, low-roofed out-house, half-cowshed and half-kitchen, with a coarse brown canvas table-cloth, and tin sconces stuck against the walls, to hold candles at supper-time." AN 13

—in Lebanon, New York: " . . . we arrived [late] at Lebanon: which is renowned for its warm baths, and for a great hotel, well adapted, I have no doubt, to the gregarious taste of those seekers after health or pleasure who repair here, but inexpressibly comfortless to me. We were shown into an immense apartment, lighted by two dim candles, called the drawing-room: from which there was a descent by a flight of steps, to another vast desert, called the dining-room: our bedchambers were among certain long rows of little whitewashed cells, which opened from either side of a dreary passage; and were so like rooms in a prison that I half expected to be locked up when I went to bed, and listened involuntarily for the turning of the key on the outside.

"There need be baths somewhere in the neighbourhood, for the other washing arrangements were on as limited a scale as I ever saw, even in America: indeed, these bedrooms were so very bare of even such common luxuries as chairs, that I should say they were not provided with enough of anything, but that I bethink myself of our having been most bountifully bitten all night." AN 15

—Planter's House, St Louis: " . . . built like an English hospital, with long passages and bare walls, and skylights above the room-doors for the free circulation of air. There were a great many boarders in it; and as many lights sparkled and glistened from the windows down into the street below, when we drove up, as if it had been illuminated on some occasion of rejoicing. It is an excellent house, and the proprietors have most bountiful notions of providing the creature comforts. Dining alone with my wife in our own room, one day, I counted fourteen dishes on the table at once." AN 12

—Tremont House, Boston: "The hotel (a very excellent one) . . . has more galleries, colonnades, piazzas, and passages than I can remember, or the reader would believe." AN 2

—in Upper Sandusky, Ohio: "The bed-chamber to which my wife and I were shown, was a large, low, ghostly room; with a quantity of withered branches on the hearth, and two doors without any fastening, opposite to each other, both opening on the black night and wild country, and so contrived, that one of them always blew the other open: a novelty in domestic architecture, which I do not remember to have seen before, and which I was somewhat disconcerted to have forced on my attention after getting into bed . . . . " AN 14

—meals

—on a canal: "At about six o'clock [PM], all the small tables were put together to form one long table, and everybody sat down to tea, coffee, bread, butter, salmon, shad, liver, steaks, potatoes, pickles, ham, chops, black-puddings, and sausages . . . .

"At eight o'clock [AM], the shelves being taken down and put away [*see —sleeping hammock*] and the tables joined together, everybody sat down to the tea, coffee, bread, butter, salmon, shad, liver, steak, potatoes, pickles, ham, chops, black-puddings, and sausages, all over again. Some were fond of compounding this variety, and having it all on their plates at once. As each gentleman got through his own personal amount of tea, coffee, bread, butter, salmon, shad, liver, steak, potatoes, pickles, ham, chops, black-puddings, and sausages, he rose up and walked off . . . . Dinner was breakfast again, without the tea and coffee; and supper and breakfast were identical." AN 10

" . . . breakfast was perhaps the least desirable meal of the day, as in addition to the many savoury odours arising from the eatables already mentioned, there were whiffs of gin, whiskey, brandy, and rum, from the little bar hard by, and a decided seasoning of stale tobacco.

"Many of the gentlemen passengers were far from particular in respect of their linen, which was in some cases as yellow as the little rivulets that had trickled from the corners of their mouths in chewing, and dried there. Nor was the atmosphere quite free from zephyr whisperings of the thirty beds which had just been cleared away, and of which we were further and more pressingly reminded by the occasional appearance on the table-cloth of a kind of Game, not mentioned in the Bill of Fare." AN 10

—convivial, on a river: "At dinner, there is nothing to drink upon the table, but great jugs full of cold water. Nobody says anything, at any meal, to anybody. All the passengers are very dismal, and seem to have tremendous secrets weighing on their minds. There is no conversation, no laughter, no cheerfulness, no sociality, except in spitting; and that is done in silent fellowship round the stove, when the meal is over.

"Every man sits down, dull and languid; swallows his fare as if breakfasts, dinners, and suppers, were necessities of nature never to be coupled with recreation or enjoyment; and having bolted his food in a gloomy silence, bolts himself, in the same state. But for these animal observances, you might suppose the whole male portion of the company to be the melancholy ghosts of departed book-keepers, who had fallen dead at the desk: such is their weary air of business and calculation. Undertakers on duty would be sprightly beside them; and a collation of funeral baked-meats in comparison with these meals, would be a sparkling festivity." ¶AN 11

—railroad: "There are no first and second class carriages as with us; but there is a gentlemen's car and a ladies' car: the main distinction between which is that in the first, everybody smokes; and in the second, nobody does. As a black man never travels with a white one, there is also a negro car; which is a great blundering clumsy chest, such as *Gulliver* put to sea in, from the kingdom of Brobdingnag. There is a great deal of jolting, a great deal of noise, a great deal of wall, nor much window, a locomotive engine, a shriek, and a bell.

"The cars are like shabby omnibuses, but larger: holding thirty, forty, fifty, people. The seats, instead of stretching from end to end, are placed crosswise. Each seat holds two persons. There is a long row of them on each side of the caravan, a narrow passage up the middle, and a door at both ends. In the centre of the carriage there is usually a stove, fed with charcoal or anthracite coal; which is for the most part red-hot. It is insufferably close; and you see the hot air fluttering between yourself and any other object you may happen to look at, like the ghost of smoke." AN 4

"Mile after mile of stunted trees: some hewn down by the axe, some blown down by the wind, some half fallen and resting on their neighbours, many mere logs half hidden in the swamp, others mouldered away to spongy chips. The very soil of the earth is made up of minute fragments such as these; each pool of stagnant water has its crust of vegetable rottenness; on every side there are the boughs, and trunks, and stumps of trees, in every possible stage of decay, decomposition, and neglect.

"Now you emerge for a few brief minutes on an open country, glittering with some bright lake or pool, broad as many an English river, but so small here that it scarcely has a name: now catch hasty glimpses of a distant town, with its clean white houses and their cool piazzas, its prim New England church and school-house; when whir-r-r-r! almost before you have seen them, comes the same dark screen: the stunted trees, the stumps, the logs, the stagnant water—all so like the last that you seem to have been transported back again by magic.

"The train calls at stations in the woods, where the wild impossibility of anybody having the smallest reason to get out, is only to be equalled by the apparently desperate hopelessness of there being anybody to get in. It rushes across the turnpike road, where there is no gate, no policeman, no signal: nothing but a rough wooden arch, on which is painted 'WHEN THE BELL RINGS, LOOK OUT FOR THE LOCOMOTIVE.' On it whirls headlong . . . suddenly awakens all the slumbering echoes in the main street of a large town, and dashes on haphazard, pell-mell, neck-or-nothing, down the middle of the road. There—with mechanics working at their trades, and people leaning from their doors and windows, and boys flying kites and playing marbles, and men smoking, and women talking, and children crawling, and pigs burrowing, and unaccustomed horses plunging and rearing, close to the very rails—there—on, on, on—tears the mad dragon of an engine with its train of cars; scattering in all directions a shower of burning sparks from its wood fire; screeching, hissing, yelling, panting; until at last the thirsty monster stops beneath a covered way to drink. The people cluster round, and you have time to breathe again." ¶AN 4

"There were three great caravans or cars attached. The ladies' car, the gentlemen's car, and the car for negroes: the latter painted black, as an appropriate compliment to its company." MC 21

—valuable property: "How the wheels clank and rattle, and the tram-road shakes, as the train rushes on! And now the engine yells, as it were lashed and tortured like a living labourer, and writhed in agony. A poor fancy; for steel and iron are of infinitely greater account, in this commonwealth, than flesh and blood. If the cunning work of man be urged beyond its power of endurance, it has within it the elements of its own revenge; whereas the wretched mechanism of the Divine Hand is dangerous with no such property, but may be tampered with, and crushed, and broken, at the driver's pleasure. Look at that engine! It shall cost a man more dollars in the way of penalty and fine, and satisfaction of the outraged law, to deface in wantonness that senseless mass of metal, than to take the lives of twenty human creatures! Thus the stars wink upon the bloody stripes; and Liberty pulls down her cap upon her eyes, and owns Oppression in its vilest aspect, for her sister." MC 21

Cabriolets and Hackney-coaches

—cab (cabriolet)

—apprehensions concerning: "Miss Tox had great experience in hackney cabs, and her starting in one was generally a work of time, as she was systematic in the preparatory arrangements.

"'Have the goodness, if you please, Towlinson,' said Miss Tox, 'first of all, to carry out a pen and ink and take his number legibly.'

"'Yes, Miss,' said Towlinson.

"'Then, if you please, Towlinson,' said Miss Tox, 'have the goodness to turn the cushion. Which,' said Miss Tox apart to Mrs Chick, 'is generally damp, my dear.'

"'Yes, Miss,' said Towlinson.

"'I'll trouble you also, if you please,' said Miss Tox, 'with this card and this shilling. He's to drive to the card, and is to understand that he will not on any account have more than the shilling.'

"'No, Miss,' said Towlinson.

"'And—I'm sorry to give you so much trouble, Towlinson,'—said Miss Tox, looking at him pensively.

"'Not at all, Miss,' said Towlinson.

"'Mention to the man, then, if you please, Towlinson,' said Miss Tox, 'that the lady's uncle is a magistrate, and that if he gives her any of his impertinence he will be punished terribly. You can pretend to say that, if you please, Towlinson, in a friendly way, and because you know it was done to another man, who died.'

"'Certainly, Miss,' said Towlinson." DS 5

—in brief: "'The Governor hisself'll be down here presently.'

"'He's a cabbin' it, I suppose?' said the father.

"'Yes, he's a havin' two mile o' danger at eight-pence,' responded the son." PP 22

—could be improved: "A London cab-stand is one of our great national, real original ill-regulated public inconveniences. As an existing buttress of our liberties, it is to be presumed that it is inseparably connected with the glory of the country, and that the country would receive a fatal shock if it were in anywise improved; but I diffidently incline to the opinion, nevertheless, that it is capable of some small changes for the better.

"It has never been clearly made out—except by prescription and precedent—why it is indispensable that a London cab should be dirty; why the palsied window-sashes must be artfully made not to fit the window; why one door must never open, and the other never shut; why there must be, at least, one broken window, replaced (in the genteeler sort of cab) with a wooden shutter; why the check-line must be broken or gone, and the bands for pulling up the glasses cropped short off; why the nose-bags of the horses must be under the seat; why there must be a view of the pavement through the chinks in the bottom; why the fare must sit in a foot-bath of foul straw; why the cab must be damp; why the driver must be dirty; why the rate of fares and distances must be nominal; why everything connected with the crazy, ricketty, jolting, ramshackle, ugly, unsavoury, cheating, dear Institution must be exactly the reverse of what it ought to be." HWC/C

—*getting in:* "Some people object to the exertion of getting into cabs, and others object to the difficulty of getting out of them; we think both these are objections which take their rise in perverse and ill-conditioned minds. The getting into a cab is a very pretty and graceful process, which, when well performed, is essentially melodramatic. First, there is the expressive pantomime of every one of the eighteen cabmen on the stand, the moment you raise your eyes from the ground. Then there is your own pantomime in reply—quite a little ballet. Four cabs immediately leave the stand, for your especial accommodation; and the evolutions of the animals who draw them are beautiful in the extreme, as they grate the wheels of the cabs against the curb-stones, and sport playfully in the kennel. You single out a particular cab, and dart swiftly towards it. One bound, and you are on the first step; turn your body lightly round to the right, and you are on the second; bend gracefully beneath the reins, working round to the left at the same time, and you are in the cab. There is no difficulty in finding a seat: the apron knocks you comfortably into it at once, and off you go." SB/LC

—*getting out:* "The getting out of a cab is, perhaps, rather more complicated in its theory, and a shade more difficult in its execution. We have studied the subject a great deal, and we think the best way is, to throw yourself out, and trust to chance for alighting on your feet. If you make the driver alight first, and then throw yourself upon him, you will find that he breaks your fall materially. In the event of your contemplating an offer of eightpence, on no account make the tender, or show the money, until you are safely on the pavement. It is very bad policy attempting to save the fourpence. You are very much in the power of a cabman, and he considers it a kind of fee not to do you any wilful damage. Any instruction, however, in the art of getting out of a cab, is wholly unnecessary if you are going any distance, because the probability is that you will be shot lightly out before you have completed the third mile." SB/LC

—*coach*

—*aristocratic:* ". . . a hackney-coachman, who seemed to have as many capes to his greasy great-coat as he was years old, packed me up in his coach and hemmed me in with a folding and jingling barrier of steps, as if he were going to take me fifty miles. His getting on his box, which I remember to have been decorated with an old weather-stained pea-green hammer-cloth, moth-eaten into rags, was quite a work of time. It was a wonderful equipage, with six great coronets outside, and ragged things behind for I don't know how many footmen to hold on by, and a harrow below them, to prevent amateur footmen from yielding to the temptation.

"I had scarcely had time to enjoy the coach and to think how like a straw-yard it was, and yet how like a rag-shop, and to wonder why the horses' nose-bags were kept inside, when I observed the coachman beginning to get down, as if we were going to stop presently." GE 20

—*a broken window:* "'Hackney-coaches, my lord [said Mrs Nickleby] are such nasty things, that it's almost better to walk at any time, for although I believe a hackney-coachman can be transported for life, if he has a broken window, still they are so reckless, that they nearly all have broken windows. I once had a swelled face for six weeks, my lord, from riding in a hackney-coach—I think it was a hackney-coach,' said Mrs Nickleby reflecting, 'though I'm not quite certain, whether it wasn't a chariot; at all events I know it was a dark green, with a very long number, beginning with a nought and ending with a nine—no, beginning with a nine, and ending with a nought, that was it, and of course the stamp-office people would know at once whether it was a coach or a chariot if any inquiries were made there—however that was, there it was with a broken window, and there was I for six weeks with a swelled face—I think that was the very same hackney-coach, that we found out afterwards, had the top open all the time, and we should never even have known it, if they hadn't charged us a shilling an hour extra for having it open, which it seems is the law, or was then, and a most shameful law it appears to be—I don't understand the subject, but I should say the Corn Laws could be nothing to *that* act of Parliament.'" NN 27

—a portrait: "There is a hackney-coach stand under the very window at which we are writing; there is only one coach on it now, but it is a fair specimen of the class of vehicles to which we have alluded—a great, lumbering, square concern of a dingy yellow colour (like a bilious brunette), with very small glasses, but very large frames; the panels are ornamented with a faded coat of arms, in shape something like a dissected bat, the axletree is red, and the majority of the wheels are green.

"The box is partially covered by an old great-coat, with a multiplicity of capes, and some extraordinary-looking clothes; and the straw, with which the canvas cushion is stuffed, is sticking up in several places, as if in rivalry of the hay, which is peeping through the chinks in the boot. The horses, with drooping heads, and each with a mane and tail as scanty and straggling as those of a worn-out rocking-horse, are standing patiently on some damp straw, occasionally wincing, and rattling the harness; and now and then one of them lifts his mouth to the ear of his companion as if he were saying, in a whisper, that he should like to assassinate the coachman. The coachman himself is in the watering-house; and the waterman, with his hands forced into his pockets as far as they can possibly go, is dancing the 'double shuffle' in front of the pump, to keep his feet warm." ¶SB/HC

—smell: " . . . a hackney coach; an institution with the peculiar smell of which the present generation is unacquainted, but to which I am again ready to swear as a combination of stable, dog with the mange, and very old bellows." CS/HH 2

—speed: "Take a regular, ponderous, rickety, London hackney-coach of the old school, and let any man have the boldness to assert, if he can, that he ever beheld any object on the face of the earth which at all resembles it, unless, indeed, it were another hackney-coach of the same date. We have recently observed on certain stands, and we say it with deep regret, rather dapper green chariots, and coaches of polished yellow, with four wheels of the same colour as the coach, whereas it is perfectly notorious to every one who has studied the subject, that every wheel ought to be of a different colour, and a different size.

"These are innovations, and, like other mis-called improvements, awful signs of the restlessness of the public mind, and the little respect paid to our time-honoured institutions. Why should hackney-coaches be clean? Our ancestors found them dirty, and left them so. Why should we, with a feverish wish to 'keep moving,' desire to roll along at the rate of six miles an hour, while they were content to rumble over the stones at four? These are solemn considerations. Hackney-coaches are part and parcel of the law of the land: they were settled by the Legislature; plated and numbered by the wisdom of Parliament.

"Then why have they been swamped by cabs and omnibuses? Or why should people be allowed to ride quickly for eightpence a mile, after Parliament had come to the solemn decision that they should pay a shilling a mile for riding slowly? We pause for a reply . . . . " ¶SB/HS

Mark Antony's pause is part of our language.

— *compared:* "Cabs, with trunks and bandboxes between the drivers' legs and outside the apron, rattle briskly up and down the streets on their way to the coach-offices or steam-packet wharfs; and the cab-drivers and hackney-coachmen who are on the stand polish up the ornamental part of their dingy vehicles—the former wondering how people can prefer 'them wild beast cariwans of homnibuses, to a riglar cab with a fast trotter,' and the latter admiring how people can trust their necks into one of 'them crazy cabs, when they can have a 'spectable 'ackney cotche with a pair of 'orses as von't run away with no vun;' a consolation unquestionably founded on fact, seeing that a hackney-coach horse never was known to run at all, 'except,' as the smart cabman in front of the rank observes, 'except one, and *he* run back'ards.'" SB/SM

"'Talk of cabs! Cabs are all very well in cases of expedition, when it's a matter of neck or nothing, life or death, your temporary home or your long one. But, besides a cab's lacking that gravity of deportment which so peculiarly distinguishes a hackney-coach, let it never be forgotten that a cab is a thing of yesterday, and that he never was anything better. A hackney-cab has always been a hackney-cab, from his first entry into life; whereas a hackney-coach is a remnant of past gentility, a victim to fashion, a hanger-on of an old English family, wearing their arms, and, in days or yore, escorted by men wearing their livery, stripped of his finery, and thrown upon the world, like a once-smart footman when he is no longer sufficiently juvenile for his office, progressing lower and lower in the scale of four-wheeled degradation, until at last it comes to—*a stand!*" SB/HC

See Indexes IV *and* VIII *for lists of cab-drivers, coachmen, drivers (private and public) and hackney drivers. Six are named, but only the great stager Tony Weller PP rates a surname. There are 124 unnamed figures.*

Chaises, Flys and Gigs

—chaise for an outing: "It was a curious little green box on four wheels, with a low place like a wine-bin for two behind, and an elevated perch for one in front, drawn by an immense brown horse . . . . " PP 5

And see LC:Words and Phrases

Mr Chester's Chair BR

—commercial: "If any bagman of that day could have caught sight of the little neck-or-nothing sort of gig, with a clay-coloured body and red wheels, and the vixenish, ill-tempered, fast-going bay mare, that looked like a cross between a butcher's horse and a two-penny post-office pony, he would have known at once, that this traveller could have been no other than Tom Smart, of the great house of Bilson and Slum, Cateaton Street, City." PP 14

—on Derby Day: "On that great occasion, an unused spectator might imagine that all London turned out. There is little perceptible difference in the bustle of its crowded streets, but all the roads leading to Epsom Downs are so thronged and blocked by every description of carriage that it is marvellous to consider how, when, and where, they were all made—out of what possible wealth they are all maintained—and by what laws the supply of horses is kept equal to the demand.

"Near the favourite bridges, and at various leading points of the leading roads, clusters of people post themselves by nine o'clock, to see the Derby people pass. Then come flitting by, barouches, phaetons, broughams, gigs, four-wheeled chaises, four-in-hands, Hansom cabs, cabs of lesser note, chaise-carts, donkey-carts, tilted vans made arborescent with green boughs and carrying no end of people, and a cask of beer—equestrians, pedestrians, horse-dealers, gentlemen, notabilities, and swindlers, by tens of thousands—gradually thickening and accumulating, until, at last, a mile short of the turnpike, they become wedged together, and are very slowly filtered through layers of police-men, mounted and a-foot, until, one by one, they pass the gate and skurry down the hill beyond.

"The most singular combinations occur in these turnpike stoppages and presses. Four-in-hand leaders look affectionately over the shoulders of ladies, in bright shawls, perched in gigs; poles of carriages appear, uninvited, in the midst of social parties in phaetons; little, fast, short-stepping ponies run up carriage-wheels before they can be stopped, and hold on behind like footmen. Now, the gentleman who is unaccustomed to public driving, gets into astonishing perplexities. Now, the Hansom cab whisks craftily in and out, and seems occasionally to fly over a waggon or so. Now the postboy on a jibbing* or a shying horse, curses the evil hour of his birth, and is ingloriously assisted by the shabby hostler out of place, who is walking down with seven shabby companions more or less equine, open to the various chances of the road.

"Now, the air if fresh, and the dust flies thick and fast. Now, the canvas-booths upon the course are seen to glisten and flutter in the distance. Now, the adventurous vehicles make cuts across, and get into ruts and gravel-pits. Now, the heather in bloom is like a field of gold, and the roar of voices is like a wind. Now, we leave the hard road and go smoothly rolling over the soft green turf, attended by an army of importunate* worshippers in red jackets and stable jackets, who make a very Juggernaut-car of our equipage, and now breathlessly call us 'My Lord,' and now, 'your Honor.'

"Now, we pass the the outer settlements of tents where pots and kettles are—where gipsy children are—where airy stabling is—where tares for horses may be bought—where water, water, water, is proclaimed—where the Tumbler in an old pea-coat, with a spangled fillet round his head, eats oysters, while his wife takes care of the golden globes, and the knives, and also of the starry little boy, their son, who lives principally upside-down. Now, we pay our one pound at the barrier, and go faster on, still Juggernaut-wise, attended by our devotees, until at last we are drawn, and rounded, and backed, and sidled, and cursed, and complimented, and vociferated into a station on the hill opposite the Grand Stand, where we presently find ourselves on foot, much bewildered, waited on by five respectful persons, who *will* brush us all at once." HWC/E

**CD's collaborator, W. H. Wills, included this piece in his book* Old Leaves (1860), *correcting apparent printer's errors at these points.*

—for hire

—to Brighton: "Mrs Pipchin [is] waiting for a fly van, going to-night to Brighton on private service, which is to call for her, by private contract and convey her home.

"Presently it comes. Mrs Pipchin's wardrobe being handed in and stowed away, Mrs Pipchin's chair is next handed in, and placed in a convenient corner among certain trusses of hay; it being the intention of the amiable woman to occupy the chair during her journey. Mrs Pipchin herself is next handed in, and grimly takes her seat. There is a snaky gleam in her hard grey eye . . . [she] almost laughs as the fly van drives off, and she composes her black bombazeen skirts, and settles herself among the cushions of her easy-chair." DS 59

—at Ramsgate: "'Fly sir?' exclaimed a chorus of fourteen men and six boys, the moment Mr Joseph Tuggs, at the head of his little party, set foot in the street.

"'Here's the gn'lm'n at last!' said one, touching his hat with mock politeness. 'Werry glad to see you sir—been a-waitin' for you these six weeks. Jump in, if you please, sir!'

"'Nice light fly and a fast trotter, sir,' said another: 'fourteen mile a hour, and surroundin' objects rendered inwisible by extreme welocity!'

"'Large fly for your luggage, sir,' cried a third. 'Werry large fly here, sir—reg'lar bluebottle!'

"'Here's *your* fly, sir!' shouted another aspiring charioteer, mounting the box, and inducing an old grey horse to indulge in some imperfect reminiscences of a canter. 'Look at him sir!—temper of a lamb and haction of a steam-ingein!'

"Resisting even the temptation of securing the services of so valuable a quadruped as the last named, Mr Joseph Tuggs beckoned to the proprietor of a dingy conveyance of a greenish hue, lined with faded striped calico; and, the luggage and the family having been deposited therein, the animal in the shafts, after describing circles in the road for a quarter of an hour, at last consented to depart in quest of lodgings." SB/TR

—*after a wedding:* ""There was some singing, too, from Miss Ledrook and Miss Bravassa, and very likely there might have been more, if the fly-driver, who stopped to drive the happy pair to the spot where they proposed to take steamboat to Ryde, had not sent in a peremptory message intimating, that if they didn't come directly he should infallibly demand eighteen-pence over and above his agreement.

"This desperate threat effectually broke up the party." NN 25

Pinch starts Homeward [in a gig] with the new Pupil MC

Omnibus

—*burdened:* ". . . waiting the arrival of a short squat omnibus, with a disproportionate heap of luggage on the roof—like a little Elephant with infinitely too much Castle—which was then the daily service between Cloisterham and external mankind." MED 6

—*praised:* "Of all the public conveyances that have been constructed since the days of the Ark—we think that is the earliest on record—to the present time, commend us to an omnibus. A long stage is not to be despised, but there you have only six insides, and the chances are, that the same people go all the way with you—there is no change, no variety. Besides, after the first twelve hours or so, people get cross and sleepy, and when you have seen a man in his nightcap, you lose all respect for him; at least, that is the case with us. Then on smooth roads people frequently get prosy, and tell long stories, and even those who don't talk, may have very unpleasant predilections.

"We once travelled four hundred miles, inside a stage-coach, with a stout man, who had a glass of rum-and-water, warm, handed in at the window at every place where we changed horses. This was decidedly unpleasant. We have also travelled occasionally, with a small boy of a pale aspect, with light hair, and no perceptible neck, coming up to town from school under the protection of the guard, and directed to be left at the Cross Keys till called for. This is, perhaps, even worse than rum-and-water in a close atmosphere.

"Then there is the whole train of evils consequent on a change of the coachman; and the misery of the discovery—which the guard is sure to make the moment you begin to doze—that he wants a brown-paper parcel, which he distinctly remembers to have deposted under the seat on which you are reposing. A great deal of bustle and groping takes place, and when you are thoroughly awakened, and severely cramped, by holding your legs up by an almost supernatural exertion, while he is looking behind them, it suddenly occurs to him that he put it in the fore-boot. Bang goes the door; the parcel is immediately found; off starts the coach again; and the guard plays the key-bugle as loud as he can play it, as if in mockery of your wretchedness.

"Now, you meet with none of these afflictions in an omnibus; sameness there can never be. The passengers change as often in the course of one journey as the figures in a kaleidoscope, and though not so glittering, are far more amusing. We believe there is no instance on record, of a man's having gone to sleep in one of these vehicles. As to long stories, would any man venture to tell a long story in an omnibus? and even if he did, where would be the harm? nobody could possibly hear what he was talking about.

"Again; children, though occasionally, are not often to be found in an omnibus; and even when they are, if the vehicle be full, as is generally the case, somebody sits upon them, and we are unconscious of their presence. Yes, after mature reflection, and considerable experience, we are decidedly of opinion that of all known vehicles, from the glass-coach in which we were taken to be christened, to the sombre caravan in which we must one day make our last earthly journey, there is nothing like an omnibus." ¶SB/O

And see 'The Admiral Napier' SB/BC *in* Vol. I p127, *and* SB/LC

Private transport

—coachman: "There were some stately footmen [in the congregation]; and there was a perfect picture of an old coachman, who looked as if he were the official representative of all the pomps and vanities that had ever been put into his coach." BH 18

—nondescript: " . . . the hooded vehicle, whatever its proper name might be . . . it was more like a gig with a tumour, than anything else . . . . " MC 5

—post-chaise to London: "The frosty night wears away, and the dawn breaks, and the post-chaise comes rolling on through the early mist, like the ghost of a chaise departed. It has plenty of spectral company, in ghosts of trees and hedges, slowly vanishing and giving place to the realities of day." BH 55

Railroad

—absence at Carrara: "But the road, the road down which the marble comes, however immense the blocks! The genius of the country, and the spirit of its institutions, pave that road: repair it, watch it, keep it going!

"Conceive a channel of water running over a rocky bed, beset with great heaps of stone of all shapes and sizes, winding down the middle of this valley; and *that* being the road—because it was the road five hundred years ago! Imagine the clumsy carts of five hundred years ago, being used to this hour, and drawn, as they used to be, five hundred years ago, by oxen, whose ancestors were worn to death five hundred years ago, as their unhappy descendants are now, in twelve months, by the suffering and agony of this cruel work!

"Two pair, four pair, ten pair, twenty pair, to one block, according to its size; down it must come, this way. In their struggling from stone to stone, with their enormous loads behind them, they die frequently upon the spot; and not they alone; for their passionate drivers, sometimes tumbling down in their energy, are crushed to death beneath the wheels. But it was good five hundred years ago, and it must be good now: and a railroad down one of these steeps (the easiest thing in the world) would be flat blasphemy." ¶PI 10

—*coach travel compared:* "'As to comfort [said Tony Weller], vere's the comfort o' sittin' in a harm-cheer lookin' at brick walls or heaps o' mud, never comin' to a public-house, never seein' a glass o' ale, never goin' through a pike, never needin' a change o' no kind (horses or othervise), but alvays comin' to a place, ven you come to one at all, the wery picter o' the last, vith the same p'leesemen standin' about, the same blessed old bell a ringin', the same unfort'-nate people standin' behind the bars, a waitin' to be let in; and everythin' the same except the name, vich is wrote up in the same sized letters as the last name, and vith the same colours.

"'As to the *h*onour and dignity o' travellin', vere can that be vithout a coachman; and wot's the rail to sich coachmen and guards as is sometimes forced to go by it, but a outrage and a insult? As to the pace, wot sort o' pace do you think I, Tony Veller, could have kept a coach goin' at, for five hundred thousand pound a mile, paid in adwance afore the coach was on the road?

"'And as to the ingein—a nasty, wheezin', creakin', gaspin', puffin', bustin' monster, alvays out o' breath, vith a shiny green-and-gold back, like a unpleasant beetle in that 'ere gas magnifier—as to the ingein as is alvays a pourin' out red-hot coals at night, and black smoke in the day, the sensiblest thing it does, in my opinion, is, ven there's somethin' in the vay, and it sets up that 'ere frightful scream vich seems to say, "Now here's two hundred and forty passengers in the wery greatest extremity o' danger, and here's their two hundred and forty screams in vun!"'" MH 11

—*and Death:* "[Mr Dombey] felt no pleasure or relief in the journey. Tortured by [his] thoughts he carried monotony with him, through the rushing landscape, and hurried headlong, not through a rich and varied country, but a wilderness of blighted plans and gnawing jealousies. The very speed at which the train was whirled along mocked the swift course of the young life that had been borne away so steadily and so inexorably to its foredoomed end. The power that forced itself upon its iron way—its own—defiant of all paths and roads, piercing through the heart of every obstacle, and dragging living creatures of all classes, ages, and degrees behind it, was a type of the triumphant monster, Death.

"Away, with a shriek, and a roar, and a rattle, from the town, burrowing among the dwellings of men and making the streets hum, flashing out into the meadows for a moment, mining in through the damp earth, booming on in darkness and heavy air, bursting out again into the sunny day so bright and wide; away, with a shriek, and a roar, and a rattle, through the fields, through the woods, through the corn, through the hay, through the chalk, through the mould, through the clay, through the rock, among objects close at hand and almost in the grasp, ever flying from the traveller, and a deceitful distance ever moving slowly within him: like as in the track of the remorseless monster, Death!

"Through the hollow, on the height, by the heath, by the orchard, by the park, by the garden, over the canal, across the river, where the sheep are feeding, where the mill is going, where the barge is floating, where the dead are lying, where the factory is smoking, where the stream is running, where the village clusters, where the great cathedral rises, where the bleak moor lies, and the wild breeze smooths or ruffles it at its inconstant will; away, with a shriek, and a roar, and a rattle, and no trace to leave behind but dust and vapour: like as in the track of the remorseless monster, Death!

"Breasting the wind and light, the shower and sunshine, away, and still away, it rolls and roars, fierce and rapid, smooth and certain, and great works and massive bridges crossing up above, fall like a beam of shadow an inch broad, upon the eye, and then are lost. Away, and still away, onward and onward ever: glimpses of cottage-homes, of houses, mansions, rich estates, of husbandry and handicraft, of people, of old roads and paths that look deserted, small, and insignificant as they are left behind: and so they do, and what else is there but such glimpses, in the track of the indomitable monster, Death!

"Away, with a shriek, and a roar, and a rattle, plunging down into the earth again, and working on in such a storm of energy and perseverance, that amidst the darkness and whirlwind the motion seems reversed, and to tend furiously backward, until a ray of light upon the wet wall shows its surface flying past like a fierce stream. Away once more into the day, and through the day, with a shrill yell of exultation, roaring, rattling, tearing on, spurning everything with its dark breath, sometimes pausing for a minute where a crowd of faces are, that in a minute more are not; sometimes lapping water greedily, and before the spout at which it drinks has ceased to drip upon the ground, shrieking, roaring, rattling through the purple distance!

"Louder and louder yet, it shrieks and cries as it comes tearing on resistless to the goal: and now its way, still like the way of Death, is strewn with ashes thickly. Everything around is blackened. There are dark pools of water, muddy lanes, and miserable habitations far below. There are jagged walls and falling houses close at hand, and through the battered roofs and broken windows, wretched rooms are seen, where want and fever hide themselves in many wretched shapes, while smoke and crowded gables, and distorted chimneys, and deformity of brick and mortar penning up deformity of mind and body, choke the murky distance. As Mr Dombey looks out of his carriage window, it is never in his thoughts that the monster who has brought him there has let the light of day in on these things: not made or caused them. It was the journey's fitting end, and might have been the end of everything; it was so ruinous and dreary." DS 20

—early travel: "We know all about that station of which we have a clear idea although we were never there; we know that if we arrive after dark we are certain to find it half a mile from the town, where the old road is sure to have been abolished, and the new road is going to be made, where the old neighbourhood has been tumbled down, and the new one is not half built up. We know all about that porter on the platform who with the best intentions in the world cannot do anything particularly efficacious with the luggage by looking at it with that bell in his hand. We know all about that particularly short omnibus, in which one is to be doubled up to the imminent danger of the crown of one's hat; and about that fly, whose leading pecularity is never to be there when it is wanted. We know, too, how instantaneously the lights of the station disappear the moment the train slips away, and about that grope to the new Railway Hotel, which will be an excellent house when the customers come, but which at present has nothing to offer but a liberal allowance of damp mortar and new lime." S/CT1

—early work: "Railroads shall soon traverse all this country, and with a rattle and a glare the engine and train shall shoot like a meteor over the wide night-landscape, turning the moon paler; but, as yet, such things are non-existent in these parts, though not wholly unexpected. Preparations are afoot, measurements are made, ground is staked out. Bridges are begun, and their not yet united piers desolately look at one another over roads and streams, like brick and mortar couples with an obstacle to their union; fragments of embankments are thrown up, and left as precipices with torrents of rusty carts and barrows tumbling over them; tripods of tall poles appear on hilltops, where there are rumours of tunnels; everything looks chaotic, and abandoned in full hopelessness. Along the freezing roads, and through the night, the post-chaise makes its way without a railroad on its mind." BH 55

And see L:Neighbourhoods—*Stagg's Gardens*

—express

—to Carlisle: "It was like all other expresses, as every express is and must be. It bore through the harvest country a smell like a large washing-day, and a sharp issue of steam as from a huge brazen tea-urn. The greatest power in nature and art combined, it yet glided over dangerous heights in the sight of people looking up from fields and roads, as smoothly and unreally as a light miniature plaything.

"Now, the engine shrieked in hysterics of such intensity, that it seemed desirable that the men who had her in charge should hold her feet, slap her hands, and bring her to; now, burrowed into tunnels with a stubborn and undemonstrative energy so confusing that the train seemed to be flying back into leagues of darkness.

"Here, were station after station, swallowed up by the express without stopping; here, stations where it fired itself in like a volley of cannon-balls, swooped away four country-people with nosegays, and three men of business with portmanteaus, and fired itself off again, bang, bang, bang!

"At long intervals were uncomfortable refreshment-rooms, made more uncomfortable by the scorn of Beauty towards Beast, the public (but to whom she never relented, as Beauty did in the story, towards the other Beast), and where sensitive stomachs were fed, with a contemptuous sharpness occasioning indigestion.

"Here, again, were stations with nothing going but a bell, and wonderful wooden razors set aloft on great posts, shaving the air. In these fields, the horses, sheep, and cattle were well used to the thundering meteor, and didn't mind; in those, they were all set scampering together, and a herd of pigs scoured after them. The pastoral country darkened, became coaly, became smoky, became infernal, got better, got worse, improved again, grew rugged, turned romantic; was a wood, a stream, a chain of hills, a gorge, a moor, a cathedral town, a fortified place, a waste.

"Now, miserable black dwellings, a black canal, and sick black towers of chimneys; now, a trim garden, where the flowers were bright and fair; now, a wilderness of hideous altars all ablaze; now, the water meadows with their fairy rings; now, the mangy patch of unlet building ground outside the stagnant town, with the larger ring where the Circus was last week. The temperature changed, the dialect changed, the people changed, faces got sharper, manner got shorter, eyes got shrewder and harder; yet all so quickly, that the spruce guard in the London uniform and silver lace, had not yet rumpled his shirt-collar, delivered half the dispatches in his shiny little pouch or read his newspaper.

"Carlisle! Idle and Goodchild had got to Carlisle." ¶LT 1

—to Folkestone: "Bang! We have let another Station off, and fly away regardless. Everything is flying. The hop-gardens turn gracefully towards me, presenting regular avenues of hops in rapid flight, then whirl away. So do the pools and rushes, haystacks, sheep, clover in full bloom delicious to the sight and smell, corn-sheaves, cherry-orchards, apple-orchards, reapers, gleaners, hedges, gates, fields that taper off into little angular corners, cottages, gardens, now and then a church.

"Bang, bang! A double-barrelled Station! Now a wood, now a bridge, now a landscape, now a cutting, now a—Bang! a single-barrelled Station—there was a cricket-match somewhere with two white tents, and then four flying cows, then turnips—now the wires of the electric telegraph are all alive, and spin, and blurr [*sic.*] their edges, and go up and down, and make the intervals between each other most irregular: contracting and expanding in the strangest manner. Now we slacken. With a screwing, and a grinding, and a smell of water thrown on ashes, now we stop!" ¶RP/F

—in France: "Anon, with no more trouble than before, I am flying again, and lazily wondering as I fly. What has the South-Eastern done with all the horrible little villages we used to pass through, in the *Diligence?* What have they done with all the summer dust, with all the winter mud, with all the dreary avenues of little trees, with all the ramshackle post-yards, with all the beggars (who used to turn out at night with bits of lighted candle, to look in at the coach windows), with all the long-tailed horses who were always biting one another, with all the big postillions in jack-boots—with all the mouldy cafes that we used to stop at, where a long mildewed table-cloth, set forth with jovial bottles of vinegar and oil, and with a Siamese arrangement of pepper and salt, was never wanting?

"Where are the grass-grown little towns, the wonderful little market-places all unconscious of markets, the shops that nobody kept, the streets that nobody trod, the churches that nobody went to, the bells that nobody rang, the tumble-down old buildings plastered with many-coloured bills that nobody read? Where are the two-and-twenty weary hours of long long day and night journey, sure to be either insupportably hot or insupportably cold? Where are the pains in my bones, where are the fidgets in my legs, where is the Frenchman with the nightcap who never *would* have the little coupe-window down, and who always fell upon me when he went to sleep, and always slept all night snoring onions?

"A voice breaks in with 'Paris! Here we are!'

"I have overflown myself, perhaps, but I can't believe it." ¶RP/F

—freight trains: "Mysterious goods trains, covered with palls and gliding on like vast weird funerals, conveying themselves guiltily away from the presence of the few lighted lamps, as if their freight had come to a secret and unlawful end. Half-miles of coal pursuing in a Detective manner, following when they lead, stopping when they stop, backing when they back.

"Red-hot embers showering out upon the ground, down this dark avenue, and down the other, as if torturing fires were being raked clear; concurrently, shrieks and groans and grinds invading the ear, as if the tortured were at the height of their suffering. Iron-barred cages full of cattle jangling by midway, the drooping beasts with horns entangled, eyes frozen with terror, and mouths too: at least they have long icicles (or what seem so) hanging from their lips.

Unknown languages in the air, conspiring in red, green, and white characters." ¶CS/MJ 1

—fuel

—coal: " . . . I beg to recommend the legal use of coke as engine-fuel, rather than the illegal use of coal; the recommendation is quite disinterested, for I was most liberally supplied with small coal on the journey, for which no charge was made. I had not only my eyes, nose, and ears filled, but my hat, and all my pockets, and my pocket-book, and my watch." UT/ST

—wood: " . . . I found abundance of entertainment for the rest of the ride in watching the effects of the wood fire, which had been invisible in the morning but were now brought out in full relief by the darkness: for we were travelling in a whirlwind of bright sparks, which showered about us like a storm of fiery snow." AN 4

—and guilt: "How long [James Carker] sat, drinking and brooding, and being dragged in imagination hither and thither, no one could have told less correctly than he. But he knew that he had been sitting a long time by candle-light, when he started up and listened, in a sudden terror.

"For now, indeed, it was no fancy. The ground shook, the house rattled, the fierce impetuous rush was in the air! He felt it come up, and go darting by; and even when he had hurried to the window, and saw what it was, he stood, shrinking from it, as if it were not safe to look.

"A curse upon the fiery devil, thundering along so smoothly, tracked through the distant valley by a glare of light and lurid smoke, and gone! He felt as if he had been plucked out of its path, and saved from being torn asunder. It made him shrink and shudder even now, when its faintest hum was hushed, and when the lines of iron road he could trace in the moonlight, running to a point, were as empty and as silent as a desert.

"Unable to rest, and irresistibly attracted—or he thought so—to this road, he went out and lounged on the brink of it, marking the way the train had gone, by the yet smoking cinders that were lying in its track.

"After a lounge of some half hour in the direction by which it had disappeared, he turned and walked the other way—still keeping to the brink of the road—past the inn garden, and a long way down; looking curiously at the bridges, signals, lamps, and wondering when another devil would come by.

"A trembling of the ground, and quick vibration in his ears; a distant shriek; a dull light advancing, quickly changed to two red eyes, and a fierce fire, dropping glowing coals; an irresistible bearing on of a great roaring and dilating mass; a high wind, and a rattle—another come and gone, and he holding to a gate, as if to save himself!

"He waited for another, and for another. He walked back to his former point, and back again to that, and still, through the wearisome vision of his journey, looked for these approaching monsters. He loitered about the station, waiting until one should stay to call there; and when one did, and was detached for water, he stood parallel with it, watching its heavy wheels and brazen front, and thinking what a cruel power and might it had. Ugh! To see the great wheels slowly turning, and to think of being run down and crushed!

"Disordered with wine and want of rest—that want which nothing, although he was so weary, would appease—these ideas and objects assumed a diseased importance in his thoughts. When he went back to his room, which was not until near midnight, they still haunted him, and he sat listening for the coming of another.

"So in his bed, whither he repaired with no hope of sleep. He still lay listening; and when he felt the trembling and vibration, got up and went to the window, to watch (as he could from its position) the dull light changing to the two red eyes, and the fierce fire dropping glowing coals, and the rush of the giant as it fled past, and the track of glare and smoke along the valley.

"Then he would glance in the direction by which he intended to depart at sunrise, as there was no rest for him there; and would lie down again, to be troubled by the vision of his journey, and the old monotony of bells and wheels and horses' feet, until another came.

"This lasted all night. So far from resuming the mastery of himself, he seemed, if possible, to lose it more and more, as the night crept on. When the dawn appeared, he was still tormented with thinking, still postponing thought until he should be in a better state; the past, present, and future, all floated confusedly before him, and he had lost all power of looking steadily at any one of them." ¶DS 54

—*impact on country town:* " . . . the first discovery I made, was, that the Station had swallowed up the playing-field.

"It was gone. The two beautiful hawthorn-trees, the hedge, the turf, and all those buttercups and daisies, had given place to the stoniest of jolting roads: while, beyond the Station, an ugly dark monster of a tunnel kept its jaws open, as if it had swallowed them and were ravenous for more destruction. The coach that had carried me away, was melodiously called Timpson's Blue-Eyed Maid, and belonged to Timpson, at the coach-office up-street; the locomotive engine that had brought me back, was called severely No. 97, and belonged to S.E.R., and was spitting ashes and hot water over the blighted ground." UT/DT

—*junction:* " . . . there were so many Lines. Gazing down upon them from a bridge at the Junction, it was as if the concentrating Companies formed a great Industrial Exhibition of the works of extraordinary ground spiders that spun iron.

"And then so many of the Lines went such wonderful ways, so crossing and curving among one another, that the eye lost them. And then some of them appeared to start with the fixed intention of going five hundred miles, and all of a sudden gave it up at any insignificant barrier, or turned off into a workshop.

"And then others, like intoxicated men, went a little way very straight, and surprisingly slued round and came back again. And then others were so chock-full of trucks of coal, others were so blocked with trucks of casks, others were so gorged with trucks of ballast, others were so set apart for wheeled objects like immense iron cotton-reels: while others were so bright and clear, and others were so delivered over to rust and ashes and idle wheelbarrows out of work, with their legs in the air (looking much like their masters on strike), that there was no beginning, middle, or end to the bewilderment.

" . . . . Then was heard a distant ringing of bells and blowing of whistles. Then, puppet-looking heads of men popped out of boxes in perspective, and popped in again. Then, prodigious wooden razors, set up on end, began shaving the atmosphere. Then, several locomotive engines in several directions began to scream and be agitated. Then, along one avenue a train came in. Then, along another two trains appeared that didn't come in, but stopped without. Then, bits of trains broke off. Then, a struggling horse became involved with them. Then, the locomotives shared the bits of trains, and ran away with the whole." CS/MJ 2

"This crashing and clashing that the train was undergoing, and this coupling on to it of a multitude of new echoes, could mean nothing less than approach to the great station. It did mean nothing less. After some stormy flashes of town lightning, in the way of swift revelations of red brick blocks of houses, high red brick chimney-shafts, vistas of red brick railway-arches, tongues of fire, blocks of smoke, valleys of canal, and hills of coal, there came the thundering in at the journey's end." CS/MJ 2

"It was a Junction-Station, where the wooden razors before-mentioned shaved the air very often, and where the sharp electric-telegraph bell was in a very restless condition. All manner of cross-lines of rails came zig-zagging into it, like a Congress of iron vipers; and, a little way out of it, a pointsman in an elevated signal-box was constantly going through the motions of drawing immense quantities of beer at a public-house bar.

"In one direction, confused perspectives of embankments and arches were to be seen from the platform; in the other, the rails soon disentangled themselves into two tracks, and shot away under a bridge, and curved round a corner. Sidings were there, in which empty luggage-vans and cattle-boxes often butted against each other as if they couldn't agree; and warehouses were there, in which great quantities of goods seemed to have taken the veil (of the consistency of tarpaulin), and to have retired from the world without any hope of getting back to it.

"Refreshment-rooms were there; one, for the hungry and thirsty Iron Locomotives where their coke and water were ready, and of good quality, for they were dangerous to play tricks with; the other, for the hungry and thirsty human Locomotives, who might take what they could get . . . . " ¶LT 3

—*night:* "By night, in its unconscious state, the Station was not so much as visible. Something in the air, like an enterprising chemist's established in business on one of the boughs of Jack's beanstalk, was all that could be discerned of it under the stars. In a moment it would break out, a constellation of gas. In another moment, twenty rival chemists, on twenty rival beanstalks, came into existence. Then, the Furies would be seen, waving their lurid torches up and down the confused perspectives of embankments and arches—would be heard, too, wailing and shrieking. Then, the Station would be full of palpitating trains, as in the day; with the heightening difference that they were not so clearly seen as in the day, whereas the Station walls, starting forward under the gas, like a hippopotamus's eyes, dazzled the human locomotives with the sauce-bottle, the cheap music, the bedstead, the distorted range of buildings where the patent safes are made, the gentleman in the rain with the registered umbrella, the lady returning from the ball with the registered respirator, and all their other embellishments.

"And now, the human locomotives, creased as to their countenances and purblind as to their eyes, would swarm forth in a heap, addressing themselves to the mysterious urns and the much-injured women; while the iron locomotives, dripping fire and water, shed their steam about plentifully, making the dull oxen in their cages, with heads depressed, and foam hanging from their mouths as their red looks glanced fearfully at the surrounding terrors, seem as though they had been drinking at half-frozen waters and were hung with icicles. Through the same steam would be caught glimpses of their fellow-travellers, the sheep, getting their white kid faces together, away from the bars, and stuffing the interstices with trembling wool. Also, down among the wheels, of the man with the sledge-hammer, ringing the axles of the fast night-train; against whom the oxen have a misgiving that he is the man with the pole-axe who is to come by-and-by, and so the nearest of them try to get back, and get a purchase for a thrust at him through the bars.

"Suddenly, the bell would ring, the steam would stop with one hiss and a yell, the chemists on the beanstalks would be busy, the avenging Furies would bestir themselves, the fast night-train would melt from eye and ear, the other trains going their ways more slowly would be heard faintly rattling in the distance like old-fashioned watches running down, the sauce-bottle and cheap music retired from view, even the bedstead went to bed, and there was no such visible thing as the Station to vex the cool wind in its blowing, or perhaps the autumn lightning, as it found out the iron rails." ¶LT 3

—killer: "[James Carker] paid the money for his journey to the country-place he had thought of; and was walking to and fro, alone, looking along the lines of iron, across the valley in one direction, and towards a dark bridge near at hand in the other; when, turning in his walk, where it was bounded by one end of the wooden stage on which he paced up and down, he saw the man from whom he had fled; emerging from the door by which he himself had entered there. And their eyes met.

"In the quick unsteadiness of the surprise, he staggered, and slipped on to the road below him. But recovering his feet immediately, he stepped back a pace or two upon that road, to interpose some wider space between them, and looked at his pursuer, breathing short and quick.

"He heard a shout—another—saw the face change from its vindictive passion to a faint sickness and terror—felt the earth tremble—knew in a moment that the rush was come—uttered a shriek—looked round—saw the red eyes, bleared and dim, in the daylight, close upon him—was beaten down, caught up, and whirled away upon a jagged mill, that spun him round and round, and struck him limb from limb, and licked his stream of life up with its fiery heat, and cast his mutilated fragments in the air.

"When the traveller, who had been recognised, recovered from a swoon, he saw them bringing from a distance something covered, that lay heavy and still, upon a board, between four men, and saw that others drove some dogs away that sniffed upon the road, and soaked his blood up, with a train of ashes." DS 55

—nostalgia for the old way: "I was returning from Manchester to London by the Mail Train, when I suddenly fell into another train—a mixed train—of reflection, occasioned by the dejected and disconsolate demeanour of the Post Office Guard.

"We were stopping at some station where they take in water, when he dismounted slowly from the little box in which he sits in ghastly mockery of his old condition with pistol and blunderbuss beside him, ready to shoot the first highwayman (or railwayman) who shall attempt to stop the horses, which now travel (when they travel at all) inside and in a portable stable invented for the purpose—he dismounted, I say, slowly and sadly, from his post, and looking mournfully about him as if in dismal recollection of the old roadside public-house—the blazing fire—the glass of foaming ale—the buxom handmaid and admiring hanger-on of tap-room and stable, all honoured by his notice; and, retiring a little apart, stood leaning against a signal-post, surveying the engine with a look of combined affliction and disgust which no words can describe.

"His scarlet coat and golden lace were tarnished with ignoble smoke; flakes of soot had fallen on his bright green shawl—his pride in days of yore—the steam condensed in the tunnel from which we had just emerged, shone upon his hat like rain. His eye betokened that he was thinking of the coachman; and as it wandered to his own seat and his own fast-fading garb, it was plain to see that he felt his office and himself had alike no business there, and were nothing but an elaborate practical joke." ¶B/FE *And see —coach travel compared*

"In the same carriage with me there sat an ancient gentleman . . . who expressed himself most mournfully as to the ruinous effects and rapid spread of railways, and was most pathetic upon the virtues of the slow-going old stage coaches. Now I, entertaining some little lingering kindness for the road, made shift to express my concurrence with the old gentleman's opinion, without any great compromise of my own. Well, we got on tolerably comfortably together; and when the engine, with a frightful screech dived into the darkness, like some strange aquatic monster, the old gentleman said this would never do, and I agreed with him. When it parted from each successive station with a shock and a shriek, as if it had had a double tooth drawn, the old gentleman shook his head, and I shook mine. When he burst forth against such new fangled notions, and said that no good could come from them, I did not contest the point. But I invariably found that when the speed of the engine was abated, or there was the slightest prolongation of our stay at any station, the old gentleman was up in arms, and his watch was instantly out of his pocket, denouncing the slowness of our progress." S/BP

—right of way: "We went to look at [our old school], only this last Midsummer, and found that the Railway had cut it up root and branch. A great trunk-line had swallowed the playground, sliced away the schoolroom, and pared off the corner of the house; which, thus curtailed of its proportions, presented itself, in a green stage of stucco, profilewise towards the road, like a forlorn flat-iron without a handle, standing on end." RP/OS

—risk of Widow: "'It wos on the rail,' said Mr [Tony] Weller, with strong emphasis; 'I wos a goin' down to Birmingham by the rail, and I wos locked up in a close carriage vith a living widder. Alone ve wos; the widder and me wos alone; and I believe it wos only because ve *wos* alone and there wos no clergyman in the conwayance, that that 'ere widder didn't marry me afore ve reached the half-way station. Ven I think how she began a screaming as ve wos a goin' under them tunnels in the dark—how she kept on a faintin' and ketchin' hold o' me—and how I trued to bust open the door as was tight-locked and perwented all escape—Ah! It was a awful thing, most awful!' . . .

"'I con-sider,' said Mr Weller, 'that the rail is unconstitootional and an inwaser o' priwileges, and I should wery much like to know what there 'ere old Carter* as once stood up for our liberties and wun 'em too—I should like to know wot he vould say, if he wos alive now, to Englishmen being locked up vith widders, or vith anybody again their wills.'" MH 11

**The reference is probably to the well-known carrier, Magna Carter.*

—spur: "In those days there was no railway to Cloisterham, and Mr Sapsea said there never would be. Mr Sapsea said more; he said there never should be. And yet, marvellous to consider, it has come to pass, in these days, that Express Trains don't think Cloisterham worth stopping at, but yell and whirl through it on their larger errands, casting the dust off their wheels as a testimony against its insignificance. Some remote fragment of Main Line to somewhere else, there was, which was going to ruin the Money Market if it failed, and Church and State if it succeeded, and (of course), the Constitution, whether or no; but even that had already so unsettled Cloisterham traffic, that the traffic, deserting the high road, came sneaking in from an unprecedented part of the country by a back stable-way, for many years labelled at the corner: 'Beware of the Dog.'" MED 6

—station stop: "The seizure of the station

with a fit of trembling, gradually deepening to a complaint of the heart, announced the train. Fire and steam, and smoke, and red light; a hiss, a crash, a bell, and a shriek; Louisa put into one carriage, Mrs Sparsit put into another: the little station a desert speck in the thunderstorm." HT ii 11

—*symbol of progress:* "Good heaven, is the house falling! Is there an earthquake in Spitalfields! Has a volcano burst out in the heart of London! What is this appalling rush and tremble?

"It is only the railroad.

"The arches of the railroad span the house; the wires of the electric telegraph stretch over the confined scene of [the weaver's] daily life; the engines fly past him on their errands, and outstrip the birds; and what can the man of prejudice and usage hope for, but to be overthrown and flung into oblivion! Look to it, gentlemen of precedent and custom standing, daintily opposed to progress, in the bag-wigs and embroidered coats of another generation, you may learn from the weaver in his shirt and trousers!" HWC/S

—*terminus before dawn:* "When there was no market, or when I wanted variety, a railway terminus with the morning mails coming in, was remunerative company. But like most of the company to be had in this world, it lasted only a very short time. The station lamps would burst out ablaze, the porters would emerge from places of concealment, the cabs and trucks would rattle to their places (the post-office carts were already in theirs), and, finally, the bell would strike up, and the train would come banging in. But there were few passengers and little luggage, and everything scuttled away with the greatest expedition. The locomotive post-offices, with their great nets—as if they had been dragging the country for bodies—would fly open as to their doors, and would disgorge a smell of lamp, an exhausted clerk, a guard in a red coat, and their bags of letters; the engine would blow and heave and perspire, like an engine wiping its forehead and saying what a run it had had; and within ten minutes the lamps were out, and I was houseless and alone again." UT/NW

—*and Time of Day:* "In the old state of the neighbourhood, if any young party was sent to the Norwich Castle to see what o'clock it was, the solid information would be brought back—say, for the sake of argument, twenty minutes to twelve. The smallest child in the neighbourhood who can tell the clock, is now convinced that it hasn't time to say twenty minutes to twelve, but comes back and jerks out, like a little Bradshaw,'Eleven forty.' Eleven forty!" HW/UN

—*wires:* "All the journey, immovable in the air though never left behind; plain to the dark eyes of [Mrs Sparsit's] mind, as the electric wires which ruled a colossal strip of music-paper out of the evening sky . . . . " HT ii 11

Ship

—*sailing*

—*cargo:* "'Think of this wine, for instance, said old Sol, 'which has been to the East Indies and back, I'm not able to say how often, and has been once round the world Think of the pitch-dark nights, the roaring winds, and rolling seas:'

"'The thunder, lightning, rain, hail, storm of all kinds,' said the boy.

"'To be sure,' said Solomon—'that this wine has passed through. Think what a straining and creaking of timbers and masts: what a whistling and howling of the gale through ropes and rigging:'

"'What a clambering aloft of men, vying with each other who shall lie out first upon the yards to furl the icy sails, while the ship rolls and pitches, like mad!' cried his nephew.

"'Exactly so,' said Solomon: 'has gone on, over the old cask that held this wine.'" DS 4

—*destroyed by storm:* "'That there unfort'nate ship met with such foul weather, out at sea [said Captain Cuttle], as don't blow once in twenty year, my darling. There was hurricanes ashore as tore up forests and blowed down towns, and there was gales at sea in them latitudes, as not the stoutest wessel ever launched could live in. Day arter day that there unfort'nate ship behaved noble, I'm told, and did her duty brave, my pretty, but at one blow a'most her bulwarks was stove in, her masts and rudder carried away, her best men swept overboard, and she left to the mercy of the storm as had no mercy but blowed harder and harder yet, while the waves dashed over her, and beat her in, and every time they come a thundering at her, broke her like a shell. Every black spot in every mountain of water that rolled away was a bit o' the ship's life or a living man, and so she went to pieces, Beauty, and no grass will never grow upon the graves of them as manned that ship.'" DS 49

—figure-head: " . . . it reached from floor to ceiling; and thrusting itself forward with that excessively wide-awake aspect, and air of somewhat obtrusive politeness, by which figure-heads are usually characterized, seemed to reduce everything else to mere pigmy proportions." OCS 62

—organizing to depart: "And the Son and Heir was in a pretty state of confusion, with sails lying all bedraggled on the wet decks, loose ropes tripping people up, men in red shirts running barefoot to and fro, casks blockading every foot of space, and, in the thickest of the fray, a black cook in a black caboose up to his eyes in vegetables and blinded with smoke." DS 19

—rigging: " . . . this great commander's ship was jammed in among some five hundred companions, whose tangled rigging looked like monstrous cobwebs half swept down . . . . " DS 23

—under way: "At length and at last, the promised wind came up in right good earnest, and away we went before it, with every stitch of canvas set, slashing through the water nobly. There was a grandeur in the motion of the splendid ship, as overshadowed by her mass of sails, she rode at a furious pace upon the waves, which filled one with an indescribable sense of pride and exultation.

"As she plunged into a foaming valley, how I loved to see the green waves, bordered deep with white, come rushing on astern, to buoy her upward at their pleasure, and curl about her as she stooped again, but always own her for their haughty mistress still!

"On, on we flew, with changing lights upon the water, being now in the blessed region of fleecy skies; a bright sun lighting us by day, and bright moon by night; the vane pointing directly homeward, alike the truthful index to the favouring wind and to our cheerful hearts . . . . " AN 16

—steam

—arrival: "The steamer, which, with its machinery on deck, looked, as it worked its long slim legs, like some enormously magnified insect or antediluvian monster—dashed at great speed up a beautiful bay; and presently they saw some heights, and islands, and a long, flat, straggling city." MC 15

—cabin: "I shall never forget the one-fourth serious and three-fourths comical astonishment, with which, on the morning of the third of January eighteen-hundred-and-forty-two, I opened the door of, and put my head into, a 'state-room' on board the 'Britannia' steam-packet [paddle-wheeler], twelve hundred tons burthen per register, bound for Halifax and Boston, and carrying Her Majesty's mails.

"That this state-room had been specially engaged for 'Charles Dickens, Esquire, and Lady,' was rendered sufficiently clear even to my scared intellect by a very small manuscript, announcing the fact, which was pinned on a very flat quilt, covering a very thin mattress, spread like a surgical plaster on a most inaccessible shelf. But that this was the state-room concerning which Charles Dickens, Esquire, and Lady, had held daily and nightly conferences for at least four months preceding: that this could by any possibility be that small snug chamber of the imagination, which Charles Dickens, Esquire, with the spirit of prophecy strong upon him, had always foretold would contain at least one little sofa, and which his lady, with a modest yet most magnificent sense of its limited dimensions, had from the first opined would not hold more than two enormous portmanteaus in some odd corner out of sight (portmanteaus which could now no more be got in at the door, not to say stowed away, than a giraffe could be persuaded or forced into a flower-pot): that this utterly impracticable, thoroughly hopeless, and profoundly preposterous box, had the remotest reference to, or connexion with, those chaste and pretty, not to say gorgeous little bowers, sketched by a masterly hand, in the highly varnished lithographic plan hanging up in the agent's counting-house in the city of London; that this room of state, in short, could be anything but a pleasant fiction and cheerful jest of the captain's, invented and put in practice for the better relish and enjoyment of the real state-room presently to be disclosed:—these were truths which I really could not, for the moment, bring my mind at all to bear upon or comprehend. And I sat down upon a kind of horsehair slab, or perch, of which there were two within; and looked, without any expression of countenance whatever, at some friends who had come on board with us, and who were crushing their faces into all manner of shapes by endeavouring to squeeze them through the small doorway." AN 1

—a gale: " . . . what the agitation of a steam-vessel is, on a bad winter's night in the wild Atlantic, it is impossible for the most vivid imagination to conceive. To say that she is flung down on her side in the waves, with her masts dipping into them, and that, springing up again, she rolls over on the other side, until a heavy sea strikes her with the noise of a hundred great guns, and hurls her back—that she stops, and staggers, and shivers, as though stunned, and then, with a violent throbbing at her heart, darts onward like a monster goaded into madness, to be beaten down, and battered, and crushed, and leaped on by the angry sea—that thunder, lightning, hail, and rain, and wind, are all in fierce contention for the mastery—that every plank has its groan, every nail its shriek, and every drop of water in the great ocean its howling voice—is nothing. To say that all is grand, and all appalling and horrible in the last degree, is nothing. Words cannot express it. Thoughts cannot convey it. Only a dream can call it up again, in all its fury, rage, and passion." AN 2

—after a gale: "Of the outrageous antics performed by that ship next morning, which made bed a practical joke, and getting up, by any process short of falling out, an impossibility, I say nothing . . . In the gale of last night the lifeboat had been crushed by one blow of the sea, like a walnut-shell; and there it hung dangling in the air, a mere fagot of crazy boards. The planking of the paddle-boxes had been torn sheer away. The wheels were exposed and bare; and they whirled and dashed their spray about the decks at random. Chimney white with crusted salt; topmast struck; storm-sails set; rigging all knotted, tangled, wet, and drooping; a gloomier picture it would be hard to look upon." AN 2

—in harbour: "There they lay, alongside of each other; hard and fast for ever, to all appearance, but designing to get out somehow, and quite confident of doing it; and in that faith shoals of passengers, and heaps of luggage, were proceeding hurriedly on board. Little steam-boats dashed up and down the stream incessantly. Tiers upon tiers of vessels, scores of masts, labyrinths of tackle, idle sails, splashing oars, gliding row-boats, lumbering barges, sunken piles, with ugly lodgings for the water-rat within their mud-discoloured nooks; church steeples, warehouses, house-roofs, arches, bridges, men and women, children, casks, cranes, boxes, horses, coaches, idlers, and hard-labourers: there they were, all jumbled up together . . . .

"In the midst of all this turmoil, there was an incessant roar from every packet's funnel, which quite expressed and carried out the uppermost emotion of the scene. They all appeared to be perspiring and bothering themselves, exactly as their passengers did; they never left off fretting and chafing, in their own hoarse manner, once; but were always panting out, without any stops, 'Come along do make haste I'm very nervous come along oh good gracious we shall never get there how late you are do make haste I'm off directly come along!' Even when they had left off, and had got safely out into the current, on the smallest provocation they began again: for the bravest packet of them all, being stopped by some entanglement in the river, would immediately begin to fume and pant afresh, 'Oh here's a stoppage what's the matter do go on there I'm in a hurry it's done on purpose did you ever oh my goodness *do* go on here!' and so, in a state of mind bordering on distraction, would be last seen drifting slowly through the mist into the summer light beyond, that made it red." MC 40

—a head-wind: "'Rather a heavy sea on, Sir, and a head-wind.'

"A head-wind! Imagine a human face upon the vessel's prow, with fifteen thousand Samsons in one bent upon driving her back, and hitting her exactly between the eyes whenever she attempts to advance an inch. Imagine the ship herself, with every pulse and artery of her huge body swollen and bursting under this maltreatment, sworn to go on or die. Imagine the wind howling, the sea roaring, the rain beating: all in furious array against her. Picture the sky both dark and wild, and the clouds, in fearful sympathy with the waves, making another ocean in the air. Add to all this, the clattering on deck and down below; the tread of hurried feet; the loud hoarse shouts of seamen; the gurgling in and out of water through the scuppers; with, every now and then, the striking of a heavy sea upon the planks above, with the deep, dead, heavy sound of thunder heard within a vault;—and there is the head-wind of that January morning." AN 2

—heavy weather: "Everything sloped the wrong way . . . . I had left the door open, a moment before, in the bosom of a gentle declivity, and, when I turned to shut it, it

was on the summit of a lofty eminence. Now every plank and timber creaked, as if the ship were made of wicker-work; and now crackled, like an enormous fire of the driest possible twigs . . . . The water-jug is plunging and leaping like a lively dolphin; all the smaller articles are afloat, except my shoes, whch are stranded on a carpet-bag, high and dry, like a couple of coal-barges. Suddenly I see them spring into the air, and behold the looking-glass, which is nailed to the wall, sticking fast upon the ceiling. At the same time the door entirely disappears, and a new one is opened in the floor. Then I begin to comprehend that the state-room is standing on its head.

"Before it is possible to make any arrangement at all compatible with this novel state of things, the ship rights. Before one can say 'Thank Heaven!' she wrongs again. Before one can cry she *is* wrong, she seems to have started forward, and to be a creature actually running of its accord, with broken knees and failing legs, through every variety of hole and pitfall, and stumbling constantly. Before one can so much as wonder, she takes a high leap into the air. Before she has well done that, she takes a deep dive into the water. Before she has gained the surface, she throws a summerset. The instant she is on her legs, she rushes backward. And so she goes on staggering, heaving, wrestling, leaping, diving, jumping, pitching, throbbing, rolling, and rocking: and going through all these movements, sometimes by turns, and sometimes altogether: until one feels disposed to roar for mercy." AN 2

—Irish: "'We have some splendid steam-vessels in Ireland,' said O'Bleary.

"'Certainly,' said Mrs Bloss, delighted to find a subject broached in which she could take part.

"'The accommodations are extraordinary,' said O'Bleary.

"'Extraordinary indeed,' returned Mrs Bloss. 'When Mr Bloss was alive, he was promiscuously obligated to go to Ireland on business. I went with him, and raly the manner in which the ladies and gentlemen were accommodated with berths, is not creditable.'" SB/BH

—lake: "She was a large vessel of five hundred tons, and handsomely fitted up, though with high-pressure engines; which always conveyed that kind of feeling to me, which I should be likely to experience, I think, if I had lodgings on the first-floor of a powder-mill." AN 14

"There is one American boat . . . superior . . . to any other in the world. This steamboat, which is called 'The Burlington,' is a perfectly exquisite achievement of neatness, elegance, and order. The decks are drawing-rooms; the cabins are boudoirs, choicely furnished and adorned with prints, pictures, and musical instruments; every nook and corner in the vessel is a perfect curiosity of graceful comfort and beautiful contrivance.

"Captain **Sherman**, her commander, to whose ingenuity and excellent taste these results are solely attributable, has bravely and worthily distinguished himself on more than one trying occasion: not least among them, in having the moral courage to carry British troops, at a time (during the Canadian rebellion) when no other conveyance was open to them. He and his vessel are held in universal respect, both by his countrymen and ours; and no man ever enjoyed the popular esteem, who, in his sphere of action, won and wore it better than this gentleman." ¶AN 15

—midwife's protest: "'Oh drat you' said Mrs Gamp, shaking her umbrella at it, 'you're a nice spluttering nisy monster for a delicate young creetur to go and be a passenger by; an't you? *You* never do no harm in that way, do you? With your hammering, and roaring, and hissing, and lamp-iling, you brute! Them Confugion steamers,' said Mrs Gamp, shaking her umbrella again, 'has done more to throw us out of our reg'lar work and bring ewents on at times when nobody counted on 'em (especially them screeching railroad ones) than all the other frights that ever was took.

"'I have heerd of one young man, a guard upon a railway, only three years opened—well does Mrs Harris know him, which indeed he is her own relation by her sister's marriage with a master sawyer—as is godfather at this present time to six-and-twenty blessed little strangers, equally unexpected, and all on 'em named after the Ingeins as was the cause. Ugh!' said Mrs Gamp, resuming her apostrophe, 'one might easy know you was a man's invention, from your disregardlessness of the weakness of our naturs, so one might, you brute!'

"It would not have been unnatural to suppose, from the first part of Mrs Gamp's lamentations, that she was connected with the stage-coaching or post-horsing trade.

She had no means of judging of the effect of her concluding remarks upon her young companion; for she interrupted herself at this point, and exclaimed:

"'There she identically goes! Poor sweet young creetur, there she goes, like a lamb to the sacrifige! If there's any illness when that wessel gets to sea,' said Mrs Gamp, prophetically, 'it's murder, and I'm the witness for the persecution.'" MC 40

—at night: " . . . 'turning in'—no sailor of seven hours' experience talks of going to bed—became the order of the night. The perpetual tramp of boot-heels on the decks gave place to a heavy silence, and the whole human freight was stowed away below . . . .

" . . . . The gloom through which the great black mass holds its direct and certain course; the rushing water, plainly heard, but dimly seen; the broad, white, glistening track, that follows in the vessel's wake; the men on the lookout forward, who would be scarcely visible against the dark sky, but for their blotting out some score of glistening stars; the helmsman at the wheel, with the illuminated card before him, shining, a speck of light amidst the darkness, like something sentient and of Divine intelligence; the melancholy sighing of the wind through block, and rope, and chain; the gleaming forth of light from every crevice, nook, and tiny piece of glass about the decks, as though the ship were filled with fire in hiding, ready to burst through any outlet, wild with its resistless power of death and ruin." AN 2

And see M:Associations, mental—*at sea*

—ocean: "And now, lying down again, awaiting the season for broiled ham and tea, I would be compelled to listen to the voice of conscience—the screw [propeller].

It might be, in some cases, no more than the voice of stomach; but I called it in my fancy by the higher name. Because it seemed to me that we were all of us, all day long, endeavouring to stifle the voice. Because it was under everybody's pillow, everybody's plate, everybody's camp-stool, everybody's book, everybody's occupation.

"Because we pretended not to hear it, especially at meal-times, evening whist, and morning conversation on deck; but it was always among us in an under monotone, not to be drowned in pea-soup, not to be shuffled with cards, not to be diverted by books, not to be knitted into any pattern, not to be walked away from.

"It was smoked in the weediest cigar, and drunk in the strongest cocktail; it was conveyed on deck at noon with limp ladies, who lay there in their wrappers until the stars shone; it waited at table with the stewards; nobody could put it out with the lights. It was considered (as on shore) ill-bred to acknowledge the voice of conscience. It was not polite to mention it. One squally day an amiable gentleman in love gave much offence to a surrounding circle, including the object of his attachment, by saying of it, after it had goaded him over two easy-chairs and a skylight, 'Screw!'

"Sometimes it would appear subdued. In fleeting moments, when bubbles of champagne pervaded the nose, or when there was 'hot pot' in the bill of fare, or when an old dish we had had regularly every day was described in that official document by a new name—under such excitements, one would almost believe it hushed.

"The ceremony of washing plates on deck, performed after every meal by a circle as of ringers of crockery triple-bob majors for a prize, would keep it down. Hauling the reel, taking the sun at noon, posting the twenty-four hours' run, altering the ship's time by the meridian, casting the waste food overboard, and attracting the eager gulls that followed in our wake—these events would suppress it for a while. But the instant any break or pause took place in any such diversion, the voice would be at it again, importuning us to the last extent . . . .

"When this terrible monitor was most severe with us was when the time approached for our retiring to our dens for the night; when the lighted candles in the saloon grew fewer and fewer; when the deserted glasses with spoons in them grew more and more numerous; when waifs of toasted cheese and strays of sardines fried in batter slid languidly to and fro in the table-racks . . . then, as we fell off one by one, and, entering our several hutches, came into a peculiar atmosphere of bilge-water and Windsor soap, the voice would shake us to the centre . . . .

"Lights out, we in our berths, and the wind rising, the voice grows angrier and deeper. Under the mattress and under the pillow, under the sofa and under the washing-stand, under the ship and under the sea, seeming to rise from the foundations under the earth with every scoop of the great Atlantic (and oh! why scoop so?), always the voice.

"Vain to deny its existence in the night season; impossible to be hard of hearing; screw, screw, screw! Sometimes it lifts out of the water, and revolves with a whirr, like a ferocious firework—except that it never expends itself, but is always ready to go off again; sometimes it seems to be in anguish, and shivers; sometimes it seems to be terrified by its last plunge, and has a fit which causes it to struggle, quiver, and for an instant stop. And now the ship sets in rolling, as only ships so fiercely screwed through time and space, day and night, fair weather and foul, *can* roll." ¶UT/AS

And see Travel—*sea voyage*

—*passengers:* "Packing-cases, portmanteaus, carpet-bags, and boxes are already passed from hand to hand, and hauled on board with breathless rapidity. The officers, smartly dressed, are at the gangway, handing the passengers up the side, and hurrying the men. In five minutes' time the little steamer is utterly deserted, and the packet is beset and overrun by its late freight, who instantly pervade the whole ship, and are to be met with by the dozen in every nook and corner: swarming down below with their own baggage, and stumbling over other people's; disposing themselves comfortably in wrong cabins, and creating a most horrible confusion by having to turn out again; madly bent upon opening locked doors, and on forcing a passage into all kinds of out-of-the way places, where there is no thoroughfare: sending wild stewards with elfin hair to and fro upon the breezy decks on unintelligible errands, impossible of execution; and, in short, creating the most extraordinary and bewildering tumult." AN 1

—*river:* " . . . these western vessels are . . . foreign to all the ideas we are accustomed to entertain of boats. I hardly know what to liken them to, or how to describe them.

"In the first place, they have no mast, cordage, tackle, rigging, or other such boat-like gear; nor have they anything in their shape at all calculated to remind one of a boat's head, stern, sides, or keel. Except that they are in the water, and display a couple of paddle-boxes, they might be intended, for anything that appears to the contrary, to perform some unknown service, high and dry, upon a mountain top.

"There is no visible deck, even: nothing but a long, black, ugly roof, covered with burn-out feathery sparks; above which tower two iron chimneys, and a hoarse escape valve, and a glass steerage-house. Then, in order as the eye descends towards the water, are the sides, and doors, and windows of the state-rooms, jumbled as oddly together as though they formed a small street, built by the varying tastes of a dozen men: the whole is supported on beams and pillars resting on a dirty barge, but a few inches above the water's edge: and in the narrow space between this upper structure and this barge's deck, are the furnace fires and machinery, open at the sides to every wind that blows, and every storm of rain it drives along its path.

"Passing one of these boats at night, and seeing the great body of fire, exposed as I have just described, that rages and roars beneath the frail pile of painted wood: the machinery, not warded off or guarded in any way, but doing its work in the midst of the crowd of idlers and emigrants and children, who throng the lower deck: under the management, too, of reckless men whose acquaintance with its mysteries may have been of six months' standing: one feels directly that the wonder is, not that there should be so many fatal accidents, but that any journey should be safely made." AN 1

" . . . we started for New York on board a great North River steamboat, which was so crowded with passengers that the upper deck was like the box lobby of a theatre between the pieces, and the lower one like Tottenham Court Road on a Saturday night." AN 15

—*saloon:* "Before descending into the bowels of the ship, we had passed from the deck into a long narrow apartment, not unlike a gigantic hearse with windows in the sides; having at the upper end a melancholy stove, at which three or four chilly stewards were warming their hands; while on either side, extending down its whole dreary length, was a long, long table, over each of which a rack, fixed to the low roof, and stuck full of drinking-glasses and cruet-stands, hinted dismally at rolling seas and heavy weather . . . the man in reply avowed the truth; the blunt, remorseless, naked truth; 'This is the saloon, Sir' . . . ." AN 1

And see Travel—*sea voyage*

Stage-coach

—*booking office:* "Here a painful consciousness of your own unimportance first rushes on your mind—the people are as cool and collected as if nobody were going out of town, or as if a journey of a hundred odd miles were a mere nothing. You enter a mouldy-looking room, ornamented with large posting-bills; the greater part of the place enclosed behind a huge lumbering rough counter, and fitted up with recesses that look like the dens of the smaller animals in a travelling menagerie, without the bars.

"Some half-dozen people are 'booking' brown-paper parcels, which one of the clerks flings into the aforesaid recesses with an air of recklessness which you, remembering the new carpet-bag you bought in the morning, feel considerably annoyed at; porters, looking like so many Atlases, keep rushing in and out, with large packages on their shoulders; and while you are waiting to make the necessary inquiries, you wonder what on earth the booking-office clerks can have been before they were booking-office clerks . . . .

"They are clearly an isolated race, evidently possessing no sympathies or feelings in common with the rest of mankind. Your turn comes at last, and having paid the fare, you tremblingly inquire—'What time will it be necessary for me to be here in the morning?'—'Six o'clock,' . . . 'Rather before than arter,' adds the man . . . with just as much ease and complacency as if the whole world got out of bed at five. You turn into the street, ruminating as you bend your steps homewards on the extent to which men become hardened in cruelty by custom." ¶SB/EC

—coachmen: special status: "'In short, Sammy [said Tony Weller], I feel that I ain't safe anyveres but on the box."

"'How are you safer there than anyveres else?' interrupted Sam [Weller].

"' 'Cos a coachman's a privileged indiwidual,' replied Mr Weller, looking fixedly at his son. ' 'Cos a coachman may do vithout suspicion wot other men may not; 'cos a coachman may be on the wery amicablest terms with eighty mile o' females, and yet nobody think that he ever means to marry any vun among 'em. And wot other man can say the same, Sammy?'

"'Vell, there's somethin' in that,' said Sam.

"'If your gov'ner had been a coachman,' reasoned Mr Weller, 'do you s'pose as that 'ere jury 'ud ever ha' conwicted him, s'posin' it possible as the matter could ha' gone to that extremity? They dustn't ha' done it.'

"'Wy not?' said Sam, rather disparagingly.

"'Wy not!' rejoined Mr Weller; ' 'cos it 'ud ha' gone agin their consciences. A reg'lar coachman's a sort o' connectin' link betwixt singleness and matrimony, and every practicable man knows it.'

"'Wot! You mean, they're gen'ral fav'rites, and nobody takes adwantage on 'em p'raps?' said Sam.

"His father nodded.

"'How it ever come to that 'ere pass,' resumed the parent Weller, 'I can't say. Wy it is that long-stage coachmen possess such insiniwations, and is alvays looked up to—adored I may say—by ev'ry young 'ooman in ev'ry town he vurks through, I don't know. I only know that so it is. It's a reg'lation of natur—a dispensary, as your poor mother-in-law used to say.'

"'A dispensation,' said Sam, correcting the old gentleman.

"'Wery good, Samivel, a dispensation, if you like it better,' returned Mr Weller; '*I* call it a dispensary, and it's alvays writ up so, at the places vere they gives you physic for nothin' in your own bottles; that's all.'" PP 52

—conveyances in France: "Then, there is the Diligence, twice or thrice a-day; with the dusty outsides in blue frocks, like butchers; and the insides in white nightcaps; and its cabriolet head on the roof, nodding and shaking, like an idiot's head; and its Young-France passengers staring out of window, with beards down to their waists, and blue spectacles awfully shading their warlike eyes, and very big sticks clenched in their National grasp. Also the Malle Poste, with only a couple of passengers, tearing along at a real good dare-devil place, and out of sight in no time." PI 2

—flight from the Terror: "'Look back, look back, and see if we are pursued!'

"'The road is clear, my dearest. So far, we are not pursued.'

"Houses in twos and threes pass by us, solitary farms, ruinous buildings, dye-works, tanneries, and the like, open country, avenues of leafless trees. The hard uneven pavement is under us, the soft deep mud is on either side. Sometimes, we strike into the skirting mud, to avoid the stones that clatter us and shake us; sometimes we stick in ruts and sloughs there. The agony of our impatience is then so great, that in our wild alarm and hurry we are for getting out and running—hiding—doing anything but stopping.

"Out of the open country, in again among ruinous buildings, solitary farms, dye-works, tanneries, and the like, cottages in twos and threes, avenues of leafless trees. Have these men deceived us, and taken us back by another road? Is not this the same place twice over? Thank Heaven, no. A village. Look back, look back, and see if we are pursued! Hush! the posting-house.

"Leisurely, our four horses are taken out; leisurely, the coach stands in the little street, bereft of horses, and with no likelihood upon it of ever moving again; leisurely, the new horses come into visible existence, one by one; leisurely, the new postilions follow, sucking and plaiting the lashes of their whips; leisurely, the old postilions count their money, make wrong additions, and arrive at dissatisfied results. All the time, our overfraught hearts are beating at a rate that would far outstrip the fastest gallop of the fastest horses ever foaled.

"At length the new postilions are in their saddles, and the old are left behind. We are through the village, up the hill, and down the hill, and on the low watery grounds. Suddenly, the postilions exchange speech with animated gesticulation, and the horses are pulled up, almost on their haunches. We are pursued?

"'Ho! Within the carriage there. Speak then!'

"'What is it?' asks Mr Lorry, looking out at window.

"'How many did they say?'

"'I do not understand you.'

"'—At the last post. How many to the Guillotine to-day?'

"'Fifty-two.'

"'I said so! A brave number! My fellow-citizen here would have it forty-two; ten more heads are worth having. The Guillotine goes handsomely. I love it. Hi forward. Whoop!'

"The night comes on dark. He [Darnay] moves more; he is beginning to revive, and to speak intelligibly; he thinks they are still together; he asks him, by his name, what he has in his hand. O pity us, kind Heaven, and help us! Look out, look out, and see if we are pursued.

"The wind is rushing after us, and the clouds are flying after us, and the moon is plunging after us, and the whole wild night is in pursuit of us; but, so far we are pursued by nothing else." TTC iii 13

—ghostly mail: "'My uncle . . . began to contemplate the mail coaches with a deal of gravity.

"'There might be a dozen of them . . .all huddled together in the most desolate condition imaginable. The doors had been torn from their hinges and removed; the linings had been stripped off: only a shred hanging here and there by a rusty nail; the lamps were gone, the poles had long since vanished, the iron-work was rusty, the paint was worn away; the wind whistled through the chinks in the bare wood work; and the rain, which had collected on the roofs, fell, drop by drop, into the insides with a hollow and melancholy sound. They were the decaying skeletons of departed mails, and in that lonely place, at that time of night, they looked chill and dismal.

"'My uncle rested his head upon his hands, and thought of the busy bustling people who had rattled about, years before, in the old coaches, and were now as silent and changed; he thought of the numbers of people to whom one of those crazy mouldering vehicles had borne, night after night, for many years, and through all weathers, the anxiously expected intelligence, the eagerly looked-for remittance, the promised assurance of health and safety, the sudden announcement of sickness and death. The merchant, the lover, the wife, the widow, the mother, the schoolboy, the very child who tottered to the door at the postman's knock—how had they all looked forward to the arrival of the old coach." PP 49

"'I wonder what these ghosts of mail coaches carry in their bags,' said the landlord, who had listened to the whole story [the Bagman's Uncle, continued] with profound attention.

"'The dead letters, of course,' said the Bagman.

"Oh, ah! To be sure,' rejoined the landlord. 'I never thought of that.'" PP 49

—to London from Salisbury: "The coach was none of your steady-going, yokel coaches, but a swaggering, rakish, dissipated London coach; up all night, and lying by all day, and leading a devil of a life. It cared no more for Salisbury than if it had been a hamlet. It rattled noisily through the best streets, defied the Cathedral, took the worst corners sharpest, went cutting in everywhere, making everything get out of its way; and spun

along the open country-road, blowing a lively defiance out of its key-bugle, as its last glad parting legacy.

" . . . . The four greys skimmed along, as if they liked it quite as well as Tom did; the bugle was in as high spirits as the greys; the coachman chimed in sometimes with his voice; the wheels hummed cheerfully in unison; the brass work on the harness was an orchestra of little bells; and thus, as they went clinking, jingling, rattling smoothly on, the whole concern, from the buckles of the leader's coupling-reins to the handle of the hind boot, was one great instrument of music.

"Yoho, past hedges, gates, and trees; past cottages and barns, and people going home from work. Yoho, past donkey-chaises, drawn aside into the ditch, and empty carts with rampant horses, shipped up at a bound upon the little watercourse, and held by struggling carters close to the five-barred gate, until the coach had passed the narrow turning in the road.

"Yoho, by churches dropped down by themselves in quiet nooks, with rustic burial-grounds about them, where the graves are green, and daisies sleep—for it is evening—on the bosoms of the dead. Yoho, past streams in which the cattle cool their feet, and where the rushes grow; past paddock-fences, farms, and rick-yards; past last year's stacks, cut, slice by slice, away, and showing, in the waning light, like ruined gables, old and brown. Yoho, down the pebbly dip, and through the merry water-splash, and up at a canter to the level road again. Yoho! Yoho! . . .

"Yoho, among the gathering shades; making of no account the deep reflections of the trees, but scampering on through light and darkness, all the same, as if the light of London fifty miles away, were quite enough to travel by, and some to spare.

"Yoho, beside the village-green, where cricket-players linger yet, and every little indentation made in the fresh grass by bat or wicket, ball or player's foot, sheds out its perfume on the night. Away with fresh horses from the Bald-faced Stag, where topers congregate about the door admiring; and the last team with traces hanging loose, go roaming off towards the pond, until observed and shouted after by a dozen throats, while volunteering boys pursue them. Now, with a clattering of hooves and striking out of fiery sparks, across the old stone bridge, and down again into the shadowy road, and through the open gate, and far away, away, into the world. Yoho! . . .

"Yoho, behind there, stop that bugle for a moment! Come creeping over to the front, along the coach-roof, guard, and make one at this basket! Not that we slacken in our pace the while, not we: we rather put the bits of blood upon their metal, for the greater glory of the snack. Ah! It is long since this bottle of old wine was brought into contact with the mellow breath of night, you may depend, and rare good stuff it is to wet a bugler's whistle with. Only try it. Don't be afraid of turning up your finger, Bill, another pull! Now, take your breath, and try the bugle, Bill. There's music! There's a tone! 'Over the hills and far away,' indeed. Yoho! The skittish mare is all alive tonight. Yoho! Yoho!

"See the bright moon! High up before we know it: making the earth reflect the objects on its breast like water. Hedges, trees, low cottages, church steeples, blighted stumps and flourishing young slips, have all grown vain upon the sudden, and mean to contemplate their own fair images till morning.

"The poplars yonder rustle that their quivering leaves may see themselves upon the ground. Not so the oak; trembling does not become *him;* and he watches himself in his stout old burly steadfastness, without the motion of a twig. The moss-grown gate, ill-poised upon its creaking hinges, crippled and decayed, swings to and fro before its glass, like some fantastic dowager; while our own ghostly likeness travels on, Yoho! Yoho! through ditch and brake, upon the ploughed land and the smooth, along the steep hill-side and steeper wall, as if it were a phantom-Hunter.

"Clouds too! And a mist upon the Hollow! Not a dull fog that hides it, but a light airy gauze-like mist, which in our eyes of modest admiration gives a new charm to the beauties it is spread before: as real gauze has done ere now, and would again, so please you, though we were the Pope. Yoho! Why now we travel like the Moon herself. Hiding this minute in a grove of trees; next minute in a patch of vapour; emerging now upon our broad clear course; withdrawing now, but always dashing on, our journey is a counterpart of hers. Yoho! A match against the Moon!

"The beauty of the night is hardly felt, when Day comes leaping up. Yoho! Two stages, and the country roads are almost changed into a continuous street. Yoho, past market-gardens, rows of houses, villas, crescents, terraces, and squares; past waggons, coaches, carts; past early workmen, late stragglers, drunken men, and sober carriers of loads; past brick and mortar in its every shape; and in among the rattling pavements, where a jaunty-seat upon a coach is not so easy to preserve! Yoho, down countless turnings, and through countless mazy ways, until an old Inn-yard is gained, and Tom Pinch, getting down, quite stunned and giddy, is in London!

"'Five minutes before the time, too!' said the driver, as he received his fee of Tom." ¶MC 36

—mail coach in 1775: "The Dover mail was in its usual genial position that the guard suspected the passengers, the passengers suspected one another and the guard, they all suspected everybody else, and the coachman was sure of nothing but the horses; as to which cattle he could with a clear conscience have taken his oath on the two Testaments that they were not fit for the journey." TTC i 2

—new-fangled in 1775: "There was no fear of old John [Willet] coming out. They could see him from the coach-roof fast asleep in his cosy bar. It was a part of John's character. He made a point of going to sleep at the coach's time. He despised gadding about; he looked upon coaches as things that ought to be indicted; as disturbers of the peace of mankind; as restless, bustling, busy, horn-blowing contrivances, quite beneath the dignity of men, and only suited to giddy girls that did nothing but chatter and go a-shopping.

"'We know nothing about coaches here, sir,' John would say, if any unlucky stranger made inquiry touching the offensive vehicles: 'we don't book for 'em; we'd rather not; they're more trouble than they're worth, with their noise and rattle. If you like to wait for 'em you can; but we don't know anything about 'em; they may call and they may not—there's a carrier—he was looked upon as quite good enough for us, when *I* was a boy.'" ¶BR 25

—by night: "The rest of the night wore away in the usual manner. Mr Pecksniff and Old Anthony [Chuzzlewit] kept tumbling against each other and waking up much terrified, or crushed their heads in opposite corners of the coach and strangely tattooed the surface of their faces—Heaven knows how—in their sleep. The coach stopped and went on, and went on and stopped, times out of number. Passengers got up and passengers got down, and fresh horses came and went and came again, with scarcely any interval between each team as it seemed to those who were dozing, and with a gap of a whole night between every one as it seemed to those who were broad awake. At length they began to jolt and rumble over horribly uneven stones, and Mr Pecksniff looking out of window said it was to-morrow morning, and they were there." MC 8

—in the old days: " . . . most of us have had experience of the extinct 'fast coaches', the 'Wonders', 'Taglionis', and 'Tallyhos', of other days . . . most of us remember certain modest post-chaises, dragging us down interminable roads through slush and mud, to little country towns with no visible populations except half a dozen men in smock frocks smoking pipes under the lee of the Town Hall; half a dozen women with umbrellas and pattens, and a washed-out dog or so shivering under the gables to complete the desolate picture." S/CT1

—punishment: "We have often wondered how many months' incessant travelling in a post-chaise it would take to kill a man; and wondering by analogy, we should very much like to know how many months of constant travelling in a succession of early coaches, an unfortunate mortal could endure. Breaking a man alive upon the wheel, would be nothing to breaking his rest, his peace, his heart—everything but his fast—upon four; and the punishment of *Ixion* (the only practical person, by-the-bye, who has discovered the secret of the perpetual motion) would sink into utter insignificance before the one we have suggested. If we had been a powerful churchman in those good times when blood was shed as freely as water, and man were mowed down like grass, in the sacred cause of religion, we would have lain by very quietly till we got hold of some especially obstinate miscreant, who positively refused to be converted to our faith, and then we would have booked him for an inside place in a small coach, which travelled day and night: and securing the remainder of the places for stout men with a slight tendency

to coughing and spitting, we would have started him forth on his last travels; leaving him mercilessly to all the tortures which the waiters, landlords, coachmen, guards, boots, chambermaids, and other familiars on his line of road, might think proper to inflict." SB/EC

—the Weller view: "'Coaches, Sammy, is like guns—they requires to be loaded with wery great care, afore they go off.'" PP 23

—a winter journey: "When I got up to the Peacock—where I found everybody drinking hot purl, in self-preservation—I asked if there were an inside seat to spare. I then discovered that, inside or out, I was the only passenger. This gave me a still livelier idea of the great inclemency of the weather, since that coach always loaded particularly well. However, I took a little purl (which I found uncommonly good), and got into the coach. When I was seated, they built me up with straw to the waist, and, conscious of making a rather ridiculous appearance, I began my journey.

"It was still dark when we left the Peacock. For a little while, pale, uncertain ghosts of houses and trees appeared and vanished, and then it was hard, black, frozen day. People were lighting their fires; smoke was mounting straight up high into the rarefied air; and we were rattling for Highgate Archway over the hardest ground I have ever heard the ring of iron shoes on.

"As we got into the country, everything seemed to have grown old and gray. The roads, the trees, thatched roofs of cottages and homesteads, the ricks in farmers' yards. Out-door work was abandoned, horse-troughs at roadside inns were frozen hard, no stragglers lounged about, doors were close shut, little turnpike houses had blazing fires inside, and children (even turnpike people have children, and seem to like them) rubbed the frost from the little panes of glass with their chubby arms, that their bright eyes might catch a glimpse of the solitary coaches going by.

"I don't know when the snow began to set in; but I know that we were changing horses somewhere when I heard the guard remark, 'That the old lady up in the sky was picking her geese pretty hard to-day.' Then, indeed, I found the white down falling fast and thick.

"The lonely day wore on, and I dozed it out, as a lonely traveller does. I was warm and valiant after eating and drinking—particularly after dinner; cold and depressed at all other times. I was always bewildered as to time and place, and always more or less out of my senses.

"The coach and horses seemed to execute in chorus Auld Lang Syne, without a moment's intermission. They kept the time and tune with the greatest regularity, and rose into the swell at the beginning of the Refrain, with a precision that worried me to death.

"While we changed horses, the guard and coachman went stumping up and down the road, printing off their shoes in the snow, and poured so much liquid consolation into themselves without being any the worse for it, that I began to confound them, as it darkened again, with two great white casks standing on end.

"Our horses tumbled down in solitary places, and we got them up—which was the pleasantest variety *I* had, for it warmed me. And it snowed and snowed, and still it snowed, and never left off snowing. All night long we went on in this manner. Thus we came round the clock, upon the Great North Road, to the performance of Auld Lang Syne all day again. And it snowed and snowed, and still it snowed, and never left off snowing.

"I forget now where we were at noon on the second day, and where we ought to have been; but I know that we were scores of miles behindhand, and that our case was growing worse every hour. The drift was becoming prodigiously deep; landmarks were getting snowed out; the road and the fields were all one; instead of having fences and hedge-rows to guide us, we went crunching on over an unbroken surface of ghastly white that might sink beneath us at any moment and drop us down a whole hillside. Still the coachman and guard—who kept together on the box, always in council, and looking well about them—made out the track with astonishing sagacity.

"When we came in sight of a town, it looked, to my fancy, like a large drawing on a slate, with abundance of slate-pencil expended on the churches and houses where the snow lay thickest. When we came within a town, and found the church clocks all stopped, the dial-faces choked with snow, and the inn-signs blotted out, it seemed as if the whole place were overgrown with white moss.

"As to the coach, it was a mere snowball; similarly, the men and boys who ran along beside us to the town's end, turning our clogged wheels and encouraging our horses, were men and boys of snow; and the bleak wild solitude to which they at last dismissed us was a snowy Sahara. One would have thought this enough: notwithstanding which, I pledge my word that it snowed and snowed, and still it snowed, and never left off snowing.

"We performed Auld Lang Syne the whole day; seeing nothing, out of towns and villages, but the track of stoats, hares, and foxes, and sometimes of birds. At nine o'clock at night, on a Yorkshire moor, a cheerful burst from our horn, and welcome sound of talking, with a glimmering and moving about of lanterns, roused me from my drowsy state. I found that we were going to change.

"They helped me out, and I said to a waiter, whose bare head became as white as King Lear's in a single minute, 'What Inn is this?'

"'The Holly-Tree, Sir,' said he.

"'Upon my word, I believe,' said I, apologetically, to the guard and coachman, 'that I must stop here.'" ¶CS/HT

Tourism

—Americans in Switzerland: "I made several American friends at that [Swiss] Inn, who all called Mont Blanc Mount Blank—except one good-humoured gentleman, of a very sociable nature, who became on such intimate terms with it that he spoke of it familiarly as 'Blank;' observing, at breakfast, 'Blank looks pretty tall this morning;' or considerably doubting in the courtyard in the evening, whether there warn't some go-ahead naters in our country, Sir, that would make out the top of Blank in a couple of hours from first start—now!" CS/HT 1

—blighting, in Rome: ". . . Little Dorrit would often ride out in a hired carriage that was left them, and alight alone and wander among the ruins of old Rome. The ruins of the vast old Amphitheatre, of the old Temples, of the old commemorative Arches, of the old trodden highways, of the old tombs, besides being what they were, to her, were ruins of the old Marshalsea—ruins of her own old life—ruins of the faces and forms that of old peopled it—ruins of its loves, hopes, cares, and joys. Two ruined spheres of action and suffering were before the solitary girl often sitting on some broken fragment; and in the lonely places, under the blue sky, she saw them both together.

"Up, then, would come Mrs General; taking all the colour out of everything, as Nature and Art had taken it out of herself; writing Prunes and Prism, in Mr **Eustace**'s text, wherever she could lay a hand; looking everywhere for Mr Eustace and company, and seeing nothing else; scratching up the driest little bones of antiquity, and bolting them whole without any human visitings—like a Ghoule in gloves." LD ii 15

—contrasting scenes, in Italy: ". . . there would be places where they stayed the week together, in splendid rooms, had banquets every day, rode out among heaps of wonders, walked through miles of palaces, and rested in dark corners of great churches; where there were winking lamps of gold and silver among pillars and arches, kneeling figures dotted about at confessionals and on the pavements; where there was the mist and scent of incense; where there were pictures, fantastic images, gaudy altars, great heights and distances, all softly lighted through stained glass, and the massive curtains that hung in the doorways.

"From these cities they would go on again, by the roads of vines and olives, through squalid villages where there was not a hovel without a gap in its filthy walls, not a window with a whole inch of glass or paper; where there seemed to be nothing to support life, nothing to eat, nothing to make, nothing to grow, nothing to hope, nothing to do but die.

"Again they would come to whole towns of palaces, whose proper inmates were all banished, and which were all changed into barracks: troops of idle soldiers leaning out of the state windows, where their accoutrements hung drying on the marble architecture, and showing to the mind like hosts of rats who were (happily) eating away the props of the edifices that supported them, and must soon, with them, be smashed on the heads of the other swarms of soldiers, and the swarms of priests, and the swarms of spies, who were all the ill-looking population left to be ruined, in the streets below." LD ii 3

And see W:Italy and things Italian, *passim.*

—English in Italy: "We often encountered, in these expeditions, a compay of English Tourists, with whom I had an ardent, but ungratified longing, to establish a speaking acquaintance. They were one Mr Davis, and a small circle of friends. It was impossible not to know Mrs Davis's name, from her being always in great request among her party, and her party being everywhere. During the Holy Week, they were in every part of every scene of every ceremony. For a fortnight or three weeks before it, they were in every tomb, and every church, and every ruin, and every Picture Gallery; and I hardly ever observed Mrs Davis to be silent for a moment. Deep underground, high up in St Peter's, out on the Campagna, and stifling in the Jews' quarter, Mrs Davis turned up, all the same.

"I don't think she saw anything, or ever looked at anything; and she had always lost something out of a straw hand-basket, and was trying to find it, with all her might and main, among an immense quantity of English halfpence, which lay, like sands on the sea-shore, at the bottom of it.

"There was a professional Cicerone always attached to the party (which had been brought over from London, fifteen or twenty strong, by contract) and if he so much as looked at Mrs Davis, she invariably cut him short by saying, 'There, God bless the man, don't worrit me! I don't understand a word you say, and shouldn't if you was to talk till you was black in the face!'

"Mr Davis always had a snuff-coloured great-coat on, and carried a great green umbrella in his hand, and had a slow curiosity constantly devouring him, which prompted him to do extraordinary things, such as taking the covers off urns in tombs, and looking in at the ashes as if they were pickles—and tracing out inscriptions with the ferrule of his umbrella, and saying, with intense thoughtfulness, 'Here's a B you see, and there's a R, and this is the way we goes on in; is it?' His antiquarian habits occasioned his being frequently in the rear of the rest; and one of the agonies of Mrs Davis, and the party in general, was an ever-present fear that Davis would be lost. This caused them to scream for him, in the strangest places, and at the most improper seasons. And when he came, slowly emerging out of some sepulchre or other, like a peaceful Ghoul, saying 'Here I am!' Mrs Davis invariably replied, 'You'll be buried alive in a foreign country, Davis, and it's no use trying to prevent you!'

"Mr and Mrs Davis, and their party, had, probably, been brought from London in about nine or ten days. Eighteen hundred years ago, the Roman legions under Claudius, protested against being led into Mr and Mrs Davis's country, urging that it lay beyond the limits of the world." PI 11

—guide-books: "We have [at Boulogne] an old walled town, rich in cool public wells of water, on the top of a hill within and above the present business-town; and if it were some hundreds of miles further from England, instead of being, on a clear day, within sight of the grass growing in the crevices of the chalk-cliffs of Dover, you would long ago have been bored to death about that town. It is more picturesque and quaint than half the innocent places which tourists, following their leader like sheep, have made impostors. To say nothing of its houses with grave courtyards, its queer by-corners, and its many-windowed streets white and quiet in the sunlight, there is an ancient belfry in it that would have been in all the Annuals and Albums, going and gone, these hundred years, if it had but been more expensive to get at.

"Happily it has escaped so well, being only in our French watering-place, that you may like it of your own accord in a natural manner, without being required to go into convulsions about it. We regard it as one of the later blessings of our life, that BILKINS, the only authority on Taste, never took any notice that we can find out, of our French watering-place. Bilkins never wrote about it, never pointed out anything to be seen in it, never measured anything in it, always left it alone. For which relief, Heaven bless the town and the memory of the immortal Bilkins likewise!" RP/FW

—led by wisdom: "Everybody was walking about St Peter's and the Vatican on somebody else's cork legs, and straining every visible object through somebody else's sieve. Nobody said what anything was, but everybody said what the Mrs Generals, Mr **Eustace**, or somebody else said it was. The whole body of travellers seemed to be a collection of voluntary human sacrifices,

bound hand and foot, and delivered over to Mr Eustace and his attendants, to have the entrails of their intellects arranged according to the taste of that sacred priesthood. Through the rugged remains of temples and tombs and palaces and senate halls and theatres and amphitheatres of ancient days, hosts of tongue-tied and blindfolded moderns were carefully feeling their way, incessantly repeating Prunes and Prism, in the endeavour to set their lips according to the received form. Mrs General was in her pure element. Nobody had an opinion. There was a formation of surface going on around her on an amazing scale, and it had not a flaw of courage or honest free speech in it." LD ii 7

And see: H:"Society"—*abroad*

—*mementos:* "Of articles collected on [Mr Meagles's] various expeditions, there was such a vast miscellany that it was like the dwelling of an amiable Corsair. There were antiquities from Central Italy, made by the best modern houses in that department of industry; bits of mummy from Egypt (and perhaps Birmingham); model gondolas from Venice; model villages from Switzerland; morsels of tesselated pavement from Herculaneum and Pompeii, like petrified minced veal; ashes out of tombs, and lava out of Vesuvius; Spanish fans, Spezzian straw hats, Moorish slippers, Tuscan hair-pins, Carrara Sculpture, Trastaverini scarves, Genoese velvets and filagree, Neapolitan coral, Roman cameos, Geneva jewellery, Arab lanterns, rosaries blest all round by the Pope himself, and an infinite variety of lumber." LD i 16

And see H:Artists and their work—*tourist's acquisitions*

Travel

—*artifacts as proxy:* "'If I have not gone to foreign countries, young man, foreign countries have come to me [said Sapsea]. They have come to me in the way of business, and I have improved upon my opportunities. Put it that I take an inventory, or make a catalogue. I see a French clock. I never saw him before, in my life, but I instantly lay my finger on him and say "Paris!" I see some cups and saucers of Chinese make, equally strangers to me personally: I put my finger on them, then and there, and I say "Pekin, Nankin, and Canton." It is the same with Japan, with Egypt, and with bamboo and sandal-wood from the East Indies; I put my finger on them all. I have put my finger on the North Pole before now, and said "Spear of Esquimaux make, for half a pint of pale sherry"'" MED 4

—*to Dover:* "Next morning's sun saw Mr Dorrit's equipage upon the Dover road, where every red-jacketed postilion was the sign of a cruel house, established for the unmerciful plundering of travellers. The whole business of the human race between London and Dover, being spoliation, Mr Dorrit was waylaid at Dartford, pillaged at Gravesend, rifled at Rochester, fleeced at Sittingbourne, and sacked at Canterbury. However, it being the Courier's business to get him out of the hands of the banditti, the Courier bought him off at every stage; and so the red-jackets went gleaming merrily along the spring landscape, rising and falling to a regular measure, between Mr Dorrit in his snug corner, and the next chalky rise in the dusty highway." LD ii 18

—*expendables:* "'Going away, Walter!' said Florence.

"'Yes, Miss Dombey,' he replied, but not so hopefully as he endeavoured: 'I have a voyage before me.'

"'And your uncle,' said Florence, looking back at Solomon. 'He is sorry you are going, I am sure. Ah! I see he is! Dear Walter, I am very sorry too.'

"'Goodness knows,' exclaimed Miss Nipper, 'there's a many we could spare instead, if numbers is a object, Mrs Pipchin as a overseer would come cheap at her weight in gold, and if a knowledge of black slavery should be required, them Blimbers is the very people for the sitiwation.'" DS 19

—*in France, of a villain:* "Shame, disappointment, and discomfiture gnawed at [James Carker's] heart; a constant apprehension of being overtaken, or met—for he was groundlessly afraid even of travellers, who came towards him by the way he was going—oppressed him heavily. The same intolerable awe and dread that had come upon him in the night, returned unweakened in the day. The monotonous ringing of the bells and tramping of the horses; the monotony of his anxiety, and useless rage; the monotonous wheel of fear, regret, and passion, he kept turning round and round; made the journey like a vision, in which nothing was quite real but his own torment.

"It was a vision of long roads; that stretched away to an horizon, always receding and never gained; of ill-paved towns, up hill and down, where faces came to dark doors and ill-glazed windows, and where rows of mud-bespattered cows and oxen were tied up for sale in the long narrow streets, butting and lowing, and receiving blows on their blunt heads from bludgeons that might have beaten them in; of bridges, crosses, churches, postyards, new horses being put in against their wills, and the horses of the last stage reeking, panting, and laying their drooping heads together dolefully at stable doors; of little cemeteries with black crosses settled sideways in the graves, and withered wreaths upon them dropping away; again of long, long roads, dragging themselves out, up hill and down, to the treacherous horizon.

"Of morning, noon, and sunset; night, and the rising of an early moon. Of long roads temporarily left behind, and a rough pavement reached; of battering and clattering over it, and looking up, among house-roofs, at a great church-tower; of getting out and eating hastily, and drinking draughts of wine that had no cheering influence; of coming forth afoot, among a host of beggars—blind men with quivering eyelids, led by old women holding candles in their faces; idiot girls; the lame, the epileptic, and the palsied—of passing through the clamour, and looking from his seat at the upturned countenances and outstretched hands, with a hurried dread of recognising some pursuer pressing forward—of galloping away again, upon the long, long road, gathered up, dull and stunned, in his corner, or rising to see where the moon shone faintly on a patch of the same endless road miles away, or looking back to see who followed . . . .

"A vision of change upon change, and still the same monotony of bells and wheels, and horses' feet and no rest. Of town and country, postyards, horses, drivers, hill and valley, light and darkness, road and pavement, height and hollow, wet weather and dry, and still the same monotony of bells and wheels, and horses' feet, and no rest. A vision of tending on at last, towards the distant capital, by busier roads, and sweeping round, by old cathedrals, and dashing through small towns and villages, less thinly scattered on the road than formerly, and sitting shrouded in his corner, with his cloak up to his face, as people passing by looked at him.

"Of rolling on and on, always postponing thought, and always racked with thinking; of being unable to reckon up the hours he had been upon the road, or to comprehend the points of time and place in his journey. Of being parched and giddy, and half mad. Of pressing on, in spite of all, as if he could not stop, and coming into Paris, where the turbid river held its swift course undisturbed, between two brawling streams of life and motion.

"A troubled vision, then, of bridges, quays, interminable streets; of wine-shops, water-carriers, great crowds of people, soldiers, coaches, military drums, arcades. Of the monotony of bells and wheels and horses' feet being at length lost in the universal din and uproar. Of the gradual subsidence of that noise as he passed out in another carriage by a different barrier from that by which he had entered. Of the restoration, as he travelled on towards the sea-coast, of the monotony of bells and wheels, and horses' feet, and no rest.

"Of sunset once again, and nightfall. Of long roads again, and dead of night, and feeble lights in windows by the roadside; and still the old monotony of bells and wheels, and horses' feet, and no rest. Of dawn, and daybreak, and the rising of the sun. Of toiling slowly up a hill, and feeling on its top the fresh sea-breeze; and seeing the morning light upon the edges of the distant waves. Of coming down into a harbour when the tide was at its full, and seeing fishing-boats float on, and glad women and children waiting for them. Of nets and seamen's clothes spread out to dry upon the shore; of busy sailors, and their voices high among ships' masts and rigging; of the buoyancy and brightness of theater, and the universal sparkling.

"Of receding from the coast, and looking back upon it from the deck when it was a haze upon the water, with here and there a little opening of bright land where the sun struck. Of the swell, and flash, and murmur of the calm sea. Of another grey line on the ocean, on the vessel's track, fast growing clearer and higher. Of cliffs and buildings, and a windmill, and a church, becoming more and more visible upon it. Of steaming on at last into smooth water, and mooring to a pier whence groups of people looked down, greeting friends on board. Of disembarking, passing among them quickly, shunning every one; and of being at last again in England." DS 55

—hotel character: infallible test: " . . . I also hold that there is no more certain index to personal character than the condition of a set of casters is to the character of any hotel. Knowing, and having often tested this theory of mine, Bullfinch resigned himself to the worst, when, laying aside any remaining veil of disguise, I held up before him in succession the cloudy oil and furry vinegar, the clogged cayenne, the dirty salt, the obscene dregs of soy, and the anchovy sauce in a flannel waistcoat of decomposition." UT/DH

—philosophy of: " . . . the sun, had just risen . . . on the morning of the thirteenth of May, one thousand eight hundred and twenty-seven, when Mr Samuel Pickwick burst like another sun from his slumbers, threw open his chamber window, and looked out upon the world beneath. Goswell Street was at his feet, Goswell Street was on his right hand—as far as the eye could reach, Goswell Street extended on his left; and the opposite side of Goswell Street was over the way. 'Such,' thought Mr Pickwick, 'are the narrow views of those philosophers who, content with examining the things that lie before them, look not to the truths which are hidden beyond. As well might I be content to gaze on Goswell Street forever, without one effort to penetrate to the hidden countries which on every side surround it.' And having given vent to this beautiful reflection, Mr Pickwick proceeded to put himself into his clothes, and his clothes into his portmanteau." PP 2

Which doubtless qualified as the neatest trick of that particular week in 1827.

—riverboat trade and truth: " . . . this was a steamboat journey, and western steamboats usually blow up one or two a week in the season . . . 'The Messenger' was the best recommended. She had been advertised to start positively, every day for a fortnight or so, and had not gone yet, nor did her captain seem to have any very fixed intention on the subject.

"But this is the custom: for if the law were to bind down a free and independent citizen to keep his word with the public, what would become of the liberty of the subject? Besides, it is in the way of trade. And if passengers be decoyed in the way of trade, and people be inconvenienced in the way of trade, what man, who is a sharp tradesman himself, shall say, 'We must put a stop to this?'" ¶AN 10

—sea voyage

—fears: "Put aside the rolling and the rush of water, and think of darting through such darkness with such velocity. Think of any other similar object coming in the opposite direction!

"Whether there may be an attraction in two such moving bodies out at sea, which may help accident to bring them into collision? Thoughts, too, arise . . . of the gulf below; of the strange unfruitful mountain ranges and deep valleys over which we are passing; of monstrous fish midway; of the ship's suddenly altering her course on her own account, and with a wild plunge settling down, and making *that* voyage with a crew of dead discoverers." UT/AS

—heavy weather: "Did she ever take a roll before like that last? Did she ever take a roll before like this worse one that is coming now? Here is the partition at my ear down in the deep on the lee side. Are we ever coming up again together? I think not; the partition and I are so long about it that I really do believe we have overdone it this time.

"Heavens, what a scoop! What a deep scoop, what a hollow scoop, what a long scoop! Will it ever end, and can we bear the heavy mass of water we have taken on board, and which has let loose all the table furniture in the officers' mess, and has beaten open the door of the little passage between the purser and me, and is swashing about, even there and even here?" ¶UT/AS

—life on board: "'Is that you, Mark [Tapley]?' asked a faint voice from another berth.

"'It's as much of me as is left, sir, after a fortnight of this work,' Mr Tapley replied. 'What with leading the life of a fly, ever since I've been abroad—for I've been perpetually holding-on to something or other, in a upside-down position—what with that, sir, and putting a very little into myself, and taking a good deal out of myself, there an't too much of me to swear by.'" MC 15

—morning view: "Then the day would break, and, descending from my berth by a graceful ladder composed of half-opened drawers beneath it, I would reopen my outer dead-light and my inner sliding window . . . and would look out at the long-rolling, lead-coloured, white-topped waves

over which the dawn, on a cold winter morning, cast a level, lonely glance, and through which the ship fought her melancholy way at a terrific rate." UT/AS

—passenger: "The observation every day at noon, and the subsequent working of the vessel's course, was, as may be supposed, a feature in our lives of paramount importance; nor were there wanting (as there never are) sagacious doubters of the captain's calculations, who, so soon as his back was turned, would, in the absence of compasses, measure the chart with bits of string, and ends of pocket-handkerchiefs, and points of snuffers, and clearly prove him to be wrong by an odd thousand miles or so.

"It was very edifying to see these unbelievers shake their heads and frown, and hear them hold forth strongly upon navigation: not that they knew anything about it, but that they always mistrusted the captain in calm weather, or when the wind was adverse.

"Indeed, the mercury itself is not so variable as this class of passengers, whom you will see, when the ship is going nobly through the water, quite pale with admiration, swearing that the captain beats all captains ever known, and even hinting at subscriptions for a piece of plate; and who, next morning, when the breeze has lulled, and all the sails hang useless in the idle air, shake their despondent heads again, and say, with screwed-up lips, they hope that captain is a sailor—but they shrewdly doubt him." AN 16

—voice of the sea: ". . . the speech of the sea is various, and wants not abundant resource of cheerfulness, hope, and lusty encouragement." RP/EW

—washing decks: ". . . I never got to sleep afterwards—with the rigging of the pump while it was yet dark, and washing down of decks. Any enormous giant at a prodigious hydropathic establishment, conscientiously undergoing the water-cure in all its departments, and extremely particular about cleaning his teeth, would make those noises. Swash, splash, scrub, rub, toothbrush, bubble, swash, splash, bubble, toothbrush, splash, splash, bubble, rub." UT/AS

—and wind: ". . . how emphatically everything by the sea declares that it has a great concern in the state of the wind. The trees blown all one way; the defences of the harbour reared highest and strongest against the raging point; the shingle flung up on the beach from the same direction; the number of arrows pointed at the common enemy; the sea tumbling in and rushing towards them as if it were inflamed by the sight." RP/OS

See —sea-sickness, Ship*—head-wind, —heavy weather and —at night; and* N:Sea

—sea-sickness: "A slight emotion on the part of the vessel, now and then, seemed to suggest the possibility of its pitching to a very uncomfortable extent in the event of its blowing harder; and every timber began to creak, as if the boat were an overladen clothes-basket. Sea-sickness, however, is like a belief in ghosts—everyone entertains some misgivings on the subject, but few will acknowledge any. The majority of the company, therefore, endeavoured to look peculiarly happy, feeling all the while especially miserable." SB/SE

"I say nothing of what may be called the domestic noises of the ship: such as the breaking of glass and crockery, the tumbling down of stewards, the gambols overhead of loose casks and truant dozens of bottled porter, and the very remarkable and far from exhilarating sounds raised in their various state-rooms by the seventy passengers who were too ill to get up to breakfast. I say nothing of them: for although I lay listening to this concert for three or four days, I don't think I heard it for more than a quarter of a minute, at the expiration of which term, I lay down again, excessively sea-sick.

"Not sea-sick, be it understood, in the ordinary acceptation of the term: I wish I had been: but in a form which I have never seen or heard described, though I have no doubt it is very common. I lay there, all the day long, quite coolly and contentedly; with no sense of weariness, with no desire to get up, or get better, or take the air; with no curiosity, or care, or regret, of any sort or degree, saving that I think I can remember, in this universal indifference, having a kind of lazy joy—of fiendish delight, if anything so lethargic can be dignified with the title—in the fact of my wife being too ill to talk to me. If I may be allowed to illustrate my state of mind by such an example, I should say that I was exactly in the condition of the elder Mr Willet, after the incursion of the rioters into his bar at Chigwell [BR 54]. Nothing would have surprised me. If, in the momentary illumination of any ray of intelligence that may have come upon me in the way of thoughts of Home, a goblin postman, with a scarlet coat and bell, had come into that little kennel before me, broad awake in broad day, and apologising for being damp through walking in the sea, had handed me a letter directed to myself, in familiar characters, I am certain I should not have felt one atom of astonishment: I should have been perfectly satisfied. If *Neptune* himself had walked in, with a toasted shark on his trident, I should have looked upon the event as one of the very commonest everyday occurrences.

"Once—once—I found myself on deck. I don't know how I got there, or what possessed me to go there, but there I was; and completely dressed too, with a huge pea-coat on, and a pair of boots such as no weak man in his senses could ever have got into.

"I found myself standing, when a gleam of consciousness came upon me, holding on to something. I don't know what. I think it was the boatswain: or it may have been the pump: or possibly the cow. I can't say how long I had been there; whether a day or a minute. I recollect trying to think about something (about anything in the whole wide world, I was not particular) without the smallest effect. I could not even make out which was the sea, and which the sky, for the horizon seemed drunk, and was flying wildly about in all directions.

"Even in that incapable state, however, I recognised the lazy gentleman standing before me; nautically clad in a suit of shaggy blue, with an oilskin hat. But I was too imbecile, although I knew it to be he, to separate him from his dress; and tried to call him, I remember, *Pilot.*

"After another interval of total unconsciousness, I found he had gone, and recognised another figure in his place. It seemed to wave and fluctuate before me as though I saw it reflected in an unsteady looking-glass; but I knew it for the captain; and such was the cheerful influence of his face, that I tried to smile: yes, even then I tried to smile.

"I saw by his gestures that he addressed me; but it was a long time before I could make out that he remonstrated against my standing up to my knees in water—as I was; of course I don't know why. I tried to thank him, but couldn't. I could only point to my boots—or wherever I supposed my boots to be—and say in a plaintive voice, 'Cork soles:' at the same time endeavouring, I am told, to sit down in the pool. Finding that I was quite insensible, and for the time a maniac, he humanely conducted me below.

"There I remained until I got better: suffering, whenever I was recommended to eat anything, an amount of anguish only second to that which is said to be endured by the apparently drowned, in the process of restoration to life." ¶AN 2

That particular crossing in the Britannia was in fact extraordinarily rough, and the difficulties overcome by the crew were immense. Dickens presided at a testimonial dinner and presentation to the captain almost immediately upon landing. S/CH

"A stout wooden wedge driven in at my right temple and out at my left, a floating deposit of lukewarm oil in my throat, and a compression of the bridge of my nose in a blunt pair of pincers—these are the personal sensations by which I know we are off, and by which I shall continue to know it until I am on the soil of France." UT/CM

"When I first made acquaintance with Calais, it was as a maundering young wretch in a clammy perspiration and dripping saline particles, who was conscious of no extremities but the one great extremity, sea-sickness—who was a mere bilious torso, with a mislaid headache somewhere in its stomach—who had been put into a horrible swing in Dover Harbour, and had tumbled giddily out of it on the French coast, or the Isle of Man, or anywhere." UT/CM

And see English Channel *and* B:Illness

—by stage-waggon: "What a soothing, luxurious, drowsy way of travelling, to lie inside that slowly-moving mountain, listening to the tinkling of the horses' bells, the occasional smacking of the carter's whip, the smooth rolling of the great broad wheels, the rattle of the harness, the cheery good-nights of passing travellers jogging past on little short-stepped horses—all made for lazy listening under, till one fell asleep! The very going to sleep, still with an indistinct idea, as the head jogged to and fro upon the pillow, of moving onward with no trouble or fatigue, and hearing all these sounds like dreamy music, lulling to the senses—and the slow waking up, and finding one's self staring out through the breezy curtain half-opened in the front, far up into the cold bright sky with its countless stars, and downward at the driver's lantern dancing on like its namesake Jack of the swamps and marshes, and sideways at the dark grim trees, and forward at the long bare road ris-

ing up, up, up, until it stopped abruptly at a sharp high ridge as if there were no more road, and all beyond was sky—and the stopping at the inn to bait,* and being helped out, and going into a room with fire and candles, and winking very much, and being agreeably reminded that the night was cold, and anxious for very comfort's sake to think it colder than it was!—What a delicious journey was that journey in the waggon!

"Then the going on again—so fresh at first, and shortly afterwards so sleepy. The waking from a sound nap as the mail came dashing past like a highway comet, with gleaming lamps and rattling hoofs, and visions of a guard behind, standing up to keep his feet warm, and of a gentleman in a fur cap opening his eyes and looking wild and stupefied—the stopping at the turnpike where the man was gone to bed, and knocking at the door until he answered with a smothered shout from under the bed-clothes in the little room above, where the faint light was burning, and presently came down, night-capped and shivering, to throw the gate wide open, and wish all waggons off the road except by day." OCS 46

**feed and water the horses*

—stories told by a bore: "Our bore has travelled. He could not possibly be a complete bore without having travelled. He rarely speaks of his travels without introducing, sometimes on his own plan of construction, morsels of the language of the country—which he always translates. You cannot name to him any little remote town in France, Italy, Germany, or Switzerland but he knows it well; stayed there a fortnight under peculiar circumstances. And talking of that little place, perhaps you know a statue over an old fountain, up a little court, which is the second—no, the third—stay—yes, the third turning on the right, after you come out of the Post-house, going up the hill towards the market?

"You *don't* know that statue? Nor that fountain? You surprise him! They are not usually seen by travellers (most extraordinary, he has never yet met with a single traveller who knew them, except one German, the most intelligent man he ever met in his life!) but he thought that YOU would have been the man to find them out. And then he describes them, in a circumstantial lecture half an hour long, generally delivered behind a door which is constantly being opened from the other side; and implores you, if you ever revisit that place, now do go and look at that statue and fountain!

"Our bore, in a similar manner, being in Italy, made a discovery of a dreadful picture, which has been the terror of a large portion of the civilised world ever since. We have seen the liveliest men paralysed by it, across a broad dining-table.

"He was lounging among the mountains, sir, basking in the mellow influences of the climate, when he came to *una piccola chiesa*—a little church—or perhaps it would be more correct to say *una piccolissima cappella*—the smallest chapel you can possibly imagine—and walked in. There was nobody inside but a *cieco*—a blind man—saying his prayers, and a *vecchio padre*—old friar—rattling a money-box.

"But, above the head of that friar, and immediately to the right of the altar as you enter—to the right of the altar? No. To the left of the altar as you enter—or say near the centre—there hung a painting (subject, Virgin and Child) so divine in its expression, so pure and yet so warm and rich in its tone, so fresh in its touch, at once so glowing in its colour and so statuesque in its repose, that our bore cried out in an ecstasy, 'That's the finest picture in Italy!'

"And so it is, sir. There is no doubt of it. It is astonishing that that picture is so little known. Even the painter is uncertain. He afterwards took Blumb, of the Royal Academy (it is to be observed that our bore takes none but eminent people to see sights, and that none but eminent people take our bore), and you never saw a man so affected in your life as Blumb was. He cried like a child! And then our bore begins his description in detail—for all this is introductory—and strangles his hearers with the folds of the purple drapery." ¶RP/B

—wayfarer: "One man, slowly moving on towards Chalons was the only visible figure in the landscape. Cain might have looked as lonely and avoided. With an old sheepskin knapsack at his back, and a rough, unbarked stick cut out of some wood in his hand; miry, footsore, his shoes and gaiters trodden out, his hair and beard untrimmed; the cloak he carried over his shoulder, and the clothes he wore, soddened with wet; limping along in pain and difficulty; he looked as if the clouds were hurrying from him, as if the wail of the wind and the shuddering of the grass were directed against him, as if the low mysterious plash-

ing of the water murmured at him, as if the fitful autumn night were disturbed by him." LD i 11

" . . . a shaggy-haired man, of almost barbarian aspect, tall, in wooden shoes that were clumsy even to the eyes of a mender of roads, grim, rough, swart, steeped in the mud and dust of many highways, dank with the marshy moisture of many low grounds, sprinkled with the thorns and leaves and moss of many byways through woods . . . .

" . . . . The bronze face, the shaggy black hair and beard, the coarse woollen red cap, the rough medley dress of the homespun stuff and hairy skins of beasts, the powerful frame attenuated by spare living, and the sullen and desperate compression of the lips in sleep, inspired the mender of roads with awe. The traveller had travelled far, and his feet were footsore, and his ankles chafed and bleeding; his great shoes, stuffed with leaves and grass, had been heavy to drag over the many long leagues, and his clothes were chafed into holes, as he himself was into sores . . . . Fortified towns with their stockades, guard-houses, gates, trenches, and drawbridges, seemed to the mender of roads, to be so much air as against this figure. And when he lifted his eyes from it to the horizon and looked around, he saw in his small fancy similar figures, stopped by no obstacle, tending to centres all over France." TTC ii 23

And see L:London—*wayfarer*

Addenda

Christened Conveyances

'Admiral Napier,' omnibus	SB/BC
Birmingham 'High-flier'	SB/EC
'Commodore', coach to Rochester	PP ch 2
Dover coach, the 'Blue-eyed Maid'	LD i 3
Exeter Telegraph, fast coach	UT/CM
'Highflyer,' coach	UT/SC
'Lads of the Village,' omnibus	SB/BC
'Timpson's Blue-Eyed Maid,' coach	UT/DT

Crossing the Channel

Does she not fear to stray,
So lone and lovely through this bleak way,
And are Erin's sons so good or so cold,
As not to be tempted by more fellow-creatures at the paddle-box or gold?
Sir Knight I feel not the least alarm,
No son of Erin will offer me harm,
For though they love fellow-creatures with umbrella down again and golden store,
Sir Knight they what a tremendous one love honour and virtue more:
For though they love Stewards with a bull's eye bright,
They'll trouble you for your ticket sir—rough passage to-night! UT/CM

(Presented in narrative form in original)

Nature

The freshness of the day, the singing of the birds, the beauty of the waving grass, the deep green leaves, the wild flowers, and the thousand exquisite scents and sounds that float in the air are deep joys to most of us, but most of all to those whose life is in a crowd or who live solitarily in great cities as in the bucket of a human well.

[OCS 15]

Air

—musty: "The very light coming through sunken windows, seemed old and gray, and the air, redolent of earth and mould, seemed laden with decay, purified by time of all its grosser particles, and sighing through arch, and aisle, and clustered pillars, like the breath of ages gone!" OCS 53

—polluted: "'First of all [said Bounderby], you see our smoke. That's meat and drink to us. It's the healthiest thing in the world in all respects, and particularly for the lungs. If you are one of those who want us to consume it, I differ from you. We are not going to wear the bottoms of our boilers out any faster than we wear 'em out now, for all the humbugging sentiment in Great Britain and Ireland.'" HT ii 2

—pollution escaped: "As Coketown cast ashes not only on its own head but on the neighbourhood's too—after the manner of those pious persons who do penance for their own sins by putting other people into sackcloth—it was customary for those who now and then thirsted for a draught of pure air, which is not absolutely the most wicked among the vanities of life, to get a few miles away by the railroad, and then begin their walk, or their lounge in the fields." HT iii 6

And see Weather—*fog; and* L:Pollution—*soot*

Animal

—alligator: " . . . with his horribly sly face, and his jaws like two great saws, was basking on the mud . . . . " HW/ET

—cat

—before a fire: "Mrs Pipchin had an old black cat, who generally lay coiled upon the centre foot of the fender, purring egotistically, and winking at the fire until the contracted pupils of his eyes were like two notes of admiration." DS 8

—fierce: "A large grey cat leaped from some neighbouring shelf on [Krook's] shoulder, and startled us all.

"'Hi! show 'em how you scratch. Hi! Tear, my lady!' said her master.

"The cat leaped down, and ripped at a bundle of rags with her tigerish claws, with a sound that it set my teeth on edge to hear.

"'She'd do as much for any one I was to set her on,' said the old man. 'I deal in cat-skins among other general matters, and hers was offered to me. It's a very fine skin, as you can see, but I didn't have it stripped off! *That* warn't like Chancery practice though, says you!'" BH 4

Lady Jane is the only named cat in CD; the most important feline is James Carker DS.

—free to roam: " . . . watch a cat in a field or garden, on a bright sunshiny day—how she crouches in the mould, rolls in the sand, basks in the grass, delights to vary the surface upon which she rests, and change the form of the substance upon which she takes her ease. Compare such surfaces and substances with the one uniform, unyielding, unnatural, unelastic, inappropriate piece of human carpentry upon which these beautiful animals [lions], with their vexed faces, pace and repace, and pass each other two hundred and fifty times an hour . . . . " HW/L

—going to bed: "Did you ever find her, or any living creature, go to bed, without re-arranging to the whim and sensation of the moment, the materials of the bed itself? Don't you, the Zoological Society, punch and poke your pillows, and settle into suitable places in your beds? Consider then, what the discomfort of these magnificent brutes [the lions] must be, to whom you leave no diversity of choice, no power of new arrangement, and as to whose unchanging and unyielding beds you begin with a form and substance that have no parallel in their natural lives." HW/L

—in Italy: " . . . fowls and cats had so taken possession of the [villa] out-buildings, that I couldn't help thinking of the fairy tales, and eyeing them with suspicion, as transformed retainers, waiting to be changed back again. One old Tom in particular: a scraggy brute, with a hungry green eye (a poor relation, in reality, I am inclined to think): came prowling round and round me, as if he half believed, for the moment, that I might be the hero come to marry the lady, and set all to-rights; but discovering his mistake, he suddenly gave a grim snarl, and walked away with such a tremendous tail, that he couldn't get into the little hole where he lived, but was obliged to wait outside, until his indignation and his tail had gone down together." PI 5

—morning in London: " . . . now and then a rakish-looking cat runs stealthily across the road and descends his own area with as much caution and slyness—bounding first on the water-butt, then on the dust-hole, and then alighting on the flag-stones—as if he were conscious that his character depended on his gallantry of the preceding

night escaping public observation." SB/SM

—in poor neighbourhoods: " . . . the cats in shy neighbourhoods exhibit a strong tendency to relapse into barbarism. Not only are they made selfishly ferocious by ruminating on the surplus population around them, and on the densely crowded state of all the avenues to cat's meat; not only is there a moral and politico-economical haggardness in them, traceable to these reflections; but they evince a physical deterioration. Their linen is not clean, and is wretchedly got up; their black turns rusty, like old mourning; they wear very indifferent fur; and take to the shabbiest cotton velvet, instead of silk velvet.

"I am on terms of recognition with several small streets of cats, about the Obelisk in Saint George's Fields, and also in the vicinity of Clerkenwell-green, and also in the back settlements of Drury-lane. In appearance, they are very like the women among whom they live. They seem to turn out of their unwholesome beds into the street, without any preparation. They leave their young families to stagger about the gutters, unassisted, while they frouzily quarrel and swear and scratch and spit, at street corners. In particular, I remark that when they are about to increase their families (an event of frequent recurrence) the resemblance is strongly expressed in a certain dusty dowdiness, down-at-heel self-neglect, and general giving up of things. I cannot honestly report that I have ever seen a feline matron of this class washing her face when in an interesting condition." ¶UT/SN

—cattle

—Arcadian: "'I assure you, Mr Dombey [said Mrs Skewton], Nature intended me for an Arcadian. I am thrown away in society. Cows are my passion. What I have ever sighed for, has been to retreat to a Swiss farm, and live entirely surrounded by cows—and china.'

"This curious association of objects, suggesting a remembrance of the celebrated bull who got by mistake into a crockery shop, was received with perfect gravity by Mr Dombey, who intimated his opinon that Nature was, no doubt, a very respectable institution." DS 21

—on home ground: "The cattle came upon me [out of the mist] with like suddenness, staring out of their eyes, and steaming out of their nostrils, 'Halloa, young thief!' One black ox, with a white cravat on—who even had to my [Pip's] awakened conscience something of a clerical air—fixed me so obstinately with his eyes, and moved his blunt head round in such an accusatory manner as I moved round, that I blubbered out to him, 'I couldn't help it, sir! It wasn't for myself I took it!' Upon which he put down his head, blew a cloud of smoke out of his nose, and vanished with a kick-up of his hindlegs, and a flourish of his tail." GE 3

"No more low wet grounds, no more dykes and sluices, no more of these grazing cattle—though they seemed, in their dull manner, to wear a more respectful air now, and to face round, in order that they might stare as long as possible at the possessor of such great expectations . . . . " GE 19

—to market: "But now, there were driven cattle on the high road near, wanting (as cattle always do) to turn into the midst of stone walls, and squeeze themselves through six inches' width of iron railing, and getting their heads down (also as cattle always do) for tossing-purchase at quite imaginary dogs, and giving themselves and every devoted creature associated with them a most extraordinary amount of unnecessary trouble." UT/NW

"To get the bullocks into their allotted stands, an incessant punishing and torturing of the miserable animals—a sticking of prongs into the tender part of their feet, and a twisting of their tails to make the whole spine teem with pain—was going on: and this seemed as much a part of the market, as the stones in its pavement. Across their horns, across their hocks, across their haunches, Mr Bovington saw the heavy blows rain thick and fast, let him look where he would. Obdurate heads of oxen, bent down in mute agony; bellowing heads of oxen lifted up, snorting out smoke and slaver; ferocious men, cursing and swearing, and belabouring oxen; made the place [Smithfield] a panorama of cruelty and suffering. By every avenue of access to the market, more oxen were pouring in: bellowing, in the confusion, and under the falling blows, as if all the church-organs in the world were wretched instruments—all there—and all being tuned together." HWC/ML *And see —oxen*

—dinosaur: "As much mud in the streets, as if the waters had but newly retired from the face of the earth, and it would not be wonderful to meet a Megalosaurus, forty feet long or so, waddling like an elephantine lizard up Holborn Hill." BH 1

—dog

—ambivalent at first: "Captain Cuttle patted Diogenes when he made allusion to him, and Diogenes met that overture graciously, half-way. During the administration of restoratives he had clearly been in two minds whether to fly at the Captain or to offer him his friendship; and he had expressed that conflict of feeling by alternate waggings of his tail, and displays of his teeth, with now and then a growl or so. But by this time his doubts were all removed. It was plain that he considered the Captain one of the most amiable of men, and a man whom it was an honour to a dog to know." DS 48

—and bad temper: "My dog knew as well when she was on the turn as I did. Before she broke out, he would give a howl, and bolt. How he knew it, was a mystery to me; but the sure and certain knowledge of it would wake him up out of his soundest sleep, and he would give a howl, and bolt. At such times I wished I was him." CS/DM 1

—bettor's: "'So he went,' said the gentleman with the gun-barrel . . . 'down to his cousin's place, and took the Dog with him by rail. Inestimable Dog. Flew at the porter fellow when he was put into the dog-box, and flew at the guard when he was taken out. He got half a dozen fellows into a Barn, and a good supply of Rats, and timed the Dog. Finding the Dog able to do it immensely, made the match, and heavily backed the Dog. When the match came off, some devil of a fellow was brought over, Sir, Dog was made drunk, Dog's master was cleaned out' . . . .

" . . . 'What did he call the Dog?'

"'Called him Lovely,' said the other gentleman. 'Said the Dog was the perfect picture of the old aunt from whom he had expecations. Found him particularly like her when hocussed.'" LD i 10

—blind man's: "Even the blind men's dogs appeared to know [Scrooge]; and when they saw him coming on, would tug their owners into doorsteps and up courts; and then would wag their tails as though they said, 'No eye at all is better than an evil eye, dark master!'" CC 1

"There is a dog residing in the Borough of Southwark who keeps a blind man. He may be seen, most days, in Oxford-street, haling the blind man away on expeditions wholly uncontemplated by, and unintelligible to, the man: wholly of the dog's conception and execution. Contrariwise, when the man has projects, the dog will sit down in a crowded thoroughfare and meditate." UT/SN

—bull-dog. "We talk of men keeping dogs, but we might often talk more expressively of dogs keeping men. I know a bull-dog in a shy corner of Hammersmith who keeps a man. He keeps him up a yard, and makes him go to the public-houses and lay wagers on him, and obliges him to lean against posts and look at him, and forces him to neglect work for him, and keeps him under rigid coercion." UT/SN

—of a condemned man: "'There is nothing more.'

"'Move forward!'

"'—Unless,' said Hugh, glancing hurriedly back—'unless any person here has a fancy for a dog; and not then, unless he means to use him well. There's one, belongs to me, at the house I came from, and it wouldn't be easy to find a better. He'll whine at first, but he'll soon get over that.—You wonder that I think about a dog just now,' he added, with a kind of laugh. 'If any man deserved it of me half as well, I'd think of *him*.'" BR 77

—country: "I noticed a country dog, only the other day, who had come up to Covent-garden Market under a cart, and had broken his cord, an end of which he still trailed along with him. He loitered about the corners of the four streets commanded by my window; and bad London dogs came up, and told him lies that he didn't believe; and worse London dogs came up, and made proposals to him to go and steal in the market, which his principles rejected; and the ways of the two confused him, and he crept aside and lay down in a doorway.

"He had scarcely got a wink of sleep, when up comes Punch with Toby. He was darting to Toby for consolation and advice, when he saw the frill, and stopped, in the middle of the street, appalled. The show was pitched, Toby retired behind the drapery, the audience formed, the drum and pipes struck up. My country dog remained immovable, intently staring at these strange appearances, until Toby opened the drama by appearing on his ledge, and to him entered Punch, who put a tobacco-pipe into Toby's mouth. At this spectacle, the country dog threw up his head, gave one terrible howl, and fled due west." ¶UT/SN

And see —Toby

—drover's: ". . . waiting for his master outside a butcher's shop, and evidently thinking about those sheep he has had upon his mind for some hours, and is happily rid of. He seems perplexed respecting three or four; can't remember where he left them; looks up and down the street, as half expecting to see them astray; suddenly pricks up his ears and remembers all about it. A thoroughly vagabond dog, accustomed to low company and public-houses; a terrific dog to sheep; ready at a whistle to scamper over their backs, and tear out mouthfuls of their wool; but an educated, improved, developed dog, who has been taught his duties and knows how to discharge them." BH 16

"I know a shaggy black and white dog who keeps a drover. He is a dog of an easy disposition, and too frequently allows this drover to get drunk. On these occasions, it is the dog's custom to sit outside the public-house, keeping his eye on a few sheep, and thinking. I have seen him with six sheep, plainly casting up in his mind how many he began with when he left the market, and at what places he has left the rest . . . .

"If I could at any time have doubted the fact that it was he who kept the drover, and not the drover who kept him, it would have been abundantly proved by his way of taking undivided charge of the six sheep, when the drover came out besmeared with red ochre and beer, and gave him wrong directions, which he calmly disregarded. He has taken the sheep entirely into his own hands, has merely remarked with respectful firmness, 'That instruction would place them under an omnibus; you had better confine your attention to yourself—you will want it all;' and has driven his charge away, with an intelligence of ears and tail, and a knowledge of business, that has left his lout of a man very, very far behind." ¶UT/SN

—effect on nerves: ". . . Miss Nipper was nervous in regard of dogs, and felt it necessary to come into the room with her skirts carefully collected about her, as if she were crossing a brook on stepping-stones; also to utter little screams and stand up on chairs when Diogenes stretched himself . . . . " DS 18

—enthusiastic: "Boxer, feeling that his attentions were due to the family in general, and must be impartially distributed, dashed in and out with bewildering inconstancy; now, describing a circle of short barks round the horse . . . now, feigning to make savage rushes at his mistress, and facetiously bringing himself to sudden stops; now eliciting a shriek from Tilly Slowboy, in the low nursing-chair near the fire, by the unexpected application of his moist nose to her countenance; now, exhibiting an obtrusive interest in the baby; now, going round and round upon the hearth, and lying down as if he had established himself for the night; now, getting up again, and taking that nothing of a fag-end of a tail of his, out into the weather, as if he had just remembered an appointment, and was off, at a round trot, to keep it . . . .

"Everybody knew him, all along the road—especially the fowls and pigs, who when they saw him approaching, with his body all on one side, and his ears pricked up inquisitively, and that knob of a tail making the most of itself in the air, immediately withdrew into remote back settlements, without waiting for the honour of a nearer acquaintance. He had business everywhere; going down all the turnings, looking into all the wells, bolting in and out of all the cottages, dashing into the midst of all the Dame-Schools, fluttering all the pigeons, magnifying the tails of all the cats, and trotting into the public houses like a regular customer." CH 2

—frantically loyal: "'Oh, Di! oh, dear, true, faithful Di, how did you come here? How could I ever leave you, Di, who would never leave me?'

"Florence bent down on the pavement, and laid his rough, old, loving, foolish head against her breast, and they got up together, and went on together; Di more off the ground than on it, endeavouring to kiss his mistress flying, tumbling over and getting up again without the least concern, dashing at big dogs in a jocose defiance of his species, terrifying with touches of his nose young housemaids who were cleaning doorsteps, and continually stopping, in the midst of a thousand extravagances, to look back at Florence, and bark until all the dogs within hearing answered, and all the dogs who could come out, came out to stare at him." DS 48

—interested in human affairs: "It was a Saturday evening, and at such a time the village dogs, always much more interested in the doings of humanity than in the affairs of their own species, were particularly active. At the general shop, at the butcher's and at the public-house, they evinced an inquiring spirit never to be satiated. Their

especial interest in the public-house would seem to imply some latent rakishness in the canine character; for little was eaten there, and they, having no taste for beer or tobacco (*Mrs Hubbard*'s dog is said to have smoked, but proof is wanting), could only have been attracted by sympathy with loose convivial habits. Moreoever a most wretched fiddle played within; a fiddle so unutterably vile, that one lean long-bodied cur, with a better ear than the rest, found himself under compulsion at intervals to go round the corner and howl. Yet even he returned to the public-house on each occasion with the tenacity of a confirmed drunkard." OMF iv 6

—irrepressible: "Boxer, feeling that his attentions were due to the family in general, and must be impartially distributed, dashed in and out with bewildering inconstancy; now, describing a circle of short barks round the horse, where he was being rubbed down at the stable-door; now, feigning to make savage rushes at his mistress, and facetiously bringing himself to sudden stops; now eliciting a shriek from Tilly Slowboy, in the low nursing-chair near the fire, by the unexpected application of his moist nose to her countenance; now, exhibiting an obtrusive interest in the baby; now, going round and round upon the hearth, and lying down as if he had established himself for the night; now, getting up again, and taking that nothing of a fag-end of a tail of his, out into the weather, as if he had just remembered an appointment, and was off, at a round trot, to keep it." CH 1

—loved though unprepossessing: "But though Diogenes was as ridiculous a dog as one would meet with on a summer's day; a blundering, ill-favoured, clumsy, bullet-headed dog, continually acting on a wrong idea that there was an enemy in the neighbourhood, whom it was meritorious to bark at; and though he was far from good-tempered, and certainly was not clever, and had hair all over his eyes, and a comic nose, and an inconsistent tail, and a gruff voice; he was dearer to Florence, in virtue of that parting remembrance of [little Paul Dombey], and that request that he might be taken care of, than the most valuable and beautiful of his kind.

"So dear, indeed, was this same ugly Diogenes, and so welcome to her, that she took the jewelled hand of Mr Toots and kissed it in her gratitude. And when Diogenes, released, came tearing up the stairs and bouncing into the room (such a business as there was first, to get him out of the cabriolet!), dived under all the furniture, and wound a long iron chain, that dangled from his neck, round legs of chairs and tables, and then tugged at it until his eyes became unnaturally visible, in consequence of their nearly starting out of his head; and when he growled at Mr Toots, who affected familiarity; and went pell-mell at Towlinson, morally convinced that he was the enemy whom he had barked at round the corner all his life and had never seen yet; Florence was as pleased with him as if he had been a miracle of discretion." DS 18

—loving: "Diogenes was broad awake upon his post, and waiting for his little mistress.

"'Oh, Di! Oh, dear Di! Love me for his sake!'

"Diogenes already loved her for her own, and didn't care how much he showed it. So he made himself vastly ridiculous by performing a variety of uncouth bounces in the antechamber, and concluded, when poor Florence was at last asleep, and dreaming of the rosy children opposite, by scratching open her bedroom door: rolling up his bed into a pillow: lying down on the boards, at the full length of his tether, with his head towards her: and looking lazily at her, upside down, out of the tops of his eyes, until from winking and winking he fell asleep himself, and dreamed, with gruff barks, of his enemy." DS 18

—making amends: "Diogenes . . . had at first objected to the admission of Edith, and, even in deference to his mistress's wish, had only permitted it under growling protest. But, emerging by little and little from the ante-room, whither he had retired in dudgeon, he soon appeared to comprehend, that with the most amiable intentions he had made one of those mistakes which will occasionally arise in the best-regulated dogs' minds; as a friendly apology for which he stuck himself up on end between the two, in a very hot place in front of the fire, and sat panting at it, with his tongue out, and a most imbecile expression of countenance, listening to the conversation." DS 35

—mastiff in unrelenting rain: "So the mastiff, dozing in his kennel, in the courtyard, with his large head on his paws, may think of the hot sunshine, when the shadows of the stable-buildings tire his patience out by changing, and leave him, at one time

of the day, no broader refuge than the shadow of his own house, where he sits on end, panting and growling short, and very much wanting something to worry, besides himself and his chain." BH 6

—*mongrel:* "I have my eye on a mongrel in Somerstown who keeps three boys. He feigns that he can bring down sparrows, and unburrow rats (he can do neither), and he takes the boys out on sporting pretences into all sorts of suburban fields. He has likewise made them believe that he possesses some mysterious knowledge of the art of fishing, and they consider themselves incompletely equipped for the Hampstead ponds, with a pickle-jar and wide-mouthed bottle, unless he is with them and barking tremendously." UT/SN

—*Newfoundland:* "I have the pleasure to know a dog in a back street in the neighbourhood of Walworth, who has greatly distinguished himself in the minor drama, and who takes his portrait with him when he makes an engagement, for the illustration of the play-bill . . . .

"He is a dog of the Newfoundland breed, for whose honesty I would be bail to any amount; but whose intellectual qualities in association with dramatic fiction, I cannot rate high. Indeed, he is too honest for the profession he has entered . . . it was in his greatest scene of all, that his honesty got the better of him. He had to enter a dense and trackless forest, on the trail of the murderer, and there to fly at the murderer when he found him resting at the foot of a tree, with his victim bound ready for slaughter.

"It was a hot night, and he came into the forest from an altogether unexpected direction, in the sweetest temper, at a very deliberate trot, not in the least excited; trotted to the foot-lights with his tongue out; and there sat down, panting, and amiably surveying the audience, with his tail beating on the boards, like a Dutch clock. Meanwhile the murderer, impatient to receive his doom, was audibly calling to him 'CO-O-OME here!' while the victim, struggling with his bonds, assailed him with the most injurious expressions." ¶UT/SN

—*noisy:* "Diogenes would lay his head upon the window-ledge, and placidly open and shut his eyes upon the street, all through a summer morning; sometimes pricking up his head to look with great significance after some noisy dog in a cart, who was barking his way along, and sometimes, with an exasperated and unaccountable recollection of his supposed enemy in the neighbourhood, rushing to the door, whence, after a deafening disturbance, he would come jogging back with a ridiculous complacency that belonged to him, and lay his jaw upon the window-ledge again, with the air of a dog who had done a public service." DS 23

—*panting:* "[Diogenes] sprung panting up again, putting out his tongue, as if he had come express to a Dispensary to be examined for his health." DS 18

—*performing poodle:* " . . . a large poodle with a pink nose . . . stood on his hind-legs presenting arms on the extreme verge of the platform . . . . This poodle wore a military shako (it is unnecessary to add, very much on one side over one eye), a little military coat, and the regulation white gaiters. He was armed with a little musket and a little sword-bayonet, and he stood presenting arms in perfect attitude . . . he remained staunch on his post, until the train was gone. He then resigned his arms to his officer, took off his shako by rubbing his paw over it, dropped on four legs, bringing his uniform coat into the absurdest relations with the overarching skies, and ran about the platform in his white gaiters, wagging his tail to an exceeding great extent. It struck me that there was more waggery than this in the poodle, and that he knew that the recruits would neither get through their exercises, nor get rid of their uniforms, as easily as he . . . . " UT/FF

—*in a poor neighbourhood:* "The dogs of shy neighbourhoods, I observe to avoid play, and to be conscious of poverty. They avoid work, too, if they can, of course; that is in the nature of all animals . . . .

"As the dogs of shy neighbourhoods usually betray a slinking consciousness of being in poor circumstances—for the most part manifested in an aspect of anxiety, an awkwardness in their play, and a misgiving that somebody is going to harness them to something, to pick up a living . . . . " UT/SN

—*pug:* " . . . rampant on one eternal door-mat, in an eternal entry long and narrow, is a puffy pug-dog, with a personal animosity towards us, who triumphs over Time. The bark of that baleful Pug, a certain radiating way he had of snapping at our undefended legs, the ghastly grinning of his moist black muzzle and white teeth, and the insolence of his crisp tail curled like a pastoral crook, all live and flourish. From an otherwise unaccountable association of him with a fiddle, we conclude that he was of French extraction, and his name *Fidele.*

"For [his owner], he would sit up and balance cake upon his nose, and not eat it until twenty had been counted. To the best of our belief we were once called in to witness this performance; when, unable, even in his milder moments, to endure our presence, he instantly made at us, cake and all." RP/OS

The Sagacious Dog PP

—sheep-dog: "And here are the sheep-dogs, sensible as ever, but with a certain French air about them—not without a suspicion of dominoes—with a kind of flavour of moustache and beard—demonstrative dogs, shaggy and loose where an English dog would be tight and close—not so troubled with business calculations as our English drovers' dogs, who have always got their sheep upon their minds, and think about their work, even resting, as you may see by their faces; but dashing, showy, rather unreliable dogs: who might worry me instead of their legitimate charges if they saw occasion—and might see it somewhat suddenly." RP/FF

—in summer: "If a dog happen to look unpleasantly warm in the summer months, and to trot about the shady side of the streets with a quarter of a yard of tongue

hanging out of his mouth, a thick leather muzzle, which has been previously prepared in compliance with the thoughtful injunctions of the Legislature, is instantly clapped over his head, by way of making him cooler, and he either looks remarkably unhappy for the next six weeks, or becomes legally insane, and goes mad, as it were, by Act of Parliament." SB/GS

—*sympathetic:* "'Such a dog as that, and one of the same breed, was the only living thing except me [aged six] that howled that day [of mother's hanging],' said Hugh. 'Out of the two thousand odd—there was a larger crowd for its being a woman—the dog and I alone had any pity. If he'd have been a man, he'd have been glad to be quit of her, for she had been forced to keep him lean and half-starved; but being a dog, and not having a man's sense, he was sorry.'" BR 23

—*terrier:* "I once knew a fancy terrier who kept a gentleman—a gentleman who had been brought up at Oxford, too. The dog kept the gentleman entirely for his glorification, and the gentleman never talked about anything but the terrier." UT/SN

—*Toby:* "In a shy street, behind Long-acre, two honest dogs live, who perform in Punch's shows. I may venture to say that I am on terms of intimacy with both, and that I never saw either guilty of the falsehood of failing to look down at the man inside the show, during the whole performance.

"The difficulty other dogs have in satisfying their minds about these dogs, appears to be never overcome by time. The same dogs must encounter them over and over again, as they trudge along in their off-minutes behind the legs of the show and beside the drum; but all dogs seem to suspect their frills and jackets, and to sniff at them as if they thought those articles of personal adornment, an eruption—a something in the nature of mange, perhaps ...." ¶UT/SN

And see —country

—donkey

—*home-loving:* "Taking a donkey towards his ordinary place of residence is a very different thing, and a feat much more easily to be accomplished, than taking him from it. It requires a great deal of foresight and presence of mind in the one case, to anticipate the numerous flights of his discursive imagination; whereas, in the other, all you have to do is to hold on, and place a blind confidence in the animal." SB/TR

—*idle:* "I have known a donkey—by sight; we were not on speaking terms—who lived over on the Surrey side of London-bridge, among the fastnesses of Jacob's Island and Dockhead.

"It was the habit of that animal, when his services were not in immediate requisition, to go out alone, idling. I have met him a mile from his place of residence, loitering about the streets; and the expression of his countenance at such times was most degraded. He was attached to the establishment of an elderly lady who sold periwinkles, and he used to stand on Saturday nights with a cartful of those delicacies outside a gin-shop, pricking up his ears when a customer came to the cart, and too evidently deriving satisfaction from the knowledge that they got bad measure . . . .

"Having been left alone with the cart of periwinkles, and forgotten, he went off idling. He prowled among his usual low haunts for some time, gratifying his depraved tastes, until, not taking the cart into his calculations, he endeavoured to turn up a narrow alley, and became greatly involved. He was taken into custody by the police . . . the stubborn sense he evinced of being . . . a blackguard, I never saw exceeded in the human subject.

"A flaring candle . . . showed him, with his ragged harness broken and his cart extensively shattered, twitching his mouth and shaking his hanging head, a picture of disgrace and obduracy. I have seen boys being taken to station-houses, who were as like him as his own brother."¶UT/SN

—*pedigreed:* "A fly was speedily found; and three donkeys—which the proprietor declared on his solemn asseveration to be 'three parts blood, and the other corn'—were engaged in the service." SB/TR

—*perverse:* "I know shy neighbourhoods where the Donkey goes in at the street-door, and appears to live up-stairs, for I have examined the back yard from over the palings, and have been unable to make him out. Gentility, nobility, royalty, would appeal to that donkey in vain to do what he does for a costermonger. Feed him with oats at the highest price, put an infant prince and princess in a pair of panniers on his back, adjust his delicate trappings to a nicety, take him to the softest slopes at Windsor, and try what pace you can get out of him. Then starve him, harness him anyhow to a truck with a flat tray on it, and see him bowl from Whitechapel to Bayswater. There appears to be no particular private understanding between birds and donkeys in a state of nature; but in the shy-neighbourhood state you shall see them always in the same hands, and always developing their very best energies for the very worst company." SB/SN

—trespassing: "Janet had gone away to get the bath ready, when my aunt, to my great alarm, became in one moment rigid with indignation, and had hardly voice to cry out, 'Janet! Donkeys!'

"Upon which, Janet came running up the stairs as if the house were in flames, darted out on a little piece of green in front, and warned off two saddle-donkeys, lady-ridden, that had presumed to set hoof upon it; while my aunt, rushing out of the house, seized the bridle of a third animal laden with a bestriding child, turned him, led him forth from those sacred precincts, and boxed the ears of the unlucky urchin in attendance who had dared to profane that hallowed ground.

"To this hour I don't know whether my aunt had any lawful right of way [*sic.*] over that patch of green; but she had settled it in her own mind that she had, and it was all the same to her. The one great outrage of her life, demanding to be constantly avenged, was the passage of a donkey over that immaculate spot. In whatever occupation she was engaged, however interesting to her the conversation in which she was taking part, a donkey turned the current of her ideas in a moment, and she was upon him straight. Jugs of water, and watering-pots, were kept in secret places ready to be discharged on the offending boys; sticks were laid in ambush behind the door; sallies were made at all hours; and incessant war prevailed. Perhaps this was an agreeable excitement to the donkey-boys; or perhaps the more sagacious of the donkeys, understanding how the case stood, delighted with constitutional obstinacy in coming that way." DC 13

—unruly: "The animal which Mr Cymon Tuggs bestrode, feeling sundry uncomfortable tugs at the bit, the intent of which he could by no means divine, abruptly sidled against a brick wall, and expressed his uneasiness by grinding Mr Cymon Tuggs's leg on the rough surface. Mrs Captain Waters's donkey, apparently under the influence of some playfulness of spirit, rushed suddenly, head first, into a hedge, and declined to come out again: and the quadruped on which Miss Tuggs was mounted, expressed his delight at this humorous proceeding by firmly planting his fore-feet against the ground, and kicking up his hind-legs in a very agile, but somewhat alarming manner." SB/TR

" . . . he desposited his rider without giving him the trouble of dismounting, by sagaciously pitching him over his head into the very doorway of the tavern . . . . It was speedily discovered, however, that [Cymon] had not sustained much more injury than the donkey—he was grazed, and the animal was grazing . . . . " SB/TR

—the Weller postboy theory: "'Wos you ever called in,' inquired Sam, glancing at the driver, after a short silence, and lowering his voice to a mysterious whisper: 'wos you ever called in, ven you wos 'prentice to a sawbones, to wisit a postboy?'

"'I don't remember that I ever was,' replied Bob Sawyer.

"'You never see a postboy in that 'ere hospital as you *walked* (as they say o' the ghosts), did you?' demanded Sam.

"'No,' replied Bob Sawyer. 'I don't think I ever did.'

"'Never know'd a churchyard where there wos a postboy's tombstone, or see a dead postboy, did you?' inquired Sam, pursuing his catechism.

"'No,' rejoined Bob, 'I never did.'

"'No!' rejoined Sam, triumphantly. 'Nor never vill; and there's another thing that no man never see . . . a dead donkey . . . .

"'Well, what has that got to do with the postboys?' asked Bob Sawyer.

"'This here,' replied Sam. 'without goin' so far as to assert, as some wery sensible people do, that postboys and donkeys is both immortal, wot *I* say is this; that wenever they feels theirselves gettin' stiff and past their work, they just rides off together, wun postboy to a pair in the usual way; wot becomes on 'em nobody knows, but it's wery probable as they starts avay to take their pleasure in some other vorld, for there ain't a man alive as ever see, either a donkey or a postboy, a takin' his pleasure in this!'" PP 51 *And see* H:Vocations—*veterinary*

—elephant

—amok: "If an elephant run mad, we are all ready for him—kill or cure—pills or bullets, calomel in conserve of roses, or lead in a musket-barrel." SB/GS

—eating habits: "[Barkis] being of a phlegmatic temperament, and not at all conversational—I offered him a cake as a mark of attention, which he ate at one gulp, exactly like an elephant, and which made no more impression on his big face than it would have done on an elephant's." DC 5

—metaphorical: " . . . the piston of the steam-engine worked monotonously up and down like the head of an elephant in a state of melancholy madness." HT i 5

" . . . no temperature made the melancholy mad elephants more mad or more sane. Their wearisome heads went up and down at the same rate, in hot weather and cold, wet weather and dry, fair weather and foul. The measured motion of their shadows on the walls, was the substitute Coketown had to show for the shadows of rustling woods . . . . " HT ii 1

—sartorial: "Thus, with the shuffling gait of the Elephant (who really does deal with the very worst trousers-maker employed by the Zoological world, and who appeared to have recommended him to Monsieur Mutuel), the old gentleman sunned himself daily when sun was to be had . . . . " CS/SL

—symbol of England: "'His capacity of intellectual development under proper training, his strength and docility, his industry, his many noble qualities, his patience and attachment under gentle treatment, and his blind resentment, when provoked too far by ill-usage, rendered him, besides, a touching symbol of the great English people; and this idea was still further expressed by his carrying trophies on his back, expressive of their enterprise and valour.'" HW/ET

—fauna in America: ""Oh!" says he, "if you should ever happen to go to bed [in Eden] . . . don't forget as to take a axe with you." I [Mark Tapley] looks at him tolerable hard. "Fleas?" says I. "And more," says he. "Wampires?" says I. "And more," says he. "Musquitoes, perhaps?" says I. "And more," says he. "What more?" says I. "Snakes more," says he; "rattlesnakes. You're right to a certain extent, stranger. There air some catawampous chawers in the small way too, as graze upon a human pretty strong; but don't mind *them*, they're company. It's snakes," he says, "as you'll object to: and whenever you wake and see one in a upright poster on your bed," he says, "like a corkscrew with the handle off a-sittin' on its bottom ring, cut him down, for he means wenom.""" MC 21

—fauna in Italy: " . . . when the sun goes down you must shut up all the windows, or the mosquitoes would tempt you to commit suicide . . . . As for the flies, you don't mind them. Nor the fleas, whose size is prodigious, and whose name is Legion, and who populate the coach-house to that extent that I daily expect to see the carriage going off bodily, drawn by myriads of industrious fleas in harness.

"The rats are kept away, quite comfortable, by scores of lean cats, who roam about the garden for that purpose. The lizards, of course, nobody cares for; they play in the sun, and don't bite. The little scorpions are merely curious. The beetles are rather late, and have not appeared yet.

"The frogs are company. There is a preserve of them in the grounds of the next villa; and after nightfall, one would think that scores upon scores of women in pattens were going up and down a wet stone pavement without a moment's cessation. That is exactly the noise they make." ¶PI 5

—hippopotamus: " . . . that impersonation of sensuality, the Hippopotamus. How do you provide for him? Could he find, on the banks of the Nile, such a villa you have built for him on the banks of the Regent's canal? Could he find, in his native Egypt, an appropriately furnished drawing-room, study, bath, wash-house, and spacious pleasure-ground, all *en suite,* and always ready? I think not." HW/L

And see TT:Railroad—*junction—night*

—horse

—abused: "There were many people on foot [in the Teetotal Procession] and many people in vehicles of various kinds . . . I never, on any occasion or under any circumstances, have beheld heavier overloading of horses than in this public show. Unless the imposition of a great van laden with from ten to twenty people on a single horse be a moderate tasking of the poor creature, then the temperate use of horses was immoderate and cruel. From the smallest and lightest horse to the largest and heaviest, there were many instances in which the beast of burden was so shamefully overladen, that the Society for the Prevention of Cruelty to Animals have frequently interposed in less gross cases." UT/TA *And see* B:Alcohol and Alcoholism—*Abstinence movement—use and abuse; and* TT:Stage-Coaches—*horses*

—admirable in England: " . . . we know little of horses; and, happily, for ourselves,

nothing of sporting; but believing in the dictum of the Natural History chapters of the Universal Spelling Book that the 'horse is a noble animal,' and that he is nowhere so noble, so well bred, so handsome, so tractable, so intelligent, so well cared for, and so well appreciated, as in this country; and that, in consequence of the national fondness for races his breed has been improved until he has attained his present excellence—believing all this, we think it quite possible to do him justice, without defiling the subject with any allusion to the knavery to which he, sometimes, innocently gives rise. Those who practise it are his vulgar parasites . . . ." HWC/E

—in ancient times: "The ancient Britons . . . were very fond of horses. The standard of Kent was the picture of a white horse. They could break them in and manage them wonderfully well. Indeed, the horses (of which they had an abundance, though they were rather small) were so well taught in those days, that they can scarcely be said to have improved since; though the men are so much wiser. They understood, and obeyed, every word of command; and would stand still by themselves, in all the din and noise of battle, while their masters went on to fight on foot." CHE 1

—a bargain: "'My life and soul . . . there is a horse for sale at Scrubbs's, which it would be a sin and a crime to lose—going, my senses' joy, for nothing.'

"'For nothing,' cried Madame, 'I am glad of that.'

"'For actually nothing,' replied Mantalini. 'A hundred guineas down will buy him; mane, and crest, and legs, and tail, all of the demdest beauty. I will ride him in the park before the very chariots of the rejected countesses. The demd old dowager will faint with grief and rage; the other two will say, "He is married, he has made away with himself, it is a demd thing, it is all up!" They will hate each other demnebly, and wish you dead and buried. Ha! ha! Demmit.'" NN 17

—benign neglect: "We take great interest in hackney-coaches, but we seldom drive, having a knack of turning ourselves over when we attempt to do so. We are as great friends to horses, hackney-coach and otherwise, as the renowned Mr **Martin**, of costermonger notoriety, and yet we never ride. We keep no horse, but a clothes-horse; enjoy no saddle so much as a saddle of mutton; and, following our own inclinations, have never followed the hounds. Leaving these fleeter means of getting over the ground, or of depositing one's-self upon it, to those who like them, by hackney-coach stands we take our stand." SB/HC

—bored in the rain: "The old roan, so famous for cross-country work, turning his large eyeball to the grated window near his rack, may remember the fresh leaves that glisten there at other times, and the scents that stream in, and may have a fine run with the hounds, while the human helper, clearing out the next stall, never stirs beyond his pitchfork and birch-broom. The grey, whose place is opposite the door, and who, with an impatient rattle of his halter, pricks his ears and turns his head so wistfully when it is opened, and to whom the opener says, 'Woa, grey, then, steady! Noabody wants you to-day!' may know it quite as well as the man. The whole seemingly monotonous and uncompanionable half-dozen, stabled together, may pass the long wet hours, when the door is shut, in livelier communication than is held in the servants' hall, or at the Dedlock Arms;—or may even beguile the time by improving (perhaps corrupting) the pony in the loose-box in the corner." BH 7

—with a cab: "'How old is that horse, my friend?' inquired Mr. Pickwick, rubbing his nose with the shilling he had reserved for the fare.

"'Forty-two,' replied the driver, eyeing him askant.

"'What!' ejaculated Mr. Pickwick, laying his hand upon his notebook. The driver reiterated his former statement. Mr. Pickwick looked very hard at the man's face, but his features were immovable, so he noted down the fact forthwith." PP 2

"'And how long do you keep him out at a time?' . . . .

"'Two or three veeks,' replied the man.

"'Weeks!' said Mr. Pickwick in astonishment . . . .

"'He lives at Pentonwil when he's at home,' observed the driver, coolly, 'but we seldom takes him home, on account of his veakness.'

"'On account of his weakness!' reiterated the perplexed Mr. Pickwick.

"'He always falls down when he's took out o' the cab,' continued the driver, 'but when he's in it, we bears him up werry tight, and takes him in werry short, so as he can't werry well fall down;' and we've got a pair o' precious large wheels on, so ven he does move, they run after him, and he must go on— he can't help it.'" PP 2

Richard ("Humanity") Martin, (1754-1834), M.P., SPCA founder, instituted checks, highly unpopular with hackeys and costermongers, on the treatment of their horses. Sam pulls the leg of a suspected informer.

—with a chaise: "'Not the slightest fear, sir,' interposed the hostler. 'Warrant him quiet, sir; a hinfant in arms might drive him.'

"'He don't shy, does he?' inquired Mr Pickwick.

"'Shy, sir?—He wouldn't shy if he was to meet a vaggin-load of monkeys with their tails burnt off." PP 5

—in a crowd: "A great annual Miner's Feast was being holden at the Inn, when I and my travelling companions presented ourselves at night among the wild crowd that were dancing before it by torchlight. We had had a break-down in the dark, on a stony morass some miles away; and I had the honour of leading one of the unharnassed [*sic.*] post-horses. If any lady or gentleman, on perusal of the present lines, will take any very tall post-horse with his traces hanging about his legs, and will conduct him by the bearing-rein into the heart of a country dance of a hundred and fifty couples, that lady or gentleman will then, and only then, form an adequate idea of the extent to which that post-horse will tread on his conductor's toes.

"Over and above which, the post-horse, finding three hundred people whirling about him, will probably rear, and also lash out with his hind legs, in a manner incompatible with dignity or self-respect on his conductor's part. With such little drawbacks on my usually impressive aspect, I appeared at this Cornish Inn, to the unutterable wonder of the Cornish Miners. It was full, and twenty times full, and nobody could be received but the post-horse,—though to get rid of that noble animal was something." ¶CS/HT 1

—defined: "'Bitzer, said Thomas Gradgrind. 'Your definition of a horse.'

"'Quadruped. Gramnivorous. Forty teeth, namely twenty-four grinders, four eye-teeth, and twelve incisive. Sheds coat in the spring; in marshy countries, sheds hoofs, too. Hoofs hard, but requiring to be shod with iron. Age known by marks in mouth.' Thus (and much more) Bitzer.

"'Now girl number twenty,' said Mr Gradgrind. 'You know what a horse is.'" HT i 1

—and dogs: "'There ain't no sort of orse that I ain't bred, and no sort of dorg. Orses and dorgs is some men's fancy. They're wittles and drink to me—lodging, wife, and children—reading, writing, and 'rithmetic—snuff, tobacker, and sleep.'

"'That ain't the sort of man to see sitting behind a coach-box, is it though?' said William in my ear, as he handled the reins.

"I construed this remark into an indication of a wish that he should have my place, so I blushingly offered to resign it.

"'Well, if you don't mind, sir,' said William, 'I think it *would* be more correct.'" DC 19

—effect on men: "The child [Nell] . . . had been thinking how strange it was that horses who were such fine honest creatures should seem to make vagabonds of all the men that drew about them . . . . " OCS 19

"[Shakers] are said to be good drivers of bargains, but to be honest and just in their transactions, and even in horse-dealing to resist those thievish tendencies which would seem, for some undiscovered reason, to be almost inseparable from that branch of traffic." AN 15

"They say that such a man was 'ruined by Horses.' ruined by Horses! They can't be open, even in that, and say he was ruined by Men; but they lay it at *our* stable-door! As if we ever ruined anybody, or were ever doing anything but being ruined ourselves, in our generous desire to fulfil the useful purposes of our existence!

"A busy little man [Phil Squod] always is, in the polishing at harness-house doors, of stirrup-irons, bits, curb-chains, harness bosses, anything in the way of a stable-yard that will take a polish: leading a life of friction." BH 66

"Between [Alfred Lammle's] room and the men there were strong points of general resemblance. Both were too gaudy, too slangy, too odorous of cigars, and too much given to horseflesh; the latter characteristic being exemplified in the room by its decorations, and in the men by their conversation. High-stepping horses seemed necessary to all Mr Lammle's friends—as necessary as their transaction of business together in a gipsy way at untimely hours of the morning and evening, and in rushes and snatches." OMF ii 4

And see H:Race Meeting

—*envied:* "The estimable Twemlow, dressing himself in his lodgings over the stable-yard in Duke Street, Saint James's, and hearing the horses at their toilet below, finds himself on the whole in a disadvantageous position as compared with the noble animals at livery. For whereas, on the one hand, he has no attendant to slap him soundingly and require him in gruff accents to come up and come over, still, on the other hand, he has no attendant at all; and the mild gentleman's finger-joints and other joints working rustily in the morning, he could deem it agreeable even to be tied up by the countenance at his chamber-door, so he were there skilfully rubbed down and slushed and sluiced and polished and clothed, while himself taking merely a passive part in these trying transactions." OMF ii 16

—*a faker:* A horse "in whom [Pecksniff's] enemies . . . pretended to detect a fanciful resemblance to his master. Not in his outward person, for he was a raw-boned, haggard horse, always on a much shorter allowance of corn than Mr. Pecksniff; but in his moral character, wherein, said they, he was full of promise, but of no performance. He was always, in a manner, going to go, and never going. When at his slowest rate of travelling, he would sometimes lift up his legs so high, and display such mighty action, that it was difficult to believe he was doing less than fourteen miles an hour; and he was for ever so perfectly satisfied with his own speed, and so little disconcerted by opportunities of comparing himself with the fastest trotters, that the illusion was the more difficult of resistance.

"He was a kind of animal who infused into the breasts of strangers a lively sense of hope, and possessed all those who knew him better with a grim despair. In what respect, having these points of character, he might be fairly likened to his master, that good man's slanderers only can explain. But it is a melancholy truth, and deplorable instance of the uncharitableness of the world, that they made the comparison." ¶MC 5

—*in a field:* " . . . the rough cart horses bestow a sleepy glance upon the smart coach team, which says, as plainly as a horse's glance can, 'It's all very fine to look at, but slow going, over a heavy field, is better than warm work like that, upon a dusty road, after all.'" PP 16

—*and gentleman:* "'And drives very beautiful horses, doesn't he?' inquired another.

"'I dare say he may, but I never saw them,' answered Kate.

"'Never saw them!' interposed Miss Knag. 'Oh, well! There it is at once you know; how can you possibly pronounce an opinion about a gentleman—hem—if you don't see him as he turns out altogether?'

"There was so much of the world—even of the little world of the country girl—in this idea of the old milliner, that Kate . . . left Miss Knag in possession of the field." NN 17

—*in a graveyard:* "The clergyman's horse, stumbling with a dull blunt sound among the graves, was cropping the grass; at once deriving orthodox consolation from the dead parishioners, and enforcing last Sunday's text that this was what all flesh came to; a lean ass who had sought to expound it also, without being qualified and ordained, was pricking his ears in an empty pound hard by, and looking with hungry eyes upon his priestly neighbour." OCS 16

—*for the inexperienced:* "Mr. Winkle . . . climbed into his saddle, with about as much difficulty as he would have experienced in getting up the side of a first-rate man-of-war.

"'All right?' inquired Mr Pickwick, with an inward presentiment that it was all wrong.

"'All right,' replied Mr. Winkle faintly. . . .

"'What makes him go sideways?' said Mr Snodgrass in the bin, to Mr Winkle in the saddle.

"'I can't imagine,' replied Mr Winkle. His horse was drifting up the street in the most mysterious manner—side first, with his head towards one side of the way, and his tail towards the other. . . .

"'Winkle, said Mr Snodgrass, as the equestrian came trotting up on the tall horse, with his hat over his ears, and shaking all over, as if he would shake to pieces, with the violence of the exercise, 'pick up the whip, there's a good fellow.' Mr Winkle pulled at the bridle of the tall horse till he was black in the face; and having at length succeeded in stopping him, dismounted, handed the whip to Mr Pickwick, and grasping the reins, prepared to remount.

"Now whether the tall horse, in the natural playfulness of his disposition, was desirous of having a little innocent recreation with Mr Winkle, or whether it occurred to him that he could perform the journey as much to his own satisfaction without a rider as with one, are points upon which, of course, we can arrive at no definite and distinct conclusion. By whatever motives the animal was actuated, certain it is that Mr Winkle had no sooner touched the reins, than he slipped them over his head, and darted backwards to their full length.

"'Poor fellow,' said Mr. Winkle, soothingly—'poor fellow—good old horse.' The 'poor fellow' was proof against flattery: the more Mr Winkle tried to get nearer him, the more he sidled away; and, notwithstanding all kinds of coaxing and wheedling, there were Mr Winkle and the horse going round and round each other for ten minutes, at the end of which time each was at precisely the same distance from the other as when they first commenced—an unsatisfactory sort of thing under any circumstances, but particularly so in a lonely road, where no assistance can be procured.

"' . . . . The horse no sooner beheld Mr Pickwick advancing towards him with the chaise whip in his hand, than he exchanged the rotatory motion in which he had previously indulged, for a retrograde movement of so very determined a character, that it at once drew Mr Winkle, who was still at the end of the bridle, at a rather quicker rate than fast walking, in the direction from which they had just come. Mr Pickwick ran to his assistance, but the faster Mr Pickwick ran forward, the faster the horse ran backward. There was a great scraping of feet, and kicking up of the dust; and at last Mr Winkle, his arms being nearly pulled out of their sockets, fairly let go his hold. The horse paused, stared, shook his head, turned round, and quietly trotted home to Rochester, leaving Mr Winkle and Mr Pickwick gazing on each other with countenances of blank dismay." PP 5

—lazy: "The carrier's horse was the laziest horse in the world, I should hope, and shuffled along, with his head down, as if he liked to keep people waiting to whom the packages were directed. I fancied, indeed, that he sometimes chuckled audibly over this reflection, but the carrier said he was only troubled with a cough." DC 3

—mail coach: " . . . the hill, and the harness, and the mud, and the mail, were all so heavy, that the horses had three times already come to a stop, besides once drawing the coach across the road, with the mutinous intent of taking it back to Blackheath. Reins and whip and coachman and guard, however, in combination, had read that article of war which forbad a purpose otherwise strongly in favour of the argument, that some brute animals are endued with Reason; and the team had capitulated and returned to duty.

"With drooping heads and tremulous tails, they mashed their way through the thick mud, floundering and stumbling between whiles, as if they were falling to pieces at the larger joints. As often as the driver rested them and brought them to a stand, with a wary 'Wo-ho! so-ho then!' the near leader violently shook his head and everything upon it—like an unusually emphatic horse, denying that the coach could be got up the hill." TTC i 2

—and man: " . . . I should describe Man [said the Horse] as an unmeaning and conceited creature, very seldom to be trusted, and not likely to make advances towards the honesty of the nobler animals. I should say that his power of warping the nobler animals to bad purposes, and damaging their reputation by his companionship, is, next to the art of growing oats, hay, carrots, and clover, one of his principal attributes. He is very unintelligible in his caprices; seldom expressing with distinctness what he wants of us; and relying greatly on our better judgment to find out. He is cruel, and fond of blood—particularly at a steeple-chase—and is very ungrateful." HW/R 3

—offered for sale: " . . . the vendor remarked to me, in an original manner, on bringing him for approval, taking his cloth off and smacking him, 'There, Sir! There's a Orse!' And when I said gallantly, 'How much do you want for him?' and when the vendor said, 'No more than sixty guineas, from you,' and when I said smartly, 'Why not more than sixty from *me?*' And when he said crushingly, 'Because upon my soul and body he'd be considered cheap at seventy, by one who understood the subject—but you don't.'" UT/RM

—ostentatious: "The horse of distinguished family, who had Capricorn for his nephew, and Cauliflower for his brother, showed himself worthy of his high relations by champing at the bit until his chest was white with foam, and rearing like a horse in

heraldry; the plated harness and the patent leather glittered in the sun; pedestrians admired; Mr Bailey was complacent, but unmoved . . . and on he went, squaring his short green arms outside the apron, as if he were hooked on to it by his armpits." MC 27

—subject of conversation: "If a man knows a Horse well, he is prouder of it than of any knowledge of himself, within the range of his limited capacity. He regards it as the sum of all human acquisition. If he is learned in a Horse, he has nothing else to learn . . . . As to making us a subject of conversation, my opinion is that we are more talked about, than history, philosophy, literature, art, and science, all put together. I have encountered innumerable gentlemen in the country, who were totally incapable of interest in anything but Horses and Dogs—except Cattle. And I have always been given to understand that they were the flower of the civilised world." HW/R 3

—in war: "The Britons could not have succeeded in their most remarkable art, without the aid of these sensible and trusty animals . . . . The horses who drew [the war chariots] were so well trained, that they would tear, at full gallop, over the most stony ways, and even through the woods; dashing down their masters' enemies beneath their hoofs . . . . In a moment, while at full speed, the horses would stop, at the driver's command. The men within would leap out, deal blows about them with their swords like hail, leap on the horses, on the pole, spring back into the chariots anyhow; and, as soon as they were safe, the horses tore away again." CHE 1

—lion

—on public-house sign: "The creaking Lion over the house-door was, therefore, to say the truth, rather a drowsy, tame, and feeble lion; and as these social representatives of a savage class are usually of a conventional character (being depicted, for the most part, in impossible attitudes and of unearthly colours) he was frequently supposed by the more ignorant and uninformed among the neighbours, to be the veritable portrait of the host as he appeared on the occasion of some great funeral ceremony or public mourning." BR 31

—in a zoo: "From day to day, I find the noble creatures patiently wearing out their weary lives in narrow spaces where they have hardly room to turn . . . . Look at those wonderfully-constructed feet, with their exquisite machinery for alighting from springs and leaps. What do you conceive to be the kind of ground to which those feet are, in the great foresight of Nature, least adapted? Bare, smooth, hard boards, perhaps, like the deck of a ship? Yes. A strange reason why you should choose that and no other flooring for their dens!" HW/L

See —cat—free to roam; and —going to bed

—menagerie: "I brought away five wonderments from the exhibition. I have wondered ever since, Whether the beasts ever do get used to those small places of confinement; Whether the monkeys have that very horrible flavour in their free state; Whether wild animals have a natural ear for time and tune, and therefore every four-footed creature began to howl in despair when the band began to play; What the giraffe does with his neck when his cart is shut up; and, Whether the elephant feels ashamed of himself when he is brought out of his den to stand on his head in the presence of the whole Collection." RP/OT

—monkey in a zoo: "They have an artificial climate carefully prepared for them. They have the blessing of congenial society carefully secured to them. They are among their own tribes and connexions. They have shelves to skip upon, and pigeon-holes to creep into. Graceful ropes dangle from the upper beams of their sitting-rooms, by which they swing, for their own enjoyment, the fascination of the fair sex, and the instruction of the enquiring minds of the rising generation." HW/L

—mouse: We recall one white mouse, who lived in the cover of a Latin dictionary, who ran up ladders, drew Roman chariots, shouldered muskets, turned wheels, and even made a very creditable appearance on the stage as the Dog of Montargis. He might have achieved greater things, but for having the misfortune to mistake his way in a triumphal procession to the Capitol, when he fell into a deep inkstand, and was dyed black and drowned." RP/OS

—mule: " . . . I deserted my German chariot for the back of a mule (in colour and consistency so very like a dusty old hair trunk I once had at school, that I half expected to see my initials in brass-headed nails on his backbone), and went up a thousand rugged ways, and looked down at a thousand woods of fir and pine, and would on the whole have preferred my mule's keeping a

little nearer to the inside, and not usually travelling with a hoof or two over the precipice—though much consoled by explanation that this was to be attributed to his great sagacity, by reason of his carrying broad loads of wood at other times, and not being clear but that I myself belonged to that station of life, and required as much room as they. He brought me safely, in his own wise way, among the passes of the Alps . . . . " UT/TA

—oxen: At Carrara: "When we stood aside, to see one of these cars drawn by only a pair of oxen (for it had but one small block of marble on it), coming down, I hailed, in my heart, the man who sat upon the heavy yoke, to keep it on the neck of the poor beasts—and who faced backwards: not before him—as the very Devil of true despotism. He had a great rod in his hand, with an iron point; and when they could plough and force their way through the loose bed of the torrent no longer, and came to a stop, he poked it into their bodies, beat it on their heads, screwed it round and round in their nostrils, got them on a yard or two, in the madness of intense pain . . . and when their writhing and smarting, and the weight behind them, bore them plunging down the precipice in a cloud of scattered water, whirled his rod above his head, and gave a great whoop and hallo, as if he had achieved something, and had no idea that they might shake him off, and blindly mash his brains upon the road, in the noon-tide of his triumph." PI 10

And see —cattle; F:The Poor, Abject*—and animals; and* TT:Railroad*—junction—night*

—pig

—disgusted: "'You are speaking of Tom [Mopes] in there?'

"'Yes.'

"'Well now,' said the Tinker, blowing the dust off his job: which was finished. 'Ain't it enough to disgust a pig, if he could give his mind to it?'

"'If he could give his mind to it,' returned the other, smiling, 'the probability is that he wouldn't be a pig.'" CS/TT 3

—a literate clubman: "Here is a solitary swine lounging homeward by himself. He has only one ear; having parted with the other to vagrant-dogs in the course of his city rambles. But he gets on very well without it; and leads a roving, gentlemanly, vagabond kind of life, somewhat answering to that of our club-men at home. He leaves his lodgings every morning at a certain hour, throws himself upon the town, gets through his day in some manner quite satisfactory to himself, and regularly appears at the door of his own house again at night, like the mysterious master of *Gil Blas.*" AN 6

See Gil Blas, Index XI part 2

And see W:France and the French—*'long'*

—man's best friend: "'It is an immense advantage to one of these poor fellows to have a pig [said Friar Bacon]. The pig consumes the refuse from the man's cottage and Allotment-garden, and the pig's refuse enriches the man's garden besides. The pig is the poor man's friend . . . .'

"The poor man's friend. Yes. I have often wondered who really was the poor man's friend among a great number of competitors, and I now clearly perceive him to be the pig. *He* never makes any flourishes about the poor man. *He* never gammons the poor man—except to his manifest advantage in the article of bacon. *He* never comes down to this house, or goes down to his constituents.

"He openly declares to the poor man, 'I want my sty, because I am a pig; I desire to have as much to eat as you can by any means stuff me with, because I am a pig.' *He* never gives the poor man a sovereign for bringing up a family. *He* never grunts the poor man's name in vain. And when he dies in the odour of porkity, he cuts up, a highly useful creature and a blessing to the poor man, from the ring in his snout to the curl in his tail. Which of the poor man's other friends can say as much. Where is the M.P. who means mere pork?" ¶AY/B

—startled: "One young gentleman (a very delicate porker with several straws sticking about his nose, betokening recent investigations in a dunghill) was walking deliberately on, profoundly thinking, when suddenly his brother, who was lying in a miry hole unseen by him, rose up immediately before his startled eyes, ghostly with damp mud.

"Never was pig's whole mass of blood so turned. He started back at least three feet, gazed for a moment, and then shot off as hard as he could go: his excessively little tail vibrating with speed and terror like a distracted pendulum. But before he had gone very far, he began to reason with himself as to the nature of this frightful appearance; and as he reasoned, he relaxed his speed by gradual degrees; until at last he stopped, and faced about.

"There was his brother, with the mud upon him glazing in the sun, yet staring out of the very same hole, perfectly amazed at his proceedings! He was no sooner assured of this; and he assured himself so carefully that one may almost say he shaded his eyes with his hand to see the better; than he came back at a round trot, pounced upon him, and summarily took off a piece of his tail; as a caution to him to be careful what he was about for the future, and never to play tricks with his family any more." AN 12

—pony

—independent: " . . . there approached towards [Kit Nubbles] a little clattering jingling four-wheeled chaise, drawn by a little obstinate-looking rough-coated pony [Whisker], and driven by a little fat placid-faced old gentleman . . . the pony was coming along at his own pace and doing exactly as he pleased with the whole concern. If the old gentleman remonstrated by shaking the reins, the pony replied by shaking his head. It was plain that the utmost the pony would consent to do, was to go in his own way up any street that the old gentleman particularly wished to traverse, but that it was an understanding between them that he must do this after his own fashion or not at all . . . .

" . . . . The pony ran off at a sharp angle to inspect a lamp-post on the opposite side of the way, and then went off at a tangent to another lamp-post on the other side. Having satisfied himself that they were of the same pattern and materials, he came to a stop apparently absorbed in meditation." OCS 14 *For another show-off, see* Pony NN

—rabbits: The staircase was sacred to rabbits. There in hutches of all shapes and kinds, made from old packing-cases, boxes, drawers, and tea-chests, they increased in a prodigious degree, and contributed their share towards that complicated whiff which, quite impartially, and without distinction of persons, saluted every nose that was put into Sweedlepipe's easy shaving-shop." MC 26

—rats, in a burning house: " . . . all this taking place—not among pitying looks and friendly murmurs of compassion, but brutal shouts and exultations, which seemed to make the very rats who stood by the old house too long, creatures with some claim upon the pity and regard of those its roof had sheltered . . . . " BR 55

—sheep, in the wind: " . . . a flock of sheep with the wool about their necks blown into such great ruffs that they looked like fleecy owls." RP/OS

And see TT:Railroad*—junction—night*

—silk-worm: " . . . [the half-pay Captain] took to breeding silk-worms, which he *would* bring in two or three times a day, in little paper boxes, to show the old lady, generally dropping a worm or two at every visit. The consequence was, that one morning a very stout silk-worm was discovered in the act of walking upstairs—probably with a view to inquiring after his friends, for, on further inspection, it appeared that some of his companions had already found their way to every room in the house. The old lady went to the seaside in despair . . . . " SB/C

And see Change*—admonitory lecture*

—snail: " . . . a steep by-street at Brighton; where . . . the houses were more than usually brittle and thin . . . and where snails were constantly discovered holding on to the street doors, and other public places they were not expected to ornament, with the tenacity of cupping-glasses." DS 8

—toad: "'I ain't superstitious about toads,' said Mark, looking round the [hut in Eden], 'but if you could prevail upon the two or three I see in company, to step out . . . my young friends, I think they'd find the open air refreshing. Not that I at all object to 'em. A very handsome animal is a toad,' said Mr Tapley, sitting down upon a stool: 'very spotted; very like a partickler style of old gentleman about the throat; very bright-eyed, very cool, and very slippy. But one sees 'em to the best advantage out of doors perhaps.'" MC 33

Bird

—in bad company: "Nothing in shy neighbourhoods perplexes my mind more than the bad company birds keep. Foreign birds often get into good society, but British birds are inseparable from low associates. There is a whole street of them in St Giles's; and I always find them in poor and immoral neighbourhoods, convenient to the public-house and the pawnbroker's. They seem to lead people into drinking, and even the man who makes their cages usually gets into a chronic state of black eye. Why is this? Also, they will do things for people in short-skirted velveteen coats with bone buttons, or in sleeved waistcoats and fur caps, which

they cannot be persuaded by the respectable orders of society to undertake." UT/SN

—*before a shoot:* "The birds, who, happily for their own peace of mind and personal comfort, were in blissful ignorance of the preparations which had been making to astonish them, on the first of September, hailed it no doubt, as one of the pleasantest mornings they had seen that season. Many a young partridge who strutted complacently among the stubble, with all the finicking coxcombry of youth, and many an older one who watched his levity out of his little round eye, with the contemptuous air of a bird of wisdom and experience, alike unconscious of their approaching doom, basked in the fresh morning air with lively and blithesome feelings, and a few hours afterwards were laid low upon the earth." PP 19

—*blackbird:* "There was not a bird of such methodical and businesslike habits in all the world as the blind blackbird, who dreamed and dozed away his days in a large snug cage, and had lost his voice from old age years before Tim [Linkinwater] first bought him." NN 37

—*bluejay:* " . . . the banks [of the Ohio River] are for the most part deep solitudes, overgrown with trees . . . nor is anything seen to move about them but the blue jay, whose colour is so bright, and yet so delicate, that it looks like a flying flower." AN 11

—*caged:* "If the bird-fancier had been at home, as he ought to have been, there would have been no great harm . . . . The shutters were down certainly; and in every pane of glass there was at least one tiny bird in a tiny bird-cage, twittering and hopping his little ballet of despair, and knocking his head against the roof: while one unhappy goldfinch who lived outside a red villa with his name on the door, drew the water for his own drinking, and mutely appealed to some good man to drop a farthing's-worth of poison in it." MC 19

—*canary:* " . . . [Miss Tox's] bird—a very high-shouldered canary, stricken in years, and much rumpled, but a piercing singer, as Princess's Place well knew . . . . " DS 29

"When Miss Clarissa [Spenlow] had shaken her head, Miss Lavinia resumed: again referring to my letter through her eye-glass. They both had little bright round twinkling eyes, by the way, which were like birds' eyes. They were not unlike birds, altogether; having a sharp, brisk sudden manner, and a little short, spruce way of adjusting themselves, like canaries." DC 41

"'You have brought your bird with you, I suppose?' said Mr Jarndyce.

"'By Heaven, he is the most astonishing bird in Europe!' replied the other . 'He *is* the most wonderful creature! I wouldn't take ten thousand guineas for that bird. I have left an annuity for his sole support, in case he should outlive me. He is, in sense and attachment, a phenomenon. And his father before him was one of the most astonishing birds that ever lived!'

"The subject of this laudation was a very little canary, who was so tame that he was brought down by Mr Boythorn's man, on his forefinger, and, after taking a gentle flight round the room, alighted on his master's head. To hear Mr Boythorn presently expressing the most implacable and passionate sentiments, with this fragile mite of a creature quietly perched on his forehead, was to have a good illustration of his character, I thought." BH 9

—*stuffed:* "The greasy door is violently pushed inward, and a boy follows it, who says, after having let it slam:

"'Come for the stuffed canary.'

"'It's three and ninepence,' returns Venus; 'have you got the money?'

"The boy produces four shillings . . . Mr Venus rescues the canary in a glass case, and shows it to the boy.

"'There!' he whispers. 'There's animation! On a twig, making up his mind to hop! Take care of him; he's a lovely specimen.—and three is four.'" OMF i 7

—*carrier pigeon:* "As carrier-pigeons, on being first let loose in a strange place, beat the air at random for a short time, before darting off towards the spot for which they are designed, so did the Marchioness flutter round and round until she believed herself in safety, and then bear swiftly down upon the port for which she was bound." OCS 65

—*cock:* " . . . hearing the cock at the little dairy in Cursitor Street go into that disinterested ecstasy of his on the subject of daylight . . . . " BH 11

—*Cock Robin:* " . . . Wegg perceives a pretty little dead bird lying on the counter, with its head drooping on one side against the rim of Mr Venus's saucer, and a long stiff wire piercing its breast. As if it were Cock Robin, the hero of the ballad, and Mr Venus were the sparrow with his bow and arrow, and Mr Wegg were the fly with his little eye." OMF i 7

—fancier: "With the exception of the staircase, and his lodger's private apartment, Poll Sweedlepipe's house was one great bird's nest. Game-cocks resided in the kitchen; pheasants wasted the brightness of their golden plumage on the garret; bantams roosted in the cellar; owls had possession of the bedroom; and specimens of all the smaller fry of birds chirrupped and twittered in the shop." MC 26

—goldfinch: " . . . I found a goldfinch drawing his own water, and drawing as much of it as if he were in a consuming fever. That goldfinch lived at a bird-shop, and offered, in writing, to barter himself against old clothes, empty bottles, or even kitchen stuff. Surely a low thing and a depraved taste in any finch!

"I bought that goldfinch for money. He was sent home, and hung upon a nail over against my table . . . . From the time of his appearance in my room, either he left off being thirsty—which was not in the bond—or he could not make up his mind to hear his little bucket drop back into his well when he let it go: a shock which in the best of times had made him tremble. He drew no water but by stealth and cloak of night.

"After an interval of futile and at length hopeless expectation, the merchant who had educated him was appealed to . . . . He sent word that he would 'look round.' He looked round, appeared in the doorway of the room, and slightly cocked up his evil eye at the goldfinch. Instantly a raging thirst beset that bird; when it was appeased, he still drew several unnecessary buckets of water; and finally, leaped about his perch and sharpened his bill, as if he had been to the nearest wine vaults and got drunk." ¶UT/SN *And see —caged*

—hummingbirds: " . . . with these feathered jewels still glittering in our vision, we cannot call them by any less delicate name than some one of the charming India terms which belong to the poetry of their associations. They shall remain in our memory under 'the pretty, fond, adoptious christendoms,'* by some of which the ancient Mexicans expressed their love for these most brilliant of living creatures. They shall be to us 'rays of the sun'—'rose-suckers'—myrtle-suckers'—'hill stars'—'hermits'—'comets'—'stars of the morning'—'tresses of the day star.'" HWC/DS

**Alls' Well that Ends Well,* I i

—lark: "Mr Carker the Manager rose with the lark, and went out walking in the summer day. His meditations . . . hardly seemed to soar as high as the lark, or to mount in that direction; rather they kept close to their nest upon the earth, and looked about, among the dust and worms. . . . As the lark rose higher, he sank deeper in thought. As the lark poured out her melody clearer and stronger, he fell into a graver and profounder silence. At length, when the lark came headlong down, with an accumulating stream of song, and dropped among the green wheat near him, rippling in the breath of the morning like a river, he sprang up from his reverie . . . . " DS 27

—linnets, etc.: "[Miss Flite] partly drew aside the curtain of the long low garret-window, and called our attention to a number of bird-cages hanging there: some containing several birds. There were larks, linnets, and goldfinches—I should think at least twenty.

"'I began to keep the little creatures,' she said, 'with an object that the wards will readily comprehend. With the intention of restoring them to liberty. When my judgment should be given. Ye-es! They die in prison, though. Their lives, poor silly things, are so short in comparison with Chancery proceedings, that, one by one, the whole collection has died over and over again. I doubt, do you know, whether one of these, though they are all young, will live to be free!'" BH 5

"'Another secret, my dear. I have added to my collection of birds' . . . .

"She nodded several times, and her face became overcast and gloomy. 'Two more. I call them the Wards in Jarndyce. They are caged up with all the others. With Hope, Joy, Youth, Peace, Rest, Life, Dust, Ashes, Waste, Want, Ruin, Despair, Madness, Death, Cunning, Folly, Words, Wigs, Rags, Sheepskin, Plunder, Precedent, Jargon, Gammon, and Spinach!'" BH 60

—owl: "I want to know why I am to be called upon to accommodate myself to . . . an owl (who is the greatest ass I have ever known) . . . . My opinion of *him* is that he blinks and stares himself into a state of such dense stupidity that he has no idea what company he is in. I have seen him, with my own eyes, blink himself, for hours, into the conviction that he was alone in a

belfry." HW/PF

"The owl shakes his head when I confide [my mission] to him, and says he doubts. He always did shake his head and doubt. Whenever he brings himself before the public, he never does anything except shake his head and doubt. I should have thought he had got himself into a sufficient mess by doing that, when he roosted for a long time in the Court of Chancery. but he can't leave off. He's always at it." HW/R 1

". . . the owl made a noise with very little resemblance in it to the noise conventionally assigned to the owl by men-poets. But it is the obstinate custom of such creatures hardly ever to say what is set down for them. " TTC ii 9

—a 'aunt: "'This gentleman wants to know,' said the landlord, 'if anything's seen at the Poplars.'

"' 'Ooded woman with a howl,' said Ikey, in a state of great freshness.

"'Do you mean a cry?'

"'I mean a bird, sir.'

"'A hooded woman with an owl. Dear me! Did you ever see her?'

"'I seen the howl.'

"'Never the woman?'

"'Not so plain as the howl, but they always keeps together' . . . .

"'Who is—or who was—the hooded woman with the owl? Do you know?'

"'Well!' said Ikey, holding up his cap with one hand while he scratched his head with the other, 'they say, in general, that she was murdered, and the howl he 'ooted the while.'" CS/HH 1

—parrot: "A gaudy parrot in a burnished cage upon the table tears at the wires with her beak, and goes walking, upside down, in its dome-top, shaking her house and screeching . . . the chafing and imprisoned bird . . . coming down into a pendant gilded hoop within the cage, like a great wedding-ring, swings in it . . . . " DS 33

"The disregarded parrot only was in action. It twisted and pulled at the wires of its cage, with its crooked beak, and crawled up to the dome, and along its roof like a fly, and down again head foremost, and shook, and bit, and rattled at every slender bar, as if it knew its master's danger, and was wild to force a passage out, and fly away to warn him of it." DS 52

" . . . there was a parrot on the outside of a golden cage holding on by its beak with its scaly legs in the air, and putting itself into many strange upside-down postures. This peculiarity has been observed in birds of quite another feather, climbing upon golden wires . . . .

"' . . . . [I] who am a child of nature if I could but show it; but so it is. Society suppresses us and dominates us—Bird, be quiet!'

"The parrot had broken into a violent fit of laughter, after twisting divers bars of his cage with his crooked bill, and licking them with his black tongue . . . .

"The sisters rose at the same time, and they all stood near the cage of the parrot, as he tore at a claw-full of biscuit and spat it out, seemed to mock them with a pompous dance of his body without moving his feet, and suddenly turned himself upside down and trailed himself all over the outside of his golden cage, with the aid of his cruel beak and his black tongue" LD i 20

"Now [said the Raven], I don't care for the parrot. I don't admire the parrot's voice—it wants hoarseness. And I despise the parrot's livery—considering black the only true wear . . . . But if you come to that, and you laugh at the parrot because the parrot says the same thing over and over again, don't you think you could get up a laugh at yourselves?

"Did you ever know a Cabinet Minister say of a flagrant job or great abuse, perfectly notorious to the whole country, that he had never heard a word of it himself, but could assure the honourable gentleman that every inquiry should be made? . . . Did you ever hear, among yourselves, anything approaching to a parrot repetition of the words, Constitution, Country, Public Service, Self-Government, Centralisation, Un-English, Capital, Balance of Power, Vested Interests, Corn, Rights of Labour, Wages, or so forth? *Did* you ever? No! Of course you never!" ¶HW/R 1

—pigeon: "There were more pigeons about the dreary [Maypole] stable yard and outbuildings than anybody but the landlord could reckon up. The wheeling and circling flights of runts, fantails, tumblers, and pouters, were perhaps not quite consistent with the grave and sober character of the building, but the monotonous cooing, which never ceased to be raised by some among them all day long, suited it exactly, and seemed to lull it to rest." BR 1

" . . . a pigeon-house, whose little apertures looked, as they do in all pigeon-houses, very much too small for the admission of the plump and swelling-breasted birds who were strutting about it, though they tried to get in never so hard." AN 13

And see H:Vocations—*illicit—bird-catching*

—poultry

—in the city: "The fowls who peck about the kennels, jerking their bodies hither and thither with a gait which none but town fowls are ever seen to adopt, and which any country cock or hen would be puzzled to understand, are perfectly in keeping with the crazy habitations of their owners. Dingy, ill-plumed drowsy flutterers, sent, like many of the neighbouring children, to get a livelihood in the streets, they hop from stone to stone, in forlorn search of some hidden eatable in the mud, and can scarcely raise a crow among them. The only one with anything approaching to a voice, is an aged bantam at the baker's; and even he is hoarse, in consequence of bad living in his last place." NN 14

"That anything born of an egg and invested with wings, should have got to the pass that it hops contentedly down a ladder into a cellar, and calls *that* going home, is a circumstance so amazing as to leave one nothing more in this connexion to wonder at. Otherwise I might wonder at the completeness with which these fowls have become separated from all the birds of the air—have taken to grovelling in bricks and mortar and mud—have forgotten all about live trees, and make roosting-places of shop-boards, barrows, oyster-tubs, bulk-heads, and door-scrapers. I wonder at nothing concerning them, and take them as they are.

"I accept as products of Nature and things of course, a reduced Bantam family of my acquaintance in the Hackney-road, who are incessantly at the pawnbroker's. I cannot say that they enjoy themselves, for they are of a melancholy temperament; but what enjoyment they are capable of, they derive from crowding together in the pawnbroker's side-entry. Here, they are always to be found in a feeble flutter, as if they were newly come down in the world, and were afraid of being identified.

"I know a low fellow, originally of a good family from Dorking, who takes his whole establishment of wives, in single file, in at the door of the Jug Department of a disorderly tavern near the Haymarket, manœuvres them among the company's legs, emerges with them at the Bottle Entrance, and so passes his life: seldom, in the season, going to bed before two in the morning.

"Over on Waterloo-bridge, there is a shabby old speckled couple (they belong to the wooden French-bedstead, washing-stand, and towel-horse-making trade), who are always trying to get in at the door of a chapel. Whether the old lady, under a delusion reminding one of Mrs Southcott, has an idea of entrusting an egg to that particular denomination, or merely understands that she has no business in the building and is consequently frantic to enter it, I cannot determine; but she is constantly endeavouring to undermine the principal door: while her partner, who is infirm upon his legs, walks up and down, encouraging her and defying the Universe.

"But, the family I have been best acquainted with, since the removal from this trying sphere of a Chinese circle at Brentford, reside in the densest part of Bethnal-green. Their abstraction from the objects among which they live, or rather their conviction that these objects have all come into existence in express subservience to fowls, has so enchanted me, that I have made them the subject of many journeys at divers hours.

"After careful observation of the two lords and the ten ladies of whom this family consists, I have come to the conclusion that their opinions are represented by the leading lord and leading lady: the latter, as I judge, an aged personage, afflicted with a paucity of feather and visibility of quill, that gives her the appearance of a bundle of office pens.

"When a railway goods van that would crush an elephant comes round the corner, tearing over these fowls, they emerge unharmed from under the horses, perfectly satisfied that the whole rush was a passing property in the air, which may have left something to eat behind it. They look upon old shoes, wrecks of kettles and saucepans, and fragments of bonnets, as a kind of meteoric discharge, for fowls to peck at. Peg-tops and hoops they account, I think, as a sort of hail; shuttlecocks, as rain, or dew.

"Gaslight comes quite as natural to them as any other light; and I have more than a suspicion that, in the minds of the two lords, the early public-house at the corner has superseded the sun. I have established it as a certain fact, that they always begin to crow when the public-house shutters begin to be taken down, and that they salute the potboy, the instant he appears to perform that duty, as if he were Phœbus in person." ¶UT/SN

—*in Flanders:* "Wonderful poultry of the French-Flemish country, why take the trouble to *be* poultry? Why not stop short at eggs in the rising generation, and die out and have done with it? Parents of chickens have I seen this day, followed by their wretched young families, scratching nothing out of the mud with an air—tottering about on legs so scraggy and weak, that the valiant word drumsticks becomes a mockery when applied to them, and the crow of the lord and master has been a mere dejected case of croup." UT/FF

—*geese in Mantua:* "Then, we went to a dismal sort of farm-yard, by which a picture-gallery was approached. The moment the gate of this retreat was opened, some five hundred geese came waddling round us, stretching out their necks, and clamouring in the most hideous manner, as if they were ejaculating, 'Oh! here's somebody come to see the Pictures! Don't go up! Don't go up!' While we went up, they waited very quietly about the door in a crowd, cackling to one another occasionally, in a subdued tone; but the instant we appeared again, their necks came out like telescopes, and setting up a great noise, which meant, I have no doubt, 'What, you would go, would you? What do you think of it? How do you like it?' they attended us to the outer gate, and cast us forth, derisively, into Mantua.

"The geese who saved the Capitol,* were, as compared to these, Pork to the learned Pig. What a gallery it was! I would take their opinion on a question of art, in preference to the discourses of Sir Joshua Reynolds." PI 9

**Legend says Gauls invading Rome in 390 BC lost the element of surprise when the cackling of the sacred geese aroused the Capitol's garrison.*

—*in unrelenting rain:* "The turkey in the poultry-yard, always troubled with a class-grievance (probably Christmas), may be reminiscent of that summer-morning wrongfully taken from him, when he got into the lane among the felled trees, where there was a barn and barley. The discontented goose, who stoops to pass under the old gateway, twenty feet high, may gabble out, if we only knew it, a waddling preference for weather when the gateway casts its shadow on the ground." BH 6

—*raven:* "'Is he old?

"'A mere boy, sir,' replied the locksmith. 'A hundred and twenty, or thereabouts. Call him down, Barnaby, my man.'

"'Call him!' echoed Barnaby, sitting upright upon the floor, and staring vacantly at Gabriel as he thrust his hair back from his face. 'But who can make him come! He calls me, and makes me go where he will. He goes on before, and I follow. He's the master, and I'm the man. Is that the truth, Grip?'

"The raven gave a short, comfortable, confidential kind of croak—a most expressive croak, which seemed to say, 'You needn't let these fellows into our secrets. We understand each other. It's all right.'" BR 6

"It was remarkable in the raven that during the whole interview he had kept his eye on his book with exactly the air of a very sly human rascal, who, under the mask of pretending to read hard, was listening to everything . . . . " BR 25

And see A:Grave—*visited by a raven*

"Grip was by no means an idle or unprofitable member of the humble household. Partly by dint of Barnaby's tuition, and partly by pursuing a species of self-instruction common to his tribe, and exerting his powers of observation to the utmost, he had acquired a degree of sagacity which rendered him famous for miles round.

"His conversational powers and surprising performances were the universal theme: and as many persons came to see the wonderful raven, and none left his exertions unrewarded—when he condescended to exhibit, which was not always, for genius is capricious—his earnings formed an important item in the common stock.

"Indeed, the bird himself appeared to know his value well; for though he was perfectly free and unrestrained in the presence of Barnaby and his mother, he maintained in public an amazing gravity, and never stooped to any other gratuitous performances than biting the ankles of vagabond boys (an exercise in which he much delighted), killing a fowl or two occasionally, and swallowing the dinners of various neighbouring dogs, of whom the boldest held him in great awe and dread." ¶BR 45

"[A raven, at Monte Cassino], croaking in answer to the bell, and uttering, at intervals, the purest Tuscan. How like a Jesuit he looks! There never was a sly and stealthy fellow so at home as is this raven, standing now at the refectory door, with his head on one side, and pretending to glance another way, while he is scrutinizing the visitors keenly, and listening with fixed attention. What a dull-headed monk the porter becomes in comparison!

"'He speaks like us!' says the porter: 'quite as plainly.' Quite as plainly, Porter. Nothing could be more expressive than his reception of the peasants who are entering the gate with baskets and burdens. There is a roll in his eye, and a chuckle in his throat, which should qualify him to be chosen Superior of an Order of Ravens. He knows all about it. 'It's all right,' he says. 'We know what we know. Come along, good people. Glad to see you!'" PI 13

"I am a Raven. I am, by nature, a sort of collector, or antiquarian . . . . I have a passion for amassing things that are of no use to me, and burying them . . . .

"What *I* want, is privacy. I want to make a collection. I desire to get a little property together." HW/R1

—rook

—clerical: "Whosoever has observed that sedate and clerical bird, the rook, may perhaps have noticed that when he wings his way homeward towards nightfall, in a sedate and clerical company, two rooks will suddenly detach themselves from the rest, will retrace their flight for some distance, and will there poise and linger; conveying to mere men the fancy that it is of some occult importance to the body politic, that this artful couple should pretend to have renounced connexion with it." MED 2

—in a graveyard: "It was a very quiet place, as such a place should be, save for the cawing of the rooks who had built their nests among the branches of some tall old trees, and were calling to one another, high up in air. First one sleek bird, hovering near his ragged house as it swung and dangled in the wind, uttered his hoarse cry, quite by chance as it would seem, and in a sober tone as though he were but talking to himself. Another answered, and he called again, but louder than before; then another spoke and then another; and each time the first, aggravated by contradiction, insisted on his case more strongly.

"Other voices, silent till now, struck in from boughs lower down and higher up and midway, and to the right and left, and from the tree-tops; and others, arriving hastily from the grey church turrets and old belfry window, joined the clamour which rose and fell, and swelled and dropped again, and still went on; and all this noisy contention amidst a skimming to and fro, and lighting on fresh branches, and frequent change of place, which satirized the old restlessness of those who lay so still beneath the moss and turf below, and the useless strife in which they had worn away their lives." ¶OCS 17

—nests: "'Why Rookery?' said Miss Betsey [Trotwood]. 'Cookery would have been more to the purpose, if you had had any practical ideas of life, either of you.'

"'The name was Mr Copperfield's choice,' returned my mother. 'When he bought the house, he liked to think that there were rooks about it' . . . .

"'Where are the birds?' asked Miss Betsey.

"'The—?' My mother had been thinking of something else.

"'The rooks—what has become of them?' asked Miss Betsey.

"'There have not been any since we have lived here,' said my mother. 'We thought—Mr Copperfield thought—it was quite a large rookery; but the nests were very old ones, and the birds have deserted them a long while.'

"'David Copperfield all over!' cried Miss Betsey. 'David Copperfield from head to foot! Calls a house a rookery when there's not a rook near it, and takes the birds on trust, because he sees the nests!'" DC 1

—noisy, at a great house: "The Rooks, swinging in their lofty houses in the elm-tree avenue, seem to discuss the question of the occupancy of the carriage as it passes underneath; some agreeing that Sir Leicester and my Lady are come down; some arguing with malcontents who won't admit it; now, all consenting to consider the question disposed of; now, all breaking out again in violent debate, incited by one obstinate and drowsy bird, who will persist in putting in a last contradictory croak. Leaving them to swing and caw, the travelling chariot rolls on . . . . " BH 12

—observant: "[Doctor Strong] had his old companions about him, too; for there were plenty of high trees in the neighbourhood, and two or three rooks were on the grass, looking after him, as if they had been written to about him by the Canterbury rooks, and were observing him closely in consequence." DC 36

—*sparrow:* "'My daughters' room. A poor first-floor to us, but a bower to them. Very neat. Very airy. Plants you observe; hyacinths; books again; birds.' These birds, by the bye, comprised, in all, one staggering old sparrow without a tail, which had been borrowed expressly from the kitchen." MC 5

"There was a tiny blink of sun peeping in from the great street round the corner, and the smoky sparrows hopped over it and back again, brightening as they passed: or bathed in it, like a stream, and became glorified sparrows, unconnected with chimneys." DS 29

"When [Dora and I] had those meetings in the garden of the square, and sat within the dingy summer-house, so happy, that I love the London sparrows to this hour, for nothing else, and see the plumage of the tropics in their smoky feathers!" DC 33

"[Staple Inn in Holborn] is one of those nooks where a few smoky sparrows twitter in smoky trees, as though they called to one another, 'Let us play at country,' and where a few feet of garden-mould and a few yards of gravel enable them to do that refreshing violence to their tiny understandings." MED 11

Change

—*admonitory lecture:* "'It's merely change of weather. We must expect change.'

"'Of weather?' asked Miss Tox, in her simplicity.

"'Of everything,' returned Mrs Chick. 'Of course we must. It's a world of change. Any one would surprise me very much, Lucretia, and would greatly alter my opinion of their understanding, if they attempted to contradict or evade what is so perfectly evident. Change!' exclaimed Mrs Chick, with severe philosophy. 'Why, my gracious me, what is there that does *not* change! even the silkworm, who I am sure might be supposed not to trouble itself about such subjects, changes into all sorts of unexpected things continually.'

"'My Louisa,' said the mild Miss Tox, 'is ever happy in her illustrations.'" DS 29

—*commercial:* "' . . . the world has gone past me [said Solomon Gills]. I don't blame it; but I no longer understand it. Tradesmen are not the same as they used to be, apprentices are not the same, business is not the same, business commodities are not the same. Seven-eighths of my stock is old-fashioned. I am an old-fashioned man in an old-fashioned shop, in a street that is not the same as I remember it. I have fallen behind the time, and am too old to catch it again. Even the noise it makes a long way ahead, confuses me.'" DS 4

—*fear of:* "In the days when Cloisterham took offence at the existence of a railroad afar off, as menacing that sensitive constitution, the property of us Britons: the odd fortune of which sacred institution it is to be in exactly equal degrees croaked about, trembled for, and boasted of, whatever happens to anything, anywhere in the world . . . . " MED 11

—*and fever:* "The changes of a fevered room are slow and fluctuating; but the changes of the fevered world are rapid and irrevocable." LD ii 33

—*human:* "Change begets change. Nothing propagates so fast. If a man habituated to a narrow circle of cares and pleasures, out of which he seldom travels, step beyond it, though for never so brief a space, his departure from the monotonous scene on which he has been an actor of importance, would seem to be the signal for instant confusion. As if, in the gap he had left, the wedge of change were driven to the head, rending what was a solid mass to fragments, things cemented and held together by the usages of years, burst asunder in as many weeks. The mine which Time has slowly dug beneath familiar objects is sprung in an instant; and what was rock before becomes but sand and dust." MC 18

—*life and death:* "'Death doesn't change us more than life, my dear.'" OCS 17

—*in nature:* "The day wore on, and all these bright colours subsided, and assumed a quieter tint, like young hopes softened down by time, or youthful features by degrees resolving into the calm and serenity of age. But they were scarcely less beautiful in their slow decline, than they had been in their prime; for nature gives to every time and season some beauties of its own; and from morning to night, as from the cradle to the grave, is but a succession of changes so gentle and easy, that we can scarcely mark their progress." NN 22

—*an old city:* "A drowsy city, Cloisterham, whose inhabitants seem to suppose, with an inconsistency more strange than rare, that all its changes lie behind it, and that there are no more to come. A queer moral to derive from antiquity, yet older than any traceable antiquity." MED 3

—*sense of time:* "So the Captain [Cuttle] sat

himself down in his altered station of life, with no company but Rob the Grinder; and losing count of time, as men do when great changes come upon them, thought musingly of Walter [Gay], and of Solomon Gills, and even of Mrs MacStinger herself, as among the things that had been." DS 25

Countryside

—to a city dweller: "A tranquil summer sunset shone upon [Arthur Clennam] as he approached the end of his walk, and passed through the meadows by the river side. He had that sense of peace, and of being lightened of a weight of care, which country quiet awakens in the breasts of dwellers in towns. Everything within his view was lovely and placid. The rich foliage of the trees, the luxuriant grass diversified with wild flowers, the little green islands in the river, the beds of rushes, the water-lilies floating on the surface of the stream, the distant voices in boats borne musically towards him on the ripple of the water and the evening air, were all expressive of rest.

"In the occasional leap of a fish, or dip of an oar, or twittering of a bird not yet at roost, or distant barking of a dog, or lowing of a cow—in all such sounds, there was the prevailing breath of rest, which seemed to encompass him in every scene that sweetened the fragrant air. The long lines of red and gold in the sky, and the glorious track of the descending sun, were all divinely calm. Upon the purple tree-tops far away, and on the green height near at hand up which the shades were slowly creeping, there was an equal hush. Between the real landscape and its shadow in the water, there was no division; both were so untroubled and clear, and, while so fraught with solemn mystery of life and death, so hopefully reassuring to the gazer's soothed heart, because so tenderly and mercifully beautiful." ¶LD i 28

" . . . although a dense vapour still enveloped the city they had left as if the very breath of its busy people hung over their schemes of gain and profit and found greater attraction there than in the quiet region above, in the open country it was clear and fair.

"Occasionally in some low spots [Nicholas Nickleby and Smike] came upon patches of mist which the sun had not yet driven from their strongholds; but these were soon passed, and as they laboured up the hills beyond, it was pleasant to look down and see how the sluggish mass rolled heavily off before the cheering influence of day.

"A broad fine honest sun lighted up the green pastures and dimpled water with the semblance of summer, while it left the travellers all the invigorating freshness of that early time of year. The ground seemed elastic under their feet; the sheep-bells were music to their ears; and exhilarated by exercise, and stimulated by hope, they pushed onwards with the strength of lions.

"The day wore on, and all these bright colours subsided, and assumed a quieter tint, like young hopes softened down by time, or youthful features by degrees resolving into the calm and serenity of age. But they were scarcely less beautiful in their slow decline than they had been in their prime; for nature gives to every time and season some beauties of his own, and from morning to night, as from the cradle to the grave, is but a succession of changes so gentle and easy, that we can scarcely mark their progress." ¶NN 22

" . . . [Snagsby] gets such a flavour of the country out of telling the two 'prentices how he *has* heard say that a brook 'as clear as crystial' once ran right down the middle of Holborn, when Turnstile really was a turnstile, leading slap away into the meadows—gets such a flavour of the country out of this, that he never wants to go there." BH 10

" . . . every day had been so bright and blue, that to ramble in the woods, and to see the light striking down among the transparent leaves, and sparkling in the beautiful interlacings of the shadows of the trees, while the birds poured out their songs, and the air was drowsy with the hum of insects, had been most delightful.

"We [John Jarndyce, Ada Clare and Esther Summerson] had one favourite spot, deep in moss and last year's leaves, where there were some felled trees from which the bark was all stripped off. Seated among these, we looked through a green vista supported by thousands of natural columns, the whitened stems of trees, upon a distant prospect made so radiant by its contrast with the shade in which we sat, and made so precious by the arched perspective through which we saw it, that it was like a glimpse of the better land." ¶BH 18

—a coastal road: "There is nothing in Italy, more beautiful to me, than the coast-road between Genoa and Spezzia [La Spezia]. On one side: sometimes far below, some-

times nearly on a level with the road, and often skirted by broken rocks of many shapes: there is the free blue sea, with here and there a picturesque felucca gliding slowly on; on the other side are lofty hills, ravines besprinkled with white cottages, patches of dark olive woods, country churches with their light open towers, and country houses gaily painted. On every bank and knoll by the wayside, the wild cactus and aloe flourish in exuberant profusion; and the gardens of the bright villages along the road, are seen, all blushing in the summer-time with clusters of the Belladonna, and are fragrant in the autumn and winter with golden oranges and lemons." PI 10

—a country county: "The conversation passed, in the Midsummer weather of no remote year of grace, down among the pleasant dales and trout-streams of a green English county. No matter what county. Enough that you may hunt there, shoot there, fish there, traverse long grass-grown Roman roads there, open ancient barrows there, see many a square mile of richly cultivated land there, and hold Arcadian talk with a bold peasantry, their country's pride, who will tell you (if you want to know) how pastoral housekeeping is done on nine shillings a week." CS/TT

—the Downs: "Onward [Nicholas Nickleby and Smike] kept with steady purpose, and entered at length upon a wide and spacious tract of downs, with every variety of little hill and plain to change their verdant surface. Here, there shot up almost perpendicularly into the sky a height so steep, as to be hardly accessible to any but the sheep and goats that fed upon its sides, and there stood a huge mound of green, sloping and tapering off so delicately, and merging so gently into the level ground, that you could scarce define its limits.

"Hills swelling above each other, and undulations shapely and uncouth, smooth and rugged, graceful and grotesque, thrown negligently side by side, bounded the view in each direction; while frequently, with unexpected noise, there uprose from the ground a flight of crows, who, cawing and wheeling round the nearest hills, as if uncertain of their course, suddenly poised themselves upon the wing and skimmed down the long vista of some opening valley with the speed of very light itself." ¶NN 22

—at the end of a working day: "The Paper Mill had stopped work for the night, and the paths and roads in its neighbourhood were sprinkled with clusters of people going home from their day's labour in it. There were men, women, and children in the groups, and there was no want of lively colour to flutter in the gentle evening wind.

"The mingling of various voices and the sound of laughter made a cheerful impression upon the ear, analogous to that of the fluttering colours upon the eye. Into the sheet of water reflecting the flushed sky in the foreground of the living picture, a knot of urchins were casting stones, and watching the expansion of the rippling circles.

"So, in the rosy evening, one might watch the ever-widening beauty of the landscape—beyond the newly-released workers wending home—beyond the silver river—beyond the deep green fields of corn, so prospering, that the loiterers in their narrow threads of pathway seemed to float immersed breast-high—beyond the hedgerows and the clumps of trees—beyond the windmills on the ridge—away to where the sky appeared to meet the earth, as if there were no immensity of space between mankind and Heaven." OMF iv 6

—enjoyed: "'Pleasant, pleasant country,' sighted the enthusiastic gentleman, as he opened his lattice window. 'Who could live to gaze from day to day on bricks and slates, who had once felt the influence of a scene like this? Who could continue to exist, where there are no cows but the cows on the chimney-pots; nothing redolent of *Pan* but pan-tiles; no crop but stone crop? Who could bear to drag out a life in such a spot? Who I ask could endure it?' and, having cross-examined solitude after the most approved precedents, at considerable length, Mr Pickwick thrust his head out of the lattice, and looked around him.

"The rich, sweet smell of the hayricks rose to his chamber window; the hundred perfumes of the little flower-garden beneath scented the air around; the deep-green meadows shone in the morning dew that glistened on every leaf as it trembled in the gentle air: and the birds sang as if every sparkling drop were a fountain of admiration to them. Mr Pickwick fell into an enchanting and delicious reverie." PP 7

"Barnaby's enjoyments were, to walk, and run, and leap, till he was tired; then to lie down in the long grass, or by the growing corn, or in the shade of some tall tree, looking upward at the light clouds as they floated over the blue surface of the sky, and listening to the lark as she poured out her brilliant song. There were wild-flowers to pluck—the bright red poppy, the gentle harebell, the cowslip, and the rose. There were birds to watch; fish; ants; worms; hares or rabbits, as they darted across the distant pathway in the wood and so were gone: millions of living things to have an interest in, and lie in wait for, and clap hands and shout in memory of, when they had disappeared. In default of these, or when they wearied, there was the merry sunlight to hunt out, as it crept in aslant through leaves and boughs of trees, and hid far down—deep, deep, in hollow places—like a silver pool, where nodding branches seemed to bathe and sport; sweet scents of summer air breathing over fields of beans or clover; the perfume of wet leaves or moss; the life of waving trees, and shadows always changing. When these or any of them tired, or in excess of pleasing tempted him to shut his eyes, there was slumber in the midst of all these soft delights, with the gentle wind murmuring like music in his ears, and everything around melting into one delicious dream." BR 45

—a hamlet: "They [Nell and her grandfather] were now in the open country; the houses were very few and scattered at long intervals, often miles apart. Occasionally they came upon a cluster of poor cottages, some with a chair or low board put across the open door to keep the scrambling children from the road, others shut up close while all the family were working in the fields. These were often the commencement of a little village: and after an interval came a wheelwright's shed or perhaps a blacksmith's forge; then a thriving farm with sleepy cows lying about the yard, and horses peering over the low wall and scampering away when harnessed horses passed upon the road, as though in triumph at their freedom.

"There were dull pigs too, turning up the ground in search of dainty food, and grunting their monotonous grumblings as they prowled about, or crossed each other in their quest; plump pigeons skimming round the roof or strutting on the eaves; and ducks and geese, far more graceful in their own conceit, waddling awkwardly about the edges of the pond or sailing glibly on its surface. The farm-yard passed, then came the little inn; the humbler beer-shop; and the village trades-man's; then the lawyer's and the parson's, at whose dread names the beer-shop trembled; the church then peeped out modestly from a clump of trees; then there were a few more cottages; then the cage, and pound, and not unfrequently, on a bank by the way-side, a deep old dusty well. Then came the trim-hedged fields on either hand, and the open road again." ¶OCS15

—industrial region: "Though the green landscape was blotted here and there with heaps of coal, it was green elsewhere, and there were trees to see, and there were larks singing (though it was Sunday), and there were pleasant scents in the air, and all was over-arched by a bright blue sky. In the distance one way, Coketown showed as a black mist; in another distance hills began to rise; in a third, there was a faint change in the light of the horizon where it shone upon the far-off sea. Under their feet, the grass was fresh; beautiful shadows of branches flickered upon it, and speckled it; hedgerows were luxuriant; everything was at peace. Engines at pits' mouths, and lean old horses that had worn the circle of their daily labour into the ground, were alike quiet; wheels had ceased for a short space to turn; and the great wheel of earth seemed to revolve without the shocks and noises of another time." HT iii 6

—in the morning: " . . . we turned into the park. The air was bright and dewy, and the sky without a cloud. The birds sang delightfully; the sparkles in the fern, the grass, and trees, were exquisite to see; the richness of the woods seemed to have increased twenty-fold since yesterday, as if, in the still night when they had looked so massively hushed in sleep, Nature, through all the minute details of every wonderful leaf, had been more wakeful than usual for the glory of that day." BH 37

—in the North of England: "Up hill and down hill, and twisting to the right, and twisting to the left, and with old Skiddaw (who has vaunted himself a great deal more than his merits deserve; but that is rather the way of the Lake country), dodging the apprentices in a picturesque and pleasant manner. Good, weather-proof, warm, pleasant houses, well white-limed, scantily dotting the road. Clean children coming out to look, carrying other clean children as big as themselves. Harvest still lying out and much rained upon; here and there, harvest still unreaped. Well-cultivated gardens attached to the cottages, with plenty of produce forced out of their hard soil.

"Lonely nooks, and wild; but people can be born, and married, and buried in such nooks, and can live and love, and be loved, there as elsewhere, thank God! . . . By-and-by, the village. Black, coarse-stoned, rough-windowed houses; some with outer staircases, like Swiss houses; a sinuous and stony gutter winding up hill and round the corner, by way of street. All the children running out directly. Women pausing in washing, to peep from doorways and very little windows." ¶LT 1

Miss Haredale walking BR

—*prairie:* "Looking towards the setting sun, there lay, stretched out before my view, a vast expanse of level ground; unbroken, save by one thin line of trees, which scarcely amounted to a scratch upon the great blank; until it met the glowing sky, wherein it seemed to dip: mingling with its rich colours, and mellowing in its distant blue.

"There it lay, a tranquil sea or lake without water, if such a simile be admissible, with the day going down upon it: a few birds wheeling here and there: and solitude and silence reigning paramount around. But the grass was not yet high; there were bare black patches on the ground; and the few wild flowers that the eye could see were poor and scanty.

"Great as the picture was, its very flatness and extent, which left nothing to the imagination, tamed it down and cramped its interest. I felt little of that sense of freedom and exhilaration which a Scottish heath inspires, or even our English downs awaken. It was lonely and wild, but oppressive in its barren monotony.

"I felt that in traversing the Prairies, I could never abandon myself to the scene, forgetful of all else; as I should do instinctively, were the heather underneath my feet, or an iron-bound coast beyond; but should often glance towards the distant and frequently-receding line of the horizon, and wish it gained and passed.

"It is not a scene to be forgotten, but it is scarcely one, I think (at all events, as I saw it), to remember with much pleasure, or to covet the looking-on again, in after-life." AN 13

—*in the rain:* "It was comfortable to see how the people coming back in open carts from Wigton market made no more of the rain than if it were sunshine; how the Wigton policeman taking a country walk of half-a-dozen miles (apparently for pleasure), in resplendent uniform, accepted saturation as his normal state; how clerks and schoolmasters in black, loitered along the road without umbrellas, getting varnished at every step; how the Cumberland girls, coming out to look after the Cumberland cows, shook the rain from their eyelashes and laughed it away; and how the rain continued to fall upon all, as it only does fall in hill countries." LT 2

—*in the sun, after rain:* "The sun burst suddenly from among the clouds; and the old battle-ground, sparkling brilliantly and cheerfully at sight of it in one green place, flashed a responsive welcome there, which spread along the country side as if a joyful beacon had been lighted up, and answered from a thousand stations.

"How beautiful the landscape kindling in the light, and that luxuriant influence passing on like a celestial presence, brightening everything! The wood, a sombre mass before, revealed its varied tints of yellow, green, brown, red: its different forms of trees, with raindrops glittering on their leaves and twinkling as they fell. The verdant meadowland, bright and glowing, seemed as if it had been blind, a minute since, and now had found a sense of sight wherewith to look up at the shining sky. Corn-fields, hedgerows, fences, homesteads, and clustered roofs, the steeple of the church, the stream, the water-mill, all sprang out of the gloomy darkness smiling. Birds sang sweetly, flowers raised their drooping heads, fresh scents arose from the invigorated ground; the blue expanse above extended and diffused itself; already the sun's slanting rays pierced mortally the sullen bank of cloud that lingered in its flight; and a rainbow, spirit of all the colours that adorned the earth and sky, spanned the whole arch with its triumphant glory." BL 3

Widow Rudge's Cottage BR

—*viewed on horseback:* "Mr Carker cantered behind the carriage, at the distance of a hundred yards or so, and watched it . . . . Whether he looked to one side of the road, or to the other—over distant landscape, with its smooth undulations, wind-mills, corn, grass, bean fields, wild-flowers, farm-yards, hayricks, and the spire among the wood—or upwards in the sunny air, where butterflies were sporting round his head, and birds wre pouring out their songs—or downward, where the shadows of the branches interlaced, and made a trembling carpet on the road—or onward, where the overhanging trees formed aisles and arches, dim with the softened light that steeped through leaves—one corner of his eye was ever on the formal head of Mr Dombey . . . . " DS 27

—*a village contrasted:* "The village street was like most other village streets: wide for its height, silent for its size, and drowsy in the dullest degree. The quietest little dwellings with the largest of window-shutters (to shut up Nothing as carefully as if it were the Mint, or the Bank of England) had called in the Doctor's house so suddenly, that his brass door-plate and three stories stood among them as conspicuous and different as the Doctor himself in his broad-cloth, among the smock-frocks of his patients.

"The village residences seemed to have gone to law with a similar absence of consideration, for a score of weak little lath-and-plaster cabins clung in confusion about the Attorney's red-brick house, which, with glaring doorsteps and a most terrific scraper, seemed to serve all manner of ejectments upon them. They were as various as labourers—high-shouldered, wry-necked, one-eyed, goggle-eyed, squinting, bow-legged, knock-kneed, rheumatic, crazy. Some of the small tradesmen's houses, such as the crockery-shop and the harness-maker's, had a Cyclops window in the middle of the gable, within an inch or two of its apex, suggesting that some forlorn rural Prentice must wriggle himself into that apartment horizontally, when he retired to rest, after the manner of the worm.

"So beautiful in its abundance was the surrounding country, and so lean and scant the village, that one might have thought the village had sown and planted everything it once possessed, to convert the same into crops. This would account for the bareness of the little shops, the bareness of the few boards and trestles designed for market purposes in a corner of the street, the bareness of the obsolete Inn and Inn Yard, with the ominous inscription 'Excise Office' not yet faded out from the gateway, as indicating the very last thing that poverty could get rid of. This would also account for the determined abandonment of the village by one stray dog, fast lessening in the perspective where the white posts and the pond were, and would explain his conduct on the hypothesis that he was going (through the act of suicide) to convert himself into manure, and become a part proprietor in turnips or mangold-wurzel." ¶CS/TT

Darkness

—*on an empty sea:* "I had thought it impossible that it could be darker than it had been, until the sun, moon, and stars should fall out of the Heavens, and Time should be destroyed; but, it had been next to light, in comparison with what it was now. The darkness was so profound, that looking into it was painful and oppressive—like looking, without a ray of light, into a dense black bandage put as close before the eyes as it could be, without touching them . . . . Few but those who have tried it can imagine the difficulty and pain of only keeping the eyes open—physically open—under such circumstances, in such darkness. They get struck by the darkness, and blinded by the darkness. They make patterns in it, and they flash in it, as if they had gone out of your head to look at you." CS/GM

—*on a teeming slum:* "Darkness rests upon Tom-all-Alone's. Dilating and dilating since the sun went down last night, it has gradually swelled until it fills every void in the place. For a time there were some dungeon lights burning, as the lamp of Life burns in Tom-all-Alone's, heavily, heavily, in the nauseous air, and winking—as that lamp, too, winks in Tom-all-Alone's—at many horrible things. But they are blotted out. The moon has eyed Tom with a dull cold stare, as admitting some puny emulation of herself in his desert region unfit for life and blasted by volcanic fires; but she has passed on, and is gone. The blackest nightmare in the infernal stables grazes on Tom-all-Alone's, and Tom is fast asleep." BH 46

Elements (the Four)

—*at a dinner-party:* "Through the various stages of rich meats and wines, continual gold and silver, dainties of earth, air, fire, and water, heaped-up fruits, and that unnecessary article in Mr Dombey's banquets—ice—the dinner slowly made its way . . . ." DS 36

—in human terms: "'Mrs William may be taken off her balance by Earth; as, for example, last Sunday week, when sloppy and greasy, and she going out to tea with her newest sister-in-law, and having a pride in herself, and wishing to appear perfectly spotless though pedestrian. Mrs William may be taken off her balance by Air; as being once over-persuaded by a friend to try a swing at Peckham Fair, which acted on her constitution instantly like a steamboat. Mrs William may be taken off her balance by Fire; as on a false alarm of engines at her mother's, when she went two miles in her nightcap. Mrs William may be taken off her balance by Water; as at Battersea, when rowed into the piers by her young nephew, Charley Swidger junior, aged twelve, which had no idea of boats whatever. But these are elements. Mrs William must be taken out of elements for the strength of her character to come into play.'" HM 1 *See* S:Feelings—*suppression relieved*

Fire

—at a chateau: "Presently the chateau began to make itself strangely visible by some light of its own, as though it were growing luminous. Then, a flickering streak played behind the architecture of the front, picking out transparent places, and showing where balustrades, arches, and windows were. Then it soared higher, and grew broader and brighter. Soon, from a score of the great windows, flames burst forth, and the stone faces awakened, stared out of fire . . . .

"The chateau was left to itself to flame and burn. In the roaring and raging of the conflagration, a red-hot wind, driving straight from the infernal regions, seemed to be blowing the edifice away. With the rising and falling of the blaze, the stone faces showed as if they were in torment. When great masses of stone and timber fell, the face with the two dints in the nose became obscured: anon struggled out of the smoke again, as if it were the face of the cruel Marquis, burning at the stake and contending with the fire.

"The chateau burned; the nearest trees, laid hold of by the fire, scorched and shrivelled; trees at a distance, fired by the four fierce figures, begirt the blazing edifice with a new forest of smoke. Molten lead and iron boiled in the marble basin of the fountain; the water ran dry; the extinguisher tops of the towers vanished like ice before the heat, and trickled down into four rugged wells of flame. Great rents and splits branched out in the solid walls, like crystallisation; stupefied birds wheeled about and dropped into the furnace; four fierce figures trudged away, East, West, North, and South, along the night-enshrouded roads, guided by the beacon they had lighted, towards their next destination." TTC ii 23

—a companion: "'See yonder there—that's *my* friend.'

"'The fire?' said the child.

"'It has been alive as long as I have,' the [furnace-watcher] made answer. 'We talk and think together all night long . . . .

"'It's like a book to me,' he said—'the only book I ever learned to read; and many an old story it tells me. It's music, for I should know its voice among a thousand, and there are other voices in its roar. It has its pictures too. You don't know how many strange faces and different scenes I trace in the red-hot coals. It's my memory, that fire, and shows me all my life . . . .

"'Yes,' he said, with a faint smile, 'it was the same when I was quite a baby, and crawled about it, till I fell asleep. My father watched it then.' . . .

"'Were you brought up here, then?' said the child.

"'Summer and winter,' he replied. 'Secretly at first, but when they found it out, they let him keep me here. So the fire nursed me—the same fire. It has never gone out.'

"'You are fond of it?' said the child.

"'Of course I am. He died before it. I saw him fall down—just there, where those ashes are burning now—and wondered, I remember, why it didn't help him.'

"'Have you been here ever since?' asked the child.

"'Ever since I came to watch it; but there was a while between, and a very cold dreary while it was. It burned all the time though, and roared and leaped when I came back, as it used to do in our play days.'" OCS 44

—at a country mansion: "The burning pile, revealing rooms and passages red hot, through gaps made in the crumbling walls; the tributary fires that licked the outer bricks and stones, with their long forked tongues, and ran up to meet the glowing mass within; the shining of the flames upon

the villains who looked on and fed them; the roaring of the angry blaze, so bright and high that it seemed in its rapacity to have swallowed up the very smoke; the living flakes the wind bore rapidly away and hurried on with, like a storm of fiery snow; the noiseless breaking of great beams of wood, which fell like feathers on the heap of ashes, and crumbled in the very act to sparks and powder; the lurid tinge that overspread the sky, and the darkness, very deep by contrast, which prevailed around . . . combined to form a scene never to be forgotten . . . . " BR 55

And see H:Mob—*burning a house*

—*and life, versus science:* "'I was encouraged [to wonder] by nothing, mother, but by looking at the red sparks dropping out of the fire, and whitening and dying. It made me think, after all, how short my life would be, and how little I could hope to do in it.'

"'Nonsense!' said Mrs Gradgrind, rendered almost energetic. 'Nonsense! Don't stand there and tell me such stuff, Louisa. . . . After the lectures you have attended, and the experiments you have seen! After I have heard you myself . . . going on with your master about combustion, and calcination, and calorification, and I may say every kind of ation that could drive a poor invalid distracted, to hear you talking in this absurd way about sparks and ashes!'" HT i 8

And see M:Parapsychology—*precognition—the mystery of the future*

—*at a party:* "The bright fire crackled and sparkled, rose and fell, as though it joined the dance itself, in right good fellowship. Sometimes, it roared as if it would make music too. Sometimes, it flashed and beamed as if it were the eye of the old room: it winked too, sometimes, like a knowing patriarch, upon the youthful whisperers in corners. Sometimes, it sported with the holly-boughs; and, shining on the leaves by fits and starts, made them look as if they were in the cold winter night again, and fluttering in the wind. Sometimes its genial humour grew obstreperous, and passed all bounds; and then it cast into the room, among the twinkling feet, with a loud burst, a shower of harmless little sparks, and in its exultation leaped and bounded, like a mad thing, up the broad old chimney . . . .

"Now, too, the fire took fresh courage, favoured by the lively wind the dance awakened, and burnt clear and high. It was the Genius of the room, and present everywhere. It shone in people's eyes, it sparkled in the jewels on the snowy necks of girls, it twinkled at their ears as if it whispered to them slyly, it flashed about their waists, it flickered on the ground and made it rosy for their feet, it bloomed upon the ceiling that its glow might set off their bright faces, and it kindled up a general illumination in Mrs Cragg's little belfry [headdress]." BL 2

—*at a prison:* "By and bye, [Rudge] saw, as he looked from his grated window, a strange glimmering on the stone walls and pavement of the yard. It was feeble at first, and came and went, as though some officers with torches were passing to and fro upon the roof of the prison. Soon it reddened, and lighted brands came whirling down, spattering the ground with fire, and burning sullenly in corners. One rolled beneath a wooden bench, and set it in a blaze; another caught a water-spout, and so went climbing up the wall, leaving a long straight track of fire behind it. After a time, a slow thick shower of burning fragments, from some upper portion of the prison which was blazing nigh, began to fall before his door. Remembering that it opened outwards, he knew that every spark which fell upon the heap, and in the act lost its bright life, and died an ugly speck of dust and rubbish, helped to entomb him in a living grave. Still, though the jail resounded with shrieks and cries for help—though the fire bounded up as if each separate flame had had a tiger's life, and roared as though, in every one, there were a hungry voice—though the heat began to grow intense, and the air suffocating, and the clamour without increased, and the danger of his situation even from one merciless element was every moment more extreme—still he was afraid to raise his voice . . . ." BR 65

—*set by a mob:* "The furniture being very dry, and rendered more combustible by wax and oil, besides the arts they had used, took fire at once. The flames roared high and fiercely, blackening the prison-wall, and twining up its lofty front like burning serpents.

"At first they crowded round the blaze, and vented their exultation only in their looks: but when it grew hotter and fiercer—when it crackled, leaped, and roared, like a great furnace—when it shone upon the opposite houses, and lighted up not only the pale and wondering faces at the windows, but the inmost corners of each habitation—when through the deep red heat and glow, the fire was seen sporting and toying with the door, now clinging to its obdurate surface, now gliding off with fierce inconstancy and soaring high into the sky, anon returning to fold it in its burning grasp and lure it to its ruin—when it shone and gleamed so brightly that the church clock of St Sepulchre's, so often pointing to the hour of death, was legible as in broad day, and the vane upon its steeple-top glittered in the unwonted light like something richly jewelled—when blackened stone and sombre brick grew ruddy in the deep reflection, and windows shone like burnished gold, dotting the longest distance in the fiery vista with their specks of brightness—when wall and tower, and roof and chimney-stack, seemed drunk, and in the flickering glare appeared to reel and stagger—when scores of objects, never seen before, burst out upon the view, and things the most familiar put on some new aspect—then the mob began to join the whirl, and with loud yells, and shouts, and clamour, such as happily is seldom heard, bestirred themselves to feed the fire, and keep it at its height.

"Although the heat was so intense that the paint on the houses over against [Newgate] prison, parched and crackled up, and swelling into boils, as it were from excess of torture, broke and crumbled away; although the glass fell from the window-sashes, and the lead and iron on the roofs blistered the incautious hand that touched them, and the sparrows in the eaves took wing, and rendered giddy by the smoke, fell fluttering down upon the blazing pile; still the fire was tended unceasingly by busy hands, and round it, men were going always." ¶BR 64

—sleepy: ". . . the fire, which had left off roaring, winked its red eyes at us . . . like a drowsy old Chancery lion." BH 3

—welcome distraction: ". . . there arose upon the night-wind the noise of distant shouting, and the roar of voices mingled in alarm and wonder. Any sound of men in that lonely place, even though it conveyed a real cause of alarm, was something to [Bill Sikes, recent murderer]. He regained his strength and energy at the prospect of personal danger; and springing to his feet, rushed into the open air.

"The broad sky seemed on fire. Rising into the air with showers of sparks, and rolling one above the other, were sheets of flame, lighting the atmosphere for miles round, and driving clouds of smoke in the direction where he stood.

"The shouts grew louder as new voices swelled the roar, and he could hear the cry of Fire! mingled with the ringing of an alarm-bell, the fall of heavy bodies, and the crackling of flames as they twined round some new obstacle, and shot aloft as though refreshed by food. The noise increased as he looked. There were people there—men and women—light, bustle. It was like new life to him. He darted onward—straight, headlong—dashing through brier and brake, and leaping gate and fence as madly as his dog, who careered with loud and sounding bark before him.

"He came upon the spot. There were half-dressed figures tearing to and fro, some endeavouring to drag the frightened horses from the stables, others driving the cattle from the yard and out-houses, and others coming laden from the burning pile, amidst a shower of falling sparks, and the tumbling down of red-hot beams.

"The apertures, where doors and windows stood an hour ago, disclosed a mass of raging fire; walls rocked and crumbled into the burning well; the molten lead and iron poured down, white hot, upon the ground. Women and children shrieked, and men encouraged each other with noisy shouts and cheers. The clanking of the engine-pumps, and the spirting and hissing of the water as it fell upon the blazing wood, added to the tremendous roar. He shouted too, till he was hoarse; and flying from memory and himself, plunged into the thickest of the throng." ¶OT 48

—and wine madness: "Men who had been into the cellars, and had staved the casks, rushed to and fro stark mad, setting fire to all they saw—often to the dresses of their own friends—and kindling the building in so many parts that some had no time for escape, and were seen, with drooping hands and blackened faces, hanging senseless on the window-sills to which they had crawled, until they were sucked and drawn into the burning gulf. The more the fire crackled and raged, the wilder and more cruel the men grew; as though moving in that element they became fiends, and changed their earthly nature for the qualities that give delight in hell." BR 55

And see Times of Day*—dawn—just before*
For CD's first professional experience of a calamitous fire see MC/HH *(1835)*

Flora

—aloes: "There were two great aloes, in tubs, on the turf outside the [Strong school] windows; the broad hard leaves of which plant (looking as if they were made of painted tin) have ever since, by association, been symbolical to me of silence and retirement." DC 16

"His office [chair of a public dinner], [CD] said, had compelled him to burst into bloom so often that he could wish there were a closer parallel between himself and the American Aloe." S/GI2 *See* Glossary, Vol. III

—box: " . . . one box-tree that had been clipped round long ago, like a pudding, and had a new growth at the top of it, out of shape and of a different colour, as if that part of the pudding had stuck to the saucepan and got burnt." GE 11

—to a city lover: "'Are there any country flowers that could interest me like these, do you think? Or do you suppose that the withering of a hundred kinds of the choicest flowers that blow, called by the hardest Latin names that were ever invented, would give me one fraction of the pain that I shall feel when those old jugs and bottles are swept away for lumber! Country!' cried Tim, with a contemptuous emphasis; 'don't you know that I couldn't have such a court under my bed-room window, anywhere, but in London?'" NN 40

—generally: "Flowers are the best picture books I know; and whenever I see them lying open at the labourer's door, I can always read in them that he is a better and happier man." S/GI2

—geraniums: "[The greenhouse] contained quite a show of beautiful geraniums. We loitered along in front of them, and Dora often stopped to admire this one or that one, and I stopped to admire the same one, and Dora, laughing, held the dog up childishly, to smell the flower; and if we were not all three in Fairyland, certainly *I* was. The scent of a geranium leaf, at this day, strikes me with a half comical, half serious wonder as to what change has come over me in a moment; and then I see a straw hat and blue ribbons, and a quantity of curls, and a little black dog being held up, in two slender arms, against a bank of blossoms and bright leaves." DC 26

—grape vines: "In Genoa, and thereabouts, they train the vines on trellis-work, supported on square clumsy pillars, which, in themselves, are anything but picturesque. But here [in the countryside between Piacenza and Parma], they twine them around trees, and let them trail among the hedges; and the vineyards are full of trees, regularly planted for this purpose, each with its own vine twining and clustering about it.

"Their leaves are now of the brightest gold and deepest red; and never was anything so enchantingly graceful and full of beauty. Through miles of these delightful forms and colours, the road winds its way. The wild festoons, the elegant wreaths, and crowns, and garlands of all shapes; the fairy nets flung over great trees, and making them prisoners in sport; the tumbled heaps and mounds of exquisite shapes upon the ground; how rich and beautiful they are! And every now and then, a long, long line of trees, will be all bound and garlanded together: as if they had taken hold of one another, and were coming dancing down the field!" ¶PI 6

—house plants: "However choice examples of their kind, too, these plants were of a kind peculiarly adapted to the embowerment of Mrs Pipchin. There were half-a-dozen specimens of the cactus, writhing round bits of lath, like hairy serpents; another specimen shooting out broad claws, like a green lobster; several creeping vegetables, possessed of sticky and adhesive leaves; and one uncomfortable flower-pot hanging to the ceiling, which appeared to have boiled over, and tickling people underneath with its long green ends, reminded them of spiders—in which Mrs Pipchin's dwelling was uncommonly prolific, though perhaps it challenged competition still more proudly, in the season, in point of earwigs." DS 8

—marigolds: "One morning [the half-pay Captain] got up early, and planted three or four roots of full-grown marigolds in every bed of her front garden, to the inconceivable astonishment of the old lady, who actually thought when she got up and looked out of the window, that it was some strange eruption which had come out in the night." SB/C

" . . . a steep by-street at Brighton; where the soil was more than usually chalky, flinty, and sterile, and . . . where the small front-gardens had the unaccountable property of producing nothing but marigolds, whatever was sown in them . . . . " DS 8

And see CD:Authorship*—similes—contented.*

CD rarely mentions flora with any favour or interest except in countryside description.

—pruning: "Miss Tox endued herself with a pair of ancient gloves, like dead leaves, in which she was accustomed to perform these avocations . . . coming round, in good time, to the plants, which generally required to be snipped here and there with a pair of scissors, for some botanical reason that was very powerful with Miss Tox." DS 29

—trees

—in America: "The eye was pained to see the stumps of great trees thickly strewn in every field of wheat, and seldom to lose the eternal swamp and dull morass, with hundreds of rotten trunks and twisted branches steeped in its unwholesome water. It was quite sad and oppressive, to come upon great tracts where settlers had been burning down the trees, and where their wounded bodies lay about, like those of murdered creatures, while here and there some charred and blackened giant reared aloft two withered arms, and seemed to call down curses on his foes." AN 10

"These stumps of trees are a curious feature in American travelling. The varying illusions they present to the unaccustomed eye as it grows dark, are quite astonishing in their number and reality. Now, there is a Grecian urn erected in the centre of a lonely field; now there is a woman weeping at a tomb; now a very commonplace old gentleman in a white waistcoat, with a thumb thrust into each arm-hole of his coat; now a student poring on a book; now a crouching negro; now, a horse, a dog, a cannon, an armed man; a hunchback throwing off his cloak and stepping forth into the light. They were often as entertaining to me as so many glasses in a magic lantern, and never took their shapes at my bidding, but seemed to force themselves upon me, whether I would or no; and strange to say, I sometimes recognised in them counterparts of figures once familiar to me in pictures attached to childish books, forgotten long ago." AN 14

—at Eden: "[Martin Chuzzlewit and Mark Tapley's] own land was mere forest. The trees had grown so thick and close that they shouldered one another out of their places, and the weakest, forced into shapes of strange distortion, languished like cripples. The best were stunted, from the pressure and the want of room; and high about the stems of all grew long rank grass, dank weeds, and frowsy underwood: not divisible into their separate kinds, but tangled all together in a heap; a jungle deep and dark, with neither earth nor water at its roots, but putrid matter, formed of the pulpy offal of the two, and of their own corruption." MC 23 *See illustration p794*

—bark: " . . . he softly rounded the trunk of one large tree, on which the obdurate bark was knotted and overlapped like the hide of a rhinoceros or some kindred monster of the ancient days before the Flood. . . . " DS 27

—in a city churchyard: "There were churches also by dozens, with many a ghostly little churchyard, all overgrown with such straggling vegetation as springs up spontaneously from damp, and graves, and rubbish. In some of these dingy resting-places, which bore much the same analogy to green churchyards, as the pots of earth for mignonette and wall-flower in the windows overlooking them did to rustic gardens, there were trees; tall trees; still putting forth their leaves in each succeeding year, with such a languishing remembrance of their kind (so one might fancy, looking on their sickly boughs) as birds in cages have of theirs." MC 9

—cut down: "The blazing fires of faggot and coal—Dedlock timber and antediluvian forest—that blaze upon the broad wide hearths, and wink in the twilight on the frowning woods, sullen to see how trees are sacrificed, do not exclude the enemy [damp cold]." BH 28

—elms: "New Haven, known also as the City of Elms, is a fine town. Many of its streets . . . are planted with rows of grand old elm-trees . . . . Even in the winter time, these groups of well-grown trees, clustering among the busy streets and houses of a thriving city, have a very quaint appearance: seeming to bring about a kind of compromise between town and country; as if each had met the other half-way, and shaken hands upon it; which is at once novel and pleasant." AN 5

"As the elms bent to one another, like giants who were whispering secrets, and after a few seconds of such repose, fell into a violent flurry, tossing their wild arms about, as if their late confidences were really too wicked for their peace of mind, some weather-beaten ragged old rooks'-nests burdening their higher branches, swung like wrecks upon a stormy sea." DC 1

And see Bird*—rook—nests*

—fallen leaves: "Around and around the house the leaves fall thick—but never fast,

for they come circling down with a dead lightness that is sombre and slow. Let the gardener sweep and sweep the turf as he will, and press the leaves into full barrows, and wheel them off, still they lie ankle-deep." BH 29

And see Weather—*wind—and leaves*

—*forest:* "In the spring, the green leaves broke out of the buds; in the summer, flourished heartily, and made deep shades; in the winter, shrivelled and blew down, and lay in brown heaps on the moss. Some trees were stately, and grew high and strong; some had fallen of themselves; some were felled by the forester's axe; some were hollow, and the rabbits burrowed at their roots; some few were struck by lightning, and stood white and bare.

"There were hill-sides covered with rich fern, on which the morning dew so beautifully sparkled; there were brooks, where the deer went down to drink, or over which the whole herd bounded, flying from the arrows of the huntsmen; there were sunny glades, and solemn places where but little light came through the rustling leaves.

"The songs of the birds in the New Forest were pleasanter to hear than the shouts of fighting men outside; and even when the Red King [Rufus: William II] and his Court came hunting through its solitudes, cursing loud and riding hard, with a jingling of stirrups and bridles and knives and daggers, they did much less harm there than among the English or Normans, and the stags died (as they lived) far easier than the people." ¶CHE 9

—*on a grim night:* "The night was very dark. A damp mist rose from the river, and the marshy ground about; and spread itself over the dreary fields. It was piercing cold, too; all was gloomy and black . . . . Oliver sat huddled together, in a corner of the cart; bewildered with alarm and apprehension; and figuring strange objects in the gaunt trees, whose branches waved grimly to and fro, as if in some fantastic joy at the desolation of the scene." OT 21

—*pruned:* "Some ancient trees before the house were still cut into fashions as formal and unnatural as the hoops and wigs and stiff skirts; but their own allotted places in the great procession of the dead were not far off, and they would soon drop into them and go the silent way of the rest." GE 33

—*on a river:* "The river has washed away its banks, and stately trees have fallen down into the stream. Some have been there so long, that they are mere dry grizzly skeletons. Some have just toppled over, and having earth yet about their roots, are bathing their green heads in the river, and putting forth new shoots and branches. Some are almost sliding down, as you look at them. And some were drowned so long ago, that their bleached arms start out from the middle of the current, and seem to try to grasp the boat, and drag it under water." AN 11

—*and Time:* "After gliding past the sombre maze of boughs for a long time, we come upon an open space where the tall trees are burning. The shape of every branch and twig is expressed in a deep red glow, and as the light wind stirs and ruffles it, they seem to vegetate in fire.

"It is such a sight as we read of in legends of enchanted forests: saving that it is sad to see these noble works wasting away so awfully, alone; and to think how many years must come and go before the magic that created them will rear their like upon this ground again.

"But the time will come; and when, in their changed ashes, the growth of centuries unborn has struck its roots, the restless men of distant ages will repair to these again unpeopled solitudes; and their fellows, in cities far away, that slumber now, perhaps, beneath the rolling sea, will read in language strange to any ears in being now, but very old to them, of primeval forests where the axe was never heard, and where the jungled ground was never trodden by a human foot." AN 11

—*a wood at dusk:* "The last rays of the sun were shining in, aslant, making a path of golden light along the stems and branches in its range, which, even as [Tigg] looked, began to die away, yielding gently to the twilight that came creeping on.

"It was so very quiet that the soft and stealthy moss about the trunks of some old trees, seemed to have grown out of the silence, and to be its proper offspring. Those other trees which were subdued by blasts of wind in winter time, had not quite tumbled down, but being caught by others, lay all bare and scathed across their leafy arms, as if unwilling to disturb the general repose by the crash of their fall.

"Vistas of silence opened everywhere, into the heart and innermost recesses of the wood; beginning with the likeness of an aisle, a cloister, or a ruin open to the sky; then tangling off into a deep green rustling mystery, through which gnarled trunks, and twisted boughs, and ivy-covered stems, and trembling leaves, and bark-stripped bodies of old trees stretched out at length, were faintly seen in beautiful confusion." ¶MC 47

Garden

—after a rain: "The superabundant moisture, trickling from everything after the late rain, set [the landlord] off well. Nothing near him was thirsty. Certain top-heavy dahlias, looking over the palings of his neat well-ordered garden, had swilled as much as they could carry—perhaps a trifle more—and may have been the worse for liquor; but the sweet-briar, roses, wall-flowers, the plants at the windows, and the leaves on the old tree, were in the beaming state of moderate company that had taken no more than was wholesome for them, and had served to develop their best qualities. Sprinkling dewy drops about them on the ground, they seemed profuse of innocent and sparkling mirth, that did good where it lighted, softening neglected corners which the steady rain could seldom reach, and hurting nothing." BL 3

—city: "Some London houses have a melancholy little plot of ground behind them, usually fenced in by four high whitewashed walls, and frowned upon by stacks of chimneys: in which there withers on, from year to year, a crippled tree, that makes a show of putting forth a few leaves late in autumn when other trees shed theirs, and, drooping in the effort, lingers on, all crackled and smoke-dried, till the following season, when it repeats the same process, and perhaps if the weather be particularly genial, even tempts some rheumatic sparrow to chirrup in its branches. People sometimes call these dark yards 'gardens;' it is not supposed that they were ever planted, but rather that they are pieces of unreclaimed land, with the withered vegetation of the original brick-field. No man thinks of walking in this desolate place, or of turning it to any account. A few hampers, half-a-dozen broken bottles, and such-like rubbish, may be thrown there, when the tenant first moves in, but nothing more; and there they remain until he goes away again: the damp straw taking just as long to moulder as it thinks proper: and mingling with the scanty box, and stunted everbrowns, and broken flower-pots, that are scattered mournfully about—a prey to 'blacks' and dirt." NN 2

" . . . a little slip of a front garden abutting on the thirsty high-road, where a few of the dustiest of leaves hung their dismal heads and led a life of choking." LD i 25

—country house: "[Mr Boythorn] lived in a pretty house, formerly the Parsonage-house, with a lawn in front, a bright flower-garden at the side, and a well-stocked orchard and kitchen-garden in the rear, enclosed with a venerable wall that had of itself a ripened ruddy look. But, indeed, everything about the place wore an aspect of maturity and abundance. The old lime-tree walk was like green cloisters, the very shadows of the cherry-trees and apple-trees were heavy with fruit, the gooseberry-bushes were so laden that their branches arched and rested on the earth, the strawberries and raspberries grew in like profusion, and the peaches basked by the hundred on the wall.

"Tumbled about among the spread nets and the glass frames sparkling and winking in the sun, there were such heaps of drooping pods, and marrows, and cucumbers, that every foot of ground appeared a vegetable treasury, while the smell of sweet herbs and all kinds of wholesome growth (to say nothing of the neighbouring meadows where the hay was carrying) made the whole air a great nosegay.

"Such stillness and composure reigned within the orderly precincts of the old red wall, that even the feathers hung in garlands to scare the birds hardly stirred; and the wall had such a ripening influence that where, here and there high up, a disused nail and scrap of list still clung to it, it was easy to fancy that they had mellowed with the changing seasons, and that they had rusted and decayed according to the common fate." ¶BH 18

—gardening: "It is not too much to say that the gardener is essential to all of us. The love of gardening is associated with all countries and all periods of time. The scholar and the statesman, men of peace and men of war, have agreed in all ages to delight in gardens. The most ancient people of the earth had gardens where there were no plants—nothing but solitary heaps of earth. The younger ancients had crowns of flowers. In China hundreds of acres were employed in gardens. When we travel by our railways we see the weaver striving for a scrap of garden, the poor man wrestling with smoke for a little bower of scarlet runners; and those who have no ground of their own will carry on their gardens in jugs and

basins. In factories and workshops, people garden; and even the prisoner is found gardening, in his lonely cell, after years and years of solitary confinement." S/GI2

And see H:Recreation—*gardening*

—*neglected:* "[The window] opened to the ground, and looked into a most miserable corner of the neglected garden; upon a rank ruin of cabbage-stalks, and one box-tree that had been clipped round long ago, like a pudding, and had a new growth at the top of it, out of shape and of a different colour, as if that part of the pudding had stuck to the saucepan and got burnt . . . .

" . . . I strolled into the garden, and strolled all over it. It was quite a wilderness, and there were old melon-frames and cucumber-frames in it, which seemed in their decline to have produced a spontaneous growth of weak attempts at pieces of old hats and boots, with now and then a weedy offshoot into the likeness of a battered saucepan." GE 11

See Times of Day—*dawn*—*brilliant*

Insect

—*bee*

—*caught:* " . . . a blundering bee, who had got himself in between the two sashes of the window, was bruising his head against the glass, endeavouring to force himself out into the fine morning, and considering himself enchanted because he couldn't do it . . . . " MC 48

—*the drone admired:* "There was honey on the table, and it led [Skimpole] into a discourse about Bees. He had no objection to honey, he said (and I should think he had not, for he seemed to like it), but he protested against the overweening assumptions of Bees. He didn't at all see why the busy Bee should be proposed as a model to him; he supposed the Bee liked to make honey, or he wouldn't do it—nobody asked him. It was not necessary for the Bee to make such a merit of his tastes.

"If every confectioner went buzzing about the world, banging against everything that came in his way, and egotistically calling upon everybody to take notice that he was going to his work and must not be interrupted, the world would be quite an unsupportable place. Then, after all, it was a ridiculous position, to be smoked out of your fortune with brimstone, as soon as you had made it. You would have a very mean opinion of a Manchester man, if he spun cotton for no other purpose.

"He must say he thought a Drone the embodiment of a pleasanter and wiser idea. The Drone said, unaffectedly, 'You will excuse me; I really cannot attend to the shop! I find myself in a world in which there is so much to see, and so short a time to see it in, that I must take the liberty of looking about me, and begging to be provided for by somebody who doesn't want to look about him.' This appeared to Mr Skimpole to be the Drone philosophy, and he thought it a very good philosophy—always supposing the Drone to be willing to be on good terms with the Bee: which, so far as he knew, the easy fellow always was, if the consequential creature would only let him, and not be so conceited about his honey!" ¶BH 8

—*how doth . . . :* "'Don't you feel how naughty it is of you,' resumed Miss Monflathers, 'to be a wax-work child, when you might have the proud consciousness of assisting, to the extent of your infant powers, the manufactures of your country; of improving your mind by the constant contemplation of the steam-engine; and of earning a comfortable and independent subsistence of from two-and-ninepence to three shillings per week? Don't you know that the harder you are at work, the happier you are?'

"'"How doth the little—"' murmured one of the teachers, in quotation from Doctor **Watts**.

"'Eh?' said Miss Monflathers, turning smartly round. 'Who said that?'

"Of course the teacher who had not said it, indicated the rival who had, whom Miss Monflathers frowningly requested to hold her peace; by that means throwing the informing teacher into raptures of joy.

"'The little busy bee,' said Miss Monflathers, drawing herself up, 'is applicable only to genteel children.

"In books, or work, or healthful play" is quite right as far as they are concerned; and the work means painting on velvet, fancy needlework, or embroidery. In such cases as these,' pointing to Nell, with her parasol, 'and in the case of all poor people's children, we should read it thus:

"In work, work, work. In work alway
Let my first years be past,
That I may give for ev'ry day
Some good account at last."'

"A deep hum of applause rose not only from the two teachers, but from all the pupils, who were equally astonished to hear

Miss Monflathers improvising after this brilliant style; for although she had been long known as a politician, she had never appeared before as an original poet. Just then somebody happened to discover that Nell was crying, and all eyes were again turned towards her." OCS 31

"'. . . there's nothing like work. Look at the bees.'

" . . . will you excuse my mentioning [said Eugene Wrayburn] that I always protest against being referred to the bees? . . .

"'I object on principle,' said Eugene, 'as a biped——'

"'As a what?' asked Mr Boffin.

"'As a two-footed creature;—I object on principle, as a two-footed creature, to being constantly referred to insects and four-footed creatures. I object to being required to model my proceedings according to the proceedings of the bee, or the dog, or the spider, or the camel. I fully admit that the camel, for instance, is an excessively temperate person; but he has several stomachs to entertain himself with, and I have only one. Besides, I am not fitted up with a convenient cool cellar to keep my drink in.'

"'But I said, you know,' urged Mr Boffin, rather at a loss for an answer, 'the bee.'

"'Exactly. And may I represent to you that it's injudicious to say the bee? For the whole case is assumed. Conceding for a moment that there is any analogy between a bee and a man in a shirt and pantaloons (which I deny), and that it is settled that the man is to learn from the bee (which I also deny), the question still remains, What is he to learn? To imitate? Or to avoid?

"'When your friends the bees worry themselves to that highly fluttered extent about their sovereign, and become perfectly distracted touching the slightest monarchical movement, are we men to learn the greatness of Tuft-hunting, or the littleness of the Court Circular? I am not clear, Mr Boffin, but that the hive may be satirical.'

"'At all events, they work,' said Mr Boffin.

"'Ye-es,' returned Eugene, disparagingly, 'they work; but don't you think they overdo it? They work so much more than they need—they make so much more than they can eat—they are so incessantly boring and buzzing at their one idea till Death comes upon them—that don't you think they overdo it?

"'And are human labourers to have no holidays, because of the bees? And am I never to have change of air, because the bees don't? Mr Boffin, I think honey excellent at breakfast; but regarded in the light of my conventional schoolmaster and moralist, I protest against the tyrannical humbug of your friend the bee." ¶OMF i 8

—blackbeetle: " . . . the blackbeetles took no notice of the agitation, and groped about the hearth in a ponderous elderly way, as if they were short-sighted and hard of hearing, and not on terms with one another." GE 11

—fire-fly: "The coast-road . . . is famous, in the warm season, especially in some parts near Genoa, for fire-flies. Walking there on a dark night, I have seen it made one sparkling firmament by these beautiful insects: so that the distant stars were pale against the flash and glitter that spangled every olive wood and hill-side, and pervaded the whole air." PI 10

" . . . the stars came out in the heavens, and the fire-flies mimicked them in the lower air, as men may feebly imitate the goodness of a better order of beings . . . . " LD i 1

—house-fly: " . . . the flies, drunk with moist sugar in the grocer's shop, forgot their wings and briskness, and baked to death in dusty corners of the window." OCS 28

" . . . Mrs Bangham, charwoman and messenger . . . had volunteered her services as fly-catcher and general attendant. The walls and ceiling were blackened with flies. Mrs Bangham, expert in sudden device, with one hand fanned the patient with a cabbage leaf, and with the other set traps of vinegar and sugar in gallipots; at the same time enunciating sentiments of an encouraging and congratulatory nature, adapted to the occasion.

"'The flies trouble you don't they, my dear?' said Mrs Bangham. 'But p'raps they'll take your mind off it, and do you good. What between the buryin ground, the grocer's, the waggon-stables, and the paunch trade, the Marshalsea flies gets very large. P'raps they're sent as a consolation, if we only know'd it.'" LD i 6

"The day was very hot, and heaps of flies, who were extending their inquisitive and adventurous perquisitions into all the glutinous little glasses near madame, fell dead at the bottom. Their decease made no impression on the other flies out promenading, who looked at them in the coolest manner (as if they themselves were elephants, or something as far removed), until they met the same fate. Curious to consider how heedless flies are!—perhaps they thought as much at Court that sunny summer day." TTC ii 16

—*moth:* "Throughout such fragments of [Diggory Chuzzlewit's] correspondence as have escaped the ravages of the moths (who, in right of their extensive absorption of the contents of deeds and papers, may be called the general registers of the Insect World . . . . " MC 1

—*spider:* "An épergne or centre-piece of some kind was . . . so heavily overhung with cobwebs that its form was quite undistinguishable; and, as I looked along the yellow expanse out of which I remember its seeming to grow, like a black fungus, I saw speckled-legged spiders with blotchy bodies running home to it, and running out from it, as if some circumstance of the greatest public importance had just transpired in the spider community." GE 11

" . . . and speckled spiders, indolent and fat with long security, swing idly to and fro in the vibration of the bells, and never loose their hold upon their thread-spun castles in the air, or climb up sailor-like in quick alarm, or drop upon the ground and ply a score of nimble legs to save one life!" C 1

—*wasp:* "In the small sunny [Flemish] shops . . . the wasps, who seemed to have taken military possession of the town, and to have placed it under wasp-martial law, executed warlike manœuvres in the windows. Other shops the wasps had entirely to themselves, and nobody cared and nobody came when I beat with a five-franc piece upon the board of custom." UT/FF

Moon and moonlight

—*a night journey:* "It was a fine dry night, and the light of a young moon, which was then just rising, shed around that peace and tranquillity which gives to evening time its most delicious charm. The lengthened shadows of the trees, softened as if reflected in still water, threw their carpet on the path the travellers pursued, and the light wind stirred yet more softly than before, as thought it were soothing Nature in her sleep." BR 14

—*on the ocean:* "The rising of the moon is more in keeping with the solitary ocean; and has an air of melancholy grandeur, which in its soft and gentle influence, seems to comfort while it saddens. I recollect when I was a very young child having a fancy that the reflection of the moon in water was a path to Heaven, trodden by the spirits of good people on their way to God; and this old feeling often came over me again, when I watched it on a tranquil night at sea." AN 16

—*on a prison:* "But the moon came slowly up in all her gentle glory, and the stars looked out, and through the small compass of the grated window, as through the narrow crevice of one good deed in a murky life of guilt, the face of Heaven shone bright and merciful. [Barnaby] raised his head; gazed upward at the quiet sky, which seemed to smile upon the earth in sadness, as if the night, more thoughtful than the day, looked down in sorrow on the sufferings and evil deeds of men; and felt its peace sink deep into his heart." BR 73

—*to a prisoner:* "'I have looked at her from my prison-window [said Doctor Manette], when I could not bear her light. I have looked at her when it has been such torture to me to think of her shining upon what I had lost, that I have beaten my head against my prison-walls. I have looked at her, in a state so dull and lethargic, that I have thought of nothing but the number of horizontal lines I could draw across her at the full, and the number of perpendicular lines with which I could intersect them.' He added in his inward and pondering manner, as he looked at the moon, 'It was twenty either way, I remember, and the twentieth was difficult to squeeze in.'" TTC ii 17

—*quiet influence:* "A very quiet night. When the moon shines very brilliantly, a solitude and stillness seem to proceed from her, that influence even crowded places full of life. Not only is it a still night on dusty high roads and on hill-summits, whence a wide expanse of country may be seen in repose, quieter and quieter as it spreads away into a fringe of trees against the sky, with the grey ghost of a bloom upon them; not only is it a still night in gardens and in woods, and on the river where the water-meadows are fresh and green, and the stream sparkles on among pleasant islands, murmuring weirs, and whispering rushes; not only does the stillness attend it as it flows where houses cluster thick, where many bridges are reflected in it, where wharves and shipping make it black and awful, where it winds from these disfigurements through marshes whose grim beacons stand like skeletons washed ashore, where it expands through the bolder region of rising grounds, rich in corn-field, wind-mill and steeple, and where it mingles with the ever-heaving sea; not only is it a still night on the deep, and on the shore where the watcher stands to see the ship with her spread wings cross the path of light that appears to be presented to only him; but even on this stranger's wilderness of London there is some rest. Its steeples and towers, and its one great dome, grow more ethereal; its smoky house-tops lose their grossness, in the pale effulgence; the noises that arise from the streets are fewer and are softened, and the foot-steps on the pavements pass more tranquilly away." BH 48

—sad: "In the sad moonlight, [Lucie Manette] clasped [Doctor Manette] by the neck, and laid her face upon his breast. In the moonlight which is always sad, as the light of the sun itself is—as the light called human life is—at its coming and going." TTC ii 17

—on the sea: "After I had said my prayers, and the candle had burnt out, I remember how I still sat looking at the moonlight on the water, as if I could hope to read my fortune in it, as in a bright book; or to see my mother with her child, coming from Heaven, along that shining path, to look upon me as she had looked when I last saw her sweet face." DC 13

And see Times of Day—*night*

Nature

—affected by the unnatural: "'There is only one change, Mr Dombey,' observed Mrs Skewton, with a mincing sigh, 'for which I really care, and that I fear I shall never be permitted to enjoy. People cannot spare one. But seclusion and contemplation are my what's-his-name . . . . Nature intended me for an Arcadian. I am thrown away in society . . . .

"'What I want,' drawled Mrs Skewton, pinching her shrivelled throat, 'is heart.' It was frightfully true in one sense, if not in that in which she used the phrase. 'What I want, is frankness, confidence, less conventionality, and freer play of soul. We are so dreadfully artificial.'

"We were, indeed.

"'In short, said Mrs Skewton, 'I want Nature everywhere. It would be so extremely charming.'" 21

"'So [Sparkler] is very impressible [said Mrs Merdle]. Not a misfortune in our natural state, I dare say, but we are not in a natural state. Much to be lamented, no doubt, particularly by myself, who am a child of nature if I could but show it; but so it is. Society suppresses us and dominates us—Bird, be quiet!' . . .

"'Adieu, Miss Dorrit, with best wishes,' said Mrs Merdle. 'If we could only come to a Millennium, or something of that sort, I for one might have the pleasure of knowing a number of charming and talented persons from whom I am at present excluded. A more primitive state of society would be delicious to me. There used to be a poem when I learnt lessons, something about Lo the poor Indian whose something mind! If a few thousand persons moving in Society, could only go and be Indians, I would put my name down directly; but as, moving in Society, we can't be Indians, unfortunately—Good morning!'" LD i 19

—to a child: "There was once a child, and he strolled about a good deal, and thought of a number of things. He had a sister, who was a child too, and his constant companion. These two used to wonder all day long. They wondered at the beauty of the flowers; they wondered at the height and blueness of the sky; they wondered at the depth of the bright water; they wondered at the goodness and the power of GOD, who made the lovely world.

"They used to say to one another, sometimes, Supposing all the children upon earth were to die, would the flowers, and the water, and the sky be sorry? They believed they would be sorry. For, said they, the buds are the children of the flowers, and the little playful streams that gambol down the hill-sides are the children of the water; and the smallest bright specks playing at hide and seek in the sky all night, must surely be the children of the stars; and they would all be grieved to see their playmates, the children of men, no more." RP/DS

—context for complacency: "The summer weather in his bosom was reflected in the breast of Nature. Through deep green vistas where the boughs arched overhead, and showed the sunlight flashing in the beautiful perspective; through dewy fern from which the startled hares leaped up, and fled at his approach; by mantled pools, and fallen trees, and down in hollow places, rustling among last year's leaves whose scent woke memory of the past; the placid Pecksniff strolled.

"By meadow gates and hedges fragrant with wild roses; and by thatched-roof cottages whose inmates humbly bowed before him as a man both good and wise; the worthy Pecksniff walked in tranquil meditation. The bee passed onward, humming of the work he had to do; the idle gnats for ever going round and round in one contracting and expanding ring, yet always going on as fast as he, danced merrily before him; the colour of the long grass came and went, as if the light clouds made it timid as they floated through the distant air. The birds, so many Pecksniff consciences, sang gaily upon every branch; and Mr Pecksniff paid his homage to the day by ruminating on his projects as he walked along." MC 30

—and family ties: "'What was it,' said Snawley, 'that made me take such a strong interest in him, when that worthy instructor of youth brought him to my house? What was it that made me burn all over with a wish to chastise him severely for cutting away from his best friends, his pastors and masters?'

"'It was parental instinct, sir,' observed Squeers.

"'That's what it was, sir,' rejoined Snawley; 'the elevated feeling, the feeling of the ancient Romans and Grecians, and of the beasts of the field and birds of the air, with the exception of rabbits and tom-cats, which sometimes devour their offspring. My heart yearned towards him. I could have—I don't know what I couldn't have done to him in the anger of a father.'

"'It only shows what Natur is, sir,' said Mr Squeers. 'She's a rum 'un, is Natur.'

"'She is a holy thing, sir,' remarked Snawley.

"'I believe you,' added Mr Squeers, with a moral sigh. 'I should like to know how we should ever get on without her. Natur,' said Mr Squeers, solemnly, 'is more easier conceived than described. Oh what a blessed thing, sir, to be in a state o' natur!'" NN 45

"' . . . . Parents who never showed their love, complain of want of natural affection in their children; children who never showed their duty, complain of want of natural feeling in their parents; law-makers who find both so miserable that their affections have never had enough of life's sun to develop them, are loud in their moralisings over parents and children too, and cry that the very ties of nature are disregarded. Natural affections and instincts, my dear sir [said Charles Cheeryble to Nicholas Nickleby], are the most beautiful of the Almighty's works, but like other beautiful works of His, they must be reared and fostered, or it is as natural that they should be wholly obscured, and that new feelings should usurp their place, as it is that the sweetest productions of the earth, left untended, should be choked with weeds and briars. I wish we could be brought to consider this, and, remember natural obligations a little more at the right time, talk about them a little less at the wrong one.'" NN 46 *And see —what is natural*

—God in: "When they rose up from the ground, and took the shady track which led them through the wood, [Nell] bounded on before; printing her tiny footsteps in the moss, which rose elastic from so light a pressure and gave it back as mirrors throw off breath; and thus she lured the old man on, with many a backward look and merry beck, now pointing stealthily to some lone bird as it perched and twittered on a branch that strayed across their path, now stopping to listen to the songs that broke the happy silence, or watch the sun as it trembled through the leaves, and stealing in among the ivied trunks of stout old trees, opened long paths of light.

"As they passed onward, parting the boughs that clustered in their way, the serenity which the child had first assumed, stole into her breast in earnest; the old man cast no longer fearful looks behind, but felt at ease and cheerful, for the further they passed into the deep green shade, the more they felt that the tranquil mind of God was there, and shed its peace on them." ¶OCS 24

—its kingdoms: " . . . [Craggs] being a cold, hard, dry man, dressed in grey and white, like flint; with small twinkles in his eyes, as if something struck sparks out of them. The three natural kingdoms, indeed, had each a fanciful representative among this brotherhood of disputants; for Snitchey was like a magpie or raven (only not so sleek), and the Doctor had a streaked face like a winter-pippin, with here and there a dimple to express the peckings of the birds, and a very little bit of pigtail behind that stood for the stalk." BL 1

—a mother: "At no Mother's knee but hers, had [Arthur Clennam] ever dwelt in his youth on hopeful promises, on playful fancies, on the harvests of tenderness and humility that lie hidden in the early-fostered seeds of the imagination; on the oaks of retreat from blighting winds, that have the germs of their strong roots in nursery

acorns." LD ii 34

—and a murderer: "All night! It is a common fancy, that nature seems to sleep by night. It is a false fancy, as who should know better than he [Jonas Chuzzlewit]?

"The fishes slumbered in the cold, bright, glistening streams and rivers, perhaps; and the birds roosted on the branches of the trees; and in their stalls and pastures beasts were quiet; and human creatures slept. But what of that, when the solemn night was watching, when it never winked, when its darkness watched no less than its light!

"The stately trees, the moon and shining stars, the softly-stirring wind, the overshadowed lane, the broad, bright countryside, they all kept watch. There was not a blade of growing grass or corn, but watched; and the quieter it was, the more intent and fixed its watch upon him seemed to be." ¶MC 47

—myth and science: "Science has gone down into the mines and coal-pits, and before the safety-lamp the Gnomes and Genii of those dark regions have disappeared. But in their stead, the process by which metals are engendered in the course of ages; the growth of plants which, hundreds of fathoms underground, and in black darkness, have still a sense of the sun's presence in the sky, and derive some portion of the subtle essence of their life from his influence; the histories of mighty forests and great tracts of land carried down into the sea, by the same process which is active in the Mississippi and such great rivers at this hour; are made familiar to us.

"Sirens, mermaids, shining cities glittering at the bottom of the quiet seas and in deep lakes, exist no longer; but in their place, Science, their destroyer, shows us whole coasts of coral reef constructed by the labours of minute creatures, points to our own chalk cliffs and limestone rocks as made of the dust of myriads of generations of infinitesimal beings that have passed away; reduces the very element of water into its constituent airs, and re-creates it at her pleasure.

"Caverns in rocks, choked with rich treasures shut up from all but the enchanted hand, Science has blown to atoms, as she can rend and rive the rocks themselves; but in those rocks she has found, and read aloud, the great stone book which is the history of the earth, even when darkness sat upon the face of the deep.

"Along their craggy sides she has traced the footprints of birds and beasts, whose shapes were never seen by man. From within them she has brought the bones, and pieced together the skeletons, of monsters that would have crushed the noted dragons of the fables at a blow." E/PS

—and Nurture

—Nature prevails: " . . . he was a man who had, deep-rooted in his nature, a belief in all the gentle and good things his life had been without. Bred in meanness and hard dealing, this had rescued him to be a man of honourable mind and open hand. Bred in coldness and severity, this had rescued him to have a warm and sympathetic heart. Bred in a creed too darkly audacious to pursue, through its process of reversing the making of man in the image of his Creator to the making of his Creator in the image of an erring man, this had rescued him to judge not, and in humility to be merciful, and have hope and charity.

"And this saved him still from the whimpering weakness and cruel selfishness of holding that because such a happiness or such a virtue had not come into his little path, or worked well for him, therefore it was not in the great scheme, but was reducible, when found in appearance, to the basest elements. A disappointed mind he had, but a mind too firm and healthy for such unwholesome air. Leaving himself in the dark, it could rise into the light, seeing it shine on others and hailing it.

"Therefore, he sat before his dying fire, sorrowful to think upon the way by which he had come to that night, yet not strewing poison on the way by which other men had come to it." LD i 13

Arthur Clennam has been raised by a woman not his mother; he never discovers this.

—Nurture prevails: "Huddled together . . . were a crowd of boys . . . with nothing natural to youth about them: with nothing frank, ingenuous, or pleasant in their faces; low-browed, vicious, cunning, wicked; abandoned of all help but [a Ragged School]; speeding downward to destruction, and UNUTTERABLY IGNORANT.

" . . . in sample of a Multitude who had within them once, and perhaps have now, the elements of men as good as you or I, and maybe infinitely better; in sample of a Multitude among whose doomed and sinful ranks . . . the child of any man upon this earth, however lofty his degree, must, as by Destiny and Fate, be found if, at its birth, it were consigned to such an infancy and nurture, as these fallen creatures had!" MP/CE

—perverted (stating the core of CD's social conscience and philosophy, with an eloquence nowhere surpassed in his work):

"Was Mr Dombey's master-vice, that ruled him so inexorably, an unnatural characteristic? It might be worth while, sometimes, to inquire what Nature is, and how men work to change her, and whether, in the enforced distortion so produced, it is not natural to be unnatural.

"Coop any son or daughter of our mighty mother within narrow range, and bind the prisoner to one idea, and foster it by servile worship of it on the part of the few timid or designing people standing round, and what is Nature to the willing captive who has never risen up upon the wings of a free mind—drooping and useless soon—to see her in her comprehensive truth!

"Alas! are there so few things in the world, about us, most unnatural, and yet most natural in being so? Hear the magistrate or judge admonish the unnatural outcasts of society; unnatural in brutal habits, unnatural in want of decency, unnatural in losing and confounding all distinctions between good and evil; unnatural in ignorance, in vice, in recklessness, in contumacy, in mind, in looks, in everything.

"But follow the good clergyman or doctor, who, with his life imperilled at every breath he draws, goes down into their dens, lying within the echoes of our carriage wheels and daily tread upon the pavement stones. Look round upon the world of odious sights—millions of immortal creatures have no other world on earth—at the lightest mention of which humanity revolts, and dainty delicacy living in the next street, stops her ears, and lisps 'I don't believe it!'

"Breathe the polluted air, foul with every impurity that is poisonous to health and life; and have every sense, conferred upon our race for its delight and happiness, offended, sickened and disgusted, and made a channel by which misery and death alone can enter. Vainly attempt to think of any simple plant, or flower, or wholesome weed, that, set in their fœtid bed, could have its natural growth, or put its little leaves off to the sun as GOD designed it.

"And then, calling up some ghastly child, with stunted form and wicked face, hold forth on its unnatural sinfulness, and lament its being, so early, far away from Heaven—but think a little of its having been conceived, and born and bred, in Hell!

"Those who study the physical sciences, and bring them to bear upon the health of Man, tell us that if the noxious particles that rise from vitiated air were palpable to the sight, we should see them lowering in a dense black cloud above such haunts, and rolling slowly on to corrupt the better portions of a town.

"But if the moral pestilence that rises with them, and in the eternal laws of outraged Nature, is inseparable from them, could be made discernible too, how terrible the revelation! Then should we see depravity, impiety, drunkenness, theft, murder, and a long train of nameless sins against the natural affections and repulsions of mankind, overhanging the devoted spots, and creeping on, to blight the innocent and spread contagion among the pure.

"Then should we see how the same poisoned fountains that flow into our hospitals and lazar-houses, inundate the jails, and make the convict-ships swim deep, and roll across the seas, and over-run vast continents with crime. Then should we stand appalled to know, that where we generate disease to strike our children down and entail itself on unborn generations, there also we breed, by the same certain process, infancy that knows no innocence, youth without modesty or shame, maturity that is mature in nothing but in suffering and guilt, blasted old age that is a scandal on the form we bear.

"Unnatural humanity! When we shall gather grapes from thorns, and figs from thistles; when fields of grain shall spring up from the offal in the bye-ways of our wicked cities, and roses bloom in the fat churchyards that they cherish; then we may look for natural humanity and find it growing from such seed.

"Oh for a good spirit who would take the house-tops off, with a more potent and benignant hand than the lame demon in the tale, and show a Christian people what dark shapes issue from amidst their homes, to swell the retinue of the Destroying Angel as he moves forth among them! For only one night's view of the pale phantoms rising from the scenes of our too-long neglect; and from the thick and sullen air where Vice and Fever propagate together, raining the tremendous social retributions which are ever pouring down, and ever coming thicker!

"Bright and blest the morning that should rise on such a night: for men, delaying no more by stumbling-blocks of their own making, which are but specks of dust upon the path between them and eternity, would then apply themselves, like creatures of one common origin, owing one duty to the Father of one family, and tending to one common end, to make the world a better place!

"Not the less bright and blest would that day be for rousing some who never have looked out upon the world of human life around them, to a knowledge of their own relation to it, and for making them acquainted with a perversion of nature in their own contracted sympathies and estimates; as great, and yet as natural in its development when once begun, as the lowest degradation known." ¶DS 47

See also H:War—*battlefield; and* FL:Past lives—*suggested by Nature*

River

—*mirror:* "The trees were bare of leaves, and the river was bare of water-lilies; but the sky was not bare of its beautiful blue, and the water reflected it, and a delicious wind ran with the stream, touching the surface crisply. Perhaps the old mirror was never yet made by human hands, which, if all the images it had in its time reflected could pass across its surface again, would fail to reveal some scene of horror or distress. But the great serene mirror of the river seemed as if it might have reproduced all it had ever reflected between those placid banks, and brought nothing to the light save what was peaceful, pastoral, and blooming." OMF iii 9

—*observer inured:* "'I should like to know where Inspector Field was born. In Ratcliff Highway, I would have answered with confidence, but for his being equally at home wherever we go. *He* does not trouble his head as I do, about the river at night. *He* does not care for its creeping, black and silent, on our right there, rushing through sluice gates, lapping at piles and posts and iron rings, hiding strange things in its mud, running away with suicides and accidentally drowned bodies faster than midnight funeral should, and acquiring such various experience between its cradle and its grave. It has no mystery for *him*. RP/DF

—*unceasing:* "Within view was the peaceful river and the ferry-boat, to moralise to all the inmates [of the Meagles house], saying: Young or old, passionate or tranquil, chafing or content, you, thus runs the current always. Let the heart swell into what discord it will, thus plays the rippling water on the prow of the ferry-boat ever the same tune. Year after year, so much allowance for the drifting of the boat, so many miles an hour the flowing of the stream, here the rushes, there the lilies, nothing uncertain or unquiet, upon this road that steadily runs away; while you, upon your flowing road of time, are so capricious and distracted." LD i 16

And see W:Rivers, *for actual streams; and* FL:Eternity—*its portal, the river*

The Sea

"' . . . the great salt field that is never sown!'" CS/MS 1

—*derisive:* "The tide is low, and seems to have thrown them together high on the bare shore. A gull comes sweeping by their heads, and flouts them. There was a golden surface on the brown cliffs but now, and behold they are only damp earth. A taunting roar comes from the sea, and the far-out rollers mount upon one another, to look at the entrapped impostors [Sophronia and Alfred Lammle], and to join in impish and exultant gambols." OMF i 10

—*at dusk:* " . . . so deep a hush was on the sea, that it scarcely whispered of the time when it shall give up its dead." LD i 1

—*after a gale:* " . . . anything like the utter dreariness and desolation that met my eyes when I literally 'tumbled up' on deck at noon, I never saw. Ocean and sky were all of one dull, heavy, uniform lead-colour. There was no extent of prospect even over the dreary waste that lay around us, for the sea ran high, and the horizon encompassed us like a large black hoop. Viewed from the air, or some tall bluff on shore, it would have been imposing and stupendous, no doubt; but seen from the wet and rolling decks, it only impressed one giddily and painfully." AN 2

—*lost at:* " . . . the influence of great privation upon the lower and less disciplined class of character, is much more bewildering and maddening at sea than on shore. The confined space, the monotonous aspect of the waves, the mournful winds, the monotonous motion, the dead uniformity of colour, the abundance of water that cannot be drunk to quench the raging thirst . . . these seem to engender a diseased mind with greater quickness and of a worse sort." HW/AV 2

—*mindless:* "'Don't you nor any other friend of mine never go to sleep with his head in a ship any more . . . . For,' said Mr [Mark] Tapley, pursuing the theme by way of soliloquy, in a low tone of voice: 'the sea is as nonsensical a thing as any going. It never knows what to do with itself. It hasn't got no employment for its mind, and is always in a state of vacancy. Like them Polar bears in the wild-beast shows as is constantly a-nodding their heads from side to side, it never can be quiet. Which is entirely owing to its uncommon stupidity.'" MC 15

—*in storm:* "'You never was at sea, my own?'

"No,' replied Florence.

"'Aye,' said the Captain, reverentially; 'it's a almighty element. There's wonders in the deep, my pretty. Think on it when the winds is roaring and the waves is rowling. Think on it when the stormy nights is so pitch dark,' said the Captain, solemnly holding up his hood, 'as you can't see your hand afore you, excepting when the wiwid lightning reweals the same; and when you drive, drive, drive through the storm and dark, as if you was a driving, head on, to the world without end, evermore, amen, and when found making a note of. Them's the times, my beauty, when a man may say to his messmate (previously a overhauling of the wollume), "A stiff nor'wester's blowing, Bill; hark, don't you hear it roar now! Lord help 'em, how I pitys all unhappy folks ashore now!"' Which quotation, as particularly applicable to the terrors of the ocean, the Captain delivered in a most impressive manner, concluding with a sonorous 'Stand by!'" DS 49

—*viewed from shore:* "Sitting on a bright September morning, among my books and papers, at my open window on the cliff overhanging the sea-beach, I have the sky and ocean framed before me like a beautiful picture. A beautiful picture, but with such movement in it, such changes of light upon the sails of ships and wake of steamboats, such dazzling gleams of silver far out at sea, such fresh touches on the crisp wave-tops as they break and roll towards me—a picture with such music in the billowy rush upon the shingle, the blowing of the morning wind through the corn-sheaves, where the farmers' waggons are busy, the singing of the larks, and the distant voices of children at play—such charms of sight and sound as all the Galleries on earth can but poorly suggest." RP/OT

"So settled and orderly was everything seaward, in the bright light of the sun and under the transparent shadows of the clouds, that it was hard to imagine the bay otherwise, for years past or to come, than it was that very day. The Tug-steamer lying a little off the shore, the Lighter lying still nearer to the shore, the boat alongside the Lighter, the regularly-turning windlass aboard the Lighter, the methodical figures at work, all slowly and regularly heaving up and down with the breathing of the sea, all seemed as much a part of the nature of the place as the tide itself." UT/S

—*its voice:* "We have a fine sea, wholesome for all people; profitable for the body, profitable for the mind. The poet's words are sometimes on its awful lips:

And the stately ships go on
To their haven under the hill;
But O for the touch of a vanished hand,
And the sound of a voice that is still.
Break, break, break,
At the foot of thy crags, O sea!
But the tender grace of a day that is dead
*Will never come back to me!**

Yet it is not always so, for the speech of the sea is various, and wants not abundant resource of cheerfulness, hope, and lusty encouragement." RP/EW

**Tennyson:* Break, Break, Break *(1842)*

—*waves, and a ship:* "On, on, on, over the countless miles of angry space roll the long heaving billows. Mountains and caves are here, and yet are not; for what is now the one, is now the other; then all is but a boiling heap of rushing water. Pursuit, and flight, and mad return of wave on wave, and savage struggle, ending in a spouting-up of foam that whitens the black night; incessant change of place, and form, and hue; constancy in nothing, but eternal strife; on, on, on, they roll, and darker grows the night, and louder howls the wind, and more clamorous and fierce become the million voices in the sea, when the wild cry goes forth upon the storm 'A ship!'

"Onward she comes, in gallant combat with the elements, her tall masts trembling, and her timbers starting on the strain; onward she comes, now high upon the curling billows, now low down in the hollows of the sea, as hiding for the moment from its fury; and every storm-voice in the air and water cries more loudly yet, 'A ship!'

"Still she comes striving on: and at her boldness and the spreading cry, the angry waves rise up above each other's hoary heads to look; and round about the vessel, far as the mariners on the decks can pierce into the gloom, they press upon her, forcing each other down, and starting up, and rushing forward from afar, in dreadful curiosity. High over her they break; and round her surge and roar; and giving place to others, moaningly depart, and dash themselves to fragments in their baffled anger. Still she comes onward bravely. And though the eager multitude crowd thick and fast upon her all the night, and dawn of day discovers the untiring train yet bearing down upon the ship in an eternity of troubled water, onward she comes, with dim lights burning in her hull, and people there, asleep: as if no deadly element were peering in at every seam and chink, and no drowned seaman's grave, with but a plank to cover it, were yawning in the unfathomable depths below." MC 15 *And see* W:Travel—*sea voyage*

Seasons

—*the round:* "Weeks, months, seasons, pass along. They seem little more than a summer day and a winter evening. Now, the Common where I walk with Dora is all in bloom, a field of bright gold; and now the unseen heather lies in mounds and bunches underneath a covering of snow. In a breath, the river that flows through our Sunday walks is sparkling in the summer sun, is ruffled by the winter wind, or thickened with drifting heaps of ice. Faster than ever river ran towards the sea, it flashes, darkens, and rolls away." DC 43

—*Spring*

—*changeable:* "It was on one of those mornings, common in early spring, when the year, fickle and changeable in its youth, like all other created things, is undecided whether to step backward into winter or forward into summer, and in its uncertainty inclines now to the one and now to the other, and now to both at once—wooing summer, in the sunshine, and lingering still with winter in the shade—it was, in short, on one of those mornings, when it is hot and cold, wet and dry, bright and lowering, sad and cheerful, withering and genial, in the compass of one short hour." BR 10

—*in the country:* "Everything was fresh and gay, as though the world were but that morning made, when Mr Chester rode at a tranquil pace along the Forest road. Though early in the season, it was warm and genial weather; the trees were budding into leaf, the hedges and the grass were green, the air was musical with songs of birds, and high above them all the lark poured out her richest melody.

"In shady spots, the morning dew sparkled on each young leaf and blade of grass; and where the sun was shining, some diamond drops yet glistened brightly, as in unwillingness to leave so fair a world, and have such brief existence. Even the light wind, whose rustling was as gentle to the ear as softly-falling water, had its hope and promise; and, leaving a pleasant fragrance in its track as it went fluttering by, whispered of its intercourse with Summer, and of his happy coming." ¶BR 29

—*March:* "It was one of those March days when the sun shines hot and the wind blows cold: when it is summer in the light, and winter in the shade." GE 54

—*May:* "The first of May! There is a merry freshness in the sound, calling to our minds a thousand thoughts of all that is pleasant in nature and beautiful in her most delightful form. What man is there, over whose mind a bright spring morning does not exercise a magic influence—carrying him back to the days of his childish sports, and conjuring up before him the old green field with its gently-waving trees, where the birds sang as he has never heard them since—where the butterfly fluttered far more gaily than he ever sees him now, in all his ramblings—where the sky seemed bluer, and the sun shone more brightly—where the air blew more freshly over greener grass, and sweeter-smelling flowers—where everything wore a richer and more brilliant hue than it is ever dressed in now! Such are the deep feelings of childhood, and such are the impressions which every lovely object stamps upon its heart! The hardy traveller wanders through the maze of thick and pathless woods, where the sun's rays never shone, and the heaven's pure air never played; he stands on the brink of the roaring waterfall, and, giddy and bewildered, watches the foaming mass as it leaps from stone to stone, and from crag to crag; he lingers in the fertile plains of a land of perpetual sunshine, and revels in the luxury of their balmy breath. But what are the deep forests, or the thundering waters, or the richest landscapes that bounteous nature ever spread, to charm the eyes, and captivate the senses of man, compared with the recollection of the old scenes of his early youth? Magic scenes indeed; for the fancies of childhood dressed them in colours brighter than the rainbow, and almost as fleeting!" SB/FM

—mid-spring: "It was a lovely evening in the spring-time of the year; and in the soft stillness of the twilight, all nature was very calm and beautiful. The day had been fine and warm; but at the coming on of night, the air grew cool, and in the mellowing distance smoke was rising gently from the cottage chimneys.

"There were a thousand pleasant scents diffused around, from young leaves and fresh buds; the cuckoo had been singing all day long, and was but just now hushed; the smell of earth newly-upturned, first breath of hope to the first labourer after his garden withered, was fragrant in the evening breeze.

"It was a time when most men cherish good resolves, and sorrow for the wasted past; when most men, looking on the shadows as they gather, think of that evening which must close on all, and that to-morrow which has none beyond.

"'Precious dull,' said Mr Jonas [Chuzzlewit], looking about. 'It's enough to make a man go melancholy mad.'" MC 20

See also S:Sensitivity

—Summer

—before air-conditioning: "It is the hottest long vacation known for many years. All the young clerks are madly in love, and, according to their various degrees, pine for bliss with the beloved object, at Margate, Ramsgate, or Gravesend. All the middle-aged clerks think their families too large. All the unowned dogs who stray into the Inns of Court, and pant about staircases and other dry places, seeking water, give short howls of aggravation. All the blind men's dogs in the streets draw their masters against pumps, or trip them over buckets. A shop with a sun-blind, and a watered pavement, and a bowl of gold and silver fish in the window, is a sanctuary. Temple Bar gets so hot, that it is, to the adjacent Strand and Fleet Street, what a heater is in an urn, and keeps them simmering all night.'" BH 19

—a country walk: "The summer weather in his bosom was reflected in the breast of Nature. Through deep green vistas where the boughs arched over-head, and showed the sunlight flashing in the beautiful perspective; through dewy fern from which the startled hares leaped up, and fled at his approach; by mantled pools, and fallen trees, and down in hollow places, rustling among last year's leaves whose scent woke memory of the past; the placid Pecksniff strolled. By meadow gates and hedges fragrant with wild roses; and by thatched-roof cottages whose inmates humbly bowed before him as a man both good and wise; the worthy Pecksniff walked in tranquil meditation. The bee passed onward, humming of the work he had to do; the idle gnats for ever going round and round in one contracting and expanding ring, yet always going on as fast as he, danced merrily before him; the colour of the long grass came and went, as if the light clouds made it timid as they floated through the distant air. The birds, so many Pecksniff consciences, sang gaily upon every branch; and Mr Pecksniff paid *his* homage to the day by ruminating on his projects as he walked along." MC 30

—by day: "Spring flew swiftly by, and summer came. If the village had been beautiful at first it was now in the full glow and luxuriance of its richness. The great trees, which had looked shrunken and bare in the earlier months, had now burst into strong life and health; and stretching forth their green arms over the thirsty ground, converted open and naked spots into choice nooks, where was a deep and pleasant shade from which to look upon the wide prospect, steeped in sunshine, which lay stretched beyond. The earth had donned her mantle of brightest green; and shed her richest perfumes abroad. It was the prime and vigour of the year; all things were glad and flourishing." OT 33

—evening: "It was a hot summer Sunday evening. The residence [the Sparklers'] at the centre of the habitable globe, at all times stuffed and close as if it had an incurable cold in its head, was that evening

particularly stifling. The bells of the churches had done their worst in the way of clanging among the unmelodious echoes of the streets, and the lighted windows of the churches had ceased to be yellow in the grey dusk, and died out opaque black." LD ii 24

—a fine morning: " . . . the morning was as fine a morning as ever was seen; and the fragrant air was kissing Ruth [Pinch] and rustling about Tom, as if it said, 'How are you, my dears: I came all this way on purpose to salute you;' and it was one of those glad times when we form, or ought to form, the wish that every one on earth were able to be happy, and catching glimpses of the summer of the heart, to feel the beauty of the summer of the year." MC 48

—August: "There is no month in the whole year, in which nature wears a more beautiful appearance than in the month of August. Spring has many beauties, and May is a fresh and blooming month, but the charms of this time of year are enhanced by their contrast with the winter season.

"August has no such advantage. It comes when we remember nothing but clear skies, green fields and sweet-smelling flowers—when the recollection of snow, and ice, and bleak winds, has faded from our minds as completely as they have disappeared from the earth—and yet what a pleasant time it is!

"Orchards and corn-fields ring with the hum of labour; trees bend beneath the thick clusters of rich fruit which bow their branches to the ground; and the corn, piled in graceful sheaves, or waving in every light breath that sweeps above it, as if it wooed the sickle, tinges the landscape with a golden hue. A mellow softness appears to hang over the whole earth; the influence of the season seems to extend itself to the very waggon, whose slow motion across the well-reaped field, is perceptible only to the eye, but strikes with no harsh sound upon the ear." ¶PP 16

And see L:Neighbourhoods—*Chancery Lane,* TP:Judge—*on vacation,* The Law—*on vacation, and* Law-clerks—*on vacation*

—the weirs: "Plashwater Weir Mill Lock looked tranquil and pretty on an evening in the summer-time. A soft air stirred the leaves of the fresh green trees, and passed like a smooth shadow over the river, and like a smoother shadow over the yielding grass. The voice of the falling water, like the voices of the sea and the wind, was an outer memory to a contemplative listener. . . . " OMF iv 1

—Autumn

—early: "In plain common-place matter-of-fact, then, it was a fine morning—so fine that you would scarcely have believed that the few months of an English summer had yet flown by. Hedges, fields, and trees, hill and moorland, presented to the eye their ever-varying shades of deep rich green; scarce a leaf had fallen, scarce a sprinkle of yellow mingled with the hues of summer, warned you that autumn had begun. The sky was cloudless, the sun shone out bright and warm; the songs of birds, and hum of myriads of summer insects, filled the air; and the cottage gardens, crowded with flowers of every rich and beautiful tint, sparkled, in the heavy dew, like beds of glittering jewels. Everything bore the stamp of summer, and none of its beautiful colours had yet faded from the dye." PP 19

—glowing: "It was a warm autumn afternoon, and there had been heavy rain. The sun burst suddenly from among the clouds; and the old battle-ground, sparkling brilliantly and cheerfully at sight of it in one green place, flashed a responsive welcome there, which spread along the country side as if a joyful beacon had been lighted up, and answered from a thousand stations.

"How beautiful the landscape kindling in the light, and that luxuriant influence passing on like a celestial presence, brightening everything! The wood, a sombre mass before, revealed its varied tints of yellow, green, brown, red: its different forms of trees, with raindrops glittering on their leaves and twinkling as they fell.

"The verdant meadowland, bright and glowing, seemed as if it had been blind, a minute since, and now had found a sense of sight wherewith to look up at the shining sky. Corn-fields, hedgerows, fences, homesteads, and clustered roofs, the steeple of the church, the stream, the water-mill, all sprang out of the gloomy darkness smiling.

"Birds sang sweetly, flowers raised their drooping heads, fresh scents arose from the invigorated ground; the blue expanse above extended and diffused itself; already the sun's slanting rays pierced mortally the sullen bank of cloud that lingered in its flight; and a rainbow, spirit of all the colours that adorned the earth and sky, spanned the whole arch with its triumphant glory." BL 3

—harvest-time: "As the coach rolls swiftly past the fields and orchards which skirt the road, groups of women and children, piling the fruit in sieves, or gathering the scattered ears of corn, pause for an instant from their labour, and shading the sun-burnt face with a still browner hand, gaze upon the passengers with curious eyes, while some stout urchin, too small to work, but too mischievous to be left at home, scrambles over the side of the basket in which he has been deposited for security, and kicks and screams with delight.

"The reaper stops in his work, and stands with folded arms, looking at the vehicle as it whirls past; and the rough cart-horses bestow a sleepy glance upon the smart coach team, which says, as plainly as a horse's glance can, 'It's all very fine to look at, but slow going, over a heavy field, is better than warm work like that, upon a dusty road, after all.' You cast a look behind you, as you turn a corner of the road. The women and children have resumed their labour: the reaper once more stoops to his work: the cart-horses have moved on: and all are again in motion." ¶PP 16

—late: "Like a sudden flash of memory or spirit kindling up the mind of an old man, [the declining sun] shed a glory upon the scene, in which its departed youth and freshness seemed to live again. The wet grass sparkled in the light; the scanty patches of verdure in the hedges—where a few green twigs yet stood together bravely, resisting to the last the tyranny of nipping winds and early frosts—took heart and brightened up; the stream which had been dull and sullen all day long, broke out into a cheerful smile; the birds began to chirp and twitter on the naked boughs, as though the hopeful creatures half believed that winter had gone by, and spring had come already.

"The vane upon the tapering spire of the old church glistened from its lofty station in sympathy with the general gladness; and from the ivy-shaded windows such gleams of light shone back upon the glowing sky, that it seemed as if the quiet buildings were the hoarding-place of twenty summers, and all their ruddiness and warmth were stored within.

"Even those tokens of the season which emphatically whispered of the coming winter, graced the landscape, and, for the moment, tinged its livelier features with no oppressive air of sadness. The fallen leaves, with which the ground was strewn, gave forth a pleasant fragrance, and subduing all harsh sounds of distant feet and wheels, created a repose in gentle unison with the light scattering of seed hither and thither by the distant husbandman, and with the noiseless passage of the plough as it turned up the rich brown earth, and wrought a graceful pattern in the stubbled fields.

"On the motionless branches of some trees, autumn berries hung like clusters of coral beads, as in those fabled orchards where the fruits were jewels; others, stripped of all their garniture, stood, each the centre of its little heap of bright red leaves, watching their slow decay; others again, still wearing theirs, had them all crunched and crackled up, as though they had been burnt; about the stems of some were piled, in ruddy mounds, the apples they had borne that year; while others (hardy evergreens this class) showed somewhat stern and gloomy in their vigour, as charged by nature with the admonition that it is not to her more sensitive and joyous favourites she grants the longest term of life." ¶MC 2

"On a healthy autumn day; when the golden fields had been reaped and ploughed again, when the summer fruits had ripened and waned, when the green perspectives of hops had been laid low by the busy pickers, when the apples clustering in the orchards were russet, and the berries of the mountain ash were crimson among the yellowing foliage. Already in the woods, glimpses of the hardy winter that was coming, were to be caught through unaccustomed openings among the boughs where the prospect shone defined and clear, free from the bloom of the drowsy summer weather, which had rested on it as the bloom lies on the plum.

"So, from the sea-shore the ocean was no longer to be seen lying asleep in the heat, but its thousand sparkling eyes were open, and its whole breadth was in joyful animation, from the cool sand on the beach to the little sails on the horizon, drifting away like autumn-tinted leaves that had drifted from the trees." ¶LD ii 34

"Not only is the day waning, but the year. The low sun is fiery and yet cold behind the monastery ruin, and the Virginia creeper on the Cathedral wall has showered half its deep-red leaves down on the pavement. There has been rain this afternoon, and a wintry shudder goes among the little pools on the cracked uneven flagstones, and through the giant elm trees as they shed a gust of tears. Their fallen leaves lie strewn thickly about. Some of these leaves, in a timid rush, seek sanctuary within the low arched Cathedral door . . . . " MED 2

—October: "It is a dull October afternoon; no blue whatever in the sky, no wind whatever in the trees. On each side of the broad high-road, the fields are puffed up into notice by a series of undulations, as if it were determined that no effort should be spared to make the greatest possible display of melancholy oaks, and red and yellow corpses, and every variety of autumn foliage which Nature has just now on hand. Dulled as we are by the dulness of the atmosphere, and little cheered by the dead leaves which make our path untidy, yet our London eyes are brightened at the first sight of a veritable five-barred gate, framed in blackberries." HWC/FE

And see B:House—*country—in Autumn*

—Winter

—congenial: "A raging winter day, that shook the old house, sometimes, as if it shivered in the blast. A day to make home doubly home. To give the chimney-corner new delights. To shed a ruddier glow upon the faces gathered round the hearth, and draw each fireside group into a closer and more social league, against the roaring elements without. Such a wild winter day as best prepares the way for shut-out night; for curtained rooms, and cheerful looks; for music, laughter, dancing, light, and jovial entertainment!" BL 2

—early and pleasant: "What better time for driving, riding, walking, moving through the air by any means, than a fresh, frosty morning, when hope runs cheerily through the veins with the brisk blood, and tingles in the frame from head to foot! This was the glad commencement of a bracing day in early winter, such as may put the languid summer season (speaking of it when it can't be had) to the blush, and shame the spring for being sometimes cold by halves.

"The sheep-bells rang as clearly in the vigorous air, as if they felt its wholesome influence like living creatures; the trees, in lieu of leaves or blossoms, shed upon the ground a frosty rime that sparkled as it fell, and might have been the dust of diamonds. . . . From cottage chimneys, smoke went streaming up high, high, as if the earth had lost its grossness, being so fair, and must not be oppressed by heavy vapour. The crust of ice on the else rippling brook was so transparent and so thin in texture, that the lively water might of its own free will have stopped . . . to look upon the lovely morning. And lest the sun should break this charm too eagerly, there moved between him and the ground, a mist like that which waits upon the moon on summer nights . . . and wooed him to dissolve it gently." ¶MC 6

—fog in January: "You couldn't see very far in the fog, of course; but you could see a great deal! It's astonishing how much you may see, in a thicker fog than that, if you will only take the trouble to look for it. Why, even to sit watching for the Fairy-rings in the fields, and for the patches of hoarfrost still lingering in the shade, near hedges and by trees, was a pleasant occupation; to make no mention of the unexpected shapes in which the trees themselves came starting out of the mist, and glided into it again." CH 2

—shelter: "One wintry evening . . . a keen north wind arose as it grew dark, and night came on with black and dismal looks. A bitter storm of sleet, sharp, dense, and icycold, swept the wet streets, and rattled on the trembling windows. Signboards, shaken past endurance in their creaking frames, fell crashing on the pavement; old tottering chimneys reeled and staggered in the blast; and many a steeple rocked again that night, as though the earth were troubled.

"It was not a time for those who could by any means get light and warmth, to brave the fury of the weather. In coffee-houses of the better sort, guests crowded round the fire, forgot to be political, and told each other with a secret gladness that the blast grew fiercer every minute. Each humble tavern by the water-side, had its group of uncouth figures round the hearth, who talked of vessels foundering at sea, and all hands lost; related many a dismal tale of shipwreck and drowned men, and hoped that some they knew were safe, and shook their heads in doubt.

"In private dwellings, children clustered near the blaze; listening with timid pleasure to tales of ghosts and goblins, and tall figures clad in white standing by bed-sides, and people who had gone to sleep in old churches and being overlooked had found themselves alone there at the dead hour of the night: until they shuddered at the thought of the dark room up-stairs, yet loved to hear the wind moan too, and hoped it would continue bravely.

"From time to time these happy indoor people stopped to listen, or one held up his finger and cried 'Hark!' and then above the rumbling in the chimney, and the fast pattering on the glass, was heard a wailing, rushing sound, which shook the walls as though a giant's hand were on them; then a hoarse roar as if the sea had risen; then such a whirl and tumult that the air seemed mad; and then, with a lengthened howl, the waves of wind swept on, and left a moment's interval of rest." ¶BR 33

—a wintry ride: "How well I [David Copperfield] recollect the wintry ride! The frozen particles of ice, brushed from the blades of grass by the wind, and borne across my face; the hard clatter of the horse's hoofs, beating a tune upon the ground; the stiff-tilled soil; the snow-drift, lightly eddying in the chalk-pit as the breeze ruffled it; the smoking team with the waggon of old hay, stopping to breathe on the hill-top, and shaking their bells musically; the whitened slopes and sweeps of Downland lying against the dark sky, as if they were drawn on a huge slate!" DC 62

And see Times of Day—*twilight—winter*

Shadow

"When twilight everywhere released the shadows, prisoned up all day, that now closed in and gathered like mustering swarms of ghosts. When they stood lowering, in corners of rooms, and frowned out from behind half-opened doors. When they had full possession of unoccupied apartments. When they danced upon the floors, and walls, and ceilings of inhabited chambers, while the fire was low, and withdrew like ebbing waters when it sprung into a blaze. When they fantastically mocked the shapes of household objects, making the nurse an ogress, the rocking-horse a monster, the wondering child half-scared and half-amused, a stranger to itself—the very tongs upon the hearth, a straddling giant with his arms a-kimbo, evidently smelling the blood of Englishmen, and wanting to grind people's bones to make his bread.

"When these shadows brought into the minds of older people, other thoughts, and showed them different images. When they stole from their retreats, in the likenesses of forms and faces from the past, from the grave, from the deep, deep gulf, where the things that might have been, and never were, are always wandering." HM 1

Sounds

—cathedral bell: " . . . a fire shines out upon the fast-darkening scene, involving in shadow the pendent masses of ivy and creeper covering the building's front. As the deep Cathedral-bell strikes the hour, a ripple of wind goes through these at their distance, like a ripple of the solemn sound that hums through tomb and tower, broken niche and defanced statue . . . . " MED 2

—an empty house: " . . . a vast blank of overgrown house looking out upon trees, sighing, wringing their hands, bowing their heads, and casting their tears upon the window-panes in monotonous depression. A labyrinth of grandeur, less the property of an old family of human beings and their ghostly likenesses, than of an old family of echoings and thunderings which start out of their hundred graves at every sound, and go resounding through the building. A waste of unused passages and staircases, in which to drop a comb upon a bedroom floor at night is to send a stealthy footfall on an errand through the house. A place where few people care to go about alone; where a maid screams if an ash drops from the fire, takes to crying at all times and seasons, becomes the victim of a low disorder of the spirits, and gives warning and departs." BH 66

—silence: "'Pickwick and principle!' exclaimed Mr Weller, in a very audible voice.

"'Sam, be quiet,' said Mr Pickwick.

"'Dumb as a drum vith a hole in it, sir,' replied Sam." PP 25

"'It's eleven o'clock striking by the bell of Saint Paul's. Listen, and you'll hear all the bells in the city jangling.'

"[Guppy and Weevle] sit silent, listening to the metal voices, near and distant, resounding from towers of various heights, in tones more various than their situations. When these at length cease, all seems more mysterious and quiet than before. One disagreeable result of whispering is, that it seems to evoke an atmosphere of silence, haunted by the ghosts of sound—strange cracks and tickings, the rustling of garments that have no substance in them, and the tread of dreadful feet, that would leave no mark on the sea-sand or the winter snow. So sensitive the two friends happen to be, that the air is full of these phantoms; and the two look over their shoulders by one consent, to see that the door is shut." BH 32

"Upon this wintry night it is so still, that listening to the intense silence is like looking at intense darkness. If any distant sound be audible in this case, it departs through the gloom like a feeble light in that, and all is heavier than before." BH 58

And see Times of Day—*night—silent*

—*at twilight:* "When the sounds that had arisen with the shadows, and come out of their lurking places at the twilight summons, seemed to make a deeper stillness all about [Redlaw]. When the wind was rumbling in the chimney, and sometimes crooning, sometimes howling, in the house. When the old trees outside were so shaken and beaten, that one querulous old rook, unable to sleep, protested now and then, in a feeble, dozy, high up 'Caw!' When, at intervals, the window trembled, the rusty vane upon the turret-top complained, the clock beneath it recorded that another quarter of an hour was gone, or the fire collapsed and fell in with a rattle." HM 1

Sun and sunlight

—*at dawn:* "That punctual servant of all work, the sun, had just arisen, and begun to strike a light . . . . " PP 2

"The night crept on apace, the moon went down, the stars grew pale and dim, and morning, cold as they, slowly approached. Then, from behind a distant hill, the noble sun rose up, driving the mists in phantom shapes before it, and clearing the earth of their ghostly forms till darkness came again." OCS 43

"When [Rigaud] started up, the Godfather Break of Day was peeping at its namesake." LD i 11

"The white face of the winter day came sluggishly on, veiled in a frosty mist; and the shadowy ships in the river slowly changed to black substances; and the sun, blood-red on the eastern marshes behind dark mast and yards, seemed filled with the ruins of a forest it had set on fire." OMF i 6

—*ephemeral in a gallery:* "Through some of the fiery windows, beautiful from without, and set, at this sunset hour, not in dull grey stone but in a glorious house of gold, the light excluded at other windows pours in, rich, lavish, overflowing like the summer plenty in the land. Then do the frozen Dedlocks thaw. Strange movements come upon their features, as the shadows of leaves play there. A dense Justice in a corner is beguiled into a wind. A staring Baronet, with a truncheon, gets a dimple in his chin. Down into the bosom of a stony shepherdess there steals a fleck of light and warmth, that would have done it good, a hundred years ago. One ancestress of Volumnia, in high-heeled shoes, very like her—casting the shadow of that virgin event before her full two centuries—shoots out into a halo and becomes a saint. A maid of honour of the court of Charles the Second, with large round eyes (and other charms to correspond), seems to bathe in glowing water, and it ripples as it glows.

"But the fire of the sun is dying. Even now the floor is dusky, and shadow slowly mounts the walls, bringing the Dedlocks down like age and death. And now, upon my Lady's picture over the great chimney-piece, a weird shade falls from some old tree, that turns it pale, and flutters it, and looks as if a great arm held a veil or hood, watching an opportunity to draw it over her. Higher and darker rises shadow on the wall—now a red gloom on the ceiling—now the fire is out." BH 40

—*on an industrial town:* "But the sun itself, however beneficent, generally, was less kind to Coketown than hard frost, and rarely looked intently into any of its closer regions without engendering more death than life. So does the eye of Heaven itself become an evil eye, when incapable or sordid hands are interposed between it and the things it looks upon to bless." HT ii 1

—*looking on and in:* "The clear cold sunshine glances into the brittle woods, and approvingly beholds the sharp wind scattering the leaves and drying the moss. It glides over the park after the moving shadows of the clouds, and chases them, and never catches them, all day. It looks in at the windows, and touches the ancestral portraits with bars and patches of brightness, never contemplated by the painters. Athwart the picture of my Lady, over the great chimney-piece, it throws a broad bend-sinister of light that strikes down crookedly into the hearth, and seems to rend it." BH 12

—*premonitory:* " . . . [Carker] turned to where the sun was rising, and beheld it, in its glory, as it broke upon the scene.

"So awful, so transcendent in its beauty, so divinely solemn. As he cast his faded eyes upon it, where it rose, tranquil and serene, unmoved by all the wrong and wickedness on which its beams had shone since the beginning of the world, who shall say that some weak sense of virtue upon Earth, and its reward in Heaven, did not manifest itself, even to him? If ever he remembered sister or brother with a touch of tenderness and remorse, who shall say it was not then?

"He needed some such touch then. Death was on him. He was marked off from the living world, and going down into his grave." DS 55

—on a prison: "'To the devil with this brigand of a Sun that never shines in here!'" LD i 1

"The last day of the appointed week touched the bars of the Marshalsea gate. Black, all night, since the gate had clashed upon Little Dorrit, its iron stripes were turned by the early-glowing sun into stripes of gold. For aslant across the city, over its jumbled roofs, and through the open tracery of its church towers, struck the long bright rays, bars of the prison of this lower world." LD ii 30

—setting: "The wide stare stared itself out for one while; the sun went down in a red, green, golden glory . . . . " LD i 1

" . . . he paused at the great western folding-door of the Cathedral, which stood open on the fine and bright, though short-lived, afternoon . . . .

"'Dear me,' said Mr Grewgious, peeping in, 'it's like looking down the throat of Old Time.'

"Old Time heaved a mouldy sigh from tomb and arch and vault; and gloomy shadows began to deepen in corners; and damps began to rise from green patches of stone; and jewels, cast upon the pavement of the nave from stained glass by the declining sun, began to perish. Within the grill-gate of the chancel, up the steps surmounted loomingly by the fast-darkening organ, white robes could be dimly seen, and one feeble voice, rising and falling in a cracked monotonous mutter, could at intervals be faintly heard. In the free outer air, the river, the green pastures, and the brown arable lands, the teeming hills and dales, were reddened by the sunset: while the distant little windows in windmills and farm homesteads, shone, patches of bright beaten gold. In the Cathedral, all became grey, murky, and sepulchral . . . . " MED 9

And see Times of Day—*sunset*

—tropical: "'Don't come too near me, for I am frightfully faint and sensitive this morning, and you smell of the Sun. You are absolutely tropical.'

"'By George, Ma'am,' said the Major, 'the time has been when Joseph Bagstock has been grilled and blistered by the Sun; the time was, when he was forced, Ma'am, into such full blow, by high hothouse heat in the West Indies, that he was known as the Flower. A man never heard of Bagstock, Ma'am, in those days; he heard of the Flower—the Flower of Ours. The Flower may have faded, more or less, Ma'am,' observed the Major . . . . " DS 26

—winter: "It was a hard frost, that day. The air was bracing, crisp, and clear. The wintry sun, though powerless for warmth, looked brightly down upon the ice it was too weak to melt, and set a radiant glory there. At other times, Trotty [Veck] might have learned a poor man's lesson from the wintry sun; but he was past that, now." C 2

And see Times of Day, *passim.;* B:Bird—*sparrow;* B:Hair—*in the sun; and* W:Cities and Towns, Actual—*Marseilles*

Tide

—low: "At low water, we are a heap of mud, with an empty channel in it where a couple of men in big boots always shovel and scoop: with what exact object, I am unable to say.

"At that time, all the stranded fishing-boats turn over on their sides, as if they were dead marine monsters; the colliers and other shipping stick disconsolate in the mud; the steamers look as if their white chimneys would never smoke more, and their red paddles never turn again; the green sea-slime and weed upon the rough stones at the entrance, seem records of obsolete high tides never more to flow; the flagstaff-halyards glare of the sun." ¶RP/OT

"Sky, sea, beach, and village, lie as still before us as if they were sitting for the picture. It is dead low-water. A ripple plays among the ripening corn upon the cliff, as if it were faintly trying from recollection to imitate the sea; and the world of butterflies hovering over the crop of radish-seed are as restless in their little way as the gulls are in their larger manner when the wind blows. But the ocean lies winking in the sunlight like a drowsy lion—its glassy waters scarcely curve upon the shore—the fishing-boats in the tiny harbour are all stranded in the mud—our two colliers . . . have not an inch of water within a quarter of a mile of them, and turn, exhausted, on their sides, like faint fish of an antediluvian species. Rusty cables and chains, ropes and rings, undermost parts of posts and piles and confused timber-defences against the waves, lie strewn about, in a brown litter of tangled sea-weed and fallen cliff which looks as if a family of giants had been making tea here for ages, and had observed an untidy custom of throwing their tea-leaves on the shore." RP/EW

And see W:Cities and Towns—*Broadstairs*

—*high:* "But the moment the tide begins to make, the Pavilionstone Harbour begins to revive. It feels the breeze of the rising water before the water comes, and begins to flutter and stir. When the little shallow waves creep in, barely overlapping one another, the vanes at the mastheads wake, and become agitated.

"As the tide rises, the fishing-boats get into good spirits and dance, the flagstaff hoists a bright red flag, the steamboat smokes, cranes creak, horses and carriages dangle in the air, stray passengers and luggage appear.

"Now, the shipping is afloat, and comes up buoyantly, to look at the wharf. Now, the carts that have come down for coals, load away as hard as they can load. Now, the steamer smokes immensely, and occasionally blows at the paddle-boxes like a vaporous whale—greatly disturbing nervous loungers.

"Now, both the tide and the breeze have risen, and you are holding your hat on . . . . Now, everything in the harbour splashes, dashes, and bobs . . . . Now, the fishing-boats that have been out, sail in at the top of the tide . . . . Now, there is not only a tide of water, but a tide of people, and a tide of luggage—all tumbling and flowing and bouncing about together." ¶RP/OT

"And since I have been idling at the window here, the tide has risen. The boats are dancing on the bubbling water; the colliers are afloat again; the white-bordered waves rush in; the children

Do chase the ebbing Neptune, and fly him
*When he comes back;**

the radiant sails are gliding past the shore, and shining on the far horizon; all the sea is sparkling, heaving, swelling up with life and beauty, this bright morning." RP/EW

**The Tempest V i*

Times of Day

—dawn

—*brilliant:* "A brilliant morning shines on the old city. Its antiquities and ruins are surpassingly beautiful, with a lusty ivy gleaming in the sun, and the rich trees waving in the balmy air. Changes of glorious light from moving boughs, songs of birds, scents from gardens, woods, and fields—or, rather, from the one great garden of the whole cultivated island in its yielding time—penetrate into the Cathedral, subdue its earthy odour, and preach the Resurrection and the Life. The cold stone tombs of centuries ago grow warm; and flecks of brightness dart into the sternest marble corners of the building, fluttering there like wings." MED 23

The chapter, entitled 'The Dawn again,' was CD's last. The foregoing words were written within two hours of his death. deF p317

—*contending with night:* "Dawn, with its passionless blank face, steals shivering to the church beneath which lies the dust of little Paul and his mother, and looks in at the windows. It is cold and dark. Night crouches yet, upon the pavement, and broods, sombre and heavy, in nooks and corners of the building . . . within doors, dawn, at first, can only peep at night, and see that it is there.

"Hovering feebly round the church, and looking in, dawn moans and weeps for its short reign, and its tears trickle on the window-glass, and the trees against the church-wall bow their heads, and wring their many hands in sympathy. Night, growing pale before it, gradually fades out of the church, but lingers in the vaults below, and sits upon the coffins. And now comes bright day, burnishing the steeple-clock, and reddening the spire, and drying up the tears of dawn, and stifling its complaining; and the scared dawn, following the night, and chasing it from its last refuge, shrinks into the vaults itself and hides, with a frightened face, among the dead, until night returns, refreshed, to drive it out." DS 31

—*as death:* "The night wore out, and, as [Carton] stood upon the bridge listening to the water as it splashed the river-walls of the Island of Paris, where the picturesque confusion of houses and cathedral shone bright in the light of the moon, the day came coldly, looking like a dead face, out of the sky. Then, the night, with the moon and the stars, turned pale and died, and for a little while it seemed as if Creation were delivered over to Death's dominion." TTC iii 9

"Day was breaking on Plashwater Weir Mill Lock. Stars were yet visible, but there was dull light in the east that was not the light of night. The moon had gone down, and a mist crept along the banks of the river, seen through which the trees were the ghosts of trees, and the water was the ghost of water. This earth looked spectral, and so did the pale stars; while the cold eastern glare, expressionless as to heat or colour, with the eye of the firmament quenched, might have been likened to the stare of the dead." OMF iv 7

—*hopeful:* "Soon, now, the distant line on the horizon brightened, the darkness faded, the sun rose red and glorious, and the chimney stacks and gables of the ancient building gleamed in the clear air, which turned the smoke and vapour of the city into a cloud of gold. The very sun-dial in his shady corner, where the wind was used to spin with such un-windy constancy, shook off the finer particles of snow that had accumulated on his dull old face in the night, and looked out at the little white wreaths eddying round and round him. Doubtless some blind groping of the morning made its way down into the forgotten crypt so cold and earthy, where the Norman arches were half buried in the ground, and stirred the dull deep sap in the lazy vegetation hanging to the walls, and quickened the slow principle of life within the little world of wonderful and delicate creation which existed there, with some faint knowledge that the sun was up." HM 3

—*peopled:* "No day yet in the sky, but there was day in the resounding stones of the streets; in the waggons, carts, and coaches; in the workers going to various occupations; in the opening of early shops; in the traffic at markets; in the stir of the river-side. There was coming day in the flaring lights, with a feebler colour in them than they would have had at another time; coming day in the increased sharpness of the air, and the ghastly dying of the night." LD i 14

—*in a prison:* "When [Little Dorrit] had stolen down-stairs, and along the empty yard, and had crept up to her own high garret, the smokeless housetops and the distant country hills were discernible over the wall in the clear morning. As she gently opened the window, and looked eastward down the prison yard, the spikes upon the wall were tipped with red, then made a sullen purple pattern on the sun as it came flaming up into the heavens. The spikes had never looked so sharp and cruel, nor the bars so heavy, nor the prison space so gloomy and contracted. She thought of the sunrise on rolling rivers, of the sunrise on wide seas, of the sunrise on rich landscapes, of the sunrise on great forests where the birds were waking and the trees were rustling; and she looked down into the living grave on which the sun had risen, with her father in it, three-and-twenty years, and said, in a burst of sorrow and compassion, 'No, no, I have never seen him in my life!'" LD i 19

—*from a window:* "It was interesting when I dressed before daylight, to peep out of window, where my candles were reflected in the black panes like two beacons, and, finding all beyond still enshrouded in the indistinctness of last night, to watch how it turned out when the day came on.

"As the prospect gradually revealed itself, and disclosed the scene over which the wind had wandered in the dark, like my memory over my life, I had a pleasure in discovering the unknown objects that had been around me in my sleep. At first they were faintly discernible in the mist, and above them the later stars still glimmered. That pale interval over, the picture began to enlarge and fill up so fast, that, at every new peep, I could have found enough to look at for an hour. Imperceptibly, my candles became the only incongruous part of the morning, the dark places in my room all melted away, and the day shone bright upon a cheerful landscape . . . . " BH 8

—*on a winter's day:* "The white face of the winter day came sluggishly on, veiled in a frosty mist; and the shadowy ships in the river slowly changed to black substances; and the sun, blood-red on the eastern marshes behind dark masts and yards, seemed filled with the ruins of a forest it had set on fire." GE i 6

See also Sun and Sunlight; Weather—*hail—at dawn; and* L: Times of Day—*daybreak*

—*dusk*

—*in an industrial town:* "[Mrs Sparsit] sat at the window, when the sun began to sink behind the smoke; she sat there, when the smoke was burning red, when the colour faded from it, when darkness seemed to rise slowly out of the ground, and creep upward, upward, up to the house-tops, up the church steeple, up to the summits of the factory chimneys, up to the sky." HT ii 1

—*in winter:* "When the wind was blowing, shrill and shrewd, with the going down of the blurred sun. When it was just so dark, as that the forms of things were indistinct and big—but not wholly lost. When sitters by the fire began to see wild faces and figures, mountains and abysses, ambuscades and armies, in the coals. When people in the streets bent down their heads and ran before the weather.

"When those who were obliged to meet it, were stopped at angry corners, stung by wandering snow-flakes alighting on the lashes of their eyes—which fell too sparingly, and were blown away too quickly, to leave a trace upon the frozen ground. When windows of private houses closed up tight and warm. When lighted gas began to burst forth in the busy and the quiet streets fast blackening otherwise. When stray pedestrians, shivering along the latter, looked down at the glowing fires in kitchens, and sharpened their sharp appetites by sniffing up the fragrance of whole miles of dinners.

"When travellers by land were bitter cold, and looked wearily on gloomy landscapes, rustling and shuddering in the blast. When mariners at sea, outlying upon icy yards, were tossed and swung above the howling ocean dreadfully. When lighthouses, on rocks and headlands, showed solitary and watchful; and benighted sea-birds breasted on against their ponderous lanterns, and fell dead . . . .

"When in rustic places, the last glimmering of daylight died away from the ends of avenues; and the trees, arching overhead, were sullen and black.

"When, in parks and woods, the high wet fern and sodden moss and beds of fallen leaves, and trunks of trees, were lost to view, in masses of impenetrable shade. When mists arose from dyke, and fen, and river. When lights in old halls and in cottage windows, were a cheerful sight. When the mill stopped, the wheelwright and the blacksmith shut their workshops, the turnpike-gate closed, the plough and harrow were left lonely in the fields, the labourer and team went home, and the striking of the church clock had a deeper sound than at noon, and the churchyard wicket would be swung no more that night." ¶HM 1

And see —twilight

—morning

—*bright:* "It was a bright and sunny morning in the pleasant time of summer. . . . Heaven above was blue, and earth beneath was green; the river glistened like a path of diamonds in the sun; the birds poured forth their songs from the shady trees; the lark soared high above the waving corn; and the deep buzz of insects filled the air." NN 6

—*depressing:* "The morning which broke upon Mr Pickwick's sight, at eight o'clock, was not at all calculated to elevate his spirits, or to lessen the depression which the unlooked-for result of his embassy inspired. The sky was dark and gloomy, the air was damp and raw, the streets were wet and sloppy. The smoke hung sluggishly above the chimney-tops as if it lacked the courage to rise, and the rain came slowly and doggedly down, as if it had not even the spirit to pour.

"A game-cock in the stable-yard, deprived of every spark of his accustomed animation, balanced himself dismally on one leg in a corner; a donkey, moping with drooping head under the narrow roof of an outhouse, appeared from his meditative and miserable countenance to be contemplating suicide. In the street, umbrellas were the only things to be seen, and the clicking of pattens and splashing of rain-drops were the only sounds to be heard." ¶PP 51

—*early:* "No period within the four-and-twenty hours of day and night is so solemn to me, as the early morning. In the summer time, I often rise very early, and repair to my room to do a day's work before breakfast, and I am always on those occasions deeply impressed by the stillness and solitude around me. Besides that there is something awful in the being surrounded by familiar faces asleep—in the knowledge that those who are dearest to us and to whom we are dearest, and profoundly unconscious of us, in an impassive state, anticipative of that mysterious condition to which we are all tending—the stopped life, the broken threads of yesterday, the deserted seat, the closed book, the unfinished but abandoned occupation, all are images of Death.

"The tranquillity of the hour is the tranquillity of Death. The colour and the chill have the same association. Even a certain air that familiar household objects take upon them when they first emerge from the shadows of the night into the morning, of being newer, and as they used to be long ago, has its counterpart in the subsidence of the worn face of maturity or age, in death, into the old youthful look" CS/HH 1.

—grumps: "It was morning; and the beautiful Aurora, of whom so much hath been written, said, and sung, did, with her rosy fingers, nip and tweak Miss Pecksniff's nose. It was the frolicsome custom of the Goddess, in her intercourse with the fair Cherry, so to do; or in more prosaic phrase, the tip of that feature in the sweet girl's countenance was always very red at breakfast time. For the most part, indeed, it wore, at that season of the day, a scraped and frosty look, as if it had been rasped; while a similar phenomenon developed itself in her humour, which was then observed to be of a sharp and acid quality, as though an extra lemon (figuratively speaking) had been squeezed into the nectar of her disposition, and had rather damaged its flavour." MC 6

—ominous: "The day comes like a phantom. Cold, colourless, and vague, it sends a warning streak before it of a deathlike hue, as if it cried out, 'Look what I am bringing you, who watch here!!' Who will tell him?'" BH 58

—rainy and grim: "The air grew colder, as day came slowly on; and the mist rolled along the ground like a dense cloud of smoke. The grass was wet; the pathways, and low places, were all mire and water; the damp breath of an unwholesome wind went languidly by, with a hollow moaning. Still, Oliver lay motionless and insensible on the spot where Sikes had left him.

"Morning drew on apace. The air became more sharp and piercing, as its first dull hue—the death of night, rather than the birth of day—glimmered faintly in the sky. The objects which had looked dim and terrible in the darkness, grew more and more defined, and gradually resolved into their familiar shapes. The rain came down, thick and fast, and pattered noisily among the leafless bushes. But Oliver felt it not, as it beat against him; for he still lay stretched, helpless and unconscious, on his bed of clay." OT 28

—soporific: "It was a cold, dry, foggy morning in early spring. A few meagre shadows flitted to and fro in the misty streets, and occasionally there loomed through the dull vapour, the heavy outline of some hackney-coach wending homewards, which, drawing slowly nearer, rolled jangling by, scattering the thin crust of frost from its whitened roof, and soon was lost again in the cloud. At intervals were heard the tread of slipshod feet, and the chilly cry of the poor sweep as he crept, shivering, to his early toil; the heavy footfall of the official watcher of the night, pacing slowly up and down and cursing the tardy hours that still intervened between him and sleep; the rumbling of ponderous carts and waggons; the roll of the lighter vehicles which carried buyers and sellers to the different markets; the sound of ineffectual knocking at the doors of heavy sleepers—all these noises fell upon the ear from time to time, but all seemed muffled by the fog, and to be rendered almost as indistinct to the ear as was every object to the sight. The sluggish darkness thickened as the day came on; and those who had the courage to rise and peep at the gloomy street from their curtained windows crept back to bed again, and coiled themselves up to sleep." NN 22

—in time of trial: "Although to restless and ardent minds, morning may be the fitting season for exertion and activity, it is not always at that time that hope is strongest or the spirit most sanguine and buoyant. In trying and doubtful positions, use, custom, a steady contemplation of the difficulties which surround us, and a familiarity with them, imperceptibly diminish our apprehensions and beget comparative indifference, if not a vague and reckless confidence in some relief, the means or nature of which we care not to foresee.

"But when we come fresh upon such things in the morning, with that dark and silent gap between us and yesterday, with every link in the brittle chain of hope to rivet afresh, our hot enthusiasm subdued, and cool calm reason substituted in its stead, doubt and misgiving revive.

"As the traveller sees farthest by day, and becomes aware of rugged mountains and trackless plains which the friendly darkness had shrouded from his sight and mind together, so the wayfarer in the toilsome path of human life sees with each returning sun some new obstacle to surmount, some new height to be attained; distances stretch out before him which last night were scarcely taken into account, and the light which gilds all nature with its cheerful beams, seems but to shine upon the weary obstacles which yet lie strewn between him and the grave." ¶NN 53

—uncommercial: "The next was a very unpropitious morning for a journey—muggy, damp, and drizzly. The horses in the stages that were going out, and had come through the city, were smoking so, that the outside passengers were invisible. The newspaper sellers looked moist, and smelt mouldy; the wet ran off the hats of the orange-venders as they thrust their heads into the coach windows, and diluted the insides in a refreshing manner. The Jews with the fifty-bladed penknives shut them up in despair; the men with the pocket-books made pocket-books of them. Watch-guards and toasting-forks were alike at a discount, and pencil-cases and sponge were a drug in the market." PP 35

And see FL:Life*—its restoration regretted, and* B:Sleep*—preferable to waking?*

—night

—before an execution: "Then came night —dark, dismal, silent night. Other watchers are glad to hear the church-clocks strike, for they tell of life and coming day. To the Jew they brought despair. The boom of every iron bell came laden with the one, deep, hollow sound—Death. What availed the noise and bustle of cheerful morning, which penetrated even there, to him? It was another form of knell, with mockery added to the warning.

"The day passed off—day!—there was no day; it was gone as soon as come—and night came on again; night so long, and yet so short; long in its dreadful silence, and short in its fleeting hours. At one time he raved and blasphemed, and at another howled and tore his hair . . . .

"Saturday night. He had only one night more to live. And as he thought of this, the day broke—Sunday . . . Eight—nine—ten. If it was not a trick to frighten him and those were the real hours treading on each other's heels, where would he be when they came round again? Eleven! Another struck before the voice of the previous hour had ceased to vibrate. At eight, he would be the only mourner in his own funeral train; at eleven—" OT 62

—country: "The rich light had faded, the sombre hues of night were falling fast upon the landscape, and a few bright stars were already twinkling overhead. The birds were all at roost; the daisies on the green had closed their fairy hoods; the honeysuckle twining round the porch exhaled its perfume in a two-fold degree, as though it lost its coyness at that silent time and loved to shed its fragrance on the night; the ivy scarcely stirred its deep green leaves. How tranquil and how beautiful it was!" BR 54

—in a country house: "Light mists arise, and the dew falls, and all the sweet scents in the garden are heavy in the air. Now, the woods settle into great masses as if they were each one profound tree. And now the moon rises, to separate them, and to glimmer here and there in horizontal lines behind their stems, and to make the avenue a pavement of light among high cathedral arches fantastically broken.

"Now, the moon is high; and the great house, needing habitation more than ever, is like a body without life. Now, it is even awful, stealing through it, to think of the live people who have slept in the solitary bedrooms: to say nothing of the dead. Now is the time for shadow, when every corner is a cavern, and every downward step a pit, when the stained glass is reflected in pale and faded hues upon the floors, when anything and everything can be made of the heavy staircase beams excepting their own proper shapes, when the armour has dull lights upon it not easily to be distinguished from stealthy movement, and when barred helmets are frightfully suggestive of heads inside." BH 40

—dead of: "It was nearly two hours before day-break; that time which, in the autumn of the year, may be truly called the dead of night; when the streets are silent and deserted; when even sounds appear to slumber, and profligacy and riot have staggered home to dream . . . . " OT 47

—ending: "No day yet in the sky, but there was day in the resounding stones of the streets; in the waggons, carts, and coaches; in the workers going to various occupations; in the opening of early shops; in the traffic at markets; in the stir of the river-side. There was coming day in the flaring lights, with a feebler colour in them than they would have had at another time; coming day in the increased sharpness of the air, and the ghastly dying of the night." LD i 14

—silent: "There was no wind; there was no passing shadow on the deep shade of the night; there was no noise. The city lay behind [Carker], lighted here and there, and

starry worlds were hidden by the masonry of spire and roof that hardly made out any shapes against the sky." DS 55

"Other sound than the owl's voice there was none, save the falling of a fountain into its stone basin; for, it was one of those dark nights that hold their breath by the hour together, and then heave a long low sigh, and hold their breath again." TTC ii 9

—sky: "It was a cold, wild night, and the trees shuddered in the wind. The rain had been thick and heavy all day, and with little intermission for many days. None was falling just then, however. The sky had partly cleared, but was very gloomy—even above us, where a few stars were shining. In the north and north-west, where the sun had set three hours before, there was a pale dead light both beautiful and awful; and into it long sullen lines of cloud waved up, like a sea stricken immovable as it was heaving. Towards London, a lurid glare overhung the whole dark waste; and the contrast between these two lights, and the fancy which the redder light engendered of an unearthly fire, gleaming on all the unseen buildings of the city, and on all the faces of its many thousands of wondering inhabitants, was as solemn as might be." BH 31 *And see* Moon and moonlight

—small hours: "The wind was blowing drearily. The lamps looked pale, and shook as if they were cold. There was a distant glimmer of something that was not quite darkness, rather than of light, in the sky; and foreboding night was shivering and restless, as the dying are who make a troubled end. Florence remembered how, as a watcher, by a sick-bed, she had noted this bleak time, and felt its influence, as if in some hidden natural antipathy to it; and now it was very, very gloomy." DS 43

"Night was still heavy in the sky. On open plains, from hill-tops, and from the decks of solitary ships at sea, a distant low-lying line, that promised by-and-by to change to light, was visible in the dim horizon; but its promise was remote and doubtful, and the moon was striving with the night-clouds busily." HM 3

"Cold on the shore, in the raw cold of that leaden crisis in the four-and-twenty hours when the vital force of all the noblest and prettiest things that live is at its lowest. . . . " OMF i 14

—three hours in France: "The stone faces on the outer walls stared blindly at the black night for three heavy hours; for three heavy hours the horses in the stables rattled at their racks, the dogs barked . . . .

"For three heavy hours, the stone faces of the chateau, lion and human, stared blindly at the night. Dead darkness lay on all the landscape, dead darkness added its own hush to the hushing dust on all the roads. The burial-place had got to the pass that its little heaps of poor grass were undistinguishable from one another; the figure on the Cross might have come down, for anything that could be seen of it. In the village, taxers and taxed were fast asleep. Dreaming, perhaps, of banquets, as the starved usually do, and of ease and rest, as the driven slave and the yoked ox may, its lean inhabitants slept soundly, and were fed and freed.

"The fountain in the village flowed unseen and unheard, and the fountain at the chateau dropped unseen and unheard—both melting away, like the minutes that were falling from the spring of Time—through three dark hours." TTC ii 9

—sunset

—in autumn: "Still athwart their darker boughs, the sunbeams struck out paths of deeper gold; and the red light, mantling in among their swarthy branches, used them as foils to set its brightness off, and aid the lustre of the dying day.

"A moment, and its glory was no more. The sun went down beneath the long dark lines of hill and cloud which piled up in the west an airy city, wall heaped on wall, and battlement on battlement; the light was all withdrawn; the shining church turned cold and dark; the stream forgot to smile; the birds were silent; and the gloom of winter dwelt on everything.

"An evening wind uprose too, and the slighter branches cracked and rattled as they moved, in skeleton dances, to its moaning music. The withering leaves no longer quiet, hurried to and fro in search of shelter from its chill pursuit; the labourer unyoked his horses, and with head bent down, trudged briskly home beside them; and from the cottage windows lights began to glance and wink upon the darkening fields." MC 2

—city and country: "The sun was getting low in the west, and, glancing out of a red mist, pierced with its rays opposite loopholes and pieces of fret-work in the spires of city churches, as if with golden arrows that struck through and through them—and far

away athwart the river and its flat banks, it was gleaming like a path of fire—and out at sea it was irradiating sails of ships—and, looked towards, from quiet churchyards, upon hill-tops in the country, it was steeping distant prospects in a flush and glow that seemed to mingle earth and sky together in one glorious suffusion . . . . " DS 49

—*murder in the air:* "The boat went on, under the arching trees, and over their tranquil shadows in the water. The bargeman [Bradley Headstone], skulking on the opposite bank of the stream, went on after it. Sparkles of light showed Riderhood when and where the rower dipped his blades, until, even as he stood idly watching, the sun went down and the landscape was dyed red. And then the red had the appearance of fading out of it and mounting up to Heaven, as we say that blood, guiltily shed, does." OMF iv 1

—*twilight*

—*in a cathedral:* " . . . all became grey, murky, and sepulchral, and the cracked monotonous mutter went on like a dying voice, until the organ and the choir burst forth, and drowned it in a sea of music. Then the sea fell, and the dying voice made another feeble effort, and then the sea rose high, and beat its life out, and lashed the roof, and surged among the arches, and pierced the heights of the great tower; and then the sea was dry, and all was still." ¶MED 9 *And see* Sun and Sunlight—*setting*

—*in winter:* "You should have seen [Redlaw] in his dwelling about twilight, in the dead winter time.

"When the wind was blowing, shrill and shrewd, with the going down of the blurred sun. When it was just so dark, as that the forms of things were indistinct and big—but not wholly lost. When sitters by the fire began to see wild faces and figures, mountains and abysses, ambuscades and armies, in the coals. When people in the streets bent down their heads and ran before the weather.

"When those who were obliged to meet it, were stopped at angry corners, stung by wandering snow-flakes alighting on the lashes of their eyes—which fell too sparingly, and were blown away too quickly, to leave a trace upon the frozen ground. When windows of private houses closed up tight and warm. When lighted gas began to burst forth in the busy and the quiet streets fast blackening otherwise. When stray pedestrians, shivering along the latter, looked down at the glowing fires in kitchens, and sharpened their sharp appetites by sniffing up the fragrance of whole miles of dinners.

"When travellers by land were bitter cold, and looked wearily on gloomy landscapes, rustling and shuddering in the blast. When mariners at sea, outlying upon icy yards, were tossed and swung above the howling ocean dreadfully. When lighthouses, on rocks and headlands, showed solitary and watchful; and benighted sea-birds breasted on against their ponderous lanterns, and fell dead. When little readers of story-books, by the firelight, trembled to think of *Cassim Baba* cut into quarters, hanging in the Robbers' Cave, or had some small misgivings that the fierce little old woman with the crutch, who used to start out of the box in the merchant *Abudah*'s bedroom, might, one of these nights, be found upon the stairs, in the long, cold, dusky journey up to bed.

"When, in rustic places, the last glimmering of daylight died away from the ends of avenues; and the trees, arching overhead, were sullen and black. When, in parks and woods, the high wet fern and sodden moss and beds of fallen leaves, and trunks of trees, were lost to view, in masses of impenetrable shade. When mists arose from dyke, and fen, and river. When lights in old halls and in cottage windows, were a cheerful sight.

"When the mill stopped, the wheelwright and the blacksmith shut their workshops, the turnpike-gate closed, the plough and harrow were left lonely in the fields, the labourer and team went home, and the striking of the church clock had a deeper sound than at noon, and the churchyard wicket would be swung no more that night." HM 1

See also —dusk, Shadow, L:Times of Day *and* FL:Time

Water

—*cold and uncomfortable:* " . . . Mrs Peerybingle filled the kettle at the water-butt. Presently returning . . . she set the kettle on the fire. In doing which she lost her temper, or mislaid it for an instant; for, the water being uncomfortably cold, and in that slippy, slushy, sleety sort of state wherein it seems to penetrate through every kind of substance, patten rings included—had laid hold of Mrs Peerybingle's toes, and even splashed her legs. And when we rather plume ourselves (with reason too) upon our legs, and keep ourselves particularly neat in point of stockings, we find this, for the moment, hard to bear." CH 1

—*seasonal perversity:* "Water is a perverse sort of element at the best of times, and in Mudfog it is particularly so. In winter, it comes oozing down the streets and tumbling over the fields—nay, rushes into the very cellars and kitchens of the houses, with a lavish prodigality that might well be dispensed with; but in the hot summer weather it *will* dry up, and turn green: and, although green is a very good colour in its way, especially in grass, still it certainly is not becoming to water; and it cannot be denied that the beauty of Mudfog is rather impaired, even by this trifling circumstance." B/T

—*in Venice:* "On we went, floating towards the heart of this strange place—with water all about us where never water was elsewhere—clusters of houses, churches, heaps of stately buildings growing out of it . . . . But close about the quays and churches, palaces and prisons: sucking at their walls, and welling up into the secret places of the town: crept the water always. Noiseless and watchful: coiled round and round it, in its many folds, like an old serpent: waiting for the time, I thought, when people should look down into its depths for any stone of the old city that had claimed to be its mistress." PI 8

—*works:* "Philadelphia is most beautifully provided with fresh water, which is showered and jerked about, and turned on, and poured off, everywhere. The Waterworks, which are on a height near the city, are no less ornamental than useful, being tastefully laid out as a public garden, and kept in the best and neatest order. The river [the Schuylkill] is dammed at this point, and forced by its own power into certain high tanks or reservoirs, whence the whole city, to the top stories of the houses, is supplied at a very trifling expense." AN 7

Weather

—*to a child:* "So [the traveller] played with that child, the whole day long, and they were very merry. The sky was so blue, the sun was so bright, the water was so sparkling, the leaves were so green, the flowers were so lovely, and they heard such singing-birds and saw so many butterflies, that everything was beautiful. This was in fine weather. When it rained, they loved to watch the falling drops, and to smell the fresh scents. When it blew, it was delightful to listen to the wind, and fancy what it said, as it came rushing from its home—where was that, they wondered!—whistling and howling, driving the clouds before it, bending the trees, rumbling in the chimneys, shaking the house, and making the sea roar in fury. But, when it snowed, that was best of all; for, they liked nothing so well as to look up at the white flakes falling fast and thick, like down from the breasts of millions of white birds; and to see how smooth and deep the drift was; and to listen to the hush upon the paths and roads." CS/CS

—*cold:* "'Well, Sam,' said Mr Pickwick as that favoured servitor entered his bedchamber with his warm water, on the morning of Christmas Day, 'Still frosty?'

"'Water in the wash-hand basin's a mask o' ice, sir,' responded Sam.

"'Severe weather, Sam,' observed Mr Pickwick.

"'Fine time for them as is well wropped up, as the Polar Bear said to himself, ven he was practising his skating,' replied Mr Weller.'" PP 30

"And a breezy, goose-skinned, blue-nosed, red-eyed, stony-toed, tooth-chattering place it was . . . . " C 1

—*fog:* "They never showed a better fog in London on Lord Mayor's day, than enwrapped the town of Mudfog [Chatham] . . . . It had risen slowly and surely from the green and stagnant water with the first light of morning, until it reached a little above the lamp-post tops; and there it had stopped, with a sleepy, sluggish obstinacy, which bade defiance to the sun, who had got up very blood-shot about the eyes, as if he had been at a drinking-party over-night, and was doing his day's work with the worst possible grace. The thick damp mist hung over the town like a huge gauze curtain. All was dim and dismal. The church steeples had bidden a temporary adieu to the world below; and every object of lesser importance—houses, barns, hedges, trees, and barges—had all taken the veil." B/T

"The hedges were tangled and bare, and waved a multitude of blighted garlands in the wind; but there was no discouragement in this. It was agreeable to contemplate; for it made the fireside warmer in possession, and the summer greener in expectancy. The river looked chilly; but it was in motion, and moving at a good pace—which was a great point. The canal was rather slow and torpid; that must be admitted. Never mind. It would freeze the sooner when the frost set fairly in, and then there would be skating, and sliding; and the heavy old barges, frozen up somewhere near a wharf, would smoke their rusty iron chimney pipes all day, and have a lazy time of it." CH 2

And see Seasons—*fog in January; and* L: Weather—*fog*

—*frost:* " . . . Mr Pickwick and his friends . . . having taken on the road quite enough of ale and brandy to enable them to bid defiance to the frost that was binding up the earth in its iron fetters, and weaving its beautiful net-work upon the trees and hedges." PP 28

—*rime:* "It was a rimy morning, and very damp. I [Pip] had seen the damp lying on the outside of my little window, as if some goblin had been crying there all night, and using the window for a pocket-handkerchief. Now I saw the damp lying on the bare hedges and spare grass, like a coarser sort of spiders' webs; hanging itself from twig to twig and blade to blade. On every rail and gate, wet lay clammy, and the marsh-mist was so thick, that the wooden finger on the post directing people to our village . . . was invisible to me until I was quite close under it. Then, as I looked up at it, while it dripped, it seemed to my oppressed conscience like a phantom devoting me to the Hulks." GE 3

—*hail*

—*at dawn:* "'Here's the hail again. See how it flies, like a troop of wild cats, at Mr Riderhood's eyes!'

"Indeed he had the full benefit of it, and it so mauled him, though he bent his head low and tried to present nothing but the mangy cap to it, that he dropped under the lee of a tier of shipping, and they lay there until it was over. The squall had come up like a spiteful messenger before the morning; there followed in its wake a ragged tier of light which ripped the dark clouds until they showed a great grey hole of day." OMF i 14

—*at noon on a July day:* " . . . the hail driving in between them like a pigmy charge of bayonets . . . . " TTC ii 23

—*and wind:* "Aslant against the hard implacable weather and the rough wind, [Riderhood] was no more to be driven back than hurried forward, but held on like an advancing Destiny. There came, when they were about midway on their journey, a heavy rush of hail, which in a few minutes pelted the streets clear, and whitened them. It made no difference to him. A man's life being to be taken and the price of it got, the hailstones to arrest the purpose must lie larger and deeper than those. He crushed through them, leaving marks in the fast-melting slush that were mere shapeless holes; one might have fancied, following, that the very fashion of humanity had departed from his feet.

"The blast went by, and the moon contended with the fast-flying clouds, and the wild disorder reigning up there made the pitiful little tumults in the streets of no account. It was not that the wind swept all the brawlers into places of shelter, as it had swept the hail still lingering in heaps wherever there was refuge for it; but that it seemed as if the streets were absorbed by the sky, and the night were all in the air." OMF i 12

Tolstoy is quoted in the Dickensian 1949 p144: *"If you sift the world's prose literature, Dickens will remain; sift Dickens,* David Copperfield *will remain; sift* David Copperfield, *the description of the storm at sea will remain."*

—*hurricane and shipwreck:* "'Don't you think that,' I asked the coachman, in the first stage out of London, 'a very remarkable sky? I don't remember to have seen one like it.'

"'Nor I—not equal to it,' he replied. 'That's wind, sir. There'll be mischief done at sea, I expect, before long.'

"It was a murky confusion—here and there blotted with a colour like the colour of the smoke from damp fuel—of flying clouds tossed up into most remarkable heaps, suggesting greater heights in the clouds than there were depths below them to the bottom of the deepest hollows in the earth, through which the wild moon seemed to plunge headlong, as if, in a dread disturbance of the laws of nature, she had lost her way and were frightened. There had been a wind all day; and it was rising then, with an extraordinary great sound. In another hour it had much increased, and the sky was more overcast, and blew hard.

"But as the night advanced, the clouds closing in and densely over-spreading the whole sky, then very dark, it came on to blow, harder and harder. It still increased, until our horses could scarcely face the wind. Many times, in the dark part of the night (it was then late in September, when the nights were not short), the leaders turned about, or came to a dead stop; and we were often in serious apprehension that the coach would be blown over. Sweeping gusts of rain came up before this storm, like showers of steel; and, at those times, when there was any shelter of trees or lee walls to be got, we were fain to stop, in a sheer impossibility of continuing the struggle.

"When the day broke, it blew harder and harder. I had been in Yarmouth when the seamen said it blew great guns, but I had never known the like of this, or anything approaching to it. We came to Ipswich—very late, having had to fight every inch of ground since we were ten miles out of London; and found a cluster of people in the market-place, who had risen from their beds in the night, fearful of falling chimneys. Some of these, congregating about the inn-yard while we changed horses, told us of great sheets of lead having been ripped off a high church-tower, and flung into a by-street, which they then blocked up. Others had to tell of country people, coming in from neighbouring villages, who had seen great trees lying torn out of the earth, and whole ricks scattered about the roads and fields. Still there was no abatement in the storm, but it blew harder.

"As we struggled on, nearer and nearer to the sea, from which this mighty wind was blowing dead on shore, its force became more and more terrific. Long before we saw the sea, its spray was on our lips, and showered salt rain upon us. The water was out, over miles and miles of the flat country adjacent to Yarmouth; and every sheet and puddle lashed its banks, and had its stress of little breakers setting heavily towards us. When we came within sight of the sea, the waves on the horizon, caught at intervals above the rolling abyss, were like glimpses of another shore with towers and buildings. When at last we got into the town, the people came out to their doors, all aslant, and with streaming hair, making a wonder of the mail that had come through such a night.

"I put up at the old inn, and went down to look at the sea; staggering along the street, which was strewn with sand and seaweed, and with flying blotches of sea-foam; afraid of falling slates and tiles; and holding by people I met, at angry corners. Coming near the beach, I saw, not only the boatmen, but half the people of the town, lurking behind buildings; some, now and then braving the fury of the storm to look away to sea, and blown sheer out of their course in trying to get zigzag back.

"Joining these groups, I found bewailing women whose husbands were away in herring or oyster boats, which there was too much reason to think might have foundered before they could run in anywhere for safety. Grizzled old sailors were among the people, shaking their heads, as they looked from water to sky, and muttering to one another; ship-owners, excited and uneasy; children, huddling together, and peering into older faces; even stout mariners, disturbed and anxious, levelling their glasses at the sea from behind places of shelter, as if they were surveying an enemy.

"The tremendous sea itself, when I could find sufficient pause to look at it, in the agitation of the blinding wind, the flying stones and sand, and the awful noise, confounded me. As the high watery walls came rolling in, and, at their highest, tumbled into surf, they looked as if the least would engulf the town. As the receding wave swept back with a hoarse roar, it seemed to scoop out deep caves in the beach, as if its purpose were to undermine the earth.

"When some white-headed billows thundered on, and dashed themselves to pieces before they reached the land, every fragment of the late whole seemed possessed by the full might of its wrath, rushing to be gathered to the composition of another monster. Undulating hills were changed to valleys, undulating valleys (with a solitary storm-bird sometimes skimming through them) were lifted up to hills; masses of water shivered and shook the beach with a booming sound; every shape tumultuously rolled on, as soon as made, to change its shape and place, and beat another shape and place away; the ideal shore on the horizon, with its towers and buildings, rose and fell; the clouds fell fast and thick; I seemed to see a rending and upheaving of all nature . . . .

" . . . . If such a wind could rise, I think it was rising. The howl and roar, the rattling of the doors and windows, the rumbling in the chimneys, the apparent rocking of the very house that sheltered me, and the prodigious tumult of the sea, were more fearful than in the morning. But there was now a great darkness besides; and that invested the storm with new terrors, real and fanciful . . . .

" . . . I made a great exertion and awoke. It was broad day—eight or nine o'clock; the storm raging, in lieu of the batteries; and some one knocking and calling at my door.

"'What is the matter?' I cried.

"'A wreck! Close by!'

"I sprung out of bed, and asked, what wreck?

"'A schooner, from Spain or Portugal, laden with fruit and wine. Make haste, sir, if you want to see her! It's thought, down on the beach, she'll go to pieces every moment.'

"The excited voice went clamouring along the staircase; and I wrapped myself in my clothes as quickly as I could, and ran into the street.

"Numbers of people were there before me, all running in one direction to the beach. I ran the same way, outstripping a good many, and soon came facing the wild sea.

"The wind might by this time have lulled a little, though not more sensibly than if the cannonading I had dreamed of had been diminished by the silencing of half-a-dozen guns out of hundreds. But the sea having upon it the additional agitation of the whole night, was infinitely more terrific than when I had seen it last. Every appearance it had then presented, bore the expression of being *swelled;* and the height to which the breakers rose, and, looking over one another, bore one another down, and rolled in, in interminable hosts, was most appalling.

"In the difficulty of hearing anything but wind and waves, and in the crowd, and the unspeakable confusion, and my first breathless efforts to stand against the weather, I was so confused that I looked out to sea for the wreck, and saw nothing but the foaming heads of the great waves. A half-dressed boatman, standing next me, pointed with his bare arm (a tattoo'd arrow on it, pointing in the same direction) to the left. Then O great Heaven, I saw it, close in upon us!

"One mast was broken short off, six or eight feet from the deck, and lay over the side, entangled in a maze of sail and rigging; and all that ruin, as the ship rolled and beat—which she did without a moment's pause, and with a violence quite inconceivable—beat the side as if it would stave it in. Some efforts were even then being made, to cut this portion of the wreck away; for as the ship, which was broadside on, turned towards us in her rolling, I plainly descried her people at work with axes, especially one active figure with long curling hair, conspicuous among the rest. But a great cry, which was audible even above the wind and water, rose from the shore at this moment; the sea, sweeping over the rolling wreck, made a clean breach, and carried men, spars, casks, planks, bulwarks, heaps of such toys, into the boiling surge.

"The second mast was yet standing, with the rags of a rent sail, and a wild confusion of broken cordage flapping to and fro. The ship had struck once, the same boatman hoarsely said in my ear, and then lifted in and struck again. I understood him to add that she was parting amidships, and I could readily suppose so, for the rolling and beating were too tremendous for any human work to suffer long. As he spoke, there was another great cry of pity from the beach; four men arose with the wreck out of the deep, clinging to the rigging of the remaining mast; uppermost, the active figure with the curling hair.

"There was a bell on board; and as the ship rolled and dashed, like a desperate creature driven mad, now showing us the whole sweep of her deck, as she turned on her beam-ends towards the shore, now nothing but her keel, as she sprung wildly over and turned towards the sea, the bell rang; and its sound, the knell of those unhappy men, was borne towards us on the wind. Again we lost her, and again she rose. Two men were gone. The agony on shore increased. Men groaned, and clasped their hands; women shrieked, and turned away their faces. Some ran wildly up and down the beach, crying for help where no help could be. I found myself one of these, frantically imploring a knot of sailors whom I knew, not to let those two lost creatures perish before our eyes.

"They were making out to me, in an agitated way—I don't know how, for the little I could hear I was scarcely composed enough to understand— that the lifeboat had been bravely manned an hour ago, and could do nothing; and that as no man would be so desperate as to attempt to wade off with a rope, and establish a communication with the shore, there was nothing left to try; when I noticed that some new sensation moved the people on the beach, and saw them part, and Ham come breaking through them to the front." DC 55

And see A:*Last Lines of Death —Ham Peggotty, and —James Steerforth*

—influence on human nature: "There are times when, the elements being in unusual commotion, those who are bent on daring enterprises, or agitated by great thoughts, whether of good or evil, feel a mysterious sympathy with the tumult of nature, and are roused into corresponding violence. In the midst of thunder, lightning, and storm, many tremendous deeds have been committed; men, self-possessed before, have given a sudden loose to passions they could no longer control. The demons of wrath and despair have striven to emulate those who ride the whirlwind and direct the storm; and man, lashed into madness with the roaring winds and boiling waters, has become for the time as wild and merciless as the elements themselves." BR 2

"'I was only disgusted,' said the Tinker.

"'Do you mean with the fine weather?'

"'With the fine weather?' repeated the Tinker, staring.

"'You told me you were not particular as to weather, and I thought—'

"'Ha, ha! How should such as me get on, if we *was* particular as to weather? We must take it as it comes, and make the best of it. There's something good in all weathers. If it don't happen to be good for my work to-day, it's good for some other man's to-day, and will come round to me to-morrow. We must all live.'

"'Pray shake hands,' said Mr Traveller." CS/TT 7

—lightning: "They spoke low, as people watching and waiting mostly do; as people in a dark room, watching and waiting for Lightning, always do." TTC ii 6

And see —storm—in the country

—mist "There was a steaming mist in all the hollows, and it had roamed in its forlornness up the hill, like an evil spirit, seeking rest and finding none. A clammy and intensely cold mist, it made its slow way through the air in ripples that visibly followed and overspread one another, as the waves of an unwholesome sea might do. It was dense enough to shut out everything from the light of the coach-lamps but these its own workings, and a few yards of road; and the reek of the labouring horses steamed into it, as if they had made it all." TTC i 1

—rain

—in the city: "Wet weather was the worst; the cold, damp, clammy wet, that wrapped him up like a moist great-coat—the only kind of great-coat Toby [Veck] owned, or could have added to his comfort by dispensing with. Wet days, when the rain came slowly, thickly, obstinately down; when the street's throat, like his own, was choked with mist; when smoking umbrellas passed and repassed, spinning round and round like so many teetotums, as they knocked against each other on the crowded footway, throwing off a little whirlpool of uncomfortable sprinklings; when gutters brawled and waterspouts were full and noisy; when the wet from the projecting stones and ledges of the church fell drip, drip, drip, on Toby, making the wisp of straw on which he stood mere mud in no time; those were the days that tried him." C 1

"We know that the same Sunday in a town or city, when pattens go clinking by upon the paving-stones—when dripping umbrellas make a dismal dance all down the street—when the shining policeman stops at the corner to throw the wet off himself, like a water-dog—when all the boys in view go slinking past, depressed, and no boy has the heart to fly over a post—when people wait under the archway, peeping ruefully out at splashed and draggled stragglers, fagging along under umbrellas: or at other stragglers who, having no umbrellas, are completely varnished from head to foot with rain—when the chimney-smoke and the little church weathercock fly round and round, bewildered to find that the wind is everywhere—when the flat little church bell seems vexed that the people won't come in, and tinkles discontentedly, while the very beadle at the door is quenched and querulous—does not inspire a lively train of thought." HWC/WR

—in city and country: "Presently the rain began to fall in slanting lines between him and those houses, and people began to collect under cover of the public passage op-

posite, and to look out hopelessly at the sky as the rain dropped thicker and faster. Then wet umbrellas began to appear, draggled skirts, and mud . . . .

" . . . . In the country, the rain would have developed a thousand fresh scents, and every drop would have had its bright association with some beautiful form of growth or life. In the city, it developed only foul stale smells, and was a sickly, lukewarm-dirt-stained, wretched addition to the gutters." LD i 3

—in the country: "The day was dawning from a patch of watery light in the east, and sullen clouds came driving up before it, from which the rain descended in a thick, wet mist. It streamed from every twig and bramble in the hedge; made little gullies in the path; ran down a hundred channels in the road; and punched innumerable holes into the face of every pond and gutter. It fell with an oozy, slushy sound among the grass; and made a muddy kennel of every furrow in the ploughed fields. No living creature was anywhere to be seen. The prospect could hardly have been more desolate if animated nature had been dissolved in water, and poured down upon the earth again in that form." MC 13

"The waters are out in Lincolnshire. An arch of the bridge in the park has been sapped and sopped away. The adjacent low-lying ground, for half a mile in breadth, is a stagnant river, with melancholy trees for islands in it, and a surface punctured all over, all day long, with falling rain.

"My Lady Dedlock's 'place' has been extremely dreary. The weather, for many a day and night, has been so wet that the trees seem wet through, and the soft loppings and prunings of the woodman's axe can make no crash or crackle as they fall. The deer, looking soaked, leave quagmires, where they pass. The shot of a rifle loses its sharpness in the moist air, and its smoke moves in a tardy little cloud towards the green rise, coppice-topped, that makes a background for the falling rain.

"The view from my Lady Dedlock's own windows is alternately a lead-coloured view, and a view in Indian ink. The vases on the stone terrace in the foreground catch the rain all day; and the heavy drops fall, drip, drip, drip, upon the broad flagged pavement, called, from old time, the Ghost's Walk, all night. On Sundays, the little church in the park is mouldy; the oaken pulpit breaks out into a cold sweat; and there is a general smell and taste as of the ancient Dedlocks in their graves." ¶BH 2

"We do not defend a wet day. We know that a wet Sunday in a country inn, when the rain falls perseveringly, between the window and the opposite haystack—when rustics lounge under penthouse roofs, or in barn or stable door-ways, festooning their smock-frocks with their pocketed hands, and yawning heavily—when we pity the people sitting at the windows over the way, and think how small and dark their houses look, forgetting that they, probably, pity us too, and think no better of the Griffin, where we have put up—is not promotive of cheerfulness." HWC/WR

And see Countryside*—in the rain*

—at sea: " . . . (the weather is always going to improve to-morrow, at sea) . . . . " AN 2

—snow: "As it grew dusk, the wind fell . . . . By degrees it lulled and died away, and then it came on to snow.

"The flakes fell fast and thick, soon covering the ground some inches deep, and spreading abroad a solemn stillness. The rolling wheels were noiseless, and the sharp ring and clatter of the horses' hoofs became a dull, muffled tramp. The life of their progress seemed to be slowly hushed, and something death-like to usurp its place." OCS 70

"There are powdered heads from time to time in the little windows of the hall, looking out at the untaxed powder falling all day from the sky . . . . " BH 58

"Full many a time, on shore [in New York], had I seen the snow come down, down, down (itself like down), until it lay deep in all the ways of men, and particularly, as it seemed, in my way, for I had not gone dry-shod many hours for months. Within two or three days last past had I watched the feather fall setting in with the ardour of a new idea, instead of dragging at the skirts of a worn-out winter, and permitting glimpses of a fresh young spring. But a bright sun and a clear sky had melted the snow in the great crucible of nature; and it had been poured out again that morning over sea and land, transformed into myriads of gold and silver sparkles." UT/AS

"In all this ashy country, there is still not a cinder visible; in all this land of smoke, not a stain upon the universal white. A very novel and curious sight is presented by the hundreds of great fires blazing in the midst of the cold dead snow. They illuminate it very little. Sometimes, the construction of a furnace, kiln, or chimney, admits of a tinge being thrown upon the pale ground near it; but, generally the fire burns in its own sullen ferocity, and the snow lies impassive and untouched. There is a glare in the sky, flickering now and then over the greater furnaces, but the earth lies stiff in its winding sheet, and the huge corpse candles burning above it affect it no more than colossal tapers of state move dead humanity." HW/F&S

And see B:Walking—*instead of riding, and* TT:Stage-coach—*a winter journey*

—*storm*

—*in the country:* "It was a melancholy time, even in the snugness of the Dragon bar. The rich expanse of corn-field, pasture-land, green slope, and gentle undulation, with its sparkling brooks, its many hedgerows, and its clumps of beautiful trees, was black and dreary, from the diamond panes of the lattice away to the far horizon, where the thunder seemed to roll along the hills. The heavy rain beat down the tender branches of vine and jessamine, and trampled on them in its fury; and when the lightning gleamed it showed the tearful leaves shivering and cowering together at the window, and tapping at it urgently, as if beseeching to be sheltered from the dismal night.

"As a mark of respect for the lightning, Mrs Lupin had removed her candle to the chimney-piece" MC 43

"It was grand to see how the wind awoke, and bent the trees, and drove the rain before it like a cloud of smoke; and to hear the solemn thunder, and to see the lightning; and while thinking with awe of the tremendous powers by which our little lives are encompassed, to consider how beneficent they are, and how upon the smallest flower and leaf there was already a freshness poured from all this seeming rage, which seemed to make creation new again." BH 18

—*at sunset*: "It had been gradually getting overcast, and now the sky was dark and lowering, save where the glory of the departing sun piled up masses of gold and burning fire, decaying embers of which gleamed here and there through the black veil, and shone redly down upon the earth. The wind began to moan in hollow murmurs, as the sun went down carrying glad day elsewhere; and a train of dull clouds coming up against it, menaced thunder and lightning. Large drops of rain soon began to fall, and, as the storm clouds came sailing onward, others supplied the void they left behind and spread over all the sky. Then was heard the low rumbling of distant thunder, then the lightning quivered, and then the darkness of an hour seemed to have gathered in an instant." OCS 29

—*thaw:* "There is no improvement in the weather. From the portico, from the eaves, from the parapet, from every ledge and post and pillar, drips the thawed snow. It has crept, as if for shelter, into the lintels of the great door—under it, into the corners of the windows, into every chink and crevice of retreat, and there wastes and dies. It is falling still; upon the roof, upon the skylight; even through the skylight, and drip, drip, drip, with the regularity of the Ghost's Walk, on the stone floor below." BH 58

—*thunder:* " . . . a rainy thunder evening. The clouds were flying fast, and the wind was coming up in gusts, banging some neighbouring shutters that had broken loose, twirling the rusty chimney-cowls and weather-cocks, and rushing round and round a confined adjacent churchyard as if it had a mind to blow the dead citizens out of their graves. The low thunder, muttering in all quarters of the sky at once, seemed to threaten vengeance for this attempted desecration, and to mutter, 'Let them rest! Let them rest!'" LD i 29

—*thunderstorm at night*

—*prelude:* "It was one of those hot, silent nights, when people sit at windows listening for the thunder which they know will shortly break; when they recall dismal tales of hurricanes and earthquakes; and of lonely travellers on open plains, and lonely ships at sea, struck by lightning. Lightning flashed and quivered on the black horizon even now; and hollow murmurings were in the wind, as though it had been blowing where the thunder rolled, and still was charged with its exhausted echoes. But the storm, though gathering swiftly, had not yet come up; and the prevailing stillness was the more solemn, from the dull intelligence that seemed to hover in the air, of noise and conflict afar off.

"It was very dark; but in the murky sky there were masses of cloud which shone with a lurid light, like monstrous heaps of copper that had been heated in a furnace, and were growing cold. These had been advancing steadily and slowly, but they were now motionless, or nearly so. As the carriage clattered round the corners of the streets, it passed at every one a knot of persons who had come there—many from their houses close at hand, without hats—to look up at that quarter of the sky. And now a very few large drops of rain began to fall, and thunder rumbled in the distance." MC 42

—thunder, lightning, rain: "The thunder rolled, the lightning flashed; the rain poured down like Heaven's wrath. Surrounded at one moment by intolerable light, and at the next by pitchy darkness, [Montague Tigg and Jonas Chuzzlewit] still pressed forward on their journey . . . .

"Louder and louder the deep thunder rolled, as through the myriad halls of some vast temple in the sky; fiercer and brighter became the lightning; more and more heavily the rain poured down. The horses (they were travelling now with a single pair) plunged and started from the rills of quivering fire that seemed to wind along the ground before them; but there these two men sat, and forward they went as if they were led on by an invisible attraction.

"The eye, partaking of the quickness of the flashing light, saw in its every gleam a multitude of objects which it could not see at steady noon in fifty times that period. Bells in steeples, with the rope and wheel that moved them; ragged nests of birds in cornices and nooks; faces full of consternation in the tilted waggons that came tearing past: their frightened teams ringing out a warning which the thunder drowned; harrows and ploughs left out in fields; miles upon miles of hedge-divided country, with the distant fringe of trees as obvious as the scarecrow in the beanfield close at hand; in a trembling, vivid, flickering instant, everything was clear and plain: then came a flush of red into the yellow light; a change to blue; a brightness so intense that there was nothing else but light; and then the deepest and profoundest darkness." MC 42

—a vision, or a pre-vision: "The lightning being very crooked and very dazzling may have presented or assisted a curious optical illusion, which suddenly rose before the startled eyes of Montague in the carriage, and as rapidly disappeared. He thought he saw Jonas with his hand lifted, and the bottle clenched in it like a hammer, making as if he would aim a blow at his head. At the same time he observed (or so believed) an expression in his face: a combination of the unnatural excitement he had shown all day, with a wild hatred and fear: which might have rendered a wolf a less terrible companion." MC 42

—wind

—blowing hard: "The wind was blowing so hard when the visitor came out at the shop-door into the darkness and dirt of Limehouse Hole, that it almost blew him in again. Doors were slamming violently, lamps were flickering or blown out, signs were rocking in their frames, the water of the kennels, wind-dispersed, flew about in drops like rain." OMF ii 13

—before a duel: " . . . a melancholy wind sounded through the deserted fields, like a distant giant whistling for his house-dog." PP 2

—dying: "As it grew dusk, the wind fell; its distant moanings were more low and mournful; and, as it came creeping up the road, and rattling covertly among the dry brambles on either hand, it seemed like some great phantom for whom the way was narrow, whose garments rustled as it stalked along. By degrees it lulled and died away . . . . " OCS 70

—in the East: "'The little Jellybys,' said Richard . . . 'are really—I can't help expressing myself strongly, sir—in a devil of a state.'

"'She means well,' said Mr Jarndyce, hastily. 'The wind's in the east.'

"'It was in the north, sir, as we came down,' observed Richard.

"'My dear Rick . . . I'll take an oath it's either in the east, or going to be. I am always conscious of an uncomfortable sensation now and then when the wind is blowing in the east.'

"'Rheumatism, sir?' said Richard.

"'I dare say it is, Rick. I believe it is. And so the little Jell—I had my doubts about 'em—are in a—oh, Lord, yes, it's easterly!' said Mr Jarndyce . . . .

" . . . 'Esther was their friend directly. Esther nursed them, coaxed them to sleep, washed and dressed them . . . . At all events, cousin John, I *will* thank you for the companion you have given me.' . . .

"'Where did you say the wind was, Rick?' asked Mr Jarndyce.

"'In the north, as we came down, sir.

"'You are right. There's no east in it. A mistake of mine.' . . .

"Ada and I agreed . . . that this caprice about the wind was a fiction; and that he used the pretence to account for any disappointment he could not conceal, rather than he would blame the real cause of it, or disparage or depreciate any one. We thought this very characteristic of his eccentric goodness; and of the difference between him and those petulant people who make the weather and the winds (particularly that unlucky wind which he had chosen for such a different purpose) the stalking-horses of their splenetic and gloomy humours." BH 6

—in Italy: "When we got on the mountain pass, which lies beyond [Radicofani], the wind . . . was so terrific, that we were obliged to take my other half out of the carriage, lest she should be blown over, carriage and all, and to hang to it, on the windy side (as well as we could for laughing), to prevent its going, Heaven knows where.

"For mere force of wind, this land-storm might have competed with an Atlantic gale, and had a reasonable chance of coming off victorious. The blast came sweeping down great gullies in a range of mountains on the right: so that we looked with positive awe at a great morass on the left, and saw that there was not a bush or twig to hold by. It seemed as if, once blown from our feet, we must be swept out to sea, or away into space.

"There was snow, and hail, and rain, and lightning, and thunder; and there were rolling mists, travelling with incredible velocity. it was dark, awful, and solitary to the last degree; there were mountains above mountains, veiled in angry clouds; and there was such a wrathful, rapid, violent, tumultuous hurry, everywhere, as rendered the scene unspeakably exciting and grand." ¶PI 10

—on a journey: "'There are many pleasanter places even in this dreary world, than Marlborough Downs when it bows hard; and if you throw in beside, a gloomy winter's evening, a miry and sloppy road, and a pelting fall of heavy rain, and try the effect, by way of experiment, in your own proper person, you will experience the full force of this observation.

"'The wind blew—not up the road or down it, though that's bad enough, but sheer across it, sending the rain slanting down like the lines they used to rule in the copy-books at school, to make the boys slope well. For a moment it would die away, and the traveller would begin to delude himself into the belief that, exhausted with its previous fury, it had quietly lain itself down to rest, when, whoo! he would hear it growling and whistling in the distance, and on it would come rushing over the hill-tops, and sweeping along the plain, gathering sound and strength as it drew nearer, until it dashed with a heavy gust against horse and man, driving the sharp rain into their ears, and its cold damp breath into their very bones; and past them it would scour, far, far away, with a stunning roar, as if in ridicule of their weakness, and triumphant in the consciousness of its own strength and power.'" PP 14

"It was a bitter day. A keen wind was blowing, and rushed against them fiercely: bleaching the hard ground, shaking the white frost from the trees and hedges, and whirling it away like dust. But, little cared Kit for weather. There was a freedom and freshness in the wind, as it came howling by, which, let it cut never so sharp, was welcome. As it swept on with its cloud of frost, bearing down the dry twigs and boughs and withered leaves, and carrying them away pell-mell, it seemed as though some general sympathy had got abroad, and everything was in a hurry, like themselves. The harder the gusts, the better progress they appeared to make. It was a good thing to go struggling and fighting forward, vanquishing them one by one; to watch them driving up, gathering strength and fury as they came along; to bend for a moment, as they whistled past; and then, to look back and see them speed away, their hoarse noise dying in the distance, and the stout trees cowering down before them." OCS 69

—and leaves: "It was small tyranny for a respectable wind to go wreaking its vengeance on such poor creatures as the fallen leaves, but this wind happening to come up with a great heap of them just after venting its humour on the insulted [Blue] Dragon [Inn], did so disperse and scatter them that they fled away, pell-mell, some here, some there, rolling over each other, whirling round and round upon their thin edges, taking frantic flights into the air, and playing all manner of extraordinary gambols in the extremity of their distress. Nor was this enough for its malicious fury: for not

content with driving them abroad, it charged small parties of them and hunted them into the wheelwright's saw-pit, and below the planks and timbers in the yard, and, scattering the sawdust in the air, it looked for them underneath, and when it did meet with any, whew! how it drove them on and followed at their heels!

"The scared leaves only flew the faster for all this, and a giddy chase it was: for they got into unfrequented places, where there was no outlet, and where their pursuer kept them eddying round and round at his pleasure; and they crept under the eaves of houses, and clung tightly to the sides of hay-ricks, like bats; and tore in at open chamber windows, and cowered close to hedges; and in short went anywhere for safety." MC 2

" . . . a wintry shudder goes among the little pools on the cracked uneven flag-stones, and through the giant elm-trees as they shed a gust of tears. Their fallen leaves lie strewn thickly about. Some of these leaves, in a timid rush, seek sanctuary within the low arched Cathedral door; but two men coming out resist them, and cast them forth again with their feet . . . . " MED 2

—mocking a corpse: "A lull, and the wind is secret and prying with him; lifts and lets fall a rag; hides palpitating under another rag; runs nimbly through his hair and beard. Then, in a rush, it cruelly taunts him. Father, was that you calling me? Was it you, the voiceless and the dead? Was it you, thus buffeted as you lie here in a heap? Was it you, thus baptized unto Death, with these flying impurities now flung upon your face? Why not speak, Father? Soaking into this filthy ground as you lie here, is your own shape. Did you never see such a shape soaked into your boat? Speak, Father. Speak to us, the winds, the only listeners left you!" ¶OMF i 14

—at night, near a church: "For the night-wind has a dismal trick of wandering round and round a building of that sort, and moaning as it goes; and of trying, with its unseen hand, the windows and the doors; and seeking out some crevices by which to enter. And when it has got in; as one not finding what it seeks, whatever that may be, it wails and howls to issue forth again: and not content with stalking through the aisles, and gliding round and round the pillars, and tempting the deep organ, soars up to the roof, and strives to rend the rafters: then flings itself despairingly upon the stones below, and passes, muttering, into the vaults.

"Anon, it comes up stealthily, and creeps along the walls, seeming to read, in whispers, the Inscriptions sacred to the Dead. At some of these, it breaks out shrilly, as with laughter; and at others, moans and cries as if it were lamenting. It has a ghostly sound too, lingering within the altar; where it seems to chaunt, in its wild way, of Wrong and Murder done, and false Gods worshipped, in defiance of the Tables of the Law, which look so fair and smooth, but are so flawed and broken. Ugh! Heaven preserve us, sitting snugly round the fire! It has an awful voice, that wind at Midnight, singing in a church!

"But, high up in the steeple! There the foul blast roars and whistles! High up in the steeple, where it is free to come and go through many an airy arch and loophole, and to twist and twine itself about the giddy stair, and twirl the groaning weather-cock, and make the very tower shake and shiver!" ¶C 1

—on the ocean: "Whither go the clouds and wind so eagerly? If, like guilty spirits, they repair to some dread conference with powers like themselves, in what wild regions do the elements hold council, or where unbend in terrible disport?

"Here! Free from that cramped prison called the earth, and out upon the waste of waters. Here, roaring, raging, shrieking, howling, all night long. Hither come the sounding voices from the caverns on the coast of that small island, sleeping, a thousand miles away, so quietly in the midst of angry waves; and hither, to meet them, rush the blasts from unknown desert places of the world. Here, in the fury of their unchecked liberty, they storm and buffet with each other, until the sea, lashed into passion like their own, leaps up, in ravings mightier than theirs, and the whole scene is madness.

"On, on, on, over the countless miles of angry space roll the long heaving billows. Mountains and caves are here, and yet are not; for what is now the one, is now the other; then all is but a boiling heap of rushing water. Pursuit, and flight, and mad return of wave on wave, and savage struggle, ending in a spouting-up of foam that whitens the black night; incessant change of place, and form, and hue; constancy in nothing, but eternal strife; on, on, on, they roll, and darker grows the night, and louder howls the wind, and more clamorous and fierce become the million voices in the sea. . . ." MC 15

And see TT:Ship—*head-wind; and —heavy weather*

—*on the river:* "We [Herbert Pocket and Pip] lived at the top of the last house, and the wind rushing up the river shook the house that night, like discharges of cannon, or breakings of a sea. When the rain came with it and dashed against the windows, I thought, raising my eyes to them as they rocked, that I might have fancied myself in a storm-beaten light-house.

"Occasionally, the smoke came rolling down the chimney as though it could not bear to go out into such a night; and when I set the doors open and looked down the staircase, the staircase lamps were blown out; and when I shaded my face with my hands and looked through the black windows (opening them, ever so little, was out of the question in the teeth of such wind and rain) I saw that the lamps in the court were blown out, and that the lamps on the bridges and the shore were shuddering, and that the coal fires in barges on the river were being carried away before the wind like red-hot splashes in the rain." GE 39

—*to waft one home:* "Some nautical authority had told me . . . 'anything with west in it, will do;' so when I darted out of bed at daylight, and throwing up the window, was saluted by a lively breeze from the northwest which had sprung up in the night, it came upon me so freshly, rustling with so many happy associations, that I conceived upon the spot a special regard for all airs blowing from that quarter of the compass, which I shall cherish, I dare say, until my own wind has breathed its last frail puff, and withdrawn itself for ever from the mortal calendar." AN 16

And see B:House—*affinity for bad weather*

—*windstorm:* "The Precincts [of the Cloisterham cathedral] are never particularly well lighted; but the strong blasts of wind blowing out many of the lamps (in some instances shattering the frames too, and bringing the glass rattling to the ground), they are unusually dark to-night. The darkness is augmented and confused, by flying dust from the earth, dry twigs from the trees, and great ragged fragments from the rooks' nests up in the tower. The trees themselves so toss and creak, as this tangible part of the darkness madly whirls about, that they seem in peril of being torn out of the earth; while ever and again a crack, and a rushing fall, denote that some large branch has yielded to the storm.

"No such power of wind has blown for many a winter night. Chimneys topple in the streets, and people hold to posts and corners, and to one another, to keep themselves upon their feet. The violent rushes abate not, but increase in frequency and fury until at midnight, when the streets are empty, the storm goes thundering along them, rattling at all the latches, and tearing at all the shutters, as if warning the people to get up and fly with it, rather than have the roofs brought down upon their brains. . . .

"All through the night the wind blows, and abates not. But early in the morning, when there is barely enough light in the east to dim the stars, it begins to lull. From that time, with occasional wild charges, like a wounded monster dying, it drops and sinks; and at full daylight it is dead." MED 14

Charles Dickens Self-Revealed

Occasionally while working with the *oeuvre,* the Editor felt the Inimitable's presence with such immediacy that the experience seemed beyond the strictly literary. It is generally agreed that CD used his life and his experiences everywhere in his work, but in a good many places the mask seems to slip. These instances, we feel, warrant creating this special, idiosyncratic chapter.

Patience, study, punctuality, determination, self-denial, training of mind and body, hours of application and seclusion to produce what one reads in seconds; correction and recorrection in the blotted manuscript, consideration, new observation, the patient massing of many reflections, experiences and imaginings for one minute purpose, and the patient separation from the heap of all the fragments that will unite to serve it. . . .

[HWC/H]

The gentleman laid his forehead against the mantelpiece, in an attitude of leap-frog, and heaved a tremendous sigh. His hair was long and lightish, and it all fell in a dusty fluff together over his eyes. When he now turned round and lifted up his head again, it all fell in a dusty fluff together over his arms. This give him a wild appearance, similar to a blasted heath.

[CS/SL 4]

America

—an initial view: "Mrs Hominy had looked on foreign countries with the eye of a perfect republican hot from the model oven; and Mrs Hominy could talk (or write) about them by the hour together. So Mrs Hominy at last came down on Martin [Chuzzlewit] heavily, and as he was fast asleep, she had it all her own way, and bruised him to her heart's content.

"It is no great matter what Mrs Hominy said, save that she had learnt it from the cant of her fellow-countrymen, who, in their every word, avow themselves to be as senseless to the high principles on which America sprang, a nation, into life, as any *Orson** in her legislative halls.

"Who are no more capable of feeling, or of caring if they did feel, that by reducing their own country to the ebb of honest men's contempt, they put in hazard the rights of nations yet unborn, and very progress of the human race, than are the swine who wallow in their streets. Who think that crying out to other nations, old in their iniquity, 'We are no worse than you!' (No worse!) is high defence and 'vantage-ground enough for that Republic, but yesterday let loose upon her noble course, and but to-day so maimed and lame, so full of sores and ulcers, foul to the eye and almost hopeless to the sense, that her best friends turn from the loathsome creature with disgust.

"Who, having by their ancestors declared and won their Independence, because they would not bend the knee to certain Public vices and corruptions, and would not abrogate the truth, run riot in the Bad, and turn their backs upon the Good; and lying down contented with the wretched boast that other Temples also are of glass, and stones which batter theirs may be flung back; show themselves, in that alone, as immeasurably behind the import of the trust they hold, and as unworthy to possess it as if the sordid hucksterings of all their little governments—each one a kingdom in its small depravity— were brought into a heap for evidence against them." ¶MC 22

**who was kidnapped in infancy by a bear and grew up a Wild Man.*

And see AN A Suppressed Introduction, Vol. I page 523

—a prejudice: "Prejudiced I am not, and never have been, otherwise than in favour of the United States. I have many friends in America, I feel a grateful interest in the country, I hope and believe it will successfully work out a problem of the highest importance to the whole human race.* To represent me as viewing AMERICA with ill-nature, coldness, or animosity, is merely to do a very foolish thing: which is always a very easy one." AN pref.

* Slavery: *see* F:Blacks *and* F:Slavery

Angry

—five bundles of rags: "I know that the unreasonable disciples of a reasonable school, demented disciples who push arithmetic and political economy beyond all bounds of sense (not to speak of such a weakness as humanity), and hold them to be all-sufficient for every case, can easily prove that such things ought to be, and that no man has any business to mind them. Without disparaging those indispensable sciences in their sanity, I utterly renounce and abominate them in their insanity; and I address people with a respect for the spirit of the New Testament, who do mind such things, and who think them infamous in our streets." HW/SL *And see* F:Homeless*—on the street outside*

—hospitalized soldiers: "My hand and my heart fail me, in writing my record of this journey. The spectacle of the soldiers in the hospital-beds of that Liverpool workhouse . . . was so shocking and so shameful, that as an Englishman I blush to remember it. It would have been simply unbearable at the time, but for the consideration and pity with which they were soothed in their sufferings.

"No punishment that our inefficient laws provide, is worthy of the name when set against the guilt of this transaction. But, if the memory of it die out unavenged, and if it do not result in the inexorable dismissal and disgrace of those who are responsible for it, their escape will be infamous to the Government (no matter of what party) that so neglects its duty, and infamous to the nation that tamely suffers such intolerable wrong to be done in its name." UT/GT

—Sabbath bill: " . . . it is a bill of blunders: it is, from beginning to end, a piece of deliberate cruelty, and crafty injustice. If the rich composed the whole population of this country, not a single comfort of one single man would be affected by it. It is directed exclusively, and without the exception of a solitary instance, against the amusements and recreations of the poor." STH/2

Authorship

—copyright

—in America: "The persons who exert themselves to mislead the American public . . . [are] those who have a strong interest in the existing system of piracy and plunder; inasmuch as, so long as it continues, they can gain a very comfortable living out of the brains of other men, while they would find it very difficult to earn bread by the exercise of their own . . . . They are, for the most part, men of very low attainments, and of more than indifferent reputation . . . ." E/IC

—in England: "'With regard to such questions as are not political,' continued Mr Gregsbury, warming; 'and which one can't be expected to care a damn about, beyond the natural care of not allowing inferior people to be as well off as ourselves—else where are our privileges?—I should wish my secretary to get together a few little flourishing speeches, of a patriotic cast.

"For instance, if any preposterous bill were brought forward for giving poor grubbing devils of authors a right to their own property, I should like to say, that I for one would never consent to opposing an insurmountable bar to the diffusion of literature among *the people*,—you understand?—that the creations of the pocket, being man's, might belong to one man, or one family; but that the creations of the brain, being God's, ought as a matter of course to belong to the people at large—and if I was pleasantly disposed, I should like to make a joke about posterity, and say that those who wrote for posterity, should be content to be rewarded by the approbation *of* posterity; it might take with the house, and could never do me any harm, because posterity can't be expected to know anything about me or my jokes either—don't you see?'

"'I see that, sir,' replied Nicholas.

"'You must always bear in mind, in such cases as this, where our interests are not affected,' said Mr Gregsbury, 'to put it very strong about the people, because it comes out very well at election-time; and you could be as funny as you liked about the authors; because I believe the greater part of them live in lodgings, and are not voters.'" ¶NN 16

—public domain: "Now it makes not the least difference to our objection whether we agree or disagree with our worthy friend, Mr Cruikshank, in the [Total Abstinence] opinions he interpolates upon an old fairy story. Whether good or bad in themselves, they are, in that relation, like the famous definition of a weed; a thing growing up in a wrong place. He has no greater moral justification in altering the harmless little books [classic fairy stories] than we should have in altering his best etchings." HW/FF

—exploited: "'Shakespeare dramatised stories which had previously appeared in print, it is true,' observed Nicholas [Nickleby].

"'Meaning Bill, sir?' said the literary gentleman. 'So he did. Bill was an adapter, certainly, so he was—and very well he adapted too—considering.'

"'I was about to say,' rejoined Nicholas, 'that Shakespeare derived some of his plots from old tales and legends in general circulation; but it seems to me, that some of the gentlemen of your craft at the present day, have shot very far beyond him—'

"'You're quite right, sir,' interrupted the literary gentleman, leaning back in his chair and exercising his toothpick. 'Human intellect, sir, has progressed since his time—is progressing—will progress—'

"'Shot beyond him, I mean,' resumed Nicholas, 'in quite another respect, for, whereas he brought within the magic circle of his genius, traditions peculiarly adapted for his purpose, and turned familiar things into constellations which should enlighten the world for ages, you drag within the magic circle of your dullness, subjects not at all adapted to the purposes of the stage, and debase as he exalted.

"'For instance, you take the uncompleted books of living authors, fresh from their hands, wet from the press, cut, hack, and carve them to the powers and capacities of your actors, and the capability of your theatres, finish unfinished works, hastily and crudely vamp up ideas not yet worked out by their original projector, but which have doubtless cost him many thoughtful days and sleepless nights; by a comparison of incidents and dialogue, down to the very last word he may have written a fortnight before, do your utmost to anticipate his plot—all this without his permission, and against his will; and then, to crown the whole proceeding, publish in some mean pamphlet, an unmeaning farrago of garbled extracts from his work, to which you put your name as author, with the honourable distinction annexed, of having perpetrated a hundred other outrages of the same description.

"Now, show me the distinction between such pilfering as this, and picking a man's pocket in the street: unless, indeed, it be, that the legislature has a regard for pocket handkerchiefs, and leaves men's brains, except when they are knocked out by violence, to take care of themselves.'

"'Men must live, sir,' said the literary gentleman, shrugging his shoulders.

"'That would be an equally fair plea in both cases,' replied Nicholas; 'but if you put it upon that ground, I have nothing more to say, than, that if I were a writer of books, and you a thirsty dramatist, I would rather pay your tavern score for six months—large as it might be—than have a niche in the Temple of Fame with you for the humblest corner of my pedestal, through six hundred generations.'" ¶NN 48

—fledgling: "I have come out in another way. I have taken with fear and trembling to authorship. I wrote a little something, in secret, and sent it to a magazine, and it was published in the magazine. Since then, I have taken heart to write a good many trifling pieces. Now, I am regularly paid for them. Altogether, I am well off; when I tell my income on the fingers of my left hand, I pass the third finger and take in the fourth to the middle joint."* DC 43

**Indicating annual income rate of £1,000*

—healing effect: "I need not say [writes Master Humphrey] what true gratification I derived from the sympathy and kindness with which this acknowledgement [*that he had been the Single Gentleman in OCS*] was received; nor how often it had risen to my lips before; nor how difficult I had found it—how impossible, when I came to those passages which touched me most, and most nearly concerned me—to sustain the character I had assumed. It is enough to say that I replaced in the clock-case the record of so many trials—sorrowfully, it is true, but with a softened sorrow which was almost pleasure; and felt that in living through the past again, and communicating to others the lesson it had helped to teach me, I had been a happier man." OCS Conclusion

And see Religion*—view of joyless*

—rewards: "'I never thought, when I used to read books, what work it was to write them.'

"'It is work enough to read them, sometimes,' I returned. 'As to the writing, it has its own charms, aunt.'

"'Ah! I see!' said my aunt. 'Ambition, love of approbation, sympathy, and much more, I suppose? Well: go along with you!'" DC 61

—similes, comical

Those of us who have attempted humourous creative writing know the temptations of this device. CD appears largely to have exorcised such facetiousness early in his writing life. The below selections are just that: there are doubtless other examples we have missed.

—brightening: "Horatio's countenance brightened up, like an old hat in a shower of rain." SB/HS

—contented: "[The Misses Crumpton] looked as happy and comfortable as a couple of marigolds run to seed." SB/S

—crestfallen: "Tom . . . caught his father's angry eye, and slunk off like a puppy convicted of petty larceny." SB/HS

—dancers by day: "their evolutions were about as inspiriting and appropriate as a country-dance in a family vault." SB/VG

—elegant: "Such a fine woman as her, so handsome and so graceful and so elegant, is like a fresh lemon on a dinner-table, ornamental wherever she goes.'" BH 53

—fluctuating: "at one moment bright, and at another dismal, like a revolving light on the sea-coast . . . . " SB/SE

—grim "as the figure-head of a man-of-war . . . . " SB/BC

—happy "as a cock on a drizzly morning." SB/HS

—in his element "as a fresh young salmon on the top of the Great Pyramid." CH 2

—listless "as happy and animated as a policeman on duty." SB/ST

—lonesome "as a kitten in a wash-house copper with the lid on . . . ." SB/BM

—out of place "as a salmon might be supposed to be on a gravel-walk." SB/BC

" . . . as a dolphin in a sentry-box." PP 6

—sad: "sighed like a gust of wind through a forest of gooseberry bushes . . . . " SB/TR

—silent: see LC:Talk

—tyro at whist: "The unlucky Miller felt as much out of his element as a dolphin in a sentry-box." PP 6

—wind and twine: "'She'll never wind and twine herself about her papa's heart like—'

"'Like the ivy?' suggested Miss Tox.

"'Like the ivy,' Mrs Chick assented. 'Never! she'll never glide and nestle into the bosom of her papa's affections like—the—'

"'Startled fawn?' . . . " DS 5

—source material: "Being accustomed to observe myself as curiously as if I were another man . . . ." UT/FL

CD's eloquent and explicit summary of the requirements of authorship (see epigraph) is in LC: Authorship—*voluntary correspondent.*

Blacking factory

—*cast out:* "I know enough of the world now, to have almost lost the capacity of being much surprised by anything; but it is matter of some surprise to me, even now, that I can have been so easily thrown away at such an age. A child of excellent abilities, and with strong powers of observation, quick, eager, delicate, and soon hurt bodily or mentally, it seems wonderful to me that nobody should have made any sign in my behalf. But none was made; and I became, at ten years old, a little labouring hind in the service of Murdstone and Grinby . . . .

"No words can express the secret agony of my soul as I sunk into this companionship [with Mick Walker and Mealy Potatoes]; compared these henceforth everyday associates with those of my happier childhood—not to say with Steerforth, Traddles, and the rest of those boys; and felt my hopes of growing up to be a learned and distinguished man crushed in my bosom. The deep remembrance of the sense I had, of being utterly without hope now; of the shame I felt in my position; of the misery it was to my young heart to believe that day by day what I had learned, and thought, and delighted in, and raised my fancy and my emulation up by, would pass away from me, little by little, never to be brought back any more; cannot be written. As often as Mick Walker went away in the course of that forenoon, I mingled my tears with the water in which I was washing the bottles; and sobbed as if there were a flaw in my own breast, and it were in danger of bursting." DC 11

" . . . a curtain had for ever fallen on my life at Murdstone and Grinby's. No one has ever raised that curtain since. I have lifted it for a moment, even in this narrative, with a reluctant hand, and dropped it gladly. The remembrance of that life is fraught with so much pain to me, with so much mental suffering and want of hope, that I have never had the courage even to examine how long I was doomed to lead it. Whether it lasted for a year, or more, or less, I do not know. I only know that it was, and ceased to be; and that I have written, and there I leave it." DC 14

"She knows he has failings, but she thinks they have grown up through his being like one cast away, for the want of something to trust in, and care for, and think well of." OMF ii 11 [Lizzie Hexam speaking of Wrayburn]

—*returned to school:* "It seemed to me so long, however, since I had been among such boys, or among any companions of my own age, except Mick Walker and Mealy Potatoes, that I felt as strange as ever I have done in all my life. I was so conscious of having passed through scenes of which they could have no knowledge, and of having acquired experiences foreign to my age, appearance, and condition as one of them, that I half believed it was an imposture to come there as an ordinary little schoolboy.

"I had become, in the Murdstone and Grinby time, however short or long it may have been, so unused to the sports and games of boys, that I knew I was awkward and inexperienced in the commonest things belonging to them. Whatever I had learnt, had so slipped away from me in the sordid cares of my life from day to night, that now, when I was examined about what I knew, I knew nothing, and was put into the lowest form of the school.

"But, troubled as I was, by my want of boyish skill, and of book-learning too, I was made infinitely more uncomfortable by the consideration that, in what I did know, I was much farther removed from my companions than in what I did not. My mind ran upon what they would think, if they knew of my familiar acquaintance with King's Bench Prison? Was there anything about me which would reveal my proceedings in connexion with the Micawber family—all those pawnings, and sellings, and suppers—in spite of myself?

"Suppose some of the boys had seen me coming through Canterbury, wayworn and ragged, and should find me out? What would they say, who made so light of money, if they could know how I had scraped my halfpence together, for the purchase of my daily saveloy and beer, or my slices of pudding? How would it affect them, who were so innocent of London life and London streets, to discover how knowing I was (and was ashamed to be) in some of the meanest phases of both?

"All this ran in my head so much, on that first day at Doctor Strong's, that I felt distrustful of my slightest look and gesture; shrunk within myself whensoever I was approached by one of my new schoolfellows;

and hurried off, the minute school was over, afraid of committing myself in my response to any friendly notice or advance." ¶DC 16

—sister's farewell: " . . . Florence ran back to throw her arms round [little Paul's] neck, and . . . hers was the last face in the doorway: turned towards him with a smile of encouragement, the brighter for the tears through which it beamed.

"It made his childish bosom heave and swell when it was gone; and sent the globes, the books, blind **Homer** and *Minerva,* swimming round the room. But they stopped, all of a sudden; and then he heard the loud clock in the hall still gravely inquiring 'how, is, my, lit, tle, friend? how, is, my, lit, tle, friend?' as it had done before.

"He sat, with folded hands, upon his pedestal, silently listening. But he might have answered 'weary, weary! very lonely, very sad!' And there, with an aching void in his young heart, and all outside so cold, and bare, and strange, Paul sat as if he had taken life unfurnished, and the upholsterer were never coming." DS 11

—swallowed up—or not: "'I have been faithful to you, and useful to you, and I am attached to you. But I can't consent, and I won't consent, and I never did consent, and I never will consent, to be lost in you. Swallow up everybody else, and welcome. The peculiarity of my temper is, ma'am, that I won't be swallowed up alive.'" LD i 15

This peculiarly over-protesting announcement by Jeremiah Flintwinch to the austere, unmotherly Mrs Clennam echoes CD's famous comment about his mother's resistance when John Dickens wanted to bring him home from the blacking factory. "I never afterwards forgot, I never shall forget, I never can forget, that my mother was warm for my being sent back." *In the fictional outcome, CD arranges for Flintwinch's refusal to knuckle under to be the means by which Blandois gains his hold upon her and she is stricken, first into confession (of an attempted disinheritance) and then into complete, permanent paralysis. A fine revenge. And how much of himself did he pour into Little Dorrit and, for that matter, 'little' Nell, who both fought to preserve their parental male relatives from the consequences of debt?*

Books

—exploration: "When the wind is blowing and the sleet or rain is driving against the dark windows, I love to sit by the fire, thinking of what I have read in books of voyage and travel. Such books have had a strong fascination for my mind from my earliest childhood; and I wonder it should have come to pass that I never have been round the world, never have been shipwrecked, ice-environed, tomahawked, or eaten.

"Sitting on my ruddy hearth in the twilight of New Year's Eve, I find incidents of travel rise around me from all the latitudes and longitudes of the globe. They observe no order or sequence, but appear and vanish as they will—'come like shadows, so depart.' **Columbus**, alone upon the sea with his disaffected crew, looks over the waste of waters from his high station on the poop of his ship, and sees the first uncertain glimmer of the light, 'rising and falling with the waves, like a torch in the bark of some fisherman,' which is the shining star of a new world. **[James] Bruce** is caged in Abyssinia, surrounded by the gory horrors which shall often startle him out of his sleep at home when years have passed away. **[Sir John] Franklin**, come to the end of his unhappy overland journey—would that it had been his last!—lies perishing of hunger with his brave companions: each emaciated figure stretched upon its miserable bed without the power to rise: all, dividing the weary days between their prayers, their remembrances of the dear ones at home, and conversation on the pleasures of eating; the last-named topic being ever present to them, likewise, in their dreams. All the African travellers, wayworn, solitary and sad, submit themselves again to drunken, murderous, man-selling despots, of the lowest order of humanity; and **Mungo Park**, fainting under a tree and succoured by a woman, gratefully remembers how his Good Samaritan has always come to him in woman's shape, the wide world over." RP/LV

—literature: "I never was in *Robinson Crusoe*'s Island, yet I frequently return there. The colony he established on it soon faded away, and it is uninhabited by any descendants of the grave and courteous Spaniards, or of *Will Atkins* and the other mutineers, and has relapsed into its original condition. Not a twig of its wicker houses remains, its goats have long run wild again, its screaming parrots would darken the sun with a cloud of many flaming colours if a gun were fired there, no face is ever reflected in the waters of the little creek which *Friday* swam across when pursued by his two brother cannibals with sharpened stomachs.

"After comparing notes with other travellers who have similarly revisited the

Island and conscientiously inspected it, I have satisfied myself that it contains no vestige of Mr Atkins's domesticity or theology, though his track on the memorable evening of his landing to set his captain ashore, when he was decoyed about and round about until it was dark, and his boat was stove, and his strengh and spirits failed him, is yet plainly to be traced. So is the hill-top on which Robinson was struck dumb with joy when the reinstated captain pointed to the ship, riding within half a mile of the shore, that was to bear him away, in the nine-and-twentieth year of his seclusion in that lonely place.

"So is the sandy beach on which the memorable footstep was impressed, and where the savages hauled up their canoes when they came ashore for those dreadful public dinners, which led to a dancing worse than speech-making. So is the cave where the flaring eyes of the old goat made such a goblin appearance in the dark. So is the site of the hut where Robinson lived with the dog and the parrot and the cat, and where he endured those first agonies of solitude, which—strange to say—never involved any ghostly fancies; a circumstance so very remarkable, that perhaps he left out something in writing his record? Round hundreds of such objects, hidden in the dense tropical foliage, the tropical sea breaks evermore; and over them the tropical sky, saving in the short rainy season, shines bright and cloudless . . . .

"I was never in the robbers' cave, where *Gil Blas* lived, but I often go back there and find the trap-door just as heavy to raise as it used to be, while that wicked old disabled Black lies everlastingly cursing in bed. I was never in *Don Quixote*'s study, where he read his books of chivalry until he rose and hacked at imaginary giants, and then refreshed himself with great draughts of water, yet you couldn't move a book in it without my knowledge, or with my consent.

"I was never (thank Heaven) in company with the little old woman who hobbled out of the chest and told the merchant *Abudah* to go in search of the Talisman of *Oromanes,* yet I make it my business to know that she is well preserved and as intolerable as ever. I was never at the school where the boy **Horatio Nelson** got out of bed to steal the pears: not because he wanted any, but because every other boy was afraid: yet I have several times been back to this Academy, to see him let down out of window with a sheet. So with Damascus, and Bagdad, and Brobdingnag (which has the curious fate of being usually misspelt when written), and Lilliput, and Laputa, and the Nile, and Abyssinia, and the Ganges, and the North Pole, and many hundreds of places—I was never at them, yet it is an affair of my life to keep them intact, and I am always going back to them." ¶UT/NS

And see LC:Books—*a lifesaver*

—*the touchstone:* "We have never grown the thousandth part of an inch out of Robinson Crusoe. He fits us just as well, and in exactly the same way, as when we were among the smallest of the small." HW/SG

No other character not created by Dickens is so frequently mentioned in his works. See Index XI

Brother and Sister

"'I may grow rich!' repeated Nicholas, with a mournful smile, 'ay, and I may grow old! But rich or poor, or old or young, we shall ever be the same to each other, and in that our comfort lies. What if we have but one home? It can never be a solitary one to you and me. What if we were to remain so true to these first impressions as to form no others? It is but one more link to the strong chain that binds us together. It seems but yesterday that we were playfellows, Kate, and it will seem but to-morrow when we are staid old people, looking back to these cares as we look back, now, to those of our childish days: and recollecting with a melancholy pleasure that the time was, when they could move us.

"'Perhaps then, when we are quaint old folks and talk of the times when our step was lighter and our hair not grey, we may be even thankful for the trials that so endeared us to each other, and turned our lives into that current, down which we shall have glided to peacefully and calmly. And having caught some inkling of our story, the young people about us—as young as you and I are now, Kate—may come to us for sympathy, and pour distresses which hope and inexperience could scarcely feel enough for, into the compassionate ears of the old bachelor brother and his maiden sister.'" NN 61

This weird fantasy gives support to the comment in PA p28 that "for Dickens himself, the relationship between brother and sister became the paradigm for human relationships in general; that loving sexless union of siblings is commemorated again and again in his novels . . . . " This is an exaggeration, but there is some evidence for it in the mutual devotion of Tom Pinch and his sister Ruth MC, and of Harriet and John Carker DS. CD was close to his only elder sibling, his sister Fanny. Ultimately, Nicholas, Kate, Ruth and Harriet all marry. The two bachelors will live with their sisters.

Chauvinist

—persevering: " . . . under the GREAT ALFRED, all the best points of the English-Saxon character were first encouraged, and in him first shown. Wherever the descendants of the Saxon race have gone, have sailed, or otherwise made their way, even to the remotest regions of the world, they have been patient, persevering, never to be broken in spirit, never to be turned aside from enterprises on which they have been resolved.

"In Europe, Asia, Africa, America, the whole world over; in the desert, in the forest, on the sea; scorched by a burning sun, or frozen by ice that never melts; the Saxon blood remains unchanged. Wheresover that race goes, there, law, and industry, and safety for life and property, and all the great results of steady perseverance, are certain to arise." CHE 3

—racism? "' . . . I have been brought up [said Neville Landless] among abject and servile dependents, of an inferior race, and I may easily have contracted some affinity with them. Sometimes, I don't know but that it may be a drop of what is tigerish in their blood.'" MED 7

See introductory remarks to Index VIII part 2 *and relevant captions therein*

—res ipsa loquitur: " . . . Leghorn [Italy] (made illustrious by SMOLLETT's grave)...." PI 10

Childhood

—debt at home: "'Lord temper the wind to you, my lamb!' said the good *Mesrour,* kneeling down, that I might have a comforting shoulder for my head to rest on, 'your Pa's dead!' . . .

"I was taken home, and there was Debt at home as well as Death, and we had a sale there. My own little bed was so superciliously looked upon by a Power unknown to me, hazily called 'The Trade,' that a brass coal-scuttle, a roasting-jack, and a birdcage, were obliged to be put into it to make a Lot of it, and then it went for a song. So I heard mentioned, and I wondered what song, and thought what a dismal song it must have been to sing!" CS/HH 2

—disillusionment: "Ah me, ah me! No other ghost has haunted the boy's room, my friends, since I have occupied it, than the ghost of my own childhood, the ghost of my own innocence, the ghost of my own airy belief. Many a time have I pursued the phantom: never with this man's stride of mine to come up with it, never with these man's hands of mine to touch it, never more to this man's heart of mine to hold it in its purity. And here you see me working out, as cheerfully and thankfully as I may, my doom of shaving in the glass a constant change of customers, and of lying down and rising up with the skeleton allotted to me for my mortal companion." CS/HH 2

—dream of a house: "Presently, the very queer small boy says, 'This is Gads-hill we are coming to, where *Falstaff* went out to rob those travellers, and ran away.'

"'You know something about Falstaff, eh?' said I.

"'All about him,' said the very queer small boy. 'I am old (I am nine), and I read all sorts of books. But *do* let us stop at the top of the hill, and look at the house there, if you please!'

"'You admire that house?' said I.

"'Bless you, sir,' said the very queer small boy, 'when I was not more than half as old as nine, it used to be a treat for me to be brought to look at it. And now, I am nine, I come by myself to look at it. And ever since I can recollect, my father, seeing me so fond of it, has often said to me, "If you were to be very persevering and were to work hard, you might some day come to live in it." Though that's impossible!' said the very queer small boy, drawing a low breath, and now staring at the house out of window with all his might.

"I was rather amazed to be told this by the very queer small boy; for that house happens to be *my* house, and I have reason to believe that what he said was true." UT/TA

—dreams: "Sauntering among the ropemaking, I am spun into a state of blissful indolence, wherein my rope of life seems to be so untwisted by the process as that I can see back to very early days indeed, when my bad dreams—they were frightful, though my more mature understanding has never made out why—were of an interminable sort of ropemaking, with long minute filaments for strands, which, when they were spun home together close to my eyes, occasioned screaming." UT/CD

—early school: "The castle of this ogress and child-queller [Mrs Pipchin] was in a steep by-street at Brighton; where the soil was more than usually chalky, flinty, and sterile, and the houses were more than usually brittle and thin . . . .

"In the winter time the air couldn't be got out of the castle, and in the summer time it couldn't be got in. There was such a continual reverberation of wind in it, that it sounded like a great shell, which the inhabitants were obliged to hold to their ears night and day, whether they liked it or no. It was not, naturally, a fresh-smelling house; and in the window of the front parlour, which was never opened, Mrs Pipchin kept a collection of plants in pots, which imparted an earthy flavour of their own to the establishment." DS 8

—father in debtor's prison: " . . . no expression of interest or amusement lighted up his thin and sickly face. [The boy's] recollections were few enough, but they were all of one kind: all connected with the poverty and misery of his parents. Hour after hour had he sat on his mother's knee, and with childish sympathy watched the tears that stole down her face, and then crept quietly away into some dark corner, and sobbed himself to sleep. The hard realities of the world, with many of its worst privations—hunger and thirst, and cold and want—had all come home to him, from the first dawnings of reason; and though the form of childhood was there, its light heart, its merry laugh, and sparkling eyes, were wanting.

"The father and mother looked on upon this, and upon each other, with thoughts of agony they dared not breathe in words. The healthy, strong-made man, who could have borne almost any fatigue of active exertion, was wasting beneath the close confinement and unhealthy atmosphere of a crowded prison. The slight and delicate woman was sinking beneath the combined effects of bodily and mental illness. The child's young heart was breaking." PP 21 *And see* A: Death—*bereavement.*

—home revisited: " . . . I was in a more charitable mood with Dullborough [Rochester] than I had been all day; and yet in my heart I had loved it all day too. Ah! who was I that I should quarrel with the town for being changed to me, when I myself had come back, so changed, to it! All my early readings and early imaginations dated from this place, and I took them away so full of innocent construction and guileless belief, and I brought them back so worn and torn, so much the wiser and so much the worse!" UT/DT *And see* Death—*premonition? and* A:Home—*revisited*

—terror: "It is a figure I once saw, just after dark, chalked upon a door in a little back lane near a country church—my first church. How young a child I may have been at the time I don't know, but it horrified me so intensely—in connexion with the churchyard, I suppose, for it smokes a pipe, and has a big hat with each of its ears sticking out in a horizontal line under the brim, and is not in itself more oppressive than a mouth from ear to ear, a pair of goggle eyes, and hands like two bunches of carrots, five in each, can make it—that it is still vaguely alarming to me to recall (as I have often done before, lying awake) the running home, the looking behind, the horror, of its following me; though whether disconnected from the door, or door and all, I can't say, and perhaps never could. It lays a disagreeable train." RP/LA

—toys: "In appalling masks; hideous, hairy, red-eyed Jacks in Boxes; Vampire Kites; demoniacal Tumblers who wouldn't lie down, and were perpetually flying forward, to stare infants out of countenance; [Tackleton's] soul perfectly revelled. They were his only relief and safety-valve. He was great in such inventions. Anything suggestive of a pony-nightmare was delicious to him. He had even lost money (and he took to that toy very kindly) by getting up goblin slides for magic-lanterns whereon the Powers of Darkness were depicted as a sort of supernatural shell-fish, with human faces.

"In intensifying the portraiture of giants, he had sunk quite a little capital; and, though no painter himself, he could indicate, for the instruction of his artists, with a piece of chalk, a certain furtive leer for the countenances of those monsters, which was safe to destroy the peace of mind of any young gentleman between the ages of six and eleven, for the whole Christmas or Midsummer Vacation . . . . " CH 1

" . . . cardboard man, who used to be hung against the wall and pulled by a string; there was a sinister expression in that nose of his; and when he got his legs round his neck (which he very often did), he was ghastly, and not a creature to be alone with."

" . . . that infernal snuff-box, out of which there sprang a demoniacal Counsellor in a black grown, with an obnoxious head of hair, and a red cloth mouth, wide open, who was not to be endured on any terms, but could not be put away either; for he used suddenly, in a highly magnified state, to fly out of Mammoth Snuff-boxes in dreams, when least expected . . . .

" . . . the frog with cobbler's wax on his tail . . . there was no knowing where he wouldn't jump; and when he flew over the candle, and came upon one's hand with that spotted back—red on a green ground—he was horrible . . . .

"When did that dreadful mask first look at me? Who put it on, and why was I so frightened that the sight of it is an era in my life? It is not a hideous visage in itself; it is even meant to be droll; why then were its stolid features so intolerable?

"Surely not because it hid the wearer's face . . . . Perhaps that fixed and set change coming over a real face, infused into my quickened heart some remote suggestion and dread of the universal change that is to come on every face, and make it still? Nothing reconciled me to it . . . . The mere recollection of that fixed face, the mere knowledge of its existence anywhere, was sufficient to awake me in the night all perspiration and horror, with, "O I know it's coming! O the mask! . . . .

"Up yonder, among the green holly and red berries, is the Tumbler with his hands in his pockets, who wouldn't lie down, but whenever he was put upon the floor, persisted in rolling his fat body about, until he rolled himself still, and brought those lobster eyes of his to bear upon me—when I affected to laugh very much, but in my heart of hearts was extremely doubtful of him." ¶CS/CT

Credulity and Incredulity

—incredulity: "[Joan of Arc] had been a solitary girl from her childhood; she had often tended sheep and cattle for whole days where no human figure was seen or human voice heard; and she had often knelt, for hours together, in the gloomy empty little village chapel, looking up at the altar and at the dim lamp burning before it, until she fancied that she saw shadowy figures standing there, and even that she heard them speak to her.

"The people in that part of France were very ignorant and superstitious, and they had many ghostly tales to tell about what they had dreamed, and what they saw among the lonely hills when the clouds and the mists were resting on them. So, they easily believed that Joan saw strange sights, and they whispered among themselves that angels and spirits talked to her . . . .

"There is no doubt, now, that Joan believed she saw and heard these things. It is very well known that such delusions are a disease which is not by any means uncommon. It is probable enough that there were figures of Saint Michael, and Saint Catherine, and Saint Margaret, in the little chapel (where they would be very likely to have shining crowns upon their heads), and that they first gave Joan the idea of those three personages. She had long been a moping, fanciful girl, and, though she was a very good girl, I dare say she was a little vain, and wishful for notoriety." ¶CHE 22 ii

And see M:Illusion *and* F:Impostor*—commemorated*

Death

—morbid association: "Of course I knew perfectly well that the large dark creature [in the Morgue] was stone dead, and that I should no more come upon him out of the place where I had seen him dead than I should come upon the Cathedral of Nôtre Dame in an entirely new situation. What troubled me was the picture of the creature; and that had so curiously and strongly painted itself upon my brain, that I could not get rid of it until it was worn out.

"I noticed the peculiarities of this possession, while it was a real discomfort to me. That very day, at dinner, some morsel on my plate looked like a piece of him, and I was glad to get up and go out . . . . What was more curious was the capriciousness with which his portrait seemed to light itself up in my mind elsewhere. I might be walking in the Palais Royal, lazily enjoying the shop windows, and might be regaling myself with one of the ready-made clothes shops that are set out there. My eyes, wandering over impossible-waisted dressing-gowns, and luminous waistcoats, would fall upon the master, or the shopman, or even the very dummy at the door, and would suggest to me, 'something like him!'—and instantly I was sickened again.

"This would happen at the theatre in the same manner. Often it would happen in the street, when I certainly was not looking for the likeness, and when probably there was no likeness there. It was not because the creature was dead that I was so haunted, because I know that I might have been (and I know it because I have been) equally attended by the image of a living aversion. This lasted about a week. The picture did not fade by degrees, in the sense that it became a whit less forcible and distinct, but in the sense that it obtruded itself less and less frequently." UT/TA

—premonition? "A few strange faces in the streets; a few other faces, half strange and half familiar, once the faces of Cloisterham [Rochester] children, now the faces of men and women who come back from the outer world at long intervals to find the city wonderfully shrunken in size, as if it had not washed by any means well in the meanwhile. To these, the striking of the Cathedral clock, and the cawing of the rooks from the Cathedral tower, are like voices of their nursery time. To such as these, it has happened in their dying hours afar off, that they have imagined their chamber-floor to be strewn with the autumnal leaves fallen from the elm-trees in the Close: so have the rustling sounds and fresh scents of their earliest impressions revived when the circle of their lives was very nearly traced, and the beginning and the end were drawing close together." MED 14

Early love

—first love: "We don't believe, we can't believe, the man who tells us he has never been in love, and can't remember with delicious, and yet melancholy distinctness, all about it. We don't care whether it was the little girl with plaited tails, in frilled trousers, and a pinafore; (though we never truly loved another) or your schoolmaster's daughter, or the lady who attended to the linen department, whom we thought a Houri, but who was, probably, some forty years of age. You may have loved Fanny, Maria, Louisa, Sarah, Martha, Harriet, or Charlotte, or fancied that you loved them since then; but in your heart of hearts you still keep the portrait of your first love, bright.

"By first love, we mean what is commonly known as 'calf love.' Our reminiscences of real first love are indissolubly connected with a disrelish for our victuals, and a wild desire to dress, regardless of expense; of dismal wailings in secret; of a demoniacal hatred of all fathers, cousins, and brothers; of hot summer days passed in green fields, staring at the birds on the boughs, and wishing—oh how devoutly wishing!—that we were twenty-one years of age." HWC/FF

—remembered: " . . . the lovers sit looking at one another, so superlatively happy, that I mind when I, turned of eighteen, went with my Angelica to a City church on account of a shower . . . and when I said to my Angelica, 'Let the blessed event, Angelica, occur at no altar but this!' and when my Angelica consented that it should occur at no other—which it certainly never did, for it never occurred anywhere. And O, Angelica, what has become of you, this present Sunday morning when I can't attend to the sermon; and, more difficult question than that, what has become of Me as I was when I sat by your side?" UT/LC

Editor

"We seek to bring into innumerable homes, from the stirring world around us, the knowledge of many social wonders, good and evil, that are not calculated to render any of us less ardently persevering in ourselves, less tolerant of one another, less faithful in the progress of mankind, less thankful for the privilege of living in the summer-dawn of time." HW/PW

Enthusiast

—across the board: "'Because I want to know,' added Thomas [Idle: Wilkie Collins], 'what you would say of it, if you were obliged to do it?'

"'It would be different then,' said Francis [Goodchild: CD]. 'It would be work, then; now, it's play.'

"'Play!' replied Thomas Idle, utterly repudiating the reply. 'Play! Here is a man goes systematically tearing himself to pieces, and putting himself through an incessant course of training, as if he were always under articles to fight a match for the champion's belt, and he calls it Play! Play!' exclaimed Thomas Idle, scornfully contemplating his one boot in the air. 'You can't play. You don't know what it is. You make work of everything.'

"The bright Goodchild amiably smiled.

"'So you do,' said Thomas. 'I mean it. To me you are an absolutely terrible fellow. You do nothing like another man. Where another fellow would fall into a footbath of action or emotion, you fall into a mine. Where any other fellow would be a painted butterfly, you are a fiery dragon. Where another man would stake a sixpence, you stake your existence. If you were to go up in a balloon, you would make for Heaven; and if you were to dive into the depths of the earth, nothing short of the other place would content you. What a fellow you are, Francis!'

"The cheerful Goodchild laughed.

"'It's all very well to laugh, but I wonder you don't feel it to be serious,' said Idle. 'A man who can do nothing by halves appears to me to be a fearful man.'

"'Tom, Tom,' returned Goodchild, 'if I can do nothing by halves, and be nothing by halves, it's pretty clear that you must take me as a whole, and make the best of me.'" LT 4

—delights of rigorous travel: ". . . there was much in this mode of travelling [by canal boat] which I heartily enjoyed at the time, and look back upon with great pleasure. Even the running up, bare-necked, at five o'-clock in the morning, from the tainted cabin to the dirty deck; scooping up the icy water, plunging one's head into it, and drawing it out, all fresh and glowing with the cold; was a good thing.

"The fast, brisk walk upon the towing-path, between that time and breakfast, when every vein and artery seemed to tingle with health; the exquisite beauty of the opening day, when light came gleaming off from everything; the lazy motion of the boat, when one lay idly on the deck, looking through, rather than at, the deep blue sky; the gliding on at night, so noiselessly, past frowning hills, sullen with dark trees, and sometimes angry in one red burning spot high up, where unseen men lay crouching round a fire; the shining out of the bright stars undisturbed by noise of wheels or steam, or any other sound than the limpid rippling of the water as the boat went on: all these were pure delights." AN 10

—on Vesuvius: "From tingeing the top of the snow above us, with a band of light, and pouring it in a stream through the valley below, while we have been ascending in the dark, the moon soon lights the whole white mountain-side, and the broad sea down below, and tiny Naples in the distance, and every village in the country round.

"The whole prospect is in this lovely state, when we come upon the platform on the mountain-top—the region of Fire—an exhausted crater formed of great masses of gigantic cinders, like blocks of stone from some tremendous waterfall, burnt up; from every chink and crevice of which, hot, sulphurous smoke is pouring out: while, from another conical-shaped hill, the present crater, rising abruptly from this platform at the end, great sheets of fire are streaming forth: reddening the night with flame, blackening it with smoke, and spotting it with red-hot stones and cinders, that fly up into the air like feathers, and fall down like lead. What words can paint the gloom and grandeur of this scene!

"The broken ground; the smoke; the sense of suffocation from the sulphur; the fear of falling down through the crevices in the yawning ground; the stopping, every now and then, for somebody who is missing in the dark (for the dense smoke now obscures the moon); the intolerable noise of the thirty [guides]; and the hoarse roaring of the mountain; make it a scene of such confusion, at the same time, that we reel again.

"But, dragging the ladies [Catherine Dickens and her sister, Georgina, on foot] through it, and across another exhausted crater to the foot of the present Volcano, we approach close to it on the windy side, and then sit down among the hot ashes at its foot, and look up in silence; faintly estimating the action that is going on within, from its being full a hundred feet higher, at this minute, than it was six weeks ago.

"There is something in the fire and roar, that generates an irresistible desire to get nearer to it. We cannot rest long, without starting off, two of us [CD and **W.B. LeGros**], on our hands and knees, accompanied by the head-guide, to climb to the brim of the flaming crater, and try to look in. Meanwhile, the thirty yell, as with one voice, that it is a dangerous proceeding, and call to us to come back; frightening the rest of the party out of their wits.

"What with their noise, and what with the trembling of the thin crust of ground, that seems about to open underneath our feet and plunge us in the burning gulf below (which is the real danger, if there be any); and what with the flashing of the fire in our faces, and the shower of red-hot ashes that is raining down, and the choking smoke and sulphur; we may well feel giddy and irrational, like drunken men. But, we contrive to climb up to the brim, and look down, for a moment, into the Hell of boiling fire below. Then we all three come rolling down; blackened, and singed, and scorched, and hot, and giddy: and each with his dress alight in half-a-dozen places." PI 16

Esoteric science

—palmistry

" . . . I am much of the same mind [that it is true] as to the subtler expressions of the hand . . . . " UT/DH

—phrenology

"I hold phrenology, within certain limits, to be true . . . . " UT/DH *And see* W: America—*Congress; and* W:Wales and the Welsh

—physiognomy

" . . . I hold physiognomy to be infallible; though all these sciences [phrenology, palmistry] demand rare qualities in the student." UT/DH

" . . . the faculty (or the habit) of correctly observing the characters of men, is a rare one. I have not even found, within my experience, that the faculty (or the habit) of correctly observing so much as the faces of men, is a general one by any means. The two commonest mistakes in judgement that I suppose to arise from the former default, are, the confounding of shyness with arrogance—a very common mistake indeed—and the not understanding that an obstinate nature exists in a perpetual struggle with itself." DS pref

"There is nothing truer than physiognomy, taken in connexion with manner. The art of reading that book of which Eternal Wisdom obliges every human creature to present his or her own page with the individual character written on it, is a difficult one, perhaps, and is little studied.

"It may require some natural aptitude, and it must require (for everything does) some patience and some pains. That these are not usually given to it—that numbers of people accept a few stock commonplace expressions of the face as the whole list of characteristics, and neither seek nor know the refinements that are truest—that You, for instance, give a great deal of time and attention to the reading of music, Greek, Latin, French, Italian, Hebrew, if you please, and do not qualify yourself to read the face of the master or mistress looking over your shoulder teaching it to you—I assume to be five hundred times more probable than improbable. Perhaps a little self-sufficiency may be at the bottom of this; facial expression requires no study from you, you think; it comes by nature to you to know enough about it, and you are not to be taken in.

"I confess, for my part, that I have been taken in, over and over again I have been taken in by acquaintances, and I have been taken in (of course) by friends; far oftener by friends than by any other class of persons. How came I to be so deceived? Had I quite misread their faces?

No. Believe me, my first impression of those people, founded on face and manner alone, was invariably true. My mistake was in suffering them to come nearer to me and explain themselves away." ¶HD 1

And see B:Facial expression

Essential ingredient

" . . . happy Sissy's happy children loving her; all children loving her; she, grown learned in childish lore; thinking no innocent and pretty fancy ever to be despised; trying hard to know her humbler fellow-creatures, and to beautify their lives of machinery and reality with those imaginative graces and delights, without which the heart of infancy will wither up, the sturdiest physical manhood will be morally stark death, and the plainest national prosperity figures can show, will be the Writing on the Wall . . . ." HT iii 9

Father

—actual: "[Micawber] was a thoroughly good-natured man, and as active a creature about everything but his own affairs as ever

existed, and never so happy as when he was busy about something that could never be of any profit to him . . . . " DC 11

—ideal: "Master Harry Walmers' father . . . was a gentleman of spirit, and good-looking, and held his head up when he walked, and had what you may call Fire about him. He wrote poetry, and he rode, and he ran, and he cricketed, and he danced, and he acted, and he done it all equally beautiful. He was uncommon proud of Master Harry as was his only child; but he didn't spoil him neither. He was a gentleman that had a will of his own and a eye of his own, and that would be minded. Consequently, though he made quite a companion of the fine bright boy, and was delighted to see him so fond of reading his fairy books, and was never tired of hearing him say my name is Norval, or hearing him sing his songs about Young May Moons is beaming love, and When he as adores thee has left but the name, and that; still, he kept the command over the child, and the child was a child, and it's be wished more of 'em was!" CS/HT 2

Feminine beauty

"The average of farmers' daughters in England are not impossible lumps of fat. One is quite as likely to find a pretty girl in a farmhouse as to find an ugly one; and we think . . . that the business of this style of art [caricature] is with the pretty one. She is not only a pleasanter object in our portfolio, but we have more interest in her. We care more about what does become her, and does not become her." E/RG

"[The Shakers] are governed by a woman, and her role is understood to be absolute, though she has the assistance of a council of elders. She lives, it is said, in strict seclusion in certain rooms above the chapel, and is never shown to profane eyes. If she at all resemble the lady who presided over the store, it is a great charity to keep her as close as possible, and I cannot too strongly express my perfect concurrence in this benevolent proceeding." AN 15

Feted in America

"Up they came in a rush. Up they came until the room was full, and, through the open door, a dismal perspective of more to come, was shown upon the stairs. One after another, one after another, dozen after dozen, score after score, more, more, more, up they came: all shaking hands with Martin [Chuzzlewit]. Such varieties of hands, the thick, the thin, the short, the long, the fat, the lean, the coarse, the fine; such differences of temperature, the hot, the cold, the dry, the moist, the flabby; such diversities of grasp, the tight, the loose, the short-lived, and the lingering! Still up, up, up, more, more, more: and ever and anon the Captain's voice was heard above the crowd: 'There's more below! there's more below. Now gentlemen, you that have been introduced to Mr. Chuzzlewit, will you clear, gentlemen? Will you clear? Will you be so good as clear, gentlemen, and make a little room for more?'

"Regardless of the Captain's cries, they didn't clear at all, but stood there, bolt upright and staring. Two gentlemen connected with the Watertoast Gazette had come express to get the matter for an article on Martin. They had agreed to divide the labour. One of them took him below the waistcoat; one above. Each stood directly in front of his subject with his head a little on one side, intent on his deportment. If Martin put one boot before the other, the lower gentleman was down upon him; he rubbed a pimple on his nose, and the upper gentleman booked it. He opened his mouth to speak, and the same gentleman was on one knee before him, looking in at his teeth, with the nice scrutiny of a dentist.

"Amateurs in the physiognomical and phrenological sciences roved about him with watchful eyes and itching fingers, and sometimes one, more daring than the rest, made a mad grasp at the back of his head, and vanished in the crowd. They had him in all points of view: in front, in profile, three-quarter face, and behind. Those who were not professional or scientific, audibly exchanged opinions on his looks. New lights shone in upon him, in respect of his nose. Contradictory rumours were abroad on the subject of his hair. And still the Captain's voice was heard—so stifled by the concourse, that he seemed to speak from underneath a feather-bed, exclaiming, 'Gentlemen, you that have been introduced to Mr. Chuzzlewit, *will* you clear?'

"Even when they began to clear it was no better; for then a stream of gentlemen, every one with a lady on each arm (exactly like the chorus to the National Anthem when Royalty goes in state to the play), came gliding in: every new group fresher than the last, and bent on staying to the latest moment. If they spoke to him, which was not often, they invariably asked the same questions, in the same tone: with no more remorse, or delicacy, or consideration, than if he had been a figure of stone, purchased, and paid for, and set up there for their delight.

"Even when, in the slow course of time, these died off, it was as bad as ever, if not worse; for then the boys grew bold, and came in as a class of themselves, and did everything that the grown-up people had done. Uncouth stragglers, too, appeared; men of a ghostly kind, who being in, didn't know how to get out again: insomuch that one silent gentleman with glazed and fishy eyes, and only one button on his waistcoat (which was a very large metal one, and shone prodigiously), got behind the door, and stood there, like a clock, long after everybody else was gone." MC ¶32

Funeral

—directive: "I emphatically direct that I be buried in an inexpensive, unostentatious, and strictly private manner, that no public announcement be made of the time or place of my burial, that, at the utmost, not more than three plain mourning-coaches be employed, and that those who attend my funeral wear no scarf, cloak, black bow, long hat-band, or other such revolting absurdity. I direct that my name be inscribed in plain English letters on my tomb, without the addition of 'Mr.' or 'Esquire.' I conjure my friends on no account to make me the subject of any monument, memorial, or testimonial whatever. I rest my claims to the remembrance of my country upon my published works, and to the remembrance of my friends upon their experience of me; in addition thereto I commit my soul to the mercy of God, through our Lord and Saviour Jesus Christ, and I exhort my dear children humbly to try to guide themselves by the teachings of the New Testament in its broad spirit, and to put no faith in any man's narrow construction of its letter here or there.

"In witness whereof, I, the said Charles Dickens, the testator, have to this my last will and testament set my hand this twelfth day of May, in the year of our Lord one thousand eight hundred and sixty-nine.

CHARLES DICKENS"

—preference: "Once I lost a friend by death, who had been troubled in his time by the Medicine-Man and the Conjuror,* and upon whose limited resources there were abundant claims. The Conjuror assured me that I must positively 'follow,' and both he and the Medicine-Man entertained no doubt that I must go in a black carriage, and must wear 'fittings.' I objected to fittings as having nothing to do with my friendship, and I objected to the black carriage as being in more senses than one a job. So it came into my mind to try what would happen if I quietly walked in my own way from my own house to my friend's burial-place, and stood beside his open grave in my own dress and person, reverently listening to the best of Services. It satisfied my mind, I found, quite as well as if I had been disguised in a hired hatband and scarf, both trailing to my very heels, and as if I had cost the orphan children, in their greatest need, ten guineas." UT/MM

**see* A:Funeral *passim*

Mrs Gamp's description

"'But who,' says I, when the bell had left off, and the train had begun to move, 'who, Mr **Wilson**, is the wild gent in the prespiration, that's been a tearing up and down all this time with a great box of papers under his arm, a talking to everybody wery indistinct, and exciting of himself dreadful?' 'Why?' says Mr Wilson, with a smile. 'Because, sir,' I says, 'he's being left behind.' 'Good God!' cries Mr Wilson, turning pale and putting out his head, 'it's your beeograffer—the Manager—and he has got the money, Mrs Gamp!'" MGS

CD claimed five feet nine inches of height. See Porter AN/WM Vol. I p539

Happy in Italy

"There is not in Italy . . . a lovelier residence than the Palazzo Peschiere, or Palace of the Fishponds . . . .

"It stands on a height within the walls of Genoa, but aloof from the town: surrounded by beautiful gardens of its own, adorned with statues, vases, fountains, marble basins, terraces, walks of orange-trees and lemon-trees, groves of roses and camellias. All its apartments are beautiful in their proportions and decorations; but the great hall, some fifty feet in height, with three large windows at the end, overlooking the whole town of Genoa, the harbour, and the neighbouring sea, affords one of the most fascinating and delightful prospects in the world . . . .

"I go back to it, in fancy, as I have done in calm reality a hundred times a day; and stand there, looking out, with the sweet scents from the garden rising up about me, in a perfect dream of happiness.

"There lies all Genoa, in beautiful confusion, with its many churches, monasteries, and convents, pointing up into the sunny sky; and down below me, just where the roofs begin, a solitary convent parapet, fashioned like a gallery, with an iron across at the end, where sometimes early in the morning, I have seen a little group of dark-veiled nuns gliding sorrowfully to and fro, and stopping now and then to peep down upon the waking world in which they have no part.

"Old Monte Faccio, brightest of hills in good weather, but sulkiest when storms are coming on, is here, upon the left. The Fort within the walls . . . commands that height upon the right. The broad sea lies beyond, in front there; and that line of coast, beginning by the lighthouse, and tapering away, a mere speck in the rosy distance, is the beautiful coast road that leads to Nice.

"The garden near at hand, among the roofs and houses: all red with roses and fresh with little fountains: is the Acqua Sola—a public promenade, where the military band plays gaily, and the white veils cluster thick, and the Genoese nobility ride round, and round, and round, in state-clothes and coaches at least, if not in absolute wisdom.

"Within a stone's-throw, as it seems, the audience of the Day Theatre sit: their faces turned this way. But as the stage is hidden, it is very odd, without a knowledge of the cause, to see their faces changed so suddenly from earnestness to laughter; and odder still, to hear the rounds upon rounds of applause, rattling in the evening air, to which the curtain falls. But, being Sunday night, they act their best and most attractive play.

"And now, the sun is going down, in such magnificent array of red, and green, and golden light, as neither pen nor pencil could depict; and to the ringing of the vesper bells, darkness sets in at once, without a twilight. Then, lights begin to shine in Genoa, and on the country road; and the revolving lantern out at sea there, flashing, for an instant, on this palace front and portico, illuminates it as if there were a bright moon bursting from behind a cloud; then, merges it in deep obscurity. And this, so far as I know, is the only reason why the Genoese avoid it after dark, and think it haunted.

"My memory will haunt it, many nights, in time to come; but nothing worse, I will engage." ¶PI 5

And see W:Cities and Towns—*Rome—the Colosseum*

Mary Hogarth

—dead: "There was a dear girl—almost a woman—never to be one—who made a mourning Christmas in a house of joy, and went her trackless way to the silent City. Do we recollect her, worn out, faintly whispering what could not be heard, and falling into that last sleep for weariness? O look upon her now! O look upon her beauty, her serenity, her changeless youth, her happiness! The daughter of *Jairus* was recalled to life, to die; but she, more blest, has heard the same voice, saying unto her, 'Arise for ever!'" CS/GO

**Mary died in CD's arms at seventeen on May 7, 1837, apparently from heart failure. "[Her death] touched him to the depths . . . [it was] the only time in his life in which he did not keep a writing commitment." FK pp92-3 "His grief was so intense, in fact, that it represented the most powerful sense of loss and pain he was ever to experience." PA p225*

—illness: "The suspense: the fearful, acute suspense: of standing idly by while the life of one we dearly love, is trembling in the balance; the racking thoughts that crowd upon the mind, and make the heart beat violently, and the breath come thick, by the force of the images they conjure up before it; the desperate anxiety *to be doing something* to relieve the pain, or lessen the danger, which we have no power to alleviate; the sinking of soul and spirit, which the sad remembrance of our helplessness produces; what tortures can equal these; what reflections or endeavours can, in the full tide and fever of the time, allay them!" OT 33

The installment which included this passage was published in June 1838.

—loss: "'I was brought here, by the most dreadful and agonising of all apprehensions,' said the young man [Harry Maylie]; 'the fear of losing the one dear being on whom my every wish and hope are fixed. You had been dying: trembling between earth and heaven. . . .

"'A creature,' continued the young man, passionately, 'a creature as fair and innocent of guile as one of God's own angels, fluttered between life and death. Oh! who could hope, when the distant world to which she was akin, half opened to her view, that she would return to the sorrow and calamity of this!

"Rose, Rose, to know that you were passing away like some soft shadow, which a light from above, casts upon the earth; to have no hope that you would be spared to those who linger here; hardly to know a reason why you should be; to feel that you belonged to that bright sphere whither so many of the fairest and the best have winged their early flight; and yet to pray, amid all these consolations, that you might be restored to those who loved you—these were distractions almost too great to bear.

"They were mine, by day and night; and with them, came such a rushing torrent of fears, and apprehensions, and selfish regrets, lest you should die, and never know how devotedly I loved you, as almost bore down sense and reason in its course." OT 35

—*what might have been:* "You recovered. Day by day, and almost hour by hour, some drop of health came back, and mingling with the spent and feeble stream of life which circulated languidly within you, swelled it again to a high and rushing tide. I have watched you change almost from death, to life, with eyes that turned blind with their eagerness and deep affection. Do not tell me that you wish I had lost this; for it has softened my heart to all mankind.'" OT 35

—*dreaming of her:* " . . . I had lost a very near and dear friend by death. Every night since, at home or away from home, I had dreamed of that friend; sometimes as still living; sometimes as returning from the world of shadows to comfort me; always as being beautiful, placid, and happy, never in association with any approach to fear or distress.

"It was at a lonely Inn in a wide moorland place, that I halted to pass the night. When I had looked from my bedroom window over the waste of snow on which the moon was shining, I sat down by my fire to write a letter. I had always, until that hour, kept it within my own breast that I dreamed every night of the dear lost one. But in the letter that I wrote I recorded the circumstance, and added that I felt much interested in proving whether the subject of my dream would still be faithful to me, travel-tired, and in that remote place.

"No. I lost the beloved figure of my vision in parting with the secret. My sleep has never looked upon it since, in sixteen years, but once. I was in Italy, and awoke (or seemed to awake), the well-remembered voice distinctly in my ears, conversing with it. I entreated it, as it rose above my bed and soared up to the vaulted roof of the old room, to answer me a question I had asked touching the Future Life. My hands were still outstretched towards it as it vanished, when I heard a bell ringing by the garden wall, and a voice in the deep stillness of the night calling on all good Christians to pray for the souls of the dead; it being All Souls' Eve." CS/HT

Loneliness

"I am not a lonely man, though I was once a lonely boy; but that was long ago." HW/RD

"Being naturally of a tender turn, I had dreadful lonely feelings on me arter this [the suicide of Mrs Marigold]. I conquered 'em at selling times, having a reputation to keep (not to mention keeping myself), but they got me down in private, and rolled upon me. That's often the way with us public characters. See us on the footboard, and you'd give pretty well anything you possess to be us. See us off the footboard, and you'd add a trifle to be off your bargain." CS/DM

And see FL:Self—*isolated*

Married life

—*begun impulsively:* "'The first mistaken impulse of an undisciplined heart.' Those words of Mrs Strong's were constantly recurring to me, at this time; were almost always present to my mind. I awoke with them, often, in the night; I remember to have even read them, in dreams, inscribed upon the walls of houses. For I knew, now, that my own heart was undisciplined when it first loved Dora; and that if it had been disciplined, it never could have felt, when we were married, what it had felt in its secret experience." DC 48

—*disparity of temperament:* "'There can be no disparity in marriage, like unsuitability of mind and purpose.' Those words I remembered too." DC 48

—*something missing:* "If I tacitly checked [Dora's] playfulness, and persisted [teaching her household accounts], she would look so scared and disconsolate, as she became more and more bewildered, that the remembrance of her natural gaiety when I first strayed into her path, and of her being my child-wife, would come reproachfully upon me; and I would lay the pencil down, and call for the guitar.

"I had a great deal of work to do, and had many anxieties, but the same considerations made me keep them to myself. I am far from sure, now, that it was right to do this, but I did it for my child-wife's sake. I search my breast, and I commit its secrets, if I know them, without any reservation to this paper. The old unhappy loss or want of something had, I am conscious, some place in my heart; but not to the embitterment of my life. When I walked alone in the fine weather, and thought of the summer days when all the air had been filled with my boyish enchantment, I did miss something of the realisation of my dreams; but I thought it was a softened glory of the Past, which nothing could have thrown upon the present time. I did feel, sometimes, for a little while, that I could have wished my wife had been my counsellor: had had more character and purpose, to sustain me, and improve me by; had been endowed with power to fill up the void which somewhere seemed to be about me; but I felt as if this were an unearthly consummation of my happiness, that never had been meant to be, and never could have been . . . .

"Thus it was that I took upon myself the toils and cares of our life, and had no partner in them." DC 44

Mealtime conviviality

—absent: "I never in my life did see such listless, heavy dulness as brooded over these meals [on an American riverboat]: the very recollection of it weighs me down, and makes me, for the moment, wretched. Reading and writing on my knee, in our little cabin, I really dreaded the coming of the hour that summoned us to table; and was as glad to escape from it again, as if it had been a penance or a punishment.

"Healthy cheerfulness and good spirits forming a part of the banquet, I could soak my crusts in the fountain with **Le Sage**'s strolling player,* and revel in their glad enjoyment: but sitting down with so many fellow-animals to ward off thirst and hunger as a business; to empty, each creature, his Yahoo's trough as quickly as he can, and then slink sullenly away; to have these social sacraments stripped of everything but the mere greedy satisfaction of the natural cravings; goes so against the grain with me, that I seriously believe the recollection of these funeral feasts will be a waking nightmare to me all my life." ¶AN 12

**Alain René Le Sage (1668-1747):* Gil Blas, *published 1715, one of CD's favourites; in the second book, the hero meets a strolling actor, has a breakfast of bread and water with him and hears his story.*

—present: "By way of beguiling the tediousness of these [shipboard] banquets, a select association was formed at the lower end of the table, below the mast, to whose distinguished president modesty forbids me to make any further allusion, which, being a very hilarious and jovial institution, was (prejudice apart) in high favour with the rest of the community, and particularly with a black steward, who lived for three weeks in a broad grin at the marvellous humour of these incorporated worthies." AN 16

Nature and Art

" . . . I have the sky and ocean framed before me like a beautiful picture. A beautiful picture, but with such movement in it, such changes of light upon the sails of ships and wake of steamboats, such dazzling gleams of silver far out at sea, such fresh touches on the crisp wave-tops as they break and roll towards me—a picture with such music in the billowy rush upon the shingle, the blowing of morning wind through the corn-sheaves where the farmers' waggons are busy, the singing of the larks, and the distant voices of children at play—such charms of sight and sound as all the Galleries on earth can but poorly suggest." RP/OT

Observation

"I looked at nothing, that I know of, but I saw everything, even to the prospect of a church upon [Traddles's] china ink-stand, as I sat down—and this, too, was a faculty confirmed in me in the old Micawber times." DC 27

Opinions

—foul language: "On Table Rock [at Horseshoe Falls], there is a cottage belonging to a Guide . . . [where] is posted: 'Visitors will please not copy nor extract the remarks and poetical effusions from the registers and albums kept here.'

"But for this intimation, I should have let them lie . . . . Curious, however, after reading this announcement, to see what kind of morsels were so carefully preserved, I turned a few leaves, and found them scrawled all over with the vilest and the filthiest ribaldry that ever human hogs delighted in.

"It is humiliating enough to know that there are among men, brutes so obscene and worthless, that they can delight in laying their miserable profanations upon the very steps of Nature's greatest altar [*see* FL: Creation]. But that these should be hoarded up for the delight of their fellow-swine, and kept in a public place where any eyes may see them, is a disgrace to the English language in which they are written (though I hope few of these entries have been made by Englishmen), and a reproach to the English side, on which they are preserved." AN 15

—joyless religion: "[The Shakers] are good farmers . . . . They are good breeders of cattle, and are kind and merciful to the brute creation . . . .

"They are said to be good drivers of bargains, but to be honest and just in their transactions . . . . In all matters they hold their own course quietly, live in their gloomy silent commonwealth, and show little desire to interfere with other people.

"This is well enough, but nevertheless I cannot, I confess, incline towards the Shakers; view them with much favour, or extend towards them any very lenient construction. I so abhor, and from my soul detest that bad spirit, no matter by what class or sect it may be entertained, which would strip life of its healthful graces, rob youth of its innocent pleasures, pluck from maturity and age their pleasant ornaments, and make existence but a narrow path towards the grave: that odious spirit which, if it could have had full scope and sway upon the earth, must have blasted and made barren the imaginations of the greatest men, and left them, in their power of raising up enduring images before their fellow-creatures yet unborn, no better than the beasts: that, in these very broad-brimmed hats and very sombre coats—in stiff-necked solemn-visaged piety, in short, no matter what its garb, whether it have cropped hair as in a Shaker village, or long nails as in a Hindoo temple—I recognise the worst among the enemies of Heaven and Earth, who turn the water at the marriage-feasts of this poor world, not into wine, but gall.

"And if there must be people vowed to crush the harmless fancies and the love of innocent delights and gaieties, which are a part of human nature: as much a part of it as any other love or hope that is our common portion: let them, for me, stand openly revealed among the ribald and licentious; the very idiots know that *they* are not on the Immortal road, and will despise them, and avoid them readily." ¶AN 15

And see S:Religion*—joyless*

—swearing: "'My God!' said the Swiss courier, speaking in French, which I do not hold (as some authors appear to do) to be such an all-sufficient excuse for a naughty word, that I have only to write it in that language to make it innocent. . . . " RD [*so betraying a modesty in CD's attainments in French*]

—tobacco: "'Do you prefer a dry smoke, or do you moisten it?'

"As unmitigated tobacco produces most disturbing effects upon my system (indeed, if I had perfect moral courage, I doubt if I should smoke at all, under any circumstances), I advocated moisture . . . . " RP/BS

Optimist

"And let us not remember Italy the less regardfully, because, in every fragment of her fallen Temples, and every stone of her deserted palaces and prisons, she helps to inculcate the lesson that the wheel of Time is rolling for an end, and that the world is, in all great essentials, better, gentler, more forbearing, and more hopeful, as it rolls!" PI 19

Parents, housed by him

"Gradually my father went off his [head], and my mother went off hers. It was in a harmless way, but it put out the family where I boarded them. The old couple, though retired, got to be wholly and solely devoted to the Cheap Jack business, and were always selling the family off. Whenever the cloth was laid for dinner, my father began rattling the plates and dishes, as we do in our line when we put up crockery for a bid, only he had lost the trick of it, and mostly let 'em drop and broke 'em . . . .

"As the old lady had been used to sit in the cart, and hand the articles out one by one to the old gentleman on the footboard to sell, just in the same way she handed him every item of the family's property, and they disposed of it in their own imaginations from morning to night." CS/DM 1

CD had to sequester his parents in the country after being repeatedly embarrassed by his father's improvidences; his mother became senile years before her death.

Perseverance

". . . [in] a patient and continuous energy which then began to be matured within me, and which I know to be the strong part of my character, if it have any strength at all . . . I find the source of my success.

"I have been very fortunate in worldly matters; many men have worked much harder, and not succeeded half so well; but I never could have done what I have done, without the habits of punctuality, order, and diligence, without the determination to concentrate myself on one object at a time, no matter how quickly its successor should come upon its heels, which I then formed. Heaven knows I write this in no spirit of self-laudation. The man who reviews his own life, as I do mine, in going on here, from page to page, had need to have been a good man indeed, if he would be spared the sharp consciousness of many talents neglected, many opportunities wasted, many erratic and perverted feelings constantly at war within his breast, and defeating him.

"I do not hold one natural gift, I dare say, that I have not abused. My meaning simply is, that whatever I have tried to do in life, I have tried with all my heart to do well; that whatever I have devoted myself to, I have devoted myself to completely; that in great aims and in small, I have always been thoroughly in earnest.

"I have never believed it possible that any natural or improved ability can claim immunity from the companionship of the steady, plain, hard-working qualities, and hope to gain its end. There is no such thing as such fulfilment on this earth. Some happy talent, and some fortunate opportunity, may form the two sides of the ladder on which some men mount, but the rounds of that ladder must be made of stuff to stand wear and tear; and there is no substitute for thorough-going, ardent, and sincere earnestness. Never to put one hand to anything on which I could throw my whole self; and never to affect depreciation of my work, whatever it was; I find, now, to have been my golden rules." ¶DC 42

The Poor

—fear of uprising: "Utilitarian economists, skeletons of schoolmasters, Commissioners of Fact, genteel and used-up infidels, gabblers of many little dog's-eared creeds, the poor you will have always with you. Cultivate in them, while there is yet time, the utmost graces of the fancies and affections, to adorn their lives so much in need of ornament; or, in the day of your triumph, when romance is utterly driven out of their souls, and they and a bare existence stand face to face, Reality will take a wolfish turn, and make an end of you." HT ii 6

—Poor Law: "I believe there has been in England, since the days of the STUARTS, no law so often infamously administered, no law so often openly violated, no law habitually so ill-supervised. In the majority of the shameful cases of disease and death from destitution that shock the Public and disgrace the country, the illegality is quite equal to the inhumanity—and known language could say no more of their lawlessness." OMF postscript

Pride in adversity

"I know that I worked from morning until night, with common men and boys, a shabby child. I know that I lounged about the streets, insufficiently and unsatisfactorily fed. I know that, but for the mercy of God, I might easily have been, for any care that was taken of me, a little robber or a little vagabond.

"Yet I held some station at Murdstone and Grinby's too. Besides that Mr Quinion did what a careless man so occupied, and dealing with a thing so anomalous, could, to treat me as one upon a different footing from the rest, I never said, to man or boy, how it was that I came to be there, or gave the least indication of being sorry that I was there.

"That I suffered in secret, and that I suffered exquisitely, no one ever knew but I. How much I suffered, it is, as I have said already, utterly beyond my power to tell. But I kept my own counsel, and I did my work. I knew from the first, that, if I could not do my work as well as any of the rest, I could not hold myself above slight and contempt.

"I soon became at least as expeditious and as skilful as either of the other boys. Though perfectly familiar with them, my conduct and manner were different enough from theirs to place a space between us. They and the men generally spoke of me as 'the little gent', or 'the young Suffolker'. A certain man named Gregory, who was foreman of the packers, and another named Tipp, who was the carman, and wore a red jacket, used to address me sometimes as 'David': but I think it was mostly when we were very confidential, and when I had made some efforts to entertain them, over our work, with some results of the old readings; which were fast perishing out of my remembrance. Mealy Potatoes uprose once, and rebelled against my being so distinguished; but Mick Walker settled him in no time." DC 11

Reading tour

The Traveller has engaged in "a pursuit (no matter what), which could be transacted by myself alone; in which I could have no help; which imposed a constant strain on the attention, memory, observation, and physical powers; and which involved an almost fabulous amount of change of place and rapid railway travelling." UT/FL

This effort is considered to have been a proximate cause of CD's death at fifty-eight.

Religion

—its cant: "Lest there should be any well-intentioned persons who do not perceive the difference . . . between religion and the cant of religion, piety and pretence of piety, a humble reverence for the great truths of Scripture and an audacious and offensive obtrusion of its letter and not its spirit in the commonest dissensions and meanest affairs of life, to the extraordinary confusion of ignorant minds, let them understand that it is always the latter, and never the former, which is satirised here. Further, that the latter is here satirised as being, according to all experience, inconsistent with the former, impossible of union with it, and one of the most evil and mischievous falsehoods existent in society . . . . It may appear unnecessary to offer a word of observation on so plain a head. But it is never out of season to protest against that coarse familiarity with sacred things which is busy on the lip, and idle in the heart; or against the confounding of Christianity with any class of persons who, in the words of **Swift**, have just enough religion to make them hate, and not enough to make them love, one another." PP pref

—disgust with conceit: "[During a period of illness] I had experiences of spiritual conceit, for which, as giving me a new warning against that curse of mankind, I shall always feel grateful to the supposition that I was too far gone to protest against playing sick lion to any stray donkey with an itching hoof. All sorts of people seemed to become vicariously religious at my expense.

"I received the most uncompromising warning that I was a Heathen; on the conclusive authority of a field preacher, who, like the most of his ignorant and vain and daring class, could not construct a tolerable sentence in his native tongue or pen a fair letter. This inspired individual called me to order roundly, and knew in the freest and easiest way where I was going to, and what would become of me if I failed to fashion myself on his bright example, and was on terms of blasphemous confidence with the Heavenly Host. He was in the secrets of my heart, and in the lowest soundings of my soul—he!—and could read the depths of my nature better than his A B C, and could turn me inside out, like his own clammy glove.

"But what is far more extraordinary than this—for such dirty water as this could alone be drawn from such a shallow and muddy source—I found, from the information of a beneficed clergyman, of whom I never heard, and whom I never saw, that I had not, as I rather supposed I had, lived a life of some reading, contemplation, and inquiry; that I had not studied, as I rather supposed I had, to inculcate some Christian lessons in books; that I had never tried, as I rather supposed I had, to turn a child or two tenderly towards the knowledge and love of our Saviour; that I had never had, as I rather supposed I had, departed friends, or stood beside open graves; but that I had lived a life of 'uninterrupted prosperity,' and that I needed this 'check, overmuch,' and that the way to turn it to account was to read these sermons and these poems, enclosed, and written and issued by my correspondent! I beg it may be understood that I relate facts of my own uncommercial experience, and no vain imaginings. The documents in proof lie near my hand." ¶UT/FL

—and the feminine principle: "The two stand in the fast-thinning throng of victims, but they speak as if they were alone. Eye to eye, voice to voice, hand to hand, heart to heart, these two children of the Universal Mother, else so wide apart and differing, have come together on the dark highway, to repair home together, and to rest in her bosom." TTC iii 14

—generally: "I should like to see the time arrive, when a man's attendance to his religious duties might be left to that religious feeling which most men possess in a greater or less degree, but which was never forced into the breast of any man by menace or restraint. I should like to see the time when Sunday might be looked forward to, as a recognised day of relaxation and enjoyment,

and when every man might feel, what few men do now, that religion is not incompatible with rational pleasure and needful recreation." STH/3

Theatre

—early impression: "It was Covent Garden Theatre that I chose; and there, from the back of a centre box, I saw *Julius Cæsar* and the new Pantomime. To have all those noble Romans alive before me, and walking in and out for my entertainment, instead of being the stern taskmasters they had been at school, was a most novel and delightful effect. But the mingled reality and mystery of the whole show, the influence upon me of the poetry, the lights, the music, the company, the smooth stupendous changes of glittering and brilliant scenery, were so dazzling, and opened up such illimitable regions of delight, that when I came out into the rainy street, at twelve o'clock at night, I felt as if I had come from the clouds, where I had been leading a romantic life for ages, to a bawling, splashing, link-lighted, umbrella-struggling, hackney-coach-jostling, patten-clinking, muddy, miserable world." DC 19

—ladies: "The lady performers pay nothing for their characters, and it is needless to add, are usually selected from one class of society . . . .

"As to the ladies (God bless them), they are quite above any formal absurdities; the mere circumstance of your being behind the scenes is a sufficient introduction to their society—for of course they know that none but strictly respectable persons would be admitted into that close fellowship with them, which acting engenders. They place implicit reliance on the manager, no doubt. . . . " SB/PT

CD had an emotionally intense (from his side), perhaps sexually consummated, relationship from 1857 until his death with the actress Ellen Ternan.

Traveller

—rough passage: "When I approached . . . with my [hot brandy and water] and was about to administer it with many consolatory expressions to the nearest sufferer, what was my dismay to see them all roll slowly down to the other end [of a long sofa]! And when I staggered to that end, and held out the glass once more, how immensely baffled were my good intentions by the ship giving another lurch, and their all rolling back again!

"I suppose I dodged them up and down this sofa for at least a quarter of an hour, without reaching them once; and by the time I did catch them, the brandy-and-water was diminished, by constant spilling, to a teaspoonful. To complete the group, it is necessary to recognise in this disconcerted dodger, an individual very pale from seasickness, who had shaved his beard and brushed his hair, last, at Liverpool: and whose only articles of dress (linen not included) were a pair of dreadnought trousers; a blue jacket, formerly admired upon the Thames at Richmond; no stockings; and one slipper." ¶AN 2

—sights seen: "'And yet,' said the voice within the great peacoat at my side, 'you'll have seen a good many rivers too, I dare say?'

"'Truly,' said I, 'when I come to think of it, not a few. From the Niagara, downward to the mountain rivers of Italy . . . . The Moselle, and the Rhine, and the Rhone; and the Seine, and the Saone; and the St Lawrence, Mississippi, and Ohio; and the Tiber, the Po, and the Arno; and the—'

"Peacoat coughing as if he had had enough of that, I said no more. I could have carried the catalogue on to a teasing length, though, if I had been in the cruel mind." RP/DT

View of Painting and Sculpture

—appreciator of realism: "The death-bed scene on board the hulks—the convict who is composing the face—and the other who is drawing the screen round the bed's head—are masterpieces, worthy of the greatest painter. The reality of the place, and the fidelity with which every minute object illustrative of it is presented, are quite surprising. But the same feature is remarkable throughout. In the trial scene at the Old Bailey the eye may wander round the court, and observe everything that is a part of the place. The very light and atmosphere of the reality are reproduced with astonishing truth. So in the gin-shop and the beer-shop; no fragment of the fact is indicated and slurred over, but every shred of it is honestly made out . . . .

"May Mr **Cruikshank** linger long behind to give us many more of such realities, and to do with simple means, such as are used here, what the whole paraphernalia and resources of Art could not effect, without a master hand!" ¶HW/DC

—art critic: "[**Donald Maclise**'s cartoon for the Fine Arts Commission, 'The Spirit of

Chivalry' is a] composition of such marvellous beauty, of such infinite variety, of such masterly design, of such vigorous and skilful drawing, of such thought and fancy, of such surprising and delicate accuracy of detail, subserving one grand harmony, and one plain purpose, that it may be questioned whether the Fine Arts in any period of their history, have known a more remarkable performance . . . .

"Eyes well accustomed to the glories of the Vatican, the galleries of Florence, all the mightiest works of art in Europe, have grown dim before it with the strong emotions it inspires . . . . " MP/SC

And see H:Artists and their work—*fresco*

"'My little reason'. . . stretching forth my hand towards stagnant pool of blacking in a frame, 'should make, even of these very works of art, an encompassing universe of beauty and happiness.' . . .

"'That policeman demanded of me, for the time being, all the best bumps in my head. Form, colour, size, proportion, distance, individuality, the true perception of every object on the face of the earth or the face of the Heavens, he insisted on my leaving at the foot of the stairs . . . . And now I find the moon to be really made of green cheese; the sun to be a yellow wafer or a little round blister; the deep wild sea to be a shallow series of slate-coloured festoons turned upside down; the human face Divine to be a smear; the whole material and immaterial universe to be sticky with treacle and polished up with blacking." ¶HW/U

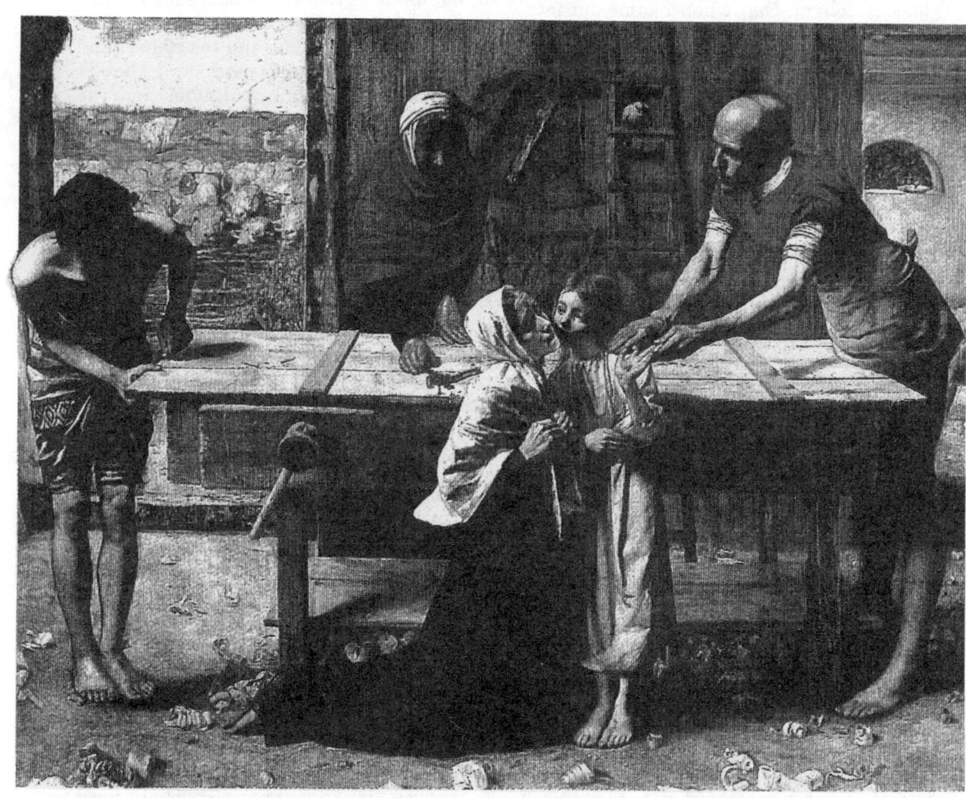

Christ in the Carpenter's Shop (detail), *by John Everett Millais (1849)*

—*hatred of the pre-Raphaelite* "You will have the goodness to discharge from your minds all Post-Raphael ideas, all religious aspirations, all elevating thoughts; all tender, awful, sorrowful, ennobling, sacred, graceful, or beautiful associations; and to prepare yourselves, as befits such a subject—pre-Raphaelly considered—for the lowest depths of what is mean, odious, repulsive, and revolting.

"You behold the interior of a carpenter's shop. In the foreground of that carpenter's shop is a hideous, wry-necked, blubbering red-headed boy, in a bed-gown, who appears to have received a poke in the hand from the stick of another boy with whom he has been playing in an adjacent gutter, and to be holding it up for the contemplation of a kneeling woman, so horrible in her ugliness, that (supposing it were possible for any human creature to exist for a moment with that dislocated throat) she would stand out from the rest of the company as a Monster, in the vilest cabaret in France, or the lowest gin-shop in England.

"Two almost naked carpenters, master and journeyman, worthy companions of this agreeable female, are working at their trade; a boy, with some small flavour of humanity in him, is entering with a vessel of water; and nobody is paying any attention to a snuffy old woman who seems to have mistaken that shop for the tobacconist's next door, and to be hopelessly waiting at the counter to be served with half an ounce of her favourite mixture.

"Wherever it is possible to express ugliness of feature, limb, or attitude, you have it expressed. Such men as the carpenters might be undressed in any hospital where dirty drunkards, in a high state of varicose veins are received. Their very toes have walked out of Saint Giles's." ¶HW/OL

—nature and grace: ***Leonardo****:* "I am not mechanically acquainted with the art of painting, and have no other means of judging of a picture than as I see it resembling and refining upon nature, and presenting graceful combinations of forms and colours. I am, therefore, no authority whatever, in reference to the 'touch' of this or that master; though I know very well . . . that few very great masters can possibly have painted, in the compass of their lives, one-half of the pictures that bear their names, and that are recognised by many aspirants to a reputation for taste, as undoubted originals. But this, by the way.

"Of the Last Supper, I would simply observe, that in its beautiful composition and arrangement, there it is, at Milan, a wonderful picture; and that, in its original colouring, or in its original expression of any single face or feature, there it is not.

"Apart from the damage it has sustained from damp, decay, or neglect, it has been . . . so retouched upon, and repainted, and that so clumsily, that many of the heads are, now, positive deformities, with patches of paint and plaster sticking upon them like wens, and utterly distorting the expression.

"Where the original artist set that impress of his genius on a face, which, almost in a line or touch, separated him from meaner painters and made him what he was, succeeding bunglers, filling up, or painting across seams and cracks, have been quite unable to imitate his hand; and putting in some scowls, or frowns, or wrinkles, of their own, have blotched and spoiled the work . . . it would be comfortable and rational for travellers and critics to arrive at a general understanding that it cannot fail to have been a work of extraordinary merit, once: when, with so few of its original beauties remaining, the grandeur of the general design is yet sufficient to sustain it, as a piece replete with interest and dignity." PI 9

"I unreservedly confess, for myself, that I cannot leave my natural perception of what is natural and true, at a palace-door, in Italy or elsewhere, as I should leave my shoes if I were travelling in the East. I cannot forget that there are certain expressions of face, natural to certain passions, and as unchangeable in their nature as the gait of a lion, or the flight of an eagle.

"I cannot dismiss from my certain knowledge, such commonplace facts as the ordinary proportion of men's arms, and legs, and heads; and when I meet with performances that do violence to these experiences and recollections, no matter where they may be, I cannot honestly admire them, and think it best to say so; in spite of high critical advice that we should sometimes feign an admiration, though we have it not.

"Therefore, I freely acknowledge that when I see a Jolly young Waterman representing a cherubim, or a **Barclay and Perkins**'s* Drayman depicted as an Evangelist, I see nothing to commend or admire in the performance, however great its reputed Painter. Neither am I partial to libellous Angels, who play on fiddles and bassoons, for the edification of sprawling monks apparently in liquor . . . .

"It seems to me, too, that the indiscriminate and determined raptures in which some critics indulge, is incompatible with the true appreciation of the really great and transcendent works. I cannot imagine, for example, how the resolute champion of undeserving pictures can soar to the amazing beauty of **Titian**'s great picture of the Assumption of the Virgin at Venice; or how the man who is truly affected by the sublimity of that exquisite production, or who is truly sensible of the beauty of **Tintoretto**'s . . . Assembly of the Blessed in the same place, can discern in **Michael Angelo**'s Last Judgment, in the Sistine chapel, any general idea, or one pervading thought, in harmony with the stupendous subject.

"He who will contemplate **Raphael**'s masterpiece, the Transfiguration, and will go away into another chamber of that same Vatican, and contemplate another design of Raphael, representing (in incredible caricature) the miraculous stopping of a great fire by Leo the Fourth—and who will say that he admires them both, as works of extraordinary genius—must, as I think, be wanting in his powers of perception in one of the two instances, and, probably, in the high and lofty one.

"It is easy to suggest a doubt, but I have a great doubt whether, sometimes, the rules of art are not too strictly observed, and whether it is quite well or agreeable that we should know before hand, where this figure will be turning round, and where that figure will be lying down, and where there will be drapery in folds, and so forth . . . .

"The exquisite grace and beauty of **Canova**'s statues; the wonderful gravity and repose of many of the ancient works in sculpture, both in the Capitol and the Vatican; and the strength and fire of many others; are, in their different ways, beyond all reach of words. They are especially impressive and delightful, after the works of **Bernini** and his disciples, in which the churches of Rome, from St Peter's downward, abound; and which are, I verily believe, the most detestable class of productions in the wide world.

"I would infinitely rather (as mere works of art) look upon the three deities of the Past, the Present, and the Future, in the Chinese Collection, than upon the best of these breezy maniacs; whose every fold of drapery is blown inside-out; whose smallest vein or artery, is as big as an ordinary forefinger; whose hair is like a nest of lively snakes; and whose attitudes put all other extravagance to shame. Insomuch that I do honestly believe, there can be no place in the world, where such intolerable abortions, begotten of the sculptor's chisel, are to be found in such profusion, as in Rome." ¶PI 11 **a prominent brewer of the period*

—reverence for the old: "At the head of the collections in the palace of Rome, the Vatican of course, with its treasures of art, its enormous galleries, and staircases, and suites upon suites of immense chambers, ranks highest and stands foremost. Many most noble statues, and wonderful pictures, are there; nor is it heresy to say that there is a considerable amount of rubbish there, too. When any old piece of sculpture dug out of the ground, finds a place in a gallery because it *is* old, and without any reference to its intrinsic merits; and finds admirers by the hundred, because it is there, and for no other reason on earth—there will be no lack of objects, very indifferent in the plain eyesight of any one who employs so vulgar a property, when he may wear the spectacles of Cant for less than nothing, and establish himself as a man of taste for the mere trouble of putting them on." PI 11

Walker and climber

—climber: "No matter that the snow and ice lie thick upon the summit of Vesuvius, or that we have been on foot all day at Pompeii, or that croakers maintain that strangers should not be on the mountain by night, in such an unusual season. Let us take advantage of the fine weather; make the best of our way to Resina, the little village at the foot of the mountain; prepare ourselves, as well as we can, on so short a notice, at the guide's house; ascend at once, and have sunset half-way up, moon-light at the top, and midnight to come down in!" PI 15

—walker: "For a while, I hid myself among some lanes and by-paths, and then struck off to walk all the way to London. For, I had by that time come to myself so far, as to consider that I could not go back to the inn and see Drummle there; that I could not bear to sit upon the coach and be spoken to; that I could do nothing half so good for myself as tire myself out." GE 44

""My last special feat was turning out of bed at two, after a hard day, pedestrian and otherwise, and walking thirty miles into the country to breakfast. The road was so lonely in the night, that I fell asleep to the monotonous sound of my own feet, doing their regular four miles an hour. Mile after mile I walked, without the slightest sense of exertion, dozing heavily and dreaming constantly.

"It was only when I made a stumble like a drunken man, or struck out into the road to avoid a horseman close upon me on the path—who had no existence—that I came to myself and looked about. The day broke mistily (it was autumn time), and I could not disembarrass myself of the idea that I had to climb those heights and banks of cloud, and that there was an Alpine Convent somewhere behind the sun, where I was going to breakfast . . . .

"My walking is of two kinds: one, straight on end to a definite goal at a round pace; one, objectless, loitering, and purely vagabond. In the latter state, no gipsy on earth is a greater vagabond than myself; it is so natural to me, and strong with me, that I think I must be the descendant, at no great distance, of some irreclaimable tramp." ¶UT/SN

"I had proceeded thus far, when I found I had been lying awake so long that the very dead began to wake too, and to crowd into my thoughts most sorrowfully. Therefore, I resolved to lie awake no more, but to get up and go out for a night walk—which resolution was an acceptable relief to me, as I dare say it may prove now to a great many more." RP/LA

And see Enthusiast; B:Walking *and* W:Italy —*the Campagna*

Young reporter

"I have pursued the calling of a reporter under circumstances of which many of my brethren at home in England here, many of my modern successors, can form no adequate conception. I have often transcribed for the printer from my shorthand notes, important public speeches in which the strictest accuracy was required, and a mistake in which would have been to a young man severely compromising, writing on the palm of my hand, by the light of a dark lantern, in a post chase and four, galloping through a wild country, all through the dead of night, at the then surprising rate of fifteen miles an hour.

"The very last time I was at Exeter, I strolled into the Castle Yard there to identify, for the amusement of a friend, the spot on which I once 'took', as we used to call it, an election speech of my noble friend **Lord Russell** [*see* MC/JR], in the midst of a lively fight maintained by all the vagabonds in that division of the county, and under such a pelting rain, that I remember two good-natured colleagues, who chanced to be at leisure, held a pocket handkerchief over my notebook after the manner of a state canopy in an ecclesiastical procession.

"I have worn my knees by writing on them on the old back row of the old gallery of the old House of Commons; and I have worn my feet by standing to write in a preposterous pen in the old House of Lords, where we used to be huddled together like so many sheep, kept in waiting, say, until the woolsack might want re-stuffing.

"I have been, in my time, belated on miry by-roads, towards the small hours, in a wheelless carriage, with exhausted horses and drunken postboys, and have got back in time for publication, to be received with never-forgotten compliments by the late Mr [**John**] **Black** [editor in chief of *The Morning Chronicle*], coming in the broadest of Scotch from the broadest of hearts I ever knew." ¶S/N5

The Mausoleum at Chesney Wold BH

First and Last Things

The light, creation's mind, was everywhere, and all things owned its power.

OCS 15

That first flood before the Deluge—Light—came rushing on Creation at the word of God.

AN 14

I stand upon a sea-shore, where the waves are years. They break and fall, and with every wave the sea is rising. I know that it will float me on this traveller's voyage at last.

[RP/LV]

Akashic records

"Chateau and hut, stone face and dangling figure, the red stain on the stone floor, and the pure water in the village well—thousands of acres of land—a whole province of France—all France itself—lay under the night sky, concentrated into a faint hair-breadth line. So does a whole world, with all its greatnesses and littlenesses, lie in a twinkling star. And as mere human knowledge can split a ray of light and analyse the manner of its composition, so, sublimer intelligences may read in the feeble shining of this earth of ours, every thought and act, every vice and virtue, of every responsible creature on it." TTC ii 15

"'In the material world, as I have long taught, nothing can be spared; no step or atom in the wondrous structure could be lost, without a blank being made in the great universe. I know, now, that it is the same with good and evil, happiness and sorrow, in the memories of men.'" HM 2

See TP:Law Courts—*criminal court—mirror*

Angel

—*a child's:* " . . . I raised my handkerchief to look upon the tiny sleeper underneath, and seemed to see a halo shine around the child through Ada's drooping hair as her pity bent her head . . . . I only thought that perhaps the Angel of the child might not be all unconscious of the woman who replaced it with so compassionate a hand . . . ." BH 8

—*a modest disclaimer:* "'My visits,' said Mr Grewgious, 'are, like those of the angels—not that I compare myself to an angel.'

"'No, sir,' said Rosa.

"'Not by any means,' assented Mr Grewgious. 'I merely refer to my visits, which are few and far between. The angels are, we know very well, upstairs.'" MED 9

—*a memory:* "'There is not an angel added to the Host of Heaven but does its blessed work on earth in those that loved it here.'" OCS 54

"'I dare say my birds sing better than other birds, and my flowers smell better than other flowers [said Jenny Wren]. For when I was a little child,' in a tone as though it were ages ago [she is thirteen], 'the children that I used to see early in the morning were very different from any others that I ever saw. They were not like me: they were not chilled, anxious, ragged, or beaten; they were never in pain. They were not like the children of the neighbours; they never made me tremble all over, by setting up shrill noises, and they never mocked me.

"'Such numbers of them, too! All in white dresses, and with something shining on the borders, and on their heads, that I have never been able to imitate with my work, though I know it so well. They used to come down in long bright slanting rows, and say all together, "Who is this in pain? Who is this in pain?" When I told them who it was, they answered, "Come and play with us!" When I said, "I never play! I can't play!" they swept about me and took me up, and made me light.

"'Then it was all delicious ease and rest till they laid me down, and said all together, "Have patience, and we will come again." Whenever they came back, I used to know they were coming before I saw the long bright rows, by hearing them ask, all together a long way off, "Who is this in pain? Who is this in pain?" And I used to cry out, "Oh, my blessed children, it's poor me! Have pity on me! Take me up and make me light!"'

"By degrees, as she progressed in this remembrance, the hand was raised, the late ecstatic look returned, and she became quite beautiful. Having so paused for a moment, silent, with a listening smile upon her face, she looked round and recalled herself." ¶OMF ii 2

It is never explained how Jenny became a cripple: Was it congenital? Was it the result of illness, carelessness or abuse? She never mentions her mother once, and her father is a confirmed drunkard whom she treats as her "child." Phoebe CS/MJ, *who had been dropped by her mother as an infant, and Sophy Marigold* CS/DM, *who died of her mother's abuse, may have been her forbears.*

—*a shared attribute:* "In the exhaustless catalogue of Heaven's mercies to mankind, the power we have of finding some germs of comfort in the hardest trials must ever occupy the foremost place; not only because it supports and upholds as when we most require to be sustained, but because in this source of consolation there is something, we have reason to believe, of the divine spirit; something of that goodness which detects, amidst our own evil doings, a redeeming quality; something which, even in our fallen nature, we possess in common with the angels; which had its being in the old time when they trod the earth, and lingers on it yet, in pity." BR 47

—*a simulacrum:* "It was no dream, no phantom conjured up by hope and fear, but

Marion, sweet Marion [Jeddler]! So beautiful, so happy, so unalloyed by care and trial, so elevated and exalted in her loveliness, that as the setting sun shone brightly on her upturned face, she might have been a spirit visiting the earth upon some healing mission." BL 3

—a sister's: "'Thou'rt an Angel [Rachael]. Bless thee, bless thee!'

"'I am, as I have told thee, Stephen, thy poor friend. Angels are not like me. Between them, and a working woman fu' of faults, there is a deep gulf set. My little sister is among them, but she is changed.'" HT i 13

CD eliminated in proof the sister's death in an industrial accident caused by unsafe working conditions.

—a visitation: "Mr Harthouse hurried into the gallery. A young woman whom he had never seen stood there. Plainly dressed, very quiet, very pretty . . . . Her face was innocent and youthful, and its expression remarkably pleasant. She was not afraid of him, or in any way disconcerted; she seemed to have her mind entirely preoccupied with the occasion of her visit, and to have substituted that consideration for herself.

"'I speak to Mr Harthouse?' she said, when they were alone.

"'To Mr Harthouse.' He added in his mind, 'And you speak to him with the most confiding eyes I ever saw, and the most earnest voice (though so quiet) I ever heard.'

"'If I do not understand—and I do not, Sir'—said Sissy [Jupe], 'what your honour as a gentleman binds you to, in other matters:' the blood really rose in his face as she began in these words: 'I am sure I may rely upon it to keep my visit secret, and to keep secret what I am going to say. I will rely upon it, if you will tell me I may so far trust—'

"'You may, I assure you.'

"'I am young, as you see; I am alone, as you see. In coming to you, Sir, I have no advice or encouragement beyond my own hope.'

"He thought, 'But that is very strong,' as he followed the momentary upward glance of her eyes. He thought besides, 'This is a very odd beginning. I don't see where we are going.'

"'I think,' said Sissy, 'you have already guessed whom I left just now! . . .

"'[Louisa] hurried [to her father's] last night. She arrived there in great agitation, and was insensible all through the night. I live at her father's, and was with her. You may be sure, Sir, you will never see her again as long as you live.'

"Mr Harthouse drew a long breath; and, if ever man found himself in the position of not knowing what to say, made the discovery beyond all question that he was so circumstanced. The child-like ingenuousness with which his visitor spoke, her modest fearlessness, her truthfulness which put all artifice aside, her entire forgetfulness of herself in her earnest quiet holding to the object with which she had come; all this, together with her reliance on his easily given promise—which in itself shamed him—presented something in which he was so inexperienced, and against which he knew any of his usual weapons would fall so powerless; that not a word could he rally to his relief.

"At last he said:

"'So startling an announcement, so confidently made, and by such lips, is really disconcerting in the last degree. May I be permitted to inquire, if you are charged to convey that information to me in those hopeless words, by the lady of whom we speak?'

"'I have no charge from her.'

"'The drowning man catches at the straw. With no disrespect for your judgment, and with no doubt of your sincerity, excuse my saying that I cling to the belief that there is yet hope that I am not condemned to perpetual exile from that lady's presence.'

"'There is not the least hope. The first object of my coming here, Sir, is to assure you that you must believe that there is no more hope of your ever speaking with her again, than there would be if she had died when she came home last night.'

"'Must believe? But if I can't—or if I should, by infirmity of nature, be obstinate—and won't—

"'It is still true. There is no hope.'

"James Harthouse looked at her with an incredulous smile upon his lips; but her mind looked over and beyond him, and the smile was quite thrown away.

"He bit his lip, and took a little time for consideration.

"'Well! If it should unhappily appear,' he said, 'after due pains and duty on my part, that I am brought to a position so desolate as this banishment, I shall not become the lady's persecutor. But you said you had no commission from her?'

"'I have only the commission of my love for her, and her love for me. I have no other trust, than that I have been with her since she came home, and that she has given me her confidence. I have no further trust, than that I know something of her character and her marriage. O Mr Harthouse, I think you had that trust too!' . . .

" . . . . He was silent for a moment; and then proceeded with a more self-possessed air, though with traces of vexation and disappointment that would not be polished out.

"'After what has been just now represented to me, in a manner I find it impossible to doubt—I know of hardly any other source from which I could have accepted it so readily—I feel bound to say to you, in whom the confidence you have mentioned has been reposed, that I cannot refuse to contemplate the possibility (however unexpected) of my seeing the lady no more. I am solely to blame for the thing having come to this—and—and, I cannot say,' he added, rather hard up for a general peroration, 'that I have any sanguine expectation of ever becoming a moral sort of fellow, or that I have any belief in any moral sort of fellow whatever.'

"Sissy's face sufficiently showed that her appeal to him was not finished.

"'You spoke,' he resumed, as she raised her eyes to him again, 'of your first object. I may assume that there is a second to be mentioned?'

"'Yes.'

"'Will you oblige me by confiding it?'

"'Mr Harthouse, returned Sissy, with a blending of gentleness and steadiness that quite defeated him, and with a simple confidence in his being bound to do what she required, that held him at a singular disadvantage, 'the only reparation that remains with you, is to leave here immediately and finally. I am quite sure that you can mitigate in no other way the wrong and harm you have done. I am quite sure that it is the only compensation you have left it in your power to make. I do not say that it is much, or that it is enough; but it is something, and it is necessary. Therefore, though without any other authority than I have given you, and even without the knowledge of any other person than yourself and myself, I ask you to depart from this place to-night, under an obligation never to return to it.'

"If she had asserted any influence over him beyond her plain faith in the truth and right of what she said; if she had concealed the least doubt or irresolution, or had harboured for the best purpose any reserve or pretence; if she had shown, or felt, the lightest trace of any sensitiveness to his ridicule or his astonishment, or any remonstrance he might offer; he would have carried it against her at this point. But he could as easily have changed a clear sky by looking at it in surprise, as affect her.

"'But do you know,' he asked, quite at a loss, 'the extent of what you ask? You probably are not aware that I am here on a public kind of business, preposterous enough in itself, but which I have gone in for, and sworn by, and am supposed to be devoted to in quite a desperate manner? You probably are not aware of that, but I assure you it's the fact.

"It had no effect on Sissy, fact or no fact.

"'Besides which,' said Mr Harthouse, taking a turn or two across the room, dubiously, 'it's so alarmingly absurd. It would make a man so ridiculous, after going in for these fellows, to back out in such an incomprehensible way.'

"'I am quite sure, repeated Sissy, 'that it is the only reparation in your power, Sir. I am quite sure, or I would not have come here' . . . .

"His leaning against the chimney piece reminded him of the night with the whelp [Tom Gradgrind]. It was the self-same chimneypiece, and somehow he felt as if *he* were the whelp to-night. He could make no way at all.

"'I suppose a man never was placed in a more ridiculous position,' he said, after looking down, and looking up, and laughing, and frowning, and walking off, and walking back again. 'But I see no way out of it. What will be, will be. *This* will be, I suppose. I must take off myself, I imagine—in short, I engage to do it.'

"Sissy rose. She was not surprised by the result, but she was happy in it, and her face beamed brightly.

"'You will permit me to say,' continued Mr James Harthouse, 'that I doubt if any other ambassador, or ambassadress, could have addressed me with the same success. I must not only regard myself as being in a very ridiculous position, but as being vanquished at all points. Will you allow me the privilege of remembering my enemy's name?'

"'*My* name?' said the ambassadress.

"'The only name I could possibly care to know, to-night.'

"'Sissy Jupe.'

"'Pardon my curiosity at parting. Related to the family?'

"'I am only a poor girl,' returned Sissy. 'I was separated from my father—he was only a stroller—and taken pity on by Mr Gradgrind. I have lived in the house ever since.'

"She was gone." HT iii 2

And see A:The Dead—*remembered*

Another plane

—edge of birth: "The father of this young gentleman had been a money-lender, who had transacted professional business with the mother of this young gentleman, when he, the latter, was waiting in the vast dark ante-chambers of the present world to be born. The lady, a widow, being unable to pay the money-lender, married him; and in due course, Fledgeby was summoned out of the vast dark ante-chambers to come and be presented to the Registrar-General. Rather a curious speculation how Fledgeby would otherwise have disposed of his leisure until Doomsday." OMF ii 5

—edge of death: "If you are not gone for good, Mr Riderhood, it would be something to know where you are hiding at present. This flabby lump of mortality that we work so hard at with such patient perseverance, yields no sign of you. If you are gone for good, Rogue, it is very solemn, and if you are coming back, it is hardly less so. Nay, in the suspense and mystery of the latter question, involving that of where you may be now, there is a solemnity even added to that of death, making us who are in attendance alike afraid to look on you and to look off you, and making those below start at the least sound of a creaking plank in the floor." OMF iii 1

Creation

—a fall of water: "We were at the foot of the American Fall [at Niagara]. I could see an immense torrent of water tearing headlong down from some great height, but had no idea of shape, or situation, or anything but vague immensity.

"When we were seated in the little ferry-boat, and were crossing the swollen river immediately before both cataracts, I began to feel what it was: but I was in a manner stunned, and unable to comprehend the vastness of the scene. It was not until I came on Table Rock, and looked—Great Heaven, on what a fall of bright-green water!—that it came upon me in its full might and majesty.

"Then, when I felt how near to my Creator I was standing, the first effect, and the enduring one—instant and lasting—of the tremendous spectacle, was Peace. Peace of Mind, tranquillity, calm recollections of the Dead, great thoughts of Eternal Rest and Happiness; nothing of gloom or terror. Niagara was at once stamped upon my heart, an Image of Beauty; to remain there, changeless and indelible, until the pulses cease to beat, for ever.

"Oh, how the strife and trouble of daily life, receded from my view, and lessened in the distance, during the ten memorable days we passed on that Enchanted Ground! What voices spoke from out the thundering water; what faces, faded from the earth, looked out upon me from its gleaming depths; what Heavenly promise glistened in those angels' tears, the drops of many hues, that showered around, and twined themselves about the gorgeous arches which the changing rainbows made!

"I never stirred in all that time from the Canadian side, whither I had gone at first. I never crossed the river again; for I knew there were people on the other shore, and in such a place it is natural to shun strange company.

"To wander to and fro all day, and see the cataracts from all points of view; to stand upon the edge of the great Horse-Shoe Fall, marking the hurried water gathering strength as it approached the verge, yet seeming, too, to pause before it shot into the gulf below; to gaze from the river's level up at the torrent as it came streaming down; to climb the neighbouring heights and watch it through the trees, and see the wreathing water in the rapids hurrying on to take its fearful plunge; to linger in the shadow of the solemn rocks three miles below; watching the river as, stirred by no visible cause, it heaved and eddied and awoke the echoes, being troubled yet, far down beneath the surface, by its giant leap; to have Niagara before me, lighted by the sun and by the moon, red in the day's decline, and grey as evening slowly fell upon it; to look upon it every day, and wake up in the night and hear its ceaseless voice: this was enough.

"I think in every quiet season now, still do those waters roll and leap, and roar and tumble, all day long; still are the rainbows spanning them, a hundred feet below. Still, when the sun is on them, do they shine and glow like molten gold. Still, when the day is gloomy, do they fall like snow, or seem to crumble away like the front of a great chalk cliff, or roll down the rock like dense white smoke.

"But always does the mighty stream appear to die as it comes down, and always from its unfathomable grave arises that tremendous ghost of spray and mist which is never laid: which has haunted this place with the same dread solemnity since Darkness brooded on the deep, and that first flood before the Deluge—Light—came rushing on Creation at the word of God." AN 14

Day of Judgment

—*anticipated:* "'I see the Spirit of the Chimes among you!' cried the old man, singling out the child, and speaking in some inspiration, which their looks conveyed to him. 'I know that our inheritance is held in store for us by Time. I know there is a sea of Time to rise one day, before which all who wrong us or oppress us will be swept away like leaves. I see it, on the flow! I know that we must trust and hope, and neither doubt ourselves, nor doubt the good in one another. I have learnt it from the creature dearest to my heart. I clasp her in my arms again. O Spirits, merciful and good, I take your lesson to my breast along with her! O Spirits, merciful and good, I am grateful!'" C

—*the child within:* "'We were all of us,' says I [Captain Ravender], 'children once; and our baby feet have strolled in green woods ashore; and our baby hands have gathered flowers in gardens, where the birds were singing. The children that we were, are not lost to the great knowledge of our Creator. Those innocent creatures will appear with us before Him, and plead for us. What we were in the best time of our generous youth will arise and go with us too. The purest of us here present are gliding. What we were then, will be as much in existence before Him, as what we are now.'" CS/GM

—*dress become paper:* "Paper! White, pure, spick and span new paper, with that fresh smell which takes us back to school and schoolbooks; can it ever come from rags like these? Is it from such bales of dusty rags, native and foreign, of every colour and of every kind, as now environ us, shutting out the summer air and putting cotton into our summer ears, that virgin paper, to be written on, and printed on, proceeds? . . . what a grave of dress this rag-store is; what a lesson of vanity it preaches. The coarse blouse of the Flemish labourer, and the fine cambric of the Parisian lady, the court dress of the Austrian jailer, and the miserable garb of the Italian peasant; the woollen petticoat of the Bavarian girl, the linen headdress of the Neapolitan woman, the priest's vestment, the player's robe, the Cardinal's hat, and the ploughman's nightcap; all dwindle down to this, and bring their littleness or greatness in fractional portions here. As it is with the worn, it shall be with the wearers; but there shall be no dust in our eyes then, though there is plenty now. Not all the great ones of the earth will raise a grain of it, and nothing but the Truth will be." HWC/PM

The Dead

—*burial at sea:* "'I am the Resurrection and the Life, saith the Lord. He raised the daughter of *Jairus* the ruler, and said she was not dead but slept. He raised the widow's son. He arose Himself, and was seen of many. He loved little children, saying, Suffer them to come unto Me, and rebuke them not, for of such is the kingdom of heaven. In His name, my friends, and committed to His merciful goodness!' With those words I laid my rough face softly on the placid little forehead, and buried the Golden Lucy in the grave of the Golden Mary." CS/GM

—*in a churchyard:* "The old church bell rang out the hour with a mournful sound, as if it had grown sad from so much communing with the dead and unheeded warning to the living; the fallen leaves rustled; the grass stirred upon the graves; all else was still and sleeping.

"Some of those dreamless sleepers lay close within the shadow of the church—touching the wall, as if they clung to it for comfort and protection. Others had chosen to lie beneath the changing shade of trees; others by the path, that footsteps might come near them; others, among the graves of little children. Some had desired to rest beneath the very ground they had trodden in their daily walks; some, where the setting sun might shine upon their beds; some, where its light would fall upon them when it rose. Perhaps not one of the imprisoned souls had been able quite to separate itself in living thought from its old companion. If any had, it had still felt for it a love like that which captives have been known to bear towards the cell in which they have been long confined, and, even at parting, hung upon its narrow bounds affectionately." OCS 52

—*communion with:* "Now, although I regard with a hushed and solemn fear, the mysteries, between which and this state of existence is interposed the barrier of the great trial and change that fall on all the things that live; and although I have not the audacity to pretend that I know anything of them; I can no more reconcile the mere banging of doors, ringing of bells, creaking of boards, and such-like insignificances, with the majestic beauty and pervading analogy of all the Divine rules that I am permitted to understand, than I had been able, a little while before, to yoke the spiritual intercourse of my fellow-traveller to the chariot of the rising sun." CS/HH 1

And see M:Memory—*of the dead*

—*condescended to:* "What a satisfaction it was to Mrs Chick—a commonplace piece of folly enough, compared with whom her sister-in-law had been a very angel of womanly intelligence and gentleness—to patronise and be tender to the memory of that lady: in exact pursuance of her conduct to her in her life-time: and to thoroughly believe herself, and take herself in, and make herself uncommonly comfortable on the strength of her toleration! What a mighty pleasant virtue toleration should be when we are right, to be so very pleasant when we are wrong, and quite unable to demonstrate how we come to be invested with the privilege of exercising it!" DS 5

—*corpses in Paris:* "Those who have never seen the Morgue may see it perfectly by presenting to themselves an indifferently paved coach-house, accessible from the street by a pair of folding-gates; on the left of the coach-house, occupying its width, any large London tailor's or linen-draper's plate-glass window, reaching to the ground; within the window, on two rows of inclined planes, what the coach-house has to show; hanging above, like irregular stalactites from the roof of a cave, a quanitity of clothes—the clothes of the dead and buried shows of the coach-house." UT/RM

" . . . a flaxen-haired boy of eighteen, with a heart hanging on his breast—'from his mother,' was engraved on it—who had come into the net across the river, with a bullet wound in his fair forehead and his hands cut with a knife, but whence or how was a blank mystery . . . a large dark man whose disfigurement by water was in a frightful manner comic, and whose expression was that of a prize-fighter who had closed his eyelids under a heavy blow, but was going immediately to open them, shake his head, and 'come up smiling' . . . [an old man] lying all alone on his cold bed, with a tap of water turned on over his grey hair, and running, drip, drip, drip, down his wretched face until it got to the corner of his mouth, where it took a turn, and made him look sly." UT/TA

"I am thinking of the [Paris] Morgue, where the bodies of all persons discovered dead, with no clue to their identity upon them, are placed to be seen by all who choose to go and look at them. All the world knows this custom, and perhaps all the world knows that the bodies lie on inclined planes within a great glass window, as though **Holbein** should represent Death, in his grim Dance, keeping a shop, and displaying his goods like a Regent Street or Boulevard linen-draper." HW/RD

—*forgotten:* "So Edith's mother lies unmentioned of her dear friends, who are deaf to the waves that are hoarse with repetition of their mystery, and blind to the dust that is piled upon the shore, and to the white arms that are beckoning, in the moonlight, to the invisible country far away. But all goes on, as it was wont, upon the margin of the unknown sea; and Edith, standing there alone, and listening to its waves, has dank weed cast up at her feet, to strew her path in life withal." DS 41

—heads on pikes: "But, in the ocean of faces where every fierce and furious expression was in vivid life, there were two groups of faces—each seven in number—so fixedly contrasting with the rest, that never did sea roll which bore more memorable wrecks with it. Seven faces of prisoners, suddenly released by the storm that had burst their tomb [the Bastille], were carried high overhead: all scared, all lost, all wondering and amazed, as if the Last Day were come, and those who rejoiced around them were lost spirits. Other seven faces there were, carried higher, seven dead faces, whose drooping eyelids and half-seen eyes awaited the Last Day. Impassive faces, yet with a suspended—not an abolished—expression on them; faces, rather, in a fearful pause, as having yet to raise the dropped lids of the eyes, and bear witness with the bloodless lips, 'THOU DIDST IT!'" TTC II 21

—as an industry: "'There'd be two sides to [graverobbing cadavers, said Jerry Cruncher]. There might be medical doctors at the present hour, a picking up their guineas where a honest tradesman don't pick up his fardens—fardens! no, nor yet his half-fardens—half fardens! no, nor yet his quarter—a banking away like smoke at Tellson's, and a cocking their medical eyes at that tradesman on the sly, a going in and going out to their own carriages—ah! equally like smoke, if not more so. Well that 'ud be imposing, too, on Tellson's.

"'For you cannot sarse the goose and not the gander. And here's Mrs Cruncher, or leastways wos in the Old England times, and would be to-morrow, if cause given, a floppin' again [praying against] the business to that degree as is ruinating—stark ruinating! Whereas them medical doctors' wives don't flop—catch 'em at it! Or, if they flop, their floppings goes in favour of more patients, and how can you rightly have one without the t'other? Then, wot with undertakers, and wot with parish clerks, and wot with sextons, and wot with private watchmen (all awaricious and all in it), a man wouldn't get much by it, even if it wos so.'" ¶TTC iii 9

—influence for good: "'And do you think,' said the schoolmaster, marking the glance she had thrown around, 'that an unvisited grave, a withered tree, a faded flower or two, are tokens of forgetfulness or cold neglect? Do you think there are no deeds, far away from here, in which these dead may be best remembered? Nell, Nell, there may be people busy in the world at this instant, in whose good actions and good thoughts these very graves—neglected as they look to us—are the chief instruments . . . .

"'There is nothing . . . no, nothing innocent or good, that dies, and is forgotten. Let us hold to that faith, or none. An infant, a prattling child, dying in its cradle, will live again in the better thoughts of those who loved it, and will play its part, through them, in the redeeming actions of the world, though its body be burnt to ashes or drowned in the deepest sea. There is not an angel added to the Host of Heaven but does its blessed work on earth in those that loved it here. Forgotten! oh, if the good deeds of human creatures could be traced to their source, how beautiful would even death appear; for how much charity, mercy, and purified affection, would be seen to have their growth in dusty graves!'" OCS 54

—and the living: "But there was one thought, scarcely shaped out to herself, yet fervent and strong within her, that upheld Florence [Dombey] when she strove, and filled her true young heart, so sorely tried, with constancy of purpose. Into her mind, as into all others contending with the great affliction of our mortal nature, there had stolen solemn wonderings and hopes, arising in the dim world beyond the present life, and murmuring, like faint music, of recognition in the far-off land between her brother and her mother: of some present consciousness in both of her: some love and commiseration for her: and some knowledge of her as she went her way upon the earth.

"It was a soothing consolation to Florence to give shelter to these thoughts, until one day—it was soon after she had last seen her father in his own room, late at night—the fancy came upon her, that, in weeping for his alienated heart, she might stir the spirits of the dead against him. Wild, weak, childish, as it may have been to think so, and to tremble at the half-formed thought, it was the impulse of her loving nature; and from that hour Florence strove against the cruel wound in her breast, and tried to think of him whose hand had made it only with hope." ¶DS 23

—looked at: "The differences of expression were not many. There was a little pity, but not much, and that mostly with a selfish touch in it—as who would say, 'Shall I, poor I, look like that, when the time comes!' There was more of a secretly brooding contemplation and curiosity, as 'That man I

don't like, and have the grudge against; would such be his appearance, if some one—not to mention names—by any chance gave him an ugly knock?' There was a wolfish stare at the object, in which the homicidal white-lead worker shone conspicuous. And there was a much more general, purposeless, vacant staring at it—like looking at waxwork, without a catalogue, and not knowing what to make of it. But all these expressions concurred in possessing the one underlying expression of *looking at something that could not return a look.*" UT/RM

—remembered: "It is an exquisite and beautiful thing in our nature, that when the heart is touched and softened by some tranquil happiness or affectionate feeling, the memory of the dead comes over it most powerfully and irresistibly. It would almost seem as though our better thoughts and sympathies were charms, in virtue of which the soul is enabled to hold some vague and mysterious intercourse with the spirits of those whom we dearly loved in life. Alas! how often and how long may those patient angels hover above us, watching for the spell which is so seldom uttered, and so soon forgotten." NN 43

—twin still growing: "'Pet had a twin sister who died when we could just see her eyes—exactly like Pet's—above the table, as she stood on tiptoe holding by it.

"'Ah! indeed, indeed?'

"'Yes, and being practical people, a result has gradually sprung up in the minds of Mrs Meagles and myself which perhaps you may—or perhaps you may not—understand. Pet and her baby sister were so exactly alike, and so completely one, that in our thoughts we have never been able to separate them since. It would be of no use to tell us that our dear child was a mere infant. We have changed that child according to the changes in the child spared to us, and always with us. As Pet has grown, that child has grown; as Pet has become more sensible and womanly, her sister has become more sensible and womanly, by just the same degrees. It would be as hard to convince me that if I was to pass into the other world tomorrow, I should not, through the mercy of God, be received there by a daughter just like Pet, as to persuade me that Pet herself is not a reality at my side.'" LD i 2

The editor's frisson, *reading this, evokes another dead sister: see* CD:Mary Hogarth

—uncomplaining: "Some of [Lady Dedlock's] old friends, principally to be found among the peachy-cheeked charmers with the skeleton throats, did once occasionally say, as they toyed in a ghastly manner with large fans—like charmers reduced to flirting with grim Death, after losing all their other beaux—did once occasionally say, that they wondered the ashes of the Dedlocks, entombed in the mausoleum, never rose against the profanation of her company. But the dead-and-gone Dedlocks take it very calmly, and have never been known to object." BH 66

—a young girl: "She was dead. No sleep so beautiful and calm, so free from trace of pain, so fair to look upon. She seemed a creature fresh from the hand of God, and waiting for the breath of life; not one who had lived and suffered death . . . . Sorrow was dead indeed in her, but peace and perfect happiness were born; imaged in her tranquil beauty and profound repose . . . . So shall we know the angels in their majesty, after death." OCS 71

See also A:Death*—dusty*

Eternity

—evocation: "The child [Nell] looked around her [in the ancient building], with that solemn feeling with which we contemplate the work of ages that have become but drops of water in the great ocean of eternity." OCS 52

—life, on its surface: "Alas, alas! [said the joyless monk] that the few bubbles on the surface of eternity—all that Heaven wills we should see of that dark deep stream—should be so lightly scattered!'" NN 6

—love: "'As I hear the sea,' says Florence, 'and sit watching it, it brings so many days into mind. It makes me think of much —'

"'Of Paul, my love. I know it does.'

"Of Paul and Walter. And the voices in the waves are always whispering to Florence, in their ceaseless murmuring, of love—of love, eternal and illimitable, not bounded by the confines of this world, or by the end of time, but ranging still, beyond the sea, beyond the sky, to the invisible country far away!" DS 57

—its portal, the river: "[Meg Veck, in a vision] sped onward to the River.

"To the rolling River, swift and dim, where Winter Night sat brooding like the last dark thoughts of many who had sought a refuge there before her. Where scattered lights upon the banks gleamed sullen, red, and dull, as torches that were burning there, to show the way to Death. Where no abode of living people cast its shadow on the deep, impenetrable, melancholy shade.

"To the River! To that portal of Eternity, her desperate footsteps tended with the swiftness of its rapid waters running to the sea . . . the wild distempered form, the fierce and terrible love, the desperation that had left all human check or hold behind, swept by him like the wind." C 4

"'Oh, the river!' [Martha Endell] cried passionately. 'Oh, the river!'

"'Hush, hush!' said I. 'Calm yourself.'

"But she still repeated the same words, continually exclaiming, 'Oh, the river!' over and over again.

"'I know it's like me!' she exclaimed. 'I know that I belong to it. I know that it's the natural company of such as I am! It comes from country places, where there was once no harm in it—and it creeps through the dismal streets, defiled and miserable—and it goes away, like my life, to a great sea, that is always troubled—and I feel that I must go with it!'

"I have never known what despair was, except in the tone of those words.

"'I can't keep away from it. I can't forget it. It haunts me day and night. It's the only thing in all the world that I am fit for, or that's fit for me. Oh, the dreadful river!'" DC 47

"In those pleasant little towns on Thames, you may hear the fall of the water over the weirs, or even, in still weather, the rustle of the rushes; and from the bridge you may see the young river, dimpled like a young child, playfully gliding away among the trees, unpolluted by the defilements that lie in wait for it on its course, and as yet out of hearing of the deep summons of the sea.

"It were too much to pretend that Betty Higden made out such thoughts; no; but she heard the tender river whispering to many like herself, 'Come to me, come to me! When the cruel shame and terror you have so long fled from, most beset you, come to me! I am the Relieving Officer appointed by eternal ordinance to do my work; I am not held in estimation according as I shirk it. My breast is softer than the pauper-nurse's; death in my arms is peacefuller than among the pauper-wards. Come to me!'" ¶OMF iii 8 *And see* Immortality

Fate

—apostrophized: "'So I'm Brass's clerk, am I?' said Dick [Swiveller]. '[Sampson] Brass's clerk, eh? And the clerk of Brass's sister—clerk to a female dragon. Very good, very good! What shall I be next? Shall I be a convict in a felt hat and a grey suit, trotting about a dockyard with my number neatly embroidered on my uniform, and the order of the garter on my leg, restrained from chafing my ankle by a twisted belcher handkerchief? Shall I be that? Will that do, or is it too genteel? Whatever you please, have it your own way of course.'

"As he was entirely alone, it may be presumed that, in these remarks, Mr Swiveller addressed himself to his fate or destiny, whom, as we learn by the precedents, it is the custom of heroes to taunt in a very bitter and ironical manner when they find themselves in situations of an unpleasant nature. This is the more probable from the circumstance of Mr Swiveller directing his observations to the ceiling, which these bodiless personages are usually supposed to inhabit—except in theatrical cases, when they live in the heart of the great chandelier.

"' . . . . Under an accumulation of staggerers, no man can be considered a free agent. No man knocks himself down; if his destiny knocks him down, his destiny must pick him up again. Then I'm very glad that mine has brought all this upon itself, and I shall be as careless as I can, and make myself quite at home to spite it. So go on, my buck,' said Mr Swiveller, taking his leave of the ceiling with a significant nod, 'and let us see which of us will be tired first!'" OCS 34

—cruelly inexorable: "'Is it possible,' cried Rose [Maylie to Nancy], 'that for such a man as this [Bill Sikes], you can resign every future hope, and the certainty of immediate rescue? It is madness.'

"'I don't know what it is,' answered the girl; 'I only know that it is so, and not with me alone, but with hundreds of others as bad and wretched as myself. I must go back. Whether it is God's wrath for the wrong I have done, I do not know; but I am drawn back to him through every suffering and ill usage; and I should be, I believe, if I knew that I was to die by his hand at last.'" OT 40

—the difference a day makes: "That was a memorable day to me [Pip], for it made great changes in me. But it is the same

with any life. Imagine one selected day struck out of it, and think how different its course would have been. Pause you who read this, and think for a moment of the long chain of iron or gold, of thorns or flowers, that would never have bound you, but for the formation of the first link on one memorable day." GE 9

—*fatalism:* "'If all goes well,' said I, 'you will be perfectly free and safe again, within a few hours.'

"'Well,' [Magwitch] returned, drawing a long breath, 'I hope so.'

"'And think so?'

"He dipped his hand in the water over the boat's gunwale, and said, smiling with that softened air upon him which was not new to me:

"'Ay, I s'pose I think so, dear boy. We'd be puzzled to be more quiet and easy-going than we are at present. But—it's a flowing so soft and pleasant through the water, p'raps, as makes me think it—I was a thinking through my smoke just then, that we can no more see to the bottom of the next few hours, than we can see to the bottom of this river what I catches hold of. Nor yet we can't no more hold their tide than I can hold this. And it's run through my fingers and gone, you see!' holding up his dripping hand." GE 54

—*in occupation:* "'I worn't always a boots, sir,' said Mr Weller, with a shake of the head. 'I wos a wagginer's boy, once.'

"'When was that?' inquired Mr Pickwick.

"'When I wos first pitched neck and crop into the world, to play at leap-frog with its troubles,' replied Sam. 'I wos a carrier's boy at startin'; then a wagginer's, then a helper, then a boots. Now I'm a gen'l'm'n's servant. I shall be a gen'l'm'n myself one of these days, perhaps with a pipe in my mouth, and a summer-house in the back-garden. Who knows? *I* shouldn't be surprised, for one.'

"'You are quite a philosopher, Sam' said Mr Pickwick." PP 16

—*ominous:* "'In our course through life we shall meet the people who are coming to meet *us,* from many strange places and by many strange roads,' was the composed reply [of Miss Wade], and what it is set to us to do to them, and what it is set to them to do to us, will all be done . . . you may be sure that there are men and women already on their road, who have their business to do with *you* [Minnie Meagles] and who will do it. Of a certainty they will do it. They may be coming hundreds, thousands, of miles over the sea there; they may be close at hand now; they may be coming, for anything you know, or anything you can do to prevent it, from the vilest sweepings of this very town.'" LD i 2

—*power of circumstances:* "[John Harmon] had lapsed into the condition in which he found himself, as many a man lapses into many a condition, without perceiving the accumulative power of its separate circumstances. When in the distrust engendered by his wretched childhood and the action for evil—never yet for good within his knowledge then—of his father and his father's wealth on all within their influence, he conceived the idea of his first deception, it was meant to be harmless, it was to last but a few hours or days, it was to involve in it only the girl so capriciously forced upon him, and upon whom he was so capriciously forced, and it was honestly meant well towards her." OMF ii 14

—*purposeful?* "Could Obenreizer be the missing man? In the unknown associations of things, was there a subtler meaning than he himself thought, in that theory so often on his lips about the smallness of the world? Had the Swiss letter presenting him followed so close on Mrs Goldstraw's revelation concerning the infant who had been taken away to Switzerland, because he was that infant grown a man? In a world where so many depths lie unsounded, it might be.

"The chances, or the laws—call them either—that had wrought out the revival of Vendale's own acquaintance with Obenreizer, and had ripened it into intimacy, and had brought them here together this present winter night, were hardly less curious; while read by such a light, they were seen to cohere towards the furtherance of a continuous and an intelligible purpose." CS/NT 3

—*the Woodman:* "It is likely enough that, rooted in the woods of France and Norway, there were [in 1775] growing trees, when that sufferer [executed for not kneeling to monks] was put to death, already marked by the Woodman, Fate, to come down and be sawn into boards, to make a certain movable framework with a sack and a knife in it, terrible in history." TTC i 1

See also Karma

Immortality

"'After a while, instead of labels, the individual letters were given to [**Laura Bridgman**] on detached bits of paper: they were arranged side by side so as to spell *book, key, &c;* then they were mixed up in a heap and a sign was made for her to arrange them herself so as to express the words *book, key &c;* and she did so.

"'Hitherto, the process had been mechanical, and the success about as great as teaching a very knowing dog a variety of tricks. The poor child had sat in mute amazement, and patiently imitated everything her teacher did; but now the truth began to flash upon her: her intellect began to work: she perceived that here was a way by which she could herself make up a sign of anything that was in her own mind, and show it to another mind; and at once her countenance lighted up with a human expression: it was no longer a dog, or parrot: it was an immortal spirit, eagerly seizing upon a new link of union with other spirits! I could almost fix upon the moment when this truth dawned upon her mind, and spread its light to her countenance . . . . '" AN 3

Karma

—eastern: "Let them be. Let them lie unspoken of, in [Edwin Drood's] breast. However distinctly or indistinctly he entertained these thoughts, he arrived at the conclusion, Let them be. Among the mighty store of wonderful chains that are for ever forging, day and night, in the vast iron-works of time and circumstance, there was one chain forged in the moment of that small conclusion, riveted to the foundations of heaven and earth, and gifted with invincible force to hold and drag." MED 13

—western: "I kept over him [Arthur Clennam] as a child, in the days of his first remembrance, my restraining and correcting hand [said Mrs Clennam]. I was stern with him, knowing that the transgressions of the parents are visited on their offspring, and that there was an angry mark upon him at his birth. I have sat with him and his father, seeing the weakness of his father yearning to unbend to him; and forcing it back, that the child might work out his release in bondage and hardship . . . .

"For his good. Not for the satisfaction of my injury. What was I, and what was the worth of that, before the curse of Heaven!" LD ii 31

Life

—analog of Nature: " . . . nature gives to every time and season some beauties of his own, and from morning to night, as from the cradle to the grave, is but a succession of changes so gentle and easy, that we can scarcely mark their progress." NN 22

—battlefield: "' . . . the greatest favour you could do me, and yourself too, I am inclined to think [said Alfred Heathfield], would be to try sometimes to forget this battlefield and others like it in that broader battlefield of Life, on which the sun looks every day . . . there are quiet victories and struggles, great sacrifices of self, and noble acts of heroism, in it—even in many of its apparent lightnesses and contradictions—not the less difficult to achieve, because they have no earthly chronicle or audience—done every day in nooks and corners, and in little households, and in men's and women's hearts—any one of which might reconcile the sternest man to such a world, and fill him with belief and hope in it, though two-fourths of its people were at war, and another fourth at law; and that's a bold word.'" BL 1

—Biblical term: "'A fine old gentleman!' repeated Jonas [Chuzzlewit], giving the crown of his hat an angry knock. 'Ah! It's time he was thinking of being drawn out a little finer too. Why, he's eighty! . . . And ecod,' cried Jonas, 'now he's gone so far without giving in, I don't see much to prevent his being ninety; no, nor even a hundred. Why, a man with any feeling ought to be ashamed of being eighty, let alone more. Where's his religion, I should like to know, when he goes flying in the face of the bible like that? Three-score-and-ten's the mark; and no man with a conscience, and a proper sense of what's expected of him, has any business to live longer.'" MC 11

—breakings-up: "Breakings-up are capital things in our school days, but in after life they are painful enough. Death, self-interest, and fortune's changes, are every day breaking up many a happy group, and scattering them far and wide; and the boys and girls never come back again." PP 30

—in brief: "'That's a melancholy tale [the five sisters of York] . . . .'

"It's a tale of life, and life is made up of such sorrows' . . . ." NN 6

"'Tuesday. D. weak and nervous. Beautiful in pallor. (Do we not remark this in moon likewise? J. M.) D., J. M., and J. took airing in carriage. J. looking out of window, and barking violently at dustman, occasioned smile to overspread features of D. (Of such slight links is chain of life composed! J.M.)" DC 38

"I think of every little trifle between me and Dora, and feel the truth, that trifles make the sum of life." DC 53

" . . . there happened to be in Coketown a considerable population of babies who had been walking against time towards the infinite world, twenty, thirty, forty, fifty years and more." HT i 8

"'Pip, dear old chap [said Joe Gargery], life is made of ever so many partings welded together, as I may say . . . . '" GE 27

"'There's no royal road to learning [said Rumty Wilfer]; and what is life but learning?'" OMF iv 5

"'"Pounds, shillings, and pence," is my next note [said Mr Grewgious]. A dry subject for a young lady, but an important subject too. Life is pounds, shillings, and pence. Death is—' A sudden recollection of the death of [Rosa's] two parents seemed to stop him, and he said in a softer tone, and evidently inserting the negative as an afterthought: 'Death is *not* pounds, shillings, and pence.'" MED 9

—the bright side: "'Come! Quit this dreary world at once [said the Genius of Despair and Suicide].'

"'I don't know,' said the baron, playing with the knife; 'it's a dreary one certainly, but I don't think yours is much better . . . .

"'Dispatch,' cried the figure, gnashing its teeth.

"'Keep off!' said the baron. 'I'll brood over miseries no longer, but put a good face on the matter, and try the fresh air and the bears again . . . . With this the baron fell into his chair and laughed so loud and boisterously that the room rang with it.

"'The figure fell back a pace or two, regarding the baron meanwhile with a look of intense terror, and when he had ceased, caught up the stake, plunged it violently into its body, uttered a frightful howl, and disappeared.

"'Von Koëldwethout never saw it again. . . . And my advice to all men is, that if ever they become hipped and melancholy from similar causes (as very many men do), they look at both sides of the question, applying a magnifying glass to the best one; and if they still feel tempted to retire without leave, that they smoke a large pipe and drink a full bottle first, and profit by the laudable example of the Baron of Grogzwig.'" NN 6

—in the city: "The freshness of the day, the singing of the birds, the beauty of the waving grass, the deep green leaves, the wild flowers, and the thousand exquisite scents and sounds that floated in the air—deep joys to most of us, but most of all to those whose life is in a crowd or who live solitarily in great cities as in the bucket of a human well—sunk into their breasts [Nell and her grandfather] and made them very glad." OCS 15

—and death: "Contrast enough between Mr Tulkinghorn shut up in his dark carriage, and Mr Bucket shut up in his. Between the immeasurable track of space beyond the little wound that has thrown the one into the fixed sleep which jolts so heavily over the stones of the streets, and the narrow track of blood which keeps the other in the watchful state expressed in every hair of his head! But it is all one to both; neither is troubled about that." BH 53

—the facts: "[Louisa] . . . concentrating her attention upon him again, said, 'Father, I have often thought that life is very short'—This was so distinctly one of his subjects that he interposed.

"'It is short, no doubt, my dear. Still, the average duration of human life is proved to have increased of late years. The calculations of various life assurance and annuity offices, among other figures which cannot go wrong, have established the fact.'" HT i 15

—first duty of: " . . . all men and women, in couples or otherwise, who fall into exclusive habits of self-indulgence, and forget their natural sympathy and close connexion with everybody and everything in the world around them, not only neglect the first duty of life, but, by a happy retributive justice, deprive themselves of its truest and best enjoyment." YC/H

—holding on: " . . . it was not easy, with the face of [Charles Darnay's] beloved wife fresh before him, to compose his mind to what it must bear. His hold on life was strong, and it was very, very hard to loosen; by gradual efforts and degrees unclosed a little here, it clenched the tighter there; and when he brought his strength to bear on that hand and it yielded, this was closed again. There was a hurry, too, in all his thoughts, a turbulent and heated working of

his heart, that contended against resignation. If, for a moment, he did feel resigned, then his wife and child who had to live after him, seemed to protest and to make it a selfish thing.

"But, all this was at first. Before long, the consideration that there was no disgrace in the fate he must meet, and that numbers went the same road wrongfully, and trod it firmly every day, sprang up to stimulate him. Next followed the thought that much of the future peace of mind enjoyable by the dear ones, depended on his quiet fortitude. So, by degrees he calmed into the better state, when he could raise his thoughts much higher, and draw comfort down." TTC iii 13

—illusion: "Look round and round upon this bare bleak plain, and see even here, upon a winter's day, how beautiful the shadows are! Alas! it is the nature of their kind to be so. The loveliest things in life . . . are but shadows; and they come and go, and change and fade away, as rapidly as these!" MC 12

—impaired by fraud: "There are degrees in murder . . . . What will not content a Begging-Letter Writer for a week, would educate a score of children for a year. Let us give all we can; let us give more than ever. Let us do all we can; let us do more than ever. But let us give, and do, with a high purpose; not to endow the scum of the earth, to its own greater corruption, with the offals of our duty." RP/BL

—insurance: "'Apart from the general human disinclination to do anything that ought to be done, I dare say [said Mr Slinkton] there is a specialty about assuring one's life. You find it like will-making. People are so superstitious, and take it for granted they will die soon afterwards.'" HD

—a joke: "'Don't you know it's always somebody's birth-day? Did you never hear how many new performers enter on this—ha! ha! ha!—it's impossible to speak gravely of it—on this preposterous and ridiculous business called Life, every minute?' . . .

"Doctor Jeddler was, as I have said, a great philosopher, and the heart and mystery of his philosophy was, to look upon the world as a gigantic practical joke; as something too absurd to be considered seriously, by any rational man . . . .

"A kind and generous man by nature, he had stumbled, by chance, over that common Philosopher's stone (much more easily discovered than the object of the alchemist's researches), which sometimes trips up kind and generous men, and has the fatal property of turning gold to dross and every precious thing to poor account." BL 1

—misery: " . . . when [Nicholas Nickleby] thought how regularly things went on from day to day in the same unvarying round—how youth and beauty died, and ugly griping age lived tottering on—how crafty avarice grew rich, and manly honest hearts were poor and sad—how few they were who tenanted the stately houses, and how many those who lay in noisome pens, or rose each day and laid them down at night, and lived and died, father and son, mother and child, race upon race, and generation upon generation, without a home to shelter them or the energies of one single man directed to their aid—how in seeking, not a luxurious and splendid life, but the bare means of a most wretched and inadequate subsistence, there were women and children in that one town, divided into classes, numbered and estimated as regularly as the noble families and folks of great degree, and reared from infancy to drive most criminal and dreadful trades—how ignorance was punished and never taught—how jail-door gaped and gallows loomed for thousands urged towards them by circumstances darkly curtaining their very cradles' heads, and but for which they might have earned their honest bread and lived in peace—how many died in soul, and had no chance of life—how many who could scarcely go astray, be they vicious as they would, turned haughtily from the crushed and stricken wretch who could scarce do otherwise, and who would have been a greater wonder had he or she done well, than even they, had they done ill—how much injustice, and misery, and wrong there was, and yet how the world rolled on from year to year, alike careless and indifferent, and no man seeking to remedy or redress it:—when he thought of all this, and selected from the mass the one slight case on which his thoughts were bent, he felt that there was little ground for hope, and little cause or reason why it should not form an atom in the huge aggregate of distress and sorrow, and add one small and unimportant unit to swell the great amount." NN 53

—its mode: "'As to our mode of life [said John Chester], every man has a right to live in the best way he can; and to make himself as comfortable as he can, or he is an

unnatural scoundrel.'" BR 15

—mystery: "'I wish I may die, if this isn't the queerest state of existence that we find ourselves forced into, without knowing why or wherefore, Mr Pecksniff! Well, never mind! Moralise as we will, the world goes on. As Hamlet says, Hercules may lay about him with his club in every possible direction, but he can't prevent the cats from making a most intolerable row on the roofs of the houses, or the dogs from being shot in the hot weather if they run about the streets unmuzzled. Life's a riddle: a most infernally hard riddle to guess, Mr Pecksniff. My own opinion is, that like that celebrated conundrum, "Why's a man in jail like a man out of jail?" there's no answer to it. Upon my soul and body, it's the queerest sort of thing altogether—but there's no use in talking about it. Ha! ha!'" MC 4

"'It's a world full of hearts,' said the Doctor [Jeddler], hugging his younger daughter, and bending across her to hug Grace—for he couldn't separate the sisters; 'and a serious world, with all its folly—even with mine, which was enough to have swamped the whole globe; and it is a world on which the sun never rises, but it looks upon a thousand bloodless battles that are some set-off against the miseries and wickedness of Battle-Fields; and it is a world we need be careful how we libel, Heaven forgive us, for it is a world of sacred mysteries, and its Creator only knows what lies beneath the surface of His lightest image!'" BL 3

"'Do you know,' simpered Cleopatra [Mrs Skewton], reversing the knave of clubs, who had come into her game with his heels uppermost, 'that if anything could tempt me to put a period to my life, it would be curiosity to find out what it's all about and what it means; there are so many provoking mysteries, really, that are hidden from us.'" DS 21

—opportunity: "'Oh! captive, bound, and double-ironed,' cried the phantom [Marley's Ghost], 'not to know that ages of incessant labour by immortal creatures for this earth must pass into eternity before the good of which it is susceptible is all developed. Not to know that any Christian spirit working kindly in its little sphere, whatever it may be, will find its mortal life too short for its vast means of usefulness. Not to know that no space of regret can make amends for one life's opportunity misused! Yet such was I! Oh! such was I!'

"'But you were always a good man of business, Jacob,' faltered Scrooge, who now began to apply this to himself.

"'Business! cried the Ghost, wringing its hands again. 'Mankind was my business. The common welfare was my business; charity, mercy, forbearance, and benevolence, were all my business. The dealings of my trade were but a drop of water in the comprehensive ocean of my business!' CC 1

And see S:Perseverance

"Thoughts of a voyager unexpectedly summoned from home, who travelled a vast distance, and could never return. Thoughts of this unhappy wayfarer in the depths of his sorrow, in the bitterness of his anguish, in the helplessness of his self-reproach, in the desperation of his desire to set right what he had left wrong, and do what he had left undone.

"For there were many many things he had neglected. Little matters while he was at home and surrounded by them, but things of mighty moment when he was at an immeasurable distance. There were many many blessings that he had inadequately felt, there were many trivial injuries that he had not forgiven, there was love that he had but poorly returned, there was friendship that he had too lightly prized: there were a million kind words that he might have spoken, a million kind looks that he might have given, uncountable slight easy deeds in which he might have been most truly great and good. O for a day (he would exclaim) for but one day to make amends! But the sun never shone upon that happy day, and out of his remote captivity he never came.

"Why does this traveller's fate obscure, on New Year's Eve, the other histories of travellers with which my mind was filled but now, and cast a solemn shadow over me! Must I one day make his journey? Even so. Who shall say, that I may not then be tortured by such late regrets: that I may not then look from my exile on my empty place and undone work? I stand upon a sea-shore, where the waves are years. They break and fall, and I may little heed them; but with every wave the sea is rising, and I know that it will float me on this traveller's voyage at last." RP/LV

And see M:Memory—*remorse*

—of paupers: "Who could help wondering why the old men lived on as they did; what grasp they had on life; what crumbs of

interest or occupation they could pick up from its bare board; whether Charley Walters had ever described to them the days when he kept company with some old pauper woman in the bud, or Billy Stevens ever told them of the time when he was a dweller in the far-off foreign land called Home!" RP/WW

—perplexities: " . . . [William Dorrit's] poor weak breast, so full of contradictions, vacillations, inconsistences, the little peevish perplexities of this ignorant life, mists which the morning without a night only can clear away." LD ii 19

—pilgrimage: "The day passed on; and again the wide stare stared itself out; and the hot night was on Marseilles; and through it the caravan of the morning, all dispersed, went their appointed ways. And thus ever, by day and night, under the sun and under the stars, climbing the dusty hills and toiling along the weary plains, journeying by land and journeying by sea, coming and going so strangely, to meet and to act and react on one another, move all we restless travellers through the pilgrimage of life." LD i 2

—precious in decline: "'I am not a young woman; and they do say, that as life steals on towards its final close, the last short remnant, worthless as it may seem to all beside, is dearer to its possessor than all the years that have gone before, connected though they be with the recollection of old friends long since dead, and young ones—children perhaps—who have fallen off from, and forgotten one as completely as if they had died too. My natural term of life cannot be many years longer, and should be dear on that account; but I would lay it down without a sigh—with cheerfulness—with joy—if what I tell you now were only false or imaginary.'" SB/BV

—present in the moment: " . . . Lord! when you come to think of yourself, you know, and what a game you have been up to ever since you was in your own cradle, and what a poor sort of a chap you are, and how it's always either Yesterday with you, or else To-morrow, and never To-day, that's where it is!" CS/HT 2

—its prison: "Black, all night, since the gate had clashed upon Little Dorrit, its iron stripes were turned by the early-glowing sun into stripes of gold. For aslant across the city, over its jumbled roofs, and through the open tracery of its church towers, struck the long bright rays, bars of the prison of this lower world." LD ii 30

—restoration regretted: "[Rogue Riderhood] is struggling to come back. Now he is almost here, now he is far away again. Now he is struggling harder to get back. And yet—like us all, when we swoon—like us all, every day of our lives when we wake—he is instinctively unwilling to be restored to the consciousness of this existence, and would be left dormant, if he could." OMF iii 3

And see B:Sleep—*preferable to waking?, and* N:Time of Day—*morning in time of trial*

—a river: "He lived on the bank of a mighty river, broad and deep, which was always silently rolling on to a vast undiscovered ocean. It had rolled on, ever since the world began. It had changed its course sometimes, and turned into new channels, leaving its old ways dry and barren; but it had ever been upon the flow, and ever was to flow until Time should be no more. Against its strong, unfathomable stream, nothing made head. No living creature, no flower, no leaf, no particle of animate or inanimate existence, ever strayed back from the undiscovered ocean. The tide of the river set resistlessly towards it; and the tide never stopped, any more than the earth stops in its circling round the sun." CS/NS

This metaphor is most conspicuous in DS: *see* Vol. I pp775-778, *where the final lines are:*

"Oh thank GOD, all who see it, for that older fashion yet, of Immortality! And look upon us, angels of young children, with regards not quite estranged, when the swift river bears us to the ocean!" DS 16

" . . . all too soon, the great black city cast its shadow on the waters, and its dark bridges spanned them as death spans life. . . . " MED 22

—sacredness: "Life must be held sacred among us in more ways than one—sacred, not merely from the murderous weapon, or the subtle poison, or the cruel blow, but sacred from preventible diseases, distortions, and pains . . . . Physical life respected, moral life comes next." RP/BL

—saved: "Doctor examines the dank carcase, and pronounces, not hopefully, that it is worth while trying to reanimate the same. All the best means are at once in action, and everybody present lends a hand, and a heart and soul. No one has the least regard for the man: with them all, he has been an object of avoidance, suspicion, and

aversion; but the spark of life within him is curiously separable from himself now, and they have a deep interest in it, probably because it *is* life, and they are living and must die . . . .

"Stay! Did that eyelid tremble? So the doctor, breathing low, and closely watching, asks himself.

"No.

"Did that nostril twitch?

"No.

"This artificial respiration ceasing, do I feel any faint flutter under my hand upon the chest?

"No.

"Over and over again. No. No. But try over and over again, nevertheless.

"See! A token of life! An indubitable token of life! The spark may smoulder and go out, or it may glow and expand, but see! The four rough fellows seeing, shed tears. Neither Riderhood in this world, nor Riderhood in the other, could draw tears from them; but a striving human soul between the two can do it easily." OMF iii 3

—its shadow: "When [Betty Higden] had spoken to the Secretary of that 'deadness that steals over me at times,' her fortitude had made too little of it. Oftener and ever oftener, it came stealing over her; darker and ever darker, like the shadow of advancing Death. That the shadow should be deep as it came on, like the shadow of an actual presence, was in accordance with the laws of the physical world, for all the Light that shone on Betty Higden lay beyond Death." OMF iii 8

—as a story: "'Our whole life, Travellers,' said I, 'is a story more or less intelligible—generally less; but we shall read it by a clearer light when it is ended. I, for one, am so divided this night between fact and fiction, that I scarce know which is which.'" CS/PT 1

—too easy: "'It's made a great deal too easy,' said Mr Craggs.

"'Law is?' asked the Doctor.

"'Yes,' said Mr Craggs, 'everything is. Everything appears to me to be made too easy, now-a-days. It's the vice of these times. If the world is a joke (I am not prepared to say it isn't), it ought to be made a very difficult joke to crack. It ought to be as hard a struggle, sir, as possible. That's the intention. But it's being made far too easy. We are oiling the gates of life. They ought to be rusty. We shall have them beginning to turn, soon, with a smooth sound. Whereas they ought to grate upon their hinges, sir.'" BL 1

—its travellers: "The post of honour and the post of shame, the general's station and the drummer's, a peer's statue in Westminster Abbey and a seaman's hammock in the bosom of the deep, the mitre and the workhouse, the woolsack and the gallows, the throne and the guillotine—the travellers to all are on the great high road; but it has wonderful divergences, and only Time shall show us whither each traveller is bound." LD i 15

—under suspicion: "And as the great black river with its dreary shores was soon lost to [Lizzie Hexam's] view in the gloom, so, she stood on the river's brink unable to see into the vast blank misery of a life suspected, and fallen away from by good and bad, but knowing that it lay there dim before her, stretching away to the great ocean, Death." OMF i 6

—its ups and downs: "Mr Plornish amiably growled, in his philosophical but not lucid manner, that there was ups you see, and there was downs. It was in wain to ask why ups, why downs; there they was, you know. He had heerd it given for a truth that accordin' as the world went round, which round it did rewolve undoubted, even the best of gentlemen must take his turn of standing with his ed upside down and all his air a flying the wrong way into what you might call Space." LD ii 27

—its use: "'No one is useless in this world,' retorted the Secretary [Rokesmith], 'who lightens the burden of it for any one else.'" OMF iii 9

—water-rate collector's despair: "'The plug of life is dry [moaned Mr Lillyvick]. Only the mud is left.'" NN 52

—and wax-work: "' . . . always the same [said Mrs Jarley], with a constantly unchanging air of coldness and gentility; and so like life, that if wax-work only spoke and walked about, you'd hardly know the difference. I won't go so far as to say, that, as it is, I've seen wax-work quite like life, but I've certainly seen some life that was exactly like wax-work.'" OCS 27

Past life

—cycle of existence: "Were this miserable mother ['Good Mrs Brown'], and this miserable daughter [Alice Marwood], only the reduction to their lowest grade, of certain social vices sometimes prevailing higher up?

In this round world of many circles within circles, do we make a weary journey from the high grade to the low, to find at last that they lie close together, that the two extremes touch, and that our journey's end is but our starting-place? Allowing for great difference of stuff and texture, was the pattern of this woof repeated among gentle blood at all?

"Say, Edith Dombey! And Cleopatra, best of mothers, let us have your testimony!" DS 34

—old soul: "'Ah! said Mr Bailey, with a wink; 'and she [Charity Pecksniff] ain't bad-looking, mind you. But her sister [Mercy] was the best. *She* was the merry one. I often used to have a bit of fun with her, in the hold times!'

"Mr Bailey spoke as if he already had a leg and three-quarters in the grave, and this had happened twenty or thirty years ago. Paul Sweedlepipe, the meek, was so perfectly confounded by his precocious self-possession, and his patronising manner, as well as by his boots, cockade, and livery, that a mist swam before his eyes, and he saw—not the Bailey of acknowledged juvenility, from Todgers's Commercial Boarding House, who had made his acquaintance within a twelve-month, by purchasing, at sundry times, small birds at two-pence each—but a highly-condensed embodiment of all the sporting grooms in London; an abstract of all the stable-knowledge of the time; a something at a high-pressure that must have had existence many years, and was fraught with terrible experiences.

"And truly, though in the cloudy atmosphere of Todgers's, Mr Bailey's genius had ever shone out brightly in this particular respect, it now eclipsed both time and space, cheated beholders of their senses, and worked on their belief in defiance of all natural laws. He walked along the tangible and real stones of Holborn Hill, an under-sized boy; and yet he winked the winks, and thought the thoughts, and did the deeds, and said the sayings of an ancient man. There was an old principle within him, and a young surface without. He became an inexplicable creature: a breeched and booted Sphinx. There was no course open to the barber but to go distracted himself, or to take Bailey for granted: and he wisely chose the latter." ¶MC 26

" . . . Smallweed; of whom it may be remarked that he is a weird changeling, to whom years are nothing. He stands pre-cociously possessed of centuries of owlish wisdom. If he ever lay in a cradle, it seems as if he must have lain there in a tail-coat.

"He has an old, old eye, has Smallweed: and he drinks and smokes, in a monkeyish way; and his neck is stiff in his collar; and he is never to be taken in; and he knows all about it, whatever it is. In short, in his bringing up, he has been so nursed by Law and Equity that he has become a kind of fossil Imp, to account for whose terrestrial existence it is reported at the public offices that his father was John Doe, and his mother the only female member of the Roe family: also that his first long-clothes were made from a blue bag." BH 20

—suggested by Nature: "Who can tell how scenes of peace and quietude sink into the minds of pain-worn dwellers in close and noisy places, and carry their own freshness, deep into their jaded hearts! Men who have lived in crowded, pent-up streets, through lives of toil, and who have never wished for change; men, to whom custom has indeed been second nature, and who have come almost to love each brick and stone that formed the narrow boundaries of their daily walks; even they, with the hand of death upon them, have been known to yearn at last for one short glimpse of Nature's face; and, carried far from the scenes of their old pains and pleasures, have seemed to pass at once into a new state of being.

"Crawling forth, from day to day, to some green sunny spot, they have had such memories wakened up within them by the sight of sky, and hill and plain, and glistening water, that a foretaste of heaven itself has soothed their quick decline, and they have sunk into their tombs, as peacefully as the sun whose setting they watched from their lonely chamber window but a few hours before, faded from their dim and feeble sight!

"The memories which peaceful country scenes call up, are not of their world, nor of its thoughts and hopes. Their gentle influence may teach us how to weave fresh garlands for the graves of those we loved: may purify our thoughts, and bear down before it old enmity and hatred; but beneath all this, there lingers, in the least reflective mind, a vague and half-formed consciousness of having held such feelings long before, in some remote and distant time, which calls up solemn thoughts of distant times to come, and bends down pride and worldliness beneath it." OT 32

—trigger of memory: "Thus, a strain of gentle music, or the rippling of water in a silent place, or the odour of a flower, or the mention of a familiar word, will sometimes call up sudden dim remembrances of scenes that never were, in this life; which vanish like a breath; which some brief memory of a happier existence, long gone by, would seem to have awakened; which no voluntary exertion of the mind can ever recall." OT 30

And see M:Parapsychology—*déjà vu*

The Self, isolated

The following may be the most remarkable passage in all of CD's work.

"A wonderful fact to reflect upon, that every human creature is constituted to be that profound secret and mystery to every other. A solemn consideration, when I enter a great city by night, that every one of those darkly clustered houses encloses its own secret; that every room in every one of them encloses its own secret; that every beating heart in the hundreds of thousands of breasts there, is, in some of its imaginings, a secret to the heart nearest it! Something of the awfulness, even of Death itself, is referable to this.

"No more can I turn the leaves of this dear book that I loved, and vainly hope in time to read it all. No more can I look into the depths of this unfathomable water, wherein, as momentary lights glanced into it, I have had glimpses of buried treasure and other things submerged. It was appointed that the book should shut with a spring, for ever and for ever, when I had read but a page. It was appointed that the water should be locked in an eternal frost, when the light was playing on its surface, and I stood in ignorance on the shore.

"My friend is dead, my neighbour is dead, my love, the darling of my soul, is dead; it is the inexorable consolidation and perpetuation of the secret that was always in that individuality, and which I shall carry in mine to my life's end. In any of the burial-places of this city through which I pass, is there a sleeper more inscrutable than its busy inhabitants are, in their innermost personality, to me, or than I am to them?

"As to this, his natural and not to be alienated inheritance, the messenger on horseback had exactly the same possessions as the King, the first Minister of State, or the richest merchant in London. So with the three passengers shut up in the narrow compass of one lumbering old mail-coach; they were mysteries to one another, as complete as if each had been in his own coach and six, or his own coach and sixty, with the breadth of a county between him and the next." ¶TTC i 3

The Stars

—admired by a hypocrite: "'Behold the wonders of the firmament, Mrs Lupin! How glorious is the scene! When I look up at those shining orbs, I think that each of them is winking to the other to take notice of the vanity of men's pursuits. My fellow-men!' cried Mr Pecksniff, shaking his head in pity; 'you are much mistaken; my wormy relatives, you are much deceived! The stars are perfectly contented (I suppose so) in their several spheres. Why are not you? Oh! do not strive and struggle to enrich yourselves, or to get the better of each other, my deluded friends, but look up there, with me!'

"Mrs Lupin shook her head, and heaved a sigh. It was very affecting." MC 44

—angels' eyes? "'Hush!' said Barnaby, laying his fingers on his lips. 'He [Edward Chester] went out to-day a wooing. I wouldn't for a light guinea that he should never go a wooing again, for if he did, some eyes would grow dim that are now as bright as—see, when I talk of eyes, the stars come out! Whose eyes are they? If they are angels' eyes, why do they look down here and see good men hurt, and only wink and sparkle all the night?'" BR 3

—astrology

—studied: "'"I read,' cried the old gentleman . . . 'I read what's going to happen, in the stars.'

"'Tom [the lamplighter] thanked him for the information, and begged to know if anything particular was going to happen in the stars, in the course of a week or so; but the old gentleman, correcting him, explained that he read in the stars what was going to happen on dry land, and that he was acquainted with all the celestial bodies.

"'"I hope they're all well, Sir," says Tom—"everybody."

"'"Hush!" cries the old gentleman. "I have consulted the book of Fate with rare and wonderful success. I am versed in the great sciences of astrology and astronomy. In my house here, I have every description of apparatus for observing the course and motion of the planets. Six months ago, I derived from this source, the knowledge that precisely as the clock struck five this afternoon a stranger would present himself—the destined husband of my young and lovely niece—in reality of illustrious and high descent, but whose birth would be enveloped in uncertainty and mystery."'" L

"'"Mr Mooney is even now watching for the precise time at which we are to come into all the riches of the earth. It will be necessary for he and I [*sic.*], alone in that silent place, to cast your nativity before the hour arrives. Put the day and minute of your birth on this piece of paper, and leave the rest to me."

"'"You don't mean to say," says Tom, doing as he was told and giving him back the paper, "that I'm to wait here long, do you? It's a precious dismal place."

"'"Hush!" says the old gentleman. "It's hallowed ground. Farewell!"

"'"Stop a minute," says Tom. "What a hurry you're in! What's in that large bottle yonder?"

"'"It's a child with three heads," says the old gentleman; "and everything else in proportion."

"'"Why don't you throw him away?" says Tom. "What do you keep such unpleasant things here for?"

"'"Throw him away!" cries the old gentleman. "We use him constantly in astrology. He's a charm."

"'"I shouldn't have thought it," says Tom, "from his appearance."'" L

" . . . his gaze wandered from the windows to the stars, as if he would have read in them something that was hidden from him. Many of us would, if we could; but none of us so much as know our letters in the stars yet—or seem likely to, in this state of existence—and few languages can be read until their alphabets are mastered." MED 17

—*superseded:* "The stars that stud the firmament by night are watched no more from lonely towers by enthusiasts or impostors, believing, or feigning to believe, those great worlds to be charged with the small destinies of individual men down here . . . . The astrologer has faded out of the castle turret-room (which overlooks a railroad now), and forebodes no longer that because the light of yonder planet is diminishing, my lord will shortly die . . . . " E/PS

"The time was once, when men as knowing as Mr Tulkinghorn would walk on turret-tops in the star-light, and look up into the sky to read their fortunes there. Hosts of stars are visible to-night, though their brilliancy is eclipsed by the splendour of the moon. If he be seeking his own star, as he methodically turns and turns upon the leads, it should be but a pale one to be so rustily represented below. If he be tracing out his destiny, that may be written in other characters nearer to his hand." BH 41

—*and fireflies:* " . . . the stars came out in the heavens, and the fireflies mimicked them in the lower air, as men may feebly imitate the goodness of a better order of beings . . . . " LD i 1

—*indifferent:* "It was a dry cold night, and the wind blew keenly, and the frost was white and hard. A man would die to-night of lying out on the marshes, I thought. And then I looked at the stars, and considered how awful it would be for a man to turn his face up to them as he froze to death, and see no help or pity in all the glittering multitude." GE 7

—*numberless:* "Nell raised her eyes to the bright stars, looking down so mildly from the wide worlds of air, and, gazing on them, found new stars burst upon her view, and more beyond, and more beyond again, until the whole great expanse sparkled with shining spheres, rising higher and higher in immeasurable space, eternal in their numbers as in their changeless and incorruptible existence. She bent over the calm river, and saw them shining in the same majestic order as when the dove beheld them gleaming through the swollen waters, upon the mountain tops down far below, and dead mankind, a million fathoms deep." OCS 42

" . . . the stars, in unimaginable millions, glittering through [the wind], from eternal space, where the world's bulk is as a grain, and its hoary age is infancy." HM 1

"All the wonderful bright colours went out of the sea and sky in a few minutes, and all the stars in the Heavens seemed to shine out together, and to look down at themselves in the sea, over one another's shoulders, millions deep." CS/EP 1

And see S:Worldliness

—*a particular Star:* "'But look up yonder, Rachael! Look aboove!'

"Following his eyes, she saw that

[Stephen Blackpool] was gazing at a star.

"'It ha' shined upon me,' he said reverently, 'in my pain and trouble down below. It ha' shined into my mind. I ha' look'n at 't and thowt o'thee, Rachael, till the muddle in my mind have cleared awa, above a bit, I hope . . . in our judgments, like as in our doins, we mun bear and forbear. In my pain an' trouble, lookin up yonder—wi' it shinin on me—I ha' seen more clear, and ha' made it my dyin prayer that aw th' world may on'y coom toogether more, an' get a better unnerstan'in o' one another, than when I were in 't my own weak seln' . . . .

"The bearers being now ready to carry him away, and the surgeon being anxious for his removal, those who had torches or lanterns, prepared to go in front of the litter. Before it was raised, and while they were arranging how to go, he said to Rachael, looking upward at the star:

"'Often as I coom to myseln, and found it shinin on me down there in my trouble, I thowt it were the star as guided to Our Saviour's home. I awmust think it be the very star!'

"They lifted him up, and he was overjoyed to find that they were about to take him in the direction whither the star seemed to him to lead . . . .

"They carried him very gently along the fields, and down the lanes, and over the wide landscape; Rachael always holding the hand in hers. Very few whispers broke the mournful silence. It was soon a funeral procession. The star had shown him where to find the God of the poor; and through humility, and sorrow, and forgiveness, he had gone to his Redeemer's rest." HT iii 6

Time

—ambivalent: "Time, which strews a man's head with silver, sometimes fills his pockets with gold." B/T

—an architectural game: "Doctor Strong looked almost as rusty, to my thinking, as the tall iron rails and gates outside the house; and almost as stiff and heavy as the great stone urns that flanked them, and were set up, on the top of the red-brick wall, at regular distances all round the court, like sublimated skittles, for Time to play at." DC 16

—benign: "Father Time is not always a hard parent, and, though he tarries for none of his children, often lays his hand lightly upon those [such as Gabriel Varden] who have used him well; making them old men and women inexorably enough, but leaving their hearts and spirits young and in full vigour. With such people the grey head is but the impression of the old fellow's hand in giving them his blessing, and every wrinkle but a notch in the quiet calendar of a well-spent life." BR 2

—relatively: "'It makes my heart ache now, even now [said Gabriel Varden], though I'm an old man, with a woman for a daughter, to think what [Mary Rudge] was and what she is. We all change, but that's with Time; Time does his work honestly, and I don't mind him. A fig for Time, sir. Use him well, and he's a hearty fellow, and scorns to have you at a disadvantage. But care and suffering (and those have changed her) are devils, sir—secret, stealthy, undermining devils—who tread down the brightest flowers in Eden, and do more havoc in a month than Time does in a year.'" BR 26

—a comfort: "'(Must not D. C. confine himself to the broad pinions of Time? J.M.)'" DC 38 *Julia Mills might have meant to say "confide."*

And see S:Self-Transformation

—dawn reflection: . The steeple-clock, perched up above the houses, emerging from beneath another of the countless ripples in the tide of time that regularly roll and break on the eternal shore, is greyly visible, like a stone beacon, recording how the sea flows on . . . . " DS 31

—and eternity: "It was on a summer morning that I [George Silverman] rose before the sun to compose myself for the crowning of my work . . . I walked down to the rocks on the shore, in order that I might behold the sun in his majesty.

"The tranquillity upon the deep, and on the firmament, the orderly withdrawal of the stars, the calm promise of coming day, the rosy suffusion of the sky and waters, the ineffable splendour that then burst forth, attuned my mind afresh after the discords of the night. Methought that all I looked on said to me, and that all I heard in the sea and in the air said to me, 'Be comforted, mortal, that thy life is so short. Our preparation for what is to follow has endured, and shall endure, for unimaginable ages.'" GSE

"Correct this [endemic Ignorance] for thyself. Be bold! Silence these voices, or virtuously lose thy power in the attempt to do it. Thou canst not sow a grain of good seed in vain. thou knowest it well. Be bold, and do thy duty!'

"The Minister shrugged his shoulders, and replied, 'It is a great wrong—BUT IT WILL LAST MY TIME.' And so he put it from him . . . .

"The Spirit [of Death], with its face concealed, summoned all the people who had used this phrase about their Time, into its presence. Then it said, beginning with the Minister of State:

"'Of what duration is *your* Time?' . . .

"'But every man, as I understand you, one and all,' said the Spirit, 'has his time?'

"'Yes!' they exclaimed together.

"'Yes,' said the Spirit: 'and it is—ETERNITY! Whosoever is a consenting party to a wrong, comforting himself with the base reflection that it will last his time, shall bear his portion of that wrong throughout ALL TIME. And, in the hour when he and I stand face to face, he shall surely know it, as my name is Death!'" HW/DV

—father and son: "On the brow of Dombey, Time and his brother Care had set some marks, as on a tree that was to come down in good time—remorseless twins they are for striding through their human forests, notching as they go—while the countenance of Son was crossed and recrossed with a thousand little creases, which the same deceitful Time would take delight in smoothing out and wearing away with the flat part of his scythe, as a preparation of the surface for his deeper operations." DS 1

—and the future: "[Louisa Gradgrind] gave [Tom] an affectionate good-night, and went out with him to the door, whence the fires of Coketown could be seen, making the distance lurid. She stood there, looking steadfastly towards them . . . when he was gone and all was quiet. It seemed as if, first in her own fire within the house, and then in the fiery haze without, she tried to discover what kind of woof Old Time, that greatest and longest-established Spinner of all, would weave from the threads he had already spun into a woman. But his factory is a secret place, his work is noiseless, and his Hands are mutes." HT i 14

—in a graveyard: " . . . the pageant of a few short hours ago was written nowhere half so legibly as in the undertaker's books.

"Not in the churchyard? Not even there. The gates were closed; the night was dark and wet; the rain fell silently, among the stagnant weeds and nettles. One new mound was there which had not been there last night. Time, burrowing like a mole below the ground, had marked his track by throwing up another heap of earth. And that was all." MC 19

—the great manufacturer: "Time went on in Coketown like its own machinery: so much material wrought up, so much fuel consumed, so many powers worn out, so much money made. But, less inexorable than iron, steel, and brass, it brought its varying seasons even into that wilderness of smoke and brick, and made the only stand that ever *was* made in the place against its direful uniformity.

"'Louisa is becoming,' said Mr Gradgrind,' almost a young woman.'

"Time, with his innumerable horse-power, worked away, not minding what anybody said . . . .

"The same great manufacturer, always with an immense variety of work on hand, in every stage of development, passed Sissy onward in his mill, and worked her up into a very pretty article indeed." HT i 14

—and humanity: "'The voice of Time,' said the Phantom, 'cries to man, Advance! Time is for his advancement and improvement; for his greater worth, his greater happiness, his better life; his progress onward to that goal within its knowledge and its view, and set there, in the period when Time and He began. Ages of darkness, wickedness, and violence, have come and gone—millions uncountable, have suffered, lived, and died—to point the way before him. Who seeks to turn him back, or stay him on his course, arrests a mighty engine which will strike the meddler dead; and be the fiercer and the wilder, ever, for its momentary check!' . . .

"'Who puts into the mouth of Time, or of its servants . . . a cry of lamentation for days which have had their trial and their failure, and have left deep traces of it which the blind may see—a cry that only serves the present time, by showing men how much it needs their help when any ears can listen to regrets for such a past—who does this, does a wrong . . . . '" C 3

—and memory: "'Another Christmas come, another year gone!' murmured the Chemist [Redlaw] with a gloomy sigh. 'More figures in the lengthening sum of recollection that we work and work at to our torment till Death idly jumbles all together, and rubs

all out.'" HM 1

—*passing quickly:* "'And talk of Time slipping by you, as if it was an animal at rustic sports with his tail soaped,' said Mr Inspector (again, a subject which nobody had approached) . . . . " OMF iv 12

—*and the past:* "'It's in vain, Trot, to recall the past, unless it works some influence upon the present.'" DC 23

" . . . the moment shot away into the plumbless depths of the past, to mingle with all the lost opportunities that are drowned there." HT i 15

—*and the railroad:* "The train rattled among the house-tops, and among the ragged sides of houses torn down to make way for it, and over the swarming streets, and under the fruitful earth, until it shot across the river: bursting over the quiet surface like a bomb-shell, and gone again as if it had exploded in the rush of smoke and steam and glare. A little more, and again it roared across the river, a great rocket: spurning the watery turnings and doublings with ineffable contempt, and going straight to its end, as Father Time goes to his. To whom it is no matter what living waters run high or low, reflect the heavenly lights and darknesses, produce their little growth of weeds and flowers, turn here, turn there, are noisy or still, are troubled or at rest, for their course has one sure termination, though their sources and devices are many." OMF iv 11 *And see* IG:Railroad—*and Time*

—*and the river:* "[Arthur Clennam] softly opened his window, and looked out upon the serene river. Year after year so much allowance for the drifting of the ferry-boat, so many miles an hour the flowing of the stream, here the rushes, there the lilies, nothing uncertain or unquiet.

"Why should he be vexed or sore at heart? It was not his weakness that he had imagined. It was nobody's, nobody's within his knowledge, why should it trouble him? And yet it did trouble him. And he thought—who has not thought for a moment, sometimes?—that it might be better to flow away monotonously, like the river, and to compound for its insensibility to happiness with its insensibility to pain." LD i 16

—*unhurried:* "The Hours did not go through any of those rosy performances, which foolish poets have ascribed to them at such [betrothal] times; neither did the clocks go any faster, or any slower, than at other seasons. The deadly statistical recorder in the Gradgrind observatory knocked every second on the head as it was born, and buried it with his accustomed regularity." HT i 16

See also A:Baby—*bran-new;* IG:Railroad—*and Time; and* N:Flora—*trees—and Time; and* N:Sun—*setting*

Truth

—*inconvenient:* "The truth has come out, as it plainly has, in a manner that there's no standing up against—and a very sublime and grand thing is truth, gentlemen, in its way, though, like other sublime and grand things, such as thunderstorms and that, we're not always over and above glad to see it." OCS 66

—*near death:* "[Mrs Gradgrind's] feeble voice sounded so far away in her bundle of shawls, and the sound of another voice addressing her seemed to take such a long time in getting down to her ears, that she might have been lying at the bottom of a well. The poor lady was nearer Truth than she ever had been: which had much to do with it." HT ii 9

—*not to meddle with:* "There is no playing fast and loose with the truth, in any game, without growing the worse for it." LD ii 6

—*a preacher's idea:* "'I hear a voice,' says Chadband; 'is it a still small voice, my friends? I fear not, though I fain would hope so ——' . . .

"'Which says, I don't know. Then I will tell you why. I say this brother [Jo], present here among us, is devoid of parents, devoid of relations, devoid of flocks and herds, devoid of gold, of silver, and of precious stones, because he is devoid of the light that shines in upon some of us. What is that light? What is it? I ask you what is that light? . . .

"'It is,' says Chadband, 'the ray of rays, the sun of suns, the moon of moons, the star of stars. It is the light of Terewth' . . . .

"'Of Terewth,' says Mr Chadband . . . 'Say not to me it is *not* the lamp of lamps. I say to you, it is. I say to you, a million times over, it is. It is! I say to you that I will proclaim it to you, whether you like it or not; nay, that the less you like it, the more I will proclaim it to you. With a speaking-trumpet! I say to you that if you rear yourself against it, you shall fall, you shall be bruised, you shall be battered, you shall be flawed, you shall be smashed.'" BH 25

—a test: "'Or, my juvenile friends, 'says Chadband, descending to the level of their comprehension, with a very obtrusive demonstration, in his greasily meek smile, of coming a long way downstairs for the purpose, 'if the master of this house was to go forth into the city and there see an eel, and was to come back, and was to call unto him the mistress of this house, and was to say, "Sarah, rejoice with me, for I have seen an elephant!" would *that* be Terewth?'

"Mrs Snagsby in tears.

"'Or put it, my juvenile friends, that he saw an elephant, and returning said "Lo, the city is barren, I have seen but an eel," would *that* be Terewth?'

"Mrs Snagsby sobbing loudly." BH 25

—the test: "'Do you remember what you told me once, about her making all the apple parsties and doing all the cooking?'

"'Yes, very well,' I returned.

"'It was as true,' said Mr Barkis, 'as turnips is. It was as true,' said Mr Barkis, nodding his night-cap, which was his only means of emphasis, 'as taxes is. And nothing's truer than them.'" DC 21

Indexes of Words and Phrases

An intelligent, well-read friend once asked the Editor for the source of the line (which he correctly, up to a point, thought was to be found in MC), "Facts must be humoured, not drove." The Editor replied that the reference was to meat, not facts, and sent his friend the extract. To which this distinguished medical man replied with thanks but said it was the wrong reference: his clear recollection insisted that the remembered language applied to Facts, not Meat. We created *Words and Phrases* for such readers (we hope they will bring open minds to it), and for those who wish to find a character, otherwise lost in the mist, by a quality like having a "gaunt and iron-bound aspect," or a "retaliative temperament," or being "perpetually around the corner."

These Indexes (*Sayings of the Characters,* and *From the Narration*) cover only text extracted in EID and the *Topicon*, except for an occasional unique or deathless phrase ("ligneous sharper"). Where entries are citable both to EID and this Volume, we have given the latter reference.

Our goal has been to be exhaustive without being repetitive: words and phrases which are captions or sub-captions in the body of this Volume will probably not be found here. In *From the Narration* we have noted words Dickens rarely used ("Belladonna," "calenture," "Dryades") even if their context is unremarkable, and readers may find it worthwhile to look for relatively rare words to see if Dickens used them (some surely are not here, given the limited purview of these Indexes). This is, to all intents and purposes, our Index of Last Resort, for it includes terms (Athanasian Creed, Cunard steamer, Esquimaux, Mississippi Momuses) which lie outside the scope of any of the Indexes in EID Volume III or the captions in this Volume.

Page numbers by themselves refer to Vol. I or (840 and up) Vol. II of EID. Quotations from EID Volume III are cited as "III p—" Numbers with column references a or b (or ab in the case of extended excerpts) refer to the *Topicon.* Citations directly to works will have "ch" or, if segmented in parts, small roman and chapter number, as "LD ii 18." Many phrases are paraphrased or otherwise abbreviated. We use / occasionally to stand for "of," "on," or "to," w to stand for "with," wo for "without" and wd for "would." For character names, consult the Indexes in Volume III.

Sayings of the Characters

'actor for the starved business' NN 311b
'actuated by maternal dictates' BH 388b
'Affection's voice is low; it waits' DC 898
'affections set on that manly brow' MHC 419
'Affliction sore long time he bore' DS 28a
'Aggerawayter' TTC 1367
'aggerawators' SB/EE 150b
'Ain't it enough to disgust a pig?' CS/TT 1483
'alien to this tenement' DC 308b
'all awaricious and all in it' TTC 1021a
'All spirits are good' HW/SB 1034
'allonging and marshonging' LD 833a
'all her acquaintance is celebrated' PP 206
'All's fish that comes to my net' BH 595a
'almost quite bright' BH 1105
'Always suspect everybody' OCS 462
'Am I insulting?' GE 1454
'amiable bull: every colour scarlet' BH 1083
'amiable Guy Fawkes' PP 178
'Amigoarawaysoo?' DC 103b
'Amusements done it' HW/GK 1135
'And how do you like that name?' BH 11a
'And this is popularity!' PP 613a
'angels are upstairs, the' MED 1015a
'anger of a father' NN 954a
'Ann Koar!' CS/NT 582b
'Anna Dominoes' TTC ii 1
'apples, cherries, hops and women' PP ch2
'appleplexy line' PP 386b
'Arcadian, Nature intended me for' DS 953a
'arcana of the Modern Babylon' DC 308a
'architectooralooral' GE 545a
'Are there no prisons?' CC 619
'Are you a princess?' NN 347
'arms o' Porpus, in the' PP ch36
'artificial, we are so dreadfully' DS 953a
'ashes, not crustiness' DS ch2
'ask for 'Melia' DS 754
'Asked and got rid of' OMF 632ab
'Aspirate the "H", We' OMF 835b
'assimilating the fragrant article!' OMF 144a
'astonishment will be your portion' HM 790
'atmosphere of evil' GE 23b
'Attendant unknowns; pokey' OMF 70b
'authors: lodgers not voters' NN 270a 988a
'autumnal fruits of the woolsack' BH 682b
'Avaunt—cat!' NN 329
'Awast, my lass, awast!' DS 745
'Aye, aye, shipmet, how fares it?' DS 744
'babes in the woods as you are!' DC 64b
'badger, end of being drawed like a' BH 1101
'balmy, murder the' OCS 444
'banking away like smoke' TTC 1021a
'bankrupt you'd be a Duck' OMF 1568
'bargain for security of possessions' LD 398a
'bargain, Mr Boffin, I never' OMF 1563
'Bashaw, you were quite a DS ch30
'Batcheetcha' for Baptista in Genoa PI ch5
'bayonetted through the body' DS 357b
'Be comforted that life is short' GSE 1034b
'be parliamentary: call him vun' MHC 417
'be somethingological directly' HT 220b
'Beast, the' CS/MJ 603a
'Beatten the schoolmeasther!' NN 340
'Bedlamite' DS 474a
'before the good is all developed' CC 1028a
'bein' only eyes, wision's limited' PP 677ab
'beloved and only child' (meant son) DS 768
'bent I hope into better shape' GE 417b
'best club in London, Commons' OMF 715b
'best-groomed woman in the stud' BH 1062
'bestowed herself on a Mendicant' OMF 1593
'better to be silly than wise as you!' BR 288a
'better-looking: so's your mother' OCS 440
'Bill [Shakspeare] was an adapter' NN 988b
'bird has all the wit, The ' BR 493
'blacks got into white satins' HWC/S 792b
'Blank looks pretty tall' CS/HT 1197
'blossom is blighted, leaf withered' DC 375a
'bluebottle! reg'lar' SB/TR 879b
'board and lodging to me, smoke is' PP 191a
'Bob swore, my ducks!' DC 842b
'Bolted. With the plate.' CS/GS 1333
'Booty with my clerk, you play' DC 467ab
'Bother Mrs Harris!' MC 581
'bottiney, noun substantive' NN 337
'bottled lightning and a corkscrew' NN 138a
'bragian little traitor, the!' MGS 707
'brave lodgings for one' PP 297a
'breast in which he revived a soul'CS/PT 42b
'Bride, five-and-forty if a day' OMF 70a
'brigand of a Sun' LD 966a
'British Judy' DC 662a
'brother to Peter the Wild Boy' MED 1693
'bubbles back, I can throw' DC 116a
'But there is One above.' C 421b
'Cackler! I wath tho muth of a' HT 610a
'calcined on our domestic hearth' DC 470ab
'calcination and calorification' HT 944a
'calculated to awaken prejudice' LD 573b
'camel excessively temperate' OMF 951a
'Canterbury Brawn, legs like' MC 603
'captivating hypocrisy' BR 381a
'care and suffering are devils' BR 1034b
'catamaran! you' NN ch53
'catawampous chawers' MC 593
'change to brother and sister' MED 1681
'charm the eye, allure the taste' BH 487b
'Child-wife, a stupid name' DC ch44
'choking eyes' BH 110a
'cholera is always coming' HW/GK 1135
'Chops, cherry-pudding for two!' CS/HT 1196

From the Narration

blood-red whirl MED 1688
Bloomer trousers CS/SL 1496
blossom-faced men OMF 1618
blot of blood and grease on History III p491
blown up, appears to have been BH 1110
blue books, abundance of HT 224a
Blue chamber and common enemy BL 691a
blue eye, with black border SB/LC 51
Blue-Eyed Maid, Timpson's UT/DT 886a
'Blue' house at elections SB/WD 857b
blunderbuss and horse-pistols TTC 594a
bluntness mistaken for sincerity SB/WT 120
boa-constrictor, said I was like a DC 906
boastfulness and bile MC 561b
bold women still children HW/FN 925
bold, haggard, flaunting, poor DC 905
bolus, force down the throat like a HT 214b
bombazeen skirts, black DS 879b
Bonbon, a stupendous PI 826b
bone, neck, nostrils; quantity of OMF 1608
bonnes in snow-white caps RP/FW 23a
bonnet like an over-ripe fig HT 1166
Boobies, Convocation of Eternal HW/OL
Booby, heavy, selfish, drifting LD 434a
Book of Roads, the S/CT1 854b
bookseller, much better thing to be OT 275b
boots laughing dryly, suspiciously GE 388a
Bore A 1 UT/AL 1421
bores, power of making UT/B 1669
born beneath Bengal star of ill omen DS 756
born to be happy, lived miserably MP/FW
borrowing eyes LD 462a
Bosom flushed: one of best effects LD 109b
bosom to hang jewels upon LD 1251
botanical account-book HT 158a
both children of the dust shine BH 1067
bottle: rather suspicious character OCS 447
Bounderby balderdash, bluster HT 449b
bountifully bitten all night AN 873b
Bourbon on English throne, vile as if UT/ST
bow out of his head, drawing a OMF 497a
Bow Street Police RP/DP
boxer, neatness of a placid GE 486a
boy in a state of somnolency PP 192
boys all blew before their time DS 743
braggadocia: three months in gaol RP/AT
Brahma in his youth, disciple of RP/HF
Bramah erysipelas or small-pox UT/C
bran-new people, bran-new baby OMF 1588
bravura concert in all languages MC 268a
brazen Colossus SB/DC 34
breakfast knife, putting edge to a NN 422a
breaking a man alive SB/EC 46
breaking rest, peace, heart PP 898a
breeding-place of fever, ague, death AN 815a
brick and mortar funeral LD 786a
bridge of light, a TTC 1349
bright long fair hair OMF 1597
brimstone, smoked out of fortune w BH 950a
Bristol-board, a few sheets of BH 560b
British female constitution CS/SL 1491
brittle chain of hope, every link in NN 970b
broad arrow, no class born to HWC/D 715a
broad-sword guards with a ruler DC 468ab
broiling in the sun one day LD 821a
broken threads of yesterday CS/HH 969b
brought in by head and shoulders DC 674a
brought up by hand GE 1444
brown hot water stiff with flour UT/RT 182a
brown, grave gentleman LD 1228
brown-paper cuirasses DC 917
bubbles and wapours CS/NT 1648
buccaneering air, defensive, prompt DC 128a
buccaneering widows CS/NT 592a
buck-baskets w half-washed linen AN 822a
Buddhist when we travelled w him RP/HF
buds are children of the flowers RP/DS 953b
built me with straw to waist CS/HT 899ab
bull in a crockery shop DS 914b
bull's-eyes melted and congealed HM 624a
Bulls of Rome HW/CB 952
Bully of humility HT 7b
bullying, decided propensity for OT 712a
bumps in my head, all the best HW/U
buried in grave of Golden Mary CS/GM 1019b
burning mountain ever at its work PI 821b
burnt-sienna natives PI 675
bursting expression HW/LT 951
business and calculation, air of AN 874a
butchery of Rome, old PI 826b
Butter-Scotch CS/MJ 799a
butterfly in the square! a NN 766b
buttoned-up man LD 1263
cabbage-leaf, cabbage-stalk dress OMF 767b
caboose, black cook in black DS 890a
Caffre would shudder BH 56b 511b
Calais burghers came out of town UT/CM
Calamity herself, as ready as LD 693b
calculation relative to number one HT 1161
calenture, a mild fit of MED 104b
California gold, nugget of UT/FF
caligraphic recreations LD 226a
calm goblin, a Shaker sort of a AN 403a
Calmucks of Tartary HT i 15
calomel in conserve of roses SB/GS 921b
came up stiff like a dead clown MC 591
Camel of Asia: symbol of fresh water HW/BV
camel of all work OMF 7b
cane like a little finger-post LD 1243
cannibalic boiled mutton UT/RT 846a
cannon, muskets, fire, smoke TTC 743ab
cap: highly aristocratic, classical III p488
capacity of easily forgetting its dead DS 29b
carbuncular potato PP 131a
Care and Complication OMF 226b
carpenter planing comes to a knot BR 183a

Index of Localities

We seek here to cover actual localities mentioned in the entire *oeuvre,* other than (unless quoted in the *Topicon*) AN, PI and the speeches, but with citations simply to works, and chapters where applicable, in cases where no page reference can be made to EID or this volume. References to captions which contain a locality name (e.g., those in the chapters *London* and *The Rest of the World*) are in **bold**. Three nations frequently mentioned—England, France and Italy—are omitted. Spellings and styles, but not the names themselves, are usually modernised. Page numbers of illustrations are in *italic.* The L and W chapter indexes should also be consulted. For references we class (fingers crossed) as fictional, *see* Volume III, Index XII.

No attempt is made here to connect localities with characters or with scenes and actions in the *oeuvre*. (An overview of the most important may be found in MMH, and LCD is excellent on London.) We have made a serious effort, however, to include all localities mentioned by CD, and each work in which any is mentioned, though without attempting to cite every instance. David Parker was of invaluable help in identifications.

As we prepared this Index, we were struck by the nearly total absence of locality names in OCS (uniquely among the novels) and in all five of the Christmas Books. Everywhere else, Dickens opted for concreteness in locating action. Overall, he names over 2,500 different localities.

*The indexes to the travel books provide citations to the works themselves. The castles, hostelries, prisons, etc. mentioned are included in the sub-indexes.

Battlefields, Castles and Forts

Hostelries

The inns and other hostelries mentioned below appear in Dickens's works under their historical names, and so are here as "actual" hostelries. See Volume III Index XII *for a list including "fictional" inns, for which CD coined names (e.g., "The Maypole" for Chigwell's King's Head).*

Places of Worship

Prisons

Ships and Other Vessels

Theatres

Adelphi UT/SE 1666 B/P YG/V E/TE1 3 4 PP ch31 MC/BF /MC /Z /YK /ZR /DS /R
Ambigû [*sic.*] Comique, Paris HWC/FP
Astley's SB/A 38 /BH 2 /LC PI 673 OCS 316b 609ab *609* SB/PT 318b AN 819b HT 1171 HW/R i BH ch21 E/TE2
Bowery, New York City AN ch6
Britannia UT/TV 319b 656b
Carl, Vienna HWC/FP
Carlo Felice, opera house in Genoa PI ch5
Colosseum MC/C /CF /RC 143 144
Covent Garden SB/HS 106 /JD YG/T AY/Q 1659 DC 1007a E/L /MB /TE1 MP/AI /TH CS/LL i HWC/FF 16a /SN
Drury Lane SB/JD /PT UT/TV 769a AF 811 HWC/DD 1322 /FF 16a /T /SN AY/Q 1659 NN ch14 YC/E YG/T RP/BS /LA /DT E/MB /TE2
Haymarket E/PB /TE2 3
Lyceum HW/SG 1028 RP/BS /PG AY/M
Marylebone E/VS MP/CP iii
Niblo's Summer; New York City AN ch6
Olympic YG/T MC/OH
Olympic, New York City AN ch6
Paris Opera UT/TV HW/RD
Park, New York City AN ch6
Pavilion E/TE2
Portsmouth NN ch23
Princess's E/TE3
Queen's MC/RP
Rochester PP ch3
Royal Coburg SB/BS
Sadler's Wells B/P 736b OT 774a
San Carlino, Naples PI 580a
San Carlo Opera, Naples PI 563b UT/TV
La Scala, Milan UT/TV 319a
St James's MC/W /BH RP/F E/TE1 2
[Standard (or The People's)] HW/AP
Strand E/TE2
Surrey B/P 736b YG/T LD i 7
Teatro Diurno, Genoa PI ch5
Théâtre de la Barrière St Martin HW/NY
—Français RP/NS E/AE HW/W?
—de la Gaieté HW/NY
—du Palais Royal HW/NY
—Royal, Drury Lane NN ch15
—St Hubert, Brussels HWC/FP
—des Variétés HW/W? /NY HWC/FP
—des Vaudevilles HW/NY
Victoria Theatre SB/SN 786b YG/T HW/AP i

American Notes

Where no locality identification beyond the name is given, it is England or London unless the context shows otherwise.

Albany, New York ch15
Allegheny Mountains, Penn. ch10
American Bottom, Missouri ch13
Auburn Prison, New York ch6
Baltimore, Maryland ch8
Barnum's Hotel, Baltimore ch9
Bath ch10
Battery Gardens, New York City ch6
Belgium ch12
Belleville, Missouri ch13
Benton County, Arkansas ch17
Big Grave Creek, on Ohio River ch11
Birmingham ch10
Black Hollow, Missouri ch13
Bloody Island, Missouri ch13
Bloody Run Valley, Virginia ch9
Boston, Mass. chs1 2 3 4
Bowery Theatre, New York City ch6
Bowery, the; New York City ch6
Boylston School, Mass. ch3
Broadway, New York City ch6
Buffalo, New York ch14
Burlington Arcade ch5
Burlington, Iowa ch17
Cairo, Illinois chs14 18
Cambridge, U. of (Harvard), Mass. ch3
Canada ch16
Cape Clear ch16
Capitol Building, Washington D.C. ch8
Carlton House Hotel, New York City ch6
Carondelet (Vide Poche), Illinois ch14
Carthage, Leake Co., Mississippi ch17
Catskill Mountains, New York ch15
Charleston, South Carolina ch8
Chatres Street, New Orleans, Louisiana ch17
Chesapeake Bay, Maryland ch9
Chigwell ch2
Cincinnati, Ohio chs10 14
City Road ch8
Clarke County, Missouri ch17
Coburg, Ontario ch15
College of Upper Canada, Toronto ch15
Columbus, Ohio ch14
Connecticut ch3
Connecticut River ch5
Connecticut State House, Hartford ch5
Dickenson's Landing, St Lawrence ch15

Pictures from Italy

Charles Dickens did not number the sections of this work. Our numbering is as follows:

1 The Reader's Passport
2 Going through France
3 Lyons, The Rhone, and the Goblin of Avignon
4 Avignon to Genoa
5 Genoa and its Neighbourhood
6 To Parma, Modena, and Bologna
7 Through Bologna and Ferrara
8 An Italian Dream [Venice]
9 By Verona, Mantua, and Milan, across the Pass of the Simplon into Switzerland [and on to London]
10 To Rome by Pisa and Siena
11 Rome
12 A Rapid Diorama—To Naples, Pompeii, Pæstum, Vesuvius, Cassino, Florence

Supplementary Index to Key Words

See *How to Use This Book* (at page xxvi), for advice on how best to search a key word or phrase, using this volume and, if available, the Indexes and Glossary in Volume III. Entries below emphasize words Dickens used relatively rarely and include phrases not to be found in *Indexes to Words and Phrases* above.

About the Editor

Until 1988, GEORGE NEWLIN had spent his professional career combining activities in law and finance with volunteer service in the arts and serious avocational musical performance. At that time, he withdrew from most of his activities in venture capital and assets management and began developing his concept for a new kind of literary anthology, beginning with the works of Charles Dickens. In 1995, his three-volume work *Everyone in Dickens* was published by Greenwood Press. He is currently working on two books of source materials intended to support high school study of the Dickens novels, *A Tale of Two Cities* and *Great Expectations*, as part of Greenwood's Literature in Context Series. He is planning a multi-volume anthology on Anthony Trollope.

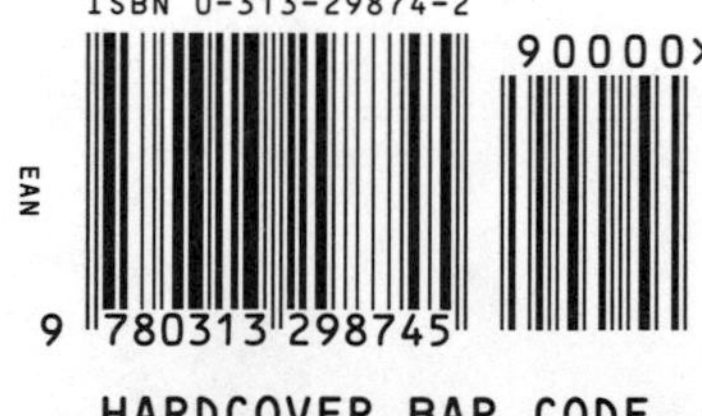
ISBN 0-313-29874-2
EAN
9 780313 298745
90000>
HARDCOVER BAR CODE